PRESENTED TO

Elkie Chafin Jr.

BY

Donna Chafin

ON

2-23-98

THIS CERTIFIES THAT

Alkie Chafin Jr.

AND

Donna Carol Pace

WERE UNITED IN

HOLY MATRIMONY

ON April THE 16th

DAY OF A.D. 1976

AT 621 Waterman

IN ACCORDANCE WITH THE LAWS OF Detroit Mi

OFFICIATING ______________________

WITNESS ______________________

WITNESS ______________________

Special Occasions to Remember

EVENT

PLACE DATE

EVENT

PLACE DATE

EVENT

PLACE DATE

EVENT

PLACE DATE

EVENT

PLACE DATE

EVENT

PLACE DATE

EVENT

PLACE DATE

FAMILY RECORD

BIRTHS

NAME ______ BORN TO ______ DATE ______

NAME ______ BORN TO ______ DATE ______

NAME ______ BORN TO ______ DATE ______

NAME ______ BORN TO ______ DATE ______

BAPTISMS

NAME ______ MINISTER ______ DATE ______

NAME ______ MINISTER ______ DATE ______

NAME ______ MINISTER ______ DATE ______

NAME ______ MINISTER ______ DATE ______

MARRIAGES

HUSBAND ______ WIFE ______ DATE ______

HUSBAND ______ WIFE ______ DATE ______

HUSBAND ______ WIFE ______ DATE ______

HUSBAND ______ WIFE ______ DATE ______

DEATHS

NAME ______ DATE ______

NAME ______ DATE ______

NAME ______ DATE ______

LIFE LESSONS *from*
THE INSPIRED WORD OF GOD

THE Inspirational STUDY BIBLE

MAX LUCADO
General Editor

LIFE LESSONS *from* THE INSPIRED WORD OF GOD

THE Inspirational STUDY BIBLE

MAX LUCADO

General Editor

New King James Version

WORD BIBLES

Dallas • London • Vancouver • Melbourne

THE INSPIRATIONAL STUDY BIBLE

Design, typesetting, and cover art by Koechel Peterson and Associates, Inc., Minneapolis, Minnesota.

Includes bibliographical references and index.
ISBN 0-8499-5123-2 (hard)

The General Editor's ACKNOWLEDGMENTS

On the title page of my Bible, I have copied two verses. The first is from Mark 12:37.

And the common people heard Him gladly.

What a compliment! "You ought to go hear this guy speak," people must have said, "It's a treat to listen to him." When Jesus spoke, people listened. And when the people listened, they listened with joy. His message was clear. His stories were stirring, and his point was unforgettable.

Wouldn't it be great if the same were true today? What if every time Jesus' words were read, the people "heard Him gladly"? What if people perked up when the Bible was opened? What if people passed out copies of the Bible saying, "You ought to read what this guy said. It's a treat."

Wouldn't that be great? I know some people who are committed to seeing it happen.

Let me introduce you to WORD Publishing. They are more than a publishing house, they are a people with a purpose. Every day they are thinking of ways to make God's Word more accessible and understandable. This Bible is the product of that desire.

The New King James Version of the Bible preserves the precise scholarship of the original King James Version while updating the literary form of the text. The most noticeable change is the deletion of seventeenth-century pronouns (*thee, thou*) and verb endings (*lovest*). The NKJV is a dependable version of the classic text in language that makes sense for today's readers.

This devotional version of the NKJV is a library worth of books in one volume. A team of diligent researchers has taken the best from hundreds of books and put it right where you need it—in the margin of your Bible.

My hat is off to the Livingstone Corporation led by Bruce Barton, Jim Galvin, Christopher Hudson, and Dave Veerman. Dave, I especially appreciate your help with the minor prophets. Only God knows the number of hours you poured into this project. But God does know, he *is not unjust to forget your work and labor of love which you have shown toward His name, in that you have ministered to the saints, and do minister* (Hebrews 6:10).

I salute my friends at WORD Publishing. What a terrific group! David Moberg deserves special mention. Without your devotion and dedication, this idea would still be that, an idea in a manila folder. Thanks for making it a reality.

Speaking of making ideas a reality, Karen Hill does that for me every day. Thanks Karen, for being more than an administrative assistant, you are a lifesaver. You put many good hours into this effort. Thanks so much.

And Denalyn, my wife, what can I say? The reason Solomon had seven hundred wives is because he was searching for someone like you.

One final word of gratitude before you turn the page. A word of thanks to you the reader. I consider you my friend. How can I do that, being that we have never met? Remember I mentioned that I have a couple of verses penned on the title page of my Bible? This is the second,

I am a companion of all who fear You, and of those who keep Your precepts (Psalm 119:63).

You must be a person who fears God, or you wouldn't be reading his Word. You must be a person who obeys his teachings, or you wouldn't be studying them. I applaud your hunger for the Bible. I commend your desire to know his Word. You are my friend. And for you, my friend, I pray as you study his message.

Max Lucado

PREFACE TO THE NEW KING JAMES VERSION

Purpose

In the preface to the 1611 edition, the translators of the Authorized Version, known popularly as the King James Bible, state that it was not their purpose "to make a new translation . . . but to make a good one better." Indebted to the earlier work of William Tyndale and others, they saw their best contribution to consist in revising and enhancing the excellence of the English versions which had sprung from the Reformation of the sixteenth century. In harmony with the purpose of the King James scholars, the translators and editors of the present work have not pursued a goal of innovation. They have perceived the Holy Bible, New King James Version, as a continuation of the labors of the earlier translators, thus unlocking for today's readers the spiritual treasures found especially in the Authorized Version of the Holy Scriptures.

A Living Legacy

For nearly four hundred years, and throughout several revisions of its English form, the King James Bible has been deeply revered among the English-speaking peoples of the world. The precision of translation for which it is historically renowned, and its majesty of style, have enabled that monumental version of the word of God to become the mainspring of the religion, language, and legal foundations of our civilization.

Although the Elizabethan period and our own era share in zeal for technical advance, the former period was more aggressively devoted to classical learning. Along with this awakened concern for the classics came a flourishing companion interest in the Scriptures, an interest that was enlivened by the conviction that the manuscripts were providentially handed down and were a trustworthy record of the inspired Word of God. The King James translators were committed to producing an English Bible that would be a precise translation, and by no means a paraphrase or a broadly approximate rendering. On the one hand, the scholars were almost as familiar with the original languages of the Bible as with their native English. On the other hand, their reverence for the divine Author and His Word assured a translation of the Scriptures in which only a principle of utmost accuracy could be accepted.

In 1786 Catholic scholar Alexander Geddes said of the King James Bible, "If accuracy and strictest attention to the letter of the text be supposed to constitute an excellent version, this is of all versions the most excellent." George Bernard Shaw became a literary legend in our century because of his severe and often humorous criticisms of our most cherished values. Surprisingly, however, Shaw pays the following tribute to the scholars commissioned by King James: "The translation was extraordinarily well done because to the translators what they were translating was not merely a curious collection of ancient books written by different authors in different stages of culture, but the Word of God divinely revealed through His chosen and expressly inspired scribes. In this conviction they carried out their work with boundless reverence and care and achieved a beautifully artistic result." History agrees with these estimates. Therefore, while seeking to unveil the excellent *form* of the traditional English Bible, special care has also been taken in the present edition to preserve the work of *precision* which is the legacy of the 1611 translators.

Complete Equivalence in Translation

Where new translation has been necessary in the New King James Version, the most complete representation of the original has been rendered by considering the history of usage and etymology of words in their contexts. This principle of complete equivalence seeks to preserve *all* of the information in the text, while presenting it in good literary form. Dynamic equivalence, a recent procedure in Bible translation, commonly results in paraphrasing where a more literal rendering is needed to reflect a specific and vital sense. For example, complete equivalence truly renders the original text in expressions such as "lifted her voice and wept" (Gen. 21:16); "I gave you cleanness of teeth" (Amos 4:6); "Jesus met them, saying, 'Rejoice!' " (Matt. 28:9); and " 'Woman, what does your concern have to do with Me?' " (John 2:4). Complete equivalence translates fully, in order to provide an English text that is both accurate and readable.

In keeping with the principle of complete equivalence, it is the policy to translate interjections which are commonly omitted in modern language renderings of the Bible. As an example, the interjection *behold,* in the older King James editions, continues to have a place in

English usage, especially in dramatically calling attention to a spectacular scene, or an event of profound importance such as the Immanuel prophecy of Isaiah 7:14. Consequently, *behold* is retained for these occasions in the present edition. However, the Hebrew and Greek originals for this word can be translated variously, depending on the circumstances in the passage. Therefore, in addition to *behold,* words such as *indeed, look, see,* and *surely* are also rendered to convey the appropriate sense suggested by the context in each case.

In faithfulness to God and to our readers, it was deemed appropriate that all participating scholars sign a statement affirming their belief in the verbal and plenary inspiration of Scripture, and in the inerrancy of the original autographs.

Devotional Quality

The King James scholars readily appreciated the intrinsic beauty of divine revelation. They accordingly disciplined their talents to render well-chosen English words of their time, as well as a graceful, often musical arrangement of language, which has stirred the hearts of Bible readers through the years. The translators, the committees, and the editors of the present edition, while sensitive to the late-twentieth-century English idiom, and while adhering faithfully to the Hebrew, Aramaic, and Greek texts, have sought to maintain those lyrical and devotional qualities that are so highly regarded in the Authorized Version. This devotional quality is especially apparent in the poetic and prophetic books, although even the relatively plain style of the Gospels and Epistles cannot strictly be likened, as sometimes suggested, to modern newspaper style. The Koine Greek of the New Testament is influenced by the Hebrew background of the writers, for whom even the gospel narratives were not merely flat utterance, but often song in various degrees of rhythm.

The Style

Students of the Bible applaud the timeless devotional character of our historic Bible. Yet it is also universally understood that our language, like all living languages, has undergone profound change since 1611. Subsequent revisions of the King James Bible have sought to keep abreast of changes in English speech. The present work is a further step toward this objective. Where obsolescence and other reading difficulties exist, present-day vocabulary, punctuation, and grammar have been carefully integrated. Words representing ancient objects, such as *chariot* and *phylactery,* have no modern substitutes and are therefore retained.

A special feature of the New King James Version is its conformity to the thought flow of the 1611 Bible. The reader discovers that the sequence and selection of words, phrases, and clauses of the new edition, while much clearer, are so close to the traditional that there is remarkable ease in listening to the reading of either edition while following with the other.

In the discipline of translating biblical and other ancient languages, a standard method of transliteration, that is, the English spelling of untranslated words, such as names of persons and places, has never been commonly adopted. In keeping with the design of the present work, the King James spelling of untranslated words is retained, although made uniform throughout. For example, instead of the spellings *Isaiah* and *Elijah* in the Old Testament, and *Esaias* and *Elias* in the New Testament, *Isaiah* and *Elijah* now appear in both Testaments.

King James doctrinal and theological terms, for example, *propitiation, justification,* and *sanctification,* are generally familiar to English-speaking peoples. Such terms have been retained except where the original language indicates need for a more precise translation.

Readers of the Authorized Version will immediately be struck by the absence of several pronouns: *thee, thou,* and *ye* are replaced by the simple *you,* while *your* and *yours* are substituted for *thy* and *thine* as applicable. *Thee, thou, thy* and *thine* were once forms of address to express a special relationship to human as well as divine persons. These pronouns are no longer part of our language. However, reverence for God in the present work is preserved by capitalizing pronouns, including *You, Your,* and *Yours,* which refer to Him. Additionally, capitalization of these pronouns benefits the reader by clearly distinguishing divine and human persons referred to in a passage. Without such capitalization the distinction is often obscure, because the antecedent of a pronoun is not always clear in the English translation.

In addition to the pronoun usages of the seventeenth century, the *-eth* and *-est* verb endings, so familiar in the earlier King James editions, are now obsolete.

Unless a speaker is schooled in these verb endings, there is common difficulty in selecting the correct form to be used with a given subject of the verb in vocal prayer. That is, should we use *love, loveth,* or *lovest? do, doeth, doest,* or *dost? have, hath,* or *hast?* Because these forms are obsolete, contemporary English usage has been substituted for the previous verb endings.

In older editions of the King James Version, the frequency of the connective *and* far exceeded the limits of present English usage. Also, biblical linguists agree that the Hebrew and Greek original words for this conjunction may commonly be translated otherwise, depending on the immediate context. Therefore, instead of *and,* alternatives such as *also, but, however, now, so, then,* and *thus* are accordingly rendered in the present edition, when the original language permits.

The real character of the Authorized Version does not reside in its archaic pronouns or verbs or other grammatical forms of the seventeenth century, but rather in the care taken by its scholars to impart the letter and spirit of the original text in a majestic and reverent style.

The Format

The format of the New King James Version is designed to enhance the vividness and devotional quality of the Holy Scriptures:

- Subject headings assist the reader to identify topics and transitions in the biblical content.
- Words or phrases in *italics* indicate expressions in the original language which require clarification by additional English words, as also done throughout the history of the King James Bible.
- *Oblique type* in the New Testament indicates a quotation from the Old Testament.
- Prose is divided into paragraphs to indicate the structure of thought.
- Poetry is structured as contemporary verse to reflect the poetic form and beauty of the passage in the original language.
- The covenant name of God was usually translated from the Hebrew as "LORD" or "GOD" (using capital letters as shown) in the King James Old Testament. This tradition is maintained. In the present edition the name is so capitalized whenever the covenant name is quoted in the New Testament from a passage in the Old Testament.

The Old Testament Text

The Hebrew Bible has come down to us through the scrupulous care of ancient scribes who copied the original text in successive generations. By the sixth century A.D. the scribes were succeeded by a group known as the Masoretes, who continued to preserve the sacred Scriptures for another five hundred years in a form known as the Masoretic Text. Babylonia, Palestine, and Tiberias were the main centers of Masoretic activity; but by the tenth century A.D. the Masoretes of Tiberias, led by the family of ben Asher, gained the ascendancy. Through subsequent editions, the ben Asher text became in the twelfth century the only recognized form of the Hebrew Scriptures.

Daniel Bomberg printed the first Rabbinic Bible in 1516–17; that work was followed in 1524–25 by a second edition prepared by Jacob ben Chayyim and also published by Bomberg. The text of ben Chayyim was adopted in most subsequent Hebrew Bibles, including those used by the King James translators. The ben Chayyim text was also used for the first two editions of Rudolph Kittel's *Biblia Hebraica* of 1906 and 1912. In 1937 Paul Kahle published a third edition of *Biblia Hebraica.* This edition was based on the oldest dated manuscript of the ben Asher text, the Leningrad Manuscript B19a (A.D. 1008), which Kahle regarded as superior to that used by ben Chayyim.

For the New King James Version the text used was the 1967/1977 Stuttgart edition of the *Biblia Hebraica,* with frequent comparisons being made with the Bomberg edition of 1524–25. The Septuagint (Greek) Version of the Old Testament and the Latin Vulgate also were consulted. In addition to referring to a variety of ancient versions of the Hebrew Scriptures, the New King James Version draws on the resources of relevant manuscripts from the Dead Sea caves. In the few places where the Hebrew was so obscure that the 1611 King James was compelled to follow one of the versions, but where information is now available to resolve the problems, the New King James Version follows the Hebrew text. Significant variations are recorded in the footnotes.

The New Testament Text

There is more manuscript support for the New Testament than for any other body of ancient literature. Over five thousand Greek, eight thousand Latin, and many more manuscripts in other languages attest the integrity of the New Testament. There is only one basic New Testament used by Protestants, Roman Catholics, and Orthodox, by conservatives and liberals. Minor variations in hand copying have appeared through the centuries, before mechanical printing began about A.D. 1450.

Some variations exist in the spelling of Greek words, in word order, and in similar details. These ordinarily do not show up in translation and do not affect the sense of the text in any way.

Other manuscript differences such as omission or inclusion of a word or a clause, and two paragraphs in the Gospels, should not overshadow the overwhelming degree of *agreement* which exists among the ancient records. Bible readers may be assured that the most important differences in English New Testaments of today are due, not to manuscript divergence, but to the way in which translators view the task of translation: How literally should the text be rendered? How does the translator view the matter of biblical inspiration? Does the translator adopt a paraphrase when a literal rendering would be quite clear and more to the point? The New King James Version follows the historic precedent of the Authorized Version in maintaining a literal approach to translation, except where the idiom of the original language cannot be translated directly into our tongue.

The King James New Testament was based on the traditional text of the Greek-speaking churches, first published in 1516, and later called the Textus Receptus or Received Text. Although based on the relatively few available manuscripts, these were representative of many more which existed at the time but only became known later. In the late nineteenth century, B. Westcott and F. Hort taught that this text had been officially edited by the fourth-century church, but a total lack of historical evidence for this event has forced a revision of the theory. It is now widely held that the Byzantine Text that largely supports the Textus Receptus has as much right as the Alexandrian or any other tradition to be weighed in determining the text of the New Testament. Those readings in the Textus Receptus which have weak support are indicated in the footnotes as being opposed by both Critical and Majority Texts (see "Footnotes").

Since the 1880s most contemporary translations of the New Testament have relied upon a relatively few manuscripts discovered chiefly in the late nineteenth and early twentieth centuries. Such translations depend primarily on two manuscripts, Codex Vaticanus and Codex Sinaiticus, because of their greater age. The Greek text obtained by using these sources and the related papyri (our most ancient manuscripts) is known as the Alexandrian Text. However, some scholars have grounds for doubting the faithfulness of Vaticanus and Sinaiticus, since they often disagree with one another, and Sinaiticus exhibits excessive omission.

A third viewpoint of New Testament scholarship holds that the best text is based on the consensus of the majority of existing Greek manuscripts. This text is called the Majority Text. Most of these manuscripts are in substantial agreement. Even though many are late, and none is earlier than the fifth century, usually their readings are verified by papyri, ancient versions, quotations from the early church fathers, or a combination of these. The Majority Text is similar to the Textus Receptus, but it corrects those readings which have little or no support in the Greek manuscript tradition.

Today, scholars agree that the science of New Testament textual criticism is in a state of flux. Very few scholars still favor the Textus Receptus as such, and then often for its historical prestige as the text of Luther, Calvin, Tyndale, and the King James Version. For about a century most have followed a Critical Text (so called because it is edited according to specific principles of textual criticism) which depends heavily upon the Alexandrian type of text. More recently many have abandoned this Critical Text (which is quite similar to the one edited by Westcott and Hort) for one that is more eclectic. Finally, a small but growing number of scholars prefer the Majority Text, which is close to the traditional text except in the Revelation.

In light of these facts, and also because the New King James Version is the fifth revision of a historic document translated from specific Greek texts, the editors decided to retain the traditional text in the body of the New Testament and to indicate major Critical and Majority Text variant readings in the footnotes. Although these variations are duly indicated in the footnotes of the present edition, it is most important to emphasize that fully eighty-five percent of the New Testament text is the same in the Textus Receptus, the Alexandrian Text, and the Majority Text.

Footnotes

Significant explanatory notes, alternate translations, and cross-references, as well as New Testament citations of Old Testament passages, are supplied in the footnotes.

Important textual variants in the Old Testament are identified in a standard form.

The textual notes in the present edition make no evaluation of readings, but do clearly indicate the manuscript sources of readings. They objectively present the facts without such tendentious remarks as "the best manuscripts omit" or "the most reliable manuscripts read." Such notes are value judgments that differ according to varying viewpoints on the text. By giving a clearly defined set of variants the New King James Version benefits readers of all textual persuasions.

Where significant variations occur in the New Testament Greek manuscripts, textual notes are classified as follows:

1. NU-Text
   These variations from the traditional text generally represent the Alexandrian or Egyptian type of text described previously in "The New Testament Text." They are found in the Critical Text published in the twenty-seventh edition of the Nestle-Aland Greek New Testament (N) and in the United Bible Societies' fourth edition (U), hence the acronym, "NU-Text."
2. M-Text
   This symbol indicates points of variation in the Majority Text from the traditional text, as also previously discussed in "The New Testament Text." It should be noted that M stands for whatever reading is printed in the published *Greek New Testament According to the Majority Text,* whether supported by overwhelming, strong, or only a divided majority textual tradition.

The textual notes reflect the scholarship of the past 150 years and will assist the reader to observe the variations between the different manuscript traditions of the New Testament. Such information is generally not available in English translations of the New Testament.

GENERAL INTRODUCTION

The Inspirational Study Bible is an exhilarating experience. As you read, you'll uncover a saga of suspense and intrigue. Flip over a few pages and find poetry and romance. Turn the page again and read tales of clashing conquerors, brave shepherds, and a captivating Carpenter. Chronicles of faith, miracles, misdeeds, and good deeds. Kings, queens, peasants—the uncommon and the commonplace. Mystery, suspense, intrigue, drama, humor, poetry, romance . . . it's all in these pages . . . stories of real people, with real problems, real joys, and a real Savior. All of that, plus some distinctive features to help you see that what happened on these pages is still happening today—that the truths of old are truths for our age.

Features

To enrich your study, this Bible has some unique features . . . some helpful tools to expand your understanding. You'll notice *Life Lessons* in the margins. Each *Life Lesson* contains a *Situation, Observation, Inspiration, Application,* and *Exploration.* The *Situation* gives a quick look into the context of the chapter: it answers the question, What's going on in this chapter?

The *Observation* goes beneath the action to explain the point of the action. What truth or lesson is noticeable in the action of these people?

The *Inspiration* takes a point or lesson found in the chapter and amplifies it. Excerpted from the writings of Christian authors, these inspirations extend the main point and give it a contemporary message that will be useful in your private devotion or for sharing with a group.

The *Application* brings the message home. "How can I use what I've learned in this chapter?" "Is there anything about my life that I should change as a result of what I've learned by reading this?"

The *Exploration* lists other Scriptures related to the same theme, for further study. Reading the *Exploration* verses provides a strong sense of the Bible as a complete story, rather than just a collection of short stories and lists of rules.

Scattered throughout the text you will discover full page devotional thoughts. These encouraging pages will reveal what God thinks about you. Use the Topical Index to Selected Readings in the back of the Bible for additional insight on similar topics.

You will also find other helpful features in this Bible. A Dictionary is located in the back of the Bible. Use this section to find a specific verse, or to look up words you wish to study further or are unfamiliar with.

The Bible's One Hundred Greatest Thoughts have been captured for you as well and are organized by topic. When you feel defeated or discouraged, turn to these pages in the back of the Bible and discover how God meets your need.

Reading Program

Designed to inspire you in your daily walk, the study-helps are streamlined for ease of use. The comments are quick, tightly-written nuggets to give you the most information in the briefest format possible, to assist your search for understanding. How do you use *The Inspirational Study Bible*? The *Life Lessons* coincide with the chapters they address. It is best to read the *Situation* first. Then read the chapter. Go to the *Observation*—is this the point you understood as you read the action? Move on to the *Inspiration*. If you're in a class, read and discuss the *Inspiration*, then use the *Application* for further discussion. If you are studying alone, keep a journal of your commitment to new goals suggested by the *Application*.

A Brief Note to Parents and Teachers

This Bible is adaptable to any age group, and is especially useful with mixed-age groups. For adults, the margin information can be used to initiate further study and discussion. For families or in children's classes, they can be used as self-contained devotionals. The *Inspirations* are particularly useful in demonstrating that people of Bible times encountered similar problems to situations occurring today . . . the same hopes, fears, desires, sins, and successes.

HOW TO STUDY THE BIBLE

by MAX LUCADO

This is a peculiar book you are holding. Words crafted in another language. Deeds done in a distant era. Events recorded in a far-off land. Counsel offered to a foreign people. This is a peculiar book.

It's surprising that anyone reads it. It's too old. Some of its writings date back five thousand years. It's too bizarre. The book speaks of incredible floods, fires, earthquakes, and people with supernatural abilities. It's too radical. The Bible calls for undying devotion to a carpenter who called himself God's Son.

Logic says this book shouldn't survive. Too old, too bizarre, too radical.

The Bible has been banned, burned, scoffed, and ridiculed. Scholars have mocked it as foolish. Kings have branded it as illegal. A thousand times over it the grave has been dug and the dirge has begun, but somehow the Bible never stays in the grave. Not only has it survived, it has thrived. It is the single most popular book in all of history. It has been the best-selling book in the world for years!

There is no way on earth to explain it. Which perhaps is the only explanation. The answer? The Bible's durability is not found on earth; it is found in heaven. For the millions who have tested its claims and claimed its promises there is but one answer—the Bible is God's book and God's voice.

As you read it, you would be wise to give some thought to two questions. What is the purpose of the Bible? and How do I study the Bible? Time spent reflecting on these two issues will greatly enhance your Bible study.

What is the purpose of the Bible?

Let the Bible itself answer that question.

From childhood you have known the Holy Scriptures, which are able to make you wise for salvation through faith which is in Christ Jesus (2 Timothy 3:15).

The purpose of the Bible? Salvation. God's highest passion is to get his children home. His book, the Bible, describes his plan of salvation. The purpose of the Bible is to proclaim God's plan and passion to save his children.

That is the reason this book has endured through the centuries. It dares to tackle the toughest questions about life: Where do I go after I die? Is there a God? What do I do with my fears? The Bible offers answers to these crucial questions. It is the treasure map that leads us to God's highest treasure, eternal life.

But how do we use the Bible? Countless copies of Scripture sit unread on bookshelves and nightstands simply because people don't know how to read it. What can we do to make the Bible real in our lives?

The clearest answer is found in the words of Jesus. *"Ask,"* he promised, *"and it will be given to you; seek and you will find; knock, and it will be opened to you"* (Matthew 7:7).

The first step in understanding the Bible is asking God to help us. We should read prayerfully. If anyone understands God's Word it is because of God and not the reader.

But the Helper, the Holy Spirit, whom the Father will send in My name, He will teach you all things, and bring to your remembrance all things that I said to you (John 14:26).

Before reading the Bible, pray. Invite God to speak to you. Don't go to Scripture looking for your idea, go searching for his.

Not only should we read the Bible prayerfully, we should read it carefully. *Seek and you will find*, is the pledge. The Bible is not a newspaper to be skimmed but rather a mine to be quarried. *If you seek her as silver, and search for her as for hidden treasures; then you will understand the fear of the LORD, and find knowledge of God* (Proverbs 2:4, 5).

Any worthy find requires effort. The Bible is no exception. To understand the Bible you don't have to be brilliant, but you must be willing to roll up your sleeves and search.

Be a worker who does not need to be ashamed, rightly dividing the word of truth (2 Timothy 2:15).

Here's a practical point. Study the Bible a bit at a time. Hunger is not satisfied by eating twenty-one meals in one sitting once a week. The body needs a steady diet to remain strong. So does the soul. When God sent food to his people in the wilderness, he didn't provide loaves already made. Instead, he sent them manna, *a small round substance, as fine as frost on the ground* (Exodus 16:14).

God gave manna in limited portions.

God sends spiritual food the same way. He opens the heavens with just enough nutrients for today's hunger. He provides, *precept upon precept, line upon line, line upon line, here a little, there a little* (Isaiah 28:10).

Don't be discouraged if your reading reaps a small harvest. Some days a lesser portion is all that is needed. What is important is to search every day for that day's message. A steady diet of God's Word over a lifetime builds a healthy soul and mind.

A little girl returned from her first day at school. Her mom asked, "Did you learn anything?" "Apparently not enough," the girl responded. "I have to go back tomorrow and the next day and the next . . ."

Such is the case with learning. And such is the case with Bible study. Understanding comes little by little over a lifetime.

There is a third step in understanding the Bible. After the asking and seeking comes the knocking. After you ask and search, then knock.

Knock, and it will be opened for you (Matthew 7:7).

To knock is to stand at God's door. To make yourself available. To climb the steps, cross the porch, stand at the doorway, and volunteer. Knocking goes beyond the realm of thinking and into the realm of acting.

To knock is to ask, What can I do? How can I obey? Where can I go?

It's one thing to know what to do. It's another to do it. But for those who do it, those who choose to obey, a special reward awaits them.

But he who looks into the perfect law of liberty and continues in it, and is not a forgetful hearer but a doer of the work, this one will be blessed in what he does (James 1:25).

What a promise. Happiness comes to those who do what they read! It's the same with medicine. If you only read the label but ignore the pills, it won't help. It's the same with food. If you only read the recipe but never cook, you won't be fed. And it's the same with the Bible. If you only read the words but never obey, you'll never know the joy God has promised.

Ask. Seek. Knock. Simple, isn't it? Why don't you give it a try? If you do, you'll see why you are holding the most remarkable book in history.

OLD TESTAMENT

NEW TESTAMENT

THE OLD TESTAMENT

The First Book of Moses Called

GENESIS

INTRODUCTION

So there you are, a teenager at your grandparents' house. You don't really want to be there, but it's one of those family things and so you're there.

You sit politely and act like you are listening as your folks and grandparents talk. Then your grandmother says something that catches your attention. She refers to your great-grandfather and the trip he made to America from the "old country."

"What?" you ask.

Grandma smiles, knowing that at some point we all wonder about our origin and here you are wondering about yours.

She unravels a tale of your family escaping persecution and settling in eastern Virginia. Next she invites you into her room, where she opens a large chest that has sat at the foot of her bed for as long as you can remember. A rush of cedar and mothballs fills the room.

"Thought you might like to see this," she explains, handing you a black-and-white photo in a large walnut frame. "It's your great-grandpa." The only thing stiffer than his collar is his expression. "Here is his father," she hands you another photo, one of a cowboy wearing a wide-brimmed hat, riding a horse.

Piece by piece, the chest tells its family tales. Soon you find yourself lost in a floor covered with old wedding gowns, photo albums, diplomas, and bronzed baby shoes. And before you leave, you find yourself the owner of something precious—a heritage. An ancestry. A beginning. An origin.

You know that you are a part of a family tree. You aren't an isolated pond, but rather a part of a river winding through a great canyon.

You leave a richer person. Knowing where you came from says much about where you are going.

Perhaps that's why the first book of the Bible is a book of beginnings. God wants us to know from where we came. Learning that will teach us much about the place we are going.

LIFE LESSON

Genesis 1:1–2:3

SITUATION The magnificent story of The Beginning revealed God's creativity, majesty, and love. Yet the most humbling, puzzling, and awe-inspiring act took place when God breathed the breath of life into humanity.

OBSERVATION God demonstrated power and love by creating. With only a spoken word God created everything around us. Then, with loving care, he formed Adam out of the ground.

INSPIRATION With one decision, history began. Existence became measurable.

Out of nothing came light.

Out of light came day.

Then came sky . . . and earth.

And on this earth? A mighty hand went to work.

Canyons were carved. Oceans were dug. Mountains erupted out of flatlands. Stars were flung. A universe sparkled.

Our sun became just one of millions. Our galaxy became just one of thousands. Planets invisibly tethered to suns roared through space at breakneck speeds. Stars blazed with heat that could melt our planet in seconds.

The hand behind it was mighty. He is mighty.

And with this might, he created. As naturally as a bird sings and a fish swims, he created. Just as an artist can't not paint and a runner can't not run, he couldn't not create. He was the Creator. Through and through, he was the Creator. A tireless dreamer and designer.

The History of Creation

In the beginning God created the heavens and the earth. [2]The earth
was without form, and void; and darkness *was*[a] on the face of
the deep. And the Spirit of God was hovering over the face of
the waters.
[3]Then God said, "Let there be light"; and there was light. [4]And God saw
the light, that *it was* good; and God divided the light from the darkness.
[5]God called the light Day, and the darkness He called Night. So the evening
and the morning were the first day.
[6]Then God said, "Let there be a firmament in the midst of the waters,
and let it divide the waters from the waters." [7]Thus God made the firmament,
and divided the waters which *were* under the firmament from the
waters which *were* above the firmament; and it was so. [8]And God called the
firmament Heaven. So the evening and the morning were the second day.
[9]Then God said, "Let the waters under the heavens be gathered together
into one place, and let the dry *land* appear"; and it was so. [10]And God called
the dry *land* Earth, and the gathering together of the waters He called Seas.
And God saw that *it was* good.
[11]Then God said, "Let the earth bring forth grass, the herb *that* yields
seed, *and* the fruit tree *that* yields fruit according to its kind, whose seed *is*
in itself, on the earth"; and it was so. [12]And the earth brought forth grass,
the herb *that* yields seed according to its kind, and the tree *that* yields fruit,
whose seed *is* in itself according to its kind. And God saw that *it was* good.
[13]So the evening and the morning were the third day.
[14]Then God said, "Let there be lights in the firmament of the heavens to
divide the day from the night; and let them be for signs and seasons, and
for days and years; [15]and let them be for lights in the firmament of the
heavens to give light on the earth"; and it was so. [16]Then God made two
great lights: the greater light to rule the day, and the lesser light to rule the
night. *He made* the stars also. [17]God set them in the firmament of the heavens
to give light on the earth, [18]and to rule over the day and over the night,
and to divide the light from the darkness. And God saw that *it was* good.
[19]So the evening and the morning were the fourth day.
[20]Then God said, "Let the waters abound with an abundance of living
creatures, and let birds fly above the earth across the face of the firmament
of the heavens." [21]So God created great sea creatures and every living
thing that moves, with which the waters abounded, according to their
kind, and every winged bird according to its kind. And God saw that *it was*
good. [22]And God blessed them, saying, "Be fruitful and multiply, and fill
the waters in the seas, and let birds multiply on the earth." [23]So the
evening and the morning were the fifth day.
[24]Then God said, "Let the earth bring forth the living creature according
to its kind: cattle and creeping thing and beast of the earth, *each* according
to its kind"; and it was so. [25]And God made the beast of the earth
according to its kind, cattle according to its kind, and everything that
creeps on the earth according to its kind. And God saw that *it was* good.
[26]Then God said, "Let Us make man in Our image, according to Our
likeness; let them have dominion over the fish of the sea, over the birds of
the air, and over the cattle, over all[b] the earth and over every creeping thing

1:2 [a] Words in italic type have been added for clarity. They are not found in the original Hebrew or Aramaic.
1:26 [b] Syriac reads *all the wild animals of.*

that creeps on the earth." 27So God created man in His *own* image; in the
image of God He created him; male and female He created them. 28Then
God blessed them, and God said to them, "Be fruitful and multiply; fill the
earth and subdue it; have dominion over the fish of the sea, over the birds
of the air, and over every living thing that moves on the earth."
29And God said, "See, I have given you every herb *that* yields seed which
is on the face of all the earth, and every tree whose fruit yields seed; to you
it shall be for food. 30Also, to every beast of the earth, to every bird of the
air, and to everything that creeps on the earth, in which *there is* life, *I have*
given every green herb for food"; and it was so. 31Then God saw everything
that He had made, and indeed *it was* very good. So the evening and the
morning were the sixth day.

2 Thus the heavens and the earth, and all the host of them, were finished.
2And on the seventh day God ended His work which He had done, and
He rested on the seventh day from all His work which He had done. 3Then
God blessed the seventh day and sanctified it, because in it He rested from
all His work which God had created and made.
4This *is* the history[c] of the heavens and the earth when they were created, in the day that the LORD God made the earth and the heavens, 5before
any plant of the field was in the earth and before any herb of the field had
grown. For the LORD God had not caused it to rain on the earth, and *there*
was no man to till the ground; 6but a mist went up from the earth and
watered the whole face of the ground.
7And the LORD God formed man *of* the dust of the ground, and breathed
into his nostrils the breath of life; and man became a living being.

Life in God's Garden

8The LORD God planted a garden eastward in Eden, and there He put the
man whom He had formed. 9And out of the ground the LORD God made
every tree grow that is pleasant to the sight and good for food. The tree of
life *was* also in the midst of the garden, and the tree of the knowledge of
good and evil.
10Now a river went out of Eden to water the garden, and from there it
parted and became four riverheads. 11The name of the first *is* Pishon; it *is*
the one which skirts the whole land of Havilah, where *there is* gold. 12And
the gold of that land *is* good. Bdellium and the onyx stone *are* there. 13The
name of the second river *is* Gihon; it *is* the one which goes around the
whole land of Cush. 14The name of the third river *is* Hiddekel;[d] it *is* the one
which goes toward the east of Assyria. The fourth river *is* the Euphrates.
15Then the LORD God took the man and put him in the garden of Eden
to tend and keep it. 16And the LORD God commanded the man, saying, "Of
every tree of the garden you may freely eat; 17but of the tree of the knowledge of good and evil you shall not eat, for in the day that you eat of it you
shall surely die."
18And the LORD God said, "*It is* not good that man should be alone; I will
make him a helper comparable to him." 19Out of the ground the LORD God
formed every beast of the field and every bird of the air, and brought *them*
to Adam to see what he would call them. And whatever Adam called each
living creature, that *was* its name. 20So Adam gave names to all cattle, to

2:4 [c] Hebrew *toledoth,* literally *generations*
2:14 [d] Or *Tigris*

From the pallet of the Ageless Artist came inimitable splendors. Before there was a person to see it, his creation was pregnant with wonder. . . .

Mundaneness found no home in his universe. . . .

Probe deep within him. Explore every corner. Search every angle. Love is all you find. Go to the beginning of every decision he has made and you'll find it. Go to the end of every story he has told and you'll see it.

Love. . . .

He created a paradise. A sinless sanctuary. A haven before fear. A home before there was a human dweller. No time. No death. No hurt. A gift built by God for his ultimate creation. And when he was through, he knew "it was very good."

But it wasn't enough.

His greatest work hadn't been completed. One final masterpiece was needed before he would stop.

Look to the canyons to see the Creator's splendor. Touch the flowers and see his delicacy. Listen to the thunder and hear his power. But gaze on [humanity]—the zenith—and witness all three . . . and more.

(From *In the Eye of the Storm* by Max Lucado)

APPLICATION Today you will encounter God's creation. When you see the beauty around you, let each detail remind you to lift your head in praise. Express your appreciation for God's creation. Encourage others to see the beauty of his creation.

EXPLORATION God the Creator—Nehemiah 9:6; Job 26:7; Psalm 102:25; Acts 14:15; Hebrews 11:3.

the birds of the air, and to every beast of the field. But for Adam there was
not found a helper comparable to him.
21 And the LORD God caused a deep sleep to fall on Adam, and he slept;
and He took one of his ribs, and closed up the flesh in its place. 22 Then the
rib which the LORD God had taken from man He made into a woman, and
He brought her to the man.
23 And Adam said:

> "This *is* now bone of my bones
> And flesh of my flesh;
> She shall be called Woman,
> Because she was taken out of Man."

24 Therefore a man shall leave his father and mother and be joined to his
wife, and they shall become one flesh.
25 And they were both naked, the man and his wife, and were not
ashamed.

The Temptation and Fall of Man

3 Now the serpent was more cunning than any beast of the field which
the LORD God had made. And he said to the woman, "Has God indeed
said, 'You shall not eat of every tree of the garden'?"
2 And the woman said to the serpent, "We may eat the fruit of the trees of
the garden; 3 but of the fruit of the tree which *is* in the midst of the garden,
God has said, 'You shall not eat it, nor shall you touch it, lest you die.' "
4 Then the serpent said to the woman, "You will not surely die. 5 For God
knows that in the day you eat of it your eyes will be opened, and you will
be like God, knowing good and evil."
6 So when the woman saw that the tree *was* good for food, that it *was*
pleasant to the eyes, and a tree desirable to make *one* wise, she took of its
fruit and ate. She also gave to her husband with her, and he ate. 7 Then the
eyes of both of them were opened, and they knew that they *were* naked;
and they sewed fig leaves together and made themselves coverings.
8 And they heard the sound of the LORD God walking in the garden in the
cool of the day, and Adam and his wife hid themselves from the presence
of the LORD God among the trees of the garden.
9 Then the LORD God called to Adam and said to him, "Where *are* you?"
10 So he said, "I heard Your voice in the garden, and I was afraid because
I was naked; and I hid myself."
11 And He said, "Who told you that you *were* naked? Have you eaten from
the tree of which I commanded you that you should not eat?"
12 Then the man said, "The woman whom You gave *to be* with me, she
gave me of the tree, and I ate."
13 And the LORD God said to the woman, "What *is* this you have done?"
The woman said, "The serpent deceived me, and I ate."
14 So the LORD God said to the serpent:

> "Because you have done this,
> You *are* cursed more than all cattle,
> And more than every beast of the field;
> On your belly you shall go,
> And you shall eat dust
> All the days of your life.

LIFE LESSON

Genesis 2:4–3:24

SITUATION God the Creator completed his masterpiece by creating man and woman. God breathed life and spirit into his special handiwork. Though sin entered the world, God also provided for redemption from sin.

OBSERVATION God created people with the freedom to choose or reject him. When his creation chose to rebel, God revealed his plan for salvation.

INSPIRATION He placed one scoop of clay upon another until a form lay lifeless on the ground. . . .

All were silent as the Creator reached in himself and removed something yet unseen. "It's called 'choice.' The seed of choice."

Creation stood in silence and gazed upon the lifeless form.

An angel spoke, "But what if he . . . ."

"What if he chooses not to love?" the Creator finished. "Come, I will show you."

Unbound by today, God and the angel walked into the realm of tomorrow. . . .

The angel gasped at what he saw. Spontaneous love. Voluntary devotion. Never had he seen anything like these. . . . The angel stood speechless as they passed through centuries of repugnance. Never had he seen such filth. Rotten hearts. Ruptured promises. Forgotten loyalties. . . .

The Creator walked on in time, further and further into the future, until he stood by a tree. A tree that would be fashioned into a cradle. Even then he could smell the hay that would surround him. . . .

"Wouldn't it be easier to not plant the seed? Wouldn't it be easier to not give the choice?"

"It would," the Creator spoke slowly. "But to remove the choice is to remove the love."

15 And I will put enmity
Between you and the woman,
And between your seed and her Seed;
He shall bruise your head,
And you shall bruise His heel."

16To the woman He said:

"I will greatly multiply your sorrow and your conception;
In pain you shall bring forth children;
Your desire *shall be* for your husband,
And he shall rule over you."

17Then to Adam He said, "Because you have heeded the voice of your wife, and have eaten from the tree of which I commanded you, saying, 'You shall not eat of it':

"Cursed *is* the ground for your sake;
In toil you shall eat *of* it
All the days of your life.
18 Both thorns and thistles it shall bring forth for you,
And you shall eat the herb of the field.
19 In the sweat of your face you shall eat bread
Till you return to the ground,
For out of it you were taken;
For dust you *are*,
And to dust you shall return."

20And Adam called his wife's name Eve, because she was the mother of all living.

21Also for Adam and his wife the LORD God made tunics of skin, and clothed them.

22Then the LORD God said, "Behold, the man has become like one of Us,
to know good and evil. And now, lest he put out his hand and take also of
the tree of life, and eat, and live forever"— 23therefore the LORD God sent
him out of the garden of Eden to till the ground from which he was taken.
24So He drove out the man; and He placed cherubim at the east of the garden of Eden, and a flaming sword which turned every way, to guard the way to the tree of life.

Cain Murders Abel

4 Now Adam knew Eve his wife, and she conceived and bore Cain, and
said, "I have acquired a man from the LORD." 2Then she bore again,
this time his brother Abel. Now Abel was a keeper of sheep, but Cain was a
tiller of the ground. 3And in the process of time it came to pass that Cain
brought an offering of the fruit of the ground to the LORD. 4Abel also
brought of the firstborn of his flock and of their fat. And the LORD respected Abel and his offering, 5but He did not respect Cain and his offering. And Cain was very angry, and his countenance fell.

6So the LORD said to Cain, "Why are you angry? And why has your countenance fallen? 7If you do well, will you not be accepted? And if you do not do well, sin lies at the door. And its desire *is* for you, but you should rule over it."

. . . They stepped into the Garden again. The Maker looked earnestly at the clay creation. A monsoon of love swelled up within him. He had died for the creation before he had made him. God's form bent over the sculptured face and breathed. Dust stirred on the lips of the new one. The chest rose, cracking the red mud. The cheeks fleshened. A finger moved. And an eye opened.

But more incredible than the moving of the flesh was the stirring of the spirit. Those who could see the unseen gasped.

Perhaps it was the wind who said it first. Perhaps what the star saw that moment is what has made it blink ever since. Maybe it was left to an angel to whisper it:

"It looks like . . . it appears so much like . . . it is him!"

The angel wasn't speaking of the face, the features, or the body. He was looking inside—at the soul.

"It's eternal!" gasped another.

Within the man, God had placed a divine seed. A seed of his self. The God of might had created earth's mightiest. The Creator had created, not a creature, but another creator. And the One who had chosen to love had created one who could love in return.

Now it's our choice.

(From *In the Eye of the Storm* by Max Lucado)

APPLICATION God did not create us as robots. Praise him for giving us the ability to serve and love him purposefully. Thank him for his gifts of freedom and creativity. Set aside time today for creative praise. Make that choice today.

EXPLORATION Human Spirit—Job 32:8; Ecclesiastes 12:7; Acts 7:59.

LIFE LESSON

Genesis 4:1–5:32

SITUATION After Adam sinned in the Garden of Eden (Gen. 3), sin affected the life and death of every living creature. Sin and death reigned in every individual. Enoch, the one notable exception to this reign of sin and death, "walked with God."

OBSERVATION Cain illustrates what happens to people who sin and then deny or justify their misbehavior. When we sin, fear, guilt, grief, anger, resentment, humiliation, loss of integrity, and even self-loathing follow. Often we choose to sin and try to ignore these consequences, but God mercifully offers us a way out.

INSPIRATION The Bible abounds with examples of men and women whose worlds crashed from self-inflicted causes, and their responses range within great extremes.

On the dark side of those extremes is the case study of Cain. Jealous of his brother, Cain killed him, denying continually that he was answerable for his attitudes and actions. As far as we know, he never brooded on the warnings that could have helped him avoid the tragedies that occurred. He appears to have ended up living a thoroughly wasted life. Cain represents the rigidity, the hardness of inner being, that can appear when the heat is on and consequences set in. Cain is not alone when it comes to those who will not accept accountability for their actions.

On the brighter side of the extremes, a woman, Mary Magdalene, came through her broken-world experience, permitting the moment to become the beginning of an entirely new life. She was one of the numerous New Testament characters who pursued

8 Now Cain talked with Abel his brother;[e] and it came to pass, when they
were in the field, that Cain rose up against Abel his brother and killed him.
9 Then the LORD said to Cain, "Where *is* Abel your brother?"
He said, "I do not know. *Am* I my brother's keeper?"
10 And He said, "What have you done? The voice of your brother's blood
cries out to Me from the ground. 11 So now you *are* cursed from the earth,
which has opened its mouth to receive your brother's blood from your
hand. 12 When you till the ground, it shall no longer yield its strength to
you. A fugitive and a vagabond you shall be on the earth."
13 And Cain said to the LORD, "My punishment *is* greater than I can bear!
14 Surely You have driven me out this day from the face of the ground; I
shall be hidden from Your face; I shall be a fugitive and a vagabond on the
earth, and it will happen *that* anyone who finds me will kill me."
15 And the LORD said to him, "Therefore,[f] whoever kills Cain, vengeance
shall be taken on him sevenfold." And the LORD set a mark on Cain, lest
anyone finding him should kill him.

The Family of Cain

16 Then Cain went out from the presence of the LORD and dwelt in the
land of Nod on the east of Eden. 17 And Cain knew his wife, and she conceived and bore Enoch. And he built a city, and called the name of the city
after the name of his son—Enoch. 18 To Enoch was born Irad; and Irad
begot Mehujael, and Mehujael begot Methushael, and Methushael begot
Lamech.
19 Then Lamech took for himself two wives: the name of one *was* Adah,
and the name of the second *was* Zillah. 20 And Adah bore Jabal. He was the
father of those who dwell in tents and have livestock. 21 His brother's name
was Jubal. He was the father of all those who play the harp and flute. 22 And
as for Zillah, she also bore Tubal-Cain, an instructor of every craftsman in
bronze and iron. And the sister of Tubal-Cain *was* Naamah.
23 Then Lamech said to his wives:

"Adah and Zillah, hear my voice;
Wives of Lamech, listen to my speech!
For I have killed a man for wounding me,
Even a young man for hurting me.
24 If Cain shall be avenged sevenfold,
Then Lamech seventy-sevenfold."

A New Son

25 And Adam knew his wife again, and she bore a son and named him
Seth, "For God has appointed another seed for me instead of Abel, whom
Cain killed." 26 And as for Seth, to him also a son was born; and he named
him Enosh.[g] Then *men* began to call on the name of the LORD.

The Family of Adam

5 This is the book of the genealogy of Adam. In the day that God created
man, He made him in the likeness of God. 2 He created them male and
female, and blessed them and called them Mankind in the day they were

4:8 [e] Samaritan Pentateuch, Septuagint, Syriac, and Vulgate add *"Let us go out to the field."*
4:15 [f] Following Masoretic Text and Targum; Septuagint, Syriac, and Vulgate read *Not so.*
4:26 [g] Greek *Enos*

created. 3And Adam lived one hundred and thirty years, and begot *a son*
in his own likeness, after his image, and named him Seth. 4After he begot
Seth, the days of Adam were eight hundred years; and he had sons and
daughters. 5So all the days that Adam lived were nine hundred and thirty
years; and he died.
6Seth lived one hundred and five years, and begot Enosh. 7After he
begot Enosh, Seth lived eight hundred and seven years, and had sons and
daughters. 8So all the days of Seth were nine hundred and twelve years;
and he died.
9Enosh lived ninety years, and begot Cainan.[h] 10After he begot Cainan,
Enosh lived eight hundred and fifteen years, and had sons and daughters.
11So all the days of Enosh were nine hundred and five years; and he died.
12Cainan lived seventy years, and begot Mahalalel. 13After he begot
Mahalalel, Cainan lived eight hundred and forty years, and had sons and
daughters. 14So all the days of Cainan were nine hundred and ten years;
and he died.
15Mahalalel lived sixty-five years, and begot Jared. 16After he begot
Jared, Mahalalel lived eight hundred and thirty years, and had sons and
daughters. 17So all the days of Mahalalel were eight hundred and ninety-
five years; and he died.
18Jared lived one hundred and sixty-two years, and begot Enoch. 19After
he begot Enoch, Jared lived eight hundred years, and had sons and daughters. 20So all the days of Jared were nine hundred and sixty-two years; and
he died.
21Enoch lived sixty-five years, and begot Methuselah. 22After he begot
Methuselah, Enoch walked with God three hundred years, and had sons
and daughters. 23So all the days of Enoch were three hundred and sixty-five
years. 24And Enoch walked with God; and he *was* not, for God took him.
25Methuselah lived one hundred and eighty-seven years, and begot
Lamech. 26After he begot Lamech, Methuselah lived seven hundred and
eighty-two years, and had sons and daughters. 27So all the days of
Methuselah were nine hundred and sixty-nine years; and he died.
28Lamech lived one hundred and eighty-two years, and had a son. 29And
he called his name Noah, saying, "This *one* will comfort us concerning our
work and the toil of our hands, because of the ground which the LORD has
cursed." 30After he begot Noah, Lamech lived five hundred and ninety-
five years, and had sons and daughters. 31So all the days of Lamech were
seven hundred and seventy-seven years; and he died.
32And Noah was five hundred years old, and Noah begot Shem, Ham,
and Japheth.

The Wickedness and Judgment of Man

6 Now it came to pass, when men began to multiply on the face of the
earth, and daughters were born to them, 2that the sons of God saw the
daughters of men, that they *were* beautiful; and they took wives for themselves of all whom they chose.
3And the LORD said, "My Spirit shall not strive[i] with man forever, for he
is indeed flesh; yet his days shall be one hundred and twenty years."
4There were giants on the earth in those days, and also afterward, when

5:9 [h] Hebrew *Qenan*
6:3 [i] Septuagint, Syriac, Targum, and Vulgate read *abide*.

lives of gross immorality and who virtually personified the energy of evil itself. She was obviously living in a kind of human bondage with no hope. No one had to tell her that her way of living was taking her downhill fast, that changes had to be made, or there would be no turning back. When Jesus offered the opportunity of liberation to her, she accepted what was given and rebuilt her broken world into something beautiful.

So there is Cain: stiff-necked and unrelenting. And there is Mary: open, unfisted, and ready to submit. All of us have seen samples, perhaps in ourselves as well as in others. . . .

When my sinful act resulted in a personal broken world, Gail and I chose to wrestle with a significant question that one of our pastoral advisors placed before us. The wording went something like this: *will you concentrate on the pain of this broken-world experience and resist it, OR will you permit the pain to become an environment in which God can clearly speak to you about matters He deems of ultimate importance? The choice is yours.*

(From *Rebuilding Your Broken World* by Gordon MacDonald)

APPLICATION Perhaps you face a similar choice as a broken-world person living with self-inflicted wounds. Or maybe you are the victim of a broken-world set of consequences. Identify the sin. Confess it. Turn from it. Avoid it at all costs. Live with a clean, forgiven conscience. Don't dwell on what God has forgotten!

EXPLORATION Broken Worlds—Exodus 2–3; 2 Samuel 11–12; Psalm 51; Jonah 1–4; Matthew 26:69-75.

LIFE LESSON

Genesis 6:1–8:22

SITUATION The size of Noah's ark ensured that it could carry tens of thousands of animals. This dramatic event demonstrated God's wrath toward sin, but also his mercy toward those who seek him.

OBSERVATION Faithfulness to God remains vital, even if everyone around us marches to a different drumbeat.

INSPIRATION "You'll never catch *me* doing *that*," one might say. "Oh yeah?"

Upright and obedient, Noah stood alone against a carousing, lustful world that drank itself silly. Who would have thought Noah would end up drunk? Abraham was ready to push obedience to the point of sacrificing his only son. Who would imagine he would lie straight-faced?

Look at Lot standing against the filthiness of Sodom. Hardly does he get delivered from the city's destruction than he falls into incest. Who would have guessed? Bold and courageous David was brave enough to go up against Goliath, the warrior giant of the Philistines; later on he made believe that he was a madman for fear of his enemies.

And consider Elijah. We take him to be a rather brave man, wielding the sword of God's vengeance against

the sons of God came in to the daughters of men and they bore *children* to
them. Those *were* the mighty men who *were* of old, men of renown.
5Then the LORD[j] saw that the wickedness of man *was* great in the earth,
and *that* every intent of the thoughts of his heart *was* only evil continually.
6And the LORD was sorry that He had made man on the earth, and He was
grieved in His heart. 7So the LORD said, "I will destroy man whom I have
created from the face of the earth, both man and beast, creeping thing and
birds of the air, for I am sorry that I have made them." 8But Noah found
grace in the eyes of the LORD.

Noah Pleases God

9This is the genealogy of Noah. Noah was a just man, perfect in his generations. Noah walked with God. 10And Noah begot three sons: Shem,
Ham, and Japheth.
11The earth also was corrupt before God, and the earth was filled with
violence. 12So God looked upon the earth, and indeed it was corrupt; for all
flesh had corrupted their way on the earth.

The Ark Prepared

13And God said to Noah, "The end of all flesh has come before Me, for
the earth is filled with violence through them; and behold, I will destroy
them with the earth. 14Make yourself an ark of gopherwood; make rooms
in the ark, and cover it inside and outside with pitch. 15And this is how you
shall make it: The length of the ark *shall be* three hundred cubits, its width
fifty cubits, and its height thirty cubits. 16You shall make a window for the
ark, and you shall finish it to a cubit from above; and set the door of the
ark in its side. You shall make it *with* lower, second, and third *decks.* 17And
behold, I Myself am bringing floodwaters on the earth, to destroy from
under heaven all flesh in which *is* the breath of life; everything that *is* on
the earth shall die. 18But I will establish My covenant with you; and you
shall go into the ark—you, your sons, your wife, and your sons' wives with
you. 19And of every living thing of all flesh you shall bring two of every *sort*
into the ark, to keep *them* alive with you; they shall be male and female. 20Of
the birds after their kind, of animals after their kind, and of every creeping
thing of the earth after its kind, two of every *kind* will come to you to keep
them alive. 21And you shall take for yourself of all food that is eaten, and
you shall gather *it* to yourself; and it shall be food for you and for them."
22Thus Noah did; according to all that God commanded him, so he did.

The Great Flood

7 Then the LORD said to Noah, "Come into the ark, you and all your
household, because I have seen *that* you *are* righteous before Me in this
generation. 2You shall take with you seven each of every clean animal, a
male and his female; two each of animals that *are* unclean, a male and his
female; 3also seven each of birds of the air, male and female, to keep the
species alive on the face of all the earth. 4For after seven more days I will
cause it to rain on the earth forty days and forty nights, and I will destroy
from the face of the earth all living things that I have made." 5And Noah
did according to all that the LORD commanded him. 6Noah *was* six hundred years old when the floodwaters were on the earth.

6:5 *j* Following Masoretic Text and Targum; Vulgate reads *God;* Septuagint reads *LORD God.*

7So Noah, with his sons, his wife, and his sons' wives, went into the ark
because of the waters of the flood. 8Of clean animals, of animals that *are*
unclean, of birds, and of everything that creeps on the earth, 9two by two
they went into the ark to Noah, male and female, as God had commanded
Noah. 10And it came to pass after seven days that the waters of the flood
were on the earth. 11In the six hundredth year of Noah's life, in the second
month, the seventeenth day of the month, on that day all the fountains of
the great deep were broken up, and the windows of heaven were opened.
12And the rain was on the earth forty days and forty nights.

13On the very same day Noah and Noah's sons, Shem, Ham, and
Japheth, and Noah's wife and the three wives of his sons with them,
entered the ark— 14they and every beast after its kind, all cattle after their
kind, every creeping thing that creeps on the earth after its kind, and every
bird after its kind, every bird of every sort. 15And they went into the ark to
Noah, two by two, of all flesh in which *is* the breath of life. 16So those that
entered, male and female of all flesh, went in as God had commanded
him; and the LORD shut him in.

17Now the flood was on the earth forty days. The waters increased and
lifted up the ark, and it rose high above the earth. 18The waters prevailed
and greatly increased on the earth, and the ark moved about on the surface of the waters. 19And the waters prevailed exceedingly on the earth, and
all the high hills under the whole heaven were covered. 20The waters prevailed fifteen cubits upward, and the mountains were covered. 21And all
flesh died that moved on the earth: birds and cattle and beasts and every
creeping thing that creeps on the earth, and every man. 22All in whose
nostrils *was* the breath of the spirit[k] of life, all that *was* on the dry *land,*
died. 23So He destroyed all living things which were on the face of the
ground: both man and cattle, creeping thing and bird of the air. They were
destroyed from the earth. Only Noah and those who *were* with him in the
ark remained *alive.* 24And the waters prevailed on the earth one hundred
and fifty days.

Noah's Deliverance

8 Then God remembered Noah, and every living thing, and all the animals that *were* with him in the ark. And God made a wind to pass over
the earth, and the waters subsided. 2The fountains of the deep and the
windows of heaven were also stopped, and the rain from heaven was
restrained. 3And the waters receded continually from the earth. At the end
of the hundred and fifty days the waters decreased. 4Then the ark rested in
the seventh month, the seventeenth day of the month, on the mountains
of Ararat. 5And the waters decreased continually until the tenth month. In
the tenth *month,* on the first *day* of the month, the tops of the mountains
were seen.

6So it came to pass, at the end of forty days, that Noah opened the window of the ark which he had made. 7Then he sent out a raven, which kept
going to and fro until the waters had dried up from the earth. 8He also sent
out from himself a dove, to see if the waters had receded from the face of
the ground. 9But the dove found no resting place for the sole of her foot,
and she returned into the ark to him, for the waters *were* on the face of the

7:22 *k* Septuagint and Vulgate omit *of the spirit.*

tens of thousands. But the threat of one woman then sends him into suicidal despair.

Peter, as part of the inner circle, followed the footsteps of Jesus closer than anyone. He ended up cursing and denying the Lord.

"These things happened to them as examples and were written down as warnings for us, on whom the fulfillment of the ages has come" (1 Corinthians 10:11).

Just when you think you know yourself, you do or say something that seems so out of character. But it's not. The character of our body of sin and death is to sin. Don't be surprised. Just be careful that you, too, don't fall.

(From *Diamonds in the Dust* by Joni Eareckson Tada)

APPLICATION God wants us to stand against sin. Sometimes we must do it all by ourselves, but it is always easier to stand with others. If you are slugging it out alone, pray for a friend—someone with whom you can share the joys and struggles of faith.

EXPLORATION Faithful to God—1 Corinthians 10:13; 15:58; Galatians 5:1; Ephesians 6:14; 2 Thessalonians 2:15; Hebrews 2:18; 12:1-3; James 1:12; 1 Peter 5:8-9.

whole earth. So he put out his hand and took her, and
drew her into the ark to himself. 10And he waited yet
another seven days, and again he sent the dove out
from the ark. 11Then the dove came to him in the
evening, and behold, a freshly plucked olive leaf *was*
in her mouth; and Noah knew that the waters had
receded from the earth. 12So he waited yet another
seven days and sent out the dove, which did not
return again to him anymore.
13And it came to pass in the six hundred and first
year, in the first *month,* the first *day* of the month, that
the waters were dried up from the earth; and Noah
removed the covering of the ark and looked, and
indeed the surface of the ground was dry. 14And in the
second month, on the twenty-seventh day of the
month, the earth was dried.
15Then God spoke to Noah, saying, 16"Go out of the
ark, you and your wife, and your sons and your sons'
wives with you. 17Bring out with you every living
thing of all flesh that *is* with you: birds and cattle and
every creeping thing that creeps on the earth, so that
they may abound on the earth, and be fruitful and
multiply on the earth." 18So Noah went out, and his
sons and his wife and his sons' wives with him.
19Every animal, every creeping thing, every bird, *and*
whatever creeps on the earth, according to their families, went out of the ark.

God's Covenant with Creation

20Then Noah built an altar to the LORD, and took of
every clean animal and of every clean bird, and
offered burnt offerings on the altar. 21And the LORD
smelled a soothing aroma. Then the LORD said in His
heart, "I will never again curse the ground for man's
sake, although the imagination of man's heart *is* evil
from his youth; nor will I again destroy every living
thing as I have done.

22 "While the earth remains,
Seedtime and harvest,
Cold and heat,
Winter and summer,
And day and night
Shall not cease."

9 So God blessed Noah and his sons, and said to
them: "Be fruitful and multiply, and fill the earth.[l]
2And the fear of you and the dread of you shall be on
every beast of the earth, on every bird of the air, on all
that move *on* the earth, and on all the fish of the sea.
They are given into your hand. 3Every moving thing
that lives shall be food for you. I have given you all
things, even as the green herbs. 4But you shall not eat
flesh with its life, *that is,* its blood. 5Surely for your
lifeblood I will demand *a reckoning;* from the hand of
every beast I will require it, and from the hand of man.
From the hand of every man's brother I will require
the life of man.

6 "Whoever sheds man's blood,
By man his blood shall be shed;
For in the image of God
He made man.
7 And as for you, be fruitful and multiply;
Bring forth abundantly in the earth
And multiply in it."

8Then God spoke to Noah and to his sons with him,
saying: 9"And as for Me, behold, I establish My
covenant with you and with your descendants[m] after
you, 10and with every living creature that *is* with you:
the birds, the cattle, and every beast of the earth with
you, of all that go out of the ark, every beast of the
earth. 11Thus I establish My covenant with you: Never
again shall all flesh be cut off by the waters of the flood;
never again shall there be a flood to destroy the earth."
12And God said: "This *is* the sign of the covenant
which I make between Me and you, and every living
creature that *is* with you, for perpetual generations:
13I set My rainbow in the cloud, and it shall be for the
sign of the covenant between Me and the earth. 14It
shall be, when I bring a cloud over the earth, that the
rainbow shall be seen in the cloud; 15and I will
remember My covenant which *is* between Me and
you and every living creature of all flesh; the waters
shall never again become a flood to destroy all flesh.
16The rainbow shall be in the cloud, and I will look on
it to remember the everlasting covenant between God
and every living creature of all flesh that *is* on the
earth." 17And God said to Noah, "This *is* the sign of
the covenant which I have established between Me
and all flesh that *is* on the earth."

Noah and His Sons

18Now the sons of Noah who went out of the ark
were Shem, Ham, and Japheth. And Ham *was* the
father of Canaan. 19These three *were* the sons of Noah,
and from these the whole earth was populated.
20And Noah began *to be* a farmer, and he planted a
vineyard. 21Then he drank of the wine and was drunk,

9:1 [l] Compare Genesis 1:28
9:9 [m] Literally *seed*

and became uncovered in his tent. [22]And Ham, the father of Canaan, saw
the nakedness of his father, and told his two brothers outside. [23]But Shem
and Japheth took a garment, laid *it* on both their shoulders, and went
backward and covered the nakedness of their father. Their faces *were*
turned away, and they did not see their father's nakedness.
[24]So Noah awoke from his wine, and knew what his younger son had
done to him. [25]Then he said:

"Cursed *be* Canaan;
A servant of servants
He shall be to his brethren."

[26]And he said:

"Blessed *be* the LORD,
The God of Shem,
And may Canaan be his servant.
27 May God enlarge Japheth,
And may he dwell in the tents of Shem;
And may Canaan be his servant."

[28]And Noah lived after the flood three hundred and fifty years. [29]So all
the days of Noah were nine hundred and fifty years; and he died.

Nations Descended from Noah

10 Now this *is* the genealogy of the sons of Noah: Shem, Ham, and
Japheth. And sons were born to them after the flood.
[2]The sons of Japheth *were* Gomer, Magog, Madai, Javan, Tubal,
Meshech, and Tiras. [3]The sons of Gomer *were* Ashkenaz, Riphath,[n] and
Togarmah. [4]The sons of Javan *were* Elishah, Tarshish, Kittim, and
Dodanim.[o] [5]From these the coastland *peoples* of the Gentiles were separated into their lands, everyone according to his language, according to
their families, into their nations.
[6]The sons of Ham *were* Cush, Mizraim, Put,[p] and Canaan. [7]The sons of
Cush *were* Seba, Havilah, Sabtah, Raamah, and Sabtechah; and the sons of
Raamah *were* Sheba and Dedan.
[8]Cush begot Nimrod; he began to be a mighty one on the earth. [9]He was
a mighty hunter before the LORD; therefore it is said, "Like Nimrod the
mighty hunter before the LORD." [10]And the beginning of his kingdom was
Babel, Erech, Accad, and Calneh, in the land of Shinar. [11]From that land he
went to Assyria and built Nineveh, Rehoboth Ir, Calah, [12]and Resen
between Nineveh and Calah (that *is* the principal city).
[13]Mizraim begot Ludim, Anamim, Lehabim, Naphtuhim, [14]Pathrusim,
and Casluhim (from whom came the Philistines and Caphtorim).
[15]Canaan begot Sidon his firstborn, and Heth; [16]the Jebusite, the
Amorite, and the Girgashite; [17]the Hivite, the Arkite, and the Sinite; [18]the
Arvadite, the Zemarite, and the Hamathite. Afterward the families of the
Canaanites were dispersed. [19]And the border of the Canaanites was from
Sidon as you go toward Gerar, as far as Gaza; then as you go toward
Sodom, Gomorrah, Admah, and Zeboiim, as far as Lasha. [20]These *were* the

10:3 [n] Spelled *Diphath* in 1 Chronicles 1:6
10:4 [o] Spelled *Rodanim* in Samaritan Pentateuch and 1 Chronicles 1:7
10:6 [p] Or *Phut*

LIFE LESSON

Genesis 9:1–10:32

SITUATION God promised that he would never again destroy the earth with a flood. A rainbow would follow rain as a reminder that God keeps his promises. Man must treat all living creatures well.

OBSERVATION God created a special covenant with humans that gave them dominance over the earth, yet made them accountable to God for each action.

INSPIRATION There's hardly a more sobering statement in Scripture than Romans 14:12: "So then, each one of us will give an account of himself to God." The words "each one of us" apply to Christians and non-Christians alike. And though believers will be saved by grace and not by works, once in Heaven our reward there will be determined on the basis of our works. The Lord will "test the quality of each man's work," and for each it will be either that "he will receive his reward" or "he will suffer loss; he himself will be saved, but only as one escaping through the flames" (1 Corinthians 3:13-15). . . .
Jesus said, "But I tell you that men will have to give account on the day of judgment for every careless word they have spoken" (Matt. 12:36).
If we must give an account to God for every word spoken, surely we must give an account for every hour spent carelessly (that is, wastefully, negligently). . . .
The wise response to such truth is to evaluate your use of time now and spend it in a way that you would like to hear at the Judgment. And if you cannot answer your conscience regarding how you use your time in the growth of Christlikeness now, how will you be able to answer God then?
(From *Spiritual Disciplines of the Christian Life* by Donald Whitney)

APPLICATION In what areas do you need accountability? Prayer time? Bible study? Sharing your faith? Pick an area in your life that needs improvement. Find someone to hold you accountable to help you make the changes God wants.

EXPLORATION Accountability —Matthew 12:38; Romans 14:10-12; Hebrews 13:17.

LIFE LESSON
Genesis 11:1-32

SITUATION People built a tower and a city called Babel as a monument to their own greatness. God thwarted this arrogant behavior by causing all the people to speak in different languages. This caused the people to scatter all over the earth.

OBSERVATION God will not permit us to replace him as supreme in the universe. We belong to him and are responsible for our actions.

INSPIRATION The scene is almost spooky: a tall, unfinished tower looming solitarily on a dusty plain. Its base is wide and strong but covered with weeds. Large stones originally intended for use in the tower lie forsaken on the ground. Buckets, hammers, and pulleys—all lie abandoned. The silhouette cast by the structure is lean and lonely.

Not too long ago, this tower was buzzing with activity. A bystander would have been impressed with the smooth-running construction of the world's first skyscraper. One group of workers stirred freshly made mortar. Another team pulled bricks out of the oven. A third group carried the bricks to the construction site while a fourth shouldered the load up a winding path to the top of the tower where it was firmly set in place.

Their dream was a tower. A tower that would be taller than anyone had ever dreamed. A tower that would punch through the clouds and scratch the heavens. And what was the purpose of the tower? To glorify God? No. To try to find God? No. To call people to look upward to God? Try again. To provide a heavenly haven of prayer? Still wrong.

The purpose of the work caused its eventual abortion. The method was right. The plan was effective. But the motive was wrong. Dead wrong. Read these minutes from the "Tower Planning Committee Meeting" and see what I mean:

"Come, let us build ourselves a city, and a tower with its top in the heavens, and [watch out] let us make a name for ourselves."

sons of Ham, according to their families, according to their languages, in
their lands *and* in their nations.
21 And *children* were born also to Shem, the father of all the children of
Eber, the brother of Japheth the elder. 22 The sons of Shem *were* Elam,
Asshur, Arphaxad, Lud, and Aram. 23 The sons of Aram *were* Uz, Hul,
Gether, and Mash.[q] 24 Arphaxad begot Salah,[r] and Salah begot Eber. 25 To
Eber were born two sons: the name of one *was* Peleg, for in his days the
earth was divided; and his brother's name *was* Joktan. 26 Joktan begot
Almodad, Sheleph, Hazarmaveth, Jerah, 27 Hadoram, Uzal, Diklah, 28 Obal,[s]
Abimael, Sheba, 29 Ophir, Havilah, and Jobab. All these *were* the sons of
Joktan. 30 And their dwelling place was from Mesha as you go toward
Sephar, the mountain of the east. 31 These *were* the sons of Shem, according to their families, according to their languages, in their lands, according to their nations.
32 These *were* the families of the sons of Noah, according to their generations, in their nations; and from these the nations were divided on the
earth after the flood.

The Tower of Babel

11 Now the whole earth had one language and one speech. 2 And it
came to pass, as they journeyed from the east, that they found a
plain in the land of Shinar, and they dwelt there. 3 Then they said to one
another, "Come, let us make bricks and bake *them* thoroughly." They had
brick for stone, and they had asphalt for mortar. 4 And they said, "Come,
let us build ourselves a city, and a tower whose top *is* in the heavens; let us
make a name for ourselves, lest we be scattered abroad over the face of the
whole earth."
5 But the LORD came down to see the city and the tower which the sons
of men had built. 6 And the LORD said, "Indeed the people *are* one and they
all have one language, and this is what they begin to do; now nothing that
they propose to do will be withheld from them. 7 Come, let Us go down and
there confuse their language, that they may not understand one another's
speech." 8 So the LORD scattered them abroad from there over the face of all
the earth, and they ceased building the city. 9 Therefore its name is called
Babel, because there the LORD confused the language of all the earth; and
from there the LORD scattered them abroad over the face of all the earth.

Shem's Descendants

10 This *is* the genealogy of Shem: Shem *was* one hundred years old, and
begot Arphaxad two years after the flood. 11 After he begot Arphaxad,
Shem lived five hundred years, and begot sons and daughters.
12 Arphaxad lived thirty-five years, and begot Salah. 13 After he begot
Salah, Arphaxad lived four hundred and three years, and begot sons and
daughters.
14 Salah lived thirty years, and begot Eber. 15 After he begot Eber, Salah
lived four hundred and three years, and begot sons and daughters.
16 Eber lived thirty-four years, and begot Peleg. 17 After he begot Peleg,
Eber lived four hundred and thirty years, and begot sons and daughters.

10:23 [q] Called *Meshech* in Septuagint and 1 Chronicles 1:17
10:24 [r] Following Masoretic Text, Vulgate, and Targum; Septuagint reads *Arphaxad begot Cainan, and Cainan begot Salah* (compare Luke 3:35, 36).
10:28 [s] Spelled *Ebal* in 1 Chronicles 1:22

18 Peleg lived thirty years, and begot Reu. 19 After he begot Reu, Peleg
lived two hundred and nine years, and begot sons and daughters.
20 Reu lived thirty-two years, and begot Serug. 21 After he begot Serug,
Reu lived two hundred and seven years, and begot sons and daughters.
22 Serug lived thirty years, and begot Nahor. 23 After he begot Nahor,
Serug lived two hundred years, and begot sons and daughters.
24 Nahor lived twenty-nine years, and begot Terah. 25 After he begot
Terah, Nahor lived one hundred and nineteen years, and begot sons and
daughters.
26 Now Terah lived seventy years, and begot Abram, Nahor, and Haran.

Terah's Descendants

27 This *is* the genealogy of Terah: Terah begot Abram, Nahor, and Haran.
Haran begot Lot. 28 And Haran died before his father Terah in his native
land, in Ur of the Chaldeans. 29 Then Abram and Nahor took wives: the
name of Abram's wife *was* Sarai, and the name of Nahor's wife, Milcah,
the daughter of Haran the father of Milcah and the father of Iscah. 30 But
Sarai was barren; she had no child.
31 And Terah took his son Abram and his grandson Lot, the son of
Haran, and his daughter-in-law Sarai, his son Abram's wife, and they
went out with them from Ur of the Chaldeans to go to the land of Canaan;
and they came to Haran and dwelt there. 32 So the days of Terah were two
hundred and five years, and Terah died in Haran.

Promises to Abram

12 Now the LORD had said to Abram:

"Get out of your country,
From your family
And from your father's house,
To a land that I will show you.
2 I will make you a great nation;
I will bless you
And make your name great;
And you shall be a blessing.
3 I will bless those who bless you,
And I will curse him who curses you;
And in you all the families of the earth shall be blessed."

4 So Abram departed as the LORD had spoken to him, and Lot went with
him. And Abram *was* seventy-five years old when he departed from
Haran. 5 Then Abram took Sarai his wife and Lot his brother's son, and all
their possessions that they had gathered, and the people whom they had
acquired in Haran, and they departed to go to the land of Canaan. So they
came to the land of Canaan. 6 Abram passed through the land to the place
of Shechem, as far as the terebinth tree of Moreh.[t] And the Canaanites *were*
then in the land.
7 Then the LORD appeared to Abram and said, "To your descendants I
will give this land." And there he built an altar to the LORD, who had appeared to him. 8 And he moved from there to the mountain east of Bethel,

12:6 [t] Hebrew *Alon Moreh*

Why was the tower being built? Selfishness. Pure, 100 percent selfishness. The bricks were made of inflated egos and the mortar was made of pride. Men were giving sweat and blood for a pillar. Why? So that somebody's name could be remembered.

We have a name for that: blind ambition.

We make heroes out of people who are ambitious.

And rightly so. This world would be in sad shape without people who dream of touching the heavens. Ambition is that grit in the soul which creates disenchantment with the ordinary and puts the dare into dreams.

But left unchecked it becomes an insatiable addition to power and prestige; a roaring hunger for achievement that devours people as a lion devours an animal, leaving behind only the skeletal remains of relationships.

Blind ambition. Distorted values.

God won't tolerate it. He didn't then and he won't now. He took the "Climb to Heaven Campaign" into his hands. With one sweep he painted the tower gray with confusion and sent workers babbling in all directions. He took man's greatest achievement and blew it into the winds like a child blows a dandelion.

Are you building any towers? Examine your motives. And remember the statement imprinted on the base of the windswept Tower of Babel: Blind ambition is a giant step away from God and one step closer to catastrophe.
(From *God Came Near* by Max Lucado)

APPLICATION What towers have you been building? Wealth? Success? Recognition? Focus on what God wants you to build. Simplify your life. Surrender your desires to him! Let him guide your efforts.

EXPLORATION Pride—Judges 8:1-3; 15:14-17; 16:17; Psalm 10:11; Luke 1:48.

LIFE LESSON

Genesis 12:1-20

SITUATION God promised Abram that many nations would come from his descendants. Abram believed God and obediently moved to an unknown land. But as he encountered danger in Egypt, Abram's faith wavered. Fear persuaded him to lie.

OBSERVATION Although old, Abram left his comfortable life in Ur with only the Lord's word as a guide. Faith means acting on our beliefs.

INSPIRATION In the Old Testament, personal relationship with God showed itself in separation, and this is symbolized in the life of Abraham by his separation from his country and from his [family]. . . .

Faith never knows where it is being led, but it loves and knows the One Who is leading. It is a life of faith, not of intellect and reason, but a life of knowing Who makes us "go." The root of faith is the knowledge of a Person, and one of the biggest snares is the idea that God is sure to lead us to success. . . .

[W]hen we pray we feel the blessing of God enwrapping us and for the time being we are changed, then we get back to the ordinary days and ways and the glory vanishes. The life of faith is not a life of mounting up with wings, but a life of walking and not fainting. It is not a question of sanctification; but . . . of faith that has been tried and proved and has stood the test. Abraham is not a type of sanctification, but a type of the life of faith, a tried faith built on a real God. "Abraham believed God."

(From *My Utmost for His Highest* by Oswald Chambers)

APPLICATION Be encouraged by the story of Abram who faithfully obeyed God in difficult situations. Today, ask God to help you be faithful under pressure.

EXPLORATION Obedient Faith—Genesis 22:2-3; Deuteronomy 26:16; Joshua 1:8; 11:15; 1 Samuel 15:22; John 14:31; Acts 5:29.

and he pitched his tent *with* Bethel on the west and Ai on the east; there he
built an altar to the LORD and called on the name of the LORD. 9So Abram
journeyed, going on still toward the South.[u]

Abram in Egypt

10Now there was a famine in the land, and Abram went down to Egypt
to dwell there, for the famine *was* severe in the land. 11And it came to pass,
when he was close to entering Egypt, that he said to Sarai his wife, "Indeed
I know that you *are* a woman of beautiful countenance. 12Therefore it will
happen, when the Egyptians see you, that they will say, 'This *is* his wife';
and they will kill me, but they will let you live. 13Please say you *are* my sister, that it may be well with me for your sake, and that I[v] may live because
of you."
14So it was, when Abram came into Egypt, that the Egyptians saw the
woman, that she *was* very beautiful. 15The princes of Pharaoh also saw her
and commended her to Pharaoh. And the woman was taken to Pharaoh's
house. 16He treated Abram well for her sake. He had sheep, oxen, male
donkeys, male and female servants, female donkeys, and camels.
17But the LORD plagued Pharaoh and his house with great plagues
because of Sarai, Abram's wife. 18And Pharaoh called Abram and said,
"What *is* this you have done to me? Why did you not tell me that she *was*
your wife? 19Why did you say, 'She *is* my sister'? I might have taken her as
my wife. Now therefore, here is your wife; take *her* and go your way." 20So
Pharaoh commanded *his* men concerning him; and they sent him away,
with his wife and all that he had.

Abram Inherits Canaan

13 Then Abram went up from Egypt, he and his wife and all that he
had, and Lot with him, to the South.[w] 2Abram *was* very rich in livestock, in silver, and in gold. 3And he went on his journey from the South
as far as Bethel, to the place where his tent had been at the beginning,
between Bethel and Ai, 4to the place of the altar which he had made there
at first. And there Abram called on the name of the LORD.
5Lot also, who went with Abram, had flocks and herds and tents. 6Now
the land was not able to support them, that they might dwell together, for
their possessions were so great that they could not dwell together. 7And
there was strife between the herdsmen of Abram's livestock and the herdsmen of Lot's livestock. The Canaanites and the Perizzites then dwelt in the
land.
8So Abram said to Lot, "Please let there be no strife between you and me,
and between my herdsmen and your herdsmen; for we *are* brethren. 9*Is* not
the whole land before you? Please separate from me. If *you take* the left,
then I will go to the right; or, if *you go* to the right, then I will go to the left."
10And Lot lifted his eyes and saw all the plain of Jordan, that it *was* well
watered everywhere (before the LORD destroyed Sodom and Gomorrah)
like the garden of the LORD, like the land of Egypt as you go toward Zoar.
11Then Lot chose for himself all the plain of Jordan, and Lot journeyed
east. And they separated from each other. 12Abram dwelt in the land of

12:9 [u] Hebrew *Negev*
12:13 [v] Literally *my soul*
13:1 [w] Hebrew *Negev*

Canaan, and Lot dwelt in the cities of the plain and pitched *his* tent even
as far as Sodom. 13But the men of Sodom *were* exceedingly wicked and sinful against the LORD.

14And the LORD said to Abram, after Lot had separated from him: "Lift
your eyes now and look from the place where you are—northward, southward, eastward, and westward; 15for all the land which you see I give to you
and your descendants[x] forever. 16And I will make your descendants as the
dust of the earth; so that if a man could number the dust of the earth, *then*
your descendants also could be numbered. 17Arise, walk in the land
through its length and its width, for I give it to you."

18Then Abram moved *his* tent, and went and dwelt by the terebinth trees
of Mamre,[y] which *are* in Hebron, and built an altar there to the LORD.

Lot's Captivity and Rescue

14 And it came to pass in the days of Amraphel king of Shinar, Arioch
king of Ellasar, Chedorlaomer king of Elam, and Tidal king of nations,[z] 2*that* they made war with Bera king of Sodom, Birsha king of
Gomorrah, Shinab king of Admah, Shemeber king of Zeboiim, and the
king of Bela (that is, Zoar). 3All these joined together in the Valley of
Siddim (that is, the Salt Sea). 4Twelve years they served Chedorlaomer, and
in the thirteenth year they rebelled.

5In the fourteenth year Chedorlaomer and the kings that *were* with him
came and attacked the Rephaim in Ashteroth Karnaim, the Zuzim in
Ham, the Emim in Shaveh Kiriathaim, 6and the Horites in their mountain
of Seir, as far as El Paran, which *is* by the wilderness. 7Then they turned
back and came to En Mishpat (that *is,* Kadesh), and attacked all the country of the Amalekites, and also the Amorites who dwelt in Hazezon Tamar.

8And the king of Sodom, the king of Gomorrah, the king of Admah, the
king of Zeboiim, and the king of Bela (that *is,* Zoar) went out and joined
together in battle in the Valley of Siddim 9against Chedorlaomer king of
Elam, Tidal king of nations,[a] Amraphel king of Shinar, and Arioch king of
Ellasar—four kings against five. 10Now the Valley of Siddim *was full of* asphalt pits; and the kings of Sodom and Gomorrah fled; *some* fell there, and
the remainder fled to the mountains. 11Then they took all the goods of
Sodom and Gomorrah, and all their provisions, and went their way. 12They
also took Lot, Abram's brother's son who dwelt in Sodom, and his goods,
and departed.

13Then one who had escaped came and told Abram the Hebrew, for he
dwelt by the terebinth trees of Mamre[b] the Amorite, brother of Eshcol and
brother of Aner; and they *were* allies with Abram. 14Now when Abram
heard that his brother was taken captive, he armed his three hundred and
eighteen trained *servants* who were born in his own house, and went in
pursuit as far as Dan. 15He divided his forces against them by night, and he
and his servants attacked them and pursued them as far as Hobah, which
is north of Damascus. 16So he brought back all the goods, and also brought
back his brother Lot and his goods, as well as the women and the people.

13:15 [x] Literally *seed,* and so throughout the book
13:18 [y] Hebrew *Alon Mamre*
14:1 [z] Hebrew *goyim*
14:9 [a] Hebrew *goyim*
14:13 [b] Hebrew *Alon Mamre*

LIFE LESSON

Genesis 13:1–14:24

SITUATION In response to God's promise to give land and descendants, Abram's family traveled from Haran through Canaan and Egypt (Genesis 11:27–12:20). God told them to avoid the land of Sodom, whose name became synonymous with gross sin (Genesis 13:13; 18:16–19:29). God would destroy that city, and Lot would barely escape.

OBSERVATION Our decisions in life bear spiritual consequences. Lot selfishly chose the lush Jordan Valley and got himself in trouble (captured by a gang of marauding kings). Abram was willing to take second choice and God blessed him.

INSPIRATION Jim spent eight years in prison for murder. He was a drug dealer. In prison, Jim found a second chance in Christ. Now a minister, Jim often speaks to high school students about the decision to take drugs. "Don't let anyone kid you," he tells them. "Drugs are fun, drugs make you feel good, and getting high is fun. You know the beginning of drugs, and it's fun. But I know the end of drugs. . . ." And then Jim tells them about the decisions that nearly ruined his life forever.

While most of us will never self-destruct in the way Jim did, we all face the choice of doing things that look like fun, but which result in a life of pain—divorce, financial disaster, disease, and relationship problems. . . .

The big question for most of us: "Is life in the fast lane where God wants me to be?"

(From *The Man in the Mirror* by Patrick Morley)

APPLICATION Would what you watch on television be popular in Sodom? Turn off shows that program you to lust or to enjoy violence. Rent movies carefully. We cannot serve God wholeheartedly and eagerly fulfill our sinful desires at the same time.

EXPLORATION Tests as Part of God's Will—Exodus 17:1-7; Matthew 4:1-11; 1 Corinthians 10:1-13; 2 Timothy 2:14–3:9; Hebrews 4:12-16; James 1.

Life Lesson

Genesis 15:1–17:27

SITUATION God promised descendants and land to the aging traveler, Abram. Despite God's promise to him, nagging doubt caused Abram to waver between shortsighted compromise and obedient faith.

OBSERVATION God keeps his promises and rewards our obedient faith. When God promises to direct our paths, we can be confident he will carefully lead us.

INSPIRATION I grew up in Southern California and my favorite activity was swimming. There was only one time I had to be rescued. When I was in ninth grade I went with some older friends to Tamarack State Beach near Oceanside, California, for a day of body-surfing. The waves were great that day. I decided to swim a little farther from shore in the hopes of catching some larger waves.

I was so intent on catching the waves I didn't notice that the waves were beginning to break in a pattern that can produce rip tides. As I was swimming farther out, I dove underneath a wave that was breaking right in front of me. Rather than immediately coming back up to the surface, I felt tremendous pressure pushing my body down and pulling me out to sea. I had no idea what was happening. My feet touched the bottom. I tried to push myself up but couldn't. I was almost out of air and I panicked. I also prayed.

I forgot what I said to God but obviously He heard me. Suddenly I found myself on the surface of the water. I was exhausted and afraid it would happen again. I heard a voice shouting to me. I turned towards the voice to see a lifeguard throwing a life preserver and hung on for dear life. With the rope in one hand the lifeguard pulled me in.

17 And the king of Sodom went out to meet him at the Valley of Shaveh (that *is,* the King's Valley), after his return from the defeat of Chedorlaomer and the kings who *were* with him.

Abram and Melchizedek

18 Then Melchizedek king of Salem brought out bread and wine; he *was* the priest of God Most High. 19 And he blessed him and said:

"Blessed be Abram of God Most High,
Possessor of heaven and earth;
20 And blessed be God Most High,
Who has delivered your enemies into your hand."

And he gave him a tithe of all.

21 Now the king of Sodom said to Abram, "Give me the persons, and take the goods for yourself."

22 But Abram said to the king of Sodom, "I have raised my hand to the LORD, God Most High, the Possessor of heaven and earth, 23 that I *will take* nothing, from a thread to a sandal strap, and that I will not take anything that *is* yours, lest you should say, 'I have made Abram rich'— 24 except only what the young men have eaten, and the portion of the men who went with me: Aner, Eshcol, and Mamre; let them take their portion."

God's Covenant with Abram

15 After these things the word of the LORD came to Abram in a vision, saying, "Do not be afraid, Abram. I *am* your shield, your exceedingly great reward."

2 But Abram said, "Lord GOD, what will You give me, seeing I go childless, and the heir of my house *is* Eliezer of Damascus?" 3 Then Abram said, "Look, You have given me no offspring; indeed one born in my house is my heir!"

4 And behold, the word of the LORD *came* to him, saying, "This one shall not be your heir, but one who will come from your own body shall be your heir." 5 Then He brought him outside and said, "Look now toward heaven, and count the stars if you are able to number them." And He said to him, "So shall your descendants be."

6 And he believed in the LORD, and He accounted it to him for righteousness.

7 Then He said to him, "I *am* the LORD, who brought you out of Ur of the Chaldeans, to give you this land to inherit it."

8 And he said, "Lord GOD, how shall I know that I will inherit it?"

9 So He said to him, "Bring Me a three-year-old heifer, a three-year-old female goat, a three-year-old ram, a turtledove, and a young pigeon." 10 Then he brought all these to Him and cut them in two, down the middle, and placed each piece opposite the other; but he did not cut the birds in two. 11 And when the vultures came down on the carcasses, Abram drove them away.

12 Now when the sun was going down, a deep sleep fell upon Abram; and behold, horror *and* great darkness fell upon him. 13 Then He said to Abram: "Know certainly that your descendants will be strangers in a land *that is* not theirs, and will serve them, and they will afflict them four hundred years. 14 And also the nation whom they serve I will judge; afterward they shall come out with great possessions. 15 Now as for you, you shall go

to your fathers in peace; you shall be buried at a good old age. 16But in the
fourth generation they shall return here, for the iniquity of the Amorites *is*
not yet complete."
17And it came to pass, when the sun went down and it was dark, that
behold, there appeared a smoking oven and a burning torch that passed
between those pieces. 18On the same day the LORD made a covenant with
Abram, saying:
"To your descendants I have given this land, from the river of Egypt to
the great river, the River Euphrates— 19the Kenites, the Kenezzites, the
Kadmonites, 20the Hittites, the Perizzites, the Rephaim, 21the Amorites, the
Canaanites, the Girgashites, and the Jebusites."

Hagar and Ishmael

16 Now Sarai, Abram's wife, had borne him no *children.* And she had
an Egyptian maidservant whose name was Hagar. 2So Sarai said to
Abram, "See now, the LORD has restrained me from bearing *children.*
Please, go in to my maid; perhaps I shall obtain children by her." And
Abram heeded the voice of Sarai. 3Then Sarai, Abram's wife, took Hagar
her maid, the Egyptian, and gave her to her husband Abram to be his wife,
after Abram had dwelt ten years in the land of Canaan. 4So he went in to
Hagar, and she conceived. And when she saw that she had conceived, her
mistress became despised in her eyes.
5Then Sarai said to Abram, "My wrong *be* upon you! I gave my maid
into your embrace; and when she saw that she had conceived, I became
despised in her eyes. The LORD judge between you and me."
6So Abram said to Sarai, "Indeed your maid *is* in your hand; do to her
as you please." And when Sarai dealt harshly with her, she fled from her
presence.
7Now the Angel of the LORD found her by a spring of water in the wilderness, by the spring on the way to Shur. 8And He said, "Hagar, Sarai's maid,
where have you come from, and where are you going?"
She said, "I am fleeing from the presence of my mistress Sarai."
9The Angel of the LORD said to her, "Return to your mistress, and submit yourself under her hand." 10Then the Angel of the LORD said to her, "I
will multiply your descendants exceedingly, so that they shall not be
counted for multitude." 11And the Angel of the LORD said to her:

"Behold, you *are* with child,
And you shall bear a son.
You shall call his name Ishmael,
Because the LORD has heard your affliction.
12 He shall be a wild man;
His hand *shall be* against every man,
And every man's hand against him.
And he shall dwell in the presence of all his brethren."

13Then she called the name of the LORD who spoke to her, You-Are-the-
God-Who-Sees; for she said, "Have I also here seen Him who sees me?"
14Therefore the well was called Beer Lahai Roi;[c] observe, *it is* between
Kadesh and Bered.

When I made it to shore I was a bit embarrassed, but most of all I was grateful. The lifeguard said he had been watching me. He could see there was rip tide condition and knew I wasn't aware of it. Before I had gone under he was already swimming towards me to warn me and, if necessary, rescue me.

Over the years I've realized that living the Christian life is a lot like the experience I had that day. Even though I wasn't aware of it, the lifeguard had his eyes on me and knew I was moving into dangerous water. He was in the water before I needed him—just in case.

God is our lifeguard. . . . God's promises are like life preservers. They keep the soul from sinking into the sea of discouragement. . . .

When your perspective becomes distorted and your problems begin to consume your entire field of vision, you need a perspective preserver. When it feels like God has deserted you and you begin to get discouraged, you will find that God's promises will always pull you out and bring you back to safety.

(From Gary Oliver, "God Is a Promise Keeper" in *What Makes a Man*)

APPLICATION Make a list of seven key promises to you from God's Word and commit them to memory, one a day for a week. Make one promise your motto for the week. Have confidence that God will do what he said. Use the promise to share your faith with someone.

EXPLORATION Justification by Faith—Romans 4; Galatians 3; Hebrews 11.

16:14 [c] Literally *Well of the One Who Lives and Sees Me*

15So Hagar bore Abram a son; and Abram named
his son, whom Hagar bore, Ishmael. 16Abram *was*
eighty-six years old when Hagar bore Ishmael to
Abram.

The Sign of the Covenant

17 When Abram was ninety-nine years old, the
LORD appeared to Abram and said to him, "I
am Almighty God; walk before Me and be blameless.
2And I will make My covenant between Me and you,
and will multiply you exceedingly." 3Then Abram fell
on his face, and God talked with him, saying: 4"As for
Me, behold, My covenant is with you, and you shall be
a father of many nations. 5No longer shall your name
be called Abram, but your name shall be Abraham;
for I have made you a father of many nations. 6I will
make you exceedingly fruitful; and I will make nations of you, and kings shall come from you. 7And I
will establish My covenant between Me and you and
your descendants after you in their generations, for
an everlasting covenant, to be God to you and your
descendants after you. 8Also I give to you and your
descendants after you the land in which you are a
stranger, all the land of Canaan, as an everlasting possession; and I will be their God."
9And God said to Abraham: "As for you, you shall
keep My covenant, you and your descendants after
you throughout their generations. 10This *is* My
covenant which you shall keep, between Me and you
and your descendants after you: Every male child
among you shall be circumcised; 11and you shall be
circumcised in the flesh of your foreskins, and it shall
be a sign of the covenant between Me and you. 12He
who is eight days old among you shall be circumcised, every male child in your generations, he who is
born in your house or bought with money from any
foreigner who is not your descendant. 13He who is
born in your house and he who is bought with your
money must be circumcised, and My covenant shall
be in your flesh for an everlasting covenant. 14And the
uncircumcised male child, who is not circumcised in
the flesh of his foreskin, that person shall be cut off
from his people; he has broken My covenant."
15Then God said to Abraham, "As for Sarai your
wife, you shall not call her name Sarai, but Sarah *shall
be* her name. 16And I will bless her and also give you a
son by her; then I will bless her, and she shall be *a
mother of* nations; kings of peoples shall be from her."
17Then Abraham fell on his face and laughed, and
said in his heart, "Shall *a child* be born to a man who
is one hundred years old? And shall Sarah, who is
ninety years old, bear *a child?*" 18And Abraham said
to God, "Oh, that Ishmael might live before You!"
19Then God said: "No, Sarah your wife shall bear
you a son, and you shall call his name Isaac; I will
establish My covenant with him for an everlasting
covenant, *and* with his descendants after him. 20And
as for Ishmael, I have heard you. Behold, I have
blessed him, and will make him fruitful, and will
multiply him exceedingly. He shall beget twelve
princes, and I will make him a great nation. 21But My
covenant I will establish with Isaac, whom Sarah
shall bear to you at this set time next year." 22Then He
finished talking with him, and God went up from
Abraham.
23So Abraham took Ishmael his son, all who were
born in his house and all who were bought with his
money, every male among the men of Abraham's
house, and circumcised the flesh of their foreskins
that very same day, as God had said to him. 24Abra-
ham *was* ninety-nine years old when he was circumcised in the flesh of his foreskin. 25And Ishmael his
son *was* thirteen years old when he was circumcised
in the flesh of his foreskin. 26That very same day
Abraham was circumcised, and his son Ishmael;
27and all the men of his house, born in the house or
bought with money from a foreigner, were circumcised with him.

The Son of Promise

18 Then the LORD appeared to him by the terebinth trees of Mamre,[d] as he was sitting in the
tent door in the heat of the day. 2So he lifted his eyes
and looked, and behold, three men were standing by
him; and when he saw *them,* he ran from the tent door
to meet them, and bowed himself to the ground, 3and
said, "My Lord, if I have now found favor in Your
sight, do not pass on by Your servant. 4Please let a little water be brought, and wash your feet, and rest
yourselves under the tree. 5And I will bring a morsel
of bread, that you may refresh your hearts. After that
you may pass by, inasmuch as you have come to your
servant."
They said, "Do as you have said."
6So Abraham hurried into the tent to Sarah and
said, "Quickly, make ready three measures of fine
meal; knead *it* and make cakes." 7And Abraham ran
to the herd, took a tender and good calf, gave *it* to a
young man, and he hastened to prepare it. 8So he took

18:1 [d] Hebrew *Alon Mamre*

butter and milk and the calf which he had prepared, and set *it* before
them; and he stood by them under the tree as they ate.
9Then they said to him, "Where *is* Sarah your wife?"
So he said, "Here, in the tent."
10And He said, "I will certainly return to you according to the time of
life, and behold, Sarah your wife shall have a son."
(Sarah was listening in the tent door which *was* behind him.) 11Now
Abraham and Sarah were old, well advanced in age; *and* Sarah had passed
the age of childbearing.[e] 12Therefore Sarah laughed within herself, saying,
"After I have grown old, shall I have pleasure, my lord being old also?"
13And the LORD said to Abraham, "Why did Sarah laugh, saying, 'Shall I
surely bear *a child,* since I am old?' 14Is anything too hard for the LORD? At
the appointed time I will return to you, according to the time of life, and
Sarah shall have a son."
15But Sarah denied *it,* saying, "I did not laugh," for she was afraid.
And He said, "No, but you did laugh!"

Abraham Intercedes for Sodom

16Then the men rose from there and looked toward Sodom, and Abraham went with them to send them on the way. 17And the LORD said, "Shall
I hide from Abraham what I am doing, 18since Abraham shall surely
become a great and mighty nation, and all the nations of the earth shall be
blessed in him? 19For I have known him, in order that he may command his
children and his household after him, that they keep the way of the LORD,
to do righteousness and justice, that the LORD may bring to Abraham what
He has spoken to him." 20And the LORD said, "Because the outcry against
Sodom and Gomorrah is great, and because their sin is very grave, 21I will
go down now and see whether they have done altogether according to the
outcry against it that has come to Me; and if not, I will know."
22Then the men turned away from there and went toward Sodom, but
Abraham still stood before the LORD. 23And Abraham came near and said,
"Would You also destroy the righteous with the wicked? 24Suppose there
were fifty righteous within the city; would You also destroy the place and
not spare *it* for the fifty righteous that were in it? 25Far be it from You to do
such a thing as this, to slay the righteous with the wicked, so that the righteous should be as the wicked; far be it from You! Shall not the Judge of all
the earth do right?"
26So the LORD said, "If I find in Sodom fifty righteous within the city,
then I will spare all the place for their sakes."
27Then Abraham answered and said, "Indeed now, I who *am but* dust
and ashes have taken it upon myself to speak to the Lord: 28Suppose there
were five less than the fifty righteous; would You destroy all of the city for
lack of five?"
So He said, "If I find there forty-five, I will not destroy *it.*"
29And he spoke to Him yet again and said, "Suppose there should be
forty found there?"
So He said, "I will not do *it* for the sake of forty."
30Then he said, "Let not the Lord be angry, and I will speak: Suppose
thirty should be found there?"

18:11 [e] Literally *the manner of women had ceased to be with Sarah*

LIFE LESSON

Genesis 18:1–20:18

SITUATION God planned to destroy Sodom and Gomorrah for their many sins. Abraham pleaded with God for Sodom in order to save Lot's life. God completely punished the city but rescued Lot by sending two angels to escort him away.

OBSERVATION God punishes sin but protects righteousness. God destroyed entire cities because the evil practiced in them was great.

INSPIRATION Though God's people often forgot their God, God didn't forget them. He kept his word. . . . He could have given up. He could have turned his back. He could have walked away from the wretched mess, but he didn't.

He didn't give up.

When he became flesh and was the victim of an assassination attempt before he was two years old, he didn't give up.

When the people from his own home town tried to push him over a cliff, he didn't give up.

When his brothers ridiculed him, he didn't give up.

When he was accused of blasphem-ing God by people who didn't fear God, he didn't give up.

When Peter worshiped him at the supper and cursed him at the fire, he didn't give up.

When people spat in his face, he didn't spit back. When the bystanders slapped him, he didn't slap them. When a whip ripped his sides, he didn't turn and command the await-ing angels to stuff that whip down that soldier's throat.

And when human hands fastened the divine hands to a cross with spikes, it wasn't the soldiers who held the hands of Jesus steady. It was God who held them steady. For those wounded hands were the same hands that had . . . brought light into thick and dreadful darkness. They had come to do it again.

(From *Six Hours One Friday* by Max Lucado)

Continued

APPLICATION Does the place where you live resemble Sodom? Stand against evil in your town or city. Be a voice for righteousness. Brainstorm with a friend how you can make a difference.

EXPLORATION God's Judgment—Deuteronomy 7:2; Judges 2:1; 1 Samuel 2:25; 1 Kings 22:34-38; 1 Chronicles 13:10-14.

So He said, "I will not do *it* if I find thirty there."
31And he said, "Indeed now, I have taken it upon myself to speak to the
Lord: Suppose twenty should be found there?"
So He said, "I will not destroy *it* for the sake of twenty."
32Then he said, "Let not the Lord be angry, and I will speak but once
more: Suppose ten should be found there?"
And He said, "I will not destroy *it* for the sake of ten." 33So the LORD went
His way as soon as He had finished speaking with Abraham; and Abraham returned to his place.

Sodom's Depravity

19 Now the two angels came to Sodom in the evening, and Lot was sitting in the gate of Sodom. When Lot saw *them,* he rose to meet them,
and he bowed himself with his face toward the ground. 2And he said,
"Here now, my lords, please turn in to your servant's house and spend the
night, and wash your feet; then you may rise early and go on your way."
And they said, "No, but we will spend the night in the open square."
3But he insisted strongly; so they turned in to him and entered his
house. Then he made them a feast, and baked unleavened bread, and
they ate.
4Now before they lay down, the men of the city, the men of Sodom, both
old and young, all the people from every quarter, surrounded the house.
5And they called to Lot and said to him, "Where are the men who came to
you tonight? Bring them out to us that we may know them *carnally.*"
6So Lot went out to them through the doorway, shut the door behind
him, 7and said, "Please, my brethren, do not do so wickedly! 8See now, I
have two daughters who have not known a man; please, let me bring
them out to you, and you may do to them as you wish; only do nothing to
these men, since this is the reason they have come under the shadow of
my roof."
9And they said, "Stand back!" Then they said, "This one came in to stay
here, and he keeps acting as a judge; now we will deal worse with you than
with them." So they pressed hard against the man Lot, and came near to
break down the door. 10But the men reached out their hands and pulled
Lot into the house with them, and shut the door. 11And they struck the
men who *were* at the doorway of the house with blindness, both small and
great, so that they became weary *trying* to find the door.

Sodom and Gomorrah Destroyed

12Then the men said to Lot, "Have you anyone else here? Son-in-law,
your sons, your daughters, and whomever you have in the city—take
them out of this place! 13For we will destroy this place, because the outcry
against them has grown great before the face of the LORD, and the LORD
has sent us to destroy it."
14So Lot went out and spoke to his sons-in-law, who had married his
daughters, and said, "Get up, get out of this place; for the LORD will destroy
this city!" But to his sons-in-law he seemed to be joking.
15When the morning dawned, the angels urged Lot to hurry, saying,
"Arise, take your wife and your two daughters who are here, lest you be
consumed in the punishment of the city." 16And while he lingered, the
men took hold of his hand, his wife's hand, and the hands of his two

daughters, the LORD being merciful to him, and they
brought him out and set him outside the city. 17So it
came to pass, when they had brought them outside,
that he[f] said, "Escape for your life! Do not look behind
you nor stay anywhere in the plain. Escape to the
mountains, lest you be destroyed."
18Then Lot said to them, "Please, no, my lords! 19In-
deed now, your servant has found favor in your sight,
and you have increased your mercy which you have
shown me by saving my life; but I cannot escape to
the mountains, lest some evil overtake me and I die.
20See now, this city *is* near *enough* to flee to, and it *is* a
little one; please let me escape there (*is* it not a little
one?) and my soul shall live."
21And he said to him, "See, I have favored you concerning this thing also, in that I will not overthrow
this city for which you have spoken. 22Hurry, escape
there. For I cannot do anything until you arrive
there."
Therefore the name of the city was called Zoar.
23The sun had risen upon the earth when Lot
entered Zoar. 24Then the LORD rained brimstone and
fire on Sodom and Gomorrah, from the LORD out of
the heavens. 25So He overthrew those cities, all the
plain, all the inhabitants of the cities, and what grew
on the ground.
26But his wife looked back behind him, and she
became a pillar of salt.
27And Abraham went early in the morning to the
place where he had stood before the LORD. 28Then he
looked toward Sodom and Gomorrah, and toward all
the land of the plain; and he saw, and behold, the
smoke of the land which went up like the smoke of a
furnace. 29And it came to pass, when God destroyed
the cities of the plain, that God remembered Abraham, and sent Lot out of the midst of the overthrow,
when He overthrew the cities in which Lot had dwelt.

The Descendants of Lot

30Then Lot went up out of Zoar and dwelt in the
mountains, and his two daughters were with him; for
he was afraid to dwell in Zoar. And he and his two
daughters dwelt in a cave. 31Now the firstborn said to
the younger, "Our father *is* old, and *there is* no man on
the earth to come in to us as is the custom of all the
earth. 32Come, let us make our father drink wine, and
we will lie with him, that we may preserve the lineage
of our father." 33So they made their father drink wine
that night. And the firstborn went in and lay with her
father, and he did not know when she lay down or
when she arose.
34It happened on the next day that the firstborn
said to the younger, "Indeed I lay with my father last
night; let us make him drink wine tonight also, and
you go in *and* lie with him, that we may preserve the
lineage of our father." 35Then they made their father
drink wine that night also. And the younger arose and
lay with him, and he did not know when she lay down
or when she arose.
36Thus both the daughters of Lot were with child by
their father. 37The firstborn bore a son and called his
name Moab; he *is* the father of the Moabites to this
day. 38And the younger, she also bore a son and called
his name Ben-Ammi; he *is* the father of the people of
Ammon to this day.

Abraham and Abimelech

20 And Abraham journeyed from there to the
South, and dwelt between Kadesh and Shur,
and stayed in Gerar. 2Now Abraham said of Sarah his
wife, "She *is* my sister." And Abimelech king of Gerar
sent and took Sarah.
3But God came to Abimelech in a dream by night,
and said to him, "Indeed you *are* a dead man because
of the woman whom you have taken, for she *is* a
man's wife."
4But Abimelech had not come near her; and he
said, "Lord, will You slay a righteous nation also? 5Did
he not say to me, 'She *is* my sister'? And she, even she
herself said, 'He *is* my brother.' In the integrity of my
heart and innocence of my hands I have done this."
6And God said to him in a dream, "Yes, I know that
you did this in the integrity of your heart. For I also
withheld you from sinning against Me; therefore I did
not let you touch her. 7Now therefore, restore the
man's wife; for he *is* a prophet, and he will pray for
you and you shall live. But if you do not restore *her*,
know that you shall surely die, you and all who *are*
yours."
8So Abimelech rose early in the morning, called all
his servants, and told all these things in their hearing;
and the men were very much afraid. 9And Abimelech
called Abraham and said to him, "What have you
done to us? How have I offended you, that you have
brought on me and on my kingdom a great sin? You
have done deeds to me that ought not to be done."
10Then Abimelech said to Abraham, "What did you
have in view, that you have done this thing?"

19:17 *f* Septuagint, Syriac, and Vulgate read *they.*

11And Abraham said, "Because I thought, surely
the fear of God *is* not in this place; and they will kill
me on account of my wife. 12But indeed *she is* truly my
sister. She *is* the daughter of my father, but not the
daughter of my mother; and she became my wife.
13And it came to pass, when God caused me to wander from my father's house, that I said to her, 'This *is*
your kindness that you should do for me: in every place,
wherever we go, say of me, "He *is* my brother." ' "
14Then Abimelech took sheep, oxen, and male and
female servants, and gave *them* to Abraham; and he
restored Sarah his wife to him. 15And Abimelech said,
"See, my land *is* before you; dwell where it pleases
you." 16Then to Sarah he said, "Behold, I have given
your brother a thousand *pieces* of silver; indeed this
vindicates you[g] before all who *are* with you and before
everybody." Thus she was rebuked.
17So Abraham prayed to God; and God healed
Abimelech, his wife, and his female servants. Then
they bore *children;* 18for the LORD had closed up all the
wombs of the house of Abimelech because of Sarah,
Abraham's wife.

Isaac Is Born

21 And the LORD visited Sarah as He had said, and
the LORD did for Sarah as He had spoken. 2For
Sarah conceived and bore Abraham a son in his old
age, at the set time of which God had spoken to him.
3And Abraham called the name of his son who was
born to him—whom Sarah bore to him—Isaac.
4Then Abraham circumcised his son Isaac when he
was eight days old, as God had commanded him.
5Now Abraham was one hundred years old when his
son Isaac was born to him. 6And Sarah said, "God has
made me laugh, *and* all who hear will laugh with me."
7She also said, "Who would have said to Abraham
that Sarah would nurse children? For I have borne
him a son in his old age."

Hagar and Ishmael Depart

8So the child grew and was weaned. And Abraham
made a great feast on the same day that Isaac was
weaned.
9And Sarah saw the son of Hagar the Egyptian,
whom she had borne to Abraham, scoffing. 10There-
fore she said to Abraham, "Cast out this bondwoman
and her son; for the son of this bondwoman shall not
be heir with my son, *namely* with Isaac." 11And the
matter was very displeasing in Abraham's sight because of his son.
12But God said to Abraham, "Do not let it be displeasing in your sight because of the lad or because of
your bondwoman. Whatever Sarah has said to you,
listen to her voice; for in Isaac your seed shall be
called. 13Yet I will also make a nation of the son of the
bondwoman, because he *is* your seed."
14So Abraham rose early in the morning, and took
bread and a skin of water; and putting *it* on her shoulder, he gave *it* and the boy to Hagar, and sent her away.
Then she departed and wandered in the Wilderness
of Beersheba. 15And the water in the skin was used up,
and she placed the boy under one of the shrubs.
16Then she went and sat down across from *him* at a
distance of about a bowshot; for she said to herself,
"Let me not see the death of the boy." So she sat opposite *him*, and lifted her voice and wept.
17And God heard the voice of the lad. Then the angel of God called to Hagar out of heaven, and said to
her, "What ails you, Hagar? Fear not, for God has
heard the voice of the lad where he *is.* 18Arise, lift up
the lad and hold him with your hand, for I will make
him a great nation."
19Then God opened her eyes, and she saw a well of
water. And she went and filled the skin with water,
and gave the lad a drink. 20So God was with the lad;
and he grew and dwelt in the wilderness, and became
an archer. 21He dwelt in the Wilderness of Paran; and
his mother took a wife for him from the land of Egypt.

A Covenant with Abimelech

22And it came to pass at that time that Abimelech
and Phichol, the commander of his army, spoke to
Abraham, saying, "God *is* with you in all that you do.
23Now therefore, swear to me by God that you will not
deal falsely with me, with my offspring, or with my
posterity; but that according to the kindness that I
have done to you, you will do to me and to the land in
which you have dwelt."
24And Abraham said, "I will swear."
25Then Abraham rebuked Abimelech because of a
well of water which Abimelech's servants had seized.
26And Abimelech said, "I do not know who has done
this thing; you did not tell me, nor had I heard *of it*
until today." 27So Abraham took sheep and oxen and
gave them to Abimelech, and the two of them made a
covenant. 28And Abraham set seven ewe lambs of the
flock by themselves.

20:16 g Literally *it is a covering of the eyes for you*

29 Then Abimelech asked Abraham, "What *is the meaning of* these seven
ewe lambs which you have set by themselves?"
30 And he said, "You will take *these* seven ewe lambs from my hand, that
they may be my witness that I have dug this well." 31 Therefore he called
that place Beersheba,[h] because the two of them swore an oath there.
32 Thus they made a covenant at Beersheba. So Abimelech rose with
Phichol, the commander of his army, and they returned to the land of the
Philistines. 33 Then *Abraham* planted a tamarisk tree in Beersheba, and
there called on the name of the LORD, the Everlasting God. 34 And Abraham
stayed in the land of the Philistines many days.

Abraham's Faith Confirmed

22 Now it came to pass after these things that God tested Abraham,
and said to him, "Abraham!"
And he said, "Here I am."
2 Then He said, "Take now your son, your only *son* Isaac, whom you love,
and go to the land of Moriah, and offer him there as a burnt offering on
one of the mountains of which I shall tell you."
3 So Abraham rose early in the morning and saddled his donkey, and
took two of his young men with him, and Isaac his son; and he split the
wood for the burnt offering, and arose and went to the place of which God
had told him. 4 Then on the third day Abraham lifted his eyes and saw the
place afar off. 5 And Abraham said to his young men, "Stay here with the
donkey; the lad[i] and I will go yonder and worship, and we will come back
to you."
6 So Abraham took the wood of the burnt offering and laid *it* on Isaac his
son; and he took the fire in his hand, and a knife, and the two of them went
together. 7 But Isaac spoke to Abraham his father and said, "My father!"
And he said, "Here I am, my son."
Then he said, "Look, the fire and the wood, but where *is* the lamb for a
burnt offering?"
8 And Abraham said, "My son, God will provide for Himself the lamb for
a burnt offering." So the two of them went together.
9 Then they came to the place of which God had told him. And Abraham
built an altar there and placed the wood in order; and he bound Isaac his
son and laid him on the altar, upon the wood. 10 And Abraham stretched
out his hand and took the knife to slay his son.
11 But the Angel of the LORD called to him from heaven and said, "Abraham, Abraham!"
So he said, "Here I am."
12 And He said, "Do not lay your hand on the lad, or do anything to him;
for now I know that you fear God, since you have not withheld your son,
your only *son,* from Me."
13 Then Abraham lifted his eyes and looked, and there behind *him was* a
ram caught in a thicket by its horns. So Abraham went and took the ram,
and offered it up for a burnt offering instead of his son. 14 And Abraham
called the name of the place, The-LORD-Will-Provide;[j] as it is said *to* this
day, "In the Mount of the LORD it shall be provided."

21:31 [h] Literally *Well of the Oath* or *Well of the Seven*
22:5 [i] Or *young man*
22:14 [j] Hebrew *YHWH Yireh*

Life Lesson

Genesis 21:1–23:20

SITUATION Even though Sarah doubted, God demonstrated his faithfulness by providing a son for her. God also took care of Hagar after she was forced to leave Abraham's camp. God fulfilled his promises when conditions appeared hopeless.

OBSERVATION God will fulfill his promises, no matter how difficult our problems. Even when we don't know how God will act, we must trust that he watches over us.

INSPIRATION Consider the case of Sarai. She is in her golden years, but God promises her a son. She gets excited. She visits the maternity shop and buys a few dresses. She plans her shower and remodels her tent . . . but no son. She eats a few birthday cakes and blows out a lot of candles . . . still no son. She goes through a decade of wall calendars . . . still no son. . . .

Finally, fourteen years later, when Abram is pushing a century of years and Sarai ninety . . . when Abram has stopped listening to Sarai's advice, and Sarai has stopped giving it . . . when the wallpaper in the nursery is faded and the baby furniture is several seasons out of date . . . when the topic of the promised child brings sighs and tears and long looks into a silent sky . . . God pays them a visit and tells them they had better select a name for their new son.

Abram and Sarai have the same response: laughter. They laugh partly because it is too good to happen and partly because it might. They laugh because they have given up hope, and hope born anew is always funny before it is real. . . .

They laugh because that is what you do when someone says he can do the impossible. They laugh a little at God, and a lot with God—for God is laughing, too. Then, with the smile still on his face, he gets busy doing what he does best—the unbelievable. . . .

He changes their faith. He changes their names. He changes the number of their tax deductions. He changes the way they define the word impossible.

Continued

But most of all, he changes Sarah's attitude about trusting God.

(From *The Applause of Heaven* by Max Lucado)

APPLICATION When you've made big mistakes and your life appears to be headed for shipwreck, who can help? Are there any promises more comforting than God's? When you feel anxious today, STOP. Pray: "God, I trust in your faithfulness to change both my attitude and my circumstances."

EXPLORATION God's Promises—Genesis 9:8-17; 16:1-3; 50:24; Exodus 6:6-8; Joshua 21:43-45; 2 Peter 1:3-4.

15Then the Angel of the LORD called to Abraham a second time out of
heaven, 16and said: "By Myself I have sworn, says the LORD, because you
have done this thing, and have not withheld your son, your only *son*—
17blessing I will bless you, and multiplying I will multiply your descendants as the stars of the heaven and as the sand which *is* on the seashore;
and your descendants shall possess the gate of their enemies. 18In your
seed all the nations of the earth shall be blessed, because you have obeyed
My voice." 19So Abraham returned to his young men, and they rose and
went together to Beersheba; and Abraham dwelt at Beersheba.

The Family of Nahor

20Now it came to pass after these things that it was told Abraham, saying, "Indeed Milcah also has borne children to your brother Nahor: 21Huz
his firstborn, Buz his brother, Kemuel the father of Aram, 22Chesed, Hazo,
Pildash, Jidlaph, and Bethuel." 23And Bethuel begot Rebekah.[k] These
eight Milcah bore to Nahor, Abraham's brother. 24His concubine, whose
name was Reumah, also bore Tebah, Gaham, Thahash, and Maachah.

Sarah's Death and Burial

23 Sarah lived one hundred and twenty-seven years; *these were* the
years of the life of Sarah. 2So Sarah died in Kirjath Arba (that *is*,
Hebron) in the land of Canaan, and Abraham came to mourn for Sarah
and to weep for her.
3Then Abraham stood up from before his dead, and spoke to the sons
of Heth, saying, 4"I *am* a foreigner and a visitor among you. Give me property for a burial place among you, that I may bury my dead out of my
sight."
5And the sons of Heth answered Abraham, saying to him, 6"Hear us, my
lord: You *are* a mighty prince among us; bury your dead in the choicest of
our burial places. None of us will withhold from you his burial place, that
you may bury your dead."
7Then Abraham stood up and bowed himself to the people of the land,
the sons of Heth. 8And he spoke with them, saying, "If it is your wish that
I bury my dead out of my sight, hear me, and meet with Ephron the son
of Zohar for me, 9that he may give me the cave of Machpelah which he has,
which *is* at the end of his field. Let him give it to me at the full price, as
property for a burial place among you."
10Now Ephron dwelt among the sons of Heth; and Ephron the Hittite
answered Abraham in the presence of the sons of Heth, all who entered at
the gate of his city, saying, 11"No, my lord, hear me: I give you the field and
the cave that *is* in it; I give it to you in the presence of the sons of my people. I give it to you. Bury your dead!"
12Then Abraham bowed himself down before the people of the land;
13and he spoke to Ephron in the hearing of the people of the land, saying,
"If you *will give it,* please hear me. I will give you money for the field; take
it from me and I will bury my dead there."
14And Ephron answered Abraham, saying to him, 15"My lord, listen to
me; the land *is worth* four hundred shekels of silver. What *is* that between
you and me? So bury your dead." 16And Abraham listened to Ephron; and

22:23 [k] Spelled *Rebecca* in Romans 9:10

Abraham weighed out the silver for Ephron which he had named in the
hearing of the sons of Heth, four hundred shekels of silver, currency of the
merchants.
17So the field of Ephron which *was* in Machpelah, which *was* before
Mamre, the field and the cave which *was* in it, and all the trees that *were* in
the field, which *were* within all the surrounding borders, were deeded 18to
Abraham as a possession in the presence of the sons of Heth, before all
who went in at the gate of his city.
19And after this, Abraham buried Sarah his wife in the cave of the field
of Machpelah, before Mamre (that *is,* Hebron) in the land of Canaan. 20So
the field and the cave that *is* in it were deeded to Abraham by the sons of
Heth as property for a burial place.

A Bride for Isaac

24 Now Abraham was old, well advanced in age; and the LORD had
blessed Abraham in all things. 2So Abraham said to the oldest servant of his house, who ruled over all that he had, "Please, put your hand
under my thigh, 3and I will make you swear by the LORD, the God of heav-
en and the God of the earth, that you will not take a wife for my son from
the daughters of the Canaanites, among whom I dwell; 4but you shall go to
my country and to my family, and take a wife for my son Isaac."
5And the servant said to him, "Perhaps the woman will not be willing to
follow me to this land. Must I take your son back to the land from which
you came?"
6But Abraham said to him, "Beware that you do not take my son back
there. 7The LORD God of heaven, who took me from my father's house and
from the land of my family, and who spoke to me and swore to me, saying, 'To your descendants[l] I give this land,' He will send His angel before
you, and you shall take a wife for my son from there. 8And if the woman is
not willing to follow you, then you will be released from this oath; only do
not take my son back there." 9So the servant put his hand under the thigh
of Abraham his master, and swore to him concerning this matter.
10Then the servant took ten of his master's camels and departed, for all
his master's goods *were in* his hand. And he arose and went to
Mesopotamia, to the city of Nahor. 11And he made his camels kneel down
outside the city by a well of water at evening time, the time when women
go out to draw *water.* 12Then he said, "O LORD God of my master Abraham,
please give me success this day, and show kindness to my master Abraham. 13Behold, *here* I stand by the well of water, and the daughters of the
men of the city are coming out to draw water. 14Now let it be that the young
woman to whom I say, 'Please let down your pitcher that I may drink,' and
she says, 'Drink, and I will also give your camels a drink'—*let* her *be the
one* You have appointed for Your servant Isaac. And by this I will know
that You have shown kindness to my master."
15And it happened, before he had finished speaking, that behold, Rebekah, who was born to Bethuel, son of Milcah, the wife of Nahor, Abraham's brother, came out with her pitcher on her shoulder. 16Now the
young woman *was* very beautiful to behold, a virgin; no man had known
her. And she went down to the well, filled her pitcher, and came up. 17And

24:7 [l] Literally *seed*

LIFE LESSON

Genesis 24:1–25:18

SITUATION Abraham obeyed God's plan. Abraham might have married Isaac to a local girl or sent him back to his family's land to find a wife. But Abraham obeyed God by selecting the right wife from the right spot. Abraham's loyal servant discerned God's will and found the right wife—Rebekah, a woman of good heart and determination.

OBSERVATION In God's will we find successful living. God's way may be harder than the world's way—but he rewards obedience!

INSPIRATION If you want God's will, give Him your total self—a living sacrifice—and that means your body and your thoughts, your mind, which He can renew from within, if you let Him. . .

The guidance of God's Word is primary, basic. It's interesting to note that many of us say we are interested in God's will, but we balk at checking our plans and habits against the plain teaching of the Bible. How can you say you are seeking God's will, if you don't know what the Bible says? This is like going to someone for advice, but not letting him talk. You actually want him to agree with everything you say. . . .

The witness of the Holy Spirit comes as you walk in the Spirit. Prayer is vital here. It's unfortunate that we have made "I'll have to pray about it" something of a cliche. Maybe we should change the phrase to "I will talk with God about it." With God, not at God. Some prayer lists sound like Christmas lists. Others sound like assignments that God should carry out because we are "so spiritual, so deserving." . . .

Take a look at outward circumstances LAST. . . .

But suppose you feel you have the Word and the Spirit lined up fairly well. How do you evaluate or act upon circumstances? This can be intriguing, exciting. For one thing you have to act in faith on what you already know. Is it evident that there are certain actions that would be worth taking? Some people call this "trying different doors." Sometimes

Continued

God will slam shut every door but the one He wants you to walk through. You may have to try several doors to learn which is the right one.

No, God's will doesn't drop out of the blue in a special delivery letter. But He has written to you—in His Word. He will talk to you, with the inner witness of His Spirit. And He will guide you as you weigh outward circumstances.

You can be "very religious" about these three checkpoints . . . or you can use them like a Christian, in faith, trust, and commitment. Then you will see from your own experience how God's ways will really satisfy you.

(From *How to Be a Christian Without Being Religious* by Fritz Ridenour)

APPLICATION As you read the Bible, ask God to show you how your plans, goals, and directions conform to his will. Ask him to reveal to you areas where you have strayed from his leading. Consult with other Christians. Ask them for help in thinking through how the Bible applies to your situation.

EXPLORATION God's Will—Exodus 40:16; Nehemiah 9:23; Psalm 16:7-8; Micah 6:8; Acts 21:13-14; 1 Thessalonians 4:3; 5:16-18.

the servant ran to meet her and said, "Please let me drink a little water
from your pitcher."
18So she said, "Drink, my lord." Then she quickly let her pitcher down to
her hand, and gave him a drink. 19And when she had finished giving him a
drink, she said, "I will draw *water* for your camels also, until they have finished drinking." 20Then she quickly emptied her pitcher into the trough,
ran back to the well to draw *water,* and drew for all his camels. 21And the
man, wondering at her, remained silent so as to know whether the LORD
had made his journey prosperous or not.
22So it was, when the camels had finished drinking, that the man took a
golden nose ring weighing half a shekel, and two bracelets for her wrists
weighing ten *shekels* of gold, 23and said, "Whose daughter *are* you? Tell me,
please, is there room *in* your father's house for us to lodge?"
24So she said to him, "I *am* the daughter of Bethuel, Milcah's son, whom
she bore to Nahor." 25Moreover she said to him, "We have both straw and
feed enough, and room to lodge."
26Then the man bowed down his head and worshiped the LORD. 27And he
said, "Blessed *be* the LORD God of my master Abraham, who has not forsaken His mercy and His truth toward my master. As for me, being on the
way, the LORD led me to the house of my master's brethren." 28So the young
woman ran and told her mother's household these things.
29Now Rebekah had a brother whose name *was* Laban, and Laban ran
out to the man by the well. 30So it came to pass, when he saw the nose ring,
and the bracelets on his sister's wrists, and when he heard the words of his
sister Rebekah, saying, "Thus the man spoke to me," that he went to the
man. And there he stood by the camels at the well. 31And he said, "Come
in, O blessed of the LORD! Why do you stand outside? For I have prepared
the house, and a place for the camels."
32Then the man came to the house. And he unloaded the camels, and
provided straw and feed for the camels, and water to wash his feet and the
feet of the men who *were* with him. 33*Food* was set before him to eat, but
he said, "I will not eat until I have told about my errand."
And he said, "Speak on."
34So he said, "I *am* Abraham's servant. 35The LORD has blessed my master greatly, and he has become great; and He has given him flocks and
herds, silver and gold, male and female servants, and camels and donkeys.
36And Sarah my master's wife bore a son to my master when she was old;
and to him he has given all that he has. 37Now my master made me swear,
saying, 'You shall not take a wife for my son from the daughters of the
Canaanites, in whose land I dwell; 38but you shall go to my father's house
and to my family, and take a wife for my son.' 39And I said to my master,
'Perhaps the woman will not follow me.' 40But he said to me, 'The LORD, before whom I walk, will send His angel with you and prosper your way; and
you shall take a wife for my son from my family and from my father's
house. 41You will be clear from this oath when you arrive among my family;
for if they will not give *her* to you, then you will be released from my oath.'
42"And this day I came to the well and said, 'O LORD God of my master
Abraham, if You will now prosper the way in which I go, 43behold, I stand
by the well of water; and it shall come to pass that when the virgin comes
out to draw *water,* and I say to her, "Please give me a little water from your
pitcher to drink," 44and she says to me, "Drink, and I will draw for your

camels also,"—*let* her *be* the woman whom the LORD
has appointed for my master's son.'
45"But before I had finished speaking in my heart,
there was Rebekah, coming out with her pitcher on
her shoulder; and she went down to the well and drew
water. And I said to her, 'Please let me drink.' 46And she
made haste and let her pitcher down from her *shoul-*
der, and said, 'Drink, and I will give your camels a
drink also.' So I drank, and she gave the camels a drink
also. 47Then I asked her, and said, 'Whose daughter *are*
you?' And she said, 'The daughter of Bethuel, Nahor's
son, whom Milcah bore to him.' So I put the nose ring
on her nose and the bracelets on her wrists. 48And I
bowed my head and worshiped the LORD, and blessed
the LORD God of my master Abraham, who had led me
in the way of truth to take the daughter of my master's
brother for his son. 49Now if you will deal kindly and
truly with my master, tell me. And if not, tell me, that
I may turn to the right hand or to the left."
50Then Laban and Bethuel answered and said, "The
thing comes from the LORD; we cannot speak to you
either bad or good. 51Here *is* Rebekah before you; take
her and go, and let her be your master's son's wife, as
the LORD has spoken."
52And it came to pass, when Abraham's servant
heard their words, that he worshiped the LORD, *bow-*
ing himself to the earth. 53Then the servant brought
out jewelry of silver, jewelry of gold, and clothing, and
gave *them* to Rebekah. He also gave precious things to
her brother and to her mother.
54And he and the men who *were* with him ate and
drank and stayed all night. Then they arose in the
morning, and he said, "Send me away to my master."
55But her brother and her mother said, "Let the
young woman stay with us *a few* days, at least ten;
after that she may go."
56And he said to them, "Do not hinder me, since the
LORD has prospered my way; send me away so that I
may go to my master."
57So they said, "We will call the young woman and
ask her personally." 58Then they called Rebekah and
said to her, "Will you go with this man?"
And she said, "I will go."
59So they sent away Rebekah their sister and her
nurse, and Abraham's servant and his men. 60And
they blessed Rebekah and said to her:

"Our sister, *may* you *become*
The mother of thousands of ten thousands;
And may your descendants possess
The gates of those who hate them."

61Then Rebekah and her maids arose, and they
rode on the camels and followed the man. So the servant took Rebekah and departed.
62Now Isaac came from the way of Beer Lahai Roi,
for he dwelt in the South. 63And Isaac went out to
meditate in the field in the evening; and he lifted his
eyes and looked, and there, the camels *were* coming.
64Then Rebekah lifted her eyes, and when she saw
Isaac she dismounted from her camel; 65for she had
said to the servant, "Who *is* this man walking in the
field to meet us?"
The servant said, "It *is* my master." So she took a
veil and covered herself.
66And the servant told Isaac all the things that he
had done. 67Then Isaac brought her into his mother
Sarah's tent; and he took Rebekah and she became his
wife, and he loved her. So Isaac was comforted after
his mother's *death.*

Abraham and Keturah

25 Abraham again took a wife, and her name *was*
Keturah. 2And she bore him Zimran, Jokshan,
Medan, Midian, Ishbak, and Shuah. 3Jokshan begot
Sheba and Dedan. And the sons of Dedan were
Asshurim, Letushim, and Leummim. 4And the sons
of Midian *were* Ephah, Epher, Hanoch, Abidah, and
Eldaah. All these *were* the children of Keturah.
5And Abraham gave all that he had to Isaac. 6But
Abraham gave gifts to the sons of the concubines
which Abraham had; and while he was still living he
sent them eastward, away from Isaac his son, to the
country of the east.

Abraham's Death and Burial

7This *is* the sum of the years of Abraham's life
which he lived: one hundred and seventy-five years.
8Then Abraham breathed his last and died in a good
old age, an old man and full *of years,* and was gathered to his people. 9And his sons Isaac and Ishmael
buried him in the cave of Machpelah, which *is* before
Mamre, in the field of Ephron the son of Zohar the
Hittite, 10the field which Abraham purchased from
the sons of Heth. There Abraham was buried, and Sarah his wife. 11And it came to pass, after the death of
Abraham, that God blessed his son Isaac. And Isaac
dwelt at Beer Lahai Roi.

The Families of Ishmael and Isaac

12Now this *is* the genealogy of Ishmael, Abraham's
son, whom Hagar the Egyptian, Sarah's maidservant,
bore to Abraham. 13And these *were* the names of the

LIFE LESSON
Genesis 25:19-34

SITUATION Rebekah gave birth to Jacob and Esau. Before they were even born, the boys were hostile to each other. Conflict between the two intensified throughout their lives. Eventually Esau threatened to kill Jacob.

OBSERVATION When Esau sold his rights as the firstborn son to Jacob for a bowl of vegetable soup, further dissension grew up between the brothers. Jacob later stole Esau's last remaining firstborn privilege: the blessing.

INSPIRATION *Anger.* It's easy to define: the noise of the soul. *Anger.* The unseen irritant of the heart. *Anger.* The relentless invader of silence. . . .

The louder it gets the more desperate we become. . . .

Some of you are thinking, Easy for you to say, Max, sitting there in your office. . . . You ought to try living with my wife. Or, You ought to have to cope with my past. Or, You ought to raise my kids. You don't know how my ex has mistreated me. You don't have any idea how hard my life has been. And you're right, I don't. But I have a very clear idea how miserable your future will be unless you deal with your anger. X-ray the world of the vengeful and behold the tumor of bitterness: black, menacing, malignant. Carcinoma of the spirit. Its fatal fibers creep around the edge of the heart and ravage it. Yesterday you can't alter, but your reaction to yesterday you can. The past you cannot change, but your response to your past you can.

(From *When God Whispers Your Name* by Max Lucado)

APPLICATION *Anger.* Does it describe how you react? Do you have a reputation for your temper? For your grudge? Are you known for desiring revenge? Ask God to help you change your response to past hurts.

EXPLORATION Forgiving Others—Genesis 33:1-11; 45:5-14; 50:15-21; 1 Samuel 24:8-12; 26:1-25; Luke 23:33-34; Acts 7:59-60; 2 Timothy 4:16.

sons of Ishmael, by their names, according to their generations: The firstborn of Ishmael, Nebajoth; then Kedar, Adbeel, Mibsam, 14Mishma,
Dumah, Massa, 15Hadar,[m] Tema, Jetur, Naphish, and Kedemah. 16These
were the sons of Ishmael and these *were* their names, by their towns and
their settlements, twelve princes according to their nations. 17These *were*
the years of the life of Ishmael: one hundred and thirty-seven years; and
he breathed his last and died, and was gathered to his people. 18(They
dwelt from Havilah as far as Shur, which *is* east of Egypt as you go toward
Assyria.) He died in the presence of all his brethren.
19This *is* the genealogy of Isaac, Abraham's son. Abraham begot Isaac.
20Isaac was forty years old when he took Rebekah as wife, the daughter of
Bethuel the Syrian of Padan Aram, the sister of Laban the Syrian. 21Now
Isaac pleaded with the LORD for his wife, because she *was* barren; and the
LORD granted his plea, and Rebekah his wife conceived. 22But the children
struggled together within her; and she said, "If *all is* well, why *am I like*
this?" So she went to inquire of the LORD.
23And the LORD said to her:

"Two nations *are* in your womb,
Two peoples shall be separated from your body;
One people shall be stronger than the other,
And the older shall serve the younger."

24So when her days were fulfilled *for her* to give birth, indeed *there were*
twins in her womb. 25And the first came out red. *He was* like a hairy garment all over; so they called his name Esau.[n] 26Afterward his brother came
out, and his hand took hold of Esau's heel; so his name was called Jacob.[o]
Isaac *was* sixty years old when she bore them.
27So the boys grew. And Esau was a skillful hunter, a man of the field; but
Jacob was a mild man, dwelling in tents. 28And Isaac loved Esau because
he ate *of his* game, but Rebekah loved Jacob.

Esau Sells His Birthright

29Now Jacob cooked a stew; and Esau came in from the field, and he *was*
weary. 30And Esau said to Jacob, "Please feed me with that same red *stew*,
for I *am* weary." Therefore his name was called Edom.[p]
31But Jacob said, "Sell me your birthright as of this day."
32And Esau said, "Look, I *am* about to die; so what *is* this birthright to
me?"
33Then Jacob said, "Swear to me as of this day."
So he swore to him, and sold his birthright to Jacob. 34And Jacob gave
Esau bread and stew of lentils; then he ate and drank, arose, and went his
way. Thus Esau despised *his* birthright.

Isaac and Abimelech

26 There was a famine in the land, besides the first famine that was in
the days of Abraham. And Isaac went to Abimelech king of the
Philistines, in Gerar.

25:15 [m] Masoretic Text reads *Hadad.*
25:25 [n] Literally *Hairy*
25:26 [o] Literally *Supplanter*
25:30 [p] Literally *Red*

2 Then the LORD appeared to him and said: "Do not go down to Egypt;
live in the land of which I shall tell you. 3 Dwell in this land, and I will be
with you and bless you; for to you and your descendants I give all these
lands, and I will perform the oath which I swore to Abraham your father.
4 And I will make your descendants multiply as the stars of heaven; I will
give to your descendants all these lands; and in your seed all the nations
of the earth shall be blessed; 5 because Abraham obeyed My voice and kept
My charge, My commandments, My statutes, and My laws."
6 So Isaac dwelt in Gerar. 7 And the men of the place asked about his wife.
And he said, "She *is* my sister"; for he was afraid to say, "*She is* my wife,"
because he thought, "lest the men of the place kill me for Rebekah, because
she *is* beautiful to behold." 8 Now it came to pass, when he had been there
a long time, that Abimelech king of the Philistines looked through a window, and saw, and there was Isaac, showing endearment to Rebekah his
wife. 9 Then Abimelech called Isaac and said, "Quite obviously she *is* your
wife; so how could you say, 'She *is* my sister'?"
Isaac said to him, "Because I said, 'Lest I die on account of her.' "
10 And Abimelech said, "What *is* this you have done to us? One of the
people might soon have lain with your wife, and you would have brought
guilt on us." 11 So Abimelech charged all *his* people, saying, "He who touches this man or his wife shall surely be put to death."
12 Then Isaac sowed in that land, and reaped in the same year a hundredfold; and the LORD blessed him. 13 The man began to prosper, and continued prospering until he became very prosperous; 14 for he had
possessions of flocks and possessions of herds and a great number of servants. So the Philistines envied him. 15 Now the Philistines had stopped up
all the wells which his father's servants had dug in the days of Abraham
his father, and they had filled them with earth. 16 And Abimelech said to
Isaac, "Go away from us, for you are much mightier than we."
17 Then Isaac departed from there and pitched his tent in the Valley of
Gerar, and dwelt there. 18 And Isaac dug again the wells of water which they
had dug in the days of Abraham his father, for the Philistines had stopped
them up after the death of Abraham. He called them by the names which
his father had called them.
19 Also Isaac's servants dug in the valley, and found a well of running
water there. 20 But the herdsmen of Gerar quarreled with Isaac's herdsmen, saying, "The water *is* ours." So he called the name of the well Esek,[q]
because they quarreled with him. 21 Then they dug another well, and they
quarreled over that *one* also. So he called its name Sitnah.[r] 22 And he moved
from there and dug another well, and they did not quarrel over it. So he
called its name Rehoboth,[s] because he said, "For now the LORD has made
room for us, and we shall be fruitful in the land."
23 Then he went up from there to Beersheba. 24 And the LORD appeared to
him the same night and said, "I *am* the God of your father Abraham; do
not fear, for I *am* with you. I will bless you and multiply your descendants
for My servant Abraham's sake." 25 So he built an altar there and called on
the name of the LORD, and he pitched his tent there; and there Isaac's servants dug a well.

26:20 [q] Literally *Quarrel*
26:21 [r] Literally *Enmity*
26:22 [s] Literally *Spaciousness*

LIFE LESSON

Genesis 26:1-35

SITUATION Despite God's clear promise to Isaac, he lacked faith. But through his encounter with Abimelech he learned to trust that God would protect him, provide for him, and fulfill his promise.

OBSERVATION God protects and provides for people who follow him. Even though we may doubt, God's faithfulness does not waver.

INSPIRATION Faith is a vital, life-changing, and creative power in human experience. It is belief in and intellectual assent to valid doctrine and acceptance of a sound theological position. But even more, faith is an in-depth assurance, a profound certainty that God will actually do what, in the Bible, He says He will do. The promises of Holy Scripture I personally believe to be true, without any doubt whatsoever.

So the reason for my strong faith is that the Bible teaches faith. Faith has demonstrated its validity in all kinds of circumstances in my life. As I have believed and practiced faith in God and in Jesus Christ, the most wonderful things have happened: peace, joy, and victory. Moreover, other people with deep faith, known to me, have experienced, unmistakably, the power of God operating in their lives. As a result, my own faith in faith as the power of God in action has become ever more certain. . . .

The Bible tells us that by faith we can move mountains of difficulty and trouble. "Verily I say unto you, If ye have faith as a grain of mustard seed, ye shall say unto this mountain, Remove hence to yonder place; and it shall remove: and nothing shall be impossible for you." This means no superficial or a soft kind of faith, but instead the kind that makes and keeps us "Strong and of good courage." It must be real, deep, positive faith. The sturdy, faith-believing, wonder-working New Testament tells us, "I can do all things through Christ which strengtheneth me."

(From *The Positive Power of Jesus Christ* by Norman Vincent Peale)

Continued

APPLICATION What causes you to feel anxious? Bills? Boss? School? Work project? Pray when these situations arise. Believe that God will be faithful to you.

EXPLORATION Trusting God—Matthew 6:33-34; 2 Corinthians 4:16-18; Hebrews 11:1.

26Then Abimelech came to him from Gerar with Ahuzzath, one of his
friends, and Phichol the commander of his army. 27And Isaac said to
them, "Why have you come to me, since you hate me and have sent me
away from you?"
28But they said, "We have certainly seen that the LORD is with you. So we
said, 'Let there now be an oath between us, between you and us; and let us
make a covenant with you, 29that you will do us no harm, since we have
not touched you, and since we have done nothing to you but good and
have sent you away in peace. You *are* now the blessed of the LORD.' "
30So he made them a feast, and they ate and drank. 31Then they arose
early in the morning and swore an oath with one another; and Isaac sent
them away, and they departed from him in peace.
32It came to pass the same day that Isaac's servants came and told him about
the well which they had dug, and said to him, "We have found water." 33So
he called it Shebah.[t] Therefore the name of the city *is* Beersheba[u] to this day.
34When Esau was forty years old, he took as wives Judith the daughter
of Beeri the Hittite, and Basemath the daughter of Elon the Hittite. 35And
they were a grief of mind to Isaac and Rebekah.

Isaac Blesses Jacob

27 Now it came to pass, when Isaac was old and his eyes were so dim
that he could not see, that he called Esau his older son and said to
him, "My son."
And he answered him, "Here I am."
2Then he said, "Behold now, I am old. I do not know the day of my
death. 3Now therefore, please take your weapons, your quiver and your
bow, and go out to the field and hunt game for me. 4And make me savory
food, such as I love, and bring *it* to me that I may eat, that my soul may
bless you before I die."
5Now Rebekah was listening when Isaac spoke to Esau his son. And
Esau went to the field to hunt game and to bring *it*. 6So Rebekah spoke to
Jacob her son, saying, "Indeed I heard your father speak to Esau your
brother, saying, 7'Bring me game and make savory food for me, that I may
eat it and bless you in the presence of the LORD before my death.' 8Now
therefore, my son, obey my voice according to what I command you. 9Go
now to the flock and bring me from there two choice kids of the goats, and
I will make savory food from them for your father, such as he loves. 10Then
you shall take *it* to your father, that he may eat *it*, and that he may bless you
before his death."
11And Jacob said to Rebekah his mother, "Look, Esau my brother *is* a
hairy man, and I *am* a smooth-*skinned* man. 12Perhaps my father will feel
me, and I shall seem to be a deceiver to him; and I shall bring a curse on
myself and not a blessing."
13But his mother said to him, "*Let* your curse *be* on me, my son; only
obey my voice, and go, get *them* for me." 14And he went and got *them* and
brought *them* to his mother, and his mother made savory food, such as his
father loved. 15Then Rebekah took the choice clothes of her elder son Esau,
which *were* with her in the house, and put them on Jacob her younger son.
16And she put the skins of the kids of the goats on his hands and on the
smooth part of his neck. 17Then she gave the savory food and the bread,
which she had prepared, into the hand of her son Jacob.

26:33 [t] Literally *Oath* or *Seven* [u] Literally *Well of the Oath* or *Well of the Seven*

18So he went to his father and said, "My father."
And he said, "Here I am. Who *are* you, my son?"
19Jacob said to his father, "I *am* Esau your firstborn; I have done just as
you told me; please arise, sit and eat of my game, that your soul may bless
me."
20But Isaac said to his son, "How *is it* that you have found *it* so quickly,
my son?"
And he said, "Because the LORD your God brought *it* to me."
21Isaac said to Jacob, "Please come near, that I may feel you, my son,
whether you *are* really my son Esau or not." 22So Jacob went near to Isaac
his father, and he felt him and said, "The voice *is* Jacob's voice, but the
hands *are* the hands of Esau." 23And he did not recognize him, because his
hands were hairy like his brother Esau's hands; so he blessed him.
24Then he said, "*Are* you really my son Esau?"
He said, "I *am*."
25He said, "Bring *it* near to me, and I will eat of my son's game, so that
my soul may bless you." So he brought *it* near to him, and he ate; and he
brought him wine, and he drank. 26Then his father Isaac said to him,
"Come near now and kiss me, my son." 27And he came near and kissed
him; and he smelled the smell of his clothing, and blessed him and said:

"Surely, the smell of my son
Is like the smell of a field
Which the LORD has blessed.
28 Therefore may God give you
Of the dew of heaven,
Of the fatness of the earth,
And plenty of grain and wine.
29 Let peoples serve you,
And nations bow down to you.
Be master over your brethren,
And let your mother's sons bow down to you.
Cursed *be* everyone who curses you,
And blessed *be* those who bless you!"

Esau's Lost Hope

30Now it happened, as soon as Isaac had finished blessing Jacob, and Jacob had scarcely gone out from the presence of Isaac his father, that Esau
his brother came in from his hunting. 31He also had made savory food,
and brought it to his father, and said to his father, "Let my father arise and
eat of his son's game, that your soul may bless me."
32And his father Isaac said to him, "Who *are* you?"
So he said, "I *am* your son, your firstborn, Esau."
33Then Isaac trembled exceedingly, and said, "Who? Where *is* the one
who hunted game and brought *it* to me? I ate all *of it* before you came, and
I have blessed him—*and* indeed he shall be blessed."
34When Esau heard the words of his father, he cried with an exceedingly great and bitter cry, and said to his father, "Bless me—me also, O my
father!"
35But he said, "Your brother came with deceit and has taken away your
blessing."

LIFE LESSON

Genesis 27:1–28:9

SITUATION After Jacob obtained Esau's birthright, their mother, Rebekah, helped Jacob trick his father into giving him his brother's blessing, too.

OBSERVATION When people choose to hurt others, God disciplines. God seeks, through his discipline, to save his children from eternal harm.

INSPIRATION As a Christian, I most certainly believe in punishment. Biblical justice demands that individuals be held accountable. Throughout the history of ancient Israel, to break God's law was to invite swift, specific, and certain punishment. When a law was broken, the resulting imbalance could be righted only when the transgressor was punished and thus made to "pay" for his wrong.

Though modern sociologists take offense at this elemental concept of retribution, it is essential. If justice means getting one's due, then justice is denied when deserved punishment is not received. And ultimately this undermines one's role as a moral, responsible human being. . . .

In this Biblical sense, punishment is not only just, it is very often redemptive—to the offender, the victim, and society at large.

(From *The God of Stones and Spiders* by Charles Colson)

APPLICATION Never discipline in anger, but always desire the best for the other person. If you are disciplined, take it joyfully. Then thank the individual for having your best interests in mind.

EXPLORATION God's Discipline—Psalm 94:12-13; 119:67; Proverbs 3:11-12; Jeremiah 46:28.

36And *Esau* said, "Is he not rightly named Jacob?
For he has supplanted me these two times. He took
away my birthright, and now look, he has taken away
my blessing!" And he said, "Have you not reserved a
blessing for me?"
37Then Isaac answered and said to Esau, "Indeed I
have made him your master, and all his brethren I have
given to him as servants; with grain and wine I have
sustained him. What shall I do now for you, my son?"
38And Esau said to his father, "Have you only one
blessing, my father? Bless me—me also, O my
father!" And Esau lifted up his voice and wept.
39Then Isaac his father answered and said to him:

"Behold, your dwelling shall be of the
fatness of the earth,
And of the dew of heaven from above.
40 By your sword you shall live,
And you shall serve your brother;
And it shall come to pass, when you
become restless,
That you shall break his yoke from your neck."

Jacob Escapes from Esau

41So Esau hated Jacob because of the blessing with
which his father blessed him, and Esau said in his
heart, "The days of mourning for my father are at
hand; then I will kill my brother Jacob."
42And the words of Esau her older son were told to
Rebekah. So she sent and called Jacob her younger
son, and said to him, "Surely your brother Esau comforts himself concerning you *by intending* to kill you.
43Now therefore, my son, obey my voice: arise, flee to
my brother Laban in Haran. 44And stay with him a
few days, until your brother's fury turns away, 45until
your brother's anger turns away from you, and he forgets what you have done to him; then I will send and
bring you from there. Why should I be bereaved also
of you both in one day?"
46And Rebekah said to Isaac, "I am weary of my life
because of the daughters of Heth; if Jacob takes a wife
of the daughters of Heth, like these *who are* the
daughters of the land, what good will my life be to
me?"

28 Then Isaac called Jacob and blessed him, and
charged him, and said to him: "You shall not
take a wife from the daughters of Canaan. 2Arise, go
to Padan Aram, to the house of Bethuel your mother's
father; and take yourself a wife from there of the
daughters of Laban your mother's brother.

3 "May God Almighty bless you,
And make you fruitful and multiply you,
That you may be an assembly of peoples;
4 And give you the blessing of Abraham,
To you and your descendants with you,
That you may inherit the land
In which you are a stranger,
Which God gave to Abraham."

5So Isaac sent Jacob away, and he went to Padan
Aram, to Laban the son of Bethuel the Syrian, the
brother of Rebekah, the mother of Jacob and Esau.

Esau Marries Mahalath

6Esau saw that Isaac had blessed Jacob and sent
him away to Padan Aram to take himself a wife from
there, *and that* as he blessed him he gave him a
charge, saying, "You shall not take a wife from the
daughters of Canaan," 7and that Jacob had obeyed his
father and his mother and had gone to Padan Aram.
8Also Esau saw that the daughters of Canaan did not
please his father Isaac. 9So Esau went to Ishmael and
took Mahalath the daughter of Ishmael, Abraham's
son, the sister of Nebajoth, to be his wife in addition
to the wives he had.

Jacob's Vow at Bethel

10Now Jacob went out from Beersheba and went
toward Haran. 11So he came to a certain place and
stayed there all night, because the sun had set. And he
took one of the stones of that place and put it at his
head, and he lay down in that place to sleep. 12Then he
dreamed, and behold, a ladder *was* set up on the
earth, and its top reached to heaven; and there the
angels of God were ascending and descending on it.
13And behold, the LORD stood above it and said: "I
am the LORD God of Abraham your father and the God
of Isaac; the land on which you lie I will give to you
and your descendants. 14Also your descendants shall
be as the dust of the earth; you shall spread abroad to
the west and the east, to the north and the south; and
in you and in your seed all the families of the earth
shall be blessed. 15Behold, I *am* with you and will keep
you wherever you go, and will bring you back to this
land; for I will not leave you until I have done what I
have spoken to you."
16Then Jacob awoke from his sleep and said,
"Surely the LORD is in this place, and I did not know
it." 17And he was afraid and said, "How awesome *is*
this place! This *is* none other than the house of God,
and this *is* the gate of heaven!"

18Then Jacob rose early in the morning, and took the stone that he had
put at his head, set it up as a pillar, and poured oil on top of it. 19And he
called the name of that place Bethel;[v] but the name of that city had been Luz
previously. 20Then Jacob made a vow, saying, "If God will be with me, and
keep me in this way that I am going, and give me bread to eat and clothing to put on, 21so that I come back to my father's house in peace, then the
LORD shall be my God. 22And this stone which I have set as a pillar shall be
God's house, and of all that You give me I will surely give a tenth to You."

Jacob Meets Rachel

29 So Jacob went on his journey and came to the land of the people of
the East. 2And he looked, and saw a well in the field; and behold,
there *were* three flocks of sheep lying by it; for out of that well they watered
the flocks. A large stone *was* on the well's mouth. 3Now all the flocks would
be gathered there; and they would roll the stone from the well's mouth,
water the sheep, and put the stone back in its place on the well's mouth.
4And Jacob said to them, "My brethren, where *are* you from?"
And they said, "We *are* from Haran."
5Then he said to them, "Do you know Laban the son of Nahor?"
And they said, "We know him."
6So he said to them, "Is he well?"
And they said, "*He is* well. And look, his daughter Rachel is coming with
the sheep."
7Then he said, "Look, *it is* still high day; *it is* not time for the cattle to be
gathered together. Water the sheep, and go and feed *them.*"
8But they said, "We cannot until all the flocks are gathered together, and
they have rolled the stone from the well's mouth; then we water the sheep."
9Now while he was still speaking with them, Rachel came with her
father's sheep, for she was a shepherdess. 10And it came to pass, when Jacob saw Rachel the daughter of Laban his mother's brother, and the sheep
of Laban his mother's brother, that Jacob went near and rolled the stone
from the well's mouth, and watered the flock of Laban his mother's brother. 11Then Jacob kissed Rachel, and lifted up his voice and wept. 12And Jacob told Rachel that he *was* her father's relative and that he *was* Rebekah's
son. So she ran and told her father.
13Then it came to pass, when Laban heard the report about Jacob his sister's son, that he ran to meet him, and embraced him and kissed him, and
brought him to his house. So he told Laban all these things. 14And Laban
said to him, "Surely you *are* my bone and my flesh." And he stayed with
him for a month.

Jacob Marries Leah and Rachel

15Then Laban said to Jacob, "Because you *are* my relative, should you
therefore serve me for nothing? Tell me, what *should* your wages *be?*"
16Now Laban had two daughters: the name of the elder *was* Leah, and the
name of the younger *was* Rachel. 17Leah's eyes *were* delicate, but Rachel
was beautiful of form and appearance.
18Now Jacob loved Rachel; so he said, "I will serve you seven years for
Rachel your younger daughter."

28:19 [v] Literally *House of God*

LIFE LESSON

Genesis 28:10–30:43

SITUATION Jacob left his home and started a four hundred-mile trip north to Haran to search for a wife. In place of the customary dowry, Jacob pledged seven years' labor (which became seven more years, thanks to Laban's deception).

OBSERVATION God remains faithful to us, just as he did to Jacob. He fulfills his promise by blessing us during trying circumstances.

INSPIRATION God is economical. He doesn't waste training or experience. He knows what we are doing, what we are learning, and how he is going to use all of that five, ten, twenty years from now.

It's easy to be disappointed when we have prepared for "the plan of God for my life," only to have the door shut in our faces.

That's because we were busy focusing on the plan when God was focusing on the preparation. Watch how he uses that preparation in a whole new way.

When the signals are blurred and you are uncertain, keep on praying, getting Christian counsel, but don't stop what you are doing. Trust him to steer you if you are on the wrong course. But don't stop!

A sailboat's rudder is useless while the sails are down. Set sail, get going. You can't get any direction until the wind fills the sails. Then when the wind changes, be ready to come about. God may have to change your course, but when he does, you will have the momentum for it.

God knows how to move you when the time comes for you to be moved. He knows what is happening to you and what should be happening for you. In other words, trust God to be God. There isn't anything he doesn't know.

(From *God Guides Your Tomorrows* by Roger C. Palms)

Continued

APPLICATION Are you frustrated because your life plan progresses slower than you like? Remember, Jacob served twice as long as he originally intended before reaching his goal. Right now, pray that God will guide you today through his plan and keep you trusting.

EXPLORATION Discouragement—Deuteronomy 1:9; Joshua 1:9; 1 Samuel 1:10-18; Psalm 62:5; Proverbs 13:12; Ephesians 3:13; James 4:13-16.

19And Laban said, "*It is* better that I give her to you than that I should give
her to another man. Stay with me." 20So Jacob served seven years for Rachel,
and they seemed *only* a few days to him because of the love he had for her.
21Then Jacob said to Laban, "Give *me* my wife, for my days are fulfilled,
that I may go in to her." 22And Laban gathered together all the men of the
place and made a feast. 23Now it came to pass in the evening, that he took
Leah his daughter and brought her to Jacob; and he went in to her. 24And
Laban gave his maid Zilpah to his daughter Leah *as* a maid. 25So it came
to pass in the morning, that behold, it *was* Leah. And he said to Laban,
"What is this you have done to me? Was it not for Rachel that I served you?
Why then have you deceived me?"
26And Laban said, "It must not be done so in our country, to give the
younger before the firstborn. 27Fulfill her week, and we will give you this one
also for the service which you will serve with me still another seven years."
28Then Jacob did so and fulfilled her week. So he gave him his daughter
Rachel as wife also. 29And Laban gave his maid Bilhah to his daughter Rachel as a maid. 30Then *Jacob* also went in to Rachel, and he also loved Rachel more than Leah. And he served with Laban still another seven years.

The Children of Jacob

31When the LORD saw that Leah *was* unloved, He opened her womb; but
Rachel *was* barren. 32So Leah conceived and bore a son, and she called his
name Reuben;[w] for she said, "The LORD has surely looked on my affliction.
Now therefore, my husband will love me." 33Then she conceived again and
bore a son, and said, "Because the LORD has heard that I *am* unloved, He
has therefore given me this *son* also." And she called his name Simeon.[x]
34She conceived again and bore a son, and said, "Now this time my husband will become attached to me, because I have borne him three sons."
Therefore his name was called Levi.[y] 35And she conceived again and bore
a son, and said, "Now I will praise the LORD." Therefore she called his
name Judah.[z] Then she stopped bearing.

30 Now when Rachel saw that she bore Jacob no children, Rachel envied her sister, and said to Jacob, "Give me children, or else I die!"
2And Jacob's anger was aroused against Rachel, and he said, "*Am* I in
the place of God, who has withheld from you the fruit of the womb?"
3So she said, "Here is my maid Bilhah; go in to her, and she will bear *a*
child on my knees, that I also may have children by her." 4Then she gave
him Bilhah her maid as wife, and Jacob went in to her. 5And Bilhah conceived and bore Jacob a son. 6Then Rachel said, "God has judged my case;
and He has also heard my voice and given me a son." Therefore she called
his name Dan.[a] 7And Rachel's maid Bilhah conceived again and bore Jacob a second son. 8Then Rachel said, "With great wrestlings I have wrestled with my sister, *and* indeed I have prevailed." So she called his name
Naphtali.[b]
9When Leah saw that she had stopped bearing, she took Zilpah her
maid and gave her to Jacob as wife. 10And Leah's maid Zilpah bore Jacob a

29:32 [w] Literally *See, a Son*
29:33 [x] Literally *Heard*
29:34 [y] Literally *Attached*
29:35 [z] Literally *Praise*
30:6 [a] Literally *Judge*
30:8 [b] Literally *My Wrestling*

son. 11 Then Leah said, "A troop comes!"[c] So she called
his name Gad.[d] 12 And Leah's maid Zilpah bore Jacob
a second son. 13 Then Leah said, "I am happy, for the
daughters will call me blessed." So she called his
name Asher.[e]

14 Now Reuben went in the days of wheat harvest
and found mandrakes in the field, and brought them
to his mother Leah. Then Rachel said to Leah, "Please
give me *some* of your son's mandrakes."

15 But she said to her, "*Is it* a small matter that you
have taken away my husband? Would you take away
my son's mandrakes also?"

And Rachel said, "Therefore he will lie with you
tonight for your son's mandrakes."

16 When Jacob came out of the field in the evening,
Leah went out to meet him and said, "You must come
in to me, for I have surely hired you with my son's
mandrakes." And he lay with her that night.

17 And God listened to Leah, and she conceived and
bore Jacob a fifth son. 18 Leah said, "God has given me
my wages, because I have given my maid to my husband." So she called his name Issachar.[f] 19 Then Leah
conceived again and bore Jacob a sixth son. 20 And
Leah said, "God has endowed me *with* a good endow-
ment; now my husband will dwell with me, because I
have borne him six sons." So she called his name
Zebulun.[g] 21 Afterward she bore a daughter, and called
her name Dinah.

22 Then God remembered Rachel, and God listened
to her and opened her womb. 23 And she conceived
and bore a son, and said, "God has taken away my
reproach." 24 So she called his name Joseph,[h] and said,
"The LORD shall add to me another son."

Jacob's Agreement with Laban

25 And it came to pass, when Rachel had borne Joseph, that Jacob said to Laban, "Send me away, that I
may go to my own place and to my country. 26 Give *me*
my wives and my children for whom I have served
you, and let me go; for you know my service which I
have done for you."

27 And Laban said to him, "Please *stay,* if I have found
favor in your eyes, *for* I have learned by experience
that the LORD has blessed me for your sake." 28 Then he
said, "Name me your wages, and I will give *it.*"

29 So *Jacob* said to him, "You know how I have
served you and how your livestock has been with me.
30 For what you had before I *came was* little, and it has
increased to a great amount; the LORD has blessed you
since my coming. And now, when shall I also provide
for my own house?"

31 So he said, "What shall I give you?"

And Jacob said, "You shall not give me anything. If
you will do this thing for me, I will again feed and
keep your flocks: 32 Let me pass through all your flock
today, removing from there all the speckled and spotted sheep, and all the brown ones among the lambs,
and the spotted and speckled among the goats; and
these shall be my wages. 33 So my righteousness will
answer for me in time to come, when the subject of
my wages comes before you: every one that *is* not
speckled and spotted among the goats, and brown
among the lambs, will be considered stolen, if *it is*
with me."

34 And Laban said, "Oh, that it were according to
your word!" 35 So he removed that day the male goats
that were speckled and spotted, all the female goats
that were speckled and spotted, every one that had
some white in it, and all the brown ones among the
lambs, and gave *them* into the hand of his sons.
36 Then he put three days' journey between himself
and Jacob, and Jacob fed the rest of Laban's flocks.

37 Now Jacob took for himself rods of green poplar
and of the almond and chestnut trees, peeled white
strips in them, and exposed the white which *was* in
the rods. 38 And the rods which he had peeled, he set
before the flocks in the gutters, in the watering
troughs where the flocks came to drink, so that they
should conceive when they came to drink. 39 So the
flocks conceived before the rods, and the flocks
brought forth streaked, speckled, and spotted. 40 Then
Jacob separated the lambs, and made the flocks face
toward the streaked and all the brown in the flock of
Laban; but he put his own flocks by themselves and
did not put them with Laban's flock.

41 And it came to pass, whenever the stronger livestock conceived, that Jacob placed the rods before the
eyes of the livestock in the gutters, that they might
conceive among the rods. 42 But when the flocks were
feeble, he did not put *them* in; so the feebler were
Laban's and the stronger Jacob's. 43 Thus the man became exceedingly prosperous, and had large flocks,
female and male servants, and camels and donkeys.

30:11 [c] Following Qere, Syriac, and Targum; Kethib, Septuagint, and Vulgate read *in fortune.* [d] Literally *Troop* or *Fortune*
30:13 [e] Literally *Happy*
30:18 [f] Literally *Wages*
30:20 [g] Literally *Dwelling*
30:24 [h] Literally *He Will Add*

LIFE LESSON

Genesis 31:1–33:20

SITUATION God commanded Jacob to return to his homeland after being mistreated by Laban. Rachel and Leah willingly followed their husband.

OBSERVATION God gave specific instructions to Jacob and led him through challenging trials and tests that increased his faith. God's covenant with Jacob guaranteed that God would always be with him.

INSPIRATION The ultimate will of God can never be finally defeated. . . . Picture some children playing in a tiny mountainside stream. They divert the stream by making little dams of mud and stones, and they float their toy boats in the puddles and ponds. But the stream continues to surge down to the river and the valley. Now picture men building great dams, changing the course of rivers with lakes and locks, diverting their flow. Yet even they cannot prevent the streams from flowing into the sea. In our lives, so many things—our sins and mistakes, the accidents of history, the sins of others against us—may divert and temporarily defeat God's plans and purposes. But even in new circumstances created by evils, ills, and accidents, God will provide other channels to carry out His ultimate will.

What is meant by the omnipotence of God? It does not mean that by sheer

Jacob Flees from Laban

31 Now *Jacob* heard the words of Laban's sons, saying, "Jacob has
taken away all that was our father's, and from what was our father's
he has acquired all this wealth." 2And Jacob saw the countenance of
Laban, and indeed it *was* not *favorable* toward him as before. 3Then the
LORD said to Jacob, "Return to the land of your fathers and to your family,
and I will be with you."
4So Jacob sent and called Rachel and Leah to the field, to his flock, 5and
said to them, "I see your father's countenance, that it *is* not *favorable*
toward me as before; but the God of my father has been with me. 6And you
know that with all my might I have served your father. 7Yet your father has
deceived me and changed my wages ten times, but God did not allow him
to hurt me. 8If he said thus: 'The speckled shall be your wages,' then all the
flocks bore speckled. And if he said thus: 'The streaked shall be your
wages,' then all the flocks bore streaked. 9So God has taken away the livestock of your father and given *them* to me.
10"And it happened, at the time when the flocks conceived, that I lifted
my eyes and saw in a dream, and behold, the rams which leaped upon the
flocks *were* streaked, speckled, and gray-spotted. 11Then the Angel of God
spoke to me in a dream, saying, 'Jacob.' And I said, 'Here I am.' 12And He
said, 'Lift your eyes now and see, all the rams which leap on the flocks *are*
streaked, speckled, and gray-spotted; for I have seen all that Laban is
doing to you. 13I *am* the God of Bethel, where you anointed the pillar *and*
where you made a vow to Me. Now arise, get out of this land, and return
to the land of your family.' "
14Then Rachel and Leah answered and said to him, "Is there still any portion or inheritance for us in our father's house? 15Are we not considered
strangers by him? For he has sold us, and also completely consumed our
money. 16For all these riches which God has taken from our father are *really* ours and our children's; now then, whatever God has said to you, do it."
17Then Jacob rose and set his sons and his wives on camels. 18And he
carried away all his livestock and all his possessions which he had gained,
his acquired livestock which he had gained in Padan Aram, to go to his
father Isaac in the land of Canaan. 19Now Laban had gone to shear his
sheep, and Rachel had stolen the household idols that were her father's.
20And Jacob stole away, unknown to Laban the Syrian, in that he did not
tell him that he intended to flee. 21So he fled with all that he had. He arose
and crossed the river, and headed toward the mountains of Gilead.

Laban Pursues Jacob

22And Laban was told on the third day that Jacob had fled. 23Then he
took his brethren with him and pursued him for seven days' journey, and
he overtook him in the mountains of Gilead. 24But God had come to Laban
the Syrian in a dream by night, and said to him, "Be careful that you speak
to Jacob neither good nor bad."
25So Laban overtook Jacob. Now Jacob had pitched his tent in the
mountains, and Laban with his brethren pitched in the mountains of
Gilead.
26And Laban said to Jacob: "What have you done, that you have stolen
away unknown to me, and carried away my daughters like captives *taken*

with the sword? 27Why did you flee away secretly, and steal away from me,
and not tell me; for I might have sent you away with joy and songs, with
timbrel and harp? 28And you did not allow me to kiss my sons and my
daughters. Now you have done foolishly in *so* doing. 29It is in my power to
do you harm, but the God of your father spoke to me last night, saying, 'Be
careful that you speak to Jacob neither good nor bad.' 30And now you have
surely gone because you greatly long for your father's house, *but* why did
you steal my gods?"

31Then Jacob answered and said to Laban, "Because I was afraid, for I
said, 'Perhaps you would take your daughters from me by force.' 32With
whomever you find your gods, do not let him live. In the presence of our
brethren, identify what I have of yours and take *it* with you." For Jacob did
not know that Rachel had stolen them.

33And Laban went into Jacob's tent, into Leah's tent, and into the two
maids' tents, but he did not find *them.* Then he went out of Leah's tent and
entered Rachel's tent. 34Now Rachel had taken the household idols, put
them in the camel's saddle, and sat on them. And Laban searched all
about the tent but did not find *them.* 35And she said to her father, "Let it
not displease my lord that I cannot rise before you, for the manner of
women *is* with me." And he searched but did not find the household idols.

36Then Jacob was angry and rebuked Laban, and Jacob answered and
said to Laban: "What *is* my trespass? What *is* my sin, that you have so
hotly pursued me? 37Although you have searched all my things, what part
of your household things have you found? Set *it* here before my brethren
and your brethren, that they may judge between us both! 38These twenty
years I *have been* with you; your ewes and your female goats have not
miscarried their young, and I have not eaten the rams of your flock. 39That
which was torn *by beasts* I did not bring to you; I bore the loss of it. You
required it from my hand, *whether* stolen by day or stolen by night. 40*There*
I was! In the day the drought consumed me, and the frost by night, and my
sleep departed from my eyes. 41Thus I have been in your house twenty
years; I served you fourteen years for your two daughters, and six years for
your flock, and you have changed my wages ten times. 42Unless the God of
my father, the God of Abraham and the Fear of Isaac, had been with me,
surely now you would have sent me away empty-handed. God has seen
my affliction and the labor of my hands, and rebuked *you* last night."

Laban's Covenant with Jacob

43And Laban answered and said to Jacob, "*These* daughters *are* my
daughters, and *these* children *are* my children, and *this* flock *is* my flock;
all that you see *is* mine. But what can I do this day to these my daughters
or to their children whom they have borne? 44Now therefore, come, let us
make a covenant, you and I, and let it be a witness between you and me."

45So Jacob took a stone and set it up *as* a pillar. 46Then Jacob said to his
brethren, "Gather stones." And they took stones and made a heap, and
they ate there on the heap. 47Laban called it Jegar Sahadutha,[i] but Jacob
called it Galeed.[j] 48And Laban said, "This heap *is* a witness between you
and me this day." Therefore its name was called Galeed, 49also Mizpah,[k]
because he said, "May the LORD watch between you and me when we are

exhibition of power God gets His own way. This would make our freedom an illusion, and moral growth an impossibility. That God has power means He has the ability to achieve His purposes. To say God is all-powerful means that nothing can happen which will ultimately defeat Him. With evil intention the establishment of Jesus' day took the innocent Son of God and crucified Him on a cross. Purely from a human standpoint, it was the most heinous crime in history. But six weeks later Christ's disciples were preaching about that very same death on the cross. God made man's crime His instrument to save the world.

Accidents, disasters, and moral evil create terrible pain. But to those of us who love God, who are called and who cooperate with His purpose, our suffering cannot separate us from His love, or defeat the working out of His purpose in our lives.

(From *Putting Away Childish Things* by David A. Seamands)

APPLICATION Do you know someone who struggles to stay faithful while facing difficulties he or she did not create? Be a friend. Call, visit, or write. Be a witness. Share an encouragement from Scripture.

EXPLORATION Persistence—Matthew 7:7-8; Luke 11:8; Philippians 3:12-14; Colossians 4:2.

31:47 [i] Literally, in Aramaic, *Heap of Witness* [j] Literally, in Hebrew, *Heap of Witness*
31:49 [k] Literally *Watch*

absent one from another. 50If you afflict my daughters, or if you take *other* wives besides my daughters,
although no man *is* with us—see, God *is* witness
between you and me!"
51Then Laban said to Jacob, "Here is this heap and
here is *this* pillar, which I have placed between you
and me. 52This heap *is* a witness, and *this* pillar *is* a
witness, that I will not pass beyond this heap to you,
and you will not pass beyond this heap and this pillar
to me, for harm. 53The God of Abraham, the God of
Nahor, and the God of their father judge between us."
And Jacob swore by the Fear of his father Isaac.
54Then Jacob offered a sacrifice on the mountain, and
called his brethren to eat bread. And they ate bread
and stayed all night on the mountain. 55And early in
the morning Laban arose, and kissed his sons and
daughters and blessed them. Then Laban departed
and returned to his place.

Esau Comes to Meet Jacob

32 So Jacob went on his way, and the angels of God
met him. 2When Jacob saw them, he said, "This
is God's camp." And he called the name of that place
Mahanaim.[l]
3Then Jacob sent messengers before him to Esau
his brother in the land of Seir, the country of Edom.
4And he commanded them, saying, "Speak thus to
my lord Esau, 'Thus your servant Jacob says: "I have
dwelt with Laban and stayed there until now. 5I have
oxen, donkeys, flocks, and male and female servants;
and I have sent to tell my lord, that I may find favor in
your sight." ' "
6Then the messengers returned to Jacob, saying,
"We came to your brother Esau, and he also is coming
to meet you, and four hundred men *are* with him."
7So Jacob was greatly afraid and distressed; and he divided the people that *were* with him, and the flocks
and herds and camels, into two companies. 8And he
said, "If Esau comes to the one company and attacks
it, then the other company which is left will escape."
9Then Jacob said, "O God of my father Abraham and
God of my father Isaac, the LORD who said to me, 'Return to your country and to your family, and I will deal
well with you': 10I am not worthy of the least of all the
mercies and of all the truth which You have shown
Your servant; for I crossed over this Jordan with my
staff, and now I have become two companies. 11Deliver
me, I pray, from the hand of my brother, from the hand
of Esau; for I fear him, lest he come and attack me *and* the
mother with the children. 12For You said, 'I will surely
treat you well, and make your descendants as the sand
of the sea, which cannot be numbered for multitude.' "
13So he lodged there that same night, and took what
came to his hand as a present for Esau his brother:
14two hundred female goats and twenty male goats,
two hundred ewes and twenty rams, 15thirty milk
camels with their colts, forty cows and ten bulls,
twenty female donkeys and ten foals. 16Then he delivered *them* to the hand of his servants, every drove by
itself, and said to his servants, "Pass over before me,
and put some distance between successive droves."
17And he commanded the first one, saying, "When
Esau my brother meets you and asks you, saying, 'To
whom do you belong, and where are you going?
Whose *are* these in front of you?' 18then you shall say,
'They *are* your servant Jacob's. It *is* a present sent to
my lord Esau; and behold, he also *is* behind us.' " 19So
he commanded the second, the third, and all who followed the droves, saying, "In this manner you shall
speak to Esau when you find him; 20and also say, 'Behold, your servant Jacob *is* behind us.' " For he said,
"I will appease him with the present that goes before
me, and afterward I will see his face; perhaps he will
accept me." 21So the present went on over before him,
but he himself lodged that night in the camp.

Wrestling with God

22And he arose that night and took his two wives,
his two female servants, and his eleven sons, and
crossed over the ford of Jabbok. 23He took them, sent
them over the brook, and sent over what he had.
24Then Jacob was left alone; and a Man wrestled with
him until the breaking of day. 25Now when He saw
that He did not prevail against him, He touched the
socket of his hip; and the socket of Jacob's hip was out
of joint as He wrestled with him. 26And He said, "Let
Me go, for the day breaks."
But he said, "I will not let You go unless You bless
me!"
27So He said to him, "What *is* your name?"
He said, "Jacob."
28And He said, "Your name shall no longer be
called Jacob, but Israel;[m] for you have struggled with
God and with men, and have prevailed."
29Then Jacob asked, saying, "Tell *me* Your name, I
pray."
And He said, "Why *is* it *that* you ask about My
name?" And He blessed him there.

32:2 [l] Literally *Double Camp*
32:28 [m] Literally *Prince with God*

[30]So Jacob called the name of the place Peniel:[n] "For
I have seen God face to face, and my life is preserved."
[31]Just as he crossed over Penuel[o] the sun rose on him,
and he limped on his hip. [32]Therefore to this day the
children of Israel do not eat the muscle that shrank,
which *is* on the hip socket, because He touched the
socket of Jacob's hip in the muscle that shrank.

Jacob and Esau Meet

33 Now Jacob lifted his eyes and looked, and there,
Esau was coming, and with him were four hundred men. So he divided the children among Leah,
Rachel, and the two maidservants. [2]And he put the
maidservants and their children in front, Leah and
her children behind, and Rachel and Joseph last.
[3]Then he crossed over before them and bowed himself to the ground seven times, until he came near to
his brother.

[4]But Esau ran to meet him, and embraced him, and
fell on his neck and kissed him, and they wept. [5]And
he lifted his eyes and saw the women and children,
and said, "Who *are* these with you?"

So he said, "The children whom God has graciously given your servant." [6]Then the maidservants came
near, they and their children, and bowed down. [7]And
Leah also came near with her children, and they
bowed down. Afterward Joseph and Rachel came
near, and they bowed down.

[8]Then Esau said, "What *do* you *mean by* all this
company which I met?"

And he said, "*These are* to find favor in the sight of
my lord."

[9]But Esau said, "I have enough, my brother; keep
what you have for yourself."

[10]And Jacob said, "No, please, if I have now found
favor in your sight, then receive my present from my
hand, inasmuch as I have seen your face as though I
had seen the face of God, and you were pleased with
me. [11]Please, take my blessing that is brought to you,
because God has dealt graciously with me, and because I have enough." So he urged him, and he took *it.*

[12]Then Esau said, "Let us take our journey; let us
go, and I will go before you."

[13]But Jacob said to him, "My lord knows that the
children *are* weak, and the flocks and herds which are
nursing *are* with me. And if the men should drive
them hard one day, all the flock will die. [14]Please let
my lord go on ahead before his servant. I will lead on
slowly at a pace which the livestock that go before me,
and the children, are able to endure, until I come to
my lord in Seir."

[15]And Esau said, "Now let me leave with you *some*
of the people who *are* with me."

But he said, "What need is there? Let me find favor
in the sight of my lord." [16]So Esau returned that day on
his way to Seir. [17]And Jacob journeyed to Succoth, built
himself a house, and made booths for his livestock.
Therefore the name of the place is called Succoth.[p]

Jacob Comes to Canaan

[18]Then Jacob came safely to the city of Shechem,
which *is* in the land of Canaan, when he came from
Padan Aram; and he pitched his tent before the city.
[19]And he bought the parcel of land, where he had
pitched his tent, from the children of Hamor,
Shechem's father, for one hundred pieces of money.
[20]Then he erected an altar there and called it El Elohe
Israel.[q]

The Dinah Incident

34 Now Dinah the daughter of Leah, whom she
had borne to Jacob, went out to see the daughters of the land. [2]And when Shechem the son of
Hamor the Hivite, prince of the country, saw her, he
took her and lay with her, and violated her. [3]His soul
was strongly attracted to Dinah the daughter of Jacob,
and he loved the young woman and spoke kindly to
the young woman. [4]So Shechem spoke to his father
Hamor, saying, "Get me this young woman as a wife."

[5]And Jacob heard that he had defiled Dinah his
daughter. Now his sons were with his livestock in the
field; so Jacob held his peace until they came. [6]Then
Hamor the father of Shechem went out to Jacob to
speak with him. [7]And the sons of Jacob came in from
the field when they heard *it;* and the men were grieved
and very angry, because he had done a disgraceful
thing in Israel by lying with Jacob's daughter, a thing
which ought not to be done. [8]But Hamor spoke with
them, saying, "The soul of my son Shechem longs for
your daughter. Please give her to him as a wife. [9]And
make marriages with us; give your daughters to us,
and take our daughters to yourselves. [10]So you shall
dwell with us, and the land shall be before you. Dwell
and trade in it, and acquire possessions for yourselves in it."

32:30 [n] Literally *Face of God*
32:31 [o] Same as *Peniel,* verse 30
33:17 [p] Literally *Booths*
33:20 [q] Literally *God, the God of Israel*

LIFE LESSON

Genesis 34:1–36:43

SITUATION Even though Shechem's rape of Dinah was wrong, Simeon and Levi overreacted and sinned. Consequently, God told Jacob to move to Bethel and Hebron.

OBSERVATION In the middle of life's continuing problems and challenges, God reminded Jacob of his new name, Israel. Through this reminder, God shows he is faithful to his promises. God's promises set believers apart.

INSPIRATION On the basis of the counseling I do, I would say that the two greatest problems among Christians are a lack of understanding their position in Christ and a lack of knowing God as their Father. They have no family image; therefore, they feel cut off from other family members—members of the Body of Christ, as well as feeling alienated from God. Our fellowship is made solid only as we renew our thinking about God. What grief it must bring to God's heart for us to cast an image on Him that is not true.

A man can be a teacher without being a father, but a true father will be a teacher. A man can be a lord without being a father, but a true father will be a good director of the home. A man can be a good provider without being a good father, but a true father will be a provider. It all fits. That is what motivates God—the delight in being a great father to His children on earth! What a joy to God's heart when we respond as Jesus did when He was in Gethsemane. It was as if He said, "I know it's going to hurt, but You are my Father, and I know You will be everything that I need. I will trust You."

In my own family the greatest times with my children have been crazy times that only a family could enjoy. Times when we just go outdoors and

11 Then Shechem said to her father and her brothers, "Let me find favor
in your eyes, and whatever you say to me I will give. 12 Ask me ever so much
dowry and gift, and I will give according to what you say to me; but give
me the young woman as a wife."
13 But the sons of Jacob answered Shechem and Hamor his father, and
spoke deceitfully, because he had defiled Dinah their sister. 14 And they said
to them, "We cannot do this thing, to give our sister to one who is uncircumcised, for that *would be* a reproach to us. 15 But on this *condition* we
will consent to you: If you will become as we *are,* if every male of you is circumcised, 16 then we will give our daughters to you, and we will take your
daughters to us; and we will dwell with you, and we will become one people. 17 But if you will not heed us and be circumcised, then we will take our
daughter and be gone."
18 And their words pleased Hamor and Shechem, Hamor's son. 19 So the
young man did not delay to do the thing, because he delighted in Jacob's
daughter. He *was* more honorable than all the household of his father.
20 And Hamor and Shechem his son came to the gate of their city, and
spoke with the men of their city, saying: 21 "These men *are* at peace with us.
Therefore let them dwell in the land and trade in it. For indeed the land *is*
large enough for them. Let us take their daughters to us as wives, and let
us give them our daughters. 22 Only on this *condition* will the men consent
to dwell with us, to be one people: if every male among us is circumcised
as they *are* circumcised. 23 *Will* not their livestock, their property, and every
animal of theirs *be* ours? Only let us consent to them, and they will dwell
with us." 24 And all who went out of the gate of his city heeded Hamor and
Shechem his son; every male was circumcised, all who went out of the gate
of his city.
25 Now it came to pass on the third day, when they were in pain, that two
of the sons of Jacob, Simeon and Levi, Dinah's brothers, each took his
sword and came boldly upon the city and killed all the males. 26 And they
killed Hamor and Shechem his son with the edge of the sword, and took
Dinah from Shechem's house, and went out. 27 The sons of Jacob came
upon the slain, and plundered the city, because their sister had been
defiled. 28 They took their sheep, their oxen, and their donkeys, what *was* in
the city and what *was* in the field, 29 and all their wealth. All their little ones
and their wives they took captive; and they plundered even all that *was* in
the houses.
30 Then Jacob said to Simeon and Levi, "You have troubled me by making me obnoxious among the inhabitants of the land, among the
Canaanites and the Perizzites; and since I *am* few in number, they will
gather themselves together against me and kill me. I shall be destroyed,
my household and I."
31 But they said, "Should he treat our sister like a harlot?"

Jacob's Return to Bethel

35 Then God said to Jacob, "Arise, go up to Bethel and dwell there; and
make an altar there to God, who appeared to you when you fled
from the face of Esau your brother."
2 And Jacob said to his household and to all who *were* with him, "Put
away the foreign gods that *are* among you, purify yourselves, and change
your garments. 3 Then let us arise and go up to Bethel; and I will make an

altar there to God, who answered me in the day of my distress and has been
with me in the way which I have gone." 4So they gave Jacob all the foreign
gods which *were* in their hands, and the earrings which *were* in their ears;
and Jacob hid them under the terebinth tree which *was* by Shechem.
5And they journeyed, and the terror of God was upon the cities that *were*
all around them, and they did not pursue the sons of Jacob. 6So Jacob
came to Luz (that *is,* Bethel), which *is* in the land of Canaan, he and all the
people who *were* with him. 7And he built an altar there and called the place
El Bethel,[r] because there God appeared to him when he fled from the face
of his brother.
8Now Deborah, Rebekah's nurse, died, and she was buried below Bethel
under the terebinth tree. So the name of it was called Allon Bachuth.[s]
9Then God appeared to Jacob again, when he came from Padan Aram,
and blessed him. 10And God said to him, "Your name *is* Jacob; your name
shall not be called Jacob anymore, but Israel shall be your name." So He
called his name Israel. 11Also God said to him: "I *am* God Almighty. Be
fruitful and multiply; a nation and a company of nations shall proceed
from you, and kings shall come from your body. 12The land which I gave
Abraham and Isaac I give to you; and to your descendants after you I give
this land." 13Then God went up from him in the place where He talked with
him. 14So Jacob set up a pillar in the place where He talked with him, a pillar
of stone; and he poured a drink offering on it, and he poured oil on it. 15And
Jacob called the name of the place where God spoke with him, Bethel.

Death of Rachel

16Then they journeyed from Bethel. And when there was but a little distance to go to Ephrath, Rachel labored *in childbirth,* and she had hard
labor. 17Now it came to pass, when she was in hard labor, that the midwife
said to her, "Do not fear; you will have this son also." 18And so it was, as
her soul was departing (for she died), that she called his name Ben-Oni;[t]
but his father called him Benjamin.[u] 19So Rachel died and was buried on
the way to Ephrath (that *is,* Bethlehem). 20And Jacob set a pillar on her
grave, which *is* the pillar of Rachel's grave to this day.
21Then Israel journeyed and pitched his tent beyond the tower of Eder.
22And it happened, when Israel dwelt in that land, that Reuben went and
lay with Bilhah his father's concubine; and Israel heard *about it.*

Jacob's Twelve Sons

Now the sons of Jacob were twelve: 23the sons of Leah *were* Reuben, Jacob's firstborn, and Simeon, Levi, Judah, Issachar, and Zebulun; 24the
sons of Rachel *were* Joseph and Benjamin; 25the sons of Bilhah, Rachel's
maidservant, *were* Dan and Naphtali; 26and the sons of Zilpah, Leah's
maidservant, *were* Gad and Asher. These *were* the sons of Jacob who were
born to him in Padan Aram.

Death of Isaac

27Then Jacob came to his father Isaac at Mamre, or Kirjath Arba[v] (that
is, Hebron), where Abraham and Isaac had dwelt. 28Now the days of Isaac

tumble through the leaves with each other. Times when my son Johnny and I have played the whole evening away with some small creative object. Times when my sons and I just grab each other and hang on each other's neck. Teachers and pupils do not do that; neither do sergeants and privates. There have been times when my little Ann, who is now nine, and I have gone on dates together. We come home with hearts so full of love for each other and so full of laughter that the joy of the Lord is our strength for days afterward. There have been times when we as a family sing at the top of our lungs. Only fathers take time for such activities.

God made us to enjoy Him. . . . God is our Father, and we are to enjoy Him forever. The family concept in heaven will be perfect in every way. Heaven on earth is the ability to bring that concept to our own hearts, friends, and churches. (Is your church characterized by a sense of family, or is it an army or a classroom?) What a comfort to enjoy God like that! I can act as a child and treat Him as a father. I am free to fail, free to speak what is a concern to me, free to be myself, free from fear, free from guilt.

(From *The God You Can Know* by Dan DeHaan)

APPLICATION Have you been wronged or harmed and responded, "I'm going to get even if it's the last thing I do!" Each time you remember the hurt, consciously turn to God for his justice and comfort. When resentment enters your mind today, say a quick silent prayer: "Not a chance! God, you are my father. Take over; I'll follow."

EXPLORATION Revenge—Judges 15; 2 Samuel 3:26-29; Matthew 5:38-45; Romans 12:17-21; 1 Peter 3:9.

35:7 [r] Literally *God of the House of God*
35:8 [s] Literally *Terebinth of Weeping*
35:18 [t] Literally *Son of My Sorrow* [u] Literally *Son of the Right Hand*
35:27 [v] Literally *Town of Arba*

were one hundred and eighty years. 29So Isaac
breathed his last and died, and was gathered to his
people, *being* old and full of days. And his sons Esau
and Jacob buried him.

The Family of Esau

36 Now this *is* the genealogy of Esau, who is
Edom. 2Esau took his wives from the daughters of Canaan: Adah the daughter of Elon the Hittite;
Aholibamah the daughter of Anah, the daughter of
Zibeon the Hivite; 3and Basemath, Ishmael's daughter, sister of Nebajoth. 4Now Adah bore Eliphaz to
Esau, and Basemath bore Reuel. 5And Aholibamah
bore Jeush, Jaalam, and Korah. These *were* the sons of
Esau who were born to him in the land of Canaan.
6Then Esau took his wives, his sons, his daughters,
and all the persons of his household, his cattle and all
his animals, and all his goods which he had gained in
the land of Canaan, and went to a country away from
the presence of his brother Jacob. 7For their possessions were too great for them to dwell together, and
the land where they were strangers could not support
them because of their livestock. 8So Esau dwelt in
Mount Seir. Esau *is* Edom.
9And this *is* the genealogy of Esau the father of the
Edomites in Mount Seir. 10These *were* the names of
Esau's sons: Eliphaz the son of Adah the wife of Esau,
and Reuel the son of Basemath the wife of Esau. 11And
the sons of Eliphaz were Teman, Omar, Zepho,[w]
Gatam, and Kenaz.
12Now Timna was the concubine of Eliphaz, Esau's
son, and she bore Amalek to Eliphaz. These *were* the
sons of Adah, Esau's wife.
13These *were* the sons of Reuel: Nahath, Zerah,
Shammah, and Mizzah. These were the sons of
Basemath, Esau's wife.
14These were the sons of Aholibamah, Esau's wife,
the daughter of Anah, the daughter of Zibeon. And
she bore to Esau: Jeush, Jaalam, and Korah.

The Chiefs of Edom

15These *were* the chiefs of the sons of Esau. The sons
of Eliphaz, the firstborn *son* of Esau, were Chief
Teman, Chief Omar, Chief Zepho, Chief Kenaz, 16Chief
Korah,[x] Chief Gatam, *and* Chief Amalek. These *were*
the chiefs of Eliphaz in the land of Edom. They *were*
the sons of Adah.
17These *were* the sons of Reuel, Esau's son: Chief
Nahath, Chief Zerah, Chief Shammah, and Chief
Mizzah. These *were* the chiefs of Reuel in the land of
Edom. These *were* the sons of Basemath, Esau's wife.
18And these *were* the sons of Aholibamah, Esau's
wife: Chief Jeush, Chief Jaalam, and Chief Korah.
These *were* the chiefs *who descended* from Aholibamah, Esau's wife, the daughter of Anah. 19These
were the sons of Esau, who is Edom, and these *were*
their chiefs.

The Sons of Seir

20These *were* the sons of Seir the Horite who inhabited the land: Lotan, Shobal, Zibeon, Anah, 21Dishon,
Ezer, and Dishan. These *were* the chiefs of the Horites,
the sons of Seir, in the land of Edom.
22And the sons of Lotan were Hori and Hemam.[y]
Lotan's sister *was* Timna.
23These *were* the sons of Shobal: Alvan,[z] Manahath,
Ebal, Shepho,[a] and Onam.
24These *were* the sons of Zibeon: both Ajah and
Anah. This *was the* Anah who found the water[b] in the
wilderness as he pastured the donkeys of his father
Zibeon. 25These *were* the children of Anah: Dishon
and Aholibamah the daughter of Anah.
26These *were* the sons of Dishon:[c] Hemdan,[d]
Eshban, Ithran, and Cheran. 27These *were* the sons of
Ezer: Bilhan, Zaavan, and Akan.[e] 28These *were* the sons
of Dishan: Uz and Aran.
29These *were* the chiefs of the Horites: Chief Lotan,
Chief Shobal, Chief Zibeon, Chief Anah, 30Chief
Dishon, Chief Ezer, and Chief Dishan. These *were* the
chiefs of the Horites, according to their chiefs in the
land of Seir.

The Kings of Edom

31Now these *were* the kings who reigned in the land
of Edom before any king reigned over the children of
Israel: 32Bela the son of Beor reigned in Edom, and
the name of his city *was* Dinhabah. 33And when Bela
died, Jobab the son of Zerah of Bozrah reigned in his
place. 34When Jobab died, Husham of the land of the
Temanites reigned in his place. 35And when Husham
died, Hadad the son of Bedad, who attacked Midian
in the field of Moab, reigned in his place. And the
name of his city *was* Avith. 36When Hadad died,

36:11 [w] Spelled *Zephi* in 1 Chronicles 1:36
36:16 [x] Samaritan Pentateuch omits *Chief Korah.*
36:22 [y] Spelled *Homam* in 1 Chronicles 1:39
36:23 [z] Spelled *Alian* in 1 Chronicles 1:40 [a] Spelled *Shephi* in 1 Chronicles 1:40
36:24 [b] Following Masoretic Text and Vulgate (*hot springs*); Septuagint reads *Jamin;* Targum reads *mighty men;* Talmud interprets as *mules.*
36:26 [c] Hebrew *Dishan* [d] Spelled *Hamran* in 1 Chronicles 1:41
36:27 [e] Spelled *Jaakan* in 1 Chronicles 1:42

Samlah of Masrekah reigned in his place. 37And when Samlah died, Saul
of Rehoboth-*by*-the-River reigned in his place. 38When Saul died, Baal-
Hanan the son of Achbor reigned in his place. 39And when Baal-Hanan the
son of Achbor died, Hadar[f] reigned in his place; and the name of his city
was Pau.[g] His wife's name *was* Mehetabel, the daughter of Matred, the
daughter of Mezahab.

The Chiefs of Esau

40And these *were* the names of the chiefs of Esau, according to their families and their places, by their names: Chief Timnah, Chief Alvah,[h] Chief
Jetheth, 41Chief Aholibamah, Chief Elah, Chief Pinon, 42Chief Kenaz, Chief
Teman, Chief Mibzar, 43Chief Magdiel, and Chief Iram. These *were* the
chiefs of Edom, according to their dwelling places in the land of their possession. Esau *was* the father of the Edomites.

Joseph Dreams of Greatness

37 Now Jacob dwelt in the land where his father was a stranger, in the
land of Canaan. 2This *is* the history of Jacob.
Joseph, *being* seventeen years old, was feeding the flock with his brothers. And the lad *was* with the sons of Bilhah and the sons of Zilpah, his
father's wives; and Joseph brought a bad report of them to his father.
3Now Israel loved Joseph more than all his children, because he *was* the
son of his old age. Also he made him a tunic of *many* colors. 4But when his
brothers saw that their father loved him more than all his brothers, they
hated him and could not speak peaceably to him.
5Now Joseph had a dream, and he told *it* to his brothers; and they hated
him even more. 6So he said to them, "Please hear this dream which I have
dreamed: 7There we were, binding sheaves in the field. Then behold, my
sheaf arose and also stood upright; and indeed your sheaves stood all
around and bowed down to my sheaf."
8And his brothers said to him, "Shall you indeed reign over us? Or shall
you indeed have dominion over us?" So they hated him even more for his
dreams and for his words.
9Then he dreamed still another dream and told it to his brothers, and
said, "Look, I have dreamed another dream. And this time, the sun, the
moon, and the eleven stars bowed down to me."
10So he told *it* to his father and his brothers; and his father rebuked him and
said to him, "What *is* this dream that you have dreamed? Shall your mother and I and your brothers indeed come to bow down to the earth before
you?" 11And his brothers envied him, but his father kept the matter *in mind.*

Joseph Sold by His Brothers

12Then his brothers went to feed their father's flock in Shechem. 13And
Israel said to Joseph, "Are not your brothers feeding *the flock* in Shechem?
Come, I will send you to them."
So he said to him, "Here I am."
14Then he said to him, "Please go and see if it is well with your brothers
and well with the flocks, and bring back word to me." So he sent him out
of the Valley of Hebron, and he went to Shechem.

36:39 [f] Spelled *Hadad* in Samaritan Pentateuch, Syriac, and 1 Chronicles 1:50 [g] Spelled *Pai* in 1 Chronicles 1:50
36:40 [h] Spelled *Aliah* in 1 Chronicles 1:51

Life Lesson

Genesis 37:1-36

SITUATION Joseph, naive, boastful, and insensitive, told his brothers of a dream that portrayed his superiority. His furious brothers plotted to murder him and hide the act from their father. But two brothers, Reuben and Judah, rescued Joseph. Instead of killing Joseph, his brothers sold him as a slave.

OBSERVATION Although we like to achieve instant success, God often develops leaders in the crucible of prolonged suffering.

INSPIRATION A man once found a cocoon of an Emperor moth and kept it with the purpose of watching the beautiful creature emerge. Finally the day came and it began to struggle through the small opening at one end of the cocoon. The struggle continued for hours, but the moth could never force its body beyond a certain point.

Finally believing that something was wrong and that the opening should have been larger, the man took a pair of scissors and carefully clipped the restraining threads. The moth emerged easily, and crawled out onto the window sill. Its body was large and swollen, its wings small and shriveled. He supposed that in a few hours the wings would develop into the beautiful objects that he had expected. But it did not happen. The moth that should have been a thing of great beauty free to float and fly, spent its short life dragging around the swollen body and shriveled wings.

The constricting threads and the struggle necessary to pass through the tiny opening had been God's method of forcing fluids from the body into the wings. The "merciful" snip of the threads was the most cruel thing possible.

Often God lets us struggle rather than stepping in like a big brother to do our fighting for us. No doubt he could make it all so easy and every moment of life so pleasant. But as we struggle, becoming exhausted almost beyond endurance, changes occur in us which could not happen otherwise: the "fluids" expand our wings, and in time we can fly. Cut the struggle short

Continued

at some crucial point and we are crippled forever . . . or until God gives another opportunity for struggle that will do what the first aborted struggle should have been allowed to do.

(From *Temptation: Help for Struggling Christians* by Charles Durham)

APPLICATION Are you experiencing a painful restriction on your lifestyle right now: a broken relationship, a betrayal of trust, a budget squeeze, some debilitating illness, jail time or some other discipline from the Lord? Can you see the plan God may have for you, turning evil into good—as he did for Joseph? Face your struggle courageously and patiently; God may be using it to prepare you to fly.

EXPLORATION God's Mysterious Actions—Esther 4–8; Job 1–3; 42; Jonah 1–4; Philippians 1; Hebrews 11–12.

15 Now a certain man found him, and there he was, wandering in the
field. And the man asked him, saying, "What are you seeking?"
16 So he said, "I am seeking my brothers. Please tell me where they are
feeding *their flocks.*"
17 And the man said, "They have departed from here, for I heard them
say, 'Let us go to Dothan.' " So Joseph went after his brothers and found
them in Dothan.
18 Now when they saw him afar off, even before he came near them, they
conspired against him to kill him. 19 Then they said to one another, "Look,
this dreamer is coming! 20 Come therefore, let us now kill him and cast him
into some pit; and we shall say, 'Some wild beast has devoured him.' We
shall see what will become of his dreams!"
21 But Reuben heard *it,* and he delivered him out of their hands, and
said, "Let us not kill him." 22 And Reuben said to them, "Shed no blood,
but cast him into this pit which *is* in the wilderness, and do not lay a hand
on him"—that he might deliver him out of their hands, and bring him
back to his father.
23 So it came to pass, when Joseph had come to his brothers, that they
stripped Joseph *of* his tunic, the tunic of *many* colors that *was* on him.
24 Then they took him and cast him into a pit. And the pit *was* empty; *there*
was no water in it.
25 And they sat down to eat a meal. Then they lifted their eyes and looked,
and there was a company of Ishmaelites, coming from Gilead with their
camels, bearing spices, balm, and myrrh, on their way to carry *them* down
to Egypt. 26 So Judah said to his brothers, "What profit *is there* if we kill our
brother and conceal his blood? 27 Come and let us sell him to the Ishmaelites,
and let not our hand be upon him, for he *is* our brother *and* our flesh."
And his brothers listened. 28 Then Midianite traders passed by; so *the*
brothers pulled Joseph up and lifted him out of the pit, and sold him to the
Ishmaelites for twenty *shekels* of silver. And they took Joseph to Egypt.
29 Then Reuben returned to the pit, and indeed Joseph *was* not in the pit;
and he tore his clothes. 30 And he returned to his brothers and said, "The
lad *is* no *more;* and I, where shall I go?"
31 So they took Joseph's tunic, killed a kid of the goats, and dipped the
tunic in the blood. 32 Then they sent the tunic of *many* colors, and they
brought *it* to their father and said, "We have found this. Do you know
whether it *is* your son's tunic or not?"
33 And he recognized it and said, "*It is* my son's tunic. A wild beast has
devoured him. Without doubt Joseph is torn to pieces." 34 Then Jacob tore
his clothes, put sackcloth on his waist, and mourned for his son many
days. 35 And all his sons and all his daughters arose to comfort him; but he
refused to be comforted, and he said, "For I shall go down into the grave
to my son in mourning." Thus his father wept for him.
36 Now the Midianites[i] had sold him in Egypt to Potiphar, an officer of
Pharaoh *and* captain of the guard.

Judah and Tamar

38 It came to pass at that time that Judah departed from his brothers,
and visited a certain Adullamite whose name *was* Hirah. 2 And Judah saw there a daughter of a certain Canaanite whose name *was* Shua,

37:36 *i* Masoretic Text reads *Medanites.*

and he married her and went in to her. 3So she conceived and bore a son,
and he called his name Er. 4She conceived again and bore a son, and she
called his name Onan. 5And she conceived yet again and bore a son, and
called his name Shelah. He was at Chezib when she bore him.
6Then Judah took a wife for Er his firstborn, and her name *was* Tamar.
7But Er, Judah's firstborn, was wicked in the sight of the LORD, and the
LORD killed him. 8And Judah said to Onan, "Go in to your brother's wife
and marry her, and raise up an heir to your brother." 9But Onan knew that
the heir would not be his; and it came to pass, when he went in to his
brother's wife, that he emitted on the ground, lest he should give an heir to
his brother. 10And the thing which he did displeased the LORD; therefore He
killed him also.
11Then Judah said to Tamar his daughter-in-law, "Remain a widow in
your father's house till my son Shelah is grown." For he said, "Lest he also
die like his brothers." And Tamar went and dwelt in her father's house.
12Now in the process of time the daughter of Shua, Judah's wife, died;
and Judah was comforted, and went up to his sheepshearers at Timnah,
he and his friend Hirah the Adullamite. 13And it was told Tamar, saying,
"Look, your father-in-law is going up to Timnah to shear his sheep." 14So
she took off her widow's garments, covered *herself* with a veil and wrapped
herself, and sat in an open place which *was* on the way to Timnah; for she
saw that Shelah was grown, and she was not given to him as a wife. 15When
Judah saw her, he thought she *was* a harlot, because she had covered her
face. 16Then he turned to her by the way, and said, "Please let me come in
to you"; for he did not know that she *was* his daughter-in-law.
So she said, "What will you give me, that you may come in to me?"
17And he said, "I will send a young goat from the flock."
So she said, "Will you give *me* a pledge till you send *it?*"
18Then he said, "What pledge shall I give you?"
So she said, "Your signet and cord, and your staff that *is* in your hand."
Then he gave *them* to her, and went in to her, and she conceived by him.
19So she arose and went away, and laid aside her veil and put on the garments of her widowhood.
20And Judah sent the young goat by the hand of his friend the
Adullamite, to receive *his* pledge from the woman's hand, but he did not
find her. 21Then he asked the men of that place, saying, "Where is the harlot who *was* openly by the roadside?"
And they said, "There was no harlot in this *place.*"
22So he returned to Judah and said, "I cannot find her. Also, the men of
the place said there was no harlot in this *place.*"
23Then Judah said, "Let her take *them* for herself, lest we be shamed; for
I sent this young goat and you have not found her."
24And it came to pass, about three months after, that Judah was told,
saying, "Tamar your daughter-in-law has played the harlot; furthermore
she *is* with child by harlotry."
So Judah said, "Bring her out and let her be burned!"
25When she *was* brought out, she sent to her father-in-law, saying, "By
the man to whom these belong, I *am* with child." And she said, "Please
determine whose these *are*—the signet and cord, and staff."
26So Judah acknowledged *them* and said, "She has been more righteous
than I, because I did not give her to Shelah my son." And he never knew
her again.

LIFE LESSON

Genesis 38:1-30

SITUATION Onan and Judah shirked their moral responsibilities to produce a child by Tamar and preserve her family line.

OBSERVATION We must trust in God's timing and restrain our natural desires in order to follow God's law.

INSPIRATION All my life, I just wanted to be a mother. Every year I received only one Christmas gift that truly counted: a doll. Not a Barbie doll or a fashion doll, but a baby doll. . . .

At thirty-five I married. I had waited, determined not to make a mistake, and though I had dated some very sharp, attractive men, it was only when Will Anderson appeared that I knew the right man had come. . . . Will and I decided we wanted to try for a baby right away. . . . Now we shared a common dream. . . .

Somehow, though, I thought the dream of having a baby would be easier to attain [than running a marathon]. That the hardest part had been waiting so many years for the right man to be my husband. But I quickly learned the word "infertility." Strictly speaking, of course, I was not infertile. I could become pregnant all right, but each time I would miscarry during the first few weeks. During one year I was hospitalized eight times with pregnancy-related problems. . . .

In this situation, no matter what medication, what shots, what torment I subjected my body to through surgeries and other procedures, I could not make a baby. I was completely stripped and broken. And I was suddenly empty enough of myself to see God in a way I had never seen Him before.

(From *Open Adoption* by Ann Kiemel Anderson)

APPLICATION Are you waiting patiently for God to work out his loving plan? Instead of trying to "make things happen," trust God's timing and submit your dreams to him.

EXPLORATION Motherhood—Deuteronomy 25:5-10; Ruth 1–4. Tamar—Ruth 4:12; 18-22; 1 Chronicles 2:4; Matthew 1:3.

Life Lesson

Genesis 39:1–40:23

SITUATION Even though Joseph's brothers sold him into slavery, God used the situation to bless Joseph. First, an Egyptian officer entrusted his household to Joseph. When Joseph rejected the sexual advances of the officer's wife, she falsely accused Joseph of rape and had him jailed. Again, even in prison, God developed Joseph's character.

OBSERVATION In order to experience God's power, leaders must often endure hardship. Then they emerge to make their contribution.

INSPIRATION [A] leader must prepare for leadership in the same way Jesus prepared: by being willing to suffer.

The words almost sound strange to modern ears. What do we know, in this wonderful country, of suffering? As a nation we have never known real want. We have not been persecuted. There has been no war on our soil during our lifetime. There have been, of course, earthquakes, floods . . . illness. There are riots and strikes and crimes. Violent death threatens us on the highways, in the cities. . . .

To suffer simply means "to bear under." A leader is [someone] who does not groan under burdens, but takes them—and with a dash of humor. He knows how to keep his mouth shut about his difficulties and how to live a day at a time, doing quietly what needs doing at the moment.

27Now it came to pass, at the time for giving birth, that behold, twins
were in her womb. 28And so it was, when she was giving birth, that *the one*
put out *his* hand; and the midwife took a scarlet *thread* and bound it on
his hand, saying, "This one came out first." 29Then it happened, as he
drew back his hand, that his brother came out unexpectedly; and she said,
"How did you break through? *This* breach *be* upon you!" Therefore his
name was called Perez.[j] 30Afterward his brother came out who had the
scarlet *thread* on his hand. And his name was called Zerah.

Joseph a Slave in Egypt

39 Now Joseph had been taken down to Egypt. And Potiphar, an officer of Pharaoh, captain of the guard, an Egyptian, bought him from
the Ishmaelites who had taken him down there. 2The LORD was with Jo-
seph, and he was a successful man; and he was in the house of his master
the Egyptian. 3And his master saw that the LORD *was* with him and that the
LORD made all he did to prosper in his hand. 4So Joseph found favor in his
sight, and served him. Then he made him overseer of his house, and all
that he had he put under his authority. 5So it was, from the time *that* he had
made him overseer of his house and all that he had, that the LORD blessed
the Egyptian's house for Joseph's sake; and the blessing of the LORD was on
all that he had in the house and in the field. 6Thus he left all that he had in
Joseph's hand, and he did not know what he had except for the bread
which he ate.

Now Joseph was handsome in form and appearance.

7And it came to pass after these things that his master's wife cast longing eyes on Joseph, and she said, "Lie with me."

8But he refused and said to his master's wife, "Look, my master does
not know what *is* with me in the house, and he has committed all that he
has to my hand. 9*There is* no one greater in this house than I, nor has he
kept back anything from me but you, because you *are* his wife. How then
can I do this great wickedness, and sin against God?"

10So it was, as she spoke to Joseph day by day, that he did not heed her, to lie with her *or* to be with her.

11But it happened about this time, when Joseph went into the house to
do his work, and none of the men of the house *was* inside, 12that she
caught him by his garment, saying, "Lie with me." But he left his garment
in her hand, and fled and ran outside. 13And so it was, when she saw that
he had left his garment in her hand and fled outside, 14that she called to the
men of her house and spoke to them, saying, "See, he has brought in to us
a Hebrew to mock us. He came in to me to lie with me, and I cried out with
a loud voice. 15And it happened, when he heard that I lifted my voice and
cried out, that he left his garment with me, and fled and went outside."

16So she kept his garment with her until his master came home. 17Then
she spoke to him with words like these, saying, "The Hebrew servant
whom you brought to us came in to me to mock me; 18so it happened, as
I lifted my voice and cried out, that he left his garment with me and fled
outside."

19So it was, when his master heard the words which his wife spoke to
him, saying, "Your servant did to me after this manner," that his anger

38:29 [j] Literally *Breach* or *Breakthrough*

was aroused. 20Then Joseph's master took him and put him into the prison, a place where the king's prisoners *were* confined. And he was there in
the prison. 21But the LORD was with Joseph and showed him mercy, and He
gave him favor in the sight of the keeper of the prison. 22And the keeper of
the prison committed to Joseph's hand all the prisoners who *were* in the
prison; whatever they did there, it was his doing. 23The keeper of the prison
did not look into anything *that was* under *Joseph's* authority,[k] because the
LORD was with him; and whatever he did, the LORD made *it* prosper.

The Prisoners' Dreams

40 It came to pass after these things *that* the butler and the baker of
the king of Egypt offended their lord, the king of Egypt. 2And
Pharaoh was angry with his two officers, the chief butler and the chief
baker. 3So he put them in custody in the house of the captain of the guard,
in the prison, the place where Joseph *was* confined. 4And the captain of the
guard charged Joseph with them, and he served them; so they were in custody for a while.

5Then the butler and the baker of the king of Egypt, who *were* confined
in the prison, had a dream, both of them, each man's dream in one night
and each man's dream with its *own* interpretation. 6And Joseph came in
to them in the morning and looked at them, and saw that they *were* sad.
7So he asked Pharaoh's officers who *were* with him in the custody of his
lord's house, saying, "Why do you look *so* sad today?"

8And they said to him, "We each have had a dream, and *there is* no interpreter of it."

So Joseph said to them, "Do not interpretations belong to God? Tell
them to me, please."

9Then the chief butler told his dream to Joseph, and said to him, "Behold, in my dream a vine *was* before me, 10and in the vine *were* three
branches; it *was* as though it budded, its blossoms shot forth, and its clusters brought forth ripe grapes. 11Then Pharaoh's cup *was* in my hand; and
I took the grapes and pressed them into Pharaoh's cup, and placed the cup
in Pharaoh's hand."

12And Joseph said to him, "This *is* the interpretation of it: The three
branches *are* three days. 13Now within three days Pharaoh will lift up your
head and restore you to your place, and you will put Pharaoh's cup in his
hand according to the former manner, when you were his butler. 14But remember me when it is well with you, and please show kindness to me;
make mention of me to Pharaoh, and get me out of this house. 15For
indeed I was stolen away from the land of the Hebrews; and also I have
done nothing here that they should put me into the dungeon."

16When the chief baker saw that the interpretation was good, he said to
Joseph, "I also *was* in my dream, and there *were* three white baskets on my
head. 17In the uppermost basket *were* all kinds of baked goods for
Pharaoh, and the birds ate them out of the basket on my head."

18So Joseph answered and said, "This *is* the interpretation of it: The
three baskets *are* three days. 19Within three days Pharaoh will lift off your
head from you and hang you on a tree; and the birds will eat your flesh
from you."

39:23 [k] Literally *his hand*

. . . [D]on't do it alone. Perhaps I seem to be belaboring the point, but lest the "rules" for leadership appear impossibly supernatural, we need to recall constantly that it is Christ who calls us; it is Christ who enables us; it is Christ who promises His presence and His strength. Who did He call to be disciples? Weren't they quite ordinary men? None was outstanding, so far as we know, before his call to discipleship. It was not unusual gifts or an unusual spirituality or any position of temporal success already gained that drew Jesus' attention to them. He spent a night in prayer to His Father, prior to the decision, and then, in accord with the Father's will, issued the call. I pray . . . that you (and others who may read this) will answer the call to be willing to suffer in order to lead, to be last in order to be first.

(From *The Mark of a Man* by Elisabeth Elliot)

APPLICATION God often develops leaders through humility and suffering. If you have a position of leadership, realize that suffering and success both come with the job. Both build character and ability. Take heart in the examples of Joseph and Jesus, two leaders who rose above suffering to lead and to love. Accept your problems today as opportunities for growth.

EXPLORATION God's Presence at All Times—Genesis 28:15; Exodus 33:14; Deuteronomy 20:1; Isaiah 43:2; Matthew 18:20; 28:20.

Life Lesson

Genesis 41:1-57

SITUATION Egypt's king had two dreams his wise men could not interpret. The king's butler told him about Joseph's ability to interpret dreams.

OBSERVATION God spoke to the king of Egypt through two dreams, alerting him to events that would soon take place. God demonstrated his faithfulness through this unusual event.

INSPIRATION That night my sleep was disturbed by a dream in which I saw our camper being towed away by a truck. The vehicle was a total wreck. In my dream, I watched the rescue truck disappear from sight taking most of our possessions with it.

I woke from that dream, lay in the darkness and, with uncharacteristic calm, prayed: "Lord, if that should happen to us, please give me the courage to cope." The prayer offered, with a peace that does not match my personality, I fell asleep.

On the following day, in high spirits, I drove from Athens to Skopje in Yugoslavia where I handed the driving over to my husband. The dream forgotten, I settled on to the back seat of the camper to read the map and relax. I don't know what made me glance up at my husband. What I do remember is the grim, gray look on his face as I watched him juggle with a steering wheel which was clearly out of control. With incredulity, I watched him drive through mid-air and head for a silver-birch tree. I heard my nine-year-old daughter scream, "No! No!" And I felt the automobile bounce off the trunk of the tree before somersaulting down the steep embankment.

Some minutes later, I lay on the grassy bank, conscious of a dull pain between my shoulder blades, aware of blood pouring from a head wound and staring at the twisted machinery before me which six months earlier had been our brand new, blue Volkswagen camper. But I was not

20Now it came to pass on the third day, *which was* Pharaoh's birthday,
that he made a feast for all his servants; and he lifted up the head of the
chief butler and of the chief baker among his servants. 21Then he restored
the chief butler to his butlership again, and he placed the cup in Pharaoh's
hand. 22But he hanged the chief baker, as Joseph had interpreted to them.
23Yet the chief butler did not remember Joseph, but forgot him.

Pharaoh's Dreams

41 Then it came to pass, at the end of two full years, that Pharaoh had
a dream; and behold, he stood by the river. 2Suddenly there came
up out of the river seven cows, fine looking and fat; and they fed in the
meadow. 3Then behold, seven other cows came up after them out of the
river, ugly and gaunt, and stood by the *other* cows on the bank of the river.
4And the ugly and gaunt cows ate up the seven fine looking and fat cows.
So Pharaoh awoke. 5He slept and dreamed a second time; and suddenly
seven heads of grain came up on one stalk, plump and good. 6Then
behold, seven thin heads, blighted by the east wind, sprang up after them.
7And the seven thin heads devoured the seven plump and full heads. So
Pharaoh awoke, and indeed, *it was* a dream. 8Now it came to pass in the
morning that his spirit was troubled, and he sent and called for all the
magicians of Egypt and all its wise men. And Pharaoh told them his
dreams, but *there was* no one who could interpret them for Pharaoh.
9Then the chief butler spoke to Pharaoh, saying: "I remember my faults
this day. 10When Pharaoh was angry with his servants, and put me in custody in the house of the captain of the guard, *both* me and the chief baker,
11we each had a dream in one night, he and I. Each of us dreamed according to the interpretation of his *own* dream. 12Now there *was* a young Hebrew man with us there, a servant of the captain of the guard. And we told
him, and he interpreted our dreams for us; to each man he interpreted
according to his *own* dream. 13And it came to pass, just as he interpreted
for us, so it happened. He restored me to my office, and he hanged him."
14Then Pharaoh sent and called Joseph, and they brought him quickly
out of the dungeon; and he shaved, changed his clothing, and came to
Pharaoh. 15And Pharaoh said to Joseph, "I have had a dream, and *there is*
no one who can interpret it. But I have heard it said of you *that* you can
understand a dream, to interpret it."
16So Joseph answered Pharaoh, saying, "*It is* not in me; God will give
Pharaoh an answer of peace."
17Then Pharaoh said to Joseph: "Behold, in my dream I stood on the
bank of the river. 18Suddenly seven cows came up out of the river, fine
looking and fat; and they fed in the meadow. 19Then behold, seven other
cows came up after them, poor and very ugly and gaunt, such ugliness as
I have never seen in all the land of Egypt. 20And the gaunt and ugly cows
ate up the first seven, the fat cows. 21When they had eaten them up, no one
would have known that they had eaten them, for they *were* just as ugly as
at the beginning. So I awoke. 22Also I saw in my dream, and suddenly
seven heads came up on one stalk, full and good. 23Then behold, seven
heads, withered, thin, *and* blighted by the east wind, sprang up after them.
24And the thin heads devoured the seven good heads. So I told *this* to the
magicians, but *there was* no one who could explain *it* to me."
25Then Joseph said to Pharaoh, "The dreams of Pharaoh *are* one; God
has shown Pharaoh what He *is* about to do: 26The seven good cows *are*

seven years, and the seven good heads *are* seven years; the dreams *are* one.
27And the seven thin and ugly cows which came up after them *are* seven
years, and the seven empty heads blighted by the east wind are seven years
of famine. 28This *is* the thing which I have spoken to Pharaoh. God has
shown Pharaoh what He *is* about to do. 29Indeed seven years of great plenty will come throughout all the land of Egypt; 30but after them seven years
of famine will arise, and all the plenty will be forgotten in the land of Egypt;
and the famine will deplete the land. 31So the plenty will not be known in
the land because of the famine following, for it *will be* very severe. 32And
the dream was repeated to Pharaoh twice because the thing *is* established
by God, and God will shortly bring it to pass.

33"Now therefore, let Pharaoh select a discerning and wise man, and set
him over the land of Egypt. 34Let Pharaoh do *this,* and let him appoint officers over the land, to collect one-fifth *of the produce* of the land of Egypt
in the seven plentiful years. 35And let them gather all the food of those
good years that are coming, and store up grain under the authority of
Pharaoh, and let them keep food in the cities. 36Then that food shall be as
a reserve for the land for the seven years of famine which shall be in the
land of Egypt, that the land may not perish during the famine."

Joseph's Rise to Power

37So the advice was good in the eyes of Pharaoh and in the eyes of all his
servants. 38And Pharaoh said to his servants, "Can we find *such a one* as
this, a man in whom *is* the Spirit of God?"
39Then Pharaoh said to Joseph, "Inasmuch as God has shown you all
this, *there is* no one as discerning and wise as you. 40You shall be over my
house, and all my people shall be ruled according to your word; only in
regard to the throne will I be greater than you." 41And Pharaoh said to Joseph, "See, I have set you over all the land of Egypt."
42Then Pharaoh took his signet ring off his hand and put it on Joseph's
hand; and he clothed him in garments of fine linen and put a gold chain
around his neck. 43And he had him ride in the second chariot which he
had; and they cried out before him, "Bow the knee!" So he set him over all
the land of Egypt. 44Pharaoh also said to Joseph, "I *am* Pharaoh, and without your consent no man may lift his hand or foot in all the land of Egypt."
45And Pharaoh called Joseph's name Zaphnath-Paaneah. And he gave him
as a wife Asenath, the daughter of Poti-Pherah priest of On. So Joseph
went out over *all* the land of Egypt.
46Joseph was thirty years old when he stood before Pharaoh king of
Egypt. And Joseph went out from the presence of Pharaoh, and went
throughout all the land of Egypt. 47Now in the seven plentiful years the
ground brought forth abundantly. 48So he gathered up all the food of the
seven years which were in the land of Egypt, and laid up the food in the
cities; he laid up in every city the food of the fields which surrounded
them. 49Joseph gathered very much grain, as the sand of the sea, until he
stopped counting, for *it was* immeasurable.
50And to Joseph were born two sons before the years of famine came,
whom Asenath, the daughter of Poti-Pherah priest of On, bore to him. 51Jo-
seph called the name of the firstborn Manasseh:[l] "For God has made me
forget all my toil and all my father's house." 52And the name of the second

41:51 [l] Literally *Making Forgetful*

surprised. Nor shaken. It was as though I had lived this moment the night before in my dream. This was simply an action replay of a familiar event. Through the trauma of the chaotic days which followed, my heart stayed at peace.

Two days later, while I lay in a primitive hospital north of Skopje wearing a crown of bandages on my injured head, a truck towed the camper containing most of our possessions to the scrap heap—just as my dream had foretold.

While I was regaining strength in this hospital, news filtered through that my father had died tragically and suddenly of a heart attack. By the time we reached home, the funeral was over. I was never able to say my final farewell to him.

My husband referred to the accident and the bereavement and the dream in a sermon on one occasion soon after we arrived back in England. A surgeon happened to be in the congregation that morning. After the service, he told my husband something which we had not appreciated at the time: that if someone was to suffer the kind of head injuries I sustained and be so quickly subjected to the added pain of bereavement, this dream was the kindest possible preparation they could have. The trust the dream engendered ensured that, at the time of the tragedies, I was relaxed, conscious that I was held by a love which would not let me go.

(From *The Joy of Listening to God* by Joyce Hugget)

APPLICATION God has sufficient power to help us face the impossible. We must stay in close contact with him. Stay alert to take the paths he points out. Thank God for his watchful care in your life.

EXPLORATION Dreams/Visions—Deuteronomy 18:21-22; Daniel 2:26-30; Matthew 1:20-24; Acts 10:1-20.

LIFE LESSON

Genesis 42:1–43:34

SITUATION Severe famine afflicted Palestine. But under Joseph's guidance, Egypt stored enough food for itself and other nations. Jacob sent his sons to Egypt to buy food.

OBSERVATION Joseph's brothers bowed before him in submission, fulfilling the dream God had given Joseph many years before. God's Word always comes true.

INSPIRATION Abraham, or Abram as he was known at the time, was finding God's promises about as easy to swallow as a chicken bone. The promise? That his descendants would be as numerous as the stars. The problem? No son. "No problem," came God's response.

Abram looked over at his wife Sarah as she shuffled by in her gown and slippers with the aid of a walker. The chicken bone stuck for a few minutes but eventually slid down his throat. Just as he was turning away to invite Sarah to a candlelight dinner he heard promise number two.

"Abram."

"Yes, Lord."

"All this land will be yours."

Imagine God telling you that your children will someday own Fifth Avenue, and you will understand Abram's hesitation.

"On that one, Father, I need a little help."

And a little help was given.

It's a curious scene.

Twilight. The sky is a soft blue ceiling with starry diamonds. The air is cool. The animals in the pasture are quiet. The trees are silhouettes. Abram dozes under a tree. His sleep is fitful.

It's as if God is allowing Abram's doubt to run its course. In his dreams Abram is forced to face the lunacy of it all. The voices of doubt speak convincingly.

he called Ephraim:[m] "For God has caused me to be fruitful in the land of
my affliction."
[53]Then the seven years of plenty which were in the land of Egypt ended,
[54]and the seven years of famine began to come, as Joseph had said. The
famine was in all lands, but in all the land of Egypt there was bread. [55]So
when all the land of Egypt was famished, the people cried to Pharaoh for
bread. Then Pharaoh said to all the Egyptians, "Go to Joseph; whatever he
says to you, do." [56]The famine was over all the face of the earth, and Joseph
opened all the storehouses[n] and sold to the Egyptians. And the famine
became severe in the land of Egypt. [57]So all countries came to Joseph in
Egypt to buy *grain,* because the famine was severe in all lands.

Joseph's Brothers Go to Egypt

42 When Jacob saw that there was grain in Egypt, Jacob said to his
sons, "Why do you look at one another?" [2]And he said, "Indeed I
have heard that there is grain in Egypt; go down to that place and buy for
us there, that we may live and not die."
[3]So Joseph's ten brothers went down to buy grain in Egypt. [4]But Jacob
did not send Joseph's brother Benjamin with his brothers, for he said,
"Lest some calamity befall him." [5]And the sons of Israel went to buy *grain*
among those who journeyed, for the famine was in the land of Canaan.
[6]Now Joseph *was* governor over the land; and it was he who sold to all
the people of the land. And Joseph's brothers came and bowed down
before him with *their* faces to the earth. [7]Joseph saw his brothers and recognized them, but he acted as a stranger to them and spoke roughly to
them. Then he said to them, "Where do you come from?"
And they said, "From the land of Canaan to buy food."
[8]So Joseph recognized his brothers, but they did not recognize him.
[9]Then Joseph remembered the dreams which he had dreamed about
them, and said to them, "You *are* spies! You have come to see the nakedness of the land!"
[10]And they said to him, "No, my lord, but your servants have come to
buy food. [11]We *are* all one man's sons; we *are* honest *men;* your servants
are not spies."
[12]But he said to them, "No, but you have come to see the nakedness of
the land."
[13]And they said, "Your servants *are* twelve brothers, the sons of one man
in the land of Canaan; and in fact, the youngest *is* with our father today,
and one *is* no more."
[14]But Joseph said to them, "It *is* as I spoke to you, saying, 'You *are* spies!'
[15]In this *manner* you shall be tested: By the life of Pharaoh, you shall not
leave this place unless your youngest brother comes here. [16]Send one of
you, and let him bring your brother; and you shall be kept in prison, that
your words may be tested to see whether *there is* any truth in you; or else,
by the life of Pharaoh, surely you *are* spies!" [17]So he put them all together
in prison three days.
[18]Then Joseph said to them the third day, "Do this and live, *for* I fear
God: [19]If you *are* honest *men,* let one of your brothers be confined to your
prison house; but you, go and carry grain for the famine of your houses.

41:52 [m] Literally *Fruitfulness*
41:56 [n] Literally *all that was in them*

20And bring your youngest brother to me; so your words will be verified,
and you shall not die."
And they did so. 21Then they said to one another, "We *are* truly guilty
concerning our brother, for we saw the anguish of his soul when he pleaded
with us, and we would not hear; therefore this distress has come upon us."
22And Reuben answered them, saying, "Did I not speak to you, saying,
'Do not sin against the boy'; and you would not listen? Therefore behold,
his blood is now required of us." 23But they did not know that Joseph
understood *them,* for he spoke to them through an interpreter. 24And he
turned himself away from them and wept. Then he returned to them
again, and talked with them. And he took Simeon from them and bound
him before their eyes.

The Brothers Return to Canaan

25Then Joseph gave a command to fill their sacks with grain, to restore
every man's money to his sack, and to give them provisions for the journey. Thus he did for them. 26So they loaded their donkeys with the grain
and departed from there. 27But as one *of them* opened his sack to give his
donkey feed at the encampment, he saw his money; and there it was, in the
mouth of his sack. 28So he said to his brothers, "My money has been restored, and there it is, in my sack!" Then their hearts failed *them* and they
were afraid, saying to one another, "What *is* this *that* God has done to us?"
29Then they went to Jacob their father in the land of Canaan and told
him all that had happened to them, saying: 30"The man *who is* lord of the
land spoke roughly to us, and took us for spies of the country. 31But we
said to him, 'We *are* honest *men;* we are not spies. 32We *are* twelve brothers, sons of our father; one *is* no *more,* and the youngest *is* with our father
this day in the land of Canaan.' 33Then the man, the lord of the country,
said to us, 'By this I will know that you *are* honest *men:* Leave one of your
brothers *here* with me, take *food for* the famine of your households, and be
gone. 34And bring your youngest brother to me; so I shall know that you
are not spies, but *that* you *are* honest *men.* I will grant your brother to you,
and you may trade in the land.' "
35Then it happened as they emptied their sacks, that surprisingly each
man's bundle of money *was* in his sack; and when they and their father
saw the bundles of money, they were afraid. 36And Jacob their father said
to them, "You have bereaved me: Joseph is no *more,* Simeon is no *more,*
and you want to take Benjamin. All these things are against me."
37Then Reuben spoke to his father, saying, "Kill my two sons if I do not
bring him *back* to you; put him in my hands, and I will bring him back to
you."
38But he said, "My son shall not go down with you, for his brother is
dead, and he is left alone. If any calamity should befall him along the way
in which you go, then you would bring down my gray hair with sorrow to
the grave."

Joseph's Brothers Return with Benjamin

43 Now the famine *was* severe in the land. 2And it came to pass, when
they had eaten up the grain which they had brought from Egypt,
that their father said to them, "Go back, buy us a little food."
3But Judah spoke to him, saying, "The man solemnly warned us, saying,
'You shall not see my face unless your brother *is* with you.' 4If you send our

How do I know God is with me?

What if this is all a hoax?

How do you know that is God who is speaking?

The thick and dreadful darkness of doubt. . . .

God had told Abram to take three animals, cut them in half, and arrange the halves facing each other. To us the command is mysterious. To Abram, it wasn't. He'd seen the ceremony before. He'd participated in it. He'd sealed many covenants by walking through the divided carcasses and stating, "May what has happened to these animals happen also to me if I fail to uphold my word."

That is why his heart must have skipped a beat when he saw the lights in the darkness passing between the carcasses. The soft golden glow from the coals in the fire pot and the courageous flames from the torch. What did they mean?

The invisible God had drawn near to make his immovable promise. "To your descendants I give this land."

And though God's people often forgot their God, God didn't forget them. He kept his word. The land became theirs.

God didn't give up. He never gives up.

(From *Six Hours One Friday* by Max Lucado)

APPLICATION Study the Bible to find God's promises to you. Thank God for each one you find. Let the promises teach you that God never gives up on you. God stands faithfully behind his promises. Let your faith increase!

EXPLORATION Promises Fulfilled—Joshua 21:43-45; 1 Kings 8:20-24; Hebrews 6:13-15; 11:11; 2 Peter 3:8-10.

brother with us, we will go down and buy you food.
5But if you will not send *him,* we will not go down; for
the man said to us, 'You shall not see my face unless
your brother *is* with you.' "
6And Israel said, "Why did you deal *so* wrongfully
with me *as* to tell the man whether you had still *another* brother?"
7But they said, "The man asked us pointedly about
ourselves and our family, saying, '*Is* your father still
alive? Have you *another* brother?' And we told him
according to these words. Could we possibly have
known that he would say, 'Bring your brother down'?"
8Then Judah said to Israel his father, "Send the lad
with me, and we will arise and go, that we may live
and not die, both we and you *and* also our little ones.
9I myself will be surety for him; from my hand you
shall require him. If I do not bring him *back* to you
and set him before you, then let me bear the blame
forever. 10For if we had not lingered, surely by now we
would have returned this second time."
11And their father Israel said to them, "If *it must be*
so, then do this: Take some of the best fruits of the
land in your vessels and carry down a present for the
man—a little balm and a little honey, spices and
myrrh, pistachio nuts and almonds. 12Take double
money in your hand, and take back in your hand the
money that was returned in the mouth of your sacks;
perhaps it was an oversight. 13Take your brother also,
and arise, go back to the man. 14And may God Almighty give you mercy before the man, that he may
release your other brother and Benjamin. If I am
bereaved, I am bereaved!"
15So the men took that present and Benjamin, and
they took double money in their hand, and arose and
went down to Egypt; and they stood before Joseph.
16When Joseph saw Benjamin with them, he said to
the steward of his house, "Take *these* men to my
home, and slaughter an animal and make ready; for
these men will dine with me at noon." 17Then the man
did as Joseph ordered, and the man brought the men
into Joseph's house.
18Now the men were afraid because they were
brought into Joseph's house; and they said, "*It is*
because of the money, which was returned in our
sacks the first time, that we are brought in, so that he
may make a case against us and seize us, to take us as
slaves with our donkeys."
19When they drew near to the steward of Joseph's
house, they talked with him at the door of the house,
20and said, "O sir, we indeed came down the first time
to buy food; 21but it happened, when we came to the
encampment, that we opened our sacks, and there,
each man's money *was* in the mouth of his sack, our
money in full weight; so we have brought it back in
our hand. 22And we have brought down other money
in our hands to buy food. We do not know who put
our money in our sacks."
23But he said, "Peace *be* with you, do not be afraid.
Your God and the God of your father has given you
treasure in your sacks; I had your money." Then he
brought Simeon out to them.
24So the man brought the men into Joseph's house
and gave *them* water, and they washed their feet; and
he gave their donkeys feed. 25Then they made the present ready for Joseph's coming at noon, for they heard
that they would eat bread there.
26And when Joseph came home, they brought him
the present which *was* in their hand into the house,
and bowed down before him to the earth. 27Then he
asked them about *their* well-being, and said, "*Is* your
father well, the old man of whom you spoke? *Is* he still
alive?"
28And they answered, "Your servant our father *is* in
good health; he *is* still alive." And they bowed their
heads down and prostrated themselves.
29Then he lifted his eyes and saw his brother Benjamin, his mother's son, and said, "*Is* this your younger
brother of whom you spoke to me?" And he said,
"God be gracious to you, my son." 30Now his heart
yearned for his brother; so Joseph made haste and
sought *somewhere* to weep. And he went into *his*
chamber and wept there. 31Then he washed his face
and came out; and he restrained himself, and said,
"Serve the bread."
32So they set him a place by himself, and them by
themselves, and the Egyptians who ate with him by
themselves; because the Egyptians could not eat food
with the Hebrews, for that *is* an abomination to the
Egyptians. 33And they sat before him, the firstborn
according to his birthright and the youngest according to his youth; and the men looked in astonishment
at one another. 34Then he took servings to them from
before him, but Benjamin's serving was five times as
much as any of theirs. So they drank and were merry
with him.

Joseph's Cup

44 And he commanded the steward of his house,
saying, "Fill the men's sacks with food, as
much as they can carry, and put each man's money in
the mouth of his sack. 2Also put my cup, the silver
cup, in the mouth of the sack of the youngest, and his

grain money." So he did according to the word that Joseph had spoken.
3As soon as the morning dawned, the men were sent away, they and their
donkeys. 4When they had gone out of the city, *and* were not *yet* far off, Joseph said to his steward, "Get up, follow the men; and when you overtake
them, say to them, 'Why have you repaid evil for good? 5*Is* not this *the one*
from which my lord drinks, and with which he indeed practices divination? You have done evil in so doing.' "
6So he overtook them, and he spoke to them these same words. 7And
they said to him, "Why does my lord say these words? Far be it from us
that your servants should do such a thing. 8Look, we brought back to you
from the land of Canaan the money which we found in the mouth of our
sacks. How then could we steal silver or gold from your lord's house?
9With whomever of your servants it is found, let him die, and we also will
be my lord's slaves."
10And he said, "Now also *let* it *be* according to your words; he with
whom it is found shall be my slave, and you shall be blameless." 11Then
each man speedily let down his sack to the ground, and each opened his
sack. 12So he searched. He began with the oldest and left off with the
youngest; and the cup was found in Benjamin's sack. 13Then they tore their
clothes, and each man loaded his donkey and returned to the city.
14So Judah and his brothers came to Joseph's house, and he *was* still
there; and they fell before him on the ground. 15And Joseph said to them,
"What deed *is* this you have done? Did you not know that such a man as I
can certainly practice divination?"
16Then Judah said, "What shall we say to my lord? What shall we speak?
Or how shall we clear ourselves? God has found out the iniquity of your
servants; here we are, my lord's slaves, both we and *he* also with whom the
cup was found."
17But he said, "Far be it from me that I should do so; the man in whose
hand the cup was found, he shall be my slave. And as for you, go up in
peace to your father."

Judah Intercedes for Benjamin

18Then Judah came near to him and said: "O my lord, please let your
servant speak a word in my lord's hearing, and do not let your anger burn
against your servant; for you *are* even like Pharaoh. 19My lord asked his
servants, saying, 'Have you a father or a brother?' 20And we said to my lord,
'We have a father, an old man, and a child of *his* old age, *who is* young; his
brother is dead, and he alone is left of his mother's children, and his father
loves him.' 21Then you said to your servants, 'Bring him down to me, that
I may set my eyes on him.' 22And we said to my lord, 'The lad cannot leave
his father, for *if* he should leave his father, *his father* would die.' 23But you
said to your servants, 'Unless your youngest brother comes down with
you, you shall see my face no more.'
24"So it was, when we went up to your servant my father, that we told
him the words of my lord. 25And our father said, 'Go back *and* buy us a little food.' 26But we said, 'We cannot go down; if our youngest brother is
with us, then we will go down; for we may not see the man's face unless
our youngest brother *is* with us.' 27Then your servant my father said to us,
'You know that my wife bore me two sons; 28and the one went out from
me, and I said, "Surely he is torn to pieces"; and I have not seen him since.

LIFE LESSON

Genesis 44:1–45:28

SITUATION Joseph tested his brothers' sincerity before he revealed himself to them. He realized that they were genuinely sorry for their sinful plot to get rid of him.

OBSERVATION Joseph exemplified God's forgiveness. We must not harbor a grudge.

INSPIRATION Joan is forty-six years old, a successful merchandiser of women's clothing, yet extremely unhappy. She resents her father to the point of hatred because she blames him that she never married. Her father so missed having a son that he pressed Joan into a too-masculine role from childhood on.

Roger, another acquaintance, is sixty, ill with a series of physical problems. He has drifted in and out of undemanding jobs beneath his ability. Roger's heart is seething with bitterness for a business partner who cheated him. Roger was the one who had to pay with a six months' jail sentence. Constantly he harks back to this so that people do not like to be with him. His face looks so angry that children are always thinking he is mad at them.

In both Joan's and Roger's situations the inability to forgive had built to a point where all the people involved are frustrated and miserable.

Most of us are aware that Christ requires us to forgive. Yet forgiving is not easy when the other person is clearly in the wrong. This is especially true in actions that violate God's and man's laws and the good that God wants for His world. . . . The rape-murder of a little girl. Ruthless exploitation of a small country by a large and powerful one. The Dachau extermination camps. Did Jesus mean that we must also forgive evil of that kind? And if He did, how can we?

For years I attached a condition to my forgiveness: if the other person saw the error of his ways, was properly sorry, and admitted his guilt, then yes, as a Christian, I was obligated to forgive him. Finally I had to face the fact that this was my pat set of conditions, not Christ's. For He said,

Continued

[29]But if you take this one also from me, and calamity befalls him, you shall
bring down my gray hair with sorrow to the grave.'
[30]"Now therefore, when I come to your servant my father, and the lad *is*
not with us, since his life is bound up in the lad's life, [31]it will happen, when
he sees that the lad *is* not *with us,* that he will die. So your servants will
bring down the gray hair of your servant our father with sorrow to the
grave. [32]For your servant became surety for the lad to my father, saying, 'If
I do not bring him *back* to you, then I shall bear the blame before my
father forever.' [33]Now therefore, please let your servant remain instead of
the lad as a slave to my lord, and let the lad go up with his brothers. [34]For
how shall I go up to my father if the lad *is* not with me, lest perhaps I see
the evil that would come upon my father?"

Joseph Revealed to His Brothers

45 Then Joseph could not restrain himself before all those who stood
by him, and he cried out, "Make everyone go out from me!" So no
one stood with him while Joseph made himself known to his brothers.
[2]And he wept aloud, and the Egyptians and the house of Pharaoh heard *it.*
[3]Then Joseph said to his brothers, "I *am* Joseph; does my father still
live?" But his brothers could not answer him, for they were dismayed in
his presence. [4]And Joseph said to his brothers, "Please come near to me."
So they came near. Then he said: "I *am* Joseph your brother, whom you
sold into Egypt. [5]But now, do not therefore be grieved or angry with yourselves because you sold me here; for God sent me before you to preserve
life. [6]For these two years the famine *has been* in the land, and *there are* still
five years in which *there will be* neither plowing nor harvesting. [7]And God
sent me before you to preserve a posterity for you in the earth, and to save
your lives by a great deliverance. [8]So now *it was* not you *who* sent me here,
but God; and He has made me a father to Pharaoh, and lord of all his
house, and a ruler throughout all the land of Egypt.
[9]"Hurry and go up to my father, and say to him, 'Thus says your son Joseph: "God has made me lord of all Egypt; come down to me, do not tarry.
[10]You shall dwell in the land of Goshen, and you shall be near to me, you
and your children, your children's children, your flocks and your herds,
and all that you have. [11]There I will provide for you, lest you and your
household, and all that you have, come to poverty; for *there are* still five
years of famine."'
[12]"And behold, your eyes and the eyes of my brother Benjamin see that
it is my mouth that speaks to you. [13]So you shall tell my father of all my
glory in Egypt, and of all that you have seen; and you shall hurry and bring
my father down here."
[14]Then he fell on his brother Benjamin's neck and wept, and Benjamin
wept on his neck. [15]Moreover he kissed all his brothers and wept over
them, and after that his brothers talked with him.
[16]Now the report of it was heard in Pharaoh's house, saying, "Joseph's
brothers have come." So it pleased Pharaoh and his servants well. [17]And
Pharaoh said to Joseph, "Say to your brothers, 'Do this: Load your animals
and depart; go to the land of Canaan. [18]Bring your father and your households and come to me; I will give you the best of the land of Egypt, and you
will eat the fat of the land. [19]Now you are commanded—do this: Take carts
out of the land of Egypt for your little ones and your wives; bring your father

"Forgive, if ye have aught against any. . . . " "Any" can have only one meaning: anybody-everybody-all-inclusive. As for the particular wrongs we are to forgive, Jesus is just as demanding on us there too. His instructions are to forgive "aught." The dictionary definition of "aught" is "anything whatsoever." Again all-inclusive.

The scope and inflexibility of Jesus' teaching on forgiveness staggered me. Obviously I was missing something. . . . How can a righteous God ask to forgive a rapist, an exploiter, or a murderer with blood on his hands? Would not forgiving the unrepentant murderer be the same as saying that all value-judgments are wrong?

(From *Something More* by Catherine Marshall)

APPLICATION What person seems impossible for you to forgive? What keeps you from fully forgiving the one who hurt you? God's love outweighs any hurtful experience. Will you obey God and forgive?

EXPLORATION Forgiveness—Matthew 18:21-35; Luke 15:11-32; Romans 5:8; Hosea 3:1-2.

and come. 20 Also do not be concerned about your goods, for the best of all
the land of Egypt *is* yours.' "
21 Then the sons of Israel did so; and Joseph gave them carts, according
to the command of Pharaoh, and he gave them provisions for the journey.
22 He gave to all of them, to each man, changes of garments; but to Benjamin he gave three hundred *pieces* of silver and five changes of garments.
23 And he sent to his father these *things:* ten donkeys loaded with the good
things of Egypt, and ten female donkeys loaded with grain, bread, and
food for his father for the journey. 24 So he sent his brothers away, and they
departed; and he said to them, "See that you do not become troubled
along the way."
25 Then they went up out of Egypt, and came to the land of Canaan to Jacob their father. 26 And they told him, saying, "Joseph *is* still alive, and he *is*
governor over all the land of Egypt." And Jacob's heart stood still, because
he did not believe them. 27 But when they told him all the words which Joseph had said to them, and when he saw the carts which Joseph had sent
to carry him, the spirit of Jacob their father revived. 28 Then Israel said, "*It*
is enough. Joseph my son *is* still alive. I will go and see him before I die."

Jacob's Journey to Egypt

46 So Israel took his journey with all that he had, and came to
Beersheba, and offered sacrifices to the God of his father Isaac.
2 Then God spoke to Israel in the visions of the night, and said, "Jacob, Jacob!"
And he said, "Here I am."
3 So He said, "I *am* God, the God of your father; do not fear to go down
to Egypt, for I will make of you a great nation there. 4 I will go down with
you to Egypt, and I will also surely bring you up *again;* and Joseph will put
his hand on your eyes."
5 Then Jacob arose from Beersheba; and the sons of Israel carried their
father Jacob, their little ones, and their wives, in the carts which Pharaoh
had sent to carry him. 6 So they took their livestock and their goods, which
they had acquired in the land of Canaan, and went to Egypt, Jacob and all
his descendants with him. 7 His sons and his sons' sons, his daughters and
his sons' daughters, and all his descendants he brought with him to Egypt.
8 Now these *were* the names of the children of Israel, Jacob and his sons,
who went to Egypt: Reuben *was* Jacob's firstborn. 9 The sons of Reuben
were Hanoch, Pallu, Hezron, and Carmi. 10 The sons of Simeon *were*
Jemuel,[o] Jamin, Ohad, Jachin,[p] Zohar,[q] and Shaul, the son of a Canaanite
woman. 11 The sons of Levi *were* Gershon, Kohath, and Merari. 12 The sons
of Judah *were* Er, Onan, Shelah, Perez, and Zerah (but Er and Onan died in
the land of Canaan). The sons of Perez were Hezron and Hamul. 13 The
sons of Issachar *were* Tola, Puvah,[r] Job,[s] and Shimron. 14 The sons of
Zebulun *were* Sered, Elon, and Jahleel. 15 These *were* the sons of Leah,
whom she bore to Jacob in Padan Aram, with his daughter Dinah. All the
persons, his sons and his daughters, *were* thirty-three.
16 The sons of Gad *were* Ziphion,[t] Haggi, Shuni, Ezbon,[u] Eri, Arodi,[v] and

46:10 [o] Spelled *Nemuel* in 1 Chronicles 4:24 [p] Called *Jarib* in 1 Chronicles 4:24 [q] Called *Zerah* in 1 Chronicles 4:24
46:13 [r] Spelled *Puah* in 1 Chronicles 7:1 [s] Same as *Jashub* in Numbers 26:24 and 1 Chronicles 7:1
46:16 [t] Spelled *Zephon* in Samaritan Pentateuch, Septuagint, and Numbers 26:15 [u] Called *Ozni* in Numbers 26:16 [v] Spelled *Arod* in Numbers 26:17

LIFE LESSON

Genesis 46:1–47:27

SITUATION At the invitation of Joseph, Jacob and his family moved to Egypt. When they settled, Joseph arranged for them to receive the best land for their herds.

OBSERVATION Although Jacob's sons had originally intended evil for Joseph, God intended good. Over a lifetime, God uses many people and circumstances to fulfill his plan for us.

INSPIRATION No pain is so bewildering as injustice or cruelty from a brother or sister in Christ. Yet if we are to be thankful to God, we cannot at the same time give way to resentment and bitterness toward those who have made themselves our enemies. A test of whether we truly understood the principle will be found in our attitude to the human "enemies" who cause our pain. If we keep this in mind, loving our enemies may not be as difficult as it would at first appear. If we can see an enemy as someone who is an unwitting instrument of our blessing, it will be much easier to be forgiving and loving toward that person.

Joseph's brothers hated him, plotted to murder him, then sold him into slavery in Egypt to face alienation from all that he loved. Later, as master of Egypt, Joseph held the power of revenge between his fingers. . . .

His brothers intended evil. And Joseph did suffer. But God intended (and delivered) only good, not just to Joseph but to millions of people. We can love our enemies if we discover that they can never truly harm us. They can only, while they may not appear to do so, be agents of God's blessing to us and to others.

(From *The Race* by John White)

APPLICATION Who are your enemies? God's love does not know any limits. Work today to bridge the gap. It's time to put past differences where they belong—in the past!

EXPLORATION Loving Enemies—Genesis 45:7-11; 50:19-21; Matthew 5:43-48; Romans 12:9-21; 1 Corinthians 13; Galatians 5:13-15; Colossians 3:12-14; James 1:2-4; 1 John 3:11-15.

LIFE LESSON

Genesis 47:28–48:22

SITUATION Jacob was ill and near death, so Joseph brought his two sons—Jacob's grandchildren—to the family patriarch for a formal blessing.

OBSERVATION Jewish patriarchs blessed their children. This action models how parents should appreciate their children today. Parents should communicate each child's high value and special strengths.

INSPIRATION Looking to modern-day Jewish homes and practices, the blessing is still an important concept in many orthodox families. At many Shabat (Sabbath) services, the parents are to bring their children in the congregation forward to receive their blessing. Acting on behalf of the parents, the rabbi will lay his hand on the head of each child and repeat words like these, "May God bless you and make you as Ephraim and Manasseh."

This blessing originally comes from Genesis 48:20, where Jacob was blessing Joseph's two sons—Jacob's *grandchildren*. . . . Even today, centuries later, in synagogues and in Jewish homes, this blessing is a favorite for parents to use with their children.

While studying how the blessing is given in modern Jewish homes, we had the privilege of speaking with several rabbis. In our interviews, we discovered that bestowing a family blessing is considered an important vehicle for communicating a sense of

Areli. 17The sons of Asher *were* Jimnah, Ishuah, Isui, Beriah, and Serah,
their sister. And the sons of Beriah *were* Heber and Malchiel. 18These *were*
the sons of Zilpah, whom Laban gave to Leah his daughter; and these she
bore to Jacob: sixteen persons.

19The sons of Rachel, Jacob's wife, *were* Joseph and Benjamin. 20And to
Joseph in the land of Egypt were born Manasseh and Ephraim, whom
Asenath, the daughter of Poti-Pherah priest of On, bore to him. 21The sons
of Benjamin *were* Belah, Becher, Ashbel, Gera, Naaman, Ehi, Rosh,
Muppim, Huppim,[w] and Ard. 22These *were* the sons of Rachel, who were
born to Jacob: fourteen persons in all.

23The son of Dan *was* Hushim.[x] 24The sons of Naphtali *were* Jahzeel,[y] Guni,
Jezer, and Shillem.[z] 25These *were* the sons of Bilhah, whom Laban gave to
Rachel his daughter, and she bore these to Jacob: seven persons in all.

26All the persons who went with Jacob to Egypt, who came from his
body, besides Jacob's sons' wives, *were* sixty-six persons in all. 27And the
sons of Joseph who were born to him in Egypt *were* two persons. All the
persons of the house of Jacob who went to Egypt were seventy.

Jacob Settles in Goshen

28Then he sent Judah before him to Joseph, to point out before him *the*
way to Goshen. And they came to the land of Goshen. 29So Joseph made
ready his chariot and went up to Goshen to meet his father Israel; and he
presented himself to him, and fell on his neck and wept on his neck a good
while.

30And Israel said to Joseph, "Now let me die, since I have seen your face,
because you *are* still alive."

31Then Joseph said to his brothers and to his father's household, "I will
go up and tell Pharaoh, and say to him, 'My brothers and those of my father's house, who *were* in the land of Canaan, have come to me. 32And the
men *are* shepherds, for their occupation has been to feed livestock; and
they have brought their flocks, their herds, and all that they have.' 33So it
shall be, when Pharaoh calls you and says, 'What is your occupation?' 34that
you shall say, 'Your servants' occupation has been with livestock from our
youth even till now, both we *and* also our fathers,' that you may dwell in the
land of Goshen; for every shepherd *is* an abomination to the Egyptians."

47 Then Joseph went and told Pharaoh, and said, "My father and my
brothers, their flocks and their herds and all that they possess, have
come from the land of Canaan; and indeed they *are* in the land of Goshen."
2And he took five men from among his brothers and presented them to
Pharaoh. 3Then Pharaoh said to his brothers, "What *is* your occupation?"

And they said to Pharaoh, "Your servants *are* shepherds, both we *and*
also our fathers." 4And they said to Pharaoh, "We have come to dwell in
the land, because your servants have no pasture for their flocks, for the
famine *is* severe in the land of Canaan. Now therefore, please let your servants dwell in the land of Goshen."

5Then Pharaoh spoke to Joseph, saying, "Your father and your brothers
have come to you. 6The land of Egypt *is* before you. Have your father and
brothers dwell in the best of the land; let them dwell in the land of Goshen.

46:21 [w] Called *Hupham* in Numbers 26:39
46:23 [x] Called *Shuham* in Numbers 26:42
46:24 [y] Spelled *Jahziel* in 1 Chronicles 7:13 [z] Spelled *Shallum* in 1 Chronicles 7:13

And if you know *any* competent men among them, then make them chief
herdsmen over my livestock."
7 Then Joseph brought in his father Jacob and set him before Pharaoh;
and Jacob blessed Pharaoh. 8 Pharaoh said to Jacob, "How old *are* you?"
9 And Jacob said to Pharaoh, "The days of the years of my pilgrimage *are*
one hundred and thirty years; few and evil have been the days of the years
of my life, and they have not attained to the days of the years of the life of
my fathers in the days of their pilgrimage." 10 So Jacob blessed Pharaoh,
and went out from before Pharaoh.
11 And Joseph situated his father and his brothers, and gave them a possession in the land of Egypt, in the best of the land, in the land of Rameses,
as Pharaoh had commanded. 12 Then Joseph provided his father, his brothers, and all his father's household with bread, according to the number in
their families.

Joseph Deals with the Famine

13 Now *there was* no bread in all the land; for the famine *was* very severe,
so that the land of Egypt and the land of Canaan languished because of the
famine. 14 And Joseph gathered up all the money that was found in the land
of Egypt and in the land of Canaan, for the grain which they bought; and
Joseph brought the money into Pharaoh's house.
15 So when the money failed in the land of Egypt and in the land of
Canaan, all the Egyptians came to Joseph and said, "Give us bread, for
why should we die in your presence? For the money has failed."
16 Then Joseph said, "Give your livestock, and I will give you *bread* for
your livestock, if the money is gone." 17 So they brought their livestock to
Joseph, and Joseph gave them bread *in exchange* for the horses, the flocks,
the cattle of the herds, and for the donkeys. Thus he fed them with bread
in exchange for all their livestock that year.
18 When that year had ended, they came to him the next year and said to
him, "We will not hide from my lord that our money is gone; my lord also
has our herds of livestock. There is nothing left in the sight of my lord but
our bodies and our lands. 19 Why should we die before your eyes, both we
and our land? Buy us and our land for bread, and we and our land will be
servants of Pharaoh; give *us* seed, that we may live and not die, that the
land may not be desolate."
20 Then Joseph bought all the land of Egypt for Pharaoh; for every man
of the Egyptians sold his field, because the famine was severe upon them.
So the land became Pharaoh's. 21 And as for the people, he moved them
into the cities,[a] from *one* end of the borders of Egypt to the *other* end.
22 Only the land of the priests he did not buy; for the priests had rations
allotted to them by Pharaoh, and they ate their rations which Pharaoh gave
them; therefore they did not sell their lands.
23 Then Joseph said to the people, "Indeed I have bought you and your
land this day for Pharaoh. Look, *here is* seed for you, and you shall sow the
land. 24 And it shall come to pass in the harvest that you shall give one-fifth
to Pharaoh. Four-fifths shall be your own, as seed for the field and for your
food, for those of your households and as food for your little ones."
25 So they said, "You have saved our lives; let us find favor in the sight of
my lord, and we will be Pharaoh's servants." 26 And Joseph made it a law

47:21 [a] Following Masoretic Text and Targum; Samaritan Pentateuch, Septuagint, and Vulgate read *made the people virtual slaves.*

identity, meaning, love, and acceptance. In fact, in many orthodox homes, a weekly blessing is given by the father to each of his children. With the ceremonial candles lit, a time of blessing begins.

Sharing special meals; kissing, hugging, or the laying on of hands; creating a word picture or using one of the Scriptures to praise a child; even asking God to provide a special future for each child are common elements of blessing children in orthodox homes today.

While the blessing is an ancient practice, it still holds important keys to granting genuine acceptance. From a blessing to the firstborn to special words of love and acceptance for each child, the blessing remains a part of Jewish family life today. For Christian parents who have the hope and reality of Jesus, the Messiah, and His love, their blessing can be even more powerful.

(From *The Blessing* by Gary Smalley and John Trent)

APPLICATION Given the significance of the blessing in Jewish homes, consider how you could extend the blessing to your children—and their children—so that they grow up convinced of God's steadfast love. Begin this week with meaningful touch, spoken words, and symbolic gestures that say, "I love you."

EXPLORATION Blessing Children—Genesis 12:2-3; 27:1-41; 49:1-28; Deuteronomy 21:15-17; Mark 10:13-16; Romans 9:6-13.

over the land of Egypt to this day, *that* Pharaoh should have one-fifth, except for the land of the priests only, *which* did not become Pharaoh's.

Joseph's Vow to Jacob

27So Israel dwelt in the land of Egypt, in the country of Goshen; and they had possessions there and grew and multiplied exceedingly. 28And Jacob lived in the land of Egypt seventeen years. So the length of Jacob's life was one hundred and forty-seven years. 29When the time drew near that Israel must die, he called his son Joseph and said to him, "Now if I have found favor in your sight, please put your hand under my thigh, and deal kindly and truly with me. Please do not bury me in Egypt, 30but let me lie with my fathers; you shall carry me out of Egypt and bury me in their burial place."

And he said, "I will do as you have said."

31Then he said, "Swear to me." And he swore to him. So Israel bowed himself on the head of the bed.

Jacob Blesses Joseph's Sons

48 Now it came to pass after these things that Joseph was told, "Indeed your father *is* sick"; and he took with him his two sons, Manasseh and Ephraim. 2And Jacob was told, "Look, your son Joseph is coming to you"; and Israel strengthened himself and sat up on the bed. 3Then Jacob said to Joseph: "God Almighty appeared to me at Luz in the land of Canaan and blessed me, 4and said to me, 'Behold, I will make you fruitful and multiply you, and I will make of you a multitude of people, and give this land to your descendants after you *as* an everlasting possession.' 5And now your two sons, Ephraim and Manasseh, who were born to you in the land of Egypt before I came to you in Egypt, *are* mine; as Reuben and Simeon, they shall be mine. 6Your offspring whom you beget after them shall be yours; they will be called by the name of their brothers in their inheritance. 7But as for me, when I came from Padan, Rachel died beside me in the land of Canaan on the way, when *there was* but a little distance to go to Ephrath; and I buried her there on the way to Ephrath (that is, Bethlehem)."

8Then Israel saw Joseph's sons, and said, "Who *are* these?"

9Joseph said to his father, "They *are* my sons, whom God has given me in this *place*."

And he said, "Please bring them to me, and I will bless them." 10Now the eyes of Israel were dim with age, *so that* he could not see. Then Joseph brought them near him, and he kissed them and embraced them. 11And Israel said to Joseph, "I had not thought to see your face; but in fact, God has also shown me your offspring!"

12So Joseph brought them from beside his knees, and he bowed down with his face to the earth. 13And Joseph took them both, Ephraim with his right hand toward Israel's left hand, and Manasseh with his left hand toward Israel's right hand, and brought *them* near him. 14Then Israel stretched out his right hand and laid *it* on Ephraim's head, who *was* the younger, and his left hand on Manasseh's head, guiding his hands knowingly, for Manasseh *was* the firstborn. 15And he blessed Joseph, and said:

"God, before whom my fathers Abraham and
Isaac walked,
The God who has fed me all my life long to
this day,
16 The Angel who has redeemed me from all evil,
Bless the lads;
Let my name be named upon them,
And the name of my fathers Abraham and
Isaac;
And let them grow into a multitude in the
midst of the earth."

17Now when Joseph saw that his father laid his right hand on the head of Ephraim, it displeased him; so he took hold of his father's hand to remove it from Ephraim's head to Manasseh's head. 18And Joseph said to his father, "Not so, my father, for this *one is* the firstborn; put your right hand on his head."

19But his father refused and said, "I know, my son, I know. He also shall become a people, and he also shall be great; but truly his younger brother shall be greater than he, and his descendants shall become a multitude of nations."

20So he blessed them that day, saying, "By you Israel will bless, saying, 'May God make you as Ephraim and as Manasseh!' " And thus he set Ephraim before Manasseh.

21Then Israel said to Joseph, "Behold, I am dying, but God will be with you and bring you back to the land of your fathers. 22Moreover I have given to you one portion above your brothers, which I took from the hand of the Amorite with my sword and my bow."

Jacob's Last Words to His Sons

49 And Jacob called his sons and said, "Gather together, that I may tell you what shall befall you in the last days:

2 "Gather together and hear, you sons of Jacob,
And listen to Israel your father.

3 "Reuben, you are my firstborn,
My might and the beginning of my strength,
The excellency of dignity and the excellency of power.
4 Unstable as water, you shall not excel,
Because you went up to your father's bed;
Then you defiled *it*—
He went up to my couch.

5 "Simeon and Levi *are* brothers;
Instruments of cruelty *are in* their dwelling place.
6 Let not my soul enter their council;
Let not my honor be united to their assembly;
For in their anger they slew a man,
And in their self-will they hamstrung an ox.
7 Cursed *be* their anger, for *it is* fierce;
And their wrath, for it is cruel!
I will divide them in Jacob
And scatter them in Israel.

8 "Judah, you *are he* whom your brothers shall praise;
Your hand *shall be* on the neck of your enemies;
Your father's children shall bow down before you.
9 Judah *is* a lion's whelp;
From the prey, my son, you have gone up.
He bows down, he lies down as a lion;
And as a lion, who shall rouse him?
10 The scepter shall not depart from Judah,
Nor a lawgiver from between his feet,
Until Shiloh comes;
And to Him *shall be* the obedience of the people.
11 Binding his donkey to the vine,
And his donkey's colt to the choice vine,
He washed his garments in wine,
And his clothes in the blood of grapes.
12 His eyes *are* darker than wine,
And his teeth whiter than milk.

13 "Zebulun shall dwell by the haven of the sea;
He *shall become* a haven for ships,
And his border shall adjoin Sidon.

14 "Issachar is a strong donkey,
Lying down between two burdens;
15 He saw that rest *was* good,
And that the land *was* pleasant;
He bowed his shoulder to bear *a burden*,
And became a band of slaves.

16 "Dan shall judge his people
As one of the tribes of Israel.
17 Dan shall be a serpent by the way,

LIFE LESSON

Genesis 49:1-33

SITUATION In previous chapters Joseph played an instrumental role in saving Egypt from the famine. In the process he revealed his identity to his brothers and called his father to join them in Egypt. As the entire family was reunited, Jacob delivered a final blessing to each of his sons.

OBSERVATION Jacob reflected upon the lives of his sons and described what they could expect in the future.

INSPIRATION Try to write through your life. In his fine autobiographies, Frederick Buechner advises us to listen to our lives, to seek those patterns and rhythms of meaning that we often miss in the living of life but can discover on looking back. Our lives are filled with significance—if only we have eyes to see.

Tell stories. We love to hear stories because they are mostly about human beings surviving trouble. And we all need the encouragement that comes from discovering that others have been afflicted as we and have found a way to the other side. In stories are pain and struggle and failure, but also laughter and wisdom and grace. Your stories will have these things as much as anyone's, and you do not have to be good with words to tell them powerfully.

A final word of advice—write letters and tell stories that are ultimately affirming. Don't settle scores or preach old sermons. Children are flesh of our flesh and bone of our bone. Their lives are and will be difficult—as yours may have been—and they need all the encouragement they can get. They might also need a kick in the seat, but there are many ways to give them that. Speak to them words of encouragement and love. They will learn, thereby, to speak such words to others.

In writing on what you care about to those you love, you will enrich the world eternally.

(From *Letters to My Children* by Daniel Taylor)

Continued

APPLICATION Write a letter or note to someone you love. Tell that person a story of what God is doing in your life. Express appreciation for what that person has done in your life.

EXPLORATION Blessings—Genesis 27:25-29; Deuteronomy 33; Joshua 14:13. Teaching Children—Deuteronomy 4:9; 6:6-9; Psalm 78:5-7; Proverbs 22:6; Isaiah 28:9.

A viper by the path,
That bites the horse's heels
So that its rider shall fall backward.
18 I have waited for Your salvation, O LORD!

19 "Gad, a troop shall tramp upon him,
But he shall triumph at last.

20 "Bread from Asher *shall be* rich,
And he shall yield royal dainties.

21 "Naphtali *is* a deer let loose;
He uses beautiful words.

22 "Joseph *is* a fruitful bough,
A fruitful bough by a well;
His branches run over the wall.
23 The archers have bitterly grieved him,
Shot *at him* and hated him.
24 But his bow remained in strength,
And the arms of his hands were made strong
By the hands of the Mighty *God* of Jacob
(From there *is* the Shepherd, the Stone of Israel),
25 By the God of your father who will help you,
And by the Almighty who will bless you
With blessings of heaven above,
Blessings of the deep that lies beneath,
Blessings of the breasts and of the womb.
26 The blessings of your father
Have excelled the blessings of my ancestors,
Up to the utmost bound of the everlasting hills.
They shall be on the head of Joseph,
And on the crown of the head of him
who was separate from his brothers.

27 "Benjamin is a ravenous wolf;
In the morning he shall devour the prey,
And at night he shall divide the spoil."

28 All these *are* the twelve tribes of Israel, and this *is* what their father spoke to them. And he blessed them; he blessed each one according to his own blessing.

Jacob's Death and Burial

29 Then he charged them and said to them: "I am to be gathered to my people; bury me with my fathers in the cave that *is* in the field of Ephron
the Hittite, 30 in the cave that *is* in the field of Machpelah, which *is* before
Mamre in the land of Canaan, which Abraham bought with the field of
Ephron the Hittite as a possession for a burial place. 31 There they buried
Abraham and Sarah his wife, there they buried Isaac and Rebekah his
wife, and there I buried Leah. 32 The field and the cave that *is* there *were*
purchased from the sons of Heth." 33 And when Jacob had finished commanding his sons, he drew his feet up into the bed and breathed his last,
and was gathered to his people.

50 Then Joseph fell on his father's face and wept over him, and kissed
him. 2And Joseph commanded his servants the physicians to embalm his father. So the physicians embalmed Israel. 3Forty days were
required for him, for such are the days required for those who are
embalmed; and the Egyptians mourned for him seventy days.
4Now when the days of his mourning were past, Joseph spoke to the
household of Pharaoh, saying, "If now I have found favor in your eyes,
please speak in the hearing of Pharaoh, saying, 5'My father made me
swear, saying, "Behold, I am dying; in my grave which I dug for myself in
the land of Canaan, there you shall bury me." Now therefore, please let me
go up and bury my father, and I will come back.' "
6And Pharaoh said, "Go up and bury your father, as he made you swear."
7So Joseph went up to bury his father; and with him went up all the servants of Pharaoh, the elders of his house, and all the elders of the land of
Egypt, 8as well as all the house of Joseph, his brothers, and his father's
house. Only their little ones, their flocks, and their herds they left in the
land of Goshen. 9And there went up with him both chariots and horsemen, and it was a very great gathering.
10Then they came to the threshing floor of Atad, which *is* beyond the Jordan, and they mourned there with a great and very solemn lamentation.
He observed seven days of mourning for his father. 11And when the inhabitants of the land, the Canaanites, saw the mourning at the threshing floor
of Atad, they said, "This *is* a deep mourning of the Egyptians." Therefore
its name was called Abel Mizraim,[b] which *is* beyond the Jordan.
12So his sons did for him just as he had commanded them. 13For his sons
carried him to the land of Canaan, and buried him in the cave of the field
of Machpelah, before Mamre, which Abraham bought with the field from
Ephron the Hittite as property for a burial place. 14And after he had buried
his father, Joseph returned to Egypt, he and his brothers and all who went
up with him to bury his father.

Joseph Reassures His Brothers

15When Joseph's brothers saw that their father was dead, they said, "Perhaps Joseph will hate us, and may actually repay us for all the evil which
we did to him." 16So they sent *messengers* to Joseph, saying, "Before your
father died he commanded, saying, 17'Thus you shall say to Joseph: "I beg
you, please forgive the trespass of your brothers and their sin; for they did
evil to you." ' Now, please, forgive the trespass of the servants of the God
of your father." And Joseph wept when they spoke to him.
18Then his brothers also went and fell down before his face, and they
said, "Behold, we *are* your servants."
19Joseph said to them, "Do not be afraid, for *am* I in the place of God?
20But as for you, you meant evil against me; *but* God meant it for good, in
order to bring it about as *it is* this day, to save many people alive. 21Now
therefore, do not be afraid; I will provide for you and your little ones." And
he comforted them and spoke kindly to them.

Death of Joseph

22So Joseph dwelt in Egypt, he and his father's household. And Joseph
lived one hundred and ten years. 23Joseph saw Ephraim's children to the

50:11 [b] Literally *Mourning of Egypt*

Life Lesson

Genesis 50:1-26

SITUATION Jacob died. Joseph mourned. His brothers feared Joseph's long-smothered revenge would break out upon them. But Joseph forgave.

OBSERVATION We face obstacles every day. We can have confidence, though, that through every struggle, God will help and guide us.

INSPIRATION Judgment is God's job.

Revenge is irreverent.

Joseph understands that. Rather than get even, he reveals his identity and has his father and the rest of the family brought to Egypt.

But then Jacob dies and the moment of truth comes. The brothers go to Joseph and plead for mercy.

"Your father gave this command before he died. . . . 'Tell Joseph to forgive you'" (Gen. 50:16-17).

Joseph's response? "When Joseph received the message, he cried" (Gen. 50:17). "What more do I have to do?" his tears implore. "I've given you a home. I've provided for your families. Why do you still mistrust my grace?"

May I restate the obvious? Revenge belongs to God!

Why? The answer is found in the second part of Joseph's statement: "You meant to hurt me, but God turned your evil into good to save the lives of many people, which is being done" (v. 20).

Forgiveness comes easier with a wide-angle lens. Joseph uses one to get the whole picture.

It always helps to see the big picture. . . .

(From *When God Whispers Your Name* by Max Lucado)

APPLICATION To forgive, what rights must you give up? What sense of personal revenge must you release to God's control? Put these feelings behind you. Be like Joseph . . . forgive!

EXPLORATION Forgiveness—Psalm 103:12; Matthew 6:14-15; Romans 12:17-21; Hebrews 10:17; 1 John 1:9.

third *generation.* The children of Machir, the son of
Manasseh, were also brought up on Joseph's knees.
24And Joseph said to his brethren, "I am dying; but
God will surely visit you, and bring you out of this land
to the land of which He swore to Abraham, to Isaac, and
to Jacob." 25Then Joseph took an oath from the children of Israel, saying, "God will surely visit you, and
you shall carry up my bones from here." 26So Joseph
died, *being* one hundred and ten years old; and they
embalmed him, and he was put in a coffin in Egypt.

The Second Book of Moses Called

EXODUS

INTRODUCTION

What follows is the greatest scene in the book of Exodus.

Risky claim, you say? Exodus is one startling scene after another. Burning bushes, dividing seas, manna falling, quail scampering. The plagues, the slaves, the pharaoh, and the fire. How could they be ranked?

Do we dare isolate one moment as the greatest?

Yes, we do.

We turn to the Hebrew slaves and stand silently as they perform an act of faith. A brush is dipped into a bowl of lamb's blood and streaked over the doorpost. Do it, they were told, and the angel of death will pass over. They obeyed. And death took an alternate route.

That's the peak of Exodus. Exodus is a book of deliverance. Liberation from slavery. The blood on the doorpost reminds us, however, that it wasn't Moses who set them free. It was God. The blood on the doorpost reminds us of blood smeared on another post.

Blood of another lamb.

The Lamb of God.

Because of his blood, we, too, are free.

Life Lesson

Exodus 1:1-22

SITUATION Exodus records how God protected the Israelites. Pharaoh enslaved and oppressed the Israelites, but they still multiplied. To control the Jewish population, Pharaoh planned to kill newborn Hebrew males. But the Hebrew midwives stayed loyal to God and refused to obey Pharaoh.

OBSERVATION If we are faithful, we will persevere and overcome the challenges placed before us. God will not abandon us in tough times, and we should not abandon him.

INSPIRATION When it comes to the major-league difficulties like death, disease, sin and disaster—you know that God cares.

But what about the smaller things? What about grouchy bosses or flat tires or lost dogs? What about broken dishes, late flights, toothaches, or a crashed hard disk? Do these matter to God?

I mean, he's got a universe to run. He's got the planets to keep balanced and presidents and kings to watch over. He's got wars to worry with and famines to fix. Who am I to tell him about my ingrown toenail?

I'm glad you asked. Let me tell you who you are. In fact, let me *proclaim* who you are.

You are an heir of God and a co-heir with Christ.

You are eternal, like an angel.

You have a crown that will last forever.

You are a holy priest, a treasured possession.

You were chosen before the creation of the world. You are destined for "praise, fame, and honor, and you will be a holy people to the Lord your God" (Deut. 26:19).

Israel's Suffering in Egypt

Now these *are* the names of the children of Israel who came
to Egypt; each man and his household came with Jacob:
2Reuben, Simeon, Levi, and Judah; 3Issachar, Zebulun, and
Benjamin; 4Dan, Naphtali, Gad, and Asher. 5All those who
were descendants[a] of Jacob were seventy[b] persons (for Joseph was in
Egypt *already*). 6And Joseph died, all his brothers, and all that generation.
7But the children of Israel were fruitful and increased abundantly, multiplied and grew exceedingly mighty; and the land was filled with them.

8Now there arose a new king over Egypt, who did not know Joseph.
9And he said to his people, "Look, the people of the children of Israel *are*
more and mightier than we; 10come, let us deal shrewdly with them, lest
they multiply, and it happen, in the event of war, that they also join our
enemies and fight against us, and *so* go up out of the land." 11Therefore
they set taskmasters over them to afflict them with their burdens. And
they built for Pharaoh supply cities, Pithom and Raamses. 12But the more
they afflicted them, the more they multiplied and grew. And they were in
dread of the children of Israel. 13So the Egyptians made the children of Israel serve with rigor. 14And they made their lives bitter with hard
bondage—in mortar, in brick, and in all manner of service in the field. All
their service in which they made them serve *was* with rigor.

15Then the king of Egypt spoke to the Hebrew midwives, of whom the
name of one *was* Shiphrah and the name of the other Puah; 16and he said,
"When you do the duties of a midwife for the Hebrew women, and see
them on the birthstools, if it *is* a son, then you shall kill him; but if it *is* a
daughter, then she shall live." 17But the midwives feared God, and did not
do as the king of Egypt commanded them, but saved the male children
alive. 18So the king of Egypt called for the midwives and said to them,
"Why have you done this thing, and saved the male children alive?"

19And the midwives said to Pharaoh, "Because the Hebrew women *are*
not like the Egyptian women; for they *are* lively and give birth before the
midwives come to them."

20Therefore God dealt well with the midwives, and the people multiplied
and grew very mighty. 21And so it was, because the midwives feared God,
that He provided households for them.

22So Pharaoh commanded all his people, saying, "Every son who is
born[c] you shall cast into the river, and every daughter you shall save alive."

Moses Is Born

2 And a man of the house of Levi went and took *as wife* a daughter of
Levi. 2So the woman conceived and bore a son. And when she saw that
he *was* a beautiful *child,* she hid him three months. 3But when she could
no longer hide him, she took an ark of bulrushes for him, daubed it with
asphalt and pitch, put the child in it, and laid *it* in the reeds by the river's
bank. 4And his sister stood afar off, to know what would be done to him.

5Then the daughter of Pharaoh came down to bathe at the river. And her
maidens walked along the riverside; and when she saw the ark among the
reeds, she sent her maid to get it. 6And when she opened *it,* she saw the

1:5 [a] Literally *who came from the loins of* [b] Dead Sea Scrolls and Septuagint read *seventy-five* (compare Acts 7:14).
1:22 [c] Samaritan Pentateuch, Septuagint, and Targum add *to the Hebrews.*

child, and behold, the baby wept. So she had compassion on him, and
said, "This is one of the Hebrews' children."
7Then his sister said to Pharaoh's daughter, "Shall I go and call a nurse
for you from the Hebrew women, that she may nurse the child for you?"
8And Pharaoh's daughter said to her, "Go." So the maiden went and
called the child's mother. 9Then Pharaoh's daughter said to her, "Take this
child away and nurse him for me, and I will give *you* your wages." So the
woman took the child and nursed him. 10And the child grew, and she
brought him to Pharaoh's daughter, and he became her son. So she called
his name Moses,[d] saying, "Because I drew him out of the water."

Moses Flees to Midian

11Now it came to pass in those days, when Moses was grown, that he
went out to his brethren and looked at their burdens. And he saw an Egyptian beating a Hebrew, one of his brethren. 12So he looked this way and
that way, and when he saw no one, he killed the Egyptian and hid him in
the sand. 13And when he went out the second day, behold, two Hebrew
men were fighting, and he said to the one who did the wrong, "Why are
you striking your companion?"
14Then he said, "Who made you a prince and a judge over us? Do you
intend to kill me as you killed the Egyptian?"
So Moses feared and said, "Surely this thing is known!" 15When Pharaoh
heard of this matter, he sought to kill Moses. But Moses fled from the face
of Pharaoh and dwelt in the land of Midian; and he sat down by a well.
16Now the priest of Midian had seven daughters. And they came and
drew water, and they filled the troughs to water their father's flock. 17Then
the shepherds came and drove them away; but Moses stood up and helped
them, and watered their flock.
18When they came to Reuel their father, he said, "How *is it that* you have
come so soon today?"
19And they said, "An Egyptian delivered us from the hand of the shepherds, and he also drew enough water for us and watered the flock."
20So he said to his daughters, "And where *is* he? Why *is* it *that* you have
left the man? Call him, that he may eat bread."
21Then Moses was content to live with the man, and he gave Zipporah
his daughter to Moses. 22And she bore *him* a son. He called his name
Gershom,[e] for he said, "I have been a stranger in a foreign land."
23Now it happened in the process of time that the king of Egypt died.
Then the children of Israel groaned because of the bondage, and they
cried out; and their cry came up to God because of the bondage. 24So God
heard their groaning, and God remembered His covenant with Abraham,
with Isaac, and with Jacob. 25And God looked upon the children of Israel,
and God acknowledged *them.*

Moses at the Burning Bush

3 Now Moses was tending the flock of Jethro his father-in-law, the priest
of Midian. And he led the flock to the back of the desert, and came to
Horeb, the mountain of God. 2And the Angel of the LORD appeared to him in
a flame of fire from the midst of a bush. So he looked, and behold, the bush

But more than any of the above—more significant than any title or position—is the simple fact that you are God's child. "The Father has loved us so much that we are called children of God. And we really are his children." I love that last phrase! "We really are his children." It's as if John knew some of us would shake our heads and say, "Naw, not me. Mother Teresa, maybe. Billy Graham, all right. But not me." If those are your feelings, John added that phrase for you.

"We *really* are his children."

As a result, if something is important to you, it's important to God. . . .

So go ahead. Tell God what hurts. Talk to him. He won't turn you away. He won't think it's silly. "For our high priest is *able to understand* our weaknesses. When he lived on earth, he was tempted in every way that we are, but he did not sin. Let us, then, feel very sure that we can come before God's throne where there is grace" (Hebrews 4:15-16, emphasis added).

Does God care about the little things in our lives? You better believe it. If it matters to you, it matters to him.

(From *He Still Moves Stones* by Max Lucado)

APPLICATION How do you respond when the going gets tough? Is there someone around to help you through those times? Let God help you when you get in a jam. He knows your limitations. When trouble arises—stop—pray—and believe God will give you the strength you need.

EXPLORATION Problems—Genesis 12:10; Exodus 5:4-9; 17:1-2; 2 Corinthians 1:8-10; James 1:2-4; 1 Peter 2:21-23.

2:10 [d] Literally *Drawn Out*
2:22 [e] Literally *Stranger There*

LIFE LESSON

Exodus 2:1–4:31

SITUATION Moses, who saved the Hebrews from bondage, was born and raised under extraordinary circumstances. Son of a Hebrew slave, he became a member of the Egyptian royal family. Later he became an outcast to the Egyptians and fled to the desert, where God prepared him for his future role.

OBSERVATION God's plans for us contain a lot of surprises. God leads and provides the means to reach his goals.

INSPIRATION Consider the rod of Moses. By this time in his life, Moses had been a shepherd as long as he had been a prince, and he'd grown accustomed to it. Herding sheep wasn't as lively as living with Egyptian royalty, but it had its moments, especially the moment God spoke to him through a burning bush that didn't burn up. God announced that Moses was his man to deliver the Israelites. Moses wasn't convinced he was the one for the job. God said that who Moses was didn't matter; what mattered was who God was. And God set out to demonstrate.

"Moses," spoke the voice from the bush, "throw down your staff."

Moses, who had walked this mountain for forty years, was not comfortable with the command.

"God, you know a lot about a lot of things, but you may not know that out here, well, you just don't go around throwing down your staff. You never know when . . ."

"Throw it down, Moses."

Moses threw it down. The rod became a snake, and Moses began to run.

"Moses!"

The old shepherd stopped.

was burning with fire, but the bush *was* not consumed. 3Then Moses said, "I
will now turn aside and see this great sight, why the bush does not burn."
4So when the LORD saw that he turned aside to look, God called to him
from the midst of the bush and said, "Moses, Moses!"
And he said, "Here I am."
5Then He said, "Do not draw near this place. Take your sandals off your
feet, for the place where you stand *is* holy ground." 6Moreover He said, "I
am the God of your father—the God of Abraham, the God of Isaac, and the
God of Jacob." And Moses hid his face, for he was afraid to look upon God.
7And the LORD said: "I have surely seen the oppression of My people who
are in Egypt, and have heard their cry because of their taskmasters, for I
know their sorrows. 8So I have come down to deliver them out of the hand
of the Egyptians, and to bring them up from that land to a good and large
land, to a land flowing with milk and honey, to the place of the Canaanites
and the Hittites and the Amorites and the Perizzites and the Hivites and
the Jebusites. 9Now therefore, behold, the cry of the children of Israel has
come to Me, and I have also seen the oppression with which the Egyptians
oppress them. 10Come now, therefore, and I will send you to Pharaoh that
you may bring My people, the children of Israel, out of Egypt."
11But Moses said to God, "Who *am* I that I should go to Pharaoh, and
that I should bring the children of Israel out of Egypt?"
12So He said, "I will certainly be with you. And this *shall be* a sign to you
that I have sent you: When you have brought the people out of Egypt, you
shall serve God on this mountain."
13Then Moses said to God, "Indeed, *when* I come to the children of Israel and say to them, 'The God of your fathers has sent me to you,' and they
say to me, 'What *is* His name?' what shall I say to them?"
14And God said to Moses, "I AM WHO I AM." And He said, "Thus you
shall say to the children of Israel, 'I AM has sent me to you.' " 15Moreover
God said to Moses, "Thus you shall say to the children of Israel: 'The LORD
God of your fathers, the God of Abraham, the God of Isaac, and the God of
Jacob, has sent me to you. This *is* My name forever, and this *is* My memorial to all generations.' 16Go and gather the elders of Israel together, and say
to them, 'The LORD God of your fathers, the God of Abraham, of Isaac, and
of Jacob, appeared to me, saying, "I have surely visited you and *seen* what
is done to you in Egypt; 17and I have said I will bring you up out of the
affliction of Egypt to the land of the Canaanites and the Hittites and the
Amorites and the Perizzites and the Hivites and the Jebusites, to a land
flowing with milk and honey." ' 18Then they will heed your voice; and you
shall come, you and the elders of Israel, to the king of Egypt; and you shall
say to him, 'The LORD God of the Hebrews has met with us; and now,
please, let us go three days' journey into the wilderness, that we may sacrifice to the LORD our God.' 19But I am sure that the king of Egypt will not
let you go, no, not even by a mighty hand. 20So I will stretch out My hand
and strike Egypt with all My wonders which I will do in its midst; and after that he will let you go. 21And I will give this people favor in the sight of
the Egyptians; and it shall be, when you go, that you shall not go empty-
handed. 22But every woman shall ask of her neighbor, namely, of her who
dwells near her house, articles of silver, articles of gold, and clothing; and
you shall put *them* on your sons and on your daughters. So you shall plunder the Egyptians."

Miraculous Signs for Pharaoh

4 Then Moses answered and said, "But suppose they will not believe me
or listen to my voice; suppose they say, 'The LORD has not appeared to
you.' "
2So the LORD said to him, "What *is* that in your hand?"
He said, "A rod."
3And He said, "Cast it on the ground." So he cast it on the ground, and
it became a serpent; and Moses fled from it. 4Then the LORD said to Moses,
"Reach out your hand and take *it* by the tail" (and he reached out his hand
and caught it, and it became a rod in his hand), 5"that they may believe
that the LORD God of their fathers, the God of Abraham, the God of Isaac,
and the God of Jacob, has appeared to you."
6Furthermore the LORD said to him, "Now put your hand in your
bosom." And he put his hand in his bosom, and when he took it out,
behold, his hand *was* leprous, like snow. 7And He said, "Put your hand in
your bosom again." So he put his hand in his bosom again, and drew it out
of his bosom, and behold, it was restored like his *other* flesh. 8"Then it will
be, if they do not believe you, nor heed the message of the first sign, that
they may believe the message of the latter sign. 9And it shall be, if they do
not believe even these two signs, or listen to your voice, that you shall take
water from the river[f] and pour *it* on the dry *land.* The water which you take
from the river will become blood on the dry *land.*"
10Then Moses said to the LORD, "O my Lord, I *am* not eloquent, neither
before nor since You have spoken to Your servant; but I *am* slow of speech
and slow of tongue."
11So the LORD said to him, "Who has made man's mouth? Or who makes
the mute, the deaf, the seeing, or the blind? *Have* not I, the LORD? 12Now
therefore, go, and I will be with your mouth and teach you what you shall
say."
13But he said, "O my Lord, please send by the hand of whomever *else*
You may send."
14So the anger of the LORD was kindled against Moses, and He said: "Is
not Aaron the Levite your brother? I know that he can speak well. And
look, he is also coming out to meet you. When he sees you, he will be glad
in his heart. 15Now you shall speak to him and put the words in his mouth.
And I will be with your mouth and with his mouth, and I will teach you
what you shall do. 16So he shall be your spokesman to the people. And he
himself shall be as a mouth for you, and you shall be to him as God. 17And
you shall take this rod in your hand, with which you shall do the signs."

Moses Goes to Egypt

18So Moses went and returned to Jethro his father-in-law, and said to
him, "Please let me go and return to my brethren who *are* in Egypt, and
see whether they are still alive."
And Jethro said to Moses, "Go in peace."
19Now the LORD said to Moses in Midian, "Go, return to Egypt; for all the
men who sought your life are dead." 20Then Moses took his wife and his
sons and set them on a donkey, and he returned to the land of Egypt. And
Moses took the rod of God in his hand.

"Pick up the snake."

Moses peered over his shoulder, first at the snake and then the bush, and then he gave the most courageous response he could muster.

"What?"

"Pick up the snake . . . by the tail." (God had to be smiling at this point.)

"God, I don't mean to object. I mean, you know a lot of things, but out here in the desert, well, you don't pick up snakes too often, and you *never* pick up snakes by the tail."

"Moses!"

"Yessir."

Just as Moses' hand touched the squirmy scales of the snake, it hardened. And Moses lifted up the rod. The same rod he would lift up in Pharaoh's court. The same rod he would lift up to divide the water and guide two million people through a desert. The rod that would remind Moses that if God can make a stick become a snake, then become a stick again—then perhaps he can do something with stubborn hearts and a stiff-necked people.

Perhaps he can do something with the common.

(From *The Applause of Heaven* by Max Lucado)

APPLICATION Have you ever been in a hopeless position at work, school, or home? Have you felt trapped and powerless to act? Remember, God hears our needs and answers prayers in the manner that will help us, serve his will, and often surprise us. Trust God in prayer right now for special guidance today.

EXPLORATION Plans—Genesis 45:4-8; Matthew 2:16-23; Mark 1:2-3; 1 Corinthians 2:7.

4:9 *f* That is, the Nile

21And the LORD said to Moses, "When you go back
to Egypt, see that you do all those wonders before
Pharaoh which I have put in your hand. But I will
harden his heart, so that he will not let the people go.
22Then you shall say to Pharaoh, 'Thus says the LORD:
"Israel *is* My son, My firstborn. 23So I say to you, let My
son go that he may serve Me. But if you refuse to let
him go, indeed I will kill your son, your firstborn." ' "
24And it came to pass on the way, at the encampment, that the LORD met him and sought to kill him.
25Then Zipporah took a sharp stone and cut off the
foreskin of her son and cast *it* at *Moses's*[g] feet, and
said, "Surely you *are* a husband of blood to me!" 26So
He let him go. Then she said, "*You are* a husband of
blood!"—because of the circumcision.
27And the LORD said to Aaron, "Go into the wilderness to meet Moses." So he went and met him on the
mountain of God, and kissed him. 28So Moses told
Aaron all the words of the LORD who had sent him,
and all the signs which He had commanded him.
29Then Moses and Aaron went and gathered together
all the elders of the children of Israel. 30And Aaron
spoke all the words which the LORD had spoken to
Moses. Then he did the signs in the sight of the people. 31So the people believed; and when they heard
that the LORD had visited the children of Israel and
that He had looked on their affliction, then they
bowed their heads and worshiped.

First Encounter with Pharaoh

5 Afterward Moses and Aaron went in and told
Pharaoh, "Thus says the LORD God of Israel: 'Let
My people go, that they may hold a feast to Me in the
wilderness.' "
2And Pharaoh said, "Who *is* the LORD, that I should
obey His voice to let Israel go? I do not know the LORD,
nor will I let Israel go."
3So they said, "The God of the Hebrews has met
with us. Please, let us go three days' journey into the
desert and sacrifice to the LORD our God, lest He fall
upon us with pestilence or with the sword."
4Then the king of Egypt said to them, "Moses and
Aaron, why do you take the people from their work?
Get *back* to your labor." 5And Pharaoh said, "Look,
the people of the land *are* many now, and you make
them rest from their labor!"
6So the same day Pharaoh commanded the taskmasters of the people and their officers, saying, 7"You shall
no longer give the people straw to make brick as before.
Let them go and gather straw for themselves. 8And you
shall lay on them the quota of bricks which they made
before. You shall not reduce it. For they are idle; therefore they cry out, saying, 'Let us go *and* sacrifice to our
God.' 9Let more work be laid on the men, that they
may labor in it, and let them not regard false words."
10And the taskmasters of the people and their officers went out and spoke to the people, saying, "Thus
says Pharaoh: 'I will not give you straw. 11Go, get yourselves straw where you can find it; yet none of your
work will be reduced.' " 12So the people were scattered
abroad throughout all the land of Egypt to gather
stubble instead of straw. 13And the taskmasters forced
them to hurry, saying, "Fulfill your work, *your* daily
quota, as when there was straw." 14Also the officers of
the children of Israel, whom Pharaoh's taskmasters
had set over them, were beaten *and* were asked, "Why
have you not fulfilled your task in making brick both
yesterday and today, as before?"
15Then the officers of the children of Israel came
and cried out to Pharaoh, saying, "Why are you dealing thus with your servants? 16There is no straw given
to your servants, and they say to us, 'Make brick!' And
indeed your servants *are* beaten, but the fault *is* in
your *own* people."
17But he said, "You *are* idle! Idle! Therefore you say,
'Let us go *and* sacrifice to the LORD.' 18Therefore go
now *and* work; for no straw shall be given you, yet you
shall deliver the quota of bricks." 19And the officers of
the children of Israel saw *that* they *were* in trouble
after it was said, "You shall not reduce *any* bricks
from your daily quota."
20Then, as they came out from Pharaoh, they met
Moses and Aaron who stood there to meet them.
21And they said to them, "Let the LORD look on you
and judge, because you have made us abhorrent in
the sight of Pharaoh and in the sight of his servants,
to put a sword in their hand to kill us."

Israel's Deliverance Assured

22So Moses returned to the LORD and said, "Lord,
why have You brought trouble on this people? Why *is*
it You have sent me? 23For since I came to Pharaoh to
speak in Your name, he has done evil to this people;
neither have You delivered Your people at all."

6 Then the LORD said to Moses, "Now you shall see
what I will do to Pharaoh. For with a strong hand
he will let them go, and with a strong hand he will
drive them out of his land."

4:25 [g] Literally *his*

2And God spoke to Moses and said to him: "I *am* the LORD. 3I appeared
to Abraham, to Isaac, and to Jacob, as God Almighty, but *by* My name
LORD[h] I was not known to them. 4I have also established My covenant with
them, to give them the land of Canaan, the land of their pilgrimage, in
which they were strangers. 5And I have also heard the groaning of the children of Israel whom the Egyptians keep in bondage, and I have remembered My covenant. 6Therefore say to the children of Israel: 'I *am* the LORD;
I will bring you out from under the burdens of the Egyptians, I will rescue
you from their bondage, and I will redeem you with an outstretched arm
and with great judgments. 7I will take you as My people, and I will be your
God. Then you shall know that I *am* the LORD your God who brings you out
from under the burdens of the Egyptians. 8And I will bring you into the
land which I swore to give to Abraham, Isaac, and Jacob; and I will give it
to you *as* a heritage: I *am* the LORD.' " 9So Moses spoke thus to the children
of Israel; but they did not heed Moses, because of anguish of spirit and
cruel bondage.

10And the LORD spoke to Moses, saying, 11"Go in, tell Pharaoh king of
Egypt to let the children of Israel go out of his land."

12And Moses spoke before the LORD, saying, "The children of Israel have
not heeded me. How then shall Pharaoh heed me, for I *am* of uncircumcised lips?"

13Then the LORD spoke to Moses and Aaron, and gave them a command
for the children of Israel and for Pharaoh king of Egypt, to bring the children of Israel out of the land of Egypt.

The Family of Moses and Aaron

14These *are* the heads of their fathers' houses: The sons of Reuben, the
firstborn of Israel, *were* Hanoch, Pallu, Hezron, and Carmi. These are the
families of Reuben. 15And the sons of Simeon *were* Jemuel,[i] Jamin, Ohad,
Jachin, Zohar, and Shaul the son of a Canaanite woman. These *are* the families of Simeon. 16These *are* the names of the sons of Levi according to their
generations: Gershon, Kohath, and Merari. And the years of the life of Levi
were one hundred and thirty-seven. 17The sons of Gershon *were* Libni and
Shimi according to their families. 18And the sons of Kohath *were* Amram,
Izhar, Hebron, and Uzziel. And the years of the life of Kohath *were* one
hundred and thirty-three. 19The sons of Merari *were* Mahli and Mushi.
These *are* the families of Levi according to their generations.

20Now Amram took for himself Jochebed, his father's sister, as wife; and
she bore him Aaron and Moses. And the years of the life of Amram *were*
one hundred and thirty-seven. 21The sons of Izhar *were* Korah, Nepheg,
and Zichri. 22And the sons of Uzziel *were* Mishael, Elzaphan, and Zithri.
23Aaron took to himself Elisheba, daughter of Amminadab, sister of
Nahshon, as wife; and she bore him Nadab, Abihu, Eleazar, and Ithamar.
24And the sons of Korah *were* Assir, Elkanah, and Abiasaph. These are the
families of the Korahites. 25Eleazar, Aaron's son, took for himself one of
the daughters of Putiel as wife; and she bore him Phinehas. These *are* the
heads of the fathers' houses of the Levites according to their families.

26These *are the same* Aaron and Moses to whom the LORD said, "Bring
out the children of Israel from the land of Egypt according to their armies."

6:3 [h] Hebrew *YHWH*, traditionally *Jehovah*
6:15 [i] Spelled *Nemuel* in Numbers 26:12

LIFE LESSON

Exodus 5:1–6:27

SITUATION Moses demanded that Pharaoh release the Hebrews so they could worship God. But Pharaoh refused and made the Hebrews work even harder. The discouraged Hebrews almost turned their backs on God. Moses asked God for guidance, and God assured him the Hebrews would leave Egypt.

OBSERVATION Just because circumstances look bleak, don't give up on God. God's plan for us includes remaining faithful through suffering and setbacks.

INSPIRATION Faithfulness is important in any relationship. A faithful person is someone we can count on during tough times, someone who is loyal and true, and someone who keeps promises and commitments.

In contrast, *unfaithfulness* has become the byword of modern culture. Husbands and wives break marriage vows, workers and employers break commitments, skilled lawyers look for loopholes in contracts, family members abuse each other, and friendships dissolve over trivialities. We long for the security and hope that faithfulness brings. . . .

While others break their commitments, God keeps his. And though everyone else deserts us, God will be there. Thank the Lord!

(From *On Eagle's Wings* by Dave Veerman)

APPLICATION Do you criticize people who are fair-weather sports fans, rooting for their favorite team only when the team wins? Don't be a fair-weather Christian by turning your back on God when having faith is hard.

EXPLORATION Faith—Psalm 118:8; Isaiah 26:3; John 20:25-28; Hebrews 11.

27 These *are* the ones who spoke to Pharaoh king of Egypt, to bring out the
children of Israel from Egypt. These *are the same* Moses and Aaron.

Aaron Is Moses' Spokesman

28 And it came to pass, on the day the LORD spoke to Moses in the land of
Egypt, 29 that the LORD spoke to Moses, saying, "I *am* the LORD. Speak to
Pharaoh king of Egypt all that I say to you."
30 But Moses said before the LORD, "Behold, I *am* of uncircumcised lips,
and how shall Pharaoh heed me?"

7 So the LORD said to Moses: "See, I have made you *as* God to Pharaoh,
and Aaron your brother shall be your prophet. 2 You shall speak all that
I command you. And Aaron your brother shall tell Pharaoh to send the
children of Israel out of his land. 3 And I will harden Pharaoh's heart, and
multiply My signs and My wonders in the land of Egypt. 4 But Pharaoh will
not heed you, so that I may lay My hand on Egypt and bring My armies
and My people, the children of Israel, out of the land of Egypt by great
judgments. 5 And the Egyptians shall know that I *am* the LORD, when I
stretch out My hand on Egypt and bring out the children of Israel from
among them."
6 Then Moses and Aaron did *so;* just as the LORD commanded them, so
they did. 7 And Moses *was* eighty years old and Aaron eighty-three years
old when they spoke to Pharaoh.

Aaron's Miraculous Rod

8 Then the LORD spoke to Moses and Aaron, saying, 9 "When Pharaoh
speaks to you, saying, 'Show a miracle for yourselves,' then you shall say
to Aaron, 'Take your rod and cast *it* before Pharaoh, *and* let it become a
serpent.' " 10 So Moses and Aaron went in to Pharaoh, and they did so, just
as the LORD commanded. And Aaron cast down his rod before Pharaoh
and before his servants, and it became a serpent.
11 But Pharaoh also called the wise men and the sorcerers; so the magicians of Egypt, they also did in like manner with their enchantments. 12 For
every man threw down his rod, and they became serpents. But Aaron's
rod swallowed up their rods. 13 And Pharaoh's heart grew hard, and he did
not heed them, as the LORD had said.

The First Plague: Waters Become Blood

14 So the LORD said to Moses: "Pharaoh's heart *is* hard; he refuses to let
the people go. 15 Go to Pharaoh in the morning, when he goes out to the water, and you shall stand by the river's bank to meet him; and the rod which
was turned to a serpent you shall take in your hand. 16 And you shall say to
him, 'The LORD God of the Hebrews has sent me to you, saying, "Let My
people go, that they may serve Me in the wilderness"; but indeed, until
now you would not hear! 17 Thus says the LORD: "By this you shall know
that I *am* the LORD. Behold, I will strike the waters which *are* in the river
with the rod that *is* in my hand, and they shall be turned to blood. 18 And
the fish that *are* in the river shall die, the river shall stink, and the Egyptians will loathe to drink the water of the river." ' "
19 Then the LORD spoke to Moses, "Say to Aaron, 'Take your rod and stretch
out your hand over the waters of Egypt, over their streams, over their rivers,
over their ponds, and over all their pools of water, that they may become

LIFE LESSON

Exodus 6:28–8:32

SITUATION The ten plagues not only drove Pharaoh to release the Israelites, but they also boosted Moses' confidence. Although he thought he could not persuade Pharaoh, Moses saw that with God, nothing is impossible.

OBSERVATION By redeeming his people from slavery, God demonstrated his love and grace.

INSPIRATION What is the purpose of grace? Primarily, to restore man's relationship with God. . . . This is what all the work of grace aims at—an ever deeper knowledge of God, and an ever closer fellowship with Him. God is drawing us sinners closer and closer to Himself.

How does God in grace prosecute this purpose? Not by shielding us from assault by the world, the flesh, and the devil, nor by protecting us from burdensome and frustrating circumstances, nor yet by shielding us from troubles created by our own temperament and psychology; but rather by exposing us to all these things, so as to overwhelm us with a sense of our inadequacy, and to drive us to cling to Him more closely. . . . When we walk along a clear road feeling fine, and someone takes our arm to help us, as likely as not we shall impatiently shake him off; but when we are caught in rough country in the dark, with a storm getting up and our strength spent, and someone takes our arm to help us, we shall thankfully lean on him. And God wants us to feel that our way through life is rough and perplexing, so that we may learn thankfully to lean on Him.

(From *Knowing God* by J. I. Packer)

APPLICATION What events cause you to worry, today? Trust God to help you with any big decisions, problems, or difficulties in your life. As your friend, he will guide you whether your life seems pleasant or painful.

EXPLORATION Redemption—Job 19:25; Psalm 31:5; 111:9; Isaiah 43:1; Romans 3:24; Galatians 3:13-14. Grace—Psalm 84:11; Daniel 9:18; Romans 9:16; Titus 3:5.

blood. And there shall be blood throughout all the
land of Egypt, both in *buckets of* wood and *pitchers of*
stone.' " 20 And Moses and Aaron did so, just as the
LORD commanded. So he lifted up the rod and struck
the waters that *were* in the river, in the sight of Pharaoh
and in the sight of his servants. And all the waters that
were in the river were turned to blood. 21 The fish that
were in the river died, the river stank, and the Egyptians could not drink the water of the river. So there
was blood throughout all the land of Egypt.
22 Then the magicians of Egypt did so with their enchantments; and Pharaoh's heart grew hard, and he
did not heed them, as the LORD had said. 23 And
Pharaoh turned and went into his house. Neither was
his heart moved by this. 24 So all the Egyptians dug all
around the river for water to drink, because they
could not drink the water of the river. 25 And seven
days passed after the LORD had struck the river.

The Second Plague: Frogs

8 And the LORD spoke to Moses, "Go to Pharaoh and
say to him, 'Thus says the LORD: "Let My people
go, that they may serve Me. 2 But if you refuse to let
them go, behold, I will smite all your territory with
frogs. 3 So the river shall bring forth frogs abundantly,
which shall go up and come into your house, into
your bedroom, on your bed, into the houses of your
servants, on your people, into your ovens, and into
your kneading bowls. 4 And the frogs shall come up on
you, on your people, and on all your servants." ' "
5 Then the LORD spoke to Moses, "Say to Aaron,
'Stretch out your hand with your rod over the streams,
over the rivers, and over the ponds, and cause frogs to
come up on the land of Egypt.' " 6 So Aaron stretched
out his hand over the waters of Egypt, and the frogs
came up and covered the land of Egypt. 7 And the magicians did so with their enchantments, and brought up
frogs on the land of Egypt.
8 Then Pharaoh called for Moses and Aaron, and
said, "Entreat the LORD that He may take away the
frogs from me and from my people; and I will let the
people go, that they may sacrifice to the LORD."
9 And Moses said to Pharaoh, "Accept the honor of
saying when I shall intercede for you, for your servants, and for your people, to destroy the frogs from
you and your houses, *that* they may remain in the
river only."
10 So he said, "Tomorrow." And he said, "*Let it be*
according to your word, that you may know that *there*
is no one like the LORD our God. 11 And the frogs shall
depart from you, from your houses, from your servants, and from your people. They shall remain in the
river only."
12 Then Moses and Aaron went out from Pharaoh.
And Moses cried out to the LORD concerning the frogs
which He had brought against Pharaoh. 13 So the LORD
did according to the word of Moses. And the frogs
died out of the houses, out of the courtyards, and out
of the fields. 14 They gathered them together in heaps,
and the land stank. 15 But when Pharaoh saw that
there was relief, he hardened his heart and did not
heed them, as the LORD had said.

The Third Plague: Lice

16 So the LORD said to Moses, "Say to Aaron, 'Stretch
out your rod, and strike the dust of the land, so that it
may become lice throughout all the land of Egypt.' "
17 And they did so. For Aaron stretched out his hand
with his rod and struck the dust of the earth, and it
became lice on man and beast. All the dust of the land
became lice throughout all the land of Egypt.
18 Now the magicians so worked with their enchantments to bring forth lice, but they could not. So there
were lice on man and beast. 19 Then the magicians said
to Pharaoh, "This *is* the finger of God." But Pharaoh's
heart grew hard, and he did not heed them, just as the
LORD had said.

The Fourth Plague: Flies

20 And the LORD said to Moses, "Rise early in the
morning and stand before Pharaoh as he comes out
to the water. Then say to him, 'Thus says the LORD:
"Let My people go, that they may serve Me. 21 Or else,
if you will not let My people go, behold, I will send
swarms *of flies* on you and your servants, on your
people and into your houses. The houses of the Egyptians shall be full of swarms *of flies*, and also the
ground on which they *stand*. 22 And in that day I will
set apart the land of Goshen, in which My people
dwell, that no swarms *of flies* shall be there, in order
that you may know that I *am* the LORD in the midst of
the land. 23 I will make a difference[j] between My people and your people. Tomorrow this sign shall be." ' "
24 And the LORD did so. Thick swarms *of flies* came into
the house of Pharaoh, *into* his servants' houses, and
into all the land of Egypt. The land was corrupted
because of the swarms *of flies*.
25 Then Pharaoh called for Moses and Aaron, and
said, "Go, sacrifice to your God in the land."

8:23 *j* Literally *set a ransom* (compare Exodus 9:4 and 11:7)

LIFE LESSON

Exodus 9:1–10:29

SITUATION Moses began to reveal the majesty of God through individual miracles and plagues. The first four plagues turned the Nile to blood and infested the country with frogs, gnats, and flies. Though the entire country of Egypt suffered these plagues, the king refused to free the Israelites.

OBSERVATION Pride makes us stubborn. Not only is pride unattractive, it can be ruinous (like it was to Pharaoh).

INSPIRATION What makes the temptation of power so seemingly irresistible? Maybe it is that power offers an easy substitute for the hard task of love. It seems easier to be God than to love God, easier to control people than to love people, easier to own life than to love life. Jesus asks, "Do you love me?" We ask, "Can we sit at your right hand and your left hand in your Kingdom?" (Matthew 20:21). Ever since the snake said, "The day you eat of this tree your eyes will be open and you will be like gods, knowing good from evil" (Genesis 3:5), we have been tempted to replace love with power. . . . The long painful history of the Church is the history of people ever and again tempted to choose power over love, control over the cross, being a leader over being led. Those who resisted this temptation to the end and thereby give us hope are true saints.

(From *In the Name of Jesus* by Henri Nouwen)

APPLICATION Choose today to serve others for Jesus: your parents, spouse, children, friend, or colleague. Love them rather than trying to control them. How can you help them meet their needs, desires, and dreams?

EXPLORATION Selfishness—Ezekiel 34:18; Matthew 25:43; Mark 10:37; Luke 10: 31-32. Service—Deuteronomy 10:12; Mark 10:43-44; Luke 6:35; John 13:14; 21:16.

26And Moses said, "It is not right to do so, for we would be sacrificing
the abomination of the Egyptians to the LORD our God. If we sacrifice the
abomination of the Egyptians before their eyes, then will they not stone
us? 27We will go three days' journey into the wilderness and sacrifice to the
LORD our God as He will command us."
28So Pharaoh said, "I will let you go, that you may sacrifice to the LORD
your God in the wilderness; only you shall not go very far away. Intercede
for me."
29Then Moses said, "Indeed I am going out from you, and I will entreat
the LORD, that the swarms *of flies* may depart tomorrow from Pharaoh,
from his servants, and from his people. But let Pharaoh not deal deceitfully anymore in not letting the people go to sacrifice to the LORD."
30So Moses went out from Pharaoh and entreated the LORD. 31And the
LORD did according to the word of Moses; He removed the swarms *of flies*
from Pharaoh, from his servants, and from his people. Not one remained.
32But Pharaoh hardened his heart at this time also; neither would he let the
people go.

The Fifth Plague: Livestock Diseased

9 Then the LORD said to Moses, "Go in to Pharaoh and tell him, 'Thus
says the LORD God of the Hebrews: "Let My people go, that they may
serve Me. 2For if you refuse to let *them* go, and still hold them, 3behold, the
hand of the LORD will be on your cattle in the field, on the horses, on the
donkeys, on the camels, on the oxen, and on the sheep—a very severe
pestilence. 4And the LORD will make a difference between the livestock of
Israel and the livestock of Egypt. So nothing shall die of all *that* belongs to
the children of Israel." ' " 5Then the LORD appointed a set time, saying,
"Tomorrow the LORD will do this thing in the land."
6So the LORD did this thing on the next day, and all the livestock of Egypt
died; but of the livestock of the children of Israel, not one died. 7Then
Pharaoh sent, and indeed, not even one of the livestock of the Israelites
was dead. But the heart of Pharaoh became hard, and he did not let the
people go.

The Sixth Plague: Boils

8So the LORD said to Moses and Aaron, "Take for yourselves handfuls of
ashes from a furnace, and let Moses scatter it toward the heavens in the
sight of Pharaoh. 9And it will become fine dust in all the land of Egypt, and
it will cause boils that break out in sores on man and beast throughout all
the land of Egypt." 10Then they took ashes from the furnace and stood before Pharaoh, and Moses scattered *them* toward heaven. And *they* caused
boils that break out in sores on man and beast. 11And the magicians could
not stand before Moses because of the boils, for the boils were on the
magicians and on all the Egyptians. 12But the LORD hardened the heart of
Pharaoh; and he did not heed them, just as the LORD had spoken to Moses.

The Seventh Plague: Hail

13Then the LORD said to Moses, "Rise early in the morning and stand
before Pharaoh, and say to him, 'Thus says the LORD God of the Hebrews:
"Let My people go, that they may serve Me, 14for at this time I will send all
My plagues to your very heart, and on your servants and on your people,

that you may know that *there is* none like Me in all the earth. 15Now if I had stretched out My hand and struck you and your people with pestilence, then you would have been cut off from the earth. 16But indeed for this *purpose* I have raised you up, that I may show My power *in* you, and that My name may be declared in all the earth. 17As yet you exalt yourself against My people in that you will not let them go. 18Behold, tomorrow about this time I will cause very heavy hail to rain down, such as has not been in Egypt since its founding until now. 19Therefore send now *and* gather your livestock and all that you have in the field, for the hail shall come down on every man and every animal which is found in the field and is not brought home; and they shall die." ' "

20He who feared the word of the LORD among the servants of Pharaoh made his servants and his livestock flee to the houses. 21But he who did not regard the word of the LORD left his servants and his livestock in the field.

22Then the LORD said to Moses, "Stretch out your hand toward heaven, that there may be hail in all the land of Egypt—on man, on beast, and on every herb of the field, throughout the land of Egypt." 23And Moses stretched out his rod toward heaven; and the LORD sent thunder and hail, and fire darted to the ground. And the LORD rained hail on the land of Egypt. 24So there was hail, and fire mingled with the hail, so very heavy that there was none like it in all the land of Egypt since it became a nation. 25And the hail struck throughout the whole land of Egypt, all that *was* in the field, both man and beast; and the hail struck every herb of the field and broke every tree of the field. 26Only in the land of Goshen, where the children of Israel *were,* there was no hail.

27And Pharaoh sent and called for Moses and Aaron, and said to them, "I have sinned this time. The LORD *is* righteous, and my people and I *are* wicked. 28Entreat the LORD, that there may be no *more* mighty thundering and hail, for *it is* enough. I will let you go, and you shall stay no longer."

29So Moses said to him, "As soon as I have gone out of the city, I will spread out my hands to the LORD; the thunder will cease, and there will be no more hail, that you may know that the earth *is* the LORD's. 30But as for you and your servants, I know that you will not yet fear the LORD God."

31Now the flax and the barley were struck, for the barley *was* in the head and the flax *was* in bud. 32But the wheat and the spelt were not struck, for they *are* late crops.

33So Moses went out of the city from Pharaoh and spread out his hands to the LORD; then the thunder and the hail ceased, and the rain was not poured on the earth. 34And when Pharaoh saw that the rain, the hail, and the thunder had ceased, he sinned yet more; and he hardened his heart, he and his servants. 35So the heart of Pharaoh was hard; neither would he let the children of Israel go, as the LORD had spoken by Moses.

The Eighth Plague: Locusts

10 Now the LORD said to Moses, "Go in to Pharaoh; for I have hardened his heart and the hearts of his servants, that I may show these signs of Mine before him, 2and that you may tell in the hearing of your son and your son's son the mighty things I have done in Egypt, and My signs which I have done among them, that you may know that I *am* the LORD."

3So Moses and Aaron came in to Pharaoh and said to him, "Thus says the LORD God of the Hebrews: 'How long will you refuse to humble yourself before Me? Let My people go, that they may serve Me. 4Or else, if you refuse to let My people go, behold, tomorrow I will bring locusts into your territory. 5And they shall cover the face of the earth, so that no one will be able to see the earth; and they shall eat the residue of what is left, which remains to you from the hail, and they shall eat every tree which grows up for you out of the field. 6They shall fill your houses, the houses of all your servants, and the houses of all the Egyptians—which neither your fathers nor your fathers' fathers have seen, since the day that they were on the earth to this day.' " And he turned and went out from Pharaoh.

7Then Pharaoh's servants said to him, "How long shall this man be a snare to us? Let the men go, that they may serve the LORD their God. Do you not yet know that Egypt is destroyed?"

8So Moses and Aaron were brought again to Pharaoh, and he said to them, "Go, serve the LORD your God. Who *are* the ones that are going?"

9And Moses said, "We will go with our young and our old; with our sons and our daughters, with our flocks and our herds we will go, for we must hold a feast to the LORD."

10Then he said to them, "The LORD had better be with you when I let you and your little ones go! Beware, for evil is ahead of you. 11Not so! Go now, you *who are* men, and serve the LORD, for that is what you desired." And they were driven out from Pharaoh's presence.

12Then the LORD said to Moses, "Stretch out your hand over the land of Egypt for the locusts, that they may come upon the land of Egypt, and eat every herb

of the land—all that the hail has left." 13So Moses
stretched out his rod over the land of Egypt, and the
LORD brought an east wind on the land all that day
and all *that* night. When it was morning, the east wind
brought the locusts. 14And the locusts went up over all
the land of Egypt and rested on all the territory of
Egypt. *They were* very severe; previously there had
been no such locusts as they, nor shall there be such
after them. 15For they covered the face of the whole
earth, so that the land was darkened; and they ate
every herb of the land and all the fruit of the trees
which the hail had left. So there remained nothing
green on the trees or on the plants of the field
throughout all the land of Egypt.
16Then Pharaoh called for Moses and Aaron in
haste, and said, "I have sinned against the LORD your
God and against you. 17Now therefore, please forgive
my sin only this once, and entreat the LORD your God,
that He may take away from me this death only." 18So
he went out from Pharaoh and entreated the LORD.
19And the LORD turned a very strong west wind, which
took the locusts away and blew them into the Red Sea.
There remained not one locust in all the territory of
Egypt. 20But the LORD hardened Pharaoh's heart, and
he did not let the children of Israel go.

The Ninth Plague: Darkness

21Then the LORD said to Moses, "Stretch out your
hand toward heaven, that there may be darkness over
the land of Egypt, darkness *which* may even be felt."
22So Moses stretched out his hand toward heaven, and
there was thick darkness in all the land of Egypt three
days. 23They did not see one another; nor did anyone
rise from his place for three days. But all the children
of Israel had light in their dwellings.
24Then Pharaoh called to Moses and said, "Go,
serve the LORD; only let your flocks and your herds be
kept back. Let your little ones also go with you."
25But Moses said, "You must also give us sacrifices
and burnt offerings, that we may sacrifice to the LORD
our God. 26Our livestock also shall go with us; not a
hoof shall be left behind. For we must take some of
them to serve the LORD our God, and even we do not
know with what we must serve the LORD until we
arrive there."
27But the LORD hardened Pharaoh's heart, and he
would not let them go. 28Then Pharaoh said to him, "Get
away from me! Take heed to yourself and see my face
no more! For in the day you see my face you shall die!"
29So Moses said, "You have spoken well. I will never
see your face again."

Death of the Firstborn Announced

11 And the LORD said to Moses, "I will bring one
more plague on Pharaoh and on Egypt. Afterward he will let you go from here. When he lets *you* go,
he will surely drive you out of here altogether. 2Speak
now in the hearing of the people, and let every man
ask from his neighbor and every woman from her
neighbor, articles of silver and articles of gold." 3And
the LORD gave the people favor in the sight of the
Egyptians. Moreover the man Moses *was* very great in
the land of Egypt, in the sight of Pharaoh's servants
and in the sight of the people.
4Then Moses said, "Thus says the LORD: 'About
midnight I will go out into the midst of Egypt; 5and all
the firstborn in the land of Egypt shall die, from the
firstborn of Pharaoh who sits on his throne, even to
the firstborn of the female servant who *is* behind the
handmill, and all the firstborn of the animals. 6Then
there shall be a great cry throughout all the land of
Egypt, such as was not like it *before,* nor shall be like
it again. 7But against none of the children of Israel
shall a dog move its tongue, against man or beast,
that you may know that the LORD does make a difference between the Egyptians and Israel.' 8And all these
your servants shall come down to me and bow down
to me, saying, 'Get out, and all the people who follow
you!' After that I will go out." Then he went out from
Pharaoh in great anger.
9But the LORD said to Moses, "Pharaoh will not
heed you, so that My wonders may be multiplied in
the land of Egypt." 10So Moses and Aaron did all these
wonders before Pharaoh; and the LORD hardened
Pharaoh's heart, and he did not let the children of Israel go out of his land.

The Passover Instituted

12 Now the LORD spoke to Moses and Aaron in the
land of Egypt, saying, 2"This month *shall be*
your beginning of months; it *shall be* the first month
of the year to you. 3Speak to all the congregation of Israel, saying: 'On the tenth of this month every man
shall take for himself a lamb, according to the house
of *his* father, a lamb for a household. 4And if the
household is too small for the lamb, let him and his
neighbor next to his house take *it* according to the
number of the persons; according to each man's need
you shall make your count for the lamb. 5Your lamb
shall be without blemish, a male of the first year. You
may take *it* from the sheep or from the goats. 6Now
you shall keep it until the fourteenth day of the same
month. Then the whole assembly of the congregation

of Israel shall kill it at twilight. 7And they shall take *some* of the blood and
put *it* on the two doorposts and on the lintel of the houses where they eat
it. 8Then they shall eat the flesh on that night; roasted in fire, with unleavened bread *and* with bitter *herbs* they shall eat it. 9Do not eat it raw, nor
boiled at all with water, but roasted in fire—its head with its legs and its
entrails. 10You shall let none of it remain until morning, and what remains
of it until morning you shall burn with fire. 11And thus you shall eat it: *with*
a belt on your waist, your sandals on your feet, and your staff in your
hand. So you shall eat it in haste. It *is* the LORD's Passover.
12'For I will pass through the land of Egypt on that night, and will strike
all the firstborn in the land of Egypt, both man and beast; and against all
the gods of Egypt I will execute judgment: I *am* the LORD. 13Now the blood
shall be a sign for you on the houses where you *are.* And when I see the
blood, I will pass over you; and the plague shall not be on you to destroy
you when I strike the land of Egypt.
14'So this day shall be to you a memorial; and you shall keep it as a feast
to the LORD throughout your generations. You shall keep it as a feast by an
everlasting ordinance. 15Seven days you shall eat unleavened bread. On the
first day you shall remove leaven from your houses. For whoever eats leavened bread from the first day until the seventh day, that person shall be
cut off from Israel. 16On the first day *there shall be* a holy convocation, and
on the seventh day there shall be a holy convocation for you. No manner
of work shall be done on them; but *that* which everyone must eat—that
only may be prepared by you. 17So you shall observe *the Feast of*
Unleavened Bread, for on this same day I will have brought your armies
out of the land of Egypt. Therefore you shall observe this day throughout
your generations as an everlasting ordinance. 18In the first *month,* on the
fourteenth day of the month at evening, you shall eat unleavened bread,
until the twenty-first day of the month at evening. 19For seven days no
leaven shall be found in your houses, since whoever eats what is leavened,
that same person shall be cut off from the congregation of Israel, whether
he is a stranger or a native of the land. 20You shall eat nothing leavened; in
all your dwellings you shall eat unleavened bread.' "
21Then Moses called for all the elders of Israel and said to them, "Pick
out and take lambs for yourselves according to your families, and kill the
Passover *lamb.* 22And you shall take a bunch of hyssop, dip *it* in the blood
that *is* in the basin, and strike the lintel and the two doorposts with the
blood that *is* in the basin. And none of you shall go out of the door of his
house until morning. 23For the LORD will pass through to strike the Egyptians; and when He sees the blood on the lintel and on the two doorposts,
the LORD will pass over the door and not allow the destroyer to come into
your houses to strike *you.* 24And you shall observe this thing as an ordinance for you and your sons forever. 25It will come to pass when you come
to the land which the LORD will give you, just as He promised, that you
shall keep this service. 26And it shall be, when your children say to you,
'What do you mean by this service?' 27that you shall say, 'It *is* the Passover
sacrifice of the LORD, who passed over the houses of the children of Israel
in Egypt when He struck the Egyptians and delivered our households.' "
So the people bowed their heads and worshiped. 28Then the children of Israel went away and did *so;* just as the LORD had commanded Moses and
Aaron, so they did.

LIFE LESSON

Exodus 11:1–12:30

SITUATION In this chapter, nine of the ten plagues in Egypt have already occurred. Pharaoh, despite the pleadings of Moses, refused to give in. God told the Israelites to prepare the Passover, which would protect his people from the final plague.

OBSERVATION God did not protect the Israelites because they were better than the Egyptians, but because they were his people. God gives grace to his followers—not based on merit but based on his loving kindness.

INSPIRATION Ancient paganism thought of each god as bound to his worshippers by bonds of self-interest, because he depended on their service and gifts for his welfare. Modern paganism has at the back of its mind a similar feeling that God is somehow obliged to love and help us, little though we deserve it. . . . But this feeling is not well founded. The God of the Bible does not depend on His human creatures for His well-being (see Psalm 50:8-13; Acts 17:25), nor, now that we have sinned, is He bound to show us favor. We can only claim from Him justice—and justice, for us, means certain condemnation. God does not owe it to anyone to stop justice taking its course. He is not obliged to pity and pardon. . . . Grace is free, in the sense of being self-originated, and of proceeding from One who was free not to be gracious. . . . The grace of God is love freely shown towards guilty sinners, contrary to their merit and indeed in defiance of their demerit. It is God showing goodness to persons who deserve only severity, and had no reason to expect anything but severity. . . . It is surely clear that, once a man is convinced that his state and need are as described, the New Testament gospel of grace cannot but sweep him off his feet with wonder and joy. For it tells how our Judge has become our Saviour.

(From *Knowing God* by J. I. Packer)

APPLICATION God has given grace to you—an unconditional gift. Receive and accept it. Look for opportunities to be "graceful" to those around you.

EXPLORATION Grace—Exodus 33:19; Proverbs 3:34; Acts 4:33; Romans 3:24; 5:15-17; Ephesians 2:8.

LIFE LESSON

Exodus 12:31–13:16

SITUATION God delivered the Israelites after four hundred years of slavery. The Passover feast would remind the Jews of this day. Moses gave them directions on how to celebrate the feast and explained its significance.

OBSERVATION Memories encourage us by reminding us of God's faithfulness. Think of all the things God has done for you.

INSPIRATION Think about the first time you ever saw him. Think about your first encounter with Christ. Robe yourself in that moment. Resurrect the relief. Recall the purity. Summon forth the passion. Can you remember?

I can. 1965. A red-headed ten-year-old with a tornado of freckles sits in a Bible class on a Wednesday night. What I remember of the class are scenes—school desks with initials carved in them. A blackboard. A dozen or so kids, some listening, some not. A teacher wearing a suit coat too tight to button around his robust belly. He is talking about Jesus. He is explaining the cross. I know I had heard it before, but that night I heard it for sure. "You can't save yourself, you need a savior." I can't explain why it connected that night as opposed to another, but it did. He

The Tenth Plague: Death of the Firstborn

29 And it came to pass at midnight that the LORD struck all the firstborn
in the land of Egypt, from the firstborn of Pharaoh who sat on his throne
to the firstborn of the captive who *was* in the dungeon, and all the firstborn of livestock. 30 So Pharaoh rose in the night, he, all his servants, and
all the Egyptians; and there was a great cry in Egypt, for *there was* not a
house where *there was* not one dead.

The Exodus

31 Then he called for Moses and Aaron by night, and said, "Rise, go out
from among my people, both you and the children of Israel. And go, serve
the LORD as you have said. 32 Also take your flocks and your herds, as you
have said, and be gone; and bless me also."

33 And the Egyptians urged the people, that they might send them out of
the land in haste. For they said, "We *shall* all *be* dead." 34 So the people took
their dough before it was leavened, having their kneading bowls bound up
in their clothes on their shoulders. 35 Now the children of Israel had done
according to the word of Moses, and they had asked from the Egyptians
articles of silver, articles of gold, and clothing. 36 And the LORD had given
the people favor in the sight of the Egyptians, so that they granted them
what they requested. Thus they plundered the Egyptians.

37 Then the children of Israel journeyed from Rameses to Succoth, about
six hundred thousand men on foot, besides children. 38 A mixed multitude
went up with them also, and flocks and herds—a great deal of livestock.
39 And they baked unleavened cakes of the dough which they had brought
out of Egypt; for it was not leavened, because they were driven out of Egypt
and could not wait, nor had they prepared provisions for themselves.

40 Now the sojourn of the children of Israel who lived in Egypt[k] *was* four
hundred and thirty years. 41 And it came to pass at the end of the four hundred and thirty years—on that very same day—it came to pass that all
the armies of the LORD went out from the land of Egypt. 42 It *is* a night of
solemn observance to the LORD for bringing them out of the land of Egypt.
This *is* that night of the LORD, a solemn observance for all the children of
Israel throughout their generations.

Passover Regulations

43 And the LORD said to Moses and Aaron, "This *is* the ordinance of the
Passover: No foreigner shall eat it. 44 But every man's servant who is
bought for money, when you have circumcised him, then he may eat it. 45 A
sojourner and a hired servant shall not eat it. 46 In one house it shall be
eaten; you shall not carry any of the flesh outside the house, nor shall you
break one of its bones. 47 All the congregation of Israel shall keep it. 48 And
when a stranger dwells with you *and wants* to keep the Passover to the
LORD, let all his males be circumcised, and then let him come near and
keep it; and he shall be as a native of the land. For no uncircumcised person shall eat it. 49 One law shall be for the native-born and for the stranger
who dwells among you."

50 Thus all the children of Israel did; as the LORD commanded Moses and
Aaron, so they did. 51 And it came to pass, on that very same day, that the

12:40 [k] Samaritan Pentateuch and Septuagint read *Egypt and Canaan.*

LORD brought the children of Israel out of the land of Egypt according to
their armies.

The Firstborn Consecrated

13 Then the LORD spoke to Moses, saying, 2“Consecrate to Me all the
firstborn, whatever opens the womb among the children of Israel,
both of man and beast; it is Mine.”

The Feast of Unleavened Bread

3And Moses said to the people: “Remember this day in which you went
out of Egypt, out of the house of bondage; for by strength of hand the LORD
brought you out of this *place.* No leavened bread shall be eaten. 4On this
day you are going out, in the month Abib. 5And it shall be, when the LORD
brings you into the land of the Canaanites and the Hittites and the
Amorites and the Hivites and the Jebusites, which He swore to your
fathers to give you, a land flowing with milk and honey, that you shall keep
this service in this month. 6Seven days you shall eat unleavened bread,
and on the seventh day *there shall be* a feast to the LORD. 7Unleavened
bread shall be eaten seven days. And no leavened bread shall be seen
among you, nor shall leaven be seen among you in all your quarters. 8And
you shall tell your son in that day, saying, ‘*This is done* because of what the
LORD did for me when I came up from Egypt.’ 9It shall be as a sign to you
on your hand and as a memorial between your eyes, that the LORD’s law
may be in your mouth; for with a strong hand the LORD has brought you
out of Egypt. 10You shall therefore keep this ordinance in its season from
year to year.

The Law of the Firstborn

11“And it shall be, when the LORD brings you into the land of the
Canaanites, as He swore to you and your fathers, and gives it to you, 12that
you shall set apart to the LORD all that open the womb, that is, every firstborn that comes from an animal which you have; the males *shall be* the
LORD’s. 13But every firstborn of a donkey you shall redeem with a lamb; and
if you will not redeem *it,* then you shall break its neck. And all the firstborn
of man among your sons you shall redeem. 14So it shall be, when your son
asks you in time to come, saying, ‘What *is* this?’ that you shall say to him,
‘By strength of hand the LORD brought us out of Egypt, out of the house of
bondage. 15And it came to pass, when Pharaoh was stubborn about letting
us go, that the LORD killed all the firstborn in the land of Egypt, both the
firstborn of man and the firstborn of beast. Therefore I sacrifice to the
LORD all males that open the womb, but all the firstborn of my sons I
redeem.’ 16It shall be as a sign on your hand and as frontlets between your
eyes, for by strength of hand the LORD brought us out of Egypt.”

The Wilderness Way

17Then it came to pass, when Pharaoh had let the people go, that God did
not lead them *by* way of the land of the Philistines, although that *was* near;
for God said, “Lest perhaps the people change their minds when they see
war, and return to Egypt.” 18So God led the people around *by* way of the
wilderness of the Red Sea. And the children of Israel went up in orderly
ranks out of the land of Egypt.

simply articulated what I was beginning to understand—I was lost—and he explained what I needed—a redeemer. From that night on, my heart belonged to Jesus.

Many would argue that a ten-year-old is too young for such a decision. And they may be right. All I know is that I never made a more earnest decision in my life. I didn’t know much about God, but what I knew was enough. I knew I wanted to go to heaven. And I knew I couldn’t do it alone.

No one had to tell me to be happy. No one had to tell me to tell others. They couldn’t keep me quiet. I told all my friends at school. I put a bumper sticker on my bicycle.

(From *Six Hours One Friday* by Max Lucado)

APPLICATION Do you remember all that God has done for you? Do you remember when you came to know him personally? When did you last thank him for all he has done for you? The Israelites were told to celebrate the Passover and explain its meaning to their children. Express what God has done for you to family and friends.

EXPLORATION Memorials—Exodus 16:32; 28:12; Joshua 4:7; Matthew 26:13; Luke 22:19.

LIFE LESSON

Exodus 13:17–15:21

SITUATION The Israelites left Egypt. As they journeyed toward Israel, God chose to lead them through a longer route, a route that protected, trained, and tested them.

OBSERVATION God can see needs and hazards we can't. He works to meet our needs and protect us. We must trust that his way is best.

INSPIRATION Is this really true? Does God lead His children in this way? I want to listen with you to that which the Holy Spirit has to tell us about guidance, for this is sometimes a problem for me, as for many people. There are many who say, "I never hear anything when asking for guidance."

But then my question is, "Do you listen?" Sometimes we have to wait for the Lord, but this waiting can be a blessing in itself, if we do it in the presence of the Lord. Our quiet time is helpful for this.

If you want to hear God's voice clearly and you are uncertain, then remain in His presence until He changes this uncertainty. Often much can happen during this waiting for the Lord. Sometimes He changes pride into humility; doubt into faith and peace; sometimes lust into purity. The Lord can and will do it.

We must also understand that sometimes the silence of the Lord is His way of letting us grow, just as a mother allows her child to fall and get up again when he is learning to walk. If at times God allows a conflict, it may be His way of training us.

(From *Not I but Christ* by Corrie ten Boom)

APPLICATION Do you get impatient with God when he takes you the longer route? Accept the path he has placed you on. Be content with God's purpose in your life. Encourage others who are dissatisfied in their own circumstances to do the same.

EXPLORATION Guidance—Isaiah 30:21; 42:16; Psalm 48:14; 139:9-10; John 16:13.

[19]And Moses took the bones of Joseph with him, for he had placed the
children of Israel under solemn oath, saying, "God will surely visit you,
and you shall carry up my bones from here with you."[l]
[20]So they took their journey from Succoth and camped in Etham at the
edge of the wilderness. [21]And the LORD went before them by day in a pillar
of cloud to lead the way, and by night in a pillar of fire to give them light,
so as to go by day and night. [22]He did not take away the pillar of cloud by
day or the pillar of fire by night *from* before the people.

The Red Sea Crossing

14 Now the LORD spoke to Moses, saying: [2]"Speak to the children of Israel, that they turn and camp before Pi Hahiroth, between Migdol
and the sea, opposite Baal Zephon; you shall camp before it by the sea.
[3]For Pharaoh will say of the children of Israel, 'They *are* bewildered by the
land; the wilderness has closed them in.' [4]Then I will harden Pharaoh's
heart, so that he will pursue them; and I will gain honor over Pharaoh and
over all his army, that the Egyptians may know that I *am* the LORD." And
they did so.
[5]Now it was told the king of Egypt that the people had fled, and the heart
of Pharaoh and his servants was turned against the people; and they said,
"Why have we done this, that we have let Israel go from serving us?" [6]So
he made ready his chariot and took his people with him. [7]Also, he took six
hundred choice chariots, and all the chariots of Egypt with captains over
every one of them. [8]And the LORD hardened the heart of Pharaoh king of
Egypt, and he pursued the children of Israel; and the children of Israel
went out with boldness. [9]So the Egyptians pursued them, all the horses
and chariots of Pharaoh, his horsemen and his army, and overtook them
camping by the sea beside Pi Hahiroth, before Baal Zephon.
[10]And when Pharaoh drew near, the children of Israel lifted their eyes,
and behold, the Egyptians marched after them. So they were very afraid,
and the children of Israel cried out to the LORD. [11]Then they said to Moses,
"Because *there were* no graves in Egypt, have you taken us away to die in
the wilderness? Why have you so dealt with us, to bring us up out of
Egypt? [12]*Is* this not the word that we told you in Egypt, saying, 'Let us alone
that we may serve the Egyptians'? For *it would have been* better for us to
serve the Egyptians than that we should die in the wilderness."
[13]And Moses said to the people, "Do not be afraid. Stand still, and see
the salvation of the LORD, which He will accomplish for you today. For the
Egyptians whom you see today, you shall see again no more forever. [14]The
LORD will fight for you, and you shall hold your peace."
[15]And the LORD said to Moses, "Why do you cry to Me? Tell the children
of Israel to go forward. [16]But lift up your rod, and stretch out your hand
over the sea and divide it. And the children of Israel shall go on dry *ground*
through the midst of the sea. [17]And I indeed will harden the hearts of the
Egyptians, and they shall follow them. So I will gain honor over Pharaoh
and over all his army, his chariots, and his horsemen. [18]Then the Egyptians shall know that I *am* the LORD, when I have gained honor for Myself
over Pharaoh, his chariots, and his horsemen."
[19]And the Angel of God, who went before the camp of Israel, moved and
went behind them; and the pillar of cloud went from before them and

13:19 [l]Genesis 50:25

stood behind them. 20 So it came between the camp of
the Egyptians and the camp of Israel. Thus it was a
cloud and darkness *to the one,* and it gave light by
night *to the other,* so that the one did not come near
the other all that night.
21 Then Moses stretched out his hand over the sea;
and the LORD caused the sea to go *back* by a strong
east wind all that night, and made the sea into dry
land, and the waters were divided. 22 So the children of
Israel went into the midst of the sea on the dry *ground,*
and the waters *were* a wall to them on their right hand
and on their left. 23 And the Egyptians pursued and
went after them into the midst of the sea, all Pharaoh's
horses, his chariots, and his horsemen.
24 Now it came to pass, in the morning watch, that the
LORD looked down upon the army of the Egyptians
through the pillar of fire and cloud, and He troubled the
army of the Egyptians. 25 And He took off[m] their chariot
wheels, so that they drove them with difficulty; and the
Egyptians said, "Let us flee from the face of Israel, for
the LORD fights for them against the Egyptians."
26 Then the LORD said to Moses, "Stretch out your
hand over the sea, that the waters may come back
upon the Egyptians, on their chariots, and on their
horsemen." 27 And Moses stretched out his hand over
the sea; and when the morning appeared, the sea returned to its full depth, while the Egyptians were fleeing into it. So the LORD overthrew the Egyptians in the
midst of the sea. 28 Then the waters returned and covered the chariots, the horsemen, *and* all the army of
Pharaoh that came into the sea after them. Not so
much as one of them remained. 29 But the children of
Israel had walked on dry *land* in the midst of the sea,
and the waters *were* a wall to them on their right hand
and on their left.
30 So the LORD saved Israel that day out of the hand of
the Egyptians, and Israel saw the Egyptians dead on
the seashore. 31 Thus Israel saw the great work which
the LORD had done in Egypt; so the people feared the
LORD, and believed the LORD and His servant Moses.

The Song of Moses

15 Then Moses and the children of Israel sang this
song to the LORD, and spoke, saying:

"I will sing to the LORD,
For He has triumphed gloriously!
The horse and its rider
He has thrown into the sea!
2 The LORD *is* my strength and song,
And He has become my salvation;
He *is* my God, and I will praise Him;
My father's God, and I will exalt Him.
3 The LORD *is* a man of war;
The LORD *is* His name.
4 Pharaoh's chariots and his army
He has cast into the sea;
His chosen captains also are drowned
in the Red Sea.
5 The depths have covered them;
They sank to the bottom like a stone.

6 "Your right hand, O LORD, has become
glorious in power;
Your right hand, O LORD, has dashed the
enemy in pieces.
7 And in the greatness of Your excellence
You have overthrown those who rose
against You;
You sent forth Your wrath;
It consumed them like stubble.
8 And with the blast of Your nostrils
The waters were gathered together;
The floods stood upright like a heap;
The depths congealed in the heart of the sea.
9 The enemy said, 'I will pursue,
I will overtake,
I will divide the spoil;
My desire shall be satisfied on them.
I will draw my sword,
My hand shall destroy them.'
10 You blew with Your wind,
The sea covered them;
They sank like lead in the mighty waters.

11 "Who *is* like You, O LORD, among the gods?
Who *is* like You, glorious in holiness,
Fearful in praises, doing wonders?
12 You stretched out Your right hand;
The earth swallowed them.
13 You in Your mercy have led forth
The people whom You have redeemed;
You have guided *them* in Your strength
To Your holy habitation.

14 "The people will hear *and* be afraid;
Sorrow will take hold of the inhabitants
of Philistia.
15 Then the chiefs of Edom will be dismayed;
The mighty men of Moab,
Trembling will take hold of them;

14:25 [m] Samaritan Pentateuch, Septuagint, and Syriac read *bound.*

LIFE LESSON

Exodus 15:22–17:7

SITUATION For centuries the Israelites had lived on fertile farm land in Goshen. What a contrast the desert was to this previous comfort. With no way to provide for themselves, the Israelites complained to God. He performed daily miracles to provide water and food for them. Manna appeared in flake form with the morning dew. The Israelites ground it like grain and cooked with it.

OBSERVATION The Israelites focused on physical needs, but God focused on their need to learn to trust him. The Israelites could not conquer the desert, but climate was not a problem for God. He sustained, tested, and encouraged them in a perfect way.

INSPIRATION In order to reach the destination, we have to say no to some requests.

Can you imagine the outcome if a parent honored each request of each child during a trip? We'd inch our bloated bellies from one ice-cream store to the next. Our priority would be popcorn and our itinerary would read like a fast-food menu. "Go to the Cherry Malt and make a right. Head north until you find the Chili Cheeseburger. Stay north for 1,300 calories and bear left at the Giant Pizza. When you see the two-for-one Chili Dog Special, take the Pepto-Bismol Turnpike east for five convenience stores. At the sixth toilet . . ."

Can you imagine the chaos if a parent indulged every indulgence?

All the inhabitants of Canaan will melt away.
16 Fear and dread will fall on them;
By the greatness of Your arm
They will be *as* still as a stone,
Till Your people pass over, O LORD,
Till the people pass over
Whom You have purchased.
17 You will bring them in and plant them
In the mountain of Your inheritance,
In the place, O LORD, *which* You have made
For Your own dwelling,
The sanctuary, O LORD, *which* Your hands have established.

18 "The LORD shall reign forever and ever."

19For the horses of Pharaoh went with his chariots and his horsemen
into the sea, and the LORD brought back the waters of the sea upon them.
But the children of Israel went on dry *land* in the midst of the sea.

The Song of Miriam

20Then Miriam the prophetess, the sister of Aaron, took the timbrel in
her hand; and all the women went out after her with timbrels and with
dances. 21And Miriam answered them:

"Sing to the LORD,
For He has triumphed gloriously!
The horse and its rider
He has thrown into the sea!"

Bitter Waters Made Sweet

22So Moses brought Israel from the Red Sea; then they went out into the
Wilderness of Shur. And they went three days in the wilderness and found
no water. 23Now when they came to Marah, they could not drink the waters
of Marah, for they *were* bitter. Therefore the name of it was called Marah.[n]
24And the people complained against Moses, saying, "What shall we
drink?" 25So he cried out to the LORD, and the LORD showed him a tree.
When he cast *it* into the waters, the waters were made sweet.

There He made a statute and an ordinance for them, and there He tested them, 26and said, "If you diligently heed the voice of the LORD your God
and do what is right in His sight, give ear to His commandments and keep
all His statutes, I will put none of the diseases on you which I have brought
on the Egyptians. For I *am* the LORD who heals you."

27Then they came to Elim, where there *were* twelve wells of water and
seventy palm trees; so they camped there by the waters.

Bread from Heaven

16 And they journeyed from Elim, and all the congregation of the children of Israel came to the Wilderness of Sin, which is between Elim
and Sinai, on the fifteenth day of the second month after they departed
from the land of Egypt. 2Then the whole congregation of the children of Israel complained against Moses and Aaron in the wilderness. 3And the

15:23 [n] Literally *Bitter*

children of Israel said to them, "Oh, that we had died by the hand of the
LORD in the land of Egypt, when we sat by the pots of meat *and* when we
ate bread to the full! For you have brought us out into this wilderness to
kill this whole assembly with hunger."
4Then the LORD said to Moses, "Behold, I will rain bread from heaven for
you. And the people shall go out and gather a certain quota every day, that I
may test them, whether they will walk in My law or not. 5And it shall be on
the sixth day that they shall prepare what they bring in, and it shall be
twice as much as they gather daily."
6Then Moses and Aaron said to all the children of Israel, "At evening
you shall know that the LORD has brought you out of the land of Egypt.
7And in the morning you shall see the glory of the LORD; for He hears your
complaints against the LORD. But what *are* we, that you complain against
us?" 8Also Moses said, "*This shall be seen* when the LORD gives you meat to
eat in the evening, and in the morning bread to the full; for the LORD hears
your complaints which you make against Him. And what *are* we? Your
complaints *are* not against us but against the LORD."
9Then Moses spoke to Aaron, "Say to all the congregation of the children of Israel, 'Come near before the LORD, for He has heard your complaints.' " 10Now it came to pass, as Aaron spoke to the whole congregation
of the children of Israel, that they looked toward the wilderness, and
behold, the glory of the LORD appeared in the cloud.
11And the LORD spoke to Moses, saying, 12"I have heard the complaints
of the children of Israel. Speak to them, saying, 'At twilight you shall eat
meat, and in the morning you shall be filled with bread. And you shall
know that I *am* the LORD your God.' "
13So it was that quails came up at evening and covered the camp, and in
the morning the dew lay all around the camp. 14And when the layer of dew
lifted, there, on the surface of the wilderness, was a small round substance,
as fine as frost on the ground. 15So when the children of Israel saw *it,* they
said to one another, "What is it?" For they did not know what it *was.*
And Moses said to them, "This *is* the bread which the LORD has given
you to eat. 16This is the thing which the LORD has commanded: 'Let every
man gather it according to each one's need, one omer for each person, *according to the* number of persons; let every man take for *those* who *are* in
his tent.' "
17Then the children of Israel did so and gathered, some more, some less.
18So when they measured *it* by omers, he who gathered much had nothing
left over, and he who gathered little had no lack. Every man had gathered
according to each one's need. 19And Moses said, "Let no one leave any of
it till morning." 20Notwithstanding they did not heed Moses. But some of
them left part of it until morning, and it bred worms and stank. And Moses was angry with them. 21So they gathered it every morning, every man
according to his need. And when the sun became hot, it melted.
22And so it was, on the sixth day, *that* they gathered twice as much
bread, two omers for each one. And all the rulers of the congregation came
and told Moses. 23Then he said to them, "This *is what* the LORD has said:
'Tomorrow *is* a Sabbath rest, a holy Sabbath to the LORD. Bake what you
will bake *today,* and boil what you will boil; and lay up for yourselves all
that remains, to be kept until morning.' " 24So they laid it up till morning,
as Moses commanded; and it did not stink, nor were there any worms in

Can you imagine the chaos if God indulged each of ours?

No is a necessary word to take on a trip. Destination has to reign over Dairy Deluxe Ice Cream Sundae.

"For God has not *destined* us [italics mine] to the terrors of judgement, but to the full attainment of salvation through our Lord Jesus Christ."

Note God's destiny for your life. Salvation.

God's overarching desire is that you reach that destiny. His itinerary includes stops that encourage your journey. He frowns on stops that deter you. When his sovereign plan and your earthly plan collide, a decision must be made. Who's in charge of this journey?

If God must choose between your earthly satisfaction and your heavenly salvation, which do you hope he chooses?

Me, too.

(From *In the Eye of the Storm* by Max Lucado)

APPLICATION What needs prompt you to pray today? Give these needs specifically to God. Pray about each one and don't worry. Trust that God, who created you, knows how to meet your needs.

EXPLORATION God Provides—Matthew 6:25; 14:18-21; Luke 12:22-31; 1 Corinthians 1:9; Philippians 4:19; 1 Peter 5:7.

it. 25Then Moses said, "Eat that today, for today *is* a Sabbath to the LORD; today you will not find it in the field. 26Six days you shall gather it, but on the seventh day, the Sabbath, there will be none."

27Now it happened *that some* of the people went out on the seventh day to gather, but they found none. 28And the LORD said to Moses, "How long do you refuse to keep My commandments and My laws? 29See! For the LORD has given you the Sabbath; therefore He gives you on the sixth day bread for two days. Let every man remain in his place; let no man go out of his place on the seventh day." 30So the people rested on the seventh day.

31And the house of Israel called its name Manna.[o] And it *was* like white coriander seed, and the taste of it *was* like wafers *made* with honey.

32Then Moses said, "This *is* the thing which the LORD has commanded: 'Fill an omer with it, to be kept for your generations, that they may see the bread with which I fed you in the wilderness, when I brought you out of the land of Egypt.' " 33And Moses said to Aaron, "Take a pot and put an omer of manna in it, and lay it up before the LORD, to be kept for your generations." 34As the LORD commanded Moses, so Aaron laid it up before the Testimony, to be kept. 35And the children of Israel ate manna forty years, until they came to an inhabited land; they ate manna until they came to the border of the land of Canaan. 36Now an omer *is* one-tenth of an ephah.

Water from the Rock

17 Then all the congregation of the children of Israel set out on their journey from the Wilderness of Sin, according to the commandment of the LORD, and camped in Rephidim; but *there was* no water for the people to drink. 2Therefore the people contended with Moses, and said, "Give us water, that we may drink."

So Moses said to them, "Why do you contend with me? Why do you tempt the LORD?"

3And the people thirsted there for water, and the people complained against Moses, and said, "Why *is* it you have brought us up out of Egypt, to kill us and our children and our livestock with thirst?"

4So Moses cried out to the LORD, saying, "What shall I do with this people? They are almost ready to stone me!"

5And the LORD said to Moses, "Go on before the people, and take with you some of the elders of Israel. Also take in your hand your rod with which you struck the river, and go. 6Behold, I will stand before you there on the rock in Horeb; and you shall strike the rock, and water will come out of it, that the people may drink."

And Moses did so in the sight of the elders of Israel. 7So he called the name of the place Massah[p] and Meribah,[q] because of the contention of the children of Israel, and because they tempted the LORD, saying, "Is the LORD among us or not?"

Victory over the Amalekites

8Now Amalek came and fought with Israel in Rephidim. 9And Moses said to Joshua, "Choose us some men and go out, fight with Amalek. Tomorrow I will stand on the top of the hill with the rod of God in my hand." 10So Joshua did as Moses said to him, and fought with Amalek. And Moses, Aaron, and Hur went up to the top of the hill. 11And so it was, when Moses held up his hand, that Israel prevailed; and when he let down his hand, Amalek prevailed. 12But Moses' hands *became* heavy; so they took a stone and put *it* under him, and he sat on it. And Aaron and Hur supported his hands, one on one side, and the other on the other side; and his hands were steady until the going down of the sun. 13So Joshua defeated Amalek and his people with the edge of the sword.

14Then the LORD said to Moses, "Write this *for* a memorial in the book and recount *it* in the hearing of Joshua, that I will utterly blot out the remembrance of Amalek from under heaven." 15And Moses built an altar and called its name, The-LORD-Is-My-Banner;[r] 16for he said, "Because the LORD has sworn: the LORD *will have* war with Amalek from generation to generation."

Jethro's Advice

18 And Jethro, the priest of Midian, Moses' father-in-law, heard of all that God had done for Moses and for Israel His people—that the LORD had brought Israel out of Egypt. 2Then Jethro, Moses' father-in-law, took Zipporah, Moses' wife, after he had sent her back, 3with her two sons, of whom the name of one *was* Gershom (for he said, "I have been a stranger in a foreign land")[s] 4and the name of the other *was* Eliezer[t] (for *he said*, "The God of my father *was* my help, and delivered me from the sword of Pharaoh");

16:31 [o] Literally *What?* (compare Exodus 16:15)
17:7 [p] Literally *Tempted* [q] Literally *Contention*
17:15 [r] Hebrew *YHWH Nissi*
18:3 [s] Compare Exodus 2:22
18:4 [t] Literally *My God Is Help*

5 and Jethro, Moses' father-in-law, came with his sons and his wife to Moses in the wilderness, where he was encamped at the mountain of God.
6 Now he had said to Moses, "I, your father-in-law Jethro, am coming to
you with your wife and her two sons with her."
7 So Moses went out to meet his father-in-law, bowed down, and kissed
him. And they asked each other about *their* well-being, and they went into
the tent. 8 And Moses told his father-in-law all that the LORD had done to
Pharaoh and to the Egyptians for Israel's sake, all the hardship that had
come upon them on the way, and *how* the LORD had delivered them. 9 Then
Jethro rejoiced for all the good which the LORD had done for Israel, whom
He had delivered out of the hand of the Egyptians. 10 And Jethro said,
"Blessed *be* the LORD, who has delivered you out of the hand of the Egyptians and out of the hand of Pharaoh, *and* who has delivered the people
from under the hand of the Egyptians. 11 Now I know that the LORD *is*
greater than all the gods; for in the very thing in which they behaved
proudly, *He was* above them." 12 Then Jethro, Moses' father-in-law, took[u] a
burnt offering and *other* sacrifices *to offer* to God. And Aaron came with
all the elders of Israel to eat bread with Moses' father-in-law before God.
13 And so it was, on the next day, that Moses sat to judge the people; and
the people stood before Moses from morning until evening. 14 So when
Moses' father-in-law saw all that he did for the people, he said, "What *is*
this thing that you are doing for the people? Why do you alone sit, and all
the people stand before you from morning until evening?"
15 And Moses said to his father-in-law, "Because the people come to me
to inquire of God. 16 When they have a difficulty, they come to me, and I
judge between one and another; and I make known the statutes of God
and His laws."
17 So Moses' father-in-law said to him, "The thing that you do *is* not
good. 18 Both you and these people who *are* with you will surely wear yourselves out. For this thing *is* too much for you; you are not able to perform
it by yourself. 19 Listen now to my voice; I will give you counsel, and God
will be with you: Stand before God for the people, so that you may bring
the difficulties to God. 20 And you shall teach them the statutes and the
laws, and show them the way in which they must walk and the work they
must do. 21 Moreover you shall select from all the people able men, such as
fear God, men of truth, hating covetousness; and place *such* over them *to*
be rulers of thousands, rulers of hundreds, rulers of fifties, and rulers of
tens. 22 And let them judge the people at all times. Then it will be *that* every
great matter they shall bring to you, but every small matter they themselves shall judge. So it will be easier for you, for they will bear *the burden*
with you. 23 If you do this thing, and God *so* commands you, then you will
be able to endure, and all this people will also go to their place in peace."
24 So Moses heeded the voice of his father-in-law and did all that he had
said. 25 And Moses chose able men out of all Israel, and made them heads
over the people: rulers of thousands, rulers of hundreds, rulers of fifties,
and rulers of tens. 26 So they judged the people at all times; the hard cases
they brought to Moses, but they judged every small case themselves.
27 Then Moses let his father-in-law depart, and he went his way to his
own land.

18:12 [u] Following Masoretic Text and Septuagint; Syriac, Targum, and Vulgate read *offered.*

LIFE LESSON

Exodus 17:8–18:27

SITUATION The Amalekites, descendants from Esau, hated the Israelites. After Moses led the victory against this enemy, he was visited by his father-in-law. The two helped each other: Jethro gave Moses wise advice about delegating responsibility, and Moses told Jethro about God's faithful care of the Israelites.

OBSERVATION Moses showed several qualities of a good leader. He relied on God and gave him credit for victory. Moses also accepted help, was teachable, and kept his priorities straight. He learned to delegate responsibility and trusted others to lead.

INSPIRATION The alternative to dictatorship in decision-making is *team leadership.* We have heard a lot about the team concept in the last couple of years. In our own organization, there is a strong movement among our field leadership groups to move toward a team emphasis. If I have heard that word once I have heard it a thousand times from the fresh young recruits. The desire to work in a team environment goes hand-in-glove with the trend away from hierarchical, top-down organizational styles. Webster defines *team* as "a number of persons associated together in work or activity; a number of persons selected to contend on one side in a match; a group of workmen each completing one of a set of operations." The word originated from the idea of a group of animals working together, as in two or more horses, oxen, or other draft animals harnessed to the same vehicle or plow. In our day we think of sports teams.

Living in Chicago, I am obviously a Chicago Bulls fan. The Bulls won three world championships under the leadership of Michael Jordan and their coach, Phil Jackson. No one doubts that the recently retired Jordan was a leader of the team. But even Michael Jordan knows that the Bulls would never have won a game without the strong support, energy, and talent of coach Jackson and the other players—like Horace Grant, Scotty Pippin, and John Paxson.

Continued

"What makes a good manager?" someone asked Yogi Berra.

"A good ball club," Yogi replied.

Leadership is teamwork, coaching, creativity—and the synergy of a group of people inspired by their leader.

(From *The Top Ten Mistakes Leaders Make* by Hans Finzel)

APPLICATION Whether you're a leader or a follower, you can follow Moses' example and the Bible's instructions for leaders. Do you rely on God, accept help in decision-making, trust and support others in leadership? How can you work better with your leaders and followers? Ask God to help you be a willing team player.

EXPLORATION Good Leadership—Jeremiah 3:15; Matthew 20:25-26; Acts 20:28; 1 Corinthians 3:4-9; 1 Timothy 3:1-13; 1 Peter 5:2-3.

Israel at Mount Sinai

19 In the third month after the children of Israel had gone out of the
land of Egypt, on the same day, they came *to* the Wilderness of Sinai. 2 For they had departed from Rephidim, had come *to* the Wilderness
of Sinai, and camped in the wilderness. So Israel camped there before the
mountain.
3 And Moses went up to God, and the LORD called to him from the mountain, saying, "Thus you shall say to the house of Jacob, and tell the children
of Israel: 4 'You have seen what I did to the Egyptians, and *how* I bore you
on eagles' wings and brought you to Myself. 5 Now therefore, if you will
indeed obey My voice and keep My covenant, then you shall be a special
treasure to Me above all people; for all the earth *is* Mine. 6 And you shall be
to Me a kingdom of priests and a holy nation.' These *are* the words which
you shall speak to the children of Israel."
7 So Moses came and called for the elders of the people, and laid before
them all these words which the LORD commanded him. 8 Then all the people answered together and said, "All that the LORD has spoken we will do."
So Moses brought back the words of the people to the LORD. 9 And the LORD
said to Moses, "Behold, I come to you in the thick cloud, that the people
may hear when I speak with you, and believe you forever."
So Moses told the words of the people to the LORD.
10 Then the LORD said to Moses, "Go to the people and consecrate them
today and tomorrow, and let them wash their clothes. 11 And let them be
ready for the third day. For on the third day the LORD will come down upon
Mount Sinai in the sight of all the people. 12 You shall set bounds for the
people all around, saying, 'Take heed to yourselves *that* you do *not* go up
to the mountain or touch its base. Whoever touches the mountain shall
surely be put to death. 13 Not a hand shall touch him, but he shall surely be
stoned or shot *with an arrow;* whether man or beast, he shall not live.'
When the trumpet sounds long, they shall come near the mountain."
14 So Moses went down from the mountain to the people and sanctified
the people, and they washed their clothes. 15 And he said to the people, "Be
ready for the third day; do not come near *your* wives."
16 Then it came to pass on the third day, in the morning, that there were
thunderings and lightnings, and a thick cloud on the mountain; and the
sound of the trumpet was very loud, so that all the people who *were* in the
camp trembled. 17 And Moses brought the people out of the camp to meet
with God, and they stood at the foot of the mountain. 18 Now Mount Sinai
was completely in smoke, because the LORD descended upon it in fire. Its
smoke ascended like the smoke of a furnace, and the whole mountain[v]
quaked greatly. 19 And when the blast of the trumpet sounded long and
became louder and louder, Moses spoke, and God answered him by voice.
20 Then the LORD came down upon Mount Sinai, on the top of the mountain. And the LORD called Moses to the top of the mountain, and Moses
went up.
21 And the LORD said to Moses, "Go down and warn the people, lest they
break through to gaze at the LORD, and many of them perish. 22 Also let the
priests who come near the LORD consecrate themselves, lest the LORD
break out against them."

19:18 [v] Septuagint reads *all the people.*

23 But Moses said to the LORD, "The people cannot come up to Mount Sinai; for You warned us, saying, 'Set bounds around the mountain and consecrate it.' "
24 Then the LORD said to him, "Away! Get down and then come up, you
and Aaron with you. But do not let the priests and the people break
through to come up to the LORD, lest He break out against them." 25 So Moses went down to the people and spoke to them.

The Ten Commandments

20 And God spoke all these words, saying:

2 "I *am* the LORD your God, who brought you out of the land of Egypt, out of the house of bondage.
3 "You shall have no other gods before Me.
4 "You shall not make for yourself a carved image—any likeness *of anything* that *is* in heaven above, or that *is* in the earth
beneath, or that *is* in the water under the earth; 5 you shall not
bow down to them nor serve them. For I, the LORD your God,
am a jealous God, visiting the iniquity of the fathers upon the children to the third and fourth *generations* of those who hate
Me, 6 but showing mercy to thousands, to those who love Me and keep My commandments.
7 "You shall not take the name of the LORD your God in vain, for the LORD will not hold *him* guiltless who takes His name in vain.
8 "Remember the Sabbath day, to keep it holy. 9 Six days you shall
labor and do all your work, 10 but the seventh day *is* the
Sabbath of the LORD your God. *In it* you shall do no work: you, nor your son, nor your daughter, nor your male servant, nor your female servant, nor your cattle, nor your stranger who *is*
within your gates. 11 For *in* six days the LORD made the heavens and the earth, the sea, and all that *is* in them, and rested the seventh day. Therefore the LORD blessed the Sabbath day and hallowed it.
12 "Honor your father and your mother, that your days may be long upon the land which the LORD your God is giving you.
13 "You shall not murder.
14 "You shall not commit adultery.
15 "You shall not steal.
16 "You shall not bear false witness against your neighbor.
17 "You shall not covet your neighbor's house; you shall not covet your neighbor's wife, nor his male servant, nor his female servant, nor his ox, nor his donkey, nor anything that *is* your neighbor's."

The People Afraid of God's Presence

18 Now all the people witnessed the thunderings, the lightning flashes, the
sound of the trumpet, and the mountain smoking; and when the people
saw *it*, they trembled and stood afar off. 19 Then they said to Moses, "You
speak with us, and we will hear; but let not God speak with us, lest we die."
20 And Moses said to the people, "Do not fear; for God has come to test you,
and that His fear may be before you, so that you may not sin." 21 So the people stood afar off, but Moses drew near the thick darkness where God *was*.

LIFE LESSON

Exodus 19:1-25

SITUATION After God rescued the Israelites from the Egyptians, he lead them into the Sinai Desert. Only God was able to keep them alive. He fed them and took care of them. Then God called for a huge prayer meeting, where he would come down to Mount Sinai in the sight of all the people.

OBSERVATION When they needed him the most, God revealed his presence.

INSPIRATION Why do all those great stories of miraculous answers to prayer come from African villages or obscure Chinese provinces? Why does it appear that God is visibly active only in the mission field? A skeptic may assume that providential drama gets added as the stories are passed along from hinterland to American Sunday school. A bigger reason, I think, is that God is most active when we are reaching out most. He stretches out when we stretch out.

Think about the classic examples. Why did George Müeller report a book full of answers to specific prayer in complacent Victorian England? He was seeking to meet the needs of two thousand orphans. Why could Hudson Taylor in remotest China report such inspiring experiences about receiving just the funds or personnel needed without ever making an appeal to any human being? He was stretching out to share the gospel where it had not been shared before. Why did God's smuggler, Brother Andrew, have such an abundance of dramatic responses to his petitions? He was given completely to a mission: taking Bibles behind the iron curtain. God is most active in the thick of it. (From *If Only God Would Answer* by Steven Mosley)

APPLICATION Over what situation in your life do you feel you have lost control? When you stop trying to run your life in your own strength, you are ready to witness God's power. Watch how he comes through for you.

EXPLORATION God Provides—Genesis 22:8; 14; Psalm 68:10; Isaiah 43:20; Jonah 1:17; 4:6-8.

The Law of the Altar

22Then the LORD said to Moses, "Thus you shall say to the children of Israel: 'You have seen that I have talked with you from heaven. 23You shall
not make *anything to be* with Me—gods of silver or gods of gold you shall
not make for yourselves. 24An altar of earth you shall make for Me, and
you shall sacrifice on it your burnt offerings and your peace offerings,
your sheep and your oxen. In every place where I record My name I will
come to you, and I will bless you. 25And if you make Me an altar of stone,
you shall not build it of hewn stone; for if you use your tool on it, you have
profaned it. 26Nor shall you go up by steps to My altar, that your nakedness
may not be exposed on it.'

The Law Concerning Servants

21 "Now these *are* the judgments which you shall set before them: 2If
you buy a Hebrew servant, he shall serve six years; and in the seventh he shall go out free and pay nothing. 3If he comes in by himself, he
shall go out by himself; if he *comes in* married, then his wife shall go out with
him. 4If his master has given him a wife, and she has borne him sons or
daughters, the wife and her children shall be her master's, and he shall go
out by himself. 5But if the servant plainly says, 'I love my master, my wife,
and my children; I will not go out free,' 6then his master shall bring him to
the judges. He shall also bring him to the door, or to the doorpost, and his
master shall pierce his ear with an awl; and he shall serve him forever.
7"And if a man sells his daughter to be a female slave, she shall not go
out as the male slaves do. 8If she does not please her master, who has betrothed her to himself, then he shall let her be redeemed. He shall have no
right to sell her to a foreign people, since he has dealt deceitfully with her.
9And if he has betrothed her to his son, he shall deal with her according to
the custom of daughters. 10If he takes another *wife,* he shall not diminish
her food, her clothing, and her marriage rights. 11And if he does not do
these three for her, then she shall go out free, without *paying* money.

The Law Concerning Violence

12"He who strikes a man so that he dies shall surely be put to death.
13However, if he did not lie in wait, but God delivered *him* into his hand,
then I will appoint for you a place where he may flee.
14"But if a man acts with premeditation against his neighbor, to kill him
by treachery, you shall take him from My altar, that he may die.
15"And he who strikes his father or his mother shall surely be put to death.
16"He who kidnaps a man and sells him, or if he is found in his hand,
shall surely be put to death.
17"And he who curses his father or his mother shall surely be put to death.
18"If men contend with each other, and one strikes the other with a stone
or with *his* fist, and he does not die but is confined to *his* bed, 19if he rises
again and walks about outside with his staff, then he who struck *him* shall
be acquitted. He shall only pay *for* the loss of his time, and shall provide
for him to be thoroughly healed.
20"And if a man beats his male or female servant with a rod, so that he
dies under his hand, he shall surely be punished. 21Notwithstanding, if he
remains alive a day or two, he shall not be punished; for he *is* his property.

LIFE LESSON

Exodus 20:1-26

SITUATION God formed a covenant with Israel at Mt. Sinai. The Ten Commandments changed history, giving us timeless truths and clear moral standards.

OBSERVATION God demands total devotion. The Ten Commandments govern the relationship between God and those who love him.

INSPIRATION The moral law does not consider our weaknesses as human beings; in fact, it does not take into account our heredity or infirmities. It simply demands that we be absolutely moral. The moral law never changes, either for the highest of society or for the weakest in the world. It is enduring and eternally the same. . . . If we are not aware of this, it is because we are less than alive. Once we do realize it, our life immediately becomes a fatal tragedy. "I was alive once without the law, but when the commandment came, sin revived and I died" (Romans 7:9). . . . Conviction of sin always brings a fearful, confining sense of the law. It makes a person hopeless—". . . sold under sin." (Romans 7:14). I, guilty sinner, can never work to get right with God—it is impossible. There is only one way by which I can get right with God, and that is through the death of Jesus Christ. I must get rid of the underlying idea that I can ever be right with God because of my obedience. Who of us could ever obey God to absolute perfection! . . . Sometimes we wish He would make us be obedient, and at other times we wish He would leave us alone. Whenever God's will is in complete control, He removes all pressure. And when we deliberately choose to obey Him, He will reach to the remotest star and to the ends of the earth to assist us with all of His mighty power. (From *My Utmost for His Highest* by Oswald Chambers)

APPLICATION Who has kept the Ten Commandments perfectly? To seek forgiveness, the Israelites offered animal sacrifices. But God provided a better way through Jesus Christ's sacrifice.

EXPLORATION God's Law—Psalm 119:12-24; Matthew 5:17-19; Luke 16:16-17; 1 John 3:19-24.

22“If men fight, and hurt a woman with child, so that she gives birth
prematurely, yet no harm follows, he shall surely be punished accordingly as the woman’s husband imposes on him; and he shall pay as the judges
determine. 23But if *any* harm follows, then you shall give life for life, 24eye
for eye, tooth for tooth, hand for hand, foot for foot, 25burn for burn, wound
for wound, stripe for stripe.
26“If a man strikes the eye of his male or female servant, and destroys it,
he shall let him go free for the sake of his eye. 27And if he knocks out the
tooth of his male or female servant, he shall let him go free for the sake of
his tooth.

Animal Control Laws

28“If an ox gores a man or a woman to death, then the ox shall surely be
stoned, and its flesh shall not be eaten; but the owner of the ox *shall be* acquitted. 29But if the ox tended to thrust with its horn in times past, and it
has been made known to his owner, and he has not kept it confined, so
that it has killed a man or a woman, the ox shall be stoned and its owner
also shall be put to death. 30If there is imposed on him a sum of money,
then he shall pay to redeem his life, whatever is imposed on him.
31Whether it has gored a son or gored a daughter, according to this judgment it shall be done to him. 32If the ox gores a male or female servant, he
shall give to their master thirty shekels of silver, and the ox shall be stoned.
33“And if a man opens a pit, or if a man digs a pit and does not cover it,
and an ox or a donkey falls in it, 34the owner of the pit shall make *it* good;
he shall give money to their owner, but the dead *animal* shall be his.
35“If one man’s ox hurts another’s, so that it dies, then they shall sell the
live ox and divide the money from it; and the dead *ox* they shall also
divide. 36Or if it was known that the ox tended to thrust in time past, and
its owner has not kept it confined, he shall surely pay ox for ox, and the
dead animal shall be his own.

Responsibility for Property

22 “If a man steals an ox or a sheep, and slaughters it or sells it, he shall
restore five oxen for an ox and four sheep for a sheep. 2If the thief is
found breaking in, and he is struck so that he dies, *there shall be* no guilt
for his bloodshed. 3If the sun has risen on him, *there shall be* guilt for his
bloodshed. He should make full restitution; if he has nothing, then he shall
be sold for his theft. 4If the theft is certainly found alive in his hand,
whether it is an ox or donkey or sheep, he shall restore double.
5“If a man causes a field or vineyard to be grazed, and lets loose his animal, and it feeds in another man’s field, he shall make restitution from the
best of his own field and the best of his own vineyard.
6“If fire breaks out and catches in thorns, so that stacked grain, standing grain, or the field is consumed, he who kindled the fire shall surely
make restitution.
7“If a man delivers to his neighbor money or articles to keep, and it is
stolen out of the man’s house, if the thief is found, he shall pay double. 8If
the thief is not found, then the master of the house shall be brought to the
judges *to see* whether he has put his hand into his neighbor’s goods.
9“For any kind of trespass, *whether it concerns* an ox, a donkey, a sheep,
or clothing, *or* for any kind of lost thing which *another* claims to be his, the

Life Lesson

Exodus 21:1–22:31

SITUATION God entrusted more laws to the Israelites: deceit, injury, slavery, robbery, property, immorality, and religion were the central themes.

OBSERVATION God provides guidelines for his people so their moral life will be pleasing to him.

INSPIRATION When I first became a Christian I was introduced to the priorities of the Christian community. I learned quickly that it was expected of me that I have a daily devotion time, a time reserved for Bible reading and prayer. I was expected to go to church. I was expected to have a kind of piety that was evident by not cursing, not drinking, not smoking, and the like. I had no idea that biblical righteousness went far beyond these things. . . .

Soon, however, I found that there was more to the Christian life than daily devotions and sanctified words. I realized that God wanted more. He wanted me to grow in my faith and obedience, to go beyond milk to meat. I also discovered that Christian jargon was an almost meaningless form of communication, both to non-Christians and Christians alike. I found myself more interested in echoing a subculture’s lingo than in finding true godliness.

My error was this: I was confusing spirituality with righteousness. I also discovered that I was not alone in this. I was caught up with a crowd who confused the means with the end. Spirituality can be a cheap substitute for righteousness. . . .

Righteousness has rules, but it is more than rules. If we care for rules without caring for people, we have missed the goal of righteousness. The scriptural rules come from God precisely because He cares about people.

We need rules to be righteous, but they must be the right rules. They must be God’s rules. We may accept no substitutes. In God’s Word we find adequate rules for pleasing God with a righteous life. And if we abide by those rules, we are not goal-less fanatics, but true children of the King.

(From *Pleasing God* by R.C. Sproul)

Continued

APPLICATION Can you distinguish God's rules from those of our Christian subculture? Make a list of ways you feel required to act within your Christian community. Check the list against God's Word. If you find the rule to be God's, glorify him by practicing it. If you cannot find the rule in the Bible, ask an older Christian why its observance is expected.

EXPLORATION Righteousness—Psalm 1:1-6; Matthew 5:17-20; 15:1-11; Romans 13:10; James 1:19-27.

cause of both parties shall come before the judges; *and* whomever the
judges condemn shall pay double to his neighbor. 10If a man delivers to his
neighbor a donkey, an ox, a sheep, or any animal to keep, and it dies, is
hurt, or driven away, no one seeing *it,* 11*then* an oath of the LORD shall be
between them both, that he has not put his hand into his neighbor's
goods; and the owner of it shall accept *that,* and he shall not make *it* good.
12But if, in fact, it is stolen from him, he shall make restitution to the owner
of it. 13If it is torn to pieces *by a beast, then* he shall bring it as evidence, *and*
he shall not make good what was torn.
14"And if a man borrows *anything* from his neighbor, and it becomes
injured or dies, the owner of it not *being* with it, he shall surely make *it*
good. 15If its owner *was* with it, he shall not make *it* good; if it *was* hired, it
came for its hire.

Moral and Ceremonial Principles

16"If a man entices a virgin who is not betrothed, and lies with her, he
shall surely pay the bride-price for her *to be* his wife. 17If her father utterly
refuses to give her to him, he shall pay money according to the bride-price
of virgins.
18"You shall not permit a sorceress to live.
19"Whoever lies with an animal shall surely be put to death.
20"He who sacrifices to *any* god, except to the LORD only, he shall be
utterly destroyed.
21"You shall neither mistreat a stranger nor oppress him, for you were
strangers in the land of Egypt.
22"You shall not afflict any widow or fatherless child. 23If you afflict them
in any way, *and* they cry at all to Me, I will surely hear their cry; 24and My
wrath will become hot, and I will kill you with the sword; your wives shall
be widows, and your children fatherless.
25"If you lend money to *any of* My people *who are* poor among you, you
shall not be like a moneylender to him; you shall not charge him interest.
26If you ever take your neighbor's garment as a pledge, you shall return it
to him before the sun goes down. 27For that *is* his only covering, it *is* his
garment for his skin. What will he sleep in? And it will be that when he
cries to Me, I will hear, for I *am* gracious.
28"You shall not revile God, nor curse a ruler of your people.
29"You shall not delay *to offer* the first of your ripe produce and your
juices. The firstborn of your sons you shall give to Me. 30Likewise you shall
do with your oxen *and* your sheep. It shall be with its mother seven days;
on the eighth day you shall give it to Me.
31"And you shall be holy men to Me: you shall not eat meat torn *by
beasts* in the field; you shall throw it to the dogs.

Justice for All

23 "You shall not circulate a false report. Do not put your hand with
the wicked to be an unrighteous witness. 2You shall not follow a
crowd to do evil; nor shall you testify in a dispute so as to turn aside after
many to pervert *justice.* 3You shall not show partiality to a poor man in his
dispute.
4"If you meet your enemy's ox or his donkey going astray, you shall
surely bring it back to him again. 5If you see the donkey of one who hates

you lying under its burden, and you would refrain from helping it, you
shall surely help him with it.
6“You shall not pervert the judgment of your poor in his dispute. 7Keep
yourself far from a false matter; do not kill the innocent and righteous. For
I will not justify the wicked. 8And you shall take no bribe, for a bribe blinds
the discerning and perverts the words of the righteous.
9“Also you shall not oppress a stranger, for you know the heart of a
stranger, because you were strangers in the land of Egypt.

The Law of Sabbaths

10“Six years you shall sow your land and gather in its produce, 11but the
seventh *year* you shall let it rest and lie fallow, that the poor of your people
may eat; and what they leave, the beasts of the field may eat. In like manner you shall do with your vineyard *and* your olive grove. 12Six days you
shall do your work, and on the seventh day you shall rest, that your ox and
your donkey may rest, and the son of your female servant and the stranger may be refreshed.
13“And in all that I have said to you, be circumspect and make no mention of the name of other gods, nor let it be heard from your mouth.

Three Annual Feasts

14“Three times you shall keep a feast to Me in the year: 15You shall keep
the Feast of Unleavened Bread (you shall eat unleavened bread seven
days, as I commanded you, at the time appointed in the month of Abib,
for in it you came out of Egypt; none shall appear before Me empty); 16and
the Feast of Harvest, the firstfruits of your labors which you have sown in
the field; and the Feast of Ingathering at the end of the year, when you have
gathered in *the fruit of* your labors from the field.
17“Three times in the year all your males shall appear before the Lord
GOD.[w]
18“You shall not offer the blood of My sacrifice with leavened bread; nor
shall the fat of My sacrifice remain until morning. 19The first of the firstfruits of your land you shall bring into the house of the LORD your God. You
shall not boil a young goat in its mother’s milk.

The Angel and the Promises

20“Behold, I send an Angel before you to keep you in the way and to
bring you into the place which I have prepared. 21Beware of Him and obey
His voice; do not provoke Him, for He will not pardon your transgressions; for My name *is* in Him. 22But if you indeed obey His voice and do all
that I speak, then I will be an enemy to your enemies and an adversary to
your adversaries. 23For My Angel will go before you and bring you in to the
Amorites and the Hittites and the Perizzites and the Canaanites and the
Hivites and the Jebusites; and I will cut them off. 24You shall not bow down
to their gods, nor serve them, nor do according to their works; but you
shall utterly overthrow them and completely break down their *sacred* pillars.
25“So you shall serve the LORD your God, and He will bless your bread
and your water. And I will take sickness away from the midst of you. 26No

23:17 [w] Hebrew *YHWH,* usually translated *LORD*

LIFE LESSON

Exodus 23:1–24:18

SITUATION God gave the Israelites guidelines for their relationships with each other and with him. These guidelines set Israel apart from the other nations. God also gave a special ceremony that confirmed the agreement between God and his people. In the ceremony blood from animals symbolized forgiveness of sins and reconciliation to God.

OBSERVATION God’s people ought to obey the standards that God lays out. One part of this is remembering their special relationship with him.

INSPIRATION The Bible makes clear . . . that unquestioning acceptance of and obedience to Jesus’ authority is the foundation of the Christian life. Everything else rests upon this. It also provides the key to understanding what is for many the great mystery of Christianity: faith.

Saving faith—that by which we are justified, made right with God—is a gift of God; and, yes, it involves a rational process as well since it comes from hearing the Word of God. . . . “All right,” the struggling Christian may say, “but practically speaking, how does my faith become real? How do I get that vibrant, strong faith of Christian maturity?”

That’s where obedience comes in. For maturing faith—faith which deepens and grows as we live our Christian life—is not just knowledge, but knowledge acted upon. It is not just belief, but belief lived out—practiced. James said we are to be doers of the Word, not just hearers. Dietrich Bonhoeffer, the German pastor martyred in a Nazi concentration camp, succinctly stated this crucial interrelationship: “Only he who believes is obedient; only he who is obedient believes.”

This may sound like a circular proposition, but many things are—in truth and in practice. Think of learning how to swim. We are told what to do. We gingerly enter the water, launch out, and promptly forget everything we’ve been told. We flail about, splashing frantically, gasping and sinking. Finally, usually at the point of utter despair, we capture for a moment the sensation of staying afloat. Realizing

Continued

it is possible, we remember our instructions and begin to follow them. They work. Like learning to balance a bicycle or mastering a foreign language, faith is a state of mind that grows out of our actions, just as it governs them.

So obedience is the key to real faith. (From *Loving God* by Charles Colson)

APPLICATION God makes several agreements with his people throughout the Bible, concluding with a new covenant in Christ. Communion reminds us that in this covenant, God forgives our sins through Christ. When you participate in communion, do not participate lightly. Be humbled by God's grace to you.

EXPLORATION Guidance of Holy Spirit—1 Kings 18:12; Psalm 143:10; Isaiah 48:16; 63:14; John 16:13; Acts 16:6-7; Romans 8:14.

one shall suffer miscarriage or be barren in your land; I will fulfill the
number of your days.
27"I will send My fear before you, I will cause confusion among all the
people to whom you come, and will make all your enemies turn *their*
backs to you. 28And I will send hornets before you, which shall drive out
the Hivite, the Canaanite, and the Hittite from before you. 29I will not drive
them out from before you in one year, lest the land become desolate and
the beasts of the field become too numerous for you. 30Little by little I will
drive them out from before you, until you have increased, and you inherit the land. 31And I will set your bounds from the Red Sea to the sea,
Philistia, and from the desert to the River.[x] For I will deliver the inhabitants of the land into your hand, and you shall drive them out before you.
32You shall make no covenant with them, nor with their gods. 33They shall
not dwell in your land, lest they make you sin against Me. For *if* you serve
their gods, it will surely be a snare to you."

Israel Affirms the Covenant

24 Now He said to Moses, "Come up to the LORD, you and Aaron,
Nadab and Abihu, and seventy of the elders of Israel, and worship
from afar. 2And Moses alone shall come near the LORD, but they shall not
come near; nor shall the people go up with him."
3So Moses came and told the people all the words of the LORD and all the
judgments. And all the people answered with one voice and said, "All the
words which the LORD has said we will do." 4And Moses wrote all the words
of the LORD. And he rose early in the morning, and built an altar at the foot
of the mountain, and twelve pillars according to the twelve tribes of Israel.
5Then he sent young men of the children of Israel, who offered burnt
offerings and sacrificed peace offerings of oxen to the LORD. 6And Moses
took half the blood and put *it* in basins, and half the blood he sprinkled on
the altar. 7Then he took the Book of the Covenant and read in the hearing
of the people. And they said, "All that the LORD has said we will do, and be
obedient." 8And Moses took the blood, sprinkled *it* on the people, and
said, "This is the blood of the covenant which the LORD has made with you
according to all these words."

On the Mountain with God

9Then Moses went up, also Aaron, Nadab, and Abihu, and seventy of
the elders of Israel, 10and they saw the God of Israel. And *there was* under
His feet as it were a paved work of sapphire stone, and it was like the very
heavens in *its* clarity. 11But on the nobles of the children of Israel He did
not lay His hand. So they saw God, and they ate and drank.
12Then the LORD said to Moses, "Come up to Me on the mountain and
be there; and I will give you tablets of stone, and the law and commandments which I have written, that you may teach them."
13So Moses arose with his assistant Joshua, and Moses went up to the
mountain of God. 14And he said to the elders, "Wait here for us until we
come back to you. Indeed, Aaron and Hur *are* with you. If any man has a
difficulty, let him go to them." 15Then Moses went up into the mountain,
and a cloud covered the mountain.
16Now the glory of the LORD rested on Mount Sinai, and the cloud covered

23:31 [x] Hebrew *Nahar,* the Euphrates

it six days. And on the seventh day He called to Moses out of the midst of
the cloud. 17The sight of the glory of the LORD *was* like a consuming fire on
the top of the mountain in the eyes of the children of Israel. 18So Moses
went into the midst of the cloud and went up into the mountain. And Moses was on the mountain forty days and forty nights.

Offerings for the Sanctuary

25 Then the LORD spoke to Moses, saying: 2"Speak to the children of Israel, that they bring Me an offering. From everyone who gives it
willingly with his heart you shall take My offering. 3And this *is* the offering
which you shall take from them: gold, silver, and bronze; 4blue, purple,
and scarlet *thread,* fine linen, and goats' *hair;* 5ram skins dyed red, badger
skins, and acacia wood; 6oil for the light, and spices for the anointing oil
and for the sweet incense; 7onyx stones, and stones to be set in the ephod
and in the breastplate. 8And let them make Me a sanctuary, that I may
dwell among them. 9According to all that I show you, *that is,* the pattern of
the tabernacle and the pattern of all its furnishings, just so you shall make *it.*

The Ark of the Testimony

10"And they shall make an ark of acacia wood; two and a half cubits *shall
be* its length, a cubit and a half its width, and a cubit and a half its height.
11And you shall overlay it with pure gold, inside and out you shall overlay
it, and shall make on it a molding of gold all around. 12You shall cast four
rings of gold for it, and put *them* in its four corners; two rings *shall be* on
one side, and two rings on the other side. 13And you shall make poles *of*
acacia wood, and overlay them with gold. 14You shall put the poles into the
rings on the sides of the ark, that the ark may be carried by them. 15The
poles shall be in the rings of the ark; they shall not be taken from it. 16And
you shall put into the ark the Testimony which I will give you.
17"You shall make a mercy seat of pure gold; two and a half cubits *shall
be* its length and a cubit and a half its width. 18And you shall make two
cherubim of gold; of hammered work you shall make them at the two ends
of the mercy seat. 19Make one cherub at one end, and the other cherub at
the other end; you shall make the cherubim at the two ends of it *of one
piece* with the mercy seat. 20And the cherubim shall stretch out *their* wings
above, covering the mercy seat with their wings, and they shall face one
another; the faces of the cherubim *shall be* toward the mercy seat. 21You
shall put the mercy seat on top of the ark, and in the ark you shall put the
Testimony that I will give you. 22And there I will meet with you, and I will
speak with you from above the mercy seat, from between the two cherubim which *are* on the ark of the Testimony, about everything which I will
give you in commandment to the children of Israel.

The Table for the Showbread

23"You shall also make a table of acacia wood; two cubits *shall be* its
length, a cubit its width, and a cubit and a half its height. 24And you shall
overlay it with pure gold, and make a molding of gold all around. 25You
shall make for it a frame of a handbreadth all around, and you shall make
a gold molding for the frame all around. 26And you shall make for it four
rings of gold, and put the rings on the four corners that *are* at its four legs.
27The rings shall be close to the frame, as holders for the poles to bear the

LIFE LESSON

Exodus 25:1–27:21

SITUATION God provided precise instructions for building the tabernacle. Detailed instructions for making the ark, the table, and the lampstand demonstrated his transcendence above the common everyday features of the world. The ark's portable nature represented God's desire to be with the Israelites wherever they traveled.

OBSERVATION Throughout the Bible, God provides ways for his people to have fellowship with him.

INSPIRATION We stream to the fellowship of our church to worship; there in that place, at that mountain of God, we are built up, established, equipped, encouraged, challenged. . . . I know that when I'm among the assembled people that God is here in our midst. The King is here seeking to rule in our hearts right now. So this concept that where two or three are gathered, there He is in our midst is a powerful truth. It challenges us because sometimes when we gather for worship, we simply go through the motions. I know I've done that a number of times, and others have told me they have done the same. But I remind myself and others that whenever the people of God gather in a theater, in an arena, or in a church for worship, God is there.

That's why I often say in an opening prayer "Lord, we don't take lightly the fact that You're here." I don't want to come into the presence of the King of kings, the Lord of lords, the Creator and Redeemer of the universe in a nonchalant, casual, and impertinent way. No, I want to come before God in all humility recognizing I am a mere creature and He is holiness. He is the Creator. (From *In This Sanctuary* by Twila Paris)

APPLICATION The diligence and care with which the Israelites built the tabernacle demonstrated their reverence for God. How do you show your reverence for him? Make your life a pure temple of faith that honors God in every action. What can you do today to tell God, "I want to honor you in all my plans"?

EXPLORATION Reverence—Psalm 34:9; Proverbs 1:7; 8:13; Ecclesiastes 12:13; 1 Peter 1:17.

table. 28And you shall make the poles of acacia wood,
and overlay them with gold, that the table may be carried with them. 29You shall make its dishes, its pans,
its pitchers, and its bowls for pouring. You shall make
them of pure gold. 30And you shall set the showbread
on the table before Me always.

The Gold Lampstand

31"You shall also make a lampstand of pure gold;
the lampstand shall be of hammered work. Its shaft,
its branches, its bowls, its *ornamental* knobs, and
flowers shall be *of one piece.* 32And six branches shall
come out of its sides: three branches of the lampstand
out of one side, and three branches of the lampstand
out of the other side. 33Three bowls *shall be* made like
almond *blossoms* on one branch, *with* an *ornamental*
knob and a flower, and three bowls made like almond
blossoms on the other branch, *with* an *ornamental*
knob and a flower—and so for the six branches that
come out of the lampstand. 34On the lampstand itself
four bowls *shall be* made like almond *blossoms, each
with* its *ornamental* knob and flower. 35And *there shall
be* a knob under the *first* two branches of the same, a
knob under the *second* two branches of the same, and
a knob under the *third* two branches of the same,
according to the six branches that extend from the
lampstand. 36Their knobs and their branches *shall be
of one piece;* all of it *shall be* one hammered piece of
pure gold. 37You shall make seven lamps for it, and
they shall arrange its lamps so that they give light in
front of it. 38And its wick-trimmers and their trays
shall be of pure gold. 39It shall be made of a talent of
pure gold, with all these utensils. 40And see to it that
you make *them* according to the pattern which was
shown you on the mountain.

The Tabernacle

26 "Moreover you shall make the tabernacle *with*
ten curtains *of* fine woven linen and blue, purple, and scarlet *thread;* with artistic designs of cherubim you shall weave them. 2The length of each curtain
shall be twenty-eight cubits, and the width of each
curtain four cubits. And every one of the curtains
shall have the same measurements. 3Five curtains shall
be coupled to one another, and *the other* five curtains
shall be coupled to one another. 4And you shall make
loops of blue *yarn* on the edge of the curtain on the
selvedge of *one* set, and likewise you shall do on the
outer edge of *the other* curtain of the second set. 5Fifty
loops you shall make in the one curtain, and fifty
loops you shall make on the edge of the curtain that *is*
on the end of the second set, that the loops may be
clasped to one another. 6And you shall make fifty
clasps of gold, and couple the curtains together with
the clasps, so that it may be one tabernacle.

7"You shall also make curtains of goats' *hair,* to be a
tent over the tabernacle. You shall make eleven curtains. 8The length of each curtain *shall be* thirty cubits,
and the width of each curtain four cubits; and the
eleven curtains shall all have the same measurements. 9And you shall couple five curtains by themselves and six curtains by themselves, and you shall
double over the sixth curtain at the forefront of the
tent. 10You shall make fifty loops on the edge of the curtain that is outermost in *one* set, and fifty loops on the
edge of the curtain of the second set. 11And you shall
make fifty bronze clasps, put the clasps into the loops,
and couple the tent together, that it may be one. 12The
remnant that remains of the curtains of the tent, the
half curtain that remains, shall hang over the back of
the tabernacle. 13And a cubit on one side and a cubit
on the other side, of what remains of the length of the
curtains of the tent, shall hang over the sides of the
tabernacle, on this side and on that side, to cover it.

14"You shall also make a covering of ram skins dyed
red for the tent, and a covering of badger skins above
that.

15"And for the tabernacle you shall make the boards
of acacia wood, standing upright. 16Ten cubits *shall be*
the length of a board, and a cubit and a half *shall be* the
width of each board. 17Two tenons *shall be* in each
board for binding one to another. Thus you shall make
for all the boards of the tabernacle. 18And you shall
make the boards for the tabernacle, twenty boards for
the south side. 19You shall make forty sockets of silver
under the twenty boards: two sockets under each of
the boards for its two tenons. 20And for the second
side of the tabernacle, the north side, *there shall be*
twenty boards 21and their forty sockets of silver: two
sockets under each of the boards. 22For the far side of
the tabernacle, westward, you shall make six boards.
23And you shall also make two boards for the two back
corners of the tabernacle. 24They shall be coupled together at the bottom and they shall be coupled together at the top by one ring. Thus it shall be for both of
them. They shall be for the two corners. 25So there
shall be eight boards with their sockets of silver—sixteen sockets—two sockets under each of the boards.

26"And you shall make bars of acacia wood: five for
the boards on one side of the tabernacle, 27five bars for
the boards on the other side of the tabernacle, and five
bars for the boards of the side of the tabernacle, for the

far side westward. 28The middle bar shall pass through
the midst of the boards from end to end. 29You shall
overlay the boards with gold, make their rings of gold
as holders for the bars, and overlay the bars with gold.
30And you shall raise up the tabernacle according to
its pattern which you were shown on the mountain.
31"You shall make a veil woven of blue, purple, and
scarlet *thread,* and fine woven linen. It shall be woven
with an artistic design of cherubim. 32You shall hang
it upon the four pillars of acacia *wood* overlaid with
gold. Their hooks *shall be* gold, upon four sockets of
silver. 33And you shall hang the veil from the clasps.
Then you shall bring the ark of the Testimony in there,
behind the veil. The veil shall be a divider for you
between the holy *place* and the Most Holy. 34You shall
put the mercy seat upon the ark of the Testimony in
the Most Holy. 35You shall set the table outside the veil,
and the lampstand across from the table on the side
of the tabernacle toward the south; and you shall put
the table on the north side.
36"You shall make a screen for the door of the tabernacle, *woven of* blue, purple, and scarlet *thread,* and
fine woven linen, made by a weaver. 37And you shall
make for the screen five pillars of acacia *wood,* and
overlay them with gold; their hooks *shall be* gold, and
you shall cast five sockets of bronze for them.

The Altar of Burnt Offering

27 "You shall make an altar of acacia wood, five
cubits long and five cubits wide—the altar
shall be square—and its height *shall be* three cubits.
2You shall make its horns on its four corners; its horns
shall be of one piece with it. And you shall overlay it
with bronze. 3Also you shall make its pans to receive
its ashes, and its shovels and its basins and its forks
and its firepans; you shall make all its utensils of bronze.
4You shall make a grate for it, a network of bronze; and
on the network you shall make four bronze rings at its
four corners. 5You shall put it under the rim of the
altar beneath, that the network may be midway up the
altar. 6And you shall make poles for the altar, poles of
acacia wood, and overlay them with bronze. 7The
poles shall be put in the rings, and the poles shall be
on the two sides of the altar to bear it. 8You shall make
it hollow with boards; as it was shown you on the
mountain, so shall they make *it.*

The Court of the Tabernacle

9"You shall also make the court of the tabernacle.
For the south side *there shall be* hangings for the court
made of fine woven linen, one hundred cubits long
for one side. 10And its twenty pillars and their twenty
sockets *shall be* bronze. The hooks of the pillars and
their bands *shall be* silver. 11Likewise along the length
of the north side *there shall be* hangings one hundred
cubits long, with its twenty pillars and their twenty
sockets of bronze, and the hooks of the pillars and
their bands of silver.
12"And along the width of the court on the west side
shall be hangings of fifty cubits, with their ten pillars
and their ten sockets. 13The width of the court on the
east side *shall be* fifty cubits. 14The hangings on *one*
side *of the gate shall be* fifteen cubits, *with* their three
pillars and their three sockets. 15And on the other side
shall be hangings of fifteen *cubits, with* their three pillars and their three sockets.
16"For the gate of the court *there shall be* a screen
twenty cubits long, *woven of* blue, purple, and scarlet
thread, and fine woven linen, made by a weaver. It
shall have four pillars and four sockets. 17All the pillars
around the court shall have bands of silver; their
hooks *shall be* of silver and their sockets of bronze.
18The length of the court *shall be* one hundred cubits, the
width fifty throughout, and the height five cubits, *made
of* fine woven linen, and its sockets of bronze. 19All the
utensils of the tabernacle for all its service, all its pegs,
and all the pegs of the court, *shall be* of bronze.

The Care of the Lampstand

20"And you shall command the children of Israel
that they bring you pure oil of pressed olives for the
light, to cause the lamp to burn continually. 21In the
tabernacle of meeting, outside the veil which *is* before
the Testimony, Aaron and his sons shall tend it from
evening until morning before the LORD. *It shall be* a
statute forever to their generations on behalf of the
children of Israel.

Garments for the Priesthood

28 "Now take Aaron your brother, and his sons
with him, from among the children of Israel,
that he may minister to Me as priest, Aaron *and* Aaron's sons: Nadab, Abihu, Eleazar, and Ithamar. 2And
you shall make holy garments for Aaron your brother,
for glory and for beauty. 3So you shall speak to all *who
are* gifted artisans, whom I have filled with the spirit
of wisdom, that they may make Aaron's garments, to
consecrate him, that he may minister to Me as priest.
4And these *are* the garments which they shall make: a
breastplate, an ephod,[y] a robe, a skillfully woven tunic,

28:4 [y] That is, an ornamented vest

LIFE LESSON

Exodus 28:1–29:46

SITUATION God instructed Aaron and his sons to become the first temple priests. These priests ministered to the people's spiritual needs and represented them before God.

OBSERVATION Priests became mediators between God and the people. The priest carried God's wisdom to the people and the people's needs to God.

INSPIRATION Each of us must see ourselves as ministers of the gospel. We don't simply attend church, consuming a religious product. Rather, our whole understanding of ourselves as members of the Body is directed toward being equipped to serve effectively in our vocation and our community—wherever God places us.

Many Christians have a bifurcated view of life: Faith is over here in this compartment, and the rest of life—work, family, leisure time, and everything else—is over there.

Like the young woman who stopped me in an airport recently, "Mr. Colson, I so admire the work that Prison Fellowship is doing. I'm a believer; I wish that I could be in full-time Christian service like you."

"What is it you do?" I asked.

"Well, I'm still in school," she said. "I'm finishing up my doctoral work in molecular biology. I had planned to teach full time. I love it. But lately I've realized I should do more for the Lord. My parents were missionaries. I'm thinking of going to Brazil as a missionary."

"You are in a tremendous position to be a missionary right where you are!" I said adamantly. "How many Christians

a turban, and a sash. So they shall make holy garments for Aaron your
brother and his sons, that he may minister to Me as priest.

The Ephod

5“They shall take the gold, blue, purple, and scarlet *thread,* and the fine
linen, 6and they shall make the ephod of gold, blue, purple, *and* scarlet
thread, and fine woven linen, artistically worked. 7It shall have two shoulder straps joined at its two edges, and *so* it shall be joined together. 8And
the intricately woven band of the ephod, which *is* on it, shall be of the same
workmanship, *made of* gold, blue, purple, and scarlet *thread,* and fine
woven linen.
9“Then you shall take two onyx stones and engrave on them the names
of the sons of Israel: 10six of their names on one stone and six names on
the other stone, in order of their birth. 11With the work of an engraver in
stone, *like* the engravings of a signet, you shall engrave the two stones with
the names of the sons of Israel. You shall set them in settings of gold. 12And
you shall put the two stones on the shoulders of the ephod *as* memorial
stones for the sons of Israel. So Aaron shall bear their names before the
LORD on his two shoulders as a memorial. 13You shall also make settings of
gold, 14and you shall make two chains of pure gold like braided cords, and
fasten the braided chains to the settings.

The Breastplate

15“You shall make the breastplate of judgment. Artistically woven
according to the workmanship of the ephod you shall make it: of gold,
blue, purple, and scarlet *thread,* and fine woven linen, you shall make it.
16It shall be doubled into a square: a span *shall be* its length, and a span
shall be its width. 17And you shall put settings of stones in it, four rows of
stones: *The first* row *shall be* a sardius, a topaz, and an emerald; *this shall
be* the first row; 18the second row *shall be* a turquoise, a sapphire, and a
diamond; 19the third row, a jacinth, an agate, and an amethyst; 20and the
fourth row, a beryl, an onyx, and a jasper. They shall be set in gold settings.
21And the stones shall have the names of the sons of Israel, twelve according to their names, *like* the engravings of a signet, each one with its own
name; they shall be according to the twelve tribes.
22“You shall make chains for the breastplate at the end, like braided
cords of pure gold. 23And you shall make two rings of gold for the breastplate, and put the two rings on the two ends of the breastplate. 24Then you
shall put the two braided *chains* of gold in the two rings which are on the
ends of the breastplate; 25and the *other* two ends of the two braided *chains*
you shall fasten to the two settings, and put them on the shoulder straps
of the ephod in the front.
26“You shall make two rings of gold, and put them on the two ends of the
breastplate, on the edge of it, which is on the inner side of the ephod.
27And two *other* rings of gold you shall make, and put them on the two
shoulder straps, underneath the ephod toward its front, right at the seam
above the intricately woven band of the ephod. 28They shall bind the
breastplate by means of its rings to the rings of the ephod, using a blue
cord, so that it is above the intricately woven band of the ephod, and so
that the breastplate does not come loose from the ephod.

29“So Aaron shall bear the names of the sons of Israel on the breastplate
of judgment over his heart, when he goes into the holy *place,* as a memorial before the LORD continually. 30And you shall put in the breastplate of
judgment the Urim and the Thummim,[z] and they shall be over Aaron’s
heart when he goes in before the LORD. So Aaron shall bear the judgment
of the children of Israel over his heart before the LORD continually.

Other Priestly Garments

31“You shall make the robe of the ephod all of blue. 32There shall be an
opening for his head in the middle of it; it shall have a woven binding all
around its opening, like the opening in a coat of mail, so that it does not
tear. 33And upon its hem you shall make pomegranates of blue, purple,
and scarlet, all around its hem, and bells of gold between them all around:
34a golden bell and a pomegranate, a golden bell and a pomegranate, upon
the hem of the robe all around. 35And it shall be upon Aaron when he ministers, and its sound will be heard when he goes into the holy *place* before
the LORD and when he comes out, that he may not die.
36“You shall also make a plate of pure gold and engrave on it, *like* the
engraving of a signet:

HOLINESS TO THE LORD.

37And you shall put it on a blue cord, that it may be on the turban; it shall
be on the front of the turban. 38So it shall be on Aaron’s forehead, that
Aaron may bear the iniquity of the holy things which the children of Israel
hallow in all their holy gifts; and it shall always be on his forehead, that
they may be accepted before the LORD.
39“You shall skillfully weave the tunic of fine linen *thread,* you shall
make the turban of fine linen, and you shall make the sash of woven work.
40“For Aaron’s sons you shall make tunics, and you shall make sashes
for them. And you shall make hats for them, for glory and beauty. 41So you
shall put them on Aaron your brother and on his sons with him. You shall
anoint them, consecrate them, and sanctify them, that they may minister
to Me as priests. 42And you shall make for them linen trousers to cover
their nakedness; they shall reach from the waist to the thighs. 43They shall
be on Aaron and on his sons when they come into the tabernacle of meeting, or when they come near the altar to minister in the holy *place,* that
they do not incur iniquity and die. *It shall be* a statute forever to him and
his descendants after him.

Aaron and His Sons Consecrated

29 “And this is what you shall do to them to hallow them for ministering to Me as priests: Take one young bull and two rams without
blemish, 2and unleavened bread, unleavened cakes mixed with oil, and
unleavened wafers anointed with oil (you shall make them of wheat flour).
3You shall put them in one basket and bring them in the basket, with the
bull and the two rams.
4“And Aaron and his sons you shall bring to the door of the tabernacle
of meeting, and you shall wash them with water. 5Then you shall take the

are there who are molecular biologists? The university needs people like you!” She looked relieved, even excited, as it sank in: She was a missionary right where she was.

There are thousands of Christians who suffer from this same kind of false understanding of the glory of vocation, and a parallel misunderstanding of how God places particular people in particular places in every arena to be salt and accomplish His preserving, flavoring purposes. . . .

In seventeenth-century London, as Reformation thinking about the church’s influences in society was making itself felt in the city, someone painted a billboard with a picture, among others, of a tailor, a cook, a porter, a blacksmith, and a saddle-maker. The inscription read: “These tradesmen are preachers in the city of London, 1647.”

Who are the preachers of America in the late twentieth century?

Each of us, as we infiltrate the arena in which God has placed us.
(From *The Body* by Charles Colson)

APPLICATION Because of Christ, we are all priests. How are you ministering to others? Pray with someone, find a way to encourage them. Be on the alert should God bring someone along your path today. Don’t get so caught up in your agenda that you miss the needs in front of you.

EXPLORATION Priests—Exodus 19:4-6; 1 Chronicles 23:28-32; John 16:23-27.

28:30 [z] Literally *the Lights and the Perfections* (compare Leviticus 8:8)

garments, put the tunic on Aaron, and the robe of the
ephod, the ephod, and the breastplate, and gird him
with the intricately woven band of the ephod. [6]You shall
put the turban on his head, and put the holy crown on
the turban. [7]And you shall take the anointing oil, pour
it on his head, and anoint him. [8]Then you shall bring
his sons and put tunics on them. [9]And you shall gird
them with sashes, Aaron and his sons, and put the hats
on them. The priesthood shall be theirs for a perpetual statute. So you shall consecrate Aaron and his sons.

[10]"You shall also have the bull brought before the
tabernacle of meeting, and Aaron and his sons shall
put their hands on the head of the bull. [11]Then you
shall kill the bull before the LORD, *by* the door of the
tabernacle of meeting. [12]You shall take *some* of the
blood of the bull and put *it* on the horns of the altar
with your finger, and pour all the blood beside the
base of the altar. [13]And you shall take all the fat that
covers the entrails, the fatty lobe *attached* to the liver,
and the two kidneys and the fat that *is* on them, and
burn *them* on the altar. [14]But the flesh of the bull, with
its skin and its offal, you shall burn with fire outside
the camp. It *is* a sin offering.

[15]"You shall also take one ram, and Aaron and his
sons shall put their hands on the head of the ram;
[16]and you shall kill the ram, and you shall take its
blood and sprinkle *it* all around on the altar. [17]Then
you shall cut the ram in pieces, wash its entrails and
its legs, and put *them* with its pieces and with its head.
[18]And you shall burn the whole ram on the altar. It *is*
a burnt offering to the LORD; it *is* a sweet aroma, an
offering made by fire to the LORD.

[19]"You shall also take the other ram, and Aaron and
his sons shall put their hands on the head of the ram.
[20]Then you shall kill the ram, and take some of its
blood and put *it* on the tip of the right ear of Aaron
and on the tip of the right ear of his sons, on the
thumb of their right hand and on the big toe of their
right foot, and sprinkle the blood all around on the
altar. [21]And you shall take some of the blood that is on
the altar, and some of the anointing oil, and sprinkle
it on Aaron and on his garments, on his sons and on
the garments of his sons with him; and he and his
garments shall be hallowed, and his sons and his
sons' garments with him.

[22]"Also you shall take the fat of the ram, the fat tail,
the fat that covers the entrails, the fatty lobe *attached to*
the liver, the two kidneys and the fat on them, the right
thigh (for it *is* a ram of consecration), [23]one loaf of
bread, one cake *made with* oil, and one wafer from the
basket of the unleavened bread that *is* before the LORD;
[24]and you shall put all these in the hands of Aaron and
in the hands of his sons, and you shall wave them *as* a
wave offering before the LORD. [25]You shall receive
them back from their hands and burn *them* on the
altar as a burnt offering, as a sweet aroma before the
LORD. It *is* an offering made by fire to the LORD.

[26]"Then you shall take the breast of the ram of Aaron's consecration and wave it *as* a wave offering before
the LORD; and it shall be your portion. [27]And from the
ram of the consecration you shall consecrate the breast
of the wave offering which is waved, and the thigh of
the heave offering which is raised, of *that* which *is* for
Aaron and of *that* which is for his sons. [28]It shall be
from the children of Israel *for* Aaron and his sons by
a statute forever. For it is a heave offering; it shall be a
heave offering from the children of Israel from the
sacrifices of their peace offerings, *that is*, their heave
offering to the LORD.

[29]"And the holy garments of Aaron shall be his
sons' after him, to be anointed in them and to be consecrated in them. [30]That son who becomes priest in his
place shall put them on for seven days, when he enters
the tabernacle of meeting to minister in the holy *place*.

[31]"And you shall take the ram of the consecration
and boil its flesh in the holy place. [32]Then Aaron and
his sons shall eat the flesh of the ram, and the bread
that *is* in the basket, *by* the door of the tabernacle of
meeting. [33]They shall eat those things with which the
atonement was made, to consecrate *and* to sanctify
them; but an outsider shall not eat *them*, because they
are holy. [34]And if any of the flesh of the consecration
offerings, or of the bread, remains until the morning,
then you shall burn the remainder with fire. It shall
not be eaten, because it *is* holy.

[35]"Thus you shall do to Aaron and his sons, according to all that I have commanded you. Seven days you
shall consecrate them. [36]And you shall offer a bull
every day *as* a sin offering for atonement. You shall
cleanse the altar when you make atonement for it,
and you shall anoint it to sanctify it. [37]Seven days you
shall make atonement for the altar and sanctify it.
And the altar shall be most holy. Whatever touches
the altar must be holy.[a]

The Daily Offerings

[38]"Now this *is* what you shall offer on the altar: two
lambs of the first year, day by day continually. [39]One

29:37 [a] Compare Numbers 4:15 and Haggai 2:11–13

lamb you shall offer in the morning, and the other lamb you shall offer at
twilight. 40With the one lamb shall be one-tenth *of an ephah* of flour mixed
with one-fourth of a hin of pressed oil, and one-fourth of a hin of wine *as*
a drink offering. 41And the other lamb you shall offer at twilight; and you
shall offer with it the grain offering and the drink offering, as in the morning, for a sweet aroma, an offering made by fire to the LORD. 42*This shall be*
a continual burnt offering throughout your generations *at* the door of the
tabernacle of meeting before the LORD, where I will meet you to speak with
you. 43And there I will meet with the children of Israel, and *the tabernacle*
shall be sanctified by My glory. 44So I will consecrate the tabernacle of
meeting and the altar. I will also consecrate both Aaron and his sons to
minister to Me as priests. 45I will dwell among the children of Israel and
will be their God. 46And they shall know that I *am* the LORD their God, who
brought them up out of the land of Egypt, that I may dwell among them. I
am the LORD their God.

The Altar of Incense

30 "You shall make an altar to burn incense on; you shall make it of
acacia wood. 2A cubit *shall be* its length and a cubit its width—it
shall be square—and two cubits *shall be* its height. Its horns *shall be* of
one piece with it. 3And you shall overlay its top, its sides all around, and
its horns with pure gold; and you shall make for it a molding of gold all
around. 4Two gold rings you shall make for it, under the molding on both
its sides. You shall place *them* on its two sides, and they will be holders for
the poles with which to bear it. 5You shall make the poles of acacia wood,
and overlay them with gold. 6And you shall put it before the veil that *is*
before the ark of the Testimony, before the mercy seat that *is* over the
Testimony, where I will meet with you.

7"Aaron shall burn on it sweet incense every morning; when he tends the
lamps, he shall burn incense on it. 8And when Aaron lights the lamps at
twilight, he shall burn incense on it, a perpetual incense before the LORD
throughout your generations. 9You shall not offer strange incense on it, or
a burnt offering, or a grain offering; nor shall you pour a drink offering on
it. 10And Aaron shall make atonement upon its horns once a year with the
blood of the sin offering of atonement; once a year he shall make atonement upon it throughout your generations. It *is* most holy to the LORD."

The Ransom Money

11Then the LORD spoke to Moses, saying: 12"When you take the census of
the children of Israel for their number, then every man shall give a ransom
for himself to the LORD, when you number them, that there may be no
plague among them when *you* number them. 13This is what everyone
among those who are numbered shall give: half a shekel according to the
shekel of the sanctuary (a shekel *is* twenty gerahs). The half-shekel *shall be*
an offering to the LORD. 14Everyone included among those who are numbered, from twenty years old and above, shall give an offering to the LORD.
15The rich shall not give more and the poor shall not give less than half a
shekel, when *you* give an offering to the LORD, to make atonement for yourselves. 16And you shall take the atonement money of the children of Israel,
and shall appoint it for the service of the tabernacle of meeting, that it may
be a memorial for the children of Israel before the LORD, to make atonement for yourselves."

LIFE LESSON

Exodus 30:1–31:18

SITUATION God instructed Moses about the rituals of the tabernacle, including burning incense, sacrificing, and anointing with oil. God commanded certain craftsmen to furnish the tabernacle with ornate wood, gold, silver, and precious stones. Finally, God called the Israelites to honor the Sabbath as a day of rest and worship.

OBSERVATION God's specific instructions to Moses reminded the people of their pact with God. God demands faithfulness from his people.

INSPIRATION The first Christians worshiped God and lived as a holy community, conforming their character to the demands of Christ rather than Caesar. They didn't purpose to turn the first-century world upside down. They did so because of *who* they were.

This character-oriented perspective is totally foreign to our achievement-oriented society, however, where we look at what people do rather than who they are. . . . Rarely do we hear believers say, "I decided to join this church because of its character as a holy community." Nor do most choose a church on the basis of its capacity to disciple and equip them for ministry. Yet that should be our very first consideration. If the church is the Body, the holy presence of Christ in the world, its most fundamental task is to build communities of holy character. And the first priority of those communities is to disciple men and women to maturity in Christ and then equip them to live their faith in every aspect of life and in every part of the world. (From *The Body* by Charles Colson)

APPLICATION Rituals can be symbols of our relationship to God. We follow these practices to show our reverence for God, but they are never more important than faith.

EXPLORATION Faithfulness—Numbers 12:7; 14:24; 1 Kings 19:18; Nehemiah 7:2; 1 Corinthians 4:17; Colossians 1:7.

The Bronze Laver

17Then the LORD spoke to Moses, saying: 18"You
shall also make a laver of bronze, with its base also of
bronze, for washing. You shall put it between the tabernacle of meeting and the altar. And you shall put water
in it, 19for Aaron and his sons shall wash their hands
and their feet in water from it. 20When they go into the
tabernacle of meeting, or when they come near the
altar to minister, to burn an offering made by fire to
the LORD, they shall wash with water, lest they die. 21So
they shall wash their hands and their feet, lest they
die. And it shall be a statute forever to them—to him
and his descendants throughout their generations."

The Holy Anointing Oil

22Moreover the LORD spoke to Moses, saying:
23"Also take for yourself quality spices—five hundred *shekels* of liquid myrrh, half as much sweet-
smelling cinnamon (two hundred and fifty *shekels*),
two hundred and fifty *shekels* of sweet-smelling cane,
24five hundred *shekels* of cassia, according to the
shekel of the sanctuary, and a hin of olive oil. 25And
you shall make from these a holy anointing oil, an
ointment compounded according to the art of the
perfumer. It shall be a holy anointing oil. 26With it you
shall anoint the tabernacle of meeting and the ark of
the Testimony; 27the table and all its utensils, the
lampstand and its utensils, and the altar of incense;
28the altar of burnt offering with all its utensils, and
the laver and its base. 29You shall consecrate them,
that they may be most holy; whatever touches them
must be holy.[b] 30And you shall anoint Aaron and his
sons, and consecrate them, that *they* may minister to
Me as priests.
31"And you shall speak to the children of Israel, saying: 'This shall be a holy anointing oil to Me throughout your generations. 32It shall not be poured on
man's flesh; nor shall you make *any other* like it,
according to its composition. It *is* holy, *and* it shall be
holy to you. 33Whoever compounds *any* like it, or
whoever puts *any* of it on an outsider, shall be cut off
from his people.' "

The Incense

34And the LORD said to Moses: "Take sweet spices,
stacte and onycha and galbanum, and pure frankincense with *these* sweet spices; there shall be equal
amounts of each. 35You shall make of these an incense,
a compound according to the art of the perfumer,
salted, pure, *and* holy. 36And you shall beat *some* of it
very fine, and put some of it before the Testimony in
the tabernacle of meeting where I will meet with you.
It shall be most holy to you. 37But *as for* the incense
which you shall make, you shall not make any for
yourselves, according to its composition. It shall be to
you holy for the LORD. 38Whoever makes *any* like it, to
smell it, he shall be cut off from his people."

Artisans for Building the Tabernacle

31 Then the LORD spoke to Moses, saying: 2"See, I
have called by name Bezalel the son of Uri, the
son of Hur, of the tribe of Judah. 3And I have filled
him with the Spirit of God, in wisdom, in understanding, in knowledge, and in all *manner of* workmanship, 4to design artistic works, to work in gold, in
silver, in bronze, 5in cutting jewels for setting, in carving wood, and to work in all *manner of* workmanship.
6"And I, indeed I, have appointed with him Aholiab
the son of Ahisamach, of the tribe of Dan; and I have
put wisdom in the hearts of all the gifted artisans, that
they may make all that I have commanded you: 7the
tabernacle of meeting, the ark of the Testimony and
the mercy seat that *is* on it, and all the furniture of the
tabernacle— 8the table and its utensils, the pure *gold*
lampstand with all its utensils, the altar of incense,
9the altar of burnt offering with all its utensils, and the
laver and its base— 10the garments of ministry,[c] the
holy garments for Aaron the priest and the garments
of his sons, to minister as priests, 11and the anointing
oil and sweet incense for the holy *place*. According to
all that I have commanded you they shall do."

The Sabbath Law

12And the LORD spoke to Moses, saying, 13"Speak
also to the children of Israel, saying: 'Surely My
Sabbaths you shall keep, for it *is* a sign between Me
and you throughout your generations, that *you* may
know that I *am* the LORD who sanctifies you. 14You
shall keep the Sabbath, therefore, for *it is* holy to you.
Everyone who profanes it shall surely be put to death;
for whoever does *any* work on it, that person shall be
cut off from among his people. 15Work shall be done
for six days, but the seventh *is* the Sabbath of rest,
holy to the LORD. Whoever does *any* work on the
Sabbath day, he shall surely be put to death. 16There-
fore the children of Israel shall keep the Sabbath, to
observe the Sabbath throughout their generations *as*

30:29 [b] Compare Numbers 4:15 and Haggai 2:11–13
31:10 [c] Or *woven garments*

a perpetual covenant. 17 It *is* a sign between Me and the children of Israel
forever; for *in* six days the LORD made the heavens and the earth, and on
the seventh day He rested and was refreshed.' "
18 And when He had made an end of speaking with him on Mount Sinai,
He gave Moses two tablets of the Testimony, tablets of stone, written with
the finger of God.

The Gold Calf

32 Now when the people saw that Moses delayed coming down from
the mountain, the people gathered together to Aaron, and said to
him, "Come, make us gods that shall go before us; for *as for* this Moses,
the man who brought us up out of the land of Egypt, we do not know what
has become of him."
2 And Aaron said to them, "Break off the golden earrings which *are* in
the ears of your wives, your sons, and your daughters, and bring *them* to
me." 3 So all the people broke off the golden earrings which *were* in their
ears, and brought *them* to Aaron. 4 And he received *the gold* from their
hand, and he fashioned it with an engraving tool, and made a molded calf.
Then they said, "This *is* your god, O Israel, that brought you out of the
land of Egypt!"
5 So when Aaron saw *it*, he built an altar before it. And Aaron made a
proclamation and said, "Tomorrow *is* a feast to the LORD." 6 Then they rose
early on the next day, offered burnt offerings, and brought peace offerings; and the people sat down to eat and drink, and rose up to play.
7 And the LORD said to Moses, "Go, get down! For your people whom you
brought out of the land of Egypt have corrupted *themselves*. 8 They have
turned aside quickly out of the way which I commanded them. They have
made themselves a molded calf, and worshiped it and sacrificed to it, and
said, 'This *is* your god, O Israel, that brought you out of the land of
Egypt!' " 9 And the LORD said to Moses, "I have seen this people, and
indeed it *is* a stiff-necked people! 10 Now therefore, let Me alone, that My
wrath may burn hot against them and I may consume them. And I will
make of you a great nation."
11 Then Moses pleaded with the LORD his God, and said: "LORD, why does
Your wrath burn hot against Your people whom You have brought out of
the land of Egypt with great power and with a mighty hand? 12 Why should
the Egyptians speak, and say, 'He brought them out to harm them, to kill
them in the mountains, and to consume them from the face of the earth'?
Turn from Your fierce wrath, and relent from this harm to Your people.
13 Remember Abraham, Isaac, and Israel, Your servants, to whom You
swore by Your own self, and said to them, 'I will multiply your descendants as the stars of heaven; and all this land that I have spoken of I give
to your descendants, and they shall inherit *it* forever.' "[d] 14 So the LORD relented from the harm which He said He would do to His people.
15 And Moses turned and went down from the mountain, and the two
tablets of the Testimony *were* in his hand. The tablets *were* written on both
sides; on the one *side* and on the other they were written. 16 Now the tablets
were the work of God, and the writing *was* the writing of God engraved on
the tablets.

32:13 *d* Genesis 13:15 and 22:17

LIFE LESSON

Exodus 32:1–34:35

SITUATION God wrote the Ten Commandments, gave them to Moses, and revealed his glory to Moses. Because Moses took so long to come down from the mountain, the people grew weary and built a new god for themselves, made of gold.

OBSERVATION We will never be able to see all of God's glory on this earth.

INSPIRATION Read carefully, very carefully, the following verses. Read to answer this question—what did Moses do in order to see God? . . .

"There is a place near me where you may stand on a rock. When my glory passes that place, I will put you in a large crack in the rock and cover you with my hand until I have passed by. Then I will take away my hand, and you will see my back. But my face must not be seen" (Exodus 33:1-23).

Did you see what Moses was to do? Neither did I. Did you note who did the work? So did I.

God did! God is active. God gave Moses a place to stand. God placed Moses in the crevice. God covered Moses with his hand. God passed by. And God revealed himself. . . .

All Moses did was ask. But, oh, how he asked. All we can do is ask. But, oh, we must ask. For only in asking do we receive. And only in seeking do we find.

And (need I make the application?) God is the one who will equip us for our eternal moment in the Son. Hasn't he given us a rock, the Lord Jesus? Hasn't he given us a cleft, his grace? And hasn't he covered us with his hand, his pierced hand?

(From *When God Whispers Your Name* by Max Lucado)

APPLICATION Do you know someone who rebels against God? Classmates? Colleagues? Neighbors? Intercede on behalf of these people today. Ask God to reveal himself to them and bring them into a relationship with him.

EXPLORATION God's Judgment—Exodus 22:24; Numbers 16:21; Deuteronomy 9:19-20; 1 Samuel 2:25; Psalm 106:23; Jeremiah 14:20-21.

17And when Joshua heard the noise of the people as
they shouted, he said to Moses, "*There is* a noise of
war in the camp."
18But he said:

"*It is* not the noise of the shout of victory,
Nor the noise of the cry of defeat,
But the sound of singing I hear."

19So it was, as soon as he came near the camp, that
he saw the calf *and* the dancing. So Moses' anger
became hot, and he cast the tablets out of his hands
and broke them at the foot of the mountain. 20Then he
took the calf which they had made, burned *it* in the
fire, and ground *it* to powder; and he scattered *it* on
the water and made the children of Israel drink *it.*
21And Moses said to Aaron, "What did this people do
to you that you have brought *so* great a sin upon
them?"
22So Aaron said, "Do not let the anger of my lord
become hot. You know the people, that they *are set* on
evil. 23For they said to me, 'Make us gods that shall go
before us; *as for* this Moses, the man who brought us
out of the land of Egypt, we do not know what has
become of him.' 24And I said to them, 'Whoever has
any gold, let them break *it* off.' So they gave *it* to me,
and I cast it into the fire, and this calf came out."
25Now when Moses saw that the people *were* unrestrained (for Aaron had not restrained them, to *their*
shame among their enemies), 26then Moses stood in
the entrance of the camp, and said, "Whoever *is* on the
LORD's side—*come* to me!" And all the sons of Levi
gathered themselves together to him. 27And he said to
them, "Thus says the LORD God of Israel: 'Let every
man put his sword on his side, and go in and out from
entrance to entrance throughout the camp, and let
every man kill his brother, every man his companion,
and every man his neighbor.' " 28So the sons of Levi
did according to the word of Moses. And about three
thousand men of the people fell that day. 29Then Moses said, "Consecrate yourselves today to the LORD,
that He may bestow on you a blessing this day, for
every man has opposed his son and his brother."
30Now it came to pass on the next day that Moses
said to the people, "You have committed a great sin.
So now I will go up to the LORD; perhaps I can make
atonement for your sin." 31Then Moses returned to
the LORD and said, "Oh, these people have committed
a great sin, and have made for themselves a god of
gold! 32Yet now, if You will forgive their sin—but if
not, I pray, blot me out of Your book which You have
written."
33And the LORD said to Moses, "Whoever has
sinned against Me, I will blot him out of My book.
34Now therefore, go, lead the people to *the place* of
which I have spoken to you. Behold, My Angel shall
go before you. Nevertheless, in the day when I visit for
punishment, I will visit punishment upon them for
their sin."
35So the LORD plagued the people because of what
they did with the calf which Aaron made.

The Command to Leave Sinai

33 Then the LORD said to Moses, "Depart *and* go
up from here, you and the people whom you
have brought out of the land of Egypt, to the land of
which I swore to Abraham, Isaac, and Jacob, saying,
'To your descendants I will give it.' 2And I will send
My Angel before you, and I will drive out the
Canaanite and the Amorite and the Hittite and the
Perizzite and the Hivite and the Jebusite. 3*Go up* to a
land flowing with milk and honey; for I will not go up
in your midst, lest I consume you on the way, for you
are a stiff-necked people."
4And when the people heard this bad news, they
mourned, and no one put on his ornaments. 5For the
LORD had said to Moses, "Say to the children of Israel,
'You *are* a stiff-necked people. I could come up into
your midst in one moment and consume you. Now
therefore, take off your ornaments, that I may know
what to do to you.' " 6So the children of Israel stripped
themselves of their ornaments by Mount Horeb.

Moses Meets with the LORD

7Moses took his tent and pitched it outside the
camp, far from the camp, and called it the tabernacle
of meeting. And it came to pass *that* everyone who
sought the LORD went out to the tabernacle of meeting
which *was* outside the camp. 8So it was, whenever
Moses went out to the tabernacle, *that* all the people
rose, and each man stood *at* his tent door and
watched Moses until he had gone into the tabernacle.
9And it came to pass, when Moses entered the tabernacle, that the pillar of cloud descended and stood *at*
the door of the tabernacle, and *the LORD* talked with
Moses. 10All the people saw the pillar of cloud standing *at* the tabernacle door, and all the people rose and
worshiped, each man *in* his tent door. 11So the LORD
spoke to Moses face to face, as a man speaks to his
friend. And he would return to the camp, but his servant Joshua the son of Nun, a young man, did not
depart from the tabernacle.

The Promise of God's Presence

[12]Then Moses said to the LORD, "See, You say to me,
'Bring up this people.' But You have not let me know
whom You will send with me. Yet You have said, 'I
know you by name, and you have also found grace in
My sight.' [13]Now therefore, I pray, if I have found
grace in Your sight, show me now Your way, that I
may know You and that I may find grace in Your
sight. And consider that this nation *is* Your people."
[14]And He said, "My Presence will go *with you,* and I
will give you rest."
[15]Then he said to Him, "If Your Presence does not
go *with us,* do not bring us up from here. [16]For how
then will it be known that Your people and I have
found grace in Your sight, except You go with us? So
we shall be separate, Your people and I, from all the
people who *are* upon the face of the earth."
[17]So the LORD said to Moses, "I will also do this
thing that you have spoken; for you have found grace
in My sight, and I know you by name."
[18]And he said, "Please, show me Your glory."
[19]Then He said, "I will make all My goodness pass
before you, and I will proclaim the name of the LORD
before you. I will be gracious to whom I will be gracious, and I will have compassion on whom I will have
compassion." [20]But He said, "You cannot see My face;
for no man shall see Me, and live." [21]And the LORD
said, "Here is a place by Me, and you shall stand on
the rock. [22]So it shall be, while My glory passes by, that
I will put you in the cleft of the rock, and will cover you
with My hand while I pass by. [23]Then I will take away
My hand, and you shall see My back; but My face shall
not be seen."

Moses Makes New Tablets

34 And the LORD said to Moses, "Cut two tablets of
stone like the first *ones,* and I will write on *these*
tablets the words that were on the first tablets which
you broke. [2]So be ready in the morning, and come up
in the morning to Mount Sinai, and present yourself
to Me there on the top of the mountain. [3]And no man
shall come up with you, and let no man be seen
throughout all the mountain; let neither flocks nor
herds feed before that mountain."
[4]So he cut two tablets of stone like the first *ones.*
Then Moses rose early in the morning and went up
Mount Sinai, as the LORD had commanded him; and
he took in his hand the two tablets of stone.
[5]Now the LORD descended in the cloud and stood
with him there, and proclaimed the name of the LORD.
[6]And the LORD passed before him and proclaimed,
"The LORD, the LORD God, merciful and gracious,
longsuffering, and abounding in goodness and truth,
[7]keeping mercy for thousands, forgiving iniquity and
transgression and sin, by no means clearing *the
guilty,* visiting the iniquity of the fathers upon the children and the children's children to the third and the
fourth generation."
[8]So Moses made haste and bowed his head toward
the earth, and worshiped. [9]Then he said, "If now I
have found grace in Your sight, O Lord, let my Lord, I
pray, go among us, even though we *are* a stiff-necked
people; and pardon our iniquity and our sin, and take
us as Your inheritance."

The Covenant Renewed

[10]And He said: "Behold, I make a covenant. Before
all your people I will do marvels such as have not
been done in all the earth, nor in any nation; and all
the people among whom you *are* shall see the work of
the LORD. For it *is* an awesome thing that I will do with
you. [11]Observe what I command you this day. Behold,
I am driving out from before you the Amorite and the
Canaanite and the Hittite and the Perizzite and the
Hivite and the Jebusite. [12]Take heed to yourself, lest
you make a covenant with the inhabitants of the land
where you are going, lest it be a snare in your midst.
[13]But you shall destroy their altars, break their *sacred*
pillars, and cut down their wooden images [14](for you
shall worship no other god, for the LORD, whose name
is Jealous, *is* a jealous God), [15]lest you make a covenant
with the inhabitants of the land, and they play the harlot with their gods and make sacrifice to their gods,
and *one of them* invites you and you eat of his sacrifice, [16]and you take of his daughters for your sons, and
his daughters play the harlot with their gods and make
your sons play the harlot with their gods.
[17]"You shall make no molded gods for yourselves.
[18]"The Feast of Unleavened Bread you shall keep.
Seven days you shall eat unleavened bread, as I commanded you, in the appointed time of the month of
Abib; for in the month of Abib you came out from
Egypt.
[19]"All that open the womb *are* Mine, and every male
firstborn among your livestock, *whether* ox or sheep.
[20]But the firstborn of a donkey you shall redeem with
a lamb. And if you will not redeem *him,* then you shall
break his neck. All the firstborn of your sons you shall
redeem.
"And none shall appear before Me empty-handed.
[21]"Six days you shall work, but on the seventh day
you shall rest; in plowing time and in harvest you
shall rest.

Life Lesson

Exodus 35:1–38:31

SITUATION Moses gave the Israelites instructions on how to build the Tabernacle. God designed each detail.

OBSERVATION God, Master Architect, designed his house. Skilled people, such as Bezalel, worked to accomplish God's plans. They wanted to honor and please God by their efforts.

INSPIRATION "The world is moved along not only by the mighty shoves of its heroes, but also by the aggregate of the tiny pushes of each honest worker." (Helen Keller)

The story is told of a man who visited a stone quarry and asked three of the workers what they were doing.

"Can't you see?" said the first one irritably. "I'm cutting a stone."

The second one replied, "I'm earning a hundred pounds a week."

But the third put down his pick and thrust out his chest proudly. "I'm building a cathedral," he said.

People view work in many different ways: as a necessary evil to keep bread on the table; as a means to a sizable bank account; as self-fulfillment and identity; as an economic obligation within society; as a means to a life of leisure.

Yet none of these represents an adequate view of work that provides ongoing or complete satisfaction for our labors. We are more than material

22"And you shall observe the Feast of Weeks, of the firstfruits of wheat
harvest, and the Feast of Ingathering at the year's end.
23"Three times in the year all your men shall appear before the Lord, the
LORD God of Israel. 24For I will cast out the nations before you and enlarge
your borders; neither will any man covet your land when you go up to
appear before the LORD your God three times in the year.
25"You shall not offer the blood of My sacrifice with leaven, nor shall the
sacrifice of the Feast of the Passover be left until morning.
26"The first of the firstfruits of your land you shall bring to the house of
the LORD your God. You shall not boil a young goat in its mother's milk."
27Then the LORD said to Moses, "Write these words, for according to the
tenor of these words I have made a covenant with you and with Israel."
28So he was there with the LORD forty days and forty nights; he neither ate
bread nor drank water. And He wrote on the tablets the words of the
covenant, the Ten Commandments.[e]

The Shining Face of Moses

29Now it was so, when Moses came down from Mount Sinai (and the two
tablets of the Testimony *were* in Moses' hand when he came down from
the mountain), that Moses did not know that the skin of his face shone
while he talked with Him. 30So when Aaron and all the children of Israel
saw Moses, behold, the skin of his face shone, and they were afraid to
come near him. 31Then Moses called to them, and Aaron and all the rulers
of the congregation returned to him; and Moses talked with them. 32After-
ward all the children of Israel came near, and he gave them as commandments all that the LORD had spoken with him on Mount Sinai. 33And when
Moses had finished speaking with them, he put a veil on his face. 34But
whenever Moses went in before the LORD to speak with Him, he would take
the veil off until he came out; and he would come out and speak to the children of Israel whatever he had been commanded. 35And whenever the
children of Israel saw the face of Moses, that the skin of Moses' face shone,
then Moses would put the veil on his face again, until he went in to speak
with Him.

Sabbath Regulations

35 Then Moses gathered all the congregation of the children of Israel
together, and said to them, "These *are* the words which the LORD has
commanded *you* to do: 2Work shall be done for six days, but the seventh
day shall be a holy day for you, a Sabbath of rest to the LORD. Whoever does
any work on it shall be put to death. 3You shall kindle no fire throughout
your dwellings on the Sabbath day."

Offerings for the Tabernacle

4And Moses spoke to all the congregation of the children of Israel, saying, "This *is* the thing which the LORD commanded, saying: 5"Take from
among you an offering to the LORD. Whoever *is* of a willing heart, let him
bring it as an offering to the LORD: gold, silver, and bronze; 6blue, purple,
and scarlet *thread,* fine linen, and goats' *hair;* 7ram skins dyed red, badger
skins, and acacia wood; 8oil for the light, and spices for the anointing oil

34:28 [e] Literally *Ten Words*

and for the sweet incense; [9]onyx stones, and stones to be set in the ephod
and in the breastplate.

Articles of the Tabernacle

[10]"All *who are* gifted artisans among you shall come and make all that
the LORD has commanded: [11]the tabernacle, its tent, its covering, its clasps,
its boards, its bars, its pillars, and its sockets; [12]the ark and its poles, *with*
the mercy seat, and the veil of the covering; [13]the table and its poles, all its
utensils, and the showbread; [14]also the lampstand for the light, its utensils,
its lamps, and the oil for the light; [15]the incense altar, its poles, the anointing oil, the sweet incense, and the screen for the door at the entrance of the
tabernacle; [16]the altar of burnt offering with its bronze grating, its poles,
all its utensils, *and* the laver and its base; [17]the hangings of the court, its pillars, their sockets, and the screen for the gate of the court; [18]the pegs of the
tabernacle, the pegs of the court, and their cords; [19]the garments of ministry,[f] for ministering in the holy *place*—the holy garments for Aaron the
priest and the garments of his sons, to minister as priests.' "

The Tabernacle Offerings Presented

[20]And all the congregation of the children of Israel departed from the
presence of Moses. [21]Then everyone came whose heart was stirred, and
everyone whose spirit was willing, *and* they brought the LORD's offering for
the work of the tabernacle of meeting, for all its service, and for the holy
garments. [22]They came, both men and women, as many as had a willing
heart, *and* brought earrings and nose rings, rings and necklaces, all jewelry of gold, that is, every man who *made* an offering of gold to the LORD.
[23]And every man, with whom was found blue, purple, and scarlet *thread*,
fine linen, goats' *hair*, red skins of rams, and badger skins, brought *them*.
[24]Everyone who offered an offering of silver or bronze brought the LORD's
offering. And everyone with whom was found acacia wood for any work
of the service, brought *it*. [25]All the women *who were* gifted artisans spun
yarn with their hands, and brought what they had spun, of blue, purple,
and scarlet, and fine linen. [26]And all the women whose hearts stirred with
wisdom spun yarn of goats' *hair*. [27]The rulers brought onyx stones, and
the stones to be set in the ephod and in the breastplate, [28]and spices and
oil for the light, for the anointing oil, and for the sweet incense. [29]The children of Israel brought a freewill offering to the LORD, all the men and
women whose hearts were willing to bring *material* for all kinds of work
which the LORD, by the hand of Moses, had commanded to be done.

The Artisans Called by God

[30]And Moses said to the children of Israel, "See, the LORD has called by
name Bezalel the son of Uri, the son of Hur, of the tribe of Judah; [31]and He
has filled him with the Spirit of God, in wisdom and understanding, in
knowledge and all manner of workmanship, [32]to design artistic works, to
work in gold and silver and bronze, [33]in cutting jewels for setting, in carving wood, and to work in all manner of artistic workmanship.
[34]"And He has put in his heart the ability to teach, *in* him and Aholiab
the son of Ahisamach, of the tribe of Dan. [35]He has filled them with skill to

35:19 *f* Or *woven garments*

beings, more than social beings, and more than cogs in the machinery of work.

We are, above all, spiritual beings, and as such we need to rediscover the moral and spiritual significance for every area and aspect of our lives, including our work.

Why, then, should we work?

Because work gives expression to our creative gifts and thus fulfills our need for meaning and purpose.

Because work is intrinsically good when done with the proper attitude and motive.

Because we are commanded to exercise stewardship over the earth, participating in the work of Creation in a way that glorifies God.

Because we are citizens of this earth and have certain responsibilities to our fellow citizen.

(From *Why America Doesn't Work* by Charles Colson and Jack Eckerd)

APPLICATION The next time you go to church, take a closer look. Ask the Lord to show you an area where you can serve. If you can't find one, ask your pastor. God receives glory when you help to build his church.

EXPLORATION God's Workmanship—Genesis 1:31; 2 Corinthians 5:17; Ephesians 2:8-10; 19-22; Colossians 1:16; Revelation 4:11. Godly Action—Colossians 3:17; 23-24.

do all manner of work of the engraver and the designer and the tapestry maker, in blue, purple, and
scarlet *thread,* and fine linen, and of the weaver—
those who do every work and those who design artistic
works.

36 "And Bezalel and Aholiab, and every gifted
artisan in whom the LORD has put wisdom and
understanding, to know how to do all manner of
work for the service of the sanctuary, shall do according to all that the LORD has commanded."

The People Give More than Enough

2Then Moses called Bezalel and Aholiab, and every
gifted artisan in whose heart the LORD had put wisdom, everyone whose heart was stirred, to come and
do the work. 3And they received from Moses all the offering which the children of Israel had brought for the
work of the service of making the sanctuary. So they
continued bringing to him freewill offerings every
morning. 4Then all the craftsmen who were doing all
the work of the sanctuary came, each from the work
he was doing, 5and they spoke to Moses, saying, "The
people bring much more than enough for the service
of the work which the LORD commanded *us* to do."
6So Moses gave a commandment, and they caused
it to be proclaimed throughout the camp, saying, "Let
neither man nor woman do any more work for the
offering of the sanctuary." And the people were
restrained from bringing, 7for the material they had
was sufficient for all the work to be done—indeed too
much.

Building the Tabernacle

8Then all the gifted artisans among them who
worked on the tabernacle made ten curtains woven of
fine linen, and of blue, purple, and scarlet thread;
with artistic designs of cherubim they made them.
9The length of each curtain *was* twenty-eight cubits,
and the width of each curtain four cubits; the curtains
were all the same size. 10And he coupled five curtains
to one another, and *the other* five curtains he coupled
to one another. 11He made loops of blue *yarn* on the
edge of the curtain on the selvedge of one set; likewise
he did on the outer edge of *the other* curtain of the second set. 12Fifty loops he made on one curtain, and fifty
loops he made on the edge of the curtain on the end
of the second set; the loops held one *curtain* to another. 13And he made fifty clasps of gold, and coupled the
curtains to one another with the clasps, that it might
be one tabernacle.
14He made curtains of goats' *hair* for the tent over
the tabernacle; he made eleven curtains. 15The length
of each curtain *was* thirty cubits, and the width of
each curtain four cubits; the eleven curtains *were* the
same size. 16He coupled five curtains by themselves
and six curtains by themselves. 17And he made fifty
loops on the edge of the curtain that is outermost in
one set, and fifty loops he made on the edge of the
curtain of the second set. 18He also made fifty bronze
clasps to couple the tent together, that it might be one.
19Then he made a covering for the tent of ram skins
dyed red, and a covering of badger skins above *that.*
20For the tabernacle he made boards of acacia
wood, standing upright. 21The length of each board
was ten cubits, and the width of each board a cubit
and a half. 22Each board had two tenons for binding
one to another. Thus he made for all the boards of the
tabernacle. 23And he made boards for the tabernacle,
twenty boards for the south side. 24Forty sockets of
silver he made to go under the twenty boards: two
sockets under each of the boards for its two tenons.
25And for the other side of the tabernacle, the north
side, he made twenty boards 26and their forty sockets
of silver: two sockets under each of the boards. 27For
the west side of the tabernacle he made six boards.
28He also made two boards for the two back corners of
the tabernacle. 29And they were coupled at the bottom
and coupled together at the top by one ring. Thus he
made both of them for the two corners. 30So there
were eight boards and their sockets—sixteen sockets
of silver—two sockets under each of the boards.
31And he made bars of acacia wood: five for the
boards on one side of the tabernacle, 32five bars for
the boards on the other side of the tabernacle, and
five bars for the boards of the tabernacle on the far
side westward. 33And he made the middle bar to pass
through the boards from one end to the other. 34He
overlaid the boards with gold, made their rings of
gold *to be* holders for the bars, and overlaid the bars
with gold.
35And he made a veil of blue, purple, and scarlet
thread, and fine woven linen; it was worked *with* an
artistic design of cherubim. 36He made for it four pillars of acacia *wood,* and overlaid them with gold, with
their hooks of gold; and he cast four sockets of silver
for them.
37He also made a screen for the tabernacle door, of
blue, purple, and scarlet *thread,* and fine woven linen,
made by a weaver, 38and its five pillars with their
hooks. And he overlaid their capitals and their rings
with gold, but their five sockets *were* bronze.

Making the Ark of the Testimony

37 Then Bezalel made the ark of acacia wood; two and a half cubits *was* its length, a cubit and a half its width, and a cubit and a half its height. [2]He overlaid it with pure gold inside and outside, and made a molding of gold all around it. [3]And he cast for it four rings of gold *to be set* in its four corners: two rings on one side, and two rings on the other side of it. [4]He made poles of acacia wood, and overlaid them with gold. [5]And he put the poles into the rings at the sides of the ark, to bear the ark. [6]He also made the mercy seat of pure gold; two and a half cubits *was* its length and a cubit and a half its width. [7]He made two cherubim of beaten gold; he made them of one piece at the two ends of the mercy seat: [8]one cherub at one end on this side, and the other cherub at the *other* end on that side. He made the cherubim at the two ends *of one piece* with the mercy seat. [9]The cherubim spread out *their* wings above, *and* covered the mercy seat with their wings. They faced one another; the faces of the cherubim were toward the mercy seat.

Making the Table for the Showbread

[10]He made the table of acacia wood; two cubits *was* its length, a cubit its width, and a cubit and a half its height. [11]And he overlaid it with pure gold, and made a molding of gold all around it. [12]Also he made a frame of a handbreadth all around it, and made a molding of gold for the frame all around it. [13]And he cast for it four rings of gold, and put the rings on the four corners that *were* at its four legs. [14]The rings were close to the frame, as holders for the poles to bear the table. [15]And he made the poles of acacia wood to bear the table, and overlaid them with gold. [16]He made of pure gold the utensils which were on the table: its dishes, its cups, its bowls, and its pitchers for pouring.

Making the Gold Lampstand

[17]He also made the lampstand of pure gold; of hammered work he made the lampstand. Its shaft, its branches, its bowls, its *ornamental* knobs, and its flowers were of the same piece. [18]And six branches came out of its sides: three branches of the lampstand out of one side, and three branches of the lampstand out of the other side. [19]There were three bowls made like almond *blossoms* on one branch, with an *ornamental* knob and a flower, and three bowls made like almond *blossoms* on the other branch, with an *ornamental* knob and a flower—and so for the six branches coming out of the lampstand. [20]And on the lampstand itself *were* four bowls made like almond *blossoms, each with* its *ornamental* knob and flower. [21]*There was* a knob under the *first* two branches of the same, a knob under the *second* two branches of the same, and a knob under the *third* two branches of the same, according to the six branches extending from it. [22]Their knobs and their branches were of one piece; all of it *was* one hammered piece of pure gold. [23]And he made its seven lamps, its wick-trimmers, and its trays of pure gold. [24]Of a talent of pure gold he made it, with all its utensils.

Making the Altar of Incense

[25]He made the incense altar of acacia wood. Its length *was* a cubit and its width a cubit—*it was* square—and two cubits *was* its height. Its horns were *of one piece* with it. [26]And he overlaid it with pure gold: its top, its sides all around, and its horns. He also made for it a molding of gold all around it. [27]He made two rings of gold for it under its molding, by its two corners on both sides, as holders for the poles with which to bear it. [28]And he made the poles of acacia wood, and overlaid them with gold.

Making the Anointing Oil and the Incense

[29]He also made the holy anointing oil and the pure incense of sweet spices, according to the work of the perfumer.

Making the Altar of Burnt Offering

38 He made the altar of burnt offering of acacia wood; five cubits *was* its length and five cubits its width—*it was* square—and its height *was* three cubits. [2]He made its horns on its four corners; the horns were *of one piece* with it. And he overlaid it with bronze. [3]He made all the utensils for the altar: the pans, the shovels, the basins, the forks, and the firepans; all its utensils he made of bronze. [4]And he made a grate of bronze network for the altar, under its rim, midway from the bottom. [5]He cast four rings for the four corners of the bronze grating, *as* holders for the poles. [6]And he made the poles of acacia wood, and overlaid them with bronze. [7]Then he put the poles into the rings on the sides of the altar, with which to bear it. He made the altar hollow with boards.

Making the Bronze Laver

[8]He made the laver of bronze and its base of bronze, from the bronze mirrors of the serving women who assembled at the door of the tabernacle of meeting.

Making the Court of the Tabernacle

9 Then he made the court on the south side; the
hangings of the court *were of* fine woven linen, one
hundred cubits long. 10 There *were* twenty pillars for
them, with twenty bronze sockets. The hooks of the
pillars and their bands *were* silver. 11 On the north side
the hangings were one hundred cubits *long,* with
twenty pillars and their twenty bronze sockets. The
hooks of the pillars and their bands *were* silver. 12 And
on the west side *there were* hangings of fifty cubits,
with ten pillars and their ten sockets. The hooks of the
pillars and their bands *were* silver. 13 For the east side
the hangings were fifty cubits. 14 The hangings of one
side *of the gate were* fifteen cubits *long, with* their
three pillars and their three sockets, 15 and the same
for the other side of the court gate; on this side and
that *were* hangings of fifteen cubits, *with* their three
pillars and their three sockets. 16 All the hangings of
the court all around *were of* fine woven linen. 17 The
sockets for the pillars *were* bronze, the hooks of the
pillars and their bands *were* silver, and the overlay of
their capitals *was* silver; and all the pillars of the court
had bands of silver. 18 The screen for the gate of the
court *was* woven of blue, purple, and scarlet *thread,*
and of fine woven linen. The length *was* twenty cubits,
and the height along its width *was* five cubits, corresponding to the hangings of the court. 19 And *there
were* four pillars *with* their four sockets of bronze;
their hooks *were* silver, and the overlay of their capitals and their bands *was* silver. 20 All the pegs of the
tabernacle, and of the court all around, *were* bronze.

Materials of the Tabernacle

21 This is the inventory of the tabernacle, the tabernacle of the Testimony, which was counted according
to the commandment of Moses, for the service of the
Levites, by the hand of Ithamar, son of Aaron the
priest.
22 Bezalel the son of Uri, the son of Hur, of the tribe
of Judah, made all that the LORD had commanded
Moses. 23 And with him *was* Aholiab the son of
Ahisamach, of the tribe of Dan, an engraver and designer, a weaver of blue, purple, and scarlet *thread,*
and of fine linen.
24 All the gold that was used in all the work of the
holy *place,* that is, the gold of the offering, was twenty-
nine talents and seven hundred and thirty shekels, according to the shekel of the sanctuary. 25 And the silver
from those who were numbered of the congregation
was one hundred talents and one thousand seven
hundred and seventy-five shekels, according to the
shekel of the sanctuary: 26 a bekah for each man (*that
is,* half a shekel, according to the shekel of the sanctuary), for everyone included in the numbering from
twenty years old and above, for six hundred and three
thousand, five hundred and fifty *men.* 27 And from the
hundred talents of silver were cast the sockets of the
sanctuary and the bases of the veil: one hundred
sockets from the hundred talents, one talent for each
socket. 28 Then from the one thousand seven hundred
and seventy-five *shekels* he made hooks for the pillars,
overlaid their capitals, and made bands for them.
29 The offering of bronze *was* seventy talents and
two thousand four hundred shekels. 30 And with it he
made the sockets for the door of the tabernacle of
meeting, the bronze altar, the bronze grating for it,
and all the utensils for the altar, 31 the sockets for the
court all around, the bases for the court gate, all the
pegs for the tabernacle, and all the pegs for the court
all around.

Making the Garments of the Priesthood

39 Of the blue, purple, and scarlet *thread* they
made garments of ministry,[g] for ministering in
the holy *place,* and made the holy garments for
Aaron, as the LORD had commanded Moses.

Making the Ephod

2 He made the ephod of gold, blue, purple, and scarlet *thread,* and of fine woven linen. 3 And they beat the
gold into thin sheets and cut *it into* threads, to work *it*
in *with* the blue, purple, and scarlet *thread,* and the
fine linen, *into* artistic designs. 4 They made shoulder
straps for it to couple *it* together; it was coupled
together at its two edges. 5 And the intricately woven
band of his ephod that *was* on it *was* of the same
workmanship, *woven of* gold, blue, purple, and scarlet *thread,* and of fine woven linen, as the LORD had
commanded Moses.
6 And they set onyx stones, enclosed in settings of
gold; they were engraved, as signets are engraved,
with the names of the sons of Israel. 7 He put them on
the shoulders of the ephod *as* memorial stones for the
sons of Israel, as the LORD had commanded Moses.

Making the Breastplate

8 And he made the breastplate, artistically woven like
the workmanship of the ephod, of gold, blue, purple,

39:1 [g] Or *woven garments*

and scarlet *thread,* and of fine woven linen. 9They made the breastplate
square by doubling it; a span *was* its length and a span its width when
doubled. 10And they set in it four rows of stones: a row with a sardius, a
topaz, and an emerald was the first row; 11the second row, a turquoise, a
sapphire, and a diamond; 12the third row, a jacinth, an agate, and an
amethyst; 13the fourth row, a beryl, an onyx, and a jasper. *They were*
enclosed in settings of gold in their mountings. 14*There were* twelve stones
according to the names of the sons of Israel: according to their names, *engraved like* a signet, each one with its own name according to the twelve
tribes. 15And they made chains for the breastplate at the ends, like braided cords of pure gold. 16They also made two settings of gold and two gold
rings, and put the two rings on the two ends of the breastplate. 17And they
put the two braided *chains* of gold in the two rings on the ends of the breastplate. 18The two ends of the two braided *chains* they fastened in the two settings, and put them on the shoulder straps of the ephod in the front. 19And
they made two rings of gold and put *them* on the two ends of the breastplate, on the edge of it, which *was* on the inward side of the ephod. 20They
made two *other* gold rings and put them on the two shoulder straps, underneath the ephod toward its front, right at the seam above the intricately
woven band of the ephod. 21And they bound the breastplate by means of its
rings to the rings of the ephod with a blue cord, so that it would be above
the intricately woven band of the ephod, and that the breastplate would
not come loose from the ephod, as the LORD had commanded Moses.

Making the Other Priestly Garments

22He made the robe of the ephod of woven work, all of blue. 23And *there
was* an opening in the middle of the robe, like the opening in a coat of mail,
with a woven binding all around the opening, so that it would not tear.
24They made on the hem of the robe pomegranates of blue, purple, and
scarlet, and of fine woven *linen.* 25And they made bells of pure gold, and
put the bells between the pomegranates on the hem of the robe all around
between the pomegranates: 26a bell and a pomegranate, a bell and a pomegranate, all around the hem of the robe to minister in, as the LORD had
commanded Moses.

27They made tunics, artistically woven of fine linen, for Aaron and his
sons, 28a turban of fine linen, exquisite hats of fine linen, short trousers of
fine woven linen, 29and a sash of fine woven linen with blue, purple, and
scarlet *thread,* made by a weaver, as the LORD had commanded Moses.

30Then they made the plate of the holy crown of pure gold, and wrote on
it an inscription *like* the engraving of a signet:

HOLINESS TO THE LORD.

31And they tied to it a blue cord, to fasten *it* above on the turban, as the
LORD had commanded Moses.

The Work Completed

32Thus all the work of the tabernacle of the tent of meeting was finished.
And the children of Israel did according to all that the LORD had commanded Moses; so they did. 33And they brought the tabernacle to Moses,
the tent and all its furnishings: its clasps, its boards, its bars, its pillars,
and its sockets; 34the covering of ram skins dyed red, the covering of badger

LIFE LESSON

Exodus 39:1–40:38

SITUATION Moses provided instructions about the priestly garments and other matters pertaining to worship and the tabernacle.

OBSERVATION Some people believe that outward appearance determines inner quality. With God, it is the other way around: outward appearance should reflect inner reality. The priestly garments reflected the holy character of the priests as they were in communion with a holy God.

INSPIRATION Character, a wise person once said, is what we do when no one is looking. It is not the same as reputation—what other people think of us. It is not the same as success or achievement. Character is not what we have done, but who we *are.* And although we often hear of tragic lapses of character, describing its absence does not tell the whole story. . . . Character cannot be developed through good resolutions and checklists. It usually requires a lot of hard work, a little pain and years of faithfulness before any of the virtues are consistently noticeable in us.

No matter how wonderful your character is, it will never be wonderful enough to earn God's approval. . . . As important as character is, it is not a way to earn salvation. That is because salvation cannot be earned—not even by courage, discipline, vision, endurance and love.

Salvation is a gift from the heavenly Father to us. It cost him everything—the death of his beloved only Son. It cost us nothing. Hard work cannot earn it; neither can good behavior or sterling character. The only way we can enjoy a relationship with God is by coming to Jesus Christ, our hands outstretched and empty, and saying, "Lord, I want to follow you. Please take me into your family, scrub me, give me new clothes and make me like you." And Jesus will do exactly that. He will take us as we are and assure us that we are his forever. Then—slowly at first, but surely—he will mold us and shape us until we resemble him.

(From *Who You Are When No One's Looking* by Bill Hybels)

Continued

APPLICATION How much time each day do you take to make yourself look good? How much time each day do you take to develop your inner character? Knowing that God cares about your inner character, get up early and start your day in prayer.

EXPLORATION God and Clothes—Matthew 6:28-30; Romans 13:14; Galatians 3:26-29; 1 Timothy 6:6-8.

skins, and the veil of the covering; 35the ark of the Testimony with its poles,
and the mercy seat; 36the table, all its utensils, and the showbread; 37the
pure *gold* lampstand with its lamps (the lamps set in order), all its utensils, and the oil for light; 38the gold altar, the anointing oil, and the sweet
incense; the screen for the tabernacle door; 39the bronze altar, its grate of
bronze, its poles, and all its utensils; the laver with its base; 40the hangings
of the court, its pillars and its sockets, the screen for the court gate, its
cords, and its pegs; all the utensils for the service of the tabernacle, for the
tent of meeting; 41and the garments of ministry,[h] to minister in the holy
place: the holy garments for Aaron the priest, and his sons' garments, to
minister as priests.
42According to all that the LORD had commanded Moses, so the children
of Israel did all the work. 43Then Moses looked over all the work, and
indeed they had done it; as the LORD had commanded, just so they had
done it. And Moses blessed them.

The Tabernacle Erected and Arranged

40 Then the LORD spoke to Moses, saying: 2"On the first day of the first
month you shall set up the tabernacle of the tent of meeting. 3You
shall put in it the ark of the Testimony, and partition off the ark with the veil.
4You shall bring in the table and arrange the things that are to be set in order
on it; and you shall bring in the lampstand and light its lamps. 5You shall
also set the altar of gold for the incense before the ark of the Testimony,
and put up the screen for the door of the tabernacle. 6Then you shall set
the altar of the burnt offering before the door of the tabernacle of the tent
of meeting. 7And you shall set the laver between the tabernacle of meeting
and the altar, and put water in it. 8You shall set up the court all around, and
hang up the screen at the court gate.
9"And you shall take the anointing oil, and anoint the tabernacle and all
that *is* in it; and you shall hallow it and all its utensils, and it shall be holy.
10You shall anoint the altar of the burnt offering and all its utensils, and
consecrate the altar. The altar shall be most holy. 11And you shall anoint
the laver and its base, and consecrate it.
12"Then you shall bring Aaron and his sons to the door of the tabernacle of meeting and wash them with water. 13You shall put the holy garments on Aaron, and anoint him and consecrate him, that he may
minister to Me as priest. 14And you shall bring his sons and clothe them
with tunics. 15You shall anoint them, as you anointed their father, that they
may minister to Me as priests; for their anointing shall surely be an everlasting priesthood throughout their generations."
16Thus Moses did; according to all that the LORD had commanded him,
so he did.
17And it came to pass in the first month of the second year, on the first
day of the month, *that* the tabernacle was raised up. 18So Moses raised up
the tabernacle, fastened its sockets, set up its boards, put in its bars, and
raised up its pillars. 19And he spread out the tent over the tabernacle and
put the covering of the tent on top of it, as the LORD had commanded Moses. 20He took the Testimony and put *it* into the ark, inserted the poles
through the rings of the ark, and put the mercy seat on top of the ark. 21And
he brought the ark into the tabernacle, hung up the veil of the covering,

39:41 [h] Or *woven garments*

and partitioned off the ark of the Testimony, as the
LORD had commanded Moses.
[22]He put the table in the tabernacle of meeting, on
the north side of the tabernacle, outside the veil; [23]and
he set the bread in order upon it before the LORD, as
the LORD had commanded Moses. [24]He put the lampstand in the tabernacle of meeting, across from the
table, on the south side of the tabernacle; [25]and he lit
the lamps before the LORD, as the LORD had commanded Moses. [26]He put the gold altar in the tabernacle of meeting in front of the veil; [27]and he burned
sweet incense on it, as the LORD had commanded Moses. [28]He hung up the screen *at* the door of the tabernacle. [29]And he put the altar of burnt offering *before*
the door of the tabernacle of the tent of meeting, and
offered upon it the burnt offering and the grain offering, as the LORD had commanded Moses. [30]He set the
laver between the tabernacle of meeting and the altar,
and put water there for washing; [31]and Moses, Aaron,
and his sons would wash their hands and their feet
with water from it. [32]Whenever they went into the
tabernacle of meeting, and when they came near the
altar, they washed, as the LORD had commanded Moses. [33]And he raised up the court all around the tabernacle and the altar, and hung up the screen of the
court gate. So Moses finished the work.

The Cloud and the Glory

[34]Then the cloud covered the tabernacle of meeting,
and the glory of the LORD filled the tabernacle. [35]And
Moses was not able to enter the tabernacle of meeting, because the cloud rested above it, and the glory of
the LORD filled the tabernacle. [36]Whenever the cloud
was taken up from above the tabernacle, the children
of Israel would go onward in all their journeys. [37]But
if the cloud was not taken up, then they did not journey till the day that it was taken up. [38]For the cloud of
the LORD *was* above the tabernacle by day, and fire was
over it by night, in the sight of all the house of Israel,
throughout all their journeys.

God's Love

When we look at the world around us, sometimes it's difficult to understand the unfairness of life. It's not fair that the young should suffer. It's not fair that the innocent should go hungry. But nor is it fair that a God would have to come to earth and hang on his own cross to protect us from the evil one. It's not fair . . . but that's *love*. And that's God.

God's love for you is not dependent on how you look, how you think, how you act, or how perfect you are. His love is absolutely nonnegotiable and nonreturnable. Ours is a faithful God.

No matter what you do, no matter how far you fall, no matter how ugly you become, God has a relentless, undying, unfathomable, unquenchable love from which you cannot be separated. Ever!

Run to Jesus. Jesus wants you to go to him. He wants to become the most important person in your life, the greatest love you'll ever know. He wants you to love him so much that there's no room in your heart and in your life for sin. Invite him to take up residence in your heart.

FATHER, we look at your plan and it's all based on love, not on our performance, and we pray that you'd help us to understand that. To be captivated by your love. To be overwhelmed by your grace. To come home to you in that beautiful path that you've already carved out for us.

You Are Worthwhile

When Jesus told the story of the missing sheep, some of the people who were listening wiped away a tear because they knew how it feels to be lost among the crowd. Jesus wanted us to understand that we have a Father who sees and cares for each one of his children—that we are all equally valuable to him.

No one is useless to God. No one, at any point in his life, is useless to God—not a little child, not the unattractive, not the clumsy, not the tired, not the discouraged. God uses his children.

Our value is inherent—it's not based on the Ph.D. after our name or the amount of money in our bank account. We have value simply because we *are*. In the eyes of God, every human has value simply because he is the creation of the almighty God.

You belong to God's eternal dream. Now you may not feel motivated, you may not feel like you have a reason for living, but you must renew your mind with the immovable fact that you are part of a commissioned people—you have a reason to be alive.

There is an eternal purpose. There is a great river of God's purpose that is moving toward an eternal home with him. You can't stop God's purpose. God's purpose is greater than you are, and if you are God's child, nothing is going to slow down God's purpose for your life.

FATHER, we know that someday you're going to take all your followers into eternal happiness. And it is to that day, Father, that we look. And it is upon our hope and confidence that you will return, that we stand.

STRENGTH

You get impatient with your own life, trying to master a habit or control a sin—and in your frustration begin to wonder where the power of God is. Be patient. God is using today's difficulties to strengthen you for tomorrow. He is *equipping* you. The God who makes things grow will help you bear fruit.

God did not leave you as an orphan. He says he will be with you always. All of us could use some more strength—who isn't trying to tackle an attitude or put away a bad habit or overcome guilt? We can't see the power, but it's real—we're not alone.

As long as we have hope, as long as we recognize that this world is not our home, as long as we recognize that some day all of our problems will be solved, that is where we will gather our strength.

FATHER, you promised that there would be faith and strength and hope to meet life's problems. Father, give that strength to those whose anxieties have buried their dreams, whose illnesses have hospitalized their hopes, whose burdens are bigger than their shoulders.

VICTORY

Sometimes life doesn't seem fair, does it? Have you ever wondered why good people have to hurt? Why the innocent suffer? Often it seems that those who have been most battered by life seem to understand Jesus best, and his assurance finds its way into the darkest corners of life, because regardless of our circumstances, God meets our needs. By surrendering to him, the ultimate victory is ours.

What is unique about the kingdom of God is that you are assured of victory. You have won! You are assured that you will someday stand before the face of God and see the King of kings. You are assured that someday you will enter a world where there will be no more pain, no more tears, no more sorrow.

If you have no faith in the future, then you have no power in the present. If you have no faith in the life beyond this life, then your present life is going to be powerless. But if you believe in the future and are assured of victory, then there should be a dance in your step and a smile on your face.

THY KINGDOM COME, Lord. Let your kingdom live in the hearts of people, let your kingdom live in society, let the church be strong, and let your kingdom come eternally.

The Third Book of Moses Called

LEVITICUS

INTRODUCTION

Suppose your father grants you a piece of land. Free. You can farm it and make a living.

There is only one condition. You first have to get the rocks out. And so you work. For hours and days you work. With time, you see the task is too great. There's just no way you can do it.

You give up.

Then your father says you've done enough. "I have another plot of land for you," he explains. "This time the stones are gone."

"Who removed them?"

"I did."

You go to the acreage and find his promise to be true. The stones are gone, and you are left to farm. And so you sow in gratitude.

Nice story Max, but what does this have to do with Leviticus?

The book of Leviticus is the deed to the farm. A rocky farm given by God to his children . . . laden with stones. Heavied with tasks. Loaded with rocky rules and regulations.

Three months after their deliverance, the children of Israel spent a year at the base of Mt. Sinai. They were nomadic people in a barren land. Suddenly forced to live together, suddenly forced to travel together, they needed guidelines for hygiene and health. They needed rules for worship and community. For that reason, God gave them Leviticus. A practical guide for community and worship. But for us, it serves a still higher purpose. Leviticus reminds us that God takes holiness seriously.

Any person who tries to be holy is soon convinced he can't. There are too many rules. Too many rocks to remove. We need help. We need a Savior. "In other words, the law was our guardian, leading us to Christ so that we could be made right with God through faith" (Galatians 3:24).

Holiness is what God desires. But holiness is what we cannot achieve. Just like the son couldn't remove the rocks, so we can't remove our sins.

But just like the father surprised the son, so our Father surprises us. He removed the rocks for us.

LIFE LESSON

Leviticus 1:1–6:7

SITUATION Blood sacrifices had great significance. Blood offered an atonement for sin, but its incompleteness required the perfect sacrifice, Jesus Christ. The sacrifices in these chapters taught the Israelites how to worship God through personal commitment.

OBSERVATION God's people must revere him, commit themselves to his laws, and show sincere dedication to him.

INSPIRATION Stories from the underground church in [the former Soviet Union] never fail to jolt us awake. I came across another one just this past week. A house church received one copy of the Gospel by Luke, the only scripture most of these Christians had ever seen. They tore it into small sections and distributed them among the body of believers. Their plan was to memorize the portion they had been given, then on the next Lord's Day they would meet and redistribute the scriptural sections. On Sunday these believers arrived inconspicuously in small groups throughout the day so as not to arouse the suspicion of KGB informers. By dusk they were all safely inside, windows closed and doors locked. They began by singing a hymn quietly but with deep emotion. Suddenly, the door was pushed open and in walked two soldiers with loaded automatic weapons at the ready. One shouted, "All right—everybody line up against the wall. If you wish to renounce your commitment to Jesus Christ, leave now!"

Two or three quickly left, then another. After a few more seconds, two more.

"This is your last chance. Either turn against your faith in Christ," he ordered, "or stay and suffer the consequences."

The Burnt Offering

Now the LORD called to Moses, and spoke to him from the tabernacle of meeting, saying, 2"Speak to the children of Israel, and say to them: 'When any one of you brings an offering to the LORD, you shall bring your offering of the livestock—of the herd and of the flock.

3'If his offering *is* a burnt sacrifice of the herd, let him offer a male without blemish; he shall offer it of his own free will at the door of the tabernacle of meeting before the LORD. 4Then he shall put his hand on the head of the burnt offering, and it will be accepted on his behalf to make atonement for him. 5He shall kill the bull before the LORD; and the priests, Aaron's sons, shall bring the blood and sprinkle the blood all around on the altar that *is by* the door of the tabernacle of meeting. 6And he shall skin the burnt offering and cut it into its pieces. 7The sons of Aaron the priest shall put fire on the altar, and lay the wood in order on the fire. 8Then the priests, Aaron's sons, shall lay the parts, the head, and the fat in order on the wood that *is* on the fire upon the altar; 9but he shall wash its entrails and its legs with water. And the priest shall burn all on the altar as a burnt sacrifice, an offering made by fire, a sweet aroma to the LORD.

10'If his offering *is* of the flocks—of the sheep or of the goats—as a burnt sacrifice, he shall bring a male without blemish. 11He shall kill it on the north side of the altar before the LORD; and the priests, Aaron's sons, shall sprinkle its blood all around on the altar. 12And he shall cut it into its pieces, with its head and its fat; and the priest shall lay them in order on the wood that *is* on the fire upon the altar; 13but he shall wash the entrails and the legs with water. Then the priest shall bring *it* all and burn *it* on the altar; it *is* a burnt sacrifice, an offering made by fire, a sweet aroma to the LORD.

14'And if the burnt sacrifice of his offering to the LORD *is* of birds, then he shall bring his offering of turtledoves or young pigeons. 15The priest shall bring it to the altar, wring off its head, and burn *it* on the altar; its blood shall be drained out at the side of the altar. 16And he shall remove its crop with its feathers and cast it beside the altar on the east side, into the place for ashes. 17Then he shall split it at its wings, *but* shall not divide *it* completely; and the priest shall burn it on the altar, on the wood that *is* on the fire. It *is* a burnt sacrifice, an offering made by fire, a sweet aroma to the LORD.

The Grain Offering

2 'When anyone offers a grain offering to the LORD, his offering shall be *of* fine flour. And he shall pour oil on it, and put frankincense on it. 2He shall bring it to Aaron's sons, the priests, one of whom shall take from it his handful of fine flour and oil with all the frankincense. And the priest shall burn *it as* a memorial on the altar, an offering made by fire, a sweet aroma to the LORD. 3The rest of the grain offering *shall be* Aaron's and his sons'. *It is* most holy of the offerings to the LORD made by fire.

4'And if you bring as an offering a grain offering baked in the oven, *it shall be* unleavened cakes of fine flour mixed with oil, or unleavened wafers anointed with oil. 5But if your offering *is* a grain offering *baked* in a pan, *it shall be of* fine flour, unleavened, mixed with oil. 6You shall break it in pieces and pour oil on it; it *is* a grain offering.

7'If your offering *is* a grain offering *baked* in a covered pan, it shall be made *of* fine flour with oil. 8You shall bring the grain offering that is made of these things to the LORD. And when it is presented to the priest, he shall

bring it to the altar. 9Then the priest shall take from the grain offering a
memorial portion, and burn *it* on the altar. *It is* an offering made by fire, a
sweet aroma to the LORD. 10And what is left of the grain offering *shall be* Aaron's and his sons'. *It is* most holy of the offerings to the LORD made by fire.
11'No grain offering which you bring to the LORD shall be made with
leaven, for you shall burn no leaven nor any honey in any offering to the
LORD made by fire. 12As for the offering of the firstfruits, you shall offer
them to the LORD, but they shall not be burned on the altar for a sweet
aroma. 13And every offering of your grain offering you shall season with
salt; you shall not allow the salt of the covenant of your God to be lacking
from your grain offering. With all your offerings you shall offer salt.
14'If you offer a grain offering of your firstfruits to the LORD, you shall
offer for the grain offering of your firstfruits green heads of grain roasted
on the fire, grain beaten from full heads. 15And you shall put oil on it, and
lay frankincense on it. It *is* a grain offering. 16Then the priest shall burn the
memorial portion: *part* of its beaten grain and *part* of its oil, with all the
frankincense, as an offering made by fire to the LORD.

The Peace Offering

3 'When his offering *is* a sacrifice of a peace offering, if he offers *it* of the
herd, whether male or female, he shall offer it without blemish before
the LORD. 2And he shall lay his hand on the head of his offering, and kill it
at the door of the tabernacle of meeting; and Aaron's sons, the priests,
shall sprinkle the blood all around on the altar. 3Then he shall offer from
the sacrifice of the peace offering an offering made by fire to the LORD. The
fat that covers the entrails and all the fat that *is* on the entrails, 4the two
kidneys and the fat that *is* on them by the flanks, and the fatty lobe *attached*
to the liver above the kidneys, he shall remove; 5and Aaron's sons shall
burn it on the altar upon the burnt sacrifice, which *is* on the wood that *is*
on the fire, *as* an offering made by fire, a sweet aroma to the LORD.
6'If his offering as a sacrifice of a peace offering to the LORD *is* of the flock,
whether male or female, he shall offer it without blemish. 7If he offers a lamb
as his offering, then he shall offer it before the LORD. 8And he shall lay his
hand on the head of his offering, and kill it before the tabernacle of meeting;
and Aaron's sons shall sprinkle its blood all around on the altar.
9'Then he shall offer from the sacrifice of the peace offering, as an offering made by fire to the LORD, its fat *and* the whole fat tail which he shall remove close to the backbone. And the fat that covers the entrails and all the
fat that *is* on the entrails, 10the two kidneys and the fat that *is* on them by
the flanks, and the fatty lobe *attached* to the liver above the kidneys, he
shall remove; 11and the priest shall burn *them* on the altar *as* food, an offering made by fire to the LORD.
12'And if his offering *is* a goat, then he shall offer it before the LORD. 13He
shall lay his hand on its head and kill it before the tabernacle of meeting;
and the sons of Aaron shall sprinkle its blood all around on the altar.
14Then he shall offer from it his offering, as an offering made by fire to the
LORD. The fat that covers the entrails and all the fat that *is* on the entrails,
15the two kidneys and the fat that *is* on them by the flanks, and the fatty
lobe *attached* to the liver above the kidneys, he shall remove; 16and the
priest shall burn them on the altar *as* food, an offering made by fire for a
sweet aroma; all the fat *is* the LORD's.

Another left. Finally, two more in embarrassed silence, their faces covered, slipped out into the night. No one else moved. Parents with small children trembling beside them looked down reassuringly. They fully expected to be gunned down or, at best, to be imprisoned.

After a few moments of complete silence, the other soldier closed the door, looked back at those who stood against the wall and said, "Keep your hands up—but this time in praise to our Lord Jesus Christ, brothers and sisters. We, too, are Christians. We were sent to another house church several weeks ago to a group of believers—"

The other soldier interrupted, ". . . but, instead, we were converted! We have learned by experience, however, that unless people are willing to die for their faith, they cannot be fully trusted."

In segments of the world where Bibles are plentiful and churches are protected, faith can run awfully shallow. Commitment can stay rather lukewarm. Eagles can learn to fly dangerously low. "What we obtain too cheap, we esteem too lightly."
(From *Living Above the Level of Mediocrity* by Charles Swindoll)

APPLICATION What difficult decisions could you face this week because of your faith? In what areas will you face ridicule? temptation? persecution? hard times? Ask God to give you courage and wisdom to face upcoming trials.

EXPLORATION Commitment —Genesis 22:1-8; Joshua 24:15; 2 Chronicles 15:14-15; Matthew 16:24-25.

17‘*This shall be* a perpetual statute throughout your
generations in all your dwellings: you shall eat neither
fat nor blood.’ ”

The Sin Offering

4 Now the LORD spoke to Moses, saying, 2“Speak to
the children of Israel, saying: ‘If a person sins
unintentionally against any of the commandments of
the LORD *in anything* which ought not to be done, and
does any of them, 3if the anointed priest sins, bringing guilt on the people, then let him offer to the LORD
for his sin which he has sinned a young bull without
blemish as a sin offering. 4He shall bring the bull to
the door of the tabernacle of meeting before the LORD,
lay his hand on the bull’s head, and kill the bull before
the LORD. 5Then the anointed priest shall take some of
the bull’s blood and bring it to the tabernacle of meeting. 6The priest shall dip his finger in the blood and
sprinkle some of the blood seven times before the
LORD, in front of the veil of the sanctuary. 7And the priest
shall put some of the blood on the horns of the altar of
sweet incense before the LORD, which is in the tabernacle of meeting; and he shall pour the remaining
blood of the bull at the base of the altar of the burnt
offering, which is at the door of the tabernacle of
meeting. 8He shall take from it all the fat of the bull as
the sin offering. The fat that covers the entrails and all
the fat which *is* on the entrails, 9the two kidneys and
the fat that *is* on them by the flanks, and the fatty lobe
attached to the liver above the kidneys, he shall remove, 10as it was taken from the bull of the sacrifice of
the peace offering; and the priest shall burn them on
the altar of the burnt offering. 11But the bull’s hide and
all its flesh, with its head and legs, its entrails and
offal— 12the whole bull he shall carry outside the
camp to a clean place, where the ashes are poured out,
and burn it on wood with fire; where the ashes are
poured out it shall be burned.

13‘Now if the whole congregation of Israel sins
unintentionally, and the thing is hidden from the eyes
of the assembly, and they have done *something*
against any of the commandments of the LORD *in any-*
thing which should not be done, and are guilty;
14when the sin which they have committed becomes
known, then the assembly shall offer a young bull for
the sin, and bring it before the tabernacle of meeting.
15And the elders of the congregation shall lay their
hands on the head of the bull before the LORD. Then
the bull shall be killed before the LORD. 16The anointed
priest shall bring some of the bull’s blood to the tabernacle of meeting. 17Then the priest shall dip his finger
in the blood and sprinkle *it* seven times before the
LORD, in front of the veil. 18And he shall put *some* of
the blood on the horns of the altar which *is* before the
LORD, which *is* in the tabernacle of meeting; and he
shall pour the remaining blood at the base of the altar
of burnt offering, which is at the door of the tabernacle of meeting. 19He shall take all the fat from it and
burn *it* on the altar. 20And he shall do with the bull as
he did with the bull as a sin offering; thus he shall do
with it. So the priest shall make atonement for them,
and it shall be forgiven them. 21Then he shall carry the
bull outside the camp, and burn it as he burned the
first bull. It *is* a sin offering for the assembly.

22‘When a ruler has sinned, and done *something*
unintentionally *against* any of the commandments of
the LORD his God *in anything* which should not be
done, and is guilty, 23or if his sin which he has committed comes to his knowledge, he shall bring as his
offering a kid of the goats, a male without blemish.
24And he shall lay his hand on the head of the goat,
and kill it at the place where they kill the burnt offering before the LORD. It *is* a sin offering. 25The priest
shall take some of the blood of the sin offering with
his finger, put *it* on the horns of the altar of burnt offering, and pour its blood at the base of the altar of
burnt offering. 26And he shall burn all its fat on the
altar, like the fat of the sacrifice of the peace offering.
So the priest shall make atonement for him concerning his sin, and it shall be forgiven him.

27‘If anyone of the common people sins unintentionally by doing *something against* any of the
commandments of the LORD *in anything* which ought
not to be done, and is guilty, 28or if his sin which he
has committed comes to his knowledge, then he shall
bring as his offering a kid of the goats, a female without blemish, for his sin which he has committed.
29And he shall lay his hand on the head of the sin offering, and kill the sin offering at the place of the
burnt offering. 30Then the priest shall take *some* of its
blood with his finger, put *it* on the horns of the altar of
burnt offering, and pour all *the remaining* blood at
the base of the altar. 31He shall remove all its fat, as fat
is removed from the sacrifice of the peace offering;
and the priest shall burn it on the altar for a sweet
aroma to the LORD. So the priest shall make atonement for him, and it shall be forgiven him.

32‘If he brings a lamb as his sin offering, he shall
bring a female without blemish. 33Then he shall lay
his hand on the head of the sin offering, and kill it as a
sin offering at the place where they kill the burnt offering. 34The priest shall take *some* of the blood of the

sin offering with his finger, put *it* on the horns of the
altar of burnt offering, and pour all *the remaining*
blood at the base of the altar. 35He shall remove all its
fat, as the fat of the lamb is removed from the sacrifice
of the peace offering. Then the priest shall burn it on
the altar, according to the offerings made by fire to the
LORD. So the priest shall make atonement for his sin
that he has committed, and it shall be forgiven him.

The Trespass Offering

5 'If a person sins in hearing the utterance of an oath,
and *is* a witness, whether he has seen or known *of
the matter*—if he does not tell *it*, he bears guilt.
2'Or if a person touches any unclean thing, whether
it is the carcass of an unclean beast, or the carcass of
unclean livestock, or the carcass of unclean creeping
things, and he is unaware of it, he also shall be unclean and guilty. 3Or if he touches human uncleanness—whatever uncleanness with which a man may
be defiled, and he is unaware of it—when he realizes
it, then he shall be guilty.
4'Or if a person swears, speaking thoughtlessly
with *his* lips to do evil or to do good, whatever *it is* that
a man may pronounce by an oath, and he is unaware
of it—when he realizes *it*, then he shall be guilty in any
of these *matters*.
5'And it shall be, when he is guilty in any of these
matters, that he shall confess that he has sinned in that
thing; 6and he shall bring his trespass offering to the
LORD for his sin which he has committed, a female
from the flock, a lamb or a kid of the goats as a sin offering. So the priest shall make atonement for him
concerning his sin.
7'If he is not able to bring a lamb, then he shall
bring to the LORD, for his trespass which he has committed, two turtledoves or two young pigeons: one as
a sin offering and the other as a burnt offering. 8And
he shall bring them to the priest, who shall offer *that*
which *is* for the sin offering first, and wring off its
head from its neck, but shall not divide *it* completely.
9Then he shall sprinkle *some* of the blood of the sin offering on the side of the altar, and the rest of the blood
shall be drained out at the base of the altar. It *is* a sin offering. 10And he shall offer the second *as* a burnt offering according to the prescribed manner. So the priest
shall make atonement on his behalf for his sin which
he has committed, and it shall be forgiven him.
11'But if he is not able to bring two turtledoves or
two young pigeons, then he who sinned shall bring
for his offering one-tenth of an ephah of fine flour as
a sin offering. He shall put no oil on it, nor shall he put
frankincense on it, for it *is* a sin offering. 12Then he
shall bring it to the priest, and the priest shall take his
handful of it as a memorial portion, and burn *it* on
the altar according to the offerings made by fire to the
LORD. It *is* a sin offering. 13The priest shall make atonement for him, for his sin that he has committed in any
of these matters; and it shall be forgiven him. *The rest*
shall be the priest's as a grain offering.' "

Offerings with Restitution

14Then the LORD spoke to Moses, saying: 15"If a person commits a trespass, and sins unintentionally in regard to the holy things of the LORD, then he shall bring
to the LORD as his trespass offering a ram without
blemish from the flocks, with your valuation in shekels
of silver according to the shekel of the sanctuary, as a
trespass offering. 16And he shall make restitution for
the harm that he has done in regard to the holy thing,
and shall add one-fifth to it and give it to the priest. So
the priest shall make atonement for him with the ram
of the trespass offering, and it shall be forgiven him.
17"If a person sins, and commits any of these things
which are forbidden to be done by the commandments of the LORD, though he does not know *it*, yet he
is guilty and shall bear his iniquity. 18And he shall
bring to the priest a ram without blemish from the
flock, with your valuation, as a trespass offering. So
the priest shall make atonement for him regarding
his ignorance in which he erred and did not know *it*,
and it shall be forgiven him. 19It is a trespass offering;
he has certainly trespassed against the LORD."

6 And the LORD spoke to Moses, saying: 2"If a person sins and commits a trespass against the LORD
by lying to his neighbor about what was delivered to
him for safekeeping, or about a pledge, or about a
robbery, or if he has extorted from his neighbor, 3or if
he has found what was lost and lies concerning it, and
swears falsely—in any one of these things that a man
may do in which he sins: 4then it shall be, because he
has sinned and is guilty, that he shall restore what he
has stolen, or the thing which he has extorted, or what
was delivered to him for safekeeping, or the lost thing
which he found, 5or all that about which he has sworn
falsely. He shall restore its full value, add one-fifth
more to it, *and* give it to whomever it belongs, on the
day of his trespass offering. 6And he shall bring his
trespass offering to the LORD, a ram without blemish
from the flock, with your valuation, as a trespass offering, to the priest. 7So the priest shall make atonement for him before the LORD, and he shall be forgiven
for any one of these things that he may have done in
which he trespasses."

LIFE LESSON

Leviticus 6:8–7:38

SITUATION God explained the proper way to bring a sacrifice. He emphasized the importance of holy living for individuals and for the community.

OBSERVATION Because God has a perfect moral nature, he requires that we approach him as persons cleansed from sin.

INSPIRATION The annual event always drew a crowd. The priest would solemnly ascend the temple steps, cradling in his arms a lamb. As the people waited outside, he would pass through the great curtain and enter the Holy of Holies. He would kill the lamb upon the altar and pray that the blood would appease God. The sins would be rolled back. And the people would sigh with relief.

A great curtain hung as a reminder of the distance between God and man. It was like a deep chasm that no one could breach. Man on his island . . . quarantined because of sin.

God could have left it like that. He could have left the people isolated. He could have washed his hands of the whole mess. He could have turned back, tossed in the towel, and started over on another planet. He *could* have, you know.

But he didn't.

God himself breached the chasm. In the darkness of an eclipsed sun, he

The Law of the Burnt Offering

8 Then the LORD spoke to Moses, saying, 9 "Command Aaron and his
sons, saying, 'This *is* the law of the burnt offering: The burnt offering *shall
be* on the hearth upon the altar all night until morning, and the fire of the
altar shall be kept burning on it. 10 And the priest shall put on his linen garment, and his linen trousers he shall put on his body, and take up the
ashes of the burnt offering which the fire has consumed on the altar, and
he shall put them beside the altar. 11 Then he shall take off his garments,
put on other garments, and carry the ashes outside the camp to a clean
place. 12 And the fire on the altar shall be kept burning on it; it shall not be
put out. And the priest shall burn wood on it every morning, and lay the
burnt offering in order on it; and he shall burn on it the fat of the peace offerings. 13 A fire shall always be burning on the altar; it shall never go out.

The Law of the Grain Offering

14 "This *is* the law of the grain offering: The sons of Aaron shall offer it on
the altar before the LORD. 15 He shall take from it his handful of the fine
flour of the grain offering, with its oil, and all the frankincense which *is* on
the grain offering, and shall burn *it* on the altar *for* a sweet aroma, as a
memorial to the LORD. 16 And the remainder of it Aaron and his sons shall
eat; with unleavened bread it shall be eaten in a holy place; in the court of
the tabernacle of meeting they shall eat it. 17 It shall not be baked with
leaven. I have given it *as* their portion of My offerings made by fire; it *is*
most holy, like the sin offering and the trespass offering. 18 All the males
among the children of Aaron may eat it. *It shall be* a statute forever in your
generations concerning the offerings made by fire to the LORD. Everyone
who touches them must be holy.' "[a]
19 And the LORD spoke to Moses, saying, 20 "This *is* the offering of Aaron
and his sons, which they shall offer to the LORD, *beginning* on the day when
he is anointed: one-tenth of an ephah of fine flour as a daily grain offering,
half of it in the morning and half of it at night. 21 It shall be made in a pan
with oil. *When it is* mixed, you shall bring it in. The baked pieces of the
grain offering you shall offer *for* a sweet aroma to the LORD. 22 The priest
from among his sons, who is anointed in his place, shall offer it. *It is* a
statute forever to the LORD. It shall be wholly burned. 23 For every grain offering for the priest shall be wholly burned. It shall not be eaten."

The Law of the Sin Offering

24 Also the LORD spoke to Moses, saying, 25 "Speak to Aaron and to his
sons, saying, 'This *is* the law of the sin offering: In the place where the
burnt offering is killed, the sin offering shall be killed before the LORD. It *is*
most holy. 26 The priest who offers it for sin shall eat it. In a holy place it
shall be eaten, in the court of the tabernacle of meeting. 27 Everyone who
touches its flesh must be holy.[b] And when its blood is sprinkled on any
garment, you shall wash that on which it was sprinkled, in a holy place.
28 But the earthen vessel in which it is boiled shall be broken. And if it is
boiled in a bronze pot, it shall be both scoured and rinsed in water. 29 All
the males among the priests may eat it. It *is* most holy. 30 But no sin offering from which *any* of the blood is brought into the tabernacle of meeting,

6:18 [a] Compare Numbers 4:15 and Haggai 2:11–13
6:27 [b] Compare Numbers 4:15 and Haggai 2:11–13

to make atonement in the holy *place*,[c] shall be eaten. It shall be burned in
the fire.

The Law of the Trespass Offering

7 1'Likewise this *is* the law of the trespass offering (it *is* most holy): 2In the
place where they kill the burnt offering they shall kill the trespass offering. And its blood he shall sprinkle all around on the altar. 3And he shall
offer from it all its fat. The fat tail and the fat that covers the entrails, 4the
two kidneys and the fat that *is* on them by the flanks, and the fatty lobe *at-*
tached to the liver above the kidneys, he shall remove; 5and the priest shall
burn them on the altar *as* an offering made by fire to the LORD. It *is* a trespass offering. 6Every male among the priests may eat it. It shall be eaten in
a holy place. It *is* most holy. 7The trespass offering *is* like the sin offering;
there is one law for them both: the priest who makes atonement with it
shall have *it*. 8And the priest who offers anyone's burnt offering, that
priest shall have for himself the skin of the burnt offering which he has offered. 9Also every grain offering that is baked in the oven and all that is
prepared in the covered pan, or in a pan, shall be the priest's who offers it.
10Every grain offering, *whether* mixed with oil or dry, shall belong to all the
sons of Aaron, to one *as much* as the other.

The Law of Peace Offerings

11'This *is* the law of the sacrifice of peace offerings which he shall offer to
the LORD: 12If he offers it for a thanksgiving, then he shall offer, with the
sacrifice of thanksgiving, unleavened cakes mixed with oil, unleavened
wafers anointed with oil, or cakes of blended flour mixed with oil. 13Be-
sides the cakes, *as* his offering he shall offer leavened bread with the sacrifice of thanksgiving of his peace offering. 14And from it he shall offer one
cake from each offering *as* a heave offering to the LORD. It shall belong to
the priest who sprinkles the blood of the peace offering.

15'The flesh of the sacrifice of his peace offering for thanksgiving shall be
eaten the same day it is offered. He shall not leave any of it until morning.
16But if the sacrifice of his offering *is* a vow or a voluntary offering, it shall
be eaten the same day that he offers his sacrifice; but on the next day the
remainder of it also may be eaten; 17the remainder of the flesh of the sacrifice on the third day must be burned with fire. 18And if *any* of the flesh of
the sacrifice of his peace offering is eaten at all on the third day, it shall not
be accepted, nor shall it be imputed to him; it shall be an abomination *to*
him who offers it, and the person who eats of it shall bear guilt.

19'The flesh that touches any unclean thing shall not be eaten. It shall be
burned with fire. And as for the *clean* flesh, all who are clean may eat of it.
20But the person who eats the flesh of the sacrifice of the peace offering
that *belongs* to the LORD, while he is unclean, that person shall be cut off
from his people. 21Moreover the person who touches any unclean thing,
such as human uncleanness, *an* unclean animal, or any abominable unclean thing,[d] and who eats the flesh of the sacrifice of the peace offering
that *belongs* to the LORD, that person shall be cut off from his people.' "

6:30 [c] *The Most Holy Place* when capitalized
7:21 [d] Following Masoretic Text, Septuagint, and Vulgate; Samaritan Pentateuch, Syriac, and Targum read *swarming thing* (compare 5:2).

and a Lamb stood in the Holy of Holies. He laid the Lamb on the altar. Not the lamb of a priest or a Jew or a shepherd, but the Lamb of God. The angels hushed as the blood of the Sufficient Sacrifice began to fall on the golden altar. Where had dripped the blood of lambs, now dripped the blood of life.

"Behold the Lamb of God."

And then it happened. God turned and looked one last time at the curtain.

"No more." And it was torn . . . from top to bottom. Ripped in two.

"No more!"

"No more lambs!"

"No more curtain!"

"No more sacrifices!"

"No more separation!"

And the sun came out.

(From *On the Anvil* by Max Lucado)

APPLICATION Is the deepest desire of your heart to have fellowship with God? Think about areas of your life where a sinful attitude or behavior has separated you from God. Renounce your sin. Commit your life to him.

EXPLORATION Holiness—Leviticus 11:45; 1 Chronicles 16:29; Romans 5:19; 1 Thessalonians 3:13; 2 Timothy 2:21; Hebrews 12:10-14; 1 Peter 3:18.

Fat and Blood May Not Be Eaten

[22]And the LORD spoke to Moses, saying, [23]"Speak to the children of Israel, saying: 'You shall not eat any fat, of ox or sheep or goat. [24]And the fat of an animal that dies *naturally*, and the fat of what is torn by wild beasts, may be used in any other way; but you shall by no means eat it. [25]For whoever eats the fat of the animal of which men offer an offering made by fire to the LORD, the person who eats *it* shall be cut off from his people. [26]Moreover you shall not eat any blood in any of your dwellings, *whether* of bird or beast. [27]Whoever eats any blood, that person shall be cut off from his people.' "

The Portion of Aaron and His Sons

[28]Then the LORD spoke to Moses, saying, [29]"Speak to the children of Israel, saying: 'He who offers the sacrifice of his peace offering to the LORD shall bring his offering to the LORD from the sacrifice of his peace offering. [30]His own hands shall bring the offerings made by fire to the LORD. The fat with the breast he shall bring, that the breast may be waved *as* a wave offering before the LORD. [31]And the priest shall burn the fat on the altar, but the breast shall be Aaron's and his sons'. [32]Also the right thigh you shall give to the priest *as* a heave offering from the sacrifices of your peace offerings. [33]He among the sons of Aaron, who offers the blood of the peace offering and the fat, shall have the right thigh for *his* part. [34]For the breast of the wave offering and the thigh of the heave offering I have taken from the children of Israel, from the sacrifices of their peace offerings, and I have given them to Aaron the priest and to his sons from the children of Israel by a statute forever.' "

[35]This *is* the consecrated portion for Aaron and his sons, from the offerings made by fire to the LORD, on the day when *Moses* presented them to minister to the LORD as priests. [36]The LORD commanded this to be given to them by the children of Israel, on the day that He anointed them, *by* a statute forever throughout their generations.

[37]This *is* the law of the burnt offering, the grain offering, the sin offering, the trespass offering, the consecrations, and the sacrifice of the peace offering, [38]which the LORD commanded Moses on Mount Sinai, on the day when He commanded the children of Israel to offer their offerings to the LORD in the Wilderness of Sinai.

Aaron and His Sons Consecrated

8 And the LORD spoke to Moses, saying: [2]"Take Aaron and his sons with him, and the garments, the anointing oil, a bull as the sin offering, two rams, and a basket of unleavened bread; [3]and gather all the congregation together at the door of the tabernacle of meeting."

[4]So Moses did as the LORD commanded him. And the congregation was gathered together at the door of the tabernacle of meeting. [5]And Moses said to the congregation, "This *is* what the LORD commanded to be done."

[6]Then Moses brought Aaron and his sons and washed them with water. [7]And he put the tunic on him, girded him with the sash, clothed him with the robe, and put the ephod on him; and he girded him with the intricately woven band of the ephod, and with it tied *the ephod* on him. [8]Then he put the breastplate on him, and he put the Urim and the Thummim[e] in the

LIFE LESSON

Leviticus 8:1–10:20

SITUATION The priests were the official communicators between God and man. God ordained priests as full-time spiritual leaders.

OBSERVATION When God calls and ordains spiritual leaders, they have a special responsibility to live obediently as they walk close to him.

INSPIRATION Let's take a look at the important balance between natural and spiritual leadership. A leader, obviously, must have some God-given natural qualities that cause others to respond to his or her influence. At the same time, the Christian leader must possess a marked degree of Spirit-directed, humble devotion to the Lord Jesus Christ . . . lest he fall into the category of a self-appointed, ambitious creature who simply loves the spotlight. It is upon this point I want to camp for a few minutes.

Dr. A. W. Tozer wrote:

> A true and safe leader is likely to be one who has no desire to lead, but is forced into a position of leadership by the inward pressure of the Holy Spirit and the press of the external situation. Such were Moses and David and the Old Testament prophets. I think there was hardly a great leader from Paul to the present day but was drafted by the Holy Spirit for the task, and commissioned by the Lord of the Church

8:8 [e] Literally *the Lights and the Perfections* (compare Exodus 28:30)

breastplate. 9And he put the turban on his head. Also on the turban, on its
front, he put the golden plate, the holy crown, as the LORD had commanded Moses.
10Also Moses took the anointing oil, and anointed the tabernacle and all
that *was* in it, and consecrated them. 11He sprinkled some of it on the altar
seven times, anointed the altar and all its utensils, and the laver and its
base, to consecrate them. 12And he poured some of the anointing oil on
Aaron's head and anointed him, to consecrate him.
13Then Moses brought Aaron's sons and put tunics on them, girded them
with sashes, and put hats on them, as the LORD had commanded Moses.
14And he brought the bull for the sin offering. Then Aaron and his sons
laid their hands on the head of the bull for the sin offering, 15and Moses
killed *it.* Then he took the blood, and put *some* on the horns of the altar all
around with his finger, and purified the altar. And he poured the blood at
the base of the altar, and consecrated it, to make atonement for it. 16Then
he took all the fat that *was* on the entrails, the fatty lobe *attached to* the liver,
and the two kidneys with their fat, and Moses burned *them* on the altar.
17But the bull, its hide, its flesh, and its offal, he burned with fire outside
the camp, as the LORD had commanded Moses.
18Then he brought the ram as the burnt offering. And Aaron and his
sons laid their hands on the head of the ram, 19and Moses killed *it.* Then he
sprinkled the blood all around on the altar. 20And he cut the ram into
pieces; and Moses burned the head, the pieces, and the fat. 21Then he
washed the entrails and the legs in water. And Moses burned the whole
ram on the altar. It *was* a burnt sacrifice for a sweet aroma, an offering
made by fire to the LORD, as the LORD had commanded Moses.
22And he brought the second ram, the ram of consecration. Then Aaron
and his sons laid their hands on the head of the ram, 23and Moses killed *it.*
Also he took *some* of its blood and put it on the tip of Aaron's right ear, on
the thumb of his right hand, and on the big toe of his right foot. 24Then he
brought Aaron's sons. And Moses put *some* of the blood on the tips of
their right ears, on the thumbs of their right hands, and on the big toes of
their right feet. And Moses sprinkled the blood all around on the altar.
25Then he took the fat and the fat tail, all the fat that *was* on the entrails, the
fatty lobe *attached to* the liver, the two kidneys and their fat, and the right
thigh; 26and from the basket of unleavened bread that was before the LORD
he took one unleavened cake, a cake of bread *anointed with* oil, and one
wafer, and put *them* on the fat and on the right thigh; 27and he put all *these*
in Aaron's hands and in his sons' hands, and waved them *as* a wave offering before the LORD. 28Then Moses took them from their hands and
burned *them* on the altar, on the burnt offering. They *were* consecration
offerings for a sweet aroma. That *was* an offering made by fire to the LORD.
29And Moses took the breast and waved it *as* a wave offering before the
LORD. It was Moses' part of the ram of consecration, as the LORD had commanded Moses.
30Then Moses took some of the anointing oil and some of the blood
which *was* on the altar, and sprinkled *it* on Aaron, on his garments, on his
sons, and on the garments of his sons with him; and he consecrated Aaron,
his garments, his sons, and the garments of his sons with him.
31And Moses said to Aaron and his sons, "Boil the flesh *at* the door of the
tabernacle of meeting, and eat it there with the bread that *is* in the basket

to fill a position he had little heart for. I believe it might be accepted as a fairly reliable rule of thumb that the man who is ambitious to lead is disqualified as a leader.

Spiritual leaders, you see, are not made by majority vote or ecclesiastical decisions, by conferences or synods. Only God can make them!

For not from the east, nor from the west,
Nor from the desert comes exaltation;
But God is the Judge;
He puts down one, and exalts another
(Psalm 75: 6-7).

This means, then, that God makes it His responsibility to prepare, nurture, train, and promote certain people to places of leadership. That's His business, not ours.

(From *Growing Strong in the Seasons of Life* by Charles Swindoll)

APPLICATION Christ desires all believers to be priests and therefore spiritual leaders. He wants us to live holy and obedient lives. Which areas of your life are less than totally dependent on him? Write down three ways you can pursue holiness before God and start practicing them.

EXPLORATION Leadership—Numbers 27:15-17; 1 Chronicles 21:8.

of consecration offerings, as I commanded, saying,
'Aaron and his sons shall eat it.' [32]What remains of
the flesh and of the bread you shall burn with fire.
[33]And you shall not go outside the door of the tabernacle of meeting *for* seven days, until the days of your
consecration are ended. For seven days he shall consecrate you. [34]As he has done this day, *so* the LORD has
commanded to do, to make atonement for you.
[35]Therefore you shall stay *at* the door of the tabernacle
of meeting day and night for seven days, and keep the
charge of the LORD, so that you may not die; for so I
have been commanded." [36]So Aaron and his sons did
all the things that the LORD had commanded by the
hand of Moses.

The Priestly Ministry Begins

9 It came to pass on the eighth day that Moses
called Aaron and his sons and the elders of Israel.
[2]And he said to Aaron, "Take for yourself a young bull
as a sin offering and a ram as a burnt offering, without
blemish, and offer *them* before the LORD. [3]And to the
children of Israel you shall speak, saying, 'Take a kid of
the goats as a sin offering, and a calf and a lamb, *both* of
the first year, without blemish, as a burnt offering,
[4]also a bull and a ram as peace offerings, to sacrifice before the LORD, and a grain offering mixed with oil; for
today the LORD will appear to you.' "

[5]So they brought what Moses commanded before
the tabernacle of meeting. And all the congregation
drew near and stood before the LORD. [6]Then Moses
said, "This *is* the thing which the LORD commanded
you to do, and the glory of the LORD will appear to
you." [7]And Moses said to Aaron, "Go to the altar, offer
your sin offering and your burnt offering, and make
atonement for yourself and for the people. Offer the
offering of the people, and make atonement for them,
as the LORD commanded."

[8]Aaron therefore went to the altar and killed the calf
of the sin offering, which *was* for himself. [9]Then the
sons of Aaron brought the blood to him. And he
dipped his finger in the blood, put *it* on the horns of
the altar, and poured the blood at the base of the altar.
[10]But the fat, the kidneys, and the fatty lobe from the
liver of the sin offering he burned on the altar, as the
LORD had commanded Moses. [11]The flesh and the hide
he burned with fire outside the camp.

[12]And he killed the burnt offering; and Aaron's sons
presented to him the blood, which he sprinkled all
around on the altar. [13]Then they presented the burnt offering to him, with its pieces and head, and he burned
them on the altar. [14]And he washed the entrails and the
legs, and burned *them* with the burnt offering on
the altar.

[15]Then he brought the people's offering, and took the
goat, which *was* the sin offering for the people, and
killed it and offered it for sin, like the first one. [16]And he
brought the burnt offering and offered it according to
the prescribed manner. [17]Then he brought the grain offering, took a handful of it, and burned *it* on the altar,
besides the burnt sacrifice of the morning.

[18]He also killed the bull and the ram *as* sacrifices of
peace offerings, which *were* for the people. And Aaron's sons presented to him the blood, which he sprinkled all around on the altar, [19]and the fat from the bull
and the ram—the fatty tail, what covers *the entrails*
and the kidneys, and the fatty lobe *attached to* the liver;
[20]and they put the fat on the breasts. Then he burned
the fat on the altar; [21]but the breasts and the right thigh
Aaron waved *as* a wave offering before the LORD, as
Moses had commanded.

[22]Then Aaron lifted his hand toward the people,
blessed them, and came down from offering the sin
offering, the burnt offering, and peace offerings.
[23]And Moses and Aaron went into the tabernacle of
meeting, and came out and blessed the people. Then
the glory of the LORD appeared to all the people, [24]and
fire came out from before the LORD and consumed the
burnt offering and the fat on the altar. When all the
people saw *it,* they shouted and fell on their faces.

The Profane Fire of Nadab and Abihu

10 Then Nadab and Abihu, the sons of Aaron,
each took his censer and put fire in it, put incense on it, and offered profane fire before the LORD,
which He had not commanded them. [2]So fire went
out from the LORD and devoured them, and they died
before the LORD. [3]And Moses said to Aaron, "This is
what the LORD spoke, saying:

'By those who come near Me
I must be regarded as holy;
And before all the people
I must be glorified.' "

So Aaron held his peace.

[4]Then Moses called Mishael and Elzaphan, the sons
of Uzziel the uncle of Aaron, and said to them, "Come
near, carry your brethren from before the sanctuary
out of the camp." [5]So they went near and carried them
by their tunics out of the camp, as Moses had said.

[6]And Moses said to Aaron, and to Eleazar and
Ithamar, his sons, "Do not uncover your heads nor

tear your clothes, lest you die, and wrath come upon all the people. But let
your brethren, the whole house of Israel, bewail the burning which the
LORD has kindled. 7You shall not go out from the door of the tabernacle of
meeting, lest you die, for the anointing oil of the LORD *is* upon you." And
they did according to the word of Moses.

Conduct Prescribed for Priests

8Then the LORD spoke to Aaron, saying: 9"Do not drink wine or intoxicating drink, you, nor your sons with you, when you go into the tabernacle
of meeting, lest you die. *It shall be* a statute forever throughout your generations, 10that you may distinguish between holy and unholy, and between
unclean and clean, 11and that you may teach the children of Israel all the
statutes which the LORD has spoken to them by the hand of Moses."
12And Moses spoke to Aaron, and to Eleazar and Ithamar, his sons who
were left: "Take the grain offering that remains of the offerings made by fire
to the LORD, and eat it without leaven beside the altar; for it *is* most holy.
13You shall eat it in a holy place, because it *is* your due and your sons' due, of
the sacrifices made by fire to the LORD; for so I have been commanded. 14The
breast of the wave offering and the thigh of the heave offering you shall eat in
a clean place, you, your sons, and your daughters with you; for *they are* your
due and your sons' due, *which* are given from the sacrifices of peace offerings of the children of Israel. 15The thigh of the heave offering and the breast
of the wave offering they shall bring with the offerings of fat made by fire, to
offer *as* a wave offering before the LORD. And it shall be yours and your sons'
with you, by a statute forever, as the LORD has commanded."
16Then Moses made careful inquiry about the goat of the sin offering,
and there it was—burned up. And he was angry with Eleazar and
Ithamar, the sons of Aaron *who were* left, saying, 17"Why have you not
eaten the sin offering in a holy place, since it *is* most holy, and *God* has
given it to you to bear the guilt of the congregation, to make atonement for
them before the LORD? 18See! Its blood was not brought inside the holy
place;[f] indeed you should have eaten it in a holy *place*, as I commanded."
19And Aaron said to Moses, "Look, this day they have offered their sin
offering and their burnt offering before the LORD, and such things have befallen me! *If* I had eaten the sin offering today, would it have been accepted
in the sight of the LORD?" 20So when Moses heard *that*, he was content.

Foods Permitted and Forbidden

11 Now the LORD spoke to Moses and Aaron, saying to them, 2"Speak to
the children of Israel, saying, 'These *are* the animals which you may
eat among all the animals that *are* on the earth: 3Among the animals, whatever divides the hoof, having cloven hooves *and* chewing the cud—that you
may eat. 4Nevertheless these you shall not eat among those that chew the
cud or those that have cloven hooves: the camel, because it chews the cud
but does not have cloven hooves, is unclean to you; 5the rock hyrax, because
it chews the cud but does not have cloven hooves, *is* unclean to you; 6the
hare, because it chews the cud but does not have cloven hooves, *is* unclean to
you; 7and the swine, though it divides the hoof, having cloven hooves, yet
does not chew the cud, *is* unclean to you. 8Their flesh you shall not eat, and
their carcasses you shall not touch. They *are* unclean to you.

10:18 *f The Most Holy Place* when capitalized

LIFE LESSON

Leviticus 11:1–15:33

SITUATION God instructed the people how to live healthy. Mildew and skin diseases were more dangerous in Bible times than today.

OBSERVATION God, through Moses and Aaron, provided the Israelites with detailed and precise instructions on clean living. He wanted them to be set apart from the peoples around them and thoroughly prepared to worship him. Holy living encompasses every part of life.

INSPIRATION We are so fussy, so eager to serve God after our own style, so prone to take up anything that another has done successfully, without staying to ask whether it is God's will for ourselves. We work so much for God, instead of waiting for Him to work through us. . . . From all such things we must cleanse ourselves. There is a defilement of the spirit as well as of the flesh. There are weights as well as sins. There are things that are not expedient, as well as those that are positively unlawful and wrong. From all we must be separate and clean. You may say that you have tried to separate yourself, but in vain; the evil clings to you like a shadow. Then fall back on the philosophy of the will. Be willing to be clean. Be willing to be made willing. . . . But do not suppose that you are always to be looking on this side of your life, on the renunciations, the excisions, the amputations. Present yourself to Jesus, as those who are alive from the dead and constrained by His mercies. You are His because He made you. . . . You are His because He redeemed you. . . . You are His because God the Father has given Him all who come to Him. . . . Will you not, therefore, present yourself to Him, that He may forgive all your sins and cleanse you from all that is unholy and inconsistent and fill you with His sacred fullness?

(From "Touch No Unclean Thing" by F. B. Meyer in *They Walked with God*)

Continued

APPLICATION Do you ever feel you've outgrown your need for spiritual guidance? If so, a warning signal should sound. Ask God to show you if there is a specific area where you are not living a spiritually healthy life. Ask a Christian who knows you to keep you accountable and to pray with you.

EXPLORATION God's People Are Special—Deuteronomy 7:6-8; 14:2; Psalm 24:3-6; 119:1-3; 135:4; 1 Peter 1:14-15; 2:9-12.

9 "These you may eat of all that *are* in the water: whatever in the water has
fins and scales, whether in the seas or in the rivers—that you may eat.
10 But all in the seas or in the rivers that do not have fins and scales, all that
move in the water or any living thing which *is* in the water, they *are* an
abomination to you. 11 They shall be an abomination to you; you shall not
eat their flesh, but you shall regard their carcasses as an abomination.
12 Whatever in the water does not have fins or scales—that *shall be* an
abomination to you.

13 "And these you shall regard as an abomination among the birds; they
shall not be eaten, they *are* an abomination: the eagle, the vulture, the buzzard, 14 the kite, and the falcon after its kind; 15 every raven after its kind,
16 the ostrich, the short-eared owl, the sea gull, and the hawk after its kind;
17 the little owl, the fisher owl, and the screech owl; 18 the white owl, the jackdaw, and the carrion vulture; 19 the stork, the heron after its kind, the
hoopoe, and the bat.

20 "All flying insects that creep on *all* fours *shall be* an abomination to
you. 21 Yet these you may eat of every flying insect that creeps on *all* fours:
those which have jointed legs above their feet with which to leap on the
earth. 22 These you may eat: the locust after its kind, the destroying locust
after its kind, the cricket after its kind, and the grasshopper after its kind.
23 But all *other* flying insects which have four feet *shall be* an abomination
to you.

Unclean Animals

24 "By these you shall become unclean; whoever touches the carcass of
any of them shall be unclean until evening; 25 whoever carries part of the
carcass of any of them shall wash his clothes and be unclean until evening:
26 *The carcass* of any animal which divides the foot, but is not cloven-
hoofed or does not chew the cud, *is* unclean to you. Everyone who touches
it shall be unclean. 27 And whatever goes on its paws, among all kinds of
animals that go on *all* fours, those *are* unclean to you. Whoever touches
any such carcass shall be unclean until evening. 28 Whoever carries *any
such* carcass shall wash his clothes and be unclean until evening. It *is* unclean to you.

29 "These also *shall be* unclean to you among the creeping things that
creep on the earth: the mole, the mouse, and the large lizard after its kind;
30 the gecko, the monitor lizard, the sand reptile, the sand lizard, and the
chameleon. 31 These *are* unclean to you among all that creep. Whoever
touches them when they are dead shall be unclean until evening.
32 Anything on which *any* of them falls, when they are dead shall be unclean,
whether *it is* any item of wood or clothing or skin or sack, whatever item *it
is,* in which *any* work is done, it must be put in water. And it shall be unclean until evening; then it shall be clean. 33 Any earthen vessel into which
any of them falls you shall break; and whatever *is* in it shall be unclean: 34 in
such a vessel, any edible food upon which water falls becomes unclean,
and any drink that may be drunk from it becomes unclean. 35 And everything on which *a part* of *any such* carcass falls shall be unclean; *whether it
is* an oven or cooking stove, it shall be broken down; *for* they *are* unclean,
and shall be unclean to you. 36 Nevertheless a spring or a cistern, *in which
there is* plenty of water, shall be clean, but whatever touches any such carcass
becomes unclean. 37 And if a part of *any such* carcass falls on any planting

seed which is to be sown, it *remains* clean. 38But if water
is put on the seed, and if *a part* of *any such* carcass falls
on it, it *becomes* unclean to you.
39'And if any animal which you may eat dies, he
who touches its carcass shall be unclean until
evening. 40He who eats of its carcass shall wash his
clothes and be unclean until evening. He also who
carries its carcass shall wash his clothes and be unclean until evening.
41'And every creeping thing that creeps on the earth
shall be an abomination. It shall not be eaten. 42What-
ever crawls on its belly, whatever goes on *all* fours, or
whatever has many feet among all creeping things
that creep on the earth—these you shall not eat, for
they *are* an abomination. 43You shall not make yourselves abominable with any creeping thing that
creeps; nor shall you make yourselves unclean with
them, lest you be defiled by them. 44For I *am* the LORD
your God. You shall therefore consecrate yourselves,
and you shall be holy; for I *am* holy. Neither shall you
defile yourselves with any creeping thing that creeps
on the earth. 45For I *am* the LORD who brings you up
out of the land of Egypt, to be your God. You shall
therefore be holy, for I *am* holy.
46'This *is* the law of the animals and the birds and
every living creature that moves in the waters, and of
every creature that creeps on the earth, 47to distinguish between the unclean and the clean, and between the animal that may be eaten and the animal
that may not be eaten.' "

The Ritual After Childbirth

12 Then the LORD spoke to Moses, saying, 2"Speak
to the children of Israel, saying: 'If a woman
has conceived, and borne a male child, then she shall
be unclean seven days; as in the days of her customary impurity she shall be unclean. 3And on the eighth
day the flesh of his foreskin shall be circumcised. 4She
shall then continue in the blood of *her* purification
thirty-three days. She shall not touch any hallowed
thing, nor come into the sanctuary until the days of
her purification are fulfilled.
5'But if she bears a female child, then she shall be
unclean two weeks, as in her customary impurity, and
she shall continue in the blood of *her* purification
sixty-six days.
6'When the days of her purification are fulfilled,
whether for a son or a daughter, she shall bring to the
priest a lamb of the first year as a burnt offering, and
a young pigeon or a turtledove as a sin offering, to the
door of the tabernacle of meeting. 7Then he shall offer
it before the LORD, and make atonement for her. And
she shall be clean from the flow of her blood. This *is*
the law for her who has borne a male or a female.
8'And if she is not able to bring a lamb, then she may
bring two turtledoves or two young pigeons—one as a
burnt offering and the other as a sin offering. So the
priest shall make atonement for her, and she will be
clean.' "

The Law Concerning Leprosy

13 And the LORD spoke to Moses and Aaron, saying: 2"When a man has on the skin of his body
a swelling, a scab, or a bright spot, and it becomes on
the skin of his body *like* a leprous[g] sore, then he shall
be brought to Aaron the priest or to one of his sons
the priests. 3The priest shall examine the sore on the
skin of the body; and if the hair on the sore has turned
white, and the sore appears *to be* deeper than the skin
of his body, it *is* a leprous sore. Then the priest shall
examine him, and pronounce him unclean. 4But if the
bright spot *is* white on the skin of his body, and does
not appear *to be* deeper than the skin, and its hair has
not turned white, then the priest shall isolate *the one
who has* the sore seven days. 5And the priest shall examine him on the seventh day; and indeed *if* the sore
appears to be as it was, *and* the sore has not spread on
the skin, then the priest shall isolate him another
seven days. 6Then the priest shall examine him again
on the seventh day; and indeed *if* the sore has faded,
and the sore has not spread on the skin, then the
priest shall pronounce him clean; it *is only* a scab, and
he shall wash his clothes and be clean. 7But if the scab
should at all spread over the skin, after he has been
seen by the priest for his cleansing, he shall be seen by
the priest again. 8And *if* the priest sees that the scab
has indeed spread on the skin, then the priest shall
pronounce him unclean. It *is* leprosy.
9"When the leprous sore is on a person, then he shall
be brought to the priest. 10And the priest shall examine
him; and indeed *if* the swelling on the skin *is* white, and
it has turned the hair white, and *there is* a spot of raw
flesh in the swelling, 11it *is* an old leprosy on the skin of
his body. The priest shall pronounce him unclean, and
shall not isolate him, for he *is* unclean.
12"And if leprosy breaks out all over the skin, and
the leprosy covers all the skin of *the one who has* the
sore, from his head to his foot, wherever the priest

13:2 *g* Hebrew *saraath,* disfiguring skin diseases, including leprosy, and so in verses 2–46 and 14:2–32

looks, 13then the priest shall consider; and indeed *if* the leprosy has covered all his body, he shall pronounce *him* clean *who has* the sore. It has all turned white. He *is* clean. 14But when raw flesh appears on him, he shall be unclean. 15And the priest shall examine the raw flesh and pronounce him to be unclean; *for* the raw flesh *is* unclean. It *is* leprosy. 16Or if the raw flesh changes and turns white again, he shall come to the priest. 17And the priest shall examine him; and indeed *if* the sore has turned white, then the priest shall pronounce *him* clean *who has* the sore. He *is* clean.

18"If the body develops a boil in the skin, and it is healed, 19and in the place of the boil there comes a white swelling or a bright spot, reddish-white, then it shall be shown to the priest; 20and *if,* when the priest sees it, it indeed *appears* deeper than the skin, and its hair has turned white, the priest shall pronounce him unclean. It *is* a leprous sore which has broken out of the boil. 21But if the priest examines it, and indeed *there are* no white hairs in it, and it *is* not deeper than the skin, but has faded, then the priest shall isolate him seven days; 22and if it should at all spread over the skin, then the priest shall pronounce him unclean. It *is* a leprous sore. 23But if the bright spot stays in one place, *and* has not spread, it *is* the scar of the boil; and the priest shall pronounce him clean.

24"Or if the body receives a burn on its skin by fire, and the raw *flesh* of the burn becomes a bright spot, reddish-white or white, 25then the priest shall examine it; and indeed *if* the hair of the bright spot has turned white, and it appears deeper than the skin, it *is* leprosy broken out in the burn. Therefore the priest shall pronounce him unclean. It *is* a leprous sore. 26But if the priest examines it, and indeed *there are* no white hairs in the bright spot, and it *is* not deeper than the skin, but has faded, then the priest shall isolate him seven days. 27And the priest shall examine him on the seventh day. If it has at all spread over the skin, then the priest shall pronounce him unclean. It *is* a leprous sore. 28But if the bright spot stays in one place, *and* has not spread on the skin, but has faded, it *is* a swelling from the burn. The priest shall pronounce him clean, for it *is* the scar from the burn.

29"If a man or woman has a sore on the head or the beard, 30then the priest shall examine the sore; and indeed if it appears deeper than the skin, *and there is* in it thin yellow hair, then the priest shall pronounce him unclean. It *is* a scaly leprosy of the head or beard. 31But if the priest examines the scaly sore, and indeed it does not appear deeper than the skin, and *there is* no black hair in it, then the priest shall isolate *the one who has* the scale seven days. 32And on the seventh day the priest shall examine the sore; and indeed *if* the scale has not spread, and there is no yellow hair in it, and the scale does not appear deeper than the skin, 33he shall shave himself, but the scale he shall not shave. And the priest shall isolate *the one who has* the scale another seven days. 34On the seventh day the priest shall examine the scale; and indeed *if* the scale has not spread over the skin, and does not appear deeper than the skin, then the priest shall pronounce him clean. He shall wash his clothes and be clean. 35But if the scale should at all spread over the skin after his cleansing, 36then the priest shall examine him; and indeed *if* the scale has spread over the skin, the priest need not seek for yellow hair. He *is* unclean. 37But if the scale appears to be at a standstill, and there is black hair grown up in it, the scale has healed. He *is* clean, and the priest shall pronounce him clean.

38"If a man or a woman has bright spots on the skin of the body, *specifically* white bright spots, 39then the priest shall look; and indeed *if* the bright spots on the skin of the body *are* dull white, it *is* a white spot *that* grows on the skin. He *is* clean.

40"As for the man whose hair has fallen from his head, he *is* bald, *but* he *is* clean. 41He whose hair has fallen from his forehead, he *is* bald on the forehead, *but* he *is* clean. 42And if there is on the bald head or bald forehead a reddish-white sore, it *is* leprosy breaking out on his bald head or his bald forehead. 43Then the priest shall examine it; and indeed *if* the swelling of the sore *is* reddish-white on his bald head or on his bald forehead, as the appearance of leprosy on the skin of the body, 44he is a leprous man. He *is* unclean. The priest shall surely pronounce him unclean; his sore *is* on his head.

45"Now the leper on whom the sore *is,* his clothes shall be torn and his head bare; and he shall cover his mustache, and cry, 'Unclean! Unclean!' 46He shall be unclean. All the days he has the sore he shall be unclean. He *is* unclean, and he shall dwell alone; his dwelling *shall be* outside the camp.

The Law Concerning Leprous Garments

47"Also, if a garment has a leprous plague[h] in it, *whether it is* a woolen garment or a linen garment, 48whether *it is* in the warp or woof of linen or wool, whether in leather or in anything made of leather,

13:47 *h* A mold, fungus, or similar infestation, and so in verses 47–59

[49]and if the plague is greenish or reddish in the garment or in the leather, whether in the warp or in the woof, or in anything made of leather, it *is* a leprous plague and shall be shown to the priest. [50]The priest shall examine the plague and isolate *that which has* the plague seven days. [51]And he shall examine the plague on the seventh day. If the plague has spread in the garment, either in the warp or in the woof, in the leather *or* in anything made of leather, the plague *is* an active leprosy. It *is* unclean. [52]He shall therefore burn that garment in which is the plague, whether warp or woof, in wool or in linen, or anything of leather, for it *is* an active leprosy; *the garment* shall be burned in the fire.

[53]"But if the priest examines *it,* and indeed the plague has not spread in the garment, either in the warp or in the woof, or in anything made of leather, [54]then the priest shall command that they wash *the thing* in which *is* the plague; and he shall isolate it another seven days. [55]Then the priest shall examine the plague after it has been washed; and indeed *if* the plague has not changed its color, though the plague has not spread, it *is* unclean, and you shall burn it in the fire; it continues eating away, *whether* the damage *is* outside or inside. [56]If the priest examines *it,* and indeed the plague has faded after washing it, then he shall tear it out of the garment, whether out of the warp or out of the woof, or out of the leather. [57]But if it appears again in the garment, either in the warp or in the woof, or in anything made of leather, it *is* a spreading *plague;* you shall burn with fire that in which is the plague. [58]And if you wash the garment, either warp or woof, or whatever is made of leather, if the plague has disappeared from it, then it shall be washed a second time, and shall be clean.

[59]"This *is* the law of the leprous plague in a garment of wool or linen, either in the warp or woof, or in anything made of leather, to pronounce it clean or to pronounce it unclean."

The Ritual for Cleansing Healed Lepers

14 Then the LORD spoke to Moses, saying, [2]"This shall be the law of the leper for the day of his cleansing: He shall be brought to the priest. [3]And the priest shall go out of the camp, and the priest shall examine *him;* and indeed, *if* the leprosy is healed in the leper, [4]then the priest shall command to take for him who is to be cleansed two living *and* clean birds, cedar wood, scarlet, and hyssop. [5]And the priest shall command that one of the birds be killed in an earthen vessel over running water. [6]As for the living bird, he shall take it, the cedar wood and the scarlet and the hyssop, and dip them and the living bird in the blood of the bird *that was* killed over the running water. [7]And he shall sprinkle it seven times on him who is to be cleansed from the leprosy, and shall pronounce him clean, and shall let the living bird loose in the open field. [8]He who is to be cleansed shall wash his clothes, shave off all his hair, and wash himself in water, that he may be clean. After that he shall come into the camp, and shall stay outside his tent seven days. [9]But on the seventh day he shall shave all the hair off his head and his beard and his eyebrows—all his hair he shall shave off. He shall wash his clothes and wash his body in water, and he shall be clean.

[10]"And on the eighth day he shall take two male lambs without blemish, one ewe lamb of the first year without blemish, three-tenths *of an ephah* of fine flour mixed with oil as a grain offering, and one log of oil. [11]Then the priest who makes *him* clean shall present the man who is to be made clean, and those things, before the LORD, *at* the door of the tabernacle of meeting. [12]And the priest shall take one male lamb and offer it as a trespass offering, and the log of oil, and wave them *as* a wave offering before the LORD. [13]Then he shall kill the lamb in the place where he kills the sin offering and the burnt offering, in a holy place; for as the sin offering *is* the priest's, so *is* the trespass offering. It *is* most holy. [14]The priest shall take *some* of the blood of the trespass offering, and the priest shall put *it* on the tip of the right ear of him who is to be cleansed, on the thumb of his right hand, and on the big toe of his right foot. [15]And the priest shall take *some* of the log of oil, and pour *it* into the palm of his own left hand. [16]Then the priest shall dip his right finger in the oil that *is* in his left hand, and shall sprinkle some of the oil with his finger seven times before the LORD. [17]And of the rest of the oil in his hand, the priest shall put *some* on the tip of the right ear of him who is to be cleansed, on the thumb of his right hand, and on the big toe of his right foot, on the blood of the trespass offering. [18]The rest of the oil that *is* in the priest's hand he shall put on the head of him who is to be cleansed. So the priest shall make atonement for him before the LORD.

[19]"Then the priest shall offer the sin offering, and make atonement for him who is to be cleansed from his uncleanness. Afterward he shall kill the burnt offering. [20]And the priest shall offer the burnt offering and the grain offering on the altar. So the priest shall make atonement for him, and he shall be clean.

[21]"But if he *is* poor and cannot afford it, then he shall take one male lamb *as* a trespass offering to be

waved, to make atonement for him, one-tenth *of an ephah* of fine flour mixed with oil as a grain offering, a log of oil, 22and two turtledoves or two young pigeons, such as he is able to afford: one shall be a sin offering and the other a burnt offering. 23He shall bring them to the priest on the eighth day for his cleansing, to the door of the tabernacle of meeting, before the LORD. 24And the priest shall take the lamb of the trespass offering and the log of oil, and the priest shall wave them *as* a wave offering before the LORD. 25Then he shall kill the lamb of the trespass offering, and the priest shall take *some* of the blood of the trespass offering and put *it* on the tip of the right ear of him who is to be cleansed, on the thumb of his right hand, and on the big toe of his right foot. 26And the priest shall pour some of the oil into the palm of his own left hand. 27Then the priest shall sprinkle with his right finger *some* of the oil that *is* in his left hand seven times before the LORD. 28And the priest shall put *some* of the oil that *is* in his hand on the tip of the right ear of him who is to be cleansed, on the thumb of the right hand, and on the big toe of his right foot, on the place of the blood of the trespass offering. 29The rest of the oil that *is* in the priest's hand he shall put on the head of him who is to be cleansed, to make atonement for him before the LORD. 30And he shall offer one of the turtledoves or young pigeons, such as he can afford— 31such as he is able to afford, the one *as* a sin offering and the other *as* a burnt offering, with the grain offering. So the priest shall make atonement for him who is to be cleansed before the LORD. 32This *is* the law *for one* who had a leprous sore, who cannot afford the usual cleansing."

The Law Concerning Leprous Houses

33And the LORD spoke to Moses and Aaron, saying: 34"When you have come into the land of Canaan, which I give you as a possession, and I put the leprous plague[i] in a house in the land of your possession, 35and he who owns the house comes and tells the priest, saying, 'It seems to me that *there is* some plague in the house,' 36then the priest shall command that they empty the house, before the priest goes *into it* to examine the plague, that all that *is* in the house may not be made unclean; and afterward the priest shall go in to examine the house. 37And he shall examine the plague; and indeed *if* the plague *is* on the walls of the house with ingrained streaks, greenish or reddish, which appear to be deep in the wall, 38then the priest shall go out of the house, to the door of the house, and shut up the house seven days. 39And the priest shall come again on the seventh day and look; and indeed *if* the plague has spread on the walls of the house, 40then the priest shall command that they take away the stones in which *is* the plague, and they shall cast them into an unclean place outside the city. 41And he shall cause the house to be scraped inside, all around, and the dust that they scrape off they shall pour out in an unclean place outside the city. 42Then they shall take other stones and put *them* in the place of *those* stones, and he shall take other mortar and plaster the house.

43"Now if the plague comes back and breaks out in the house, after he has taken away the stones, after he has scraped the house, and after it is plastered, 44then the priest shall come and look; and indeed *if* the plague has spread in the house, it *is* an active leprosy in the house. It *is* unclean. 45And he shall break down the house, its stones, its timber, and all the plaster of the house, and he shall carry *them* outside the city to an unclean place. 46Moreover he who goes into the house at all while it is shut up shall be unclean until evening. 47And he who lies down in the house shall wash his clothes, and he who eats in the house shall wash his clothes.

48"But if the priest comes in and examines *it,* and indeed the plague has not spread in the house after the house was plastered, then the priest shall pronounce the house clean, because the plague is healed. 49And he shall take, to cleanse the house, two birds, cedar wood, scarlet, and hyssop. 50Then he shall kill one of the birds in an earthen vessel over running water; 51and he shall take the cedar wood, the hyssop, the scarlet, and the living bird, and dip them in the blood of the slain bird and in the running water, and sprinkle the house seven times. 52And he shall cleanse the house with the blood of the bird and the running water and the living bird, with the cedar wood, the hyssop, and the scarlet. 53Then he shall let the living bird loose outside the city in the open field, and make atonement for the house, and it shall be clean.

54"This *is* the law for any leprous sore and scale, 55for the leprosy of a garment and of a house, 56for a swelling and a scab and a bright spot, 57to teach when *it is* unclean and when *it is* clean. This *is* the law of leprosy."

The Law Concerning Bodily Discharges

15 And the LORD spoke to Moses and Aaron, saying, 2"Speak to the children of Israel, and say to them: 'When any man has a discharge from his body,

14:34 [i] Decomposition by mildew, mold, dry rot, etc., and so in verses 34–53

his discharge *is* unclean. 3And this shall be his
uncleanness in regard to his discharge—whether his
body runs with his discharge, or his body is stopped
up by his discharge, it *is* his uncleanness. 4Every bed
is unclean on which he who has the discharge lies,
and everything on which he sits shall be unclean.
5And whoever touches his bed shall wash his clothes
and bathe in water, and be unclean until evening. 6He
who sits on anything on which he who has the discharge sat shall wash his clothes and bathe in water,
and be unclean until evening. 7And he who touches
the body of him who has the discharge shall wash his
clothes and bathe in water, and be unclean until
evening. 8If he who has the discharge spits on him
who is clean, then he shall wash his clothes and bathe
in water, and be unclean until evening. 9Any saddle on
which he who has the discharge rides shall be unclean. 10Whoever touches anything that was under
him shall be unclean until evening. He who carries
any of those things shall wash his clothes and bathe in
water, and be unclean until evening. 11And whomever
the one who has the discharge touches, and has not
rinsed his hands in water, he shall wash his clothes
and bathe in water, and be unclean until evening.
12The vessel of earth that he who has the discharge
touches shall be broken, and every vessel of wood
shall be rinsed in water.

13'And when he who has a discharge is cleansed of
his discharge, then he shall count for himself seven
days for his cleansing, wash his clothes, and bathe his
body in running water; then he shall be clean. 14On the
eighth day he shall take for himself two turtledoves or
two young pigeons, and come before the LORD, to the
door of the tabernacle of meeting, and give them to
the priest. 15Then the priest shall offer them, the one
as a sin offering and the other *as* a burnt offering. So
the priest shall make atonement for him before the
LORD because of his discharge.

16'If any man has an emission of semen, then he
shall wash all his body in water, and be unclean until
evening. 17And any garment and any leather on which
there is semen, it shall be washed with water, and be
unclean until evening. 18Also, when a woman lies with
a man, and *there is* an emission of semen, they shall
bathe in water, and be unclean until evening.

19'If a woman has a discharge, *and* the discharge
from her body is blood, she shall be set apart seven
days; and whoever touches her shall be unclean until
evening. 20Everything that she lies on during her impurity shall be unclean; also everything that she sits
on shall be unclean. 21Whoever touches her bed shall
wash his clothes and bathe in water, and be unclean
until evening. 22And whoever touches anything that
she sat on shall wash his clothes and bathe in water,
and be unclean until evening. 23If *anything* is on *her*
bed or on anything on which she sits, when he
touches it, he shall be unclean until evening. 24And if
any man lies with her at all, so that her impurity is on
him, he shall be unclean seven days; and every bed on
which he lies shall be unclean.

25'If a woman has a discharge of blood for many
days, other than at the time of her *customary* impurity, or if it runs beyond her *usual time of* impurity, all
the days of her unclean discharge shall be as the days
of her *customary* impurity. She *shall be* unclean.
26Every bed on which she lies all the days of her discharge shall be to her as the bed of her impurity; and
whatever she sits on shall be unclean, as the uncleanness of her impurity. 27Whoever touches those things
shall be unclean; he shall wash his clothes and bathe
in water, and be unclean until evening.

28'But if she is cleansed of her discharge, then she
shall count for herself seven days, and after that she
shall be clean. 29And on the eighth day she shall take
for herself two turtledoves or two young pigeons, and
bring them to the priest, to the door of the tabernacle
of meeting. 30Then the priest shall offer the one *as* a
sin offering and the other *as* a burnt offering, and the
priest shall make atonement for her before the LORD
for the discharge of her uncleanness.

31'Thus you shall separate the children of Israel
from their uncleanness, lest they die in their uncleanness when they defile My tabernacle that *is* among
them. 32This *is* the law for one who has a discharge,
and *for him* who emits semen and is unclean thereby,
33and for her who is indisposed because of her *cus-*
tomary impurity, and for one who has a discharge, either man or woman, and for him who lies with her
who is unclean.' "

The Day of Atonement

16 Now the LORD spoke to Moses after the death of
the two sons of Aaron, when they offered *pro-*
fane fire before the LORD, and died; 2and the LORD said
to Moses: "Tell Aaron your brother not to come at *just*
any time into the Holy *Place* inside the veil, before the
mercy seat which *is* on the ark, lest he die; for I will appear in the cloud above the mercy seat.

3"Thus Aaron shall come into the Holy *Place:* with
the blood of a young bull as a sin offering, and *of* a ram
as a burnt offering. 4He shall put the holy linen tunic
and the linen trousers on his body; he shall be girded

with a linen sash, and with the linen turban he shall be attired. These *are*
holy garments. Therefore he shall wash his body in water, and put them
on. 5And he shall take from the congregation of the children of Israel two
kids of the goats as a sin offering, and one ram as a burnt offering.
6"Aaron shall offer the bull as a sin offering, which *is* for himself, and
make atonement for himself and for his house. 7He shall take the two goats
and present them before the LORD *at* the door of the tabernacle of meeting.
8Then Aaron shall cast lots for the two goats: one lot for the LORD and the
other lot for the scapegoat. 9And Aaron shall bring the goat on which the
LORD's lot fell, and offer it *as* a sin offering. 10But the goat on which the lot fell
to be the scapegoat shall be presented alive before the LORD, to make atonement upon it, *and* to let it go as the scapegoat into the wilderness.
11"And Aaron shall bring the bull of the sin offering, which is for himself, and make atonement for himself and for his house, and shall kill the
bull as the sin offering which *is* for himself. 12Then he shall take a censer
full of burning coals of fire from the altar before the LORD, with his hands
full of sweet incense beaten fine, and bring *it* inside the veil. 13And he shall
put the incense on the fire before the LORD, that the cloud of incense may
cover the mercy seat that *is* on the Testimony, lest he die. 14He shall take
some of the blood of the bull and sprinkle *it* with his finger on the mercy
seat on the east *side;* and before the mercy seat he shall sprinkle some of
the blood with his finger seven times.
15"Then he shall kill the goat of the sin offering, which *is* for the people,
bring its blood inside the veil, do with that blood as he did with the blood
of the bull, and sprinkle it on the mercy seat and before the mercy seat.
16So he shall make atonement for the Holy *Place,* because of the uncleanness of the children of Israel, and because of their transgressions, for all
their sins; and so he shall do for the tabernacle of meeting which remains
among them in the midst of their uncleanness. 17There shall be no man in
the tabernacle of meeting when he goes in to make atonement in the Holy
Place, until he comes out, that he may make atonement for himself, for his
household, and for all the assembly of Israel. 18And he shall go out to the
altar that *is* before the LORD, and make atonement for it, and shall take
some of the blood of the bull and some of the blood of the goat, and put it
on the horns of the altar all around. 19Then he shall sprinkle some of the
blood on it with his finger seven times, cleanse it, and consecrate it from
the uncleanness of the children of Israel.
20"And when he has made an end of atoning for the Holy *Place,* the
tabernacle of meeting, and the altar, he shall bring the live goat. 21Aaron
shall lay both his hands on the head of the live goat, confess over it all the
iniquities of the children of Israel, and all their transgressions, concerning
all their sins, putting them on the head of the goat, and shall send *it* away
into the wilderness by the hand of a suitable man. 22The goat shall bear on
itself all their iniquities to an uninhabited land; and he shall release the
goat in the wilderness.
23"Then Aaron shall come into the tabernacle of meeting, shall take off
the linen garments which he put on when he went into the Holy *Place,* and
shall leave them there. 24And he shall wash his body with water in a holy
place, put on his garments, come out and offer his burnt offering and the
burnt offering of the people, and make atonement for himself and for the
people. 25The fat of the sin offering he shall burn on the altar. 26And he who

LIFE LESSON

Leviticus 16:1–17:16

SITUATION The Day of Atonement was the holiest day for the Israelites. God's strict guidelines showed the priests and people how to stay faithful to God while living among pagans.

OBSERVATION We must be holy in order to have a relationship with a holy God. Sin cannot have a hold on us. Sin cannot stand in the presence of God.

INSPIRATION In the Old Testament, worship centered around the altar with the presentations of sacrifices offered to God. For the most part these sacrifices of animals and various grains were made as sin offerings. In themselves the animal sacrifices had no power to atone for sins. They were symbols that pointed forward to the one great sacrifice that would be made on the cross. After the perfect Lamb was slain, the altar sacrifices ceased. The Christian church has no provision for animal sacrifices anymore because it has no need for such sacrifices. To offer them now would be to insult the perfection of the sacrifice of Christ. Because the days of animal sacrifices are over, many assume that all sacrifices offered to God are abhorrent to Him. This is simply not true. . . . We are to sacrifice not our grains or our animals, but we are to give ourselves to God. This new sacrifice is not an act of atonement; neither is it a sin offering. The sacrifice of our bodies to God is a thank offering.

(*The Holiness of God* by R. C. Sproul)

APPLICATION What value would a sacrifice have if it cost us little or could be of inferior quality? The greatest sacrifice possible has been made for you. How highly do you value it? Thank God for this sacrifice and live differently today because you are thankful.

EXPLORATION Blood and Atonement—Exodus 12:1-13; Leviticus 9:7; Matthew 26:28; Acts 20:28; Romans 3:24-25; Ephesians 1:7; Hebrews 9:22; 13:12.

released the goat as the scapegoat shall wash his clothes
and bathe his body in water, and afterward he may come
into the camp. [27]The bull *for* the sin offering and the goat
for the sin offering, whose blood was brought in to make
atonement in the Holy *Place*, shall be carried outside the
camp. And they shall burn in the fire their skins, their
flesh, and their offal. [28]Then he who burns them shall
wash his clothes and bathe his body in water, and afterward he may come into the camp.

[29]"*This* shall be a statute forever for you: In the seventh month, on the tenth *day* of the month, you shall
afflict your souls, and do no work at all, *whether* a native of your own country or a stranger who dwells
among you. [30]For on that day *the priest* shall make
atonement for you, to cleanse you, *that* you may be
clean from all your sins before the LORD. [31]It *is* a sabbath
of solemn rest for you, and you shall afflict your souls.
It is a statute forever. [32]And the priest, who is anointed
and consecrated to minister as priest in his father's
place, shall make atonement, and put on the linen
clothes, the holy garments; [33]then he shall make atonement for the Holy Sanctuary,[j] and he shall make
atonement for the tabernacle of meeting and for the
altar, and he shall make atonement for the priests and
for all the people of the assembly. [34]This shall be an
everlasting statute for you, to make atonement for the
children of Israel, for all their sins, once a year." And
he did as the LORD commanded Moses.

The Sanctity of Blood

17 And the LORD spoke to Moses, saying, [2]"Speak
to Aaron, to his sons, and to all the children of
Israel, and say to them, 'This *is* the thing which the
LORD has commanded, saying: [3]"Whatever man of the
house of Israel who kills an ox or lamb or goat in the
camp, or who kills *it* outside the camp, [4]and does not
bring it to the door of the tabernacle of meeting to offer
an offering to the LORD before the tabernacle of the
LORD, the guilt of bloodshed shall be imputed to that
man. He has shed blood; and that man shall be cut off
from among his people, [5]to the end that the children of
Israel may bring their sacrifices which they offer in the
open field, that they may bring them to the LORD at the
door of the tabernacle of meeting, to the priest, and
offer them *as* peace offerings to the LORD. [6]And the
priest shall sprinkle the blood on the altar of the LORD *at*
the door of the tabernacle of meeting, and burn the fat
for a sweet aroma to the LORD. [7]They shall no more offer
their sacrifices to demons, after whom they have
played the harlot. This shall be a statute forever for
them throughout their generations." '

[8]"Also you shall say to them: 'Whatever man of the
house of Israel, or of the strangers who dwell among
you, who offers a burnt offering or sacrifice, [9]and
does not bring it to the door of the tabernacle of meeting, to offer it to the LORD, that man shall be cut off
from among his people.

[10]'And whatever man of the house of Israel, or of
the strangers who dwell among you, who eats any
blood, I will set My face against that person who eats
blood, and will cut him off from among his people.
[11]For the life of the flesh *is* in the blood, and I have
given it to you upon the altar to make atonement for
your souls; for it *is* the blood *that* makes atonement
for the soul.' [12]Therefore I said to the children of Israel, 'No one among you shall eat blood, nor shall any
stranger who dwells among you eat blood.'

[13]"Whatever man of the children of Israel, or of the
strangers who dwell among you, who hunts and
catches any animal or bird that may be eaten, he shall
pour out its blood and cover it with dust; [14]for *it is* the
life of all flesh. Its blood sustains its life. Therefore I
said to the children of Israel, 'You shall not eat the
blood of any flesh, for the life of all flesh is its blood.
Whoever eats it shall be cut off.'

[15]"And every person who eats what died *naturally* or
what was torn *by beasts, whether he is* a native of your
own country or a stranger, he shall both wash his clothes
and bathe in water, and be unclean until evening. Then
he shall be clean. [16]But if he does not wash *them* or bathe
his body, then he shall bear his guilt."

Laws of Sexual Morality

18 Then the LORD spoke to Moses, saying, [2]"Speak
to the children of Israel, and say to them: 'I am
the LORD your God. [3]According to the doings of the
land of Egypt, where you dwelt, you shall not do; and
according to the doings of the land of Canaan, where I
am bringing you, you shall not do; nor shall you walk
in their ordinances. [4]You shall observe My judgments
and keep My ordinances, to walk in them: I *am* the
LORD your God. [5]You shall therefore keep My statutes
and My judgments, which if a man does, he shall live
by them: I *am* the LORD.

[6]'None of you shall approach anyone who is near of
kin to him, to uncover his nakedness: I *am* the LORD.
[7]The nakedness of your father or the nakedness of
your mother you shall not uncover. She *is* your

16:33 *j* That is, the Most Holy Place

mother; you shall not uncover her nakedness. 8The nakedness of your father's wife you shall not uncover; it *is* your father's nakedness. 9The nakedness of your sister, the daughter of your father, or the daughter of your
mother, *whether* born at home or elsewhere, their nakedness you shall not
uncover. 10The nakedness of your son's daughter or your daughter's
daughter, their nakedness you shall not uncover; for theirs *is* your own
nakedness. 11The nakedness of your father's wife's daughter, begotten by
your father—she *is* your sister—you shall not uncover her nakedness.
12You shall not uncover the nakedness of your father's sister; she *is* near of
kin to your father. 13You shall not uncover the nakedness of your mother's
sister, for she *is* near of kin to your mother. 14You shall not uncover the
nakedness of your father's brother. You shall not approach his wife; she *is*
your aunt. 15You shall not uncover the nakedness of your daughter-in-
law—she *is* your son's wife—you shall not uncover her nakedness. 16You
shall not uncover the nakedness of your brother's wife; it *is* your brother's
nakedness. 17You shall not uncover the nakedness of a woman and her
daughter, nor shall you take her son's daughter or her daughter's daughter, to uncover her nakedness. They *are* near of kin to her. It *is* wickedness.
18Nor shall you take a woman as a rival to her sister, to uncover her nakedness while the other is alive.

19'Also you shall not approach a woman to uncover her nakedness as
long as she is in her *customary* impurity. 20Moreover you shall not lie carnally with your neighbor's wife, to defile yourself with her. 21And you shall
not let any of your descendants pass through *the fire* to Molech, nor shall
you profane the name of your God: I *am* the LORD. 22You shall not lie with a
male as with a woman. It *is* an abomination. 23Nor shall you mate with any
animal, to defile yourself with it. Nor shall any woman stand before an animal to mate with it. It *is* perversion.

24'Do not defile yourselves with any of these things; for by all these the
nations are defiled, which I am casting out before you. 25For the land is defiled; therefore I visit the punishment of its iniquity upon it, and the land
vomits out its inhabitants. 26You shall therefore keep My statutes and My
judgments, and shall not commit *any* of these abominations, *either* any of
your own nation or any stranger who dwells among you 27(for all these
abominations the men of the land have done, who *were* before you, and
thus the land is defiled), 28lest the land vomit you out also when you defile
it, as it vomited out the nations that *were* before you. 29For whoever commits any of these abominations, the persons who commit *them* shall be
cut off from among their people.

30'Therefore you shall keep My ordinance, so that *you* do not commit
any of these abominable customs which were committed before you, and
that you do not defile yourselves by them: I *am* the LORD your God.' "

Moral and Ceremonial Laws

19 And the LORD spoke to Moses, saying, 2"Speak to all the congregation
of the children of Israel, and say to them: 'You shall be holy, for I the
LORD your God *am* holy.

3'Every one of you shall revere his mother and his father, and keep My
Sabbaths: I *am* the LORD your God.

4'Do not turn to idols, nor make for yourselves molded gods: I *am* the
LORD your God.

LIFE LESSON

Leviticus 18:1–20:27

SITUATION God was leading the Israelites from one pagan culture (Egypt) to another (Canaan). God wanted the people to follow his guidelines for sexual practices. He wanted them to abhor the sexual sins of the pagan cultures.

OBSERVATION To obey God means fulfilling our sexual desires only with our spouse, as God intends.

INSPIRATION Perhaps it is clear to you already that the strongest protection a marriage can have against adultery is in the *attitude* of the partners toward the marriage and toward each other. No one—absolutely no one, male or female—who has vowed faithfulness to another human deserves sexual satisfaction outside the marriage bond. Yet self-centered adulterers have justified their sin by the premise that sexual satisfaction is somehow their right—because God made them this way and they can't help it; because the world makes so much of sexual experience; because they don't receive enough "loving" from their spouses.

But in fact, the marriage vow subordinates one's individual satisfactions in all areas to one's marital partner—declaring publicly that sex is less important than one's spouse, less important than the health of the relationship. Sexual satisfaction is no longer a right, but a *blessing*, a gift of the relationship *to* its partners. This attitude, then—that the health of the relationship is infinitely more important than one's own desires, and that the sweet fulfillment of one's desires is an undeserved bounty within that

5'And if you offer a sacrifice of a peace offering to the LORD, you shall
offer it of your own free will. 6It shall be eaten the same day you offer *it*,
and on the next day. And if any remains until the third day, it shall be
burned in the fire. 7And if it is eaten at all on the third day, it *is* an
abomination. It shall not be accepted. 8Therefore *everyone* who eats it shall
bear his iniquity, because he has profaned the hallowed *offering* of the
LORD; and that person shall be cut off from his people.
9'When you reap the harvest of your land, you shall not wholly reap the
corners of your field, nor shall you gather the gleanings of your harvest.
10And you shall not glean your vineyard, nor shall you gather *every* grape
of your vineyard; you shall leave them for the poor and the stranger: I *am*
the LORD your God.
11'You shall not steal, nor deal falsely, nor lie to one another. 12And you
shall not swear by My name falsely, nor shall you profane the name of your
God: I *am* the LORD.
13'You shall not cheat your neighbor, nor rob *him*. The wages of him who
is hired shall not remain with you all night until morning. 14You shall not
curse the deaf, nor put a stumbling block before the blind, but shall fear
your God: I *am* the LORD.
15'You shall do no injustice in judgment. You shall not be partial to the
poor, nor honor the person of the mighty. In righteousness you shall judge
your neighbor. 16You shall not go about *as* a talebearer among your people;
nor shall you take a stand against the life of your neighbor: I *am* the LORD.
17'You shall not hate your brother in your heart. You shall surely rebuke
your neighbor, and not bear sin because of him. 18You shall not take
vengeance, nor bear any grudge against the children of your people, but
you shall love your neighbor as yourself: I *am* the LORD.
19'You shall keep My statutes. You shall not let your livestock breed with
another kind. You shall not sow your field with mixed seed. Nor shall a
garment of mixed linen and wool come upon you.
20'Whoever lies carnally with a woman who *is* betrothed to a man as a
concubine, and who has not at all been redeemed nor given her freedom,
for this there shall be scourging; *but* they shall not be put to death, because
she was not free. 21And he shall bring his trespass offering to the LORD, to
the door of the tabernacle of meeting, a ram as a trespass offering. 22The
priest shall make atonement for him with the ram of the trespass offering
before the LORD for his sin which he has committed. And the sin which he
has committed shall be forgiven him.
23'When you come into the land, and have planted all kinds of trees for
food, then you shall count their fruit as uncircumcised. Three years it shall
be as uncircumcised to you. *It* shall not be eaten. 24But in the fourth year all
its fruit shall be holy, a praise to the LORD. 25And in the fifth year you may eat
its fruit, that it may yield to you its increase: I *am* the LORD your God.
26'You shall not eat *anything* with the blood, nor shall you practice divination or soothsaying. 27You shall not shave around the sides of your head, nor
shall you disfigure the edges of your beard. 28You shall not make any cuttings in your flesh for the dead, nor tattoo any marks on you: I *am* the LORD.
29'Do not prostitute your daughter, to cause her to be a harlot, lest the
land fall into harlotry, and the land become full of wickedness.
30'You shall keep My Sabbaths and reverence My sanctuary: I *am* the LORD.
31'Give no regard to mediums and familiar spirits; do not seek after

relationship—not only closes the door to adulteries, but abolishes the door and the thought altogether.

He who worships anything of himself is a candidate for extra-marital sex. His marriage is vulnerable. His desires have become his privileges. So long as he is his own god, he feels himself free to obey nothing and no one *but* himself.

But he who takes seriously his declared commitment to the mutual relationship with his spouse, will guard the marriage even against the assaults of his own desires. His attitude sensitizes him, making him careful, wary, and aware. He will be able to identify as threats those desires that are purely personal and merely self-satisfying. He will recognize them already when they are weak and small, before they grow monstrous and demanding; and then he will not nurse them to size, but, while he can, cut them off and quench them.

(From *As for Me and My House* by Walter Wangerin, Jr.)

APPLICATION The world promotes sex without restrictions as the key to happiness. Avoid that lie. Eliminate its deceitful influence. Build solid friendships and an active social life on a foundation of sexual purity. If you are married, renew your commitment to your spouse.

EXPLORATION Sexual Purity—Exodus 20:14; Deuteronomy 23:17; Proverbs 23:26-28; Romans 13:13-14; 1 Corinthians 6:15-20; 1 Thessalonians 4:3-5.

them, to be defiled by them: I *am* the LORD your God.
32‘You shall rise before the gray headed and honor
the presence of an old man, and fear your God: I *am*
the LORD.
33‘And if a stranger dwells with you in your land,
you shall not mistreat him. 34The stranger who dwells
among you shall be to you as one born among you,
and you shall love him as yourself; for you were strangers in the land of Egypt: I *am* the LORD your God.
35‘You shall do no injustice in judgment, in mea-
surement of length, weight, or volume. 36You shall
have honest scales, honest weights, an honest ephah,
and an honest hin: I *am* the LORD your God, who
brought you out of the land of Egypt.
37‘Therefore you shall observe all My statutes and all
My judgments, and perform them: I *am* the LORD.’ ”

Penalties for Breaking the Law

20 Then the LORD spoke to Moses, saying,
2“Again, you shall say to the children of Israel:
‘Whoever of the children of Israel, or of the strangers
who dwell in Israel, who gives *any* of his descendants
to Molech, he shall surely be put to death. The people
of the land shall stone him with stones. 3I will set My
face against that man, and will cut him off from his
people, because he has given *some* of his descendants
to Molech, to defile My sanctuary and profane My
holy name. 4And if the people of the land should in
any way hide their eyes from the man, when he gives
some of his descendants to Molech, and they do not
kill him, 5then I will set My face against that man and
against his family; and I will cut him off from his people, and all who prostitute themselves with him to
commit harlotry with Molech.
6‘And the person who turns to mediums and familiar
spirits, to prostitute himself with them, I will set My face
against that person and cut him off from his people.
7Consecrate yourselves therefore, and be holy, for I *am*
the LORD your God. 8And you shall keep My statutes, and
perform them: I *am* the LORD who sanctifies you.
9‘For everyone who curses his father or his mother
shall surely be put to death. He has cursed his father
or his mother. His blood *shall be* upon him.
10‘The man who commits adultery with *another*
man’s wife, *he* who commits adultery with his neighbor’s wife, the adulterer and the adulteress, shall
surely be put to death. 11The man who lies with his father’s wife has uncovered his father’s nakedness; both
of them shall surely be put to death. Their blood *shall*
be upon them. 12If a man lies with his daughter-in-
law, both of them shall surely be put to death. They
have committed perversion. Their blood *shall be* upon
them. 13If a man lies with a male as he lies with a
woman, both of them have committed an abomination. They shall surely be put to death. Their blood *shall*
be upon them. 14If a man marries a woman and her
mother, it *is* wickedness. They shall be burned with
fire, both he and they, that there may be no wickedness
among you. 15If a man mates with an animal, he shall
surely be put to death, and you shall kill the animal. 16If
a woman approaches any animal and mates with it,
you shall kill the woman and the animal. They shall
surely be put to death. Their blood *is* upon them.
17‘If a man takes his sister, his father’s daughter or
his mother’s daughter, and sees her nakedness and
she sees his nakedness, it *is* a wicked thing. And they
shall be cut off in the sight of their people. He has
uncovered his sister’s nakedness. He shall bear his
guilt. 18If a man lies with a woman during her sickness and uncovers her nakedness, he has exposed her
flow, and she has uncovered the flow of her blood.
Both of them shall be cut off from their people.
19‘You shall not uncover the nakedness of your
mother’s sister nor of your father’s sister, for that
would uncover his near of kin. They shall bear their
guilt. 20If a man lies with his uncle’s wife, he has
uncovered his uncle’s nakedness. They shall bear
their sin; they shall die childless. 21If a man takes his
brother’s wife, it *is* an unclean thing. He has uncovered his brother’s nakedness. They shall be childless.
22‘You shall therefore keep all My statutes and all My
judgments, and perform them, that the land where I
am bringing you to dwell may not vomit you out.
23And you shall not walk in the statutes of the nation
which I am casting out before you; for they commit all
these things, and therefore I abhor them. 24But I have
said to you, “You shall inherit their land, and I will give
it to you to possess, a land flowing with milk and
honey.” I *am* the LORD your God, who has separated
you from the peoples. 25You shall therefore distinguish
between clean animals and unclean, between unclean
birds and clean, and you shall not make yourselves
abominable by beast or by bird, or by any kind of living thing that creeps on the ground, which I have separated from you as unclean. 26And you shall be holy to
Me, for I the LORD *am* holy, and have separated you
from the peoples, that you should be Mine.
27‘A man or a woman who is a medium, or who has
familiar spirits, shall surely be put to death; they shall
stone them with stones. Their blood *shall be* upon
them.’ ”

Regulations for Conduct of Priests

21 And the LORD said to Moses, "Speak to the priests, the sons of
Aaron, and say to them: 'None shall defile himself for the dead
among his people, 2except for his relatives who are nearest to him: his
mother, his father, his son, his daughter, and his brother; 3also his virgin
sister who is near to him, who has had no husband, for her he may defile
himself. 4*Otherwise* he shall not defile himself, *being* a chief man among
his people, to profane himself.
5'They shall not make any bald *place* on their heads, nor shall they
shave the edges of their beards nor make any cuttings in their flesh. 6They
shall be holy to their God and not profane the name of their God, for they
offer the offerings of the LORD made by fire, *and* the bread of their God;
therefore they shall be holy. 7They shall not take a wife *who is* a harlot or a
defiled woman, nor shall they take a woman divorced from her husband;
for *the priest*[k] is holy to his God. 8Therefore you shall consecrate him, for
he offers the bread of your God. He shall be holy to you, for I the LORD,
who sanctify you, *am* holy. 9The daughter of any priest, if she profanes
herself by playing the harlot, she profanes her father. She shall be burned
with fire.
10'*He who is* the high priest among his brethren, on whose head the
anointing oil was poured and who is consecrated to wear the garments,
shall not uncover his head nor tear his clothes; 11nor shall he go near any
dead body, nor defile himself for his father or his mother; 12nor shall he go
out of the sanctuary, nor profane the sanctuary of his God; for the consecration of the anointing oil of his God *is* upon him: I *am* the LORD. 13And he
shall take a wife in her virginity. 14A widow or a divorced woman or a defiled woman *or* a harlot—these he shall not marry; but he shall take a virgin of his own people as wife. 15Nor shall he profane his posterity among
his people, for I the LORD sanctify him.' "
16And the LORD spoke to Moses, saying, 17"Speak to Aaron, saying: 'No
man of your descendants in *succeeding* generations, who has *any* defect,
may approach to offer the bread of his God. 18For any man who has a defect shall not approach: a man blind or lame, who has a marred *face* or any
limb too long, 19a man who has a broken foot or broken hand, 20or is a
hunchback or a dwarf, or *a man* who has a defect in his eye, or eczema or
scab, or is a eunuch. 21No man of the descendants of Aaron the priest, who
has a defect, shall come near to offer the offerings made by fire to the
LORD. He has a defect; he shall not come near to offer the bread of his God.
22He may eat the bread of his God, *both* the most holy and the holy; 23only
he shall not go near the veil or approach the altar, because he has a defect,
lest he profane My sanctuaries; for I the LORD sanctify them.' "
24And Moses told *it* to Aaron and his sons, and to all the children of Israel.

22 Then the LORD spoke to Moses, saying, 2"Speak to Aaron and his
sons, that they separate themselves from the holy things of the children of Israel, and that they do not profane My holy name *by* what they
dedicate to Me: I *am* the LORD. 3Say to them: 'Whoever of all your descendants throughout your generations, who goes near the holy things which
the children of Israel dedicate to the LORD, while he has uncleanness upon
him, that person shall be cut off from My presence: I *am* the LORD.

21:7 [k] Literally *he*

LIFE LESSON

Leviticus 21:1–22:33

SITUATION God gave instructions to Moses about the priesthood and sacrifices, and gave a code of moral principles.

OBSERVATION Those who serve God must be totally dedicated, because he deserves only the best.

INSPIRATION Purity, even purity of heart, is the main thing to be aimed at. We need to be made clean within through the Spirit and the Word, and then we shall be clean without consecration and obedience. Here is a close connection between the affections and the understanding: if we love evil we cannot understand that which is good. If the heart is foul, the eye will be dim. How can those men see a holy God who love unholy things?

What a privilege it is to see God here! A glimpse of Him is Heaven below! In Christ Jesus the pure in heart behold the Father. We see Him, His truth, His love, His purpose, His sovereignty, His covenant character, yea, we see Himself in Christ. But this is only apprehended as sin is kept out of the heart. Only those who aim at godliness can cry, "Mine eyes are ever towards the Lord." The desire of Moses, "I beseech thee, show me thy glory," can only be fulfilled in us as we purify ourselves from all iniquity. We shall "see him as he is"; and "every one that has this hope in him purifieth himself." The enjoyment of present fellowship and the hope of the beatific vision are urgent motives for purity of heart and life. Lord, make us pure in heart, that we may see Thee!

(From *Faith's Checkbook* by Charles H. Spurgeon)

APPLICATION To arrive at holiness we must trust in Jesus Christ, who has become our great sacrifice. Every area of our lives must be placed in subjection to his lordship, every decision made with him taken into account, and every word honoring to him. Believe in him today and so begin the adventure of faith, hope, and love.

EXPLORATION Holiness—Leviticus 20:7-8; Isaiah 6:3; Hebrews 7:26; 1 Peter 1:15-16.

4“Whatever man of the descendants of Aaron, who
is a leper or has a discharge, shall not eat the holy offerings until he is clean. And whoever touches anything made unclean *by* a corpse, or a man who has
had an emission of semen, 5or whoever touches any
creeping thing by which he would be made unclean,
or any person by whom he would become unclean,
whatever his uncleanness may be— 6the person who
has touched any such thing shall be unclean until
evening, and shall not eat the holy *offerings* unless he
washes his body with water. 7And when the sun goes
down he shall be clean; and afterward he may eat the
holy *offerings,* because it *is* his food. 8Whatever dies
naturally or is torn *by beasts* he shall not eat, to defile
himself with it: I *am* the LORD.

9“They shall therefore keep My ordinance, lest they
bear sin for it and die thereby, if they profane it: I the
LORD sanctify them.

10“No outsider shall eat the holy *offering;* one who
dwells with the priest, or a hired servant, shall not eat
the holy thing. 11But if the priest buys a person with
his money, he may eat it; and one who is born in his
house may eat his food. 12If the priest’s daughter is
married to an outsider, she may not eat of the holy offerings. 13But if the priest’s daughter is a widow or divorced, and has no child, and has returned to her
father’s house as in her youth, she may eat her father’s
food; but no outsider shall eat it.

14“And if a man eats the holy *offering* unintentionally, then he shall restore a holy *offering* to the
priest, and add one-fifth to it. 15They shall not profane
the holy *offerings* of the children of Israel, which they
offer to the LORD, 16or allow them to bear the guilt of
trespass when they eat their holy *offerings;* for I the
LORD sanctify them.’ ”

Offerings Accepted and Not Accepted

17And the LORD spoke to Moses, saying, 18“Speak to
Aaron and his sons, and to all the children of Israel,
and say to them: ‘Whatever man of the house of Israel, or of the strangers in Israel, who offers his sacrifice for any of his vows or for any of his freewill
offerings, which they offer to the LORD as a burnt offering— 19*you shall offer* of your own free will a male
without blemish from the cattle, from the sheep, or
from the goats. 20Whatever has a defect, you shall not
offer, for it shall not be acceptable on your behalf.
21And whoever offers a sacrifice of a peace offering to
the LORD, to fulfill *his* vow, or a freewill offering from
the cattle or the sheep, it must be perfect to be accepted; there shall be no defect in it. 22Those *that are*
blind or broken or maimed, or have an ulcer or
eczema or scabs, you shall not offer to the LORD, nor
make an offering by fire of them on the altar to the
LORD. 23Either a bull or a lamb that has any limb too
long or too short you may offer *as* a freewill offering,
but for a vow it shall not be accepted.

24“You shall not offer to the LORD what is bruised or
crushed, or torn or cut; nor shall you make *any offering
of them* in your land. 25Nor from a foreigner’s hand
shall you offer any of these as the bread of your God,
because their corruption *is* in them, *and* defects *are* in
them. They shall not be accepted on your behalf.’ ”

26And the LORD spoke to Moses, saying: 27“When a
bull or a sheep or a goat is born, it shall be seven days
with its mother; and from the eighth day and thereafter
it shall be accepted as an offering made by fire to the
LORD. 28*Whether it is* a cow or ewe, do not kill both her
and her young on the same day. 29And when you offer a
sacrifice of thanksgiving to the LORD, offer *it* of your
own free will. 30On the same day it shall be eaten; you
shall leave none of it until morning: I *am* the LORD.

31“Therefore you shall keep My commandments,
and perform them: I *am* the LORD. 32You shall not profane My holy name, but I will be hallowed among the
children of Israel. I *am* the LORD who sanctifies you,
33who brought you out of the land of Egypt, to be your
God: I *am* the LORD.”

Feasts of the LORD

23 And the LORD spoke to Moses, saying, 2“Speak
to the children of Israel, and say to them: ‘The
feasts of the LORD, which you shall proclaim *to be* holy
convocations, these *are* My feasts.

The Sabbath

3‘Six days shall work be done, but the seventh day *is*
a Sabbath of solemn rest, a holy convocation. You
shall do no work *on it;* it *is* the Sabbath of the LORD in
all your dwellings.

The Passover and Unleavened Bread

4‘These *are* the feasts of the LORD, holy convocations
which you shall proclaim at their appointed times.
5On the fourteenth *day* of the first month at twilight *is*
the LORD’s Passover. 6And on the fifteenth day of the
same month *is* the Feast of Unleavened Bread to the
LORD; seven days you must eat unleavened bread. 7On
the first day you shall have a holy convocation; you
shall do no customary work on it. 8But you shall offer
an offering made by fire to the LORD for seven days.
The seventh day *shall be* a holy convocation; you shall
do no customary work *on it.*’ ”

The Feast of Firstfruits

9And the LORD spoke to Moses, saying, 10"Speak to the children of Israel, and say to them: 'When you come into the land which I give to you, and reap its harvest, then you shall bring a sheaf of the firstfruits of your harvest to the priest. 11He shall wave the sheaf before the LORD, to be accepted on your behalf; on the day after the Sabbath the priest shall wave it. 12And you shall offer on that day, when you wave the sheaf, a male lamb of the first year, without blemish, as a burnt offering to the LORD. 13Its grain offering *shall be* two-tenths *of an ephah* of fine flour mixed with oil, an offering made by fire to the LORD, for a sweet aroma; and its drink offering *shall be* of wine, one-fourth of a hin. 14You shall eat neither bread nor parched grain nor fresh grain until the same day that you have brought an offering to your God; *it shall be* a statute forever throughout your generations in all your dwellings.

The Feast of Weeks

15'And you shall count for yourselves from the day after the Sabbath, from the day that you brought the sheaf of the wave offering: seven Sabbaths shall be completed. 16Count fifty days to the day after the seventh Sabbath; then you shall offer a new grain offering to the LORD. 17You shall bring from your dwellings two wave *loaves* of two-tenths *of an ephah.* They shall be of fine flour; they shall be baked with leaven. *They are* the firstfruits to the LORD. 18And you shall offer with the bread seven lambs of the first year, without blemish, one young bull, and two rams. They shall be *as* a burnt offering to the LORD, with their grain offering and their drink offerings, an offering made by fire for a sweet aroma to the LORD. 19Then you shall sacrifice one kid of the goats as a sin offering, and two male lambs of the first year as a sacrifice of a peace offering. 20The priest shall wave them with the bread of the firstfruits *as* a wave offering before the LORD, with the two lambs. They shall be holy to the LORD for the priest. 21And you shall proclaim on the same day *that* it is a holy convocation to you. You shall do no customary work *on it. It shall be* a statute forever in all your dwellings throughout your generations.

22'When you reap the harvest of your land, you shall not wholly reap the corners of your field when you reap, nor shall you gather any gleaning from your harvest. You shall leave them for the poor and for the stranger: I *am* the LORD your God.' "

The Feast of Trumpets

23Then the LORD spoke to Moses, saying, 24"Speak to the children of Israel, saying: 'In the seventh month, on the first *day* of the month, you shall have a sabbath-*rest,* a memorial of blowing of trumpets, a holy convocation. 25You shall do no customary work *on it;* and you shall offer an offering made by fire to the LORD.' "

The Day of Atonement

26And the LORD spoke to Moses, saying: 27"Also the tenth *day* of this seventh month *shall be* the Day of Atonement. It shall be a holy convocation for you; you shall afflict your souls, and offer an offering made by fire to the LORD. 28And you shall do no work on that same day, for it *is* the Day of

LIFE LESSON

Leviticus 23:1–25:55

SITUATION God established several holidays that symbolized the Israelites' special relationship with him. He also gave rules that governed interpersonal relationships.

OBSERVATION Special holidays remind us of the past. Feasts help renew our commitment. In the New Testament, the celebration of the Lord's Supper reminds us of Christ's sacrificial death on the cross for our sins and calls us to renewed commitment.

INSPIRATION A party was the last thing Mary Magdalene expected as she approached the tomb on that Sunday morning. The last few days had brought nothing to celebrate. The Jews could celebrate—Jesus was out of the way. The soldiers could celebrate—their work was done. But Mary couldn't celebrate. To her the last few days had brought nothing but tragedy. . . .

A gray sky gives way to gold as she walks up the narrow trail. As she rounds the final bend, she gasps. The rock in front of the grave is pushed back.

"Someone took the body." She runs to awaken Peter and John. They rush to see for themselves. She tries to keep up with them but can't.

Peter comes out of the tomb bewildered and John comes out believing, but Mary just sits in front of it weeping. The two men go home and leave her alone with her grief.

But something tells her she is not alone. Maybe she hears a noise. Maybe she hears a whisper. Or maybe she just hears her own heart tell her to take a look for herself.

Whatever the reason, she does. She stoops down, sticks her head into the hewn entrance and waits for her eyes to adjust to the dark.

"Why are you crying?" She sees what looks to be a man, but he's white—radiantly white. He is one of two lights on either end of the vacant slab. Two candles blazing on an altar.

"Why are you crying?" An uncommon question to be asked in a cemetery. In

Continued

fact, the question is rude. That is, unless the questioner knows something the questionee doesn't. . . .

"Why are you crying? Who is it you are looking for?"

He doesn't leave her wondering long, just long enough to remind us that he loves to surprise us. He waits for us to despair of human strength and then intervenes with heavenly. God waits for us to give up and then—surprise!

And listen to the surprise as Mary's name is spoken by a man she loved—a man she had buried.

"Miriam."

God appearing at the strangest of places. . . . "Miriam," he said softly, "surprise!"

Mary was shocked. It's not often you hear your name spoken by an eternal tongue. But when she did, she recognized it. And when she did, she responded correctly. She worshiped him.

The scene had all the elements of a surprise party—secrecy, wide eyes, amazement, gratitude. But this celebration is timid in comparison with the one that is being planned for the future. It will be similar to Mary's but a lot bigger. Many more graves will open. Many more names will be called. Many more knees will bow. And many more seekers will celebrate.

It's going to be some party. I plan to make sure my name is on the guest list. How about you?

(From *Six Hours One Friday* by Max Lucado)

APPLICATION Approach this Sunday as a real holiday. Celebrate it with all your heart. Remember the past. Renew for the future. Jesus is risen! God has conquered death! Be glad.

EXPLORATION Celebrations—Exodus 20:8-11; Numbers 36:4; 1 Corinthians 5:7; 16:8.

Atonement, to make atonement for you before the LORD your God. 29For
any person who is not afflicted *in soul* on that same day shall be cut off
from his people. 30And any person who does any work on that same day,
that person I will destroy from among his people. 31You shall do no manner of work; *it shall be* a statute forever throughout your generations in all
your dwellings. 32It *shall be* to you a sabbath of *solemn* rest, and you shall
afflict your souls; on the ninth *day* of the month at evening, from evening
to evening, you shall celebrate your sabbath."

The Feast of Tabernacles

33Then the LORD spoke to Moses, saying, 34"Speak to the children of Israel,
saying: 'The fifteenth day of this seventh month *shall be* the Feast of
Tabernacles *for* seven days to the LORD. 35On the first day *there shall be* a holy
convocation. You shall do no customary work *on it.* 36*For* seven days you
shall offer an offering made by fire to the LORD. On the eighth day you shall
have a holy convocation, and you shall offer an offering made by fire to the
LORD. It *is* a sacred assembly, *and* you shall do no customary work *on it.*
37'These *are* the feasts of the LORD which you shall proclaim *to be* holy convocations, to offer an offering made by fire to the LORD, a burnt offering and
a grain offering, a sacrifice and drink offerings, everything on its day—
38besides the Sabbaths of the LORD, besides your gifts, besides all your vows,
and besides all your freewill offerings which you give to the LORD.
39'Also on the fifteenth day of the seventh month, when you have gathered in the fruit of the land, you shall keep the feast of the LORD *for* seven
days; on the first day *there shall be* a sabbath-*rest,* and on the eighth day a
sabbath-*rest.* 40And you shall take for yourselves on the first day the fruit of
beautiful trees, branches of palm trees, the boughs of leafy trees, and willows of the brook; and you shall rejoice before the LORD your God for seven
days. 41You shall keep it as a feast to the LORD for seven days in the year. *It
shall be* a statute forever in your generations. You shall celebrate it in the
seventh month. 42You shall dwell in booths for seven days. All who are native Israelites shall dwell in booths, 43that your generations may know that
I made the children of Israel dwell in booths when I brought them out of
the land of Egypt: I *am* the LORD your God.' "
44So Moses declared to the children of Israel the feasts of the LORD.

Care of the Tabernacle Lamps

24 Then the LORD spoke to Moses, saying: 2"Command the children of
Israel that they bring to you pure oil of pressed olives for the light,
to make the lamps burn continually. 3Outside the veil of the Testimony, in
the tabernacle of meeting, Aaron shall be in charge of it from evening until
morning before the LORD continually; *it shall be* a statute forever in your
generations. 4He shall be in charge of the lamps on the pure *gold* lampstand before the LORD continually.

The Bread of the Tabernacle

5"And you shall take fine flour and bake twelve cakes with it. Two-
tenths *of an ephah* shall be in each cake. 6You shall set them in two rows,
six in a row, on the pure *gold* table before the LORD. 7And you shall put pure
frankincense on *each* row, that it may be on the bread for a memorial, an
offering made by fire to the LORD. 8Every Sabbath he shall set it in order be-

fore the LORD continually, *being taken* from the children of Israel by an everlasting covenant. 9And it shall
be for Aaron and his sons, and they shall eat it in a
holy place; for it *is* most holy to him from the offerings of the LORD made by fire, by a perpetual statute."

The Penalty for Blasphemy

10Now the son of an Israelite woman, whose father
was an Egyptian, went out among the children of Israel; and this Israelite *woman's* son and a man of Israel
fought each other in the camp. 11And the Israelite
woman's son blasphemed the name *of the LORD* and
cursed; and so they brought him to Moses. (His
mother's name *was* Shelomith the daughter of Dibri,
of the tribe of Dan.) 12Then they put him in custody,
that the mind of the LORD might be shown to them.
13And the LORD spoke to Moses, saying, 14"Take outside the camp him who has cursed; then let all who
heard *him* lay their hands on his head, and let all the
congregation stone him.
15"Then you shall speak to the children of Israel,
saying: 'Whoever curses his God shall bear his sin.
16And whoever blasphemes the name of the LORD shall
surely be put to death. All the congregation shall certainly stone him, the stranger as well as him who is
born in the land. When he blasphemes the name *of
the LORD*, he shall be put to death.
17'Whoever kills any man shall surely be put to
death. 18Whoever kills an animal shall make it good,
animal for animal.
19'If a man causes disfigurement of his neighbor, as
he has done, so shall it be done to him— 20fracture
for fracture, eye for eye, tooth for tooth; as he has
caused disfigurement of a man, so shall it be done to
him. 21And whoever kills an animal shall restore it;
but whoever kills a man shall be put to death. 22You
shall have the same law for the stranger and for one
from your own country; for I *am* the LORD your God.' "
23Then Moses spoke to the children of Israel; and
they took outside the camp him who had cursed, and
stoned him with stones. So the children of Israel did
as the LORD commanded Moses.

The Sabbath of the Seventh Year

25 And the LORD spoke to Moses on Mount Sinai,
saying, 2"Speak to the children of Israel, and
say to them: 'When you come into the land which I
give you, then the land shall keep a sabbath to the
LORD. 3Six years you shall sow your field, and six years
you shall prune your vineyard, and gather its fruit;
4but in the seventh year there shall be a sabbath of
solemn rest for the land, a sabbath to the LORD. You
shall neither sow your field nor prune your vineyard.
5What grows of its own accord of your harvest you
shall not reap, nor gather the grapes of your untended
vine, *for* it is a year of rest for the land. 6And the sabbath *produce* of the land shall be food for you: for you,
your male and female servants, your hired man, and
the stranger who dwells with you, 7for your livestock
and the beasts that *are* in your land—all its produce
shall be for food.

The Year of Jubilee

8'And you shall count seven sabbaths of years for
yourself, seven times seven years; and the time of the
seven sabbaths of years shall be to you forty-nine
years. 9Then you shall cause the trumpet of the Jubilee
to sound on the tenth *day* of the seventh month; on
the Day of Atonement you shall make the trumpet to
sound throughout all your land. 10And you shall consecrate the fiftieth year, and proclaim liberty throughout *all* the land to all its inhabitants. It shall be a
Jubilee for you; and each of you shall return to his
possession, and each of you shall return to his family.
11That fiftieth year shall be a Jubilee to you; in it you
shall neither sow nor reap what grows of its own accord, nor gather *the grapes* of your untended vine.
12For it *is* the Jubilee; it shall be holy to you; you shall
eat its produce from the field.
13'In this Year of Jubilee, each of you shall return to
his possession. 14And if you sell anything to your
neighbor or buy from your neighbor's hand, you shall
not oppress one another. 15According to the number
of years after the Jubilee you shall buy from your
neighbor, and according to the number of years of
crops he shall sell to you. 16According to the multitude
of years you shall increase its price, and according to
the fewer number of years you shall diminish its
price; for he sells to you *according* to the number *of
the years* of the crops. 17Therefore you shall not oppress one another, but you shall fear your God; for I
am the LORD your God.

Provisions for the Seventh Year

18'So you shall observe My statutes and keep My
judgments, and perform them; and you will dwell in
the land in safety. 19Then the land will yield its fruit,
and you will eat your fill, and dwell there in safety.
20'And if you say, "What shall we eat in the seventh
year, since we shall not sow nor gather in our produce?" 21Then I will command My blessing on you in
the sixth year, and it will bring forth produce enough

for three years. 22And you shall sow in the eighth year,
and eat old produce until the ninth year; until its produce comes in, you shall eat *of* the old *harvest.*

Redemption of Property

23'The land shall not be sold permanently, for the
land *is* Mine; for you *are* strangers and sojourners
with Me. 24And in all the land of your possession you
shall grant redemption of the land.

25'If one of your brethren becomes poor, and has
sold *some* of his possession, and if his redeeming relative comes to redeem it, then he may redeem what
his brother sold. 26Or if the man has no one to redeem
it, but he himself becomes able to redeem it, 27then let
him count the years since its sale, and restore the remainder to the man to whom he sold it, that he may
return to his possession. 28But if he is not able to have
it restored to himself, then what was sold shall remain in the hand of him who bought it until the Year
of Jubilee; and in the Jubilee it shall be released, and
he shall return to his possession.

29'If a man sells a house in a walled city, then he may
redeem it within a whole year after it is sold; *within* a
full year he may redeem it. 30But if it is not redeemed
within the space of a full year, then the house in the
walled city shall belong permanently to him who
bought it, throughout his generations. It shall not be
released in the Jubilee. 31However the houses of villages which have no wall around them shall be
counted as the fields of the country. They may be redeemed, and they shall be released in the Jubilee.
32Nevertheless the cities of the Levites, *and* the houses
in the cities of their possession, the Levites may redeem at any time. 33And if a man purchases a house
from the Levites, then the house that was sold in the
city of his possession shall be released in the Jubilee;
for the houses in the cities of the Levites *are* their possession among the children of Israel. 34But the field of
the common-land of their cities may not be sold, for it
is their perpetual possession.

Lending to the Poor

35'If one of your brethren becomes poor, and falls
into poverty among you, then you shall help him, like
a stranger or a sojourner, that he may live with you.
36Take no usury or interest from him; but fear your
God, that your brother may live with you. 37You shall
not lend him your money for usury, nor lend him
your food at a profit. 38I *am* the LORD your God, who
brought you out of the land of Egypt, to give you the
land of Canaan *and* to be your God.

The Law Concerning Slavery

39'And if *one of* your brethren *who dwells* by you becomes poor, and sells himself to you, you shall not
compel him to serve as a slave. 40As a hired servant
and a sojourner he shall be with you, *and* shall serve
you until the Year of Jubilee. 41And *then* he shall depart from you—he and his children with him—and
shall return to his own family. He shall return to the
possession of his fathers. 42For they *are* My servants,
whom I brought out of the land of Egypt; they shall
not be sold as slaves. 43You shall not rule over him
with rigor, but you shall fear your God. 44And as for
your male and female slaves whom you may have—
from the nations that are around you, from them you
may buy male and female slaves. 45Moreover you may
buy the children of the strangers who dwell among
you, and their families who are with you, which they
beget in your land; and they shall become your property. 46And you may take them as an inheritance for
your children after you, to inherit *them as* a possession; they shall be your permanent slaves. But regarding your brethren, the children of Israel, you shall not
rule over one another with rigor.

47'Now if a sojourner or stranger close to you becomes rich, and *one of* your brethren *who dwells* by
him becomes poor, and sells himself to the stranger
or sojourner close to you, or to a member of the stranger's family, 48after he is sold he may be redeemed
again. One of his brothers may redeem him; 49or his
uncle or his uncle's son may redeem him; or *anyone*
who is near of kin to him in his family may redeem
him; or if he is able he may redeem himself. 50Thus he
shall reckon with him who bought him: The price of
his release shall be according to the number of years,
from the year that he was sold to him until the Year of
Jubilee; *it shall be* according to the time of a hired servant for him. 51If *there are* still many years *remaining,*
according to them he shall repay the price of his redemption from the money with which he was bought.
52And if there remain but a few years until the Year of
Jubilee, then he shall reckon with him, *and* according
to his years he shall repay him the price of his redemption. 53He shall be with him as a yearly hired servant,
and he shall not rule with rigor over him in your sight.
54And if he is not redeemed in these *years,* then he
shall be released in the Year of Jubilee—he and his
children with him. 55For the children of Israel *are* servants to Me; they *are* My servants whom I brought out
of the land of Egypt: I *am* the LORD your God.

Promise of Blessing and Retribution

26 'You shall not make idols for yourselves;
neither a carved image nor a *sacred* pillar shall you
rear up for yourselves;
nor shall you set up an engraved stone in your land,
to bow down to it;
for I *am* the LORD your God.
2 You shall keep My Sabbaths and reverence My sanctuary:
I *am* the LORD.

3 'If you walk in My statutes and keep My commandments,
and perform them,
4 then I will give you rain in its season, the land shall yield its
produce, and the trees of the field shall yield their fruit.
5 Your threshing shall last till the time of vintage,
and the vintage shall last till the time of sowing;
you shall eat your bread to the full, and dwell in your land safely.
6 I will give peace in the land, and you shall lie down,
and none will make *you* afraid;
I will rid the land of evil beasts,
and the sword will not go through your land.
7 You will chase your enemies, and they shall
fall by the sword before you.
8 Five of you shall chase a hundred, and a hundred of you
shall put ten thousand to flight;
your enemies shall fall by the sword before you.

9 'For I will look on you favorably and make you fruitful, multiply you
and confirm My covenant with you.
10 You shall eat the old harvest, and clear out
the old because of the new.
11 I will set My tabernacle among you, and My
soul shall not abhor you.
12 I will walk among you and be your God, and you shall be My people.
13 I *am* the LORD your God, who brought you out of the land of Egypt,
that *you* should not be their slaves;
I have broken the bands of your yoke and made you walk upright.

14 'But if you do not obey Me, and do not
observe all these commandments,
15 and if you despise My statutes, or if your soul abhors
My judgments, so that you do not perform all
My commandments, *but* break My covenant,
16 I also will do this to you:
I will even appoint terror over you, wasting disease and fever which
shall consume the eyes and cause sorrow of heart.
And you shall sow your seed in vain, for your enemies shall eat it.
17 I will set My face against you, and you shall be
defeated by your enemies.

Life Lesson

Leviticus 26:1–27:34

SITUATION God, through Moses, presented blessings as a reward for obedience and cursings as a punishment for habitual sin. This led the people to confess and reiterate their devotion to God with vows and tithes.

OBSERVATION God sets boundaries for our own good. We suffer when we break them. We must respond to his love so that we will not have to face his discipline.

INSPIRATION I once owned a ewe. . . . She was one of the most attractive sheep that ever belonged to me. Her body was beautifully proportioned. She had a strong constitution and an excellent coat of wool. Her head was clean, alert, well-set with bright eyes. She bore sturdy lambs that matured rapidly.

But in spite of all these attributes, she had one pronounced fault. She was restless—discontented—a fence crawler.

So much so that I came to call her "Mrs. Gad-about."

This one ewe produced more problems for me than almost all the rest of the flock combined.

No matter what field or pasture the sheep were in, she would search all along the fences or shoreline (we lived by the sea) looking for a loophole she could crawl through and start to feed on the other side.

It was not that she lacked pasturage. My fields were my joy and delight. No sheep in the district had better grazing.

With "Mrs. Gad-about" it was an ingrained habit. She was simply never contented with things as they were. Often when she had forced her way through some such spot in a fence or found a way around the end of the wire at low tide on the beaches, she would end up feeding on bare, brown, burned-up pasturage of a most inferior sort.

But she never learned her lesson and continued to fence crawl time after time.

Now it would have been bad enough if she was the only one who did this.

Continued

It was a sufficient problem to find her and bring her back. But the further point was that she taught her lambs the same tricks. They simply followed her example and soon were as skilled at escaping as their mother.

Even worse, however, was the example she set for other sheep. In a short time she began to lead others over the same holes and over the same dangerous paths down by the sea.

After putting up with her perverseness for a summer I finally came to the conclusion that to save the rest of the flock from becoming unsettled, she would have to go. I could not allow one obstinate, discontented ewe to ruin the whole ranch operation.

It was a difficult decision to make, for I loved her in the same way I loved the rest. Her strength and beauty and alertness were a delight to the eye.

But one morning I took the killing knife in hand and butchered her. Her career of fence crawling was cut short. It was the only solution to the dilemma.

She was a sheep, who in spite of all that I had done to give her the very best care—still wanted something else.

(From *A Shepherd Looks at Psalm 23* by Phillip Keller)

APPLICATION Consider all that God has done for you in redeeming you from sin's captivity and providing you with blessing. In what areas do you overstep God's boundaries? Consider the consequences. Stop in your tracks. Flee from tempting circumstances. Return to the Lord, the Good Shepherd.

EXPLORATION On Blessing and Cursing—Deuteronomy 11; Ezekiel 14:12-21.

Those who hate you shall reign over you, and you shall flee
when no one pursues you.

18 'And after all this, if you do not obey Me, then I will punish you
seven times more for your sins.
19 I will break the pride of your power;
I will make your heavens like iron and your earth like bronze.
20 And your strength shall be spent in vain;
for your land shall not yield its produce, nor shall the trees of the
land yield their fruit.

21 'Then, if you walk contrary to Me, and are not willing to obey Me, I
will bring on you seven times more plagues,
according to your sins.
22 I will also send wild beasts among you, which shall rob you of
your children, destroy your livestock,
and make you few in number;
and your highways shall be desolate.

23 'And if by these things you are not reformed by Me,
but walk contrary to Me,
24 then I also will walk contrary to you, and I will punish you
yet seven times for your sins.
25 And I will bring a sword against you that will execute
the vengeance of the covenant;
when you are gathered together within your cities
I will send pestilence among you;
and you shall be delivered into the hand of the enemy.
26 When I have cut off your supply of bread, ten women shall bake
your bread in one oven, and they shall bring back your bread by
weight, and you shall eat and not be satisfied.

27 'And after all this, if you do not obey Me, but walk contrary to Me,
28 then I also will walk contrary to you in fury;
and I, even I, will chastise you seven times for your sins.
29 You shall eat the flesh of your sons, and you shall eat
the flesh of your daughters.
30 I will destroy your high places, cut down your incense altars, and
cast your carcasses on the lifeless forms of your idols;
and My soul shall abhor you.
31 I will lay your cities waste and bring your sanctuaries to desolation,
and I will not smell the fragrance of your sweet aromas.
32 I will bring the land to desolation, and your enemies who dwell in it
shall be astonished at it.
33 I will scatter you among the nations and draw out a sword after you;
your land shall be desolate and your cities waste.
34 Then the land shall enjoy its sabbaths as long as it lies desolate and
you *are* in your enemies' land;
then the land shall rest and enjoy its sabbaths.
35 As long as *it* lies desolate it shall rest—
for the time it did not rest on your sabbaths when you dwelt in it.

36 'And as for those of you who are left, I will send
faintness into their hearts in the lands of
their enemies;
the sound of a shaken leaf shall cause them
to flee;
they shall flee as though fleeing from a sword,
and they shall fall when no one pursues.
37 They shall stumble over one another, as it were
before a sword, when no one pursues;
and you shall have no *power* to stand before
your enemies.
38 You shall perish among the nations, and the
land of your enemies shall eat you up.
39 And those of you who are left shall waste away
in their iniquity in your enemies' lands;
also in their fathers' iniquities, which are with
them, they shall waste away.

40 '*But* if they confess their iniquity and the iniquity of their fathers, with their unfaithfulness in which they were unfaithful to Me,
and that they also have walked contrary
to Me,
41 and *that* I also have walked contrary to them
and have brought them into the land of
their enemies;
if their uncircumcised hearts are humbled,
and they accept their guilt—
42 then I will remember My covenant with Jacob,
and My covenant with Isaac and My
covenant with Abraham I will remember;
I will remember the land.
43 The land also shall be left empty by them, and
will enjoy its sabbaths while it lies desolate
without them;
they will accept their guilt, because they despised My judgments and because their
soul abhorred My statutes.
44 Yet for all that, when they are in the land of
their enemies, I will not cast them away,
nor shall I abhor them, to utterly destroy
them and break My covenant with them;
for I *am* the LORD their God.
45 But for their sake I will remember the
covenant of their ancestors, whom I
brought out of the land of Egypt in the sight
of the nations, that I might be their God:
I *am* the LORD.' "

46 These *are* the statutes and judgments and laws
which the LORD made between Himself and the children of Israel on Mount Sinai by the hand of Moses.

Redeeming Persons and Property Dedicated to God

27 Now the LORD spoke to Moses, saying, 2 "Speak
to the children of Israel, and say to them:
'When a man consecrates by a vow certain persons to
the LORD, according to your valuation, 3 if your valuation is of a male from twenty years old up to sixty
years old, then your valuation shall be fifty shekels of
silver, according to the shekel of the sanctuary. 4 If it *is*
a female, then your valuation shall be thirty shekels;
5 and if from five years old up to twenty years old, then
your valuation for a male shall be twenty shekels, and
for a female ten shekels; 6 and if from a month old up
to five years old, then your valuation for a male shall
be five shekels of silver, and for a female your valuation shall be three shekels of silver; 7 and if from sixty
years old and above, if *it is* a male, then your valuation
shall be fifteen shekels, and for a female ten shekels.
8 'But if he is too poor to pay your valuation, then he
shall present himself before the priest, and the priest
shall set a value for him; according to the ability of
him who vowed, the priest shall value him.
9 'If *it is* an animal that men may bring as an offering to the LORD, all that *anyone* gives to the LORD shall
be holy. 10 He shall not substitute it or exchange it,
good for bad or bad for good; and if he at all exchanges animal for animal, then both it and the one
exchanged for it shall be holy. 11 If *it is* an unclean animal which they do not offer as a sacrifice to the LORD,
then he shall present the animal before the priest;
12 and the priest shall set a value for it, whether it is
good or bad; as you, the priest, value it, so it shall be.
13 But if he *wants* at all *to* redeem it, then he must add
one-fifth to your valuation.
14 'And when a man dedicates his house *to be* holy to
the LORD, then the priest shall set a value for it,
whether it is good or bad; as the priest values it, so it
shall stand. 15 If he who dedicated it *wants to* redeem
his house, then he must add one-fifth of the money of
your valuation to it, and it shall be his.
16 'If a man dedicates to the LORD *part* of a field of his
possession, then your valuation shall be according to
the seed for it. A homer of barley seed *shall be valued*
at fifty shekels of silver. 17 If he dedicates his field from
the Year of Jubilee, according to your valuation it shall
stand. 18 But if he dedicates his field after the Jubilee,
then the priest shall reckon to him the money due according to the years that remain till the Year of Jubilee,
and it shall be deducted from your valuation. 19 And if
he who dedicates the field ever wishes to redeem it,

then he must add one-fifth of the money of your valuation to it, and it shall belong to him. [20]But if he does not want to redeem the field, or if he has sold the field to another man, it shall not be redeemed anymore; [21]but the field, when it is released in the Jubilee, shall be holy to the LORD, as a devoted field; it shall be the possession of the priest.

[22]'And if a man dedicates to the LORD a field which he has bought, which is not the field of his possession, [23]then the priest shall reckon to him the worth of your valuation, up to the Year of Jubilee, and he shall give your valuation on that day *as* a holy *offering* to the LORD. [24]In the Year of Jubilee the field shall return to him from whom it was bought, to the one who *owned* the land as a possession. [25]And all your valuations shall be according to the shekel of the sanctuary: twenty gerahs to the shekel.

[26]'But the firstborn of the animals, which should be the LORD's firstborn, no man shall dedicate; whether *it is* an ox or sheep, it *is* the LORD's. [27]And if *it is* an unclean animal, then he shall redeem *it* according to your valuation, and shall add one-fifth to it; or if it is not redeemed, then it shall be sold according to your valuation.

[28]'Nevertheless no devoted *offering* that a man may devote to the LORD of all that he has, *both* man and beast, or the field of his possession, shall be sold or redeemed; every devoted *offering is* most holy to the LORD. [29]No person under the ban, who may become doomed to destruction among men, shall be redeemed, *but* shall surely be put to death. [30]And all the tithe of the land, *whether* of the seed of the land *or* of the fruit of the tree, *is* the LORD's. It *is* holy to the LORD. [31]If a man wants at all to redeem *any* of his tithes, he shall add one-fifth to it. [32]And concerning the tithe of the herd or the flock, of whatever passes under the rod, the tenth one shall be holy to the LORD. [33]He shall not inquire whether it is good or bad, nor shall he exchange it; and if he exchanges it at all, then both it and the one exchanged for it shall be holy; it shall not be redeemed.' "

[34]These *are* the commandments which the LORD commanded Moses for the children of Israel on Mount Sinai.

The Fourth Book of Moses Called

NUMBERS

INTRODUCTION

Every life is a pilgrimage.

Every person is on a journey.

Every journey has its challenges.

The Book of Numbers is a travel diary. Two million ex-slaves weaving their way through a desert. The trip from Egypt to the promised land can be made in nine days (Deuteronomy 1:2). It took the Israelites thirty-eight years.

What they should have done, they didn't. And what they didn't do, they should have. So God decided they needed some time to rethink a few things.

He took them the long way.

Maybe you're on a detour in your journey. Things seem slow. Road seems dark. Maybe God is wanting to teach you a few things. Pay attention.

You don't want to spend thirty-eight years missing the point.

LIFE LESSON

Numbers 1:1–2:34

SITUATION God directed Moses and others to take a census of the Israelites and to organize the tribes for specific duties.

OBSERVATION Moses counted all of God's people and assigned certain people to lead in worship. Each role helped to shape the community.

INSPIRATION Jonathan Edwards was one man who made a difference. Born in 1703, he was perhaps the most brilliant mind America ever produced. A pastor, writer, and later, president of Princeton, he and his wife had eleven children. Of his known male descendants:

More than 300 became pastors, missionaries, or theological professors;

120 were professors at various universities;

110 became attorneys;

60 were prominent authors;

30 were judges;

14 served as president of universities and colleges;

3 served in the U.S. Congress, and

The First Census of Israel

Now the LORD spoke to Moses in the Wilderness of Sinai, in
the tabernacle of meeting, on the first *day* of the second
month, in the second year after they had come out of the
land of Egypt, saying: 2"Take a census of all the congregation
of the children of Israel, by their families, by their fathers' houses, according to the number of names, every male individually, 3from twenty years
old and above—all who *are able to* go to war in Israel. You and Aaron shall
number them by their armies. 4And with you there shall be a man from
every tribe, each one the head of his father's house.
5"These are the names of the men who shall stand with you: from Reuben, Elizur the son of Shedeur; 6from Simeon, Shelumiel the son of
Zurishaddai; 7from Judah, Nahshon the son of Amminadab; 8from
Issachar, Nethanel the son of Zuar; 9from Zebulun, Eliab the son of Helon;
10from the sons of Joseph: from Ephraim, Elishama the son of Ammihud;
from Manasseh, Gamaliel the son of Pedahzur; 11from Benjamin, Abidan
the son of Gideoni; 12from Dan, Ahiezer the son of Ammishaddai; 13from
Asher, Pagiel the son of Ocran; 14from Gad, Eliasaph the son of Deuel;[a]
15from Naphtali, Ahira the son of Enan." 16These *were* chosen from the congregation, leaders of their fathers' tribes, heads of the divisions in Israel.
17Then Moses and Aaron took these men who had been mentioned by
name, 18and they assembled all the congregation together on the first *day*
of the second month; and they recited their ancestry by families, by their
fathers' houses, according to the number of names, from twenty years old
and above, each one individually. 19As the LORD commanded Moses, so he
numbered them in the Wilderness of Sinai.
20Now the children of Reuben, Israel's oldest son, their genealogies by
their families, by their fathers' house, according to the number of names,
every male individually, from twenty years old and above, all who *were able
to* go to war: 21those who were numbered of the tribe of Reuben *were* forty-six
thousand five hundred.
22From the children of Simeon, their genealogies by their families, by
their fathers' house, of those who were numbered, according to the number of names, every male individually, from twenty years old and above,
all who *were able to* go to war: 23those who were numbered of the tribe of
Simeon *were* fifty-nine thousand three hundred.
24From the children of Gad, their genealogies by their families, by their
fathers' house, according to the number of names, from twenty years old
and above, all who *were able to* go to war: 25those who were numbered of
the tribe of Gad *were* forty-five thousand six hundred and fifty.
26From the children of Judah, their genealogies by their families, by
their fathers' house, according to the number of names, from twenty years
old and above, all who *were able to* go to war: 27those who were numbered
of the tribe of Judah *were* seventy-four thousand six hundred.
28From the children of Issachar, their genealogies by their families, by
their fathers' house, according to the number of names, from twenty years
old and above, all who *were able to* go to war: 29those who were numbered
of the tribe of Issachar *were* fifty-four thousand four hundred.
30From the children of Zebulun, their genealogies by their families, by
their fathers' house, according to the number of names, from twenty years

1:14 [a] Spelled *Reuel* in 2:14

old and above, all who *were able to* go to war: [31]those who were numbered of the tribe of Zebulun *were* fifty-seven thousand four hundred.

[32]From the sons of Joseph, the children of Ephraim, their genealogies by their families, by their fathers' house, according to the number of names, from twenty years old and above, all who *were able to* go to war: [33]those who were numbered of the tribe of Ephraim *were* forty thousand five hundred.

[34]From the children of Manasseh, their genealogies by their families, by their fathers' house, according to the number of names, from twenty years old and above, all who *were able to* go to war: [35]those who were numbered of the tribe of Manasseh *were* thirty-two thousand two hundred.

[36]From the children of Benjamin, their genealogies by their families, by their fathers' house, according to the number of names, from twenty years old and above, all who *were able to* go to war: [37]those who were numbered of the tribe of Benjamin *were* thirty-five thousand four hundred.

[38]From the children of Dan, their genealogies by their families, by their fathers' house, according to the number of names, from twenty years old and above, all who *were able to* go to war: [39]those who were numbered of the tribe of Dan *were* sixty-two thousand seven hundred.

[40]From the children of Asher, their genealogies by their families, by their fathers' house, according to the number of names, from twenty years old and above, all who *were able to* go to war: [41]those who were numbered of the tribe of Asher *were* forty-one thousand five hundred.

[42]From the children of Naphtali, their genealogies by their families, by their fathers' house, according to the number of names, from twenty years old and above, all who *were able to* go to war: [43]those who were numbered of the tribe of Naphtali *were* fifty-three thousand four hundred.

[44]These are the ones who were numbered, whom Moses and Aaron numbered, with the leaders of Israel, twelve men, each one representing his father's house. [45]So all who were numbered of the children of Israel, by their fathers' houses, from twenty years old and above, all who *were able to* go to war in Israel— [46]all who were numbered were six hundred and three thousand five hundred and fifty.

[47]But the Levites were not numbered among them by their fathers' tribe; [48]for the LORD had spoken to Moses, saying: [49]"Only the tribe of Levi you shall not number, nor take a census of them among the children of Israel; [50]but you shall appoint the Levites over the tabernacle of the Testimony, over all its furnishings, and over all things that belong to it; they shall carry the tabernacle and all its furnishings; they shall attend to it and camp around the tabernacle. [51]And when the tabernacle is to go forward, the Levites shall take it down; and when the tabernacle is to be set up, the Levites shall set it up. The outsider who comes near shall be put to death. [52]The children of Israel shall pitch their tents, everyone by his own camp, everyone by his own standard, according to their armies; [53]but the Levites shall camp around the tabernacle of the Testimony, that there may be no wrath on the congregation of the children of Israel; and the Levites shall keep charge of the tabernacle of the Testimony."

[54]Thus the children of Israel did; according to all that the LORD commanded Moses, so they did.

one became vice-president of the United States.

Jonathan Edwards . . . was just one man, but he positively affected hundreds and even thousands of his descendants after his death. . . . The destiny of those future generations is in your hands. The choices you make with your family today will determine the quality of life in your family tree for generations to come. That's why one man can make a difference.

(From *Point Man* by Steve Farrar)

APPLICATION You can make a difference in the lives of your children and grandchildren by serving God and dedicating your children to his service. The next time your family comes together, share about the "point people" who have most affected your life for the Lord. Help instill a vision for service in the kingdom of God. Then share with your children how they can pass along that vision.

EXPLORATION Influencing Future Generations—Genesis 17; Numbers 26; Joshua 24; 1 Kings 8.

The Tribes and Leaders by Armies

2 And the LORD spoke to Moses and Aaron, saying:
2“Everyone of the children of Israel shall camp by
his own standard, beside the emblems of his father’s
house; they shall camp some distance from the tabernacle of meeting. 3On the east side, toward the rising
of the sun, those of the standard of the forces with Judah shall camp according to their armies; and
Nahshon the son of Amminadab *shall be* the leader of
the children of Judah.” 4And his army was numbered
at seventy-four thousand six hundred.
5“Those who camp next to him *shall be* the tribe of
Issachar, and Nethanel the son of Zuar *shall be* the
leader of the children of Issachar.” 6And his army was
numbered at fifty-four thousand four hundred.
7“Then *comes* the tribe of Zebulun, and Eliab the
son of Helon *shall be* the leader of the children of
Zebulun.” 8And his army was numbered at fifty-
seven thousand four hundred. 9“All who were numbered according to their armies of the forces with
Judah, one hundred and eighty-six thousand four
hundred—these shall break camp first.
10“On the south side *shall be* the standard of the
forces with Reuben according to their armies, and the
leader of the children of Reuben *shall be* Elizur the
son of Shedeur.” 11And his army was numbered at
forty-six thousand five hundred.
12“Those who camp next to him *shall be* the tribe of
Simeon, and the leader of the children of Simeon *shall*
be Shelumiel the son of Zurishaddai.” 13And his army
was numbered at fifty-nine thousand three hundred.
14“Then *comes* the tribe of Gad, and the leader of the
children of Gad *shall be* Eliasaph the son of Reuel.”[b]
15And his army was numbered at forty-five thousand
six hundred and fifty. 16“All who were numbered according to their armies of the forces with Reuben, one
hundred and fifty-one thousand four hundred and
fifty—they shall be the second to break camp.
17“And the tabernacle of meeting shall move out
with the camp of the Levites in the middle of the
camps; as they camp, so they shall move out, everyone in his place, by their standards.
18“On the west side *shall be* the standard of the
forces with Ephraim according to their armies, and
the leader of the children of Ephraim *shall be*
Elishama the son of Ammihud.” 19And his army was
numbered at forty thousand five hundred.
20“Next to him *comes* the tribe of Manasseh, and
the leader of the children of Manasseh *shall be*
Gamaliel the son of Pedahzur.” 21And his army was
numbered at thirty-two thousand two hundred.
22“Then *comes* the tribe of Benjamin, and the
leader of the children of Benjamin *shall be* Abidan the
son of Gideoni.” 23And his army was numbered at
thirty-five thousand four hundred. 24“All who were
numbered according to their armies of the forces
with Ephraim, one hundred and eight thousand one
hundred—they shall be the third to break camp.
25“The standard of the forces with Dan *shall be* on
the north side according to their armies, and the
leader of the children of Dan *shall be* Ahiezer the son
of Ammishaddai.” 26And his army was numbered at
sixty-two thousand seven hundred.
27“Those who camp next to him *shall be* the tribe of
Asher, and the leader of the children of Asher *shall be*
Pagiel the son of Ocran.” 28And his army was numbered at forty-one thousand five hundred.
29“Then *comes* the tribe of Naphtali, and the leader
of the children of Naphtali *shall be* Ahira the son of
Enan.” 30And his army was numbered at fifty-three
thousand four hundred. 31“All who were numbered
of the forces with Dan, one hundred and fifty-seven
thousand six hundred—they shall break camp last,
with their standards.”
32These *are* the ones who were numbered of the
children of Israel by their fathers’ houses. All who
were numbered according to their armies of the
forces *were* six hundred and three thousand five hundred and fifty. 33But the Levites were not numbered
among the children of Israel, just as the LORD commanded Moses.
34Thus the children of Israel did according to all
that the LORD commanded Moses; so they camped by
their standards and so they broke camp, each one by
his family, according to their fathers’ houses.

The Sons of Aaron

3 Now these *are* the records of Aaron and Moses
when the LORD spoke with Moses on Mount Sinai.
2And these *are* the names of the sons of Aaron: Nadab,
the firstborn, and Abihu, Eleazar, and Ithamar.
3These *are* the names of the sons of Aaron, the
anointed priests, whom he consecrated to minister as
priests. 4Nadab and Abihu had died before the LORD
when they offered profane fire before the LORD in the
Wilderness of Sinai; and they had no children. So
Eleazar and Ithamar ministered as priests in the
presence of Aaron their father.

2:14 [b] Spelled *Deuel* in 1:14 and 7:42

The Levites Serve in the Tabernacle

5And the LORD spoke to Moses, saying: 6"Bring the tribe of Levi near,
and present them before Aaron the priest, that they may serve him. 7And
they shall attend to his needs and the needs of the whole congregation before the tabernacle of meeting, to do the work of the tabernacle. 8Also they
shall attend to all the furnishings of the tabernacle of meeting, and to the
needs of the children of Israel, to do the work of the tabernacle. 9And you
shall give the Levites to Aaron and his sons; they *are* given entirely to him[c]
from among the children of Israel. 10So you shall appoint Aaron and his
sons, and they shall attend to their priesthood; but the outsider who
comes near shall be put to death."
11Then the LORD spoke to Moses, saying: 12"Now behold, I Myself have
taken the Levites from among the children of Israel instead of every firstborn who opens the womb among the children of Israel. Therefore the
Levites shall be Mine, 13because all the firstborn *are* Mine. On the day that
I struck all the firstborn in the land of Egypt, I sanctified to Myself all the
firstborn in Israel, both man and beast. They shall be Mine: I *am* the LORD."

Census of the Levites Commanded

14Then the LORD spoke to Moses in the Wilderness of Sinai, saying:
15"Number the children of Levi by their fathers' houses, by their families;
you shall number every male from a month old and above."
16So Moses numbered them according to the word of the LORD, as he was
commanded. 17These were the sons of Levi by their names: Gershon,
Kohath, and Merari. 18And these *are* the names of the sons of Gershon by
their families: Libni and Shimei. 19And the sons of Kohath by their families: Amram, Izehar, Hebron, and Uzziel. 20And the sons of Merari by their
families: Mahli and Mushi. These *are* the families of the Levites by their fathers' houses.
21From Gershon *came* the family of the Libnites and the family of the
Shimites; these *were* the families of the Gershonites. 22Those who were
numbered, according to the number of all the males from a month old
and above—of those who were numbered *there were* seven thousand five
hundred. 23The families of the Gershonites were to camp behind the tabernacle westward. 24And the leader of the father's house of the Gershonites
was Eliasaph the son of Lael. 25The duties of the children of Gershon in the
tabernacle of meeting *included* the tabernacle, the tent with its covering,
the screen for the door of the tabernacle of meeting, 26the screen for the
door of the court, the hangings of the court which *are* around the tabernacle and the altar, and their cords, according to all the work relating to them.
27From Kohath *came* the family of the Amramites, the family of the
Izharites, the family of the Hebronites, and the family of the Uzzielites;
these *were* the families of the Kohathites. 28According to the number of all
the males, from a month old and above, *there were* eight thousand six[d]
hundred keeping charge of the sanctuary. 29The families of the children of
Kohath were to camp on the south side of the tabernacle. 30And the leader
of the fathers' house of the families of the Kohathites *was* Elizaphan the
son of Uzziel. 31Their duty *included* the ark, the table, the lampstand, the

3:9 [c] Samaritan Pentateuch and Septuagint read *Me*.
3:28 [d] Some manuscripts of the Septuagint read *three*.

LIFE LESSON

Numbers 3:1–5:31

SITUATION God established the Levites as the tribe responsible for providing priests and caring for the tabernacle. God gave different tribes specific responsibilities to meet certain needs. Anyone entering the sanctuary other than Moses and Aaron or his sons was punished by death.

OBSERVATION The Old Testament covenant (or agreement) between God and his people required special intermediaries—the priests. Now, Christ is the only intermediary needed for forgiveness of sins. We can go straight to him ourselves.

INSPIRATION The crowd is waiting outside the temple in silence. The signal has already been given. The high priest has gone into the Holy of Holies and, for the only time in the year allowed, has spoken the sacred name of God. At that signal the Jews assembled outside in the courtyard fall to their faces in respect and fear, since the priest and presumably the temple will be destroyed if he has spoken "the name" with impure lips.

The crowd awaits the high priest's return to the front of the temple with the announcement that the sacrifice has been accepted and that full forgiveness has been granted. The sacrifice he offers is for his sins and for the sins of the people. If he returns, all is well. If he does not return, the crowd outside will know that he has been struck down in the temple and they will remain guilty, unclean, hopeless. He is their only hope.

In the book of Hebrews, the writer presents Jesus as our High Priest. The high priest in the Old Testament offered up blood that was "not his own," a lifeless sacrifice, but Jesus offered His own blood. His sacrifice was better because it was a living sacrifice, which was offered "once for all," not every year. And unlike the high priest, who served only for a specific period of time, Jesus' is an eternal priesthood (the order of Melchizedek).

Even as Jesus is our High Priest, so we are in the same position as those early Israelites. We wait expectantly, but without fear, for our High Priest's

Continued

return, for "He will appear a second time, not to bear sin, but to bring salvation to those who are waiting for Him." The relief the children of Israel had at seeing their high priest return is nothing in comparison to the relief we will have at seeing the clouds roll back and Jesus, our High Priest, appear again.

(From *Immanuel* by Michael Card)

APPLICATION Under the old covenant, only the priests could approach God. Today, all who believe in Christ can approach God as members of the priesthood. Are you fully enjoying this privilege with God? Be thankful for Christ's sacrifice which gives direct access to God at all times. Use the freedom often. Pray today for people who need help, for political leaders who need wisdom.

EXPLORATION Relationship with God—Genesis 28:10-15; Exodus 19:20-24; Deuteronomy 10:16-17; Romans 8:34; Hebrews 4:14-16; 10:11-14.

altars, the utensils of the sanctuary with which they ministered, the
screen, and all the work relating to them.
32 And Eleazar the son of Aaron the priest *was to be* chief over the leaders
of the Levites, *with* oversight of those who kept charge of the sanctuary.
33 From Merari *came* the family of the Mahlites and the family of the
Mushites; these *were* the families of Merari. 34 And those who were numbered, according to the number of all the males from a month old and
above, *were* six thousand two hundred. 35 The leader of the fathers' house
of the families of Merari *was* Zuriel the son of Abihail. These *were* to camp
on the north side of the tabernacle. 36 And the appointed duty of the children of Merari *included* the boards of the tabernacle, its bars, its pillars, its
sockets, its utensils, all the work relating to them, 37 and the pillars of the
court all around, with their sockets, their pegs, and their cords.
38 Moreover those who were to camp before the tabernacle on the east,
before the tabernacle of meeting, *were* Moses, Aaron, and his sons, keeping charge of the sanctuary, to meet the needs of the children of Israel; but
the outsider who came near was to be put to death. 39 All who were numbered of the Levites, whom Moses and Aaron numbered at the commandment of the LORD, by their families, all the males from a month old and
above, *were* twenty-two thousand.

Levites Dedicated Instead of the Firstborn

40 Then the LORD said to Moses: "Number all the firstborn males of the
children of Israel from a month old and above, and take the number of
their names. 41 And you shall take the Levites for Me—I *am* the LORD—instead of all the firstborn among the children of Israel, and the livestock of
the Levites instead of all the firstborn among the livestock of the children
of Israel." 42 So Moses numbered all the firstborn among the children of Israel, as the LORD commanded him. 43 And all the firstborn males, according to the number of names from a month old and above, of those who
were numbered of them, were twenty-two thousand two hundred and
seventy-three.
44 Then the LORD spoke to Moses, saying: 45 "Take the Levites instead of all
the firstborn among the children of Israel, and the livestock of the Levites
instead of their livestock. The Levites shall be Mine: I *am* the LORD. 46 And
for the redemption of the two hundred and seventy-three of the firstborn
of the children of Israel, who are more than the number of the Levites,
47 you shall take five shekels for each one individually; you shall take *them*
in the currency of the shekel of the sanctuary, the shekel of twenty gerahs.
48 And you shall give the money, with which the excess number of them is
redeemed, to Aaron and his sons."
49 So Moses took the redemption money from those who were over and
above those who were redeemed by the Levites. 50 From the firstborn of the
children of Israel he took the money, one thousand three hundred and
sixty-five *shekels,* according to the shekel of the sanctuary. 51 And Moses
gave their redemption money to Aaron and his sons, according to the
word of the LORD, as the LORD commanded Moses.

Duties of the Sons of Kohath

4 Then the LORD spoke to Moses and Aaron, saying: 2 "Take a census of
the sons of Kohath from among the children of Levi, by their families,

by their fathers' house, 3from thirty years old and
above, even to fifty years old, all who enter the service
to do the work in the tabernacle of meeting.
4"This *is* the service of the sons of Kohath in the
tabernacle of meeting, *relating to* the most holy
things: 5When the camp prepares to journey, Aaron
and his sons shall come, and they shall take down the
covering veil and cover the ark of the Testimony with
it. 6Then they shall put on it a covering of badger
skins, and spread over *that* a cloth entirely of blue;
and they shall insert its poles.
7"On the table of showbread they shall spread a
blue cloth, and put on it the dishes, the pans, the
bowls, and the pitchers for pouring; and the showbread[e] shall be on it. 8They shall spread over them a
scarlet cloth, and cover the same with a covering of
badger skins; and they shall insert its poles. 9And they
shall take a blue cloth and cover the lampstand of the
light, with its lamps, its wick-trimmers, its trays, and
all its oil vessels, with which they service it. 10Then
they shall put it with all its utensils in a covering of
badger skins, and put *it* on a carrying beam.
11"Over the golden altar they shall spread a blue
cloth, and cover it with a covering of badger skins;
and they shall insert its poles. 12Then they shall take
all the utensils of service with which they minister in
the sanctuary, put *them* in a blue cloth, cover them
with a covering of badger skins, and put *them* on a
carrying beam. 13Also they shall take away the ashes
from the altar, and spread a purple cloth over it.
14They shall put on it all its implements with which
they minister there—the firepans, the forks, the
shovels, the basins, and all the utensils of the altar—
and they shall spread on it a covering of badger skins,
and insert its poles. 15And when Aaron and his sons
have finished covering the sanctuary and all the furnishings of the sanctuary, when the camp is set to go,
then the sons of Kohath shall come to carry *them;* but
they shall not touch any holy thing, lest they die.
"These *are* the things in the tabernacle of meeting
which the sons of Kohath are to carry.
16"The appointed duty of Eleazar the son of Aaron
the priest *is* the oil for the light, the sweet incense, the
daily grain offering, the anointing oil, the oversight of
all the tabernacle, of all that *is* in it, with the sanctuary
and its furnishings."
17Then the LORD spoke to Moses and Aaron, saying:
18"Do not cut off the tribe of the families of the
Kohathites from among the Levites; 19but do this in
regard to them, that they may live and not die when
they approach the most holy things: Aaron and his
sons shall go in and appoint each of them to his service and his task. 20But they shall not go in to watch
while the holy things are being covered, lest they die."

Duties of the Sons of Gershon

21Then the LORD spoke to Moses, saying: 22"Also take
a census of the sons of Gershon, by their fathers' house,
by their families. 23From thirty years old and above,
even to fifty years old, you shall number them, all who
enter to perform the service, to do the work in the
tabernacle of meeting. 24This *is* the service of the families of the Gershonites, in serving and carrying: 25They
shall carry the curtains of the tabernacle and the tabernacle of meeting *with* its covering, the covering of badger skins that *is* on it, the screen for the door of the
tabernacle of meeting, 26the screen for the door of the
gate of the court, the hangings of the court which *are*
around the tabernacle and altar, and their cords, all
the furnishings for their service and all that is made
for these things: so shall they serve.
27"Aaron and his sons shall assign all the service of
the sons of the Gershonites, all their tasks and all their
service. And you shall appoint to them all their tasks
as their duty. 28This *is* the service of the families of the
sons of Gershon in the tabernacle of meeting. And
their duties *shall be* under the authority[f] of Ithamar
the son of Aaron the priest.

Duties of the Sons of Merari

29"*As for* the sons of Merari, you shall number them
by their families and by their fathers' house. 30From
thirty years old and above, even to fifty years old, you
shall number them, everyone who enters the service
to do the work of the tabernacle of meeting. 31And this
is what they must carry as all their service for the
tabernacle of meeting: the boards of the tabernacle,
its bars, its pillars, its sockets, 32and the pillars around
the court with their sockets, pegs, and cords, with all
their furnishings and all their service; and you shall
assign *to each man* by name the items he must carry.
33This *is* the service of the families of the sons of
Merari, as all their service for the tabernacle of meeting, under the authority[g] of Ithamar the son of Aaron
the priest."

4:7 [e] Literally *the continual bread*
4:28 [f] Literally *hand*
4:33 [g] Literally *hand*

Census of the Levites

[34]And Moses, Aaron, and the leaders of the congregation numbered the sons of the Kohathites by their
families and by their fathers' house, [35]from thirty
years old and above, even to fifty years old, everyone
who entered the service for work in the tabernacle of
meeting; [36]and those who were numbered by their
families were two thousand seven hundred and fifty.
[37]These *were* the ones who were numbered of the families of the Kohathites, all who might serve in the
tabernacle of meeting, whom Moses and Aaron numbered according to the commandment of the LORD by
the hand of Moses.

[38]And those who were numbered of the sons of
Gershon, by their families and by their fathers' house,
[39]from thirty years old and above, even to fifty years
old, everyone who entered the service for work in the
tabernacle of meeting— [40]those who were numbered
by their families, by their fathers' house, were two
thousand six hundred and thirty. [41]These *are* the ones
who were numbered of the families of the sons of
Gershon, of all who might serve in the tabernacle of
meeting, whom Moses and Aaron numbered according to the commandment of the LORD.

[42]Those of the families of the sons of Merari who
were numbered, by their families, by their fathers'
house, [43]from thirty years old and above, even to fifty
years old, everyone who entered the service for work
in the tabernacle of meeting— [44]those who were
numbered by their families were three thousand two
hundred. [45]These *are* the ones who were numbered of
the families of the sons of Merari, whom Moses and
Aaron numbered according to the word of the LORD
by the hand of Moses.

[46]All who were numbered of the Levites, whom
Moses, Aaron, and the leaders of Israel numbered, by
their families and by their fathers' houses, [47]from
thirty years old and above, even to fifty years old,
everyone who came to do the work of service and the
work of bearing burdens in the tabernacle of meeting— [48]those who were numbered were eight thousand five hundred and eighty.

[49]According to the commandment of the LORD they
were numbered by the hand of Moses, each according
to his service and according to his task; thus were they
numbered by him, as the LORD commanded Moses.

Ceremonially Unclean Persons Isolated

5 And the LORD spoke to Moses, saying: [2]"Command the children of Israel that they put out of the
camp every leper, everyone who has a discharge, and
whoever becomes defiled by a corpse. [3]You shall put
out both male and female; you shall put them outside
the camp, that they may not defile their camps in the
midst of which I dwell." [4]And the children of Israel
did so, and put them outside the camp; as the LORD
spoke to Moses, so the children of Israel did.

Confession and Restitution

[5]Then the LORD spoke to Moses, saying, [6]"Speak to
the children of Israel: 'When a man or woman commits any sin that men commit in unfaithfulness
against the LORD, and that person is guilty, [7]then he
shall confess the sin which he has committed. He
shall make restitution for his trespass in full, plus
one-fifth of it, and give *it* to the one he has wronged.
[8]But if the man has no relative to whom restitution
may be made for the wrong, the restitution for the
wrong *must go* to the LORD for the priest, in addition
to the ram of the atonement with which atonement is
made for him. [9]Every offering of all the holy things of
the children of Israel, which they bring to the priest,
shall be his. [10]And every man's holy things shall be
his; whatever any man gives the priest shall be his.' "

Concerning Unfaithful Wives

[11]And the LORD spoke to Moses, saying, [12]"Speak to
the children of Israel, and say to them: 'If any man's
wife goes astray and behaves unfaithfully toward
him, [13]and a man lies with her carnally, and it is hidden from the eyes of her husband, and it is concealed
that she has defiled herself, and *there was* no witness
against her, nor was she caught— [14]if the spirit of jealousy comes upon him and he becomes jealous of his
wife, who has defiled herself; or if the spirit of jealousy comes upon him and he becomes jealous of his
wife, although she has not defiled herself— [15]then the
man shall bring his wife to the priest. He shall bring
the offering required for her, one-tenth of an ephah of
barley meal; he shall pour no oil on it and put no
frankincense on it, because it *is* a grain offering of
jealousy, an offering for remembering, for bringing
iniquity to remembrance.

[16]'And the priest shall bring her near, and set her
before the LORD. [17]The priest shall take holy water in
an earthen vessel, and take some of the dust that is on
the floor of the tabernacle and put *it* into the water.
[18]Then the priest shall stand the woman before the
LORD, uncover the woman's head, and put the offering
for remembering in her hands, which *is* the grain offering of jealousy. And the priest shall have in his

hand the bitter water that brings a curse. 19And the priest shall put her under oath, and say to the woman, "If no man has lain with you, and if you have not gone astray to uncleanness *while* under your husband's *authority,* be free from this bitter water that brings a curse. 20But if you have gone astray *while* under your husband's *authority,* and if you have defiled yourself and some man other than your husband has lain with you"— 21then the priest shall put the woman under the oath of the curse, and he shall say to the woman—"the LORD make you a curse and an oath among your people, when the LORD makes your thigh rot and your belly swell; 22and may this water that causes the curse go into your stomach, and make *your* belly swell and *your* thigh rot."

'Then the woman shall say, "Amen, so be it."

23'Then the priest shall write these curses in a book, and he shall scrape *them* off into the bitter water. 24And he shall make the woman drink the bitter water that brings a curse, and the water that brings the curse shall enter her *to become* bitter. 25Then the priest shall take the grain offering of jealousy from the woman's hand, shall wave the offering before the LORD, and bring it to the altar; 26and the priest shall take a handful of the offering, as its memorial portion, burn *it* on the altar, and afterward make the woman drink the water. 27When he has made her drink the water, then it shall be, if she has defiled herself and behaved unfaithfully toward her husband, that the water that brings a curse will enter her *and become* bitter, and her belly will swell, her thigh will rot, and the woman will become a curse among her people. 28But if the woman has not defiled herself, and is clean, then she shall be free and may conceive children.

29'This *is* the law of jealousy, when a wife, *while* under her husband's *authority,* goes astray and defiles herself, 30or when the spirit of jealousy comes upon a man, and he becomes jealous of his wife; then he shall stand the woman before the LORD, and the priest shall execute all this law upon her. 31Then the man shall be free from iniquity, but that woman shall bear her guilt.'"

The Law of the Nazirite

6 Then the LORD spoke to Moses, saying, 2"Speak to the children of Israel, and say to them: 'When either a man or woman consecrates an offering to take the vow of a Nazirite, to separate himself to the LORD, 3he shall separate himself from wine and *similar* drink; he shall drink neither vinegar made from wine nor vinegar made from *similar* drink; neither shall he drink any grape juice, nor eat fresh grapes or raisins. 4All the days of his separation he shall eat nothing that is produced by the grapevine, from seed to skin.

5'All the days of the vow of his separation no razor shall come upon his head; until the days are fulfilled for which he separated himself to the LORD, he shall be holy. *Then* he shall let the locks of the hair of his head grow. 6All the days that he separates himself to the LORD he shall not go near a dead body. 7He shall not make himself unclean even for his father or his mother, for his brother or his sister, when they die, because his separation to God *is* on his head. 8All the days of his separation he shall be holy to the LORD.

9'And if anyone dies very suddenly beside him, and he defiles his consecrated head, then he shall shave his head on the day of his cleansing; on the

LIFE LESSON

Numbers 6:1-27

SITUATION God established the Nazirite vow to form a small group who would serve God. The restrictions (abstaining from wine, cutting or shaving hair, and touching a dead body) were intended to keep a Nazirite's life holy and clean.

OBSERVATION The Nazirites followed special rules to be closer in mind and spirit to God. They provide examples for us of dedication to God. Religious rules should only be followed by people who have a sincere heart.

INSPIRATION The leading religious party members of the day quickly labeled Jesus an adversary because He had the capacity to do the one thing that terrified them most: expose the inner person. They were reasonably good people, but they put a premium on decorating the exterior of life with words, robes, and rituals and camouflaging the interior of life where the scenery was spoiled.

But others were actually drawn to Him because they sensed an overriding safety in being transparent with Him. Instead of heaping shame upon them as others did, He gave grace. That's it: self-disclosure always resulted in grace in the presence of Jesus. And grace meant reclamation from spoiledness. Grace meant a new start. . . .

A powerful example of this is Zacchaeus, the Jericho tax collector who climbed a tree to be above the crowd and get a glimpse of Jesus. Why did the Lord stop and choose to visit at Zacchaeus's house that day? It's clear that He saw what no one else could see: the man known for his exploitation of people was ready to acknowledge the inner spoiledness that, in this case, was out-and-out greed. The grace of Christ was drawn to the openness of the sinner.

What is the point of all this? That Christ-following always involves exposure and renovation of the inner life. And not just a small part of the inner life, but an ever-enlarging section of it.

(From *Christ Followers in the Real World* by Gordon MacDonald)

Continued

APPLICATION We do not need to become Nazirites to serve Christ. Follow God's Word and pray for God's wisdom so you can better serve him in your family and work. Find a way to say to someone today, "God cares about you."

EXPLORATION Dedication to Service—1 Chronicles. 6:31; 2 Chronicles 7:4-5; Luke 9:62; Romans 12:1-2.

seventh day he shall shave it. 10Then on the eighth day he shall bring two
turtledoves or two young pigeons to the priest, to the door of the tabernacle of meeting; 11and the priest shall offer one as a sin offering and *the*
other as a burnt offering, and make atonement for him, because he sinned
in regard to the corpse; and he shall sanctify his head that same day. 12He
shall consecrate to the LORD the days of his separation, and bring a male
lamb in its first year as a trespass offering; but the former days shall be
lost, because his separation was defiled.

13"Now this *is* the law of the Nazirite: When the days of his separation are
fulfilled, he shall be brought to the door of the tabernacle of meeting.
14And he shall present his offering to the LORD: one male lamb in its first
year without blemish as a burnt offering, one ewe lamb in its first year
without blemish as a sin offering, one ram without blemish as a peace offering, 15a basket of unleavened bread, cakes of fine flour mixed with oil,
unleavened wafers anointed with oil, and their grain offering with their
drink offerings.

16"Then the priest shall bring *them* before the LORD and offer his sin offering and his burnt offering; 17and he shall offer the ram as a sacrifice of a
peace offering to the LORD, with the basket of unleavened bread; the priest
shall also offer its grain offering and its drink offering. 18Then the Nazirite
shall shave his consecrated head *at* the door of the tabernacle of meeting,
and shall take the hair from his consecrated head and put *it* on the fire
which is under the sacrifice of the peace offering.

19"And the priest shall take the boiled shoulder of the ram, one unleavened cake from the basket, and one unleavened wafer, and put *them* upon
the hands of the Nazirite after he has shaved his consecrated *hair,* 20and the
priest shall wave them as a wave offering before the LORD; they *are* holy for
the priest, together with the breast of the wave offering and the thigh of the
heave offering. After that the Nazirite may drink wine.'

21"This is the law of the Nazirite who vows to the LORD the offering for
his separation, and besides that, whatever else his hand is able to provide;
according to the vow which he takes, so he must do according to the law of
his separation."

The Priestly Blessing

22And the LORD spoke to Moses, saying: 23"Speak to Aaron and his sons,
saying, 'This is the way you shall bless the children of Israel. Say to them:

24 "The LORD bless you and keep you;
25 The LORD make His face shine upon you,
And be gracious to you;
26 The LORD lift up His countenance upon you,
And give you peace." '

27"So they shall put My name on the children of Israel, and I will bless
them."

Offerings of the Leaders

7 Now it came to pass, when Moses had finished setting up the tabernacle, that he anointed it and consecrated it and all its furnishings, and
the altar and all its utensils; so he anointed them and consecrated them.
2Then the leaders of Israel, the heads of their fathers' houses, who *were* the

leaders of the tribes and over those who were numbered, made an offering. 3And they brought their offering before the LORD, six covered carts
and twelve oxen, a cart for *every* two of the leaders, and for each one an ox;
and they presented them before the tabernacle.
4Then the LORD spoke to Moses, saying, 5"Accept *these* from them, that
they may be used in doing the work of the tabernacle of meeting; and you
shall give them to the Levites, *to* every man according to his service." 6So
Moses took the carts and the oxen, and gave them to the Levites. 7Two carts
and four oxen he gave to the sons of Gershon, according to their service;
8and four carts and eight oxen he gave to the sons of Merari, according to
their service, under the authority[h] of Ithamar the son of Aaron the priest.
9But to the sons of Kohath he gave none, because theirs *was* the service of
the holy things, *which* they carried on their shoulders.
10Now the leaders offered the dedication *offering* for the altar when it
was anointed; so the leaders offered their offering before the altar. 11For the
LORD said to Moses, "They shall offer their offering, one leader each day,
for the dedication of the altar."
12And the one who offered his offering on the first day *was* Nahshon the
son of Amminadab, from the tribe of Judah. 13His offering *was* one silver
platter, the weight of which *was* one hundred and thirty *shekels,* and one
silver bowl of seventy shekels, according to the shekel of the sanctuary,
both of them full of fine flour mixed with oil as a grain offering; 14one gold
pan of ten *shekels,* full of incense; 15one young bull, one ram, and one male
lamb in its first year, as a burnt offering; 16one kid of the goats as a sin offering; 17and for the sacrifice of peace offerings: two oxen, five rams, five
male goats, and five male lambs in their first year. This *was* the offering of
Nahshon the son of Amminadab.
18On the second day Nethanel the son of Zuar, leader of Issachar, presented *an offering.* 19*For* his offering he offered one silver platter, the weight
of which *was* one hundred and thirty *shekels,* and one silver bowl of seventy shekels, according to the shekel of the sanctuary, both of them full of
fine flour mixed with oil as a grain offering; 20one gold pan of ten *shekels,*
full of incense; 21one young bull, one ram, and one male lamb in its first
year, as a burnt offering; 22one kid of the goats as a sin offering; 23and as
the sacrifice of peace offerings: two oxen, five rams, five male goats, and
five male lambs in their first year. This *was* the offering of Nethanel the
son of Zuar.
24On the third day Eliab the son of Helon, leader of the children of
Zebulun, *presented an offering.* 25His offering *was* one silver platter, the
weight of which *was* one hundred and thirty *shekels,* and one silver bowl of
seventy shekels, according to the shekel of the sanctuary, both of them full
of fine flour mixed with oil as a grain offering; 26one gold pan of ten
shekels, full of incense; 27one young bull, one ram, and one male lamb in
its first year, as a burnt offering; 28one kid of the goats as a sin offering;
29and for the sacrifice of peace offerings: two oxen, five rams, five male
goats, and five male lambs in their first year. This *was* the offering of Eliab
the son of Helon.
30On the fourth day Elizur the son of Shedeur, leader of the children of
Reuben, *presented an offering.* 31His offering *was* one silver platter, the

7:8 [h] Literally *hand*

LIFE LESSON

Numbers 7:1–9:14

SITUATION Moses consecrated and anointed the completed temple. The people brought gifts and offerings for the tabernacle.

OBSERVATION In order to truly know God, we must worship him.

INSPIRATION The Bible tells us that God speaks to us in four different ways.

1. God reveals himself in nature. Psalm 19 describes this kind of revelation. . . . Romans 1:20 also speaks of the revelation of God in nature. . . . Anyone who has seen nature knows enough about God to seek him out.

. . . Although this is a true revelation, it is doesn't tell us anything of God's moral character. More important, it doesn't tell us anything of his love. . . .

2. God reveals himself in history. In the Old Testament, God spoke to people personally and intervened in a miraculous way by altering the rules of nature. For example, in delivering the Jews from Egypt, he revealed his character and his moral law. He delivered the Israelites from bondage so they would follow him and obey his commandments.

The chief revelation of God in history is Jesus Christ. . . . In Jesus Christ we discover things about God we don't learn from nature. We learn that God is a person, that God is loving. Above all we find the way of salvation through Christ's death and resurrection.

3. God reveals himself in the Bible. God's written revelation is crucial because whatever we say about God is based on his revelation in the Bible. The Bible is the record of what God has done, focusing on what he has done through Jesus Christ. The Old Testament anticipates Christ's coming. The four Gospels detail his earthly ministry. The Epistles and the other books of the New Testament explain the rest of the Bible for our benefit. More than nature and history, the Bible leads us to seek God.

Continued

4. *God reveals himself through the Holy Spirit.* Through the illumination of the Holy Spirit a person experiences rebirth. This is the most personal form of God's revelation. Without the Spirit, we cannot understand spiritual things. . . . But the Holy Spirit makes us alive in Christ. He gives us a new nature. He gives us a new capacity to see God in nature and history and to read the Bible with new understanding.

A non-Christian will attend a Bible study, but nothing makes sense. Then suddenly something clicks and it becomes clear. The Holy Spirit has revealed to him in a personal way that Jesus Christ is God and that Jesus Christ is the Savior. He can now see what he couldn't see before. The person has been born again through the work of the Holy Spirit.

(From "God Speaks to Us Today" by James Boice in *Practical Christianity*)

APPLICATION What rituals, symbols, or observances in your church tell you about God or help you worship? Are there some that you don't understand? Take time to find out what they mean. Let them be God's message for you.

EXPLORATION Public Worship—Psalm 95:6; John 4:23-24; Acts 2:42-47; Hebrews 10:25.

weight of which *was* one hundred and thirty *shekels,* and one silver bowl of
seventy shekels, according to the shekel of the sanctuary, both of them full
of fine flour mixed with oil as a grain offering; [32]one gold pan of ten
shekels, full of incense; [33]one young bull, one ram, and one male lamb in
its first year, as a burnt offering; [34]one kid of the goats as a sin offering;
[35]and as the sacrifice of peace offerings: two oxen, five rams, five male
goats, and five male lambs in their first year. This *was* the offering of Elizur
the son of Shedeur.
[36]On the fifth day Shelumiel the son of Zurishaddai, leader of the children of Simeon, *presented an offering.* [37]His offering *was* one silver platter,
the weight of which *was* one hundred and thirty *shekels,* and one silver
bowl of seventy shekels, according to the shekel of the sanctuary, both of
them full of fine flour mixed with oil as a grain offering; [38]one gold pan of
ten *shekels,* full of incense; [39]one young bull, one ram, and one male lamb
in its first year, as a burnt offering; [40]one kid of the goats as a sin offering;
[41]and as the sacrifice of peace offerings: two oxen, five rams, five male
goats, and five male lambs in their first year. This *was* the offering of
Shelumiel the son of Zurishaddai.
[42]On the sixth day Eliasaph the son of Deuel,[i] leader of the children of
Gad, *presented an offering.* [43]His offering *was* one silver platter, the weight
of which *was* one hundred and thirty *shekels,* and one silver bowl of seventy
shekels, according to the shekel of the sanctuary, both of them full of fine
flour mixed with oil as a grain offering; [44]one gold pan of ten *shekels,* full of
incense; [45]one young bull, one ram, and one male lamb in its first year, as a
burnt offering; [46]one kid of the goats as a sin offering; [47]and as the sacrifice
of peace offerings: two oxen, five rams, five male goats, and five male
lambs in their first year. This *was* the offering of Eliasaph the son of Deuel.
[48]On the seventh day Elishama the son of Ammihud, leader of the children of Ephraim, *presented an offering.* [49]His offering *was* one silver platter, the weight of which *was* one hundred and thirty *shekels,* and one silver
bowl of seventy shekels, according to the shekel of the sanctuary, both of
them full of fine flour mixed with oil as a grain offering; [50]one gold pan of
ten *shekels,* full of incense; [51]one young bull, one ram, and one male lamb
in its first year, as a burnt offering; [52]one kid of the goats as a sin offering;
[53]and as the sacrifice of peace offerings: two oxen, five rams, five male
goats, and five male lambs in their first year. This *was* the offering of
Elishama the son of Ammihud.
[54]On the eighth day Gamaliel the son of Pedahzur, leader of the children
of Manasseh, *presented an offering.* [55]His offering *was* one silver platter, the
weight of which *was* one hundred and thirty *shekels,* and one silver bowl of
seventy shekels, according to the shekel of the sanctuary, both of them full
of fine flour mixed with oil as a grain offering; [56]one gold pan of ten
shekels, full of incense; [57]one young bull, one ram, and one male lamb in
its first year, as a burnt offering; [58]one kid of the goats as a sin offering;
[59]and as the sacrifice of peace offerings: two oxen, five rams, five male
goats, and five male lambs in their first year. This *was* the offering of
Gamaliel the son of Pedahzur.
[60]On the ninth day Abidan the son of Gideoni, leader of the children of
Benjamin, *presented an offering.* [61]His offering *was* one silver platter, the

7:42 *i* Spelled *Reuel* in 2:14

weight of which *was* one hundred and thirty *shekels,*
and one silver bowl of seventy shekels, according to
the shekel of the sanctuary, both of them full of fine
flour mixed with oil as a grain offering; 62one gold pan
of ten *shekels,* full of incense; 63one young bull, one
ram, and one male lamb in its first year, as a burnt offering; 64one kid of the goats as a sin offering; 65and as
the sacrifice of peace offerings: two oxen, five rams,
five male goats, and five male lambs in their first year.
This *was* the offering of Abidan the son of Gideoni.
66On the tenth day Ahiezer the son of Ammishaddai, leader of the children of Dan, *presented an
offering.* 67His offering *was* one silver platter, the
weight of which *was* one hundred and thirty *shekels,*
and one silver bowl of seventy shekels, according to
the shekel of the sanctuary, both of them full of fine
flour mixed with oil as a grain offering; 68one gold pan
of ten *shekels,* full of incense; 69one young bull, one
ram, and one male lamb in its first year, as a burnt offering; 70one kid of the goats as a sin offering; 71and as
the sacrifice of peace offerings: two oxen, five rams,
five male goats, and five male lambs in their first year.
This *was* the offering of Ahiezer the son of
Ammishaddai.
72On the eleventh day Pagiel the son of Ocran,
leader of the children of Asher, *presented an offering.*
73His offering *was* one silver platter, the weight of
which *was* one hundred and thirty *shekels,* and one
silver bowl of seventy shekels, according to the shekel
of the sanctuary, both of them full of fine flour mixed
with oil as a grain offering; 74one gold pan of ten
shekels, full of incense; 75one young bull, one ram, and
one male lamb in its first year, as a burnt offering;
76one kid of the goats as a sin offering; 77and as the
sacrifice of peace offerings: two oxen, five rams, five
male goats, and five male lambs in their first year.
This *was* the offering of Pagiel the son of Ocran.
78On the twelfth day Ahira the son of Enan, leader
of the children of Naphtali, *presented an offering.* 79His
offering *was* one silver platter, the weight of which *was*
one hundred and thirty *shekels,* and one silver bowl of
seventy shekels, according to the shekel of the sanctuary, both of them full of fine flour mixed with oil as a
grain offering; 80one gold pan of ten *shekels,* full of incense; 81one young bull, one ram, and one male lamb
in its first year, as a burnt offering; 82one kid of the
goats as a sin offering; 83and as the sacrifice of peace
offerings: two oxen, five rams, five male goats, and
five male lambs in their first year. This *was* the offering of Ahira the son of Enan.
84This *was* the dedication *offering* for the altar from
the leaders of Israel, when it was anointed: twelve silver platters, twelve silver bowls, and twelve gold pans.
85Each silver platter *weighed* one hundred and thirty
shekels and each bowl seventy *shekels.* All the silver of
the vessels *weighed* two thousand four hundred
shekels, according to the shekel of the sanctuary. 86The
twelve gold pans full of incense *weighed* ten *shekels*
apiece, according to the shekel of the sanctuary; all
the gold of the pans *weighed* one hundred and twenty
shekels. 87All the oxen for the burnt offering *were*
twelve young bulls, the rams twelve, the male lambs
in their first year twelve, with their grain offering, and
the kids of the goats as a sin offering twelve. 88And all
the oxen for the sacrifice of peace offerings were
twenty-four bulls, the rams sixty, the male goats sixty,
and the lambs in their first year sixty. This *was* the
dedication *offering* for the altar after it was anointed.
89Now when Moses went into the tabernacle of
meeting to speak with Him, he heard the voice of One
speaking to him from above the mercy seat that *was*
on the ark of the Testimony, from between the two
cherubim; thus He spoke to him.

Arrangement of the Lamps

8 And the LORD spoke to Moses, saying: 2"Speak to
Aaron, and say to him, 'When you arrange the
lamps, the seven lamps shall give light in front of the
lampstand.' " 3And Aaron did so; he arranged the
lamps to face toward the front of the lampstand, as
the LORD commanded Moses. 4Now this workmanship of the lampstand *was* hammered gold; from its
shaft to its flowers it *was* hammered work. According
to the pattern which the LORD had shown Moses, so he
made the lampstand.

Cleansing and Dedication of the Levites

5Then the LORD spoke to Moses, saying: 6"Take the
Levites from among the children of Israel and cleanse
them *ceremonially.* 7Thus you shall do to them to
cleanse them: Sprinkle water of purification on them,
and let them shave all their body, and let them wash
their clothes, and *so* make themselves clean. 8Then let
them take a young bull with its grain offering of fine
flour mixed with oil, and you shall take another
young bull as a sin offering. 9And you shall bring the
Levites before the tabernacle of meeting, and you
shall gather together the whole congregation of the
children of Israel. 10So you shall bring the Levites before the LORD, and the children of Israel shall lay their
hands on the Levites; 11and Aaron shall offer the
Levites before the LORD *like* a wave offering from the

LIFE LESSON

Numbers 9:15–10:10

SITUATION God guided the Israelites in the wilderness with a cloud by day and a pillar of fire by night. The cloud and fire moved according to God's will. When they moved, the people moved; where they stopped, the people stopped.

OBSERVATION When we follow God's guidance, we please him. Although his plan may not always be clear to us, we must follow.

INSPIRATION Does God guide? Yes. Most times, I believe, he guides in subtle ways, by feeding ideas into our minds, speaking through a nagging sensation of dissatisfaction, inspiring us to choose better than we otherwise would have done, bringing to the surface hidden dangers of temptation, and perhaps by rearranging certain circumstances.

. . . Sociologist Bronislaw Malinowski suggested a distinction between magic and religion. Magic, he said, is when we manipulate the deities so that they perform our wishes; religion is when we subject ourselves to the will of the deities. True guidance cannot resemble magic, a way for God to give us shortcuts and genie bottles. It must, rather, fall under Malinowski's definition of religion. If so, it will occur in the context of a committed relationship between a Christian and God.

. . . A picture is being painted, for me, for all who are called the sons and daughters of God. Yet it does not take shape until enough time passes for me to stand up and look back on what colors and designs have been laid down. If I saw the pattern in advance, a sort of schema for "paint-by-numbers," that would leave no room for faith. And, besides, God does not paint numbers.

(From *Guidance: Making Sense of God's Direction* by Phillip Yancey)

APPLICATION How easily do you change direction? Are you willing to adapt to God's will? Ask God to make his plans for you clear and to move you toward his will for the future.

EXPLORATION Guidance—Exodus 15:13; Psalm 23:1-4; Isaiah 58:11.

children of Israel, that they may perform the work of the LORD.
12Then the
Levites shall lay their hands on the heads of the young bulls, and you shall offer one as a sin offering and the other as a burnt offering to the LORD, to make atonement for the Levites.
13"And you shall stand the Levites before Aaron and his sons, and then offer them *like* a wave offering to the LORD.
14Thus you shall separate the Levites from among the children of Israel, and the Levites shall be Mine.
15After that the Levites shall go in to service the tabernacle of meeting. So you shall cleanse them and offer them *like* a wave offering.
16For they *are* wholly given to Me from among the children of Israel; I have taken them for Myself instead of all who open the womb, the firstborn of all the children of Israel.
17For all the firstborn among the children of Israel *are* Mine, *both* man and beast; on the day that I struck all the firstborn in the land of Egypt I sanctified them to Myself.
18I have taken the Levites instead of all the firstborn of the children of Israel.
19And I have given the Levites as a gift to Aaron and his sons from among the children of Israel, to do the work for the children of Israel in the tabernacle of meeting, and to make atonement for the children of Israel, that there be no plague among the children of Israel when the children of Israel come near the sanctuary."
20Thus Moses and Aaron and all the congregation of the children of Israel did to the Levites; according to all that the LORD commanded Moses concerning the Levites, so the children of Israel did to them.
21And the
Levites purified themselves and washed their clothes; then Aaron presented them *like* a wave offering before the LORD, and Aaron made atonement for them to cleanse them.
22After that the Levites went in to do their work in the tabernacle of meeting before Aaron and his sons; as the LORD commanded Moses concerning the Levites, so they did to them.
23Then the LORD spoke to Moses, saying,
24"This *is* what *pertains* to the Levites: From twenty-five years old and above one may enter to perform service in the work of the tabernacle of meeting;
25and at the age of fifty years they must cease performing this work, and shall work no more.
26They may minister with their brethren in the tabernacle of meeting, to attend to needs, but they *themselves* shall do no work. Thus you shall do to the Levites regarding their duties."

The Second Passover

9 Now the LORD spoke to Moses in the Wilderness of Sinai, in the first month of the second year after they had come out of the land of Egypt, saying:
2"Let the children of Israel keep the Passover at its appointed time.
3On the fourteenth day of this month, at twilight, you shall keep it at its appointed time. According to all its rites and ceremonies you shall keep it."
4So Moses told the children of Israel that they should keep the Passover.
5And they kept the Passover on the fourteenth day of the first month, at twilight, in the Wilderness of Sinai; according to all that the LORD commanded Moses, so the children of Israel did.
6Now there were *certain* men who were defiled by a human corpse, so that they could not keep the Passover on that day; and they came before Moses and Aaron that day.
7And those men said to him, "We *became* defiled by a human corpse. Why are we kept from presenting the offering of the LORD at its appointed time among the children of Israel?"

8And Moses said to them, "Stand still, that I may
hear what the LORD will command concerning you."
9Then the LORD spoke to Moses, saying, 10"Speak to
the children of Israel, saying: 'If anyone of you or your
posterity is unclean because of a corpse, or *is* far away
on a journey, he may still keep the LORD's Passover.
11On the fourteenth day of the second month, at twilight, they may keep it. They shall eat it with unleavened bread and bitter herbs. 12They shall leave none of
it until morning, nor break one of its bones. According to all the ordinances of the Passover they shall
keep it. 13But the man who *is* clean and is not on a
journey, and ceases to keep the Passover, that same
person shall be cut off from among his people, because he did not bring the offering of the LORD at its
appointed time; that man shall bear his sin.
14'And if a stranger dwells among you, and would
keep the LORD's Passover, he must do so according to
the rite of the Passover and according to its ceremony;
you shall have one ordinance, both for the stranger
and the native of the land.' "

The Cloud and the Fire

15Now on the day that the tabernacle was raised up,
the cloud covered the tabernacle, the tent of the
Testimony; from evening until morning it was above
the tabernacle like the appearance of fire. 16So it was
always: the cloud covered it *by day,* and the appearance of fire by night. 17Whenever the cloud was taken
up from above the tabernacle, after that the children
of Israel would journey; and in the place where the
cloud settled, there the children of Israel would pitch
their tents. 18At the command of the LORD the children
of Israel would journey, and at the command of the
LORD they would camp; as long as the cloud stayed
above the tabernacle they remained encamped.
19Even when the cloud continued long, many days
above the tabernacle, the children of Israel kept the
charge of the LORD and did not journey. 20So it was,
when the cloud was above the tabernacle a few days:
according to the command of the LORD they would remain encamped, and according to the command of
the LORD they would journey. 21So it was, when the
cloud remained only from evening until morning:
when the cloud was taken up in the morning, then
they would journey; whether by day or by night,
whenever the cloud was taken up, they would journey.
22*Whether it was* two days, a month, or a year that the
cloud remained above the tabernacle, the children of
Israel would remain encamped and not journey; but
when it was taken up, they would journey. 23At the
command of the LORD they remained encamped, and
at the command of the LORD they journeyed; they kept
the charge of the LORD, at the command of the LORD by
the hand of Moses.

Two Silver Trumpets

10 And the LORD spoke to Moses, saying: 2"Make
two silver trumpets for yourself; you shall
make them of hammered work; you shall use them
for calling the congregation and for directing the
movement of the camps. 3When they blow both of
them, all the congregation shall gather before you at
the door of the tabernacle of meeting. 4But if they
blow *only* one, then the leaders, the heads of the divisions of Israel, shall gather to you. 5When you sound
the advance, the camps that lie on the east side shall
then begin their journey. 6When you sound the advance the second time, then the camps that lie on the
south side shall begin their journey; they shall sound
the call for them to begin their journeys. 7And when
the assembly is to be gathered together, you shall
blow, but not sound the advance. 8The sons of Aaron,
the priests, shall blow the trumpets; and these shall be
to you as an ordinance forever throughout your generations.
9"When you go to war in your land against the
enemy who oppresses you, then you shall sound an
alarm with the trumpets, and you will be remembered before the LORD your God, and you will be saved
from your enemies. 10Also in the day of your gladness,
in your appointed feasts, and at the beginning of your
months, you shall blow the trumpets over your burnt
offerings and over the sacrifices of your peace offerings; and they shall be a memorial for you before your
God: I *am* the LORD your God."

Departure from Sinai

11Now it came to pass on the twentieth *day* of the
second month, in the second year, that the cloud was
taken up from above the tabernacle of the Testimony.
12And the children of Israel set out from the Wilderness of Sinai on their journeys; then the cloud settled
down in the Wilderness of Paran. 13So they started out
for the first time according to the command of the
LORD by the hand of Moses.
14The standard of the camp of the children of Judah
set out first according to their armies; over their army
was Nahshon the son of Amminadab. 15Over the army
of the tribe of the children of Issachar *was* Nethanel
the son of Zuar. 16And over the army of the tribe of the
children of Zebulun *was* Eliab the son of Helon.

LIFE LESSON

Numbers 10:11–11:35

SITUATION Approximately two years passed since the departure of the Israelites from Egypt. During this time at Mount Sinai, God gave them the tabernacle, ceremonial and ritual laws, and travel instructions. Then they traveled from Mount Sinai into the wilderness of Paran en route to the Promised Land. When they faced many hardships, they forgot about God's provision and protection and began to curse and complain. God punished them for their lack of faith.

OBSERVATION Follow God's lead without complaining. Pride (sin) causes us to question God, and we feel as if we could do better than Almighty God.

INSPIRATION If you came to me complaining that your church was not meeting your needs, the first thing I'd ask is what your needs are. . . . Take a sheet of paper and list your needs. Before you pray about them, ask yourself how these needs can realistically be met. . . .

Often as people write out and analyze their needs, all of a sudden they see that the church is not at fault. For example, you may have a need for close friendship with someone. You go to church expecting the church as a whole to become your close friend. This is unlikely. There may be people within the church who could meet your need, but you have an important part to play as well. You need to be able to initiate friendship as well as to respond to others. . . .

17 Then the tabernacle was taken down; and the sons of Gershon and the
sons of Merari set out, carrying the tabernacle.
18 And the standard of the camp of Reuben set out according to their
armies; over their army *was* Elizur the son of Shedeur. 19 Over the army of
the tribe of the children of Simeon *was* Shelumiel the son of Zurishaddai.
20 And over the army of the tribe of the children of Gad *was* Eliasaph the
son of Deuel.
21 Then the Kohathites set out, carrying the holy things. (The tabernacle
would be prepared for their arrival.)
22 And the standard of the camp of the children of Ephraim set out according to their armies; over their army *was* Elishama the son of
Ammihud. 23 Over the army of the tribe of the children of Manasseh *was*
Gamaliel the son of Pedahzur. 24 And over the army of the tribe of the children of Benjamin *was* Abidan the son of Gideoni.
25 Then the standard of the camp of the children of Dan (the rear guard
of all the camps) set out according to their armies; over their army *was*
Ahiezer the son of Ammishaddai. 26 Over the army of the tribe of the children of Asher *was* Pagiel the son of Ocran. 27 And over the army of the tribe
of the children of Naphtali *was* Ahira the son of Enan.
28 Thus *was* the order of march of the children of Israel, according to
their armies, when they began their journey.
29 Now Moses said to Hobab the son of Reuel[j] the Midianite, Moses' father-
in-law, "We are setting out for the place of which the LORD said, 'I will give
it to you.' Come with us, and we will treat you well; for the LORD has promised
good things to Israel."
30 And he said to him, "I will not go, but I will depart to my *own* land and
to my relatives."
31 So *Moses* said, "Please do not leave, inasmuch as you know how we are
to camp in the wilderness, and you can be our eyes. 32 And it shall be, if you
go with us—indeed it shall be—that whatever good the LORD will do to us,
the same we will do to you."
33 So they departed from the mountain of the LORD on a journey of three
days; and the ark of the covenant of the LORD went before them for the
three days' journey, to search out a resting place for them. 34 And the cloud
of the LORD *was* above them by day when they went out from the camp.
35 So it was, whenever the ark set out, that Moses said:

"Rise up, O LORD!
Let Your enemies be scattered,
And let those who hate You flee before You."

36 And when it rested, he said:

"Return, O LORD,
To the many thousands of Israel."

The People Complain

11 Now *when* the people complained, it displeased the LORD; for the
LORD heard *it,* and His anger was aroused. So the fire of the LORD
burned among them, and consumed *some* in the outskirts of the camp.
2 Then the people cried out to Moses, and when Moses prayed to the LORD,

10:29 [j] Septuagint reads *Raguel* (compare Exodus 2:18).

the fire was quenched. 3So he called the name of the place Taberah,[k] because the fire of the LORD had burned among them.
4Now the mixed multitude who were among them yielded to intense
craving; so the children of Israel also wept again and said: "Who will give
us meat to eat? 5We remember the fish which we ate freely in Egypt, the cucumbers, the melons, the leeks, the onions, and the garlic; 6but now our
whole being *is* dried up; *there is* nothing at all except this manna *before* our
eyes!"
7Now the manna *was* like coriander seed, and its color like the color of
bdellium. 8The people went about and gathered *it,* ground *it* on millstones
or beat *it* in the mortar, cooked *it* in pans, and made cakes of it; and its
taste was like the taste of pastry prepared with oil. 9And when the dew fell
on the camp in the night, the manna fell on it.
10Then Moses heard the people weeping throughout their families,
everyone at the door of his tent; and the anger of the LORD was greatly
aroused; Moses also was displeased. 11So Moses said to the LORD, "Why
have You afflicted Your servant? And why have I not found favor in Your
sight, that You have laid the burden of all these people on me? 12Did I conceive all these people? Did I beget them, that You should say to me, 'Carry
them in your bosom, as a guardian carries a nursing child,' to the land
which You swore to their fathers? 13Where am I to get meat to give to all
these people? For they weep all over me, saying, 'Give us meat, that we may
eat.' 14I am not able to bear all these people alone, because the burden *is* too
heavy for me. 15If You treat me like this, please kill me here and now—if I
have found favor in Your sight—and do not let me see my wretchedness!"

The Seventy Elders

16So the LORD said to Moses: "Gather to Me seventy men of the elders of
Israel, whom you know to be the elders of the people and officers over
them; bring them to the tabernacle of meeting, that they may stand there
with you. 17Then I will come down and talk with you there. I will take of the
Spirit that *is* upon you and will put *the same* upon them; and they shall
bear the burden of the people with you, that you may not bear *it* yourself
alone. 18Then you shall say to the people, 'Consecrate yourselves for tomorrow, and you shall eat meat; for you have wept in the hearing of the
LORD, saying, "Who will give us meat to eat? For *it was* well with us in
Egypt." Therefore the LORD will give you meat, and you shall eat. 19You
shall eat, not one day, nor two days, nor five days, nor ten days, nor twenty
days, 20but *for* a whole month, until it comes out of your nostrils and becomes loathsome to you, because you have despised the LORD who is
among you, and have wept before Him, saying, "Why did we ever come up
out of Egypt?" ' "
21And Moses said, "The people whom I *am* among *are* six hundred
thousand men on foot; yet You have said, 'I will give them meat, that they
may eat *for* a whole month.' 22Shall flocks and herds be slaughtered for
them, to provide enough for them? Or shall all the fish of the sea be gathered together for them, to provide enough for them?"
23And the LORD said to Moses, "Has the LORD's arm been shortened?
Now you shall see whether what I say will happen to you or not."

11:3 [k] Literally *Burning*

Second, I'd ask if you are personally spending time in the Word of God. The first place God will meet your needs is on a one-to-one level, in the Scriptures. Too often we don't get into the Scriptures ourselves; we don't let God meet us on a personal, intimate basis. Then we go to church and feel bad because the church is unable to meet our needs. . . .

Third, I'd ask if you are praying for your church and your pastor by name. I have found that when people pray specifically and individually for someone or something, they become more realistic in their expectations.

Fourth, I'd suggest that you seek counsel from your pastor and others. Go to your pastor and share your needs and frustrations. He may be able to give you some tremendous insight into the situation. Go to other church leaders as well—an elder, perhaps, or a Sunday school teacher. The Bible says, "For lack of guidance a nation falls, but many advisers make victory sure" (Proverbs 11:14). This is true of an individual also. Seek those advisers and get help.

(From "What Are Your Needs?" by Josh McDowell in *Practical Christianity)*

APPLICATION Try the four-point action plan above. Better yet, try it with a small group of friends so you can talk about the results.

EXPLORATION Complaining—Exodus 14:10-11; 17:2; Numbers 11:4-6; 1 Corinthians 10:10; Philippians 2:14-16.

LIFE LESSON

Numbers 12:1-16

SITUATION After being freed from Egypt, Israel traveled in the desert for over two years. Although they had food and safety, they continued to grumble against Moses and God.

OBSERVATION Living and cooperating with others requires God's help.

INSPIRATION We have glamorized vice and minimized virtue. We have played down gentleness, manners, and morals—while we have played up rudeness, savagery, and vice. We have reverted to the barbaric era of "tooth and claw," "the survival of the fittest," and the philosophy of "might is right."… We have heard the modern expression "Don't fight it—it's bigger than both of us." Those who are meek do not fight back at life. They learn the secret of surrender, of yielding to God. He then fights for us!

The Bible says: "For as ye have yielded your members servants to uncleanness and to iniquity … even so now yield your members servants unto holiness" (Romans 6:19).

Instead of filling your mind with resentments, abusing your body by sinful diversions, and damaging your soul by willfulness, humbly give all over to God. Your conflicts will disappear and your inner tension will vanish into thin air.

Then your life will begin to count for something. It will begin to yield, to produce, to bear fruit. You will have the feeling of belonging to life. Boredom will melt away, and you will become vibrant with hope and expectation. Because you are meekly yielded, you will begin to "inherit the earth" of good things which God holds in store for those who trust Him with their all. …

(From *The Secret of Happiness* by Billy Graham)

APPLICATION Are there people in your life who cause conflict? Encourage them today with a letter or phone call. Let them know of your love for God and your commitment to them.

EXPLORATION Meekness—Isaiah 53:7; Zephaniah 2:3; Matthew 11:29; Luke 6:29; Galatians 5:22-23; Ephesians 4:2; Colossians 3:13; 2 Timothy 2:25; 1 Peter 2:23; 3:4.

24So Moses went out and told the people the words of the LORD, and he
gathered the seventy men of the elders of the people and placed them
around the tabernacle. 25Then the LORD came down in the cloud, and
spoke to him, and took of the Spirit that *was* upon him, and placed *the
same* upon the seventy elders; and it happened, when the Spirit rested
upon them, that they prophesied, although they never did *so* again.[l]
26But two men had remained in the camp: the name of one *was* Eldad,
and the name of the other Medad. And the Spirit rested upon them. Now
they *were* among those listed, but who had not gone out to the tabernacle;
yet they prophesied in the camp. 27And a young man ran and told Moses,
and said, "Eldad and Medad are prophesying in the camp."
28So Joshua the son of Nun, Moses' assistant, *one* of his choice men, answered and said, "Moses my lord, forbid them!"
29Then Moses said to him, "Are you zealous for my sake? Oh, that all the
LORD's people were prophets *and* that the LORD would put His Spirit upon
them!" 30And Moses returned to the camp, he and the elders of Israel.

The LORD Sends Quail

31Now a wind went out from the LORD, and it brought quail from the sea
and left *them* fluttering near the camp, about a day's journey on this side
and about a day's journey on the other side, all around the camp, and
about two cubits above the surface of the ground. 32And the people stayed
up all that day, all night, and all the next day, and gathered the quail (he
who gathered least gathered ten homers); and they spread *them* out for
themselves all around the camp. 33But while the meat *was* still between
their teeth, before it was chewed, the wrath of the LORD was aroused
against the people, and the LORD struck the people with a very great
plague. 34So he called the name of that place Kibroth Hattaavah,[m] because
there they buried the people who had yielded to craving.
35From Kibroth Hattaavah the people moved to Hazeroth, and camped
at Hazeroth.

Dissension of Aaron and Miriam

12 Then Miriam and Aaron spoke against Moses because of the Ethiopian woman whom he had married; for he had married an Ethiopian woman. 2So they said, "Has the LORD indeed spoken only through
Moses? Has He not spoken through us also?" And the LORD heard *it.* 3(Now
the man Moses *was* very humble, more than all men who *were* on the face
of the earth.)
4Suddenly the LORD said to Moses, Aaron, and Miriam, "Come out, you
three, to the tabernacle of meeting!" So the three came out. 5Then the LORD
came down in the pillar of cloud and stood *in* the door of the tabernacle,
and called Aaron and Miriam. And they both went forward. 6Then He
said,

"Hear now My words:
If there is a prophet among you,
I, the LORD, make Myself known to him in a vision;
I speak to him in a dream.

11:25 [l] Targum and Vulgate read *did not cease.*
11:34 [m] Literally *Graves of Craving*

7 Not so with My servant Moses;
He *is* faithful in all My house.
8 I speak with him face to face,
Even plainly, and not in dark sayings;
And he sees the form of the LORD.
Why then were you not afraid
To speak against My servant Moses?"

9So the anger of the LORD was aroused against them, and He departed.
10And when the cloud departed from above the tabernacle, suddenly Miriam *became* leprous, as *white as* snow. Then Aaron turned toward Miriam, and there she was, a leper. 11So Aaron said to Moses, "Oh, my lord!
Please do not lay *this* sin on us, in which we have done foolishly and in
which we have sinned. 12Please do not let her be as one dead, whose flesh
is half consumed when he comes out of his mother's womb!"
13So Moses cried out to the LORD, saying, "Please heal her, O God, I pray!"
14Then the LORD said to Moses, "If her father had but spit in her face,
would she not be shamed seven days? Let her be shut out of the camp
seven days, and afterward she may be received *again.*" 15So Miriam was
shut out of the camp seven days, and the people did not journey till Miriam was brought in *again.* 16And afterward the people moved from
Hazeroth and camped in the Wilderness of Paran.

Spies Sent into Canaan

13 And the LORD spoke to Moses, saying, 2"Send men to spy out the land
of Canaan, which I am giving to the children of Israel; from each
tribe of their fathers you shall send a man, every one a leader among them."
3So Moses sent them from the Wilderness of Paran according to the
command of the LORD, all of them men who *were* heads of the children of
Israel. 4Now these *were* their names: from the tribe of Reuben, Shammua
the son of Zaccur; 5from the tribe of Simeon, Shaphat the son of Hori;
6from the tribe of Judah, Caleb the son of Jephunneh; 7from the tribe of
Issachar, Igal the son of Joseph; 8from the tribe of Ephraim, Hoshea[n] the
son of Nun; 9from the tribe of Benjamin, Palti the son of Raphu; 10from the
tribe of Zebulun, Gaddiel the son of Sodi; 11from the tribe of Joseph, *that is,*
from the tribe of Manasseh, Gaddi the son of Susi; 12from the tribe of Dan,
Ammiel the son of Gemalli; 13from the tribe of Asher, Sethur the son of Michael; 14from the tribe of Naphtali, Nahbi the son of Vophsi; 15from the
tribe of Gad, Geuel the son of Machi.
16These *are* the names of the men whom Moses sent to spy out the land.
And Moses called Hoshea[o] the son of Nun, Joshua.
17Then Moses sent them to spy out the land of Canaan, and said to them,
"Go up this *way* into the South, and go up to the mountains, 18and see what
the land is like: whether the people who dwell in it *are* strong or weak, few
or many; 19whether the land they dwell in *is* good or bad; whether the cities
they inhabit *are* like camps or strongholds; 20whether the land *is* rich or
poor; and whether there are forests there or not. Be of good courage. And
bring some of the fruit of the land." Now the time *was* the season of the
first ripe grapes.

13:8 [n] Septuagint and Vulgate read *Oshea.*
13:16 [o] Septuagint and Vulgate read *Oshea.*

LIFE LESSON

Numbers 13:1–14:45

SITUATION The Bible called the Promised Land, Canaan, a land flowing with milk and honey because of the abundance of figs, dates, and nuts there. The land also contained many imposing cities with tall, thick walls.

OBSERVATION God expects Believers to exercise faith and obey his leading, even when they face challenging obstacles. Although we might not find a way, God can. Faithful disciples wait patiently for him to work.

INSPIRATION For many people, it is less difficult to commit the future to the Lord than to commit the present. Many recognize that we are helpless in regard to the future, but we feel as if the present is in our own hands and must be carried on our own shoulders.

I knew a Christian woman who had a great "burden" in her life. Her concern caused her to lose sleep and her appetite, and soon her health was in danger of breaking down. . . . She recognized, however, that she could in no way alter her circumstances and therefore resolved to try a new plan.

She took her circumstances to the Lord. She handed them over to His management. Then she simply believed from that very moment that He took them. She decided to leave all responsibility, and her mental worrying and anxious feelings, with Him, too.

Of course, all of these tormenting things tried time and again to return. And each time, she took them back to the Lord. As a result—although the outward circumstances did not change—her soul began to experience perfect peace in the midst of trouble.

She rejoiced at having entered into such a practical secret of the spiritual life. And from that time, she set this as her goal: Never to carry her own burdens nor to manage her own affairs, but to hand them over as fast as they arose to the divine Burdenbearer.

Continued

21So they went up and spied out the land from the Wilderness of Zin as
far as Rehob, near the entrance of Hamath. 22And they went up through
the South and came to Hebron; Ahiman, Sheshai, and Talmai, the descendants of Anak, *were* there. (Now Hebron was built seven years before Zoan
in Egypt.) 23Then they came to the Valley of Eshcol, and there cut down a
branch with one cluster of grapes; they carried it between two of them on
a pole. *They* also *brought* some of the pomegranates and figs. 24The place
was called the Valley of Eshcol,[p] because of the cluster which the men of Israel cut down there. 25And they returned from spying out the land after
forty days.

26Now they departed and came back to Moses and Aaron and all the
congregation of the children of Israel in the Wilderness of Paran, at Kadesh; they brought back word to them and to all the congregation, and
showed them the fruit of the land. 27Then they told him, and said: "We
went to the land where you sent us. It truly flows with milk and honey, and
this *is* its fruit. 28Nevertheless the people who dwell in the land *are* strong;
the cities *are* fortified *and* very large; moreover we saw the descendants of
Anak there. 29The Amalekites dwell in the land of the South; the Hittites,
the Jebusites, and the Amorites dwell in the mountains; and the
Canaanites dwell by the sea and along the banks of the Jordan."

30Then Caleb quieted the people before Moses, and said, "Let us go up at
once and take possession, for we are well able to overcome it."

31But the men who had gone up with him said, "We are not able to go up
against the people, for they *are* stronger than we." 32And they gave the children of Israel a bad report of the land which they had spied out, saying,
"The land through which we have gone as spies *is* a land that devours its
inhabitants, and all the people whom we saw in it *are* men of *great* stature.
33There we saw the giants[q] (the descendants of Anak came from the giants); and we were like grasshoppers in our own sight, and so we were in
their sight."

Israel Refuses to Enter Canaan

14 So all the congregation lifted up their voices and cried, and the people wept that night. 2And all the children of Israel complained
against Moses and Aaron, and the whole congregation said to them, "If
only we had died in the land of Egypt! Or if only we had died in this wilderness! 3Why has the LORD brought us to this land to fall by the sword, that
our wives and children should become victims? Would it not be better for
us to return to Egypt?" 4So they said to one another, "Let us select a leader
and return to Egypt."

5Then Moses and Aaron fell on their faces before all the assembly of the
congregation of the children of Israel.

6But Joshua the son of Nun and Caleb the son of Jephunneh, *who were*
among those who had spied out the land, tore their clothes; 7and they
spoke to all the congregation of the children of Israel, saying: "The land we
passed through to spy out *is* an exceedingly good land. 8If the LORD delights in us, then He will bring us into this land and give it to us, 'a land
which flows with milk and honey.'[r] 9Only do not rebel against the LORD,

13:24 [p] Literally *Cluster*
13:33 [q] Hebrew *nephilim*
14:8 [r] Exodus 3:8

This same secret, which was so effective in dealing with outward circumstances, she began to apply to her inward life—because, in fact, her moods and emotions were even more utterly unmanageable. So she abandoned her whole self to the Lord, all that she was, as well as all that she had. She believed that He took what she committed to Him, and determined that she would cease fretting and worrying.

And so she felt a new light dawning within, and felt flooded with the gladness that comes when we know we belong to God. By applying this simple secret, she discovered it is possible to obey God's loving commandment, contained in the words: "Do not worry about anything."

The inevitable result is that the peace of God, which comes when we step beyond our understanding and into trust, will take hold of our heart and mind.

(From "The Christian's Secret of a Happy Life" by Hannah W. Smith in *Safe Within Your Love*)

APPLICATION What are your big concerns and worries? However imposing they may be, commit them to the Lord. Begin a conversation today with a close friend by explaining how God is working in your life. Ask the friend to pray with you.

EXPLORATION Testing God—Deuteronomy 6:16; Psalm 95:8-9; Isaiah 7:10-13; Matthew 16:1; Acts 15:10; 1 Corinthians 10:9.

nor fear the people of the land, for they *are* our bread;
their protection has departed from them, and the
LORD *is* with us. Do not fear them."
10 And all the congregation said to stone them with
stones. Now the glory of the LORD appeared in the
tabernacle of meeting before all the children of Israel.

Moses Intercedes for the People

11 Then the LORD said to Moses: "How long will these
people reject Me? And how long will they not believe
Me, with all the signs which I have performed among
them? 12 I will strike them with the pestilence and
disinherit them, and I will make of you a nation
greater and mightier than they."
13 And Moses said to the LORD: "Then the Egyptians
will hear *it*, for by Your might You brought these people up from among them, 14 and they will tell *it* to the
inhabitants of this land. They have heard that You,
LORD, *are* among these people; that You, LORD, are
seen face to face and Your cloud stands above them,
and You go before them in a pillar of cloud by day and
in a pillar of fire by night. 15 Now *if* You kill these people as one man, then the nations which have heard of
Your fame will speak, saying, 16 'Because the LORD was
not able to bring this people to the land which He
swore to give them, therefore He killed them in the
wilderness.' 17 And now, I pray, let the power of my
Lord be great, just as You have spoken, saying, 18 'The
LORD is longsuffering and abundant in mercy, forgiving iniquity and transgression; but He by no means
clears *the guilty*, visiting the iniquity of the fathers on
the children to the third and fourth *generation*.'[s] 19 Pardon the iniquity of this people, I pray, according to the
greatness of Your mercy, just as You have forgiven this
people, from Egypt even until now."
20 Then the LORD said: "I have pardoned, according to
your word; 21 but truly, as I live, all the earth shall be
filled with the glory of the LORD— 22 because all these
men who have seen My glory and the signs which I did
in Egypt and in the wilderness, and have put Me to the
test now these ten times, and have not heeded My voice,
23 they certainly shall not see the land of which I swore
to their fathers, nor shall any of those who rejected Me
see it. 24 But My servant Caleb, because he has a different
spirit in him and has followed Me fully, I will bring
into the land where he went, and his descendants shall
inherit it. 25 Now the Amalekites and the Canaanites
dwell in the valley; tomorrow turn and move out into
the wilderness by the Way of the Red Sea."

Death Sentence on the Rebels

26 And the LORD spoke to Moses and Aaron, saying,
27 "How long *shall I bear with* this evil congregation
who complain against Me? I have heard the complaints which the children of Israel make against Me.
28 Say to them, 'As I live,' says the LORD, 'just as you
have spoken in My hearing, so I will do to you: 29 The
carcasses of you who have complained against Me
shall fall in this wilderness, all of you who were numbered, according to your entire number, from twenty
years old and above. 30 Except for Caleb the son of
Jephunneh and Joshua the son of Nun, you shall by
no means enter the land which I swore I would make
you dwell in. 31 But your little ones, whom you said
would be victims, I will bring in, and they shall know
the land which you have despised. 32 But *as for* you,
your carcasses shall fall in this wilderness. 33 And your
sons shall be shepherds in the wilderness forty years,
and bear the brunt of your infidelity, until your carcasses are consumed in the wilderness. 34 According
to the number of the days in which you spied out the
land, forty days, for each day you shall bear your guilt
one year, *namely* forty years, and you shall know My
rejection. 35 I the LORD have spoken this. I will surely
do so to all this evil congregation who are gathered together against Me. In this wilderness they shall be
consumed, and there they shall die.'"
36 Now the men whom Moses sent to spy out the
land, who returned and made all the congregation
complain against him by bringing a bad report of the
land, 37 those very men who brought the evil report
about the land, died by the plague before the LORD.
38 But Joshua the son of Nun and Caleb the son of
Jephunneh remained alive, of the men who went to
spy out the land.

A Futile Invasion Attempt

39 Then Moses told these words to all the children of
Israel, and the people mourned greatly. 40 And they
rose early in the morning and went up to the top of
the mountain, saying, "Here we are, and we will go up
to the place which the LORD has promised, for we have
sinned!"
41 And Moses said, "Now why do you transgress the
command of the LORD? For this will not succeed. 42 Do
not go up, lest you be defeated by your enemies, for
the LORD *is* not among you. 43 For the Amalekites and
the Canaanites *are* there before you, and you shall fall

14:18 [s] Exodus 34:6, 7

LIFE LESSON

Numbers 15:1-41

SITUATION God used tassels on garments as a visual reminder of his presence. Israel's religion contrasted with the pagan idol worship of other people in the land, worship that led to self-centeredness and pride.

OBSERVATION God still pointed his people toward the Promised Land, even after their rebellion in the desert. God has a purpose, and he will fulfill it. Follow him without grumbling.

INSPIRATION God declares that He will faithfully remove the created things which can be shaken—the shakeable kingdom. Why? So that the unshakeable may remain. Created things give cultural Christianity its toehold. Created things defeat us and choke the Word—the worries of this life and the deceitfulness of wealth. (Matthew 13:22).

When we cross over the line and refuse Him who speaks, He will separate us from the created things—the idols, the shakeable kingdom—which dilute our devotion to him. If we cannot remain obedient, if we cannot be holy, then He will discipline us for our own good, "that we may share in his holiness."...

Do not be alarmed if God shakes up your world. Though your first natural thought will disagree, it is a blessing. It is not a sign that you are unworthy—every one of us is unworthy. It is not a sign of hatred, but love. If He did not

by the sword; because you have turned away from the LORD, the LORD will
not be with you."
44But they presumed to go up to the mountaintop. Nevertheless, neither
the ark of the covenant of the LORD nor Moses departed from the camp.
45Then the Amalekites and the Canaanites who dwelt in that mountain
came down and attacked them, and drove them back as far as Hormah.

Laws of Grain and Drink Offerings

15 And the LORD spoke to Moses, saying, 2"Speak to the children of Israel, and say to them: 'When you have come into the land you are to
inhabit, which I am giving to you, 3and you make an offering by fire to the
LORD, a burnt offering or a sacrifice, to fulfill a vow or as a freewill offering
or in your appointed feasts, to make a sweet aroma to the LORD, from the
herd or the flock, 4then he who presents his offering to the LORD shall bring
a grain offering of one-tenth *of an ephah* of fine flour mixed with one-
fourth of a hin of oil; 5and one-fourth of a hin of wine as a drink offering
you shall prepare with the burnt offering or the sacrifice, for each lamb.
6Or for a ram you shall prepare as a grain offering two-tenths *of an ephah*
of fine flour mixed with one-third of a hin of oil; 7and as a drink offering
you shall offer one-third of a hin of wine as a sweet aroma to the LORD.
8And when you prepare a young bull as a burnt offering, or as a sacrifice to
fulfill a vow, or as a peace offering to the LORD, 9then shall be offered with
the young bull a grain offering of three-tenths *of an ephah* of fine flour
mixed with half a hin of oil; 10and you shall bring as the drink offering half
a hin of wine as an offering made by fire, a sweet aroma to the LORD.
11'Thus it shall be done for each young bull, for each ram, or for each
lamb or young goat. 12According to the number that you prepare, so you
shall do with everyone according to their number. 13All who are native-
born shall do these things in this manner, in presenting an offering made
by fire, a sweet aroma to the LORD. 14And if a stranger dwells with you, or
whoever *is* among you throughout your generations, and would present
an offering made by fire, a sweet aroma to the LORD, just as you do, so shall
he do. 15One ordinance *shall be* for you of the assembly and for the stranger
who dwells *with you,* an ordinance forever throughout your generations;
as you are, so shall the stranger be before the LORD. 16One law and one custom shall be for you and for the stranger who dwells with you.' "[t]
17Again the LORD spoke to Moses, saying, 18"Speak to the children of Israel, and say to them: 'When you come into the land to which I bring you,
19then it will be, when you eat of the bread of the land, that you shall offer
up a heave offering to the LORD. 20You shall offer up a cake of the first of
your ground meal *as* a heave offering; as a heave offering of the threshing
floor, so shall you offer it up. 21Of the first of your ground meal you shall
give to the LORD a heave offering throughout your generations.

Laws Concerning Unintentional Sin

22'If you sin unintentionally, and do not observe all these commandments which the LORD has spoken to Moses— 23all that the LORD has commanded you by the hand of Moses, from the day the LORD gave
commandment and onward throughout your generations— 24then it will

15:16 [t] Compare Exodus 12:49

be, if it is unintentionally committed, without the knowledge of the congregation, that the whole congregation shall offer one young bull as a
burnt offering, as a sweet aroma to the LORD, with its grain offering and
its drink offering, according to the ordinance, and one kid of the goats as
a sin offering. 25So the priest shall make atonement for the whole congregation of the children of Israel, and it shall be forgiven them, for it
was unintentional; they shall bring their offering, an offering made by
fire to the LORD, and their sin offering before the LORD, for their unin-
tended sin. 26It shall be forgiven the whole congregation of the children
of Israel and the stranger who dwells among them, because all the people *did it* unintentionally.

27'And if a person sins unintentionally, then he shall bring a female goat
in its first year as a sin offering. 28So the priest shall make atonement for the
person who sins unintentionally, when he sins unintentionally before the
LORD, to make atonement for him; and it shall be forgiven him. 29You shall
have one law for him who sins unintentionally, *for* him who is native-born
among the children of Israel and for the stranger who dwells among them.

Law Concerning Presumptuous Sin

30'But the person who does *anything* presumptuously, *whether he is*
native-born or a stranger, that one brings reproach on the LORD, and he
shall be cut off from among his people. 31Because he has despised the
word of the LORD, and has broken His commandment, that person shall
be completely cut off; his guilt *shall be* upon him.' "

Penalty for Violating the Sabbath

32Now while the children of Israel were in the wilderness, they found a
man gathering sticks on the Sabbath day. 33And those who found him
gathering sticks brought him to Moses and Aaron, and to all the congregation. 34They put him under guard, because it had not been explained
what should be done to him.

35Then the LORD said to Moses, "The man must surely be put to death;
all the congregation shall stone him with stones outside the camp." 36So,
as the LORD commanded Moses, all the congregation brought him outside
the camp and stoned him with stones, and he died.

Tassels on Garments

37Again the LORD spoke to Moses, saying, 38"Speak to the children of Israel: Tell them to make tassels on the corners of their garments throughout their generations, and to put a blue thread in the tassels of the corners.
39And you shall have the tassel, that you may look upon it and remember
all the commandments of the LORD and do them, and that you *may* not follow the harlotry to which your own heart and your own eyes are inclined,
40and that you may remember and do all My commandments, and be holy
for your God. 41I *am* the LORD your God, who brought you out of the land of
Egypt, to be your God: I *am* the LORD your God."

Rebellion Against Moses and Aaron

16 Now Korah the son of Izhar, the son of Kohath, the son of Levi, with
Dathan and Abiram the sons of Eliab, and On the son of Peleth, sons
of Reuben, took *men;* 2and they rose up before Moses with some of the

love you, He would let you completely self-destruct. As it is, He cleanses your life from sin. . . .

When God disciplines you by removing created things, by shaking up your temporal kingdom, rejoice and be glad. Created things divide our affections from God and become competition to our devotion. They lure us into the wrong race. They consume our creativity and deflect our thoughts away from the Lord Jesus.

I became a cultural Christian. Created things became idols and divided me from complete, faithful devotion to our Lord. God removed most of the created things I accumulated. I built a shakeable kingdom, and God shook it. Words are inadequate to express the joy and gratitude I feel toward God for the wounds He faithfully inflicted. It may be the single greatest blessing of my spiritual pilgrimage.

(From *Walking with Christ in the Details of Life* by Patrick M. Morley)

APPLICATION What is your ideal day? Go ahead, dream a little. Does God have a place in it? If he is off to the side, you need realignment. Do something today to give God a greater share of your life.

EXPLORATION Objects of Hope—Job 13:15; Psalm 25:3; 33:20-22; 119:43; Isaiah 42:4; Jeremiah 14:22; Romans 4:17-18; 1 Timothy 6:17.

LIFE LESSON

Numbers 16:1–17:13

SITUATION God directed the Israelites back into the desert for forty years because of disobedience and unbelief. The people resisted this tough directive. Some of the Levites became disgruntled with Moses' leadership. Korah, one of the Levites, led a disastrous rebellion.

OBSERVATION Leaders deserve our respect and support, even during trying times. We must not take part in a rebellion or gossip against a leader.

INSPIRATION Recently, my wife and I had the pleasure of spending an evening with former astronaut General Charles M. Duke. All of us in the room sat in rapt fascination as the man told of the *Apollo 16* mission to the moon, including some interesting tidbits related to driving "Rover," the lunar vehicle, and actually walking on the surface of the planet. We were full of questions which General Duke patiently and carefully answered one after another.

I asked, "Once you were there, weren't you free to make your own decisions and carry out some of your own experiments . . . you know, sort of do as you pleased—maybe stay a little longer if you liked?" He smiled

children of Israel, two hundred and fifty leaders of the congregation, representatives of the congregation, men of renown. 3They gathered together
against Moses and Aaron, and said to them, "*You take* too much upon
yourselves, for all the congregation *is* holy, every one of them, and the
LORD *is* among them. Why then do you exalt yourselves above the assembly of the LORD?"
4So when Moses heard *it,* he fell on his face; 5and he spoke to Korah and
all his company, saying, "Tomorrow morning the LORD will show who *is*
His and *who is* holy, and will cause *him* to come near to Him. That one
whom He chooses He will cause to come near to Him. 6Do this: Take
censers, Korah and all your company; 7put fire in them and put incense in
them before the LORD tomorrow, and it shall be *that* the man whom the
LORD chooses *is* the holy one. *You take* too much upon yourselves, you
sons of Levi!"
8Then Moses said to Korah, "Hear now, you sons of Levi: 9*Is it* a small
thing to you that the God of Israel has separated you from the congregation of Israel, to bring you near to Himself, to do the work of the tabernacle of the LORD, and to stand before the congregation to serve them; 10and
that He has brought you near *to Himself,* you and all your brethren, the
sons of Levi, with you? And are you seeking the priesthood also? 11There-
fore you and all your company *are* gathered together against the LORD.
And what *is* Aaron that you complain against him?"
12And Moses sent to call Dathan and Abiram the sons of Eliab, but they
said, "We will not come up! 13*Is it* a small thing that you have brought us
up out of a land flowing with milk and honey, to kill us in the wilderness,
that you should keep acting like a prince over us? 14Moreover you have not
brought us into a land flowing with milk and honey, nor given us inheritance of fields and vineyards. Will you put out the eyes of these men? We
will not come up!"
15Then Moses was very angry, and said to the LORD, "Do not respect their
offering. I have not taken one donkey from them, nor have I hurt one of
them."
16And Moses said to Korah, "Tomorrow, you and all your company be
present before the LORD—you and they, as well as Aaron. 17Let each take
his censer and put incense in it, and each of you bring his censer before
the LORD, two hundred and fifty censers; both you and Aaron, each *with*
his censer." 18So every man took his censer, put fire in it, laid incense on it,
and stood at the door of the tabernacle of meeting with Moses and Aaron.
19And Korah gathered all the congregation against them at the door of the
tabernacle of meeting. Then the glory of the LORD appeared to all the congregation.
20And the LORD spoke to Moses and Aaron, saying, 21"Separate yourselves
from among this congregation, that I may consume them in a moment."
22Then they fell on their faces, and said, "O God, the God of the spirits of
all flesh, shall one man sin, and You be angry with all the congregation?"
23So the LORD spoke to Moses, saying, 24"Speak to the congregation, saying, 'Get away from the tents of Korah, Dathan, and Abiram.' "
25Then Moses rose and went to Dathan and Abiram, and the elders of
Israel followed him. 26And he spoke to the congregation, saying, "Depart
now from the tents of these wicked men! Touch nothing of theirs, lest you
be consumed in all their sins." 27So they got away from around the tents of

Korah, Dathan, and Abiram; and Dathan and Abiram came out and stood
at the door of their tents, with their wives, their sons, and their little children.
28And Moses said: "By this you shall know that the LORD has sent me to
do all these works, for *I have* not *done them* of my own will. 29If these men
die naturally like all men, or if they are visited by the common fate of all
men, *then* the LORD has not sent me. 30But if the LORD creates a new thing,
and the earth opens its mouth and swallows them up with all that belongs
to them, and they go down alive into the pit, then you will understand that
these men have rejected the LORD."
31Now it came to pass, as he finished speaking all these words, that the
ground split apart under them, 32and the earth opened its mouth and
swallowed them up, with their households and all the men with Korah,
with all *their* goods. 33So they and all those with them went down alive into
the pit; the earth closed over them, and they perished from among the assembly. 34Then all Israel who *were* around them fled at their cry, for they
said, "Lest the earth swallow us up *also!*"
35And a fire came out from the LORD and consumed the two hundred
and fifty men who were offering incense.
36Then the LORD spoke to Moses, saying: 37"Tell Eleazar, the son of Aaron
the priest, to pick up the censers out of the blaze, for they are holy, and
scatter the fire some distance away. 38The censers of these men who sinned
against their own souls, let them be made into hammered plates as a covering for the altar. Because they presented them before the LORD, therefore
they are holy; and they shall be a sign to the children of Israel." 39So
Eleazar the priest took the bronze censers, which those who were burned
up had presented, and they were hammered out as a covering on the altar,
40*to be* a memorial to the children of Israel that no outsider, who *is* not a
descendant of Aaron, should come near to offer incense before the LORD,
that he might not become like Korah and his companions, just as the LORD
had said to him through Moses.

Complaints of the People

41On the next day all the congregation of the children of Israel complained against Moses and Aaron, saying, "You have killed the people of
the LORD." 42Now it happened, when the congregation had gathered
against Moses and Aaron, that they turned toward the tabernacle of meeting; and suddenly the cloud covered it, and the glory of the LORD appeared.
43Then Moses and Aaron came before the tabernacle of meeting.
44And the LORD spoke to Moses, saying, 45"Get away from among this
congregation, that I may consume them in a moment."
And they fell on their faces.
46So Moses said to Aaron, "Take a censer and put fire in it from the altar,
put incense *on it,* and take it quickly to the congregation and make atonement for them; for wrath has gone out from the LORD. The plague has
begun." 47Then Aaron took *it* as Moses commanded, and ran into the
midst of the assembly; and already the plague had begun among the people. So he put in the incense and made atonement for the people. 48And he
stood between the dead and the living; so the plague was stopped. 49Now
those who died in the plague were fourteen thousand seven hundred, besides those who died in the Korah incident. 50So Aaron returned to Moses
at the door of the tabernacle of meeting, for the plague had stopped.

back, "Sure, Chuck, if we didn't want to return to earth!"

He then described the intricate plan, the exact and precise instructions, the essential discipline, the instant obedience that was needed right down to the split second. By the way, he said they had landed somewhat "heavy" when they touched down on the moon. He was referring to their fuel supply. They had plenty left. Guess how much. One minute. They landed with sixty seconds of fuel remaining. Talk about being exact! I got the distinct impression that a rebel spirit doesn't fit inside a space suit. Whoever represents the United States in the space program must have an unconditional respect for authority. (From *Strengthening Your Grip* by Charles Swindoll)

APPLICATION Today, show loyalty to God when the way is rough and the future less bright than you want. Stay loyal to our great leader, who surely knows the way home.

EXPLORATION Rebellion—Numbers 12:1-15. Submission to Authority—Romans 13:1-6; Hebrews 13:17.

LIFE LESSON

Numbers 18:1–19:22

SITUATION The Lord gave instructions concerning the duties of the Levites: how sacrifices should be conducted.

OBSERVATION The elaborate method of cleansing from sin using the blood of animals demonstrated the need for purity in our relationship with God. God has provided for our cleansing through the washing of the blood of Christ (Titus 2:5-8).

INSPIRATION "What is that?" "It's a refinery," Dad answered.

A jungle of pipes and tanks and tubes and generators—heaters, pumps, pipes, filters, valves, hoses, conduits, switches, circuits. . . .

The function of that maze of machinery is defined by its name: It refines. Gasoline, oil, chemicals—the refinery takes whatever comes in and purifies it so that it's ready to go out.

The refinery does for petroleum and other products what your heart should do for you. It takes out the bad and utilizes the good.

We tend to think of the heart as the seat of emotion. We speak of "heart-throbs," "heartaches," and "broken hearts."

But when Jesus said, "Blessed are the pure in heart," he was speaking in a different context. To Jesus' listeners, the heart was the totality of the inner person—the control tower, the cockpit. The heart was thought of as the seat of the character—the origin of desires, affections, perceptions, thoughts, reasoning, imagination, conscience, intentions, purpose, will, and faith.

Thus a proverb admonished, "Above all else, guard your heart, for it is the wellspring of life."

To the Hebrew mind, the heart is a freeway clover-leaf where all emotions and prejudices and wisdom converge. It is a switch house that receives

The Budding of Aaron's Rod

17 And the LORD spoke to Moses, saying: 2"Speak to the children of Israel, and get from them a rod from each father's house, all their leaders according to their fathers' houses—twelve rods. Write each man's
name on his rod. 3And you shall write Aaron's name on the rod of Levi.
For there shall be one rod for the head of *each* father's house. 4Then you
shall place them in the tabernacle of meeting before the Testimony, where
I meet with you. 5And it shall be *that* the rod of the man whom I choose
will blossom; thus I will rid Myself of the complaints of the children of Israel, which they make against you."
6So Moses spoke to the children of Israel, and each of their leaders gave
him a rod apiece, for each leader according to their fathers' houses, twelve
rods; and the rod of Aaron *was* among their rods. 7And Moses placed the
rods before the LORD in the tabernacle of witness.
8Now it came to pass on the next day that Moses went into the tabernacle of witness, and behold, the rod of Aaron, of the house of Levi, had
sprouted and put forth buds, had produced blossoms and yielded ripe almonds. 9Then Moses brought out all the rods from before the LORD to all
the children of Israel; and they looked, and each man took his rod.
10And the LORD said to Moses, "Bring Aaron's rod back before the
Testimony, to be kept as a sign against the rebels, that you may put their
complaints away from Me, lest they die." 11Thus did Moses; just as the
LORD had commanded him, so he did.
12So the children of Israel spoke to Moses, saying, "Surely we die, we
perish, we all perish! 13Whoever even comes near the tabernacle of the
LORD must die. Shall we all utterly die?"

Duties of Priests and Levites

18 Then the LORD said to Aaron: "You and your sons and your father's
house with you shall bear the iniquity *related to* the sanctuary, and
you and your sons with you shall bear the iniquity *associated with* your
priesthood. 2Also bring with you your brethren of the tribe of Levi, the
tribe of your father, that they may be joined with you and serve you while
you and your sons *are* with you before the tabernacle of witness. 3They
shall attend to your needs and all the needs of the tabernacle; but they shall
not come near the articles of the sanctuary and the altar, lest they die—
they and you also. 4They shall be joined with you and attend to the needs of
the tabernacle of meeting, for all the work of the tabernacle; but an outsider shall not come near you. 5And you shall attend to the duties of the
sanctuary and the duties of the altar, that there *may* be no more wrath on
the children of Israel. 6Behold, I Myself have taken your brethren the
Levites from among the children of Israel; *they are* a gift to you, given by
the LORD, to do the work of the tabernacle of meeting. 7Therefore you and
your sons with you shall attend to your priesthood for everything at the
altar and behind the veil; and you shall serve. I give your priesthood *to you*
as a gift for service, but the outsider who comes near shall be put to death."

Offerings for Support of the Priests

8And the LORD spoke to Aaron: "Here, I Myself have also given you
charge of My heave offerings, all the holy gifts of the children of Israel; I

have given them as a portion to you and your sons, as an ordinance forever. 9This shall be yours of the most holy things *reserved* from the fire:
every offering of theirs, every grain offering and every sin offering and every
trespass offering which they render to Me, *shall be* most holy for you and
your sons. 10In a most holy *place* you shall eat it; every male shall eat it. It
shall be holy to you.
11"This also *is* yours: the heave offering of their gift, with all the wave offerings of the children of Israel; I have given them to you, and your sons
and daughters with you, as an ordinance forever. Everyone who is clean in
your house may eat it.
12"All the best of the oil, all the best of the new wine and the grain, their
firstfruits which they offer to the LORD, I have given them to you. 13What-
ever first ripe fruit is in their land, which they bring to the LORD, shall be
yours. Everyone who is clean in your house may eat it.
14"Every devoted thing in Israel shall be yours.
15"Everything that first opens the womb of all flesh, which they bring to
the LORD, whether man or beast, shall be yours; nevertheless the firstborn
of man you shall surely redeem, and the firstborn of unclean animals you
shall redeem. 16And those redeemed of the devoted things you shall redeem when one month old, according to your valuation, for five shekels of
silver, according to the shekel of the sanctuary, which *is* twenty gerahs.
17But the firstborn of a cow, the firstborn of a sheep, or the firstborn of a
goat you shall not redeem; they *are* holy. You shall sprinkle their blood on
the altar, and burn their fat *as* an offering made by fire for a sweet aroma to
the LORD. 18And their flesh shall be yours, just as the wave breast and the
right thigh are yours.
19"All the heave offerings of the holy things, which the children of Israel
offer to the LORD, I have given to you and your sons and daughters with
you as an ordinance forever; it *is* a covenant of salt forever before the LORD
with you and your descendants with you."
20Then the LORD said to Aaron: "You shall have no inheritance in their
land, nor shall you have any portion among them; I *am* your portion and
your inheritance among the children of Israel.

Tithes for Support of the Levites

21"Behold, I have given the children of Levi all the tithes in Israel as an
inheritance in return for the work which they perform, the work of the
tabernacle of meeting. 22Hereafter the children of Israel shall not come
near the tabernacle of meeting, lest they bear sin and die. 23But the Levites
shall perform the work of the tabernacle of meeting, and they shall bear
their iniquity; *it shall be* a statute forever, throughout your generations,
that among the children of Israel they shall have no inheritance. 24For the
tithes of the children of Israel, which they offer up *as* a heave offering to
the LORD, I have given to the Levites as an inheritance; therefore I have said
to them, 'Among the children of Israel they shall have no inheritance.' "

The Tithe of the Levites

25Then the LORD spoke to Moses, saying, 26"Speak thus to the Levites,
and say to them: 'When you take from the children of Israel the tithes
which I have given you from them as your inheritance, then you shall offer
up a heave offering of it to the LORD, a tenth of the tithe. 27And your heave

freight cars loaded with moods, dead emotions and convictions and puts them on the right track.

And just as low-grade oil or alloyed gasoline would cause you to question the performance of a refinery, evil acts and impure thoughts cause us to question the condition of our hearts. . . .

The heart is the center of the spiritual life. If the fruit of a tree is bad, you don't try to fix the fruit; you treat the roots. And if a person's actions are evil, it's not enough to change habits; you have to go deeper. You have to go to the heart of the problem, which is the problem of the heart.

That is why the state of the heart is so critical. What is the state of yours? . . . The state of your heart dictates whether you harbor a grudge or give grace, seek self-pity or seek Christ, drink human misery or taste God's mercy. No wonder, then, the wise man begs, "Above all else, guard your heart."

David's prayer should be ours: "Create in me a pure heart, O God."

And Jesus' statement rings true: "Blessed are the pure in heart, for they shall see God."

Note the order of this beatitude: first purify the heart, then you will see God. Clean the refinery, and the result will be a pure product.

(From *The Applause of Heaven* by Max Lucado)

APPLICATION Have you taken the step the Bible describes as being washed in Christ's blood? It is the step of faith we take when we trust in Jesus alone to save us from sin's penalty and to lead us into eternal life. Do it today.

EXPLORATION Cleansing of Sin—Psalm 51:1-7; Hebrews 9:11-14; 10:19-22; 1 John 1:7-9.

offering shall be reckoned to you as though *it were* the grain of the threshing floor and as the fullness of the winepress. 28Thus you shall also offer a heave offering to the LORD from all your tithes which you receive from the children of Israel, and you shall give the LORD's heave offering from it to Aaron the priest. 29Of all your gifts you shall offer up every heave offering due to the LORD, from all the best of them, the consecrated part of them.' 30Therefore you shall say to them: 'When you have lifted up the best of it, then *the rest* shall be accounted to the Levites as the produce of the threshing floor and as the produce of the winepress. 31You may eat it in any place, you and your households, for it *is* your reward for your work in the tabernacle of meeting. 32And you shall bear no sin because of it, when you have lifted up the best of it. But you shall not profane the holy gifts of the children of Israel, lest you die.' "

Laws of Purification

19 Now the LORD spoke to Moses and Aaron, saying, 2"This *is* the ordinance of the law which the LORD has commanded, saying: 'Speak to the children of Israel, that they bring you a red heifer without blemish, in which there *is* no defect *and* on which a yoke has never come. 3You shall give it to Eleazar the priest, that he may take it outside the camp, and it shall be slaughtered before him; 4and Eleazar the priest shall take some of its blood with his finger, and sprinkle some of its blood seven times directly in front of the tabernacle of meeting. 5Then the heifer shall be burned in his sight: its hide, its flesh, its blood, and its offal shall be burned. 6And the priest shall take cedar wood and hyssop and scarlet, and cast *them* into the midst of the fire burning the heifer. 7Then the priest shall wash his clothes, he shall bathe in water, and afterward he shall come into the camp; the priest shall be unclean until evening. 8And the one who burns it shall wash his clothes in water, bathe in water, and shall be unclean until evening. 9Then a man *who is* clean shall gather up the ashes of the heifer, and store *them* outside the camp in a clean place; and they shall be kept for the congregation of the children of Israel for the water of purification;[u] it *is* for purifying from sin. 10And the one who gathers the ashes of the heifer shall wash his clothes, and be unclean until evening. It shall be a statute forever to the children of Israel and to the stranger who dwells among them.

11'He who touches the dead body of anyone shall be unclean seven days. 12He shall purify himself with the water on the third day and on the seventh day; *then* he will be clean. But if he does not purify himself on the third day and on the seventh day, he will not be clean. 13Whoever touches the body of anyone who has died, and does not purify himself, defiles the tabernacle of the LORD. That person shall be cut off from Israel. He shall be unclean, because the water of purification was not sprinkled on him; his uncleanness *is* still on him.

14'This *is* the law when a man dies in a tent: All who come into the tent and all who *are* in the tent shall be unclean seven days; 15and every open vessel, which has no cover fastened on it, *is* unclean. 16Whoever in the open field touches one who is slain by a sword or who has died, or a bone of a man, or a grave, shall be unclean seven days.

17'And for an unclean *person* they shall take some of the ashes of the heifer burnt for purification from sin, and running water shall be put on them in a vessel. 18A clean person shall take hyssop and dip *it* in the water, sprinkle *it* on the tent, on all the vessels, on the persons who were there, or on the one who touched a bone, the slain, the dead, or a grave. 19The clean *person* shall sprinkle the unclean on the third day and on the seventh day; and on the seventh day he shall purify himself, wash his clothes, and bathe in water; and at evening he shall be clean.

20'But the man who is unclean and does not purify himself, that person shall be cut off from among the assembly, because he has defiled the sanctuary of the LORD. The water of purification has not been sprinkled on him; he *is* unclean. 21It shall be a perpetual statute for them. He who sprinkles the water of purification shall wash his clothes; and he who touches the water of purification shall be unclean until evening. 22Whatever the unclean *person* touches shall be unclean; and the person who touches *it* shall be unclean until evening.' "

Moses' Error at Kadesh

20 Then the children of Israel, the whole congregation, came into the Wilderness of Zin in the first month, and the people stayed in Kadesh; and Miriam died there and was buried there.

2Now there was no water for the congregation; so they gathered together against Moses and Aaron. 3And the people contended with Moses and spoke, saying: "If only we had died when our brethren died

19:9 [u] Literally *impurity*

before the LORD! [4]Why have you brought up the assembly of the LORD into
this wilderness, that we and our animals should die here? [5]And why have
you made us come up out of Egypt, to bring us to this evil place? It *is* not a
place of grain or figs or vines or pomegranates; nor *is* there any water to
drink." [6]So Moses and Aaron went from the presence of the assembly to
the door of the tabernacle of meeting, and they fell on their faces. And the
glory of the LORD appeared to them.
[7]Then the LORD spoke to Moses, saying, [8]"Take the rod; you and your
brother Aaron gather the congregation together. Speak to the rock before
their eyes, and it will yield its water; thus you shall bring water for them
out of the rock, and give drink to the congregation and their animals." [9]So
Moses took the rod from before the LORD as He commanded him.
[10]And Moses and Aaron gathered the assembly together before the rock;
and he said to them, "Hear now, you rebels! Must we bring water for you
out of this rock?" [11]Then Moses lifted his hand and struck the rock twice
with his rod; and water came out abundantly, and the congregation and
their animals drank.
[12]Then the LORD spoke to Moses and Aaron, "Because you did not believe Me, to hallow Me in the eyes of the children of Israel, therefore you
shall not bring this assembly into the land which I have given them."
[13]This *was* the water of Meribah,[v] because the children of Israel contended with the LORD, and He was hallowed among them.

Passage Through Edom Refused

[14]Now Moses sent messengers from Kadesh to the king of Edom. "Thus
says your brother Israel: 'You know all the hardship that has befallen us,
[15]how our fathers went down to Egypt, and we dwelt in Egypt a long time,
and the Egyptians afflicted us and our fathers. [16]When we cried out to the
LORD, He heard our voice and sent the Angel and brought us up out of
Egypt; now here we are in Kadesh, a city on the edge of your border.
[17]Please let us pass through your country. We will not pass through fields
or vineyards, nor will we drink water from wells; we will go along the
King's Highway; we will not turn aside to the right hand or to the left until
we have passed through your territory.' "
[18]Then Edom said to him, "You shall not pass through my *land,* lest I
come out against you with the sword."
[19]So the children of Israel said to him, "We will go by the Highway, and if
I or my livestock drink any of your water, then I will pay for it; let me only
pass through on foot, nothing *more.*"
[20]Then he said, "You shall not pass through." So Edom came out against
them with many men and with a strong hand. [21]Thus Edom refused to
give Israel passage through his territory; so Israel turned away from him.

Death of Aaron

[22]Now the children of Israel, the whole congregation, journeyed from
Kadesh and came to Mount Hor. [23]And the LORD spoke to Moses and
Aaron in Mount Hor by the border of the land of Edom, saying: [24]"Aaron
shall be gathered to his people, for he shall not enter the land which I have
given to the children of Israel, because you rebelled against My word at the

20:13 [v] Literally *Contention*

LIFE LESSON

Numbers 20:1–21:35

SITUATION The Israelites returned to Kadesh thirty-seven years after the disappointing spy mission. Nearly all of the generation that left Egypt had died. Moses felt the people were ready for a fresh start toward the Promised Land.

OBSERVATION God continued to be in control as he led his people, even to the extent of denying the leaders, Moses and Aaron, entrance into the Promised Land. When the people entered the land without these great men, God showed that his power does not depend on any dynamic leader.

INSPIRATION Human nature begs to construct a picture of what we think God is like, a kind of spiritual box we can fit Him into. We want a fix on God. The how-to formulas are actually comforting—tangible evidence that things will work out the way we want them to.

The kind of disappointment or letdown that jars our faith, though, also causes the walls of that box to dissolve. The spiritual territory here is uncharted and sometimes frightening. Perhaps you took a wrong turn to arrive at such a place. You don't know what else lurks in the darkness. As one friend said, "Suddenly, I realized that if the thing I feared had happened, then almost anything else was possible, too. I no longer felt safe."

Can't I just return to the days when faith seemed sure and simple? Can't I just go back to where I was? These are natural questions to ask. We long for a Bible study or spiritual retreat or earnest effort or *something* that promises that old certainty. We long for faith to lose its tentative feel—to cease to feel like faith.

There is no going back, though. Our manageable belief system no longer works so well. The walls of the box begin to crumble. God often seems strangely absent, as though He has left us on our own to sort things out. Yet, in reality, what we are experiencing is this pain and confusion of letting go, not of God, but of the safe, secure, confines we built to house our concept of Him. God is not a concept

Continued

water of Meribah. 25Take Aaron and Eleazar his son, and bring them up to Mount Hor; 26and strip Aaron of his garments and put them on Eleazar his son; for Aaron shall be gathered *to his people* and die there." 27So Moses did just as the LORD commanded, and they went up to Mount Hor in the sight of all the congregation. 28Moses stripped Aaron of his garments and put them on Eleazar his son; and Aaron died there on the top of the mountain. Then Moses and Eleazar came down from the mountain. 29Now when all the congregation saw that Aaron was dead, all the house of Israel mourned for Aaron thirty days.

Canaanites Defeated at Hormah

21 The king of Arad, the Canaanite, who dwelt in the South, heard that Israel was coming on the road to Atharim. Then he fought against Israel and took *some* of them prisoners. 2So Israel made a vow to the LORD, and said, "If You will indeed deliver this people into my hand, then I will utterly destroy their cities." 3And the LORD listened to the voice of Israel and delivered up the Canaanites, and they utterly destroyed them and their cities. So the name of that place was called Hormah.[w]

The Bronze Serpent

4Then they journeyed from Mount Hor by the Way of the Red Sea, to go around the land of Edom; and the soul of the people became very discouraged on the way. 5And the people spoke against God and against Moses: "Why have you brought us up out of Egypt to die in the wilderness? For *there is* no food and no water, and our soul loathes this worthless bread." 6So the LORD sent fiery serpents among the people, and they bit the people; and many of the people of Israel died.

7Therefore the people came to Moses, and said, "We have sinned, for we have spoken against the LORD and against you; pray to the LORD that He take away the serpents from us." So Moses prayed for the people.

8Then the LORD said to Moses, "Make a fiery *serpent,* and set it on a pole; and it shall be that everyone who is bitten, when he looks at it, shall live." 9So Moses made a bronze serpent, and put it on a pole; and so it was, if a serpent had bitten anyone, when he looked at the bronze serpent, he lived.

From Mount Hor to Moab

10Now the children of Israel moved on and camped in Oboth. 11And they journeyed from Oboth and camped at Ije Abarim, in the wilderness which *is* east of Moab, toward the sunrise. 12From there they moved and camped in the Valley of Zered. 13From there they moved and camped on the other side of the Arnon, which *is* in the wilderness that extends from the border of the Amorites; for the Arnon *is* the border of Moab, between Moab and the Amorites. 14Therefore it is said in the Book of the Wars of the LORD:

"Waheb in Suphah,[x]
The brooks of the Arnon,
15 And the slope of the brooks
That reaches to the dwelling of Ar,
And lies on the border of Moab."

21:3 [w] Literally *Utter Destruction*
21:14 [x] Ancient unknown places; Vulgate reads *What He did in the Red Sea.*

---

to be mastered, a set of prescriptions we can control. He shows Himself to be much different than we thought—more loving, more exacting, more faithful.

(From *The Cleavers Don't Live Here Anymore* by Paula Rinehart)

APPLICATION Do you have a major decision or important step of faith to take? What role have you let God play? Pray today that barriers to God's will in your life will be torn down. Be open to God's plan for you.

EXPLORATION God's Will—Genesis 45:4-7; 50:19-20; Isaiah 46:8-11; Micah 6:8; Matthew 25:34; Ephesians 3:11; 1 Thessalonians 4:3; 5:16-18.

[16]From there *they went* to Beer, which *is* the well
where the LORD said to Moses, "Gather the people together, and I will give them water." [17]Then Israel sang
this song:

"Spring up, O well!
All of you sing to it—
18 The well the leaders sank,
Dug by the nation's nobles,
By the lawgiver, with their staves."

And from the wilderness *they went* to Mattanah,
[19]from Mattanah to Nahaliel, from Nahaliel to
Bamoth, [20]and from Bamoth, *in* the valley that *is* in
the country of Moab, to the top of Pisgah which looks
down on the wasteland.[y]

King Sihon Defeated

[21]Then Israel sent messengers to Sihon king of the
Amorites, saying, [22]"Let me pass through your land.
We will not turn aside into fields or vineyards; we will
not drink water from wells. We will go by the King's
Highway until we have passed through your territory." [23]But Sihon would not allow Israel to pass
through his territory. So Sihon gathered all his people
together and went out against Israel in the wilderness, and he came to Jahaz and fought against Israel.
[24]Then Israel defeated him with the edge of the
sword, and took possession of his land from the
Arnon to the Jabbok, as far as the people of Ammon;
for the border of the people of Ammon *was* fortified.
[25]So Israel took all these cities, and Israel dwelt in all
the cities of the Amorites, in Heshbon and in all its
villages. [26]For Heshbon *was* the city of Sihon king of
the Amorites, who had fought against the former
king of Moab, and had taken all his land from his
hand as far as the Arnon. [27]Therefore those who
speak in proverbs say:

"Come to Heshbon, let it be built;
Let the city of Sihon be repaired.
28 "For fire went out from Heshbon,
A flame from the city of Sihon;
It consumed Ar of Moab,
The lords of the heights of the Arnon.
29 Woe to you, Moab!
You have perished, O people of Chemosh!
He has given his sons as fugitives,
And his daughters into captivity,
To Sihon king of the Amorites.
30 "But we have shot at them;
Heshbon has perished as far as Dibon.
Then we laid waste as far as Nophah,
Which *reaches* to Medeba."

[31]Thus Israel dwelt in the land of the Amorites.
[32]Then Moses sent to spy out Jazer; and they took its
villages and drove out the Amorites who *were* there.

King Og Defeated

[33]And they turned and went up by the way to
Bashan. So Og king of Bashan went out against them,
he and all his people, to battle at Edrei. [34]Then the
LORD said to Moses, "Do not fear him, for I have delivered him into your hand, with all his people and his
land; and you shall do to him as you did to Sihon king
of the Amorites, who dwelt at Heshbon." [35]So they defeated him, his sons, and all his people, until there
was no survivor left him; and they took possession of
his land.

Balak Sends for Balaam

22 Then the children of Israel moved, and camped
in the plains of Moab on the side of the Jordan
across from Jericho.

[2]Now Balak the son of Zippor saw all that Israel
had done to the Amorites. [3]And Moab was exceedingly afraid of the people because they *were* many,
and Moab was sick with dread because of the children of Israel. [4]So Moab said to the elders of Midian,
"Now this company will lick up everything around
us, as an ox licks up the grass of the field." And Balak
the son of Zippor *was* king of the Moabites at that
time. [5]Then he sent messengers to Balaam the son of
Beor at Pethor, which *is* near the River[z] in the land of
the sons of his people,[a] to call him, saying: "Look, a
people has come from Egypt. See, they cover the face
of the earth, and are settling next to me! [6]Therefore
please come at once, curse this people for me, for
they *are* too mighty for me. Perhaps I shall be able to
defeat them and drive them out of the land, for I
know that he whom you bless *is* blessed, and he
whom you curse is cursed."

[7]So the elders of Moab and the elders of Midian departed with the diviner's fee in their hand, and they
came to Balaam and spoke to him the words of Balak.
[8]And he said to them, "Lodge here tonight, and I will
bring back word to you, as the LORD speaks to me." So
the princes of Moab stayed with Balaam.

21:20 [y] Hebrew *Jeshimon*
22:5 [z] That is, the Euphrates [a] Or *the people of Amau*

LIFE LESSON

Numbers 22:1–25:18

SITUATION People in Old Testament times commonly believed in curses and blessings. Balak and the Moabites wanted the sorcerer, Balaam, to use his supposed influence with Israel's God to curse the Israelites and halt their progress into Canaan.

OBSERVATION God evaluates both motives and actions. Individuals' inner heart attitudes, such as Balaam's desire for power and money, will eventually be revealed no matter what outward disguise they use.

INSPIRATION Character is what we truly are, compared with what we seem to be. You can appear to be generous even when your heart is that of a skinflint.

Character is different from piety. By piety, I mean a personal relationship with God. By character, I mean the quality of the person. Even so, they are certainly inseparable; God is quite interested in character, and there is something wrong if a pious person does not have a good moral character. . . .

When considering what makes for good moral character, the word *virtue* comes to mind. The ancient Greeks used the word to mean "excellence." I would like to consider the classic definition of virtue as part of our description of character.

In the Greek catalog, there were four cardinal virtues—four things that you should never leave home without. The first is *discernment*. Unless you are able to discern what is really going on in a situation, what people are feeling, and what is important, you will always make wrong decisions. My theory is that the greatest moral disputes of any age are differences not so much in moral theory as in the power of discernment. This virtue is the essence of Paul's advice: "Do not conform any longer to the pattern of this world, but be transformed by the renewing of your mind. Then you will be able to test and approve what God's will is—his good, pleasing and perfect will" (Romans 12:2).

The second virtue is *courage*. It is the power to do well when the air is turbulent and the going gets tough. It is

9 Then God came to Balaam and said, "Who *are* these men with you?"
10 So Balaam said to God, "Balak the son of Zippor, king of Moab, has
sent to me, *saying,* 11 'Look, a people has come out of Egypt, and they cover
the face of the earth. Come now, curse them for me; perhaps I shall be able
to overpower them and drive them out.' "
12 And God said to Balaam, "You shall not go with them; you shall not
curse the people, for they *are* blessed."
13 So Balaam rose in the morning and said to the princes of Balak, "Go
back to your land, for the LORD has refused to give me permission to go
with you."
14 And the princes of Moab rose and went to Balak, and said, "Balaam
refuses to come with us."
15 Then Balak again sent princes, more numerous and more honorable
than they. 16 And they came to Balaam and said to him, "Thus says Balak
the son of Zippor: 'Please let nothing hinder you from coming to me; 17 for
I will certainly honor you greatly, and I will do whatever you say to me.
Therefore please come, curse this people for me.' "
18 Then Balaam answered and said to the servants of Balak, "Though
Balak were to give me his house full of silver and gold, I could not go beyond the word of the LORD my God, to do less or more. 19 Now therefore,
please, you also stay here tonight, that I may know what more the LORD
will say to me."
20 And God came to Balaam at night and said to him, "If the men come
to call you, rise *and* go with them; but only the word which I speak to
you—that you shall do." 21 So Balaam rose in the morning, saddled his
donkey, and went with the princes of Moab.

Balaam, the Donkey, and the Angel

22 Then God's anger was aroused because he went, and the Angel of the
LORD took His stand in the way as an adversary against him. And he was
riding on his donkey, and his two servants *were* with him. 23 Now the donkey saw the Angel of the LORD standing in the way with His drawn sword in
His hand, and the donkey turned aside out of the way and went into the
field. So Balaam struck the donkey to turn her back onto the road. 24 Then
the Angel of the LORD stood in a narrow path between the vineyards, *with* a
wall on this side and a wall on that side. 25 And when the donkey saw the
Angel of the LORD, she pushed herself against the wall and crushed
Balaam's foot against the wall; so he struck her again. 26 Then the Angel of
the LORD went further, and stood in a narrow place where there *was* no way
to turn either to the right hand or to the left. 27 And when the donkey saw
the Angel of the LORD, she lay down under Balaam; so Balaam's anger was
aroused, and he struck the donkey with his staff.
28 Then the LORD opened the mouth of the donkey, and she said to
Balaam, "What have I done to you, that you have struck me these three
times?"
29 And Balaam said to the donkey, "Because you have abused me. I wish
there were a sword in my hand, for now I would kill you!"
30 So the donkey said to Balaam, "*Am* I not your donkey on which you
have ridden, ever since *I became* yours, to this day? Was I ever disposed to
do this to you?"
And he said, "No."

[31]Then the LORD opened Balaam's eyes, and he saw the Angel of the LORD
standing in the way with His drawn sword in His hand; and he bowed his
head and fell flat on his face. [32]And the Angel of the LORD said to him, "Why
have you struck your donkey these three times? Behold, I have come out to
stand against you, because *your* way is perverse before Me. [33]The donkey
saw Me and turned aside from Me these three times. If she had not turned
aside from Me, surely I would also have killed you by now, and let her live."
[34]And Balaam said to the Angel of the LORD, "I have sinned, for I did not
know You stood in the way against me. Now therefore, if it displeases You,
I will turn back."
[35]Then the Angel of the LORD said to Balaam, "Go with the men, but only
the word that I speak to you, that you shall speak." So Balaam went with
the princes of Balak.
[36]Now when Balak heard that Balaam was coming, he went out to meet
him at the city of Moab, which *is* on the border at the Arnon, the boundary of the territory. [37]Then Balak said to Balaam, "Did I not earnestly send
to you, calling for you? Why did you not come to me? Am I not able to
honor you?"
[38]And Balaam said to Balak, "Look, I have come to you! Now, have I any
power at all to say anything? The word that God puts in my mouth, that I
must speak." [39]So Balaam went with Balak, and they came to Kirjath
Huzoth. [40]Then Balak offered oxen and sheep, and he sent *some* to Balaam
and to the princes who *were* with him.

Balaam's First Prophecy

[41]So it was, the next day, that Balak took Balaam and brought him up to
the high places of Baal, that from there he might observe the extent of the
people.

23

Then Balaam said to Balak, "Build seven altars for me here, and
prepare for me here seven bulls and seven rams."
[2]And Balak did just as Balaam had spoken, and Balak and Balaam offered a bull and a ram on *each* altar. [3]Then Balaam said to Balak, "Stand by
your burnt offering, and I will go; perhaps the LORD will come to meet me,
and whatever He shows me I will tell you." So he went to a desolate height.
[4]And God met Balaam, and he said to Him, "I have prepared the seven altars, and I have offered on *each* altar a bull and a ram."
[5]Then the LORD put a word in Balaam's mouth, and said, "Return to
Balak, and thus you shall speak." [6]So he returned to him, and there he
was, standing by his burnt offering, he and all the princes of Moab.
[7]And he took up his oracle and said:

"Balak the king of Moab has brought me from Aram,
From the mountains of the east.
'Come, curse Jacob for me,
And come, denounce Israel!'

8 "How shall I curse whom God has not cursed?
And how shall I denounce *whom* the LORD has not denounced?
9 For from the top of the rocks I see him,
And from the hills I behold him;

having the character to do well when things are tempting, when things are painful. It is easy to be a mother when a baby is cooing and gurgling over breakfast; it takes courage to be a mother when the child suffers from a terrible and incurable handicap. Courage is the power to do well in the face of a threat—to your life, to your security, to your future, to the things you hold dear. The Old Testament is a symphony of variations on the theme of courage.

Temperance is the third virtue. It means being in charge of your own life. To manage, to control, to be able to orchestrate all the stuff that is going on inside. Of course, by control of one's life, I do not mean that a Christian gallops ahead on his own, oblivious of Christ's lordship. A temperate person gives control to God, and in turn accepts genuine responsibility as a challenge from God. The temperate person does not let circumstances, substances, or other people control him. Like other gifts of the Spirit, temperance needs to be practiced, lest we lose it.

The fourth virtue is *justice*. The person of justice determines always to be fair and does not treat one person differently from another. It is rejecting questions such as Whose wheel is squeaking the loudest? or Who will reward me the most? The prophets called out for justice, stating God's case against Israel: "He has showed you, O man, what is good. And what does the Lord require of you? To act justly and to love mercy and to walk humbly with your God" (Micah 6:8). . . . In the long run, God will not ask how happy you were. He will ask, What sort of person were you?

(From "Basic Moral Characteristics" by Lewis Smedes in *Practical Christianity)*

APPLICATION Which of these virtues do you most want to develop? Commit yourself during the next month to develop that virtue. Write a note to remind yourself of this goal. Put it on your mirror, in your locker, or car. Think about ways to develop virtue in your life.

EXPLORATION Heart and Ethics—Deuteronomy 30:17; 1 Kings 8:58; 2 Chronicles 29:31; Psalm 141:4; Matthew 5:8; 6:21; James 3:14.

There! A people dwelling alone,
Not reckoning itself among the nations.
10 "Who can count the dust[b] of Jacob,
Or number one-fourth of Israel?
Let me die the death of the righteous,
And let my end be like his!"

11Then Balak said to Balaam, "What have you done
to me? I took you to curse my enemies, and look, you
have blessed *them* bountifully!"
12So he answered and said, "Must I not take heed to
speak what the LORD has put in my mouth?"

Balaam's Second Prophecy

13Then Balak said to him, "Please come with me to
another place from which you may see them; you
shall see only the outer part of them, and shall not see
them all; curse them for me from there." 14So he
brought him to the field of Zophim, to the top of
Pisgah, and built seven altars, and offered a bull and a
ram on *each* altar.
15And he said to Balak, "Stand here by your burnt
offering while I meet[c] *the LORD* over there."
16Then the LORD met Balaam, and put a word in his
mouth, and said, "Go back to Balak, and thus you
shall speak." 17So he came to him, and there he was,
standing by his burnt offering, and the princes of
Moab were with him. And Balak said to him, "What
has the LORD spoken?"
18Then he took up his oracle and said:

"Rise up, Balak, and hear!
Listen to me, son of Zippor!
19 "God *is* not a man, that He should lie,
Nor a son of man, that He should repent.
Has He said, and will He not do?
Or has He spoken, and will He not make it good?
20 Behold, I have received *a command* to bless;
He has blessed, and I cannot reverse it.

21 "He has not observed iniquity in Jacob,
Nor has He seen wickedness in Israel.
The LORD his God *is* with him,
And the shout of a King *is* among them.
22 God brings them out of Egypt;
He has strength like a wild ox.

23 "For *there is* no sorcery against Jacob,
Nor any divination against Israel.
It now must be said of Jacob
And of Israel, 'Oh, what God has done!'
24 Look, a people rises like a lioness,
And lifts itself up like a lion;
It shall not lie down until it devours the prey,
And drinks the blood of the slain."

25Then Balak said to Balaam, "Neither curse them
at all, nor bless them at all!"
26So Balaam answered and said to Balak, "Did I not
tell you, saying, 'All that the LORD speaks, that I
must do'?"

Balaam's Third Prophecy

27Then Balak said to Balaam, "Please come, I will
take you to another place; perhaps it will please God
that you may curse them for me from there." 28So
Balak took Balaam to the top of Peor, that overlooks
the wasteland.[d] 29Then Balaam said to Balak, "Build for
me here seven altars, and prepare for me here seven
bulls and seven rams." 30And Balak did as Balaam
had said, and offered a bull and a ram on *every* altar.

24 Now when Balaam saw that it pleased the LORD
to bless Israel, he did not go as at other times,
to seek to use sorcery, but he set his face toward the
wilderness. 2And Balaam raised his eyes, and saw Israel encamped according to their tribes; and the
Spirit of God came upon him.
3Then he took up his oracle and said:

"The utterance of Balaam the son of Beor,
The utterance of the man whose eyes
are opened,
4 The utterance of him who hears the
words of God,
Who sees the vision of the Almighty,
Who falls down, with eyes wide open:

5 "How lovely are your tents, O Jacob!
Your dwellings, O Israel!
6 Like valleys that stretch out,
Like gardens by the riverside,
Like aloes planted by the LORD,
Like cedars beside the waters.
7 He shall pour water from his buckets,
And his seed *shall be* in many waters.

"His king shall be higher than Agag,
And his kingdom shall be exalted.

23:10 [b] Or *dust cloud*
23:15 [c] Following Masoretic Text, Targum, and Vulgate; Syriac reads *call;* Septuagint reads *go and ask God.*
23:28 [d] Hebrew *Jeshimon*

8 "God brings him out of Egypt;
He has strength like a wild ox;
He shall consume the nations, his enemies;
He shall break their bones
And pierce *them* with his arrows.
9 'He bows down, he lies down as a lion;
And as a lion, who shall rouse him?'[e]

"Blessed *is* he who blesses you,
And cursed *is* he who curses you."

10 Then Balak's anger was aroused against Balaam,
and he struck his hands together; and Balak said to
Balaam, "I called you to curse my enemies, and look,
you have bountifully blessed *them* these three times!
11 Now therefore, flee to your place. I said I would
greatly honor you, but in fact, the LORD has kept you
back from honor."

12 So Balaam said to Balak, "Did I not also speak to
your messengers whom you sent to me, saying, 13 'If
Balak were to give me his house full of silver and gold,
I could not go beyond the word of the LORD, to do
good or bad of my own will. What the LORD says, that
I must speak'? 14 And now, indeed, I am going to my
people. Come, I will advise you what this people will
do to your people in the latter days."

Balaam's Fourth Prophecy

15 So he took up his oracle and said:

"The utterance of Balaam the son of Beor,
And the utterance of the man whose eyes
are opened;
16 The utterance of him who hears the
words of God,
And has the knowledge of the Most High,
Who sees the vision of the Almighty,
Who falls down, with eyes wide open:

17 "I see Him, but not now;
I behold Him, but not near;
A Star shall come out of Jacob;
A Scepter shall rise out of Israel,
And batter the brow of Moab,
And destroy all the sons of tumult.[f]

18 "And Edom shall be a possession;
Seir also, his enemies, shall be a possession,
While Israel does valiantly.
19 Out of Jacob One shall have dominion,
And destroy the remains of the city."

20 Then he looked on Amalek, and he took up his oracle and said:

"Amalek *was* first among the nations,
But *shall be* last until he perishes."

21 Then he looked on the Kenites, and he took up his
oracle and said:

"Firm is your dwelling place,
And your nest is set in the rock;
22 Nevertheless Kain shall be burned.
How long until Asshur carries you
away captive?"

23 Then he took up his oracle and said:

"Alas! Who shall live when God does this?
24 But ships *shall come* from the coasts
of Cyprus,[g]
And they shall afflict Asshur and afflict Eber,
And so shall *Amalek*,[h] until he perishes."

25 So Balaam rose and departed and returned to his
place; Balak also went his way.

Israel's Harlotry in Moab

25 Now Israel remained in Acacia Grove,[i] and the
people began to commit harlotry with the
women of Moab. 2 They invited the people to the sacrifices of their gods, and the people ate and bowed
down to their gods. 3 So Israel was joined to Baal of
Peor, and the anger of the LORD was aroused against
Israel.

4 Then the LORD said to Moses, "Take all the leaders
of the people and hang the offenders before the LORD,
out in the sun, that the fierce anger of the LORD may
turn away from Israel."

5 So Moses said to the judges of Israel, "Every one of
you kill his men who were joined to Baal of Peor."

6 And indeed, one of the children of Israel came and
presented to his brethren a Midianite woman in the
sight of Moses and in the sight of all the congregation
of the children of Israel, who *were* weeping at the door
of the tabernacle of meeting. 7 Now when Phinehas the
son of Eleazar, the son of Aaron the priest, saw *it*, he
rose from among the congregation and took a javelin

24:9 [e] Genesis 49:9
24:17 [f] Hebrew *Sheth* (compare Jeremiah 48:45)
24:24 [g] Hebrew *Kittim* [h] Literally *he* or *that one*
25:1 [i] Hebrew *Shittim*

Life Lesson

Numbers 26:1–27:23

SITUATION Israel needed a new census because everyone over age twenty at the previous census had died. Census-taking demonstrated that God was keeping his people united and organized.

OBSERVATION From the appointment of Joshua as his successor to the taking of a new census, Moses demonstrated consistency in following God. Leaders today can learn from his example.

INSPIRATION Two great problems in serving others are both problems of human nature, of focusing on our relationship with people instead of our relationship with Christ. The first problem is that people will expect too much of you; and the second, you will expect too much of them. Both of these problems are problems of unrealistic expectations. Expectations must be focused on Christ, not each other. He is the only One who will consistently not let us down.

The milk of human sympathy will undernourish your soul. No amount of human gratitude will properly compensate your effort to improve the human condition. When we focus on serving the person, we are inevitably disappointed. And what's more, we will disappoint them. Serving people for the sake of their gratitude is a guaranteed formula for disappointment. Just when you begin to feel good about your labors, someone lets you down. Or, more likely, someone will expect too much from you and accuse you of letting them down. Either way, your destiny is to be terribly discouraged. . . .

The key is the personal relationship with Christ. The focus must not be on serving others or on being served.

in his hand; 8and he went after the man of Israel into the tent and thrust
both of them through, the man of Israel, and the woman through her
body. So the plague was stopped among the children of Israel. 9And those
who died in the plague were twenty-four thousand.
10Then the LORD spoke to Moses, saying: 11"Phinehas the son of Eleazar,
the son of Aaron the priest, has turned back My wrath from the children of
Israel, because he was zealous with My zeal among them, so that I did not
consume the children of Israel in My zeal. 12Therefore say, 'Behold, I give
to him My covenant of peace; 13and it shall be to him and his descendants
after him a covenant of an everlasting priesthood, because he was zealous
for his God, and made atonement for the children of Israel.' "
14Now the name of the Israelite who was killed, who was killed with the
Midianite woman, *was* Zimri the son of Salu, a leader of a father's house
among the Simeonites. 15And the name of the Midianite woman who was
killed *was* Cozbi the daughter of Zur; he *was* head of the people of a father's
house in Midian.
16Then the LORD spoke to Moses, saying: 17"Harass the Midianites, and
attack them; 18for they harassed you with their schemes by which they seduced
you in the matter of Peor and in the matter of Cozbi, the daughter of
a leader of Midian, their sister, who was killed in the day of the plague because
of Peor."

The Second Census of Israel

26 And it came to pass, after the plague, that the LORD spoke to Moses
and Eleazar the son of Aaron the priest, saying: 2"Take a census of
all the congregation of the children of Israel from twenty years old and
above, by their fathers' houses, all who are able to go to war in Israel." 3So
Moses and Eleazar the priest spoke with them in the plains of Moab by the
Jordan, *across from* Jericho, saying: 4"*Take a census of the people* from
twenty years old and above, just as the LORD commanded Moses and the
children of Israel who came out of the land of Egypt."
5Reuben *was* the firstborn of Israel. The children of Reuben *were: of*
Hanoch, the family of the Hanochites; *of* Pallu, the family of the
Palluites; 6*of* Hezron, the family of the Hezronites; *of* Carmi, the family
of the Carmites. 7These *are* the families of the Reubenites: those who
were numbered of them were forty-three thousand seven hundred and
thirty. 8And the son of Pallu *was* Eliab. 9The sons of Eliab *were* Nemuel,
Dathan, and Abiram. These *are* the Dathan and Abiram, representatives
of the congregation, who contended against Moses and Aaron in
the company of Korah, when they contended against the LORD; 10and the
earth opened its mouth and swallowed them up together with Korah
when that company died, when the fire devoured two hundred and fifty
men; and they became a sign. 11Nevertheless the children of Korah did
not die.
12The sons of Simeon according to their families *were: of* Nemuel,[j] the
family of the Nemuelites; *of* Jamin, the family of the Jaminites; *of* Jachin,[k]
the family of the Jachinites; 13*of* Zerah,[l] the family of the Zarhites; *of* Shaul,
the family of the Shaulites. 14These *are* the families of the Simeonites:
twenty-two thousand two hundred.

26:12 [j] Spelled *Jemuel* in Genesis 46:10 and Exodus 6:15 [k] Called *Jarib* in 1 Chronicles 4:24
26:13 [l] Called *Zohar* in Genesis 46:10

15The sons of Gad according to their families *were: of* Zephon,[m] the family of the Zephonites; *of* Haggi, the family of the Haggites; *of* Shuni, the
family of the Shunites; 16*of* Ozni,[n] the family of the Oznites; *of* Eri, the family of the Erites; 17*of* Arod,[o] the family of the Arodites; *of* Areli, the family of
the Arelites. 18These *are* the families of the sons of Gad according to those
who were numbered of them: forty thousand five hundred.
19The sons of Judah *were* Er and Onan; and Er and Onan died in the land
of Canaan. 20And the sons of Judah according to their families were: *of*
Shelah, the family of the Shelanites; *of* Perez, the family of the Parzites; *of*
Zerah, the family of the Zarhites. 21And the sons of Perez were: *of* Hezron,
the family of the Hezronites; *of* Hamul, the family of the Hamulites.
22These *are* the families of Judah according to those who were numbered
of them: seventy-six thousand five hundred.
23The sons of Issachar according to their families *were: of* Tola, the family of the Tolaites; of Puah,[p] the family of the Punites;[q] 24of Jashub, the family
of the Jashubites; of Shimron, the family of the Shimronites. 25These *are*
the families of Issachar according to those who were numbered of them:
sixty-four thousand three hundred.
26The sons of Zebulun according to their families *were:* of Sered, the
family of the Sardites; of Elon, the family of the Elonites; of Jahleel, the
family of the Jahleelites. 27These *are* the families of the Zebulunites according to those who were numbered of them: sixty thousand five hundred.
28The sons of Joseph according to their families, by Manasseh and
Ephraim, *were:* 29The sons of Manasseh: of Machir, the family of the Mach-
irites; and Machir begot Gilead; of Gilead, the family of the Gileadites.
30These *are* the sons of Gilead: *of* Jeezer,[r] the family of the Jeezerites; of
Helek, the family of the Helekites; 31*of* Asriel, the family of the Asrielites; *of*
Shechem, the family of the Shechemites; 32*of* Shemida, the family of the
Shemidaites; *of* Hepher, the family of the Hepherites. 33Now Zelophehad
the son of Hepher had no sons, but daughters; and the names of the
daughters of Zelophehad *were* Mahlah, Noah, Hoglah, Milcah, and Tirzah.
34These *are* the families of Manasseh; and those who were numbered of
them *were* fifty-two thousand seven hundred.
35These *are* the sons of Ephraim according to their families: of
Shuthelah, the family of the Shuthalhites; of Becher,[s] the family of the
Bachrites; of Tahan, the family of the Tahanites. 36And these *are* the sons of
Shuthelah: of Eran, the family of the Eranites. 37These *are* the families of the
sons of Ephraim according to those who were numbered of them: thirty-
two thousand five hundred.
These *are* the sons of Joseph according to their families.
38The sons of Benjamin according to their families were: of Bela, the
family of the Belaites; of Ashbel, the family of the Ashbelites; of Ahiram,
the family of the Ahiramites; 39of Shupham,[t] the family of the Shuph-
amites; of Hupham,[u] the family of the Huphamites. 40And the sons of Bela

The focus must be on Jesus, on becoming so absorbed in the relationship with Him that every other thing is a response to our relationship. We don't serve men; we serve God. Have no expectations of men. Focus on the personal relationship with Him, and there will be an overflow available for others.

Look to Christ alone for gratitude. If you serve Christ, then you will remember to look to Him for your approval, not to the milk of human sympathy. He will reward you for serving others; in fact, He is the reward.

When someone feels you let them down, you can surrender that relationship to Christ. You are serving Him only; He will give you the strength to serve that person more. You may want to flee from the ingratitude—the insatiable demands of other people—but Christ will empower you to be a servant if you take on His attitude. It can only come by devotion to the personal relationship.

The personal relationship with Christ is the oasis in the desert of human relations. When people begin to wear you down, let it remind you that you are not in the overflow. It is time to drink of Christ.

(From *Walking with Christ in the Details of Life* by Patrick Morley)

APPLICATION Take a motivation inventory. Do you serve others for the praise you receive or for the pleasure of serving Christ? When you have an opportunity to serve, ask God to help you have the right motives. Ask yourself: *Why would I do this?*

EXPLORATION Steadfastness —Psalm 37:31; 112:7; 125:1; Colossians 2:5; 2 Thessalonians 2:15; Hebrews 10:23.

26:15 [m] Called *Ziphion* in Genesis 46:16
26:16 [n] Called *Ezbon* in Genesis 46:16
26:17 [o] Spelled *Arodi* in Samaritan Pentateuch, Syriac, and Genesis 46:16
26:23 [p] Hebrew *Puvah* (compare Genesis 46:13 and 1 Chronicles 7:1); Samaritan Pentateuch, Septuagint, Syriac, and Vulgate read *Puah.* [q] Samaritan Pentateuch, Septuagint, Syriac, and Vulgate read *Puaites.*
26:30 [r] Called *Abiezer* in Joshua 17:2
26:35 [s] Called *Bered* in 1 Chronicles 7:20
26:39 [t] Masoretic Text reads *Shephupham,* spelled *Shephuphan* in 1 Chronicles 8:5. [u] Called *Huppim* in Genesis 46:21

were Ard[v] and Naaman: *of Ard,* the family of the
Ardites; of Naaman, the family of the Naamites.
41These *are* the sons of Benjamin according to their
families; and those who were numbered of them *were*
forty-five thousand six hundred.

42These *are* the sons of Dan according to their families: of Shuham,[w] the family of the Shuhamites. These
are the families of Dan according to their families.
43All the families of the Shuhamites, according to
those who were numbered of them, *were* sixty-four
thousand four hundred.

44The sons of Asher according to their families
were: of Jimna, the family of the Jimnites; of Jesui, the
family of the Jesuites; of Beriah, the family of the
Beriites. 45Of the sons of Beriah: of Heber, the family
of the Heberites; of Malchiel, the family of the
Malchielites. 46And the name of the daughter of Asher
was Serah. 47These *are* the families of the sons of
Asher according to those who were numbered of
them: fifty-three thousand four hundred.

48The sons of Naphtali according to their families
were: of Jahzeel,[x] the family of the Jahzeelites; of Guni,
the family of the Gunites; 49of Jezer, the family of the
Jezerites; of Shillem, the family of the Shillemites.
50These *are* the families of Naphtali according to their
families; and those who were numbered of them *were*
forty-five thousand four hundred.

51These *are* those who were numbered of the children of Israel: six hundred and one thousand seven
hundred and thirty.

52Then the LORD spoke to Moses, saying: 53"To these
the land shall be divided as an inheritance, according
to the number of names. 54To a large *tribe* you shall
give a larger inheritance, and to a small *tribe* you shall
give a smaller inheritance. Each shall be given its inheritance according to those who were numbered of
them. 55But the land shall be divided by lot; they shall
inherit according to the names of the tribes of their fathers. 56According to the lot their inheritance shall be
divided between the larger and the smaller."

57And these *are* those who were numbered of the
Levites according to their families: of Gershon, the
family of the Gershonites; of Kohath, the family of the
Kohathites; of Merari, the family of the Merarites.
58These *are* the families of the Levites: the family of the
Libnites, the family of the Hebronites, the family of
the Mahlites, the family of the Mushites, and the family of the Korathites. And Kohath begot Amram. 59The
name of Amram's wife *was* Jochebed the daughter of
Levi, who was born to Levi in Egypt; and to Amram
she bore Aaron and Moses and their sister Miriam.
60To Aaron were born Nadab and Abihu, Eleazar and
Ithamar. 61And Nadab and Abihu died when they offered profane fire before the LORD.

62Now those who were numbered of them were
twenty-three thousand, every male from a month old
and above; for they were not numbered among the
other children of Israel, because there was no inheritance given to them among the children of Israel.

63These *are* those who were numbered by Moses
and Eleazar the priest, who numbered the children of
Israel in the plains of Moab by the Jordan, *across from*
Jericho. 64But among these there was not a man of
those who were numbered by Moses and Aaron the
priest when they numbered the children of Israel in
the Wilderness of Sinai. 65For the LORD had said of
them, "They shall surely die in the wilderness." So
there was not left a man of them, except Caleb the son
of Jephunneh and Joshua the son of Nun.

Inheritance Laws

27 Then came the daughters of Zelophehad the
son of Hepher, the son of Gilead, the son of
Machir, the son of Manasseh, from the families of
Manasseh the son of Joseph; and these *were* the
names of his daughters: Mahlah, Noah, Hoglah,
Milcah, and Tirzah. 2And they stood before Moses,
before Eleazar the priest, and before the leaders and
all the congregation, *by* the doorway of the tabernacle
of meeting, saying: 3"Our father died in the wilderness; but he was not in the company of those who
gathered together against the LORD, in company with
Korah, but he died in his own sin; and he had no sons.
4Why should the name of our father be removed from
among his family because he had no son? Give us a
possession among our father's brothers."

5So Moses brought their case before the LORD.

6And the LORD spoke to Moses, saying: 7"The
daughters of Zelophehad speak *what is* right; you
shall surely give them a possession of inheritance
among their father's brothers, and cause the inheritance of their father to pass to them. 8And you shall
speak to the children of Israel, saying: 'If a man dies
and has no son, then you shall cause his inheritance
to pass to his daughter. 9If he has no daughter, then
you shall give his inheritance to his brothers. 10If he

26:40 [v] Called *Addar* in 1 Chronicles 8:3
26:42 [w] Called *Hushim* in Genesis 46:23
26:48 [x] Spelled *Jahziel* in 1 Chronicles 7:13

has no brothers, then you shall give his inheritance to his father's brothers.
11And if his father has no brothers, then you shall give his inheritance to
the relative closest to him in his family, and he shall possess it.'" And it
shall be to the children of Israel a statute of judgment, just as the LORD
commanded Moses.

Joshua the Next Leader of Israel

12Now the LORD said to Moses: "Go up into this Mount Abarim, and see
the land which I have given to the children of Israel. 13And when you have
seen it, you also shall be gathered to your people, as Aaron your brother
was gathered. 14For in the Wilderness of Zin, during the strife of the congregation, you rebelled against My command to hallow Me at the waters
before their eyes." (These *are* the waters of Meribah, at Kadesh in the
Wilderness of Zin.)

15Then Moses spoke to the LORD, saying: 16"Let the LORD, the God of the
spirits of all flesh, set a man over the congregation, 17who may go out before them and go in before them, who may lead them out and bring them
in, that the congregation of the LORD may not be like sheep which have no
shepherd."

18And the LORD said to Moses: "Take Joshua the son of Nun with you, a
man in whom *is* the Spirit, and lay your hand on him; 19set him before
Eleazar the priest and before all the congregation, and inaugurate him in
their sight. 20And you shall give *some* of your authority to him, that all the
congregation of the children of Israel may be obedient. 21He shall stand
before Eleazar the priest, who shall inquire before the LORD for him by the
judgment of the Urim. At his word they shall go out, and at his word they
shall come in, he and all the children of Israel with him—all the congregation."

22So Moses did as the LORD commanded him. He took Joshua and set
him before Eleazar the priest and before all the congregation. 23And he
laid his hands on him and inaugurated him, just as the LORD commanded
by the hand of Moses.

Daily Offerings

28 Now the LORD spoke to Moses, saying, 2"Command the children of
Israel, and say to them, 'My offering, My food for My offerings
made by fire as a sweet aroma to Me, you shall be careful to offer to Me at
their appointed time.'

3"And you shall say to them, 'This *is* the offering made by fire which
you shall offer to the LORD: two male lambs in their first year without
blemish, day by day, as a regular burnt offering. 4The one lamb you shall
offer in the morning, the other lamb you shall offer in the evening, 5and
one-tenth of an ephah of fine flour as a grain offering mixed with one-
fourth of a hin of pressed oil. 6*It is* a regular burnt offering which was ordained at Mount Sinai for a sweet aroma, an offering made by fire to the
LORD. 7And its drink offering *shall be* one-fourth of a hin for each lamb; in
a holy *place* you shall pour out the drink to the LORD as an offering. 8The
other lamb you shall offer in the evening; as the morning grain offering
and its drink offering, you shall offer *it* as an offering made by fire, a
sweet aroma to the LORD.

LIFE LESSON

Numbers 28:1–30:16

SITUATION God commanded the Israelites to remember him. To do this, he assigned daily, weekly, and monthly offerings, as well as five annual events: Passover, Feast of Weeks, Feast of Trumpets, Feast of Tabernacles, and the Day of Atonement.

OBSERVATION God wants his people to be thankful to him. We can honor him by giving regular offerings. This reminds us to keep him the first priority in our lives.

INSPIRATION The renowned British educator, Edward Thring, said, "The mighty leisure hours with their occupations are all-powerful. . . . The mighty question of leisure hours ought to be the most important question of all, since it affects our character most. . . . Leisure hours are the hinge on which true education turns." This eminent authority in the field of education had seen that noble character and authentic being come first; after that, as a second, the training of skill and strength. He had seen, too, that though a teacher can do much by high belief and true work to stimulate and to guide, every student has to develop his own character. It is in the leisure hours, when free from constraint and observation, that the student shows what is really uppermost within him. . . .

In spiritual life this is intensely true. . . .When the time of relaxation comes, and one is free to do exactly as one likes, many a student finds that the morning watch and its fellowship with God had not become so natural, so necessary for spiritual life and joy. Therefore, observance is not included with vacation pleasure. . . . The question of leisure hours is crucial. In them one turns freely and naturally to what he loves most. In them one proves and increases the power to keep what he has. . . .

During vacation we are set free from the school laws under which we live during our stay there. But there are *other* laws: laws of morality, laws of health, from which there is no relaxation. Warn the student that the call to daily fellowship with God belongs

Continued

not to the former but the latter category. As much as he needs during the vacation to daily eat and breathe, he needs to daily eat the bread and breathe the air of heaven.

Emphasize that the morning watch is not only a duty, but an unspeakable privilege and pleasure. Fellowship with God, abiding in Christ, loving the Word and meditating on it all the day are life and strength, health and gladness to the new nature. They should look upon them in this light, believe in the power of the new nature within, and act upon it. If they count it a joy, it will become a joy to them. . . .

God has created and redeemed you that through you He may, as through the sun He illuminates the world, shine His light and life and love upon men. You need to be in communication with the fountain of all light daily. Do not think of asking for a vacation relief from this communion, much less take it. Prize your vacation for the special opportunity of more fellowship with the Father and the Son. Don't allow it to become a snare, and exhaust all your energy in just keeping from losing ground. Prize the vacation as a blessed time for grace and victory over self and the world, of great increase of grace and strength, of being blessed and being made a blessing.

(From *The Believer's Daily Renewal* by Andrew Murray)

APPLICATION It takes time and effort to grow in our relationship with God. In what ways do you make God your daily priority? Think about the joy you have received from your growing friendship with the Lord; then decide how your daily worship needs to change to encourage a deeper and more joyful relationship with him.

EXPLORATION Life and Faith—Deuteronomy 6:5-9; Psalm 1:2; 5:3; 16:8; Daniel 6:10; John 4:24; Romans 12:1; Colossians 3:17; 1 Timothy 5:5; 1 Peter 2:5.

Sabbath Offerings

9‘And on the Sabbath day two lambs in their first year, without blemish,
and two-tenths *of an ephah* of fine flour as a grain offering, mixed with oil,
with its drink offering— 10*this is* the burnt offering for every Sabbath, besides the regular burnt offering with its drink offering.

Monthly Offerings

11‘At the beginnings of your months you shall present a burnt offering
to the LORD: two young bulls, one ram, and seven lambs in their first year,
without blemish; 12three-tenths *of an ephah* of fine flour as a grain offering, mixed with oil, for each bull; two-tenths *of an ephah* of fine flour as a
grain offering, mixed with oil, for the one ram; 13and one-tenth *of an ephah*
of fine flour, mixed with oil, as a grain offering for each lamb, as a burnt
offering of sweet aroma, an offering made by fire to the LORD. 14Their drink
offering shall be half a hin of wine for a bull, one-third of a hin for a ram,
and one-fourth of a hin for a lamb; this *is* the burnt offering for each
month throughout the months of the year. 15Also one kid of the goats as a
sin offering to the LORD shall be offered, besides the regular burnt offering
and its drink offering.

Offerings at Passover

16‘On the fourteenth day of the first month *is* the Passover of the LORD.
17And on the fifteenth day of this month *is* the feast; unleavened bread
shall be eaten for seven days. 18On the first day *you shall have* a holy convocation. You shall do no customary work. 19And you shall present an offering made by fire as a burnt offering to the LORD: two young bulls, one
ram, and seven lambs in their first year. Be sure they are without blemish. 20Their grain offering shall be of fine flour mixed with oil: three-tenths *of an ephah* you shall offer for a bull, and two-tenths for a ram;
21you shall offer one-tenth *of an ephah* for each of the seven lambs; 22also
one goat *as* a sin offering, to make atonement for you. 23You shall offer
these besides the burnt offering of the morning, which *is* for a regular
burnt offering. 24In this manner you shall offer the food of the offering
made by fire daily for seven days, as a sweet aroma to the LORD; it shall be
offered besides the regular burnt offering and its drink offering. 25And on
the seventh day you shall have a holy convocation. You shall do no customary work.

Offerings at the Feast of Weeks

26‘Also on the day of the firstfruits, when you bring a new grain offering
to the LORD at your *Feast of* Weeks, you shall have a holy convocation. You
shall do no customary work. 27You shall present a burnt offering as a sweet
aroma to the LORD: two young bulls, one ram, and seven lambs in their
first year, 28with their grain offering of fine flour mixed with oil: three-tenths *of an ephah* for each bull, two-tenths for the one ram, 29and one-tenth for each of the seven lambs; 30*also* one kid of the goats, to make
atonement for you. 31Be sure they are without blemish. You shall present
them with their drink offerings, besides the regular burnt offering with its
grain offering.

Offerings at the Feast of Trumpets

29 'And in the seventh month, on the first *day* of
the month, you shall have a holy convocation.
You shall do no customary work. For you it is a day
of blowing the trumpets. 2You shall offer a burnt offering as a sweet aroma to the LORD: one young bull,
one ram, *and* seven lambs in their first year, without
blemish. 3Their grain offering *shall be* fine flour
mixed with oil: three-tenths *of an ephah* for the bull,
two-tenths for the ram, 4and one-tenth for each of
the seven lambs; 5also one kid of the goats *as* a sin
offering, to make atonement for you; 6besides the
burnt offering with its grain offering for the New
Moon, the regular burnt offering with its grain offering, and their drink offerings, according to their ordinance, as a sweet aroma, an offering made by fire
to the LORD.

Offerings on the Day of Atonement

7'On the tenth *day* of this seventh month you shall
have a holy convocation. You shall afflict your souls;
you shall not do any work. 8You shall present a burnt
offering to the LORD *as* a sweet aroma: one young bull,
one ram, *and* seven lambs in their first year. Be sure
they are without blemish. 9Their grain offering *shall
be of* fine flour mixed with oil: three-tenths *of an
ephah* for the bull, two-tenths for the one ram, 10and
one-tenth for each of the seven lambs; 11also one kid
of the goats *as* a sin offering, besides the sin offering
for atonement, the regular burnt offering with its
grain offering, and their drink offerings.

Offerings at the Feast of Tabernacles

12'On the fifteenth day of the seventh month you
shall have a holy convocation. You shall do no customary work, and you shall keep a feast to the LORD
seven days. 13You shall present a burnt offering, an offering made by fire as a sweet aroma to the LORD: thirteen young bulls, two rams, *and* fourteen lambs in
their first year. They shall be without blemish. 14Their
grain offering *shall be of* fine flour mixed with oil:
three-tenths *of an ephah* for each of the thirteen bulls,
two-tenths for each of the two rams, 15and one-tenth
for each of the fourteen lambs; 16also one kid of the
goats *as* a sin offering, besides the regular burnt offering, its grain offering, and its drink offering.
17'On the second day *present* twelve young bulls, two
rams, fourteen lambs in their first year without blemish, 18and their grain offering and their drink offerings for the bulls, for the rams, and for the lambs, by
their number, according to the ordinance; 19also one
kid of the goats *as* a sin offering, besides the regular
burnt offering with its grain offering, and their drink
offerings.
20'On the third day *present* eleven bulls, two rams,
fourteen lambs in their first year without blemish,
21and their grain offering and their drink offerings for
the bulls, for the rams, and for the lambs, by their
number, according to the ordinance; 22also one goat
as a sin offering, besides the regular burnt offering, its
grain offering, and its drink offering.
23'On the fourth day *present* ten bulls, two rams, *and*
fourteen lambs in their first year, without blemish,
24and their grain offering and their drink offerings for
the bulls, for the rams, and for the lambs, by their
number, according to the ordinance; 25also one kid of
the goats *as* a sin offering, besides the regular burnt
offering, its grain offering, and its drink offering.
26'On the fifth day *present* nine bulls, two rams, *and*
fourteen lambs in their first year without blemish,
27and their grain offering and their drink offerings for
the bulls, for the rams, and for the lambs, by their
number, according to the ordinance; 28also one goat
as a sin offering, besides the regular burnt offering, its
grain offering, and its drink offering.
29'On the sixth day *present* eight bulls, two rams,
and fourteen lambs in their first year without blemish, 30and their grain offering and their drink offerings for the bulls, for the rams, and for the lambs, by
their number, according to the ordinance; 31also one
goat *as* a sin offering, besides the regular burnt offering, its grain offering, and its drink offering.
32'On the seventh day *present* seven bulls, two rams,
and fourteen lambs in their first year without blemish, 33and their grain offering and their drink offerings for the bulls, for the rams, and for the lambs, by
their number, according to the ordinance; 34also one
goat *as* a sin offering, besides the regular burnt offering, its grain offering, and its drink offering.
35'On the eighth day you shall have a sacred assembly. You shall do no customary work. 36You shall present a burnt offering, an offering made by fire as a
sweet aroma to the LORD: one bull, one ram, seven
lambs in their first year without blemish, 37and their
grain offering and their drink offerings for the bull,
for the ram, and for the lambs, by their number, according to the ordinance; 38also one goat *as* a sin offering, besides the regular burnt offering, its grain
offering, and its drink offering.
39'These you shall present to the LORD at your appointed feasts (besides your vowed offerings and

LIFE LESSON

Numbers 30:16–31:54

SITUATION The Midianites tried to turn the Israelites away from God. Because of this, the two nomadic nations became enemies despite their common lineage, for the Midianites were descendants of Abraham and his second wife.

OBSERVATION God's purpose in destroying this group of Midianites was to keep the people of Israel free from sin and ungodly influences. God desired moral purity in his followers. Not only were sinful influences to be completely destroyed, but the spoils of war—blessings to the people—were to be purified as well.

INSPIRATION If you were to list on a chalkboard the ways by which we become more like Jesus, what would you write? The following might top your list: We become patient. Loving. Sympathetic. Wise. More pure. More sensitive. More discerning.

But in fact, because Christ was sinless, we become most like Him when we sin less. That's why a "hatred of sin" should top the list of qualities that make us most like Christ.

Jesus squared off against sin because He knew it was the ruin of those He loved. We feel His love most when He makes us most conscious of our rebellion. If you desire to become more like Jesus, if you want to get closer and know Him better, then be prepared to have Him uproot sin from your life.

(From *Diamonds in the Dust* by Joni Eareckson Tada)

APPLICATION How have you seen God remove sin from your life? It may have felt unpleasant, unreasonable, or even unfair. Remember that whatever God allows into your life or withholds from you is in your best interest. Focus today on God's love for you and his goal of making you like him—pure and holy.

EXPLORATION Holiness—Leviticus 11:45; Matthew 5:8; 1 Corinthians 1:30; 2 Corinthians 7:1; Ephesians 5:27; Titus 2:11-12; Hebrews 12:14; 1 Peter 1:16; 2 Peter 3:14; 1 John 3:3.

your freewill offerings) as your burnt offerings and your grain offerings,
as your drink offerings and your peace offerings.' "
40So Moses told the children of Israel everything, just as the LORD commanded Moses.

The Law Concerning Vows

30 Then Moses spoke to the heads of the tribes concerning the children of Israel, saying, "This *is* the thing which the LORD has commanded: 2If a man makes a vow to the LORD, or swears an oath to bind
himself by some agreement, he shall not break his word; he shall do according to all that proceeds out of his mouth.
3"Or if a woman makes a vow to the LORD, and binds *herself* by some
agreement while in her father's house in her youth, 4and her father hears
her vow and the agreement by which she has bound herself, and her father
holds his peace, then all her vows shall stand, and every agreement with
which she has bound herself shall stand. 5But if her father overrules her on
the day that he hears, then none of her vows nor her agreements by which
she has bound herself shall stand; and the LORD will release her, because
her father overruled her.
6"If indeed she takes a husband, while bound by her vows or by a rash
utterance from her lips by which she bound herself, 7and her husband
hears *it,* and makes no response to her on the day that he hears, then her
vows shall stand, and her agreements by which she bound herself shall
stand. 8But if her husband overrules her on the day that he hears *it,* he shall
make void her vow which she took and what she uttered with her lips, by
which she bound herself, and the LORD will release her.
9"Also any vow of a widow or a divorced woman, by which she has
bound herself, shall stand against her.
10"If she vowed in her husband's house, or bound herself by an agreement with an oath, 11and her husband heard *it,* and made no response to
her *and* did not overrule her, then all her vows shall stand, and every agreement by which she bound herself shall stand. 12But if her husband truly
made them void on the day he heard *them,* then whatever proceeded from
her lips concerning her vows or concerning the agreement binding her, it
shall not stand; her husband has made them void, and the LORD will release
her. 13Every vow and every binding oath to afflict her soul, her husband may
confirm it, or her husband may make it void. 14Now if her husband makes
no response whatever to her from day to day, then he confirms all her vows
or all the agreements that bind her; he confirms them, because he made
no response to her on the day that he heard *them.* 15But if he does make
them void after he has heard *them,* then he shall bear her guilt."
16These *are* the statutes which the LORD commanded Moses, between a
man and his wife, and between a father and his daughter in her youth in
her father's house.

Vengeance on the Midianites

31 And the LORD spoke to Moses, saying: 2"Take vengeance on the
Midianites for the children of Israel. Afterward you shall be gathered
to your people."
3So Moses spoke to the people, saying, "Arm some of yourselves for
war, and let them go against the Midianites to take vengeance for the LORD

on Midian. 4A thousand from each tribe of all the
tribes of Israel you shall send to the war."
5So there were recruited from the divisions of Israel
one thousand from *each* tribe, twelve thousand
armed for war. 6Then Moses sent them to the war, one
thousand from *each* tribe; he sent them to the war
with Phinehas the son of Eleazar the priest, with the
holy articles and the signal trumpets in his hand.
7And they warred against the Midianites, just as the
LORD commanded Moses, and they killed all the
males. 8They killed the kings of Midian with *the rest of*
those who were killed—Evi, Rekem, Zur, Hur, and
Reba, the five kings of Midian. Balaam the son of
Beor they also killed with the sword.
9And the children of Israel took the women of
Midian captive, with their little ones, and took as spoil
all their cattle, all their flocks, and all their goods.
10They also burned with fire all the cities where they
dwelt, and all their forts. 11And they took all the spoil
and all the booty—of man and beast.

Return from the War

12Then they brought the captives, the booty, and the
spoil to Moses, to Eleazar the priest, and to the congregation of the children of Israel, to the camp in the
plains of Moab by the Jordan, *across from* Jericho.
13And Moses, Eleazar the priest, and all the leaders of
the congregation, went to meet them outside the
camp. 14But Moses was angry with the officers of the
army, *with* the captains over thousands and captains
over hundreds, who had come from the battle.
15And Moses said to them: "Have you kept all the
women alive? 16Look, these *women* caused the children of Israel, through the counsel of Balaam, to trespass against the LORD in the incident of Peor, and
there was a plague among the congregation of the
LORD. 17Now therefore, kill every male among the little
ones, and kill every woman who has known a man intimately. 18But keep alive for yourselves all the young
girls who have not known a man intimately. 19And as
for you, remain outside the camp seven days; whoever has killed any person, and whoever has touched
any slain, purify yourselves and your captives on the
third day and on the seventh day. 20Purify every garment, everything made of leather, everything woven
of goats' *hair*, and everything made of wood."
21Then Eleazar the priest said to the men of war
who had gone to the battle, "This *is* the ordinance of
the law which the LORD commanded Moses: 22"Only
the gold, the silver, the bronze, the iron, the tin, and
the lead, 23everything that can endure fire, you shall
put through the fire, and it shall be clean; and it shall
be purified with the water of purification. But all that
cannot endure fire you shall put through water. 24And
you shall wash your clothes on the seventh day and be
clean, and afterward you may come into the camp."

Division of the Plunder

25Now the LORD spoke to Moses, saying: 26"Count
up the plunder that was taken—of man and beast—
you and Eleazar the priest and the chief fathers of the
congregation; 27and divide the plunder into two parts,
between those who took part in the war, who went out
to battle, and all the congregation. 28And levy a tribute
for the LORD on the men of war who went out to battle:
one of every five hundred of the persons, the cattle,
the donkeys, and the sheep; 29take *it* from their half,
and give *it* to Eleazar the priest as a heave offering to
the LORD. 30And from the children of Israel's half you
shall take one of every fifty, drawn from the persons,
the cattle, the donkeys, and the sheep, from all the
livestock, and give them to the Levites who keep
charge of the tabernacle of the LORD." 31So Moses
and Eleazar the priest did as the LORD commanded
Moses.
32The booty remaining from the plunder, which the
men of war had taken, was six hundred and seventy-
five thousand sheep, 33seventy-two thousand cattle,
34sixty-one thousand donkeys, 35and thirty-two thousand persons in all, of women who had not known a
man intimately. 36And the half, the portion for those
who had gone out to war, was in number three hundred and thirty-seven thousand five hundred sheep;
37and the LORD's tribute of the sheep was six hundred
and seventy-five. 38The cattle *were* thirty-six thousand, of which the LORD's tribute *was* seventy-two.
39The donkeys *were* thirty thousand five hundred, of
which the LORD's tribute *was* sixty-one. 40The persons
were sixteen thousand, of which the LORD's tribute
was thirty-two persons. 41So Moses gave the tribute
which was the LORD's heave offering to Eleazar the
priest, as the LORD commanded Moses.
42And from the children of Israel's half, which Moses separated from the men who fought— 43now the
half belonging to the congregation was three hundred
and thirty-seven thousand five hundred sheep,
44thirty-six thousand cattle, 45thirty thousand five
hundred donkeys, 46and sixteen thousand persons—
47and from the children of Israel's half Moses took one
of every fifty, drawn from man and beast, and gave
them to the Levites, who kept charge of the tabernacle
of the LORD, as the LORD commanded Moses.

48Then the officers who *were* over thousands of the army, the captains of
thousands and captains of hundreds, came near to Moses; 49and they said
to Moses, "Your servants have taken a count of the men of war who *are*
under our command, and not a man of us is missing. 50Therefore we have
brought an offering for the LORD, what every man found of ornaments of
gold: armlets and bracelets and signet rings and earrings and necklaces,
to make atonement for ourselves before the LORD." 51So Moses and Eleazar
the priest received the gold from them, all the fashioned ornaments. 52And
all the gold of the offering that they offered to the LORD, from the captains
of thousands and captains of hundreds, was sixteen thousand seven hundred and fifty shekels. 53(The men of war had taken spoil, every man for
himself.) 54And Moses and Eleazar the priest received the gold from the
captains of thousands and of hundreds, and brought it into the tabernacle
of meeting as a memorial for the children of Israel before the LORD.

The Tribes Settling East of the Jordan

32 Now the children of Reuben and the children of Gad had a very great
multitude of livestock; and when they saw the land of Jazer and the
land of Gilead, that indeed the region *was* a place for livestock, 2the children of Gad and the children of Reuben came and spoke to Moses, to
Eleazar the priest, and to the leaders of the congregation, saying,
3"Ataroth, Dibon, Jazer, Nimrah, Heshbon, Elealeh, Shebam, Nebo, and
Beon, 4the country which the LORD defeated before the congregation of Israel, *is* a land for livestock, and your servants have livestock." 5Therefore
they said, "If we have found favor in your sight, let this land be given to
your servants as a possession. Do not take us over the Jordan."
6And Moses said to the children of Gad and to the children of Reuben:
"Shall your brethren go to war while you sit here? 7Now why will you discourage the heart of the children of Israel from going over into the land
which the LORD has given them? 8Thus your fathers did when I sent them
away from Kadesh Barnea to see the land. 9For when they went up to the
Valley of Eshcol and saw the land, they discouraged the heart of the children of Israel, so that they did not go into the land which the LORD had
given them. 10So the LORD's anger was aroused on that day, and He swore
an oath, saying, 11'Surely none of the men who came up from Egypt, from
twenty years old and above, shall see the land of which I swore to Abraham, Isaac, and Jacob, because they have not wholly followed Me, 12except
Caleb the son of Jephunneh, the Kenizzite, and Joshua the son of Nun, for
they have wholly followed the LORD.' 13So the LORD's anger was aroused
against Israel, and He made them wander in the wilderness forty years,
until all the generation that had done evil in the sight of the LORD was gone.
14And look! You have risen in your fathers' place, a brood of sinful men, to
increase still more the fierce anger of the LORD against Israel. 15For if you
turn away from following Him, He will once again leave them in the
wilderness, and you will destroy all these people."
16Then they came near to him and said: "We will build sheepfolds here
for our livestock, and cities for our little ones, 17but we ourselves will be
armed, ready *to go* before the children of Israel until we have brought
them to their place; and our little ones will dwell in the fortified cities because of the inhabitants of the land. 18We will not return to our homes until
every one of the children of Israel has received his inheritance. 19For we will

LIFE LESSON

Numbers 32:1-42

SITUATION Three tribes asked to reside east rather than west of the Jordan in order to secure their flocks in simple livestock pens. The pens' four stone walls would be built tall enough to keep out predatory animals and thieves. Then the men of the tribes would be free to help the other nine tribes west of the Jordan.

OBSERVATION The three tribes showed selfless effort in helping the other tribes west of the Jordan. We should help others finish a job, even if by doing so we receive no direct benefit.

INSPIRATION Many people these days are accepting Christianity as an explanation of life, but they're not willing to accept it as a way of life. . . . Christ calls us not only to accept an explanation, but to practice a way. That's tougher.

For one thing, it means meshing your life as closely as possible with other believers. No snobbery. No privileges. All together, sharing the same ideas (the apostles' doctrine), the same friends (fellowship), the same practices (breaking of bread), and the same religious habits (public prayers).

One of the young wives in our church was talking to me recently. She said, "Jerry and I have been praying over the passage that says if you have two coats, to give to him who has none. We discovered that we're now over the median income of our church members, so we're two-coat people, and that gives us responsibility of caring for others."

not inherit with them on the other side of the Jordan and beyond, because
our inheritance has fallen to us on this eastern side of the Jordan."
20Then Moses said to them: "If you do this thing, if you arm yourselves
before the LORD for the war, 21and all your armed men cross over the Jordan before the LORD until He has driven out His enemies from before Him,
22and the land is subdued before the LORD, then afterward you may return
and be blameless before the LORD and before Israel; and this land shall be
your possession before the LORD. 23But if you do not do so, then take note,
you have sinned against the LORD; and be sure your sin will find you out.
24Build cities for your little ones and folds for your sheep, and do what has
proceeded out of your mouth."
25And the children of Gad and the children of Reuben spoke to Moses,
saying: "Your servants will do as my lord commands. 26Our little ones, our
wives, our flocks, and all our livestock will be there in the cities of Gilead;
27but your servants will cross over, every man armed for war, before the
LORD to battle, just as my lord says."
28So Moses gave command concerning them to Eleazar the priest, to
Joshua the son of Nun, and to the chief fathers of the tribes of the children
of Israel. 29And Moses said to them: "If the children of Gad and the children
of Reuben cross over the Jordan with you, every man armed for battle before the LORD, and the land is subdued before you, then you shall give them
the land of Gilead as a possession. 30But if they do not cross over armed
with you, they shall have possessions among you in the land of Canaan."
31Then the children of Gad and the children of Reuben answered, saying: "As the LORD has said to your servants, so we will do. 32We will cross
over armed before the LORD into the land of Canaan, but the possession of
our inheritance *shall remain* with us on this side of the Jordan."
33So Moses gave to the children of Gad, to the children of Reuben, and to
half the tribe of Manasseh the son of Joseph, the kingdom of Sihon king of
the Amorites and the kingdom of Og king of Bashan, the land with its cities
within the borders, the cities of the surrounding country. 34And the children of Gad built Dibon and Ataroth and Aroer, 35Atroth and Shophan and
Jazer and Jogbehah, 36Beth Nimrah and Beth Haran, fortified cities, and
folds for sheep. 37And the children of Reuben built Heshbon and Elealeh
and Kirjathaim, 38Nebo and Baal Meon (*their* names being changed) and
Shibmah; and they gave *other* names to the cities which they built.
39And the children of Machir the son of Manasseh went to Gilead and
took it, and dispossessed the Amorites who *were* in it. 40So Moses gave
Gilead to Machir the son of Manasseh, and he dwelt in it. 41Also Jair the
son of Manasseh went and took its small towns, and called them Havoth
Jair.[y] 42Then Nobah went and took Kenath and its villages, and he called it
Nobah, after his own name.

Israel's Journey from Egypt Reviewed

33 These *are* the journeys of the children of Israel, who went out of the
land of Egypt by their armies under the hand of Moses and Aaron.
2Now Moses wrote down the starting points of their journeys at the command of the LORD. And these *are* their journeys according to their starting
points:

32:41 [y] Literally *Towns of Jair*

I said to her, "Do you remember, Linda, several years ago when Jerry was going through seminary, you were the no-coat ones; and how often believers would lovingly slip you money, or put a bag of groceries in the back door?"

She said, "Oh, *yes!* How could we forget? And now that it's the other way, we've upped our church giving, and we're also looking for the ones who need our help. They're all around us, and the Lord has already pointed out the first one."

She named a single mother raising teenagers, and she told gleefully about a sneaky plan to meet one of her needs anonymously. I couldn't help being tickled because she was so tickled!

Sharing in the family of God is a sure sign of authenticity. I love it when we get so comfortable with each other that we can think, "I do believe Sharon would look better in this sweater than I do; I think I'll offer it to her!" It's not a matter of charity as we now use the word—it's not who's richer and who's poorer; it's charity in its old usage—just pure love in the Body!

(From *Discipling One Another* by Anne Ortlund)

APPLICATION In what ways are you a "two-coater"? Look for someone today with whom you can share some of your resources in Jesus' name.

EXPLORATION Generosity—Proverbs 14:21; Psalm 15:5; Romans 15:2; 13:8-10; James 2:8.

LIFE LESSON

Numbers 33:1-56

SITUATION God ordered the Israelites to destroy the Canaanites because of their wickedness. God wished to prevent the Canaanites' sinful practices from affecting the Israelites.

OBSERVATION Learn to avoid sinful practices. Don't rub shoulders with those hostile to God. They will have a negative affect on you.

INSPIRATION Suppose you gave yourself to the Lord—to be wholly and altogether His, made and molded according to His own divine purpose, determined to follow Him wherever He may lead you. It is just at this point that you are faced with a new and very practical difficulty.

How are you to know the voice of the Good Shepherd, whom you have pledged to follow?

Many Christians live in constant doubt and confusion as to His will for them.

And this confusion is further compounded. Maybe there are certain "paths" into which God seems to be calling you, of which your friends disapprove—and it may be that these disapproving friends are older than yourself in the Christian life. You can hardly bear to disagree with them, or to see the distress on their faces.

The first thing you must do is to ask the Lord to help you quietly examine the motives of your heart. Be sure that you really have set your will to obey the Lord in every respect. If this is your purpose then, and your soul is merely waiting to know the will of God in order to consent to it, then you have done your part.

From this point, you can be certain that He will make His mind known to you

3They departed from Rameses in the first month, on the fifteenth day of
the first month; on the day after the Passover the children of Israel went
out with boldness in the sight of all the Egyptians. 4For the Egyptians were
burying all *their* firstborn, whom the LORD had killed among them. Also
on their gods the LORD had executed judgments.
5Then the children of Israel moved from Rameses and camped at
Succoth. 6They departed from Succoth and camped at Etham, which *is* on
the edge of the wilderness. 7They moved from Etham and turned back to
Pi Hahiroth, which *is* east of Baal Zephon; and they camped near Migdol.
8They departed from before Hahiroth[z] and passed through the midst of
the sea into the wilderness, went three days' journey in the Wilderness of
Etham, and camped at Marah. 9They moved from Marah and came to
Elim. At Elim *were* twelve springs of water and seventy palm trees; so they
camped there.
10They moved from Elim and camped by the Red Sea. 11They moved
from the Red Sea and camped in the Wilderness of Sin. 12They journeyed
from the Wilderness of Sin and camped at Dophkah. 13They departed
from Dophkah and camped at Alush. 14They moved from Alush and
camped at Rephidim, where there was no water for the people to drink.
15They departed from Rephidim and camped in the Wilderness of Sinai.
16They moved from the Wilderness of Sinai and camped at Kibroth
Hattaavah. 17They departed from Kibroth Hattaavah and camped at
Hazeroth. 18They departed from Hazeroth and camped at Rithmah. 19They
departed from Rithmah and camped at Rimmon Perez. 20They departed
from Rimmon Perez and camped at Libnah. 21They moved from Libnah
and camped at Rissah. 22They journeyed from Rissah and camped at
Kehelathah. 23They went from Kehelathah and camped at Mount Shepher.
24They moved from Mount Shepher and camped at Haradah. 25They
moved from Haradah and camped at Makheloth. 26They moved from
Makheloth and camped at Tahath. 27They departed from Tahath and
camped at Terah. 28They moved from Terah and camped at Mithkah.
29They went from Mithkah and camped at Hashmonah. 30They departed
from Hashmonah and camped at Moseroth. 31They departed from
Moseroth and camped at Bene Jaakan. 32They moved from Bene Jaakan
and camped at Hor Hagidgad. 33They went from Hor Hagidgad and
camped at Jotbathah. 34They moved from Jotbathah and camped at
Abronah. 35They departed from Abronah and camped at Ezion Geber.
36They moved from Ezion Geber and camped in the Wilderness of Zin,
which *is* Kadesh. 37They moved from Kadesh and camped at Mount Hor,
on the boundary of the land of Edom.
38Then Aaron the priest went up to Mount Hor at the command of the
LORD, and died there in the fortieth year after the children of Israel had
come out of the land of Egypt, on the first *day* of the fifth month. 39Aaron
was one hundred and twenty-three years old when he died on Mount Hor.
40Now the king of Arad, the Canaanite, who dwelt in the South in the
land of Canaan, heard of the coming of the children of Israel.
41So they departed from Mount Hor and camped at Zalmonah. 42They
departed from Zalmonah and camped at Punon. 43They departed from
Punon and camped at Oboth. 44They departed from Oboth and camped at

33:8 [z] Many Hebrew manuscripts, Samaritan Pentateuch, Syriac, Targum, and Vulgate read *from Pi Hahiroth* (compare verse 7).

Ije Abarim, at the border of Moab. 45They departed from Ijim[a] and
camped at Dibon Gad. 46They moved from Dibon Gad and camped at
Almon Diblathaim. 47They moved from Almon Diblathaim and camped in
the mountains of Abarim, before Nebo. 48They departed from the mountains of Abarim and camped in the plains of Moab by the Jordan, *across*
from Jericho. 49They camped by the Jordan, from Beth Jesimoth as far as
the Abel Acacia Grove[b] in the plains of Moab.

Instructions for the Conquest of Canaan

50Now the LORD spoke to Moses in the plains of Moab by the Jordan,
across from Jericho, saying, 51"Speak to the children of Israel, and say to
them: 'When you have crossed the Jordan into the land of Canaan, 52then
you shall drive out all the inhabitants of the land from before you, destroy
all their engraved stones, destroy all their molded images, and demolish
all their high places; 53you shall dispossess *the inhabitants of* the land and
dwell in it, for I have given you the land to possess. 54And you shall divide
the land by lot as an inheritance among your families; to the larger you
shall give a larger inheritance, and to the smaller you shall give a smaller
inheritance; there everyone's *inheritance* shall be whatever falls to him by
lot. You shall inherit according to the tribes of your fathers. 55But if you do
not drive out the inhabitants of the land from before you, then it shall be
that those whom you let remain *shall be* irritants in your eyes and thorns
in your sides, and they shall harass you in the land where you dwell.
56Moreover it shall be *that* I will do to you as I thought to do to them.' "

The Appointed Boundaries of Canaan

34 Then the LORD spoke to Moses, saying, 2"Command the children of
Israel, and say to them: 'When you come into the land of Canaan,
this *is* the land that shall fall to you as an inheritance—the land of Canaan to
its boundaries. 3Your southern border shall be from the Wilderness of Zin
along the border of Edom; then your southern border shall extend eastward to the end of the Salt Sea; 4your border shall turn from the southern
side of the Ascent of Akrabbim, continue to Zin, and be on the south of
Kadesh Barnea; then it shall go on to Hazar Addar, and continue to
Azmon; 5the border shall turn from Azmon to the Brook of Egypt, and it
shall end at the Sea.

6'As for the western border, you shall have the Great Sea for a border;
this shall be your western border.

7'And this shall be your northern border: From the Great Sea you shall
mark out your *border* line to Mount Hor; 8from Mount Hor you shall mark
out *your border* to the entrance of Hamath; then the direction of the border shall be toward Zedad; 9the border shall proceed to Ziphron, and it
shall end at Hazar Enan. This shall be your northern border.

10'You shall mark out your eastern border from Hazar Enan to
Shepham; 11the border shall go down from Shepham to Riblah on the east
side of Ain; the border shall go down and reach to the eastern side of the
Sea of Chinnereth; 12the border shall go down along the Jordan, and it
shall end at the Salt Sea. This shall be your land with its surrounding
boundaries.' "

33:45 [a] Same as *Ije Abarim,* verse 44
33:49 [b] Hebrew *Abel Shittim*

and will guide you on the right paths, for "He calls his own sheep by name, and leads them out . . . he goes on ahead of them, and his sheep follow him because they know his voice" (John 10:3-4). . . . And, "If any of you lacks wisdom, he should ask God, who gives generously to all without finding fault, and it will be given him" (James 1:5). Let no hint of doubt turn you from a steadfast faith in God's willingness and ability to guide you.

Remember this though: Our God has all knowledge and all wisdom. Therefore it is very possible He may guide you into paths wherein He knows great blessings are awaiting you just around the next fearsome turn—paths on which, to our short-sighted human eyes, there seems to be only confusion and loss.

You must become settled on this spiritual fact: God's thoughts are not like man's thoughts, nor are His ways like our ways. He alone, who knows the end of things from their beginning, is able to determine what the results of any course of action may be.

(From "The Christian's Secret of a Happy Life" by Hannah W. Smith in *Safe Within Your Love*)

APPLICATION Do you keep a devotional journal? If not, try it for three weeks. Write down thoughts from your daily study or devotional time with God. If you already keep a journal, look back and read what God has been showing you recently.

EXPLORATION Listening—Deuteronomy 5:1; 1 Kings 19:11-13; Proverbs 1:23-28; Mark 4:9; Luke 6:49; Hebrews 2:1-3.

13Then Moses commanded the children of Israel,
saying: "This *is* the land which you shall inherit by lot,
which the LORD has commanded to give to the nine
tribes and to the half-tribe. 14For the tribe of the children of Reuben according to the house of their fathers, and the tribe of the children of Gad according
to the house of their fathers, have received *their inheritance;* and the half-tribe of Manasseh has received its
inheritance. 15The two tribes and the half-tribe have
received their inheritance on this side of the Jordan,
across from Jericho eastward, toward the sunrise."

The Leaders Appointed to Divide the Land

16And the LORD spoke to Moses, saying, 17"These *are*
the names of the men who shall divide the land
among you as an inheritance: Eleazar the priest and
Joshua the son of Nun. 18And you shall take one leader
of every tribe to divide the land for the inheritance.
19These *are* the names of the men: from the tribe of Judah, Caleb the son of Jephunneh; 20from the tribe of
the children of Simeon, Shemuel the son of
Ammihud; 21from the tribe of Benjamin, Elidad the
son of Chislon; 22a leader from the tribe of the children of Dan, Bukki the son of Jogli; 23from the sons of
Joseph: a leader from the tribe of the children of
Manasseh, Hanniel the son of Ephod, 24and a leader
from the tribe of the children of Ephraim, Kemuel the
son of Shiphtan; 25a leader from the tribe of the children of Zebulun, Elizaphan the son of Parnach; 26a
leader from the tribe of the children of Issachar,
Paltiel the son of Azzan; 27a leader from the tribe of the
children of Asher, Ahihud the son of Shelomi; 28and a
leader from the tribe of the children of Naphtali,
Pedahel the son of Ammihud."

29These *are* the ones the LORD commanded to divide
the inheritance among the children of Israel in the
land of Canaan.

Cities for the Levites

35 And the LORD spoke to Moses in the plains of
Moab by the Jordan *across from* Jericho, saying:
2"Command the children of Israel that they give the
Levites cities to dwell in from the inheritance of their
possession, and you shall *also* give the Levites common-
land around the cities. 3They shall have the cities to
dwell in; and their common-land shall be for their
cattle, for their herds, and for all their animals. 4The
common-land of the cities which you will give the
Levites *shall extend* from the wall of the city outward a
thousand cubits all around. 5And you shall measure
outside the city on the east side two thousand cubits,
on the south side two thousand cubits, on the west
side two thousand cubits, and on the north side two
thousand cubits. The city *shall be* in the middle. This
shall belong to them as common-land for the cities.

6"Now among the cities which you will give to the
Levites *you shall appoint* six cities of refuge, to which
a manslayer may flee. And to these you shall add
forty-two cities. 7So all the cities you will give to the
Levites *shall be* forty-eight; these *you shall give* with
their common-land. 8And the cities which you will
give *shall be* from the possession of the children of Israel; from the larger *tribe* you shall give many, from
the smaller you shall give few. Each shall give some of
its cities to the Levites, in proportion to the inheritance that each receives."

Cities of Refuge

9Then the LORD spoke to Moses, saying, 10"Speak to
the children of Israel, and say to them: 'When you
cross the Jordan into the land of Canaan, 11then you
shall appoint cities to be cities of refuge for you, that
the manslayer who kills any person accidentally may
flee there. 12They shall be cities of refuge for you from
the avenger, that the manslayer may not die until he
stands before the congregation in judgment. 13And of
the cities which you give, you shall have six cities of
refuge. 14You shall appoint three cities on this side of
the Jordan, and three cities you shall appoint in the
land of Canaan, *which* will be cities of refuge. 15These
six cities shall be for refuge for the children of Israel,
for the stranger, and for the sojourner among them,
that anyone who kills a person accidentally may flee
there.

16'But if he strikes him with an iron implement, so
that he dies, he *is* a murderer; the murderer shall
surely be put to death. 17And if he strikes him with a
stone in the hand, by which one could die, and he
does die, he *is* a murderer; the murderer shall surely
be put to death. 18Or *if* he strikes him with a wooden
hand weapon, by which one could die, and he does
die, he *is* a murderer; the murderer shall surely be put
to death. 19The avenger of blood himself shall put the
murderer to death; when he meets him, he shall put
him to death. 20If he pushes him out of hatred or,
while lying in wait, hurls something at him so that he
dies, 21or in enmity he strikes him with his hand so
that he dies, the one who struck *him* shall surely be
put to death. He *is* a murderer. The avenger of blood
shall put the murderer to death when he meets him.

22'However, if he pushes him suddenly without enmity, or throws anything at him without lying in wait,

23or uses a stone, by which a man could die, throwing
it at him without seeing *him,* so that he dies, while he
was not his enemy or seeking his harm, 24then the congregation shall judge between the manslayer and the
avenger of blood according to these judgments. 25So
the congregation shall deliver the manslayer from the
hand of the avenger of blood, and the congregation
shall return him to the city of refuge where he had fled,
and he shall remain there until the death of the high
priest who was anointed with the holy oil. 26But if the
manslayer at any time goes outside the limits of the
city of refuge where he fled, 27and the avenger of blood
finds him outside the limits of his city of refuge, and
the avenger of blood kills the manslayer, he shall not
be guilty of blood, 28because he should have remained
in his city of refuge until the death of the high priest.
But after the death of the high priest the manslayer
may return to the land of his possession.

29"And these *things* shall be a statute of judgment to
you throughout your generations in all your dwellings.
30Whoever kills a person, the murderer shall be put to
death on the testimony of witnesses; but one witness
is not *sufficient* testimony against a person for the
death *penalty.* 31Moreover you shall take no ransom
for the life of a murderer who *is* guilty of death, but he
shall surely be put to death. 32And you shall take no
ransom for him who has fled to his city of refuge, that
he may return to dwell in the land before the death of
the priest. 33So you shall not pollute the land where
you *are;* for blood defiles the land, and no atonement
can be made for the land, for the blood that is shed on
it, except by the blood of him who shed it. 34Therefore
do not defile the land which you inhabit, in the midst
of which I dwell; for I the LORD dwell among the children of Israel.' "

Marriage of Female Heirs

36 Now the chief fathers of the families of the children of Gilead the son of Machir, the son of
Manasseh, of the families of the sons of Joseph, came
near and spoke before Moses and before the leaders,
the chief fathers of the children of Israel. 2And they
said: "The LORD commanded my lord *Moses* to give
the land as an inheritance by lot to the children of Israel, and my lord was commanded by the LORD to give
the inheritance of our brother Zelophehad to his
daughters. 3Now if they are married to any of the sons
of the *other* tribes of the children of Israel, then their
inheritance will be taken from the inheritance of our
fathers, and it will be added to the inheritance of the
tribe into which they marry; so it will be taken from
the lot of our inheritance. 4And when the Jubilee of the
children of Israel comes, then their inheritance will be
added to the inheritance of the tribe into which they
marry; so their inheritance will be taken away from
the inheritance of the tribe of our fathers."

5Then Moses commanded the children of Israel according to the word of the LORD, saying: "What the
tribe of the sons of Joseph speaks is right. 6This *is*
what the LORD commands concerning the daughters
of Zelophehad, saying, 'Let them marry whom they
think best, but they may marry only within the family
of their father's tribe.' 7So the inheritance of the children of Israel shall not change hands from tribe to
tribe, for every one of the children of Israel shall keep
the inheritance of the tribe of his fathers. 8And every
daughter who possesses an inheritance in any tribe of
the children of Israel shall be the wife of one of the
family of her father's tribe, so that the children of Israel each may possess the inheritance of his fathers.
9Thus no inheritance shall change hands from *one*
tribe to another, but every tribe of the children of Israel shall keep its own inheritance."

10Just as the LORD commanded Moses, so did the
daughters of Zelophehad; 11for Mahlah, Tirzah,
Hoglah, Milcah, and Noah, the daughters of Zelophehad, were married to the sons of their father's
brothers. 12They were married into the families of the
children of Manasseh the son of Joseph, and their inheritance remained in the tribe of their father's family.

13These *are* the commandments and the judgments
which the LORD commanded the children of Israel by
the hand of Moses in the plains of Moab by the Jordan, *across from* Jericho.

The Fifth Book of Moses Called

DEUTERONOMY

INTRODUCTION

If you've ever been a part of the following scene, you know you'll never forget it.

Inside the house is a quiet bedroom. Last spring's prom photo sits on the bedside table. A dried homecoming mum hangs from the bulletin board. Outside the house is a packed car. Both trunk and seat are full of clothes, books, and stereo. What was in the room is now in the car. The one who used to live in the room is about to drive the car ... to college.

Both parent and child are stunned by the moment. What happened to childhood? Who fast-forwarded the years? Why, just yesterday this child was filling the house with cartwheels and playdough—now look. He's so tall. She's such a beauty. The child is grown.

The grown child is equally stunned. The road ahead looks lonely and long. There is safety in these walls. Protection. Security. Those pleas for independence so recently voiced are unheard today. "Just say the word, Dad, I'll stay. Just ask me, Mom, I won't leave."

But Mom and Dad know better. They know that love releases the loved. They know the training is over. The last bell has rung. The class is dismissed, and the application has begun.

And so parent and child hesitate at the side of the car. There's no time to teach new truths. There's no time to instill values or lay foundations. There is only one word that can be said,—*remember*. Remember who loves you. Remember what matters. Remember what is right and what is wrong.

Remember.

In Deuteronomy God tells his children to *remember.*

Israel is about to make a transition. For forty years they have wandered. Now they are about to settle down in a new land. It's a time of transition. From Moses to Joshua. From the wilderness to the promised land. From nomads to farmers. From people with no land to people of the land.

God wants them to stay faithful. Stay distinctive. For forty days Moses teaches the words you are about to read. God repeats what he has already taught. *Deutero* means second. *Nomos* means law. Deuteronomy is a second hearing of the law.

God didn't want them to forget.

LIFE LESSON

Deuteronomy 1:1–3:29

SITUATION In Moab, Moses recounted the struggles and victories that God had given the Israelites while they wandered for forty years. This book reviews Israel's history and restates God's covenant with his people.

OBSERVATION The Lord demonstrated his faithfulness to the Israelites by providing great leaders and a land for them. He also gave them his law to govern their religious, civil, and personal life.

INSPIRATION Have you ever noticed how people who experienced the Depression years keep harking back to them? They do so with a kind of pride. If you are not irritated by such people, you may be able to observe that the effect of the Depression on them was to toughen and strengthen them and that thinking back to the lean years reinforces their resilience.

If you never thought about it, you might expect that positive and beautiful memories would be the ones to increase our faith. I always believed, for instance, that one or two really dramatic or miraculous answers to prayer would increase my faith

The Previous Command to Enter Canaan

These *are* the words which Moses spoke to all Israel on this
side of the Jordan in the wilderness, in the plain[a] opposite
Suph,[b] between Paran, Tophel, Laban, Hazeroth, and Dizahab.
2*It is* eleven days' *journey* from Horeb by way of Mount Seir to
Kadesh Barnea. 3Now it came to pass in the fortieth year, in the eleventh
month, on the first *day* of the month, *that* Moses spoke to the children of
Israel according to all that the LORD had given him as commandments to
them, 4after he had killed Sihon king of the Amorites, who dwelt in Heshbon,
and Og king of Bashan, who dwelt at Ashtaroth in[c] Edrei.
5On this side of the Jordan in the land of Moab, Moses began to explain
this law, saying, 6"The LORD our God spoke to us in Horeb, saying: 'You
have dwelt long enough at this mountain. 7Turn and take your journey,
and go to the mountains of the Amorites, to all the neighboring *places* in
the plain,[d] in the mountains and in the lowland, in the South and on the
seacoast, to the land of the Canaanites and to Lebanon, as far as the great
river, the River Euphrates. 8See, I have set the land before you; go in and
possess the land which the LORD swore to your fathers—to Abraham,
Isaac, and Jacob—to give to them and their descendants after them.'

Tribal Leaders Appointed

9"And I spoke to you at that time, saying: 'I alone am not able to bear
you. 10The LORD your God has multiplied you, and here you *are* today, as
the stars of heaven in multitude. 11May the LORD God of your fathers make
you a thousand times more numerous than you are, and bless you as He
has promised you! 12How can I alone bear your problems and your burdens and your complaints? 13Choose wise, understanding, and knowledgeable men from among your tribes, and I will make them heads over
you.' 14And you answered me and said, 'The thing which you have told *us*
to do *is* good.' 15So I took the heads of your tribes, wise and knowledgeable
men, and made them heads over you, leaders of thousands, leaders of
hundreds, leaders of fifties, leaders of tens, and officers for your tribes.
16"Then I commanded your judges at that time, saying, 'Hear *the cases*
between your brethren, and judge righteously between a man and his
brother or the stranger who is with him. 17You shall not show partiality in
judgment; you shall hear the small as well as the great; you shall not be
afraid in any man's presence, for the judgment *is* God's. The case that is
too hard for you, bring to me, and I will hear it.' 18And I commanded you
at that time all the things which you should do.

Israel's Refusal to Enter the Land

19"So we departed from Horeb, and went through all that great and terrible wilderness which you saw on the way to the mountains of the
Amorites, as the LORD our God had commanded us. Then we came to
Kadesh Barnea. 20And I said to you, 'You have come to the mountains of
the Amorites, which the LORD our God is giving us. 21Look, the LORD your
God has set the land before you; go up *and* possess *it,* as the LORD God of
your fathers has spoken to you; do not fear or be discouraged.'

1:1 [a] Hebrew *arabah* [b] One manuscript of the Septuagint, also Targum and Vulgate, read *Red Sea.*
1:4 [c] Septuagint, Syriac, and Vulgate read *and* (compare Joshua 12:4).
1:7 [d] Hebrew *arabah*

22"And every one of you came near to me and said, 'Let us send men before us, and let them search out the land for us, and bring back word to us
of the way by which we should go up, and of the cities into which we shall
come.'
23"The plan pleased me well; so I took twelve of your men, one man
from *each* tribe. 24And they departed and went up into the mountains, and
came to the Valley of Eshcol, and spied it out. 25They also took *some* of the
fruit of the land in their hands and brought *it* down to us; and they
brought back word to us, saying, '*It is* a good land which the LORD our God
is giving us.'
26"Nevertheless you would not go up, but rebelled against the command of the LORD your God; 27and you complained in your tents, and said,
'Because the LORD hates us, He has brought us out of the land of Egypt to
deliver us into the hand of the Amorites, to destroy us. 28Where can we go
up? Our brethren have discouraged our hearts, saying, "The people *are*
greater and taller than we; the cities *are* great and fortified up to heaven;
moreover we have seen the sons of the Anakim there." '
29"Then I said to you, 'Do not be terrified, or afraid of them. 30The LORD
your God, who goes before you, He will fight for you, according to all He
did for you in Egypt before your eyes, 31and in the wilderness where you
saw how the LORD your God carried you, as a man carries his son, in all the
way that you went until you came to this place.' 32Yet, for all that, you did
not believe the LORD your God, 33who went in the way before you to search
out a place for you to pitch your tents, to show you the way you should go,
in the fire by night and in the cloud by day.

The Penalty for Israel's Rebellion

34"And the LORD heard the sound of your words, and was angry, and
took an oath, saying, 35'Surely not one of these men of this evil generation
shall see that good land of which I swore to give to your fathers, 36except
Caleb the son of Jephunneh; he shall see it, and to him and his children I
am giving the land on which he walked, because he wholly followed the
LORD.' 37The LORD was also angry with me for your sakes, saying, 'Even you
shall not go in there. 38Joshua the son of Nun, who stands before you, he
shall go in there. Encourage him, for he shall cause Israel to inherit it.
39'Moreover your little ones and your children, who you say will be victims, who today have no knowledge of good and evil, they shall go in there;
to them I will give it, and they shall possess it. 40But *as for* you, turn and
take your journey into the wilderness by the Way of the Red Sea.'
41"Then you answered and said to me, 'We have sinned against the
LORD; we will go up and fight, just as the LORD our God commanded us.'
And when everyone of you had girded on his weapons of war, you were
ready to go up into the mountain.
42"And the LORD said to me, 'Tell them, "Do not go up nor fight, for I *am*
not among you; lest you be defeated before your enemies." ' 43So I spoke to
you; yet you would not listen, but rebelled against the command of the
LORD, and presumptuously went up into the mountain. 44And the
Amorites who dwelt in that mountain came out against you and chased
you as bees do, and drove you back from Seir to Hormah. 45Then you returned and wept before the LORD, but the LORD would not listen to your
voice nor give ear to you.

immeasurably. Yet it hasn't worked out that way. . . . Tough times, of course, do one of two things to you. They either break you or make you. If you are not utterly crushed by them (in which case you will do all you can to bury their memory), you will be enlarged by them. . . . If you have only just come to Christ, your rough time may not yet have taken place. But if you've been longer on the way—think back. . . . Think well on the rough times in your Christian past. (From *The Fight* by John White)

APPLICATION Set aside time this week for reflection. Write down as many examples as you can of how the Lord has led you and of the Lord's faithfulness. Start a journal of events as they occur. Share these examples, as you are able, with your loved ones. Also, use them to begin a conversation with an unbeliever as you recount God's faithfulness.

EXPLORATION God's Faithfulness—Lamentations 3:19-26; Psalm 103:14; 111:5; 1 Chronicles 16:14-18.

46“So you remained in Kadesh many days, according to the days that you spent *there.*

The Desert Years

2 “Then we turned and journeyed into the wilderness of the Way of the Red Sea, as the LORD spoke
to me, and we skirted Mount Seir for many days.
2“And the LORD spoke to me, saying: 3‘You have
skirted this mountain long enough; turn northward.
4And command the people, saying, “You *are about to*
pass through the territory of your brethren, the descendants of Esau, who live in Seir; and they will be
afraid of you. Therefore watch yourselves carefully.
5Do not meddle with them, for I will not give you *any*
of their land, no, not so much as one footstep, because
I have given Mount Seir to Esau *as* a possession. 6You
shall buy food from them with money, that you may
eat; and you shall also buy water from them with
money, that you may drink.
7“For the LORD your God has blessed you in all the
work of your hand. He knows your trudging through
this great wilderness. These forty years the LORD your
God *has been* with you; you have lacked nothing.” ’
8“And when we passed beyond our brethren, the
descendants of Esau who dwell in Seir, away from the
road of the plain, away from Elath and Ezion Geber, we
turned and passed by way of the Wilderness of Moab.
9Then the LORD said to me, ‘Do not harass Moab, nor
contend with them in battle, for I will not give you *any*
of their land *as* a possession, because I have given Ar
to the descendants of Lot *as* a possession.’ ”
10(The Emim had dwelt there in times past, a people as great and numerous and tall as the Anakim.
11They were also regarded as giants,[e] like the Anakim,
but the Moabites call them Emim. 12The Horites formerly dwelt in Seir, but the descendants of Esau
dispossessed them and destroyed them from before
them, and dwelt in their place, just as Israel did to the
land of their possession which the LORD gave them.)
13“ ‘Now rise and cross over the Valley of the Zered.’
So we crossed over the Valley of the Zered. 14And the
time we took to come from Kadesh Barnea until we
crossed over the Valley of the Zered *was* thirty-eight
years, until all the generation of the men of war was
consumed from the midst of the camp, just as the
LORD had sworn to them. 15For indeed the hand of the
LORD was against them, to destroy them from the
midst of the camp until they were consumed.
16“So it was, when all the men of war had finally
perished from among the people, 17that the LORD
spoke to me, saying: 18‘This day you are to cross over
at Ar, the boundary of Moab. 19And *when* you come
near the people of Ammon, do not harass them or
meddle with them, for I will not give you *any* of the
land of the people of Ammon *as* a possession, because I have given it to the descendants of Lot *as* a
possession.’ ”
20(That was also regarded as a land of giants;[f] giants formerly dwelt there. But the Ammonites call
them Zamzummim, 21a people as great and numerous and tall as the Anakim. But the LORD destroyed
them before them, and they dispossessed them and
dwelt in their place, 22just as He had done for the descendants of Esau, who dwelt in Seir, when He destroyed the Horites from before them. They
dispossessed them and dwelt in their place, even to
this day. 23And the Avim, who dwelt in villages as far
as Gaza—the Caphtorim, who came from Caphtor,
destroyed them and dwelt in their place.)
24“ ‘Rise, take your journey, and cross over the
River Arnon. Look, I have given into your hand Sihon
the Amorite, king of Heshbon, and his land. Begin to
possess *it,* and engage him in battle. 25This day I will
begin to put the dread and fear of you upon the nations under the whole heaven, who shall hear the report of you, and shall tremble and be in anguish
because of you.’

King Sihon Defeated

26“And I sent messengers from the Wilderness of
Kedemoth to Sihon king of Heshbon, with words of
peace, saying, 27‘Let me pass through your land; I will
keep strictly to the road, and I will turn neither to the
right nor to the left. 28You shall sell me food for
money, that I may eat, and give me water for money,
that I may drink; only let me pass through on foot,
29just as the descendants of Esau who dwell in Seir
and the Moabites who dwell in Ar did for me, until I
cross the Jordan to the land which the LORD our God is
giving us.’
30“But Sihon king of Heshbon would not let us pass
through, for the LORD your God hardened his spirit
and made his heart obstinate, that He might deliver
him into your hand, as *it is* this day.
31“And the LORD said to me, ‘See, I have begun to
give Sihon and his land over to you. Begin to possess
it, that you may inherit his land.’ 32Then Sihon and all
his people came out against us to fight at Jahaz. 33And

2:11 [e] Hebrew *rephaim*
2:20 [f] Hebrew *rephaim*

the LORD our God delivered him over to us; so we defeated him, his sons, and all his people. 34We took all
his cities at that time, and we utterly destroyed the
men, women, and little ones of every city; we left none
remaining. 35We took only the livestock as plunder for
ourselves, with the spoil of the cities which we took.
36From Aroer, which *is* on the bank of the River
Arnon, and *from* the city that *is* in the ravine, as far as
Gilead, there was not one city too strong for us; the
LORD our God delivered all to us. 37Only you did not go
near the land of the people of Ammon—anywhere
along the River Jabbok, or to the cities of the mountains, or wherever the LORD our God had forbidden us.

King Og Defeated

3 "Then we turned and went up the road to Bashan;
and Og king of Bashan came out against us, he
and all his people, to battle at Edrei. 2And the LORD
said to me, 'Do not fear him, for I have delivered him
and all his people and his land into your hand; you
shall do to him as you did to Sihon king of the
Amorites, who dwelt at Heshbon.'
3"So the LORD our God also delivered into our
hands Og king of Bashan, with all his people, and we
attacked him until he had no survivors remaining.
4And we took all his cities at that time; there was not a
city which we did not take from them: sixty cities, all
the region of Argob, the kingdom of Og in Bashan.
5All these cities *were* fortified with high walls, gates,
and bars, besides a great many rural towns. 6And we
utterly destroyed them, as we did to Sihon king of
Heshbon, utterly destroying the men, women, and
children of every city. 7But all the livestock and the
spoil of the cities we took as booty for ourselves.
8"And at that time we took the land from the hand
of the two kings of the Amorites who *were* on this side
of the Jordan, from the River Arnon to Mount
Hermon 9(the Sidonians call Hermon Sirion, and the
Amorites call it Senir), 10all the cities of the plain, all
Gilead, and all Bashan, as far as Salcah and Edrei,
cities of the kingdom of Og in Bashan.
11"For only Og king of Bashan remained of the remnant of the giants.[g] Indeed his bedstead *was* an iron
bedstead. (*Is* it not in Rabbah of the people of
Ammon?) Nine cubits *is* its length and four cubits its
width, according to the standard cubit.

The Land East of the Jordan Divided

12"And this land, *which* we possessed at that time,
from Aroer, which *is* by the River Arnon, and half the
mountains of Gilead and its cities, I gave to the
Reubenites and the Gadites. 13The rest of Gilead, and
all Bashan, the kingdom of Og, I gave to half the tribe
of Manasseh. (All the region of Argob, with all
Bashan, was called the land of the giants.[h] 14Jair the
son of Manasseh took all the region of Argob, as far as
the border of the Geshurites and the Maachathites,
and called Bashan after his own name, Havoth Jair,[i] to
this day.)
15"Also I gave Gilead to Machir. 16And to the
Reubenites and the Gadites I gave from Gilead as far
as the River Arnon, the middle of the river as *the* border, as far as the River Jabbok, the border of the people
of Ammon; 17the plain also, with the Jordan as *the* border, from Chinnereth as far as the east side of the Sea
of the Arabah (the Salt Sea), below the slopes of Pisgah.
18"Then I commanded you at that time, saying:
'The LORD your God has given you this land to possess. All you men of valor shall cross over armed before your brethren, the children of Israel. 19But your
wives, your little ones, and your livestock (I know that
you have much livestock) shall stay in your cities
which I have given you, 20until the LORD has given rest
to your brethren as to you, and they also possess the
land which the LORD your God is giving them beyond
the Jordan. Then each of you may return to his possession which I have given you.'
21"And I commanded Joshua at that time, saying,
'Your eyes have seen all that the LORD your God has
done to these two kings; so will the LORD do to all the
kingdoms through which you pass. 22You must not fear
them, for the LORD your God Himself fights for you.'

Moses Forbidden to Enter the Land

23"Then I pleaded with the LORD at that time, saying: 24'O Lord GOD, You have begun to show Your servant Your greatness and Your mighty hand, for what
god *is there* in heaven or on earth who can do *anything*
like Your works and Your mighty *deeds*? 25I pray, let
me cross over and see the good land beyond the Jordan, those pleasant mountains, and Lebanon.'
26"But the LORD was angry with me on your account, and would not listen to me. So the LORD said to
me: 'Enough of that! Speak no more to Me of this
matter. 27Go up to the top of Pisgah, and lift your eyes
toward the west, the north, the south, and the east; behold *it* with your eyes, for you shall not cross over this

3:11 [g] Hebrew *rephaim*
3:13 [h] Hebrew *rephaim*
3:14 [i] Literally *Towns of Jair*

Jordan. 28But command Joshua, and encourage him and strengthen him;
for he shall go over before this people, and he shall cause them to inherit
the land which you will see.'
29"So we stayed in the valley opposite Beth Peor.

Moses Commands Obedience

4 "Now, O Israel, listen to the statutes and the judgments which I teach
you to observe, that you may live, and go in and possess the land
which the LORD God of your fathers is giving you. 2You shall not add to the
word which I command you, nor take from it, that you may keep the commandments of the LORD your God which I command you. 3Your eyes have
seen what the LORD did at Baal Peor; for the LORD your God has destroyed
from among you all the men who followed Baal of Peor. 4But you who held
fast to the LORD your God *are* alive today, every one of you.
5"Surely I have taught you statutes and judgments, just as the LORD my
God commanded me, that you should act according *to them* in the land
which you go to possess. 6Therefore be careful to observe *them;* for this *is*
your wisdom and your understanding in the sight of the peoples who will
hear all these statutes, and say, 'Surely this great nation *is* a wise and understanding people.'
7"For what great nation *is there* that has God *so* near to it, as the LORD our
God *is* to us, for whatever *reason* we may call upon Him? 8And what great
nation *is there* that has *such* statutes and righteous judgments as are in all
this law which I set before you this day? 9Only take heed to yourself, and
diligently keep yourself, lest you forget the things your eyes have seen, and
lest they depart from your heart all the days of your life. And teach them to
your children and your grandchildren, 10*especially concerning* the day you
stood before the LORD your God in Horeb, when the LORD said to me, 'Gather
the people to Me, and I will let them hear My words, that they may learn to
fear Me all the days they live on the earth, and *that* they may teach their
children.'
11"Then you came near and stood at the foot of the mountain, and the
mountain burned with fire to the midst of heaven, with darkness, cloud,
and thick darkness. 12And the LORD spoke to you out of the midst of the fire.
You heard the sound of the words, but saw no form; *you* only *heard* a voice.
13So He declared to you His covenant which He commanded you to perform,
the Ten Commandments; and He wrote them on two tablets of stone. 14And
the LORD commanded me at that time to teach you statutes and judgments,
that you might observe them in the land which you cross over to possess.

Beware of Idolatry

15"Take careful heed to yourselves, for you saw no form when the LORD
spoke to you at Horeb out of the midst of the fire, 16lest you act corruptly
and make for yourselves a carved image in the form of any figure: the likeness of male or female, 17the likeness of any animal that *is* on the earth or
the likeness of any winged bird that flies in the air, 18the likeness of anything that creeps on the ground or the likeness of any fish that *is* in the
water beneath the earth. 19And *take heed,* lest you lift your eyes to heaven,
and *when* you see the sun, the moon, and the stars, all the host of heaven,
you feel driven to worship them and serve them, which the LORD your God
has given to all the peoples under the whole heaven as a heritage. 20But the
LORD has taken you and brought you out of the iron furnace, out of Egypt,

LIFE LESSON

Deuteronomy 4:1-43

SITUATION After forty years of wandering in the desert, Moses carried out God's instructions to teach the people and prepare them to enter the Promised Land.

OBSERVATION God loves his people with a jealous love that leaves no room for idolatry or other sin.

INSPIRATION In the midst of playing baseball in the backyard, Jim's six-year-old son's best friend, and next door neighbor, came out of his house. "Dad, can I go play with Brad?" he asked. "But son, we're playing baseball. Don't you want to play with me?" Jim asked, not really wanting to hear the answer he knew was coming. "Nah, I'd rather play with Brad," his son replied, all too honestly. Jim had a rival for his son's affection, and he was a six-year-old. As he struggled with that thought, knowing that he'd better get a handle on it because it was only going to escalate, he suddenly was reminded that God felt the same way about him. He jealously desires our affection and attention as well. It breaks his heart when we show more interest in cars, sports, newspapers, television, yard work, hobbies, books, and family activities than we do in reading his word and prayer. It saddens him when we are more committed to serving ourselves and pursuing our own interests than we are in serving him.

If God were to examine your heart today, what rivals for his attention would he find?

(From *A Dad's Blessing* by Gary Smalley and John Trent)

APPLICATION Idolatry makes anything but God the highest priority in life. Do you value your relationship with God more than anything else? Or have you allowed money, leisure, friendships—or anything else—to rule your life? Smash the idols in your life and make a fresh commitment to put God first. He alone is worthy of this position!

EXPLORATION God's Jealousy—Exodus 20:4-6; 34:14; Joshua 24:19-20.

to be His people, an inheritance, as you are this day. 21Furthermore the
LORD was angry with me for your sakes, and swore that I would not cross
over the Jordan, and that I would not enter the good land which the LORD
your God is giving you as an inheritance. 22But I must die in this land, I
must not cross over the Jordan; but you shall cross over and possess that
good land. 23Take heed to yourselves, lest you forget the covenant of the
LORD your God which He made with you, and make for yourselves a
carved image in the form of anything which the LORD your God has forbidden you. 24For the LORD your God *is* a consuming fire, a jealous God.
25"When you beget children and grandchildren and have grown old in
the land, and act corruptly and make a carved image in the form of anything, and do evil in the sight of the LORD your God to provoke Him to
anger, 26I call heaven and earth to witness against you this day, that you
will soon utterly perish from the land which you cross over the Jordan to
possess; you will not prolong *your* days in it, but will be utterly destroyed.
27And the LORD will scatter you among the peoples, and you will be left few
in number among the nations where the LORD will drive you. 28And there
you will serve gods, the work of men's hands, wood and stone, which neither
see nor hear nor eat nor smell. 29But from there you will seek the LORD your
God, and you will find *Him* if you seek Him with all your heart and with all
your soul. 30When you are in distress, and all these things come upon you
in the latter days, when you turn to the LORD your God and obey His voice
31(for the LORD your God *is* a merciful God), He will not forsake you nor destroy you, nor forget the covenant of your fathers which He swore to them.
32"For ask now concerning the days that are past, which were before
you, since the day that God created man on the earth, and *ask* from one
end of heaven to the other, whether *any* great *thing* like this has happened,
or *anything* like it has been heard. 33Did *any* people *ever* hear the voice of
God speaking out of the midst of the fire, as you have heard, and live? 34Or
did God *ever* try to go *and* take for Himself a nation from the midst of *another* nation, by trials, by signs, by wonders, by war, by a mighty hand and
an outstretched arm, and by great terrors, according to all that the LORD
your God did for you in Egypt before your eyes? 35To you it was shown, that
you might know that the LORD Himself *is* God; *there is* none other besides
Him. 36Out of heaven He let you hear His voice, that He might instruct you;
on earth He showed you His great fire, and you heard His words out of the
midst of the fire. 37And because He loved your fathers, therefore He chose
their descendants after them; and He brought you out of Egypt with His
Presence, with His mighty power, 38driving out from before you nations
greater and mightier than you, to bring you in, to give you their land *as* an
inheritance, as *it is* this day. 39Therefore know this day, and consider *it* in
your heart, that the LORD Himself *is* God in heaven above and on the earth
beneath; *there is* no other. 40You shall therefore keep His statutes and His
commandments which I command you today, that it may go well with you
and with your children after you, and that you may prolong *your* days in
the land which the LORD your God is giving you for all time."

Cities of Refuge East of the Jordan

41Then Moses set apart three cities on this side of the Jordan, toward the
rising of the sun, 42that the manslayer might flee there, who kills his neighbor unintentionally, without having hated him in time past, and that by
fleeing to one of these cities he might live: 43Bezer in the wilderness on the

LIFE LESSON

Deuteronomy 4:44–5:33

SITUATION Finally. The fortieth year of the Exodus from Egypt. Many Israelites had died since God gave the commandments at Mt. Sinai. God held the entire nation responsible for obeying the commandments.

OBSERVATION God longs for his people to abide by his stipulations, so that all will be well with them and the generations that follow them. It pleases him when his people profess willingness to obey his commandments, but he knows their hearts will lead them to disobey.

INSPIRATION You lose your temper. You lust. You fall. You take a drag. You buy a drink. You kiss the woman. You follow the crowd. You rationalize. You say yes. You sign your name. You forget who you are. You walk into her room. You look in the window. You break your promise. You buy the magazine. You lie. You covet. You stomp your feet and demand your way. You deny your Master.

It's David disrobing Bathsheba. It's Adam accepting the fruit from Eve. It's Abraham lying about Sarah. It's Peter denying that he ever knew Jesus. It's Noah, drunk and naked in his tent. It's Lot in bed with his own daughter. It's your worst nightmare. It's sudden. It's sin.

Satan numbs our awareness and short-circuits our self-control. We know what we are doing and yet can't believe that we are doing it. In the fog of weakness we want to stop but haven't the will to do so. We want to turn around, but our feet won't move. We want to run and, pitifully, we want to stay. . . .

No one who is reading these words is free from the treachery of sudden sin. No one is immune to this trick of perdition. This demon of hell can scale the highest monastery wall, penetrate the deepest faith, and desecrate the purest home.

Some of you know exactly what I mean. You could write these words better than I, couldn't you? Some of you, like me, have tumbled so often that the stench of Satan's breath is far from a novelty. You've asked for

Continued

God's forgiveness so often that you worry that the well of mercy might run dry. . . .

Romans chapter 7 is the Emancipation Proclamation for those of us who have a tendency to tumble. Look at verse 15: "I do not understand what I do. For what I want to do I do not do, but what I hate I do."

Sound familiar? Read on. Verses 18-19: "For I have the desire to do what is good, but I cannot carry it out. For what I do is not the good I want to do; no, the evil I do not want to do—this I keep on doing."

Man, that fellow has been reading my diary!

"What a wretched man I am! Who will rescue me from the body of death?" (v. 24).

Please, Paul, don't stop there! Is there no oasis in this barrenness of guilt? There is. Thank God and drink deeply as you read verse 25 and verse 12 of chapter 8: "Thanks be to God—through Jesus Christ our Lord! . . . Therefore there is now no condemnation for those who are in Christ Jesus."

Amen. There it is. You read it right. Underline it if you wish. For those in Christ there is *no* condemnation. Absolutely none. Claim the promise. Memorize the words. Accept the cleansing. Throw out the guilt. Praise the Lord.

(From *On the Anvil* by Max Lucado)

APPLICATION Every Christian has suffered from the guilt that comes after sin. Remember, Christ's forgiveness covers every sin, every time. Don't let guilt drag you down after you have been forgiven. Believe it when he says you're forgiven!

EXPLORATION Confessing Sin—Luke 15:11-32; James 5:16; 1John 1:8-10.

plateau for the Reubenites, Ramoth in Gilead for the Gadites, and Golan in
Bashan for the Manassites.

Introduction to God's Law

44 Now this *is* the law which Moses set before the children of Israel.
45 These *are* the testimonies, the statutes, and the judgments which Moses
spoke to the children of Israel after they came out of Egypt, 46 on this side
of the Jordan, in the valley opposite Beth Peor, in the land of Sihon king of
the Amorites, who dwelt at Heshbon, whom Moses and the children of Israel defeated after they came out of Egypt. 47 And they took possession of
his land and the land of Og king of Bashan, two kings of the Amorites, who
were on this side of the Jordan, toward the rising of the sun, 48 from Aroer,
which *is* on the bank of the River Arnon, even to Mount Sion[j] (that is,
Hermon), 49 and all the plain on the east side of the Jordan as far as the Sea
of the Arabah, below the slopes of Pisgah.

The Ten Commandments Reviewed

5 And Moses called all Israel, and said to them: "Hear, O Israel, the
statutes and judgments which I speak in your hearing today, that you
may learn them and be careful to observe them. 2 The LORD our God made
a covenant with us in Horeb. 3 The LORD did not make this covenant with
our fathers, but with us, those who *are* here today, all of us who *are* alive.
4 The LORD talked with you face to face on the mountain from the midst of
the fire. 5 I stood between the LORD and you at that time, to declare to you
the word of the LORD; for you were afraid because of the fire, and you did
not go up the mountain. *He* said:

6 'I *am* the LORD your God who brought you out of the land of Egypt,
out of the house of bondage.

7 'You shall have no other gods before Me.

8 'You shall not make for yourself a carved image—any likeness *of*
anything that *is* in heaven above, or that *is* in the earth beneath, or that *is* in the water under the earth; 9 you shall not
bow down to them nor serve them. For I, the LORD your God,
am a jealous God, visiting the iniquity of the fathers upon the
children to the third and fourth *generations* of those who hate
Me, 10 but showing mercy to thousands, to those who love Me
and keep My commandments.

11 'You shall not take the name of the LORD your God in vain, for the
LORD will not hold *him* guiltless who takes His name in vain.

12 'Observe the Sabbath day, to keep it holy, as the LORD your God
commanded you. 13 Six days you shall labor and do all your
work, 14 but the seventh day *is* the Sabbath of the LORD your
God. *In it* you shall do no work: you, nor your son, nor your
daughter, nor your male servant, nor your female servant, nor
your ox, nor your donkey, nor any of your cattle, nor your
stranger who *is* within your gates, that your male servant and
your female servant may rest as well as you. 15 And remember
that you were a slave in the land of Egypt, and the LORD your
God brought you out from there by a mighty hand and by an
outstretched arm; therefore the LORD your God commanded
you to keep the Sabbath day.

4:48 [j] Syriac reads *Sirion* (compare 3:9).

16 'Honor your father and your mother, as the LORD your God has
commanded you, that your days may be long, and that it may
be well with you in the land which the LORD your God is giving
you.
17 'You shall not murder.
18 'You shall not commit adultery.
19 'You shall not steal.
20 'You shall not bear false witness against your neighbor.
21 'You shall not covet your neighbor's wife; and you shall not desire
your neighbor's house, his field, his male servant, his female
servant, his ox, his donkey, or anything that *is* your neighbor's.'
22 "These words the LORD spoke to all your assembly, in the mountain
from the midst of the fire, the cloud, and the thick darkness, with a loud
voice; and He added no more. And He wrote them on two tablets of stone
and gave them to me.

The People Afraid of God's Presence

23 "So it was, when you heard the voice from the midst of the darkness,
while the mountain was burning with fire, that you came near to me, all
the heads of your tribes and your elders.
24 And you said: 'Surely the LORD
our God has shown us His glory and His greatness, and we have heard His
voice from the midst of the fire. We have seen this day that God speaks
with man; yet he *still* lives.
25 Now therefore, why should we die? For this
great fire will consume us; if we hear the voice of the LORD our God anymore, then we shall die.
26 For who *is there* of all flesh who has heard the
voice of the living God speaking from the midst of the fire, as we *have*, and
lived?
27 You go near and hear all that the LORD our God may say, and tell us
all that the LORD our God says to you, and we will hear and do *it*.'
28 "Then the LORD heard the voice of your words when you spoke to me,
and the LORD said to me: 'I have heard the voice of the words of this people
which they have spoken to you. They are right *in* all that they have spoken.
29 Oh, that they had such a heart in them that they would fear Me and always
keep all My commandments, that it might be well with them and with
their children forever!
30 Go and say to them, "Return to your tents."
31 But
as for you, stand here by Me, and I will speak to you all the commandments, the statutes, and the judgments which you shall teach them, that
they may observe *them* in the land which I am giving them to possess.'
32 "Therefore you shall be careful to do as the LORD your God has commanded you; you shall not turn aside to the right hand or to the left.
33 You
shall walk in all the ways which the LORD your God has commanded you,
that you may live and *that it may be* well with you, and *that* you may prolong *your* days in the land which you shall possess.

The Greatest Commandment

6 "Now this *is* the commandment, *and these are* the statutes and judgments which the LORD your God has commanded to teach you, that
you may observe *them* in the land which you are crossing over to possess,
2 that you may fear the LORD your God, to keep all His statutes and His commandments which I command you, you and your son and your grandson,
all the days of your life, and that your days may be prolonged.
3 Therefore

LIFE LESSON

Deuteronomy 6:1–7:26

SITUATION God repeated these commands because of their importance. God wanted the parents to teach his commandments to their children.

OBSERVATION God gives parents the responsibility to teach his commandments to their children. This requires spending time with children daily and telling them about the commands of God.

INSPIRATION Living as we did in a congested and bustling city, my mother arranged with a teenage girl who lived next door to walk me home at the end of the day. For this arduous responsibility, the girl was paid five cents a day, or a grand total of a quarter a week. In second grade, I became irritated that our poor family was giving this neighbor girl so much money, and I offered a deal to my mom. "Look," I said, "I'll walk myself to school and, if you give me a nickel a week, I will be extra careful. You can keep the other twenty cents and we'll all be better off." I pleaded and begged, and eventually my mother gave in to my proposal. For the next two years I walked to and from school all by myself. It was an eight-block walk with many streets to cross, but I crossed them all with great care. I didn't talk to any strangers. I always kept on the appointed path. I always did as I promised and I did it alone—or at least I thought I did.

Years later when we were enjoying a family party, I bragged about my characteristic independence and, in a grandiose fashion, reminded my family of how I had been able to take care of myself even as a small boy. I recalled the arrangements for going to and from school that I had worked out with Mom. It was then that my mother laughed and told me the whole story. "Did you really think you were alone?" she asked. "Every morning when you left for school, I left with you. I walked behind you all the way. When you got out of school at 3:30 in the afternoon, I was there. I always kept myself hidden, but I was

Continued

there and I followed you all the way home. I just wanted to be there for you in case you needed me."

Mom *was* always there for me, and Mom always believed in me. . . . My mother also had a way of minimizing my failures and accentuating my accomplishments. Over and over again she told me how proud she was of anything I did that had any value. I don't ever remember her saying, "You could have done better." . . .

Every day as I left the house, the last thing she would say to me was "Remember! You can go over the top for Jesus!" We joked about that, but the last conversation I had with her before she died ended with those exact words. My mother made me feel special. She made me feel that I could do great things. She convinced me that, with Jesus, any limitations in my background could be overcome. . .

(From *What My Parents Did Right* by Tony Campolo)

APPLICATION We must spend time with our children, instructing them in the ways of God, modeling for them a Christ-centered lifestyle. On the other hand, children must honor their parents. Should you stray away from these commitments, ask God to be relentless about bringing you back on that track.

EXPLORATION Commandments to Children—Exodus 20:12; Proverbs 1:8; 3:1-3; 23:22; Colossians 3:20.

hear, O Israel, and be careful to observe *it*, that it may be well with you, and
that you may multiply greatly as the LORD God of your fathers has
promised you—'a land flowing with milk and honey.'[k]
[4]"Hear, O Israel: The LORD our God, the LORD *is* one![l] [5]You shall love the
LORD your God with all your heart, with all your soul, and with all your
strength.
[6]"And these words which I command you today shall be in your heart.
[7]You shall teach them diligently to your children, and shall talk of them
when you sit in your house, when you walk by the way, when you lie down,
and when you rise up. [8]You shall bind them as a sign on your hand, and
they shall be as frontlets between your eyes. [9]You shall write them on the
doorposts of your house and on your gates.

Caution Against Disobedience

[10]"So it shall be, when the LORD your God brings you into the land of
which He swore to your fathers, to Abraham, Isaac, and Jacob, to give you
large and beautiful cities which you did not build, [11]houses full of all good
things, which you did not fill, hewn-out wells which you did not dig, vineyards and olive trees which you did not plant—when you have eaten and
are full— [12]*then* beware, lest you forget the LORD who brought you out of
the land of Egypt, from the house of bondage. [13]You shall fear the LORD
your God and serve Him, and shall take oaths in His name. [14]You shall not
go after other gods, the gods of the peoples who *are* all around you [15](for
the LORD your God *is* a jealous God among you), lest the anger of the LORD
your God be aroused against you and destroy you from the face of the earth.
[16]"You shall not tempt the LORD your God as you tempted *Him* in
Massah. [17]You shall diligently keep the commandments of the LORD your
God, His testimonies, and His statutes which He has commanded you.
[18]And you shall do *what is* right and good in the sight of the LORD, that it
may be well with you, and that you may go in and possess the good land of
which the LORD swore to your fathers, [19]to cast out all your enemies from
before you, as the LORD has spoken.
[20]"When your son asks you in time to come, saying, 'What *is the meaning of* the testimonies, the statutes, and the judgments which the LORD our
God has commanded you?' [21]then you shall say to your son: 'We were
slaves of Pharaoh in Egypt, and the LORD brought us out of Egypt with a
mighty hand; [22]and the LORD showed signs and wonders before our eyes,
great and severe, against Egypt, Pharaoh, and all his household. [23]Then He
brought us out from there, that He might bring us in, to give us the land of
which He swore to our fathers. [24]And the LORD commanded us to observe
all these statutes, to fear the LORD our God, for our good always, that He
might preserve us alive, as *it is* this day. [25]Then it will be righteousness for
us, if we are careful to observe all these commandments before the LORD
our God, as He has commanded us.'

A Chosen People

7 "When the LORD your God brings you into the land which you go to
possess, and has cast out many nations before you, the Hittites and the
Girgashites and the Amorites and the Canaanites and the Perizzites and

6:3 [k] Exodus 3:8
6:4 [l] Or *The LORD is our God, the LORD alone* (that is, the only one)

the Hivites and the Jebusites, seven nations greater and mightier than you, 2and when the LORD your God delivers them over to you, you shall conquer them *and* utterly destroy them. You shall make no covenant with them nor show mercy to them. 3Nor shall you make marriages with them. You shall not give your daughter to their son, nor take their daughter for your son. 4For they will turn your sons away from following Me, to serve other gods; so the anger of the LORD will be aroused against you and destroy you suddenly. 5But thus you shall deal with them: you shall destroy their altars, and break down their *sacred* pillars, and cut down their wooden images,[m] and burn their carved images with fire.

6"For you *are* a holy people to the LORD your God; the LORD your God has chosen you to be a people for Himself, a special treasure above all the peoples on the face of the earth. 7The LORD did not set His love on you nor choose you because you were more in number than any other people, for you were the least of all peoples; 8but because the LORD loves you, and because He would keep the oath which He swore to your fathers, the LORD has brought you out with a mighty hand, and redeemed you from the house of bondage, from the hand of Pharaoh king of Egypt.

9"Therefore know that the LORD your God, He *is* God, the faithful God who keeps covenant and mercy for a thousand generations with those who love Him and keep His commandments; 10and He repays those who hate Him to their face, to destroy them. He will not be slack with him who hates Him; He will repay him to his face. 11Therefore you shall keep the commandment, the statutes, and the judgments which I command you today, to observe them.

Blessings of Obedience

12"Then it shall come to pass, because you listen to these judgments, and keep and do them, that the LORD your God will keep with you the covenant and the mercy which He swore to your fathers. 13And He will love you and bless you and multiply you; He will also bless the fruit of your womb and the fruit of your land, your grain and your new wine and your oil, the increase of your cattle and the offspring of your flock, in the land of which He swore to your fathers to give you. 14You shall be blessed above all peoples; there shall not be a male or female barren among you or among your livestock. 15And the LORD will take away from you all sickness, and will afflict you with none of the terrible diseases of Egypt which you have known, but will lay *them* on all those who hate you. 16Also you shall destroy all the peoples whom the LORD your God delivers over to you; your eye shall have no pity on them; nor shall you serve their gods, for that *will be* a snare to you.

17"If you should say in your heart, 'These nations are greater than I; how can I dispossess them?'— 18you shall not be afraid of them, *but* you shall remember well what the LORD your God did to Pharaoh and to all Egypt: 19the great trials which your eyes saw, the signs and the wonders, the mighty hand and the outstretched arm, by which the LORD your God brought you out. So shall the LORD your God do to all the peoples of whom you are afraid. 20Moreover the LORD your God will send the hornet among them until those who are left, who hide themselves from you, are destroyed. 21You shall not be terrified of them; for the LORD your God, the great and awesome God, *is* among you. 22And the LORD your God will drive out those nations before you little by little; you will be unable to destroy them at once, lest the beasts of the field become *too* numerous for you. 23But the LORD your God will deliver them over to you, and will inflict defeat upon them until they are destroyed. 24And He will deliver their kings into your hand, and you will destroy their name from under heaven; no one shall be able to stand against you until you have destroyed them. 25You shall burn the carved images of their gods with fire; you shall not covet the silver or gold *that is* on them, nor take *it* for yourselves, lest you be snared by it; for it *is* an abomination to the LORD your God. 26Nor shall you bring an abomination into your house, lest you be doomed to destruction like it. You shall utterly detest it and utterly abhor it, for it *is* an accursed thing.

Remember the LORD Your God

8 "Every commandment which I command you today you must be careful to observe, that you may live and multiply, and go in and possess the land of which the LORD swore to your fathers. 2And you shall remember that the LORD your God led you all the way these forty years in the wilderness, to humble you *and* test you, to know what *was* in your heart, whether you would keep His commandments or not. 3So He humbled you, allowed you to hunger, and fed you with manna which you did not know nor did your fathers know, that He might make you know that man shall not live by bread alone; but man lives by every *word* that proceeds from the mouth of the LORD. 4Your garments did not wear out on you, nor did your foot

7:5 [m] Hebrew *Asherim,* Canaanite deities

LIFE LESSON
Deuteronomy 8:1–9:29

SITUATION The Israelites were about to enter the promised land. They had experienced important victories, enjoyed unprecedented prosperity, and achieved a homeland. But with these blessings came certain risks that the people would forget God, that they would lose their belief and develop false pride of self-achievement. To avoid these dangers the people had to remember their past and how God had helped them. That would keep them properly focused.

OBSERVATION Remember God's protection and bountiful provisions. Let these memories keep you humble, thankful, and full of belief.

INSPIRATION It is not unusual for persons in their early twenties to defect from their early teaching. The reasons are many. Perhaps their exposure to unbelief "took" better than their exposure to belief. This is often the case, for the Bible says, "The heart of man is deceitful above all things." The human heart is as prepared by sin to accept unbelief as faith. Some person they regard very highly has undoubtedly influenced their thinking; and for the time being they look on their early training as "bunk." As someone has said, "A little learning may take a man away from God, but full understanding will bring him back." Some of the staunchest Christians I know are people who had periods in their life when they questioned the Bible, Christ, and God. But as they continued to examine the matter, there was overwhelming evidence that only "the fool hath said in his heart, There is no God."

(From *Day by Day with Billy Graham* by Joan W. Brown)

APPLICATION How are your beliefs changing? Growing or dissolving? Maturing or disintegrating? Hang on to the elements in your life that promote growth. Cut off activities and relationships that cause you to sin and replace them with ones that help you grow.

EXPLORATION Unbelief—Exodus 11:9-10; Deuteronomy 9:23; Romans 4:20; 11:20; Hebrews 3:19.

swell these forty years. 5You should know in your heart that as a man chastens his son, *so* the LORD your God chastens you.
6"Therefore you shall keep the commandments of the LORD your God, to
walk in His ways and to fear Him. 7For the LORD your God is bringing you
into a good land, a land of brooks of water, of fountains and springs, that
flow out of valleys and hills; 8a land of wheat and barley, of vines and fig
trees and pomegranates, a land of olive oil and honey; 9a land in which you
will eat bread without scarcity, in which you will lack nothing; a land
whose stones *are* iron and out of whose hills you can dig copper. 10When
you have eaten and are full, then you shall bless the LORD your God for the
good land which He has given you.
11"Beware that you do not forget the LORD your God by not keeping His
commandments, His judgments, and His statutes which I command you
today, 12lest—*when* you have eaten and are full, and have built beautiful
houses and dwell *in them;* 13and *when* your herds and your flocks multiply,
and your silver and your gold are multiplied, and all that you have is multiplied; 14when your heart is lifted up, and you forget the LORD your God
who brought you out of the land of Egypt, from the house of bondage;
15who led you through that great and terrible wilderness, *in which were*
fiery serpents and scorpions and thirsty land where there was no water;
who brought water for you out of the flinty rock; 16who fed you in the
wilderness with manna, which your fathers did not know, that He might
humble you and that He might test you, to do you good in the end—
17then you say in your heart, 'My power and the might of my hand have
gained me this wealth.'
18"And you shall remember the LORD your God, for *it is* He who gives
you power to get wealth, that He may establish His covenant which He
swore to your fathers, as *it is* this day. 19Then it shall be, if you by any
means forget the LORD your God, and follow other gods, and serve them
and worship them, I testify against you this day that you shall surely perish. 20As the nations which the LORD destroys before you, so you shall perish, because you would not be obedient to the voice of the LORD your God.

Israel's Rebellions Reviewed

9 "Hear, O Israel: You *are* to cross over the Jordan today, and go in to
dispossess nations greater and mightier than yourself, cities great and
fortified up to heaven, 2a people great and tall, the descendants of the
Anakim, whom you know, and *of whom* you heard *it said,* 'Who can stand
before the descendants of Anak?' 3Therefore understand today that the
LORD your God *is* He who goes over before you *as* a consuming fire. He will
destroy them and bring them down before you; so you shall drive them
out and destroy them quickly, as the LORD has said to you.
4"Do not think in your heart, after the LORD your God has cast them out
before you, saying, 'Because of my righteousness the LORD has brought me
in to possess this land'; but *it is* because of the wickedness of these nations
that the LORD is driving them out from before you. 5*It is* not because of
your righteousness or the uprightness of your heart *that* you go in to possess their land, but because of the wickedness of these nations *that* the
LORD your God drives them out from before you, and that He may fulfill
the word which the LORD swore to your fathers, to Abraham, Isaac, and Jacob. 6Therefore understand that the LORD your God is not giving you this

good land to possess because of your righteousness,
for you *are* a stiff-necked people.
7“Remember! Do not forget how you provoked the
LORD your God to wrath in the wilderness. From the
day that you departed from the land of Egypt until
you came to this place, you have been rebellious
against the LORD. 8Also in Horeb you provoked the
LORD to wrath, so that the LORD was angry *enough*
with you to have destroyed you. 9When I went up into
the mountain to receive the tablets of stone, the
tablets of the covenant which the LORD made with
you, then I stayed on the mountain forty days and
forty nights. I neither ate bread nor drank water.
10Then the LORD delivered to me two tablets of stone
written with the finger of God, and on them *were* all
the words which the LORD had spoken to you on the
mountain from the midst of the fire in the day of the
assembly. 11And it came to pass, at the end of forty
days and forty nights, *that* the LORD gave me the two
tablets of stone, the tablets of the covenant.
12“Then the LORD said to me, ‘Arise, go down
quickly from here, for your people whom you
brought out of Egypt have acted corruptly; they have
quickly turned aside from the way which I commanded them; they have made themselves a molded
image.’
13“Furthermore the LORD spoke to me, saying, ‘I
have seen this people, and indeed they are a stiff-necked people. 14Let Me alone, that I may destroy
them and blot out their name from under heaven;
and I will make of you a nation mightier and greater
than they.’
15“So I turned and came down from the mountain,
and the mountain burned with fire; and the two
tablets of the covenant *were* in my two hands. 16And I
looked, and behold, you had sinned against the LORD
your God—had made for yourselves a molded calf!
You had turned aside quickly from the way which the
LORD had commanded you. 17Then I took the two
tablets and threw them out of my two hands and
broke them before your eyes. 18And I fell down before
the LORD, as at the first, forty days and forty nights; I
neither ate bread nor drank water, because of all your
sin which you committed in doing wickedly in the
sight of the LORD, to provoke Him to anger. 19For I was
afraid of the anger and hot displeasure with which the
LORD was angry with you, to destroy you. But the LORD
listened to me at that time also. 20And the LORD was
very angry with Aaron *and* would have destroyed
him; so I prayed for Aaron also at the same time.
21Then I took your sin, the calf which you had made,
and burned it with fire and crushed it *and* ground *it*
very small, until it was as fine as dust; and I threw its
dust into the brook that descended from the mountain.
22“Also at Taberah and Massah and Kibroth
Hattaavah you provoked the LORD to wrath. 23Likewise, when the LORD sent you from Kadesh Barnea,
saying, ‘Go up and possess the land which I have
given you,’ then you rebelled against the commandment of the LORD your God, and you did not believe
Him nor obey His voice. 24You have been rebellious
against the LORD from the day that I knew you.
25“Thus I prostrated myself before the LORD; forty
days and forty nights I kept prostrating myself, because the LORD had said He would destroy you.
26Therefore I prayed to the LORD, and said: ‘O Lord
GOD, do not destroy Your people and Your inheritance
whom You have redeemed through Your greatness,
whom You have brought out of Egypt with a mighty
hand. 27Remember Your servants, Abraham, Isaac,
and Jacob; do not look on the stubbornness of this
people, or on their wickedness or their sin, 28lest the
land from which You brought us should say, “Because
the LORD was not able to bring them to the land which
He promised them, and because He hated them, He
has brought them out to kill them in the wilderness.”
29Yet they *are* Your people and Your inheritance,
whom You brought out by Your mighty power and by
Your outstretched arm.’

The Second Pair of Tablets

10 “At that time the LORD said to me, ‘Hew for
yourself two tablets of stone like the first, and
come up to Me on the mountain and make yourself
an ark of wood. 2And I will write on the tablets the
words that were on the first tablets, which you broke;
and you shall put them in the ark.’
3“So I made an ark of acacia wood, hewed two
tablets of stone like the first, and went up the mountain, having the two tablets in my hand. 4And He
wrote on the tablets according to the first writing, the
Ten Commandments, which the LORD had spoken to
you in the mountain from the midst of the fire in the
day of the assembly; and the LORD gave them to me.
5Then I turned and came down from the mountain,
and put the tablets in the ark which I had made; and
there they are, just as the LORD commanded me.”
6(Now the children of Israel journeyed from the
wells of Bene Jaakan to Moserah, where Aaron died,
and where he was buried; and Eleazar his son ministered as priest in his stead. 7From there they journeyed to Gudgodah, and from Gudgodah to

LIFE LESSON

Deuteronomy 10:1–11:32

SITUATION Moses continued to emphasize the requirements for a personal relationship with a holy God. He reminded the Israelites that God gave moral laws. Obeying God's laws would bring prosperity, and disobeying them would bring punishment.

OBSERVATION Obedience to God's Word and submission to his will result in spiritual prosperity. Disobedience and rejection lead to judgment and poverty.

INSPIRATION J. Hudson Taylor, the great missionary statesman and founder of the China Inland Mission, prepared himself for missionary service by doing "gospel work" in London among the people "in the lowest part of the town." On one occasion, as he was finishing up his work late at night, he was stopped by a man who asked if he would come and pray with his sick wife. The man explained that he had sought to find a priest, but was told that he would need a payment of eighteen pence, which the man did not have. Indeed the man confessed that he did not even have money to buy food for his starving family.

Taylor agreed to go to his home, but immediately his conscience was stricken. He too was living on virtually a starvation diet, but he had money—a half crown—in his pocket. It was all the money he had, and his own food was running out. "If only I had two shillings and a sixpence," he contemplated, "instead of this half-crown, how gladly would I give these poor people a shilling!" But to give all his money to a stranger—that was unthinkable.

Finally they arrived at the tenement. "Up a miserable flight of stairs into a wretched room he led me, and oh, what a sight there presented itself! Four or five children stood about, their sunken cheeks and temples telling

Jotbathah, a land of rivers of water. 8At that time the LORD separated the
tribe of Levi to bear the ark of the covenant of the LORD, to stand before the
LORD to minister to Him and to bless in His name, to this day. 9Therefore
Levi has no portion nor inheritance with his brethren; the LORD *is* his inheritance, just as the LORD your God promised him.)

10"As at the first time, I stayed in the mountain forty days and forty
nights; the LORD also heard me at that time, *and* the LORD chose not to destroy you. 11Then the LORD said to me, 'Arise, begin *your* journey before the
people, that they may go in and possess the land which I swore to their fathers to give them.'

The Essence of the Law

12"And now, Israel, what does the LORD your God require of you, but to
fear the LORD your God, to walk in all His ways and to love Him, to serve the
LORD your God with all your heart and with all your soul, 13*and* to keep the
commandments of the LORD and His statutes which I command you today
for your good? 14Indeed heaven and the highest heavens belong to the LORD
your God, *also* the earth with all that *is* in it. 15The LORD delighted only in
your fathers, to love them; and He chose their descendants after them, you
above all peoples, as *it is* this day. 16Therefore circumcise the foreskin of
your heart, and be stiff-necked no longer. 17For the LORD your God *is* God
of gods and Lord of lords, the great God, mighty and awesome, who shows
no partiality nor takes a bribe. 18He administers justice for the fatherless
and the widow, and loves the stranger, giving him food and clothing.
19Therefore love the stranger, for you were strangers in the land of Egypt.
20You shall fear the LORD your God; you shall serve Him, and to Him you
shall hold fast, and take oaths in His name. 21He *is* your praise, and He *is*
your God, who has done for you these great and awesome things which
your eyes have seen. 22Your fathers went down to Egypt with seventy persons, and now the LORD your God has made you as the stars of heaven in
multitude.

Love and Obedience Rewarded

11 "Therefore you shall love the LORD your God, and keep His charge,
His statutes, His judgments, and His commandments always.
2Know today that *I do* not *speak* with your children, who have not known
and who have not seen the chastening of the LORD your God, His greatness
and His mighty hand and His outstretched arm— 3His signs and His acts
which He did in the midst of Egypt, to Pharaoh king of Egypt, and to all his
land; 4what He did to the army of Egypt, to their horses and their chariots:
how He made the waters of the Red Sea overflow them as they pursued
you, and *how* the LORD has destroyed them to this day; 5what He did for
you in the wilderness until you came to this place; 6and what He did to
Dathan and Abiram the sons of Eliab, the son of Reuben: how the earth
opened its mouth and swallowed them up, their households, their tents,
and all the substance that *was* in their possession, in the midst of all Israel— 7but your eyes have seen every great act of the LORD which He did.
8"Therefore you shall keep every commandment which I command you
today, that you may be strong, and go in and possess the land which you
cross over to possess, 9and that you may prolong *your* days in the land
which the LORD swore to give your fathers, to them and their descendants,

'a land flowing with milk and honey.'[n] 10 For the land which you go to possess *is* not like the land of Egypt from which you have come, where you
sowed your seed and watered *it* by foot, as a vegetable garden; 11 but the
land which you cross over to possess *is* a land of hills and valleys, which
drinks water from the rain of heaven, 12 a land for which the LORD your God
cares; the eyes of the LORD your God *are* always on it, from the beginning of
the year to the very end of the year.

13 "And it shall be that if you earnestly obey My commandments which I
command you today, to love the LORD your God and serve Him with all
your heart and with all your soul, 14 then I[o] will give *you* the rain for your
land in its season, the early rain and the latter rain, that you may gather in
your grain, your new wine, and your oil. 15 And I will send grass in your
fields for your livestock, that you may eat and be filled.' 16 Take heed to
yourselves, lest your heart be deceived, and you turn aside and serve other
gods and worship them, 17 lest the LORD's anger be aroused against you,
and He shut up the heavens so that there be no rain, and the land yield no
produce, and you perish quickly from the good land which the LORD is giving you.

18 "Therefore you shall lay up these words of mine in your heart and in
your soul, and bind them as a sign on your hand, and they shall be as
frontlets between your eyes. 19 You shall teach them to your children,
speaking of them when you sit in your house, when you walk by the way,
when you lie down, and when you rise up. 20 And you shall write them on
the doorposts of your house and on your gates, 21 that your days and the days
of your children may be multiplied in the land of which the LORD swore to
your fathers to give them, like the days of the heavens above the earth.

22 "For if you carefully keep all these commandments which I command
you to do—to love the LORD your God, to walk in all His ways, and to hold
fast to Him— 23 then the LORD will drive out all these nations from before
you, and you will dispossess greater and mightier nations than yourselves. 24 Every place on which the sole of your foot treads shall be yours:
from the wilderness and Lebanon, from the river, the River Euphrates,
even to the Western Sea,[p] shall be your territory. 25 No man shall be able to
stand against you; the LORD your God will put the dread of you and the fear
of you upon all the land where you tread, just as He has said to you.

26 "Behold, I set before you today a blessing and a curse: 27 the blessing, if
you obey the commandments of the LORD your God which I command
you today; 28 and the curse, if you do not obey the commandments of the
LORD your God, but turn aside from the way which I command you today,
to go after other gods which you have not known. 29 Now it shall be, when
the LORD your God has brought you into the land which you go to possess,
that you shall put the blessing on Mount Gerizim and the curse on Mount
Ebal. 30 *Are* they not on the other side of the Jordan, toward the setting sun,
in the land of the Canaanites who dwell in the plain opposite Gilgal, beside
the terebinth trees of Moreh? 31 For you will cross over the Jordan and go in
to possess the land which the LORD your God is giving you, and you will
possess it and dwell in it. 32 And you shall be careful to observe all the
statutes and judgments which I set before you today.

11:9 [n] Exodus 3:8
11:14 [o] Following Masoretic Text and Targum; Samaritan Pentateuch, Septuagint, and Vulgate read *He*.
11:24 [p] That is, the Mediterranean

unmistakably the story of slow starvation, and lying on a wretched pallet was a poor, exhausted mother, with a tiny infant thirty-six hours-old moaning rather than crying at her side."

Taylor spoke to them, trying to bring comfort and encouragement, but the words stuck in his throat. "Something within me cried, 'You hypocrite! telling these unconverted people about a kind and loving Father in heaven, and not prepared yourself to trust him without half a crown.'" With nothing to say, Taylor determined to get the visit over quickly so he offered to pray as the man had initially requested. "But no sooner had I opened my lips with, 'Our Father who art in heaven,' than conscience said within, 'Dare you mock God? Dare you kneel down and call him "Father" with that half-crown in your pocket?'"

When Taylor got up from his knees he was so distraught that the man asked him what was wrong. The man could never have understood, but Taylor himself knew what was wrong and there was only one remedy. He dug deep into his pocket for his half-crown and gave it to the man. "And how the joy came back in full flood tide to my heart! . . . Not only was the poor woman's life saved, but my life as fully realized had been saved too." (From *Sacred Stories* by Ruth A. Tucker)

APPLICATION Many times in our life we may have asked the question, "What does God want of me?" Moses tells us that God wants us to walk in his ways and serve him with our heart and soul. Thank God that he has made plain his will for us and that he will help us to do it.

EXPLORATION Obedience—Genesis 2:16-17; 3:14-19; Joshua 1:6-8; Ephesians 6:1-2; Romans 13:1-6.

LIFE LESSON

Deuteronomy 12:1–13:18

SITUATION Moses continued to prepare the Israelites to inhabit their new land. He reminded them of the Ten Commandments, their special place in God's eyes, and all the wondrous blessings God would give them.

OBSERVATION The Israelites demonstrated that worship of God must be free from idolatry.

INSPIRATION The highest expression of the will of God in this age is the church which He purchased with His own blood. . . . According to the Scriptures the church is the habitation of God through the Spirit, and as such is the most important organism beneath the sun. She is not one more good institute along with the home, the state, and the school; she is the most vital of all institutions—the only one that can claim a heavenly origin.

The cynic may inquire which church we mean, and may remind us that the Christian church is so divided that it is impossible to tell which is the true one, even if such a one exists. But we are not too troubled by the suppressed smile of the doubter. Being inside the church we are probably as well aware of her faults as any person on the outside could possibly be. And we believe in her nevertheless wherever she manifests herself in a world of darkness and unbelief.

The church is found wherever the Holy Spirit has drawn together a few persons who trust Christ for their salvation, worship God in spirit and have

A Prescribed Place of Worship

12 "These *are* the statutes and judgments which you shall be careful to
observe in the land which the LORD God of your fathers is giving you
to possess, all the days that you live on the earth. 2You shall utterly destroy
all the places where the nations which you shall dispossess served their
gods, on the high mountains and on the hills and under every green tree.
3And you shall destroy their altars, break their *sacred* pillars, and burn
their wooden images with fire; you shall cut down the carved images of
their gods and destroy their names from that place. 4You shall not worship
the LORD your God *with* such *things*.
5"But you shall seek the place where the LORD your God chooses, out of
all your tribes, to put His name for His dwelling place; and there you shall
go. 6There you shall take your burnt offerings, your sacrifices, your tithes,
the heave offerings of your hand, your vowed offerings, your freewill offerings, and the firstborn of your herds and flocks. 7And there you shall eat
before the LORD your God, and you shall rejoice in all to which you have
put your hand, you and your households, in which the LORD your God has
blessed you.
8"You shall not at all do as we are doing here today—every man doing
whatever *is* right in his own eyes— 9for as yet you have not come to the
rest and the inheritance which the LORD your God is giving you. 10But *when*
you cross over the Jordan and dwell in the land which the LORD your God is
giving you to inherit, and He gives you rest from all your enemies round
about, so that you dwell in safety, 11then there will be the place where the
LORD your God chooses to make His name abide. There you shall bring all
that I command you: your burnt offerings, your sacrifices, your tithes, the
heave offerings of your hand, and all your choice offerings which you vow
to the LORD. 12And you shall rejoice before the LORD your God, you and
your sons and your daughters, your male and female servants, and the
Levite who *is* within your gates, since he has no portion nor inheritance
with you. 13Take heed to yourself that you do not offer your burnt offerings
in every place that you see; 14but in the place which the LORD chooses, in
one of your tribes, there you shall offer your burnt offerings, and there you
shall do all that I command you.
15"However, you may slaughter and eat meat within all your gates, whatever your heart desires, according to the blessing of the LORD your God
which He has given you; the unclean and the clean may eat of it, of the
gazelle and the deer alike. 16Only you shall not eat the blood; you shall pour
it on the earth like water. 17You may not eat within your gates the tithe of
your grain or your new wine or your oil, of the firstborn of your herd or
your flock, of any of your offerings which you vow, of your freewill offerings, or of the heave offering of your hand. 18But you must eat them before
the LORD your God in the place which the LORD your God chooses, you and
your son and your daughter, your male servant and your female servant,
and the Levite who *is* within your gates; and you shall rejoice before the
LORD your God in all to which you put your hands. 19Take heed to yourself
that you do not forsake the Levite as long as you live in your land.
20"When the LORD your God enlarges your border as He has promised
you, and you say, 'Let me eat meat,' because you long to eat meat, you may
eat as much meat as your heart desires. 21If the place where the LORD your

God chooses to put His name is too far from you, then you may slaughter
from your herd and from your flock which the LORD has given you, just as
I have commanded you, and you may eat within your gates as much as
your heart desires. [22]Just as the gazelle and the deer are eaten, so you may
eat them; the unclean and the clean alike may eat them. [23]Only be sure that
you do not eat the blood, for the blood *is* the life; you may not eat the life
with the meat. [24]You shall not eat it; you shall pour it on the earth like
water. [25]You shall not eat it, that it may go well with you and your children
after you, when you do *what is* right in the sight of the LORD. [26]Only the holy
things which you have, and your vowed offerings, you shall take and go to
the place which the LORD chooses. [27]And you shall offer your burnt offerings, the meat and the blood, on the altar of the LORD your God; and the
blood of your sacrifices shall be poured out on the altar of the LORD your
God, and you shall eat the meat. [28]Observe and obey all these words which
I command you, that it may go well with you and your children after you
forever, when you do *what is* good and right in the sight of the LORD your
God.

Beware of False Gods

[29]"When the LORD your God cuts off from before you the nations which
you go to dispossess, and you displace them and dwell in their land, [30]take
heed to yourself that you are not ensnared to follow them, after they are
destroyed from before you, and that you do not inquire after their gods,
saying, 'How did these nations serve their gods? I also will do likewise.'
[31]You shall not worship the LORD your God in that way; for every abomination to the LORD which He hates they have done to their gods; for they burn
even their sons and daughters in the fire to their gods.
[32]"Whatever I command you, be careful to observe it; you shall not add
to it nor take away from it.

Punishment of Apostates

13 "If there arises among you a prophet or a dreamer of dreams, and
he gives you a sign or a wonder, [2]and the sign or the wonder comes
to pass, of which he spoke to you, saying, 'Let us go after other gods'—
which you have not known—'and let us serve them,' [3]you shall not listen
to the words of that prophet or that dreamer of dreams, for the LORD your
God is testing you to know whether you love the LORD your God with all
your heart and with all your soul. [4]You shall walk after the LORD your God
and fear Him, and keep His commandments and obey His voice; you shall
serve Him and hold fast to Him. [5]But that prophet or that dreamer of
dreams shall be put to death, because he has spoken in order to turn *you*
away from the LORD your God, who brought you out of the land of Egypt
and redeemed you from the house of bondage, to entice you from the way
in which the LORD your God commanded you to walk. So you shall put
away the evil from your midst.
[6]"If your brother, the son of your mother, your son or your daughter, the
wife of your bosom, or your friend who is as your own soul, secretly entices you, saying, 'Let us go and serve other gods,' which you have not
known, neither you nor your fathers, [7]of the gods of the people which *are*
all around you, near to you or far off from you, from *one* end of the earth to
the *other* end of the earth, [8]you shall not consent to him or listen to him,

no dealings with the world and the flesh. The members may by necessity be scattered over the surface of the earth and separated by distance and circumstances, but in every true member of the church is the homing instinct and the longing of the sheep for the fold and the shepherd. Give a few real Christians half a chance and they will get together and organize and plan regular meetings for prayer and worship. In these meetings they will hear the Scriptures expounded, break bread together in one form or another according to their light, and try as far as possible to spread the saving gospel to the lost world.

Such groups are cells in the Body of Christ, and each one is a true church, a real part of the greater church. It is in and through these cells that the Spirit does His work on earth. Whoever scorns the local church scorns the Body of Christ.

The church is still to be reckoned with. "The gates of hell shall not prevail against her."

(From *Best of Tozer* Compiled by Warren Wiersbe)

APPLICATION Are you involved in a local church? Decide today to make a greater commitment to that church. Find out how you can help. Participate. Pray for the church and love the people in the church.

EXPLORATION House of God—Psalm 27:4; 84:10; Matthew 16:18; Acts 20:28; Ephesians 1:22; Hebrews 10:25.

LIFE LESSON

Deuteronomy 14:1–16:20

SITUATION God prepared Israel to inhabit the Promised Land. Everything he told the Israelites was designed to protect them from forgetting God and turning to idolatry.

OBSERVATION God gave the Israelites rules that helped them keep his priorities. The principles we follow today also help us keep perspectives right.

INSPIRATION One of the celebrated heroes of our century has been Mohandas Gandhi, the Indian leader who sparked the flame of independence for his country. Those who have read his biography or who have seen his story so brilliantly told upon the screen are often impressed with the tranquil spirit that "India's George Washington" displayed. . . . How could Gandhi maintain his private sense of order, his appropriate humility, and his base wisdom and judgment? How did he avoid losing his own identity and spirit of conviction as he moved between those enormous extremes? Where did the emotional and spiritual force come from?

Perhaps the beginning of an answer to those questions lies in Gandhi's fascination with the simple spinning wheel. The wheel seems to have always been at the center of his life. Gandhi appears to have often returned from public exposure to his humble dwellings where he would, in Indian fashion, sit upon the floor and engage in the simple act of spinning the wool from which his clothes were made. . . .

Gandhi's spinning wheel was his center of gravity in life. It was the great

nor shall your eye pity him, nor shall you spare him or conceal him; 9but
you shall surely kill him; your hand shall be first against him to put him to
death, and afterward the hand of all the people. 10And you shall stone him
with stones until he dies, because he sought to entice you away from the
LORD your God, who brought you out of the land of Egypt, from the house
of bondage. 11So all Israel shall hear and fear, and not again do such
wickedness as this among you.

12"If you hear someone in one of your cities, which the LORD your God
gives you to dwell in, saying, 13'Corrupt men have gone out from among
you and enticed the inhabitants of their city, saying, "Let us go and serve
other gods" '—which you have not known— 14then you shall inquire,
search out, and ask diligently. And *if it is* indeed true *and* certain *that* such
an abomination was committed among you, 15you shall surely strike the
inhabitants of that city with the edge of the sword, utterly destroying it, all
that is in it and its livestock—with the edge of the sword. 16And you shall
gather all its plunder into the middle of the street, and completely burn
with fire the city and all its plunder, for the LORD your God. It shall be a
heap forever; it shall not be built again. 17So none of the accursed things
shall remain in your hand, that the LORD may turn from the fierceness of
His anger and show you mercy, have compassion on you and multiply
you, just as He swore to your fathers, 18because you have listened to the
voice of the LORD your God, to keep all His commandments which I command you today, to do *what is* right in the eyes of the LORD your God.

Improper Mourning

14 "You *are* the children of the LORD your God; you shall not cut yourselves nor shave the front of your head for the dead. 2For you *are* a
holy people to the LORD your God, and the LORD has chosen you to be a
people for Himself, a special treasure above all the peoples who *are* on the
face of the earth.

Clean and Unclean Meat

3"You shall not eat any detestable thing. 4These *are* the animals which
you may eat: the ox, the sheep, the goat, 5the deer, the gazelle, the roe deer,
the wild goat, the mountain goat,[q] the antelope, and the mountain sheep.
6And you may eat every animal with cloven hooves, having the hoof split
into two parts, *and that* chews the cud, among the animals. 7Nevertheless,
of those that chew the cud or have cloven hooves, you shall not eat, *such as*
these: the camel, the hare, and the rock hyrax; for they chew the cud but do
not have cloven hooves; they *are* unclean for you. 8Also the swine is unclean for you, because it has cloven hooves, yet *does* not *chew* the cud; you
shall not eat their flesh or touch their dead carcasses.

9"These you may eat of all that *are* in the waters: you may eat all that
have fins and scales. 10And whatever does not have fins and scales you
shall not eat; it *is* unclean for you.

11"All clean birds you may eat. 12But these you shall not eat: the eagle, the
vulture, the buzzard, 13the red kite, the falcon, and the kite after their
kinds; 14every raven after its kind; 15the ostrich, the short-eared owl, the sea
gull, and the hawk after their kinds; 16the little owl, the screech owl, the
white owl, 17the jackdaw, the carrion vulture, the fisher owl, 18the stork, the
heron after its kind, and the hoopoe and the bat.

14:5 q Or *addax*

19“Also every creeping thing that flies is unclean for you; they shall not
be eaten.
20“You may eat all clean birds.
21“You shall not eat anything that dies *of itself;* you may give it to the
alien who *is* within your gates, that he may eat it, or you may sell it to a foreigner; for you *are* a holy people to the LORD your God.
“You shall not boil a young goat in its mother’s milk.

Tithing Principles

22“You shall truly tithe all the increase of your grain that the field produces year by year. 23And you shall eat before the LORD your God, in the
place where He chooses to make His name abide, the tithe of your grain
and your new wine and your oil, of the firstborn of your herds and your
flocks, that you may learn to fear the LORD your God always. 24But if the
journey is too long for you, so that you are not able to carry *the tithe, or* if
the place where the LORD your God chooses to put His name is too far from
you, when the LORD your God has blessed you, 25then you shall exchange *it*
for money, take the money in your hand, and go to the place which the
LORD your God chooses. 26And you shall spend that money for whatever
your heart desires: for oxen or sheep, for wine or similar drink, for whatever your heart desires; you shall eat there before the LORD your God, and
you shall rejoice, you and your household. 27You shall not forsake the
Levite who *is* within your gates, for he has no part nor inheritance with
you.
28“At the end of *every* third year you shall bring out the tithe of your produce of that year and store *it* up within your gates. 29And the Levite, because he has no portion nor inheritance with you, and the stranger and
the fatherless and the widow who *are* within your gates, may come and eat
and be satisfied, that the LORD your God may bless you in all the work of
your hand which you do.

Debts Canceled Every Seven Years

15 “At the end of *every* seven years you shall grant a release *of debts.*
2And this *is* the form of the release: Every creditor who has lent *any-*
thing to his neighbor shall release *it;* he shall not require *it* of his neighbor
or his brother, because it is called the LORD’s release. 3Of a foreigner you
may require *it;* but you shall give up your claim to what is owed by your
brother, 4except when there may be no poor among you; for the LORD will
greatly bless you in the land which the LORD your God is giving you to possess *as* an inheritance— 5only if you carefully obey the voice of the LORD
your God, to observe with care all these commandments which I command you today. 6For the LORD your God will bless you just as He
promised you; you shall lend to many nations, but you shall not borrow;
you shall reign over many nations, but they shall not reign over you.

Generosity to the Poor

7“If there is among you a poor man of your brethren, within any of the
gates in your land which the LORD your God is giving you, you shall not
harden your heart nor shut your hand from your poor brother, 8but you
shall open your hand wide to him and willingly lend him sufficient for his
need, whatever he needs. 9Beware lest there be a wicked thought in your

leveler in his human experience. When he returned from the great public moments in his life, the spinning-wheel experience restored him to his proper sense of proportion, so that he was not falsely swelled with pride due to the cheers of the people. . . .

Gandhi was by no means a Christian, but what he was doing at the wheel is an indispensable lesson for any healthy Christian. For he shows us what every man or woman who wants to move in a public world without being pressed into its mold needs to do. We, too, need the spinning-wheel experience—the ordering of our private worlds so that they are constantly restructured with strength and vitality. . . .

When we come from an experience at the spinning wheel, where all is returned to proper proportion and value, the public world can be managed and properly touched. Relationships with family and friends, with business associates, neighbors and even enemies take on a new and healthier perspective. It becomes possible to forgive, to serve, to not seek vengeance, to be generous.

(From *Ordering Your Private World* by Gordon MacDonald)

APPLICATION Remind yourself of what is important. Take a walk with your family. Send money to someone in need. Be a volunteer. Spend time worshiping God. Allow your perspective to be refocused.

EXPLORATION Giving—Deuteronomy 15:7; Proverbs 25:21; Matthew 6:3; Luke 12:33; Romans 12:8; 2 Corinthians 9:7.

LIFE LESSON

Deuteronomy 16:21–18:22

SITUATION Moses gave civil laws for ruling the nation. Even in this area, strict compliance with God's rules was necessary in order to avoid harsh punishment. Worshiping other gods would not be tolerated. The people were to comply with instructions from courts, kings, priests, and prophets. They were to be wary of kings who were tempted by wealth and power, and prophets whose predictions were not fulfilled.

OBSERVATION God provided precise instructions to the Israelites for governing themselves and honoring the divine moral code.

INSPIRATION As the Constitution is the highest law of the land, so the Bible is the highest law of God. For it is in the Bible that God sets forth His spiritual laws. It is in the Bible that God makes His enduring promises. It is in the Bible that God reveals the plan of redemption for the human race. . . .

The laws of our land find their genesis in the Ten Commandments. And Sir William Blackstone, the great English jurist, wrote: "The Bible has always been regarded as part of the Common Law of England."

Christianity finds all its doctrines stated in the Bible, and Christianity denies no part, nor attempts to add anything to the Word of God. While the Constitution of the United States may be amended from time to time, no amendment is ever necessary for the Bible. We truly believe that the men who wrote the Bible were guided by the Holy Spirit, both in the thoughts they expressed and in their choice of words. As Peter said, "For the prophecy came not in old time by the will of man: but holy men of God spake as they were moved by the Holy Ghost."

In setting down their forthright messages, biblical scribes have never attempted to gloss over the realities of life. The sins of the great and small

heart, saying, 'The seventh year, the year of release, is at hand,' and your
eye be evil against your poor brother and you give him nothing, and he cry
out to the LORD against you, and it become sin among you. 10You shall
surely give to him, and your heart should not be grieved when you give to
him, because for this thing the LORD your God will bless you in all your
works and in all to which you put your hand. 11For the poor will never
cease from the land; therefore I command you, saying, 'You shall open
your hand wide to your brother, to your poor and your needy, in your
land.'

The Law Concerning Bondservants

12"If your brother, a Hebrew man, or a Hebrew woman, is sold to you
and serves you six years, then in the seventh year you shall let him go free
from you. 13And when you send him away free from you, you shall not let
him go away empty-handed; 14you shall supply him liberally from your
flock, from your threshing floor, and from your winepress. *From what* the
LORD has blessed you with, you shall give to him. 15You shall remember
that you were a slave in the land of Egypt, and the LORD your God redeemed you; therefore I command you this thing today. 16And if it happens that he says to you, 'I will not go away from you,' because he loves you
and your house, since he prospers with you, 17then you shall take an awl
and thrust *it* through his ear to the door, and he shall be your servant forever. Also to your female servant you shall do likewise. 18It shall not seem
hard to you when you send him away free from you; for he has been worth
a double hired servant in serving you six years. Then the LORD your God
will bless you in all that you do.

The Law Concerning Firstborn Animals

19"All the firstborn males that come from your herd and your flock you
shall sanctify to the LORD your God; you shall do no work with the firstborn of your herd, nor shear the firstborn of your flock. 20You and your
household shall eat *it* before the LORD your God year by year in the place
which the LORD chooses. 21But if there is a defect in it, *if it is* lame or blind
or has any serious defect, you shall not sacrifice it to the LORD your God.
22You may eat it within your gates; the unclean and the clean *person* alike
may eat it, as *if it were* a gazelle or a deer. 23Only you shall not eat its blood;
you shall pour it on the ground like water.

The Passover Reviewed

16 "Observe the month of Abib, and keep the Passover to the LORD your
God, for in the month of Abib the LORD your God brought you out of
Egypt by night. 2Therefore you shall sacrifice the Passover to the LORD your
God, from the flock and the herd, in the place where the LORD chooses to
put His name. 3You shall eat no leavened bread with it; seven days you
shall eat unleavened bread with it, *that is,* the bread of affliction (for you
came out of the land of Egypt in haste), that you may remember the day in
which you came out of the land of Egypt all the days of your life. 4And no
leaven shall be seen among you in all your territory for seven days, nor
shall *any* of the meat which you sacrifice the first day at twilight remain
overnight until morning.

5"You may not sacrifice the Passover within any of your gates which the

LORD your God gives you; 6but at the place where the LORD your God
chooses to make His name abide, there you shall sacrifice the Passover at
twilight, at the going down of the sun, at the time you came out of Egypt.
7And you shall roast and eat *it* in the place which the LORD your God
chooses, and in the morning you shall turn and go to your tents. 8Six days
you shall eat unleavened bread, and on the seventh day there *shall be* a sacred assembly to the LORD your God. You shall do no work *on it.*

The Feast of Weeks Reviewed

9"You shall count seven weeks for yourself; begin to count the seven
weeks from *the time* you begin *to put* the sickle to the grain. 10Then you
shall keep the Feast of Weeks to the LORD your God with the tribute of a
freewill offering from your hand, which you shall give as the LORD your
God blesses you. 11You shall rejoice before the LORD your God, you and
your son and your daughter, your male servant and your female servant,
the Levite who *is* within your gates, the stranger and the fatherless and the
widow who *are* among you, at the place where the LORD your God chooses
to make His name abide. 12And you shall remember that you were a slave
in Egypt, and you shall be careful to observe these statutes.

The Feast of Tabernacles Reviewed

13"You shall observe the Feast of Tabernacles seven days, when you have
gathered from your threshing floor and from your winepress. 14And you
shall rejoice in your feast, you and your son and your daughter, your male
servant and your female servant and the Levite, the stranger and the fatherless and the widow, who *are* within your gates. 15Seven days you shall
keep a sacred feast to the LORD your God in the place which the LORD
chooses, because the LORD your God will bless you in all your produce and
in all the work of your hands, so that you surely rejoice.
16"Three times a year all your males shall appear before the LORD your
God in the place which He chooses: at the Feast of Unleavened Bread, at
the Feast of Weeks, and at the Feast of Tabernacles; and they shall not appear before the LORD empty-handed. 17Every man *shall give* as he is able,
according to the blessing of the LORD your God which He has given you.

Justice Must Be Administered

18"You shall appoint judges and officers in all your gates, which the LORD
your God gives you, according to your tribes, and they shall judge the people with just judgment. 19You shall not pervert justice; you shall not show
partiality, nor take a bribe, for a bribe blinds the eyes of the wise and twists
the words of the righteous. 20You shall follow what is altogether just, that
you may live and inherit the land which the LORD your God is giving you.
21"You shall not plant for yourself any tree, as a wooden image, near the
altar which you build for yourself to the LORD your God. 22You shall not set
up a sacred pillar, which the LORD your God hates.

17 "You shall not sacrifice to the LORD your God a bull or sheep which
has any blemish *or* defect, for that *is* an abomination to the LORD
your God.
2"If there is found among you, within any of your gates which the LORD
your God gives you, a man or a woman who has been wicked in the sight
of the LORD your God, in transgressing His covenant, 3who has gone and

are freely admitted, the weaknesses of human nature are acknowledged, and life in biblical times is recorded as it was lived. The startling thing is that the lives and motivations of these people who lived so long ago have such a modern flavor! As we read, the pages seem like mirrors held up before our own minds and hearts, reflecting our own prides and prejudices, our own failures and humiliations, our own sins and sorrows.

Truth is timeless. Truth does not differ from one age to another, from one people to another, from one geographical location to another. Men's ideas may differ, men's customs may change, men's moral codes may vary, but the great all-prevailing Truth stands for time and eternity.

The message of Jesus Christ, our Savior, is the story of the Bible—it is the story of salvation. Profound students of the Bible have traced the story of Jesus Christ from the beginning of the Old Testament, for He is the true theme of the Old as well as the New Testament.

The fact of Jesus Christ is the eternal message of the Bible. It is the story of life, peace, eternity, and heaven. The Bible has no hidden purpose. It has no need for special interpretation. It has a single, clear, bold message for every living being—the message of Christ and His offer of peace with God.

(From *Peace with God* by Billy Graham)

APPLICATION We like to rebel against laws when they limit our freedom. But God's law blesses us because it protects us and simplifies our decision-making. How do you view God's rules? If you view them as moral guideposts, your trail through life will have fewer twists and dead ends.

EXPLORATION Law of God—Exodus 15:25; Leviticus 19:10-35; Psalm 31:8; Galatians 2:15-16.

served other gods and worshiped them, either the sun
or moon or any of the host of heaven, which I have not
commanded, 4and it is told you, and you hear *of it,*
then you shall inquire diligently. And if *it is* indeed
true *and* certain that such an abomination has been
committed in Israel, 5then you shall bring out to your
gates that man or woman who has committed that
wicked thing, and shall stone to death that man or
woman with stones. 6Whoever is deserving of death
shall be put to death on the testimony of two or three
witnesses; he shall not be put to death on the testimony of one witness. 7The hands of the witnesses
shall be the first against him to put him to death, and
afterward the hands of all the people. So you shall put
away the evil from among you.
8"If a matter arises which is too hard for you to
judge, between degrees of guilt for bloodshed, between one judgment or another, or between one punishment or another, matters of controversy within
your gates, then you shall arise and go up to the place
which the LORD your God chooses. 9And you shall
come to the priests, the Levites, and to the judge *there*
in those days, and inquire *of them;* they shall pronounce upon you the sentence of judgment. 10You
shall do according to the sentence which they pronounce upon you in that place which the LORD
chooses. And you shall be careful to do according to
all that they order you. 11According to the sentence of
the law in which they instruct you, according to the
judgment which they tell you, you shall do; you shall
not turn aside *to* the right hand or *to* the left from the
sentence which they pronounce upon you. 12Now the
man who acts presumptuously and will not heed the
priest who stands to minister there before the LORD
your God, or the judge, that man shall die. So you
shall put away the evil from Israel. 13And all the people
shall hear and fear, and no longer act presumptuously.

Principles Governing Kings

14"When you come to the land which the LORD your
God is giving you, and possess it and dwell in it, and
say, 'I will set a king over me like all the nations that
are around me,' 15you shall surely set a king over you
whom the LORD your God chooses; *one* from among
your brethren you shall set as king over you; you may
not set a foreigner over you, who *is* not your brother.
16But he shall not multiply horses for himself, nor
cause the people to return to Egypt to multiply
horses, for the LORD has said to you, 'You shall not return that way again.' 17Neither shall he multiply wives
for himself, lest his heart turn away; nor shall he
greatly multiply silver and gold for himself.
18"Also it shall be, when he sits on the throne of his
kingdom, that he shall write for himself a copy of this
law in a book, from *the one* before the priests, the
Levites. 19And it shall be with him, and he shall read it
all the days of his life, that he may learn to fear the
LORD his God and be careful to observe all the words
of this law and these statutes, 20that his heart may not
be lifted above his brethren, that he may not turn
aside from the commandment *to* the right hand or *to*
the left, and that he may prolong *his* days in his kingdom, he and his children in the midst of Israel.

The Portion of the Priests and Levites

18 "The priests, the Levites—all the tribe of
Levi—shall have no part nor inheritance with
Israel; they shall eat the offerings of the LORD made by
fire, and His portion. 2Therefore they shall have no inheritance among their brethren; the LORD is their inheritance, as He said to them.
3"And this shall be the priest's due from the people,
from those who offer a sacrifice, whether *it is* bull or
sheep: they shall give to the priest the shoulder, the
cheeks, and the stomach. 4The firstfruits of your grain
and your new wine and your oil, and the first of the
fleece of your sheep, you shall give him. 5For the LORD
your God has chosen him out of all your tribes to
stand to minister in the name of the LORD, him and his
sons forever.
6"So if a Levite comes from any of your gates, from
where he dwells among all Israel, and comes with all
the desire of his mind to the place which the LORD
chooses, 7then he may serve in the name of the LORD
his God as all his brethren the Levites *do,* who stand
there before the LORD. 8They shall have equal portions
to eat, besides what comes from the sale of his inheritance.

Avoid Wicked Customs

9"When you come into the land which the LORD
your God is giving you, you shall not learn to follow
the abominations of those nations. 10There shall not
be found among you *anyone* who makes his son or his
daughter pass through the fire, *or one* who practices
witchcraft, *or* a soothsayer, or one who interprets
omens, or a sorcerer, 11or one who conjures spells, or
a medium, or a spiritist, or one who calls up the dead.
12For all who do these things *are* an abomination to
the LORD, and because of these abominations the
LORD your God drives them out from before you. 13You

shall be blameless before the LORD your God. 14For these nations which
you will dispossess listened to soothsayers and diviners; but as for you,
the LORD your God has not appointed such for you.

A New Prophet Like Moses

15"The LORD your God will raise up for you a Prophet like me from your
midst, from your brethren. Him you shall hear, 16according to all you desired of the LORD your God in Horeb in the day of the assembly, saying, 'Let
me not hear again the voice of the LORD my God, nor let me see this great
fire anymore, lest I die.'
17"And the LORD said to me: 'What they have spoken is good. 18I will raise
up for them a Prophet like you from among their brethren, and will put
My words in His mouth, and He shall speak to them all that I command
Him. 19And it shall be *that* whoever will not hear My words, which He
speaks in My name, I will require *it* of him. 20But the prophet who pre-
sumes to speak a word in My name, which I have not commanded him to
speak, or who speaks in the name of other gods, that prophet shall die.'
21And if you say in your heart, 'How shall we know the word which the
LORD has not spoken?'— 22when a prophet speaks in the name of the LORD,
if the thing does not happen or come to pass, that *is* the thing which the
LORD has not spoken; the prophet has spoken it presumptuously; you shall
not be afraid of him.

Three Cities of Refuge

19 "When the LORD your God has cut off the nations whose land the
LORD your God is giving you, and you dispossess them and dwell in
their cities and in their houses, 2you shall separate three cities for yourself
in the midst of your land which the LORD your God is giving you to possess.
3You shall prepare roads for yourself, and divide into three parts the territory of your land which the LORD your God is giving you to inherit, that any
manslayer may flee there.
4"And this *is* the case of the manslayer who flees there, that he may live:
Whoever kills his neighbor unintentionally, not having hated him in time
past— 5as when *a man* goes to the woods with his neighbor to cut timber,
and his hand swings a stroke with the ax to cut down the tree, and the head
slips from the handle and strikes his neighbor so that he dies—he shall
flee to one of these cities and live; 6lest the avenger of blood, while his
anger is hot, pursue the manslayer and overtake him, because the way is
long, and kill him, though he *was* not deserving of death, since he had not
hated the victim in time past. 7Therefore I command you, saying, 'You
shall separate three cities for yourself.'
8"Now if the LORD your God enlarges your territory, as He swore to your
fathers, and gives you the land which He promised to give to your fathers,
9and if you keep all these commandments and do them, which I command you today, to love the LORD your God and to walk always in His ways,
then you shall add three more cities for yourself besides these three, 10lest
innocent blood be shed in the midst of your land which the LORD your God
is giving you *as* an inheritance, and *thus* guilt of bloodshed be upon you.
11"But if anyone hates his neighbor, lies in wait for him, rises against
him and strikes him mortally, so that he dies, and he flees to one of these
cities, 12then the elders of his city shall send and bring him from there, and

LIFE LESSON

Deuteronomy 19:1–20:20

SITUATION Moses gave the people of Israel God's laws for ruling the nation. God's law stressed issues of safety, justice, and dealing with conflict. God promised to go with them in battle.

OBSERVATION God knows that standing for truth is not easy. He promises to stand with his people and to bring victory.

INSPIRATION God never leaves us with only one line of comfort, there are many always at hand. There is one that I have not often heard mentioned, and yet there is help to be found in it. "Thou shalt not be given into the hand of the men of whom thou art afraid." What is the thing that you most fear and most earnestly pray about, the thing of all other things that you dread? If you love your Lord, and yet know your own weakness, is it not that something may happen to sweep you off your feet, or that your strength may be drained and you may yield and fall, and fail Him at the end? I have known many whose lives were shadowed by this fear.

Oh, take comfort. God . . . knows our hearts, too. He knows who the men are (What the forces of trial are) of whom we are afraid; and he assures us and reassures us, "Thou shalt not be given into the hand of the men of whom thou art afraid."

(From *Thou Givest, They Gather* by Amy Carmichael)

APPLICATION As you read the newspaper, notice how often you read about war or revolution. Remind yourself that you fight a spiritual battle. Have confidence when you face trials, because you know God stands with you.

EXPLORATION God and the World—John 16:33. God's Values—Micah 6:8; Mark 12:28-31. God and the Mind—Romans 12:1-2.

deliver him over to the hand of the avenger of blood,
that he may die. [13]Your eye shall not pity him, but you
shall put away *the guilt of* innocent blood from Israel,
that it may go well with you.

Property Boundaries

[14]"You shall not remove your neighbor's landmark,
which the men of old have set, in your inheritance
which you will inherit in the land that the LORD your
God is giving you to possess.

The Law Concerning Witnesses

[15]"One witness shall not rise against a man concerning any iniquity or any sin that he commits; by
the mouth of two or three witnesses the matter shall
be established. [16]If a false witness rises against any
man to testify against him of wrongdoing, [17]then both
men in the controversy shall stand before the LORD,
before the priests and the judges who serve in those
days. [18]And the judges shall make careful inquiry, and
indeed, *if* the witness *is* a false witness, who has testified falsely against his brother, [19]then you shall do to
him as he thought to have done to his brother; so you
shall put away the evil from among you. [20]And those
who remain shall hear and fear, and hereafter they
shall not again commit such evil among you. [21]Your
eye shall not pity: life *shall be* for life, eye for eye, tooth
for tooth, hand for hand, foot for foot.

Principles Governing Warfare

20 "When you go out to battle against your enemies, and see horses and chariots *and* people
more numerous than you, do not be afraid of them;
for the LORD your God *is* with you, who brought you
up from the land of Egypt. [2]So it shall be, when you
are on the verge of battle, that the priest shall approach
and speak to the people. [3]And he shall say to them,
'Hear, O Israel: Today you are on the verge of battle with
your enemies. Do not let your heart faint, do not be
afraid, and do not tremble or be terrified because of
them; [4]for the LORD your God *is* He who goes with you,
to fight for you against your enemies, to save you.'
[5]"Then the officers shall speak to the people, saying: 'What man *is there* who has built a new house and
has not dedicated it? Let him go and return to his
house, lest he die in the battle and another man dedicate it. [6]Also what man *is there* who has planted a
vineyard and has not eaten of it? Let him go and return to his house, lest he die in the battle and another
man eat of it. [7]And what man *is there* who is betrothed
to a woman and has not married her? Let him go and
return to his house, lest he die in the battle and another man marry her.'
[8]"The officers shall speak further to the people, and
say, 'What man *is there who is* fearful and fainthearted? Let him go and return to his house, lest the
heart of his brethren faint[r] like his heart.' [9]And so it
shall be, when the officers have finished speaking to
the people, that they shall make captains of the
armies to lead the people.
[10]"When you go near a city to fight against it, then
proclaim an offer of peace to it. [11]And it shall be that if
they accept your offer of peace, and open to you, then
all the people *who are* found in it shall be placed
under tribute to you, and serve you. [12]Now if *the city*
will not make peace with you, but war against you,
then you shall besiege it. [13]And when the LORD your
God delivers it into your hands, you shall strike every
male in it with the edge of the sword. [14]But the
women, the little ones, the livestock, and all that is in
the city, all its spoil, you shall plunder for yourself;
and you shall eat the enemies' plunder which the
LORD your God gives you. [15]Thus you shall do to all the
cities *which are* very far from you, which *are* not of the
cities of these nations.
[16]"But of the cities of these peoples which the LORD
your God gives you *as* an inheritance, you shall let
nothing that breathes remain alive, [17]but you shall utterly destroy them: the Hittite and the Amorite and
the Canaanite and the Perizzite and the Hivite and the
Jebusite, just as the LORD your God has commanded
you, [18]lest they teach you to do according to all their
abominations which they have done for their gods,
and you sin against the LORD your God.
[19]"When you besiege a city for a long time, while
making war against it to take it, you shall not destroy
its trees by wielding an ax against them; if you can eat
of them, do not cut them down to use in the siege, for
the tree of the field *is* man's *food*. [20]Only the trees
which you know *are* not trees for food you may destroy and cut down, to build siegeworks against the
city that makes war with you, until it is subdued.

The Law Concerning Unsolved Murder

21 "If *anyone* is found slain, lying in the field in
the land which the LORD your God is giving you
to possess, *and* it is not known who killed him, [2]then
your elders and your judges shall go out and measure
the distance from the slain man to the surrounding

20:8 [r] Following Masoretic Text and Targum; Samaritan Pentateuch, Septuagint, Syriac, and Vulgate read *lest he make his brother's heart faint.*

cities. 3And it shall be *that* the elders of the city nearest to the slain man
will take a heifer which has not been worked *and* which has not pulled
with a yoke. 4The elders of that city shall bring the heifer down to a valley
with flowing water, which is neither plowed nor sown, and they shall break
the heifer's neck there in the valley. 5Then the priests, the sons of Levi, shall
come near, for the LORD your God has chosen them to minister to Him and
to bless in the name of the LORD; by their word every controversy and every
assault shall be *settled.* 6And all the elders of that city nearest to the slain
man shall wash their hands over the heifer whose neck was broken in the
valley. 7Then they shall answer and say, 'Our hands have not shed this
blood, nor have our eyes seen *it.* 8Provide atonement, O LORD, for Your
people Israel, whom You have redeemed, and do not lay innocent blood to
the charge of Your people Israel.' And atonement shall be provided on
their behalf for the blood. 9So you shall put away the *guilt of* innocent
blood from among you when you do *what is* right in the sight of the LORD.

Female Captives

10"When you go out to war against your enemies, and the LORD your God
delivers them into your hand, and you take them captive, 11and you see
among the captives a beautiful woman, and desire her and would take her
for your wife, 12then you shall bring her home to your house, and she shall
shave her head and trim her nails. 13She shall put off the clothes of her captivity, remain in your house, and mourn her father and her mother a full
month; after that you may go in to her and be her husband, and she shall
be your wife. 14And it shall be, if you have no delight in her, then you shall
set her free, but you certainly shall not sell her for money; you shall not
treat her brutally, because you have humbled her.

Firstborn Inheritance Rights

15"If a man has two wives, one loved and the other unloved, and they
have borne him children, *both* the loved and the unloved, and *if* the firstborn son is of her who is unloved, 16then it shall be, on the day he be-
queaths his possessions to his sons, *that* he must not bestow firstborn
status on the son of the loved wife in preference to the son of the unloved,
the *true* firstborn. 17But he shall acknowledge the son of the unloved wife
as the firstborn by giving him a double portion of all that he has, for he *is*
the beginning of his strength; the right of the firstborn *is* his.

The Rebellious Son

18"If a man has a stubborn and rebellious son who will not obey the
voice of his father or the voice of his mother, and *who,* when they have
chastened him, will not heed them, 19then his father and his mother shall
take hold of him and bring him out to the elders of his city, to the gate of
his city. 20And they shall say to the elders of his city, 'This son of ours is
stubborn and rebellious; he will not obey our voice; he is a glutton and a
drunkard.' 21Then all the men of his city shall stone him to death with
stones; so you shall put away the evil from among you, and all Israel shall
hear and fear.

Miscellaneous Laws

22"If a man has committed a sin deserving of death, and he is put to
death, and you hang him on a tree, 23his body shall not remain overnight

LIFE LESSON

Deuteronomy 21:1–22:30

SITUATION Moses gave the people laws on incest, murder, adultery, fornication, inheritance, discipline of children, and social responsibilities.

OBSERVATION Obeying the principles God lays out will protect us from the consequences of sin. We honor God by obeying him and living peacefully with each other.

INSPIRATION We live in an upside down world. Men hate when they should love, men quarrel when they should be friendly, men fight when they should be peaceful, men wound when they should heal, men steal when they should share, men do wrong when they should do right. I once saw a toy clown with a weight in its head. No matter what position you put it in, it invariably assumed an upside-down position. Put it on its feet or on its side, and when you let it go it flipped back on its head. Man in his unregenerate state is just like that! Do what you may with him, and he always reverts to an upside-down position. That is why the disciples to the world were misfits. To an upside down man, a right-side up man seems upside down. To a sinner, a righteous man is an oddity and an abnormality. A Christian's goodness is a rebuke to the wicked; his being right-side up is a reflection upon the world's inverted position.

(From *Day by Day with Billy Graham* by Joan W. Brown)

APPLICATION What evils do you see in your community that are similar to those mentioned in the passage? What evil activity has become so popular that it is considered normal? Have you been desensitized to how wicked it really is? Treat sin as God does. Allow no room for it in your life.

EXPLORATION Shun Evil—Psalm 34:14-16; 97:10; Colossians 3:5; Romans 12:9; 1 Peter 3:11.

on the tree, but you shall surely bury him that day, so that you do not defile the land which the LORD your God is giving you *as* an inheritance; for he who is hanged *is* accursed of God.

22 "You shall not see your brother's ox or his sheep going astray, and hide yourself from them; you shall certainly bring them back to your brother. 2And if your brother *is* not near you, or if you do not know him, then you shall bring it to your own house, and it shall remain with you until your brother seeks it; then you shall restore it to him. 3You shall do the same with his donkey, and so shall you do with his garment; with any lost thing of your brother's, which he has lost and you have found, you shall do likewise; you must not hide yourself.

4"You shall not see your brother's donkey or his ox fall down along the road, and hide yourself from them; you shall surely help him lift *them* up again.

5"A woman shall not wear anything that pertains to a man, nor shall a man put on a woman's garment, for all who do so *are* an abomination to the LORD your God.

6"If a bird's nest happens to be before you along the way, in any tree or on the ground, with young ones or eggs, with the mother sitting on the young or on the eggs, you shall not take the mother with the young; 7you shall surely let the mother go, and take the young for yourself, that it may be well with you and *that* you may prolong *your* days.

8"When you build a new house, then you shall make a parapet for your roof, that you may not bring guilt of bloodshed on your household if anyone falls from it.

9"You shall not sow your vineyard with different kinds of seed, lest the yield of the seed which you have sown and the fruit of your vineyard be defiled.

10"You shall not plow with an ox and a donkey together.

11"You shall not wear a garment of different sorts, *such as* wool and linen mixed together.

12"You shall make tassels on the four corners of the clothing with which you cover *yourself.*

Laws of Sexual Morality

13"If any man takes a wife, and goes in to her, and detests her, 14and charges her with shameful conduct, and brings a bad name on her, and says, 'I took this woman, and when I came to her I found she *was* not a virgin,' 15then the father and mother of the young woman shall take and bring out *the evidence of* the young woman's virginity to the elders of the city at the gate. 16And the young woman's father shall say to the elders, 'I gave my daughter to this man as wife, and he detests her. 17Now he has charged her with shameful conduct, saying, "I found your daughter *was* not a virgin," and yet these *are the evidences of* my daughter's virginity.' And they shall spread the cloth before the elders of the city. 18Then the elders of that city shall take that man and punish him; 19and they shall fine him one hundred *shekels* of silver and give *them* to the father of the young woman, because he has brought a bad name on a virgin of Israel. And she shall be his wife; he cannot divorce her all his days.

20"But if the thing is true, *and evidences of* virginity are not found for the young woman, 21then they shall bring out the young woman to the door of her father's house, and the men of her city shall stone her to death with stones, because she has done a disgraceful thing in Israel, to play the harlot in her father's house. So you shall put away the evil from among you.

22"If a man is found lying with a woman married to a husband, then both of them shall die—the man that lay with the woman, and the woman; so you shall put away the evil from Israel.

23"If a young woman *who is* a virgin is betrothed to a husband, and a man finds her in the city and lies with her, 24then you shall bring them both out to the gate of that city, and you shall stone them to death with stones, the young woman because she did not cry out in the city, and the man because he humbled his neighbor's wife; so you shall put away the evil from among you.

25"But if a man finds a betrothed young woman in the countryside, and the man forces her and lies with her, then only the man who lay with her shall die. 26But you shall do nothing to the young woman; *there is* in the young woman no sin *deserving* of death, for just as when a man rises against his neighbor and kills him, even so *is* this matter. 27For he found her in the countryside, *and* the betrothed young woman cried out, but *there was* no one to save her.

28"If a man finds a young woman *who is* a virgin, who is not betrothed, and he seizes her and lies with her, and they are found out, 29then the man who lay with her shall give to the young woman's father fifty *shekels* of silver, and she shall be his wife because he has humbled her; he shall not be permitted to divorce her all his days.

30"A man shall not take his father's wife, nor uncover his father's bed.

Those Excluded from the Congregation

23 "He who is emasculated by crushing or mutilation shall not enter the assembly of the LORD.

2“One of illegitimate birth shall not enter the assembly of the LORD; even
to the tenth generation none of his *descendants* shall enter the assembly of
the LORD.
3“An Ammonite or Moabite shall not enter the assembly of the LORD;
even to the tenth generation none of his *descendants* shall enter the assembly of the LORD forever, 4because they did not meet you with bread and
water on the road when you came out of Egypt, and because they hired
against you Balaam the son of Beor from Pethor of Mesopotamia,[s] to curse
you. 5Nevertheless the LORD your God would not listen to Balaam, but the
LORD your God turned the curse into a blessing for you, because the LORD
your God loves you. 6You shall not seek their peace nor their prosperity all
your days forever.
7“You shall not abhor an Edomite, for he *is* your brother. You shall not
abhor an Egyptian, because you were an alien in his land. 8The children of
the third generation born to them may enter the assembly of the LORD.

Cleanliness of the Camp Site

9“When the army goes out against your enemies, then keep yourself
from every wicked thing. 10If there is any man among you who becomes
unclean by some occurrence in the night, then he shall go outside the
camp; he shall not come inside the camp. 11But it shall be, when evening
comes, that he shall wash with water; and when the sun sets, he may come
into the camp.
12“Also you shall have a place outside the camp, where you may go out;
13and you shall have an implement among your equipment, and when you
sit down outside, you shall dig with it and turn and cover your refuse.
14For the LORD your God walks in the midst of your camp, to deliver you
and give your enemies over to you; therefore your camp shall be holy, that
He may see no unclean thing among you, and turn away from you.

Miscellaneous Laws

15“You shall not give back to his master the slave who has escaped from
his master to you. 16He may dwell with you in your midst, in the place
which he chooses within one of your gates, where it seems best to him; you
shall not oppress him.
17“There shall be no *ritual* harlot[t] of the daughters of Israel, or a perverted[u] one of the sons of Israel. 18You shall not bring the wages of a harlot
or the price of a dog to the house of the LORD your God for any vowed offering, for both of these *are* an abomination to the LORD your God.
19“You shall not charge interest to your brother—interest on money *or*
food *or* anything that is lent out at interest. 20To a foreigner you may
charge interest, but to your brother you shall not charge interest, that the
LORD your God may bless you in all to which you set your hand in the land
which you are entering to possess.
21“When you make a vow to the LORD your God, you shall not delay to
pay it; for the LORD your God will surely require it of you, and it would be
sin to you. 22But if you abstain from vowing, it shall not be sin to you.
23That which has gone from your lips you shall keep and perform, for you

23:4 [s] Hebrew *Aram Naharaim*
23:17 [t] Hebrew *qedeshah,* feminine of *qadesh* (see following note) [u] Hebrew *qadesh,* that is, one practicing sodomy and prostitution in religious rituals

LIFE LESSON

Deuteronomy 23:1–25:19

SITUATION God continued to give laws to his people. He wanted them to treat each other with respect.

OBSERVATION God revealed his concern for families. For God's people, family responsibilities should be a higher priority than civil responsibilities.

INSPIRATION I appeal to the young people: It is a very beautiful gift of God for a young man to love a young woman, and a young woman to love a young man, but you must love each other with a clean heart. The greatest gift you can give to each other on the day you get married is a pure heart—a virgin body, a virgin heart. And you need to pray for this purity.

A few weeks ago, two young people came to our house in Calcutta, and they offered me lots of money to feed our people (because we cook every day for 9,000 people). We asked them, “Where did you get this money?” And they said, “We were married two days ago. But we decided beforehand that we would not buy wedding clothes or have a wedding feast—we would give you the money instead.” And again we asked, “But why are you doing this?” They answered, “We loved each other so much that we wanted to give something special to each other and begin our married life with a deep demonstration of our love for each other.” It was wonderful to see the true love and respect these two young people had for each other.

And I repeat: Young people, especially nowadays when “love” is shown so easily in the streets, don't belittle the gift of God. Give the love of a clean heart to each other, and keep yourselves for each other so that God may always be with you; for a clean heart will always see God. He loves a heart that is totally given to him. And my prayer is that you may grow in holiness through this love for each other.

(From *Who Is for Life?* by Mother Theresa)

Continued

APPLICATION If you are married, schedule regular time to spend with your spouse. Communicate often. Don't let even good things take a higher priority. If you are not married, look for ways to serve others in your immediate family or your church family. Ask God to help you have a pure heart.

EXPLORATION Marriage—Genesis 2:18-25; 24; Song of Solomon 4:15; 5:2-8; Hebrews 13:4.

voluntarily vowed to the LORD your God what you have promised with
your mouth.
24"When you come into your neighbor's vineyard, you may eat your fill
of grapes at your pleasure, but you shall not put *any* in your container.
25When you come into your neighbor's standing grain, you may pluck the
heads with your hand, but you shall not use a sickle on your neighbor's
standing grain.

Law Concerning Divorce

24 "When a man takes a wife and marries her, and it happens that she
finds no favor in his eyes because he has found some uncleanness
in her, and he writes her a certificate of divorce, puts *it* in her hand, and
sends her out of his house, 2when she has departed from his house, and
goes and becomes another man's *wife*, 3*if* the latter husband detests her
and writes her a certificate of divorce, puts *it* in her hand, and sends her
out of his house, or if the latter husband dies who took her as his wife,
4*then* her former husband who divorced her must not take her back to be
his wife after she has been defiled; for that *is* an abomination before the
LORD, and you shall not bring sin on the land which the LORD your God is
giving you *as* an inheritance.

Miscellaneous Laws

5"When a man has taken a new wife, he shall not go out to war or be
charged with any business; he shall be free at home one year, and bring
happiness to his wife whom he has taken.
6"No man shall take the lower or the upper millstone in pledge, for he
takes *one's* living in pledge.
7"If a man is found kidnapping any of his brethren of the children of Israel, and mistreats him or sells him, then that kidnapper shall die; and
you shall put away the evil from among you.
8"Take heed in an outbreak of leprosy, that you carefully observe and do
according to all that the priests, the Levites, shall teach you; just as I commanded them, *so* you shall be careful to do. 9Remember what the LORD
your God did to Miriam on the way when you came out of Egypt!
10"When you lend your brother anything, you shall not go into his house
to get his pledge. 11You shall stand outside, and the man to whom you lend
shall bring the pledge out to you. 12And if the man *is* poor, you shall not
keep his pledge overnight. 13You shall in any case return the pledge to him
again when the sun goes down, that he may sleep in his own garment and
bless you; and it shall be righteousness to you before the LORD your God.
14"You shall not oppress a hired servant *who is* poor and needy, *whether*
one of your brethren or one of the aliens who *is* in your land within your
gates. 15Each day you shall give *him* his wages, and not let the sun go down
on it, for he *is* poor and has set his heart on it; lest he cry out against you to
the LORD, and it be sin to you.
16"Fathers shall not be put to death for *their* children, nor shall children be
put to death for *their* fathers; a person shall be put to death for his own sin.
17"You shall not pervert justice due the stranger or the fatherless, nor
take a widow's garment as a pledge. 18But you shall remember that you
were a slave in Egypt, and the LORD your God redeemed you from there;
therefore I command you to do this thing.
19"When you reap your harvest in your field, and forget a sheaf in the

field, you shall not go back to get it; it shall be for the
stranger, the fatherless, and the widow, that the LORD
your God may bless you in all the work of your hands.
[20]When you beat your olive trees, you shall not go over
the boughs again; it shall be for the stranger, the fatherless, and the widow. [21]When you gather the grapes
of your vineyard, you shall not glean *it* afterward; it
shall be for the stranger, the fatherless, and the widow.
[22]And you shall remember that you were a slave in the
land of Egypt; therefore I command you to do this
thing.

25 "If there is a dispute between men, and they
come to court, that *the judges* may judge them,
and they justify the righteous and condemn the
wicked, [2]then it shall be, if the wicked man deserves to
be beaten, that the judge will cause him to lie down
and be beaten in his presence, according to his guilt,
with a certain number of blows. [3]Forty blows he may
give him *and* no more, lest he should exceed this and
beat him with many blows above these, and your
brother be humiliated in your sight.
[4]"You shall not muzzle an ox while it treads out *the
grain.*

Marriage Duty of the Surviving Brother

[5]"If brothers dwell together, and one of them dies
and has no son, the widow of the dead man shall not
be *married* to a stranger outside *the family;* her husband's brother shall go in to her, take her as his wife,
and perform the duty of a husband's brother to her.
[6]And it shall be *that* the firstborn son which she bears
will succeed to the name of his dead brother, that his
name may not be blotted out of Israel. [7]But if the man
does not want to take his brother's wife, then let his
brother's wife go up to the gate to the elders, and say,
'My husband's brother refuses to raise up a name to
his brother in Israel; he will not perform the duty of
my husband's brother.' [8]Then the elders of his city
shall call him and speak to him. But *if* he stands firm
and says, 'I do not want to take her,' [9]then his
brother's wife shall come to him in the presence of the
elders, remove his sandal from his foot, spit in his
face, and answer and say, 'So shall it be done to the
man who will not build up his brother's house.' [10]And
his name shall be called in Israel, 'The house of him
who had his sandal removed.'

Miscellaneous Laws

[11]"If *two* men fight together, and the wife of one
draws near to rescue her husband from the hand of
the one attacking him, and puts out her hand and
seizes him by the genitals, [12]then you shall cut off her
hand; your eye shall not pity *her.*
[13]"You shall not have in your bag differing weights,
a heavy and a light. [14]You shall not have in your house
differing measures, a large and a small. [15]You shall
have a perfect and just weight, a perfect and just measure, that your days may be lengthened in the land
which the LORD your God is giving you. [16]For all who
do such things, all who behave unrighteously, *are* an
abomination to the LORD your God.

Destroy the Amalekites

[17]"Remember what Amalek did to you on the way
as you were coming out of Egypt, [18]how he met you on
the way and attacked your rear ranks, all the strag-
glers at your rear, when you *were* tired and weary; and
he did not fear God. [19]Therefore it shall be, when the
LORD your God has given you rest from your enemies
all around, in the land which the LORD your God is giving you to possess *as* an inheritance, *that* you will blot
out the remembrance of Amalek from under heaven.
You shall not forget.

Offerings of Firstfruits and Tithes

26 "And it shall be, when you come into the land
which the LORD your God is giving you *as* an
inheritance, and you possess it and dwell in it, [2]that
you shall take some of the first of all the produce of
the ground, which you shall bring from your land that
the LORD your God is giving you, and put *it* in a basket
and go to the place where the LORD your God chooses
to make His name abide. [3]And you shall go to the one
who is priest in those days, and say to him, 'I declare
today to the LORD your[v] God that I have come to the
country which the LORD swore to our fathers to give
us.'
[4]"Then the priest shall take the basket out of your
hand and set it down before the altar of the LORD your
God. [5]And you shall answer and say before the LORD
your God: 'My father *was* a Syrian,[w] about to perish,
and he went down to Egypt and dwelt there, few in
number; and there he became a nation, great, mighty,
and populous. [6]But the Egyptians mistreated us, afflicted us, and laid hard bondage on us. [7]Then we
cried out to the LORD God of our fathers, and the LORD
heard our voice and looked on our affliction and our
labor and our oppression. [8]So the LORD brought us

26:3 [v] Septuagint reads *my.*
26:5 [w] Or *Aramean*

LIFE LESSON

Deuteronomy 26:1-19

SITUATION God reminded the Israelites how he had faithfully provided for all their needs. They were also instructed to give the first portion of each harvest to God, and he would bless them in the land.

OBSERVATION God's Word reminds us to honor him by giving back a portion of what he has provided for us.

INSPIRATION According to the dictionary, the original definition of tithe was one-tenth of the annual produce of one's land or of one's annual income. According to the Bible, that is merely the starting place of giving to the Lord. The Malachi passage refers to "tithes and offerings." One might say, then, that there is no offering until the tithe has been paid; it is the expected, minimum amount.

So a lot of people who practice this critical spiritual law give more than 10 percent of their income to the Lord's work. It's all His anyhow, they recognize. . . . Therefore, many people ignore any 10 percent cutoff and give out of the abundance of their provision. I know one New Jersey florist who had been thoroughly blessed by the Lord as he exercised the principles we are exploring in this book, and he frequently gave 90 percent of his annual income to the service of God. And the prosperity simply mounted. He was not able to outgive the Lord. That law is built into the kingdom. It never changes.

(From *The Secret Kingdom* by Pat Robertson)

APPLICATION Do you give money to God's work regularly? Is there money set apart in your budget so that he gets the first cut from your paycheck? Rework your budget or create one that will allow you to give to God's work before anything else. God deserves our firstfruits, not whatever is left at the end.

EXPLORATION Giving—Proverbs 3:9; 11:24-5; Luke 6:38; 1John 3:17.

out of Egypt with a mighty hand and with an outstretched arm, with great
terror and with signs and wonders. 9He has brought us to this place and
has given us this land, "a land flowing with milk and honey";[x] 10and now,
behold, I have brought the firstfruits of the land which you, O LORD, have
given me.'

"Then you shall set it before the LORD your God, and worship before the
LORD your God. 11So you shall rejoice in every good *thing* which the LORD
your God has given to you and your house, you and the Levite and the
stranger who *is* among you.

12"When you have finished laying aside all the tithe of your increase in
the third year—the year of tithing—and have given *it* to the Levite, the
stranger, the fatherless, and the widow, so that they may eat within your
gates and be filled, 13then you shall say before the LORD your God: 'I have
removed the holy *tithe* from *my* house, and also have given them to the
Levite, the stranger, the fatherless, and the widow, according to all Your
commandments which You have commanded me; I have not transgressed Your commandments, nor have I forgotten *them.* 14I have not
eaten any of it when in mourning, nor have I removed *any* of it for an unclean *use,* nor given *any* of it for the dead. I have obeyed the voice of the
LORD my God, and have done according to all that You have commanded
me. 15Look down from Your holy habitation, from heaven, and bless Your
people Israel and the land which You have given us, just as You swore to
our fathers, "a land flowing with milk and honey." '[y]

A Special People of God

16"This day the LORD your God commands you to observe these statutes
and judgments; therefore you shall be careful to observe them with all
your heart and with all your soul. 17Today you have proclaimed the LORD to
be your God, and that you will walk in His ways and keep His statutes, His
commandments, and His judgments, and that you will obey His voice.
18Also today the LORD has proclaimed you to be His special people, just as
He promised you, that *you* should keep all His commandments, 19and that
He will set you high above all nations which He has made, in praise, in
name, and in honor, and that you may be a holy people to the LORD your
God, just as He has spoken."

The Law Inscribed on Stones

27 Now Moses, with the elders of Israel, commanded the people, saying: "Keep all the commandments which I command you today.
2And it shall be, on the day when you cross over the Jordan to the land
which the LORD your God is giving you, that you shall set up for yourselves
large stones, and whitewash them with lime. 3You shall write on them all
the words of this law, when you have crossed over, that you may enter the
land which the LORD your God is giving you, 'a land flowing with milk and
honey,'[z] just as the LORD God of your fathers promised you. 4Therefore it
shall be, when you have crossed over the Jordan, *that* on Mount Ebal you
shall set up these stones, which I command you today, and you shall
whitewash them with lime. 5And there you shall build an altar to the LORD
your God, an altar of stones; you shall not use an iron *tool* on them. 6You

26:9 [x] Exodus 3:8
26:15 [y] Exodus 3:8
27:3 [z] Exodus 3:8

shall build with whole stones the altar of the LORD your God, and offer
burnt offerings on it to the LORD your God. 7You shall offer peace offerings,
and shall eat there, and rejoice before the LORD your God. 8And you shall
write very plainly on the stones all the words of this law."
9Then Moses and the priests, the Levites, spoke to all Israel, saying,
"Take heed and listen, O Israel: This day you have become the people of
the LORD your God. 10Therefore you shall obey the voice of the LORD your
God, and observe His commandments and His statutes which I command
you today."

Curses Pronounced from Mount Ebal

11And Moses commanded the people on the same day, saying, 12"These
shall stand on Mount Gerizim to bless the people, when you have crossed
over the Jordan: Simeon, Levi, Judah, Issachar, Joseph, and Benjamin;
13and these shall stand on Mount Ebal to curse: Reuben, Gad, Asher,
Zebulun, Dan, and Naphtali.
14"And the Levites shall speak with a loud voice and say to all the men of
Israel: 15'Cursed *is* the one who makes a carved or molded image, an
abomination to the LORD, the work of the hands of the craftsman, and sets
it up in secret.'
"And all the people shall answer and say, 'Amen!'
16'Cursed *is* the one who treats his father or his mother with contempt.'
"And all the people shall say, 'Amen!'
17'Cursed *is* the one who moves his neighbor's landmark.'
"And all the people shall say, 'Amen!'
18'Cursed *is* the one who makes the blind to wander off the road.'
"And all the people shall say, 'Amen!'
19'Cursed *is* the one who perverts the justice due the stranger, the fatherless, and widow.'
"And all the people shall say, 'Amen!'
20'Cursed *is* the one who lies with his father's wife, because he has
uncovered his father's bed.'
"And all the people shall say, 'Amen!'
21'Cursed *is* the one who lies with any kind of animal.'
"And all the people shall say, 'Amen!'
22'Cursed *is* the one who lies with his sister, the daughter of his father or
the daughter of his mother.'
"And all the people shall say, 'Amen!'
23'Cursed *is* the one who lies with his mother-in-law.'
"And all the people shall say, 'Amen!'
24'Cursed *is* the one who attacks his neighbor secretly.'
"And all the people shall say, 'Amen!'
25'Cursed *is* the one who takes a bribe to slay an innocent person.'
"And all the people shall say, 'Amen!'
26'Cursed *is* the one who does not confirm *all* the words of this law.'
"And all the people shall say, 'Amen!' "

Blessings on Obedience

28 "Now it shall come to pass, if you diligently obey the voice of the
LORD your God, to observe carefully all His commandments which
I command you today, that the LORD your God will set you high above all

LIFE LESSON

Deuteronomy 27:1–28:68

SITUATION The altar at Mount Ebal was to serve as a reminder of the blessings of obedience and the curses of disobedience.

OBSERVATION Actions have consequences. Because the Israelites neglected to obey God, they fell into the hands of Assyria and Babylon.

INSPIRATION The *partially surrendered life* may be Christian in spirit, but it is secular in practice. It may save one's soul, but it hardly leaves a noticeable ripple on one's lifestyle, life view, or the world and culture in which we live. Of what earthly value is Christianity if it leaves no indelible mark on one's lifestyle? It is of no value (in this life) to be Christian if you do not think Christianly—if you do not have a Christian life view.

We live in a broken generation. One doesn't need to be a rocket scientist to make this observation, but the obvious question, of course, is *Why?* Many think the answer is confusing, but it is not. It is found throughout the record of Scripture—it is *disobedience.* It is to lead a partially surrendered, or worse, an unsurrendered, unyielded life. How can we learn to be obedient? We must learn how to surrender, to submit to Christ in the details of daily life.

Over the past few decades, many of us started off on the wrong foot with Jesus Christ. It is the proposition that Jesus can be *Savior* without being *Lord.* It is the idea that one can *add* Christ, but not *subtract* sin. Many of us have merely added Christ to our lives as another interest in an already busy and otherwise overcrowded schedule. This sort of thinking has watered down the meaning of a personal relationship with Christ.

The problem is that we often seek the God we want, but do not know the God who is. Many men and women I have met express complete, utter frustration about leading this kind of defeated (sometimes counterfeit), partially surrendered life—the life of a cultural Christian.

How did this come about? The *low demands* of cultural Christianity have

Continued

nations of the earth. 2And all these blessings shall come upon you and
overtake you, because you obey the voice of the LORD your God:
3"Blessed *shall* you *be* in the city, and blessed *shall* you *be* in the country.
4"Blessed *shall be* the fruit of your body, the produce of your ground and
the increase of your herds, the increase of your cattle and the offspring of
your flocks.
5"Blessed *shall be* your basket and your kneading bowl.
6"Blessed *shall* you *be* when you come in, and blessed *shall* you *be* when
you go out.
7"The LORD will cause your enemies who rise against you to be defeated
before your face; they shall come out against you one way and flee before
you seven ways.
8"The LORD will command the blessing on you in your storehouses and
in all to which you set your hand, and He will bless you in the land which
the LORD your God is giving you.
9"The LORD will establish you as a holy people to Himself, just as He has
sworn to you, if you keep the commandments of the LORD your God and
walk in His ways. 10Then all peoples of the earth shall see that you are
called by the name of the LORD, and they shall be afraid of you. 11And the
LORD will grant you plenty of goods, in the fruit of your body, in the increase of your livestock, and in the produce of your ground, in the land of
which the LORD swore to your fathers to give you. 12The LORD will open to
you His good treasure, the heavens, to give the rain to your land in its season, and to bless all the work of your hand. You shall lend to many nations,
but you shall not borrow. 13And the LORD will make you the head and not
the tail; you shall be above only, and not be beneath, if you heed the commandments of the LORD your God, which I command you today, and are
careful to observe *them.* 14So you shall not turn aside from any of the
words which I command you this day, *to* the right or the left, to go after
other gods to serve them.

Curses on Disobedience

15"But it shall come to pass, if you do not obey the voice of the LORD your
God, to observe carefully all His commandments and His statutes which I
command you today, that all these curses will come upon you and overtake you:
16"Cursed *shall* you *be* in the city, and cursed *shall* you *be* in the country.
17"Cursed *shall be* your basket and your kneading bowl.
18"Cursed *shall be* the fruit of your body and the produce of your land,
the increase of your cattle and the offspring of your flocks.
19"Cursed *shall* you *be* when you come in, and cursed *shall* you *be* when
you go out.
20"The LORD will send on you cursing, confusion, and rebuke in all that
you set your hand to do, until you are destroyed and until you perish
quickly, because of the wickedness of your doings in which you have forsaken Me. 21The LORD will make the plague cling to you until He has consumed you from the land which you are going to possess. 22The LORD will
strike you with consumption, with fever, with inflammation, with severe
burning fever, with the sword, with scorching, and with mildew; they shall
pursue you until you perish. 23And your heavens which *are* over your head
shall be bronze, and the earth which is under you *shall be* iron. 24The LORD

led to a *low response*—it has become the norm. But the Bible calls men and women to a *turning point*, to a radical, life-transforming change. This turning point is no mean challenge, but a full surrender to history's most ideal, most radical leader: the Lord Jesus Christ.

(From *Walking with Christ in the Details of Life* by Patrick Morley)

APPLICATION God wants your life marked by obedience and integrity. How do you justify avoiding God? Because of money? Because some Christian has done you wrong? Because Sundays are for sports? Evaluate, adjust, and begin a fresh walk with God.

EXPLORATION Warnings—Numbers 14:11-12; 20:12; 2 Kings 17:14; Romans 11:19-21; Hebrews 2:1-3; 10:37-38.

will change the rain of your land to powder and dust;
from the heaven it shall come down on you until you
are destroyed.
25"The LORD will cause you to be defeated before
your enemies; you shall go out one way against them
and flee seven ways before them; and you shall become troublesome to all the kingdoms of the earth.
26Your carcasses shall be food for all the birds of the
air and the beasts of the earth, and no one shall
frighten *them* away. 27The LORD will strike you with the
boils of Egypt, with tumors, with the scab, and with
the itch, from which you cannot be healed. 28The LORD
will strike you with madness and blindness and confusion of heart. 29And you shall grope at noonday, as a
blind man gropes in darkness; you shall not prosper
in your ways; you shall be only oppressed and plundered continually, and no one shall save *you.*
30"You shall betroth a wife, but another man shall
lie with her; you shall build a house, but you shall not
dwell in it; you shall plant a vineyard, but shall not
gather its grapes. 31Your ox *shall be* slaughtered before
your eyes, but you shall not eat of it; your donkey *shall
be* violently taken away from before you, and shall not
be restored to you; your sheep *shall be* given to your
enemies, and you shall have no one to rescue *them.*
32Your sons and your daughters *shall be* given to another people, and your eyes shall look and fail *with
longing* for them all day long; and *there shall be* no
strength in your hand. 33A nation whom you have not
known shall eat the fruit of your land and the produce
of your labor, and you shall be only oppressed and
crushed continually. 34So you shall be driven mad because of the sight which your eyes see. 35The LORD will
strike you in the knees and on the legs with severe
boils which cannot be healed, and from the sole of
your foot to the top of your head.
36"The LORD will bring you and the king whom you
set over you to a nation which neither you nor your fathers have known, and there you shall serve other
gods—wood and stone. 37And you shall become an
astonishment, a proverb, and a byword among all nations where the LORD will drive you.
38"You shall carry much seed out to the field but
gather little in, for the locust shall consume it. 39You
shall plant vineyards and tend *them,* but you shall
neither drink *of* the wine nor gather the *grapes;* for the
worms shall eat them. 40You shall have olive trees
throughout all your territory, but you shall not anoint
yourself with the oil; for your olives shall drop off.
41You shall beget sons and daughters, but they shall not
be yours; for they shall go into captivity. 42Locusts
shall consume all your trees and the produce of your
land.
43"The alien who *is* among you shall rise higher and
higher above you, and you shall come down lower
and lower. 44He shall lend to you, but you shall not lend
to him; he shall be the head, and you shall be the tail.
45"Moreover all these curses shall come upon you
and pursue and overtake you, until you are destroyed,
because you did not obey the voice of the LORD your
God, to keep His commandments and His statutes
which He commanded you. 46And they shall be upon
you for a sign and a wonder, and on your descendants
forever.
47"Because you did not serve the LORD your God
with joy and gladness of heart, for the abundance of
everything, 48therefore you shall serve your enemies,
whom the LORD will send against you, in hunger, in
thirst, in nakedness, and in need of everything; and
He will put a yoke of iron on your neck until He has
destroyed you. 49The LORD will bring a nation against
you from afar, from the end of the earth, *as swift* as the
eagle flies, a nation whose language you will not understand, 50a nation of fierce countenance, which
does not respect the elderly nor show favor to the
young. 51And they shall eat the increase of your livestock and the produce of your land, until you are destroyed; they shall not leave you grain or new wine or
oil, *or* the increase of your cattle or the offspring of
your flocks, until they have destroyed you.
52"They shall besiege you at all your gates until your
high and fortified walls, in which you trust, come
down throughout all your land; and they shall besiege
you at all your gates throughout all your land which
the LORD your God has given you. 53You shall eat the
fruit of your own body, the flesh of your sons and your
daughters whom the LORD your God has given you, in
the siege and desperate straits in which your enemy
shall distress you. 54The sensitive and very refined
man among you will be hostile toward his brother, toward the wife of his bosom, and toward the rest of his
children whom he leaves behind, 55so that he will not
give any of them the flesh of his children whom he
will eat, because he has nothing left in the siege and
desperate straits in which your enemy shall distress
you at all your gates. 56The tender and delicate woman
among you, who would not venture to set the sole of
her foot on the ground because of her delicateness
and sensitivity, will refuse[a] to the husband of her
bosom, and to her son and her daughter, 57her

28:56 [a] Literally *her eye shall be evil toward*

placenta which comes out from between her feet and her children whom
she bears; for she will eat them secretly for lack of everything in the siege and
desperate straits in which your enemy shall distress you at all your gates.
58“If you do not carefully observe all the words of this law that are written in this book, that you may fear this glorious and awesome name, THE
LORD YOUR GOD, 59then the LORD will bring upon you and your descendants extraordinary plagues—great and prolonged plagues—and serious and prolonged sicknesses. 60Moreover He will bring back on you all
the diseases of Egypt, of which you were afraid, and they shall cling to you.
61Also every sickness and every plague, which *is* not written in this Book of
the Law, will the LORD bring upon you until you are destroyed. 62You shall
be left few in number, whereas you were as the stars of heaven in multitude, because you would not obey the voice of the LORD your God. 63And it
shall be, *that* just as the LORD rejoiced over you to do you good and multiply
you, so the LORD will rejoice over you to destroy you and bring you to nothing; and you shall be plucked from off the land which you go to possess.
64“Then the LORD will scatter you among all peoples, from one end of the
earth to the other, and there you shall serve other gods, which neither you
nor your fathers have known—wood and stone. 65And among those nations you shall find no rest, nor shall the sole of your foot have a resting
place; but there the LORD will give you a trembling heart, failing eyes, and
anguish of soul. 66Your life shall hang in doubt before you; you shall fear
day and night, and have no assurance of life. 67In the morning you shall
say, ‘Oh, that it were evening!’ And at evening you shall say, ‘Oh, that it
were morning!’ because of the fear which terrifies your heart, and because
of the sight which your eyes see.
68“And the LORD will take you back to Egypt in ships, by the way of which
I said to you, ‘You shall never see it again.’ And there you shall be offered
for sale to your enemies as male and female slaves, but no one will buy
you.”

The Covenant Renewed in Moab

29 These *are* the words of the covenant which the LORD commanded
Moses to make with the children of Israel in the land of Moab, besides the covenant which He made with them in Horeb.
2Now Moses called all Israel and said to them: “You have seen all that
the LORD did before your eyes in the land of Egypt, to Pharaoh and to all his
servants and to all his land— 3the great trials which your eyes have seen,
the signs, and those great wonders. 4Yet the LORD has not given you a heart
to perceive and eyes to see and ears to hear, to this *very* day. 5And I have led
you forty years in the wilderness. Your clothes have not worn out on you,
and your sandals have not worn out on your feet. 6You have not eaten
bread, nor have you drunk wine or *similar* drink, that you may know that
I *am* the LORD your God. 7And when you came to this place, Sihon king of
Heshbon and Og king of Bashan came out against us to battle, and we conquered them. 8We took their land and gave it as an inheritance to the
Reubenites, to the Gadites, and to half the tribe of Manasseh. 9Therefore
keep the words of this covenant, and do them, that you may prosper in all
that you do.
10“All of you stand today before the LORD your God: your leaders and
your tribes and your elders and your officers, all the men of Israel, 11your

LIFE LESSON

Deuteronomy 29:1–30:20

SITUATION Moses summarized God’s guidance and provision for the Israelites during the previous forty years. The adults who originally escaped from Egypt had all died in the desert, but God’s covenant included their descendants. Many times throughout the Old Testament God renewed his covenant with them. Though all Israelites were invited to take part in God’s covenant, only those who chose to obey the covenant received his blessings.

OBSERVATION To choose against God brings emptiness and pain—death. To choose God brings blessings and fulfillment—life.

INSPIRATION Do you remember when you said “yes” to Jesus? How long ago was it? A few months, maybe years? I said “yes” to the Lord in November 1964 when I was a teenager. But I also said “yes” to Him just the other day.

After a row with Ken, I escaped to the shopping mall with a friend to get my mind off the quarrel. While meandering past a sales rack of blouses, I could no longer contain my self-pity. I began sobbing right next to a couple of mannequins. I couldn’t hide my face in a tissue, and my wheelchair was too big for me to escape behind several clothes racks. All I could do was sit there, cry, and stare at the mannequins with the plastic smiles.

little ones and your wives—also the stranger who *is* in your camp, from the
one who cuts your wood to the one who draws your water— 12 that you may
enter into covenant with the LORD your God, and into His oath, which the
LORD your God makes with you today, 13 that He may establish you today as a
people for Himself, and *that* He may be God to you, just as He has spoken to
you, and just as He has sworn to your fathers, to Abraham, Isaac, and Jacob.
14 "I make this covenant and this oath, not with you alone, 15 but with
him who stands here with us today before the LORD our God, as well as
with *him* who *is* not here with us today 16 (for you know that we dwelt in the
land of Egypt and that we came through the nations which you passed by,
17 and you saw their abominations and their idols which *were* among
them—wood and stone and silver and gold); 18 so that there may not be
among you man or woman or family or tribe, whose heart turns away
today from the LORD our God, to go *and* serve the gods of these nations,
and that there may not be among you a root bearing bitterness or wormwood; 19 and so it may not happen, when he hears the words of this curse,
that he blesses himself in his heart, saying, 'I shall have peace, even though
I follow the dictates[b] of my heart'—as though the drunkard could be included with the sober.
20 "The LORD would not spare him; for then the anger of the LORD and His
jealousy would burn against that man, and every curse that is written in
this book would settle on him, and the LORD would blot out his name from
under heaven. 21 And the LORD would separate him from all the tribes of Israel for adversity, according to all the curses of the covenant that are written in this Book of the Law, 22 so that the coming generation of your
children who rise up after you, and the foreigner who comes from a far
land, would say, when they see the plagues of that land and the sicknesses
which the LORD has laid on it:
23 'The whole land *is* brimstone, salt, and burning; it is not sown, nor
does it bear, nor does any grass grow there, like the overthrow of Sodom
and Gomorrah, Admah, and Zeboiim, which the LORD overthrew in His
anger and His wrath.' 24 All nations would say, 'Why has the LORD done so
to this land? What does the heat of this great anger mean?' 25 Then *people*
would say: 'Because they have forsaken the covenant of the LORD God of
their fathers, which He made with them when He brought them out of the
land of Egypt; 26 for they went and served other gods and worshiped them,
gods that they did not know and that He had not given to them. 27 Then the
anger of the LORD was aroused against this land, to bring on it every curse
that is written in this book. 28 And the LORD uprooted them from their land
in anger, in wrath, and in great indignation, and cast them into another
land, as *it is* this day.'
29 "The secret *things belong* to the LORD our God, but those *things which*
are revealed *belong* to us and to our children forever, that *we* may do all the
words of this law.

The Blessing of Returning to God

30 "Now it shall come to pass, when all these things come upon you,
the blessing and the curse which I have set before you, and you call
them to mind among all the nations where the LORD your God drives you,

29:19 *b* Or *stubbornness*

While wiping my eyes with the backside of my hand splint, I knew what I had to do. In between sobs, I said out loud what I've said so many times before, "Yes, Jesus, I choose you. I don't choose self-pity or resentment. I say 'yes' to you!"

Even though my face was still wet, my heart filled with peace. Nothing about my husband had changed. Shoppers on the other side of the store still picked through the racks . . . teenagers still ambled by, giggling, and eating popcorn . . . but *everything* was different because of my peaceful heart. Because I said "yes" to Jesus.

(From *Diamonds in the Dust* by Joni Eareckson Tada)

APPLICATION Have you made a commitment to God? He offers a relationship open to all people. Today, accept Jesus Christ as Lord of your life, then you can experience his promises.

EXPLORATION Commitment to God—Joshua 24:15; 1 Kings 18:21; 2 Kings 23:3; Matthew 19:27; Mark 12:30; Luke 9:23-24; John 6:67-68; Romans 12:1; Philippians 3:8-9.

LIFE LESSON

Deuteronomy 31:1-29

SITUATION God instructed the Levites to read his laws to the people. Joshua took over the leadership from Moses.

OBSERVATION God's word benefits our lives. Because we need reminders to obey, we need to read the Bible and apply it often.

INSPIRATION If we are to be Christians whose hearts beat and break with the rhythm of the heart of God, we must take on his whole Word wholeheartedly. That means reading the Bible, studying it, committing it to memory, allowing his words to dwell richly in our minds. It means understanding Scripture in its historic, classical context. It means accepting Christ as Savior and allowing his rule to permeate our thoughts, decisions, and actions.

If the church is to be the church in a darkening age, it must take its stand on the solid ground of biblical revelation and the historic confession of Christian truth. Another word for this is orthodoxy or dogma. While it seems the dry and dusty stuff of theologians, dogma is actually the only bulwark that allows the church to both judge itself and stand fast against the currents of cultural trends. As surely as we yield the ground staked out for the church, the barbarians will advance to claim the terrain.

(From *Against the Night: Living in the New Dark Ages* by Charles Colson)

APPLICATION Make God's Word a vital part of your day. Memorize a verse (try Deuteronomy 31:6) and think about it often.

EXPLORATION Scripture—Deuteronomy 17:18-20; Psalm 119:9-11; Isaiah 8:16; Jeremiah 23:28; Luke 4:1-13; 24:25-27; 2 Timothy 3:16-17; 2 Peter 1:20-21.

2and you return to the LORD your God and obey His voice, according to all
that I command you today, you and your children, with all your heart and
with all your soul, 3that the LORD your God will bring you back from captivity, and have compassion on you, and gather you again from all the nations where the LORD your God has scattered you. 4If *any* of you are driven
out to the farthest *parts* under heaven, from there the LORD your God will
gather you, and from there He will bring you. 5Then the LORD your God will
bring you to the land which your fathers possessed, and you shall possess
it. He will prosper you and multiply you more than your fathers. 6And the
LORD your God will circumcise your heart and the heart of your descendants, to love the LORD your God with all your heart and with all your soul,
that you may live.
7"Also the LORD your God will put all these curses on your enemies and
on those who hate you, who persecuted you. 8And you will again obey the
voice of the LORD and do all His commandments which I command you
today. 9The LORD your God will make you abound in all the work of your
hand, in the fruit of your body, in the increase of your livestock, and in the
produce of your land for good. For the LORD will again rejoice over you for
good as He rejoiced over your fathers, 10if you obey the voice of the LORD
your God, to keep His commandments and His statutes which are written
in this Book of the Law, *and* if you turn to the LORD your God with all your
heart and with all your soul.

The Choice of Life or Death

11"For this commandment which I command you today *is* not *too* mysterious for you, nor *is* it far off. 12It *is* not in heaven, that you should say,
'Who will ascend into heaven for us and bring it to us, that we may hear it
and do it?' 13Nor *is* it beyond the sea, that you should say, 'Who will go over
the sea for us and bring it to us, that we may hear it and do it?' 14But the
word *is* very near you, in your mouth and in your heart, that you may do it.
15"See, I have set before you today life and good, death and evil, 16in that
I command you today to love the LORD your God, to walk in His ways, and
to keep His commandments, His statutes, and His judgments, that you
may live and multiply; and the LORD your God will bless you in the land
which you go to possess. 17But if your heart turns away so that you do not
hear, and are drawn away, and worship other gods and serve them, 18I announce to you today that you shall surely perish; you shall not prolong
your days in the land which you cross over the Jordan to go in and possess.
19I call heaven and earth as witnesses today against you, *that* I have set before you life and death, blessing and cursing; therefore choose life, that
both you and your descendants may live; 20that you may love the LORD
your God, that you may obey His voice, and that you may cling to Him, for
He *is* your life and the length of your days; and that you may dwell in the
land which the LORD swore to your fathers, to Abraham, Isaac, and Jacob,
to give them."

Joshua the New Leader of Israel

31 Then Moses went and spoke these words to all Israel. 2And he said to
them: "I *am* one hundred and twenty years old today. I can no
longer go out and come in. Also the LORD has said to me, 'You shall not
cross over this Jordan.' 3The LORD your God Himself crosses over before

you; He will destroy these nations from before you, and you shall dispossess them. Joshua himself crosses over before you, just as the LORD has said. 4And the LORD will do to them as He did to Sihon and Og, the kings of the Amorites and their land, when He destroyed them. 5The LORD will give them over to you, that you may do to them according to every commandment which I have commanded you. 6Be strong and of good courage, do not fear nor be afraid of them; for the LORD your God, He *is* the One who goes with you. He will not leave you nor forsake you."

7Then Moses called Joshua and said to him in the sight of all Israel, "Be strong and of good courage, for you must go with this people to the land which the LORD has sworn to their fathers to give them, and you shall cause them to inherit it. 8And the LORD, He *is* the One who goes before you. He will be with you, He will not leave you nor forsake you; do not fear nor be dismayed."

The Law to Be Read Every Seven Years

9So Moses wrote this law and delivered it to the priests, the sons of Levi, who bore the ark of the covenant of the LORD, and to all the elders of Israel. 10And Moses commanded them, saying: "At the end of *every* seven years, at the appointed time in the year of release, at the Feast of Tabernacles, 11when all Israel comes to appear before the LORD your God in the place which He chooses, you shall read this law before all Israel in their hearing. 12Gather the people together, men and women and little ones, and the stranger who *is* within your gates, that they may hear and that they may learn to fear the LORD your God and carefully observe all the words of this law, 13and *that* their children, who have not known it, may hear and learn to fear the LORD your God as long as you live in the land which you cross the Jordan to possess."

Prediction of Israel's Rebellion

14Then the LORD said to Moses, "Behold, the days approach when you must die; call Joshua, and present yourselves in the tabernacle of meeting, that I may inaugurate him."

So Moses and Joshua went and presented themselves in the tabernacle of meeting. 15Now the LORD appeared at the tabernacle in a pillar of cloud, and the pillar of cloud stood above the door of the tabernacle.

16And the LORD said to Moses: "Behold, you will rest with your fathers; and this people will rise and play the harlot with the gods of the foreigners of the land, where they go *to be* among them, and they will forsake Me and break My covenant which I have made with them. 17Then My anger shall be aroused against them in that day, and I will forsake them, and I will hide My face from them, and they shall be devoured. And many evils and troubles shall befall them, so that they will say in that day, 'Have not these evils come upon us because our God *is* not among us?' 18And I will surely hide My face in that day because of all the evil which they have done, in that they have turned to other gods.

19"Now therefore, write down this song for yourselves, and teach it to the children of Israel; put it in their mouths, that this song may be a witness for Me against the children of Israel. 20When I have brought them to the land flowing with milk and honey, of which I swore to their fathers, and they have eaten and filled themselves and grown fat, then they will turn to other gods and serve them; and they will provoke Me and break My covenant. 21Then it shall be, when many evils and troubles have come upon them, that this song will testify against them as a witness; for it will not be forgotten in the mouths of their descendants, for I know the inclination of their behavior today, even before I have brought them to the land of which I swore *to give them.*"

22Therefore Moses wrote this song the same day, and taught it to the children of Israel. 23Then He inaugurated Joshua the son of Nun, and said, "Be strong and of good courage; for you shall bring the children of Israel into the land of which I swore to them, and I will be with you."

24So it was, when Moses had completed writing the words of this law in a book, when they were finished, 25that Moses commanded the Levites, who bore the ark of the covenant of the LORD, saying: 26"Take this Book of the Law, and put it beside the ark of the covenant of the LORD your God, that it may be there as a witness against you; 27for I know your rebellion and your stiff neck. *If* today, while I am yet alive with you, you have been rebellious against the LORD, then how much more after my death? 28Gather to me all the elders of your tribes, and your officers, that I may speak these words in their hearing and call heaven and earth to witness against them. 29For I know that after my death you will become utterly corrupt, and turn aside from the way which I have commanded you. And evil will befall you in the latter days, because you will do evil in the sight of the LORD, to provoke Him to anger through the work of your hands."

The Song of Moses

30Then Moses spoke in the hearing of all the assembly of Israel the words of this song until they were ended:

LIFE LESSON

Deuteronomy 31:30–32:52

SITUATION Moses' death was near. He gave his last sermon in the form of a song. He reminded the people of their history and warned them not to repeat their mistakes but instead to trust the Lord. He prophesied their future disloyalty and punishment, as well as God's forgiveness and mercy.

OBSERVATION We have no excuse for abandoning God. He protects, provides, and leads us like a shepherd. We must always put our faith and trust in Him.

INSPIRATION To know the will of God is the highest of all wisdom. Living in the center of God's will rules out all falseness of religion and puts the stamp of true sincerity upon our service to God. You can be miserable with much, if you are out of His will; but you can have peace in your heart with little, if you are in the will of God. You can be wretched with wealth and fame, out of His will; but you can have joy in obscurity, if you are in the will of God. You can have agony in good health, out of His will; but you can be happy in the midst of suffering, if you are in God's will. You can be miserable and defeated in the midst of acclaim, if you are out of His will; but you can be calm and at peace in the midst of persecution, as long as you are in the will of God. The Bible reveals that God has a plan for every life, and that if we live in constant fellowship with Him, He will direct and lead us in the fulfillment of His plan.
(From *Day by Day with Billy Graham* by Joan W. Brown)

APPLICATION Plans rarely turn out as intended. Accidents happen. People move, die, or grow cold toward us. What is your anchor in a changing world? Thank God today for the immense security he provides. Take comfort in God's promises to you.

EXPLORATION Trust—
Proverbs 3:5-6; Psalm 62:5-8;
Romans 3:21-29; Hebrews 3:15-4:3.

32 "Give ear, O heavens, and I will speak;
And hear, O earth, the words of my mouth.
2 Let my teaching drop as the rain,
My speech distill as the dew,
As raindrops on the tender herb,
And as showers on the grass.
3 For I proclaim the name of the LORD:
Ascribe greatness to our God.
4 *He is* the Rock, His work *is* perfect;
For all His ways *are* justice,
A God of truth and without injustice;
Righteous and upright *is* He.

5 "They have corrupted themselves;
They are not His children,
Because of their blemish:
A perverse and crooked generation.
6 Do you thus deal with the LORD,
O foolish and unwise people?
Is He not your Father, *who* bought you?
Has He not made you and established you?

7 "Remember the days of old,
Consider the years of many generations.
Ask your father, and he will show you;
Your elders, and they will tell you:
8 When the Most High divided their inheritance to the nations,
When He separated the sons of Adam,
He set the boundaries of the peoples
According to the number of the children of Israel.
9 For the LORD's portion *is* His people;
Jacob *is* the place of His inheritance.

10 "He found him in a desert land
And in the wasteland, a howling wilderness;
He encircled him, He instructed him,
He kept him as the apple of His eye.
11 As an eagle stirs up its nest,
Hovers over its young,
Spreading out its wings, taking them up,
Carrying them on its wings,
12 *So* the LORD alone led him,
And *there was* no foreign god with him.

13 "He made him ride in the heights of the earth,
That he might eat the produce of the fields;
He made him draw honey from the rock,
And oil from the flinty rock;
14 Curds from the cattle, and milk of the flock,
With fat of lambs;
And rams of the breed of Bashan, and goats,
With the choicest wheat;
And you drank wine, the blood of the grapes.

15 "But Jeshurun grew fat and kicked;
You grew fat, you grew thick,
You are obese!
Then he forsook God *who* made him,
And scornfully esteemed the Rock of his
salvation.
16 They provoked Him to jealousy with
foreign *gods;*
With abominations they provoked Him
to anger.
17 They sacrificed to demons, not to God,
To gods they did not know,
To new *gods,* new arrivals
That your fathers did not fear.
18 Of the Rock *who* begot you, you
are unmindful,
And have forgotten the God who fathered you.

19 "And when the LORD saw *it,* He spurned *them,*
Because of the provocation of His sons and
His daughters.
20 And He said: 'I will hide My face from them,
I will see what their end *will be,*
For they *are* a perverse generation,
Children in whom *is* no faith.
21 They have provoked Me to jealousy by
what is not God;
They have moved Me to anger by their
foolish idols.
But I will provoke them to jealousy by *those*
who are not a nation;
I will move them to anger by a foolish nation.
22 For a fire is kindled in My anger,
And shall burn to the lowest hell;
It shall consume the earth with her increase,
And set on fire the foundations of
the mountains.

23 'I will heap disasters on them;
I will spend My arrows on them.
24 *They shall be* wasted with hunger,
Devoured by pestilence and bitter destruction;
I will also send against them the teeth
of beasts,
With the poison of serpents of the dust.
25 The sword shall destroy outside;
There shall be terror within
For the young man and virgin,
The nursing child with the man of gray hairs.
26 I would have said, "I will dash them in pieces,
I will make the memory of them to cease from
among men,"
27 Had I not feared the wrath of the enemy,
Lest their adversaries should misunderstand,
Lest they should say, "Our hand *is* high;
And it is not the LORD who has done all this." '

28 "For they *are* a nation void of counsel,
Nor *is there any* understanding in them.
29 Oh, that they were wise, *that* they
understood this,
That they would consider their latter end!
30 How could one chase a thousand,
And two put ten thousand to flight,
Unless their Rock had sold them,
And the LORD had surrendered them?
31 For their rock *is* not like our Rock,
Even our enemies themselves *being* judges.
32 For their vine *is* of the vine of Sodom
And of the fields of Gomorrah;
Their grapes *are* grapes of gall,
Their clusters *are* bitter.
33 Their wine *is* the poison of serpents,
And the cruel venom of cobras.

34 '*Is* this not laid up in store with Me,
Sealed up among My treasures?
35 Vengeance is Mine, and recompense;
Their foot shall slip in *due* time;
For the day of their calamity *is* at hand,
And the things to come hasten upon them.'

36 "For the LORD will judge His people
And have compassion on His servants,
When He sees that *their* power is gone,
And *there is* no one *remaining,* bond or free.
37 He will say: 'Where *are* their gods,
The rock in which they sought refuge?
38 Who ate the fat of their sacrifices,
And drank the wine of their drink offering?
Let them rise and help you,
And be your refuge.

39 'Now see that I, *even* I, *am* He,
And *there is* no God besides Me;
I kill and I make alive;
I wound and I heal;
Nor *is there any* who can deliver from
My hand.
40 For I raise My hand to heaven,
And say, "*As* I live forever,
41 If I whet My glittering sword,
And My hand takes hold on judgment,
I will render vengeance to My enemies,
And repay those who hate Me.

LIFE LESSON

Deuteronomy 33:1–34:12

SITUATION These blessings pointed to a great and glorious future for the nation of Israel. Each blessing drew out the unique talents or characteristics of each tribe. All the blessings were necessary to fulfill God's plan for the nation.

OBSERVATION God gives blessings to people according to his will. Be grateful for all the blessings God has given you.

INSPIRATION David and Svea Flood, a young Swedish missionary couple, were on fire for God when they arrived in Africa in 1921. They were determined that they would do pioneer work among unreached people, but the Africans were hostile and the climate was deadly. Soon after the birth of their second child, Svea died. The pain was too much for David. Doubts consumed him. Why had God let them down when they had sacrificed everything for Him? Had God forgotten them? Were they on a fool's errand? For all their work they had only one convert, and he was a child.

David was in this mindset when he left Africa with his young son, leaving behind his baby girl who was too weak to travel. A missionary couple took her in and when they subsequently died, she was passed on to another missionary couple, who later raised her in America. In the meantime, David, who was living in Sweden, turned his back on the church and his thoughts were far from the spiritual realm. After his second marriage dissolved, he began living with a mistress. He thought little about the daughter whom he had not seen since infancy.

42 I will make My arrows drunk with blood,
And My sword shall devour flesh,
With the blood of the slain and the captives,
From the heads of the leaders of the enemy."'

43 "Rejoice, O Gentiles, *with* His people;[c]
For He will avenge the blood of His servants,
And render vengeance to His adversaries;
He will provide atonement for His land *and* His people."

44So Moses came with Joshua[d] the son of Nun and spoke all the words of
this song in the hearing of the people. 45Moses finished speaking all these
words to all Israel, 46and he said to them: "Set your hearts on all the words
which I testify among you today, which you shall command your children
to be careful to observe—all the words of this law. 47For it *is* not a futile
thing for you, because it *is* your life, and by this word you shall prolong
your days in the land which you cross over the Jordan to possess."

Moses to Die on Mount Nebo

48Then the LORD spoke to Moses that very same day, saying: 49"Go up
this mountain of the Abarim, Mount Nebo, which *is* in the land of Moab,
across from Jericho; view the land of Canaan, which I give to the children
of Israel as a possession; 50and die on the mountain which you ascend,
and be gathered to your people, just as Aaron your brother died on Mount
Hor and was gathered to his people; 51because you trespassed against Me
among the children of Israel at the waters of Meribah Kadesh, in the
Wilderness of Zin, because you did not hallow Me in the midst of the children of Israel. 52Yet you shall see the land before *you,* though you shall not
go there, into the land which I am giving to the children of Israel."

Moses' Final Blessing on Israel

33 Now this *is* the blessing with which Moses the man of God blessed
the children of Israel before his death. 2And he said:

"The LORD came from Sinai,
And dawned on them from Seir;
He shone forth from Mount Paran,
And He came with ten thousands of saints;
From His right hand
Came a fiery law for them.
3 Yes, He loves the people;
All His saints *are* in Your hand;
They sit down at Your feet;
Everyone receives Your words.
4 Moses commanded a law for us,
A heritage of the congregation of Jacob.
5 And He was King in Jeshurun,
When the leaders of the people were gathered,
All the tribes of Israel together.

32:43 [c] A Dead Sea Scroll fragment adds *And let all the gods (angels) worship Him* (compare Septuagint and Hebrews 1:6).
32:44 [d] Hebrew *Hoshea* (compare Numbers 13:8, 16)

6 "Let Reuben live, and not die,
Nor let his men be few."

7 And this he said of Judah:

"Hear, LORD, the voice of Judah,
And bring him to his people;
Let his hands be sufficient for him,
And may You be a help against his enemies."

8 And of Levi he said:

"*Let* Your Thummim and Your Urim *be* with Your holy one,
Whom You tested at Massah,
And with whom You contended at the waters of Meribah,
9 Who says of his father and mother,
'I have not seen them';
Nor did he acknowledge his brothers,
Or know his own children;
For they have observed Your word
And kept Your covenant.
10 They shall teach Jacob Your judgments,
And Israel Your law.
They shall put incense before You,
And a whole burnt sacrifice on Your altar.
11 Bless his substance, LORD,
And accept the work of his hands;
Strike the loins of those who rise against him,
And of those who hate him, that they rise not again."

12 Of Benjamin he said:

"The beloved of the LORD shall dwell in safety by Him,
Who shelters him all the day long;
And he shall dwell between His shoulders."

13 And of Joseph he said:

"Blessed of the LORD *is* his land,
With the precious things of heaven, with the dew,
And the deep lying beneath,
14 With the precious fruits of the sun,
With the precious produce of the months,
15 With the best things of the ancient mountains,
With the precious things of the everlasting hills,
16 With the precious things of the earth and its fullness,
And the favor of Him who dwelt in the bush.
Let *the blessing* come 'on the head of Joseph,
And on the crown of the head of him *who was* separate
from his brothers.'[e]
17 His glory *is like* a firstborn bull,
And his horns *like* the horns of the wild ox;
Together with them
He shall push the peoples

33:16 [e] Genesis 49:26

His daughter Aggie, however, thought about him often. She had learned about the work he and her mother had begun in Africa, and she wanted to talk about it with him. After high school and further study at North Central Bible College, she married Dewey Hurst and together they served in various ministries with the Assemblies of God. But she longed to visit her father and her homeland of Sweden.

Finally, she was able to make the trip to Stockholm where she found her seventy-three-year-old bedridden father in a run-down apartment with liquor bottles lining the window sills. She took him in her arms and told him she loved him and that God had taken care of her through the years.

Indeed, God had done far more than that. There in his grimy bed with tobacco juice running down his unshaven face, her father heard for the first time that the little boy who had been converted through his and Svea's ministry had won his village of 600 people to Christ, and had gone on to be a great leader in the church. It was an emotional moment for him, and through his daughter's urging, he recommitted his life to God. There was joy in that tiny apartment that day, and neither of them could know that David had only six months more to live.

(From *Stories of Faith* by Ruth A. Tucker)

APPLICATION God wants to love, protect, and bless us if only we will let him. Our pride, envy, stubbornness, and disobedience deprive us of God's eternal blessings. Confess your sins before God. Don't let anything hinder your relationship with him.

EXPLORATION Blessings—1 Samuel 2:21; 2 Kings 4:6; 5:9-15; Nehemiah 9:35; Psalm 34:1; 95:11; Ephesians 3:14-15; James 2:2-4.

To the ends of the earth;
They *are* the ten thousands of Ephraim,
And they *are* the thousands of Manasseh."

18 And of Zebulun he said:

"Rejoice, Zebulun, in your going out,
And Issachar in your tents!
19 They shall call the peoples *to* the mountain;
There they shall offer sacrifices of righteousness;
For they shall partake *of* the abundance of the seas
And *of* treasures hidden in the sand."

20 And of Gad he said:

"Blessed *is* he who enlarges Gad;
He dwells as a lion,
And tears the arm and the crown of his head.
21 He provided the first *part* for himself,
Because a lawgiver's portion was reserved there.
He came *with* the heads of the people;
He administered the justice of the LORD,
And His judgments with Israel."

22 And of Dan he said:

"Dan *is* a lion's whelp;
He shall leap from Bashan."

23 And of Naphtali he said:

"O Naphtali, satisfied with favor,
And full of the blessing of the LORD,
Possess the west and the south."

24 And of Asher he said:

"Asher *is* most blessed of sons;
Let him be favored by his brothers,
And let him dip his foot in oil.
25 Your sandals *shall be* iron and bronze;
As your days, *so shall* your strength *be*.
26 "*There is* no one like the God of Jeshurun,
Who rides the heavens to help you,
And in His excellency on the clouds.
27 The eternal God *is your* refuge,
And underneath *are* the everlasting arms;
He will thrust out the enemy from before you,
And will say, 'Destroy!'
28 Then Israel shall dwell in safety,
The fountain of Jacob alone,
In a land of grain and new wine;
His heavens shall also drop dew.
29 Happy *are* you, O Israel!
Who *is* like you, a people saved by the LORD,
The shield of your help
And the sword of your majesty!
Your enemies shall submit to you,
And you shall tread down their high places."

Moses Dies on Mount Nebo

34 Then Moses went up from the plains of Moab
to Mount Nebo, to the top of Pisgah, which is
across from Jericho. And the LORD showed him all the
land of Gilead as far as Dan, 2 all Naphtali and the land
of Ephraim and Manasseh, all the land of Judah as far
as the Western Sea,[f] 3 the South, and the plain of the
Valley of Jericho, the city of palm trees, as far as Zoar.
4 Then the LORD said to him, "This *is* the land of which
I swore to give Abraham, Isaac, and Jacob, saying, 'I
will give it to your descendants.' I have caused you to
see *it* with your eyes, but you shall not cross over
there."

5 So Moses the servant of the LORD died there in the
land of Moab, according to the word of the LORD.
6 And He buried him in a valley in the land of Moab,
opposite Beth Peor; but no one knows his grave to
this day. 7 Moses *was* one hundred and twenty years
old when he died. His eyes were not dim nor his natural vigor diminished. 8 And the children of Israel
wept for Moses in the plains of Moab thirty days. So
the days of weeping *and* mourning for Moses ended.

9 Now Joshua the son of Nun was full of the spirit of
wisdom, for Moses had laid his hands on him; so the
children of Israel heeded him, and did as the LORD
had commanded Moses.

10 But since then there has not arisen in Israel a
prophet like Moses, whom the LORD knew face to face,
11 in all the signs and wonders which the LORD sent
him to do in the land of Egypt, before Pharaoh, before
all his servants, and in all his land, 12 and by all that
mighty power and all the great terror which Moses
performed in the sight of all Israel.

34:2 [f] That is, the Mediterranean

The Book of JOSHUA

INTRODUCTION

May I describe a few battles?

Let's say that you have a problem with a person—a rotten person. A scoundrel who has taken advantage of your kindness. Because of him you have less money, more headaches, and a bitter heart.

Let's also say that you've got the goods on this guy. Caught him. Aha! Red-handed. You can turn him in. Make a spectacle. Get even and get out. Give him what he deserves.

But something won't let you. A verse from your past tethers your heart. "Vengeance is mine," says the Lord. "I will repay."

Within you the battle rages. *Let vengeance be mine, Lord,* you pray. *Just once. Let me get even.* But the Word won't let you. And with time, you drop your fists to your side and just trust.

Here's another battle.

Let's say you have a problem with money. Every month you just barely make it. Each paycheck is spent before it's cashed. If just one month you could get a break. Just some cushion. That's all you need.

Poof, your prayer is answered. Unexpected bonus. An extra month's salary. Finally, some breathing room. First, pay off the credit card, next repay my sister, then get the bumper fixed and . . . uh-oh—my giving. "Surely God doesn't want me to give 10 percent of the bonus? I mean, I give every month . . . Surely, he'll understand if I use this for something else . . ."

But the words challenge faintly yet firmly, "Honor the Lord with the firstfruits of your labor . . ." Within you the battle rages. One side says, "Believe." The other, "Be real." Finally, a truce is called and a white flag is waved and a check is written and placed in the plate.

But even as you give, you confess, "Doesn't make sense, but because you say so . . ."

Let's go one more. This time let's really stretch it. Let's say you are a general. A General in the Israeli Army. Moses is dead, the Jordan has been crossed, the mantle passed, and you are wearing it.

God has promised that you will take Jericho. But as you look at the city, you have to wonder . . . the walls are high. The people are armed. The challenge is great.

But God has a plan.

You can't wait to hear it. "Surely, he'll give us more soldiers, stronger weapons, mightier swords. His plan must include this and more."

So you sit and listen as God explains. As he talks you are stunned, "What? Walk around the city seven times, blow some trumpets and . . . Wait a minute, God, this doesn't make sense."

The Book of Joshua is a book of battles. A book for soldiers. A book for people who would dare win God's way. What applied then, applies today. It is the faithful who conquer. Those who follow the strategy win, those who don't—don't.

LIFE LESSON

Joshua 1:1–2:24

SITUATION The story of Joshua begins after the death of Moses. God appointed Joshua to lead the Israelites across the Jordan River into the land of Canaan.

OBSERVATION God establishes leaders to fulfill his plan. God brings success when we follow his appointed leader.

INSPIRATION Leaders don't lead forever, even godly leaders like Moses. There comes a time in every ministry when God calls for a new beginning with a new generation and new leadership. Except for Joshua and Caleb, the old generation of Jews had perished during the nation's wanderings in the wilderness; and Joshua was commissioned to lead the new generation into a new challenge: entering and conquering the Promised Land. "God buries His workmen, but His work goes on." It was God who had chosen Joshua, and everybody in Israel knew that he was their new leader.

Over the years I've seen churches and parachurch ministries flounder and almost destroy themselves in futile attempts to embalm the past and escape the future. Their theme song was "As it was in the beginning, so shall it ever be, world without end." Often I've prayed with and for godly Christian leaders who were criticized, persecuted, and attacked

God's Commission to Joshua

After the death of Moses the servant of the LORD, it came to pass
that the LORD spoke to Joshua the son of Nun, Moses' assistant,
saying: 2"Moses My servant is dead. Now therefore, arise, go
over this Jordan, you and all this people, to the land which I am
giving to them—the children of Israel. 3Every place that the sole of your
foot will tread upon I have given you, as I said to Moses. 4From the wilderness and this Lebanon as far as the great river, the River Euphrates, all the
land of the Hittites, and to the Great Sea toward the going down of the sun,
shall be your territory. 5No man shall *be able to* stand before you all the days
of your life; as I was with Moses, *so* I will be with you. I will not leave you
nor forsake you. 6Be strong and of good courage, for to this people you shall
divide as an inheritance the land which I swore to their fathers to give
them. 7Only be strong and very courageous, that you may observe to do
according to all the law which Moses My servant commanded you; do not
turn from it to the right hand or to the left, that you may prosper wherever
you go. 8This Book of the Law shall not depart from your mouth, but you
shall meditate in it day and night, that you may observe to do according to
all that is written in it. For then you will make your way prosperous, and
then you will have good success. 9Have I not commanded you? Be strong
and of good courage; do not be afraid, nor be dismayed, for the LORD your
God *is* with you wherever you go."

The Order to Cross the Jordan

10Then Joshua commanded the officers of the people, saying, 11"Pass
through the camp and command the people, saying, 'Prepare provisions
for yourselves, for within three days you will cross over this Jordan, to go
in to possess the land which the LORD your God is giving you to possess.' "
12And to the Reubenites, the Gadites, and half the tribe of Manasseh
Joshua spoke, saying, 13"Remember the word which Moses the servant of
the LORD commanded you, saying, 'The LORD your God is giving you rest
and is giving you this land.' 14Your wives, your little ones, and your livestock shall remain in the land which Moses gave you on this side of the
Jordan. But you shall pass before your brethren armed, all your mighty
men of valor, and help them, 15until the LORD has given your brethren rest,
as He *gave* you, and they also have taken possession of the land which the
LORD your God is giving them. Then you shall return to the land of your
possession and enjoy it, which Moses the LORD's servant gave you on this
side of the Jordan toward the sunrise."

16So they answered Joshua, saying, "All that you command us we will
do, and wherever you send us we will go. 17Just as we heeded Moses in all
things, so we will heed you. Only the LORD your God be with you, as He was
with Moses. 18Whoever rebels against your command and does not heed
your words, in all that you command him, shall be put to death. Only be
strong and of good courage."

Rahab Hides the Spies

2 Now Joshua the son of Nun sent out two men from Acacia Grove[a] to
spy secretly, saying, "Go, view the land, especially Jericho."

So they went, and came to the house of a harlot named Rahab, and
lodged there. 2And it was told the king of Jericho, saying, "Behold, men have

2:1 [a] Hebrew *Shittim*

come here tonight from the children of Israel to search out the country."
3So the king of Jericho sent to Rahab, saying, "Bring out the men who
have come to you, who have entered your house, for they have come to
search out all the country."
4Then the woman took the two men and hid them. So she said, "Yes, the
men came to me, but I did not know where they *were* from. 5And it happened as the gate was being shut, when it was dark, that the men went out.
Where the men went I do not know; pursue them quickly, for you may
overtake them." 6(But she had brought them up to the roof and hidden
them with the stalks of flax, which she had laid in order on the roof.) 7Then
the men pursued them by the road to the Jordan, to the fords. And as soon
as those who pursued them had gone out, they shut the gate.
8Now before they lay down, she came up to them on the roof, 9and said
to the men: "I know that the LORD has given you the land, that the terror of
you has fallen on us, and that all the inhabitants of the land are fainthearted because of you. 10For we have heard how the LORD dried up the
water of the Red Sea for you when you came out of Egypt, and what you
did to the two kings of the Amorites who *were* on the other side of the Jordan, Sihon and Og, whom you utterly destroyed. 11And as soon as we
heard *these things,* our hearts melted; neither did there remain any more
courage in anyone because of you, for the LORD your God, He *is* God in
heaven above and on earth beneath. 12Now therefore, I beg you, swear to
me by the LORD, since I have shown you kindness, that you also will show
kindness to my father's house, and give me a true token, 13and spare my
father, my mother, my brothers, my sisters, and all that they have, and deliver our lives from death."
14So the men answered her, "Our lives for yours, if none of you tell this
business of ours. And it shall be, when the LORD has given us the land, that
we will deal kindly and truly with you."
15Then she let them down by a rope through the window, for her house
was on the city wall; she dwelt on the wall. 16And she said to them, "Get to
the mountain, lest the pursuers meet you. Hide there three days, until the
pursuers have returned. Afterward you may go your way."
17So the men said to her: "We *will be* blameless of this oath of yours
which you have made us swear, 18unless, *when* we come into the land, you
bind this line of scarlet cord in the window through which you let us down,
and unless you bring your father, your mother, your brothers, and all your
father's household to your own home. 19So it shall be *that* whoever goes outside the doors of your house into the street, his blood *shall be* on his own
head, and we *will be* guiltless. And whoever is with you in the house, his
blood *shall be* on our head if a hand is laid on him. 20And if you tell this business of ours, then we will be free from your oath which you made us swear."
21Then she said, "According to your words, so *be* it." And she sent them
away, and they departed. And she bound the scarlet cord in the window.
22They departed and went to the mountain, and stayed there three days
until the pursuers returned. The pursuers sought *them* all along the way,
but did not find *them.* 23So the two men returned, descended from the
mountain, and crossed over; and they came to Joshua the son of Nun, and
told him all that had befallen them. 24And they said to Joshua, "Truly the
LORD has delivered all the land into our hands, for indeed all the inhabitants of the country are fainthearted because of us."

simply because, like Joshua, they had a divine commission to lead a ministry into new fields of conquest; but the people would not follow. . . .

A wise leader doesn't completely abandon the past but builds on it as he or she moves towards the future. Moses is mentioned fifty-seven times in the Book of Joshua, evidence that Joshua respected Moses and what he had done for Israel. Joshua worshipped the same God that Moses had worshipped, and he obeyed the same Word that Moses had given to the nation. There was continuity from one leader to the next, but there wasn't always conformity; for each leader is different and must maintain his or her individuality. Twice in these verses Moses is called God's servant, but Joshua was also the servant of God (24:29). The important thing is not the servant but the Master.

(From *Be Strong* by Warren Wiersbe)

APPLICATION Think of church leaders who have recently taken on new responsibilities and pray for them; ask for the Lord's strength and wisdom in their ministry. Then follow up your prayers with words and deeds of encouragement and help.

EXPLORATION Respect for Leaders—Philippians 2:29-30; 1 Thessalonians 5:12-13; 1 Timothy 5:17-19; Hebrews 13:17.

LIFE LESSON

Joshua 3:1–5:12

SITUATION As God guided the Israelites into the Promised Land he instructed them to purify themselves before crossing the Jordan River. In another powerful miracle, God stopped the Jordan River in flood stage so that the people easily crossed into Canaan. The Ark of the Covenant and the priests led this procession.

OBSERVATION God guided the Israelites into the Promised Land as they continued to trust in him.

INSPIRATION In reading carefully through the New Testament to see just what kind of an experience you can expect, I find that the New Testament sets forth only one. There is just one experience for which you can look—only one feeling you can expect—and that is the experience of faith. Believing is an experience as real as any experience, yet many are looking for something more—some dramatic sensation that will bring a physical thrill, while others look for some spectacular manifestation. Many have been told to look for such sensations, but the Bible says that a man is "justified by faith" and not by feeling. A man is saved by trusting in the finished work of Christ on the cross and not by physical excitement or religious ecstasy.

Israel Crosses the Jordan

3 Then Joshua rose early in the morning; and they set out from Acacia
Grove[b] and came to the Jordan, he and all the children of Israel, and
lodged there before they crossed over. 2So it was, after three days, that the
officers went through the camp; 3and they commanded the people, saying, "When you see the ark of the covenant of the LORD your God, and the
priests, the Levites, bearing it, then you shall set out from your place and
go after it. 4Yet there shall be a space between you and it, about two thousand cubits by measure. Do not come near it, that you may know the way
by which you must go, for you have not passed *this* way before."
5And Joshua said to the people, "Sanctify yourselves, for tomorrow the
LORD will do wonders among you." 6Then Joshua spoke to the priests, saying, "Take up the ark of the covenant and cross over before the people."
So they took up the ark of the covenant and went before the people.
7And the LORD said to Joshua, "This day I will begin to exalt you in the
sight of all Israel, that they may know that, as I was with Moses, *so* I will be
with you. 8You shall command the priests who bear the ark of the
covenant, saying, 'When you have come to the edge of the water of the Jordan, you shall stand in the Jordan.'"
9So Joshua said to the children of Israel, "Come here, and hear the
words of the LORD your God." 10And Joshua said, "By this you shall know
that the living God *is* among you, and *that* He will without fail drive out
from before you the Canaanites and the Hittites and the Hivites and the
Perizzites and the Girgashites and the Amorites and the Jebusites: 11Be-
hold, the ark of the covenant of the Lord of all the earth is crossing over before you into the Jordan. 12Now therefore, take for yourselves twelve men
from the tribes of Israel, one man from every tribe. 13And it shall come to
pass, as soon as the soles of the feet of the priests who bear the ark of the
LORD, the Lord of all the earth, shall rest in the waters of the Jordan, *that* the
waters of the Jordan shall be cut off, the waters that come down from upstream, and they shall stand as a heap."
14So it was, when the people set out from their camp to cross over the
Jordan, with the priests bearing the ark of the covenant before the people,
15and as those who bore the ark came to the Jordan, and the feet of the
priests who bore the ark dipped in the edge of the water (for the Jordan
overflows all its banks during the whole time of harvest), 16that the waters
which came down from upstream stood *still, and* rose in a heap very far
away at Adam, the city that *is* beside Zaretan. So the waters that went down
into the Sea of the Arabah, the Salt Sea, failed, *and* were cut off; and the
people crossed over opposite Jericho. 17Then the priests who bore the ark
of the covenant of the LORD stood firm on dry ground in the midst of the
Jordan; and all Israel crossed over on dry ground, until all the people had
crossed completely over the Jordan.

The Memorial Stones

4 And it came to pass, when all the people had completely crossed over
the Jordan, that the LORD spoke to Joshua, saying: 2"Take for yourselves
twelve men from the people, one man from every tribe, 3and command

3:1 [b] Hebrew *Shittim*

GRACE

What is the grace of God? The grace of God says you serve God *because* you're saved, not in order to *be* saved. You love people *because* you're saved, and not in order to *be* saved. You're not trying to keep a legalistic system, you're responding to a system of love and peace.

What is grace? It's what someone gives us out of the goodness of his heart, not out of the perfection of ours. The story of grace is the good news that says that when we come, he gives. That's what grace is.

Grace is a pleasant surprise. Grace is a kind gesture. Grace is something you did not expect. It is something you certainly could never earn. But grace is something you'd never turn down.

You know what happens when someone sees the grace of God? When someone really tastes the forgiving and liberating grace of God? Someone who tastes God's grace is the hardest worker, the most morally pure individual, and the person most willing to forgive.

Always remember that Jesus says, "My grace is deeper than your sins."

FATHER, how holy and great is your promise. You've been so good to us, but somehow, Father, we find things about which to complain even though we've been given life eternal. Renew our vision; help us to see heaven. Help us to be busy about the right business—the business of serving you.

FREEDOM

Freedom is an elusive thing—it's the carrot on the end of the stick that causes a lot of us mules to do the things we do. Jesus spoke of freedom, but he spoke of a different kind of freedom: the type of freedom that comes not through power but through submission. Not through control but through surrender. Not through possessions but through open hands.

God wants to emancipate his people; he wants to set them free. He wants his people to be not slaves but sons. He wants them governed not by law but by love.

We have been liberated from our own guilt and our own legalism. We have the freedom to pray and the freedom to love the God of our heart. And we have been forgiven by the only one who could condemn us. We are truly free!

THANK YOU *for setting us free. May we be spurred on by your love to do great works, yet never substituting those works for your great grace. May we always hear your voice. Keep us free from our own legalism, our own systems. Keep us amazed and mesmerized by what you have done for us.*

GOD

Do you wonder where you can go for encouragement and motivation? Go back to that moment when you first saw the love of Jesus Christ. Remember the day when you were separated from Christ? You knew only guilt and confusion and then—a light. Someone opened a door and light came into your darkness, and you said in your heart, "I am redeemed!"

Can you recall the moment you first believed? You felt a flame in your heart that was dancing so hot that you knew even death couldn't put it out. Is that flame still there? If it is, then fan it, bring it to life. Stand face to face with the only hope this earth knows.

Jesus described for his followers what he came to do. He came to build a relationship with people. He came to take away enmity, to take away the strife, to take away the isolation that existed between God and man. Once he bridged that, once he overcame that, he said, "I will call you friends."

I've noticed that those who serve God most joyfully are the ones who know him most personally. Those who are quickest to speak about Jesus are those who realize how great has been their own redemption.

God is an exalted friend, a holy Father, and an elevated King. How do we approach him—as king, as father, or as friend? The answer: yes!

GOD OF HEAVEN, we see your hand stretching as far as the east is from the west. Put your hands and your arms around us and embrace us, Father. Take us home. May we be yours forever.

REPENTANCE

No one is happier than the one who has sincerely repented of wrong. Repentance is the decision to turn from selfish desires and seek God. It is a genuine, sincere regret that creates sorrow and moves us to admit wrong and desire to do better.

Genuine repentance is a moving condition of the heart that is testified and demonstrated by our deeds. It's an inward conviction that expresses itself in outward actions.

You look at the love of God and you can't believe he's loved you like he has, and it motivates you to change your life. That is the nature of repentance.

YOU'VE GIVEN *us such a great promise, the promise of salvation. Forgive us, Father, when we sometimes put more hope in the things of this earth than in the incredible promises of your heaven.*

them, saying, 'Take for yourselves twelve stones from here, out of the
midst of the Jordan, from the place where the priests' feet stood firm. You
shall carry them over with you and leave them in the lodging place where
you lodge tonight.' "
4Then Joshua called the twelve men whom he had appointed from the
children of Israel, one man from every tribe; 5and Joshua said to them:
"Cross over before the ark of the LORD your God into the midst of the Jordan, and each one of you take up a stone on his shoulder, according to the
number of the tribes of the children of Israel, 6that this may be a sign
among you when your children ask in time to come, saying, 'What do
these stones *mean* to you?' 7Then you shall answer them that the waters of
the Jordan were cut off before the ark of the covenant of the LORD; when it
crossed over the Jordan, the waters of the Jordan were cut off. And these
stones shall be for a memorial to the children of Israel forever."
8And the children of Israel did so, just as Joshua commanded, and took
up twelve stones from the midst of the Jordan, as the LORD had spoken to
Joshua, according to the number of the tribes of the children of Israel, and
carried them over with them to the place where they lodged, and laid them
down there. 9Then Joshua set up twelve stones in the midst of the Jordan,
in the place where the feet of the priests who bore the ark of the covenant
stood; and they are there to this day.
10So the priests who bore the ark stood in the midst of the Jordan until
everything was finished that the LORD had commanded Joshua to speak to
the people, according to all that Moses had commanded Joshua; and the
people hurried and crossed over. 11Then it came to pass, when all the people
had completely crossed over, that the ark of the LORD and the priests
crossed over in the presence of the people. 12And the men of Reuben, the
men of Gad, and half the tribe of Manasseh crossed over armed before the
children of Israel, as Moses had spoken to them. 13About forty thousand
prepared for war crossed over before the LORD for battle, to the plains of
Jericho. 14On that day the LORD exalted Joshua in the sight of all Israel; and
they feared him, as they had feared Moses, all the days of his life.
15Then the LORD spoke to Joshua, saying, 16"Command the priests who
bear the ark of the Testimony to come up from the Jordan." 17Joshua
therefore commanded the priests, saying, "Come up from the Jordan."
18And it came to pass, when the priests who bore the ark of the covenant of
the LORD had come from the midst of the Jordan, *and* the soles of the
priests' feet touched the dry land, that the waters of the Jordan returned to
their place and overflowed all its banks as before.
19Now the people came up from the Jordan on the tenth *day* of the first
month, and they camped in Gilgal on the east border of Jericho. 20And
those twelve stones which they took out of the Jordan, Joshua set up in
Gilgal. 21Then he spoke to the children of Israel, saying: "When your children ask their fathers in time to come, saying, 'What *are* these stones?'
22then you shall let your children know, saying, 'Israel crossed over this
Jordan on dry land'; 23for the LORD your God dried up the waters of the Jordan before you until you had crossed over, as the LORD your God did to the
Red Sea, which He dried up before us until we had crossed over, 24that all
the peoples of the earth may know the hand of the LORD, that it *is* mighty,
that you may fear the LORD your God forever."

But you may say to me, "What about feeling? Is there no place in saving faith for any feeling?" Certainly there is room for feeling in saving faith, but we are not saved by it. Whatever feeling there may be is only the result of saving faith, but it in itself is not what does the saving! . . .

Finally, someone may say, "I believe the historic facts of the gospel, but still I am not saved." Perhaps so, for the faith that saves has one distinguishing quality—saving faith is a faith that produces obedience, it is a faith that brings about a way of life. Some have quite successfully imitated this way of life for a time, but for those who trust Christ for salvation, that faith brings about in them a desire to live out that inward experience of faith. It is a power that results in godly living and surrender.

(From *Peace with God* by Billy Graham)

APPLICATION What steps are you taking to fulfill God's will? Often our efforts seem uncertain or risky. Put your trust in God to guide.

EXPLORATION Faith Defined—Matthew 13:44; Romans 10:9; 12:3; Ephesians 1:11; 3:16; 6:16; 1 Thessalonians 1:3; 5:8; Hebrews 11:1; Jude 20-21.

LIFE LESSON

Joshua 5:13–6:27

SITUATION Although God had promised him victory, Joshua stared at an impenetrable city. God intervened and the Israelites conquered the city. Joshua believed God and led the Israelites in victorious assault.

OBSERVATION No defense is too strong for God. No barrier will keep God from fulfilling his word.

INSPIRATION When we call God the Almighty, we call Him by His name because He has all might. He is all-powerful. There is nothing that He cannot do. He is the Lord God omnipotent. . . .

The power of God is seen in the creation of the universe and the creation of human kind. He created the heavens and earth instantly, out of nothing, without tools, by a word. Think of the power that spangled the heavens with stars, planets, and galaxies that are spread out in space for billions of light-years. Consider the power that creates the human body in the mother's womb. Then think of the power that holds matter together, the power of God in sustaining the universe, in maintaining the planets in their orbits, in preserving His creatures, and in answering prayer.

We see divine omnipotence in floods, fires, earthquakes, volcanic eruptions, storms, winds, and waves. We see it in the salvation of a sinner, in the healing of diseases, in the judgement of the wicked. . . .

Our hearts should be filled with worship and the fear of the Lord when we meditate on the omnipotence of our Lord. . . . There are very practical lessons to be learned from the omnipotence of God. The first lesson is that an individual cannot fight suc-

The Second Generation Circumcised

5 So it was, when all the kings of the Amorites who *were* on the west side
of the Jordan, and all the kings of the Canaanites who *were* by the sea,
heard that the LORD had dried up the waters of the Jordan from before the
children of Israel until we[c] had crossed over, that their heart melted; and
there was no spirit in them any longer because of the children of Israel.
2At that time the LORD said to Joshua, "Make flint knives for yourself,
and circumcise the sons of Israel again the second time." 3So Joshua made
flint knives for himself, and circumcised the sons of Israel at the hill of the
foreskins.[d] 4And this *is* the reason why Joshua circumcised them: All the
people who came out of Egypt *who were* males, all the men of war, had
died in the wilderness on the way, after they had come out of Egypt. 5For all
the people who came out had been circumcised, but all the people born in
the wilderness, on the way as they came out of Egypt, had not been circumcised. 6For the children of Israel walked forty years in the wilderness,
till all the people *who were* men of war, who came out of Egypt, were consumed, because they did not obey the voice of the LORD—to whom the
LORD swore that He would not show them the land which the LORD had
sworn to their fathers that He would give us, "a land flowing with milk and
honey."[e] 7Then Joshua circumcised their sons *whom* He raised up in their
place; for they were uncircumcised, because they had not been circumcised on the way.
8So it was, when they had finished circumcising all the people, that they
stayed in their places in the camp till they were healed. 9Then the LORD said
to Joshua, "This day I have rolled away the reproach of Egypt from you."
Therefore the name of the place is called Gilgal[f] to this day.
10Now the children of Israel camped in Gilgal, and kept the Passover on
the fourteenth day of the month at twilight on the plains of Jericho. 11And
they ate of the produce of the land on the day after the Passover, unleavened bread and parched grain, on the very same day. 12Then the manna
ceased on the day after they had eaten the produce of the land; and the
children of Israel no longer had manna, but they ate the food of the land of
Canaan that year.

The Commander of the Army of the LORD

13And it came to pass, when Joshua was by Jericho, that he lifted his eyes
and looked, and behold, a Man stood opposite him with His sword drawn
in His hand. And Joshua went to Him and said to Him, "*Are* You for us or
for our adversaries?"
14So He said, "No, but *as* Commander of the army of the LORD I have
now come."
And Joshua fell on his face to the earth and worshiped, and said to Him,
"What does my Lord say to His servant?"
15Then the Commander of the LORD's army said to Joshua, "Take your
sandal off your foot, for the place where you stand *is* holy." And Joshua did
so.

5:1 [c] Following Kethib; Qere, some Hebrew manuscripts and editions, Septuagint, Syriac, Targum, and Vulgate read *they.*
5:3 [d] Hebrew *Gibeath Haaraloth*
5:6 [e] Exodus 3:8
5:9 [f] Literally *Rolling*

The Destruction of Jericho

6 Now Jericho was securely shut up because of the children of Israel;
none went out, and none came in. 2And the LORD said to Joshua: "See!
I have given Jericho into your hand, its king, *and* the mighty men of valor.
3You shall march around the city, all *you* men of war; you shall go all
around the city once. This you shall do six days. 4And seven priests shall
bear seven trumpets of rams' horns before the ark. But the seventh day
you shall march around the city seven times, and the priests shall blow the
trumpets. 5It shall come to pass, when they make a long *blast* with the
ram's horn, *and* when you hear the sound of the trumpet, that all the people shall shout with a great shout; then the wall of the city will fall down
flat. And the people shall go up every man straight before him."
6Then Joshua the son of Nun called the priests and said to them, "Take
up the ark of the covenant, and let seven priests bear seven trumpets of
rams' horns before the ark of the LORD." 7And he said to the people, "Proceed, and march around the city, and let him who is armed advance before
the ark of the LORD."
8So it was, when Joshua had spoken to the people, that the seven priests
bearing the seven trumpets of rams' horns before the LORD advanced and
blew the trumpets, and the ark of the covenant of the LORD followed them.
9The armed men went before the priests who blew the trumpets, and the
rear guard came after the ark, while *the priests* continued blowing the
trumpets. 10Now Joshua had commanded the people, saying, "You shall
not shout or make any noise with your voice, nor shall a word proceed out
of your mouth, until the day I say to you, 'Shout!' Then you shall shout."
11So he had the ark of the LORD circle the city, going around *it* once. Then
they came into the camp and lodged in the camp.
12And Joshua rose early in the morning, and the priests took up the ark
of the LORD. 13Then seven priests bearing seven trumpets of rams' horns
before the ark of the LORD went on continually and blew with the trumpets. And the armed men went before them. But the rear guard came after
the ark of the LORD, while *the priests* continued blowing the trumpets.
14And the second day they marched around the city once and returned to
the camp. So they did six days.
15But it came to pass on the seventh day that they rose early, about the
dawning of the day, and marched around the city seven times in the same
manner. On that day only they marched around the city seven times. 16And
the seventh time it happened, when the priests blew the trumpets, that
Joshua said to the people: "Shout, for the LORD has given you the city!
17Now the city shall be doomed by the LORD to destruction, it and all who
are in it. Only Rahab the harlot shall live, she and all who *are* with her in the
house, because she hid the messengers that we sent. 18And you, by all
means abstain from the accursed things, lest you become accursed when
you take of the accursed things, and make the camp of Israel a curse, and
trouble it. 19But all the silver and gold, and vessels of bronze and iron, *are*
consecrated to the LORD; they shall come into the treasury of the LORD."
20So the people shouted when *the priests* blew the trumpets. And it happened when the people heard the sound of the trumpet, and the people
shouted with a great shout, that the wall fell down flat. Then the people went
up into the city, every man straight before him, and they took the city. 21And

cessfully against God. It would be like a gnat trying to fight against a blast furnace in a steel mill. . . .

A second lesson is that those who are friends of God are on the side of divine omnipotence and therefore on the winning side. At any particular time the waves may seem to be against us, but the tide is sure to win. We need not fear what others can do to us. . . .

The final lesson that I will mention is that the omnipotence of God serves as comfort and encouragement to His people. What a consolation to know that our God can do anything, that nothing is impossible for Him! . . . . Although *He* has no problems, He is able to cope with any problem *we* may be facing. . . .

I sing the mighty pow'r of God
That made the mountains rise,
That spread the flowing seas abroad
And filled the lofty skies.
I sing the wisdom that ordained
The sun to rule the day;
The moon shines full at His command,
And all the stars obey.

(From *Alone in Majesty* by William MacDonald)

APPLICATION What impassable barriers do you face? Do you believe God can deliver you? Get together with a Christian friend. Share your obstacle and ask that person to pray with you for confidence.

EXPLORATION God is Able—Luke 1:37; Acts 20:32; 2 Corinthians 9:8; Philippians 3:20-21; Hebrews 2:18; 7:25; Jude 24.

they utterly destroyed all that *was* in the city, both man and woman, young and
old, ox and sheep and donkey, with the edge of the sword.
[22]But Joshua had said to the two men who had spied out the country, "Go
into the harlot's house, and from there bring out the woman and all that she
has, as you swore to her." [23]And the young men who had been spies went in
and brought out Rahab, her father, her mother, her brothers, and all that she
had. So they brought out all her relatives and left them outside the camp of
Israel. [24]But they burned the city and all that *was* in it with fire. Only the silver and gold, and the vessels of bronze and iron, they put into the treasury
of the house of the LORD. [25]And Joshua spared Rahab the harlot, her father's household, and all that she had. So she dwells in Israel to this day,
because she hid the messengers whom Joshua sent to spy out Jericho.
[26]Then Joshua charged *them* at that time, saying, "Cursed *be* the man before the LORD who rises up and builds this city Jericho; he shall lay its foundation with his firstborn, and with his youngest he shall set up its gates."
[27]So the LORD was with Joshua, and his fame spread throughout all the
country.

Defeat at Ai

7 But the children of Israel committed a trespass regarding the accursed
things, for Achan the son of Carmi, the son of Zabdi,[g] the son of Zerah,
of the tribe of Judah, took of the accursed things; so the anger of the LORD
burned against the children of Israel.
[2]Now Joshua sent men from Jericho to Ai, which *is* beside Beth Aven, on
the east side of Bethel, and spoke to them, saying, "Go up and spy out the
country." So the men went up and spied out Ai. [3]And they returned to
Joshua and said to him, "Do not let all the people go up, but let about two
or three thousand men go up and attack Ai. Do not weary all the people
there, for *the people of Ai are* few." [4]So about three thousand men went up
there from the people, but they fled before the men of Ai. [5]And the men of
Ai struck down about thirty-six men, for they chased them *from* before the
gate as far as Shebarim, and struck them down on the descent; therefore
the hearts of the people melted and became like water.
[6]Then Joshua tore his clothes, and fell to the earth on his face before the
ark of the LORD until evening, he and the elders of Israel; and they put dust
on their heads. [7]And Joshua said, "Alas, Lord GOD, why have You brought
this people over the Jordan at all—to deliver us into the hand of the
Amorites, to destroy us? Oh, that we had been content, and dwelt on the
other side of the Jordan! [8]O Lord, what shall I say when Israel turns its
back before its enemies? [9]For the Canaanites and all the inhabitants of the
land will hear *it*, and surround us, and cut off our name from the earth.
Then what will You do for Your great name?"

The Sin of Achan

[10]So the LORD said to Joshua: "Get up! Why do you lie thus on your face?
[11]Israel has sinned, and they have also transgressed My covenant which I
commanded them. For they have even taken some of the accursed things,
and have both stolen and deceived; and they have also put *it* among their
own stuff. [12]Therefore the children of Israel could not stand before their
enemies, *but* turned *their* backs before their enemies, because they have

7:1 [g] Called *Zimri* in 1 Chronicles 2:6

Life Lesson

Joshua 7:1-26

SITUATION After dreaming of a homeland for forty years and tasting victory in Jericho, Israel received a stunning defeat at Ai. One man, Achan, stole plunder from Jericho and brought God's judgment on all the people. God helped Israel conquer Ai after the sinful man and his family were destroyed.

OBSERVATION God insists on obedience to his commands no matter how small or strict they may seem. Only then can we enjoy his blessing.

INSPIRATION There are times when you cannot understand why you cannot do what you want to do. When God brings the blank space, see that you do not fill it in, but wait. The blank space may come in order to teach you what sanctification means, or it may come after sanctification to teach you what service means. Never run before God's guidance. If there is the slightest doubt, then He is not guiding. Whenever there is doubt—*don't*.

In the beginning you may see clearly what God's will is—the severance of a friendship, the breaking off of a business relationship, something you feel distinctly before God is His will for you to do, never do it on the impulse of that feeling. If you do, you will end in making difficulties that will take years of time to put right. Wait for God's time to bring it round and He will do it without any heartbreak or disappointment. When it is a question of the providential will of God, wait for God to move.

(From *My Utmost for His Highest* by Oswald Chambers)

APPLICATION God does not seek partial compliance with his instructions. We must obey him completely. Did you participate in a questionable activity during the last week? Was it sin? Evaluate honestly. If you are unsure, avoid the activity next time.

EXPLORATION Obedience—Genesis 3:11-13; 17:1; 22:3; 1 Samuel 31:13; 2 Kings 23:4-8; John 14:23-24; 2 John 1:6.

become doomed to destruction. Neither will I be with you anymore, unless you destroy the accursed from among you. 13Get up, sanctify the people, and say, 'Sanctify yourselves for tomorrow, because thus says the LORD God of Israel: "*There is* an accursed thing in your midst, O Israel; you cannot stand before your enemies until you take away the accursed thing from among you." 14In the morning therefore you shall be brought according to your tribes. And it shall be *that* the tribe which the LORD takes shall come according to families; and the family which the LORD takes shall come by households; and the household which the LORD takes shall come man by man. 15Then it shall be *that* he who is taken with the accursed thing shall be burned with fire, he and all that he has, because he has transgressed the covenant of the LORD, and because he has done a disgraceful thing in Israel.' "

16So Joshua rose early in the morning and brought Israel by their tribes, and the tribe of Judah was taken. 17He brought the clan of Judah, and he took the family of the Zarhites; and he brought the family of the Zarhites man by man, and Zabdi was taken. 18Then he brought his household man by man, and Achan the son of Carmi, the son of Zabdi, the son of Zerah, of the tribe of Judah, was taken.

19Now Joshua said to Achan, "My son, I beg you, give glory to the LORD God of Israel, and make confession to Him, and tell me now what you have done; do not hide *it* from me."

20And Achan answered Joshua and said, "Indeed I have sinned against the LORD God of Israel, and this is what I have done: 21When I saw among the spoils a beautiful Babylonian garment, two hundred shekels of silver, and a wedge of gold weighing fifty shekels, I coveted them and took them. And there they are, hidden in the earth in the midst of my tent, with the silver under it."

22So Joshua sent messengers, and they ran to the tent; and there it was, hidden in his tent, with the silver under it. 23And they took them from the midst of the tent, brought them to Joshua and to all the children of Israel, and laid them out before the LORD. 24Then Joshua, and all Israel with him, took Achan the son of Zerah, the silver, the garment, the wedge of gold, his sons, his daughters, his oxen, his donkeys, his sheep, his tent, and all that he had, and they brought them to the Valley of Achor. 25And Joshua said, "Why have you troubled us? The LORD will trouble you this day." So all Israel stoned him with stones; and they burned them with fire after they had stoned them with stones.

26Then they raised over him a great heap of stones, still there to this day. So the LORD turned from the fierceness of His anger. Therefore the name of that place has been called the Valley of Achor[h] to this day.

The Fall of Ai

8 Now the LORD said to Joshua: "Do not be afraid, nor be dismayed; take all the people of war with you, and arise, go up to Ai. See, I have given into your hand the king of Ai, his people, his city, and his land. 2And you shall do to Ai and its king as you did to Jericho and its king. Only its spoil and its cattle you shall take as booty for yourselves. Lay an ambush for the city behind it."

3So Joshua arose, and all the people of war, to go up against Ai; and

7:26 [h] Literally *Trouble*

LIFE LESSON

Joshua 8:1-35

SITUATION After Achan's sin, Joshua carefully obeyed all of God's instructions. Joshua completely destroyed Ai and built an altar to the Lord.

OBSERVATION After the war, Joshua took time to honor God. Through the trial of battle, he trusted God.

INSPIRATION We think of war as ugly—and so it is. Throughout history no war has been fought without terror, barbarity, cruelty, the agony of the dying and the hopeless sobbing of enslaved and bereaved men, women and children. Modern warfare with its potential for indiscriminate mass destruction has assumed an unreal, nightmare quality. We do well to pray and to work for peace on earth.

Yet in our modern revulsion against war we are inclined to forget that the same wars that gave rise to atrocities and barbarism also produced the noblest and best in man. I would not justify war, yet what I say is a fact. Unnatural courage, unbelievable self-sacrifice, devotion, loyalty and love, resourcefulness in the face of impossible odds, endurance beyond the limits of human strength: these, too, are part of the picture. . . .

But earthly warfare is not the real warfare. It is but a faint, ugly reflection of the real thing. It is into the *real* war that the Christian is to plunge. Wars on earth are but tremors felt from an earthquake light-years away. The Christian's war takes place at the epicenter of the earthquake. It is infinitely more deadly, while the issues that hang on it make earth's most momentous questions no more than village gossip.

(From *The Fight* by John White)

APPLICATION To battle successfully in the spiritual realm, you must train your spirit. To train yourself, read God's word each day, pray often, get together with other Christians, and memorize Scripture. Arrange time in your schedule to do all of these.

EXPLORATION Spiritual Warfare—Ephesians 6:12; 1 Thessalonians 5:8.

Joshua chose thirty thousand mighty men of valor
and sent them away by night. 4And he commanded
them, saying: "Behold, you shall lie in ambush
against the city, behind the city. Do not go very far
from the city, but all of you be ready. 5Then I and all
the people who *are* with me will approach the city;
and it will come about, when they come out against
us as at the first, that we shall flee before them. 6For
they will come out after us till we have drawn them
from the city, for they will say, '*They are* fleeing before
us as at the first.' Therefore we will flee before them.
7Then you shall rise from the ambush and seize the
city, for the LORD your God will deliver it into your
hand. 8And it will be, when you have taken the city,
that you shall set the city on fire. According to the
commandment of the LORD you shall do. See, I have
commanded you."

9Joshua therefore sent them out; and they went to
lie in ambush, and stayed between Bethel and Ai, on
the west side of Ai; but Joshua lodged that night
among the people. 10Then Joshua rose up early in the
morning and mustered the people, and went up, he
and the elders of Israel, before the people to Ai. 11And
all the people of war who *were* with him went up and
drew near; and they came before the city and camped
on the north side of Ai. Now a valley *lay* between them
and Ai. 12So he took about five thousand men and set
them in ambush between Bethel and Ai, on the west
side of the city. 13And when they had set the people, all
the army that *was* on the north of the city, and its rear
guard on the west of the city, Joshua went that night
into the midst of the valley.

14Now it happened, when the king of Ai saw *it*, that
the men of the city hurried and rose early and went
out against Israel to battle, he and all his people, at an
appointed place before the plain. But he did not know
that *there was* an ambush against him behind the city.
15And Joshua and all Israel made as if they were
beaten before them, and fled by the way of the wilderness. 16So all the people who *were* in Ai were called together to pursue them. And they pursued Joshua and
were drawn away from the city. 17There was not a man
left in Ai or Bethel who did not go out after Israel. So
they left the city open and pursued Israel.

18Then the LORD said to Joshua, "Stretch out the
spear that *is* in your hand toward Ai, for I will give it
into your hand." And Joshua stretched out the spear
that *was* in his hand toward the city. 19So *those in* ambush arose quickly out of their place; they ran as soon
as he had stretched out his hand, and they entered the
city and took it, and hurried to set the city on fire.
20And when the men of Ai looked behind them, they
saw, and behold, the smoke of the city ascended to
heaven. So they had no power to flee this way or that
way, and the people who had fled to the wilderness
turned back on the pursuers.

21Now when Joshua and all Israel saw that the ambush had taken the city and that the smoke of the city
ascended, they turned back and struck down the men
of Ai. 22Then the others came out of the city against
them; so they were *caught* in the midst of Israel, some
on this side and some on that side. And they struck
them down, so that they let none of them remain or
escape. 23But the king of Ai they took alive, and
brought him to Joshua.

24And it came to pass when Israel had made an end
of slaying all the inhabitants of Ai in the field, in the
wilderness where they pursued them, and when they
all had fallen by the edge of the sword until they were
consumed, that all the Israelites returned to Ai and
struck it with the edge of the sword. 25So it was *that* all
who fell that day, both men and women, *were* twelve
thousand—all the people of Ai. 26For Joshua did not
draw back his hand, with which he stretched out the
spear, until he had utterly destroyed all the inhabitants of Ai. 27Only the livestock and the spoil of that
city Israel took as booty for themselves, according to
the word of the LORD which He had commanded
Joshua. 28So Joshua burned Ai and made it a heap forever, a desolation to this day. 29And the king of Ai he
hanged on a tree until evening. And as soon as the
sun was down, Joshua commanded that they should
take his corpse down from the tree, cast it at the entrance of the gate of the city, and raise over it a great
heap of stones *that remains* to this day.

Joshua Renews the Covenant

30Now Joshua built an altar to the LORD God of Israel in Mount Ebal, 31as Moses the servant of the LORD
had commanded the children of Israel, as it is written
in the Book of the Law of Moses: "an altar of whole
stones over which no man has wielded an iron *tool*."[i]
And they offered on it burnt offerings to the LORD, and
sacrificed peace offerings. 32And there, in the presence of the children of Israel, he wrote on the stones a
copy of the law of Moses, which he had written.
33Then all Israel, with their elders and officers and
judges, stood on either side of the ark before the
priests, the Levites, who bore the ark of the covenant

8:31 *i* Deuteronomy 27:5, 6

of the LORD, the stranger as well as he who was born among them. Half of
them *were* in front of Mount Gerizim and half of them in front of Mount
Ebal, as Moses the servant of the LORD had commanded before, that they
should bless the people of Israel. 34And afterward he read all the words of
the law, the blessings and the cursings, according to all that is written in
the Book of the Law. 35There was not a word of all that Moses had commanded which Joshua did not read before all the assembly of Israel, with
the women, the little ones, and the strangers who were living among them.

The Treaty with the Gibeonites

9 And it came to pass when all the kings who *were* on this side of the Jordan, in the hills and in the lowland and in all the coasts of the Great Sea
toward Lebanon—the Hittite, the Amorite, the Canaanite, the Perizzite,
the Hivite, and the Jebusite—heard *about it,* 2that they gathered together
to fight with Joshua and Israel with one accord.
3But when the inhabitants of Gibeon heard what Joshua had done to Jericho and Ai, 4they worked craftily, and went and pretended to be ambassadors.
And they took old sacks on their donkeys, old wineskins torn and mended,
5old and patched sandals on their feet, and old garments on themselves; and
all the bread of their provision was dry *and* moldy. 6And they went to Joshua,
to the camp at Gilgal, and said to him and to the men of Israel, "We have come
from a far country; now therefore, make a covenant with us."
7Then the men of Israel said to the Hivites, "Perhaps you dwell among
us; so how can we make a covenant with you?"
8But they said to Joshua, "We *are* your servants."
And Joshua said to them, "Who *are* you, and where do you come from?"
9So they said to him: "From a very far country your servants have come,
because of the name of the LORD your God; for we have heard of His fame,
and all that He did in Egypt, 10and all that He did to the two kings of the
Amorites who *were* beyond the Jordan—to Sihon king of Heshbon, and
Og king of Bashan, who was at Ashtaroth. 11Therefore our elders and all
the inhabitants of our country spoke to us, saying, 'Take provisions with
you for the journey, and go to meet them, and say to them, "We *are* your
servants; now therefore, make a covenant with us." ' 12This bread of ours
we took hot *for* our provision from our houses on the day we departed to
come to you. But now look, it is dry and moldy. 13And these wineskins
which we filled *were* new, and see, they are torn; and these our garments
and our sandals have become old because of the very long journey."
14Then the men of Israel took some of their provisions; but they did not
ask counsel of the LORD. 15So Joshua made peace with them, and made a
covenant with them to let them live; and the rulers of the congregation
swore to them.
16And it happened at the end of three days, after they had made a
covenant with them, that they heard that they *were* their neighbors who
dwelt near them. 17Then the children of Israel journeyed and came to their
cities on the third day. Now their cities *were* Gibeon, Chephirah, Beeroth,
and Kirjath Jearim. 18But the children of Israel did not attack them, because the rulers of the congregation had sworn to them by the LORD God of
Israel. And all the congregation complained against the rulers.
19Then all the rulers said to all the congregation, "We have sworn to
them by the LORD God of Israel; now therefore, we may not touch them.

Life Lesson

Joshua 9:1–10:43

SITUATION God did not promise the Israelites the land without giving them the strength to conquer it. God helped Joshua lead the people into possession of their land.

OBSERVATION God does not give us commands or lead us to decisions and leave us to fight the obstacles in our own strength. He strengthens us and guides us in every detail.

INSPIRATION If I found I had driven into a bog, I should know I had missed the road. But this knowledge would not be of much comfort if I then had to stand helpless watching the car sink and vanish: the damage would be done, and that would be that. Is it the same when a Christian wakes up to the fact that he has missed God's guidance and taken the wrong way? Is the damage irrevocable? Must he now be put off course for life? Thank God, no. Our God is a God who not merely restores, but takes up our mistakes and follies into His plan for us and brings good out of them. This is part of the wonder of His gracious sovereignty. . . .

Guidance, like all God's acts of blessing under the covenant of grace, is a sovereign act. Not merely does God will to guide us in the sense of showing us His way, that we may tread it; He wills also to guide us in the more fundamental sense of ensuring that, whatever happens, whatever mistakes we may make, we shall come safely home. Slipping and straying there will be, no doubt, but the everlasting arms are beneath us; we shall be caught, rescued, restored. This is God's promise; this is how good He is. Thus it appears that the right context of discussing guidance is one of confidence in the God who will not let us ruin our souls.

(From *Knowing God* by J. I. Packer)

APPLICATION Do you know someone who is suffering from unwise decisions? Is that person having trouble putting life back together? Contact that individual. What can you do to help? Be available for God to work through your service.

Continued

EXPLORATION Consequences of Sin—Leviticus 26:23-24; Deuteronomy 28:15; Job 5:12; Proverbs 23:21; Ecclesiastes 2:26; Jeremiah 18:15-17; Romans 2:9; Philippians 3:18-19.

20This we will do to them: We will let them live, lest wrath be upon us because of the oath which we swore to them." 21And the rulers said to them,
"Let them live, but let them be woodcutters and water carriers for all the
congregation, as the rulers had promised them."
22Then Joshua called for them, and he spoke to them, saying, "Why have
you deceived us, saying, 'We *are* very far from you,' when you dwell near
us? 23Now therefore, you *are* cursed, and none of you shall be freed from
being slaves—woodcutters and water carriers for the house of my God."
24So they answered Joshua and said, "Because your servants were
clearly told that the LORD your God commanded His servant Moses to give
you all the land, and to destroy all the inhabitants of the land from before
you; therefore we were very much afraid for our lives because of you, and
have done this thing. 25And now, here we are, in your hands; do with us as
it seems good and right to do to us." 26So he did to them, and delivered
them out of the hand of the children of Israel, so that they did not kill
them. 27And that day Joshua made them woodcutters and water carriers
for the congregation and for the altar of the LORD, in the place which He
would choose, even to this day.

The Sun Stands Still

10 Now it came to pass when Adoni-Zedek king of Jerusalem heard
how Joshua had taken Ai and had utterly destroyed it—as he had
done to Jericho and its king, so he had done to Ai and its king—and how
the inhabitants of Gibeon had made peace with Israel and were among
them, 2that they feared greatly, because Gibeon *was* a great city, like one of
the royal cities, and because it *was* greater than Ai, and all its men *were*
mighty. 3Therefore Adoni-Zedek king of Jerusalem sent to Hoham king of
Hebron, Piram king of Jarmuth, Japhia king of Lachish, and Debir king of
Eglon, saying, 4"Come up to me and help me, that we may attack Gibeon,
for it has made peace with Joshua and with the children of Israel." 5There-
fore the five kings of the Amorites, the king of Jerusalem, the king of
Hebron, the king of Jarmuth, the king of Lachish, *and* the king of Eglon,
gathered together and went up, they and all their armies, and camped before Gibeon and made war against it.
6And the men of Gibeon sent to Joshua at the camp at Gilgal, saying,
"Do not forsake your servants; come up to us quickly, save us and help us,
for all the kings of the Amorites who dwell in the mountains have gathered
together against us."
7So Joshua ascended from Gilgal, he and all the people of war with him,
and all the mighty men of valor. 8And the LORD said to Joshua, "Do not fear
them, for I have delivered them into your hand; not a man of them shall
stand before you." 9Joshua therefore came upon them suddenly, having
marched all night from Gilgal. 10So the LORD routed them before Israel,
killed them with a great slaughter at Gibeon, chased them along the road
that goes to Beth Horon, and struck them down as far as Azekah and
Makkedah. 11And it happened, as they fled before Israel *and* were on the
descent of Beth Horon, that the LORD cast down large hailstones from
heaven on them as far as Azekah, and they died. *There were* more who died
from the hailstones than the children of Israel killed with the sword.
12Then Joshua spoke to the LORD in the day when the LORD delivered up
the Amorites before the children of Israel, and he said in the sight of Israel:

“Sun, stand still over Gibeon;
And Moon, in the Valley of Aijalon.”
13 So the sun stood still,
And the moon stopped,
Till the people had revenge
Upon their enemies.

Is this not written in the Book of Jasher? So the sun
stood still in the midst of heaven, and did not hasten to
go *down* for about a whole day. 14And there has been no
day like that, before it or after it, that the LORD heeded
the voice of a man; for the LORD fought for Israel.
15Then Joshua returned, and all Israel with him, to
the camp at Gilgal.

The Amorite Kings Executed

16But these five kings had fled and hidden themselves in a cave at Makkedah. 17And it was told Joshua,
saying, “The five kings have been found hidden in the
cave at Makkedah.”
18So Joshua said, “Roll large stones against the
mouth of the cave, and set men by it to guard them.
19And do not stay *there* yourselves, *but* pursue your
enemies, and attack their rear *guard*. Do not allow
them to enter their cities, for the LORD your God has
delivered them into your hand.” 20Then it happened,
while Joshua and the children of Israel made an end
of slaying them with a very great slaughter, till they
had finished, that those who escaped entered fortified
cities. 21And all the people returned to the camp, to
Joshua at Makkedah, in peace.
No one moved his tongue against any of the children of Israel.
22Then Joshua said, “Open the mouth of the cave,
and bring out those five kings to me from the cave.”
23And they did so, and brought out those five kings to
him from the cave: the king of Jerusalem, the king of
Hebron, the king of Jarmuth, the king of Lachish, *and*
the king of Eglon.
24So it was, when they brought out those kings to
Joshua, that Joshua called for all the men of Israel,
and said to the captains of the men of war who went
with him, “Come near, put your feet on the necks of
these kings.” And they drew near and put their feet on
their necks. 25Then Joshua said to them, “Do not be
afraid, nor be dismayed; be strong and of good
courage, for thus the LORD will do to all your enemies
against whom you fight.” 26And afterward Joshua
struck them and killed them, and hanged them on
five trees; and they were hanging on the trees until
evening. 27So it was at the time of the going down of
the sun *that* Joshua commanded, and they took them
down from the trees, cast them into the cave where
they had been hidden, and laid large stones against
the cave’s mouth, *which remain* until this very day.

Conquest of the Southland

28On that day Joshua took Makkedah, and struck it
and its king with the edge of the sword. He utterly destroyed them[j]—all the people who *were* in it. He let
none remain. He also did to the king of Makkedah as
he had done to the king of Jericho.
29Then Joshua passed from Makkedah, and all Israel with him, to Libnah; and they fought against
Libnah. 30And the LORD also delivered it and its king
into the hand of Israel; he struck it and all the people
who *were* in it with the edge of the sword. He let none
remain in it, but did to its king as he had done to the
king of Jericho.
31Then Joshua passed from Libnah, and all Israel
with him, to Lachish; and they encamped against it
and fought against it. 32And the LORD delivered
Lachish into the hand of Israel, who took it on the second day, and struck it and all the people who *were* in it
with the edge of the sword, according to all that he
had done to Libnah. 33Then Horam king of Gezer
came up to help Lachish; and Joshua struck him and
his people, until he left him none remaining.
34From Lachish Joshua passed to Eglon, and all Israel with him; and they encamped against it and
fought against it. 35They took it on that day and struck
it with the edge of the sword; all the people who *were*
in it he utterly destroyed that day, according to all that
he had done to Lachish.
36So Joshua went up from Eglon, and all Israel with
him, to Hebron; and they fought against it. 37And they
took it and struck it with the edge of the sword—its
king, all its cities, and all the people who *were* in it; he
left none remaining, according to all that he had done
to Eglon, but utterly destroyed it and all the people
who *were* in it.
38Then Joshua returned, and all Israel with him, to
Debir; and they fought against it. 39And he took it and
its king and all its cities; they struck them with the
edge of the sword and utterly destroyed all the people
who *were* in it. He left none remaining; as he had done
to Hebron, so he did to Debir and its king, as he had
done also to Libnah and its king.

10:28 *j* Following Masoretic Text and most authorities; many Hebrew manuscripts, some manuscripts of the Septuagint, and some manuscripts of the Targum read *it*.

LIFE LESSON

Joshua 11:1–12:24

SITUATION Joshua led Israel's army to many victories over the Canaanites. Though the Israelites were outnumbered, God is never outnumbered. He encouraged, supported, and brought victory to them. After seven years of campaigning, the Israelites destroyed the alliance of Canaanite tribes.

OBSERVATION The Israelites obeyed God. As a result of their obedience, God granted the Israelites success.

INSPIRATION I don't want to give the impression that because I [committed my career to the Lord,] God had somehow guaranteed my [professional] baseball success. He didn't give me mastery over some great new pitch no one could hit. He didn't magically speed up my fastball or slow down the opposing hitter's swings. But several beneficial things did happen as a result of committing my career to the Lord. From that day on, I knew I had to concern myself only with my own effort and then trust the Lord with the results. If those results were good, it would be great, if they were bad, I would still believe He wasn't going to make His first mistake with me.

If God was ultimately in charge of my career as well as my life, I didn't have to worry about what might happen as a result of my performance, because God was in charge of my future whether it was in baseball or not.

With that attitude, the gut-wrenching pressure disappeared. I felt a peace and a freedom I never felt before. All I had to do was give my best, and that's what I did.

(From *Major League Dad* by Tim and Christine Burke)

APPLICATION Are you impatient to have your prayers answered immediately or to win easy victories over sin? Be patient and obedient to God's directions for you. He will decide what is best for you. Take a step today, in faith, and trust God for another step tomorrow.

EXPLORATION Obedience—Genesis 22:1-8; Leviticus 9:22-23; 1 Samuel 13:11-12; 15:22; Psalm 27:14.

40So Joshua conquered all the land: the mountain country and the
South[k] and the lowland and the wilderness slopes, and all their kings; he
left none remaining, but utterly destroyed all that breathed, as the LORD
God of Israel had commanded. 41And Joshua conquered them from
Kadesh Barnea as far as Gaza, and all the country of Goshen, even as far as
Gibeon. 42All these kings and their land Joshua took at one time, because
the LORD God of Israel fought for Israel. 43Then Joshua returned, and all Is-
rael with him, to the camp at Gilgal.

The Northern Conquest

11 And it came to pass, when Jabin king of Hazor heard *these things,*
that he sent to Jobab king of Madon, to the king of Shimron, to the
king of Achshaph, 2and to the kings who *were* from the north, in the
mountains, in the plain south of Chinneroth, in the lowland, and in the
heights of Dor on the west, 3to the Canaanites in the east and in the west,
the Amorite, the Hittite, the Perizzite, the Jebusite in the mountains, and
the Hivite below Hermon in the land of Mizpah. 4So they went out, they
and all their armies with them, *as* many people *as* the sand that *is* on the
seashore in multitude, with very many horses and chariots. 5And when all
these kings had met together, they came and camped together at the waters of Merom to fight against Israel.

6But the LORD said to Joshua, "Do not be afraid because of them, for tomorrow about this time I will deliver all of them slain before Israel. You shall hamstring their horses and burn their chariots with fire." 7So Joshua and all the
people of war with him came against them suddenly by the waters of Merom,
and they attacked them. 8And the LORD delivered them into the hand of Israel,
who defeated them and chased them to Greater Sidon, to the Brook
Misrephoth,[l] and to the Valley of Mizpah eastward; they attacked them until
they left none of them remaining. 9So Joshua did to them as the LORD had told
him: he hamstrung their horses and burned their chariots with fire.

10Joshua turned back at that time and took Hazor, and struck its king with
the sword; for Hazor was formerly the head of all those kingdoms. 11And they
struck all the people who *were* in it with the edge of the sword, utterly destroying *them.* There was none left breathing. Then he burned Hazor with fire.

12So all the cities of those kings, and all their kings, Joshua took and
struck with the edge of the sword. He utterly destroyed them, as Moses the
servant of the LORD had commanded. 13But *as for* the cities that stood on
their mounds,[m] Israel burned none of them, except Hazor only, *which*
Joshua burned. 14And all the spoil of these cities and the livestock, the children of Israel took as booty for themselves; but they struck every man
with the edge of the sword until they had destroyed them, and they left
none breathing. 15As the LORD had commanded Moses his servant, so Moses commanded Joshua, and so Joshua did. He left nothing undone of all
that the LORD had commanded Moses.

Summary of Joshua's Conquests

16Thus Joshua took all this land: the mountain country, all the South, all
the land of Goshen, the lowland, and the Jordan plain[n]—the mountains of

10:40 [k] Hebrew *Negev,* and so throughout this book
11:8 [l] Hebrew *Misrephoth Maim*
11:13 [m] Hebrew *tel,* a heap of successive city ruins
11:16 [n] Hebrew *arabah*

Israel and its lowlands, 17from Mount Halak and the ascent to Seir, even as far as Baal Gad in the Valley of Lebanon below Mount Hermon. He captured all their kings, and struck them down and killed them. 18Joshua made war a long time with all those kings. 19There was not a city that made peace with the children of Israel, except the Hivites, the inhabitants of Gibeon. All *the others* they took in battle. 20For it was of the LORD to harden their hearts, that they should come against Israel in battle, that He might utterly destroy them, *and* that they might receive no mercy, but that He might destroy them, as the LORD had commanded Moses.

21And at that time Joshua came and cut off the Anakim from the mountains: from Hebron, from Debir, from Anab, from all the mountains of Judah, and from all the mountains of Israel; Joshua utterly destroyed them with their cities. 22None of the Anakim were left in the land of the children of Israel; they remained only in Gaza, in Gath, and in Ashdod.

23So Joshua took the whole land, according to all that the LORD had said to Moses; and Joshua gave it as an inheritance to Israel according to their divisions by their tribes. Then the land rested from war.

The Kings Conquered by Moses

12 These *are* the kings of the land whom the children of Israel defeated, and whose land they possessed on the other side of the Jordan toward the rising of the sun, from the River Arnon to Mount Hermon, and all the eastern Jordan plain: 2*One king was* Sihon king of the Amorites, who dwelt in Heshbon *and* ruled half of Gilead, from Aroer, which is on the bank of the River Arnon, from the middle of that river, even as far as the River Jabbok, *which is* the border of the Ammonites, 3and the eastern Jordan plain from the Sea of Chinneroth as far as the Sea of the Arabah (the Salt Sea), the road to Beth Jeshimoth, and southward below the slopes of Pisgah. 4*The other king was* Og king of Bashan and his territory, *who was* of the remnant of the giants, who dwelt at Ashtaroth and at Edrei, 5and reigned over Mount Hermon, over Salcah, over all Bashan, as far as the border of the Geshurites and the Maachathites, and over half of Gilead *to* the border of Sihon king of Heshbon.

6These Moses the servant of the LORD and the children of Israel had conquered; and Moses the servant of the LORD had given it *as* a possession to the Reubenites, the Gadites, and half the tribe of Manasseh.

The Kings Conquered by Joshua

7And these *are* the kings of the country which Joshua and the children of Israel conquered on this side of the Jordan, on the west, from Baal Gad in the Valley of Lebanon as far as Mount Halak and the ascent to Seir, which Joshua gave to the tribes of Israel *as* a possession according to their divisions, 8in the mountain country, in the lowlands, in the *Jordan* plain, in the slopes, in the wilderness, and in the South—the Hittites, the Amorites, the Canaanites, the Perizzites, the Hivites, and the Jebusites: 9the king of Jericho, one; the king of Ai, which *is* beside Bethel, one; 10the king of Jerusalem, one; the king of Hebron, one; 11the king of Jarmuth, one; the king of Lachish, one; 12the king of Eglon, one; the king of Gezer, one; 13the king of Debir, one; the king of Geder, one; 14the king of Hormah, one; the king of Arad, one; 15the king of Libnah, one; the king of Adullam, one; 16the king of Makkedah, one; the king of Bethel, one; 17the king of Tappuah, one; the king of Hepher, one; 18the king of Aphek, one; the king of Lasharon, one; 19the king of Madon, one; the king of Hazor, one; 20the king of Shimron Meron, one; the king of Achshaph, one; 21the king of Taanach, one; the king of Megiddo, one; 22the king of Kedesh, one; the king of Jokneam in Carmel, one; 23the king of Dor in the heights of Dor, one; the king of the people of Gilgal, one; 24the king of Tirzah, one—all the kings, thirty-one.

Remaining Land to Be Conquered

13 Now Joshua was old, advanced in years. And the LORD said to him: "You are old, advanced in years, and there remains very much land yet to be possessed. 2This is the land that yet remains: all the territory of the Philistines and all *that of* the Geshurites, 3from Sihor, which *is* east of Egypt, as far as the border of Ekron northward (*which* is counted as Canaanite); the five lords of the Philistines—the Gazites, the Ashdodites, the Ashkelonites, the Gittites, and the Ekronites; also the Avites; 4from the south, all the land of the Canaanites, and Mearah that belongs to the Sidonians as far as Aphek, to the border of the Amorites; 5the land of the Gebalites,[o] and all Lebanon, toward the sunrise, from Baal Gad below Mount Hermon as far as the entrance to Hamath; 6all the inhabitants of the mountains from Lebanon as far as the Brook Misrephoth,[p] *and* all the Sidonians—them I will drive out from before the children of Israel; only divide it by lot to Israel as an inheritance, as I have

13:5 *o* Or *Giblites*
13:6 *p* Hebrew *Misrephoth Maim*

commanded you. 7Now therefore, divide this land as an inheritance to the
nine tribes and half the tribe of Manasseh."

The Land Divided East of the Jordan

8With the other half-tribe the Reubenites and the Gadites received their
inheritance, which Moses had given them, beyond the Jordan eastward, as
Moses the servant of the LORD had given them: 9from Aroer which *is* on the
bank of the River Arnon, and the town that *is* in the midst of the ravine,
and all the plain of Medeba as far as Dibon; 10all the cities of Sihon king of
the Amorites, who reigned in Heshbon, as far as the border of the children
of Ammon; 11Gilead, and the border of the Geshurites and Maachathites,
all Mount Hermon, and all Bashan as far as Salcah; 12all the kingdom of Og
in Bashan, who reigned in Ashtaroth and Edrei, who remained of the
remnant of the giants; for Moses had defeated and cast out these.
13Nevertheless the children of Israel did not drive out the Geshurites or
the Maachathites, but the Geshurites and the Maachathites dwell among
the Israelites until this day.
14Only to the tribe of Levi he had given no inheritance; the sacrifices of the
LORD God of Israel made by fire *are* their inheritance, as He said to them.

The Land of Reuben

15And Moses had given to the tribe of the children of Reuben *an inheritance*
according to their families. 16Their territory was from Aroer, which *is* on the
bank of the River Arnon, and the city that *is* in the midst of the ravine, and all
the plain by Medeba; 17Heshbon and all its cities that *are* in the plain: Dibon,
Bamoth Baal, Beth Baal Meon, 18Jahaza, Kedemoth, Mephaath, 19Kirjathaim,
Sibmah, Zereth Shahar on the mountain of the valley, 20Beth Peor, the slopes
of Pisgah, and Beth Jeshimoth— 21all the cities of the plain and all the kingdom of Sihon king of the Amorites, who reigned in Heshbon, whom Moses
had struck with the princes of Midian: Evi, Rekem, Zur, Hur, and Reba, who
were princes of Sihon dwelling in the country. 22The children of Israel also
killed with the sword Balaam the son of Beor, the soothsayer, among those
who were killed by them. 23And the border of the children of Reuben was the
bank of the Jordan. This *was* the inheritance of the children of Reuben according to their families, the cities and their villages.

The Land of Gad

24Moses also had given *an inheritance* to the tribe of Gad, to the children of
Gad according to their families. 25Their territory was Jazer, and all the cities of
Gilead, and half the land of the Ammonites as far as Aroer, which *is* before
Rabbah, 26and from Heshbon to Ramath Mizpah and Betonim, and from
Mahanaim to the border of Debir, 27and in the valley Beth Haram, Beth
Nimrah, Succoth, and Zaphon, the rest of the kingdom of Sihon king of
Heshbon, with the Jordan as *its* border, as far as the edge of the Sea of
Chinnereth, on the other side of the Jordan eastward. 28This *is* the inheritance
of the children of Gad according to their families, the cities and their villages.

Half the Tribe of Manasseh (East)

29Moses also had given *an inheritance* to half the tribe of Manasseh; it
was for half the tribe of the children of Manasseh according to their fami-

LIFE LESSON

Joshua 13:1–17:18

SITUATION The twelve tribes of Israel divided the conquered lands according to God's wishes. Joshua dismissed the army, leaving additional conquests as each tribe's responsibility.

OBSERVATION God rewards his people for following through on what he says. In these chapters, the Israelites were rewarded with a homeland.

INSPIRATION God gives us "the real life" through His Son, Christ. And only through His Son. Please get that straight. That's the basis of the gospel. That's why Christ is the pre-eminent message—not good works, not positive thinking, not good books, not being widely traveled or earning a good education (as fine as all those things may be). Christ, and Christ alone, will give you the life of God, and He's from outside this galaxy. He's not within it. . . .

Life from God is supernatural power now—not a vague force limited to a long time ago. You know, the greatest evidence of power is change. Take a trip to Hoover Dam and look at that massive amount of water; it's really impressive. But you don't say, "My! Look at that power." What you see is not the greatest evidence of power. That's just water going over a dam. If you want to see the evidence of power at Hoover Dam, you need to drive to a residential section in a nearby city that draws its source of electricity from the dam . . . walk into

lies: 30Their territory was from Mahanaim, all Bashan, all the kingdom of
Og king of Bashan, and all the towns of Jair which are in Bashan, sixty
cities; 31half of Gilead, and Ashtaroth and Edrei, cities of the kingdom of
Og in Bashan, *were* for the children of Machir the son of Manasseh, for half
of the children of Machir according to their families.
32These *are the areas* which Moses had distributed as an inheritance in
the plains of Moab on the other side of the Jordan, by Jericho eastward.
33But to the tribe of Levi Moses had given no inheritance; the LORD God of
Israel *was* their inheritance, as He had said to them.

The Land Divided West of the Jordan

14 These *are the areas* which the children of Israel inherited in the land
of Canaan, which Eleazar the priest, Joshua the son of Nun, and the
heads of the fathers of the tribes of the children of Israel distributed as an
inheritance to them. 2Their inheritance *was* by lot, as the LORD had commanded by the hand of Moses, for the nine tribes and the half-tribe. 3For
Moses had given the inheritance of the two tribes and the half-tribe on the
other side of the Jordan; but to the Levites he had given no inheritance
among them. 4For the children of Joseph were two tribes: Manasseh and
Ephraim. And they gave no part to the Levites in the land, except cities to
dwell *in,* with their common-lands for their livestock and their property.
5As the LORD had commanded Moses, so the children of Israel did; and
they divided the land.

Caleb Inherits Hebron

6Then the children of Judah came to Joshua in Gilgal. And Caleb the son
of Jephunneh the Kenizzite said to him: "You know the word which the
LORD said to Moses the man of God concerning you and me in Kadesh
Barnea. 7I *was* forty years old when Moses the servant of the LORD sent me
from Kadesh Barnea to spy out the land, and I brought back word to him
as *it was* in my heart. 8Nevertheless my brethren who went up with me
made the heart of the people melt, but I wholly followed the LORD my God.
9So Moses swore on that day, saying, 'Surely the land where your foot has
trodden shall be your inheritance and your children's forever, because you
have wholly followed the LORD my God.' 10And now, behold, the LORD has
kept me alive, as He said, these forty-five years, ever since the LORD spoke
this word to Moses while Israel wandered in the wilderness; and now, here
I am this day, eighty-five years old. 11As yet I *am as* strong this day as on
the day that Moses sent me; just as my strength *was* then, so now *is* my
strength for war, both for going out and for coming in. 12Now therefore,
give me this mountain of which the LORD spoke in that day; for you heard
in that day how the Anakim *were* there, and *that* the cities *were* great *and*
fortified. It may be that the LORD *will be* with me, and I shall be able to
drive them out as the LORD said."
13And Joshua blessed him, and gave Hebron to Caleb the son of
Jephunneh as an inheritance. 14Hebron therefore became the inheritance
of Caleb the son of Jephunneh the Kenizzite to this day, because he wholly
followed the LORD God of Israel. 15And the name of Hebron formerly was
Kirjath Arba (*Arba was* the greatest man among the Anakim).
Then the land had rest from war.

a darkened room in the middle of the night and flip on the light. In one simple "click" you've got the greatest evidence of the power at that massive dam. It's able to change darkness into light. It's able to transform a cold house into a warm home.

Now, the wonderful news is that God dispenses His supernatural power to anyone who says, "I want it." It doesn't cost you a thing. You don't have to see a film. You don't have to visit a territory of the country. There are no Meccas. You don't have to read a series of books. You don't have to be on probation for a year and a half. You don't have to keep going to a church to earn your way in. You don't have to pray a whole lot. . . . Whether you're the richest of the rich, the poorest of the poor, or anywhere between, all you have to do is take a gift. And the gift is the power of God, through faith in His Son.

(From *Living on the Ragged Edge* by Charles Swindoll)

APPLICATION What "promised lands" have you inherited in recent years: Studies completed? Relationships secured? Reflect on God's help. Thank him today. Stretch your faith for tomorrow.

EXPLORATION Promises—Genesis 21:7; Exodus 2:23-25; Joshua 21:43-45; 23:14; Psalm 119:62; Hebrews 10:27.

The Land of Judah

15 So *this* was the lot of the tribe of the children of Judah according to their families:
The border of Edom at the Wilderness of Zin southward *was* the extreme southern boundary. 2And their
southern border began at the shore of the Salt Sea, from
the bay that faces southward. 3Then it went out to the
southern side of the Ascent of Akrabbim, passed along
to Zin, ascended on the south side of Kadesh Barnea,
passed along to Hezron, went up to Adar, and went
around to Karkaa. 4*From there* it passed toward Azmon
and went out to the Brook of Egypt; and the border
ended at the sea. This shall be your southern border.
5The east border *was* the Salt Sea as far as the
mouth of the Jordan.
And the border on the northern quarter *began* at
the bay of the sea at the mouth of the Jordan. 6The
border went up to Beth Hoglah and passed north of
Beth Arabah; and the border went up to the stone of
Bohan the son of Reuben. 7Then the border went up
toward Debir from the Valley of Achor, and it turned
northward toward Gilgal, which *is* before the Ascent
of Adummim, which *is* on the south side of the valley.
The border continued toward the waters of En
Shemesh and ended at En Rogel. 8And the border
went up by the Valley of the Son of Hinnom to the
southern slope of the Jebusite *city* (which *is* Jerusalem). The border went up to the top of the mountain
that *lies* before the Valley of Hinnom westward, which
is at the end of the Valley of Rephaim[q] northward.
9Then the border went around from the top of the hill
to the fountain of the water of Nephtoah, and extended
to the cities of Mount Ephron. And the border went
around to Baalah (which *is* Kirjath Jearim). 10Then the
border turned westward from Baalah to Mount Seir,
passed along to the side of Mount Jearim on the north
(which *is* Chesalon), went down to Beth Shemesh, and
passed on to Timnah. 11And the border went out to the
side of Ekron northward. Then the border went
around to Shicron, passed along to Mount Baalah, and
extended to Jabneel; and the border ended at the sea.
12The west border *was* the coastline of the Great Sea.
This *is* the boundary of the children of Judah all
around according to their families.

Caleb Occupies Hebron and Debir

13Now to Caleb the son of Jephunneh he gave a
share among the children of Judah, according to the
commandment of the LORD to Joshua, *namely,*
Kirjath Arba, which *is* Hebron (*Arba was* the father of
Anak). 14Caleb drove out the three sons of Anak from
there: Sheshai, Ahiman, and Talmai, the children of
Anak. 15Then he went up from there to the inhabitants of Debir (formerly the name of Debir *was*
Kirjath Sepher).
16And Caleb said, "He who attacks Kirjath Sepher
and takes it, to him I will give Achsah my daughter as
wife." 17So Othniel the son of Kenaz, the brother of Caleb, took it; and he gave him Achsah his daughter as
wife. 18Now it was so, when she came *to him,* that she
persuaded him to ask her father for a field. So she dismounted from *her* donkey, and Caleb said to her,
"What do you wish?" 19She answered, "Give me a
blessing; since you have given me land in the South,
give me also springs of water." So he gave her the
upper springs and the lower springs.

The Cities of Judah

20This *was* the inheritance of the tribe of the chil-
dren of Judah according to their families:
21The cities at the limits of the tribe of the children
of Judah, toward the border of Edom in the South,
were Kabzeel, Eder, Jagur, 22Kinah, Dimonah,
Adadah, 23Kedesh, Hazor, Ithnan, 24Ziph, Telem,
Bealoth, 25Hazor, Hadattah, Kerioth, Hezron (which *is*
Hazor), 26Amam, Shema, Moladah, 27Hazar Gaddah,
Heshmon, Beth Pelet, 28Hazar Shual, Beersheba,
Bizjothjah, 29Baalah, Ijim, Ezem, 30Eltolad, Chesil,
Hormah, 31Ziklag, Madmannah, Sansannah,
32Lebaoth, Shilhim, Ain, and Rimmon: all the cities
are twenty-nine, with their villages.
33In the lowland: Eshtaol, Zorah, Ashnah, 34Zanoah,
En Gannim, Tappuah, Enam, 35Jarmuth, Adullam,
Socoh, Azekah, 36Sharaim, Adithaim, Gederah, and
Gederothaim: fourteen cities with their villages;
37Zenan, Hadashah, Migdal Gad, 38Dilean, Mizpah,
Joktheel, 39Lachish, Bozkath, Eglon, 40Cabbon,
Lahmas,[r] Kithlish, 41Gederoth, Beth Dagon, Naamah,
and Makkedah: sixteen cities with their villages;
42Libnah, Ether, Ashan, 43Jiphtah, Ashnah, Nezib,
44Keilah, Achzib, and Mareshah: nine cities with their
villages; 45Ekron, with its towns and villages; 46from
Ekron to the sea, all that *lay* near Ashdod, with their villages; 47Ashdod with its towns and villages, Gaza with
its towns and villages—as far as the Brook of Egypt
and the Great Sea with *its* coastline.
48And in the mountain country: Shamir, Jattir,

15:8 [q] Literally *Giants*
15:40 [r] Or *Lahmam*

Sochoh, 49 Dannah, Kirjath Sannah (which *is* Debir),
50 Anab, Eshtemoh, Anim, 51 Goshen, Holon, and
Giloh: eleven cities with their villages; 52 Arab, Dumah,
Eshean, 53 Janum, Beth Tappuah, Aphekah, 54 Humtah,
Kirjath Arba (which *is* Hebron), and Zior: nine cities
with their villages; 55 Maon, Carmel, Ziph, Juttah,
56 Jezreel, Jokdeam, Zanoah, 57 Kain, Gibeah, and
Timnah: ten cities with their villages; 58 Halhul, Beth
Zur, Gedor, 59 Maarath, Beth Anoth, and Eltekon: six
cities with their villages; 60 Kirjath Baal (which *is* Kirjath
Jearim) and Rabbah: two cities with their villages.

61 In the wilderness: Beth Arabah, Middin, Secacah,
62 Nibshan, the City of Salt, and En Gedi: six cities with
their villages.

63 As for the Jebusites, the inhabitants of Jerusalem,
the children of Judah could not drive them out; but
the Jebusites dwell with the children of Judah at Jerusalem to this day.

Ephraim and West Manasseh

16 The lot fell to the children of Joseph from the
Jordan, by Jericho, to the waters of Jericho on
the east, to the wilderness that goes up from Jericho
through the mountains to Bethel, 2 then went out from
Bethel to Luz,[s] passed along to the border of the
Archites at Ataroth, 3 and went down westward to the
boundary of the Japhletites, as far as the boundary of
Lower Beth Horon to Gezer; and it ended at the sea.

4 So the children of Joseph, Manasseh and Ephraim,
took their inheritance.

The Land of Ephraim

5 The border of the children of Ephraim, according
to their families, was *thus:* The border of their inheritance on the east side was Ataroth Addar as far as
Upper Beth Horon.

6 And the border went out toward the sea on the
north side of Michmethath; then the border went
around eastward to Taanath Shiloh, and passed by it
on the east of Janohah. 7 Then it went down from
Janohah to Ataroth and Naarah,[t] reached to Jericho,
and came out at the Jordan.

8 The border went out from Tappuah westward to the
Brook Kanah, and it ended at the sea. This *was* the inheritance of the tribe of the children of Ephraim according to their families. 9 The separate cities for the
children of Ephraim *were* among the inheritance of the
children of Manasseh, all the cities with their villages.

10 And they did not drive out the Canaanites who
dwelt in Gezer; but the Canaanites dwell among the
Ephraimites to this day and have become forced
laborers.

The Other Half-Tribe of Manasseh (West)

17 There was also a lot for the tribe of Manasseh,
for he *was* the firstborn of Joseph: *namely* for
Machir the firstborn of Manasseh, the father of
Gilead, because he was a man of war; therefore he was
given Gilead and Bashan. 2 And there was *a lot* for the
rest of the children of Manasseh according to their
families: for the children of Abiezer,[u] the children of
Helek, the children of Asriel, the children of Shechem,
the children of Hepher, and the children of Shemida;
these *were* the male children of Manasseh the son of
Joseph according to their families.

3 But Zelophehad the son of Hepher, the son of
Gilead, the son of Machir, the son of Manasseh, had
no sons, but only daughters. And these *are* the names
of his daughters: Mahlah, Noah, Hoglah, Milcah, and
Tirzah. 4 And they came near before Eleazar the priest,
before Joshua the son of Nun, and before the rulers,
saying, "The LORD commanded Moses to give us an
inheritance among our brothers." Therefore, according to the commandment of the LORD, he gave them
an inheritance among their father's brothers. 5 Ten
shares fell to Manasseh, besides the land of Gilead
and Bashan, which *were* on the other side of the Jordan, 6 because the daughters of Manasseh received an
inheritance among his sons; and the rest of
Manasseh's sons had the land of Gilead.

7 And the territory of Manasseh was from Asher to
Michmethath, that *lies* east of Shechem; and the border went along south to the inhabitants of En
Tappuah. 8 Manasseh had the land of Tappuah, but
Tappuah on the border of Manasseh *belonged* to the
children of Ephraim. 9 And the border descended to
the Brook Kanah, southward to the brook. These
cities of Ephraim *are* among the cities of Manasseh.
The border of Manasseh *was* on the north side of the
brook; and it ended at the sea.

10 Southward *it was* Ephraim's, northward *it was*
Manasseh's, and the sea was its border. Manasseh's
territory was adjoining Asher on the north and
Issachar on the east. 11 And in Issachar and in Asher,
Manasseh had Beth Shean and its towns, Ibleam and
its towns, the inhabitants of Dor and its towns, the inhabitants of En Dor and its towns, the inhabitants of

16:2 [s] Septuagint reads *Bethel* (that is, Luz).
16:7 [t] Or *Naaran* (compare 1 Chronicles 7:28)
17:2 [u] Called *Jeezer* in Numbers 26:30

Taanach and its towns, and the inhabitants of Megiddo and its towns—
three hilly regions. 12Yet the children of Manasseh could not drive out *the*
inhabitants of those cities, but the Canaanites were determined to dwell in
that land. 13And it happened, when the children of Israel grew strong, that
they put the Canaanites to forced labor, but did not utterly drive them out.

More Land for Ephraim and Manasseh

14Then the children of Joseph spoke to Joshua, saying, "Why have you
given us *only* one lot and one share to inherit, since we *are* a great people,
inasmuch as the LORD has blessed us until now?"
15So Joshua answered them, "If you *are* a great people, *then* go up to the
forest *country* and clear a place for yourself there in the land of the
Perizzites and the giants, since the mountains of Ephraim are too confined for you."
16But the children of Joseph said, "The mountain country is not enough
for us; and all the Canaanites who dwell in the land of the valley have chariots of iron, *both those* who *are* of Beth Shean and its towns and *those* who
are of the Valley of Jezreel."
17And Joshua spoke to the house of Joseph—to Ephraim and Manasseh—saying, "You *are* a great people and have great power; you shall
not have *only* one lot, 18but the mountain country shall be yours. Although
it *is* wooded, you shall cut it down, and its farthest extent shall be yours;
for you shall drive out the Canaanites, though they have iron chariots *and*
are strong."

The Remainder of the Land Divided

18 Now the whole congregation of the children of Israel assembled together at Shiloh, and set up the tabernacle of meeting there. And the
land was subdued before them. 2But there remained among the children
of Israel seven tribes which had not yet received their inheritance.
3Then Joshua said to the children of Israel: "How long will you neglect to
go and possess the land which the LORD God of your fathers has given you?
4Pick out from among you three men for *each* tribe, and I will send them;
they shall rise and go through the land, survey it according to their inheritance, and come *back* to me. 5And they shall divide it into seven parts. Judah
shall remain in their territory on the south, and the house of Joseph shall remain in their territory on the north. 6You shall therefore survey the land in
seven parts and bring *the survey* here to me, that I may cast lots for you here
before the LORD our God. 7But the Levites have no part among you, for the
priesthood of the LORD *is* their inheritance. And Gad, Reuben, and half the
tribe of Manasseh have received their inheritance beyond the Jordan on the
east, which Moses the servant of the LORD gave them."
8Then the men arose to go away; and Joshua charged those who went to
survey the land, saying, "Go, walk through the land, survey it, and come
back to me, that I may cast lots for you here before the LORD in Shiloh." 9So
the men went, passed through the land, and wrote the survey in a book in
seven parts by cities; and they came to Joshua at the camp in Shiloh. 10Then
Joshua cast lots for them in Shiloh before the LORD, and there Joshua divided
the land to the children of Israel according to their divisions.

The Land of Benjamin

11Now the lot of the tribe of the children of Benjamin came up according

Life Lesson

Joshua 18:1–19:51

SITUATION Seven more tribes received their inheritance, which was administered by Joshua. He also took possession of the town, Timnath.

OBSERVATION The children of Israel could not exercise full dominion over the land as its new tenants until each tribe had been assigned its portions. When this occurred, then the nation as a whole began to rule and have authority on the earth as God's representatives.

INSPIRATION I was praying and fasting some years ago, seeking to understand God's purpose more fully. I heard his voice, level and conversational, "What do I desire for man?"

A bit surprised, I replied, "I don't know, Lord. You know." Then the Lord directed me to open my Bible. "Look at Genesis, and you will see, he said."

Genesis is one of the longest books in the Bible, but I opened it at the beginning. As I read along, my eyes fell on this passage:

And God said, let us make man in our image, after our likeness: and let them have dominion over the fish of the sea, and over the fowl of the air, and over the cattle, and over all the earth, and over every creeping thing that creeps upon the earth. So God created man.

"Let them have dominion." My eyes went over it several times. Then I knew the Lord's purpose. He wanted man to have dominion—then and now.

It was very clear. This was a kingdom law. God wants man to have authority

to their families, and the territory of their lot came out between the children
of Judah and the children of Joseph. [12]Their border on the north side began
at the Jordan, and the border went up to the side of Jericho on the north, and
went up through the mountains westward; it ended at the Wilderness of
Beth Aven. [13]The border went over from there toward Luz, to the side of Luz
(which *is* Bethel) southward; and the border descended to Ataroth Addar,
near the hill that *lies* on the south side of Lower Beth Horon.
[14]Then the border extended around the west side to the south, from the hill
that *lies* before Beth Horon southward; and it ended at Kirjath Baal (which *is*
Kirjath Jearim), a city of the children of Judah. This *was* the west side.
[15]The south side *began* at the end of Kirjath Jearim, and the border extended on the west and went out to the spring of the waters of Nephtoah.
[16]Then the border came down to the end of the mountain that *lies* before
the Valley of the Son of Hinnom, which *is* in the Valley of the Rephaim[v] on
the north, descended to the Valley of Hinnom, to the side of the Jebusite
city on the south, and descended to En Rogel. [17]And it went around from
the north, went out to En Shemesh, and extended toward Geliloth, which
is before the Ascent of Adummim, and descended to the stone of Bohan
the son of Reuben. [18]Then it passed along toward the north side of
Arabah,[w] and went down to Arabah. [19]And the border passed along to the
north side of Beth Hoglah; then the border ended at the north bay at the
Salt Sea, at the south end of the Jordan. This *was* the southern boundary.
[20]The Jordan was its border on the east side. This *was* the inheritance of
the children of Benjamin, according to its boundaries all around, according to their families.
[21]Now the cities of the tribe of the children of Benjamin, according to their
families, were Jericho, Beth Hoglah, Emek Keziz, [22]Beth Arabah, Zemaraim,
Bethel, [23]Avim, Parah, Ophrah, [24]Chephar Haammoni, Ophni, and Gaba:
twelve cities with their villages; [25]Gibeon, Ramah, Beeroth, [26]Mizpah,
Chephirah, Mozah, [27]Rekem, Irpeel, Taralah, [28]Zelah, Eleph, Jebus (which *is*
Jerusalem), Gibeath, *and* Kirjath: fourteen cities with their villages. This was
the inheritance of the children of Benjamin according to their families.

Simeon's Inheritance with Judah

19 The second lot came out for Simeon, for the tribe of the children of
Simeon according to their families. And their inheritance was within
the inheritance of the children of Judah. [2]They had in their inheritance
Beersheba (Sheba), Moladah, [3]Hazar Shual, Balah, Ezem, [4]Eltolad, Bethul,
Hormah, [5]Ziklag, Beth Marcaboth, Hazar Susah, [6]Beth Lebaoth, and
Sharuhen: thirteen cities and their villages; [7]Ain, Rimmon, Ether, and
Ashan: four cities and their villages; [8]and all the villages that *were* all around
these cities as far as Baalath Beer, Ramah of the South. This *was* the inheritance of the tribe of the children of Simeon according to their families.
[9]The inheritance of the children of Simeon *was included* in the share of
the children of Judah, for the share of the children of Judah was too much
for them. Therefore the children of Simeon had *their* inheritance within
the inheritance of that people.

The Land of Zebulun

[10]The third lot came out for the children of Zebulun according to their

over the earth. He wants him to rule the way he was created to rule. . . . Almighty God wants us to recapture the dominion man held in the beginning. He has gone to great lengths to make that possible, sending His own Son as the second Adam to restore what was lost in Eden. . . .

God gives man the authority to govern all that is willing to be governed. . . . He grants man authority over the untamed and rebellious. God gave man a sweeping and total mandate of dominion over this planet and everything in it.

But stewardship requires responsibility. And implicit in the grant was a requirement that man order the planet according to God's will and for God's purposes. This was a grant of freedom, not of license. As subsequent history proved, God's intention was that His world be governed and subdued by those who themselves were governed by God.

(From *The Secret Kingdom* by Pat Robertson)

APPLICATION Are you a faithful steward of what God has given you? Do you spend money carefully? Do you take care of your environment? Be a faithful steward this week: recycle more, waste less. Don't overlook the little details that can add up to tremendous waste.

EXPLORATION Man's Dominion—Genesis 1:26; 9:2; Daniel 2:38; Hebrews 2:7.

18:16 [v] Literally *Giants*
18:18 [w] Or *Beth Arabah* (compare 15:6 and 18:22)

families, and the border of their inheritance was as far
as Sarid. 11Their border went toward the west and to
Maralah, went to Dabbasheth, and extended along
the brook that is east of Jokneam. 12Then from Sarid it
went eastward toward the sunrise along the border of
Chisloth Tabor, and went out toward Daberath,
bypassing Japhia. 13And from there it passed along on
the east of Gath Hepher, toward Eth Kazin, and extended to Rimmon, which borders on Neah. 14Then
the border went around it on the north side of
Hannathon, and it ended in the Valley of Jiphthah El.
15Included were Kattath, Nahallal, Shimron, Idalah,
and Bethlehem: twelve cities with their villages. 16This
was the inheritance of the children of Zebulun according to their families, these cities with their villages.

The Land of Issachar

17The fourth lot came out to Issachar, for the children of Issachar according to their families. 18And
their territory went to Jezreel, and *included*
Chesulloth, Shunem, 19Haphraim, Shion, Anaharath,
20Rabbith, Kishion, Abez, 21Remeth, En Gannim, En
Haddah, and Beth Pazzez. 22And the border reached
to Tabor, Shahazimah, and Beth Shemesh; their border ended at the Jordan: sixteen cities with their villages. 23This *was* the inheritance of the tribe of the
children of Issachar according to their families, the
cities and their villages.

The Land of Asher

24The fifth lot came out for the tribe of the children
of Asher according to their families. 25And their terri-
tory included Helkath, Hali, Beten, Achshaph,
26Alammelech, Amad, and Mishal; it reached to
Mount Carmel westward, along *the Brook* Shihor
Libnath. 27It turned toward the sunrise to Beth
Dagon; and it reached to Zebulun and to the Valley of
Jiphthah El, then northward beyond Beth Emek and
Neiel, bypassing Cabul *which was* on the left, 28includ-
ing Ebron,[x] Rehob, Hammon, and Kanah, as far as
Greater Sidon. 29And the border turned to Ramah and
to the fortified city of Tyre; then the border turned to
Hosah, and ended at the sea by the region of Achzib.
30Also Ummah, Aphek, and Rehob *were included:*
twenty-two cities with their villages. 31This *was* the inheritance of the tribe of the children of Asher according to their families, these cities with their villages.

The Land of Naphtali

32The sixth lot came out to the children of Naphtali,
for the children of Naphtali according to their families. 33And their border began at Heleph, enclosing
the territory from the terebinth tree in Zaanannim,
Adami Nekeb, and Jabneel, as far as Lakkum; it
ended at the Jordan. 34From Heleph the border extended westward to Aznoth Tabor, and went out from
there toward Hukkok; it adjoined Zebulun on the
south side and Asher on the west side, and ended at
Judah by the Jordan toward the sunrise. 35And the fortified cities *are* Ziddim, Zer, Hammath, Rakkath,
Chinnereth, 36Adamah, Ramah, Hazor, 37Kedesh,
Edrei, En Hazor, 38Iron, Migdal El, Horem, Beth
Anath, and Beth Shemesh: nineteen cities with their
villages. 39This *was* the inheritance of the tribe of the
children of Naphtali according to their families, the
cities and their villages.

The Land of Dan

40The seventh lot came out for the tribe of the children
of Dan according to their families. 41And the territory of
their inheritance was Zorah, Eshtaol, Ir Shemesh,
42Shaalabbin, Aijalon, Jethlah, 43Elon, Timnah, Ekron,
44Eltekeh, Gibbethon, Baalath, 45Jehud, Bene Berak,
Gath Rimmon, 46Me Jarkon, and Rakkon, with the region near Joppa. 47And the border of the children of
Dan went beyond these, because the children of Dan
went up to fight against Leshem and took it; and they
struck it with the edge of the sword, took possession of
it, and dwelt in it. They called Leshem, Dan, after the
name of Dan their father. 48This *is* the inheritance of the
tribe of the children of Dan according to their families,
these cities with their villages.

Joshua's Inheritance

49When they had made an end of dividing the land
as an inheritance according to their borders, the children of Israel gave an inheritance among them to
Joshua the son of Nun. 50According to the word of the
LORD they gave him the city which he asked for,
Timnath Serah in the mountains of Ephraim; and he
built the city and dwelt in it.

51These *were* the inheritances which Eleazar the
priest, Joshua the son of Nun, and the heads of the fathers of the tribes of the children of Israel divided as
an inheritance by lot in Shiloh before the LORD, at the
door of the tabernacle of meeting. So they made an
end of dividing the country.

The Cities of Refuge

20 The LORD also spoke to Joshua, saying, 2"Speak
to the children of Israel, saying: 'Appoint for

19:28 [x] Following Masoretic Text, Targum, and Vulgate; a few Hebrew manuscripts read *Abdon* (compare 21:30 and 1 Chronicles 6:74).

yourselves cities of refuge, of which I spoke to you through Moses, 3that
the slayer who kills a person accidentally *or* unintentionally may flee there;
and they shall be your refuge from the avenger of blood. 4And when he
flees to one of those cities, and stands at the entrance of the gate of the city,
and declares his case in the hearing of the elders of that city, they shall take
him into the city as one of them, and give him a place, that he may dwell
among them. 5Then if the avenger of blood pursues him, they shall not deliver the slayer into his hand, because he struck his neighbor unintentionally,
but did not hate him beforehand. 6And he shall dwell in that city until he
stands before the congregation for judgment, *and* until the death of the
one who is high priest in those days. Then the slayer may return and come
to his own city and his own house, to the city from which he fled.' "
7So they appointed Kedesh in Galilee, in the mountains of Naphtali,
Shechem in the mountains of Ephraim, and Kirjath Arba (which *is* Hebron)
in the mountains of Judah. 8And on the other side of the Jordan, by Jericho
eastward, they assigned Bezer in the wilderness on the plain, from the tribe
of Reuben, Ramoth in Gilead, from the tribe of Gad, and Golan in Bashan,
from the tribe of Manasseh. 9These were the cities appointed for all the children of Israel and for the stranger who dwelt among them, that whoever
killed a person accidentally might flee there, and not die by the hand of the
avenger of blood until he stood before the congregation.

Cities of the Levites

21 Then the heads of the fathers' *houses* of the Levites came near to
Eleazar the priest, to Joshua the son of Nun, and to the heads of the fathers' *houses* of the tribes of the children of Israel. 2And they spoke to them
at Shiloh in the land of Canaan, saying, "The LORD commanded through
Moses to give us cities to dwell in, with their common-lands for our livestock." 3So the children of Israel gave to the Levites from their inheritance, at
the commandment of the LORD, these cities and their common-lands:
4Now the lot came out for the families of the Kohathites. And the children of Aaron the priest, *who were* of the Levites, had thirteen cities by lot
from the tribe of Judah, from the tribe of Simeon, and from the tribe of
Benjamin. 5The rest of the children of Kohath had ten cities by lot from the
families of the tribe of Ephraim, from the tribe of Dan, and from the half-
tribe of Manasseh.
6And the children of Gershon had thirteen cities by lot from the families
of the tribe of Issachar, from the tribe of Asher, from the tribe of Naphtali,
and from the half-tribe of Manasseh in Bashan.
7The children of Merari according to their families had twelve cities from
the tribe of Reuben, from the tribe of Gad, and from the tribe of Zebulun.
8And the children of Israel gave these cities with their common-lands
by lot to the Levites, as the LORD had commanded by the hand of Moses.
9So they gave from the tribe of the children of Judah and from the tribe
of the children of Simeon these cities which are designated by name,
10which were for the children of Aaron, one of the families of the
Kohathites, *who were* of the children of Levi; for the lot was theirs first.
11And they gave them Kirjath Arba (*Arba was* the father of Anak), which *is*
Hebron, in the mountains of Judah, with the common-land surrounding
it. 12But the fields of the city and its villages they gave to Caleb the son of
Jephunneh as his possession.

LIFE LESSON

Joshua 20:1–21:45

SITUATION God set up cities of refuge to protect the innocent and consecrated the Levites for service to him. Because of the Levites' position, they were not eligible to inherit land, but Joshua assigned them towns and pasturelands to provide for their needs.

OBSERVATION The Lord, in justice and love for his people, provides for all their needs, even for unforeseen accidents.

INSPIRATION To recognize God as Lord is to acknowledge that he is sovereign and supreme in the universe. To accept him as Savior is to accept his gift of salvation offered on the cross. To regard him as a Father is to go a step further. Ideally, a father is the one in your life who provides and protects. That is exactly what God has done.

He has provided for your needs. He has protected you from harm. He had adopted you. And he has given you his name.

God has proven himself as a faithful father. Now it falls to us to be trusting children. Let God give you what your family doesn't. Let him fill the void others have left. Rely upon him for your affirmation and encouragement. Look at Paul's words: "You are God's child and *God will give you the blessing promised*, because you are his child" (Gal. 4:7, emphasis added).

(From *He Still Moves Stones* by Max Lucado)

APPLICATION As God's children we have confidence in his provision for all our needs. We know that he even notices the unforeseen problems and our smallest concerns. Approach God as you would a loving father.

EXPLORATION God Provides—Psalm 103:3; 128:2; Proverbs 10:22; Isaiah 43:20; Matthew 6:26.

13Thus to the children of Aaron the priest they gave Hebron with its common-land (a city of refuge for the slayer), Libnah with its common-land, 14Jattir with its common-land, Eshtemoa with its common-land, 15Holon with its common-land, Debir with its common-land, 16Ain with its common-land, Juttah with its common-land, and Beth Shemesh with its common-land: nine cities from those two tribes; 17and from the tribe of Benjamin, Gibeon with its common-land, Geba with its common-land, 18Anathoth with its common-land, and Almon with its common-land: four cities. 19All the cities of the children of Aaron, the priests, *were* thirteen cities with their common-lands.

20And the families of the children of Kohath, the Levites, the rest of the children of Kohath, even they had the cities of their lot from the tribe of Ephraim. 21For they gave them Shechem with its common-land in the mountains of Ephraim (a city of refuge for the slayer), Gezer with its common-land, 22Kibzaim with its common-land, and Beth Horon with its common-land: four cities; 23and from the tribe of Dan, Eltekeh with its common-land, Gibbethon with its common-land, 24Aijalon with its common-land, *and* Gath Rimmon with its common-land: four cities; 25and from the half-tribe of Manasseh, Tanach with its common-land and Gath Rimmon with its common-land: two cities. 26All the ten cities with their common-lands were for the rest of the families of the children of Kohath.

27Also to the children of Gershon, of the families of the Levites, from the *other* half-tribe of Manasseh, *they gave* Golan in Bashan with its common-land (a city of refuge for the slayer), and Be Eshterah with its common-land: two cities; 28and from the tribe of Issachar, Kishion with its common-land, Daberath with its common-land, 29Jarmuth with its common-land, *and* En Gannim with its common-land: four cities; 30and from the tribe of Asher, Mishal with its common-land, Abdon with its common-land, 31Helkath with its common-land, and Rehob with its common-land: four cities; 32and from the tribe of Naphtali, Kedesh in Galilee with its common-land (a city of refuge for the slayer), Hammoth Dor with its common-land, and Kartan with its common-land: three cities. 33All the cities of the Gershonites according to their families *were* thirteen cities with their common-lands.

34And to the families of the children of Merari, the rest of the Levites, from the tribe of Zebulun, Jokneam with its common-land, Kartah with its common-land, 35Dimnah with its common-land, *and* Nahalal with its common-land: four cities; 36and from the tribe of Reuben, Bezer with its common-land, Jahaz with its common-land, 37Kedemoth with its common-land, and Mephaath with its common-land: four cities;[y] 38and from the tribe of Gad, Ramoth in Gilead with its common-land (a city of refuge for the slayer), Mahanaim with its common-land, 39Heshbon with its common-land, *and* Jazer with its common-land: four cities in all. 40So all the cities for the children of Merari according to their families, the rest of the families of the Levites, were *by* their lot twelve cities.

41All the cities of the Levites within the possession of the children of Israel *were* forty-eight cities with their common-lands. 42Every one of these cities had its common-land surrounding it; thus *were* all these cities.

The Promise Fulfilled

43So the LORD gave to Israel all the land of which He had sworn to give to their fathers, and they took possession of it and dwelt in it. 44The LORD gave them rest all around, according to all that He had sworn to their fathers. And not a man of all their enemies stood against them; the LORD delivered all their enemies into their hand. 45Not a word failed of any good thing which the LORD had spoken to the house of Israel. All came to pass.

Eastern Tribes Return to Their Lands

22 Then Joshua called the Reubenites, the Gadites, and half the tribe of Manasseh, 2and said to them: "You have kept all that Moses the servant of the LORD commanded you, and have obeyed my voice in all that I commanded you. 3You have not left your brethren these many days, up to this day, but have kept the charge of the commandment of the LORD your God. 4And now the LORD your God has given rest to your brethren, as He promised them; now therefore, return and go to your tents *and* to the land of your possession, which Moses the servant of the LORD gave you on the other side of the Jordan. 5But take careful heed to do the commandment and the law which Moses the servant of the LORD commanded you, to love the LORD your God, to walk in all His ways, to keep His commandments, to hold fast to Him, and to serve Him with all your heart and with all your soul." 6So Joshua blessed them and sent them away, and they went to their tents.

7Now to half the tribe of Manasseh Moses had given a possession in Bashan, but to the *other* half of it

21:37 *y* Following Septuagint and Vulgate (compare 1 Chronicles 6:78, 79); Masoretic Text, Bomberg, and Targum omit verses 36 and 37.

Joshua gave *a possession* among their brethren on this side of the Jordan, westward. And indeed, when Joshua sent them away to their tents, he blessed them, 8and spoke to them, saying, "Return with much riches to your tents, with very much livestock, with silver, with gold, with bronze, with iron, and with very much clothing. Divide the spoil of your enemies with your brethren."

9So the children of Reuben, the children of Gad, and half the tribe of Manasseh returned, and departed from the children of Israel at Shiloh, which *is* in the land of Canaan, to go to the country of Gilead, to the land of their possession, which they had obtained according to the word of the LORD by the hand of Moses.

An Altar by the Jordan

10And when they came to the region of the Jordan which *is* in the land of Canaan, the children of Reuben, the children of Gad, and half the tribe of Manasseh built an altar there by the Jordan—a great, impressive altar. 11Now the children of Israel heard *someone* say, "Behold, the children of Reuben, the children of Gad, and half the tribe of Manasseh have built an altar on the frontier of the land of Canaan, in the region of the Jordan—on the children of Israel's side." 12And when the children of Israel heard *of it,* the whole congregation of the children of Israel gathered together at Shiloh to go to war against them.

13Then the children of Israel sent Phinehas the son of Eleazar the priest to the children of Reuben, to the children of Gad, and to half the tribe of Manasseh, into the land of Gilead, 14and with him ten rulers, one ruler each from the chief house of every tribe of Israel; and each one *was* the head of the house of his father among the divisions[z] of Israel. 15Then they came to the children of Reuben, to the children of Gad, and to half the tribe of Manasseh, to the land of Gilead, and they spoke with them, saying, 16"Thus says the whole congregation of the LORD: 'What treachery *is* this that you have committed against the God of Israel, to turn away this day from following the LORD, in that you have built for yourselves an altar, that you might rebel this day against the LORD? 17*Is* the iniquity of Peor not enough for us, from which we are not cleansed till this day, although there was a plague in the congregation of the LORD, 18but that you must turn away this day from following the LORD? And it shall be, if you rebel today against the LORD, that tomorrow He will be angry with the whole congregation of Israel. 19Nevertheless, if the land of your possession *is* unclean, *then* cross over to the land of the possession of the LORD, where the LORD's tabernacle stands, and take possession among us; but do not rebel against the LORD, nor rebel against us, by building yourselves an altar besides the altar of the LORD our God. 20Did not Achan the son of Zerah commit a trespass in the accursed thing, and wrath fell on all the congregation of Israel? And that man did not perish alone in his iniquity.' "

21Then the children of Reuben, the children of Gad, and half the tribe of Manasseh answered and said to the heads of the divisions[a] of Israel: 22"The LORD God of gods, the LORD God of gods, He knows, and let Israel itself know—if *it is* in rebellion, or if in treachery against the LORD, do not

22:14 [z] Literally *thousands*
22:21 [a] Literally *thousands*

Life Lesson

Joshua 22:1-34

SITUATION The Israelites conquered and possessed the land. Reuben, Gad, and Manasseh fulfilled their obligations to conquer the western side of Jordan. Returning to the eastern side, the three tribes built an altar patterned after the Lord's altar. They were accused of idolatry and rebellion. But Phinehas declared that the altar was a token of solidarity with the rest of Israel and a reminder to the rest of the tribes that they all worshiped one God.

OBSERVATION When conflict occurs we must not jump to a hasty conclusion, but listen to both sides of the story in order to make a wise decision.

INSPIRATION These are ten questions you'll want to ask yourself and pray about when you're faced with a decision. The first five are generic. They represent moral issues and godly wisdom that are normative for all times. The next five are questions that you need to ask when facing a change in direction. Let's take a look at what each question entails.

First, have you prayed about it? The Lord's Prayer begins with a petition for His will. Prayer was never intended to be a fourth-down punting situation in which we ask God to bail us out of our hasty decisions. It was intended to be a first-down huddle. We aren't supposed to ask God to bless our plans; we are supposed to ask God for His plans.

. . . Second, is it consistent with the Word of God? In our culture ignorance is no excuse since resources abound. I believe every home should have at least a concordance, Bible dictionary, topical Bible, a good commentary and a study Bible with notes.

. . . Third, can I do it and be a positive Christian witness?

. . . Fourth, will the Lord be glorified? . . . Am I seeking the glory of man or glory of God? Am I doing this to be noticed by man or am I seeking to please the Lord?

. . . Fifth, am I acting responsibly? God doesn't bail us out of our irresponsibility. He will let us suffer the

Continued

consequences of our sins and irresponsible choices. But when we are faithful in little things, he will put us in charge of greater things.

. . . Sixth, is it reasonable? God expects us to think. His guidance may transcend human reasoning, but it never excludes it. God doesn't bypass our mind. . . . We are warned in Scripture not to put our mind in neutral. We are to think and practice what we know to be true (Philippians 4:8,9). Seventh, does a realistic opportunity exist? Closed doors are not meant to be knocked down. If you have a hopeless scheme let it go. If it isn't God's timing, wait. If a realistic opportunity exists, and all the other factors are in agreement, then take the plunge.

. . . Eighth, are unbiased, spiritually sensitive associates in agreement? Be careful not to consult only those who will agree with you. Give your advisors permission to ask hard questions. Don't be afraid of no answers. If it isn't God's will, don't you want to know before you make the mistake of acting impulsively?

Ninth, do I have a sanctified desire? Don't think that being in the will of God must always be an unpleasant task. The joy of the Lord should be our strength. . . . Is this a desire to satisfy a lust of the flesh, or a Spirit-filled desire to see God's kingdom established and people helped?

Tenth, do I have a peace about it? This is an inner peace. In the world you will have tribulation, but in Christ we have assurance of overcoming the world. Is the peace of God guarding your heart and your mind?

If you have been able to answer yes to all ten deciding factors, what are you waiting for?

(From *Walking in the Light* by Neil Anderson)

APPLICATION Rewrite the ten questions listed above. Which questions have you neglected to consider? Are you facing a key decision? Evaluate your choice in light of these questions.

EXPLORATION Decisions—Proverbs 18:13, 15, 17; Matthew 1:19; James 1:5-8.

save us this day. 23If we have built ourselves an altar to turn from following the LORD, or if to offer on it burnt offerings or grain offerings, or if to offer peace offerings on it, let the LORD Himself require *an account.* 24But in fact we have done it for fear, for a reason, saying, 'In time to come your descendants may speak to our descendants, saying, "What have you to do with the LORD God of Israel? 25For the LORD has made the Jordan a border between you and us, *you* children of Reuben and children of Gad. You have no part in the LORD." So your descendants would make our descendants cease fearing the LORD.' 26Therefore we said, 'Let us now prepare to build ourselves an altar, not for burnt offering nor for sacrifice, 27but *that* it *may be* a witness between you and us and our generations after us, that we may perform the service of the LORD before Him with our burnt offerings, with our sacrifices, and with our peace offerings; that your descendants may not say to our descendants in time to come, "You have no part in the LORD."' 28Therefore we said that it will be, when they say *this* to us or to our generations in time to come, that we may say, 'Here is the replica of the altar of the LORD which our fathers made, though not for burnt offerings nor for sacrifices; but it *is* a witness between you and us.' 29Far be it from us that we should rebel against the LORD, and turn from following the LORD this day, to build an altar for burnt offerings, for grain offerings, or for sacrifices, besides the altar of the LORD our God which *is* before His tabernacle."

30Now when Phinehas the priest and the rulers of the congregation, the heads of the divisions[b] of Israel who *were* with him, heard the words that the children of Reuben, the children of Gad, and the children of Manasseh spoke, it pleased them. 31Then Phinehas the son of Eleazar the priest said to the children of Reuben, the children of Gad, and the children of Manasseh, "This day we perceive that the LORD *is* among us, because you have not committed this treachery against the LORD. Now you have delivered the children of Israel out of the hand of the LORD."

32And Phinehas the son of Eleazar the priest, and the rulers, returned from the children of Reuben and the children of Gad, from the land of Gilead to the land of Canaan, to the children of Israel, and brought back word to them. 33So the thing pleased the children of Israel, and the children of Israel blessed God; they spoke no more of going against them in battle, to destroy the land where the children of Reuben and Gad dwelt.

34The children of Reuben and the children of Gad[c] called the altar, *Witness,* "For *it is* a witness between us that the LORD *is* God."

Joshua's Farewell Address

23 Now it came to pass, a long time after the LORD had given rest to Israel from all their enemies round about, that Joshua was old, advanced in age. 2And Joshua called for all Israel, for their elders, for their heads, for their judges, and for their officers, and said to them:

"I am old, advanced in age. 3You have seen all that the LORD your God has done to all these nations because of you, for the LORD your God *is* He who has fought for you. 4See, I have divided to you by lot these nations that remain, to be an inheritance for your tribes, from the Jordan, with all the nations that I have cut off, as far as the Great Sea westward. 5And the LORD your God will expel them from before you and drive them out of your

22:30 [b] Literally *thousands*
22:34 [c] Septuagint adds *and half the tribe of Manasseh*

sight. So you shall possess their land, as the LORD your God promised you.
6Therefore be very courageous to keep and to do all that is written in the
Book of the Law of Moses, lest you turn aside from it to the right hand or
to the left, 7*and* lest you go among these nations, these who remain among
you. You shall not make mention of the name of their gods, nor cause *any-*
one to swear *by them;* you shall not serve them nor bow down to them, 8but
you shall hold fast to the LORD your God, as you have done to this day. 9For
the LORD has driven out from before you great and strong nations; but *as*
for you, no one has been able to stand against you to this day. 10One man of
you shall chase a thousand, for the LORD your God *is* He who fights for you,
as He promised you. 11Therefore take careful heed to yourselves, that you
love the LORD your God. 12Or else, if indeed you do go back, and cling to the
remnant of these nations—these that remain among you—and make
marriages with them, and go in to them and they to you, 13know for certain
that the LORD your God will no longer drive out these nations from before
you. But they shall be snares and traps to you, and scourges on your sides
and thorns in your eyes, until you perish from this good land which the
LORD your God has given you.

14"Behold, this day I *am* going the way of all the earth. And you know in all
your hearts and in all your souls that not one thing has failed of all the good
things which the LORD your God spoke concerning you. All have come to
pass for you; not one word of them has failed. 15Therefore it shall come to
pass, that as all the good things have come upon you which the LORD your
God promised you, so the LORD will bring upon you all harmful things, until
He has destroyed you from this good land which the LORD your God has
given you. 16When you have transgressed the covenant of the LORD your God,
which He commanded you, and have gone and served other gods, and
bowed down to them, then the anger of the LORD will burn against you, and
you shall perish quickly from the good land which He has given you."

The Covenant at Shechem

24 Then Joshua gathered all the tribes of Israel to Shechem and called
for the elders of Israel, for their heads, for their judges, and for their
officers; and they presented themselves before God. 2And Joshua said to
all the people, "Thus says the LORD God of Israel: 'Your fathers, *including*
Terah, the father of Abraham and the father of Nahor, dwelt on the other
side of the River[d] in old times; and they served other gods. 3Then I took
your father Abraham from the other side of the River, led him throughout
all the land of Canaan, and multiplied his descendants and gave him
Isaac. 4To Isaac I gave Jacob and Esau. To Esau I gave the mountains of Seir
to possess, but Jacob and his children went down to Egypt. 5Also I sent
Moses and Aaron, and I plagued Egypt, according to what I did among
them. Afterward I brought you out.

6'Then I brought your fathers out of Egypt, and you came to the sea; and
the Egyptians pursued your fathers with chariots and horsemen to the
Red Sea. 7So they cried out to the LORD; and He put darkness between you
and the Egyptians, brought the sea upon them, and covered them. And
your eyes saw what I did in Egypt. Then you dwelt in the wilderness a long
time. 8And I brought you into the land of the Amorites, who dwelt on the

LIFE LESSON

Joshua 23:1–24:33

SITUATION God gave the people of Israel rest from all their enemies. In his farewell address, Joshua reminded the people of God's bountiful grace and mercy. He gave the Israelites commands to help them avoid falling into most likely areas of temptation.

OBSERVATION We must resist the temptation to sin and live in loving obedience to God.

INSPIRATION Several men went on a mission trip to Haiti where they met a nineteen-year-old boy who loved Christ deeply. He impressed them so profoundly that they invited him to visit the United States.

Upon arrival a whole new world opened up before this young Haitian's eyes. He had never slept between sheets, never had three meals on the same day, never used indoor plumbing, and never tasted McDonald's.

While traveling the U.S., this godly young man made many new friends. At the end of a six-week-long visit, his sponsors hosted a farewell dinner in his honor. After dinner several members of the group offered warm parting remarks. Then they asked the young Haitian if he would like to say anything.

"Yes," he said as he rose, "I would. I want to thank you so much for inviting me here. I have really enjoyed this time in the United States. But I am also very glad to be going home. You have so much in America, that I'm beginning to lose my grip on my day-to-day dependency on Christ."

Do you have "so much" that you find it hard to keep a grip on your day-to-day dependency on Christ? Or worse, have you lost your grip?

When we don't need to depend on Christ, we will not. . . . Our natural tendency is to depend on self, not Christ. Depending on Christ is an act of the will by faith, not the natural disposition of our heart.

I have prayed that God will always keep some major unmet need in my life so that I will always depend upon Him. To be really in need, like the

Continued

24:2 *d* Hebrew *Nahar,* the Euphrates, and so in verses 3, 14, and 15

widow in 1 Timothy 5:5, creates dependency. To have so much, as the young Haitian observed, creates self-sufficiency. When our lives prosper, the natural tendency is to lose our grip.

Someone called my prayer courageous. I disagree. It is not of courage, but of fear—the fear of a holy God. For God has the power to give us what we deserve, whether good or bad. I have come to fear, with reverence and awe, the God who is, for He is a consuming fire.

(From *Walking with Christ in the Details of Life* by Patrick Morley)

APPLICATION Have your abundant resources kept you from depending on God? Have you lost your grip on God's help? Focus on a special need that only God can meet. Seek his help today.

EXPLORATION Dependence—2 Chronicles 13:18; 16:8; Psalm 33:4; John 8:26.

other side of the Jordan, and they fought with you. But I gave them into
your hand, that you might possess their land, and I destroyed them from
before you. 9Then Balak the son of Zippor, king of Moab, arose to make
war against Israel, and sent and called Balaam the son of Beor to curse
you. 10But I would not listen to Balaam; therefore he continued to bless
you. So I delivered you out of his hand. 11Then you went over the Jordan
and came to Jericho. And the men of Jericho fought against you—*also* the
Amorites, the Perizzites, the Canaanites, the Hittites, the Girgashites, the
Hivites, and the Jebusites. But I delivered them into your hand. 12I sent the
hornet before you which drove them out from before you, *also* the two
kings of the Amorites, *but* not with your sword or with your bow. 13I have
given you a land for which you did not labor, and cities which you did not
build, and you dwell in them; you eat of the vineyards and olive groves
which you did not plant.'

14"Now therefore, fear the LORD, serve Him in sincerity and in truth, and
put away the gods which your fathers served on the other side of the River
and in Egypt. Serve the LORD! 15And if it seems evil to you to serve the LORD,
choose for yourselves this day whom you will serve, whether the gods
which your fathers served that *were* on the other side of the River, or the
gods of the Amorites, in whose land you dwell. But as for me and my
house, we will serve the LORD."

16So the people answered and said: "Far be it from us that we should forsake the LORD to serve other gods; 17for the LORD our God *is* He who brought
us and our fathers up out of the land of Egypt, from the house of bondage,
who did those great signs in our sight, and preserved us in all the way that
we went and among all the people through whom we passed. 18And the LORD
drove out from before us all the people, including the Amorites who dwelt in
the land. We also will serve the LORD, for He *is* our God."

19But Joshua said to the people, "You cannot serve the LORD, for He *is* a
holy God. He *is* a jealous God; He will not forgive your transgressions nor
your sins. 20If you forsake the LORD and serve foreign gods, then He will
turn and do you harm and consume you, after He has done you good."

21And the people said to Joshua, "No, but we will serve the LORD!"

22So Joshua said to the people, "You *are* witnesses against yourselves
that you have chosen the LORD for yourselves, to serve Him."

And they said, "*We are* witnesses!"

23"Now therefore," *he said,* "put away the foreign gods which *are* among
you, and incline your heart to the LORD God of Israel."

24And the people said to Joshua, "The LORD our God we will serve, and
His voice we will obey!"

25So Joshua made a covenant with the people that day, and made for
them a statute and an ordinance in Shechem.

26Then Joshua wrote these words in the Book of the Law of God. And he
took a large stone, and set it up there under the oak that *was* by the sanctuary of the LORD. 27And Joshua said to all the people, "Behold, this stone
shall be a witness to us, for it has heard all the words of the LORD which He
spoke to us. It shall therefore be a witness to you, lest you deny your God."
28So Joshua let the people depart, each to his own inheritance.

Death of Joshua and Eleazar

29Now it came to pass after these things that Joshua the son of Nun, the

servant of the LORD, died, *being* one hundred and ten
years old. 30And they buried him within the border of
his inheritance at Timnath Serah, which *is* in the
mountains of Ephraim, on the north side of Mount
Gaash.

31Israel served the LORD all the days of Joshua, and
all the days of the elders who outlived Joshua, who
had known all the works of the LORD which He had
done for Israel.

32The bones of Joseph, which the children of Israel
had brought up out of Egypt, they buried at Shechem,
in the plot of ground which Jacob had bought from
the sons of Hamor the father of Shechem for one hundred pieces of silver, and which had become an inheritance of the children of Joseph.

33And Eleazar the son of Aaron died. They buried
him in a hill *belonging to* Phinehas his son, which was
given to him in the mountains of Ephraim.

The Book of JUDGES

INTRODUCTION

It was a nation born out of a passion for religious freedom. Free practice of faith had been oppressed and forbidden in the old country. The people longed to be in a place where they could worship God as they desired.

So they left. Willing to battle the fears of the unknown in exchange for freedom. Only a small portion of those who began the journey survived it.

When the travelers reached the new country they celebrated. They gave thanks to God and praised him for guiding them to their new home.

But their new home was not a peaceful place. Nearby enemies attacked and years of battles ensued. The settlers, however, were men and women of faith and courage. With time they sank their roots in the new land and began a new life.

The first generation of settlers were hearty people. Though the hardships were great, their faith was greater. God answered their prayers and established them in the new land.

With time the new land was divided into states, and leaders were assigned to each region. The population grew, and the boundary of the country expanded.

But with the growth of the land and the passage of the decades, two troubling trends began.

The first was the disappearance of values. Early settlers had a common conviction as to what was right and wrong. The family was the core of society. Religion was the source of faith. Education was the highest task.

But by the end of the first hundred years in the new land, these virtues had begun to wane . . . the family was under attack; sophisticated thinkers mocked religion.

The second alarming trend was the inconsistency of moral leadership. Early leaders—capable military and skillful politicians—were also men of God. Men prone to spend time in prayer and meditation. Men who listened to God and earnestly tried to follow his will.

Such leadership became rare, however. The nation we look at now lacks moral leadership. Leaders squabble and steal. Others are lazy and spoiled. There are even cases of national leaders accused of making sexual advances to women.

Though the nation has a glorious past, it is hidden in a cloudy present.

Sound familiar? Sound like any nation you know? Sound like us? It sounds like ours, could be ours, might be ours, but I didn't get the profile out of the newspaper. I read it in the Bible. In the Book of Judges.

Judges chronicles the dark ages of Israel, the death of Israel. The death of the heart. A three hundred-year era in which "everyone did what seemed right" (Judges 21:25).

Not a pretty story. Not intended to be. It's intended to be a warning. A warning of what happens when God is ignored and passions are worshiped.

A warning for our times.

LIFE LESSON

Judges 1:1–2:5

SITUATION God commanded Israel to destroy every enemy in the promised land. Yet, Israel decided to leave some "harmless" enemies alone. Not only was Israel disobedient, but the "harmless" residents of the land of Israel rose up to become dangerous enemies.

OBSERVATION God foresees potential danger in our lives. He gives commands that, if followed, can protect us from dangerous consequences. If we neglect certain commands, we may reap painful consequences later.

INSPIRATION The tables turned! Instead of the Hebrews' keeping the upper hand, they loosened their grip on absolute obedience, they talked themselves out of Joshua's game plan, they opted for compromise with wrong . . . and they became victims instead of victors.

Compromises like that never work. We always get burned. Even though we rationalize around our weak decisions and tell ourselves that wicked associations really won't harm us ("They'll get better, our good will rub off on their bad!"), we get soiled in the process.

If you put on a pair of clean white gloves on a rainy day and then go out

The Continuing Conquest of Canaan

Now after the death of Joshua it came to pass that the children of Israel asked the LORD, saying, "Who shall be first to go up for us against the Canaanites to fight against them?" 2And the LORD said, "Judah shall go up. Indeed I have delivered the land into his hand."

3So Judah said to Simeon his brother, "Come up with me to my allotted territory, that we may fight against the Canaanites; and I will likewise go with you to your allotted territory." And Simeon went with him. 4Then Judah went up, and the LORD delivered the Canaanites and the Perizzites into their hand; and they killed ten thousand men at Bezek. 5And they found Adoni-Bezek in Bezek, and fought against him; and they defeated the Canaanites and the Perizzites. 6Then Adoni-Bezek fled, and they pursued him and caught him and cut off his thumbs and big toes. 7And Adoni-Bezek said, "Seventy kings with their thumbs and big toes cut off used to gather *scraps* under my table; as I have done, so God has repaid me." Then they brought him to Jerusalem, and there he died.

8Now the children of Judah fought against Jerusalem and took it; they struck it with the edge of the sword and set the city on fire. 9And afterward the children of Judah went down to fight against the Canaanites who dwelt in the mountains, in the South,[a] and in the lowland. 10Then Judah went against the Canaanites who dwelt in Hebron. (Now the name of Hebron *was* formerly Kirjath Arba.) And they killed Sheshai, Ahiman, and Talmai. 11From there they went against the inhabitants of Debir. (The name of Debir *was* formerly Kirjath Sepher.)

12Then Caleb said, "Whoever attacks Kirjath Sepher and takes it, to him I will give my daughter Achsah as wife." 13And Othniel the son of Kenaz, Caleb's younger brother, took it; so he gave him his daughter Achsah as wife. 14Now it happened, when she came *to him,* that she urged him[b] to ask her father for a field. And she dismounted from *her* donkey, and Caleb said to her, "What do you wish?" 15So she said to him, "Give me a blessing; since you have given me land in the South, give me also springs of water." And Caleb gave her the upper springs and the lower springs.

16Now the children of the Kenite, Moses' father-in-law, went up from the City of Palms with the children of Judah into the Wilderness of Judah, which *lies* in the South *near* Arad; and they went and dwelt among the people. 17And Judah went with his brother Simeon, and they attacked the Canaanites who inhabited Zephath, and utterly destroyed it. So the name of the city was called Hormah. 18Also Judah took Gaza with its territory, Ashkelon with its territory, and Ekron with its territory. 19So the LORD was with Judah. And they drove out the mountaineers, but they could not drive out the inhabitants of the lowland, because they had chariots of iron. 20And they gave Hebron to Caleb, as Moses had said. Then he expelled from there the three sons of Anak. 21But the children of Benjamin did not drive out the Jebusites who inhabited Jerusalem; so the Jebusites dwell with the children of Benjamin in Jerusalem to this day.

22And the house of Joseph also went up against Bethel, and the LORD *was* with them. 23So the house of Joseph sent men to spy out Bethel. (The name of the city *was* formerly Luz.) 24And when the spies saw a man coming out

1:9 [a] Hebrew *Negev,* and so throughout this book
1:14 [b] Septuagint and Vulgate read *he urged her.*

of the city, they said to him, "Please show us the entrance to the city, and
we will show you mercy." 25So he showed them the entrance to the city, and
they struck the city with the edge of the sword; but they let the man and all
his family go. 26And the man went to the land of the Hittites, built a city,
and called its name Luz, which *is* its name to this day.

Incomplete Conquest of the Land

27However, Manasseh did not drive out *the inhabitants of* Beth Shean
and its villages, or Taanach and its villages, or the inhabitants of Dor and
its villages, or the inhabitants of Ibleam and its villages, or the inhabitants
of Megiddo and its villages; for the Canaanites were determined to dwell in
that land. 28And it came to pass, when Israel was strong, that they put the
Canaanites under tribute, but did not completely drive them out.
29Nor did Ephraim drive out the Canaanites who dwelt in Gezer; so the
Canaanites dwelt in Gezer among them.
30Nor did Zebulun drive out the inhabitants of Kitron or the inhabitants
of Nahalol; so the Canaanites dwelt among them, and were put under tribute.
31Nor did Asher drive out the inhabitants of Acco or the inhabitants of
Sidon, or of Ahlab, Achzib, Helbah, Aphik, or Rehob. 32So the Asherites
dwelt among the Canaanites, the inhabitants of the land; for they did not
drive them out.
33Nor did Naphtali drive out the inhabitants of Beth Shemesh or the inhabitants of Beth Anath; but they dwelt among the Canaanites, the inhabitants of the land. Nevertheless the inhabitants of Beth Shemesh and Beth
Anath were put under tribute to them.
34And the Amorites forced the children of Dan into the mountains, for they
would not allow them to come down to the valley; 35and the Amorites were
determined to dwell in Mount Heres, in Aijalon, and in Shaalbim;[c] yet when the
strength of the house of Joseph became greater, they were put under tribute.
36Now the boundary of the Amorites *was* from the Ascent of Akrabbim,
from Sela, and upward.

Israel's Disobedience

2 Then the Angel of the LORD came up from Gilgal to Bochim, and said:
"I led you up from Egypt and brought you to the land of which I swore
to your fathers; and I said, 'I will never break My covenant with you. 2And
you shall make no covenant with the inhabitants of this land; you shall
tear down their altars.' But you have not obeyed My voice. Why have you
done this? 3Therefore I also said, 'I will not drive them out before you; but
they shall be *thorns* in your side,[d] and their gods shall be a snare to you.' "
4So it was, when the Angel of the LORD spoke these words to all the children
of Israel, that the people lifted up their voices and wept.
5Then they called the name of that place Bochim;[e] and they sacrificed
there to the LORD. 6And when Joshua had dismissed the people, the children of Israel went each to his own inheritance to possess the land.

Death of Joshua

7So the people served the LORD all the days of Joshua, and all the days of
the elders who outlived Joshua, who had seen all the great works of the

1:35 [c] Spelled *Shaalabbin* in Joshua 19:42
2:3 [d] Septuagint, Targum, and Vulgate read *enemies to you.*
2:5 [e] Literally *Weeping*

into the back yard to the flower bed and pick up a glob of mud, trust me, the mud will never get "glovey." The gloves will definitely get muddy. Every time. In all my forty nine years on earth, I have never seen glovey mud. Not once. In simple terms that is what 1 Corinthians 15:33 is saying: "Do not be deceived: bad company corrupts good morals."

. . . Just as the human body cannot grow and survive unless disease is removed . . . and just as the national body of Israel could not remain strong and healthy unless Canaanite lifestyle was removed, so it is in the body of Christ. If our resistance breaks down, alien germs will cause us to lose our health and hinder our ability to function.

(From *Dropping Your Guard* by Charles Swindoll)

APPLICATION What sin did you purposely commit yesterday or today? Learn from Israel: Compromise can be deadly! Decide today to be totally faithful and obedient to God.

EXPLORATION Compromise—Genesis 19; Exodus 8:25-29; Numbers 25:1; 1 Kings 11:4; Proverbs 12:3; Daniel 1:8-16; Mark 15:15; 2 Corinthians 6:14-18; Galatians 2:11; Revelation 2:2.

LIFE LESSON

Judges 2:6–3:6

SITUATION A new generation of Israelites neglected their relationship with God. They did not see God's hand at work like their parents had. When they turned away from God, God disciplined them.

OBSERVATION Failing to teach our children to love and obey God will bring disaster on them.

INSPIRATION Have you ever thought about what you are going to leave behind when you die? Most people think in terms of possessions—property, money, stocks and bonds, and so forth. But let's think in terms of what kind of spiritual heritage, what kind of lifestyle, what kind of understanding of who God is and of what the Scriptures say will be your legacy?

You may say, "Wait a minute. You can't give someone else your faith. That is something everyone has to experience on a personal basis. You can't really give your faith away." You cannot give away your experience, I admit, but you can hand down your faith. You can leave your sense of moral values, your understanding of the principles of Scripture, those principles of the Word of God that have guided you and led you as you made your decisions in life. . . .

If you are a godly parent, look at what you have to give to your children. You may not be able to leave them even a small amount of money but if you have loved God and practiced the principles of Scripture, if you have loved your children and listened to them, you will leave them a faith to sustain them through every difficulty, every heartache, and every trial of life.

My challenge to you is to build a strong Christian home. If you will purpose to do so, you will keep your kids on your team.

(From *How to Keep Your Kids on Your Team* by Charles Stanley)

APPLICATION Pray daily with your children and discipline them. Speak to them from your heart about the Lord.

EXPLORATION Handing Down Your Faith—Deuteronomy 6:4-7; 11:18-21; 32:46; Proverbs 20:7; 22:6; Isaiah 38:19; Ephesians 6:4; 2 Timothy 1:1-9; 3:14-15.

LORD which He had done for Israel. 8Now Joshua the son of Nun, the servant of the LORD, died *when he was* one hundred and ten years old. 9And
they buried him within the border of his inheritance at Timnath Heres, in
the mountains of Ephraim, on the north side of Mount Gaash. 10When all
that generation had been gathered to their fathers, another generation
arose after them who did not know the LORD nor the work which He had
done for Israel.

Israel's Unfaithfulness

11Then the children of Israel did evil in the sight of the LORD, and served
the Baals; 12and they forsook the LORD God of their fathers, who had
brought them out of the land of Egypt; and they followed other gods from
among the gods of the people who *were* all around them, and they bowed
down to them; and they provoked the LORD to anger. 13They forsook the
LORD and served Baal and the Ashtoreths.[f] 14And the anger of the LORD was
hot against Israel. So He delivered them into the hands of plunderers who
despoiled them; and He sold them into the hands of their enemies all
around, so that they could no longer stand before their enemies. 15Wher-
ever they went out, the hand of the LORD was against them for calamity, as
the LORD had said, and as the LORD had sworn to them. And they were
greatly distressed.
16Nevertheless, the LORD raised up judges who delivered them out of the
hand of those who plundered them. 17Yet they would not listen to their
judges, but they played the harlot with other gods, and bowed down to
them. They turned quickly from the way in which their fathers walked, in
obeying the commandments of the LORD; they did not do so. 18And when
the LORD raised up judges for them, the LORD was with the judge and delivered them out of the hand of their enemies all the days of the judge; for the
LORD was moved to pity by their groaning because of those who oppressed
them and harassed them. 19And it came to pass, when the judge was dead,
that they reverted and behaved more corruptly than their fathers, by following other gods, to serve them and bow down to them. They did not
cease from their own doings nor from their stubborn way.
20Then the anger of the LORD was hot against Israel; and He said, "Because this nation has transgressed My covenant which I commanded
their fathers, and has not heeded My voice, 21I also will no longer drive out
before them any of the nations which Joshua left when he died, 22so that
through them I may test Israel, whether they will keep the ways of the
LORD, to walk in them as their fathers kept *them,* or not." 23Therefore the
LORD left those nations, without driving them out immediately; nor did He
deliver them into the hand of Joshua.

The Nations Remaining in the Land

3 Now these *are* the nations which the LORD left, that He might test Israel
by them, *that is,* all who had not known any of the wars in Canaan 2(*this
was* only so that the generations of the children of Israel might be taught
to know war, at least those who had not formerly known it), 3*namely,* five
lords of the Philistines, all the Canaanites, the Sidonians, and the Hivites
who dwelt in Mount Lebanon, from Mount Baal Hermon to the entrance
of Hamath. 4And they were *left, that He might* test Israel by them, to know

2:13 *f* Canaanite goddesses

whether they would obey the commandments of the LORD, which He had
commanded their fathers by the hand of Moses.
5Thus the children of Israel dwelt among the Canaanites, the Hittites,
the Amorites, the Perizzites, the Hivites, and the Jebusites. 6And they took
their daughters to be their wives, and gave their daughters to their sons;
and they served their gods.

Othniel

7So the children of Israel did evil in the sight of the LORD. They forgot the
LORD their God, and served the Baals and Asherahs.[g] 8Therefore the anger
of the LORD was hot against Israel, and He sold them into the hand of
Cushan-Rishathaim king of Mesopotamia; and the children of Israel
served Cushan-Rishathaim eight years. 9When the children of Israel cried
out to the LORD, the LORD raised up a deliverer for the children of Israel,
who delivered them: Othniel the son of Kenaz, Caleb's younger brother.
10The Spirit of the LORD came upon him, and he judged Israel. He went out
to war, and the LORD delivered Cushan-Rishathaim king of Mesopotamia
into his hand; and his hand prevailed over Cushan-Rishathaim. 11So the
land had rest for forty years. Then Othniel the son of Kenaz died.

Ehud

12And the children of Israel again did evil in the sight of the LORD. So the
LORD strengthened Eglon king of Moab against Israel, because they had
done evil in the sight of the LORD. 13Then he gathered to himself the people of
Ammon and Amalek, went and defeated Israel, and took possession of the
City of Palms. 14So the children of Israel served Eglon king of Moab eighteen
years.
15But when the children of Israel cried out to the LORD, the LORD raised
up a deliverer for them: Ehud the son of Gera, the Benjamite, a left-handed
man. By him the children of Israel sent tribute to Eglon king of Moab.
16Now Ehud made himself a dagger (it was double-edged and a cubit in
length) and fastened it under his clothes on his right thigh. 17So he brought
the tribute to Eglon king of Moab. (Now Eglon *was* a very fat man.) 18And
when he had finished presenting the tribute, he sent away the people who
had carried the tribute. 19But he himself turned back from the stone images that *were* at Gilgal, and said, "I have a secret message for you, O king."
He said, "Keep silence!" And all who attended him went out from him.
20So Ehud came to him (now he was sitting upstairs in his cool private
chamber). Then Ehud said, "I have a message from God for you." So he
arose from *his* seat. 21Then Ehud reached with his left hand, took the dagger
from his right thigh, and thrust it into his belly. 22Even the hilt went in after
the blade, and the fat closed over the blade, for he did not draw the dagger
out of his belly; and his entrails came out. 23Then Ehud went out through the
porch and shut the doors of the upper room behind him and locked them.
24When he had gone out, *Eglon's*[h] servants came to look, and *to their*
surprise, the doors of the upper room were locked. So they said, "He is
probably attending to his needs in the cool chamber." 25So they waited till
they were embarrassed, and still he had not opened the doors of the upper
room. Therefore they took the key and opened *them.* And there was their
master, fallen dead on the floor.

3:7 [g] Name or symbol for Canaanite goddesses
3:24 [h] Literally *his*

LIFE LESSON

Judges 3:7-31

SITUATION The Israelites rebelled against God. He used their enemies to exercise his discipline.

OBSERVATION Othniel delivered Israel. Later, Ehud liberated Israel using a surprising tactic.

INSPIRATION In the *Canaan Times* the headlines scream: "MONARCH MURDERED BY LEFT-HANDED KILLER . . . Eglon, . . . king of Moab, died today after a knife attack by an Israelite terrorist. First reports indicate that . . ."

Of the abundant details which flow over from the front page to the next, the most memorable may be that Eglon is "a very fat man" (3:17), but the most significant is that Ehud is left-handed (3:15). We can get an idea of what that implies for the Bible writers if we piece together some of the verses where the words right hand are used. A concordance will list them for us, and will draw our attention especially to the Lord's own right hand. By it he swears to bless his people, and with it he destroys their enemies. At his right hand are pleasures for evermore, and there his Chosen One sits. It is the hand of power, glory, and blessing.

So if we had been told that the Lord, the Judge, stretching out his right hand to rescue Israel raised up a deliverer who likewise lifted his right hand to brandish the sword of liberation, we should have observed "How apt!" And when we are told instead that the deliverer cannot use his right hand, we shall say "How odd"—for this is not what the pattern of Othniel will have led us to expect.

. . . God's chosen deliverer, when he comes, turns out to be a man who cannot use his right hand. This is what the Hebrew phrase means. It is not making the positive statement that Ehud naturally uses his left hand, but the negative one that he is "bound" or restricted in the use of the right. Perhaps it is deformed or paralyzed in some way. As an added irony, he belongs to the tribe of Benjamin, whose name means "son of the right hand."

Continued

. . . We, the readers, can see the irony of the call of such a man. . . . But we must also realize that at the time it must have been a perplexing and mind-stretching experience for Israel. God's ultimate objectives do not change: He will do what he has said. But how he will do it is another matter. . . .

. . . We are not to be surprised if he chooses the most unlikely methods, even if we find that such left-handed things as deprivation or illness, frustration or failure, become the instruments of his rule. After all, who would have expected that he would choose to work through such a left-handed crowd of people as the Christian church? Who would have predicted that when the Judge came himself in the flesh, he would come as such a "left-handed" person, with "no form or comeliness that we should look at him, and no beauty that we should desire him . . . despised and rejected by men"?

(From *The Message of Judges* by M. Wilcox)

APPLICATION Are there Christians you don't like? Why do you think God can't use them—physical appearance? Ethnic background? Worship preference? Ask God to help you accept and value those people. Choose to become a friend to a Christian who is tough for you to love.

EXPLORATION God Uses Unlikely People—1 Samuel 16:6-7; Psalm 8:2; 1 Corinthians 1:26-29; 2 Corinthians 12:9-10; Hebrews 11:32-34.

26 But Ehud had escaped while they delayed, and passed beyond the
stone images and escaped to Seirah. 27 And it happened, when he arrived,
that he blew the trumpet in the mountains of Ephraim, and the children of
Israel went down with him from the mountains; and he led them. 28 Then
he said to them, "Follow *me,* for the LORD has delivered your enemies the
Moabites into your hand." So they went down after him, seized the fords
of the Jordan leading to Moab, and did not allow anyone to cross over.
29 And at that time they killed about ten thousand men of Moab, all stout
men of valor; not a man escaped. 30 So Moab was subdued that day under
the hand of Israel. And the land had rest for eighty years.

Shamgar

31 After him was Shamgar the son of Anath, who killed six hundred men
of the Philistines with an ox goad; and he also delivered Israel.

Deborah

4 When Ehud was dead, the children of Israel again did evil in the sight
of the LORD. 2 So the LORD sold them into the hand of Jabin king of
Canaan, who reigned in Hazor. The commander of his army *was* Sisera,
who dwelt in Harosheth Hagoyim. 3 And the children of Israel cried out to
the LORD; for Jabin had nine hundred chariots of iron, and for twenty years
he had harshly oppressed the children of Israel.
4 Now Deborah, a prophetess, the wife of Lapidoth, was judging Israel at
that time. 5 And she would sit under the palm tree of Deborah between
Ramah and Bethel in the mountains of Ephraim. And the children of Israel came up to her for judgment. 6 Then she sent and called for Barak the
son of Abinoam from Kedesh in Naphtali, and said to him, "Has not the
LORD God of Israel commanded, 'Go and deploy *troops* at Mount Tabor;
take with you ten thousand men of the sons of Naphtali and of the sons of
Zebulun; 7 and against you I will deploy Sisera, the commander of Jabin's
army, with his chariots and his multitude at the River Kishon; and I will
deliver him into your hand'?"
8 And Barak said to her, "If you will go with me, then I will go; but if you
will not go with me, I will not go!"
9 So she said, "I will surely go with you; nevertheless there will be no
glory for you in the journey you are taking, for the LORD will sell Sisera into
the hand of a woman." Then Deborah arose and went with Barak to Kedesh.
10 And Barak called Zebulun and Naphtali to Kedesh; he went up with ten
thousand men under his command,[i] and Deborah went up with him.
11 Now Heber the Kenite, of the children of Hobab the father-in-law of
Moses, had separated himself from the Kenites and pitched his tent near
the terebinth tree at Zaanaim, which *is* beside Kedesh.
12 And they reported to Sisera that Barak the son of Abinoam had gone
up to Mount Tabor. 13 So Sisera gathered together all his chariots, nine
hundred chariots of iron, and all the people who *were* with him, from
Harosheth Hagoyim to the River Kishon.
14 Then Deborah said to Barak, "Up! For this *is* the day in which the LORD
has delivered Sisera into your hand. Has not the LORD gone out before
you?" So Barak went down from Mount Tabor with ten thousand men following him. 15 And the LORD routed Sisera and all *his* chariots and all *his*

4:10 [i] Literally *at his feet*

army with the edge of the sword before Barak; and Sisera alighted from *his*
chariot and fled away on foot. 16But Barak pursued the chariots and the
army as far as Harosheth Hagoyim, and all the army of Sisera fell by the
edge of the sword; not a man was left.
17However, Sisera had fled away on foot to the tent of Jael, the wife of
Heber the Kenite; for *there was* peace between Jabin king of Hazor and the
house of Heber the Kenite. 18And Jael went out to meet Sisera, and said to
him, "Turn aside, my lord, turn aside to me; do not fear." And when he
had turned aside with her into the tent, she covered him with a blanket.
19Then he said to her, "Please give me a little water to drink, for I am
thirsty." So she opened a jug of milk, gave him a drink, and covered him.
20And he said to her, "Stand at the door of the tent, and if any man comes
and inquires of you, and says, 'Is there any man here?' you shall say, 'No.' "
21Then Jael, Heber's wife, took a tent peg and took a hammer in her
hand, and went softly to him and drove the peg into his temple, and it
went down into the ground; for he was fast asleep and weary. So he died.
22And then, as Barak pursued Sisera, Jael came out to meet him, and said
to him, "Come, I will show you the man whom you seek." And when he
went into her *tent,* there lay Sisera, dead with the peg in his temple.
23So on that day God subdued Jabin king of Canaan in the presence of
the children of Israel. 24And the hand of the children of Israel grew
stronger and stronger against Jabin king of Canaan, until they had destroyed Jabin king of Canaan.

The Song of Deborah

5 Then Deborah and Barak the son of Abinoam sang on that day, saying:

2 "When leaders lead in Israel,
When the people willingly offer themselves,
Bless the LORD!

3 "Hear, O kings! Give ear, O princes!
I, *even* I, will sing to the LORD;
I will sing praise to the LORD God of Israel.

4 "LORD, when You went out from Seir,
When You marched from the field of Edom,
The earth trembled and the heavens poured,
The clouds also poured water;
5 The mountains gushed before the LORD,
This Sinai, before the LORD God of Israel.

6 "In the days of Shamgar, son of Anath,
In the days of Jael,
The highways were deserted,
And the travelers walked along the byways.
7 Village life ceased, it ceased in Israel,
Until I, Deborah, arose,
Arose a mother in Israel.
8 They chose new gods;
Then *there was* war in the gates;
Not a shield or spear was seen among forty thousand in Israel.

LIFE LESSON

Judges 4:1–5:31

SITUATION Now the Israelites' enemy (the Canaanites) came from within their own territory. Deborah rose to national leadership.

OBSERVATION God chooses the person with the strongest character to lead his people to victory at crucial times. The key elements for such leadership are faith, trust, and worship.

INSPIRATION In the Older Testament almost every man and woman did the faith-oriented things for which we credit them *not* in religious environments but in real-world environments. Moses did most of his work in the Pharaoh's conference rooms and in the deserts. Esther did hers in a king's palace. Nehemiah did his on a construction project. These men and women were administrators, scholars, builders, warriors, and merchants. For the most part, they were not clergy. They were the people of the streets, and their faith was defined in terms of a God who wanted to be active in the streets.

Their faith language, recorded in the Bible, was the language of the streets; but we have taken it away from there and made it a religious language. Their jobs were the work of the streets; but we, in our lack of imagination, have taken these men and women off the streets (figuratively speaking) and made them seem like theologians and full-time religious workers. The problems to which they addressed themselves were usually the problems of the streets; but we have taken the problems and spiritualized them.

In short, we have tended to tame these men and women of the Bible, making them smaller than life. It is not that we have not admired them and revered them as heroes. And it is not that we have not wanted to be like them. But it has not occurred to us often enough to wonder if they could have been construction workers on a highway project, manufacturers, franchisees, secretaries, and managers in our day. The result? I'll say it one more time: we do not fully appreciate that their faith was a faith for the real

Continued

world and not for the restricted environment of professional religion.

(From *Christ Followers in the Real World* by Gordon MacDonald)

APPLICATION Take time this week to study a leader in the Bible (Esther, Elijah, Paul . . .). What made that person successful? How did that leader honor God? What made that individual unique? As you develop your own character, imitate the godly characteristics you find.

EXPLORATION Women Leaders—Exodus 15:20; 2 Kings 11:1-16; 22:14-20; Esther 2:17; Luke 1:41-45; 2:36-38.

9 My heart *is* with the rulers of Israel
Who offered themselves willingly with the people.
Bless the LORD!

10 "Speak, you who ride on white donkeys,
Who sit in judges' attire,
And who walk along the road.
11 Far from the noise of the archers, among the watering places,
There they shall recount the righteous acts of the LORD,
The righteous acts *for* His villagers in Israel;
Then the people of the LORD shall go down to the gates.

12 "Awake, awake, Deborah!
Awake, awake, sing a song!
Arise, Barak, and lead your captives away,
O son of Abinoam!

13 "Then the survivors came down, the people against the nobles;
The LORD came down for me against the mighty.
14 From Ephraim *were* those whose roots were in Amalek.
After you, Benjamin, with your peoples,
From Machir rulers came down,
And from Zebulun those who bear the recruiter's staff.
15 And the princes of Issachar[j] *were* with Deborah;
As Issachar, so *was* Barak
Sent into the valley under his command;[k]
Among the divisions of Reuben
There were great resolves of heart.
16 Why did you sit among the sheepfolds,
To hear the pipings for the flocks?
The divisions of Reuben have great searchings of heart.
17 Gilead stayed beyond the Jordan,
And why did Dan remain on ships?[l]
Asher continued at the seashore,
And stayed by his inlets.
18 Zebulun *is* a people *who* jeopardized their lives
to the point of death,
Naphtali also, on the heights of the battlefield.

19 "The kings came *and* fought,
Then the kings of Canaan fought
In Taanach, by the waters of Megiddo;
They took no spoils of silver.
20 They fought from the heavens;
The stars from their courses fought against Sisera.
21 The torrent of Kishon swept them away,
That ancient torrent, the torrent of Kishon.
O my soul, march on in strength!
22 Then the horses' hooves pounded,
The galloping, galloping of his steeds.

5:15 *j* Following Septuagint, Syriac, Targum, and Vulgate; Masoretic Text reads *And my princes in Issachar.* *k* Literally *at his feet*
5:17 *l* Or *at ease*

23 'Curse Meroz,' said the angel[m] of the LORD,
'Curse its inhabitants bitterly,
Because they did not come to the help of the LORD,
To the help of the LORD against the mighty.'
24 "Most blessed among women is Jael,
The wife of Heber the Kenite;
Blessed is she among women in tents.
25 He asked for water, she gave milk;
She brought out cream in a lordly bowl.
26 She stretched her hand to the tent peg,
Her right hand to the workmen's hammer;
She pounded Sisera, she pierced his head,
She split and struck through his temple.
27 At her feet he sank, he fell, he lay still;
At her feet he sank, he fell;
Where he sank, there he fell dead.
28 "The mother of Sisera looked through the window,
And cried out through the lattice,
'Why is his chariot *so* long in coming?
Why tarries the clatter of his chariots?'
29 Her wisest ladies answered her,
Yes, she answered herself,
30 'Are they not finding and dividing the spoil:
To every man a girl *or* two;
For Sisera, plunder of dyed garments,
Plunder of garments embroidered and dyed,
Two pieces of dyed embroidery for the neck of the looter?'

31 "Thus let all Your enemies perish, O LORD!
But *let* those who love Him *be* like the sun
When it comes out in full strength."
So the land had rest for forty years.

Midianites Oppress Israel

6 Then the children of Israel did evil in the sight of the LORD. So the LORD
delivered them into the hand of Midian for seven years, 2and the hand
of Midian prevailed against Israel. Because of the Midianites, the children
of Israel made for themselves the dens, the caves, and the strongholds
which *are* in the mountains. 3So it was, whenever Israel had sown,
Midianites would come up; also Amalekites and the people of the East
would come up against them. 4Then they would encamp against them and
destroy the produce of the earth as far as Gaza, and leave no sustenance
for Israel, neither sheep nor ox nor donkey. 5For they would come up with
their livestock and their tents, coming in as numerous as locusts; both
they and their camels were without number; and they would enter the
land to destroy it. 6So Israel was greatly impoverished because of the
Midianites, and the children of Israel cried out to the LORD.
7And it came to pass, when the children of Israel cried out to the LORD
because of the Midianites, 8that the LORD sent a prophet to the children of

5:23 [m] Or *Angel*

LIFE LESSON

Judges 6:1–7:25

SITUATION The Midianites were desert marauders related to the Israelites through Abraham's second wife, Keturah, and her son, Midian. For centuries they were at odds with Israel, especially during this fourth period of Judges.

OBSERVATION God expands our abilities and resources when he calls us into ministry. This happens in spite of our doubts, as it did with Gideon.

INSPIRATION Fear of rejection is there because of a broken relationship with a holy God. Many attempt to please God and thus receive His acceptance. Many become more religious. But in the shadow of their religion stands a tall, ugly figure called "Rejection." Many churches are filled with people working hard to escape this figure, but the fear of rejection can never be escaped by religion.

Revival always awakens man to the true basis of acceptance. Acceptance can be found only through faith. Martin Luther understood that "the just shall live by faith," and he shook the world for God's glory. He did not experience some new faith. He came to know and experience the faith of the spiritual giants of centuries past. His faith was the same as Abraham's, Isaac's, and Jacob's. It was the faith of Paul, Peter, and John. True faith is simply *our acceptance of His acceptance of us based on what Jesus did on the cross.*

Old Testament believers found acceptance by looking forward to the Messiah. We find our acceptance by looking back to the cross. One word gushes forth from the cross: *grace.* Rejection has to flee when that word is spoken. Hallelujah! I have been accepted! By grace I have been accepted! Sin separated many from God. But God entered human history uniquely through Jesus. He was unique. He was so much God that it was as though He was not man. And yet, He was so much man that it was as though He was not God. He was Son of God and Son of Man. He was the God-man. He crashed through the wall of sin that separates man from

Continued

God. He has become the door through that wall. He forever stands as the doorway to God's acceptance. And when we have been accepted by the Father, we have really been accepted! That causes us to bow before the Father to love and worship Him in simplicity and devotion. He has met the deepest need of our lives though His Son, Jesus.

We have a new power to accept ourselves as we are. That enables us to accept others in a revolutionary way.

We can witness for Christ powerfully and boldly without fear of rejection.

But most important, we have peace and contentment. That security gives us the ability to stand alone. If the whole world rejects us, we can stand alone for God. We have been accepted by Him, and that is all that matters.

(From *Fire in Your Heart* by Sammy Tippit)

APPLICATION What specific fear holds you back from accepting new opportunities at school, work, home, or at church? Ask God to help you overcome it. This week, use God's resources against your fear. Share the discoveries with a small group.

EXPLORATION Resources Available—Exodus 3:10–4:17; 2 Kings 6:16-17; Ezra 1:2; Matthew 14:19-21; Luke 12:48; John 6:5-7.

Israel, who said to them, "Thus says the LORD God of Israel: 'I brought you up from Egypt and brought you out of the house of bondage; 9and I delivered you out of the hand of the Egyptians and out of the hand of all who oppressed you, and drove them out before you and gave you their land. 10Also I said to you, "I *am* the LORD your God; do not fear the gods of the Amorites, in whose land you dwell." But you have not obeyed My voice.' "

Gideon

11Now the Angel of the LORD came and sat under the terebinth tree which *was* in Ophrah, which *belonged* to Joash the Abiezrite, while his son Gideon threshed wheat in the winepress, in order to hide *it* from the Midianites. 12And the Angel of the LORD appeared to him, and said to him, "The LORD *is* with you, you mighty man of valor!"

13Gideon said to Him, "O my lord,[n] if the LORD is with us, why then has all this happened to us? And where *are* all His miracles which our fathers told us about, saying, 'Did not the LORD bring us up from Egypt?' But now the LORD has forsaken us and delivered us into the hands of the Midianites."

14Then the LORD turned to him and said, "Go in this might of yours, and you shall save Israel from the hand of the Midianites. Have I not sent you?"

15So he said to Him, "O my Lord,[o] how can I save Israel? Indeed my clan *is* the weakest in Manasseh, and I *am* the least in my father's house."

16And the LORD said to him, "Surely I will be with you, and you shall defeat the Midianites as one man."

17Then he said to Him, "If now I have found favor in Your sight, then show me a sign that it is You who talk with me. 18Do not depart from here, I pray, until I come to You and bring out my offering and set *it* before You."

And He said, "I will wait until you come back."

19So Gideon went in and prepared a young goat, and unleavened bread from an ephah of flour. The meat he put in a basket, and he put the broth in a pot; and he brought *them* out to Him under the terebinth tree and presented *them*. 20The Angel of God said to him, "Take the meat and the unleavened bread and lay *them* on this rock, and pour out the broth." And he did so.

21Then the Angel of the LORD put out the end of the staff that *was* in His hand, and touched the meat and the unleavened bread; and fire rose out of the rock and consumed the meat and the unleavened bread. And the Angel of the LORD departed out of his sight.

22Now Gideon perceived that He *was* the Angel of the LORD. So Gideon said, "Alas, O Lord GOD! For I have seen the Angel of the LORD face to face."

23Then the LORD said to him, "Peace *be* with you; do not fear, you shall not die." 24So Gideon built an altar there to the LORD, and called it The-LORD-*Is*-Peace.[p] To this day it *is* still in Ophrah of the Abiezrites.

25Now it came to pass the same night that the LORD said to him, "Take your father's young bull, the second bull of seven years old, and tear down the altar of Baal that your father has, and cut down the wooden image[q] that *is* beside it; 26and build an altar to the LORD your God on top of this rock in the proper arrangement, and take the second bull and offer a

6:13 [n] Hebrew *adoni,* used of man
6:15 [o] Hebrew *Adonai,* used of God
6:24 [p] Hebrew *YHWH Shalom*
6:25 [q] Hebrew *Asherah,* a Canaanite goddess

burnt sacrifice with the wood of the image which you
shall cut down." 27So Gideon took ten men from
among his servants and did as the LORD had said to
him. But because he feared his father's household and
the men of the city too much to do *it* by day, he did *it*
by night.

Gideon Destroys the Altar of Baal

28And when the men of the city arose early in the
morning, there was the altar of Baal, torn down; and
the wooden image that *was* beside it was cut down,
and the second bull was being offered on the altar
which had been built. 29So they said to one another,
"Who has done this thing?" And when they had inquired and asked, they said, "Gideon the son of Joash
has done this thing." 30Then the men of the city said
to Joash, "Bring out your son, that he may die, because he has torn down the altar of Baal, and because
he has cut down the wooden image that *was* beside
it."

31But Joash said to all who stood against him,
"Would you plead for Baal? Would you save him? Let
the one who would plead for him be put to death by
morning! If he *is* a god, let him plead for himself, because his altar has been torn down!" 32Therefore on
that day he called him Jerubbaal,[r] saying, "Let Baal
plead against him, because he has torn down his
altar."

33Then all the Midianites and Amalekites, the people of the East, gathered together; and they crossed
over and encamped in the Valley of Jezreel. 34But the
Spirit of the LORD came upon Gideon; then he blew the
trumpet, and the Abiezrites gathered behind him.
35And he sent messengers throughout all Manasseh,
who also gathered behind him. He also sent messengers to Asher, Zebulun, and Naphtali; and they came
up to meet them.

The Sign of the Fleece

36So Gideon said to God, "If You will save Israel by
my hand as You have said— 37look, I shall put a fleece
of wool on the threshing floor; if there is dew on the
fleece only, and *it is* dry on all the ground, then I shall
know that You will save Israel by my hand, as You
have said." 38And it was so. When he rose early the
next morning and squeezed the fleece together, he
wrung the dew out of the fleece, a bowlful of water.
39Then Gideon said to God, "Do not be angry with me,
but let me speak just once more: Let me test, I pray,
just once more with the fleece; let it now be dry only
on the fleece, but on all the ground let there be dew."
40And God did so that night. It was dry on the fleece
only, but there was dew on all the ground.

Gideon's Valiant Three Hundred

7 Then Jerubbaal (that *is,* Gideon) and all the people
who *were* with him rose early and encamped beside the well of Harod, so that the camp of the
Midianites was on the north side of them by the hill of
Moreh in the valley.

2And the LORD said to Gideon, "The people who *are*
with you *are* too many for Me to give the Midianites
into their hands, lest Israel claim glory for itself
against Me, saying, 'My own hand has saved me.'
3Now therefore, proclaim in the hearing of the people,
saying, 'Whoever *is* fearful and afraid, let him turn
and depart at once from Mount Gilead.'" And
twenty-two thousand of the people returned, and ten
thousand remained.

4But the LORD said to Gideon, "The people *are* still
too many; bring them down to the water, and I will
test them for you there. Then it will be, *that* of whom I
say to you, 'This one shall go with you,' the same shall
go with you; and of whomever I say to you, 'This one
shall not go with you,' the same shall not go." 5So he
brought the people down to the water. And the LORD
said to Gideon, "Everyone who laps from the water
with his tongue, as a dog laps, you shall set apart by
himself; likewise everyone who gets down on his
knees to drink." 6And the number of those who
lapped, *putting* their hand to their mouth, was three
hundred men; but all the rest of the people got down
on their knees to drink water. 7Then the LORD said to
Gideon, "By the three hundred men who lapped I will
save you, and deliver the Midianites into your hand.
Let all the *other* people go, every man to his place."
8So the people took provisions and their trumpets in
their hands. And he sent away all *the rest of* Israel,
every man to his tent, and retained those three hundred men. Now the camp of Midian was below him in
the valley.

9It happened on the same night that the LORD said
to him, "Arise, go down against the camp, for I have
delivered it into your hand. 10But if you are afraid to
go down, go down to the camp with Purah your servant, 11and you shall hear what they say; and afterward your hands shall be strengthened to go down
against the camp." Then he went down with Purah

6:32 [r] Literally *Let Baal Plead*

LIFE LESSON

Judges 8:1–9:57

SITUATION Gideon and his army, though greatly outnumbered, defeated the Midianite invaders with God's blessing. Yet after Gideon died, the Israelites again abandoned God and worshiped Baal. The Israelites foolishly made Abimelech the king, helping him murder sixty-nine of his seventy brothers. God repaid the treachery and idolatry of Abimelech and the town of Shechem with death and destruction.

OBSERVATION Sin will always be judged by God. Consequences from our past sins often come back to haunt us.

INSPIRATION Sin entered the human race through Adam, and the human race has been trying without success to get rid of it ever since. And, short of that, mankind has been seeking in vain to reverse the curse. The Bible teaches that God warned Adam before he sinned that if he ate of the tree of knowledge he would surely die. The Bible also tells us that God instructed Adam and Eve to be fruitful and to multiply and to replenish the earth. But although they had been created in the image of God, after the Fall Adam and Eve gave birth to children after their own likeness and image. Consequently Cain and Abel were infected with the death-dealing disease of sin, which they inherited from their parents and which has been passed on to every generation since. We are all sinners by inheritance, and try as we will, we cannot escape our birthright.

We have resorted to every means to win back the position that Adam lost. We have tried through education, through philosophy, through religion, through governments to throw off our yoke of depravity and sin. We have sought to accomplish with our sin-limited minds the things that God intended to do with the clear vision that can come only from on high. Our motives have been good and some of our attempts have been commendable, but they have all fallen far, far short of the goal. All our knowledge, all our inventions, all our developments and ambitious plans move us ahead only a

his servant to the outpost of the armed men who *were* in the camp. 12 Now
the Midianites and Amalekites, all the people of the East, were lying in the
valley as numerous as locusts; and their camels *were* without number, as
the sand by the seashore in multitude.
13 And when Gideon had come, there was a man telling a dream to his
companion. He said, "I have had a dream: *To my* surprise, a loaf of barley
bread tumbled into the camp of Midian; it came to a tent and struck it so
that it fell and overturned, and the tent collapsed."
14 Then his companion answered and said, "This *is* nothing else but the
sword of Gideon the son of Joash, a man of Israel! Into his hand God has
delivered Midian and the whole camp."
15 And so it was, when Gideon heard the telling of the dream and its interpretation, that he worshiped. He returned to the camp of Israel, and
said, "Arise, for the LORD has delivered the camp of Midian into your
hand." 16 Then he divided the three hundred men *into* three companies,
and he put a trumpet into every man's hand, with empty pitchers, and
torches inside the pitchers. 17 And he said to them, "Look at me and do likewise; watch, and when I come to the edge of the camp you shall do as I do:
18 When I blow the trumpet, I and all who *are* with me, then you also blow
the trumpets on every side of the whole camp, and say, '*The sword of* the
LORD and of Gideon!' "
19 So Gideon and the hundred men who *were* with him came to the outpost of the camp at the beginning of the middle watch, just as they had
posted the watch; and they blew the trumpets and broke the pitchers that
were in their hands. 20 Then the three companies blew the trumpets and
broke the pitchers—they held the torches in their left hands and the trumpets in their right hands for blowing—and they cried, "The sword of the
LORD and of Gideon!" 21 And every man stood in his place all around the
camp; and the whole army ran and cried out and fled. 22 When the three
hundred blew the trumpets, the LORD set every man's sword against his
companion throughout the whole camp; and the army fled to Beth
Acacia,[s] toward Zererah, as far as the border of Abel Meholah, by Tabbath.
23 And the men of Israel gathered together from Naphtali, Asher, and all
Manasseh, and pursued the Midianites.
24 Then Gideon sent messengers throughout all the mountains of
Ephraim, saying, "Come down against the Midianites, and seize from
them the watering places as far as Beth Barah and the Jordan." Then all the
men of Ephraim gathered together and seized the watering places as far as
Beth Barah and the Jordan. 25 And they captured two princes of the
Midianites, Oreb and Zeeb. They killed Oreb at the rock of Oreb, and Zeeb
they killed at the winepress of Zeeb. They pursued Midian and brought the
heads of Oreb and Zeeb to Gideon on the other side of the Jordan.

Gideon Subdues the Midianites

8 Now the men of Ephraim said to him, "Why have you done this to us
by not calling us when you went to fight with the Midianites?" And
they reprimanded him sharply.
2 So he said to them, "What have I done now in comparison with you? *Is*
not the gleaning *of the grapes* of Ephraim better than the vintage of
Abiezer? 3 God has delivered into your hands the princes of Midian, Oreb

7:22 [s] Hebrew *Beth Shittah*

and Zeeb. And what was I able to do in comparison with you?" Then their
anger toward him subsided when he said that.
4When Gideon came to the Jordan, he and the three hundred men who
were with him crossed over, exhausted but still in pursuit. 5Then he said to
the men of Succoth, "Please give loaves of bread to the people who follow
me, for they are exhausted, and I am pursuing Zebah and Zalmunna,
kings of Midian."
6And the leaders of Succoth said, "*Are* the hands of Zebah and
Zalmunna now in your hand, that we should give bread to your army?"
7So Gideon said, "For this cause, when the LORD has delivered Zebah
and Zalmunna into my hand, then I will tear your flesh with the thorns of
the wilderness and with briers!" 8Then he went up from there to Penuel
and spoke to them in the same way. And the men of Penuel answered him
as the men of Succoth had answered. 9So he also spoke to the men of
Penuel, saying, "When I come back in peace, I will tear down this tower!"
10Now Zebah and Zalmunna *were* at Karkor, and their armies with
them, about fifteen thousand, all who were left of all the army of the people of the East; for one hundred and twenty thousand men who drew the
sword had fallen. 11Then Gideon went up by the road of those who dwell in
tents on the east of Nobah and Jogbehah; and he attacked the army while
the camp felt secure. 12When Zebah and Zalmunna fled, he pursued them;
and he took the two kings of Midian, Zebah and Zalmunna, and routed the
whole army.
13Then Gideon the son of Joash returned from battle, from the Ascent of
Heres. 14And he caught a young man of the men of Succoth and interro-
gated him; and he wrote down for him the leaders of Succoth and its elders, seventy-seven men. 15Then he came to the men of Succoth and said,
"Here are Zebah and Zalmunna, about whom you ridiculed me, saying,
'*Are* the hands of Zebah and Zalmunna now in your hand, that we should
give bread to your weary men?' " 16And he took the elders of the city, and
thorns of the wilderness and briers, and with them he taught the men of
Succoth. 17Then he tore down the tower of Penuel and killed the men of the
city.
18And he said to Zebah and Zalmunna, "What kind of men *were they*
whom you killed at Tabor?"
So they answered, "As you *are,* so *were* they; each one resembled the son
of a king."
19Then he said, "They *were* my brothers, the sons of my mother. *As* the
LORD lives, if you had let them live, I would not kill you." 20And he said to
Jether his firstborn, "Rise, kill them!" But the youth would not draw his
sword; for he was afraid, because he *was* still a youth.
21So Zebah and Zalmunna said, "Rise yourself, and kill us; for as a man
is, so is his strength." So Gideon arose and killed Zebah and Zalmunna,
and took the crescent ornaments that *were* on their camels' necks.

Gideon's Ephod

22Then the men of Israel said to Gideon, "Rule over us, both you and
your son, and your grandson also; for you have delivered us from the hand
of Midian."
23But Gideon said to them, "I will not rule over you, nor shall my son
rule over you; the LORD shall rule over you." 24Then Gideon said to them, "I

very little before we drop back again to the point from which we started. For we are still making the same mistake that Adam made—we are still trying to be king in our own right, and with our own power, instead of obeying God's laws. . . .

Man's only salvation from sin stands on a lonely, barren, skull-shaped hill: a thief hangs on one cross, a murderer on another, and between them, a Man with a crown of thorns. . . .

And who is this tortured figure, who is this Man whom other men seek to humiliate and kill? He is the Son of God, the Prince of Peace, heaven's own appointed Messenger to the sin-ridden earth.

Who inflicted this hideous torture upon the Man who came to teach us love? You did and I did, for it was for your sin and my sin that Jesus was nailed to the cross. . . .

But sin overreached itself on the cross. Man's hideous injustice that crucified Christ became the means that opened the way for man to become free. Sin's masterpiece of shame and hate became God's masterpiece of mercy and forgiveness. Through the death of Christ upon the cross, sin itself was crucified for those who believe in Him. Sin was conquered on the cross. His death is the foundation of our hope, the promise of our triumph! Christ bore in His own body on the tree the sins that shackle us. He died for us and rose again. He proved the truth of all God's promises to man; and if you will accept Christ by faith today, you, too, can be forgiven for your sins. You can stand secure and free in the knowledge that through the love of Christ your soul is cleansed of sin and saved from damnation.

(From *Peace with God* by Billy Graham)

APPLICATION Sin brings judgment. Turn away from the sin that you enjoy. Seek help to remove the sin that reoccurs in your life. Don't let patterns of sinfulness destroy your life; repent and seek Christ's help.

EXPLORATION Sin—Genesis 3:6-7; 9:20-27; Exodus 2:12-14; 34:7; Deuteronomy 7:2; Nehemiah 31:14-16.

would like to make a request of you, that each of you
would give me the earrings from his plunder." For
they had golden earrings, because they *were*
Ishmaelites.
25So they answered, "We will gladly give *them.*"
And they spread out a garment, and each man threw
into it the earrings from his plunder. 26Now the weight
of the gold earrings that he requested was one thousand seven hundred *shekels* of gold, besides the crescent ornaments, pendants, and purple robes which
were on the kings of Midian, and besides the chains
that *were* around their camels' necks. 27Then Gideon
made it into an ephod and set it up in his city, Ophrah.
And all Israel played the harlot with it there. It became a snare to Gideon and to his house.
28Thus Midian was subdued before the children of
Israel, so that they lifted their heads no more. And the
country was quiet for forty years in the days of Gideon.

Death of Gideon

29Then Jerubbaal the son of Joash went and dwelt
in his own house. 30Gideon had seventy sons who
were his own offspring, for he had many wives. 31And
his concubine who *was* in Shechem also bore him a
son, whose name he called Abimelech. 32Now Gideon
the son of Joash died at a good old age, and was
buried in the tomb of Joash his father, in Ophrah of
the Abiezrites.
33So it was, as soon as Gideon was dead, that the
children of Israel again played the harlot with the
Baals, and made Baal-Berith their god. 34Thus the
children of Israel did not remember the LORD their
God, who had delivered them from the hands of all
their enemies on every side; 35nor did they show kindness to the house of Jerubbaal (Gideon) in accordance with the good he had done for Israel.

Abimelech's Conspiracy

9 Then Abimelech the son of Jerubbaal went to
Shechem, to his mother's brothers, and spoke
with them and with all the family of the house of his
mother's father, saying, 2"Please speak in the hearing
of all the men of Shechem: 'Which is better for you,
that all seventy of the sons of Jerubbaal reign over
you, or that one reign over you?' Remember that I *am*
your own flesh and bone."
3And his mother's brothers spoke all these words
concerning him in the hearing of all the men of
Shechem; and their heart was inclined to follow
Abimelech, for they said, "He is our brother." 4So they
gave him seventy *shekels* of silver from the temple of
Baal-Berith, with which Abimelech hired worthless
and reckless men; and they followed him. 5Then he
went to his father's house at Ophrah and killed his
brothers, the seventy sons of Jerubbaal, on one stone.
But Jotham the youngest son of Jerubbaal was left,
because he hid himself. 6And all the men of Shechem
gathered together, all of Beth Millo, and they went and
made Abimelech king beside the terebinth tree at the
pillar that *was* in Shechem.

The Parable of the Trees

7Now when they told Jotham, he went and stood on
top of Mount Gerizim, and lifted his voice and cried
out. And he said to them:

"Listen to me, you men of Shechem,
That God may listen to you!
8 "The trees once went forth to anoint a king
over them.
And they said to the olive tree,
'Reign over us!'
9 But the olive tree said to them,
'Should I cease giving my oil,
With which they honor God and men,
And go to sway over trees?'
10 "Then the trees said to the fig tree,
'You come *and* reign over us!'
11 But the fig tree said to them,
'Should I cease my sweetness and my
good fruit,
And go to sway over trees?'
12 "Then the trees said to the vine,
'You come *and* reign over us!'
13 But the vine said to them,
'Should I cease my new wine,
Which cheers *both* God and men,
And go to sway over trees?'
14 "Then all the trees said to the bramble,
'You come *and* reign over us!'
15 And the bramble said to the trees,
'If in truth you anoint me as king over you,
Then come *and* take shelter in my shade;
But if not, let fire come out of the bramble
And devour the cedars of Lebanon!'

16"Now therefore, if you have acted in truth and sincerity in making Abimelech king, and if you have
dealt well with Jerubbaal and his house, and have
done to him as he deserves— 17for my father fought

for you, risked his life, and delivered you out of the
hand of Midian; [18]but you have risen up against my
father's house this day, and killed his seventy sons on
one stone, and made Abimelech, the son of his female
servant, king over the men of Shechem, because he is
your brother— [19]if then you have acted in truth and
sincerity with Jerubbaal and with his house this day,
then rejoice in Abimelech, and let him also rejoice in
you. [20]But if not, let fire come from Abimelech and
devour the men of Shechem and Beth Millo; and let
fire come from the men of Shechem and from Beth
Millo and devour Abimelech!" [21]And Jotham ran
away and fled; and he went to Beer and dwelt there,
for fear of Abimelech his brother.

Downfall of Abimelech

[22]After Abimelech had reigned over Israel three
years, [23]God sent a spirit of ill will between Abimelech
and the men of Shechem; and the men of Shechem
dealt treacherously with Abimelech, [24]that the crime
done to the seventy sons of Jerubbaal might be settled
and their blood be laid on Abimelech their brother,
who killed them, and on the men of Shechem, who
aided him in the killing of his brothers. [25]And the men
of Shechem set men in ambush against him on the
tops of the mountains, and they robbed all who passed
by them along that way; and it was told Abimelech.

[26]Now Gaal the son of Ebed came with his brothers
and went over to Shechem; and the men of Shechem
put their confidence in him. [27]So they went out into
the fields, and gathered *grapes* from their vineyards
and trod *them,* and made merry. And they went into
the house of their god, and ate and drank, and cursed
Abimelech. [28]Then Gaal the son of Ebed said, "Who *is*
Abimelech, and who *is* Shechem, that we should serve
him? *Is he* not the son of Jerubbaal, and *is not* Zebul
his officer? Serve the men of Hamor the father of
Shechem; but why should we serve him? [29]If only this
people were under my authority![t] Then I would remove Abimelech." So he[u] said to Abimelech, "Increase your army and come out!"

[30]When Zebul, the ruler of the city, heard the words
of Gaal the son of Ebed, his anger was aroused. [31]And
he sent messengers to Abimelech secretly, saying,
"Take note! Gaal the son of Ebed and his brothers
have come to Shechem; and here they are, fortifying
the city against you. [32]Now therefore, get up by night,
you and the people who *are* with you, and lie in wait in
the field. [33]And it shall be, as soon as the sun is up in the
morning, *that* you shall rise early and rush upon the
city; and *when* he and the people who are with him
come out against you, you may then do to them as you
find opportunity."

[34]So Abimelech and all the people who *were* with
him rose by night, and lay in wait against Shechem in
four companies. [35]When Gaal the son of Ebed went
out and stood in the entrance to the city gate,
Abimelech and the people who *were* with him rose
from lying in wait. [36]And when Gaal saw the people,
he said to Zebul, "Look, people are coming down
from the tops of the mountains!"

But Zebul said to him, "You see the shadows of the
mountains as *if they were* men."

[37]So Gaal spoke again and said, "See, people are
coming down from the center of the land, and another company is coming from the Diviners'[v]
Terebinth Tree."

[38]Then Zebul said to him, "Where indeed *is* your
mouth now, with which you said, 'Who is Abimelech,
that we should serve him?' *Are* not these the people
whom you despised? Go out, if you will, and fight with
them now."

[39]So Gaal went out, leading the men of Shechem,
and fought with Abimelech. [40]And Abimelech chased
him, and he fled from him; and many fell wounded, to
the *very* entrance of the gate. [41]Then Abimelech dwelt
at Arumah, and Zebul drove out Gaal and his brothers, so that they would not dwell in Shechem.

[42]And it came about on the next day that the people
went out into the field, and they told Abimelech. [43]So
he took his people, divided them into three companies, and lay in wait in the field. And he looked, and
there were the people, coming out of the city; and he
rose against them and attacked them. [44]Then
Abimelech and the company that *was* with him
rushed forward and stood at the entrance of the gate
of the city; and the *other* two companies rushed upon
all who *were* in the fields and killed them. [45]So
Abimelech fought against the city all that day; he took
the city and killed the people who *were* in it; and he
demolished the city and sowed it with salt.

[46]Now when all the men of the tower of Shechem
had heard *that,* they entered the stronghold of the
temple of the god Berith. [47]And it was told Abimelech
that all the men of the tower of Shechem were gathered together. [48]Then Abimelech went up to Mount
Zalmon, he and all the people who *were* with him.
And Abimelech took an ax in his hand and cut down

9:29 [t] Literally *hand* [u] Following Masoretic Text and Targum; Dead Sea Scrolls read *they;* Septuagint reads *I.*
9:37 [v] Hebrew *Meonenim*

LIFE LESSON
Judges 10:1–12:15

SITUATION Turning away from God, the idol-worshiping Israelites suffered foreign invasion and devastation. Desperate for relief, they turned to God. God provided a military leader, Jephthah of Gilead, who triumphed over the invading Ammonites and became the leader of Gilead. To insure victory, he made a foolish vow before God, which caused grief.

OBSERVATION Don't be foolish by making spiritual deals with God. God doesn't want our promises for the future but, rather, our obedience today.

INSPIRATION Our Lord never insists on having authority; He never says—Thou shalt. He leaves us perfectly free—so free that we can spit in His face, as men did; so free that we can put Him to death, as men did; and He will never say a word. But when His life has been created in me by His Redemption, I instantly recognize His right to absolute authority over me. It is a moral domination—"Thou art worthy. . .". It is only the unworthy in me that refuses to bow down to the worthy. If when I meet a man who is more holy than myself, I do not recognize his worthiness and obey what comes through him, it is a revelation of the unworthy in me. God educates us by means of people who are a little better than we are, not intellectually but "holily," until we get

a bough from the trees, and took it and laid *it* on his shoulder; then he said
to the people who were with him, "What you have seen me do, make haste
and do as I *have done*." 49So each of the people likewise cut down his own
bough and followed Abimelech, put *them* against the stronghold, and set
the stronghold on fire above them, so that all the people of the tower of
Shechem died, about a thousand men and women.

50Then Abimelech went to Thebez, and he encamped against Thebez
and took it. 51But there was a strong tower in the city, and all the men and
women—all the people of the city—fled there and shut themselves in;
then they went up to the top of the tower. 52So Abimelech came as far as the
tower and fought against it; and he drew near the door of the tower to burn
it with fire. 53But a certain woman dropped an upper millstone on
Abimelech's head and crushed his skull. 54Then he called quickly to the
young man, his armorbearer, and said to him, "Draw your sword and kill
me, lest men say of me, 'A woman killed him.' " So his young man thrust
him through, and he died. 55And when the men of Israel saw that
Abimelech was dead, they departed, every man to his place.

56Thus God repaid the wickedness of Abimelech, which he had done to
his father by killing his seventy brothers. 57And all the evil of the men of
Shechem God returned on their own heads, and on them came the curse
of Jotham the son of Jerubbaal.

Tola

10 After Abimelech there arose to save Israel Tola the son of Puah, the
son of Dodo, a man of Issachar; and he dwelt in Shamir in the
mountains of Ephraim. 2He judged Israel twenty-three years; and he died
and was buried in Shamir.

Jair

3After him arose Jair, a Gileadite; and he judged Israel twenty-two years.
4Now he had thirty sons who rode on thirty donkeys; they also had thirty
towns, which are called "Havoth Jair"[w] to this day, which *are* in the land of
Gilead. 5And Jair died and was buried in Camon.

Israel Oppressed Again

6Then the children of Israel again did evil in the sight of the LORD, and
served the Baals and the Ashtoreths, the gods of Syria, the gods of Sidon,
the gods of Moab, the gods of the people of Ammon, and the gods of the
Philistines; and they forsook the LORD and did not serve Him. 7So the
anger of the LORD was hot against Israel; and He sold them into the hands
of the Philistines and into the hands of the people of Ammon. 8From that
year they harassed and oppressed the children of Israel for eighteen
years—all the children of Israel who *were* on the other side of the Jordan
in the land of the Amorites, in Gilead. 9Moreover the people of Ammon
crossed over the Jordan to fight against Judah also, against Benjamin, and
against the house of Ephraim, so that Israel was severely distressed.

10And the children of Israel cried out to the LORD, saying, "We have
sinned against You, because we have both forsaken our God and served
the Baals!"

11So the LORD said to the children of Israel, "*Did I* not *deliver you* from
the Egyptians and from the Amorites and from the people of Ammon and

10:4 [w] Literally *Towns of Jair* (compare Numbers 32:41 and Deuteronomy 3:14)

from the Philistines? 12Also the Sidonians and Amalekites and Maonites[x]
oppressed you; and you cried out to Me, and I delivered you from their
hand. 13Yet you have forsaken Me and served other gods. Therefore I will
deliver you no more. 14Go and cry out to the gods which you have chosen;
let them deliver you in your time of distress."
15And the children of Israel said to the LORD, "We have sinned! Do to us
whatever seems best to You; only deliver us this day, we pray." 16So they
put away the foreign gods from among them and served the LORD. And His
soul could no longer endure the misery of Israel.
17Then the people of Ammon gathered together and encamped in
Gilead. And the children of Israel assembled together and encamped in
Mizpah. 18And the people, the leaders of Gilead, said to one another, "Who
is the man who will begin the fight against the people of Ammon? He shall
be head over all the inhabitants of Gilead."

Jephthah

11 Now Jephthah the Gileadite was a mighty man of valor, but he *was*
the son of a harlot; and Gilead begot Jephthah. 2Gilead's wife bore
sons; and when his wife's sons grew up, they drove Jephthah out, and said
to him, "You shall have no inheritance in our father's house, for you *are* the
son of another woman." 3Then Jephthah fled from his brothers and dwelt
in the land of Tob; and worthless men banded together with Jephthah and
went out *raiding* with him.
4It came to pass after a time that the people of Ammon made war
against Israel. 5And so it was, when the people of Ammon made war
against Israel, that the elders of Gilead went to get Jephthah from the land
of Tob. 6Then they said to Jephthah, "Come and be our commander, that
we may fight against the people of Ammon."
7So Jephthah said to the elders of Gilead, "Did you not hate me, and
expel me from my father's house? Why have you come to me now when
you are in distress?"
8And the elders of Gilead said to Jephthah, "That is why we have turned
again to you now, that you may go with us and fight against the people of
Ammon, and be our head over all the inhabitants of Gilead."
9So Jephthah said to the elders of Gilead, "If you take me back home to
fight against the people of Ammon, and the LORD delivers them to me,
shall I be your head?"
10And the elders of Gilead said to Jephthah, "The LORD will be a witness
between us, if we do not do according to your words." 11Then Jephthah
went with the elders of Gilead, and the people made him head and commander over them; and Jephthah spoke all his words before the LORD in
Mizpah.
12Now Jephthah sent messengers to the king of the people of Ammon,
saying, "What do you have against me, that you have come to fight against
me in my land?"
13And the king of the people of Ammon answered the messengers of
Jephthah, "Because Israel took away my land when they came up out of
Egypt, from the Arnon as far as the Jabbok, and to the Jordan. Now therefore, restore those *lands* peaceably."
14So Jephthah again sent messengers to the king of the people of

10:12 [x] Some Septuagint manuscripts read *Midianites.*

under the domination of the Lord Himself, and then the whole attitude of the life is one of obedience to Him. If Our Lord insisted upon obedience He would become a taskmaster, and He would cease to have any authority. He never insists on obedience, but when we do see Him we obey Him instantly, He is easily Lord, and we live in adoration of Him from morning till night. The revelation of my growth in grace is the way in which I look upon obedience. We have to rescue the word "obedience" from the mire. Obedience is only possible between equals; it is the relationship between father and son, not between master and servant. "I and My Father are one." "Though He were a Son, yet learned He obedience by the things which He suffered." The Son's obedience was as Redeemer, *because He was Son*, not in order to be Son.

(From *My Utmost for His Highest* by Oswald Chambers)

APPLICATION Have you ever promised to do something for the Lord if he will grant your request? God doesn't work that way. He wants us to be loyal and obedient constantly. His answer to our prayers reflects his perfect will for us.

EXPLORATION Obedience—Genesis 2:16-17; Exodus 8:25-29; Joshua 11:15; 1 Samuel 15:9; Matthew 23:23-24; Romans 6:17.

Ammon, [15]and said to him, "Thus says Jephthah: 'Israel did not take away the land of Moab, nor the land of the people of Ammon; [16]for when Israel came up from Egypt, they walked through the wilderness as far as the Red Sea and came to Kadesh. [17]Then Israel sent messengers to the king of Edom, saying, "Please let me pass through your land." But the king of Edom would not heed. And in like manner they sent to the king of Moab, but he would not *consent.* So Israel remained in Kadesh. [18]And they went along through the wilderness and bypassed the land of Edom and the land of Moab, came to the east side of the land of Moab, and encamped on the other side of the Arnon. But they did not enter the border of Moab, for the Arnon *was* the border of Moab. [19]Then Israel sent messengers to Sihon king of the Amorites, king of Heshbon; and Israel said to him, "Please let us pass through your land into our place." [20]But Sihon did not trust Israel to pass through his territory. So Sihon gathered all his people together, encamped in Jahaz, and fought against Israel. [21]And the LORD God of Israel delivered Sihon and all his people into the hand of Israel, and they defeated them. Thus Israel gained possession of all the land of the Amorites, who inhabited that country. [22]They took possession of all the territory of the Amorites, from the Arnon to the Jabbok and from the wilderness to the Jordan.

[23]'And now the LORD God of Israel has dispossessed the Amorites from before His people Israel; should you then possess it? [24]Will you not possess whatever Chemosh your god gives you to possess? So whatever the LORD our God takes possession of before us, we will possess. [25]And now, *are* you any better than Balak the son of Zippor, king of Moab? Did he ever strive against Israel? Did he ever fight against them? [26]While Israel dwelt in Heshbon and its villages, in Aroer and its villages, and in all the cities along the banks of the Arnon, for three hundred years, why did you not recover *them* within that time? [27]Therefore I have not sinned against you, but you wronged me by fighting against me. May the LORD, the Judge, render judgment this day between the children of Israel and the people of Ammon.' " [28]However, the king of the people of Ammon did not heed the words which Jephthah sent him.

Jephthah's Vow and Victory

[29]Then the Spirit of the LORD came upon Jephthah, and he passed through Gilead and Manasseh, and passed through Mizpah of Gilead; and from Mizpah of Gilead he advanced *toward* the people of Ammon. [30]And Jephthah made a vow to the LORD, and said, "If You will indeed deliver the people of Ammon into my hands, [31]then it will be that whatever comes out of the doors of my house to meet me, when I return in peace from the people of Ammon, shall surely be the LORD's, and I will offer it up as a burnt offering."

[32]So Jephthah advanced toward the people of Ammon to fight against them, and the LORD delivered them into his hands. [33]And he defeated them from Aroer as far as Minnith—twenty cities—and to Abel Keramim,[y] with a very great slaughter. Thus the people of Ammon were subdued before the children of Israel.

Jephthah's Daughter

[34]When Jephthah came to his house at Mizpah, there was his daughter, coming out to meet him with timbrels and dancing; and she *was his* only child. Besides her he had neither son nor daughter. [35]And it came to pass, when he saw her, that he tore his clothes, and said, "Alas, my daughter! You have brought me very low! You are among those who trouble me! For I have given my word to the LORD, and I cannot go back on it."

[36]So she said to him, "My father, *if* you have given your word to the LORD, do to me according to what has gone out of your mouth, because the LORD has avenged you of your enemies, the people of Ammon." [37]Then she said to her father, "Let this thing be done for me: let me alone for two months, that I may go and wander on the mountains and bewail my virginity, my friends and I."

[38]So he said, "Go." And he sent her away *for* two months; and she went with her friends, and bewailed her virginity on the mountains. [39]And it was so at the end of two months that she returned to her father, and he carried out his vow with her which he had vowed. She knew no man.

And it became a custom in Israel [40]*that* the daughters of Israel went four days each year to lament the daughter of Jephthah the Gileadite.

Jephthah's Conflict with Ephraim

12 Then the men of Ephraim gathered together, crossed over toward Zaphon, and said to Jephthah, "Why did you cross over to fight against the people of Ammon, and did not call us to go with you? We will burn your house down on you with fire!"

[2]And Jephthah said to them, "My people and I were in a great struggle with the people of Ammon; and when I called you, you did not deliver me out of their

11:33 [y] Literally *Plain of Vineyards*

hands. 3So when I saw that you would not deliver *me*, I took my life in my
hands and crossed over against the people of Ammon; and the LORD delivered them into my hand. Why then have you come up to me this day to
fight against me?" 4Now Jephthah gathered together all the men of Gilead
and fought against Ephraim. And the men of Gilead defeated Ephraim, because they said, "You Gileadites *are* fugitives of Ephraim among the
Ephraimites *and* among the Manassites." 5The Gileadites seized the fords
of the Jordan before the Ephraimites *arrived*. And when *any* Ephraimite
who escaped said, "Let me cross over," the men of Gilead would say to
him, "*Are* you an Ephraimite?" If he said, "No," 6then they would say to
him, "Then say, 'Shibboleth'!" And he would say, "Sibboleth," for he could
not pronounce *it* right. Then they would take him and kill him at the fords
of the Jordan. There fell at that time forty-two thousand Ephraimites.
7And Jephthah judged Israel six years. Then Jephthah the Gileadite died
and was buried among the cities of Gilead.

Ibzan, Elon, and Abdon

8After him, Ibzan of Bethlehem judged Israel. 9He had thirty sons. And
he gave away thirty daughters in marriage, and brought in thirty daughters from elsewhere for his sons. He judged Israel seven years. 10Then
Ibzan died and was buried at Bethlehem.
11After him, Elon the Zebulunite judged Israel. He judged Israel ten
years. 12And Elon the Zebulunite died and was buried at Aijalon in the
country of Zebulun.
13After him, Abdon the son of Hillel the Pirathonite judged Israel. 14He
had forty sons and thirty grandsons, who rode on seventy young donkeys.
He judged Israel eight years. 15Then Abdon the son of Hillel the
Pirathonite died and was buried in Pirathon in the land of Ephraim, in the
mountains of the Amalekites.

The Birth of Samson

13 Again the children of Israel did evil in the sight of the LORD, and the
LORD delivered them into the hand of the Philistines for forty years.
2Now there was a certain man from Zorah, of the family of the Danites,
whose name *was* Manoah; and his wife *was* barren and had no children.
3And the Angel of the LORD appeared to the woman and said to her, "Indeed
now, you are barren and have borne no children, but you shall conceive and
bear a son. 4Now therefore, please be careful not to drink wine or *similar*
drink, and not to eat anything unclean. 5For behold, you shall conceive
and bear a son. And no razor shall come upon his head, for the child shall be
a Nazirite to God from the womb; and he shall begin to deliver Israel out of
the hand of the Philistines."
6So the woman came and told her husband, saying, "A Man of God
came to me, and His countenance *was* like the countenance of the Angel of
God, very awesome; but I did not ask Him where He *was* from, and He did
not tell me His name. 7And He said to me, 'Behold, you shall conceive and
bear a son. Now drink no wine or *similar* drink, nor eat anything unclean, for
the child shall be a Nazirite to God from the womb to the day of his death.' "
8Then Manoah prayed to the LORD, and said, "O my Lord, please let the
Man of God whom You sent come to us again and teach us what we shall
do for the child who will be born."
9And God listened to the voice of Manoah, and the Angel of God came to

LIFE LESSON

Judges:13:1-25

SITUATION As the Israelites settled into Palestine, they faced a struggle to retain their own identity as the Chosen Ones. Again and again they disregarded the commandments of God. Punishment often resulted. Yet, God retained his covenant with these obstinate people. At the time of the Judges, he provided a deliverer. A baby was promised to a childless couple. He was to deliver his people from the oppression of the Philistines. When he was born he was named Samson.

OBSERVATION Pride makes us drift from God's commands. We feel "I can do it on my own," or we become confident in our own ability to handle each day. Yet, like Israel, we often remember to turn to God when life suddenly gets hard. Pride is idolatry—the idol is self.

INSPIRATION In the rough and tumble of our abrasive twentieth century, humility is scarcely considered a virtue. Such qualities as meekness and gentleness are not the sort that most people seek in order to succeed. We are fast moving, masterful, permissive people who from the cradle learn to shove and push and scream and scramble to get ahead—to plant our proud feet on the top of the totem pole.

Fiercely we contend for our rights, believing the strange philosophy that to be big and bold and brazen is best. We subscribe to the idea that since no one else will blow my horn for me, I must blow my own bugle loudly and long. We are completely convinced that unless we make our own mark in the world we will be forgotten in the crush—obliterated from memory by the milling masses around us.

From the hour we begin to take our first feeble, frightened steps as tiny tots we are exhorted to "stand on your own feet." We are urged and encouraged to "make it on your own." We are told to "make your own decisions." We are stimulated to be aggressive, self-assertive, and very self-assured. All of these attributes we are sure will lead to ultimate greatness.

Continued

In the face of all this it comes to us as a distinct shock to hear our Lord declare: "whosoever therefore shall humble himself as this little child, the same is greatest in the kingdom of heaven." . . .

The selfless, self-effacing character of God's love simply does not permit it to strut and parade itself pompously. It will have no part of such a performance. It is not proud, arrogant, puffed up with its own importance. (From *A Gardener Looks at the Fruits of the Spirit* by Phillip Keller)

APPLICATION Has your pride led you away from God? Have you become self-reliant rather than following God's advice? Follow his advice in every area of your life.

EXPLORATION Obedience to God—Leviticus 25:18; Job 22:23-29; 1 Samuel 15:22.

the woman again as she was sitting in the field; but Manoah her husband
was not with her. 10Then the woman ran in haste and told her husband,
and said to him, "Look, the Man who came to me the *other* day has just
now appeared to me!"
11So Manoah arose and followed his wife. When he came to the Man, he
said to Him, "Are You the Man who spoke to this woman?"
And He said, "I *am.*"
12Manoah said, "Now let Your words come *to pass!* What will be the
boy's rule of life, and his work?"
13So the Angel of the LORD said to Manoah, "Of all that I said to the
woman let her be careful. 14She may not eat anything that comes from the
vine, nor may she drink wine or *similar* drink, nor eat anything unclean.
All that I commanded her let her observe."
15Then Manoah said to the Angel of the LORD, "Please let us detain You,
and we will prepare a young goat for You."
16And the Angel of the LORD said to Manoah, "Though you detain Me, I
will not eat your food. But if you offer a burnt offering, you must offer it to
the LORD." (For Manoah did not know He *was* the Angel of the LORD.)
17Then Manoah said to the Angel of the LORD, "What *is* Your name, that
when Your words come *to pass* we may honor You?"
18And the Angel of the LORD said to him, "Why do you ask My name,
seeing it *is* wonderful?"
19So Manoah took the young goat with the grain offering, and offered it
upon the rock to the LORD. And He did a wondrous thing while Manoah
and his wife looked on— 20it happened as the flame went up toward
heaven from the altar—the Angel of the LORD ascended in the flame of the
altar! When Manoah and his wife saw *this,* they fell on their faces to the
ground. 21When the Angel of the LORD appeared no more to Manoah and
his wife, then Manoah knew that He *was* the Angel of the LORD.
22And Manoah said to his wife, "We shall surely die, because we have
seen God!"
23But his wife said to him, "If the LORD had desired to kill us, He would
not have accepted a burnt offering and a grain offering from our hands,
nor would He have shown us all these *things,* nor would He have told us
such things as these at this time."
24So the woman bore a son and called his name Samson; and the child
grew, and the LORD blessed him. 25And the Spirit of the LORD began to
move upon him at Mahaneh Dan[z] between Zorah and Eshtaol.

Samson's Philistine Wife

14 Now Samson went down to Timnah, and saw a woman in Timnah
of the daughters of the Philistines. 2So he went up and told his father
and mother, saying, "I have seen a woman in Timnah of the daughters of
the Philistines; now therefore, get her for me as a wife."
3Then his father and mother said to him, "*Is there* no woman among the
daughters of your brethren, or among all my people, that you must go and
get a wife from the uncircumcised Philistines?"
And Samson said to his father, "Get her for me, for she pleases me well."
4But his father and mother did not know that it was of the LORD—that
He was seeking an occasion to move against the Philistines. For at that
time the Philistines had dominion over Israel.

13:25 [z] Literally *Camp of Dan* (compare 18:12)

[5]So Samson went down to Timnah with his father and mother, and
came to the vineyards of Timnah.
Now *to his* surprise, a young lion *came* roaring against him. [6]And the
Spirit of the LORD came mightily upon him, and he tore the lion apart as
one would have torn apart a young goat, though *he had* nothing in his
hand. But he did not tell his father or his mother what he had done.
[7]Then he went down and talked with the woman; and she pleased Samson
well. [8]After some time, when he returned to get her, he turned aside to see the
carcass of the lion. And behold, a swarm of bees and honey *were* in the
carcass of the lion. [9]He took some of it in his hands and went along, eating.
When he came to his father and mother, he gave *some* to them, and they also
ate. But he did not tell them that he had taken the honey out of the carcass of
the lion.
[10]So his father went down to the woman. And Samson gave a feast there,
for young men used to do so. [11]And it happened, when they saw him, that
they brought thirty companions to be with him.
[12]Then Samson said to them, "Let me pose a riddle to you. If you can
correctly solve and explain it to me within the seven days of the feast, then
I will give you thirty linen garments and thirty changes of clothing. [13]But if
you cannot explain *it* to me, then you shall give me thirty linen garments
and thirty changes of clothing."
And they said to him, "Pose your riddle, that we may hear it."
[14]So he said to them:

"Out of the eater came something to eat,
And out of the strong came something sweet."

Now for three days they could not explain the riddle.
[15]But it came to pass on the seventh[a] day that they said to Samson's wife,
"Entice your husband, that he may explain the riddle to us, or else we will
burn you and your father's house with fire. Have you invited us in order to
take what is ours? *Is that* not *so*?"
[16]Then Samson's wife wept on him, and said, "You only hate me! You do
not love me! You have posed a riddle to the sons of my people, but you
have not explained *it* to me."
And he said to her, "Look, I have not explained *it* to my father or my
mother; so should I explain *it* to you?" [17]Now she had wept on him the
seven days while their feast lasted. And it happened on the seventh day
that he told her, because she pressed him so much. Then she explained the
riddle to the sons of her people. [18]So the men of the city said to him on the
seventh day before the sun went down:

"What *is* sweeter than honey?
And what *is* stronger than a lion?"

And he said to them:

"If you had not plowed with my heifer,
You would not have solved my riddle!"

[19]Then the Spirit of the LORD came upon him mightily, and he went down

LIFE LESSON

Judges 14:1-20

SITUATION The Philistines ruled over Israel. The Israelites cried to God to save them. God provided a leader called Samson.

OBSERVATION God always provides strength to do his will. In Samson's case, God supplied extraordinary physical power.

INSPIRATION People who have moved the world have been Spirit-filled. Filled with the Spirit, the first disciples "turned the world upside down." Filled with the Spirit, the reformers started the spiritual blaze which became the Reformation. Filled with the Spirit, Francis Asbury, George Fox, Jonathan Edwards, Charles Finney, and David Brainerd set the mountains and prairies of America aglow with the fires of real Christianity. Filled with the Spirit, D. L. Moody and Ira Sankey shook two continents out of their spiritual lethargy. Corrie ten Boom and Mother Teresa impacted their world greatly.

The tides of civilization have risen, the courses of history have been brightened by people who have been filled with the Spirit of God. . . .

Have you yielded your life to Christ without reserve, asking Him to fill you and use you for His glory?

(From *The Secret of Happiness* by Billy Graham)

APPLICATION Pray for strength to do your work. Pray for yourself and others close to you: your family, pastor, friends. Let the Holy Spirit do extraordinary work in you.

EXPLORATION Source of Strength—Psalm 28:7; Zechariah 4:6; Acts 1:8.

14:15 [a] Following Masoretic Text, Targum, and Vulgate; Septuagint and Syriac read *fourth*.

Life Lesson

Judges 15:1–16:31

SITUATION Samson lost his betrothed wife to his best man. Obviously angry, Samson took revenge on the Philistines. Eventually, he died as a result of revealing the secret of his strength to Delilah.

OBSERVATION Samson initiated a cycle of violence and revenge between himself and the Philistines. This vicious cycle continued to grow in scope.

INSPIRATION Grudge is one of those words that defines itself. Its very sound betrays its meaning.

Say it slowly : "Grr-uuuud-ge."

It starts with a growl. "Grr . . . " Like a bear with bad breath coming out of hibernation or a mangy mongrel defending his bone in an alley. "Grr. . . . "

Being near a resentful person and petting a growling dog are equally enjoyable.

Don't you just love being next to people who are nursing a grudge? Isn't it a delight to listen to them sing their songs of woe? They are so optimistic! They are so full of hope. They are bubbling with life.

You know better. You know as well as I that if they are bubbling with anything it is anger. And if they are full of any-

to Ashkelon and killed thirty of their men, took their apparel, and gave the
changes *of clothing* to those who had explained the riddle. So his anger
was aroused, and he went back up to his father's house. 20 And Samson's
wife was *given* to his companion, who had been his best man.

Samson Defeats the Philistines

15 After a while, in the time of wheat harvest, it happened that Samson
visited his wife with a young goat. And he said, "Let me go in to my
wife, into *her* room." But her father would not permit him to go in.
2 Her father said, "I really thought that you thoroughly hated her; therefore I gave her to your companion. *Is* not her younger sister better than
she? Please, take her instead."
3 And Samson said to them, "This time I shall be blameless regarding
the Philistines if I harm them!" 4 Then Samson went and caught three hundred foxes; and he took torches, turned *the foxes* tail to tail, and put a torch
between each pair of tails. 5 When he had set the torches on fire, he let *the*
foxes go into the standing grain of the Philistines, and burned up both the
shocks and the standing grain, as well as the vineyards *and* olive groves.
6 Then the Philistines said, "Who has done this?"
And they answered, "Samson, the son-in-law of the Timnite, because
he has taken his wife and given her to his companion." So the Philistines
came up and burned her and her father with fire.
7 Samson said to them, "Since you would do a thing like this, I will surely
take revenge on you, and after that I will cease." 8 So he attacked them hip
and thigh with a great slaughter; then he went down and dwelt in the cleft
of the rock of Etam.
9 Now the Philistines went up, encamped in Judah, and deployed themselves against Lehi. 10 And the men of Judah said, "Why have you come up
against us?"
So they answered, "We have come up to arrest Samson, to do to him as
he has done to us."
11 Then three thousand men of Judah went down to the cleft of the rock
of Etam, and said to Samson, "Do you not know that the Philistines rule
over us? What *is* this you have done to us?"
And he said to them, "As they did to me, so I have done to them."
12 But they said to him, "We have come down to arrest you, that we may
deliver you into the hand of the Philistines."
Then Samson said to them, "Swear to me that you will not kill me yourselves."
13 So they spoke to him, saying, "No, but we will tie you securely and deliver you into their hand; but we will surely not kill you." And they bound
him with two new ropes and brought him up from the rock.
14 When he came to Lehi, the Philistines came shouting against him.
Then the Spirit of the LORD came mightily upon him; and the ropes that *were* on
his arms became like flax that is burned with fire, and his bonds broke
loose from his hands. 15 He found a fresh jawbone of a donkey, reached out his
hand and took it, and killed a thousand men with it. 16 Then Samson said:

"With the jawbone of a donkey,
Heaps upon heaps,
With the jawbone of a donkey
I have slain a thousand men!"

17And so it was, when he had finished speaking, that he threw the jawbone
from his hand, and called that place Ramath Lehi.[b]
18Then he became very thirsty; so he cried out to the LORD and said, "You
have given this great deliverance by the hand of Your servant; and now
shall I die of thirst and fall into the hand of the uncircumcised?" 19So God
split the hollow place that *is* in Lehi,[c] and water came out, and he drank;
and his spirit returned, and he revived. Therefore he called its name En
Hakkore,[d] which is in Lehi to this day. 20And he judged Israel twenty years
in the days of the Philistines.

Samson and Delilah

16 Now Samson went to Gaza and saw a harlot there, and went in to
her. 2*When* the Gazites *were told,* "Samson has come here!" they surrounded *the place* and lay in wait for him all night at the gate of the city.
They were quiet all night, saying, "In the morning, when it is daylight, we
will kill him." 3And Samson lay *low* till midnight; then he arose at midnight, took hold of the doors of the gate of the city and the two gateposts,
pulled them up, bar and all, put *them* on his shoulders, and carried them
to the top of the hill that faces Hebron.
4Afterward it happened that he loved a woman in the Valley of Sorek,
whose name *was* Delilah. 5And the lords of the Philistines came up to her
and said to her, "Entice him, and find out where his great strength *lies,* and
by what *means* we may overpower him, that we may bind him to afflict
him; and every one of us will give you eleven hundred *pieces* of silver."
6So Delilah said to Samson, "Please tell me where your great strength
lies, and with what you may be bound to afflict you."
7And Samson said to her, "If they bind me with seven fresh bowstrings,
not yet dried, then I shall become weak, and be like any *other* man."
8So the lords of the Philistines brought up to her seven fresh bowstrings,
not yet dried, and she bound him with them. 9Now *men were* lying in wait,
staying with her in the room. And she said to him, "The Philistines *are*
upon you, Samson!" But he broke the bowstrings as a strand of yarn
breaks when it touches fire. So the secret of his strength was not known.
10Then Delilah said to Samson, "Look, you have mocked me and told
me lies. Now, please tell me what you may be bound with."
11So he said to her, "If they bind me securely with new ropes that have
never been used, then I shall become weak, and be like any *other* man."
12Therefore Delilah took new ropes and bound him with them, and said
to him, "The Philistines *are* upon you, Samson!" And *men were* lying in
wait, staying in the room. But he broke them off his arms like a thread.
13Delilah said to Samson, "Until now you have mocked me and told me
lies. Tell me what you may be bound with."
And he said to her, "If you weave the seven locks of my head into the
web of the loom"—
14So she wove *it* tightly with the batten of the loom, and said to him, "The
Philistines *are* upon you, Samson!" But he awoke from his sleep, and
pulled out the batten and the web from the loom.
15Then she said to him, "How can you say, 'I love you,' when your heart
is not with me? You have mocked me these three times, and have not told

thing, it is poisonous barbs of condemnation for all the people who have hurt them. Grudge bearers and angry animals are a lot alike. Both are irritable. Both are explosive. Both can be rabid. Someone needs to make a sign that can be worn around the neck of the resentful: "Beware of the Grrrrrrudge Bearer."

Add an M to the second part of the word , and you will see what grudge bearers throw. Mud. It's not enough to accuse; the other person's character must be attacked. It's insufficient to point a finger; a rifle must be aimed. Slander is slung. Names are called. Circles are drawn. Walls are built. And enemies are made. . . .

Is this the way you are coping with your hurts?

(From *The Applause of Heaven* by Max Lucado)

APPLICATION Grudges can create emotional walls in families, between friends, at work or at church—places where people step on and over each other. Are you holding a grudge? It is a negative factor in your life. Pray for help to change your attitude.

EXPLORATION Revenge—Leviticus 19:18; Proverbs 20:22; 24:29; Matthew 5:39; Romans 12:19-20.

15:17 [b] Literally *Jawbone Height*
15:19 [c] Literally *Jawbone* (compare verse 14) [d] Literally *Spring of the Caller*

me where your great strength *lies*." 16And it came to
pass, when she pestered him daily with her words and
pressed him, *so* that his soul was vexed to death, 17that
he told her all his heart, and said to her, "No razor has
ever come upon my head, for I *have been* a Nazirite to
God from my mother's womb. If I am shaven, then
my strength will leave me, and I shall become weak,
and be like any *other* man."

18When Delilah saw that he had told her all his heart,
she sent and called for the lords of the Philistines, saying, "Come up once more, for he has told me all his
heart." So the lords of the Philistines came up to her
and brought the money in their hand. 19Then she lulled
him to sleep on her knees, and called for a man and
had him shave off the seven locks of his head. Then
she began to torment him,[e] and his strength left him.
20And she said, "The Philistines *are* upon you, Samson!" So he awoke from his sleep, and said, "I will go
out as before, at other times, and shake myself free!"
But he did not know that the LORD had departed from
him.

21Then the Philistines took him and put out his
eyes, and brought him down to Gaza. They bound
him with bronze fetters, and he became a grinder in
the prison. 22However, the hair of his head began to
grow again after it had been shaven.

Samson Dies with the Philistines

23Now the lords of the Philistines gathered together
to offer a great sacrifice to Dagon their god, and to rejoice. And they said:

"Our god has delivered into our hands
Samson our enemy!"

24When the people saw him, they praised their god;
for they said:

"Our god has delivered into our hands our
enemy,
The destroyer of our land,
And the one who multiplied our dead."

25So it happened, when their hearts were merry, that
they said, "Call for Samson, that he may perform for
us." So they called for Samson from the prison, and
he performed for them. And they stationed him between the pillars. 26Then Samson said to the lad who
held him by the hand, "Let me feel the pillars which
support the temple, so that I can lean on them." 27Now
the temple was full of men and women. All the lords
of the Philistines *were* there—about three thousand
men and women on the roof watching while Samson
performed.

28Then Samson called to the LORD, saying, "O Lord
GOD, remember me, I pray! Strengthen me, I pray, just
this once, O God, that I may with one *blow* take
vengeance on the Philistines for my two eyes!" 29And
Samson took hold of the two middle pillars which
supported the temple, and he braced himself against
them, one on his right and the other on his left. 30Then
Samson said, "Let me die with the Philistines!" And
he pushed with *all his* might, and the temple fell on
the lords and all the people who *were* in it. So the dead
that he killed at his death were more than he had
killed in his life.

31And his brothers and all his father's household
came down and took him, and brought *him* up and
buried him between Zorah and Eshtaol in the tomb of
his father Manoah. He had judged Israel twenty years.

Micah's Idolatry

17 Now there was a man from the mountains of
Ephraim, whose name *was* Micah. 2And he said
to his mother, "The eleven hundred *shekels* of silver
that were taken from you, and on which you put a
curse, even saying it in my ears—here *is* the silver
with me; I took it."

And his mother said, "*May you be* blessed by the
LORD, my son!" 3So when he had returned the eleven
hundred *shekels* of silver to his mother, his mother
said, "I had wholly dedicated the silver from my hand
to the LORD for my son, to make a carved image and a
molded image; now therefore, I will return it to you."
4Thus he returned the silver to his mother. Then his
mother took two hundred *shekels* of silver and gave
them to the silversmith, and he made it into a carved
image and a molded image; and they were in the
house of Micah.

5The man Micah had a shrine, and made an ephod
and household idols;[f] and he consecrated one of his
sons, who became his priest. 6In those days *there was*
no king in Israel; everyone did *what was* right in his
own eyes.

7Now there was a young man from Bethlehem in
Judah, of the family of Judah; he *was* a Levite, and was
staying there. 8The man departed from the city of
Bethlehem in Judah to stay wherever he could find *a*

16:19 [e] Following Masoretic Text, Targum, and Vulgate; Septuagint reads *he began to be weak.*
17:5 [f] Hebrew *teraphim*

place. Then he came to the mountains of Ephraim, to the house of Micah,
as he journeyed. 9And Micah said to him, "Where do you come from?"
So he said to him, "I *am* a Levite from Bethlehem in Judah, and I am on
my way to find *a place* to stay."
10Micah said to him, "Dwell with me, and be a father and a priest to me,
and I will give you ten *shekels* of silver per year, a suit of clothes, and your
sustenance." So the Levite went in. 11Then the Levite was content to dwell
with the man; and the young man became like one of his sons to him. 12So
Micah consecrated the Levite, and the young man became his priest, and
lived in the house of Micah. 13Then Micah said, "Now I know that the LORD
will be good to me, since I have a Levite as priest!"

The Danites Adopt Micah's Idolatry

18 In those days *there was* no king in Israel. And in those days the tribe
of the Danites was seeking an inheritance for itself to dwell in; for
until that day *their* inheritance among the tribes of Israel had not fallen to
them. 2So the children of Dan sent five men of their family from their territory, men of valor from Zorah and Eshtaol, to spy out the land and
search it. They said to them, "Go, search the land." So they went to the
mountains of Ephraim, to the house of Micah, and lodged there. 3While
they *were* at the house of Micah, they recognized the voice of the young
Levite. They turned aside and said to him, "Who brought you here? What
are you doing in this *place?* What do you have here?"
4He said to them, "Thus and so Micah did for me. He has hired me, and
I have become his priest."
5So they said to him, "Please inquire of God, that we may know whether
the journey on which we go will be prosperous."
6And the priest said to them, "Go in peace. The presence of the LORD *be*
with you on your way."
7So the five men departed and went to Laish. They saw the people who
were there, how they dwelt safely, in the manner of the Sidonians, quiet
and secure. *There were* no rulers in the land who might put *them* to shame
for anything. They *were* far from the Sidonians, and they had no ties with
anyone.[g]
8Then *the spies* came back to their brethren at Zorah and Eshtaol, and
their brethren said to them, "What *is* your *report?*"
9So they said, "Arise, let us go up against them. For we have seen the
land, and indeed it *is* very good. *Would* you *do* nothing? Do not hesitate to
go, *and* enter to possess the land. 10When you go, you will come to a secure
people and a large land. For God has given it into your hands, a place
where *there is* no lack of anything that *is* on the earth."
11And six hundred men of the family of the Danites went from there,
from Zorah and Eshtaol, armed with weapons of war. 12Then they went up
and encamped in Kirjath Jearim in Judah. (Therefore they call that place
Mahaneh Dan[h] to this day. There *it is,* west of Kirjath Jearim.) 13And they
passed from there to the mountains of Ephraim, and came to the house of
Micah.
14Then the five men who had gone to spy out the country of Laish answered and said to their brethren, "Do you know that there are in these

18:7 [g] Following Masoretic Text, Targum, and Vulgate; Septuagint reads *with Syria.*
18:12 [h] Literally *Camp of Dan*

LIFE LESSON

Judges 17:1–18:31

SITUATION Micah, a man who stole money from his mother, decided to confess when he heard his mother calling down curses upon the thief who stole her money. His mother blessed and forgave him. Micah's mother made an idol from the money to try to atone for the sin her son committed.

OBSERVATION False religion seeks peace of heart through all the wrong ways. A true relationship with God requires whole hearted obedience, not a token sacrifice.

INSPIRATION "Lord," I said, "I want to be your man, not my own. So to you I give my money, my car—even my home."

Then, smug and content, I relaxed with a smile and whispered to God, "I bet it's been a while since anyone has given so much—so freely?"
His answer surprised me. He replied, "Not really."

Not a day has gone by since the beginning of time, that someone hasn't offered meager nickels and dimes, golden alters and crosses, contributions and penance, stone monuments and steeples; but why not repentance?

"The money, the statues, the cathedrals you've built, do you really think I need your offering of guilt?

"What good is money that's meant only to salve the hurting conscience that so many of you have?

"Your lips know no prayers. Your eyes, no compassion.

But you will go to church (when church going's in fashion).

"Just give me a tear—a heart ready to mold.

And I'll give you a mission, a message so bold—

That a fire will be stirred where there was only death,

And your heart will be flamed by my life and my breath."

I stuck my hands in my pockets and kicked at the dirt.

It's tough to be corrected (I guess my feelings were hurt).

Continued

But it was worth the struggle to realize the thought.

That the cross isn't for sale and Christ's blood can't be bought.
(From *On the Anvil* by Max Lucado)

APPLICATION Are you trying to win God's favor? Instead, accept his gift of salvation. God has no price tag attached to his mercy. Jesus paid the price himself.

EXPLORATION Obedience Not Sacrifice—Proverbs 21:3; Hosea 6:6; 1 Samuel 15:22.

houses an ephod, household idols, a carved image, and a molded image?
Now therefore, consider what you should do." 15 So they turned aside
there, and came to the house of the young Levite man—to the house of
Micah—and greeted him. 16 The six hundred men armed with their
weapons of war, who *were* of the children of Dan, stood by the entrance of
the gate. 17 Then the five men who had gone to spy out the land went up.
Entering there, they took the carved image, the ephod, the household
idols, and the molded image. The priest stood at the entrance of the gate
with the six hundred men *who were* armed with weapons of war.

18 When these went into Micah's house and took the carved image, the
ephod, the household idols, and the molded image, the priest said to
them, "What are you doing?"

19 And they said to him, "Be quiet, put your hand over your mouth, and
come with us; be a father and a priest to us. *Is it* better for you to be a priest
to the household of one man, or that you be a priest to a tribe and a family
in Israel?" 20 So the priest's heart was glad; and he took the ephod, the household idols, and the carved image, and took his place among the people.

21 Then they turned and departed, and put the little ones, the livestock,
and the goods in front of them. 22 When they were a good way from the
house of Micah, the men who *were* in the houses near Micah's house gathered together and overtook the children of Dan. 23 And they called out to
the children of Dan. So they turned around and said to Micah, "What ails
you, that you have gathered such a company?"

24 So he said, "You have taken away my gods which I made, and the
priest, and you have gone away. Now what more do I have? How can you
say to me, 'What ails you?' "

25 And the children of Dan said to him, "Do not let your voice be heard
among us, lest angry men fall upon you, and you lose your life, with the
lives of your household!" 26 Then the children of Dan went their way. And
when Micah saw that they *were* too strong for him, he turned and went
back to his house.

Danites Settle in Laish

27 So they took *the things* Micah had made, and the priest who had belonged to him, and went to Laish, to a people quiet and secure; and they
struck them with the edge of the sword and burned the city with fire.
28 *There was* no deliverer, because it *was* far from Sidon, and they had no
ties with anyone. It was in the valley that belongs to Beth Rehob. So they
rebuilt the city and dwelt there. 29 And they called the name of the city Dan,
after the name of Dan their father, who was born to Israel. However, the
name of the city formerly *was* Laish.

30 Then the children of Dan set up for themselves the carved image; and
Jonathan the son of Gershom, the son of Manasseh,[i] and his sons were
priests to the tribe of Dan until the day of the captivity of the land. 31 So they
set up for themselves Micah's carved image which he made, all the time
that the house of God was in Shiloh.

The Levite's Concubine

19 And it came to pass in those days, when *there was* no king in Israel,
that there was a certain Levite staying in the remote mountains of

18:30 [i] Septuagint and Vulgate read *Moses*.

Ephraim. He took for himself a concubine from Bethlehem in Judah. 2But
his concubine played the harlot against him, and went away from him to
her father's house at Bethlehem in Judah, and was there four whole
months. 3Then her husband arose and went after her, to speak kindly to
her *and* bring her back, having his servant and a couple of donkeys with
him. So she brought him into her father's house; and when the father of the
young woman saw him, he was glad to meet him. 4Now his father-in-law,
the young woman's father, detained him; and he stayed with him three
days. So they ate and drank and lodged there.
5Then it came to pass on the fourth day that they arose early in the
morning, and he stood to depart; but the young woman's father said to his
son-in-law, "Refresh your heart with a morsel of bread, and afterward go
your way."
6So they sat down, and the two of them ate and drank together. Then the
young woman's father said to the man, "Please be content to stay all night,
and let your heart be merry." 7And when the man stood to depart, his father-
in-law urged him; so he lodged there again. 8Then he arose early in the
morning on the fifth day to depart, but the young woman's father said,
"Please refresh your heart." So they delayed until afternoon; and both of
them ate.
9And when the man stood to depart—he and his concubine and his servant—his father-in-law, the young woman's father, said to him, "Look, the
day is now drawing toward evening; please spend the night. See, the day is
coming to an end; lodge here, that your heart may be merry. Tomorrow go
your way early, so that you may get home."
10However, the man was not willing to spend that night; so he rose and
departed, and came opposite Jebus (that *is,* Jerusalem). With him were
the two saddled donkeys; his concubine *was* also with him. 11They *were*
near Jebus, and the day was far spent; and the servant said to his master,
"Come, please, and let us turn aside into this city of the Jebusites and
lodge in it."
12But his master said to him, "We will not turn aside here into a city of
foreigners, who *are* not of the children of Israel; we will go on to Gibeah."
13So he said to his servant, "Come, let us draw near to one of these places,
and spend the night in Gibeah or in Ramah." 14And they passed by and
went their way; and the sun went down on them near Gibeah, which belongs to Benjamin. 15They turned aside there to go in to lodge in Gibeah.
And when he went in, he sat down in the open square of the city, for no one
would take them into *his* house to spend the night.
16Just then an old man came in from his work in the field at evening,
who also *was* from the mountains of Ephraim; he was staying in Gibeah,
whereas the men of the place *were* Benjamites. 17And when he raised his
eyes, he saw the traveler in the open square of the city; and the old man
said, "Where are you going, and where do you come from?"
18So he said to him, "We *are* passing from Bethlehem in Judah toward
the remote mountains of Ephraim; I *am* from there. I went to Bethlehem
in Judah; *now* I am going to the house of the LORD. But there *is* no one who
will take me into his house, 19although we have both straw and fodder for
our donkeys, and bread and wine for myself, for your female servant, and
for the young man *who is* with your servant; *there is* no lack of anything."
20And the old man said, "Peace *be* with you! However, *let* all your needs

LIFE LESSON

Judges 19:1–21:25

SITUATION A Levite priest cruelly and unjustly handed over his concubine to be abused by wicked men living in Gibeah, a village of the Benjamites. When he got home, the priest cut her corpse into twelve parts and sent each tribe in Israel a part to dramatize the shamefulness of the act perpetrated by the men of Gibeah.

OBSERVATION We must protect the helpless and vulnerable, as we trust God to protect us.

INSPIRATION That was the night God gave me real compassion for whites—the night those Mississippi police officers beat me almost to death.

It was Saturday, February 7, 1970, about 6:30 p.m. Here's how I described the scene later in the court trial: "When I got to the jail and saw the people in jail, of course I was horrified as to why we were arrested and when I got in the jail Sheriff Jonathan Edwards came over to me right away and said, "This is the smart nigger, and this is a new ballgame. You're not in Simpson county now; you are in Brandon. He began to beat me, and from that time on they continued beating me."

It got worse as the night wore on. One officer brought a fork over to me and said, "Do you see this?" And he jammed it up my nose. Then he crammed it down my throat. Then they beat me to the ground again and stomped on me.

. . . I remember their faces—so twisted with hate. It was like looking at white faced demons. For the first time I saw what hate had done to those people. These policemen were poor. They saw themselves as failures. The only way they knew how to find a sense of self worth was by beating us. Their racism made them feel like "somebody."

My beating and the frustration and bitterness that followed took their toll. In July of 1970 I had a heart attack. I was hospitalized in Mound Bayou, a small black community where I had helped organize some co-ops. After a partial recovery I found myself back in

Continued

the same hospital with ulcers. Dr. Harvey Sanders, a black doctor, had to take out two thirds of my stomach.

Lying in that hospital bed I had a lot of time to think. I thought about blacks and whites. About how, in a country that claimed to stand for "liberty and justice for all," a black man in Mississippi could get no justice. I thought about how in Mississippi, "Christians" were the most racist whites of all.

. . . The Spirit of God worked on me as I lay in that bed. An image formed in my mind—the image of a cross, of Christ on the cross. This Jesus knew what I had suffered. He understood. He cared. Because he had gone through it all himself.

I read Matthew 6:14-15 again and again in that bed: "For if you forgive men for their transgressions, your heavenly Father will also forgive you. But if you do not forgive men, then your heavenly Father will not forgive your transgressions." To receive God's forgiveness I was going to have to forgive those who had hurt me. As I prayed, the faces of those policemen passed before me one by one and I forgave each one. Faces of other white people from the past came before me, and I forgave them. I could sense that God was working a deep inner healing in me that went back beyond February 7, 1970. It went clear back to my earliest memories of childhood. God was healing all those wounds that had kept me from loving whites. How sweet God's forgiveness and healing was!

(From *With Justice for All* by John Perkins)

APPLICATION Read Matthew 6:14-15 and 18:21-35. Think about one or two people who have hurt you. Pray for them. Do not excuse what they did, but pray that God will help you forgive them as God forgave you.

EXPLORATION Injustice—Exodus 22:21; Psalm 43:1; Zephaniah 3:5; Luke 16:10.

be my responsibility; only do not spend the night in the open square." 21So
he brought him into his house, and gave fodder to the donkeys. And they
washed their feet, and ate and drank.

Gibeah's Crime

22As they were enjoying themselves, suddenly certain men of the city,
perverted men,[j] surrounded the house *and* beat on the door. They spoke to
the master of the house, the old man, saying, "Bring out the man who
came to your house, that we may know him *carnally!*"
23But the man, the master of the house, went out to them and said to
them, "No, my brethren! I beg you, do not act *so* wickedly! Seeing this man
has come into my house, do not commit this outrage. 24Look, *here is* my
virgin daughter and *the man's*[k] concubine; let me bring them out now.
Humble them, and do with them as you please; but to this man do not do
such a vile thing!" 25But the men would not heed him. So the man took his
concubine and brought *her* out to them. And they knew her and abused
her all night until morning; and when the day began to break, they let her
go.
26Then the woman came as the day was dawning, and fell down at the
door of the man's house where her master *was,* till it was light.
27When her master arose in the morning, and opened the doors of the
house and went out to go his way, there was his concubine, fallen *at* the
door of the house with her hands on the threshold. 28And he said to her,
"Get up and let us be going." But there was no answer. So the man lifted
her onto the donkey; and the man got up and went to his place.
29When he entered his house he took a knife, laid hold of his concubine,
and divided her into twelve pieces, limb by limb,[l] and sent her throughout
all the territory of Israel. 30And so it was that all who saw it said, "No such
deed has been done or seen from the day that the children of Israel came
up from the land of Egypt until this day. Consider it, confer, and speak
up!"

Israel's War with the Benjamites

20 So all the children of Israel came out, from Dan to Beersheba, as
well as from the land of Gilead, and the congregation gathered together as one man before the LORD at Mizpah. 2And the leaders of all the
people, all the tribes of Israel, presented themselves in the assembly of the
people of God, four hundred thousand foot soldiers who drew the sword.
3(Now the children of Benjamin heard that the children of Israel had gone
up to Mizpah.)
Then the children of Israel said, "Tell *us,* how did this wicked deed happen?"
4So the Levite, the husband of the woman who was murdered, answered
and said, "My concubine and I went into Gibeah, which belongs to Benjamin, to spend the night. 5And the men of Gibeah rose against me, and surrounded the house at night because of me. They intended to kill me, but
instead they ravished my concubine so that she died. 6So I took hold of my
concubine, cut her in pieces, and sent her throughout all the territory of

19:22 [j] Literally *sons of Belial*
19:24 [k] Literally *his*
19:29 [l] Literally *with her bones*

the inheritance of Israel, because they committed
lewdness and outrage in Israel. 7 Look! All of you *are*
children of Israel; give your advice and counsel here
and now!"
8 So all the people arose as one man, saying, "None
of us will go to his tent, nor will any turn back to his
house; 9 but now this *is* the thing which we will do to
Gibeah: *We will go up* against it by lot. 10 We will take
ten men out of *every* hundred throughout all the
tribes of Israel, a hundred out of *every* thousand, and
a thousand out of *every* ten thousand, to make provisions for the people, that when they come to Gibeah in
Benjamin, they may repay all the vileness that they
have done in Israel." 11 So all the men of Israel were
gathered against the city, united together as one man.
12 Then the tribes of Israel sent men through all the
tribe of Benjamin, saying, "What *is* this wickedness
that has occurred among you? 13 Now therefore, deliver up the men, the perverted men[m] who *are* in
Gibeah, that we may put them to death and remove the
evil from Israel!" But the children of Benjamin would
not listen to the voice of their brethren, the children of
Israel. 14 Instead, the children of Benjamin gathered
together from their cities to Gibeah, to go to battle
against the children of Israel. 15 And from their cities at
that time the children of Benjamin numbered twenty-
six thousand men who drew the sword, besides the
inhabitants of Gibeah, who numbered seven hundred
select men. 16 Among all this people *were* seven hundred select men *who were* left-handed; every one could
sling a stone at a hair's *breadth* and not miss. 17 Now
besides Benjamin, the men of Israel numbered four
hundred thousand men who drew the sword; all of
these *were* men of war.
18 Then the children of Israel arose and went up to
the house of God[n] to inquire of God. They said,
"Which of us shall go up first to battle against the children of Benjamin?"
The LORD said, "Judah first!"
19 So the children of Israel rose in the morning and
encamped against Gibeah. 20 And the men of Israel
went out to battle against Benjamin, and the men of
Israel put themselves in battle array to fight against
them at Gibeah. 21 Then the children of Benjamin
came out of Gibeah, and on that day cut down to the
ground twenty-two thousand men of the Israelites.
22 And the people, that is, the men of Israel, encouraged themselves and again formed the battle line at
the place where they had put themselves in array on
the first day. 23 Then the children of Israel went up and
wept before the LORD until evening, and asked counsel of the LORD, saying, "Shall I again draw near for
battle against the children of my brother Benjamin?"
And the LORD said, "Go up against him."
24 So the children of Israel approached the children
of Benjamin on the second day. 25 And Benjamin went
out against them from Gibeah on the second day, and
cut down to the ground eighteen thousand more of
the children of Israel; all these drew the sword.
26 Then all the children of Israel, that is, all the people, went up and came to the house of God[o] and wept.
They sat there before the LORD and fasted that day
until evening; and they offered burnt offerings and
peace offerings before the LORD. 27 So the children of
Israel inquired of the LORD (the ark of the covenant of
God *was* there in those days, 28 and Phinehas the son
of Eleazar, the son of Aaron, stood before it in those
days), saying, "Shall I yet again go out to battle against
the children of my brother Benjamin, or shall I
cease?"
And the LORD said, "Go up, for tomorrow I will deliver them into your hand."
29 Then Israel set men in ambush all around Gibeah.
30 And the children of Israel went up against the children of Benjamin on the third day, and put themselves in battle array against Gibeah as at the other
times. 31 So the children of Benjamin went out against
the people, *and* were drawn away from the city. They
began to strike down *and* kill some of the people, as at
the other times, in the highways (one of which goes
up to Bethel and the other to Gibeah) and in the field,
about thirty men of Israel. 32 And the children of Benjamin said, "They *are* defeated before us, as at first."
But the children of Israel said, "Let us flee and
draw them away from the city to the highways." 33 So
all the men of Israel rose from their place and put
themselves in battle array at Baal Tamar. Then Israel's
men in ambush burst forth from their position in the
plain of Geba. 34 And ten thousand select men from all
Israel came against Gibeah, and the battle was fierce.
But *the Benjamites*[p] did not know that disaster *was*
upon them. 35 The LORD defeated Benjamin before Israel. And the children of Israel destroyed that day
twenty-five thousand one hundred Benjamites; all
these drew the sword.
36 So the children of Benjamin saw that they were

20:13 [m] Literally *sons of Belial*
20:18 [n] Or *Bethel*
20:26 [o] Or *Bethel*
20:34 [p] Literally *they*

defeated. The men of Israel had given ground to the
Benjamites, because they relied on the men in ambush
whom they had set against Gibeah. 37 And the men in
ambush quickly rushed upon Gibeah; the men in ambush spread out and struck the whole city with the
edge of the sword. 38 Now the appointed signal between the men of Israel and the men in ambush was
that they would make a great cloud of smoke rise up
from the city, 39 whereupon the men of Israel would
turn in battle. Now Benjamin had begun to strike *and*
kill about thirty of the men of Israel. For they said,
"Surely they are defeated before us, as *in* the first battle." 40 But when the cloud began to rise from the city
in a column of smoke, the Benjamites looked behind
them, and there was the whole city going up *in smoke*
to heaven. 41 And when the men of Israel turned back,
the men of Benjamin panicked, for they saw that disaster had come upon them. 42 Therefore they turned
their backs before the men of Israel in the direction of
the wilderness; but the battle overtook them, and
whoever *came* out of the cities they destroyed in their
midst. 43 They surrounded the Benjamites, chased
them, *and* easily trampled them down as far as the
front of Gibeah toward the east. 44 And eighteen thousand men of Benjamin fell; all these *were* men of
valor. 45 Then they[q] turned and fled toward the wilderness to the rock of Rimmon; and they cut down five
thousand of them on the highways. Then they pursued them relentlessly up to Gidom, and killed two
thousand of them. 46 So all who fell of Benjamin that
day were twenty-five thousand men who drew the
sword; all these *were* men of valor.

47 But six hundred men turned and fled toward the
wilderness to the rock of Rimmon, and they stayed at
the rock of Rimmon for four months. 48 And the men
of Israel turned back against the children of Benjamin,
and struck them down with the edge of the sword—
from *every* city, men and beasts, all who were found.
They also set fire to all the cities they came to.

Wives Provided for the Benjamites

21 Now the men of Israel had sworn an oath at
Mizpah, saying, "None of us shall give his
daughter to Benjamin as a wife." 2 Then the people
came to the house of God,[r] and remained there before
God till evening. They lifted up their voices and wept
bitterly, 3 and said, "O LORD God of Israel, why has this
come to pass in Israel, that today there should be one
tribe *missing* in Israel?"

4 So it was, on the next morning, that the people
rose early and built an altar there, and offered burnt
offerings and peace offerings. 5 The children of Israel
said, "Who *is there* among all the tribes of Israel who
did not come up with the assembly to the LORD?" For
they had made a great oath concerning anyone who
had not come up to the LORD at Mizpah, saying, "He
shall surely be put to death." 6 And the children of Israel grieved for Benjamin their brother, and said,
"One tribe is cut off from Israel today. 7 What shall we
do for wives for those who remain, seeing we have
sworn by the LORD that we will not give them our
daughters as wives?"

8 And they said, "What one *is there* from the tribes
of Israel who did not come up to Mizpah to the LORD?"
And, in fact, no one had come to the camp from Jabesh
Gilead to the assembly. 9 For when the people were
counted, indeed, not one of the inhabitants of Jabesh
Gilead *was* there. 10 So the congregation sent out there
twelve thousand of their most valiant men, and commanded them, saying, "Go and strike the inhabitants of Jabesh Gilead with the edge of the sword,
including the women and children. 11 And this *is* the
thing that you shall do: You shall utterly destroy every
male, and every woman who has known a man intimately." 12 So they found among the inhabitants of
Jabesh Gilead four hundred young virgins who had
not known a man intimately; and they brought them
to the camp at Shiloh, which is in the land of Canaan.

13 Then the whole congregation sent *word* to the children of Benjamin who *were* at the rock of Rimmon,
and announced peace to them. 14 So Benjamin came
back at that time, and they gave them the women
whom they had saved alive of the women of Jabesh
Gilead; and yet they had not found enough for them.

15 And the people grieved for Benjamin, because the
LORD had made a void in the tribes of Israel.

16 Then the elders of the congregation said, "What
shall we do for wives for those who remain, since the
women of Benjamin have been destroyed?" 17 And
they said, "*There must be* an inheritance for the survivors of Benjamin, that a tribe may not be destroyed
from Israel. 18 However, we cannot give them wives
from our daughters, for the children of Israel have
sworn an oath, saying, 'Cursed *be* the one who gives a
wife to Benjamin.' " 19 Then they said, "In fact, *there is*
a yearly feast of the LORD in Shiloh, which *is* north of
Bethel, on the east side of the highway that goes up
from Bethel to Shechem, and south of Lebonah."

20:45 [q] Septuagint reads *the rest.*
21:2 [r] Or *Bethel*

[20]Therefore they instructed the children of Benjamin, saying, "Go, lie in wait in the vineyards, [21]and
watch; and just when the daughters of Shiloh come
out to perform their dances, then come out from the
vineyards, and every man catch a wife for himself
from the daughters of Shiloh; then go to the land of
Benjamin. [22]Then it shall be, when their fathers or
their brothers come to us to complain, that we will say
to them, 'Be kind to them for our sakes, because we
did not take a wife for any of them in the war; for *it is*
not *as though* you have given the *women* to them at
this time, making yourselves guilty of your oath.' "

[23]And the children of Benjamin did so; they took
enough wives for their number from those who
danced, whom they caught. Then they went and returned to their inheritance, and they rebuilt the cities
and dwelt in them. [24]So the children of Israel departed
from there at that time, every man to his tribe and
family; they went out from there, every man to his inheritance.

[25]In those days *there was* no king in Israel; everyone
did *what was* right in his own eyes.

The Book of

RUTH

INTRODUCTION

Here is a play with four characters.

Character number one is a prostitute.

Character number two is her son. By the time we meet him he is wealthy, powerful, and single. (We wonder if his bachelorhood has anything to do with being the son of a prostitute.)

Character number three is a foreign widow in a clannish culture. Everything about her is different. Speaks with an accent. Wears a different name. Eats different food. Has a different way. Her only friend is her mother-in-law who happens also to be a widow and happens to be:

Character number four. She is older than the first widow. Too old to have kids. When her two sons die and her husband dies, she is left alone. With only a foreigner as a friend.

Four people. Each rejected. Each alone. Four frazzled strings in the bottom of the knitting basket. Left untouched, awaiting the toss of the master-weaver. But he doesn't discard them.

He picks them up and weaves them together.

The result? The unmarried son of the prostitute meets the foreign widow who left her homeland to accompany her mother-in-law. The mother-in-law recognizes the bachelor as a relative and urges her daughter-in-law to make herself available. She does, the two marry, and the single bachelor has a wife—the young widow has a husband and the older widow has a grandson and we have a story of providential romance.

Such is the story of Ruth.

You'll recognize her as the younger widow. The older is named Naomi. Boaz is the son of the prostitute. And the prostitute? Well, she isn't mentioned in this book. But she is mentioned in, of all places, the Gospel of Matthew.

Read the words in parenthesis of chapter one verse five. Go ahead and flip over there, I'll wait for you.

Did you see it? Salmon was the father of Boaz. (Boaz's mother was Rahab.)

Who would've thought? A harlot on Jesus' family tree.

But these kind of things happen in the Bible. Aren't we glad they do? Aren't we glad the master-weaver has a place in his plan for each of us?

LIFE LESSON

Ruth 1:1-22

SITUATION The story of Ruth took place sometime during the rule of the Judges. Those were dark days for Israel, when "everyone did as he saw fit" (Judges 17:6). But during those dark days and evil times many remained faithful to God.

OBSERVATION Naomi and Ruth portrayed beautiful examples of loyalty, friendship, and commitment to each other and to God.

INSPIRATION One relationship of this caliber can buoy us through the fiercest storms. It was the Beatles who sang, "Will you still need me, will you still feed me, when I'm sixty-four?" Oh, the agony of being sixty-four (or any age, for that matter) and having no one to care for you or need you. Happy are those who have one companion, one relationship that is not based on looks or performance. Every person is in dire need of at least one faithful friend, or a mate who will look him in the eye and say, "I will never leave you. You may grow old and gray, but I'll never leave you. Your face may wrinkle and your body may ruin, but I'll never leave you. The years may be cruel and the times may be hard, but I'll be here. I will never leave you."

(From *On the Anvil* by Max Lucado)

APPLICATION Think for a minute about the people in your world. What do they think of your commitment to them? How would they rate your faithfulness? Does your loyalty ever waver? With whom are you a friend forever? Pray for that person(s) today.

EXPLORATION Commitment—Esther 4:16; 1 Samuel 20:16-17; 2 Chronicles 15:14-15; Psalm 37:5; Proverbs 17:17; Luke 9:23-27.

Elimelech's Family Goes to Moab

Now it came to pass, in the days when the judges ruled, that
there was a famine in the land. And a certain man of Bethlehem, Judah, went to dwell in the country of Moab, he and his
wife and his two sons. 2 The name of the man *was* Elimelech,
the name of his wife *was* Naomi, and the names of his two sons *were* Mahlon
and Chilion—Ephrathites of Bethlehem, Judah. And they went to the country of Moab and remained there. 3 Then Elimelech, Naomi's husband, died;
and she was left, and her two sons. 4 Now they took wives of the women of
Moab: the name of the one *was* Orpah, and the name of the other Ruth.
And they dwelt there about ten years. 5 Then both Mahlon and Chilion also
died; so the woman survived her two sons and her husband.

Naomi Returns with Ruth

6 Then she arose with her daughters-in-law that she might return from
the country of Moab, for she had heard in the country of Moab that the
LORD had visited His people by giving them bread. 7 Therefore she went out
from the place where she was, and her two daughters-in-law with her; and
they went on the way to return to the land of Judah. 8 And Naomi said to
her two daughters-in-law, "Go, return each to her mother's house. The
LORD deal kindly with you, as you have dealt with the dead and with me.
9 The LORD grant that you may find rest, each in the house of her husband."
So she kissed them, and they lifted up their voices and wept. 10 And they
said to her, "Surely we will return with you to your people."
11 But Naomi said, "Turn back, my daughters; why will you go with me?
Are there still sons in my womb, that they may be your husbands? 12 Turn
back, my daughters, go—for I am too old to have a husband. If I should say
I have hope, *if* I should have a husband tonight and should also bear sons,
13 would you wait for them till they were grown? Would you restrain yourselves from having husbands? No, my daughters; for it grieves me very
much for your sakes that the hand of the LORD has gone out against me!"
14 Then they lifted up their voices and wept again; and Orpah kissed her
mother-in-law, but Ruth clung to her.
15 And she said, "Look, your sister-in-law has gone back to her people
and to her gods; return after your sister-in-law."
16 But Ruth said:

"Entreat me not to leave you,
Or to turn back from following after you;
For wherever you go, I will go;
And wherever you lodge, I will lodge;
Your people *shall be* my people,
And your God, my God.
17 Where you die, I will die,
And there will I be buried.
The LORD do so to me, and more also,
If *anything but* death parts you and me."

18 When she saw that she was determined to go with her, she stopped
speaking to her.
19 Now the two of them went until they came to Bethlehem. And it happened, when they had come to Bethlehem, that all the city was excited because of them; and the women said, "*Is* this Naomi?"

20But she said to them, "Do not call me Naomi;[a] call me Mara,[b] for the
Almighty has dealt very bitterly with me. 21I went out full, and the LORD has
brought me home again empty. Why do you call me Naomi, since the LORD
has testified against me, and the Almighty has afflicted me?"
22So Naomi returned, and Ruth the Moabitess her daughter-in-law with
her, who returned from the country of Moab. Now they came to Bethlehem at the beginning of barley harvest.

Ruth Meets Boaz

2 There was a relative of Naomi's husband, a man of great wealth, of the
family of Elimelech. His name *was* Boaz. 2So Ruth the Moabitess said
to Naomi, "Please let me go to the field, and glean heads of grain after *him*
in whose sight I may find favor."
And she said to her, "Go, my daughter."
3Then she left, and went and gleaned in the field after the reapers. And
she happened to come to the part of the field *belonging* to Boaz, who *was* of
the family of Elimelech.
4Now behold, Boaz came from Bethlehem, and said to the reapers, "The
LORD *be* with you!"
And they answered him, "The LORD bless you!"
5Then Boaz said to his servant who was in charge of the reapers,
"Whose young woman *is* this?"
6So the servant who was in charge of the reapers answered and said, "It
is the young Moabite woman who came back with Naomi from the country of Moab. 7And she said, 'Please let me glean and gather after the
reapers among the sheaves.' So she came and has continued from morning until now, though she rested a little in the house."
8Then Boaz said to Ruth, "You will listen, my daughter, will you not? Do
not go to glean in another field, nor go from here, but stay close by my
young women. 9*Let* your eyes *be* on the field which they reap, and go after
them. Have I not commanded the young men not to touch you? And when
you are thirsty, go to the vessels and drink from what the young men have
drawn."
10So she fell on her face, bowed down to the ground, and said to him,
"Why have I found favor in your eyes, that you should take notice of me,
since I *am* a foreigner?"
11And Boaz answered and said to her, "It has been fully reported to me,
all that you have done for your mother-in-law since the death of your husband, and *how* you have left your father and your mother and the land of
your birth, and have come to a people whom you did not know before.
12The LORD repay your work, and a full reward be given you by the LORD
God of Israel, under whose wings you have come for refuge."
13Then she said, "Let me find favor in your sight, my lord; for you have
comforted me, and have spoken kindly to your maidservant, though I am
not like one of your maidservants."
14Now Boaz said to her at mealtime, "Come here, and eat of the bread,
and dip your piece of bread in the vinegar." So she sat beside the reapers,
and he passed parched *grain* to her; and she ate and was satisfied, and kept
some back. 15And when she rose up to glean, Boaz commanded his young

1:20 [a] Literally *Pleasant* [b] Literally *Bitter*

LIFE LESSON

Ruth 2:1-23

SITUATION God rewarded Ruth's loyalty to Naomi when she went to glean barley in the fields of Boaz. Boaz recognized her as a woman of worth and made sure his workers left extra barley stalks for her. Even though Ruth had to work hard, she was thankful for what she had; she was not bitter and despondent.

OBSERVATION Boaz exhibited small acts of kindness. These small acts produced great rewards.

INSPIRATION Sometimes people think that the only significant things they do are those for which they receive public recognition. . . . We think that in order to do something of ultimate importance we must write the great American novel or paint some artistic masterpiece. There is a common notion that significance in life depends on some kind of public recognition. But such is not the case. Really gratifying deeds are often done quietly and with hardly any recognition. . . .

Some of the most important things we do in life are often neither dramatic nor memorable. Happily, on Judgment Day, Jesus will reward a lot of people who hardly remember the important things for which they will be honored. Sending a card of appreciation to someone who is a bit down and needs a lift, visiting a shut-in who is lonely, baby-sitting for a harried mother who needs a few hours off, calling someone on the phone to show that you care, and giving a glass of cool water in the name of Christ are not the sorts of things that we even remember doing after they are done. But the people we do them for often remember, and I know that Jesus never forgets.

(From *Who Switched the Price Tags?* by Tony Campolo)

APPLICATION When life throws a curve ball to a friend, do you stand ready to help? Ask God to help you explore ways to lighten someone's load.

EXPLORATION Character—Genesis 5:18-24; 1 Samuel 16:7; Romans 5:3-4.

men, saying, "Let her glean even among the sheaves, and do not reproach
her. [16]Also let *grain* from the bundles fall purposely for her; leave *it* that she
may glean, and do not rebuke her."
[17]So she gleaned in the field until evening, and beat out what she had
gleaned, and it was about an ephah of barley. [18]Then she took *it* up and
went into the city, and her mother-in-law saw what she had gleaned. So
she brought out and gave to her what she had kept back after she had been
satisfied.
[19]And her mother-in-law said to her, "Where have you gleaned today?
And where did you work? Blessed be the one who took notice of you."
So she told her mother-in-law with whom she had worked, and said,
"The man's name with whom I worked today *is* Boaz."
[20]Then Naomi said to her daughter-in-law, "Blessed *be* he of the LORD,
who has not forsaken His kindness to the living and the dead!" And Naomi
said to her, "This man *is* a relation of ours, one of our close relatives."
[21]Ruth the Moabitess said, "He also said to me, 'You shall stay close by
my young men until they have finished all my harvest.' "
[22]And Naomi said to Ruth her daughter-in-law, "*It is* good, my daughter, that you go out with his young women, and that people do not meet
you in any other field." [23]So she stayed close by the young women of Boaz,
to glean until the end of barley harvest and wheat harvest; and she dwelt
with her mother-in-law.

Ruth's Redemption Assured

3 Then Naomi her mother-in-law said to her, "My daughter, shall I not
seek security for you, that it may be well with you? [2]Now Boaz, whose
young women you were with, *is he* not our relative? In fact, he is winnowing barley tonight at the threshing floor. [3]Therefore wash yourself and
anoint yourself, put on your *best* garment and go down to the threshing
floor; *but* do not make yourself known to the man until he has finished
eating and drinking. [4]Then it shall be, when he lies down, that you shall
notice the place where he lies; and you shall go in, uncover his feet, and lie
down; and he will tell you what you should do."
[5]And she said to her, "All that you say to me I will do."
[6]So she went down to the threshing floor and did according to all that
her mother-in-law instructed her. [7]And after Boaz had eaten and drunk,
and his heart was cheerful, he went to lie down at the end of the heap of
grain; and she came softly, uncovered his feet, and lay down.
[8]Now it happened at midnight that the man was startled, and turned
himself; and there, a woman was lying at his feet. [9]And he said, "Who *are*
you?"
So she answered, "I *am* Ruth, your maidservant. Take your maidservant under your wing,[c] for you are a close relative."
[10]Then he said, "Blessed *are* you of the LORD, my daughter! For you have
shown more kindness at the end than at the beginning, in that you did not
go after young men, whether poor or rich. [11]And now, my daughter, do not
fear. I will do for you all that you request, for all the people of my town know
that you *are* a virtuous woman. [12]Now it is true that I *am* a close relative;
however, there is a relative closer than I. [13]Stay this night, and in the morn-

3:9 [c] Or *Spread the corner of your garment over your maidservant*

LIFE LESSON

Ruth 3:1-18

SITUATION Naomi sought to find a husband for Ruth. She selected Boaz, a relative and a good hearted man, to be someone who would care for Ruth, possibly even marry her according to custom. Ruth diligently followed Naomi's instructions and lay at the feet of Boaz at night as a servant would. Her loyalty met with Boaz's approval.

OBSERVATION Both Ruth and Boaz were persons of high moral integrity who selflessly honored the customs and traditions of their people.

INSPIRATION I don't see life divided into public and private, secular and sacred. It is all an open place of service before our God. My hope is to see this generation produce a group of Christians who will infiltrate our society—in fact, our entire world—with a pure, beautiful message of grace and honesty in the marketplace. Recently I had a delightful talk with a keen-thinking young man following one of the worship services at our church. As we visited, I asked about his future plans. "Well, I've just graduated from law school," he said. "I want to be a man of integrity who practices law." What refreshing words! They reflected the right priority. There is not a career worth pursuing where you cannot have integrity. Every vocation cries out for it. (From *Simple Faith* by Charles Swindoll)

APPLICATION Can you be trusted to perform duties assigned? Today, try one over-and-above-the-call-of-duty task. Surprise someone: your boss, a fellow employee, a friend, or your spouse.

EXPLORATION Integrity—Genesis 43:12; Psalm 25:21; Proverbs 12:3; 19:1.

ing it shall be *that* if he will perform the duty of a close relative for you—
good; let him do it. But if he does not want to perform the duty for you, then
I will perform the duty for you, *as* the LORD lives! Lie down until morning."
14So she lay at his feet until morning, and she arose before one could recognize another. Then he said, "Do not let it be known that the woman
came to the threshing floor." 15Also he said, "Bring the shawl that *is* on you
and hold it." And when she held it, he measured six *ephahs* of barley, and
laid *it* on her. Then she[d] went into the city.
16When she came to her mother-in-law, she said, "*Is* that you, my
daughter?"
Then she told her all that the man had done for her. 17And she said,
"These six *ephahs* of barley he gave me; for he said to me, 'Do not go
empty-handed to your mother-in-law.' "
18Then she said, "Sit still, my daughter, until you know how the matter
will turn out; for the man will not rest until he has concluded the matter
this day."

Boaz Redeems Ruth

4 Now Boaz went up to the gate and sat down there; and behold, the
close relative of whom Boaz had spoken came by. So Boaz said, "Come
aside, friend,[e] sit down here." So he came aside and sat down. 2And he
took ten men of the elders of the city, and said, "Sit down here." So they sat
down. 3Then he said to the close relative, "Naomi, who has come back
from the country of Moab, sold the piece of land which *belonged* to our
brother Elimelech. 4And I thought to inform you, saying, 'Buy *it* back in
the presence of the inhabitants and the elders of my people. If you will redeem *it,* redeem *it;* but if you[f] will not redeem *it, then* tell me, that I may
know; for *there is* no one but you to redeem *it,* and I *am* next after you.' "
And he said, "I will redeem *it.*"
5Then Boaz said, "On the day you buy the field from the hand of Naomi,
you must also buy *it* from Ruth the Moabitess, the wife of the dead, to perpetuate[g] the name of the dead through his inheritance."
6And the close relative said, "I cannot redeem *it* for myself, lest I ruin
my own inheritance. You redeem my right of redemption for yourself, for
I cannot redeem *it.*"
7Now this *was the custom* in former times in Israel concerning redeeming and exchanging, to confirm anything: one man took off his sandal and
gave *it* to the other, and this *was* a confirmation in Israel.
8Therefore the close relative said to Boaz, "Buy *it* for yourself." So he
took off his sandal. 9And Boaz said to the elders and all the people, "You
are witnesses this day that I have bought all that was Elimelech's, and all
that *was* Chilion's and Mahlon's, from the hand of Naomi. 10Moreover,
Ruth the Moabitess, the widow of Mahlon, I have acquired as my wife, to
perpetuate the name of the dead through his inheritance, that the name of
the dead may not be cut off from among his brethren and from his position at the gate.[h] You *are* witnesses this day."

3:15 [d] Many Hebrew manuscripts, Syriac, and Vulgate read *she;* Masoretic Text, Septuagint, and Targum read *he.*
4:1 [e] Hebrew *peloni almoni;* literally *so and so*
4:4 [f] Following many Hebrew manuscripts, Septuagint, Syriac, Targum, and Vulgate; Masoretic Text reads *he.*
4:5 [g] Literally *raise up*
4:10 [h] Probably his civic office

LIFE LESSON

Ruth 4:1-22

SITUATION Naomi and Ruth waited for the decision of their close relatives. God blessed Ruth with marriage and children. David and Jesus were her descendants.

OBSERVATION When life takes a negative turn, God can turn heartache (Ruth 1:21) into blessing (Ruth 4:14-15).

INSPIRATION How long must the agony continue? My license to practice law was gone, my son imprisoned, my dad gone, my compatriots freed and over two years of a three-year sentence still staring me in the face. Though I knew I could not give up, those next days were the most difficult of any that I had spent in prison, probably the most difficult of my life.

. . . On Tuesday, January 28, Al Quie called: "Chuck . . . I've been thinking." There was a long pause. "There's an old statute someone told me about. I'm going to ask the President if I could serve the rest of your term for you."

Stunned, I could only stammer a protest. Al Quie with twenty years in Congress, was the sixth-ranking Republican in the House, senior minority member of the Education and Labor Committee, and one of the most respected public figures in Washington. He could not be serious.

"I mean it, Chuck," he said. "I haven't come to this decision lightly."

. . . It was that night in the quiet of my room that I made the total surrender, completing what had begun in Tom Phillips's driveway eighteen months before: "Lord, if this is what it's all about," I said, "then I thank You. I praise You for leaving me in prison, for letting them take away my license to practice law, yes—even for my son being arrested. I praise You for giving me your love through these men, for being God, just letting me walk with Jesus."

. . . Forty-eight hours later, five o'clock on Friday afternoon, Judge Gesell phoned David Shapiro: because of family problems—what had happened to [my son]—an order was being prepared to release Charles Colson from prison immediately.

Continued

Hours later, Jack, the marshal who had been so sympathetic, ran over to us as Patty and I were standing at the front gate at Holibird, bidding good-bye to the small band of inmates.

"The Lord really takes care of His own men," Jack said. "I kind of knew He would set you free today."

"Thank you, brother," I said, "but He did it two nights ago."

(From *Born Again* by Charles Colson)

APPLICATION Do you feel like God has abandoned you? Don't give up! Pray that he will give you patience to see the situation through, and thank him in advance for what he is going to do.

EXPLORATION God's Way—Genesis 50:20; Job 42:2-3; Isaiah 38:17; 55:8; Micah 4:11-12; Romans 8:28.

11 And all the people who *were* at the gate, and the elders, said, "*We are*
witnesses. The LORD make the woman who is coming to your house like
Rachel and Leah, the two who built the house of Israel; and may you prosper in Ephrathah and be famous in Bethlehem. 12 May your house be like
the house of Perez, whom Tamar bore to Judah, because of the offspring
which the LORD will give you from this young woman."

Descendants of Boaz and Ruth

13 So Boaz took Ruth and she became his wife; and when he went in to
her, the LORD gave her conception, and she bore a son. 14 Then the women
said to Naomi, "Blessed *be* the LORD, who has not left you this day without
a close relative; and may his name be famous in Israel! 15 And may he be to
you a restorer of life and a nourisher of your old age; for your daughter-in-
law, who loves you, who is better to you than seven sons, has borne him."
16 Then Naomi took the child and laid him on her bosom, and became a
nurse to him. 17 Also the neighbor women gave him a name, saying, "There
is a son born to Naomi." And they called his name Obed. He *is* the father of
Jesse, the father of David.

18 Now this *is* the genealogy of Perez: Perez begot Hezron; 19 Hezron begot
Ram, and Ram begot Amminadab; 20 Amminadab begot Nahshon, and
Nahshon begot Salmon;[i] 21 Salmon begot Boaz, and Boaz begot Obed;
22 Obed begot Jesse, and Jesse begot David.

4:20 [i] Hebrew *Salmah*

The First Book of

SAMUEL

INTRODUCTION

It's the end of the race that matters.

Trophies aren't given for great starts. Medals aren't awarded for entering the race. A good start is crucial, but in the end, the end is all that matters.

First Samuel is a book of good starts but bad finishes.

It seems that every key character put his best foot forward and ended up in last place.

Take Eli for example. A sterling religious leader. A man with a heart for God. Perceptive and strong, the last of the great priests. But look at the end of his life. The ark of the covenant has been captured. Two of his rebellious sons are killed. When he hears of their deaths, he falls over and breaks his neck.

Samuel is another case. Dedicated to God's service by Hannah, his mother, he anointed Israel's first kings. But he didn't learn from Eli's mistakes. Just like his mentor, he failed to train his family and his sons turned away from God.

But the most dramatic example is Saul, Israel's first king. He seemed to be the perfect man—handsome and meek, brave and victorious in battle. But success led to disobedience, and he slid from prominence to paranoia to suicide.

Why are these stories in the Bible? To remind us that we too are in a race. And that race isn't over. How we started isn't nearly as important as how we finish.

Life Lesson

1 Samuel 1:1–2:11

SITUATION As the book of 1 Samuel opens, judges had ruled Israel for more than two hundred years. Eli and Samuel were the last two judges, and Samuel was the first priest and prophet to serve when Israel had a king (Saul, David).

OBSERVATION God rewards persevering faith. For example, Samuel's mother Hannah persevered in prayer, and God gave her a son. Faithful to her promise, she gave her son back to God.

INSPIRATION Without continuance the prayer may go unanswered. Importunity is made up of the ability to hold on, to press on, to wait with unrelaxed and unrelaxable grasp, restless desire, and restful patience. Importunate prayer is not an incident but the main thing, not a performance but a passion, not a need but a necessity.

Prayer in its highest form and grandest success assumes the attitude of a wrestler with God. It is the contest, trial, and victory of faith; a victory not secured from an enemy, but from Him who tries our faith that He may enlarge it, who tests our strength to make us stronger. Few things give such quickened and permanent vigor to the soul as a long exhaustive search of importunate prayer. It makes an experience, an epoch, a new calendar for the spirit, a new life to religion, a

The Family of Elkanah

Now there was a certain man of Ramathaim Zophim, of the
mountains of Ephraim, and his name *was* Elkanah the son
of Jeroham, the son of Elihu,[a] the son of Tohu,[b] the son of
Zuph, an Ephraimite. 2And he had two wives: the name of one
was Hannah, and the name of the other Peninnah. Peninnah had children, but
Hannah had no children. 3This man went up from his city yearly to worship
and sacrifice to the LORD of hosts in Shiloh. Also the two sons of Eli, Hophni
and Phinehas, the priests of the LORD, *were* there. 4And whenever the time came
for Elkanah to make an offering, he would give portions to Peninnah his wife
and to all her sons and daughters. 5But to Hannah he would give a double
portion, for he loved Hannah, although the LORD had closed her womb. 6And
her rival also provoked her severely, to make her miserable, because the LORD
had closed her womb. 7So it was, year by year, when she went up to the house
of the LORD, that she provoked her; therefore she wept and did not eat.

Hannah's Vow

8Then Elkanah her husband said to her, "Hannah, why do you weep?
Why do you not eat? And why is your heart grieved? *Am* I not better to you
than ten sons?"
9So Hannah arose after they had finished eating and drinking in Shiloh.
Now Eli the priest was sitting on the seat by the doorpost of the tabernacle[c]
of the LORD. 10And she *was* in bitterness of soul, and prayed to the LORD and
wept in anguish. 11Then she made a vow and said, "O LORD of hosts, if You
will indeed look on the affliction of Your maidservant and remember me,
and not forget Your maidservant, but will give Your maidservant a male
child, then I will give him to the LORD all the days of his life, and no razor
shall come upon his head."
12And it happened, as she continued praying before the LORD, that Eli
watched her mouth. 13Now Hannah spoke in her heart; only her lips moved,
but her voice was not heard. Therefore Eli thought she was drunk. 14So Eli
said to her, "How long will you be drunk? Put your wine away from you!"
15But Hannah answered and said, "No, my lord, I *am* a woman of sorrowful spirit. I have drunk neither wine nor intoxicating drink, but have
poured out my soul before the LORD. 16Do not consider your maidservant a
wicked woman,[d] for out of the abundance of my complaint and grief I
have spoken until now."
17Then Eli answered and said, "Go in peace, and the God of Israel grant
your petition which you have asked of Him."
18And she said, "Let your maidservant find favor in your sight." So the
woman went her way and ate, and her face was no longer *sad.*

Samuel Is Born and Dedicated

19Then they rose early in the morning and worshiped before the LORD,
and returned and came to their house at Ramah. And Elkanah knew
Hannah his wife, and the LORD remembered her. 20So it came to pass in the
process of time that Hannah conceived and bore a son, and called his
name Samuel,[e] *saying,* "Because I have asked for him from the LORD."

1:1 [a] Spelled *Eliel* in 1 Chronicles 6:34 [b] Spelled *Toah* in 1 Chronicles 6:34
1:9 [c] Hebrew *heykal,* palace or temple
1:16 [d] Literally *daughter of Belial*
1:20 [e] Literally *Heard by God*

21 Now the man Elkanah and all his house went up to offer to the LORD
the yearly sacrifice and his vow. 22 But Hannah did not go up, for she said to
her husband, "*Not* until the child is weaned; then I will take him, that he
may appear before the LORD and remain there forever."
23 So Elkanah her husband said to her, "Do what seems best to you; wait
until you have weaned him. Only let the LORD establish His[f] word." Then
the woman stayed and nursed her son until she had weaned him.
24 Now when she had weaned him, she took him up with her, with three
bulls,[g] one ephah of flour, and a skin of wine, and brought him to the house
of the LORD in Shiloh. And the child *was* young. 25 Then they slaughtered a
bull, and brought the child to Eli. 26 And she said, "O my lord! As your soul
lives, my lord, I *am* the woman who stood by you here, praying to the
LORD. 27 For this child I prayed, and the LORD has granted me my petition
which I asked of Him. 28 Therefore I also have lent him to the LORD; as long
as he lives he shall be lent to the LORD." So they worshiped the LORD there.

Hannah's Prayer

2 And Hannah prayed and said:

"My heart rejoices in the LORD;
My horn[h] is exalted in the LORD.
I smile at my enemies,
Because I rejoice in Your salvation.

2 "No one is holy like the LORD,
For *there is* none besides You,
Nor *is there* any rock like our God.

3 "Talk no more so very proudly;
Let no arrogance come from your mouth,
For the LORD *is* the God of knowledge;
And by Him actions are weighed.

4 "The bows of the mighty men *are* broken,
And those who stumbled are girded with strength.
5 *Those who were* full have hired themselves out for bread,
And the hungry have ceased *to hunger.*
Even the barren has borne seven,
And she who has many children has become feeble.

6 "The LORD kills and makes alive;
He brings down to the grave and brings up.
7 The LORD makes poor and makes rich;
He brings low and lifts up.
8 He raises the poor from the dust
And lifts the beggar from the ash heap,
To set *them* among princes
And make them inherit the throne of glory.

"For the pillars of the earth *are* the LORD's,
And He has set the world upon them.
9 He will guard the feet of His saints,
But the wicked shall be silent in darkness.

1:23 [f] Following Masoretic Text, Targum, and Vulgate; Dead Sea Scrolls, Septuagint, and Syriac read *your*.
1:24 [g] Dead Sea Scrolls, Septuagint, and Syriac read *a three-year-old bull.*
2:1 [h] That is, strength

soldierly training. The Bible never wearies in its pressure and illustration of the fact that the highest spiritual good is secured as the return of the out-going of the highest form of spiritual effort. There is neither encouragement nor room in Bible religion for feeble desires, listless efforts, lazy attitudes; all must be strenuous, urgent, ardent. Inflamed desires, impassioned, unwearied insistence delight heaven. God would have His children incorrigibly in earnest and persistently bold in their efforts. . . . Our seasons of importunate prayer cut themselves, like the print of a diamond, into our hardest places, and mark with ineffaceable traces our characters. They are the salient periods of our lives, the memorial stones which endure and to which we turn. . . . Pray and never faint is the motto Christ gives us for praying. It is the test of our faith; and the severer the trial and the longer the waiting, the more glorious the result.

(From *Purpose in Prayer* by E. M. Bounds)

APPLICATION How long do you hang on when it comes to praying for a specific need or desire? Do you give up or persevere? Try keeping a list: (1) what you pray for and when; (2) how God answers and when.

EXPLORATION Patience in Prayer—Psalm 5:1-3; 40:1; 55:17; 116:2; Luke 11:5-10; 18:1-8; Ephesians 6:18.

LIFE LESSON

1 Samuel 2:12–3:21

SITUATION Contempt, arrogance, and disobedience marked Eli's sons. Eli dealt with them poorly himself. These major factors contributed to the bleak spiritual climate during Samuel's childhood. For three centuries no prophet had spoken God's Word until Samuel was chosen.

OBSERVATION God honors and wants to use people, such as Samuel, who honor him. But those who flagrantly disobey, such as Eli's sons, God will judge.

INSPIRATION It is not only the greatness of the blessings promised by Jesus that encourages us in His service. Their security encourages us too. The young man turned away from Christ because he was unwilling to part with his possessions, but it is an irony of the story that he turned from possessions that were certain to possessions that were at best uncertain. Maybe he lost those possessions before the year was out. Maybe his gold was stolen. His land could have been taken. As in the prodigal's case, his friends could have grown cold and abandoned him.

This point can be made even stronger. God often allows the ungodly to amass great wealth—to their destruction. But if you are one with whom God is dealing and if you put the pursuit of riches (or anything else) before service to Christ, God may take away those riches (and other things) until you turn to Him.

Some years ago Donald Grey Barnhouse was counseling a young woman on the sidewalk in front of Tenth Presbyterian Church following an evening service. She said she was a Christian and that she wanted to

"For by strength no man shall prevail.
10 The adversaries of the LORD shall be broken in pieces;
From heaven He will thunder against them.
The LORD will judge the ends of the earth.
"He will give strength to His king,
And exalt the horn of His anointed."

11Then Elkanah went to his house at Ramah. But the child ministered to
the LORD before Eli the priest.

The Wicked Sons of Eli

12Now the sons of Eli *were* corrupt;[i] they did not know the LORD. 13And
the priests' custom with the people *was that* when any man offered a sacrifice, the priest's servant would come with a three-pronged fleshhook in
his hand while the meat was boiling. 14Then he would thrust *it* into the
pan, or kettle, or caldron, or pot; and the priest would take for himself all
that the fleshhook brought up. So they did in Shiloh to all the Israelites
who came there. 15Also, before they burned the fat, the priest's servant
would come and say to the man who sacrificed, "Give meat for roasting to
the priest, for he will not take boiled meat from you, but raw."
16And *if* the man said to him, "They should really burn the fat first; *then*
you may take *as much* as your heart desires," he would then answer him,
"*No,* but you must give *it* now; and if not, I will take *it* by force."
17Therefore the sin of the young men was very great before the LORD, for
men abhorred the offering of the LORD.

Samuel's Childhood Ministry

18But Samuel ministered before the LORD, *even as* a child, wearing a
linen ephod. 19Moreover his mother used to make him a little robe, and
bring *it* to him year by year when she came up with her husband to offer
the yearly sacrifice. 20And Eli would bless Elkanah and his wife, and say,
"The LORD give you descendants from this woman for the loan that was
given to the LORD." Then they would go to their own home.
21And the LORD visited Hannah, so that she conceived and bore three
sons and two daughters. Meanwhile the child Samuel grew before the LORD.

Prophecy Against Eli's Household

22Now Eli was very old; and he heard everything his sons did to all Israel,[j] and how they lay with the women who assembled at the door of the
tabernacle of meeting. 23So he said to them, "Why do you do such
things? For I hear of your evil dealings from all the people. 24No, my
sons! For *it is* not a good report that I hear. You make the LORD's people
transgress. 25If one man sins against another, God will judge him. But if
a man sins against the LORD, who will intercede for him?" Nevertheless
they did not heed the voice of their father, because the LORD desired to
kill them.
26And the child Samuel grew in stature, and in favor both with the LORD
and men.

2:12 [i] Literally *sons of Belial*
2:22 [j] Following Masoretic Text, Targum, and Vulgate; Dead Sea Scrolls and Septuagint omit the rest of this verse.

27Then a man of God came to Eli and said to him, "Thus says the LORD:
'Did I not clearly reveal Myself to the house of your father when they were
in Egypt in Pharaoh's house? 28Did I not choose him out of all the tribes of
Israel *to be* My priest, to offer upon My altar, to burn incense, and to wear
an ephod before Me? And did I not give to the house of your father all the
offerings of the children of Israel made by fire? 29Why do you kick at My
sacrifice and My offering which I have commanded *in My* dwelling place,
and honor your sons more than Me, to make yourselves fat with the best
of all the offerings of Israel My people?' 30Therefore the LORD God of Israel
says: 'I said indeed *that* your house and the house of your father would
walk before Me forever.' But now the LORD says: 'Far be it from Me; for
those who honor Me I will honor, and those who despise Me shall be
lightly esteemed. 31Behold, the days are coming that I will cut off your arm
and the arm of your father's house, so that there will not be an old man in
your house. 32And you will see an enemy *in My* dwelling place, *despite* all
the good which God does for Israel. And there shall not be an old man in
your house forever. 33But any of your men *whom* I do not cut off from My
altar shall consume your eyes and grieve your heart. And all the descendants of your house shall die in the flower of their age. 34Now this *shall be* a
sign to you that will come upon your two sons, on Hophni and Phinehas:
in one day they shall die, both of them. 35Then I will raise up for Myself a
faithful priest *who* shall do according to what *is* in My heart and in My
mind. I will build him a sure house, and he shall walk before My anointed
forever. 36And it shall come to pass that everyone who is left in your house
will come *and* bow down to him for a piece of silver and a morsel of bread,
and say, "Please, put me in one of the priestly positions, that I may eat a
piece of bread." ' "

Samuel's First Prophecy

3 Now the boy Samuel ministered to the LORD before Eli. And the word of
the LORD was rare in those days; *there was* no widespread revelation.
2And it came to pass at that time, while Eli *was* lying down in his place, and
when his eyes had begun to grow so dim that he could not see, 3and before
the lamp of God went out in the tabernacle[k] of the LORD where the ark of
God *was*, and while Samuel was lying down, 4that the LORD called Samuel.
And he answered, "Here I am!" 5So he ran to Eli and said, "Here I am, for
you called me."

And he said, "I did not call; lie down again." And he went and lay down.
6Then the LORD called yet again, "Samuel!"

So Samuel arose and went to Eli, and said, "Here I am, for you called
me." He answered, "I did not call, my son; lie down again." 7(Now Samuel did not yet know the LORD, nor was the word of the LORD yet revealed
to him.)

8And the LORD called Samuel again the third time. So he arose and went
to Eli, and said, "Here I am, for you did call me."

Then Eli perceived that the LORD had called the boy. 9Therefore Eli said
to Samuel, "Go, lie down; and it shall be, if He calls you, that you must say,
'Speak, LORD, for Your servant hears.' " So Samuel went and lay down in
his place.

follow Christ. But she wanted to be famous too. She wanted to pursue a stage career in New York. "After I have made it in the theater, I'll follow Christ completely," she said.

Barnhouse took a key out of his pocket and scratched a mark on a postal box standing on the corner. "That is what God will let you do," he said. "God will let you scratch the surface of success. He will let you get close enough to the top to know what it is, but He will never let you have it, because He will never let one of His children have anything rather than Himself."

Years later he met the girl again, and she confessed that this had indeed been her life story. She had dabbled in the stage. Once her picture had been in a national magazine. But she had never quite made it. She told Barnhouse, "I can't tell you how many times in my discouragement I have closed my eyes and seen you scratching on that postal box with your key. God let me scratch the edges, but He gave me nothing in place of Himself."

How different for those who deny themselves, take up their crosses, and follow Jesus. Their path begins with denial but ends in fulfillment, and the blessings given cannot be snatched away.

(From *Christ's Call to Discipleship* by James M. Boice)

APPLICATION What is your attitude when it comes to success? Is reaching the pinnacle your real god? Ask God to show you what has first place in your heart. Pray today, with first place given to God.

EXPLORATION Arrogance—Judges 8:1-3; 2 Samuel 17:11; 2 Chronicles 26:16; Psalm 10:11; Acts 12:23; Ephesians 2:11-13.

3:3 [k] Hebrew *heykal*, palace or temple

LIFE LESSON

1 Samuel 4:1–5:12

SITUATION When the Israelites improperly brought the ark of the covenant into battle with the Philistines, they were routed and the ark captured. Eli, who had grown lazy in his position, died when he heard that the battle had been lost and his sons killed. The Israelites thought God had abandoned them. At the same time, the Philistines endured plagues when they set the Ark among their idols.

OBSERVATION God's power and support for us is not based on a lucky charm or holy object like the Ark, but on our constant faithfulness to him.

INSPIRATION Whenever God appears to people, His glory is veiled. It would be impossible for unredeemed humanity to look on God's unveiled glory and live. Jacob was surprised that he survived after seeing God. And yet the Savior promised that the pure in heart will see God.

That brings us to the inevitable question, If God is Spirit and therefore invisible, will we see God in heaven? The simplest answer is that Jesus is God, and we will certainly see Jesus in heaven.

But perhaps there is more. In heaven the limitations of this earthly body will

[10]Now the LORD came and stood and called as at other times, "Samuel!
Samuel!"
And Samuel answered, "Speak, for Your servant hears."
[11]Then the LORD said to Samuel: "Behold, I will do something in Israel at
which both ears of everyone who hears it will tingle. [12]In that day I will perform against Eli all that I have spoken concerning his house, from beginning to end. [13]For I have told him that I will judge his house forever for the
iniquity which he knows, because his sons made themselves vile, and he
did not restrain them. [14]And therefore I have sworn to the house of Eli that
the iniquity of Eli's house shall not be atoned for by sacrifice or offering
forever."
[15]So Samuel lay down until morning,[l] and opened the doors of the
house of the LORD. And Samuel was afraid to tell Eli the vision. [16]Then Eli
called Samuel and said, "Samuel, my son!"
He answered, "Here I am."
[17]And he said, "What *is* the word that *the LORD* spoke to you? Please do
not hide *it* from me. God do so to you, and more also, if you hide anything
from me of all the things that He said to you." [18]Then Samuel told him
everything, and hid nothing from him. And he said, "It *is* the LORD. Let
Him do what seems good to Him."
[19]So Samuel grew, and the LORD was with him and let none of his words
fall to the ground. [20]And all Israel from Dan to Beersheba knew that Samuel *had been* established as a prophet of the LORD. [21]Then the LORD appeared again in Shiloh. For the LORD revealed Himself to Samuel in Shiloh
by the word of the LORD.
4 And the word of Samuel came to all Israel.[m]

The Ark of God Captured

Now Israel went out to battle against the Philistines, and encamped beside Ebenezer; and the Philistines encamped in Aphek. [2]Then the
Philistines put themselves in battle array against Israel. And when they
joined battle, Israel was defeated by the Philistines, who killed about four
thousand men of the army in the field. [3]And when the people had come
into the camp, the elders of Israel said, "Why has the LORD defeated us
today before the Philistines? Let us bring the ark of the covenant of the
LORD from Shiloh to us, that when it comes among us it may save us from
the hand of our enemies." [4]So the people sent to Shiloh, that they might
bring from there the ark of the covenant of the LORD of hosts, who dwells
between the cherubim. And the two sons of Eli, Hophni and Phinehas,
were there with the ark of the covenant of God.
[5]And when the ark of the covenant of the LORD came into the camp, all
Israel shouted so loudly that the earth shook. [6]Now when the Philistines
heard the noise of the shout, they said, "What *does* the sound of this great
shout in the camp of the Hebrews *mean?*" Then they understood that the
ark of the LORD had come into the camp. [7]So the Philistines were afraid, for
they said, "God has come into the camp!" And they said, "Woe to us! For
such a thing has never happened before. [8]Woe to us! Who will deliver us

3:15 [l] Following Masoretic Text, Targum, and Vulgate; Septuagint adds *and he arose in the morning.*
4:1 [m] Following Masoretic Text and Targum; Septuagint and Vulgate add *And it came to pass in those days that the Philistines gathered themselves together to fight;* Septuagint adds further *against Israel.*

from the hand of these mighty gods? These *are* the gods who struck the
Egyptians with all the plagues in the wilderness. 9Be strong and conduct
yourselves like men, you Philistines, that you do not become servants of the
Hebrews, as they have been to you. Conduct yourselves like men, and fight!"
10So the Philistines fought, and Israel was defeated, and every man fled
to his tent. There was a very great slaughter, and there fell of Israel thirty
thousand foot soldiers. 11Also the ark of God was captured; and the two
sons of Eli, Hophni and Phinehas, died.

Death of Eli

12Then a man of Benjamin ran from the battle line the same day, and
came to Shiloh with his clothes torn and dirt on his head. 13Now when he
came, there was Eli, sitting on a seat by the wayside watching,[n] for his heart
trembled for the ark of God. And when the man came into the city and told
it, all the city cried out. 14When Eli heard the noise of the outcry, he said,
"What *does* the sound of this tumult *mean?*" And the man came quickly
and told Eli. 15Eli was ninety-eight years old, and his eyes were so dim that
he could not see.
16Then the man said to Eli, "I *am* he who came from the battle. And I fled
today from the battle line."
And he said, "What happened, my son?"
17So the messenger answered and said, "Israel has fled before the
Philistines, and there has been a great slaughter among the people. Also
your two sons, Hophni and Phinehas, are dead; and the ark of God has
been captured."
18Then it happened, when he made mention of the ark of God, that Eli fell
off the seat backward by the side of the gate; and his neck was broken and he
died, for the man was old and heavy. And he had judged Israel forty years.

Ichabod

19Now his daughter-in-law, Phinehas' wife, was with child, *due* to be delivered; and when she heard the news that the ark of God was captured,
and that her father-in-law and her husband were dead, she bowed herself
and gave birth, for her labor pains came upon her. 20And about the time of
her death the women who stood by her said to her, "Do not fear, for you
have borne a son." But she did not answer, nor did she regard *it.* 21Then
she named the child Ichabod,[o] saying, "The glory has departed from Israel!" because the ark of God had been captured and because of her father-
in-law and her husband. 22And she said, "The glory has departed from
Israel, for the ark of God has been captured."

The Philistines and the Ark

5 Then the Philistines took the ark of God and brought it from Ebenezer
to Ashdod. 2When the Philistines took the ark of God, they brought it
into the house of Dagon[p] and set it by Dagon. 3And when the people of
Ashdod arose early in the morning, there was Dagon, fallen on its face to
the earth before the ark of the LORD. So they took Dagon and set it in its
place again. 4And when they arose early the next morning, there was

4:13 [n] Following Masoretic Text and Vulgate; Septuagint reads *beside the gate watching the road.*
4:21 [o] Literally *Inglorious*
5:2 [p] A Philistine idol

be set aside. We will have powers that we cannot imagine now. Although we cannot see God with these mortal eyes, is it not possible that, as one youngster suggested, we will have bigger eyes in heaven? We cannot be wrong in claiming the absolute promise of the Lord Jesus: "Blessed are the pure in heart, for they shall see God." . . . True worship is not confined to any place or building on earth. It is not concerned with stained-glass windows, ecclesiastical garments, candles, liturgies, or incense. Rather, in genuine worship we pass from earth to heaven by faith, and there, in the presence of God, we pour out our souls in thanksgiving, praise, and homage to the Lord for all He is and for all He has done for us.

(From *Alone in Majesty* by William MacDonald)

APPLICATION The Israelites worshiped the ark, rather than God himself. Is there an "ark" in your life? Does something get more attention than God? If so, turn your focus to the ever-present God, whose power transcends any object.

EXPLORATION Worship—Deuteronomy 5:7; Judges 17:6; 2 Chronicles 4:11-16; 2 Kings 18:4.

LIFE LESSON

1 Samuel 6:1–7:17

SITUATION Afflicted by plagues of rats and tumors, the Philistines returned the Ark to Israel. The Israelites rejoiced and under Samuel's direction discarded their idols and former arrogance. Later, when the Philistines invaded, Samuel offered up prayer and sacrifice to God and the Philistines were routed. Israel lived in peace for many years under Samuel's wise leadership.

OBSERVATION When we place our trust in God and relinquish control of our lives to him, he provides for our needs and takes care of us.

INSPIRATION Notion your mind with the idea that God is there. If once the mind is notioned along that line, then when you are in difficulties it is as easy as breathing to remember—Why, my Father knows all about it! It is not an effort, it comes naturally when perplexities press. Before, you used to go to this person and that, but now the notion of the Divine control is forming so powerfully in you that you go to God about it. Jesus is laying down the rules of conduct for those who have His Spirit, and it works on this principle—God is my Father, He loves me, I shall never think of anything He will forget, why should I worry?

Dagon, fallen on its face to the ground before the ark of the LORD. The head
of Dagon and both the palms of its hands *were* broken off on the threshold; only Dagon's torso[q] was left of it. 5Therefore neither the priests of
Dagon nor any who come into Dagon's house tread on the threshold of
Dagon in Ashdod to this day.
6But the hand of the LORD was heavy on the people of Ashdod, and He
ravaged them and struck them with tumors,[r] *both* Ashdod and its territory. 7And when the men of Ashdod saw how *it was,* they said, "The ark of
the God of Israel must not remain with us, for His hand is harsh toward us
and Dagon our god." 8Therefore they sent and gathered to themselves all
the lords of the Philistines, and said, "What shall we do with the ark of the
God of Israel?"
And they answered, "Let the ark of the God of Israel be carried away to
Gath." So they carried the ark of the God of Israel away. 9So it was, after
they had carried it away, that the hand of the LORD was against the city with
a very great destruction; and He struck the men of the city, both small and
great, and tumors broke out on them.
10Therefore they sent the ark of God to Ekron. So it was, as the ark of God
came to Ekron, that the Ekronites cried out, saying, "They have brought
the ark of the God of Israel to us, to kill us and our people!" 11So they sent
and gathered together all the lords of the Philistines, and said, "Send away
the ark of the God of Israel, and let it go back to its own place, so that it
does not kill us and our people." For there was a deadly destruction
throughout all the city; the hand of God was very heavy there. 12And the
men who did not die were stricken with the tumors, and the cry of the city
went up to heaven.

The Ark Returned to Israel

6 Now the ark of the LORD was in the country of the Philistines seven
months. 2And the Philistines called for the priests and the diviners,
saying, "What shall we do with the ark of the LORD? Tell us how we should
send it to its place."
3So they said, "If you send away the ark of the God of Israel, do not send
it empty; but by all means return *it* to Him *with* a trespass offering. Then
you will be healed, and it will be known to you why His hand is not removed from you."
4Then they said, "What *is* the trespass offering which we shall return to
Him?"
They answered, "Five golden tumors and five golden rats, *according to*
the number of the lords of the Philistines. For the same plague *was* on all
of you and on your lords. 5Therefore you shall make images of your tumors and images of your rats that ravage the land, and you shall give glory
to the God of Israel; perhaps He will lighten His hand from you, from your
gods, and from your land. 6Why then do you harden your hearts as the
Egyptians and Pharaoh hardened their hearts? When He did mighty
things among them, did they not let the people go, that they might depart?
7Now therefore, make a new cart, take two milk cows which have never
been yoked, and hitch the cows to the cart; and take their calves home,

5:4 [q] Following Septuagint, Syriac, Targum, and Vulgate; Masoretic Text reads *Dagon.*
5:6 [r] Probably bubonic plague. Septuagint and Vulgate add here *And in the midst of their land rats sprang up, and there was a great death panic in the city.*

away from them. 8Then take the ark of the LORD and set it on the cart; and
put the articles of gold which you are returning to Him *as* a trespass offering in a chest by its side. Then send it away, and let it go. 9And watch: if it
goes up the road to its own territory, to Beth Shemesh, *then* He has done us
this great evil. But if not, then we shall know that *it is* not His hand *that*
struck us—it happened to us by chance."
10Then the men did so; they took two milk cows and hitched them to the
cart, and shut up their calves at home. 11And they set the ark of the LORD on
the cart, and the chest with the gold rats and the images of their tumors.
12Then the cows headed straight for the road to Beth Shemesh, *and* went
along the highway, lowing as they went, and did not turn aside to the right
hand or the left. And the lords of the Philistines went after them to the border of Beth Shemesh.
13Now *the people of* Beth Shemesh *were* reaping their wheat harvest in
the valley; and they lifted their eyes and saw the ark, and rejoiced to see *it.*
14Then the cart came into the field of Joshua of Beth Shemesh, and stood
there; a large stone *was* there. So they split the wood of the cart and offered
the cows as a burnt offering to the LORD. 15The Levites took down the ark of the
LORD and the chest that *was* with it, in which *were* the articles of gold, and
put *them* on the large stone. Then the men of Beth Shemesh offered burnt
offerings and made sacrifices the same day to the LORD. 16So when the five
lords of the Philistines had seen *it,* they returned to Ekron the same day.
17These *are* the golden tumors which the Philistines returned *as* a trespass offering to the LORD: one for Ashdod, one for Gaza, one for Ashkelon,
one for Gath, one for Ekron; 18and the golden rats, *according to* the number of all the cities of the Philistines *belonging* to the five lords, *both* fortified cities and country villages, even as far as the large *stone of* Abel on
which they set the ark of the LORD, *which stone remains* to this day in the
field of Joshua of Beth Shemesh.
19Then He struck the men of Beth Shemesh, because they had looked
into the ark of the LORD. He struck fifty thousand and seventy men[s] of the
people, and the people lamented because the LORD had struck the people
with a great slaughter.

The Ark at Kirjath Jearim

20And the men of Beth Shemesh said, "Who is able to stand before this
holy LORD God? And to whom shall it go up from us?" 21So they sent messengers to the inhabitants of Kirjath Jearim, saying, "The Philistines have
brought back the ark of the LORD; come down *and* take it up with you."

7 Then the men of Kirjath Jearim came and took the ark of the LORD, and
brought it into the house of Abinadab on the hill, and consecrated
Eleazar his son to keep the ark of the LORD.

Samuel Judges Israel

2So it was that the ark remained in Kirjath Jearim a long time; it was
there twenty years. And all the house of Israel lamented after the LORD.
3Then Samuel spoke to all the house of Israel, saying, "If you return to
the LORD with all your hearts, *then* put away the foreign gods and the
Ashtoreths[t] from among you, and prepare your hearts for the LORD, and

6:19 [s] Or *He struck seventy men of the people and fifty oxen of a man*
7:3 [t] Canaanite goddesses

There are times, says Jesus, when God cannot lift the darkness from you, but trust Him. God will appear like an unkind friend, but He is not; He will appear like an unnatural Father, but He is not; He will appear like an unjust judge, but He is not. Keep the notion of the mind of God behind all things strong and growing. Nothing happens in any particular unless God's will is behind it, therefore you can rest in perfect confidence in Him. Prayer is not only asking, but an attitude of mind which produces the atmosphere in which asking is perfectly natural. "Ask, and it shall be given you."

(From *My Utmost for His Highest* by Oswald Chambers)

APPLICATION The Israelites believed they could harness God's power by simply controlling the Ark, but they were wrong. Don't allow yourself to believe you can control God. He directs the universe, and we must seek his will rather than our own. When you make your plans, evaluate: Do God's plans fit mine? Or do my plans fit God's?

EXPLORATION Control—Joshua 24:15; Psalm 60:6-10; Matthew 4:17; Mark 14:27; Romans 6:6.

Life Lesson

1 Samuel 8:1-22

SITUATION When Samuel retired, Israel rejected his sons as judges and asked for a king, in spite of God's warning against this. Their request for a king was based on a desire to be like all the other nations.

OBSERVATION Israel demonstrates that our desire to imitate the world may seem righteous at first, but the final result will be destruction.

INSPIRATION We need to show how cold, black, hard, and ugly we are, to get motivated to stay in that fire. Unless we do, we will never hate sin and fear sin and be repelled by sin enough to stay in the fire. (Says Tozer, "The Holy Spirit is first of all a moral flame.") . . .

I see how, when liberalism waned and we evangelicals rose to popularity and were listened to, we could have given our authentic message and cried to the world, "Repent! Be radically cleansed of your sin! Receive Jesus Christ's purity and holiness for your lives!"

But instead, in that time of golden opportunity, we lost our courage. We Madison-Avenue-trivialized our glorious gospel. And we stained ourselves with the world's adulteries and fornications.

We must weep; we must mourn! We must hate what He hates! Let us ask Him to forgive our unwashed praises before Him, our sillinesses, our ignorances.

Let us see how our coldness, blackness, hardness, ugliness become colder, blacker, harder, uglier—unless in terror we wrench ourselves free and rush to His precious Fire!

(From *My Sacrifice, His Fire* by Anne Ortlund)

APPLICATION How deeply do you care about fitting in and being like the world? What are the areas of your life where you blend in with those around you when you should not? Ask God to give you the courage and conviction to stand apart when you should.

EXPLORATION Separation from the World—Isaiah 52:11; John 17:14; Romans 12:2; Galatians 1:10; Hebrews 11:24-26; James 1:27; 1 John 2:15-17.

serve Him only; and He will deliver you from the hand of the Philistines." 4So the children of Israel put away the Baals and the Ashtoreths,[u] and served the LORD only.

5And Samuel said, "Gather all Israel to Mizpah, and I will pray to the LORD for you." 6So they gathered together at Mizpah, drew water, and poured *it* out before the LORD. And they fasted that day, and said there, "We have sinned against the LORD." And Samuel judged the children of Israel at Mizpah.

7Now when the Philistines heard that the children of Israel had gathered together at Mizpah, the lords of the Philistines went up against Israel. And when the children of Israel heard *of it,* they were afraid of the Philistines. 8So the children of Israel said to Samuel, "Do not cease to cry out to the LORD our God for us, that He may save us from the hand of the Philistines."

9And Samuel took a suckling lamb and offered *it as* a whole burnt offering to the LORD. Then Samuel cried out to the LORD for Israel, and the LORD answered him. 10Now as Samuel was offering up the burnt offering, the Philistines drew near to battle against Israel. But the LORD thundered with a loud thunder upon the Philistines that day, and so confused them that they were overcome before Israel. 11And the men of Israel went out of Mizpah and pursued the Philistines, and drove them back as far as below Beth Car. 12Then Samuel took a stone and set *it* up between Mizpah and Shen, and called its name Ebenezer,[v] saying, "Thus far the LORD has helped us."

13So the Philistines were subdued, and they did not come anymore into the territory of Israel. And the hand of the LORD was against the Philistines all the days of Samuel. 14Then the cities which the Philistines had taken from Israel were restored to Israel, from Ekron to Gath; and Israel recovered its territory from the hands of the Philistines. Also there was peace between Israel and the Amorites.

15And Samuel judged Israel all the days of his life. 16He went from year to year on a circuit to Bethel, Gilgal, and Mizpah, and judged Israel in all those places. 17But he always returned to Ramah, for his home *was* there. There he judged Israel, and there he built an altar to the LORD.

Israel Demands a King

8 Now it came to pass when Samuel was old that he made his sons judges over Israel. 2The name of his firstborn was Joel, and the name of his second, Abijah; *they were* judges in Beersheba. 3But his sons did not walk in his ways; they turned aside after dishonest gain, took bribes, and perverted justice.

4Then all the elders of Israel gathered together and came to Samuel at Ramah, 5and said to him, "Look, you are old, and your sons do not walk in your ways. Now make us a king to judge us like all the nations."

6But the thing displeased Samuel when they said, "Give us a king to judge us." So Samuel prayed to the LORD. 7And the LORD said to Samuel, "Heed the voice of the people in all that they say to you; for they have not rejected you, but they have rejected Me, that I should not reign over them. 8According to all the works which they have done since the day that I brought them up out of Egypt, even to this day—with which they have forsaken Me and served other gods—so they are doing to you also. 9Now

7:4 [u] Canaanite goddesses
7:12 [v] Literally *Stone of Help*

therefore, heed their voice. However, you shall solemnly forewarn them,
and show them the behavior of the king who will reign over them."
10 So Samuel told all the words of the LORD to the people who asked him
for a king. 11 And he said, "This will be the behavior of the king who will
reign over you: He will take your sons and appoint *them* for his own chariots and *to be* his horsemen, and *some* will run before his chariots. 12 He
will appoint captains over his thousands and captains over his fifties, *will*
set some to plow his ground and reap his harvest, and *some* to make his
weapons of war and equipment for his chariots. 13 He will take your daughters *to be* perfumers, cooks, and bakers. 14 And he will take the best of your
fields, your vineyards, and your olive groves, and give *them* to his servants. 15 He will take a tenth of your grain and your vintage, and give it to
his officers and servants. 16 And he will take your male servants, your female servants, your finest young men,[w] and your donkeys, and put *them*
to his work. 17 He will take a tenth of your sheep. And you will be his servants. 18 And you will cry out in that day because of your king whom you
have chosen for yourselves, and the LORD will not hear you in that day."
19 Nevertheless the people refused to obey the voice of Samuel; and they
said, "No, but we will have a king over us, 20 that we also may be like all the
nations, and that our king may judge us and go out before us and fight our
battles."
21 And Samuel heard all the words of the people, and he repeated them in
the hearing of the LORD. 22 So the LORD said to Samuel, "Heed their voice,
and make them a king."
And Samuel said to the men of Israel, "Every man go to his city."

Saul Chosen to Be King

9 There was a man of Benjamin whose name *was* Kish the son of Abiel,
the son of Zeror, the son of Bechorath, the son of Aphiah, a Benjamite,
a mighty man of power. 2 And he had a choice and handsome son whose
name *was* Saul. *There was* not a more handsome person than he among
the children of Israel. From his shoulders upward *he was* taller than any of
the people.
3 Now the donkeys of Kish, Saul's father, were lost. And Kish said to his
son Saul, "Please take one of the servants with you, and arise, go and look
for the donkeys." 4 So he passed through the mountains of Ephraim and
through the land of Shalisha, but they did not find *them*. Then they passed
through the land of Shaalim, and *they were* not *there*. Then he passed through
the land of the Benjamites, but they did not find *them*.
5 When they had come to the land of Zuph, Saul said to his servant who
was with him, "Come, let us return, lest my father cease *caring* about the
donkeys and become worried about us."
6 And he said to him, "Look now, *there is* in this city a man of God, and *he*
is an honorable man; all that he says surely comes to pass. So let us go
there; perhaps he can show us the way that we should go."
7 Then Saul said to his servant, "But look, *if* we go, what shall we bring
the man? For the bread in our vessels is all gone, and *there is* no present to
bring to the man of God. What do we have?"
8 And the servant answered Saul again and said, "Look, I have here at
hand one-fourth of a shekel of silver. I will give *that* to the man of God, to

8:16 [w] Septuagint reads *cattle*.

LIFE LESSON

1 Samuel 9:1–10:27

SITUATION Samuel had been an exceptional judge over Israel. But when it was time for him to retire, his sons were corrupt and inadequate for leading the nation. The people failed to recognize that God alone was their king and that their disobedience to him was the reason for their problems. God knew that Israel's desire for a king was based on her reliance on human rather than divine strength.

OBSERVATION In the life of Saul, we learn the important lesson that seeking God and being obedient to him is far more important than all of the human strengths we may possess.

INSPIRATION Pick at random a score of great saints whose lives and testimonies are widely known. Let them be Bible characters or well-known Christians of post-biblical times. You will be struck instantly with the fact that the saints were not alike. Sometimes the unlikenesses were so great as to be positively glaring. How different, for example, was Moses from Isaiah; how different was Elijah from David; how unlike each other were John and Paul, St. Francis and Luther, Finney and Thomas à Kempis. The differences are as wide as human life itself—differences of race, nationality, education, temperament, habit and personal qualities. Yet they all walked, each in his day, upon a high road of spiritual living far above the common way.

Their differences must have been incidental and in the eyes of God of no significance. In some vital quality they must have been alike. What was it?

I venture to suggest that the one vital quality which they had in common was spiritual receptivity. Something in them was open to heaven, something which urged them Godward. Without attempting anything like a profound analysis, I shall say simply that they went on to cultivate it until it became the biggest thing in their lives. They differed from the average person in that when they felt the inward longing, they did something about it. They acquired the lifelong habit of spiritual response. They were not disobedient to the heavenly vision. As David put it

Continued

neatly, "When thou saidst, Seek ye my face; my heart said unto thee, Thy face, Lord, will I seek" (Ps. 27:8).

(From *The Pursuit of God* by A. W. Tozer)

APPLICATION If you want to be used by God, what do you see as the source of your potential success? Are you relying too heavily on your human strengths or doubting because of your human weaknesses? Remember, only God's power can make us useful for service in his kingdom, and with his power we are more than conquerors.

EXPLORATION Necessity of Divine Power—Exodus 3:11-12; Judges 6:12-14; 2 Chronicles 14:11; Ezra 1:2; Psalm 20:6-7; 2 Corinthians 12:9.

tell us our way." 9(Formerly in Israel, when a man went to inquire of God,
he spoke thus: "Come, let us go to the seer"; for *he who is* now *called* a
prophet was formerly called a seer.)
10Then Saul said to his servant, "Well said; come, let us go." So they went
to the city where the man of God *was.*
11As they went up the hill to the city, they met some young women going
out to draw water, and said to them, "Is the seer here?"
12And they answered them and said, "Yes, there he is, just ahead of you.
Hurry now; for today he came to this city, because there is a sacrifice of the
people today on the high place. 13As soon as you come into the city, you
will surely find him before he goes up to the high place to eat. For the people will not eat until he comes, because he must bless the sacrifice; afterward those who are invited will eat. Now therefore, go up, for about this
time you will find him." 14So they went up to the city. As they were coming
into the city, there was Samuel, coming out toward them on his way up to
the high place.
15Now the LORD had told Samuel in his ear the day before Saul came,
saying, 16"Tomorrow about this time I will send you a man from the land
of Benjamin, and you shall anoint him commander over My people Israel,
that he may save My people from the hand of the Philistines; for I have
looked upon My people, because their cry has come to Me."
17So when Samuel saw Saul, the LORD said to him, "There he is, the man
of whom I spoke to you. This one shall reign over My people." 18Then Saul
drew near to Samuel in the gate, and said, "Please tell me, where *is* the
seer's house?"
19Samuel answered Saul and said, "I *am* the seer. Go up before me to the
high place, for you shall eat with me today; and tomorrow I will let you go
and will tell you all that *is* in your heart. 20But as for your donkeys that were
lost three days ago, do not be anxious about them, for they have been
found. And on whom *is* all the desire of Israel? *Is it* not on you and on all
your father's house?"
21And Saul answered and said, "*Am* I not a Benjamite, of the smallest of
the tribes of Israel, and my family the least of all the families of the tribe[x] of
Benjamin? Why then do you speak like this to me?"
22Now Samuel took Saul and his servant and brought them into the hall,
and had them sit in the place of honor among those who were invited;
there *were* about thirty persons. 23And Samuel said to the cook, "Bring the
portion which I gave you, of which I said to you, 'Set it apart.'" 24So the
cook took up the thigh with its upper part and set *it* before Saul. And *Samuel* said, "Here it is, what was kept back. *It* was set apart for you. Eat; for
until this time it has been kept for you, since I said I invited the people." So
Saul ate with Samuel that day.
25When they had come down from the high place into the city, *Samuel*
spoke with Saul on the top of the house.[y] 26They arose early; and it was
about the dawning of the day that Samuel called to Saul on the top of the
house, saying, "Get up, that I may send you on your way." And Saul arose,
and both of them went outside, he and Samuel.

9:21 [x] Literally *tribes*

9:25 [y] Following Masoretic Text and Targum; Septuagint omits *He spoke with Saul on the top of the house;* Septuagint and Vulgate add *And he prepared a bed for Saul on the top of the house, and he slept.*

Saul Anointed King

[27]As they were going down to the outskirts of the city, Samuel said to Saul, "Tell the servant to go on ahead of us." And he went on. "But you stand here awhile, that I may announce to you the word of God."

10 Then Samuel took a flask of oil and poured *it* on his head, and kissed him and said: "*Is it* not because the LORD has anointed you commander over His inheritance?[z] [2]When you have departed from me today, you will find two men by Rachel's tomb in the territory of Benjamin at Zelzah; and they will say to you, 'The donkeys which you went to look for have been found. And now your father has ceased caring about the donkeys and is worrying about you, saying, "What shall I do about my son?"' [3]Then you shall go on forward from there and come to the terebinth tree of Tabor. There three men going up to God at Bethel will meet you, one carrying three young goats, another carrying three loaves of bread, and another carrying a skin of wine. [4]And they will greet you and give you two *loaves* of bread, which you shall receive from their hands. [5]After that you shall come to the hill of God where the Philistine garrison *is.* And it will happen, when you have come there to the city, that you will meet a group of prophets coming down from the high place with a stringed instrument, a tambourine, a flute, and a harp before them; and they will be prophesying. [6]Then the Spirit of the LORD will come upon you, and you will prophesy with them and be turned into another man. [7]And let it be, when these signs come to you, *that* you do as the occasion demands; for God *is* with you. [8]You shall go down before me to Gilgal; and surely I will come down to you to offer burnt offerings *and* make sacrifices of peace offerings. Seven days you shall wait, till I come to you and show you what you should do."

[9]So it was, when he had turned his back to go from Samuel, that God gave him another heart; and all those signs came to pass that day. [10]When they came there to the hill, there was a group of prophets to meet him; then the Spirit of God came upon him, and he prophesied among them. [11]And it happened, when all who knew him formerly saw that he indeed prophesied among the prophets, that the people said to one another, "What *is* this *that* has come upon the son of Kish? *Is* Saul also among the prophets?" [12]Then a man from there answered and said, "But who *is* their father?" Therefore it became a proverb: "*Is* Saul also among the prophets?" [13]And when he had finished prophesying, he went to the high place.

[14]Then Saul's uncle said to him and his servant, "Where did you go?"

So he said, "To look for the donkeys. When we saw that *they were* nowhere *to be found,* we went to Samuel."

[15]And Saul's uncle said, "Tell me, please, what Samuel said to you."

[16]So Saul said to his uncle, "He told us plainly that the donkeys had been found." But about the matter of the kingdom, he did not tell him what Samuel had said.

Saul Proclaimed King

[17]Then Samuel called the people together to the LORD at Mizpah, [18]and said to the children of Israel, "Thus says the LORD God of Israel: 'I brought up Israel out of Egypt, and delivered you from the hand of the Egyptians *and* from the hand of all kingdoms and from those who oppressed you.' [19]But you have today rejected your God, who Himself saved you from all your adversities and your tribulations; and you have said to Him, 'No, set a king over us!' Now therefore, present yourselves before the LORD by your tribes and by your clans."[a]

[20]And when Samuel had caused all the tribes of Israel to come near, the tribe of Benjamin was chosen. [21]When he had caused the tribe of Benjamin to come near by their families, the family of Matri was chosen. And Saul the son of Kish was chosen. But when they sought him, he could not be found. [22]Therefore they inquired of the LORD further, "Has the man come here yet?"

And the LORD answered, "There he is, hidden among the equipment."

[23]So they ran and brought him from there; and when he stood among the people, he was taller than any of the people from his shoulders upward. [24]And Samuel said to all the people, "Do you see him whom the LORD has chosen, that *there is* no one like him among all the people?"

So all the people shouted and said, "Long live the king!"

[25]Then Samuel explained to the people the behavior of royalty, and wrote *it* in a book and laid *it* up before the LORD. And Samuel sent all the people away, every man to his house. [26]And Saul also went home to Gibeah; and valiant *men* went with him, whose hearts God had touched. [27]But some rebels said, "How can

10:1 [z] Following Masoretic Text, Targum, and Vulgate; Septuagint reads *His people Israel; and you shall rule the people of the Lord;* Septuagint and Vulgate add *And you shall deliver His people from the hands of their enemies all around them. And this shall be a sign to you, that God has anointed you to be a prince.*
10:19 [a] Literally *thousands*

Life Lesson

1 Samuel 11:1–12:25

SITUATION Saul's strength and resolve as a ruler were tested soon after he was anointed by Samuel. Though some doubted whether Saul should be king, he acted to rescue Jabesh Gilead and united his people against the Ammonites. These events confirmed for the people his place as king.

OBSERVATION Saul stepped out and took a risk to fulfill God's plan. He exemplifies that God protects us as we take intelligent risks to accomplish his will.

INSPIRATION It is true that there are great possibilities for failure [when taking risks] and, if you fail, there will be those who will mock you. But mockers are not important. Those who like to point when the risk-takers stumble don't count. The criticisms of those who sit back, observe, and offer smug suggestions can be discounted. The Promised Land belongs to the person who takes the risks, whose face is marred with dust and sweat, who strives valiantly while daring everything, who may err and fall, but who has done his or her best. This person's place shall never be with those cold and timid souls who know neither victory nor defeat.

Oh, if only I could persuade timid souls I meet to listen to that inner voice of the Spirit, which challenges us to attempt great things for God and expect great things from God. Oh, if only I could inspire them to heed that inner urging that tells them "Go for it!" I cannot say what a person should do with life, but I can say what a person should not do with it. No one should devote one's life to safety, to a course of action that offers no challenge and no fun.

(From *Who Switched the Price Tags?* by Tony Campolo)

APPLICATION Be encouraged to take risks for the sake of others. God honors those who follow his call to risk-taking. Seek his peace and "go for it"!

EXPLORATION Risk Taking—Judges 2:15; 3:9; 9:17; 13:5; 1 Samuel 9:16; Nehemiah 9:27.

this man save us?" So they despised him, and brought him no presents.
But he held his peace.

Saul Saves Jabesh Gilead

11 Then Nahash the Ammonite came up and encamped against Jabesh
Gilead; and all the men of Jabesh said to Nahash, "Make a covenant
with us, and we will serve you."
2And Nahash the Ammonite answered them, "On this *condition* I will
make *a covenant* with you, that I may put out all your right eyes, and bring
reproach on all Israel."
3Then the elders of Jabesh said to him, "Hold off for seven days, that we
may send messengers to all the territory of Israel. And then, if *there is* no
one to save us, we will come out to you."
4So the messengers came to Gibeah of Saul and told the news in the
hearing of the people. And all the people lifted up their voices and wept.
5Now there was Saul, coming behind the herd from the field; and Saul
said, "What *troubles* the people, that they weep?" And they told him the
words of the men of Jabesh. 6Then the Spirit of God came upon Saul when
he heard this news, and his anger was greatly aroused. 7So he took a yoke
of oxen and cut them in pieces, and sent *them* throughout all the territory
of Israel by the hands of messengers, saying, "Whoever does not go out
with Saul and Samuel to battle, so it shall be done to his oxen."
And the fear of the LORD fell on the people, and they came out with one
consent. 8When he numbered them in Bezek, the children of Israel were
three hundred thousand, and the men of Judah thirty thousand. 9And
they said to the messengers who came, "Thus you shall say to the men of
Jabesh Gilead: 'Tomorrow, by *the time* the sun is hot, you shall have help.' "
Then the messengers came and reported *it* to the men of Jabesh, and they
were glad. 10Therefore the men of Jabesh said, "Tomorrow we will come
out to you, and you may do with us whatever seems good to you."
11So it was, on the next day, that Saul put the people in three companies;
and they came into the midst of the camp in the morning watch, and killed
Ammonites until the heat of the day. And it happened that those who survived were scattered, so that no two of them were left together.
12Then the people said to Samuel, "Who *is* he who said, 'Shall Saul reign
over us?' Bring the men, that we may put them to death."
13But Saul said, "Not a man shall be put to death this day, for today the
LORD has accomplished salvation in Israel."
14Then Samuel said to the people, "Come, let us go to Gilgal and renew the
kingdom there." 15So all the people went to Gilgal, and there they made Saul
king before the LORD in Gilgal. There they made sacrifices of peace offerings
before the LORD, and there Saul and all the men of Israel rejoiced greatly.

Samuel's Address at Saul's Coronation

12 Now Samuel said to all Israel: "Indeed I have heeded your voice in
all that you said to me, and have made a king over you. 2And now
here is the king, walking before you; and I am old and gray headed, and
look, my sons *are* with you. I have walked before you from my childhood
to this day. 3Here I am. Witness against me before the LORD and before His
anointed: Whose ox have I taken, or whose donkey have I taken, or whom

have I cheated? Whom have I oppressed, or from whose hand have I received *any* bribe with which to blind my eyes? I will restore *it* to you."
4 And they said, "You have not cheated us or oppressed us, nor have you
taken anything from any man's hand."
5 Then he said to them, "The LORD *is* witness against you, and His
anointed *is* witness this day, that you have not found anything in my hand."
And they answered, "*He is* witness."
6 Then Samuel said to the people, "*It is* the LORD who raised up Moses
and Aaron, and who brought your fathers up from the land of Egypt. 7 Now
therefore, stand still, that I may reason with you before the LORD concerning all the righteous acts of the LORD which He did to you and your fathers:
8 When Jacob had gone into Egypt,[b] and your fathers cried out to the LORD,
then the LORD sent Moses and Aaron, who brought your fathers out of
Egypt and made them dwell in this place. 9 And when they forgot the LORD
their God, He sold them into the hand of Sisera, commander of the army
of Hazor, into the hand of the Philistines, and into the hand of the king of
Moab; and they fought against them. 10 Then they cried out to the LORD,
and said, 'We have sinned, because we have forsaken the LORD and served
the Baals and Ashtoreths;[c] but now deliver us from the hand of our enemies, and we will serve You.' 11 And the LORD sent Jerubbaal,[d] Bedan,[e]
Jephthah, and Samuel,[f] and delivered you out of the hand of your enemies
on every side; and you dwelt in safety. 12 And when you saw that Nahash
king of the Ammonites came against you, you said to me, 'No, but a king
shall reign over us,' when the LORD your God *was* your king.
13 "Now therefore, here is the king whom you have chosen *and* whom you
have desired. And take note, the LORD has set a king over you. 14 If you fear the
LORD and serve Him and obey His voice, and do not rebel against the commandment of the LORD, then both you and the king who reigns over you
will continue following the LORD your God. 15 However, if you do not obey
the voice of the LORD, but rebel against the commandment of the LORD,
then the hand of the LORD will be against you, as *it was* against your fathers.
16 "Now therefore, stand and see this great thing which the LORD will do
before your eyes: 17 *Is* today not the wheat harvest? I will call to the LORD,
and He will send thunder and rain, that you may perceive and see that
your wickedness *is* great, which you have done in the sight of the LORD, in
asking a king for yourselves."
18 So Samuel called to the LORD, and the LORD sent thunder and rain that
day; and all the people greatly feared the LORD and Samuel.
19 And all the people said to Samuel, "Pray for your servants to the LORD
your God, that we may not die; for we have added to all our sins the evil of
asking a king for ourselves."
20 Then Samuel said to the people, "Do not fear. You have done all this
wickedness; yet do not turn aside from following the LORD, but serve the
LORD with all your heart. 21 And do not turn aside; for *then you would go*
after empty things which cannot profit or deliver, for they *are* nothing. 22 For
the LORD will not forsake His people, for His great name's sake, because it
has pleased the LORD to make you His people. 23 Moreover, as for me, far be
it from me that I should sin against the LORD in ceasing to pray for you; but

12:8 [b] Following Masoretic Text, Targum, and Vulgate; Septuagint adds *and the Egyptians afflicted them.*
12:10 [c] Canaanite goddesses
12:11 [d] Syriac reads *Deborah;* Targum reads *Gideon.* [e] Septuagint and Syriac read *Barak;* Targum reads *Simson.* [f] Syriac reads *Simson.*

LIFE LESSON

1 Samuel 13:1–15:35

SITUATION When the Philistines gathered to attack Israel at Geba, the Israelites were badly outnumbered. King Saul grew tired of waiting for Samuel to instruct him about the battle at hand. Samuel delayed, and Saul's men began to desert; but he erred in his panic.

OBSERVATION Obey God's command in all circumstances. Saul lost his kingdom because he disobeyed God. Saul was pressured to act before all his men deserted. Lack of patience cost him everything.

INSPIRATION Have you heard the American's prayer?

"Lord, give me patience . . . , And I want it right now!"

It's awfully hard for a country that exists on frozen dinners, instant mashed potatoes, powdered orange juice, packaged cake mixes, instant-print cameras, and freeway express lanes to teach its young how to wait. In fact, it's next to impossible.

One evening I was fussing about seeds in the grapes my wife had served for supper. After crunching into another seed, I laid down the law. "No more grapes served in the Swindoll home unless they are seedless!" I announced with characteristic dogmatism. Later, when nobody else was around to hear her reproof, Cynthia edged up to me and quietly asked: "Do you know why seeds in grapes bug you?"

"Sure," I said, "because I bite into those bitter little things and they scatter all over my mouth!"

"No." She smiled. "It's because you're too impatient to dig them out first. The purple grapes really taste better . . . but they take a little more time."

There I stood, riveted to the pantry door by a very true (yet painful) set of facts. I was too busy, too much in a hurry to split open a grape and pull out the seeds. Wow! No wonder waiting is such a difficult hassle for me to handle.

Wouldn't you rather do anything than wait? If the truth were known, some of us would rather do the wrong thing than wait.

Continued

I have found, however, that waiting is the rule rather than the exception in life. The exception is an open door; when you have one—go! They don't happen very often! But waiting, when the door is closed doesn't mean you're out of the will of God. You could be right in the center of His will.

The open door is the exception. The burst of green lights happen just a few seconds in life. The rest of the time is filled with a few yellow lights, and mostly red lights that flash, "Wait, wait, wait!"

(From *Three Steps Forward and Two Steps Back* by Charles Swindoll)

APPLICATION It's easy to compromise when people are waiting for you to act. Determine that no matter the pressure, no matter the cost, no matter the delay, you will act only when your response honors God. Never compromise your integrity to satisfy others.

EXPLORATION Waiting—Psalm 27; 37:5-7.

I will teach you the good and the right way. [24]Only fear the LORD, and serve
Him in truth with all your heart; for consider what great things He has
done for you. [25]But if you still do wickedly, you shall be swept away, both
you and your king."

Saul's Unlawful Sacrifice

13 Saul reigned one year; and when he had reigned two years over Israel,[g] [2]Saul chose for himself three thousand *men* of Israel. Two
thousand were with Saul in Michmash and in the mountains of Bethel,
and a thousand were with Jonathan in Gibeah of Benjamin. The rest of the
people he sent away, every man to his tent.
[3]And Jonathan attacked the garrison of the Philistines that *was* in Geba,
and the Philistines heard *of it.* Then Saul blew the trumpet throughout all
the land, saying, "Let the Hebrews hear!" [4]Now all Israel heard it said *that* Saul
had attacked a garrison of the Philistines, and *that* Israel had also become
an abomination to the Philistines. And the people were called together to
Saul at Gilgal.
[5]Then the Philistines gathered together to fight with Israel, thirty[h] thousand chariots and six thousand horsemen, and people as the sand which
is on the seashore in multitude. And they came up and encamped in
Michmash, to the east of Beth Aven. [6]When the men of Israel saw that they
were in danger (for the people were distressed), then the people hid in
caves, in thickets, in rocks, in holes, and in pits. [7]And *some of* the Hebrews
crossed over the Jordan to the land of Gad and Gilead.
As for Saul, he *was* still in Gilgal, and all the people followed him trembling. [8]Then he waited seven days, according to the time set by Samuel.
But Samuel did not come to Gilgal; and the people were scattered from
him. [9]So Saul said, "Bring a burnt offering and peace offerings here to
me." And he offered the burnt offering. [10]Now it happened, as soon as he
had finished presenting the burnt offering, that Samuel came; and Saul
went out to meet him, that he might greet him.
[11]And Samuel said, "What have you done?"
Saul said, "When I saw that the people were scattered from me, and *that*
you did not come within the days appointed, and *that* the Philistines gathered together at Michmash, [12]then I said, 'The Philistines will now come
down on me at Gilgal, and I have not made supplication to the LORD.'
Therefore I felt compelled, and offered a burnt offering."
[13]And Samuel said to Saul, "You have done foolishly. You have not kept
the commandment of the LORD your God, which He commanded you. For
now the LORD would have established your kingdom over Israel forever.
[14]But now your kingdom shall not continue. The LORD has sought for
Himself a man after His own heart, and the LORD has commanded him *to
be* commander over His people, because you have not kept what the LORD
commanded you."
[15]Then Samuel arose and went up from Gilgal to Gibeah of Benjamin.[i]
And Saul numbered the people present with him, about six hundred men.

13:1 [g] The Hebrew is difficult (compare 2 Samuel 5:4; 2 Kings 14:2; see also 2 Samuel 2:10; Acts 13:21).
13:5 [h] Following Masoretic Text, Septuagint, Targum, and Vulgate; Syriac and some manuscripts of the Septuagint read *three.*
13:15 [i] Following Masoretic Text and Targum; Septuagint and Vulgate add *And the rest of the people went up after Saul to meet the people who fought against them, going from Gilgal to Gibeah in the hill of Benjamin.*

No Weapons for the Army

16 Saul, Jonathan his son, and the people present
with them remained in Gibeah of Benjamin. But the
Philistines encamped in Michmash. 17 Then raiders
came out of the camp of the Philistines in three companies. One company turned onto the road to
Ophrah, to the land of Shual, 18 another company
turned to the road *to* Beth Horon, and another company turned *to* the road of the border that overlooks
the Valley of Zeboim toward the wilderness.
19 Now there was no blacksmith to be found
throughout all the land of Israel, for the Philistines
said, "Lest the Hebrews make swords or spears." 20 But
all the Israelites would go down to the Philistines to
sharpen each man's plowshare, his mattock, his ax,
and his sickle; 21 and the charge for a sharpening was a
pim[j] for the plowshares, the mattocks, the forks, and
the axes, and to set the points of the goads. 22 So it
came about, on the day of battle, that there was neither sword nor spear found in the hand of any of the
people who *were* with Saul and Jonathan. But they
were found with Saul and Jonathan his son.
23 And the garrison of the Philistines went out to the
pass of Michmash.

Jonathan Defeats the Philistines

14 Now it happened one day that Jonathan the son
of Saul said to the young man who bore his
armor, "Come, let us go over to the Philistines' garrison
that *is* on the other side." But he did not tell his father.
2 And Saul was sitting in the outskirts of Gibeah under
a pomegranate tree which *is* in Migron. The people
who *were* with him *were* about six hundred men.
3 Ahijah the son of Ahitub, Ichabod's brother, the son
of Phinehas, the son of Eli, the LORD's priest in Shiloh,
was wearing an ephod. But the people did not know
that Jonathan had gone.
4 Between the passes, by which Jonathan sought to
go over to the Philistines' garrison, *there was* a sharp
rock on one side and a sharp rock on the other side.
And the name of one *was* Bozez, and the name of the
other Seneh. 5 The front of one faced northward opposite Michmash, and the other southward opposite
Gibeah.
6 Then Jonathan said to the young man who bore
his armor, "Come, let us go over to the garrison of
these uncircumcised; it may be that the LORD will
work for us. For nothing restrains the LORD from saving by many or by few."
7 So his armorbearer said to him, "Do all that is in
your heart. Go then; here I am with you, according to
your heart."
8 Then Jonathan said, "Very well, let us cross over to
these men, and we will show ourselves to them. 9 If
they say thus to us, 'Wait until we come to you,' then
we will stand still in our place and not go up to them.
10 But if they say thus, 'Come up to us,' then we will go
up. For the LORD has delivered them into our hand,
and this *will be* a sign to us."
11 So both of them showed themselves to the garrison of the Philistines. And the Philistines said, "Look,
the Hebrews are coming out of the holes where they
have hidden." 12 Then the men of the garrison called to
Jonathan and his armorbearer, and said, "Come up to
us, and we will show you something."
Jonathan said to his armorbearer, "Come up after
me, for the LORD has delivered them into the hand of
Israel." 13 And Jonathan climbed up on his hands and
knees with his armorbearer after him; and they fell
before Jonathan. And as he came after him, his armorbearer killed them. 14 That first slaughter which
Jonathan and his armorbearer made was about
twenty men within about half an acre of land.[k]
15 And there was trembling in the camp, in the field,
and among all the people. The garrison and the
raiders also trembled; and the earth quaked, so that it
was a very great trembling. 16 Now the watchmen of
Saul in Gibeah of Benjamin looked, and *there* was the
multitude, melting away; and they went here and
there. 17 Then Saul said to the people who *were* with
him, "Now call the roll and see who has gone from
us." And when they had called the roll, surprisingly,
Jonathan and his armorbearer *were* not *there.* 18 And
Saul said to Ahijah, "Bring the ark[l] of God here" (for
at that time the ark[m] of God was with the children of
Israel). 19 Now it happened, while Saul talked to the
priest, that the noise which *was* in the camp of the
Philistines continued to increase; so Saul said to the
priest, "Withdraw your hand." 20 Then Saul and all the
people who *were* with him assembled, and they went
to the battle; and indeed every man's sword was
against his neighbor, *and there was* very great confusion. 21 Moreover the Hebrews *who* were with the
Philistines before that time, who went up with them
into the camp *from the* surrounding *country,* they also

13:21 [j] About two-thirds shekel weight
14:14 [k] Literally *half the area plowed by a yoke* (of oxen in a day)
14:18 [l] Following Masoretic Text, Targum, and Vulgate; Septuagint reads *ephod.* [m] Following Masoretic Text, Targum, and Vulgate; Septuagint reads *ephod.*

joined the Israelites who *were* with Saul and Jonathan.
22Likewise all the men of Israel who had hidden in the
mountains of Ephraim, *when* they heard that the
Philistines fled, they also followed hard after them in
the battle. 23So the LORD saved Israel that day, and the
battle shifted to Beth Aven.

Saul's Rash Oath

24And the men of Israel were distressed that day, for
Saul had placed the people under oath, saying,
"Cursed *is* the man who eats *any* food until evening,
before I have taken vengeance on my enemies." So
none of the people tasted food. 25Now all *the people* of
the land came to a forest; and there was honey on the
ground. 26And when the people had come into the
woods, there was the honey, dripping; but no one put
his hand to his mouth, for the people feared the oath.
27But Jonathan had not heard his father charge the
people with the oath; therefore he stretched out the
end of the rod that *was* in his hand and dipped it in a
honeycomb, and put his hand to his mouth; and his
countenance brightened. 28Then one of the people
said, "Your father strictly charged the people with an
oath, saying, 'Cursed *is* the man who eats food this
day.'" And the people were faint.
29But Jonathan said, "My father has troubled the
land. Look now, how my countenance has brightened
because I tasted a little of this honey. 30How much better if the people had eaten freely today of the spoil of
their enemies which they found! For now would there
not have been a much greater slaughter among the
Philistines?"
31Now they had driven back the Philistines that day
from Michmash to Aijalon. So the people were very
faint. 32And the people rushed on the spoil, and took
sheep, oxen, and calves, and slaughtered *them* on the
ground; and the people ate *them* with the blood.
33Then they told Saul, saying, "Look, the people are
sinning against the LORD by eating with the blood!"
So he said, "You have dealt treacherously; roll a
large stone to me this day." 34Then Saul said, "Disperse yourselves among the people, and say to them,
'Bring me here every man's ox and every man's sheep,
slaughter *them* here, and eat; and do not sin against
the LORD by eating with the blood.'" So every one of
the people brought his ox with him that night, and
slaughtered *it* there. 35Then Saul built an altar to the
LORD. This was the first altar that he built to the LORD.
36Now Saul said, "Let us go down after the Philistines
by night, and plunder them until the morning light;
and let us not leave a man of them."
And they said, "Do whatever seems good to you."
Then the priest said, "Let us draw near to God here."
37So Saul asked counsel of God, "Shall I go down
after the Philistines? Will You deliver them into the
hand of Israel?" But He did not answer him that day.
38And Saul said, "Come over here, all you chiefs of the
people, and know and see what this sin was today.
39For *as* the LORD lives, who saves Israel, though it be
in Jonathan my son, he shall surely die." But not a
man among all the people answered him. 40Then he
said to all Israel, "You be on one side, and my son Jonathan and I will be on the other side."
And the people said to Saul, "Do what seems good
to you."
41Therefore Saul said to the LORD God of Israel,
"Give a perfect *lot*."[n] So Saul and Jonathan were
taken, but the people escaped. 42And Saul said, "Cast
lots between my son Jonathan and me." So Jonathan
was taken. 43Then Saul said to Jonathan, "Tell me
what you have done."
And Jonathan told him, and said, "I only tasted a
little honey with the end of the rod that *was* in my
hand. So now I must die!"
44Saul answered, "God do so and more also; for you
shall surely die, Jonathan."
45But the people said to Saul, "Shall Jonathan die,
who has accomplished this great deliverance in Israel? Certainly not! *As* the LORD lives, not one hair of
his head shall fall to the ground, for he has worked
with God this day." So the people rescued Jonathan,
and he did not die.
46Then Saul returned from pursuing the Philistines, and the Philistines went to their own place.

Saul's Continuing Wars

47So Saul established his sovereignty over Israel,
and fought against all his enemies on every side,
against Moab, against the people of Ammon, against
Edom, against the kings of Zobah, and against the
Philistines. Wherever he turned, he harassed *them*.[o]
48And he gathered an army and attacked the
Amalekites, and delivered Israel from the hands of
those who plundered them.
49The sons of Saul were Jonathan, Jishui,[p] and
Malchishua. And the names of his two daughters *were*

14:41 [n] Following Masoretic Text and Targum; Septuagint and Vulgate read *Why do You not answer Your servant today? If the injustice is with me or Jonathan my son, O LORD God of Israel, give proof; and if You say it is with Your people Israel, give holiness.*
14:47 [o] Septuagint and Vulgate read *prospered.*
14:49 [p] Called *Abinadab* in 1 Chronicles 8:33 and 9:39

these: the name of the firstborn Merab, and the name of the younger Michal. 50The name of Saul's wife *was* Ahinoam the daughter of Ahimaaz. And the name of the commander of his army *was* Abner the son of Ner, Saul's uncle. 51Kish *was* the father of Saul, and Ner the father of Abner *was* the son of Abiel.

52Now there was fierce war with the Philistines all the days of Saul. And when Saul saw any strong man or any valiant man, he took him for himself.

Saul Spares King Agag

15 Samuel also said to Saul, "The LORD sent me to anoint you king over His people, over Israel. Now therefore, heed the voice of the words of the LORD. 2Thus says the LORD of hosts: 'I will punish Amalek *for* what he did to Israel, how he ambushed him on the way when he came up from Egypt. 3Now go and attack Amalek, and utterly destroy all that they have, and do not spare them. But kill both man and woman, infant and nursing child, ox and sheep, camel and donkey.' "

4So Saul gathered the people together and numbered them in Telaim, two hundred thousand foot soldiers and ten thousand men of Judah. 5And Saul came to a city of Amalek, and lay in wait in the valley.

6Then Saul said to the Kenites, "Go, depart, get down from among the Amalekites, lest I destroy you with them. For you showed kindness to all the children of Israel when they came up out of Egypt." So the Kenites departed from among the Amalekites. 7And Saul attacked the Amalekites, from Havilah all the way to Shur, which is east of Egypt. 8He also took Agag king of the Amalekites alive, and utterly destroyed all the people with the edge of the sword. 9But Saul and the people spared Agag and the best of the sheep, the oxen, the fatlings, the lambs, and all *that was* good, and were unwilling to utterly destroy them. But everything despised and worthless, that they utterly destroyed.

Saul Rejected as King

10Now the word of the LORD came to Samuel, saying, 11"I greatly regret that I have set up Saul *as* king, for he has turned back from following Me, and has not performed My commandments." And it grieved Samuel, and he cried out to the LORD all night. 12So when Samuel rose early in the morning to meet Saul, it was told Samuel, saying, "Saul went to Carmel, and indeed, he set up a monument for himself; and he has gone on around, passed by, and gone down to Gilgal." 13Then Samuel went to Saul, and Saul said to him, "Blessed *are* you of the LORD! I have performed the commandment of the LORD."

14But Samuel said, "What then *is* this bleating of the sheep in my ears, and the lowing of the oxen which I hear?"

15And Saul said, "They have brought them from the Amalekites; for the people spared the best of the sheep and the oxen, to sacrifice to the LORD your God; and the rest we have utterly destroyed."

16Then Samuel said to Saul, "Be quiet! And I will tell you what the LORD said to me last night."

And he said to him, "Speak on."

17So Samuel said, "When you *were* little in your own eyes, *were* you not head of the tribes of Israel? And did not the LORD anoint you king over Israel? 18Now the LORD sent you on a mission, and said, 'Go, and utterly destroy the sinners, the Amalekites, and fight against them until they are consumed.' 19Why then did you not obey the voice of the LORD? Why did you swoop down on the spoil, and do evil in the sight of the LORD?"

20And Saul said to Samuel, "But I have obeyed the voice of the LORD, and gone on the mission on which the LORD sent me, and brought back Agag king of Amalek; I have utterly destroyed the Amalekites. 21But the people took of the plunder, sheep and oxen, the best of the things which should have been utterly destroyed, to sacrifice to the LORD your God in Gilgal."

22So Samuel said:

"Has the LORD *as great* delight in burnt
offerings and sacrifices,
As in obeying the voice of the LORD?
Behold, to obey is better than sacrifice,
And to heed than the fat of rams.
23 For rebellion *is as* the sin of witchcraft,
And stubbornness *is as* iniquity and idolatry.
Because you have rejected the word of
the LORD,
He also has rejected you from *being* king."

24Then Saul said to Samuel, "I have sinned, for I have transgressed the commandment of the LORD and your words, because I feared the people and obeyed their voice. 25Now therefore, please pardon my sin, and return with me, that I may worship the LORD."

26But Samuel said to Saul, "I will not return with you, for you have rejected the word of the LORD, and the LORD has rejected you from being king over Israel."

27And as Samuel turned around to go away, *Saul* seized the edge of his robe, and it tore. 28So Samuel said to him, "The LORD has torn the kingdom of Israel from you today, and has given it to a neighbor of

LIFE LESSON

1 Samuel 16:1-23

SITUATION God sent Samuel to Bethlehem to anoint one of Jesse's sons as king. This new king would replace King Saul, who had failed to obey God.

OBSERVATION God does not see or judge in the same way that humans do. People look at the outside appearance or qualifications, but God looks at the heart. He evaluates our inner disposition and character.

INSPIRATION None were more shunned by their culture than the blind, the lame, the lepers, and the deaf. They had no place. No name. No value. Canker sores on the culture. Excess baggage on the side of the road. But those whom the people called trash, Jesus called treasures.

In my closet hangs a sweater that I seldom wear. It is too small. The sleeves are too short, the shoulders too tight. Some of the buttons are missing, and the thread is frazzled. I should throw that sweater away. I have no use for it. I'll never wear it again. Logic says I should clear out the space and get rid of the sweater.

That's what logic says.

But love won't let me.

Something unique about the sweater makes me keep it. What is unusual about it? For one thing, it has no label. Nowhere on the garment will you find a tag that reads, "Made In Taiwan," or "Wash in Cold Water." It has no tag because it wasn't made in a factory. It has no label because it wasn't produced on an assembly line. It isn't the product of a nameless employee earning a living. It's the creation of a devoted mother expressing her love.

That sweater is unique. One of a kind.

yours, *who is* better than you. 29And also the Strength of Israel will not lie
nor relent. For He *is* not a man, that He should relent."
30Then he said, "I have sinned; *yet* honor me now, please, before the elders of my people and before Israel, and return with me, that I may worship the LORD your God." 31So Samuel turned back after Saul, and Saul
worshiped the LORD.
32Then Samuel said, "Bring Agag king of the Amalekites here to me." So
Agag came to him cautiously.
And Agag said, "Surely the bitterness of death is past."
33But Samuel said, "As your sword has made women childless, so shall
your mother be childless among women." And Samuel hacked Agag in
pieces before the LORD in Gilgal.
34Then Samuel went to Ramah, and Saul went up to his house at Gibeah
of Saul. 35And Samuel went no more to see Saul until the day of his death.
Nevertheless Samuel mourned for Saul, and the LORD regretted that He
had made Saul king over Israel.

David Anointed King

16 Now the LORD said to Samuel, "How long will you mourn for Saul,
seeing I have rejected him from reigning over Israel? Fill your horn
with oil, and go; I am sending you to Jesse the Bethlehemite. For I have
provided Myself a king among his sons."
2And Samuel said, "How can I go? If Saul hears *it*, he will kill me."
But the LORD said, "Take a heifer with you, and say, 'I have come to sacrifice to the LORD.' 3Then invite Jesse to the sacrifice, and I will show you
what you shall do; you shall anoint for Me the one I name to you."
4So Samuel did what the LORD said, and went to Bethlehem. And the
elders of the town trembled at his coming, and said, "Do you come
peaceably?"
5And he said, "Peaceably; I have come to sacrifice to the LORD. Sanctify
yourselves, and come with me to the sacrifice." Then he consecrated Jesse
and his sons, and invited them to the sacrifice.
6So it was, when they came, that he looked at Eliab and said, "Surely the
LORD's anointed *is* before Him!"
7But the LORD said to Samuel, "Do not look at his appearance or at his
physical stature, because I have refused him. For *the LORD does* not *see* as
man sees;[q] for man looks at the outward appearance, but the LORD looks at
the heart."
8So Jesse called Abinadab, and made him pass before Samuel. And he
said, "Neither has the LORD chosen this one." 9Then Jesse made Shammah
pass by. And he said, "Neither has the LORD chosen this one." 10Thus Jesse
made seven of his sons pass before Samuel. And Samuel said to Jesse,
"The LORD has not chosen these." 11And Samuel said to Jesse, "Are all the
young men here?" Then he said, "There remains yet the youngest, and
there he is, keeping the sheep."
And Samuel said to Jesse, "Send and bring him. For we will not sit
down[r] till he comes here." 12So he sent and brought him in. Now he *was*
ruddy, with bright eyes, and good-looking. And the LORD said, "Arise,

16:7 [q] Septuagint reads *For God does not see as man sees;* Targum reads *It is not by the appearance of a man;* Vulgate reads *Nor do I judge according to the looks of a man.*
16:11 [r] Following Septuagint and Vulgate; Masoretic Text reads *turn around;* Targum and Syriac read *turn away.*

anoint him; for this *is* the one!" 13 Then Samuel took the horn of oil and
anointed him in the midst of his brothers; and the Spirit of the LORD came
upon David from that day forward. So Samuel arose and went to Ramah.

A Distressing Spirit Troubles Saul

14 But the Spirit of the LORD departed from Saul, and a distressing spirit
from the LORD troubled him. 15 And Saul's servants said to him, "Surely, a
distressing spirit from God is troubling you. 16 Let our master now command your servants, *who are* before you, to seek out a man *who is* a skillful player on the harp. And it shall be that he will play it with his hand
when the distressing spirit from God is upon you, and you shall be well."
17 So Saul said to his servants, "Provide me now a man who can play
well, and bring *him* to me."
18 Then one of the servants answered and said, "Look, I have seen a son
of Jesse the Bethlehemite, *who is* skillful in playing, a mighty man of
valor, a man of war, prudent in speech, and a handsome person; and the
LORD *is* with him."
19 Therefore Saul sent messengers to Jesse, and said, "Send me your son
David, who *is* with the sheep." 20 And Jesse took a donkey *loaded with*
bread, a skin of wine, and a young goat, and sent *them* by his son David to
Saul. 21 So David came to Saul and stood before him. And he loved him
greatly, and he became his armorbearer. 22 Then Saul sent to Jesse, saying,
"Please let David stand before me, for he has found favor in my sight."
23 And so it was, whenever the spirit from God was upon Saul, that David
would take a harp and play *it* with his hand. Then Saul would become refreshed and well, and the distressing spirit would depart from him.

David and Goliath

17 Now the Philistines gathered their armies together to battle, and
were gathered at Sochoh, which *belongs* to Judah; they encamped
between Sochoh and Azekah, in Ephes Dammim. 2 And Saul and the men
of Israel were gathered together, and they encamped in the Valley of Elah,
and drew up in battle array against the Philistines. 3 The Philistines stood
on a mountain on one side, and Israel stood on a mountain on the other
side, with a valley between them.
4 And a champion went out from the camp of the Philistines, named Goliath, from Gath, whose height *was* six cubits and a span. 5 *He had* a bronze
helmet on his head, and he *was* armed with a coat of mail, and the weight
of the coat *was* five thousand shekels of bronze. 6 And *he had* bronze armor
on his legs and a bronze javelin between his shoulders. 7 Now the staff of
his spear *was* like a weaver's beam, and his iron spearhead *weighed* six
hundred shekels; and a shield-bearer went before him. 8 Then he stood
and cried out to the armies of Israel, and said to them, "Why have you
come out to line up for battle? *Am* I not a Philistine, and you the servants
of Saul? Choose a man for yourselves, and let him come down to me. 9 If he
is able to fight with me and kill me, then we will be your servants. But if I
prevail against him and kill him, then you shall be our servants and serve
us." 10 And the Philistine said, "I defy the armies of Israel this day; give me
a man, that we may fight together." 11 When Saul and all Israel heard these
words of the Philistine, they were dismayed and greatly afraid.
12 Now David *was* the son of that Ephrathite of Bethlehem Judah, whose

It can't be replaced. Each strand was chosen with care. Each thread was selected with affection.

And though the sweater has lost all of its use, it has lost none of its value. It is valuable not because of its function, but because of its maker.

That must have been what the psalmist had in mind when he wrote, "You knit me together in my mother's womb."

Think on those words. You were knitted together. You aren't an accident. You weren't mass produced. You aren't an assembly-line product. You were deliberately planned, specifically gifted, and lovingly positioned on this earth by the Master Craftsman.

"For we are God's workmanship, created in Christ Jesus to do good works, which God prepared in advance for us to do."

In a society that has little room for second fiddles, that's good news. In a culture where the door of opportunity opens only once and then slams shut, that is a revelation. In a system that ranks the value of a human by the figures of his salary or the shape of her legs . . . let me tell you something: Jesus' plan is a reason for joy! Jesus told John that a new kingdom was coming—a kingdom where people have value not because of what they do, but because of whose they are.

(From *The Applause of Heaven* by Max Lucado)

APPLICATION We often pick leaders by credentials rather than character. Next time you must select a leader, ask questions about character—not about resumé. Spend more time cultivating your character than your references.

EXPLORATION God's Insight—1 Chronicles 28:9; Exodus 4:10-16; Jeremiah 1:6-7; 17:9-10.

LIFE LESSON

1 Samuel 17:1-58

SITUATION Earlier passages confirmed that Goliath came from an area that had many tall people. Even though it wasn't unusual for two armies to send out their best soldiers to fight in place of an all-out war, the Israelites had no one to compare to nine-foot tall Goliath.

OBSERVATION Though the Israelites feared losing to Goliath, they forgot who had called them to enter the Promised Land. Though they had seen God fight for them in many previous battles, they neglected to trust him in this one. David's focus was not on the size of the enemy, but on God.

INSPIRATION There are certain things anyone knows not to do. . . . You don't fight a lion with a toothpick. You don't sneeze into the wind. You don't go bear hunting with a cork gun. And you don't send a shepherd boy to battle a giant.

You don't, that is, unless you are out of options. Saul was. And it is when we are out of options that we are most ready for God's surprises.

Was Saul ever surprised!

The king tried to give David some equipment. "What do you want, boy? Shield? Sword? Grenades? Rifles? A helicopter? We'll make a Rambo out of you."

David had something else in mind. Five smooth stones and an ordinary leather sling.

The soldiers gasped. Saul sighed. Goliath jeered. David swung. And God made his point. "Anyone who underestimates what God can do with the ordinary has rocks in his head."

(From *The Applause of Heaven* by Max Lucado)

APPLICATION What battle are you facing this week? Even if it's bigger than you can handle, it's not bigger than God can handle. Proceed with his backing.

EXPLORATION Don't Be Afraid—Deuteronomy 31:6; Isaiah 46:4; Daniel 6:27; Matthew 10:28-31; John 14:27; 2 Corinthians 1:10; Philippians 4:6; Hebrews 13:6.

name *was* Jesse, and who had eight sons. And the man was old, advanced
in years, in the days of Saul. 13The three oldest sons of Jesse had gone to follow Saul to the battle. The names of his three sons who went to the battle
were Eliab the firstborn, next to him Abinadab, and the third Shammah.
14David *was* the youngest. And the three oldest followed Saul. 15But David
occasionally went and returned from Saul to feed his father's sheep at
Bethlehem.

16And the Philistine drew near and presented himself forty days, morning and evening.

17Then Jesse said to his son David, "Take now for your brothers an
ephah of this dried *grain* and these ten loaves, and run to your brothers at
the camp. 18And carry these ten cheeses to the captain of *their* thousand,
and see how your brothers fare, and bring back news of them." 19Now Saul
and they and all the men of Israel *were* in the Valley of Elah, fighting with
the Philistines.

20So David rose early in the morning, left the sheep with a keeper, and
took *the things* and went as Jesse had commanded him. And he came to
the camp as the army was going out to the fight and shouting for the battle. 21For Israel and the Philistines had drawn up in battle array, army
against army. 22And David left his supplies in the hand of the supply
keeper, ran to the army, and came and greeted his brothers. 23Then as he
talked with them, there was the champion, the Philistine of Gath, Goliath
by name, coming up from the armies of the Philistines; and he spoke according to the same words. So David heard *them.* 24And all the men of Israel, when they saw the man, fled from him and were dreadfully afraid.
25So the men of Israel said, "Have you seen this man who has come up?
Surely he has come up to defy Israel; and it shall be *that* the man who kills
him the king will enrich with great riches, will give him his daughter, and
give his father's house exemption *from taxes* in Israel."

26Then David spoke to the men who stood by him, saying, "What shall
be done for the man who kills this Philistine and takes away the reproach
from Israel? For who *is* this uncircumcised Philistine, that he should defy
the armies of the living God?"

27And the people answered him in this manner, saying, "So shall it be
done for the man who kills him."

28Now Eliab his oldest brother heard when he spoke to the men; and
Eliab's anger was aroused against David, and he said, "Why did you come
down here? And with whom have you left those few sheep in the wilderness? I know your pride and the insolence of your heart, for you have
come down to see the battle."

29And David said, "What have I done now? Is *there* not a cause?" 30Then
he turned from him toward another and said the same thing; and these
people answered him as the first ones *did.*

31Now when the words which David spoke were heard, they reported
them to Saul; and he sent for him. 32Then David said to Saul, "Let no man's
heart fail because of him; your servant will go and fight with this
Philistine."

33And Saul said to David, "You are not able to go against this Philistine to
fight with him; for you *are* a youth, and he a man of war from his youth."

34But David said to Saul, "Your servant used to keep his father's sheep,
and when a lion or a bear came and took a lamb out of the flock, 35I went

out after it and struck it, and delivered *the lamb* from its mouth; and when
it arose against me, I caught *it* by its beard, and struck and killed it. 36Your
servant has killed both lion and bear; and this uncircumcised Philistine
will be like one of them, seeing he has defied the armies of the living God."
37Moreover David said, "The LORD, who delivered me from the paw of the
lion and from the paw of the bear, He will deliver me from the hand of this
Philistine."

And Saul said to David, "Go, and the LORD be with you!"
38So Saul clothed David with his armor, and he put a bronze helmet on
his head; he also clothed him with a coat of mail. 39David fastened his
sword to his armor and tried to walk, for he had not tested *them*. And David said to Saul, "I cannot walk with these, for I have not tested *them*." So
David took them off.
40Then he took his staff in his hand; and he chose for himself five
smooth stones from the brook, and put them in a shepherd's bag, in a
pouch which he had, and his sling was in his hand. And he drew near to
the Philistine. 41So the Philistine came, and began drawing near to David,
and the man who bore the shield *went* before him. 42And when the
Philistine looked about and saw David, he disdained him; for he was *only*
a youth, ruddy and good-looking. 43So the Philistine said to David, "*Am* I
a dog, that you come to me with sticks?" And the Philistine cursed David
by his gods. 44And the Philistine said to David, "Come to me, and I will
give your flesh to the birds of the air and the beasts of the field!"
45Then David said to the Philistine, "You come to me with a sword, with
a spear, and with a javelin. But I come to you in the name of the LORD of
hosts, the God of the armies of Israel, whom you have defied. 46This day
the LORD will deliver you into my hand, and I will strike you and take your
head from you. And this day I will give the carcasses of the camp of the
Philistines to the birds of the air and the wild beasts of the earth, that all
the earth may know that there is a God in Israel. 47Then all this assembly
shall know that the LORD does not save with sword and spear; for the battle
is the LORD's, and He will give you into our hands."
48So it was, when the Philistine arose and came and drew near to meet
David, that David hurried and ran toward the army to meet the Philistine.
49Then David put his hand in his bag and took out a stone; and he slung *it*
and struck the Philistine in his forehead, so that the stone sank into his
forehead, and he fell on his face to the earth. 50So David prevailed over the
Philistine with a sling and a stone, and struck the Philistine and killed
him. But *there was* no sword in the hand of David. 51Therefore David ran
and stood over the Philistine, took his sword and drew it out of its sheath
and killed him, and cut off his head with it.

And when the Philistines saw that their champion was dead, they fled.
52Now the men of Israel and Judah arose and shouted, and pursued the
Philistines as far as the entrance of the valley[s] and to the gates of Ekron.
And the wounded of the Philistines fell along the road to Shaaraim, even
as far as Gath and Ekron. 53Then the children of Israel returned from
chasing the Philistines, and they plundered their tents. 54And David took
the head of the Philistine and brought it to Jerusalem, but he put his
armor in his tent.

17:52 [s] Following Masoretic Text, Syriac, Targum, and Vulgate; Septuagint reads *Gath*.

Life Lesson

Samuel 18:1–20:42

SITUATION Though Saul was king and his son Jonathan first in line for succession, God had appointed David as the next king of Israel. David waited for God's timing and did not try to dethrone Saul or eliminate the heir to the throne. Saul's goal was to protect his family line at any cost.

OBSERVATION Saul chose jealousy over God's will. Jonathan chose obedience to God's plan and friendship with David over jealousy. Though Jonathan was not given the throne—despite his obedience and godly attitude—he did have peace of heart and knew his priorities were straight.

INSPIRATION I saw a man in the supermarket yesterday using a new sporty wheelchair. When he zipped down the aisle, his chair didn't make a squeak. I looked down at my big clunky twenty-year-old model with dirt on the frame and threadbare padding. Little wonder I looked with envy at his high-tech wheels.

I'd like a trade-in on my wheelchair. Perhaps you would like a trade-in on your old car. Perhaps the grass seems greener down the street where they are building brand new homes. Yes, an automatic garage door opener and a trash compactor would be great to have. But sometimes when we compile our desires up against God's desires for us, I wonder how many match.

The apostle Paul says that he has learned the secret of remaining content despite either plenty or poverty. What was the secret Paul had learned? He gave it away in his next breath when he said that he was ready for anything *through the strength of the One who lived inside him.*

Contentment is found not in circumstances. Contentment is found in a Person, the Lord Jesus.

It requires a special act of grace to accommodate ourselves to every condition of life, to carry an equal temper of mind through every circumstance. On the one hand, only in Christ can we face poverty contentedly, that is, without losing our comfort in God. On the other hand, only in Christ can we face plenty and not be filled with pride.

Continued

Lord, there are many things I desire, but I really don't need. Subtract my desires and keep me from adding my own wants. Help me to find satisfaction in You, for only then will I find real and lasting contentment.
(*From Diamonds in the Dust* by Joni Eareckson Tada)

APPLICATION Are you content with what God is doing for you? It can be hard to accept that God's will for you may be less money, a lower position, a long wait. Ask God to make you like Jonathan and David and to develop in you contentment in trusting and obeying him. Be satisfied with where God has placed you.

EXPLORATION Contentment —Psalm 16:5-6; 119:165; Proverbs 30:7-9; Isaiah 26:3; 2 Corinthians 12:7-10; Philippians 4:11-13; 1 Timothy 6:6; Hebrews 13:5.

55When Saul saw David going out against the Philistine, he said to
Abner, the commander of the army, "Abner, whose son *is* this youth?"
And Abner said, "As your soul lives, O king, I do not know."
56So the king said, "Inquire whose son this young man *is*."
57Then, as David returned from the slaughter of the Philistine, Abner
took him and brought him before Saul with the head of the Philistine in
his hand. 58And Saul said to him, "Whose son *are* you, young man?"
So David answered, "*I am* the son of your servant Jesse the Bethlehemite."

Saul Resents David

18 Now when he had finished speaking to Saul, the soul of Jonathan
was knit to the soul of David, and Jonathan loved him as his own
soul. 2Saul took him that day, and would not let him go home to his father's
house anymore. 3Then Jonathan and David made a covenant, because he
loved him as his own soul. 4And Jonathan took off the robe that *was* on
him and gave it to David, with his armor, even to his sword and his bow
and his belt.
5So David went out wherever Saul sent him, *and* behaved wisely. And
Saul set him over the men of war, and he was accepted in the sight of all the
people and also in the sight of Saul's servants. 6Now it had happened as
they were coming *home,* when David was returning from the slaughter of
the Philistine, that the women had come out of all the cities of Israel,
singing and dancing, to meet King Saul, with tambourines, with joy, and
with musical instruments. 7So the women sang as they danced, and said:

"Saul has slain his thousands,
And David his ten thousands."

8Then Saul was very angry, and the saying displeased him; and he said,
"They have ascribed to David ten thousands, and to me they have ascribed
only thousands. Now *what* more can he have but the kingdom?" 9So Saul
eyed David from that day forward.
10And it happened on the next day that the distressing spirit from God
came upon Saul, and he prophesied inside the house. So David played *music* with his hand, as at other times; but *there was* a spear in Saul's hand.
11And Saul cast the spear, for he said, "I will pin David to the wall!" But David escaped his presence twice.
12Now Saul was afraid of David, because the LORD was with him, but had
departed from Saul. 13Therefore Saul removed him from his presence, and
made him his captain over a thousand; and he went out and came in before the people. 14And David behaved wisely in all his ways, and the LORD
was with him. 15Therefore, when Saul saw that he behaved very wisely, he
was afraid of him. 16But all Israel and Judah loved David, because he went
out and came in before them.

David Marries Michal

17Then Saul said to David, "Here is my older daughter Merab; I will give
her to you as a wife. Only be valiant for me, and fight the LORD's battles."
For Saul thought, "Let my hand not be against him, but let the hand of the
Philistines be against him."

18So David said to Saul, "Who *am* I, and what *is* my life *or* my father's family in Israel, that I should be son-in-law to the king?" 19But it happened at the time when Merab, Saul's daughter, should have been given to David, that she was given to Adriel the Meholathite as a wife.

20Now Michal, Saul's daughter, loved David. And they told Saul, and the thing pleased him. 21So Saul said, "I will give her to him, that she may be a snare to him, and that the hand of the Philistines may be against him." Therefore Saul said to David a second time, "You shall be my son-in-law today."

22And Saul commanded his servants, "Communicate with David secretly, and say, 'Look, the king has delight in you, and all his servants love you. Now therefore, become the king's son-in-law.' "

23So Saul's servants spoke those words in the hearing of David. And David said, "Does it seem to you *a* light *thing* to be a king's son-in-law, seeing I *am* a poor and lightly esteemed man?" 24And the servants of Saul told him, saying, "In this manner David spoke."

25Then Saul said, "Thus you shall say to David: 'The king does not desire any dowry but one hundred foreskins of the Philistines, to take vengeance on the king's enemies.' " But Saul thought to make David fall by the hand of the Philistines. 26So when his servants told David these words, it pleased David well to become the king's son-in-law. Now the days had not expired; 27therefore David arose and went, he and his men, and killed two hundred men of the Philistines. And David brought their foreskins, and they gave them in full count to the king, that he might become the king's son-in-law. Then Saul gave him Michal his daughter as a wife.

28Thus Saul saw and knew that the LORD *was* with David, and *that* Michal, Saul's daughter, loved him; 29and Saul was still more afraid of David. So Saul became David's enemy continually. 30Then the princes of the Philistines went out *to war.* And so it was, whenever they went out, *that* David behaved more wisely than all the servants of Saul, so that his name became highly esteemed.

Saul Persecutes David

19 Now Saul spoke to Jonathan his son and to all his servants, that they should kill David; but Jonathan, Saul's son, delighted greatly in David. 2So Jonathan told David, saying, "My father Saul seeks to kill you. Therefore please be on your guard until morning, and stay in a secret *place* and hide. 3And I will go out and stand beside my father in the field where you *are,* and I will speak with my father about you. Then what I observe, I will tell you."

4Thus Jonathan spoke well of David to Saul his father, and said to him, "Let not the king sin against his servant, against David, because he has not sinned against you, and because his works *have been* very good toward you. 5For he took his life in his hands and killed the Philistine, and the LORD brought about a great deliverance for all Israel. You saw *it* and rejoiced. Why then will you sin against innocent blood, to kill David without a cause?"

6So Saul heeded the voice of Jonathan, and Saul swore, "*As* the LORD lives, he shall not be killed." 7Then Jonathan called David, and Jonathan told him all these things. So Jonathan brought David to Saul, and he was in his presence as in times past.

8And there was war again; and David went out and fought with the Philistines, and struck them with a mighty blow, and they fled from him.

9Now the distressing spirit from the LORD came upon Saul as he sat in his house with his spear in his hand. And David was playing *music* with *his* hand. 10Then Saul sought to pin David to the wall with the spear, but he slipped away from Saul's presence; and he drove the spear into the wall. So David fled and escaped that night.

11Saul also sent messengers to David's house to watch him and to kill him in the morning. And Michal, David's wife, told him, saying, "If you do not save your life tonight, tomorrow you will be killed." 12So Michal let David down through a window. And he went and fled and escaped. 13And Michal took an image and laid *it* in the bed, put a cover of goats' *hair* for his head, and covered *it* with clothes. 14So when Saul sent messengers to take David, she said, "He *is* sick."

15Then Saul sent the messengers *back* to see David, saying, "Bring him up to me in the bed, that I may kill him." 16And when the messengers had come in, there was the image in the bed, with a cover of goats' *hair* for his head. 17Then Saul said to Michal, "Why have you deceived me like this, and sent my enemy away, so that he has escaped?"

And Michal answered Saul, "He said to me, 'Let me go! Why should I kill you?' "

18So David fled and escaped, and went to Samuel at Ramah, and told him all that Saul had done to him. And he and Samuel went and stayed in Naioth. 19Now

19:24 *t* Compare 1 Samuel 10:12

it was told Saul, saying, "Take note, David *is* at Naioth in Ramah!" [20]Then Saul sent messengers to take David. And when they saw the group of prophets prophesying, and Samuel standing *as* leader over them, the Spirit of God came upon the messengers of Saul, and they also prophesied. [21]And when Saul was told, he sent other messengers, and they prophesied likewise. Then Saul sent messengers again the third time, and they prophesied also. [22]Then he also went to Ramah, and came to the great well that *is* at Sechu. So he asked, and said, "Where *are* Samuel and David?"

And *someone* said, "Indeed *they are* at Naioth in Ramah." [23]So he went there to Naioth in Ramah. Then the Spirit of God was upon him also, and he went on and prophesied until he came to Naioth in Ramah. [24]And he also stripped off his clothes and prophesied before Samuel in like manner, and lay down naked all that day and all that night. Therefore they say, "*Is* Saul also among the prophets?"[t]

Jonathan's Loyalty to David

20 Then David fled from Naioth in Ramah, and went and said to Jonathan, "What have I done? What *is* my iniquity, and what *is* my sin before your father, that he seeks my life?"

[2]So Jonathan said to him, "By no means! You shall not die! Indeed, my father will do nothing either great or small without first telling me. And why should my father hide this thing from me? It *is* not *so!*"

[3]Then David took an oath again, and said, "Your father certainly knows that I have found favor in your eyes, and he has said, 'Do not let Jonathan know this, lest he be grieved.' But truly, *as* the LORD lives and *as* your soul lives, *there is* but a step between me and death."

[4]So Jonathan said to David, "Whatever you yourself desire, I will do *it* for you."

[5]And David said to Jonathan, "Indeed tomorrow *is* the New Moon, and I should not fail to sit with the king to eat. But let me go, that I may hide in the field until the third *day* at evening. [6]If your father misses me at all, then say, 'David earnestly asked *permission* of me that he might run over to Bethlehem, his city, for *there is* a yearly sacrifice there for all the family.' [7]If he says thus: '*It is* well,' your servant will be safe. But if he is very angry, be sure that evil is determined by him. [8]Therefore you shall deal kindly with your servant, for you have brought your servant into a covenant of the LORD with you. Nevertheless, if there is iniquity in me, kill me yourself, for why should you bring me to your father?"

[9]But Jonathan said, "Far be it from you! For if I knew certainly that evil was determined by my father to come upon you, then would I not tell you?"

[10]Then David said to Jonathan, "Who will tell me, or what *if* your father answers you roughly?"

[11]And Jonathan said to David, "Come, let us go out into the field." So both of them went out into the field. [12]Then Jonathan said to David: "The LORD God of Israel *is witness!* When I have sounded out my father sometime tomorrow, *or* the third *day,* and indeed *there is* good toward David, and I do not send to you and tell you, [13]may the LORD do so and much more to Jonathan. But if it pleases my father *to do* you evil, then I will report it to you and send you away, that you may go in safety. And the LORD be with you as He has been with my father. [14]And you shall not only show me the kindness of the LORD while I still live, that I may not die; [15]but you shall not cut off your kindness from my house forever, no, not when the LORD has cut off every one of the enemies of David from the face of the earth." [16]So Jonathan made *a covenant* with the house of David, *saying,* "Let the LORD require *it* at the hand of David's enemies."

[17]Now Jonathan again caused David to vow, because he loved him; for he loved him as he loved his own soul. [18]Then Jonathan said to David, "Tomorrow *is* the New Moon; and you will be missed, because your seat will be empty. [19]And *when* you have stayed three days, go down quickly and come to the place where you hid on the day of the deed; and remain by the stone Ezel. [20]Then I will shoot three arrows to the side, as though I shot at a target; [21]and there I will send a lad, *saying,* 'Go, find the arrows.' If I expressly say to the lad, 'Look, the arrows *are* on this side of you; get them and come'—then, as the LORD lives, *there is* safety for you and no harm. [22]But if I say thus to the young man, 'Look, the arrows *are* beyond you'—go your way, for the LORD has sent you away. [23]And as for the matter which you and I have spoken of, indeed the LORD *be* between you and me forever."

[24]Then David hid in the field. And when the New Moon had come, the king sat down to eat the feast. [25]Now the king sat on his seat, as at other times, on a seat by the wall. And Jonathan arose,[u] and Abner sat by Saul's side, but David's place was empty. [26]Nevertheless Saul did not say anything that day, for he thought, "Something has happened to him; he *is* un-

20:25 [u] Following Masoretic Text, Syriac, Targum, and Vulgate; Septuagint reads *he sat across from Jonathan.*

clean, surely he *is* unclean." 27And it happened the next day, the second *day*
of the month, that David's place was empty. And Saul said to Jonathan his
son, "Why has the son of Jesse not come to eat, either yesterday or today?"
28So Jonathan answered Saul, "David earnestly asked *permission* of me
to go to Bethlehem. 29And he said, 'Please let me go, for our family has a
sacrifice in the city, and my brother has commanded me *to be there.* And
now, if I have found favor in your eyes, please let me get away and see my
brothers.' Therefore he has not come to the king's table."
30Then Saul's anger was aroused against Jonathan, and he said to him,
"You son of a perverse, rebellious *woman!* Do I not know that you have
chosen the son of Jesse to your own shame and to the shame of your
mother's nakedness? 31For as long as the son of Jesse lives on the earth,
you shall not be established, nor your kingdom. Now therefore, send and
bring him to me, for he shall surely die."
32And Jonathan answered Saul his father, and said to him, "Why should
he be killed? What has he done?" 33Then Saul cast a spear at him to kill him,
by which Jonathan knew that it was determined by his father to kill David.
34So Jonathan arose from the table in fierce anger, and ate no food the
second day of the month, for he was grieved for David, because his father
had treated him shamefully.
35And so it was, in the morning, that Jonathan went out into the field at
the time appointed with David, and a little lad *was* with him. 36Then he
said to his lad, "Now run, find the arrows which I shoot." As the lad ran, he
shot an arrow beyond him. 37When the lad had come to the place where
the arrow was which Jonathan had shot, Jonathan cried out after the lad
and said, "*Is* not the arrow beyond you?" 38And Jonathan cried out after
the lad, "Make haste, hurry, do not delay!" So Jonathan's lad gathered up
the arrows and came back to his master. 39But the lad did not know anything. Only Jonathan and David knew of the matter. 40Then Jonathan gave
his weapons to his lad, and said to him, "Go, carry *them* to the city."
41As soon as the lad had gone, David arose from *a place* toward the
south, fell on his face to the ground, and bowed down three times. And
they kissed one another; and they wept together, but David more so.
42Then Jonathan said to David, "Go in peace, since we have both sworn in
the name of the LORD, saying, 'May the LORD be between you and me, and
between your descendants and my descendants, forever.' " So he arose
and departed, and Jonathan went into the city.

David and the Holy Bread

21 Now David came to Nob, to Ahimelech the priest. And Ahimelech
was afraid when he met David, and said to him, "Why *are* you alone,
and no one is with you?"
2So David said to Ahimelech the priest, "The king has ordered me on
some business, and said to me, 'Do not let anyone know anything about
the business on which I send you, or what I have commanded you.' And I
have directed *my* young men to such and such a place. 3Now therefore,
what have you on hand? Give *me* five *loaves of* bread in my hand, or whatever can be found."
4And the priest answered David and said, "*There is* no common bread
on hand; but there is holy bread, if the young men have at least kept themselves from women."

LIFE LESSON

1 Samuel 21:1–22:23

SITUATION David, pursued by Saul, sought rest at the town of Nob. Ahimelech the priest cared for David and his men. When Saul discovered David had been at Nob, he condemned the priests who aided David. Fearful of a conspiracy against himself, Saul ordered eighty-five priests killed and the town of Nob destroyed. Only one son of Ahimelech escaped to join David.

OBSERVATION Saul's fear and resentment of David caused him to stray farther from God, committing rash crimes. Saul chose to disregard God's plan and God's priests.

INSPIRATION Sharing your personal testimony may not necessarily be convicting.

I discovered this recently when talking with an acquaintance who happens to be a prominent journalist. . . .

It's wonderful that you've found peace and fulfillment through Jesus, he said in effect, but I don't believe in Jesus. He told me he had friends in the New Age movement who had found spirituality too; it had worked for them as well as Christ had "worked" for me.

So I shifted gears and began to talk about eternal life. This man had had some health problems in the past; surely he had done some thinking about his own mortality.

Again he cut me off. Death was simply the end, he said. When we die we are just like a tree or an animal: we return to the dust. No such thing as an afterlife.

I talked about the Bible. He put his hand up, palm outward. "All legends," he said firmly.

What could I say? He didn't care about God's plan for his life, getting into heaven, or what the Bible said.

Perhaps it's when we are caught short—when our canned answers don't work—that God uses us most effectively. For even as I was fumbling with my fork and my facts, an idea popped into my head.

"Have you seen Woody Allen's *Crimes and Misdemeanors*?" I asked.

He had, and we talked about it for a few minutes. Then, catching him off guard,

Continued

I asked, "Are you Judah Rosenthal?"

He laughed, but it was a nervous laugh.

"You may think this life is all there is," I said, "but if so, then there is still an issue at hand—how do you live with yourself while you're here? I know you have a conscience. So how do you deal with that when you know you do wrong?"

He picked at his food and told me that very issue gave him a lot of problems. Then somehow we moved into a discussion of Leo Tolstoy's novel, *War and Peace*, in which Pierre, the central character, cries out, *Why is it that I know what is right but do what is wrong*? That in turn led us to C.S. Lewis' concept of the natural law ingrained in all of us, and then to the central point of Romans 1: That we all are imbued with a conscience, run from it though we might, and that conscience itself points to questions which can only be answered outside of ourselves.

I don't know what's going to happen to this friend. My hunch is he's going to come to Christ, because I believe the Holy Spirit is hounding him. But I know one thing: without Woody Allen, Leo Tolstoy, and C.S. Lewis, I wouldn't have found a common ground and language with which to discuss the spiritual realm.

What does this tell us? Well, first of all, it does not mean that we must all run out to the video store and rent *Crimes and Misdemeanors* or slog through *War and Peace*. But it does mean that to evangelize today we must address the human condition at its point of felt need—conscience, guilt, dealing with others, finding a purpose for staying alive. Talking about the abundant life everlasting or Bible promises often just won't do it.

(From *The Body* by Charles Colson)

APPLICATION Sometimes our anger or fear causes us to act rashly and to displease God. Such acts separate us from our eternal Father and strain our relationship with him. What did you fear or get angry about yesterday? Repent and ask for God's forgiveness.

EXPLORATION Separation—Isaiah 1:4-9; 2 Thessalonians 1:7-9; Revelation 14:11.

5 Then David answered the priest, and said to him, "Truly, women *have been* kept from us about three days since I came out. And the vessels of the young men are holy, and *the bread is* in effect common, even though it was consecrated in the vessel this day."
6 So the priest gave him holy *bread;* for there was no bread there but the showbread which had been taken from before the LORD, in order to put hot bread *in its place* on the day when it was taken away.
7 Now a certain man of the servants of Saul *was* there that day, detained before the LORD. And his name *was* Doeg, an Edomite, the chief of the herdsmen who *belonged* to Saul.
8 And David said to Ahimelech, "Is there not here on hand a spear or a sword? For I have brought neither my sword nor my weapons with me, because the king's business required haste."
9 So the priest said, "The sword of Goliath the Philistine, whom you killed in the Valley of Elah, there it is, wrapped in a cloth behind the ephod. If you will take that, take *it*. For *there is* no other except that one here."
And David said, "*There is* none like it; give it to me."

David Flees to Gath

10 Then David arose and fled that day from before Saul, and went to
Achish the king of Gath. 11 And the servants of Achish said to him, "*Is* this
not David the king of the land? Did they not sing of him to one another in dances, saying:

'Saul has slain his thousands,
And David his ten thousands'?"[v]

12 Now David took these words to heart, and was very much afraid of
Achish the king of Gath. 13 So he changed his behavior before them, pretended madness in their hands, scratched on the doors of the gate, and let
his saliva fall down on his beard. 14 Then Achish said to his servants,
"Look, you see the man is insane. Why have you brought him to me?
15 Have I need of madmen, that you have brought this *fellow* to play the madman in my presence? Shall this *fellow* come into my house?"

David's Four Hundred Men

22 David therefore departed from there and escaped to the cave of Adullam. So when his brothers and all his father's house heard *it*,
they went down there to him. 2 And everyone *who was* in distress, everyone
who *was* in debt, and everyone *who was* discontented gathered to him. So he became captain over them. And there were about four hundred men with him.
3 Then David went from there to Mizpah of Moab; and he said to the king of Moab, "Please let my father and mother come here with you, till I know
what God will do for me." 4 So he brought them before the king of Moab, and they dwelt with him all the time that David was in the stronghold.
5 Now the prophet Gad said to David, "Do not stay in the stronghold; depart, and go to the land of Judah." So David departed and went into the forest of Hereth.

21:11 [v] Compare 1 Samuel 18:7

Saul Murders the Priests

6When Saul heard that David and the men who
were with him had been discovered—now Saul was
staying in Gibeah under a tamarisk tree in Ramah,
with his spear in his hand, and all his servants standing about him— 7then Saul said to his servants who
stood about him, "Hear now, you Benjamites! Will the
son of Jesse give every one of you fields and vineyards, *and* make you all captains of thousands and
captains of hundreds? 8All of you have conspired
against me, and *there is* no one who reveals to me that
my son has made a covenant with the son of Jesse;
and *there is* not one of you who is sorry for me or reveals to me that my son has stirred up my servant
against me, to lie in wait, as *it is* this day."
9Then answered Doeg the Edomite, who was set
over the servants of Saul, and said, "I saw the son of
Jesse going to Nob, to Ahimelech the son of Ahitub.
10And he inquired of the LORD for him, gave him
provisions, and gave him the sword of Goliath the
Philistine."
11So the king sent to call Ahimelech the priest, the
son of Ahitub, and all his father's house, the priests
who *were* in Nob. And they all came to the king. 12And
Saul said, "Hear now, son of Ahitub!"
He answered, "Here I am, my lord."
13Then Saul said to him, "Why have you conspired
against me, you and the son of Jesse, in that you have
given him bread and a sword, and have inquired of
God for him, that he should rise against me, to lie in
wait, as it is this day?"
14So Ahimelech answered the king and said, "And
who among all your servants *is as* faithful as David,
who is the king's son-in-law, who goes at your bidding, and is honorable in your house? 15Did I then
begin to inquire of God for him? Far be it from me! Let
not the king impute anything to his servant, *or* to any
in the house of my father. For your servant knew
nothing of all this, little or much."
16And the king said, "You shall surely die, Ahimelech, you and all your father's house!" 17Then the
king said to the guards who stood about him, "Turn
and kill the priests of the LORD, because their hand
also *is* with David, and because they knew when he
fled and did not tell it to me." But the servants of the
king would not lift their hands to strike the priests of
the LORD. 18And the king said to Doeg, "You turn and
kill the priests!" So Doeg the Edomite turned and
struck the priests, and killed on that day eighty-five
men who wore a linen ephod. 19Also Nob, the city of
the priests, he struck with the edge of the sword, both
men and women, children and nursing infants, oxen
and donkeys and sheep—with the edge of the sword.
20Now one of the sons of Ahimelech the son of
Ahitub, named Abiathar, escaped and fled after David. 21And Abiathar told David that Saul had killed the
LORD's priests. 22So David said to Abiathar, "I knew
that day, when Doeg the Edomite *was* there, that he
would surely tell Saul. I have caused *the death* of all
the persons of your father's house. 23Stay with me; do
not fear. For he who seeks my life seeks your life, but
with me you *shall be* safe."

David Saves the City of Keilah

23 Then they told David, saying, "Look, the
Philistines are fighting against Keilah, and
they are robbing the threshing floors."
2Therefore David inquired of the LORD, saying,
"Shall I go and attack these Philistines?"
And the LORD said to David, "Go and attack the
Philistines, and save Keilah."
3But David's men said to him, "Look, we are afraid
here in Judah. How much more then if we go to Keilah
against the armies of the Philistines?" 4Then David inquired of the LORD once again.
And the LORD answered him and said, "Arise, go
down to Keilah. For I will deliver the Philistines into
your hand." 5And David and his men went to Keilah
and fought with the Philistines, struck them with a
mighty blow, and took away their livestock. So David
saved the inhabitants of Keilah.
6Now it happened, when Abiathar the son of
Ahimelech fled to David at Keilah, *that* he went down
with an ephod in his hand.
7And Saul was told that David had gone to Keilah.
So Saul said, "God has delivered him into my hand,
for he has shut himself in by entering a town that has
gates and bars." 8Then Saul called all the people together for war, to go down to Keilah to besiege David
and his men.
9When David knew that Saul plotted evil against
him, he said to Abiathar the priest, "Bring the ephod
here." 10Then David said, "O LORD God of Israel, Your
servant has certainly heard that Saul seeks to come to
Keilah to destroy the city for my sake. 11Will the men
of Keilah deliver me into his hand? Will Saul come
down, as Your servant has heard? O LORD God of Israel, I pray, tell Your servant."
And the LORD said, "He will come down."
12Then David said, "Will the men of Keilah deliver
me and my men into the hand of Saul?"

LIFE LESSON

1 Samuel 23:1–24:22

SITUATION David, hotly pursued by King Saul, proved his honorable motivations by *not* killing Saul in the cave. Although his own men pressured him, he would not kill God's king.

OBSERVATION By maintaining right priorities in life, you can withstand the fiery trials and temptations.

INSPIRATION "Careful!" the craftsman exclaimed. "Please don't touch the pottery on that shelf. You'll ruin it." Then he surprised us when he said, "Why don't you touch the ones on the other shelf?" Needless to say, we were curious as to why some vases could be touched and not others.

Glancing at the "do-not-touch" shelf, he explained, "These haven't been fired yet." The potter told us then that there was more to masterpieces than just making blobs into beautiful shapes. If he stopped at that point, they would quickly be marred and misshapen. Without the fire, the potter's work is still beautiful, but too fragile.

The other vases could be touched because they had twice been baked in his kiln at temperatures of more than 2,000 degrees! "The fire makes the

And the LORD said, "They will deliver *you.*"
13So David and his men, about six hundred, arose and departed from
Keilah and went wherever they could go. Then it was told Saul that David
had escaped from Keilah; so he halted the expedition.

David in Wilderness Strongholds

14And David stayed in strongholds in the wilderness, and remained in
the mountains in the Wilderness of Ziph. Saul sought him every day, but
God did not deliver him into his hand. 15So David saw that Saul had come
out to seek his life. And David *was* in the Wilderness of Ziph in a forest.[w]
16Then Jonathan, Saul's son, arose and went to David in the woods and
strengthened his hand in God. 17And he said to him, "Do not fear, for the
hand of Saul my father shall not find you. You shall be king over Israel, and
I shall be next to you. Even my father Saul knows that." 18So the two of
them made a covenant before the LORD. And David stayed in the woods,
and Jonathan went to his own house.
19Then the Ziphites came up to Saul at Gibeah, saying, "Is David not hiding with us in strongholds in the woods, in the hill of Hachilah, which *is* on
the south of Jeshimon? 20Now therefore, O king, come down according to
all the desire of your soul to come down; and our part *shall be* to deliver
him into the king's hand."
21And Saul said, "Blessed *are* you of the LORD, for you have compassion
on me. 22Please go and find out for sure, and see the place where his hideout is, *and* who has seen him there. For I am told he is very crafty. 23See
therefore, and take knowledge of all the lurking places where he hides; and
come back to me with certainty, and I will go with you. And it shall be, if he
is in the land, that I will search for him throughout all the clans[x] of Judah."
24So they arose and went to Ziph before Saul. But David and his men
were in the Wilderness of Maon, in the plain on the south of Jeshimon.
25When Saul and his men went to seek *him,* they told David. Therefore he
went down to the rock, and stayed in the Wilderness of Maon. And when
Saul heard *that,* he pursued David in the Wilderness of Maon. 26Then Saul
went on one side of the mountain, and David and his men on the other
side of the mountain. So David made haste to get away from Saul, for Saul
and his men were encircling David and his men to take them.
27But a messenger came to Saul, saying, "Hurry and come, for the
Philistines have invaded the land!" 28Therefore Saul returned from pursuing David, and went against the Philistines; so they called that place the
Rock of Escape.[y] 29Then David went up from there and dwelt in strongholds at En Gedi.

David Spares Saul

24 Now it happened, when Saul had returned from following the
Philistines, that it was told him, saying, "Take note! David *is* in the
Wilderness of En Gedi." 2Then Saul took three thousand chosen men
from all Israel, and went to seek David and his men on the Rocks of the
Wild Goats. 3So he came to the sheepfolds by the road, where there *was* a
cave; and Saul went in to attend to his needs. (David and his men were
staying in the recesses of the cave.) 4Then the men of David said to him,

23:15 [w] Or *in Horesh*
23:23 [x] Literally *thousands*
23:28 [y] Hebrew *Sela Hammahlekoth*

"This is the day of which the LORD said to you, 'Behold, I will deliver your
enemy into your hand, that you may do to him as it seems good to you.' "
And David arose and secretly cut off a corner of Saul's robe. 5Now it happened afterward that David's heart troubled him because he had cut Saul's
robe. 6And he said to his men, "The LORD forbid that I should do this thing
to my master, the LORD's anointed, to stretch out my hand against him,
seeing he *is* the anointed of the LORD." 7So David restrained his servants
with *these* words, and did not allow them to rise against Saul. And Saul got
up from the cave and went on *his* way.
8David also arose afterward, went out of the cave, and called out to Saul,
saying, "My lord the king!" And when Saul looked behind him, David
stooped with his face to the earth, and bowed down. 9And David said to
Saul: "Why do you listen to the words of men who say, 'Indeed David
seeks your harm'? 10Look, this day your eyes have seen that the LORD delivered you today into my hand in the cave, and *someone* urged *me* to kill
you. But *my eye* spared you, and I said, 'I will not stretch out my hand
against my lord, for he *is* the LORD's anointed.' 11Moreover, my father, see!
Yes, see the corner of your robe in my hand! For in that I cut off the corner
of your robe, and did not kill you, know and see that *there is* neither evil
nor rebellion in my hand, and I have not sinned against you. Yet you hunt
my life to take it. 12Let the LORD judge between you and me, and let the
LORD avenge me on you. But my hand shall not be against you. 13As the
proverb of the ancients says, 'Wickedness proceeds from the wicked.' But
my hand shall not be against you. 14After whom has the king of Israel
come out? Whom do you pursue? A dead dog? A flea? 15Therefore let the
LORD be judge, and judge between you and me, and see and plead my case,
and deliver me out of your hand."
16So it was, when David had finished speaking these words to Saul, that
Saul said, "*Is* this your voice, my son David?" And Saul lifted up his voice
and wept. 17Then he said to David: "You *are* more righteous than I; for you
have rewarded me with good, whereas I have rewarded you with evil.
18And you have shown this day how you have dealt well with me; for when
the LORD delivered me into your hand, you did not kill me. 19For if a man
finds his enemy, will he let him get away safely? Therefore may the LORD
reward you with good for what you have done to me this day. 20And now I
know indeed that you shall surely be king, and that the kingdom of Israel
shall be established in your hand. 21Therefore swear now to me by the LORD
that you will not cut off my descendants after me, and that you will not destroy my name from my father's house."
22So David swore to Saul. And Saul went home, but David and his men
went up to the stronghold.

Death of Samuel

25 Then Samuel died; and the Israelites gathered together and lamented for him, and buried him at his home in Ramah. And David
arose and went down to the Wilderness of Paran.[z]

David and the Wife of Nabal

2Now *there was* a man in Maon whose business *was* in Carmel, and the
man *was* very rich. He had three thousand sheep and a thousand goats.

25:1 [z] Following Masoretic Text, Syriac, Targum, and Vulgate; Septuagint reads *Maon.*

clay firm and strong," our host concluded. "Fire makes the beauty last."

That was the trigger. My thoughts raced to Peter's words: "All kinds of trials . . . have come so that your faith—of greater worth than gold, which perishes even though refined by fire—may be proved genuine." (1 Peter 1:6-7).

Both Peter and the potter were talking to me about a fire that increases the value of something precious. Having spent my adult years in an oven—a pressure cooker to be exact—I knew about fire. Much of it could be traced to my overheated schedule and overcommitted lifestyle. That heat was my own fault.

But there is another fire that comes, not from me, but from the Master Potter. There is, to be sure, a heat that burns, and another heat that beautifies.

(From *Peaceful Living in a Stressful World* by Ron Hutchcraft)

APPLICATION Grow a plant in an earthenware pot. Let it serve as a reminder that in the midst of stress, "there is a heat that beautifies." Praise God for his gracious help while growing in your spiritual walk.

EXPLORATION Peace—John 14:27; Galatians 5:22. Pressure—Philippians 3:12-14.

LIFE LESSON

1 Samuel 25:1–26:25

SITUATION As an outcast, David lived by his wits in order to evade death at the hands of King Saul. During this time, David went to Nabal (a rich man he had aided in the past) for help. Nabal insulted David and his men, but through Abigail, Nabal's wife, God constrained David from killing Nabal. David had an opportunity to kill Saul but respected his position instead.

OBSERVATION God leads us through difficult moral choices and personal hardships to train us for leadership in his kingdom.

INSPIRATION Some Christians have been taught that all one has to do to get things from God is to speak the word of faith, believe, and receive. That comes close to the truth, but it neglects the universal Law of Perseverance. God slowly yields the good things of the kingdom and the world to those who struggle. Jacob, for instance, wrestled all night with an angel before he became Israel, a prince with God. Abraham waited a hundred years before he received Isaac, the child of promise. The people of Judah waited and struggled seventy years in captivity before God brought them home.

And he was shearing his sheep in Carmel. 3The name of the man *was*
Nabal, and the name of his wife Abigail. And *she was* a woman of good understanding and beautiful appearance; but the man *was* harsh and evil in
his doings. He *was of the house of* Caleb.
4When David heard in the wilderness that Nabal was shearing his sheep,
5David sent ten young men; and David said to the young men, "Go up to
Carmel, go to Nabal, and greet him in my name. 6And thus you shall say to
him who lives *in prosperity:* 'Peace *be* to you, peace to your house, and
peace to all that you have! 7Now I have heard that you have shearers. Your
shepherds were with us, and we did not hurt them, nor was there anything
missing from them all the while they were in Carmel. 8Ask your young
men, and they will tell you. Therefore let *my* young men find favor in your
eyes, for we come on a feast day. Please give whatever comes to your hand
to your servants and to your son David.' "
9So when David's young men came, they spoke to Nabal according to all
these words in the name of David, and waited.
10Then Nabal answered David's servants, and said, "Who *is* David, and
who *is* the son of Jesse? There are many servants nowadays who break
away each one from his master. 11Shall I then take my bread and my water
and my meat that I have killed for my shearers, and give *it* to men when I
do not know where they *are* from?"
12So David's young men turned on their heels and went back; and they
came and told him all these words. 13Then David said to his men, "Every
man gird on his sword." So every man girded on his sword, and David
also girded on his sword. And about four hundred men went with David,
and two hundred stayed with the supplies.
14Now one of the young men told Abigail, Nabal's wife, saying, "Look,
David sent messengers from the wilderness to greet our master; and he reviled them. 15But the men *were* very good to us, and we were not hurt, nor
did we miss anything as long as we accompanied them, when we were in
the fields. 16They were a wall to us both by night and day, all the time we
were with them keeping the sheep. 17Now therefore, know and consider
what you will do, for harm is determined against our master and against all
his household. For he *is such* a scoundrel[a] that *one* cannot speak to him."
18Then Abigail made haste and took two hundred *loaves* of bread, two
skins of wine, five sheep already dressed, five seahs of roasted *grain,* one
hundred clusters of raisins, and two hundred cakes of figs, and loaded
them on donkeys. 19And she said to her servants, "Go on before me; see, I
am coming after you." But she did not tell her husband Nabal.
20So it was, *as* she rode on the donkey, that she went down under cover
of the hill; and there were David and his men, coming down toward her,
and she met them. 21Now David had said, "Surely in vain I have protected
all that this *fellow* has in the wilderness, so that nothing was missed of all
that *belongs* to him. And he has repaid me evil for good. 22May God do so,
and more also, to the enemies of David, if I leave one male of all who *be-*
long to him by morning light."
23Now when Abigail saw David, she dismounted quickly from the donkey, fell on her face before David, and bowed down to the ground. 24So she
fell at his feet and said: "On me, my lord, *on* me *let* this iniquity *be!* And

25:17 [a] Literally *son of Belial*

please let your maidservant speak in your ears, and hear the words of your
maidservant. [25]Please, let not my lord regard this scoundrel Nabal. For as
his name *is,* so *is* he: Nabal[b] *is* his name, and folly *is* with him! But I, your
maidservant, did not see the young men of my lord whom you sent. [26]Now
therefore, my lord, *as* the LORD lives and *as* your soul lives, since the LORD
has held you back from coming to bloodshed and from avenging yourself
with your own hand, now then, let your enemies and those who seek harm
for my lord be as Nabal. [27]And now this present which your maidservant
has brought to my lord, let it be given to the young men who follow my
lord. [28]Please forgive the trespass of your maidservant. For the LORD will
certainly make for my lord an enduring house, because my lord fights the
battles of the LORD, and evil is not found in you throughout your days. [29]Yet
a man has risen to pursue you and seek your life, but the life of my lord
shall be bound in the bundle of the living with the LORD your God; and the
lives of your enemies He shall sling out, *as from* the pocket of a sling. [30]And
it shall come to pass, when the LORD has done for my lord according to all
the good that He has spoken concerning you, and has appointed you ruler
over Israel, [31]that this will be no grief to you, nor offense of heart to my
lord, either that you have shed blood without cause, or that my lord has
avenged himself. But when the LORD has dealt well with my lord, then remember your maidservant."

[32]Then David said to Abigail: "Blessed *is* the LORD God of Israel, who
sent you this day to meet me! [33]And blessed *is* your advice and blessed *are*
you, because you have kept me this day from coming to bloodshed and
from avenging myself with my own hand. [34]For indeed, *as* the LORD God of
Israel lives, who has kept me back from hurting you, unless you had hurried and come to meet me, surely by morning light no males would have
been left to Nabal!" [35]So David received from her hand what she had
brought him, and said to her, "Go up in peace to your house. See, I have
heeded your voice and respected your person."

[36]Now Abigail went to Nabal, and there he was, holding a feast in his
house, like the feast of a king. And Nabal's heart *was* merry within him, for
he *was* very drunk; therefore she told him nothing, little or much, until
morning light. [37]So it was, in the morning, when the wine had gone from
Nabal, and his wife had told him these things, that his heart died within
him, and he became *like* a stone. [38]Then it happened, *after* about ten days,
that the LORD struck Nabal, and he died.

[39]So when David heard that Nabal was dead, he said, "Blessed *be* the
LORD, who has pleaded the cause of my reproach from the hand of Nabal,
and has kept His servant from evil! For the LORD has returned the wickedness of Nabal on his own head."

And David sent and proposed to Abigail, to take her as his wife. [40]When
the servants of David had come to Abigail at Carmel, they spoke to her saying, "David sent us to you, to ask you to become his wife."

[41]Then she arose, bowed her face to the earth, and said, "Here is your
maidservant, a servant to wash the feet of the servants of my lord." [42]So
Abigail rose in haste and rode on a donkey, attended by five of her maidens; and she followed the messengers of David, and became his wife. [43]Da-
vid also took Ahinoam of Jezreel, and so both of them were his wives.

25:25 [b] Literally *Fool*

This does not negate the necessity for asking in faith, the believing, and the receiving. But many times those steps are only the beginning of the process. The fulfillment may take years. . . .

Jesus knew men inside out. He knew our tendency to give up quickly, to become inconsistent and lackadaisical. Yet he pleaded with us to persist, in prayer and in all aspects of life. . . .

Keep on asking, he said, keep on seeking, and keep on knocking. Don't be afraid even to make a ruckus. God prefers persistence much more than slothfulness and indolence. He wants people who will travail and perhaps stumble a bit, but keep on going forward, just like a toddler who's trying to learn to walk. The child builds muscles and learns. One day he will run.

(From *The Secret Kingdom* by Pat Robertson)

APPLICATION What tasks are hard for you to finish? What attitudes make finishing difficult? Boredom? Indifference? Loneliness? Ask a close friend to be firm with you when your motivation falters. Pray for perseverance.

EXPLORATION Perseverance—Psalm 37:24; Proverbs 4:18; Jeremiah 32:40; 1 Corinthians 16:13; Hebrews 10:23.

44 But Saul had given Michal his daughter, David's wife, to Palti[c] the son of Laish, who *was* from Gallim.

David Spares Saul a Second Time

26 Now the Ziphites came to Saul at Gibeah, saying, "Is David not hiding in the hill of Hachilah, opposite Jeshimon?" 2 Then Saul arose and went down to the Wilderness of Ziph, having three thousand chosen men of Israel with him, to seek David in the Wilderness of Ziph. 3 And Saul encamped in the hill of Hachilah, which *is* opposite Jeshimon, by the road. But David stayed in the wilderness, and he saw that Saul came after him into the wilderness. 4 David therefore sent out spies, and understood that Saul had indeed come.

5 So David arose and came to the place where Saul had encamped. And David saw the place where Saul lay, and Abner the son of Ner, the commander of his army. Now Saul lay within the camp, with the people encamped all around him. 6 Then David answered, and said to Ahimelech the Hittite and to Abishai the son of Zeruiah, brother of Joab, saying, "Who will go down with me to Saul in the camp?"

And Abishai said, "I will go down with you."

7 So David and Abishai came to the people by night; and there Saul lay sleeping within the camp, with his spear stuck in the ground by his head. And Abner and the people lay all around him. 8 Then Abishai said to David, "God has delivered your enemy into your hand this day. Now therefore, please, let me strike him at once with the spear, right to the earth; and I will not *have to strike* him a second time!"

9 But David said to Abishai, "Do not destroy him; for who can stretch out his hand against the LORD's anointed, and be guiltless?" 10 David said furthermore, "*As* the LORD lives, the LORD shall strike him, or his day shall come to die, or he shall go out to battle and perish. 11 The LORD forbid that I should stretch out my hand against the LORD's anointed. But please, take now the spear and the jug of water that *are* by his head, and let us go." 12 So David took the spear and the jug of water *by* Saul's head, and they got away; and no man saw or knew *it* or awoke. For they *were* all asleep, because a deep sleep from the LORD had fallen on them.

13 Now David went over to the other side, and stood on the top of a hill afar off, a great distance *being* between them. 14 And David called out to the people and to Abner the son of Ner, saying, "Do you not answer, Abner?"

Then Abner answered and said, "Who *are* you, calling out to the king?"

15 So David said to Abner, "*Are* you not a man? And who *is* like you in Israel? Why then have you not guarded your lord the king? For one of the people came in to destroy your lord the king. 16 This thing that you have done *is* not good. *As* the LORD lives, you deserve to die, because you have not guarded your master, the LORD's anointed. And now see where the king's spear *is,* and the jug of water that *was* by his head."

17 Then Saul knew David's voice, and said, "*Is* that your voice, my son David?"

David said, "*It is* my voice, my lord, O king." 18 And he said, "Why does my lord thus pursue his servant? For what have I done, or what evil *is* in my hand? 19 Now therefore, please, let my lord the king hear the words of his servant: If the LORD has stirred you up against me, let Him accept an offering. But if *it is* the children of men, *may* they *be* cursed before the LORD, for they have driven me out this day from sharing in the inheritance of the LORD, saying, 'Go, serve other gods.' 20 So now, do not let my blood fall to the earth before the face of the LORD. For the king of Israel has come out to seek a flea, as when one hunts a partridge in the mountains."

21 Then Saul said, "I have sinned. Return, my son David. For I will harm you no more, because my life was precious in your eyes this day. Indeed I have played the fool and erred exceedingly."

22 And David answered and said, "Here is the king's spear. Let one of the young men come over and get it. 23 May the LORD repay every man *for* his righteousness and his faithfulness; for the LORD delivered you into *my* hand today, but I would not stretch out my hand against the LORD's anointed. 24 And indeed, as your life was valued much this day in my eyes, so let my life be valued much in the eyes of the LORD, and let Him deliver me out of all tribulation."

25 Then Saul said to David, "*May* you *be* blessed, my son David! You shall both do great things and also still prevail."

So David went on his way, and Saul returned to his place.

David Allied with the Philistines

27 And David said in his heart, "Now I shall perish someday by the hand of Saul. *There is* nothing better for me than that I should speedily escape to the land of the Philistines; and Saul will despair of me,

25:44 [c] Spelled *Paltiel* in 2 Samuel 3:15

to seek me anymore in any part of Israel. So I shall escape out of his
hand." 2Then David arose and went over with the six hundred men who
were with him to Achish the son of Maoch, king of Gath. 3So David dwelt
with Achish at Gath, he and his men, each man with his household, *and*
David with his two wives, Ahinoam the Jezreelitess, and Abigail the
Carmelitess, Nabal's widow. 4And it was told Saul that David had fled to
Gath; so he sought him no more.

5Then David said to Achish, "If I have now found favor in your eyes, let
them give me a place in some town in the country, that I may dwell there.
For why should your servant dwell in the royal city with you?" 6So Achish
gave him Ziklag that day. Therefore Ziklag has belonged to the kings of Judah to this day. 7Now the time that David dwelt in the country of the
Philistines was one full year and four months.

8And David and his men went up and raided the Geshurites, the Girzites,[d]
and the Amalekites. For those nations were the inhabitants of the land from
of old, as you go to Shur, even as far as the land of Egypt. 9Whenever David
attacked the land, he left neither man nor woman alive, but took away the
sheep, the oxen, the donkeys, the camels, and the apparel, and returned and
came to Achish. 10Then Achish would say, "Where have you made a raid
today?" And David would say, "Against the southern *area* of Judah, or
against the southern *area* of the Jerahmeelites, or against the southern *area*
of the Kenites." 11David would save neither man nor woman alive, to bring
news to Gath, saying, "Lest they should inform on us, saying, 'Thus David
did.' " And thus *was* his behavior all the time he dwelt in the country of the
Philistines. 12So Achish believed David, saying, "He has made his people
Israel utterly abhor him; therefore he will be my servant forever."

28 Now it happened in those days that the Philistines gathered their
armies together for war, to fight with Israel. And Achish said to David, "You assuredly know that you will go out with me to battle, you and
your men."

2So David said to Achish, "Surely you know what your servant can do."
And Achish said to David, "Therefore I will make you one of my chief
guardians forever."

Saul Consults a Medium

3Now Samuel had died, and all Israel had lamented for him and buried
him in Ramah, in his own city. And Saul had put the mediums and the
spiritists out of the land.

4Then the Philistines gathered together, and came and encamped at
Shunem. So Saul gathered all Israel together, and they encamped at Gilboa.
5When Saul saw the army of the Philistines, he was afraid, and his heart
trembled greatly. 6And when Saul inquired of the LORD, the LORD did not
answer him, either by dreams or by Urim or by the prophets.

7Then Saul said to his servants, "Find me a woman who is a medium,
that I may go to her and inquire of her."

And his servants said to him, "In fact, *there is* a woman who is a
medium at En Dor."

8So Saul disguised himself and put on other clothes, and he went, and
two men with him; and they came to the woman by night. And he said,

27:8 [d] Or *Gezrites*

LIFE LESSON

1 Samuel 27:1-12

SITUATION David knew that his life was in jeopardy as long as Saul was alive. David's problems drove him so far from his homeland and heritage that he resorted to an alliance with the Philistine king who allowed him to survive as an outlaw.

OBSERVATION Troubles and conflicts sometimes cause us to make accomodations we normally find unacceptable.

INSPIRATION Jesus said that out of the nature of the heart a man speaks. There's nothing like a good thump to reveal the nature of a heart. The true character of a person is seen not in momentary heroics, but in the thump-packed humdrum of day-to-day living. . . .

Begin by thanking God for thumps. I don't mean a half-hearted thank you. I mean a "rejoicing, jumping for joy" thank you from the bottom of your heart. Chances are that God is doing the thumping. And he's doing it for your own good. So every thump is a reminder that God is molding you. . . .

Beware of "thump-slump" times. Know your pressure periods. For me, Mondays are infamous for causing thump-slumps. Fridays can be just as bad. For all of us there are times during the week that we can anticipate an unusual amount of thumping. The best way to handle thump-slump times? Bolster yourself with extra prayer and don't give up.

Remember, no thump is disastrous. All thumps work for good if we are living for and obeying God.

(From *On the Anvil* by Max Lucado)

APPLICATION The problems and obstacles we encounter in life are meant to cultivate faith, wisdom, patience, and confidence. We can profit from facing such obstacles as we allow God to shape our character through them. What events today could bring obstacles into your path? Ask God to increase your faith through those difficulties.

EXPLORATION Trials—Job 23:10; Psalm 94:12; Proverbs 3:11; Romans 5:3; 1 Peter 1:7.

LIFE LESSON

1 Samuel 28:1-25

SITUATION Saul discovered the Philistines massing for an attack. Unsure of his ability to lead the nation to victory, Saul turned to the witch of En Dor for help.

OBSERVATION Sometimes, in a struggle to solve our problems, we are tempted to turn away from God's help. Saul's life demonstrated the disastrous results of seeking help by means of spiritual forces other than God.

INSPIRATION So there are external spiritual forces which are at work in this world, seeking to keep us from God and His will. . . .

And this is not just external to us. This battle goes on inside of us. . . . Maybe your sin is wrong sexual desires, pride, gluttony, laziness, or anger, or some other besetting sin. . . . But you feel the inner struggle. Sometimes you conclude just as Paul did in Romans 7:22-24. ["What a struggle!"]

But don't stop there! Note Paul's glorious conclusion in verse 25 and 8:2. . . . "Thanks be to God through Jesus Christ our Lord! . . . For the law of the Spirit of life in Christ Jesus has set you free from the law of sin and death."

(From *The Holy Spirit* by Billy Graham)

APPLICATION Pride, insecurity, and fear will rise up and assert themselves, prompting us to live independently of God. We must anticipate this temptation and resist, allowing faith in Christ to lead us toward God and all of his resources.

EXPLORATION Victory—Matthew 26:41; John 2:16; Romans 8:8; 1 Corinthians 15:50; Ephesians 6:12.

"Please conduct a séance for me, and bring up for me the one I shall name to you."

9Then the woman said to him, "Look, you know what Saul has done, how he has cut off the mediums and the spiritists from the land. Why then do you lay a snare for my life, to cause me to die?"

10And Saul swore to her by the LORD, saying, "*As* the LORD lives, no punishment shall come upon you for this thing."

11Then the woman said, "Whom shall I bring up for you?"

And he said, "Bring up Samuel for me."

12When the woman saw Samuel, she cried out with a loud voice. And the woman spoke to Saul, saying, "Why have you deceived me? For you *are* Saul!"

13And the king said to her, "Do not be afraid. What did you see?"

And the woman said to Saul, "I saw a spirit[e] ascending out of the earth."

14So he said to her, "What *is* his form?"

And she said, "An old man is coming up, and he *is* covered with a mantle." And Saul perceived that it *was* Samuel, and he stooped with *his* face to the ground and bowed down.

15Now Samuel said to Saul, "Why have you disturbed me by bringing me up?"

And Saul answered, "I am deeply distressed; for the Philistines make war against me, and God has departed from me and does not answer me anymore, neither by prophets nor by dreams. Therefore I have called you, that you may reveal to me what I should do."

16Then Samuel said: "So why do you ask me, seeing the LORD has departed from you and has become your enemy? 17And the LORD has done for Himself[f] as He spoke by me. For the LORD has torn the kingdom out of your hand and given it to your neighbor, David. 18Because you did not obey the voice of the LORD nor execute His fierce wrath upon Amalek, therefore the LORD has done this thing to you this day. 19Moreover the LORD will also deliver Israel with you into the hand of the Philistines. And tomorrow you and your sons *will be* with me. The LORD will also deliver the army of Israel into the hand of the Philistines."

20Immediately Saul fell full length on the ground, and was dreadfully afraid because of the words of Samuel. And there was no strength in him, for he had eaten no food all day or all night.

21And the woman came to Saul and saw that he was severely troubled, and said to him, "Look, your maidservant has obeyed your voice, and I have put my life in my hands and heeded the words which you spoke to me. 22Now therefore, please, heed also the voice of your maidservant, and let me set a piece of bread before you; and eat, that you may have strength when you go on *your* way."

23But he refused and said, "I will not eat."

So his servants, together with the woman, urged him; and he heeded their voice. Then he arose from the ground and sat on the bed. 24Now the woman had a fatted calf in the house, and she hastened to kill it. And she took flour and kneaded *it*, and baked unleavened bread from it. 25So she brought *it* before Saul and his servants, and they ate. Then they rose and went away that night.

28:13 [e] Hebrew *elohim*
28:17 [f] Or *him*, that is, David

The Philistines Reject David

29 Then the Philistines gathered together all their armies at Aphek, and
the Israelites encamped by a fountain which *is* in Jezreel. 2And the
lords of the Philistines passed in review by hundreds and by thousands,
but David and his men passed in review at the rear with Achish. 3Then the
princes of the Philistines said, "What *are* these Hebrews *doing here?*"
And Achish said to the princes of the Philistines, "*Is* this not David, the
servant of Saul king of Israel, who has been with me these days, or these
years? And to this day I have found no fault in him since he defected *to me.*"
4But the princes of the Philistines were angry with him; so the princes of
the Philistines said to him, "Make this fellow return, that he may go back
to the place which you have appointed for him, and do not let him go down
with us to battle, lest in the battle he become our adversary. For with what
could he reconcile himself to his master, if not with the heads of these men?
5*Is* this not David, of whom they sang to one another in dances, saying:

'Saul has slain his thousands,
And David his ten thousands'?"[g]

6Then Achish called David and said to him, "Surely, *as* the LORD lives,
you have been upright, and your going out and your coming in with me in
the army *is* good in my sight. For to this day I have not found evil in you
since the day of your coming to me. Nevertheless the lords do not favor
you. 7Therefore return now, and go in peace, that you may not displease
the lords of the Philistines."
8So David said to Achish, "But what have I done? And to this day what
have you found in your servant as long as I have been with you, that I may
not go and fight against the enemies of my lord the king?"
9Then Achish answered and said to David, "I know that you *are* as good
in my sight as an angel of God; nevertheless the princes of the Philistines
have said, 'He shall not go up with us to the battle.' 10Now therefore, rise
early in the morning with your master's servants who have come with you.[h]
And as soon as you are up early in the morning and have light, depart."
11So David and his men rose early to depart in the morning, to return to
the land of the Philistines. And the Philistines went up to Jezreel.

David's Conflict with the Amalekites

30 Now it happened, when David and his men came to Ziklag, on the
third day, that the Amalekites had invaded the South and Ziklag, attacked Ziklag and burned it with fire, 2and had taken captive the women
and those who *were* there, from small to great; they did not kill anyone,
but carried *them* away and went their way. 3So David and his men came to
the city, and there it was, burned with fire; and their wives, their sons, and
their daughters had been taken captive. 4Then David and the people who
were with him lifted up their voices and wept, until they had no more
power to weep. 5And David's two wives, Ahinoam the Jezreelitess, and
Abigail the widow of Nabal the Carmelite, had been taken captive. 6Now
David was greatly distressed, for the people spoke of stoning him, because

LIFE LESSON

1 Samuel 29:1-11

SITUATION David and his refugee warriors prepared to fight with the Philistines against Saul's army. But the Philistines feared David would turn traitor against them, and they refused his assistance.

OBSERVATION God helps us avoid situations that would divide our loyalties and break our hearts.

INSPIRATION "Give me a word picture to describe a relative in your life who really bugs you." . . .

"Tar baby in Brer Rabbit," someone responded. Everyone understood the reference except me. I didn't remember the story of Brer Rabbit. I asked for the short version. Wily Fox played a trick on Brer Rabbit. The fox made a doll out of tar and stuck it on the side of the road. When Rabbit saw the tar baby, he thought it was a person and stopped to visit.

It was a one-sided conversation. The tar baby's silence bothered the rabbit. . . . So in his frustration he hit the tar baby and stuck to it. He hit the tar baby again with the other hand and, you guessed it, the other hand got stuck.

"That's how we are with difficult relatives," my fable-using friend explained. "We're stuck to someone we can't communicate with." . . .

You've probably got a tar baby in your life, someone you can't talk to and can't walk away from. A mother who whines, an uncle who slurps his soup, or a sister who flaunts her figure. . . .

Tar-baby relationships—stuck together but falling apart. . . .

I can't assure you that your family will ever give you the blessing you seek, but I know God will. Let God give you what your family doesn't. If your earthly father doesn't affirm you, then let your heavenly Father take his place. . . .

(From *He Still Moves Stones* by Max Lucado)

APPLICATION God knows the pain of conflict with people close to us.

EXPLORATION God and Conflict—Genesis 13:5-9; Luke 12:51-53; John 14:27-29; Acts 15:37-39; Ephesians 4:25-32.

29:5 [g] Compare 1 Samuel 18:7
29:10 [h] Following Masoretic Text, Targum, and Vulgate; Septuagint adds *and go to the place which I have selected for you there; and set no bothersome word in your heart, for you are good before me. And rise on your way.*

LIFE LESSON

1 Samuel 30:1–31:13

SITUATION When his own village was raided by the Amalekites, David pursued the raiders. But first he averted a mutiny by his warriors and sought God's wisdom. After destroying the Amalekite band, David brought back the captured women, children, and plunder. He divided the plunder equally among those who had fought and those who had stayed behind. Elsewhere, Saul killed himself in a losing battle with the Philistines, who hung his headless body on a city wall as an insult to the defeated Israelites.

OBSERVATION In times of trouble, David turned to God for wisdom and help, while Saul consistently turned away from God, even at his death.

INSPIRATION You came home cranky because a deadline got moved up. She came home grumpy because the day care forgot to give your five-year-old her throat medicine. Each of you was wanting a little sympathy from the other, but neither got any. So there you sit at the dinner table—cranky and grumpy—with little Emily. Emily folds her hands to pray (as she has been taught), and the two of you bow your heads (but not your hearts) and listen. From where this prayer comes, God only knows.

"God, it's Emily. How are you? I'm fine, thank you. Mom and Dad are

the soul of all the people was grieved, every man for his sons and his
daughters. But David strengthened himself in the LORD his God.
[7]Then David said to Abiathar the priest, Ahimelech's son, "Please bring
the ephod here to me." And Abiathar brought the ephod to David. [8]So David inquired of the LORD, saying, "Shall I pursue this troop? Shall I overtake them?"

And He answered him, "Pursue, for you shall surely overtake *them* and without fail recover *all*."

[9]So David went, he and the six hundred men who *were* with him, and
came to the Brook Besor, where those stayed who were left behind. [10]But
David pursued, he and four hundred men; for two hundred stayed *behind*,
who were so weary that they could not cross the Brook Besor.

[11]Then they found an Egyptian in the field, and brought him to David;
and they gave him bread and he ate, and they let him drink water. [12]And
they gave him a piece of a cake of figs and two clusters of raisins. So when
he had eaten, his strength came back to him; for he had eaten no bread nor
drunk water for three days and three nights. [13]Then David said to him, "To
whom do you *belong*, and where *are* you from?"

And he said, "I *am* a young man from Egypt, servant of an Amalekite;
and my master left me behind, because three days ago I fell sick. [14]We
made an invasion of the southern *area* of the Cherethites, in the *territory*
which *belongs* to Judah, and of the southern *area* of Caleb; and we burned
Ziklag with fire."

[15]And David said to him, "Can you take me down to this troop?"

So he said, "Swear to me by God that you will neither kill me nor deliver me into the hands of my master, and I will take you down to this troop."

[16]And when he had brought him down, there they were, spread out over
all the land, eating and drinking and dancing, because of all the great spoil
which they had taken from the land of the Philistines and from the land of
Judah. [17]Then David attacked them from twilight until the evening of the
next day. Not a man of them escaped, except four hundred young men
who rode on camels and fled. [18]So David recovered all that the Amalekites
had carried away, and David rescued his two wives. [19]And nothing of
theirs was lacking, either small or great, sons or daughters, spoil or anything which they had taken from them; David recovered all. [20]Then David
took all the flocks and herds they had driven before those *other* livestock,
and said, "This *is* David's spoil."

[21]Now David came to the two hundred men who had been so weary that
they could not follow David, whom they also had made to stay at the Brook
Besor. So they went out to meet David and to meet the people who *were*
with him. And when David came near the people, he greeted them. [22]Then
all the wicked and worthless men[i] of those who went with David answered
and said, "Because they did not go with us, we will not give them *any* of the
spoil that we have recovered, except for every man's wife and children,
that they may lead *them* away and depart."

[23]But David said, "My brethren, you shall not do so with what the LORD
has given us, who has preserved us and delivered into our hand the troop
that came against us. [24]For who will heed you in this matter? But as his
part *is* who goes down to the battle, so *shall* his part *be* who stays by the

30:22 [i] Literally *men of Belial*

supplies; they shall share alike." [25]So it was, from that day forward; he
made it a statute and an ordinance for Israel to this day.
[26]Now when David came to Ziklag, he sent *some* of the spoil to the elders
of Judah, to his friends, saying, "Here is a present for you from the spoil of
the enemies of the LORD"— [27]to *those* who *were* in Bethel, *those* who *were*
in Ramoth of the South, *those* who *were* in Jattir, [28]*those* who *were* in Aroer,
those who *were* in Siphmoth, *those* who *were* in Eshtemoa, [29]*those* who *were*
in Rachal, *those* who *were* in the cities of the Jerahmeelites, *those* who *were* in
the cities of the Kenites, [30]*those* who *were* in Hormah, *those* who *were* in
Chorashan,[j] *those* who *were* in Athach, [31]*those* who *were* in Hebron, and to
all the places where David himself and his men were accustomed to rove.

The Tragic End of Saul and His Sons

31 Now the Philistines fought against Israel; and the men of Israel fled
from before the Philistines, and fell slain on Mount Gilboa. [2]Then
the Philistines followed hard after Saul and his sons. And the Philistines
killed Jonathan, Abinadab, and Malchishua, Saul's sons. [3]The battle became fierce against Saul. The archers hit him, and he was severely
wounded by the archers.
[4]Then Saul said to his armorbearer, "Draw your sword, and thrust me
through with it, lest these uncircumcised men come and thrust me through
and abuse me."
But his armorbearer would not, for he was greatly afraid. Therefore
Saul took a sword and fell on it. [5]And when his armorbearer saw that Saul
was dead, he also fell on his sword, and died with him. [6]So Saul, his three
sons, his armorbearer, and all his men died together that same day.
[7]And when the men of Israel who *were* on the other side of the valley,
and *those* who *were* on the other side of the Jordan, saw that the men of Israel had fled and that Saul and his sons were dead, they forsook the cities
and fled; and the Philistines came and dwelt in them. [8]So it happened the
next day, when the Philistines came to strip the slain, that they found Saul
and his three sons fallen on Mount Gilboa. [9]And they cut off his head and
stripped off his armor, and sent *word* throughout the land of the
Philistines, to proclaim *it in* the temple of their idols and among the people. [10]Then they put his armor in the temple of the Ashtoreths, and they
fastened his body to the wall of Beth Shan.[k]
[11]Now when the inhabitants of Jabesh Gilead heard what the Philistines
had done to Saul, [12]all the valiant men arose and traveled all night, and
took the body of Saul and the bodies of his sons from the wall of Beth
Shan; and they came to Jabesh and burned them there. [13]Then they took
their bones and buried *them* under the tamarisk tree at Jabesh, and fasted
seven days.

mad. I don't know why. We've got birds and toys and mash potatoes and each other. Maybe you can get them to stop being mad? Please do, or it's just gonna be you and me having any fun tonight. Amen."

The prayer is answered before it's finished, you both look up in the middle and laugh at the end and shake your heads and say you're sorry. And you both thank God for the little voice who reminded you about what matters.

That's what "lovebursts" do . . . Lovebursts. Spontaneous affection. Tender moments of radiant love. Ignited devotion. Explosions of tenderness . . . They remind you about what matters. A telegram delivered to the back door of the familiar, telling you to treasure the treasure you've got while you've got it. A whisper from an angel, or someone who sounds like one, reminding you that what you have is greater than what you want and that what is urgent is not always what matters.

(From *He Still Moves Stones* by Max Lucado)

APPLICATION How do you react to problems and pressures? Ask God to help you lighten up with laughter, forgiveness, and trust—that God will give you all the energy you need.

EXPLORATION Listening to God—Exodus 9:12; 1 Kings 19:11-13; Proverbs 1:23-28; Mark 4:9; Hebrews 2:1-3.

30:30 [j] Or *Borashan*
31:10 [k] Spelled *Beth Shean* in Joshua 17:11 and elsewhere

The Second Book of

SAMUEL

INTRODUCTION

King David.

In the first ten chapters of Second Samuel he can do no wrong. He is never defeated in battle. Never wrong in judgment. He begins his reign in prayer (2:1) and continues in faith. Enemies are subdued, the nation is unified, the capitol secured, and the boundary extends from six thousand to sixty thousand square miles.

But that is the first ten chapters.

Chapter eleven is a hinge on which hangs the cellar door. David opens it and down he falls. By the time he lands on the cellar floor, he is bruised, confused, and staring into the darkness.

You know what happened. On a lazy afternoon his wandering eyes found a forbidden maiden. Testosterone surged and evil urged so he summoned her, slept with her, and then sent her home.

A rendezvous. So fast. So impulsive. So passionate. So pregnant.

Rather than repent, he connives and lies and leaves a soldier dead and a widow weeping and all of us wondering: Is this the same David? Is this the shepherd? Is this the boy of faith? The man of prayer? Is this the man after God's own heart?

With time, confession comes and forgiveness is given, but the scars remain. Nathan's prophecy proves true: the sword never departed from David's house (12:10). Bloodshed stained his home from then on.

Some of the final words written about David are some of the saddest, "Now King David was old, advanced in years; and they put covers on him, but he could not get warm" (1 Kings 1:1).

Mark it down. Compromise chills the soul.

If only David hadn't opened that cellar door.

The Report of Saul's Death

Now it came to pass after the death of
Saul, when David had returned from
the slaughter of the Amalekites, and David had stayed two days in Ziklag, 2on the
third day, behold, it happened that a man came from
Saul's camp with his clothes torn and dust on his
head. So it was, when he came to David, that he fell to
the ground and prostrated himself.
3And David said to him, "Where have you come
from?"
So he said to him, "I have escaped from the camp of
Israel."
4Then David said to him, "How did the matter go?
Please tell me."
And he answered, "The people have fled from the
battle, many of the people are fallen and dead, and
Saul and Jonathan his son are dead also."
5So David said to the young man who told him,
"How do you know that Saul and Jonathan his son are
dead?"
6Then the young man who told him said, "As I happened by chance *to be* on Mount Gilboa, there was Saul,
leaning on his spear; and indeed the chariots and
horsemen followed hard after him. 7Now when he
looked behind him, he saw me and called to me. And I
answered, 'Here I am.' 8And he said to me, 'Who *are*
you?' So I answered him, 'I *am* an Amalekite.' 9He said
to me again, 'Please stand over me and kill me, for anguish has come upon me, but my life still *remains* in
me.' 10So I stood over him and killed him, because I was
sure that he could not live after he had fallen. And I took
the crown that *was* on his head and the bracelet that *was*
on his arm, and have brought them here to my lord."
11Therefore David took hold of his own clothes and
tore them, and *so did* all the men who *were* with him.
12And they mourned and wept and fasted until
evening for Saul and for Jonathan his son, for the people of the LORD and for the house of Israel, because
they had fallen by the sword.
13Then David said to the young man who told him,
"Where *are* you from?"
And he answered, "I *am* the son of an alien, an
Amalekite."
14So David said to him, "How was it you were not
afraid to put forth your hand to destroy the LORD's
anointed?" 15Then David called one of the young men
and said, "Go near, *and* execute him!" And he struck
him so that he died. 16So David said to him, "Your blood
is on your own head, for your own mouth has testified
against you, saying, 'I have killed the LORD's anointed.'"

The Song of the Bow

17Then David lamented with this lamentation over
Saul and over Jonathan his son, 18and he told *them* to
teach the children of Judah *the Song of* the Bow; indeed
it is written in the Book of Jasher:

19 "The beauty of Israel is slain on your
high places!
How the mighty have fallen!
20 Tell *it* not in Gath,
Proclaim *it* not in the streets of Ashkelon—
Lest the daughters of the Philistines rejoice,
Lest the daughters of the uncircumcised
triumph.

21 "O mountains of Gilboa,
Let there be no dew nor rain upon you,
Nor fields of offerings.
For the shield of the mighty is cast away there!
The shield of Saul, not anointed with oil.
22 From the blood of the slain,
From the fat of the mighty,
The bow of Jonathan did not turn back,
And the sword of Saul did not return empty.

23 "Saul and Jonathan *were* beloved and pleasant
in their lives,
And in their death they were not divided;
They were swifter than eagles,
They were stronger than lions.

24 "O daughters of Israel, weep over Saul,
Who clothed you in scarlet, with luxury;
Who put ornaments of gold on your apparel.

25 "How the mighty have fallen in the midst of the
battle!
Jonathan *was* slain in your high places.
26 I am distressed for you, my brother Jonathan;
You have been very pleasant to me;
Your love to me was wonderful,
Surpassing the love of women.

27 "How the mighty have fallen,
And the weapons of war perished!"

David Anointed King of Judah

2 It happened after this that David inquired of the
LORD, saying, "Shall I go up to any of the cities of
Judah?"
And the LORD said to him, "Go up."
David said, "Where shall I go up?"
And He said, "To Hebron."
2So David went up there, and his two wives also,

Ahinoam the Jezreelitess, and Abigail the widow of Nabal the Carmelite.
3And David brought up the men who *were* with him, every man with his
household. So they dwelt in the cities of Hebron.
4Then the men of Judah came, and there they anointed David king over
the house of Judah. And they told David, saying, "The men of Jabesh
Gilead *were the ones* who buried Saul." 5So David sent messengers to the
men of Jabesh Gilead, and said to them, "You *are* blessed of the LORD, for
you have shown this kindness to your lord, to Saul, and have buried him.
6And now may the LORD show kindness and truth to you. I also will repay
you this kindness, because you have done this thing. 7Now therefore, let
your hands be strengthened, and be valiant; for your master Saul is dead,
and also the house of Judah has anointed me king over them."

Ishbosheth Made King of Israel

8But Abner the son of Ner, commander of Saul's army, took Ishbosheth[a]
the son of Saul and brought him over to Mahanaim; 9and he made him
king over Gilead, over the Ashurites, over Jezreel, over Ephraim, over Benjamin, and over all Israel. 10Ishbosheth, Saul's son, *was* forty years old
when he began to reign over Israel, and he reigned two years. Only the
house of Judah followed David. 11And the time that David was king in
Hebron over the house of Judah was seven years and six months.

Israel and Judah at War

12Now Abner the son of Ner, and the servants of Ishbosheth the son of
Saul, went out from Mahanaim to Gibeon. 13And Joab the son of Zeruiah,
and the servants of David, went out and met them by the pool of Gibeon.
So they sat down, one on one side of the pool and the other on the other
side of the pool. 14Then Abner said to Joab, "Let the young men now arise
and compete before us."
And Joab said, "Let them arise."
15So they arose and went over by number, twelve from Benjamin, *followers* of Ishbosheth the son of Saul, and twelve from the servants of David. 16And each one grasped his opponent by the head and *thrust* his
sword in his opponent's side; so they fell down together. Therefore that
place was called the Field of Sharp Swords,[b] which *is* in Gibeon. 17So there
was a very fierce battle that day, and Abner and the men of Israel were
beaten before the servants of David.
18Now the three sons of Zeruiah were there: Joab and Abishai and
Asahel. And Asahel *was as* fleet of foot as a wild gazelle. 19So Asahel pursued Abner, and in going he did not turn to the right hand or to the left
from following Abner.
20Then Abner looked behind him and said, "*Are* you Asahel?"
He answered, "I *am*."
21And Abner said to him, "Turn aside to your right hand or to your left,
and lay hold on one of the young men and take his armor for yourself."
But Asahel would not turn aside from following him. 22So Abner said
again to Asahel, "Turn aside from following me. Why should I strike you
to the ground? How then could I face your brother Joab?" 23However, he refused to turn aside. Therefore Abner struck him in the stomach with the

2:8 [a] Called *Esh-Baal* in 1 Chronicles 8:33 and 9:39
2:16 [b] Hebrew *Helkath Hazzurim*

LIFE LESSON

2 Samuel 2:1–3:5

SITUATION When David was crowned king, conflict arose between those who had followed Saul and David's followers. God provided victory for David.

OBSERVATION David followed God's plan as well as he could. Even through dangers and distractions, God delivers on his promises.

INSPIRATION Citizenship of the Kingdom looks beyond this life. When this life comes to an end, when we die, life is not finished. There is a life to come. And the kind of life we have lived here will make all the difference to the kind of life we'll live in the world to come. In school we cannot move up to a higher class until we have faithfully done the work of a lower class. Unless we had faithfully done the tasks of the lower class we would not be fit for the higher tasks of the higher class. Life is like that. To die is like moving up to a higher class. . . . In that world to come we will be very directly in God's presence. That must mean that we can be happy there only if we have done God's will. And so to do God's will is not only the thing which brings us happiness in this life; it brings us happiness also in the life to come. That is why it is so important to become a citizen of the Kingdom. It is worth much to be happy in this life. It is worth still more to be useful to others; but it is worth most of all to find happiness in the life to come which is to last forever. And we can only find these things when our will is God's will and God's will is our will; that is, when we are really and truly citizens of his Kingdom.

(From *The King and the Kingdom* by William Barclay)

APPLICATION Are you discouraged by temporary setbacks? Remember that ultimate victory comes only in Christ when we will live with him forever. What areas of your life are too focused on this world's happiness? Consider God's ultimate plan and revise your goals.

EXPLORATION Obeying God—Leviticus 25:18; Acts 5:29; Ephesians 5:10-14.

LIFE LESSON
2 Samuel 3:6–4:12

SITUATION David welcomed Abner to join him in battle. All of his men did not share his enthusiasm, and Joab killed Abner. David sought justice for his murder.

OBSERVATION David not only battled the house of Saul, but battled sin. Leaders can suffer from sinful decisions others make.

INSPIRATION Real change is an inside job. You might alter things a day or two with money and systems, but the heart of the matter is and always will be, the matter of the heart.

Allow me to get specific. Our problem is sin. Not finances. Not budgets. Not overcrowded prisons or drug dealers. Our problem is sin. We are in rebellion against our Creator. We are separated from our Father. We are cut off from the source of life. A new president or policy won't fix that. It can only be solved by God.

That's why the Bible uses drastic terms like *conversion*, *repentance*, and *lost* and *found*. Society may renovate, but only God re-creates.

Here is a practical exercise to put this truth into practice. The next time alarms go off in your world, ask yourself three questions.

1. Is there any unconfessed sin in my life? . . .

2. Are there any unresolved conflicts in my world? . . .

3. Are there any unsurrendered worries in my heart? . . .

Alarms serve a purpose. They signal a problem. Sometimes the problem is out there. More often it's in here. So before you peek outside, take a good look inside.

(From *When God Whispers Your Name* by Max Lucado)

APPLICATION Ask yourself the three questions above. What alarms are sounding? Take a peek inside and turn those alarms off!

EXPLORATION Submission to God—Deuteronomy 4:29; 1 Chronicles 16:11; 22:19; Psalm 25:4; 27:4-14; Romans 6:13-20; 12:1-2; James 4:8.

blunt end of the spear, so that the spear came out of his back; and he fell down there and died on the spot. So it was *that* as many as came to the place where Asahel fell down and died, stood still.
24Joab and Abishai also pursued Abner. And the sun was going down when they came to the hill of Ammah, which *is* before Giah by the road to the Wilderness of Gibeon. 25Now the children of Benjamin gathered together behind Abner and became a unit, and took their stand on top of a hill. 26Then Abner called to Joab and said, "Shall the sword devour forever? Do you not know that it will be bitter in the latter end? How long will it be then until you tell the people to return from pursuing their brethren?"
27And Joab said, "*As* God lives, unless you had spoken, surely then by morning all the people would have given up pursuing their brethren." 28So Joab blew a trumpet; and all the people stood still and did not pursue Israel anymore, nor did they fight anymore. 29Then Abner and his men went on all that night through the plain, crossed over the Jordan, and went through all Bithron; and they came to Mahanaim.
30So Joab returned from pursuing Abner. And when he had gathered all the people together, there were missing of David's servants nineteen men and Asahel. 31But the servants of David had struck down, of Benjamin and Abner's men, three hundred and sixty men who died. 32Then they took up Asahel and buried him in his father's tomb, which *was in* Bethlehem. And Joab and his men went all night, and they came to Hebron at daybreak.

3 Now there was a long war between the house of Saul and the house of David. But David grew stronger and stronger, and the house of Saul grew weaker and weaker.

Sons of David

2Sons were born to David in Hebron: His firstborn was Amnon by Ahinoam the Jezreelitess; 3his second, Chileab, by Abigail the widow of Nabal the Carmelite; the third, Absalom the son of Maacah, the daughter of Talmai, king of Geshur; 4the fourth, Adonijah the son of Haggith; the fifth, Shephatiah the son of Abital; 5and the sixth, Ithream, by David's wife Eglah. These were born to David in Hebron.

Abner Joins Forces with David

6Now it was so, while there was war between the house of Saul and the house of David, that Abner was strengthening *his hold* on the house of Saul.
7And Saul had a concubine, whose name *was* Rizpah, the daughter of Aiah. So *Ishbosheth* said to Abner, "Why have you gone in to my father's concubine?"
8Then Abner became very angry at the words of Ishbosheth, and said, "*Am* I a dog's head that belongs to Judah? Today I show loyalty to the house of Saul your father, to his brothers, and to his friends, and have not delivered you into the hand of David; and you charge me today with a fault concerning this woman? 9May God do so to Abner, and more also, if I do not do for David as the LORD has sworn to him— 10to transfer the kingdom from the house of Saul, and set up the throne of David over Israel and over Judah, from Dan to Beersheba." 11And he could not answer Abner another word, because he feared him.
12Then Abner sent messengers on his behalf to David, saying, "Whose *is* the land?" saying *also,* "Make your covenant with me, and indeed my hand *shall be* with you to bring all Israel to you."

13And *David* said, "Good, I will make a covenant with you. But one thing I require of you: you shall not see my face unless you first bring Michal, Saul's daughter, when you come to see my face." 14So David sent messengers to Ishbosheth, Saul's son, saying, "Give *me* my wife Michal, whom I betrothed to myself for a hundred foreskins of the Philistines." 15And Ishbosheth sent and took her from *her* husband, from Paltiel[c] the son of Laish. 16Then her husband went along with her to Bahurim, weeping behind her. So Abner said to him, "Go, return!" And he returned.

17Now Abner had communicated with the elders of Israel, saying, "In time past you were seeking for David *to be* king over you. 18Now then, do *it!* For the LORD has spoken of David, saying, 'By the hand of My servant David, I[d] will save My people Israel from the hand of the Philistines and the hand of all their enemies.' " 19And Abner also spoke in the hearing of Benjamin. Then Abner also went to speak in the hearing of David in Hebron all that seemed good to Israel and the whole house of Benjamin.

20So Abner and twenty men with him came to David at Hebron. And David made a feast for Abner and the men who *were* with him. 21Then Abner said to David, "I will arise and go, and gather all Israel to my lord the king, that they may make a covenant with you, and that you may reign over all that your heart desires." So David sent Abner away, and he went in peace.

Joab Murders Abner

22At that moment the servants of David and Joab came from a raid and brought much spoil with them. But Abner *was* not with David in Hebron, for he had sent him away, and he had gone in peace. 23When Joab and all the troops that *were* with him had come, they told Joab, saying, "Abner the son of Ner came to the king, and he sent him away, and he has gone in peace." 24Then Joab came to the king and said, "What have you done? Look, Abner came to you; why *is* it *that* you sent him away, and he has already gone? 25Surely you realize that Abner the son of Ner came to deceive you, to know your going out and your coming in, and to know all that you are doing."

26And when Joab had gone from David's presence, he sent messengers after Abner, who brought him back from the well of Sirah. But David did not know *it.* 27Now when Abner had returned to Hebron, Joab took him aside in the gate to speak with him privately, and there stabbed him in the stomach, so that he died for the blood of Asahel his brother.

28Afterward, when David heard *it,* he said, "My kingdom and I *are* guiltless before the LORD forever of the blood of Abner the son of Ner. 29Let it rest on the head of Joab and on all his father's house; and let there never fail to be in the house of Joab one who has a discharge or is a leper, who leans on a staff or falls by the sword, or who lacks bread." 30So Joab and Abishai his brother killed Abner, because he had killed their brother Asahel at Gibeon in the battle.

David's Mourning for Abner

31Then David said to Joab and to all the people who were with him, "Tear your clothes, gird yourselves with sackcloth, and mourn for Abner." And King David followed the coffin. 32So they buried Abner in Hebron; and the king lifted up his voice and wept at the grave of Abner, and all the people wept. 33And the king sang *a lament* over Abner and said:

"Should Abner die as a fool dies?
34 Your hands were not bound
Nor your feet put into fetters;
As a man falls before wicked men, *so* you fell."

Then all the people wept over him again.

35And when all the people came to persuade David to eat food while it was still day, David took an oath, saying, "God do so to me, and more also, if I taste bread or anything else till the sun goes down!" 36Now all the people took note *of it,* and it pleased them, since whatever the king did pleased all the people. 37For all the people and all Israel understood that day that it had not been the king's *intent* to kill Abner the son of Ner. 38Then the king said to his servants, "Do you not know that a prince and a great man has fallen this day in Israel? 39And I *am* weak today, though anointed king; and these men, the sons of Zeruiah, *are* too harsh for me. The LORD shall repay the evildoer according to his wickedness."

Ishbosheth Is Murdered

4 When Saul's son[e] heard that Abner had died in Hebron, he lost heart, and all Israel was troubled. 2Now Saul's son *had* two men *who were* captains of troops. The name of one *was* Baanah and the name of the other Rechab, the sons of Rimmon the Beerothite, of the children of Benjamin. (For Beeroth also was *part* of Benjamin, 3because the Beerothites fled to Gittaim and have been sojourners there until this day.)

3:15 [c] Spelled *Palti* in 1 Samuel 25:44
3:18 [d] Following many Hebrew manuscripts, Septuagint, Syriac, and Targum; Masoretic Text reads *he.*
4:1 [e] That is, Ishbosheth

LIFE LESSON

2 Samuel 5:1–6:23

SITUATION At the beginning of David's reign, God enabled him to conquer Jerusalem and bring the Ark of God to this holy city. These accomplishments filled David with joy.

OBSERVATION Through the high and low points of our lives, God graciously provides for our needs. As we experience this, our lives can be filled with joyful expressions of praise to him.

INSPIRATION A heart filled with God's heart is free both to glorify and to enjoy God. There is no grimness in David's relationship with God. He could weep out his loneliness and fear to the Lord, but he could also dance with unrestrained fervor. When we love God with all our heart we can openly express our emotions to him, and then to others. He wants us to be real with him. When we are in the valley of despair or the mountain peaks of sublime joy, we can express it.

David's abandoned freedom to express his praise is contrasted with his wife Michal's reserve and contempt. . . . Michal was like her father Saul. Her emotional energy was not guided by firm beliefs about God's sovereignty and grace. There was little in her mind about God's loving-kindness, and therefore, little capacity of emotional delight in him. . . .

There are Michals in all our lives, people whose minds are starved for liberating truth about God and whose emotions are stunted by malnutrition of lively belief. The conviction of God's grace results in the expression of joy. . . . The tragedy of religion is that it produces more Michals than Davids. . . . A heart that has never felt God's presence in sorrow or pain will seldom express his delight in adoration and praise.

(From *Lord of the Impossible* by Lloyd John Ogilvie)

APPLICATION Keep a prayer journal. Be completely honest with God. Write down disappointments, then devote pages to successes.

EXPLORATION Joy—1 Thessalonians 5:16-22. Unity—Romans 15:5-6. Love—Romans 12:9-21.

4Jonathan, Saul's son, had a son *who was* lame in *his* feet. He was five
years old when the news about Saul and Jonathan came from Jezreel; and
his nurse took him up and fled. And it happened, as she made haste to
flee, that he fell and became lame. His name *was* Mephibosheth.[f]
5Then the sons of Rimmon the Beerothite, Rechab and Baanah, set out
and came at about the heat of the day to the house of Ishbosheth, who was
lying on his bed at noon. 6And they came there, all the way into the house,
as though to get wheat, and they stabbed him in the stomach. Then Rechab
and Baanah his brother escaped. 7For when they came into the house, he
was lying on his bed in his bedroom; then they struck him and killed him,
beheaded him and took his head, and were all night escaping through the
plain. 8And they brought the head of Ishbosheth to David at Hebron, and
said to the king, "Here is the head of Ishbosheth, the son of Saul your
enemy, who sought your life; and the LORD has avenged my lord the king
this day of Saul and his descendants."
9But David answered Rechab and Baanah his brother, the sons of
Rimmon the Beerothite, and said to them, "*As* the LORD lives, who has redeemed my life from all adversity, 10when someone told me, saying, 'Look,
Saul is dead,' thinking to have brought good news, I arrested him and had
him executed in Ziklag—the one who *thought* I would give him a reward
for *his* news. 11How much more, when wicked men have killed a righteous
person in his own house on his bed? Therefore, shall I not now require his
blood at your hand and remove you from the earth?" 12So David commanded his young men, and they executed them, cut off their hands and
feet, and hanged *them* by the pool in Hebron. But they took the head of
Ishbosheth and buried *it* in the tomb of Abner in Hebron.

David Reigns over All Israel

5 Then all the tribes of Israel came to David at Hebron and spoke, saying,
"Indeed we *are* your bone and your flesh. 2Also, in time past, when
Saul was king over us, you were the one who led Israel out and brought
them in; and the LORD said to you, 'You shall shepherd My people Israel,
and be ruler over Israel.' " 3Therefore all the elders of Israel came to the
king at Hebron, and King David made a covenant with them at Hebron before the LORD. And they anointed David king over Israel. 4David *was* thirty
years old when he began to reign, *and* he reigned forty years. 5In Hebron
he reigned over Judah seven years and six months, and in Jerusalem he
reigned thirty-three years over all Israel and Judah.

The Conquest of Jerusalem

6And the king and his men went to Jerusalem against the Jebusites, the
inhabitants of the land, who spoke to David, saying, "You shall not come
in here; but the blind and the lame will repel you," thinking, "David cannot come in here." 7Nevertheless David took the stronghold of Zion (that
is, the City of David).
8Now David said on that day, "Whoever climbs up by way of the water
shaft and defeats the Jebusites (the lame and the blind, *who are* hated by
David's soul), *he shall be chief and captain.*"[g] Therefore they say, "The blind
and the lame shall not come into the house."

4:4 [f]Called *Merib-Baal* in 1 Chronicles 8:34 and 9:40
5:8 [g]Compare 1 Chronicles 11:6

9Then David dwelt in the stronghold, and called it
the City of David. And David built all around from the
Millo[h] and inward. 10So David went on and became
great, and the LORD God of hosts *was* with him.
11Then Hiram king of Tyre sent messengers to David, and cedar trees, and carpenters and masons.
And they built David a house. 12So David knew that
the LORD had established him as king over Israel, and
that He had exalted His kingdom for the sake of His
people Israel.
13And David took more concubines and wives from
Jerusalem, after he had come from Hebron. Also
more sons and daughters were born to David. 14Now
these *are* the names of those who were born to him in
Jerusalem: Shammua,[i] Shobab, Nathan, Solomon,
15Ibhar, Elishua,[j] Nepheg, Japhia, 16Elishama, Eliada,
and Eliphelet.

The Philistines Defeated

17Now when the Philistines heard that they had
anointed David king over Israel, all the Philistines
went up to search for David. And David heard *of it*
and went down to the stronghold. 18The Philistines
also went and deployed themselves in the Valley of
Rephaim. 19So David inquired of the LORD, saying,
"Shall I go up against the Philistines? Will You deliver
them into my hand?"
And the LORD said to David, "Go up, for I will
doubtless deliver the Philistines into your hand."
20So David went to Baal Perazim, and David defeated them there; and he said, "The LORD has broken
through my enemies before me, like a breakthrough
of water." Therefore he called the name of that place
Baal Perazim.[k] 21And they left their images there, and
David and his men carried them away.
22Then the Philistines went up once again and deployed themselves in the Valley of Rephaim. 23There-
fore David inquired of the LORD, and He said, "You
shall not go up; circle around behind them, and come
upon them in front of the mulberry trees. 24And it
shall be, when you hear the sound of marching in the
tops of the mulberry trees, then you shall advance
quickly. For then the LORD will go out before you to
strike the camp of the Philistines." 25And David did
so, as the LORD commanded him; and he drove back
the Philistines from Geba[l] as far as Gezer.

The Ark Brought to Jerusalem

6 Again David gathered all *the* choice *men* of Israel,
thirty thousand. 2And David arose and went with
all the people who *were* with him from Baale Judah to
bring up from there the ark of God, whose name is
called by the Name,[m] the LORD of Hosts, who dwells
between the cherubim. 3So they set the ark of God on a
new cart, and brought it out of the house of
Abinadab, which *was* on the hill; and Uzzah and Ahio,
the sons of Abinadab, drove the new cart.[n] 4And they
brought it out of the house of Abinadab, which *was* on
the hill, accompanying the ark of God; and Ahio went
before the ark. 5Then David and all the house of Israel
played *music* before the LORD on all kinds of *instruments of* fir wood, on harps, on stringed instruments,
on tambourines, on sistrums, and on cymbals.
6And when they came to Nachon's threshing floor,
Uzzah put out his *hand* to the ark of God and took
hold of it, for the oxen stumbled. 7Then the anger of
the LORD was aroused against Uzzah, and God struck
him there for *his* error; and he died there by the ark of
God. 8And David became angry because of the LORD's
outbreak against Uzzah; and he called the name of the
place Perez Uzzah[o] to this day.
9David was afraid of the LORD that day; and he said,
"How can the ark of the LORD come to me?" 10So David
would not move the ark of the LORD with him into the
City of David; but David took it aside into the house of
Obed-Edom the Gittite. 11The ark of the LORD remained in
the house of Obed-Edom the Gittite three months. And
the LORD blessed Obed-Edom and all his household.
12Now it was told King David, saying, "The LORD has
blessed the house of Obed-Edom and all that *belongs* to
him, because of the ark of God." So David went and
brought up the ark of God from the house of Obed-
Edom to the City of David with gladness. 13And so it
was, when those bearing the ark of the LORD had gone
six paces, that he sacrificed oxen and fatted sheep.
14Then David danced before the LORD with all *his* might;
and David *was* wearing a linen ephod. 15So David and
all the house of Israel brought up the ark of the LORD
with shouting and with the sound of the trumpet.

5:9 [h] Literally *The Landfill*
5:14 [i] Spelled *Shimea* in 1 Chronicles 3:5
5:15 [j] Spelled *Elishama* in 1 Chronicles 3:6
5:20 [k] Literally *Master of Breakthroughs*
5:25 [l] Following Masoretic Text, Targum, and Vulgate; Septuagint reads *Gibeon.*
6:2 [m] Septuagint, Targum, and Vulgate omit *by the Name;* many Hebrew manuscripts and Syriac read *there.*
6:3 [n] Septuagint adds *with the ark.*
6:8 [o] Literally *Outburst Against Uzzah*

LIFE LESSON
2 Samuel 7:1-29

SITUATION David sought to honor God, and God rewarded him with promises for his future. David's response was humble, worshipful prayer.

OBSERVATION David not only knew about God, he fellowshiped with God. David shows us the value of knowing God better.

INSPIRATION Do we know Him? Do we know that God of Jesus Christ? Maybe we think that there are other things more important in the Christian walk than knowing God—like loving God, praising Him, thanking Him, keeping the commandments, living a good life. There are many things that make up a truly Christian life, but all of them are rooted in authentic knowledge of God.

Perhaps we think that because we are Christians and read the Bible and know a great deal *about* God, that therefore we know God. Nothing could be further from the truth. It does us little good to memorize chapter and verse, to master the language of the Bible, if we have nothing to share in that language, no *experiential knowledge* of God in our lives.

Maybe that doesn't happen because we pray so little, so infrequently, and so poorly. For everything else we have plenty of leisure time. Visits, get-togethers, movies, the Olympics, concerts, and evening with friends, an invitation we can't decline—and these things are good because it is right and natural to come together with friends. But most of our lives we are, as Søren Kierkegaard noted, "so busy" with other things that we don't have time to wait patiently to hear the

16Now as the ark of the LORD came into the City of David, Michal, Saul's
daughter, looked through a window and saw King David leaping and
whirling before the LORD; and she despised him in her heart. 17So they
brought the ark of the LORD, and set it in its place in the midst of the tabernacle that David had erected for it. Then David offered burnt offerings and
peace offerings before the LORD. 18And when David had finished offering
burnt offerings and peace offerings, he blessed the people in the name of
the LORD of hosts. 19Then he distributed among all the people, among the
whole multitude of Israel, both the women and the men, to everyone a loaf
of bread, a piece *of meat,* and a cake of raisins. So all the people departed,
everyone to his house.
20Then David returned to bless his household. And Michal the daughter
of Saul came out to meet David, and said, "How glorious was the king of
Israel today, uncovering himself today in the eyes of the maids of his servants, as one of the base fellows shamelessly uncovers himself!"
21So David said to Michal, "*It was* before the LORD, who chose me instead of your father and all his house, to appoint me ruler over the people
of the LORD, over Israel. Therefore I will play *music* before the LORD. 22And
I will be even more undignified than this, and will be humble in my own
sight. But as for the maidservants of whom you have spoken, by them I
will be held in honor."
23Therefore Michal the daughter of Saul had no children to the day of
her death.

God's Covenant with David

7 Now it came to pass when the king was dwelling in his house, and the
LORD had given him rest from all his enemies all around, 2that the king
said to Nathan the prophet, "See now, I dwell in a house of cedar, but the
ark of God dwells inside tent curtains."
3Then Nathan said to the king, "Go, do all that *is* in your heart, for the
LORD *is* with you."
4But it happened that night that the word of the LORD came to Nathan,
saying, 5"Go and tell My servant David, 'Thus says the LORD: "Would you
build a house for Me to dwell in? 6For I have not dwelt in a house since the
time that I brought the children of Israel up from Egypt, even to this day,
but have moved about in a tent and in a tabernacle. 7Wherever I have
moved about with all the children of Israel, have I ever spoken a word to
anyone from the tribes of Israel, whom I commanded to shepherd My
people Israel, saying, 'Why have you not built Me a house of cedar?' " '
8Now therefore, thus shall you say to My servant David, 'Thus says the
LORD of hosts: "I took you from the sheepfold, from following the sheep, to
be ruler over My people, over Israel. 9And I have been with you wherever
you have gone, and have cut off all your enemies from before you, and
have made you a great name, like the name of the great men who *are* on
the earth. 10Moreover I will appoint a place for My people Israel, and will
plant them, that they may dwell in a place of their own and move no more;
nor shall the sons of wickedness oppress them anymore, as previously,
11since the time that I commanded judges *to be* over My people Israel, and
have caused you to rest from all your enemies. Also the LORD tells you that
He will make you a house.[p]

7:11 [p] That is, a royal dynasty

12“When your days are fulfilled and you rest with your fathers, I will set
up your seed after you, who will come from your body, and I will establish
his kingdom. 13He shall build a house for My name, and I will establish the
throne of his kingdom forever. 14I will be his Father, and he shall be My
son. If he commits iniquity, I will chasten him with the rod of men and
with the blows of the sons of men. 15But My mercy shall not depart from
him, as I took *it* from Saul, whom I removed from before you. 16And your
house and your kingdom shall be established forever before you.[q] Your
throne shall be established forever.” ’ ”

17According to all these words and according to all this vision, so Nathan spoke to David.

David’s Thanksgiving to God

18Then King David went in and sat before the LORD; and he said: “Who
am I, O Lord GOD? And what is my house, that You have brought me this
far? 19And yet this was a small thing in Your sight, O Lord GOD; and You
have also spoken of Your servant’s house for a great while to come. *Is* this
the manner of man, O Lord GOD? 20Now what more can David say to You?
For You, Lord GOD, know Your servant. 21For Your word’s sake, and according to Your own heart, You have done all these great things, to make
Your servant know *them.* 22Therefore You are great, O Lord GOD.[r] For *there*
is none like You, nor *is there any* God besides You, according to all that we
have heard with our ears. 23And who *is* like Your people, like Israel, the one
nation on the earth whom God went to redeem for Himself as a people, to
make for Himself a name—and to do for Yourself great and awesome
deeds for Your land—before Your people whom You redeemed for
Yourself from Egypt, the nations, and their gods? 24For You have made
Your people Israel Your very own people forever; and You, LORD, have become their God.

25“Now, O LORD God, the word which You have spoken concerning Your
servant and concerning his house, establish *it* forever and do as You have
said. 26So let Your name be magnified forever, saying, ‘The LORD of hosts *is*
the God over Israel.’ And let the house of Your servant David be established before You. 27For You, O LORD of hosts, God of Israel, have revealed
this to Your servant, saying, ‘I will build you a house.’ Therefore Your servant has found it in his heart to pray this prayer to You.

28“And now, O Lord GOD, You are God, and Your words are true, and You
have promised this goodness to Your servant. 29Now therefore, let it please
You to bless the house of Your servant, that it may continue before You forever; for You, O Lord GOD, have spoken *it,* and with Your blessing let the
house of Your servant be blessed forever.”

David’s Further Conquests

8 After this it came to pass that David attacked the Philistines and subdued them. And David took Metheg Ammah from the hand of the
Philistines.

2Then he defeated Moab. Forcing them down to the ground, he measured
them off with a line. With two lines he measured off those to be put to death,
and with one full line those to be kept alive. So the Moabites became David’s
servants, *and* brought tribute.

7:16 q Septuagint reads *Me.*
7:22 r Targum and Syriac read *O LORD God.*

voice of the God of Jesus within us. An appointment with the barber or hairdresser is inviolable, but when God lays claim to our time, we balk. The most important thing that ever happens in prayer is letting ourselves be loved by God. “Be still, and know that I am God” (Psalm 46:10). It’s like slipping into a tub of hot water and letting God’s love wash over us, enfold us. Prayer is like sunbathing. When you spend a lot of time in the sun, people notice it. They say, “You’ve been at the beach.” You look like you’ve been out in the sun because you’ve got a tan. Prayer—or bathing in the Son of God’s love (Son-bathing?)—makes you look different. The awareness of being loved brings a touch of lightness and a tint of brightness and sometimes, for no apparent reason, a smile plays at the corner of your mouth. Through prayer you not only know God’s love, you realize it, you are in conscious communion with it.

(From *Lion and Lamb* by Brennan Manning)

APPLICATION Do you feel like you communicate with God when you pray? Or do your prayers merely fulfill an obligation? Next time you pray, talk to God as you would a friend. Put any fancy prayer words aside and let God know how you feel.

EXPLORATION Hindrances to Prayer—Micah 3:4; Philippians 4:6; 1 Peter 3:7.

LIFE LESSON

2 Samuel 8:1–10:19

SITUATION David defeated the Edomites, Moabites, Ammonites, and Philistines. These nations had been a constant military and religious threat to Israel.

OBSERVATION God gave David victory wherever he went. David's military success was not his own making. It was God's victory. God fulfilled his promises to David. He made him great by helping him conquer Israel's enemies.

INSPIRATION When you face an impossibility, leave it in the hands of the specialist. Refuse to calculate. Refuse to doubt. Refuse to work it out by yourself. Refuse to worry or encourage others to worry.

Instead, say, "Lord, I'm carrying around something I cannot handle. Because You are not only able but also willing and anxious, take this off my hands. It's impossible to me, but it is as nothing with You." Persevering through the pressures of impossibilities calls for that kind of confidence.

Now, our problem is that we hold onto our problems. If your Swiss watch stops working, you don't sit down at home with a screwdriver and start working on it yourself. You take it to a specialist.

What if you do work on that watch and *then* you take it to a specialist? "Sir, my watch stopped working."

"Oh really. Let me take a look at it. . . . What in the world have you done to this lovely watch?"

The problem is that the Lord gets all the leftovers. We make all the mistakes and get things tied into nineteen granny knots, then dump it in His lap and say, "Here, Lord."

No! Right at first, say, "It's impossible: I can't handle it. Lord, before I foul it up, it's yours." He is able to handle it.

(From *Three Steps Forward and Two Steps Back* by Charles Swindoll)

APPLICATION Do you face an impossible challenge? Remember the battle belongs to the Lord!

EXPLORATION God's Victory—Exodus 14:13-14; 1 Samuel 17:47; 2 Chronicles 20:16-20; Isaiah 41:10-11; Acts 12:1-23; 2 Corinthians 2:14.

3David also defeated Hadadezer the son of Rehob, king of Zobah, as he
went to recover his territory at the River Euphrates. 4David took from him
one thousand *chariots,* seven hundred[s] horsemen, and twenty thousand
foot soldiers. Also David hamstrung all the chariot horses, except that he
spared *enough* of them for one hundred chariots.
5When the Syrians of Damascus came to help Hadadezer king of
Zobah, David killed twenty-two thousand of the Syrians. 6Then David put
garrisons in Syria of Damascus; and the Syrians became David's servants,
and brought tribute. So the LORD preserved David wherever he
went. 7And David took the shields of gold that had belonged to the servants
of Hadadezer, and brought them to Jerusalem. 8Also from Betah[t]
and from Berothai, cities of Hadadezer, King David took a large amount
of bronze.
9When Toi[u] king of Hamath heard that David had defeated all the army
of Hadadezer, 10then Toi sent Joram[v] his son to King David, to greet him
and bless him, because he had fought against Hadadezer and defeated
him (for Hadadezer had been at war with Toi); and *Joram* brought with
him articles of silver, articles of gold, and articles of bronze. 11King David
also dedicated these to the LORD, along with the silver and gold that he had
dedicated from all the nations which he had subdued— 12from Syria,[w]
from Moab, from the people of Ammon, from the Philistines, from
Amalek, and from the spoil of Hadadezer the son of Rehob, king of Zobah.
13And David made *himself* a name when he returned from killing eighteen
thousand Syrians[x] in the Valley of Salt. 14He also put garrisons in
Edom; throughout all Edom he put garrisons, and all the Edomites became
David's servants. And the LORD preserved David wherever he went.

David's Administration

15So David reigned over all Israel; and David administered judgment
and justice to all his people. 16Joab the son of Zeruiah *was* over the army;
Jehoshaphat the son of Ahilud *was* recorder; 17Zadok the son of Ahitub
and Ahimelech the son of Abiathar *were* the priests; Seraiah[y] *was* the
scribe; 18Benaiah the son of Jehoiada *was over* both the Cherethites and the
Pelethites; and David's sons were chief ministers.

David's Kindness to Mephibosheth

9 Now David said, "Is there still anyone who is left of the house of Saul,
that I may show him kindness for Jonathan's sake?"
2And *there was* a servant of the house of Saul whose name *was* Ziba. So
when they had called him to David, the king said to him, "*Are* you Ziba?"
He said, "At your service!"
3Then the king said, "*Is* there not still someone of the house of Saul, to
whom I may show the kindness of God?"
And Ziba said to the king, "There is still a son of Jonathan *who is* lame in
his feet."
4So the king said to him, "Where *is* he?"

8:4 [s] Or *seven thousand* (compare 1 Chronicles 18:4)
8:8 [t] Spelled *Tibhath* in 1 Chronicles 18:8
8:9 [u] Spelled *Tou* in 1 Chronicles 18:9
8:10 [v] Spelled *Hadoram* in 1 Chronicles 18:10
8:12 [w] Septuagint, Syriac, and some Hebrew manuscripts read *Edom.*
8:13 [x] Septuagint, Syriac, and some Hebrew manuscripts read *Edomites* (compare 1 Chronicles 18:12).
8:17 [y] Spelled *Shavsha* in 1 Chronicles 18:16

And Ziba said to the king, "Indeed he *is* in the
house of Machir the son of Ammiel, in Lo Debar."
5Then King David sent and brought him out of the
house of Machir the son of Ammiel, from Lo Debar.
6Now when Mephibosheth the son of Jonathan, the
son of Saul, had come to David, he fell on his face and
prostrated himself. Then David said, "Mephibosheth?"
And he answered, "Here is your servant!"
7So David said to him, "Do not fear, for I will surely
show you kindness for Jonathan your father's sake, and
will restore to you all the land of Saul your grandfather; and you shall eat bread at my table continually."
8Then he bowed himself, and said, "What *is* your
servant, that you should look upon such a dead dog
as I?"
9And the king called to Ziba, Saul's servant, and
said to him, "I have given to your master's son all that
belonged to Saul and to all his house. 10You therefore,
and your sons and your servants, shall work the land
for him, and you shall bring in *the harvest,* that your
master's son may have food to eat. But Mephibosheth
your master's son shall eat bread at my table always."
Now Ziba had fifteen sons and twenty servants.
11Then Ziba said to the king, "According to all that
my lord the king has commanded his servant, so will
your servant do."
"As for Mephibosheth," *said the king,* "he shall eat
at my table[z] like one of the king's sons." 12Mephibosheth
had a young son whose name *was* Micha. And all who
dwelt in the house of Ziba *were* servants of Mephibosheth. 13So Mephibosheth dwelt in Jerusalem, for
he ate continually at the king's table. And he was lame
in both his feet.

The Ammonites and Syrians Defeated

10 It happened after this that the king of the people of Ammon died, and Hanun his son reigned
in his place. 2Then David said, "I will show kindness
to Hanun the son of Nahash, as his father showed
kindness to me."
So David sent by the hand of his servants to comfort him concerning his father. And David's servants
came into the land of the people of Ammon. 3And the
princes of the people of Ammon said to Hanun their
lord, "Do you think that David really honors your father because he has sent comforters to you? Has David not *rather* sent his servants to you to search the
city, to spy it out, and to overthrow it?"
4Therefore Hanun took David's servants, shaved off
half of their beards, cut off their garments in the middle, at their buttocks, and sent them away. 5When they
told David, he sent to meet them, because the men
were greatly ashamed. And the king said, "Wait at Jericho until your beards have grown, and *then* return."
6When the people of Ammon saw that they had
made themselves repulsive to David, the people of
Ammon sent and hired the Syrians of Beth Rehob
and the Syrians of Zoba, twenty thousand foot soldiers; and from the king of Maacah one thousand
men, and from Ish-Tob twelve thousand men. 7Now
when David heard *of it,* he sent Joab and all the army
of the mighty men. 8Then the people of Ammon came
out and put themselves in battle array at the entrance
of the gate. And the Syrians of Zoba, Beth Rehob, Ish-
Tob, and Maacah *were* by themselves in the field.
9When Joab saw that the battle line was against him
before and behind, he chose some of Israel's best and
put *them* in battle array against the Syrians. 10And the
rest of the people he put under the command of
Abishai his brother, that he might set *them* in battle
array against the people of Ammon. 11Then he said,
"If the Syrians are too strong for me, then you shall
help me; but if the people of Ammon are too strong
for you, then I will come and help you. 12Be of good
courage, and let us be strong for our people and for
the cities of our God. And may the LORD do *what is*
good in His sight."
13So Joab and the people who *were* with him drew
near for the battle against the Syrians, and they fled
before him. 14When the people of Ammon saw that
the Syrians were fleeing, they also fled before Abishai,
and entered the city. So Joab returned from the people
of Ammon and went to Jerusalem.
15When the Syrians saw that they had been defeated
by Israel, they gathered together. 16Then Hadadezer[a]
sent and brought out the Syrians who *were* beyond
the River,[b] and they came to Helam. And Shobach the
commander of Hadadezer's army *went* before them.
17When it was told David, he gathered all Israel,
crossed over the Jordan, and came to Helam. And the
Syrians set themselves in battle array against David
and fought with him. 18Then the Syrians fled before
Israel; and David killed seven hundred charioteers
and forty thousand horsemen of the Syrians, and
struck Shobach the commander of their army, who
died there. 19And when all the kings *who were* servants
to Hadadezer[c] saw that they were defeated by Israel,

9:11 [z] Septuagint reads *David's table.*
10:16 [a] Hebrew *Hadarezer* [b] That is, the Euphrates
10:19 [c] Hebrew *Hadarezer*

they made peace with Israel and served them. So the Syrians were afraid
to help the people of Ammon anymore.

David, Bathsheba, and Uriah

11 It happened in the spring of the year, at the time when kings go out
to battle, that David sent Joab and his servants with him, and all Israel; and they destroyed the people of Ammon and besieged Rabbah. But
David remained at Jerusalem.
2Then it happened one evening that David arose from his bed and
walked on the roof of the king's house. And from the roof he saw a woman
bathing, and the woman *was* very beautiful to behold. 3So David sent and
inquired about the woman. And *someone* said, "*Is* this not Bathsheba, the
daughter of Eliam, the wife of Uriah the Hittite?" 4Then David sent messengers, and took her; and she came to him, and he lay with her, for she
was cleansed from her impurity; and she returned to her house. 5And the
woman conceived; so she sent and told David, and said, "I *am* with child."
6Then David sent to Joab, *saying,* "Send me Uriah the Hittite." And Joab
sent Uriah to David. 7When Uriah had come to him, David asked how Joab
was doing, and how the people were doing, and how the war prospered. 8And
David said to Uriah, "Go down to your house and wash your feet." So Uriah
departed from the king's house, and a gift *of food* from the king followed him.
9But Uriah slept at the door of the king's house with all the servants of his lord,
and did not go down to his house. 10So when they told David, saying, "Uriah
did not go down to his house," David said to Uriah, "Did you not come from
a journey? Why did you not go down to your house?"
11And Uriah said to David, "The ark and Israel and Judah are dwelling
in tents, and my lord Joab and the servants of my lord are encamped in
the open fields. Shall I then go to my house to eat and drink, and to lie with
my wife? *As* you live, and *as* your soul lives, I will not do this thing."
12Then David said to Uriah, "Wait here today also, and tomorrow I will
let you depart." So Uriah remained in Jerusalem that day and the next.
13Now when David called him, he ate and drank before him; and he made
him drunk. And at evening he went out to lie on his bed with the servants
of his lord, but he did not go down to his house.
14In the morning it happened that David wrote a letter to Joab and sent
it by the hand of Uriah. 15And he wrote in the letter, saying, "Set Uriah in
the forefront of the hottest battle, and retreat from him, that he may be
struck down and die." 16So it was, while Joab besieged the city, that he assigned Uriah to a place where he knew there *were* valiant men. 17Then the
men of the city came out and fought with Joab. And *some* of the people of
the servants of David fell; and Uriah the Hittite died also.
18Then Joab sent and told David all the things concerning the war, 19and
charged the messenger, saying, "When you have finished telling the matters of the war to the king, 20if it happens that the king's wrath rises, and he
says to you: 'Why did you approach so near to the city when you fought?
Did you not know that they would shoot from the wall? 21Who struck
Abimelech the son of Jerubbesheth?[d] Was it not a woman who cast a piece
of a millstone on him from the wall, so that he died in Thebez? Why did
you go near the wall?'—then you shall say, 'Your servant Uriah the Hittite
is dead also.'"

11:21 *d* Same as *Jerubbaal* (Gideon), Judges 6:32ff

LIFE LESSON

2 Samuel 11:1–12:31

SITUATION David became king of Israel after Saul's death. Although a successful commander of Israel's army, he let himself be conquered by lust. He committed adultery with Bathsheba, then arranged to have her husband murdered.

OBSERVATION David was not immune to temptation. When he sinned, God held him accountable for his actions.

INSPIRATION As to our personal evil and the pain that comes from present sin, it was sin precisely like our sin that killed Christ, for sin is always the anxious pride of the creature by which we try to be our own god. . . . Each man, each nation, each era must make its own choice under new options, yet the options in essence do not change, for always the alternatives are man's futile will or God's overruling will. . . .

As for the mystery of pain—why the snake appears in our natural world and as seducer in our world of human decision—the mystery remains: We do not know, though we do know that we cannot shelve responsibility for our choice.

The pain that comes of sin is the focal item in the whole "problem" and in the midst of it stand a Cross and a Resurrection. . . . Of us, you and me, the prayer is spoken, "Father, forgive them; for they know not what they do." . . . Yes, the prayer is spoken of us. Yet because God raised him from the dead the prayer is already answered for us. We are forgiven!

(From *God, Pain, and Evil* by George Arthur Buttrick)

APPLICATION God has forgiven us. But, many times we have done something that is so painful it is difficult to forgive ourselves. You are sorry for what you have done. You have tried to make amends. Now, forgive yourself and begin to live life anew.

EXPLORATION Put off Sin—Isaiah 59; Proverbs 3:11-12; Romans 6:15-23; Hebrews 12:1.

22So the messenger went, and came and told David all that Joab had sent by him. 23And the messenger said to David, "Surely the men prevailed against us and came out to us in the field; then we drove them back as far as the entrance of the gate. 24The archers shot from the wall at your servants; and *some* of the king's servants are dead, and your servant Uriah the Hittite is dead also."

25Then David said to the messenger, "Thus you shall say to Joab: 'Do not let this thing displease you, for the sword devours one as well as another. Strengthen your attack against the city, and overthrow it.' So encourage him."

26When the wife of Uriah heard that Uriah her husband was dead, she mourned for her husband. 27And when her mourning was over, David sent and brought her to his house, and she became his wife and bore him a son. But the thing that David had done displeased the LORD.

Nathan's Parable and David's Confession

12 Then the LORD sent Nathan to David. And he came to him, and said to him: "There were two men in one city, one rich and the other poor. 2The rich *man* had exceedingly many flocks and herds. 3But the poor *man* had nothing, except one little ewe lamb which he had bought and nourished; and it grew up together with him and with his children. It ate of his own food and drank from his own cup and lay in his bosom; and it was like a daughter to him. 4And a traveler came to the rich man, who refused to take from his own flock and from his own herd to prepare one for the wayfaring man who had come to him; but he took the poor man's lamb and prepared it for the man who had come to him."

5So David's anger was greatly aroused against the man, and he said to Nathan, "*As* the LORD lives, the man who has done this shall surely die! 6And he shall restore fourfold for the lamb, because he did this thing and because he had no pity."

7Then Nathan said to David, "You *are* the man! Thus says the LORD God of Israel: 'I anointed you king over Israel, and I delivered you from the hand of Saul. 8I gave you your master's house and your master's wives into your keeping, and gave you the house of Israel and Judah. And if *that had been* too little, I also would have given you much more! 9Why have you despised the commandment of the LORD, to do evil in His sight? You have killed Uriah the Hittite with the sword; you have taken his wife *to be* your wife, and have killed him with the sword of the people of Ammon. 10Now therefore, the sword shall never depart from your house, because you have despised Me, and have taken the wife of Uriah the Hittite to be your wife.' 11Thus says the LORD: 'Behold, I will raise up adversity against you from your own house; and I will take your wives before your eyes and give *them* to your neighbor, and he shall lie with your wives in the sight of this sun. 12For you did *it* secretly, but I will do this thing before all Israel, before the sun.' "

13So David said to Nathan, "I have sinned against the LORD."

And Nathan said to David, "The LORD also has put away your sin; you shall not die. 14However, because by this deed you have given great occasion to the enemies of the LORD to blaspheme, the child also *who is* born to you shall surely die." 15Then Nathan departed to his house.

The Death of David's Son

And the LORD struck the child that Uriah's wife bore to David, and it became ill. 16David therefore pleaded with God for the child, and David fasted and went in and lay all night on the ground. 17So the elders of his house arose *and went* to him, to raise him up from the ground. But he would not, nor did he eat food with them. 18Then on the seventh day it came to pass that the child died. And the servants of David were afraid to tell him that the child was dead. For they said, "Indeed, while the child was alive, we spoke to him, and he would not heed our voice. How can we tell him that the child is dead? He may do some harm!"

19When David saw that his servants were whispering, David perceived that the child was dead. Therefore David said to his servants, "Is the child dead?"

And they said, "He is dead."

20So David arose from the ground, washed and anointed himself, and changed his clothes; and he went into the house of the LORD and worshiped. Then he went to his own house; and when he requested, they set food before him, and he ate. 21Then his servants said to him, "What *is* this that you have done? You fasted and wept for the child *while he was* alive, but when the child died, you arose and ate food."

22And he said, "While the child was alive, I fasted and wept; for I said, 'Who can tell *whether* the LORD[e] will be gracious to me, that the child may live?' 23But now he is dead; why should I fast? Can I bring him back again? I shall go to him, but he shall not return to me."

12:22 [e] A few Hebrew manuscripts and Syriac read *God.*

LIFE LESSON

2 Samuel 13:1–14:33

SITUATION David's family was in conflict. His eldest son, Amnon, raped Tamar, his own half sister. Absalom, Tamar's brother, murdered Amnon in revenge.

OBSERVATION Sexual sin produces disastrous consequences in a family.

INSPIRATION What do you do with your failures? Our mistakes come to us as pebbles; small stones that serve as souvenirs of our stumbles. . . . Here are some failures that have been drug into my office.

Unfaithfulness. He wanted to try again. She said "No way." He wanted a second chance. She said, "You blew your chance." He admitted that he made a mistake by seeing another woman. He sees now that the mistake was fatal to his marriage.

Homosexuality. His wrists bore the scars of a suicide attempt. His arms had tracks from countless needles. His eyes reflected the spirit of one hell-bent on self-destruction. His words were those of a prisoner grimly resigned to the judge's sentence. "I'm gay. My dad says I'm queer. I guess he's right. . . . "

Immorality. She came to church with a pregnant womb and a repentant spirit. "I can't have a child," she pleaded. "We'll find a home for it," she was assured. She agreed. Then she changed her mind. Her boyfriend funded the abortion. "Can God ever forgive me?" she asked.

Could you do it all over again, you'd do it differently. You'd be a different person. You'd be more patient. You'd control your tongue. You'd finish what you started. You'd turn the other cheek instead of slapping his. You'd get married first. You wouldn't marry at all. You'd be honest. You'd resist the temptation. . . .

But you can't. And as many times as you tell yourself, "What's done is done," what you did can't be undone.

That's part of what Paul meant when he said, "The wages of sin is death."

Solomon Is Born

24Then David comforted Bathsheba his wife, and went in to her and lay with her. So she bore a son, and he[f] called his name Solomon. Now the LORD loved him, 25and He sent *word* by the hand of Nathan the prophet: So he[g] called his name Jedidiah,[h] because of the LORD.

Rabbah Is Captured

26Now Joab fought against Rabbah of the people of Ammon, and took the royal city. 27And Joab sent messengers to David, and said, "I have fought against Rabbah, and I have taken the city's water *supply.* 28Now therefore, gather the rest of the people together and encamp against the city and take it, lest I take the city and it be called after my name." 29So David gathered all the people together and went to Rabbah, fought against it, and took it. 30Then he took their king's crown from his head. Its weight *was* a talent of gold, with precious stones. And it was *set* on David's head. Also he brought out the spoil of the city in great abundance. 31And he brought out the people who *were* in it, and put *them to work* with saws and iron picks and iron axes, and made them cross over to the brick works. So he did to all the cities of the people of Ammon. Then David and all the people returned to Jerusalem.

Amnon and Tamar

13 After this Absalom the son of David had a lovely sister, whose name *was* Tamar; and Amnon the son of David loved her. 2Amnon was so distressed over his sister Tamar that he became sick; for she *was* a virgin. And it was improper for Amnon to do anything to her. 3But Amnon had a friend whose name *was* Jonadab the son of Shimeah, David's brother. Now Jonadab *was* a very crafty man. 4And he said to him, "Why *are* you, the king's son, becoming thinner day after day? Will you not tell me?"

Amnon said to him, "I love Tamar, my brother Absalom's sister."

5So Jonadab said to him, "Lie down on your bed and pretend to be ill. And when your father comes to see you, say to him, 'Please let my sister Tamar come and give me food, and prepare the food in my sight, that I may see *it* and eat it from her hand.' " 6Then Amnon lay down and pretended to be ill; and when the king came to see him, Amnon said to the king, "Please let Tamar my sister come and make a couple of cakes for me in my sight, that I may eat from her hand."

7And David sent home to Tamar, saying, "Now go to your brother Amnon's house, and prepare food for him." 8So Tamar went to her brother Amnon's house; and he was lying down. Then she took flour and kneaded *it,* made cakes in his sight, and baked the cakes. 9And she took the pan and placed *them* out before him, but he refused to eat. Then Amnon said, "Have everyone go out from me." And they all went out from him. 10Then Amnon said to Tamar, "Bring the food into the bedroom, that I may eat from your hand." And Tamar took the cakes which she had made, and brought *them* to Amnon her brother in the bedroom. 11Now when she had brought *them* to him to eat, he took hold of her and said to her, "Come, lie with me, my sister."

12:24 [f] Following Kethib, Septuagint, and Vulgate; Qere, a few Hebrew manuscripts, Syriac, and Targum read *she.*
12:25 [g] Qere, some Hebrew manuscripts, Syriac, and Targum read *she.* [h] Literally *Beloved of the LORD*

12 But she answered him, "No, my brother, do not force me, for no such
thing should be done in Israel. Do not do this disgraceful thing! 13 And I,
where could I take my shame? And as for you, you would be like one of the
fools in Israel. Now therefore, please speak to the king; for he will not withhold me from you." 14 However, he would not heed her voice; and being
stronger than she, he forced her and lay with her.
15 Then Amnon hated her exceedingly, so that the hatred with which he
hated her *was* greater than the love with which he had loved her. And
Amnon said to her, "Arise, be gone!"
16 So she said to him, "No, indeed! This evil of sending me away *is* worse
than the other that you did to me."
But he would not listen to her. 17 Then he called his servant who attended
him, and said, "Here! Put this *woman* out, away from me, and bolt the
door behind her." 18 Now she had on a robe of many colors, for the king's
virgin daughters wore such apparel. And his servant put her out and
bolted the door behind her.
19 Then Tamar put ashes on her head, and tore her robe of many colors
that *was* on her, and laid her hand on her head and went away crying bitterly. 20 And Absalom her brother said to her, "Has Amnon your brother
been with you? But now hold your peace, my sister. He *is* your brother; do
not take this thing to heart." So Tamar remained desolate in her brother
Absalom's house.
21 But when King David heard of all these things, he was very angry.
22 And Absalom spoke to his brother Amnon neither good nor bad. For
Absalom hated Amnon, because he had forced his sister Tamar.

Absalom Murders Amnon

23 And it came to pass, after two full years, that Absalom had sheepshearers in Baal Hazor, which *is* near Ephraim; so Absalom invited all the king's
sons. 24 Then Absalom came to the king and said, "Kindly note, your servant has sheepshearers; please, let the king and his servants go with your
servant."
25 But the king said to Absalom, "No, my son, let us not all go now, lest
we be a burden to you." Then he urged him, but he would not go; and he
blessed him.
26 Then Absalom said, "If not, please let my brother Amnon go with us."
And the king said to him, "Why should he go with you?" 27 But Absalom
urged him; so he let Amnon and all the king's sons go with him.
28 Now Absalom had commanded his servants, saying, "Watch now,
when Amnon's heart is merry with wine, and when I say to you, 'Strike
Amnon!' then kill him. Do not be afraid. Have I not commanded you? Be
courageous and valiant." 29 So the servants of Absalom did to Amnon as
Absalom had commanded. Then all the king's sons arose, and each one
got on his mule and fled.
30 And it came to pass, while they were on the way, that news came to David,
saying, "Absalom has killed all the king's sons, and not one of them is left!"
31 So the king arose and tore his garments and lay on the ground, and all his
servants stood by with their clothes torn. 32 Then Jonadab the son of Shimeah,
David's brother, answered and said, "Let not my lord suppose they have killed
all the young men, the king's sons, for only Amnon is dead. For by the command of Absalom this has been determined from the day that he forced

He didn't say, "The wages of sin is a bad mood." Or, "The wages of sin is a hard day." Nor, "The wages of sin is depression." Read it again. "The wages of sin is death." Sin is fatal.

Can anything be done with it? . . . What do you do with the stones from life's stumbles?

My oldest daughter, Jenna, is four years old. Some time ago she came to me with a confession. "Daddy, I took a crayon and drew on the wall." (Kids amaze me with their honesty.)

I sat down and lifted her up into my lap and tried to be wise. "Is that a good thing to do?" I asked her.

"No."

"What does Daddy do when you write on the wall?"

"You spank me."

"What do you think Daddy should do this time?"

"Love."

Don't we all want that? Don't we all long for a father who even though our mistakes are written all over the wall, will love us anyway? Don't we want a father who cares for us in spite of our failures?

We do have that type of a father. A father who is at his best when we are at our worst. A father whose grace is strongest when our devotion is weakest. If your bag is bulky, then you're in for some thrilling news: Your failures are not fatal.

(From *Six Hours One Friday* by Max Lucado)

APPLICATION What price have you paid for sin? Remember, God does not want you to live in guilt or defeat. Embrace Christ for healing and hope. Trust Christ for tomorrow. In faith, begin to heal wounds today.

EXPLORATION Consequences of Sin—Genesis 4:1-16; Exodus 34:6-7; Joshua 7:24-25; Hebrews 12: 4-17; Revelation 2:20-23.

his sister Tamar. 33Now therefore, let not my lord the
king take the thing to his heart, to think that all the
king's sons are dead. For only Amnon is dead."

Absalom Flees to Geshur

34Then Absalom fled. And the young man who was
keeping watch lifted his eyes and looked, and there,
many people were coming from the road on the hillside behind him.[i] 35And Jonadab said to the king,
"Look, the king's sons are coming; as your servant
said, so it is." 36So it was, as soon as he had finished
speaking, that the king's sons indeed came, and they
lifted up their voice and wept. Also the king and all his
servants wept very bitterly.

37But Absalom fled and went to Talmai the son of
Ammihud, king of Geshur. And *David* mourned for
his son every day. 38So Absalom fled and went to
Geshur, and was there three years. 39And King David[j]
longed to go to[k] Absalom. For he had been comforted
concerning Amnon, because he was dead.

Absalom Returns to Jerusalem

14 So Joab the son of Zeruiah perceived that the
king's heart *was* concerned about Absalom.
2And Joab sent to Tekoa and brought from there a
wise woman, and said to her, "Please pretend to be a
mourner, and put on mourning apparel; do not
anoint yourself with oil, but act like a woman who has
been mourning a long time for the dead. 3Go to the
king and speak to him in this manner." So Joab put
the words in her mouth.

4And when the woman of Tekoa spoke[l] to the king,
she fell on her face to the ground and prostrated herself, and said, "Help, O king!"

5Then the king said to her, "What troubles you?"

And she answered, "Indeed I *am* a widow, my husband is dead. 6Now your maidservant had two sons;
and the two fought with each other in the field, and
there was no one to part them, but the one struck the
other and killed him. 7And now the whole family has
risen up against your maidservant, and they said,
'Deliver him who struck his brother, that we may execute him for the life of his brother whom he killed;
and we will destroy the heir also.' So they would extin-
guish my ember that is left, and leave to my husband
neither name nor remnant on the earth."

8Then the king said to the woman, "Go to your
house, and I will give orders concerning you."

9And the woman of Tekoa said to the king, "My lord,
O king, *let* the iniquity *be* on me and on my father's
house, and the king and his throne *be* guiltless."

10So the king said, "Whoever says *anything* to you,
bring him to me, and he shall not touch you anymore."

11Then she said, "Please let the king remember the
LORD your God, and do not permit the avenger of
blood to destroy anymore, lest they destroy my son."

And he said, "*As* the LORD lives, not one hair of your
son shall fall to the ground."

12Therefore the woman said, "Please, let your
maidservant speak *another* word to my lord the king."

And he said, "Say on."

13So the woman said: "Why then have you schemed
such a thing against the people of God? For the king
speaks this thing as one who is guilty, *in that* the king
does not bring his banished one home again. 14For we
will surely die and *become* like water spilled on the
ground, which cannot be gathered up again. Yet God
does not take away a life; but He devises means, so
that His banished ones are not expelled from Him.
15Now therefore, I have come to speak of this thing to
my lord the king because the people have made me
afraid. And your maidservant said, 'I will now speak
to the king; it may be that the king will perform the request of his maidservant. 16For the king will hear and
deliver his maidservant from the hand of the man
who would destroy me and my son together from the
inheritance of God.' 17Your maidservant said, 'The
word of my lord the king will now be comforting; for
as the angel of God, so *is* my lord the king in discerning good and evil. And may the LORD your God be
with you.'"

18Then the king answered and said to the woman,
"Please do not hide from me anything that I ask you."

And the woman said, "Please, let my lord the king
speak."

19So the king said, "*Is* the hand of Joab with you in
all this?" And the woman answered and said, "*As* you
live, my lord the king, no one can turn to the right
hand or to the left from anything that my lord the
king has spoken. For your servant Joab commanded
me, and he put all these words in the mouth of your
maidservant. 20To bring about this change of affairs

13:34 [i] Septuagint adds *And the watchman went and told the king, and said, "I see men from the way of Horonaim, from the regions of the mountains."*
13:39 [j] Following Masoretic Text, Syriac, and Vulgate; Septuagint reads *the spirit of the king;* Targum reads *the soul of King David.* [k] Following Masoretic Text and Targum; Septuagint and Vulgate read *ceased to pursue after.*
14:4 [l] Many Hebrew manuscripts, Septuagint, Syriac, and Vulgate read *came.*

your servant Joab has done this thing; but my lord *is* wise, according to the
wisdom of the angel of God, to know everything that *is* in the earth."
21 And the king said to Joab, "All right, I have granted this thing. Go
therefore, bring back the young man Absalom."
22 Then Joab fell to the ground on his face and bowed himself, and
thanked the king. And Joab said, "Today your servant knows that I have
found favor in your sight, my lord, O king, in that the king has fulfilled the
request of his servant." 23 So Joab arose and went to Geshur, and brought
Absalom to Jerusalem. 24 And the king said, "Let him return to his own
house, but do not let him see my face." So Absalom returned to his own
house, but did not see the king's face.

David Forgives Absalom

25 Now in all Israel there was no one who was praised as much as Absalom
for his good looks. From the sole of his foot to the crown of his head there
was no blemish in him. 26 And when he cut the hair of his head—at the end
of every year he cut *it* because it was heavy on him—when he cut it, he
weighed the hair of his head at two hundred shekels according to the king's
standard. 27 To Absalom were born three sons, and one daughter whose
name *was* Tamar. She was a woman of beautiful appearance.
28 And Absalom dwelt two full years in Jerusalem, but did not see the
king's face. 29 Therefore Absalom sent for Joab, to send him to the king, but
he would not come to him. And when he sent again the second time, he
would not come. 30 So he said to his servants, "See, Joab's field is near
mine, and he has barley there; go and set it on fire." And Absalom's servants set the field on fire.
31 Then Joab arose and came to Absalom's house, and said to him, "Why
have your servants set my field on fire?"
32 And Absalom answered Joab, "Look, I sent to you, saying, 'Come here,
so that I may send you to the king, to say, "Why have I come from Geshur?
It would be better for me *to be* there still." ' Now therefore, let me see the
king's face; but if there is iniquity in me, let him execute me."
33 So Joab went to the king and told him. And when he had called for
Absalom, he came to the king and bowed himself on his face to the ground
before the king. Then the king kissed Absalom.

Absalom's Treason

15 After this it happened that Absalom provided himself with chariots and horses, and fifty men to run before him. 2 Now Absalom
would rise early and stand beside the way to the gate. *So* it was, whenever
anyone who had a lawsuit came to the king for a decision, that Absalom
would call to him and say, "What city *are* you from?" And he would say,
"Your servant *is* from such and such a tribe of Israel." 3 Then Absalom
would say to him, "Look, your case *is* good and right; but *there is* no deputy of the king to hear you." 4 Moreover Absalom would say, "Oh, that I
were made judge in the land, and everyone who has any suit or cause
would come to me; then I would give him justice." 5 And *so* it was, whenever anyone came near to bow down to him, that he would put out his
hand and take him and kiss him. 6 In this manner Absalom acted toward
all Israel who came to the king for judgment. So Absalom stole the hearts
of the men of Israel.

LIFE LESSON

2 Samuel 15:1–16:14

SITUATION Absalom's charisma and charm won over many followers. His rebellion became so strong and widespread that David fled rather than engage in a long, bloody opposition.

OBSERVATION Even though God had forgiven David, David's sins brought painful consequences. Believers today should also be prepared for trials, realizing that past sin can bring difficult consequences.

INSPIRATION For one week every year I go fishing in Minnesota. I try a variety of artificial lures to catch walleyes and northerns.

Some days the fish strike one lure, some days another. But there is one particular lure that they go for every time. They can't resist it. That lure is chewed where so many fish have fought to dislodge the hook but couldn't. Those fish have a weakness, and I know what it is. Because I know, I can catch them.

Satan knows the weakness of every one of us too. He has a lot of different lures to dangle in front of us and may try them. But for each of us, he has a favorite lure and he knows how to use it.

Occasionally a fish will pull loose, ripping its skin, and with mouth hanging down off it goes to heal. But the scars will always be there. Sometimes we can pull away from Satan too, but not before some painful tearing occurs causing scars that will remain for the rest of our lives. For even when we are made whole again by receiving and accepting forgiveness, the physical and sometimes the emotional results of what we did won't go away. Christians get emotionally, physically and spiritually hurt, and they hurt others too.

There are so many painful ways for the people of God to stumble, and Satan knows every one of them. As he studies believers, he knows that he probably cannot make us denounce Christ—but he can tempt us into a compromise with sin. Satan knows exactly how to make each one of us fall. Our weaknesses are no secret to him.

Knowing what we are like and how our minds work, Satan will aim where

Continued

we are vulnerable. A person may not be tempted with greed, but might be tempted with the pride that grows out of not being greedy. The person who can't stand the taste of liquor will probably not become an alcoholic—but he might lust for food. Satan knows how to get to our weak spots. He knows where they are.

Three things are certain about messing up our lives. First, we don't have to yield to temptation. God has made a way of escape. Second, if we do slip we don't have to wallow in our mistakes. There is deliverance. Third, we can use the lesson learned from falling not only to avoid falling again, but to help some other person who is facing similar pressures.

(From *God Guides Your Tomorrows* by Roger C. Palms)

APPLICATION Today, don't make excuses for yourself. Don't tell all your problems to the world. Turn from a focus of how bad things are to something new: how good God is. Let today mark a new direction for your life.

EXPLORATION Rebellion—Numbers 16; 1 Kings 1–2; 12:16-20; 15:27–16:7; Hosea 9:15; 13:16.

7Now it came to pass after forty[m] years that Absalom said to the king,
"Please, let me go to Hebron and pay the vow which I made to the LORD.
8For your servant took a vow while I dwelt at Geshur in Syria, saying, 'If the
LORD indeed brings me back to Jerusalem, then I will serve the LORD.' "
9And the king said to him, "Go in peace." So he arose and went to
Hebron.
10Then Absalom sent spies throughout all the tribes of Israel, saying,
"As soon as you hear the sound of the trumpet, then you shall say,
'Absalom reigns in Hebron!' " 11And with Absalom went two hundred
men invited from Jerusalem, and they went along innocently and did not
know anything. 12Then Absalom sent for Ahithophel the Gilonite, David's
counselor, from his city—from Giloh—while he offered sacrifices. And
the conspiracy grew strong, for the people with Absalom continually increased in number.

David Escapes from Jerusalem

13Now a messenger came to David, saying, "The hearts of the men of Israel are with Absalom."
14So David said to all his servants who *were* with him at Jerusalem,
"Arise, and let us flee, or we shall not escape from Absalom. Make haste to
depart, lest he overtake us suddenly and bring disaster upon us, and strike
the city with the edge of the sword."
15And the king's servants said to the king, "We *are* your servants, *ready
to do* whatever my lord the king commands." 16Then the king went out
with all his household after him. But the king left ten women, concubines,
to keep the house. 17And the king went out with all the people after him,
and stopped at the outskirts. 18Then all his servants passed before him;
and all the Cherethites, all the Pelethites, and all the Gittites, six hundred
men who had followed him from Gath, passed before the king.
19Then the king said to Ittai the Gittite, "Why are you also going with us?
Return and remain with the king. For you *are* a foreigner and also an exile
from your own place. 20In fact, you came *only* yesterday. Should I make
you wander up and down with us today, since I go I know not where?
Return, and take your brethren back. Mercy and truth *be* with you."
21But Ittai answered the king and said, "*As* the LORD lives, and *as* my lord
the king lives, surely in whatever place my lord the king shall be, whether
in death or life, even there also your servant will be."
22So David said to Ittai, "Go, and cross over." Then Ittai the Gittite and all
his men and all the little ones who *were* with him crossed over. 23And all
the country wept with a loud voice, and all the people crossed over. The
king himself also crossed over the Brook Kidron, and all the people
crossed over toward the way of the wilderness.
24There was Zadok also, and all the Levites with him, bearing the ark of
the covenant of God. And they set down the ark of God, and Abiathar went
up until all the people had finished crossing over from the city. 25Then the
king said to Zadok, "Carry the ark of God back into the city. If I find favor
in the eyes of the LORD, He will bring me back and show me *both* it and His
dwelling place. 26But if He says thus: 'I have no delight in you,' here I am,
let Him do to me as seems good to Him." 27The king also said to Zadok the

15:7 [m] Septuagint manuscripts, Syriac, and Josephus read *four.*

priest, "*Are* you *not* a seer? Return to the city in peace, and your two sons
with you, Ahimaaz your son, and Jonathan the son of Abiathar. 28See, I will
wait in the plains of the wilderness until word comes from you to inform
me." 29Therefore Zadok and Abiathar carried the ark of God back to Jerusalem. And they remained there.

30So David went up by the Ascent of the *Mount of* Olives, and wept as he
went up; and he had his head covered and went barefoot. And all the people who *were* with him covered their heads and went up, weeping as they
went up. 31Then *someone* told David, saying, "Ahithophel *is* among the
conspirators with Absalom." And David said, "O LORD, I pray, turn the
counsel of Ahithophel into foolishness!"

32Now it happened when David had come to the top *of the mountain,*
where he worshiped God—there was Hushai the Archite coming to meet
him with his robe torn and dust on his head. 33David said to him, "If you
go on with me, then you will become a burden to me. 34But if you return to
the city, and say to Absalom, 'I will be your servant, O king; *as* I *was* your
father's servant previously, so I *will* now also *be* your servant,' then you
may defeat the counsel of Ahithophel for me. 35And *do* you not *have* Zadok
and Abiathar the priests with you there? Therefore it will be *that* whatever
you hear from the king's house, you shall tell to Zadok and Abiathar the
priests. 36Indeed *they have* there with them their two sons, Ahimaaz,
Zadok's *son,* and Jonathan, Abiathar's *son;* and by them you shall send me
everything you hear."

37So Hushai, David's friend, went into the city. And Absalom came into
Jerusalem.

Mephibosheth's Servant

16 When David was a little past the top *of the mountain,* there was Ziba
the servant of Mephibosheth, who met him with a couple of saddled
donkeys, and on them two hundred *loaves* of bread, one hundred clusters
of raisins, one hundred summer fruits, and a skin of wine. 2And the king
said to Ziba, "What do you mean to do with these?"

So Ziba said, "The donkeys *are* for the king's household to ride on, the
bread and summer fruit for the young men to eat, and the wine for those
who are faint in the wilderness to drink."

3Then the king said, "And where *is* your master's son?"

And Ziba said to the king, "Indeed he is staying in Jerusalem, for he said,
'Today the house of Israel will restore the kingdom of my father to me.' "

4So the king said to Ziba, "Here, all that *belongs* to Mephibosheth *is*
yours."

And Ziba said, "I humbly bow before you, *that* I may find favor in your
sight, my lord, O king!"

Shimei Curses David

5Now when King David came to Bahurim, there was a man from the
family of the house of Saul, whose name *was* Shimei the son of Gera, coming from there. He came out, cursing continuously as he came. 6And he
threw stones at David and at all the servants of King David. And all the
people and all the mighty men *were* on his right hand and on his left. 7Also
Shimei said thus when he cursed: "Come out! Come out! You bloodthirsty
man, you rogue! 8The LORD has brought upon you all the blood of the

LIFE LESSON

2 Samuel 16:15–19:43

SITUATION Ahithophel and Hushai competed as advisors to Absalom during the revolution. Most leaders in those times relied on advisors to make important policy decisions.

OBSERVATION God enables his chosen leaders (such as David) to prevail, even through the most complex and adverse circumstances.

INSPIRATION In our day-to-day experience it is sometimes difficult to determine the source of our adversity. Adversity related to our personal sin is usually easy to identify. Beyond that, though, things begin to run together. We certainly do not want to rebuke the devil for something God is behind. Neither do we want to just grin and bear it if there is something we can do to put an end to our suffering.

The Bible does not give us three simple steps to aid us in determining the source of our adversity. This used to really bother me. For a long time, when I faced adversity, I would pray and pray for God to give me some indication as to why I was suffering. Then I realized why those kinds of prayers rarely seemed to be answered. There was and is a much more important issue at stake.

Far more important than the *source* of adversity is the *response* to adversity. Why? Because adversity, regardless of the source, is God's most effective tool for deepening your faith and commitment to Him. The areas in which you are experiencing the most adversity are the areas in which God is at work. When someone says, "God is not doing anything in my life," my response is always, "So, you don't have any problems?" Why? Because the best way to identify God's involvement in your life is to consider your response to adversity. God uses adversity, regardless of the source. But your response to adversity determines whether or not God is able to use it to accomplish His purpose. . . .

As much as we all want to know the answer to the *why* question, it is really not the most significant question. The real question each of us needs to ask is, "*How* should I respond?" To spend too much time trying to

Continued

answer the *why* question is to run the risk of missing what God wants to teach us.

(From *How to Handle Adversity* by Charles Stanley)

APPLICATION Isolate a major problem you will face today. Choose a Christian response to it, check out your solution with a trusted friend, and put your idea into action.

EXPLORATION Purposes of God—Genesis 45:4-7; 50:19-20; Isaiah 46:8-11; Matthew 25:34; 2 Timothy 1:8-9.

house of Saul, in whose place you have reigned; and the LORD has delivered the kingdom into the hand of Absalom your son. So now you *are*
caught in your own evil, because you are a bloodthirsty man!"
9 Then Abishai the son of Zeruiah said to the king, "Why should this dead
dog curse my lord the king? Please, let me go over and take off his head!"
10 But the king said, "What have I to do with you, you sons of Zeruiah? So
let him curse, because the LORD has said to him, 'Curse David.' Who then
shall say, 'Why have you done so?' "
11 And David said to Abishai and all his servants, "See how my son who
came from my own body seeks my life. How much more now *may this*
Benjamite? Let him alone, and let him curse; for so the LORD has ordered him.
12 It may be that the LORD will look on my affliction,[n] and that the LORD will repay me with good for his cursing this day." 13 And as David and his men went
along the road, Shimei went along the hillside opposite him and cursed as he
went, threw stones at him and kicked up dust. 14 Now the king and all the people who *were* with him became weary; so they refreshed themselves there.

The Advice of Ahithophel

15 Meanwhile Absalom and all the people, the men of Israel, came to Jerusalem; and Ahithophel *was* with him. 16 And so it was, when Hushai the
Archite, David's friend, came to Absalom, that Hushai said to Absalom,
"*Long* live the king! *Long* live the king!"
17 So Absalom said to Hushai, "*Is* this your loyalty to your friend? Why
did you not go with your friend?"
18 And Hushai said to Absalom, "No, but whom the LORD and this people
and all the men of Israel choose, his I will be, and with him I will remain.
19 "Furthermore, whom should I serve? *Should I* not *serve* in the presence
of his son? As I have served in your father's presence, so will I be in your
presence."
20 Then Absalom said to Ahithophel, "Give advice as to what we should do."
21 And Ahithophel said to Absalom, "Go in to your father's concubines,
whom he has left to keep the house; and all Israel will hear that you are abhorred by your father. Then the hands of all who are with you will be
strong." 22 So they pitched a tent for Absalom on the top of the house, and
Absalom went in to his father's concubines in the sight of all Israel.
23 Now the advice of Ahithophel, which he gave in those days, *was* as if
one had inquired at the oracle of God. So *was* all the advice of Ahithophel
both with David and with Absalom.
17 Moreover Ahithophel said to Absalom, "Now let me choose twelve
thousand men, and I will arise and pursue David tonight. 2 I will
come upon him while he *is* weary and weak, and make him afraid. And all
the people who *are* with him will flee, and I will strike only the king. 3 Then
I will bring back all the people to you. When all return except the man
whom you seek, all the people will be at peace." 4 And the saying pleased
Absalom and all the elders of Israel.

The Advice of Hushai

5 Then Absalom said, "Now call Hushai the Archite also, and let us hear
what he says too." 6 And when Hushai came to Absalom, Absalom spoke to

16:12 [n] Following Kethib, Septuagint, Syriac, and Vulgate; Qere reads *my eyes;* Targum reads *tears of my eyes.*

him, saying, "Ahithophel has spoken in this manner.
Shall we do as he says? If not, speak up."
7So Hushai said to Absalom: "The advice that
Ahithophel has given *is* not good at this time. 8For,"
said Hushai, "you know your father and his men, that
they *are* mighty men, and they *are* enraged in their
minds, like a bear robbed of her cubs in the field; and
your father *is* a man of war, and will not camp with the
people. 9Surely by now he is hidden in some pit, or in
some *other* place. And it will be, when some of them
are overthrown at the first, that whoever hears *it* will
say, 'There is a slaughter among the people who follow Absalom.' 10And even he *who is* valiant, whose
heart *is* like the heart of a lion, will melt completely.
For all Israel knows that your father *is* a mighty man,
and *those* who *are* with him *are* valiant men. 11There-
fore I advise that all Israel be fully gathered to you,
from Dan to Beersheba, like the sand that *is* by the sea
for multitude, and that you go to battle in person. 12So
we will come upon him in some place where he may
be found, and we will fall on him as the dew falls on
the ground. And of him and all the men who *are* with
him there shall not be left so much as one. 13Moreover,
if he has withdrawn into a city, then all Israel shall
bring ropes to that city; and we will pull it into the
river, until there is not one small stone found there."
14So Absalom and all the men of Israel said, "The
advice of Hushai the Archite *is* better than the advice
of Ahithophel." For the LORD had purposed to defeat
the good advice of Ahithophel, to the intent that the
LORD might bring disaster on Absalom.

Hushai Warns David to Escape

15Then Hushai said to Zadok and Abiathar the
priests, "Thus and so Ahithophel advised Absalom
and the elders of Israel, and thus and so I have advised. 16Now therefore, send quickly and tell David,
saying, 'Do not spend this night in the plains of the
wilderness, but speedily cross over, lest the king and
all the people who *are* with him be swallowed up.' "
17Now Jonathan and Ahimaaz stayed at En Rogel, for
they dared not be seen coming into the city; so a female servant would come and tell them, and they
would go and tell King David. 18Nevertheless a lad saw
them, and told Absalom. But both of them went away
quickly and came to a man's house in Bahurim, who
had a well in his court; and they went down into it.
19Then the woman took and spread a covering over
the well's mouth, and spread ground grain on it; and
the thing was not known. 20And when Absalom's servants came to the woman at the house, they said,
"Where *are* Ahimaaz and Jonathan?"
So the woman said to them, "They have gone over
the water brook."
And when they had searched and could not find
them, they returned to Jerusalem. 21Now it came to
pass, after they had departed, that they came up out of
the well and went and told King David, and said to
David, "Arise and cross over the water quickly. For
thus has Ahithophel advised against you." 22So David
and all the people who *were* with him arose and
crossed over the Jordan. By morning light not one of
them was left who had not gone over the Jordan.
23Now when Ahithophel saw that his advice was not
followed, he saddled a donkey, and arose and went
home to his house, to his city. Then he put his household in order, and hanged himself, and died; and he
was buried in his father's tomb.
24Then David went to Mahanaim. And Absalom
crossed over the Jordan, he and all the men of Israel
with him. 25And Absalom made Amasa captain of the
army instead of Joab. This Amasa *was* the son of a
man whose name *was* Jithra,[o] an Israelite,[p] who had
gone in to Abigail the daughter of Nahash, sister of
Zeruiah, Joab's mother. 26So Israel and Absalom encamped in the land of Gilead.
27Now it happened, when David had come to
Mahanaim, that Shobi the son of Nahash from Rabbah
of the people of Ammon, Machir the son of Ammiel
from Lo Debar, and Barzillai the Gileadite from
Rogelim, 28brought beds and basins, earthen vessels
and wheat, barley and flour, parched *grain* and beans,
lentils and parched *seeds,* 29honey and curds, sheep
and cheese of the herd, for David and the people who
were with him to eat. For they said, "The people are
hungry and weary and thirsty in the wilderness."

Absalom's Defeat and Death

18 And David numbered the people who *were* with
him, and set captains of thousands and captains of hundreds over them. 2Then David sent out
one third of the people under the hand of Joab, one
third under the hand of Abishai the son of Zeruiah,
Joab's brother, and one third under the hand of Ittai
the Gittite. And the king said to the people, "I also will
surely go out with you myself."

17:25 [o] Spelled *Jether* in 1 Chronicles 2:17 and elsewhere [p] Following Masoretic Text, some manuscripts of the Septuagint, and Targum; some manuscripts of the Septuagint read *Ishmaelite* (compare 1 Chronicles 2:17); Vulgate reads *of Jezrael.*

3But the people answered, "You shall not go out!
For if we flee away, they will not care about us; nor if
half of us die, will they care about us. But *you are*
worth ten thousand of us now. For you are now more
help to us in the city."
4Then the king said to them, "Whatever seems best
to you I will do." So the king stood beside the gate, and
all the people went out by hundreds and by thousands.
5Now the king had commanded Joab, Abishai, and
Ittai, saying, "*Deal* gently for my sake with the young
man Absalom." And all the people heard when the
king gave all the captains orders concerning Absalom.
6So the people went out into the field of battle
against Israel. And the battle was in the woods of
Ephraim. 7The people of Israel were overthrown there
before the servants of David, and a great slaughter of
twenty thousand took place there that day. 8For the
battle there was scattered over the face of the whole
countryside, and the woods devoured more people
that day than the sword devoured.
9Then Absalom met the servants of David.
Absalom rode on a mule. The mule went under the
thick boughs of a great terebinth tree, and his head
caught in the terebinth; so he was left hanging between heaven and earth. And the mule which *was*
under him went on. 10Now a certain man saw *it* and
told Joab, and said, "I just saw Absalom hanging in a
terebinth tree!"
11So Joab said to the man who told him, "You just
saw *him!* And why did you not strike him there to the
ground? I would have given you ten *shekels* of silver
and a belt."
12But the man said to Joab, "Though I were to receive a thousand *shekels* of silver in my hand, I would
not raise my hand against the king's son. For in our
hearing the king commanded you and Abishai and
Ittai, saying, 'Beware lest anyone *touch* the young
man Absalom!'[q] 13Otherwise I would have dealt falsely
against my own life. For there is nothing hidden from
the king, and you yourself would have set yourself
against *me*."
14Then Joab said, "I cannot linger with you." And
he took three spears in his hand and thrust them
through Absalom's heart, while he was *still* alive in the
midst of the terebinth tree. 15And ten young men who
bore Joab's armor surrounded Absalom, and struck
and killed him.
16So Joab blew the trumpet, and the people returned
from pursuing Israel. For Joab held back the people.
17And they took Absalom and cast him into a large pit
in the woods, and laid a very large heap of stones over
him. Then all Israel fled, everyone to his tent.
18Now Absalom in his lifetime had taken and set up
a pillar for himself, which *is* in the King's Valley. For
he said, "I have no son to keep my name in remembrance." He called the pillar after his own name. And
to this day it is called Absalom's Monument.

David Hears of Absalom's Death

19Then Ahimaaz the son of Zadok said, "Let me run
now and take the news to the king, how the LORD has
avenged him of his enemies."
20And Joab said to him, "You shall not take the
news this day, for you shall take the news another day.
But today you shall take no news, because the king's
son is dead." 21Then Joab said to the Cushite, "Go, tell
the king what you have seen." So the Cushite bowed
himself to Joab and ran.
22And Ahimaaz the son of Zadok said again to Joab,
"But whatever happens, please let me also run after
the Cushite."
So Joab said, "Why will you run, my son, since you
have no news ready?"
23"But whatever happens," *he said,* "let me run."
So he said to him, "Run." Then Ahimaaz ran by
way of the plain, and outran the Cushite.
24Now David was sitting between the two gates. And
the watchman went up to the roof over the gate, to the
wall, lifted his eyes and looked, and there was a man,
running alone. 25Then the watchman cried out and told
the king. And the king said, "If he *is* alone, *there is* news
in his mouth." And he came rapidly and drew near.
26Then the watchman saw *another* man running,
and the watchman called to the gatekeeper and said,
"There is *another* man, running alone!"
And the king said, "He also brings news."
27So the watchman said, "I think the running of the
first is like the running of Ahimaaz the son of Zadok."
And the king said, "He *is* a good man, and comes
with good news."
28So Ahimaaz called out and said to the king, "All is
well!" Then he bowed down with his face to the earth
before the king, and said, "Blessed *be* the LORD your
God, who has delivered up the men who raised their
hand against my lord the king!"
29The king said, "Is the young man Absalom safe?"
Ahimaaz answered, "When Joab sent the king's
servant and *me* your servant, I saw a great tumult, but
I did not know what *it was about*."

18:12 q The ancient versions read '*Protect the young man Absalom for me!*'

30And the king said, "Turn aside *and* stand here."
So he turned aside and stood still.
31Just then the Cushite came, and the Cushite said,
"There is good news, my lord the king! For the LORD
has avenged you this day of all those who rose against
you."
32And the king said to the Cushite, "Is the young
man Absalom safe?"
So the Cushite answered, "May the enemies of my
lord the king, and all who rise against you to do harm,
be like *that* young man!"

David's Mourning for Absalom

33Then the king was deeply moved, and went up to
the chamber over the gate, and wept. And as he went, he
said thus: "O my son Absalom—my son, my son
Absalom—if only I had died in your place! O Absalom
my son, my son!"
19 And Joab was told, "Behold, the king is weeping
and mourning for Absalom." 2So the victory
that day was *turned* into mourning for all the people.
For the people heard it said that day, "The king is
grieved for his son." 3And the people stole back into
the city that day, as people who are ashamed steal
away when they flee in battle. 4But the king covered
his face, and the king cried out with a loud voice, "O
my son Absalom! O Absalom, my son, my son!"
5Then Joab came into the house to the king, and said,
"Today you have disgraced all your servants who today
have saved your life, the lives of your sons and daughters, the lives of your wives and the lives of your concubines, 6in that you love your enemies and hate your
friends. For you have declared today that you regard
neither princes nor servants; for today I perceive that if
Absalom had lived and all of us had died today, then it
would have pleased you well. 7Now therefore, arise, go
out and speak comfort to your servants. For I swear by
the LORD, if you do not go out, not one will stay with you
this night. And that will be worse for you than all the
evil that has befallen you from your youth until now."
8Then the king arose and sat in the gate. And they told
all the people, saying, "There is the king, sitting in the
gate." So all the people came before the king.
For everyone of Israel had fled to his tent.

David Returns to Jerusalem

9Now all the people were in a dispute throughout all
the tribes of Israel, saying, "The king saved us from
the hand of our enemies, he delivered us from the
hand of the Philistines, and now he has fled from the
land because of Absalom. 10But Absalom, whom we
anointed over us, has died in battle. Now therefore,
why do you say nothing about bringing back the king?"
11So King David sent to Zadok and Abiathar the
priests, saying, "Speak to the elders of Judah, saying,
'Why are you the last to bring the king back to his
house, since the words of all Israel have come to the
king, to his *very* house? 12You *are* my brethren, you *are*
my bone and my flesh. Why then are you the last to
bring back the king?' 13And say to Amasa, '*Are* you not
my bone and my flesh? God do so to me, and more
also, if you are not commander of the army before me
continually in place of Joab.' " 14So he swayed the
hearts of all the men of Judah, just as *the heart of* one
man, so that they sent *this word* to the king: "Return,
you and all your servants!"
15Then the king returned and came to the Jordan.
And Judah came to Gilgal, to go to meet the king, to
escort the king across the Jordan. 16And Shimei the
son of Gera, a Benjamite, who *was* from Bahurim,
hurried and came down with the men of Judah to
meet King David. 17*There were* a thousand men of
Benjamin with him, and Ziba the servant of the house
of Saul, and his fifteen sons and his twenty servants
with him; and they went over the Jordan before the
king. 18Then a ferryboat went across to carry over the
king's household, and to do what he thought good.

David's Mercy to Shimei

Now Shimei the son of Gera fell down before the
king when he had crossed the Jordan. 19Then he said
to the king, "Do not let my lord impute iniquity to me,
or remember what wrong your servant did on the day
that my lord the king left Jerusalem, that the king
should take *it* to heart. 20For I, your servant, know that
I have sinned. Therefore here I am, the first to come
today of all the house of Joseph to go down to meet
my lord the king."
21But Abishai the son of Zeruiah answered and
said, "Shall not Shimei be put to death for this, because he cursed the LORD's anointed?"
22And David said, "What have I to do with you, you
sons of Zeruiah, that you should be adversaries to me
today? Shall any man be put to death today in Israel?
For do I not know that today I *am* king over Israel?"
23Therefore the king said to Shimei, "You shall not
die." And the king swore to him.

David and Mephibosheth Meet

24Now Mephibosheth the son of Saul came down to
meet the king. And he had not cared for his feet, nor
trimmed his mustache, nor washed his clothes, from

the day the king departed until the day he returned in
peace. 25So it was, when he had come to Jerusalem to
meet the king, that the king said to him, "Why did you
not go with me, Mephibosheth?"
26And he answered, "My lord, O king, my servant deceived me. For your servant said, 'I will saddle a donkey for myself, that I may ride on it and go to the king,'
because your servant *is* lame. 27And he has slandered
your servant to my lord the king, but my lord the king
is like the angel of God. Therefore do *what is* good in
your eyes. 28For all my father's house were but dead
men before my lord the king. Yet you set your servant
among those who eat at your own table. Therefore
what right have I still to cry out anymore to the king?"
29So the king said to him, "Why do you speak anymore of your matters? I have said, 'You and Ziba divide the land.'"
30Then Mephibosheth said to the king, "Rather, let
him take it all, inasmuch as my lord the king has
come back in peace to his own house."

David's Kindness to Barzillai

31And Barzillai the Gileadite came down from
Rogelim and went across the Jordan with the king, to
escort him across the Jordan. 32Now Barzillai was a
very aged man, eighty years old. And he had provided
the king with supplies while he stayed at Mahanaim,
for he *was* a very rich man. 33And the king said to
Barzillai, "Come across with me, and I will provide
for you while you are with me in Jerusalem."
34But Barzillai said to the king, "How long have I to
live, that I should go up with the king to Jerusalem? 35I
am today eighty years old. Can I discern between the
good and bad? Can your servant taste what I eat or
what I drink? Can I hear any longer the voice of
singing men and singing women? Why then should
your servant be a further burden to my lord the king?
36Your servant will go a little way across the Jordan
with the king. And why should the king repay me *with*
such a reward? 37Please let your servant turn back
again, that I may die in my own city, near the grave of
my father and mother. But here is your servant
Chimham; let him cross over with my lord the king,
and do for him what seems good to you."
38And the king answered, "Chimham shall cross
over with me, and I will do for him what seems good to
you. Now whatever you request of me, I will do for you."
39Then all the people went over the Jordan. And when
the king had crossed over, the king kissed Barzillai and
blessed him, and he returned to his own place.

The Quarrel About the King

40Now the king went on to Gilgal, and Chimham[r]
went on with him. And all the people of Judah escorted
the king, and also half the people of Israel. 41Just then
all the men of Israel came to the king, and said to the
king, "Why have our brethren, the men of Judah,
stolen you away and brought the king, his household,
and all David's men with him across the Jordan?"
42So all the men of Judah answered the men of Israel,
"Because the king *is* a close relative of ours. Why then
are you angry over this matter? Have we ever eaten at
the king's *expense?* Or has he given us any gift?"
43And the men of Israel answered the men of Judah, and said, "We have ten shares in the king; therefore we also have more *right* to David than you. Why
then do you despise us—were we not the first to advise bringing back our king?"
Yet the words of the men of Judah were fiercer than
the words of the men of Israel.

The Rebellion of Sheba

20 And there happened to be there a rebel,[s] whose
name *was* Sheba the son of Bichri, a Benjamite.
And he blew a trumpet, and said:

"We have no share in David,
Nor do we have inheritance in the son of Jesse;
Every man to his tents, O Israel!"

2So every man of Israel deserted David, *and* followed
Sheba the son of Bichri. But the men of Judah, from the
Jordan as far as Jerusalem, remained loyal to their king.
3Now David came to his house at Jerusalem. And the
king took the ten women, his concubines whom he had
left to keep the house, and put them in seclusion and
supported them, but did not go in to them. So they were
shut up to the day of their death, living in widowhood.
4And the king said to Amasa, "Assemble the men
of Judah for me within three days, and be present
here yourself." 5So Amasa went to assemble *the men
of* Judah. But he delayed longer than the set time
which David had appointed him. 6And David said to
Abishai, "Now Sheba the son of Bichri will do us more
harm than Absalom. Take your lord's servants and
pursue him, lest he find for himself fortified cities,
and escape us." 7So Joab's men, with the Cherethites,

19:40 [r] Masoretic Text reads *Chimhan.*
20:1 [s] Literally *man of Belial*

SUFFERING

When Jesus healed the woman in Matthew 9, he told her that her faith had made her well. He was also saying to her, "You're very special to me, daughter. I know you don't have anything to offer me; I know you've been rejected by society, but your Father has not forgotten you." Our Savior says the same to us when we need his healing hand.

Jesus and his disciples saw a blind man while walking down the road. The disciples said, "Jesus, who sinned?" Jesus said, "No one sinned." Then Jesus healed the man. And he eternally answered that our pain is not a result of our sin. God is not so small that he would zap us for making a mistake. This passage teaches just the opposite: Our Savior is not asleep; Jesus is alive and interested in our pain.

We have a Father who is filled with compassion, a feeling Father who hurts when his children hurt. We serve a God who says that even when we're under pressure and feel like nothing is going to go right, he's waiting for us, to embrace us whether we succeed or fail.

He doesn't come quarreling and wrangling and forcing his way into anyone's heart. He comes into our hearts like a gentle lamb, not a roaring lion.

FATHER, *forgive us for the times that we have questioned you; forgive us for the times we have doubted you; forgive us for the times we've shaken our heads and pounded our fists against the earth and cried, "Where are you?" For Father, we know that you have been here—you've carried us through the valley, and you've given us strength.*

PROBLEMS

Sometimes it seems that the more we try to do something good, the more bad things happen. It's tough to have problems when you are trying to be a faithful servant of God, or trying to be loyal to your family. Life was not designed to be problem free, but with the hope promised us by the Father, we can handle the problems that come into our daily life.

If you're facing a problem, perhaps what you need to do is just simply calm down, settle down, and start thinking. Don't try to douse it, don't try to rationalize it. Don't try to escape it. Just think it through, with God's help.

Don't retire your brain when you become a follower of Christ. Be a thinker. Jesus told his followers to be shrewd as snakes. The first thing you need to do to solve problems is to get your brain in gear! That may not sound very spiritual, but it's a very practical principle. You need to use your head.

HERE WE ARE, Father. We call ourselves your people, yet we carry the baggage of a week of concerns. We come to you just as we are, without trying to hide our mistakes. Father, mend us and make us better than we could be alone. Take that which is broken in our lives and make it stronger at the broken places. And use that new strength in your kingdom.

STRUGGLES

Something happens to us when we struggle with physical or emotional or financial problems. Either we can become paralyzed by our problems, turning inward and getting hooked on the "angel dust" of pity, or we can defeat the inclination to turn inward and allow God to help us grow through these difficulties.

Struggling with life's difficulties makes us a little wiser, a little more capable, enabling us to comfort others who experience pain.

Any difficulties we face in life are short-lived; all rewards are eternal. A divine inheritance will be our reward for faithfulness to our heavenly Father. Our faithfulness to the Father is something we should renew daily—a priority for beginning our day.

FATHER, thank you for carrying us when we struggle. We're grateful that you don't turn your back when we're in trouble. Help us not to minimize our struggles; yet, at the same time, help us recognize that any struggle we have is small in comparison to the great God we serve.

REACH OUT

Our biblical act of worship is not what we do on Sunday mornings in coats and ties, but our act of worship is a lifelong, seven-days-a-week process of placing ourselves upon an altar of sacrifice. Worship is living the principles of Christ in everything we do. You're worshiping God by what you do all week long.

What's the difference between a Christian who's reaching out to people, trying to help people—and a Christian who sits like a fat cat on a pew? Well, maybe the Christian who's reaching out realizes the urgency and remembers what it was like before he knew about Jesus. Maybe he realizes that when people need help, they need Jesus above all else.

When you take food to the poor, that's an act of worship. When you give a word of kindness to someone who needs it, that's an act of worship. When you write someone a letter to encourage them or sit down and open your Bible with someone to teach them, that's an act of worship.

We're in a fast-moving, fast-paced society. We need to build bridges between our hearts and those of people we see who need a friend—and allow Jesus to cross that bridge of friendship and walk into their hearts.

We know the importance of a friend. All of us need friends, don't we? Whether or not you are friendly could determine whether or not someone hears about Jesus Christ. Your handshake, your warmth, your walk, your friendliness could make the difference in someone's life.

LIFT UP OUR EYES, Father, that we might see our world as you see it. Help us respond as you respond to the hurts around us.

the Pelethites, and all the mighty men, went out after him. And they went
out of Jerusalem to pursue Sheba the son of Bichri. 8When they *were* at the
large stone which *is* in Gibeon, Amasa came before them. Now Joab was
dressed in battle armor; on it was a belt *with* a sword fastened in its sheath
at his hips; and as he was going forward, it fell out. 9Then Joab said to
Amasa, "*Are* you in health, my brother?" And Joab took Amasa by the
beard with his right hand to kiss him. 10But Amasa did not notice the
sword that *was* in Joab's hand. And he struck him with it in the stomach,
and his entrails poured out on the ground; and he did not *strike* him again.
Thus he died.

Then Joab and Abishai his brother pursued Sheba the son of Bichri.
11Meanwhile one of Joab's men stood near Amasa, and said, "Whoever favors Joab and whoever *is* for David—follow Joab!" 12But Amasa wallowed
in *his* blood in the middle of the highway. And when the man saw that all
the people stood still, he moved Amasa from the highway to the field and
threw a garment over him, when he saw that everyone who came upon
him halted. 13When he was removed from the highway, all the people went
on after Joab to pursue Sheba the son of Bichri.

14And he went through all the tribes of Israel to Abel and Beth Maachah
and all the Berites. So they were gathered together and also went after
Sheba.[t] 15Then they came and besieged him in Abel of Beth Maachah; and
they cast up a siege mound against the city, and it stood by the rampart.
And all the people who *were* with Joab battered the wall to throw it down.

16Then a wise woman cried out from the city, "Hear, hear! Please say to
Joab, 'Come nearby, that I may speak with you.'" 17When he had come
near to her, the woman said, "*Are* you Joab?"

He answered, "I *am.*"

Then she said to him, "Hear the words of your maidservant."

And he answered, "I am listening."

18So she spoke, saying, "They used to talk in former times, saying, 'They
shall surely seek *guidance* at Abel,' and so they would end *disputes.* 19I *am*
among the peaceable *and* faithful in Israel. You seek to destroy a city and a
mother in Israel. Why would you swallow up the inheritance of the LORD?"

20And Joab answered and said, "Far be it, far be it from me, that I should
swallow up or destroy! 21That *is* not so. But a man from the mountains of
Ephraim, Sheba the son of Bichri by name, has raised his hand against the
king, against David. Deliver him only, and I will depart from the city."

So the woman said to Joab, "Watch, his head will be thrown to you over
the wall." 22Then the woman in her wisdom went to all the people. And
they cut off the head of Sheba the son of Bichri, and threw *it* out to Joab.
Then he blew a trumpet, and they withdrew from the city, every man to his
tent. So Joab returned to the king at Jerusalem.

David's Government Officers

23And Joab *was* over all the army of Israel; Benaiah the son of Jehoiada *was*
over the Cherethites and the Pelethites; 24Adoram *was* in charge of revenue;
Jehoshaphat the son of Ahilud *was* recorder; 25Sheva *was* scribe; Zadok
and Abiathar *were* the priests; 26and Ira the Jairite was a chief minister
under David.

20:14 [t] Literally *him*

LIFE LESSON

2 Samuel 20:1-26

SITUATION Sheba, a Benjamite, called upon the Israelites to follow him and rebel against king David. David, who had just defeated Absalom's rebellion, put down Sheba's rebellion as well.

OBSERVATION The house of Benjamin had been a rival of David since he became King of Israel. Old jealousies and bitterness prompted Sheba to call for a revolt against David. In doing so, Sheba hoped to take the monarchy by force and return it to the house of Benjamin.

INSPIRATION Black and cold, bitterness denies easy escape. The sides are slippery with resentment. A floor of muddy anger stills the feet. The stench of betrayal fills the air and stings the eyes. A cloud of self-pity blocks the view of the tiny exit above. . . .

You can choose, like many, to chain yourself to your hurt.

Or you can choose, like some, to put away your hurts before they become hates. You can choose to go to the party. You have a place there. Your name is beside a plate. If you are a child of God, no one can take away your sonship.

Which is precisely what the father said to the older son. "Son, you are always with me, and all that I have is yours."

And that is precisely what the Father says to you. How does God deal with your bitter heart? He reminds you that what you have is more important than what you don't have. You still have your relationship with God. No one can take that. No one can touch it.

(From *He Still Moves Stones* by Max Lucado)

APPLICATION Who or what can evoke a bitter response from you? Put the past behind you. Trust God for the strength to forgive.

EXPLORATION Jealousy—Proverbs 6:34; Romans 13:13; 1 Corinthians 13:4.

David Avenges the Gibeonites

21 Now there was a famine in the days of David for three years, year
after year; and David inquired of the LORD. And the LORD answered,
"*It is* because of Saul and *his* bloodthirsty house, because he killed the
Gibeonites." 2So the king called the Gibeonites and spoke to them. Now
the Gibeonites *were* not of the children of Israel, but of the remnant of the
Amorites; the children of Israel had sworn protection to them, but Saul
had sought to kill them in his zeal for the children of Israel and Judah.
3Therefore David said to the Gibeonites, "What shall I do for you? And with
what shall I make atonement, that you may bless the inheritance of the LORD?"
4And the Gibeonites said to him, "We will have no silver or gold from
Saul or from his house, nor shall you kill any man in Israel for us."
So he said, "Whatever you say, I will do for you."
5Then they answered the king, "As for the man who consumed us and
plotted against us, *that* we should be destroyed from remaining in any of the
territories of Israel, 6let seven men of his descendants be delivered to us, and
we will hang them before the LORD in Gibeah of Saul, *whom* the LORD chose."
And the king said, "I will give *them.*"
7But the king spared Mephibosheth the son of Jonathan, the son of Saul,
because of the LORD's oath that *was* between them, between David and
Jonathan the son of Saul. 8So the king took Armoni and Mephibosheth,
the two sons of Rizpah the daughter of Aiah, whom she bore to Saul, and
the five sons of Michal[u] the daughter of Saul, whom she brought up for
Adriel the son of Barzillai the Meholathite; 9and he delivered them into the
hands of the Gibeonites, and they hanged them on the hill before the LORD.
So they fell, *all* seven together, and were put to death in the days of harvest,
in the first *days,* in the beginning of barley harvest.
10Now Rizpah the daughter of Aiah took sackcloth and spread it for herself on the rock, from the beginning of harvest until the late rains poured
on them from heaven. And she did not allow the birds of the air to rest on
them by day nor the beasts of the field by night.
11And David was told what Rizpah the daughter of Aiah, the concubine
of Saul, had done. 12Then David went and took the bones of Saul, and the
bones of Jonathan his son, from the men of Jabesh Gilead who had stolen
them from the street of Beth Shan,[v] where the Philistines had hung them
up, after the Philistines had struck down Saul in Gilboa. 13So he brought up
the bones of Saul and the bones of Jonathan his son from there; and they
gathered the bones of those who had been hanged. 14They buried the
bones of Saul and Jonathan his son in the country of Benjamin in Zelah, in
the tomb of Kish his father. So they performed all that the king commanded. And after that God heeded the prayer for the land.

Philistine Giants Destroyed

15When the Philistines were at war again with Israel, David and his servants with him went down and fought against the Philistines; and David
grew faint. 16Then Ishbi-Benob, who *was* one of the sons of the giant, the
weight of whose bronze spear *was* three hundred *shekels,* who was bearing
a new *sword,* thought he could kill David. 17But Abishai the son of Zeruiah
came to his aid, and struck the Philistine and killed him. Then the men of

21:8 [u] Or *Merab* (compare 1 Samuel 18:19 and 25:44; 2 Samuel 3:14 and 6:23)
21:12 [v] Spelled *Beth Shean* in Joshua 17:11 and elsewhere

LIFE LESSON

2 Samuel 21:1-22

SITUATION A three year famine ravaged Israel. David turned to God for relief and insight.

OBSERVATION God revealed his answer to David after three years of waiting. God used famine to judge the nation of Israel because of injustices Saul had done against the Gibeonites.

INSPIRATION Prayer. . . . Often there is a wrestle. A thousand invisible enemies will seem to fill the air and crowd between you and your Lord. Each of them has a stinging or depressing word. . . . Our wrestling is with these whispering or shouting spiritual foes. We must press through, fight through, and the sword with which to fight is the blessed word of God. . . .

Sometimes we cannot find words. We are not always meant to find them. I have been greatly comforted in the word that says we are not heard for our much speaking. We are not pledged to pour out words for half an hour. Words fail us at times . . . So do not be afraid of silence in your prayer time. It may be that you are meant to listen, not to speak. So wait before the Lord. Wait in stillness. Wait as David waited when he "sat before the Lord." And in that stillness, assurance will come to you. You will know that you are heard; you will know that your Lord ponders the voice of your humble desires; you will hear quiet words spoken to you yourself, perhaps to your grateful surprise and refresh-ment. And you will know that the power of your Lord will be great.

(From *Thou Givest, They Gather* by Amy Carmichael)

APPLICATION Spend a couple of minutes in silent prayer. Simply be quiet before God. Then speak, know-ing that he listens.

EXPLORATION Be Quiet Before God—1 Kings 19:11-13; Psalm 37:7; 46:10.

David swore to him, saying, "You shall go out no more with us to battle,
lest you quench the lamp of Israel."
18Now it happened afterward that there was again a battle with the
Philistines at Gob. Then Sibbechai the Hushathite killed Saph,[w] who *was*
one of the sons of the giant. 19Again there was war at Gob with the
Philistines, where Elhanan the son of Jaare-Oregim[x] the Bethlehemite
killed *the brother of* Goliath the Gittite, the shaft of whose spear *was* like a
weaver's beam.
20Yet again there was war at Gath, where there was a man of *great*
stature, who had six fingers on each hand and six toes on each foot,
twenty-four in number; and he also was born to the giant. 21So when he
defied Israel, Jonathan the son of Shimea,[y] David's brother, killed him.
22These four were born to the giant in Gath, and fell by the hand of David
and by the hand of his servants.

Praise for God's Deliverance

22 Then David spoke to the LORD the words of this song, on the day
when the LORD had delivered him from the hand of all his enemies,
and from the hand of Saul. 2And he said:[z]

"The LORD *is* my rock and my fortress and my deliverer;
3 The God of my strength, in whom I will trust;
My shield and the horn of my salvation,
My stronghold and my refuge;
My Savior, You save me from violence.
4 I will call upon the LORD, *who is worthy* to be praised;
So shall I be saved from my enemies.

5 "When the waves of death surrounded me,
The floods of ungodliness made me afraid.
6 The sorrows of Sheol surrounded me;
The snares of death confronted me.
7 In my distress I called upon the LORD,
And cried out to my God;
He heard my voice from His temple,
And my cry *entered* His ears.

8 "Then the earth shook and trembled;
The foundations of heaven[a] quaked
and were shaken,
Because He was angry.
9 Smoke went up from His nostrils,
And devouring fire from His mouth;
Coals were kindled by it.
10 He bowed the heavens also, and came down
With darkness under His feet.
11 He rode upon a cherub, and flew;

LIFE LESSON

2 Samuel 22:1–23:7

SITUATION David praised God for the close attention God had given him during his reign. David humbly praised God for his care and help.

OBSERVATION God knows the needs and concerns of his people and ensures that his people are cared for. Nothing can stop God from showing his commitment to those he loves.

INSPIRATION When I see a flock of sheep I see exactly that, a flock. A rabble of wool. A herd of hooves. I don't see *a* sheep. I see sheep. All alike. None different. That's what I see.

But not so with the shepherd. To him every sheep is different. Every face is special. Every face has a story. And every sheep has a name. *The one with the sad eyes, that's Droopy. And the fellow with one ear up and the other down, I call him Oscar. And the small one with the black patch on his leg, he's an orphan with no brothers. I call him Joseph.*

The shepherd knows his sheep. He calls them by name.

When we see a crowd, we see exactly that, a crowd. Filling a stadium or flooding a mall. When we see a crowd, we see people, not persons, but people. A herd of humans. A flock of faces. That's what we see.

But not so with the Shepherd. To him every face is different. Every face is a story. Every face is a child. Every child has a name. *The one with the sad eyes, that's Sally. The old fellow with one eyebrow up and the other down, Harry's his name. And the young one with the limp? He's an orphan with no brothers. I call him Joey.*

The shepherd knows his sheep. He knows each one by name. The Shepherd knows you. He knows your name. And he will never forget it. *I have written your name on my hand* (Isaiah 49:16).

Quite a thought, isn't it? Your name on God's hand. Your name on God's lips. Maybe you've seen your name in some special places. On an award or diploma or walnut door. Or maybe you've heard your name from some important people—a coach, a celebrity, a teacher.

Continued

21:18 [w] Spelled *Sippai* in 1 Chronicles 20:4
21:19 [x] Spelled *Jair* in 1 Chronicles 20:5
21:21 [y] Spelled *Shammah* in 1 Samuel 16:9 and elsewhere
22:2 [z] Compare Psalm 18
22:8 [a] Following Masoretic Text, Septuagint, and Targum; Syriac and Vulgate read *hills* (compare Psalm 18:7).

But to think that your name is on God's hand, on God's lips . . . my, could it be?

Or perhaps you've never seen your name honored. And you can't remember when you heard it spoken with kindness. If so, it may be more difficult for you to believe that God knows your name.

But he does, written on his hand. Spoken by his mouth. Whispered by his lips. Your name.

(From *When God Whispers Your Name* by Max Lucado)

APPLICATION Are you surprised that God thinks of you? That he even cares about you? Throughout your daily activities, imagine Jesus watching you. When you stop and pray, imagine him listening carefully. God watches and listens constantly.

EXPLORATION God's Thoughts to You—Psalm 139:17; Isaiah 43:4; 2 Corinthians 5:21; 1 Peter 2:4.

And He was seen[b] upon the wings of the wind.
12 He made darkness canopies around Him,
Dark waters *and* thick clouds of the skies.
13 From the brightness before Him
Coals of fire were kindled.

14 "The LORD thundered from heaven,
And the Most High uttered His voice.
15 He sent out arrows and scattered them;
Lightning bolts, and He vanquished them.
16 Then the channels of the sea were seen,
The foundations of the world were uncovered,
At the rebuke of the LORD,
At the blast of the breath of His nostrils.

17 "He sent from above, He took me,
He drew me out of many waters.
18 He delivered me from my strong enemy,
From those who hated me;
For they were too strong for me.
19 They confronted me in the day of my calamity,
But the LORD was my support.
20 He also brought me out into a broad place;
He delivered me because He delighted in me.

21 "The LORD rewarded me according to my righteousness;
According to the cleanness of my hands
He has recompensed me.
22 For I have kept the ways of the LORD,
And have not wickedly departed from my God.
23 For all His judgments *were* before me;
And *as for* His statutes, I did not depart from them.
24 I was also blameless before Him,
And I kept myself from my iniquity.
25 Therefore the LORD has recompensed me according
to my righteousness,
According to my cleanness in His eyes.[c]

26 "With the merciful You will show Yourself merciful;
With a blameless man You will show Yourself blameless;
27 With the pure You will show Yourself pure;
And with the devious You will show Yourself shrewd.
28 You will save the humble people;
But Your eyes *are* on the haughty, *that* You may bring *them* down.

29 "For You *are* my lamp, O LORD;
The LORD shall enlighten my darkness.
30 For by You I can run against a troop;
By my God I can leap over a wall.
31 *As for* God, His way *is* perfect;

22:11 [b] Following Masoretic Text and Septuagint; many Hebrew manuscripts, Syriac, and Vulgate read *He flew* (compare Psalm 18:10); Targum reads *He spoke with power.*
22:25 [c] Septuagint, Syriac, and Vulgate read *the cleanness of my hands in His sight* (compare Psalm 18:24); Targum reads *my cleanness before His word.*

The word of the LORD *is* proven;
He *is* a shield to all who trust in Him.

32 "For who *is* God, except the LORD?
And who *is* a rock, except our God?
33 God *is* my strength *and* power,[d]
And He makes my[e] way perfect.
34 He makes my[f] feet like the *feet* of deer,
And sets me on my high places.
35 He teaches my hands to make war,
So that my arms can bend a bow of bronze.

36 "You have also given me the shield of
Your salvation;
Your gentleness has made me great.
37 You enlarged my path under me;
So my feet did not slip.

38 "I have pursued my enemies and
destroyed them;
Neither did I turn back again till they
were destroyed.
39 And I have destroyed them and
wounded them,
So that they could not rise;
They have fallen under my feet.
40 For You have armed me with strength for
the battle;
You have subdued under me those who rose
against me.
41 You have also given me the necks of
my enemies,
So that I destroyed those who hated me.
42 They looked, but *there was* none to save;
Even to the LORD, but He did not answer them.
43 Then I beat them as fine as the dust of
the earth;
I trod them like dirt in the streets,
And I spread them out.

44 "You have also delivered me from the strivings
of my people;
You have kept me as the head of the nations.
A people I have not known shall serve me.
45 The foreigners submit to me;
As soon as they hear, they obey me.
46 The foreigners fade away,
And come frightened[g] from their hideouts.

47 "The LORD lives!
Blessed *be* my Rock!
Let God be exalted,
The Rock of my salvation!
48 *It is* God who avenges me,
And subdues the peoples under me;
49 He delivers me from my enemies.
You also lift me up above those who rise
against me;
You have delivered me from the violent man.
50 Therefore I will give thanks to You, O LORD,
among the Gentiles,
And sing praises to Your name.

51 *He is* the tower of salvation to His king,
And shows mercy to His anointed,
To David and his descendants
forevermore."

David's Last Words

23 Now these *are* the last words of David.

Thus says David the son of Jesse;
Thus says the man raised up on high,
The anointed of the God of Jacob,
And the sweet psalmist of Israel:

2 "The Spirit of the LORD spoke by me,
And His word *was* on my tongue.
3 The God of Israel said,
The Rock of Israel spoke to me:
'He who rules over men *must be* just,
Ruling in the fear of God.
4 And *he shall be* like the light of the morning
when the sun rises,
A morning without clouds,
Like the tender grass *springing* out of
the earth,
By clear shining after rain.'

5 "Although my house *is* not so with God,
Yet He has made with me an
everlasting covenant,
Ordered in all *things* and secure.
For *this is* all my salvation and all *my* desire;
Will He not make *it* increase?
6 But *the sons* of rebellion *shall* all *be* as thorns
thrust away,
Because they cannot be taken with hands.
7 But the man *who* touches them

22:33 [d] Dead Sea Scrolls, Septuagint, Syriac, and Vulgate read *It is God who arms me with strength* (compare Psalm 18:32); Targum reads *It is God who sustains me with strength.* [e] Following Qere, Septuagint, Syriac, Targum, and Vulgate (compare Psalm 18:32); Kethib reads *His.*
22:34 [f] Following Qere, Septuagint, Syriac, Targum, and Vulgate (compare Psalm 18:33); Kethib reads *His.*
22:46 [g] Following Septuagint, Targum, and Vulgate (compare Psalm 18:45); Masoretic Text reads *gird themselves.*

Must be armed with iron and the shaft of a spear,
And they shall be utterly burned with fire in *their* place."

David's Mighty Men

8These *are* the names of the mighty men whom David had: Josheb-Basshebeth[h] the Tachmonite, chief among the captains.[i] He was called Adino the Eznite, because he had killed eight hundred men at one time. 9And after him *was* Eleazar the son of Dodo,[j] the Ahohite, *one* of the three mighty men with David when they defied the Philistines *who* were gathered there for battle, and the men of Israel had retreated. 10He arose and attacked the Philistines until his hand was weary, and his hand stuck to the sword. The LORD brought about a great victory that day; and the people returned after him only to plunder. 11And after him *was* Shammah the son of Agee the Hararite. The Philistines had gathered together into a troop where there was a piece of ground full of lentils. So the people fled from the Philistines. 12But he stationed himself in the middle of the field, defended it, and killed the Philistines. So the LORD brought about a great victory.

13Then three of the thirty chief men went down at harvest time and came to David at the cave of Adullam. And the troop of Philistines encamped in the Valley of Rephaim. 14David *was* then in the stronghold, and the garrison of the Philistines *was* then *in* Bethlehem. 15And David said with longing, "Oh, that someone would give me a drink of the water from the well of Bethlehem, which *is* by the gate!" 16So the three mighty men broke through the camp of the Philistines, drew water from the well of Bethlehem that *was* by the gate, and took it and brought *it* to David. Nevertheless he would not drink it, but poured it out to the LORD. 17And he said, "Far be it from me, O LORD, that I should do this! Is *this not* the blood of the men who went in *jeopardy of* their lives?" Therefore he would not drink it.

These things were done by the three mighty men.

18Now Abishai the brother of Joab, the son of Zeruiah, was chief of *another* three.[k] He lifted his spear against three hundred *men*, killed *them*, and won a name among *these* three. 19Was he not the most honored of three? Therefore he became their captain. However, he did not attain to the *first* three.

20Benaiah *was* the son of Jehoiada, the son of a valiant man from Kabzeel, who had done many deeds. He had killed two lion-like heroes of Moab. He also had gone down and killed a lion in the midst of a pit on a snowy day. 21And he killed an Egyptian, a spectacular man. The Egyptian *had* a spear in his hand; so he went down to him with a staff, wrested the spear out of the Egyptian's hand, and killed him with his own spear. 22These *things* Benaiah the son of Jehoiada did, and won a name among three mighty men. 23He was more honored than the thirty, but he did not attain to the *first* three. And David appointed him over his guard.

24Asahel the brother of Joab *was* one of the thirty; Elhanan the son of Dodo of Bethlehem, 25Shammah the Harodite, Elika the Harodite, 26Helez the Paltite, Ira the son of Ikkesh the Tekoite, 27Abiezer the Anathothite, Mebunnai the Hushathite, 28Zalmon the Ahohite, Maharai the Netophathite, 29Heleb the son of Baanah (the Netophathite), Ittai the son of Ribai from

23:8 [h] Literally *One Who Sits in the Seat* (compare 1 Chronicles 11:11) [i] Following Masoretic Text and Targum; Septuagint and Vulgate read *the three.*
23:9 [j] Spelled *Dodai* in 1 Chronicles 27:4
23:18 [k] Following Masoretic Text, Septuagint, and Vulgate; some Hebrew manuscripts and Syriac read *thirty;* Targum reads *the mighty men.*

LIFE LESSON

2 Samuel 23:8–24:25

SITUATION David's reign brought great peace, prosperity, and military success. David and the people began to be proud, and God punished them for this sin.

OBSERVATION We must find our strength and security only in God and never in worldly possessions.

INSPIRATION Do you think anything concerning you right now is too small?

Your house or apartment? Your personal reputation? Your influence? Your job? Your family? (You want to add a spouse or children)? Your circle of friends? Your salary? Your life?

Until I paid attention to Psalm 131, I chafed. Then I discovered that God's leash wasn't too tight—my heart was too proud! I thought I "deserved" more; my self-image had greater expectations, and that attitude was the very grease on which I slid into self-pity, discontent, ungratefulness, misery.

Then I fixed my eyes on Jesus and in my own eyes I became smaller and smaller. What was my stature, my purity, my power, my excellence compared with His?

I felt foolish, embarrassed, very small.

And now what did I deserve? Nothing—nothing at all. I was an "unworthy servant" (Luke 17:10).

Now I looked at all that the Lord God in His incredible grace had lavished on me—with such love and joy—and it was like Christmas in July!

(From *My Sacrifice, His Fire* by Anne Ortlund)

APPLICATION What gives your life security or significance apart from God: Money? Status? Position? Possessions? Imagine that you lost them all. How would you feel? Learn to see all that you have as a gift from God to be used only for him, not for personal pride.

EXPLORATION Pride—Judges 7:2; 1 Samuel 2:3; Proverbs 18:11-12; Jeremiah 9:23-24; Zechariah 4:6; Romans 12:3; 1 Corinthians 4:6-10; 2 Corinthians 10:12; Galatians 6:3; Revelation 3:17.

Gibeah of the children of Benjamin, 30Benaiah a Pirathonite, Hiddai from the brooks of Gaash, 31Abi-Albon the Arbathite, Azmaveth the Barhumite, 32Eliahba the Shaalbonite (of the sons of Jashen), Jonathan, 33Shammah the Hararite, Ahiam the son of Sharar the Hararite, 34Eliphelet the son of Ahasbai, the son of the Maachathite, Eliam the son of Ahithophel the Gilonite, 35Hezrai[l] the Carmelite, Paarai the Arbite, 36Igal the son of Nathan of Zobah, Bani the Gadite, 37Zelek the Ammonite, Naharai the Beerothite (armorbearer of Joab the son of Zeruiah), 38Ira the Ithrite, Gareb the Ithrite, 39*and* Uriah the Hittite: thirty-seven in all.

David's Census of Israel and Judah

24 Again the anger of the LORD was aroused against Israel, and He moved David against them to say, "Go, number Israel and Judah."

2So the king said to Joab the commander of the army who *was* with him, "Now go throughout all the tribes of Israel, from Dan to Beersheba, and count the people, that I may know the number of the people."

3And Joab said to the king, "Now may the LORD your God add to the people a hundred times more than there are, and may the eyes of my lord the king see *it.* But why does my lord the king desire this thing?" 4Nevertheless the king's word prevailed against Joab and against the captains of the army. Therefore Joab and the captains of the army went out from the presence of the king to count the people of Israel.

5And they crossed over the Jordan and camped in Aroer, on the right side of the town which *is* in the midst of the ravine of Gad, and toward Jazer. 6Then they came to Gilead and to the land of Tahtim Hodshi; they came to Dan Jaan and around to Sidon; 7and they came to the stronghold of Tyre and to all the cities of the Hivites and the Canaanites. Then they went out to South Judah *as far as* Beersheba. 8So when they had gone through all the land, they came to Jerusalem at the end of nine months and twenty days. 9Then Joab gave the sum of the number of the people to the king. And there were in Israel eight hundred thousand valiant men who drew the sword, and the men of Judah were five hundred thousand men.

The Judgment on David's Sin

10And David's heart condemned him after he had numbered the people. So David said to the LORD, "I have sinned greatly in what I have done; but now, I pray, O LORD, take away the iniquity of Your servant, for I have done very foolishly."

11Now when David arose in the morning, the word of the LORD came to the prophet Gad, David's seer, saying, 12"Go and tell David, 'Thus says the LORD: "I offer you three *things;* choose one of them for yourself, that I may do *it* to you." ' " 13So Gad came to David and told him; and he said to him, "Shall seven[m] years of famine come to you in your land? Or shall you flee three months before your enemies, while they pursue you? Or shall there be three days' plague in your land? Now consider and see what answer I should take back to Him who sent me."

14And David said to Gad, "I am in great distress. Please let us fall into the hand of the LORD, for His mercies *are* great; but do not let me fall into the hand of man."

15So the LORD sent a plague upon Israel from the morning till the appointed time. From Dan to Beersheba seventy thousand men of the people died. 16And when the angel[n] stretched out His hand over Jerusalem to destroy it, the LORD relented from the destruction, and said to the angel who was destroying the people, "It is enough; now restrain your hand." And the angel of the LORD was by the threshing floor of Araunah[o] the Jebusite.

17Then David spoke to the LORD when he saw the angel who was striking the people, and said, "Surely I have sinned, and I have done wickedly; but these sheep, what have they done? Let Your hand, I pray, be against me and against my father's house."

The Altar on the Threshing Floor

18And Gad came that day to David and said to him, "Go up, erect an altar to the LORD on the threshing floor of Araunah the Jebusite." 19So David, according to the word of Gad, went up as the LORD commanded. 20Now Araunah looked, and saw the king and his servants coming toward him. So Araunah went out and bowed before the king with his face to the ground.

21Then Araunah said, "Why has my lord the king come to his servant?"

And David said, "To buy the threshing floor from you, to build an altar to the LORD, that the plague may be withdrawn from the people."

22Now Araunah said to David, "Let my lord the king take and offer up whatever *seems* good to him. Look, *here are* oxen for burnt sacrifice, and threshing

23:35 *l* Spelled *Hezro* in 1 Chronicles 11:37
24:13 *m* Following Masoretic Text, Syriac, Targum, and Vulgate; Septuagint reads *three* (compare 1 Chronicles 21:12).
24:16 *n* Or *Angel* *o* Spelled *Ornan* in 1 Chronicles 21:15

implements and the yokes of the oxen for wood. 23All
these, O king, Araunah has given to the king."
And Araunah said to the king, "May the LORD your
God accept you."
24Then the king said to Araunah, "No, but I will
surely buy *it* from you for a price; nor will I offer burnt
offerings to the LORD my God with that which costs me
nothing." So David bought the threshing floor and the
oxen for fifty shekels of silver. 25And David built there
an altar to the LORD, and offered burnt offerings and
peace offerings. So the LORD heeded the prayers for the
land, and the plague was withdrawn from Israel.

The First Book of the KINGS

INTRODUCTION

The book starts with Solomon and ends with Elijah. The difference between the two gives you an idea as to what lies between.

Solomon might never have been born had it not been for the palace scandal between David and Bathsheba. Not the best of beginnings. He picked up some of his father's traits, both good and bad. Like his dad, he got off to a good start. But like his dad, he had a weakness for women that undid him.

You have to wonder what it was like growing up in a house where your father had several wives and your siblings wore swords to the dinner table. Solomon did well at first, praying for wisdom and building a temple that would have bankrupted most nations.

He took seven years building it. But then he spent thirteen years building a palace for himself. Somewhere around mid-life he got off track. His taste for wives (he was known to have accumulated some seven hundred or so) led him to worship whom they worshiped. This, in turn, led him away from God. His nation followed suit, and even the preaching of Elijah couldn't bring them back.

Not that Elijah didn't try. Toward the end of this book you'll read of the contest between Elijah and the prophets of Baal. In a classic my-God-is-greater-than-yours encounter, Jehovah won hands down. God was exalted. But Queen Jezebel, a leading Baal-worshiper, was infuriated.

She ordered Elijah's death, so Elijah ran. He ran until he was so tired and discouraged that he sat down under a bush and said, "take my life" (19:4).

What does God do with tired servants who want to quit? In a tender moment the God who'd brought fire on the mountain sent food to the prophet and whispered his affection in a "still small voice" (19:12).

What a Father.

What a book! In between Solomon and Elijah, you'll find it all. Rebellion, corruption, courage, faith. You'll see that their world is much like ours. Things haven't changed much.

And God? God hasn't changed at all. The quiet, gentle sound that encouraged Elijah? Listen as you read. It will encourage you.

LIFE LESSON

1 Kings 1:1-53

SITUATION When David's life and reign drew to a close, his sons competed for his throne. David appointed Solomon as his heir.

OBSERVATION Although David served well as a king, he often failed as a parent. We can be successful in our public life and a failure in private. Our families should be our first ministry priority.

INSPIRATION When Daddy came to tuck me in, he would sit on the bed, and I would often kneel, reaching up to put my hands on his knees. With his huge hands on mine he prayed for me. . . . The biggest decisions of his life—his salvation, his marriage, his life's work—were made on the basis of eternal, not temporal value. . . .

As Christ's submission to His Father meant also His submission to the needs of His disciples, so a father's submission to a Heavenly Father means submission to the needs of his children, in other words, sacrifice and humble service, always the conditions of Godlike authority. "I am among you as one who serves," Jesus said (Luke 22:27 RSV). . . .

It is sad to read that the average father nowadays spends three minutes per week with each child. Home, frankly, is just "not his scene". He'd rather be elsewhere. What does he do with the

Adonijah Presumes to Be King

Now King David was old, advanced in years; and they put
covers on him, but he could not get warm. 2Therefore his
servants said to him, "Let a young woman, a virgin, be
sought for our lord the king, and let her stand before the king,
and let her care for him; and let her lie in your bosom, that our lord the
king may be warm." 3So they sought for a lovely young woman throughout all the territory of Israel, and found Abishag the Shunammite, and
brought her to the king. 4The young woman *was* very lovely; and she cared
for the king, and served him; but the king did not know her.
5Then Adonijah the son of Haggith exalted himself, saying, "I will be
king"; and he prepared for himself chariots and horsemen, and fifty men
to run before him. 6(And his father had not rebuked him at any time by
saying, "Why have you done so?" He *was* also very good-looking. *His
mother* had borne him after Absalom.) 7Then he conferred with Joab the
son of Zeruiah and with Abiathar the priest, and they followed and helped
Adonijah. 8But Zadok the priest, Benaiah the son of Jehoiada, Nathan the
prophet, Shimei, Rei, and the mighty men who *belonged* to David were not
with Adonijah.
9And Adonijah sacrificed sheep and oxen and fattened cattle by the stone
of Zoheleth, which *is* by En Rogel; he also invited all his brothers, the king's
sons, and all the men of Judah, the king's servants. 10But he did not invite
Nathan the prophet, Benaiah, the mighty men, or Solomon his brother.
11So Nathan spoke to Bathsheba the mother of Solomon, saying, "Have
you not heard that Adonijah the son of Haggith has become king, and David our lord does not know *it?* 12Come, please, let me now give you advice,
that you may save your own life and the life of your son Solomon. 13Go immediately to King David and say to him, 'Did you not, my lord, O king,
swear to your maidservant, saying, "Assuredly your son Solomon shall
reign after me, and he shall sit on my throne"? Why then has Adonijah become king?' 14Then, while you are still talking there with the king, I also
will come in after you and confirm your words."
15So Bathsheba went into the chamber to the king. (Now the king was
very old, and Abishag the Shunammite was serving the king.) 16And
Bathsheba bowed and did homage to the king. Then the king said, "What
is your wish?"
17Then she said to him, "My lord, you swore by the LORD your God to
your maidservant, *saying,* 'Assuredly Solomon your son shall reign after
me, and he shall sit on my throne.' 18So now, look! Adonijah has become
king; and now, my lord the king, you do not know about *it.* 19He has sacrificed oxen and fattened cattle and sheep in abundance, and has invited all
the sons of the king, Abiathar the priest, and Joab the commander of the
army; but Solomon your servant he has not invited. 20And as for you, my
lord, O king, the eyes of all Israel *are* on you, that you should tell them who
will sit on the throne of my lord the king after him. 21Otherwise it will happen, when my lord the king rests with his fathers, that I and my son Solomon will be counted as offenders."
22And just then, while she was still talking with the king, Nathan the
prophet also came in. 23So they told the king, saying, "Here is Nathan the
prophet." And when he came in before the king, he bowed down before
the king with his face to the ground. 24And Nathan said, "My lord, O king,

have you said, 'Adonijah shall reign after me, and he shall sit on my
throne'? 25For he has gone down today, and has sacrificed oxen and fattened cattle and sheep in abundance, and has invited all the king's sons,
and the commanders of the army, and Abiathar the priest; and look! They
are eating and drinking before him; and they say, '*Long* live King
Adonijah!' 26But he has not invited me—me your servant—nor Zadok the
priest, nor Benaiah the son of Jehoiada, nor your servant Solomon. 27Has
this thing been done by my lord the king, and you have not told your servant who should sit on the throne of my lord the king after him?"

David Proclaims Solomon King

28Then King David answered and said, "Call Bathsheba to me." So she
came into the king's presence and stood before the king. 29And the king
took an oath and said, "*As* the LORD lives, who has redeemed my life from
every distress, 30just as I swore to you by the LORD God of Israel, saying,
'Assuredly Solomon your son shall be king after me, and he shall sit on my
throne in my place,' so I certainly will do this day."
31Then Bathsheba bowed with *her* face to the earth, and paid homage to
the king, and said, "Let my lord King David live forever!"
32And King David said, "Call to me Zadok the priest, Nathan the prophet,
and Benaiah the son of Jehoiada." So they came before the king. 33The king
also said to them, "Take with you the servants of your lord, and have Solomon my son ride on my own mule, and take him down to Gihon. 34There
let Zadok the priest and Nathan the prophet anoint him king over Israel; and
blow the horn, and say, '*Long* live King Solomon!' 35Then you shall come up
after him, and he shall come and sit on my throne, and he shall be king in
my place. For I have appointed him to be ruler over Israel and Judah."
36Benaiah the son of Jehoiada answered the king and said, "Amen! May
the LORD God of my lord the king say so *too.* 37As the LORD has been with
my lord the king, even so may He be with Solomon, and make his throne
greater than the throne of my lord King David."
38So Zadok the priest, Nathan the prophet, Benaiah the son of Jehoiada,
the Cherethites, and the Pelethites went down and had Solomon ride on
King David's mule, and took him to Gihon. 39Then Zadok the priest took a
horn of oil from the tabernacle and anointed Solomon. And they blew the
horn, and all the people said, "*Long* live King Solomon!" 40And all the people went up after him; and the people played the flutes and rejoiced with
great joy, so that the earth *seemed to* split with their sound.
41Now Adonijah and all the guests who *were* with him heard *it* as they
finished eating. And when Joab heard the sound of the horn, he said,
"Why *is* the city in such a noisy uproar?" 42While he was still speaking,
there came Jonathan, the son of Abiathar the priest. And Adonijah said to
him, "Come in, for you *are* a prominent man, and bring good news."
43Then Jonathan answered and said to Adonijah, "No! Our lord King
David has made Solomon king. 44The king has sent with him Zadok the
priest, Nathan the prophet, Benaiah the son of Jehoiada, the Cherethites,
and the Pelethites; and they have made him ride on the king's mule. 45So
Zadok the priest and Nathan the prophet have anointed him king at
Gihon; and they have gone up from there rejoicing, so that the city is in an
uproar. This *is* the noise that you have heard. 46Also Solomon sits on the
throne of the kingdom. 47And moreover the king's servants have gone to

rest of his time? Is it a relentless frantic scramble to earn money five or six days a week, with a frantic scramble on weekends to "relax" and enjoy himself, often in expensive and sometimes dangerous ways? Can this really be what God wants for Christian families? If there were the willingness to be content with less money, fewer activities which eat into the budget and take the family away from home, fewer possessions; if there were the willingness to "be content with such things as you have," would we not sooner find the truth of God's Word, "A man's real life in no way depends upon the number of his possessions" (Luke 12:15)? The willingness to be and to have just what God wants us to be and to have, nothing more, nothing less, and nothing else, would set our hearts at rest, and we would discover that the simpler the life the greater the peace.

(From *The Shaping of a Christian Family* by Elisabeth Elliot)

APPLICATION If you are a parent, take time with each child today: listen, talk, and care. As a son or daughter, plan to spend time with your parents. Be concerned for their needs. Be eager to pray for family needs.

EXPLORATION Family Responsibility—Deuteronomy 6:4-7; 11:18-21; 32:46; Psalm 127:3; Proverbs 20:7; 22:6; Isaiah 38:19; Matthew 19:14; Ephesians 6:4; 1 Timothy 3:14-15; 2 Timothy 1:3-7; 1 Thessalonians 2:10-12.

LIFE LESSON

1 Kings 2:1-46

SITUATION David gave final instructions to Solomon that would ensure success. At David's death, Solomon consolidated his power and administration.

OBSERVATION At his death, the great King David exhorted his son: obey God, follow him, and be kind to others.

INSPIRATION Successful people are at the right place at the right time to a great extent because they have learned how to take certain action steps in proper sequence. They have learned that scriptural truth, "To everything there is a season, A time for every purpose under heaven." They know that everything they desire has an appropriate place and time for accomplishment, and toward that end, they set their priorities in certain orders, prepare themselves in certain ways, and refuse to give in to discouragement or failures along the way.

What about those who are unsuccessful?

Some fail because they lack dreams or they don't believe in the possibility of their dreams becoming reality.

Some fail to reach their full potential of a rewarding harvest in life because they have not turned their dreams into specific goals and plans of action for reaching those goals. Many others fail, however, because they are out of sync with time and place:

bless our lord King David, saying, 'May God make the name of Solomon
better than your name, and may He make his throne greater than your
throne.' Then the king bowed himself on the bed. 48Also the king said thus,
'Blessed *be* the LORD God of Israel, who has given *one* to sit on my throne
this day, while my eyes see *it!*' "
49So all the guests who were with Adonijah were afraid, and arose, and
each one went his way.
50Now Adonijah was afraid of Solomon; so he arose, and went and took
hold of the horns of the altar. 51And it was told Solomon, saying, "Indeed
Adonijah is afraid of King Solomon; for look, he has taken hold of the
horns of the altar, saying, 'Let King Solomon swear to me today that he will
not put his servant to death with the sword.' "
52Then Solomon said, "If he proves himself a worthy man, not one hair
of him shall fall to the earth; but if wickedness is found in him, he shall
die." 53So King Solomon sent them to bring him down from the altar. And
he came and fell down before King Solomon; and Solomon said to him,
"Go to your house."

David's Instructions to Solomon

2 Now the days of David drew near that he should die, and he charged
Solomon his son, saying: 2"I go the way of all the earth; be strong, therefore, and prove yourself a man. 3And keep the charge of the LORD your God:
to walk in His ways, to keep His statutes, His commandments, His judgments, and His testimonies, as it is written in the Law of Moses, that you
may prosper in all that you do and wherever you turn; 4that the LORD may
fulfill His word which He spoke concerning me, saying, 'If your sons take
heed to their way, to walk before Me in truth with all their heart and with all
their soul,' He said, 'you shall not lack a man on the throne of Israel.'
5"Moreover you know also what Joab the son of Zeruiah did to me, *and*
what he did to the two commanders of the armies of Israel, to Abner the son
of Ner and Amasa the son of Jether, whom he killed. And he shed the blood
of war in peacetime, and put the blood of war on his belt that *was* around his
waist, and on his sandals that *were* on his feet. 6Therefore do according to
your wisdom, and do not let his gray hair go down to the grave in peace.
7"But show kindness to the sons of Barzillai the Gileadite, and let them
be among those who eat at your table, for so they came to me when I fled
from Absalom your brother.
8"And see, *you have* with you Shimei the son of Gera, a Benjamite from
Bahurim, who cursed me with a malicious curse in the day when I went to
Mahanaim. But he came down to meet me at the Jordan, and I swore to him
by the LORD, saying, 'I will not put you to death with the sword.' 9Now therefore, do not hold him guiltless, for you *are* a wise man and know what you
ought to do to him; but bring his gray hair down to the grave with blood."

Death of David

10So David rested with his fathers, and was buried in the City of David.
11The period that David reigned over Israel *was* forty years; seven years he
reigned in Hebron, and in Jerusalem he reigned thirty-three years. 12Then
Solomon sat on the throne of his father David; and his kingdom was
firmly established.

Solomon Executes Adonijah

13 Now Adonijah the son of Haggith came to Bathsheba the mother of
Solomon. So she said, "Do you come peaceably?"
And he said, "Peaceably." 14 Moreover he said, "I have something *to say*
to you."
And she said, "Say it."
15 Then he said, "You know that the kingdom was mine, and all Israel
had set their expectations on me, that I should reign. However, the kingdom has been turned over, and has become my brother's; for it was his
from the LORD. 16 Now I ask one petition of you; do not deny me."
And she said to him, "Say it."
17 Then he said, "Please speak to King Solomon, for he will not refuse
you, that he may give me Abishag the Shunammite as wife."
18 So Bathsheba said, "Very well, I will speak for you to the king."
19 Bathsheba therefore went to King Solomon, to speak to him for
Adonijah. And the king rose up to meet her and bowed down to her, and
sat down on his throne and had a throne set for the king's mother; so she
sat at his right hand. 20 Then she said, "I desire one small petition of you;
do not refuse me."
And the king said to her, "Ask it, my mother, for I will not refuse you."
21 So she said, "Let Abishag the Shunammite be given to Adonijah your
brother as wife."
22 And King Solomon answered and said to his mother, "Now why do
you ask Abishag the Shunammite for Adonijah? Ask for him the kingdom
also—for he *is* my older brother—for him, and for Abiathar the priest,
and for Joab the son of Zeruiah." 23 Then King Solomon swore by the LORD,
saying, "May God do so to me, and more also, if Adonijah has not spoken
this word against his own life! 24 Now therefore, *as* the LORD lives, who has
confirmed me and set me on the throne of David my father, and who has
established a house[a] for me, as He promised, Adonijah shall be put to
death today!"
25 So King Solomon sent by the hand of Benaiah the son of Jehoiada; and
he struck him down, and he died.

Abiathar Exiled, Joab Executed

26 And to Abiathar the priest the king said, "Go to Anathoth, to your
own fields, for you *are* deserving of death; but I will not put you to death
at this time, because you carried the ark of the Lord GOD before my father
David, and because you were afflicted every time my father was afflicted."
27 So Solomon removed Abiathar from being priest to the LORD, that he
might fulfill the word of the LORD which He spoke concerning the house
of Eli at Shiloh.
28 Then news came to Joab, for Joab had defected to Adonijah, though he
had not defected to Absalom. So Joab fled to the tabernacle of the LORD,
and took hold of the horns of the altar. 29 And King Solomon was told,
"Joab has fled to the tabernacle of the LORD; there *he is*, by the altar." Then
Solomon sent Benaiah the son of Jehoiada, saying, "Go, strike him down."
30 So Benaiah went to the tabernacle of the LORD, and said to him, "Thus
says the king, 'Come out!' "

2:24 [a] That is, a royal dynasty

- They planted or fertilized their goals in the wrong season.
- They planted before they fully planned.
- They attempted to harvest a goal before it was fully developed.

Such failures arise not from a lack of determination or willingness to keep trying but from efforts that are out of proper sequence. The result is that those who fail because of their improper alignment of time and place soon become frustrated, begin to believe that it's impossible for them to achieve anything significant, or allow their disappointments to develop into a failure-anticipating mind-set.

. . . The opportunity for success is yours. Believe it. Regardless of what you experienced in your past, the future can hold success for you.
(From *Timing Is Everything* by Denis Waitley)

APPLICATION If you want success in life, then all your activities must reflect God's will. Today, make God the center of your life. Ask God to show you what successful living means for you. Then, rest easy in God's peace and his plans.

EXPLORATION Success—Joshua 1:6-8; 2 Samuel 5:12; 1 Chronicles 18:13; Proverbs 3:6; 16:3; Matthew 6:33-34.

LIFE LESSON

1 Kings 3:1–4:34

SITUATION Solomon carefully lived by God's rules, and God gave him success. Solomon asked God for wisdom, and with it, God gave him economic prosperity and fame.

OBSERVATION God expects all people to use their gifts to do his will. When they do, everyone else benefits.

INSPIRATION The enemy emphasizes the past, with its mistakes and heartaches; the Comforter exalts the present help of our Lord (Ps. 46:1). The devil delights in taunting us with our weaknesses, and the Lord reminds us of the wealth of His riches in grace. Condemnation concerns itself with our failures; conviction shows us the faithfulness of God. The tempter teases us with immediate gain, at any cost; the Trustworthy One tells us of eternal gain, and reminds us of Passion and Patience in Bunyan's House of the Interpreter. The father of lies magnifies our problems, by showing their hopelessness, impossibility, and pain; the God of all grace reminds us of the promises, whereby we can hope against hope; for "suffering produces perseverance; perseverance, character; and character, hope; and hope does not disappoint us" (Rom. 5:3-5). Thus we know that pain can mean gain.

The false angel of light would have us walk by sight and earthly wisdom ("the counsel of the ungodly," Ps. 1:1); the Lord of life, who sees the end from the beginning, would have us walk by faith (2 Cor. 5:7), and thereby please our heavenly Father (Heb. 11:6). The enemy would have us see the hosts of evil against us rather than the hillsides covered with ministering spirits (2 Kings 6:15-17). He would keep us dwelling upon the injuries from others, until we become ineffective in service, rather than forgetting the things that

And he said, "No, but I will die here." And Benaiah brought back word
to the king, saying, "Thus said Joab, and thus he answered me."
31Then the king said to him, "Do as he has said, and strike him down and
bury him, that you may take away from me and from the house of my father the innocent blood which Joab shed. 32So the LORD will return his blood
on his head, because he struck down two men more righteous and better
than he, and killed them with the sword—Abner the son of Ner, the commander of the army of Israel, and Amasa the son of Jether, the commander
of the army of Judah—though my father David did not know *it.* 33Their
blood shall therefore return upon the head of Joab and upon the head of his
descendants forever. But upon David and his descendants, upon his house
and his throne, there shall be peace forever from the LORD."
34So Benaiah the son of Jehoiada went up and struck and killed him;
and he was buried in his own house in the wilderness. 35The king put
Benaiah the son of Jehoiada in his place over the army, and the king put
Zadok the priest in the place of Abiathar.

Shimei Executed

36Then the king sent and called for Shimei, and said to him, "Build
yourself a house in Jerusalem and dwell there, and do not go out from
there anywhere. 37For it shall be, on the day you go out and cross the Brook
Kidron, know for certain you shall surely die; your blood shall be on your
own head."
38And Shimei said to the king, "The saying *is* good. As my lord the king
has said, so your servant will do." So Shimei dwelt in Jerusalem many days.
39Now it happened at the end of three years, that two slaves of Shimei
ran away to Achish the son of Maachah, king of Gath. And they told
Shimei, saying, "Look, your slaves *are* in Gath!" 40So Shimei arose, saddled
his donkey, and went to Achish at Gath to seek his slaves. And Shimei went
and brought his slaves from Gath. 41And Solomon was told that Shimei
had gone from Jerusalem to Gath and had come back. 42Then the king sent
and called for Shimei, and said to him, "Did I not make you swear by the
LORD, and warn you, saying, 'Know for certain that on the day you go out
and travel anywhere, you shall surely die'? And you said to me, 'The word
I have heard *is* good.' 43Why then have you not kept the oath of the LORD
and the commandment that I gave you?" 44The king said moreover to
Shimei, "You know, as your heart acknowledges, all the wickedness that
you did to my father David; therefore the LORD will return your wickedness
on your own head. 45But King Solomon *shall be* blessed, and the throne of
David shall be established before the LORD forever."
46So the king commanded Benaiah the son of Jehoiada; and he went out
and struck him down, and he died. Thus the kingdom was established in
the hand of Solomon.

Solomon Requests Wisdom

3 Now Solomon made a treaty with Pharaoh king of Egypt, and married
Pharaoh's daughter; then he brought her to the City of David until he
had finished building his own house, and the house of the LORD, and the
wall all around Jerusalem. 2Meanwhile the people sacrificed at the high
places, because there was no house built for the name of the LORD until
those days. 3And Solomon loved the LORD, walking in the statutes of his father David, except that he sacrificed and burned incense at the high places

4Now the king went to Gibeon to sacrifice there, for that *was* the great
high place: Solomon offered a thousand burnt offerings on that altar. 5At
Gibeon the LORD appeared to Solomon in a dream by night; and God said,
"Ask! What shall I give you?"
6And Solomon said: "You have shown great mercy to Your servant David my father, because he walked before You in truth, in righteousness,
and in uprightness of heart with You; You have continued this great kindness for him, and You have given him a son to sit on his throne, as *it is* this
day. 7Now, O LORD my God, You have made Your servant king instead of
my father David, but I *am* a little child; I do not know *how* to go out or
come in. 8And Your servant *is* in the midst of Your people whom You have
chosen, a great people, too numerous to be numbered or counted. 9There-
fore give to Your servant an understanding heart to judge Your people,
that I may discern between good and evil. For who is able to judge this
great people of Yours?"
10The speech pleased the LORD, that Solomon had asked this thing.
11Then God said to him: "Because you have asked this thing, and have not
asked long life for yourself, nor have asked riches for yourself, nor have
asked the life of your enemies, but have asked for yourself understanding
to discern justice, 12behold, I have done according to your words; see, I
have given you a wise and understanding heart, so that there has not been
anyone like you before you, nor shall any like you arise after you. 13And I
have also given you what you have not asked: both riches and honor, so
that there shall not be anyone like you among the kings all your days. 14So
if you walk in My ways, to keep My statutes and My commandments, as
your father David walked, then I will lengthen your days."
15Then Solomon awoke; and indeed it had been a dream. And he came
to Jerusalem and stood before the ark of the covenant of the LORD, offered
up burnt offerings, offered peace offerings, and made a feast for all his
servants.

Solomon's Wise Judgment

16Now two women *who were* harlots came to the king, and stood before
him. 17And one woman said, "O my lord, this woman and I dwell in the
same house; and I gave birth while she *was* in the house. 18Then it happened, the third day after I had given birth, that this woman also gave
birth. And we *were* together; no one *was* with us in the house, except the
two of us in the house. 19And this woman's son died in the night, because
she lay on him. 20So she arose in the middle of the night and took my son
from my side, while your maidservant slept, and laid him in her bosom,
and laid her dead child in my bosom. 21And when I rose in the morning to
nurse my son, there he was, dead. But when I had examined him in the
morning, indeed, he was not my son whom I had borne."
22Then the other woman said, "No! But the living one *is* my son, and the
dead one *is* your son."
And the first woman said, "No! But the dead one *is* your son, and the living one *is* my son."
Thus they spoke before the king.
23And the king said, "The one says, 'This *is* my son, who lives, and your
son *is* the dead one'; and the other says, 'No! But your son *is* the dead one,
and my son *is* the living one.' " 24Then the king said, "Bring me a sword."

are behind and pressing forward (Phil. 3:13,14) in the spirit of Him who said, "Father, forgive them." The Vanquished would have us feel the nails and the thorns, the Victor would have us see the triumph of Calvary's tree.

The discipline of discernment requires that we follow the tenets of divine revelation, lest we fall before the wrath of the tempter. We are to meet his subtlety, selfishness and sophistry in the same way as did the Captain of our salvation, with the unequivocal statement, "It is written" (Matt. 4:4, 7, 10). We also are to live by the Word of God, are not to tempt the Lord our God, and are to worship Him only. We are to believe that as we commit our way unto the Lord and trust also in Him, He brings to pass His will (Ps. 37:5). We are to trust that He is able to fill us with the knowledge of His will (Col. 1:9), and to protect us from ways of the destroyer. "When the enemy shall come in like a flood, the Spirit of the Lord shall lift up a standard against him" (Isa. 59: 19). As we submit ourselves without reservation unto God, and resist the devil, the latter will flee from us (Jas. 4:7).

By the Word, by the Spirit, by faith, by submission to the divine will, and by resistance to any appeal to self and sin we discern between the way of God and the path of the destroyer.

(From *The Disciplines of Life* by V. Raymond Edman)

APPLICATION If you were given Solomon's opportunity to ask for anything, what would you choose? Would your requests benefit others if God granted them? In your prayers today, ask God for your heart's desire. Trust in God's generosity to you.

EXPLORATION Wisdom—Job 28:13; Psalm 119:97-104; Proverbs 1:7-9; 23-28; 2:9-10; Ecclesiastes 8:1.

So they brought a sword before the king. 25 And the king said, "Divide the living child in two, and give half to one, and half to the other."

26 Then the woman whose son *was* living spoke to the king, for she yearned with compassion for her son; and she said, "O my lord, give her the living child, and by no means kill him!"

But the other said, "Let him be neither mine nor yours, *but* divide *him.*"

27 So the king answered and said, "Give the first woman the living child, and by no means kill him; she *is* his mother."

28 And all Israel heard of the judgment which the king had rendered; and they feared the king, for they saw that the wisdom of God *was* in him to administer justice.

Solomon's Administration

4 So King Solomon was king over all Israel. 2 And these *were* his officials: Azariah the son of Zadok, the priest; 3 Elihoreph and Ahijah, the sons of Shisha, scribes; Jehoshaphat the son of Ahilud, the recorder; 4 Benaiah the son of Jehoiada, over the army; Zadok and Abiathar, the priests; 5 Azariah the son of Nathan, over the officers; Zabud the son of Nathan, a priest *and* the king's friend; 6 Ahishar, over the household; and Adoniram the son of Abda, over the labor force.

7 And Solomon had twelve governors over all Israel, who provided food for the king and his household; each one made provision for one month of the year. 8 These *are* their names: Ben-Hur,[b] in the mountains of Ephraim; 9 Ben-Deker,[c] in Makaz, Shaalbim, Beth Shemesh, and Elon Beth Hanan; 10 Ben-Hesed,[d] in Arubboth; to him *belonged* Sochoh and all the land of Hepher; 11 Ben-Abinadab,[e] *in* all the regions of Dor; he had Taphath the daughter of Solomon as wife; 12 Baana the son of Ahilud, *in* Taanach, Megiddo, and all Beth Shean, which *is* beside Zaretan below Jezreel, from Beth Shean to Abel Meholah, as far as the other side of Jokneam; 13 Ben-Geber,[f] in Ramoth Gilead; to him *belonged* the towns of Jair the son of Manasseh, in Gilead; to him *also belonged* the region of Argob in Bashan—sixty large cities with walls and bronze gate-bars; 14 Ahinadab the son of Iddo, *in* Mahanaim; 15 Ahimaaz, in Naphtali; he also took Basemath the daughter of Solomon as wife; 16 Baanah the son of Hushai, in Asher and Aloth; 17 Jehoshaphat the son of Paruah, in Issachar; 18 Shimei the son of Elah, in Benjamin; 19 Geber the son of Uri, in the land of Gilead, *in* the country of Sihon king of the Amorites, and of Og king of Bashan. *He was* the only governor who *was* in the land.

Prosperity and Wisdom of Solomon's Reign

20 Judah and Israel *were* as numerous as the sand by the sea in multitude, eating and drinking and rejoicing. 21 So Solomon reigned over all kingdoms from the River[g] *to* the land of the Philistines, as far as the border of Egypt. *They* brought tribute and served Solomon all the days of his life.

22 Now Solomon's provision for one day was thirty kors of fine flour, sixty kors of meal, 23 ten fatted oxen, twenty oxen from the pastures, and one hundred sheep, besides deer, gazelles, roebucks, and fatted fowl.

24 For he had dominion over all *the region* on this side of the River[h] from Tiphsah even to Gaza, namely over all the kings on this side of the River; and he had peace on every side all around him. 25 And Judah and Israel dwelt safely, each man under his vine and his fig tree, from Dan as far as Beersheba, all the days of Solomon.

26 Solomon had forty[i] thousand stalls of horses for his chariots, and twelve thousand horsemen. 27 And these governors, each man in his month, provided food for King Solomon and for all who came to King Solomon's table. There was no lack in their supply. 28 They also brought barley and straw to the proper place, for the horses and steeds, each man according to his charge.

29 And God gave Solomon wisdom and exceedingly great understanding, and largeness of heart like the sand on the seashore. 30 Thus Solomon's wisdom excelled the wisdom of all the men of the East and all the wisdom of Egypt. 31 For he was wiser than all men—than Ethan the Ezrahite, and Heman, Chalcol, and Darda, the sons of Mahol; and his fame was in all the surrounding nations. 32 He spoke three thousand proverbs, and his songs were one thousand and five. 33 Also he spoke of trees, from the cedar tree of Lebanon even to the hyssop that springs out of the wall; he

4:8 [b] Literally *Son of Hur*
4:9 [c] Literally *Son of Deker*
4:10 [d] Literally *Son of Hesed*
4:11 [e] Literally *Son of Abinadab*
4:13 [f] Literally *Son of Geber*
4:21 [g] That is, the Euphrates
4:24 [h] That is, the Euphrates
4:26 [i] Following Masoretic Text and most other authorities; some manuscripts of the Septuagint read *four* (compare 2 Chronicles 9:25).

spoke also of animals, of birds, of creeping things, and of fish. 34And men of all nations, from all the kings of the earth who had heard of his wisdom, came to hear the wisdom of Solomon.

Solomon Prepares to Build the Temple

5 Now Hiram king of Tyre sent his servants to Solomon, because he heard that they had anointed him king in place of his father, for Hiram had always loved David. 2Then Solomon sent to Hiram, saying:

3 You know how my father David could not build a house for the name of the LORD his God because of the wars which were fought against him on every side, until the LORD put *his foes*[j] under the soles of his feet.
4 But now the LORD my God has given me rest on every side; *there is* neither adversary nor evil occurrence.
5 And behold, I propose to build a house for the name of the LORD my God, as the LORD spoke to my father David, saying, "Your son, whom I will set on your throne in your place, he shall build the house for My name."
6 Now therefore, command that they cut down cedars for me from Lebanon; and my servants will be with your servants, and I will pay you wages for your servants according to whatever you say. For you know *there is* none among us who has skill to cut timber like the Sidonians.

7So it was, when Hiram heard the words of Solomon, that he rejoiced greatly and said,

Blessed *be* the LORD this day, for He has given David a wise son over this great people!

8Then Hiram sent to Solomon, saying:

I have considered *the message* which you sent me, *and* I will do all you desire concerning the cedar and cypress logs.
9 My servants shall bring *them* down from Lebanon to the sea; I will float them in rafts by sea to the place you indicate to me, and will have them broken apart there; then you can take *them* away. And you shall fulfill my desire by giving food for my household.

10Then Hiram gave Solomon cedar and cypress logs *according to* all his desire. 11And Solomon gave Hiram twenty thousand kors of wheat *as* food for his household, and twenty[k] kors of pressed oil. Thus Solomon gave to Hiram year by year.

12So the LORD gave Solomon wisdom, as He had promised him; and there was peace between Hiram and Solomon, and the two of them made a treaty together.

13Then King Solomon raised up a labor force out of all Israel; and the labor force was thirty thousand men. 14And he sent them to Lebanon, ten thousand a month in shifts: they were one month in Lebanon *and* two months at home; Adoniram *was* in charge of the labor force. 15Solomon had seventy thousand who carried burdens, and eighty thousand who

5:3 *j* Literally *them*
5:11 *k* Following Masoretic Text, Targum, and Vulgate; Septuagint and Syriac read *twenty thousand.*

LIFE LESSON

1 Kings 5:1–6:38

SITUATION Solomon thoughtfully prepared to build the great temple in Jerusalem. The King of Tyre allowed the wood from his forest to be used for building materials. In order to keep family ties strong, Solomon rotated the workmen so that only one-third of the work force lived away from home at a time.

OBSERVATION Solomon's paternalism toward workers demonstrated wisdom and compassion.

INSPIRATION Waldo strolled down the city sidewalk, lost in thought. He was going to church. . . . He trod toward the stone church on the corner; its spires and towers stretching to the sky. . . . He walked up the steps and into the church.

He halted inside the door to let his eyes adjust from sunlight to the subdued lighting of the church.

"Will you be coming in?"

The voice startled Waldo. . . . He turned in the direction from which the voice had come. He saw a small, slightly hunched woman with gray hair gathered in a bun at the back of her head. . . .

"Uh, yes," Waldo answered. "Yes, I will."

"Your brains, please."

Waldo was sure he misunderstood her. . . .

"My brains?"

"Yes. You're entering the church, aren't you?"

Waldo nodded.

"You've decided to follow Christ? Become a Christian?"

"Yes," He said.

"Well, then you must check your brains here. You won't be needing them anymore. We'll label them with your name. They'll be safe here. Don't worry, this is the way it's done. If you're going to become a Christian, you check your brains at the door."

Waldo's experience is, of course, fictional. But it reflects how many people feel and think about Christian conversion. They think that becoming a Christian requires you to "check your brains at the door," to sacrifice your

Continued

intellect and ignore your rational processes.

That's a myth.

Many of the greatest minds in history have belonged to Christians. The Apostle Paul. Augustine. Martin Luther. John Calvin. John Bunyan. Deitrich Bonhoeffer. Francis Schaeffer.

Christian conversion does not compromise a person's intellect. It completes it. Becoming a Christian often prompts an "Aha!" reaction, as a person sees pieces of life's puzzle slipping into place.

In his autobiography, C. S. Lewis tells how he avoided and violently resisted the gospel as a young man because he considered Christianity an unintellectual system. His resistance broke, however, and he was "surprised by joy." He found that conversion *ignited* his imaginative and creative powers. He became most famous for his writings, books like *The Screwtape Letters* and the acclaimed six-part Chronicles of Narnia. . . .

British trial lawyer Frank Morison intended to write a book disproving the resurrection of Jesus Christ. He conducted intensive research, gathered historical evidence, and worked devotedly at his task. Finally, his intellect and work brought him to the unavoidable conclusion that Jesus had risen from the dead! He became a Christian.

The gospel does not require that you check your brains at the door. On the contrary, it demands the full use of your intellect until you can say with the confidence of Paul, "I am not ashamed of the gospel, because it is the power of God for the salvation of everyone who believes" (Romans 1:16). (From *Don't Check Your Brains at the Door* by Josh McDowell)

APPLICATION When you think the challenge you face is too big, ask God for help and wisdom. Trust God to care for your needs. Don't be anxious. Then, think of ways you can meet the challenge.

EXPLORATION God's Perspective—Deuteronomy 27:2-9; Isaiah 55:8-9; Matthew 16:23.

quarried *stone* in the mountains, 16 besides three thousand three hundred[l]
from the chiefs of Solomon's deputies, who supervised the people who labored in the work. 17 And the king commanded them to quarry large
stones, costly stones, *and* hewn stones, to lay the foundation of the temple.[m] 18 So Solomon's builders, Hiram's builders, and the Gebalites quarried *them;* and they prepared timber and stones to build the temple.

Solomon Builds the Temple

6 And it came to pass in the four hundred and eightieth[n] year after the
children of Israel had come out of the land of Egypt, in the fourth year
of Solomon's reign over Israel, in the month of Ziv, which *is* the second
month, that he began to build the house of the LORD. 2 Now the house
which King Solomon built for the LORD, its length *was* sixty cubits, its
width twenty, and its height thirty cubits. 3 The vestibule in front of the
sanctuary[o] of the house *was* twenty cubits long across the width of the
house, *and* the width of *the vestibule*[p] *extended* ten cubits from the front of
the house. 4 And he made for the house windows with beveled frames.
5 Against the wall of the temple he built chambers all around, *against* the
walls of the temple, all around the sanctuary and the inner sanctuary.[q]
Thus he made side chambers all around it. 6 The lowest chamber *was* five
cubits wide, the middle *was* six cubits wide, and the third *was* seven cubits
wide; for he made narrow ledges around the outside of the temple, so that
the support beams would not be fastened into the walls of the temple. 7 And
the temple, when it was being built, was built with stone finished at the
quarry, so that no hammer or chisel *or* any iron tool was heard in the temple while it was being built. 8 The doorway for the middle story[r] *was* on the
right side of the temple. They went up by stairs to the middle *story,* and
from the middle to the third.
9 So he built the temple and finished it, and he paneled the temple with
beams and boards of cedar. 10 And he built side chambers against the entire temple, each five cubits high; they were attached to the temple with
cedar beams.
11 Then the word of the LORD came to Solomon, saying: 12 "*Concerning* this
temple which you are building, if you walk in My statutes, execute My judgments, keep all My commandments, and walk in them, then I will perform
My word with you, which I spoke to your father David. 13 And I will dwell
among the children of Israel, and will not forsake My people Israel."
14 So Solomon built the temple and finished it. 15 And he built the inside
walls of the temple with cedar boards; from the floor of the temple to the
ceiling he paneled the inside with wood; and he covered the floor of the
temple with planks of cypress. 16 Then he built the twenty-cubit room at
the rear of the temple, from floor to ceiling, with cedar boards; he built *it*
inside as the inner sanctuary, as the Most Holy *Place.* 17 And in front of it
the temple sanctuary was forty cubits *long.* 18 The inside of the temple was
cedar, carved with ornamental buds and open flowers. All *was* cedar; there
was no stone *to be* seen.

5:16 [l] Following Masoretic Text, Targum, and Vulgate; Septuagint reads *three thousand six hundred.*
5:17 [m] Literally *house,* and so frequently throughout this book
6:1 [n] Following Masoretic Text, Targum, and Vulgate; Septuagint reads *fortieth.*
6:3 [o] Hebrew *heykal;* here the main room of the temple, elsewhere called the holy place (compare Exodus 26:33 and Ezekiel 41:1) [p] Literally *it*
6:5 [q] Hebrew *debir;* here the inner room of the temple, elsewhere called the Most Holy Place (compare verse 16)
6:8 [r] Following Masoretic Text and Vulgate; Septuagint reads *upper story;* Targum reads *ground story.*

19 And he prepared the inner sanctuary inside the temple, to set the ark
of the covenant of the LORD there. 20 The inner sanctuary *was* twenty cubits
long, twenty cubits wide, and twenty cubits high. He overlaid it with pure
gold, and overlaid the altar of cedar. 21 So Solomon overlaid the inside of
the temple with pure gold. He stretched gold chains across the front of the
inner sanctuary, and overlaid it with gold. 22 The whole temple he overlaid
with gold, until he had finished all the temple; also he overlaid with gold
the entire altar that *was* by the inner sanctuary.
23 Inside the inner sanctuary he made two cherubim *of* olive wood, *each*
ten cubits high. 24 One wing of the cherub *was* five cubits, and the other
wing of the cherub five cubits: ten cubits from the tip of one wing to the tip
of the other. 25 And the other cherub *was* ten cubits; both cherubim *were* of
the same size and shape. 26 The height of one cherub *was* ten cubits, and so
was the other cherub. 27 Then he set the cherubim inside the inner room;[s]
and they stretched out the wings of the cherubim so that the wing of the
one touched *one* wall, and the wing of the other cherub touched the other
wall. And their wings touched each other in the middle of the room. 28 Also
he overlaid the cherubim with gold.
29 Then he carved all the walls of the temple all around, both the inner
and outer *sanctuaries,* with carved figures of cherubim, palm trees, and
open flowers. 30 And the floor of the temple he overlaid with gold, both the
inner and outer *sanctuaries.*
31 For the entrance of the inner sanctuary he made doors *of* olive wood;
the lintel *and* doorposts *were* one-fifth *of the wall.* 32 The two doors *were of*
olive wood; and he carved on them figures of cherubim, palm trees, and
open flowers, and overlaid *them* with gold; and he spread gold on the
cherubim and on the palm trees. 33 So for the door of the sanctuary he also
made doorposts *of* olive wood, one-fourth *of the wall.* 34 And the two doors
were of cypress wood; two panels *comprised* one folding door, and two
panels *comprised* the other folding door. 35 Then he carved cherubim, palm
trees, and open flowers *on them,* and overlaid *them* with gold applied
evenly on the carved work.
36 And he built the inner court with three rows of hewn stone and a row
of cedar beams.
37 In the fourth year the foundation of the house of the LORD was laid, in
the month of Ziv. 38 And in the eleventh year, in the month of Bul, which is
the eighth month, the house was finished in all its details and according to
all its plans. So he was seven years in building it.

Solomon's Other Buildings

7 But Solomon took thirteen years to build his own house; so he finished
all his house.
2 He also built the House of the Forest of Lebanon; its length *was* one
hundred cubits, its width fifty cubits, and its height thirty cubits, with four
rows of cedar pillars, and cedar beams on the pillars. 3 And *it was* paneled
with cedar above the beams that *were* on forty-five pillars, fifteen *to* a row.
4 *There were* windows *with beveled frames in* three rows, and window *was*
opposite window *in* three tiers. 5 And all the doorways and doorposts *had*
rectangular frames; and window *was* opposite window *in* three tiers.

6:27 [s] Literally *house*

LIFE LESSON

1 Kings 7:1–8:66

SITUATION After lavishly constructing and decorating the temple, Solomon offered a prayer of thanksgiving and blessing to God. He praised God and prayed for his people.

OBSERVATION The temple symbolized Israel's devotion and thankfulness to God for his blessings upon them.

INSPIRATION "I love the church!" Ray exclaimed to me recently. I know it's true. He loves the grandparents, the children, the middle-agers, the young people; he loves the mystics, the pragmatists, the theologians, the simplists, the immature and the deep, the visionaries and the plodders, the faithful committee workers who make it happen and the laggards who have to be cajoled. Ray loves the church! I can't pray he'll back off; I can only pray he'll have the body and heart to love it for a long, long time.

And as his wife, I see what the church has done for Ray—deep things I never could have done.

I told this recently to a young wife, who didn't want her husband to serve on one of our church committees. "Let your husband go," I said. "Don't try to overpossess him. If you don't sense that he's deliberately escaping from his family—which is another matter—then (I know this sounds heretical) let him plunge into all the church life he wants to. His heart may need it. Encourage lots of exposure to godly people. He'll be a far better husband and father as a result!"

I told her how the multifaceted, richly diverse Body of Christ has stretched and challenged Ray in a thousand ways I couldn't—ever—as one human being. Sometimes when he's come home, for all the fatigue, there's a look of splendor shining in his eyes. And when he does come home, in less time he's a far more effective husband and father. Oh, yes! The children and I wouldn't trade.

The miracle of the church! Who can explain it? We need all the relationships God will give us.

(From *My Sacrifice, His Fire* by Anne Ortlund)

Continued

APPLICATION Church membership and participation is an important part of the Christian walk. If you do not attend a church, find one and attend regularly. If you are inactive in church, find ways to serve. If you are disappointed in church and with Christians, get busy and love God anew.

EXPLORATION Temple—Ezekiel 5:11; Acts 7:44-50; 1 Corinthians 3:6; 6:19.

6 He also made the Hall of Pillars: its length *was* fifty cubits, and its width
thirty cubits; and in front of them *was* a portico with pillars, and a canopy
was in front of them.
7 Then he made a hall for the throne, the Hall of Judgment, where he
might judge; and *it was* paneled with cedar from floor to ceiling.[t]
8 And the house where he dwelt *had* another court inside the hall, of like
workmanship. Solomon also made a house like this hall for Pharaoh's
daughter, whom he had taken *as wife*.
9 All these *were of* costly stones cut to size, trimmed with saws, inside
and out, from the foundation to the eaves, and also on the outside to the
great court. 10 The foundation *was of* costly stones, large stones, some ten
cubits and some eight cubits. 11 And above *were* costly stones, hewn to size,
and cedar wood. 12 The great court *was* enclosed with three rows of hewn
stones and a row of cedar beams. So were the inner court of the house of
the LORD and the vestibule of the temple.

Hiram the Craftsman

13 Now King Solomon sent and brought Huram[u] from Tyre. 14 He *was* the
son of a widow from the tribe of Naphtali, and his father *was* a man of
Tyre, a bronze worker; he was filled with wisdom and understanding and
skill in working with all kinds of bronze work. So he came to King Solomon and did all his work.

The Bronze Pillars for the Temple

15 And he cast two pillars of bronze, each one eighteen cubits high, and a
line of twelve cubits measured the circumference of each. 16 Then he made
two capitals *of* cast bronze, to set on the tops of the pillars. The height of
one capital *was* five cubits, and the height of the other capital *was* five cubits. 17 *He made* a lattice network, with wreaths of chainwork, for the capitals which *were* on top of the pillars: seven chains for one capital and seven
for the other capital. 18 So he made the pillars, and two rows of pomegranates above the network all around to cover the capitals that *were* on top;
and thus he did for the other capital.
19 The capitals which *were* on top of the pillars in the hall *were* in the
shape of lilies, four cubits. 20 The capitals on the two pillars also *had pomegranates* above, by the convex surface which *was* next to the network; and
there *were* two hundred such pomegranates in rows on each of the capitals
all around.
21 Then he set up the pillars by the vestibule of the temple; he set up the
pillar on the right and called its name Jachin, and he set up the pillar on
the left and called its name Boaz. 22 The tops of the pillars were in the shape
of lilies. So the work of the pillars was finished.

The Sea and the Oxen

23 And he made the Sea of cast bronze, ten cubits from one brim to the
other; *it was* completely round. Its height *was* five cubits, and a line of
thirty cubits measured its circumference.
24 Below its brim *were* ornamental buds encircling it all around, ten to a
cubit, all the way around the Sea. The ornamental buds *were* cast in two

7:7 [t] Literally *floor*, that is, of the upper level
7:13 [u] Hebrew *Hiram* (compare 2 Chronicles 2:13, 14)

rows when it was cast. 25It stood on twelve oxen: three
looking toward the north, three looking toward the
west, three looking toward the south, and three looking toward the east; the Sea *was set* upon them, and all
their back parts *pointed* inward. 26It *was* a handbreadth thick; and its brim was shaped like the brim
of a cup, *like* a lily blossom. It contained two thousand[v] baths.

The Carts and the Lavers

27He also made ten carts of bronze; four cubits *was*
the length of each cart, four cubits its width, and
three cubits its height. 28And this *was* the design of
the carts: They had panels, and the panels *were* between frames; 29on the panels that *were* between the
frames *were* lions, oxen, and cherubim. And on the
frames *was* a pedestal on top. Below the lions and
oxen *were* wreaths of plaited work. 30Every cart had
four bronze wheels and axles of bronze, and its four
feet had supports. Under the laver *were* supports of
cast *bronze* beside each wreath. 31Its opening inside
the crown at the top *was* one cubit in diameter; and
the opening *was* round, shaped *like* a pedestal, one
and a half cubits in outside diameter; and also on
the opening *were* engravings, but the panels were
square, not round. 32Under the panels *were* the four
wheels, and the axles of the wheels *were joined* to the
cart. The height of a wheel *was* one and a half cubits.
33The workmanship of the wheels *was* like the workmanship of a chariot wheel; their axle pins, their
rims, their spokes, and their hubs *were* all of cast
bronze. 34And *there were* four supports at the four
corners of each cart; its supports *were* part of the
cart itself. 35On the top of the cart, at the height of
half a cubit, *it was* perfectly round. And on the top of
the cart, its flanges and its panels *were* of the same
casting. 36On the plates of its flanges and on its panels he engraved cherubim, lions, and palm trees,
wherever there was a clear space on each, with
wreaths all around. 37Thus he made the ten carts. All
of them were of the same mold, one measure, *and*
one shape.

38Then he made ten lavers of bronze; each laver
contained forty baths, *and* each laver *was* four cubits.
On each of the ten carts *was* a laver. 39And he put five
carts on the right side of the house, and five on the left
side of the house. He set the Sea on the right side of
the house, toward the southeast.

Furnishings of the Temple

40Huram[w] made the lavers and the shovels and the
bowls. So Huram finished doing all the work that he
was to do for King Solomon *for* the house of the LORD:
41the two pillars, the *two* bowl-shaped capitals that
were on top of the two pillars; the two networks covering the two bowl-shaped capitals which *were* on top of
the pillars; 42four hundred pomegranates for the two
networks (two rows of pomegranates for each network, to cover the two bowl-shaped capitals that *were*
on top of the pillars); 43the ten carts, and ten lavers on
the carts; 44one Sea, and twelve oxen under the Sea;
45the pots, the shovels, and the bowls.

All these articles which Huram[x] made for King Solomon *for* the house of the LORD *were of* burnished
bronze. 46In the plain of Jordan the king had them
cast in clay molds, between Succoth and Zaretan.
47And Solomon did not weigh all the articles, because
there were so many; the weight of the bronze was not
determined.

48Thus Solomon had all the furnishings made for
the house of the LORD: the altar of gold, and the table
of gold on which *was* the showbread; 49the lampstands of pure gold, five on the right *side* and five on
the left in front of the inner sanctuary, with the flowers and the lamps and the wick-trimmers of gold;
50the basins, the trimmers, the bowls, the ladles, and
the censers of pure gold; and the hinges of gold, *both*
for the doors of the inner room (the Most Holy *Place*)
and for the doors of the main hall of the temple.

51So all the work that King Solomon had done for
the house of the LORD was finished; and Solomon
brought in the things which his father David had dedicated: the silver and the gold and the furnishings. He
put them in the treasuries of the house of the LORD.

The Ark Brought into the Temple

8 Now Solomon assembled the elders of Israel and
all the heads of the tribes, the chief fathers of the
children of Israel, to King Solomon in Jerusalem, that
they might bring up the ark of the covenant of the
LORD from the City of David, which *is* Zion. 2Therefore
all the men of Israel assembled with King Solomon at
the feast in the month of Ethanim, which *is* the seventh month. 3So all the elders of Israel came, and the
priests took up the ark. 4Then they brought up the ark
of the LORD, the tabernacle of meeting, and all the holy
furnishings that *were* in the tabernacle. The priests

7:26 [v] Or *three thousand* (compare 2 Chronicles 4:5)
7:40 [w] Hebrew *Hiram* (compare 2 Chronicles 2:13, 14)
7:45 [x] Hebrew *Hiram* (compare 2 Chronicles 2:13, 14)

and the Levites brought them up. 5Also King Solomon,
and all the congregation of Israel who were assembled
with him, *were* with him before the ark, sacrificing
sheep and oxen that could not be counted or numbered for multitude. 6Then the priests brought in the
ark of the covenant of the LORD to its place, into the inner
sanctuary of the temple, to the Most Holy *Place,* under
the wings of the cherubim. 7For the cherubim spread
their two wings over the place of the ark, and the cherubim overshadowed the ark and its poles. 8The poles
extended so that the ends of the poles could be seen
from the holy *place,* in front of the inner sanctuary;
but they could not be seen from outside. And they are
there to this day. 9Nothing *was* in the ark except the
two tablets of stone which Moses put there at Horeb,
when the LORD made *a covenant* with the children of
Israel, when they came out of the land of Egypt.

10And it came to pass, when the priests came out of
the holy *place,* that the cloud filled the house of the
LORD, 11so that the priests could not continue ministering because of the cloud; for the glory of the LORD
filled the house of the LORD.

12Then Solomon spoke:

"The LORD said He would dwell in
the dark cloud.
13 I have surely built You an exalted house,
And a place for You to dwell in forever."

Solomon's Speech at Completion of the Work

14Then the king turned around and blessed the whole
assembly of Israel, while all the assembly of Israel
was standing. 15And he said: "Blessed *be* the LORD God
of Israel, who spoke with His mouth to my father David, and with His hand has fulfilled *it,* saying, 16'Since
the day that I brought My people Israel out of Egypt, I
have chosen no city from any tribe of Israel *in which*
to build a house, that My name might be there; but I
chose David to be over My people Israel.' 17Now it was
in the heart of my father David to build a temple[y] for
the name of the LORD God of Israel. 18But the LORD said
to my father David, 'Whereas it was in your heart to
build a temple for My name, you did well that it was in
your heart. 19Nevertheless you shall not build the temple, but your son who will come from your body, he
shall build the temple for My name.' 20So the LORD has
fulfilled His word which He spoke; and I have filled
the position of my father David, and sit on the throne
of Israel, as the LORD promised; and I have built a
temple for the name of the LORD God of Israel. 21And
there I have made a place for the ark, in which *is* the
covenant of the LORD which He made with our fathers,
when He brought them out of the land of Egypt."

Solomon's Prayer of Dedication

22Then Solomon stood before the altar of the LORD
in the presence of all the assembly of Israel, and
spread out his hands toward heaven; 23and he said:
"LORD God of Israel, *there is* no God in heaven above
or on earth below like You, who keep *Your* covenant
and mercy with Your servants who walk before You
with all their hearts. 24You have kept what You
promised Your servant David my father; You have
both spoken with Your mouth and fulfilled *it* with
Your hand, as *it is* this day. 25Therefore, LORD God of
Israel, now keep what You promised Your servant David my father, saying, 'You shall not fail to have a man
sit before Me on the throne of Israel, only if your sons
take heed to their way, that they walk before Me as you
have walked before Me.' 26And now I pray, O God of
Israel, let Your word come true, which You have spoken to Your servant David my father.

27"But will God indeed dwell on the earth? Behold,
heaven and the heaven of heavens cannot contain
You. How much less this temple which I have built!
28Yet regard the prayer of Your servant and his supplication, O LORD my God, and listen to the cry and the
prayer which Your servant is praying before You
today: 29that Your eyes may be open toward this temple night and day, toward the place of which You said,
'My name shall be there,' that You may hear the
prayer which Your servant makes toward this place.
30And may You hear the supplication of Your servant
and of Your people Israel, when they pray toward this
place. Hear in heaven Your dwelling place; and when
You hear, forgive.

31"When anyone sins against his neighbor, and is
forced to take an oath, and comes *and* takes an oath
before Your altar in this temple, 32then hear in heaven,
and act, and judge Your servants, condemning the
wicked, bringing his way on his head, and justifying the
righteous by giving him according to his righteousness.

33"When Your people Israel are defeated before an
enemy because they have sinned against You, and
when they turn back to You and confess Your name,
and pray and make supplication to You in this temple, 34then hear in heaven, and forgive the sin of Your
people Israel, and bring them back to the land which
You gave to their fathers.

8:17 [y] Literally *house,* and so in verses 18–20

35“When the heavens are shut up and there is no rain
because they have sinned against You, when they pray
toward this place and confess Your name, and turn
from their sin because You afflict them, 36then hear in
heaven, and forgive the sin of Your servants, Your people Israel, that You may teach them the good way in
which they should walk; and send rain on Your land
which You have given to Your people as an inheritance.
37“When there is famine in the land, pestilence *or*
blight *or* mildew, locusts *or* grasshoppers; when their
enemy besieges them in the land of their cities; whatever plague or whatever sickness *there is;* 38whatever
prayer, whatever supplication is made by anyone, *or* by
all Your people Israel, when each one knows the plague
of his own heart, and spreads out his hands toward
this temple: 39then hear in heaven Your dwelling place,
and forgive, and act, and give to everyone according
to all his ways, whose heart You know (for You alone
know the hearts of all the sons of men), 40that they
may fear You all the days that they live in the land
which You gave to our fathers.
41“Moreover, concerning a foreigner, who *is* not of
Your people Israel, but has come from a far country for
Your name’s sake 42(for they will hear of Your great
name and Your strong hand and Your outstretched
arm), when he comes and prays toward this temple,
43hear in heaven Your dwelling place, and do according
to all for which the foreigner calls to You, that all peoples of the earth may know Your name and fear You, as
do Your people Israel, and that they may know that
this temple which I have built is called by Your name.
44“When Your people go out to battle against their
enemy, wherever You send them, and when they pray
to the LORD toward the city which You have chosen
and the temple which I have built for Your name,
45then hear in heaven their prayer and their supplication, and maintain their cause.
46“When they sin against You (for *there is* no one
who does not sin), and You become angry with them
and deliver them to the enemy, and they take them
captive to the land of the enemy, far or near; 47*yet*
when they come to themselves in the land where they
were carried captive, and repent, and make supplication to You in the land of those who took them captive, saying, ‘We have sinned and done wrong, we
have committed wickedness’; 48and *when* they return
to You with all their heart and with all their soul in the
land of their enemies who led them away captive, and
pray to You toward their land which You gave to their
fathers, the city which You have chosen and the temple which I have built for Your name: 49then hear in
heaven Your dwelling place their prayer and their
supplication, and maintain their cause, 50and forgive
Your people who have sinned against You, and all
their transgressions which they have transgressed
against You; and grant them compassion before those
who took them captive, that they may have compassion on them 51(for they *are* Your people and Your inheritance, whom You brought out of Egypt, out of the
iron furnace), 52that Your eyes may be open to the
supplication of Your servant and the supplication of
Your people Israel, to listen to them whenever they
call to You. 53For You separated them from among all
the peoples of the earth *to be* Your inheritance, as You
spoke by Your servant Moses, when You brought our
fathers out of Egypt, O Lord GOD.”

Solomon Blesses the Assembly

54And so it was, when Solomon had finished praying all this prayer and supplication to the LORD, that
he arose from before the altar of the LORD, from kneeling on his knees with his hands spread up to heaven.
55Then he stood and blessed all the assembly of Israel
with a loud voice, saying: 56“Blessed *be* the LORD, who
has given rest to His people Israel, according to all
that He promised. There has not failed one word of all
His good promise, which He promised through His
servant Moses. 57May the LORD our God be with us, as
He was with our fathers. May He not leave us nor forsake us, 58that He may incline our hearts to Himself,
to walk in all His ways, and to keep His commandments and His statutes and His judgments, which He
commanded our fathers. 59And may these words of
mine, with which I have made supplication before the
LORD, be near the LORD our God day and night, that He
may maintain the cause of His servant and the cause
of His people Israel, as each day may require, 60that all
the peoples of the earth may know that the LORD *is*
God; *there is* no other. 61Let your heart therefore be
loyal to the LORD our God, to walk in His statutes and
keep His commandments, as at this day.”

Solomon Dedicates the Temple

62Then the king and all Israel with him offered sacrifices before the LORD. 63And Solomon offered a sacrifice of peace offerings, which he offered to the LORD,
twenty-two thousand bulls and one hundred and
twenty thousand sheep. So the king and all the children of Israel dedicated the house of the LORD. 64On
the same day the king consecrated the middle of the
court that *was* in front of the house of the LORD; for
there he offered burnt offerings, grain offerings, and

LIFE LESSON

1 Kings 9:1–11:43

SITUATION This is the story of Solomon's greatness and decline. God appeared to Solomon and promised blessing in exchange for obedience. The Queen of Sheba heard of Solomon's wisdom and came to see if the reports were true. Finally, toward the end of his life, Solomon's many wives influenced him to turn away from God.

OBSERVATION Solomon's sin did not catch God off guard. Although God knew Solomon would sin, he continued to bless Solomon because of God's promise to David.

INSPIRATION God is outside and above the Time-line. In that case, what we call "tomorrow" is visible to Him in just the same way as what we call "today." All the days are "now" for him. He does not remember you doing things yesterday; He simply sees you doing because, though you have lost yesterday, He has not. He does not "foresee" you doing things tomorrow; He simply sees you doing them: because, though tomorrow is not yet here for you, it is for Him. You must never suppose that your actions at this moment are any less free because God knows what you are doing.
(From *The Quotable Lewis* edited by Wayne Martindale and Jerry Root)

APPLICATION What gifts has God given you? Money? Musical talent? Outgoing personality? Intelligence, sensitivity, or discipline? Find a way to use your gifts in service to God so that he receives the glory.

EXPLORATION Purpose of Gifts—Romans 12:3-6; 1 Corinthians 12:12; 14:26; Ephesians 4:11-16; 1 Timothy 4:14; 2 Timothy 1:6.

the fat of the peace offerings, because the bronze altar that *was* before the
LORD *was* too small to receive the burnt offerings, the grain offerings, and
the fat of the peace offerings.
65At that time Solomon held a feast, and all Israel with him, a great assembly from the entrance of Hamath to the Brook of Egypt, before the
LORD our God, seven days and seven *more* days—fourteen days. 66On the
eighth day he sent the people away; and they blessed the king, and went to
their tents joyful and glad of heart for all the good that the LORD had done
for His servant David, and for Israel His people.

God's Second Appearance to Solomon

9 And it came to pass, when Solomon had finished building the house of
the LORD and the king's house, and all Solomon's desire which he
wanted to do, 2that the LORD appeared to Solomon the second time, as He
had appeared to him at Gibeon. 3And the LORD said to him: "I have heard
your prayer and your supplication that you have made before Me; I have
consecrated this house which you have built to put My name there forever,
and My eyes and My heart will be there perpetually. 4Now if you walk before Me as your father David walked, in integrity of heart and in uprightness, to do according to all that I have commanded you, *and* if you keep
My statutes and My judgments, 5then I will establish the throne of your
kingdom over Israel forever, as I promised David your father, saying, 'You
shall not fail to have a man on the throne of Israel.' 6*But* if you or your sons
at all turn from following Me, and do not keep My commandments *and*
My statutes which I have set before you, but go and serve other gods and
worship them, 7then I will cut off Israel from the land which I have given
them; and this house which I have consecrated for My name I will cast out
of My sight. Israel will be a proverb and a byword among all peoples. 8And
as for this house, *which* is exalted, everyone who passes by it will be astonished and will hiss, and say, 'Why has the LORD done thus to this land and
to this house?' 9Then they will answer, 'Because they forsook the LORD their
God, who brought their fathers out of the land of Egypt, and have embraced other gods, and worshiped them and served them; therefore the
LORD has brought all this calamity on them.' "

Solomon and Hiram Exchange Gifts

10Now it happened at the end of twenty years, when Solomon had built
the two houses, the house of the LORD and the king's house 11(Hiram the
king of Tyre had supplied Solomon with cedar and cypress and gold, as
much as he desired), *that* King Solomon then gave Hiram twenty cities in
the land of Galilee. 12Then Hiram went from Tyre to see the cities which
Solomon had given him, but they did not please him. 13So he said, "What
kind of cities *are* these which you have given me, my brother?" And he
called them the land of Cabul,[z] as they are to this day. 14Then Hiram sent
the king one hundred and twenty talents of gold.

Solomon's Additional Achievements

15And this *is* the reason for the labor force which King Solomon raised: to
build the house of the LORD, his own house, the Millo,[a] the wall of Jerusalem,

9:13 [z] Literally *Good for Nothing*
9:15 [a] Literally *The Landfill*

Hazor, Megiddo, and Gezer. 16(Pharaoh king of Egypt had gone up and taken Gezer and burned it with fire, had killed the Canaanites who dwelt in the city, and had given it *as* a dowry to his daughter, Solomon's wife.) 17And Solomon built Gezer, Lower Beth Horon, 18Baalath, and Tadmor in the wilderness, in the land *of Judah,* 19all the storage cities that Solomon had, cities for his chariots and cities for his cavalry, and whatever Solomon desired to build in Jerusalem, in Lebanon, and in all the land of his dominion.

20All the people *who were* left of the Amorites, Hittites, Perizzites, Hivites, and Jebusites, who *were* not of the children of Israel— 21that is, their descendants who were left in the land after them, whom the children of Israel had not been able to destroy completely—from these Solomon raised forced labor, as it is to this day. 22But of the children of Israel Solomon made no forced laborers, because they *were* men of war and his servants: his officers, his captains, commanders of his chariots, and his cavalry.

23Others *were* chiefs of the officials who *were* over Solomon's work: five hundred and fifty, who ruled over the people who did the work.

24But Pharaoh's daughter came up from the City of David to her house which *Solomon*[b] had built for her. Then he built the Millo.

25Now three times a year Solomon offered burnt offerings and peace offerings on the altar which he had built for the LORD, and he burned incense with them *on the altar* that *was* before the LORD. So he finished the temple.

26King Solomon also built a fleet of ships at Ezion Geber, which *is* near Elath[c] on the shore of the Red Sea, in the land of Edom. 27Then Hiram sent his servants with the fleet, seamen who knew the sea, to work with the servants of Solomon. 28And they went to Ophir, and acquired four hundred and twenty talents of gold from there, and brought *it* to King Solomon.

The Queen of Sheba's Praise of Solomon

10 Now when the queen of Sheba heard of the fame of Solomon concerning the name of the LORD, she came to test him with hard questions. 2She came to Jerusalem with a very great retinue, with camels that bore spices, very much gold, and precious stones; and when she came to Solomon, she spoke with him about all that was in her heart. 3So Solomon answered all her questions; there was nothing so difficult for the king that he could not explain *it* to her. 4And when the queen of Sheba had seen all the wisdom of Solomon, the house that he had built, 5the food on his table, the seating of his servants, the service of his waiters and their apparel, his cupbearers, and his entryway by which he went up to the house of the LORD, there was no more spirit in her. 6Then she said to the king: "It was a true report which I heard in my own land about your words and your wisdom. 7However I did not believe the words until I came and saw with my own eyes; and indeed the half was not told me. Your wisdom and prosperity exceed the fame of which I heard. 8Happy *are* your men and happy *are* these your servants, who stand continually before you *and* hear your wisdom! 9Blessed be the LORD your God, who delighted in you, setting you on the throne of Israel! Because the LORD has loved Israel forever, therefore He made you king, to do justice and righteousness."

10Then she gave the king one hundred and twenty talents of gold, spices in great quantity, and precious stones. There never again came such abundance of spices as the queen of Sheba gave to King Solomon. 11Also, the ships of Hiram, which brought gold from Ophir, brought great *quantities* of almug[d] wood and precious stones from Ophir. 12And the king made steps of the almug wood for the house of the LORD and for the king's house, also harps and stringed instruments for singers. There never again came such almug wood, nor has the like been seen to this day.

13Now King Solomon gave the queen of Sheba all she desired, whatever she asked, besides what Solomon had given her according to the royal generosity. So she turned and went to her own country, she and her servants.

Solomon's Great Wealth

14The weight of gold that came to Solomon yearly was six hundred and sixty-six talents of gold, 15besides *that* from the traveling merchants, from the income of traders, from all the kings of Arabia, and from the governors of the country.

16And King Solomon made two hundred large shields *of* hammered gold; six hundred *shekels* of gold went into each shield. 17He also *made* three hundred shields *of* hammered gold; three minas of gold went into each shield. The king put them in the House of the Forest of Lebanon.

18Moreover the king made a great throne of ivory,

9:24 [b] Literally *he* (compare 2 Chronicles 8:11)
9:26 [c] Hebrew *Eloth* (compare 2 Kings 14:22)
10:11 [d] Or *algum* (compare 2 Chronicles 9:10, 11)

and overlaid it with pure gold. 19The throne had six steps, and the top of the throne *was* round at the back; *there were* armrests on either side of the place of the seat, and two lions stood beside the armrests. 20Twelve lions stood there, one on each side of the six steps; nothing like *this* had been made for any *other* kingdom.

21All King Solomon's drinking vessels *were* gold, and all the vessels of the House of the Forest of Lebanon *were* pure gold. Not *one was* silver, for this was accounted as nothing in the days of Solomon. 22For the king had merchant ships[e] at sea with the fleet of Hiram. Once every three years the merchant ships came bringing gold, silver, ivory, apes, and monkeys.[f] 23So King Solomon surpassed all the kings of the earth in riches and wisdom.

24Now all the earth sought the presence of Solomon to hear his wisdom, which God had put in his heart. 25Each man brought his present: articles of silver and gold, garments, armor, spices, horses, and mules, at a set rate year by year.

26And Solomon gathered chariots and horsemen; he had one thousand four hundred chariots and twelve thousand horsemen, whom he stationed[g] in the chariot cities and with the king at Jerusalem. 27The king made silver *as common* in Jerusalem as stones, and he made cedar trees as abundant as the sycamores which *are* in the lowland.

28Also Solomon had horses imported from Egypt and Keveh; the king's merchants bought them in Keveh at the *current* price. 29Now a chariot that was imported from Egypt cost six hundred *shekels* of silver, and a horse one hundred and fifty; and thus, through their agents,[h] they exported *them* to all the kings of the Hittites and the kings of Syria.

Solomon's Heart Turns from the Lord

11 But King Solomon loved many foreign women, as well as the daughter of Pharaoh: women of the Moabites, Ammonites, Edomites, Sidonians, *and* Hittites— 2from the nations of whom the LORD had said to the children of Israel, "You shall not intermarry with them, nor they with you. Surely they will turn away your hearts after their gods." Solomon clung to these in love. 3And he had seven hundred wives, princesses, and three hundred concubines; and his wives turned away his heart. 4For it was so, when Solomon was old, that his wives turned his heart after other gods; and his heart was not loyal to the LORD his God, as *was* the heart of his father David. 5For Solomon went after Ashtoreth the goddess of the Sidonians, and after Milcom the abomination of the Ammonites. 6Solomon did evil in the sight of the LORD, and did not fully follow the LORD, as *did* his father David. 7Then Solomon built a high place for Chemosh the abomination of Moab, on the hill that *is* east of Jerusalem, and for Molech the abomination of the people of Ammon. 8And he did likewise for all his foreign wives, who burned incense and sacrificed to their gods.

9So the LORD became angry with Solomon, because his heart had turned from the LORD God of Israel, who had appeared to him twice, 10and had commanded him concerning this thing, that he should not go after other gods; but he did not keep what the LORD had commanded. 11Therefore the LORD said to Solomon, "Because you have done this, and have not kept My covenant and My statutes, which I have commanded you, I will surely tear the kingdom away from you and give it to your servant. 12Nevertheless I will not do it in your days, for the sake of your father David; I will tear it out of the hand of your son. 13However I will not tear away the whole kingdom; I will give one tribe to your son for the sake of My servant David, and for the sake of Jerusalem which I have chosen."

Adversaries of Solomon

14Now the LORD raised up an adversary against Solomon, Hadad the Edomite; he *was* a descendant of the king in Edom. 15For it happened, when David was in Edom, and Joab the commander of the army had gone up to bury the slain, after he had killed every male in Edom 16(because for six months Joab remained there with all Israel, until he had cut down every male in Edom), 17that Hadad fled to go to Egypt, he and certain Edomites of his father's servants with him. Hadad *was* still a little child. 18Then they arose from Midian and came to Paran; and they took men with them from Paran and came to Egypt, to Pharaoh king of Egypt, who gave him a house, apportioned food for him, and gave him land. 19And Hadad found great favor in the sight of Pharaoh, so that he gave him as wife the sister of his own wife, that is, the sister of Queen Tahpenes. 20Then the sister of Tahpenes bore him Genubath his son, whom Tahpenes weaned in Pharaoh's house. And Genubath was in Pharaoh's household among the sons of Pharaoh.

10:22 [e] Literally *ships of Tarshish,* deep-sea vessels [f] *Or* peacocks
10:26 [g] Following Septuagint, Syriac, Targum, and Vulgate (compare 2 Chronicles 9:25); Masoretic Text reads *led.*
10:29 [h] Literally *by their hands*

21So when Hadad heard in Egypt that David rested
with his fathers, and that Joab the commander of the
army was dead, Hadad said to Pharaoh, "Let me depart, that I may go to my own country."
22Then Pharaoh said to him, "But what have you
lacked with me, that suddenly you seek to go to your
own country?"
So he answered, "Nothing, but do let me go anyway."
23And God raised up *another* adversary against
him, Rezon the son of Eliadah, who had fled from his
lord, Hadadezer king of Zobah. 24So he gathered men
to him and became captain over a band *of raiders,*
when David killed those *of Zobah.* And they went to
Damascus and dwelt there, and reigned in Damascus.
25He was an adversary of Israel all the days of Solomon (besides the trouble that Hadad *caused*); and
he abhorred Israel, and reigned over Syria.

Jeroboam's Rebellion

26Then Solomon's servant, Jeroboam the son of Nebat,
an Ephraimite from Zereda, whose mother's name
was Zeruah, a widow, also rebelled against the king.
27And this *is* what caused him to rebel against the
king: Solomon had built the Millo *and* repaired the
damages to the City of David his father. 28The man
Jeroboam *was* a mighty man of valor; and Solomon,
seeing that the young man was industrious, made him
the officer over all the labor force of the house of Joseph.
29Now it happened at that time, when Jeroboam
went out of Jerusalem, that the prophet Ahijah the
Shilonite met him on the way; and he had clothed
himself with a new garment, and the two *were* alone
in the field. 30Then Ahijah took hold of the new garment that *was* on him, and tore it *into* twelve pieces.
31And he said to Jeroboam, "Take for yourself ten
pieces, for thus says the LORD, the God of Israel: 'Behold, I will tear the kingdom out of the hand of Solomon and will give ten tribes to you 32(but he shall
have one tribe for the sake of My servant David, and
for the sake of Jerusalem, the city which I have chosen out of all the tribes of Israel), 33because they have[i]
forsaken Me, and worshiped Ashtoreth the goddess
of the Sidonians, Chemosh the god of the Moabites,
and Milcom the god of the people of Ammon, and
have not walked in My ways to do *what is* right in My
eyes and *keep* My statutes and My judgments, as *did*
his father David. 34However I will not take the whole
kingdom out of his hand, because I have made him
ruler all the days of his life for the sake of My servant
David, whom I chose because he kept My commandments and My statutes. 35But I will take the kingdom
out of his son's hand and give it to you—ten tribes.
36And to his son I will give one tribe, that My servant
David may always have a lamp before Me in Jerusalem, the city which I have chosen for Myself, to put
My name there. 37So I will take you, and you shall
reign over all your heart desires, and you shall be
king over Israel. 38Then it shall be, if you heed all that
I command you, walk in My ways, and do *what is*
right in My sight, to keep My statutes and My commandments, as My servant David did, then I will be
with you and build for you an enduring house, as I
built for David, and will give Israel to you. 39And I will
afflict the descendants of David because of this, but
not forever.' "
40Solomon therefore sought to kill Jeroboam. But
Jeroboam arose and fled to Egypt, to Shishak king of
Egypt, and was in Egypt until the death of Solomon.

Death of Solomon

41Now the rest of the acts of Solomon, all that he
did, and his wisdom, *are* they not written in the book
of the acts of Solomon? 42And the period that Solomon
reigned in Jerusalem over all Israel *was* forty years.
43Then Solomon rested with his fathers, and was
buried in the City of David his father. And Rehoboam
his son reigned in his place.

The Revolt Against Rehoboam

12 And Rehoboam went to Shechem, for all Israel
had gone to Shechem to make him king. 2So it
happened, when Jeroboam the son of Nebat heard *it*
(he was still in Egypt, for he had fled from the presence of King Solomon and had been dwelling in
Egypt), 3that they sent and called him. Then
Jeroboam and the whole assembly of Israel came and
spoke to Rehoboam, saying, 4"Your father made our
yoke heavy; now therefore, lighten the burdensome
service of your father, and his heavy yoke which he
put on us, and we will serve you."
5So he said to them, "Depart *for* three days, then
come back to me." And the people departed.
6Then King Rehoboam consulted the elders who
stood before his father Solomon while he still lived,
and he said, "How do you advise *me* to answer these
people?"
7And they spoke to him, saying, "If you will be a
servant to these people today, and serve them, and

11:33 [i] Following Masoretic Text and Targum; Septuagint, Syriac, and Vulgate read *he has.*

LIFE LESSON

1 Kings 12:1-33

SITUATION Rehoboam, Solomon's heir, rejected the advice of experienced elders in favor of the harsh counsel of friends. This action placed such a burden on the country that the Northern Kingdom (Israel) chose to rebel, expressing its rebellion through idolatry.

OBSERVATION God provides elders to help us lead well. The older and more experienced person often speaks with wisdom.

INSPIRATION Cattle are driven; sheep are led; and our Lord compares His people to sheep, not to cattle.

He did not and does not drive his people; rather He leads the way Himself and enables His followers to come after Him. He suffered at the hands of men and can therefore fairly ask His people to suffer as He did. While He lived on earth He went about doing good, walking in dignified poverty, and it is no injustice when He calls His followers to lives of frugality and simplicity. He lived in the bosom of the Father even while here below (John 1:18), and led the way for us so we may do the same. He bore His cross and died upon it, so the New Testament requirement of personal crucifixion for all believers is morally logical. Finally, He arose and ascended to sit in heavenly places and thus give foundation to Paul's words in Colossians: "Since, then, you have been raised with Christ, set your hearts on things above, where Christ is seated at the right hand of God. Set your minds on things above, not on earthly things. For you died, and your life is now hidden with Christ in God" (3:1-3).

(From *The Price of Neglect* by A. W. Tozer)

APPLICATION You don't have to be a king to have influence. Pray that God would develop your own character.

EXPLORATION Shepherding—Job 12:12; Matthew 23:4-12; Acts 20:28; Titus 2:1-8.

answer them, and speak good words to them, then they will be your servants forever."
8But he rejected the advice which the elders had given him, and consulted the young men who had grown up with him, who stood before him.
9And he said to them, "What advice do you give? How should we answer
this people who have spoken to me, saying, 'Lighten the yoke which your
father put on us'?"
10Then the young men who had grown up with him spoke to him, saying, "Thus you should speak to this people who have spoken to you, saying, 'Your father made our yoke heavy, but you make *it* lighter on
us'—thus you shall say to them: 'My little *finger* shall be thicker than my
father's waist! 11And now, whereas my father put a heavy yoke on you, I will
add to your yoke; my father chastised you with whips, but I will chastise
you with scourges!' "[j]
12So Jeroboam and all the people came to Rehoboam the third day, as
the king had directed, saying, "Come back to me the third day." 13Then the
king answered the people roughly, and rejected the advice which the elders had given him; 14and he spoke to them according to the advice of the
young men, saying, "My father made your yoke heavy, but I will add to
your yoke; my father chastised you with whips, but I will chastise you with
scourges!"[k] 15So the king did not listen to the people; for the turn *of events*
was from the LORD, that He might fulfill His word, which the LORD had spoken by Ahijah the Shilonite to Jeroboam the son of Nebat.
16Now when all Israel saw that the king did not listen to them, the people
answered the king, saying:

"What share have we in David?
We have no inheritance in the son of Jesse.
To your tents, O Israel!
Now, see to your own house, O David!"

So Israel departed to their tents. 17But Rehoboam reigned over the children of Israel who dwelt in the cities of Judah.
18Then King Rehoboam sent Adoram, who *was* in charge of the revenue;
but all Israel stoned him with stones, and he died. Therefore King
Rehoboam mounted his chariot in haste to flee to Jerusalem. 19So Israel
has been in rebellion against the house of David to this day.
20Now it came to pass when all Israel heard that Jeroboam had come
back, they sent for him and called him to the congregation, and made him
king over all Israel. There was none who followed the house of David, but
the tribe of Judah only.
21And when Rehoboam came to Jerusalem, he assembled all the house
of Judah with the tribe of Benjamin, one hundred and eighty thousand
chosen *men* who were warriors, to fight against the house of Israel, that he
might restore the kingdom to Rehoboam the son of Solomon. 22But the
word of God came to Shemaiah the man of God, saying, 23"Speak to
Rehoboam the son of Solomon, king of Judah, to all the house of Judah
and Benjamin, and to the rest of the people, saying, 24'Thus says the LORD:
"You shall not go up nor fight against your brethren the children of Israel.
Let every man return to his house, for this thing is from Me." ' " Therefore

12:11 [j] Literally *scorpions*
12:14 [k] Literally *scorpions*

they obeyed the word of the LORD, and turned back, according to the word
of the LORD.

Jeroboam's Gold Calves

25Then Jeroboam built Shechem in the mountains of Ephraim, and
dwelt there. Also he went out from there and built Penuel. 26And Jeroboam
said in his heart, "Now the kingdom may return to the house of David: 27If
these people go up to offer sacrifices in the house of the LORD at Jerusalem,
then the heart of this people will turn back to their lord, Rehoboam king of
Judah, and they will kill me and go back to Rehoboam king of Judah."
28Therefore the king asked advice, made two calves of gold, and said to
the people, "It is too much for you to go up to Jerusalem. Here are your
gods, O Israel, which brought you up from the land of Egypt!" 29And he set
up one in Bethel, and the other he put in Dan. 30Now this thing became a
sin, for the people went *to worship* before the one as far as Dan. 31He made
shrines[l] on the high places, and made priests from every class of people,
who were not of the sons of Levi.
32Jeroboam ordained a feast on the fifteenth day of the eighth month,
like the feast that *was* in Judah, and offered sacrifices on the altar. So he did
at Bethel, sacrificing to the calves that he had made. And at Bethel he installed the priests of the high places which he had made. 33So he made offerings on the altar which he had made at Bethel on the fifteenth day of the
eighth month, in the month which he had devised in his own heart. And
he ordained a feast for the children of Israel, and offered sacrifices on the
altar and burned incense.

The Message of the Man of God

13 And behold, a man of God went from Judah to Bethel by the word of
the LORD, and Jeroboam stood by the altar to burn incense. 2Then he
cried out against the altar by the word of the LORD, and said, "O altar, altar!
Thus says the LORD: 'Behold, a child, Josiah by name, shall be born to the
house of David; and on you he shall sacrifice the priests of the high places
who burn incense on you, and men's bones shall be burned on you.' "
3And he gave a sign the same day, saying, "This *is* the sign which the LORD
has spoken: Surely the altar shall split apart, and the ashes on it shall be
poured out."
4So it came to pass when King Jeroboam heard the saying of the man of
God, who cried out against the altar in Bethel, that he stretched out his
hand from the altar, saying, "Arrest him!" Then his hand, which he
stretched out toward him, withered, so that he could not pull it back to
himself. 5The altar also was split apart, and the ashes poured out from the
altar, according to the sign which the man of God had given by the word of
the LORD. 6Then the king answered and said to the man of God, "Please entreat the favor of the LORD your God, and pray for me, that my hand may be
restored to me."
So the man of God entreated the LORD, and the king's hand was restored
to him, and became as before. 7Then the king said to the man of God,
"Come home with me and refresh yourself, and I will give you a reward."
8But the man of God said to the king, "If you were to give me half your

12:31 [l] Literally *a house*

LIFE LESSON

1 Kings 13:1–14:31

SITUATION After Solomon's death, Israel quickly declined due to disobedience and immorality.

OBSERVATION Disobedience to God brings destruction. Individuals may try to avoid his judgment, but God cannot be out-maneuvered.

INSPIRATION Our family used to go to Cape Cod every summer. Many times when the tide was low we looked eyeball to eyeball at some little sea creature in his shell. He wasn't a bit afraid of us; we were the ones who were afraid! There we were with all our sixty-nine hundred square inches apiece of exposed skin—and all his possible bites and pinches. But he was safe. He knew, as long as he stayed retracted in that nice, strong shell, that we couldn't get to him.

And as far as all eternity is concerned, you're safe in Christ.

As far as all the hassles in your life are concerned, you're safe in Him.

As far as all your unknowns are concerned, you're safe.

As far as all the world, the flesh and the devil are concerned—you're safe.

But what if that little fellow, instead of staying safe in his shell, comes right out and he's sunning himself on our hand, totally unconcerned? Now he's vulnerable to anything, everything.

If you refuse to learn what it means to abide in Christ; if you insist on living out there where you worry and you strive and you're insecure and even disobedient; if you deliberately choose to live as if you were not in Christ at all—you're totally vulnerable, and you're in deep trouble with yourself and with God.

He commands you to learn to abide in Him and stay there. He requires that you settle down and shelter yourself in Him and trust Him absolutely. He insists on your living your life in Him; with its resulting rest and joy. If you don't, He loves you too much to neglect you. He'll childtrain you and chastise you until you consciously come into Him.

You need the "holy habit" of saying to the Father under any circumstances, "You are my hiding place"—saying it

Continued

continually, and saying it in peace and stability and joy.

(From *My Sacrifice, His Fire* by Anne Ortlund)

APPLICATION In a small group, explore the topic: "I am most likely to be disobedient when I . . . ." Then talk about what safeguards you can establish to insure obedience to God.

EXPLORATION Disobedience —Genesis 3:14-19; Numbers 20:12; 1 Samuel 15:17-23; Matthew 23:23-24; 1 John 2:3-6.

house, I would not go in with you; nor would I eat bread nor drink water in
this place. 9For so it was commanded me by the word of the LORD, saying,
'You shall not eat bread, nor drink water, nor return by the same way you
came.' " 10So he went another way and did not return by the way he came
to Bethel.

Death of the Man of God

11Now an old prophet dwelt in Bethel, and his sons came and told him
all the works that the man of God had done that day in Bethel; they also
told their father the words which he had spoken to the king. 12And their father said to them, "Which way did he go?" For his sons had seen[m] which
way the man of God went who came from Judah. 13Then he said to his
sons, "Saddle the donkey for me." So they saddled the donkey for him;
and he rode on it, 14and went after the man of God, and found him sitting
under an oak. Then he said to him, "*Are* you the man of God who came
from Judah?"

And he said, "I *am*."

15Then he said to him, "Come home with me and eat bread."

16And he said, "I cannot return with you nor go in with you; neither can
I eat bread nor drink water with you in this place. 17For I have been told by
the word of the LORD, 'You shall not eat bread nor drink water there, nor
return by going the way you came.' "

18He said to him, "I too *am* a prophet as you *are*, and an angel spoke to
me by the word of the LORD, saying, 'Bring him back with you to your
house, that he may eat bread and drink water.' " (He was lying to him.)

19So he went back with him, and ate bread in his house, and drank water.

20Now it happened, as they sat at the table, that the word of the LORD
came to the prophet who had brought him back; 21and he cried out to the
man of God who came from Judah, saying, "Thus says the LORD: 'Because
you have disobeyed the word of the LORD, and have not kept the commandment which the LORD your God commanded you, 22but you came
back, ate bread, and drank water in the place of which *the LORD* said to you,
"Eat no bread and drink no water," your corpse shall not come to the tomb
of your fathers.' "

23So it was, after he had eaten bread and after he had drunk, that he saddled the donkey for him, the prophet whom he had brought back. 24When
he was gone, a lion met him on the road and killed him. And his corpse
was thrown on the road, and the donkey stood by it. The lion also stood by
the corpse. 25And there, men passed by and saw the corpse thrown on the
road, and the lion standing by the corpse. Then they went and told *it* in the
city where the old prophet dwelt.

26Now when the prophet who had brought him back from the way heard
it, he said, "It *is* the man of God who was disobedient to the word of the
LORD. Therefore the LORD has delivered him to the lion, which has torn
him and killed him, according to the word of the LORD which He spoke to
him." 27And he spoke to his sons, saying, "Saddle the donkey for me." So
they saddled *it*. 28Then he went and found his corpse thrown on the road,
and the donkey and the lion standing by the corpse. The lion had not eaten
the corpse nor torn the donkey. 29And the prophet took up the corpse of

13:12 [m] Septuagint, Syriac, Targum, and Vulgate read *showed him.*

the man of God, laid it on the donkey, and brought it
back. So the old prophet came to the city to mourn,
and to bury him. [30]Then he laid the corpse in his own
tomb; and they mourned over him, *saying,* "Alas, my
brother!" [31]So it was, after he had buried him, that he
spoke to his sons, saying, "When I am dead, then
bury me in the tomb where the man of God *is* buried;
lay my bones beside his bones. [32]For the saying which
he cried out by the word of the LORD against the altar
in Bethel, and against all the shrines[n] on the high
places which *are* in the cities of Samaria, will surely
come to pass."

[33]After this event Jeroboam did not turn from his
evil way, but again he made priests from every class of
people for the high places; whoever wished, he consecrated him, and he became *one* of the priests of the
high places. [34]And this thing was the sin of the house
of Jeroboam, so as to exterminate and destroy *it* from
the face of the earth.

Judgment on the House of Jeroboam

14 At that time Abijah the son of Jeroboam became sick. [2]And Jeroboam said to his wife,
"Please arise, and disguise yourself, that they may not
recognize you as the wife of Jeroboam, and go to
Shiloh. Indeed, Ahijah the prophet *is* there, who told
me that *I would be* king over this people. [3]Also take
with you ten loaves, *some* cakes, and a jar of honey,
and go to him; he will tell you what will become of the
child." [4]And Jeroboam's wife did so; she arose and
went to Shiloh, and came to the house of Ahijah. But
Ahijah could not see, for his eyes were glazed by reason of his age.

[5]Now the LORD had said to Ahijah, "Here is the wife
of Jeroboam, coming to ask you something about her
son, for he *is* sick. Thus and thus you shall say to her;
for it will be, when she comes in, that she will pretend
to be another *woman.*"

[6]And so it was, when Ahijah heard the sound of her
footsteps as she came through the door, he said,
"Come in, wife of Jeroboam. Why do you pretend *to be*
another *person?* For I *have been* sent to you *with* bad
news. [7]Go, tell Jeroboam, 'Thus says the LORD God of
Israel: "Because I exalted you from among the people,
and made you ruler over My people Israel, [8]and tore
the kingdom away from the house of David, and gave
it to you; and *yet* you have not been as My servant David, who kept My commandments and who followed
Me with all his heart, to do only *what was* right in My
eyes; [9]but you have done more evil than all who were
before you, for you have gone and made for yourself
other gods and molded images to provoke Me to
anger, and have cast Me behind your back— [10]there-
fore behold! I will bring disaster on the house of
Jeroboam, and will cut off from Jeroboam every male
in Israel, bond and free; I will take away the remnant
of the house of Jeroboam, as one takes away refuse
until it is all gone. [11]The dogs shall eat whoever belongs
to Jeroboam and dies in the city, and the birds of the
air shall eat whoever dies in the field; for the LORD has
spoken!"' [12]Arise therefore, go to your own house.
When your feet enter the city, the child shall die. [13]And
all Israel shall mourn for him and bury him, for he is
the only one of Jeroboam who shall come to the grave,
because in him there is found something good toward
the LORD God of Israel in the house of Jeroboam.

[14]"Moreover the LORD will raise up for Himself a
king over Israel who shall cut off the house of
Jeroboam; this is the day. What? Even now! [15]For the
LORD will strike Israel, as a reed is shaken in the water.
He will uproot Israel from this good land which He
gave to their fathers, and will scatter them beyond the
River,[o] because they have made their wooden
images,[p] provoking the LORD to anger. [16]And He will
give Israel up because of the sins of Jeroboam, who
sinned and who made Israel sin."

[17]Then Jeroboam's wife arose and departed, and
came to Tirzah. When she came to the threshold of
the house, the child died. [18]And they buried him; and
all Israel mourned for him, according to the word of
the LORD which He spoke through His servant Ahijah
the prophet.

Death of Jeroboam

[19]Now the rest of the acts of Jeroboam, how he
made war and how he reigned, indeed they *are* written
in the book of the chronicles of the kings of Israel.
[20]The period that Jeroboam reigned *was* twenty-two
years. So he rested with his fathers. Then Nadab his
son reigned in his place.

Rehoboam Reigns in Judah

[21]And Rehoboam the son of Solomon reigned in Judah. Rehoboam *was* forty-one years old when he became king. He reigned seventeen years in Jerusalem,
the city which the LORD had chosen out of all the tribes
of Israel, to put His name there. His mother's name
was Naamah, an Ammonitess. [22]Now Judah did evil

13:32 [n] Literally *houses*
14:15 [o] That is, the Euphrates [p] Hebrew *Asherim,* Canaanite deities

LIFE LESSON

1 Kings 15:1–16:34

SITUATION The author of First Kings recounted the lives of seven evil kings. Only one king, Asa, did what was right in God's eyes. God blessed him with long life.

OBSERVATION Asa undoubtedly faced opposition as he tore down the nation's idols. He made unpopular decisions, but remained faithful to God all his life.

INSPIRATION We develop toughness or fortitude by repeatedly being tested and *prevailing.* The more tests we pass, the tougher we become. As a boxer engages in bout after bout, he toughens and becomes wiser and stronger. After a time he develops such fortitude, perseverance, and staying power that he can take on the best. There is no way a fighter, or any of us, can develop toughness without testing! The endurance and fortitude of the Apostle Paul or William Carey or Corrie ten Boom did not come overnight and did not come apart from trials. . . .

Nature teaches us the same principle. Free a butterfly from its chrysalis, and thus from the struggle of liberating itself, and you destroy its life, for it will never develop the strength to soar as it should.

(From *James* by R. Kent Hughes)

APPLICATION Are you willing to stand up for your faith? Think about the people and circumstances that might challenge your standards of humor, entertainment, or activities, and plan how you can respond.

EXPLORATION Choosing—Joshua 24:15; Ruth 1:16; 1 Kings 18:21; 2 Kings 17:41; Matthew 6:24.

in the sight of the LORD, and they provoked Him to jealousy with their sins
which they committed, more than all that their fathers had done. [23]For
they also built for themselves high places, *sacred* pillars, and wooden images on every high hill and under every green tree. [24]And there were also
perverted persons[q] in the land. They did according to all the abominations
of the nations which the LORD had cast out before the children of Israel.
[25]It happened in the fifth year of King Rehoboam *that* Shishak king of
Egypt came up against Jerusalem. [26]And he took away the treasures of the
house of the LORD and the treasures of the king's house; he took away everything. He also took away all the gold shields which Solomon had made.
[27]Then King Rehoboam made bronze shields in their place, and committed
them to the hands of the captains of the guard, who guarded the doorway of
the king's house. [28]And whenever the king entered the house of the LORD,
the guards carried them, then brought them back into the guardroom.
[29]Now the rest of the acts of Rehoboam, and all that he did, *are* they not
written in the book of the chronicles of the kings of Judah? [30]And there was
war between Rehoboam and Jeroboam all *their* days. [31]So Rehoboam
rested with his fathers, and was buried with his fathers in the City of David. His mother's name *was* Naamah, an Ammonitess. Then Abijam[r] his
son reigned in his place.

Abijam Reigns in Judah

15 In the eighteenth year of King Jeroboam the son of Nebat, Abijam
became king over Judah. [2]He reigned three years in Jerusalem. His
mother's name *was* Maachah the granddaughter of Abishalom. [3]And he
walked in all the sins of his father, which he had done before him; his heart
was not loyal to the LORD his God, as was the heart of his father David. [4]Nev-
ertheless for David's sake the LORD his God gave him a lamp in Jerusalem,
by setting up his son after him and by establishing Jerusalem; [5]because David did *what was* right in the eyes of the LORD, and had not turned aside
from anything that He commanded him all the days of his life, except in
the matter of Uriah the Hittite. [6]And there was war between Rehoboam[s]
and Jeroboam all the days of his life. [7]Now the rest of the acts of Abijam,
and all that he did, *are* they not written in the book of the chronicles of the
kings of Judah? And there was war between Abijam and Jeroboam.
[8]So Abijam rested with his fathers, and they buried him in the City of
David. Then Asa his son reigned in his place.

Asa Reigns in Judah

[9]In the twentieth year of Jeroboam king of Israel, Asa became king over
Judah. [10]And he reigned forty-one years in Jerusalem. His grandmother's
name *was* Maachah the granddaughter of Abishalom. [11]Asa did *what was*
right in the eyes of the LORD, as *did* his father David. [12]And he banished the
perverted persons[t] from the land, and removed all the idols that his fathers had made. [13]Also he removed Maachah his grandmother from *being*
queen mother, because she had made an obscene image of Asherah.[u] And
Asa cut down her obscene image and burned *it* by the Brook Kidron. [14]But
the high places were not removed. Nevertheless Asa's heart was loyal to

14:24 [q] Hebrew *qadesh,* that is, one practicing sodomy and prostitution in religious rituals
14:31 [r] Spelled *Abijah* in 2 Chronicles 12:16ff
15:6 [s] Following Masoretic Text, Septuagint, Targum, and Vulgate; some Hebrew manuscripts and Syriac read *Abijam.*

the LORD all his days. 15He also brought into the house
of the LORD the things which his father had dedicated,
and the things which he himself had dedicated: silver
and gold and utensils.
16Now there was war between Asa and Baasha king
of Israel all their days. 17And Baasha king of Israel came
up against Judah, and built Ramah, that he might let
none go out or come in to Asa king of Judah. 18Then
Asa took all the silver and gold *that was* left in the treasuries of the house of the LORD and the treasuries of the
king's house, and delivered them into the hand of his
servants. And King Asa sent them to Ben-Hadad the
son of Tabrimmon, the son of Hezion, king of Syria,
who dwelt in Damascus, saying, 19"*Let there be* a treaty
between you and me, as there was between my father
and your father. See, I have sent you a present of silver
and gold. Come and break your treaty with Baasha
king of Israel, so that he will withdraw from me."
20So Ben-Hadad heeded King Asa, and sent the
captains of his armies against the cities of Israel. He
attacked Ijon, Dan, Abel Beth Maachah, and all
Chinneroth, with all the land of Naphtali. 21Now it
happened, when Baasha heard *it*, that he stopped
building Ramah, and remained in Tirzah.
22Then King Asa made a proclamation throughout
all Judah; none *was* exempted. And they took away the
stones and timber of Ramah, which Baasha had used
for building; and with them King Asa built Geba of
Benjamin, and Mizpah.
23The rest of all the acts of Asa, all his might, all that
he did, and the cities which he built, *are* they not written in the book of the chronicles of the kings of Judah?
But in the time of his old age he was diseased in his
feet. 24So Asa rested with his fathers, and was buried
with his fathers in the City of David his father. Then
Jehoshaphat his son reigned in his place.

Nadab Reigns in Israel

25Now Nadab the son of Jeroboam became king
over Israel in the second year of Asa king of Judah,
and he reigned over Israel two years. 26And he did evil
in the sight of the LORD, and walked in the way of his
father, and in his sin by which he had made Israel sin.
27Then Baasha the son of Ahijah, of the house of
Issachar, conspired against him. And Baasha killed
him at Gibbethon, which *belonged* to the Philistines,
while Nadab and all Israel laid siege to Gibbethon.
28Baasha killed him in the third year of Asa king of Judah, and reigned in his place. 29And it was so, when he
became king, *that* he killed all the house of Jeroboam.
He did not leave to Jeroboam anyone that breathed,
until he had destroyed him, according to the word of
the LORD which He had spoken by His servant Ahijah
the Shilonite, 30because of the sins of Jeroboam,
which he had sinned and by which he had made Israel
sin, because of his provocation with which he had
provoked the LORD God of Israel to anger.
31Now the rest of the acts of Nadab, and all that he
did, *are* they not written in the book of the chronicles
of the kings of Israel? 32And there was war between
Asa and Baasha king of Israel all their days.

Baasha Reigns in Israel

33In the third year of Asa king of Judah, Baasha the
son of Ahijah became king over all Israel in Tirzah, and
reigned twenty-four years. 34He did evil in the sight of
the LORD, and walked in the way of Jeroboam, and in
his sin by which he had made Israel sin.

16 Then the word of the LORD came to Jehu the son
of Hanani, against Baasha, saying: 2"Inasmuch
as I lifted you out of the dust and made you ruler over
My people Israel, and you have walked in the way of
Jeroboam, and have made My people Israel sin, to
provoke Me to anger with their sins, 3surely I will
take away the posterity of Baasha and the posterity of
his house, and I will make your house like the house
of Jeroboam the son of Nebat. 4The dogs shall eat
whoever belongs to Baasha and dies in the city, and
the birds of the air shall eat whoever dies in the fields."
5Now the rest of the acts of Baasha, what he did,
and his might, *are* they not written in the book of the
chronicles of the kings of Israel? 6So Baasha rested
with his fathers and was buried in Tirzah. Then Elah
his son reigned in his place.
7And also the word of the LORD came by the prophet
Jehu the son of Hanani against Baasha and his house,
because of all the evil that he did in the sight of the
LORD in provoking Him to anger with the work of his
hands, in being like the house of Jeroboam, and because he killed them.

Elah Reigns in Israel

8In the twenty-sixth year of Asa king of Judah, Elah
the son of Baasha became king over Israel, *and*
reigned two years in Tirzah. 9Now his servant Zimri,
commander of half *his* chariots, conspired against
him as he was in Tirzah drinking himself drunk in the
house of Arza, steward of *his* house in Tirzah. 10And
Zimri went in and struck him and killed him in the

15:12 [t] Hebrew *qedeshim,* that is, those practicing sodomy and prostitution in religious rituals
15:13 [u] A Canaanite goddess

twenty-seventh year of Asa king of Judah, and reigned
in his place.
11 Then it came to pass, when he began to reign, as
soon as he was seated on his throne, *that* he killed all
the household of Baasha; he did not leave him one
male, neither of his relatives nor of his friends. 12 Thus
Zimri destroyed all the household of Baasha, according to the word of the LORD, which He spoke against
Baasha by Jehu the prophet, 13 for all the sins of Baasha
and the sins of Elah his son, by which they had sinned
and by which they had made Israel sin, in provoking
the LORD God of Israel to anger with their idols.
14 Now the rest of the acts of Elah, and all that he did,
are they not written in the book of the chronicles of
the kings of Israel?

Zimri Reigns in Israel

15 In the twenty-seventh year of Asa king of Judah,
Zimri had reigned in Tirzah seven days. And the people *were* encamped against Gibbethon, which *belonged* to the Philistines. 16 Now the people *who were*
encamped heard it said, "Zimri has conspired and
also has killed the king." So all Israel made Omri, the
commander of the army, king over Israel that day in
the camp. 17 Then Omri and all Israel with him went
up from Gibbethon, and they besieged Tirzah. 18 And
it happened, when Zimri saw that the city was taken,
that he went into the citadel of the king's house and
burned the king's house down upon himself with fire,
and died, 19 because of the sins which he had committed in doing evil in the sight of the LORD, in walking in
the way of Jeroboam, and in his sin which he had
committed to make Israel sin.
20 Now the rest of the acts of Zimri, and the treason
he committed, *are* they not written in the book of the
chronicles of the kings of Israel?

Omri Reigns in Israel

21 Then the people of Israel were divided into two
parts: half of the people followed Tibni the son of
Ginath, to make him king, and half followed Omri.
22 But the people who followed Omri prevailed over
the people who followed Tibni the son of Ginath. So
Tibni died and Omri reigned. 23 In the thirty-first year
of Asa king of Judah, Omri became king over Israel,
and reigned twelve years. Six years he reigned in
Tirzah. 24 And he bought the hill of Samaria from
Shemer for two talents of silver; then he built on the
hill, and called the name of the city which he built,
Samaria, after the name of Shemer, owner of the hill.
25 Omri did evil in the eyes of the LORD, and did worse
than all who *were* before him. 26 For he walked in all
the ways of Jeroboam the son of Nebat, and in his sin
by which he had made Israel sin, provoking the LORD
God of Israel to anger with their idols.
27 Now the rest of the acts of Omri which he did, and
the might that he showed, *are* they not written in the
book of the chronicles of the kings of Israel?
28 So Omri rested with his fathers and was buried in
Samaria. Then Ahab his son reigned in his place.

Ahab Reigns in Israel

29 In the thirty-eighth year of Asa king of Judah,
Ahab the son of Omri became king over Israel; and
Ahab the son of Omri reigned over Israel in Samaria
twenty-two years. 30 Now Ahab the son of Omri did
evil in the sight of the LORD, more than all who *were*
before him. 31 And it came to pass, as though it had
been a trivial thing for him to walk in the sins of
Jeroboam the son of Nebat, that he took as wife
Jezebel the daughter of Ethbaal, king of the Sidonians;
and he went and served Baal and worshiped him.
32 Then he set up an altar for Baal in the temple of Baal,
which he had built in Samaria. 33 And Ahab made a
wooden image.[v] Ahab did more to provoke the LORD
God of Israel to anger than all the kings of Israel who
were before him. 34 In his days Hiel of Bethel built Jericho. He laid its foundation with Abiram his firstborn,
and with his youngest *son* Segub he set up its gates, according to the word of the LORD, which He had spoken
through Joshua the son of Nun.[w]

Elijah Proclaims a Drought

17 And Elijah the Tishbite, of the inhabitants of
Gilead, said to Ahab, "*As* the LORD God of Israel
lives, before whom I stand, there shall not be dew nor
rain these years, except at my word."
2 Then the word of the LORD came to him, saying,
3 "Get away from here and turn eastward, and hide by
the Brook Cherith, which flows into the Jordan. 4 And
it will be *that* you shall drink from the brook, and I
have commanded the ravens to feed you there."
5 So he went and did according to the word of the
LORD, for he went and stayed by the Brook Cherith,
which flows into the Jordan. 6 The ravens brought him
bread and meat in the morning, and bread and meat
in the evening; and he drank from the brook. 7 And it
happened after a while that the brook dried up, because
there had been no rain in the land.

16:33 [v] Hebrew *Asherah,* a Canaanite goddess
16:34 [w] Compare Joshua 6:26

Elijah and the Widow

8Then the word of the LORD came to him, saying, 9"Arise, go to
Zarephath, which *belongs* to Sidon, and dwell there. See, I have commanded a widow there to provide for you." 10So he arose and went to
Zarephath. And when he came to the gate of the city, indeed a widow *was*
there gathering sticks. And he called to her and said, "Please bring me a
little water in a cup, that I may drink." 11And as she was going to get *it*, he
called to her and said, "Please bring me a morsel of bread in your hand."
12So she said, "As the LORD your God lives, I do not have bread, only a
handful of flour in a bin, and a little oil in a jar; and see, I *am* gathering a
couple of sticks that I may go in and prepare it for myself and my son, that
we may eat it, and die."
13And Elijah said to her, "Do not fear; go *and* do as you have said, but
make me a small cake from it first, and bring *it* to me; and afterward make
some for yourself and your son. 14For thus says the LORD God of Israel: 'The
bin of flour shall not be used up, nor shall the jar of oil run dry, until the
day the LORD sends rain on the earth.' "
15So she went away and did according to the word of Elijah; and she and
he and her household ate for *many* days. 16The bin of flour was not used
up, nor did the jar of oil run dry, according to the word of the LORD which
He spoke by Elijah.

Elijah Revives the Widow's Son

17Now it happened after these things *that* the son of the woman who
owned the house became sick. And his sickness was so serious that there
was no breath left in him. 18So she said to Elijah, "What have I to do with
you, O man of God? Have you come to me to bring my sin to remembrance, and to kill my son?"
19And he said to her, "Give me your son." So he took him out of her arms
and carried him to the upper room where he was staying, and laid him on
his own bed. 20Then he cried out to the LORD and said, "O LORD my God,
have You also brought tragedy on the widow with whom I lodge, by killing
her son?" 21And he stretched himself out on the child three times, and
cried out to the LORD and said, "O LORD my God, I pray, let this child's soul
come back to him." 22Then the LORD heard the voice of Elijah; and the soul
of the child came back to him, and he revived.
23And Elijah took the child and brought him down from the upper room
into the house, and gave him to his mother. And Elijah said, "See, your son
lives!"
24Then the woman said to Elijah, "Now by this I know that you *are* a man
of God, *and* that the word of the LORD in your mouth *is* the truth."

Elijah's Message to Ahab

18 And it came to pass *after* many days that the word of the LORD came
to Elijah, in the third year, saying, "Go, present yourself to Ahab,
and I will send rain on the earth."
2So Elijah went to present himself to Ahab; and *there was* a severe
famine in Samaria. 3And Ahab had called Obadiah, who *was* in charge of
his house. (Now Obadiah feared the LORD greatly. 4For so it was, while
Jezebel massacred the prophets of the LORD, that Obadiah had taken one

LIFE LESSON

1 Kings 17:1-24

SITUATION Elijah was the first of many important prophets God sent to warn Israel and Judah as the two kingdoms fell away from God. Israel especially needed these prophets because of an evil king and unfaithful priests.

OBSERVATION God used miraculous signs and means to provide for his servants and confirm that he remained with them.

INSPIRATION The Paris doctor warned us that the baby would never reach full term. And without an abortion, he warned, my own life would be in danger.

Our ears took in the words; our minds refused them. Destroy the child we'd waited for? Thus, after three years of roaming Europe as travel writers, John and I hurried home to the specialist my anxious family had located in New York City.

Only to confront a second crisis. Two major New York newspapers had recently folded; scores of expert writers were out of work. The jobs we applied for had waiting periods before we could even get on a list.

Doctors' bills were mounting and the one resource we had, our writing experience, was worth nothing. The one resource, that is, that we knew about. . . . We had no idea, back then in 1950, about the all-sufficiency of God.

Our anxiety had reached the desperation point when John found a stop-gap job. Just until something better turned up, he was to be a reporter for a little sixteen-page religious pamphlet published out of a couple of hotel rooms. He thought the name was *Guideposts.*

"Religious?" I asked incredulously. "Did you tell them we don't go to church or anything?"

He had, but the editor, a man named Len LeSourd, had simply smiled. "God has a plan for you, John, no matter how hard you try to run from it."

The baby was born, full-term and healthy—our son John Scott, now thirty-nine, a country-music writer, a husband and father himself.

And John and I were launched on a lifetime of Christian writing—and the

Continued

biggest travel adventure of all: the journey of faith. "God has a plan for you . . ." It's true of every human being. Sometimes, when you're as deaf as John and I were, it takes seeming disaster to point it out.

(From *Glimpses of His Glory* by John and Elizabeth Sherrill)

APPLICATION Some miracles we can only see in retrospect. How has God worked in your life in the last six weeks beyond your expectations? Share his provision with a friend during the next week.

EXPLORATION Purpose of Miracles—Exodus 3:1-6; Deuteronomy 4:34; Joshua 4:23-24; Psalm 105:4-5; John 20:30; Acts 4:13-20.

hundred prophets and hidden them, fifty to a cave, and had fed them with
bread and water.) 5And Ahab had said to Obadiah, "Go into the land to all
the springs of water and to all the brooks; perhaps we may find grass to
keep the horses and mules alive, so that we will not have to kill any livestock." 6So they divided the land between them to explore it; Ahab went
one way by himself, and Obadiah went another way by himself.
7Now as Obadiah was on his way, suddenly Elijah met him; and he recognized him, and fell on his face, and said, "*Is* that you, my lord Elijah?"
8And he answered him, "*It is* I. Go, tell your master, 'Elijah *is here.*' "
9So he said, "How have I sinned, that you are delivering your servant
into the hand of Ahab, to kill me? 10*As* the LORD your God lives, there is no
nation or kingdom where my master has not sent someone to hunt for
you; and when they said, '*He is* not *here*,' he took an oath from the kingdom or nation that they could not find you. 11And now you say, 'Go, tell
your master, "Elijah *is here*" '! 12And it shall come to pass, *as soon as* I am
gone from you, that the Spirit of the LORD will carry you to a place I do not
know; so when I go and tell Ahab, and he cannot find you, he will kill me.
But I your servant have feared the LORD from my youth. 13Was it not reported to my lord what I did when Jezebel killed the prophets of the LORD,
how I hid one hundred men of the LORD's prophets, fifty to a cave, and fed
them with bread and water? 14And now you say, 'Go, tell your master,
"Elijah *is here.*" ' He will kill me!"
15Then Elijah said, "*As* the LORD of hosts lives, before whom I stand, I
will surely present myself to him today."
16So Obadiah went to meet Ahab, and told him; and Ahab went to meet
Elijah.
17Then it happened, when Ahab saw Elijah, that Ahab said to him, "*Is
that* you, O troubler of Israel?"
18And he answered, "I have not troubled Israel, but you and your father's house *have,* in that you have forsaken the commandments of the
LORD and have followed the Baals. 19Now therefore, send *and* gather all Israel to me on Mount Carmel, the four hundred and fifty prophets of Baal,
and the four hundred prophets of Asherah,[x] who eat at Jezebel's table."

Elijah's Mount Carmel Victory

20So Ahab sent for all the children of Israel, and gathered the prophets
together on Mount Carmel. 21And Elijah came to all the people, and said,
"How long will you falter between two opinions? If the LORD *is* God, follow
Him; but if Baal, follow him." But the people answered him not a word.
22Then Elijah said to the people, "I alone am left a prophet of the LORD; but
Baal's prophets *are* four hundred and fifty men. 23Therefore let them give
us two bulls; and let them choose one bull for themselves, cut it in pieces,
and lay *it* on the wood, but put no fire *under it;* and I will prepare the other
bull, and lay *it* on the wood, but put no fire *under it.* 24Then you call on the
name of your gods, and I will call on the name of the LORD; and the God
who answers by fire, He is God."
So all the people answered and said, "It is well spoken."
25Now Elijah said to the prophets of Baal, "Choose one bull for yourselves and prepare *it* first, for you *are* many; and call on the name of your
god, but put no fire *under it.*"

18:19 [x] A Canaanite goddess

26So they took the bull which was given them, and they prepared *it,* and
called on the name of Baal from morning even till noon, saying, "O Baal,
hear us!" But *there was* no voice; no one answered. Then they leaped about
the altar which they had made.
27And so it was, at noon, that Elijah mocked them and said, "Cry aloud,
for he *is* a god; either he is meditating, or he is busy, or he is on a journey,
or perhaps he is sleeping and must be awakened." 28So they cried aloud,
and cut themselves, as was their custom, with knives and lances, until the
blood gushed out on them. 29And when midday was past, they prophesied
until the *time* of the offering of the *evening* sacrifice. But *there was* no
voice; no one answered, no one paid attention.
30Then Elijah said to all the people, "Come near to me." So all the people
came near to him. And he repaired the altar of the LORD *that was* broken
down. 31And Elijah took twelve stones, according to the number of the
tribes of the sons of Jacob, to whom the word of the LORD had come, saying, "Israel shall be your name."[y] 32Then with the stones he built an altar in
the name of the LORD; and he made a trench around the altar large enough
to hold two seahs of seed. 33And he put the wood in order, cut the bull in
pieces, and laid *it* on the wood, and said, "Fill four waterpots with water,
and pour *it* on the burnt sacrifice and on the wood." 34Then he said, "Do *it*
a second time," and they did *it* a second time; and he said, "Do *it* a third
time," and they did *it* a third time. 35So the water ran all around the altar;
and he also filled the trench with water.
36And it came to pass, at *the time of* the offering of the *evening* sacrifice,
that Elijah the prophet came near and said, "LORD God of Abraham, Isaac,
and Israel, let it be known this day that You *are* God in Israel and I *am* Your
servant, and *that* I have done all these things at Your word. 37Hear me, O
LORD, hear me, that this people may know that You *are* the LORD God, and
that You have turned their hearts back *to You* again."
38Then the fire of the LORD fell and consumed the burnt sacrifice, and
the wood and the stones and the dust, and it licked up the water that *was* in
the trench. 39Now when all the people saw *it,* they fell on their faces; and
they said, "The LORD, He *is* God! The LORD, He *is* God!"
40And Elijah said to them, "Seize the prophets of Baal! Do not let one of
them escape!" So they seized them; and Elijah brought them down to the
Brook Kishon and executed them there.

The Drought Ends

41Then Elijah said to Ahab, "Go up, eat and drink; for *there is* the sound
of abundance of rain." 42So Ahab went up to eat and drink. And Elijah
went up to the top of Carmel; then he bowed down on the ground, and put
his face between his knees, 43and said to his servant, "Go up now, look toward the sea."
So he went up and looked, and said, "*There is* nothing." And seven
times he said, "Go again."
44Then it came to pass the seventh *time,* that he said, "There is a cloud,
as small as a man's hand, rising out of the sea!" So he said, "Go up, say to
Ahab, 'Prepare *your chariot,* and go down before the rain stops you.' "
45Now it happened in the meantime that the sky became black with

18:31 [y] Genesis 32:28

LIFE LESSON

1 Kings 18:1-46

SITUATION King Ahab and his wife Jezebel worshiped Baal, the most popular Canaanite god. Baal idols were often cast in the form of a bull, which represented lust, power, and fertility. Baals were believed to supply rain for crops—an irony during this time of God-appointed drought.

OBSERVATION God demonstrated, powerfully and dramatically, his superiority to all false gods and their prophets.

INSPIRATION Fifty-six times in the Bible the word *almighty* is used. Always it is used of God; never of anyone else. God is all powerful, or omnipotent. Again we are forced to use a negative to explain the concept—there is nothing He can't do. That is a staggering idea. He has no bounds to His energy.

God can do one thing as easily as He can do another. It is no more difficult for God to create a universe than it is for Him to make a butterfly, and He does everything without losing any of His strength. Isaiah 40:28 says, "The Everlasting God, the Lord, the Creator of the ends of the earth does not become weary or tired." God never needs to be replenished. Where would He go for more strength? There is no power outside of God.

Built into absolute power is the authority to use it. God not only has the power but He has the authority to do anything He wants to do. While God can do anything He wants to do, however, His will is totally consistent with His nature. That's why, for example, He cannot lie and will not tolerate sin. It is also why He shows grace and mercy. Psalm 115:3 says, "Our God is in the heavens; He does whatever He pleases." Have you ever asked the question, "Why did God do this?" He did it because He wanted to. If this doesn't seem like a sufficient answer to you, it's because you don't understand God. . . .

We worship an unchanging, all-powerful God. If that makes Him seem far beyond your ability to comprehend, that is good. If you think of God as someone simple enough for

Continued

the human mind to understand, your god is not the true God.

What is your concept of God? Do you see Him as a timeless, infinite, all-powerful, unchanging, glorious being? Or do you, like many, tend to minimize God's greatness, preferring to think of Him as one who may be manipulated or fooled by human hypocrisy, or one who may be mandated to do what we want? Such a view of God is utterly pagan.

A vision of the steadfastness of our immutable God brings a sense of security and stability to our unsettled lives. And the understanding that His power is unlimited and undiminishing strengthens and encourages even the weakest believer. The natural response to that is praise and adoration that overflows in a life that worships.

(From *The Ultimate Priority* by John MacArthur, Jr.)

APPLICATION Is your God too small? Take a moment to pray as you contemplate God's almighty power. Ask him to help you realize his greatness and worship him.

EXPLORATION God Is All Powerful—Genesis 18:14; Exodus 15:6; 1 Samuel 14:6; Psalm 93:4; 115:3; Matthew 19:26; Luke 1:37; Revelation 19:6.

clouds and wind, and there was a heavy rain. So Ahab rode away and went
to Jezreel. 46 Then the hand of the LORD came upon Elijah; and he girded up
his loins and ran ahead of Ahab to the entrance of Jezreel.

Elijah Escapes from Jezebel

19 And Ahab told Jezebel all that Elijah had done, also how he had executed all the prophets with the sword. 2 Then Jezebel sent a messenger to Elijah, saying, "So let the gods do *to me,* and more also, if I do not
make your life as the life of one of them by tomorrow about this time."
3 And when he saw *that,* he arose and ran for his life, and went to
Beersheba, which *belongs* to Judah, and left his servant there.
4 But he himself went a day's journey into the wilderness, and came and
sat down under a broom tree. And he prayed that he might die, and said,
"It is enough! Now, LORD, take my life, for I *am* no better than my fathers!"
5 Then as he lay and slept under a broom tree, suddenly an angel[z] touched
him, and said to him, "Arise *and* eat." 6 Then he looked, and there by his
head *was* a cake baked on coals, and a jar of water. So he ate and drank, and
lay down again. 7 And the angel[a] of the LORD came back the second time, and
touched him, and said, "Arise *and* eat, because the journey *is* too great for
you." 8 So he arose, and ate and drank; and he went in the strength of that
food forty days and forty nights as far as Horeb, the mountain of God.
9 And there he went into a cave, and spent the night in that place; and behold, the word of the LORD *came* to him, and He said to him, "What are you
doing here, Elijah?"
10 So he said, "I have been very zealous for the LORD God of hosts; for the
children of Israel have forsaken Your covenant, torn down Your altars,
and killed Your prophets with the sword. I alone am left; and they seek to
take my life."

God's Revelation to Elijah

11 Then He said, "Go out, and stand on the mountain before the LORD."
And behold, the LORD passed by, and a great and strong wind tore into the
mountains and broke the rocks in pieces before the LORD, *but* the LORD *was*
not in the wind; and after the wind an earthquake, *but* the LORD *was* not in
the earthquake; 12 and after the earthquake a fire, *but* the LORD *was* not in the
fire; and after the fire a still small voice.
13 So it was, when Elijah heard *it,* that he wrapped his face in his mantle
and went out and stood in the entrance of the cave. Suddenly a voice *came*
to him, and said, "What are you doing here, Elijah?"
14 And he said, "I have been very zealous for the LORD God of hosts; because the children of Israel have forsaken Your covenant, torn down Your
altars, and killed Your prophets with the sword. I alone am left; and they
seek to take my life."
15 Then the LORD said to him: "Go, return on your way to the Wilderness
of Damascus; and when you arrive, anoint Hazael *as* king over Syria.
16 Also you shall anoint Jehu the son of Nimshi *as* king over Israel. And
Elisha the son of Shaphat of Abel Meholah you shall anoint *as* prophet in
your place. 17 It shall be *that* whoever escapes the sword of Hazael, Jehu will kill;
and whoever escapes the sword of Jehu, Elisha will kill. 18 Yet I have reserved

19:5 [z] Or *Angel*
19:7 [a] Or *Angel*

seven thousand in Israel, all whose knees have not bowed to Baal, and
every mouth that has not kissed him."

Elisha Follows Elijah

19 So he departed from there, and found Elisha the son of Shaphat, who
was plowing *with* twelve yoke *of oxen* before him, and he was with the
twelfth. Then Elijah passed by him and threw his mantle on him. 20 And he
left the oxen and ran after Elijah, and said, "Please let me kiss my father
and my mother, and *then* I will follow you."
And he said to him, "Go back again, for what have I done to you?"
21 So *Elisha* turned back from him, and took a yoke of oxen and slaughtered them and boiled their flesh, using the oxen's equipment, and gave it
to the people, and they ate. Then he arose and followed Elijah, and became
his servant.

Ahab Defeats the Syrians

20 Now Ben-Hadad the king of Syria gathered all his forces together;
thirty-two kings *were* with him, with horses and chariots. And he
went up and besieged Samaria, and made war against it. 2 Then he sent
messengers into the city to Ahab king of Israel, and said to him, "Thus
says Ben-Hadad: 3 'Your silver and your gold *are* mine; your loveliest wives
and children are mine.' "
4 And the king of Israel answered and said, "My lord, O king, just as you
say, I and all that I have *are* yours."
5 Then the messengers came back and said, "Thus speaks Ben-Hadad,
saying, 'Indeed I have sent to you, saying, "You shall deliver to me your silver and your gold, your wives and your children"; 6 but I will send my servants to you tomorrow about this time, and they shall search your house
and the houses of your servants. And it shall be, *that* whatever is pleasant
in your eyes, they will put *it* in their hands and take *it*.' "
7 So the king of Israel called all the elders of the land, and said, "Notice,
please, and see how this *man* seeks trouble, for he sent to me for my wives,
my children, my silver, and my gold; and I did not deny him."
8 And all the elders and all the people said to him, "Do not listen or consent."
9 Therefore he said to the messengers of Ben-Hadad, "Tell my lord the
king, 'All that you sent for to your servant the first time I will do, but this
thing I cannot do.' "
And the messengers departed and brought back word to him.
10 Then Ben-Hadad sent to him and said, "The gods do so to me, and
more also, if enough dust is left of Samaria for a handful for each of the
people who follow me."
11 So the king of Israel answered and said, "Tell *him*, 'Let not the one who
puts on *his armor* boast like the one who takes *it off*.' "
12 And it happened when *Ben-Hadad* heard this message, as he and the
kings *were* drinking at the command post, that he said to his servants,
"Get ready." And they got ready to attack the city.
13 Suddenly a prophet approached Ahab king of Israel, saying, "Thus
says the LORD: 'Have you seen all this great multitude? Behold, I will deliver it into your hand today, and you shall know that I *am* the LORD.' "
14 So Ahab said, "By whom?"

LIFE LESSON

1 Kings 19:1–20:43

SITUATION In one moment God displayed his power, and Elijah triumphed over the prophets of Baal. In the next, God's prophet ran for his life from Jezebel who sought revenge. He hid in the desert.

OBSERVATION God cares for his servants both in moments of triumph and defeat. He remains present with those who trust Him.

INSPIRATION In the barren prairie, the hiker huddles down. The cold northerly sweeps over him, stinging his face and numbing his fingers. The whistle of the wind is deafening. The hiker hugs his knees to his chest, yearning for warmth.

He doesn't move. The sky is orange with dirt. His teeth are grainy, his eyes sooty. He thinks of quitting. Going home. Home to the mountains.

"Ahh. The mountains." The spirit that moved him in the mountains seems so far away. For a moment, his mind wanders back to his homeland. Green country. Mountain trails. Fresh water. Hikers hiking on well marked trails. No surprises, few fears, rich companionship.

One day, while on a brisk hike, he had stopped to look out from the mountains across the neighboring dessert. He felt strangely pulled to the sweeping barrenness that lay before him. The next day he paused again. And the next, and the next. "Shouldn't someone try to take life to the desert?" Slowly the flicker in his heart became a flame.

Many agreed that someone should go, but no one volunteered.

Uncharted land, fearful storms, loneliness.

But the hiker, spurred by the enthusiasm of others, determined to go. After careful preparation, he set out, alone. With the cheers of his friends behind him, he descended the grassy highlands and entered the desolate wilderness.

The first few days his steps were springy and his eye was keen. He yearned to do his part to bring life to the desert. Then came the heat. The scorpions. The monotony. The snakes. Slowly, the fire diminished. And

Continued

now . . . the storm. The endless roar of the wind. The relentless, cursed cold.

"I don't know how much more I can take." Weary and beaten, the hiker considers going back. "At least I got this far." Knees tucked under him, head bowed, almost touching the ground. "Will it ever stop?"

Grimly he laughs at the irony of the situation. "Some hiker. Too tired to go on, yet too ashamed to go home."

Deep, deep is the struggle. No longer can he hear the voices of friends. Long gone is the romance of his mission. No longer does he float on the fancifulness of a dream.

"Maybe someone else should do this. I'm too young, too inexperienced."

The winds of discouragement and fear whip at his fire, exhausting what is left of the flame. But the coals remain, hidden and hot.

The hiker, now almost the storm's victim, looks one last time for the fire. (Is there any greater challenge than of stirring a spirit while in the clutches of defeat?) Yearning and clawing, the temptation to quit is gradually overcome by the urge to go on. Blowing on the coals, the hiker once again hears the call to the desert. Though faint, the call is clear.

With all the strength he can summon, the hiker rises to his feet, bows his head, and takes his first step into the wind.

(From *On the Anvil* by Max Lucado)

APPLICATION Are you facing a life challenge? Are you discouraged and wondering why circumstances have suddenly taken a turn for the worst? Where is God? Run to God to help you! Everywhere, anytime, God has resources to help you.

EXPLORATION Desert Experiences—Matthew 4:1-11; 28:19; Acts 5:1-32; 16:16-24; Hebrews 13:5-8.

And he said, "Thus says the LORD: 'By the young leaders of the provinces.' "
Then he said, "Who will set the battle in order?"
And he answered, "You."
15Then he mustered the young leaders of the provinces, and there were
two hundred and thirty-two; and after them he mustered all the people, all
the children of Israel—seven thousand.
16So they went out at noon. Meanwhile Ben-Hadad and the thirty-two
kings helping him were getting drunk at the command post. 17The young
leaders of the provinces went out first. And Ben-Hadad sent out *a patrol,*
and they told him, saying, "Men are coming out of Samaria!" 18So he said,
"If they have come out for peace, take them alive; and if they have come
out for war, take them alive."
19Then these young leaders of the provinces went out of the city with the
army which followed them. 20And each one killed his man; so the Syrians
fled, and Israel pursued them; and Ben-Hadad the king of Syria escaped
on a horse with the cavalry. 21Then the king of Israel went out and attacked
the horses and chariots, and killed the Syrians with a great slaughter.
22And the prophet came to the king of Israel and said to him, "Go,
strengthen yourself; take note, and see what you should do, for in the
spring of the year the king of Syria will come up against you."

The Syrians Again Defeated

23Then the servants of the king of Syria said to him, "Their gods *are* gods
of the hills. Therefore they were stronger than we; but if we fight against
them in the plain, surely we will be stronger than they. 24So do this thing:
Dismiss the kings, each from his position, and put captains in their places;
25and you shall muster an army like the army that you have lost, horse for
horse and chariot for chariot. Then we will fight against them in the plain;
surely we will be stronger than they."
And he listened to their voice and did so.
26So it was, in the spring of the year, that Ben-Hadad mustered the Syrians and went up to Aphek to fight against Israel. 27And the children of Israel
were mustered and given provisions, and they went against them. Now the
children of Israel encamped before them like two little flocks of goats,
while the Syrians filled the countryside.
28Then a man of God came and spoke to the king of Israel, and said,
"Thus says the LORD: 'Because the Syrians have said, "The LORD *is* God of
the hills, but He *is* not God of the valleys," therefore I will deliver all this
great multitude into your hand, and you shall know that I *am* the LORD.' "
29And they encamped opposite each other for seven days. So it was that on
the seventh day the battle was joined; and the children of Israel killed one
hundred thousand foot soldiers *of* the Syrians in one day. 30But the rest
fled to Aphek, into the city; then a wall fell on twenty-seven thousand of
the men *who were* left.
And Ben-Hadad fled and went into the city, into an inner chamber.

Ahab's Treaty with Ben-Hadad

31Then his servants said to him, "Look now, we have heard that the kings
of the house of Israel *are* merciful kings. Please, let us put sackcloth around
our waists and ropes around our heads, and go out to the king of Israel;
perhaps he will spare your life." 32So they wore sackcloth around their

waists and *put* ropes around their heads, and came to
the king of Israel and said, "Your servant Ben-Hadad
says, 'Please let me live.' "
And he said, "*Is* he still alive? He *is* my brother."
33Now the men were watching closely to see
whether *any sign of mercy would come* from him; and
they quickly grasped *at this word* and said, "Your
brother Ben-Hadad."
So he said, "Go, bring him." Then Ben-Hadad came
out to him; and he had him come up into the chariot.
34So *Ben-Hadad* said to him, "The cities which my
father took from your father I will restore; and you
may set up marketplaces for yourself in Damascus, as
my father did in Samaria."
Then *Ahab said,* "I will send you away with this
treaty." So he made a treaty with him and sent him away.

Ahab Condemned

35Now a certain man of the sons of the prophets
said to his neighbor by the word of the LORD, "Strike
me, please." And the man refused to strike him.
36Then he said to him, "Because you have not obeyed
the voice of the LORD, surely, as soon as you depart
from me, a lion shall kill you." And as soon as he left
him, a lion found him and killed him.
37And he found another man, and said, "Strike me,
please." So the man struck him, inflicting a wound.
38Then the prophet departed and waited for the king
by the road, and disguised himself with a bandage
over his eyes. 39Now as the king passed by, he cried out
to the king and said, "Your servant went out into the
midst of the battle; and there, a man came over and
brought a man to me, and said, 'Guard this man; if by
any means he is missing, your life shall be for his life,
or else you shall pay a talent of silver.' 40While your
servant was busy here and there, he was gone."
Then the king of Israel said to him, "So *shall* your
judgment *be;* you yourself have decided *it.*"
41And he hastened to take the bandage away from
his eyes; and the king of Israel recognized him as one of
the prophets. 42Then he said to him, "Thus says the LORD:
'Because you have let slip out of *your* hand a man
whom I appointed to utter destruction, therefore your
life shall go for his life, and your people for his people.' "
43So the king of Israel went to his house sullen and
displeased, and came to Samaria.

Naboth Is Murdered for His Vineyard

21 And it came to pass after these things *that*
Naboth the Jezreelite had a vineyard which *was*
in Jezreel, next to the palace of Ahab king of Samaria.
2So Ahab spoke to Naboth, saying, "Give me your
vineyard, that I may have it for a vegetable garden, because it *is* near, next to my house; and for it I will give
you a vineyard better than it. *Or,* if it seems good to
you, I will give you its worth in money."
3But Naboth said to Ahab, "The LORD forbid that I
should give the inheritance of my fathers to you!"
4So Ahab went into his house sullen and displeased
because of the word which Naboth the Jezreelite had
spoken to him; for he had said, "I will not give you the
inheritance of my fathers." And he lay down on his
bed, and turned away his face, and would eat no food.
5But Jezebel his wife came to him, and said to him,
"Why is your spirit so sullen that you eat no food?"
6He said to her, "Because I spoke to Naboth the
Jezreelite, and said to him, 'Give me your vineyard for
money; or else, if it pleases you, I will give you *another*
vineyard for it.' And he answered, 'I will not give you
my vineyard.' "
7Then Jezebel his wife said to him, "You now exercise authority over Israel! Arise, eat food, and let your
heart be cheerful; I will give you the vineyard of
Naboth the Jezreelite."
8And she wrote letters in Ahab's name, sealed *them*
with his seal, and sent the letters to the elders and the
nobles who *were* dwelling in the city with Naboth.
9She wrote in the letters, saying,

> Proclaim a fast, and seat Naboth with high
> honor among the people; 10and seat two men,
> scoundrels, before him to bear witness
> against him, saying, You have blasphemed
> God and the king. *Then* take him out, and
> stone him, that he may die.

11So the men of his city, the elders and nobles who
were inhabitants of his city, did as Jezebel had sent to
them, as it *was* written in the letters which she had
sent to them. 12They proclaimed a fast, and seated
Naboth with high honor among the people. 13And two
men, scoundrels, came in and sat before him; and the
scoundrels witnessed against him, against Naboth, in
the presence of the people, saying, "Naboth has blasphemed God and the king!" Then they took him outside the city and stoned him with stones, so that he
died. 14Then they sent to Jezebel, saying, "Naboth has
been stoned and is dead."
15And it came to pass, when Jezebel heard that
Naboth had been stoned and was dead, that Jezebel
said to Ahab, "Arise, take possession of the vineyard
of Naboth the Jezreelite, which he refused to give you
for money; for Naboth is not alive, but dead." 16So it

was, when Ahab heard that Naboth was dead, that
Ahab got up and went down to take possession of the
vineyard of Naboth the Jezreelite.

The LORD Condemns Ahab

17 Then the word of the LORD came to Elijah the
Tishbite, saying, 18 "Arise, go down to meet Ahab king
of Israel, who *lives* in Samaria. There *he is,* in the vineyard of Naboth, where he has gone down to take possession of it. 19 You shall speak to him, saying, 'Thus
says the LORD: "Have you murdered and also taken possession?" ' And you shall speak to him, saying, 'Thus
says the LORD: "In the place where dogs licked the blood
of Naboth, dogs shall lick your blood, even yours." ' "
20 So Ahab said to Elijah, "Have you found me, O my
enemy?"
And he answered, "I have found *you,* because you
have sold yourself to do evil in the sight of the LORD:
21 'Behold, I will bring calamity on you. I will take away
your posterity, and will cut off from Ahab every male
in Israel, both bond and free. 22 I will make your house
like the house of Jeroboam the son of Nebat, and like
the house of Baasha the son of Ahijah, because of the
provocation with which you have provoked *Me* to
anger, and made Israel sin.' 23 And concerning Jezebel
the LORD also spoke, saying, 'The dogs shall eat
Jezebel by the wall[b] of Jezreel.' 24 The dogs shall eat
whoever belongs to Ahab and dies in the city, and the
birds of the air shall eat whoever dies in the field."
25 But there was no one like Ahab who sold himself
to do wickedness in the sight of the LORD, because
Jezebel his wife stirred him up. 26 And he behaved very
abominably in following idols, according to all *that*
the Amorites had done, whom the LORD had cast out
before the children of Israel.
27 So it was, when Ahab heard those words, that he
tore his clothes and put sackcloth on his body, and
fasted and lay in sackcloth, and went about mourning.
28 And the word of the LORD came to Elijah the Tishbite, saying, 29 "See how Ahab has humbled himself
before Me? Because he has humbled himself before
Me, I will not bring the calamity in his days. In the
days of his son I will bring the calamity on his house."

Micaiah Warns Ahab

22 Now three years passed without war between
Syria and Israel. 2 Then it came to pass, in the
third year, that Jehoshaphat the king of Judah went
down to *visit* the king of Israel.
3 And the king of Israel said to his servants, "Do you
know that Ramoth in Gilead *is* ours, but we hesitate to
take it out of the hand of the king of Syria?" 4 So he
said to Jehoshaphat, "Will you go with me to fight at
Ramoth Gilead?"
Jehoshaphat said to the king of Israel, "I *am* as you
are, my people as your people, my horses as your
horses." 5 Also Jehoshaphat said to the king of Israel,
"Please inquire for the word of the LORD today."
6 Then the king of Israel gathered the prophets together,
about four hundred men, and said to them, "Shall I
go against Ramoth Gilead to fight, or shall I refrain?"
So they said, "Go up, for the Lord will deliver *it* into
the hand of the king."
7 And Jehoshaphat said, "*Is there* not still a prophet
of the LORD here, that we may inquire of Him?"[c]
8 So the king of Israel said to Jehoshaphat, "*There is*
still one man, Micaiah the son of Imlah, by whom we
may inquire of the LORD; but I hate him, because he
does not prophesy good concerning me, but evil."
And Jehoshaphat said, "Let not the king say such
things!"
9 Then the king of Israel called an officer and said,
"Bring Micaiah the son of Imlah quickly!"
10 The king of Israel and Jehoshaphat the king of Judah, having put on *their* robes, sat each on his throne,
at a threshing floor at the entrance of the gate of Samaria; and all the prophets prophesied before them.
11 Now Zedekiah the son of Chenaanah had made
horns of iron for himself; and he said, "Thus says the
LORD: 'With these you shall gore the Syrians until they
are destroyed.' " 12 And all the prophets prophesied so,
saying, "Go up to Ramoth Gilead and prosper, for the
LORD will deliver *it* into the king's hand."
13 Then the messenger who had gone to call Micaiah
spoke to him, saying, "Now listen, the words of the
prophets with one accord encourage the king. Please,
let your word be like the word of one of them, and
speak encouragement."
14 And Micaiah said, "*As* the LORD lives, whatever
the LORD says to me, that I will speak."
15 Then he came to the king; and the king said to
him, "Micaiah, shall we go to war against Ramoth
Gilead, or shall we refrain?"
And he answered him, "Go and prosper, for the
LORD will deliver *it* into the hand of the king!"
16 So the king said to him, "How many times shall I
make you swear that you tell me nothing but the truth
in the name of the LORD?"

21:23 [b] Following Masoretic Text and Septuagint; some Hebrew manuscripts, Syriac, Targum, and Vulgate read *plot of ground* (compare 2 Kings 9:36).
22:7 [c] Or *him*

17 Then he said, "I saw all Israel scattered on the
mountains, as sheep that have no shepherd. And the
LORD said, 'These have no master. Let each return to
his house in peace.' "
18 And the king of Israel said to Jehoshaphat, "Did I
not tell you he would not prophesy good concerning
me, but evil?"
19 Then *Micaiah* said, "Therefore hear the word of
the LORD: I saw the LORD sitting on His throne, and all
the host of heaven standing by, on His right hand and
on His left. 20 And the LORD said, 'Who will persuade
Ahab to go up, that he may fall at Ramoth Gilead?' So
one spoke in this manner, and another spoke in that
manner. 21 Then a spirit came forward and stood before the LORD, and said, 'I will persuade him.' 22 The
LORD said to him, 'In what way?' So he said, 'I will go
out and be a lying spirit in the mouth of all his
prophets.' And the LORD said, 'You shall persuade
him, and also prevail. Go out and do so.' 23 Therefore
look! The LORD has put a lying spirit in the mouth of
all these prophets of yours, and the LORD has declared
disaster against you."
24 Now Zedekiah the son of Chenaanah went near
and struck Micaiah on the cheek, and said, "Which
way did the spirit from the LORD go from me to speak
to you?"
25 And Micaiah said, "Indeed, you shall see on that
day when you go into an inner chamber to hide!"
26 So the king of Israel said, "Take Micaiah, and return him to Amon the governor of the city and to
Joash the king's son; 27 and say, 'Thus says the king:
"Put this *fellow* in prison, and feed him with bread of
affliction and water of affliction, until I come in
peace." ' "
28 But Micaiah said, "If you ever return in peace, the
LORD has not spoken by me." And he said, "Take heed,
all you people!"

Ahab Dies in Battle

29 So the king of Israel and Jehoshaphat the king of
Judah went up to Ramoth Gilead. 30 And the king of Israel said to Jehoshaphat, "I will disguise myself and
go into battle; but you put on your robes." So the king
of Israel disguised himself and went into battle.
31 Now the king of Syria had commanded the thirty-
two captains of his chariots, saying, "Fight with no
one small or great, but only with the king of Israel."
32 So it was, when the captains of the chariots saw Jehoshaphat, that they said, "Surely it *is* the king of Israel!"
Therefore they turned aside to fight against him, and
Jehoshaphat cried out. 33 And it happened, when the
captains of the chariots saw that it *was* not the king of
Israel, that they turned back from pursuing him.
34 Now a *certain* man drew a bow at random, and
struck the king of Israel between the joints of his
armor. So he said to the driver of his chariot, "Turn
around and take me out of the battle, for I am
wounded."
35 The battle increased that day; and the king was
propped up in his chariot, facing the Syrians, and
died at evening. The blood ran out from the wound
onto the floor of the chariot. 36 Then, as the sun was
going down, a shout went throughout the army, saying, "Every man to his city, and every man to his own
country!"
37 So the king died, and was brought to Samaria.
And they buried the king in Samaria. 38 Then *someone*
washed the chariot at a pool in Samaria, and the dogs
licked up his blood while the harlots bathed,[d] according to the word of the LORD which He had spoken.
39 Now the rest of the acts of Ahab, and all that he
did, the ivory house which he built and all the cities
that he built, *are* they not written in the book of the
chronicles of the kings of Israel? 40 So Ahab rested with
his fathers. Then Ahaziah his son reigned in his place.

Jehoshaphat Reigns in Judah

41 Jehoshaphat the son of Asa had become king over
Judah in the fourth year of Ahab king of Israel.
42 Jehoshaphat *was* thirty-five years old when he became king, and he reigned twenty-five years in Jerusalem. His mother's name *was* Azubah the daughter
of Shilhi. 43 And he walked in all the ways of his father
Asa. He did not turn aside from them, doing *what was*
right in the eyes of the LORD. Nevertheless the high
places were not taken away, *for* the people offered sacrifices and burned incense on the high places. 44 Also
Jehoshaphat made peace with the king of Israel.
45 Now the rest of the acts of Jehoshaphat, the might
that he showed, and how he made war, *are* they not
written in the book of the chronicles of the kings of Judah? 46 And the rest of the perverted persons,[e] who remained in the days of his father Asa, he banished
from the land. 47 *There was* then no king in Edom, only
a deputy of the king.
48 Jehoshaphat made merchant ships[f] to go to Ophir
for gold; but they never sailed, for the ships were
wrecked at Ezion Geber. 49 Then Ahaziah the son of

22:38 [d] Syriac and Targum read *they washed his armor.*
22:46 [e] Hebrew *qadesh,* that is, one practicing sodomy and prostitution in religious rituals
22:48 [f] Or *ships of Tarshish*

Ahab said to Jehoshaphat, "Let my servants go with
your servants in the ships." But Jehoshaphat would not.
50 And Jehoshaphat rested with his fathers, and was
buried with his fathers in the City of David his father.
Then Jehoram his son reigned in his place.

Ahaziah Reigns in Israel

51 Ahaziah the son of Ahab became king over Israel
in Samaria in the seventeenth year of Jehoshaphat
king of Judah, and reigned two years over Israel. 52 He
did evil in the sight of the LORD, and walked in the way
of his father and in the way of his mother and in the
way of Jeroboam the son of Nebat, who had made Israel sin; 53 for he served Baal and worshiped him, and
provoked the LORD God of Israel to anger, according
to all that his father had done.

The Second Book of the KINGS

INTRODUCTION

The tone for the book is set in the first two verses.

Moab rebelled against Israel after the death of Ahab. Now Ahaziah fell through the lattice of his upper room in Samaria, and was injured; so he sent messengers and said to them, "Go, inquire of Baal-Zebub, the god of Ekron, whether I shall recover from this injury" (1:1-2).

In those inaugural words you find death (Ahab died), rebellion (Moab broke away), calamity (Ahaziah fell down), and superstition (Go ask . . . the god of Ekron).

What a beginning. It doesn't get any better. Second Kings is not a book for the faint of heart. But is a book for the serious disciple. Its message is embossed at the top of every page: "The way of transgressors is hard."

Remember what Paul said about the wages of sin being death? This book proves his point. Twenty-five chapters of people reaping the harvest of sin. Story after story of people learning firsthand the eternal truth: *The consequence of persistent sin is pain.* Pain, not just in your life but in the lives of those you love.

The book relates the decline of two powers.

The Northern Kingdom, Israel, was headquartered in Samaria. Nineteen kings led this nation. Not one was godly. Not one! In spite of strong prophets like Jonah, Amos, Hosea, Elijah, and Elisha, the kings didn't listen.

The Southern Kingdom, Judah, used Jerusalem as its capitol. Of its twenty sovereigns, only eight walked with God. Again powerful prophets challenged them. Obadiah, Joel, Isaiah, and Jeremiah were just a few of the men who proclaimed God's message.

But the people didn't listen. They slipped from conviction to compromise into captivity. The book ends with the battered nations of Israel and Judah dragged behind the horses of their conquerors. God will leave them in captivity for seventy years. Plenty of time for them to ponder the lesson: *Do not be deceived, God is not mocked; for whatever a man sows, that he will also reap* (Galatians 6:7).

It took these people several decades to get the point. I hope we are better listeners.

LIFE LESSON

2 Kings 1:1-18

SITUATION Ahaziah served as king of the Northern Kingdom (Israel) for two years. As an evil king, he followed Baal.

OBSERVATION Pagan deities are no help, and God is offended when we think otherwise.

INSPIRATION There are two sorts of jealousy among men, and only one of them is a vice. Vicious jealousy is an expression of an attitude, "I want what you've got, and I hate you because I haven't got it." It is an infantile resentment springing from unmortified covetousness, which expresses itself in envy, malice, and meanness of action. . . .

But there is another sort of jealousy—zeal to protect a love relationship, or to avenge it when broken. . . . This sort of jealousy is a positive virtue, for it shows a grasp of the true meaning of the husband-wife relationship, together with a proper zeal to keep it intact.

Now, Scripture consistently views God's jealousy as being of this latter kind: that is, an aspect of His covenantal love for His own people. The Old Testament regards God's covenant as His marriage with Israel, carrying with it a demand for unqualified love and loyalty. . . .

One further point must be made, if we are to view this matter in its true light. God's jealousy over His people, as we have seen, presupposes His covenantal love; and this love is no transitory affection, accidental and aimless, but is the expression of a sovereign purpose. The goal of the covenant love of God is that He should have a people on earth as long as history lasts, and after that have all His faithful ones of every age with Him in glory. Covenant love is the heart of God's plan for the world.

(From *Knowing God* by J. I. Packer)

APPLICATION Thank God for his unfailing love for you. He is the best friend you will ever have.

EXPLORATION Jealousy of God—Exodus 20:5; Deuteronomy 4:24; Ezekiel 39:25; Nahum 1:2; 1 Corinthians 10:22; James 4:5.

God Judges Ahaziah

Moab rebelled against Israel after the death of Ahab.
2Now Ahaziah fell through the lattice of his upper room in
Samaria, and was injured; so he sent messengers and said to
them, "Go, inquire of Baal-Zebub, the god of Ekron, whether
I shall recover from this injury." 3But the angel[a] of the LORD said to Elijah the
Tishbite, "Arise, go up to meet the messengers of the king of Samaria, and
say to them, '*Is it* because *there is* no God in Israel that you are going to inquire of Baal-Zebub, the god of Ekron?' 4Now therefore, thus says the LORD:
'You shall not come down from the bed to which you have gone up, but you
shall surely die.' " So Elijah departed.
5And when the messengers returned to him, he said to them, "Why
have you come back?"
6So they said to him, "A man came up to meet us, and said to us, 'Go, return to the king who sent you, and say to him, "Thus says the LORD: '*Is it*
because *there is* no God in Israel *that* you are sending to inquire of Baal-
Zebub, the god of Ekron? Therefore you shall not come down from the bed
to which you have gone up, but you shall surely die.' " ' "
7Then he said to them, "What kind of man *was it* who came up to meet
you and told you these words?"
8So they answered him, "A hairy man wearing a leather belt around his
waist."
And he said, "It *is* Elijah the Tishbite."
9Then the king sent to him a captain of fifty with his fifty men. So he
went up to him; and there he was, sitting on the top of a hill. And he spoke
to him: "Man of God, the king has said, 'Come down!' "
10So Elijah answered and said to the captain of fifty, "If I *am* a man of
God, then let fire come down from heaven and consume you and your fifty
men." And fire came down from heaven and consumed him and his fifty.
11Then he sent to him another captain of fifty with his fifty men.
And he answered and said to him: "Man of God, thus has the king said,
'Come down quickly!' "
12So Elijah answered and said to them, "If I *am* a man of God, let fire
come down from heaven and consume you and your fifty men." And the
fire of God came down from heaven and consumed him and his fifty.
13Again, he sent a third captain of fifty with his fifty men. And the third
captain of fifty went up, and came and fell on his knees before Elijah, and
pleaded with him, and said to him: "Man of God, please let my life and the
life of these fifty servants of yours be precious in your sight. 14Look, fire
has come down from heaven and burned up the first two captains of fifties
with their fifties. But let my life now be precious in your sight."
15And the angel[b] of the LORD said to Elijah, "Go down with him; do not
be afraid of him." So he arose and went down with him to the king. 16Then
he said to him, "Thus says the LORD: 'Because you have sent messengers to
inquire of Baal-Zebub, the god of Ekron, *is it* because *there is* no God in Israel
to inquire of His word? Therefore you shall not come down from the bed
to which you have gone up, but you shall surely die.' "
17So *Ahaziah* died according to the word of the LORD which Elijah had

1:3 [a] Or *Angel*
1:15 [b] Or *Angel*

spoken. Because he had no son, Jehoram[c] became king in his place, in the
second year of Jehoram the son of Jehoshaphat, king of Judah.
18Now the rest of the acts of Ahaziah which he did, *are* they not written in
the book of the chronicles of the kings of Israel?

Elijah Ascends to Heaven

2 And it came to pass, when the LORD was about to take up Elijah into heaven
by a whirlwind, that Elijah went with Elisha from Gilgal. 2Then Elijah said
to Elisha, "Stay here, please, for the LORD has sent me on to Bethel."
But Elisha said, "*As* the LORD lives, and *as* your soul lives, I will not leave
you!" So they went down to Bethel.
3Now the sons of the prophets who *were* at Bethel came out to Elisha,
and said to him, "Do you know that the LORD will take away your master
from over you today?"
And he said, "Yes, I know; keep silent!"
4Then Elijah said to him, "Elisha, stay here, please, for the LORD has sent
me on to Jericho."
But he said, "*As* the LORD lives, and *as* your soul lives, I will not leave
you!" So they came to Jericho.
5Now the sons of the prophets who *were* at Jericho came to Elisha and
said to him, "Do you know that the LORD will take away your master from
over you today?"
So he answered, "Yes, I know; keep silent!"
6Then Elijah said to him, "Stay here, please, for the LORD has sent me on
to the Jordan."
But he said, "*As* the LORD lives, and *as* your soul lives, I will not leave
you!" So the two of them went on. 7And fifty men of the sons of the
prophets went and stood facing *them* at a distance, while the two of them
stood by the Jordan. 8Now Elijah took his mantle, rolled *it* up, and struck
the water; and it was divided this way and that, so that the two of them
crossed over on dry ground.
9And so it was, when they had crossed over, that Elijah said to Elisha,
"Ask! What may I do for you, before I am taken away from you?"
Elisha said, "Please let a double portion of your spirit be upon me."
10So he said, "You have asked a hard thing. *Nevertheless,* if you see me
when I am taken from you, it shall be so for you; but if not, it shall not be
so." 11Then it happened, as they continued on and talked, that suddenly a
chariot of fire *appeared* with horses of fire, and separated the two of them;
and Elijah went up by a whirlwind into heaven.
12And Elisha saw *it,* and he cried out, "My father, my father, the chariot
of Israel and its horsemen!" So he saw him no more. And he took hold of
his own clothes and tore them into two pieces. 13He also took up the mantle of Elijah that had fallen from him, and went back and stood by the bank
of the Jordan. 14Then he took the mantle of Elijah that had fallen from him,
and struck the water, and said, "Where *is* the LORD God of Elijah?" And
when he also had struck the water, it was divided this way and that; and
Elisha crossed over.
15Now when the sons of the prophets who *were* from Jericho saw him,
they said, "The spirit of Elijah rests on Elisha." And they came to meet

1:17 *c* The son of Ahab king of Israel (compare 3:1)

LIFE LESSON

2 Kings 2:1–3:27

SITUATION Elijah's ministry drew to an end. Elisha requested a double portion of the Holy Spirit that rested upon Elijah. Elisha's request demonstrated his willingness to be God's prophet, no matter the cost.

OBSERVATION Because Elisha had followed Elijah for so long, he knew that being a prophet of God was not an easy job. Even so, he desired to serve God in this way, and God granted his request.

INSPIRATION The future is hard to figure out. We know that . . . the seeds of repentance and renewal will fall on different kinds of soil. Some who receive these seeds will be superficial in their commitment and, lacking depth, will turn away from radical Christianity. . . .

But every so often, and more often than one might think, there will be those individuals who get a handle on the message, realize what is involved, and go with it all the way. As the prophetic seeds take root in them, they will seek to do the works of righteousness (Matt. 5:6). In hard and forgotten places they will try to do what must be done for justice to roll down and for *shalom* to thrive. What they try to accomplish will often leave them frustrated, but they will learn from their frustrations. The people they try to serve will hurt them many times, but they will learn to see Jesus in these people anyway. What they achieve will be limited in the world's eyes, but they *will* learn how to overcome the world (John 16:33). And in the end they will bear fruit. Eventually their efforts will come to greatness. Even the seemingly little things that they do will have their rewards (Matt. 10:42). And when these people come together, they will be a presence that the world will not be able to ignore. They will be a new people who will shake the foundations of the old order. They will be a leaven in society. They will be the salt of the earth. They will be the beginning of a new Kingdom, even as the old . . . passes away.

(From *Wake Up America* by Tony Campolo)

Continued

APPLICATION Jesus has called his people to be the salt of the earth. Get involved with a ministry through your church or a Christian organization.

EXPLORATION Willing Servants—Matthew 20:26-28; Luke 10:25-37; 2 Corinthians 9:10-14; Galatians 5:13-14; Colossians 3:23; Hebrews 6:10.

him, and bowed to the ground before him. 16Then they said to him, "Look
now, there are fifty strong men with your servants. Please let them go and
search for your master, lest perhaps the Spirit of the LORD has taken him
up and cast him upon some mountain or into some valley."
And he said, "You shall not send anyone."
17But when they urged him till he was ashamed, he said, "Send *them!*"
Therefore they sent fifty men, and they searched for three days but did not
find him. 18And when they came back to him, for he had stayed in Jericho,
he said to them, "Did I not say to you, 'Do not go'?"

Elisha Performs Miracles

19Then the men of the city said to Elisha, "Please notice, the situation of
this city *is* pleasant, as my lord sees; but the water *is* bad, and the ground
barren."
20And he said, "Bring me a new bowl, and put salt in it." So they brought
it to him. 21Then he went out to the source of the water, and cast in the salt
there, and said, "Thus says the LORD: 'I have healed this water; from it
there shall be no more death or barrenness.' " 22So the water remains
healed to this day, according to the word of Elisha which he spoke.
23Then he went up from there to Bethel; and as he was going up the road,
some youths came from the city and mocked him, and said to him, "Go
up, you baldhead! Go up, you baldhead!"
24So he turned around and looked at them, and pronounced a curse on
them in the name of the LORD. And two female bears came out of the
woods and mauled forty-two of the youths.
25Then he went from there to Mount Carmel, and from there he returned to Samaria.

Moab Rebels Against Israel

3 Now Jehoram the son of Ahab became king over Israel at Samaria in
the eighteenth year of Jehoshaphat king of Judah, and reigned twelve
years. 2And he did evil in the sight of the LORD, but not like his father and
mother; for he put away the *sacred* pillar of Baal that his father had made.
3Nevertheless he persisted in the sins of Jeroboam the son of Nebat, who
had made Israel sin; he did not depart from them.
4Now Mesha king of Moab was a sheepbreeder, and he regularly paid
the king of Israel one hundred thousand lambs and the wool of one hundred thousand rams. 5But it happened, when Ahab died, that the king of
Moab rebelled against the king of Israel.
6So King Jehoram went out of Samaria at that time and mustered all Israel. 7Then he went and sent to Jehoshaphat king of Judah, saying, "The
king of Moab has rebelled against me. Will you go with me to fight against
Moab?"
And he said, "I will go up; I *am* as you *are*, my people as your people, my
horses as your horses." 8Then he said, "Which way shall we go up?"
And he answered, "By way of the Wilderness of Edom."
9So the king of Israel went with the king of Judah and the king of Edom,
and they marched on that roundabout route seven days; and there was no
water for the army, nor for the animals that followed them. 10And the king
of Israel said, "Alas! For the LORD has called these three kings together to
deliver them into the hand of Moab."

11 But Jehoshaphat said, "*Is there* no prophet of the LORD here, that we
may inquire of the LORD by him?"
So one of the servants of the king of Israel answered and said, "Elisha
the son of Shaphat *is* here, who poured water on the hands of Elijah."
12 And Jehoshaphat said, "The word of the LORD is with him." So the king
of Israel and Jehoshaphat and the king of Edom went down to him.
13 Then Elisha said to the king of Israel, "What have I to do with you? Go
to the prophets of your father and the prophets of your mother."
But the king of Israel said to him, "No, for the LORD has called these
three kings *together* to deliver them into the hand of Moab."
14 And Elisha said, "*As* the LORD of hosts lives, before whom I stand,
surely were it not that I regard the presence of Jehoshaphat king of Judah,
I would not look at you, nor see you. 15 But now bring me a musician."
Then it happened, when the musician played, that the hand of the LORD
came upon him. 16 And he said, "Thus says the LORD: 'Make this valley full
of ditches.' 17 For thus says the LORD: 'You shall not see wind, nor shall you
see rain; yet that valley shall be filled with water, so that you, your cattle,
and your animals may drink.' 18 And this is a simple matter in the sight of
the LORD; He will also deliver the Moabites into your hand. 19 Also you shall
attack every fortified city and every choice city, and shall cut down every
good tree, and stop up every spring of water, and ruin every good piece of
land with stones."
20 Now it happened in the morning, when the grain offering was offered, that
suddenly water came by way of Edom, and the land was filled with water.
21 And when all the Moabites heard that the kings had come up to fight
against them, all who were able to bear arms and older were gathered; and
they stood at the border. 22 Then they rose up early in the morning, and the sun
was shining on the water; and the Moabites saw the water on the other side *as*
red as blood. 23 And they said, "This is blood; the kings have surely struck
swords and have killed one another; now therefore, Moab, to the spoil!"
24 So when they came to the camp of Israel, Israel rose up and attacked the
Moabites, so that they fled before them; and they entered *their* land, killing
the Moabites. 25 Then they destroyed the cities, and each man threw a stone
on every good piece of land and filled it; and they stopped up all the springs
of water and cut down all the good trees. But they left the stones of Kir
Haraseth *intact.* However the slingers surrounded and attacked it.
26 And when the king of Moab saw that the battle was too fierce for him,
he took with him seven hundred men who drew swords, to break through
to the king of Edom, but they could not. 27 Then he took his eldest son who
would have reigned in his place, and offered him *as* a burnt offering upon
the wall; and there was great indignation against Israel. So they departed
from him and returned to *their own* land.

Elisha and the Widow's Oil

4 A certain woman of the wives of the sons of the prophets cried out to
Elisha, saying, "Your servant my husband is dead, and you know that
your servant feared the LORD. And the creditor is coming to take my two
sons to be his slaves."
2 So Elisha said to her, "What shall I do for you? Tell me, what do you
have in the house?" And she said, "Your maidservant has nothing in the
house but a jar of oil."

LIFE LESSON

2 Kings 4:1–6:7

SITUATION God used Elisha to express divine power and concern by working wonders through this faithful servant. The miracles in this passage not only benefitted the Israelites but also helped people whom the Israelites considered ungodly and unworthy of God's attention.

OBSERVATION Miraculous interventions are just one way God expresses compassion to those he loves. Though people sometimes misunderstand God as harsh and judging, he has a loving nature and shows concern even in the small details of our lives.

INSPIRATION The car gave a violent lurch and came to a stop. "What was that!" the children cried. Tib looked down into the deep draw below us. "I think we've gone through the bridge," she said.

It was true. As soon as I stepped out onto the narrow log-and-dirt bridge straddling the steep gully, I saw that our rear wheel had plunged through the rotten timbers up to the axle.

Tib took the three kids back to solid ground. Gingerly, I jacked up the car, intending to fill the hole, then let the rear wheels back down and drive off. But searching that barren landscape produced nothing but small twigs and pebbles which fell right through the break in the bridge. Nowhere could we find rocks or logs big enough to plug the hole.

Since we had come to Africa we had never been in clearer need of guidance. We were still fifteen miles from the village where we planned to spend the night. Behind us were miles of empty bush; all afternoon we had met one car on the winding dirt track we were following in this little-traveled district of Uganda. Thunderclouds were building up over the Nile, and night would be upon us in half an hour. We couldn't spend the night in the car for fear the rest of the bridge would go. We couldn't stay out of the car: this was lion country. A mile back we had passed a fresh hippo carcass.

Continued

And so in this emergency we did what we had done frequently since arriving on this unpredictable continent. We asked God what to do. We used a principle we had used before, thanking Him ahead of time for the answer which we confidently expected would come. Then we simply waited. And in the strange calm which follows this attitude, the answer was there, simple and perfect. I got out the spare tire, slipped it beneath the jacked-up wheel and found that it straddled the hole exactly. I let the car back down and, to the cheers of the children, drove off the bridge. Just in time too, for with nightfall came the first wave of a driving tropical rainstorm.

Now it would be possible, of course, to say that we had not received guidance at all, we were just using common sense. Once I would have been inclined to agree. But not today. For our African year, from beginning to end, was above all else an adventure in guidance. There where so much was strange, we found ourselves daily, hourly, sometimes minute-by-minute asking God's direction.

(From *Glimpses of His Glory* by John and Elizabeth Sherrill)

APPLICATION Are you convinced of God's love for you—enough that you expect and trust that he will intervene when you need him to? Are you facing a difficult situation? Find the courage to bring it to God in faith. Ask him to help you in the way he knows is best; then wait and see how God intervenes.

EXPLORATION God's Intervention—Exodus 19:4; Psalm 34:6-7; Proverbs 16:9; Isaiah 41:10; 65:24; Matthew 20:28; Luke 5:12-13; Romans 5:6; Colossians 2:13.

3 Then he said, "Go, borrow vessels from everywhere, from all your
neighbors—empty vessels; do not gather just a few. 4 And when you have
come in, you shall shut the door behind you and your sons; then pour it
into all those vessels, and set aside the full ones."
5 So she went from him and shut the door behind her and her sons, who
brought *the vessels* to her; and she poured *it* out. 6 Now it came to pass, when
the vessels were full, that she said to her son, "Bring me another vessel."
And he said to her, "*There is* not another vessel." So the oil ceased. 7 Then
she came and told the man of God. And he said, "Go, sell the oil and pay
your debt; and you *and* your sons live on the rest."

Elisha Raises the Shunammite's Son

8 Now it happened one day that Elisha went to Shunem, where there *was*
a notable woman, and she persuaded him to eat some food. So it was, as
often as he passed by, he would turn in there to eat some food. 9 And she
said to her husband, "Look now, I know that this *is* a holy man of God,
who passes by us regularly. 10 Please, let us make a small upper room on
the wall; and let us put a bed for him there, and a table and a chair and a
lampstand; so it will be, whenever he comes to us, he can turn in there."
11 And it happened one day that he came there, and he turned in to the
upper room and lay down there. 12 Then he said to Gehazi his servant, "Call
this Shunammite woman." When he had called her, she stood before him.
13 And he said to him, "Say now to her, 'Look, you have been concerned for
us with all this care. What *can I* do for you? Do you want me to speak on
your behalf to the king or to the commander of the army?' "
She answered, "I dwell among my own people."
14 So he said, "What then *is* to be done for her?"
And Gehazi answered, "Actually, she has no son, and her husband is old."
15 So he said, "Call her." When he had called her, she stood in the doorway. 16 Then he said, "About this time next year you shall embrace a son."
And she said, "No, my lord. Man of God, do not lie to your maidservant!"
17 But the woman conceived, and bore a son when the appointed time
had come, of which Elisha had told her.
18 And the child grew. Now it happened one day that he went out to his
father, to the reapers. 19 And he said to his father, "My head, my head!"
So he said to a servant, "Carry him to his mother." 20 When he had taken
him and brought him to his mother, he sat on her knees till noon, and *then*
died. 21 And she went up and laid him on the bed of the man of God, shut
the door upon him, and went out. 22 Then she called to her husband, and
said, "Please send me one of the young men and one of the donkeys, that I
may run to the man of God and come back."
23 So he said, "Why are you going to him today? *It is* neither the New
Moon nor the Sabbath."
And she said, "*It is* well." 24 Then she saddled a donkey, and said to her
servant, "Drive, and go forward; do not slacken the pace for me unless I tell
you." 25 And so she departed, and went to the man of God at Mount Carmel.
So it was, when the man of God saw her afar off, that he said to his servant Gehazi, "Look, the Shunammite woman! 26 Please run now to meet
her, and say to her, '*Is it* well with you? *Is it* well with your husband? *Is it*
well with the child?' "
And she answered, "*It is* well." 27 Now when she came to the man of God at

the hill, she caught him by the feet, but Gehazi came
near to push her away. But the man of God said, "Let
her alone; for her soul *is* in deep distress, and the LORD
has hidden *it* from me, and has not told me."
28 So she said, "Did I ask a son of my lord? Did I not
say, 'Do not deceive me'?"
29 Then he said to Gehazi, "Get yourself ready, and
take my staff in your hand, and be on your way. If you
meet anyone, do not greet him; and if anyone greets
you, do not answer him; but lay my staff on the face of
the child."
30 And the mother of the child said, "*As* the LORD
lives, and *as* your soul lives, I will not leave you." So he
arose and followed her. 31 Now Gehazi went on ahead
of them, and laid the staff on the face of the child; but
there was neither voice nor hearing. Therefore he went
back to meet him, and told him, saying, "The child
has not awakened."
32 When Elisha came into the house, there was the
child, lying dead on his bed. 33 He went in therefore,
shut the door behind the two of them, and prayed to
the LORD. 34 And he went up and lay on the child, and
put his mouth on his mouth, his eyes on his eyes, and
his hands on his hands; and he stretched himself out
on the child, and the flesh of the child became warm.
35 He returned and walked back and forth in the
house, and again went up and stretched himself out
on him; then the child sneezed seven times, and the
child opened his eyes. 36 And he called Gehazi and
said, "Call this Shunammite woman." So he called
her. And when she came in to him, he said, "Pick up
your son." 37 So she went in, fell at his feet, and bowed to
the ground; then she picked up her son and went out.

Elisha Purifies the Pot of Stew

38 And Elisha returned to Gilgal, and *there was* a
famine in the land. Now the sons of the prophets *were*
sitting before him; and he said to his servant, "Put on
the large pot, and boil stew for the sons of the
prophets." 39 So one went out into the field to gather
herbs, and found a wild vine, and gathered from it a
lapful of wild gourds, and came and sliced *them* into
the pot of stew, though they did not know *what they
were.* 40 Then they served it to the men to eat. Now it
happened, as they were eating the stew, that they cried
out and said, "Man of God, *there is* death in the pot!"
And they could not eat *it*.
41 So he said, "Then bring some flour." And he put *it*
into the pot, and said, "Serve *it* to the people, that they
may eat." And there was nothing harmful in the pot.

Elisha Feeds One Hundred Men

42 Then a man came from Baal Shalisha, and
brought the man of God bread of the firstfruits, twenty
loaves of barley bread, and newly ripened grain in his
knapsack. And he said, "Give *it* to the people, that they
may eat."
43 But his servant said, "What? Shall I set this before
one hundred men?"
He said again, "Give it to the people, that they may
eat; for thus says the LORD: 'They shall eat and have
some left over.' " 44 So he set *it* before them; and they
ate and had *some* left over, according to the word of
the LORD.

Naaman's Leprosy Healed

5 Now Naaman, commander of the army of the king
of Syria, was a great and honorable man in the
eyes of his master, because by him the LORD had given
victory to Syria. He was also a mighty man of valor,
but a leper. 2 And the Syrians had gone out on raids,
and had brought back captive a young girl from the
land of Israel. She waited on Naaman's wife. 3 Then
she said to her mistress, "If only my master *were* with
the prophet who *is* in Samaria! For he would heal him
of his leprosy." 4 And *Naaman* went in and told his
master, saying, "Thus and thus said the girl who *is*
from the land of Israel."
5 Then the king of Syria said, "Go now, and I will
send a letter to the king of Israel."
So he departed and took with him ten talents of silver, six thousand *shekels* of gold, and ten changes of
clothing. 6 Then he brought the letter to the king of Israel, which said,

> Now be advised, when this letter comes to
> you, that I have sent Naaman my servant to
> you, that you may heal him of his leprosy.

7 And it happened, when the king of Israel read the letter, that he tore his clothes and said, "*Am* I God, to kill
and make alive, that this man sends a man to me to
heal him of his leprosy? Therefore please consider,
and see how he seeks a quarrel with me."
8 So it was, when Elisha the man of God heard that
the king of Israel had torn his clothes, that he sent to
the king, saying, "Why have you torn your clothes?
Please let him come to me, and he shall know that
there is a prophet in Israel."
9 Then Naaman went with his horses and chariot,
and he stood at the door of Elisha's house. 10 And
Elisha sent a messenger to him, saying, "Go and wash
in the Jordan seven times, and your flesh shall be re-

stored to you, and *you shall* be clean." 11But Naaman
became furious, and went away and said, "Indeed, I
said to myself, 'He will surely come out *to me*, and
stand and call on the name of the LORD his God, and
wave his hand over the place, and heal the leprosy.'
12*Are* not the Abanah[d] and the Pharpar, the rivers of
Damascus, better than all the waters of Israel? Could I
not wash in them and be clean?" So he turned and
went away in a rage. 13And his servants came near and
spoke to him, and said, "My father, *if* the prophet had
told you *to do* something great, would you not have
done *it*? How much more then, when he says to you,
'Wash, and be clean'?" 14So he went down and dipped
seven times in the Jordan, according to the saying of
the man of God; and his flesh was restored like the
flesh of a little child, and he was clean.

15And he returned to the man of God, he and all his
aides, and came and stood before him; and he said,
"Indeed, now I know that *there is* no God in all the
earth, except in Israel; now therefore, please take a
gift from your servant."

16But he said, "*As* the LORD lives, before whom I
stand, I will receive nothing." And he urged him to
take *it*, but he refused.

17So Naaman said, "Then, if not, please let your servant be given two mule-loads of earth; for your servant will no longer offer either burnt offering or
sacrifice to other gods, but to the LORD. 18Yet in this
thing may the LORD pardon your servant: when my
master goes into the temple of Rimmon to worship
there, and he leans on my hand, and I bow down in
the temple of Rimmon—when I bow down in the
temple of Rimmon, may the LORD please pardon your
servant in this thing."

19Then he said to him, "Go in peace." So he departed from him a short distance.

Gehazi's Greed

20But Gehazi, the servant of Elisha the man of God,
said, "Look, my master has spared Naaman this Syrian,
while not receiving from his hands what he brought; but
as the LORD lives, I will run after him and take something
from him." 21So Gehazi pursued Naaman. When
Naaman saw *him* running after him, he got down from
the chariot to meet him, and said, "*Is* all well?"

22And he said, "All *is* well. My master has sent me,
saying, 'Indeed, just now two young men of the sons of
the prophets have come to me from the mountains of
Ephraim. Please give them a talent of silver and two
changes of garments.' "

23So Naaman said, "Please, take two talents." And
he urged him, and bound two talents of silver in two
bags, with two changes of garments, and handed
them to two of his servants; and they carried *them* on
ahead of him. 24When he came to the citadel, he took
them from their hand, and stored *them* away in the
house; then he let the men go, and they departed.
25Now he went in and stood before his master. Elisha
said to him, "Where *did you go*, Gehazi?"

And he said, "Your servant did not go anywhere."

26Then he said to him, "Did not my heart go *with
you* when the man turned back from his chariot to
meet you? *Is it* time to receive money and to receive
clothing, olive groves and vineyards, sheep and oxen,
male and female servants? 27Therefore the leprosy of
Naaman shall cling to you and your descendants forever." And he went out from his presence leprous, *as
white* as snow.

The Floating Ax Head

6 And the sons of the prophets said to Elisha, "See
now, the place where we dwell with you is too
small for us. 2Please, let us go to the Jordan, and let
every man take a beam from there, and let us make
there a place where we may dwell."

So he answered, "Go."

3Then one said, "Please consent to go with your
servants."

And he answered, "I will go." 4So he went with
them. And when they came to the Jordan, they cut
down trees. 5But as one was cutting down a tree, the
iron *ax head* fell into the water; and he cried out and
said, "Alas, master! For it was borrowed."

6So the man of God said, "Where did it fall?" And
he showed him the place. So he cut off a stick, and
threw *it* in there; and he made the iron float. 7There-
fore he said, "Pick *it* up for yourself." So he reached
out his hand and took it.

The Blinded Syrians Captured

8Now the king of Syria was making war against Israel; and he consulted with his servants, saying, "My
camp *will be* in such and such a place." 9And the man
of God sent to the king of Israel, saying, "Beware that
you do not pass this place, for the Syrians are coming
down there." 10Then the king of Israel sent *someone* to
the place of which the man of God had told him. Thus
he warned him, and he was watchful there, not just
once or twice.

5:12 *d* Following Kethib, Septuagint, and Vulgate; Qere, Syriac, and Targum read *Amanah*.

11Therefore the heart of the king of Syria was greatly troubled by this
thing; and he called his servants and said to them, "Will you not show me
which of us *is* for the king of Israel?"
12And one of his servants said, "None, my lord, O king; but Elisha, the
prophet who *is* in Israel, tells the king of Israel the words that you speak in
your bedroom."
13So he said, "Go and see where he *is,* that I may send and get him."
And it was told him, saying, "Surely *he is* in Dothan."
14Therefore he sent horses and chariots and a great army there, and they
came by night and surrounded the city. 15And when the servant of the man
of God arose early and went out, there was an army, surrounding the city
with horses and chariots. And his servant said to him, "Alas, my master!
What shall we do?"
16So he answered, "Do not fear, for those who *are* with us *are* more than
those who *are* with them." 17And Elisha prayed, and said, "LORD, I pray, open
his eyes that he may see." Then the LORD opened the eyes of the young man,
and he saw. And behold, the mountain *was* full of horses and chariots of fire
all around Elisha. 18So when *the Syrians* came down to him, Elisha prayed to
the LORD, and said, "Strike this people, I pray, with blindness." And He
struck them with blindness according to the word of Elisha.
19Now Elisha said to them, "This *is* not the way, nor *is* this the city. Follow me,
and I will bring you to the man whom you seek." But he led them to Samaria.
20So it was, when they had come to Samaria, that Elisha said, "LORD,
open the eyes of these *men,* that they may see." And the LORD opened their
eyes, and they saw; and there *they were,* inside Samaria!
21Now when the king of Israel saw them, he said to Elisha, "My father,
shall I kill *them?* Shall I kill *them?*"
22But he answered, "You shall not kill *them.* Would you kill those whom
you have taken captive with your sword and your bow? Set food and water
before them, that they may eat and drink and go to their master." 23Then
he prepared a great feast for them; and after they ate and drank, he sent
them away and they went to their master. So the bands of Syrian *raiders*
came no more into the land of Israel.

Syria Besieges Samaria in Famine

24And it happened after this that Ben-Hadad king of Syria gathered all
his army, and went up and besieged Samaria. 25And there was a great famine in Samaria; and indeed they besieged it until a donkey's head was *sold*
for eighty *shekels* of silver, and one-fourth of a kab of dove droppings for
five *shekels* of silver.
26Then, as the king of Israel was passing by on the wall, a woman cried
out to him, saying, "Help, my lord, O king!"
27And he said, "If the LORD does not help you, where can I find help for
you? From the threshing floor or from the winepress?" 28Then the king
said to her, "What is troubling you?"

And she answered, "This woman said to me, 'Give your son, that we
may eat him today, and we will eat my son tomorrow.' 29So we boiled my
son, and ate him. And I said to her on the next day, 'Give your son, that we
may eat him'; but she has hidden her son."
30Now it happened, when the king heard the words of the woman, that
he tore his clothes; and as he passed by on the wall, the people looked, and

Life Lesson

2 Kings 6:8–8:15

SITUATION Aram was a region in southern Syria. The kings of Aram and Israel frequently fought each other, with tenuous times of peace between the battles.

OBSERVATION Though God used hard times such as famine to prompt the Israelites to return to him, he also provided miraculous protection for his people. God's ways of working are often invisible to human eyes.

INSPIRATION The local sheriff had decided to tighten the requirements for his deputies. Each man had to qualify on the firing range, and the distance had been extended from fifteen yards to twenty-five yards. So the deputies gathered to try their hand at hitting the target at the increased distance. Each man had eighteen seconds to get off twelve shots.

The best shot in the area is also a personal friend, George Burgin, who, together with his wife, Corenne, keeps an eye on Bill and me. The day before the trials he had been fitted with his first pair of trifocals. When his time came to shoot, he drew a bead on the target.

"Suddenly," as he told me later, "I began to perspire. And when I perspire, my glasses fog up. There I was with a bead drawn on the target, and all I could see was fog."

"Then I remembered what our old Navy instructor had taught us: 'If (for some reason) you ever lose sight of the target,' he said, 'just remember your position.'"

"So," our friend said, "I just held my position and pulled the trigger as fast as I could. By then I had less than eighteen seconds, but I got off all twelve shots. When I took off my glasses and wiped them, I had hit the bull's-eye every time."

There are times when we, for some reason, lose sight of our target—which is to glorify our Lord. The world is too much with us. Tears blur our vision. Unexplained tragedy raises questions that cannot be answered and shakes our faith to its foundations.

Continued

Then we must remember our position, for the Christian's position is "in Christ." As if we were tired or hurt children, He will gather both us and our loads.

Though we may not, for some reason, see the target, if we just "remember our position," we won't miss.

(From *The Legacy of a Pack Rat* by Ruth Bell Graham)

APPLICATION When God feels far away, don't despair. He is actually just as close as the times when you sense his presence. Ask God to open your eyes to his invisible work in your life. Trust that he is working in ways you might not be able to see. Each day remember that you are his special child.

EXPLORATION Trusting God's Invisible Work—Job 5:9; Psalm 37:7; 119:18; Habakkuk 3:17-19; Luke 17:5; 2 Corinthians 4:18; Ephesians 6:12; Hebrews 11:27; 12:2; 2 Peter 3:8-9.

there underneath *he had* sackcloth on his body. 31Then he said, "God do so
to me and more also, if the head of Elisha the son of Shaphat remains on
him today!"
32But Elisha was sitting in his house, and the elders were sitting with
him. And *the king* sent a man ahead of him, but before the messenger came
to him, he said to the elders, "Do you see how this son of a murderer has
sent someone to take away my head? Look, when the messenger comes,
shut the door, and hold him fast at the door. *Is* not the sound of his master's
feet behind him?" 33And while he was still talking with them, there was the
messenger, coming down to him; and then *the king* said, "Surely this
calamity *is* from the LORD; why should I wait for the LORD any longer?"
7 Then Elisha said, "Hear the word of the LORD. Thus says the LORD: 'Tomorrow about this time a seah of fine flour *shall be sold* for a shekel,
and two seahs of barley for a shekel, at the gate of Samaria.' "
2So an officer on whose hand the king leaned answered the man of God
and said, "Look, *if* the LORD would make windows in heaven, could this
thing be?"
And he said, "In fact, you shall see *it* with your eyes, but you shall not eat
of it."

The Syrians Flee

3Now there were four leprous men at the entrance of the gate; and they
said to one another, "Why are we sitting here until we die? 4If we say, 'We
will enter the city,' the famine *is* in the city, and we shall die there. And if we
sit here, we die also. Now therefore, come, let us surrender to the army of
the Syrians. If they keep us alive, we shall live; and if they kill us, we shall
only die." 5And they rose at twilight to go to the camp of the Syrians; and
when they had come to the outskirts of the Syrian camp, to their surprise
no one *was* there. 6For the LORD had caused the army of the Syrians to hear
the noise of chariots and the noise of horses—the noise of a great army;
so they said to one another, "Look, the king of Israel has hired against us
the kings of the Hittites and the kings of the Egyptians to attack us!"
7Therefore they arose and fled at twilight, and left the camp intact—their
tents, their horses, and their donkeys—and they fled for their lives. 8And
when these lepers came to the outskirts of the camp, they went into one
tent and ate and drank, and carried from it silver and gold and clothing,
and went and hid *them;* then they came back and entered another tent,
and carried *some* from there *also,* and went and hid *it.*
9Then they said to one another, "We are not doing right. This day *is* a
day of good news, and we remain silent. If we wait until morning light,
some punishment will come upon us. Now therefore, come, let us go and
tell the king's household." 10So they went and called to the gatekeepers of
the city, and told them, saying, "We went to the Syrian camp, and surprisingly no one *was* there, not a human sound—only horses and donkeys
tied, and the tents intact." 11And the gatekeepers called out, and they told
it to the king's household inside.
12So the king arose in the night and said to his servants, "Let me now tell
you what the Syrians have done to us. They know that we *are* hungry;
therefore they have gone out of the camp to hide themselves in the field,
saying, 'When they come out of the city, we shall catch them alive, and get
into the city.' "

13 And one of his servants answered and said, "Please, let several *men*
take five of the remaining horses which are left in the city. Look, they *may*
either become like all the multitude of Israel that are left in it; or indeed, *I*
say, they *may become* like all the multitude of Israel left from those who are
consumed; so let us send them and see." 14 Therefore they took two chariots with horses; and the king sent them in the direction of the Syrian army,
saying, "Go and see." 15 And they went after them to the Jordan; and indeed
all the road *was* full of garments and weapons which the Syrians had
thrown away in their haste. So the messengers returned and told the king.
16 Then the people went out and plundered the tents of the Syrians. So a
seah of fine flour was *sold* for a shekel, and two seahs of barley for a shekel,
according to the word of the LORD.

17 Now the king had appointed the officer on whose hand he leaned to
have charge of the gate. But the people trampled him in the gate, and he
died, just as the man of God had said, who spoke when the king came
down to him. 18 So it happened just as the man of God had spoken to the
king, saying, "Two seahs of barley for a shekel, and a seah of fine flour for
a shekel, shall be *sold* tomorrow about this time in the gate of Samaria."

19 Then that officer had answered the man of God, and said, "Now look,
if the LORD would make windows in heaven, could such a thing be?"

And he had said, "In fact, you shall see *it* with your eyes, but you shall
not eat of it." 20 And so it happened to him, for the people trampled him in
the gate, and he died.

The King Restores the Shunammite's Land

8 Then Elisha spoke to the woman whose son he had restored to life,
saying, "Arise and go, you and your household, and stay wherever you
can; for the LORD has called for a famine, and furthermore, it will come
upon the land for seven years." 2 So the woman arose and did according to
the saying of the man of God, and she went with her household and dwelt
in the land of the Philistines seven years.

3 It came to pass, at the end of seven years, that the woman returned from
the land of the Philistines; and she went to make an appeal to the king for
her house and for her land. 4 Then the king talked with Gehazi, the servant
of the man of God, saying, "Tell me, please, all the great things Elisha has
done." 5 Now it happened, as he was telling the king how he had restored the
dead to life, that there was the woman whose son he had restored to life, appealing to the king for her house and for her land. And Gehazi said, "My
lord, O king, this *is* the woman, and this *is* her son whom Elisha restored to
life." 6 And when the king asked the woman, she told him.

So the king appointed a certain officer for her, saying, "Restore all that
was hers, and all the proceeds of the field from the day that she left the land
until now."

Death of Ben-Hadad

7 Then Elisha went to Damascus, and Ben-Hadad king of Syria was sick;
and it was told him, saying, "The man of God has come here." 8 And the
king said to Hazael, "Take a present in your hand, and go to meet the man
of God, and inquire of the LORD by him, saying, 'Shall I recover from this
disease?' " 9 So Hazael went to meet him and took a present with him, of
every good thing of Damascus, forty camel-loads; and he came and stood

LIFE LESSON

2 Kings 8:16–9:37

SITUATION With Jehoshaphat as a father, Jehoram had a good example to follow. When he became king, however, he foolishly chose to marry the daughter of Ahab and Jezebel (probably as a political alliance). This daughter, Athaliah, brought evil practices and the need for God's judgment to the Southern Kingdom.

OBSERVATION If we purposely ignore God's desire for us, we will find ourselves candidates for his discipline.

INSPIRATION In our less consistent moments we almost unconsciously see the conflict between God and Satan as an arm-wrestling match. Their wrists go first this way, then that; God's arm is on top one moment, Satan's the next. We remind ourselves that God will win in the end because He's slightly stronger and can hold out longer. But, we reason, it's going to take much time, effort, and a few close calls. We almost think Satan's schemes throw a monkey wrench into God's plans, catch Him off guard, and present Him with problems He wishes wouldn't happen.

That's silly. The truth is, God is infinitely more powerful than Satan. God, the One who is in you, is greater than Satan, the one who is in the world. Satan owes his very existence to God—he is a created being, an angel, and a fallen one at that. Satan had to receive God's permission before afflicting Job, and even then he was under definite restrictions. Satan's demonic hordes feared Jesus and obeyed Jesus' commands. And the Bible is clear that when our Lord is ready, He will crush the Evil One forever.

No, Satan doesn't sneak out and cause pneumonia and cancer while God happens to be looking the other way listening to the prayers of His saints. He can only do what our all-powerful and all-knowing God allows him to do.

Lord Jesus, I have nothing to fear, knowing that You are in control. There is no accident, injury, or circumstance that can happen beyond Your sovereign

Continued

will. I recognize that the Devil cannot touch my life, that he cannot even tempt me without gaining Your permission. Help me to realize just how great and powerful You really are! (From *Diamonds in the Dust* by Joni Eareckson Tada)

APPLICATION Are you troubled by the evil that surrounds you? Leaders or managers who don't honor God? The suffering of the innocent? The influence of sin?—All of these can weigh you down and make you doubt God's ability to intervene. Remember: God has perfect timing. He has a plan to judge and punish evil. Bring your discouragement to him and rely on his victory.

EXPLORATION Evil Defeated—Psalm 44:2-8; Romans 8:37-39; 1 Corinthians 15:55-57; Colossians 2:13-15; 2 Thessalonians 2:8; Hebrews 2:14-15; 1 John 4:4; 5:4; Jude 6; Revelation 19:20.

before him, and said, "Your son Ben-Hadad king of Syria has sent me to
you, saying, 'Shall I recover from this disease?' "
10 And Elisha said to him, "Go, say to him, 'You shall certainly recover.'
However the LORD has shown me that he will really die." 11 Then he set his
countenance in a stare until he was ashamed; and the man of God wept.
12 And Hazael said, "Why is my lord weeping?"
He answered, "Because I know the evil that you will do to the children of
Israel: Their strongholds you will set on fire, and their young men you will
kill with the sword; and you will dash their children, and rip open their
women with child."
13 So Hazael said, "But what *is* your servant—a dog, that he should do
this gross thing?"
And Elisha answered, "The LORD has shown me that you *will become*
king over Syria."
14 Then he departed from Elisha, and came to his master, who said to
him, "What did Elisha say to you?" And he answered, "He told me you
would surely recover." 15 But it happened on the next day that he took a
thick cloth and dipped *it* in water, and spread *it* over his face so that he
died; and Hazael reigned in his place.

Jehoram Reigns in Judah

16 Now in the fifth year of Joram the son of Ahab, king of Israel,
Jehoshaphat *having been* king of Judah, Jehoram the son of Jehoshaphat
began to reign as king of Judah. 17 He was thirty-two years old when he became king, and he reigned eight years in Jerusalem. 18 And he walked in the
way of the kings of Israel, just as the house of Ahab had done, for the
daughter of Ahab was his wife; and he did evil in the sight of the LORD. 19 Yet
the LORD would not destroy Judah, for the sake of His servant David, as He
promised him to give a lamp to him *and* his sons forever.
20 In his days Edom revolted against Judah's authority, and made a king
over themselves. 21 So Joram[e] went to Zair, and all his chariots with him.
Then he rose by night and attacked the Edomites who had surrounded
him and the captains of the chariots; and the troops fled to their tents.
22 Thus Edom has been in revolt against Judah's authority to this day. And
Libnah revolted at that time.
23 Now the rest of the acts of Joram, and all that he did, *are* they not written in the book of the chronicles of the kings of Judah? 24 So Joram rested
with his fathers, and was buried with his fathers in the City of David. Then
Ahaziah his son reigned in his place.

Ahaziah Reigns in Judah

25 In the twelfth year of Joram the son of Ahab, king of Israel, Ahaziah the
son of Jehoram, king of Judah, began to reign. 26 Ahaziah *was* twenty-two
years old when he became king, and he reigned one year in Jerusalem. His
mother's name *was* Athaliah the granddaughter of Omri, king of Israel. 27 And
he walked in the way of the house of Ahab, and did evil in the sight of the LORD,
like the house of Ahab, for he *was* the son-in-law of the house of Ahab.
28 Now he went with Joram the son of Ahab to war against Hazael king of
Syria at Ramoth Gilead; and the Syrians wounded Joram. 29 Then King
Joram went back to Jezreel to recover from the wounds which the Syrians

8:21 [e] Spelled *Jehoram* in verse 16

had inflicted on him at Ramah, when he fought
against Hazael king of Syria. And Ahaziah the son of
Jehoram, king of Judah, went down to see Joram the
son of Ahab in Jezreel, because he was sick.

Jehu Anointed King of Israel

9 And Elisha the prophet called one of the sons of the
prophets, and said to him, "Get yourself ready, take
this flask of oil in your hand, and go to Ramoth Gilead.
2Now when you arrive at that place, look there for Jehu
the son of Jehoshaphat, the son of Nimshi, and go in
and make him rise up from among his associates, and
take him to an inner room. 3Then take the flask of oil,
and pour *it* on his head, and say, 'Thus says the LORD: "I
have anointed you king over Israel." ' Then open the
door and flee, and do not delay."
4So the young man, the servant of the prophet, went
to Ramoth Gilead. 5And when he arrived, there *were*
the captains of the army sitting; and he said, "I have a
message for you, Commander."
Jehu said, "For which *one* of us?"
And he said, "For you, Commander." 6Then he
arose and went into the house. And he poured the oil
on his head, and said to him, "Thus says the LORD God
of Israel: 'I have anointed you king over the people of
the LORD, over Israel. 7You shall strike down the house
of Ahab your master, that I may avenge the blood of
My servants the prophets, and the blood of all the servants of the LORD, at the hand of Jezebel. 8For the
whole house of Ahab shall perish; and I will cut off
from Ahab all the males in Israel, both bond and free.
9So I will make the house of Ahab like the house of
Jeroboam the son of Nebat, and like the house of
Baasha the son of Ahijah. 10The dogs shall eat Jezebel
on the plot *of ground* at Jezreel, and *there shall be* none
to bury *her.*' " And he opened the door and fled.
11Then Jehu came out to the servants of his master,
and *one* said to him, "*Is* all well? Why did this madman come to you?"
And he said to them, "You know the man and his
babble."
12And they said, "A lie! Tell us now."
So he said, "Thus and thus he spoke to me, saying,
'Thus says the LORD: "I have anointed you king over
Israel." ' "
13Then each man hastened to take his garment and
put *it* under him on the top of the steps; and they blew
trumpets, saying, "Jehu is king!"

Joram of Israel Killed

14So Jehu the son of Jehoshaphat, the son of
Nimshi, conspired against Joram. (Now Joram had
been defending Ramoth Gilead, he and all Israel,
against Hazael king of Syria. 15But King Joram had returned to Jezreel to recover from the wounds which
the Syrians had inflicted on him when he fought with
Hazael king of Syria.) And Jehu said, "If you are so
minded, let no one leave *or* escape from the city to go
and tell *it* in Jezreel." 16So Jehu rode in a chariot and
went to Jezreel, for Joram was laid up there; and
Ahaziah king of Judah had come down to see Joram.
17Now a watchman stood on the tower in Jezreel,
and he saw the company of Jehu as he came, and said,
"I see a company of men."
And Joram said, "Get a horseman and send him to
meet them, and let him say, '*Is it* peace?' "
18So the horseman went to meet him, and said,
"Thus says the king: '*Is it* peace?' "
And Jehu said, "What have you to do with peace?
Turn around and follow me."
So the watchman reported, saying, "The messenger
went to them, but is not coming back."
19Then he sent out a second horseman who came to
them, and said, "Thus says the king: '*Is it* peace?' "
And Jehu answered, "What have you to do with
peace? Turn around and follow me."
20So the watchman reported, saying, "He went up
to them and is not coming back; and the driving *is* like
the driving of Jehu the son of Nimshi, for he drives
furiously!"
21Then Joram said, "Make ready." And his chariot
was made ready. Then Joram king of Israel and
Ahaziah king of Judah went out, each in his chariot;
and they went out to meet Jehu, and met him on the
property of Naboth the Jezreelite. 22Now it happened,
when Joram saw Jehu, that he said, "*Is it* peace, Jehu?"
So he answered, "What peace, as long as the harlotries of your mother Jezebel and her witchcraft *are*
so many?"
23Then Joram turned around and fled, and said to
Ahaziah, "Treachery, Ahaziah!" 24Now Jehu drew his
bow with full strength and shot Jehoram between his
arms; and the arrow came out at his heart, and he
sank down in his chariot. 25Then *Jehu* said to Bidkar
his captain, "Pick *him* up, *and* throw him into the
tract of the field of Naboth the Jezreelite; for remember, when you and I were riding together behind Ahab
his father, that the LORD laid this burden upon him:
26'Surely I saw yesterday the blood of Naboth and the
blood of his sons,' says the LORD, 'and I will repay you
in this plot,' says the LORD. Now therefore, take *and*
throw him on the plot *of ground,* according to the
word of the LORD."

LIFE LESSON

2 Kings 10:1-36

SITUATION King Jehu drastically reformed society. He spoke out against practices that disregarded God's law and called the people back to God's standards. He killed wicked Ahab's household and the prophets of Baal. Although he led the way in these reforms, he failed to finish the job—he did not remove the idols set up in Dan and Bethel.

OBSERVATION Jehu passionately opposed practices that were dishonoring to God, but some of his own efforts were sinful (Hosea 1:4-5).

INSPIRATION It seems a couple of prowlers broke into a department store in a large city . . . They took nothing. Absolutely nothing. No merchandise was stolen. No items were removed. But what they did was ridiculous.

Instead of stealing anything, they changed the cost of everything. Price tags were swapped. Values were exchanged. These clever pranksters took the tag off a $395 camera and stuck it on a $5.00 box of stationery. The $5.95 sticker on a paperback book was removed and placed on an outboard motor. They repriced everything in the store!

Crazy? You bet. But the craziest part of this story took place the next morning. The store opened as usual. Employees went to work. Customers began to shop. The place functioned as normal for four hours before anyone noticed what had happened.

Four hours! Some people got some great bargains. Others got fleeced. For four solid hours no one noticed that all the values had been swapped.

Hard to believe? It shouldn't be—we see the same thing happening every day. We are deluged by a distorted value system. We see the most valuable things in our lives peddled for pennies and we see the cheapest smut go for millions.

The salesman who defended his illegal practices by saying, "Let's not confuse business with ethics."

The military men who sold top-secret information (as well as their integrity) for $6,000.

Ahaziah of Judah Killed

27But when Ahaziah king of Judah saw *this,* he fled by the road to Beth
Haggan.[f] So Jehu pursued him, and said, "Shoot him also in the chariot." *And
they shot him* at the Ascent of Gur, which is by Ibleam. Then he fled to
Megiddo, and died there. 28And his servants carried him in the chariot to Jerusalem, and buried him in his tomb with his fathers in the City of David. 29In the
eleventh year of Joram the son of Ahab, Ahaziah had become king over Judah.

Jezebel's Violent Death

30Now when Jehu had come to Jezreel, Jezebel heard *of it;* and she put paint
on her eyes and adorned her head, and looked through a window. 31Then, as
Jehu entered at the gate, she said, "*Is it* peace, Zimri, murderer of your master?"
32And he looked up at the window, and said, "Who *is* on my side? Who?"
So two *or* three eunuchs looked out at him. 33Then he said, "Throw her
down." So they threw her down, and *some* of her blood spattered on the
wall and on the horses; and he trampled her underfoot. 34And when he had
gone in, he ate and drank. Then he said, "Go now, see to this accursed
woman, and bury her, for she was a king's daughter." 35So they went to
bury her, but they found no more of her than the skull and the feet and the
palms of *her* hands. 36Therefore they came back and told him. And he said,
"This *is* the word of the LORD, which He spoke by His servant Elijah the
Tishbite, saying, 'On the plot *of ground* at Jezreel dogs shall eat the flesh of
Jezebel;[g] 37and the corpse of Jezebel shall be as refuse on the surface of the
field, in the plot at Jezreel, so that they shall not say, "Here *lies* Jezebel." ' "

Ahab's Seventy Sons Killed

10 Now Ahab had seventy sons in Samaria. And Jehu wrote and sent
letters to Samaria, to the rulers of Jezreel,[h] to the elders, and to those
who reared Ahab's *sons,* saying:

2 Now as soon as this letter comes to you, since your master's sons
are with you, and you have chariots and horses, a fortified city
also, and weapons, 3choose the best qualified of your master's
sons, set *him* on his father's throne, and fight for your
master's house.

4But they were exceedingly afraid, and said, "Look, two kings could not
stand up to him; how then can we stand?" 5And he who *was* in charge of
the house, and he who *was* in charge of the city, the elders also, and those
who reared *the sons,* sent to Jehu, saying, "We *are* your servants, we will do
all you tell us; but we will not make anyone king. Do *what is* good in your
sight." 6Then he wrote a second letter to them, saying:

If you *are* for me and will obey my voice, take the heads of the men,
your master's sons, and come to me at Jezreel by this time
tomorrow.

Now the king's sons, seventy persons, *were* with the great men of the
city, *who* were rearing them. 7So it was, when the letter came to them, that
they took the king's sons and slaughtered seventy persons, put their heads
in baskets and sent *them* to him at Jezreel.

9:27 [f] Literally *The Garden House*
9:36 [g] 1 Kings 21:23
10:1 [h] Following Masoretic Text, Syriac, and Targum; Septuagint reads *Samaria;* Vulgate reads *city.*

8 Then a messenger came and told him, saying, "They have brought the
heads of the king's sons."
And he said, "Lay them in two heaps at the entrance of the gate until
morning."
9 So it was, in the morning, that he went out and stood, and said to all the
people, "You *are* righteous. Indeed I conspired against my master and
killed him; but who killed all these? 10 Know now that nothing shall fall to
the earth of the word of the LORD which the LORD spoke concerning the
house of Ahab; for the LORD has done what He spoke by His servant
Elijah." 11 So Jehu killed all who remained of the house of Ahab in Jezreel,
and all his great men and his close acquaintances and his priests, until he
left him none remaining.

Ahaziah's Forty-two Brothers Killed

12 And he arose and departed and went to Samaria. On the way, at Beth
Eked[i] of the Shepherds, 13 Jehu met with the brothers of Ahaziah king of Judah, and said, "Who *are* you?"
So they answered, "We *are* the brothers of Ahaziah; we have come down
to greet the sons of the king and the sons of the queen mother."
14 And he said, "Take them alive!" So they took them alive, and killed
them at the well of Beth Eked, forty-two men; and he left none of them.

The Rest of Ahab's Family Killed

15 Now when he departed from there, he met Jehonadab the son of
Rechab, *coming* to meet him; and he greeted him and said to him, "Is your
heart right, as my heart *is* toward your heart?"
And Jehonadab answered, "It is."
Jehu said, "If it is, give *me* your hand." So he gave *him* his hand, and he
took him up to him into the chariot. 16 Then he said, "Come with me, and
see my zeal for the LORD." So they had him ride in his chariot. 17 And when
he came to Samaria, he killed all who remained to Ahab in Samaria, till he
had destroyed them, according to the word of the LORD which He spoke to
Elijah.

Worshipers of Baal Killed

18 Then Jehu gathered all the people together, and said to them, "Ahab
served Baal a little, Jehu will serve him much. 19 Now therefore, call to me
all the prophets of Baal, all his servants, and all his priests. Let no one be
missing, for I have a great sacrifice for Baal. Whoever is missing shall not
live." But Jehu acted deceptively, with the intent of destroying the worshipers of Baal. 20 And Jehu said, "Proclaim a solemn assembly for Baal."
So they proclaimed *it.* 21 Then Jehu sent throughout all Israel; and all the
worshipers of Baal came, so that there was not a man left who did not
come. So they came into the temple[j] of Baal, and the temple of Baal was
full from one end to the other. 22 And he said to the one in charge of the
wardrobe, "Bring out vestments for all the worshipers of Baal." So he
brought out vestments for them. 23 Then Jehu and Jehonadab the son of
Rechab went into the temple of Baal, and said to the worshipers of Baal,

10:12 [i] Or *The Shearing House*
10:21 [j] Literally *house,* and so elsewhere in this chapter

The cabinet member of a large nation who was caught illegally dealing in semi-precious stones. His cabinet position? Minister of *Justice.*

The father who confessed to the murder of his twelve-year-old daughter. The reason he killed her? She refused to go to bed with him.

Why do we do what we do? Why do we take blatantly black-and-white and paint it gray? Why are priceless mores trashed while senseless standards are obeyed? What causes us to elevate the body and degrade the soul? What causes us to pamper the skin while we pollute the heart?

Our values are messed up. Someone broke into the store and exchanged all the price tags. Thrills are going for top dollar and the value of human beings is at an all-time low. . . .

And you've seen the results of this. Our system goes haywire. We feel useless and worthless. We freak out. We play games. We create false value systems. We say that you are valuable if you are pretty. We say that you are valuable if you can produce. . . .

Now please understand, this is man's value system. It is not God's. . . .

In God's book man is heading somewhere. He has an amazing destiny. We are being prepared to walk down the church aisle and become the bride of Jesus. We are going to live with him. Share the throne with him. Reign with him. We count. We are valuable. And what's more, our worth is built in! Our value is inborn.
(From *No Wonder They Call Him the Savior* by Max Lucado)

APPLICATION Make a list of things the world values (money, good looks, nice cars.) When you've completed your list, ask yourself, "Which of these do I value? Which does God value? How can I spend my time and money better to reflect what God values?"

EXPLORATION Distorted Values—Job 21:14; Psalm 82:5; Proverbs 14:12; 30:20; Isaiah 44:18-20; Jeremiah 9:3-6; Zephaniah 3:5; John 1:5; Romans 1:21-32; Ephesians 4:18; 2 Peter 2:19.

Life Lesson

2 Kings 11:1–12:21

SITUATION Joash, under the guidance of the priest Jehoiada, purged the land of idolatry. Joash collected money and ordered the priests to repair the temple. When they failed, he brought in other workmen to complete the task.

OBSERVATION God uses people other than priests and pastors. Sometimes the most effective workers God uses are just ordinary people.

INSPIRATION Recently, I read a sociological study that has great significance for those of us who are trying to respond to champions of the yuppies value system. In this particular study fifty people over the age of ninety-five were asked one question: "If you could live your life over again, what would you do differently?" . . . Three answers constantly re-emerged and dominated the results of that study. . . .

1. If I had it to do over again, I would reflect more.

2. If I had it to do over again, I would risk more.

3. If I had it to do over again, I would do more things that would live on after I am dead.

I think that these elderly people have a good handle on what life is all about. I believe that their perspective gives better direction on how to live life with joy and satisfaction than we can gain from listening to the new kids on the block. . . . I am convinced that people who want to have fun in life would do well to consider the observations of those whom time has made wise.

(From *Who Switched the Price Tags?* by Tony Campolo)

APPLICATION Don't let your lack of theological training or position stop you from serving God in your work. Become an active participant in church. Talk about Christ with your neighbors, co-workers, family members, and friends. Be a witness right where you are.

EXPLORATION Lay People—Exodus 39:42; Joshua 1:16; 2 Kings 10:30-31; 2 Chronicles 30:15.

"Search and see that no servants of the LORD are here with you, but only
the worshipers of Baal." 24So they went in to offer sacrifices and burnt offerings. Now Jehu had appointed for himself eighty men on the outside,
and had said, "*If* any of the men whom I have brought into your hands escapes, *whoever lets him escape, it shall be* his life for the life of the other."
25Now it happened, as soon as he had made an end of offering the burnt
offering, that Jehu said to the guard and to the captains, "Go in *and* kill
them; let no one come out!" And they killed them with the edge of the
sword; then the guards and the officers threw *them* out, and went into the
inner room of the temple of Baal. 26And they brought the *sacred* pillars out
of the temple of Baal and burned them. 27Then they broke down the *sacred*
pillar of Baal, and tore down the temple of Baal and made it a refuse dump
to this day. 28Thus Jehu destroyed Baal from Israel.
29However Jehu did not turn away from the sins of Jeroboam the son of
Nebat, who had made Israel sin, *that is,* from the golden calves that *were* at
Bethel and Dan. 30And the LORD said to Jehu, "Because you have done well
in doing *what is* right in My sight, *and* have done to the house of Ahab all
that *was* in My heart, your sons shall sit on the throne of Israel to the
fourth *generation.*" 31But Jehu took no heed to walk in the law of the LORD
God of Israel with all his heart; for he did not depart from the sins of
Jeroboam, who had made Israel sin.

Death of Jehu

32In those days the LORD began to cut off *parts* of Israel; and Hazael conquered them in all the territory of Israel 33from the Jordan eastward: all the
land of Gilead—Gad, Reuben, and Manasseh—from Aroer, which *is* by
the River Arnon, including Gilead and Bashan.
34Now the rest of the acts of Jehu, all that he did, and all his might, *are*
they not written in the book of the chronicles of the kings of Israel? 35So
Jehu rested with his fathers, and they buried him in Samaria. Then
Jehoahaz his son reigned in his place. 36And the period that Jehu reigned
over Israel in Samaria *was* twenty-eight years.

Athaliah Reigns in Judah

11 When Athaliah the mother of Ahaziah saw that her son was dead,
she arose and destroyed all the royal heirs. 2But Jehosheba, the
daughter of King Joram, sister of Ahaziah, took Joash the son of Ahaziah,
and stole him away from among the king's sons *who were* being murdered; and they hid him and his nurse in the bedroom, from Athaliah, so
that he was not killed. 3So he was hidden with her in the house of the LORD
for six years, while Athaliah reigned over the land.

Joash Crowned King of Judah

4In the seventh year Jehoiada sent and brought the captains of hundreds—of the bodyguards and the escorts—and brought them into the
house of the LORD to him. And he made a covenant with them and took an
oath from them in the house of the LORD, and showed them the king's son.
5Then he commanded them, saying, "This *is* what you shall do: One-third
of you who come on duty on the Sabbath shall be keeping watch over the
king's house, 6one-third *shall be* at the gate of Sur, and one-third at the gate
behind the escorts. You shall keep the watch of the house, lest it be broken

down. 7The two contingents of you who go off duty on
the Sabbath shall keep the watch of the house of the
LORD for the king. 8But you shall surround the king on
all sides, every man with his weapons in his hand;
and whoever comes within range, let him be put to
death. You are to be with the king as he goes out and
as he comes in."

9So the captains of the hundreds did according to
all that Jehoiada the priest commanded. Each of them
took his men who were to be on duty on the Sabbath,
with those who were going off duty on the Sabbath,
and came to Jehoiada the priest. 10And the priest gave
the captains of hundreds the spears and shields
which *had belonged* to King David, that were in the
temple of the LORD. 11Then the escorts stood, every
man with his weapons in his hand, all around the
king, from the right side of the temple to the left side
of the temple, by the altar and the house. 12And he
brought out the king's son, put the crown on him, and
gave him the Testimony;[k] they made him king and
anointed him, and they clapped their hands and said,
"Long live the king!"

Death of Athaliah

13Now when Athaliah heard the noise of the escorts
and the people, she came to the people *in* the temple
of the LORD. 14When she looked, there was the king
standing by a pillar according to custom; and the
leaders and the trumpeters were by the king. All the
people of the land were rejoicing and blowing trumpets. So Athaliah tore her clothes and cried out,
"Treason! Treason!"

15And Jehoiada the priest commanded the captains
of the hundreds, the officers of the army, and said to
them, "Take her outside under guard, and slay with
the sword whoever follows her." For the priest had
said, "Do not let her be killed in the house of the
LORD." 16So they seized her; and she went by way of the
horses' entrance *into* the king's house, and there she
was killed.

17Then Jehoiada made a covenant between the
LORD, the king, and the people, that they should be the
LORD's people, and *also* between the king and the people. 18And all the people of the land went to the temple
of Baal, and tore it down. They thoroughly broke in
pieces its altars and images, and killed Mattan the
priest of Baal before the altars. And the priest appointed officers over the house of the LORD. 19Then he
took the captains of hundreds, the bodyguards, the
escorts, and all the people of the land; and they
brought the king down from the house of the LORD,
and went by way of the gate of the escorts to the king's
house. Then he sat on the throne of the kings. 20So all
the people of the land rejoiced; and the city was quiet,
for they had slain Athaliah with the sword *in* the
king's house. 21Jehoash *was* seven years old when he
became king.

Jehoash Repairs the Temple

12 In the seventh year of Jehu, Jehoash[l] became
king, and he reigned forty years in Jerusalem.
His mother's name *was* Zibiah of Beersheba. 2Jehoash
did *what was* right in the sight of the LORD all the days
in which Jehoiada the priest instructed him. 3But the
high places were not taken away; the people still sacrificed and burned incense on the high places.

4And Jehoash said to the priests, "All the money of
the dedicated gifts that are brought into the house of
the LORD—each man's census money, each man's assessment money[m]—*and* all the money that a man
purposes in his heart to bring into the house of the
LORD, 5let the priests take *it* themselves, each from his
constituency; and let them repair the damages of the
temple, wherever any dilapidation is found."

6Now it was so, by the twenty-third year of King
Jehoash, *that* the priests had not repaired the damages of the temple. 7So King Jehoash called Jehoiada
the priest and the *other* priests, and said to them,
"Why have you not repaired the damages of the temple? Now therefore, do not take *more* money from
your constituency, but deliver it for repairing the
damages of the temple." 8And the priests agreed that
they would neither receive *more* money from the people, nor repair the damages of the temple.

9Then Jehoiada the priest took a chest, bored a hole
in its lid, and set it beside the altar, on the right side as
one comes into the house of the LORD; and the priests
who kept the door put there all the money brought
into the house of the LORD. 10So it was, whenever they
saw that *there was* much money in the chest, that the
king's scribe and the high priest came up and put it in
bags, and counted the money that was found in the
house of the LORD. 11Then they gave the money, which
had been apportioned, into the hands of those who
did the work, who had the oversight of the house of
the LORD; and they paid it out to the carpenters and

11:12 [k] That is, the Law (compare Exodus 25:16, 21 and Deuteronomy 31:9)
12:1 [l] Spelled *Joash* in 11:2ff
12:4 [m] Compare Leviticus 27:2ff

LIFE LESSON
2 Kings 13:1–14:29

SITUATION Under the domination of Syria, Israel became helpless. The Israelites lost the power to rule themselves and degraded their belief in God by corrupting their religion. Yet, when Jehoahaz prayed to God for the first time in seventeen years, God listened.

OBSERVATION God always listens to a person who sincerely repents and returns to a life of obedience. God wants more than just an outward show of faith. He seeks true devotion.

INSPIRATION Out of all the people of the earth, they [Israel] believed God had chosen them to be his own particular people. They described their unique relationship with God as a covenant or binding agreement. The covenant was not something that they invented. On the contrary, it was a gift of God's grace. It was offered to them purely out of God's love for them and for all men. As long as they remained faithful to their covenant with God, life was rich and moved in a purposive direction. But any reader of the Old Testament is familiar with the record of broken covenants, of unfaithfulness, and of growing estrangement between Israel and God. One of the astounding

builders who worked on the house of the LORD, [12]and to masons and
stonecutters, and for buying timber and hewn stone, to repair the damage
of the house of the LORD, and for all that was paid out to repair the temple.
[13]However there were not made for the house of the LORD basins of silver,
trimmers, sprinkling-bowls, trumpets, any articles of gold or articles of silver, from the money brought into the house of the LORD. [14]But they gave that
to the workmen, and they repaired the house of the LORD with it. [15]Moreover
they did not require an account from the men into whose hand they delivered the money to be paid to workmen, for they dealt faithfully. [16]The money
from the trespass offerings and the money from the sin offerings was not
brought into the house of the LORD. It belonged to the priests.

Hazael Threatens Jerusalem

[17]Hazael king of Syria went up and fought against Gath, and took it; then
Hazael set his face to go up to Jerusalem. [18]And Jehoash king of Judah took all
the sacred things that his fathers, Jehoshaphat and Jehoram and Ahaziah,
kings of Judah, had dedicated, and his own sacred things, and all the gold
found in the treasuries of the house of the LORD and in the king's house, and
sent *them* to Hazael king of Syria. Then he went away from Jerusalem.

Death of Joash

[19]Now the rest of the acts of Joash,[n] and all that he did, *are* they not written in the book of the chronicles of the kings of Judah?
[20]And his servants arose and formed a conspiracy, and killed Joash in
the house of the Millo,[o] which goes down to Silla. [21]For Jozachar[p] the son of
Shimeath and Jehozabad the son of Shomer,[q] his servants, struck him. So
he died, and they buried him with his fathers in the City of David. Then
Amaziah his son reigned in his place.

Jehoahaz Reigns in Israel

13 In the twenty-third year of Joash[r] the son of Ahaziah, king of Judah,
Jehoahaz the son of Jehu became king over Israel in Samaria, *and
reigned* seventeen years. [2]And he did evil in the sight of the LORD, and followed the sins of Jeroboam the son of Nebat, who had made Israel sin. He
did not depart from them.
[3]Then the anger of the LORD was aroused against Israel, and He delivered them into the hand of Hazael king of Syria, and into the hand of Ben-
Hadad the son of Hazael, all *their* days. [4]So Jehoahaz pleaded with the
LORD, and the LORD listened to him; for He saw the oppression of Israel, because the king of Syria oppressed them. [5]Then the LORD gave Israel a deliverer, so that they escaped from under the hand of the Syrians; and the
children of Israel dwelt in their tents as before. [6]Nevertheless they did not
depart from the sins of the house of Jeroboam, who had made Israel sin,
but walked in them; and the wooden image[s] also remained in Samaria.
[7]For He left of the army of Jehoahaz only fifty horsemen, ten chariots, and
ten thousand foot soldiers; for the king of Syria had destroyed them and
made them like the dust at threshing.

12:19 [n] Spelled *Jehoash* in 12:1ff
12:20 [o] Literally *The Landfill*
12:21 [p] Called *Zabad* in 2 Chronicles 24:26 [q] Called *Shimrith* in 2 Chronicles 24:26
13:1 [r] Spelled *Jehoash* in 12:1ff
13:6 [s] Hebrew *Asherah,* a Canaanite goddess

8Now the rest of the acts of Jehoahaz, all that he did, and his might, *are*
they not written in the book of the chronicles of the kings of Israel? 9So
Jehoahaz rested with his fathers, and they buried him in Samaria. Then
Joash his son reigned in his place.

Jehoash Reigns in Israel

10In the thirty-seventh year of Joash king of Judah, Jehoash[t] the son of
Jehoahaz became king over Israel in Samaria, *and reigned* sixteen years.
11And he did evil in the sight of the LORD. He did not depart from all the sins
of Jeroboam the son of Nebat, who made Israel sin, *but* walked in them.
12Now the rest of the acts of Joash, all that he did, and his might with
which he fought against Amaziah king of Judah, *are* they not written in the
book of the chronicles of the kings of Israel? 13So Joash rested with his fathers. Then Jeroboam sat on his throne. And Joash was buried in Samaria
with the kings of Israel.

Death of Elisha

14Elisha had become sick with the illness of which he would die. Then
Joash the king of Israel came down to him, and wept over his face, and
said, "O my father, my father, the chariots of Israel and their horsemen!"
15And Elisha said to him, "Take a bow and some arrows." So he took
himself a bow and some arrows. 16Then he said to the king of Israel, "Put
your hand on the bow." So he put his hand *on it*, and Elisha put his hands
on the king's hands. 17And he said, "Open the east window"; and he
opened *it*. Then Elisha said, "Shoot"; and he shot. And he said, "The arrow
of the LORD's deliverance and the arrow of deliverance from Syria; for you
must strike the Syrians at Aphek till you have destroyed *them*." 18Then he
said, "Take the arrows"; so he took *them*. And he said to the king of Israel,
"Strike the ground"; so he struck three times, and stopped. 19And the man
of God was angry with him, and said, "You should have struck five or six
times; then you would have struck Syria till you had destroyed *it!* But now
you will strike Syria *only* three times."
20Then Elisha died, and they buried him. And the *raiding* bands from
Moab invaded the land in the spring of the year. 21So it was, as they were
burying a man, that suddenly they spied a band *of raiders;* and they put
the man in the tomb of Elisha; and when the man was let down and
touched the bones of Elisha, he revived and stood on his feet.

Israel Recaptures Cities from Syria

22And Hazael king of Syria oppressed Israel all the days of Jehoahaz.
23But the LORD was gracious to them, had compassion on them, and regarded them, because of His covenant with Abraham, Isaac, and Jacob,
and would not yet destroy them or cast them from His presence.
24Now Hazael king of Syria died. Then Ben-Hadad his son reigned in his
place. 25And Jehoash[u] the son of Jehoahaz recaptured from the hand of
Ben-Hadad, the son of Hazael, the cities which he had taken out of the
hand of Jehoahaz his father by war. Three times Joash defeated him and
recaptured the cities of Israel.

things about human life is that even when we know that the purpose of life is realized in relationship with God, we choose to rebel and try to walk alone. It has been this way from the beginning.

. . . If one part of the Old Testament is a record of broken covenants and unfaithfulness, the other is a story of continuing forgiveness and renewal. God continued to call man into relationship with himself even in the face of continuing rejection. To our astonishment the Old Testament ends with a promise that God's purpose will soon be even more clearly revealed in a Messiah, one whose life will be the supreme revelation of what every man's life is intended to be.

(From *Beyond Belief* by Edward W. Bauman)

APPLICATION Do your actions represent your heart? Do you put on your best behavior on Sunday and then do wrong on Monday? Be honest with yourself and with others. Ask God to help you live a godly life all week.

EXPLORATION Faith—Psalm 136; 2 Samuel 22; Romans 2:17-18; Luke 24:47-48; 1 John 1:8-10.

13:10 [t] Spelled *Joash* in verse 9
13:25 [u] Spelled *Joash* in verses 12–14, 25

Amaziah Reigns in Judah

14 In the second year of Joash the son of Jehoahaz,
king of Israel, Amaziah the son of Joash, king of
Judah, became king. 2He was twenty-five years old
when he became king, and he reigned twenty-nine
years in Jerusalem. His mother's name was
Jehoaddan of Jerusalem. 3And he did *what was* right
in the sight of the LORD, yet not like his father David; he
did everything as his father Joash had done. 4However
the high places were not taken away, and the people still
sacrificed and burned incense on the high places.

5Now it happened, as soon as the kingdom was established in his hand, that he executed his servants
who had murdered his father the king. 6But the children of the murderers he did not execute, according
to what is written in the Book of the Law of Moses, in
which the LORD commanded, saying, "Fathers shall
not be put to death for their children, nor shall children be put to death for their fathers; but a person
shall be put to death for his own sin."[v]

7He killed ten thousand Edomites in the Valley of
Salt, and took Sela by war, and called its name
Joktheel to this day.

8Then Amaziah sent messengers to Jehoash[w] the
son of Jehoahaz, the son of Jehu, king of Israel, saying, "Come, let us face one another *in battle.*" 9And
Jehoash king of Israel sent to Amaziah king of Judah,
saying, "The thistle that *was* in Lebanon sent to the
cedar that *was* in Lebanon, saying, 'Give your daughter to my son as wife'; and a wild beast that *was* in
Lebanon passed by and trampled the thistle. 10You
have indeed defeated Edom, and your heart has lifted
you up. Glory *in that,* and stay at home; for why
should you meddle with trouble so that you fall—you
and Judah with you?"

11But Amaziah would not heed. Therefore Jehoash
king of Israel went out; so he and Amaziah king of Judah faced one another at Beth Shemesh, which *belongs* to Judah. 12And Judah was defeated by Israel,
and every man fled to his tent. 13Then Jehoash king of
Israel captured Amaziah king of Judah, the son of
Jehoash, the son of Ahaziah, at Beth Shemesh; and he
went to Jerusalem, and broke down the wall of Jerusalem from the Gate of Ephraim to the Corner Gate—
four hundred cubits. 14And he took all the gold and
silver, all the articles that were found in the house of
the LORD and in the treasuries of the king's house, and
hostages, and returned to Samaria.

15Now the rest of the acts of Jehoash which he did—
his might, and how he fought with Amaziah king of Judah—*are* they not written in the book of the chronicles
of the kings of Israel? 16So Jehoash rested with his fathers, and was buried in Samaria with the kings of Israel. Then Jeroboam his son reigned in his place.

17Amaziah the son of Joash, king of Judah, lived fifteen years after the death of Jehoash the son of Jehoahaz,
king of Israel. 18Now the rest of the acts of Amaziah, *are*
they not written in the book of the chronicles of the
kings of Judah? 19And they formed a conspiracy against
him in Jerusalem, and he fled to Lachish; but they sent
after him to Lachish and killed him there. 20Then they
brought him on horses, and he was buried at Jerusalem
with his fathers in the City of David.

21And all the people of Judah took Azariah,[x] who
was sixteen years old, and made him king instead of
his father Amaziah. 22He built Elath and restored it to
Judah, after the king rested with his fathers.

Jeroboam II Reigns in Israel

23In the fifteenth year of Amaziah the son of Joash,
king of Judah, Jeroboam the son of Joash, king of Israel, became king in Samaria, *and reigned* forty-one
years. 24And he did evil in the sight of the LORD; he did
not depart from all the sins of Jeroboam the son of
Nebat, who had made Israel sin. 25He restored the territory of Israel from the entrance of Hamath to the
Sea of the Arabah, according to the word of the LORD
God of Israel, which He had spoken through His servant Jonah the son of Amittai, the prophet who *was*
from Gath Hepher. 26For the LORD saw *that* the affliction of Israel *was* very bitter; and whether bond or
free, there was no helper for Israel. 27And the LORD did
not say that He would blot out the name of Israel from
under heaven; but He saved them by the hand of
Jeroboam the son of Joash.

28Now the rest of the acts of Jeroboam, and all that
he did—his might, how he made war, and how he
recaptured for Israel, from Damascus and Hamath,
what had belonged to Judah—*are* they not written in
the book of the chronicles of the kings of Israel? 29So
Jeroboam rested with his fathers, the kings of Israel.
Then Zechariah his son reigned in his place.

Azariah Reigns in Judah

15 In the twenty-seventh year of Jeroboam king of
Israel, Azariah the son of Amaziah, king of Judah,

14:6 [v] Deuteronomy 24:16
14:8 [w] Spelled *Joash* in 13:12ff and 2 Chronicles 25:17ff
14:21 [x] Called *Uzziah* in 2 Chronicles 26:1ff, Isaiah 6:1, and elsewhere

became king. 2He was sixteen years old when he became king, and he reigned fifty-two years in Jerusalem. His mother's name *was* Jecholiah of Jerusalem. 3And he did *what was* right in the sight of the LORD, according to all that his father Amaziah had done, 4except that the high places were not removed; the people still sacrificed and burned incense on the high places. 5Then the LORD struck the king, so that he was a leper until the day of his death; so he dwelt in an isolated house. And Jotham the king's son *was* over the *royal* house, judging the people of the land.

6Now the rest of the acts of Azariah, and all that he did, *are* they not written in the book of the chronicles of the kings of Judah? 7So Azariah rested with his fathers, and they buried him with his fathers in the City of David. Then Jotham his son reigned in his place.

Zechariah Reigns in Israel

8In the thirty-eighth year of Azariah king of Judah, Zechariah the son of Jeroboam reigned over Israel in Samaria six months. 9And he did evil in the sight of the LORD, as his fathers had done; he did not depart from the sins of Jeroboam the son of Nebat, who had made Israel sin. 10Then Shallum the son of Jabesh conspired against him, and struck and killed him in front of the people; and he reigned in his place.

11Now the rest of the acts of Zechariah, indeed they *are* written in the book of the chronicles of the kings of Israel.

12This *was* the word of the LORD which He spoke to Jehu, saying, "Your sons shall sit on the throne of Israel to the fourth *generation*."[y] And so it was.

Shallum Reigns in Israel

13Shallum the son of Jabesh became king in the thirty-ninth year of Uzziah[z] king of Judah; and he reigned a full month in Samaria. 14For Menahem the son of Gadi went up from Tirzah, came to Samaria, and struck Shallum the son of Jabesh in Samaria and killed him; and he reigned in his place.

15Now the rest of the acts of Shallum, and the conspiracy which he led, indeed they *are* written in the book of the chronicles of the kings of Israel. 16Then from Tirzah, Menahem attacked Tiphsah, all who *were* there, and its territory. Because they did not surrender, therefore he attacked *it.* All the women there who were with child he ripped open.

Menahem Reigns in Israel

17In the thirty-ninth year of Azariah king of Judah, Menahem the son of Gadi became king over Israel, *and reigned* ten years in Samaria. 18And he did evil in the sight of the LORD; he did not depart all his days from the sins of Jeroboam the son of Nebat, who had made Israel sin. 19Pul[a] king of Assyria came against the land; and Menahem gave Pul a thousand talents of silver, that his hand might be with him to strengthen the kingdom under his control. 20And Menahem exacted the money from Israel, from all the very wealthy, from each man fifty shekels of silver, to give to the king of Assyria. So the king of Assyria turned back, and did not stay there in the land.

21Now the rest of the acts of Menahem, and all that he did, *are* they not written in the book of the chronicles of the kings of Israel? 22So Menahem rested with his fathers. Then Pekahiah his son reigned in his place.

15:12 [y] 2 Kings 10:30
15:13 [z] Called *Azariah* in 14:21ff and 15:1ff
15:19 [a] That is, Tiglath-Pileser III (compare verse 29)

LIFE LESSON

2 Kings 15:1–16:20

SITUATION During this time, all the kings of Israel did what God said was wrong. On the other hand, the kings of Judah did what God said was right. The one exception was Ahaz, who even dedicated his son to false gods. God used many prophets to speak to these rebellious kings: Jonah, Amos, Hosea, Micah, and Isaiah.

OBSERVATION God loves his people even when they are unfaithful children. Israel and Judah remained God's chosen people despite their spiritual adultery.

INSPIRATION Now God raised up the prophets, burned into their consciousness a lively awareness of his presence, and sent them to reveal him in a warmer, more passionate manner. Though Israel had played the prostitute whoring after false gods, the prophets cry the constancy of God in the face of human infidelity: "Israel, don't ever be so foolish as to measure my love for you in terms of your love for me! Don't ever compare your thin, pallid, wavering, and moody love with my love, for I am God, not man."

Human love will always be a faint shadow of God's love. Not because it is too sugary or sentimental but simply because it can never compare from whence it comes. Human love with all its passion and emotion is a thin echo of the passion/emotion love of Yahweh.

In the Sinai wilderness the covenant-God was faithful and just. Israel was faithful. They were related. But if Israel became unfaithful, logic and human justice required no further pursuit of Yahweh. He sees the contract broken, picks up his briefcase, and walks out of court. The relationship ended.

But we cannot apply human logic and justice to the living God. Human logic is based on human experience and human nature. Yahweh does not conform to this model. If Israel is unfaithful, God remains faithful against all logic and all limits of justice because *he is.* Love clarifies the happy irra-

Continued

tionality of God's conduct. Love tends to be irrational at times. It pursues despite infidelity. It blossoms into jealousy and anger—which betrays keen interest. The more complex and emotional the image of God becomes in the Bible, the bigger he grows, and the more we approach the mystery of his indefinability.

(From *The Ragamuffin Gospel* by Brennan Manning)

APPLICATION Thank God for his faithfulness to you. Make that faithfulness the model for all your relationships: Concerning family members, how can you serve them? Concerning coworkers, how can you help them perform better? Concerning friends, how can you show your loyalty? All without regard for anything in return.

EXPLORATION Spiritual Adultery—Isaiah 1:21-22; 57:3-13; Hosea 1-3; Mark 8:38.

Pekahiah Reigns in Israel

[23]In the fiftieth year of Azariah king of Judah, Pekahiah the son of
Menahem became king over Israel in Samaria, *and reigned* two years.
[24]And he did evil in the sight of the LORD; he did not depart from the sins of
Jeroboam the son of Nebat, who had made Israel sin. [25]Then Pekah the son
of Remaliah, an officer of his, conspired against him and killed him in Samaria, in the citadel of the king's house, along with Argob and Arieh; and
with him were fifty men of Gilead. He killed him and reigned in his place.
[26]Now the rest of the acts of Pekahiah, and all that he did, indeed they *are*
written in the book of the chronicles of the kings of Israel.

Pekah Reigns in Israel

[27]In the fifty-second year of Azariah king of Judah, Pekah the son of
Remaliah became king over Israel in Samaria, *and reigned* twenty years.
[28]And he did evil in the sight of the LORD; he did not depart from the sins of
Jeroboam the son of Nebat, who had made Israel sin. [29]In the days of
Pekah king of Israel, Tiglath-Pileser king of Assyria came and took Ijon,
Abel Beth Maachah, Janoah, Kedesh, Hazor, Gilead, and Galilee, all the
land of Naphtali; and he carried them captive to Assyria. [30]Then Hoshea
the son of Elah led a conspiracy against Pekah the son of Remaliah, and
struck and killed him; so he reigned in his place in the twentieth year of
Jotham the son of Uzziah.
[31]Now the rest of the acts of Pekah, and all that he did, indeed they *are*
written in the book of the chronicles of the kings of Israel.

Jotham Reigns in Judah

[32]In the second year of Pekah the son of Remaliah, king of Israel,
Jotham the son of Uzziah, king of Judah, began to reign. [33]He was twenty-
five years old when he became king, and he reigned sixteen years in Jerusalem. His mother's name *was* Jerusha[b] the daughter of Zadok. [34]And he
did *what was* right in the sight of the LORD; he did according to all that his
father Uzziah had done. [35]However the high places were not removed; the
people still sacrificed and burned incense on the high places. He built the
Upper Gate of the house of the LORD.
[36]Now the rest of the acts of Jotham, and all that he did, *are* they not written in the book of the chronicles of the kings of Judah? [37]In those days the
LORD began to send Rezin king of Syria and Pekah the son of Remaliah
against Judah. [38]So Jotham rested with his fathers, and was buried with his
fathers in the City of David his father. Then Ahaz his son reigned in his place.

Ahaz Reigns in Judah

16 In the seventeenth year of Pekah the son of Remaliah, Ahaz the son of
Jotham, king of Judah, began to reign. [2]Ahaz *was* twenty years old
when he became king, and he reigned sixteen years in Jerusalem; and he did
not do *what was* right in the sight of the LORD his God, as his father David *had
done.* [3]But he walked in the way of the kings of Israel; indeed he made his son
pass through the fire, according to the abominations of the nations whom the
LORD had cast out from before the children of Israel. [4]And he sacrificed and
burned incense on the high places, on the hills, and under every green tree.

15:33 [b] Spelled *Jerushah* in 2 Chronicles 27:1

[5]Then Rezin king of Syria and Pekah the son of Remaliah, king of Israel,
came up to Jerusalem to *make* war; and they besieged Ahaz but could not
overcome *him.* [6]At that time Rezin king of Syria captured Elath for Syria,
and drove the men of Judah from Elath. Then the Edomites[c] went to Elath,
and dwell there to this day.
[7]So Ahaz sent messengers to Tiglath-Pileser king of Assyria, saying, "I *am*
your servant and your son. Come up and save me from the hand of the king of
Syria and from the hand of the king of Israel, who rise up against me." [8]And
Ahaz took the silver and gold that was found in the house of the LORD, and in
the treasuries of the king's house, and sent *it as* a present to the king of Assyria.
[9]So the king of Assyria heeded him; for the king of Assyria went up against Damascus and took it, carried *its people* captive to Kir, and killed Rezin.
[10]Now King Ahaz went to Damascus to meet Tiglath-Pileser king of Assyria, and saw an altar that *was* at Damascus; and King Ahaz sent to Urijah
the priest the design of the altar and its pattern, according to all its workmanship. [11]Then Urijah the priest built an altar according to all that King
Ahaz had sent from Damascus. So Urijah the priest made *it* before King
Ahaz came back from Damascus. [12]And when the king came back from
Damascus, the king saw the altar; and the king approached the altar and
made offerings on it. [13]So he burned his burnt offering and his grain offering; and he poured his drink offering and sprinkled the blood of his peace
offerings on the altar. [14]He also brought the bronze altar which *was* before
the LORD, from the front of the temple—from between the *new* altar and
the house of the LORD—and put it on the north side of the *new* altar.
[15]Then King Ahaz commanded Urijah the priest, saying, "On the great *new*
altar burn the morning burnt offering, the evening grain offering, the
king's burnt sacrifice, and his grain offering, with the burnt offering of all
the people of the land, their grain offering, and their drink offerings; and
sprinkle on it all the blood of the burnt offering and all the blood of the
sacrifice. And the bronze altar shall be for me to inquire *by.*" [16]Thus did
Urijah the priest, according to all that King Ahaz commanded.
[17]And King Ahaz cut off the panels of the carts, and removed the lavers
from them; and he took down the Sea from the bronze oxen that *were* under
it, and put it on a pavement of stones. [18]Also he removed the Sabbath pavilion which they had built in the temple, and he removed the king's outer entrance from the house of the LORD, on account of the king of Assyria.
[19]Now the rest of the acts of Ahaz which he did, *are* they not written in
the book of the chronicles of the kings of Judah? [20]So Ahaz rested with his
fathers, and was buried with his fathers in the City of David. Then
Hezekiah his son reigned in his place.

Hoshea Reigns in Israel

17 In the twelfth year of Ahaz king of Judah, Hoshea the son of Elah became king of Israel in Samaria, *and he reigned* nine years. [2]And he did
evil in the sight of the LORD, but not as the kings of Israel who were before him.
[3]Shalmaneser king of Assyria came up against him; and Hoshea became his
vassal, and paid him tribute money. [4]And the king of Assyria uncovered a
conspiracy by Hoshea; for he had sent messengers to So, king of Egypt, and
brought no tribute to the king of Assyria, as *he had done* year by year.
Therefore the king of Assyria shut him up, and bound him in prison.

16:6 [c] Some ancient authorities read *Syrians.*

LIFE LESSON

2 Kings 17:1-41

SITUATION Because of its long history of sin and rebellion, the Northern Kingdom was invaded, beaten, and exiled. Foreigners settled the vacant land and practiced idolatry.

OBSERVATION God consciously disciplines his people. He knows that it is the only way they can learn certain lessons.

INSPIRATION The essential meaning of exile is that we are where we don't want to be. We are separated from home. We are not permitted to reside in the place where we comprehend and appreciate our surroundings. We are forced to be away from that which is most congenial to us. It is an experience of dislocation—everything is out of joint; nothing fits together. The thousand details that have been built up through the years that give a sense of at-home—gestures, customs, rituals, phrases—are all gone. Life is ripped out of the familiar soil of generations of language, habit, weather, story-telling, and rudely and unceremoniously dropped into some unfamiliar spot of earth. The place of exile may boast a higher standard of living. It may be more pleasant in its weather. That doesn't matter. It isn't home.

But this very strangeness can open up new reality to us. An accident, a tragedy, a disaster of any kind can force the realization that the world is not predictable, that reality is far more extensive than our habitual perception of it. With the pain and in the midst of alienation a sense of freedom can occur.

(From *Run with the Horses* by Eugene Peterson)

APPLICATION God permits some hard times into our lives to teach us. When hardship comes, thank God for this demonstration of love. Then ask him to help you learn from the situation.

EXPLORATION Discipline—Deuteronomy 8:5; 2 Samuel 7:14-15; Hebrews 12:3-11; Revelation 3:19.

Israel Carried Captive to Assyria

5Now the king of Assyria went throughout all the
land, and went up to Samaria and besieged it for
three years. 6In the ninth year of Hoshea, the king of
Assyria took Samaria and carried Israel away to Assyria, and placed them in Halah and by the Habor, the
River of Gozan, and in the cities of the Medes.

7For so it was that the children of Israel had sinned
against the LORD their God, who had brought them up
out of the land of Egypt, from under the hand of
Pharaoh king of Egypt; and they had feared other
gods, 8and had walked in the statutes of the nations
whom the LORD had cast out from before the children
of Israel, and of the kings of Israel, which they had
made. 9Also the children of Israel secretly did against
the LORD their God things that *were* not right, and they
built for themselves high places in all their cities,
from watchtower to fortified city. 10They set up for
themselves *sacred* pillars and wooden images[d] on
every high hill and under every green tree. 11There
they burned incense on all the high places, like the nations whom the LORD had carried away before them;
and they did wicked things to provoke the LORD to
anger, 12for they served idols, of which the LORD had
said to them, "You shall not do this thing."

13Yet the LORD testified against Israel and against
Judah, by all of His prophets, every seer, saying, "Turn
from your evil ways, and keep My commandments
and My statutes, according to all the law which I commanded your fathers, and which I sent to you by My
servants the prophets." 14Nevertheless they would not
hear, but stiffened their necks, like the necks of their
fathers, who did not believe in the LORD their God.
15And they rejected His statutes and His covenant that
He had made with their fathers, and His testimonies
which He had testified against them; they followed
idols, became idolaters, and *went* after the nations
who *were* all around them, *concerning* whom the LORD
had charged them that they should not do like them.
16So they left all the commandments of the LORD their
God, made for themselves a molded image *and* two
calves, made a wooden image and worshiped all the
host of heaven, and served Baal. 17And they caused
their sons and daughters to pass through the fire,
practiced witchcraft and soothsaying, and sold themselves to do evil in the sight of the LORD, to provoke
Him to anger. 18Therefore the LORD was very angry
with Israel, and removed them from His sight; there
was none left but the tribe of Judah alone.

19Also Judah did not keep the commandments of
the LORD their God, but walked in the statutes of Israel
which they made. 20And the LORD rejected all the descendants of Israel, afflicted them, and delivered
them into the hand of plunderers, until He had cast
them from His sight. 21For He tore Israel from the
house of David, and they made Jeroboam the son of
Nebat king. Then Jeroboam drove Israel from following the LORD, and made them commit a great sin.
22For the children of Israel walked in all the sins of
Jeroboam which he did; they did not depart from
them, 23until the LORD removed Israel out of His sight,
as He had said by all His servants the prophets. So Israel was carried away from their own land to Assyria,
as it is to this day.

Assyria Resettles Samaria

24Then the king of Assyria brought *people* from
Babylon, Cuthah, Ava, Hamath, and from Sepharvaim, and placed *them* in the cities of Samaria instead of the children of Israel; and they took
possession of Samaria and dwelt in its cities. 25And it
was so, at the beginning of their dwelling there, *that*
they did not fear the LORD; therefore the LORD sent
lions among them, which killed *some* of them. 26So
they spoke to the king of Assyria, saying, "The nations
whom you have removed and placed in the cities of
Samaria do not know the rituals of the God of the
land; therefore He has sent lions among them, and indeed, they are killing them because they do not know
the rituals of the God of the land." 27Then the king of
Assyria commanded, saying, "Send there one of the
priests whom you brought from there; let him go and
dwell there, and let him teach them the rituals of the
God of the land." 28Then one of the priests whom they
had carried away from Samaria came and dwelt in
Bethel, and taught them how they should fear the
LORD.

29However every nation continued to make gods of
its own, and put *them* in the shrines on the high
places which the Samaritans had made, *every* nation
in the cities where they dwelt. 30The men of Babylon
made Succoth Benoth, the men of Cuth made Nergal,
the men of Hamath made Ashima, 31and the Avites
made Nibhaz and Tartak; and the Sepharvites burned
their children in fire to Adrammelech and
Anammelech, the gods of Sepharvaim. 32So they
feared the LORD, and from every class they appointed
for themselves priests of the high places, who sacrificed for them in the shrines of the high places. 33They

17:10 [d] Hebrew *Asherim,* Canaanite deities

feared the LORD, yet served their own gods—according to the rituals of the
nations from among whom they were carried away.
34To this day they continue practicing the former rituals; they do not
fear the LORD, nor do they follow their statutes or their ordinances, or the
law and commandment which the LORD had commanded the children of
Jacob, whom He named Israel, 35with whom the LORD had made a
covenant and charged them, saying: "You shall not fear other gods, nor
bow down to them nor serve them nor sacrifice to them; 36but the LORD,
who brought you up from the land of Egypt with great power and an outstretched arm, Him you shall fear, Him you shall worship, and to Him you
shall offer sacrifice. 37And the statutes, the ordinances, the law, and the
commandment which He wrote for you, you shall be careful to observe
forever; you shall not fear other gods. 38And the covenant that I have made
with you, you shall not forget, nor shall you fear other gods. 39But the LORD
your God you shall fear; and He will deliver you from the hand of all your
enemies." 40However they did not obey, but they followed their former rituals. 41So these nations feared the LORD, yet served their carved images;
also their children and their children's children have continued doing as
their fathers did, even to this day.

Hezekiah Reigns in Judah

18 Now it came to pass in the third year of Hoshea the son of Elah, king
of Israel, *that* Hezekiah the son of Ahaz, king of Judah, began to
reign. 2He was twenty-five years old when he became king, and he reigned
twenty-nine years in Jerusalem. His mother's name *was* Abi[e] the daughter
of Zechariah. 3And he did *what was* right in the sight of the LORD, according to all that his father David had done.
4He removed the high places and broke the *sacred* pillars, cut down the
wooden image[f] and broke in pieces the bronze serpent that Moses had
made; for until those days the children of Israel burned incense to it, and
called it Nehushtan.[g] 5He trusted in the LORD God of Israel, so that after
him was none like him among all the kings of Judah, nor who were before
him. 6For he held fast to the LORD; he did not depart from following Him,
but kept His commandments, which the LORD had commanded Moses.
7The LORD was with him; he prospered wherever he went. And he rebelled
against the king of Assyria and did not serve him. 8He subdued the
Philistines, as far as Gaza and its territory, from watchtower to fortified city.
9Now it came to pass in the fourth year of King Hezekiah, which *was* the
seventh year of Hoshea the son of Elah, king of Israel, *that* Shalmaneser
king of Assyria came up against Samaria and besieged it. 10And at the end
of three years they took it. In the sixth year of Hezekiah, that *is,* the ninth
year of Hoshea king of Israel, Samaria was taken. 11Then the king of Assyria
carried Israel away captive to Assyria, and put them in Halah and by the
Habor, the River of Gozan, and in the cities of the Medes, 12because they
did not obey the voice of the LORD their God, but transgressed His
covenant *and* all that Moses the servant of the LORD had commanded; and
they would neither hear nor do *them.*
13And in the fourteenth year of King Hezekiah, Sennacherib king of Assyria came up against all the fortified cities of Judah and took them.

18:2 [e] Called *Abijah* in 2 Chronicles 29:1ff
18:4 [f] Hebrew *Asherah,* a Canaanite goddess [g] Literally *Bronze Thing*

LIFE LESSON

2 Kings 18:1–19:37

SITUATION Assyria defeated Israel. The Assyrian general, Sennacherib, led his troops through Israel into Judah. He laid siege to Jerusalem. Though outnumbered, King Hezekiah trusted God.

OBSERVATION The contest between Sennacherib and Hezekiah was a contest between gods. Hezekiah trusted in the true God, and he was proven right. The defeat of Sennacherib demonstrates that God acts on behalf of those who trust in him.

INSPIRATION A chronic menstrual disorder. A perpetual issue of blood. Such a condition would be difficult for any woman of any era. But for a Jewess, nothing could be worse. No part of her life was left unaffected.

Sexually . . . she could not touch her husband.

Maternally . . . she could not bear children.

Domestically . . . anything she touched was considered unclean. No washing dishes. No sweeping floors.

Spiritually . . . she was not allowed to enter the temple.

She was physically exhausted and socially ostracized.

She had sought help "under the care of many doctors" . . .

She was a bruised reed. She awoke daily in a body that no one wanted. She is down to her last prayer. And on the day we encounter her, she's about to pray it.

By the time she gets to Jesus, he is surrounded by people. He's on his way to help the daughter of Jairus, the most important man in the community. What are the odds that he will interrupt an urgent mission with a high official to help the likes of her? Very few. But what are the odds that she will survive if she doesn't take a chance? Fewer still. So she takes a chance.

"If I can just touch his clothes," she thinks, "I will be healed."

Risky decision. To touch him, she will have to touch the people. If one of

Continued

them recognizes her. . . . But what choice does she have? She has no money, no clout, no friends, no solutions. All she has is a crazy hunch that Jesus can help and a high hope that he will. . . .

There was no guarantee, of course. She hoped he'd respond . . . she longed for it . . . but she didn't know if he would. All she knew was that he was good. That's faith.

Faith is not the belief that God will do what you want. Faith is the belief that God will do what is right.

"Blessed are the dirt-poor, nothing-to-give, trapped-in-a-corner, destitute, diseased," Jesus said, "for theirs is the kingdom of heaven" (Matt. 5:6, my translation).

God's economy is upside down (or rightside up and ours is upside down!). God says that the more hopeless your circumstance, the more likely your salvation. The greater your cares, the more genuine your prayers. The darker the room, the greater the need for light.

A healthy lady never would have appreciated the power of a touch of the hem of his robe. But this woman was sick . . . and when her dilemma met his dedication, a miracle occurred.

Her part in the healing was very small. All she did was extend her arm through the crowd.

"If only I can touch him." . . .

Healing begins when we do something. Healing begins when we reach out. Healing starts when we take a step.

(From *He still Moves Stones* by Max Lucado)

APPLICATION In what situations is your faith being tested? Hezekiah took his problem to God and trusted him with it. Entrust your problems to God through prayer. Have faith that he will care for you.

EXPLORATION Trust—
1 Samuel 17:42-51; 14:8-13;
2 Chronicles 20:1-24; Acts 5:18-29;
Hebrews 11:29-33.

14 Then Hezekiah king of Judah sent to the king of Assyria at Lachish, saying, "I have done wrong; turn away from me; whatever you impose on me I will pay." And the king of Assyria assessed Hezekiah king of Judah three hundred talents of silver and thirty talents of gold.
15 So Hezekiah gave *him* all the silver that was found in the house of the LORD and in the treasuries of the king's house.
16 At that time Hezekiah stripped *the gold from* the doors of the temple of the LORD, and *from* the pillars which Hezekiah king of Judah had overlaid, and gave it to the king of Assyria.

Sennacherib Boasts Against the LORD

17 Then the king of Assyria sent *the* Tartan,[h] *the* Rabsaris,[i] *and the* Rabshakeh[j] from Lachish, with a great army against Jerusalem, to King Hezekiah. And they went up and came to Jerusalem. When they had come up, they went and stood by the aqueduct from the upper pool, which *was* on the highway to the Fuller's Field.
18 And when they had called to the king, Eliakim the son of Hilkiah, who *was* over the household, Shebna the scribe, and Joah the son of Asaph, the recorder, came out to them.
19 Then *the* Rabshakeh said to them, "Say now to Hezekiah, 'Thus says the great king, the king of Assyria: "What confidence *is* this in which you trust?
20 You speak of *having* plans and power for war; but *they are* mere words. And in whom do you trust, that you rebel against me?
21 Now look! You are trusting in the staff of this broken reed, Egypt, on which if a man leans, it will go into his hand and pierce it. So *is* Pharaoh king of Egypt to all who trust in him.
22 But if you say to me, 'We trust in the LORD our God,' *is* it not He whose high places and whose altars Hezekiah has taken away, and said to Judah and Jerusalem, 'You shall worship before this altar in Jerusalem'?" '
23 Now therefore, I urge you, give a pledge to my master the king of Assyria, and I will give you two thousand horses—if you are able on your part to put riders on them!
24 How then will you repel one captain of the least of my master's servants, and put your trust in Egypt for chariots and horsemen?
25 Have I now come up without the LORD against this place to destroy it? The LORD said to me, 'Go up against this land, and destroy it.' "

26 Then Eliakim the son of Hilkiah, Shebna, and Joah said to *the* Rabshakeh, "Please speak to your servants in Aramaic, for we understand *it;* and do not speak to us in Hebrew[k] in the hearing of the people who *are* on the wall."

27 But *the* Rabshakeh said to them, "Has my master sent me to your master and to you to speak these words, and not to the men who sit on the wall, who will eat and drink their own waste with you?"

28 Then *the* Rabshakeh stood and called out with a loud voice in Hebrew, and spoke, saying, "Hear the word of the great king, the king of Assyria!
29 Thus says the king: 'Do not let Hezekiah deceive you, for he shall not be able to deliver you from his hand;
30 nor let Hezekiah make you trust in the LORD, saying, "The LORD will surely deliver us; this city shall not be given into the hand of the king of Assyria." '
31 Do not listen to Hezekiah; for thus says the king of Assyria: 'Make *peace* with me by a present and come out to me; and every one of you eat from his own vine and every one from his

18:17 [h] A title, probably *Commander in Chief* [i] A title, probably *Chief Officer* [j] A title, probably *Chief of Staff* or *Governor*
18:26 [k] Literally *Judean*

own fig tree, and every one of you drink the waters of
his own cistern; 32until I come and take you away to a
land like your own land, a land of grain and new wine,
a land of bread and vineyards, a land of olive groves
and honey, that you may live and not die. But do not
listen to Hezekiah, lest he persuade you, saying, "The
LORD will deliver us." 33Has any of the gods of the nations at all delivered its land from the hand of the king
of Assyria? 34Where *are* the gods of Hamath and Arpad?
Where *are* the gods of Sepharvaim and Hena and Ivah?
Indeed, have they delivered Samaria from my hand?
35Who among all the gods of the lands have delivered
their countries from my hand, that the LORD should deliver Jerusalem from my hand?' "

36But the people held their peace and answered him
not a word; for the king's commandment was, "Do
not answer him." 37Then Eliakim the son of Hilkiah,
who *was* over the household, Shebna the scribe, and
Joah the son of Asaph, the recorder, came to Hezekiah
with *their* clothes torn, and told him the words of *the*
Rabshakeh.

Isaiah Assures Deliverance

19 And so it was, when King Hezekiah heard *it,*
that he tore his clothes, covered himself with
sackcloth, and went into the house of the LORD. 2Then
he sent Eliakim, who *was* over the household, Shebna
the scribe, and the elders of the priests, covered with
sackcloth, to Isaiah the prophet, the son of Amoz.
3And they said to him, "Thus says Hezekiah: 'This day
is a day of trouble, and rebuke, and blasphemy; for
the children have come to birth, but *there is* no
strength to bring them forth. 4It may be that the LORD
your God will hear all the words of *the* Rabshakeh,
whom his master the king of Assyria has sent to reproach the living God, and will rebuke the words
which the LORD your God has heard. Therefore lift up
your prayer for the remnant that is left.' "

5So the servants of King Hezekiah came to Isaiah.
6And Isaiah said to them, "Thus you shall say to your
master, 'Thus says the LORD: "Do not be afraid of the
words which you have heard, with which the servants
of the king of Assyria have blasphemed Me. 7Surely I
will send a spirit upon him, and he shall hear a rumor
and return to his own land; and I will cause him to fall
by the sword in his own land." ' "

Sennacherib's Threat and Hezekiah's Prayer

8Then *the* Rabshakeh returned and found the king
of Assyria warring against Libnah, for he heard that
he had departed from Lachish. 9And the king heard
concerning Tirhakah king of Ethiopia, "Look, he has
come out to make war with you." So he again sent
messengers to Hezekiah, saying, 10"Thus you shall
speak to Hezekiah king of Judah, saying: 'Do not let
your God in whom you trust deceive you, saying, "Jerusalem shall not be given into the hand of the king of
Assyria." 11Look! You have heard what the kings of
Assyria have done to all lands by utterly destroying
them; and shall you be delivered? 12Have the gods of
the nations delivered those whom my fathers have
destroyed, Gozan and Haran and Rezeph, and the
people of Eden who *were* in Telassar? 13Where *is* the
king of Hamath, the king of Arpad, and the king of the
city of Sepharvaim, Hena, and Ivah?' "

14And Hezekiah received the letter from the hand of
the messengers, and read it; and Hezekiah went up to
the house of the LORD, and spread it before the LORD.
15Then Hezekiah prayed before the LORD, and said: "O
LORD God of Israel, *the One* who dwells *between* the
cherubim, You are God, You alone, of all the kingdoms of the earth. You have made heaven and earth.
16Incline Your ear, O LORD, and hear; open Your eyes, O
LORD, and see; and hear the words of Sennacherib,
which he has sent to reproach the living God. 17Truly,
LORD, the kings of Assyria have laid waste the nations
and their lands, 18and have cast their gods into the
fire; for they *were* not gods, but the work of men's
hands—wood and stone. Therefore they destroyed
them. 19Now therefore, O LORD our God, I pray, save us
from his hand, that all the kingdoms of the earth may
know that You *are* the LORD God, You alone."

The Word of the LORD Concerning Sennacherib

20Then Isaiah the son of Amoz sent to Hezekiah,
saying, "Thus says the LORD God of Israel: 'Because
you have prayed to Me against Sennacherib king of
Assyria, I have heard.' 21This *is* the word which the
LORD has spoken concerning him:

'The virgin, the daughter of Zion,
Has despised you, laughed you to scorn;
The daughter of Jerusalem
Has shaken *her* head behind your back!

22 'Whom have you reproached and blasphemed?
Against whom have you raised *your* voice,
And lifted up your eyes on high?
Against the Holy *One* of Israel.
23 By your messengers you have reproached the
Lord,
And said: "By the multitude of my chariots
I have come up to the height of the mountains,

To the limits of Lebanon;
I will cut down its tall cedars
And its choice cypress trees;
I will enter the extremity of its borders,
To its fruitful forest.
24 I have dug and drunk strange water,
And with the soles of my feet I have dried up
All the brooks of defense."

25 'Did you not hear long ago
How I made it,
From ancient times that I formed it?
Now I have brought it to pass,
That you should be
For crushing fortified cities *into* heaps
of ruins.
26 Therefore their inhabitants had little power;
They were dismayed and confounded;
They were *as* the grass of the field
And the green herb,
As the grass on the housetops
And *grain* blighted before it is grown.

27 'But I know your dwelling place,
Your going out and your coming in,
And your rage against Me.
28 Because your rage against Me and
your tumult
Have come up to My ears,
Therefore I will put My hook in your nose
And My bridle in your lips,
And I will turn you back
By the way which you came.

29 'This *shall be* a sign to you:

You shall eat this year such as grows of itself,
And in the second year what springs from
the same;
Also in the third year sow and reap,
Plant vineyards and eat the fruit of them.
30 And the remnant who have escaped of the
house of Judah
Shall again take root downward,
And bear fruit upward.
31 For out of Jerusalem shall go a remnant,
And those who escape from Mount Zion.
The zeal of the LORD of hosts[l] will do this.'

32 "Therefore thus says the LORD concerning the
king of Assyria:

'He shall not come into this city,
Nor shoot an arrow there,
Nor come before it with shield,
Nor build a siege mound against it.
33 By the way that he came,
By the same shall he return;
And he shall not come into this city,'
Says the LORD.
34 'For I will defend this city, to save it
For My own sake and for My servant David's
sake.' "

Sennacherib's Defeat and Death

35 And it came to pass on a certain night that the angel[m] of the LORD went out, and killed in the camp of
the Assyrians one hundred and eighty-five thousand;
and when *people* arose early in the morning, there
were the corpses—all dead. 36 So Sennacherib king of
Assyria departed and went away, returned *home,* and
remained at Nineveh. 37 Now it came to pass, as he was
worshiping in the temple of Nisroch his god, that his
sons Adrammelech and Sharezer struck him down
with the sword; and they escaped into the land of
Ararat. Then Esarhaddon his son reigned in his place.

Hezekiah's Life Extended

20 In those days Hezekiah was sick and near
death. And Isaiah the prophet, the son of Amoz,
went to him and said to him, "Thus says the LORD: 'Set
your house in order, for you shall die, and not live.' "
2 Then he turned his face toward the wall, and
prayed to the LORD, saying, 3 "Remember now, O LORD,
I pray, how I have walked before You in truth and with
a loyal heart, and have done *what was* good in Your
sight." And Hezekiah wept bitterly.
4 And it happened, before Isaiah had gone out into
the middle court, that the word of the LORD came to
him, saying, 5 "Return and tell Hezekiah the leader of
My people, 'Thus says the LORD, the God of David
your father: "I have heard your prayer, I have seen
your tears; surely I will heal you. On the third day you
shall go up to the house of the LORD. 6 And I will add to
your days fifteen years. I will deliver you and this city
from the hand of the king of Assyria; and I will defend this city for My own sake, and for the sake of My
servant David." ' "
7 Then Isaiah said, "Take a lump of figs." So they
took and laid *it* on the boil, and he recovered.

19:31 [l] Following many Hebrew manuscripts and ancient versions (compare Isaiah 37:32); Masoretic Text omits *of hosts.*
19:35 [m] Or *Angel*

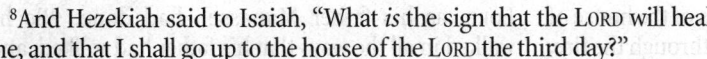

[8]And Hezekiah said to Isaiah, "What *is* the sign that the LORD will heal
me, and that I shall go up to the house of the LORD the third day?"
[9]Then Isaiah said, "This is the sign to you from the LORD, that the LORD
will do the thing which He has spoken: *shall* the shadow go forward ten degrees or go backward ten degrees?"
[10]And Hezekiah answered, "It is an easy thing for the shadow to go
down ten degrees; no, but let the shadow go backward ten degrees."
[11]So Isaiah the prophet cried out to the LORD, and He brought the shadow
ten degrees backward, by which it had gone down on the sundial of Ahaz.

The Babylonian Envoys

[12]At that time Berodach-Baladan[n] the son of Baladan, king of Babylon,
sent letters and a present to Hezekiah, for he heard that Hezekiah had
been sick. [13]And Hezekiah was attentive to them, and showed them all the
house of his treasures—the silver and gold, the spices and precious ointment, and all[o] his armory—all that was found among his treasures. There
was nothing in his house or in all his dominion that Hezekiah did not
show them.
[14]Then Isaiah the prophet went to King Hezekiah, and said to him,
"What did these men say, and from where did they come to you?"
So Hezekiah said, "They came from a far country, from Babylon."
[15]And he said, "What have they seen in your house?"
So Hezekiah answered, "They have seen all that *is* in my house; there is
nothing among my treasures that I have not shown them."
[16]Then Isaiah said to Hezekiah, "Hear the word of the LORD: [17]'Behold,
the days are coming when all that *is* in your house, and what your fathers
have accumulated until this day, shall be carried to Babylon; nothing shall
be left,' says the LORD. [18]'And they shall take away some of your sons who
will descend from you, whom you will beget; and they shall be eunuchs in
the palace of the king of Babylon.' "
[19]So Hezekiah said to Isaiah, "The word of the LORD which you have spoken
is good!" For he said, "Will there not be peace and truth at least in my days?"

Death of Hezekiah

[20]Now the rest of the acts of Hezekiah—all his might, and how he made
a pool and a tunnel and brought water into the city—*are* they not written
in the book of the chronicles of the kings of Judah? [21]So Hezekiah rested
with his fathers. Then Manasseh his son reigned in his place.

Manasseh Reigns in Judah

21 Manasseh *was* twelve years old when he became king, and he
reigned fifty-five years in Jerusalem. His mother's name *was*
Hephzibah. [2]And he did evil in the sight of the LORD, according to the
abominations of the nations whom the LORD had cast out before the children of Israel. [3]For he rebuilt the high places which Hezekiah his father
had destroyed; he raised up altars for Baal, and made a wooden image,[p] as
Ahab king of Israel had done; and he worshiped all the host of heaven[q] and
served them. [4]He also built altars in the house of the LORD, of which the
LORD had said, "In Jerusalem I will put My name." [5]And he built altars for

LIFE LESSON

2 Kings 20:1–21:26

SITUATION Because God loved Hezekiah, he healed him. Hezekiah prayed, God healed, and the king lived. Manasseh, the next king, led Israel into sin.

OBSERVATION Although Hezekiah made mistakes, God still demonstrated love to him.

INSPIRATION The God and Father of our Lord Jesus Christ is gracious. His love is gratuitous in a way that defies our imagination.

It is for this reason that we can proclaim with theological certainty in the power of the Word: *God loves you as you are and not as you should be!* Do you believe this? That God loves you beyond worthiness and unworthiness, beyond fidelity and infidelity, that He loves you in the morning sun and the evening rain, that He loves you without caution, regret, boundary, limit, or breaking point?

I am *not* asking: Do you believe in love? That is abstract ideology. Agnostics and atheists can say that. What I am asking is: can you say with conviction what the apostle John writes in his first letter: "I have come to know and believe in the love *God has for me."* The last four words—God has for me—turn an abstract proposition into a personal relationship. This love is the content of our faith: it is a magnificent summary of all we believe. "The love God has for us" constitutes ultimate meaning and brings the peace and joy the world cannot give.

(From *Lion and Lamb* by Brennan Manning)

APPLICATION God's example is the one we need to follow: to love people as they are and not as they should be. Forgive the person who offends you. Accept the child who disappoints you. Do something lovely for someone the world says is unlovely.

EXPLORATION Healing—Exodus 15:26; 2 Kings 5:1-14; Matthew 4:23-24; James 5:14-16.

20:12 [n] Spelled *Merodach-Baladan* in Isaiah 39:1
20:13 [o] Following many Hebrew manuscripts, Syriac, and Targum; Masoretic Text omits *all.*
21:3 [p] Hebrew *Asherah,* a Canaanite goddess [q] The gods of the Assryians

all the host of heaven in the two courts of the house of the LORD. 6Also he made his son pass through the fire, practiced soothsaying, used witchcraft, and consulted spiritists and mediums. He did much evil in the sight of the LORD, to provoke *Him* to anger. 7He even set a carved image of Asherah[r] that he had made, in the house of which the LORD had said to David and to Solomon his son, "In this house and in Jerusalem, which I have chosen out of all the tribes of Israel, I will put My name forever; 8and I will not make the feet of Israel wander anymore from the land which I gave their fathers—only if they are careful to do according to all that I have commanded them, and according to all the law that My servant Moses commanded them." 9But they paid no attention, and Manasseh seduced them to do more evil than the nations whom the LORD had destroyed before the children of Israel.

10And the LORD spoke by His servants the prophets, saying, 11"Because Manasseh king of Judah has done these abominations (he has acted more wickedly than all the Amorites who *were* before him, and has also made Judah sin with his idols), 12therefore thus says the LORD God of Israel: 'Behold, *I* am bringing *such* calamity upon Jerusalem and Judah, that whoever hears of it, both his ears will tingle. 13And I will stretch over Jerusalem the measuring line of Samaria and the plummet of the house of Ahab; I will wipe Jerusalem as *one* wipes a dish, wiping *it* and turning *it* upside down. 14So I will forsake the remnant of My inheritance and deliver them into the hand of their enemies; and they shall become victims of plunder to all their enemies, 15because they have done evil in My sight, and have provoked Me to anger since the day their fathers came out of Egypt, even to this day.' "

16Moreover Manasseh shed very much innocent blood, till he had filled Jerusalem from one end to another, besides his sin by which he made Judah sin, in doing evil in the sight of the LORD.

17Now the rest of the acts of Manasseh—all that he did, and the sin that he committed—*are* they not written in the book of the chronicles of the kings of Judah? 18So Manasseh rested with his fathers, and was buried in the garden of his own house, in the garden of Uzza. Then his son Amon reigned in his place.

Amon's Reign and Death

19Amon *was* twenty-two years old when he became king, and he reigned two years in Jerusalem. His mother's name *was* Meshullemeth the daughter of Haruz of Jotbah. 20And he did evil in the sight of the LORD, as his father Manasseh had done. 21So he walked in all the ways that his father had walked; and he served the idols that his father had served, and worshiped them. 22He forsook the LORD God of his fathers, and did not walk in the way of the LORD.

23Then the servants of Amon conspired against him, and killed the king in his own house. 24But the people of the land executed all those who had conspired against King Amon. Then the people of the land made his son Josiah king in his place.

25Now the rest of the acts of Amon which he did, *are* they not written in the book of the chronicles of the kings of Judah? 26And he was buried in his tomb in the garden of Uzza. Then Josiah his son reigned in his place.

Josiah Reigns in Judah

22 Josiah *was* eight years old when he became king, and he reigned thirty-one years in Jerusalem. His mother's name *was* Jedidah the daughter of Adaiah of Bozkath. 2And he did *what was* right in the sight of the LORD, and walked in all the ways of his father David; he did not turn aside to the right hand or to the left.

Hilkiah Finds the Book of the Law

3Now it came to pass, in the eighteenth year of King Josiah, *that* the king sent Shaphan the scribe, the son of Azaliah, the son of Meshullam, to the house of the LORD, saying: 4"Go up to Hilkiah the high priest, that he may count the money which has been brought into the house of the LORD, which the doorkeepers have gathered from the people. 5And let them deliver it into the hand of those doing the work, who are the overseers in the house of the LORD; let them give it to those who *are* in the house of the LORD doing the work, to repair the damages of the house— 6to carpenters and builders and masons—and to buy timber and hewn stone to repair the house. 7However there need be no accounting made with them of the money delivered into their hand, because they deal faithfully."

8Then Hilkiah the high priest said to Shaphan the scribe, "I have found the Book of the Law in the house of the LORD." And Hilkiah gave the book to Shaphan, and he read it. 9So Shaphan the scribe went to the king, bringing the king word, saying, "Your servants have gathered the money that was found in the house, and have delivered it into the hand of those who do the work, who oversee the house of the LORD." 10Then Shaphan the scribe showed the king, saying, "Hilkiah the priest has given me a book." And Shaphan read it before the king.

21:7 [r] A Canaanite goddess

11Now it happened, when the king heard the words of the Book of the
Law, that he tore his clothes. 12Then the king commanded Hilkiah the
priest, Ahikam the son of Shaphan, Achbor[s] the son of Michaiah, Shaphan
the scribe, and Asaiah a servant of the king, saying, 13"Go, inquire of the
LORD for me, for the people and for all Judah, concerning the words of this
book that has been found; for great *is* the wrath of the LORD that is aroused
against us, because our fathers have not obeyed the words of this book, to
do according to all that is written concerning us."
14So Hilkiah the priest, Ahikam, Achbor, Shaphan, and Asaiah went to
Huldah the prophetess, the wife of Shallum the son of Tikvah, the son of
Harhas, keeper of the wardrobe. (She dwelt in Jerusalem in the Second
Quarter.) And they spoke with her. 15Then she said to them, "Thus says the
LORD God of Israel, 'Tell the man who sent you to Me, 16"Thus says the
LORD: 'Behold, I will bring calamity on this place and on its inhabitants—
all the words of the book which the king of Judah has read— 17because
they have forsaken Me and burned incense to other gods, that they might
provoke Me to anger with all the works of their hands. Therefore My wrath
shall be aroused against this place and shall not be quenched.' " ' 18But as
for the king of Judah, who sent you to inquire of the LORD, in this manner
you shall speak to him, 'Thus says the LORD God of Israel: "*Concerning* the
words which you have heard— 19because your heart was tender, and you
humbled yourself before the LORD when you heard what I spoke against
this place and against its inhabitants, that they would become a desolation
and a curse, and you tore your clothes and wept before Me, I also have
heard *you*," says the LORD. 20Surely, therefore, I will gather you to your fathers, and you shall be gathered to your grave in peace; and your eyes shall
not see all the calamity which I will bring on this place." ' " So they
brought back word to the king.

Josiah Restores True Worship

23 Now the king sent them to gather all the elders of Judah and Jerusalem to him. 2The king went up to the house of the LORD with all the
men of Judah, and with him all the inhabitants of Jerusalem—the priests
and the prophets and all the people, both small and great. And he read in
their hearing all the words of the Book of the Covenant which had been
found in the house of the LORD.
3Then the king stood by a pillar and made a covenant before the LORD, to
follow the LORD and to keep His commandments and His testimonies and
His statutes, with all *his* heart and all *his* soul, to perform the words of this
covenant that were written in this book. And all the people took a stand for
the covenant. 4And the king commanded Hilkiah the high priest, the
priests of the second order, and the doorkeepers, to bring out of the temple of the LORD all the articles that were made for Baal, for Asherah,[t] and
for all the host of heaven;[u] and he burned them outside Jerusalem in the
fields of Kidron, and carried their ashes to Bethel. 5Then he removed the
idolatrous priests whom the kings of Judah had ordained to burn incense
on the high places in the cities of Judah and in the places all around Jerusalem, and those who burned incense to Baal, to the sun, to the moon, to
the constellations, and to all the host of heaven. 6And he brought out the

22:12 [s] *Abdon the son of Micah* in 2 Chronicles 34:20
23:4 [t] A Canaanite goddess [u] The gods of the Assyrians

LIFE LESSON

2 Kings 22:1–23:35

SITUATION Josiah obeyed God with undivided devotion and initiated thorough reforms. While repairing the formerly neglected temple, God's Word was found. Josiah used God's Word to bring drastic changes to the nation's life-style.

OBSERVATION God used one man to bring a revival to an entire nation.

INSPIRATION Maybe your past isn't much to brag about. Maybe you've seen raw evil. And now you, like Josiah, have to make a choice. Do you rise above the past and make a difference? Or do you remain controlled by the past and make excuses?

Many choose the latter.

Many choose the convalescent homes of the heart. Healthy bodies. Sharp minds. But retired dreams. Back and forth they rock in the chair of regret, repeating the terms of surrender. Lean closely and you will hear them: "If only." The white flag of the heart.

"If only . . ."

"If only I'd been born somewhere else . . . "

"If only I'd been treated fairly . . . "

"If only I'd had kinder parents, more money, greater opportunities . . . "

"If only I'd been potty-trained sooner, spanked less, or taught to eat without slurping."

Maybe you've used those words. Maybe you have every right to use them. Perhaps you, like Josiah, were hearing the ten count before you even got into the ring. For you to find an ancestor worth imitating, you, like Josiah, have to flip way back in your family album.

If such is the case, let me show you where to turn. Put down the scrapbook and pick up your Bible. Go to John's Gospel and read Jesus' words: "Human life comes from human parents, but spiritual life comes from the Spirit" (John 3:6).

Think about that. Spiritual life comes from the Spirit! Your parents may

Continued

have given you genes, but God gives you grace. Your parents may be responsible for your body, but God has taken charge of your soul. You may get your looks from your mother, but you get eternity from your Father, your heavenly Father. . . .

God has not left you adrift on a sea of heredity. Just like Josiah, you cannot control the way your forefathers responded to God. But you can control the way you respond to him. The past does not have to be your prison. You have a voice in your destiny. You have a say in your life. You have a choice in the path you take.

Choose well and someday—generations from now—your grandchildren and great-grandchildren will thank God for the seeds you sowed.

(From *When God Whispers Your Name* by Max Lucado)

APPLICATION How many times during the last week did you read your Bible? Develop an action plan for making God's message all-important in your life. Equip yourself to pass on a righteous legacy.

EXPLORATION Scripture—Deuteronomy 17:18-20; 2 Kings 22:11; Job 4:7-8; Psalm 119:19; 105; 2 Timothy 3:15-17.

wooden image[v] from the house of the LORD, to the Brook Kidron outside Jerusalem, burned it at the Brook Kidron and ground *it* to ashes, and threw its ashes on the graves of the common people. [7]Then he tore down the *ritual* booths of the perverted persons[w] that *were* in the house of the LORD, where the women wove hangings for the wooden image. [8]And he brought all the priests from the cities of Judah, and defiled the high places where the priests had burned incense, from Geba to Beersheba; also he broke down the high places at the gates which *were* at the entrance of the Gate of Joshua the governor of the city, which *were* to the left of the city gate. [9]Nevertheless the priests of the high places did not come up to the altar of the LORD in Jerusalem, but they ate unleavened bread among their brethren.

[10]And he defiled Topheth, which *is* in the Valley of the Son[x] of Hinnom, that no man might make his son or his daughter pass through the fire to Molech. [11]Then he removed the horses that the kings of Judah had dedicated to the sun, at the entrance to the house of the LORD, by the chamber of Nathan-Melech, the officer who *was* in the court; and he burned the chariots of the sun with fire. [12]The altars that *were* on the roof, the upper chamber of Ahaz, which the kings of Judah had made, and the altars which Manasseh had made in the two courts of the house of the LORD, the king broke down and pulverized there, and threw their dust into the Brook Kidron. [13]Then the king defiled the high places that *were* east of Jerusalem, which *were* on the south of the Mount of Corruption, which Solomon king of Israel had built for Ashtoreth the abomination of the Sidonians, for Chemosh the abomination of the Moabites, and for Milcom the abomination of the people of Ammon. [14]And he broke in pieces the *sacred* pillars and cut down the wooden images, and filled their places with the bones of men.

[15]Moreover the altar that *was* at Bethel, *and* the high place which Jeroboam the son of Nebat, who made Israel sin, had made, both that altar and the high place he broke down; and he burned the high place *and* crushed *it* to powder, and burned the wooden image. [16]As Josiah turned, he saw the tombs that *were* there on the mountain. And he sent and took the bones out of the tombs and burned *them* on the altar, and defiled it according to the word of the LORD which the man of God proclaimed, who proclaimed these words. [17]Then he said, "What gravestone *is* this that I see?"

So the men of the city told him, "*It is* the tomb of the man of God who came from Judah and proclaimed these things which you have done against the altar of Bethel."

[18]And he said, "Let him alone; let no one move his bones." So they let his bones alone, with the bones of the prophet who came from Samaria.

[19]Now Josiah also took away all the shrines of the high places that *were* in the cities of Samaria, which the kings of Israel had made to provoke the LORD[y] to anger; and he did to them according to all the deeds he had done in Bethel. [20]He executed all the priests of the high places who *were* there, on the altars, and burned men's bones on them; and he returned to Jerusalem.

[21]Then the king commanded all the people, saying, "Keep the Passover to the LORD your God, as *it is* written in this Book of the Covenant." [22]Such a Passover surely had never been held since the days of the judges who

23:6 [v] Hebrew *Asherah,* a Canaanite goddess
23:7 [w] Hebrew *qedeshim,* that is, those practicing sodomy and prostitution in religious rituals
23:10 [x] Kethib reads *Sons.*
23:19 [y] Following Septuagint, Syriac, and Vulgate; Masoretic Text and Targum omit *the LORD.*

judged Israel, nor in all the days of the kings of Israel and the kings of Judah. 23But in the eighteenth year of King Josiah this Passover was held before the LORD in Jerusalem. 24Moreover Josiah put away those who
consulted mediums and spiritists, the household gods and idols, all the
abominations that were seen in the land of Judah and in Jerusalem, that
he might perform the words of the law which were written in the book that
Hilkiah the priest found in the house of the LORD. 25Now before him there
was no king like him, who turned to the LORD with all his heart, with all his
soul, and with all his might, according to all the Law of Moses; nor after
him did *any* arise like him.

Impending Judgment on Judah

26Nevertheless the LORD did not turn from the fierceness of His great
wrath, with which His anger was aroused against Judah, because of all the
provocations with which Manasseh had provoked Him. 27And the LORD
said, "I will also remove Judah from My sight, as I have removed Israel,
and will cast off this city Jerusalem which I have chosen, and the house of
which I said, 'My name shall be there.' "[z]

Josiah Dies in Battle

28Now the rest of the acts of Josiah, and all that he did, *are* they not written in the book of the chronicles of the kings of Judah? 29In his days
Pharaoh Necho king of Egypt went to the aid of the king of Assyria, to the
River Euphrates; and King Josiah went against him. And *Pharaoh Necho*
killed him at Megiddo when he confronted him. 30Then his servants
moved his body in a chariot from Megiddo, brought him to Jerusalem,
and buried him in his own tomb. And the people of the land took Jehoahaz
the son of Josiah, anointed him, and made him king in his father's place.

The Reign and Captivity of Jehoahaz

31Jehoahaz *was* twenty-three years old when he became king, and he
reigned three months in Jerusalem. His mother's name *was* Hamutal the
daughter of Jeremiah of Libnah. 32And he did evil in the sight of the LORD,
according to all that his fathers had done. 33Now Pharaoh Necho put him
in prison at Riblah in the land of Hamath, that he might not reign in Jerusalem; and he imposed on the land a tribute of one hundred talents of silver and a talent of gold. 34Then Pharaoh Necho made Eliakim the son of
Josiah king in place of his father Josiah, and changed his name to Jehoiakim.
And *Pharaoh* took Jehoahaz and went to Egypt, and he[a] died there.

Jehoiakim Reigns in Judah

35So Jehoiakim gave the silver and gold to Pharaoh; but he taxed the
land to give money according to the command of Pharaoh; he exacted the
silver and gold from the people of the land, from every one according to
his assessment, to give *it* to Pharaoh Necho. 36Jehoiakim *was* twenty-five
years old when he became king, and he reigned eleven years in Jerusalem.
His mother's name *was* Zebudah the daughter of Pedaiah of Rumah.
37And he did evil in the sight of the LORD, according to all that his fathers
had done.

23:27 [z] 1 Kings 8:29
23:34 [a] That is, Jehoahaz

LIFE LESSON

2 Kings 23:36–25:30

SITUATION Each of the last three kings of Judah rebelled against the Babylonians. Each time, Babylon brought quick and severe retribution. They displaced people, looted the temple, and destroyed Jerusalem. Even though Israel's captivity had been foretold for over a century by various prophets, the people and their leaders refused to listen and stop sinning.

OBSERVATION God warned the people for over one hundred years that continued disobedience would lead to disaster.

INSPIRATION As long as men and women seek to gain their sense of significance and self-worth from anything other than God, they will be set up for temptation. Certain people, places, or things will always have an inordinate ability to lure them into sin. Until they change their definition of significance and until they transfer their security to Someone who can give them real security, they will never experience lasting victory in their lives. . . .

Making the switch from your present set of values to God's involves two steps. First of all, you must identify the things and people from which you draw your identity. I call this step of the process reviewing your life. . . .

A second step in making this switch involves renewing your mind to the truth. To renew your mind, you must remove the old ways of thinking and replace them with the truth. . . . The truth is that all of your security and significance is wrapped up in your relationship with God through Jesus Christ.

(From *Winning the War Within* by Charles Stanley)

APPLICATION Are you most likely to disobey God with certain friends? At certain places? In certain moods? Ask Jesus to take charge of your relationships, desires, and moods. Then choose to spend your time wisely.

EXPLORATION Disobedience—Genesis 3:14-19; Exodus 8:15; Numbers 20:3-5; 1 Chronicles 10:13-14; Isaiah 3:1-3.

Judah Overrun by Enemies

24 In his days Nebuchadnezzar king of Babylon
came up, and Jehoiakim became his vassal *for*
three years. Then he turned and rebelled against him.
2And the LORD sent against him *raiding* bands of
Chaldeans, bands of Syrians, bands of Moabites, and
bands of the people of Ammon; He sent them against
Judah to destroy it, according to the word of the LORD
which He had spoken by His servants the prophets.
3Surely at the commandment of the LORD *this* came
upon Judah, to remove *them* from His sight because
of the sins of Manasseh, according to all that he had
done, 4and also because of the innocent blood that he
had shed; for he had filled Jerusalem with innocent
blood, which the LORD would not pardon.

5Now the rest of the acts of Jehoiakim, and all that he
did, *are* they not written in the book of the chronicles of
the kings of Judah? 6So Jehoiakim rested with his fathers. Then Jehoiachin his son reigned in his place.

7And the king of Egypt did not come out of his land
anymore, for the king of Babylon had taken all that
belonged to the king of Egypt from the Brook of Egypt
to the River Euphrates.

The Reign and Captivity of Jehoiachin

8Jehoiachin *was* eighteen years old when he became
king, and he reigned in Jerusalem three months. His
mother's name *was* Nehushta the daughter of
Elnathan of Jerusalem. 9And he did evil in the sight of
the LORD, according to all that his father had done.

10At that time the servants of Nebuchadnezzar king
of Babylon came up against Jerusalem, and the city
was besieged. 11And Nebuchadnezzar king of Babylon
came against the city, as his servants were besieging
it. 12Then Jehoiachin king of Judah, his mother, his
servants, his princes, and his officers went out to the
king of Babylon; and the king of Babylon, in the
eighth year of his reign, took him prisoner.

The Captivity of Jerusalem

13And he carried out from there all the treasures of
the house of the LORD and the treasures of the king's
house, and he cut in pieces all the articles of gold which
Solomon king of Israel had made in the temple of the
LORD, as the LORD had said. 14Also he carried into captivity all Jerusalem: all the captains and all the mighty
men of valor, ten thousand captives, and all the craftsmen and smiths. None remained except the poorest
people of the land. 15And he carried Jehoiachin captive to Babylon. The king's mother, the king's wives,
his officers, and the mighty of the land he carried into
captivity from Jerusalem to Babylon. 16All the valiant
men, seven thousand, and craftsmen and smiths, one
thousand, all *who were* strong *and* fit for war, these the
king of Babylon brought captive to Babylon.

Zedekiah Reigns in Judah

17Then the king of Babylon made Mattaniah,
Jehoiachin's[b] uncle, king in his place, and changed his
name to Zedekiah.

18Zedekiah *was* twenty-one years old when he became king, and he reigned eleven years in Jerusalem.
His mother's name *was* Hamutal the daughter of
Jeremiah of Libnah. 19He also did evil in the sight of
the LORD, according to all that Jehoiakim had done.
20For because of the anger of the LORD *this* happened
in Jerusalem and Judah, that He finally cast them out
from His presence. Then Zedekiah rebelled against
the king of Babylon.

The Fall and Captivity of Judah

25 Now it came to pass in the ninth year of his
reign, in the tenth month, on the tenth *day* of
the month, *that* Nebuchadnezzar king of Babylon and
all his army came against Jerusalem and encamped
against it; and they built a siege wall against it all
around. 2So the city was besieged until the eleventh
year of King Zedekiah. 3By the ninth *day* of the *fourth*
month the famine had become so severe in the city
that there was no food for the people of the land.

4Then the city wall was broken through, and all the
men of war *fled* at night by way of the gate between
two walls, which was by the king's garden, even
though the Chaldeans *were* still encamped all around
against the city. And *the king*[c] went by way of the
plain.[d] 5But the army of the Chaldeans pursued the
king, and they overtook him in the plains of Jericho.
All his army was scattered from him. 6So they took the
king and brought him up to the king of Babylon at
Riblah, and they pronounced judgment on him.
7Then they killed the sons of Zedekiah before his eyes,
put out the eyes of Zedekiah, bound him with bronze
fetters, and took him to Babylon.

8And in the fifth month, on the seventh *day* of the
month (which *was* the nineteenth year of King Nebuchadnezzar king of Babylon), Nebuzaradan the captain
of the guard, a servant of the king of Babylon, came to

24:17 [b] Literally *his*
25:4 [c] Literally *he* [d] Or *Arabah,* that is, the Jordan Valley

Jerusalem. 9He burned the house of the LORD and the
king's house; all the houses of Jerusalem, that is, all the
houses of the great, he burned with fire. 10And all the
army of the Chaldeans who *were with* the captain of the
guard broke down the walls of Jerusalem all around.
11Then Nebuzaradan the captain of the guard carried away captive the rest of the people *who* remained
in the city and the defectors who had deserted to the
king of Babylon, with the rest of the multitude. 12But
the captain of the guard left *some* of the poor of the
land as vinedressers and farmers. 13The bronze pillars
that *were* in the house of the LORD, and the carts and
the bronze Sea that *were* in the house of the LORD, the
Chaldeans broke in pieces, and carried their bronze to
Babylon. 14They also took away the pots, the shovels,
the trimmers, the spoons, and all the bronze utensils
with which the priests ministered. 15The firepans and
the basins, the things of solid gold and solid silver, the
captain of the guard took away. 16The two pillars, one
Sea, and the carts, which Solomon had made for the
house of the LORD, the bronze of all these articles was
beyond measure. 17The height of one pillar *was* eighteen cubits, and the capital on it *was* of bronze. The
height of the capital was three cubits, and the network
and pomegranates all around the capital were all of
bronze. The second pillar was the same, with a network.
18And the captain of the guard took Seraiah the chief
priest, Zephaniah the second priest, and the three doorkeepers. 19He also took out of the city an officer who had
charge of the men of war, five men of the king's close associates who were found in the city, the chief recruiting
officer of the army, who mustered the people of the land,
and sixty men of the people of the land *who were* found
in the city. 20So Nebuzaradan, captain of the guard, took
these and brought them to the king of Babylon at Riblah.
21Then the king of Babylon struck them and put them
to death at Riblah in the land of Hamath. Thus Judah
was carried away captive from its own land.

Gedaliah Made Governor of Judah

22Then he made Gedaliah the son of Ahikam, the
son of Shaphan, governor over the people who remained in the land of Judah, whom Nebuchadnezzar
king of Babylon had left. 23Now when all the captains
of the armies, they and *their* men, heard that the king
of Babylon had made Gedaliah governor, they came
to Gedaliah at Mizpah—Ishmael the son of
Nethaniah, Johanan the son of Careah, Seraiah the
son of Tanhumeth the Netophathite, and Jaazaniah[e]
the son of a Maachathite, they and their men. 24And
Gedaliah took an oath before them and their men,
and said to them, "Do not be afraid of the servants of
the Chaldeans. Dwell in the land and serve the king of
Babylon, and it shall be well with you."
25But it happened in the seventh month that Ishmael
the son of Nethaniah, the son of Elishama, of the royal
family, came with ten men and struck and killed
Gedaliah, the Jews, as well as the Chaldeans who were
with him at Mizpah. 26And all the people, small and
great, and the captains of the armies, arose and went to
Egypt; for they were afraid of the Chaldeans.

Jehoiachin Released from Prison

27Now it came to pass in the thirty-seventh year of
the captivity of Jehoiachin king of Judah, in the
twelfth month, on the twenty-seventh *day* of the
month, *that* Evil-Merodach[f] king of Babylon, in the
year that he began to reign, released Jehoiachin king
of Judah from prison. 28He spoke kindly to him, and
gave him a more prominent seat than those of the
kings who *were* with him in Babylon. 29So Jehoiachin
changed from his prison garments, and he ate bread
regularly before the king all the days of his life. 30And
as for his provisions, *there was* a regular ration given
him by the king, a portion for each day, all the days of
his life.

25:23 [e] Spelled *Jezaniah* in Jeremiah 40:8
25:27 [f] Literally *Man of Marduk*

The First Book of the CHRONICLES

INTRODUCTION

Ever been held up by a grandparent?

You naively ask how the grandkids are, and before you know it the purse opens and out pops a billfold thick with pictures.

"This is Joey in the third grade holding his puppy named Snapper. And this is Joey in the fourth grade on his little league team where he played second base. And this is Joey in the fifth grade. The kid behind him is his cousin Terry who is living in Seattle with his dad. I've got some pictures of them I'll show you in just a minute. But first let me show you Joey in the seventh grade wearing his football uniform . . ."

Yawn.

Hard to stay interested hearing names of people you'll never see who live in places you'll never know.

Such is the case with the Book of Chronicles. Full of names, many hard to pronounce. Full of places, most of which you'll never see. The book won't keep you on the edge of your seat. It wasn't intended to. It will, however, provide you with a catalog of facts and names of people who matter to God.

Which reminds us of an encouraging truth: God keeps up with his children. He knows their names and keeps them in a book. What may be dry to us matters to him, because they are his kids. By the way, he's working on a new volume. This one is entitled the Book of Life.

Is your name in it?

LIFE LESSON

1 Chronicles 1:1–3:24

SITUATION Chronicles was written after the exile to help those returning to Israel understand how to worship God. The history focused on the Southern Kingdom—the tribes of Judah, Benjamin, and Levi. These tribes tended to be more faithful to God.

OBSERVATION God knows every person who has ever lived. We are not just faceless numbers among the thousands of years of humanity. God concerns himself with every person and detail. We should never feel insignificant.

INSPIRATION We can learn much about a person by looking at his or her track record, checking out how he or she has related to others in the past.

We can learn much about God by taking a close look at how he has acted in the past and how he has related to his people, the children of Israel. What we find is that God is profoundly loving. In fact, time after time when Israel would disobey his commands and even begin to worship idols, God would be slow to punish them and would take them back as soon as they turned from their sin.

The fact that God is "slow to anger" should not encourage us to take him for granted. Instead, we should remember his unending love and determine to live for him and close to him.

Thank God for what he has done in the past, for Israel and for you. And live in the light of his gracious and compassionate love.

(From *On Eagles' Wings* by Dave Veerman)

APPLICATION God knows your name, your history, your dreams, your future, your thoughts, and every detail of your life. Are you tempted to feel insignificant? Remember that he loves you intensely.

EXPLORATION Important to God—Isaiah 43:1; 49:16; Jeremiah 31:3; Luke 12:6-7; John 10:3; Romans 8:27; 1 John 3:1.

The Family of Adam—Seth to Abraham

Adam, Seth, Enosh, 2Cainan,[a] Mahalalel, Jared, 3Enoch, Methuselah, Lamech, 4Noah,[b] Shem, Ham, and Japheth.

5The sons of Japheth *were* Gomer, Magog, Madai, Javan, Tubal, Meshech, and Tiras. 6The sons of Gomer *were* Ashkenaz, Diphath,[c] and Togarmah. 7The sons of Javan *were* Elishah, Tarshishah,[d] Kittim, and Rodanim.[e]

8The sons of Ham *were* Cush, Mizraim, Put, and Canaan. 9The sons of Cush *were* Seba, Havilah, Sabta,[f] Raama,[g] and Sabtecha. The sons of Raama *were* Sheba and Dedan. 10Cush begot Nimrod; he began to be a mighty one on the earth. 11Mizraim begot Ludim, Anamim, Lehabim, Naphtuhim, 12Pathrusim, Casluhim (from whom came the Philistines and the Caphtorim). 13Canaan begot Sidon, his firstborn, and Heth; 14the Jebusite, the Amorite, and the Girgashite; 15the Hivite, the Arkite, and the Sinite; 16the Arvadite, the Zemarite, and the Hamathite.

17The sons of Shem *were* Elam, Asshur, Arphaxad, Lud, Aram, Uz, Hul, Gether, and Meshech.[h] 18Arphaxad begot Shelah, and Shelah begot Eber. 19To Eber were born two sons: the name of one *was* Peleg,[i] for in his days the earth was divided; and his brother's name *was* Joktan. 20Joktan begot Almodad, Sheleph, Hazarmaveth, Jerah, 21Hadoram, Uzal, Diklah, 22Ebal,[j] Abimael, Sheba, 23Ophir, Havilah, and Jobab. All these *were* the sons of Joktan.

24Shem, Arphaxad, Shelah, 25Eber, Peleg, Reu, 26Serug, Nahor, Terah, 27and Abram, who *is* Abraham. 28The sons of Abraham *were* Isaac and Ishmael.

The Family of Ishmael

29These *are* their genealogies: The firstborn of Ishmael *was* Nebajoth; then Kedar, Adbeel, Mibsam, 30Mishma, Dumah, Massa, Hadad,[k] Tema, 31Jetur, Naphish, and Kedemah. These *were* the sons of Ishmael.

The Family of Keturah

32Now the sons born to Keturah, Abraham's concubine, *were* Zimran, Jokshan, Medan, Midian, Ishbak, and Shuah. The sons of Jokshan *were* Sheba and Dedan. 33The sons of Midian *were* Ephah, Epher, Hanoch, Abida, and Eldaah. All these were the children of Keturah.

The Family of Isaac

34And Abraham begot Isaac. The sons of Isaac *were* Esau and Israel. 35The sons of Esau *were* Eliphaz, Reuel, Jeush, Jaalam, and Korah. 36And the sons of Eliphaz *were* Teman, Omar, Zephi,[l] Gatam, *and* Kenaz; and *by* Timna,[m] Amalek. 37The sons of Reuel *were* Nahath, Zerah, Shammah, and Mizzah.

The Family of Seir

38The sons of Seir *were* Lotan, Shobal, Zibeon, Anah, Dishon, Ezer, and Dishan. 39And the sons of Lotan *were* Hori and Homam; Lotan's sister *was*

1:2 [a] Hebrew *Qenan*
1:4 [b] Following Masoretic Text and Vulgate; Septuagint adds *the sons of Noah.*
1:6 [c] Spelled *Riphath* in Genesis 10:3
1:7 [d] Spelled *Tarshish* in Genesis 10:4 [e] Spelled *Dodanim* in Genesis 10:4
1:9 [f] Spelled *Sabtah* in Genesis 10:7 [g] Spelled *Raamah* in Genesis 10:7
1:17 [h] Spelled *Mash* in Genesis 10:23
1:19 [i] Literally *Division*
1:22 [j] Spelled *Obal* in Genesis 10:28
1:30 [k] Spelled *Hadar* in Genesis 25:15
1:36 [l] Spelled *Zepho* in Genesis 36:11 [m] Compare Genesis 36:12

Timna. 40 The sons of Shobal *were* Alian,[n] Manahath, Ebal, Shephi,[o] and Onam. The sons of Zibeon *were* Ajah and Anah. 41 The son of Anah *was* Dishon. The sons of Dishon *were* Hamran,[p] Eshban, Ithran, and Cheran. 42 The sons of Ezer *were* Bilhan, Zaavan, *and* Jaakan.[q] The sons of Dishan *were* Uz and Aran.

The Kings of Edom

43 Now these *were* the kings who reigned in the land of Edom before a king reigned over the children of Israel: Bela the son of Beor, and the name of his city was Dinhabah. 44 And when Bela died, Jobab the son of Zerah of Bozrah reigned in his place. 45 When Jobab died, Husham of the land of the Temanites reigned in his place. 46 And when Husham died, Hadad the son of Bedad, who attacked Midian in the field of Moab, reigned in his place. The name of his city *was* Avith. 47 When Hadad died, Samlah of Masrekah reigned in his place. 48 And when Samlah died, Saul of Rehoboth-by-the-River reigned in his place. 49 When Saul died, Baal-Hanan the son of Achbor reigned in his place. 50 And when Baal-Hanan died, Hadad[r] reigned in his place; and the name of his city was Pai.[s] His wife's name was Mehetabel the daughter of Matred, the daughter of Mezahab. 51 Hadad died also. And the chiefs of Edom were Chief Timnah, Chief Aliah,[t] Chief Jetheth, 52 Chief Aholibamah, Chief Elah, Chief Pinon, 53 Chief Kenaz, Chief Teman, Chief Mibzar, 54 Chief Magdiel, and Chief Iram. These *were* the chiefs of Edom.

The Family of Israel

2 These *were* the sons of Israel: Reuben, Simeon, Levi, Judah, Issachar, Zebulun, 2 Dan, Joseph, Benjamin, Naphtali, Gad, and Asher.

From Judah to David

3 The sons of Judah *were* Er, Onan, and Shelah. *These* three were born to him by the daughter of Shua, the Canaanitess. Er, the firstborn of Judah, was wicked in the sight of the LORD; so He killed him. 4 And Tamar, his daughter-in-law, bore him Perez and Zerah. All the sons of Judah *were* five.

5 The sons of Perez *were* Hezron and Hamul. 6 The sons of Zerah *were* Zimri, Ethan, Heman, Calcol, and Dara—five of them in all.

7 The son of Carmi *was* Achar,[u] the troubler of Israel, who transgressed in the accursed thing.

8 The son of Ethan *was* Azariah.

9 Also the sons of Hezron who were born to him *were* Jerahmeel, Ram, and Chelubai.[v] 10 Ram begot Amminadab, and Amminadab begot Nahshon, leader of the children of Judah; 11 Nahshon begot Salma,[w] and Salma begot Boaz; 12 Boaz begot Obed, and Obed begot Jesse; 13 Jesse begot Eliab his firstborn, Abinadab the second, Shimea[x] the third, 14 Nethanel the fourth, Raddai the fifth, 15 Ozem the sixth, *and* David the seventh.

16 Now their sisters *were* Zeruiah and Abigail. And the sons of Zeruiah *were* Abishai, Joab, and Asahel—three. 17 Abigail bore Amasa; and the father of Amasa *was* Jether the Ishmaelite.[y]

The Family of Hezron

18 Caleb the son of Hezron had children by Azubah, *his* wife, and by Jerioth. Now these were her sons: Jesher, Shobab, and Ardon. 19 When Azubah died, Caleb took Ephrath[z] as his wife, who bore him Hur. 20 And Hur begot Uri, and Uri begot Bezalel.

21 Now afterward Hezron went in to the daughter of Machir the father of Gilead, whom he married when he *was* sixty years old; and she bore him Segub. 22 Segub begot Jair, who had twenty-three cities in the land of Gilead. 23 (Geshur and Syria took from them the towns of Jair, with Kenath and its towns—sixty towns.) All these *belonged to* the sons of Machir the father of Gilead. 24 After Hezron died in Caleb Ephrathah, Hezron's wife Abijah bore him Ashhur the father of Tekoa.

The Family of Jerahmeel

25 The sons of Jerahmeel, the firstborn of Hezron, *were* Ram, the firstborn, and Bunah, Oren, Ozem, *and* Ahijah. 26 Jerahmeel had another wife, whose name was Atarah; she was the mother of Onam. 27 The sons of Ram, the firstborn of Jerahmeel, were Maaz, Jamin,

1:40 [n] Spelled *Alvan* in Genesis 36:23 [o] Spelled *Shepho* in Genesis 36:23
1:41 [p] Spelled *Hemdan* in Genesis 36:26
1:42 [q] Spelled *Akan* in Genesis 36:27
1:50 [r] Spelled *Hadar* in Genesis 36:39 [s] Spelled *Pau* in Genesis 36:39
1:51 [t] Spelled *Alvah* in Genesis 36:40
2:7 [u] Spelled *Achan* in Joshua 7:1 and elsewhere
2:9 [v] Spelled *Caleb* in 2:18, 42
2:11 [w] Spelled *Salmon* in Ruth 4:21 and Luke 3:32
2:13 [x] Spelled *Shammah* in 1 Samuel 16:9 and elsewhere
2:17 [y] Compare 2 Samuel 17:25
2:19 [z] Spelled *Ephrathah* elsewhere

and Eker. 28The sons of Onam were Shammai and Jada.
The sons of Shammai *were* Nadab and Abishur.
29And the name of the wife of Abishur *was* Abihail,
and she bore him Ahban and Molid. 30The sons of Nadab
were Seled and Appaim; Seled died without children.
31The son of Appaim *was* Ishi, the son of Ishi *was*
Sheshan, and Sheshan's son *was* Ahlai. 32The sons of
Jada, the brother of Shammai, *were* Jether and Jonathan;
Jether died without children. 33The sons of Jonathan *were*
Peleth and Zaza. These were the sons of Jerahmeel.
34Now Sheshan had no sons, only daughters. And
Sheshan had an Egyptian servant whose name *was*
Jarha. 35Sheshan gave his daughter to Jarha his servant as wife, and she bore him Attai. 36Attai begot Nathan, and Nathan begot Zabad; 37Zabad begot Ephlal,
and Ephlal begot Obed; 38Obed begot Jehu, and Jehu
begot Azariah; 39Azariah begot Helez, and Helez
begot Eleasah; 40Eleasah begot Sismai, and Sismai
begot Shallum; 41Shallum begot Jekamiah, and
Jekamiah begot Elishama.

The Family of Caleb

42The descendants of Caleb the brother of Jerahmeel
were Mesha, his firstborn, who was the father of Ziph,
and the sons of Mareshah the father of Hebron. 43The
sons of Hebron *were* Korah, Tappuah, Rekem, and
Shema. 44Shema begot Raham the father of Jorkoam,
and Rekem begot Shammai. 45And the son of Shammai
was Maon, and Maon *was* the father of Beth Zur.
46Ephah, Caleb's concubine, bore Haran, Moza, and
Gazez; and Haran begot Gazez. 47And the sons of Jahdai
were Regem, Jotham, Geshan, Pelet, Ephah, and Shaaph.
48Maachah, Caleb's concubine, bore Sheber and
Tirhanah. 49She also bore Shaaph the father of
Madmannah, Sheva the father of Machbenah and the
father of Gibea. And the daughter of Caleb *was* Achsah.
50These were the descendants of Caleb: The sons of
Hur, the firstborn of Ephrathah, *were* Shobal the father of Kirjath Jearim, 51Salma the father of Bethlehem, *and* Hareph the father of Beth Gader.
52And Shobal the father of Kirjath Jearim had descendants: Haroeh, *and* half of the *families of* Manuhoth.[a]
53The families of Kirjath Jearim *were* the Ithrites, the
Puthites, the Shumathites, and the Mishraites. From
these came the Zorathites and the Eshtaolites.
54The sons of Salma *were* Bethlehem, the Netophathites, Atroth Beth Joab, half of the Manahethites,
and the Zorites.
55And the families of the scribes who dwelt at Jabez
were the Tirathites, the Shimeathites, *and* the
Suchathites. These *were* the Kenites who came from
Hammath, the father of the house of Rechab.

The Family of David

3 Now these were the sons of David who were born to
him in Hebron: The firstborn *was* Amnon, by
Ahinoam the Jezreelitess; the second, Daniel,[b] by Abigail
the Carmelitess; 2the third, Absalom the son of Maacah,
the daughter of Talmai, king of Geshur; the fourth,
Adonijah the son of Haggith; 3the fifth, Shephatiah, by
Abital; the sixth, Ithream, by his wife Eglah.
4*These* six were born to him in Hebron. There he
reigned seven years and six months, and in Jerusalem he reigned thirty-three years. 5And these were
born to him in Jerusalem: Shimea,[c] Shobab, Nathan,
and Solomon—four by Bathshua[d] the daughter of
Ammiel.[e] 6Also *there* were Ibhar, Elishama,[f] Eliphelet,[g]
7Nogah, Nepheg, Japhia, 8Elishama, Eliada,[h] and
Eliphelet—nine *in all.* 9*These were* all the sons of David, besides the sons of the concubines, and Tamar
their sister.

The Family of Solomon

10Solomon's son *was* Rehoboam; Abijah[i] *was* his son,
Asa his son, Jehoshaphat his son, 11Joram[j] his son,
Ahaziah his son, Joash[k] his son, 12Amaziah his son,
Azariah[l] his son, Jotham his son, 13Ahaz his son,
Hezekiah his son, Manasseh his son, 14Amon his son,
and Josiah his son. 15The sons of Josiah *were* Johanan the
firstborn, the second Jehoiakim, the third Zedekiah,
and the fourth Shallum.[m] 16The sons of Jehoiakim *were*
Jeconiah his son *and* Zedekiah[n] his son.

The Family of Jeconiah

17And the sons of Jeconiah[o] *were* Assir,[p] Shealtiel his
son, 18*and* Malchiram, Pedaiah, Shenazzar, Jecamiah,

2:52 [a] Same as *the Manahethites,* verse 54
3:1 [b] Called *Chileab* in 2 Samuel 3:3
3:5 [c] Spelled *Shammua* in 14:4 and 2 Samuel 5:14 [d] Spelled *Bathsheba* in 2 Samuel 11:3 [e] Called *Eliam* in 2 Samuel 11:3
3:6 [f] Spelled *Elishua* in 14:5 and 2 Samuel 5:15 [g] Spelled *Elpelet* in 14:5
3:8 [h] Spelled *Beeliada* in 14:7
3:10 [i] Spelled *Abijam* in 1 Kings 15:1
3:11 [j] Spelled *Jehoram* in 2 Kings 1:17 and 8:16 [k] Spelled *Jehoash* in 2 Kings 12:1
3:12 [l] Called *Uzziah* in Isaiah 6:1
3:15 [m] Called *Jehoahaz* in 2 Kings 23:31
3:16 [n] Compare 2 Kings 24:17
3:17 [o] Also called *Coniah* in Jeremiah 22:24 and *Jehoiachin* in 2 Kings 24:8 [p] Or *Jeconiah the captive were*

Hoshama, and Nedabiah. [19]The sons of Pedaiah *were* Zerubbabel and Shimei. The sons of Zerubbabel *were* Meshullam, Hananiah, Shelomith their sister, [20]and Hashubah, Ohel, Berechiah, Hasadiah, and Jushab-Hesed—five *in all.*

[21]The sons of Hananiah *were* Pelatiah and Jeshaiah, the sons of Rephaiah, the sons of Arnan, the sons of Obadiah, and the sons of Shechaniah. [22]The son of Shechaniah was Shemaiah. The sons of Shemaiah *were* Hattush, Igal, Bariah, Neariah, and Shaphat—six *in all.* [23]The sons of Neariah *were* Elioenai, Hezekiah, and Azrikam—three *in all.* [24]The sons of Elioenai *were* Hodaviah, Eliashib, Pelaiah, Akkub, Johanan, Delaiah, and Anani—seven *in all.*

The Family of Judah

4 The sons of Judah *were* Perez, Hezron, Carmi, Hur, and Shobal. [2]And Reaiah the son of Shobal begot Jahath, and Jahath begot Ahumai and Lahad. These *were* the families of the Zorathites. [3]These *were* the sons *of the father* of Etam: Jezreel, Ishma, and Idbash; and the name of their sister *was* Hazelelponi; [4]and Penuel *was* the father of Gedor, and Ezer *was the* father of Hushah.

These *were* the sons of Hur, the firstborn of Ephrathah the father of Bethlehem.

[5]And Ashhur the father of Tekoa had two wives, Helah and Naarah. [6]Naarah bore him Ahuzzam, Hepher, Temeni, and Haahashtari. These *were* the sons of Naarah. [7]The sons of Helah *were* Zereth, Zohar, and Ethnan; [8]and Koz begot Anub, Zobebah, and the families of Aharhel the son of Harum.

[9]Now Jabez was more honorable than his brothers, and his mother called his name Jabez,[q] saying, "Because I bore *him* in pain." [10]And Jabez called on the God of Israel saying, "Oh, that You would bless me indeed, and enlarge my territory, that Your hand would be with me, and that You would keep *me* from evil, that I may not cause pain!" So God granted him what he requested.

[11]Chelub the brother of Shuhah begot Mehir, who *was* the father of Eshton. [12]And Eshton begot Beth-Rapha, Paseah, and Tehinnah the father of Ir-Nahash. These *were* the men of Rechah.

[13]The sons of Kenaz *were* Othniel and Seraiah. The sons of Othniel *were* Hathath,[r] [14]and Meonothai *who* begot Ophrah. Seraiah begot Joab the father of Ge Harashim,[s] for they were craftsmen. [15]The sons of Caleb the son of Jephunneh *were* Iru, Elah, and Naam. The son of Elah *was* Kenaz. [16]The sons of Jehallelel *were* Ziph, Ziphah, Tiria, and Asarel. [17]The sons of Ezrah *were* Jether, Mered, Epher, and Jalon. And *Mered's wife*[t] *bore* Miriam, Shammai, and Ishbah the father of Eshtemoa. [18](His wife Jehudijah[u] bore Jered the father of Gedor, Heber the father of Sochoh, and Jekuthiel the father of Zanoah.) And these were the sons of Bithiah the daughter of Pharaoh, whom Mered took.

[19]The sons of Hodiah's wife, the sister of Naham, *were* the fathers of Keilah the Garmite and of Eshtemoa the Maachathite. [20]And the sons of

4:9 [q] Literally *He Will Cause Pain*
4:13 [r] Septuagint and Vulgate add *and Meonothai.*
4:14 [s] Literally *Valley of Craftsmen*
4:17 [t] Literally *she*
4:18 [u] Or *His Judean wife*

Life Lesson

1 Chronicles 4:1–9:1

SITUATION An individual's lineage was very important in Bible times. A person's tribe determined where that person would live or what occupation he or she would pursue (for example, Levites served in the temple). Prophecies stated that the Messiah would come from the line of David. Though careful records were kept, the genealogical listings in Chronicles were considered a condensed version, with certain names, lines, and generations omitted.

OBSERVATION Rather than merely listing names, several times the genealogy reveals glimpses into individuals' lives. It mentions small acts of faith, small deeds of kindness, and even "small" sins. Many of these people used their years on earth to serve God.

INSPIRATION A hospital is a microcosm of the world.

Why? Let me explain.

On the surface, a hospital appears to be a great place. The sheets are clean and the staff is friendly. Nurses come and go with warm smiles. Doctors periodically appear wearing nice loafers, a tie, and a kind face. Friends and family visit bringing pretty plants and friendly words.

There's a curiously large number of smiles here. I've walked the halls and been greeted by the smiling Candy Stripers pushing the coffee cart. The gift shop downstairs is full of magazines with smiling people on the covers. The lady selling them smiled broadly at me when I bought one. The receptionist at the front desk smiles when you pass by. . . .

Smiles, efficiency, distraction. I've seen some resorts that don't offer this kind of treatment. My, you almost forget where you are. . . .

But just when you relax—just when you begin to smile to yourself . . . a siren reminds you. The scream of the patient next door reminds you. Paramedics rushing a stretcher toward the emergency room remind you.

And the reminder is sobering. This is a hospital. The sole function of this

Continued

building is to bargain with death. The walls can't be white enough nor the staff polite enough to hide the stark reality of the bottom line: People come here to give all they have to postpone the inevitable.

We give it our best shot. We put up the best we have—the best technology, the best minds, the best equipment; and yet, at best we walk away with an extension, never a solution. And though we may walk or be wheeled out with smiles and waves of victory, down deep we know it is just a matter of time until the best we have won't be enough and the enemy will conquer. . . .

Our world is identical to a hospital. Have you ever noticed the endless extremes to which a person will go to hide the realities of life?

Take age for example. Do you know anyone who has not aged? Do you know anyone who is younger today than when you met him? Aging is a universal condition. But the way we try to hide it, you would think it was a plague! . . .

Dentures bring youth to the mouth, wrinkle cream brings youth to the face, and color in a bottle brings youth to the hair.

All to hide what everyone already knows—we're getting older.

Death is another lump in the carpet. We don't like it. (If you ever want to stall a conversation at a party just say, "How are you feeling about your approaching death?" It won't put much life into the conversation.)

I have a friend who has cancer. At present the cancer is in remission. Recently he had to go to the doctor for a physical. A nurse, apparently unaware of his condition, was asking him questions for his medical record. "Are you presently ill?"

"Well, yes. I have cancer."

She dropped her pencil and looked up at him. "Are you terminal?" she asked.

"Yes, aren't we all?"

You'd think we weren't, the way the subject is kept hush-hush. . . .

But this obsession with fleeing the facts is as maddening as it is futile. For, as in the case of the hospital, the truth always surfaces. A siren sounds causing reality to shock us out of our sleep.

Shimon *were* Amnon, Rinnah, Ben-Hanan, and Tilon. And the sons of
Ishi *were* Zoheth and Ben-Zoheth.
21The sons of Shelah the son of Judah *were* Er the father of Lecah,
Laadah the father of Mareshah, and the families of the house of the linen
workers of the house of Ashbea; 22also Jokim, the men of Chozeba, and
Joash; Saraph, who ruled in Moab, and Jashubi-Lehem. Now the records
are ancient. 23These *were* the potters and those who dwell at Netaim[v] and
Gederah;[w] there they dwelt with the king for his work.

The Family of Simeon

24The sons of Simeon *were* Nemuel, Jamin, Jarib,[x] Zerah,[y] *and* Shaul,
25Shallum his son, Mibsam his son, and Mishma his son. 26And the sons of
Mishma *were* Hamuel his son, Zacchur his son, and Shimei his son.
27Shimei had sixteen sons and six daughters; but his brothers did not have
many children, nor did any of their families multiply as much as the children of Judah.
28They dwelt at Beersheba, Moladah, Hazar Shual, 29Bilhah, Ezem,
Tolad, 30Bethuel, Hormah, Ziklag, 31Beth Marcaboth, Hazar Susim, Beth
Biri, and at Shaaraim. These *were* their cities until the reign of David.
32And their villages *were* Etam, Ain, Rimmon, Tochen, and Ashan—five
cities— 33and all the villages that *were* around these cities as far as Baal.[z]
These *were* their dwelling places, and they maintained their genealogy:
34Meshobab, Jamlech, and Joshah the son of Amaziah; 35Joel, and Jehu the
son of Joshibiah, the son of Seraiah, the son of Asiel; 36Elioenai, Jaakobah,
Jeshohaiah, Asaiah, Adiel, Jesimiel, and Benaiah; 37Ziza the son of Shiphi,
the son of Allon, the son of Jedaiah, the son of Shimri, the son of
Shemaiah— 38these mentioned by name *were* leaders in their families,
and their father's house increased greatly.
39So they went to the entrance of Gedor, as far as the east side of the valley, to seek pasture for their flocks. 40And they found rich, good pasture,
and the land *was* broad, quiet, and peaceful; for some Hamites formerly
lived there.
41These recorded by name came in the days of Hezekiah king of Judah;
and they attacked their tents and the Meunites who were found there, and
utterly destroyed them, as it is to this day. So they dwelt in their place, because *there was* pasture for their flocks there. 42Now *some* of them, five
hundred men of the sons of Simeon, went to Mount Seir, having as their
captains Pelatiah, Neariah, Rephaiah, and Uzziel, the sons of Ishi. 43And
they defeated the rest of the Amalekites who had escaped. They have dwelt
there to this day.

The Family of Reuben

5 Now the sons of Reuben the firstborn of Israel—he *was* indeed the firstborn, but because he defiled his father's bed, his birthright was given to
the sons of Joseph, the son of Israel, so that the genealogy is not listed according to the birthright; 2yet Judah prevailed over his brothers, and from
him *came* a ruler, although the birthright was Joseph's— 3the sons of Reuben the firstborn of Israel were Hanoch, Pallu, Hezron, and Carmi.

4:23 [v] Literally *Plants* [w] Literally *Hedges*
4:24 [x] Called *Jachin* in Genesis 46:10 [y] Called *Zohar* in Genesis 46:10
4:33 [z] Or *Baalath Beer* (compare Joshua 19:8)

4The sons of Joel *were* Shemaiah his son, Gog his son, Shimei his son,
5Micah his son, Reaiah his son, Baal his son, 6and Beerah his son, whom
Tiglath-Pileser[a] king of Assyria carried into captivity. He *was* leader of the
Reubenites. 7And his brethren by their families, when the genealogy of
their generations was registered: the chief, Jeiel, and Zechariah, 8and Bela
the son of Azaz, the son of Shema, the son of Joel, who dwelt in Aroer, as
far as Nebo and Baal Meon. 9Eastward they settled as far as the entrance of
the wilderness this side of the River Euphrates, because their cattle had
multiplied in the land of Gilead.
10Now in the days of Saul they made war with the Hagrites, who fell by their
hand; and they dwelt in their tents throughout the entire *area* east of Gilead.

The Family of Gad

11And the children of Gad dwelt next to them in the land of Bashan as far
as Salcah: 12Joel *was* the chief, Shapham the next, then Jaanai and Shaphat
in Bashan, 13and their brethren of their father's house: Michael,
Meshullam, Sheba, Jorai, Jachan, Zia, and Eber—seven *in all.* 14These *were*
the children of Abihail the son of Huri, the son of Jaroah, the son of Gilead,
the son of Michael, the son of Jeshishai, the son of Jahdo, the son of Buz;
15Ahi the son of Abdiel, the son of Guni, *was* chief of their father's house.
16And *the Gadites* dwelt in Gilead, in Bashan and in its villages, and in all
the common-lands of Sharon within their borders. 17All these were registered by genealogies in the days of Jotham king of Judah, and in the days
of Jeroboam king of Israel.
18The sons of Reuben, the Gadites, and half the tribe of Manasseh *had*
forty-four thousand seven hundred and sixty valiant men, men able to
bear shield and sword, to shoot with the bow, and skillful in war, who
went to war. 19They made war with the Hagrites, Jetur, Naphish, and
Nodab. 20And they were helped against them, and the Hagrites were delivered into their hand, and all who *were* with them, for they cried out to
God in the battle. He heeded their prayer, because they put their trust in
Him. 21Then they took away their livestock—fifty thousand of their
camels, two hundred and fifty thousand of their sheep, and two thousand of their donkeys—also one hundred thousand of their men; 22for
many fell dead, because the war *was* God's. And they dwelt in their place
until the captivity.

The Family of Manasseh (East)

23So the children of the half-tribe of Manasseh dwelt in the land. Their
numbers increased from Bashan to Baal Hermon, that is, to Senir, or
Mount Hermon. 24These *were* the heads of their fathers' houses: Epher,
Ishi, Eliel, Azriel, Jeremiah, Hodaviah, and Jahdiel. They were mighty men
of valor, famous men, *and* heads of their fathers' houses.
25And they were unfaithful to the God of their fathers, and played the
harlot after the gods of the peoples of the land, whom God had destroyed
before them. 26So the God of Israel stirred up the spirit of Pul king of Assyria, that is, Tiglath-Pileser[b] king of Assyria. He carried the Reubenites,
the Gadites, and the half-tribe of Manasseh into captivity. He took them to
Halah, Habor, Hara, and the river of Gozan to this day.

An old college roomie retires and you have to admit that if he is in the autumn of his life, you must be too.

You walk your daughter down the aisle. "When did she grow up?"...

Be the event pleasant or painful, the result is the same. Reality breaks through the papier-maché mask and screams at you like a Marine drill sergeant. "You *are* getting old! You *are* going to die! You *can't* be someone you are not!" . . .

The best thing for you to do now is pause and think. Take a good look at the facts. And while you're looking at them, it would be wise to take a good look at him. To those perched on the peak of Mount Perspective, His Majesty takes on special significance. Jesus does his best work at such moments. Just when the truth about life sinks in, his truth starts to surface. He takes us by the hand and dares us not to sweep the facts under the rug but to confront them with him at our side.

Aging? A necessary process to pass on to a better world.

Death? Merely a brief passage, a tunnel.

Self? Designed and created for a purpose, purchased by God himself.

There, was that so bad?

Funerals, divorces, illnesses, and stays in the hospital—you can't lie about life at such times. Maybe that's why he's always present at such moments. The next time you find yourself alone in a dark alley facing the undeniables of life, don't cover them with a blanket, or ignore them with a nervous grin. Don't turn up the TV and pretend they aren't there. Instead, stand still, whisper his name, and listen. He is nearer than you think.

(From *God Came Near* by Max Lucado)

APPLICATION What could you do for God this week? What are some ways you could serve that hardly seem worth mentioning (but could meet a real need)? Take the time to do even small deeds. They could be more important than the larger tasks you plan.

EXPLORATION Small Acts of Faith—Matthew 10:42; 25:34-40; Mark 14:8-9; Luke 10:33-35; Acts 28:2; Hebrews 11:20-24, 30-34.

5:6 [a] Hebrew *Tilgath-Pilneser*
5:26 [b] Hebrew *Tilgath-Pilneser*

The Family of Levi

6 The sons of Levi *were* Gershon, Kohath, and Merari. 2The sons of Kohath *were* Amram, Izhar, Hebron, and Uzziel. 3The children of Amram *were* Aaron, Moses, and Miriam. And the sons of Aaron *were* Nadab, Abihu, Eleazar, and Ithamar. 4Eleazar begot Phinehas, *and* Phinehas begot Abishua; 5Abishua begot Bukki, and Bukki begot Uzzi; 6Uzzi begot Zerahiah, and Zerahiah begot Meraioth; 7Meraioth begot Amariah, and Amariah begot Ahitub; 8Ahitub begot Zadok, and Zadok begot Ahimaaz; 9Ahimaaz begot Azariah, and Azariah begot Johanan; 10Johanan begot Azariah (it was he who ministered as priest in the temple that Solomon built in Jerusalem); 11Azariah begot Amariah, and Amariah begot Ahitub; 12Ahitub begot Zadok, and Zadok begot Shallum; 13Shallum begot Hilkiah, and Hilkiah begot Azariah; 14Azariah begot Seraiah, and Seraiah begot Jehozadak. 15Jehozadak went *into captivity* when the LORD carried Judah and Jerusalem into captivity by the hand of Nebuchadnezzar.

16The sons of Levi *were* Gershon,[c] Kohath, and Merari. 17These are the names of the sons of Gershon: Libni and Shimei. 18The sons of Kohath *were* Amram, Izhar, Hebron, and Uzziel. 19The sons of Merari *were* Mahli and Mushi. Now these *are* the families of the Levites according to their fathers: 20Of Gershon *were* Libni his son, Jahath his son, Zimmah his son, 21Joah his son, Iddo his son, Zerah his son, *and* Jeatherai his son. 22The sons of Kohath *were* Amminadab his son, Korah his son, Assir his son, 23Elkanah his son, Ebiasaph his son, Assir his son, 24Tahath his son, Uriel his son, Uzziah his son, and Shaul his son. 25The sons of Elkanah *were* Amasai and Ahimoth. 26*As for* Elkanah,[d] the sons of Elkanah *were* Zophai[e] his son, Nahath[f] his son, 27Eliab[g] his son, Jeroham his son, *and* Elkanah his son. 28The sons of Samuel *were* Joel[h] the firstborn, and Abijah the second.[i] 29The sons of Merari *were* Mahli, Libni his son, Shimei his son, Uzzah his son, 30Shimea his son, Haggiah his son, *and* Asaiah his son.

Musicians in the House of the LORD

31Now these are the men whom David appointed over the service of song in the house of the LORD, after the ark came to rest. 32They were ministering with music before the dwelling place of the tabernacle of meeting, until Solomon had built the house of the LORD in Jerusalem, and they served in their office according to their order.

33And these *are* the ones who ministered with their sons: Of the sons of the Kohathites *were* Heman the singer, the son of Joel, the son of Samuel, 34the son of Elkanah, the son of Jeroham, the son of Eliel,[j] the son of Toah,[k] 35the son of Zuph, the son of Elkanah, the son of Mahath, the son of Amasai, 36the son of Elkanah, the son of Joel, the son of Azariah, the son of Zephaniah, 37the son of Tahath, the son of Assir, the son of Ebiasaph, the son of Korah, 38the son of Izhar, the son of Kohath, the son of Levi, the son of Israel. 39And his brother Asaph, who stood at his right hand, *was* Asaph the son of Berachiah, the son of Shimea, 40the son of Michael, the son of Baaseiah, the son of Malchijah, 41the son of Ethni, the son of Zerah, the son of Adaiah, 42the son of Ethan, the son of Zimmah, the son of Shimei, 43the son of Jahath, the son of Gershon, the son of Levi.

44Their brethren, the sons of Merari, on the left hand, *were* Ethan the son of Kishi, the son of Abdi, the son of Malluch, 45the son of Hashabiah, the son of Amaziah, the son of Hilkiah, 46the son of Amzi, the son of Bani, the son of Shamer, 47the son of Mahli, the son of Mushi, the son of Merari, the son of Levi.

48And their brethren, the Levites, *were* appointed to every kind of service of the tabernacle of the house of God.

The Family of Aaron

49But Aaron and his sons offered sacrifices on the altar of burnt offering and on the altar of incense, for all the work of the Most Holy *Place,* and to make atonement for Israel, according to all that Moses the servant of God had commanded. 50Now these *are* the sons of Aaron: Eleazar his son, Phinehas his son, Abishua his son, 51Bukki his son, Uzzi his son, Zerahiah his son, 52Meraioth his son, Amariah his son, Ahitub his son, 53Zadok his son, *and* Ahimaaz his son.

Dwelling Places of the Levites

54Now these *are* their dwelling places throughout their settlements in their territory, for they were *given* by lot to the sons of Aaron, of the family of the

6:16 [c] Hebrew *Gershom* (alternate spelling of *Gershon,* as in verses 1, 17, 20, 43, 62, and 71)
6:26 [d] Compare verse 35 [e] Spelled *Zuph* in verse 35 and 1 Samuel 1:1 [f] Compare verse 34
6:27 [g] Compare verse 34
6:28 [h] Following Septuagint, Syriac, and Arabic (compare verse 33 and 1 Samuel 8:2) [i] Hebrew *Vasheni*
6:34 [j] Spelled *Elihu* in 1 Samuel 1:1 [k] Spelled *Tohu* in 1 Samuel 1:1

Kohathites: 55They gave them Hebron in the land of
Judah, with its surrounding common-lands. 56But the
fields of the city and its villages they gave to Caleb the
son of Jephunneh. 57And to the sons of Aaron they
gave *one of* the cities of refuge, Hebron; also Libnah
with its common-lands, Jattir, Eshtemoa with its
common-lands, 58Hilen[l] with its common-lands,
Debir with its common-lands, 59Ashan[m] with its
common-lands, and Beth Shemesh with its common-
lands. 60And from the tribe of Benjamin: Geba with its
common-lands, Alemeth[n] with its common-lands,
and Anathoth with its common-lands. All their cities
among their families *were* thirteen.

61To the rest of the family of the tribe of the
Kohathites *they gave* by lot ten cities from half the
tribe of Manasseh. 62And to the sons of Gershon,
throughout their families, *they gave* thirteen cities
from the tribe of Issachar, from the tribe of Asher,
from the tribe of Naphtali, and from the tribe of
Manasseh in Bashan. 63To the sons of Merari,
throughout their families, *they gave* twelve cities from
the tribe of Reuben, from the tribe of Gad, and from
the tribe of Zebulun. 64So the children of Israel gave
these cities with their common-lands to the Levites.
65And they gave by lot from the tribe of the children of
Judah, from the tribe of the children of Simeon, and
from the tribe of the children of Benjamin these cities
which are called by *their* names.

66Now some of the families of the sons of Kohath
were given cities as their territory from the tribe of
Ephraim. 67And they gave them *one of* the cities of
refuge, Shechem with its common-lands, in the
mountains of Ephraim, also Gezer with its common-
lands, 68Jokmeam with its common-lands, Beth
Horon with its common-lands, 69Aijalon with its
common-lands, and Gath Rimmon with its common-
lands. 70And from the half-tribe of Manasseh: Aner
with its common-lands and Bileam with its common-
lands, for the rest of the family of the sons of Kohath.

71From the family of the half-tribe of Manasseh the
sons of Gershon *were given* Golan in Bashan with its
common-lands and Ashtaroth with its common-
lands. 72And from the tribe of Issachar: Kedesh with
its common-lands, Daberath with its common-lands,
73Ramoth with its common-lands, and Anem with its
common-lands. 74And from the tribe of Asher: Mashal
with its common-lands, Abdon with its common-
lands, 75Hukok with its common-lands, and Rehob
with its common-lands. 76And from the tribe of
Naphtali: Kedesh in Galilee with its common-lands,
Hammon with its common-lands, and Kirjathaim
with its common-lands.

77From the tribe of Zebulun the rest of the children
of Merari *were given* Rimmon[o] with its common-
lands and Tabor with its common-lands. 78And on the
other side of the Jordan, across from Jericho, on the
east side of the Jordan, *they were given* from the tribe
of Reuben: Bezer in the wilderness with its common-
lands, Jahzah with its common-lands, 79Kedemoth
with its common-lands, and Mephaath with its
common-lands. 80And from the tribe of Gad: Ramoth
in Gilead with its common-lands, Mahanaim with its
common-lands, 81Heshbon with its common-lands,
and Jazer with its common-lands.

The Family of Issachar

7 The sons of Issachar *were* Tola, Puah,[p] Jashub, and
Shimron—four *in all.* 2The sons of Tola *were* Uzzi,
Rephaiah, Jeriel, Jahmai, Jibsam, and Shemuel, heads
of their father's house. *The sons* of Tola *were* mighty
men of valor in their generations; their number in the
days of David *was* twenty-two thousand six hundred.
3The son of Uzzi *was* Izrahiah, and the sons of
Izrahiah *were* Michael, Obadiah, Joel, and Ishiah. All
five of them *were* chief men. 4And with them, by their
generations, according to their fathers' houses, *were*
thirty-six thousand troops ready for war; for they had
many wives and sons.

5Now their brethren among all the families of Issachar
were mighty men of valor, listed by their genealogies,
eighty-seven thousand in all.

The Family of Benjamin

6*The sons* of Benjamin *were* Bela, Becher, and
Jediael—three *in all.* 7The sons of Bela were Ezbon,
Uzzi, Uzziel, Jerimoth, and Iri—five *in all.* They *were*
heads of *their* fathers' houses, and they were listed by
their genealogies, twenty-two thousand and thirty-
four mighty men of valor.

8The sons of Becher *were* Zemirah, Joash, Eliezer,
Elioenai, Omri, Jerimoth, Abijah, Anathoth, and
Alemeth. All these *are* the sons of Becher. 9And they were

6:58 [l] Spelled *Holon* in Joshua 21:15
6:59 [m] Spelled *Ain* in Joshua 21:16
6:60 [n] Spelled *Almon* in Joshua 21:18
6:77 [o] Hebrew *Rimmono,* alternate spelling of *Rimmon;* see 4:32
7:1 [p] Spelled *Puvah* in Genesis 46:13

recorded by genealogy according to their generations, heads of their fathers' houses, twenty thousand two hundred mighty men of valor. 10The son of Jediael *was* Bilhan, and the sons of Bilhan *were* Jeush, Benjamin, Ehud, Chenaanah, Zethan, Tharshish, and Ahishahar.

11All these sons of Jediael *were* heads of their fathers' houses; *there were* seventeen thousand two hundred mighty men of valor fit to go out for war *and* battle. 12Shuppim and Huppim[q] *were* the sons of Ir, *and* Hushim *was* the son of Aher.

The Family of Naphtali

13The sons of Naphtali *were* Jahziel,[r] Guni, Jezer, and Shallum,[s] the sons of Bilhah.

The Family of Manasseh (West)

14The descendants of Manasseh: his Syrian concubine bore him Machir the father of Gilead, the father of Asriel.[t] 15Machir took as his wife *the sister* of Huppim and Shuppim,[u] whose name *was* Maachah. The name of *Gilead's* grandson[v] *was* Zelophehad,[w] but Zelophehad begot only daughters. 16(Maachah the wife of Machir bore a son, and she called his name Peresh. The name of his brother *was* Sheresh, and his sons *were* Ulam and Rakem. 17The son of Ulam *was* Bedan.) These *were* the descendants of Gilead the son of Machir, the son of Manasseh.

18His sister Hammoleketh bore Ishhod, Abiezer, and Mahlah.

19And the sons of Shemida were Ahian, Shechem, Likhi, and Aniam.

The Family of Ephraim

20The sons of Ephraim *were* Shuthelah, Bered his son, Tahath his son, Eladah his son, Tahath his son, 21Zabad his son, Shuthelah his son, and Ezer and Elead. The men of Gath who were born in *that* land killed *them* because they came down to take away their cattle. 22Then Ephraim their father mourned many days, and his brethren came to comfort him.

23And when he went in to his wife, she conceived and bore a son; and he called his name Beriah,[x] because tragedy had come upon his house. 24Now his daughter *was* Sheerah, who built Lower and Upper Beth Horon and Uzzen Sheerah; 25and Rephah *was* his son, *as well* as Resheph, and Telah his son, Tahan his son, 26Laadan his son, Ammihud his son, Elishama his son, 27Nun[y] his son, and Joshua his son.

28Now their possessions and dwelling places *were* Bethel and its towns: to the east Naaran, to the west Gezer and its towns, and Shechem and its towns, as far as Ayyah[z] and its towns; 29and by the borders of the children of Manasseh *were* Beth Shean and its towns, Taanach and its towns, Megiddo and its towns, Dor and its towns. In these dwelt the children of Joseph, the son of Israel.

The Family of Asher

30The sons of Asher *were* Imnah, Ishvah, Ishvi, Beriah, and their sister Serah. 31The sons of Beriah *were* Heber and Malchiel, who was the father of Birzaith.[a] 32And Heber begot Japhlet, Shomer,[b] Hotham,[c] and their sister Shua. 33The sons of Japhlet *were* Pasach, Bimhal, and Ashvath. These *were* the children of Japhlet. 34The sons of Shemer *were* Ahi, Rohgah, Jehubbah, and Aram. 35And the sons of his brother Helem *were* Zophah, Imna, Shelesh, and Amal. 36The sons of Zophah *were* Suah, Harnepher, Shual, Beri, Imrah, 37Bezer, Hod, Shamma, Shilshah, Jithran,[d] and Beera. 38The sons of Jether *were* Jephunneh, Pispah, and Ara. 39The sons of Ulla *were* Arah, Haniel, and Rizia.

40All these *were* the children of Asher, heads of *their* fathers' houses, choice men, mighty men of valor, chief leaders. And they were recorded by genealogies among the army fit for battle; their number *was* twenty-six thousand.

The Family Tree of King Saul of Benjamin

8 Now Benjamin begot Bela his firstborn, Ashbel the second, Aharah[e] the third, 2Nohah the fourth, and Rapha the fifth. 3The sons of Bela *were* Addar,[f] Gera, Abihud, 4Abishua, Naaman, Ahoah, 5Gera, Shephuphan, and Huram.

7:12 [q] Called *Hupham* in Numbers 26:39
7:13 [r] Spelled *Jahzeel* in Genesis 46:24 [s] Spelled *Shillem* in Genesis 46:24
7:14 [t] The son of Gilead (compare Numbers 26:30, 31)
7:15 [u] Compare verse 12 [v] Literally *the second* [w] Compare Numbers 26:30–33
7:23 [x] Literally *In Tragedy*
7:27 [y] Hebrew *Non*
7:28 [z] Many Hebrew manuscripts, Bomberg, Septuagint, Targum, and Vulgate read *Gazza.*
7:31 [a] Or *Birzavith* or *Birzoth*
7:32 [b] Spelled *Shemer* in verse 34 [c] *Spelled* Helem *in verse 35*
7:37 [d] Spelled *Jether* in verse 38
8:1 [e] Spelled *Ahiram* in Numbers 26:38
8:3 [f] Called *Ard* in Numbers 26:40

6These *are* the sons of Ehud, who were the heads of the fathers' *houses* of
the inhabitants of Geba, and who forced them to move to Manahath:
7Naaman, Ahijah, and Gera who forced them to move. He begot Uzza and
Ahihud.
8Also Shaharaim had children in the country of Moab, after he had sent
away Hushim and Baara his wives. 9By Hodesh his wife he begot Jobab,
Zibia, Mesha, Malcam, 10Jeuz, Sachiah, and Mirmah. These *were* his sons,
heads of their fathers' *houses.*
11And by Hushim he begot Abitub and Elpaal. 12The sons of Elpaal *were*
Eber, Misham, and Shemed, who built Ono and Lod with its towns; 13and
Beriah and Shema, who *were* heads of their fathers' *houses* of the inhabitants
of Aijalon, who drove out the inhabitants of Gath. 14Ahio, Shashak,
Jeremoth, 15Zebadiah, Arad, Eder, 16Michael, Ispah, and Joha *were* the sons
of Beriah. 17Zebadiah, Meshullam, Hizki, Heber, 18Ishmerai, Jizliah, and
Jobab *were* the sons of Elpaal. 19Jakim, Zichri, Zabdi, 20Elienai, Zillethai,
Eliel, 21Adaiah, Beraiah, and Shimrath *were* the sons of Shimei. 22Ishpan,
Eber, Eliel, 23Abdon, Zichri, Hanan, 24Hananiah, Elam, Antothijah,
25Iphdeiah, and Penuel *were* the sons of Shashak. 26Shamsherai, Shehariah,
Athaliah, 27Jaareshiah, Elijah, and Zichri *were* the sons of Jeroham.
28These *were* heads of the fathers' *houses* by their generations, chief men.
These dwelt in Jerusalem.
29Now the father of Gibeon, whose wife's name *was* Maacah, dwelt at
Gibeon. 30And his firstborn son *was* Abdon, then Zur, Kish, Baal, Nadab,
31Gedor, Ahio, Zecher, 32and Mikloth, *who* begot Shimeah.[g] They also dwelt
alongside their relatives in Jerusalem, with their brethren. 33Ner[h] begot
Kish, Kish begot Saul, and Saul begot Jonathan, Malchishua, Abinadab,[i]
and Esh-Baal.[j] 34The son of Jonathan *was* Merib-Baal,[k] and Merib-Baal
begot Micah. 35The sons of Micah *were* Pithon, Melech, Tarea, and Ahaz.
36And Ahaz begot Jehoaddah;[l] Jehoaddah begot Alemeth, Azmaveth, and
Zimri; and Zimri begot Moza. 37Moza begot Binea, Raphah[m] his son,
Eleasah his son, *and* Azel his son.
38Azel had six sons whose names *were* these: Azrikam, Bocheru,
Ishmael, Sheariah, Obadiah, and Hanan. All these *were* the sons of Azel.
39And the sons of Eshek his brother *were* Ulam his firstborn, Jeush the second, and Eliphelet the third.
40The sons of Ulam were mighty men of valor—archers. *They* had
many sons and grandsons, one hundred and fifty *in all.* These *were* all
sons of Benjamin.

9 So all Israel was recorded by genealogies, and indeed, they *were* inscribed in the book of the kings of Israel. But Judah was carried away
captive to Babylon because of their unfaithfulness. 2And the first inhabitants who *dwelt* in their possessions in their cities *were* Israelites, priests,
Levites, and the Nethinim.

Dwellers in Jerusalem

3Now in Jerusalem the children of Judah dwelt, and some of the children of Benjamin, and of the children of Ephraim and Manasseh: 4Uthai

LIFE LESSON

1 Chronicles 9:2-44

SITUATION The families of Israel who lived in Jerusalem after the captivity were recorded.

OBSERVATION God holds his people accountable for the stewardship of their belongings. Each person must contribute to God's work and to the upkeep of his house.

INSPIRATION You have a responsibility to build up your church and help it to be and do what Jesus created it to be and do. You could do so much for your church if you would just give yourself and your church a chance. For instance, if your church has a weekly prayer meeting, you could get your whole youth group together and show up. It would be wild if you didn't tell your pastor in advance. You would blow his mind. Have you ever thought of doing that? Or, have you thought of going to a church business meeting to share your beliefs and convictions about how the church can minister to the world? Your church needs your input. If you come in a loving and humble manner, the faithful workers in the church will be thrilled to see you taking an active part in the life of the church. You will be a source of encouragement to everyone.

You need the church and the church desperately needs you. If you are not affiliated with the church, you have denied yourself one of the major means through which God wants to keep you faithful to Him.

(From *You Can Make a Difference* by Tony Campolo)

APPLICATION Do you participate in church? Use your God-given gifts, and temperament to help build the church. Help out in the nursery, with Sunday school, in a fellowship group . . .

EXPLORATION The Spiritual House of God—Matthew 16:18; Ephesians 1:22; Hebrews 3:6; 1 Peter 2:5.

8:32 [g] Spelled *Shimeam* in 9:38
8:33 [h] Also the son of Gibeon (compare 9:36, 39) [i] Called *Jishui* in 1 Samuel 14:49 [j] Called *Ishbosheth* in 2 Samuel 2:8 and elsewhere
8:34 [k] Called *Mephibosheth* in 2 Samuel 4:4
8:36 [l] Spelled *Jarah* in 9:42
8:37 [m] Spelled *Rephaiah* in 9:43

the son of Ammihud, the son of Omri, the son of Imri, the son of Bani, of the descendants of Perez, the son of Judah. 5Of the Shilonites: Asaiah the firstborn and his sons. 6Of the sons of Zerah: Jeuel, and their brethren—six hundred and ninety. 7Of the sons of Benjamin: Sallu the son of Meshullam, the son of Hodaviah, the son of Hassenuah; 8Ibneiah the son of Jeroham; Elah the son of Uzzi, the son of Michri; Meshullam the son of Shephatiah, the son of Reuel, the son of Ibnijah; 9and their brethren, according to their generations—nine hundred and fifty-six. All these men *were* heads of a father's *house* in their fathers' houses.

The Priests at Jerusalem

10Of the priests: Jedaiah, Jehoiarib, and Jachin; 11Azariah the son of Hilkiah, the son of Meshullam, the son of Zadok, the son of Meraioth, the son of Ahitub, the officer over the house of God; 12Adaiah the son of Jeroham, the son of Pashur, the son of Malchijah; Maasai the son of Adiel, the son of Jahzerah, the son of Meshullam, the son of Meshillemith, the son of Immer; 13and their brethren, heads of their fathers' *houses*—one thousand seven hundred and sixty. *They were* very able men for the work of the service of the house of God.

The Levites at Jerusalem

14Of the Levites: Shemaiah the son of Hasshub, the son of Azrikam, the son of Hashabiah, of the sons of Merari; 15Bakbakkar, Heresh, Galal, and Mattaniah the son of Micah, the son of Zichri, the son of Asaph; 16Obadiah the son of Shemaiah, the son of Galal, the son of Jeduthun; and Berechiah the son of Asa, the son of Elkanah, who lived in the villages of the Netophathites.

The Levite Gatekeepers

17And the gatekeepers *were* Shallum, Akkub, Talmon, Ahiman, and their brethren. Shallum *was* the chief. 18Until then *they had been* gatekeepers for the camps of the children of Levi at the King's Gate on the east.

19Shallum the son of Kore, the son of Ebiasaph, the son of Korah, and his brethren, from his father's house, the Korahites, *were* in charge of the work of the service, gatekeepers of the tabernacle. Their fathers had been keepers of the entrance to the camp of the LORD. 20And Phinehas the son of Eleazar had been the officer over them in time past; the LORD *was* with him. 21Zechariah the son of Meshelemiah *was* keeper of the door of the tabernacle of meeting.

22All those chosen as gatekeepers *were* two hundred and twelve. They were recorded by their genealogy, in their villages. David and Samuel the seer had appointed them to their trusted office. 23So they and their children *were* in charge of the gates of the house of the LORD, the house of the tabernacle, by assignment. 24The gatekeepers were assigned to the four directions: the east, west, north, and south. 25And their brethren in their villages *had* to come with them from time to time for seven days. 26For in this trusted office *were* four chief gatekeepers; they were Levites. And they had charge over the chambers and treasuries of the house of God. 27And they lodged *all* around the house of God because they *had* the responsibility, and they *were* in charge of opening *it* every morning.

Other Levite Responsibilities

28Now *some* of them were in charge of the serving vessels, for they brought them in and took them out by count. 29*Some* of them *were* appointed over the furnishings and over all the implements of the sanctuary, and over the fine flour and the wine and the oil and the incense and the spices. 30And *some* of the sons of the priests made the ointment of the spices.

31Mattithiah of the Levites, the firstborn of Shallum the Korahite, had the trusted office over the things that were baked in the pans. 32And some of their brethren of the sons of the Kohathites *were* in charge of preparing the showbread for every Sabbath.

33These are the singers, heads of the fathers' *houses* of the Levites, *who lodged* in the chambers, *and were* free *from other duties;* for they were employed in *that* work day and night. 34These heads of the fathers' *houses* of the Levites *were* heads throughout their generations. They dwelt at Jerusalem.

The Family of King Saul

35Jeiel the father of Gibeon, whose wife's name *was* Maacah, dwelt at Gibeon. 36His firstborn son *was* Abdon, then Zur, Kish, Baal, Ner, Nadab, 37Gedor, Ahio, Zechariah,[n] and Mikloth. 38And Mikloth begot Shimeam.[o] They also dwelt alongside their relatives in Jerusalem, with their brethren. 39Ner begot Kish, Kish begot Saul, and Saul begot Jonathan, Malchishua, Abinadab, and Esh-Baal. 40The son of Jonathan *was* Merib-Baal, and Merib-Baal begot Micah. 41The sons of Micah *were* Pithon, Melech,

9:37 *n* Called *Zecher* in 8:31
9:38 *o* Spelled *Shimeah* in 8:32

Tahrea,[p] *and Ahaz.*[q] 42And Ahaz begot Jarah;[r] Jarah begot Alemeth,
Azmaveth, and Zimri; and Zimri begot Moza; 43Moza begot Binea,
Rephaiah[s] his son, Eleasah his son, and Azel his son.
44And Azel had six sons whose names *were* these: Azrikam, Bocheru,
Ishmael, Sheariah, Obadiah, and Hanan; these *were* the sons of Azel.

Tragic End of Saul and His Sons

10 Now the Philistines fought against Israel; and the men of Israel fled
from before the Philistines, and fell slain on Mount Gilboa. 2Then
the Philistines followed hard after Saul and his sons. And the Philistines
killed Jonathan, Abinadab, and Malchishua, Saul's sons. 3The battle became fierce against Saul. The archers hit him, and he was wounded by the
archers. 4Then Saul said to his armorbearer, "Draw your sword, and thrust
me through with it, lest these uncircumcised men come and abuse me." But
his armorbearer would not, for he was greatly afraid. Therefore Saul took a
sword and fell on it. 5And when his armorbearer saw that Saul was dead, he
also fell on his sword and died. 6So Saul and his three sons died, and all his
house died together. 7And when all the men of Israel who *were* in the valley
saw that they had fled and that Saul and his sons were dead, they forsook
their cities and fled; then the Philistines came and dwelt in them.
8So it happened the next day, when the Philistines came to strip the
slain, that they found Saul and his sons fallen on Mount Gilboa. 9And they
stripped him and took his head and his armor, and sent word *throughout*
the land of the Philistines to proclaim the news *in the temple* of their idols
and among the people. 10Then they put his armor in the temple of their
gods, and fastened his head in the temple of Dagon.
11And when all Jabesh Gilead heard all that the Philistines had done to
Saul, 12all the valiant men arose and took the body of Saul and the bodies
of his sons; and they brought them to Jabesh, and buried their bones
under the tamarisk tree at Jabesh, and fasted seven days.
13So Saul died for his unfaithfulness which he had committed against the
LORD, because he did not keep the word of the LORD, and also because he consulted a medium for guidance. 14But *he* did not inquire of the LORD; therefore
He killed him, and turned the kingdom over to David the son of Jesse.

David Made King over All Israel

11 Then all Israel came together to David at Hebron, saying, "Indeed
we *are* your bone and your flesh. 2Also, in time past, even when Saul
was king, you *were* the one who led Israel out and brought them in; and the
LORD your God said to you, 'You shall shepherd My people Israel, and be
ruler over My people Israel.' " 3Therefore all the elders of Israel came to
the king at Hebron, and David made a covenant with them at Hebron before the LORD. And they anointed David king over Israel, according to the
word of the LORD by Samuel.

The City of David

4And David and all Israel went to Jerusalem, which is Jebus, where the
Jebusites *were,* the inhabitants of the land. 5But the inhabitants of Jebus

LIFE LESSON

1 Chronicles 10:1–12:40

SITUATION After Saul's death, David was anointed king of Judah. Even so, it was more than seven years later before he ruled over all of Israel. That seven year period was marked by civil war and Philistine domination.

OBSERVATION Failure results when people forsake God. We must choose to follow and fight for the kingdom that follows God rather than the one that forsakes him.

INSPIRATION On the very spot where the evil ambitions of the Third Reich were born, we came to proclaim the gospel of Jesus Christ. The Nazis had promised the German people a thousand-year regime of military might and power and awful judgment; I spoke to them of the good news of forgiveness and the love of God. It was a different time. It was a message for a people struggling between the failures of history and ideology and their hopes for peace and security.

The entire world watched via satellite when the Berlin Wall came down. I suspect a large part of the shock expressed by the world was not because the hideous wall had at last fallen, but that the emotional and political barriers to peace were being taken away, stone by stone. . . .

The place where I stood to address the German people on that afternoon in March 1990 was only yards away from the shattered section of the Berlin Wall where workers with saws and torches were ripping out the bars that supported the barriers. By a show of hands, I learned that more than half of the fifteen thousand to seventeen thousand people who came out to brave the wind and rain were from East Germany. They listened attentively and hopefully, and I wanted to give them a message of peace, a message as big as their dreams.

I told these expectant men and women that the world was watching them by satellite and that Christians everywhere were praying for them. I said it was "with tears of rejoicing and happiness as we watched you coming through the wall." Because of

Continued

9:41 [p] Spelled *Tarea* in 8:35 [q] Following Arabic, Syriac, Targum, and Vulgate (compare 8:35); Masoretic Text and Septuagint omit *and Ahaz.*
9:42 [r] Spelled *Jehoaddah* in 8:36
9:43 [s] Spelled *Raphah* in 8:37

these events, there was a new "hope that peace was on its way to our world." "God has answered our prayers," I assured them, and the changes taking place in the world prove that He cares for us.

(From *Storm Warning* by Billy Graham)

APPLICATION Which side are you on? Which kingdom do you fight for? Speak for? Pray for? Pray for the fortitude to stand for God's kingdom, even if it brings personal loss to you.

EXPLORATION Serve God—Exodus 23:22; Joshua 24:15; Galatians 6:7.

said to David, "You shall not come in here!" Nevertheless David took the
stronghold of Zion (that is, the City of David). [6]Now David said, "Whoever
attacks the Jebusites first shall be chief and captain." And Joab the son of
Zeruiah went up first, and became chief. [7]Then David dwelt in the stronghold; therefore they called it the City of David. [8]And he built the city
around it, from the Millo[t] to the surrounding area. Joab repaired the rest
of the city. [9]So David went on and became great, and the LORD of hosts *was*
with him.

The Mighty Men of David

[10]Now these *were* the heads of the mighty men whom David had, who
strengthened themselves with him in his kingdom, with all Israel, to make
him king, according to the word of the LORD concerning Israel.
[11]And this *is* the number of the mighty men whom David had:
Jashobeam the son of a Hachmonite, chief of the captains;[u] he had lifted
up his spear against three hundred, killed *by him* at one time.
[12]After him *was* Eleazar the son of Dodo, the Ahohite, who *was one* of the
three mighty men. [13]He was with David at Pasdammim. Now there the
Philistines were gathered for battle, and there was a piece of ground full of
barley. So the people fled from the Philistines. [14]But they stationed themselves in the middle of *that* field, defended it, and killed the Philistines. So
the LORD brought about a great victory.
[15]Now three of the thirty chief men went down to the rock to David, into
the cave of Adullam; and the army of the Philistines encamped in the
Valley of Rephaim. [16]David *was* then in the stronghold, and the garrison of
the Philistines *was* then in Bethlehem. [17]And David said with longing, "Oh,
that someone would give me a drink of water from the well of Bethlehem,
which is by the gate!" [18]So the three broke through the camp of the
Philistines, drew water from the well of Bethlehem that *was* by the gate,
and took *it* and brought *it* to David. Nevertheless David would not drink it,
but poured it out to the LORD. [19]And he said, "Far be it from me, O my God,
that I should do this! Shall I drink the blood of these men *who have put*
their lives *in jeopardy?* For at the risk of their lives they brought it."
Therefore he would not drink it. These things were done by the three
mighty men.
[20]Abishai the brother of Joab was chief of *another* three.[v] He had lifted
up his spear against three hundred *men,* killed *them,* and won a name
among *these* three. [21]Of the three he was more honored than the other two
men. Therefore he became their captain. However he did not attain to the
first three.
[22]Benaiah was the son of Jehoiada, the son of a valiant man from
Kabzeel, who had done many deeds. He had killed two lion-like heroes of
Moab. He also had gone down and killed a lion in the midst of a pit on a
snowy day. [23]And he killed an Egyptian, a man of *great* height, five cubits
tall. In the Egyptian's hand *there was* a spear like a weaver's beam; and he
went down to him with a staff, wrested the spear out of the Egyptian's
hand, and killed him with his own spear. [24]These *things* Benaiah the son of
Jehoiada did, and won a name among three mighty men. [25]Indeed he was

11:8 [t] Literally *The Landfill*
11:11 [u] Following Qere; Kethib, Septuagint, and Vulgate read *the thirty* (compare 2 Samuel 23:8).
11:20 [v] Following Masoretic Text, Septuagint, and Vulgate; Syriac reads *thirty*.

more honored than the thirty, but he did not attain to the
first three. And David appointed him over his guard.
26 Also the mighty warriors *were* Asahel the brother
of Joab, Elhanan the son of Dodo of Bethlehem,
27 Shammoth the Harorite,[w] Helez the Pelonite,[x] 28 Ira
the son of Ikkesh the Tekoite, Abiezer the Anathothite,
29 Sibbechai the Hushathite, Ilai the Ahohite,
30 Maharai the Netophathite, Heled[y] the son of Baanah
the Netophathite, 31 Ithai[z] the son of Ribai of Gibeah,
of the sons of Benjamin, Benaiah the Pirathonite,
32 Hurai[a] of the brooks of Gaash, Abiel[b] the Arbathite,
33 Azmaveth the Baharumite,[c] Eliahba the
Shaalbonite, 34 the sons of Hashem the Gizonite, Jonathan the son of Shageh the Hararite, 35 Ahiam the son
of Sacar the Hararite, Eliphal the son of Ur, 36 Hepher
the Mecherathite, Ahijah the Pelonite, 37 Hezro the
Carmelite, Naarai the son of Ezbai, 38 Joel the brother
of Nathan, Mibhar the son of Hagri, 39 Zelek the
Ammonite, Naharai the Berothite[d] (the armorbearer
of Joab the son of Zeruiah), 40 Ira the Ithrite, Gareb the
Ithrite, 41 Uriah the Hittite, Zabad the son of Ahlai,
42 Adina the son of Shiza the Reubenite (a chief of the
Reubenites) and thirty with him, 43 Hanan the son of
Maachah, Joshaphat the Mithnite, 44 Uzzia the
Ashterathite, Shama and Jeiel the sons of Hotham the
Aroerite, 45 Jediael the son of Shimri, and Joha his
brother, the Tizite, 46 Eliel the Mahavite, Jeribai and
Joshaviah the sons of Elnaam, Ithmah the Moabite,
47 Eliel, Obed, and Jaasiel the Mezobaite.

The Growth of David's Army

12 Now these *were* the men who came to David at
Ziklag while he was still a fugitive from Saul the
son of Kish; and they *were* among the mighty men,
helpers in the war, 2 armed with bows, using both the
right hand and the left in *hurling* stones and *shooting*
arrows with the bow. *They were* of Benjamin, Saul's
brethren.
3 The chief *was* Ahiezer, then Joash, the sons of
Shemaah the Gibeathite; Jeziel and Pelet the sons of
Azmaveth; Berachah, and Jehu the Anathothite;
4 Ishmaiah the Gibeonite, a mighty man among the
thirty, and over the thirty; Jeremiah, Jahaziel,
Johanan, and Jozabad the Gederathite; 5 Eluzai,
Jerimoth, Bealiah, Shemariah, and Shephatiah the
Haruphite; 6 Elkanah, Jisshiah, Azarel, Joezer, and
Jashobeam, the Korahites; 7 and Joelah and Zebadiah
the sons of Jeroham of Gedor.
8 *Some* Gadites joined David at the stronghold in the
wilderness, mighty men of valor, men trained for battle, who could handle shield and spear, whose faces
were like the faces of lions, and *were* as swift as gazelles
on the mountains: 9 Ezer the first, Obadiah the second,
Eliab the third, 10 Mishmannah the fourth, Jeremiah the
fifth, 11 Attai the sixth, Eliel the seventh, 12 Johanan the
eighth, Elzabad the ninth, 13 Jeremiah the tenth, and
Machbanai the eleventh. 14 These *were* from the sons of
Gad, captains of the army; the least was over a hundred, and the greatest was over a thousand. 15 These *are*
the ones who crossed the Jordan in the first month,
when it had overflowed all its banks; and they put to
flight all *those* in the valleys, to the east and to the west.
16 Then some of the sons of Benjamin and Judah
came to David at the stronghold. 17 And David went
out to meet them, and answered and said to them, "If
you have come peaceably to me to help me, my heart
will be united with you; but if to betray me to my enemies, since *there is* no wrong in my hands, may the
God of our fathers look and bring judgment." 18 Then
the Spirit came upon Amasai, chief of the captains,
and he said:

"*We are* yours, O David;
We *are* on your side, O son of Jesse!
Peace, peace to you,
And peace to your helpers!
For your God helps you."

So David received them, and made them captains of
the troop.
19 And *some* from Manasseh defected to David when
he was going with the Philistines to battle against Saul;
but they did not help them, for the lords of the
Philistines sent him away by agreement, saying, "He
may defect to his master Saul *and endanger* our heads."
20 When he went to Ziklag, those of Manasseh who defected to him were Adnah, Jozabad, Jediael, Michael,
Jozabad, Elihu, and Zillethai, captains of the thousands
who *were* from Manasseh. 21 And they helped David
against the bands *of raiders*, for they *were* all mighty
men of valor, and they were captains in the army. 22 For
at *that* time they came to David day by day to help him,
until *it was* a great army, like the army of God.

11:27 [w] Spelled *Harodite* in 2 Samuel 23:25 [x] Called *Paltite* in 2 Samuel 23:26
11:30 [y] Spelled *Heleb* in 2 Samuel 23:29 and *Heldai* in 1 Chronicles 27:15
11:31 [z] Spelled *Ittai* in 2 Samuel 23:29
11:32 [a] Spelled *Hiddai* in 2 Samuel 23:30 [b] Spelled *Abi-Albon* in 2 Samuel 23:31
11:33 [c] Spelled *Barhumite* in 2 Samuel 23:31
11:39 [d] Spelled *Beerothite* in 2 Samuel 23:37

LIFE LESSON

1 Chronicles 13:1–14:17

SITUATION God had given specific instructions concerning the sacred objects (Num. 4:15). God said he would put to death anyone who touched the Ark.

OBSERVATION David became angry at God. Yet, it was David's own neglect that brought God's severe action.

INSPIRATION Some time ago, I took my family to the bicycle store to purchase a bike for five-year-old Jenna. She picked out a shiny "Starlett" with a banana seat and training wheels. And Andrea, age three, decided she wanted one as well.

. . . I told her she was still having trouble with a tricycle and was too small for a two-wheeler. No luck; she still wanted a bike. . . .

Finally I sighed and said this time her daddy knew best. Her response? . . .

"Then I want a *new* daddy!"

Though the words were from a child's mouth, they carried an adult's sentiments.

. . . When we don't agree with the One who calls the shots, our reaction is often the same as Andrea's—the same as John's. . . . "Are you the one? Should we look for another?"

. . . John couldn't believe that anything less than his release would be for the best interest of all involved. . . . But the One who had the power was "sitting on his hands."

. . . You may learn, as John did, that the problem is not as much in God's silence as it is in your ability to hear.

(From *The Applause of Heaven* by Max Lucado)

APPLICATION God helps us avoid future mistakes by sending people to correct us. When you are corrected, use the opportunity to learn and improve your attitude and work!

EXPLORATION Obedience—Exodus 24:7; Psalm 143:10; Isaiah 1:19; Matthew 12:50; John 14:15, 23, 31.

David's Army at Hebron

23Now these *were* the numbers of the divisions *that were* equipped for
war, *and* came to David at Hebron to turn *over* the kingdom of Saul to him,
according to the word of the LORD: 24of the sons of Judah bearing shield
and spear, six thousand eight hundred armed for war; 25of the sons of
Simeon, mighty men of valor fit for war, seven thousand one hundred; 26of
the sons of Levi four thousand six hundred; 27Jehoiada, the leader of the
Aaronites, and with him three thousand seven hundred; 28Zadok, a young
man, a valiant warrior, and from his father's house twenty-two captains;
29of the sons of Benjamin, relatives of Saul, three thousand (until then the
greatest part of them had remained loyal to the house of Saul); 30of the
sons of Ephraim twenty thousand eight hundred, mighty men of valor, famous men throughout their father's house; 31of the half-tribe of Manasseh
eighteen thousand, who were designated by name to come and make David king; 32of the sons of Issachar who had understanding of the times, to
know what Israel ought to do, their chiefs were two hundred; and all their
brethren were at their command; 33of Zebulun there were fifty thousand
who went out to battle, expert in war with all weapons of war, stouthearted
men who could keep ranks; 34of Naphtali one thousand captains, and with
them thirty-seven thousand with shield and spear; 35of the Danites who
could keep battle formation, twenty-eight thousand six hundred; 36of
Asher, those who could go out to war, able to keep battle formation, forty
thousand; 37of the Reubenites and the Gadites and the half-tribe of
Manasseh, from the other side of the Jordan, one hundred and twenty
thousand armed for battle with every *kind* of weapon of war.

38All these men of war, who could keep ranks, came to Hebron with a loyal
heart, to make David king over all Israel; and all the rest of Israel *were* of one
mind to make David king. 39And they were there with David three days, eating and drinking, for their brethren had prepared for them. 40Moreover
those who were near to them, from as far away as Issachar and Zebulun and
Naphtali, were bringing food on donkeys and camels, on mules and oxen—
provisions of flour and cakes of figs and cakes of raisins, wine and oil and
oxen and sheep abundantly, for *there was* joy in Israel.

The Ark Brought from Kirjath Jearim

13 Then David consulted with the captains of thousands and hundreds, *and* with every leader. 2And David said to all the assembly of
Israel, "If *it seems* good to you, and if it is of the LORD our God, let us send
out to our brethren everywhere *who are* left in all the land of Israel, and with
them to the priests and Levites *who are* in their cities *and* their common-lands, that they may gather together to us; 3and let us bring the ark of our
God back to us, for we have not inquired at it since the days of Saul." 4Then
all the assembly said that they would do so, for the thing was right in the
eyes of all the people.

5So David gathered all Israel together, from Shihor in Egypt to as far as
the entrance of Hamath, to bring the ark of God from Kirjath Jearim. 6And
David and all Israel went up to Baalah,[e] to Kirjath Jearim, which belonged
to Judah, to bring up from there the ark of God the LORD, who dwells *between* the cherubim, where *His* name is proclaimed. 7So they carried the

13:6 [e] Called *Baale Judah* in 2 Samuel 6:2

ark of God on a new cart from the house of Abinadab, and Uzza and Ahio drove the cart. 8 Then David and all Israel played *music* before God with all *their* might, with singing, on harps, on stringed instruments, on tambourines, on cymbals, and with trumpets.

9 And when they came to Chidon's[f] threshing floor, Uzza put out his hand to hold the ark, for the oxen stumbled. 10 Then the anger of the LORD was aroused against Uzza, and He struck him because he put his hand to the ark; and he died there before God. 11 And David became angry because of the LORD's outbreak against Uzza; therefore that place is called Perez Uzza[g] to this day. 12 David was afraid of God that day, saying, "How can I bring the ark of God to me?"

13 So David would not move the ark with him into the City of David, but took it aside into the house of Obed-Edom the Gittite. 14 The ark of God remained with the family of Obed-Edom in his house three months. And the LORD blessed the house of Obed-Edom and all that he had.

David Established at Jerusalem

14 Now Hiram king of Tyre sent messengers to David, and cedar trees, with masons and carpenters, to build him a house. 2 So David knew that the LORD had established him as king over Israel, for his kingdom was highly exalted for the sake of His people Israel.

3 Then David took more wives in Jerusalem, and David begot more sons and daughters. 4 And these are the names of his children whom he had in Jerusalem: Shammua,[h] Shobab, Nathan, Solomon, 5 Ibhar, Elishua,[i] Elpelet,[j] 6 Nogah, Nepheg, Japhia, 7 Elishama, Beeliada,[k] and Eliphelet.

The Philistines Defeated

8 Now when the Philistines heard that David had been anointed king over all Israel, all the Philistines went up to search for David. And David heard *of it* and went out against them. 9 Then the Philistines went and made a raid on the Valley of Rephaim. 10 And David inquired of God, saying, "Shall I go up against the Philistines? Will You deliver them into my hand?"

The LORD said to him, "Go up, for I will deliver them into your hand."

11 So they went up to Baal Perazim, and David defeated them there. Then David said, "God has broken through my enemies by my hand like a breakthrough of water." Therefore they called the name of that place Baal Perazim.[l] 12 And when they left their gods there, David gave a commandment, and they were burned with fire.

13 Then the Philistines once again made a raid on the valley. 14 Therefore David inquired again of God, and God said to him, "You shall not go up after them; circle around them, and come upon them in front of the mulberry trees. 15 And it shall be, when you hear a sound of marching in the tops of the mulberry trees, then you shall go out to battle, for God has gone out before you to strike the camp of the Philistines." 16 So David did as God commanded him, and they drove back the army of the Philistines from Gibeon as far as Gezer. 17 Then the fame of David went out into all lands, and the LORD brought the fear of him upon all nations.

The Ark Brought to Jerusalem

15 *David* built houses for himself in the City of David; and he prepared a place for the ark of God, and pitched a tent for it. 2 Then David said, "No one may carry the ark of God but the Levites, for the LORD has chosen them to carry the ark of God and to minister before Him forever." 3 And David gathered all Israel together at Jerusalem, to bring up the ark of the LORD to its place, which he had prepared for it. 4 Then David assembled the children of Aaron and the Levites: 5 of the sons of Kohath, Uriel the chief, and one hundred and twenty of his brethren; 6 of the sons of Merari, Asaiah the chief, and two hundred and twenty of his brethren; 7 of the sons of Gershom, Joel the chief, and one hundred and thirty of his brethren; 8 of the sons of Elizaphan, Shemaiah the chief, and two hundred of his brethren; 9 of the sons of Hebron, Eliel the chief, and eighty of his brethren; 10 of the sons of Uzziel, Amminadab the chief, and one hundred and twelve of his brethren.

11 And David called for Zadok and Abiathar the priests, and for the Levites: for Uriel, Asaiah, Joel, Shemaiah, Eliel, and Amminadab. 12 He said to them, "You *are* the heads of the fathers' *houses* of the Levites; sanctify yourselves, you and your brethren, that you may bring up the ark of the LORD God of Israel to *the place* I have prepared for it. 13 For because you *did* not *do it* the first *time,* the LORD our God

13:9 [f] Called *Nachon* in 2 Samuel 6:6
13:11 [g] Literally *Outburst Against Uzza*
14:4 [h] Spelled *Shimea* in 3:5
14:5 [i] Spelled *Elishama* in 3:6 [j] Spelled *Eliphelet* in 3:6
14:7 [k] Spelled *Eliada* in 3:8
14:11 [l] Literally *Master of Breakthroughs*

LIFE LESSON

1 Chronicles 15:1–17:27

SITUATION David learned from his previous mistake. When they moved the Ark, David and his men carefully followed God's instructions.

OBSERVATION David's praise-filled reception of God's Ark demonstrates genuine spiritual worship. God showed that he was greatly pleased with such worship and honor.

INSPIRATION Although it is intensely personal, there is nothing self-centered about genuine worship. If believers are to maintain a consistent life-style of continuous worship, they need the fellowship and encouragement of other believers as they assemble for group worship. Individual worship and corporate worship feed each other. So on the one hand, I need the fellowship of the saints. On the other hand, the community of saints needs me to live a consistent life of worship.

The source of most of the problems people have in their Christian lives relates to two things: either they are not worshiping six days a week with their life, or they are not worshiping one day a week with the assembly of the saints. We need both.

If you go to church only when it is convenient, you will never be victorious and productive as a Christian. You can't succeed on your own; you need to have the spiritual stimulation of fellow believers. We live in such an easy-come, easy-go, casual, flippant society that people don't make consistent, faithful commitments, and then they wonder why they fail. The answer is clear. Spiritual success requires commitment to others. . . .

A pastor went to see a man who didn't attend church very faithfully. The man was sitting before a fire, watching the

broke out against us, because we did not consult Him about the proper
order."
[14]So the priests and the Levites sanctified themselves to bring up the ark
of the LORD God of Israel. [15]And the children of the Levites bore the ark of
God on their shoulders, by its poles, as Moses had commanded according
to the word of the LORD.
[16]Then David spoke to the leaders of the Levites to appoint their
brethren *to be* the singers accompanied by instruments of music, stringed
instruments, harps, and cymbals, by raising the voice with resounding
joy. [17]So the Levites appointed Heman the son of Joel; and of his brethren,
Asaph the son of Berechiah; and of their brethren, the sons of Merari,
Ethan the son of Kushaiah; [18]and with them their brethren of the second
rank: Zechariah, Ben,[m] Jaaziel, Shemiramoth, Jehiel, Unni, Eliab, Benaiah,
Maaseiah, Mattithiah, Elipheleh, Mikneiah, Obed-Edom, and Jeiel, the
gatekeepers; [19]the singers, Heman, Asaph, and Ethan, *were* to sound the
cymbals of bronze; [20]Zechariah, Aziel, Shemiramoth, Jehiel, Unni, Eliab,
Maaseiah, and Benaiah, with strings according to Alamoth; [21]Mattithiah,
Elipheleh, Mikneiah, Obed-Edom, Jeiel, and Azaziah, to direct with harps
on the Sheminith; [22]Chenaniah, leader of the Levites, was instructor *in
charge of* the music, because he *was* skillful; [23]Berechiah and Elkanah *were*
doorkeepers for the ark; [24]Shebaniah, Joshaphat, Nethanel, Amasai,
Zechariah, Benaiah, and Eliezer, the priests, were to blow the trumpets before the ark of God; and Obed-Edom and Jehiah, doorkeepers for the ark.
[25]So David, the elders of Israel, and the captains over thousands went to
bring up the ark of the covenant of the LORD from the house of Obed-
Edom with joy. [26]And so it was, when God helped the Levites who bore the
ark of the covenant of the LORD, that they offered seven bulls and seven
rams. [27]David was clothed with a robe of fine linen, as were all the Levites
who bore the ark, the singers, and Chenaniah the music master *with* the
singers. David also wore a linen ephod. [28]Thus all Israel brought up the
ark of the covenant of the LORD with shouting and with the sound of the
horn, with trumpets and with cymbals, making music with stringed instruments and harps.
[29]And it happened, *as* the ark of the covenant of the LORD came to the City
of David, that Michal, Saul's daughter, looked through a window and saw
King David whirling and playing music; and she despised him in her heart.

The Ark Placed in the Tabernacle

16 So they brought the ark of God, and set it in the midst of the tabernacle that David had erected for it. Then they offered burnt offerings
and peace offerings before God. [2]And when David had finished offering the
burnt offerings and the peace offerings, he blessed the people in the name
of the LORD. [3]Then he distributed to everyone of Israel, both man and
woman, to everyone a loaf of bread, a piece *of meat,* and a cake of raisins.
[4]And he appointed some of the Levites to minister before the ark of the
LORD, to commemorate, to thank, and to praise the LORD God of Israel:
[5]Asaph the chief, and next to him Zechariah, *then* Jeiel, Shemiramoth, Jehiel,
Mattithiah, Eliab, Benaiah, and Obed-Edom: Jeiel with stringed instruments
and harps, but Asaph made music with cymbals; [6]Benaiah and Jahaziel the
priests regularly *blew* the trumpets before the ark of the covenant of God.

15:18 *m* Following Masoretic Text and Vulgate; Septuagint omits *Ben.*

David's Song of Thanksgiving

7 On that day David first delivered *this psalm* into the hand of Asaph and his brethren, to thank the LORD:

8 Oh, give thanks to the LORD!
Call upon His name;
Make known His deeds among the peoples!
9 Sing to Him, sing psalms to Him;
Talk of all His wondrous works!
10 Glory in His holy name;
Let the hearts of those rejoice who seek the LORD!
11 Seek the LORD and His strength;
Seek His face evermore!
12 Remember His marvelous works which He has done,
His wonders, and the judgments of His mouth,
13 O seed of Israel His servant,
You children of Jacob, His chosen ones!

14 He *is* the LORD our God;
His judgments *are* in all the earth.
15 Remember His covenant forever,
The word which He commanded, for a thousand generations,
16 *The covenant which* He made with Abraham,
And His oath to Isaac,
17 And confirmed it to Jacob for a statute,
To Israel *for* an everlasting covenant,
18 Saying, "To you I will give the land of Canaan
As the allotment of your inheritance,"
19 When you were few in number,
Indeed very few, and strangers in it.

20 When they went from one nation to another,
And from *one* kingdom to another people,
21 He permitted no man to do them wrong;
Yes, He rebuked kings for their sakes,
22 *Saying,* "Do not touch My anointed ones,
And do My prophets no harm."[n]

23 Sing to the LORD, all the earth;
Proclaim the good news of His salvation from day to day.
24 Declare His glory among the nations,
His wonders among all peoples.

25 For the LORD *is* great and greatly to be praised;
He *is* also to be feared above all gods.
26 For all the gods of the peoples *are* idols,
But the LORD made the heavens.
27 Honor and majesty *are* before Him;
Strength and gladness are in His place.

warm glow of the coals. It was a cold winter day, but the coals were red hot, and the fire was warm. The pastor pleaded with the man to be more faithful in meeting with the people of God, but the man didn't seem to be getting the message.

So the pastor took the tongs beside the fireplace, pulled open the screen, and reached in and began to separate all the coals. When none of the coals was touching the others, he stood and watched in silence. In a matter of moments, they were all cold. "That's what's happening in your life," he told the man. "As soon as you isolate yourself from God's people, the fire goes out." The man got the message.

The church is not the brick-and-mortar building in which the assembly meets; it is God's people in whom He dwells. In the church—among God's people, the true worshipers—we must bring a worshiping heart to stimulate others while being stimulated to love and good works. As that stimulation affects our souls we do good and share. The cycle is complete when we live out the overflow of praise and a continual heart of thanksgiving. Then worship is a way of life. For that we were redeemed.

(From *The Ultimate Priority* by John MacArthur, Jr.)

APPLICATION Plan for a special day this Sunday. On Saturday night, start preparing your heart and mind for worship. On Sunday, anticipate worship.

EXPLORATION Attitude of Worship—Psalm 27:4; 51:6; 84:1-3; 1 Chronicles 29:9; John 4:23-24; Romans 12:1; Philippians 3:3; Hebrews 10:1-10.

16:22 *n* Compare verses 8–22 with Psalm 105:1–15

28 Give to the LORD, O families of the peoples,
Give to the LORD glory and strength.
29 Give to the LORD the glory *due* His name;
Bring an offering, and come before Him.
Oh, worship the LORD in the beauty
of holiness!
30 Tremble before Him, all the earth.
The world also is firmly established,
It shall not be moved.

31 Let the heavens rejoice, and let the earth
be glad;
And let them say among the nations, "The
LORD reigns."
32 Let the sea roar, and all its fullness;
Let the field rejoice, and all that *is* in it.
33 Then the trees of the woods shall rejoice
before the LORD,
For He is coming to judge the earth.[o]
34 Oh, give thanks to the LORD, for *He is* good!
For His mercy *endures* forever.[p]
35 And say, "Save us, O God of our salvation;
Gather us together, and deliver us from
the Gentiles,
To give thanks to Your holy name,
To triumph in Your praise."
36 Blessed *be* the LORD God of Israel
From everlasting to everlasting![q]

And all the people said, "Amen!" and praised the LORD.

Regular Worship Maintained

37So he left Asaph and his brothers there before the
ark of the covenant of the LORD to minister before the
ark regularly, as every day's work required; 38and
Obed-Edom with his sixty-eight brethren, including
Obed-Edom the son of Jeduthun, and Hosah, *to be*
gatekeepers; 39and Zadok the priest and his brethren
the priests, before the tabernacle of the LORD at the
high place that *was* at Gibeon, 40to offer burnt offerings to the LORD on the altar of burnt offering regularly morning and evening, and *to do* according to all
that is written in the Law of the LORD which He commanded Israel; 41and with them Heman and
Jeduthun and the rest who were chosen, who were
designated by name, to give thanks to the LORD, because His mercy *endures* forever; 42and with them
Heman and Jeduthun, to sound aloud with trumpets
and cymbals and the musical instruments of God.
Now the sons of Jeduthun *were* gatekeepers.
43Then all the people departed, every man to his
house; and David returned to bless his house.

God's Covenant with David

17 Now it came to pass, when David was dwelling
in his house, that David said to Nathan the
prophet, "See now, I dwell in a house of cedar, but the
ark of the covenant of the LORD *is* under tent curtains."
2Then Nathan said to David, "Do all that *is* in your
heart, for God *is* with you."
3But it happened that night that the word of God came
to Nathan, saying, 4"Go and tell My servant David,
'Thus says the LORD: "You shall not build Me a house
to dwell in. 5For I have not dwelt in a house since the
time that I brought up Israel, even to this day, but
have gone from tent to tent, and from *one* tabernacle *to*
another. 6Wherever I have moved about with all Israel,
have I ever spoken a word to any of the judges of Israel,
whom I commanded to shepherd My people, saying,
'Why have you not built Me a house of cedar?' " ' 7Now
therefore, thus shall you say to My servant David, 'Thus
says the LORD of hosts: "I took you from the sheepfold,
from following the sheep, to be ruler over My people
Israel. 8And I have been with you wherever you have
gone, and have cut off all your enemies from before you,
and have made you a name like the name of the great
men who *are* on the earth. 9Moreover I will appoint a
place for My people Israel, and will plant them, that
they may dwell in a place of their own and move no
more; nor shall the sons of wickedness oppress them
anymore, as previously, 10since the time that I commanded judges *to be* over My people Israel. Also I will
subdue all your enemies. Furthermore I tell you that
the LORD will build you a house.[r] 11And it shall be,
when your days are fulfilled, when you must go *to be*
with your fathers, that I will set up your seed after you,
who will be of your sons; and I will establish his kingdom. 12He shall build Me a house, and I will establish
his throne forever. 13I will be his Father, and he shall
be My son; and I will not take My mercy away from
him, as I took *it* from *him* who was before you. 14And
I will establish him in My house and in My kingdom
forever; and his throne shall be established forever." ' "
15According to all these words and according to all
this vision, so Nathan spoke to David.

16:33 [o] Compare verses 23–33 with Psalm 96:1–13
16:34 [p] Compare verse 34 with Psalm 106:1
16:36 [q] Compare verses 35, 36 with Psalm 106:47, 48
17:10 [r] That is, a royal dynasty

16Then King David went in and sat before the LORD; and he said: "Who
am I, O LORD God? And what is my house, that You have brought me this
far? 17And *yet* this was a small thing in Your sight, O God; and You have *also*
spoken of Your servant's house for a great while to come, and have regarded me according to the rank of a man of high degree, O LORD God.
18What more can David *say* to You for the honor of Your servant? For You
know Your servant. 19O LORD, for Your servant's sake, and according to Your
own heart, You have done all this greatness, in making known all these great
things. 20O LORD, *there is* none like You, nor *is there any* God besides You, according to all that we have heard with our ears. 21And who *is* like Your people
Israel, the one nation on the earth whom God went to redeem for Himself *as*
a people—to make for Yourself a name by great and awesome deeds, by driving out nations from before Your people whom You redeemed from Egypt?
22For You have made Your people Israel Your very own people forever; and
You, LORD, have become their God.

23"And now, O LORD, the word which You have spoken concerning Your
servant and concerning his house, *let it* be established forever, and do as
You have said. 24So let it be established, that Your name may be magnified
forever, saying, 'The LORD of hosts, the God of Israel, *is* Israel's God.' And
let the house of Your servant David be established before You. 25For You, O
my God, have revealed to Your servant that You will build him a house.
Therefore Your servant has found it *in his heart* to pray before You. 26And
now, LORD, You are God, and have promised this goodness to Your servant.
27Now You have been pleased to bless the house of Your servant, that it
may continue before You forever; for You have blessed it, O LORD, and *it
shall be* blessed forever."

David's Further Conquests

18 After this it came to pass that David attacked the Philistines, subdued them, and took Gath and its towns from the hand of the
Philistines. 2Then he defeated Moab, and the Moabites became David's
servants, *and* brought tribute.

3And David defeated Hadadezer[s] king of Zobah *as far as* Hamath, as he
went to establish his power by the River Euphrates. 4David took from him
one thousand chariots, seven thousand[t] horsemen, and twenty thousand
foot soldiers. Also David hamstrung all the chariot *horses,* except that he
spared enough of them for one hundred chariots.

5When the Syrians of Damascus came to help Hadadezer king of Zobah,
David killed twenty-two thousand of the Syrians. 6Then David put *garrisons* in Syria of Damascus; and the Syrians became David's servants, *and*
brought tribute. So the LORD preserved David wherever he went. 7And David took the shields of gold that were on the servants of Hadadezer, and
brought them to Jerusalem. 8Also from Tibhath[u] and from Chun, cities of
Hadadezer, David brought a large amount of bronze, with which Solomon
made the bronze Sea, the pillars, and the articles of bronze.

9Now when Tou[v] king of Hamath heard that David had defeated all the
army of Hadadezer king of Zobah, 10he sent Hadoram[w] his son to King David,

18:3 [s] Hebrew *Hadarezer,* and so throughout chapters 18 and 19
18:4 [t] Or *seven hundred* (compare 2 Samuel 8:4)
18:8 [u] Spelled *Betah* in 2 Samuel 8:8
18:9 [v] Spelled *Toi* in 2 Samuel 8:9, 10
18:10 [w] Spelled *Joram* in 2 Samuel 8:10

LIFE LESSON

1 Chronicles 18:1–22:1

SITUATION God gave David victory over the surrounding kings. David congratulated himself by taking a census of the people to portray his power.

OBSERVATION When David repented, he displayed how a leader can set an example through humility.

INSPIRATION We can have overflowing hearts that worship in spirit. First of all *we must be yielded to the Holy Spirit.* Before we can worship God in our spirit, the Holy Spirit has to be there to produce true worship. First Corinthians 2:11 says, "The thoughts of God no one knows except the Spirit of God." If you don't have the Spirit of God prompting your heart, motivating your heart, cleansing your heart, instructing your heart, you cannot worship God, because you cannot even know Him.

"No one can say, 'Jesus is Lord,' except by the Holy Spirit" (1 Corinthians 12:3). In other words, without the Holy Spirit, a person cannot truly affirm the Lordship of Christ. To worship Christ as sovereign requires prodding by the Holy Spirit. And we receive the Holy Spirit only upon the reception of Jesus as Savior and Lord. . . .

David was a king. He had more than a few things to worry about. And yet he sought to worship God with an undivided heart. In Psalm 86:11 David prayed, "Unite my heart to fear Thy name." (The expression "fear Thy name" is equivalent to the word *worship.*)

In Psalm 57:7, David wrote, "My heart is steadfast, O God, my heart is steadfast; I will sing, yes, I will sing praises." In other words, the music of praise rises out of a steadfast heart. In Psalm 108 we find the same thought. Verse 1 says, "My heart is steadfast, O God; I will sing, I will sing praises, even with my soul." Worship comes from a steadfast heart, a resolute heart, a determined heart, a heart focused solely on God.

Finally, *we must be repentant.* All sin must be dealt with. When we talk about worship we must talk about cleansing,

Continued

purging, purifying, confessing, repenting—because the only person who can enter into communion with an utterly holy God is one whose sin is dealt with. . . .

Maybe the reason we have difficulty really abandoning ourselves in worship to God, the reason we do not experience the nearness of God, is that we have areas in our lives that are not pure in the sight of God. We all have our blind spots and deficiencies only God knows. We must be open, willing to ask God to turn on the searchlight and expose whatever is in the shadows. We must yield our spirits to the Holy Spirit who fills us with His presence and power. We ask Him to cleanse every corner of our lives—and then the flow of worship can occur. (From *The Ultimate Priority* by John MacArthur, Jr.)

APPLICATION Do you have time for God? Are you too busy being successful to thank God for your skills or for otherwise helping you accomplish all you have so far? Do you need to reconsider your priorities? Memorize Psalm 139:23-24.

EXPLORATION Devotion—Psalm 25:4-5; 118:17-19; 143:5; Isaiah 40:31; Luke 2:25; Philippians 3:12-14; Hebrews 11:6.

to greet him and bless him, because he had fought against Hadadezer and
defeated him (for Hadadezer had been at war with Tou); and *Hadoram*
brought with him all kinds of articles of gold, silver, and bronze. [11]King David also dedicated these to the LORD, along with the silver and gold that he
had brought from all *these* nations—from Edom, from Moab, from the
people of Ammon, from the Philistines, and from Amalek.
[12]Moreover Abishai the son of Zeruiah killed eighteen thousand
Edomites[x] in the Valley of Salt. [13]He also put garrisons in Edom, and all the
Edomites became David's servants. And the LORD preserved David wherever he went.

David's Administration

[14]So David reigned over all Israel, and administered judgment and justice to all his people. [15]Joab the son of Zeruiah *was* over the army;
Jehoshaphat the son of Ahilud *was* recorder; [16]Zadok the son of Ahitub
and Abimelech the son of Abiathar *were* the priests; Shavsha[y] *was* the
scribe; [17]Benaiah the son of Jehoiada *was* over the Cherethites and the
Pelethites; and David's sons *were* chief ministers at the king's side.

The Ammonites and Syrians Defeated

19 It happened after this that Nahash the king of the people of Ammon
died, and his son reigned in his place. [2]Then David said, "I will show
kindness to Hanun the son of Nahash, because his father showed kindness to me." So David sent messengers to comfort him concerning his father. And David's servants came to Hanun in the land of the people of
Ammon to comfort him.
[3]And the princes of the people of Ammon said to Hanun, "Do you think
that David really honors your father because he has sent comforters to
you? Did his servants not come to you to search and to overthrow and to
spy out the land?"
[4]Therefore Hanun took David's servants, shaved them, and cut off their
garments in the middle, at their buttocks, and sent them away. [5]Then *some*
went and told David about the men; and he sent to meet them, because the
men were greatly ashamed. And the king said, "Wait at Jericho until your
beards have grown, and *then* return."
[6]When the people of Ammon saw that they had made themselves repulsive to David, Hanun and the people of Ammon sent a thousand talents of
silver to hire for themselves chariots and horsemen from Mesopotamia,[z]
from Syrian Maacah, and from Zobah.[a] [7]So they hired for themselves
thirty-two thousand chariots, with the king of Maacah and his people,
who came and encamped before Medeba. Also the people of Ammon
gathered together from their cities, and came to battle.
[8]Now when David heard *of it,* he sent Joab and all the army of the
mighty men. [9]Then the people of Ammon came out and put themselves in
battle array before the gate of the city, and the kings who had come *were* by
themselves in the field.
[10]When Joab saw that the battle line was against him before and behind, he
chose some of Israel's best, and put *them* in battle array against the Syrians.

18:12 [x] Or *Syrians* (compare 2 Samuel 8:13)
18:16 [y] Spelled *Seraiah* in 2 Samuel 8:17
19:6 [z] Hebrew *Aram Naharaim* [a] Spelled *Zoba* in 2 Samuel 10:6

11And the rest of the people he put under the command of Abishai his brother, and they set *themselves*
in battle array against the people of Ammon. 12Then
he said, "If the Syrians are too strong for me, then you
shall help me; but if the people of Ammon are too
strong for you, then I will help you. 13Be of good
courage, and let us be strong for our people and for
the cities of our God. And may the LORD do *what is*
good in His sight."

14So Joab and the people who *were* with him drew
near for the battle against the Syrians, and they fled before him. 15When the people of Ammon saw that the
Syrians were fleeing, they also fled before Abishai his
brother, and entered the city. So Joab went to Jerusalem.

16Now when the Syrians saw that they had been defeated by Israel, they sent messengers and brought
the Syrians who were beyond the River,[b] and
Shophach[c] the commander of Hadadezer's army
went before them. 17When it was told David, he gathered all Israel, crossed over the Jordan and came
upon them, and set up in battle array against them. So
when David had set up in *battle* array against the Syrians, they fought with him. 18Then the Syrians fled
before Israel; and David killed seven thousand[d] charioteers and forty thousand foot soldiers[e] of the Syrians, and killed Shophach the commander of the
army. 19And when the servants of Hadadezer saw that
they were defeated by Israel, they made peace with
David and became his servants. So the Syrians were
not willing to help the people of Ammon anymore.

Rabbah Is Conquered

20 It happened in the spring of the year, at the time
kings go out *to battle,* that Joab led out the armed
forces and ravaged the country of the people of Ammon,
and came and besieged Rabbah. But David stayed at Jerusalem. And Joab defeated Rabbah and overthrew it.
2Then David took their king's crown from his head, and
found it to weigh a talent of gold, and *there were* precious
stones in it. And it was set on David's head. Also he
brought out the spoil of the city in great abundance.
3And he brought out the people who *were* in it, and put
them to work[f] with saws, with iron picks, and with axes.
So David did to all the cities of the people of Ammon.
Then David and all the people returned *to* Jerusalem.

Philistine Giants Destroyed

4Now it happened afterward that war broke out at
Gezer with the Philistines, at which time Sibbechai
the Hushathite killed Sippai,[g] *who was one* of the sons
of the giant. And they were subdued.

5Again there was war with the Philistines, and Elhanan
the son of Jair[h] killed Lahmi the brother of Goliath the
Gittite, the shaft of whose spear *was* like a weaver's beam.

6Yet again there was war at Gath, where there was a
man of *great* stature, with twenty-four fingers and
toes, six *on each hand* and six *on each foot;* and he also
was born to the giant. 7So when he defied Israel, Jonathan the son of Shimea,[i] David's brother, killed him.

8These were born to the giant in Gath, and they fell
by the hand of David and by the hand of his servants.

The Census of Israel and Judah

21 Now Satan stood up against Israel, and moved
David to number Israel. 2So David said to Joab
and to the leaders of the people, "Go, number Israel
from Beersheba to Dan, and bring the number of
them to me that I may know *it.*"

3And Joab answered, "May the LORD make His people a hundred times more than they are. But, my lord
the king, *are* they not all my lord's servants? Why then
does my lord require this thing? Why should he be a
cause of guilt in Israel?"

4Nevertheless the king's word prevailed against
Joab. Therefore Joab departed and went throughout
all Israel and came to Jerusalem. 5Then Joab gave the
sum of the number of the people to David. All Israel
had one million one hundred thousand men who
drew the sword, and Judah *had* four hundred and
seventy thousand men who drew the sword. 6But he
did not count Levi and Benjamin among them, for the
king's word was abominable to Joab.

7And God was displeased with this thing; therefore
He struck Israel. 8So David said to God, "I have sinned
greatly, because I have done this thing; but now, I
pray, take away the iniquity of Your servant, for I have
done very foolishly."

9Then the LORD spoke to Gad, David's seer, saying,
10"Go and tell David, saying, 'Thus says the LORD: "I
offer you three *things;* choose one of them for yourself, that I may do *it* to you." ' "

11So Gad came to David and said to him, "Thus says

19:16 [b] That is, the Euphrates [c] Spelled *Shobach* in 2 Samuel 10:16
19:18 [d] Or *seven hundred* (compare 2 Samuel 10:18) [e] Or *horsemen* (compare 2 Samuel 10:18)
20:3 [f] Septuagint reads *cut them.*
20:4 [g] Spelled *Saph* in 2 Samuel 21:18
20:5 [h] Spelled *Jaare-Oregim* in 2 Samuel 21:19
20:7 [i] Spelled *Shimeah* in 2 Samuel 21:21 and *Shammah* in 1 Samuel 16:9

the LORD: 'Choose for yourself, [12]either three[j] years of famine, or three months to be defeated by your foes with the sword of your enemies overtaking *you,* or else for three days the sword of the LORD—the plague in the land, with the angel[k] of the LORD destroying throughout all the territory of Israel.' Now consider what answer I should take back to Him who sent me."

[13]And David said to Gad, "I am in great distress. Please let me fall into the hand of the LORD, for His mercies *are* very great; but do not let me fall into the hand of man."

[14]So the LORD sent a plague upon Israel, and seventy thousand men of Israel fell. [15]And God sent an angel to Jerusalem to destroy it. As he[l] was destroying, the LORD looked and relented of the disaster, and said to the angel who was destroying, "It is enough; now restrain your[m] hand." And the angel of the LORD stood by the threshing floor of Ornan[n] the Jebusite.

[16]Then David lifted his eyes and saw the angel of the LORD standing between earth and heaven, having in his hand a drawn sword stretched out over Jerusalem. So David and the elders, clothed in sackcloth, fell on their faces. [17]And David said to God, "Was it not I who commanded the people to be numbered? I am the one who has sinned and done evil indeed; but these sheep, what have they done? Let Your hand, I pray, O LORD my God, be against me and my father's house, but not against Your people that they should be plagued."

[18]Therefore, the angel of the LORD commanded Gad to say to David that David should go and erect an altar to the LORD on the threshing floor of Ornan the Jebusite. [19]So David went up at the word of Gad, which he had spoken in the name of the LORD. [20]Now Ornan turned and saw the angel; and his four sons *who were* with him hid themselves, but Ornan continued threshing wheat. [21]So David came to Ornan, and Ornan looked and saw David. And he went out from the threshing floor, and bowed before David with *his* face to the ground. [22]Then David said to Ornan, "Grant me the place of *this* threshing floor, that I may build an altar on it to the LORD. You shall grant it to me at the full price, that the plague may be withdrawn from the people."

[23]But Ornan said to David, "Take *it* to yourself, and let my lord the king do *what is* good in his eyes. Look, I *also* give *you* the oxen for burnt offerings, the threshing implements for wood, and the wheat for the grain offering; I give *it* all."

[24]Then King David said to Ornan, "No, but I will surely buy *it* for the full price, for I will not take what is yours for the LORD, nor offer burnt offerings with *that which* costs *me* nothing." [25]So David gave Ornan six hundred shekels of gold by weight for the place. [26]And David built there an altar to the LORD, and offered burnt offerings and peace offerings, and called on the LORD; and He answered him from heaven by fire on the altar of burnt offering.

[27]So the LORD commanded the angel, and he returned his sword to its sheath.

[28]At that time, when David saw that the LORD had answered him on the threshing floor of Ornan the Jebusite, he sacrificed there. [29]For the tabernacle of the LORD and the altar of the burnt offering, which Moses had made in the wilderness, *were* at that time at the high place in Gibeon. [30]But David could not go before it to inquire of God, for he was afraid of the sword of the angel of the LORD.

David Prepares to Build the Temple

22 Then David said, "This *is* the house of the LORD God, and this *is* the altar of burnt offering for Israel." [2]So David commanded to gather the aliens who *were* in the land of Israel; and he appointed masons to cut hewn stones to build the house of God. [3]And David prepared iron in abundance for the nails of the doors of the gates and for the joints, and bronze in abundance beyond measure, [4]and cedar trees in abundance; for the Sidonians and those from Tyre brought much cedar wood to David.

[5]Now David said, "Solomon my son *is* young and inexperienced, and the house to be built for the LORD *must be* exceedingly magnificent, famous and glorious throughout all countries. I will now make preparation for it." So David made abundant preparations before his death.

[6]Then he called for his son Solomon, and charged him to build a house for the LORD God of Israel. [7]And David said to Solomon: "My son, as for me, it was in my mind to build a house to the name of the LORD my God; [8]but the word of the LORD came to me, saying, 'You have shed much blood and have made great wars; you shall not build a house for My name, because you have shed much blood on the earth in My sight. [9]Behold, a son shall be born to you, who shall be a man of rest; and I will give him rest from all his enemies all around. His name shall be Solomon,[o] for I will give peace and quietness to Israel in his days. [10]He

21:12 [j] Or *seven* (compare 2 Samuel 24:13) [k] Or *Angel*, and so elsewhere in this chapter
21:15 [l] Or *He* [m] Or *Your* [n] Spelled *Araunah* in 2 Samuel 24:16
22:9 [o] Literally *Peaceful*

shall build a house for My name, and he shall be My son, and I *will be* his
Father; and I will establish the throne of his kingdom over Israel forever.'
11Now, my son, may the LORD be with you; and may you prosper, and build
the house of the LORD your God, as He has said to you. 12Only may the LORD
give you wisdom and understanding, and give you charge concerning Israel, that you may keep the law of the LORD your God. 13Then you will prosper, if you take care to fulfill the statutes and judgments with which the
LORD charged Moses concerning Israel. Be strong and of good courage; do
not fear nor be dismayed. 14Indeed I have taken much trouble to prepare for
the house of the LORD one hundred thousand talents of gold and one million talents of silver, and bronze and iron beyond measure, for it is so abundant. I have prepared timber and stone also, and you may add to them.
15Moreover *there are* workmen with you in abundance: woodsmen and
stonecutters, and all types of skillful men for every kind of work. 16Of gold
and silver and bronze and iron *there is* no limit. Arise and begin working,
and the LORD be with you."
17David also commanded all the leaders of Israel to help Solomon his son,
saying, 18"*Is* not the LORD your God with you? And has He *not* given you rest on
every side? For He has given the inhabitants of the land into my hand, and the
land is subdued before the LORD and before His people. 19Now set your heart
and your soul to seek the LORD your God. Therefore arise and build the sanctuary of the LORD God, to bring the ark of the covenant of the LORD and the
holy articles of God into the house that is to be built for the name of the LORD."

The Divisions of the Levites

23 So when David was old and full of days, he made his son Solomon
king over Israel.
2And he gathered together all the leaders of Israel, with the priests and
the Levites. 3Now the Levites were numbered from the age of thirty years
and above; and the number of individual males was thirty-eight thousand. 4Of these, twenty-four thousand *were* to look after the work of the
house of the LORD, six thousand *were* officers and judges, 5four thousand
were gatekeepers, and four thousand praised the LORD with *musical* instruments, "which I made," *said David,* "for giving praise."
6Also David separated them into divisions among the sons of Levi:
Gershon, Kohath, and Merari.
7Of the Gershonites: Laadan[p] and Shimei. 8The sons of Laadan: the first
Jehiel, then Zetham and Joel—three *in all.* 9The sons of Shimei:
Shelomith, Haziel, and Haran—three *in all.* These were the heads of the
fathers' *houses* of Laadan. 10And the sons of Shimei: Jahath, Zina,[q] Jeush,
and Beriah. These *were* the four sons of Shimei. 11Jahath was the first and
Zizah the second. But Jeush and Beriah did not have many sons; therefore
they were assigned as one father's house.
12The sons of Kohath: Amram, Izhar, Hebron, and Uzziel—four *in all.*
13The sons of Amram: Aaron and Moses; and Aaron was set apart, he and
his sons forever, that he should sanctify the most holy things, to burn incense before the LORD, to minister to Him, and to give the blessing in His
name forever. 14Now the sons of Moses the man of God were reckoned to
the tribe of Levi. 15The sons of Moses *were* Gershon[r] and Eliezer. 16Of the

23:7 [p] Spelled *Libni* in Exodus 6:17
23:10 [q] Septuagint and Vulgate read *Zizah* (compare verse 11).

LIFE LESSON

1 Chronicles 22:2–24:31

SITUATION David planned the temple. After the exile, these dimensions were used to rebuild the temple.

OBSERVATION In service to God, everyone's job remains important. Each person's part honors God.

INSPIRATION When we compare the present day churches to the original blueprint it is strikingly apparent that many deviations have been permitted which have been detrimental to the life of the church. Through the centuries the church gradually turned away from the simple provisions which made it such a powerful and compelling force in its early years, and there came in terrible distortions from which we are suffering greatly today. The popular thinking fastened upon the building as the identifying symbol and emphasis was put upon great imposing structures and massive cathedrals. In the beginning, "working in the church" meant to exercise a gift or perform a ministry among Christian people wherever they were, but gradually it came to mean doing some religious act within a building.

Along with this came a gradual transfer of responsibility from the people to what was termed "the clergy," which is a term derived from the Latin *clericus* meaning a priest. The scriptural concept that every believer is a priest before God was gradually lost and a special body of super-Christians emerged who were looked to for practically everything and so came to be termed "the ministry." . . .

When the ministry was thus left to the professionals there was nothing left for the people to do other than come to church and listen. They were told it was their responsibility to bring the world into the church building to hear the pastor preach the gospel. Soon Christianity became nothing but a spectator sport, very much akin to the definition of football—22 men down on the field, desperately in need of rest, and 20 thousand in the grandstands, desperately in need of exercise!

This unbiblical distortion has placed pastors under an unbearable burden. They have proved completely unequal

Continued

to the task of evangelizing the world, counseling the distressed and brokenhearted, ministering to the poor and needy, relieving the oppressed and afflicted, expounding the Scriptures, and challenging the entrenched forces of evil in an increasingly darkened world. They were never meant to do it. . . .

Nothing is more desperately needed than to return to the dynamic of the early church. . . .

Again it is the entire body of believers who must attempt the work of the ministry, equipped and guided by gifted men who are able to expound and apply the Scriptures with such wisdom that even the least believer discovers and begins to exercise the gift or gifts the Holy Spirit has given him. The whole body then stirs with resurrection power. Boldness and power again become the trademarks of the church of Jesus Christ.

(From *Body Life* by Ray C. Stedman)

APPLICATION How can you begin to serve God? Perhaps you can help lead a Bible study for new believers or even open your home so someone else can. Look for a way you can lift the load from someone else.

EXPLORATION Body of Believers—Romans 12:3-6; 1 Corinthians 12:4-27; 14:3-5; Ephesians 2:21; 4:11-12, 15-16.

sons of Gershon, Shebuel[s] *was* the first. 17Of the descendants of Eliezer,
Rehabiah was the first. And Eliezer had no other sons, but the sons of
Rehabiah were very many. 18Of the sons of Izhar, Shelomith *was* the first.
19Of the sons of Hebron, Jeriah *was* the first, Amariah the second, Jahaziel
the third, and Jekameam the fourth. 20Of the sons of Uzziel, Michah *was*
the first and Jesshiah the second.

21The sons of Merari *were* Mahli and Mushi. The sons of Mahli *were*
Eleazar and Kish. 22And Eleazar died, and had no sons, but only daughters; and their brethren, the sons of Kish, took them *as wives.* 23The sons of
Mushi *were* Mahli, Eder, and Jeremoth—three *in all.*

24These *were* the sons of Levi by their fathers' houses—the heads of the fathers' *houses* as they were counted individually by the number of their names, who did the work for the service of the house of the LORD, from the age of twenty years and above.

25For David said, "The LORD God of Israel has given rest to His people,
that they may dwell in Jerusalem forever"; 26and also to the Levites, "They
shall no longer carry the tabernacle, or any of the articles for its service."
27For by the last words of David the Levites *were* numbered from twenty
years old and above; 28because their duty *was* to help the sons of Aaron in the service of the house of the LORD, in the courts and in the chambers, in the purifying of all holy things and the work of the service of the house of
God, 29both with the showbread and the fine flour for the grain offering, with the unleavened cakes and *what is baked in* the pan, with what is mixed
and with all kinds of measures and sizes; 30to stand every morning to thank
and praise the LORD, and likewise at evening; 31and at every presentation of a burnt offering to the LORD on the Sabbaths and on the New Moons and on the set feasts, by number according to the ordinance governing them, regularly before the LORD; 32and that they should attend to the needs of the tabernacle of meeting, the needs of the holy *place,* and the needs of the sons of Aaron their brethren in the work of the house of the LORD.

The Divisions of the Priests

24 Now *these are* the divisions of the sons of Aaron. The sons of Aaron
were Nadab, Abihu, Eleazar, and Ithamar. 2And Nadab and Abihu
died before their father, and had no children; therefore Eleazar and
Ithamar ministered as priests. 3Then David with Zadok of the sons of
Eleazar, and Ahimelech of the sons of Ithamar, divided them according to the schedule of their service.

4There were more leaders found of the sons of Eleazar than of the sons of Ithamar, and *thus* they were divided. Among the sons of Eleazar *were* sixteen heads of *their* fathers' houses, and eight heads of their fathers'
houses among the sons of Ithamar. 5Thus they were divided by lot, one group as another, for there were officials of the sanctuary and officials *of the house* of God, from the sons of Eleazar and from the sons of Ithamar.
6And the scribe, Shemaiah the son of Nethanel, *one of* the Levites, wrote them down before the king, the leaders, Zadok the priest, Ahimelech the son of Abiathar, and the heads of the fathers' *houses* of the priests and Levites, one father's house taken for Eleazar and *one* for Ithamar.

7Now the first lot fell to Jehoiarib, the second to Jedaiah, 8the third to

23:15 [r] Hebrew *Gershom* (compare 6:16)
23:16 [s] Spelled *Shubael* in 24:20

Harim, the fourth to Seorim, [9]the fifth to Malchijah, the sixth to Mijamin, [10]the seventh to Hakkoz, the eighth to Abijah, [11]the ninth to Jeshua, the tenth to Shecaniah, [12]the eleventh to Eliashib, the twelfth to Jakim, [13]the thirteenth to Huppah, the fourteenth to Jeshebeab, [14]the fifteenth to Bilgah, the sixteenth to Immer, [15]the seventeenth to Hezir, the eighteenth to Happizzez,[t] [16]the nineteenth to Pethahiah, the twentieth to Jehezekel,[u] [17]the twenty-first to Jachin, the twenty-second to Gamul, [18]the twenty-third to Delaiah, the twenty-fourth to Maaziah.

[19]This *was* the schedule of their service for coming into the house of the LORD according to their ordinance by the hand of Aaron their father, as the LORD God of Israel had commanded him.

Other Levites

[20]And the rest of the sons of Levi: of the sons of Amram, Shubael;[v] of the sons of Shubael, Jehdeiah. [21]Concerning Rehabiah, of the sons of Rehabiah, the first *was* Isshiah. [22]Of the Izharites, Shelomoth;[w] of the sons of Shelomoth, Jahath. [23]Of the sons *of Hebron,*[x] Jeriah *was the first,*[y] Amariah the second, Jahaziel the third, *and* Jekameam the fourth. [24]*Of* the sons of Uzziel, Michah; of the sons of Michah, Shamir. [25]The brother of Michah, Isshiah; of the sons of Isshiah, Zechariah. [26]The sons of Merari *were* Mahli and Mushi; the son of Jaaziah, Beno. [27]The sons of Merari by Jaaziah *were* Beno, Shoham, Zaccur, and Ibri. [28]Of Mahli: Eleazar, who had no sons. [29]Of Kish: the son of Kish, Jerahmeel.

[30]Also the sons of Mushi *were* Mahli, Eder, and Jerimoth. These *were* the sons of the Levites according to their fathers' houses.

[31]These also cast lots just as their brothers the sons of Aaron did, in the presence of King David, Zadok, Ahimelech, and the heads of the fathers' *houses* of the priests and Levites. The chief fathers *did* just as their younger brethren.

The Musicians

25 Moreover David and the captains of the army separated for the service *some* of the sons of Asaph, of Heman, and of Jeduthun, who *should* prophesy with harps, stringed instruments, and cymbals. And the number of the skilled men performing their service was: [2]Of the sons of Asaph: Zaccur, Joseph, Nethaniah, and Asharelah;[z] the sons of Asaph *were* under the direction of Asaph, who prophesied according to the order of the king. [3]Of Jeduthun, the sons of Jeduthun: Gedaliah, Zeri,[a] Jeshaiah, Shimei, Hashabiah, and Mattithiah, six,[b] under the direction of their father Jeduthun, who prophesied with a harp to give thanks and to praise the LORD. [4]Of Heman, the sons of Heman: Bukkiah, Mattaniah, Uzziel,[c] Shebuel,[d] Jerimoth,[e] Hananiah, Hanani, Eliathah, Giddalti, Romamti-Ezer, Joshbekashah, Mallothi, Hothir, *and* Mahazioth. [5]All these *were* the sons of Heman the king's seer in the words of God, to exalt his horn.[f] For God gave Heman fourteen sons and three daughters.

24:15 [t] Septuagint and Vulgate read *Aphses.*
24:16 [u] Masoretic Text reads *Jehezkel.*
24:20 [v] Spelled *Shebuel* in 23:16
24:22 [w] Spelled *Shelomith* in 23:18
24:23 [x] Supplied from 23:19 (following some Hebrew manuscripts and Septuagint manuscripts)
[y] Supplied from 23:19 (following some Hebrew manuscripts and Septuagint manuscripts)
25:2 [z] Spelled *Jesharelah* in verse 14
25:3 [a] Spelled *Jizri* in verse 11 [b] *Shimei,* appearing in one Hebrew and several Septuagint manuscripts, completes the total of six sons (compare verse 17).
25:4 [c] Spelled *Azarel* in verse 18 [d] Spelled *Shubael* in verse 20 [e] Spelled *Jeremoth* in verse 22
25:5 [f] That is, to increase his power or influence

LIFE LESSON

1 Chronicles 25:1–27:34

SITUATION King David hoped to build the temple for God. In addition to planning and funding the temple, David spent time preparing the temple servants to be ready when Solomon finished the temple.

OBSERVATION David developed a plan so that operations would go smoothly. Each person fulfilled his or her role, working for the common good of God's people.

INSPIRATION At a recent conference, I shared the platform with my friend, Camille. Actually, she doesn't speak. Camille is an interpreter for the deaf who often travels with me to sign my messages. As I talked, her hands were working a mile a minute just to keep up. I spoke for almost an hour, got a sore throat, and had to pop a lozenge.

During break time I noticed my friend Francie sitting with Camille, giving her hands a deep massage. Camille signed, "Joni, your throat may be sore, but my hands are sore from your talk. My tendons are tight and this handrub is as soothing as—well, that lozenge on your throat."

It never occurred to me that Camille's hands could get tired of talking, or I should say, signing. As I watched Francie give Camille back the "voice" in her hands, I thought, *What a beautiful picture of the body of Christ working together.* One part can't do the job alone. When I speak, I need someone else's hands to push my chair to the platform. My deaf friends who are present can't hear unless Camille offers her hands to interpret. And Camille can't use her hands very long unless someone else gives her wrists and fingers a massage.

When it comes to giving the Gospel, it's always a cooperative effort of love and support. The Lord takes delight when His body works that way.

Someone needs you today. You could be the hands or the ears or the voice of someone who needs help. We're in this together so find a part of the body that can't be complete without you.

(From *Diamonds in the Dust* by Joni Eareckson Tada)

Continued

APPLICATION The Holy Spirit has assigned gifts and opportunities for service to each believer. How are you serving God with your abilities? Look for an opportunity today to honor God by giving of yourself to others.

EXPLORATION Serving God—Isaiah 45:9; Luke 12:47; Acts 13:2; 26:16; Romans 9:20-21; 1 Corinthians 12:7; Ephesians 6:7.

6 All these *were* under the direction of their father for the music *in* the
house of the LORD, with cymbals, stringed instruments, and harps, for the
service of the house of God. Asaph, Jeduthun, and Heman *were* under the
authority of the king. 7 So the number of them, with their brethren who
were instructed in the songs of the LORD, all who were skillful, *was* two
hundred and eighty-eight.

8 And they cast lots for their duty, the small as well as the great, the
teacher with the student.

9 Now the first lot for Asaph came out for Joseph; the second for
Gedaliah, him with his brethren and sons, twelve; 10 the third for Zaccur,
his sons and his brethren, twelve; 11 the fourth for Jizri,[g] his sons and his
brethren, twelve; 12 the fifth for Nethaniah, his sons and his brethren,
twelve; 13 the sixth for Bukkiah, his sons and his brethren, twelve; 14 the seventh for Jesharelah,[h] his sons and his brethren, twelve; 15 the eighth for
Jeshaiah, his sons and his brethren, twelve; 16 the ninth for Mattaniah, his
sons and his brethren, twelve; 17 the tenth for Shimei, his sons and his
brethren, twelve; 18 the eleventh for Azarel,[i] his sons and his brethren,
twelve; 19 the twelfth for Hashabiah, his sons and his brethren, twelve; 20 the
thirteenth for Shubael,[j] his sons and his brethren, twelve; 21 the fourteenth
for Mattithiah, his sons and his brethren, twelve; 22 the fifteenth for
Jeremoth,[k] his sons and his brethren, twelve; 23 the sixteenth for Hananiah,
his sons and his brethren, twelve; 24 the seventeenth for Joshbekashah, his
sons and his brethren, twelve; 25 the eighteenth for Hanani, his sons and
his brethren, twelve; 26 the nineteenth for Mallothi, his sons and his
brethren, twelve; 27 the twentieth for Eliathah, his sons and his brethren,
twelve; 28 the twenty-first for Hothir, his sons and his brethren, twelve;
29 the twenty-second for Giddalti, his sons and his brethren, twelve; 30 the
twenty-third for Mahazioth, his sons and his brethren, twelve; 31 the
twenty-fourth for Romamti-Ezer, his sons and his brethren, twelve.

The Gatekeepers

26 Concerning the divisions of the gatekeepers: of the Korahites,
Meshelemiah the son of Kore, of the sons of Asaph. 2 And the sons
of Meshelemiah *were* Zechariah the firstborn, Jediael the second,
Zebadiah the third, Jathniel the fourth, 3 Elam the fifth, Jehohanan the
sixth, Eliehoenai the seventh.

4 Moreover the sons of Obed-Edom *were* Shemaiah the firstborn,
Jehozabad the second, Joah the third, Sacar the fourth, Nethanel the fifth,
5 Ammiel the sixth, Issachar the seventh, Peulthai the eighth; for God
blessed him.

6 Also to Shemaiah his son were sons born who governed their fathers'
houses, because they *were* men of great ability. 7 The sons of Shemaiah *were*
Othni, Rephael, Obed, and Elzabad, whose brothers Elihu and Semachiah
were able men.

8 All these *were* of the sons of Obed-Edom, they and their sons and their
brethren, able men with strength for the work: sixty-two of Obed-Edom.

25:11 [g] Spelled *Zeri* in verse 3
25:14 [h] Spelled *Asharelah* in verse 2
25:18 [i] Spelled *Uzziel* in verse 4
25:20 [j] Spelled *Shebuel* in verse 4
25:22 [k] Spelled *Jerimoth* in verse 4

9And Meshelemiah had sons and brethren, eighteen able men.
10Also Hosah, of the children of Merari, had sons:
Shimri the first (for *though* he was not the firstborn,
his father made him the first), 11Hilkiah the second,
Tebaliah the third, Zechariah the fourth; all the sons
and brethren of Hosah *were* thirteen.
12Among these *were* the divisions of the gatekeepers,
among the chief men, *having* duties just like their
brethren, to serve in the house of the LORD. 13And they
cast lots for each gate, the small as well as the great, according to their father's house. 14The lot for the East *Gate*
fell to Shelemiah. Then they cast lots *for* his son
Zechariah, a wise counselor, and his lot came out for the
North Gate; 15to Obed-Edom the South Gate, and to his
sons the storehouse.[l] 16To Shuppim and Hosah *the lot*
came out for the West Gate, with the Shallecheth Gate on
the ascending highway—watchman opposite watchman. 17On the east were *six* Levites, on the north four
each day, on the south four each day, and for the storehouse[m] two by two. 18As for the Parbar[n] on the west,
there were four on the highway *and* two at the Parbar.
19These were the divisions of the gatekeepers among the
sons of Korah and among the sons of Merari.

The Treasuries and Other Duties

20Of the Levites, Ahijah *was* over the treasuries of
the house of God and over the treasuries of the dedicated things. 21The sons of Laadan, the descendants of
the Gershonites of Laadan, heads of their fathers'
houses, of Laadan the Gershonite: Jehieli. 22The sons
of Jehieli, Zetham and Joel his brother, *were* over the
treasuries of the house of the LORD. 23Of the
Amramites, the Izharites, the Hebronites, and the
Uzzielites: 24Shebuel the son of Gershom, the son of
Moses, *was* overseer of the treasuries. 25And his
brethren by Eliezer *were* Rehabiah his son, Jeshaiah
his son, Joram his son, Zichri his son, and Shelomith
his son.
26This Shelomith and his brethren *were* over all the
treasuries of the dedicated things which King David
and the heads of fathers' *houses,* the captains over
thousands and hundreds, and the captains of the
army, had dedicated. 27Some of the spoils won in battles they dedicated to maintain the house of the LORD.
28And all that Samuel the seer, Saul the son of Kish,
Abner the son of Ner, and Joab the son of Zeruiah had
dedicated, every dedicated *thing,* was under the hand
of Shelomith and his brethren.
29Of the Izharites, Chenaniah and his sons *per-*
formed duties as officials and judges over Israel outside Jerusalem.
30Of the Hebronites, Hashabiah and his brethren,
one thousand seven hundred able men, had the oversight of Israel on the west side of the Jordan for all the
business of the LORD, and in the service of the king.
31Among the Hebronites, Jerijah *was* head of the
Hebronites according to his genealogy of the fathers.
In the fortieth year of the reign of David they were
sought, and there were found among them capable
men at Jazer of Gilead. 32And his brethren *were* two
thousand seven hundred able men, heads of fathers'
houses, whom King David made officials over the
Reubenites, the Gadites, and the half-tribe of
Manasseh, for every matter pertaining to God and the
affairs of the king.

The Military Divisions

27 And the children of Israel, according to their
number, the heads of fathers' *houses,* the captains of thousands and hundreds and their officers,
served the king in every matter of the *military* divisions. *These divisions* came in and went out month by
month throughout all the months of the year, each
division *having* twenty-four thousand.
2Over the first division for the first month *was*
Jashobeam the son of Zabdiel, and in his division
were twenty-four thousand; 3*he was* of the children of
Perez, and the chief of all the captains of the army for
the first month. 4Over the division of the second
month *was* Dodai[o] an Ahohite, and of his division
Mikloth also *was* the leader; in his division *were*
twenty-four thousand. 5The third captain of the army
for the third month *was* Benaiah, the son of Jehoiada
the priest, who was chief; in his division *were* twenty-
four thousand. 6This was the Benaiah *who was*
mighty *among* the thirty, and was over the thirty; in
his division *was* Ammizabad his son. 7The fourth *cap-*
tain for the fourth month *was* Asahel the brother of
Joab, and Zebadiah his son after him; in his division
were twenty-four thousand. 8The fifth *captain* for the
fifth month *was* Shamhuth[p] the Izrahite; in his division were twenty-four thousand. 9The sixth *captain*
for the sixth month *was* Ira the son of Ikkesh the

26:15 [l] Hebrew *asuppim*
26:17 [m] Hebrew *asuppim*
26:18 [n] Probably a court or colonnade extending west of the temple
27:4 [o] Hebrew *Dodai,* usually spelled *Dodo* (compare 2 Samuel 23:9)
27:8 [p] Spelled *Shammoth* in 11:27 and *Shammah* in 2 Samuel 23:11

Tekoite; in his division *were* twenty-four thousand. [10]The seventh *captain* for the seventh month *was* Helez the Pelonite, of the children of Ephraim; in his division *were* twenty-four thousand. [11]The eighth *captain* for the eighth month *was* Sibbechai the Hushathite, of the Zarhites; in his division *were* twenty-four thousand. [12]The ninth *captain* for the ninth month *was* Abiezer the Anathothite, of the Benjamites; in his division *were* twenty-four thousand. [13]The tenth *captain* for the tenth month *was* Maharai the Netophathite, of the Zarhites; in his division *were* twenty-four thousand. [14]The eleventh *captain* for the eleventh month *was* Benaiah the Pirathonite, of the children of Ephraim; in his division *were* twenty-four thousand. [15]The twelfth *captain* for the twelfth month *was* Heldai[q] the Netophathite, of Othniel; in his division *were* twenty-four thousand.

Leaders of Tribes

[16]Furthermore, over the tribes of Israel: the officer over the Reubenites *was* Eliezer the son of Zichri; over the Simeonites, Shephatiah the son of Maachah; [17]*over* the Levites, Hashabiah the son of Kemuel; over the Aaronites, Zadok; [18]*over* Judah, Elihu, *one* of David's brothers; *over* Issachar, Omri the son of Michael; [19]*over* Zebulun, Ishmaiah the son of Obadiah; *over* Naphtali, Jerimoth the son of Azriel; [20]*over* the children of Ephraim, Hoshea the son of Azaziah; *over* the half-tribe of Manasseh, Joel the son of Pedaiah; [21]*over* the half-*tribe* of Manasseh in Gilead, Iddo the son of Zechariah; *over* Benjamin, Jaasiel the son of Abner; [22]*over* Dan, Azarel the son of Jeroham. These *were* the leaders of the tribes of Israel.

[23]But David did not take the number of those twenty years old and under, because the LORD had said He would multiply Israel like the stars of the heavens. [24]Joab the son of Zeruiah began a census, but he did not finish, for wrath came upon Israel because of this census; nor was the number recorded in the account of the chronicles of King David.

Other State Officials

[25]And Azmaveth the son of Adiel *was* over the king's treasuries; and Jehonathan the son of Uzziah was over the storehouses in the field, in the cities, in the villages, and in the fortresses. [26]Ezri the son of Chelub was over those who did the work of the field for tilling the ground. [27]And Shimei the Ramathite *was* over the vineyards, and Zabdi the Shiphmite was over the produce of the vineyards for the supply of wine. [28]Baal-Hanan the Gederite was over the olive trees and the sycamore trees that *were* in the lowlands, and Joash *was* over the store of oil. [29]And Shitrai the Sharonite *was* over the herds that fed in Sharon, and Shaphat the son of Adlai was over the herds *that were* in the valleys. [30]Obil the Ishmaelite *was* over the camels, Jehdeiah the Meronothite *was* over the donkeys, [31]and Jaziz the Hagrite *was* over the flocks. All these *were* the officials over King David's property.

[32]Also Jehonathan, David's uncle, *was* a counselor, a wise man, and a scribe; and Jehiel the son of Hachmoni *was* with the king's sons. [33]Ahithophel *was* the king's counselor, and Hushai the Archite *was* the king's companion. [34]After Ahithophel *was* Jehoiada the son of Benaiah, then Abiathar. And the general of the king's army *was* Joab.

Solomon Instructed to Build the Temple

28 Now David assembled at Jerusalem all the leaders of Israel: the officers of the tribes and the captains of the divisions who served the king, the captains over thousands and captains over hundreds, and the stewards over all the substance and possessions of the king and of his sons, with the officials, the valiant men, and all the mighty men of valor.

[2]Then King David rose to his feet and said, "Hear me, my brethren and my people: I *had* it in my heart to build a house of rest for the ark of the covenant of the LORD, and for the footstool of our God, and had made preparations to build it. [3]But God said to me, 'You shall not build a house for My name, because you *have been* a man of war and have shed blood.' [4]However the LORD God of Israel chose me above all the house of my father to be king over Israel forever, for He has chosen Judah *to be* the ruler. And of the house of Judah, the house of my father, and among the sons of my father, He was pleased with me to make *me* king over all Israel. [5]And of all my sons (for the LORD has given me many sons) He has chosen my son Solomon to sit on the throne of the kingdom of the LORD over Israel. [6]Now He said to me, 'It is your son Solomon *who* shall build My house and My courts; for I have chosen him *to be* My son, and I will be his Father. [7]Moreover I will establish his kingdom forever, if he is steadfast to observe My commandments and My judgments, as it is this day.' [8]Now therefore, in the sight of all Israel, the assembly of the LORD, and in the hearing of our God, be careful to seek

27:15 [q] Spelled *Heled* in 11:30 and *Heleb* in 2 Samuel 23:29

out all the commandments of the LORD your God, that you may possess this
good land, and leave *it* as an inheritance for your children after you forever.
9“As for you, my son Solomon, know the God of your father, and serve
Him with a loyal heart and with a willing mind; for the LORD searches all
hearts and understands all the intent of the thoughts. If you seek Him, He
will be found by you; but if you forsake Him, He will cast you off forever.
10Consider now, for the LORD has chosen you to build a house for the sanctuary; be strong, and do it.”
11Then David gave his son Solomon the plans for the vestibule, its
houses, its treasuries, its upper chambers, its inner chambers, and the
place of the mercy seat; 12and the plans for all that he had by the Spirit, of
the courts of the house of the LORD, of all the chambers all around, of the
treasuries of the house of God, and of the treasuries for the dedicated
things; 13also for the division of the priests and the Levites, for all the work
of the service of the house of the LORD, and for all the articles of service in
the house of the LORD. 14*He gave* gold by weight for *things* of gold, for all articles used in every kind of service; also *silver* for all articles of silver by
weight, for all articles used in every kind of service; 15the weight for the
lampstands of gold, and their lamps of gold, by weight for each lampstand
and its lamps; for the lampstands of silver by weight, for the lampstand and
its lamps, according to the use of each lampstand. 16And by weight *he gave*
gold for the tables of the showbread, for each table, and silver for the tables
of silver; 17also pure gold for the forks, the basins, the pitchers of pure gold,
and the golden bowls—*he gave gold* by weight for every bowl; and for the
silver bowls, *silver* by weight for every bowl; 18and refined gold by weight for
the altar of incense, and for the construction of the chariot, that is, the gold
cherubim that spread *their wings* and overshadowed the ark of the
covenant of the LORD. 19“All *this,*” *said David,* “the LORD made me understand in writing, by *His* hand upon me, all the works of these plans.”
20And David said to his son Solomon, “Be strong and of good courage,
and do *it;* do not fear nor be dismayed, for the LORD God—my God—*will
be* with you. He will not leave you nor forsake you, until you have finished
all the work for the service of the house of the LORD. 21*Here are* the divisions
of the priests and the Levites for all the service of the house of God; and
every willing craftsman *will be* with you for all manner of workmanship,
for every kind of service; also the leaders and all the people *will be* completely at your command.”

Offerings for Building the Temple

29 Furthermore King David said to all the assembly: “My son Solomon, whom alone God has chosen, *is* young and inexperienced;
and the work *is* great, because the temple[r] *is* not for man but for the LORD
God. 2Now for the house of my God I have prepared with all my might:
gold for *things to be made of* gold, silver for *things of* silver, bronze for
things of bronze, iron for *things of* iron, wood for *things of* wood, onyx
stones, *stones* to be set, glistening stones of various colors, all kinds of precious stones, and marble slabs in abundance. 3Moreover, because I have
set my affection on the house of my God, I have given to the house of my
God, over and above all that I have prepared for the holy house, my own

29:1 [r] Literally *palace*

LIFE LESSON

1 Chronicles 28:1–29:30

SITUATION As David grew old, he handed the temple building plans to his son Solomon. God chose Solomon to reign after David (even though he wasn’t the oldest son). David also gave Solomon wise advice about his relationship with God.

OBSERVATION God reveals himself to those who search for him. God often communicates his desires for us by the wise counsel of parents and mentors.

INSPIRATION The cat had kittens on the trundle bed in the downstairs guest room.

We didn’t think that was such a good idea, so we collected them and placed them on rags in a cardboard box in front of the kitchen fireplace until we could come up with something more suitable.

But the mother cat had a mind of her own. We watched with amusement as she entered the kitchen silently, stood on her back legs, front legs on the box, sniffing for her babies. Then leaping nimbly over the side, she checked them over, picked one up by the back of the neck, leaped out, and quietly returned it to the trundle bed. This was repeated till all that was left was the runt of the litter.

She did not come back. She may have been exhausted from her efforts, or she may have been busy playing lunch counter to the others.

We waited.

Finally the tiny scrap in the bottom of the box let out more of a squeak than a mew. It was almost a nonsound.

Instantly, soundlessly, the mother cat appeared, bounded in and out of the box, the littlest kitten in her mouth, and carried it back to the guest room.

Three doors, two rooms, and two hallways away, and yet she heard.

The Great Dane had her first litter of pups (two, to be exact) under the lilac bush outside the kitchen window.

After second thoughts she picked up the larger one and carried it to the

Continued

dog house (around two sides of the house), but being irresponsible, she forgot to return for the second.

After awhile number two pup got hungry. It made the sort of noise newborn pups make, and a very weak one at that.

I could hear the mother coming before I saw her. Galloping like a clap of thunder, she skidded to a stop, and gently lifting the little left-behind by the back of its what-was-supposed-to-be neck, she carried it to join the other. In neither case was it even a full-fledged cry. . . .

Nor are our prayers necessarily full-fledged prayers—or even articulated cries for help.

According to the Bible, God responds to our sighs, our tears, our murmurs—even our longings can be interpreted as prayer.

(From *The Legacy of a Pack Rat* by Ruth Bell Graham)

APPLICATION God knows our hearts. When you call to him for help, he faithfully cares for you. In what ways can you seek God's help for family disputes? Career paths? College choice? Dating? Tell God about your needs and longings.

EXPLORATION Seeking God—Deuteronomy 4:29; 2 Chronicles 15:15; Psalm 145:18-19; Isaiah 55:6; Jeremiah 29:13; Matthew 6:33; 7:7-8; Acts 17:27; Hebrews 11:6.

special treasure of gold and silver: 4three thousand talents of gold, of the
gold of Ophir, and seven thousand talents of refined silver, to overlay the
walls of the houses; 5the gold for *things of* gold and the silver for *things of*
silver, and for all kinds of work *to be done* by the hands of craftsmen. Who
then is willing to consecrate himself this day to the LORD?"
6Then the leaders of the fathers' *houses,* leaders of the tribes of Israel, the
captains of thousands and of hundreds, with the officers over the king's
work, offered willingly. 7They gave for the work of the house of God five
thousand talents and ten thousand darics of gold, ten thousand talents of
silver, eighteen thousand talents of bronze, and one hundred thousand
talents of iron. 8And whoever had *precious* stones gave *them* to the treasury of the house of the LORD, into the hand of Jehiel[s] the Gershonite.
9Then the people rejoiced, for they had offered willingly, because with a
loyal heart they had offered willingly to the LORD; and King David also rejoiced greatly.

David's Praise to God

10Therefore David blessed the LORD before all the assembly; and David
said:

"Blessed are You, LORD God of Israel, our Father, forever and ever.
11 Yours, O LORD, *is* the greatness,
The power and the glory,
The victory and the majesty;
For all *that is* in heaven and in earth *is Yours;*
Yours *is* the kingdom, O LORD,
And You are exalted as head over all.
12 Both riches and honor *come* from You,
And You reign over all.
In Your hand *is* power and might;
In Your hand *it is* to make great
And to give strength to all.

13 "Now therefore, our God,
We thank You
And praise Your glorious name.
14 But who *am* I, and who *are* my people,
That we should be able to offer so willingly as this?
For all things *come* from You,
And of Your own we have given You.
15 For we *are* aliens and pilgrims before You,
As *were* all our fathers;
Our days on earth *are* as a shadow,
And without hope.

16"O LORD our God, all this abundance that we have prepared to build
You a house for Your holy name is from Your hand, and *is* all Your own. 17I
know also, my God, that You test the heart and have pleasure in uprightness. As for me, in the uprightness of my heart I have willingly offered all
these *things;* and now with joy I have seen Your people, who are present
here to offer willingly to You. 18O LORD God of Abraham, Isaac, and Israel,

29:8 [s] Possibly the same as *Jehieli* (compare 26:21, 22)

our fathers, keep this forever in the intent of the
thoughts of the heart of Your people, and fix their
heart toward You. [19]And give my son Solomon a loyal
heart to keep Your commandments and Your testimonies and Your statutes, to do all *these things,* and to
build the temple[t] for which I have made provision."
[20]Then David said to all the assembly, "Now bless
the LORD your God." So all the assembly blessed the
LORD God of their fathers, and bowed their heads and
prostrated themselves before the LORD and the king.

Solomon Anointed King

[21]And they made sacrifices to the LORD and offered
burnt offerings to the LORD on the next day: a thousand bulls, a thousand rams, a thousand lambs, with
their drink offerings, and sacrifices in abundance for
all Israel. [22]So they ate and drank before the LORD with
great gladness on that day. And they made Solomon
the son of David king the second time, and anointed
him before the LORD *to be* the leader, and Zadok *to be*
priest. [23]Then Solomon sat on the throne of the LORD
as king instead of David his father, and prospered;
and all Israel obeyed him. [24]All the leaders and the
mighty men, and also all the sons of King David, submitted themselves to King Solomon. [25]So the LORD exalted Solomon exceedingly in the sight of all Israel,
and bestowed on him *such* royal majesty as had not
been on any king before him in Israel.

The Close of David's Reign

[26]Thus David the son of Jesse reigned over all Israel.
[27]And the period that he reigned over Israel *was* forty
years; seven years he reigned in Hebron, and thirty-
three *years* he reigned in Jerusalem. [28]So he died in a
good old age, full of days and riches and honor; and
Solomon his son reigned in his place. [29]Now the acts
of King David, first and last, indeed they *are* written in
the book of Samuel the seer, in the book of Nathan the
prophet, and in the book of Gad the seer, [30]with all his
reign and his might, and the events that happened to
him, to Israel, and to all the kingdoms of the lands.

29:19 [t] Literally *palace*

The Second Book of the

CHRONICLES

INTRODUCTION

A friend tells me of the time his five-year-old daughter took inventory of her friends.

Seems she took a tumble down the stairs and banged her head on the wall. Her mom rushed her to the emergency room and, though the injury wasn't severe, the doctor felt it wise to keep her overnight for observation. So the little girl spent the night in the hospital.

The next morning they took her home, and the dad carried her upstairs and put her in bed for a nap. As he closed the door he heard her voice. At first he thought she was speaking to him, so he stopped to listen.

"Sleepy? Grumpy? Dopey?"

My friend smiled. Painted on his daughter's bedroom wall were the characters from the Snow White story. For his daughter they were more than characters, however, they were friends. Every day she spent time talking to them. The dad knew what she was doing. "She was taking inventory of her friends," he said. "She'd been through a rough night and just wanted to make sure they were okay."

God has been known to do that. His people have a tendency to take tumbles. Some of those tumbles are severe. Second Chronicles will give you a few examples.

They aren't very pretty.

Some are very shameful. Still, they are his children and every so often he takes inventory of those who matter to him.

Buried in this large quarry called Chronicles are several jewels worth mining.

Here are two of the finest:

If My people who are called by My name will humble themselves, and pray and seek My face, and turn from their wicked ways, then I will hear from heaven, and will forgive their sin and heal their land (7:14).

For the eyes of the LORD run to and fro throughout the whole earth, to show Himself strong on behalf of those whose heart is loyal to Him (16:9).

Keep those verses in your hip pocket. You never know when you may take a spill yourself. Those words might be just what you need to get back on your feet.

Life Lesson

2 Chronicles 1:1-17

SITUATION Solomon became king over Israel. God gave him an opportunity to ask for anything.

OBSERVATION Put God first, and he will provide other needed resources.

INSPIRATION Ever have trouble determining God's will for your future? You are not alone. "Do I move to Mobile or Minnesota?" "Do I retire or keep working?" "An engineer at IBM or a clerk at Sears?" "Do I marry or stay single?" The questions are endless. One follows another. Every new responsibility brings new decisions. "What college should my son attend?" . . .

How in the world do we know what God wants? Do we set out a fleece? Seek advice? Pray? Read the Bible? All these are right yet there is one decision that must be made first. (Hang on, it's a tough one.)

To know God's will, we must totally surrender to God's will. Our tendency is to make God's decision for him. I used to do that with my mom. As a child, I hated to get the flu for two reasons: (1) it hurt; (2) my mom was a nurse. Since she was an RN, she knew the fastest way to tackle the flu bug was with a needle . . . in my bottom. Ouch! (I grew up thinking penicillin was a dirty word.)

Solomon Requests Wisdom

Now Solomon the son of David was strengthened in his kingdom, and the LORD his God *was* with him and exalted him exceedingly.

2And Solomon spoke to all Israel, to the captains of thousands and of hundreds, to the judges, and to every leader in all Israel, the heads of the fathers' *houses.* 3Then Solomon, and all the assembly with him, went to the high place that *was* at Gibeon; for the tabernacle of meeting with God was there, which Moses the servant of the LORD had made in the wilderness. 4But David had brought up the ark of God from Kirjath Jearim to *the place* David had prepared for it, for he had pitched a tent for it at Jerusalem. 5Now the bronze altar that Bezalel the son of Uri, the son of Hur, had made, he put[a] before the tabernacle of the LORD; Solomon and the assembly sought Him *there.* 6And Solomon went up there to the bronze altar before the LORD, which *was* at the tabernacle of meeting, and offered a thousand burnt offerings on it.

7On that night God appeared to Solomon, and said to him, "Ask! What shall I give you?"

8And Solomon said to God: "You have shown great mercy to David my father, and have made me king in his place. 9Now, O LORD God, let Your promise to David my father be established, for You have made me king over a people like the dust of the earth in multitude. 10Now give me wisdom and knowledge, that I may go out and come in before this people; for who can judge this great people of Yours?"

11Then God said to Solomon: "Because this was in your heart, and you have not asked riches or wealth or honor or the life of your enemies, nor have you asked long life—but have asked wisdom and knowledge for yourself, that you may judge My people over whom I have made you king— 12wisdom and knowledge *are* granted to you; and I will give you riches and wealth and honor, such as none of the kings have had who *were* before you, nor shall any after you have the like."

Solomon's Military and Economic Power

13So Solomon came to Jerusalem from the high place that *was* at Gibeon, from before the tabernacle of meeting, and reigned over Israel. 14And Solomon gathered chariots and horsemen; he had one thousand four hundred chariots and twelve thousand horsemen, whom he stationed in the chariot cities and with the king in Jerusalem. 15Also the king made silver and gold as common in Jerusalem as stones, and he made cedars as abundant as the sycamores which *are* in the lowland. 16And Solomon had horses imported from Egypt and Keveh; the king's merchants bought them in Keveh at the *current* price. 17They also acquired and imported from Egypt a chariot for six hundred *shekels* of silver, and a horse for one hundred and fifty; thus, through their agents,[b] they exported them to all the kings of the Hittites and the kings of Syria.

Solomon Prepares to Build the Temple

2 Then Solomon determined to build a temple for the name of the LORD, and a royal house for himself. 2Solomon selected seventy thousand

1:5 [a] Some authorities read *it was there.*
1:17 [b] Literally *by their hands*

men to bear burdens, eighty thousand to quarry *stone* in the mountains,
and three thousand six hundred to oversee them.
3Then Solomon sent to Hiram[c] king of Tyre, saying:

As you have dealt with David my father, and sent him cedars to
build himself a house to dwell in, *so deal with me.* 4Behold, I am
building a temple for the name of the LORD my God, to dedicate *it*
to Him, to burn before Him sweet incense, for the continual
showbread, for the burnt offerings morning and evening, on the
Sabbaths, on the New Moons, and on the set feasts of the LORD
our God. This *is an ordinance* forever to Israel.

5 And the temple which I build *will be* great, for our God is greater
than all gods. 6But who is able to build Him a temple, since heaven
and the heaven of heavens cannot contain Him? Who *am* I then, that
I should build Him a temple, except to burn sacrifice before Him?

7 Therefore send me at once a man skillful to work in gold and silver,
in bronze and iron, in purple and crimson and blue, who has skill
to engrave with the skillful men who are with me in Judah and
Jerusalem, whom David my father provided. 8Also send me cedar
and cypress and algum logs from Lebanon, for I know that your
servants have skill to cut timber in Lebanon; and indeed my
servants *will be* with your servants, 9to prepare timber for me in
abundance, for the temple which I am about to build *shall be* great
and wonderful.

10 And indeed I will give to your servants, the woodsmen who cut
timber, twenty thousand kors of ground wheat, twenty thousand
kors of barley, twenty thousand baths of wine, and twenty
thousand baths of oil.

11Then Hiram king of Tyre answered in writing, which he sent to Solomon:

Because the LORD loves His people, He has made you king over
them.

12Hiram[d] also said:

Blessed *be* the LORD God of Israel, who made heaven and earth, for
He has given King David a wise son, endowed with prudence and
understanding, who will build a temple for the LORD and a royal
house for himself!

13 And now I have sent a skillful man, endowed with understanding,
Huram[e] my master[f] *craftsman* 14(the son of a woman of the
daughters of Dan, and his father was a man of Tyre), skilled to
work in gold and silver, bronze and iron, stone and wood, purple
and blue, fine linen and crimson, and to make any engraving and
to accomplish any plan which may be given to him, with your
skillful men and with the skillful men of my lord David your father.

15 Now therefore, the wheat, the barley, the oil, and the wine which
my lord has spoken of, let him send to his servants. 16And we will

2:3 [c] Hebrew *Huram* (compare 1 Kings 5:1)
2:12 [d] Hebrew *Huram* (compare 1 Kings 5:1)
2:13 [e] Spelled *Hiram* in 1 Kings 7:13 [f] Literally *father* (compare 1 Kings 7:13, 14)

When she would tell me "to go get the medicine," I would get everything but the dreaded needle. I'd come back with an armful: aspirin, Pepto Bismol, ear drops, nose drops, ankle wraps—anything but penicillin. But as good moms do, she always got her point across. "Now you know better," she'd say with a smile, and would go get the (gulp) needle.

Here's the point. Don't go to God with options and expect him to choose one of your preferences. Go to him with empty hands—no hidden agendas, no crossed fingers, nothing behind your back. Go to him with a willingness to do whatever he says. If you surrender your will, then he will "equip you with everything good for doing his will" (Hebrews 13:21). It's a promise. (From *On the Anvil* by Max Lucado)

APPLICATION If God asked you for a wish list, what would be your top three items? Pray about these priorities today—for God to refine the list to include items he desires for you.

EXPLORATION Asking—Matthew 6:33; 7:7-8; Luke 18:1-8; John 14:13-14.

LIFE LESSON

2 Chronicles 2:1–5:1

SITUATION Solomon prepared to build a temple in Jerusalem according to the plans his father, David, had given him. Only the best wood and precious metals were used for God's house.

OBSERVATION God deserves the best we can give. God deserves our finest possessions, our most valuable time, and our precious money.

INSPIRATION You don't give for God's sake. You give for your sake. "The purpose of tithing is to teach you to always put God first in your lives" (Deut. 14:23 TLB). How does tithing teach you? Consider the simple act of writing a check for the offering. First you enter the date. Already you are reminded that you are a time-bound creature and every possession you have will rust or burn. Best to give it while you can.

Then you enter the name of the one to whom you are giving the money. If the bank would cash it, you'd write God. But they won't, so you write the name of the church or group that has earned your trust.

Next comes the amount. Ahh, the moment of truth. You're more than a person with a checkbook. You're David, placing a stone in the sling. You're Peter, one foot on the boat, one foot on the lake. You're a little boy in a big crowd. A picnic lunch is all the Teacher needs, but it's all you have.

cut wood from Lebanon, as much as you need; we will bring it to
you in rafts by sea to Joppa, and you will carry it up to Jerusalem.

17 Then Solomon numbered all the aliens who *were* in the land of Israel,
after the census in which David his father had numbered them; and there
were found to be one hundred and fifty-three thousand six hundred.
18 And he made seventy thousand of them bearers of burdens, eighty thousand stonecutters in the mountain, and three thousand six hundred overseers to make the people work.

Solomon Builds the Temple

3 Now Solomon began to build the house of the LORD at Jerusalem on
Mount Moriah, where *the LORD*[g] had appeared to his father David, at
the place that David had prepared on the threshing floor of Ornan[h] the
Jebusite. 2 And he began to build on the second *day* of the second month in
the fourth year of his reign.

3 This is the foundation which Solomon laid for building the house of
God: The length *was* sixty cubits (by cubits according to the former measure) and the width twenty cubits. 4 And the vestibule that *was* in front *of*
the sanctuary[i] was twenty cubits long across the width of the house, and
the height was one hundred and[j] twenty. He overlaid the inside with pure
gold. 5 The larger room[k] he paneled with cypress which he overlaid with
fine gold, and he carved palm trees and chainwork on it. 6 And he decorated the house with precious stones for beauty, and the gold was gold
from Parvaim. 7 He also overlaid the house—the beams and doorposts, its
walls and doors—with gold; and he carved cherubim on the walls.

8 And he made the Most Holy Place. Its length was according to the
width of the house, twenty cubits, and its width twenty cubits. He overlaid
it with six hundred talents of fine gold. 9 The weight of the nails *was* fifty
shekels of gold; and he overlaid the upper area with gold. 10 In the Most
Holy Place he made two cherubim, fashioned by carving, and overlaid
them with gold. 11 The wings of the cherubim *were* twenty cubits in *overall*
length: one wing *of the one cherub was* five cubits, touching the wall of the
room, and the other wing *was* five cubits, touching the wing of the other
cherub; 12 *one* wing of the other cherub *was* five cubits, touching the wall of
the room, and the other wing *also was* five cubits, touching the wing of the
other cherub. 13 The wings of these cherubim spanned twenty cubits overall. They stood on their feet, and they faced inward. 14 And he made the veil
of blue, purple, crimson, and fine linen, and wove cherubim into it.

15 Also he made in front of the temple[l] two pillars thirty-five[m] cubits high,
and the capital that *was* on the top of each of *them* was five cubits. 16 He
made wreaths of chainwork, as in the inner sanctuary, and put *them* on top
of the pillars; and he made one hundred pomegranates, and put *them* on
the wreaths of chainwork. 17 Then he set up the pillars before the temple,
one on the right hand and the other on the left; he called the name of the
one on the right hand Jachin, and the name of the one on the left Boaz.

3:1 [g] Literally *He,* following Masoretic Text and Vulgate; Septuagint reads *the LORD;* Targum reads *the Angel of the LORD.* [h] Spelled *Araunah* in 2 Samuel 24:16ff
3:4 [i] The main room of the temple; elsewhere called the holy place (compare 1 Kings 6:3) [j] Following Masoretic Text, Septuagint, and Vulgate; Arabic, some manuscripts of the Septuagint, and Syriac omit *one hundred and.*
3:5 [k] Literally *house*
3:15 [l] Literally *house* [m] Or *eighteen* (compare 1 Kings 7:15; 2 Kings 25:17; and Jeremiah 52:21)

Furnishings of the Temple

4 Moreover he made a bronze altar: twenty cubits was its length, twenty
cubits its width, and ten cubits its height.
2Then he made the Sea of cast *bronze,* ten cubits from one brim to the
other; *it was* completely round. Its height *was* five cubits, and a line of
thirty cubits measured its circumference. 3And under it *was* the likeness
of oxen encircling it all around, ten to a cubit, all the way around the Sea.
The oxen *were* cast in two rows, when it was cast. 4It stood on twelve oxen:
three looking toward the north, three looking toward the west, three looking toward the south, and three looking toward the east; the Sea *was set*
upon them, and all their back parts *pointed* inward. 5It *was* a handbreadth
thick; and its brim was shaped like the brim of a cup, *like* a lily blossom. It
contained three thousand[n] baths.
6He also made ten lavers, and put five on the right side and five on the
left, to wash in them; such things as they offered for the burnt offering they
would wash in them, but the Sea *was* for the priests to wash in. 7And he
made ten lampstands of gold according to their design, and set *them* in
the temple, five on the right side and five on the left. 8He also made ten tables, and placed *them* in the temple, five on the right side and five on the
left. And he made one hundred bowls of gold.
9Furthermore he made the court of the priests, and the great court and
doors for the court; and he overlaid these doors with bronze. 10He set the
Sea on the right side, toward the southeast.
11Then Huram made the pots and the shovels and the bowls. So Huram
finished doing the work that he was to do for King Solomon for the house
of God: 12the two pillars and the bowl-shaped capitals *that were* on top of
the two pillars; the two networks covering the two bowl-shaped capitals
which *were* on top of the pillars; 13four hundred pomegranates for the two
networks (two rows of pomegranates for each network, to cover the two
bowl-shaped capitals that *were* on the pillars); 14he also made carts and the
lavers on the carts; 15one Sea and twelve oxen under it; 16also the pots, the
shovels, the forks—and all their articles Huram his master[o] *craftsman*
made of burnished bronze for King Solomon for the house of the LORD.
17In the plain of Jordan the king had them cast in clay molds, between
Succoth and Zeredah.[p] 18And Solomon had all these articles made in such
great abundance that the weight of the bronze was not determined.
19Thus Solomon had all the furnishings made for the house of God: the
altar of gold and the tables on which *was* the showbread; 20the lampstands
with their lamps of pure gold, to burn in the prescribed manner in front of
the inner sanctuary, 21with the flowers and the lamps and the wick-trimmers of gold, of purest gold; 22the trimmers, the bowls, the ladles, and the
censers of pure gold. As for the entry of the sanctuary, its inner doors to the
Most Holy *Place,* and the doors of the main hall of the temple, *were* gold.
5 So all the work that Solomon had done for the house of the LORD was
finished; and Solomon brought in the things which his father David
had dedicated: the silver and the gold and all the furnishings. And he put
them in the treasuries of the house of God.

4:5 *n* Or *two thousand* (compare 1 Kings 7:26)
4:16 *o* Literally *father*
4:17 *p* Spelled *Zaretan* in 1 Kings 7:46

What will you do? Sling the Stone? Take the Step? Give the Meal?

Careful now, don't move too quickly. You aren't just entering an amount... you are making a confession. A confession that God owns it all anyway.

And then the line in the lower left-hand corner on which you write what the check is for. Hard to know what to put. It's for the light bills and literature. A little bit of outreach. A little bit of salary.

Better yet, it's partial payment for what the church has done to help you raise your family . . . keep your own priorities sorted out . . . tune you in to his ever-nearness.

Or, perhaps, best yet, it's for you. It's a moment for you to clip yet another strand from the rope of earth so that when he returns you won't be tied up. (From *When God Whispers Your Name* by Max Lucado)

APPLICATION Name the charities to which you give. What do you know about their financial integrity? How much of every dollar goes to fundraising or administration? Call your charity and ask for this information. Good stewardship requires careful giving.

EXPLORATION Preparations—Proverbs 20:18; 15:22; Luke 14:28-32; 2 Corinthians 1:17.

LIFE LESSON

2 Chronicles 5:2–7:22

SITUATION Solomon dedicated the new temple in Jerusalem. He invited tribal elders and chiefs from throughout Israel. While the sacred furnishings from the Meeting Tent were moved inside the temple, sacrifices began. Amid song, praise, and music, God's glory filled the temple.

OBSERVATION The temple symbolized a special relationship between God and the Israelites. As such, it became a holy and honored place.

INSPIRATION Many Christians have been infected with the most virulent virus of modern American life, what sociologist Robert Bellah calls "radical individualism." They concentrate on personal obedience to Christ as if all that matters is "Jesus and me," but in so doing miss the point altogether. For Christianity is not a solitary belief system. Any genuine resurgence of Christianity, as history demonstrates, depends on a reawakening and renewal of that which is the essence of the faith—that is, the people of God, the new society, the body of Christ, which is made manifest in the world—the church. . . .

The church is not incidental to the great cosmic struggle for the hearts and souls of modern men and women. It is the instrument God has chosen for that battle—a battle we are called to by virtue of being members of His body. To bring hope and truth to a needy world, the church *must be the church*. . . .

We cannot give what we do not have. We cannot impart values we do not hold. We cannot do until we are. To be the church—our highest calling—depends on understanding the very character of the body of Christ on earth. Only then can we understand what it means to live as the people of God, serving God in today's world.

(From *The Body* by Charles Colson)

APPLICATION Become an active member of a local church. Love the people, serve the Lord. Don't wait until your schedule clears. Do it this week.

EXPLORATION Temple—1 Kings 6:13; 8:15-21; 2 Chronicles 7:4-5; Ezekiel 5:11.

The Ark Brought into the Temple

2Now Solomon assembled the elders of Israel and all the heads of the
tribes, the chief fathers of the children of Israel, in Jerusalem, that they
might bring the ark of the covenant of the LORD up from the City of David,
which *is* Zion. 3Therefore all the men of Israel assembled with the king at
the feast, which *was* in the seventh month. 4So all the elders of Israel came,
and the Levites took up the ark. 5Then they brought up the ark, the tabernacle of meeting, and all the holy furnishings that *were* in the tabernacle.
The priests and the Levites brought them up. 6Also King Solomon, and all
the congregation of Israel who were assembled with him before the ark,
were sacrificing sheep and oxen that could not be counted or numbered
for multitude. 7Then the priests brought in the ark of the covenant of the
LORD to its place, into the inner sanctuary of the temple,[q] to the Most Holy
Place, under the wings of the cherubim. 8For the cherubim spread *their*
wings over the place of the ark, and the cherubim overshadowed the ark and
its poles. 9The poles extended so that the ends of the poles of the ark could be
seen from *the holy place,* in front of the inner sanctuary; but they could not
be seen from outside. And they are there to this day. 10Nothing was in the ark
except the two tablets which Moses put *there* at Horeb, when the LORD made
a covenant with the children of Israel, when they had come out of Egypt.
11And it came to pass when the priests came out of the *Most* Holy *Place*
(for all the priests who *were* present had sanctified themselves, without
keeping to their divisions), 12and the Levites *who were* the singers, all those
of Asaph and Heman and Jeduthun, with their sons and their brethren,
stood at the east end of the altar, clothed in white linen, having cymbals,
stringed instruments and harps, and with them one hundred and twenty
priests sounding with trumpets— 13indeed it came to pass, when the
trumpeters and singers *were* as one, to make one sound to be heard in
praising and thanking the LORD, and when they lifted up their voice with
the trumpets and cymbals and instruments of music, and praised the
LORD, *saying:*

"*For He is* good,
For His mercy *endures* forever,"[r]

that the house, the house of the LORD, was filled with a cloud, 14so that the
priests could not continue ministering because of the cloud; for the glory
of the LORD filled the house of God.

6 Then Solomon spoke:

"The LORD said He would dwell in the dark cloud.
2 I have surely built You an exalted house,
And a place for You to dwell in forever."

Solomon's Speech upon Completion of the Work

3Then the king turned around and blessed the whole assembly of Israel,
while all the assembly of Israel was standing. 4And he said: "Blessed *be* the
LORD God of Israel, who has fulfilled with His hands *what* He spoke with
His mouth to my father David, saying, 5'Since the day that I brought My

5:7 [q] Literally *house*
5:13 [r] Compare Psalm 106:1

people out of the land of Egypt, I have chosen no city
from any tribe of Israel *in which* to build a house, that
My name might be there, nor did I choose any man to
be a ruler over My people Israel. 6Yet I have chosen Jerusalem, that My name may be there, and I have chosen David to be over My people Israel.' 7Now it was in
the heart of my father David to build a temple[s] for the
name of the LORD God of Israel. 8But the LORD said to
my father David, 'Whereas it was in your heart to
build a temple for My name, you did well in that it was
in your heart. 9Nevertheless you shall not build the
temple, but your son who will come from your body,
he shall build the temple for My name.' 10So the LORD
has fulfilled His word which He spoke, and I have
filled the position of my father David, and sit on the
throne of Israel, as the LORD promised; and I have
built the temple for the name of the LORD God of Israel. 11And there I have put the ark, in which *is* the
covenant of the LORD which He made with the children of Israel."

Solomon's Prayer of Dedication

12Then *Solomon*[t] stood before the altar of the LORD
in the presence of all the assembly of Israel, and
spread out his hands 13(for Solomon had made a
bronze platform five cubits long, five cubits wide, and
three cubits high, and had set it in the midst of the
court; and he stood on it, knelt down on his knees before all the assembly of Israel, and spread out his
hands toward heaven); 14and he said: "LORD God of Israel, *there is* no God in heaven or on earth like You,
who keep *Your* covenant and mercy with Your servants who walk before You with all their hearts. 15You
have kept what You promised Your servant David my
father; You have both spoken with Your mouth and
fulfilled *it* with Your hand, as *it is* this day. 16Therefore,
LORD God of Israel, now keep what You promised
Your servant David my father, saying, 'You shall not
fail to have a man sit before Me on the throne of Israel, only if your sons take heed to their way, that they
walk in My law as you have walked before Me.' 17And
now, O LORD God of Israel, let Your word come true,
which You have spoken to Your servant David.

18"But will God indeed dwell with men on the
earth? Behold, heaven and the heaven of heavens cannot contain You. How much less this temple[u] which I
have built! 19Yet regard the prayer of Your servant and
his supplication, O LORD my God, and listen to the cry
and the prayer which Your servant is praying before
You: 20that Your eyes may be open toward this temple
day and night, toward the place where *You* said *You
would* put Your name, that You may hear the prayer
which Your servant makes toward this place. 21And
may You hear the supplications of Your servant and of
Your people Israel, when they pray toward this place.
Hear from heaven Your dwelling place, and when You
hear, forgive.

22"If anyone sins against his neighbor, and is forced
to take an oath, and comes *and* takes an oath before
Your altar in this temple, 23then hear from heaven,
and act, and judge Your servants, bringing retribution on the wicked by bringing his way on his own
head, and justifying the righteous by giving him according to his righteousness.

24"Or if Your people Israel are defeated before an
enemy because they have sinned against You, and return and confess Your name, and pray and make supplication before You in this temple, 25then hear from
heaven and forgive the sin of Your people Israel, and
bring them back to the land which You gave to them
and their fathers.

26"When the heavens are shut up and there is no rain
because they have sinned against You, when they pray
toward this place and confess Your name, and turn
from their sin because You afflict them, 27then hear *in*
heaven, and forgive the sin of Your servants, Your people Israel, that You may teach them the good way in
which they should walk; and send rain on Your land
which You have given to Your people as an inheritance.

28"When there is famine in the land, pestilence or
blight or mildew, locusts or grasshoppers; when their
enemies besiege them in the land of their cities; whatever plague or whatever sickness *there is;* 29whatever
prayer, whatever supplication is *made* by anyone, or
by all Your people Israel, when each one knows his
own burden and his own grief, and spreads out his
hands to this temple: 30then hear from heaven Your
dwelling place, and forgive, and give to everyone according to all his ways, whose heart You know (for
You alone know the hearts of the sons of men), 31that
they may fear You, to walk in Your ways as long as they
live in the land which You gave to our fathers.

32"Moreover, concerning a foreigner, who is not of
Your people Israel, but has come from a far country
for the sake of Your great name and Your mighty hand
and Your outstretched arm, when they come and pray

6:7 [s] Literally *house,* and so in verses 8–10
6:12 [t] Literally *he* (compare 1 Kings 8:22)
6:18 [u] Literally *house*

in this temple; 33then hear from heaven Your dwelling place, and do according to all for which the foreigner calls to You, that all peoples of the earth may know Your name and fear You, as *do* Your people Israel, and that they may know that this temple which I have built is called by Your name.

34"When Your people go out to battle against their enemies, wherever You send them, and when they pray to You toward this city which You have chosen and the temple which I have built for Your name, 35then hear from heaven their prayer and their supplication, and maintain their cause.

36"When they sin against You (for *there is* no one who does not sin), and You become angry with them and deliver them to the enemy, and they take them captive to a land far or near; 37*yet* when they come to themselves in the land where they were carried captive, and repent, and make supplication to You in the land of their captivity, saying, 'We have sinned, we have done wrong, and have committed wickedness'; 38and *when* they return to You with all their heart and with all their soul in the land of their captivity, where they have been carried captive, and pray toward their land which You gave to their fathers, the city which You have chosen, and toward the temple which I have built for Your name: 39then hear from heaven Your dwelling place their prayer and their supplications, and maintain their cause, and forgive Your people who have sinned against You. 40Now, my God, I pray, let Your eyes be open and *let* Your ears *be* attentive to the prayer *made* in this place.

41 "Now therefore,
Arise, O LORD God, to Your resting place,
You and the ark of Your strength.
Let Your priests, O LORD God, be clothed with
salvation,
And let Your saints rejoice in goodness.

42 "O LORD God, do not turn away the face of Your
Anointed;
Remember the mercies of Your servant
David."[v]

Solomon Dedicates the Temple

7 When Solomon had finished praying, fire came down from heaven and consumed the burnt offering and the sacrifices; and the glory of the LORD filled the temple.[w] 2And the priests could not enter the house of the LORD, because the glory of the LORD had filled the LORD's house. 3When all the children of Israel saw how the fire came down, and the glory of the LORD on the temple, they bowed their faces to the ground on the pavement, and worshiped and praised the LORD, *saying:*

"For *He is* good,
For His mercy *endures* forever."[x]

4Then the king and all the people offered sacrifices before the LORD. 5King Solomon offered a sacrifice of twenty-two thousand bulls and one hundred and twenty thousand sheep. So the king and all the people dedicated the house of God. 6And the priests attended to their services; the Levites also with instruments of the music of the LORD, which King David had made to praise the LORD, saying, "For His mercy *endures* forever,"[y] whenever David offered praise by their ministry. The priests sounded trumpets opposite them, while all Israel stood.

7Furthermore Solomon consecrated the middle of the court that *was* in front of the house of the LORD; for there he offered burnt offerings and the fat of the peace offerings, because the bronze altar which Solomon had made was not able to receive the burnt offerings, the grain offerings, and the fat.

8At that time Solomon kept the feast seven days, and all Israel with him, a very great assembly from the entrance of Hamath to the Brook of Egypt.[z] 9And on the eighth day they held a sacred assembly, for they observed the dedication of the altar seven days, and the feast seven days. 10On the twenty-third day of the seventh month he sent the people away to their tents, joyful and glad of heart for the good that the LORD had done for David, for Solomon, and for His people Israel. 11Thus Solomon finished the house of the LORD and the king's house; and Solomon successfully accomplished all that came into his heart to make in the house of the LORD and in his own house.

God's Second Appearance to Solomon

12Then the LORD appeared to Solomon by night, and said to him: "I have heard your prayer, and have chosen this place for Myself as a house of sacrifice. 13When I shut up heaven and there is no rain, or command the locusts to devour the land, or send pesti-

6:42 [v] Compare Psalm 132:8–10
7:1 [w] Literally *house*
7:3 [x] Compare Psalm 106:1
7:6 [y] Compare Psalm 106:1
7:8 [z] That is, the Shihor (compare 1 Chronicles 13:5)

lence among My people, 14if My people who are called by My name will
humble themselves, and pray and seek My face, and turn from their
wicked ways, then I will hear from heaven, and will forgive their sin and
heal their land. 15Now My eyes will be open and My ears attentive to prayer
made in this place. 16For now I have chosen and sanctified this house, that
My name may be there forever; and My eyes and My heart will be there
perpetually. 17As for you, if you walk before Me as your father David
walked, and do according to all that I have commanded you, and if you
keep My statutes and My judgments, 18then I will establish the throne of
your kingdom, as I covenanted with David your father, saying, 'You shall
not fail *to have* a man as ruler in Israel.'

19"But if you turn away and forsake My statutes and My commandments which I have set before you, and go and serve other gods, and worship them, 20then I will uproot them from My land which I have given
them; and this house which I have sanctified for My name I will cast out of
My sight, and will make it a proverb and a byword among all peoples.

21"And *as for* this house, which is exalted, everyone who passes by it will
be astonished and say, 'Why has the LORD done thus to this land and this
house?' 22Then they will answer, 'Because they forsook the LORD God of
their fathers, who brought them out of the land of Egypt, and embraced
other gods, and worshiped them and served them; therefore He has
brought all this calamity on them.' "

Solomon's Additional Achievements

8 It came to pass at the end of twenty years, when Solomon had built the
house of the LORD and his own house, 2that the cities which Hiram[a]
had given to Solomon, Solomon built them; and he settled the children of
Israel there. 3And Solomon went to Hamath Zobah and seized it. 4He also
built Tadmor in the wilderness, and all the storage cities which he built in
Hamath. 5He built Upper Beth Horon and Lower Beth Horon, fortified
cities *with* walls, gates, and bars, 6also Baalath and all the storage cities
that Solomon had, and all the chariot cities and the cities of the cavalry,
and all that Solomon desired to build in Jerusalem, in Lebanon, and in all
the land of his dominion.

7All the people *who were* left of the Hittites, Amorites, Perizzites, Hivites,
and Jebusites, who *were* not of Israel— 8that is, their descendants who
were left in the land after them, whom the children of Israel did not destroy—from these Solomon raised forced labor, as it is to this day. 9But
Solomon did not make the children of Israel servants for his work. Some
were men of war, captains of his officers, captains of his chariots, and his
cavalry. 10And others *were* chiefs of the officials of King Solomon: two hundred and fifty, who ruled over the people.

11Now Solomon brought the daughter of Pharaoh up from the City of
David to the house he had built for her, for he said, "My wife shall not dwell
in the house of David king of Israel, because *the places* to which the ark of
the LORD has come are holy."

12Then Solomon offered burnt offerings to the LORD on the altar of the
LORD which he had built before the vestibule, 13according to the daily rate,
offering according to the commandment of Moses, for the Sabbaths, the

8:2 [a] Hebrew *Huram* (compare 2 Chronicles 2:3)

LIFE LESSON

2 Chronicles 8:1–9:31

SITUATION Solomon built Israel into a wealthy and powerful nation. Neighboring rulers came to visit him and sought to learn from his great wisdom. Solomon became caught up in worldly affairs, eventually marrying pagan women.

OBSERVATION Solomon used his God-given wisdom to make Israel strong. But as Solomon became wealthy, he grew distant from God.

INSPIRATION From the looks of things, you're pretty impressive. You've got a nice place. And I suppose your neighbors would agree that you're a hard worker . . . climbing right on up that ladder toward success, right? I realize you're not into big bucks; but face it, nobody's going hungry. Far from it. Your job is fairly secure. Making more money than ever, you're on your way. But wait, I want to know about the "other half." These things I've mentioned are all external—physical and material stuff. What I want to know is how things are internally.

You look secure and successful, but the half has not been told, right? Part of you is insecure and fearful. Underneath, you're pretty weak. You appear to be happy, easy-going, and fulfilled; but the half has not been told, has it? You wonder about where all this is leading you. Your restless drive for more and your desire for calm, peaceful contentment seem poles apart . . . because they are poles apart. Deep down, nothing within you smiles.

Your salary is good and your material possessions are growing in number, but again, the half has not been told. The truth is that you are empty on the inside and you're faking it on the outside. Not one thing you own in all your "kingdom" has brought you the happiness you long for. So you're thinking, "Maybe if I could land that better job," or "get into that bigger house," or . . . or . . .

But don't allow the smoke screen of more money to blind your eyes to the truth. There's a lot more to being rich than making more money. Seneca, the Roman, was right, "Money has

Continued

never yet made anyone rich." Do you want riches? Then listen to Jesus: But seek first His kingdom and His righteousness, and all these things shall be added to you.

For the real riches, try switching kingdoms.

(From *Living on the Ragged Edge* by Charles Swindoll)

APPLICATION Is wealth your aim? Put that dream aside and give priority to God. Do something today to curb the appetite for money, and be content with what you have.

EXPLORATION True Wealth—Deuteronomy 4:40; Mark 10:17-31; Luke 12:33; 16:1-13.

New Moons, and the three appointed yearly feasts—the Feast of
Unleavened Bread, the Feast of Weeks, and the Feast of Tabernacles.
14 And, according to the order of David his father, he appointed the divisions of the priests for their service, the Levites for their duties (to praise
and serve before the priests) as the duty of each day required, and the gatekeepers by their divisions at each gate; for so David the man of God had
commanded. 15 They did not depart from the command of the king to the
priests and Levites concerning any matter or concerning the treasuries.
16 Now all the work of Solomon was well-ordered from[b] the day of the
foundation of the house of the LORD until it was finished. So the house of
the LORD was completed.
17 Then Solomon went to Ezion Geber and Elath[c] on the seacoast, in the
land of Edom. 18 And Hiram sent him ships by the hand of his servants,
and servants who knew the sea. They went with the servants of Solomon
to Ophir, and acquired four hundred and fifty talents of gold from there,
and brought it to King Solomon.

The Queen of Sheba's Praise of Solomon

9 Now when the queen of Sheba heard of the fame of Solomon, she came
to Jerusalem to test Solomon with hard questions, *having* a very great
retinue, camels that bore spices, gold in abundance, and precious stones;
and when she came to Solomon, she spoke with him about all that was in
her heart. 2 So Solomon answered all her questions; there was nothing so difficult for Solomon that he could not explain it to her. 3 And when the queen of
Sheba had seen the wisdom of Solomon, the house that he had built, 4 the
food on his table, the seating of his servants, the service of his waiters and
their apparel, his cupbearers and their apparel, and his entryway by which
he went up to the house of the LORD, there was no more spirit in her.
5 Then she said to the king: "*It was* a true report which I heard in my own
land about your words and your wisdom. 6 However I did not believe their
words until I came and saw with my own eyes; and indeed the half of the
greatness of your wisdom was not told me. You exceed the fame of which I
heard. 7 Happy *are* your men and happy *are* these your servants, who stand
continually before you and hear your wisdom! 8 Blessed be the LORD your
God, who delighted in you, setting you on His throne *to be* king for the LORD
your God! Because your God has loved Israel, to establish them forever,
therefore He made you king over them, to do justice and righteousness."
9 And she gave the king one hundred and twenty talents of gold, spices
in great abundance, and precious stones; there never were any spices such
as those the queen of Sheba gave to King Solomon.
10 Also, the servants of Hiram and the servants of Solomon, who brought
gold from Ophir, brought algum[d] wood and precious stones. 11 And the
king made walkways *of* the algum[e] wood for the house of the LORD and for
the king's house, also harps and stringed instruments for singers; and
there were none such *as these* seen before in the land of Judah.
12 Now King Solomon gave to the queen of Sheba all she desired, whatever she asked, *much more* than she had brought to the king. So she turned
and went to her own country, she and her servants.

8:16 [b] Following Septuagint, Syriac, and Vulgate; Masoretic Text reads *as far as*.
8:17 [c] Hebrew *Eloth* (compare 2 Kings 14:22)
9:10 [d] Or *almug* (compare 1 Kings 10:11, 12)
9:11 [e] Or *almug* (compare 1 Kings 10:11, 12)

Solomon's Great Wealth

13The weight of gold that came to Solomon yearly was six hundred and
sixty-six talents of gold, 14besides *what* the traveling merchants and
traders brought. And all the kings of Arabia and governors of the country
brought gold and silver to Solomon. 15And King Solomon made two hundred large shields of hammered gold; six hundred *shekels* of hammered
gold went into each shield. 16*He* also *made* three hundred shields of hammered gold; three hundred *shekels*[f] of gold went into each shield. The king
put them in the House of the Forest of Lebanon.
17Moreover the king made a great throne of ivory, and overlaid it with
pure gold. 18The throne *had* six steps, with a footstool of gold, *which were*
fastened to the throne; there were armrests on either side of the place of
the seat, and two lions stood beside the armrests. 19Twelve lions stood
there, one on each side of the six steps; nothing like *this* had been made for
any *other* kingdom.
20All King Solomon's drinking vessels *were* gold, and all the vessels of
the House of the Forest of Lebanon *were* pure gold. Not *one was* silver, for
this was accounted as nothing in the days of Solomon. 21For the king's
ships went to Tarshish with the servants of Hiram.[g] Once every three
years the merchant ships[h] came, bringing gold, silver, ivory, apes, and
monkeys.[i]
22So King Solomon surpassed all the kings of the earth in riches and
wisdom. 23And all the kings of the earth sought the presence of Solomon
to hear his wisdom, which God had put in his heart. 24Each man brought
his present: articles of silver and gold, garments, armor, spices, horses,
and mules, at a set rate year by year.
25Solomon had four thousand stalls for horses and chariots, and twelve
thousand horsemen whom he stationed in the chariot cities and with the
king at Jerusalem.
26So he reigned over all the kings from the River[j] to the land of the
Philistines, as far as the border of Egypt. 27The king made silver *as com-*
mon in Jerusalem as stones, and he made cedar trees as abundant as the
sycamores which *are* in the lowland. 28And they brought horses to Solomon from Egypt and from all lands.

Death of Solomon

29Now the rest of the acts of Solomon, first and last, *are* they not written
in the book of Nathan the prophet, in the prophecy of Ahijah the Shilonite,
and in the visions of Iddo the seer concerning Jeroboam the son of Nebat?
30Solomon reigned in Jerusalem over all Israel forty years. 31Then Solomon rested with his fathers, and was buried in the City of David his father. And Rehoboam his son reigned in his place.

The Revolt Against Rehoboam

10 And Rehoboam went to Shechem, for all Israel had gone to
Shechem to make him king. 2So it happened, when Jeroboam the
son of Nebat heard *it* (he was in Egypt, where he had fled from the presence of King Solomon), that Jeroboam returned from Egypt. 3Then they

Life Lesson

2 Chronicles 10:1–11:17

SITUATION King Solomon died. Rehoboam, in prideful youth, turned down the wisdom of older counselors. His blunder sparked the division of Israel.

OBSERVATION God used Rehoboam's pride to accomplish his divine plan. Due to Solomon's sin, God planned to divide the kingdom. God uses our sinful decisions to accomplish his plan.

INSPIRATION My kids pulled a fast one on me one Christmas years ago. They teamed up, pooled their vast financial resources, and bought me a little motto to set on my desk. It was more than cute . . . it was convicting. In bold, black letters it read:

Diets Are For People Who Are Thick And Tired Of It

At first you thmile . . . then it makes you thad. Especially if you're not thick of being thick!

There's another thickness that's just as bad. We could call it an "inner thickness." I'm referring to insensitivity . . . being unaware, out of touch, lacking insight, failing to pay attention. The Hebrew Scriptures occasionally mention those who are foolish and simple, as in the book of Proverbs (1:22-33). The original term means "thick, dull, sluggish." It's the picture of mental dullness, one who is virtually blind toward others . . . failing to feel others' feelings, think others' thoughts, sense others' needs.

Professional insensitivity is painfully common. To some physicians you're case number twenty-three today . . . a body, weighing so much . . . a mouth, saying words . . . a gall bladder, needing removal.

And how about insensitive teachers or speakers? Talk about painful! A block of information is dumped into your ears from their mouth. Whether it's interesting or well thought through is unimportant. The whole episode is about as memorable as changing a flat.

And have you come across an insensitive sales person lately? You can feel the thickness. Your exasperation leads to gross impatience . . . and then, finally, confusion. You're not

Continued

9:16 [f] Or *three minas* (compare 1 Kings 10:17)
9:21 [g] Hebrew *Huram* (compare 1 Kings 10:22) [h] Literally *ships of Tarshish,* deep-sea vessels [i] Or *peacocks*
9:26 [j] That is, the Euphrates

sure if the individual only understands Swahili . . . or is recovering from advanced lockjaw.

Perhaps the most tragic shades of insensitivity occur in the home. Between mates, to begin with. Needs in the heart of a wife long to be discovered by her husband. She hides them until an appropriate moment . . . but it never arrives. He's "too busy." What cursed words! "Other things are more important." Oh, really? Name one.

A husband wrestles with a matter down deep . . . in the "combat zone" of his mind. Lacking perception, the preoccupied wife drives on—never pausing, never looking into his eyes, his soul-gate, reading the signs that spell I A-M H-U-R-T-I-N-G.

. . . To be thick is understandable. To be thick and tired of it is commendable. To be thick and tired of it but unwilling to change—is inexcusable.

(From *Come Before Winter* by Charles Swindoll)

APPLICATION What is your reputation with family and friends? Do they see you as a sensitive person, or as a selfish person who has little time for their needs and concerns? Listen and be sensitive to their needs. Ask God for the opportunity to spend time with someone this week who needs a listening ear. Be prepared to respond when God sends someone.

EXPLORATION Concern for Others—Psalm 103:13; Luke 10:25-37; Acts 20:35; Galatians 6:2; Philippians 2:3-4; Hebrews 4:15; James 1:27.

sent for him and called him. And Jeroboam and all Israel came and spoke
to Rehoboam, saying, 4"Your father made our yoke heavy; now therefore,
lighten the burdensome service of your father and his heavy yoke which he
put on us, and we will serve you."
5So he said to them, "Come back to me after three days." And the people
departed.
6Then King Rehoboam consulted the elders who stood before his father
Solomon while he still lived, saying, "How do you advise *me* to answer
these people?"
7And they spoke to him, saying, "If you are kind to these people, and
please them, and speak good words to them, they will be your servants
forever."
8But he rejected the advice which the elders had given him, and consulted the young men who had grown up with him, who stood before him.
9And he said to them, "What advice do you give? How should we answer
this people who have spoken to me, saying, 'Lighten the yoke which your
father put on us'?"
10Then the young men who had grown up with him spoke to him, saying, "Thus you should speak to the people who have spoken to you, saying, 'Your father made our yoke heavy, but you make *it* lighter on
us'—thus you shall say to them: 'My little *finger* shall be thicker than my
father's waist! 11And now, whereas my father put a heavy yoke on you, I will
add to your yoke; my father chastised you with whips, but I *will chastise*
you with scourges!' "[k]
12So Jeroboam and all the people came to Rehoboam on the third day, as
the king had directed, saying, "Come back to me the third day." 13Then the
king answered them roughly. King Rehoboam rejected the advice of the
elders, 14and he spoke to them according to the advice of the young men,
saying, "My father[l] made your yoke heavy, but I will add to it; my father
chastised you with whips, but I *will chastise you* with scourges!"[m] 15So the
king did not listen to the people; for the turn *of events* was from God, that
the LORD might fulfill His word, which He had spoken by the hand of
Ahijah the Shilonite to Jeroboam the son of Nebat.
16Now when all Israel *saw* that the king did not listen to them, the people
answered the king, saying:

"What share have we in David?
We have no inheritance in the son of Jesse.
Every man to your tents, O Israel!
Now see to your own house, O David!"

So all Israel departed to their tents. 17But Rehoboam reigned over the
children of Israel who dwelt in the cities of Judah.
18Then King Rehoboam sent Hadoram, who *was* in charge of revenue;
but the children of Israel stoned him with stones, and he died. Therefore
King Rehoboam mounted *his* chariot in haste to flee to Jerusalem. 19So Israel has been in rebellion against the house of David to this day.

11 Now when Rehoboam came to Jerusalem, he assembled from the
house of Judah and Benjamin one hundred and eighty thousand

10:11 [k] Literally *scorpions*
10:14 [l] Following many Hebrew manuscripts, Septuagint, Syriac, and Vulgate (compare verse 10 and 1 Kings 12:14); Masoretic Text reads *I.* [m] Literally *scorpions*

chosen *men* who were warriors, to fight against Israel, that he might restore the kingdom to Rehoboam.
2But the word of the LORD came to Shemaiah the man of God, saying,
3"Speak to Rehoboam the son of Solomon, king of Judah, and to all Israel
in Judah and Benjamin, saying, 4'Thus says the LORD: "You shall not go up
or fight against your brethren! Let every man return to his house, for this
thing is from Me." ' " Therefore they obeyed the words of the LORD, and
turned back from attacking Jeroboam.

Rehoboam Fortifies the Cities

5So Rehoboam dwelt in Jerusalem, and built cities for defense in Judah.
6And he built Bethlehem, Etam, Tekoa, 7Beth Zur, Sochoh, Adullam, 8Gath,
Mareshah, Ziph, 9Adoraim, Lachish, Azekah, 10Zorah, Aijalon, and
Hebron, which are in Judah and Benjamin, fortified cities. 11And he fortified the strongholds, and put captains in them, and stores of food, oil, and
wine. 12Also in every city *he put* shields and spears, and made them very
strong, having Judah and Benjamin on his side.

Priests and Levites Move to Judah

13And from all their territories the priests and the Levites who *were* in all
Israel took their stand with him. 14For the Levites left their common-lands
and their possessions and came to Judah and Jerusalem, for Jeroboam
and his sons had rejected them from serving as priests to the LORD. 15Then
he appointed for himself priests for the high places, for the demons, and
the calf idols which he had made. 16And after *the Levites left,*[n] those from all
the tribes of Israel, such as set their heart to seek the LORD God of Israel,
came to Jerusalem to sacrifice to the LORD God of their fathers. 17So they
strengthened the kingdom of Judah, and made Rehoboam the son of Solomon strong for three years, because they walked in the way of David and
Solomon for three years.

The Family of Rehoboam

18Then Rehoboam took for himself as wife Mahalath the daughter of
Jerimoth the son of David, *and of* Abihail the daughter of Eliah the son of
Jesse. 19And she bore him children: Jeush, Shamariah, and Zaham. 20After
her he took Maachah the granddaughter[o] of Absalom; and she bore him
Abijah, Attai, Ziza, and Shelomith. 21Now Rehoboam loved Maachah the
granddaughter of Absalom more than all his wives and his concubines;
for he took eighteen wives and sixty concubines, and begot twenty-eight
sons and sixty daughters. 22And Rehoboam appointed Abijah the son of
Maachah as chief, *to be* leader among his brothers; for he *intended* to make
him king. 23He dealt wisely, and dispersed some of his sons throughout all
the territories of Judah and Benjamin, to every fortified city; and he gave
them provisions in abundance. He also sought many wives *for them.*

Egypt Attacks Judah

12 Now it came to pass, when Rehoboam had established the kingdom
and had strengthened himself, that he forsook the law of the LORD,
and all Israel along with him. 2And it happened in the fifth year of King

11:16 [n] Literally *after them*
11:20 [o] Literally *daughter,* but in the broader sense of granddaughter (compare 2 Chronicles 13:2)

LIFE LESSON

2 Chronicles 11:18–14:1

SITUATION King Rehoboam showed wisdom after Israel and Judah split. He sought to honor God as his father and grandfather had done. But after becoming well established, Rehoboam stopped depending on God. God used the ambitious king of Egypt to cause Rehoboam to look to God again. But the consequences of Rehoboam's decisions still followed him and affected the whole nation.

OBSERVATION No matter what circumstance or temptation causes us to drift away from God, he still loves us and wants us back. God forgives us and calls us back to himself. Sometimes God uses a difficult situation to call us back, as in the case of Rehoboam. When we repent, we may still bear the consequences of our sin, but God forgives and restores us.

INSPIRATION What poses the greatest risk to not continuing in Christ? The greatest risk is the crisis of values which inexorably comes when we follow hollow and deceptive philosophy. It may not come until we have traveled for many years down the road of self-deceit, but it will come.

The crisis of values is no less than a bad case of the -ism's—materialism, relativism, humanism, hedonism, liberalism, legalism, secularism and so on. I doubt few of us ever set out to become a materialist or a relativist or whatever. It is more that without self-examination we atrophy from the Christian value system into something less. Not that we abandon the spiritual connection, but slowly, almost imperceptibly, we undo the moral knowledge to which we pledged ourselves. When once we redraw the line, there is less pressure against redrawing it, and less and less each time thereafter. . . .

God wants us to make a comeback. He wants us to make a comeback more than we do. . . .

How can someone start a comeback? From the belly of the great fish Jonah cried out, "When my life was ebbing away, I remembered you, Lord, and my prayer rose to you, to your holy temple. Those who cling to worthless idols [the -ism's] forfeit the grace that could be theirs" (Jonah 2:7-8). Jonah

Continued

could not know it, but when he humbled himself, God initiated his comeback. When we humble ourselves and turn back, God initiates our comeback.

At the point Jonah turned back, how did God respond? Did He call for a celebration? No, He did not. Once we have been swallowed up, the first step back is merely to make it back to dry land. "And the Lord commanded the fish, and it vomited Jonah onto dry land" (Jonah 2:10).

When we start on the comeback, we start from where we have been—in the belly of the world which swallowed us up. God spits us up onto the shore by His grace; it is an inauspicious starting point from which to make a comeback.

The comeback will be embarrassing. The odor of where we have been remains until we cleanse ourselves. The people we hurt will not trust us at first. We must still work through the human consequences of having untied the moral knot—of being taken captive by hollow and deceptive philosophy. Painful and embarrassing it may be, but He does let us come back.

Do you have a case of the *-ism's*? Have you been taken captive, swallowed up into the belly of the world? If you have been swallowed up, are you ready yet to humble yourself? Are you ready to start your comeback? If you are willing, He is willing.

(From *Walking with Christ in the Details of Life* by Patrick Morley)

APPLICATION Have you developed any habits or attitudes that stand between you and God? Are you noticing any of society's immoral values infiltrating your faith? If you have been gradually easing away from God, what can you change to head back in the right direction?

EXPLORATION Repentance—2 Chronicles 7:14; Psalm 51:17; 107:10-14, 17-20; Joel 2:13; Acts 8:22; 2 Corinthians 7:10; 1 John 1:9.

Rehoboam *that* Shishak king of Egypt came up against Jerusalem, because they had transgressed against the LORD, 3with twelve hundred chariots, sixty thousand horsemen, and people without number who came
with him out of Egypt—the Lubim and the Sukkiim and the Ethiopians.
4And he took the fortified cities of Judah and came to Jerusalem.
5Then Shemaiah the prophet came to Rehoboam and the leaders of Judah, who were gathered together in Jerusalem because of Shishak, and
said to them, "Thus says the LORD: 'You have forsaken Me, and therefore I
also have left you in the hand of Shishak.' "

6So the leaders of Israel and the king humbled themselves; and they
said, "The LORD *is* righteous."

7Now when the LORD saw that they humbled themselves, the word of the
LORD came to Shemaiah, saying, "They have humbled themselves; *therefore* I will not destroy them, but I will grant them some deliverance. My
wrath shall not be poured out on Jerusalem by the hand of Shishak. 8Nev-
ertheless they will be his servants, that they may distinguish My service
from the service of the kingdoms of the nations."

9So Shishak king of Egypt came up against Jerusalem, and took away
the treasures of the house of the LORD and the treasures of the king's
house; he took everything. He also carried away the gold shields which
Solomon had made. 10Then King Rehoboam made bronze shields in their
place, and committed *them* to the hands of the captains of the guard, who
guarded the doorway of the king's house. 11And whenever the king entered
the house of the LORD, the guard would go and bring them out; then they
would take them back into the guardroom. 12When he humbled himself,
the wrath of the LORD turned from him, so as not to destroy *him* completely; and things also went well in Judah.

The End of Rehoboam's Reign

13Thus King Rehoboam strengthened himself in Jerusalem and
reigned. Now Rehoboam *was* forty-one years old when he became king;
and he reigned seventeen years in Jerusalem, the city which the LORD had
chosen out of all the tribes of Israel, to put His name there. His mother's
name *was* Naamah, an Ammonitess. 14And he did evil, because he did not
prepare his heart to seek the LORD.

15The acts of Rehoboam, first and last, *are* they not written in the book of
Shemaiah the prophet, and of Iddo the seer concerning genealogies? And
there were wars between Rehoboam and Jeroboam all their days. 16So
Rehoboam rested with his fathers, and was buried in the City of David.
Then Abijah[p] his son reigned in his place.

Abijah Reigns in Judah

13 In the eighteenth year of King Jeroboam, Abijah became king over
Judah. 2He reigned three years in Jerusalem. His mother's name
was Michaiah[q] the daughter of Uriel of Gibeah.

And there was war between Abijah and Jeroboam. 3Abijah set the battle
in order with an army of valiant warriors, four hundred thousand choice
men. Jeroboam also drew up in battle formation against him with eight
hundred thousand choice men, mighty men of valor.

12:16 [p] Spelled *Abijam* in 1 Kings 14:31
13:2 [q] Spelled *Maachah* in 11:20, 21 and 1 Kings 15:2

ETERNAL LIFE

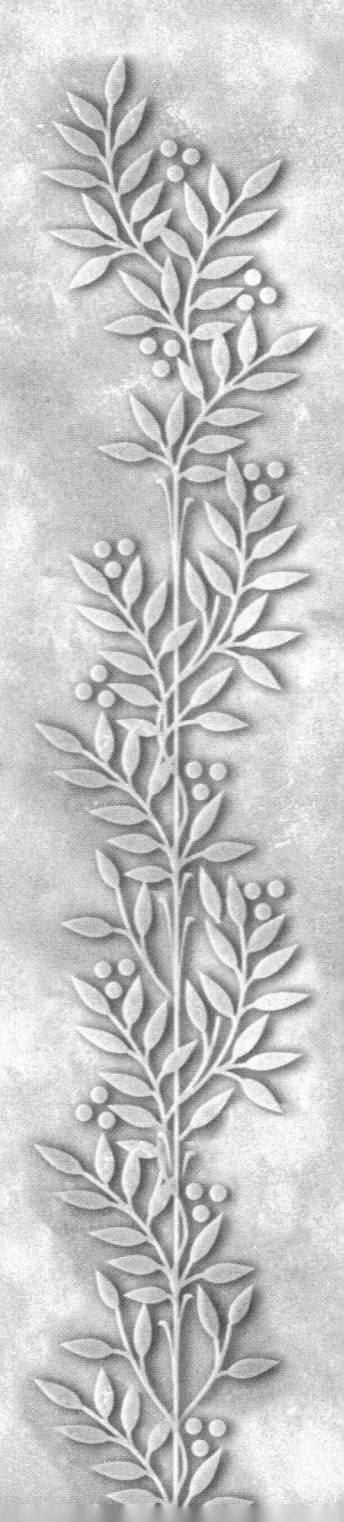

We know that someday our heavenly Father is going to take all those who follow him into eternal happiness. It's to that day that we look. It's upon our hope and confidence that he will return that we stand. Our prayer should be that our Father will help us make decisions that will set us on the course of eternal life.

Listen to the Christ rather than to the voices of men. Jesus says you can't please men and still be a servant of God. Those who listen and follow Christ will be received into heaven by the pierced hands of the one who knows the freedom of giving up what you cannot own in order to receive what no one can take from you—eternal life.

HEAVENLY FATHER, may your name be praised. Lord, may we see the joy that is before us. Would you pull back the eternal curtain and give us a glimpse into the everlasting? Would you hear the secret yearnings of our hearts? Will you keep us close to you this day?

GOD'S LOVE

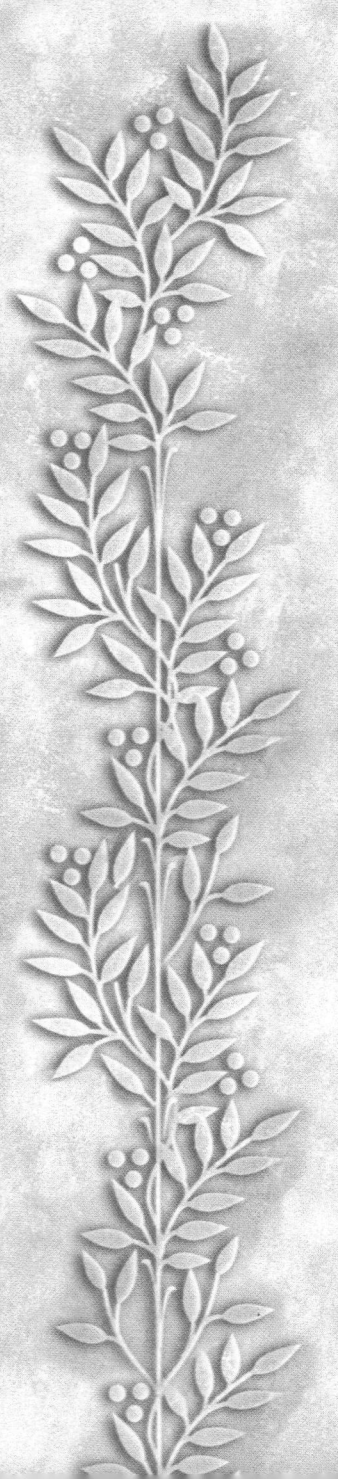

Don't think that God always has goose bumps and happy feelings toward his people. That same God is the God who once wondered if he should have ever made this thing called the human race. But it's the same God who assures us that "you are my people and I will be your God." It's not based on feelings or perfection; it's based on a covenant of love.

Once we see how much God cares for his people, then we begin to see how much his heart must have broken when the hand of man reached out and took the goblet of sin offered by Satan. Because God is perfect, he cannot dwell with a sinful being. He must have wept so much the tears were like a flood and showered the creation.

The love of Christ compels us to do what we never thought we could do and go to heights we never thought we could reach. Precious is the name of Jesus!

LORD, let us not pretend to be something we're not.
You know us early in the morning; you know us late at night.
You know us when we're weak; you know us when we're strong.
Father, remind us that you still care and that you still love us.

REST

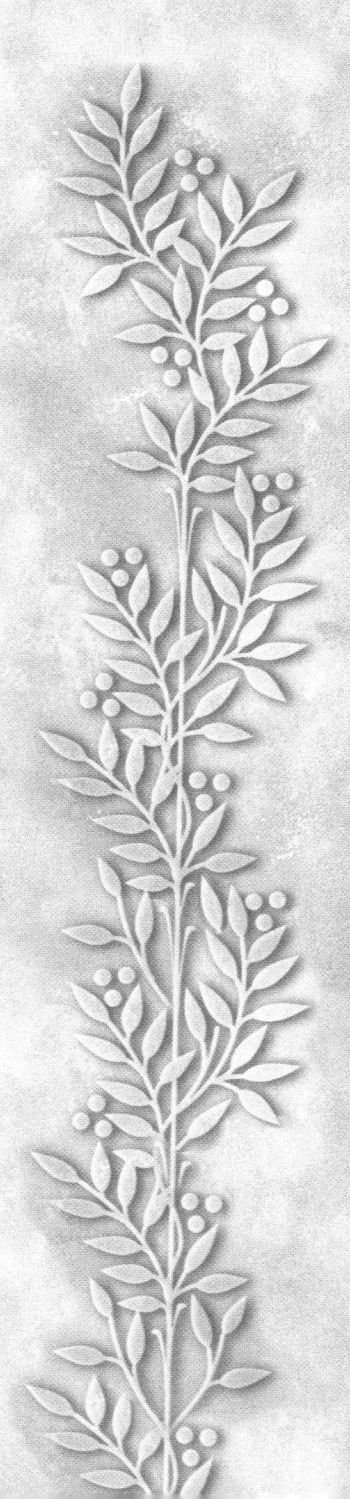

In this fast-paced world in which we live, the very thing we need to do is what we often don't do: We need simply to sit still and open our heart to the counsel of God. Then we will be well prepared for whatever the day brings.

Sometimes the most godly thing we can do for ourselves is go to sleep. Sometimes the most godly thing we can do for our family and friends is to take a break and regather our strength.

Perhaps the words of the carpenter, promising rest, are so compelling because of our endless desire and quest to rest—not just to rest in the body, but to rest the heart, to find peace, to finally settle down in a valley fertile with contentment.

Do you know where to find rest? Where you find a clean conscience? Where you find the ability to sleep at night and live with yourself? By living in the pleasure of the Father who made you.

If you want to bring under control a fast-paced life-style, you must eliminate the unnecessary; if you want to be where God wants you to be, you must concentrate on the necessary.

FATHER, help us to use our time wisely, to take advantage of the opportunities we have to be just the type of Christians you want us to be. When it seems like we don't have enough time to do what we need to do, increase our gratitude for the challenges of each day. And help us meet those challenges in ways that please you.

TRUST GOD

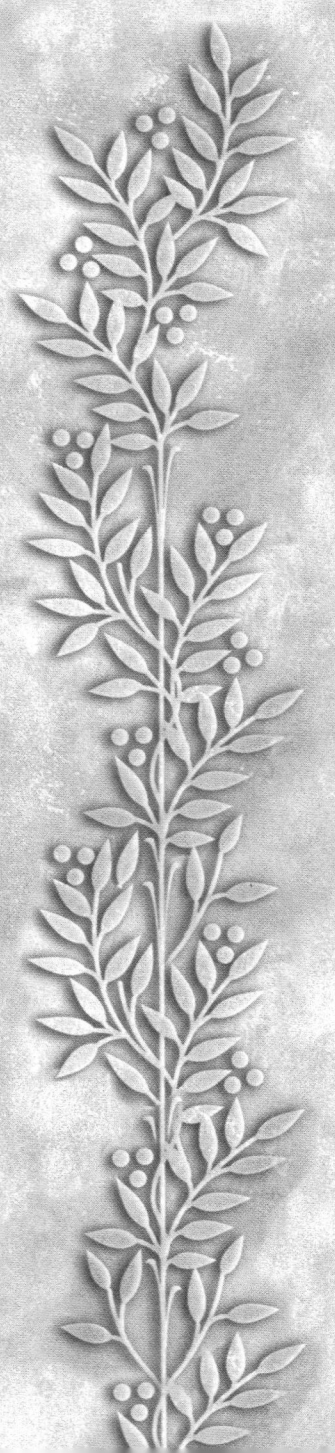

I believe that many of us go through life sucking on pacifiers. Oh, we don't see them because they're in our bank. Or they're parked in our garage. Or we live in them.

Don't put your hope into things that change—relationships, money, talents, beauty, even health. Set your sights on the one thing that can never change: trust in your heavenly Father.

God loves those who need him most, who rely on him, depend on him, and trust him in everything. Little he cares whether you've been as pure as John or as sinful as Mary Magdalene; all that matters is your trust in him.

FATHER, help us today to maintain our promise of faithfulness to you, even in times when we're not surrounded by people who agree with us and encourage and understand our devotion to you. Give us great courage as we face the challenges of each new day.

4Then Abijah stood on Mount Zemaraim, which *is*
in the mountains of Ephraim, and said, "Hear me,
Jeroboam and all Israel: 5Should you not know that
the LORD God of Israel gave the dominion over Israel
to David forever, to him and his sons, by a covenant of
salt? 6Yet Jeroboam the son of Nebat, the servant of
Solomon the son of David, rose up and rebelled
against his lord. 7Then worthless rogues gathered to
him, and strengthened themselves against
Rehoboam the son of Solomon, when Rehoboam was
young and inexperienced and could not withstand
them. 8And now you think to withstand the kingdom
of the LORD, which is in the hand of the sons of David;
and you *are* a great multitude, and with you are the
gold calves which Jeroboam made for you as gods.
9Have you not cast out the priests of the LORD, the sons
of Aaron, and the Levites, and made for yourselves
priests, like the peoples of *other* lands, so that whoever
comes to consecrate himself with a young bull and
seven rams may be a priest of *things that are* not gods?
10But as for us, the LORD *is* our God, and we have not
forsaken Him; and the priests who minister to the
LORD *are* the sons of Aaron, and the Levites *attend* to
their duties. 11And they burn to the LORD every morning and every evening burnt sacrifices and sweet incense; *they* also *set* the showbread *in order on* the pure
gold table, and the lampstand of gold with its lamps to
burn every evening; for we keep the command of the
LORD our God, but you have forsaken Him. 12Now look,
God Himself is with us as *our* head, and His priests
with sounding trumpets to sound the alarm against
you. O children of Israel, do not fight against the LORD
God of your fathers, for you shall not prosper!"
13But Jeroboam caused an ambush to go around
behind them; so they were in front of Judah, and the
ambush *was* behind them. 14And when Judah looked
around, to their surprise the battle line *was* at both
front and rear; and they cried out to the LORD, and the
priests sounded the trumpets. 15Then the men of Judah gave a shout; and as the men of Judah shouted, it
happened that God struck Jeroboam and all Israel before Abijah and Judah. 16And the children of Israel
fled before Judah, and God delivered them into their
hand. 17Then Abijah and his people struck them with
a great slaughter; so five hundred thousand choice
men of Israel fell slain. 18Thus the children of Israel
were subdued at that time; and the children of Judah
prevailed, because they relied on the LORD God of
their fathers.
19And Abijah pursued Jeroboam and took cities
from him: Bethel with its villages, Jeshanah with its
villages, and Ephrain[r] with its villages. 20So Jeroboam
did not recover strength again in the days of Abijah;
and the LORD struck him, and he died.
21But Abijah grew mighty, married fourteen wives,
and begot twenty-two sons and sixteen daughters.
22Now the rest of the acts of Abijah, his ways, and his
sayings *are* written in the annals of the prophet Iddo.

14 So Abijah rested with his fathers, and they
buried him in the City of David. Then Asa his
son reigned in his place. In his days the land was quiet
for ten years.

Asa Reigns in Judah

2Asa did *what was* good and right in the eyes of the
LORD his God, 3for he removed the altars of the foreign
gods and the high places, and broke down the *sacred*
pillars and cut down the wooden images. 4He commanded Judah to seek the LORD God of their fathers,
and to observe the law and the commandment. 5He
also removed the high places and the incense altars
from all the cities of Judah, and the kingdom was
quiet under him. 6And he built fortified cities in Judah, for the land had rest; he had no war in those
years, because the LORD had given him rest. 7There-
fore he said to Judah, "Let us build these cities and
make walls around *them,* and towers, gates, and bars,
while the land *is* yet before us, because we have
sought the LORD our God; we have sought *Him,* and
He has given us rest on every side." So they built and
prospered. 8And Asa had an army of three hundred
thousand from Judah who carried shields and spears,
and from Benjamin two hundred and eighty thousand men who carried shields and drew bows; all
these *were* mighty men of valor.
9Then Zerah the Ethiopian came out against them
with an army of a million men and three hundred
chariots, and he came to Mareshah. 10So Asa went out
against him, and they set the troops in battle array in
the Valley of Zephathah at Mareshah. 11And Asa cried
out to the LORD his God, and said, "LORD, *it is* nothing
for You to help, whether with many or with those who
have no power; help us, O LORD our God, for we rest on
You, and in Your name we go against this multitude.
O LORD, You *are* our God; do not let man prevail
against You!"
12So the LORD struck the Ethiopians before Asa and
Judah, and the Ethiopians fled. 13And Asa and the

13:19 [r] Or *Ephron*

LIFE LESSON

2 Chronicles 14:2–16:14

SITUATION King Asa wholeheartedly followed God. God rewarded him with wealth, advice, and a peaceful kingdom. But in his security, Asa started relying on his own wisdom and strength.

OBSERVATION Though hard times bring frustration, easy times can cause us to forget God and depend on ourselves. Because he loves us, God may let difficult situations enter our lives to redirect our attention to him.

INSPIRATION February 15, 1921. New York City. The operating room of the Kane Summit Hospital. A doctor is performing an appendectomy. In many ways the events leading to the surgery are uneventful. The patient has complained of severe abdominal pain. The diagnosis is clear: an inflamed appendix. Dr. Evan O'Neill Kane is performing the surgery. In his distinguished thirty-seven-year medical career, he has performed nearly four thousand appendectomies, so this surgery will be uneventful in all ways except two.

The first novelty of this operation? The use of local anesthesia in major surgery. Dr. Kane is a crusader against the hazards of general anesthesia. He contends that a local application is far safer. Many of his colleagues agree with him in principle, but in order for them to agree in practice, they will have to see the theory applied.

Dr. Kane searches for a volunteer, a patient who is willing to undergo surgery while under local anesthesia. A volunteer is not easily found. Many are squeamish at the thought of being awake during their own surgery. Others are fearful that the anesthesia might wear off too soon. Eventually, however, Dr. Kane finds a candidate. On Tuesday morning, February 15, the historic operation occurs.

people who *were* with him pursued them to Gerar. So the Ethiopians were
overthrown, and they could not recover, for they were broken before the
LORD and His army. And they carried away very much spoil. 14Then they
defeated all the cities around Gerar, for the fear of the LORD came upon
them; and they plundered all the cities, for there was exceedingly much
spoil in them. 15They also attacked the livestock enclosures, and carried off
sheep and camels in abundance, and returned to Jerusalem.

The Reforms of Asa

15 Now the Spirit of God came upon Azariah the son of Oded. 2And he
went out to meet Asa, and said to him: "Hear me, Asa, and all Judah
and Benjamin. The LORD *is* with you while you are with Him. If you seek
Him, He will be found by you; but if you forsake Him, He will forsake you.
3For a long time Israel *has been* without the true God, without a teaching
priest, and without law; 4but when in their trouble they turned to the LORD
God of Israel, and sought Him, He was found by them. 5And in those times
there was no peace to the one who went out, nor to the one who came in,
but great turmoil *was* on all the inhabitants of the lands. 6So nation was
destroyed by nation, and city by city, for God troubled them with every adversity. 7But you, be strong and do not let your hands be weak, for your
work shall be rewarded!"

8And when Asa heard these words and the prophecy of Oded[s] the
prophet, he took courage, and removed the abominable idols from all the
land of Judah and Benjamin and from the cities which he had taken in the
mountains of Ephraim; and he restored the altar of the LORD that *was* before the vestibule of the LORD. 9Then he gathered all Judah and Benjamin,
and those who dwelt with them from Ephraim, Manasseh, and Simeon,
for they came over to him in great numbers from Israel when they saw that
the LORD his God was with him.

10So they gathered together at Jerusalem in the third month, in the fifteenth year of the reign of Asa. 11And they offered to the LORD at that time
seven hundred bulls and seven thousand sheep from the spoil they had
brought. 12Then they entered into a covenant to seek the LORD God of their
fathers with all their heart and with all their soul; 13and whoever would not
seek the LORD God of Israel was to be put to death, whether small or great,
whether man or woman. 14Then they took an oath before the LORD with a
loud voice, with shouting and trumpets and rams' horns. 15And all Judah
rejoiced at the oath, for they had sworn with all their heart and sought Him
with all their soul; and He was found by them, and the LORD gave them rest
all around.

16Also he removed Maachah, the mother of Asa the king, from *being*
queen mother, because she had made an obscene image of Asherah;[t] and
Asa cut down her obscene image, then crushed and burned *it* by the Brook
Kidron. 17But the high places were not removed from Israel. Nevertheless
the heart of Asa was loyal all his days.

18He also brought into the house of God the things that his father had
dedicated and that he himself had dedicated: silver and gold and utensils.
19And there was no war until the thirty-fifth year of the reign of Asa.

15:8 [s] Following Masoretic Text and Septuagint; Syriac and Vulgate read *Azariah the son of Oded* (compare verse 1).

15:16 [t] A Canaanite deity

Asa's Treaty with Syria

16 In the thirty-sixth year of the reign of Asa, Baasha king of Israel
came up against Judah and built Ramah, that he might let none go
out or come in to Asa king of Judah. 2Then Asa brought silver and gold
from the treasuries of the house of the LORD and of the king's house, and
sent to Ben-Hadad king of Syria, who dwelt in Damascus, saying, 3"*Let*
there be a treaty between you and me, as there was between my father and
your father. See, I have sent you silver and gold; come, break your treaty
with Baasha king of Israel, so that he will withdraw from me."
4So Ben-Hadad heeded King Asa, and sent the captains of his armies
against the cities of Israel. They attacked Ijon, Dan, Abel Maim, and all the
storage cities of Naphtali. 5Now it happened, when Baasha heard *it,* that he
stopped building Ramah and ceased his work. 6Then King Asa took all Judah, and they carried away the stones and timber of Ramah, which
Baasha had used for building; and with them he built Geba and Mizpah.

Hanani's Message to Asa

7And at that time Hanani the seer came to Asa king of Judah, and said to
him: "Because you have relied on the king of Syria, and have not relied on
the LORD your God, therefore the army of the king of Syria has escaped
from your hand. 8Were the Ethiopians and the Lubim not a huge army
with very many chariots and horsemen? Yet, because you relied on the
LORD, He delivered them into your hand. 9For the eyes of the LORD run to
and fro throughout the whole earth, to show Himself strong on behalf of
those whose heart *is* loyal to Him. In this you have done foolishly; therefore
from now on you shall have wars." 10Then Asa was angry with the seer, and
put him in prison, for *he was* enraged at him because of this. And Asa oppressed *some* of the people at that time.

Illness and Death of Asa

11Note that the acts of Asa, first and last, are indeed written in the book
of the kings of Judah and Israel. 12And in the thirty-ninth year of his reign,
Asa became diseased in his feet, and his malady was severe; yet in his disease he did not seek the LORD, but the physicians.
13So Asa rested with his fathers; he died in the forty-first year of his
reign. 14They buried him in his own tomb, which he had made for himself
in the City of David; and they laid him in the bed which was filled with
spices and various ingredients prepared in a mixture of ointments. They
made a very great burning for him.

Jehoshaphat Reigns in Judah

17 Then Jehoshaphat his son reigned in his place, and strengthened
himself against Israel. 2And he placed troops in all the fortified cities
of Judah, and set garrisons in the land of Judah and in the cities of
Ephraim which Asa his father had taken. 3Now the LORD was with
Jehoshaphat, because he walked in the former ways of his father David; he
did not seek the Baals, 4but sought the God[u] of his father, and walked in
His commandments and not according to the acts of Israel. 5Therefore the
LORD established the kingdom in his hand; and all Judah gave presents to

17:4 [u] Septuagint reads *LORD God.*

The patient is prepped and wheeled into the operating room. A local anesthetic is applied. As he has done thousands of times, Dr. Kane dissects the superficial tissues and locates the appendix. He skillfully excises it and concludes the surgery. During the procedure, the patient complains of only minor discomfort. . . .

Dr. Kane has proven his theory. . . .

But I said there were two facts that made the surgery unique. I've told you the first: the use of local anesthesia. The second is the patient. The courageous candidate for surgery by Dr. Kane was Dr. Kane.

To prove his point, Dr. Kane operated on himself!

A wise move. The doctor became a patient in order to convince the patients to trust the doctor.

. . . The story of the doctor who became his own patient is mild compared to the story of the God who became human. But Jesus did. So that you and I would believe that the Healer knows our hurts, he voluntarily became one of us. He placed himself in our position. He suffered our pains and felt our fears.

Rejection? He felt it. Temptation? He knew it. Loneliness? He experienced it. Death? He tasted it.

And stress? He could write a best-selling book about it.

Why did he do it? One reason. So that when you hurt you will go to him—your Father and your Physician—and let him heal.

(From *In the Eye of the Storm* by Max Lucado)

APPLICATION What desires or goals do you have that may be weakening your faith? What comforts or successes cause you to depend less on God? When a difficult situation arises today, turn to God before trying to decide on a solution.

EXPLORATION Dependence on God—Deuteronomy 6:10-12; 2 Chronicles 20:12; Psalm 20:7; Isaiah 31:1; Zechariah 4:6; 2 Corinthians 3:5; 12:9-10.

LIFE LESSON

2 Chronicles 17:1–19:3

SITUATION Jehoshaphat feared and loved God. But he foolishly made an alliance with Ahab, the wicked king of Israel. Judah adopted Israel's evil practices, which led to judgment on both nations.

OBSERVATION Partnerships with non-Christians can bring compromise if the believer does not constantly guard against this danger.

INSPIRATION We live in an age in which everything is working against the things we hold dear. Think about it. What force in our society is working to help you remain faithful to your partner? None that I can think of. The message of our world is just the opposite. What force in our society is working to help your kids remain true to principles the Bible sets forth in regard to sexual purity, honesty, loyalty, and the priority of character development? None! The message our kids are bombarded with is, "Acquire all you can and do whatever feels good." We don't live in a neutral world that beckons us to choose between right and wrong. The world we face everyday is one in which right has become wrong. . . .

In addressing the believers of this city, Paul advised them to make the most of their time. That is, they should use their time carefully. Paul realized that it required absolutely no effort on their part to become like the world. They did not have to study or set goals or even make any plans to become worldly. All they had to do was get out in the world and live. If they took no precautions, it would be just a matter of time before they looked, acted, and thought just like the world. And that applies to us, too.

. . . In this evil day we need constant reminders of the truth. If we are not careful with our time, we will allow others to fill it up for us. There will be

Jehoshaphat, and he had riches and honor in abundance. 6And his heart
took delight in the ways of the LORD; moreover he removed the high places
and wooden images from Judah.
7Also in the third year of his reign he sent his leaders, Ben-Hail, Obadiah,
Zechariah, Nethanel, and Michaiah, to teach in the cities of Judah. 8And
with them *he sent* Levites: Shemaiah, Nethaniah, Zebadiah, Asahel,
Shemiramoth, Jehonathan, Adonijah, Tobijah, and Tobadonijah—the
Levites; and with them Elishama and Jehoram, the priests. 9So they taught
in Judah, and *had* the Book of the Law of the LORD with them; they went
throughout all the cities of Judah and taught the people.
10And the fear of the LORD fell on all the kingdoms of the lands that *were*
around Judah, so that they did not make war against Jehoshaphat. 11Also
some of the Philistines brought Jehoshaphat presents and silver as tribute;
and the Arabians brought him flocks, seven thousand seven hundred
rams and seven thousand seven hundred male goats.
12So Jehoshaphat became increasingly powerful, and he built fortresses
and storage cities in Judah. 13He had much property in the cities of Judah;
and the men of war, mighty men of valor, *were* in Jerusalem.
14These *are* their numbers, according to their fathers' houses. Of Judah,
the captains of thousands: Adnah the captain, and with him three hundred
thousand mighty men of valor; 15and next to him *was* Jehohanan the captain, and with him two hundred and eighty thousand; 16and next to him
was Amasiah the son of Zichri, who willingly offered himself to the LORD,
and with him two hundred thousand mighty men of valor. 17Of Benjamin:
Eliada a mighty man of valor, and with him two hundred thousand men
armed with bow and shield; 18and next to him *was* Jehozabad, and with
him one hundred and eighty thousand prepared for war. 19These served the
king, besides those the king put in the fortified cities throughout all Judah.

Micaiah Warns Ahab

18 Jehoshaphat had riches and honor in abundance; and by marriage
he allied himself with Ahab. 2After some years he went down to *visit*
Ahab in Samaria; and Ahab killed sheep and oxen in abundance for him
and the people who were with him, and persuaded him to go up *with him*
to Ramoth Gilead. 3So Ahab king of Israel said to Jehoshaphat king of Judah, "Will you go with me *against* Ramoth Gilead?"
And he answered him, "I *am* as you *are,* and my people as your people;
we will be with you in the war."
4Also Jehoshaphat said to the king of Israel, "Please inquire for the word
of the LORD today."
5Then the king of Israel gathered the prophets together, four hundred
men, and said to them, "Shall we go to war against Ramoth Gilead, or shall
I refrain?"
So they said, "Go up, for God will deliver it into the king's hand."
6But Jehoshaphat said, "*Is there* not still a prophet of the LORD here, that
we may inquire of Him?"[v]
7So the king of Israel said to Jehoshaphat, "*There is* still one man by
whom we may inquire of the LORD; but I hate him, because he never prophesies good concerning me, but always evil. He *is* Micaiah the son of Imla."

18:6 [v] Or *him*

And Jehoshaphat said, "Let not the king say such things!"
8 Then the king of Israel called one *of his* officers and said, "Bring
Micaiah the son of Imla quickly!"
9 The king of Israel and Jehoshaphat king of Judah, clothed in *their*
robes, sat each on his throne; and they sat at a threshing floor at the entrance of the gate of Samaria; and all the prophets prophesied before
them. 10 Now Zedekiah the son of Chenaanah had made horns of iron for
himself; and he said, "Thus says the LORD: 'With these you shall gore the
Syrians until they are destroyed.' "
11 And all the prophets prophesied so, saying, "Go up to Ramoth Gilead
and prosper, for the LORD will deliver *it* into the king's hand."
12 Then the messenger who had gone to call Micaiah spoke to him, saying, "Now listen, the words of the prophets with one accord encourage the
king. Therefore please let your word be like *the word of* one of them, and
speak encouragement."
13 And Micaiah said, "*As* the LORD lives, whatever my God says, that I will
speak."
14 Then he came to the king; and the king said to him, "Micaiah, shall we
go to war against Ramoth Gilead, or shall I refrain?"
And he said, "Go and prosper, and they shall be delivered into your
hand!"
15 So the king said to him, "How many times shall I make you swear that
you tell me nothing but the truth in the name of the LORD?"
16 Then he said, "I saw all Israel scattered on the mountains, as sheep
that have no shepherd. And the LORD said, 'These have no master. Let each
return to his house in peace.' "
17 And the king of Israel said to Jehoshaphat, "Did I not tell you he would
not prophesy good concerning me, but evil?"
18 Then *Micaiah* said, "Therefore hear the word of the LORD: I saw the
LORD sitting on His throne, and all the host of heaven standing on His right
hand and His left. 19 And the LORD said, 'Who will persuade Ahab king of
Israel to go up, that he may fall at Ramoth Gilead?' So one spoke in this
manner, and another spoke in that manner. 20 Then a spirit came forward
and stood before the LORD, and said, 'I will persuade him.' The LORD said
to him, 'In what way?' 21 So he said, 'I will go out and be a lying spirit in the
mouth of all his prophets.' And *the LORD* said, 'You shall persuade *him* and
also prevail; go out and do so.' 22 Therefore look! The LORD has put a lying
spirit in the mouth of these prophets of yours, and the LORD has declared
disaster against you."
23 Then Zedekiah the son of Chenaanah went near and struck Micaiah
on the cheek, and said, "Which way did the spirit from the LORD go from
me to speak to you?"
24 And Micaiah said, "Indeed you shall see on that day when you go into
an inner chamber to hide!"
25 Then the king of Israel said, "Take Micaiah, and return him to Amon
the governor of the city and to Joash the king's son; 26 and say, 'Thus says
the king: "Put this *fellow* in prison, and feed him with bread of affliction
and water of affliction, until I return in peace." ' "
27 But Micaiah said, "If you ever return in peace, the LORD has not spoken by me." And he said, "Take heed, all you people!"

no time for God. . . . Wise men and women are careful with their time. They use their extra time to draw close to God. . . .

If doing business with certain individuals or groups puts you in a position that causes you to violate your convictions time and time again, quit doing business with them. If watching certain television shows causes you to lust, don't excuse them because of their entertainment value. Just quit watching them. If being with a particular group of people causes you to stumble, don't rationalize by saying, "But they are my friends." Get some new friends!

In every area of life, face up to what God would have you do. As long as you play games, as long as you ignore what you know in your heart God would have you do, you set yourself up to fail. . . .

God wants control over every area of your life. Not partial control, total control. He wants you to be victorious over temptation. But He wants you to be victorious for His purposes, not yours. You may not have achieved victory over temptation because you are holding to the reins of your life and trying to get God to intervene in the rough spots. That isn't the way God works. He wants all of you. And when He knows you are His, He will do whatever He needs to make you into an effective servant for His kingdom. (From *Winning the War Within* by Charles Stanley)

APPLICATION Evaluate your alliances in career, leisure, and finances. Which "allies" tempt you to compromise? Which "allies" help you know the Bible? Pray? Add a spiritual ally this week.

EXPLORATION Alliances—Numbers 25:1; 1 Kings 3:1; Isaiah 52:11; 2 Corinthians 6:14-18; Ephesians 5:7; Revelation 18:4.

LIFE LESSON

2 Chronicles 19:4–21:3

SITUATION Jehoshaphat concentrated on administration by appointing loyal, faithful, capable, and God-fearing judges throughout the land. To ensure justice, he laid down rules for judging the people.

OBSERVATION Godly leaders focus on God's power and answer to God for their judgments.

INSPIRATION For many years I couldn't talk without stammering and hesitating. This was very humiliating to me. That changed when I was forty-five years old, after I had known the Lord for twenty-five years.

I had been on the mission field for nearly twenty years when the Lord told me I must now learn to talk like the people in heaven. That meant I mustn't grumble and complain anymore. I mustn't talk about other people's faults. I mustn't say things behind their backs that I wouldn't like them to say about me.

At that time I was accustomed to saying to a fellow missionary, "Let's have a little prayer together to help you change, to see if God will help you stop stumbling." The Lord Jesus said to me, "In heaven we don't talk about faults. When you pray like that, I have to get up quietly and go out of the room. That leaves you talking to the four walls."

I said, "Lord, I'm forty-five years old and my habits are fixed, but you help me alter them."

Ahab Dies in Battle

28So the king of Israel and Jehoshaphat the king of Judah went up to
Ramoth Gilead. 29And the king of Israel said to Jehoshaphat, "I will disguise myself and go into battle; but you put on your robes." So the king of
Israel disguised himself, and they went into battle.
30Now the king of Syria had commanded the captains of the chariots
who *were* with him, saying, "Fight with no one small or great, but only
with the king of Israel."
31So it was, when the captains of the chariots saw Jehoshaphat, that
they said, "It *is* the king of Israel!" Therefore they surrounded him to attack; but Jehoshaphat cried out, and the LORD helped him, and God di-
verted them from him. 32For so it was, when the captains of the chariots
saw that it was not the king of Israel, that they turned back from pursuing him. 33Now a certain man drew a bow at random, and struck the king
of Israel between the joints of his armor. So he said to the driver of his
chariot, "Turn around and take me out of the battle, for I am wounded."
34The battle increased that day, and the king of Israel propped *himself* up
in *his* chariot facing the Syrians until evening; and about the time of sunset he died.

19 Then Jehoshaphat the king of Judah returned safely to his house in
Jerusalem. 2And Jehu the son of Hanani the seer went out to meet
him, and said to King Jehoshaphat, "Should you help the wicked and love
those who hate the LORD? Therefore the wrath of the LORD *is* upon you.
3Nevertheless good things are found in you, in that you have removed the
wooden images from the land, and have prepared your heart to seek God."

The Reforms of Jehoshaphat

4So Jehoshaphat dwelt at Jerusalem; and he went out again among the
people from Beersheba to the mountains of Ephraim, and brought them
back to the LORD God of their fathers. 5Then he set judges in the land
throughout all the fortified cities of Judah, city by city, 6and said to the
judges, "Take heed to what you are doing, for you do not judge for man but
for the LORD, who *is* with you in the judgment. 7Now therefore, let the fear
of the LORD be upon you; take care and do *it,* for *there is* no iniquity with
the LORD our God, no partiality, nor taking of bribes."
8Moreover in Jerusalem, for the judgment of the LORD and for contro-
versies, Jehoshaphat appointed some of the Levites and priests, and some
of the chief fathers of Israel, when they returned to Jerusalem.[w] 9And he
commanded them, saying, "Thus you shall act in the fear of the LORD,
faithfully and with a loyal heart: 10Whatever case comes to you from your
brethren who dwell in their cities, whether of bloodshed or offenses
against law or commandment, against statutes or ordinances, you shall
warn them, lest they trespass against the LORD and wrath come upon you
and your brethren. Do this, and you will not be guilty. 11And take notice:
Amariah the chief priest *is* over you in all matters of the LORD; and
Zebadiah the son of Ishmael, the ruler of the house of Judah, for all the
king's matters; also the Levites *will be* officials before you. Behave courageously, and the LORD will be with the good."

19:8 [w] Septuagint and Vulgate read *for the inhabitants of Jerusalem.*

Ammon, Moab, and Mount Seir Defeated

20 It happened after this *that* the people of Moab with the people of
Ammon, and *others* with them besides the Ammonites,[x] came to
battle against Jehoshaphat. 2Then some came and told Jehoshaphat, saying, "A great multitude is coming against you from beyond the sea, from
Syria;[y] and they are in Hazazon Tamar" (which *is* En Gedi). 3And
Jehoshaphat feared, and set himself to seek the LORD, and proclaimed a
fast throughout all Judah. 4So Judah gathered together to ask *help* from the
LORD; and from all the cities of Judah they came to seek the LORD.
5Then Jehoshaphat stood in the assembly of Judah and Jerusalem, in
the house of the LORD, before the new court, 6and said: "O LORD God of our
fathers, *are* You not God in heaven, and do You *not* rule over all the kingdoms of the nations, and in Your hand *is there not* power and might, so
that no one is able to withstand You? 7*Are* You not our God, *who* drove out
the inhabitants of this land before Your people Israel, and gave it to the descendants of Abraham Your friend forever? 8And they dwell in it, and have
built You a sanctuary in it for Your name, saying, 9'If disaster comes upon
us—sword, judgment, pestilence, or famine—we will stand before this
temple and in Your presence (for Your name *is* in this temple), and cry out
to You in our affliction, and You will hear and save.' 10And now, here are the
people of Ammon, Moab, and Mount Seir—whom You would not let Israel invade when they came out of the land of Egypt, but they turned from
them and did not destroy them— 11here they are, rewarding us by coming
to throw us out of Your possession which You have given us to inherit. 12O
our God, will You not judge them? For we have no power against this great
multitude that is coming against us; nor do we know what to do, but our
eyes *are* upon You."
13Now all Judah, with their little ones, their wives, and their children,
stood before the LORD.
14Then the Spirit of the LORD came upon Jahaziel the son of Zechariah,
the son of Benaiah, the son of Jeiel, the son of Mattaniah, a Levite of the
sons of Asaph, in the midst of the assembly. 15And he said, "Listen, all you
of Judah and you inhabitants of Jerusalem, and you, King Jehoshaphat!
Thus says the LORD to you: 'Do not be afraid nor dismayed because of this
great multitude, for the battle *is* not yours, but God's. 16Tomorrow go down
against them. They will surely come up by the Ascent of Ziz, and you will
find them at the end of the brook before the Wilderness of Jeruel. 17You will
not *need* to fight in this *battle*. Position yourselves, stand still and see the
salvation of the LORD, who is with you, O Judah and Jerusalem!' Do not fear
or be dismayed; tomorrow go out against them, for the LORD *is* with you."
18And Jehoshaphat bowed his head with *his* face to the ground, and all
Judah and the inhabitants of Jerusalem bowed before the LORD, worshiping the LORD. 19Then the Levites of the children of the Kohathites and of the
children of the Korahites stood up to praise the LORD God of Israel with
voices loud and high.
20So they rose early in the morning and went out into the Wilderness of
Tekoa; and as they went out, Jehoshaphat stood and said, "Hear me, O Judah and you inhabitants of Jerusalem: Believe in the LORD your God, and

20:1 [x] Following Masoretic Text and Vulgate; Septuagint reads *Meunites* (compare 26:7).
20:2 [y] Following Masoretic Text, Septuagint, and Vulgate; some Hebrew manuscripts and Old Latin read *Edom*.

He said, "Hannah, you're an addict. You find fault and talk about people's faults and criticize others all the time. There are plenty of other people to talk about faults—I don't need you to do so. But you are like an alcoholic. You don't dare give in to it once. If you promise not to make any exceptions, I'll help you."

"Well," I said, "only your grace could do that, Lord."

And the Lord said, "I'm going to ask for one of the heavenly beings to take a coal from off the altar and to touch your lips with it."

Jesus then told me all the things I should say—the kind, helpful good things they talk about in heaven. The language of heaven is called blessing. He taught me how lovely it is always to draw attention to what is good. Whenever Jesus spoke, the people "were amazed at the gracious words that came from his lips" (Luke 4:22).

(From "The Language of Heaven" by Hannah Hurnard in *Practical Christianity*)

APPLICATION We spend our whole life making judgments and judging various situations and actions. How do you go about making these judgments? Josiah gives us some pointers: realize we are judging for the Lord; judge impartially, without injustice; serve faithfully and in the fear of the Lord (19:6-7, 9).

EXPLORATION Judging Others—1 Samuel 16:7; Isaiah 11:3-5; Matthew 7:1-5; Luke 3:2; John 8:7; Acts 11:2-18; 1 Corinthians 5:12-13.

you shall be established; believe His prophets, and
you shall prosper." 21And when he had consulted with
the people, he appointed those who should sing to the
LORD, and who should praise the beauty of holiness,
as they went out before the army and were saying:

"Praise the LORD,
For His mercy *endures* forever."[z]

22Now when they began to sing and to praise, the
LORD set ambushes against the people of Ammon,
Moab, and Mount Seir, who had come against Judah;
and they were defeated. 23For the people of Ammon
and Moab stood up against the inhabitants of Mount
Seir to utterly kill and destroy *them*. And when they
had made an end of the inhabitants of Seir, they
helped to destroy one another.

24So when Judah came to a place overlooking the
wilderness, they looked toward the multitude; and
there *were* their dead bodies, fallen on the earth. No
one had escaped.

25When Jehoshaphat and his people came to take
away their spoil, they found among them an abundance of valuables on the dead bodies,[a] and precious
jewelry, which they stripped off for themselves, more
than they could carry away; and they were three days
gathering the spoil because there was so much. 26And
on the fourth day they assembled in the Valley of
Berachah, for there they blessed the LORD; therefore
the name of that place was called The Valley of Berachah[b] until this day. 27Then they returned, every man
of Judah and Jerusalem, with Jehoshaphat in front of
them, to go back to Jerusalem with joy, for the LORD
had made them rejoice over their enemies. 28So they
came to Jerusalem, with stringed instruments and
harps and trumpets, to the house of the LORD. 29And
the fear of God was on all the kingdoms of *those* countries when they heard that the LORD had fought
against the enemies of Israel. 30Then the realm of
Jehoshaphat was quiet, for his God gave him rest all
around.

The End of Jehoshaphat's Reign

31So Jehoshaphat was king over Judah. *He was*
thirty-five years old when he became king, and he
reigned twenty-five years in Jerusalem. His mother's
name *was* Azubah the daughter of Shilhi. 32And he
walked in the way of his father Asa, and did not turn
aside from it, doing *what was* right in the sight of the
LORD. 33Nevertheless the high places were not taken
away, for as yet the people had not directed their
hearts to the God of their fathers.

34Now the rest of the acts of Jehoshaphat, first and
last, indeed they *are* written in the book of Jehu the
son of Hanani, which *is* mentioned in the book of the
kings of Israel.

35After this Jehoshaphat king of Judah allied himself with Ahaziah king of Israel, who acted very wickedly. 36And he allied himself with him to make ships
to go to Tarshish, and they made the ships in Ezion
Geber. 37But Eliezer the son of Dodavah of Mareshah
prophesied against Jehoshaphat, saying, "Because
you have allied yourself with Ahaziah, the LORD has
destroyed your works." Then the ships were wrecked,
so that they were not able to go to Tarshish.

Jehoram Reigns in Judah

21 And Jehoshaphat rested with his fathers, and
was buried with his fathers in the City of David.
Then Jehoram his son reigned in his place. 2He had
brothers, the sons of Jehoshaphat: Azariah, Jehiel,
Zechariah, Azaryahu, Michael, and Shephatiah; all
these *were* the sons of Jehoshaphat king of Israel.
3Their father gave them great gifts of silver and gold
and precious things, with fortified cities in Judah; but
he gave the kingdom to Jehoram, because he *was* the
firstborn.

4Now when Jehoram was established over the kingdom of his father, he strengthened himself and killed
all his brothers with the sword, and also *others* of the
princes of Israel.

5Jehoram *was* thirty-two years old when he became
king, and he reigned eight years in Jerusalem. 6And
he walked in the way of the kings of Israel, just as the
house of Ahab had done, for he had the daughter of
Ahab as a wife; and he did evil in the sight of the LORD.
7Yet the LORD would not destroy the house of David,
because of the covenant that He had made with David, and since He had promised to give a lamp to him
and to his sons forever.

8In his days Edom revolted against Judah's authority, and made a king over themselves. 9So Jehoram
went out with his officers, and all his chariots with
him. And he rose by night and attacked the Edomites
who had surrounded him and the captains of the
chariots. 10Thus Edom has been in revolt against Judah's authority to this day. At that time Libnah re-

20:21 [z] Compare Psalm 106:1
20:25 [a] A few Hebrew manuscripts, Old Latin, and Vulgate read *garments;* Septuagint reads *armor.*
20:26 [b] Literally *Blessing*

volted against his rule, because he had forsaken the LORD God of his fathers. 11Moreover he made high places in the mountains of Judah, and
caused the inhabitants of Jerusalem to commit harlotry, and led Judah
astray.
12And a letter came to him from Elijah the prophet, saying,

> Thus says the LORD God of your father David:
> Because you have not walked in the ways of Jehoshaphat your
> father, or in the ways of Asa king of Judah, 13but have walked in
> the way of the kings of Israel, and have made Judah and the
> inhabitants of Jerusalem to play the harlot like the harlotry of the
> house of Ahab, and also have killed your brothers, those of your
> father's household, *who were* better than yourself, 14behold, the LORD
> will strike your people with a serious affliction—your children,
> your wives, and all your possessions; 15and you *will become* very
> sick with a disease of your intestines, until your intestines come
> out by reason of the sickness, day by day.

16Moreover the LORD stirred up against Jehoram the spirit of the
Philistines and the Arabians who *were* near the Ethiopians. 17And they
came up into Judah and invaded it, and carried away all the possessions
that were found in the king's house, and also his sons and his wives, so that
there was not a son left to him except Jehoahaz,[c] the youngest of his sons.
18After all this the LORD struck him in his intestines with an incurable
disease. 19Then it happened in the course of time, after the end of two
years, that his intestines came out because of his sickness; so he died in severe pain. And his people made no burning for him, like the burning for
his fathers.
20He was thirty-two years old when he became king. He reigned in Jerusalem eight years and, to no one's sorrow, departed. However they buried
him in the City of David, but not in the tombs of the kings.

Ahaziah Reigns in Judah

22 Then the inhabitants of Jerusalem made Ahaziah his youngest son
king in his place, for the raiders who came with the Arabians into
the camp had killed all the older *sons*. So Ahaziah the son of Jehoram, king
of Judah, reigned. 2Ahaziah *was* forty-two[d] years old when he became
king, and he reigned one year in Jerusalem. His mother's name *was*
Athaliah the granddaughter of Omri. 3He also walked in the ways of the
house of Ahab, for his mother advised him to do wickedly. 4Therefore he
did evil in the sight of the LORD, like the house of Ahab; for they were his
counselors after the death of his father, to his destruction. 5He also followed their advice, and went with Jehoram[e] the son of Ahab king of Israel
to war against Hazael king of Syria at Ramoth Gilead; and the Syrians
wounded Joram. 6Then he returned to Jezreel to recover from the wounds
which he had received at Ramah, when he fought against Hazael king of
Syria. And Azariah[f] the son of Jehoram, king of Judah, went down to see
Jehoram the son of Ahab in Jezreel, because he was sick.
7His going to Joram was God's occasion for Ahaziah's downfall; for

21:17 [c] Elsewhere called *Ahaziah* (compare 2 Chronicles 22:1)
22:2 [d] Or *twenty-two* (compare 2 Kings 8:26)
22:5 [e] Also spelled *Joram* (compare verses 5 and 7; 2 Kings 8:28; and elsewhere)
22:6 [f] Some Hebrew manuscripts, Septuagint, Syriac, Vulgate, and 2 Kings 8:29 read *Ahaziah*.

LIFE LESSON

2 Chronicles 21:4–24:27

SITUATION Under the guidance of Jehoiada the priest, Joash restored worship in the temple and destroyed the altars of Baal. When Jehoiada died, Joash turned his back on God and felt God's punishment.

OBSERVATION Surrounded by company that honored God, Joash made God-honoring decisions. When his counselor died, he failed to replace this voice in his life. When Joash sinned, God gave him many chances to repent.

INSPIRATION I don't believe it is possible for a person to be regenerated until the Holy Spirit has convicted that person of sin. Man can't be moral on his own. Given a choice, we will always choose the sinful way. I thought I was a moral person, but it wasn't until the moral person died that the Spirit of God could come to work in me. I love what William James said: "The death of a moral man is his spiritual birthday."

The conviction of sin by the Holy Spirit is the beginning. Without it, we cannot understand our need for God, and we cannot understand God's grace. We must not ever leave that out of our preaching, teaching, or understanding of Christianity. To omit it is to trivialize the work of Christ on the cross.

. . . If I were asked today to name the one doctrine of the Christian faith being preached about the least, I would have to say repentance. Repentance means change, and we don't want to threaten people with the need to change.

Repentance is commonly thought of as breast-beating, but it is not that at all. The Greek word used in the New Testament means simply, "change of mind." When you come to God, you have a change of mind, from exalting yourself to exalting Christ. Repentance means turning from man's ways to embrace God's ways. It means a desire to be different, to belong to Christ and to live as he commands us to live. Repentance, then, is the longing to turn away from the old self and to live a new life in Christ.

In my own life, repentance meant that I wanted to adopt new values. I wanted

Continued

when he arrived, he went out with Jehoram against Jehu the son of
Nimshi, whom the LORD had anointed to cut off the house of Ahab. 8And it
happened, when Jehu was executing judgment on the house of Ahab, and
found the princes of Judah and the sons of Ahaziah's brothers who served
Ahaziah, that he killed them. 9Then he searched for Ahaziah; and they
caught him (he was hiding in Samaria), and brought him to Jehu. When
they had killed him, they buried him, "because," they said, "he is the son
of Jehoshaphat, who sought the LORD with all his heart."
So the house of Ahaziah had no one to assume power over the kingdom.

Athaliah Reigns in Judah

10Now when Athaliah the mother of Ahaziah saw that her son was dead,
she arose and destroyed all the royal heirs of the house of Judah. 11But
Jehoshabeath,[g] the daughter of the king, took Joash the son of Ahaziah,
and stole him away from among the king's sons who were being murdered, and put him and his nurse in a bedroom. So Jehoshabeath, the
daughter of King Jehoram, the wife of Jehoiada the priest (for she was the
sister of Ahaziah), hid him from Athaliah so that she did not kill him.
12And he was hidden with them in the house of God for six years, while
Athaliah reigned over the land.

Joash Crowned King of Judah

23 In the seventh year Jehoiada strengthened himself, *and made a*
covenant with the captains of hundreds: Azariah the son of
Jeroham, Ishmael the son of Jehohanan, Azariah the son of Obed,
Maaseiah the son of Adaiah, and Elishaphat the son of Zichri. 2And they
went throughout Judah and gathered the Levites from all the cities of Judah, and the chief fathers of Israel, and they came to Jerusalem.
3Then all the assembly made a covenant with the king in the house of
God. And he said to them, "Behold, the king's son shall reign, as the LORD
has said of the sons of David. 4This *is* what you shall do: One-third of you
entering on the Sabbath, of the priests and the Levites, *shall be* keeping
watch over the doors; 5one-third *shall be* at the king's house; and one-third
at the Gate of the Foundation. All the people *shall be* in the courts of the
house of the LORD. 6But let no one come into the house of the LORD except
the priests and those of the Levites who serve. They may go in, for they *are*
holy; but all the people shall keep the watch of the LORD. 7And the Levites
shall surround the king on all sides, every man with his weapons in his
hand; and whoever comes into the house, let him be put to death. You are
to be with the king when he comes in and when he goes out."
8So the Levites and all Judah did according to all that Jehoiada the priest
commanded. And each man took his men who were to be on duty on the
Sabbath, with those who were going *off duty* on the Sabbath; for Jehoiada
the priest had not dismissed the divisions. 9And Jehoiada the priest gave
to the captains of hundreds the spears and the large and small shields
which *had belonged* to King David, that *were* in the temple of God. 10Then
he set all the people, every man with his weapon in his hand, from the
right side of the temple to the left side of the temple, along by the altar and
by the temple, all around the king. 11And they brought out the king's son,
put the crown on him, *gave him* the Testimony,[h] and made him king. Then

to be forgiven of what I'd done in the past and not continue doing those things, but rather be led by the Spirit to the kinds of things that God wants from my life. There is a certain sorrow that goes with repentance, a sorrow over your sins, a desire to restore where you have done harm in the past. One thing I did was to apologize to some of the people I had hurt in politics. I went to them to seek their forgiveness because I realized that God had forgiven me and I should seek to restore my relationships with people I had injured. Some of them remained cynical about me. They had been political enemies, and they thought my seeking forgiveness was some sort of ploy. Some did not understand it. Others were deeply affected by it. And some people had trouble accepting my repentance. They would say, "Sure I forgive you," but they were very uncomfortable because it convicted them as well.

A prime case of repentance leading to restoration is the well-known case of Cathleen Webb, who falsely accused Gary Dotson of raping her. When she came under the conviction of sin—six years later—she realized that she had to recant her story and tell the truth. You can just imagine the pain that was involved for that young girl in coming forward with the truth. I met with her, and I know that her decision was a moving of the Spirit. She was left with no choice but to confess.

That's what happens when the conviction of sin leads to repentance. The yearning for God's cleansing is so strong that we cannot find peace until we have accepted that "change of mind" and begin to walk in the new life with the Lord.

(From "What it Means to Repent" by Charles Colson in *Practical Christianity*)

APPLICATION What would be the hardest part of true repentance for you? What would be the most liberating part? Seek help from Christian friends who will pray with you through the process.

EXPLORATION Repentance—Ezra 10:2-4, 11; 1 Kings 21:29; 1 Chronicles 21:8; Psalm 80:3, 7, 19; Matthew 3:1-6; 2 Corinthians 7:10; Luke 3:8-9; 19:1-8; Acts 3:19.

22:11 [g] Spelled *Jehosheba* in 2 Kings 11:2
23:11 [h] That is, the Law (compare Exodus 25:16, 21; 31:18)

Jehoiada and his sons anointed him, and said, "*Long*
live the king!"

Death of Athaliah

12Now when Athaliah heard the noise of the people
running and praising the king, she came to the people
in the temple of the LORD. 13*When* she looked, there
was the king standing by his pillar at the entrance;
and the leaders and the trumpeters *were* by the king.
All the people of the land were rejoicing and blowing
trumpets, also the singers with musical instruments,
and those who led in praise. So Athaliah tore her
clothes and said, "Treason! Treason!"
14And Jehoiada the priest brought out the captains
of hundreds who were set over the army, and said to
them, "Take her outside under guard, and slay with
the sword whoever follows her." For the priest had
said, "Do not kill her in the house of the LORD."
15So they seized her; and she went by way of the entrance of the Horse Gate *into* the king's house, and
they killed her there.
16Then Jehoiada made a covenant between himself,
the people, and the king, that they should be the LORD's
people. 17And all the people went to the temple[i] of Baal,
and tore it down. They broke in pieces its altars and
images, and killed Mattan the priest of Baal before the
altars. 18Also Jehoiada appointed the oversight of the
house of the LORD to the hand of the priests, the
Levites, whom David had assigned in the house of the
LORD, to offer the burnt offerings of the LORD, as *it is*
written in the Law of Moses, with rejoicing and with
singing, *as it was established* by David. 19And he set the
gatekeepers at the gates of the house of the LORD, so
that no one *who was* in any way unclean should enter.
20Then he took the captains of hundreds, the nobles,
the governors of the people, and all the people of the
land, and brought the king down from the house of the
LORD; and they went through the Upper Gate to the
king's house, and set the king on the throne of the kingdom. 21So all the people of the land rejoiced; and the city
was quiet, for they had slain Athaliah with the sword.

Joash Repairs the Temple

24 Joash *was* seven years old when he became
king, and he reigned forty years in Jerusalem.
His mother's name *was* Zibiah of Beersheba. 2Joash
did *what was* right in the sight of the LORD all the days
of Jehoiada the priest. 3And Jehoiada took two wives
for him, and he had sons and daughters.
4Now it happened after this *that* Joash set his heart
on repairing the house of the LORD. 5Then he gathered
the priests and the Levites, and said to them, "Go out
to the cities of Judah, and gather from all Israel
money to repair the house of your God from year to
year, and see that you do it quickly."
However the Levites did not do it quickly. 6So the
king called Jehoiada the chief *priest,* and said to him,
"Why have you not required the Levites to bring in
from Judah and from Jerusalem the collection, *according to the commandment* of Moses the servant of
the LORD and of the assembly of Israel, for the tabernacle of witness?" 7For the sons of Athaliah, that
wicked woman, had broken into the house of God,
and had also presented all the dedicated things of the
house of the LORD to the Baals.
8Then at the king's command they made a chest,
and set it outside at the gate of the house of the LORD.
9And they made a proclamation throughout Judah
and Jerusalem to bring to the LORD the collection *that*
Moses the servant of God *had imposed* on Israel in the
wilderness. 10Then all the leaders and all the people
rejoiced, brought their contributions, and put *them*
into the chest until all had given. 11So it was, at that
time, when the chest was brought to the king's official
by the hand of the Levites, and when they saw that
there was much money, that the king's scribe and the
high priest's officer came and emptied the chest, and
took it and returned it to its place. Thus they did day
by day, and gathered money in abundance.
12The king and Jehoiada gave it to those who did the
work of the service of the house of the LORD; and they
hired masons and carpenters to repair the house of
the LORD, and also those who worked in iron and
bronze to restore the house of the LORD. 13So the workmen labored, and the work was completed by them;
they restored the house of God to its original condition and reinforced it. 14When they had finished, they
brought the rest of the money before the king and
Jehoiada; they made from it articles for the house of
the LORD, articles for serving and offering, spoons and
vessels of gold and silver. And they offered burnt offerings in the house of the LORD continually all the
days of Jehoiada.

Apostasy of Joash

15But Jehoiada grew old and was full of days, and he
died; *he was* one hundred and thirty years old when
he died. 16And they buried him in the City of David

23:17 [i] Literally *house*

among the kings, because he had done good in Israel, both toward God and His house.

17Now after the death of Jehoiada the leaders of Judah came and bowed down to the king. And the king listened to them. 18Therefore they left the house of the LORD God of their fathers, and served wooden images and idols; and wrath came upon Judah and Jerusalem because of their trespass. 19Yet He sent prophets to them, to bring them back to the LORD; and they testified against them, but they would not listen.

20Then the Spirit of God came upon Zechariah the son of Jehoiada the priest, who stood above the people, and said to them, "Thus says God: 'Why do you transgress the commandments of the LORD, so that you cannot prosper? Because you have forsaken the LORD, He also has forsaken you.' " 21So they conspired against him, and at the command of the king they stoned him with stones in the court of the house of the LORD. 22Thus Joash the king did not remember the kindness which Jehoiada his father had done to him, but killed his son; and as he died, he said, "The LORD look on *it*, and repay!"

Death of Joash

23So it happened in the spring of the year *that* the army of Syria came up against him; and they came to Judah and Jerusalem, and destroyed all the leaders of the people from among the people, and sent all their spoil to the king of Damascus. 24For the army of the Syrians came with a small company of men; but the LORD delivered a very great army into their hand, because they had forsaken the LORD God of their fathers. So they executed judgment against Joash. 25And when they had withdrawn from him (for they left him severely wounded), his own servants conspired against him because of the blood of the sons[j] of Jehoiada the priest, and killed him on his bed. So he died. And they buried him in the City of David, but they did not bury him in the tombs of the kings.

26These are the ones who conspired against him: Zabad[k] the son of Shimeath the Ammonitess, and Jehozabad the son of Shimrith[l] the Moabitess. 27Now *concerning* his sons, and the many oracles about him, and the repairing of the house of God, indeed they *are* written in the annals of the book of the kings. Then Amaziah his son reigned in his place.

Amaziah Reigns in Judah

25 Amaziah *was* twenty-five years old *when* he became king, and he reigned twenty-nine years in Jerusalem. His mother's name *was* Jehoaddan of Jerusalem. 2And he did *what was* right in the sight of the LORD, but not with a loyal heart.

3Now it happened, as soon as the kingdom was established for him, that he executed his servants who had murdered his father the king. 4However he did not execute their children, but *did* as *it is* written in the Law in the Book of Moses, where the LORD commanded, saying, "The fathers shall not be put to death for their children, nor shall the children be put to death for their fathers; but a person shall die for his own sin."[m]

LIFE LESSON

2 Chronicles 25:1–26:23

SITUATION Both Amaziah and Uzziah were God-fearing kings. As long as they acknowledged God's part in their achievements, they prospered. When ambition and pride caused them to forget God, they paid the price for their sin.

OBSERVATION Pride causes us to set ourselves up as gods. Because of pride, we sin without regard to God's standards.

INSPIRATION Do not be ashamed to serve others because of your love for Jesus Christ, or to appear poor in the world's eyes.

Do not count on your own strength; trust God. Do what you can, and God will supply the difference.

Take glory neither in money, if you have some, nor in influential friends, but in God who gives you everything and above all wants to give you himself.

Avoid boasting about the size or beauty of your body, which a little illness can disfigure or destroy.

Have no pride in your native wit and talent; that would displease God who gave you every good thing that you naturally possess.

24:25 [j] Septuagint and Vulgate read *son* (compare verses 20–22).
24:26 [k] Or *Jozachar* (compare 2 Kings 12:21) [l] Or *Shomer* (compare 2 Kings 12:21)
25:4 [m] Deuteronomy 24:16

The War Against Edom

5Moreover Amaziah gathered Judah together and set over them captains of thousands and captains of hundreds, according to *their* fathers'
houses, throughout all Judah and Benjamin; and he numbered them from
twenty years old and above, and found them to be three hundred thousand choice *men, able* to go to war, who could handle spear and shield.
6He also hired one hundred thousand mighty men of valor from Israel for
one hundred talents of silver. 7But a man of God came to him, saying, "O
king, do not let the army of Israel go with you, for the LORD *is* not with Israel—*not with* any of the children of Ephraim. 8But if you go, be gone! Be
strong in battle! *Even so,* God shall make you fall before the enemy; for God
has power to help and to overthrow."
9Then Amaziah said to the man of God, "But what *shall we* do about the
hundred talents which I have given to the troops of Israel?"
And the man of God answered, "The LORD is able to give you much
more than this." 10So Amaziah discharged the troops that had come to
him from Ephraim, to go back home. Therefore their anger was greatly
aroused against Judah, and they returned home in great anger.
11Then Amaziah strengthened himself, and leading his people, he went
to the Valley of Salt and killed ten thousand of the people of Seir. 12Also the
children of Judah took captive ten thousand alive, brought them to the top
of the rock, and cast them down from the top of the rock, so that they all
were dashed in pieces.
13But as for the soldiers of the army which Amaziah had discharged, so
that they would not go with him to battle, they raided the cities of Judah
from Samaria to Beth Horon, killed three thousand in them, and took
much spoil.
14Now it was so, after Amaziah came from the slaughter of the Edomites,
that he brought the gods of the people of Seir, set them up *to be* his gods,
and bowed down before them and burned incense to them. 15Therefore
the anger of the LORD was aroused against Amaziah, and He sent him a
prophet who said to him, "Why have you sought the gods of the people,
which could not rescue their own people from your hand?"
16So it was, as he talked with him, that *the king* said to him, "Have we
made you the king's counselor? Cease! Why should you be killed?"
Then the prophet ceased, and said, "I know that God has determined to
destroy you, because you have done this and have not heeded my advice."

Israel Defeats Judah

17Now Amaziah king of Judah asked advice and sent to Joash*n* the son of
Jehoahaz, the son of Jehu, king of Israel, saying, "Come, let us face one another *in battle.*"
18And Joash king of Israel sent to Amaziah king of Judah, saying, "The
thistle that *was* in Lebanon sent to the cedar that was in Lebanon, saying,
'Give your daughter to my son as wife'; and a wild beast that *was* in Lebanon passed by and trampled the thistle. 19Indeed you say that you have defeated the Edomites, and your heart is lifted up to boast. Stay at home now;
why should you meddle with trouble, that you should fall—you and Judah with you?"

Reject the thought that you are better than anyone else. If you think such haughty thoughts, God (who knows what is in you) will consider you worse than they.

Pride about our good deeds is pointless. God has his own ideas regarding what is good, and he does not always agree with us. If there is anything good about you, believe better things of others. This will keep you humble.

It will not hurt you at all to consider yourself less righteous than others, but it will be disastrous for you to consider yourself better than even one person.

The humble are always at peace; the proud are often envious and angry.

(From *The Imitation of Christ* by Thomas à Kempis)

APPLICATION Pride and ambition may creep in and sweep away our devotion to God. Success often tries to squeeze God out of our mind. Check your attitudes. Resist pride. Focus on Christ.

EXPLORATION Pride—Numbers 16:8-10; Judges 8:1-3; 17:6; Mark 9:34; Luke 18:11-14; Ephesians 2:11-13.

25:17 *n* Spelled *Jehoash* in 2 Kings 14:8ff

20But Amaziah would not heed, for it *came* from
God, that He might give them into the hand *of their en-*
emies, because they sought the gods of Edom. 21So
Joash king of Israel went out; and he and Amaziah
king of Judah faced one another at Beth Shemesh,
which *belongs* to Judah. 22And Judah was defeated by
Israel, and every man fled to his tent. 23Then Joash the
king of Israel captured Amaziah king of Judah, the son
of Joash, the son of Jehoahaz, at Beth Shemesh; and he
brought him to Jerusalem, and broke down the wall of
Jerusalem from the Gate of Ephraim to the Corner
Gate—four hundred cubits. 24And *he took* all the gold
and silver, all the articles that were found in the house
of God with Obed-Edom, the treasures of the king's
house, and hostages, and returned to Samaria.

Death of Amaziah

25Amaziah the son of Joash, king of Judah, lived fifteen years after the death of Joash the son of Jehoahaz,
king of Israel. 26Now the rest of the acts of Amaziah,
from first to last, indeed *are* they not written in the
book of the kings of Judah and Israel? 27After the time
that Amaziah turned away from following the LORD,
they made a conspiracy against him in Jerusalem,
and he fled to Lachish; but they sent after him to
Lachish and killed him there. 28Then they brought
him on horses and buried him with his fathers in the
City of Judah.

Uzziah Reigns in Judah

26 Now all the people of Judah took Uzziah,[o] who
was sixteen years old, and made him king instead of his father Amaziah. 2He built Elath[p] and restored it to Judah, after the king rested with his fathers.
3Uzziah *was* sixteen years old when he became
king, and he reigned fifty-two years in Jerusalem. His
mother's name was Jecholiah of Jerusalem. 4And he
did *what was* right in the sight of the LORD, according
to all that his father Amaziah had done. 5He sought
God in the days of Zechariah, who had understanding
in the visions[q] of God; and as long as he sought the
LORD, God made him prosper.
6Now he went out and made war against the
Philistines, and broke down the wall of Gath, the wall
of Jabneh, and the wall of Ashdod; and he built cities
around Ashdod and among the Philistines. 7God
helped him against the Philistines, against the Arabians who lived in Gur Baal, and against the
Meunites. 8Also the Ammonites brought tribute to
Uzziah. His fame spread as far as the entrance of
Egypt, for he became exceedingly strong.
9And Uzziah built towers in Jerusalem at the Corner Gate, at the Valley Gate, and at the corner buttress
of the wall; then he fortified them. 10Also he built towers in the desert. He dug many wells, for he had much
livestock, both in the lowlands and in the plains; *he*
also had farmers and vinedressers in the mountains
and in Carmel, for he loved the soil.
11Moreover Uzziah had an army of fighting men who
went out to war by companies, according to the number on their roll as prepared by Jeiel the scribe and
Maaseiah the officer, under the hand of Hananiah, *one*
of the king's captains. 12The total number of chief officers[r] of the mighty men of valor *was* two thousand six
hundred. 13And under their authority *was* an army of
three hundred and seven thousand five hundred, that
made war with mighty power, to help the king against
the enemy. 14Then Uzziah prepared for them, for the
entire army, shields, spears, helmets, body armor,
bows, and slings *to cast* stones. 15And he made devices
in Jerusalem, invented by skillful men, to be on the
towers and the corners, to shoot arrows and large
stones. So his fame spread far and wide, for he was
marvelously helped till he became strong.

The Penalty for Uzziah's Pride

16But when he was strong his heart was lifted up, to
his destruction, for he transgressed against the LORD
his God by entering the temple of the LORD to burn incense on the altar of incense. 17So Azariah the priest
went in after him, and with him were eighty priests of
the LORD—valiant men. 18And they withstood King
Uzziah, and said to him, "*It is* not for you, Uzziah, to
burn incense to the LORD, but for the priests, the sons
of Aaron, who are consecrated to burn incense. Get
out of the sanctuary, for you have trespassed! You
shall have no honor from the LORD God."
19Then Uzziah became furious; and he *had* a censer
in his hand to burn incense. And while he was angry
with the priests, leprosy broke out on his forehead,
before the priests in the house of the LORD, beside the
incense altar. 20And Azariah the chief priest and all
the priests looked at him, and there, on his forehead,
he *was* leprous; so they thrust him out of that place.
Indeed he also hurried to get out, because the LORD
had struck him.

26:1 [o] Called *Azariah* in 2 Kings 14:21ff
26:2 [p] Hebrew *Eloth*
26:5 [q] Several Hebrew manuscripts, Septuagint, Syriac, Targum, and Arabic read *fear.*
26:12 [r] Literally *chief fathers*

21 King Uzziah was a leper until the day of his death. He dwelt in an isolated house, because he was a leper; for he was cut off from the house of
the LORD. Then Jotham his son *was* over the king's house, judging the people of the land.
22 Now the rest of the acts of Uzziah, from first to last, the prophet Isaiah
the son of Amoz wrote. 23 So Uzziah rested with his fathers, and they buried
him with his fathers in the field of burial which *belonged* to the kings, for
they said, "He is a leper." Then Jotham his son reigned in his place.

Jotham Reigns in Judah

27 Jotham *was* twenty-five years old when he became king, and he
reigned sixteen years in Jerusalem. His mother's name *was*
Jerushah[s] the daughter of Zadok. 2 And he did *what was* right in the sight of
the LORD, according to all that his father Uzziah had done (although he did
not enter the temple of the LORD). But still the people acted corruptly.
3 He built the Upper Gate of the house of the LORD, and he built exten-
sively on the wall of Ophel. 4 Moreover he built cities in the mountains of
Judah, and in the forests he built fortresses and towers. 5 He also fought
with the king of the Ammonites and defeated them. And the people of
Ammon gave him in that year one hundred talents of silver, ten thousand
kors of wheat, and ten thousand of barley. The people of Ammon paid this
to him in the second and third years also. 6 So Jotham became mighty, because he prepared his ways before the LORD his God.
7 Now the rest of the acts of Jotham, and all his wars and his ways, indeed they *are* written in the book of the kings of Israel and Judah. 8 He was
twenty-five years old when he became king, and he reigned sixteen years
in Jerusalem. 9 So Jotham rested with his fathers, and they buried him in
the City of David. Then Ahaz his son reigned in his place.

Ahaz Reigns in Judah

28 Ahaz *was* twenty years old when he became king, and he reigned
sixteen years in Jerusalem; and he did not do *what was* right in the
sight of the LORD, as his father David *had done.* 2 For he walked in the ways
of the kings of Israel, and made molded images for the Baals. 3 He burned
incense in the Valley of the Son of Hinnom, and burned his children in the
fire, according to the abominations of the nations whom the LORD had cast
out before the children of Israel. 4 And he sacrificed and burned incense on
the high places, on the hills, and under every green tree.

Syria and Israel Defeat Judah

5 Therefore the LORD his God delivered him into the hand of the king of
Syria. They defeated him, and carried away a great multitude of them as
captives, and brought *them* to Damascus. Then he was also delivered into
the hand of the king of Israel, who defeated him with a great slaughter.
6 For Pekah the son of Remaliah killed one hundred and twenty thousand
in Judah in one day, all valiant men, because they had forsaken the LORD
God of their fathers. 7 Zichri, a mighty man of Ephraim, killed Maaseiah
the king's son, Azrikam the officer over the house, and Elkanah *who was*
second to the king. 8 And the children of Israel carried away captive of their

27:1 [s] Spelled *Jerusha* in 2 Kings 15:33

LIFE LESSON

2 Chronicles 27:1–28:27

SITUATION Although King Jotham obeyed God, his subjects did not. It seems he never encouraged them to walk in God's way.

OBSERVATION God places people around us who can benefit from our influence.

INSPIRATION Christianity roared across the civilized world because of integrity, not image. The best growth rates were the years without legal recognition or social clout. Why? Because God blessed authentic faith! Then, after the Edict of Constantine, when the Church received legal status and began to jockey for the support of political power, the Christian movement began to lose its steam.

We sometimes rely on "ministry by charisma." We want preachers that can "wow" the audience. Let Christ be represented by a real charmer, someone who can bring in the crowds and excite the masses. Now, there is nothing wrong in utilizing God-given gifts of communication. But there is something wrong, even idolatrous, in replacing God's Holy Spirit with the force of human personality, or scholarship, or reputation. . . .

We sometimes operate as if we expect kingdom growth through political posturing. We want to headline Christians who can impress. Wouldn't it be great if the governor was a part of our church? Wouldn't it be something if we could get a movie star to testify at our services? Or how about a converted porno publisher?

The truth is, all people need the gospel. And God doesn't need just the "influential" to carry His message. If He has succeeded in communicating through donkeys and tornadoes, He can probably use ordinary Joes like us.

Some of us may occasionally be guilty of intimidation by information as we go out to blow away people with the Bible. We may fire off our barrage of biblical bullets from six feet above criticism, quoting our repertoire of verses and packaged answers ready-made for any situation. . . .

The difference between the prophet

Continued

in the Bible and the professional in the limelight dangerously resembles the difference between authentic Christianity and insincerity. . . .

Possibly prophets are needed more urgently than professionals—prophets who deny themselves rather than professionals who exalt themselves; prophets who are weak rather than professionals who are polished; prophets who may get stoned rather than professionals who get pampered; prophets walking with Christ, who hunger for God in prayer and who weep over sins. Prophets! Not more slick professionals with Teflon exteriors that slough off the messy painful side of life.

An authentic walk with Christ makes us hunger for God in prayer and weep over sins. God draws us toward the holiness of heaven.

(From *Heaven Came Down* by Lynn Anderson)

APPLICATION You can encourage other believers today! You can help unbelievers find Christ! How? Look for the hurting. Look for the lost. Watch for needs. Opportunities are plentiful. Accept the challenge of an opportunity and pray that God will help you be successful.

EXPLORATION Influence—Genesis 6:9; Matthew 5:13; Romans 1:5; 1 Peter 3:1-2.

brethren two hundred thousand women, sons, and daughters; and they also took away much spoil from them, and brought the spoil to Samaria.

Israel Returns the Captives

9But a prophet of the LORD was there, whose name *was* Oded; and he
went out before the army that came to Samaria, and said to them: "Look,
because the LORD God of your fathers was angry with Judah, He has delivered them into your hand; but you have killed them in a rage *that* reaches
up to heaven. 10And now you propose to force the children of Judah and Jerusalem to be your male and female slaves; *but are* you not also guilty before the LORD your God? 11Now hear me, therefore, and return the captives,
whom you have taken captive from your brethren, for the fierce wrath of
the LORD *is* upon you."

12Then some of the heads of the children of Ephraim, Azariah the son of
Johanan, Berechiah the son of Meshillemoth, Jehizkiah the son of
Shallum, and Amasa the son of Hadlai, stood up against those who came
from the war, 13and said to them, "You shall not bring the captives here, for
we *already* have offended the LORD. You intend to add to our sins and to
our guilt; for our guilt is great, and *there is* fierce wrath against Israel." 14So
the armed men left the captives and the spoil before the leaders and all the
assembly. 15Then the men who were designated by name rose up and took
the captives, and from the spoil they clothed all who were naked among
them, dressed them and gave them sandals, gave them food and drink,
and anointed them; and they let all the feeble ones ride on donkeys. So
they brought them to their brethren at Jericho, the city of palm trees. Then
they returned to Samaria.

Assyria Refuses to Help Judah

16At the same time King Ahaz sent to the kings[t] of Assyria to help him.
17For again the Edomites had come, attacked Judah, and carried away captives. 18The Philistines also had invaded the cities of the lowland and of the
South of Judah, and had taken Beth Shemesh, Aijalon, Gederoth, Sochoh
with its villages, Timnah with its villages, and Gimzo with its villages; and
they dwelt there. 19For the LORD brought Judah low because of Ahaz king of
Israel, for he had encouraged moral decline in Judah and had been continually unfaithful to the LORD. 20Also Tiglath-Pileser[u] king of Assyria came to
him and distressed him, and did not assist him. 21For Ahaz took part *of the*
treasures from the house of the LORD, from the house of the king, and from
the leaders, and he gave *it* to the king of Assyria; but he did not help him.

Apostasy and Death of Ahaz

22Now in the time of his distress King Ahaz became increasingly
unfaithful to the LORD. This *is that* King Ahaz. 23For he sacrificed to the
gods of Damascus which had defeated him, saying, "Because the gods of
the kings of Syria help them, I will sacrifice to them that they may help
me." But they were the ruin of him and of all Israel. 24So Ahaz gathered the
articles of the house of God, cut in pieces the articles of the house of God,
shut up the doors of the house of the LORD, and made for himself altars in
every corner of Jerusalem. 25And in every single city of Judah he made

28:16 [t] Septuagint, Syriac, and Vulgate read *king* (compare verse 20).
28:20 [u] Hebrew *Tilgath-Pilneser*

high places to burn incense to other gods, and provoked to anger the LORD
God of his fathers.
26Now the rest of his acts and all his ways, from first to last, indeed they
are written in the book of the kings of Judah and Israel. 27So Ahaz rested
with his fathers, and they buried him in the city, in Jerusalem; but they did
not bring him into the tombs of the kings of Israel. Then Hezekiah his son
reigned in his place.

Hezekiah Reigns in Judah

29 Hezekiah became king *when he was* twenty-five years old, and he
reigned twenty-nine years in Jerusalem. His mother's name *was*
Abijah[v] the daughter of Zechariah. 2And he did *what was* right in the sight
of the LORD, according to all that his father David had done.

Hezekiah Cleanses the Temple

3In the first year of his reign, in the first month, he opened the doors of
the house of the LORD and repaired them. 4Then he brought in the priests
and the Levites, and gathered them in the East Square, 5and said to them:
"Hear me, Levites! Now sanctify yourselves, sanctify the house of the LORD
God of your fathers, and carry out the rubbish from the holy *place.* 6For
our fathers have trespassed and done evil in the eyes of the LORD our God;
they have forsaken Him, have turned their faces away from the dwelling
place of the LORD, and turned *their* backs *on Him.* 7They have also shut up
the doors of the vestibule, put out the lamps, and have not burned incense
or offered burnt offerings in the holy *place* to the God of Israel. 8Therefore
the wrath of the LORD fell upon Judah and Jerusalem, and He has given
them up to trouble, to desolation, and to jeering, as you see with your eyes.
9For indeed, because of this our fathers have fallen by the sword; and our
sons, our daughters, and our wives *are* in captivity.
10"Now *it is* in my heart to make a covenant with the LORD God of Israel,
that His fierce wrath may turn away from us. 11My sons, do not be negligent now, for the LORD has chosen you to stand before Him, to serve Him,
and that you should minister to Him and burn incense."
12Then these Levites arose: Mahath the son of Amasai and Joel the son of
Azariah, of the sons of the Kohathites; of the sons of Merari, Kish the son
of Abdi and Azariah the son of Jehallelel; of the Gershonites, Joah the son of
Zimmah and Eden the son of Joah; 13of the sons of Elizaphan, Shimri and
Jeiel; of the sons of Asaph, Zechariah and Mattaniah; 14of the sons of Heman,
Jehiel and Shimei; and of the sons of Jeduthun, Shemaiah and Uzziel.
15And they gathered their brethren, sanctified themselves, and went according to the commandment of the king, at the words of the LORD, to
cleanse the house of the LORD. 16Then the priests went into the inner part of
the house of the LORD to cleanse *it,* and brought out all the debris that they
found in the temple of the LORD to the court of the house of the LORD. And
the Levites took *it* out and carried *it* to the Brook Kidron.
17Now they began to sanctify on the first *day* of the first month, and on
the eighth day of the month they came to the vestibule of the LORD. So they
sanctified the house of the LORD in eight days, and on the sixteenth day of
the first month they finished.

29:1 [v] Spelled *Abi* in 2 Kings 18:2

LIFE LESSON

2 Chronicles 29:1–32:23

SITUATION Kings who worshiped false gods ruled Judah. Hezekiah, however, followed God and desired to please him. He destroyed the pagan temples and altars that had become common in Judah and reopened the temple in Jerusalem. He brought about a religious revival and sought to restore the nation to God.

OBSERVATION God does not tolerate compromise with the pagans. The longer compromise goes unchecked, the harder it becomes to turn back.

INSPIRATION Hezekiah, king of Israel, stirrer of religious revival in the land, calls upon the people to abandon false Gods and return to the true God. He calls upon the people to come to Jerusalem to celebrate the Passover. But there are two problems.

One, it has been so long since the people partook of the Passover that no one is ceremonially clean. No one is prepared to partake. Even the priests have been worshiping idols and have failed to observe the necessary rituals for purity.

Two, God had commanded that the Passover be celebrated on the fourteenth day of the first month. By the time Hezekiah can assemble the people it is the second month.

So the Passover was kept a month late by impure participants.

Hezekiah prayed for them: "LORD, you are good. . . . Please forgive all those who try to obey you even if they did not make themselves clean as the rules of the Temple command."

Do you see the dilemma?

What does God do when the motive is pure but the method is poor?

"The LORD listened to Hezekiah's prayer, and he healed the people."

The right heart with the wrong ritual is better than the wrong heart with the right ritual. . . .

Some of you are scowling. "Wait a minute, Max. Are you saying that the method we use to approach God is immaterial? Are you saying that the only thing that matters is why we go

Continued

to God and that how we approach him is relative?"

No, that's not what I'm saying. . . . Ideally, we approach God with the right motive and the right method. And sometimes we do. Sometimes the words of our prayer are as beautiful as the motive behind the prayer. Sometimes the way we sing is as strong as the reason we sing.

But many times it isn't. Many times our words falter. Many times our music suffers. Many times our worship is less than what we want it to be. . . . God didn't tell Hezekiah to shut down the celebration. . . . Hezekiah did the best [he] could with what [he] had—and that was enough.

"You will search for me," God declared. "And when you search for me with all your heart, you will find me! I will let you find me."

What a promise!

(From *And the Angels Were Silent* by Max Lucado)

APPLICATION Pray for national leaders today, local leaders tomorrow, world leaders the next day. Keep your prayer habit strong.

EXPLORATION Righteousness in Life and Prayer—Genesis 6:9; 2 Kings 19:1-7; Isaiah 26:7; James 5:16.

[18]Then they went in to King Hezekiah and said, "We have cleansed all the house of the LORD, the altar of burnt offerings with all its articles, and the table of the showbread with all its articles. [19]Moreover all the articles which King Ahaz in his reign had cast aside in his transgression we have prepared and sanctified; and there they *are,* before the altar of the LORD."

Hezekiah Restores Temple Worship

[20]Then King Hezekiah rose early, gathered the rulers of the city, and went up to the house of the LORD. [21]And they brought seven bulls, seven rams, seven lambs, and seven male goats for a sin offering for the kingdom, for the sanctuary, and for Judah. Then he commanded the priests, the sons of Aaron, to offer *them* on the altar of the LORD. [22]So they killed the bulls, and the priests received the blood and sprinkled *it* on the altar. Likewise they killed the rams and sprinkled the blood on the altar. They also killed the lambs and sprinkled the blood on the altar. [23]Then they brought out the male goats *for* the sin offering before the king and the assembly, and they laid their hands on them. [24]And the priests killed them; and they presented their blood on the altar as a sin offering to make an atonement for all Israel, for the king commanded *that* the burnt offering and the sin offering *be made* for all Israel.

[25]And he stationed the Levites in the house of the LORD with cymbals, with stringed instruments, and with harps, according to the commandment of David, of Gad the king's seer, and of Nathan the prophet; for thus *was* the commandment of the LORD by His prophets. [26]The Levites stood with the instruments of David, and the priests with the trumpets. [27]Then Hezekiah commanded *them* to offer the burnt offering on the altar. And when the burnt offering began, the song of the LORD *also* began, with the trumpets and with the instruments of David king of Israel. [28]So all the assembly worshiped, the singers sang, and the trumpeters sounded; all *this continued* until the burnt offering was finished. [29]And when they had finished offering, the king and all who were present with him bowed and worshiped. [30]Moreover King Hezekiah and the leaders commanded the Levites to sing praise to the LORD with the words of David and of Asaph the seer. So they sang praises with gladness, and they bowed their heads and worshiped.

[31]Then Hezekiah answered and said, "Now *that* you have consecrated yourselves to the LORD, come near, and bring sacrifices and thank offerings into the house of the LORD." So the assembly brought in sacrifices and thank offerings, and as many as were of a willing heart *brought* burnt offerings. [32]And the number of the burnt offerings which the assembly brought was seventy bulls, one hundred rams, *and* two hundred lambs; all these *were* for a burnt offering to the LORD. [33]The consecrated things *were* six hundred bulls and three thousand sheep. [34]But the priests were too few, so that they could not skin all the burnt offerings; therefore their brethren the Levites helped them until the work was ended and until the *other* priests had sanctified themselves, for the Levites were more diligent in sanctifying themselves than the priests. [35]Also the burnt offerings *were* in abundance, with the fat of the peace offerings and *with* the drink offerings for *every* burnt offering.

So the service of the house of the LORD was set in order. [36]Then Hezekiah and all the people rejoiced that God had prepared the people, since the events took place so suddenly.

Hezekiah Keeps the Passover

30 And Hezekiah sent to all Israel and Judah, and also wrote letters to Ephraim and Manasseh, that they should come to the house of the LORD at Jerusalem, to keep the Passover to the LORD God of Israel. 2For the king and his leaders and all the assembly in Jerusalem had agreed to keep the Passover in the second month. 3For they could not keep it at the regular time,[w] because a sufficient number of priests had not consecrated themselves, nor had the people gathered together at Jerusalem. 4And the matter pleased the king and all the assembly. 5So they resolved to make a proclamation throughout all Israel, from Beersheba to Dan, that they should come to keep the Passover to the LORD God of Israel at Jerusalem, since they had not done *it* for a long *time* in the *prescribed* manner.

6Then the runners went throughout all Israel and Judah with the letters from the king and his leaders, and spoke according to the command of the king: "Children of Israel, return to the LORD God of Abraham, Isaac, and Israel; then He will return to the remnant of you who have escaped from the hand of the kings of Assyria. 7And do not be like your fathers and your brethren, who trespassed against the LORD God of their fathers, so that He gave them up to desolation, as you see. 8Now do not be stiff-necked, as your fathers *were, but* yield yourselves to the LORD; and enter His sanctuary, which He has sanctified forever, and serve the LORD your God, that the fierceness of His wrath may turn away from you. 9For if you return to the LORD, your brethren and your children *will be treated* with compassion by those who lead them captive, so that they may come back to this land; for the LORD your God *is* gracious and merciful, and will not turn *His* face from you if you return to Him."

10So the runners passed from city to city through the country of Ephraim and Manasseh, as far as Zebulun; but they laughed at them and mocked them. 11Nevertheless some from Asher, Manasseh, and Zebulun humbled themselves and came to Jerusalem. 12Also the hand of God was on Judah to give them singleness of heart to obey the command of the king and the leaders, at the word of the LORD.

13Now many people, a very great assembly, gathered at Jerusalem to keep the Feast of Unleavened Bread in the second month. 14They arose and took away the altars that *were* in Jerusalem, and they took away all the incense altars and cast *them* into the Brook Kidron. 15Then they slaughtered the Passover *lambs* on the fourteenth *day* of the second month. The priests and the Levites were ashamed, and sanctified themselves, and brought the burnt offerings to the house of the LORD. 16They stood in their place according to their custom, according to the Law of Moses the man of God; the priests sprinkled the blood *received* from the hand of the Levites. 17For *there were* many in the assembly who had not sanctified themselves; therefore the Levites had charge of the slaughter of the Passover *lambs* for everyone *who was* not clean, to sanctify *them* to the LORD. 18For a multitude of the people, many from Ephraim, Manasseh, Issachar, and Zebulun, had not cleansed themselves, yet they ate the Passover contrary to what was written. But Hezekiah prayed for them, saying, "May the good LORD provide atonement for everyone 19*who* prepares his heart to seek God, the LORD God of his fathers, though *he is* not *cleansed* according to the purification of the sanctuary." 20And the LORD listened to Hezekiah and healed the people.

21So the children of Israel who were present at Jerusalem kept the Feast of Unleavened Bread seven days with great gladness; and the Levites and the priests praised the LORD day by day, *singing* to the LORD, accompanied by loud instruments. 22And Hezekiah gave encouragement to all the Levites who taught the good knowledge of the LORD; and they ate throughout the feast seven days, offering peace offerings and making confession to the LORD God of their fathers.

23Then the whole assembly agreed to keep *the feast* another seven days, and they kept it *another* seven days with gladness. 24For Hezekiah king of Judah gave to the assembly a thousand bulls and seven thousand sheep, and the leaders gave to the assembly a thousand bulls and ten thousand sheep; and a great number of priests sanctified themselves. 25The whole assembly of Judah rejoiced, also the priests and Levites, all the assembly that came from Israel, the sojourners who came from the land of Israel, and those who dwelt in Judah. 26So there was great joy in Jerusalem, for since the time of Solomon the son of David, king of Israel, *there had* been nothing like this in Jerusalem. 27Then the priests, the Levites, arose and blessed the people, and their voice was heard; and their prayer came *up* to His holy dwelling place, to heaven.

30:3 [w] That is, the first month (compare Leviticus 23:5); literally *at that time*

The Reforms of Hezekiah

31 Now when all this was finished, all Israel who
were present went out to the cities of Judah and
broke the sacred pillars in pieces, cut down the
wooden images, and threw down the high places and
the altars—from all Judah, Benjamin, Ephraim, and
Manasseh—until they had utterly destroyed them all.
Then all the children of Israel returned to their own
cities, every man to his possession.
2And Hezekiah appointed the divisions of the
priests and the Levites according to their divisions,
each man according to his service, the priests and
Levites for burnt offerings and peace offerings, to
serve, to give thanks, and to praise in the gates of the
camp[x] of the LORD. 3The king also *appointed* a portion
of his possessions for the burnt offerings: for the
morning and evening burnt offerings, the burnt offerings for the Sabbaths and the New Moons and the
set feasts, as *it is* written in the Law of the LORD.
4Moreover he commanded the people who dwelt in
Jerusalem to contribute support for the priests and
the Levites, that they might devote themselves to the
Law of the LORD.
5As soon as the commandment was circulated, the
children of Israel brought in abundance the firstfruits of grain and wine, oil and honey, and of all the
produce of the field; and they brought in abundantly
the tithe of everything. 6And the children of Israel
and Judah, who dwelt in the cities of Judah, brought
the tithe of oxen and sheep; also the tithe of holy
things which were consecrated to the LORD their God
they laid in heaps.
7In the third month they began laying them in
heaps, and they finished in the seventh month. 8And
when Hezekiah and the leaders came and saw the
heaps, they blessed the LORD and His people Israel.
9Then Hezekiah questioned the priests and the
Levites concerning the heaps. 10And Azariah the chief
priest, from the house of Zadok, answered him and
said, "Since *the people* began to bring the offerings
into the house of the LORD, we have had enough to eat
and have plenty left, for the LORD has blessed His people; and what is left *is* this great abundance."
11Now Hezekiah commanded *them* to prepare
rooms in the house of the LORD, and they prepared
them. 12Then they faithfully brought in the offerings,
the tithes, and the dedicated things; Cononiah the
Levite had charge of them, and Shimei his brother
was the next. 13Jehiel, Azaziah, Nahath, Asahel,
Jerimoth, Jozabad, Eliel, Ismachiah, Mahath, and
Benaiah *were* overseers under the hand of Cononiah
and Shimei his brother, at the commandment of
Hezekiah the king and Azariah the ruler of the house
of God. 14Kore the son of Imnah the Levite, the keeper
of the East Gate, *was* over the freewill offerings to God,
to distribute the offerings of the LORD and the most
holy things. 15And under him *were* Eden, Miniamin,
Jeshua, Shemaiah, Amariah, and Shecaniah, *his* faithful assistants in the cities of the priests, to distribute
allotments to their brethren by divisions, to the great
as well as the small.
16Besides those males from three years old and up
who were written in the genealogy, they distributed
to everyone who entered the house of the LORD his
daily portion for the work of his service, by his division, 17and to the priests who were written in the genealogy according to their father's house, and to the
Levites from twenty years old and up according to
their work, by their divisions, 18and to all who were
written in the genealogy—their little ones and their
wives, their sons and daughters, the whole company
of them—for in their faithfulness they sanctified
themselves in holiness.
19Also for the sons of Aaron the priests, *who were* in
the fields of the common-lands of their cities, in every
single city, *there were* men who were designated by
name to distribute portions to all the males among
the priests and to all who were listed by genealogies
among the Levites.
20Thus Hezekiah did throughout all Judah, and he
did what *was* good and right and true before the LORD
his God. 21And in every work that he began in the service of the house of God, in the law and in the commandment, to seek his God, he did *it* with all his
heart. So he prospered.

Sennacherib Boasts Against the LORD

32 After these deeds of faithfulness, Sennacherib
king of Assyria came and entered Judah; he encamped against the fortified cities, thinking to win
them over to himself. 2And when Hezekiah saw that
Sennacherib had come, and that his purpose was to
make war against Jerusalem, 3he consulted with his
leaders and commanders[y] to stop the water from the
springs which *were* outside the city; and they helped
him. 4Thus many people gathered together who
stopped all the springs and the brook that ran

31:2 [x] That is, the temple
32:3 [y] Literally *mighty men*

through the land, saying, "Why should the kings[z] of Assyria come and
find much water?" 5And he strengthened himself, built up all the wall that
was broken, raised *it* up to the towers, and *built* another wall outside; also
he repaired the Millo[a] *in* the City of David, and made weapons and
shields in abundance. 6Then he set military captains over the people,
gathered them together to him in the open square of the city gate, and
gave them encouragement, saying, 7"Be strong and courageous; do not
be afraid nor dismayed before the king of Assyria, nor before all the multitude that *is* with him; for *there are* more with us than with him. 8With
him *is* an arm of flesh; but with us *is* the LORD our God, to help us and to
fight our battles." And the people were strengthened by the words of
Hezekiah king of Judah.
9After this Sennacherib king of Assyria sent his servants to Jerusalem
(but he and all the forces with him *laid siege* against Lachish), to Hezekiah
king of Judah, and to all Judah who *were* in Jerusalem, saying, 10"Thus says
Sennacherib king of Assyria: 'In what do you trust, that you remain under
siege in Jerusalem? 11Does not Hezekiah persuade you to give yourselves
over to die by famine and by thirst, saying, "The LORD our God will deliver
us from the hand of the king of Assyria"? 12Has not the same Hezekiah
taken away His high places and His altars, and commanded Judah and Jerusalem, saying, "You shall worship before one altar and burn incense on
it"? 13Do you not know what I and my fathers have done to all the peoples
of *other* lands? Were the gods of the nations of those lands in any way able
to deliver their lands out of my hand? 14Who *was there* among all the gods
of those nations that my fathers utterly destroyed that could deliver his
people from my hand, that your God should be able to deliver you from
my hand? 15Now therefore, do not let Hezekiah deceive you or persuade
you like this, and do not believe him; for no god of any nation or kingdom
was able to deliver his people from my hand or the hand of my fathers.
How much less will your God deliver you from my hand?' "
16Furthermore, his servants spoke against the LORD God and against His
servant Hezekiah.
17He also wrote letters to revile the LORD God of Israel, and to speak
against Him, saying, "As the gods of the nations of *other* lands have not
delivered their people from my hand, so the God of Hezekiah will not deliver His people from my hand." 18Then they called out with a loud voice in
Hebrew[b] to the people of Jerusalem who *were* on the wall, to frighten them
and trouble them, that they might take the city. 19And they spoke against
the God of Jerusalem, as against the gods of the people of the earth—the
work of men's hands.

Sennacherib's Defeat and Death

20Now because of this King Hezekiah and the prophet Isaiah, the son of
Amoz, prayed and cried out to heaven. 21Then the LORD sent an angel who
cut down every mighty man of valor, leader, and captain in the camp of the
king of Assyria. So he returned shamefaced to his own land. And when he
had gone into the temple of his god, some of his own offspring struck him
down with the sword there.

32:4 [z] Following Masoretic Text and Vulgate; Arabic, Septuagint, and Syriac read *king*.
32:5 [a] Literally *The Landfill*
32:18 [b] Literally *Judean*

LIFE LESSON

2 Chronicles 32:24–33:25

SITUATION Hezekiah's son Manasseh succeeded him. Manasseh worshiped false gods as his ancestors had done. But God caused him to turn from his sin.

OBSERVATION It was out of his great need that Manasseh turned to God. The Lord hears our prayers and shows great mercy.

INSPIRATION You know the story of Peter, the first sailor. Let me tell you about the second, whose name was John.

He had served on the seas since he was eleven years old. His father, an English shipmaster in the Mediterranean, took him aboard and trained him well for a life in the Royal Navy.

Yet what John gained in experience, he lacked in discipline. He mocked authority. Ran with the wrong crowd. Indulged in the sinful ways of a sailor. Although his training would have qualified him to serve as an officer, his behavior caused him to be flogged and demoted.

In his early twenties, he made his way to Africa, where he became intrigued with the lucrative slave trade. At age twenty-one, he made his living on the *Greyhound*, a slave ship crossing the Atlantic Ocean.

John ridiculed the moral and poked fun at the religious. He even made jokes about a book that would eventually help reshape his life: *The Imitation of Christ*. In fact, he was degrading that book a few hours before his ship sailed into an angry storm.

That night the waves pummeled the *Greyhound*, spinning the ship one minute on the top of a wave. Plunging her the next into a watery valley.

John awakened to find his cabin filled with water. A side of the *Greyhound* had collapsed. Ordinarily such damage would have sent a ship to the bottom in a matter of minutes. The *Greyhound*, however, was carrying buoyant cargo and remained afloat.

John worked at the pumps all night. For nine hours, he and the other sailors struggled to keep the ship from sinking. But he knew that it was a losing cause. Finally, when his

Continued

22Thus the LORD saved Hezekiah and the inhabitants of Jerusalem from
the hand of Sennacherib the king of Assyria, and from the hand of all *oth-*
ers, and guided them[c] on every side. 23And many brought gifts to the LORD
at Jerusalem, and presents to Hezekiah king of Judah, so that he was exalted in the sight of all nations thereafter.

Hezekiah Humbles Himself

24In those days Hezekiah was sick and near death, and he prayed to the
LORD; and He spoke to him and gave him a sign. 25But Hezekiah did not
repay according to the favor *shown* him, for his heart was lifted up; therefore wrath was looming over him and over Judah and Jerusalem. 26Then
Hezekiah humbled himself for the pride of his heart, he and the inhabitants of Jerusalem, so that the wrath of the LORD did not come upon them
in the days of Hezekiah.

Hezekiah's Wealth and Honor

27Hezekiah had very great riches and honor. And he made himself treasuries for silver, for gold, for precious stones, for spices, for shields, and
for all kinds of desirable items; 28storehouses for the harvest of grain,
wine, and oil; and stalls for all kinds of livestock, and folds for flocks.[d]
29Moreover he provided cities for himself, and possessions of flocks and
herds in abundance; for God had given him very much property. 30This
same Hezekiah also stopped the water outlet of Upper Gihon, and brought
the water by tunnel[e] to the west side of the City of David. Hezekiah prospered in all his works.

31However, *regarding* the ambassadors of the princes of Babylon, whom
they sent to him to inquire about the wonder that was *done* in the land,
God withdrew from him, in order to test him, that He might know all *that*
was in his heart.

Death of Hezekiah

32Now the rest of the acts of Hezekiah, and his goodness, indeed they *are*
written in the vision of Isaiah the prophet, the son of Amoz, *and* in the
book of the kings of Judah and Israel. 33So Hezekiah rested with his fathers, and they buried him in the upper tombs of the sons of David; and all
Judah and the inhabitants of Jerusalem honored him at his death. Then
Manasseh his son reigned in his place.

Manasseh Reigns in Judah

33 Manasseh *was* twelve years old when he became king, and he
reigned fifty-five years in Jerusalem. 2But he did evil in the sight of
the LORD, according to the abominations of the nations whom the LORD had
cast out before the children of Israel. 3For he rebuilt the high places which
Hezekiah his father had broken down; he raised up altars for the Baals, and
made wooden images; and he worshiped all the host of heaven[f] and served
them. 4He also built altars in the house of the LORD, of which the LORD had
said, "In Jerusalem shall My name be forever." 5And he built altars for all

32:22 [c] Septuagint reads *gave them rest;* Vulgate reads *gave them treasures.*
32:28 [d] Following Septuagint and Vulgate; Arabic and Syriac omit *folds for flocks;* Masoretic Text reads *flocks for sheepfolds.*
32:30 [e] Literally *brought it straight* (compare 2 Kings 20:20)
33:3 [f] The gods of the Assyrians

hopes were more battered than the vessel, he threw himself on the salt-water-soaked deck and pleaded, "If this will not do, then Lord have mercy on us all."

John didn't deserve mercy, but he received it. The *Greyhound* and her crew survived.

John never forgot God's mercy shown on that tempestuous day in the roaring Atlantic. He returned to England where he became a prolific composer. You've sung his songs, like this one:

Amazing grace! how sweet the sound,
That saved a wretch like me!
I once was lost, but now am found,
was blind, but now I see.

This slave-trader-turned-songwriter was John Newton.

Along with his hymn writing, he also became a powerful pulpiteer. For nearly fifty years, he filled pulpits and churches with the story of the Savior who meets you and me in the storm.

(From *In the Eye of the Storm* by Max Lucado)

APPLICATION Take the troubles you face today—disease, alcohol, kids in trouble, cash flow—and wrap them in a prayer: "Lord, have mercy, and teach me to see your way through the storm."

EXPLORATION God Hears Us—Psalm 18:6; Isaiah 41:10; Hebrews 13:6.

the host of heaven in the two courts of the house of the
LORD. [6]Also he caused his sons to pass through the fire
in the Valley of the Son of Hinnom; he practiced
soothsaying, used witchcraft and sorcery, and consulted mediums and spiritists. He did much evil in the
sight of the LORD, to provoke Him to anger. [7]He even
set a carved image, the idol which he had made, in the
house of God, of which God had said to David and to
Solomon his son, "In this house and in Jerusalem,
which I have chosen out of all the tribes of Israel, I will
put My name forever; [8]and I will not again remove the
foot of Israel from the land which I have appointed for
your fathers—only if they are careful to do all that I
have commanded them, according to the whole law
and the statutes and the ordinances by the hand of Moses." [9]So Manasseh seduced Judah and the inhabitants
of Jerusalem to do more evil than the nations whom
the LORD had destroyed before the children of Israel.

Manasseh Restored After Repentance

[10]And the LORD spoke to Manasseh and his people,
but they would not listen. [11]Therefore the LORD
brought upon them the captains of the army of the
king of Assyria, who took Manasseh with hooks,[g]
bound him with bronze *fetters,* and carried him off to
Babylon. [12]Now when he was in affliction, he implored
the LORD his God, and humbled himself greatly before
the God of his fathers, [13]and prayed to Him; and He received his entreaty, heard his supplication, and
brought him back to Jerusalem into his kingdom.
Then Manasseh knew that the LORD *was* God.
[14]After this he built a wall outside the City of David
on the west side of Gihon, in the valley, as far as the
entrance of the Fish Gate; and *it* enclosed Ophel, and
he raised it to a very great height. Then he put military
captains in all the fortified cities of Judah. [15]He took
away the foreign gods and the idol from the house of
the LORD, and all the altars that he had built in the
mount of the house of the LORD and in Jerusalem; and
he cast *them* out of the city. [16]He also repaired the altar
of the LORD, sacrificed peace offerings and thank offerings on it, and commanded Judah to serve the LORD
God of Israel. [17]Nevertheless the people still sacrificed
on the high places, *but* only to the LORD their God.

Death of Manasseh

[18]Now the rest of the acts of Manasseh, his prayer to
his God, and the words of the seers who spoke to him
in the name of the LORD God of Israel, indeed they *are*
written in the book[h] of the kings of Israel. [19]Also his
prayer and *how God* received his entreaty, and all his
sin and trespass, and the sites where he built high
places and set up wooden images and carved images,
before he was humbled, indeed they *are* written
among the sayings of Hozai.[i] [20]So Manasseh rested
with his fathers, and they buried him in his own
house. Then his son Amon reigned in his place.

Amon's Reign and Death

[21]Amon *was* twenty-two years old when he became
king, and he reigned two years in Jerusalem. [22]But he
did evil in the sight of the LORD, as his father
Manasseh had done; for Amon sacrificed to all the
carved images which his father Manasseh had made,
and served them. [23]And he did not humble himself
before the LORD, as his father Manasseh had humbled
himself; but Amon trespassed more and more.
[24]Then his servants conspired against him, and
killed him in his own house. [25]But the people of the
land executed all those who had conspired against
King Amon. Then the people of the land made his son
Josiah king in his place.

Josiah Reigns in Judah

34 Josiah *was* eight years old when he became
king, and he reigned thirty-one years in Jerusalem. [2]And he did *what was* right in the sight of the
LORD, and walked in the ways of his father David; *he*
did *not* turn aside to the right hand or to the left.
[3]For in the eighth year of his reign, while he was still
young, he began to seek the God of his father David;
and in the twelfth year he began to purge Judah and
Jerusalem of the high places, the wooden images, the
carved images, and the molded images. [4]They broke
down the altars of the Baals in his presence, and the
incense altars which *were* above them he cut down;
and the wooden images, the carved images, and the
molded images he broke in pieces, and made dust of
them and scattered *it* on the graves of those who had
sacrificed to them. [5]He also burned the bones of the
priests on their altars, and cleansed Judah and Jerusalem. [6]And *so he did* in the cities of Manasseh,
Ephraim, and Simeon, as far as Naphtali and all
around, with axes.[j] [7]When he had broken down the altars and the wooden images, had beaten the carved

33:11 [g] That is, nose hooks (compare 2 Kings 19:28)
33:18 [h] Literally *words*
33:19 [i] Septuagint reads *the seers.*
34:6 [j] Literally *swords*

LIFE LESSON

2 Chronicles 34:1–36:1

SITUATION As king of Judah, Josiah led his people in committing their lives to God. He discovered the Mosaic law and celebrated the Passover on the plains of Megiddo.

OBSERVATION Josiah modeled an earnest attempt to honor God.

INSPIRATION I wanted to be loved. Nothing unusual about that, nothing to separate my generation from any other.

But I wanted something deeper. Down among all the foolishness in my diary, thoughts like chaff which the wind of the Spirit can drive away, there was some wheat. There was an honest-to-God longing for the "fixed heart" that the collect speaks of. A thousand questions cluttered my mind, the same ones I find today in the letters I receive. I had thought some of mine were new. My correspondents think the same. They aren't. But the question to preceed all others, which finally determines the course of our lives, is What do I really want? Was it to love what God commands, . . . and to desire what he promises? Did I want what I wanted, or did I want what He wanted, no matter what it might cost?

Until the will and the affections are brought under the authority of Christ, we have not begun to understand, let alone to accept, His lordship. The Cross . . . will reveal the heart's truth. My heart, I knew, would be forever a lonely hunter unless settled "where true joys are to be found." . . .

(From *Passion and Purity* by Elisabeth Elliot)

APPLICATION Decide what you will desire most in life. Make your choice. Bring to mind the things, people, and loyalties that you have not yet given to Jesus. As you hand them over to his control, be glad for the opportunity of trusting him.

EXPLORATION Pursuing God—Genesis 6:8-9; Psalm 27:4; 42:1-2; Philippians 3:7-14.

images into powder, and cut down all the incense altars throughout all the
land of Israel, he returned to Jerusalem.

Hilkiah Finds the Book of the Law

8In the eighteenth year of his reign, when he had purged the land and
the temple,[k] he sent Shaphan the son of Azaliah, Maaseiah the governor of
the city, and Joah the son of Joahaz the recorder, to repair the house of the
LORD his God. 9When they came to Hilkiah the high priest, they delivered
the money that was brought into the house of God, which the Levites who
kept the doors had gathered from the hand of Manasseh and Ephraim,
from all the remnant of Israel, from all Judah and Benjamin, and *which*
they had brought back to Jerusalem. 10Then they put *it* in the hand of the
foremen who had the oversight of the house of the LORD; and they gave it to
the workmen who worked in the house of the LORD, to repair and restore
the house. 11They gave *it* to the craftsmen and builders to buy hewn stone
and timber for beams, and to floor the houses which the kings of Judah
had destroyed. 12And the men did the work faithfully. Their overseers *were*
Jahath and Obadiah the Levites, of the sons of Merari, and Zechariah and
Meshullam, of the sons of the Kohathites, to supervise. *Others of* the
Levites, all of whom were skillful with instruments of music, 13*were* over
the burden bearers and *were* overseers of all who did work in any kind of
service. And *some* of the Levites *were* scribes, officers, and gatekeepers.
14Now when they brought out the money that was brought into the
house of the LORD, Hilkiah the priest found the Book of the Law of the LORD
given by Moses. 15Then Hilkiah answered and said to Shaphan the scribe,
"I have found the Book of the Law in the house of the LORD." And Hilkiah
gave the book to Shaphan. 16So Shaphan carried the book to the king,
bringing the king word, saying, "All that was committed to your servants
they are doing. 17And they have gathered the money that was found in the
house of the LORD, and have delivered it into the hand of the overseers and
the workmen." 18Then Shaphan the scribe told the king, saying, "Hilkiah
the priest has given me a book." And Shaphan read it before the king.
19Thus it happened, when the king heard the words of the Law, that he
tore his clothes. 20Then the king commanded Hilkiah, Ahikam the son of
Shaphan, Abdon[l] the son of Micah, Shaphan the scribe, and Asaiah a servant of the king, saying, 21"Go, inquire of the LORD for me, and for those
who are left in Israel and Judah, concerning the words of the book that is
found; for great *is* the wrath of the LORD that is poured out on us, because
our fathers have not kept the word of the LORD, to do according to all that is
written in this book."
22So Hilkiah and those the king *had appointed* went to Huldah the
prophetess, the wife of Shallum the son of Tokhath,[m] the son of Hasrah,[n]
keeper of the wardrobe. (She dwelt in Jerusalem in the Second Quarter.)
And they spoke to her to that *effect*.
23Then she answered them, "Thus says the LORD God of Israel, 'Tell the
man who sent you to Me, 24"Thus says the LORD: 'Behold, I will bring
calamity on this place and on its inhabitants, all the curses that are written
in the book which they have read before the king of Judah, 25because they

34:8 [k] Literally *house*
34:20 [l] *Achbor the son of Michaiah* in 2 Kings 22:12
34:22 [m] Spelled *Tikvah* in 2 Kings 22:14 [n] Spelled *Harhas* in 2 Kings 22:14

have forsaken Me and burned incense to other gods,
that they might provoke Me to anger with all the works
of their hands. Therefore My wrath will be poured out
on this place, and not be quenched.' " ' 26But as for the
king of Judah, who sent you to inquire of the LORD, in
this manner you shall speak to him, 'Thus says the
LORD God of Israel: "*Concerning* the words which you
have heard— 27because your heart was tender, and
you humbled yourself before God when you heard His
words against this place and against its inhabitants,
and you humbled yourself before Me, and you tore
your clothes and wept before Me, I also have heard
you," says the LORD. 28"Surely I will gather you to your
fathers, and you shall be gathered to your grave in
peace; and your eyes shall not see all the calamity
which I will bring on this place and its inhabitants." ' "
So they brought back word to the king.

Josiah Restores True Worship

29Then the king sent and gathered all the elders of
Judah and Jerusalem. 30The king went up to the house
of the LORD, with all the men of Judah and the inhabitants of Jerusalem—the priests and the Levites, and
all the people, great and small. And he read in their
hearing all the words of the Book of the Covenant
which had been found in the house of the LORD.
31Then the king stood in his place and made a
covenant before the LORD, to follow the LORD, and to
keep His commandments and His testimonies and
His statutes with all his heart and all his soul, to perform the words of the covenant that were written in
this book. 32And he made all who were present in Jerusalem and Benjamin take a stand. So the inhabitants of Jerusalem did according to the covenant of
God, the God of their fathers. 33Thus Josiah removed
all the abominations from all the country that *belonged* to the children of Israel, and made all who
were present in Israel diligently serve the LORD their
God. All his days they did not depart from following
the LORD God of their fathers.

Josiah Keeps the Passover

35 Now Josiah kept a Passover to the LORD in Jerusalem, and they slaughtered the Passover *lambs*
on the fourteenth *day* of the first month. 2And he set
the priests in their duties and encouraged them for
the service of the house of the LORD. 3Then he said to
the Levites who taught all Israel, who were holy to the
LORD: "Put the holy ark in the house which Solomon
the son of David, king of Israel, built. *It shall* no longer
be a burden on *your* shoulders. Now serve the LORD
your God and His people Israel. 4Prepare *yourselves*
according to your fathers' houses, according to your
divisions, following the written instruction of David
king of Israel and the written instruction of Solomon
his son. 5And stand in the holy *place* according to the
divisions of the fathers' houses of your brethren the
lay people, and *according to* the division of the father's house of the Levites. 6So slaughter the Passover
offerings, consecrate yourselves, and prepare *them* for
your brethren, that *they* may do according to the word
of the LORD by the hand of Moses."

7Then Josiah gave the *lay* people lambs and young
goats from the flock, all for Passover *offerings* for all
who were present, to the number of thirty thousand,
as well as three thousand cattle; these *were* from the
king's possessions. 8And his leaders gave willingly to
the people, to the priests, and to the Levites. Hilkiah,
Zechariah, and Jehiel, rulers of the house of God, gave
to the priests for the Passover *offerings* two thousand
six hundred *from the flock*, and three hundred cattle.
9Also Conaniah, his brothers Shemaiah and Nethanel,
and Hashabiah and Jeiel and Jozabad, chief of the
Levites, gave to the Levites for Passover *offerings* five
thousand *from the flock* and five hundred cattle.

10So the service was prepared, and the priests stood
in their places, and the Levites in their divisions, according to the king's command. 11And they slaughtered the Passover *offerings;* and the priests sprinkled
the blood with their hands, while the Levites skinned
the animals. 12Then they removed the burnt offerings
that *they* might give them to the divisions of the fathers' houses of the *lay* people, to offer to the LORD, as
it is written in the Book of Moses. And so *they did* with
the cattle. 13Also they roasted the Passover *offerings*
with fire according to the ordinance; but the *other*
holy *offerings* they boiled in pots, in caldrons, and in
pans, and divided *them* quickly among all the *lay* people. 14Then afterward they prepared portions for
themselves and for the priests, because the priests,
the sons of Aaron, *were busy* in offering burnt offerings and fat until night; therefore the Levites prepared
portions for themselves and for the priests, the sons
of Aaron. 15And the singers, the sons of Asaph, *were* in
their places, according to the command of David,
Asaph, Heman, and Jeduthun the king's seer. Also the
gatekeepers were at each gate; they did not have to
leave their position, because their brethren the
Levites prepared portions for them.

16So all the service of the LORD was prepared the
same day, to keep the Passover and to offer burnt offerings on the altar of the LORD, according to the command

of King Josiah. 17And the children of Israel who were
present kept the Passover at that time, and the Feast
of Unleavened Bread for seven days. 18There had
been no Passover kept in Israel like that since the
days of Samuel the prophet; and none of the kings of
Israel had kept such a Passover as Josiah kept, with
the priests and the Levites, all Judah and Israel who
were present, and the inhabitants of Jerusalem. 19In
the eighteenth year of the reign of Josiah this Passover
was kept.

Josiah Dies in Battle

20After all this, when Josiah had prepared the temple, Necho king of Egypt came up to fight against
Carchemish by the Euphrates; and Josiah went out
against him. 21But he sent messengers to him, saying,
"What have I to do with you, king of Judah? *I have* not
come against you this day, but against the house with
which I have war; for God commanded me to make
haste. Refrain *from meddling with* God, who *is* with
me, lest He destroy you." 22Nevertheless Josiah would
not turn his face from him, but disguised himself so
that he might fight with him, and did not heed the
words of Necho from the mouth of God. So he came to
fight in the Valley of Megiddo.
23And the archers shot King Josiah; and the king
said to his servants, "Take me away, for I am severely
wounded." 24His servants therefore took him out of
that chariot and put him in the second chariot that he
had, and they brought him to Jerusalem. So he died,
and was buried in *one of* the tombs of his fathers. And
all Judah and Jerusalem mourned for Josiah.
25Jeremiah also lamented for Josiah. And to this day
all the singing men and the singing women speak of
Josiah in their lamentations. They made it a custom in
Israel; and indeed they *are* written in the Laments.
26Now the rest of the acts of Josiah and his goodness, according to *what was* written in the Law of the
LORD, 27and his deeds from first to last, indeed they *are*
written in the book of the kings of Israel and Judah.

The Reign and Captivity of Jehoahaz

36 Then the people of the land took Jehoahaz the
son of Josiah, and made him king in his father's place in Jerusalem. 2Jehoahaz[o] *was* twenty-
three years old when he became king, and he reigned
three months in Jerusalem. 3Now the king of Egypt
deposed him at Jerusalem; and he imposed on the
land a tribute of one hundred talents of silver and a talent of gold. 4Then the king of Egypt made *Jehoahaz's*[p]
brother Eliakim king over Judah and Jerusalem, and
changed his name to Jehoiakim. And Necho took
Jehoahaz[q] his brother and carried him off to Egypt.

The Reign and Captivity of Jehoiakim

5Jehoiakim *was* twenty-five years old when he became king, and he reigned eleven years in Jerusalem.
And he did evil in the sight of the LORD his God.
6Nebuchadnezzar king of Babylon came up against
him, and bound him in bronze *fetters* to carry him off
to Babylon. 7Nebuchadnezzar also carried off *some* of
the articles from the house of the LORD to Babylon,
and put them in his temple at Babylon. 8Now the rest
of the acts of Jehoiakim, the abominations which he
did, and what was found against him, indeed they *are*
written in the book of the kings of Israel and Judah.
Then Jehoiachin his son reigned in his place.

The Reign and Captivity of Jehoiachin

9Jehoiachin *was* eight[r] years old when he became
king, and he reigned in Jerusalem three months and
ten days. And he did evil in the sight of the LORD. 10At
the turn of the year King Nebuchadnezzar summoned *him* and took him to Babylon, with the costly
articles from the house of the LORD, and made
Zedekiah, *Jehoiakim's*[s] brother, king over Judah and
Jerusalem.

Zedekiah Reigns in Judah

11Zedekiah *was* twenty-one years old when he became king, and he reigned eleven years in Jerusalem.
12He did evil in the sight of the LORD his God, *and* did
not humble himself before Jeremiah the prophet, *who
spoke* from the mouth of the LORD. 13And he also rebelled against King Nebuchadnezzar, who had made
him swear *an oath* by God; but he stiffened his neck
and hardened his heart against turning to the LORD
God of Israel. 14Moreover all the leaders of the priests
and the people transgressed more and more, *according* to all the abominations of the nations, and defiled
the house of the LORD which He had consecrated in Jerusalem.

The Fall of Jerusalem

15And the LORD God of their fathers sent *warnings* to
them by His messengers, rising up early and sending

36:2 [o] Masoretic Text reads *Joahaz.*
36:4 [p] Literally *his* [q] Masoretic Text reads *Joahaz.*
36:9 [r] Some Hebrew manuscripts, Septuagint, Syriac, and 2 Kings 24:8 read *eighteen.*
36:10 [s] Literally *his* (compare 2 Kings 24:17)

them, because He had compassion on His people and
on His dwelling place. [16]But they mocked the messengers of God, despised His words, and scoffed at His
prophets, until the wrath of the LORD arose against His
people, till *there was* no remedy.
[17]Therefore He brought against them the king of the
Chaldeans, who killed their young men with the
sword in the house of their sanctuary, and had no
compassion on young man or virgin, on the aged or
the weak; He gave *them* all into his hand. [18]And all the
articles from the house of God, great and small, the
treasures of the house of the LORD, and the treasures
of the king and of his leaders, all *these* he took to
Babylon. [19]Then they burned the house of God, broke
down the wall of Jerusalem, burned all its palaces
with fire, and destroyed all its precious possessions.
[20]And those who escaped from the sword he carried
away to Babylon, where they became servants to him
and his sons until the rule of the kingdom of Persia,
[21]to fulfill the word of the LORD by the mouth of
Jeremiah, until the land had enjoyed her Sabbaths. As
long as she lay desolate she kept Sabbath, to fulfill seventy years.

The Proclamation of Cyrus

[22]Now in the first year of Cyrus king of Persia, that
the word of the LORD by the mouth of Jeremiah might
be fulfilled, the LORD stirred up the spirit of Cyrus king
of Persia, so that he made a proclamation throughout
all his kingdom, and also *put it* in writing, saying,

[23] Thus says Cyrus king of Persia:
All the kingdoms of the earth the LORD God of
heaven has given me. And He has commanded
me to build Him a house at Jerusalem which
is in Judah. Who *is* among you of all His people?
May the LORD his God *be* with him, and let
him go up!

The Book of

EZRA

INTRODUCTION

Martin Luther you've heard of. Philipp Melanchthon, probably not. But Luther knew Melanchthon. And Luther was a better man as a result.

Melanchthon was the intellectual of the Reformation. He authored the Augsburg Confession. He was the first to put into writing an evangelical theology.

He was only eleven when his father died, only twelve when his grandfather presented him with a Bible and a Greek grammar. The next fifty years the three were inseparable. Melanchthon's one great love was to teach the Word of God.

He didn't just read the Bible, he devoured it. By the age of seventeen he was a faculty member at the University of Wittenberg. Though he was small of frame and frail of health, he was keen of mind.

And even more important, he was keen of purpose.

He lived to study and teach the Bible. He commanded the respect of Martin Luther. "I was born to fight," he said, "but Master Philipp, he comes along sowing with joy."

The prophet Ezra was the Philipp Melanchthon of his day.

Ezra was the second of three key leaders to leave Babylon for the reconstruction of Jerusalem. Zerubbabel was first. Then Ezra and then Nehemiah. Zerubbabel reconstructed the Temple, Nehemiah rebuilt the walls, and Ezra restored the worship.

Any person who has tackled the task of presenting the Bible to people will find a friend in Ezra. He was a student. He was an interpreter. In fact, the clearest Old Testament reference to exposition is attributed to Ezra. He was the head of the Levites who "read distinctly from the book, in the Law of God; and they gave the sense, and helped them to understand the reading" (Nehemiah 8:8).

Don't you appreciate that last phrase, "and helped them to understand the reading . . ."? Don't you appreciate the person who can take the Word and reveal it for your life?

Perhaps you can do that. If so, stay faithful. There is no higher task.

Perhaps you have a teacher like that. If so, be grateful. There is no greater friend.

LIFE LESSON

Ezra 1:1–2:70

SITUATION Cyrus, King of Persia, allowed the captive Jews to return to Jerusalem and rebuild the temple. Cyrus blessed the venture and subsidized the journey back to their homeland.

OBSERVATION Although Cyrus was not Jewish, God used this Persian king to restore his people and to rebuild Jerusalem.

INSPIRATION The cross is the focal point in the life and ministry of Jesus Christ. Some think that God didn't want Christ to die, but was forced to adjust His plans to adapt to it. Scripture makes it very clear, however, that the cross was no afterthought with God. Christ was "delivered up by the predetermined plan and foreknowledge of God" (Acts 2:23).

God designed the cross to defeat Satan, who by deception had obtained squatters' rights to the title deed of the world. When Satan with all of his clever promises separated man from God in the Garden of Eden, he was more than the deceiver of Adam and Eve. In some mysterious manner he began to exert a kind of pseudosovereignty over man. In his arrogant violence, Satan unleashed his fiercest attack to stop Christ's ministry by seeing that He was murdered. But Satan was stopped by God and caught in his own trap. He hadn't realized that God loved the world so intensely that He could let His own Son be subjected to the worst Satan could do. . .

(From *How to Be Born Again* by Billy Graham)

APPLICATION Have you ever seen a good result come from something bad? Think of an episode in your life where God's will was revealed through an unlikely agent. Today, if you are buried under a set of problems, be encouraged that none of them is too complex for God to solve.

EXPLORATION God's Will—Genesis 18:14; 20:6; 50:20; Exodus 3:2; Esther 4:13-14; Matthew 1:1-17.

End of the Babylonian Captivity

Now in the first year of Cyrus king of Persia, that the word of the LORD by the mouth of Jeremiah might be fulfilled, the LORD stirred up the spirit of Cyrus king of Persia, so that he made a proclamation throughout all his kingdom, and also *put it* in writing, saying,

2 Thus says Cyrus king of Persia:
All the kingdoms of the earth the LORD God of heaven has given me. And He has commanded me to build Him a house at Jerusalem which *is* in Judah. [3]Who *is* among you of all His people? May his God be with him, and let him go up to Jerusalem which *is* in Judah, and build the house of the LORD God of Israel (He *is* God), which *is* in Jerusalem. [4]And whoever is left in any place where he dwells, let the men of his place help him with silver and gold, with goods and livestock, besides the freewill offerings for the house of God which *is* in Jerusalem.

[5]Then the heads of the fathers' *houses* of Judah and Benjamin, and the priests and the Levites, with all whose spirits God had moved, arose to go up and build the house of the LORD which *is* in Jerusalem. [6]And all those who *were* around them encouraged them with articles of silver and gold, with goods and livestock, and with precious things, besides all *that* was willingly offered.

[7]King Cyrus also brought out the articles of the house of the LORD, which Nebuchadnezzar had taken from Jerusalem and put in the temple of his gods; [8]and Cyrus king of Persia brought them out by the hand of Mithredath the treasurer, and counted them out to Sheshbazzar the prince of Judah. [9]This *is* the number of them: thirty gold platters, one thousand silver platters, twenty-nine knives, [10]thirty gold basins, four hundred and ten silver basins of a similar *kind, and* one thousand other articles. [11]All the articles of gold and silver *were* five thousand four hundred. All *these* Sheshbazzar took with the captives who were brought from Babylon to Jerusalem.

The Captives Who Returned to Jerusalem

2 Now[a] these *are* the people of the province who came back from the captivity, of those who had been carried away, whom Nebuchadnezzar the king of Babylon had carried away to Babylon, and who returned to Jerusalem and Judah, everyone to his *own* city.

[2]*Those* who came with Zerubbabel *were* Jeshua, Nehemiah, Seraiah, Reelaiah, Mordecai, Bilshan, Mispar,[b] Bigvai, Rehum,[c] *and* Baanah. The number of the men of the people of Israel: [3]the people of Parosh, two thousand one hundred and seventy-two; [4]the people of Shephatiah, three hundred and seventy-two; [5]the people of Arah, seven hundred and seventy-five; [6]the people of Pahath-Moab, of the people of Jeshua *and* Joab, two thousand eight hundred and twelve; [7]the people of Elam, one thousand two hundred and fifty-four; [8]the people of Zattu, nine hundred and forty-five; [9]the people of Zaccai, seven hundred and sixty; [10]the people of Bani,[d] six hundred and forty-two; [11]the people of Bebai, six hundred

2:1 [a] Compare this chapter with Nehemiah 7:6–73.
2:2 [b] Spelled *Mispereth* in Nehemiah 7:7 [c] Spelled *Nehum* in Nehemiah 7:7
2:10 [d] Spelled *Binnui* in Nehemiah 7:15

and twenty-three; 12the people of Azgad, one thousand two hundred and
twenty-two; 13the people of Adonikam, six hundred and sixty-six; 14the
people of Bigvai, two thousand and fifty-six; 15the people of Adin, four
hundred and fifty-four; 16the people of Ater of Hezekiah, ninety-eight;
17the people of Bezai, three hundred and twenty-three; 18the people of
Jorah,[e] one hundred and twelve; 19the people of Hashum, two hundred and
twenty-three; 20the people of Gibbar,[f] ninety-five; 21the people of Bethlehem,
one hundred and twenty-three; 22the men of Netophah, fifty-six; 23the men
of Anathoth, one hundred and twenty-eight; 24the people of Azmaveth,[g]
forty-two; 25the people of Kirjath Arim,[h] Chephirah, and Beeroth, seven
hundred and forty-three; 26the people of Ramah and Geba, six hundred
and twenty-one; 27the men of Michmas, one hundred and twenty-two; 28the
men of Bethel and Ai, two hundred and twenty-three; 29the people of Nebo,
fifty-two; 30the people of Magbish, one hundred and fifty-six; 31the people
of the other Elam, one thousand two hundred and fifty-four; 32the people
of Harim, three hundred and twenty; 33the people of Lod, Hadid, and Ono,
seven hundred and twenty-five; 34the people of Jericho, three hundred and
forty-five; 35the people of Senaah, three thousand six hundred and thirty.

36The priests: the sons of Jedaiah, of the house of Jeshua, nine hundred
and seventy-three; 37the sons of Immer, one thousand and fifty-two; 38the
sons of Pashhur, one thousand two hundred and forty-seven; 39the sons of
Harim, one thousand and seventeen.

40The Levites: the sons of Jeshua and Kadmiel, of the sons of Hodaviah,[i]
seventy-four.

41The singers: the sons of Asaph, one hundred and twenty-eight.

42The sons of the gatekeepers: the sons of Shallum, the sons of Ater, the
sons of Talmon, the sons of Akkub, the sons of Hatita, and the sons of
Shobai, one hundred and thirty-nine *in* all.

43The Nethinim: the sons of Ziha, the sons of Hasupha, the sons of
Tabbaoth, 44the sons of Keros, the sons of Siaha,[j] the sons of Padon, 45the
sons of Lebanah, the sons of Hagabah, the sons of Akkub, 46the sons of
Hagab, the sons of Shalmai, the sons of Hanan, 47the sons of Giddel, the
sons of Gahar, the sons of Reaiah, 48the sons of Rezin, the sons of Nekoda,
the sons of Gazzam, 49the sons of Uzza, the sons of Paseah, the sons of
Besai, 50the sons of Asnah, the sons of Meunim, the sons of Nephusim,[k]
51the sons of Bakbuk, the sons of Hakupha, the sons of Harhur, 52the sons
of Bazluth,[l] the sons of Mehida, the sons of Harsha, 53the sons of Barkos,
the sons of Sisera, the sons of Tamah, 54the sons of Neziah, and the sons of
Hatipha.

55The sons of Solomon's servants: the sons of Sotai, the sons of
Sophereth, the sons of Peruda,[m] 56the sons of Jaala, the sons of Darkon, the
sons of Giddel, 57the sons of Shephatiah, the sons of Hattil, the sons of
Pochereth of Zebaim, and the sons of Ami.[n] 58All the Nethinim and the
children of Solomon's servants were three hundred and ninety-two.

2:18 [e] Called *Hariph* in Nehemiah 7:24
2:20 [f] Called *Gibeon* in Nehemiah 7:25
2:24 [g] Called *Beth Azmaveth* in Nehemiah 7:28
2:25 [h] Called *Kirjath Jearim* in Nehemiah 7:29
2:40 [i] Spelled *Hodevah* in Nehemiah 7:43
2:44 [j] Spelled *Sia* in Nehemiah 7:47
2:50 [k] Spelled *Nephishesim* in Nehemiah 7:52
2:52 [l] Spelled *Bazlith* in Nehemiah 7:54
2:55 [m] Spelled *Perida* in Nehemiah 7:57
2:57 [n] Spelled *Amon* in Nehemiah 7:59

LIFE LESSON

Ezra 3:1–4:24

SITUATION Judah's jealous enemies to the north conspired to put an end to the rebuilding of Jerusalem. For several years, these enemies worked to hinder the Jews. Finally, they persuaded the Persian King, Artaxerxes, to stop the building.

OBSERVATION Satan always challenges God's followers. Even though Satan occasionally appears victorious, he cannot triumph as long as we stand strong in our faith.

INSPIRATION Deadly erosion has plunged our world into frighteningly deep darkness. Some Christians have distanced themselves so far from the lifestyle of the unbeliever that they don't have a clue how dark the world system really is. They don't see its boredom, its flat tastelessness, its terror and its stark hopelessness. There is the inescapable threat of AIDS, along with the abduction of children, alcoholism, fears of growing old, of financial reversal, of marital infidelity, of emotional breakdown. Such darkness surfaces only briefly, then runs and hides its face in the valley of death.

One morning when I had a few extra minutes, I thumbed through a few pages of a local newspaper. . . . Do you have any idea what that kind of news does to the average citizen? If it doesn't scare the life out of him, it can make him strangely apathetic. Then he gets hardened to it . . . shrugs it off, and says, "Who gives a rip?" So it goes in the darkness.

(From *Simple Faith* by Charles Swindoll)

APPLICATION Important projects at work or home or even at church run into problems: injuries strike, the cash flow dries up, arguments arise. Work to resolve the problems you can. Pray for wisdom for the problems you cannot resolve.

EXPLORATION Negative Events—Leviticus 19:10-35; Deuteronomy 1:23-40.

59And these *were* the ones who came up from Tel Melah, Tel Harsha, Cherub, Addan,[o] and Immer; but they could not identify their father's house or their genealogy,[p] whether they *were* of Israel: 60the sons of Delaiah, the sons of Tobiah, and the sons of Nekoda, six hundred and fifty-two; 61and of the sons of the priests: the sons of Habaiah, the sons of Koz,[q] and the sons of Barzillai, who took a wife of the daughters of Barzillai the Gileadite, and was called by their name. 62These sought their listing *among* those who were registered by genealogy, but they were not found; therefore they *were excluded* from the priesthood as defiled. 63And the governor[r] said to them that they should not eat of the most holy things till a priest could consult with the Urim and Thummim.

64The whole assembly together *was* forty-two thousand three hundred *and* sixty, 65besides their male and female servants, of whom *there were* seven thousand three hundred and thirty-seven; and they had two hundred men and women singers. 66Their horses *were* seven hundred and thirty-six, their mules two hundred and forty-five, 67their camels four hundred and thirty-five, and *their* donkeys six thousand seven hundred and twenty.

68*Some* of the heads of the fathers' *houses,* when they came to the house of the LORD which *is* in Jerusalem, offered freely for the house of God, to erect it in its place: 69According to their ability, they gave to the treasury for the work sixty-one thousand gold drachmas, five thousand minas of silver, and one hundred priestly garments.

70So the priests and the Levites, *some* of the people, the singers, the gatekeepers, and the Nethinim, dwelt in their cities, and all Israel in their cities.

Worship Restored at Jerusalem

3 And when the seventh month had come, and the children of Israel *were* in the cities, the people gathered together as one man to Jerusalem. 2Then Jeshua the son of Jozadak[s] and his brethren the priests, and Zerubbabel the son of Shealtiel and his brethren, arose and built the altar of the God of Israel, to offer burnt offerings on it, as *it is* written in the Law of Moses the man of God. 3Though fear *had come* upon them because of the people of those countries, they set the altar on its bases; and they offered burnt offerings on it to the LORD, *both* the morning and evening burnt offerings. 4They also kept the Feast of Tabernacles, as *it is* written, and *offered* the daily burnt offerings in the number required by ordinance for each day. 5Afterwards *they offered* the regular burnt offering, and *those* for New Moons and for all the appointed feasts of the LORD that were consecrated, and *those* of everyone who willingly offered a freewill offering to the LORD. 6From the first day of the seventh month they began to offer burnt offerings to the LORD, although the foundation of the temple of the LORD had not been laid. 7They also gave money to the masons and the carpenters, and food, drink, and oil to the people of Sidon and Tyre to bring cedar logs from Lebanon to the sea, to Joppa, according to the permission which they had from Cyrus king of Persia.

Restoration of the Temple Begins

8Now in the second month of the second year of their coming to the house of God at Jerusalem, Zerubbabel the son of Shealtiel, Jeshua the son of Jozadak,[t] and the rest of their brethren the priests and the Levites, and all those who had come out of the captivity to Jerusalem, began *work* and appointed the Levites from twenty years old and above to oversee the work of the house of the LORD. 9Then Jeshua *with* his sons and brothers, Kadmiel *with* his sons, and the sons of Judah,[u] arose as one to oversee those working on the house of God: the sons of Henadad *with* their sons and their brethren the Levites.

10When the builders laid the foundation of the temple of the LORD, the priests stood[v] in their apparel with trumpets, and the Levites, the sons of Asaph, with cymbals, to praise the LORD, according to the ordinance of David king of Israel. 11And they sang responsively, praising and giving thanks to the LORD:

"For *He is* good,
For His mercy *endures* forever toward Israel."[w]

Then all the people shouted with a great shout, when they praised the LORD, because the foundation of the house of the LORD was laid.

12But many of the priests and Levites and heads of the fathers' *houses,* old men who had seen the first

2:59 [o] Spelled *Addon* in Nehemiah 7:61 [p] Literally *seed*
2:61 [q] Or *Hakkoz*
2:63 [r] Hebrew *Tirshatha*
3:2 [s] Spelled *Jehozadak* in 1 Chronicles 6:14
3:8 [t] Spelled *Jehozadak* in 1 Chronicles 6:14
3:9 [u] Or *Hodaviah* (compare 2:40)
3:10 [v] Following Septuagint, Syriac, and Vulgate; Masoretic Text reads *they stationed the priests.*
3:11 [w] Compare Psalm 136:1

temple, wept with a loud voice when the foundation
of this temple was laid before their eyes. Yet many
shouted aloud for joy, 13 so that the people could not
discern the noise of the shout of joy from the noise of
the weeping of the people, for the people shouted with
a loud shout, and the sound was heard afar off.

Resistance to Rebuilding the Temple

4 Now when the adversaries of Judah and Benjamin
heard that the descendants of the captivity were
building the temple of the LORD God of Israel, 2 they
came to Zerubbabel and the heads of the fathers'
houses, and said to them, "Let us build with you, for
we seek your God as you *do;* and we have sacrificed to
Him since the days of Esarhaddon king of Assyria,
who brought us here." 3 But Zerubbabel and Jeshua
and the rest of the heads of the fathers' *houses* of Israel
said to them, "You may do nothing with us to build a
house for our God; but we alone will build to the LORD
God of Israel, as King Cyrus the king of Persia has
commanded us." 4 Then the people of the land tried to
discourage the people of Judah. They troubled them
in building, 5 and hired counselors against them to
frustrate their purpose all the days of Cyrus king of
Persia, even until the reign of Darius king of Persia.

Rebuilding of Jerusalem Opposed

6 In the reign of Ahasuerus, in the beginning of his
reign, they wrote an accusation against the inhabitants of Judah and Jerusalem.
7 In the days of Artaxerxes also, Bishlam, Mithredath,
Tabel, and the rest of their companions wrote to
Artaxerxes king of Persia; and the letter *was* written in
Aramaic script, and translated into the Aramaic language. 8 Rehum[x] the commander and Shimshai the
scribe wrote a letter against Jerusalem to King
Artaxerxes in this fashion:

9 From[y] Rehum the commander, Shimshai the
scribe, and the rest of their companions—
representatives of the Dinaites, the
Apharsathchites, the Tarpelites, the people of
Persia and Erech and Babylon and Shushan,[z]
the Dehavites, the Elamites, 10 and the rest of
the nations whom the great and noble
Osnapper took captive and settled in the cities
of Samaria and the remainder beyond the
River[a]—and so forth.[b]

11 (This *is* a copy of the letter that they sent him)

To King Artaxerxes from your servants, the
men *of the region* beyond the River, and so
forth:[c]

12 Let it be known to the king that the Jews who
came up from you have come to us at Jerusalem,
and are building the rebellious and evil city,
and are finishing *its* walls and repairing the
foundations. 13 Let it now be known to the king
that, if this city is built and the walls completed,
they will not pay tax, tribute, or custom, and
the king's treasury will be diminished. 14 Now
because we receive support from the palace, it
was not proper for us to see the king's dishonor;
therefore we have sent and informed the king,
15 that search may be made in the book of the
records of your fathers. And you will find in
the book of the records and know that this city
is a rebellious city, harmful to kings and
provinces, and that they have incited sedition
within the city in former times, for which
cause this city was destroyed.

16 We inform the king that if this city is rebuilt and
its walls are completed, the result will be that
you will have no dominion beyond the River.

17 The king sent an answer:

To Rehum the commander, *to* Shimshai the
scribe, *to* the rest of their companions who
dwell in Samaria, and *to* the remainder
beyond the River:

Peace, and so forth.[d]

18 The letter which you sent to us has been
clearly read before me. 19 And I gave the
command, and a search has been made, and
it was found that this city in former times has
revolted against kings, and rebellion and
sedition have been fostered in it. 20 There have
also been mighty kings over Jerusalem, who
have ruled over all *the region* beyond the River;
and tax, tribute, and custom were paid to them.

4:8 [x] The original language of Ezra 4:8 through 6:18 is Aramaic.
4:9 [y] Literally *Then* [z] Or *Susa*
4:10 [a] That is, the Euphrates [b] Literally *and now*
4:11 [c] Literally *and now*
4:17 [d] Literally *and now*

LIFE LESSON

Ezra 5:1–6:22

SITUATION The Gentiles in the area of Judah and Jerusalem tried to block the rebuilding of the temple. But God used elders and prophets to secure permission to resume building.

OBSERVATION God's influence supersedes the actions of secular authorities to accomplish his desires.

INSPIRATION Nowadays, much of the time, life seems to have gone out of control. Several nations have the nuclear bomb, and several more will be developing it soon. History seems senseless. Men kill and order others to kill. Armies destroy and hurt. World leaders seem to do Satan's will, and Christians may wonder if God has lost control of his world.

He has not!

Although Satan is the prince of this world (John 12:31), he has been judged and condemned (John 16:11). God is sovereign over all men and nations, and all must make a final account with him. At the time of the final reckoning, every problem—personal and national—will be set right. But as of now, evil is a terrible thing, and until it is destroyed, life will sometimes appear out of control.

The trouble is that evil has burrowed into the human personality. It is in all of us. We don't always act in the best interest of others. Feeling coerced by the political system, or by what others will think of us, or by the values of those around us, we surrender our Christian freedom and choose to do what we know is wrong. At the end of World War II, the world was horrified

21 Now give the command to make these men cease, that this city
may not be built until the command is given by me.

22 Take heed now that you do not fail to do this. Why should damage
increase to the hurt of the kings?

23 Now when the copy of King Artaxerxes' letter *was* read before Rehum,
Shimshai the scribe, and their companions, they went up in haste to Jerusalem against the Jews, and by force of arms made them cease. 24 Thus the
work of the house of God which *is* at Jerusalem ceased, and it was discon-
tinued until the second year of the reign of Darius king of Persia.

Restoration of the Temple Resumed

5 Then the prophet Haggai and Zechariah the son of Iddo, prophets,
prophesied to the Jews who *were* in Judah and Jerusalem, in the name
of the God of Israel, *who was* over them. 2 So Zerubbabel the son of
Shealtiel and Jeshua the son of Jozadak[e] rose up and began to build the
house of God which *is* in Jerusalem; and the prophets of God *were* with
them, helping them.
3 At the same time Tattenai the governor of *the region* beyond the River[f]
and Shethar-Boznai and their companions came to them and spoke thus
to them: "Who has commanded you to build this temple and finish this
wall?" 4 Then, accordingly, we told them the names of the men who were
constructing this building. 5 But the eye of their God was upon the elders of
the Jews, so that they could not make them cease till a report could go to
Darius. Then a written answer was returned concerning this *matter.* 6 This
is a copy of the letter that Tattenai sent:

The governor of *the region* beyond the River, and Shethar-Boznai, and his companions, the Persians who *were in the region* beyond the River, to Darius the king.

7 (They sent a letter to him, in which was written thus)

To Darius the king:

All peace.

8 Let it be known to the king that we went into the province of Judea, to the temple of the great God, which is being built with heavy stones, and timber is being laid in the walls; and this work goes on diligently and prospers in their hands.

9 Then we asked those elders, *and* spoke thus to them: "Who
commanded you to build this temple and to finish these walls?"
10 We also asked them their names to inform you, that we might
write the names of the men who *were* chief among them.

11 And thus they returned us an answer, saying: "We are the servants of the God of heaven and earth, and we are rebuilding the temple that was built many years ago, which a great king of Israel built

5:2 [e] Spelled *Jehozadak* in 1 Chronicles 6:14
5:3 [f] That is, the Euphrates

and completed. 12But because our fathers provoked the God of
heaven to wrath, He gave them into the hand of Nebuchadnezzar
king of Babylon, the Chaldean, *who* destroyed this temple and
carried the people away to Babylon. 13However, in the first year of
Cyrus king of Babylon, King Cyrus issued a decree to build this
house of God. 14Also, the gold and silver articles of the house of
God, which Nebuchadnezzar had taken from the temple that *was*
in Jerusalem and carried into the temple of Babylon—those King
Cyrus took from the temple of Babylon, and they were given to one
named Sheshbazzar, whom he had made governor. 15And he said
to him, 'Take these articles; go, carry them to the temple *site* that *is*
in Jerusalem, and let the house of God be rebuilt on its former
site.' 16Then the same Sheshbazzar came *and* laid the foundation of
the house of God which *is* in Jerusalem; but from that time even
until now it has been under construction, and it is not finished."

17 Now therefore, if *it seems* good to the king, let a search be made in
the king's treasure house, which *is* there in Babylon, whether it is
so that a decree was issued by King Cyrus to build this house of
God at Jerusalem, and let the king send us his pleasure concerning
this *matter.*

The Decree of Darius

6 Then King Darius issued a decree, and a search was made in the ar-
chives,[g] where the treasures were stored in Babylon. 2And at
Achmetha,[h] in the palace that *is* in the province of Media, a scroll was
found, and in it a record *was* written thus:

3 In the first year of King Cyrus, King Cyrus issued a decree *concerning*
the house of God at Jerusalem: "Let the house be rebuilt, the place
where they offered sacrifices; and let the foundations of it be firmly
laid, its height sixty cubits *and* its width sixty cubits, 4*with* three rows
of heavy stones and one row of new timber. Let the expenses be
paid from the king's treasury. 5Also let the gold and silver articles of
the house of God, which Nebuchadnezzar took from the temple
which *is* in Jerusalem and brought to Babylon, be restored and
taken back to the temple which *is* in Jerusalem, *each* to its place;
and deposit *them* in the house of God"—

6 Now *therefore,* Tattenai, governor of *the region* beyond the River,
and Shethar-Boznai, and your companions the Persians who *are*
beyond the River, keep yourselves far from there. 7Let the work of
this house of God alone; let the governor of the Jews and the elders
of the Jews build this house of God on its site.

8 Moreover I issue a decree *as to* what you shall do for the elders of
these Jews, for the building of this house of God: Let the cost be
paid at the king's expense from taxes *on the region* beyond the
River; this is to be given immediately to these men, so that they are
not hindered. 9And whatever they need—young bulls, rams, and

6:1 *g* Literally *house of the scrolls*
6:2 *h* Probably *Ecbatana,* the ancient capital of Media

to discover that brilliant men with PhDs could build gas chambers. Their level of intelligence had nothing to do with their ability to choose to do right. One military leader after another at the Nuremberg trials said, "I was only taking orders."

How can I say God is in control when all around me I see evil? Consider the ending of the book of Habakkuk. The prophet is living in a time of natural and military calamities. "Destruction and violence are before me; there is strife, and conflict abounds. Therefore the law is paralyzed, and justice never prevails. The wicked hem in the righteous, so that justice is perverted" (1:3,4).

But Habakkuk had faith that, in the end, the Lord will save his people. He describes the future day of judgement when "you came out to deliver your people" (3:13), and he proclaims his faith that God is in control in spite of appearances. . . . No matter how things look, we can have faith that God will never abandon his world. He is always sovereign in this universe.

(From "God Is in Control" by Calvin Miller in *Practical Christianity*)

APPLICATION Governmental leaders, whether or not they are Christians, need our support. Do you honor those in government? Don't be quick to cut them down. Pray regularly for those in positions of authority.

EXPLORATION Opposition to God—Isaiah 14:13-14; Acts 13:10; 26:17-18; Romans 16:20; 1 Thessalonians 2:18.

LIFE LESSON

Ezra 7:1–8:36

SITUATION Sixty years elapsed between the events of Ezra 6 and 7. Although Ezra had previously remained in Babylon compiling a historical record, he obtained permission to return to Jerusalem. He led the Jews to a spiritual renewal.

OBSERVATION Ezra's careful study of Scripture throughout his life enabled him to be an effective minister to those in need.

INSPIRATION There is a well-known local coach in Fullerton, California, whose thirty-five-plus years in athletics have been eminently successful. . . . His incredible career in Southern California speaks for itself. When he was interviewed by the *Los Angeles Times*, the sportswriter wanted to know his secret. What was it that made him so successful? Without hesitation Coach Sherbeck said that his credo could best be stated in words written by an anonymous author. Ever since he was a boy growing up in Big Sandy, Montana, he has lived by these words:

Press on.
Nothing in the world
Can take the place of persistence.
Talent will not;
Nothing is more common
Than unsuccessful men
With talent.
Genius will not;
Unrewarded genius
Is almost a proverb.
Education will not;
The world is full of
Educated derelicts.
Persistence and determination
Alone are omnipotent.

lambs for the burnt offerings of the God of heaven, wheat, salt,
wine, and oil, according to the request of the priests who *are* in
Jerusalem—let it be given them day by day without fail, [10]that they
may offer sacrifices of sweet aroma to the God of heaven, and pray
for the life of the king and his sons.

11 Also I issue a decree that whoever alters this edict, let a timber be
pulled from his house and erected, and let him be hanged on it;
and let his house be made a refuse heap because of this. [12]And
may the God who causes His name to dwell there destroy any king
or people who put their hand to alter it, or to destroy this house of
God which is in Jerusalem. I Darius issue a decree; let it be done
diligently.

The Temple Completed and Dedicated

[13]Then Tattenai, governor of *the region* beyond the River, Shethar-
Boznai, and their companions diligently did according to what King
Darius had sent. [14]So the elders of the Jews built, and they prospered
through the prophesying of Haggai the prophet and Zechariah the son of
Iddo. And they built and finished *it,* according to the commandment of
the God of Israel, and according to the command of Cyrus, Darius, and
Artaxerxes king of Persia. [15]Now the temple was finished on the third day
of the month of Adar, which was in the sixth year of the reign of King
Darius. [16]Then the children of Israel, the priests and the Levites and the
rest of the descendants of the captivity, celebrated the dedication of this
house of God with joy. [17]And they offered sacrifices at the dedication of
this house of God, one hundred bulls, two hundred rams, four hundred
lambs, and as a sin offering for all Israel twelve male goats, according to
the number of the tribes of Israel. [18]They assigned the priests to their divisions and the Levites to their divisions, over the service of God in Jerusalem, as it is written in the Book of Moses.

The Passover Celebrated

[19]And the descendants of the captivity kept the Passover on the fourteenth *day* of the first month. [20]For the priests and the Levites had purified
themselves; all of them *were ritually* clean. And they slaughtered the
Passover *lambs* for all the descendants of the captivity, for their brethren
the priests, and for themselves. [21]Then the children of Israel who had returned from the captivity ate together with all who had separated themselves from the filth of the nations of the land in order to seek the LORD
God of Israel. [22]And they kept the Feast of Unleavened Bread seven days
with joy; for the LORD made them joyful, and turned the heart of the king of
Assyria toward them, to strengthen their hands in the work of the house of
God, the God of Israel.

The Arrival of Ezra

7 Now after these things, in the reign of Artaxerxes king of Persia, Ezra
the son of Seraiah, the son of Azariah, the son of Hilkiah, [2]the son of
Shallum, the son of Zadok, the son of Ahitub, [3]the son of Amariah, the son
of Azariah, the son of Meraioth, [4]the son of Zerahiah, the son of Uzzi, the

son of Bukki, 5the son of Abishua, the son of Phinehas, the son of Eleazar,
the son of Aaron the chief priest— 6this Ezra came up from Babylon; and
he *was* a skilled scribe in the Law of Moses, which the LORD God of Israel
had given. The king granted him all his request, according to the hand of
the LORD his God upon him. 7*Some* of the children of Israel, the priests, the
Levites, the singers, the gatekeepers, and the Nethinim came up to Jerusalem in the seventh year of King Artaxerxes. 8And Ezra came to Jerusalem
in the fifth month, which *was* in the seventh year of the king. 9On the first
day of the first month he began *his* journey from Babylon, and on the first
day of the fifth month he came to Jerusalem, according to the good hand
of his God upon him. 10For Ezra had prepared his heart to seek the Law of
the LORD, and to do *it,* and to teach statutes and ordinances in Israel.

The Letter of Artaxerxes to Ezra

11This *is* a copy of the letter that King Artaxerxes gave Ezra the priest, the
scribe, expert in the words of the commandments of the LORD, and of His
statutes to Israel:

12 Artaxerxes,[i] king of kings,

To Ezra the priest, a scribe of the Law of the God of heaven:

Perfect *peace,* and so forth.[j]

13 I issue a decree that all those of the people of Israel and the priests
and Levites in my realm, who volunteer to go up to Jerusalem, may
go with you. 14And whereas you are being sent by the king and his
seven counselors to inquire concerning Judah and Jerusalem, with
regard to the Law of your God which *is* in your hand; 15and *whereas
you are* to carry the silver and gold which the king and his counselors
have freely offered to the God of Israel, whose dwelling *is* in
Jerusalem; 16and *whereas* all the silver and gold that you may find
in all the province of Babylon, along with the freewill offering of
the people and the priests, *are to be* freely offered for the house of
their God in Jerusalem— 17now therefore, be careful to buy with
this money bulls, rams, and lambs, with their grain offerings and
their drink offerings, and offer them on the altar of the house of
your God in Jerusalem.

18 And whatever seems good to you and your brethren to do with the
rest of the silver and the gold, do it according to the will of your God.
19Also the articles that are given to you for the service of the house
of your God, deliver in full before the God of Jerusalem. 20And
whatever more may be needed for the house of your God, which you
may have occasion to provide, pay *for it* from the king's treasury.

21 And I, *even* I, Artaxerxes the king, issue a decree to all the treasurers
who *are in the region* beyond the River, that whatever Ezra the priest,
the scribe of the Law of the God of heaven, may require of you, let
it be done diligently, 22up to one hundred talents of silver, one
hundred kors of wheat, one hundred baths of wine, one hundred
baths of oil, and salt without prescribed limit. 23Whatever is
commanded by the God of heaven, let it diligently be done for the

7:12 [i] The original language of Ezra 7:12–26 is Aramaic. [j] Literally *and now*

Coach Sherbeck had no quick and easy formula for success; he lives by his strong commitment to persistence and determination.

Don't misunderstand. I have in mind being determined to accomplish what is right. . . . When the objective is good and the motive is pure, there is nothing more valuable in the pathway leading to genuine success than persistence and determination. Following one's dream requires these disciplines. . . . The thing that makes for greatness is determination, persisting in the right direction over the long haul, following your dream, staying at the task. Just as there is no thing such as instant failure, neither is there automatic or instant success. But success is the direct result of a process that is long, arduous, and often unappreciated by others. It also includes a willingness to sacrifice. . . . In our world of instant everything, these thoughts are not very popular. . . . If we really want to soar like an eagle, we must keep on continually pursuing—we must keep on seeking. (From *Living Above the Level of Mediocrity* by Charles Swindoll)

APPLICATION Is there a specific goal you recently gave up? Reexamine your motive for doing so. Is it possible that you gave up too soon? Would God want you to persist? If so, recommit yourself to the task. Talk to a friend who can encourage you to reach your goal.

EXPLORATION Excellence in Obedience—Leviticus 25:18-19; Joshua 23:6; Psalm 1:1-2; 18:21-23; 2 Corinthians 8:7; James 1:25.

house of the God of heaven. For why should
there be wrath against the realm of the king
and his sons?

24 Also we inform you that it shall not be lawful
to impose tax, tribute, or custom *on* any of the
priests, Levites, singers, gatekeepers, Nethinim,
or servants of this house of God. 25And you, Ezra,
according to your God-given wisdom, set
magistrates and judges who may judge all the
people who *are in the region* beyond the River,
all such as know the laws of your God; and teach
those who do not know *them.* 26Whoever will
not observe the law of your God and the law of
the king, let judgment be executed speedily on
him, whether *it be* death, or banishment, or
confiscation of goods, or imprisonment.

27Blessed *be* the LORD God of our fathers, who has
put *such a thing* as this in the king's heart, to beautify
the house of the LORD which *is* in Jerusalem, 28and has
extended mercy to me before the king and his counselors, and before all the king's mighty princes.

So I was encouraged, as the hand of the LORD my
God *was* upon me; and I gathered leading men of Israel to go up with me.

Heads of Families Who Returned with Ezra

8 These *are* the heads of their fathers' *houses,* and
this is the genealogy of those who went up with
me from Babylon, in the reign of King Artaxerxes: 2of
the sons of Phinehas, Gershom; of the sons of
Ithamar, Daniel; of the sons of David, Hattush; 3of the
sons of Shecaniah, of the sons of Parosh, Zechariah;
and registered with him *were* one hundred and fifty
males; 4of the sons of Pahath-Moab, Eliehoenai the
son of Zerahiah, and with him two hundred males;
5of the sons of Shechaniah,[k] Ben-Jahaziel, and with
him three hundred males; 6of the sons of Adin, Ebed
the son of Jonathan, and with him fifty males; 7of the
sons of Elam, Jeshaiah the son of Athaliah, and with
him seventy males; 8of the sons of Shephatiah,
Zebadiah the son of Michael, and with him eighty
males; 9of the sons of Joab, Obadiah the son of Jehiel,
and with him two hundred and eighteen males; 10of the
sons of Shelomith,[l] Ben-Josiphiah, and with him one
hundred and sixty males; 11of the sons of Bebai,
Zechariah the son of Bebai, and with him twenty-
eight males; 12of the sons of Azgad, Johanan the son of
Hakkatan, and with him one hundred and ten males;
13of the last sons of Adonikam, whose names *are*
these—Eliphelet, Jeiel, and Shemaiah—and with
them sixty males; 14also of the sons of Bigvai, Uthai
and Zabbud, and with them seventy males.

Servants for the Temple

15Now I gathered them by the river that flows to
Ahava, and we camped there three days. And I looked
among the people and the priests, and found none of
the sons of Levi there. 16Then I sent for Eliezer, Ariel,
Shemaiah, Elnathan, Jarib, Elnathan, Nathan,
Zechariah, and Meshullam, leaders; also for Joiarib
and Elnathan, men of understanding. 17And I gave
them a command for Iddo the chief man at the place
Casiphia, and I told them what they should say to
Iddo *and* his brethren[m] the Nethinim at the place
Casiphia—that they should bring us servants for the
house of our God. 18Then, by the good hand of our
God upon us, they brought us a man of understanding, of the sons of Mahli the son of Levi, the son of Israel, namely Sherebiah, with his sons and brothers,
eighteen men; 19and Hashabiah, and with him Jeshaiah
of the sons of Merari, his brothers and their sons,
twenty men; 20also of the Nethinim, whom David and
the leaders had appointed for the service of the
Levites, two hundred and twenty Nethinim. All of them
were designated by name.

Fasting and Prayer for Protection

21Then I proclaimed a fast there at the river of
Ahava, that we might humble ourselves before our
God, to seek from Him the right way for us and our little ones and all our possessions. 22For I was ashamed
to request of the king an escort of soldiers and horsemen to help us against the enemy on the road, because we had spoken to the king, saying, "The hand of
our God *is* upon all those for good who seek Him, but
His power and His wrath *are* against all those who forsake Him." 23So we fasted and entreated our God for
this, and He answered our prayer.

Gifts for the Temple

24And I separated twelve of the leaders of the
priests—Sherebiah, Hashabiah, and ten of their
brethren with them— 25and weighed out to them the
silver, the gold, and the articles, the offering for the
house of our God which the king and his counselors

8:5 [k] Following Masoretic Text and Vulgate; Septuagint reads *the sons of Zatho, Shechaniah.*
8:10 [l] Following Masoretic Text and Vulgate; Septuagint reads *the sons of Banni, Shelomith.*
8:17 [m] Following Vulgate; Masoretic Text reads *to Iddo his brother;* Septuagint reads *to their brethren.*

and his princes, and all Israel *who were* present, had offered. 26I weighed into their hand six hundred and fifty
talents of silver, silver articles *weighing* one hundred
talents, one hundred talents of gold, 27twenty gold
basins *worth* a thousand drachmas, and two vessels of
fine polished bronze, precious as gold. 28And I said to
them, "You *are* holy to the Lord; the articles *are* holy
also; and the silver and the gold *are* a freewill offering to
the Lord God of your fathers. 29Watch and keep *them*
until you weigh *them* before the leaders of the priests
and the Levites and heads of the fathers' *houses* of Israel
in Jerusalem, *in* the chambers of the house of the
Lord." 30So the priests and the Levites received the silver and the gold and the articles by weight, to bring
them to Jerusalem to the house of our God.

The Return to Jerusalem

31Then we departed from the river of Ahava on the
twelfth *day* of the first month, to go to Jerusalem. And
the hand of our God was upon us, and He delivered us
from the hand of the enemy and from ambush along
the road. 32So we came to Jerusalem, and stayed there
three days.

33Now on the fourth day the silver and the gold and
the articles were weighed in the house of our God by
the hand of Meremoth the son of Uriah the priest, and
with him *was* Eleazar the son of Phinehas; with them
were the Levites, Jozabad the son of Jeshua and
Noadiah the son of Binnui, 34with the number *and*
weight of everything. All the weight was written down
at that time.

35The children of those who had been carried away
captive, who had come from the captivity, offered
burnt offerings to the God of Israel: twelve bulls for all
Israel, ninety-six rams, seventy-seven lambs, and
twelve male goats *as* a sin offering. All *this was* a burnt
offering to the Lord.

36And they delivered the king's orders to the king's
satraps and the governors *in the region* beyond the
River. So they gave support to the people and the
house of God.

Intermarriage with Pagans

9 When these things were done, the leaders came to
me, saying, "The people of Israel and the priests
and the Levites have not separated themselves from
the peoples of the lands, with respect to the abominations of the Canaanites, the Hittites, the Perizzites, the
Jebusites, the Ammonites, the Moabites, the Egyptians, and the Amorites. 2For they have taken some of
their daughters *as wives* for themselves and their
sons, so that the holy seed is mixed with the peoples
of *those* lands. Indeed, the hand of the leaders and
rulers has been foremost in this trespass." 3So when I
heard this thing, I tore my garment and my robe, and
plucked out some of the hair of my head and beard,
and sat down astonished. 4Then everyone who trembled at the words of the God of Israel assembled to
me, because of the transgression of those who had
been carried away captive, and I sat astonished until
the evening sacrifice.

5At the evening sacrifice I arose from my fasting;
and having torn my garment and my robe, I fell on
my knees and spread out my hands to the Lord my
God. 6And I said: "O my God, I am too ashamed and
humiliated to lift up my face to You, my God; for our
iniquities have risen higher than *our* heads, and our
guilt has grown up to the heavens. 7Since the days of
our fathers to this day we *have been* very guilty, and
for our iniquities we, our kings, *and* our priests have
been delivered into the hand of the kings of the lands,
to the sword, to captivity, to plunder, and to humiliation, as *it is* this day. 8And now for a little while grace
has been *shown* from the Lord our God, to leave us a
remnant to escape, and to give us a peg in His holy
place, that our God may enlighten our eyes and give
us a measure of revival in our bondage. 9For we *were*
slaves. Yet our God did not forsake us in our bondage;
but He extended mercy to us in the sight of the kings
of Persia, to revive us, to repair the house of our God,
to rebuild its ruins, and to give us a wall in Judah and
Jerusalem. 10And now, O our God, what shall we say
after this? For we have forsaken Your commandments, 11which You commanded by Your servants the
prophets, saying, 'The land which you are entering to
possess is an unclean land, with the uncleanness of
the peoples of the lands, with their abominations
which have filled it from one end to another with their
impurity. 12Now therefore, do not give your daughters
as wives for their sons, nor take their daughters to
your sons; and never seek their peace or prosperity,
that you may be strong and eat the good of the land,
and leave *it* as an inheritance to your children forever.' 13And after all that has come upon us for our evil
deeds and for our great guilt, since You our God have
punished us less than our iniquities *deserve,* and have
given us *such* deliverance as this, 14should we again
break Your commandments, and join in marriage
with the people *committing* these abominations?
Would You not be angry with us until You had consumed *us,* so that *there would be* no remnant or survivor? 15O Lord God of Israel, You *are* righteous, for we

are left as a remnant, as *it is* this day. Here we *are* before You, in our guilt, though no one can stand before
You because of this!"

Confession of Improper Marriages

10 Now while Ezra was praying, and while he was
confessing, weeping, and bowing down before
the house of God, a very large assembly of men,
women, and children gathered to him from Israel; for
the people wept very bitterly. 2And Shechaniah the
son of Jehiel, *one* of the sons of Elam, spoke up and
said to Ezra, "We have trespassed against our God,
and have taken pagan wives from the peoples of the
land; yet now there is hope in Israel in spite of this.
3Now therefore, let us make a covenant with our God
to put away all these wives and those who have been
born to them, according to the advice of my master
and of those who tremble at the commandment of
our God; and let it be done according to the law.
4Arise, for *this* matter *is* your *responsibility.* We also *are*
with you. Be of good courage, and do *it.*"

5Then Ezra arose, and made the leaders of the
priests, the Levites, and all Israel swear an oath that
they would do according to this word. So they swore
an oath. 6Then Ezra rose up from before the house of
God, and went into the chamber of Jehohanan the son
of Eliashib; and *when* he came there, he ate no bread
and drank no water, for he mourned because of the
guilt of those from the captivity.

7And they issued a proclamation throughout Judah
and Jerusalem to all the descendants of the captivity,
that they must gather at Jerusalem, 8and that whoever
would not come within three days, according to the
instructions of the leaders and elders, all his property
would be confiscated, and he himself would be separated from the assembly of those from the captivity.

9So all the men of Judah and Benjamin gathered at
Jerusalem within three days. It *was* the ninth month,
on the twentieth of the month; and all the people sat
in the open square of the house of God, trembling because of *this* matter and because of heavy rain. 10Then
Ezra the priest stood up and said to them, "You have
transgressed and have taken pagan wives, adding to
the guilt of Israel. 11Now therefore, make confession
to the LORD God of your fathers, and do His will; separate yourselves from the peoples of the land, and from
the pagan wives."

12Then all the assembly answered and said with a
loud voice, "Yes! As you have said, so we must do.
13But *there are* many people; *it is* the season for heavy
rain, and we are not able to stand outside. Nor *is this*
the work of one or two days, for *there are* many of us
who have transgressed in this matter. 14Please, let the
leaders of our entire assembly stand; and let all those
in our cities who have taken pagan wives come at appointed times, together with the elders and judges of
their cities, until the fierce wrath of our God is turned
away from us in this matter." 15Only Jonathan the son
of Asahel and Jahaziah the son of Tikvah opposed this,
and Meshullam and Shabbethai the Levite gave them
support.

16Then the descendants of the captivity did so. And
Ezra the priest, *with* certain heads of the fathers'
households, were set apart by the fathers' *households,*
each of them by name; and they sat down on the first
day of the tenth month to examine the matter. 17By the
first day of the first month they finished *questioning*
all the men who had taken pagan wives.

Pagan Wives Put Away

18And among the sons of the priests who had taken
pagan wives *the following* were found of the sons of
Jeshua the son of Jozadak,[n] and his brothers: Maaseiah,
Eliezer, Jarib, and Gedaliah. 19And they gave their
promise that they would put away their wives; and *being* guilty, *they presented* a ram of the flock as their
trespass offering.

20Also of the sons of Immer: Hanani and Zebadiah;
21of the sons of Harim: Maaseiah, Elijah, Shemaiah,
Jehiel, and Uzziah; 22of the sons of Pashhur: Elioenai,
Maaseiah, Ishmael, Nethanel, Jozabad, and Elasah.

23Also of the Levites: Jozabad, Shimei, Kelaiah (the
same *is* Kelita), Pethahiah, Judah, and Eliezer.

24Also of the singers: Eliashib; and of the gatekeepers: Shallum, Telem, and Uri.

25And others of Israel: of the sons of Parosh: Ramiah,
Jeziah, Malchiah, Mijamin, Eleazar, Malchijah, and
Benaiah; 26of the sons of Elam: Mattaniah, Zechariah,
Jehiel, Abdi, Jeremoth, and Eliah; 27of the sons of Zattu:
Elioenai, Eliashib, Mattaniah, Jeremoth, Zabad, and
Aziza; 28of the sons of Bebai: Jehohanan, Hananiah,
Zabbai, *and* Athlai; 29of the sons of Bani: Meshullam,
Malluch, Adaiah, Jashub, Sheal, *and* Ramoth;[o] 30of the
sons of Pahath-Moab: Adna, Chelal, Benaiah, Maase-
iah, Mattaniah, Bezalel, Binnui, and Manasseh; 31*of* the
sons of Harim: Eliezer, Ishijah, Malchijah, Shemaiah,
Shimeon, 32Benjamin, Malluch, *and* Shemariah; 33of the
sons of Hashum: Mattenai, Mattattah, Zabad, Eliphelet,

10:18 [n] Spelled *Jehozadak* in 1 Chronicles 6:14
10:29 [o] Or *Jeremoth*

Jeremai, Manasseh, *and* Shimei; 34of the sons of Bani:
Maadai, Amram, Uel, 35Benaiah, Bedeiah, Cheluh,[p]
36Vaniah, Meremoth, Eliashib, 37Mattaniah, Mattenai,
Jaasai,[q] 38Bani, Binnui, Shimei, 39Shelemiah, Nathan,
Adaiah, 40Machnadebai, Shashai, Sharai, 41Azarel,
Shelemiah, Shemariah, 42Shallum, Amariah, *and* Jo-
seph; 43of the sons of Nebo: Jeiel, Mattithiah, Zabad,
Zebina, Jaddai,[r] Joel, *and* Benaiah.

44All these had taken pagan wives, and *some* of them had wives *by whom* they had children.

10:35 [p] Or *Cheluhi,* or *Cheluhu*
10:37 [q] Or *Jaasu*
10:43 [r] Or *Jaddu*

The Book of NEHEMIAH

INTRODUCTION

You are about to meet the Abraham Lincoln of the Old Testament. A respected leader with a tender heart. You will see his tears in the oval office as he weeps for people oppressed and vulnerable.

You are about to meet the General George Patton of the Old Testament. A rugged leader. Intolerant of compromise. Relentless in demanding perfection. He punished those who were soft by pushing them down and cursing their names.

You are about to meet the Winston Churchill of the Old Testament. A statesman. Tested and tried. Resisting the enemies who seek to lure him away from the task. Rising above the squabbling factions who could distract him.

The tenderness of Lincoln. The fire of Patton. The savvy of Churchill. All found in the same man.

Nehemiah.

When we meet him he is wearing the robe of royalty. He is the king's cupbearer. But though he was in a position of power, his heart beat for people in Israel. He was a Hebrew in Persia. When word reached him that the Temple was being reconstructed, he grew anxious. He knew there was no wall to protect it.

Nehemiah invited God to use him to save the city. God answered his prayer by softening the heart of the Persian king. Artaxerxes gave not only his blessing, but also supplies to be used in the project.

Nehemiah exchanged the royal robe for coveralls and got to work. The project took twelve years and was uphill all the way. He was accused of everything from allowing faulty construction to being power-hungry. In spite of grumpy workers and lurking enemies, he made it. With the wall built and the enemy silent, the people rejoiced and Nehemiah went back to Persia.

After twelve years he returned. The walls were strong, but the people had gone to pot. Faith was forgotten and discipline was a bad word. So Nehemiah got busy again.

He went to his closet, hung up his royal robe, bypassed his coveralls, and dusted off his frock and set about the task of teaching the people a few things about morality. He didn't mince words. "So I contended with them and cursed them, struck some of them and pulled out their hair. . ." (13:25). Not what you'd call a typical Bible class.

But Nehemiah wasn't what you'd call a typical fellow.

LIFE LESSON

Nehemiah 1:1–2:10

SITUATION Nehemiah, a Jew displaced by the Babylonian captivity, served in the king's court. When he heard of the decrepit condition of the gates and walls of Jerusalem, he wept and asked the king to send him to rebuild the walls.

OBSERVATION When Nehemiah heard bad news, he prayed. After praying, he developed a plan.

INSPIRATION Nehemiah 1 is a blend of prayer and action. . . . Why is prayer so important? Here are the four shortest reasons I know.

. . . Prayer forces me to leave the situation with God; *it makes me wait.* Secondly, prayer *clears my vision.* . . . When you first face a situation, is it foggy? Prayer will "burn through." Your vision will clear so you can see through God's eyes.

Thirdly, prayer *quiets my heart.* I cannot worry and pray at the same time. . . .

Fourthly, prayer *activates my faith.* After praying I am more prone to trust God. . . . Prayer sets faith on fire.

Don't just fill the margins in your Bible with words and thoughts about ways a leader prays. Do it! . . . Pray! Prayer was the first major step Nehemiah took in his journey to effective leadership. . . .

. . . The Lord is the Specialist we need for those uncrossable and impossible experiences. He delights in accomplishing what we cannot pull off. But He awaits our cry. He listens for our request. . . .

(From *Hand Me Another Brick* by Charles Swindoll)

APPLICATION What was your first response to an unexpected medical bill, a car breakdown, or a layoff at work? Did you respond in anger, by worrying and complaining, or did you first go to God and ask for his help and guidance through the hardship?

EXPLORATION Prayer During Difficult Times—1 Samuel 7:7-9; 1 Kings 17:17-24; Psalm 34:4-7; 61:1-2; 2 Corinthians 12:7-9.

Nehemiah Prays for His People

The words of Nehemiah the son of Hachaliah.
It came to pass in the month of Chislev, *in* the twentieth year, as
I was in Shushan[a] the citadel, 2that Hanani one of my brethren
came with men from Judah; and I asked them concerning the Jews
who had escaped, who had survived the captivity, and concerning Jerusalem. 3And they said to me, "The survivors who are left from the captivity in
the province *are* there in great distress and reproach. The wall of Jerusalem *is* also broken down, and its gates *are* burned with fire."
4So it was, when I heard these words, that I sat down and wept, and
mourned *for many* days; I was fasting and praying before the God of heaven.
5And I said: "I pray, LORD God of heaven, O great and awesome God, *You*
who keep *Your* covenant and mercy with those who love You[b] and observe
Your[c] commandments, 6please let Your ear be attentive and Your eyes
open, that You may hear the prayer of Your servant which I pray before
You now, day and night, for the children of Israel Your servants, and confess the sins of the children of Israel which we have sinned against You.
Both my father's house and I have sinned. 7We have acted very corruptly
against You, and have not kept the commandments, the statutes, nor the
ordinances which You commanded Your servant Moses. 8Remember, I
pray, the word that You commanded Your servant Moses, saying, '*If* you are
unfaithful, I will scatter you among the nations;[d] 9but *if* you return to Me,
and keep My commandments and do them, though some of you were cast
out to the farthest part of the heavens, *yet* I will gather them from there,
and bring them to the place which I have chosen as a dwelling for My
name.'[e] 10Now these *are* Your servants and Your people, whom You have
redeemed by Your great power, and by Your strong hand. 11O Lord, I pray,
please let Your ear be attentive to the prayer of Your servant, and to the
prayer of Your servants who desire to fear Your name; and let Your servant
prosper this day, I pray, and grant him mercy in the sight of this man."
For I was the king's cupbearer.

Nehemiah Sent to Judah

2 And it came to pass in the month of Nisan, in the twentieth year of
King Artaxerxes, *when* wine *was* before him, that I took the wine and
gave it to the king. Now I had never been sad in his presence before.
2Therefore the king said to me, "Why *is* your face sad, since you *are* not
sick? This *is* nothing but sorrow of heart."
So I became dreadfully afraid, 3and said to the king, "May the king live
forever! Why should my face not be sad, when the city, the place of my fathers' tombs, *lies* waste, and its gates are burned with fire?"
4Then the king said to me, "What do you request?"
So I prayed to the God of heaven. 5And I said to the king, "If it pleases
the king, and if your servant has found favor in your sight, I ask that you
send me to Judah, to the city of my fathers' tombs, that I may rebuild it."
6Then the king said to me (the queen also sitting beside him), "How
long will your journey be? And when will you return?" So it pleased the
king to send me; and I set him a time.

1:1 [a] Or *Susa*
1:5 [b] Literally *Him* [c] Literally *His*
1:8 [d] Leviticus 26:33
1:9 [e] Deuteronomy 30:2–5

7Furthermore I said to the king, "If it pleases the king, let letters be given
to me for the governors *of the region* beyond the River,[f] that they must permit me to pass through till I come to Judah, 8and a letter to Asaph the
keeper of the king's forest, that he must give me timber to make beams for
the gates of the citadel which *pertains* to the temple,[g] for the city wall, and
for the house that I will occupy." And the king granted *them* to me according to the good hand of my God upon me.
9Then I went to the governors *in the region* beyond the River, and gave
them the king's letters. Now the king had sent captains of the army and
horsemen with me. 10When Sanballat the Horonite and Tobiah the
Ammonite official[h] heard *of it,* they were deeply disturbed that a man had
come to seek the well-being of the children of Israel.

Nehemiah Views the Wall of Jerusalem

11So I came to Jerusalem and was there three days. 12Then I arose in the
night, I and a few men with me; I told no one what my God had put in my
heart to do at Jerusalem; nor was there any animal with me, except the one
on which I rode. 13And I went out by night through the Valley Gate to the
Serpent Well and the Refuse Gate, and viewed the walls of Jerusalem
which were broken down and its gates which were burned with fire.
14Then I went on to the Fountain Gate and to the King's Pool, but *there was*
no room for the animal under me to pass. 15So I went up in the night by the
valley, and viewed the wall; then I turned back and entered by the Valley
Gate, and so returned. 16And the officials did not know where I had gone
or what I had done; I had not yet told the Jews, the priests, the nobles, the
officials, or the others who did the work.
17Then I said to them, "You see the distress that we *are* in, how Jerusalem *lies* waste, and its gates are burned with fire. Come and let us build the
wall of Jerusalem, that we may no longer be a reproach." 18And I told them
of the hand of my God which had been good upon me, and also of the
king's words that he had spoken to me.
So they said, "Let us rise up and build." Then they set their hands to *this*
good *work.*
19But when Sanballat the Horonite, Tobiah the Ammonite official, and
Geshem the Arab heard *of it,* they laughed at us and despised us, and said,
"What *is* this thing that you are doing? Will you rebel against the king?"
20So I answered them, and said to them, "The God of heaven Himself
will prosper us; therefore we His servants will arise and build, but you
have no heritage or right or memorial in Jerusalem."

Rebuilding the Wall

3 Then Eliashib the high priest rose up with his brethren the priests and
built the Sheep Gate; they consecrated it and hung its doors. They built
as far as the Tower of the Hundred,[i] *and* consecrated it, then as far as the
Tower of Hananel. 2Next to *Eliashib*[j] the men of Jericho built. And next to
them Zaccur the son of Imri built.
3Also the sons of Hassenaah built the Fish Gate; they laid its beams and

2:7 [f] That is, the Euphrates, and so elsewhere in this book
2:8 [g] Literally *house*
2:10 [h] Literally *servant,* and so elsewhere in this book
3:1 [i] Hebrew *Hammeah,* also at 12:39
3:2 [j] Literally *On his hand*

LIFE LESSON

Nehemiah 2:11–3:32

SITUATION The king gave Nehemiah permission to travel to Jerusalem and rebuild the walls of the city. In spite of opposition from the surrounding nations, Nehemiah led the people to complete the reconstruction.

OBSERVATION We can trust in God to help us accomplish his will.

INSPIRATION What does a child say when he is face to face with the neighborhood bully? "My brother is bigger than your brother." "My dad is stronger than your dad." Then adults get into the act. . . .

What does a three-year-old do when he gets a knot in his shoelaces? He runs to Daddy. What does a five-year-old girl do when she falls and skins her knee? She cries to Mommy for comfort.

When faced with a problem, danger, difficulty or sadness, we naturally go to someone who is bigger, stronger, and more powerful. Just as a child wants to crawl up on Daddy's lap or have Mommy's arms wrapped around him, so we go to our heavenly Father. His is the fortress that protects us from attack, the refuge that grants us asylum from persecution, the safe harbor that shelters us from the storms of life.

(From *A Dad's Blessing* by Gary Smalley and John Trent)

APPLICATION Do you feel like you are being attacked? Are you up against a difficult situation or an imposing problem? Run to God and know that he is with you and will protect you. Thank him for protecting you in every circumstance—especially the one you are facing right now.

EXPLORATION God's Protection—Proverbs 18:10; Psalm 4:8; Isaiah 41:10; John 17:11-12; 2 Thessalonians 3:3; Hebrews 13:6.

hung its doors with its bolts and bars. [4]And next to them Meremoth the son of Urijah, the son of Koz,[k] made repairs. Next to them Meshullam the son of Berechiah, the son of Meshezabel, made repairs. Next to them Zadok the son of Baana made repairs. [5]Next to them the Tekoites made repairs; but their nobles did not put their shoulders[l] to the work of their Lord.

[6]Moreover Jehoiada the son of Paseah and Meshullam the son of Besodeiah repaired the Old Gate; they laid its beams and hung its doors, with its bolts and bars. [7]And next to them Melatiah the Gibeonite, Jadon the Meronothite, the men of Gibeon and Mizpah, repaired the residence[m] of the governor *of the region* beyond the River. [8]Next to him Uzziel the son of Harhaiah, one of the goldsmiths, made repairs. Also next to him Hananiah, one[n] of the perfumers, made repairs; and they fortified Jerusalem as far as the Broad Wall. [9]And next to them Rephaiah the son of Hur, leader of half the district of Jerusalem, made repairs. [10]Next to them Jedaiah the son of Harumaph made repairs in front of his house. And next to him Hattush the son of Hashabniah made repairs.

[11]Malchijah the son of Harim and Hashub the son of Pahath-Moab repaired another section, as well as the Tower of the Ovens. [12]And next to him was Shallum the son of Hallohesh, leader of half the district of Jerusalem; he and his daughters made repairs.

[13]Hanun and the inhabitants of Zanoah repaired the Valley Gate. They built it, hung its doors with its bolts and bars, and *repaired* a thousand cubits of the wall as far as the Refuse Gate.

[14]Malchijah the son of Rechab, leader of the district of Beth Haccerem, repaired the Refuse Gate; he built it and hung its doors with its bolts and bars.

[15]Shallun the son of Col-Hozeh, leader of the district of Mizpah, repaired the Fountain Gate; he built it, covered it, hung its doors with its bolts and bars, and repaired the wall of the Pool of Shelah by the King's Garden, as far as the stairs that go down from the City of David. [16]After him Nehemiah the son of Azbuk, leader of half the district of Beth Zur, made repairs as far as *the place* in front of the tombs[o] of David, to the man-made pool, and as far as the House of the Mighty.

[17]After him the Levites, *under* Rehum the son of Bani, made repairs. Next to him Hashabiah, leader of half the district of Keilah, made repairs for his district. [18]After him their brethren, *under* Bavai[p] the son of Henadad, leader of the *other* half of the district of Keilah, made repairs. [19]And next to him Ezer the son of Jeshua, the leader of Mizpah, repaired another section in front of the Ascent to the Armory at the buttress. [20]After him Baruch the son of Zabbai[q] carefully repaired the other section, from the buttress to the door of the house of Eliashib the high priest. [21]After him Meremoth the son of Urijah, the son of Koz,[r] repaired another section, from the door of the house of Eliashib to the end of the house of Eliashib.

[22]And after him the priests, the men of the plain, made repairs. [23]After him Benjamin and Hasshub made repairs opposite their house. After them Azariah the son of Maaseiah, the son of Ananiah, made repairs by his house. [24]After him Binnui the son of Henadad repaired another section, from the house of Azariah to the buttress, even as far as the corner. [25]Palal the son of Uzai *made repairs* opposite the buttress, and on the tower which projects from the king's upper house that *was* by the court of the prison. After him Pedaiah the son of Parosh *made repairs.*

[26]Moreover the Nethinim who dwelt in Ophel *made repairs* as far as *the place* in front of the Water Gate toward the east, and on the projecting tower. [27]After them the Tekoites repaired another section, next to the great projecting tower, and as far as the wall of Ophel.

[28]Beyond the Horse Gate the priests made repairs, each in front of his *own* house. [29]After them Zadok the son of Immer made repairs in front of his *own* house. After him Shemaiah the son of Shechaniah, the keeper of the East Gate, made repairs. [30]After him Hananiah the son of Shelemiah, and Hanun, the sixth son of Zalaph, repaired another section. After him Meshullam the son of Berechiah made repairs in front of his dwelling. [31]After him Malchijah, one of the goldsmiths, made repairs as far as the house of the Nethinim and of the merchants, in front of the Miphkad[s] Gate, and as far as the upper room at the corner. [32]And between the upper room at the corner, as far as the Sheep Gate, the goldsmiths and the merchants made repairs.

3:4 [k] Or *Hakkoz*
3:5 [l] Literally *necks*
3:7 [m] Literally *throne*
3:8 [n] Literally *the son*
3:16 [o] Septuagint, Syriac, and Vulgate read *tomb.*
3:18 [p] Following Masoretic Text and Vulgate; some Hebrew manuscripts, Septuagint, and Syriac read *Binnui* (compare verse 24).
3:20 [q] A few Hebrew manuscripts, Syriac, and Vulgate read *Zaccai.*
3:21 [r] Or *Hakkoz*
3:31 [s] Literally *Inspection* or *Recruiting*

The Wall Defended Against Enemies

4 But it so happened, when Sanballat heard that we were rebuilding the
wall, that he was furious and very indignant, and mocked the Jews.
[2]And he spoke before his brethren and the army of Samaria, and said,
"What are these feeble Jews doing? Will they fortify themselves? Will they
offer sacrifices? Will they complete it in a day? Will they revive the stones
from the heaps of rubbish—*stones* that are burned?"
[3]Now Tobiah the Ammonite *was* beside him, and he said, "Whatever
they build, if even a fox goes up *on it,* he will break down their stone wall."
[4]Hear, O our God, for we are despised; turn their reproach on their own
heads, and give them as plunder to a land of captivity! [5]Do not cover their
iniquity, and do not let their sin be blotted out from before You; for they
have provoked *You* to anger before the builders.
[6]So we built the wall, and the entire wall was joined together up to half
its *height,* for the people had a mind to work.
[7]Now it happened, when Sanballat, Tobiah, the Arabs, the Ammonites,
and the Ashdodites heard that the walls of Jerusalem were being restored
and the gaps were beginning to be closed, that they became very angry,
[8]and all of them conspired together to come *and* attack Jerusalem and create confusion. [9]Nevertheless we made our prayer to our God, and because
of them we set a watch against them day and night.
[10]Then Judah said, "The strength of the laborers is failing, and *there is* so
much rubbish that we are not able to build the wall."
[11]And our adversaries said, "They will neither know nor see anything,
till we come into their midst and kill them and cause the work to cease."
[12]So it was, when the Jews who dwelt near them came, that they told us
ten times, "From whatever place you turn, *they will be* upon us."
[13]Therefore I positioned *men* behind the lower parts of the wall, at the
openings; and I set the people according to their families, with their swords,
their spears, and their bows. [14]And I looked, and arose and said to the nobles, to the leaders, and to the rest of the people, "Do not be afraid of them.
Remember the Lord, great and awesome, and fight for your brethren, your
sons, your daughters, your wives, and your houses."
[15]And it happened, when our enemies heard that it was known to us, and
that God had brought their plot to nothing, that all of us returned to the wall,
everyone to his work. [16]So it was, from that time on, *that* half of my servants
worked at construction, while the other half held the spears, the shields, the
bows, and *wore* armor; and the leaders *were* behind all the house of Judah.
[17]Those who built on the wall, and those who carried burdens, loaded themselves so that with one hand they worked at construction, and with the other
held a weapon. [18]Every one of the builders had his sword girded at his side as
he built. And the one who sounded the trumpet *was* beside me.
[19]Then I said to the nobles, the rulers, and the rest of the people, "The
work *is* great and extensive, and we are separated far from one another on
the wall. [20]Wherever you hear the sound of the trumpet, rally to us there.
Our God will fight for us."
[21]So we labored in the work, and half of *the men*[t] held the spears from
daybreak until the stars appeared. [22]At the same time I also said to the
people, "Let each man and his servant stay at night in Jerusalem, that they

4:21 [t] Literally *them*

LIFE LESSON

Nehemiah 4:1-23

SITUATION Sanballat and Tobiah were leaders in surrounding cities who wanted to spread their influence into Jerusalem. When the rebuilding of Jerusalem's wall continued, they responded with opposition.

OBSERVATION Taunted, ridiculed, threatened. Instead of giving in, Nehemiah and the Israelites chose to find new strength and determination through their faith in God.

INSPIRATION After I spoke at a women's retreat recently, a darling gal rushed up to me saying, "Oh, Barb, you are just SO LUCKY! You have come through all your trials with so much joy and victory! . . .

I laughed and told the lady that I didn't believe there was any such thing as luck for Christians. . . .

Look at it this way: One family out of 500,000 lost a son in Vietnam . . . we are one of those families. One family out of every 800 has a child killed by a drunk driver . . . we experienced that, too. Statistics say that one family out of every ten will have a homosexual child . . . we know all about that. And recently I became part of another set of statistics, namely that out of every forty women over middle-age, one will develop adult-onset diabetes.

This is something that is brand new in my life. Although it is considered milder than juvenile-onset, it carries with it all the life-threatening complications. . . . I said a lot more, but the main thrust was that I chose to look at what seemed *good* to me rather than to anticipate all the gruesome complications that can happen at some point. . . . We are all going to have pain, but *misery is optional.* We can decide how we will react to the pain that inevitably comes to us all.

(From *Stick a Geranium in Your Hat and Be Happy* by Barbara Johnson)

APPLICATION The Israelites teach us to regard God as our only source of confidence! Today, when your life encounters friction, pray first and believe that God will smooth the road.

EXPLORATION Confidence—Joshua 1:9; Jeremiah 29:11; James 1:2-4.

Life Lesson

Nehemiah 5:1-19

SITUATION When some of the people began exploiting the poor, Nehemiah cried foul. He considered the poor to be valuable members of society, and he protected them.

OBSERVATION God concerns himself with poor and helpless people. People who have no power in society are not less important or less valuable but have great worth in God's eyes.

INSPIRATION When Jesus chose his disciples, the persons who were to carry on his mission, all except Matthew were fishermen and other common folk. Those who think that only the rich and powerful change history continue to take offense at Jesus' preoccupation with the poor and weak.

Again we must oppose the view that God never uses rich, powerful people as his chosen instruments. He has and does. But we always choose such people. God, on the other hand, frequently selects the poor to carry out his most important tasks. He sees potential that we do not. And when the task is done, the poor and weak are less likely to boast that they deserve the credit. God's selection of the lowly to be his special messengers of salvation to the world is striking evidence of his special concern for them. And his incarnation as a poor Galilean suggests that the frequent use of the poor as his special instruments is not insignificant historical trivia. It points to something significant about the very nature of God.

(From *Rich Christians in an Age of Hunger* by Ronald Sider)

APPLICATION What can you do in the next month to help the poor? Consider giving your time or money to help a friend, a relative, or even a stranger who needs something you can spare. Volunteer in a homeless shelter, give money to your church's benevolent fund, or help a friend or relative with a purchase they are struggling to make.

EXPLORATION God and the Poor—Job 34:28; 9:18; 14:4-7; 40:17; Zechariah 7:10.

may be our guard by night and a working party by day." 23So neither I, my brethren, my servants, nor the men of the guard who followed me took off our clothes, *except* that everyone took them off for washing.

Nehemiah Deals with Oppression

5 And there was a great outcry of the people and their wives against their Jewish brethren. 2For there were those who said, "We, our sons, and our daughters *are* many; therefore let us get grain, that we may eat and live."

3There were also *some* who said, "We have mortgaged our lands and vineyards and houses, that we might buy grain because of the famine."

4There were also those who said, "We have borrowed money for the king's tax *on* our lands and vineyards. 5Yet now our flesh *is* as the flesh of our brethren, our children as their children; and indeed we are forcing our sons and our daughters to be slaves, and *some* of our daughters have been brought into slavery. *It is* not in our power *to redeem them,* for other men have our lands and vineyards."

6And I became very angry when I heard their outcry and these words. 7After serious thought, I rebuked the nobles and rulers, and said to them, "Each of you is exacting usury from his brother." So I called a great assembly against them. 8And I said to them, "According to our ability we have redeemed our Jewish brethren who were sold to the nations. Now indeed, will you even sell your brethren? Or should they be sold to us?"

Then they were silenced and found nothing *to say.* 9Then I said, "What you are doing *is* not good. Should you not walk in the fear of our God because of the reproach of the nations, our enemies? 10I also, *with* my brethren and my servants, am lending them money and grain. Please, let us stop this usury! 11Restore now to them, even this day, their lands, their vineyards, their olive groves, and their houses, also a hundredth of the money and the grain, the new wine and the oil, that you have charged them."

12So they said, "We will restore *it,* and will require nothing from them; we will do as you say."

Then I called the priests, and required an oath from them that they would do according to this promise. 13Then I shook out the fold of my garment[u] and said, "So may God shake out each man from his house, and from his property, who does not perform this promise. Even thus may he be shaken out and emptied."

And all the assembly said, "Amen!" and praised the LORD. Then the people did according to this promise.

The Generosity of Nehemiah

14Moreover, from the time that I was appointed to be their governor in the land of Judah, from the twentieth year until the thirty-second year of King Artaxerxes, twelve years, neither I nor my brothers ate the governor's provisions. 15But the former governors who *were* before me laid burdens on the people, and took from them bread and wine, besides forty shekels of silver. Yes, even their servants bore rule over the people, but I did not do so, because of the fear of God. 16Indeed, I also continued the work on this wall, and we[v] did not buy any land. All my servants *were* gathered there for the work.

5:13 [u] Literally *my lap*
5:16 [v] Following Masoretic Text; Septuagint, Syriac, and Vulgate read *I.*

17And at my table *were* one hundred and fifty Jews and rulers, besides
those who came to us from the nations around us. 18Now *that* which was
prepared daily *was* one ox *and* six choice sheep. Also fowl were prepared
for me, and once every ten days an abundance of all kinds of wine. Yet in
spite of this I did not demand the governor's provisions, because the
bondage was heavy on this people.
19Remember me, my God, for good, *according to* all that I have done for
this people.

Conspiracy Against Nehemiah

6 Now it happened when Sanballat, Tobiah, Geshem the Arab, and the
rest of our enemies heard that I had rebuilt the wall, and *that* there
were no breaks left in it (though at that time I had not hung the doors in
the gates), 2that Sanballat and Geshem sent to me, saying, "Come, let us
meet together among the villages in the plain of Ono." But they thought to
do me harm.
3So I sent messengers to them, saying, "I *am* doing a great work, so that
I cannot come down. Why should the work cease while I leave it and go
down to you?"
4But they sent me this message four times, and I answered them in the
same manner.
5Then Sanballat sent his servant to me as before, the fifth time, with an
open letter in his hand. 6In it *was* written:

> It is reported among the nations, and Geshem[w] says, *that* you and
> the Jews plan to rebel; therefore, according to these rumors, you
> are rebuilding the wall, that you may be their king. 7And you have
> also appointed prophets to proclaim concerning you at Jerusalem,
> saying, "*There is* a king in Judah!" Now these matters will be reported
> to the king. So come, therefore, and let us consult together.

8Then I sent to him, saying, "No such things as you say are being done,
but you invent them in your own heart."
9For they all *were trying to* make us afraid, saying, "Their hands will be
weakened in the work, and it will not be done."
Now therefore, *O God,* strengthen my hands.
10Afterward I came to the house of Shemaiah the son of Delaiah, the son of
Mehetabel, who *was* a secret informer; and he said, "Let us meet together in
the house of God, within the temple, and let us close the doors of the temple,
for they are coming to kill you; indeed, at night they will come to kill you."
11And I said, "Should such a man as I flee? And who *is there* such as I
who would go into the temple to save his life? I will not go in!" 12Then I perceived that God had not sent him at all, but that he pronounced *this*
prophecy against me because Tobiah and Sanballat had hired him. 13For
this reason he *was* hired, that I should be afraid and act that way and sin, so
that they might have *cause* for an evil report, that they might reproach me.
14My God, remember Tobiah and Sanballat, according to these their
works, and the prophetess Noadiah and the rest of the prophets who
would have made me afraid.

LIFE LESSON

Nehemiah 6:1–7:73

SITUATION Despite much opposition from Sanballat, Tobiah, and Geshem, Nehemiah and the Israelites finished the wall of Jerusalem.

OBSERVATION Satan tries to discourage us. But we can survive setbacks if we stay focused and fulfill God's purposes.

INSPIRATION An altogether different person was the man who was my seatmate on a flight to St. Louis. . . .

"I happen to be facing a crisis at this time," went on my seatmate. "Just what it is, is irrelevant, but to get ready for it my mind must be working at maximum, so I follow a procedure. First, I sharpen my mind by reading [the Bible]. . . .

"Then I affirm God's presence. I remind myself that the Lord is with me, for He said: 'I am with you always.' I spend a moment sensing and feeling the Lord's actual presence . . . Next, I pray that my decisions will be right.

"Having completed those procedures, I then practice one of the wisest bits of advice in the Bible. Know what that is?"

"You tell me," I urged.

"'Having done all, to stand.' When you've done all you can do, what more can you do? Just put everything confidently into God's hands. He will bring it out OK."

(From *The Positive Power of Jesus Christ* by Norman Vincent Peale)

APPLICATION What crises threaten to discourage you? The next time you face a crisis, imitate the person who discovered how to stay focused on God: read, meditate, pray, act, and wait.

EXPLORATION Examples of Faith—Job 13:15; 19:25; Psalm 13:5; Daniel 3:1-30; 6:7-23; Matthew 9:18-25; Luke 7:36-50; Romans 4:18-24; Hebrews 11.

6:6 [w] Hebrew *Gashmu*

The Wall Completed

15 So the wall was finished on the twenty-fifth *day* of
Elul, in fifty-two days. 16 And it happened, when all our
enemies heard *of it,* and all the nations around us saw
these things, that they were very disheartened in their
own eyes; for they perceived that this work was done
by our God.
17 Also in those days the nobles of Judah sent many
letters to Tobiah, and *the letters of* Tobiah came to
them. 18 For many in Judah were pledged to him, because he was the son-in-law of Shechaniah the son of
Arah, and his son Jehohanan had married the daughter of Meshullam the son of Berechiah. 19 Also they reported his good deeds before me, and reported my
words to him. Tobiah sent letters to frighten me.

7 Then it was, when the wall was built and I had
hung the doors, when the gatekeepers, the singers,
and the Levites had been appointed, 2 that I gave the
charge of Jerusalem to my brother Hanani, and
Hananiah the leader of the citadel, for he *was* a faithful man and feared God more than many.
3 And I said to them, "Do not let the gates of Jerusalem be opened until the sun is hot; and while they
stand *guard,* let them shut and bar the doors; and appoint guards from among the inhabitants of Jerusalem, one at his watch station and another in front of
his own house."

The Captives Who Returned to Jerusalem

4 Now the city *was* large and spacious, but the people in it *were* few, and the houses *were* not rebuilt.
5 Then my God put it into my heart to gather the nobles, the rulers, and the people, that they might be
registered by genealogy. And I found a register of the
genealogy of those who had come up in the first *return,* and found written in it:

6 These[x] *are* the people of the province who
came back from the captivity, of those who
had been carried away, whom
Nebuchadnezzar the king of Babylon had carried away, and who returned to Jerusalem and
Judah, everyone to his city.

7 Those who came with Zerubbabel *were*
Jeshua, Nehemiah, Azariah, Raamiah,
Nahamani, Mordecai, Bilshan, Mispereth,[y]
Bigvai, Nehum, and Baanah.

The number of the men of the people of Israel:
8 the sons of Parosh, two thousand one hundred
and seventy-two;
9 the sons of Shephatiah, three hundred and
seventy-two;
10 the sons of Arah, six hundred and fifty-two;
11 the sons of Pahath-Moab, of the sons of
Jeshua and Joab, two thousand eight hundred
and eighteen;
12 the sons of Elam, one thousand two hundred
and fifty-four;
13 the sons of Zattu, eight hundred and
forty-five;
14 the sons of Zaccai, seven hundred and sixty;
15 the sons of Binnui,[z] six hundred and
forty-eight;
16 the sons of Bebai, six hundred and
twenty-eight;
17 the sons of Azgad, two thousand three
hundred and twenty-two;
18 the sons of Adonikam, six hundred and
sixty-seven;
19 the sons of Bigvai, two thousand and
sixty-seven;
20 the sons of Adin, six hundred and fifty-five;
21 the sons of Ater of Hezekiah, ninety-eight;
22 the sons of Hashum, three hundred and
twenty-eight;
23 the sons of Bezai, three hundred and
twenty-four;
24 the sons of Hariph,[a] one hundred and twelve;
25 the sons of Gibeon,[b] ninety-five;
26 the men of Bethlehem and Netophah, one
hundred and eighty-eight;
27 the men of Anathoth, one hundred and
twenty-eight;
28 the men of Beth Azmaveth,[c] forty-two;
29 the men of Kirjath Jearim, Chephirah, and
Beeroth, seven hundred and forty-three;
30 the men of Ramah and Geba, six hundred
and twenty-one;
31 the men of Michmas, one hundred and
twenty-two;
32 the men of Bethel and Ai, one hundred and
twenty-three;
33 the men of the other Nebo, fifty-two;

7:6 [x] Compare verses 6–72 with Ezra 2:1–70
7:7 [y] Spelled *Mispar* in Ezra 2:2
7:15 [z] Spelled *Bani* in Ezra 2:10
7:24 [a] Called *Jorah* in Ezra 2:18
7:25 [b] Called *Gibbar* in Ezra 2:20
7:28 [c] Called *Azmaveth* in Ezra 2:24

[34]the sons of the other Elam, one thousand
two hundred and fifty-four;
[35]the sons of Harim, three hundred and twenty;
[36]the sons of Jericho, three hundred and
forty-five;
[37]the sons of Lod, Hadid, and Ono, seven
hundred and twenty-one;
[38]the sons of Senaah, three thousand nine
hundred and thirty.

39 The priests: the sons of Jedaiah, of the house
of Jeshua, nine hundred and seventy-three;
[40]the sons of Immer, one thousand and
fifty-two;
[41]the sons of Pashhur, one thousand two
hundred and forty-seven;
[42]the sons of Harim, one thousand and
seventeen.

43 The Levites: the sons of Jeshua, of Kadmiel,
and of the sons of Hodevah,[d] seventy-four.

44 The singers: the sons of Asaph, one hundred
and forty-eight.

45 The gatekeepers: the sons of Shallum,
the sons of Ater,
the sons of Talmon,
the sons of Akkub,
the sons of Hatita,
the sons of Shobai, one hundred and
thirty-eight.

46 The Nethinim: the sons of Ziha,
the sons of Hasupha,
the sons of Tabbaoth,
[47]the sons of Keros,
the sons of Sia,[e]
the sons of Padon,
[48]the sons of Lebana,[f]
the sons of Hagaba,[g]
the sons of Salmai,[h]
[49]the sons of Hanan,
the sons of Giddel,
the sons of Gahar,
[50]the sons of Reaiah,
the sons of Rezin,
the sons of Nekoda,
[51]the sons of Gazzam,
the sons of Uzza,
the sons of Paseah,
[52]the sons of Besai,
the sons of Meunim,
the sons of Nephishesim,[i]
[53]the sons of Bakbuk,
the sons of Hakupha,
the sons of Harhur,
[54]the sons of Bazlith,[j]
the sons of Mehida,
the sons of Harsha,
[55]the sons of Barkos,
the sons of Sisera,
the sons of Tamah,
[56]the sons of Neziah,
and the sons of Hatipha.

57 The sons of Solomon's servants: the sons of Sotai,
the sons of Sophereth,
the sons of Perida,[k]
[58]the sons of Jaala,
the sons of Darkon,
the sons of Giddel,
[59]the sons of Shephatiah,
the sons of Hattil,
the sons of Pochereth of Zebaim,
and the sons of Amon.[l]
[60]All the Nethinim, and the sons of Solomon's
servants, *were* three hundred and ninety-two.

61 And these *were* the ones who came up from
Tel Melah, Tel Harsha, Cherub, Addon,[m] and
Immer, but they could not identify their father's
house nor their lineage, whether they *were* of
Israel: [62]the sons of Delaiah,
the sons of Tobiah,
the sons of Nekoda, six hundred and forty-two;
[63]and of the priests: the sons of Habaiah,
the sons of Koz,[n]

7:43 [d] Spelled *Hodaviah* in Ezra 2:40
7:47 [e] Spelled *Siaha* in Ezra 2:44
7:48 [f] Masoretic Text reads *Lebanah.* [g] Masoretic Text reads *Hogabah.* [h] Or *Shalmai,* or *Shamlai*
7:52 [i] Spelled *Nephusim* in Ezra 2:50
7:54 [j] Spelled *Bazluth* in Ezra 2:52
7:57 [k] Spelled *Peruda* in Ezra 2:55
7:59 [l] Spelled *Ami* in Ezra 2:57
7:61 [m] Spelled *Addan* in Ezra 2:59
7:63 [n] Or *Hakkoz*

LIFE LESSON

Nehemiah 8:1-18

SITUATION Nehemiah and Ezra assembled the people in Jerusalem to hear the Laws of Moses. Many wept when they realized how disobedient they had been. The assembly became a festive time when the people reclaimed their legacy as God's chosen people.

OBSERVATION Nehemiah and Ezra reintroduced God's laws and customs to the former exiles so that God would give his favor.

INSPIRATION Love is the only law you need. . . .

To love your neighbor as yourself. Keep this command, this law, and you automatically keep all the others. If you are really concerned with keeping the law of love, it is the only law you really need. Then civil laws are not problems or objects of protests and demonstrations. Civil laws are only guidelines to help you achieve your aim: loving others as you love yourself and thereby fulfilling all of God's requirements. . . .

The Christian who lives by the law of love does not see authority as a threat. Nor does he see imperfections or even gross errors in government as reason to riot or demonstrate unlawfully. The Christian is not a bystander in his society. Actually, he should be in the thick of the battle for justice, morality and the right. But the Christian operates with a different motive. He seeks justice for all, yes, but justice is primarily a negative concept, based on avoiding or preventing the doing of wrongs to others. The law of love goes beyond justice. The law of love seeks the positive doing of good to others. It is the only law a Christian needs.

(From *How to Be a Christian Without Being Religious* by Fritz Ridenour)

APPLICATION Look around you—who do you see at work? At home? On the road? In church? Give them your time, your attention, your love, and your respect.

EXPLORATION God's Law—Exodus 31:18; Leviticus 19:9-10; Deuteronomy 4:15-19; Matthew 5;19; 22:37-40.

the sons of Barzillai, who took a wife of the daughters of Barzillai
the Gileadite, and was called by their name.
64 These sought their listing *among* those who were registered by
genealogy, but it was not found; therefore they were excluded from
the priesthood as defiled.
65 And the governor[o] said to them that they should not eat of the most
holy things till a priest could consult with the Urim and Thummim.

66 Altogether the whole assembly *was* forty-two thousand three
hundred and sixty, 67 besides their male and female servants, of
whom *there were* seven thousand three hundred and thirty-seven;
and they had two hundred and forty-five men and women singers.
68 Their horses were seven hundred and thirty-six, their mules two
hundred and forty-five, 69 *their* camels four hundred and thirty-five,
and donkeys six thousand seven hundred and twenty.

70 And some of the heads of the fathers' houses gave to the work. The
governor[p] gave to the treasury one thousand gold drachmas, fifty
basins, and five hundred and thirty priestly garments. 71 Some of
the heads of the fathers' *houses* gave to the treasury of the work
twenty thousand gold drachmas, and two thousand two hundred
silver minas. 72 And that which the rest of the people gave *was*
twenty thousand gold drachmas, two thousand silver minas, and
sixty-seven priestly garments.

73 So the priests, the Levites, the gatekeepers, the singers, *some* of the
people, the Nethinim, and all Israel dwelt in their cities.

Ezra Reads the Law

When the seventh month came, the children of Israel *were* in their
cities.

8 Now all the people gathered together as one man in the open square
that *was* in front of the Water Gate; and they told Ezra the scribe to
bring the Book of the Law of Moses, which the LORD had commanded Israel. 2 So Ezra the priest brought the Law before the assembly of men and
women and all who *could* hear with understanding on the first day of the
seventh month. 3 Then he read from it in the open square that *was* in front
of the Water Gate from morning until midday, before the men and women
and those who could understand; and the ears of all the people *were attentive* to the Book of the Law.
4 So Ezra the scribe stood on a platform of wood which they had made
for the purpose; and beside him, at his right hand, stood Mattithiah, Shema,
Anaiah, Urijah, Hilkiah, and Maaseiah; and at his left hand Pedaiah,
Mishael, Malchijah, Hashum, Hashbadana, Zechariah, *and* Meshullam.
5 And Ezra opened the book in the sight of all the people, for he was *standing*
above all the people; and when he opened it, all the people stood up. 6 And
Ezra blessed the LORD, the great God.
Then all the people answered, "Amen, Amen!" while lifting up their
hands. And they bowed their heads and worshiped the LORD with *their*
faces to the ground.

7:65 [o] Hebrew *Tirshatha*
7:70 [p] Hebrew *Tirshatha*

[7]Also Jeshua, Bani, Sherebiah, Jamin, Akkub, Shabbethai, Hodijah, Maaseiah, Kelita, Azariah, Jozabad, Hanan, Pelaiah, and the Levites, helped the people to understand the Law; and the people *stood* in their place. [8]So they read distinctly from the book, in the Law of God; and they gave the sense, and helped *them* to understand the reading.

[9]And Nehemiah, who *was* the governor,[q] Ezra the priest *and* scribe, and the Levites who taught the people said to all the people, "This day *is* holy to the LORD your God; do not mourn nor weep." For all the people wept, when they heard the words of the Law.

[10]Then he said to them, "Go your way, eat the fat, drink the sweet, and send portions to those for whom nothing is prepared; for *this* day *is* holy to our Lord. Do not sorrow, for the joy of the LORD is your strength."

[11]So the Levites quieted all the people, saying, "Be still, for the day *is* holy; do not be grieved." [12]And all the people went their way to eat and drink, to send portions and rejoice greatly, because they understood the words that were declared to them.

The Feast of Tabernacles

[13]Now on the second day the heads of the fathers' *houses* of all the people, with the priests and Levites, were gathered to Ezra the scribe, in order to understand the words of the Law. [14]And they found written in the Law, which the LORD had commanded by Moses, that the children of Israel should dwell in booths during the feast of the seventh month, [15]and that they should announce and proclaim in all their cities and in Jerusalem, saying, "Go out to the mountain, and bring olive branches, branches of oil trees, myrtle branches, palm branches, and branches of leafy trees, to make booths, as *it is* written."

[16]Then the people went out and brought *them* and made themselves booths, each one on the roof of his house, or in their courtyards or the courts of the house of God, and in the open square of the Water Gate and in the open square of the Gate of Ephraim. [17]So the whole assembly of those who had returned from the captivity made booths and sat under the booths; for since the days of Joshua the son of Nun until that day the children of Israel had not done so. And there was very great gladness. [18]Also day by day, from the first day until the last day, he read from the Book of the Law of God. And they kept the feast seven days; and on the eighth day *there was* a sacred assembly, according to the *prescribed* manner.

The People Confess Their Sins

9 Now on the twenty-fourth day of this month the children of Israel were assembled with fasting, in sackcloth, and with dust on their heads.[r] [2]Then those of Israelite lineage separated themselves from all foreigners; and they stood and confessed their sins and the iniquities of their fathers. [3]And they stood up in their place and read from the Book of the Law of the LORD their God *for one*-fourth of the day; and *for another* fourth they confessed and worshiped the LORD their God.

[4]Then Jeshua, Bani, Kadmiel, Shebaniah, Bunni, Sherebiah, Bani, *and* Chenani stood on the stairs of the Levites and cried out with a loud voice to the LORD their God. [5]And the Levites, Jeshua, Kadmiel, Bani, Hashabniah, Sherebiah, Hodijah, Shebaniah, *and* Pethahiah, said:

"Stand up *and* bless the LORD your God
Forever and ever!

"Blessed be Your glorious name,
Which is exalted above all blessing and praise!
6 You alone *are* the LORD;
You have made heaven,
The heaven of heavens, with all their host,
The earth and everything on it,
The seas and all that is in them,
And You preserve them all.
The host of heaven worships You.

7 "You *are* the LORD God,
Who chose Abram,
And brought him out of Ur of the Chaldeans,
And gave him the name Abraham;
8 You found his heart faithful before You,
And made a covenant with him
To give the land of the Canaanites,
The Hittites, the Amorites,
The Perizzites, the Jebusites,
And the Girgashites—
To give *it* to his descendants.
You have performed Your words,
For You *are* righteous.

9 "You saw the affliction of our fathers in Egypt,
And heard their cry by the Red Sea.
10 You showed signs and wonders against
Pharaoh,
Against all his servants,
And against all the people of his land.

8:9 *q* Hebrew *Tirshatha*
9:1 *r* Literally *earth on them*

LIFE LESSON

Nehemiah 9:1–10:39

SITUATION Nehemiah helped the people to learn God's Law and to confess their sins. The people agreed to honor God in every aspect of their lives. They sought to eliminate relationships that would contaminate their culture and faith.

OBSERVATION As the walls of Jerusalem were restored, the people renewed their devotion to God and his covenant.

INSPIRATION Jesus told us we must be born again. The infinitive be is passive. It shows that it is something that must be done for us. No man can "born" himself. He must be born. The new birth is wholly foreign to our will. In other words, the new birth is a divine work—we are born of God.

Even though the new birth seems mysterious, that does not make it untrue. We may not understand the how of electricity, but we know that it lights our homes, runs our television and radio sets. We do not understand how the sheep grows wool, the cow grows hair, or the fowl grows feathers—but we know they do. We do not understand many mysteries, but we accept by faith the fact that at the moment we repent of sin and turn by faith to Jesus Christ we are born again.

It is the infusion of divine life into the human soul. It is the implementation or impartation of divine nature into the human soul whereby we become the children of God. We receive the

For You knew that they acted proudly against them.
So You made a name for Yourself, as *it is* this day.
11 And You divided the sea before them,
So that they went through the midst of the sea on the dry land;
And their persecutors You threw into the deep,
As a stone into the mighty waters.
12 Moreover You led them by day with a cloudy pillar,
And by night with a pillar of fire,
To give them light on the road
Which they should travel.

13 "You came down also on Mount Sinai,
And spoke with them from heaven,
And gave them just ordinances and true laws,
Good statutes and commandments.
14 You made known to them Your holy Sabbath,
And commanded them precepts, statutes and laws,
By the hand of Moses Your servant.
15 You gave them bread from heaven for their hunger,
And brought them water out of the rock for their thirst,
And told them to go in to possess the land
Which You had sworn to give them.

16 "But they and our fathers acted proudly,
Hardened their necks,
And did not heed Your commandments.
17 They refused to obey,
And they were not mindful of Your wonders
That You did among them.
But they hardened their necks,
And in their rebellion[s]
They appointed a leader
To return to their bondage.
But You *are* God,
Ready to pardon,
Gracious and merciful,
Slow to anger,
Abundant in kindness,
And did not forsake them.

18 "Even when they made a molded calf for themselves,
And said, 'This *is* your god
That brought you up out of Egypt,'
And worked great provocations,
19 Yet in Your manifold mercies
You did not forsake them in the wilderness.
The pillar of the cloud did not depart from them by day,
To lead them on the road;
Nor the pillar of fire by night,
To show them light,
And the way they should go.

9:17 [s] Following Masoretic Text and Vulgate; Septuagint reads *in Egypt.*

20 You also gave Your good Spirit to instruct them,
And did not withhold Your manna from their mouth,
And gave them water for their thirst.
21 Forty years You sustained them in the wilderness;
They lacked nothing;
Their clothes did not wear out[t]
And their feet did not swell.

22 "Moreover You gave them kingdoms and nations,
And divided them into districts.[u]
So they took possession of the land of Sihon,
The land of[v] the king of Heshbon,
And the land of Og king of Bashan.
23 You also multiplied their children as the stars of heaven,
And brought them into the land
Which You had told their fathers
To go in and possess.
24 So the people went in
And possessed the land;
You subdued before them the inhabitants of the land,
The Canaanites,
And gave them into their hands,
With their kings
And the people of the land,
That they might do with them as they wished.
25 And they took strong cities and a rich land,
And possessed houses full of all goods,
Cisterns *already* dug, vineyards, olive groves,
And fruit trees in abundance.
So they ate and were filled and grew fat,
And delighted themselves in Your great goodness.

26 "Nevertheless they were disobedient
And rebelled against You,
Cast Your law behind their backs
And killed Your prophets, who testified against them
To turn them to Yourself;
And they worked great provocations.
27 Therefore You delivered them into the hand of their enemies,
Who oppressed them;
And in the time of their trouble,
When they cried to You,
You heard from heaven;
And according to Your abundant mercies
You gave them deliverers who saved them
From the hand of their enemies.

28 "But after they had rest,
They again did evil before You.
Therefore You left them in the hand of their enemies,

breath of God. Christ through the Holy Spirit takes up residence in our hearts. We are attached to God for eternity. That means that if you have been born again, you will live as long as God lives, because you are now sharing His very life. The long-lost fellowship man had with God in the Garden of Eden has been restored. . . .

This new nature that you receive from God is bent to the will of God. You will want to do only His will. You are utterly and completely devoted to Him. There is a new self-determination, inclination, disposition, a new principle of living, new choices. You seek to glorify God. You seek fellowship with other Christians in the church. You love the Bible. You love to spend time in prayer with God. Your whole disposition is changed. Whereas your life once was filled with unbelief, the root and foundation of all sin, and you once doubted God, now you believe Him. Now you have utmost confidence and faith in God and His Word.

(From *Peace with God* by Billy Graham)

APPLICATION God saves us without expecting any additional payment. Those who love God, however, want to obey him. Repentance is the first step in placing our lives under his authority. What area of life do you want to turn over to God?

EXPLORATION Covenant—Genesis 17:2-8; Deuteronomy 5:1-3; Isaiah 61:8; Matthew 26:28.

9:21 [t] Compare Deuteronomy 29:5
9:22 [u] Literally *corners* [v] Following Masoretic Text and Vulgate; Septuagint omits *The land of.*

So that they had dominion over them;
Yet when they returned and cried out to You,
You heard from heaven;
And many times You delivered them
according to Your mercies,
29 And testified against them,
That You might bring them back to Your law.
Yet they acted proudly,
And did not heed Your commandments,
But sinned against Your judgments,
'Which if a man does, he shall live by them.'[w]
And they shrugged their shoulders,
Stiffened their necks,
And would not hear.
30 Yet for many years You had patience with them,
And testified against them by Your Spirit in
Your prophets.
Yet they would not listen;
Therefore You gave them into the hand of the
peoples of the lands.
31 Nevertheless in Your great mercy
You did not utterly consume them nor
forsake them;
For You *are* God, gracious and merciful.

32 "Now therefore, our God,
The great, the mighty, and awesome God,
Who keeps covenant and mercy:
Do not let all the trouble seem small before You
That has come upon us,
Our kings and our princes,
Our priests and our prophets,
Our fathers and on all Your people,
From the days of the kings of Assyria
until this day.
33 However You *are* just in all that has befallen us;
For You have dealt faithfully,
But we have done wickedly.
34 Neither our kings nor our princes,
Our priests nor our fathers,
Have kept Your law,
Nor heeded Your commandments
and Your testimonies,
With which You testified against them.
35 For they have not served You in their kingdom,
Or in the many good *things* that You gave them,
Or in the large and rich land which You set
before them;
Nor did they turn from their wicked works.

36 "Here we *are*, servants today!
And the land that You gave to our fathers,
To eat its fruit and its bounty,
Here we *are*, servants in it!
37 And it yields much increase to the kings
You have set over us,
Because of our sins;
Also they have dominion over our bodies
and our cattle
At their pleasure;
And we *are* in great distress.

38 "And because of all this,
We make a sure *covenant* and write *it;*
Our leaders, our Levites, *and* our priests
seal *it*."

The People Who Sealed the Covenant

10 Now those who placed *their* seal on *the document were:*
Nehemiah the governor, the son of Hacaliah, and
Zedekiah, 2Seraiah, Azariah, Jeremiah, 3Pashhur,
Amariah, Malchijah, 4Hattush, Shebaniah, Malluch,
5Harim, Meremoth, Obadiah, 6Daniel, Ginnethon,
Baruch, 7Meshullam, Abijah, Mijamin, 8Maaziah,
Bilgai, *and* Shemaiah. These *were* the priests.
9The Levites: Jeshua the son of Azaniah, Binnui of
the sons of Henadad, *and* Kadmiel.
10Their brethren: Shebaniah, Hodijah, Kelita,
Pelaiah, Hanan, 11Micha, Rehob, Hashabiah, 12Zaccur,
Sherebiah, Shebaniah, 13Hodijah, Bani, *and* Beninu.
14The leaders of the people: Parosh, Pahath-Moab,
Elam, Zattu, Bani, 15Bunni, Azgad, Bebai, 16Adonijah,
Bigvai, Adin, 17Ater, Hezekiah, Azzur, 18Hodijah,
Hashum, Bezai, 19Hariph, Anathoth, Nebai, 20Magpi-
ash, Meshullam, Hezir, 21Meshezabel, Zadok, Jaddua,
22Pelatiah, Hanan, Anaiah, 23Hoshea, Hananiah, Hasshub, 24Hallohesh, Pilha, Shobek, 25Rehum, Hashab-
nah, Maaseiah, 26Ahijah, Hanan, Anan, 27Malluch,
Harim, *and* Baanah.

The Covenant That Was Sealed

28Now the rest of the people—the priests, the Levites,
the gatekeepers, the singers, the Nethinim, and all those
who had separated themselves from the peoples of the
lands to the Law of God, their wives, their sons, and their
daughters, everyone who had knowledge and understanding— 29these joined with their brethren, their nobles, and entered into a curse and an oath to walk in
God's Law, which was given by Moses the servant of
God, and to observe and do all the commandments of
the LORD our Lord, and His ordinances and His statutes:

9:29 [w] Leviticus 18:5

[30]We would not give our daughters as wives to the peoples of the land, nor take their daughters for our sons; [31]*if*
the peoples of the land brought wares or any grain to sell
on the Sabbath day, we would not buy it from them on
the Sabbath, or on a holy day; and we would forego the
seventh year's *produce* and the exacting of every debt.
[32]Also we made ordinances for ourselves, to exact
from ourselves yearly one-third of a shekel for the
service of the house of our God: [33]for the showbread,
for the regular grain offering, for the regular burnt offering of the Sabbaths, the New Moons, and the set
feasts; for the holy things, for the sin offerings to make
atonement for Israel, and all the work of the house of
our God. [34]We cast lots among the priests, the Levites,
and the people, for *bringing* the wood offering into the
house of our God, according to our fathers' houses, at
the appointed times year by year, to burn on the altar
of the LORD our God as *it is* written in the Law.
[35]And *we made ordinances* to bring the firstfruits of
our ground and the firstfruits of all fruit of all trees,
year by year, to the house of the LORD; [36]to bring the
firstborn of our sons and our cattle, as *it is* written in
the Law, and the firstborn of our herds and our flocks,
to the house of our God, to the priests who minister in
the house of our God; [37]to bring the firstfruits of our
dough, our offerings, the fruit from all kinds of trees,
the new wine and oil, to the priests, to the storerooms
of the house of our God; and to bring the tithes of our
land to the Levites, for the Levites should receive the
tithes in all our farming communities. [38]And the priest,
the descendant of Aaron, shall be with the Levites when
the Levites receive tithes; and the Levites shall bring
up a tenth of the tithes to the house of our God, to the
rooms of the storehouse.
[39]For the children of Israel and the children of Levi
shall bring the offering of the grain, of the new wine
and the oil, to the storerooms where the articles of the
sanctuary *are, where* the priests who minister and the
gatekeepers and the singers *are;* and we will not neglect the house of our God.

The People Dwelling in Jerusalem

11 Now the leaders of the people dwelt at Jerusalem;
the rest of the people cast lots to bring one out
of ten to dwell in Jerusalem, the holy city, and nine-
tenths *were to dwell* in *other* cities. [2]And the people
blessed all the men who willingly offered themselves
to dwell at Jerusalem.
[3]These *are* the heads of the province who dwelt in
Jerusalem. (But in the cities of Judah everyone dwelt
in his own possession in their cities—Israelites,
priests, Levites, Nethinim, and descendants of Solomon's servants.) [4]Also in Jerusalem dwelt *some* of
the children of Judah and of the children of Benjamin.
The children of Judah: Athaiah the son of Uzziah,
the son of Zechariah, the son of Amariah, the son of
Shephatiah, the son of Mahalalel, of the children of
Perez; [5]and Maaseiah the son of Baruch, the son of
Col-Hozeh, the son of Hazaiah, the son of Adaiah, the
son of Joiarib, the son of Zechariah, the son of Shiloni.
[6]All the sons of Perez who dwelt at Jerusalem *were*
four hundred and sixty-eight valiant men.
[7]And these are the sons of Benjamin: Sallu the son
of Meshullam, the son of Joed, the son of Pedaiah, the
son of Kolaiah, the son of Maaseiah, the son of Ithiel,
the son of Jeshaiah; [8]and after him Gabbai *and* Sallai,
nine hundred and twenty-eight. [9]Joel the son of Zichri
was their overseer, and Judah the son of Senuah[x] *was*
second over the city.
[10]Of the priests: Jedaiah the son of Joiarib, and
Jachin; [11]Seraiah the son of Hilkiah, the son of
Meshullam, the son of Zadok, the son of Meraioth,
the son of Ahitub, *was* the leader of the house of God.
[12]Their brethren who did the work of the house *were*
eight hundred and twenty-two; and Adaiah the son of
Jeroham, the son of Pelaliah, the son of Amzi, the son of
Zechariah, the son of Pashhur, the son of Malchijah,
[13]and his brethren, heads of the fathers' *houses, were*
two hundred and forty-two; and Amashai the son of
Azarel, the son of Ahzai, the son of Meshillemoth, the
son of Immer, [14]and their brethren, mighty men of
valor, *were* one hundred and twenty-eight. Their overseer *was* Zabdiel the son of *one of* the great men.[y]
[15]Also of the Levites: Shemaiah the son of Hasshub,
the son of Azrikam, the son of Hashabiah, the son of
Bunni; [16]Shabbethai and Jozabad, of the heads of the
Levites, *had* the oversight of the business outside of
the house of God; [17]Mattaniah the son of Micha,[z] the
son of Zabdi, the son of Asaph, the leader *who* began
the thanksgiving with prayer; Bakbukiah, the second
among his brethren; and Abda the son of Shammua,
the son of Galal, the son of Jeduthun. [18]All the Levites
in the holy city *were* two hundred and eighty-four.
[19]Moreover the gatekeepers, Akkub, Talmon, and
their brethren who kept the gates, *were* one hundred
and seventy-two.

11:9 [x] Or *Hassenuah*
11:14 [y] Or *the son of Haggedolim*
11:17 [z] Or *Michah*

LIFE LESSON
Nehemiah 11:1–13:31

SITUATION To resettle Jerusalem, Nehemiah required ten percent of the people to move from their villages to the city. Many people disliked this plan because it forced them to move.

OBSERVATION For the good of the whole community, Nehemiah required some people to sacrifice.

INSPIRATION "I am ready to be offered." It is a transaction of will, not of sentiment. Tell God you are ready to be offered; then let the consequences be what they may, there is no strand of complaint now, no matter what God chooses. God puts you through the crisis in private, no one person can help another. Externally, the life may be the same; the difference is in will. Go through the crisis in will, then when it comes externally there will be no thought of the cost. If you do not transact in will with God along this line, you will end in awakening sympathy for yourself.

"Bind the sacrifice with cords, even unto the horns of the altar." The altar means fire—burning and purification and insulation for one purpose only, the destruction of every affinity that God has not started and of every attachment that is not an attachment in God. You do not destroy it, God does; you bind the sacrifice to the horns of the altar; and see that you do not give way to self-pity when the fire begins. After this way of fire, there is nothing that oppresses or depresses. When the crisis arises, you realize that things cannot touch you as they used to do. What is your way of fire?

Tell God you are ready to be offered, and God will prove Himself to be all you ever dreamed He would be. (From *My Utmost for His Highest* by Oswald Chambers)

APPLICATION What are you willing to give up? Would you be willing to move? Change jobs? Face new challenges? Be flexible so that God can move you easily.

EXPLORATION Sacrifice—Leviticus 1:2; 1 Samuel 15:22; Psalm 4:5; Isaiah 1:10-14.

[20]And the rest of Israel, of the priests *and* Levites, *were* in all the cities of
Judah, everyone in his inheritance. [21]But the Nethinim dwelt in Ophel.
And Ziha and Gishpa *were* over the Nethinim.
[22]Also the overseer of the Levites at Jerusalem *was* Uzzi the son of Bani,
the son of Hashabiah, the son of Mattaniah, the son of Micha, of the sons
of Asaph, the singers in charge of the service of the house of God. [23]For *it*
was the king's command concerning them that a certain portion should
be for the singers, a quota day by day. [24]Pethahiah the son of Meshezabel,
of the children of Zerah the son of Judah, *was* the king's deputy[a] in all matters concerning the people.

The People Dwelling Outside Jerusalem

[25]And as for the villages with their fields, *some* of the children of Judah
dwelt in Kirjath Arba and its villages, Dibon and its villages, Jekabzeel and its
villages; [26]in Jeshua, Moladah, Beth Pelet, [27]Hazar Shual, and Beersheba and
its villages; [28]in Ziklag and Meconah and its villages; [29]in En Rimmon, Zorah,
Jarmuth, [30]Zanoah, Adullam, and their villages; in Lachish and its fields; in
Azekah and its villages. They dwelt from Beersheba to the Valley of Hinnom.
[31]Also the children of Benjamin from Geba *dwelt* in Michmash, Aija, and
Bethel, and their villages; [32]in Anathoth, Nob, Ananiah; [33]in Hazor, Ramah,
Gittaim; [34]in Hadid, Zeboim, Neballat; [35]in Lod, Ono, *and* the Valley of
Craftsmen. [36]Some of the Judean divisions of Levites *were* in Benjamin.

The Priests and Levites

12 Now these *are* the priests and the Levites who came up with
Zerubbabel the son of Shealtiel, and Jeshua: Seraiah, Jeremiah, Ezra,
[2]Amariah, Malluch, Hattush, [3]Shechaniah, Rehum, Meremoth, [4]Iddo, Ginnethoi,[b] Abijah, [5]Mijamin, Maadiah, Bilgah, [6]Shemaiah, Joiarib, Jedaiah,
[7]Sallu, Amok, Hilkiah, *and* Jedaiah.
These *were* the heads of the priests and their brethren in the days of
Jeshua.
[8]Moreover the Levites *were* Jeshua, Binnui, Kadmiel, Sherebiah, Judah,
and Mattaniah *who led* the thanksgiving *psalms,* he and his brethren. [9]Also
Bakbukiah and Unni, their brethren, *stood* across from them in *their* duties.
[10]Jeshua begot Joiakim, Joiakim begot Eliashib, Eliashib begot Joiada,
[11]Joiada begot Jonathan, and Jonathan begot Jaddua.
[12]Now in the days of Joiakim, the priests, the heads of the fathers' *houses*
were: of Seraiah, Meraiah; of Jeremiah, Hananiah; [13]of Ezra, Meshullam; of
Amariah, Jehohanan; [14]of Melichu,[c] Jonathan; of Shebaniah,[d] Joseph; [15]of
Harim,[e] Adna; of Meraioth,[f] Helkai; [16]of Iddo, Zechariah; of Ginnethon,
Meshullam; [17]of Abijah, Zichri; *the son* of Minjamin;[g] of Moadiah,[h] Piltai;
[18]of Bilgah, Shammua; of Shemaiah, Jehonathan; [19]of Joiarib, Mattenai; of
Jedaiah, Uzzi; [20]of Sallai,[i] Kallai; of Amok, Eber; [21]of Hilkiah, Hashabiah;
and of Jedaiah, Nethanel.
[22]During the reign of Darius the Persian, a record *was also kept* of the
Levites and priests *who had been* heads of their fathers' *houses* in the days of

11:24 [a] Literally *at the king's hand*
12:4 [b] Or *Ginnethon* (compare verse 16)
12:14 [c] Or *Malluch* (compare verse 2) [d] Or *Shechaniah* (compare verse 3)
12:15 [e] Or *Rehum* (compare verse 3) [f] Or *Meremoth* (compare verse 3)
12:17 [g] Or *Mijamin* (compare verse 5) [h] Or *Maadiah* (compare verse 5)
12:20 [i] Or *Sallu* (compare verse 7)

Eliashib, Joiada, Johanan, and Jaddua. 23The sons of
Levi, the heads of the fathers' *houses* until the days of
Johanan the son of Eliashib, *were* written in the book
of the chronicles.
24And the heads of the Levites *were* Hashabiah,
Sherebiah, and Jeshua the son of Kadmiel, with their
brothers across from them, to praise *and* give thanks,
group alternating with group, according to the command of David the man of God. 25Mattaniah, Bakbukiah, Obadiah, Meshullam, Talmon, and Akkub *were*
gatekeepers keeping the watch at the storerooms of the
gates. 26These *lived* in the days of Joiakim the son of
Jeshua, the son of Jozadak,[j] and in the days of Nehemiah
the governor, and of Ezra the priest, the scribe.

Nehemiah Dedicates the Wall

27Now at the dedication of the wall of Jerusalem they
sought out the Levites in all their places, to bring them
to Jerusalem to celebrate the dedication with gladness, both with thanksgivings and singing, *with* cymbals and stringed instruments and harps. 28And the
sons of the singers gathered together from the countryside around Jerusalem, from the villages of the
Netophathites, 29from the house of Gilgal, and from
the fields of Geba and Azmaveth; for the singers had
built themselves villages all around Jerusalem. 30Then
the priests and Levites purified themselves, and purified the people, the gates, and the wall.
31So I brought the leaders of Judah up on the wall,
and appointed two large thanksgiving choirs. *One*
went to the right hand on the wall toward the Refuse
Gate. 32After them went Hoshaiah and half of the leaders of Judah, 33and Azariah, Ezra, Meshullam, 34Ju-
dah, Benjamin, Shemaiah, Jeremiah, 35and some of
the priests' sons with trumpets—Zechariah the son of
Jonathan, the son of Shemaiah, the son of Mattaniah,
the son of Michaiah, the son of Zaccur, the son of
Asaph, 36and his brethren, Shemaiah, Azarel, Milalai,
Gilalai, Maai, Nethanel, Judah, *and* Hanani, with the
musical instruments of David the man of God. And
Ezra the scribe *went* before them. 37By the Fountain
Gate, in front of them, they went up the stairs of the
City of David, on the stairway of the wall, beyond the
house of David, as far as the Water Gate eastward.
38The other thanksgiving choir went the opposite
way, and I *was* behind them with half of the people on
the wall, going past the Tower of the Ovens as far as
the Broad Wall, 39and above the Gate of Ephraim,
above the Old Gate, above the Fish Gate, the Tower of
Hananel, the Tower of the Hundred, as far as the Sheep
Gate; and they stopped by the Gate of the Prison.
40So the two thanksgiving choirs stood in the house
of God, likewise I and the half of the rulers with me;
41and the priests, Eliakim, Maaseiah, Minjamin,[k]
Michaiah, Elioenai, Zechariah, *and* Hananiah, with
trumpets; 42also Maaseiah, Shemaiah, Eleazar, Uzzi,
Jehohanan, Malchijah, Elam, and Ezer. The singers
sang loudly with Jezrahiah the director.
43Also that day they offered great sacrifices, and rejoiced, for God had made them rejoice with great joy;
the women and the children also rejoiced, so that the
joy of Jerusalem was heard afar off.

Temple Responsibilities

44And at the same time some were appointed over
the rooms of the storehouse for the offerings, the
firstfruits, and the tithes, to gather into them from the
fields of the cities the portions specified by the Law
for the priests and Levites; for Judah rejoiced over the
priests and Levites who ministered. 45Both the singers
and the gatekeepers kept the charge of their God and
the charge of the purification, according to the command of David *and* Solomon his son. 46For in the days
of David and Asaph of old *there were* chiefs of the
singers, and songs of praise and thanksgiving to God.
47In the days of Zerubbabel and in the days of
Nehemiah all Israel gave the portions for the singers
and the gatekeepers, a portion for each day. They also
consecrated *holy things* for the Levites, and the
Levites consecrated *them* for the children of Aaron.

Principles of Separation

13 On that day they read from the Book of Moses
in the hearing of the people, and in it was found
written that no Ammonite or Moabite should ever
come into the assembly of God, 2because they had not
met the children of Israel with bread and water, but
hired Balaam against them to curse them. However,
our God turned the curse into a blessing. 3So it was,
when they had heard the Law, that they separated all
the mixed multitude from Israel.

The Reforms of Nehemiah

4Now before this, Eliashib the priest, having authority
over the storerooms of the house of our God, *was* allied
with Tobiah. 5And he had prepared for him a large room,
where previously they had stored the grain offerings,
the frankincense, the articles, the tithes of grain, the new
wine and oil, which were commanded *to be given* to the

12:26 [j] Spelled *Jehozadak* in 1 Chronicles 6:14
12:41 [k] Or *Mijamin* (compare verse 5)

Levites and singers and gatekeepers, and the offerings
for the priests. 6But during all this I was not in Jerusalem,
for in the thirty-second year of Artaxerxes king of Babylon I had returned to the king. Then after certain days
I obtained leave from the king, 7and I came to Jerusalem and discovered the evil that Eliashib had done for
Tobiah, in preparing a room for him in the courts of
the house of God. 8And it grieved me bitterly; therefore
I threw all the household goods of Tobiah out of the
room. 9Then I commanded them to cleanse the rooms;
and I brought back into them the articles of the house
of God, with the grain offering and the frankincense.

10I also realized that the portions for the Levites had
not been given *them;* for each of the Levites and the
singers who did the work had gone back to his field.
11So I contended with the rulers, and said, "Why is the
house of God forsaken?" And I gathered them together
and set them in their place. 12Then all Judah brought
the tithe of the grain and the new wine and the oil to
the storehouse. 13And I appointed as treasurers over the
storehouse Shelemiah the priest and Zadok the
scribe, and of the Levites, Pedaiah; and next to them
was Hanan the son of Zaccur, the son of Mattaniah;
for they were considered faithful, and their task *was*
to distribute to their brethren.

14Remember me, O my God, concerning this, and
do not wipe out my good deeds that I have done for
the house of my God, and for its services!

15In those days I saw *people* in Judah treading wine
presses on the Sabbath, and bringing in sheaves, and
loading donkeys with wine, grapes, figs, and all *kinds
of* burdens, which they brought into Jerusalem on the
Sabbath day. And I warned *them* about the day on
which they were selling provisions. 16Men of Tyre
dwelt there also, who brought in fish and all kinds of
goods, and sold *them* on the Sabbath to the children
of Judah, and in Jerusalem.

17Then I contended with the nobles of Judah, and
said to them, "What evil thing *is* this that you do, by
which you profane the Sabbath day? 18Did not your fathers do thus, and did not our God bring all this disaster
on us and on this city? Yet you bring added wrath on
Israel by profaning the Sabbath."

19So it was, at the gates of Jerusalem, as it began to
be dark before the Sabbath, that I commanded the
gates to be shut, and charged that they must not be
opened till after the Sabbath. Then I posted *some* of
my servants at the gates, *so that* no burdens would be
brought in on the Sabbath day. 20Now the merchants
and sellers of all kinds of wares lodged outside Jerusalem once or twice.

21Then I warned them, and said to them, "Why do
you spend the night around the wall? If you do *so*
again, I will lay hands on you!" From that time on they
came no *more* on the Sabbath. 22And I commanded
the Levites that they should cleanse themselves, and
that they should go and guard the gates, to sanctify
the Sabbath day.

Remember me, O my God, *concerning* this also, and
spare me according to the greatness of Your mercy!

23In those days I also saw Jews *who* had married
women of Ashdod, Ammon, *and* Moab. 24And half of
their children spoke the language of Ashdod, and could
not speak the language of Judah, but spoke according
to the language of one or the other people.

25So I contended with them and cursed them,
struck some of them and pulled out their hair, and
made them swear by God, *saying,* "You shall not give
your daughters as wives to their sons, nor take their
daughters for your sons or yourselves. 26Did not Solomon king of Israel sin by these things? Yet among
many nations there was no king like him, who was
beloved of his God; and God made him king over all
Israel. Nevertheless pagan women caused even him
to sin. 27Should we then hear of your doing all this
great evil, transgressing against our God by marrying
pagan women?"

28And *one* of the sons of Joiada, the son of Eliashib
the high priest, *was* a son-in-law of Sanballat the
Horonite; therefore I drove him from me.

29Remember them, O my God, because they have
defiled the priesthood and the covenant of the priesthood and the Levites.

30Thus I cleansed them of everything pagan. I also
assigned duties to the priests and the Levites, each to
his service, 31and *to bringing* the wood offering and
the firstfruits at appointed times.

Remember me, O my God, for good!

The Book of ESTHER

INTRODUCTION

The Book of Esther. Some things about it you love. Some things you admire. But there is one thing about it that leaves you scratching your head.

You love the story. A Jewish girl raised in Persia by a cousin named Mordecai. She becomes the wife of the king by winning the Miss Persia contest. Her husband is Xerxes. (Better known to some as Ahasuerus, which sounds like something you do when you have a bad cold.)

It's a rags-to-riches romance, though you've got to wonder how much romance could occur when you are married to a guy who would chop your head off if you popped into his office without an appointment. But that's what Esther did. She took the chance at the chance it would save her nation.

That is the part of Esther you admire. Aside from being a beauty, she was gutsy. Xerxes's right-hand man is Haman. (A name that, as you'll soon see, sounds curiously close to "hangman.") Haman was a raging Nazi. Nothing would suit him better than annihilation of the Jews. One day he got his chance. Mordecai, Esther's foster father, refused to bow before Haman. Haman was so mad he convinced Xerxes to let him do away with the whole nation.

That's where Esther comes in. Literally. She comes into the king's chambers uninvited but not unprepared. After getting the Jews to pray and fast for three days, she puts on her royal robes and stands at the door. Xerxes likes what he sees and invites her in. One invitation leads to another, and by the time she finishes, Xerxes not only agrees to call off the massacre but orders Haman to hang from the same gallows Haman had built for Mordecai.

Whew! Quite a lady, this Esther. You have to admire her courage. You have to love her story. But there is one thing that is tough to figure. God's name never appears in the entire book. His actions do. His thoughts do. His plan does. His fingerprints are on every page. But his name never appears. Could it be that God is more concerned about getting the job done than getting credit?

LIFE LESSON

Esther 1:1–2:23

SITUATION Trouble brewed in Persia. Queen Vashti refused to obey King Xerxes. In anger, the king banished the queen and got a new one. Esther, an adopted Jewish orphan, became queen of Persia because of her beauty.

OBSERVATION God uses unlikely people in unusual situations to preserve his people.

INSPIRATION John Egglen had never preached a sermon in his life. Never.

Wasn't that he didn't want to, just never needed to. But then one morning he did. The snow left his town of Colchester, England, buried in white. When he awoke on that January Sunday in 1850, he thought of staying home. Who would go to church in such weather?

But he reconsidered. He was, after all, a deacon. And if the deacons didn't go, who would? So he put on his boots, hat, and coat and walked the six miles to the Methodist Church.

He wasn't the only member who considered staying home. In fact, he was one of the few who came. Only thirteen people were present. Twelve members and one visitor. Even the minister was snowed in. Someone suggested they go home. Egglen would hear none of that. They'd come this far; they would have a service. Besides, they had a visitor. A thirteen-year-old boy.

The King Dethrones Queen Vashti

Now it came to pass in the days of Ahasuerus[a] (this *was* the
Ahasuerus who reigned over one hundred and twenty-
seven provinces, from India to Ethiopia), [2]in those days
when King Ahasuerus sat on the throne of his kingdom,
which *was* in Shushan[b] the citadel, [3]*that* in the third year of his reign he
made a feast for all his officials and servants—the powers of Persia and
Media, the nobles, and the princes of the provinces *being* before him—
[4]when he showed the riches of his glorious kingdom and the splendor of
his excellent majesty for many days, one hundred and eighty days *in all.*
[5]And when these days were completed, the king made a feast lasting
seven days for all the people who were present in Shushan the citadel,
from great to small, in the court of the garden of the king's palace. [6]*There*
were white and blue linen *curtains* fastened with cords of fine linen and
purple on silver rods and marble pillars; *and the* couches *were* of gold and
silver on a *mosaic* pavement of alabaster, turquoise, and white and black
marble. [7]And they served drinks in golden vessels, each vessel being different from the other, with royal wine in abundance, according to the generosity of the king. [8]In accordance with the law, the drinking was not
compulsory; for so the king had ordered all the officers of his household,
that they should do according to each man's pleasure.
[9]Queen Vashti also made a feast for the women *in* the royal palace which
belonged to King Ahasuerus.
[10]On the seventh day, when the heart of the king was merry with wine, he
commanded Mehuman, Biztha, Harbona, Bigtha, Abagtha, Zethar, and
Carcas, seven eunuchs who served in the presence of King Ahasuerus, [11]to
bring Queen Vashti before the king, *wearing* her royal crown, in order to
show her beauty to the people and the officials, for she *was* beautiful to behold. [12]But Queen Vashti refused to come at the king's command *brought*
by *his* eunuchs; therefore the king was furious, and his anger burned
within him.
[13]Then the king said to the wise men who understood the times (for this
was the king's manner toward all who knew law and justice, [14]those closest
to him *being* Carshena, Shethar, Admatha, Tarshish, Meres, Marsena, and
Memucan, the seven princes of Persia and Media, who had access to the
king's presence, *and* who ranked highest in the kingdom): [15]"What *shall*
we do to Queen Vashti, according to law, because she did not obey the
command of King Ahasuerus *brought to her* by the eunuchs?"
[16]And Memucan answered before the king and the princes: "Queen
Vashti has not only wronged the king, but also all the princes, and all the
people who *are* in all the provinces of King Ahasuerus. [17]For the queen's
behavior will become known to all women, so that they will despise their
husbands in their eyes, when they report, 'King Ahasuerus commanded
Queen Vashti to be brought in before him, but she did not come.' [18]This
very day the *noble* ladies of Persia and Media will say to all the king's officials that they have heard of the behavior of the queen. Thus *there will be*
excessive contempt and wrath. [19]If it pleases the king, let a royal decree go
out from him, and let it be recorded in the laws of the Persians and the
Medes, so that it will not be altered, that Vashti shall come no more before

1:1 [a] Generally identified with Xerxes I (485–464 B.C.)
1:2 [b] Or *Susa,* and so throughout this book

King Ahasuerus; and let the king give her royal position to another who is
better than she. 20When the king's decree which he will make is proclaimed throughout all his empire (for it is great), all wives will honor
their husbands, both great and small."
21And the reply pleased the king and the princes, and the king did according to the word of Memucan. 22Then he sent letters to all the king's
provinces, to each province in its own script, and to every people in their
own language, that each man should be master in his own house, and
speak in the language of his own people.

Esther Becomes Queen

2 After these things, when the wrath of King Ahasuerus subsided, he remembered Vashti, what she had done, and what had been decreed
against her. 2Then the king's servants who attended him said: "Let beautiful young virgins be sought for the king; 3and let the king appoint officers
in all the provinces of his kingdom, that they may gather all the beautiful
young virgins to Shushan the citadel, into the women's quarters, under
the custody of Hegai[c] the king's eunuch, custodian of the women. And let
beauty preparations be given *them.* 4Then let the young woman who
pleases the king be queen instead of Vashti."
This thing pleased the king, and he did so.
5In Shushan the citadel there was a certain Jew whose name *was*
Mordecai the son of Jair, the son of Shimei, the son of Kish, a Benjamite.
6*Kish*[d] had been carried away from Jerusalem with the captives who had
been captured with Jeconiah[e] king of Judah, whom Nebuchadnezzar the
king of Babylon had carried away. 7And *Mordecai* had brought up
Hadassah, that *is,* Esther, his uncle's daughter, for she had neither father
nor mother. The young woman *was* lovely and beautiful. When her father
and mother died, Mordecai took her as his own daughter.
8So it was, when the king's command and decree were heard, and when
many young women were gathered at Shushan the citadel, *under* the custody of Hegai, that Esther also was taken to the king's palace, into the care
of Hegai the custodian of the women. 9Now the young woman pleased
him, and she obtained his favor; so he readily gave beauty preparations to
her, besides her allowance. Then seven choice maidservants were provided
for her from the king's palace, and he moved her and her maidservants to
the best *place* in the house of the women.
10Esther had not revealed her people or family, for Mordecai had
charged her not to reveal *it.* 11And every day Mordecai paced in front of the
court of the women's quarters, to learn of Esther's welfare and what was
happening to her.
12Each young woman's turn came to go in to King Ahasuerus after she
had completed twelve months' preparation, according to the regulations
for the women, for thus were the days of their preparation apportioned:
six months with oil of myrrh, and six months with perfumes and preparations for beautifying women. 13Thus *prepared, each* young woman went
to the king, and she was given whatever she desired to take with her from
the women's quarters to the king's palace. 14In the evening she went, and

2:3 [c] Hebrew *Hege*
2:6 [d] Literally *Who* [e] Same as *Jehoiachin,* 2 Kings 24:6 and elsewhere

But who would preach? Egglen was the only deacon. It fell to him.

And so he did. His sermon lasted only ten minutes. It drifted and wandered and made no point in an effort to make several. But at the end, an uncharacteristic courage settled upon the man. He lifted his eyes and looked straight at the boy and challenged: "Young man, look to Jesus. Look! Look! Look!"

Did the challenge make a difference? Let the boy, now a man, answer. "I did look, and then and there the cloud on my heart lifted, the darkness rolled away, and at that moment I saw the sun."

The boy's name? Charles Haddon Spurgeon. England's prince of preachers.

(From *When God Whispers Your Name* by Max Lucado)

APPLICATION God raised Esther to a royal position to save her people. Look at your surroundings. How could God use you? Perhaps he has placed you in your job, school, or family to reach someone for Jesus. Be bold (but not brash). Share your faith. Encourage others to look to Jesus.

EXPLORATION Respect Authority—Ephesians 5:21-26; 1 Peter 3:1-7; 5:5-6; Hebrews 13:17.

LIFE LESSON

Esther 3:1–4:17

SITUATION Haman conspired to destroy all of the Jews. Mordecai learned of Haman's plot and urged Esther to intercede on behalf of the Jews.

OBSERVATION Esther and Mordecai could have tried to save only themselves, but chose instead to risk their lives in order to save their people. Esther realized that God had placed her as queen for this reason.

INSPIRATION We shall all feel very much ashamed if we do not yield to Jesus on the point He has asked us to yield to Him. Paul says—"My determination is to be my utmost for His Highest." To get there is a question of will, not of debate nor of reasoning, but a surrender of will, an absolute and irrevocable surrender on that point. An overweening consideration for ourselves is the thing that keeps us from that decision, though we put it that we are considering others. When we consider what it will cost others if we obey the call of Jesus, we tell God He does not know what our obedience will mean. Keep to the point; He does know. Shut out every other consideration and keep yourself before God for this one thing only—My Utmost for His Highest. I am determined to be absolutely and entirely for Him and for Him alone. . . .

God's order has to work up to a crisis in our lives because we will not heed the gentler way. He brings us to the place where He asks us to be our utmost for Him, and we begin to debate; then He produces a providential crisis where we have to decide—for or against, and from that point the "Great Divide" begins.

If the crisis has come to you on any line, surrender your will to Him absolutely and irrevocably.

(From *My Utmost for His Highest* by Oswald Chambers)

APPLICATION Has someone harassed you or persecuted you because you are a Christian? Stay loyal to God, even when it may be dangerous or embarrassing to do so.

EXPLORATION Choosing God—Joshua 24:15; 1 Samuel 7:3-4; Matthew 6:24; 12:30.

in the morning she returned to the second house of the women, to the custody of Shaashgaz, the king's eunuch who kept the concubines. She would not go in to the king again unless the king delighted in her and called for her by name.

[15]Now when the turn came for Esther the daughter of Abihail the uncle
of Mordecai, who had taken her as his daughter, to go in to the king, she
requested nothing but what Hegai the king's eunuch, the custodian of the
women, advised. And Esther obtained favor in the sight of all who saw her.
[16]So Esther was taken to King Ahasuerus, into his royal palace, in the tenth
month, which *is* the month of Tebeth, in the seventh year of his reign.
[17]The king loved Esther more than all the *other* women, and she obtained
grace and favor in his sight more than all the virgins; so he set the royal
crown upon her head and made her queen instead of Vashti. [18]Then the
king made a great feast, the Feast of Esther, for all his officials and servants; and he proclaimed a holiday in the provinces and gave gifts according to the generosity of a king.

Mordecai Discovers a Plot

[19]When virgins were gathered together a second time, Mordecai sat
within the king's gate. [20]*Now* Esther had not revealed her family and her
people, just as Mordecai had charged her, for Esther obeyed the command of Mordecai as when she was brought up by him.

[21]In those days, while Mordecai sat within the king's gate, two of the
king's eunuchs, Bigthan and Teresh, doorkeepers, became furious and
sought to lay hands on King Ahasuerus. [22]So the matter became known to
Mordecai, who told Queen Esther, and Esther informed the king in
Mordecai's name. [23]And when an inquiry was made into the matter, it was
confirmed, and both were hanged on a gallows; and it was written in the book of the chronicles in the presence of the king.

Haman's Conspiracy Against the Jews

3 After these things King Ahasuerus promoted Haman, the son of Hammedatha the Agagite, and advanced him and set his seat above all
the princes who *were* with him. [2]And all the king's servants who *were*
within the king's gate bowed and paid homage to Haman, for so the king had commanded concerning him. But Mordecai would not bow or pay
homage. [3]Then the king's servants who *were* within the king's gate said to
Mordecai, "Why do you transgress the king's command?" [4]Now it hap-
pened, when they spoke to him daily and he would not listen to them, that they told *it* to Haman, to see whether Mordecai's words would stand; for
Mordecai had told them that he *was* a Jew. [5]When Haman saw that Mordecai
did not bow or pay him homage, Haman was filled with wrath. [6]But he dis-
dained to lay hands on Mordecai alone, for they had told him of the people of Mordecai. Instead, Haman sought to destroy all the Jews who *were* throughout the whole kingdom of Ahasuerus—the people of Mordecai.

[7]In the first month, which is the month of Nisan, in the twelfth year of
King Ahasuerus, they cast Pur (that *is,* the lot), before Haman to determine the day and the month,[f] until *it fell on the* twelfth *month,*[g] which *is* the month of Adar.

3:7 [f] Septuagint adds *to destroy the people of Mordecai in one day;* Vulgate adds *the nation of the Jews should be destroyed.* [g] Following Masoretic Text and Vulgate; Septuagint reads *and the lot fell on the fourteenth of the month.*

8 Then Haman said to King Ahasuerus, "There is a
certain people scattered and dispersed among the
people in all the provinces of your kingdom; their
laws *are* different from all *other* people's, and they do
not keep the king's laws. Therefore it *is* not fitting for
the king to let them remain. 9 If it pleases the king, let *a*
decree be written that they be destroyed, and I will pay
ten thousand talents of silver into the hands of those
who do the work, to bring *it* into the king's treasuries."
10 So the king took his signet ring from his hand and
gave it to Haman, the son of Hammedatha the
Agagite, the enemy of the Jews. 11 And the king said to
Haman, "The money and the people *are* given to you,
to do with them as seems good to you."
12 Then the king's scribes were called on the thirteenth day of the first month, and *a decree* was written
according to all that Haman commanded—to the
king's satraps, to the governors who *were* over each
province, to the officials of all people, to every
province according to its script, and to every people
in their language. In the name of King Ahasuerus it
was written, and sealed with the king's signet ring.
13 And the letters were sent by couriers into all the
king's provinces, to destroy, to kill, and to annihilate
all the Jews, both young and old, little children and
women, in one day, on the thirteenth *day* of the
twelfth *month,* which *is* the month of Adar, and to
plunder their possessions.[h] 14 A copy of the document
was to be issued as law in every province, being published for all people, that they should be ready for that
day. 15 The couriers went out, hastened by the king's
command; and the decree was proclaimed in
Shushan the citadel. So the king and Haman sat down
to drink, but the city of Shushan was perplexed.

Esther Agrees to Help the Jews

4 When Mordecai learned all that had happened, he
tore his clothes and put on sackcloth and ashes,
and went out into the midst of the city. He cried out
with a loud and bitter cry. 2 He went as far as the front of
the king's gate, for no one *might* enter the king's gate
clothed with sackcloth. 3 And in every province where
the king's command and decree arrived, *there was*
great mourning among the Jews, with fasting, weeping,
and wailing; and many lay in sackcloth and ashes.
4 So Esther's maids and eunuchs came and told her,
and the queen was deeply distressed. Then she sent
garments to clothe Mordecai and take his sackcloth
away from him, but he would not accept *them.* 5 Then
Esther called Hathach, *one* of the king's eunuchs
whom he had appointed to attend her, and she gave
him a command concerning Mordecai, to learn what
and why this *was.* 6 So Hathach went out to Mordecai
in the city square that *was* in front of the king's gate.
7 And Mordecai told him all that had happened to
him, and the sum of money that Haman had
promised to pay into the king's treasuries to destroy
the Jews. 8 He also gave him a copy of the written decree for their destruction, which was given at
Shushan, that he might show it to Esther and explain
it to her, and that he might command her to go in to
the king to make supplication to him and plead before him for her people. 9 So Hathach returned and
told Esther the words of Mordecai.
10 Then Esther spoke to Hathach, and gave him a
command for Mordecai: 11 "All the king's servants and
the people of the king's provinces know that any man
or woman who goes into the inner court to the king,
who has not been called, *he has* but one law: put *all* to
death, except the one to whom the king holds out the
golden scepter, that he may live. Yet I myself have not
been called to go in to the king these thirty days." 12 So
they told Mordecai Esther's words.
13 And Mordecai told *them* to answer Esther: "Do
not think in your heart that you will escape in the
king's palace any more than all the other Jews. 14 For if
you remain completely silent at this time, relief and
deliverance will arise for the Jews from another place,
but you and your father's house will perish. Yet who
knows whether you have come to the kingdom for
such a time as this?"
15 Then Esther told *them* to reply to Mordecai: 16 "Go,
gather all the Jews who are present in Shushan, and
fast for me; neither eat nor drink for three days, night
or day. My maids and I will fast likewise. And so I will
go to the king, which *is* against the law; and if I perish,
I perish!"
17 So Mordecai went his way and did according to all
that Esther commanded him.[i]

Esther's Banquet

5 Now it happened on the third day that Esther put
on *her* royal *robes* and stood in the inner court of
the king's palace, across from the king's house, while
the king sat on his royal throne in the royal house, facing the entrance of the house.[j] 2 So it was, when the

3:13 [h] Septuagint adds the text of the letter here.
4:17 [i] Septuagint adds a prayer of Mordecai here.
5:1 [j] Septuagint adds many extra details in verses 1 and 2.

LIFE LESSON

Esther 5:1–6:14

SITUATION Esther gained an audience with King Xerxes, but delayed her request. Meanwhile, Haman unwittingly orchestrated his own death.

OBSERVATION Esther's discretion contrasted with Haman's reckless conceit.

INSPIRATION We must realize that the battle for self-control is fought primarily within our own minds; it is a battle with our passions, thoughts, and desires. In those areas where we have failed to curb our appetites and emotions, we seem to have invisible antennae sensitively attuned to the corresponding temptations. The proverbial "chip on his shoulder" describes the person whose antennae is constantly searching for the minor incident that he can magnify into an occasion for losing his temper. The person who habitually yields to some bodily appetite or lust is constantly alert for opportunities to indulge that carnal desire. We must learn to say no to those passions when they first enter our minds. Above all, we must pray for the inner strength of will necessary to curb our passions and desires. It is God who works in us to will and to act. Our own particular areas of vulnerability must be made the subject of earnest,

king saw Queen Esther standing in the court, *that* she found favor in his
sight, and the king held out to Esther the golden scepter that *was* in his
hand. Then Esther went near and touched the top of the scepter.
3And the king said to her, "What do you wish, Queen Esther? What *is*
your request? It shall be given to you—up to half the kingdom!"
4So Esther answered, "If it pleases the king, let the king and Haman
come today to the banquet that I have prepared for him."
5Then the king said, "Bring Haman quickly, that he may do as Esther has
said." So the king and Haman went to the banquet that Esther had prepared.
6At the banquet of wine the king said to Esther, "What *is* your petition? It
shall be granted you. What *is* your request, up to half the kingdom? It shall
be done!"
7Then Esther answered and said, "My petition and request *is this:* 8If I have
found favor in the sight of the king, and if it pleases the king to grant my petition and fulfill my request, then let the king and Haman come to the banquet
which I will prepare for them, and tomorrow I will do as the king has said."

Haman's Plot Against Mordecai

9So Haman went out that day joyful and with a glad heart; but when
Haman saw Mordecai in the king's gate, and that he did not stand or tremble
before him, he was filled with indignation against Mordecai. 10Nevertheless
Haman restrained himself and went home, and he sent and called for his
friends and his wife Zeresh. 11Then Haman told them of his great riches, the
multitude of his children, everything in which the king had promoted him,
and how he had advanced him above the officials and servants of the king.
12Moreover Haman said, "Besides, Queen Esther invited no one but me
to come in with the king to the banquet that she prepared; and tomorrow
I am again invited by her, along with the king. 13Yet all this avails me nothing, so long as I see Mordecai the Jew sitting at the king's gate."
14Then his wife Zeresh and all his friends said to him, "Let a gallows be
made, fifty cubits high, and in the morning suggest to the king that
Mordecai be hanged on it; then go merrily with the king to the banquet."
And the thing pleased Haman; so he had the gallows made.

The King Honors Mordecai

6 That night the king could not sleep. So one was commanded to bring
the book of the records of the chronicles; and they were read before the
king. 2And it was found written that Mordecai had told of Bigthana and
Teresh, two of the king's eunuchs, the doorkeepers who had sought to lay
hands on King Ahasuerus. 3Then the king said, "What honor or dignity
has been bestowed on Mordecai for this?"
And the king's servants who attended him said, "Nothing has been
done for him."
4So the king said, "Who *is* in the court?" Now Haman had *just* entered
the outer court of the king's palace to suggest that the king hang Mordecai
on the gallows that he had prepared for him.
5The king's servants said to him, "Haman is there, standing in the court."
And the king said, "Let him come in."
6So Haman came in, and the king asked him, "What shall be done for
the man whom the king delights to honor?"
Now Haman thought in his heart, "Whom would the king delight to
honor more than me?" 7And Haman answered the king, "*For* the man

whom the king delights to honor, 8let a royal robe be brought which the
king has worn, and a horse on which the king has ridden, which has a
royal crest placed on its head. 9Then let this robe and horse be delivered to
the hand of one of the king's most noble princes, that he may array the
man whom the king delights to honor. Then parade him on horseback
through the city square, and proclaim before him: 'Thus shall it be done to
the man whom the king delights to honor!' "
10Then the king said to Haman, "Hurry, take the robe and the horse, as
you have suggested, and do so for Mordecai the Jew who sits within the
king's gate! Leave nothing undone of all that you have spoken."
11So Haman took the robe and the horse, arrayed Mordecai and led him
on horseback through the city square, and proclaimed before him, "Thus
shall it be done to the man whom the king delights to honor!"
12Afterward Mordecai went back to the king's gate. But Haman hurried
to his house, mourning and with his head covered. 13When Haman told
his wife Zeresh and all his friends everything that had happened to him,
his wise men and his wife Zeresh said to him, "If Mordecai, before whom
you have begun to fall, is of Jewish descent, you will not prevail against
him but will surely fall before him."
14While they *were* still talking with him, the king's eunuchs came, and
hastened to bring Haman to the banquet which Esther had prepared.

Haman Hanged Instead of Mordecai

7 So the king and Haman went to dine with Queen Esther. 2And on the
second day, at the banquet of wine, the king again said to Esther,
"What *is* your petition, Queen Esther? It shall be granted you. And what *is*
your request, up to half the kingdom? It shall be done!"
3Then Queen Esther answered and said, "If I have found favor in your
sight, O king, and if it pleases the king, let my life be given me at my petition, and my people at my request. 4For we have been sold, my people and
I, to be destroyed, to be killed, and to be annihilated. Had we been sold as
male and female slaves, I would have held my tongue, although the enemy
could never compensate for the king's loss."
5So King Ahasuerus answered and said to Queen Esther, "Who is he,
and where is he, who would dare presume in his heart to do such a thing?"
6And Esther said, "The adversary and enemy *is* this wicked Haman!"
So Haman was terrified before the king and queen.
7Then the king arose in his wrath from the banquet of wine *and went*
into the palace garden; but Haman stood before Queen Esther, pleading
for his life, for he saw that evil was determined against him by the king.
8When the king returned from the palace garden to the place of the banquet of wine, Haman had fallen across the couch where Esther *was.* Then
the king said, "Will he also assault the queen while I *am* in the house?"
As the word left the king's mouth, they covered Haman's face. 9Now
Harbonah, one of the eunuchs, said to the king, "Look! The gallows, fifty
cubits high, which Haman made for Mordecai, who spoke good on the
king's behalf, is standing at the house of Haman."
Then the king said, "Hang him on it!"
10So they hanged Haman on the gallows that he had prepared for
Mordecai. Then the king's wrath subsided.

beseeching prayer for God's grace to work in our wills. At the same time we must realize that the will is strengthened by obedience. The more we say no to sinful desires, the more we will be able to say no. But to experience this, we must persevere through many failures. A large part of learning self-control is breaking bad habits and replacing them with good ones. . . .

As we grow in the grace of self-control, we will experience the liberation of those who, under the guidance and grace of the Holy Spirit, are freed from the shackles of self-indulgence and are brought into the freedom of true spiritual discipline.

(From *The Practice of Godliness* by Jerry Bridges)

APPLICATION Are you disciplined even under difficult circumstances? Say no to the temptation to indulge every appetite. Substitute an old habit with a new one: praise, don't complain; support, don't argue; encourage, don't brag.

EXPLORATION Self-Control—Proverbs 1:2-4; 21:23; Ecclesiastes 5:1-2; Acts 24:25; Galatians 5:22-23.

Life Lesson

Esther 7:1–8:17

SITUATION Esther asked that her people be allowed to live. King Xerxes granted her request and had Haman hanged. The Jews were rescued.

OBSERVATION God used individual people and governments to enact his will.

INSPIRATION If you find yourself dealing with people who are not playing by the biblical rules, who are underhanded, deceptive, dishonest, and self-serving, can you learn to see the advantage you have over them? In refusing to use their tactics and choosing to abide by biblical principles, you are under God's protection, and He has promised to honor you and to prosper you.

A few years ago, while in the process of purchasing a newly built home, I found myself engaged in a conflict with one of the employees of the building firm. She was arrogant, rude, and terribly disrespectful to me, the customer. I responded as I knew a businessperson should: I was assertive, refused to talk to her, went to a higher authority, and demanded my rights. . . .

Instead of raising my voice and demanding my rights, I could have been just as assertive by calmly repeating my concerns, refusing to allow the conversation to deteriorate to that low level. I could have been kind and polite; I could have stopped and quickly prayed for the woman; I

Esther Saves the Jews

8 On that day King Ahasuerus gave Queen Esther the house of Haman,
the enemy of the Jews. And Mordecai came before the king, for Esther
had told how he *was related* to her. 2So the king took off his signet ring,
which he had taken from Haman, and gave it to Mordecai; and Esther appointed Mordecai over the house of Haman.
3Now Esther spoke again to the king, fell down at his feet, and implored
him with tears to counteract the evil of Haman the Agagite, and the
scheme which he had devised against the Jews. 4And the king held out the
golden scepter toward Esther. So Esther arose and stood before the king,
5and said, "If it pleases the king, and if I have found favor in his sight and
the thing *seems* right to the king and I am pleasing in his eyes, let it be written to revoke the letters devised by Haman, the son of Hammedatha the
Agagite, which he wrote to annihilate the Jews who *are* in all the king's
provinces. 6For how can I endure to see the evil that will come to my people? Or how can I endure to see the destruction of my countrymen?"
7Then King Ahasuerus said to Queen Esther and Mordecai the Jew, "Indeed, I have given Esther the house of Haman, and they have hanged him
on the gallows because he *tried to* lay his hand on the Jews. 8You yourselves
write *a decree* concerning the Jews, as you please, in the king's name, and
seal *it* with the king's signet ring; for whatever is written in the king's name
and sealed with the king's signet ring no one can revoke."
9So the king's scribes were called at that time, in the third month, which
is the month of Sivan, on the twenty-third *day;* and it was written, according to all that Mordecai commanded, to the Jews, the satraps, the governors, and the princes of the provinces from India to Ethiopia, one
hundred and twenty-seven provinces *in all,* to every province in its own
script, to every people in their own language, and to the Jews in their own
script and language. 10And he wrote in the name of King Ahasuerus,
sealed *it* with the king's signet ring, and sent letters by couriers on horseback, riding on royal horses bred from swift steeds.[k]
11By these letters the king permitted the Jews who *were* in every city to
gather together and protect their lives—to destroy, kill, and annihilate all
the forces of any people or province that would assault them, *both* little
children and women, and to plunder their possessions, 12on one day in all
the provinces of King Ahasuerus, on the thirteenth *day* of the twelfth
month, which *is* the month of Adar.[l] 13A copy of the document was to be issued as a decree in every province and published for all people, so that the
Jews would be ready on that day to avenge themselves on their enemies.
14The couriers who rode on royal horses went out, hastened and pressed on
by the king's command. And the decree was issued in Shushan the citadel.
15So Mordecai went out from the presence of the king in royal apparel of
blue and white, with a great crown of gold and a garment of fine linen and
purple; and the city of Shushan rejoiced and was glad. 16The Jews had light
and gladness, joy and honor. 17And in every province and city, wherever
the king's command and decree came, the Jews had joy and gladness, a
feast and a holiday. Then many of the people of the land became Jews, because fear of the Jews fell upon them.

8:10 [k] Literally *sons of the swift horses*
8:12 [l] Septuagint adds the text of the letter here.

The Jews Destroy Their Tormentors

9 Now in the twelfth month, that *is,* the month of Adar, on the thirteenth
day, *the time* came for the king's command and his decree to be executed. On the day that the enemies of the Jews had hoped to overpower
them, the opposite occurred, in that the Jews themselves overpowered
those who hated them. [2]The Jews gathered together in their cities throughout all the provinces of King Ahasuerus to lay hands on those who sought
their harm. And no one could withstand them, because fear of them fell
upon all people. [3]And all the officials of the provinces, the satraps, the governors, and all those doing the king's work, helped the Jews, because the
fear of Mordecai fell upon them. [4]For Mordecai *was* great in the king's
palace, and his fame spread throughout all the provinces; for this man
Mordecai became increasingly prominent. [5]Thus the Jews defeated all
their enemies with the stroke of the sword, with slaughter and destruction, and did what they pleased with those who hated them.
[6]And in Shushan the citadel the Jews killed and destroyed five hundred
men. [7]Also Parshandatha, Dalphon, Aspatha, [8]Poratha, Adalia, Aridatha,
[9]Parmashta, Arisai, Aridai, and Vajezatha— [10]the ten sons of Haman the
son of Hammedatha, the enemy of the Jews—they killed; but they did not
lay a hand on the plunder.
[11]On that day the number of those who were killed in Shushan the citadel was brought to the king. [12]And the king said to Queen Esther, "The
Jews have killed and destroyed five hundred men in Shushan the citadel,
and the ten sons of Haman. What have they done in the rest of the king's
provinces? Now what *is* your petition? It shall be granted to you. Or what *is*
your further request? It shall be done."
[13]Then Esther said, "If it pleases the king, let it be granted to the Jews
who *are* in Shushan to do again tomorrow according to today's decree,
and let Haman's ten sons be hanged on the gallows."
[14]So the king commanded this to be done; the decree was issued in
Shushan, and they hanged Haman's ten sons.
[15]And the Jews who *were* in Shushan gathered together again on the
fourteenth day of the month of Adar and killed three hundred men at
Shushan; but they did not lay a hand on the plunder.
[16]The remainder of the Jews in the king's provinces gathered together and
protected their lives, had rest from their enemies, and killed seventy-five
thousand of their enemies; but they did not lay a hand on the plunder. [17]*This
was* on the thirteenth day of the month of Adar. And on the fourteenth of *the
month*[m] they rested and made it a day of feasting and gladness.

The Feast of Purim

[18]But the Jews who *were* at Shushan assembled together on the thirteenth *day,* as well as on the fourteenth; and on the fifteenth of *the month*[n]
they rested, and made it a day of feasting and gladness. [19]Therefore the
Jews of the villages who dwelt in the unwalled towns celebrated the fourteenth day of the month of Adar *with* gladness and feasting, as a holiday,
and for sending presents to one another.
[20]And Mordecai wrote these things and sent letters to all the Jews, near
and far, who *were* in all the provinces of King Ahasuerus, [21]to establish

could have thought about what bitterness and anger there was inside her to cause her to behave the way she did and allowed God to give me compassion for her. I could have done all that, but I missed the opportunity because I was too concerned with the way she was treating me.

I'm not suggesting we become doormats, but when we can control our reactions and respond in a Christlike manner, we actually have the advantage over the other person. When we take the world's way out, we often lose our Christian advantage, not to mention our testimony for Christ. When our business dealings are guided by biblical principles, it gives us a great advantage in the marketplace, because God created the marketplace and He knows what works!

(From *Workday Meditations* by Mary Whelchel)

APPLICATION Don't get so busy securing your rights or accomplishing your agenda that you miss the opportunity to serve. Look up from your responsibilities and find an opportunity to reach out.

EXPLORATION Living Honorably—Ephesians 2:10; Colossians 1:10; 1 Thessalonians 2:10-12; James 4:7-10.

9:17 [m] Literally *it*
9:18 [n] Literally *it*

LIFE LESSON

Esther 9:1–10:3

SITUATION Israel defeated its enemies and initiated the feast of Purim to commemorate its deliverance.

OBSERVATION God is always faithful to his people.

INSPIRATION Upon God's faithfulness rests our whole hope of future blessedness. Only as He is faithful will His covenants stand and His promises be honored. Only as we have complete assurance that He is faithful may we live in peace and look forward with assurance to the life to come.

Every heart can make its own application of this truth and draw from it such conclusions as the truth suggests and its own needs bring into focus. The tempted, the anxious, the fearful, the discouraged may all find new hope and good cheer in the knowledge that our Heavenly Father is faithful. He will ever be true to His pledged word. The hard-pressed sons of the covenant may be sure that He will never remove His loving-kindness from them nor suffer His faithfulness to fail.

Happy the man whose hopes rely
On Israel's God; He made the sky,
And earth, and seas, with all their train;
His truth forever stands secure;
He saves the oppressed, He feeds the poor,
And none shall find His promise vain.

Isaac Watts

(From *The Knowledge of the Holy* by A. W. Tozer)

APPLICATION What causes you to feel anxious, fearful, or discouraged? Remember that God faithfully loves you, faithfully cares for you, and faithfully provides for you. God is faithful in everything. Celebrate!

EXPLORATION Faithfulness—Psalm 73:25-26; 139; Isaiah 54:10; Lamentations 3:22-24; Zephaniah 3:17; 1 Corinthians 1:8-9.

among them that they should celebrate yearly the fourteenth and fifteenth
days of the month of Adar, 22as the days on which the Jews had rest from
their enemies, as the month which was turned from sorrow to joy for
them, and from mourning to a holiday; that they should make them days
of feasting and joy, of sending presents to one another and gifts to the
poor. 23So the Jews accepted the custom which they had begun, as
Mordecai had written to them, 24because Haman, the son of Hammedatha
the Agagite, the enemy of all the Jews, had plotted against the Jews to annihilate them, and had cast Pur (that *is,* the lot), to consume them and destroy them; 25but when *Esther*[o] came before the king, he commanded by
letter that this[p] wicked plot which *Haman* had devised against the Jews
should return on his own head, and that he and his sons should be hanged
on the gallows.

26So they called these days Purim, after the name Pur. Therefore, because of all the words of this letter, what they had seen concerning this
matter, and what had happened to them, 27the Jews established and imposed it upon themselves and their descendants and all who would join
them, that without fail they should celebrate these two days every year, according to the written *instructions* and according to the *prescribed* time,
28*that* these days *should be* remembered and kept throughout every generation, every family, every province, and every city, that these days of Purim
should not fail *to be observed* among the Jews, and *that* the memory of
them should not perish among their descendants.

29Then Queen Esther, the daughter of Abihail, with Mordecai the Jew,
wrote with full authority to confirm this second letter about Purim. 30And
Mordecai sent letters to all the Jews, to the one hundred and twenty-seven
provinces of the kingdom of Ahasuerus, *with* words of peace and truth,
31to confirm these days of Purim at their *appointed* time, as Mordecai the
Jew and Queen Esther had prescribed for them, and as they had decreed
for themselves and their descendants concerning matters of their fasting
and lamenting. 32So the decree of Esther confirmed these matters of
Purim, and it was written in the book.

Mordecai's Advancement

10 And King Ahasuerus imposed tribute on the land and *on* the islands of the sea. 2Now all the acts of his power and his might, and
the account of the greatness of Mordecai, to which the king advanced him,
are they not written in the book of the chronicles of the kings of Media and
Persia? 3For Mordecai the Jew *was* second to King Ahasuerus, and was
great among the Jews and well received by the multitude of his brethren,
seeking the good of his people and speaking peace to all his countrymen.[q]

9:25 [o] Literally *she* or *it* [p] Literally *his*
10:3 [q] Literally *seed.* Septuagint and Vulgate add a dream of Mordecai here; Vulgate adds six more chapters.

The Book of

JOB

INTRODUCTION

It's easy to thank God when he does what we want. But God doesn't always do what we want. Ask Job.

His empire collapsed, his children were killed, and what was a healthy body became a rage of boils. From whence came this torrent? From whence will come any help?

Not from his wife. You can't blame her for telling Job to curse God. But to curse God and die?

Then come his friends. They mean well, but they comfort poorly. They tell him he must have been pretty bad to get it so bad.

"With friends like you guys . . . ," Job says and then tells them to take their theology back to the dime store where they bought it. Getting no comfort from family or friend, he goes straight to God and pleads his case. His head hurts. His body hurts. His heart hurts. And he can't tolerate anymore half-baked answers. "Why is this happening to me?" he demands.

And God answers. Not with answers but with questions. An ocean of questions. Space doesn't permit their listing, but one or two will convey the point. "*Can you lift up your voice to the clouds, that an abundance of water may cover you? Can you send out lightnings, that they may go, and say to you, 'Here we are!'?*" (38:34–35).

After several dozen of these, Job is left on the beach drenched and wide-eyed, knowing he will never argue with the ocean again. He lifts his hand and cries, "Enough." He has gotten the point. What is it?

God owes no one anything. No reasons. No explanations. Nothing. If he gave them, we couldn't understand them.

Which makes the conclusion of the book all the more moving. Even though God owed Job nothing, he gave him everything. New health, new business, new family. And most of all, new insight.

God is God. He knows what he is doing. When you can't trace his hand, trust his heart.

LIFE LESSON

Job 1:1–2:13

SITUATION Satan hoped to convince God that Job only was righteous because of his comfortable life. God allowed Satan to bring disaster upon Job, but Job stayed loyal to God.

OBSERVATION God allows people to be tested and endure hardships, but his love for them never diminishes. In the end he is glorified, and they are made more mature.

INSPIRATION The Bible is certainly not oblivious to difficulty. But it is critical that we begin to understand Scripture's message that difficulty and joy are not exclusive entities, but mutual friends. . . .

Most of the greatest thoughts of the greatest thinkers of all time had to pass through the fire. Bunyan wrote *Pilgrim's Progress* from jail. Florence Nightingale, too ill to move from her bed, reorganized the hospitals of England. Semiparalyzed and under the constant menace of apoplexy, Pasteur was tireless in his attack on disease. During the greater part of his life, American historian Francis Parkman suffered so acutely that he could not work for more than five minutes at a time. His eyesight was so wretched that he could scrawl only a few gigantic words on a manuscript, yet he contrived to write twenty magnificent volumes of history. Sometimes it seems that when God is about to make preeminent use of a man, he puts him through the fire.

Many people live as though they regret God's incredible invitation to life. Avoiding pain becomes their chief occupation. And few of them realize that avoidance of difficulty only produces more pain in the long run.

(From *You Gotta Keep Dancin'* by Tim Hansel)

APPLICATION Don't get angry at God. Use problems to strengthen your character and to bring glory to God.

EXPLORATION Resist Temptation—Genesis 14:23; Joshua 23:7-8; Jeremiah 35:6; Daniel 1:8; Luke 4:5-8; 1 Corinthians 15:58; Galatians 5:1; Philippians 1:27; 1 Peter 5:9; 2 Peter 3:17.

Job and His Family in Uz

There was a man in the land of Uz, whose name *was* Job; and
that man was blameless and upright, and one who feared God
and shunned evil. 2And seven sons and three daughters were born
to him. 3Also, his possessions were seven thousand sheep, three
thousand camels, five hundred yoke of oxen, five hundred female donkeys, and a very large household, so that this man was the greatest of all
the people of the East.
4And his sons would go and feast *in their* houses, each on his *appointed*
day, and would send and invite their three sisters to eat and drink with
them. 5So it was, when the days of feasting had run their course, that Job
would send and sanctify them, and he would rise early in the morning and
offer burnt offerings *according to* the number of them all. For Job said, "It
may be that my sons have sinned and cursed[a] God in their hearts." Thus
Job did regularly.

Satan Attacks Job's Character

6Now there was a day when the sons of God came to present themselves
before the LORD, and Satan[b] also came among them. 7And the LORD said to
Satan, "From where do you come?"
So Satan answered the LORD and said, "From going to and fro on the
earth, and from walking back and forth on it."
8Then the LORD said to Satan, "Have you considered My servant Job,
that *there is* none like him on the earth, a blameless and upright man, one
who fears God and shuns evil?"
9So Satan answered the LORD and said, "Does Job fear God for nothing?
10Have You not made a hedge around him, around his household, and around
all that he has on every side? You have blessed the work of his hands, and
his possessions have increased in the land. 11But now, stretch out Your
hand and touch all that he has, and he will surely curse You to Your face!"
12And the LORD said to Satan, "Behold, all that he has *is* in your power;
only do not lay a hand on his *person*."
So Satan went out from the presence of the LORD.

Job Loses His Property and Children

13Now there was a day when his sons and daughters *were* eating and
drinking wine in their oldest brother's house; 14and a messenger came to
Job and said, "The oxen were plowing and the donkeys feeding beside them,
15when the Sabeans[c] raided *them* and took them away—indeed they have
killed the servants with the edge of the sword; and I alone have escaped to
tell you!"
16While he *was* still speaking, another also came and said, "The fire of
God fell from heaven and burned up the sheep and the servants, and consumed them; and I alone have escaped to tell you!"
17While he *was* still speaking, another also came and said, "The Chaldeans formed three bands, raided the camels and took them away, yes, and
killed the servants with the edge of the sword; and I alone have escaped to
tell you!"

1:5 [a] Literally *blessed,* but used here in the evil sense, and so in verse 11 and 2:5, 9
1:6 [b] Literally *the Adversary,* and so throughout this book
1:15 [c] Literally *Sheba* (compare 6:19)

18While he *was* still speaking, another also came and said, "Your sons
and daughters *were* eating and drinking wine in their oldest brother's
house, 19and suddenly a great wind came from across[d] the wilderness and
struck the four corners of the house, and it fell on the young people, and
they are dead; and I alone have escaped to tell you!"
20Then Job arose, tore his robe, and shaved his head; and he fell to the
ground and worshiped. 21And he said:

"Naked I came from my mother's womb,
And naked shall I return there.
The LORD gave, and the LORD has taken away;
Blessed be the name of the LORD."

22In all this Job did not sin nor charge God with wrong.

Satan Attacks Job's Health

2 Again there was a day when the sons of God came to present themselves
before the LORD, and Satan came also among them to present himself
before the LORD. 2And the LORD said to Satan, "From where do you come?"
Satan answered the LORD and said, "From going to and fro on the earth,
and from walking back and forth on it."
3Then the LORD said to Satan, "Have you considered My servant Job,
that *there is* none like him on the earth, a blameless and upright man, one
who fears God and shuns evil? And still he holds fast to his integrity, although you incited Me against him, to destroy him without cause."
4So Satan answered the LORD and said, "Skin for skin! Yes, all that a man
has he will give for his life. 5But stretch out Your hand now, and touch his
bone and his flesh, and he will surely curse You to Your face!"
6And the LORD said to Satan, "Behold, he *is* in your hand, but spare his
life."
7So Satan went out from the presence of the LORD, and struck Job with
painful boils from the sole of his foot to the crown of his head. 8And he
took for himself a potsherd with which to scrape himself while he sat in
the midst of the ashes.
9Then his wife said to him, "Do you still hold fast to your integrity? Curse
God and die!"
10But he said to her, "You speak as one of the foolish women speaks.
Shall we indeed accept good from God, and shall we not accept adversity?"
In all this Job did not sin with his lips.

Job's Three Friends

11Now when Job's three friends heard of all this adversity that had come
upon him, each one came from his own place—Eliphaz the Temanite,
Bildad the Shuhite, and Zophar the Naamathite. For they had made an appointment together to come and mourn with him, and to comfort him.
12And when they raised their eyes from afar, and did not recognize him,
they lifted their voices and wept; and each one tore his robe and sprinkled
dust on his head toward heaven. 13So they sat down with him on the
ground seven days and seven nights, and no one spoke a word to him, for
they saw that *his* grief was very great.

1:19 *d* Septuagint omits *across.*

LIFE LESSON

Job 3:1-26

SITUATION His wealth, gone. Children, dead. Health, failed. Despite these disasters, Job still held firmly to his faith. Friends came to visit and exhort him. Before they spoke, Job cursed the day he was born.

OBSERVATION No matter how powerfully troubles crush, God's hold is more powerful.

INSPIRATION Once the apostle Paul directly addressed the question of disappointment with God. He told the Corinthians that, in spite of incredible hardships, he did not "lose heart": "Though outwardly we are wasting away, yet inwardly we are being renewed day by day. For our light and momentary [!] troubles are achieving for us an eternal glory that far outweighs them all. So we fix our eyes not on what is seen, but on what is unseen. For what is seen is temporary, but what is unseen is eternal."

Paul endured trials and died a martyr, still anticipating his reward. Job endured trials, but received a fine reward in this life. So what, exactly, can we expect from God? Perhaps the best way to view the ending in Job is to see it not as a blueprint for what will happen to us in this life, but rather as a sign of what is to come. It stands as a sweet, satisfying symbol, a solution to one man's disappointment that offers us all a foretaste of the future. . . .

The worst mistake of all would be to conclude that God is somehow content to make a few minor adjustments to this tragic, unfair world.

Some people stake all their faith on a miracle, as if a miracle would eliminate all disappointment with God. It wouldn't! . . . Miracles serve as signs pointing on to the future. They are appetizers that awaken a longing for something more, something permanent. . . . The good news at the end of Job and the good news of Easter at the end of the Gospels are previews of the good news described at the end of Revelation.

(From *Disappointment with God* by Philip Yancey)

Continued

APPLICATION Place your hope in God's eternal home, not heaven-on-earth. Read Hebrews 11:32-40 and Revelation 21:1–22:21 several times, and thank God for eternal rewards.

EXPLORATION God's Power—Psalm 8; Matthew 19:26; James 1:16-18.

Job Deplores His Birth

3 After this Job opened his mouth and cursed the day of his *birth.* 2 And
Job spoke, and said:

3 "May the day perish on which I was born,
And the night *in which* it was said,
'A male child is conceived.'
4 May that day be darkness;
May God above not seek it,
Nor the light shine upon it.
5 May darkness and the shadow of death claim it;
May a cloud settle on it;
May the blackness of the day terrify it.
6 *As for* that night, may darkness seize it;
May it not rejoice[e] among the days of the year,
May it not come into the number of the months.
7 Oh, may that night be barren!
May no joyful shout come into it!
8 May those curse it who curse the day,
Those who are ready to arouse Leviathan.
9 May the stars of its morning be dark;
May it look for light, but *have* none,
And not see the dawning of the day;
10 Because it did not shut up the doors of my *mother's* womb,
Nor hide sorrow from my eyes.

11 "Why did I not die at birth?
Why did I *not* perish when I came from the womb?
12 Why did the knees receive me?
Or why the breasts, that I should nurse?
13 For now I would have lain still and been quiet,
I would have been asleep;
Then I would have been at rest
14 With kings and counselors of the earth,
Who built ruins for themselves,
15 Or with princes who had gold,
Who filled their houses *with* silver;
16 Or *why* was I not hidden like a stillborn child,
Like infants who never saw light?
17 There the wicked cease *from* troubling,
And there the weary are at rest.
18 *There* the prisoners rest together;
They do not hear the voice of the oppressor.
19 The small and great are there,
And the servant *is* free from his master.

20 "Why is light given to him who is in misery,
And life to the bitter of soul,
21 Who long for death, but it does not *come,*
And search for it more than hidden treasures;
22 Who rejoice exceedingly,

3:6 [e] Septuagint, Syriac, Targum, and Vulgate read *be joined.*

And are glad when they can find the grave?
23 *Why is light given* to a man whose way is hidden,
And whom God has hedged in?
24 For my sighing comes before I eat,[f]
And my groanings pour out like water.
25 For the thing I greatly feared has come upon me,
And what I dreaded has happened to me.
26 I am not at ease, nor am I quiet;
I have no rest, for trouble comes."

Eliphaz: Job Has Sinned

4 Then Eliphaz the Temanite answered and said:

2 "*If* one attempts a word with you, will you become weary?
But who can withhold himself from speaking?
3 Surely you have instructed many,
And you have strengthened weak hands.
4 Your words have upheld him who was stumbling,
And you have strengthened the feeble knees;
5 But now it comes upon you, and you are weary;
It touches you, and you are troubled.
6 *Is* not your reverence your confidence?
And the integrity of your ways your hope?

7 "Remember now, who *ever* perished being innocent?
Or where were the upright *ever* cut off?
8 Even as I have seen,
Those who plow iniquity
And sow trouble reap the same.
9 By the blast of God they perish,
And by the breath of His anger they are consumed.
10 The roaring of the lion,
The voice of the fierce lion,
And the teeth of the young lions are broken.
11 The old lion perishes for lack of prey,
And the cubs of the lioness are scattered.

12 "Now a word was secretly brought to me,
And my ear received a whisper of it.
13 In disquieting thoughts from the visions of the night,
When deep sleep falls on men,
14 Fear came upon me, and trembling,
Which made all my bones shake.
15 Then a spirit passed before my face;
The hair on my body stood up.
16 It stood still,
But I could not discern its appearance.
A form *was* before my eyes;
There was silence;
Then I heard a voice *saying:*
17 'Can a mortal be more righteous than God?

3:24 *f* Literally *my bread*

Life Lesson

Job 4:1–7:21

SITUATION Job's friends failed to understand his situation and wrongly accused him of bringing his troubles upon himself through sin. Job defended himself against these accusations.

OBSERVATION Be careful in your assumptions. Don't judge too quickly, because only God knows all the details of every situation.

INSPIRATION It is overpowering to think of all the knowledge of God. In our generation, we have witnessed an enormous knowledge explosion. In science, literature, philosophy, geography, history, and every other sphere, new books pour out in seemingly endless procession. Our libraries are glutted. Specialization is the name of the game. Experts are proficient in only a small field; they can never hope to cover the spectrum. But God has full knowledge of everything in heaven and on earth, and He doles this knowledge out to people in thimblefuls. Whenever He does, these people are promptly acclaimed as discoverers.

But there is still so much we do *not* know. Though we can travel to the moon, we can't understand how a bee can fly. Though we can transplant human hearts, we can't cure the common cold. We can conquer outer space, but we cannot conquer inner space. We can make war, but we cannot make peace. We know so much, and yet we know so little. With God there are no mysteries, no insoluble problems, no puzzles. . . .

This attribute of God should have a profound effect on our lives. How we should honor the Lord as we muse on the infinite dimensions of His knowledge! How we should sing his praises!

(From *Alone in Majesty* by William MacDonald)

APPLICATION Are you knowledgeable in a certain area? Do people ask you for help, advice, or an opinion? Refuse to be proud. Use your knowledge as a gift from God for the good of others. Praise God because of this gift.

EXPLORATION Trust in God—Psalm 37:3-7; Proverbs 3:5-6; Matthew 10:16-39; Romans 11:33.

Can a man be more pure than his Maker?
18 If He puts no trust in His servants,
If He charges His angels with error,
19 How much more those who dwell in houses of clay,
Whose foundation is in the dust,
Who are crushed before a moth?
20 They are broken in pieces from morning till evening;
They perish forever, with no one regarding.
21 Does not their own excellence go away?
They die, even without wisdom.'

Eliphaz: Job Is Chastened by God

5 "Call out now;
Is there anyone who will answer you?
And to which of the holy ones will you turn?
2 For wrath kills a foolish man,
And envy slays a simple one.
3 I have seen the foolish taking root,
But suddenly I cursed his dwelling place.
4 His sons are far from safety,
They are crushed in the gate,
And *there is* no deliverer.
5 Because the hungry eat up his harvest,
Taking it even from the thorns,[g]
And a snare snatches their substance.[h]
6 For affliction does not come from the dust,
Nor does trouble spring from the ground;
7 Yet man is born to trouble,
As the sparks fly upward.

8 "But as for me, I would seek God,
And to God I would commit my cause—
9 Who does great things, and unsearchable,
Marvelous things without number.
10 He gives rain on the earth,
And sends waters on the fields.
11 He sets on high those who are lowly,
And those who mourn are lifted to safety.
12 He frustrates the devices of the crafty,
So that their hands cannot carry out their plans.
13 He catches the wise in their own craftiness,
And the counsel of the cunning comes quickly upon them.
14 They meet with darkness in the daytime,
And grope at noontime as in the night.
15 But He saves the needy from the sword,
From the mouth of the mighty,
And from their hand.
16 So the poor have hope,
And injustice shuts her mouth.

17 "Behold, happy *is* the man whom God corrects;
Therefore do not despise the chastening of the Almighty.
18 For He bruises, but He binds up;
He wounds, but His hands make whole.
19 He shall deliver you in six troubles,
Yes, in seven no evil shall touch you.
20 In famine He shall redeem you from death,
And in war from the power of the sword.
21 You shall be hidden from the scourge of the tongue,
And you shall not be afraid of destruction when it comes.
22 You shall laugh at destruction and famine,
And you shall not be afraid of the beasts of the earth.
23 For you shall have a covenant with the stones of the field,
And the beasts of the field shall be at peace with you.
24 You shall know that your tent *is* in peace;
You shall visit your dwelling and find nothing amiss.
25 You shall also know that your descendants *shall be* many,
And your offspring like the grass of the earth.
26 You shall come to the grave at a full age,
As a sheaf of grain ripens in its season.
27 Behold, this we have searched out;
It *is* true.
Hear it, and know for yourself."

Job: My Complaint Is Just

6 Then Job answered and said:
2 "Oh, that my grief were fully weighed,
And my calamity laid with it on the scales!
3 For then it would be heavier than the sand of the sea—
Therefore my words have been rash.
4 For the arrows of the Almighty *are* within me;
My spirit drinks in their poison;
The terrors of God are arrayed against me.
5 Does the wild donkey bray when it has grass,
Or does the ox low over its fodder?

5:5 [g] Septuagint reads *They shall not be taken from evil men;* Vulgate reads *And the armed man shall take him by violence.* [h] Septuagint reads *The might shall draw them off;* Vulgate reads *And the thirsty shall drink up their riches.*

6 Can flavorless food be eaten without salt?
Or is there *any* taste in the white of an egg?
7 My soul refuses to touch them;
They *are* as loathsome food to me.

8 "Oh, that I might have my request,
That God would grant *me* the thing
that I long for!
9 That it would please God to crush me,
That He would loose His hand and cut me off!
10 Then I would still have comfort;
Though in anguish I would exult,
He will not spare;
For I have not concealed the words
of the Holy One.

11 "What strength do I have, that I should hope?
And what *is* my end, that I should
prolong my life?
12 *Is* my strength the strength of stones?
Or is my flesh bronze?
13 *Is* my help not within me?
And is success driven from me?

14 "To him who is afflicted, kindness *should be
shown* by his friend,
Even though he forsakes the
fear of the Almighty.
15 My brothers have dealt deceitfully like a brook,
Like the streams of the brooks that pass away,
16 Which are dark because of the ice,
And into which the snow vanishes.
17 When it is warm, they cease to flow;
When it is hot, they vanish from their place.
18 The paths of their way turn aside,
They go nowhere and perish.
19 The caravans of Tema look,
The travelers of Sheba hope for them.
20 They are disappointed because
they were confident;
They come there and are confused.
21 For now you are nothing,
You see terror and are afraid.
22 Did I ever say, 'Bring *something* to me'?
Or, 'Offer a bribe for me from your wealth'?
23 Or, 'Deliver me from the enemy's hand'?
Or, 'Redeem me from the hand of oppressors'?

24 "Teach me, and I will hold my tongue;
Cause me to understand wherein I have erred.
25 How forceful are right words!
But what does your arguing prove?
26 Do you intend to rebuke *my* words,
And the speeches of a desperate one,
which are as wind?
27 Yes, you overwhelm the fatherless,
And you undermine your friend.
28 Now therefore, be pleased to look at me;
For I would never lie to your face.
29 Yield now, let there be no injustice!
Yes, concede, my righteousness still stands!
30 Is there injustice on my tongue?
Cannot my taste discern the unsavory?

Job: My Suffering Is Comfortless

7 "*Is there* not a time of hard service for man on
earth?
Are not his days also like the days
of a hired man?
2 Like a servant who earnestly
desires the shade,
And like a hired man who eagerly
looks for his wages,
3 So I have been allotted months of futility,
And wearisome nights have been
appointed to me.
4 When I lie down, I say, 'When shall I arise,
And the night be ended?'
For I have had my fill of tossing till dawn.
5 My flesh is caked with worms and dust,
My skin is cracked and breaks out afresh.

6 "My days are swifter than a weaver's shuttle,
And are spent without hope.
7 Oh, remember that my life *is* a breath!
My eye will never again see good.
8 The eye of him who sees me will
see me no *more;*
While your *eyes* are upon me, I
shall no longer *be.*
9 *As* the cloud disappears and vanishes away,
So he who goes down to the grave does not
come up.
10 He shall never return to his house,
Nor shall his place know him anymore.

11 "Therefore I will not restrain my mouth;
I will speak in the anguish of my spirit;
I will complain in the bitterness of my soul.
12 *Am* I a sea, or a sea serpent,
That You set a guard over me?
13 When I say, 'My bed will comfort me,
My couch will ease my complaint,'
14 Then You scare me with dreams
And terrify me with visions,

LIFE LESSON

Job 8:1–10:22

SITUATION Bildad told Job that his children had died because they sinned against God. Bildad believed that if Job repented, God would restore his wealth.

OBSERVATION Bildad's ignorance proved that not all advice is worth heeding. Be careful to choose counselors who can listen as well as advise.

INSPIRATION Some time ago Denalyn [my wife] was gone for a couple of days and left me alone with the girls. Though the time was not without the typical children's quarrels and occasional misbehavior, it went fine.

"How were the girls?" Denalyn asked when she got home.

"Good. No problem at all."

Jenna overheard my response. "We weren't good, Daddy," she objected. "We fought once, we didn't do what you said once. We weren't good. How can you say we were good?"

Jenna and I had different perceptions of what pleases a father. She thought it depended upon what she did. It didn't. We think the same about God. We think his love rises and falls with our performance. It doesn't. I don't love Jenna for what she does. I love her for whose she is. She is mine.

15 So that my soul chooses strangling
And death rather than my body.[i]
16 I loathe *my life;*
I would not live forever.
Let me alone,
For my days *are but* a breath.

17 "What *is* man, that You should exalt him,
That You should set Your heart on him,
18 That You should visit him every morning,
And test him every moment?
19 How long?
Will You not look away from me,
And let me alone till I swallow my saliva?
20 Have I sinned?
What have I done to You, O watcher of men?
Why have You set me as Your target,
So that I am a burden to myself?[j]
21 Why then do You not pardon my transgression,
And take away my iniquity?
For now I will lie down in the dust,
And You will seek me diligently,
But I *will* no longer *be.*"

Bildad: Job Should Repent

8 Then Bildad the Shuhite answered and said:

2 "How long will you speak these *things,*
And the words of your mouth *be like* a strong wind?
3 Does God subvert judgment?
Or does the Almighty pervert justice?
4 If your sons have sinned against Him,
He has cast them away for their transgression.
5 If you would earnestly seek God
And make your supplication to the Almighty,
6 If you *were* pure and upright,
Surely now He would awake for you,
And prosper your rightful dwelling place.
7 Though your beginning was small,
Yet your latter end would increase abundantly.

8 "For inquire, please, of the former age,
And consider the things discovered by their fathers;
9 For we *were born* yesterday, and know nothing,
Because our days on earth *are* a shadow.
10 Will they not teach you and tell you,
And utter words from their heart?

11 "Can the papyrus grow up without a marsh?
Can the reeds flourish without water?

7:15 [i] Literally *my bones*
7:20 [j] Following Masoretic Text, Targum, and Vulgate; Septuagint and Jewish tradition read *to You.*

12 While it *is* yet green *and* not cut down,
It withers before any *other* plant.
13 So *are* the paths of all who forget God;
And the hope of the hypocrite shall perish,
14 Whose confidence shall be cut off,
And whose trust *is* a spider's web.
15 He leans on his house, but it does not stand.
He holds it fast, but it does not endure.
16 He grows green in the sun,
And his branches spread out in his garden.
17 His roots wrap around the rock heap,
And look for a place in the stones.
18 If he is destroyed from his place,
Then *it* will deny him, *saying*, 'I have not seen you.'

19 "Behold, this is the joy of His way,
And out of the earth others will grow.
20 Behold, God will not cast away the blameless,
Nor will He uphold the evildoers.
21 He will yet fill your mouth with laughing,
And your lips with rejoicing.
22 Those who hate you will be clothed with shame,
And the dwelling place of the wicked
will come to nothing."[k]

Job: There Is No Mediator

9 Then Job answered and said:

2 "Truly I know *it is* so,
But how can a man be righteous before God?
3 If one wished to contend with Him,
He could not answer Him one time out of a thousand.
4 *God is* wise in heart and mighty in strength.
Who has hardened *himself* against Him and prospered?
5 He removes the mountains, and they do not know
When He overturns them in His anger;
6 He shakes the earth out of its place,
And its pillars tremble;
7 He commands the sun, and it does not rise;
He seals off the stars;
8 He alone spreads out the heavens,
And treads on the waves of the sea;
9 He made the Bear, Orion, and the Pleiades,
And the chambers of the south;
10 He does great things past finding out,
Yes, wonders without number.
11 If He goes by me, I do not see *Him;*
If He moves past, I do not perceive Him;
12 If He takes away, who can hinder Him?
Who can say to Him, 'What are You doing?'

God loves you for the same reason. He loves you for whose you are, you are his child. It was this love that pursued the Israelites. It was this love that sent the prophets. It was this love which wrapped itself in human flesh and descended the birth canal of Mary. It was this love which walked the hard trails of Galilee and spoke to the hard hearts of the religious.

"This is not normal, Lord GOD," David exclaimed as he considered God's love. You are right, David. God's love is not normal love. It's not normal to love a murderer and adulterer, but God did when he loved David. It isn't normal to love a man who takes his eyes off you, but such was God's love for Solomon. It isn't normal to love people who love stone idols more than they love you, but God did when he refused to give up on Israel.

(From *And the Angels Were Silent* by Max Lucado)

APPLICATION Do you wonder if God really cares? Do you feel like he has left you to face your problems alone? Trust God to work in your life day by day. Let God be your source of security.

EXPLORATION Faithfulness of God—2 Kings 13:23; Isaiah 42:16; Hosea 2:19.

8:22 *k* Literally *will not be*

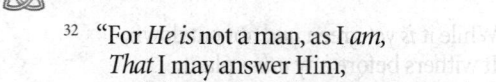

13 God will not withdraw His anger,
The allies of the proud[l] lie prostrate beneath Him.

14 "How then can I answer Him,
And choose my words *to reason* with Him?
15 For though I were righteous, I could not answer Him;
I would beg mercy of my Judge.
16 If I called and He answered me,
I would not believe that He was listening to my voice.
17 For He crushes me with a tempest,
And multiplies my wounds without cause.
18 He will not allow me to catch my breath,
But fills me with bitterness.
19 If *it is a matter* of strength, indeed *He is* strong;
And if of justice, who will appoint my day *in court?*
20 Though I were righteous, my own mouth would condemn me;
Though I *were* blameless, it would prove me perverse.

21 "I am blameless, yet I do not know myself;
I despise my life.
22 It *is* all one *thing;*
Therefore I say, 'He destroys the blameless and the wicked.'
23 If the scourge slays suddenly,
He laughs at the plight of the innocent.
24 The earth is given into the hand of the wicked.
He covers the faces of its judges.
If it is not *He,* who else could it be?

25 "Now my days are swifter than a runner;
They flee away, they see no good.
26 They pass by like swift ships,
Like an eagle swooping on its prey.
27 If I say, 'I will forget my complaint,
I will put off my sad face and wear a smile,'
28 I am afraid of all my sufferings;
I know that You will not hold me innocent.
29 *If* I am condemned,
Why then do I labor in vain?
30 If I wash myself with snow water,
And cleanse my hands with soap,
31 Yet You will plunge me into the pit,
And my own clothes will abhor me.

32 "For *He is* not a man, as I *am,*
That I may answer Him,
And that we should go to court together.
33 Nor is there any mediator between us,
Who may lay his hand on us both.
34 Let Him take His rod away from me,
And do not let dread of Him terrify me.
35 *Then* I would speak and not fear Him,
But it is not so with me.

Job: I Would Plead with God

10 "My soul loathes my life;
I will give free course to my complaint,
I will speak in the bitterness of my soul.
2 I will say to God, 'Do not condemn me;
Show me why You contend with me.
3 *Does it* seem good to You that You should oppress,
That You should despise the work of Your hands,
And smile on the counsel of the wicked?
4 Do You have eyes of flesh?
Or do You see as man sees?
5 *Are* Your days like the days of a mortal man?
Are Your years like the days of a mighty man,
6 That You should seek for my iniquity
And search out my sin,
7 Although You know that I am not wicked,
And *there is* no one who can deliver from Your hand?

8 'Your hands have made me and fashioned me,
An intricate unity;
Yet You would destroy me.
9 Remember, I pray, that You have made me like clay.
And will You turn me into dust again?
10 Did You not pour me out like milk,
And curdle me like cheese,
11 Clothe me with skin and flesh,
And knit me together with bones and sinews?
12 You have granted me life and favor,
And Your care has preserved my spirit.

13 'And these *things* You have hidden in Your heart;
I know that this *was* with You:
14 If I sin, then You mark me,
And will not acquit me of my iniquity.
15 If I am wicked, woe to me;
Even *if* I am righteous, I cannot lift up my head.
I am full of disgrace;

9:13 [l] Hebrew *rahab*

See my misery!
16 If *my head* is exalted,
You hunt me like a fierce lion,
And again You show Yourself awesome against me.
17 You renew Your witnesses against me,
And increase Your indignation toward me;
Changes and war are *ever* with me.

18 'Why then have You brought me out of the womb?
Oh, that I had perished and no eye had seen me!
19 I would have been as though I had not been.
I would have been carried from the womb to the grave.
20 Are not my days few?
Cease! Leave me alone, that I may take a little comfort,
21 Before I go *to the place from which* I shall not return,
To the land of darkness and the shadow of death,
22 A land as dark as darkness *itself*,
As the shadow of death, without any order,
Where even the light *is* like darkness.' "

Zophar Urges Job to Repent

11 Then Zophar the Naamathite answered and said:

2 "Should not the multitude of words be answered?
And should a man full of talk be vindicated?
3 Should your empty talk make men hold their peace?
And when you mock, should no one rebuke you?
4 For you have said,
'My doctrine *is* pure,
And I am clean in your eyes.'
5 But oh, that God would speak,
And open His lips against you,
6 That He would show you the secrets of wisdom!
For *they would* double *your* prudence.
Know therefore that God exacts from you
Less than your iniquity *deserves*.

7 "Can you search out the deep things of God?
Can you find out the limits of the Almighty?
8 *They are* higher than heaven— what can you do?
Deeper than Sheol— what can you know?
9 Their measure *is* longer than the earth
And broader than the sea.

10 "If He passes by, imprisons, and
gathers *to judgment*,
Then who can hinder Him?
11 For He knows deceitful men;
He sees wickedness also.
Will He not then consider *it*?
12 For an empty-headed man will be wise,
When a wild donkey's colt is born a man.

LIFE LESSON

Job 11:1-20

SITUATION Unsympathetic, Zophar tried to convince Job that his troubles stemmed from a hidden sin. Zophar believed that God was punishing Job for this sin.

OBSERVATION No one can claim complete understanding of God's ways.

INSPIRATION Once there was an old man who lived in a tiny village. Although poor, he was envied by all, for he owned a beautiful white horse. Even the king coveted his treasure. A horse like this had never been seen before—such was its splendor, its majesty, its strength.

People offered fabulous prices for the steed, but the old man always refused. "This horse is not a horse to me," he would tell them. "It is a person. How could you sell a person? He is a friend, not a possession. How could you sell a friend?" The man was poor and the temptation was great. But he never sold the horse.

One morning he found that the horse was not in the stable. All the village came to see him. "You old fool," they scoffed, "we told you that someone would steal your horse. We warned you that you would be robbed. You are so poor. How could you ever hope to protect such a valuable animal? It would have been better to have sold him. You could have gotten whatever price you wanted. No amount would have been too high. Now the horse is gone, and you've been cursed with misfortune."

The old man responded, "Don't speak too quickly. Say only that the horse is not in the stable. That is all we know; the rest is judgment. If I've been cursed or not, how can you know? How can you judge?"

The people contested, "Don't make us out to be fools! We may not be philosophers, but great philosophy is not needed. The simple fact that your horse is gone is a curse."

The old man spoke again. "All I know is that the stable is empty, and the horse is gone. The rest I don't know. Whether it be a curse or a blessing, I can't say. All we can see is a fragment. Who can say what will come next?"

Continued

The people of the village laughed. They thought that the man was crazy. They had always thought he was a fool; if he wasn't, he would have sold the horse and lived off the money. But instead, he was a poor woodcutter, an old man still cutting firewood and dragging it out of the forest and selling it. He lived hand to mouth in the misery of poverty. Now he had proven that he was, indeed, a fool.

After fifteen days, the horse returned. He hadn't been stolen; he had run away into the forest. Not only had he returned, he had brought a dozen wild horses with him. Once again the village people gathered around the woodcutter and spoke. "Old man, you were right and we were wrong. What we thought was a curse was a blessing. Please forgive us."

The man responded, "Once again, you go too far. Say only that the horse is back. State only that a dozen horses returned with him, but don't judge. How do you know if this is a blessing or not? You see only a fragment. Unless you know the whole story, how can you judge? You read only one page of a book. Can you judge the whole book? You read only one word of a phrase. Can you understand the entire phrase?

"Life is so vast, yet you judge all of life with one page or one word. All you have is a fragment! Don't say that this is a blessing. No one knows. I am content with what I know. I am not perturbed by what I don't."

"Maybe the old man is right," they said to one another. So they said little. But down deep, they knew he was wrong. They knew it was a blessing. Twelve wild horses had returned with one horse. With a little bit of work, the animals could be broken and trained and sold for much money.

The old man had a son, an only son. The young man began to break the wild horses. After a few days, he fell from one of the horses and broke both legs. Once again the villagers gathered around the old man and cast their judgments.

"You were right," they said. "You proved you were right. The dozen horses were not a blessing. They

13 "If you would prepare your heart,
And stretch out your hands toward Him;
14 If iniquity *were* in your hand, *and you* put it far away,
And would not let wickedness dwell in your tents;
15 Then surely you could lift up your face without spot;
Yes, you could be steadfast, and not fear;
16 Because you would forget *your* misery,
And remember *it* as waters *that have* passed away,
17 And *your* life would be brighter than noonday.
Though you were dark, you would be like the morning.
18 And you would be secure, because there is hope;
Yes, you would dig *around you, and* take your rest in safety.
19 You would also lie down, and no one would make *you* afraid;
Yes, many would court your favor.
20 But the eyes of the wicked will fail,
And they shall not escape,
And their hope—loss of life!"

Job Answers His Critics

12 Then Job answered and said:

2 "No doubt you *are* the people,
And wisdom will die with you!
3 But I have understanding as well as you;
I *am* not inferior to you.
Indeed, who does not *know* such things as these?

4 "I am one mocked by his friends,
Who called on God, and He answered him,
The just and blameless *who is* ridiculed.
5 A lamp[m] is despised in the thought of one who is at ease;
It is made ready for those whose feet slip.
6 The tents of robbers prosper,
And those who provoke God are secure—
In what God provides by His hand.

7 "But now ask the beasts, and they will teach you;
And the birds of the air, and they will tell you;
8 Or speak to the earth, and it will teach you;
And the fish of the sea will explain to you.
9 Who among all these does not know
That the hand of the LORD has done this,
10 In whose hand *is* the life of every living thing,
And the breath of all mankind?
11 Does not the ear test words
And the mouth taste its food?
12 Wisdom *is* with aged men,
And with length of days, understanding.

13 "With Him *are* wisdom and strength,
He has counsel and understanding.

12:5 [m] Or *disaster*

14 If He breaks *a thing* down, it cannot be rebuilt;
If He imprisons a man, there can be no release.
15 If He withholds the waters, they dry up;
If He sends them out, they overwhelm the earth.
16 With Him *are* strength and prudence.
The deceived and the deceiver *are* His.
17 He leads counselors away plundered,
And makes fools of the judges.
18 He loosens the bonds of kings,
And binds their waist with a belt.
19 He leads princes[n] away plundered,
And overthrows the mighty.
20 He deprives the trusted ones of speech,
And takes away the discernment of the elders.
21 He pours contempt on princes,
And disarms the mighty.
22 He uncovers deep things out of darkness,
And brings the shadow of death to light.
23 He makes nations great, and destroys them;
He enlarges nations, and guides them.
24 He takes away the understanding[o] of the chiefs of the people of the earth,
And makes them wander in a pathless wilderness.
25 They grope in the dark without light,
And He makes them stagger like a drunken *man*.

13 "Behold, my eye has seen all *this*,
My ear has heard and understood it.
2 What you know, I also know;
I *am* not inferior to you.
3 But I would speak to the Almighty,
And I desire to reason with God.
4 But you forgers of lies,
You *are* all worthless physicians.
5 Oh, that you would be silent,
And it would be your wisdom!
6 Now hear my reasoning,
And heed the pleadings of my lips.
7 Will you speak wickedly for God,
And talk deceitfully for Him?
8 Will you show partiality for Him?
Will you contend for God?
9 Will it be well when He searches you out?
Or can you mock Him as one mocks a man?
10 He will surely rebuke you
If you secretly show partiality.
11 Will not His excellence make you afraid,
And the dread of Him fall upon you?

12:19 [n] Literally *priests*, but not in a technical sense
12:24 [o] Literally *heart*

were a curse. Your only son has broken his legs, and now in your old age you have no one to help you. Now you are poorer than ever."

The old man spoke again. "You people are obsessed with judging. Don't go so far. Say only that my son broke his legs. Who knows if it is a blessing or a curse? No one knows. We only have a fragment. Life comes in fragments."

It so happened that a few weeks later the country engaged in war against a neighboring country. All the young men of the village were required to join the army. Only the son of the old man was excluded, because he was injured. Once again the people gathered around the old man, crying and screaming because their sons had been taken. There was little chance that they would return. The enemy was strong, and the war would be a losing struggle. They would never see their sons again.

"You were right, old man," they wept. "God knows you were right. This proves it. Your son's accident was a blessing. His legs may be broken, but at least he is with you. Our sons are gone forever."

The old man spoke again. "It is impossible to talk with you. You always draw conclusions. No one knows. Say only this. Your sons had to go to war, and mine did not. No one knows if it is a blessing or a curse. No one is wise enough to know. Only God knows."

(From *In the Eye of the Storm* by Max Lucado)

APPLICATION When someone else suffers, ask God for wisdom to be an instrument of healing. Remember that no matter what you feel, God is always good!

EXPLORATION God Is Incomprehensible—Deuteronomy 29:29; Ecclesiastes 3:11; Isaiah 40:12-14; 55:8-9; Proverbs 25:2; 1 Corinthians 2:16. God Is Compassionate—Exodus 22:27; 34:6; Psalm 65:3; 78:38; 103:3; 106:1.

12 Your platitudes *are* proverbs of ashes,
Your defenses are defenses of clay.

13 "Hold your peace with me, and let me speak,
Then let come on me what *may!*
14 Why do I take my flesh in my teeth,
And put my life in my hands?
15 Though He slay me, yet will I trust Him.
Even so, I will defend my own ways before Him.
16 He also *shall* be my salvation,
For a hypocrite could not come before Him.
17 Listen carefully to my speech,
And to my declaration with your ears.
18 See now, I have prepared *my* case,
I know that I shall be vindicated.
19 Who *is* he *who* will contend with me?
If now I hold my tongue, I perish.

Job's Despondent Prayer

20 "Only two *things* do not do to me,
Then I will not hide myself from You:
21 Withdraw Your hand far from me,
And let not the dread of You make me afraid.
22 Then call, and I will answer;
Or let me speak, then You respond to me.
23 How many *are* my iniquities and sins?
Make me know my transgression and my sin.
24 Why do You hide Your face,
And regard me as Your enemy?
25 Will You frighten a leaf driven to and fro?
And will You pursue dry stubble?
26 For You write bitter things against me,
And make me inherit the iniquities
of my youth.
27 You put my feet in the stocks,
And watch closely all my paths.
You set a limit[p] for the soles of my feet.

28 "*Man*[q] decays like a rotten thing,
Like a garment that is moth-eaten.

14 "Man *who is* born of woman
Is of few days and full of trouble.
2 He comes forth like a flower and fades away;
He flees like a shadow and does not continue.
3 And do You open Your eyes on such a one,
And bring me[r] to judgment with Yourself?
4 Who can bring a clean *thing* out of an unclean?
No one!
5 Since his days *are* determined,
The number of his months *is* with You;
You have appointed his limits, so that he
cannot pass.
6 Look away from him that he may rest,
Till like a hired man he finishes his day.

7 "For there is hope for a tree,
If it is cut down, that it will sprout again,
And that its tender shoots will not cease.
8 Though its root may grow old in the earth,
And its stump may die in the ground,
9 *Yet* at the scent of water it will bud
And bring forth branches like a plant.
10 But man dies and is laid away;
Indeed he breathes his last
And where *is* he?
11 *As* water disappears from the sea,
And a river becomes parched and dries up,
12 So man lies down and does not rise.
Till the heavens *are* no more,
They will not awake
Nor be roused from their sleep.

13 "Oh, that You would hide me in the grave,
That You would conceal me until
Your wrath is past,
That You would appoint me a set time,
and remember me!
14 If a man dies, shall he live *again?*
All the days of my hard service I will wait,
Till my change comes.
15 You shall call, and I will answer You;
You shall desire the work of Your hands.
16 For now You number my steps,
But do not watch over my sin.
17 My transgression *is* sealed up in a bag,
And You cover[s] my iniquity.

18 "But *as* a mountain falls *and* crumbles away,
And *as* a rock is moved from its place;
19 *As* water wears away stones,
And as torrents wash away the soil of the earth;
So You destroy the hope of man.
20 You prevail forever against him,
and he passes on;
You change his countenance and send him away.
21 His sons come to honor, and he
does not know *it;*

13:27 [p] Literally *inscribe a print*
13:28 [q] Literally *He*
14:3 [r] Septuagint, Syriac, and Vulgate read *him.*
14:17 [s] Literally *plaster over*

They are brought low, and he does not perceive *it*.
22 But his flesh will be in pain over it,
And his soul will mourn over it."

Eliphaz Accuses Job of Folly

15 Then Eliphaz the Temanite answered and said:
2 "Should a wise man answer with empty knowledge,
And fill himself with the east wind?
3 Should he reason with unprofitable talk,
Or by speeches with which he can do no good?
4 Yes, you cast off fear,
And restrain prayer before God.
5 For your iniquity teaches your mouth,
And you choose the tongue of the crafty.
6 Your own mouth condemns you, and not I;
Yes, your own lips testify against you.

7 "*Are* you the first man *who* was born?
Or were you made before the hills?
8 Have you heard the counsel of God?
Do you limit wisdom to yourself?
9 What do you know that we do not know?
What do you understand that *is* not in us?
10 Both the gray-haired and the aged *are* among us,
Much older than your father.
11 *Are* the consolations of God too small for you,
And the word *spoken* gently[t] with you?
12 Why does your heart carry you away,
And what do your eyes wink at,
13 That you turn your spirit against God,
And let *such* words go out of your mouth?

14 "What *is* man, that he could be pure?
And *he who is* born of a woman, that he could be righteous?
15 If *God* puts no trust in His saints,
And the heavens are not pure in His sight,
16 How much less man, *who is* abominable and filthy,
Who drinks iniquity like water!

17 "I will tell you, hear me;
What I have seen I will declare,
18 What wise men have told,
Not hiding *anything received* from their fathers,
19 To whom alone the land was given,
And no alien passed among them:
20 The wicked man writhes with pain all *his* days,
And the number of years is hidden from the oppressor.
21 Dreadful sounds *are* in his ears;
In prosperity the destroyer comes upon him.
22 He does not believe that he will return from darkness,

15:11 [t] Septuagint reads *a secret thing*.

LIFE LESSON

Job 15:1–17:16

SITUATION Job's four friends gave their opinions concerning the reason for his troubles. Eliphaz argued that suffering resulted from sin. Job answered, hurt and grieved by his friend's harsh words.

OBSERVATION Suffering is never easy to understand. Because he assumed that suffering resulted from sin, Eliphaz could not comfort his friend.

INSPIRATION Some people see sin in every sickness. They make their friends miserable by probing for hidden sins whenever suffering enters their lives. Although there may be truth in their questioning, it also could be a cruel response to another's time of pain. They are like Job's so-called friends who pointed out all of his wrongs. Job called them "miserable comforters."...

It is unkind to attribute every accident, every illness and sorrow to God's punishment for wrong behavior. It is appalling how many Christians approach suffering friends with that principle. They visit first with words of comfort, and then leave a load of guilt behind ("What could you have done to deserve this?") or pious advice ("Perhaps you need to pray harder").

Suffering people can be tormented with questions of guilt; however, if all suffering is punishment for sin, then God's signals must be mixed, for accidents occur at random and disease strikes without any relationship to a person's moral or immoral lifestyle.

God's teaching does not attribute all suffering to sin or punishment for human mistakes. I have no right to tell a suffering person that it is because he sinned that his child died, or that he has cancer, or that his house burned.

In John 9, the followers of Jesus pointed to a man born blind and asked, "Who sinned, this man or his parents?" Jesus told them that neither the man nor his parents sinned, "But this happened so that the work of God might be displayed in his life." The disciples wanted to look back, to probe into the

Continued

behavior of the blind man or his parents, but Jesus pointed them to the future and the hope that even suffering can be used to glorify God.
(From *Hope for the Troubled Heart* by Billy Graham)

APPLICATION Who among your friends, family, or co-workers needs comforting? Call, write a note, or pay a visit to let that person know you care.

EXPLORATION Suffering—John 9:2-3; Romans 8:18; Philippians 1:29; Hebrews 2:18; 1 Peter 5:10.

For a sword is waiting for him.
23 He wanders about for bread, *saying,* 'Where *is it?*'
He knows that a day of darkness is ready at his hand.
24 Trouble and anguish make him afraid;
They overpower him, like a king ready for battle.
25 For he stretches out his hand against God,
And acts defiantly against the Almighty,
26 Running stubbornly against Him
With his strong, embossed shield.

27 "Though he has covered his face with his fatness,
And made *his* waist heavy with fat,
28 He dwells in desolate cities,
In houses which no one inhabits,
Which are destined to become ruins.
29 He will not be rich,
Nor will his wealth continue,
Nor will his possessions overspread the earth.
30 He will not depart from darkness;
The flame will dry out his branches,
And by the breath of His mouth he will go away.
31 Let him not trust in futile *things,* deceiving himself,
For futility will be his reward.
32 It will be accomplished before his time,
And his branch will not be green.
33 He will shake off his unripe grape like a vine,
And cast off his blossom like an olive tree.
34 For the company of hypocrites *will be* barren,
And fire will consume the tents of bribery.
35 They conceive trouble and bring forth futility;
Their womb prepares deceit."

Job Reproaches His Pitiless Friends

16 Then Job answered and said:

2 "I have heard many such things;
Miserable comforters *are* you all!
3 Shall words of wind have an end?
Or what provokes you that you answer?
4 I also could speak as you *do,*
If your soul were in my soul's place.
I could heap up words against you,
And shake my head at you;
5 *But* I would strengthen you with my mouth,
And the comfort of my lips would relieve *your grief.*

6 "Though I speak, my grief is not relieved;
And *if* I remain silent, how am I eased?
7 But now He has worn me out;
You have made desolate all my company.
8 You have shriveled me up,
And it is a witness *against me;*

My leanness rises up against me
And bears witness to my face.
9 He tears *me* in His wrath, and hates me;
He gnashes at me with His teeth;
My adversary sharpens His gaze on me.
10 They gape at me with their mouth,
They strike me reproachfully on the cheek,
They gather together against me.
11 God has delivered me to the ungodly,
And turned me over to the hands of the wicked.
12 I was at ease, but He has shattered me;
He also has taken *me* by my neck, and shaken
me to pieces;
He has set me up for His target,
13 His archers surround me.
He pierces my heart[u] and does not pity;
He pours out my gall on the ground.
14 He breaks me with wound upon wound;
He runs at me like a warrior.[v]

15 "I have sewn sackcloth over my skin,
And laid my head[w] in the dust.
16 My face is flushed from weeping,
And on my eyelids *is* the shadow of death;
17 Although no violence *is* in my hands,
And my prayer *is* pure.

18 "O earth, do not cover my blood,
And let my cry have no *resting* place!
19 Surely even now my witness *is* in heaven,
And my evidence *is* on high.
20 My friends scorn me;
My eyes pour out *tears* to God.
21 Oh, that one might plead for a man with God,
As a man *pleads* for his neighbor!
22 For when a few years are finished,
I shall go the way of no return.

Job Prays for Relief

17 "My spirit is broken,
My days are extinguished,
The grave *is ready* for me.
2 *Are* not mockers with me?
And does not my eye dwell on their provocation?

3 "Now put down a pledge for me with Yourself.
Who *is* he *who* will shake hands with me?
4 For You have hidden their heart
from understanding;
Therefore You will not exalt *them*.
5 He who speaks flattery to *his* friends,
Even the eyes of his children will fail.

6 "But He has made me a byword of the people,
And I have become one in whose face men spit.
7 My eye has also grown dim because of sorrow,
And all my members *are* like shadows.
8 Upright *men* are astonished at this,
And the innocent stirs himself up
against the hypocrite.
9 Yet the righteous will hold to his way,
And he who has clean hands will be stronger
and stronger.

10 "But please, come back again, all of you,[x]
For I shall not find *one* wise *man* among you.
11 My days are past,
My purposes are broken off,
Even the thoughts of my heart.
12 They change the night into day;
'The light *is* near,' *they say*, in the
face of darkness.
13 If I wait *for* the grave *as* my house,
If I make my bed in the darkness,
14 If I say to corruption, 'You *are* my father,'
And to the worm, 'You *are* my
mother and my sister,'
15 Where then *is* my hope?
As for my hope, who can see it?
16 *Will* they go down to the gates of Sheol?
Shall *we have* rest together in the dust?"

Bildad: The Wicked Are Punished

18 Then Bildad the Shuhite answered and said:

2 "How long *till* you put an end to words?
Gain understanding, and afterward
we will speak.
3 Why are we counted as beasts,
And regarded as stupid in your sight?
4 You who tear yourself in anger,
Shall the earth be forsaken for you?
Or shall the rock be removed from its place?

5 "The light of the wicked indeed goes out,
And the flame of his fire does not shine.
6 The light is dark in his tent,
And his lamp beside him is put out.

16:13 [u] Literally *kidneys*
16:14 [v] Vulgate reads *giant.*
16:15 [w] Literally *horn*
17:10 [x] Following some Hebrew manuscripts, Septuagint, Syriac, and Vulgate; Masoretic Text and Targum read *all of them*.

LIFE LESSON

Job 18:1–19:29

SITUATION Because Job rejected his advice, Bildad grew frustrated. In an effort to convince Job, he told of the horrible fate of sinners. Job firmly believed that in the end God would vindicate him because of his innocence.

OBSERVATION Job listened to Bildad, even though he knew Bildad was incorrect. Only when Bildad was finished speaking did Job answer.

INSPIRATION Let me introduce you to several kinds of people who express various forms of destructive criticism. First are the blamers. They avoid accepting responsibility for their actions by criticizing other people or blaming past experiences which cannot be changed or undone. . . .

Another negative critic is the hurtful joker. Humor is a positive method of relating to others. . . . But hurtful jokers make others the butt of their humor. They specialize in laughing at people instead of laughing with them. . . .

A third kind of critic is the fault-finder. This person seems to have an insatiable need to point out others' defects. . . . And do you know what is so maddening about this person? He usually does what he does with a smile, saying, "I'm just trying to be helpful." . . .

Another kind of critic at large in the world today is the cannibal. These people don't criticize in a joking manner or settle for mere nitpicking. They go for the jugular. . . . They attack through the most severe forms of personal criticism and put downs with complete disregard for the feelings of others. . . .

Destructive critics may say they are only interested in remodeling you into a better person by sharing a little constructive criticism. But in reality, [these] critics . . . are intent on putting you down, tearing you down, punishing you, and manipulating you. Their brand of criticism does not nourish; it poisons. . . .

7 The steps of his strength are shortened,
And his own counsel casts him down.
8 For he is cast into a net by his own feet,
And he walks into a snare.
9 The net takes *him* by the heel,
And a snare lays hold of him.
10 A noose *is* hidden for him on the ground,
And a trap for him in the road.
11 Terrors frighten him on every side,
And drive him to his feet.
12 His strength is starved,
And destruction *is* ready at his side.
13 It devours patches of his skin;
The firstborn of death devours his limbs.
14 He is uprooted from the shelter of his tent,
And they parade him before the king of terrors.
15 They dwell in his tent *who are* none of his;
Brimstone is scattered on his dwelling.
16 His roots are dried out below,
And his branch withers above.
17 The memory of him perishes from the earth,
And he has no name among the renowned.[y]
18 He is driven from light into darkness,
And chased out of the world.
19 He has neither son nor posterity among his people,
Nor any remaining in his dwellings.
20 Those in the west are astonished at his day,
As those in the east are frightened.
21 Surely such *are* the dwellings of the wicked,
And this *is* the place *of him who* does not know God."

Job Trusts in His Redeemer

19 Then Job answered and said:

2 "How long will you torment my soul,
And break me in pieces with words?
3 These ten times you have reproached me;
You are not ashamed *that* you have wronged me.[z]
4 And if indeed I have erred,
My error remains with me.
5 If indeed you exalt *yourselves* against me,
And plead my disgrace against me,
6 Know then that God has wronged me,
And has surrounded me with His net.

7 "If I cry out concerning wrong, I am not heard.
If I cry aloud, *there is* no justice.
8 He has fenced up my way, so that I cannot pass;
And He has set darkness in my paths.

18:17 [y] Literally *before the outside,* meaning distinguished, famous
19:3 [z] A Jewish tradition reads *make yourselves strange to me.*

9 He has stripped me of my glory,
And taken the crown *from* my head.
10 He breaks me down on every side,
And I am gone;
My hope He has uprooted like a tree.
11 He has also kindled His wrath against me,
And He counts me as *one of* His enemies.
12 His troops come together
And build up their road against me;
They encamp all around my tent.

13 "He has removed my brothers far from me,
And my acquaintances are completely
estranged from me.
14 My relatives have failed,
And my close friends have forgotten me.
15 Those who dwell in my house,
and my maidservants,
Count me as a stranger;
I am an alien in their sight.
16 I call my servant, but he gives no answer;
I beg him with my mouth.
17 My breath is offensive to my wife,
And I am repulsive to the children of my own body.
18 Even young children despise me;
I arise, and they speak against me.
19 All my close friends abhor me,
And those whom I love have turned against me.
20 My bone clings to my skin and to my flesh,
And I have escaped by the skin of my teeth.

21 "Have pity on me, have pity on me, O you my friends,
For the hand of God has struck me!
22 Why do you persecute me as God *does,*
And are not satisfied with my flesh?

23 "Oh, that my words were written!
Oh, that they were inscribed in a book!
24 That they were engraved on a rock
With an iron pen and lead, forever!
25 For I know *that* my Redeemer lives,
And He shall stand at last on the earth;
26 And after my skin is destroyed, this *I know,*
That in my flesh I shall see God,
27 Whom I shall see for myself,
And my eyes shall behold, and not another.
How my heart yearns within me!
28 If you should say, 'How shall we persecute him?'—
Since the root of the matter is found in me,
29 Be afraid of the sword for yourselves;
For wrath *brings* the punishment of the sword,
That you may know *there is* a judgment."

When you are the target of another person's destructive criticism, the natural response is to become defensive. But in reality, the least effective way to respond to criticism is to defend yourself, make excuses, or counterattack. . . .

Remind yourself that you are responsible to answer to God and to yourself, not to the critical person. Being responsible to God, you look to Him for direction and approval. Being responsible to yourself, you take ownership of your feelings, attitudes, and behavior. If you are aligned with God and with what He wants you to be, you don't need to fear criticism or try to justify your position. You have the power to make your own choices and grow through the experience of criticism.

As a nondefensive person, you respect and feel good about yourself. You believe in your worth and your capabilities. You possess your own identity and sense of security. Being nondefensive, you can listen to others more objectively and evaluate better what they are saying, even when they express themselves in a negative manner. You can accept the critical person for who he is, even if you don't agree with him. You can accept his right to see the world as he sees it, whether or not it coincides with your view. You're able to relate to him without making disparaging comments or negative judgments about him.

(From *How to Get Along with Almost Anyone* by H. Norman Wright)

APPLICATION What is your first response to criticism? Are you thin-skinned, touchy, or sensitive? Ask God to help you listen with interest. Take the criticism, evaluate it, and apply what will be helpful.

EXPLORATION Criticism—Job 6:24; 19: 3-5; Proverbs 10:17; 27:6.

Life Lesson

Job 20:1–21:34

SITUATION Zophar joined Bildad in telling about the fate of the wicked. His assumed Job was a hypocrite.

OBSERVATION Zophar and Bildad mistakenly equated all prosperity with God's blessings and all suffering with judgment.

INSPIRATION Sin incurs the death penalty and no man has the ability in himself to save himself from its penalty or to cleanse his own heart of its corruption. . . .

Man's only salvation from sin stands on a lonely, barren, skull-shaped hill; a thief hangs on one cross, a murderer on another and between them, a Man with a crown of thorns. Blood flows from His hands and feet, it pours from His side, it drops down his face—while those who stand looking on sneer and mock him.

And who is this tortured figure, who is this Man whom other men seek to humiliate and kill? He is the Son of God, the Prince of Peace, heaven's own appointed Messenger to the sin-ridden earth. This is He, before whom angels fall down and veil their faces. And yet He hangs bleeding and forsaken upon the cross.

Zophar's Sermon on the Wicked Man

20 Then Zophar the Naamathite answered and said:

2 "Therefore my anxious thoughts make me answer,
Because of the turmoil within me.
3 I have heard the rebuke that reproaches me,
And the spirit of my understanding causes me to answer.

4 "Do you *not* know this of old,
Since man was placed on earth,
5 That the triumphing of the wicked is short,
And the joy of the hypocrite is *but* for a moment?
6 Though his haughtiness mounts up to the heavens,
And his head reaches to the clouds,
7 *Yet* he will perish forever like his own refuse;
Those who have seen him will say, 'Where is he?'
8 He will fly away like a dream, and not be found;
Yes, he will be chased away like a vision of the night.
9 The eye *that* saw him will *see him* no more,
Nor will his place behold him anymore.
10 His children will seek the favor of the poor,
And his hands will restore his wealth.
11 His bones are full of his youthful vigor,
But it will lie down with him in the dust.

12 "Though evil is sweet in his mouth,
And he hides it under his tongue,
13 *Though* he spares it and does not forsake it,
But still keeps it in his mouth,
14 *Yet* his food in his stomach turns sour;
It becomes cobra venom within him.
15 He swallows down riches
And vomits them up again;
God casts them out of his belly.
16 He will suck the poison of cobras;
The viper's tongue will slay him.
17 He will not see the streams,
The rivers flowing with honey and cream.
18 He will restore that for which he labored,
And will not swallow *it* down;
From the proceeds of business
He will get no enjoyment.
19 For he has oppressed *and* forsaken the poor,
He has violently seized a house which he did not build.

20 "Because he knows no quietness in his heart,[a]
He will not save anything he desires.
21 Nothing is left for him to eat;
Therefore his well-being will not last.
22 In his self-sufficiency he will be in distress;
Every hand of misery will come against him.

20:20 [a] Literally *belly*

23 *When* he is about to fill his stomach,
God will cast on him the fury of His wrath,
And will rain *it* on him while he is eating.
24 He will flee from the iron weapon;
A bronze bow will pierce him through.
25 It is drawn, and comes out of the body;
Yes, the glittering *point comes* out of his gall.
Terrors *come* upon him;
26 Total darkness *is* reserved for his treasures.
An unfanned fire will consume him;
It shall go ill with him who is left in his tent.
27 The heavens will reveal his iniquity,
And the earth will rise up against him.
28 The increase of his house will depart,
And his goods will flow away in the day of His wrath.
29 This *is* the portion from God for a wicked man,
The heritage appointed to him by God."

Job's Discourse on the Wicked

21 Then Job answered and said:

2 "Listen carefully to my speech,
And let this be your consolation.
3 Bear with me that I may speak,
And after I have spoken, keep mocking.

4 "As for me, *is* my complaint against man?
And if *it were*, why should I not be impatient?
5 Look at me and be astonished;
Put *your* hand over *your* mouth.
6 Even when I remember I am terrified,
And trembling takes hold of my flesh.
7 Why do the wicked live *and* become old,
Yes, become mighty in power?
8 Their descendants are established with them in their sight,
And their offspring before their eyes.
9 Their houses *are* safe from fear,
Neither *is* the rod of God upon them.
10 Their bull breeds without failure;
Their cow calves without miscarriage.
11 They send forth their little ones like a flock,
And their children dance.
12 They sing to the tambourine and harp,
And rejoice to the sound of the flute.
13 They spend their days in wealth,
And in a moment go down to the grave.[b]
14 Yet they say to God, 'Depart from us,
For we do not desire the knowledge of Your ways.
15 Who *is* the Almighty, that we should serve Him?
And what profit do we have if we pray to Him?'

What brought Him to this place of horrors? Who inflicted that hideous torture upon the Man who came to teach us love? You did and I did, for it was for your sin and my sin that Jesus was nailed to the cross. In this immortal moment the human race experienced the darkest reaches of sin, it sank to its lowest depths, it touched its foulest limits. No wonder that the sun could not endure and veiled its face!

. . . But sin overreached itself on the cross. Man's hideous injustice that crucified Christ became the means that opened the way for man to become free. Sin's masterpiece of shame and hate became God's masterpiece of mercy and forgiveness.

(From *Peace with God* by Billy Graham)

APPLICATION Write your personal plan for success. What traits do you aspire to? Be quick to be fair, tell the truth, and put others first.

EXPLORATION Confused Values—Genesis 3:17-19; Psalm 36:1-4; Proverbs 1:10-19; Isaiah 5:8-25; Matthew 5:29-30; John 12:4-6; Romans 1:18.

21:13 *b* Or *Sheol*

16 Indeed their prosperity *is* not in their hand;
The counsel of the wicked is far from me.

17 "How often is the lamp of the wicked put out?
How often does their destruction
come upon them,
The sorrows *God* distributes in His anger?
18 They are like straw before the wind,
And like chaff that a storm carries away.
19 *They say,* 'God lays up one's[c] iniquity
for his children';
Let Him recompense him, that he may know *it.*
20 Let his eyes see his destruction,
And let him drink of the wrath
of the Almighty.
21 For what does he care about his
household after him,
When the number of his months is cut in half?

22 "Can *anyone* teach God knowledge,
Since He judges those on high?
23 One dies in his full strength,
Being wholly at ease and secure;
24 His pails[d] are full of milk,
And the marrow of his bones is moist.
25 Another man dies in the bitterness of his soul,
Never having eaten with pleasure.
26 They lie down alike in the dust,
And worms cover them.

27 "Look, I know your thoughts,
And the schemes *with which* you
would wrong me.
28 For you say,
'Where *is* the house of the prince?
And where *is* the tent,[e]
The dwelling place of the wicked?'
29 Have you not asked those who travel the road?
And do you not know their signs?
30 For the wicked are reserved for
the day of doom;
They shall be brought out on the day of wrath.
31 Who condemns his way to his face?
And who repays him *for what* he has done?
32 Yet he shall be brought to the grave,
And a vigil kept over the tomb.
33 The clods of the valley shall be sweet to him;
Everyone shall follow him,
As countless *have gone* before him.
34 How then can you comfort me with
empty words,
Since falsehood remains in your answers?"

Eliphaz Accuses Job of Wickedness

22 Then Eliphaz the Temanite answered and said:

2 "Can a man be profitable to God,
Though he who is wise may be
profitable to himself?
3 *Is it* any pleasure to the Almighty that
you are righteous?
Or *is it* gain *to Him* that you make
your ways blameless?

4 "Is it because of your fear of Him that
He corrects you,
And enters into judgment with you?
5 *Is* not your wickedness great,
And your iniquity without end?
6 For you have taken pledges from your brother
for no reason,
And stripped the naked of their clothing.
7 You have not given the weary water to drink,
And you have withheld bread from the hungry.
8 But the mighty man possessed the land,
And the honorable man dwelt in it.
9 You have sent widows away empty,
And the strength of the fatherless was crushed.
10 Therefore snares *are* all around you,
And sudden fear troubles you,
11 Or darkness *so that* you cannot see;
And an abundance of water covers you.

12 "Is not God in the height of heaven?
And see the highest stars, how lofty they are!
13 And you say, 'What does God know?
Can He judge through the deep darkness?
14 Thick clouds cover Him, so that
He cannot see,
And He walks above the circle of heaven.'
15 Will you keep to the old way
Which wicked men have trod,
16 Who were cut down before their time,
Whose foundations were swept away by a flood?
17 They said to God, 'Depart from us!
What can the Almighty do to them?'[f]
18 Yet He filled their houses with good *things;*
But the counsel of the wicked is far from me.

21:19 [c] Literally *his*
21:24 [d] Septuagint and Vulgate read *bowels;* Syriac reads *sides;* Targum reads *breasts.*
21:28 [e] Vulgate omits *the tent.*
22:17 [f] Septuagint and Syriac read *us.*

19 "The righteous see *it* and are glad,
And the innocent laugh at them:
20 'Surely our adversaries[g] are cut down,
And the fire consumes their remnant.'

21 "Now acquaint yourself with Him, and be at peace;
Thereby good will come to you.
22 Receive, please, instruction from His mouth,
And lay up His words in your heart.
23 If you return to the Almighty, you will be built up;
You will remove iniquity far from your tents.
24 Then you will lay your gold in the dust,
And the *gold* of Ophir among the stones of the brooks.
25 Yes, the Almighty will be your gold[h]
And your precious silver;
26 For then you will have your delight in the Almighty,
And lift up your face to God.
27 You will make your prayer to Him,
He will hear you,
And you will pay your vows.
28 You will also declare a thing,
And it will be established for you;
So light will shine on your ways.
29 When they cast *you* down, and you say, 'Exaltation *will come!*'
Then He will save the humble *person.*
30 He will *even* deliver one who is not innocent;
Yes, he will be delivered by the purity of your hands."

Job Proclaims God's Righteous Judgments

23 Then Job answered and said:

2 "Even today my complaint is bitter;
My[i] hand is listless because of my groaning.
3 Oh, that I knew where I might find Him,
That I might come to His seat!
4 I would present *my* case before Him,
And fill my mouth with arguments.
5 I would know the words *which* He would answer me,
And understand what He would say to me.
6 Would He contend with me in His great power?
No! But He would take *note* of me.
7 There the upright could reason with Him,
And I would be delivered forever from my Judge.

8 "Look, I go forward, but He is not *there,*
And backward, but I cannot perceive Him;
9 When He works on the left hand, I cannot behold *Him;*
When He turns to the right hand, I cannot see *Him.*
10 But He knows the way that I take;

22:20 [g] Septuagint reads *substance.*
22:25 [h] The ancient versions suggest *defense;* Hebrew reads *gold* as in verse 24.
23:2 [i] Following Masoretic Text, Targum, and Vulgate; Septuagint and Syriac read *His.*

LIFE LESSON

Job 22:1–24:25

SITUATION Eliphaz exhorted Job to admit that his sufferings resulted from sin. Job disagreed. He began to question whether or not God had treated him fairly.

OBSERVATION Job knew he was righteous before God. Job wondered why he had been afflicted and if God cared for him.

INSPIRATION Most of us tend to have this idea that since God is sovereign, He's supposed to make everything work out perfectly. Nothing is supposed to touch us as long as we're walking with Him.

This is the very problem that leads many Christians to despair when they go through trials. They can't imagine how God could ever let anything bad happen to them. They turn His sovereignty into a magic genie that's supposed to push all problems, trials, difficulties, and irritations away the moment we say "Go!" As a result, when we suddenly find ourselves in the midst of terrible circumstances, we crumble, blame God, and accuse Him of not caring, not being just, not acting in a loving manner, not having our best interests in mind.

We must come back to the truth that while God is in absolute control of all life, He is not the cause of all life's mishaps. Rather, His plan *allows* those mishaps for the great purpose of raising up "many brethren conformed to the image of Christ" (Romans 8:29).

Job's trial exposed this important misinterpretation on Job's part. . . . He couldn't understand how God could allow these things to continue—let alone happen. . . . We can all identify with Job. . . . The reason we see things this way is because we don't understand how God thinks; we can't comprehend the nature of His wisdom. "His thoughts are not our thoughts; His ways are not our ways," said Isaiah (55:8). When we're new in the faith, or immature, we tend to think that God will always do what is best for us. Indeed, He will. But what *we* think is best and what *He* does are as

Continued

different as whipped cream and concrete. We think He'll make us happy. In effect, we envision these warm, fuzzy feelings. But He plans to make us holy. That often calls for plenty of knocks and raps. . . .

Job's problem was just like ours. We have one plan and God has another. But God's plan is the one that will be put into operation. And when those plans turn into real life circumstances, we can feel as though we've been drawn, quartered, and fed to the crows.

But it's through gaining God's perspective that we begin to see true wisdom. That was what God was bringing Job to understand.
(From *When God Seems Far Away* by Mark R. Littleton)

APPLICATION It is easy to question God in times of struggle. When you feel afflicted turn toward God, not away from him. Seek the counsel of Christian friends and remain active in your church.

EXPLORATION Suffering Has a Purpose—Mark 8:31-32; Luke 24:46-47; Romans 8:17-18; 1 Peter 2:21; 4:12-13.

When He has tested me, I shall come forth as gold.
11 My foot has held fast to His steps;
I have kept His way and not turned aside.
12 I have not departed from the commandment of His lips;
I have treasured the words of His mouth
More than my necessary *food.*

13 "But He *is* unique, and who can make Him change?
And *whatever* His soul desires, *that* He does.
14 For He performs *what is* appointed for me,
And many such *things are* with Him.
15 Therefore I am terrified at His presence;
When I consider *this,* I am afraid of Him.
16 For God made my heart weak,
And the Almighty terrifies me;
17 Because I was not cut off from the presence of darkness,
And He did *not* hide deep darkness from my face.

Job Complains of Violence on the Earth

24 "*Since* times are not hidden from the Almighty,
Why do those who know Him see not His days?

2 "*Some* remove landmarks;
They seize flocks violently and feed *on them;*
3 They drive away the donkey of the fatherless;
They take the widow's ox as a pledge.
4 They push the needy off the road;
All the poor of the land are forced to hide.
5 Indeed, *like* wild donkeys in the desert,
They go out to their work, searching for food.
The wilderness *yields* food for them *and* for *their* children.
6 They gather their fodder in the field
And glean in the vineyard of the wicked.
7 They spend the night naked, without clothing,
And have no covering in the cold.
8 They are wet with the showers of the mountains,
And huddle around the rock for want of shelter.

9 "*Some* snatch the fatherless from the breast,
And take a pledge from the poor.
10 They cause *the poor* to go naked, without clothing;
And they take away the sheaves from the hungry.
11 They press out oil within their walls,
And tread winepresses, yet suffer thirst.
12 The dying groan in the city,
And the souls of the wounded cry out;
Yet God does not charge *them* with wrong.

13 "There are those who rebel against the light;
They do not know its ways
Nor abide in its paths.
14 The murderer rises with the light;
He kills the poor and needy;

And in the night he is like a thief.
15 The eye of the adulterer waits for the twilight,
Saying, 'No eye will see me';
And he disguises *his* face.
16 In the dark they break into houses
Which they marked for themselves in the daytime;
They do not know the light.
17 For the morning is the same to them as the shadow of death;
If *someone* recognizes *them,*
They are in the terrors of the shadow of death.

18 "They *should be* swift on the face of the waters,
Their portion *should be* cursed in the earth,
So that no *one would* turn into the way of their vineyards.
19 As drought and heat consume the snow waters,
So the grave[j] *consumes those who* have sinned.
20 The womb *should* forget him,
The worm *should* feed sweetly on him;
He *should* be remembered no more,
And wickedness *should* be broken like a tree.
21 For he preys on the barren *who* do not bear,
And does no good for the widow.

22 "But *God* draws the mighty away with His power;
He rises up, but no *man* is sure of life.
23 He gives them security, and they rely *on it;*
Yet His eyes *are* on their ways.
24 They are exalted for a little while,
Then they are gone.
They are brought low;
They are taken out of the way like all *others;*
They dry out like the heads of grain.

25 "Now if *it is* not *so,* who will prove me a liar,
And make my speech worth nothing?"

Bildad: How Can Man Be Righteous?

25 Then Bildad the Shuhite answered and said:

2 "Dominion and fear *belong* to Him;
He makes peace in His high places.
3 Is there any number to His armies?
Upon whom does His light not rise?
4 How then can man be righteous before God?
Or how can he be pure *who is*
born of a woman?
5 If even the moon does not shine,
And the stars are not pure in His sight,
6 How much less man, *who is* a maggot,
And a son of man, *who is* a worm?"

24:19 *j* Or *Sheol*

LIFE LESSON

Job 25:1–26:14

SITUATION The discussion between Job and his friends continued. Bildad replied to Job's claim of innocence. Job responded sarcastically to Bildad (26:2-4) because his advice lacked consolation.

OBSERVATION Man cannot be compared with God. God's immensity cannot be measured.

INSPIRATION Ever get a song on your mind? . . . It happened to me last week. . . . I found myself listening to what Watts wrote over two centuries ago:

Alas! and did my Savior bleed?
And did my Sovereign die?
Would he devote that sacred head
For such a worm as I?

I frowned as that last line faded away. "A worm"? Does God see people as "worms"? When Christ died did He "devote that sacred head" for *worms*? Now, obviously, Watts wanted to portray a vivid illustration of sinful mankind—lost, undeserving, spiritually worthless, wicked within. Dipping his brush in Job 25 and Isaiah 41, the hymnist painted such a picture, using the very term Scripture uses—*worm.* He was biblical and therefore justified his choice of terms for the text. Frankly, we were worm-like when our righteous God found us—lowly, wandering, dirty, unattractive, grubby creatures. But that doesn't mean we work hard at making ourselves into worms now. *A child of God is not a worm.* If God had wanted you to be a worm, He could have very easily made you one! . . . When Watts wrote of worms he was merely using a word picture. Many others, however, have framed it as a model to follow, calling it humility. This "worm theology" creates enormous problems.

It wears many faces—all sad. It crawls out from between the mattress and springs in the morning, telling itself, "I'm nothing. I'm a worm. Woe, woe. I can't do anything and even if I appear to be doing something, it's not really me. Woe! I must annihilate self-respect . . . crucify all motivation and ambition. . . . I'm a worm. Good for

Continued

nothing except crawling very slowly, drowning in mud puddles, or getting stepped on. Woe, woe, woe."

There's one main problem with this sort of thinking—*it's phony.* No matter how diligently we labor to appear genuinely humble, it amounts to nothing more than trying to look good in another way. . . .

And therin lies the ugly sin: PRIDE. Heretical though it may sound, no one who actually hates himself can adequately share the love of Christ. Our Lord taught that we were to love our neighbors *as we love ourselves.* . . .

Have you taken time this week to consider before your Lord who you really are? . . .

Sinful? Oh yes. Undeserving? Absolutely. Imperfect? Who isn't. Selfish? Indeed! Wrong? More often than not.

But a *worm*? Useless? Unimportant? Spineless? Meaningless? No, not that. God declared us righteous. He lifted us out of miry clay and set us upon a rock. He invites us to approach him with boldness. And he means it!

(From *Growing Strong in the Seasons of Life* by Charles Swindoll)

APPLICATION Although God has vast power, he still cares greatly for his children. Explore the verses below. Copy two on an index card and place the card where you will see it often. Remember that God never forgets who you are and what you are facing.

EXPLORATION Value of People—Genesis 1:26; Job 32:8; John 3:16; 1 Peter 1:18-19; Revelation 1:5.

Job: Man's Frailty and God's Majesty

26 But Job answered and said:

2 "How have you helped *him who is* without power?
How have you saved the arm *that has* no strength?
3 How have you counseled *one who has* no wisdom?
And *how* have you declared sound advice to many?
4 To whom have you uttered words?
And whose spirit came from you?

5 "The dead tremble,
Those under the waters and those inhabiting them.
6 Sheol *is* naked before Him,
And Destruction has no covering.
7 He stretches out the north over empty space;
He hangs the earth on nothing.
8 He binds up the water in His thick clouds,
Yet the clouds are not broken under it.
9 He covers the face of *His* throne,
And spreads His cloud over it.
10 He drew a circular horizon on the face of the waters,
At the boundary of light and darkness.
11 The pillars of heaven tremble,
And are astonished at His rebuke.
12 He stirs up the sea with His power,
And by His understanding He breaks up the storm.
13 By His Spirit He adorned the heavens;
His hand pierced the fleeing serpent.
14 Indeed these *are* the mere edges of His ways,
And how small a whisper we hear of Him!
But the thunder of His power who can understand?"

Job Maintains His Integrity

27 Moreover Job continued his discourse, and said:

2 "*As* God lives, *who* has taken away my justice,
And the Almighty, *who* has made my soul bitter,
3 As long as my breath *is* in me,
And the breath of God in my nostrils,
4 My lips will not speak wickedness,
Nor my tongue utter deceit.
5 Far be it from me
That I should say you are right;
Till I die I will not put away my integrity from me.
6 My righteousness I hold fast, and will not let it go;
My heart shall not reproach *me* as long as I live.

7 "May my enemy be like the wicked,
And he who rises up against me like the unrighteous.
8 For what is the hope of the hypocrite,
Though he may gain *much*,
If God takes away his life?

9 Will God hear his cry
When trouble comes upon him?
10 Will he delight himself in the Almighty?
Will he always call on God?

11 "I will teach you about the hand of God;
What *is* with the Almighty I will not conceal.
12 Surely all of you have seen *it;*
Why then do you behave with complete nonsense?

13 "This is the portion of a wicked man with God,
And the heritage of oppressors, received from the Almighty:
14 If his children are multiplied, *it is* for the sword;
And his offspring shall not be satisfied with bread.
15 Those who survive him shall be buried in death,
And their[k] widows shall not weep,
16 Though he heaps up silver like dust,
And piles up clothing like clay—
17 He may pile *it* up, but the just will wear *it,*
And the innocent will divide the silver.
18 He builds his house like a moth,[l]
Like a booth *which* a watchman makes.
19 The rich man will lie down,
But not be gathered *up;*[m]
He opens his eyes,
And he *is* no more.
20 Terrors overtake him like a flood;
A tempest steals him away in the night.
21 The east wind carries him away, and he is gone;
It sweeps him out of his place.
22 It hurls against him and does not spare;
He flees desperately from its power.
23 *Men* shall clap their hands at him,
And shall hiss him out of his place.

Job's Discourse on Wisdom

28 "Surely there is a mine for silver,
And a place *where* gold is refined.
2 Iron is taken from the earth,
And copper *is* smelted *from* ore.
3 *Man* puts an end to darkness,
And searches every recess
For ore in the darkness and the shadow of death.
4 He breaks open a shaft away from people;
In places forgotten by feet
They hang far away from men;
They swing to and fro.
5 *As for* the earth, from it comes bread,

27:15 [k] Literally *his*
27:18 [l] Following Masoretic Text and Vulgate; Septuagint and Syriac read *spider* (compare 8:14); Targum reads *decay.*
27:19 [m] Following Masoretic Text and Targum; Septuagint and Syriac read *But shall not add* (that is, do it again); Vulgate reads *But take away nothing.*

LIFE LESSON

Job 27:1-23

SITUATION When Job claimed that his suffering did not result from sin, Bildad accused him of pride. Job responded with a passionate declaration of his integrity.

OBSERVATION Despite the accusations being hurled at him, Job recognized that he had a clear conscience.

INSPIRATION A few weeks ago, Roger's family was shopping for groceries. As they rounded a corner, he looked down at his two-year-old daughter who was riding in the basket. She was holding the carton of eggs. The carton was open and revealed that several of the eggs were broken and others were cracked. His first thought was, "Let's just put the carton back and get another. No one will notice."

Sometimes the same temptation occurs when one stays overnight in a motel. Occasionally, the thought comes to mind, "Why not watch one of those late night cable channels? Who's going to know?"

In both of these instances, and in countless others, it is helpful to ask yourself the question, "Who am I when no one's looking? Am I consistent, or do I act differently? Am I the same person Monday through Saturday that I am on Sunday? Will I be blameless and holy when I meet the Lord?"

(From *A Dad's Blessing* by Gary Smalley and John Trent)

APPLICATION Do you act differently when no one is looking? Is your conscience clear? If not, ask God to forgive your sin and help you live a life of integrity. Tell a trusted friend of any problem areas. Ask that person to hold you accountable.

EXPLORATION Clear Conscience—Acts 24:16; Romans 9:1; 1 Timothy 3:9; Hebrews 9:14; 1 Peter 3:16.

But underneath it is turned up as by fire;
6 Its stones *are* the source of sapphires,
And it contains gold dust.
7 *That* path no bird knows,
Nor has the falcon's eye seen it.
8 The proud lions[n] have not trodden it,
Nor has the fierce lion passed over it.
9 He puts his hand on the flint;
He overturns the mountains at the roots.
10 He cuts out channels in the rocks,
And his eye sees every precious thing.
11 He dams up the streams from trickling;
What is hidden he brings forth to light.

12 "But where can wisdom be found?
And where *is* the place of understanding?
13 Man does not know its value,
Nor is it found in the land of the living.
14 The deep says, '*It is* not in me';
And the sea says, '*It is* not with me.'
15 It cannot be purchased for gold,
Nor can silver be weighed *for* its price.
16 It cannot be valued in the gold of Ophir,
In precious onyx or sapphire.
17 Neither gold nor crystal can equal it,
Nor can it be exchanged for jewelry of fine gold.
18 No mention shall be made of coral or quartz,
For the price of wisdom *is* above rubies.
19 The topaz of Ethiopia cannot equal it,
Nor can it be valued in pure gold.

20 "From where then does wisdom come?
And where *is* the place of understanding?
21 It is hidden from the eyes of all living,
And concealed from the birds of the air.
22 Destruction and Death say,
'We have heard a report about it with our ears.'
23 God understands its way,
And He knows its place.
24 For He looks to the ends of the earth,
And sees under the whole heavens,
25 To establish a weight for the wind,
And apportion the waters by measure.
26 When He made a law for the rain,
And a path for the thunderbolt,
27 Then He saw *wisdom*[o] and declared it;
He prepared it, indeed, He searched it out.
28 And to man He said,
'Behold, the fear of the Lord, that *is* wisdom,
And to depart from evil *is* understanding.' "

28:8 [n] Literally *sons of pride,* figurative of the great lions
28:27 [o] Literally *it*

LIFE LESSON

Job 28:1-28

SITUATION Job continued his long reply to Bildad and his other friends. In his speech, Job claimed that God's wisdom supersedes all human wisdom.

OBSERVATION Nature cannot tell everything about God's wisdom. For further insight we must look at God's Word.

INSPIRATION God knows me! He knows every tear I cry. "Thou hast taken account of my wanderings; put my tears in Thy bottle" [Psalm 56:8]. God knows every trial we go through, and His wisdom allows each to happen. . . .

God is perfect in His wisdom. As the sun cannot be without light, neither can God be without wisdom. He was wisdom *originally.* Men acquire wisdom through experience; God has it by essence. He does not have to study or gain more experience. God has wisdom *perfectly.* He has absolutely no ignorance. He has wisdom *universally.* Men are wise in various things. God is wise in all things. He has wisdom *perpetually.* Man's wisdom fades near death. God's wisdom is perpetual. His wisdom is *incomprehensible.* The wisdom of one man may be comprehended by another. "Canst thou by searching find out God?" [Job 11:7, KJV] His wisdom is *infallible.* Even the wisest men fall short of their goals. God never fails.

(From *The God You Can Know* by Dan DeHaan)

APPLICATION To know more of God's wisdom, we must study the Bible. Develop a plan for daily study. Memorize one verse by rewriting it each day for a week. Reflect on your selected verse throughout the day.

EXPLORATION Wisdom of God—Daniel 2:19-23; Luke 4:14-15; Romans 16:27; 1 Corinthians 1:21-24; Colossians 2:2-3.

Job's Summary Defense

29 Job further continued his discourse, and said:

2 "Oh, that I were as *in* months past,
As *in* the days *when* God watched over me;
3 When His lamp shone upon my head,
And when by His light I walked *through* darkness;
4 Just as I was in the days of my prime,
When the friendly counsel of God *was* over my tent;
5 When the Almighty *was* yet with me,
When my children *were* around me;
6 When my steps were bathed with cream,[p]
And the rock poured out rivers of oil for me!

7 "When I went out to the gate by the city,
When I took my seat in the open square,
8 The young men saw me and hid,
And the aged arose *and* stood;
9 The princes refrained from talking,
And put *their* hand on their mouth;
10 The voice of nobles was hushed,
And their tongue stuck to the roof of their mouth.
11 When the ear heard, then it blessed me,
And when the eye saw, then it approved me;
12 Because I delivered the poor who cried out,
The fatherless and *the one who* had no helper.
13 The blessing of a perishing *man* came upon me,
And I caused the widow's heart to sing for joy.
14 I put on righteousness, and it clothed me;
My justice *was* like a robe and a turban.
15 I *was* eyes to the blind,
And I *was* feet to the lame.
16 I *was* a father to the poor,
And I searched out the case *that* I did not know.
17 I broke the fangs of the wicked,
And plucked the victim from his teeth.

18 "Then I said, 'I shall die in my nest,
And multiply *my* days as the sand.
19 My root *is* spread out to the waters,
And the dew lies all night on my branch.
20 My glory *is* fresh within me,
And my bow is renewed in my hand.'

21 "*Men* listened to me and waited,
And kept silence for my counsel.
22 After my words they did not speak again,
And my speech settled on them *as dew.*
23 They waited for me *as* for the rain,
And they opened their mouth wide *as* for the spring rain.
24 *If* I mocked at them, they did not believe *it*,

29:6 *p* Masoretic Text reads *wrath;* ancient versions and some Hebrew manuscripts read *cream* (compare 20:17).

Life Lesson

Job 29:1–31:40

SITUATION Job described his role in the community. He may have been a judge or city official. In his position he sought justice and cared for the needy.

OBSERVATION Be careful to avoid pride because of your status. Job did not use his position for evil.

INSPIRATION The little house made me think of pictures I'd seen of the United States during the Depression. Unlit kerosene lanterns (no electricity). Basins of water to wash up in (no running water). A wall lined with well-worn hoes, shovels, and picks (no modern equipment). The kitchen was a separate hut that sat next to the front door of the house. I was intrigued by the stove. It was made of hard, backed mud, molded in a long narrow piece about four feet long and three feet tall. A four or five inch trough ran down the center to hold the wood. The ever-present pots cooking the beans and rice straddled the hot trough. I felt a long way from Rio.

Senor José took me on a tour through his segment of the world. For thirty-seven years he had plowed and tilled his two acres. It was obvious that he knew every hole and turn.

"I fed fourteen mouths off this land," he smiled, fingering a lettuce plant. "Where did you say you were from?"

"The U.S."

"What do you do there?"

I explained a bit about my work. . . .

"A missionary, huh? Your job must be pretty easy."

"How's that?" I asked.

"I have no trouble believing in God. After I see what he has done on my little farm, year after year, it is easy to believe." He smiled another toothless grin and yelled to his wife to bring out some beans.

As we drove home, I couldn't help thinking about Senor José. My, what a simple life. No traffic jams, airline schedules, or long lines. Far removed from Wall Street, IRS, and mortgages. Unacquainted with Johannine theology, Martin Luther, or Christian evidences.

Continued

I thought of his faith, his ability to believe, and his surprise that there were some who couldn't. I compared his faith with others I knew had more difficulty believing; a university student, a wealthy import-export man, an engineer. There was such a difference between José and the others.

His faith was rooted in the simple miracles that he witnessed every day:

A small seed becoming a towering tree.

A thin stalk pushing back the earth.

A rainbow arching in the midst of the thundercloud.

It was easy for him to believe. I can see why. Someone who witnesses God's daily display of majesty doesn't find the secret of Easter absurd. Someone who depends upon the mysteries of nature for his livelihood doesn't find it difficult to depend on an unseen God for his salvation. . . . God's testimony. When was the last time you witnessed it? A stroll though knee-high grass in a green meadow. An hour listening to seagulls or looking at seashells on the beach. Or witnessing the shafts of sunlight brighten the snow on a crisp winter dawn. Miracles that almost match the magnitude of the empty tomb happen all around us; we only have to pay attention. (From *No Wonder They Call Him the Savior* by Max Lucado)

APPLICATION Look around. What can you observe that speaks mightily about God's care and concern in your family, in nature, and in world events? Use your simple discovery in a conversation with a younger person this week. Help that person to build trust in God.

EXPLORATION Truth—Psalm 10:17-18; Proverbs 23:10-11; 2 Corinthians 10:5; 1 Peter 3:15.

And the light of my countenance they did not cast down.
25 I chose the way for them, and sat as chief;
So I dwelt as a king in the army,
As one *who* comforts mourners.

30 "But now they mock at me, *men* younger than I,
Whose fathers I disdained to put with the dogs of my flock.
2 Indeed, what *profit* is the strength of their hands to me?
Their vigor has perished.
3 *They are* gaunt from want and famine,
Fleeing late to the wilderness, desolate and waste,
4 Who pluck mallow by the bushes,
And broom tree roots *for* their food.
5 They were driven out from among *men*,
They shouted at them as *at* a thief.
6 *They had* to live in the clefts of the valleys,
In caves of the earth and the rocks.
7 Among the bushes they brayed,
Under the nettles they nestled.
8 *They were* sons of fools,
Yes, sons of vile men;
They were scourged from the land.

9 "And now I am their taunting song;
Yes, I am their byword.
10 They abhor me, they keep far from me;
They do not hesitate to spit in my face.
11 Because He has loosed my[q] bowstring and afflicted me,
They have cast off restraint before me.
12 At *my* right *hand* the rabble arises;
They push away my feet,
And they raise against me their ways of destruction.
13 They break up my path,
They promote my calamity;
They have no helper.
14 They come as broad breakers;
Under the ruinous storm they roll along.
15 Terrors are turned upon me;
They pursue my honor as the wind,
And my prosperity has passed like a cloud.

16 "And now my soul is poured out because of my *plight;*
The days of affliction take hold of me.
17 My bones are pierced in me at night,
And my gnawing pains take no rest.
18 By great force my garment is disfigured;
It binds me about as the collar of my coat.
19 He has cast me into the mire,
And I have become like dust and ashes.

20 "I cry out to You, but You do not answer me;
I stand up, and You regard me.

30:11 [q] Following Masoretic Text, Syriac, and Targum; Septuagint and Vulgate read *His*.

21 *But* You have become cruel to me;
With the strength of Your hand You oppose me.
22 You lift me up to the wind and cause me to ride *on it;*
You spoil my success.
23 For I know *that* You will bring me *to* death,
And *to* the house appointed for all living.

24 "Surely He would not stretch out *His* hand against a heap of ruins,
If they cry out when He destroys *it.*
25 Have I not wept for him who was in trouble?
Has *not* my soul grieved for the poor?
26 But when I looked for good, evil came *to me;*
And when I waited for light, then came darkness.
27 My heart is in turmoil and cannot rest;
Days of affliction confront me.
28 I go about mourning, but not in the sun;
I stand up in the assembly *and* cry out for help.
29 I am a brother of jackals,
And a companion of ostriches.
30 My skin grows black and falls from me;
My bones burn with fever.
31 My harp is *turned* to mourning,
And my flute to the voice of those who weep.

31 "I have made a covenant with my eyes;
Why then should I look upon a young woman?
2 For what *is* the allotment of God from above,
And the inheritance of the Almighty from on high?
3 *Is* it not destruction for the wicked,
And disaster for the workers of iniquity?
4 Does He not see my ways,
And count all my steps?

5 "If I have walked with falsehood,
Or if my foot has hastened to deceit,
6 Let me be weighed on honest scales,
That God may know my integrity.
7 If my step has turned from the way,
Or my heart walked after my eyes,
Or if any spot adheres to my hands,
8 *Then* let me sow, and another eat;
Yes, let my harvest be rooted out.

9 "If my heart has been enticed by a woman,
Or *if* I have lurked at my neighbor's door,
10 *Then* let my wife grind for another,
And let others bow down over her.
11 For that *would be* wickedness;
Yes, it *would be* iniquity *deserving of* judgment.
12 For that *would be* a fire *that* consumes to destruction,
And would root out all my increase.

13 "If I have despised the cause of my male or female servant
When they complained against me,
14 What then shall I do when God rises up?
When He punishes, how shall I answer Him?
15 Did not He who made me in the womb make them?
Did not the same One fashion us in the womb?

16 "If I have kept the poor from *their* desire,
Or caused the eyes of the widow to fail,
17 Or eaten my morsel by myself,
So that the fatherless could not eat of it
18 (But from my youth I reared him as a father,
And from my mother's womb I guided *the widow*[r]);
19 If I have seen anyone perish for lack of clothing,
Or any poor *man* without covering;
20 If his heart[s] has not blessed me,
And *if* he was *not* warmed with the fleece of my sheep;
21 If I have raised my hand against the fatherless,
When I saw I had help in the gate;
22 *Then* let my arm fall from my shoulder,
Let my arm be torn from the socket.
23 For destruction *from* God *is* a terror to me,
And because of His magnificence I cannot endure.

24 "If I have made gold my hope,
Or said to fine gold, '*You are* my confidence';
25 If I have rejoiced because my wealth *was* great,
And because my hand had gained much;
26 If I have observed the sun[t] when it shines,
Or the moon moving *in* brightness,
27 So that my heart has been secretly enticed,
And my mouth has kissed my hand;
28 This also *would be* an iniquity *deserving of* judgment,
For I would have denied God *who is* above.

29 "If I have rejoiced at the destruction of him who hated me,

31:18 [r] Literally *her* (compare verse 16)
31:20 [s] Literally *loins*
31:26 [t] Literally *light*

Or lifted myself up when evil found him
30 (Indeed I have not allowed my mouth to sin
By asking for a curse on his soul);
31 If the men of my tent have not said,
'Who is there that has not been satisfied
with his meat?'
32 (*But* no sojourner had to lodge in the street,
For I have opened my doors to the traveler[u]);
33 If I have covered my transgressions as Adam,
By hiding my iniquity in my bosom,
34 Because I feared the great multitude,
And dreaded the contempt of families,
So that I kept silence
And did not go out of the door—
35 Oh, that I had one to hear me!
Here is my mark.
Oh, that the Almighty would answer me,
That my Prosecutor had written a book!
36 Surely I would carry it on my shoulder,
And bind it on me *like* a crown;
37 I would declare to Him the number of my steps;
Like a prince I would approach Him.

38 "If my land cries out against me,
And its furrows weep together;
39 If I have eaten its fruit[v] without money,
Or caused its owners to lose their lives;
40 *Then* let thistles grow instead of wheat,
And weeds instead of barley."

The words of Job are ended.

Elihu Contradicts Job's Friends

32 So these three men ceased answering Job, because
he *was* righteous in his own eyes. 2 Then the wrath
of Elihu, the son of Barachel the Buzite, of the family of
Ram, was aroused against Job; his wrath was aroused
because he justified himself rather than God. 3 Also
against his three friends his wrath was aroused, because
they had found no answer, and *yet* had condemned Job.
4 Now because they *were* years older than he, Elihu
had waited to speak to Job.[w] 5 When Elihu saw that *there*
was no answer in the mouth of these three men, his
wrath was aroused.
6 So Elihu, the son of Barachel the Buzite, answered
and said:

"I *am* young in years, and you *are* very old;
Therefore I was afraid,
And dared not declare my opinion to you.
7 I said, 'Age[x] should speak,
And multitude of years should teach wisdom.'
8 But *there is* a spirit in man,
And the breath of the Almighty gives
him understanding.
9 Great men[y] are not *always* wise,
Nor do the aged *always* understand justice.

10 "Therefore I say, 'Listen to me,
I also will declare my opinion.'
11 Indeed I waited for your words,
I listened to your reasonings, while you
searched out what to say.
12 I paid close attention to you;
And surely not one of you convinced Job,
Or answered his words—
13 Lest you say,
'We have found wisdom';
God will vanquish him, not man.
14 Now he has not directed *his* words against me;
So I will not answer him with your words.

15 "They are dismayed and answer no more;
Words escape them.
16 And I have waited, because they did not speak,
Because they stood still *and* answered no more.
17 I also will answer my part,
I too will declare my opinion.
18 For I am full of words;
The spirit within me compels me.
19 Indeed my belly *is* like wine *that* has no vent;
It is ready to burst like new wineskins.
20 I will speak, that I may find relief;
I must open my lips and answer.
21 Let me not, I pray, show partiality to anyone;
Nor let me flatter any man.
22 For I do not know how to flatter,
Else my Maker would soon take me away.

Elihu Contradicts Job

33 "But please, Job, hear my speech,
And listen to all my words.
2 Now, I open my mouth;
My tongue speaks in my mouth.
3 My words *come* from my upright heart;
My lips utter pure knowledge.
4 The Spirit of God has made me,

31:32 [u] Following Septuagint, Syriac, Targum, and Vulgate; Masoretic Text reads *road.*
31:39 [v] Literally *its strength*
32:4 [w] Vulgate reads *till Job had spoken.*
32:7 [x] Literally *Days,* that is, years
32:9 [y] Or *Men of many years*

And the breath of the Almighty gives me life.
5 If you can answer me,
Set *your words* in order before me;
Take your stand.
6 Truly I *am* as your spokesman[z] before God;
I also have been formed out of clay.
7 Surely no fear of me will terrify you,
Nor will my hand be heavy on you.

8 "Surely you have spoken in my hearing,
And I have heard the sound of
your words, *saying,*
9 'I *am* pure, without transgression;
I *am* innocent, and *there is* no iniquity in me.
10 Yet He finds occasions against me,
He counts me as His enemy;
11 He puts my feet in the stocks,
He watches all my paths.'

12 "Look, *in* this you are not righteous.
I will answer you,
For God is greater than man.
13 Why do you contend with Him?
For He does not give an accounting
of any of His words.
14 For God may speak in one way, or in another,
Yet man does not perceive it.
15 In a dream, in a vision of the night,
When deep sleep falls upon men,
While slumbering on their beds,
16 Then He opens the ears of men,
And seals their instruction.
17 In order to turn man *from his* deed,
And conceal pride from man,
18 He keeps back his soul from the Pit,
And his life from perishing by the sword.

19 "*Man* is also chastened with pain on his bed,
And with strong *pain* in many of his bones,
20 So that his life abhors bread,
And his soul succulent food.
21 His flesh wastes away from sight,
And his bones stick out *which*
once were not seen.
22 Yes, his soul draws near the Pit,
And his life to the executioners.

23 "If there is a messenger for him,
A mediator, one among a thousand,
To show man His uprightness,
24 Then He is gracious to him, and says,
'Deliver him from going down to the Pit;
I have found a ransom';
25 His flesh shall be young like a child's,
He shall return to the days of his youth.
26 He shall pray to God, and He
will delight in him,
He shall see His face with joy,
For He restores to man His righteousness.
27 Then he looks at men and says,
'I have sinned, and perverted *what was* right,
And it did not profit me.'
28 He will redeem his[a] soul from going
down to the Pit,
And his[b] life shall see the light.

29 "Behold, God works all these *things,*
Twice, *in fact,* three *times* with a man,
30 To bring back his soul from the Pit,
That he may be enlightened with
the light of life.

31 "Give ear, Job, listen to me;
Hold your peace, and I will speak.
32 If you have anything to say, answer me;
Speak, for I desire to justify you.
33 If not, listen to me;
Hold your peace, and I will teach you wisdom."

Elihu Proclaims God's Justice

34 Elihu further answered and said:

2 "Hear my words, you wise *men;*
Give ear to me, you who have knowledge.
3 For the ear tests words
As the palate tastes food.
4 Let us choose justice for ourselves;
Let us know among ourselves what *is* good.

5 "For Job has said, 'I am righteous,
But God has taken away my justice;
6 Should I lie concerning my right?
My wound *is* incurable, *though I am*
without transgression.'
7 What man *is* like Job,
Who drinks scorn like water,
8 Who goes in company with the
workers of iniquity,
And walks with wicked men?
9 For he has said, 'It profits a man nothing
That he should delight in God.'

33:6 [z] Literally *as your mouth*
33:28 [a] Or *my* (Kethib) [b] Or *my* (Kethib)

10 "Therefore listen to me, you
men of understanding:
Far be it from God *to do* wickedness,
And *from* the Almighty to *commit* iniquity.
11 For He repays man *according to* his work,
And makes man to find a reward
according to *his* way.
12 Surely God will never do wickedly,
Nor will the Almighty pervert justice.
13 Who gave Him charge over the earth?
Or who appointed *Him over* the whole world?
14 If He should set His heart on it,
If He should gather to Himself His
Spirit and His breath,
15 All flesh would perish together,
And man would return to dust.

16 "If *you have* understanding, hear this;
Listen to the sound of my words:
17 Should one who hates justice govern?
Will you condemn *Him who is* most just?
18 *Is it fitting* to say to a king, '*You are* worthless,'
And to nobles, '*You are* wicked'?
19 Yet He is not partial to princes,
Nor does He regard the rich more than the poor;
For they *are* all the work of His hands.
20 In a moment they die, in the middle of the night;
The people are shaken and pass away;
The mighty are taken away without a hand.

21 "For His eyes *are* on the ways of man,
And He sees all his steps.
22 There is no darkness nor shadow of death
Where the workers of iniquity may
hide themselves.
23 For He need not further consider a man,
That he should go before God in judgment.
24 He breaks in pieces mighty
men without inquiry,
And sets others in their place.
25 Therefore He knows their works;
He overthrows *them* in the night,
And they are crushed.
26 He strikes them as wicked *men*
In the open sight of others,
27 Because they turned back from Him,
And would not consider any of His ways,
28 So that they caused the cry of the poor to
come to Him;
For He hears the cry of the afflicted.
29 When He gives quietness, who then
can make trouble?
And when He hides *His* face, who
then can see Him,
Whether *it is* against a nation or a man alone?—
30 That the hypocrite should not reign,
Lest the people be ensnared.

31 "For has *anyone* said to God,
'I have borne *chastening;*
I will offend no more;
32 Teach me *what* I do not see;
If I have done iniquity, I will do no more'?
33 Should He repay *it* according to your *terms,*
Just because you disavow it?
You must choose, and not I;
Therefore speak what you know.

34 "Men of understanding say to me,
Wise men who listen to me:
35 'Job speaks without knowledge,
His words *are* without wisdom.'
36 Oh, that Job were tried to the utmost,
Because *his* answers *are like* those
of wicked men!
37 For he adds rebellion to his sin;
He claps *his hands* among us,
And multiplies his words against God."

Elihu Condemns Self-Righteousness

35 Moreover Elihu answered and said:

2 "Do you think this is right?
Do you say,
'My righteousness is more than God's'?
3 For you say,
'What advantage will it be to You?
What profit shall I have, more than
if I had sinned?'

4 "I will answer you,
And your companions with you.
5 Look to the heavens and see;
And behold the clouds—
They are higher than you.
6 If you sin, what do you accomplish against Him?
Or, *if* your transgressions are multiplied, what
do you do to Him?
7 If you are righteous, what do you give Him?
Or what does He receive from your hand?
8 Your wickedness affects a man such as you,
And your righteousness a son of man.

9 "Because of the multitude of oppressions
they cry out;

They cry out for help because of the
arm of the mighty.
10 But no one says, 'Where *is* God my Maker,
Who gives songs in the night,
11 Who teaches us more than the beasts of the earth,
And makes us wiser than the birds of heaven?'
12 There they cry out, but He does not answer,
Because of the pride of evil men.
13 Surely God will not listen to empty *talk*,
Nor will the Almighty regard it.
14 Although you say you do not see Him,
Yet justice *is* before Him, and you must wait for Him.
15 And now, because He has not punished in His anger,
Nor taken much notice of folly,
16 Therefore Job opens his mouth in vain;
He multiplies words without knowledge."

Elihu Proclaims God's Goodness

36 Elihu also proceeded and said:

2 "Bear with me a little, and I will show you
That *there are* yet words to speak on God's behalf.
3 I will fetch my knowledge from afar;
I will ascribe righteousness to my Maker.
4 For truly my words *are* not false;
One who is perfect in knowledge *is* with you.

5 "Behold, God *is* mighty, but despises *no one;*
He is mighty in strength of understanding.
6 He does not preserve the life of the wicked,
But gives justice to the oppressed.
7 He does not withdraw His eyes from the righteous;
But *they are* on the throne with kings,
For He has seated them forever,
And they are exalted.
8 And if *they are* bound in fetters,
Held in the cords of affliction,
9 Then He tells them their work and their transgressions—
That they have acted defiantly.
10 He also opens their ear to instruction,
And commands that they turn from iniquity.
11 If they obey and serve *Him*,
They shall spend their days in prosperity,
And their years in pleasures.
12 But if they do not obey,
They shall perish by the sword,
And they shall die without knowledge.[c]

13 "But the hypocrites in heart store up wrath;
They do not cry for help when He binds them.
14 They die in youth,

LIFE LESSON

Job 32:1–37:24

SITUATION Elihu, the youngest of Job's friends, confronted Job. Elihu knew the advice of the other friends was wrong. Yet, he could not fully arrive at the right conclusion either.

OBSERVATION Elihu gave the best answer he could. Only God knew all the facts.

INSPIRATION Most of the time, when we muster the courage to confront, we will not lose a friend. The few times I have risked confronting a beloved friend over serious sins in his or her life, far from becoming enemies, we now have deeper trust and deeper respect for each other. And I think more, not less, of the people who have loved me enough to painfully confront me. I know these people really care, because they have invested value into my life.
. . . As you read this book, you may be agonizing over something that has gone wrong in your life. You desperately want it resolved, but you cannot find the courage to say anything. Since no one but you knows, there is [no one] to confront you. Maybe the Holy Spirit is confronting you this very moment, through me.

Or possibly you know something sinful in the life of a beloved brother or sister. You have known it for some time, but you felt it was none of your business, or you lacked courage, or you did not know what to do. Let these lines say to you: Before God, care enough to confront.

. . . When you need to confront someone, and you fear the risk, remember: The Holy Spirit can give you the wisdom to do it lovingly and the courage to care enough.
(From *Finding the Heart to Go On* by Lynn Anderson)

APPLICATION Learn to confront people with love and firmness. Ask others how they have learned to confront successfully (pastors, police, school administrators, sports officials). Apply the lessons they have learned.

EXPLORATION Confrontation— Genesis 3:1-13; 4:1-15; 2 Samuel 12:1-22.

36:12 [c] Masoretic Text reads *as one without knowledge.*

And their life *ends* among the
perverted persons.[d]
15 He delivers the poor in their affliction,
And opens their ears in oppression.

16 "Indeed He would have brought
you out of dire distress,
Into a broad place where *there is* no restraint;
And what is set on your table *would*
be full of richness.
17 But you are filled with the judgment
due the wicked;
Judgment and justice take hold *of you.*
18 Because *there is* wrath, *beware* lest He take you
away with *one* blow;
For a large ransom would not help you avoid *it.*
19 Will your riches,
Or all the mighty forces,
Keep you from distress?
20 Do not desire the night,
When people are cut off in their place.
21 Take heed, do not turn to iniquity,
For you have chosen this rather than affliction.

22 "Behold, God is exalted by His power;
Who teaches like Him?
23 Who has assigned Him His way,
Or who has said, 'You have done wrong'?

Elihu Proclaims God's Majesty

24 "Remember to magnify His work,
Of which men have sung.
25 Everyone has seen it;
Man looks on *it* from afar.

26 "Behold, God *is* great, and we do not know *Him;*
Nor can the number of His years *be* discovered.
27 For He draws up drops of water,
Which distill as rain from the mist,
28 Which the clouds drop down
And pour abundantly on man.
29 Indeed, can *anyone* understand the
spreading of clouds,
The thunder from His canopy?
30 Look, He scatters His light upon it,
And covers the depths of the sea.
31 For by these He judges the peoples;
He gives food in abundance.
32 He covers *His* hands with lightning,
And commands it to strike.
33 His thunder declares it,
The cattle also, concerning the rising *storm.*

37 "At this also my heart trembles,
And leaps from its place.
2 Hear attentively the thunder of His voice,
And the rumbling *that* comes from His mouth.
3 He sends it forth under the whole heaven,
His lightning to the ends of the earth.
4 After it a voice roars;
He thunders with His majestic voice,
And He does not restrain them when His
voice is heard.
5 God thunders marvelously with His voice;
He does great things which we cannot
comprehend.
6 For He says to the snow, 'Fall *on* the earth';
Likewise to the gentle rain and the heavy rain
of His strength.
7 He seals the hand of every man,
That all men may know His work.
8 The beasts go into dens,
And remain in their lairs.
9 From the chamber *of the south* comes
the whirlwind,
And cold from the scattering winds *of the north.*
10 By the breath of God ice is given,
And the broad waters are frozen.
11 Also with moisture He saturates
the thick clouds;
He scatters His bright clouds.
12 And they swirl about, being turned
by His guidance,
That they may do whatever He
commands them
On the face of the whole earth.[e]
13 He causes it to come,
Whether for correction,
Or for His land,
Or for mercy.

14 "Listen to this, O Job;
Stand still and consider the wondrous
works of God.
15 Do you know when God dispatches them,
And causes the light of His cloud to shine?
16 Do you know how the clouds are balanced,
Those wondrous works of Him who is perfect
in knowledge?
17 Why *are* your garments hot,

36:14 [d] Hebrew *qedeshim,* that is, those practicing sodomy and prostitution in religious rituals
37:12 [e] Literally *the world of the earth*

When He quiets the earth by the south *wind?*
18 With Him, have you spread out the skies,
Strong as a cast metal mirror?

19 "Teach us what we should say to Him,
For we can prepare nothing because
of the darkness.
20 Should He be told that I *wish to* speak?
If a man were to speak, surely he would be
swallowed up.
21 Even now *men* cannot look at the light *when it*
is bright in the skies,
When the wind has passed and cleared them.
22 He comes from the north *as* golden *splendor;*
With God *is* awesome majesty.
23 *As for* the Almighty, we cannot find Him;
He is excellent in power,
In judgment and abundant justice;
He does not oppress.
24 Therefore men fear Him;
He shows no partiality to any *who*
are wise of heart."

The LORD *Reveals His Omnipotence to Job*

38 Then the LORD answered Job out of the whirlwind, and said:

2 "Who *is* this who darkens counsel
By words without knowledge?
3 Now prepare yourself like a man;
I will question you, and you shall answer Me.

4 "Where were you when I laid the foundations
of the earth?
Tell *Me,* if you have understanding.
5 Who determined its measurements?
Surely you know!
Or who stretched the line upon it?
6 To what were its foundations fastened?
Or who laid its cornerstone,
7 When the morning stars sang together,
And all the sons of God shouted for joy?

8 "Or *who* shut in the sea with doors,
When it burst forth *and* issued from the womb;
9 When I made the clouds its garment,
And thick darkness its swaddling band;
10 When I fixed My limit for it,
And set bars and doors;
11 When I said,
'This far you may come, but no farther,
And here your proud waves must stop!'

12 "Have you commanded the morning since
your days *began,*
And caused the dawn to know its place,
13 That it might take hold of the ends of the earth,
And the wicked be shaken out of it?
14 It takes on form like clay *under* a seal,
And stands out like a garment.
15 From the wicked their light is withheld,
And the upraised arm is broken.

16 "Have you entered the springs of the sea?
Or have you walked in search of the depths?
17 Have the gates of death been revealed to you?
Or have you seen the doors of the
shadow of death?
18 Have you comprehended the breadth
of the earth?
Tell *Me,* if you know all this.

19 "Where *is* the way *to* the dwelling of light?
And darkness, where *is* its place,
20 That you may take it to its territory,
That you may know the paths *to* its home?
21 Do you know *it,* because you were born then,
Or *because* the number of your days *is* great?

22 "Have you entered the treasury of snow,
Or have you seen the treasury of hail,
23 Which I have reserved for the time of trouble,
For the day of battle and war?
24 By what way is light diffused,
Or the east wind scattered over the earth?

25 "Who has divided a channel for the
overflowing *water,*
Or a path for the thunderbolt,
26 To cause it to rain on a land *where*
there is no one,
A wilderness in which *there is* no man;
27 To satisfy the desolate waste,
And cause to spring forth the growth
of tender grass?
28 Has the rain a father?
Or who has begotten the drops of dew?
29 From whose womb comes the ice?
And the frost of heaven, who gives it birth?
30 The waters harden like stone,
And the surface of the deep is frozen.

31 "Can you bind the cluster of the Pleiades,
Or loose the belt of Orion?
32 Can you bring out Mazzaroth[f] in its season?

38:32 *f* Literally *Constellations*

LIFE LESSON

Job 38:1–41:34

SITUATION Job could not require God to give answers. Instead, through rhetorical questions, God revealed his power and perfection to Job. Job and his friends needed to decide how they would respond to God.

OBSERVATION Elihu told Job that God was too powerful to communicate with people. God proved Elihu wrong by speaking to Job.

INSPIRATION "God, why is this happening to me?"

So God speaks.

Out of the thunder, he speaks. Out of the sky, he speaks. For all of us who would put ditto marks under Job's question and sign our names to it, he speaks. . . .

He speaks out of the storm and into the storm, for that is where Job is. That is where God is best heard. God's voice thunders in the room. Elihu sits down. Job sits up. And the two will never be the same again.

"Who is this that darkens my counsel with words without knowledge?"

Job doesn't respond.

"Brace yourself like a man; I will question you, and you shall answer me."

"Where were you when I laid the foundations of the earth? Tell me, if you know so much."

One question would have been enough for Job, but it isn't enough for God.

"Do you know how its dimensions were determined and who did the surveying?" God asks. "What supports its foundations, and who laid its cornerstone, as the morning stars sang together and all the angels shouted for joy?"

Questions rush forth. They pour like sheets of rain out of the clouds. They splatter in the chambers of Job's

Or can you guide the Great Bear with its cubs?
33 Do you know the ordinances of the heavens?
Can you set their dominion over the earth?

34 "Can you lift up your voice to the clouds,
That an abundance of water may cover you?
35 Can you send out lightnings, that they may go,
And say to you, 'Here we *are!*'?
36 Who has put wisdom in the mind?[g]
Or who has given understanding to the heart?
37 Who can number the clouds by wisdom?
Or who can pour out the bottles of heaven,
38 When the dust hardens in clumps,
And the clods cling together?

39 "Can you hunt the prey for the lion,
Or satisfy the appetite of the young lions,
40 When they crouch in *their* dens,
Or lurk in their lairs to lie in wait?
41 Who provides food for the raven,
When its young ones cry to God,
And wander about for lack of food?

39 "Do you know the time when the wild mountain goats bear young?
Or can you mark when the deer gives birth?
2 Can you number the months *that* they fulfill?
Or do you know the time when they bear young?
3 They bow down,
They bring forth their young,
They deliver their offspring.[h]
4 Their young ones are healthy,
They grow strong with grain;
They depart and do not return to them.

5 "Who set the wild donkey free?
Who loosed the bonds of the onager,
6 Whose home I have made the wilderness,
And the barren land his dwelling?
7 He scorns the tumult of the city;
He does not heed the shouts of the driver.
8 The range of the mountains *is* his pasture,
And he searches after every green thing.

9 "Will the wild ox be willing to serve you?
Will he bed by your manger?
10 Can you bind the wild ox in the furrow with ropes?
Or will he plow the valleys behind you?
11 Will you trust him because his strength *is* great?
Or will you leave your labor to him?
12 Will you trust him to bring home your grain,
And gather it to your threshing floor?

38:36 [g] Literally *inward parts*
39:3 [h] Literally *pangs*, figurative of offspring

13 "The wings of the ostrich wave proudly,
But are her wings and pinions *like the* kindly stork's?
14 For she leaves her eggs on the ground,
And warms them in the dust;
15 She forgets that a foot may crush them,
Or that a wild beast may break them.
16 She treats her young harshly, as though *they were* not hers;
Her labor is in vain, without concern,
17 Because God deprived her of wisdom,
And did not endow her with understanding.
18 When she lifts herself on high,
She scorns the horse and its rider.

19 "Have you given the horse strength?
Have you clothed his neck with thunder?[i]
20 Can you frighten him like a locust?
His majestic snorting strikes terror.
21 He paws in the valley, and rejoices in *his* strength;
He gallops into the clash of arms.
22 He mocks at fear, and is not frightened;
Nor does he turn back from the sword.
23 The quiver rattles against him,
The glittering spear and javelin.
24 He devours the distance with fierceness and rage;
Nor does he come to a halt because the
trumpet *has* sounded.
25 At *the blast of* the trumpet he says, 'Aha!'
He smells the battle from afar,
The thunder of captains and shouting.

26 "Does the hawk fly by your wisdom,
And spread its wings toward the south?
27 Does the eagle mount up at your command,
And make its nest on high?
28 On the rock it dwells and resides,
On the crag of the rock and the stronghold.
29 From there it spies out the prey;
Its eyes observe from afar.
30 Its young ones suck up blood;
And where the slain *are,* there it *is.*"

40 Moreover the LORD answered Job, and said:

2 "Shall the one who contends with the Almighty correct *Him?*
He who rebukes God, let him answer it."

Job's Response to God

3 Then Job answered the LORD and said:

4 "Behold, I am vile;
What shall I answer You?
I lay my hand over my mouth.

39:19 *i* Or *a mane*

heart with a wildness and a beauty and a terror that leave every Job who has ever lived drenched and speechless, watching the Master redefine who is who in the universe. . . .

God's questions aren't intended to teach; they are intended to stun. They aren't intended to enlighten; they are intended to awaken. They aren't intended to stir the mind; they are intended to bend the knees. . . .

Finally Job's feeble hand lifts, and God stops long enough for him to respond. "I am nothing—how could I ever find the answers? I lay my hand upon my mouth in silence. I have said too much already." . . .

"I owe no one anything," God declares in the crescendo of the wind. "Everything under the heaven is mine."

Job couldn't argue. God owes no one anything. No explanations. No excuses. No help. God has no debt, no outstanding balance, no favors to return. God owes no man anything.

Which makes the fact that he gave us everything even more astounding.

(From *In the Eye of the Storm* by Max Lucado)

APPLICATION Consider your understanding of God. Do you acknowledge God as the almighty creator and absolute authority? Can you accept his love and special concern for you? Today, take note of events or insights that remind you of these truths. Tonight, prayerfully reflect on God's greatness.

EXPLORATION God and People—Genesis 1:27; Exodus 15:11; Nehemiah 9:6; Psalm 103:13-18; Jeremiah 31:3; Zephaniah 3:17; Romans 3:23; Philippians 2:7; Hebrews 1:10-12; 1 John 3:1; Revelation 1:8.

5 Once I have spoken, but I will not answer;
Yes, twice, but I will proceed no further."

God's Challenge to Job

6Then the LORD answered Job out of the whirlwind, and said:

7 "Now prepare yourself like a man;
I will question you, and you shall answer Me:

8 "Would you indeed annul My judgment?
Would you condemn Me that you may be justified?
9 Have you an arm like God?
Or can you thunder with a voice like His?
10 Then adorn yourself *with* majesty and splendor,
And array yourself with glory and beauty.
11 Disperse the rage of your wrath;
Look on everyone *who is* proud, and humble him.
12 Look on everyone *who is* proud, *and* bring him low;
Tread down the wicked in their place.
13 Hide them in the dust together,
Bind their faces in hidden *darkness.*
14 Then I will also confess to you
That your own right hand can save you.

15 "Look now at the behemoth,[j] which I made *along* with you;
He eats grass like an ox.
16 See now, his strength *is* in his hips,
And his power *is* in his stomach muscles.
17 He moves his tail like a cedar;
The sinews of his thighs are tightly knit.
18 His bones *are like* beams of bronze,
His ribs like bars of iron.
19 He *is* the first of the ways of God;
Only He who made him can bring near His sword.
20 Surely the mountains yield food for him,
And all the beasts of the field play there.
21 He lies under the lotus trees,
In a covert of reeds and marsh.
22 The lotus trees cover him *with* their shade;
The willows by the brook surround him.
23 Indeed the river may rage,
Yet he is not disturbed;
He is confident, though the Jordan gushes into his mouth,
24 *Though* he takes it in his eyes,
Or one pierces *his* nose with a snare.

41 "Can you draw out Leviathan[k] with a hook,
Or *snare* his tongue with a line *which* you lower?
2 Can you put a reed through his nose,
Or pierce his jaw with a hook?
3 Will he make many supplications to you?
Will he speak softly to you?
4 Will he make a covenant with you?
Will you take him as a servant forever?
5 Will you play with him as *with* a bird,
Or will you leash him for your maidens?
6 Will *your* companions make a banquet[l] of him?
Will they apportion him among the merchants?
7 Can you fill his skin with harpoons,
Or his head with fishing spears?
8 Lay your hand on him;
Remember the battle—
Never do it again!
9 Indeed, *any* hope of *overcoming* him is false;
Shall *one not* be overwhelmed at the sight of him?
10 No one *is so* fierce that he would dare stir him up.
Who then is able to stand against Me?
11 Who has preceded Me, that I should pay *him?*
Everything under heaven is Mine.

12 "I will not conceal[m] his limbs,
His mighty power, or his graceful proportions.
13 Who can remove his outer coat?
Who can approach *him* with a double bridle?
14 Who can open the doors of his face,
With his terrible teeth all around?
15 *His* rows of scales are *his* pride,
Shut up tightly *as with* a seal;
16 One is so near another
That no air can come between them;
17 They are joined one to another,
They stick together and cannot be parted.
18 His sneezings flash forth light,
And his eyes *are* like the eyelids of the morning.
19 Out of his mouth go burning lights;
Sparks of fire shoot out.
20 Smoke goes out of his nostrils,

40:15 [j] A large animal, exact identity unknown
41:1 [k] A large sea creature, exact identity unknown
41:6 [l] Or *bargain over him*
41:12 [m] Literally *keep silent about*

As *from* a boiling pot and burning rushes.
21 His breath kindles coals,
And a flame goes out of his mouth.
22 Strength dwells in his neck,
And sorrow dances before him.
23 The folds of his flesh are joined together;
They are firm on him and cannot be moved.
24 His heart is as hard as stone,
Even as hard as the lower *millstone.*
25 When he raises himself up, the mighty are afraid;
Because of his crashings they are beside[n] themselves.
26 *Though* the sword reaches him, it cannot avail;
Nor does spear, dart, or javelin.
27 He regards iron as straw,
And bronze as rotten wood.
28 The arrow cannot make him flee;
Slingstones become like stubble to him.
29 Darts are regarded as straw;
He laughs at the threat of javelins.
30 His undersides *are* like sharp potsherds;
He spreads pointed *marks* in the mire.
31 He makes the deep boil like a pot;
He makes the sea like a pot of ointment.
32 He leaves a shining wake behind him;
One would think the deep had white hair.
33 On earth there is nothing like him,
Which is made without fear.
34 He beholds every high *thing;*
He *is* king over all the children of pride."

Job's Repentance and Restoration

42 Then Job answered the LORD and said:

2 "I know that You can do everything,
And that no purpose *of Yours* can be withheld from You.
3 *You asked,* 'Who *is* this who hides counsel without knowledge?'
Therefore I have uttered what I did not understand,
Things too wonderful for me, which I did not know.
4 Listen, please, and let me speak;
You said, 'I will question you, and you shall answer Me.'

5 "I have heard of You by the hearing of the ear,
But now my eye sees You.
6 Therefore I abhor *myself,*
And repent in dust and ashes."

7And so it was, after the LORD had spoken these words to Job, that the
LORD said to Eliphaz the Temanite, "My wrath is aroused against you and
your two friends, for you have not spoken of Me *what is* right, as My servant
Job *has.* 8Now therefore, take for yourselves seven bulls and seven rams, go
to My servant Job, and offer up for yourselves a burnt offering; and My

41:25 *n* Or *purify themselves*

LIFE LESSON

Job 42:1-17

SITUATION Job learned of God's greatness and humbly prayed. God graciously restored Job's material blessings and family.

OBSERVATION We are better able to appreciate blessings if we endure hardship.

INSPIRATION All his life, Job had been a good man. All his life, he had believed in God. All his life, he had discussed God, had notions about him, and had prayed to him.

But in the storm Job sees him!

He sees Hope. Lover. Destroyer. Giver. Taker. Dreamer. Deliverer. Job sees the tender anger of a God whose unending love is often received with peculiar mistrust. Job stands as a blade of grass against the consuming fire of God's splendor. Job's demands melt like wax as God pulls back the curtain and heaven's light falls uneclipsed across the earth.

Job sees God.

God could turn away at this point. The gavel has been slammed, the verdict has been rendered. The Eternal Judge has spoken.

Ah, but God is not angry with Job. Firm? Yes. Direct? No doubt. Clear and convincing? Absolutely. But angry? No.

God is never irritated by the candle of an honest seeker.

If you underline any passage in the Book of Job, underline this one: "I had heard about you before, but now I have seen you."

Job sees God—and that is enough.

But it isn't enough for God.

The years to come find Job once again sitting behind his mahogany desk with health restored and profits up. His lap is once again full of children and grandchildren and great-grandchildren—for four generations!

If Job ever wonders why God doesn't bring back the children he had taken away, he doesn't ask. Maybe he doesn't ask because he knows that his children could never be happier than they are in the presence of this One he has seen so briefly.

Continued

Something tells me that Job would do it all again, if that's what it took to hear God's voice and stand in the Presence. Even if God left him with his bedsores and bills, Job would do it again.

For God gave Job more than Job ever dreamed. God gave Job Himself.

(From *In the Eye of the Storm* by Max Lucado)

APPLICATION How have personal problems hindered your spiritual progress? What steps are you taking to know God better? Stand still and experience God's presence.

EXPLORATION Knowing God—Jeremiah 9:24; John 15:13-15; 17:3; James 4:8; 1 John 2:14; 4:7-8.

servant Job shall pray for you. For I will accept him, lest I deal with you *according to your* folly; because you have not spoken of Me *what is* right, as
My servant Job *has*."
9 So Eliphaz the Temanite and Bildad the Shuhite *and* Zophar the Naamathite went and did as the LORD commanded them; for the LORD had accepted
Job. 10 And the LORD restored Job's losses[o] when he prayed for his friends.
Indeed the LORD gave Job twice as much as he had before. 11 Then all his
brothers, all his sisters, and all those who had been his acquaintances before, came to him and ate food with him in his house; and they consoled
him and comforted him for all the adversity that the LORD had brought
upon him. Each one gave him a piece of silver and each a ring of gold.
12 Now the LORD blessed the latter *days* of Job more than his beginning;
for he had fourteen thousand sheep, six thousand camels, one thousand
yoke of oxen, and one thousand female donkeys. 13 He also had seven sons
and three daughters. 14 And he called the name of the first Jemimah, the
name of the second Keziah, and the name of the third Keren-Happuch.
15 In all the land were found no women *so* beautiful as the daughters of Job;
and their father gave them an inheritance among their brothers.
16 After this Job lived one hundred and forty years, and saw his children
and grandchildren *for* four generations. 17 So Job died, old and full of days.

42:10 [o] Literally *Job's captivity,* that is, what was captured from Job

The Book of

PSALMS

INTRODUCTION

Worship. In two thousand years we haven't worked out the kinks. We still struggle for the right words in prayer. We still fumble over Scripture. We don't know when to kneel. We don't know when to stand. We don't know how to pray.

Worship is a daunting task.

For that reason, God gave us the Psalms—a praisebook for God's people. The Psalms could be titled *God's Book of Common Prayer.* This collection of hymns and petitions are strung together by one thread—a heart hungry for God.

Some are defiant. Others are reverent. Some are to be sung. Others are to be prayed. Some are intensely personal. Others are written as if the whole world would use them. Some were penned in caves, others in temples.

But all have one purpose—to give us the words to say when we stand before God.

The very variety should remind us that worship is personal. No secret formula exists. What moves you may stymie another. Each worships differently. But each should worship.

This book will help you do just that.

Here is a hint. Don't just read the prayers of these saints, pray them. Experience their energy. Imitate their honesty. Enjoy their creativity. Let these souls lead you in worship.

And let's remember. The language of worship is not polished, perfect, or advanced. It's just honest.

LIFE LESSON

Psalm 1:1-6

SITUATION Life offers two roads to travel, the way of the righteous or the way of the wicked. God provides, protects, and nourishes the righteous.

OBSERVATION Follow the faithful road. God's rewards supersede the benefits of the wicked.

INSPIRATION One marked difference between the faith of our fathers as conceived by the fathers and the same faith as understood and lived by their children is that the fathers were concerned with the root of the matter, while their present-day descendants seem concerned only with the fruit. . . .

Our fathers looked well to the root of the tree and were willing to wait with patience for the fruit to appear. We demand the fruit immediately even though the root may be weak and knobby or missing altogether. Impatient Christians today explain away the simple beliefs of the saints of other days and smile off their serious-minded approach to God and sacred things. They were victims of their own limited religious outlook, but great and sturdy souls withal who managed to achieve a satisfying spiritual experience and do a lot of good in the world in spite of their handicaps. . . .

. . . The bough that breaks off from the tree in a storm may bloom briefly and give to the unthinking passer-by the impression that it is a healthy and fruitful branch, but its tender blossoms will soon perish and the bough itself wither and die. There is no lasting life apart from the root.

Book One: Psalms 1—41

PSALM 1

The Way of the Righteous and the End of the Ungodly

Blessed *is* the man
Who walks not in the counsel of the ungodly,
Nor stands in the path of sinners,
Nor sits in the seat of the scornful;
2 But his delight *is* in the law of the LORD,
And in His law he meditates day and night.
3 He shall be like a tree
Planted by the rivers of water,
That brings forth its fruit in its season,
Whose leaf also shall not wither;
And whatever he does shall prosper.

4 The ungodly *are* not so,
But *are* like the chaff which the wind drives away.
5 Therefore the ungodly shall not stand in the judgment,
Nor sinners in the congregation of the righteous.

6 For the LORD knows the way of the righteous,
But the way of the ungodly shall perish.

PSALM 2

The Messiah's Triumph and Kingdom

Why do the nations rage,
And the people plot a vain thing?
2 The kings of the earth set themselves,
And the rulers take counsel together,
Against the LORD and against His Anointed, *saying,*
3 "Let us break Their bonds in pieces
And cast away Their cords from us."

4 He who sits in the heavens shall laugh;
The LORD shall hold them in derision.
5 Then He shall speak to them in His wrath,
And distress them in His deep displeasure:
6 "Yet I have set My King
On My holy hill of Zion."

7 "I will declare the decree:
The LORD has said to Me,
'You *are* My Son,
Today I have begotten You.
8 Ask of Me, and I will give *You*
The nations *for* Your inheritance,
And the ends of the earth *for* Your possession.
9 You shall break[a] them with a rod of iron;
You shall dash them to pieces like a potter's vessel.' "

2:9 [a]Following Masoretic Text and Targum; Septuagint, Syriac, and Vulgate read *rule* (compare Revelation 2:27).

10 Now therefore, be wise, O kings;
Be instructed, you judges of the earth.
11 Serve the LORD with fear,
And rejoice with trembling.
12 Kiss the Son,[b] lest He[c] be angry,
And you perish *in* the way,
When His wrath is kindled but a little.
Blessed *are* all those who put their trust in Him.

PSALM 3

The LORD Helps His Troubled People

A Psalm of David when he fled from Absalom his son.

LORD, how they have increased who trouble me!
Many *are* they who rise up against me.
2 Many *are* they who say of me,
"*There is* no help for him in God." Selah

3 But You, O LORD, *are* a shield for me,
My glory and the One who lifts up my head.
4 I cried to the LORD with my voice,
And He heard me from His holy hill. Selah

5 I lay down and slept;
I awoke, for the LORD sustained me.
6 I will not be afraid of ten thousands of people
Who have set *themselves* against me all around.

7 Arise, O LORD;
Save me, O my God!
For You have struck all my enemies on the cheekbone;
You have broken the teeth of the ungodly.
8 Salvation *belongs* to the LORD.
Your blessing *is* upon Your people. Selah

PSALM 4

The Safety of the Faithful

To the Chief Musician. With stringed instruments. A Psalm of David.

Hear me when I call, O God of my righteousness!
You have relieved me in *my* distress;
Have mercy on me, and hear my prayer.

2 How long, O you sons of men,
Will you turn my glory to shame?
How long will you love worthlessness
And seek falsehood? Selah
3 But know that the LORD has set apart[d] for
Himself him who is godly;
The LORD will hear when I call to Him.

2:12 [b] Septuagint and Vulgate read *Embrace discipline;* Targum reads *Receive instruction.* [c] Septuagint reads *the LORD.*
4:3 [d] Many Hebrew manuscripts, Septuagint, Targum, and Vulgate read *made wonderful.*

Much that passes for Christianity today is the brief bright effort of the severed branch to bring forth its fruit in its season. But the deep laws of life are against it. Preoccupation with appearances and a corresponding neglect of the out-of-sight root of the true spiritual life are prophetic signs which go unheeded. Immediate "results" are all that matter, quick proofs of present success without a thought of next week or next year. . . . There is but one test for the religious leader: success. Everything is forgiven him except failure. . . .

The whole Bible and all the great saints of the past join to tell us the same thing. "Take nothing for granted," they say to us. "Go back to the grass roots. Open your hearts and search the Scriptures. Bear your cross, follow your Lord and pay no heed to the passing religious vogue. The masses are always wrong. In every generation the number of the righteous is small. Be sure you are among them."

(From *The Best of Tozer* compiled by Warren Wiersbe)

APPLICATION What kind of people do you associate with? Who do you turn to for advice? Is God's Word a priority in your decision making? Let these areas of your life honor God. Thank him for giving his word to guide you.

EXPLORATION Fruitfulness—Matthew 3:8; 25:14-28; John 15:4-8; Philippians 1:9-11; Galatians 5:22-23; 2 Peter 1:5-6.

LIFE LESSON

Psalms 4:1–6:10

SITUATION David rejoiced because of God's protection and peace. He encouraged others to trust in God.

OBSERVATION Godly people can place their confidence in God because he listens to them and puts joy in their hearts.

INSPIRATION In August of 1930, forty-five-year-old Joseph Crater waved good-bye to friends after an evening meal in a New York restaurant, flagged down a taxi, and rode off. He was never seen or heard from again. . . .

A search of his apartment revealed one clue. It was a note attached to a check, and both were left for his wife. The check was for a sizable amount and the note simply read, "I am very weary. Love, Joe."

The note could have been nothing more than a thought at the end of a hard day. Or it could have meant a great deal more—the epitaph of a despairing man.

Weariness is tough. I don't mean the physical weariness that comes with mowing the lawn, or the mental weariness that follows a hard day of decisions and thinking. No, the weariness that attacked Judge Crater is much worse. It's the weariness that comes just before you give up. That feeling of honest desperation. It's the dispirited father, the abandoned child, or the retiree with time on his hands. It's that stage in life when motivation disappears; the children grow up, a job is lost, a wife dies. The result is weariness—deep, lonely, frustrated weariness.

Only one man in history has claimed to have an answer for it. He stands before all the Joseph Craters of the world with the same promise: "Come to me, all you who are weary . . . and I will give you rest" (Matt. 11:28).

(From *On the Anvil* by Max Lucado)

APPLICATION Ask God for a new sense of joy and love. When tension mounts, pause to thank God for his love.

EXPLORATION Joy—Psalm 16:9; Matthew 5:3-12; John 15:11; Philippians 4:4.

4 Be angry, and do not sin.
Meditate within your heart on your bed, and be still. Selah
5 Offer the sacrifices of righteousness,
And put your trust in the LORD.

6 *There are* many who say,
"Who will show us *any* good?"
LORD, lift up the light of Your countenance upon us.
7 You have put gladness in my heart,
More than in the season that their grain and wine increased.
8 I will both lie down in peace, and sleep;
For You alone, O LORD, make me dwell in safety.

PSALM 5

A Prayer for Guidance

To the Chief Musician. With flutes.[e] A Psalm of David.

Give ear to my words, O LORD,
Consider my meditation.
2 Give heed to the voice of my cry,
My King and my God,
For to You I will pray.
3 My voice You shall hear in the morning, O LORD;
In the morning I will direct *it* to You,
And I will look up.

4 For You *are* not a God who takes pleasure in wickedness,
Nor shall evil dwell with You.
5 The boastful shall not stand in Your sight;
You hate all workers of iniquity.
6 You shall destroy those who speak falsehood;
The LORD abhors the bloodthirsty and deceitful man.

7 But as for me, I will come into Your house
in the multitude of Your mercy;
In fear of You I will worship toward Your holy temple.
8 Lead me, O LORD, in Your righteousness
because of my enemies;
Make Your way straight before my face.

9 For *there is* no faithfulness in their mouth;
Their inward part *is* destruction;
Their throat *is* an open tomb;
They flatter with their tongue.
10 Pronounce them guilty, O God!
Let them fall by their own counsels;
Cast them out in the multitude of their transgressions,
For they have rebelled against You.

11 But let all those rejoice who put their trust in You;
Let them ever shout for joy, because You defend them;
Let those also who love Your name
Be joyful in You.

5:title [e] Hebrew *nehiloth*

12 For You, O LORD, will bless the righteous;
With favor You will surround him as *with* a shield.

PSALM 6

A Prayer of Faith in Time of Distress

To the Chief Musician. With stringed instruments. On an eight-stringed harp.[f] A Psalm of David.

O LORD, do not rebuke me in Your anger,
Nor chasten me in Your hot displeasure.
2 Have mercy on me, O LORD, for I *am* weak;
O LORD, heal me, for my bones are troubled.
3 My soul also is greatly troubled;
But You, O LORD—how long?

4 Return, O LORD, deliver me!
Oh, save me for Your mercies' sake!
5 For in death *there is* no remembrance of You;
In the grave who will give You thanks?

6 I am weary with my groaning;
All night I make my bed swim;
I drench my couch with my tears.
7 My eye wastes away because of grief;
It grows old because of all my enemies.

8 Depart from me, all you workers of iniquity;
For the LORD has heard the voice of my weeping.
9 The LORD has heard my supplication;
The LORD will receive my prayer.
10 Let all my enemies be ashamed and greatly troubled;
Let them turn back *and* be ashamed suddenly.

PSALM 7

Prayer and Praise for Deliverance from Enemies

A Meditation[g] of David, which he sang to the LORD concerning the words of Cush, a Benjamite.

O LORD my God, in You I put my trust;
Save me from all those who persecute me;
And deliver me,
2 Lest they tear me like a lion,
Rending *me* in pieces, while *there is* none to deliver.

3 O LORD my God, if I have done this:
If there is iniquity in my hands,
4 If I have repaid evil to him who was at peace with me,
Or have plundered my enemy without cause,
5 Let the enemy pursue me and overtake *me;*
Yes, let him trample my life to the earth,
And lay my honor in the dust. Selah

LIFE LESSON

Psalms 7:1–8:9

SITUATION This psalm may have been David's response to slanderous accusations. Some accused him of trying to kill King Saul and seize the throne (1 Samuel 24:9-11).

OBSERVATION Depend on God to bring justice. God judges perfectly when you are falsely accused.

INSPIRATION God's power to take the most negative situations and turn them into positive realities worthy of His praise is demonstrated throughout biblical history. There is not a crisis that goes beyond the bounds of God's creative power. Whether the difficulties come from Satan or other people, or are self-inflicted, or are experienced in the process of our obedience, it is the prerogative of God to rearrange, reconstruct, reinterpret, and realign the situation to bring glory and praise to His name. . . . Even Christ's death on the cross was transformed by the power of God into positive results and residual benefits of the redemption that many of us have come to know and enjoy. Since God is just, all that He permits is consistent with His justice. . . . God's justice guarantees that ultimately all that is unfair will be dealt with. We are naive to assume that all of life in its fallen condition is fair and just. It is only safe to realize that God is just and that in His time and in His own way He will deal with both the injustice and those who have been unjust. (From *The Upside of Down* by Joseph Stowell)

APPLICATION Think of a time when you were falsely accused. What did you do? Did you turn to God as David did, or did you take matters into your own hands? The next time you face injustice, remember that God perfectly judges all difficult matters. Turn the injustices over to him.

EXPLORATION Justice of God—Exodus 34:6-7; Deuteronomy 32:4; Job 34:17-30; Psalm 58:11; 140:12; Luke 18:7-8.

6:title [f] Hebrew *sheminith*
7:title [g] Hebrew *Shiggaion*

6 Arise, O LORD, in Your anger;
Lift Yourself up because of the rage
of my enemies;
Rise up for me[h] *to* the judgment
You have commanded!
7 So the congregation of the peoples
shall surround You;
For their sakes, therefore, return on high.
8 The LORD shall judge the peoples;
Judge me, O LORD, according
to my righteousness,
And according to my integrity within me.

9 Oh, let the wickedness of the wicked
come to an end,
But establish the just;
For the righteous God tests the hearts and minds.
10 My defense *is* of God,
Who saves the upright in heart.
11 God *is* a just judge,
And God is angry *with the wicked* every day.
12 If he does not turn back,
He will sharpen His sword;
He bends His bow and makes it ready.
13 He also prepares for Himself
instruments of death;
He makes His arrows into fiery shafts.

14 Behold, *the wicked* brings forth iniquity;
Yes, he conceives trouble and brings
forth falsehood.
15 He made a pit and dug it out,
And has fallen into the ditch *which* he made.
16 His trouble shall return upon his own head,
And his violent dealing shall come down on
his own crown.

17 I will praise the LORD according to His
righteousness,
And will sing praise to the name of the
LORD Most High.

PSALM 8

The Glory of the LORD in Creation

To the Chief Musician. On the instrument of Gath.[i] A Psalm of David.

O LORD, our Lord,
How excellent *is* Your name in all the earth,
Who have set Your glory above the heavens!

2 Out of the mouth of babes and nursing infants
You have ordained strength,
Because of Your enemies,
That You may silence the enemy
and the avenger.

3 When I consider Your heavens, the work
of Your fingers,
The moon and the stars, which
You have ordained,
4 What is man that You are mindful of him,
And the son of man that You visit him?
5 For You have made him a little lower
than the angels,[j]
And You have crowned him with
glory and honor.

6 You have made him to have dominion over
the works of Your hands;
You have put all *things* under his feet,
7 All sheep and oxen—
Even the beasts of the field,
8 The birds of the air,
And the fish of the sea
That pass through the paths of the seas.

9 O LORD, our Lord,
How excellent *is* Your name in all the earth!

PSALM 9

Prayer and Thanksgiving for the LORD's Righteous Judgments

To the Chief Musician. To *the tune of* "Death of the Son."[k] A Psalm of David.

I will praise *You,* O LORD, with my whole heart;
I will tell of all Your marvelous works.
2 I will be glad and rejoice in You;
I will sing praise to Your name, O Most High.

3 When my enemies turn back,
They shall fall and perish at Your presence.
4 For You have maintained my right
and my cause;
You sat on the throne judging in
righteousness.
5 You have rebuked the nations,
You have destroyed the wicked;
You have blotted out their name
forever and ever.

7:6 [h] Following Masoretic Text, Targum, and Vulgate; Septuagint reads *O LORD my God.*
8:title [i] Hebrew *Al Gittith*
8:5 [j] Hebrew *Elohim, God;* Septuagint, Syriac, Targum, and Jewish tradition translate as *angels.*
9:title [k] Hebrew *Muth Labben*

6 O enemy, destructions are finished forever!
And you have destroyed cities;
Even their memory has perished.
7 But the LORD shall endure forever;
He has prepared His throne for judgment.
8 He shall judge the world in righteousness,
And He shall administer judgment for the peoples in uprightness.

9 The LORD also will be a refuge for the oppressed,
A refuge in times of trouble.
10 And those who know Your name will put their trust in You;
For You, LORD, have not forsaken those who seek You.

11 Sing praises to the LORD, who dwells in Zion!
Declare His deeds among the people.
12 When He avenges blood, He remembers them;
He does not forget the cry of the humble.

13 Have mercy on me, O LORD!
Consider my trouble from those who hate me,
You who lift me up from the gates of death,
14 That I may tell of all Your praise
In the gates of the daughter of Zion.
I will rejoice in Your salvation.

15 The nations have sunk down in the pit *which* they made;
In the net which they hid, their own foot is caught.
16 The LORD is known *by* the judgment He executes;
The wicked is snared in the work of his own hands.
Meditation.[1] Selah

17 The wicked shall be turned into hell,
And all the nations that forget God.
18 For the needy shall not always be forgotten;
The expectation of the poor shall *not* perish forever.

19 Arise, O LORD,
Do not let man prevail;
Let the nations be judged in Your sight.
20 Put them in fear, O LORD,
That the nations may know themselves *to be but* men. Selah

PSALM 10

A Song of Confidence in God's Triumph over Evil

Why do You stand afar off, O LORD?
Why do You hide in times of trouble?
2 The wicked in *his* pride persecutes the poor;
Let them be caught in the plots which they have devised.

3 For the wicked boasts of his heart's desire;
He blesses the greedy *and* renounces the LORD.
4 The wicked in his proud countenance does not seek *God;*
God *is* in none of his thoughts.

9:16 [1] Hebrew *Higgaion*

LIFE LESSON

Psalms 9:1–10:18

SITUATION David praised God as a way of saying thank you. God helped David and the Israelites. David knew God would show his constant care in the future, too.

OBSERVATION God is never deaf to his children's cries for help.

INSPIRATION The Bible is a Christian's guidebook, and I believe the knowledge it sheds on pain and suffering is the great antidote to fear for suffering people. . . .

When I suffer pain over any length of time I try to reflect on the good which the Bible has promised pain is producing in me. . . .

"How does suffering accomplish this?" I ask myself. It produces perseverance, or steadiness, by slowing me down, by forcing me to turn to God, by proving to me that I can survive a crisis. . . .

The Bible is filled with resources available to one trying to stave off fears and helplessness. Reading Job's thrashings in fear about God's seeming lack of concern can make mine easier to bear. . . . And knowledge about prayer to a loving God can ward off frenzied efforts to "muster up faith" in hopes of impressing God—prayer does not work that way, as the Bible shows. God is already full of loving concern; we do not need to impress Him with spiritual calisthenics. . . .

Attitudes of fear and helplessness affect the quantity of suffering. At least we have the inspiring examples of those who have proved that the human spirit can ascend through the words of circumstances. And because man is both body and spirit, Christianity can offer a true and healing hope.

(From *Where Is God When It Hurts* by Philip Yancey)

APPLICATION Whenever you face a trial, pray for God's help. Pray that God will be glorified in the situation. And thank him for the care he shows.

EXPLORATION God as Help—Psalm 30:10; 33:20; 54:4; 70:5; 115:9; 146:5.

Life Lesson

Psalms 11:1–13:6

SITUATION David complained to God about the evil in society. The wicked seemed to prosper, while the righteous suffered.

OBSERVATION God will punish evil at the proper time. Until then, he will protect us.

INSPIRATION There are snowstorms. There are hailstorms. There are rainstorms. And there are doubtstorms.

Every so often a doubtstorm rolls into my life, bringing with it a flurry of questions and gale-force winds of fear. And, soon after it comes, a light shines through it.

Sometimes the storm comes after the evening news. Some nights I wonder why I watch it. Some nights it's just too much. From the steps of the Supreme Court to the steppes of South Africa, the news is usually gloomy . . . thirty minutes of bite-sized tragedies. A handsome man in a nice suit with a warm voice gives bad news. They call him the anchorman. Good title. One needs an anchor in today's tempestuous waters.

Sometimes the storm comes when I'm at work. Story after story of homes that won't heal and hearts that won't melt. Always more hunger than food. More needs than money. More questions than answers. On Sundays I stand before a church with a three-point outline in my hand, thirty minutes on the clock, and a prayer on my lips. I do my best to say something that will convince a stranger that an unseen God still hears.

And I sometimes wonder why so many hearts have to hurt.

Do you ever get doubtstorms? Some of you don't, I know. I've talked to you. Some of you have a "Davidish" optimism that defies any Goliath. I used to think that you were naive at best and phony at worst.

I don't think that anymore.

I think you are gifted. You are gifted with faith. You can see the rainbow before the clouds part. If you have this gift, then skip this chapter. I won't say anything you need to hear.

5 His ways are always prospering;
Your judgments *are* far above, out of his sight;
As for all his enemies, he sneers at them.
6 He has said in his heart, "I shall not be moved;
I shall never be in adversity."
7 His mouth is full of cursing and deceit and oppression;
Under his tongue *is* trouble and iniquity.

8 He sits in the lurking places of the villages;
In the secret places he murders the innocent;
His eyes are secretly fixed on the helpless.
9 He lies in wait secretly, as a lion in his den;
He lies in wait to catch the poor;
He catches the poor when he draws him into his net.
10 So he crouches, he lies low,
That the helpless may fall by his strength.
11 He has said in his heart,
"God has forgotten;
He hides His face;
He will never see."

12 Arise, O LORD!
O God, lift up Your hand!
Do not forget the humble.
13 Why do the wicked renounce God?
He has said in his heart,
"You will not require *an account.*"

14 But You have seen, for You observe trouble and grief,
To repay *it* by Your hand.
The helpless commits himself to You;
You are the helper of the fatherless.
15 Break the arm of the wicked and the evil *man;*
Seek out his wickedness *until* You find none.

16 The LORD *is* King forever and ever;
The nations have perished out of His land.
17 LORD, You have heard the desire of the humble;
You will prepare their heart;
You will cause Your ear to hear,
18 To do justice to the fatherless and the oppressed,
That the man of the earth may oppress no more.

PSALM 11

Faith in the LORD's Righteousness

To the Chief Musician. A Psalm of David.

In the LORD I put my trust;
How can you say to my soul,
"Flee *as* a bird to your mountain"?
2 For look! The wicked bend *their* bow,
They make ready their arrow on the string,
That they may shoot secretly at the upright in heart.

3 If the foundations are destroyed,
What can the righteous do?

4 The LORD *is* in His holy temple,
The LORD's throne *is* in heaven;
His eyes behold,
His eyelids test the sons of men.
5 The LORD tests the righteous,
But the wicked and the one who loves violence His soul hates.
6 Upon the wicked He will rain coals;
Fire and brimstone and a burning wind
Shall be the portion of their cup.

7 For the LORD *is* righteous,
He loves righteousness;
His countenance beholds the upright.[m]

PSALM 12

Man's Treachery and God's Constancy

To the Chief Musician. On an eight-stringed harp.[n] A Psalm of David.

Help, LORD, for the godly man ceases!
For the faithful disappear from among the sons of men.
2 They speak idly everyone with his neighbor;
With flattering lips *and* a double heart they speak.

3 May the LORD cut off all flattering lips,
And the tongue that speaks proud things,
4 Who have said,
"With our tongue we will prevail;
Our lips *are* our own;
Who *is* lord over us?"

5 "For the oppression of the poor, for the sighing of the needy,
Now I will arise," says the LORD;
"I will set *him* in the safety for which he yearns."
6 The words of the LORD *are* pure words,
Like silver tried in a furnace of earth,
Purified seven times.
7 You shall keep them, O LORD,
You shall preserve them from this generation forever.

8 The wicked prowl on every side,
When vileness is exalted among the sons of men.

PSALM 13

Trust in the Salvation of the LORD

To the Chief Musician. A Psalm of David.

How long, O LORD? Will You forget me forever?
How long will You hide Your face from me?
2 How long shall I take counsel in my soul,

11:7 [m] Or *The upright beholds His countenance*
12:title [n] Hebrew *sheminith*

But others of you wonder . . .

You wonder what others know that you don't. You wonder if you are blind or if they are. You wonder why some proclaim "Eureka" before the gold is found. You wonder why some shout "Land ho" before the fog has cleared. You wonder how some people believe so confidently while you believe so reluctantly.

As a result, you are a bit uncomfortable on the padded pew of blind belief. Your Bible hero is Thomas. Your middle name is Caution. Your queries are the bane of every Sunday school teacher.

"If God is so good, why do I sometimes feel so bad?"

"If his message is so clear, why do I get so confused?"

"If the Father is in control, why do good people have gut-wrenching problems?"

You wonder if it is a blessing or a curse to have a mind that never rests. . . .

Tough questions. Throw-in-the-towel questions. Questions the disciples must have asked. . . .

Where is God when his world is stormy?

Doubtstorms: turbulent days when the enemy is too big, the task too great, the future too bleak, and the answers too few. . . .

"When God comes," we doubters think, "all pain will flee. Life will be tranquil. No questions will remain."

And because we look for the bonfire, we miss the candle. Because we listen for the shout, we miss the whisper.

But it is in burnished candles that God comes, and through whispered promises he speaks: "When you doubt, look around; I am closer than you think."

(From *In the Eye of the Storm* by Max Lucado)

APPLICATION In what ways do you see evil people prospering and righteous people suffering? Your challenge is to *wait*; to *trust* that God will one day balance the scales.

EXPLORATION God Judges the Wicked—Zephaniah 3:1-8; Malachi 3:13–4:3; 2 Peter 2:1-13; Revelation 20:1-15.

Having sorrow in my heart daily?
How long will my enemy be exalted over me?

3 Consider *and* hear me, O LORD my God;
Enlighten my eyes,
Lest I sleep the *sleep of* death;
4 Lest my enemy say,
"I have prevailed against him";
Lest those who trouble me rejoice when I am moved.

5 But I have trusted in Your mercy;
My heart shall rejoice in Your salvation.
6 I will sing to the LORD,
Because He has dealt bountifully with me.

PSALM 14

Folly of the Godless, and God's Final Triumph

To the Chief Musician. A Psalm of David.

The fool has said in his heart,
"*There is* no God."
They are corrupt,
They have done abominable works,
There is none who does good.

2 The LORD looks down from heaven upon the children of men,
To see if there are any who understand, who seek God.
3 They have all turned aside,
They have together become corrupt;
There is none who does good,
No, not one.

4 Have all the workers of iniquity no knowledge,
Who eat up my people *as* they eat bread,
And do not call on the LORD?
5 There they are in great fear,
For God *is* with the generation of the righteous.
6 You shame the counsel of the poor,
But the LORD *is* his refuge.

7 Oh, that the salvation of Israel *would come* out of Zion!
When the LORD brings back the captivity of His people,
Let Jacob rejoice *and* Israel be glad.

PSALM 15

The Character of Those Who May Dwell with the LORD

A Psalm of David.

LORD, who may abide in Your tabernacle?
Who may dwell in Your holy hill?

LIFE LESSON

Psalms 14:1–15:5

SITUATION David mourned or lamented. He may have written Psalm 14 when enemies pressed in on him. David wrote Psalm 15 in a liturgical style. Perhaps he taught this song to the Israelites as a reminder of godly living.

OBSERVATION Evil, wickedness, and deceit define how a world without God behaves. Yet the righteous live according to God's commands. Truth, justice, and a passion for righteousness please God.

INSPIRATION The goal of Christian growth is the achievement of righteousness. In the Christian world today such a statement may sound radical. Christians hardly ever talk about righteousness. The word has almost become a swear word. Nearly any other term is preferred to the word righteousness. I have never had a student, a parishioner, or any other person come to me and ask, "How can I become righteous?"

To be spiritual has only one real purpose. It is a means to an end, not the end itself. The goal of all spiritual exercise must be the goal of righteousness. God calls us to be holy. Christ sets the priority of the Christian life: "Seek ye first the kingdom of God, and his righteousness; and all these things shall be added unto you." The goal is righteousness.

(From *The Holiness of God* by R. C. Sproul)

APPLICATION Live according to God's high moral standards. Make decisions as if God were your companion in all your activities—for he is!

EXPLORATION Righteousness—Daniel 4:27; Hosea 10:12; Matthew 5:20; Ephesians 6:14; Philippians 1:11; 1 Timothy 6:11; 2 Peter 3:11.

2 He who walks uprightly,
And works righteousness,
And speaks the truth in his heart;
3 He *who* does not backbite with his tongue,
Nor does evil to his neighbor,
Nor does he take up a reproach against his friend;
4 In whose eyes a vile person is despised,
But he honors those who fear the LORD;
He *who* swears to his own hurt and does not change;
5 He *who* does not put out his money at usury,
Nor does he take a bribe against the innocent.

He who does these *things* shall never be moved.

PSALM 16

The Hope of the Faithful, and the Messiah's Victory

A Michtam of David.

Preserve me, O God, for in You I put my trust.

2 *O my soul,* you have said to the LORD,
"You *are* my Lord,
My goodness is nothing apart from You."
3 As for the saints who *are* on the earth,
"They are the excellent ones, in whom is all my delight."

4 Their sorrows shall be multiplied who hasten *after* another *god;*
Their drink offerings of blood I will not offer,
Nor take up their names on my lips.

5 O LORD, *You are* the portion of my inheritance and my cup;
You maintain my lot.
6 The lines have fallen to me in pleasant *places;*
Yes, I have a good inheritance.

7 I will bless the LORD who has given me counsel;
My heart also instructs me in the night seasons.
8 I have set the LORD always before me;
Because *He is* at my right hand I shall not be moved.

9 Therefore my heart is glad, and my glory rejoices;
My flesh also will rest in hope.
10 For You will not leave my soul in Sheol,
Nor will You allow Your Holy One to see corruption.
11 You will show me the path of life;
In Your presence *is* fullness of joy;
At Your right hand *are* pleasures forevermore.

PSALM 17

Prayer with Confidence in Final Salvation

A Prayer of David.

Hear a just cause, O LORD,
Attend to my cry;
Give ear to my prayer *which is* not from deceitful lips.

LIFE LESSON

Psalms 16:1–17:15

SITUATION David's prayers revealed his trust in and reliance upon God, both in this life and the life to come.

OBSERVATION David's trust in God inspires Christians today.

INSPIRATION The Bible tells us our God is so trustworthy that we are to throw our confidence on Him, not leaning on our own understanding (Proverbs 3:5). God has already proved how much His love can be trusted by sending Christ to die for us. Wasn't that enough? Not for me. I always wanted to be on the inside looking out—sitting with the Lord up in the control tower instead of down on the confusing ground level. He couldn't be trusted unless I was there to oversee things! What a low view of my Master and Creator I had held all these years! How could I have dared to assume that almighty God owed me explanations! Did I think that because I had done God the "favor" of becoming a Christian, He must now check things out with me? Was the Lord of the universe under obligation to show me how the trials of every human being fit into the tapestry of life? Had I never read Deuteronomy 29:29, "There are secrets the Lord your God has not revealed to us" (LB)? What made me think that even if He explained all His ways to me I would be able to understand them? It would be like pouring million-gallon truths into my one-ounce brain.

(From *A Step Further* by Joni Eareckson Tada)

APPLICATION Find an enticing jigsaw puzzle and try putting it together. As you experience the challenge and frustration of finding the right pieces, stop and read these psalms again. Note the connections you can make with these psalms, the puzzle, and your life. Rest in the fact that God has already put together the "big picture" of your life.

EXPLORATION Trust—Proverbs 3:5-7; Victory—1 Timothy 1:18; 6:12; 2 Timothy 4:7.

LIFE LESSON

Psalm 18:1-50

SITUATION King David cried out to God in great distress. God helped him by his mighty power.

OBSERVATION David knew that help comes only from God, so he quickly asked for God's help. God answered.

INSPIRATION The one hundredth anniversary of the Statue of Liberty was a glorious experience and a reminder that America is an immigrant nation. Nearly all of us can trace our roots to another land.

After the Vietnam war, tens of thousands of immigrants came to America as refugees. Many more went to other free countries. The refugees were looking for safe havens for themselves and their families, away from wars and hunger and need. America has provided a safe haven for millions, a place where immigrants can pursue their hopes and dreams.

Like the torch held by the Lady in the harbor, God's light shines to signify that He is a refuge for all who wish to flee from the storms of life, "a helper in the time of storms," as the hymn says.

My wife once heard this story about a poor woman who went up to the foothills in a Chinese town to cut the grass. Her baby was tied to her back and a little child walked beside her. In her hand was a sickle to cut the grass.

2 Let my vindication come from Your presence;
Let Your eyes look on the things that are upright.

3 You have tested my heart;
You have visited *me* in the night;
You have tried me and have found nothing;
I have purposed that my mouth shall not transgress.
4 Concerning the works of men,
By the word of Your lips,
I have kept away from the paths of the destroyer.
5 Uphold my steps in Your paths,
That my footsteps may not slip.

6 I have called upon You, for You will hear me, O God;
Incline Your ear to me, *and* hear my speech.
7 Show Your marvelous lovingkindness by Your right hand,
O You who save those who trust *in You*
From those who rise up *against them.*
8 Keep me as the apple of Your eye;
Hide me under the shadow of Your wings,
9 From the wicked who oppress me,
From my deadly enemies who surround me.

10 They have closed up their fat *hearts;*
With their mouths they speak proudly.
11 They have now surrounded us in our steps;
They have set their eyes, crouching down to the earth,
12 As a lion is eager to tear his prey,
And like a young lion lurking in secret places.

13 Arise, O LORD,
Confront him, cast him down;
Deliver my life from the wicked with Your sword,
14 With Your hand from men, O LORD,
From men of the world *who have* their portion in *this* life,
And whose belly You fill with Your hidden treasure.
They are satisfied with children,
And leave the rest of their *possession* for their babes.

15 As for me, I will see Your face in righteousness;
I shall be satisfied when I awake in Your likeness.

PSALM 18

God the Sovereign Savior

To the Chief Musician. A Psalm of David the servant of the LORD, who spoke to the LORD the words of this song on the day that the LORD delivered him from the hand of all his enemies and from the hand of Saul. And he said:

I will love You, O LORD, my strength.
2 The LORD is my rock and my fortress and my deliverer;
My God, my strength, in whom I will trust;
My shield and the horn of my salvation, my stronghold.
3 I will call upon the LORD, *who is worthy* to be praised;
So shall I be saved from my enemies.

4 The pangs of death surrounded me,
And the floods of ungodliness made me afraid.
5 The sorrows of Sheol surrounded me;
The snares of death confronted me.
6 In my distress I called upon the LORD,
And cried out to my God;
He heard my voice from His temple,
And my cry came before Him, *even* to His ears.
7 Then the earth shook and trembled;
The foundations of the hills also quaked and were shaken,
Because He was angry.
8 Smoke went up from His nostrils,
And devouring fire from His mouth;
Coals were kindled by it.
9 He bowed the heavens also, and came down
With darkness under His feet.
10 And He rode upon a cherub, and flew;
He flew upon the wings of the wind.
11 He made darkness His secret place;
His canopy around Him *was* dark waters
And thick clouds of the skies.
12 From the brightness before Him,
His thick clouds passed with hailstones and coals of fire.

13 The LORD thundered from heaven,
And the Most High uttered His voice,
Hailstones and coals of fire.[o]
14 He sent out His arrows and scattered the foe,
Lightnings in abundance, and He vanquished them.
15 Then the channels of the sea were seen,
The foundations of the world were uncovered
At Your rebuke, O LORD,
At the blast of the breath of Your nostrils.

16 He sent from above, He took me;
He drew me out of many waters.
17 He delivered me from my strong enemy,
From those who hated me,
For they were too strong for me.
18 They confronted me in the day of my calamity,
But the LORD was my support.
19 He also brought me out into a broad place;
He delivered me because He delighted in me.

20 The LORD rewarded me according to my righteousness;
According to the cleanness of my hands
He has recompensed me.
21 For I have kept the ways of the LORD,
And have not wickedly departed from my God.

Just as she reached the top of a hill, she heard a roar. Frightened, she turned and saw a mother tigress springing at her, followed by her two cubs.

The illiterate Chinese woman had never attended school or church, but a missionary once told her about Jesus, "who is able to help you when you are in trouble." As the tiger's claws tore into her arm, the woman cried out, "O Jesus, help me!" The tiger, instead of attacking again, suddenly turned and ran away.

The Bible says, "He will give his angels charge of you to guard you in all your ways" (Psalm 91:11, RSV). What "beasts" are attacking you? Chances are you will never be attacked by a wild beast, but you will be attacked by doubts, by fears of other kinds, by worry, by loneliness, by despair.

Cry out to Jesus, and He will answer you just as surely as the Chinese woman's desperate cry was heard and answered.

(From *Unto the Hills* by Billy Graham)

APPLICATION Whenever you feel swamped by pressure or problems or crises, ask God to help you. He will respond.

EXPLORATION God, Our Rock—Deuteronomy 32:4; 2 Samuel 22:2-3.

18:13 [o] Following Masoretic Text, Targum, and Vulgate; a few Hebrew manuscripts and Septuagint omit *Hailstones and coals of fire.*

22 For all His judgments *were* before me,
And I did not put away His statutes from me.
23 I was also blameless before Him,
And I kept myself from my iniquity.
24 Therefore the LORD has recompensed me
according to my righteousness,
According to the cleanness of my
hands in His sight.

25 With the merciful You will show
Yourself merciful;
With a blameless man You will show
Yourself blameless;
26 With the pure You will show Yourself pure;
And with the devious You will show
Yourself shrewd.
27 For You will save the humble people,
But will bring down haughty looks.

28 For You will light my lamp;
The LORD my God will enlighten
my darkness.
29 For by You I can run against a troop,
By my God I can leap over a wall.
30 *As for* God, His way *is* perfect;
The word of the LORD is proven;
He *is* a shield to all who trust in Him.

31 For who *is* God, except the LORD?
And who *is* a rock, except our God?
32 *It is* God who arms me with strength,
And makes my way perfect.
33 He makes my feet like the *feet of* deer,
And sets me on my high places.
34 He teaches my hands to make war,
So that my arms can bend a bow of bronze.

35 You have also given me the shield
of Your salvation;
Your right hand has held me up,
Your gentleness has made me great.
36 You enlarged my path under me,
So my feet did not slip.

37 I have pursued my enemies and
overtaken them;
Neither did I turn back again till
they were destroyed.
38 I have wounded them,
So that they could not rise;
They have fallen under my feet.
39 For You have armed me with strength
for the battle;
You have subdued under me those who rose
up against me.
40 You have also given me the necks
of my enemies,
So that I destroyed those who hated me.
41 They cried out, but *there was* none to save;
Even to the LORD, but He did not answer them.
42 Then I beat them as fine as the dust
before the wind;
I cast them out like dirt in the streets.

43 You have delivered me from the strivings of
the people;
You have made me the head of the nations;
A people I have not known shall serve me.
44 As soon as they hear of me they obey me;
The foreigners submit to me.
45 The foreigners fade away,
And come frightened from their hideouts.

46 The LORD lives!
Blessed *be* my Rock!
Let the God of my salvation be exalted.
47 *It is* God who avenges me,
And subdues the peoples under me;
48 He delivers me from my enemies.
You also lift me up above those who
rise against me;
You have delivered me from
the violent man.
49 Therefore I will give thanks to You, O LORD,
among the Gentiles,
And sing praises to Your name.

50 Great deliverance He gives to His king,
And shows mercy to His anointed,
To David and his descendants forevermore.

PSALM 19

The Perfect Revelation of the LORD

To the Chief Musician. A Psalm of David.

The heavens declare the glory of God;
And the firmament shows His handiwork.
2 Day unto day utters speech,
And night unto night reveals knowledge.
3 *There is* no speech nor language
Where their voice is not heard.
4 Their line[p] has gone out through all the earth,
And their words to the end of the world.

19:4 [p] Septuagint, Syriac, and Vulgate read *sound;* Targum reads *business.*

In them He has set a tabernacle for the sun,
5 Which *is* like a bridegroom coming out of his chamber,
And rejoices like a strong man to run its race.
6 Its rising *is* from one end of heaven,
And its circuit to the other end;
And there is nothing hidden from its heat.

7 The law of the LORD *is* perfect, converting the soul;
The testimony of the LORD *is* sure, making wise the simple;
8 The statutes of the LORD *are* right, rejoicing the heart;
The commandment of the LORD *is* pure, enlightening the eyes;
9 The fear of the LORD *is* clean, enduring forever;
The judgments of the LORD *are* true *and* righteous altogether.
10 More to be desired *are they* than gold,
Yea, than much fine gold;
Sweeter also than honey and the honeycomb.
11 Moreover by them Your servant is warned,
And in keeping them *there is* great reward.

12 Who can understand *his* errors?
Cleanse me from secret *faults.*
13 Keep back Your servant also from presumptuous *sins;*
Let them not have dominion over me.
Then I shall be blameless,
And I shall be innocent of great transgression.

14 Let the words of my mouth and the meditation of my heart
Be acceptable in Your sight,
O LORD, my strength and my Redeemer.

PSALM 20

The Assurance of God's Saving Work

To the Chief Musician. A Psalm of David.

May the LORD answer you in the day of trouble;
May the name of the God of Jacob defend you;
2 May He send you help from the sanctuary,
And strengthen you out of Zion;
3 May He remember all your offerings,
And accept your burnt sacrifice. Selah

4 May He grant you according to your heart's *desire,*
And fulfill all your purpose.
5 We will rejoice in your salvation,
And in the name of our God we will set up *our* banners!
May the LORD fulfill all your petitions.

6 Now I know that the LORD saves His anointed;
He will answer him from His holy heaven
With the saving strength of His right hand.

7 Some *trust* in chariots, and some in horses;
But we will remember the name of the LORD our God.
8 They have bowed down and fallen;

LIFE LESSON

Psalm 19:1-14

SITUATION David praised God for the beauty of nature. David believed that rather than inhibiting actions, God's laws pointed out shortfalls and sins.

OBSERVATION God's law helps us avoid sin and enjoy fellowship with him. The law does not prevent enjoyment but encourages it.

INSPIRATION The Ten Commandments tell us not to covet or lust. However, all moral law is more than a test; it's for our own good. Every law which God has given has been for our benefit. If a person breaks it, he is not only rebelling against God, he is hurting himself. God gave "the law" because he loves man. It is for man's benefit. God's commandments were given to protect and promote man's happiness, not to restrict it. God wants the best for man. To ask God to revise his commandments would be to ask him to stop loving man. . . .

In our universe, we live under God's law. In the physical realm, the planets move in split-second precision. There is no guesswork in the galaxies. We see in nature that everything is part of a plan which is harmonious, orderly, and obedient. Could a God who made the physical universe be any less exacting in the higher spiritual and moral order? God loves us with an infinite love, but he cannot and will not approve of disorder. Consequently, he has laid down spiritual laws which, if obeyed, bring harmony and fulfillment, but, if disobeyed, bring discord and disorder.

(From *How to Be Born Again* by Billy Graham)

APPLICATION Think of a few laws in your town. Rewrite a few that begin with "Do not" to begin with "You must." Write them so that keeping them brings law-abiding citizens enjoyment. Harder than you thought? Thank God today for laws that promote justice and peace. Write a letter of encouragement to your mayor or police chief.

EXPLORATION Law of God—Exodus 15:26; 20:1-17; Leviticus 20:22-23; Galatians 2:16.

LIFE LESSON
Psalms 20:1–22:31

SITUATION Jesus quoted the first line of Psalm 22 when he suffered on the cross.

OBSERVATION This psalm prophesied Jesus' suffering on the cross. It described his emotional, spiritual, and physical anguish.

INSPIRATION Lord?

Yes.

I may be stepping out of line by saying this, but I need to tell you something that's been on my mind.

Go ahead.

I don't like this verse: "My God, my God, why have you abandoned me?" It doesn't sound like you; it doesn't sound like something you would say.

Usually I love it when you speak. I listen when you speak. I imagine the power of your voice, the thunder of your commands, the dynamism in your dictates.

That's what I like to hear.

Remember the creation song you sang into the soundless eternity? Ah, now that's you. That was the act of a God!

And when you ordained the waves to splash and they roared, when you declared that the stars be flung and they flew, when you proclaimed that life be alive and it all began? . . . Or the whisper of breath into the clay-caked Adam? That was you at your best. That's the way I like to hear you. That's the voice I love to hear.

That's why I don't like this verse. . . . Look at the sentence. There is a "why" at the beginning and a question mark at the end. You don't ask questions. . . .

And as long as I'm shooting straight with you—I don't like to see the word *abandon,* either. The source of life . . . abandoned? The giver of love . . . alone? The father of it all . . . isolated?

Come on. Surely you don't mean it. Could deity feel abandoned?

Could we change the sentence a bit? Not much. Just the verb.

What would you suggest?

How about *challenge*? "My God, my God, why did you challenge me?"

But we have risen and stand upright.
9 Save, LORD!
May the King answer us when we call.

PSALM 21

Joy in the Salvation of the LORD

To the Chief Musician. A Psalm of David.

The king shall have joy in Your strength, O LORD;
And in Your salvation how greatly shall he rejoice!
2 You have given him his heart's desire,
And have not withheld the request of his lips. Selah

3 For You meet him with the blessings of goodness;
You set a crown of pure gold upon his head.
4 He asked life from You, *and* You gave *it* to him—
Length of days forever and ever.
5 His glory *is* great in Your salvation;
Honor and majesty You have placed upon him.
6 For You have made him most blessed forever;
You have made him exceedingly glad with Your presence.
7 For the king trusts in the LORD,
And through the mercy of the Most High he shall not be moved.

8 Your hand will find all Your enemies;
Your right hand will find those who hate You.
9 You shall make them as a fiery oven in the time of Your anger;
The LORD shall swallow them up in His wrath,
And the fire shall devour them.
10 Their offspring You shall destroy from the earth,
And their descendants from among the sons of men.
11 For they intended evil against You;
They devised a plot *which* they are not able *to perform.*
12 Therefore You will make them turn their back;
You will make ready *Your arrows* on Your string toward their faces.

13 Be exalted, O LORD, in Your own strength!
We will sing and praise Your power.

PSALM 22

The Suffering, Praise, and Posterity of the Messiah

To the Chief Musician. Set to "The Deer of the Dawn."[q] A Psalm of David.

My God, My God, why have You forsaken Me?
Why are You so far from helping Me,
And from the words of My groaning?
2 O My God, I cry in the daytime, but You do not hear;
And in the night season, and am not silent.

3 But You *are* holy,
Enthroned in the praises of Israel.

22:title [q] Hebrew *Aijeleth Hashahar*

Worry

The same God that gave us commandments such as "Do not commit adultery, do not murder" said, "Do not worry." It's a violation of our relationship to God to question his authority by worrying.

Has any good ever come out of any worrying that you've ever done? Worry only compartmentalizes us and makes us unable to do what we set out to do. If you are worried about a problem, what you need to do is simply trust the Lord and do good.

The word *worry* comes from a word that means "to divide." When you worry, you divide your energy. Do you worry? I worry about you if you don't worry! All of us worry, but we shouldn't. Jesus commands us half a dozen times, "Do not worry." When we worry about a situation, the problem gets us instead of us getting it.

Jesus is not afraid of the things that cause us fear. He never said, "Don't bring your fears to me; I'm too busy." Instead, he said, "I'm not afraid of the things that cause you fear. Bring your fears to me."

WE DON'T LOOK like we're afraid, Father—calm on the outside. But Father, we have our hidden fears. You know them. We're afraid of being alone. We're afraid of being jobless. We're afraid of pain. Father, we offer these fears to you and ask you to give us more courage as we look at you, the One who knows no fear.

TEMPTATION

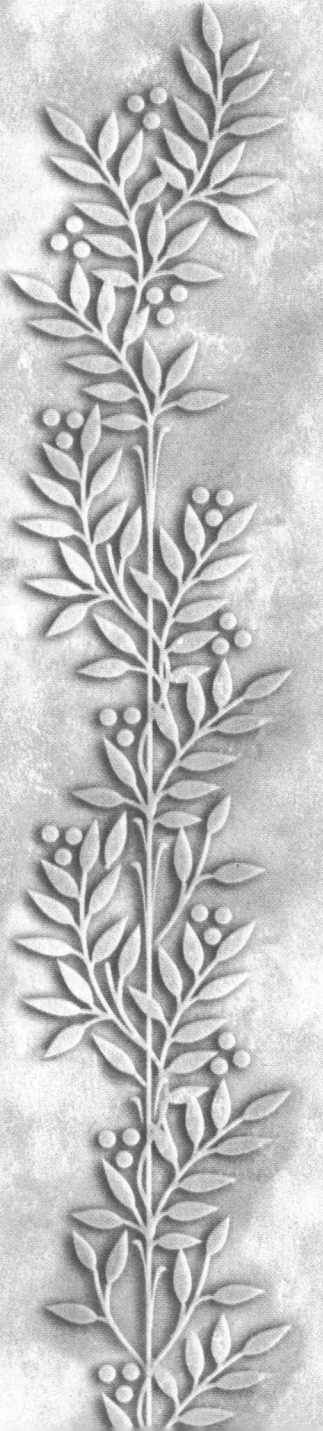

I am terribly concerned as I hear more and more about how people flirt with immorality and how people dance with materialism and how they consider themselves invulnerable to Satan. We are not invulnerable to Satan—he's wise, he's crafty . . . and just as God wishes you to spend forever with him in heaven, Satan wishes you to spend eternity separated from God. Guard your heart!

When you think of the temptation with which you struggle most in your life, you can deal with it boldly. You can have the confidence that God has given you a spirit of self-discipline. It's up to you to tap into that gift.

FATHER, when we confront temptation, when we stand face to face with evil, we pray that you would give us strength and that you would use your power to block the path of evil. Thank you for your promise that if we do what is right, eventually truth and justice and goodness will prevail. As we face the dilemmas and options of this time, remind us that good does reign supreme.

WHY?

A misconception people have in dealing with life's troubles is that it's wrong to ask *why*—that a Christian simply accepts and never questions. Abraham, Moses, and David all interceded and struggled to understand God. But the lives of these men model for us a total reliance on God, even in the midst of questioning.

It's not a sin to doubt. Disbelief is sin, but questioning—sincerely seeking—is acceptable to God, because in the presence of God you may ask any question you want.

God never turns his back on those who ask honest questions. He never did in the Old Testament; he never did in the New Testament. So if you are asking honest questions of God, he will not turn away from you.

Perhaps the reason that God doesn't always give us the answer to the *whys* of our existence is that he knows we haven't got the capacity to understand the answer. In learning to depend on God, we must accept that we may not know all the answers, but we know *who* knows the answers.

WE PRAY, O Father, that in the hours when we find ourselves in the dungeons of doubt, that you would hear our questions. Forgive us for demanding that you answer our questions like we want them to be answered. Forgive us for having certain expectations that we think you should meet.

God Forgives

A lot of us live with a hidden fear that God is angry at us. Somewhere, sometime, some Sunday school class or some television show convinced us that God has a whip behind his back, a paddle in his back pocket, and he's going to nail us when we've gone too far. No concept could be more wrong! Your Savior's Father is very fond of you and only wants to share his love with you.

Could you use the genuine fresh air of God's forgiveness? Would you love to stand in the approval of God again? How do you do it? By genuinely admitting to God that you've made a mistake, knowing that God loves you more than he hates your mistakes. And knowing that he will forgive those mistakes.

Does the Word of God say, "There is *limited* condemnation for those who are in Christ Jesus"? No. Does it say, "There is *some* condemnation . . . "? No. It says, "There is *no* condemnation for those who are in Christ Jesus." Think of it—regardless of our sin, we are not guilty!

WE'RE NOT perfect, Father, but we are yours. We're not what we should be, but we do claim your salvation and your grace. We ask you to make us every day more and more into the image of Jesus Christ. We stand amazed that you would have such mercy upon us to forgive us time and time again. Thank you for the immeasurable depth of your grace.

4 Our fathers trusted in You;
They trusted, and You delivered them.
5 They cried to You, and were delivered;
They trusted in You, and were not ashamed.

6 But I *am* a worm, and no man;
A reproach of men, and despised by the people.
7 All those who see Me ridicule Me;
They shoot out the lip, they shake the head, *saying*,
8 "He trusted[r] in the LORD, let Him rescue Him;
Let Him deliver Him, since He delights in Him!"

9 But You *are* He who took Me out of the womb;
You made Me trust *while* on My mother's breasts.
10 I was cast upon You from birth.
From My mother's womb
You *have been* My God.
11 Be not far from Me,
For trouble *is* near;
For *there is* none to help.

12 Many bulls have surrounded Me;
Strong *bulls* of Bashan have encircled Me.
13 They gape at Me *with* their mouths,
Like a raging and roaring lion.

14 I am poured out like water,
And all My bones are out of joint;
My heart is like wax;
It has melted within Me.
15 My strength is dried up like a potsherd,
And My tongue clings to My jaws;
You have brought Me to the dust of death.

16 For dogs have surrounded Me;
The congregation of the wicked has enclosed Me.
They pierced[s] My hands and My feet;
17 I can count all My bones.
They look *and* stare at Me.
18 They divide My garments among them,
And for My clothing they cast lots.

19 But You, O LORD, do not be far from Me;
O My Strength, hasten to help Me!
20 Deliver Me from the sword,
My precious *life* from the power of the dog.
21 Save Me from the lion's mouth
And from the horns of the wild oxen!

You have answered Me.

22 I will declare Your name to My brethren;
In the midst of the assembly I will praise You.

Isn't that better? Now we can applaud. Now we can lift banners for your dedication. Now we can explain it to our children. It makes sense now. You see, that makes you a hero. A hero. History is full of heroes.

And who is a hero but someone who survives a challenge?

Or, if that's not acceptable, I have another one. Why not *afflict*? "My God, my God, why did you afflict me?" Yes, that's it. Now you are a martyr, taking a stand for truth. A patriot, pierced by evil. A noble soldier who took the sword all the way to the hilt; bloody and beaten, but victorious.

Afflicted is much better than *abandoned.* You are a martyr. Right up there with Patrick Henry and Abraham Lincoln.

You are God, Jesus! You couldn't be abandoned. You couldn't be left alone. You couldn't be deserted in your most painful moment.

Abandonment. That is the punishment for a criminal. Abandonment. That is the suffering borne by the most evil. Abandonment. That's for the vile—not for you. Not you, the King of kings. Not you, the Beginning and the End. Not you, the One Unborn. After all, didn't John call you the Lamb of God? . . .

"Who has come to take away the sins of the world." Wait a minute. "To take away the sins . . . " I'd never thought about those words.

I'd read them but never thought about them. I thought you just, I don't know, sent sin away. Banished it. I thought you'd just stood in front of the mountains of our sins and told them to begone. Just like you did to the demons. Just like you did to the hypocrites in the temple.

I just thought you commanded the evil out. I never noticed that you took it out. It never occurred to me that you actually touched it—or worse still that it touched you.

That must have been a horrible moment. I know what it's like to be touched by sin. I know what it's like to smell the stench of that stuff. Remember what I used to be like? Before I knew you, I wallowed in that mire. I didn't just touch sin, I loved it. I drank it. I danced with it. I was in the middle of it.

22:8 [r] Septuagint, Syriac, and Vulgate read *hoped;* Targum reads *praised.*
22:16 [s] Following some Hebrew manuscripts, Septuagint, Syriac, Vulgate; Masoretic Text reads *Like a lion.*

Continued

But why am I telling you? You remember. You were the one who saw me. You were the one who found me. I was lonely. I was afraid. Remember? "Why? Why me? Why has all this hurt happened?"

I know it wasn't much of a question. It wasn't the right question. But it was all I knew to ask. You see, God, I felt so confused. So desolate. Sin will do that to you. Sin leaves you shipwrecked, orphaned, adrift. Sin leaves you aban—

Oh. Oh, my.

My goodness, God. Is that what happened? You mean sin did the same to you that it did to me?

Oh, I'm sorry. I'm so sorry. I didn't know. I didn't understand. You really were alone, weren't you?

Your question was real, wasn't it, Jesus? You really were afraid. You really were alone. Just like I was. Only, I deserved it. You didn't.

Forgive me, I spoke out of turn. (From *And the Angels Were Silent* by Max Lucado)

APPLICATION When was the last time you felt lonely? The next time you feel that way, look around. Everyone else may have deserted you, but God remains at your side.

EXPLORATION Victory Is the Lord's—1 Samuel 17:47; Proverbs 3:5-6; Psalm18:1-6; 28:7; Romans 8:37; Hebrews 12:2.

23 You who fear the LORD, praise Him!
All you descendants of Jacob, glorify Him,
And fear Him, all you offspring of Israel!
24 For He has not despised nor abhorred the affliction of the afflicted;
Nor has He hidden His face from Him;
But when He cried to Him, He heard.

25 My praise *shall be* of You in the great assembly;
I will pay My vows before those who fear Him.
26 The poor shall eat and be satisfied;
Those who seek Him will praise the LORD.
Let your heart live forever!

27 All the ends of the world
Shall remember and turn to the LORD,
And all the families of the nations
Shall worship before You.[t]
28 For the kingdom *is* the LORD's,
And He rules over the nations.

29 All the prosperous of the earth
Shall eat and worship;
All those who go down to the dust
Shall bow before Him,
Even he who cannot keep himself alive.

30 A posterity shall serve Him.
It will be recounted of the Lord to the *next* generation,
31 They will come and declare His righteousness
to a people who will be born,
That He has done *this*.

PSALM 23

The LORD the Shepherd of His People

A Psalm of David.

The LORD *is* my shepherd;
I shall not want.
2 He makes me to lie down in green pastures;
He leads me beside the still waters.
3 He restores my soul;
He leads me in the paths of righteousness
For His name's sake.

4 Yea, though I walk through the valley of the shadow of death,
I will fear no evil;
For You *are* with me;
Your rod and Your staff, they comfort me.

5 You prepare a table before me in the presence of my enemies;
You anoint my head with oil;
My cup runs over.

22:27 [t] Following Masoretic Text, Septuagint, and Targum; Arabic, Syriac, and Vulgate read *Him*.

6 Surely goodness and mercy shall follow me
All the days of my life;
And I will dwell[u] in the house of the LORD
Forever.

PSALM 24

The King of Glory and His Kingdom

A Psalm of David.

The earth *is* the LORD's, and all its fullness,
The world and those who dwell therein.
2 For He has founded it upon the seas,
And established it upon the waters.

3 Who may ascend into the hill of the LORD?
Or who may stand in His holy place?
4 He who has clean hands and a pure heart,
Who has not lifted up his soul to an idol,
Nor sworn deceitfully.
5 He shall receive blessing from the LORD,
And righteousness from the God of his salvation.
6 This *is* Jacob, the generation of those who seek Him,
Who seek Your face. Selah

7 Lift up your heads, O you gates!
And be lifted up, you everlasting doors!
And the King of glory shall come in.
8 Who *is* this King of glory?
The LORD strong and mighty,
The LORD mighty in battle.
9 Lift up your heads, O you gates!
Lift up, you everlasting doors!
And the King of glory shall come in.
10 Who is this King of glory?
The LORD of hosts,
He *is* the King of glory. Selah

PSALM 25

A Plea for Deliverance and Forgiveness

A Psalm of David.

To You, O LORD, I lift up my soul.
2 O my God, I trust in You;
Let me not be ashamed;
Let not my enemies triumph over me.
3 Indeed, let no one who waits on You be ashamed;
Let those be ashamed who deal treacherously without cause.

4 Show me Your ways, O LORD;
Teach me Your paths.

23:6 [u] Following Septuagint, Syriac, Targum, and Vulgate; Masoretic Text reads *return.*

LIFE LESSON

Psalms 23:1–24:10

SITUATION David portrayed God as a caring shepherd. This shepherd protected his sheep from harm.

OBSERVATION Although we may face stressful situations, God leads us safely through as a shepherd would do for his sheep.

INSPIRATION "She'll not live a day," a physician told an attending nurse. Concerned, the nurse befriended the dying woman and in a few hours had won her confidence.

Motioning for the nurse to come near, the old woman said sorrowfully, "I have traveled all the way from California by myself, stopping at every city of importance between San Francisco and Boston. In each city I visit just two places: the police station and the hospital. You see, my boy ran away from home and I have no idea where he is. I've got to find him. . . ."

The mother's eyes seemed to flash a ray of hope as she added, "Someday he may even come into this very hospital, and if he does, please promise me you'll tell him his two best friends never gave up on him." . . .

Bending over the dying mother, the nurse whispered softly, "Tell me the names of those two friends so I can tell your son if I ever see him."

With trembling lips and her eyes filled with tears the mother responded, "Tell him those two friends were God and his mother," and she closed her eyes and died.

God, even more than a forgiving mother, never gives up on one of His children. His forgiveness is uniquely infinite. . . . And since God is the quintessence of forgiveness, to think on God is to immerse oneself in thoughts of forgiveness rather than failure.
(From *Living and Praying in Jesus' Name* by Dick Eastman and Jack Hayford)

APPLICATION Find your bearings today by following the Good Shepherd. Trust Jesus today to lead you to an eternal home.

EXPLORATION Shepherd—Genesis 48:15; Psalm 78:71-72; Mark 6:34; John 10:26-29.

LIFE LESSON

Psalms 25:1–26:12

SITUATION David prayed for God to give him mercy. He not only asked for forgiveness but for help to do right.

OBSERVATION Trust God to forgive your sins. He shows us the right path to take and protects us from evil.

INSPIRATION Poor memories are a part of the human condition. And so when God tells us that He will remember our sins no more, I'm puzzled. How could God possibly forget? That's our job! . . .

Then why do we feel so bad about our past sins? Because we confuse sin with its impression. Got a notepad nearby? Let me show you how this can be so. Write the word "sin" on the page. Press hard. Now tear off that sheet of paper, crumple it up, and throw it across the room. That's how God forgets your sin.

Now take your pencil and rub it on the new page at an angle, back and forth, over the same location where you wrote. And guess what: The ghost of the word "sin" appears.

That's what our flawed memories do. We go back over the deep impression left by the transgressions in our life, and we feel just as guilty. It's as if the sin never left. But be encouraged, the impression of sin is not the same thing as sin. And with David you can cry out, "I can't forget my scars, it seems, Lord. But you have forgotten their cause. Look upon me with loving, kind eyes."

It's your choice. Will you continue to work over forgiven sin as with a pencil? Or will you let the Holy Spirit work His lovingkindness?

(From *Diamonds in the Dust* by Joni Eareckson Tada)

APPLICATION Is there a sin in your past that you keep remembering, regretting, and confessing to God? Decide today to do with that sin what God does with all sin that he forgives—forget it!

EXPLORATION Forgiveness—Psalm 103:12; Isaiah 43:25; Micah 7:18-19; Hebrews 8:12; 1 John 1:9.

---

5 Lead me in Your truth and teach me,
For You *are* the God of my salvation;
On You I wait all the day.

6 Remember, O LORD, Your tender mercies
and Your lovingkindnesses,
For they *are* from of old.
7 Do not remember the sins of my youth, nor my transgressions;
According to Your mercy remember me,
For Your goodness' sake, O LORD.

8 Good and upright *is* the LORD;
Therefore He teaches sinners in the way.
9 The humble He guides in justice,
And the humble He teaches His way.
10 All the paths of the LORD *are* mercy and truth,
To such as keep His covenant and His testimonies.
11 For Your name's sake, O LORD,
Pardon my iniquity, for it *is* great.

12 Who *is* the man that fears the LORD?
Him shall He[v] teach in the way He[w] chooses.
13 He himself shall dwell in prosperity,
And his descendants shall inherit the earth.
14 The secret of the LORD *is* with those who fear Him,
And He will show them His covenant.
15 My eyes *are* ever toward the LORD,
For He shall pluck my feet out of the net.

16 Turn Yourself to me, and have mercy on me,
For I *am* desolate and afflicted.
17 The troubles of my heart have enlarged;
Bring me out of my distresses!
18 Look on my affliction and my pain,
And forgive all my sins.
19 Consider my enemies, for they are many;
And they hate me with cruel hatred.
20 Keep my soul, and deliver me;
Let me not be ashamed, for I put my trust in You.
21 Let integrity and uprightness preserve me,
For I wait for You.

22 Redeem Israel, O God,
Out of all their troubles!

PSALM 26

A Prayer for Divine Scrutiny and Redemption

A Psalm of David.

Vindicate me, O LORD,
For I have walked in my integrity.
I have also trusted in the LORD;
I shall not slip.

25:12 [v] Or *he* [w] Or *he*

2 Examine me, O LORD, and prove me;
Try my mind and my heart.
3 For Your lovingkindness *is* before my eyes,
And I have walked in Your truth.
4 I have not sat with idolatrous mortals,
Nor will I go in with hypocrites.
5 I have hated the assembly of evildoers,
And will not sit with the wicked.

6 I will wash my hands in innocence;
So I will go about Your altar, O LORD,
7 That I may proclaim with the voice of thanksgiving,
And tell of all Your wondrous works.
8 LORD, I have loved the habitation of Your house,
And the place where Your glory dwells.

9 Do not gather my soul with sinners,
Nor my life with bloodthirsty men,
10 In whose hands *is* a sinister scheme,
And whose right hand is full of bribes.

11 But as for me, I will walk in my integrity;
Redeem me and be merciful to me.
12 My foot stands in an even place;
In the congregations I will bless the LORD.

PSALM 27

An Exuberant Declaration of Faith

A Psalm of David.

The LORD *is* my light and my salvation;
Whom shall I fear?
The LORD *is* the strength of my life;
Of whom shall I be afraid?
2 When the wicked came against me
To eat up my flesh,
My enemies and foes,
They stumbled and fell.
3 Though an army may encamp against me,
My heart shall not fear;
Though war may rise against me,
In this I *will be* confident.

4 One *thing* I have desired of the LORD,
That will I seek:
That I may dwell in the house of the LORD
All the days of my life,
To behold the beauty of the LORD,
And to inquire in His temple.
5 For in the time of trouble
He shall hide me in His pavilion;
In the secret place of His tabernacle
He shall hide me;
He shall set me high upon a rock.

LIFE LESSON

Psalms 27:1–28:9

SITUATION David sought to be close to God. He asked God for instruction and waited patiently for God to act. God sustained, protected, helped, and taught him.

OBSERVATION Recognize that only God can assist when we stand helpless.

INSPIRATION Waiting certainly plays an enormous role in the unfolding story of God's relationship to man. It is God's oft-repeated way of teaching us that His power is real and that He can answer our prayers without interference and manipulation from us.

But we have such trouble getting *our* will, *our* time schedules out of the way. Much of the time we act like a child who brings a broken toy to his father to be mended. The father gladly takes the toy and begins work. Then after a while, childlike impatience takes over. Why is it taking so long?

The child stands by, getting his hands in the father's way, offering a lot of meaningless advice and some rather silly criticism. Finally in desperation, he snatches the toy from the father's hands and walks off with it, saying rather bitterly that he hadn't really thought his father could fix it anyway. Perhaps it isn't even "his will" to mend toys.

On the other hand, whenever we are trustful enough to leave our "broken toy" with the Father, not only do we eventually get it back gloriously restored, but are also handed a surprising plus. We find for ourselves what the saints and mystics affirm, that during the dark waiting period when self-effort had ceased, a spurt of astonishing spiritual growth took place in us. Afterwards, we have qualities like more patience, more love for the Lord and those around us, more ability to hear His voice, greater willingness to obey.

(From *Adventures in Prayer* by Catherine Marshall)

Continued

APPLICATION Do you catch yourself being impatient with God? Do you think you know the best way to handle a problem? While waiting, don't stew over your problem. Praise God for his solution to the problem. Instead of focusing on yourself and your problem, focus on God's care for you.

EXPLORATION Waiting—Psalm 40:1; Hosea 12:6; Micah 7:7; 2 Peter 3:8-9. Seeking the Lord—Psalm 145:18; Isaiah 55:6; Hosea 10:12; Matthew 6:33.

6 And now my head shall be lifted up above
my enemies all around me;
Therefore I will offer sacrifices of joy in His tabernacle;
I will sing, yes, I will sing praises to the LORD.

7 Hear, O LORD, *when* I cry with my voice!
Have mercy also upon me, and answer me.
8 *When You said,* "Seek My face,"
My heart said to You, "Your face, LORD, I will seek."
9 Do not hide Your face from me;
Do not turn Your servant away in anger;
You have been my help;
Do not leave me nor forsake me,
O God of my salvation.
10 When my father and my mother forsake me,
Then the LORD will take care of me.

11 Teach me Your way, O LORD,
And lead me in a smooth path, because of my enemies.
12 Do not deliver me to the will of my adversaries;
For false witnesses have risen against me,
And such as breathe out violence.
13 *I would have lost heart,* unless I had believed
That I would see the goodness of the LORD
In the land of the living.

14 Wait on the LORD;
Be of good courage,
And He shall strengthen your heart;
Wait, I say, on the LORD!

PSALM 28

Rejoicing in Answered Prayer

A Psalm of David.

To You I will cry, O LORD my Rock:
Do not be silent to me,
Lest, if You *are* silent to me,
I become like those who go down to the pit.
2 Hear the voice of my supplications
When I cry to You,
When I lift up my hands toward Your holy sanctuary.

3 Do not take me away with the wicked
And with the workers of iniquity,
Who speak peace to their neighbors,
But evil *is* in their hearts.
4 Give them according to their deeds,
And according to the wickedness of their endeavors;
Give them according to the work of their hands;
Render to them what they deserve.

5 Because they do not regard the works of the LORD,
Nor the operation of His hands,
He shall destroy them
And not build them up.

6 Blessed *be* the LORD,
Because He has heard the voice of my supplications!
7 The LORD *is* my strength and my shield;
My heart trusted in Him, and I am helped;
Therefore my heart greatly rejoices,
And with my song I will praise Him.

8 The LORD *is* their strength,[x]
And He *is* the saving refuge of His anointed.
9 Save Your people,
And bless Your inheritance;
Shepherd them also,
And bear them up forever.

PSALM 29

Praise to God in His Holiness and Majesty

A Psalm of David.

Give unto the LORD, O you mighty ones,
Give unto the LORD glory and strength.
2 Give unto the LORD the glory due to His name;
Worship the LORD in the beauty of holiness.

3 The voice of the LORD *is* over the waters;
The God of glory thunders;
The LORD *is* over many waters.
4 The voice of the LORD *is* powerful;
The voice of the LORD *is* full of majesty.

5 The voice of the LORD breaks the cedars,
Yes, the LORD splinters the cedars of Lebanon.
6 He makes them also skip like a calf,
Lebanon and Sirion like a young wild ox.
7 The voice of the LORD divides the flames of fire.

8 The voice of the LORD shakes the wilderness;
The LORD shakes the Wilderness of Kadesh.
9 The voice of the LORD makes the deer give birth,
And strips the forests bare;
And in His temple everyone says, "Glory!"

10 The LORD sat *enthroned* at the Flood,
And the LORD sits as King forever.
11 The LORD will give strength to His people;
The LORD will bless His people with peace.

28:8 [x] Following Masoretic Text and Targum; Septuagint, Syriac, and Vulgate read *the strength of His people.*

LIFE LESSON

Psalms 29:1–30:12

SITUATION David applauded God for his protection and help. Though David still had problems, he knew that God was powerful and faithful and always worthy of praise.

OBSERVATION God satisfies us because he holds all the power and protection we need. Trusting him brings contentment.

INSPIRATION Satisfied? That is one thing we are not. We are not satisfied. . . .

We push back from the Thanksgiving table and pat our round bellies. "I'm satisfied," we declare. But look at us a few hours later, back in the kitchen picking the meat from the bone.

We take a vacation of a lifetime. For years we planned. For years we saved. And off we go. We satiate ourselves with sun, fun, and good food. But we are not even on the way home before we dread the end of the trip and begin planning another.

We are not satisfied.

As a child we say, "If only I were a teenager." As a teen we say, "If only I were an adult." As an adult, "If only I were married." As a spouse, "If only I had kids." As a parent, "If only my kids were grown." In an empty house, "If only the kids would visit." As a retiree in the rocking chair with stiff joints and fading sight, "If only I were a child again."

We are not satisfied. Contentment is a difficult virtue. Why?

Because there is nothing on earth that can satisfy our deepest longing. We long to see God. The leaves of life are rustling with the rumor that we will—and we won't be satisfied until we do.

(From *When God Whispers Your Name* by Max Lucado)

APPLICATION Enjoy your age, job, friends, and lifestyle. When you are tempted to be dissatisfied, pray, "God, help me to find my contentment in you."

EXPLORATION Contentment —Exodus 20:17; Psalm 17:13-15; Matthew 6:24; Philippians 4:10-14.

LIFE LESSON

Psalm 31:1-24

SITUATION Although the writer of this psalm was grieved, his complete dedication to God caused him to thank God.

OBSERVATION Throughout trials God provides a place of refuge. God provides stability in a broken world.

INSPIRATION Anyone who has read my books or heard me speak knows the profound impact William Wilberforce has had on my Christian life. That's why I refer so consistently to his radical stand for Christ in his culture and why I quote so often from a letter written by John Wesley to Wilberforce—then a recent convert. Wesley, who was to die only days later, commissioned Wilberforce to lead the radical campaign against slavery. I've carried this excerpt from Wesley's letter in my Bible for the past seven years:

"Unless the Divine Power has raised you up to be as Athanasius, *Contra Mundum*, I see not how you can go through your glorious enterprise in opposing that execrable villainy which is the scandal of religion, of England, and of human nature. Unless God has raised you up for this very thing, you will be worn out by the opposition of

PSALM 30

The Blessedness of Answered Prayer

A Psalm. A Song at the dedication of the house of David.

I will extol You, O LORD, for You have lifted me up,
And have not let my foes rejoice over me.
2 O LORD my God, I cried out to You,
And You healed me.
3 O LORD, You brought my soul up from the grave;
You have kept me alive, that I should not go down to the pit.[y]

4 Sing praise to the LORD, you saints of His,
And give thanks at the remembrance of His holy name.[z]
5 For His anger *is but for* a moment,
His favor *is for* life;
Weeping may endure for a night,
But joy *comes* in the morning.

6 Now in my prosperity I said,
"I shall never be moved."
7 LORD, by Your favor You have made my mountain stand strong;
You hid Your face, *and* I was troubled.

8 I cried out to You, O LORD;
And to the LORD I made supplication:
9 "What profit *is there* in my blood,
When I go down to the pit?
Will the dust praise You?
Will it declare Your truth?
10 Hear, O LORD, and have mercy on me;
LORD, be my helper!"

11 You have turned for me my mourning into dancing;
You have put off my sackcloth and clothed me with gladness,
12 To the end that *my* glory may sing praise to
You and not be silent.
O LORD my God, I will give thanks to You forever.

PSALM 31

The LORD a Fortress in Adversity

To the Chief Musician. A Psalm of David.

In You, O LORD, I put my trust;
Let me never be ashamed;
Deliver me in Your righteousness.
2 Bow down Your ear to me,
Deliver me speedily;
Be my rock of refuge,
A fortress of defense to save me.

30:3 [y] Following Qere and Targum; Kethib, Septuagint, Syriac, and Vulgate read *from those who descend to the pit.*
30:4 [z] Or *His holiness*

3 For You *are* my rock and my fortress;
Therefore, for Your name's sake,
Lead me and guide me.
4 Pull me out of the net which they have secretly laid for me,
For You *are* my strength.
5 Into Your hand I commit my spirit;
You have redeemed me, O LORD God of truth.

6 I have hated those who regard useless idols;
But I trust in the LORD.
7 I will be glad and rejoice in Your mercy,
For You have considered my trouble;
You have known my soul in adversities,
8 And have not shut me up into the hand of the enemy;
You have set my feet in a wide place.

9 Have mercy on me, O LORD, for I am in trouble;
My eye wastes away with grief,
Yes, my soul and my body!
10 For my life is spent with grief,
And my years with sighing;
My strength fails because of my iniquity,
And my bones waste away.
11 I am a reproach among all my enemies,
But especially among my neighbors,
And *am* repulsive to my acquaintances;
Those who see me outside flee from me.
12 I am forgotten like a dead man, out of mind;
I am like a broken vessel.
13 For I hear the slander of many;
Fear *is* on every side;
While they take counsel together against me,
They scheme to take away my life.

14 But as for me, I trust in You, O LORD;
I say, "You *are* my God."
15 My times *are* in Your hand;
Deliver me from the hand of my enemies,
And from those who persecute me.
16 Make Your face shine upon Your servant;
Save me for Your mercies' sake.
17 Do not let me be ashamed, O LORD, for I have called upon You;
Let the wicked be ashamed;
Let them be silent in the grave.
18 Let the lying lips be put to silence,
Which speak insolent things proudly and
contemptuously against the righteous.

19 Oh, how great *is* Your goodness,
Which You have laid up for those who fear You,
Which You have prepared for those who trust in You
In the presence of the sons of men!
20 You shall hide them in the secret place of Your presence

men and devils, but if God be for you, who can be against you? Are all of them stronger than God? Oh, be not weary in well doing. Go on, in the name of God and in the power of His might, till even American slavery, the vilest that ever saw the sun, shall vanish away before it."

Wilberforce took his stand, at first but a single, lonely voice against a business that was the mainstay of the lucrative West Indies trade, employing some 5,500 sailors and 160 ships worth 6,000,000 pounds sterling a year. For twenty years the radical Wilberforce . . . fought the economic and political might of the British Empire. In the end, righteousness prevailed, and for the next half century a mighty revival swept across England and the Western world. *Contra mundum.* Against the world. Radicals.
(From *Loving God* by Charles Colson)

APPLICATION Find a Christian who works for a worthy cause. Encourage the person. Pray for him or her. Help however you can. Praise God for his faithfulness.

EXPLORATION God's Faithfulness—Lamentations 3:19-23; Trust—Proverbs 3:5-6; Assurance in Suffering—1 John 4:4.

LIFE LESSON

Psalms 32:1–33:22

SITUATION Psalm 32 records the relief and joy David found in God's forgiveness. In Psalm 33, an anonymous author calls all the people to praise and thank God.

OBSERVATION God forgives the sins of those who repent. Confession brings relief.

INSPIRATION To say "I believe in Jesus" is not enough. You must be willing to acknowledge Him as the most important person in your life. You must be willing to say, "I will do what He wants me to do above all else and above any demands that others may place upon me." If you will make that decision, I have great news for you—I can promise you a very positive self-image. When Jesus is the most important person in your life, you will soon come to define yourself in the same way that Jesus defines you. You will begin to think of yourself as He thinks of you. And here's more good news: Jesus thinks you're great! He thinks you're terrific. He really does.

You say, "Not me, Tony. You don't know me or the sin in my life. There are things that I can never tell you. If you knew them it would cause you to view me with contempt."

We could compare horror stories. You could tell me how rotten you are and I could tell you how rotten I am and we could try to see which of us is worse. Both of us would end up in despair. But that's not what Jesus wants us to do. He wants us to realize that once we accept Him as our Savior and Lord, we stand before Him as perfect people. . . . The Bible says that my sin is blotted out. It is buried in the deepest sea; it is remembered no more.

(From *It's Friday, but Sunday's Comin'* by Tony Campolo)

APPLICATION What sin haunts your mind? Have you repented? If so . . . God forgives you. Now forgive yourself.

EXPLORATION Repentance—Exodus 34:7; Psalm 51; Romans 4:7-8.

From the plots of man;
You shall keep them secretly in a pavilion
From the strife of tongues.

21 Blessed *be* the LORD,
For He has shown me His marvelous kindness in a strong city!
22 For I said in my haste,
"I am cut off from before Your eyes";
Nevertheless You heard the voice of my supplications
When I cried out to You.

23 Oh, love the LORD, all you His saints!
For the LORD preserves the faithful,
And fully repays the proud person.
24 Be of good courage,
And He shall strengthen your heart,
All you who hope in the LORD.

PSALM 32

The Joy of Forgiveness

A Psalm of David. A Contemplation.[a]

Blessed *is he whose* transgression *is* forgiven,
Whose sin *is* covered.
2 Blessed *is* the man to whom the LORD does not impute iniquity,
And in whose spirit *there is* no deceit.

3 When I kept silent, my bones grew old
Through my groaning all the day long.
4 For day and night Your hand was heavy upon me;
My vitality was turned into the drought of summer. Selah
5 I acknowledged my sin to You,
And my iniquity I have not hidden.
I said, "I will confess my transgressions to the LORD,"
And You forgave the iniquity of my sin. Selah

6 For this cause everyone who is godly shall pray to You
In a time when You may be found;
Surely in a flood of great waters
They shall not come near him.
7 You *are* my hiding place;
You shall preserve me from trouble;
You shall surround me with songs of deliverance. Selah

8 I will instruct you and teach you in the way you should go;
I will guide you with My eye.
9 Do not be like the horse *or* like the mule,
Which have no understanding,
Which must be harnessed with bit and bridle,
Else they will not come near you.

10 Many sorrows *shall be* to the wicked;
But he who trusts in the LORD, mercy shall surround him.

32:title [a] Hebrew *Maschil*

11 Be glad in the LORD and rejoice, you righteous;
And shout for joy, all *you* upright in heart!

PSALM 33

The Sovereignty of the LORD in Creation and History

Rejoice in the LORD, O you righteous!
For praise from the upright is beautiful.
2 Praise the LORD with the harp;
Make melody to Him with an instrument of ten strings.
3 Sing to Him a new song;
Play skillfully with a shout of joy.

4 For the word of the LORD *is* right,
And all His work *is done* in truth.
5 He loves righteousness and justice;
The earth is full of the goodness of the LORD.

6 By the word of the LORD the heavens were made,
And all the host of them by the breath of His mouth.
7 He gathers the waters of the sea together as a heap;[b]
He lays up the deep in storehouses.

8 Let all the earth fear the LORD;
Let all the inhabitants of the world stand in awe of Him.
9 For He spoke, and it was *done;*
He commanded, and it stood fast.

10 The LORD brings the counsel of the nations to nothing;
He makes the plans of the peoples of no effect.
11 The counsel of the LORD stands forever,
The plans of His heart to all generations.
12 Blessed *is* the nation whose God *is* the LORD,
The people He has chosen as His own inheritance.

13 The LORD looks from heaven;
He sees all the sons of men.
14 From the place of His dwelling He looks
On all the inhabitants of the earth;
15 He fashions their hearts individually;
He considers all their works.

16 No king *is* saved by the multitude of an army;
A mighty man is not delivered by great strength.
17 A horse *is* a vain hope for safety;
Neither shall it deliver *any* by its great strength.

18 Behold, the eye of the LORD *is* on those who fear Him,
On those who hope in His mercy,
19 To deliver their soul from death,
And to keep them alive in famine.

20 Our soul waits for the LORD;
He *is* our help and our shield.

33:7 *b* Septuagint, Targum, and Vulgate read *in a vessel.*

LIFE LESSON

Psalm 34:1-22

SITUATION David composed this psalm after he escaped King Achish in Gath by pretending to be insane (1 Samuel 21:10-15). David told how faithful God remained during a time of trouble.

OBSERVATION God delivers those who persevere in their faith.

INSPIRATION You may have heard it said that a person does not really know who his friends are until the bottom drops out. I think there is great truth to that. All of us have experienced the pain of discovering that people we thought would be faithful—no matter what—were simply "fair-weather friends." You know, friends whose loyalty hinges upon the climate or circumstances. As long as the relationship is enjoyable, they are with you all the way. But when it begins to demand some sacrifice on their part, they are hard to find. The ultimate measure of friends is not where they stand in times of comfort and convenience, but where they stand in times of challenge and controversy. That being the case, apart from adversity of some kind, we would never know who our faithful friends really are.

In the same way, we will never know in a personal way the faithfulness of Christ apart from adversity. As a result, our faith in Him would never increase. It would remain static. One of the primary reasons God allows us to face adversity is so that He can demonstrate His faithfulness and in turn increase our faith. If you are a believer, you have made a decision to trust Christ with your eternal destiny. But you will not experience His faithfulness in that particular area until you die. God wants more from you and for you than simple intellectual acknowledgement of His faithfulness. It is His will that you *experience* it now.

If our lives are free from pain, turmoil, and sorrow, our knowledge of God will remain purely academic. Our relationship with Him could be compared with that of a great-great-grandfather about whom we have heard stories, yet never met personally. We would have great admiration, but

Continued

no intimacy, no fellowship. There would always be a sense of distance and mystery.

That is not the kind of relationship God wants with His children. Through the death of Christ, God has opened the way for us to have direct access to Him. He went to great lengths to clear the way so that nothing stands between Him and His children. There is potential now for intimacy between us and our Creator. . . .

God is in the process of engineering circumstances through which He can reveal Himself to each of us. And both history as well as our personal testimonies bear witness to the fact that it is in times of adversity that we come to a greater realization of God's incredible faithfulness to us.

(From *How to Handle Adversity* by Charles Stanley)

APPLICATION Can you remember a time when you were in desperate circumstances? What was the cry of your heart? When you have the opportunity, do as David did—praise God. Tell someone else what you learned. Memorize verses 17-22.

EXPLORATION Goodness of God—2 Chronicles 5:13; 6:41; Psalm 31:19; 52:9; Matthew 19:17; Romans 8:32; James 1:17.

21 For our heart shall rejoice in Him,
Because we have trusted in His holy name.
22 Let Your mercy, O LORD, be upon us,
Just as we hope in You.

PSALM 34

The Happiness of Those Who Trust in God

A Psalm of David when he pretended madness before Abimelech, who drove him away, and he departed.

I will bless the LORD at all times;
His praise *shall* continually *be* in my mouth.
2 My soul shall make its boast in the LORD;
The humble shall hear *of it* and be glad.
3 Oh, magnify the LORD with me,
And let us exalt His name together.

4 I sought the LORD, and He heard me,
And delivered me from all my fears.
5 They looked to Him and were radiant,
And their faces were not ashamed.
6 This poor man cried out, and the LORD heard *him,*
And saved him out of all his troubles.
7 The angel[c] of the LORD encamps all around those who fear Him,
And delivers them.

8 Oh, taste and see that the LORD *is* good;
Blessed *is* the man *who* trusts in Him!
9 Oh, fear the LORD, you His saints!
There is no want to those who fear Him.
10 The young lions lack and suffer hunger;
But those who seek the LORD shall not lack any good *thing.*

11 Come, you children, listen to me;
I will teach you the fear of the LORD.
12 Who *is* the man *who* desires life,
And loves *many* days, that he may see good?
13 Keep your tongue from evil,
And your lips from speaking deceit.
14 Depart from evil and do good;
Seek peace and pursue it.

15 The eyes of the LORD *are* on the righteous,
And His ears *are open* to their cry.
16 The face of the LORD *is* against those who do evil,
To cut off the remembrance of them from the earth.

17 *The righteous* cry out, and the LORD hears,
And delivers them out of all their troubles.
18 The LORD *is* near to those who have a broken heart,
And saves such as have a contrite spirit.

34:7 [c] Or *Angel*

19 Many *are* the afflictions of the righteous,
But the LORD delivers him out of them all.
20 He guards all his bones;
Not one of them is broken.
21 Evil shall slay the wicked,
And those who hate the righteous shall be condemned.
22 The LORD redeems the soul of His servants,
And none of those who trust in Him shall be condemned.

PSALM 35

The LORD the Avenger of His People

A Psalm of David.

Plead *my cause,* O LORD, with those who strive with me;
Fight against those who fight against me.
2 Take hold of shield and buckler,
And stand up for my help.
3 Also draw out the spear,
And stop those who pursue me.
Say to my soul,
"I *am* your salvation."
4 Let those be put to shame and brought to dishonor
Who seek after my life;
Let those be turned back and brought to confusion
Who plot my hurt.
5 Let them be like chaff before the wind,
And let the angel[d] of the LORD chase *them.*
6 Let their way be dark and slippery,
And let the angel of the LORD pursue them.
7 For without cause they have hidden their net for me *in* a pit,
Which they have dug without cause for my life.
8 Let destruction come upon him unexpectedly,
And let his net that he has hidden catch himself;
Into that very destruction let him fall.

9 And my soul shall be joyful in the LORD;
It shall rejoice in His salvation.
10 All my bones shall say,
"LORD, who *is* like You,
Delivering the poor from him who is too strong for him,
Yes, the poor and the needy from him who plunders him?"

11 Fierce witnesses rise up;
They ask me *things* that I do not know.
12 They reward me evil for good,
To the sorrow of my soul.
13 But as for me, when they were sick,
My clothing *was* sackcloth;
I humbled myself with fasting;
And my prayer would return to my own heart.

35:5 [d] Or *Angel*

LIFE LESSON

Psalms 35:1–36:12

SITUATION David begged God to rescue him from those who sought his demise. He recognized the wickedness of his enemies and asked God to intervene.

OBSERVATION God fights on behalf of his children.

INSPIRATION You feel unsafe, unsure.

You don't like to be alone.

You're frightened, and fear limits the joy you experience in your life. You're trapped in an adventureless existence. What are you afraid of? Pain? Rejection? Are you afraid of making a mistake? Of getting hurt? Of being robbed or killed? Of getting a disease?

. . . Did you know I am never afraid, worried, frenzied or never driven with terror? Did you know that your Lord is at peace always? Did you know my Spirit—the same as is in Me—lives in you?

I have built a wall of protection around you so that the invisible dragons of the night will not harm you. . . . I save you from the troubles and dangers of the daytime. I am for you. Who can be against you?

But you worry.

You worry because of past experiences when you were hurt. You are afraid to be hurt again. You are afraid I won't keep my word. You are afraid I don't care about you. But I do care. Every hair on your head is numbered.

. . . See Me surrounding you and keeping you from evil. See Me bringing you up out of a horrible pit, lifting you gently out of the miry clay of fear and worry. See yourself completely safe, with your feet upon a rock, established in the ways of God.

(From *His Thoughts Toward Me* by Marie Chapian)

APPLICATION When you face battles in life, write them in a prayer journal. Wait on your Defender and record his victory in your journal. This will build your faith.

EXPLORATION Fighting—Exodus 14:13-14; 1 Samuel 17:45-47; 2 Chronicles 20:15-17; Nehemiah 4:20; Romans 12:19.

14 I paced about as though *he were*
my friend *or* brother;
I bowed down heavily, as one who
mourns *for his* mother.
15 But in my adversity they rejoiced
And gathered together;
Attackers gathered against me,
And I did not know *it;*
They tore *at me* and did not cease;
16 With ungodly mockers at feasts
They gnashed at me with their teeth.

17 Lord, how long will You look on?
Rescue me from their destructions,
My precious *life* from the lions.
18 I will give You thanks in the
great assembly;
I will praise You among many people.

19 Let them not rejoice over me who are
wrongfully my enemies;
Nor let them wink with the eye who hate me
without a cause.
20 For they do not speak peace,
But they devise deceitful matters
Against *the* quiet ones in the land.
21 They also opened their mouth wide against me,
And said, "Aha, aha!
Our eyes have seen *it.*"

22 *This* You have seen, O LORD;
Do not keep silence.
O Lord, do not be far from me.
23 Stir up Yourself, and awake to my vindication,
To my cause, my God and my Lord.
24 Vindicate me, O LORD my God, according
to Your righteousness;
And let them not rejoice over me.
25 Let them not say in their hearts, "Ah, so we
would have it!"
Let them not say, "We have swallowed him up."

26 Let them be ashamed and brought
to mutual confusion
Who rejoice at my hurt;
Let them be clothed with shame
and dishonor
Who exalt themselves against me.

27 Let them shout for joy and be glad,
Who favor my righteous cause;
And let them say continually,
"Let the LORD be magnified,
Who has pleasure in the prosperity
of His servant."
28 And my tongue shall speak
of Your righteousness
And of Your praise all the day long.

PSALM 36

Man's Wickedness and God's Perfections

To the Chief Musician. A Psalm of David the servant of the LORD.

An oracle within my heart concerning the
transgression of the wicked:
There is no fear of God before his eyes.
2 For he flatters himself in his own eyes,
When he finds out his iniquity
and when he hates.
3 The words of his mouth *are*
wickedness and deceit;
He has ceased to be wise *and* to do good.
4 He devises wickedness on his bed;
He sets himself in a way *that is* not good;
He does not abhor evil.

5 Your mercy, O LORD, *is* in the heavens;
Your faithfulness *reaches* to the clouds.
6 Your righteousness *is* like
the great mountains;
Your judgments *are* a great deep;
O LORD, You preserve man and beast.

7 How precious *is* Your lovingkindness, O God!
Therefore the children of men put their trust
under the shadow of Your wings.
8 They are abundantly satisfied with the
fullness of Your house,
And You give them drink from the
river of Your pleasures.
9 For with You *is* the fountain of life;
In Your light we see light.

10 Oh, continue Your lovingkindness to those
who know You,
And Your righteousness to the
upright in heart.
11 Let not the foot of pride come against me,
And let not the hand of the
wicked drive me away.
12 There the workers of iniquity have fallen;
They have been cast down and
are not able to rise.

PSALM 37

The Heritage of the Righteous and the Calamity of the Wicked

A Psalm of David.

Do not fret because of evildoers,
Nor be envious of the workers of iniquity.
2 For they shall soon be cut down like the grass,
And wither as the green herb.

3 Trust in the LORD, and do good;
Dwell in the land, and feed on His faithfulness.
4 Delight yourself also in the LORD,
And He shall give you the desires of your heart.

5 Commit your way to the LORD,
Trust also in Him,
And He shall bring *it* to pass.
6 He shall bring forth your righteousness as the light,
And your justice as the noonday.

7 Rest in the LORD, and wait patiently for Him;
Do not fret because of him who prospers in his way,
Because of the man who brings wicked schemes to pass.
8 Cease from anger, and forsake wrath;
Do not fret—*it* only *causes* harm.

9 For evildoers shall be cut off;
But those who wait on the LORD,
They shall inherit the earth.
10 For yet a little while and the wicked *shall be* no *more;*
Indeed, you will look carefully for his place,
But it *shall be* no *more.*
11 But the meek shall inherit the earth,
And shall delight themselves in the abundance of peace.

12 The wicked plots against the just,
And gnashes at him with his teeth.
13 The Lord laughs at him,
For He sees that his day is coming.
14 The wicked have drawn the sword
And have bent their bow,
To cast down the poor and needy,
To slay those who are of upright conduct.
15 Their sword shall enter their own heart,
And their bows shall be broken.

16 A little that a righteous man has
Is better than the riches of many wicked.
17 For the arms of the wicked shall be broken,
But the LORD upholds the righteous.

18 The LORD knows the days of the upright,
And their inheritance shall be forever.
19 They shall not be ashamed in the evil time,
And in the days of famine they shall be satisfied.

LIFE LESSON

Psalm 37:1-40

SITUATION Who would prosper—the wicked or the righteous? David encouraged the people to live a life that modeled justice, wisdom, and integrity.

OBSERVATION God's people must learn to trust him with all their affairs. Trust involves commitment, patience, delight in the Lord, and obedience.

INSPIRATION In 1857 a tightrope walker named Blondin stretched a two-inch steel cable across the gorge of the Niagara Falls, attracting a large crowd. He said to the onlookers, "How many of you believe that I can carry the weight of a man on my shoulders across this gorge?" The crowd shouted and cheered their belief that he could do it. Sure enough, Blondin picked up a sack of sand weighing about 180 pounds and carried it across the falls.

Then Blondin said, "How many of you believe that I can actually carry a person across the gorge?" Many people in the crowd indicated that they thought he could do it. Then Blondin called out, "Which one of you will climb on my shoulders and let me carry you across the falls?"

Suddenly there was silence. Everyone wanted to see Blondin carry a person across the gorge and many believed he could. But nobody wanted to put his life in Blondin's hands.

Some time later Blondin did carry a man across Niagara Falls. The man was Blondin's manager, who had known the tightrope walker personally for many years. "You must not trust your own feelings, but mine," Blondin told his manager as they prepared for the crossing. "You will feel like turning when we don't need to turn. And if you trust your feelings, we will both fall. You must become part of me."

This is what faith in Jesus is: knowing Him personally and entrusting our eternal life into His hands.

(From *Won by One* by Ron Rand)

Continued

APPLICATION Is God calling you to trust him to carry you over some dangerous impasses in your Christian pilgrimage? What do you need to trust him for—your next job, a fragile marriage, a bad habit, a new ministry? Take a step of faith this week that demonstrates you have put your faith on the line.

EXPLORATION Trust/Faith—Genesis 22; Joshua 3; Habakkuk 2:4; 3:17-19; 2 Timothy 2:1-13; Hebrews 11.

20 But the wicked shall perish;
And the enemies of the LORD,
Like the splendor of the meadows, shall vanish.
Into smoke they shall vanish away.

21 The wicked borrows and does not repay,
But the righteous shows mercy and gives.
22 For *those* blessed by Him shall inherit the earth,
But *those* cursed by Him shall be cut off.

23 The steps of a *good* man are ordered by the LORD,
And He delights in his way.
24 Though he fall, he shall not be utterly cast down;
For the LORD upholds *him with* His hand.

25 I have been young, and *now* am old;
Yet I have not seen the righteous forsaken,
Nor his descendants begging bread.
26 *He is* ever merciful, and lends;
And his descendants *are* blessed.

27 Depart from evil, and do good;
And dwell forevermore.
28 For the LORD loves justice,
And does not forsake His saints;
They are preserved forever,
But the descendants of the wicked shall be cut off.
29 The righteous shall inherit the land,
And dwell in it forever.

30 The mouth of the righteous speaks wisdom,
And his tongue talks of justice.
31 The law of his God *is* in his heart;
None of his steps shall slide.

32 The wicked watches the righteous,
And seeks to slay him.
33 The LORD will not leave him in his hand,
Nor condemn him when he is judged.

34 Wait on the LORD,
And keep His way,
And He shall exalt you to inherit the land;
When the wicked are cut off, you shall see *it.*
35 I have seen the wicked in great power,
And spreading himself like a native green tree.
36 Yet he passed away,[e] and behold, he *was* no *more;*
Indeed I sought him, but he could not be found.

37 Mark the blameless *man,* and observe the upright;
For the future of *that* man *is* peace.
38 But the transgressors shall be destroyed together;
The future of the wicked shall be cut off.

37:36 [e] Following Masoretic Text, Septuagint, and Targum; Syriac and Vulgate read *I passed by.*

39 But the salvation of the righteous *is* from the LORD;
He is their strength in the time of trouble.
40 And the LORD shall help them and deliver them;
He shall deliver them from the wicked,
And save them,
Because they trust in Him.

PSALM 38

Prayer in Time of Chastening

A Psalm of David. To bring to remembrance.

O LORD, do not rebuke me in Your wrath,
Nor chasten me in Your hot displeasure!
2 For Your arrows pierce me deeply,
And Your hand presses me down.

3 *There is* no soundness in my flesh
Because of Your anger,
Nor *any* health in my bones
Because of my sin.
4 For my iniquities have gone over my head;
Like a heavy burden they are too heavy for me.
5 My wounds are foul *and* festering
Because of my foolishness.

6 I am troubled, I am bowed down greatly;
I go mourning all the day long.
7 For my loins are full of inflammation,
And *there is* no soundness in my flesh.
8 I am feeble and severely broken;
I groan because of the turmoil of my heart.

9 Lord, all my desire *is* before You;
And my sighing is not hidden from You.
10 My heart pants, my strength fails me;
As for the light of my eyes, it also has gone from me.

11 My loved ones and my friends stand aloof from my plague,
And my relatives stand afar off.
12 Those also who seek my life lay snares *for me;*
Those who seek my hurt speak of destruction,
And plan deception all the day long.

13 But I, like a deaf *man,* do not hear;
And *I am* like a mute *who* does not open his mouth.
14 Thus I am like a man who does not hear,
And in whose mouth *is* no response.

15 For in You, O LORD, I hope;
You will hear, O Lord my God.
16 For I said, "*Hear me,* lest they rejoice over me,
Lest, when my foot slips, they exalt *themselves* against me."
17 For I *am* ready to fall,

LIFE LESSON

Psalms 38:1–39:13

SITUATION David prayed when he suffered. He knew only God could bring forgiveness and healing.

OBSERVATION Whether we suffer because of sin or righteousness, we can rejoice that God pardons our sin and defends us from our enemies.

INSPIRATION When we wallow in guilt, remorse, and shame over real or imagined sins of the past we are disdaining God's gift of grace.

Preoccupation with self is always a major component of unhealthy guilt and recrimination. It stirs our emotions, churning in self-destructive ways, closes us in upon the mighty citadel of self, leads to depression and despair and preempts the presence of a compassionate God. The language of unhealthy guilt is harsh. It is demanding, abusing, criticizing, rejecting, accusing, blaming, condemning, reproaching, and scolding. It is one of impatience and chastisement. Christians are shocked and horrified because they have failed. Unhealthy guilt becomes bigger than life. The image of the childhood story "Chicken Little" comes to mind. Guilt becomes the experience in which people feel the sky is falling.

Yes, we feel guilt over sins, but healthy guilt is one which acknowledges the wrong done and feels remorse, but then is free to embrace the forgiveness that has been offered. Healthy guilt focuses on the realization that all has been forgiven, the wrong has been redeemed.

(From *The Ragamuffin Gospel* by Brennan Manning)

APPLICATION When you sin, do you casually say "I'm sorry" or do you feel like David did? Do not take God's forgiveness for granted. Humbly repent of your sins. Then, go in confidence knowing that you are forgiven!

EXPLORATION Prayer—Psalm 6; 17:6; 116:2; 1 Thessalonians 5:17.

And my sorrow *is* continually before me.
18 For I will declare my iniquity;
I will be in anguish over my sin.
19 But my enemies *are* vigorous, *and* they are strong;
And those who hate me wrongfully have multiplied.
20 Those also who render evil for good,
They are my adversaries, because I follow *what is* good.

21 Do not forsake me, O LORD;
O my God, be not far from me!
22 Make haste to help me,
O Lord, my salvation!

PSALM 39

Prayer for Wisdom and Forgiveness

To the Chief Musician. To Jeduthun. A Psalm of David.

I said, "I will guard my ways,
Lest I sin with my tongue;
I will restrain my mouth with a muzzle,
While the wicked are before me."
2 I was mute with silence,
I held my peace *even* from good;
And my sorrow was stirred up.
3 My heart was hot within me;
While I was musing, the fire burned.
Then I spoke with my tongue:

4 "LORD, make me to know my end,
And what *is* the measure of my days,
That I may know how frail I *am*.
5 Indeed, You have made my days *as* handbreadths,
And my age *is* as nothing before You;
Certainly every man at his best state *is* but vapor. Selah
6 Surely every man walks about like a shadow;
Surely they busy themselves in vain;
He heaps up *riches*,
And does not know who will gather them.

7 "And now, Lord, what do I wait for?
My hope *is* in You.
8 Deliver me from all my transgressions;
Do not make me the reproach of the foolish.
9 I was mute, I did not open my mouth,
Because it was You who did *it*.
10 Remove Your plague from me;
I am consumed by the blow of Your hand.
11 When with rebukes You correct man for iniquity,
You make his beauty melt away like a moth;
Surely every man *is* vapor. Selah

12 "Hear my prayer, O LORD,
And give ear to my cry;
Do not be silent at my tears;
For I *am* a stranger with You,
A sojourner, as all my fathers *were*.
13 Remove Your gaze from me, that I may regain strength,
Before I go away and am no more."

PSALM 40

Faith Persevering in Trial

To the Chief Musician. A Psalm of David.

I waited patiently for the LORD;
And He inclined to me,
And heard my cry.
2 He also brought me up out of a horrible pit,
Out of the miry clay,
And set my feet upon a rock,
And established my steps.
3 He has put a new song in my mouth—
Praise to our God;
Many will see *it* and fear,
And will trust in the LORD.

4 Blessed *is* that man who makes the LORD his trust,
And does not respect the proud, nor such as turn aside to lies.
5 Many, O LORD my God, *are* Your wonderful works
Which You have done;
And Your thoughts toward us
Cannot be recounted to You in order;
If I would declare and speak *of them*,
They are more than can be numbered.

6 Sacrifice and offering You did not desire;
My ears You have opened.
Burnt offering and sin offering You did not require.
7 Then I said, "Behold, I come;
In the scroll of the book *it is* written of me.
8 I delight to do Your will, O my God,
And Your law *is* within my heart."
9 I have proclaimed the good news of righteousness

In the great assembly;
Indeed, I do not restrain my lips,
O LORD, You Yourself know.
10 I have not hidden Your righteousness within my heart;
I have declared Your faithfulness and Your salvation;
I have not concealed Your lovingkindness and Your truth
From the great assembly.

11 Do not withhold Your tender mercies from me, O LORD;
Let Your lovingkindness and Your truth continually preserve me.
12 For innumerable evils have surrounded me;
My iniquities have overtaken me, so that I am not able to look up;
They are more than the hairs of my head;
Therefore my heart fails me.

13 Be pleased, O LORD, to deliver me;
O LORD, make haste to help me!
14 Let them be ashamed and brought to mutual confusion
Who seek to destroy my life;
Let them be driven backward and brought to dishonor
Who wish me evil.
15 Let them be confounded because of their shame,
Who say to me, "Aha, aha!"

16 Let all those who seek You rejoice and be glad in You;
Let such as love Your salvation say continually,
"The LORD be magnified!"
17 But I *am* poor and needy;
Yet the LORD thinks upon me.
You *are* my help and my deliverer;
Do not delay, O my God.

PSALM 41

The Blessing and Suffering of the Godly

To the Chief Musician. A Psalm of David.

Blessed *is* he who considers the poor;
The LORD will deliver him in time of trouble.
2 The LORD will preserve him and keep him alive,
And he will be blessed on the earth;
You will not deliver him to the will of his enemies.
3 The LORD will strengthen him on his bed of illness;
You will sustain him on his sickbed.

4 I said, "LORD, be merciful to me;
Heal my soul, for I have sinned against You."
5 My enemies speak evil of me:
"When will he die, and his name perish?"
6 And if he comes to see *me,* he speaks lies;
His heart gathers iniquity to itself;
When he goes out, he tells *it.*
7 All who hate me whisper together against me;

LIFE LESSON

Psalms 40:1–41:13

SITUATION David fled from Saul prior to replacing him as king.

OBSERVATION God delivers us from trouble. The wait may be difficult, but we can be thankful for the outcome and can tell others about it.

INSPIRATION An old man walks down a Florida beach. The sun sets like an orange ball on the horizon. The waves slap the sand. The smell of saltwater stings the air. The beach is vacant. No sun to entice the sunbathers. Not enough light for the fishermen. So, aside from a few joggers and strollers, the gentleman is alone.

He carries a bucket in his bony hand. A bucket of shrimp. It's not for him. It's not for the fish. It's for the sea gulls.

He walks to an isolated pier cast in gold by the setting sun. He steps out to the end of the pier. The time has come for the weekly ritual.

He stands and waits.

Soon the sky becomes a mass of dancing dots. The evening silence gives way to the screeching of birds. They fill the sky and then cover the moorings. They are on a pilgrimage to meet the old man.

For a half hour or so, the bushy-browed, shoulder-bent gentleman will stand on the pier, surrounded by the birds of the sea, until his bucket is empty.

But even after the food is gone, his feathered friends still linger. They linger as if they're attracted to more than just food. They perch on his hat. They walk on the pier. And they all share a moment together. . . .

The old man on the pier couldn't go a week without saying "thank you."

His name was Eddie Rickenbacker. If you were alive in October 1943, you probably remember the day that he was reported missing at sea.

He had been sent on a mission to deliver a message to Gen. Douglas MacArthur. With a handpicked crew in a B-17 known as the "Flying Fortress," he set off across the South Pacific. Somewhere the crew became lost, the fuel ran out, and the plane went down.

Continued

All eight crew members escaped into the life rafts. They battled the weather, the water, the sharks, and the sun. But most of all, they battled the hunger. After eight days, their rations were gone. They ran out of options. It would take a miracle for them to survive.

And a miracle occurred.

After an afternoon devotional service, the men said a prayer and tried to rest. As Rickenbacker was dozing with his hat over his eyes, something landed on his head. He would later say that he knew it was a sea gull. He didn't know how he knew; he just knew. That gull meant food . . . if he could catch it. And he did.

The flesh was eaten. The intestines were used as fish bait. And the crew survived.

What was a sea gull doing hundreds of miles away from land?

Only God knows.

But whatever the reason, Rickenbacker was thankful. As a result, every Friday evening this old captain walked to the pier, his bucket full of shrimp and his heart full of thanks.

We'd be wise to do the same. We've much in common with Rickenbacker. We, too, were saved by a Sacrificial Visitor.

We, too, were rescued by One who journeyed far from only God knows where.

And we, like the captain, have every reason to look into the sky . . . and worship.

(From *In the Eye of the Storm* by Max Lucado)

APPLICATION Tired of waiting for a career break? A loving spouse? Children? Pray through this psalm when you feel impatient. Let God know your feelings, and tell him your frustrations.

EXPLORATION Waiting—Psalm 5:3; 27:14; 130:5-6; Isaiah 30:18; Micah 7:7; Luke 12:35-40; James 5:7-8.

Against me they devise my hurt.
8 "An evil disease," *they say,* "clings to him.
And *now* that he lies down, he will rise up no more."
9 Even my own familiar friend in whom I trusted,
Who ate my bread,
Has lifted up *his* heel against me.

10 But You, O LORD, be merciful to me, and raise me up,
That I may repay them.
11 By this I know that You are well pleased with me,
Because my enemy does not triumph over me.
12 As for me, You uphold me in my integrity,
And set me before Your face forever.

13 Blessed *be* the LORD God of Israel
From everlasting to everlasting!
Amen and Amen.

Book Two: Psalms 42—72

PSALM 42

Yearning for God in the Midst of Distresses

To the Chief Musician. A Contemplation[f] of the sons of Korah.

As the deer pants for the water brooks,
So pants my soul for You, O God.
2 My soul thirsts for God, for the living God.
When shall I come and appear before God?[g]
3 My tears have been my food day and night,
While they continually say to me,
"Where *is* your God?"

4 When I remember these *things,*
I pour out my soul within me.
For I used to go with the multitude;
I went with them to the house of God,
With the voice of joy and praise,
With a multitude that kept a pilgrim feast.

5 Why are you cast down, O my soul?
And *why* are you disquieted within me?
Hope in God, for I shall yet praise Him
For the help of His countenance.[h]

6 O my God,[i] my soul is cast down within me;
Therefore I will remember You from the land of the Jordan,
And from the heights of Hermon,
From the Hill Mizar.
7 Deep calls unto deep at the noise of Your waterfalls;

42:title [f] Hebrew *Maschil*

42:2 [g] Following Masoretic Text and Vulgate; some Hebrew manuscripts, Septuagint, Syriac, and Targum read *I see the face of God.*

42:5 [h] Following Masoretic Text and Targum; a few Hebrew manuscripts, Septuagint, Syriac, and Vulgate read *The help of my countenance, my God.*

42:6 [i] Following Masoretic Text and Targum; a few Hebrew manuscripts, Septuagint, Syriac, and Vulgate put *my God* at the end of verse 5.

All Your waves and billows have gone over me.
8 The LORD will command His lovingkindness in the daytime,
And in the night His song *shall be* with me—
A prayer to the God of my life.

9 I will say to God my Rock,
"Why have You forgotten me?
Why do I go mourning because of the oppression of the enemy?"
10 *As* with a breaking of my bones,
My enemies reproach me,
While they say to me all day long,
"Where *is* your God?"

11 Why are you cast down, O my soul?
And why are you disquieted within me?
Hope in God;
For I shall yet praise Him,
The help of my countenance and my God.

PSALM 43

Prayer to God in Time of Trouble

Vindicate me, O God,
And plead my cause against an ungodly nation;
Oh, deliver me from the deceitful and unjust man!
2 For You *are* the God of my strength;
Why do You cast me off?
Why do I go mourning because of the oppression of the enemy?

3 Oh, send out Your light and Your truth!
Let them lead me;
Let them bring me to Your holy hill
And to Your tabernacle.
4 Then I will go to the altar of God,
To God my exceeding joy;
And on the harp I will praise You,
O God, my God.

5 Why are you cast down, O my soul?
And why are you disquieted within me?
Hope in God;
For I shall yet praise Him,
The help of my countenance and my God.

PSALM 44

Redemption Remembered in Present Dishonor

To the Chief Musician. A Contemplation[j] of the sons of Korah.

We have heard with our ears, O God,
Our fathers have told us,
The deeds You did in their days,
In days of old:

44:title *j* Hebrew *Maschil*

LIFE LESSON
Psalms 42:1–43:5

SITUATION Psalms 42 and 43 were probably written as one psalm. Though the writer felt separated from God, he expressed hope in God through prayer.

OBSERVATION Seek God even in times of discouragement, and he will provide hope.

INSPIRATION Bart decided to ask God to shape his character. He surrendered his own will to the will of God. At the time, Bart's business floundered on the verge of failure. "Should I throw in the towel, or keep trying to hang on?" Bart wondered.

God replies, "You need to persevere." After we have done the will of God, then we will receive our reward. God's will is for us to demonstrate to a hurting world how wonderfully His power can work within the person who perseveres.

Certainly, there are days when we feel like we will die, or maybe even wish we could, but we keep going. Why? Why do we keep going? Because *when* we have done the will of God we *will* receive what He has promised.

Will persevering guarantee we will succeed in the worldly sense of success? Is that what He has promised? Does it mean we will not go out of business if we hang on? No, but we can state emphatically that if we don't persevere we will not succeed in any sense. Not persevering guarantees we will fail. . . .

Beyond succeeding in a worldly sense, though, God wants our character to succeed more than our circumstances to succeed. He will adjust our circumstances in such a way that our character eventually succeeds, for that is His highest aim, His will.

(From *Walking with Christ in the Details of Life* by Patrick Morley)

APPLICATION Do you feel distant from God? Remember, God remains as close as a prayer.

EXPLORATION Prayer—Psalm 5:1-3; Matthew 6:5-13; Romans 12:10-13; Philippians 4:6-7; Colossians 4:2.

LIFE LESSON

Psalm 44:1-26

SITUATION The Sons of Korah wrote this psalm after Israel lost a war. The Israelites did not understand what caused them to lose.

OBSERVATION Although disappointed and confused, Israel kept trusting in God. They praised him and knew that he continued to be strong.

INSPIRATION Two-year-old Sara sits on my lap. We are watching a comedy on television about a guy who has a mouse in his room. He is asleep. He opens one eye and finds himself peering into the face of the rodent. . . .

I laugh, but Sara panics. She turns away from the screen and buries her face in my shoulder. Her arms encircle my neck and clamp like a vise. Her little body grows rigid. She thinks the mouse is going to get her.

"It's ok, Sara," I assure her. . . .

She is afraid.

But with time, I convince her. . . . Sara has gone from white-faced fear to peaceful chuckles in a few moments. Why? Because her father spoke and she believed.

Would that we would do the same. Got any giant mice on your screen? Got any fears that won't go away? . . .

I wish the fears were just television images. They aren't. They lurk in hospital rooms and funeral homes. They stare at us from divorce papers and eviction notices. They glare through the eyes of cruel parents or an abusive mate. . . .

There are times when mice roar. There are times when we need a strong pair of arms. You need to know that the arms of God are there.

(From *Tell Me the Story* by Max Lucado)

APPLICATION What problem or fear do you need to trust God with today? Remember that God already knows your problem and wants you to trust him for strength to solve it. Tell God about your need.

EXPLORATION Trust God—Proverbs 3:5; Isaiah 26:3-4; 50:10; Jeremiah 17:7-8; Habakkuk 3:17-19; Romans 15:13; Hebrews 6:18-19.

2 You drove out the nations with Your hand,
But them You planted;
You afflicted the peoples, and cast them out.
3 For they did not gain possession of the land by their own sword,
Nor did their own arm save them;
But it was Your right hand, Your arm, and
the light of Your countenance,
Because You favored them.

4 You are my King, O God;[k]
Command[l] victories for Jacob.
5 Through You we will push down our enemies;
Through Your name we will trample those who rise up against us.
6 For I will not trust in my bow,
Nor shall my sword save me.
7 But You have saved us from our enemies,
And have put to shame those who hated us.
8 In God we boast all day long,
And praise Your name forever. Selah

9 But You have cast *us* off and put us to shame,
And You do not go out with our armies.
10 You make us turn back from the enemy,
And those who hate us have taken spoil for themselves.
11 You have given us up like sheep *intended* for food,
And have scattered us among the nations.
12 You sell Your people for *next to* nothing,
And are not enriched by selling them.

13 You make us a reproach to our neighbors,
A scorn and a derision to those all around us.
14 You make us a byword among the nations,
A shaking of the head among the peoples.
15 My dishonor *is* continually before me,
And the shame of my face has covered me,
16 Because of the voice of him who reproaches and reviles,
Because of the enemy and the avenger.

17 All this has come upon us;
But we have not forgotten You,
Nor have we dealt falsely with Your covenant.
18 Our heart has not turned back,
Nor have our steps departed from Your way;
19 But You have severely broken us in the place of jackals,
And covered us with the shadow of death.

20 If we had forgotten the name of our God,
Or stretched out our hands to a foreign god,
21 Would not God search this out?
For He knows the secrets of the heart.

44:4 [k] Following Masoretic Text and Targum; Septuagint and Vulgate read *and my God.* [l] Following Masoretic Text and Targum; Septuagint, Syriac, and Vulgate read *Who commands.*

22 Yet for Your sake we are killed all day long;
We are accounted as sheep for the slaughter.

23 Awake! Why do You sleep, O Lord?
Arise! Do not cast *us* off forever.
24 Why do You hide Your face,
And forget our affliction and our oppression?
25 For our soul is bowed down to the dust;
Our body clings to the ground.
26 Arise for our help,
And redeem us for Your mercies' sake.

PSALM 45

The Glories of the Messiah and His Bride

To the Chief Musician. Set to "The Lilies."[m] A Contemplation[n] of the sons of Korah. A Song of Love.

My heart is overflowing with a good theme;
I recite my composition concerning the King;
My tongue *is* the pen of a ready writer.

2 You are fairer than the sons of men;
Grace is poured upon Your lips;
Therefore God has blessed You forever.
3 Gird Your sword upon *Your* thigh, O Mighty One,
With Your glory and Your majesty.
4 And in Your majesty ride prosperously because of truth,
humility, *and* righteousness;
And Your right hand shall teach You awesome things.
5 Your arrows *are* sharp in the heart of the King's enemies;
The peoples fall under You.

6 Your throne, O God, *is* forever and ever;
A scepter of righteousness *is* the scepter of Your kingdom.
7 You love righteousness and hate wickedness;
Therefore God, Your God, has anointed You
With the oil of gladness more than Your companions.
8 All Your garments are scented with myrrh and aloes *and* cassia,
Out of the ivory palaces, by which they have made You glad.
9 Kings' daughters *are* among Your honorable women;
At Your right hand stands the queen in gold from Ophir.

10 Listen, O daughter,
Consider and incline your ear;
Forget your own people also, and your father's house;
11 So the King will greatly desire your beauty;
Because He *is* your Lord, worship Him.
12 And the daughter of Tyre *will come* with a gift;
The rich among the people will seek your favor.

13 The royal daughter *is* all glorious within *the palace;*
Her clothing *is* woven with gold.

45:title [m] Hebrew *Shoshannim* [n] Hebrew *Maschil*

LIFE LESSON

Psalms 45:1–46:11

SITUATION God's strength provided safety, security, and peace. His power guaranteed victory. (Psalm 45 may have been written for a wedding).

OBSERVATION Nothing occurs beyond the reach of God's power. Awareness of God's power provides rest and encouragement to Christians.

INSPIRATION America is in a hurry. Time has skyrocketed in value. The value of any commodity depends on its scarcity. And time that once was abundant now is going to the highest bidder.

. . . "Time," according to pollster Louis Harris, "may have become the most precious commodity in the land."

Do we really have less time? Or is it just our imagination?

In 1965 a testimony before a Senate subcommittee claimed the future looked bright for free time in America. By 1985, predicted the report, Americans would be working twenty-two hours a week and would be able to retire at age thirty-eight.

The reason? The computer age would usher in a gleaming array of advances that would do our work for us while stabilizing our economy.

Take the household, they cited. Microwaves, quick-fix foods, and food processors will pave the way into the carefree future. And the office? Well, you know that old stencil machine? It'll be replaced by a copier. And the files? Computers are the files of the future. And that electric typewriter? Don't get too attached to it; a computer will do its work, too.

And now, years later, we have everything the report promised. The computers are byting, the VCRs are recording, the fax machines are faxing. Yet the clocks are still ticking, and people are still running. The truth is, the average amount of leisure time has *shrunk* 37 percent since 1973. The average work week has *increased* from forty-one to forty-seven hours. (And, for many of you, forty-seven hours would be a calm week.)

Why didn't the forecast come true? What did the committee overlook?

Continued

They misjudged the appetite of the consumer. As the individualism of the sixties led to the materialism of the eighties, the free time gained for us by technology didn't make us relax; it made us run. Gadgets provided more time . . . more time meant more potential money . . . more potential money meant more time needed . . . and round and round it went. Lives grew louder as demands became greater. And as demands became greater, lives grew emptier.

"I've got so many irons in the fire, I can't keep any of them hot," complained one young father.

Can you relate?

When I was ten years old, my mother enrolled me in piano lessons. Now, many youngsters excel at the keyboard. Not me. Spending thirty minutes every afternoon tethered to a piano bench was a torture just one level away from swallowing broken glass. The metronome inspected each second with glacial slowness before it was allowed to pass.

Some of the music, though, I learned to enjoy. I hammered the staccatos. I belabored the crescendos. The thundering finishes I kettle-drummed. But there was one instruction in the music I could never obey to my teacher's satisfaction. The rest. The zigzagged command to do nothing. Nothing! What sense does that make? Why sit at the piano and pause when you can pound?

"Because," my teacher patiently explained, "music is always sweeter after a rest."

It didn't make sense to me at age ten. But now, a few decades later, the words ring with wisdom—divine wisdom.

(From *The Applause of Heaven* by Max Lucado)

APPLICATION Are you weary? Look to the protection and strength of God. The world can be overwhelming at times, but remember that God has everything under control. Relax in him.

EXPLORATION God's Strength for Us—Exodus 15:2; 2 Samuel 22:33; Psalm 28:8; 73:26; 81:1; 89:21.

14 She shall be brought to the King in robes of many colors;
The virgins, her companions who follow her,
shall be brought to You.
15 With gladness and rejoicing they shall be brought;
They shall enter the King's palace.

16 Instead of Your fathers shall be Your sons,
Whom You shall make princes in all the earth.
17 I will make Your name to be remembered in all generations;
Therefore the people shall praise You forever and ever.

PSALM 46

God the Refuge of His People and Conqueror of the Nations

To the Chief Musician. A Psalm of the sons of Korah. A Song for Alamoth.

God *is* our refuge and strength,
A very present help in trouble.
2 Therefore we will not fear,
Even though the earth be removed,
And though the mountains be carried into the midst of the sea;
3 *Though* its waters roar *and* be troubled,
Though the mountains shake with its swelling. Selah

4 *There is* a river whose streams shall make glad the city of God,
The holy *place* of the tabernacle of the Most High.
5 God *is* in the midst of her, she shall not be moved;
God shall help her, just at the break of dawn.
6 The nations raged, the kingdoms were moved;
He uttered His voice, the earth melted.

7 The LORD of hosts *is* with us;
The God of Jacob *is* our refuge. Selah

8 Come, behold the works of the LORD,
Who has made desolations in the earth.
9 He makes wars cease to the end of the earth;
He breaks the bow and cuts the spear in two;
He burns the chariot in the fire.

10 Be still, and know that I *am* God;
I will be exalted among the nations,
I will be exalted in the earth!

11 The LORD of hosts *is* with us;
The God of Jacob *is* our refuge. Selah

PSALM 47

Praise to God, the Ruler of the Earth

To the Chief Musician. A Psalm of the sons of Korah.

Oh, clap your hands, all you peoples!
Shout to God with the voice of triumph!
2 For the LORD Most High *is* awesome;
He is a great King over all the earth.

3 He will subdue the peoples under us,
And the nations under our feet.
4 He will choose our inheritance for us,
The excellence of Jacob whom He loves. Selah

5 God has gone up with a shout,
The LORD with the sound of a trumpet.
6 Sing praises to God, sing praises!
Sing praises to our King, sing praises!
7 For God *is* the King of all the earth;
Sing praises with understanding.

8 God reigns over the nations;
God sits on His holy throne.
9 The princes of the people have gathered together,
The people of the God of Abraham.
For the shields of the earth *belong* to God;
He is greatly exalted.

PSALM 48

The Glory of God in Zion

A Song. A Psalm of the sons of Korah.

Great *is* the LORD, and greatly to be praised
In the city of our God,
In His holy mountain.
2 Beautiful in elevation,
The joy of the whole earth,
Is Mount Zion *on* the sides of the north,
The city of the great King.
3 God *is* in her palaces;
He is known as her refuge.

4 For behold, the kings assembled,
They passed by together.
5 They saw *it, and* so they marveled;
They were troubled, they hastened away.
6 Fear took hold of them there,
And pain, as of a woman in birth pangs,
7 *As when* You break the ships of Tarshish
With an east wind.

8 As we have heard,
So we have seen
In the city of the LORD of hosts,
In the city of our God:
God will establish it forever. Selah

9 We have thought, O God, on Your lovingkindness,
In the midst of Your temple.
10 According to Your name, O God,
So *is* Your praise to the ends of the earth;
Your right hand is full of righteousness.

LIFE LESSON

Psalms 47:1–48:14

SITUATION This festive song celebrated the universal reign of God.

OBSERVATION God reigns over all the earth and every nation. He deserves our adoration.

INSPIRATION Do you hunger for Jesus Christ? Do you yearn to spend time alone with Him in prayer? Is He the most important person in your life? . . . Do you eagerly turn to His . . . Gospels to learn more of Him? Are you making the effort to die to anything and everything that would inhibit, diminish, or threaten your friendship?

To discern where you really are with the Lord, recall what has saddened you recently. Was it the realization that you don't love Jesus enough? . . . That you can't honestly say that the greatest thing that ever happened in your life is that Jesus came to you and you heard His voice? . . .

Or have you been saddened and depressed over a lack of human respect, criticism from an authority figure, financial problems, lack of friends, your bulging waistline?

On the other hand, what has gladdened you recently? Reflection on your election to the Christian community? . . . The afternoon you stole away with the Gospel as your only companion? The thrilling awareness that God loves you unconditionally just as you are and not as you should be? . . .

When our lives are governed not by a network of laws but by the fire of the Spirit that burns within, . . . when we respond to the call of Jesus, which is not, "Come to the ice cream party," but "*Come to Me*," then the limitless power of the Holy Sprit will be unleashed with astonishing force. (From *Lion and Lamb* by Brennan Manning)

APPLICATION Take a Saturday or Sunday afternoon retreat. Grab your Bible, a notebook, and a blanket and spend the day in the park. Read through a Gospel. Read a handful of psalms. Pray. Do it soon.

EXPLORATION Sovereignty of God—Daniel 4:32; Acts 4:24-29; Revelation 19:16.

11 Let Mount Zion rejoice,
Let the daughters of Judah be glad,
Because of Your judgments.

12 Walk about Zion,
And go all around her.
Count her towers;
13 Mark well her bulwarks;
Consider her palaces;
That you may tell *it* to the generation following.
14 For this *is* God,
Our God forever and ever;
He will be our guide
Even to death.[o]

PSALM 49

The Confidence of the Foolish

To the Chief Musician. A Psalm of the sons of Korah.

Hear this, all peoples;
Give ear, all inhabitants of the world,
2 Both low and high,
Rich and poor together.
3 My mouth shall speak wisdom,
And the meditation of my heart *shall give* understanding.
4 I will incline my ear to a proverb;
I will disclose my dark saying on the harp.

5 Why should I fear in the days of evil,
When the iniquity at my heels surrounds me?
6 Those who trust in their wealth
And boast in the multitude of their riches,
7 None *of them* can by any means redeem *his* brother,
Nor give to God a ransom for him—
8 For the redemption of their souls *is* costly,
And it shall cease forever—
9 That he should continue to live eternally,
And not see the Pit.

10 For he sees wise men die;
Likewise the fool and the senseless person perish,
And leave their wealth to others.
11 Their inner thought *is that* their houses *will last* forever,[p]
Their dwelling places to all generations;
They call *their* lands after their own names.
12 Nevertheless man, *though* in honor, does not remain;[q]
He is like the beasts *that* perish.

13 This is the way of those who *are* foolish,
And of their posterity who approve their sayings. Selah

LIFE LESSON

Psalms 49:1–50:23

SITUATION David's song instructed those who consider their material wealth more important than their spiritual wealth. David cautioned the people against greed.

OBSERVATION The benefits of material wealth are too short-lived. Only treasures stored in heaven endure.

INSPIRATION Adding to the uncertainty is the problem of materialism. I asked some young persons their definition of success. They indicated that they and their friends believe that being successful means "being able to have whatever you want whenever you want it." That is probably the best definition of materialism I know.

Many people believe if they live by this philosophy, they will be able to meet all of life's needs, and they will be happy. This idea, of course, is illusory. As philosophers throughout the centuries, including Solomon . . . have warned, "Materialism will never bring happiness."

Judy and I took a trip to Africa several years ago with some friends. On that trip we went into the bush country in Kenya to visit with an African pastor. One of his five children played nearby with her only toy, a used flashlight battery, as we had tea outside his mud hut. Some in our group asked him, "What is the greatest barrier to the spread of the gospel in this part of Africa?"

His response was very insightful but astounding to each of us. I would have expected him to say something about the lack of communication, transportation, or literacy. In fact, he said, the greatest barrier to the spread of the gospel there was materialism. When we asked him to explain further, he said that if a man

48:14 [o] Following Masoretic Text and Syriac; Septuagint and Vulgate read *Forever.*
49:11 [p] Septuagint, Syriac, Targum, and Vulgate read *Their graves shall be their houses forever.*
49:12 [q] Following Masoretic Text and Targum; Septuagint, Syriac, and Vulgate read *understand* (compare verse 20).

14 Like sheep they are laid in the grave;
Death shall feed on them;
The upright shall have dominion over them in the morning;
And their beauty shall be consumed in the grave,
far from their dwelling.
15 But God will redeem my soul from the power of the grave,
For He shall receive me. Selah

16 Do not be afraid when one becomes rich,
When the glory of his house is increased;
17 For when he dies he shall carry nothing away;
His glory shall not descend after him.
18 Though while he lives he blesses himself
(For *men* will praise you when you do well for yourself),
19 He shall go to the generation of his fathers;
They shall never see light.
20 A man *who is* in honor, yet does not understand,
Is like the beasts *that* perish.

PSALM 50

God the Righteous Judge

A Psalm of Asaph.

The Mighty One, God the LORD,
Has spoken and called the earth
From the rising of the sun to its going down.
2 Out of Zion, the perfection of beauty,
God will shine forth.
3 Our God shall come, and shall not keep silent;
A fire shall devour before Him,
And it shall be very tempestuous all around Him.

4 He shall call to the heavens from above,
And to the earth, that He may judge His people:
5 "Gather My saints together to Me,
Those who have made a covenant with Me by sacrifice."
6 Let the heavens declare His righteousness,
For God Himself *is* Judge. Selah

7 "Hear, O My people, and I will speak,
O Israel, and I will testify against you;
I *am* God, your God!
8 I will not rebuke you for your sacrifices
Or your burnt offerings,
Which are continually before Me.
9 I will not take a bull from your house,
Nor goats out of your folds.
10 For every beast of the forest *is* Mine,
And the cattle on a thousand hills.
11 I know all the birds of the mountains,
And the wild beasts of the field *are* Mine.

12 "If I were hungry, I would not tell you;
For the world *is* Mine, and all its fullness.

has one wife, he wants two wives; if he has a cow manure hut, he wants a mud hut; if he has a thatch roof, he wants a tin roof on his hut; if he has one acre of ground, he wants two acres of ground; if he has one cow, he wants two cows; and on and on.

His comments indicated to us that materialism is not indigenous to the United States. Instead materialism is indigenous to the human heart and replaces the thought with a vain and empty philosophy—one that promises much but delivers *nothing.* Materialism cannot provide true satisfaction, purpose and accomplishment, factors that are so essential in life.

Even though we know intuitively that materialism will not satisfy our innermost desires, as a family and as a nation we have developed a short-term perspective on all financial decisions, leading ultimately to our massive national and personal debts. We really believe that there are no limits on what we can spend, because if we can afford it now, the future will take care of itself. We are living blindly, ignoring the long-term consequences of the poor decisions we make.

(From *Raising Money-Smart Kids* by Ron and Judy Blue)

APPLICATION Do you desire a promotion at work more than serving unnoticed at church? Would you rather help at a church work day or put in extra hours at the office? Put your material possessions in perspective. Instead of using your money, car, or house to feel good about yourself, use them to reach out to those in need.

EXPLORATION Wealth—Psalm 17:13-15; Matthew 19:24; Mark 10:23; 1 Timothy 6:10; James 1:10-11.

LIFE LESSON

Psalms 51:1–52:9

SITUATION David repented after Nathan confronted him. Nathan rightly pointed to David's sin of adultery and murder (2 Samuel 11–12).

OBSERVATION David pled for restoration and renewal. He asked that God would purify his heart.

INSPIRATION When I was ten years old, I had a puppy named Tina. You would have loved her. She was the perfect pet. An irresistible, pug-nosed Pekingese pup. One ear fell over and the other ear stood straight up. She never tired of playing and yet never got in the way.

Her mother died when she was born so the rearing of the puppy fell to me. I fed her milk from a doll bottle and used to sneak out at night to see if she was warm. I'll never forget the night I took her to bed with me only to have her mess on my pillow. We made quite a pair. My first brush with parenthood.

One day I went into the backyard to give Tina her dinner. I looked around and spotted her in a corner near the fence. She had cornered a butterfly (as much as a butterfly can be cornered) and was playfully yelping and jumping in the air trying to catch the butterfly in her mouth. Amused, I watched her for a few minutes and then called to her.

"Tina! Come here, girl! It's time to eat!" What happened next surprised me. Tina stopped her playing and looked at me. But instead of immediately scampering in my direction, she sat back on her haunches. Then she tilted her head back toward the butterfly, looked back at me, then back to the butterfly, and then back to me. For the first time in her life, she had to make a decision. . . .

And do you know what she did? She chased the butterfly! Scurrying and barking, she ignored my call and chased that silly thing until it flew over the fence.

That is when the guilt hit.

She stopped at the fence for a long time, sitting back on her hind legs looking up in the air where the butterfly

13 Will I eat the flesh of bulls,
Or drink the blood of goats?
14 Offer to God thanksgiving,
And pay your vows to the Most High.
15 Call upon Me in the day of trouble;
I will deliver you, and you shall glorify Me."

16 But to the wicked God says:
"What *right* have you to declare My statutes,
Or take My covenant in your mouth,
17 Seeing you hate instruction
And cast My words behind you?
18 When you saw a thief, you consented[r] with him,
And have been a partaker with adulterers.
19 You give your mouth to evil,
And your tongue frames deceit.
20 You sit *and* speak against your brother;
You slander your own mother's son.
21 These *things* you have done, and I kept silent;
You thought that I was altogether like you;
But I will rebuke you,
And set *them* in order before your eyes.

22 "Now consider this, you who forget God,
Lest I tear *you* in pieces,
And *there be* none to deliver:
23 Whoever offers praise glorifies Me;
And to him who orders *his* conduct *aright*
I will show the salvation of God."

PSALM 51

A Prayer of Repentance

To the Chief Musician. A Psalm of David when Nathan the prophet went to him, after he had gone in to Bathsheba.

Have mercy upon me, O God,
According to Your lovingkindness;
According to the multitude of Your tender mercies,
Blot out my transgressions.
2 Wash me thoroughly from my iniquity,
And cleanse me from my sin.

3 For I acknowledge my transgressions,
And my sin *is* always before me.
4 Against You, You only, have I sinned,
And done *this* evil in Your sight—
That You may be found just when You speak,[s]
And blameless when You judge.

5 Behold, I was brought forth in iniquity,
And in sin my mother conceived me.

50:18 [r] Septuagint, Syriac, Targum, and Vulgate read *ran.*
51:4 [s] Septuagint, Targum, and Vulgate read *in Your words.*

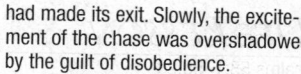

6 Behold, You desire truth in the inward parts,
And in the hidden *part* You will make me to know wisdom.

7 Purge me with hyssop, and I shall be clean;
Wash me, and I shall be whiter than snow.
8 Make me hear joy and gladness,
That the bones You have broken may rejoice.
9 Hide Your face from my sins,
And blot out all my iniquities.

10 Create in me a clean heart, O God,
And renew a steadfast spirit within me.
11 Do not cast me away from Your presence,
And do not take Your Holy Spirit from me.

12 Restore to me the joy of Your salvation,
And uphold me *by Your* generous Spirit.
13 *Then* I will teach transgressors Your ways,
And sinners shall be converted to You.

14 Deliver me from the guilt of bloodshed, O God,
The God of my salvation,
And my tongue shall sing aloud of Your righteousness.
15 O Lord, open my lips,
And my mouth shall show forth Your praise.
16 For You do not desire sacrifice, or else I would give *it;*
You do not delight in burnt offering.
17 The sacrifices of God *are* a broken spirit,
A broken and a contrite heart—
These, O God, You will not despise.

18 Do good in Your good pleasure to Zion;
Build the walls of Jerusalem.
19 Then You shall be pleased with the
sacrifices of righteousness,
With burnt offering and whole burnt offering;
Then they shall offer bulls on Your altar.

PSALM 52

The End of the Wicked and the Peace of the Godly

To the Chief Musician. A Contemplation[t] of David when Doeg the Edomite went and told Saul, and said to him, "David has gone to the house of Ahimelech."

Why do you boast in evil, O mighty man?
The goodness of God *endures* continually.
2 Your tongue devises destruction,
Like a sharp razor, working deceitfully.
3 You love evil more than good,
Lying rather than speaking righteousness. Selah

4 You love all devouring words,
You deceitful tongue.

had made its exit. Slowly, the excitement of the chase was overshadowed by the guilt of disobedience.

She turned painfully and walked back to encounter her owner. (To be honest, I was a little miffed.) Her head was ducked as she regretfully trudged across the yard.

For the first time in her life, she felt guilty.

She had violated her "should" and had given in to her "want." My heart melted, however, and I called her name again. Sensing forgiveness, Tina darted into my hands. (I always was a softy.)

Now, I may be overdoing it a bit. I don't know if a dog can really feel guilty or not. But I do know a human can. And whether the sin is as slight as chasing a butterfly or as serious as sleeping with another man's wife, the effects are the same. . . .

Man cannot cope with guilt alone. . . .

. . . I don't care how many worship services you attend or good deeds you do, your goodness is insufficient. You *can't* be good enough to deserve forgiveness. No one bats a thousand. No one bowls three hundred. No one. Not you, not me, not anyone. . . .

. . . Listen. Quit trying to quench your own guilt. You can't do it. There's no way. Not with a bottle of whiskey or perfect Sunday School attendance. Sorry. I don't care how bad you are. You can't be bad enough to forget it. And I don't care how good you are. You can't be good enough to overcome it. You need a Savior.

(From *No Wonder They Call Him the Savior* by Max Lucado)

APPLICATION Do you think you have committed too great a sin for God to forget it? Do you think you have waited too long to ask for his pardon? Read this psalm to God as your own prayer. Experience God's forgiving grace as David did.

EXPLORATION Confession of Sin—Ezra 9:5-7; 10:1; Nehemiah 1:5-7; Psalm 32:5; 41:4; Luke 3:3; Acts 3:19; 1 John 1:9.

52:title [t] Hebrew *Maschil*

5 God shall likewise destroy you forever;
He shall take you away, and pluck you out of *your* dwelling place,
And uproot you from the land of the living. Selah
6 The righteous also shall see and fear,
And shall laugh at him, *saying,*
7 "Here is the man *who* did not make God his strength,
But trusted in the abundance of his riches,
And strengthened himself in his wickedness."

8 But I *am* like a green olive tree in the house of God;
I trust in the mercy of God forever and ever.
9 I will praise You forever,
Because You have done *it;*
And in the presence of Your saints
I will wait on Your name, for *it is* good.

LIFE LESSON

Psalms 53:1–55:23

SITUATION People who denied God were foolish, for they denied the one who could save them. David prayed for salvation to reach his people. He praised God for giving favor to an unworthy nation.

OBSERVATION Denying God doesn't detract from his majesty, but it does separate you from your divine Father. Avoid this tragedy!

INSPIRATION One Sunday afternoon I was reading a biography of Bill Borden, a Yale University student many years ago.

. . . [Bill's] father had been a millionaire and had left his fortune to Bill. But I was unsettled when I learned that Bill gave away his inheritance to missionary societies . . . so that more people would hear and accept the good news. . . . I read that Bill had decided to become a missionary.

As I read on . . . I learned that only a few weeks after arriving in Cairo to begin his work as a missionary . . . [Bill] woke up one morning feeling sick . . . because of a high fever. The fever didn't go away, but became worse.

I had heard and read enough missionary stories to know how God sometimes heals people, so I was completely unprepared to find out that God didn't heal Bill. Instead, Bill died. I was utterly shocked. . . .

God was unfair. God was ungrateful. *I would never serve a God like that,* I thought. So I decided, as I sat there

PSALM 53

Folly of the Godless, and the Restoration of Israel

To the Chief Musician. Set to "Mahalath." A Contemplation[u] of David.

The fool has said in his heart,
"*There is* no God."
They are corrupt, and have done abominable iniquity;
There is none who does good.

2 God looks down from heaven upon the children of men,
To see if there are *any* who understand, who seek God.
3 Every one of them has turned aside;
They have together become corrupt;
There is none who does good,
No, not one.

4 Have the workers of iniquity no knowledge,
Who eat up my people *as* they eat bread,
And do not call upon God?
5 There they are in great fear
Where no fear was,
For God has scattered the bones of him who encamps against you;
You have put *them* to shame,
Because God has despised them.

6 Oh, that the salvation of Israel would come out of Zion!
When God brings back the captivity of His people,
Let Jacob rejoice *and* Israel be glad.

PSALM 54

Answered Prayer for Deliverance from Adversaries

To the Chief Musician. With stringed instruments.[v] A Contemplation[w] of David when the Ziphites went and said to Saul, "Is David not hiding with us?"

Save me, O God, by Your name,
And vindicate me by Your strength.

53:title [u] Hebrew *Maschil*
54:title [v] Hebrew *neginoth* [w] Hebrew *Maschil*

2 Hear my prayer, O God;
Give ear to the words of my mouth.
3 For strangers have risen up against me,
And oppressors have sought after my life;
They have not set God before them. Selah

4 Behold, God *is* my helper;
The Lord *is* with those who uphold my life.
5 He will repay my enemies for their evil.
Cut them off in Your truth.

6 I will freely sacrifice to You;
I will praise Your name, O LORD, for *it is* good.
7 For He has delivered me out of all trouble;
And my eye has seen *its desire* upon my enemies.

PSALM 55

Trust in God Concerning the Treachery of Friends

To the Chief Musician. With stringed instruments.[x] A Contemplation[y] of David.

Give ear to my prayer, O God,
And do not hide Yourself from my supplication.
2 Attend to me, and hear me;
I am restless in my complaint, and moan noisily,
3 Because of the voice of the enemy,
Because of the oppression of the wicked;
For they bring down trouble upon me,
And in wrath they hate me.

4 My heart is severely pained within me,
And the terrors of death have fallen upon me.
5 Fearfulness and trembling have come upon me,
And horror has overwhelmed me.
6 So I said, "Oh, that I had wings like a dove!
I would fly away and be at rest.
7 Indeed, I would wander far off,
And remain in the wilderness. Selah
8 I would hasten my escape
From the windy storm *and* tempest."

9 Destroy, O Lord, *and* divide their tongues,
For I have seen violence and strife in the city.
10 Day and night they go around it on its walls;
Iniquity and trouble *are* also in the midst of it.
11 Destruction *is* in its midst;
Oppression and deceit do not depart from its streets.

12 For *it is* not an enemy *who* reproaches me;
Then I could bear *it*.
Nor *is it* one *who* hates me who has exalted *himself* against me;
Then I could hide from him.

55:title [x] Hebrew *neginoth* [y] Hebrew *Maschil*

reading, to go my own way and run my own life. . . .

Then a strange thing happened. God had mercy on me. Even as I was defying Him and deciding to go my own way and do my own thing, my mind changed and I saw the fatal foolishness of that decision. A moment later I was down on my knees beside the chair where I had been reading. And I found myself praying and telling God that He could have my life, and I would do whatever He wanted me to do. It was as though He reached out for me as I was going over the edge and pulled me back and gave me a second chance.

From then on, although with some bumps, relapses, and detours along the way, I have stuck to my goal: to belong to Him alone and to be what He wants me to be, to do what He tells me to do. What happiness and joy I have had as a result!
(From *Next Steps for New Christians* by Kenneth Taylor)

APPLICATION Humanity has built tall buildings, gone to the moon, and transplanted organs. But we haven't overcome the penalty of sin. Such a challenge escapes us. Who has the cure for sin or for death? Open your heart to God today. Watch God accomplish changes in areas you have not been able to change.

EXPLORATION Denying God—Exodus 11:9-10; Matthew 10:32-33; 2 Timothy 2:12.

13 But *it was* you, a man my equal,
My companion and my acquaintance.
14 We took sweet counsel together,
And walked to the house of God in the throng.

15 Let death seize them;
Let them go down alive into hell,
For wickedness *is* in their dwellings *and* among them.

16 As for me, I will call upon God,
And the LORD shall save me.
17 Evening and morning and at noon
I will pray, and cry aloud,
And He shall hear my voice.
18 He has redeemed my soul in peace from
the battle *that was* against me,
For there were many against me.
19 God will hear, and afflict them,
Even He who abides from of old. Selah
Because they do not change,
Therefore they do not fear God.

20 He has put forth his hands against those
who were at peace with him;
He has broken his covenant.
21 *The words* of his mouth were smoother than butter,
But war *was* in his heart;
His words were softer than oil,
Yet they *were* drawn swords.

22 Cast your burden on the LORD,
And He shall sustain you;
He shall never permit the righteous to be moved.

23 But You, O God, shall bring them down
to the pit of destruction;
Bloodthirsty and deceitful men shall not live out half their days;
But I will trust in You.

PSALM 56

Prayer for Relief from Tormentors

To the Chief Musician. Set to "The Silent Dove in Distant Lands."[z] A Michtam of David when the Philistines captured him in Gath.

Be merciful to me, O God, for man would swallow me up;
Fighting all day he oppresses me.
2 My enemies would hound *me* all day,
For *there are* many who fight against me, O Most High.

3 Whenever I am afraid,
I will trust in You.

56:title [z] Hebrew *Jonath Elem Rechokim*

LIFE LESSON

Psalms 56:1–57:11

SITUATION David wrote Psalm 56 when the Philistines captured him in Gath (1 Samuel 21:10-15). He wrote Psalm 57 while hiding in a cave.

OBSERVATION God is trustworthy. He is a rock, a hiding place, a fortress. We have safety and comfort in him.

INSPIRATION Many years ago, Frederick Nolan was fleeing from his enemies during the North African persecution. Hounded by his pursuers over hill and valley with no place to hide, he fell exhausted into a wayside cave where he fully expected to be found. Awaiting his death, he saw a spider weaving a web. Within minutes, the little bug had woven a beautiful web across the mouth of the cave. The pursuers arrived and wondered if Nolan was hiding in there; but they thought it impossible for him to have entered the cave without dismantling the web. And so they went on. Having escaped, Nolan emerged from his hiding place and proclaimed, "Where God is, a spider's web is like a wall. Where God is not, a wall is like a spider's web."

God is our wall of defense. He is the one who delivers us from those who want to hurt us. He is the one who gives us the comfort and strength we need to be courageous and to endure the trials and trouble that enter our lives.

(From *A Dad's Blessing* by Gary Smalley and John Trent)

APPLICATION Christians will be persecuted. In what ways are you persecuted? Who opposes you? When life gets hard, look to your refuge—God.

EXPLORATION God as Refuge—2 Samuel 22:31; Psalm 46:1; 59:16; 62:7; Isaiah 25:4; Jeremiah 16:19; Joel 3:16; Nahum 1:7.

4 In God (I will praise His word),
In God I have put my trust;
I will not fear.
What can flesh do to me?

5 All day they twist my words;
All their thoughts *are* against me for evil.
6 They gather together,
They hide, they mark my steps,
When they lie in wait for my life.
7 Shall they escape by iniquity?
In anger cast down the peoples, O God!

8 You number my wanderings;
Put my tears into Your bottle;
Are they not in Your book?
9 When I cry out *to You,*
Then my enemies will turn back;
This I know, because God *is* for me.
10 In God (I will praise *His* word),
In the LORD (I will praise *His* word),
11 In God I have put my trust;
I will not be afraid.
What can man do to me?

12 Vows *made* to You *are binding*
upon me, O God;
I will render praises to You,
13 For You have delivered my soul from death.
Have You not *kept* my feet from falling,
That I may walk before God
In the light of the living?

PSALM 57

Prayer for Safety from Enemies

To the Chief Musician. Set to "Do Not Destroy."[a] A Michtam of David when he fled from Saul into the cave.

Be merciful to me, O God, be merciful to me!
For my soul trusts in You;
And in the shadow of Your wings I
will make my refuge,
Until *these* calamities have passed by.

2 I will cry out to God Most High,
To God who performs *all things* for me.
3 He shall send from heaven and save me;
He reproaches the one who would
swallow me up. Selah
God shall send forth His mercy and His truth.

4 My soul *is* among lions;
I lie *among* the sons of men
Who are set on fire,
Whose teeth *are* spears and arrows,
And their tongue a sharp sword.
5 Be exalted, O God, above the heavens;
Let Your glory *be* above all the earth.

6 They have prepared a net for my steps;
My soul is bowed down;
They have dug a pit before me;
Into the midst of it they *themselves* have fallen.
Selah

7 My heart is steadfast, O God,
my heart is steadfast;
I will sing and give praise.
8 Awake, my glory!
Awake, lute and harp!
I will awaken the dawn.

9 I will praise You, O Lord, among the peoples;
I will sing to You among the nations.
10 For Your mercy reaches unto the heavens,
And Your truth unto the clouds.

11 Be exalted, O God, above the heavens;
Let Your glory *be* above all the earth.

PSALM 58

The Just Judgment of the Wicked

To the Chief Musician. Set to "Do Not Destroy."[b] A Michtam of David.

Do you indeed speak righteousness,
you silent ones?
Do you judge uprightly, you sons of men?
2 No, in heart you work wickedness;
You weigh out the violence of your
hands in the earth.

3 The wicked are estranged from the womb;
They go astray as soon as they are born,
speaking lies.
4 Their poison *is* like the poison of a serpent;
They are like the deaf cobra *that* stops its ear,
5 Which will not heed the voice of charmers,
Charming ever so skillfully.

6 Break their teeth in their mouth, O God!
Break out the fangs of the young lions, O LORD!

57:title [a] Hebrew *Al Tashcheth*
58:title [b] Hebrew *Al Tashcheth*

Life Lesson

Psalms 58:1–59:17

SITUATION David sang to God for his protection and justice. He asked God to stop the assault of evil people on the righteous.

OBSERVATION God cares for people who try to live a life set apart for his service. He will bring the unrepentant to justice.

INSPIRATION Many non-Christians try to convince themselves that they believe neither in the supernatural nor in the hereafter. Try as they will, however, there lingers the nagging, irrepressible realization that we have not been created just for time. We instinctively know that justice alone demands some judgment day. Unless we have knowingly settled the question of our sinful guilt, we are chronically beset by this fear. Until you acknowledge this fact, your fears will worsen. If you admit the possibility of the supernatural and acknowledge the facts of the gospel as they apply to your own life, you would find the fear of death removed and the glorious peace of believing present as a part of your life.

You can have peace in your heart and the personal and perennial assurance of salvation if you will humbly acknowledge yourself as a sinner in God's sight, ask for His forgiveness and cleansing by the blood of Christ shed on the cross, and trust in Jesus, God's Son, as your Savior and Lord. Christ died to do all this. . . .

. . . This can be your experience today as you turn in faith to Christ and give your life to Him. Don't let another day go by without committing your life to Christ.

(From *Storm Warning* by Billy Graham)

APPLICATION Commit your life to Christ. First, appeal to God's mercy in prayer, then ask Jesus to enter your life as Lord and Savior. Develop a relationship with him.

EXPLORATION Judgment—Matthew 12:36; Romans 14:10-12; 2 Corinthians 5:10; Revelation 20:11-15. Salvation—John 3:16; Romans 3:23; 5:8; 6:23; 10:9-10.

7 Let them flow away as waters *which* run continually;
When he bends *his bow,*
Let his arrows be as if cut in pieces.
8 *Let them be* like a snail which melts away as it goes,
Like a stillborn child of a woman, that they may not see the sun.

9 Before your pots can feel *the burning* thorns,
He shall take them away as with a whirlwind,
As in His living and burning wrath.
10 The righteous shall rejoice when he sees the vengeance;
He shall wash his feet in the blood of the wicked,
11 So that men will say,
"Surely *there is* a reward for the righteous;
Surely He is God who judges in the earth."

PSALM 59

The Assured Judgment of the Wicked

To the Chief Musician. Set to "Do Not Destroy."[c] A Michtam of David when Saul sent men, and they watched the house in order to kill him.

Deliver me from my enemies, O my God;
Defend me from those who rise up against me.
2 Deliver me from the workers of iniquity,
And save me from bloodthirsty men.

3 For look, they lie in wait for my life;
The mighty gather against me,
Not *for* my transgression nor *for* my sin, O LORD.
4 They run and prepare themselves through no fault *of mine.*

Awake to help me, and behold!
5 You therefore, O LORD God of hosts, the God of Israel,
Awake to punish all the nations;
Do not be merciful to any wicked transgressors. Selah

6 At evening they return,
They growl like a dog,
And go all around the city.
7 Indeed, they belch with their mouth;
Swords *are* in their lips;
For *they say,* "Who hears?"

8 But You, O LORD, shall laugh at them;
You shall have all the nations in derision.
9 I will wait for You, O You his Strength;[d]
For God *is* my defense.
10 My God of mercy[e] shall come to meet me;
God shall let me see *my desire* on my enemies.

59:title [c] Hebrew *Al Tashcheth*
59:9 [d] Following Masoretic Text and Syriac; some Hebrew manuscripts, Septuagint, Targum, and Vulgate read *my Strength.*
59:10 [e] Following Qere; some Hebrew manuscripts, Septuagint, and Vulgate read *My God, His mercy;* Kethib, some Hebrew manuscripts and Targum read *O God, my mercy;* Syriac reads *O God, Your mercy.*

11 Do not slay them, lest my people forget;
Scatter them by Your power,
And bring them down,
O Lord our shield.
12 *For* the sin of their mouth *and* the words of their lips,
Let them even be taken in their pride,
And for the cursing and lying *which* they speak.
13 Consume *them* in wrath, consume *them,*
That they *may* not *be;*
And let them know that God rules in Jacob
To the ends of the earth. Selah

14 And at evening they return,
They growl like a dog,
And go all around the city.
15 They wander up and down for food,
And howl[f] if they are not satisfied.

16 But I will sing of Your power;
Yes, I will sing aloud of Your mercy in the morning;
For You have been my defense
And refuge in the day of my trouble.
17 To You, O my Strength, I will sing praises;
For God *is* my defense,
My God of mercy.

PSALM 60

Urgent Prayer for the Restored Favor of God

To the Chief Musician. Set to "Lily of the Testimony."[g] A Michtam of David. For teaching. When he fought against Mesopotamia and Syria of Zobah, and Joab returned and killed twelve thousand Edomites in the Valley of Salt.

O God, You have cast us off;
You have broken us down;
You have been displeased;
Oh, restore us again!
2 You have made the earth tremble;
You have broken it;
Heal its breaches, for it is shaking.
3 You have shown Your people hard things;
You have made us drink the wine of confusion.

4 You have given a banner to those who fear You,
That it may be displayed because of the truth. Selah
5 That Your beloved may be delivered,
Save *with* Your right hand, and hear me.

6 God has spoken in His holiness:
"I will rejoice;
I will divide Shechem
And measure out the Valley of Succoth.

LIFE LESSON

Psalms 60:1–62:12

SITUATION Life on earth was difficult for David. He found satisfaction only in his relationship with God. God refreshed and fulfilled him.

OBSERVATION To find joy and fulfillment, we should pursue fellowship with God.

INSPIRATION The only ultimate disaster that can befall us, I have come to realize, is to feel ourselves to be home on earth. As long as we are aliens, we cannot forget our true homeland.

Unhappiness on earth cultivates a hunger for heaven. By gracing us with a deep dissatisfaction, God holds our attention. The only tragedy, then, is to be satisfied prematurely. To settle for earth. To be content in a strange land. . . .

We are not happy here because we are not at home here. We are not happy here because we are not supposed to be happy here. We are "like foreigners and strangers in this world" (1 Pet. 2:11).

Take a fish and place him on the beach. Watch his gills gasp and scales dry. Is he happy? No! How do you make him happy? Do you cover him with a mountain of cash? Do you get a beach chair and sunglasses? Do you bring him a *Playfish* magazine and martini? Do you wardrobe him in double breasted fins and people-skinned shoes?

Of course not. Then how do you make him happy? You put him back in his element. You put him back in the water. He will never be happy on the beach simply because he was not made for the beach.

And you will never be completely happy on earth simply because you were not made for earth. Oh, you will have moments of joy. You will catch glimpses of light. You will know moments or even days of peace. But they simply do not compare with the happiness that lies ahead.

(From *When God Whispers Your Name* by Max Lucado)

Continued

59:15 *f* Following Septuagint and Vulgate; Masoretic Text, Syriac, and Targum read *spend the night.*
60:title *g* Hebrew *Shushan Eduth*

APPLICATION Where do you seek fulfillment? Love? Work? Money? Entertainment? Education? Refreshment and contentment can be found only in God. Memorize Psalm 62:1-2 and share it with a fellow believer.

EXPLORATION Rest—Psalm 55:22; 91:1; 116:7; Jeremiah 6:16; Matthew 6:25-34; Hebrews 4:9; 1 Peter 5:7; 1 John 3:19.

7 Gilead *is* Mine, and Manasseh *is* Mine;
Ephraim also *is* the helmet for My head;
Judah *is* My lawgiver.
8 Moab *is* My washpot;
Over Edom I will cast My shoe;
Philistia, shout in triumph because of Me."

9 Who will bring me *to* the strong city?
Who will lead me to Edom?
10 *Is it* not You, O God, *who* cast us off?
And You, O God, *who* did not go out with our armies?
11 Give us help from trouble,
For the help of man *is* useless.
12 Through God we will do valiantly,
For *it is* He *who* shall tread down our enemies.[h]

PSALM 61

Assurance of God's Eternal Protection

To the Chief Musician. On a stringed instrument.[i] A Psalm of David.

Hear my cry, O God;
Attend to my prayer.
2 From the end of the earth I will cry to You,
When my heart is overwhelmed;
Lead me to the rock that is higher than I.

3 For You have been a shelter for me,
A strong tower from the enemy.
4 I will abide in Your tabernacle forever;
I will trust in the shelter of Your wings. Selah

5 For You, O God, have heard my vows;
You have given *me* the heritage of those who fear Your name.
6 You will prolong the king's life,
His years as many generations.
7 He shall abide before God forever.
Oh, prepare mercy and truth, *which* may preserve him!

8 So I will sing praise to Your name forever,
That I may daily perform my vows.

PSALM 62

A Calm Resolve to Wait for the Salvation of God

To the Chief Musician. To Jeduthun. A Psalm of David.

Truly my soul silently *waits* for God;
From Him *comes* my salvation.
2 He only *is* my rock and my salvation;
He is my defense;
I shall not be greatly moved.

60:12 *h* Compare verses 5–12 with 108:6–13
61:title *i* Hebrew *neginah*

3 How long will you attack a man?
You shall be slain, all of you,
Like a leaning wall and a tottering fence.
4 They only consult to cast *him* down from his high position;
They delight in lies;
They bless with their mouth,
But they curse inwardly. Selah

5 My soul, wait silently for God alone,
For my expectation *is* from Him.
6 He only *is* my rock and my salvation;
He is my defense;
I shall not be moved.
7 In God *is* my salvation and my glory;
The rock of my strength,
And my refuge, *is* in God.

8 Trust in Him at all times, you people;
Pour out your heart before Him;
God *is* a refuge for us. Selah

9 Surely men of low degree *are* a vapor,
Men of high degree *are* a lie;
If they are weighed on the scales,
They *are* altogether *lighter* than vapor.
10 Do not trust in oppression,
Nor vainly hope in robbery;
If riches increase,
Do not set *your* heart *on them.*

11 God has spoken once,
Twice I have heard this:
That power *belongs* to God.
12 Also to You, O Lord, *belongs* mercy;
For You render to each one according to his work.

PSALM 63

Joy in the Fellowship of God

A Psalm of David when he was in the wilderness of Judah.

O God, You *are* my God;
Early will I seek You;
My soul thirsts for You;
My flesh longs for You
In a dry and thirsty land
Where there is no water.
2 So I have looked for You in the sanctuary,
To see Your power and Your glory.

3 Because Your lovingkindness *is* better than life,
My lips shall praise You.
4 Thus I will bless You while I live;
I will lift up my hands in Your name.

LIFE LESSON

Psalms 63:1–65:13

SITUATION David expressed joy and praise to God. He also wrote of his hope for God's protection from evildoers.

OBSERVATION God meets every need and satisfies fully. You cannot improve on God's work.

INSPIRATION It is . . . weariness that makes the words of the carpenter so compelling. Listen to them. "Come to me, all you who are weary and burdened and I will give you rest."

Come to me. . . . The invitation is to come to him. Why him?

He offers the invitation as a penniless rabbi in an oppressed nation. He has no political office, no connections with the authorities in Rome. He hasn't written a best-seller or earned a diploma.

Yet, he dares to look into the leathery faces of farmers and tired faces of housewives and offer rest. He looks into the disillusioned eyes of a preacher or two from Jerusalem. He gazes into the cynical stare of a banker and the hungry eyes of a bartender and makes this paradoxical promise: "Take my yoke upon you and learn from me, for I am gentle and humble in heart, and you will find rest for your souls."

The people came. They came out of the cul-de-sacs and office complexes of their day. They brought him the burdens of their existence and he gave them, not religion, not doctrine, not systems, but rest.

As a result, they called him Lord.

As a result, they called him Savior.

Not so much because of what he said, but because of what he did.

What he did on the cross during six hours, one Friday. . . .

Jesus was the only man to walk God's earth who claimed to have an answer for man's burdens. "Come to me," he invited them.

My prayer is that you, too, will find rest. And that you will sleep like a baby.

(From *Six Hours One Friday* by Max Lucado)

Continued

APPLICATION Make a list of five ways God has provided for you this past week. Go to God and praise him for those blessings.

EXPLORATION Provision—Genesis 28:15; Exodus 19:4; Psalm 121:1-8; Isaiah 41:10; Matthew 28:20; Hebrews 7:25.

5 My soul shall be satisfied as with marrow and fatness,
And my mouth shall praise You with joyful lips.

6 When I remember You on my bed,
I meditate on You in the *night* watches.
7 Because You have been my help,
Therefore in the shadow of Your wings I will rejoice.
8 My soul follows close behind You;
Your right hand upholds me.

9 But those *who* seek my life, to destroy *it,*
Shall go into the lower parts of the earth.
10 They shall fall by the sword;
They shall be a portion for jackals.

11 But the king shall rejoice in God;
Everyone who swears by Him shall glory;
But the mouth of those who speak lies shall be stopped.

PSALM 64

Oppressed by the Wicked but Rejoicing in the LORD

To the Chief Musician. A Psalm of David.

Hear my voice, O God, in my meditation;
Preserve my life from fear of the enemy.
2 Hide me from the secret plots of the wicked,
From the rebellion of the workers of iniquity,
3 Who sharpen their tongue like a sword,
And bend *their bows to shoot* their arrows—bitter words,
4 That they may shoot in secret at the blameless;
Suddenly they shoot at him and do not fear.

5 They encourage themselves *in* an evil matter;
They talk of laying snares secretly;
They say, "Who will see them?"
6 They devise iniquities:
"We have perfected a shrewd scheme."
Both the inward thought and the heart of man are deep.

7 But God shall shoot at them *with* an arrow;
Suddenly they shall be wounded.
8 So He will make them stumble over their own tongue;
All who see them shall flee away.
9 All men shall fear,
And shall declare the work of God;
For they shall wisely consider His doing.

10 The righteous shall be glad in the LORD, and trust in Him.
And all the upright in heart shall glory.

PSALM 65

Praise to God for His Salvation and Providence

To the Chief Musician. A Psalm of David. A Song.

Praise is awaiting You, O God, in Zion;
And to You the vow shall be performed.

2 O You who hear prayer,
To You all flesh will come.
3 Iniquities prevail against me;
As for our transgressions,
You will provide atonement for them.

4 Blessed *is the man* You choose,
And cause to approach *You,*
That he may dwell in Your courts.
We shall be satisfied with the goodness of Your house,
Of Your holy temple.

5 *By* awesome deeds in righteousness You will answer us,
O God of our salvation,
You who are the confidence of all the ends of the earth,
And of the far-off seas;
6 Who established the mountains by His strength,
Being clothed with power;
7 You who still the noise of the seas,
The noise of their waves,
And the tumult of the peoples.
8 They also who dwell in the farthest parts are afraid of Your signs;
You make the outgoings of the morning and evening rejoice.

9 You visit the earth and water it,
You greatly enrich it;
The river of God is full of water;
You provide their grain,
For so You have prepared it.
10 You water its ridges abundantly,
You settle its furrows;
You make it soft with showers,
You bless its growth.

11 You crown the year with Your goodness,
And Your paths drip *with* abundance.
12 They drop *on* the pastures of the wilderness,
And the little hills rejoice on every side.
13 The pastures are clothed with flocks;
The valleys also are covered with grain;
They shout for joy, they also sing.

PSALM 66

Praise to God for His Awesome Works

To the Chief Musician. A Song. A Psalm.

Make a joyful shout to God, all the earth!
2 Sing out the honor of His name;
Make His praise glorious.
3 Say to God,
"How awesome are Your works!
Through the greatness of Your power
Your enemies shall submit themselves to You.

LIFE LESSON

Psalms 66:1–67:7

SITUATION This songwriter praised God for blessing the people. The writer promised to praise and offer sacrifice to God because God had always remained faithful.

OBSERVATION God is worthy of praise. He not only grants us our life, but he guides us as well.

INSPIRATION We are living in a time when more and more Christians direct their prayers to Jesus. I do not remember any occasion in the Scriptures where people prayed to the Son of God, so I suggest we follow His instructions. . . . When [Jesus] taught His followers to pray, it was always to the Father. So if you wish to be absolutely biblical about it, pray to the Father and call Him that. It will help you in praying to picture Him in your mind as Father more than Friend, or more than just a distant Deity. But of all the titles we could choose to use, Father says it best. He is our heavenly Father. He cares for His children. He knows how to handle His family. . . . I urge you to slow your pace, to approach His "hallowed name" thoughtfully. Take time! Give Him the respect He deserves. Wait on God. In return, He will give you a clearer vision. Furthermore, He will soften your will and make you want to know and do His will.

(From *Simple Faith* by Charles Swindoll)

APPLICATION Make this your "thank God" day. Focus on the blessings, whether they are as simple as a beautiful tree or as profound as peace of mind. Perhaps you could thank him for your older neighbor, your stubborn child, your gas-guzzling car, your boss—thank God for all things.

EXPLORATION Praise—1 Chronicles 16:4; 2 Chronicles 5:13; Psalm 61:8; Isaiah 12:1; Acts 16:22-25.

4 All the earth shall worship You
And sing praises to You;
They shall sing praises *to* Your name."
Selah

5 Come and see the works of God;
He is awesome *in His* doing toward the
sons of men.
6 He turned the sea into dry *land;*
They went through the river on foot.
There we will rejoice in Him.
7 He rules by His power forever;
His eyes observe the nations;
Do not let the rebellious exalt themselves.
Selah

8 Oh, bless our God, you peoples!
And make the voice of His praise to be heard,
9 Who keeps our soul among the living,
And does not allow our feet to be moved.
10 For You, O God, have tested us;
You have refined us as silver is refined.
11 You brought us into the net;
You laid affliction on our backs.
12 You have caused men to ride over our heads;
We went through fire and through water;
But You brought us out to rich *fulfillment.*

13 I will go into Your house with burnt offerings;
I will pay You my vows,
14 Which my lips have uttered
And my mouth has spoken
when I was in trouble.
15 I will offer You burnt sacrifices of fat animals,
With the sweet aroma of rams;
I will offer bulls with goats. Selah

16 Come *and* hear, all you who fear God,
And I will declare what He has
done for my soul.
17 I cried to Him with my mouth,
And He was extolled with my tongue.
18 If I regard iniquity in my heart,
The Lord will not hear.
19 *But* certainly God has heard *me;*
He has attended to the voice of my prayer.

20 Blessed *be* God,
Who has not turned away my prayer,
Nor His mercy from me!

PSALM 67

An Invocation and a Doxology

To the Chief Musician. On stringed instruments.[j] A Psalm. A Song.

God be merciful to us and bless us,
And cause His face to shine upon us, Selah
2 That Your way may be known on earth,
Your salvation among all nations.

3 Let the peoples praise You, O God;
Let all the peoples praise You.
4 Oh, let the nations be glad and sing for joy!
For You shall judge the people righteously,
And govern the nations on earth. Selah

5 Let the peoples praise You, O God;
Let all the peoples praise You.
6 *Then* the earth shall yield her increase;
God, our own God, shall bless us.
7 God shall bless us,
And all the ends of the earth shall fear Him.

PSALM 68

The Glory of God in His Goodness to Israel

To the Chief Musician. A Psalm of David. A Song.

Let God arise,
Let His enemies be scattered;
Let those also who hate Him flee before Him.
2 As smoke is driven away,
So drive *them* away;
As wax melts before the fire,
So let the wicked perish at the presence of God.
3 But let the righteous be glad;
Let them rejoice before God;
Yes, let them rejoice exceedingly.

4 Sing to God, sing praises to His name;
Extol Him who rides on the clouds,[k]
By His name YAH,
And rejoice before Him.

5 A father of the fatherless, a defender of widows,
Is God in His holy habitation.
6 God sets the solitary in families;
He brings out those who are
bound into prosperity;
But the rebellious dwell in a dry *land.*

67:title [j] Hebrew *neginoth*
68:4 [k] Masoretic Text reads *deserts;* Targum reads *heavens* (compare verse 34 and Isaiah 19:1).

7 O God, when You went out before Your people,
When You marched through the wilderness, Selah
8 The earth shook;
The heavens also dropped *rain* at the presence of God;
Sinai itself *was moved* at the presence of God, the God of Israel.
9 You, O God, sent a plentiful rain,
Whereby You confirmed Your inheritance,
When it was weary.
10 Your congregation dwelt in it;
You, O God, provided from Your goodness for the poor.

11 The Lord gave the word;
Great *was* the company of those who proclaimed *it*:
12 "Kings of armies flee, they flee,
And she who remains at home divides the spoil.
13 Though you lie down among the sheepfolds,
You will be like the wings of a dove covered with silver,
And her feathers with yellow gold."
14 When the Almighty scattered kings in it,
It was *white* as snow in Zalmon.

15 A mountain of God *is* the mountain of Bashan;
A mountain *of many* peaks *is* the mountain of Bashan.
16 Why do you fume with envy, you mountains of *many* peaks?
This is the mountain *which* God desires to dwell in;
Yes, the LORD will dwell *in it* forever.

17 The chariots of God *are* twenty thousand,
Even thousands of thousands;
The Lord is among them *as in* Sinai, in the Holy *Place*.
18 You have ascended on high,
You have led captivity captive;
You have received gifts among men,
Even *from* the rebellious,
That the LORD God might dwell *there*.

19 Blessed *be* the Lord,
Who daily loads us *with benefits*,
The God of our salvation! Selah
20 Our God *is* the God of salvation;
And to GOD the Lord *belong* escapes from death.

21 But God will wound the head of His enemies,
The hairy scalp of the one who still goes on in his trespasses.
22 The Lord said, "I will bring back from Bashan,
I will bring *them* back from the depths of the sea,
23 That your foot may crush *them*[l] in blood,
And the tongues of your dogs *may have*
their portion from *your* enemies."

24 They have seen Your procession, O God,
The procession of my God, my King, into the sanctuary.

68:23 [l] Septuagint, Syriac, Targum, and Vulgate read *you may dip your foot.*

LIFE LESSON

Psalm 68:1-35

SITUATION David led a joyful procession when the ark of God came to Jerusalem (2 Sam. 6:11-15).

OBSERVATION Praise God for the provision and protection he gives his people throughout all time.

INSPIRATION How precious are the promises when we lie sick, gazing into an empty month, sorely tried and tempted through pain and weariness! All depressing circumstances lose their power for evil when our faith takes hold upon the promises of God. . . .

If such be the greatness and value of the promises, let us joyfully accept and believe them. Shall I urge the child of God to do this? No, I will not so dishonor Him; surely He will believe His own Father! Surely, surely, it ought to be the easiest thing in the world for the sons and daughters of the Most High to believe in Him who gave them the power to become the children of God! . . .

Furthermore, let us know the promises. Should we not carry them at our fingers' ends? Should we not know them better than anything else? The promises should be the classics of all believers. . . . We ought to be so versed in Scripture as always to have at the tip of our tongue the promise that most exactly meets our case. We ought to be transcripts of Scripture; the divine promise should be as much written upon our hearts as upon the pages of the Book.

(From "The Valuation of the Promises" by Charles H. Spurgeon in *They Walked with God)*

APPLICATION Have you ever praised God for what he has done for his church? Isn't it easier to present your requests? During the next week, balance specific requests with specific thanks for deeds he has done.

EXPLORATION Power of God—Exodus 9:16; 15:6; Joshua 4:24; Psalm 111:6; 135:5; Luke 1:37; Romans 4:20-21; Revelation 4:8.

LIFE LESSON

Psalm 69:1-36

SITUATION Despite overwhelming misfortunes, David cried to God in trust and hope. He knew that only God can give eternal gladness and joy. This psalm has been called a Messianic Psalm because it portrays the humiliation and rejection of Jesus.

OBSERVATION People might growl their disapproval; but God, our faithful protector, gives us joy and strength.

INSPIRATION There are various ways of being happy, and every man has the capacity to make his life what it needs to be for him to have a reasonable amount of peace in it. Why then do we persecute ourselves with illusory demands, never content until we feel we have conformed to some standard of happiness that is not good for us only, but for everyone? Why can we not be content with the secret gift of the happiness that God offers us, without consulting the rest of the world? Why do we insist, rather, on a happiness that is approved by the magazines and TV? Perhaps because we do not believe in a happiness that is given to us for nothing. We do not think we can be happy with a happiness that has no price tag on it.

25 The singers went before, the players on instruments *followed* after;
Among *them were* the maidens playing timbrels.
26 Bless God in the congregations,
The Lord, from the fountain of Israel.
27 There *is* little Benjamin, their leader,
The princes of Judah *and* their company,
The princes of Zebulun *and* the princes of Naphtali.

28 Your God has commanded[m] your strength;
Strengthen, O God, what You have done for us.
29 Because of Your temple at Jerusalem,
Kings will bring presents to You.
30 Rebuke the beasts of the reeds,
The herd of bulls with the calves of the peoples,
Till everyone submits himself with pieces of silver.
Scatter the peoples *who* delight in war.
31 Envoys will come out of Egypt;
Ethiopia will quickly stretch out her hands to God.

32 Sing to God, you kingdoms of the earth;
Oh, sing praises to the Lord, Selah
33 To Him who rides on the heaven of heavens, *which were* of old!
Indeed, He sends out His voice, a mighty voice.
34 Ascribe strength to God;
His excellence *is* over Israel,
And His strength *is* in the clouds.
35 O God, *You are* more awesome than Your holy places.
The God of Israel *is* He who gives strength
and power to *His* people.

Blessed *be* God!

PSALM 69

An Urgent Plea for Help in Trouble

To the Chief Musician. Set to "The Lilies."[n] A Psalm of David.

Save me, O God!
For the waters have come up to *my* neck.
2 I sink in deep mire,
Where *there is* no standing;
I have come into deep waters,
Where the floods overflow me.
3 I am weary with my crying;
My throat is dry;
My eyes fail while I wait for my God.

4 Those who hate me without a cause
Are more than the hairs of my head;
They are mighty who would destroy me,
Being my enemies wrongfully;
Though I have stolen nothing,
I *still* must restore *it.*

68:28 [m] Septuagint, Syriac, Targum, and Vulgate read *Command, O God.*
69:title [n] Hebrew *Shoshannim*

5 O God, You know my foolishness;
And my sins are not hidden from You.
6 Let not those who wait for You, O Lord GOD of hosts,
be ashamed because of me;
Let not those who seek You be confounded because
of me, O God of Israel.
7 Because for Your sake I have borne reproach;
Shame has covered my face.
8 I have become a stranger to my brothers,
And an alien to my mother's children;
9 Because zeal for Your house has eaten me up,
And the reproaches of those who reproach You have fallen on me.
10 When I wept *and chastened* my soul with fasting,
That became my reproach.
11 I also made sackcloth my garment;
I became a byword to them.
12 Those who sit in the gate speak against me,
And I *am* the song of the drunkards.

13 But as for me, my prayer *is* to You,
O LORD, *in* the acceptable time;
O God, in the multitude of Your mercy,
Hear me in the truth of Your salvation.
14 Deliver me out of the mire,
And let me not sink;
Let me be delivered from those who hate me,
And out of the deep waters.
15 Let not the floodwater overflow me,
Nor let the deep swallow me up;
And let not the pit shut its mouth on me.

16 Hear me, O LORD, for Your lovingkindness *is* good;
Turn to me according to the multitude of Your tender mercies.
17 And do not hide Your face from Your servant,
For I am in trouble;
Hear me speedily.
18 Draw near to my soul, *and* redeem it;
Deliver me because of my enemies.

19 You know my reproach, my shame, and my dishonor;
My adversaries *are* all before You.
20 Reproach has broken my heart,
And I am full of heaviness;
I looked *for someone* to take pity, but *there was* none;
And for comforters, but I found none.
21 They also gave me gall for my food,
And for my thirst they gave me vinegar to drink.

22 Let their table become a snare before them,
And their well-being a trap.
23 Let their eyes be darkened, so that they do not see;
And make their loins shake continually.
24 Pour out Your indignation upon them,
And let Your wrathful anger take hold of them.

If we are fools enough to remain at the mercy of the people who want to sell us happiness, it will be impossible for us ever to be content with anything. How would they profit if we became content? We would no longer need their new product.

The last thing the salesman wants is for the buyer to become content. You are of no use in our affluent society unless you are always just about to grasp what you never have. . . .

God gives us freedom to make our own lives within the situation which is the gift of His love to us, and by means of the power His love grants us.

(From *Conjectures of a Guilty Bystander* by Thomas Merton)

APPLICATION What is your reputation at work? Do your colleagues see you as joyful? Do you find the good among all the bad? Or are you a complainer, a whiner, always ready to share your life's crises? Share the good. Be joyful. Be encouraging to those around you instead of depressing.

EXPLORATION Happiness—Psalm 16:7-11; 17:15; Ecclesiastes 2:10-11; 18-26; Matthew 5:3-12.

LIFE LESSON

Psalms 70:1–71:24

SITUATION David wrote these psalms as a cry for help in his old age. David longed to be a testimony of God's faithfulness and a useful part of God's work.

OBSERVATION In the later years of his life, David looked for God's hand just as surely as he had during his younger years. His dependence on God did not lessen with age.

INSPIRATION God had been [David's] trust and his hope from his youth—a remarkable distinction. His defense was God. His hope was God. In God he placed his trust.

This is what youth is seeking today: something that gives meaning to life, something to trust, a confident relationship with a protector, hope for an otherwise dull life. Youth has to feel his way through a maze of problems; and in finding himself, he needs a trust that does not waver.

25 Let their dwelling place be desolate;
Let no one live in their tents.
26 For they persecute the *ones* You have struck,
And talk of the grief of those You have wounded.
27 Add iniquity to their iniquity,
And let them not come into Your righteousness.
28 Let them be blotted out of the book of the living,
And not be written with the righteous.

29 But I *am* poor and sorrowful;
Let Your salvation, O God, set me up on high.
30 I will praise the name of God with a song,
And will magnify Him with thanksgiving.
31 *This* also shall please the LORD better than an ox *or* bull,
Which has horns and hooves.
32 The humble shall see *this and* be glad;
And you who seek God, your hearts shall live.
33 For the LORD hears the poor,
And does not despise His prisoners.

34 Let heaven and earth praise Him,
The seas and everything that moves in them.
35 For God will save Zion
And build the cities of Judah,
That they may dwell there and possess it.
36 Also, the descendants of His servants shall inherit it,
And those who love His name shall dwell in it.

PSALM 70

Prayer for Relief from Adversaries

To the Chief Musician. *A Psalm* of David. To bring to remembrance.

M*ake haste,* O God, to deliver me!
Make haste to help me, O LORD!

2 Let them be ashamed and confounded
Who seek my life;
Let them be turned back[o] and confused
Who desire my hurt.
3 Let them be turned back because of their shame,
Who say, "Aha, aha!"

4 Let all those who seek You rejoice and be glad in You;
And let those who love Your salvation say continually,
"Let God be magnified!"

5 But I *am* poor and needy;
Make haste to me, O God!
You *are* my help and my deliverer;
O LORD, do not delay.

70:2 *o* Following Masoretic Text, Septuagint, Targum, and Vulgate; some Hebrew manuscripts and Syriac read *be appalled* (compare 40:15).

PSALM 71

God the Rock of Salvation

In You, O LORD, I put my trust;
Let me never be put to shame.
2 Deliver me in Your righteousness, and cause me to escape;
Incline Your ear to me, and save me.
3 Be my strong refuge,
To which I may resort continually;
You have given the commandment to save me,
For You *are* my rock and my fortress.

4 Deliver me, O my God, out of the hand of the wicked,
Out of the hand of the unrighteous and cruel man.
5 For You are my hope, O Lord GOD;
You are my trust from my youth.
6 By You I have been upheld from birth;
You are He who took me out of my mother's womb.
My praise *shall be* continually of You.

7 I have become as a wonder to many,
But You *are* my strong refuge.
8 Let my mouth be filled *with* Your praise
And with Your glory all the day.

9 Do not cast me off in the time of old age;
Do not forsake me when my strength fails.
10 For my enemies speak against me;
And those who lie in wait for my life take counsel together,
11 Saying, "God has forsaken him;
Pursue and take him, for *there is* none to deliver *him*."

12 O God, do not be far from me;
O my God, make haste to help me!
13 Let them be confounded *and* consumed
Who are adversaries of my life;
Let them be covered *with* reproach and dishonor
Who seek my hurt.

14 But I will hope continually,
And will praise You yet more and more.
15 My mouth shall tell of Your righteousness
And Your salvation all the day,
For I do not know *their* limits.
16 I will go in the strength of the Lord GOD;
I will make mention of Your righteousness, of Yours only.

17 O God, You have taught me from my youth;
And to this *day* I declare Your wondrous works.
18 Now also when *I am* old and grayheaded,
O God, do not forsake me,
Until I declare Your strength to *this* generation,
Your power to everyone *who* is to come.

19 Also Your righteousness, O God, *is* very high,

Youth is a time filled with potentials. Every hour of it trembles with destiny. It would be tragic to twist and warp a life so soon begun. For its formation it should be given to God, like clay is given to the potter, for His own shaping and molding. The Scriptures bear out this suggestion. . . .

Unless real quality is ingrained in youth's fiber, the years will expose them as ordinary stuff. Like cheap cloth assumes a different appearance when washed, they too will shrink and fade when later tested and run through the wringer.

(From *A Psalm In My Heart* by Leroy Brownlow)

APPLICATION Are you young and looking for something to believe in? Are you older and looking for God's hand anew? God answers both needs. Look to him and no further.

EXPLORATION Encouragement and Examples for Old and Young—Psalm 119:9; Proverbs 16:31; Ecclesiastes 11:9; 12:1; Isaiah 46:4; Lamentations 3:27; 1 Timothy 4:12; Titus 2:2-3.

LIFE LESSON

Psalm 72:1-20

SITUATION Solomon asked God to grant his son wisdom. In his prayer, he looked forward to the eternal, perfect reign of Christ.

OBSERVATION Solomon asked God for sound judgment and goodness. The kings of Israel were called to help the poor. Even Jesus, the King of kings, ministered to those bound by oppression and poverty.

INSPIRATION George is an evangelist in Malawi who uses an old badly battered wheelchair. Not long ago he wrote to ask me to send him my husband's used shirts—his were wearing out, and he wanted to dress his best as an ambassador for Christ.

George wheels himself from village to village over bumpy, rutted dirt roads that connect the small towns in Malawi. . . . Despite sore muscles and calluses on his hands, he keeps going. His deepest desire is to share Christ with others who are handicapped, to tell them that despite their poverty, God is in control for their good and His glory.

George is dirt poor. The people to whom he ministers are even more poor. But there is none so rich in faith as George.

Remember, Christ willed to be born poor, and he chose disciples who were living, for the most part, in poverty. Christ made Himself a servant of poor people. And he reminds us that whatever we do to help the least of the brethren—those most poor—we are personally ministering to Him.

(From *Diamonds in the Dust* by Joni Eareckson Tada)

APPLICATION Are you following the example of Jesus? Do you reach out to the poor? Find a way to help someone this week in a personal and material way. Take that person out for a meal. Anonymously provide a bag of groceries. Help that person work on his or her car. Watch for an opportunity.

EXPLORATION Helping the Poor—Proverbs 14:31; 19:17; Matthew 25:35-40; Luke 4:18; 1 John 3:17.

You who have done great things;
O God, who *is* like You?
20 *You,* who have shown me great and severe troubles,
Shall revive me again,
And bring me up again from the depths of the earth.
21 You shall increase my greatness,
And comfort me on every side.

22 Also with the lute I will praise You—
And Your faithfulness, O my God!
To You I will sing with the harp,
O Holy One of Israel.
23 My lips shall greatly rejoice when I sing to You,
And my soul, which You have redeemed.
24 My tongue also shall talk of Your righteousness all
the day long;
For they are confounded,
For they are brought to shame
Who seek my hurt.

PSALM 72

Glory and Universality of the Messiah's Reign

A Psalm of Solomon.

Give the king Your judgments, O God,
And Your righteousness to the king's Son.
2 He will judge Your people with righteousness,
And Your poor with justice.
3 The mountains will bring peace to the people,
And the little hills, by righteousness.
4 He will bring justice to the poor of the people;
He will save the children of the needy,
And will break in pieces the oppressor.

5 They shall fear You[p]
As long as the sun and moon endure,
Throughout all generations.
6 He shall come down like rain upon the grass before mowing,
Like showers *that* water the earth.
7 In His days the righteous shall flourish,
And abundance of peace,
Until the moon is no more.

8 He shall have dominion also from sea to sea,
And from the River to the ends of the earth.
9 Those who dwell in the wilderness will bow before Him,
And His enemies will lick the dust.
10 The kings of Tarshish and of the isles
Will bring presents;
The kings of Sheba and Seba
Will offer gifts.

72:5 *p* Following Masoretic Text and Targum; Septuagint and Vulgate read *They shall continue.*

11 Yes, all kings shall fall down before Him;
All nations shall serve Him.

12 For He will deliver the needy when he cries,
The poor also, and *him* who has no helper.
13 He will spare the poor and needy,
And will save the souls of the needy.
14 He will redeem their life from oppression and violence;
And precious shall be their blood in His sight.

15 And He shall live;
And the gold of Sheba will be given to Him;
Prayer also will be made for Him continually,
And daily He shall be praised.

16 There will be an abundance of grain in the earth,
On the top of the mountains;
Its fruit shall wave like Lebanon;
And *those* of the city shall flourish like grass of the earth.

17 His name shall endure forever;
His name shall continue as long as the sun.
And *men* shall be blessed in Him;
All nations shall call Him blessed.

18 Blessed *be* the LORD God, the God of Israel,
Who only does wondrous things!
19 And blessed *be* His glorious name forever!
And let the whole earth be filled *with* His glory.
Amen and Amen.

20 The prayers of David the son of Jesse are ended.

Book Three: Psalms 73—89

PSALM 73

The Tragedy of the Wicked, and the Blessedness of Trust in God

A Psalm of Asaph.

Truly God *is* good to Israel,
To such as are pure in heart.
2 But as for me, my feet had almost stumbled;
My steps had nearly slipped.
3 For I *was* envious of the boastful,
When I saw the prosperity of the wicked.

4 For *there are* no pangs in their death,
But their strength *is* firm.
5 They *are* not in trouble *as other* men,
Nor are they plagued like *other* men.
6 Therefore pride serves as their necklace;
Violence covers them *like* a garment.
7 Their eyes bulge[q] with abundance;

LIFE LESSON
Psalm 73:1-28

SITUATION Asaph, a choir director, questioned God's wisdom. Asaph saw the wicked prospering and the righteous suffering.

OBSERVATION Looking at circumstances from God's perspective shows that the eternal rewards of the righteous far outweigh the temporary prosperity of the wicked.

INSPIRATION The story is told of two prisoners in one small cell with no light except what came through a tiny window three feet above eye level. Both prisoners spent a great deal of time looking at that window. One of them saw the bars—obvious, ugly, metallic reminders of reality. From day to day he grew increasingly discouraged, bitter, angry, and hopeless. By contrast, the other prisoner looked through the window to the stars beyond. Hope welled up in that prisoner as he began to think of starting a new life in freedom.

The prisoners were looking at the same window, but one saw bars while the other saw stars. And the difference in their vision made a huge difference in their lives.

. . . Vision, like courage and discipline, is a character trait that can be stimulated and developed in anyone who is willing to understand what it really is and then to work hard at making it part of everyday life. Everyone can choose to look at bars or stars. In fact, everyone makes that choice several times every day.

(From *Who You Are When No One Is Looking* by Bill Hybels)

APPLICATION When you look at your life, which do you see: trouble or opportunity? Develop an eye to see God's blessing even in your darkest hour.

EXPLORATION Vision—2 Kings 6:8-17. Wisdom—Ecclesiastes 8:17; Isaiah 55:6-9. Values—Philippians 3:8. Guidance—Psalm 48:14. Perseverance—Hebrews 10:19-25.

73:7 q Targum reads *face bulges;* Septuagint, Syriac, and Vulgate read *iniquity bulges.*

LIFE LESSON

Psalm 74:1-23

SITUATION Asaph was tired of being stepped on. He felt rejected, defeated, and forgotten. He prayed that God would restore Israel and grant revenge.

OBSERVATION We want revenge. But only God can bring about justice.

INSPIRATION Bernhard Goetz was an American fantasy come true. He did what every citizen wants to do. He fought back. He "kicked the bully in the shins." He "punched the villain in the nose." He "clobbered evil over the head." This unassuming hero embodied a nationwide, even world-wide anger: a passion for revenge.

The outpouring of support gives clear evidence. People are mad. People are angry. There is a pent-up, boiling rage that causes us to toast a man who fearlessly says, "I ain't taking it no more!" and then comes out with a hot pistol in each hand. . . .

Anger. It's a peculiar yet predictable emotion. It begins as a drop of water. An irritant. A frustration. Nothing big, just an aggravation. Someone gets your parking place. Someone pulls in front of you on the freeway. A waitress is slow and you are in a hurry. The toast burns. Drops of water. Drip. Drip. Drip. Drip.

Yet, get enough of these seemingly innocent drops of anger and before long you've got a bucket full of rage. . . .

Reality makes us ask the questions: What good was done? Is that really the way to reduce the crime rate? . . . No. Anger doesn't do that. Anger only feeds a primitive lust for revenge that feeds our anger. . . .

Yet, what do we do? . . . Jesus speaks about the mob that killed. "Father forgive them, for they do not know what they are doing."

Have you ever wondered how Jesus kept from retaliating? . . . Here's the answer. It's the second part of the statement, "for they do not know what they are doing. . . ." It's as if Jesus considered this bloodthirsty, death-hungry crowd not as murderers, but as victims. It's . . . as [if they were] "sheep without a shepherd."

They have more than heart could wish.
8 They scoff and speak wickedly *concerning* oppression;
They speak loftily.
9 They set their mouth against the heavens,
And their tongue walks through the earth.

10 Therefore his people return here,
And waters of a full *cup* are drained by them.
11 And they say, "How does God know?
And is there knowledge in the Most High?"
12 Behold, these *are* the ungodly,
Who are always at ease;
They increase *in* riches.
13 Surely I have cleansed my heart *in* vain,
And washed my hands in innocence.
14 For all day long I have been plagued,
And chastened every morning.

15 If I had said, "I will speak thus,"
Behold, I would have been untrue to the generation
of Your children.
16 When I thought *how* to understand this,
It *was* too painful for me—
17 Until I went into the sanctuary of God;
Then I understood their end.

18 Surely You set them in slippery places;
You cast them down to destruction.
19 Oh, how they are *brought* to desolation, as in a moment!
They are utterly consumed with terrors.
20 As a dream when *one* awakes,
So, Lord, when You awake,
You shall despise their image.

21 Thus my heart was grieved,
And I was vexed in my mind.
22 I *was* so foolish and ignorant;
I was *like* a beast before You.
23 Nevertheless I *am* continually with You;
You hold *me* by my right hand.
24 You will guide me with Your counsel,
And afterward receive me *to* glory.

25 Whom have I in heaven *but You?*
And *there is* none upon earth *that* I desire besides You.
26 My flesh and my heart fail;
But God *is* the strength of my heart and my portion forever.

27 For indeed, those who are far from You shall perish;
You have destroyed all those who desert You for harlotry.
28 But *it is* good for me to draw near to God;
I have put my trust in the Lord GOD,
That I may declare all Your works.

PSALM 74

A Plea for Relief from Oppressors

A Contemplation[r] of Asaph.

O God, why have You cast *us* off forever?
Why does Your anger smoke against the sheep of Your pasture?
2 Remember Your congregation, *which* You have purchased of old,
The tribe of Your inheritance, *which* You have redeemed—
This Mount Zion where You have dwelt.
3 Lift up Your feet to the perpetual desolations.
The enemy has damaged everything in the sanctuary.
4 Your enemies roar in the midst of Your meeting place;
They set up their banners *for* signs.
5 They seem like men who lift up
Axes among the thick trees.
6 And now they break down its carved work, all at once,
With axes and hammers.
7 They have set fire to Your sanctuary;
They have defiled the dwelling place of Your name to the ground.
8 They said in their hearts,
"Let us destroy them altogether."
They have burned up all the meeting places of God in the land.

9 We do not see our signs;
There is no longer any prophet;
Nor *is there* any among us who knows how long.
10 O God, how long will the adversary reproach?
Will the enemy blaspheme Your name forever?
11 Why do You withdraw Your hand, even Your right hand?
Take it out of Your bosom and destroy *them.*
12 For God *is* my King from of old,
Working salvation in the midst of the earth.
13 You divided the sea by Your strength;
You broke the heads of the sea serpents in the waters.
14 You broke the heads of Leviathan in pieces,
And gave him *as* food to the people inhabiting the wilderness.
15 You broke open the fountain and the flood;
You dried up mighty rivers.
16 The day *is* Yours, the night also *is* Yours;
You have prepared the light and the sun.
17 You have set all the borders of the earth;
You have made summer and winter.

18 Remember this, *that* the enemy has reproached, O LORD,
And *that* a foolish people has blasphemed Your name.
19 Oh, do not deliver the life of Your turtledove to the wild beast!
Do not forget the life of Your poor forever.
20 Have respect to the covenant;
For the dark places of the earth are full of the haunts of cruelty.
21 Oh, do not let the oppressed return ashamed!
Let the poor and needy praise Your name.

74:title [r] Hebrew *Maschil*

"They don't know what they are doing."

And when you think about it, they didn't . . .

And for the most part, neither do we. We are still, as much as we hate to admit it, shepherdless sheep. All we know is that we were born out of one eternity and are frighteningly close to another. . . .

My point is this: Uncontrolled anger won't better our world, but sympathetic understanding will. Once we see the world and ourselves for what we are, we can help. Once we understand ourselves, we begin to operate not from a posture of anger but one of compassion and concern. We look at the world not with bitter frowns but with extended hands. We realize that the lights are out and a lot of people are stumbling in the darkness. So we light the candles. . . .

Instead of fighting back we help out. We go to the ghettos. We teach in the schools. We build hospitals and help orphans . . . we put away our guns.

"They do not know what they are doing."

There is something about understanding the world that makes us want to save it, even to die for it. Anger? Anger never did anyone any good. Understanding? Well, the results are not as quick as the vigilante's bullet, but they are certainly much more constructive.

(From *No Wonder They Call Him the Savior* by Max Lucado)

APPLICATION As you watch the news, what makes you angry? What makes you want to get revenge? Next time you are tempted to seek revenge, stop. See aggressors as people who need God. Pray that God will meet that need.

EXPLORATION Revenge is God's—Dueteronomy 32:43; Psalm 58:10; 94:1; Nahum 1:2.

LIFE LESSON

Psalms 75:1–76:12

SITUATION Asaph grew in confidence that God would bring the wicked to judgment. God would not let anyone deserving judgment slip free unnoticed.

OBSERVATION God's holiness contrasts with our sinfulness. Without mercy from God, we all would be judged.

INSPIRATION According to legend, the first American Indian to see the Grand Canyon tied himself to a tree in terror. According to Scripture, any man privileged to peek at God has felt the same.

Sheer terror. Remember the words of Isaiah after his vision of God? "Oh, no! I will be destroyed. I am not pure, and I live among people who are not pure, but I have seen the King, the Lord All-Powerful" (Isa. 6:5).

Upon seeing God, Isaiah was terrified. Why such fear? Why did he tremble so? Because he was wax before the sun. A candle in a hurricane. A minnow at Niagara. God's glory was too great. His purity too sterling. His power too mighty.

(From *When God Whispers Your Name* by Max Lucado)

APPLICATION God is much more than a cosmic buddy. Be careful not to think too little of God. When you pray, approach him with a respectful, humble attitude.

EXPLORATION Cup of God's Judgment—Isaiah 51:17; Jeremiah 25:15; 49:12; Habakkuk 2:16; Revelation 14:10; 16:19; 18:6.

22 Arise, O God, plead Your own cause;
Remember how the foolish man reproaches You daily.
23 Do not forget the voice of Your enemies;
The tumult of those who rise up against You increases continually.

PSALM 75

Thanksgiving for God's Righteous Judgment

To the Chief Musician. Set to "Do Not Destroy."[s] A Psalm of Asaph. A Song.

We give thanks to You, O God, we give thanks!
For Your wondrous works declare *that* Your name is near.

2 "When I choose the proper time,
I will judge uprightly.
3 The earth and all its inhabitants are dissolved;
I set up its pillars firmly. Selah

4 "I said to the boastful, 'Do not deal boastfully,'
And to the wicked, 'Do not lift up the horn.
5 Do not lift up your horn on high;
Do *not* speak with a stiff neck.' "

6 For exaltation *comes* neither from the east
Nor from the west nor from the south.
7 But God *is* the Judge:
He puts down one,
And exalts another.
8 For in the hand of the LORD *there is* a cup,
And the wine is red;
It is fully mixed, and He pours it out;
Surely its dregs shall all the wicked of the earth
Drain *and* drink down.

9 But I will declare forever,
I will sing praises to the God of Jacob.

10 "All the horns of the wicked I will also cut off,
But the horns of the righteous shall be exalted."

PSALM 76

The Majesty of God in Judgment

To the Chief Musician. On stringed instruments.[t] A Psalm of Asaph. A Song.

In Judah God *is* known;
His name *is* great in Israel.
2 In Salem[u] also is His tabernacle,
And His dwelling place in Zion.
3 There He broke the arrows of the bow,
The shield and sword of battle. Selah

4 You *are* more glorious and excellent

75:title [s] Hebrew *Al Tashcheth*
76:title [t] Hebrew *neginoth*
76:2 [u] That is, Jerusalem

Than the mountains of prey.
5 The stouthearted were plundered;
They have sunk into their sleep;
And none of the mighty men have found the use of their hands.
6 At Your rebuke, O God of Jacob,
Both the chariot and horse were cast into a dead sleep.

7 You, Yourself, *are* to be feared;
And who may stand in Your presence
When once You are angry?
8 You caused judgment to be heard from heaven;
The earth feared and was still,
9 When God arose to judgment,
To deliver all the oppressed of the earth. Selah

10 Surely the wrath of man shall praise You;
With the remainder of wrath You shall gird Yourself.

11 Make vows to the LORD your God, and pay *them;*
Let all who are around Him bring presents to Him who
ought to be feared.
12 He shall cut off the spirit of princes;
He is awesome to the kings of the earth.

PSALM 77

The Consoling Memory of God's Redemptive Works

To the Chief Musician. To Jeduthun. A Psalm of Asaph.

I cried out to God with my voice—
To God with my voice;
And He gave ear to me.
2 In the day of my trouble I sought the Lord;
My hand was stretched out in the night without ceasing;
My soul refused to be comforted.
3 I remembered God, and was troubled;
I complained, and my spirit was overwhelmed. Selah

4 You hold my eyelids *open;*
I am so troubled that I cannot speak.
5 I have considered the days of old,
The years of ancient times.
6 I call to remembrance my song in the night;
I meditate within my heart,
And my spirit makes diligent search.

7 Will the Lord cast off forever?
And will He be favorable no more?
8 Has His mercy ceased forever?
Has *His* promise failed forevermore?
9 Has God forgotten to be gracious?
Has He in anger shut up His tender mercies? Selah

10 And I said, "This *is* my anguish;
But I will remember the years of the right hand of the Most High."

LIFE LESSON

Psalm 77:1-20

SITUATION Asaph reviewed God's past miracles and mighty works on behalf of the Israelites when they went to the Promised Land. Asaph needed courage during a time of personal distress.

OBSERVATION Remembering and meditating upon God's previous works can provide believers with courage during difficult times of struggle and trial.

INSPIRATION What are we to do when even our trust in God seems shaky? When answers are not immediate and God seems far away? When we do not know how to tap His help and are left to wait passively for Him to answer, wishing for some spectacular flurry of divine activity to deliver us? What are we to do when that rescue doesn't come, and unfulfilled expectations for help from Him turn our hearts toward doubt? When we begin to slip back to the "Whys?"—"Why me? Why not them? Why now?"—and tend to doubt His goodness and may even then doubt that He actually does love and care for us. . . .

Before that happens, we must turn to the entity over which we exercise exclusive control, our wills, to the choices we have to think correctly and respond constructively. . . . If we choose not to cultivate our hope in Him, where will we place our hope? Is there anything greater, more just, more equitable, more powerful, more reliable, more true than God?

(From *The Upside of Down* by Joseph Stowell)

APPLICATION Does stress keep you from sleeping? Next time, when you are awake and miserable, do what Asaph did. Remember God's faithfulness to you and to others. Praise him for what he has done.

EXPLORATION Miracles—Deuteronomy 34:10-12; 1 Kings 18:36-39; Psalm 105:4-5; John 10:37-38; 14:11; Hebrews 2:2-4.

LIFE LESSON

Psalm 78:1-72

SITUATION Asaph recounted Israel's history from slavery in Egypt until the reign of King David. He retold the story in order that the Jewish people would remember their past and be reminded of the mercy that God had shown them.

OBSERVATION While the Israelites continually complained and were unfaithful, God faithfully blessed them. God cared for his people even as they dishonored him.

INSPIRATION We should banish from our minds forever the common but erroneous notion that justice and judgment characterize the God of Israel, while mercy and grace belong to the Lord of the Church. Actually there is in principle no difference between the Old Testament and the New. In the New Testament Scriptures there is a fuller development of redemptive truth, but one God speaks in both dispensations, and what He speaks agrees with what He is. Wherever and whenever God appears to men, He acts like Himself. Whether in the Garden of Eden or the Garden of Gethsemane, God is merciful as well as just. He has always dealt in mercy with mankind and will always deal in justice when His mercy is despised. Thus He did in antediluvian times; thus when Christ walked among men; thus He is doing today and will continue always to do for no other reason than that He is God. . . .

11 I will remember the works of the LORD;
Surely I will remember Your wonders of old.
12 I will also meditate on all Your work,
And talk of Your deeds.
13 Your way, O God, *is* in the sanctuary;
Who *is* so great a God as *our* God?
14 You *are* the God who does wonders;
You have declared Your strength among the peoples.
15 You have with *Your* arm redeemed Your people,
The sons of Jacob and Joseph. Selah

16 The waters saw You, O God;
The waters saw You, they were afraid;
The depths also trembled.
17 The clouds poured out water;
The skies sent out a sound;
Your arrows also flashed about.
18 The voice of Your thunder *was* in the whirlwind;
The lightnings lit up the world;
The earth trembled and shook.
19 Your way *was* in the sea,
Your path in the great waters,
And Your footsteps were not known.
20 You led Your people like a flock
By the hand of Moses and Aaron.

PSALM 78

God's Kindness to Rebellious Israel

A Contemplation[v] of Asaph.

Give ear, O my people, *to* my law;
Incline your ears to the words of my mouth.
2 I will open my mouth in a parable;
I will utter dark sayings of old,
3 Which we have heard and known,
And our fathers have told us.
4 We will not hide *them* from their children,
Telling to the generation to come the praises of the LORD,
And His strength and His wonderful works that He has done.

5 For He established a testimony in Jacob,
And appointed a law in Israel,
Which He commanded our fathers,
That they should make them known to their children;
6 That the generation to come might know *them,*
The children *who* would be born,
That they may arise and declare *them* to their children,
7 That they may set their hope in God,
And not forget the works of God,
But keep His commandments;
8 And may not be like their fathers,

78:title [v] Hebrew *Maschil*

A stubborn and rebellious generation,
A generation *that* did not set its heart aright,
And whose spirit was not faithful to God.

9 The children of Ephraim, *being* armed *and* carrying bows,
Turned back in the day of battle.
10 They did not keep the covenant of God;
They refused to walk in His law,
11 And forgot His works
And His wonders that He had shown them.

12 Marvelous things He did in the sight of their fathers,
In the land of Egypt, *in* the field of Zoan.
13 He divided the sea and caused them to pass through;
And He made the waters stand up like a heap.
14 In the daytime also He led them with the cloud,
And all the night with a light of fire.
15 He split the rocks in the wilderness,
And gave *them* drink in abundance like the depths.
16 He also brought streams out of the rock,
And caused waters to run down like rivers.

17 But they sinned even more against Him
By rebelling against the Most High in the wilderness.
18 And they tested God in their heart
By asking for the food of their fancy.
19 Yes, they spoke against God:
They said, "Can God prepare a table in the wilderness?
20 Behold, He struck the rock,
So that the waters gushed out,
And the streams overflowed.
Can He give bread also?
Can He provide meat for His people? "

21 Therefore the LORD heard *this* and was furious;
So a fire was kindled against Jacob,
And anger also came up against Israel,
22 Because they did not believe in God,
And did not trust in His salvation.
23 Yet He had commanded the clouds above,
And opened the doors of heaven,
24 Had rained down manna on them to eat,
And given them of the bread of heaven.
25 Men ate angels' food;
He sent them food to the full.

26 He caused an east wind to blow in the heavens;
And by His power He brought in the south wind.
27 He also rained meat on them like the dust,
Feathered fowl like the sand of the seas;
28 And He let *them* fall in the midst of their camp,
All around their dwellings.
29 So they ate and were well filled,

As judgment is God's justice confronting moral inequity, so mercy is the goodness of God confronting human suffering and guilt. Were there no guilt in the world, no pain and no tears, God would yet be infinitely merciful; but His mercy might well remain hidden in His heart, unknown to the created universe. No voice would be raised to celebrate the mercy of which none felt the need. It is human misery and sin that call forth the divine mercy.

(From *The Knowledge of the Holy* by A. W. Tozer)

APPLICATION Don't forget to praise God and thank him for what he has done. Prayerfully remember the stepping stones in your life. Thank God for molding you as he has seen fit throughout the years.

EXPLORATION God's Unfailing Mercy—2 Samuel 24:14; Nehemiah 9:31; Psalm 25:6; 57:1; Isaiah 63:9; Ephesians 2:4-7; Hebrews 4:16; 1 Peter 1:3.

For He gave them their own desire.
30 They were not deprived of their craving;
But while their food *was* still in their mouths,
31 The wrath of God came against them,
And slew the stoutest of them,
And struck down the choice *men* of Israel.

32 In spite of this they still sinned,
And did not believe in His wondrous works.
33 Therefore their days He consumed in futility,
And their years in fear.

34 When He slew them, then they sought Him;
And they returned and sought earnestly
for God.
35 Then they remembered that God *was*
their rock,
And the Most High God their Redeemer.
36 Nevertheless they flattered Him with
their mouth,
And they lied to Him with their tongue;
37 For their heart was not steadfast with Him,
Nor were they faithful in His covenant.
38 But He, *being* full of compassion, forgave
their iniquity,
And did not destroy *them.*
Yes, many a time He turned His anger away,
And did not stir up all His wrath;
39 For He remembered that they *were but* flesh,
A breath that passes away and does not
come again.

40 How often they provoked Him in
the wilderness,
And grieved Him in the desert!
41 Yes, again and again they tempted God,
And limited the Holy One of Israel.
42 They did not remember His power:
The day when He redeemed them from
the enemy,
43 When He worked His signs in Egypt,
And His wonders in the field of Zoan;
44 Turned their rivers into blood,
And their streams, that they could not drink.
45 He sent swarms of flies among them, which
devoured them,
And frogs, which destroyed them.
46 He also gave their crops to the caterpillar,
And their labor to the locust.
47 He destroyed their vines with hail,
And their sycamore trees with frost.
48 He also gave up their cattle to the hail,
And their flocks to fiery lightning.
49 He cast on them the fierceness of His anger,
Wrath, indignation, and trouble,
By sending angels of destruction
among them.
50 He made a path for His anger;
He did not spare their soul from death,
But gave their life over to the plague,
51 And destroyed all the firstborn in Egypt,
The first of *their* strength in the tents of Ham.
52 But He made His own people go forth
like sheep,
And guided them in the wilderness
like a flock;
53 And He led them on safely, so that they
did not fear;
But the sea overwhelmed their enemies.
54 And He brought them to His holy border,
This mountain *which* His right hand
had acquired.
55 He also drove out the nations before them,
Allotted them an inheritance by survey,
And made the tribes of Israel dwell in
their tents.

56 Yet they tested and provoked the Most
High God,
And did not keep His testimonies,
57 But turned back and acted unfaithfully like
their fathers;
They were turned aside like a deceitful bow.
58 For they provoked Him to anger with their
high places,
And moved Him to jealousy with their
carved images.
59 When God heard *this,* He was furious,
And greatly abhorred Israel,
60 So that He forsook the tabernacle of Shiloh,
The tent He had placed among men,
61 And delivered His strength into captivity,
And His glory into the enemy's hand.
62 He also gave His people over to the sword,
And was furious with His inheritance.
63 The fire consumed their young men,
And their maidens were not given
in marriage.
64 Their priests fell by the sword,
And their widows made no lamentation.

65 Then the Lord awoke as *from* sleep,
Like a mighty man who shouts because
of wine.

66 And He beat back His enemies;
He put them to a perpetual reproach.
67 Moreover He rejected the tent of Joseph,
And did not choose the tribe of Ephraim,
68 But chose the tribe of Judah,
Mount Zion which He loved.
69 And He built His sanctuary like the heights,
Like the earth which He has established forever.
70 He also chose David His servant,
And took him from the sheepfolds;
71 From following the ewes that had young He brought him,
To shepherd Jacob His people,
And Israel His inheritance.
72 So he shepherded them according to the integrity of his heart,
And guided them by the skillfulness of his hands.

PSALM 79

A Dirge and a Prayer for Israel, Destroyed by Enemies

A Psalm of Asaph.

O God, the nations have come into Your inheritance;
Your holy temple they have defiled;
They have laid Jerusalem in heaps.
2 The dead bodies of Your servants
They have given *as* food for the birds of the heavens,
The flesh of Your saints to the beasts of the earth.
3 Their blood they have shed like water all around Jerusalem,
And *there was* no one to bury *them.*
4 We have become a reproach to our neighbors,
A scorn and derision to those who are around us.

5 How long, LORD?
Will You be angry forever?
Will Your jealousy burn like fire?
6 Pour out Your wrath on the nations that do not know You,
And on the kingdoms that do not call on Your name.
7 For they have devoured Jacob,
And laid waste his dwelling place.

8 Oh, do not remember former iniquities against us!
Let Your tender mercies come speedily to meet us,
For we have been brought very low.
9 Help us, O God of our salvation,
For the glory of Your name;
And deliver us, and provide atonement for our sins,
For Your name's sake!
10 Why should the nations say,
"Where *is* their God?"
Let there be known among the nations in our sight
The avenging of the blood of Your servants *which has been* shed.

11 Let the groaning of the prisoner come before You;

LIFE LESSON

Psalms 79:1–80:19

SITUATION Israel was attacked by a heathen nation. God's people cried out for divine intervention and judgment upon their persecutors.

OBSERVATION Stress helps us realize how much we need God to steady our lives.

INSPIRATION When you recognize God as Creator, you will admire him. When you recognize his wisdom, you will learn from him. When you discover his strength, you will rely on him. But only when he saves you will you worship him.

It's a "before and after" scenario. Before your rescue, you could easily keep God at a distance. Comfortably dismissed. Neatly shelved. Sure he was important, but so was your career. Your status. Your salary. He was high on your priority list, but he shared the spot with others.

Then came the storm . . . the rage . . . the fight . . . the ripped moorings . . . the starless night. Despair fell like a fog; your bearings were gone. In your heart, you knew there was no exit.

Turn to your career for help? Only if you want to hide from the storm . . . not escape it. Lean on your status for strength? A storm isn't impressed with your title. Rely on your salary for rescue? Many try . . . genuinely ask . . . he will come.

And from that moment on, he is not just a deity to admire, a teacher to observe, or a master to obey. He is the Savior. The Savior to be worshiped. . . .

(From *In the Eye of the Storm* by Max Lucado)

APPLICATION Name your current hardships and trials. What lessons could you learn from them? How could God use these circumstances to draw you closer to him? Make the most of your trials. Let them be opportunities for increased spiritual growth and faith.

EXPLORATION God is Our Strength and Salvation—Psalm 106:8; 121:1-2; Jeremiah 3:23; Malachi 4:2.

According to the greatness of Your power
Preserve those who are appointed to die;
12 And return to our neighbors sevenfold into their bosom
Their reproach with which they have reproached You, O Lord.

13 So we, Your people and sheep of Your pasture,
Will give You thanks forever;
We will show forth Your praise to all generations.

PSALM 80

Prayer for Israel's Restoration

To the Chief Musician. Set to "The Lilies."[w] A Testimony[x] of Asaph. A Psalm.

Give ear, O Shepherd of Israel,
You who lead Joseph like a flock;
You who dwell *between* the cherubim, shine forth!
2 Before Ephraim, Benjamin, and Manasseh,
Stir up Your strength,
And come *and* save us!

3 Restore us, O God;
Cause Your face to shine,
And we shall be saved!

4 O LORD God of hosts,
How long will You be angry
Against the prayer of Your people?
5 You have fed them with the bread of tears,
And given them tears to drink in great measure.
6 You have made us a strife to our neighbors,
And our enemies laugh among themselves.

7 Restore us, O God of hosts;
Cause Your face to shine,
And we shall be saved!

8 You have brought a vine out of Egypt;
You have cast out the nations, and planted it.
9 You prepared *room* for it,
And caused it to take deep root,
And it filled the land.
10 The hills were covered with its shadow,
And the mighty cedars with its boughs.
11 She sent out her boughs to the Sea,[y]
And her branches to the River.[z]
12 Why have You broken down her hedges,
So that all who pass by the way pluck her *fruit?*
13 The boar out of the woods uproots it,
And the wild beast of the field devours it.

14 Return, we beseech You, O God of hosts;
Look down from heaven and see,
And visit this vine
15 And the vineyard which Your right hand has planted,
And the branch *that* You made strong for Yourself.
16 *It is* burned with fire, *it is* cut down;
They perish at the rebuke of Your countenance.
17 Let Your hand be upon the man of Your right hand,
Upon the son of man *whom* You made strong for Yourself.
18 Then we will not turn back from You;
Revive us, and we will call upon Your name.

19 Restore us, O LORD God of hosts;
Cause Your face to shine,
And we shall be saved!

PSALM 81

An Appeal for Israel's Repentance

To the Chief Musician. On an instrument of Gath.[a] A Psalm of Asaph.

Sing aloud to God our strength;
Make a joyful shout to the God of Jacob.
2 Raise a song and strike the timbrel,
The pleasant harp with the lute.

3 Blow the trumpet at the time of the New Moon,
At the full moon, on our solemn feast day.
4 For this *is* a statute for Israel,
A law of the God of Jacob.
5 This He established in Joseph *as* a testimony,
When He went throughout the land of Egypt,
Where I heard a language I did not understand.

6 "I removed his shoulder from the burden;
His hands were freed from the baskets.

80:title [w] Hebrew *Shoshannim* [x] Hebrew *Eduth*
80:11 [y] That is, the Mediterranean [z] That is, the Euphrates
81:title [a] Hebrew *Al Gittith*

7 You called in trouble, and I delivered you;
I answered you in the secret place of thunder;
I tested you at the waters of Meribah. Selah

8 "Hear, O My people, and I will admonish you!
O Israel, if you will listen to Me!
9 There shall be no foreign god among you;
Nor shall you worship any foreign god.
10 I *am* the LORD your God,
Who brought you out of the land of Egypt;
Open your mouth wide, and I will fill it.

11 "But My people would not heed My voice,
And Israel would *have* none of Me.
12 So I gave them over to their own stubborn heart,
To walk in their own counsels.

13 "Oh, that My people would listen to Me,
That Israel would walk in My ways!
14 I would soon subdue their enemies,
And turn My hand against their adversaries.
15 The haters of the LORD would pretend submission to Him,
But their fate would endure forever.
16 He would have fed them also with the finest of wheat;
And with honey from the rock I would have satisfied you."

PSALM 82

A Plea for Justice

A Psalm of Asaph.

God stands in the congregation of the mighty;
He judges among the gods.[b]
2 How long will you judge unjustly,
And show partiality to the wicked? Selah
3 Defend the poor and fatherless;
Do justice to the afflicted and needy.
4 Deliver the poor and needy;
Free *them* from the hand of the wicked.

5 They do not know, nor do they understand;
They walk about in darkness;
All the foundations of the earth are unstable.
6 I said, "You *are* gods,[c]
And all of you *are* children of the Most High.
7 But you shall die like men,
And fall like one of the princes."

8 Arise, O God, judge the earth;
For You shall inherit all nations.

82:1 [b] Hebrew *elohim, mighty ones;* that is, the judges
82:6 [c] Hebrew *elohim, mighty ones;* that is, the judges

LIFE LESSON

Psalms 81:1–82:8

SITUATION Asaph called Israel to sing praises to God and to obey God. The song was probably used as a hymn in the temple.

OBSERVATION "Please listen to me!" God pleaded with Israel to listen, but Israel ignored him.

INSPIRATION Just because I have listened carefully and intently to one thing from God does not mean that I will listen to everything He says. I show God my lack of love and respect of Him by the insensitivity of my heart and mind toward what He says. If I love my friend, I will instinctively understand what he wants. And Jesus said, "You are My friends. . . ." (John 15:14). . . . But most of us show incredible disrespect to God because we don't even hear Him. He might as well never have spoken to us.

The goal of my spiritual life is such close identification with Jesus Christ that I will always hear God and know that God always hears me (see John 11:41). If I am united with Jesus Christ, I hear God all the time through the devotion of hearing. A flower, a tree or a servant of God may convey God's message to me. What hinders me from hearing is my attention to other things. It is not that I don't want to hear God, but I am not devoted in the right areas of my life. . . . God may say whatever He wants, but I just don't hear Him. The attitude of a child of God should always be "Speak, for Your servant hears." If I have not developed and nurtured this devotion of hearing, I can only hear God's voice at certain times. . . . This is not living the life of a child of God. Have you heard God's voice today?

(From *My Utmost for His Highest* by Oswald Chambers)

APPLICATION Do you take time to listen to God? What is God telling you to do? What is God asking you to change? The Israelites missed God's best for them when they failed to listen. Take time out each day to read and think about God's Word.

EXPLORATION Listen and Obey—Exodus 15:26; Isaiah 65:12; Hosea 9:17; John 14:21-23.

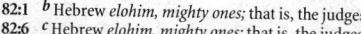

LIFE LESSON

Psalms 83:1–84:12

SITUATION These songs celebrated God's strength, grace, and glory.

OBSERVATION The blessings of God surely come to those who serve and trust in him.

INSPIRATION Celebration praises God for His power and works, and it reinforces our confidence in Him to intervene in our lives.

With tears of joy, my friend Lori related, "I recently bought a house and last night three friends gave me a housewarming party to celebrate my new home. Looking around the room at the people who had gathered, I was in awe. God has been so good to me! I have a beautiful home and friends who really care about me. How much He has done for me! He has intervened in my life, time and time again, and has brought these people into my life. I am overwhelmed with love and gratitude for His kindness and for these friends!"

Celebrations not only praise God, but also they honor your friend for her desire to follow Jesus and her ability to make decisions or take steps that have brought positive changes in her life by His power.

Lori continued, "As I opened the housewarming gifts, I realized that the evening would never have occurred if I had not allowed Jesus to work in my life. Most of the people gathered were friends I had made because of my decision to follow Jesus. The party was not just a celebration of a new home, but for me, it was a celebration of a new way of life!"

(From *The Counsel of a Friend* by Lynda D. Elliott)

APPLICATION Praise God for the friends he has brought you. Be a friend that someone would praise God for. If you do not have a friend, ask God to give you one.

EXPLORATION Joy in God Our Strength—Exodus 15:2; 2 Samuel 22:33; Psalm 28:8; 46:1; 73:26; 81:1; 89:21.

PSALM 83

Prayer to Frustrate Conspiracy Against Israel

A Song. A Psalm of Asaph.

Do not keep silent, O God!
Do not hold Your peace,
And do not be still, O God!
2 For behold, Your enemies make a tumult;
And those who hate You have lifted up their head.
3 They have taken crafty counsel against Your people,
And consulted together against Your sheltered ones.
4 They have said, "Come, and let us cut them off from *being* a nation,
That the name of Israel may be remembered no more."

5 For they have consulted together with one consent;
They form a confederacy against You:
6 The tents of Edom and the Ishmaelites;
Moab and the Hagrites;
7 Gebal, Ammon, and Amalek;
Philistia with the inhabitants of Tyre;
8 Assyria also has joined with them;
They have helped the children of Lot. Selah

9 Deal with them as *with* Midian,
As *with* Sisera,
As *with* Jabin at the Brook Kishon,
10 Who perished at En Dor,
Who became *as* refuse on the earth.
11 Make their nobles like Oreb and like Zeeb,
Yes, all their princes like Zebah and Zalmunna,
12 Who said, "Let us take for ourselves
The pastures of God for a possession."

13 O my God, make them like the whirling dust,
Like the chaff before the wind!
14 As the fire burns the woods,
And as the flame sets the mountains on fire,
15 So pursue them with Your tempest,
And frighten them with Your storm.
16 Fill their faces with shame,
That they may seek Your name, O LORD.
17 Let them be confounded and dismayed forever;
Yes, let them be put to shame and perish,
18 That they may know that You, whose name alone *is* the LORD,
Are the Most High over all the earth.

PSALM 84

The Blessedness of Dwelling in the House of God

To the Chief Musician. On an instrument of Gath.[d] A Psalm of the sons of Korah.

How lovely *is* Your tabernacle,
O LORD of hosts!

84:title [d] Hebrew *Al Gittith*

2 My soul longs, yes, even faints
For the courts of the LORD;
My heart and my flesh cry out for the living God.
3 Even the sparrow has found a home,
And the swallow a nest for herself,
Where she may lay her young—
Even Your altars, O LORD of hosts,
My King and my God.
4 Blessed *are* those who dwell in Your house;
They will still be praising You. Selah

5 Blessed *is* the man whose strength *is* in You,
Whose heart *is* set on pilgrimage.
6 *As they* pass through the Valley of Baca,
They make it a spring;
The rain also covers it with pools.
7 They go from strength to strength;
Each one appears before God in Zion.[e]

8 O LORD God of hosts, hear my prayer;
Give ear, O God of Jacob! Selah
9 O God, behold our shield,
And look upon the face of Your anointed.

10 For a day in Your courts *is* better than a thousand.
I would rather be a doorkeeper in the house of my God
Than dwell in the tents of wickedness.
11 For the LORD God *is* a sun and shield;
The LORD will give grace and glory;
No good *thing* will He withhold
From those who walk uprightly.

12 O LORD of hosts,
Blessed *is* the man who trusts in You!

PSALM 85

Prayer that the LORD Will Restore Favor to the Land

To the Chief Musician. A Psalm of the sons of Korah.

LORD, You have been favorable to Your land;
You have brought back the captivity of Jacob.
2 You have forgiven the iniquity of Your people;
You have covered all their sin. Selah
3 You have taken away all Your wrath;
You have turned from the fierceness of Your anger.

4 Restore us, O God of our salvation,
And cause Your anger toward us to cease.
5 Will You be angry with us forever?
Will You prolong Your anger to all generations?
6 Will You not revive us again,

84:7 [e] Septuagint, Syriac, and Vulgate read *The God of gods shall be seen*.

LIFE LESSON

Psalms 85:1–86:17

SITUATION God confirmed that he had plans for Israel's future. No matter how difficult the circumstances, he promised to support them.

OBSERVATION God faithfully restores his people after times of difficulty. We must be diligent by reading God's word.

INSPIRATION Be confident of this very thing, that the Father, who has begun a wonderful and good work in you will continue to work it in you and through you until He sends Me to the earth again to gather up My children.

Your heavenly Father never leaves a job half done, never walks away from a thing He has originated, leaving it unfinished.

I am the Alpha and Omega,

the beginning and the end.

I am altogether perfect.

My dealings with you are perfect. . . . When you drink in My word and keep it in your mind continually, meditating on it day and night to observe and do according to all that is written in it, then you shall make your way prosperous, and then you shall deal wisely and have good success.

(From *His Thoughts Toward Me* by Marie Chapian)

APPLICATION The world trains you to think that success comes from demonstrating personal power and desire, and by networking with the right people. God says true success comes from knowing, contemplating, and memorizing his Word. Choose the best time for you to read your Bible and pray. Then do it faithfully every day.

EXPLORATION Restoration—Psalm 91:14-16; Isaiah 40:10-11; 58:11; 1 Corinthians 1:8-9; Philippians 1:6.

That Your people may rejoice in You?
7 Show us Your mercy, LORD,
And grant us Your salvation.

8 I will hear what God the LORD will speak,
For He will speak peace
To His people and to His saints;
But let them not turn back to folly.
9 Surely His salvation *is* near to those who fear Him,
That glory may dwell in our land.

10 Mercy and truth have met together;
Righteousness and peace have kissed.
11 Truth shall spring out of the earth,
And righteousness shall look down from heaven.
12 Yes, the LORD will give *what is* good;
And our land will yield its increase.
13 Righteousness will go before Him,
And shall make His footsteps *our* pathway.

PSALM 86

Prayer for Mercy, with Meditation on the Excellencies of the LORD

A Prayer of David.

Bow down Your ear, O LORD, hear me;
For I *am* poor and needy.
2 Preserve my life, for I *am* holy;
You are my God;
Save Your servant who trusts in You!
3 Be merciful to me, O Lord,
For I cry to You all day long.
4 Rejoice the soul of Your servant,
For to You, O Lord, I lift up my soul.
5 For You, Lord, *are* good, and ready to forgive,
And abundant in mercy to all those who call upon You.

6 Give ear, O LORD, to my prayer;
And attend to the voice of my supplications.
7 In the day of my trouble I will call upon You,
For You will answer me.

8 Among the gods *there is* none like You, O Lord;
Nor *are there any works* like Your works.
9 All nations whom You have made
Shall come and worship before You, O Lord,
And shall glorify Your name.
10 For You *are* great, and do wondrous things;
You alone *are* God.

11 Teach me Your way, O LORD;
I will walk in Your truth;
Unite my heart to fear Your name.
12 I will praise You, O Lord my God, with all my heart,
And I will glorify Your name forevermore.
13 For great *is* Your mercy toward me,
And You have delivered my soul from the depths of Sheol.

14 O God, the proud have risen against me,
And a mob of violent *men* have sought my life,
And have not set You before them.
15 But You, O Lord, *are* a God full of compassion, and gracious,
Longsuffering and abundant in mercy and truth.

16 Oh, turn to me, and have mercy on me!
Give Your strength to Your servant,
And save the son of Your maidservant.
17 Show me a sign for good,
That those who hate me may see *it* and be ashamed,
Because You, LORD, have helped me and comforted me.

PSALM 87

The Glories of the City of God

A Psalm of the sons of Korah. A Song.

His foundation *is* in the holy mountains.
2 The LORD loves the gates of Zion
More than all the dwellings of Jacob.
3 Glorious things are spoken of you,
O city of God! Selah

4 "I will make mention of Rahab and Babylon to those who know Me;
Behold, O Philistia and Tyre, with Ethiopia:
'This *one* was born there.' "

5 And of Zion it will be said,
"This *one* and that *one* were born in her;
And the Most High Himself shall establish her."
6 The LORD will record,
When He registers the peoples:
"This *one* was born there." Selah

7 Both the singers and the players on instruments *say,*
"All my springs *are* in you."

PSALM 88

A Prayer for Help in Despondency

A Song. A Psalm of the sons of Korah. To the Chief Musician. Set to "Mahalath Leannoth." A Contemplation[f] of Heman the Ezrahite.

O LORD, God of my salvation,
I have cried out day and night before You.
2 Let my prayer come before You;
Incline Your ear to my cry.

3 For my soul is full of troubles,
And my life draws near to the grave.
4 I am counted with those who go down to the pit;
I am like a man *who has* no strength,
5 Adrift among the dead,
Like the slain who lie in the grave,
Whom You remember no more,
And who are cut off from Your hand.

6 You have laid me in the lowest pit,
In darkness, in the depths.
7 Your wrath lies heavy upon me,
And You have afflicted *me* with all Your waves. Selah
8 You have put away my acquaintances far from me;
You have made me an abomination to them;
I am shut up, and I cannot get out;
9 My eye wastes away because of affliction.

LORD, I have called daily upon You;
I have stretched out my hands to You.
10 Will You work wonders for the dead?
Shall the dead arise *and* praise You? Selah
11 Shall Your lovingkindness be declared in the grave?
Or Your faithfulness in the place of destruction?
12 Shall Your wonders be known in the dark?
And Your righteousness in the land of forgetfulness?

13 But to You I have cried out, O LORD,
And in the morning my prayer comes before You.
14 LORD, why do You cast off my soul?
Why do You hide Your face from me?
15 I *have been* afflicted and ready to die from *my* youth;
I suffer Your terrors;
I am distraught.
16 Your fierce wrath has gone over me;
Your terrors have cut me off.
17 They came around me all day long like water;
They engulfed me altogether.
18 Loved one and friend You have put far from me,
And my acquaintances into darkness.

88:title *f* Hebrew *Maschil*

LIFE LESSON

Psalms 87:1–88:18

SITUATION God was devoted to Zion (Psalm 87). This psalm of celebration contrasted the heavy and sad tone of the subsequent psalm, which spoke of death and despair (Psalm 88).

OBSERVATION God will hear your tearful prayers and heal your deepest wounds. His perfect love will reduce or take away anxiety.

INSPIRATION When Becky Smith-Greer was growing up in North Carolina, she pretended she was Princess Rose and would someday marry the man of her dreams. Following a college romance, she married Sonny Smith, who became more than the husband of her fairy-tale fantasy. Sonny became her best friend and the loving father of their two children.

The Smiths became teachers in the Hendersonville, North Carolina, area. Sonny was the high school band director, and Becky taught kindergarten. Then Becky's idyllic life was shattered when she heard the words, "There's been an accident!"

In one swift moment, she lost half her family—her husband and her 12-year-old son, Greg—in a plane crash. Two others also perished: Sonny's 26-year-old nephew, Richard, and his brother-in-law, Jack, the pilot of the single-engine craft. . . .

Our story begins [twelve] months later.

. . . My will to survive was almost gone. . . . When I tried to sleep, visions of blood and twisted metal often invaded my dreams. . . .

Finally I threw back the covers and stumbled through the darkness to Greg's room. . . . In utter desperation, I screamed aloud, "God, if You're there, and if You're real, You've got to help me! I can't go on like this!"

. . . Not long after that frightful night, God did come to visit me in an unexpected time and place. He slipped quietly beside me on the steps of my classroom and used a little boy named Mark to teach me about Himself. . . .

I looked up to see Mark chasing several girls with a stick.

Continued

Mark was so tiny, I didn't think he had the strength to hurt them. Actually, I was glad to see him interacting at any level. Mark was my puzzle and challenge. His frail body was spaghetti thin, his brown eyes hauntingly blank. In the classroom, he usually sat on the floor, folded his bony knees together, and stared at the carpet. The only way I could look into his eyes was to pull him to me and cup his face in my hands. Even then, he would not look directly at me.

"You know, Mark, I had a little boy just like you. His name was Greg, but I don't have him anymore. He died." Mark looked up at me now as I talked. "Greg loved Matchbox cars. Do you like those cars?"

He nodded his head vigorously.

"I'll tell you what I'm going to do. Tomorrow I'll bring you one of Greg's cars. Would you like that? I know Greg would like you to have one."

Mark nodded again and gently relaxed. I felt some of the fight drain out of him. I began to hum and rock. In a while, his body went limp as he fell asleep. I cradled him in my arms and wiped the perspiration from his tiny forehead.

Ever so quietly, God crept into my heart and whispered to softly, "Becky, you're just like Mark. I've tried to talk with you all these months, but you kicked and screamed so loudly you couldn't hear me. It's okay. I know you're hurt. I've just had to hold you tightly until you calm down. If you let Me now, I'll cradle you in My arms, and you can rest. You can trust me. I won't let you go."

(From *Keepsakes for the Heart* by Becky Smith-Greer)

APPLICATION Picture yourself climbing up into God's lap, feeling his arms wrap around you, and receiving his hug. Tell him of your grief, anger, and despair. Share with one other trusted friend this week what you told God in the darkness.

EXPLORATION Overcoming Spiritual Depression—Job 42:1-6; Psalms 42–43; Romans 8:18-38; 1 Corinthians 15:12-19; 2 Corinthians 1:3-11; 1 Peter 1; Revelation 21:1-8.

PSALM 89

Remembering the Covenant with David, and Sorrow for Lost Blessings

A Contemplation[g] of Ethan the Ezrahite.

I will sing of the mercies of the LORD forever;
With my mouth will I make known Your
faithfulness to all generations.
2 For I have said, "Mercy shall be built up forever;
Your faithfulness You shall establish in the very heavens."

3 "I have made a covenant with My chosen,
I have sworn to My servant David:
4 'Your seed I will establish forever,
And build up your throne to all generations.' " Selah

5 And the heavens will praise Your wonders, O LORD;
Your faithfulness also in the assembly of the saints.
6 For who in the heavens can be compared to the LORD?
Who among the sons of the mighty can be likened to the LORD?
7 God is greatly to be feared in the assembly of the saints,
And to be held in reverence by all *those* around Him.
8 O LORD God of hosts,
Who *is* mighty like You, O LORD?
Your faithfulness also surrounds You.
9 You rule the raging of the sea;
When its waves rise, You still them.
10 You have broken Rahab in pieces, as one who is slain;
You have scattered Your enemies with Your mighty arm.

11 The heavens *are* Yours, the earth also *is* Yours;
The world and all its fullness, You have founded them.
12 The north and the south, You have created them;
Tabor and Hermon rejoice in Your name.
13 You have a mighty arm;
Strong is Your hand, *and* high is Your right hand.
14 Righteousness and justice *are* the foundation of Your throne;
Mercy and truth go before Your face.
15 Blessed *are* the people who know the joyful sound!
They walk, O LORD, in the light of Your countenance.
16 In Your name they rejoice all day long,
And in Your righteousness they are exalted.
17 For You *are* the glory of their strength,
And in Your favor our horn is exalted.
18 For our shield *belongs* to the LORD,
And our king to the Holy One of Israel.

19 Then You spoke in a vision to Your holy one,[h]
And said: "I have given help to *one who is* mighty;
I have exalted one chosen from the people.

89:title [g] Hebrew *Maschil*
89:19 [h] Following many Hebrew manuscripts; Masoretic Text, Septuagint, Targum, and Vulgate read *holy ones.*

20 I have found My servant David;
With My holy oil I have anointed him,
21 With whom My hand shall be established;
Also My arm shall strengthen him.
22 The enemy shall not outwit him,
Nor the son of wickedness afflict him.
23 I will beat down his foes before his face,
And plague those who hate him.

24 "But My faithfulness and My mercy *shall be* with him,
And in My name his horn shall be exalted.
25 Also I will set his hand over the sea,
And his right hand over the rivers.
26 He shall cry to Me, 'You *are* my Father,
My God, and the rock of my salvation.'
27 Also I will make him *My* firstborn,
The highest of the kings of the earth.
28 My mercy I will keep for him forever,
And My covenant shall stand firm with him.
29 His seed also I will make *to endure* forever,
And his throne as the days of heaven.

30 "If his sons forsake My law
And do not walk in My judgments,
31 If they break My statutes
And do not keep My commandments,
32 Then I will punish their transgression with the rod,
And their iniquity with stripes.
33 Nevertheless My lovingkindness I will not utterly take from him,
Nor allow My faithfulness to fail.
34 My covenant I will not break,
Nor alter the word that has gone out of My lips.
35 Once I have sworn by My holiness;
I will not lie to David:
36 His seed shall endure forever,
And his throne as the sun before Me;
37 It shall be established forever like the moon,
Even *like* the faithful witness in the sky." Selah

38 But You have cast off and abhorred,
You have been furious with Your anointed.
39 You have renounced the covenant of Your servant;
You have profaned his crown *by casting it* to the ground.
40 You have broken down all his hedges;
You have brought his strongholds to ruin.
41 All who pass by the way plunder him;
He is a reproach to his neighbors.
42 You have exalted the right hand of his adversaries;
You have made all his enemies rejoice.
43 You have also turned back the edge of his sword,
And have not sustained him in the battle.
44 You have made his glory cease,

LIFE LESSON

Psalm 89:1-52

SITUATION This psalm celebrated David's glorious reign. David's reign was successful because God sustained him.

OBSERVATION One of David's descendants (Jesus Christ) would reign over God's people forever.

INSPIRATION Children love to swing. There's nothing like it. Thrusting your feet toward the sky, leaning so far backward that everything looks upside down. Spinning trees, a stomach that jumps into your throat. Ah, swinging. . . .

I learned a lot about trust on a swing. As a child, I only trusted certain people to push my swing. If I was being pushed by people I trusted (like Dad or Mom), they could do anything they wanted. They could twist me, turn me, stop me . . . But let a stranger push my swing (which often happened at family reunions and Fourth of July picnics), and it was *hang on, baby!* Who knew what this newcomer would do? When a stranger pushes your swing, you tense up, ball up, and hang on. . . .

We live in a stormy world. At this writing, wars rage in both hemispheres of our globe. World conflict is threatening all humanity. Jobs are getting scarce. Money continues to get tight. Families are coming apart at the seams. . . .

We must remember who is pushing the swing. We must put our trust in him. We can't grow fearful. He won't let us tumble out.

(From *On the Anvil* by Max Lucado)

APPLICATION When do you feel safe? When your spouse is with you? When the doors are locked? When the alarm is on? When you have enough money for any situation? All of these securities can fail. Ask God to help you depend on him for your security.

EXPLORATION God as Security—Genesis 15:1; Deuteronomy 33:29; 2 Samuel 22:3; Psalm 7:10; 28:7; 33:20; 59:11; 84:11; 115:9; 144:2; Proverbs 30:5.

LIFE LESSON

Psalms 90:1–91:16

SITUATION Moses remembered his pain over the sins of the people (see Exodus 32:9-14).

OBSERVATION Moses prayed that God would show favor and blessing to his weak people.

INSPIRATION Psalm 90 is the only psalm specifically attributed to Moses. He may have written others, but we know for sure he wrote this one. Remember Moses? Most think of him as a man of action, an aggressive leader, point man in the exodus, outspoken giver of the law. But it is easy to overlook the repetitious, monotonous routine he endured. Between ages forty and eighty, Moses led his father-in-law's flock of sheep in the desert. Following the exodus, he led the Hebrews for another forty years as they wandered across and around the wilderness. I'd say he knew about the blahs. Same terrain, same scenes, same route, same ornery people, same negative outlook, same complaints, same miserable weather, same everything! The prayer he wrote could have been his means of maintaining sanity! . . .
Frequently, our problem with boredom begins when we fall under monotony's "spell." . . . How to cope? We must direct our attention (as Moses does) to (a) the right object and (b) the right perspective. . . .

And cast his throne down to the ground.
45 The days of his youth You have shortened;
You have covered him with shame. Selah

46 How long, LORD?
Will You hide Yourself forever?
Will Your wrath burn like fire?
47 Remember how short my time is;
For what futility have You created all the children of men?
48 What man can live and not see death?
Can he deliver his life from the power of the grave? Selah

49 Lord, where *are* Your former lovingkindnesses,
Which You swore to David in Your truth?
50 Remember, Lord, the reproach of Your servants—
How I bear in my bosom *the reproach of* all the many peoples,
51 With which Your enemies have reproached, O LORD,
With which they have reproached the footsteps of Your anointed.

52 Blessed *be* the LORD forevermore!
Amen and Amen.

Book Four: Psalms 90—106

PSALM 90

The Eternity of God, and Man's Frailty

A Prayer of Moses the man of God.

LORD, You have been our dwelling place[i]
in all generations.
2 Before the mountains were brought forth,
Or ever You had formed the earth and the world,
Even from everlasting to everlasting, You *are* God.

3 You turn man to destruction,
And say, "Return, O children of men."
4 For a thousand years in Your sight
Are like yesterday when it is past,
And *like* a watch in the night.
5 You carry them away *like* a flood;
They are like a sleep.
In the morning they are like grass *which* grows up:
6 In the morning it flourishes and grows up;
In the evening it is cut down and withers.

7 For we have been consumed by Your anger,
And by Your wrath we are terrified.
8 You have set our iniquities before You,
Our secret *sins* in the light of Your countenance.
9 For all our days have passed away in Your wrath;
We finish our years like a sigh.

90:1 [i] Septuagint, Targum, and Vulgate read *refuge*.

10 The days of our lives *are* seventy years;
And if by reason of strength *they are* eighty years,
Yet their boast *is* only labor and sorrow;
For it is soon cut off, and we fly away.
11 Who knows the power of Your anger?
For as the fear of You, *so is* Your wrath.
12 So teach *us* to number our days,
That we may gain a heart of wisdom.

13 Return, O LORD!
How long?
And have compassion on Your servants.
14 Oh, satisfy us early with Your mercy,
That we may rejoice and be glad all our days!
15 Make us glad according to the days *in which* You have afflicted us,
The years *in which* we have seen evil.
16 Let Your work appear to Your servants,
And Your glory to their children.
17 And let the beauty of the LORD our God be upon us,
And establish the work of our hands for us;
Yes, establish the work of our hands.

PSALM 91

Safety of Abiding in the Presence of God

He who dwells in the secret place of the Most High
Shall abide under the shadow of the Almighty.
2 I will say of the LORD, "*He is* my refuge and my fortress;
My God, in Him I will trust."

3 Surely He shall deliver you from the snare of the fowler[j]
And from the perilous pestilence.
4 He shall cover you with His feathers,
And under His wings you shall take refuge;
His truth *shall be your* shield and buckler.
5 You shall not be afraid of the terror by night,
Nor of the arrow *that* flies by day,
6 *Nor* of the pestilence *that* walks in darkness,
Nor of the destruction *that* lays waste at noonday.

7 A thousand may fall at your side,
And ten thousand at your right hand;
But it shall not come near you.
8 Only with your eyes shall you look,
And see the reward of the wicked.

9 Because you have made the LORD, *who is* my refuge,
Even the Most High, your dwelling place,
10 No evil shall befall you,
Nor shall any plague come near your dwelling;
11 For He shall give His angels charge over you,
To keep you in all your ways.

91:3 *j* That is, one who catches birds in a trap or snare

As I probe my soul during times of such wrestling, almost without exception, I find three thoughts washing around in my head. First, I think: Life is so short. . . . Look again at Moses' prayer. He brings a second thought that plagues me when the blahs come: My sins are so obvious. . . .

Yes, life is short. Yes, our sins are obvious. . . . And if those thoughts aren't hard enough to handle, there's a third feeling: My days are so empty. . . . After the satisfaction that comes from fresh joy in the morning, there is restoration. . . . God has a way of balancing out the good with the bad. (From *Living Above the Level of Mediocrity* by Charles Swindoll)

APPLICATION What would you like to do before you die? What fulfillment will it bring you? When you die what lasting effects, if any, will it have? Invest your time in people and projects that will live on after you die: be a friend, share the gospel, give someone a Bible, donate time or money to a Christian ministry.

EXPLORATION Humans Are Finite—Genesis 6:3; Job 34:14-15; Psalm 78:39; Isaiah 40:6-8; Matthew 26:41.

12 In *their* hands they shall bear you up,
Lest you dash your foot against a stone.
13 You shall tread upon the lion and the cobra,
The young lion and the serpent you shall trample underfoot.

14 "Because he has set his love upon Me, therefore I will deliver him;
I will set him on high, because he has known My name.
15 He shall call upon Me, and I will answer him;
I *will be* with him in trouble;
I will deliver him and honor him.
16 With long life I will satisfy him,
And show him My salvation."

PSALM 92

Praise to the LORD for His Love and Faithfulness

A Psalm. A Song for the Sabbath day.

It is good to give thanks to the LORD,
And to sing praises to Your name, O Most High;
2 To declare Your lovingkindness in the morning,
And Your faithfulness every night,
3 On an instrument of ten strings,
On the lute,
And on the harp,
With harmonious sound.
4 For You, LORD, have made me glad through Your work;
I will triumph in the works of Your hands.

5 O LORD, how great are Your works!
Your thoughts are very deep.
6 A senseless man does not know,
Nor does a fool understand this.
7 When the wicked spring up like grass,
And when all the workers of iniquity flourish,
It is that they may be destroyed forever.

8 But You, LORD, *are* on high forevermore.
9 For behold, Your enemies, O LORD,
For behold, Your enemies shall perish;
All the workers of iniquity shall be scattered.

10 But my horn You have exalted like a wild ox;
I have been anointed with fresh oil.
11 My eye also has seen *my desire* on my enemies;
My ears hear *my desire* on the wicked
Who rise up against me.

12 The righteous shall flourish like a palm tree,
He shall grow like a cedar in Lebanon.
13 Those who are planted in the house of the LORD
Shall flourish in the courts of our God.
14 They shall still bear fruit in old age;
They shall be fresh and flourishing,

LIFE LESSON

Psalms 92:1–93:5

SITUATION As king, David discerned between evil and righteousness by using God's character as the criterion.

OBSERVATION God rules his creation perfectly. We must be thankful and faithful to him.

INSPIRATION We know that God will fulfill every promise made to the prophets; we know that sinners will someday be cleansed out of the earth; we know that a ransomed company will enter into the joy of God and that the righteous will shine forth in the kingdom of their Father; we know that God's perfections will yet receive universal acclamation, that all created intelligences will own Jesus Christ as Lord to the glory of God the Father, that the present imperfect order will be done away, and a new heaven and a new earth be established forever.

Toward all this God is moving with infinite wisdom and perfect precision of action. No one can dissuade Him from His purposes; nothing can turn Him aside from His plans. Since he is omniscient, there can be no unforeseen circumstances, no accidents. As he is sovereign, there can be no countermanded orders, no breakdown in authority; and as he is omnipotent, there can be no want of power to achieve His chosen ends. God is sufficient unto Himself for all these things.

(From *The Knowledge of the Holy* by A. W. Tozer)

APPLICATION Where in your life do you insist on calling the shots? In the kind of movies you watch? The employees you hire? Your spouse's behavior? Every choice your children make? Hand your need to control over to God—you'll be relieved by his loving administration!

EXPLORATION Sovereignty—Psalm 1:1-6; 103:19-22; Romans 11:33-36; Revelation 1:5.

15 To declare that the LORD is upright;
He is my rock, and *there is* no unrighteousness in Him.

PSALM 93

The Eternal Reign of the LORD

The LORD reigns, He is clothed with majesty;
The LORD is clothed,
He has girded Himself with strength.
Surely the world is established, so that it cannot be moved.
2 Your throne *is* established from of old;
You *are* from everlasting.

3 The floods have lifted up, O LORD,
The floods have lifted up their voice;
The floods lift up their waves.
4 The LORD on high *is* mightier
Than the noise of many waters,
Than the mighty waves of the sea.

5 Your testimonies are very sure;
Holiness adorns Your house,
O LORD, forever.

PSALM 94

God the Refuge of the Righteous

O LORD God, to whom vengeance belongs—
O God, to whom vengeance belongs, shine forth!
2 Rise up, O Judge of the earth;
Render punishment to the proud.
3 LORD, how long will the wicked,
How long will the wicked triumph?

4 They utter speech, *and* speak insolent things;
All the workers of iniquity boast in themselves.
5 They break in pieces Your people, O LORD,
And afflict Your heritage.
6 They slay the widow and the stranger,
And murder the fatherless.
7 Yet they say, "The LORD does not see,
Nor does the God of Jacob understand."

8 Understand, you senseless among the people;
And *you* fools, when will you be wise?
9 He who planted the ear, shall He not hear?
He who formed the eye, shall He not see?
10 He who instructs the nations, shall He not correct,
He who teaches man knowledge?
11 The LORD knows the thoughts of man,
That they *are* futile.

12 Blessed *is* the man whom You instruct, O LORD,
And teach out of Your law,

LIFE LESSON

Psalm 94:1-23

SITUATION The psalm writer felt surrounded by people who did not seek after God. He rejoiced that God would protect and care for the righteous.

OBSERVATION It is easy to grow weary and discouraged when we are surrounded by those who do not seek God. But God promises to be a shelter to those who are his children.

INSPIRATION Where do *you* turn when the bottom drops out of *your* life? Or when you face an issue that is embarrassing . . . maybe even scandalous? . . . What do you need when circumstances puncture your fragile dikes and threaten to engulf your life with pain and confusion?

You need a shelter. A listener. Someone who understands.

But to whom do you turn when there's no one to tell your troubles to? Where do you find encouragement? . . .

Discouraged people don't need critics. They hurt enough already. They don't need more guilt or piled-on distress. They need encouragement. They need a refuge.

A place to hide and heal.

A willing, caring, available someone. A confidant and comrade-at-arms. Can't find one? Why not share David's shelter? The One he called My Strength, Mighty Rock, Fortress, Stronghold, and High Tower.

David's Refuge *never* failed. Not even once. And he never regretted the times he dropped his heavy load and ran for cover.

Neither will you.

(From *Growing Old in the Seasons of Life* by Charles Swindoll)

APPLICATION Do you ever feel alone and discouraged in your faith? Become a part of a church and befriend a few other Believers—people who will shelter you when you're facing life's storms.

EXPLORATION God's Protection—Deuteronomy 33:27; 2 Samuel 22:3; Psalm 17:8; 91:4; Proverbs 14:26; Luke 13:34.

13 That You may give him rest from the days of adversity,
Until the pit is dug for the wicked.
14 For the LORD will not cast off His people,
Nor will He forsake His inheritance.
15 But judgment will return to righteousness,
And all the upright in heart will follow it.

16 Who will rise up for me against the evildoers?
Who will stand up for me against the workers of iniquity?
17 Unless the LORD *had been* my help,
My soul would soon have settled in silence.
18 If I say, "My foot slips,"
Your mercy, O LORD, will hold me up.
19 In the multitude of my anxieties within me,
Your comforts delight my soul.

20 Shall the throne of iniquity, which devises evil by law,
Have fellowship with You?
21 They gather together against the life of the righteous,
And condemn innocent blood.
22 But the LORD has been my defense,
And my God the rock of my refuge.
23 He has brought on them their own iniquity,
And shall cut them off in their own wickedness;
The LORD our God shall cut them off.

PSALM 95

A Call to Worship and Obedience

Oh come, let us sing to the LORD!
Let us shout joyfully to the Rock of our salvation.
2 Let us come before His presence with thanksgiving;
Let us shout joyfully to Him with psalms.
3 For the LORD *is* the great God,
And the great King above all gods.
4 In His hand *are* the deep places of the earth;
The heights of the hills *are* His also.
5 The sea *is* His, for He made it;
And His hands formed the dry *land*.

6 Oh come, let us worship and bow down;
Let us kneel before the LORD our Maker.
7 For He *is* our God,
And we *are* the people of His pasture,
And the sheep of His hand.

Today, if you will hear His voice:
8 "Do not harden your hearts, as in the rebellion,[k]
As *in* the day of trial[l] in the wilderness,
9 When your fathers tested Me;
They tried Me, though they saw My work.
10 For forty years I was grieved with *that* generation,

LIFE LESSON

Psalms 95:1–96:13

SITUATION Everything that has been created gives glory to God. The psalm writer encouraged the people to bring an offering of worship to God.

OBSERVATION As Creator, God calls for submission from his creation.

INSPIRATION Devotion to God is the first aspect of Godliness; Godlike character is the second. There may be some question about whether or not humility is a Godlike quality, since humility is a trait befitting the creature, not the Creator. But there is no question that God commends humility and delights in it in his people. . . .

Not only does God commend humility in his people; our Lord displayed it in his humanity. "And being found in appearance as a man, he humbled himself and became obedient to death—even death on a cross!" (Philippians 2:8). Jesus Christ exemplified humility in its utmost through his death for us. But he also exemplified humility throughout his life. He was born in the humblest of circumstances; he was obedient to his earthly parents; he called people to himself as one who was "gentle and humble in heart"; he said, "I am among you as one who serves"; he washed the disciples' feet on the very night of his betrayal; and he taught, "he who humbles himself will be exalted." If we question whether humility is a Godlike trait (as we view God in his majesty), we certainly cannot question that it is a Christlike trait. And we are to be imitators of him as he lived out his human life on earth.

(From *The Practice of Godliness* by Jerry Bridges)

APPLICATION Read an episode from the life of Christ. What were some of his character traits? Try to be more like Christ in these areas.

EXPLORATION Submission—Isaiah 66:1-2; Matthew 26:57-63; James 4:7-10; 1 Peter 5:6.

95:8 [k] Or *Meribah* [l] Or *Massah*

And said, 'It *is* a people who go astray in their hearts,
And they do not know My ways.'
11 So I swore in My wrath,
'They shall not enter My rest.' "

PSALM 96

A Song of Praise to God Coming in Judgment

Oh, sing to the LORD a new song!
Sing to the LORD, all the earth.
2 Sing to the LORD, bless His name;
Proclaim the good news of His salvation from day to day.
3 Declare His glory among the nations,
His wonders among all peoples.

4 For the LORD *is* great and greatly to be praised;
He *is* to be feared above all gods.
5 For all the gods of the peoples *are* idols,
But the LORD made the heavens.
6 Honor and majesty *are* before Him;
Strength and beauty *are* in His sanctuary.

7 Give to the LORD, O families of the peoples,
Give to the LORD glory and strength.
8 Give to the LORD the glory *due* His name;
Bring an offering, and come into His courts.
9 Oh, worship the LORD in the beauty of holiness!
Tremble before Him, all the earth.

10 Say among the nations, "The LORD reigns;
The world also is firmly established,
It shall not be moved;
He shall judge the peoples righteously."

11 Let the heavens rejoice, and let the earth be glad;
Let the sea roar, and all its fullness;
12 Let the field be joyful, and all that *is* in it.
Then all the trees of the woods will rejoice before the LORD.
13 For He is coming, for He is coming to judge the earth.
He shall judge the world with righteousness,
And the peoples with His truth.

PSALM 97

A Song of Praise to the Sovereign LORD

The LORD reigns;
Let the earth rejoice;
Let the multitude of isles be glad!

2 Clouds and darkness surround Him;
Righteousness and justice *are* the foundation of His throne.
3 A fire goes before Him,
And burns up His enemies round about.
4 His lightnings light the world;

LIFE LESSON

Psalms 97:1–98:9

SITUATION Like many psalms used at Jewish festivals, these psalms celebrated God's reign.

OBSERVATION God reigns. He brings justice, victory, and righteousness.

INSPIRATION The Christian's instincts of trust and worship are stimulated very powerfully by knowledge of the greatness of God. But this is knowledge which Christians today largely lack: And that is one reason why our faith is so feeble and our worship so flabby. . . . A recent book was called *Your God Is Too Small*; it was a timely title. We are poles apart from our evangelical forefathers at this point, even when we confess our faith in their words. When you start reading Luther, or Edwards, or Whitefield, though your doctrine may be theirs, you soon find yourself wondering whether you have any acquaintance at all with the mighty God whom they knew so intimately.

Today, vast stress is laid on the thought that God is *personal*, but this truth is so stated as to leave the impression that God is a person of the same sort as we are—weak, inadequate, ineffective, a little pathetic. But this is not the God of the Bible! . . . Like us, He is personal; but unlike us, He is *great*. In all its constant stress on the reality of God's personal concern for His people, and on the gentleness, tenderness, sympathy, patience, and yearning compassion that He shows towards them, the Bible never lets us lose sight of His majesty, and His unlimited dominion over all His creatures.

(From *Knowing God* by J. I. Packer)

APPLICATION Which has a higher priority for you: obeying God or reaching your goals? Which do you spend more time and energy trying to attain? Any loyalty greater than one to God is idolatry. Don't let anything take God's place in your heart, mind, and daily events.

EXPLORATION The Greatness of God—Deuteronomy 3:24; 2 Samuel 7:22; Psalm 77:13-20; 95:3-5; 104.

The earth sees and trembles.
5 The mountains melt like wax at the presence of the LORD,
At the presence of the Lord of the whole earth.
6 The heavens declare His righteousness,
And all the peoples see His glory.

7 Let all be put to shame who serve carved images,
Who boast of idols.
Worship Him, all *you* gods.
8 Zion hears and is glad,
And the daughters of Judah rejoice
Because of Your judgments, O LORD.
9 For You, LORD, *are* most high above all the earth;
You are exalted far above all gods.

10 You who love the LORD, hate evil!
He preserves the souls of His saints;
He delivers them out of the hand of the wicked.
11 Light is sown for the righteous,
And gladness for the upright in heart.
12 Rejoice in the LORD, you righteous,
And give thanks at the remembrance of His holy name.[m]

PSALM 98

A Song of Praise to the LORD for His Salvation and Judgment

A Psalm.

Oh, sing to the LORD a new song!
For He has done marvelous things;
His right hand and His holy arm have gained Him the victory.
2 The LORD has made known His salvation;
His righteousness He has revealed in the sight of the nations.
3 He has remembered His mercy and His faithfulness to the house of Israel;
All the ends of the earth have seen the salvation of our God.

4 Shout joyfully to the LORD, all the earth;
Break forth in song, rejoice, and sing praises.
5 Sing to the LORD with the harp,
With the harp and the sound of a psalm,
6 With trumpets and the sound of a horn;
Shout joyfully before the LORD, the King.

7 Let the sea roar, and all its fullness,
The world and those who dwell in it;
8 Let the rivers clap *their* hands;
Let the hills be joyful together before the LORD,
9 For He is coming to judge the earth.
With righteousness He shall judge the world,
And the peoples with equity.

PSALM 99

Praise to the LORD for His Holiness

The LORD reigns;
Let the peoples tremble!
He dwells *between* the cherubim;
Let the earth be moved!
2 The LORD *is* great in Zion,
And He *is* high above all the peoples.
3 Let them praise Your great and awesome name—
He *is* holy.

4 The King's strength also loves justice;
You have established equity;
You have executed justice and righteousness in Jacob.
5 Exalt the LORD our God,
And worship at His footstool—
He *is* holy.

6 Moses and Aaron were among His priests,
And Samuel was among those who called upon His name;
They called upon the LORD, and He answered them.
7 He spoke to them in the cloudy pillar;
They kept His testimonies and the ordinance He gave them.

8 You answered them, O LORD our God;
You were to them God-Who-Forgives,
Though You took vengeance on their deeds.
9 Exalt the LORD our God,
And worship at His holy hill;
For the LORD our God *is* holy.

PSALM 100

A Song of Praise for the LORD's Faithfulness to His People

A Psalm of Thanksgiving.

Make a joyful shout to the LORD, all you lands!

97:12 [m] Or *His holiness*

2 Serve the LORD with gladness;
Come before His presence with singing.
3 Know that the LORD, He *is* God;
It is He *who* has made us, and not we ourselves;[n]
We are His people and the sheep of His pasture.

4 Enter into His gates with thanksgiving,
And into His courts with praise.
Be thankful to Him, *and* bless His name.
5 For the LORD *is* good;
His mercy *is* everlasting,
And His truth *endures* to all generations.

PSALM 101

Promised Faithfulness to the LORD

A Psalm of David.

I will sing of mercy and justice;
To You, O LORD, I will sing praises.

2 I will behave wisely in a perfect way.
Oh, when will You come to me?
I will walk within my house with a perfect heart.

3 I will set nothing wicked before my eyes;
I hate the work of those who fall away;
It shall not cling to me.
4 A perverse heart shall depart from me;
I will not know wickedness.

5 Whoever secretly slanders his neighbor,
Him I will destroy;
The one who has a haughty look and a proud heart,
Him I will not endure.

6 My eyes *shall be* on the faithful of the land,
That they may dwell with me;
He who walks in a perfect way,
He shall serve me.
7 He who works deceit shall not dwell within my house;
He who tells lies shall not continue in my presence.
8 Early I will destroy all the wicked of the land,
That I may cut off all the evildoers from the city of the LORD.

PSALM 102

The LORD's Eternal Love

A Prayer of the afflicted, when he is overwhelmed and pours out his complaint before the LORD.

Hear my prayer, O LORD,
And let my cry come to You.
2 Do not hide Your face from me in the day of my trouble;

100:3 [n]Following Kethib, Septuagint, and Vulgate; Qere, many Hebrew manuscripts, and Targum read *we are His.*

LIFE LESSON

Psalms 99:1–101:8

SITUATION Although Psalms 99–100 have unknown authors, Psalm 101 was written by David. Early in his reign, he recorded the standards of conduct he wanted to follow.

OBSERVATION God can be praised and trusted by Believers because he is holy, good, and perfect. All Believers should be motivated to honorable conduct.

INSPIRATION At some point in life, each one of us must decide what is his highest joy; for the thing that delights us directs us. Generally speaking, a child finds his delight in what he has; a youth in what he does; and an adult in what he is. The first lives for possessions, the second for the experiences, and the third for character. We do not condemn the child or the youth for so living, because neither has reached maturity; but we would certainly wonder at an adult who lived on those lower levels. . . .

So, every person has an outlook on life; he is seeking his highest joy. Outlook determines outcome. Abraham lifted up his eyes and saw the stars and became the friend of God by faith. Lot lifted up his eyes and saw Sodom and became the friend of the world. Abraham inherited the city prepared for him by God, the city he had been seeking (Hebrews 11:13-16); but Lot lost everything when Sodom went up in smoke.
If life is to be rich and meaningful, then our joys must be the highest possible; and Jesus tells us that the highest joy possible is to see God.
(From *Live Like a King* by Warren Wiersbe)

APPLICATION Take time to assess and write down your priorities and what they reveal about your trust in God.

EXPLORATION God Is Trustworthy—Deuteronomy 7:9; 1 Kings 8:56; Psalm 33:4; 89:2; 138:8; Lamentations 3:22-23; 1 Corinthians 1:9; 1 Thessalonians 5:23-24; Hebrews 10:23.

LIFE LESSON

Psalm 102:1-28

SITUATION The psalmist's distress is not hopeless. Through faith he saw a glorious future for unborn generations.

OBSERVATION God will never die or forget about us. He will protect and restore his people today as in the past.

INSPIRATION A brighter prospect is before the true believer—*restoration.* God has no intention of leaving His investment in a shambles. There will be a divine housecleaning. That is a foregone conclusion. This is the message of all the prophets. *But housecleaning is followed by restoration.*

We know for instance that we are going to have a cleansed and restored heavens. We have filled the air with violence, brutality, and threat. We know that the brute creation is to be restored to dignity—that ". . . the wolf and the lamb will feed together . . . ."

I think the most encouraging sign I have seen this year—a sign that is becoming more and more evident in a catalogue of different places—*is a dawning consciousness that we need something more than religious activity.* . . . You can feel a stirring. It's coming . . . not reformation, but restoration. It must come! . . .

There will be a new day for the oil and wine of the gospel. The presence of the Holy Spirit and the "good news" of abundant grace of God are the power of the gospel. Revival is not spurious, jazzed-up religious activity. . . . God is about to have his say in this world—and He is going to start with His Church.

(From *Revivaltime Pulpit* by C. M. Ward)

APPLICATION Don't suffer alone. When you feel attacked or overwhelmed, tell God. Then, look to another friend or family member who will help carry you through.

EXPLORATION Restoration—Exodus 30:11-16; Numbers 5:5-8; Psalm 126: 5-6; Matthew 8:2-3; 2 Corinthians 2:5-11; Ephesians 4:15-16.

Incline Your ear to me;
In the day that I call, answer me speedily.

3 For my days are consumed like smoke,
And my bones are burned like a hearth.
4 My heart is stricken and withered like grass,
So that I forget to eat my bread.
5 Because of the sound of my groaning
My bones cling to my skin.
6 I am like a pelican of the wilderness;
I am like an owl of the desert.
7 I lie awake,
And am like a sparrow alone on the housetop.

8 My enemies reproach me all day long;
Those who deride me swear an oath against me.
9 For I have eaten ashes like bread,
And mingled my drink with weeping,
10 Because of Your indignation and Your wrath;
For You have lifted me up and cast me away.
11 My days *are* like a shadow that lengthens,
And I wither away like grass.

12 But You, O LORD, shall endure forever,
And the remembrance of Your name to all generations.
13 You will arise *and* have mercy on Zion;
For the time to favor her,
Yes, the set time, has come.
14 For Your servants take pleasure in her stones,
And show favor to her dust.
15 So the nations shall fear the name of the LORD,
And all the kings of the earth Your glory.
16 For the LORD shall build up Zion;
He shall appear in His glory.
17 He shall regard the prayer of the destitute,
And shall not despise their prayer.

18 This will be written for the generation to come,
That a people yet to be created may praise the LORD.
19 For He looked down from the height of His sanctuary;
From heaven the LORD viewed the earth,
20 To hear the groaning of the prisoner,
To release those appointed to death,
21 To declare the name of the LORD in Zion,
And His praise in Jerusalem,
22 When the peoples are gathered together,
And the kingdoms, to serve the LORD.

23 He weakened my strength in the way;
He shortened my days.
24 I said, "O my God,
Do not take me away in the midst of my days;
Your years *are* throughout all generations.
25 Of old You laid the foundation of the earth,

And the heavens *are* the work of Your hands.
26 They will perish, but You will endure;
Yes, they will all grow old like a garment;
Like a cloak You will change them,
And they will be changed.
27 But You *are* the same,
And Your years will have no end.
28 The children of Your servants will continue,
And their descendants will be established before You."

PSALM 103

Praise for the LORD's Mercies

A Psalm of David.

Bless the LORD, O my soul;
And all that is within me, *bless* His holy name!
2 Bless the LORD, O my soul,
And forget not all His benefits:
3 Who forgives all your iniquities,
Who heals all your diseases,
4 Who redeems your life from destruction,
Who crowns you with lovingkindness and tender mercies,
5 Who satisfies your mouth with good *things,*
So that your youth is renewed like the eagle's.

6 The LORD executes righteousness
And justice for all who are oppressed.
7 He made known His ways to Moses,
His acts to the children of Israel.
8 The LORD *is* merciful and gracious,
Slow to anger, and abounding in mercy.
9 He will not always strive *with us,*
Nor will He keep *His anger* forever.
10 He has not dealt with us according to our sins,
Nor punished us according to our iniquities.

11 For as the heavens are high above the earth,
So great is His mercy toward those who fear Him;
12 As far as the east is from the west,
So far has He removed our transgressions from us.
13 As a father pities *his* children,
So the LORD pities those who fear Him.
14 For He knows our frame;
He remembers that we *are* dust.

15 *As for* man, his days *are* like grass;
As a flower of the field, so he flourishes.
16 For the wind passes over it, and it is gone,
And its place remembers it no more.[o]
17 But the mercy of the LORD *is* from everlasting to everlasting
On those who fear Him,

103:16 [o] Compare Job 7:10

LIFE LESSON

Psalms 103:1-22

SITUATION David urged everyone to praise God. He told of God's faithfulness and praised him.

OBSERVATION The first few verses set the tone for this psalm. David urged the reader to avoid allowing God to become so commonplace that he forgot to praise him.

INSPIRATION Abraham Lincoln once listened to the pleas of the mother of a soldier who'd been sentenced to hang for treason. She begged the President to grant a pardon. Lincoln agreed. Yet, he's reported to have left the lady with the following words: "Still, I wish we could teach him a lesson. I wish we could give him just a little bit of hangin'."

I think I know what the old railsplitter had in mind. Yesterday, I got a little bit of hangin'.

We were having Sunday lunch at the home of a fellow missionary family. It was after the meal. . . . Their three-year-old daughter Beth Ann was playing with our two-year-old Jenna in the front yard. All of a sudden Beth Ann rushed in with a look of panic on her face. "Jenna is in the pool!"

Paul was the first to arrive at the poolside . . . [and] lifted her up out of the water to the extended hands of her mother. Jenna was simultaneously choking, crying, and coughing. She vomited a bellyful of water. I held her as she cried. Denalyn began to weep. I began to sweat.

For the rest of the day I couldn't hold her enough, nor could we thank Beth Ann enough. . . . I still can't thank God enough.

It was a little bit of hangin'. . . . Because of it, I came face to face with one of the underground's slyest agents—the agent of familiarity. . . .

To say that this agent of familiarity breeds contempt is to let him off easy. Contempt is just one of his offspring. He also sires broken hearts, wasted hours, and an insatiable desire for more. . . . He won't take your children, he'll just make you too busy to notice them. His whispers to procrastinate are seductive. There is

Continued

always next summer to coach the team, next month to go to the lake, and next week to teach Johnny how to pray. He'll make you forget that the faces around your table will soon be at tables of their own. Hence, books will go unread, games will go unplayed, hearts will go unnurtured, and opportunities will go ignored. All because the poison of the ordinary has deadened your senses to the magic of the moment. . . .

On a shelf above my desk is a picture of two little girls. They're holding hands and standing in front of a swimming pool, the same pool from which the younger of the two had been pulled only minutes before. I put the picture where I would see it daily so I would remember what God doesn't want me to forget.

And you can bet this time I'm going to remember. I don't want any more hangin'. Not even a little bit.

(From *God Came Near* by Max Lucado)

APPLICATION Make Psalm 103 your prayer. Pray this prayer throughout the day. Maintain an attitude of praise in all your activities.

EXPLORATION Cautions about Forgetting God—Deuteronomy 4:9; 6:10-12; Psalm 9:17; 50:22; Isaiah 17:10; 51:13; Jeremiah 3:21.

And His righteousness to children's children,
18 To such as keep His covenant,
And to those who remember His commandments to do them.

19 The LORD has established His throne in heaven,
And His kingdom rules over all.

20 Bless the LORD, you His angels,
Who excel in strength, who do His word,
Heeding the voice of His word.
21 Bless the LORD, all *you* His hosts,
You ministers of His, who do His pleasure.
22 Bless the LORD, all His works,
In all places of His dominion.

Bless the LORD, O my soul!

PSALM 104

Praise to the Sovereign LORD for His Creation and Providence

Bless the LORD, O my soul!

O LORD my God, You are very great:
You are clothed with honor and majesty,
2 Who cover *Yourself* with light as *with* a garment,
Who stretch out the heavens like a curtain.

3 He lays the beams of His upper chambers in the waters,
Who makes the clouds His chariot,
Who walks on the wings of the wind,
4 Who makes His angels spirits,
His ministers a flame of fire.

5 *You who* laid the foundations of the earth,
So *that* it should not be moved forever,
6 You covered it with the deep as *with* a garment;
The waters stood above the mountains.
7 At Your rebuke they fled;
At the voice of Your thunder they hastened away.
8 They went up over the mountains;
They went down into the valleys,
To the place which You founded for them.
9 You have set a boundary that they may not pass over,
That they may not return to cover the earth.

10 He sends the springs into the valleys;
They flow among the hills.
11 They give drink to every beast of the field;
The wild donkeys quench their thirst.
12 By them the birds of the heavens have their home;
They sing among the branches.
13 He waters the hills from His upper chambers;
The earth is satisfied with the fruit of Your works.

14 He causes the grass to grow for the cattle,
And vegetation for the service of man,
That he may bring forth food from the earth,
15 And wine *that* makes glad the heart of man,
Oil to make *his* face shine,
And bread *which* strengthens man's heart.
16 The trees of the LORD are full *of sap,*
The cedars of Lebanon which He planted,
17 Where the birds make their nests;
The stork has her home in the fir trees.
18 The high hills *are* for the wild goats;
The cliffs are a refuge for the rock badgers.[p]

19 He appointed the moon for seasons;
The sun knows its going down.
20 You make darkness, and it is night,
In which all the beasts of the forest creep about.
21 The young lions roar after their prey,
And seek their food from God.
22 *When* the sun rises, they gather together
And lie down in their dens.
23 Man goes out to his work
And to his labor until the evening.

24 O LORD, how manifold are Your works!
In wisdom You have made them all.
The earth is full of Your possessions—
25 This great and wide sea,
In which *are* innumerable teeming things,
Living things both small and great.
26 There the ships sail about;
There is that Leviathan
Which You have made to play there.

27 These all wait for You,
That You may give *them* their food in due season.
28 *What* You give them they gather in;
You open Your hand, they are filled with good.
29 You hide Your face, they are troubled;
You take away their breath, they die and return to their dust.
30 You send forth Your Spirit, they are created;
And You renew the face of the earth.

31 May the glory of the LORD endure forever;
May the LORD rejoice in His works.
32 He looks on the earth, and it trembles;
He touches the hills, and they smoke.

33 I will sing to the LORD as long as I live;
I will sing praise to my God while I have my being.
34 May my meditation be sweet to Him;
I will be glad in the LORD.

104:18 *p* Or *rock hyrax* (compare Leviticus 11:5)

LIFE LESSON

Psalm 104:1-35

SITUATION This anonymous songwriter appreciated God's creation. God created and sustains the universe.

OBSERVATION The universe bears witness to God's majesty, splendor, and Lordship.

INSPIRATION Look next at the world. Consider the size of it, the variety and complexity of it; think of the three thousand-odd millions who populate it, and of the vast sky above it. What puny figures you and I are, by comparison with the whole planet on which we live! Yet what is this whole mighty planet by comparison to God? "It is he that sitteth upon (above) the circle of the earth, and the inhabitants thereof are as grasshoppers; that stretcheth out the heavens as a curtain, and spreadeth them out as a tent to dwell in" (Isaiah 40:22). The world dwarfs us all, but God dwarfs the world. The world is His footstool, above which He sits secure. . . . Behold your God!

(From *Knowing God* by J. I. Packer)

APPLICATION Take a walk in a park. Gaze out the window at the clouds. Get away from the noise and listen to the sounds of nature. As you enjoy the beauty of creation, thank and praise God for his handiwork.

EXPLORATION God the Creator—Genesis 1–2; Nehemiah 9:6; Job 26:7; 38-39; Psalm 8:3-4; 102:25; Acts 14:15; Hebrews 11:3.

LIFE LESSON

Psalm 105:1-45

SITUATION David reminded the people of God's mighty deeds. God's past miracles encouraged Believers to remain loyal to him.

OBSERVATION By recounting God's work in history, Christians can be encouraged to praise God—because he is trustworthy.

INSPIRATION "In the beginning God *created* the heavens and the earth." It doesn't say, "God *made* the heavens and the earth." Nor does it say that he "Xeroxed" the heavens and the earth. Or "built" or "developed" or "mass-produced." No, the word is "created."

And that one word says a lot. Creating is something far different than constructing. The difference is pretty obvious. Constructing something engages only the hands while creating engages the heart and the soul. . . .

Now, imagine God's creativity. Of all we don't know about the creation, there is one thing we do know—he did it with a smile. He must've had a blast. Painting the stripes on the zebra, hanging the stars in the sky, putting the gold in the sunset. What creativity! Stretching the neck of the giraffe, putting the flutter in the mockingbird's wings, planting the giggle in the hyena.

What a time he had. Like a whistling carpenter in his workshop, he loved every bit of it. He poured himself into the work. . . .

And then, as a finale to a brilliant performance, he made man. With his typical creative flair, he began with a useless mound of dirt and ended up with an invaluable species called a human. A human who had the unique honor to bear the stamp, "in His Image."

At this point in the story one would be tempted to jump and clap. "Bravo!" "Encore!" "Unmatchable!" "Beautiful!"

But the applause would be premature. The Divine Artist has yet to unveil his greatest creation.

As the story unfolds, a devil of a snake feeds man a line and an apple, and gullible Adam swallows them both. This one act of rebellion sets in motion a dramatic and erratic

35 May sinners be consumed from the earth,
And the wicked be no more.

Bless the LORD, O my soul!
Praise the LORD!

PSALM 105

The Eternal Faithfulness of the LORD

Oh, give thanks to the LORD!
Call upon His name;
Make known His deeds among the peoples!
2 Sing to Him, sing psalms to Him;
Talk of all His wondrous works!
3 Glory in His holy name;
Let the hearts of those rejoice who seek the LORD!
4 Seek the LORD and His strength;
Seek His face evermore!
5 Remember His marvelous works which He has done,
His wonders, and the judgments of His mouth,
6 O seed of Abraham His servant,
You children of Jacob, His chosen ones!

7 He *is* the LORD our God;
His judgments *are* in all the earth.
8 He remembers His covenant forever,
The word *which* He commanded, for a thousand generations,
9 *The covenant* which He made with Abraham,
And His oath to Isaac,
10 And confirmed it to Jacob for a statute,
To Israel *as* an everlasting covenant,
11 Saying, "To you I will give the land of Canaan
As the allotment of your inheritance,"
12 When they were few in number,
Indeed very few, and strangers in it.

13 When they went from one nation to another,
From *one* kingdom to another people,
14 He permitted no one to do them wrong;
Yes, He rebuked kings for their sakes,
15 *Saying,* "Do not touch My anointed ones,
And do My prophets no harm."

16 Moreover He called for a famine in the land;
He destroyed all the provision of bread.
17 He sent a man before them—
Joseph—*who* was sold as a slave.
18 They hurt his feet with fetters,
He was laid in irons.
19 Until the time that his word came to pass,
The word of the LORD tested him.
20 The king sent and released him,
The ruler of the people let him go free.
21 He made him lord of his house,

And ruler of all his possessions,
22 To bind his princes at his pleasure,
And teach his elders wisdom.

23 Israel also came into Egypt,
And Jacob dwelt in the land of Ham.
24 He increased His people greatly,
And made them stronger than their enemies.
25 He turned their heart to hate His people,
To deal craftily with His servants.

26 He sent Moses His servant,
And Aaron whom He had chosen.
27 They performed His signs among them,
And wonders in the land of Ham.
28 He sent darkness, and made *it* dark;
And they did not rebel against His word.
29 He turned their waters into blood,
And killed their fish.
30 Their land abounded with frogs,
Even in the chambers of their kings.
31 He spoke, and there came swarms of flies,
And lice in all their territory.
32 He gave them hail for rain,
And flaming fire in their land.
33 He struck their vines also, and their fig trees,
And splintered the trees of their territory.
34 He spoke, and locusts came,
Young locusts without number,
35 And ate up all the vegetation in their land,
And devoured the fruit of their ground.
36 He also destroyed all the firstborn in their land,
The first of all their strength.

37 He also brought them out with silver and gold,
And *there was* none feeble among His tribes.
38 Egypt was glad when they departed,
For the fear of them had fallen upon them.
39 He spread a cloud for a covering,
And fire to give light in the night.
40 *The people* asked, and He brought quail,
And satisfied them with the bread of heaven.
41 He opened the rock, and water gushed out;
It ran in the dry places *like* a river.

42 For He remembered His holy promise,
And Abraham His servant.
43 He brought out His people with joy,
His chosen ones with gladness.
44 He gave them the lands of the Gentiles,
And they inherited the labor of the nations,
45 That they might observe His statutes
And keep His laws.

Praise the LORD!

courtship between God and man. Though the characters and scenes change, the scenario repeats itself endlessly. God, still the compassionate Creator, woos his creation. Man, the creation, alternately reaches out in repentance and runs in rebellion.

It is within this simple script that God's creativity flourishes. If you thought he was imaginative with the sea and stars, just wait until you read what he does to get his creation to listen to him!

For example:

A ninety year old woman gets pregnant.

Another woman turns to salt.

A flood blankets the earth.

A bush burns (but doesn't burn up!)

The Red Sea splits in two.

The walls of Jericho fall.

The sky rains fire.

A donkey talks.

You talk about special effects! But these acts, be they very ingenious, still couldn't compare with what was to come.

Nearing the climax of the story, God, motivated by love and directed by divinity, surprised everyone. He became a man. In an untouchable mystery, he disguised himself as a carpenter and lived in a dusty Judean village. Determined to prove his love for his creation, he walked incognito through his own world. His callused hands touched wounds and his compassionate tongue touched hearts. He became one of us.

(From *No Wonder They Call Him the Savior* by Max Lucado)

APPLICATION Take a blank piece of paper and write "God is faithful" at the top. Then write as many instances as you can remember that show God's faithfulness to you. Use biblical examples and personal experiences. Don't stop until your page is full. Praise God for his faithfulness to you!

EXPLORATION Praise the Faithful God—Psalm 31:21; 57:91; 59:16; 63:3; 86:12; 89:1; 100:4; 108:3; 117:1-2; 138:2.

LIFE LESSON

Psalm 106:1-48

SITUATION Israel's rebellion and divine patience—this common theme in the Old Testament is detailed in Psalm 106.

OBSERVATION Because God forgives us, we can rejoice and sing about it.

INSPIRATION Imagine the exhilaration of a former resident of death row who has just been pardoned by the governor. Condemned to death, he has been forgiven by the state and is released. Instead of waiting execution, he is free to leave and to live. He has been turned from death to life!

Sin drives a wedge in our relationship with God. Our disobedience breaks fellowship and scars our souls. And we sinners stand guilty, awaiting our deserved punishment. Like condemned murderers, we know that the just sentence is death.

But we can be pardoned, forgiven, set free. That's why David exclaims enthusiastically that we are *blessed*.

If you have given your life to Christ and are trusting in him alone for salvation, your transgressions are forgiven, your sins are covered by his blood. Thank God for his love and justice, and rejoice in your freedom.
(From *On Eagles' Wings* by Dave Veerman)

APPLICATION Confess your sins to God. Accept his forgiveness through Jesus Christ. Respond to his mercy with heart-filled praise. Find a new way to worship God by singing a song or writing a poem.

EXPLORATION God's Forgiveness—Psalm 78:38; 103:3; Isaiah 43:25; Joel 2:13; Micah 7:18-19; Ephesians 1:7; Colossians 1:13-14; 1 John 1:9.

PSALM 106

Joy in Forgiveness of Israel's Sins

Praise the LORD!

Oh, give thanks to the LORD, for *He is* good!
For His mercy *endures* forever.

2 Who can utter the mighty acts of the LORD?
Who can declare all His praise?
3 Blessed *are* those who keep justice,
And he who does[q] righteousness at all times!

4 Remember me, O LORD, with the favor *You have toward*
Your people.
Oh, visit me with Your salvation,
5 That I may see the benefit of Your chosen ones,
That I may rejoice in the gladness of Your nation,
That I may glory with Your inheritance.

6 We have sinned with our fathers,
We have committed iniquity,
We have done wickedly.
7 Our fathers in Egypt did not understand Your wonders;
They did not remember the multitude of Your mercies,
But rebelled by the sea—the Red Sea.

8 Nevertheless He saved them for His name's sake,
That He might make His mighty power known.
9 He rebuked the Red Sea also, and it dried up;
So He led them through the depths,
As through the wilderness.
10 He saved them from the hand of him who hated *them*,
And redeemed them from the hand of the enemy.
11 The waters covered their enemies;
There was not one of them left.
12 Then they believed His words;
They sang His praise.

13 They soon forgot His works;
They did not wait for His counsel,
14 But lusted exceedingly in the wilderness,
And tested God in the desert.
15 And He gave them their request,
But sent leanness into their soul.

16 When they envied Moses in the camp,
And Aaron the saint of the LORD,
17 The earth opened up and swallowed Dathan,
And covered the faction of Abiram.
18 A fire was kindled in their company;
The flame burned up the wicked.

106:3 [q] Septuagint, Syriac, Targum, and Vulgate read *those who do.*

19 They made a calf in Horeb,
And worshiped the molded image.
20 Thus they changed their glory
Into the image of an ox that eats grass.
21 They forgot God their Savior,
Who had done great things in Egypt,
22 Wondrous works in the land of Ham,
Awesome things by the Red Sea.
23 Therefore He said that He would destroy them,
Had not Moses His chosen one stood before
Him in the breach,
To turn away His wrath, lest He destroy *them.*

24 Then they despised the pleasant land;
They did not believe His word,
25 But complained in their tents,
And did not heed the voice of the LORD.
26 Therefore He raised His hand *in an oath*
against them,
To overthrow them in the wilderness,
27 To overthrow their descendants among
the nations,
And to scatter them in the lands.

28 They joined themselves also to Baal of Peor,
And ate sacrifices made to the dead.
29 Thus they provoked *Him* to anger with
their deeds,
And the plague broke out among them.
30 Then Phinehas stood up and intervened,
And the plague was stopped.
31 And that was accounted to him
for righteousness
To all generations forevermore.

32 They angered *Him* also at the waters of strife,[r]
So that it went ill with Moses on account
of them;
33 Because they rebelled against His Spirit,
So that he spoke rashly with his lips.

34 They did not destroy the peoples,
Concerning whom the LORD had
commanded them,
35 But they mingled with the Gentiles
And learned their works;
36 They served their idols,
Which became a snare to them.
37 They even sacrificed their sons
And their daughters to demons,
38 And shed innocent blood,
The blood of their sons and daughters,
Whom they sacrificed to the idols of Canaan;
And the land was polluted with blood.
39 Thus they were defiled by their own works,
And played the harlot by their own deeds.

40 Therefore the wrath of the LORD was kindled
against His people,
So that He abhorred His own inheritance.
41 And He gave them into the hand of
the Gentiles,
And those who hated them ruled over them.
42 Their enemies also oppressed them,
And they were brought into subjection
under their hand.
43 Many times He delivered them;
But they rebelled in their counsel,
And were brought low for their iniquity.
44 Nevertheless He regarded their affliction,
When He heard their cry;
45 And for their sake He remembered
His covenant,
And relented according to the multitude of
His mercies.
46 He also made them to be pitied
By all those who carried them
away captive.

47 Save us, O LORD our God,
And gather us from among the Gentiles,
To give thanks to Your holy name,
To triumph in Your praise.

48 Blessed *be* the LORD God of Israel
From everlasting to everlasting!
And let all the people say, "Amen!"

Praise the LORD!

Book Five: Psalms 107—150

PSALM 107

Thanksgiving to the LORD for His Great Works of Deliverance

Oh, give thanks to the LORD, for *He is* good!
For His mercy *endures* forever.
2 Let the redeemed of the LORD say *so,*
Whom He has redeemed from the hand
of the enemy,
3 And gathered out of the lands,

106:32 [r] Or *Meribah*

LIFE LESSON

Psalm 107:1-43

SITUATION Wanderers, prisoners, sick and storm-tossed people all suffered but were saved when they called upon God. This psalm tells why people should give thanks and praise to their Savior and Deliverer.

OBSERVATION God will rescue us from trials if we are faithful to ask him for help.

INSPIRATION "If we confess our sins, He is faithful and just to forgive us our sins and to cleanse us from all unrighteousness." How wonderful is this provision! God knows our weaknesses, and Christ's death for our sins included the sins we commit in the new life, as well as those before we came to Him for our salvation.

. . . He is faithful, that is, He doesn't break His promise. And His promise to His Son is that all who receive His Son as Savior become God's children, adopted into His own family. When a child does wrong, he isn't kicked out of the family, though he may be disciplined. . . . He is faithful to His promise to His Son and to us to forgive us when we sin.

. . . To be just is to be fair. Is it really fair of God to forgive us no matter what sins we have committed? Don't we have to be good enough to be saved?

From the east and from the west,
From the north and from the south.

4 They wandered in the wilderness in a desolate way;
They found no city to dwell in.
5 Hungry and thirsty,
Their soul fainted in them.
6 Then they cried out to the LORD in their trouble,
And He delivered them out of their distresses.
7 And He led them forth by the right way,
That they might go to a city for a dwelling place.
8 Oh, that *men* would give thanks to the LORD *for* His goodness,
And *for* His wonderful works to the children of men!
9 For He satisfies the longing soul,
And fills the hungry soul with goodness.

10 Those who sat in darkness and in the shadow of death,
Bound in affliction and irons—
11 Because they rebelled against the words of God,
And despised the counsel of the Most High,
12 Therefore He brought down their heart with labor;
They fell down, and *there was* none to help.
13 Then they cried out to the LORD in their trouble,
And He saved them out of their distresses.
14 He brought them out of darkness and the shadow of death,
And broke their chains in pieces.
15 Oh, that *men* would give thanks to the LORD *for* His goodness,
And *for* His wonderful works to the children of men!
16 For He has broken the gates of bronze,
And cut the bars of iron in two.

17 Fools, because of their transgression,
And because of their iniquities, were afflicted.
18 Their soul abhorred all manner of food,
And they drew near to the gates of death.
19 Then they cried out to the LORD in their trouble,
And He saved them out of their distresses.
20 He sent His word and healed them,
And delivered *them* from their destructions.
21 Oh, that *men* would give thanks to the LORD *for* His goodness,
And *for* His wonderful works to the children of men!
22 Let them sacrifice the sacrifices of thanksgiving,
And declare His works with rejoicing.

23 Those who go down to the sea in ships,
Who do business on great waters,
24 They see the works of the LORD,
And His wonders in the deep.
25 For He commands and raises the stormy wind,
Which lifts up the waves of the sea.
26 They mount up to the heavens,
They go down again to the depths;
Their soul melts because of trouble.
27 They reel to and fro, and stagger like a drunken man,

And are at their wits' end.
28 Then they cry out to the LORD in their trouble,
And He brings them out of their distresses.
29 He calms the storm,
So that its waves are still.
30 Then they are glad because they are quiet;
So He guides them to their desired haven.
31 Oh, that *men* would give thanks to the LORD *for* His goodness,
And *for* His wonderful works to the children of men!
32 Let them exalt Him also in the assembly of the people,
And praise Him in the company of the elders.

33 He turns rivers into a wilderness,
And the watersprings into dry ground;
34 A fruitful land into barrenness,
For the wickedness of those who dwell in it.
35 He turns a wilderness into pools of water,
And dry land into watersprings.
36 There He makes the hungry dwell,
That they may establish a city for a dwelling place,
37 And sow fields and plant vineyards,
That they may yield a fruitful harvest.
38 He also blesses them, and they multiply greatly;
And He does not let their cattle decrease.

39 When they are diminished and brought low
Through oppression, affliction and sorrow,
40 He pours contempt on princes,
And causes them to wander in the wilderness
where there is no way;
41 Yet He sets the poor on high, far from affliction,
And makes *their* families like a flock.
42 The righteous see *it* and rejoice,
And all iniquity stops its mouth.

43 Whoever *is* wise will observe these *things*,
And they will understand the lovingkindness of the LORD.

PSALM 108

Assurance of God's Victory over Enemies

A Song. A Psalm of David.

O God, my heart is steadfast;
I will sing and give praise, even with my glory.
2 Awake, lute and harp!
I will awaken the dawn.
3 I will praise You, O LORD, among the peoples,
And I will sing praises to You among the nations.
4 For Your mercy *is* great above the heavens,
And Your truth *reaches* to the clouds.

5 Be exalted, O God, above the heavens,
And Your glory above all the earth;

No, I hope this is very clear to you by now—no one is good enough to claim a right to heaven. Christ died for us to make us good in the sight of God. Because of what Christ did for us in dying on the cross and rising again from the dead, God has taken away all our guilt. The Scriptures declare, "As far as the east is from the west, so far has He removed our transgressions from us."

Though we had no right whatever, Christ has made a road to heaven for us, and He takes us with Him right into the throne room of God, right into His holy presence. There Christ presents each of us to His Father as a new child of God, as Christ's new brother or sister. God welcomes us with warmth and excitement and joy as new members of His family.

(From *Next Steps for New Christians* by Kenneth Taylor)

APPLICATION Are any of the trials in this psalm yours? Are you without money for food? Are you discouraged? Miserable? In jail? In trouble? Find your answer in the psalm, too. Let God save you, give you peace, and work a miracle in your life.

EXPLORATION God's Faithfulness—Deuteronomy 7:9; 1 Kings 8:56; Lamentations 3:22-23.

6 That Your beloved may be delivered,
Save *with* Your right hand, and hear me.

7 God has spoken in His holiness:
"I will rejoice;
I will divide Shechem
And measure out the Valley of Succoth.
8 Gilead *is* Mine; Manasseh *is* Mine;
Ephraim also *is* the helmet for My head;
Judah *is* My lawgiver.
9 Moab *is* My washpot;
Over Edom I will cast My shoe;
Over Philistia I will triumph."

10 Who will bring me *into* the strong city?
Who will lead me to Edom?
11 *Is it* not *You,* O God, *who* cast us off?
And *You,* O God, *who* did not go out with our armies?
12 Give us help from trouble,
For the help of man is useless.
13 Through God we will do valiantly,
For *it is* He *who* shall tread down our enemies.[s]

PSALM 109

Plea for Judgment of False Accusers

To the Chief Musician. A Psalm of David.

Do not keep silent,
O God of my praise!
2 For the mouth of the wicked and the mouth of the deceitful
Have opened against me;
They have spoken against me with a lying tongue.
3 They have also surrounded me with words of hatred,
And fought against me without a cause.
4 In return for my love they are my accusers,
But I *give myself to* prayer.
5 Thus they have rewarded me evil for good,
And hatred for my love.

6 Set a wicked man over him,
And let an accuser[t] stand at his right hand.
7 When he is judged, let him be found guilty,
And let his prayer become sin.
8 Let his days be few,
And let another take his office.
9 Let his children be fatherless,
And his wife a widow.
10 Let his children continually be vagabonds, and beg;
Let them seek *their bread*[u] also from their desolate places.

LIFE LESSON

Psalms 108:1–109:31

SITUATION Psalm 57:7-11 and Psalm 60:5-12 were combined to form Psalm 108. David celebrated his victory. He knew that without God, he would have been defeated.

OBSERVATION With God on our side, we can do more than we think possible. God provides victory. We ought to praise God in both victory and defeat.

INSPIRATION Christians are to rejoice. To do that, you need only to think of the great things God has done for you. Then we are told not to be anxious, but in our prayers to make our requests known to God. In your biggest problems, you have One that you can go to; and before Him you can pour out your heart with the assurance that He will not leave you without an answer to that great problem. Then we are to fill our minds with those things that are good. They are mentioned in the Scriptures as being things that are true, honorable, just, pure, lovely, of good report, and of virtue. It is upon these things that we are to think. Live positively, not negatively. Once you learn that secret, God will have given you the victory.

(From *Day by Day with Billy Graham* by Joan W. Brown)

APPLICATION When were you worried last? When you received relief, did you praise God? Next time God gives you a victory, give him praise.

EXPLORATION Victory—
1 Chronicles 18:13; 2 Chronicles 25:14; 1 Samuel 4:5-8; Psalm 98:1-3; Ephesians 4:8; Colossians 2:15; Hebrews 11:32-35; 1 John 3:8-9; 4:4; 5:4.

108:13 [s] Compare verses 6–13 with 60:5–12
109:6 [t] Hebrew *satan*
109:10 [u] Following Masoretic Text and Targum; Septuagint and Vulgate read *be cast out.*

11 Let the creditor seize all that he has,
And let strangers plunder his labor.
12 Let there be none to extend mercy to him,
Nor let there be any to favor his
fatherless children.
13 Let his posterity be cut off,
And in the generation following let their name
be blotted out.

14 Let the iniquity of his fathers be remembered
before the LORD,
And let not the sin of his mother be
blotted out.
15 Let them be continually before the LORD,
That He may cut off the memory of them
from the earth;
16 Because he did not remember to show mercy,
But persecuted the poor and needy man,
That he might even slay the broken in heart.
17 As he loved cursing, so let it come to him;
As he did not delight in blessing, so let it
be far from him.
18 As he clothed himself with cursing as with
his garment,
So let it enter his body like water,
And like oil into his bones.
19 Let it be to him like the garment which
covers him,
And for a belt with which he girds
himself continually.
20 *Let* this *be* the LORD's reward to my accusers,
And to those who speak evil against
my person.

21 But You, O GOD the Lord,
Deal with me for Your name's sake;
Because Your mercy *is* good, deliver me.
22 For I *am* poor and needy,
And my heart is wounded within me.
23 I am gone like a shadow when it lengthens;
I am shaken off like a locust.
24 My knees are weak through fasting,
And my flesh is feeble from lack of fatness.
25 I also have become a reproach to them;
When they look at me, they shake their heads.

26 Help me, O LORD my God!
Oh, save me according to Your mercy,
27 That they may know that this *is* Your hand—
That You, LORD, have done it!
28 Let them curse, but You bless;
When they arise, let them be ashamed,
But let Your servant rejoice.
29 Let my accusers be clothed with shame,
And let them cover themselves with their own
disgrace as with a mantle.

30 I will greatly praise the LORD with my mouth;
Yes, I will praise Him among the multitude.
31 For He shall stand at the right hand of
the poor,
To save *him* from those who condemn him.

PSALM 110

Announcement of the Messiah's Reign

A Psalm of David.

The LORD said to my Lord,
"Sit at My right hand,
Till I make Your enemies Your footstool."
2 The LORD shall send the rod of Your strength
out of Zion.
Rule in the midst of Your enemies!

3 Your people *shall be* volunteers
In the day of Your power;
In the beauties of holiness, from the womb of
the morning,
You have the dew of Your youth.
4 The LORD has sworn
And will not relent,
"You *are* a priest forever
According to the order of Melchizedek."
5 The Lord *is* at Your right hand;
He shall execute kings in the day of His wrath.
6 He shall judge among the nations,
He shall fill *the places* with dead bodies,
He shall execute the heads of many countries.
7 He shall drink of the brook by the wayside;
Therefore He shall lift up the head.

PSALM 111

Praise to God for His Faithfulness and Justice

Praise the LORD!

I will praise the LORD with *my* whole heart,
In the assembly of the upright and
in the congregation.

2 The works of the LORD *are* great,
Studied by all who have pleasure in them.
3 His work *is* honorable and glorious,
And His righteousness endures forever.
4 He has made His wonderful works
to be remembered;

LIFE LESSON

Psalms 110:1–112:10

SITUATION Although the Jews lived near nations that worshiped idols, God reminded Israel to worship him only. God promised to send the Messiah, indicating that full deliverance was yet to come. Psalms 111 and 112 begin each phrase with a successive letter of the Hebrew alphabet.

OBSERVATION Praise the true God! Reading Scripture helps us know God better. When we know him better, we are equipped to worship him more earnestly.

INSPIRATION The apostle Paul points out in Romans 1 that everyone knows that there is a God. His existence is revealed in creation; creation demands a Creator, and design demands a Designer. And it is revealed in conscience; we all have an innate consciousness of right and wrong. . . .

The heathen do not *want* to retain the true God in their knowledge. They know that belief in such a God would cramp their life-styles. So they turn to idolatry. They make images of people, birds, animals, and snakes and then worship them. Since each successive image represents a downward step in the scale of creation, it follows that they feel less and less responsible to live clean lives. If their god is a snake, it doesn't really matter how they live. This explains the close link between idolatry and immorality. Idols made by human beings do not make moral demands on their worshipers. . . .

Belief determines behavior. That is why it is so important to have true views of God. The higher our thoughts of Him, the more our lives will be exalted, holy, and glorious.

(From *Alone in Majesty* by William MacDonald)

APPLICATION Who is God? Answer the question by making a list of God's attributes from these psalms. Circle three from your list. Over the next three days, reflect on one attribute each day. As the day goes by, discover how this reality about God affects you.

EXPLORATION Knowing God—Hosea 6:3; Matthew 22:29; John 4:24; 7:16-17; 8:31-2; Romans 1:21-25; Ephesians 4:14-15, 18; 2 Peter 3:18.

The LORD *is* gracious and full of compassion.
5 He has given food to those who fear Him;
He will ever be mindful of His covenant.
6 He has declared to His people the power of
His works,
In giving them the heritage of the nations.

7 The works of His hands *are* verity and justice;
All His precepts *are* sure.
8 They stand fast forever and ever,
And are done in truth and uprightness.
9 He has sent redemption to His people;
He has commanded His covenant forever:
Holy and awesome *is* His name.
10 The fear of the LORD *is* the beginning of wisdom;
A good understanding have all those who do
His commandments.
His praise endures forever.

PSALM 112

The Blessed State of the Righteous

Praise the LORD!

Blessed *is* the man *who* fears the LORD,
Who delights greatly in His commandments.
2 His descendants will be mighty on earth;
The generation of the upright will be blessed.
3 Wealth and riches *will be* in his house,
And his righteousness endures forever.
4 Unto the upright there arises light in
the darkness;
He is gracious, and full of compassion,
and righteous.
5 A good man deals graciously and lends;
He will guide his affairs with discretion.
6 Surely he will never be shaken;
The righteous will be in everlasting remembrance.
7 He will not be afraid of evil tidings;
His heart is steadfast, trusting in the LORD.
8 His heart *is* established;
He will not be afraid,
Until he sees *his desire* upon his enemies.

9 He has dispersed abroad,
He has given to the poor;
His righteousness endures forever;
His horn will be exalted with honor.
10 The wicked will see *it* and be grieved;
He will gnash his teeth and melt away;
The desire of the wicked shall perish.

PSALM 113

The Majesty and Condescension of God

Praise the LORD!

Praise, O servants of the LORD,
Praise the name of the LORD!
2 Blessed be the name of the LORD
From this time forth and forevermore!
3 From the rising of the sun to
its going down
The LORD's name *is* to be praised.

4 The LORD *is* high above all nations,
His glory above the heavens.
5 Who *is* like the LORD our God,
Who dwells on high,
6 Who humbles Himself to behold
The things that are in the heavens and
in the earth?

7 He raises the poor out of the dust,
And lifts the needy out of the ash heap,
8 That He may seat *him* with princes—
With the princes of His people.
9 He grants the barren woman a home,
Like a joyful mother of children.

Praise the LORD!

PSALM 114

The Power of God in His Deliverance of Israel

When Israel went out of Egypt,
The house of Jacob from a people of
strange language,
2 Judah became His sanctuary,
And Israel His dominion.

3 The sea saw *it* and fled;
Jordan turned back.
4 The mountains skipped like rams,
The little hills like lambs.
5 What ails you, O sea, that you fled?
O Jordan, *that* you turned back?
6 O mountains, *that* you skipped like rams?
O little hills, like lambs?

7 Tremble, O earth, at the presence
of the Lord,
At the presence of the God of Jacob,
8 Who turned the rock *into* a pool of water,
The flint into a fountain of waters.

LIFE LESSON

Psalms 113:1–115:18

SITUATION The next six psalms were used during the Passover, the Feast of Tabernacles, and other traditional Jewish festivals.

OBSERVATION Although the Israelites set aside one day a week to revere God, they used many Scriptures to encourage them to have a thankful, loving attitude toward God.

INSPIRATION I had no problem recognizing the command to worship. My problem was understanding and obeying. . . . For years—too many years—I was content to let my local church define "worship" for me, accepting worship as practiced by my adult role models.

The word was used almost exclusively to refer to our Sunday morning services, which seemed to mark the last day of the week—an afterthought—rather than the first. There was a specific time and a place for worship. It happened on Sundays, it happened from 11:00 A.M. to noon, and it happened in "the sanctuary."

As time passed, I became vaguely uneasy. Surely there had to be more to it than I and my role models understood.

Eventually, God's patient and quickening Spirit moved me from a vague and passive acknowledgment of worship to a proactive pilgrimage of discovery. I began to explore worship in the Bible and to mull over the writing of others who were on this same quest long before I was. . . .

I saw that real worship is much more than a Sunday experience. First as an intellectual acknowledgment and then sinking eighteen inches down into my heart as a deep-seated experience: Worship occurs throughout the week in a variety of ways. . . .

So what? Does it make any difference?

For an answer, look at the people around you. Unless you live in a Christian cocoon—and even there you are probably not exempt—you are surrounded by those for whom high times bring hedonism, low times bring languidness, and in-between times bring the blahs. Offend them, and whether they're on a high, a low, or an in-between, out comes profanity.

Continued

Now consider David, in the Old Testament. Whether he was on a high, a low, or an in-between, out came psalms! From boyhood to mature adult, it was the same. While not ignoring his well-chronicled humanity, observe that worship permeated his life and overflowed from his heart, saturating his lifestyle. No wonder God considered him a man after His own heart (Acts 13:22)!

In return, God took this man whose lifestyle of worship separated him from the ordinary, run-of-the-mill lifestyles of those around him and gave him a significant, fulfilling leadership role in His plan for Israel. (From *Lifestyle Worship* by John Garmo)

APPLICATION Learn to continually praise God. Praise God while you do dishes and while you drive your car. Fill everyday moments with praise.

EXPLORATION Unceasing Praise—Psalm 71:14; Romans 12:1; Colossians 3:17; 1 Thessalonians 5:16-18; Hebrews 13:15; Revelation 4:8.

PSALM 115

The Futility of Idols and the Trustworthiness of God

Not unto us, O LORD, not unto us,
But to Your name give glory,
Because of Your mercy,
Because of Your truth.
2 Why should the Gentiles say,
"So where *is* their God?"

3 But our God *is* in heaven;
He does whatever He pleases.
4 Their idols *are* silver and gold,
The work of men's hands.
5 They have mouths, but they do not speak;
Eyes they have, but they do not see;
6 They have ears, but they do not hear;
Noses they have, but they do not smell;
7 They have hands, but they do not handle;
Feet they have, but they do not walk;
Nor do they mutter through their throat.
8 Those who make them are like them;
So is everyone who trusts in them.

9 O Israel, trust in the LORD;
He *is* their help and their shield.
10 O house of Aaron, trust in the LORD;
He *is* their help and their shield.
11 You who fear the LORD, trust in the LORD;
He *is* their help and their shield.

12 The LORD has been mindful of *us;*
He will bless us;
He will bless the house of Israel;
He will bless the house of Aaron.
13 He will bless those who fear the LORD,
Both small and great.

14 May the LORD give you increase
more and more,
You and your children.
15 *May* you *be* blessed by the LORD,
Who made heaven and earth.

16 The heaven, *even* the heavens, *are* the LORD's;
But the earth He has given to the
children of men.
17 The dead do not praise the LORD,
Nor any who go down into silence.
18 But we will bless the LORD
From this time forth and forevermore.

Praise the LORD!

PSALM 116

Thanksgiving for Deliverance from Death

I love the LORD, because He has heard
My voice *and* my supplications.
2 Because He has inclined His ear to me,
Therefore I will call *upon Him* as long as I live.

3 The pains of death surrounded me,
And the pangs of Sheol laid hold of me;
I found trouble and sorrow.
4 Then I called upon the name of the LORD:
"O LORD, I implore You, deliver my soul!"

5 Gracious *is* the LORD, and righteous;
Yes, our God *is* merciful.
6 The LORD preserves the simple;
I was brought low, and He saved me.
7 Return to your rest, O my soul,
For the LORD has dealt bountifully with you.

8 For You have delivered my soul from death,
My eyes from tears,
And my feet from falling.
9 I will walk before the LORD
In the land of the living.
10 I believed, therefore I spoke,
"I am greatly afflicted."
11 I said in my haste,
"All men *are* liars."

12 What shall I render to the LORD
For all His benefits toward me?
13 I will take up the cup of salvation,
And call upon the name of the LORD.
14 I will pay my vows to the LORD
Now in the presence of all His people.

15 Precious in the sight of the LORD
Is the death of His saints.

16 O LORD, truly I *am* Your servant;
I *am* Your servant, the son of
Your maidservant;
You have loosed my bonds.
17 I will offer to You the sacrifice of thanksgiving,
And will call upon the name of the LORD.

18 I will pay my vows to the LORD
Now in the presence of all His people,
19 In the courts of the LORD's house,
In the midst of you, O Jerusalem.

Praise the LORD!

LIFE LESSON

Psalms 116:1–117:2

SITUATION After a close call with death, this unknown psalmist thanked God for answering his prayers and praised God for his deliverance.

OBSERVATION Praise should be the natural result of answered prayer.

INSPIRATION Worshiping in spirit is the opposite of worshiping in merely external ways. It is the opposite of empty formalism and traditionalism. Worshiping in truth is the opposite of worship based on an inadequate view of God. Worship must have heart and head. Worship must engage emotions and thought.

Truth without emotion produces dead orthodoxy and a church full (or half-full) of artificial admirers (like people who write generic anniversary cards for a living). On the other hand, emotion without truth produces empty frenzy and cultivates shallow people who refuse the discipline of rigorous thought. But true worship comes from people who are deeply emotional and who love deep and sound doctrine. Strong affections for God rooted in truth are the bone and marrow of biblical worship.

Perhaps we can tie things together with this picture: The fuel of worship is the truth of God, the furnace of worship is the spirit of man, and the heat of worship is the vital affections of reverence, contrition, trust, gratitude, and joy.

But there is something missing from this picture. There is furnace, fuel and heat, but no *fire*. The fuel of truth in the furnace of our spirit does not automatically produce the heat of worship. There must be ignition and fire. This is the Holy Spirit. . . .

Now we can complete our picture. The fuel of worship is a true vision of the greatness of God; the fire that makes the fuel burn white-hot is the quickening of the Holy Spirit; the furnace made alive and warm by the flame of the truth is our renewed spirit; and the resulting heat of our affections is powerful worship, pushing its way out in confessions, longings, acclamations, tears, songs, shouts, bowed heads, lifted hands and obedient lives.

(From *Desiring God* by John Piper)

Continued

APPLICATION Have you ever been in a desperate situation? Did you ever thank God for saving you? It is never too late. Thank him. If you are at a loss for words, read this psalm as your prayer to God.

EXPLORATION Thankfulness —2 Chronicles 7:3; Psalm 8:2; 30:11-12; 107:31-32; Luke 17:15-16; 1 Corinthians 15:56-57; 2 Corinthians 1:10-11; Ephesians 5:19-20.

PSALM 117

Let All Peoples Praise the LORD

Praise the LORD, all you Gentiles!
Laud Him, all you peoples!
2 For His merciful kindness is great toward us,
And the truth of the LORD *endures* forever.

Praise the LORD!

PSALM 118

Praise to God for His Everlasting Mercy

Oh, give thanks to the LORD, for *He is* good!
For His mercy *endures* forever.

2 Let Israel now say,
"His mercy *endures* forever."
3 Let the house of Aaron now say,
"His mercy *endures* forever."
4 Let those who fear the LORD now say,
"His mercy *endures* forever."

5 I called on the LORD in distress;
The LORD answered me *and set me* in a broad place.
6 The LORD *is* on my side;
I will not fear.
What can man do to me?
7 The LORD is for me among those who help me;
Therefore I shall see *my desire* on those who hate me.
8 *It is* better to trust in the LORD
Than to put confidence in man.
9 *It is* better to trust in the LORD
Than to put confidence in princes.

10 All nations surrounded me,
But in the name of the LORD I will destroy them.
11 They surrounded me,
Yes, they surrounded me;
But in the name of the LORD I will destroy them.
12 They surrounded me like bees;
They were quenched like a fire of thorns;
For in the name of the LORD I will destroy them.
13 You pushed me violently, that I might fall,
But the LORD helped me.
14 The LORD *is* my strength and song,
And He has become my salvation.[v]

15 The voice of rejoicing and salvation
Is in the tents of the righteous;
The right hand of the LORD does valiantly.
16 The right hand of the LORD is exalted;
The right hand of the LORD does valiantly.

118:14 [v] Compare Exodus 15:2

17 I shall not die, but live,
And declare the works of the LORD.
18 The LORD has chastened me severely,
But He has not given me over to death.

19 Open to me the gates of righteousness;
I will go through them,
And I will praise the LORD.
20 This is the gate of the LORD,
Through which the righteous shall enter.

21 I will praise You,
For You have answered me,
And have become my salvation.

22 The stone *which* the builders rejected
Has become the chief cornerstone.
23 This was the LORD's doing;
It *is* marvelous in our eyes.
24 This *is* the day the LORD has made;
We will rejoice and be glad in it.

25 Save now, I pray, O LORD;
O LORD, I pray, send now prosperity.
26 Blessed *is* he who comes in the name of the LORD!
We have blessed you from the house of the LORD.
27 God *is* the LORD,
And He has given us light;
Bind the sacrifice with cords to the horns of the altar.
28 You *are* my God, and I will praise You;
You are my God, I will exalt You.

29 Oh, give thanks to the LORD, for *He is* good!
For His mercy *endures* forever.

PSALM 119

Meditations on the Excellencies of the Word of God

א ALEPH

Blessed *are* the undefiled in the way,
Who walk in the law of the LORD!
2 Blessed *are* those who keep His testimonies,
Who seek Him with the whole heart!
3 They also do no iniquity;
They walk in His ways.
4 You have commanded *us*
To keep Your precepts diligently.
5 Oh, that my ways were directed
To keep Your statutes!
6 Then I would not be ashamed,
When I look into all Your commandments.
7 I will praise You with uprightness of heart,
When I learn Your righteous judgments.

LIFE LESSON

Psalm 118:1-29

SITUATION The psalmist understood that in the midst of calamity, God was with him. God promised to guard and cherish his people forever.

OBSERVATION We can live in assurance and calm. Despite troubles around us, if we love and trust God, he will be with us. We have nothing to fear if we put our trust in our Guardian.

INSPIRATION We have the assurance that in the storms of life today, Jesus Himself will be standing just outside the door waiting to be invited in. He is waiting to share a meal with us, waiting to share our sorrows, to renew our courage, to come in and talk intimately.

We are not alone. We never shall be. He has to be there; all we need do is open the door to Him. What is your need today? Do you need comfort in your personal trials? Christ is waiting. Do you need forgiveness for your sins? He is knocking. Do you need to make a new commitment to serve God with your life? Whatever your spiritual need, right now Christ is knocking at the door of your heart. He is Lord of the universe, and He wants to be Lord of your life as well.

(From *Storm Warning* by Billy Graham)

APPLICATION What will you depend on today for your needs? Although you may be tempted to trust earthly means more than God, have more confidence in God than anything else.

EXPLORATION Assurance—Psalm 46:1-3; Isaiah 43:1-7; Jeremiah 1:6-8; 1 Corinthians 2:4.

Life Lesson

Psalm 119:1-176

SITUATION This testimony exalted the Word of God—the complete and perfect standard of truth, values, reality, and behavior.

OBSERVATION God's Word is wholly sufficient for godly living. By grasping its powerful message, God's children can be pure.

INSPIRATION We need sound doctrine. The Spirit of holiness is also the Spirit of truth. Truth and righteousness go together. . . .

Why? Why is sound doctrine necessary for sanctification? For real sanctification to occur in the Christian life at least three absolute changes are necessary. There must be a change in our consciousness. There must be a change in our convictions. There must be a change in our conscience. Consciousness, conviction, and conscience—these three are all vital to our sanctification.

Consciousness involves knowledge. Before we can willfully do what God commands and what pleases Him, we must first understand what it is that God requires. From the law comes a knowledge of sin. Also from the law comes a knowledge of righteousness.

A person could "accidentally" obey the law without doing so consciously. But such an action would have no moral virtue to it. Suppose a man enjoys driving his car at fifty miles an hour. It pleases him to ride at that rate of speed. He drives his car at fifty miles an hour in fifty-five-mile-per-hour zones and in fifteen-mile-per-hour zones. When he drives in the fifty-five-mile-per-hour zone, he is within the speed limit. He is obeying the law. But when he goes fifty in a fifteen-mile-per-hour-zone, he is a menace to those around him.

8 I will keep Your statutes;
Oh, do not forsake me utterly!

ב Beth

9 How can a young man cleanse his way?
By taking heed according to Your word.
10 With my whole heart I have sought You;
Oh, let me not wander from Your commandments!
11 Your word I have hidden in my heart,
That I might not sin against You.
12 Blessed *are* You, O Lord!
Teach me Your statutes.
13 With my lips I have declared
All the judgments of Your mouth.
14 I have rejoiced in the way of Your testimonies,
As *much as* in all riches.
15 I will meditate on Your precepts,
And contemplate Your ways.
16 I will delight myself in Your statutes;
I will not forget Your word.

ג Gimel

17 Deal bountifully with Your servant,
That I may live and keep Your word.
18 Open my eyes, that I may see
Wondrous things from Your law.
19 I *am* a stranger in the earth;
Do not hide Your commandments from me.
20 My soul breaks with longing
For Your judgments at all times.
21 You rebuke the proud—the cursed,
Who stray from Your commandments.
22 Remove from me reproach and contempt,
For I have kept Your testimonies.
23 Princes also sit *and* speak against me,
But Your servant meditates on Your statutes.
24 Your testimonies also *are* my delight
And my counselors.

ד Daleth

25 My soul clings to the dust;
Revive me according to Your word.
26 I have declared my ways, and You answered me;
Teach me Your statutes.
27 Make me understand the way of Your precepts;
So shall I meditate on Your wonderful works.
28 My soul melts from heaviness;
Strengthen me according to Your word.
29 Remove from me the way of lying,
And grant me Your law graciously.
30 I have chosen the way of truth;
Your judgments I have laid *before me.*

31 I cling to Your testimonies;
O LORD, do not put me to shame!
32 I will run the course of Your commandments,
For You shall enlarge my heart.

ה HE

33 Teach me, O LORD, the way of Your statutes,
And I shall keep it *to* the end.
34 Give me understanding, and I shall keep Your law;
Indeed, I shall observe it with *my* whole heart.
35 Make me walk in the path of Your commandments,
For I delight in it.
36 Incline my heart to Your testimonies,
And not to covetousness.
37 Turn away my eyes from looking at worthless things,
And revive me in Your way.[w]
38 Establish Your word to Your servant,
Who *is devoted* to fearing You.
39 Turn away my reproach which I dread,
For Your judgments *are* good.
40 Behold, I long for Your precepts;
Revive me in Your righteousness.

ו WAW

41 Let Your mercies come also to me, O LORD—
Your salvation according to Your word.
42 So shall I have an answer for him who reproaches me,
For I trust in Your word.
43 And take not the word of truth utterly out of my mouth,
For I have hoped in Your ordinances.
44 So shall I keep Your law continually,
Forever and ever.
45 And I will walk at liberty,
For I seek Your precepts.
46 I will speak of Your testimonies also before kings,
And will not be ashamed.
47 And I will delight myself in Your commandments,
Which I love.
48 My hands also I will lift up to Your commandments,
Which I love,
And I will meditate on Your statutes.

ז ZAYIN

49 Remember the word to Your servant,
Upon which You have caused me to hope.
50 This *is* my comfort in my affliction,
For Your word has given me life.
51 The proud have me in great derision,
Yet I do not turn aside from Your law.
52 I remembered Your judgments of old, O LORD,
And have comforted myself.

Suppose our mythical driver systematically refuses to look at speed limit signs. He averts his gaze from any sign that even appears to mark a speed limit. He keeps himself purposely unconscious of speed limits. At times he "happens" to obey the law, but purely by coincidence. If the man wants to achieve moral virtue as a driver and always drive within the speed limit, he must first become aware, he must become conscious of the law.

But consciousness is not enough. We all have seen people who are quite conscious of the speed limits while they are violating them. We don't have to look beyond ourselves to discover the culprits. For our behavior to change we must move beyond consciousness to conviction. Conviction is a matter of depth and intensity. It is one thing to be aware that a certain action is right. It is another to have a conviction about it. It is a lot easier for us to compromise our knowledge than to act against convictions. A conviction is knowledge that is settled. It has a firm hold on us. It goes beyond our brains and penetrates the conscience.

Our conscience acts as a kind of governor upon our behavior. It is the inner voice that either accuses or excuses us. It monitors our behavior by way of approval or disapproval. The problem is that our conscience doesn't always tell us the truth. We are adept at training it in the direction of self-approval. . . .

For the conscience to function in a godly way it must be influenced by godly convictions. To gain godly consciences, our consciousness of what is right and what is wrong must be sharpened. This involves the mind. It is a matter of doctrine.

(From *Pleasing God* by R. C. Sproul)

APPLICATION God's Word teaches us sound doctrine. When was the last time you memorized a verse? Memorize Psalm 119:105. Consider memorizing one verse a week.

EXPLORATION God's Word—2 Samuel 22:31; Psalm 12:6; Proverbs 30:5; 2 Timothy 3:16-17; Hebrews 4:12.

119:37 [w] Following Masoretic Text, Septuagint, and Vulgate; Targum reads *Your words.*

53 Indignation has taken hold of me
Because of the wicked, who forsake Your law.
54 Your statutes have been my songs
In the house of my pilgrimage.
55 I remember Your name in the night, O LORD,
And I keep Your law.
56 This has become mine,
Because I kept Your precepts.

ח HETH

57 *You are* my portion, O LORD;
I have said that I would keep Your words.
58 I entreated Your favor with *my* whole heart;
Be merciful to me according to Your word.
59 I thought about my ways,
And turned my feet to Your testimonies.
60 I made haste, and did not delay
To keep Your commandments.
61 The cords of the wicked have bound me,
But I have not forgotten Your law.
62 At midnight I will rise to give thanks to You,
Because of Your righteous judgments.
63 I *am* a companion of all who fear You,
And of those who keep Your precepts.
64 The earth, O LORD, is full of Your mercy;
Teach me Your statutes.

ט TETH

65 You have dealt well with Your servant,
O LORD, according to Your word.
66 Teach me good judgment and knowledge,
For I believe Your commandments.
67 Before I was afflicted I went astray,
But now I keep Your word.
68 You *are* good, and do good;
Teach me Your statutes.
69 The proud have forged a lie against me,
But I will keep Your precepts with *my*
whole heart.
70 Their heart is as fat as grease,
But I delight in Your law.
71 *It is* good for me that I have been afflicted,
That I may learn Your statutes.
72 The law of Your mouth *is* better to me
Than thousands of *coins of* gold and silver.

י YOD

73 Your hands have made me and fashioned me;
Give me understanding, that I may learn
Your commandments.
74 Those who fear You will be glad
when they see me,
Because I have hoped in Your word.
75 I know, O LORD, that Your judgments *are* right,
And *that* in faithfulness You have afflicted me.
76 Let, I pray, Your merciful kindness be for
my comfort,
According to Your word to Your servant.
77 Let Your tender mercies come to me, that I
may live;
For Your law *is* my delight.
78 Let the proud be ashamed,
For they treated me wrongfully with falsehood;
But I will meditate on Your precepts.
79 Let those who fear You turn to me,
Those who know Your testimonies.
80 Let my heart be blameless regarding
Your statutes,
That I may not be ashamed.

כ KAPH

81 My soul faints for Your salvation,
But I hope in Your word.
82 My eyes fail *from searching* Your word,
Saying, "When will You comfort me?"
83 For I have become like a wineskin in smoke,
Yet I do not forget Your statutes.
84 How many *are* the days of Your servant?
When will You execute judgment on those
who persecute me?
85 The proud have dug pits for me,
Which *is* not according to Your law.
86 All Your commandments *are* faithful;
They persecute me wrongfully;
Help me!
87 They almost made an end of me on earth,
But I did not forsake Your precepts.
88 Revive me according to Your lovingkindness,
So that I may keep the testimony of
Your mouth.

ל LAMED

89 Forever, O LORD,
Your word is settled in heaven.
90 Your faithfulness *endures* to all generations;
You established the earth, and it abides.
91 They continue this day according to
Your ordinances,
For all *are* Your servants.
92 Unless Your law *had been* my delight,
I would then have perished in my affliction.
93 I will never forget Your precepts,
For by them You have given me life.
94 I *am* Yours, save me;

For I have sought Your precepts.
95 The wicked wait for me to destroy me,
But I will consider Your testimonies.
96 I have seen the consummation of all perfection,
But Your commandment *is* exceedingly broad.

מ MEM

97 Oh, how I love Your law!
It *is* my meditation all the day.
98 You, through Your commandments, make me wiser than my enemies;
For they *are* ever with me.
99 I have more understanding than all my teachers,
For Your testimonies *are* my meditation.
100 I understand more than the ancients,
Because I keep Your precepts.
101 I have restrained my feet from every evil way,
That I may keep Your word.
102 I have not departed from Your judgments,
For You Yourself have taught me.
103 How sweet are Your words to my taste,
Sweeter than honey to my mouth!
104 Through Your precepts I get understanding;
Therefore I hate every false way.

נ NUN

105 Your word *is* a lamp to my feet
And a light to my path.
106 I have sworn and confirmed
That I will keep Your righteous judgments.
107 I am afflicted very much;
Revive me, O LORD, according to Your word.
108 Accept, I pray, the freewill offerings of my mouth, O LORD,
And teach me Your judgments.
109 My life *is* continually in my hand,
Yet I do not forget Your law.
110 The wicked have laid a snare for me,
Yet I have not strayed from Your precepts.
111 Your testimonies I have taken as a heritage forever,
For they *are* the rejoicing of my heart.
112 I have inclined my heart to perform Your statutes
Forever, to the very end.

ס SAMEK

113 I hate the double-minded,
But I love Your law.
114 You *are* my hiding place and my shield;
I hope in Your word.
115 Depart from me, you evildoers,
For I will keep the commandments of my God!
116 Uphold me according to Your word, that I may live;
And do not let me be ashamed of my hope.
117 Hold me up, and I shall be safe,
And I shall observe Your statutes continually.
118 You reject all those who stray from Your statutes,
For their deceit *is* falsehood.
119 You put away all the wicked of the earth *like* dross;
Therefore I love Your testimonies.
120 My flesh trembles for fear of You,
And I am afraid of Your judgments.

ע AYIN

121 I have done justice and righteousness;
Do not leave me to my oppressors.
122 Be surety for Your servant for good;
Do not let the proud oppress me.
123 My eyes fail *from seeking* Your salvation
And Your righteous word.
124 Deal with Your servant according to Your mercy,
And teach me Your statutes.
125 I *am* Your servant;
Give me understanding,
That I may know Your testimonies.
126 *It is* time for *You* to act, O LORD,
For they have regarded Your law as void.
127 Therefore I love Your commandments
More than gold, yes, than fine gold!
128 Therefore all *Your* precepts *concerning* all *things*
I consider *to be* right;
I hate every false way.

פ PE

129 Your testimonies are wonderful;
Therefore my soul keeps them.
130 The entrance of Your words gives light;
It gives understanding to the simple.
131 I opened my mouth and panted,
For I longed for Your commandments.
132 Look upon me and be merciful to me,
As Your custom *is* toward those who love Your name.
133 Direct my steps by Your word,

And let no iniquity have dominion over me.
134 Redeem me from the oppression of man,
That I may keep Your precepts.
135 Make Your face shine upon Your servant,
And teach me Your statutes.
136 Rivers of water run down from my eyes,
Because *men* do not keep Your law.

צ TSADDE

137 Righteous *are* You, O LORD,
And upright *are* Your judgments.
138 Your testimonies, *which* You
have commanded,
Are righteous and very faithful.
139 My zeal has consumed me,
Because my enemies have forgotten
Your words.
140 Your word *is* very pure;
Therefore Your servant loves it.
141 I *am* small and despised,
Yet I do not forget Your precepts.
142 Your righteousness *is* an everlasting
righteousness,
And Your law *is* truth.
143 Trouble and anguish have overtaken me,
Yet Your commandments *are* my delights.
144 The righteousness of Your testimonies
is everlasting;
Give me understanding, and I shall live.

ק QOPH

145 I cry out with *my* whole heart;
Hear me, O LORD!
I will keep Your statutes.
146 I cry out to You;
Save me, and I will keep Your testimonies.
147 I rise before the dawning of the morning,
And cry for help;
I hope in Your word.
148 My eyes are awake through the *night* watches,
That I may meditate on Your word.
149 Hear my voice according to
Your lovingkindness;
O LORD, revive me according to Your justice.
150 They draw near who follow
after wickedness;
They are far from Your law.
151 You *are* near, O LORD,
And all Your commandments *are* truth.
152 Concerning Your testimonies,
I have known of old that You have founded
them forever.

ר RESH

153 Consider my affliction and deliver me,
For I do not forget Your law.
154 Plead my cause and redeem me;
Revive me according to Your word.
155 Salvation *is* far from the wicked,
For they do not seek Your statutes.
156 Great *are* Your tender mercies, O LORD;
Revive me according to Your judgments.
157 Many *are* my persecutors and my enemies,
Yet I do not turn from Your testimonies.
158 I see the treacherous, and am disgusted,
Because they do not keep Your word.
159 Consider how I love Your precepts;
Revive me, O LORD, according to
Your lovingkindness.
160 The entirety of Your word *is* truth,
And every one of Your righteous judgments
endures forever.

ש SHIN

161 Princes persecute me without a cause,
But my heart stands in awe of Your word.
162 I rejoice at Your word
As one who finds great treasure.
163 I hate and abhor lying,
But I love Your law.
164 Seven times a day I praise You,
Because of Your righteous judgments.
165 Great peace have those who love Your law,
And nothing causes them to stumble.
166 LORD, I hope for Your salvation,
And I do Your commandments.
167 My soul keeps Your testimonies,
And I love them exceedingly.
168 I keep Your precepts and Your testimonies,
For all my ways *are* before You.

ת TAU

169 Let my cry come before You, O LORD;
Give me understanding according to
Your word.
170 Let my supplication come before You;
Deliver me according to Your word.
171 My lips shall utter praise,
For You teach me Your statutes.
172 My tongue shall speak of Your word,
For all Your commandments
are righteousness.
173 Let Your hand become my help,
For I have chosen Your precepts.

174 I long for Your salvation, O LORD,
And Your law *is* my delight.
175 Let my soul live, and it shall praise You;
And let Your judgments help me.
176 I have gone astray like a lost sheep;
Seek Your servant,
For I do not forget Your commandments.

PSALM 120

Plea for Relief from Bitter Foes

A Song of Ascents.

In my distress I cried to the LORD,
And He heard me.
2 Deliver my soul, O LORD, from lying lips
And from a deceitful tongue.

3 What shall be given to you,
Or what shall be done to you,
You false tongue?
4 Sharp arrows of the warrior,
With coals of the broom tree!

5 Woe is me, that I dwell in Meshech,
That I dwell among the tents of Kedar!
6 My soul has dwelt too long
With one who hates peace.
7 I *am for* peace;
But when I speak, they *are* for war.

PSALM 121

God the Help of Those Who Seek Him

A Song of Ascents.

I will lift up my eyes to the hills—
From whence comes my help?
2 My help *comes* from the LORD,
Who made heaven and earth.

3 He will not allow your foot to be moved;
He who keeps you will not slumber.
4 Behold, He who keeps Israel
Shall neither slumber nor sleep.

5 The LORD *is* your keeper;
The LORD *is* your shade at your right hand.
6 The sun shall not strike you by day,
Nor the moon by night.

7 The LORD shall preserve you from all evil;
He shall preserve your soul.
8 The LORD shall preserve your going out and your coming in
From this time forth, and even forevermore.

LIFE LESSON

Psalms 120:1–123:4

SITUATION Psalms 120–135 were sung during annual feasts. Pilgrims would also recite these psalms as they journeyed to the temple in Jerusalem.

OBSERVATION The writer (some believe Hezekiah) asked God to rescue him from false accusers.

INSPIRATION All of us at times find ourselves and our futures seemingly in the hands of other people. Their decisions or their actions determine whether we get a good grade or a poor one, whether we are promoted or fired, whether our careers blossom or fold. I am not overlooking our own responsibility in these situations, but all of us know that even when we have, so to speak, done our best, we are still dependent upon the favor or frown of that teacher or boss or commanding officer. We are, from a human point of view, often at the mercy of other people and their decisions or actions. . . .

Can we trust God that He can and will work in the heart of that individual to bring about His plan for us? Or consider the instance when someone is out to harm us, to ruin our reputation, or jeopardize our career: Can we trust God to intervene in the heart of that person so that he does not carry out his evil intent? According to the Bible, the answer in both instances is yes. We can trust God.

(From *Trusting God* by Jerry Bridges)

APPLICATION Do you know someone who stirs up trouble? Have you seen that person develop enemies? What can you do? Can you help clear up a misunderstanding? Can you help make peace? If it is possible to resolve the conflict, be a peacemaker.

EXPLORATION Deceit—Exodus 20:16; Job 11:11; Psalm 5:6; 43:1; Proverbs 12:22; Acts 5:7-9; Ephesians 4:25; Colossians 3:9.

LIFE LESSON

Psalms 124:1–127:5

SITUATION God rescued the Israelites from their enemies. Although the odds were against God's people, he saved them.

OBSERVATION We should not seek strength in weapons, economic might, or political strength. Real power comes from God.

INSPIRATION God has done everything possible to bring you salvation; you can add nothing to what He has done. He has shown us the vision of the coming storm to give advance warning of the judgment so that we can flee from His wrath and come to Him. If you wish to be saved and go to heaven, you can, by believing in the Lord Jesus Christ as your Savior.

Jesus Christ rose from the dead to be alive forever. Because He is alive and because He can be everywhere at once, He is right there where you're reading. All you have to do is take Him, receive Him, accept Him personally into your heart as your Lord and Savior. . . .

What more could you desire, ask, or ever hope for than that the grace of our Lord Jesus Christ be with you forever? (From *Storm Warning* by Billy Graham)

APPLICATION How do you relieve stress? Do you take a nap, reach for a drink, read a book, or play a round of golf? Put a bookmark in this psalm. When you feel swamped with problems, call on a friend to help you avoid inappropriate ways to relieve stress. Review this psalm when you feel pressured. Then face the problem with God's help.

EXPLORATION Deliverance—Exodus 12:17, 23; Exodus 14:21-31; Judges 4:3; Mark 4:38-40.

PSALM 122

The Joy of Going to the House of the LORD

A Song of Ascents. Of David.

I was glad when they said to me,
"Let us go into the house of the LORD."
2 Our feet have been standing
Within your gates, O Jerusalem!

3 Jerusalem is built
As a city that is compact together,
4 Where the tribes go up,
The tribes of the LORD,
To the Testimony of Israel,
To give thanks to the name of the LORD.
5 For thrones are set there for judgment,
The thrones of the house of David.

6 Pray for the peace of Jerusalem:
"May they prosper who love you.
7 Peace be within your walls,
Prosperity within your palaces."
8 For the sake of my brethren and companions,
I will now say, "Peace *be* within you."
9 Because of the house of the LORD our God
I will seek your good.

PSALM 123

Prayer for Relief from Contempt

A Song of Ascents.

Unto You I lift up my eyes,
O You who dwell in the heavens.
2 Behold, as the eyes of servants *look* to the hand of their masters,
As the eyes of a maid to the hand of her mistress,
So our eyes *look* to the LORD our God,
Until He has mercy on us.

3 Have mercy on us, O LORD, have mercy on us!
For we are exceedingly filled with contempt.
4 Our soul is exceedingly filled
With the scorn of those who are at ease,
With the contempt of the proud.

PSALM 124

The LORD the Defense of His People

A Song of Ascents. Of David.

"If it had not been the LORD who was on our side,"
Let Israel now say—
2 "If it had not been the LORD who was on our side,

When men rose up against us,
3 Then they would have swallowed us alive,
When their wrath was kindled against us;
4 Then the waters would have overwhelmed us,
The stream would have gone over our soul;
5 Then the swollen waters
Would have gone over our soul."

6 Blessed *be* the LORD,
Who has not given us *as* prey to their teeth.
7 Our soul has escaped as a bird from the snare
of the fowlers;[x]
The snare is broken, and we have escaped.
8 Our help *is* in the name of the LORD,
Who made heaven and earth.

PSALM 125

The LORD the Strength of His People

A Song of Ascents.

Those who trust in the LORD
Are like Mount Zion,
Which cannot be moved, *but* abides forever.
2 As the mountains surround Jerusalem,
So the LORD surrounds His people
From this time forth and forever.

3 For the scepter of wickedness shall not rest
On the land allotted to the righteous,
Lest the righteous reach out their hands
to iniquity.

4 Do good, O LORD, to *those who are* good,
And to *those who are* upright in their hearts.

5 As for such as turn aside to their
crooked ways,
The LORD shall lead them away
With the workers of iniquity.

Peace *be* upon Israel!

PSALM 126

A Joyful Return to Zion

A Song of Ascents.

When the LORD brought back the captivity
of Zion,
We were like those who dream.
2 Then our mouth was filled with laughter,
And our tongue with singing.
Then they said among the nations,
"The LORD has done great things for them."
3 The LORD has done great things for us,
And we are glad.

4 Bring back our captivity, O LORD,
As the streams in the South.

5 Those who sow in tears
Shall reap in joy.
6 He who continually goes forth weeping,
Bearing seed for sowing,
Shall doubtless come again with rejoicing,
Bringing his sheaves *with him.*

PSALM 127

Laboring and Prospering with the LORD

A Song of Ascents. Of Solomon.

Unless the LORD builds the house,
They labor in vain who build it;
Unless the LORD guards the city,
The watchman stays awake in vain.
2 *It is* vain for you to rise up early,
To sit up late,
To eat the bread of sorrows;
For so He gives His beloved sleep.

3 Behold, children *are* a heritage from
the LORD,
The fruit of the womb *is* a reward.
4 Like arrows in the hand of a warrior,
So *are* the children of one's youth.
5 Happy *is* the man who has his quiver
full of them;
They shall not be ashamed,
But shall speak with their enemies in the gate.

PSALM 128

Blessings of Those Who Fear the LORD

A Song of Ascents.

Blessed *is* every one who fears the LORD,
Who walks in His ways.

2 When you eat the labor of your hands,
You *shall be* happy, and *it shall be* well
with you.
3 Your wife *shall be* like a fruitful vine
In the very heart of your house,
Your children like olive plants
All around your table.

124:7 [x] That is, persons who catch birds in a trap or snare

Life Lesson

Psalms 128:1–131:3

SITUATION Possibly written by King Hezekiah, these lyrics were often sung at Israelite weddings.

OBSERVATION If you allow God to be head of your home, he will bless your family life.

INSPIRATION Perhaps the most taxing of all, are the years a family finds itself in and out of crisis situations. Little babies that cooed and gurgled grow up into challenging, independent-thinking adolescents. The protective, sheltered environment of the home is broken into by the school, new friends, alien philosophies, financial strain, illness, accidents, hard questions, constant decisions, and busy schedules . . . and it isn't difficult to feel the pressure mounting—especially when you add dating, new drivers in the family, leaving for college, talk of marriage, and moving out. Whew! And what does God say about these years? . . .

He says we'll be "blessed." We'll be "happy." It will "be well" with us during these years. . . . In the family portrayed on this scriptural canvas, "the Lord" is still central. . . .

4 Behold, thus shall the man be blessed
Who fears the LORD.
5 The LORD bless you out of Zion,
And may you see the good of Jerusalem
All the days of your life.
6 Yes, may you see your children's children.

Peace *be* upon Israel!

PSALM 129

Song of Victory over Zion's Enemies

A Song of Ascents.

"Many a time they have afflicted me from my youth,"
Let Israel now say—
2 "Many a time they have afflicted me from my youth;
Yet they have not prevailed against me.
3 The plowers plowed on my back;
They made their furrows long."
4 The LORD *is* righteous;
He has cut in pieces the cords of the wicked.

5 Let all those who hate Zion
Be put to shame and turned back.
6 Let them be as the grass *on* the housetops,
Which withers before it grows up,
7 With which the reaper does not fill his hand,
Nor he who binds sheaves, his arms.
8 Neither let those who pass by them say,
"The blessing of the LORD *be* upon you;
We bless you in the name of the LORD!"

PSALM 130

Waiting for the Redemption of the LORD

A Song of Ascents.

Out of the depths I have cried to You,
O LORD;
2 Lord, hear my voice!
Let Your ears be attentive
To the voice of my supplications.

3 If You, LORD, should mark iniquities,
O Lord, who could stand?
4 But *there is* forgiveness with You,
That You may be feared.

5 I wait for the LORD, my soul waits,
And in His word I do hope.
6 My soul *waits* for the Lord
More than those who watch for the morning—
Yes, more than those who watch for the morning.

7 O Israel, hope in the LORD;
For with the LORD *there is* mercy,
And with Him *is* abundant redemption.
8 And He shall redeem Israel
From all his iniquities.

PSALM 131

Simple Trust in the LORD

A Song of Ascents. Of David.

LORD, my heart is not haughty,
Nor my eyes lofty.
Neither do I concern myself with great matters,
Nor with things too profound for me.

2 Surely I have calmed and quieted my soul,
Like a weaned child with his mother;
Like a weaned child *is* my soul within me.

3 O Israel, hope in the LORD
From this time forth and forever.

PSALM 132

The Eternal Dwelling of God in Zion

A Song of Ascents.

LORD, remember David
And all his afflictions;
2 How he swore to the LORD,
And vowed to the Mighty One of Jacob:
3 "Surely I will not go into the chamber of my house,
Or go up to the comfort of my bed;
4 I will not give sleep to my eyes
Or slumber to my eyelids,
5 Until I find a place for the LORD,
A dwelling place for the Mighty One of Jacob."

6 Behold, we heard of it in Ephrathah;
We found it in the fields of the woods.[y]
7 Let us go into His tabernacle;
Let us worship at His footstool.
8 Arise, O LORD, to Your resting place,
You and the ark of Your strength.
9 Let Your priests be clothed with righteousness,
And let Your saints shout for joy.

10 For Your servant David's sake,
Do not turn away the face of Your Anointed.

11 The LORD has sworn *in* truth to David;
He will not turn from it:
"I will set upon your throne the fruit of your body.

132:6 [y] Hebrew *Jaar*

Even before you finish, . . . it may be the right time for you to come to terms with the truth regarding your family. I must be honest with you, in most of the family conflicts I have dealt with involving trouble with teenagers, the problem has been more with parents who were either too liberal and permissive or too inflexible, distant, rigid (and sometimes hypocritical) than with teenagers who were unwilling to cooperate. When the modeling is as it should be, there is seldom much trouble from those who fall under the shadow of the leader. Strengthening your grip on the family may start with an unguarded appraisal of the leadership your family is expected to follow.

(From *Strengthening Your Grip* by Charles Swindoll)

APPLICATION Do you look forward to going home or do you dread it? Is God the head of your home? Pray for your family daily. Memorize a favorite psalm as a family. After dinner, read a chapter from the Bible every day for a month.

EXPLORATION Marriage and Family—Genesis 2:18-25; Exodus 20:12; Matthew 19:5-6; Mark 7:9-13; Ephesians 5:22-33.

LIFE LESSON

Psalms 132:1–134:3

SITUATION These songs of worship, written by various writers, were also sung by pilgrims on their way to the temple.

OBSERVATION Honoring and worshiping God not only causes God's people to rejoice, it also unifies them.

INSPIRATION I had a vision one day while our church was worshiping. As I looked around at the people I have come to love, I saw that each was an earthen vessel, a real mud pot. . . . But as I continued to look, in prayer and worship, I looked "into" each mud pot, and what I saw was exquisite molten gold. Each person, frail, vulnerable, and half-fashioned, had a treasure inside. But then I saw something more—each pot was cracked. Finally I looked again and saw something miraculous: the molten gold was oozing through the cracks. That is how ministry comes into the world, not poured out of expensive vases, but through the orifice of the faults and weaknesses of real people who are being transfigured by Christ. . . .

Relational life is not a mere accessory to spirituality or ministry, but the heart of it. Finding unity within diversity because of the diversity, and not in spite of it, is an important link with the unity within God himself and is both a mark of spirituality and true ministry.

(From *Disciplines of the Hungry Heart* by Paul Stevens)

APPLICATION Work to become unified. Don't avoid conversations that are necessary to make peace, but resist the temptation to become angry. Be quick to forgive and careful in your response. Hear the whole story first, then respond. Your opinions may differ, but part as friends.

EXPLORATION God as Potter—Isaiah 64:8; God's People as Clay—2 Corinthians 4:7-11; God's Love and Ours—1 John 4:7-21

12 If your sons will keep My covenant
And My testimony which I shall teach them,
Their sons also shall sit upon your throne forevermore."

13 For the LORD has chosen Zion;
He has desired *it* for His dwelling place:
14 "This *is* My resting place forever;
Here I will dwell, for I have desired it.
15 I will abundantly bless her provision;
I will satisfy her poor with bread.
16 I will also clothe her priests with salvation,
And her saints shall shout aloud for joy.
17 There I will make the horn of David grow;
I will prepare a lamp for My Anointed.
18 His enemies I will clothe with shame,
But upon Himself His crown shall flourish."

PSALM 133

Blessed Unity of the People of God

A Song of Ascents. Of David.

Behold, how good and how pleasant *it is*
For brethren to dwell together in unity!

2 *It is* like the precious oil upon the head,
Running down on the beard,
The beard of Aaron,
Running down on the edge of his garments.
3 *It is* like the dew of Hermon,
Descending upon the mountains of Zion;
For there the LORD commanded the blessing—
Life forevermore.

PSALM 134

Praising the LORD in His House at Night

A Song of Ascents.

Behold, bless the LORD,
All *you* servants of the LORD,
Who by night stand in the house of the LORD!
2 Lift up your hands *in* the sanctuary,
And bless the LORD.

3 The LORD who made heaven and earth
Bless you from Zion!

PSALM 135

Praise to God in Creation and Redemption

Praise the LORD!

Praise the name of the LORD;
Praise *Him,* O you servants of the LORD!

2 You who stand in the house of the LORD,
In the courts of the house of our God,
3 Praise the LORD, for the LORD *is* good;
Sing praises to His name, for *it is* pleasant.
4 For the LORD has chosen Jacob for Himself,
Israel for His special treasure.

5 For I know that the LORD *is* great,
And our Lord *is* above all gods.
6 Whatever the LORD pleases He does,
In heaven and in earth,
In the seas and in all deep places.
7 He causes the vapors to ascend from the
ends of the earth;
He makes lightning for the rain;
He brings the wind out of His treasuries.

8 He destroyed the firstborn of Egypt,
Both of man and beast.
9 He sent signs and wonders into the
midst of you, O Egypt,
Upon Pharaoh and all his servants.
10 He defeated many nations
And slew mighty kings—
11 Sihon king of the Amorites,
Og king of Bashan,
And all the kingdoms of Canaan—
12 And gave their land *as* a heritage,
A heritage to Israel His people.

13 Your name, O LORD, *endures* forever,
Your fame, O LORD, throughout
all generations.
14 For the LORD will judge His people,
And He will have compassion on His servants.

15 The idols of the nations *are* silver and gold,
The work of men's hands.
16 They have mouths, but they do not speak;
Eyes they have, but they do not see;
17 They have ears, but they do not hear;
Nor is there *any* breath in their mouths.
18 Those who make them are like them;
So is everyone who trusts in them.

19 Bless the LORD, O house of Israel!
Bless the LORD, O house of Aaron!
20 Bless the LORD, O house of Levi!
You who fear the LORD, bless the LORD!
21 Blessed be the LORD out of Zion,
Who dwells in Jerusalem!

Praise the LORD!

LIFE LESSON

Psalm 135:1-21

SITUATION This writer praised God because God chose Israel as his people, God created a beautiful world, and God has greater power than any other god.

OBSERVATION God's children worship only him, while the heathen worship idols in vain.

INSPIRATION We usually think of an idol as a religious figure carved out of wood or stone, perhaps in some primitive tribe, far removed from civilization. But we have our "idols" today, because an idol is something that you worship in place of the living God. Some people worship the idol of beauty or sexual pleasure. Some people worship the idol of money and security—although I have observed that the more money some people have the more insecure they become. Some people worship at the shrine of power, constantly scheming for ways they can dominate others.

. . . What is your idol? What really, honestly, dominates your life? What are your priorities, and what are the real (although perhaps hidden) motives in your everyday living? Is Christ on the throne of your life, or is it self? You don't have to practice voodoo or be a follower of a strange cult to have been deceived. . . . Anything that entices you away from a wholehearted commitment to Christ is being used of Satan to deceive you. (From *Approaching Hoofbeats* by Billy Graham)

APPLICATION What inhibits your relationship with God? Get rid of distractions: pay off your credit cards, turn off the television for a night, and leave the motor home parked for the weekend. Take time to improve your friendship with God this week.

EXPLORATION Idols—Deuteronomy 32:16; Psalm 96:5; Isaiah 2:8-9; Colossians 3:5-6; Revelation 9:20.

LIFE LESSON

Psalm 136:1-26

SITUATION People cannot put a limit on God's patient care. He painstakingly created every detail of the universe and patiently provides for his people.

OBSERVATION Thank God because he has more resources than we can ever exhaust.

INSPIRATION We should never take any blessing for granted, but accept everything as a gift from the Father of Lights. Whole days may be spent occasionally in the holy practice of being thankful. We should write on a tablet one by one the things for which we are grateful to God and to our fellow men. And a constant return to this thought during the day as our minds get free will serve to fix the habit in our hearts. . . .

In trying to count our many blessings, the difficulty is not to find things to count, but to find time to enumerate them all. Personally, I have gotten great help from the practice of talking over with God the many kindnesses I have received from my fellow men. To my parents I owe my life and my upbringing. To my teachers I owe that patient line-upon-line instruction that took me when I was a young, ignorant pagan and enabled me to read and write. To the patriots and statesmen of the past I owe the liberties I now enjoy. To numerous and unknown soldiers who shed their blood to keep our country free I owe a debt I can never pay. And I please God and enlarge my own heart when I remind the Lord that I am grateful for them. For every man and woman of every race and nationality who may have contributed anything to my peace and welfare I am grateful, and I shall not let God forget that I am.

(From *The Root of Righteousness* by A. W. Tozer)

APPLICATION How has God blessed you? How have others contributed to your life? Take time to thank God for ten blessings today.

EXPLORATION Thanksgiving —2 Chronicles 20:21-22; Psalm 103:1-5; Revelation 4:9-11.

PSALM 136

Thanksgiving to God for His Enduring Mercy

Oh, give thanks to the LORD, for *He is* good!
For His mercy *endures* forever.
2 Oh, give thanks to the God of gods!
For His mercy *endures* forever.
3 Oh, give thanks to the Lord of lords!
For His mercy *endures* forever:

4 To Him who alone does great wonders,
For His mercy *endures* forever;
5 To Him who by wisdom made the heavens,
For His mercy *endures* forever;
6 To Him who laid out the earth above the waters,
For His mercy *endures* forever;
7 To Him who made great lights,
For His mercy *endures* forever—
8 The sun to rule by day,
For His mercy *endures* forever;
9 The moon and stars to rule by night,
For His mercy *endures* forever.

10 To Him who struck Egypt in their firstborn,
For His mercy *endures* forever;
11 And brought out Israel from among them,
For His mercy *endures* forever;
12 With a strong hand, and with an outstretched arm,
For His mercy *endures* forever;
13 To Him who divided the Red Sea in two,
For His mercy *endures* forever;
14 And made Israel pass through the midst of it,
For His mercy *endures* forever;
15 But overthrew Pharaoh and his army in the Red Sea,
For His mercy *endures* forever;
16 To Him who led His people through the wilderness,
For His mercy *endures* forever;
17 To Him who struck down great kings,
For His mercy *endures* forever;
18 And slew famous kings,
For His mercy *endures* forever—
19 Sihon king of the Amorites,
For His mercy *endures* forever;
20 And Og king of Bashan,
For His mercy *endures* forever—
21 And gave their land as a heritage,
For His mercy *endures* forever;
22 A heritage to Israel His servant,
For His mercy *endures* forever.

23 Who remembered us in our lowly state,
For His mercy *endures* forever;

24 And rescued us from our enemies,
For His mercy *endures* forever;
25 Who gives food to all flesh,
For His mercy *endures* forever.

26 Oh, give thanks to the God of heaven!
For His mercy *endures* forever.

PSALM 137

Longing for Zion in a Foreign Land

By the rivers of Babylon,
There we sat down, yea, we wept
When we remembered Zion.
2 We hung our harps
Upon the willows in the midst of it.
3 For there those who carried us away captive
asked of us a song,
And those who plundered us *requested* mirth,
Saying, "Sing us *one* of the songs of Zion!"

4 How shall we sing the LORD's song
In a foreign land?
5 If I forget you, O Jerusalem,
Let my right hand forget *its skill!*
6 If I do not remember you,
Let my tongue cling to the roof of my mouth—
If I do not exalt Jerusalem
Above my chief joy.

7 Remember, O LORD, against the sons of Edom
The day of Jerusalem,
Who said, "Raze *it,* raze *it,*
To its very foundation!"

8 O daughter of Babylon, who are to be destroyed,
Happy the one who repays you as you have served us!
9 Happy the one who takes and dashes
Your little ones against the rock!

PSALM 138

The LORD's Goodness to the Faithful

A Psalm of David.

I will praise You with my whole heart;
Before the gods I will sing praises to You.
2 I will worship toward Your holy temple,
And praise Your name
For Your lovingkindness and Your truth;
For You have magnified Your word above all Your name.
3 In the day when I cried out, You answered me,
And made me bold *with* strength in my soul.

LIFE LESSON

Psalms 137:1–138:8

SITUATION During the Babylon captivity, the Israelites mourned for their lost land.

OBSERVATION In times of trouble it is easy to wonder if God hears us. God does hear our prayers, and he carries us through the difficulties.

INSPIRATION Since God is more moved by our hurt than our eloquence, he respond[s]. That's what fathers do.

That's exactly what Jim Redmond did.

His son Derek, a twenty-six-year-old Briton, was favored to win the four-hundred-meter race in the 1992 Barcelona Olympics. Halfway into his semifinal heat, a fiery pain seared through his right leg. He crumpled to the track with a torn hamstring.

As the medical attendants were approaching, Redmond fought to his feet. "It was animal instinct," he would later say. He set out hopping, pushing away the coaches in a crazed attempt to finish the race.

When he reached the stretch, a big man pushed through the crowd. He was wearing a t-shirt that read "Have you hugged your child today?" and a hat that challenged, "Just Do It." The man was Jim Redmond, Derek's father.

"You don't have to do this," he told his weeping son.

"Yes, I do," Derek declared.

"Well, then," said Jim, "we're going to finish this together."

And they did. Jim wrapped Derek's arm around his shoulder and helped him hobble to the finish line. Fighting off security men, the son's head sometimes buried in the father's shoulder, they stayed in Derek's lane to the end.

The crowd clapped, then stood, then cheered, and then wept as the father and the son finished the race.

What made the father do it? What made the father leave the stands to meet his son on the track? Was it the strength of his child? No, it was the pain of his child. His son was hurt and fighting to complete the race. So the father came to help him finish.

Continued

God does the same. Our prayers may be awkward. Our attempts may be feeble. But since the power of prayer is in the one who hears it and not the one who says it, our prayers do make a difference.

(From *He Still Moves Stones* by Max Lucado)

APPLICATION God wants us to pray to him without getting bogged down in proper words and phrases. Forget the fancy words and eloquent phrases. Don't get caught up using the right prayer words. Pour out your joys, fears, concerns, and requests. He hears and will aid and comfort you.

EXPLORATION God Hears His People—Exodus 2:23-25; 22:27; Psalm 18:6; 145:18; Isaiah 65:24; Jeremiah 33:3; Romans 10:12-13.

4 All the kings of the earth shall praise You, O LORD,
When they hear the words of Your mouth.
5 Yes, they shall sing of the ways of the LORD,
For great *is* the glory of the LORD.
6 Though the LORD *is* on high,
Yet He regards the lowly;
But the proud He knows from afar.

7 Though I walk in the midst of trouble, You will revive me;
You will stretch out Your hand
Against the wrath of my enemies,
And Your right hand will save me.
8 The LORD will perfect *that which* concerns me;
Your mercy, O LORD, *endures* forever;
Do not forsake the works of Your hands.

PSALM 139

God's Perfect Knowledge of Man

For the Chief Musician. A Psalm of David.

O LORD, You have searched me and
known *me*.
2 You know my sitting down and my rising up;
You understand my thought afar off.
3 You comprehend my path and my lying down,
And are acquainted with all my ways.
4 For *there is* not a word on my tongue,
But behold, O LORD, You know it altogether.
5 You have hedged me behind and before,
And laid Your hand upon me.
6 *Such* knowledge *is* too wonderful for me;
It is high, I cannot *attain* it.

7 Where can I go from Your Spirit?
Or where can I flee from Your presence?
8 If I ascend into heaven, You *are* there;
If I make my bed in hell, behold, You *are there.*
9 *If* I take the wings of the morning,
And dwell in the uttermost parts of the sea,
10 Even there Your hand shall lead me,
And Your right hand shall hold me.
11 If I say, "Surely the darkness shall fall[z] on me,"
Even the night shall be light about me;
12 Indeed, the darkness shall not hide from You,
But the night shines as the day;
The darkness and the light *are* both alike *to You.*

13 For You formed my inward parts;
You covered me in my mother's womb.
14 I will praise You, for I am fearfully *and* wonderfully made;[a]

139:11 [z] Vulgate and Symmachus read *cover.*
139:14 [a] Following Masoretic Text and Targum; Septuagint, Syriac, and Vulgate read *You are fearfully wonderful.*

Marvelous are Your works,
And *that* my soul knows very well.
15 My frame was not hidden from You,
When I was made in secret,
And skillfully wrought in the lowest parts of the earth.
16 Your eyes saw my substance, being yet unformed.
And in Your book they all were written,
The days fashioned for me,
When *as yet there were* none of them.

17 How precious also are Your thoughts to me, O God!
How great is the sum of them!
18 *If* I should count them, they would be more in number
than the sand;
When I awake, I am still with You.

19 Oh, that You would slay the wicked, O God!
Depart from me, therefore, you bloodthirsty men.
20 For they speak against You wickedly;
Your enemies take *Your name* in vain.[b]
21 Do I not hate them, O LORD, who hate You?
And do I not loathe those who rise up against You?
22 I hate them with perfect hatred;
I count them my enemies.

23 Search me, O God, and know my heart;
Try me, and know my anxieties;
24 And see if *there is any* wicked way in me,
And lead me in the way everlasting.

PSALM 140

Prayer for Deliverance from Evil Men

To the Chief Musician. A Psalm of David.

Deliver me, O LORD, from evil men;
Preserve me from violent men,
2 Who plan evil things in *their* hearts;
They continually gather together *for* war.
3 They sharpen their tongues like a serpent;
The poison of asps *is* under their lips. Selah

4 Keep me, O LORD, from the hands of the wicked;
Preserve me from violent men,
Who have purposed to make my steps stumble.
5 The proud have hidden a snare for me, and cords;
They have spread a net by the wayside;
They have set traps for me. Selah

6 I said to the LORD: "You *are* my God;
Hear the voice of my supplications, O LORD.
7 O GOD the Lord, the strength of my salvation,
You have covered my head in the day of battle.

139:20 *b* Septuagint and Vulgate read *They take your cities in vain.*

LIFE LESSON

Psalm 139:1-24

SITUATION David acknowledged that God knows everything and nothing can overpower him. Because of this, God not only knew all of David's sins but could forgive him.

OBSERVATION God knows everything about us—our thoughts, fears, hopes—and yet he loves us in spite of them.

INSPIRATION Weary of assemblies, hearings, conferences, and investigations designed to reveal the root causes of state difficulties, David turned his face to the altar of God. He prayed earnestly for God to begin the revival of his nation by kindling the fires of revival in his own heart. . . . His heart yearned, as indeed our hearts yearn today, for a personal, vital intimacy with God. In short, he was praying for a new, definite, real experience with his God.

Unless God is revealed to us through personal experience, we can never really know God. Most of us know *about* God, but that is quite different from really *knowing* God.

Is it not logical to believe that the only One who can re-create us is the One who created us in the first place? Our spiritual problems can only be solved by the God who created us originally. He created us in His own image and likeness; today by the grace of His Son, He can re-create us in the likeness of His resurrection. Through faith in Jesus Christ, we are re-created and become partakers of His life.

(From *Unto the Hills* by Billy Graham)

APPLICATION Write your own psalm. It doesn't need to be poetic, or have meter and rhyme. Just write a short message to God. Tell him of your desire to know him, confess your sins, and look to him as your refuge.

EXPLORATION Known by God—1 Chronicles 28:9; Psalm 17:3; Proverbs 20:27; John 10:27-28; 2 Corinthians 5:17; Hebrews 4:13.

8 Do not grant, O LORD, the desires of the wicked;
Do not further his *wicked* scheme,
Lest they be exalted. Selah

9 "*As for* the head of those who surround me,
Let the evil of their lips cover them;
10 Let burning coals fall upon them;
Let them be cast into the fire,
Into deep pits, that they rise not up again.
11 Let not a slanderer be established in the earth;
Let evil hunt the violent man to overthrow *him*."

12 I know that the LORD will maintain
The cause of the afflicted,
And justice for the poor.
13 Surely the righteous shall give thanks to Your name;
The upright shall dwell in Your presence.

PSALM 141

Prayer for Safekeeping from Wickedness

A Psalm of David.

LORD, I cry out to You;
Make haste to me!
Give ear to my voice when I cry out to You.
2 Let my prayer be set before You *as* incense,
The lifting up of my hands *as* the evening sacrifice.

3 Set a guard, O LORD, over my mouth;
Keep watch over the door of my lips.
4 Do not incline my heart to any evil thing,
To practice wicked works
With men who work iniquity;
And do not let me eat of their delicacies.

5 Let the righteous strike me;
It shall be a kindness.
And let him rebuke me;
It shall be as excellent oil;
Let my head not refuse it.

For still my prayer *is* against the deeds of the wicked.
6 Their judges are overthrown by the sides of the cliff,
And they hear my words, for they are sweet.
7 Our bones are scattered at the mouth of the grave,
As when one plows and breaks up the earth.

8 But my eyes *are* upon You, O GOD the Lord;
In You I take refuge;
Do not leave my soul destitute.
9 Keep me from the snares they have laid for me,
And from the traps of the workers of iniquity.
10 Let the wicked fall into their own nets,
While I escape safely.

LIFE LESSON

Psalms 140:1–142:7

SITUATION David prayed for God's strength when he felt overwhelmed.

OBSERVATION God gives us the endurance we need to face whatever situation life brings us.

INSPIRATION When I was a boy . . . I told people that my father was stronger than anyone else in the world. . . .

So I would go out on the front porch and roar to the neighborhood: "My daddy's arm is as strong as trucks! The strongest man in the world." . . . In those days a cherry tree grew in our backyard. This was my hiding place. Ten feet above the ground a stout limb made a horizontal fork, a cradle on which I could lie face-down, reading, thinking, being alone. Nobody bothered me here. Even my parents didn't know where I went to hide. Sometimes Daddy would come out and call, "Wally? Wally?" but he didn't see me in the leaves.

I felt very tricky.

Then came the thunderstorm . . . One day suddenly, a wind tore through the backyard and struck my cherry tree with such force that it ripped the book from my hands and nearly threw me from the limb. I locked my arms around the forking branches and hung on. My head hung down between them. I tried to wind my legs around the limb, but the whole tree was wallowing in the wind. . . .

"Daddeeeeeeee !"

There he was. . . . The branches swept up and down, like huge waves on an ocean—and Daddy saw me, and right away he came out into the wind and the weather, and I felt so relieved because I just took it for granted that he would climb right up the tree to get me.

But that wasn't his plan at all.

PSALM 142

A Plea for Relief from Persecutors

A Contemplation[c] of David. A Prayer when he was in the cave.

I cry out to the LORD with my voice;
With my voice to the LORD I make my supplication.
2 I pour out my complaint before Him;
I declare before Him my trouble.

3 When my spirit was overwhelmed within me,
Then You knew my path.
In the way in which I walk
They have secretly set a snare for me.
4 Look on *my* right hand and see,
For *there is* no one who acknowledges me;
Refuge has failed me;
No one cares for my soul.

5 I cried out to You, O LORD:
I said, "You *are* my refuge,
My portion in the land of the living.
6 Attend to my cry,
For I am brought very low;
Deliver me from my persecutors,
For they are stronger than I.
7 Bring my soul out of prison,
That I may praise Your name;
The righteous shall surround me,
For You shall deal bountifully with me."

PSALM 143

An Earnest Appeal for Guidance and Deliverance

A Psalm of David.

Hear my prayer, O LORD,
Give ear to my supplications!
In Your faithfulness answer me,
And in Your righteousness.
2 Do not enter into judgment with Your servant,
For in Your sight no one living is righteous.

3 For the enemy has persecuted my soul;
He has crushed my life to the ground;
He has made me dwell in darkness,
Like those who have long been dead.
4 Therefore my spirit is overwhelmed within me;
My heart within me is distressed.

5 I remember the days of old;
I meditate on all Your works;
I muse on the work of Your hands.

142:title [c] Hebrew *Maschil*

He came to a spot right below me and lifted his arms and shouted, "Jump."

"What?"

"Jump. I'll catch you."

Jump? I had a crazy man for a father. He was standing six or seven miles beneath me, holding up two skinny arms and telling me to jump. If I jumped, he'd miss. I'd hit the ground and die. . . .

But the wind and the rain slapped that cherry tree, bent it back, and cracked my limb at the trunk. I dropped a foot. My eyes flew open. Then the wood whined and splintered and sank, and so did I, in bloody terror.

No, I did not jump. I let go. I surrendered.

I fell.

In a fast, eternal moment I despaired and plummeted. *This,* I thought, *is what it's like to die—*

But my father caught me. . . .

Now, in such a storm the tree which was our stable world is shaken, and instinct makes us grab it tighter: by our own strength we grip the habits that have helped us in the past, repeating them, believing them. We'd rather trust what *is* than what *might be* : that is, our power, our reason and feeling and endurance. . . . We spend a long time screaming *No!* . . .

But always, God is present. God has always been present. And it is God who says, "Jump."

(From *Mourning Into Dancing* by Walt Wangerin, Jr.)

APPLICATION What is your endurance quota? Do you need to improve it? Perhaps you need more patience, or strength to face a physical challenge. God can help you to endure all of life's struggles.

EXPLORATION God Our Help—Deuteronomy 33:26-29; Psalm 30:2; 46:1; Isaiah 41:9-10; Jonah 2:2.

LIFE LESSON

Psalms 143:1–144:15

SITUATION Whether David felt afraid or joyful, he found strength by reading God's Word and praying.

OBSERVATION David knew life went by too quickly to neglect his relationship with God. Regardless of the situation, David put his relationship with God first.

INSPIRATION God's way is to take some word in His Book and make it spirit and life. Then, relying upon that word, it is possible for us to go on from strength to strength. There is always something new in our lives which calls for vital faith, if we are to go on with God; but there is always the word waiting in His Book which will meet us just where we are and carry us further on. It will be a fight to the end—"the good fight of faith" is His word about it—but full provision is made for victory in that fight, and whether the matter that negates us has to do with our inner life or the outer, there is nothing to fear. It is our Father's good pleasure to give us the Kingdom. We need never—by his grace we *shall* never—be defeated.
(From *Thou Givest, They Gather* by Amy Carmichael)

APPLICATION Out of all the minutes in a day, how many do you devote to God? Consider setting your alarm earlier tomorrow so that you can spend time praying and reading God's Word.

EXPLORATION Morning Prayer—Psalm 5:3; Mark 1:35.

6 I spread out my hands to You;
My soul *longs* for You like a thirsty land. Selah

7 Answer me speedily, O LORD;
My spirit fails!
Do not hide Your face from me,
Lest I be like those who go down into the pit.
8 Cause me to hear Your lovingkindness in the morning,
For in You do I trust;
Cause me to know the way in which I should walk,
For I lift up my soul to You.

9 Deliver me, O LORD, from my enemies;
In You I take shelter.[d]
10 Teach me to do Your will,
For You *are* my God;
Your Spirit *is* good.
Lead me in the land of uprightness.

11 Revive me, O LORD, for Your name's sake!
For Your righteousness' sake bring my soul out of trouble.
12 In Your mercy cut off my enemies,
And destroy all those who afflict my soul;
For I *am* Your servant.

PSALM 144

A Song to the LORD Who Preserves and Prospers His People

A Psalm of David.

Blessed *be* the LORD my Rock,
Who trains my hands for war,
And my fingers for battle—
2 My lovingkindness and my fortress,
My high tower and my deliverer,
My shield and *the One* in whom I take refuge,
Who subdues my people[e] under me.

3 LORD, what *is* man, that You take knowledge of him?
Or the son of man, that You are mindful of him?
4 Man is like a breath;
His days *are* like a passing shadow.

5 Bow down Your heavens, O LORD, and come down;
Touch the mountains, and they shall smoke.
6 Flash forth lightning and scatter them;
Shoot out Your arrows and destroy them.
7 Stretch out Your hand from above;
Rescue me and deliver me out of great waters,
From the hand of foreigners,
8 Whose mouth speaks lying words,
And whose right hand *is* a right hand of falsehood.

143:9 [d] Septuagint and Vulgate read *To You I flee.*
144:2 [e] Following Masoretic Text, Septuagint, and Vulgate; Syriac and Targum read *the peoples* (compare 18:47).

9 I will sing a new song to You, O God;
On a harp of ten strings I will sing praises to You,
10 *The One* who gives salvation to kings,
Who delivers David His servant
From the deadly sword.

11 Rescue me and deliver me from the hand of foreigners,
Whose mouth speaks lying words,
And whose right hand *is* a right hand of falsehood—
12 That our sons *may be* as plants grown up in their youth;
That our daughters *may be* as pillars,
Sculptured in palace style;
13 *That* our barns *may be* full,
Supplying all kinds of produce;
That our sheep may bring forth thousands
And ten thousands in our fields;
14 *That* our oxen *may be* well laden;
That there be no breaking in or going out;
That there be no outcry in our streets.
15 Happy *are* the people who are in such a state;
Happy *are* the people whose God *is* the LORD!

PSALM 145

A Song of God's Majesty and Love

A Praise of David.

I will extol You, my God, O King;
And I will bless Your name forever and ever.
2 Every day I will bless You,
And I will praise Your name forever and ever.
3 Great *is* the LORD, and greatly to be praised;
And His greatness *is* unsearchable.

4 One generation shall praise Your works to another,
And shall declare Your mighty acts.
5 I[f] will meditate on the glorious splendor of Your majesty,
And on Your wondrous works.[g]
6 *Men* shall speak of the might of Your awesome acts,
And I will declare Your greatness.
7 They shall utter the memory of Your great goodness,
And shall sing of Your righteousness.

8 The LORD *is* gracious and full of compassion,
Slow to anger and great in mercy.
9 The LORD *is* good to all,
And His tender mercies *are* over all His works.

10 All Your works shall praise You, O LORD,
And Your saints shall bless You.
11 They shall speak of the glory of Your kingdom,
And talk of Your power,

145:5 *f* Following Masoretic Text and Targum; Dead Sea Scrolls, Septuagint, Syriac, and Vulgate read *They*. *g* Literally *on the words of Your wondrous works.*

LIFE LESSON

Psalms 145:1–150:6

SITUATION Some psalms directed people to praise God. The last four psalms were directed to God. They begin and end with *hallelujah,* the Hebrew word for "Praise the LORD."

OBSERVATION Praise God for his abundant provision, his greatness, and his love.

INSPIRATION "The people," Matthew wrote, "were amazed when they saw the mute speaking, the crippled made well, the lame walking and the blind seeing."

. . . Then Matthew, still the great economizer of words, gave us another phrase on which I wish he would have elaborated:

"They praised the God of Israel."

I wonder how they did that? I feel more certain of what they *didn't* do than of what they did do. I feel confident that they didn't form a praise committee. I feel confident that they didn't make any robes. I feel confident that they didn't sit in rows and stare at the back of each other's heads.

I doubt seriously if they wrote a creed on how they were to praise this God they had never before worshiped. I can't picture them getting into an argument over technicalities. I doubt if they felt it had to be done indoors.

And I know they didn't wait until the Sabbath to do it. . . .

I can imagine throngs of people pushing and shoving. Wanting to get close. Not to request anything or demand anything, but just to say "thank you."

. . . However they did it, they did it. And Jesus was touched, so touched that he insisted they stay for a meal before they left. . . .

Worship is the "thank you" that refuses to be silenced.

We have tried to make a science out of worship. We can't do that. We can't do that any more than we can "sell love" or "negotiate peace."

Worship is a voluntary act of gratitude offered by the saved to the Savior, by the healed to the Healer, and by the delivered to the Deliverer.

(From *In the Eye of the Storm* by Max Lucado)

Continued

APPLICATION Find a new way to praise God. Learn to play an instrument. Take up a new activity that will help you learn more about God or his creation. Sing a song of praise in your car. Praise the Lord!

EXPLORATION Spontaneous Praise—Nehemiah 8:5-6; Isaiah 12:6; 55:12; Luke 2:20; 19:37-40; 1 Thessalonians 5:18; Hebrews 13:15; Revelation 7:9-12.

12 To make known to the sons of men His mighty acts,
And the glorious majesty of His kingdom.
13 Your kingdom *is* an everlasting kingdom,
And Your dominion *endures* throughout all generations.[h]

14 The LORD upholds all who fall,
And raises up all *who are* bowed down.
15 The eyes of all look expectantly to You,
And You give them their food in due season.
16 You open Your hand
And satisfy the desire of every living thing.

17 The LORD *is* righteous in all His ways,
Gracious in all His works.
18 The LORD *is* near to all who call upon Him,
To all who call upon Him in truth.
19 He will fulfill the desire of those who fear Him;
He also will hear their cry and save them.
20 The LORD preserves all who love Him,
But all the wicked He will destroy.
21 My mouth shall speak the praise of the LORD,
And all flesh shall bless His holy name
Forever and ever.

PSALM 146

The Happiness of Those Whose Help Is the LORD

Praise the LORD!

Praise the LORD, O my soul!
2 While I live I will praise the LORD;
I will sing praises to my God while I have my being.

3 Do not put your trust in princes,
Nor in a son of man, in whom *there is* no help.
4 His spirit departs, he returns to his earth;
In that very day his plans perish.

5 Happy *is he* who *has* the God of Jacob for his help,
Whose hope *is* in the LORD his God,
6 Who made heaven and earth,
The sea, and all that *is* in them;
Who keeps truth forever,
7 Who executes justice for the oppressed,
Who gives food to the hungry.
The LORD gives freedom to the prisoners.

8 The LORD opens *the eyes of* the blind;
The LORD raises those who are bowed down;
The LORD loves the righteous.
9 The LORD watches over the strangers;
He relieves the fatherless and widow;

145:13 [h] Following Masoretic Text and Targum; Dead Sea Scrolls, Septuagint, Syriac, and Vulgate add *The LORD is faithful in all His words, And holy in all His works.*

But the way of the wicked He turns
upside down.

10 The LORD shall reign forever—
Your God, O Zion, to all generations.

Praise the LORD!

PSALM 147

Praise to God for His Word and Providence

Praise the LORD!
For *it is* good to sing praises to our God;
For *it is* pleasant, *and* praise is beautiful.

2 The LORD builds up Jerusalem;
He gathers together the outcasts of Israel.
3 He heals the brokenhearted
And binds up their wounds.
4 He counts the number of the stars;
He calls them all by name.
5 Great *is* our Lord, and mighty in power;
His understanding *is* infinite.
6 The LORD lifts up the humble;
He casts the wicked down to the ground.

7 Sing to the LORD with thanksgiving;
Sing praises on the harp to our God,
8 Who covers the heavens with clouds,
Who prepares rain for the earth,
Who makes grass to grow on the mountains.
9 He gives to the beast its food,
And to the young ravens that cry.

10 He does not delight in the strength of
the horse;
He takes no pleasure in the legs of a man.
11 The LORD takes pleasure in those who
fear Him,
In those who hope in His mercy.

12 Praise the LORD, O Jerusalem!
Praise your God, O Zion!
13 For He has strengthened the bars of
your gates;
He has blessed your children within you.
14 He makes peace *in* your borders,
And fills you with the finest wheat.

15 He sends out His command *to the* earth;
His word runs very swiftly.
16 He gives snow like wool;
He scatters the frost like ashes;
17 He casts out His hail like morsels;
Who can stand before His cold?
18 He sends out His word and melts them;
He causes His wind to blow, *and* the
waters flow.

19 He declares His word to Jacob,
His statutes and His judgments to Israel.
20 He has not dealt thus with any nation;
And *as for His* judgments, they have not
known them.

Praise the LORD!

PSALM 148

Praise to the LORD from Creation

Praise the LORD!

Praise the LORD from the heavens;
Praise Him in the heights!
2 Praise Him, all His angels;
Praise Him, all His hosts!
3 Praise Him, sun and moon;
Praise Him, all you stars of light!
4 Praise Him, you heavens of heavens,
And you waters above the heavens!

5 Let them praise the name of the LORD,
For He commanded and they were created.
6 He also established them forever and ever;
He made a decree which shall not pass away.

7 Praise the LORD from the earth,
You great sea creatures and all the depths;
8 Fire and hail, snow and clouds;
Stormy wind, fulfilling His word;
9 Mountains and all hills;
Fruitful trees and all cedars;
10 Beasts and all cattle;
Creeping things and flying fowl;
11 Kings of the earth and all peoples;
Princes and all judges of the earth;
12 Both young men and maidens;
Old men and children.

13 Let them praise the name of the LORD,
For His name alone is exalted;
His glory *is* above the earth and heaven.
14 And He has exalted the horn of His people,
The praise of all His saints—
Of the children of Israel,
A people near to Him.

Praise the LORD!

PSALM 149

Praise to God for His Salvation and Judgment

Praise the LORD!

Sing to the LORD a new song,
And His praise in the assembly of saints.
2 Let Israel rejoice in their Maker;
Let the children of Zion be joyful in their King.
3 Let them praise His name with the dance;
Let them sing praises to Him with the timbrel and harp.
4 For the LORD takes pleasure in His people;
He will beautify the humble with salvation.

5 Let the saints be joyful in glory;
Let them sing aloud on their beds.
6 *Let* the high praises of God *be* in their mouth,
And a two-edged sword in their hand,
7 To execute vengeance on the nations,
And punishments on the peoples;
8 To bind their kings with chains,
And their nobles with fetters of iron;
9 To execute on them the written judgment—
This honor have all His saints.

Praise the LORD!

PSALM 150

Let All Things Praise the LORD

Praise the LORD!

Praise God in His sanctuary;
Praise Him in His mighty firmament!
2 Praise Him for His mighty acts;
Praise Him according to His excellent greatness!

3 Praise Him with the sound of the trumpet;
Praise Him with the lute and harp!
4 Praise Him with the timbrel and dance;
Praise Him with stringed instruments and flutes!
5 Praise Him with loud cymbals;
Praise Him with clashing cymbals!

6 Let everything that has breath praise the LORD.

Praise the LORD!

The Book of *PROVERBS*

INTRODUCTION

Proverbs is a collection of lamps.

Not spotlights that blind. Not bonfires that blaze. But lamps. Lamps that do for your heart what the lamps in your house do for your eyes. They chase away the darkness.

"The commandment is a lamp," wrote Solomon, "and the law a light; reproofs of instruction are the way of life" (6:23).

Reading Proverbs turns on the lamps in the dark corners of life.

Corners such as: Foolishness. Wisdom. Pride. Humility. Fear. Insecurity. Wealth. Mercy. Lust. Diligence. Laziness. Prudence. Anger. Flattery. Gossip. Violence.

And that's just a start.

Having trouble with an enemy? Turn on the lamp of patience:

A soft answer turns away wrath, but a harsh word stirs up anger (15:1).

Having trouble with greed? Flip the switch of prudence:

Better is a life with the fear of the LORD, than great treasure with trouble (15:16).

Anxious about tomorrow? Sit under the light of trust:

Commit your works to the LORD, and your thoughts will be established (16:3).

See what I mean? Time spent with Proverbs makes a heart wise. It's a practical guide for getting along with others. Whereas Psalms tells you how to get along with God, Proverbs tells you how to get along with people. Whereas Psalms is a book for Sunday, Proverbs is a book for Monday.

Why don't you flip on a few lights and see for yourself?

LIFE LESSON
Proverbs 1:1-33

SITUATION Proverbs provide wisdom and guidance for living an obedient life. Simple words and common sense give us guidelines for daily life.

OBSERVATION The Proverbs contain many instructions to help steer readers away from sin. Listen to this advice and grow in wisdom.

INSPIRATION I've thought about what the Scriptures are teaching on wisdom and I've come up with this: Wisdom is the God-given ability to see life with rare objectivity and to handle life with rare stability.

When we operate in the sphere of the wisdom of God, when it is at work in our mind and in our life, we look at life through lenses of perception, and we respond to it in calm confidence. There's a remarkable absence of fear. We are not seized with panic. We can either lose our jobs or we can be promoted in our work, and neither will derail us. Why? Because we see it with God-given objectivity. And we handle it in His wisdom.

We can dip into an unexpected valley or we can soar to the pinnacle of prosperity, and we can cope with both extremes. His wisdom provides us the necessary objectivity and stability. That's the way life is when it is lived in the palm of His hand. This is not some dreamland fantasy. It is reality. It is the ability to live above the drag of human opinion and horizontal perspective. It is what happens within us when wisdom goes to work.

(From *Living on the Ragged Edge* by Charles Swindoll)

APPLICATION Today you may be bombarded by people giving advice—talk show hosts, psychics, psychologists. Take more time to listen to God than to television. At the end of the day, assess which words of wisdom you applied (or should have).

EXPLORATION Wisdom—1 Kings 3:6-12; Proverbs 1:7; 4:7-8; Luke 2:40.

The Beginning of Knowledge

The proverbs of Solomon the son of David, king of Israel:

2 To know wisdom and instruction,
To perceive the words of understanding,
3 To receive the instruction of wisdom,
Justice, judgment, and equity;
4 To give prudence to the simple,
To the young man knowledge and discretion—
5 A wise *man* will hear and increase learning,
And a man of understanding will attain wise counsel,
6 To understand a proverb and an enigma,
The words of the wise and their riddles.

7 The fear of the LORD *is* the beginning of knowledge,
But fools despise wisdom and instruction.

Shun Evil Counsel

8 My son, hear the instruction of your father,
And do not forsake the law of your mother;
9 For they *will be* a graceful ornament on your head,
And chains about your neck.

10 My son, if sinners entice you,
Do not consent.
11 If they say, "Come with us,
Let us lie in wait to *shed* blood;
Let us lurk secretly for the innocent without cause;
12 Let us swallow them alive like Sheol,[a]
And whole, like those who go down to the Pit;
13 We shall find all *kinds* of precious possessions,
We shall fill our houses with spoil;
14 Cast in your lot among us,
Let us all have one purse"—
15 My son, do not walk in the way with them,
Keep your foot from their path;
16 For their feet run to evil,
And they make haste to shed blood.
17 Surely, in vain the net is spread
In the sight of any bird;
18 But they lie in wait for their *own* blood,
They lurk secretly for their *own* lives.
19 So *are* the ways of everyone who is greedy for gain;
It takes away the life of its owners.

The Call of Wisdom

20 Wisdom calls aloud outside;
She raises her voice in the open squares.
21 She cries out in the chief concourses,[b]
At the openings of the gates in the city

1:12 [a] Or *the grave*
1:21 [b] Septuagint, Syriac, and Targum read *top of the walls;* Vulgate reads *the head of multitudes.*

She speaks her words:
22 "How long, you simple ones, will you love simplicity?
For scorners delight in their scorning,
And fools hate knowledge.
23 Turn at my rebuke;
Surely I will pour out my spirit on you;
I will make my words known to you.
24 Because I have called and you refused,
I have stretched out my hand and no one regarded,
25 Because you disdained all my counsel,
And would have none of my rebuke,
26 I also will laugh at your calamity;
I will mock when your terror comes,
27 When your terror comes like a storm,
And your destruction comes like a whirlwind,
When distress and anguish come upon you.

28 "Then they will call on me, but I will not answer;
They will seek me diligently, but they will not find me.
29 Because they hated knowledge
And did not choose the fear of the LORD,
30 They would have none of my counsel
And despised my every rebuke.
31 Therefore they shall eat the fruit of their own way,
And be filled to the full with their own fancies.
32 For the turning away of the simple will slay them,
And the complacency of fools will destroy them;
33 But whoever listens to me will dwell safely,
And will be secure, without fear of evil."

The Value of Wisdom

2 My son, if you receive my words,
And treasure my commands within you,
2 So that you incline your ear to wisdom,
And apply your heart to understanding;
3 Yes, if you cry out for discernment,
And lift up your voice for understanding,
4 If you seek her as silver,
And search for her as *for* hidden treasures;
5 Then you will understand the fear of the LORD,
And find the knowledge of God.
6 For the LORD gives wisdom;
From His mouth *come* knowledge and understanding;
7 He stores up sound wisdom for the upright;
He is a shield to those who walk uprightly;
8 He guards the paths of justice,
And preserves the way of His saints.
9 Then you will understand righteousness and justice,
Equity *and* every good path.

10 When wisdom enters your heart,
And knowledge is pleasant to your soul,

LIFE LESSON

Proverbs 2:1-22

SITUATION Solomon warned his readers to heed God's word. He exhorted them to learn about God, who would help them to choose the right path.

OBSERVATION Rebelling against God's wisdom leads to immorality and spiritual death. God's wisdom keeps us from living an immoral and defeated life.

INSPIRATION The secret is making the right choices. Here's what I mean. In the light of truth, you and I are able to see both truth and lie, both light and darkness—that which is simple, pure, and clear and that which is deceptive. But enslaved to darkness and plunged into the pit of the lie, we no longer see the truth. We have no other option but to believe the lie. We become victimized in our addiction—in "sin's foul bondage."

The secret, of course, is making the right choices every day. So? Watch those choices! Watch your decisions! . . .

We need to keep asking ourselves, Does this honor the Savior? Does this exalt my Lord? Does this bring glory to His name? Does this lift Him up? How powerful is our focus! . . .

Once you decide to trust God in simple faith and allow Him complete freedom to carry out His plan and purpose in you as well as through you, you need only relax and count on Him to take care of things you once tried to keep under control.

(From *Simple Faith* by Charles Swindoll)

APPLICATION As you read the Bible this week, select a Proverb each day that will help you make wise decisions. Make a list of these Proverbs. Carry the list with you so you can remind yourself to use this wisdom.

EXPLORATION Moral Choices—Exodus 23:24-25; 2 Kings 17:27-29; 2 Chronicles 13:8; Romans 1:25; 1 Corinthians 6:19-20.

Life Lesson

Proverbs 3:1-35

SITUATION God promises to guide those who obey and trust him. Those who obey must actively explore God's Word.

OBSERVATION Depend on God in every part of your life, and he will guide, protect, and comfort you.

INSPIRATION This expression "God's guidance," or "God's will," is really quite confusing. It seems so far removed from selling insurance, cleaning house, or taking the dog to the vet for his shot. It seems to imply being constantly ecstatic over "finding Jesus," or living on Cloud Nine without interruption. I suppose this could be part of it. But so many Christians, new and old alike, drape so much glamorous ecclesiastical jargon around it, that it gives the impression of being for an elite few "spiritual" or "saintly" people. That would leave out most of us, wouldn't it, God? . . . Jesus told His disciples that He was going away and would send someone to carry on for Him. This one would be a Comforter, a Helper, to remind and to guide. If He wasn't supposed to guide us in all things, how would we know when He was guiding and when He wasn't?

It occurs to me that if I'm tuned in to You, Jesus, I'm guided in everything I do. It could include simple things at the office, housework, even answering the presumptuous ring of the telephone to give some lonely forgotten soul a bit of myself.

11 Discretion will preserve you;
Understanding will keep you,
12 To deliver you from the way of evil,
From the man who speaks perverse things,
13 From those who leave the paths of uprightness
To walk in the ways of darkness;
14 Who rejoice in doing evil,
And delight in the perversity of the wicked;
15 Whose ways *are* crooked,
And *who are* devious in their paths;
16 To deliver you from the immoral woman,
From the seductress *who* flatters with her words,
17 Who forsakes the companion of her youth,
And forgets the covenant of her God.
18 For her house leads down to death,
And her paths to the dead;
19 None who go to her return,
Nor do they regain the paths of life—
20 So you may walk in the way of goodness,
And keep *to* the paths of righteousness.
21 For the upright will dwell in the land,
And the blameless will remain in it;
22 But the wicked will be cut off from the earth,
And the unfaithful will be uprooted from it.

Guidance for the Young

3 My son, do not forget my law,
But let your heart keep my commands;
2 For length of days and long life
And peace they will add to you.

3 Let not mercy and truth forsake you;
Bind them around your neck,
Write them on the tablet of your heart,
4 *And* so find favor and high esteem
In the sight of God and man.

5 Trust in the LORD with all your heart,
And lean not on your own understanding;
6 In all your ways acknowledge Him,
And He shall direct[c] your paths.

7 Do not be wise in your own eyes;
Fear the LORD and depart from evil.
8 It will be health to your flesh,[d]
And strength[e] to your bones.

9 Honor the LORD with your possessions,
And with the firstfruits of all your increase;
10 So your barns will be filled with plenty,
And your vats will overflow with new wine.

3:6 [c] Or *make smooth* or *straight*
3:8 [d] Literally *navel,* figurative of the body [e] Literally *drink* or *refreshment*

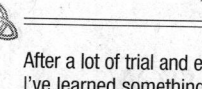

11 My son, do not despise the chastening of the LORD,
Nor detest His correction;
12 For whom the LORD loves He corrects,
Just as a father the son *in whom* he delights.

13 Happy *is* the man *who* finds wisdom,
And the man *who* gains understanding;
14 For her proceeds *are* better than the profits of silver,
And her gain than fine gold.
15 She *is* more precious than rubies,
And all the things you may desire cannot compare with her.
16 Length of days *is* in her right hand,
In her left hand riches and honor.
17 Her ways *are* ways of pleasantness,
And all her paths *are* peace.
18 She *is* a tree of life to those who take hold of her,
And happy *are all* who retain her.

19 The LORD by wisdom founded the earth;
By understanding He established the heavens;
20 By His knowledge the depths were broken up,
And clouds drop down the dew.

21 My son, let them not depart from your eyes—
Keep sound wisdom and discretion;
22 So they will be life to your soul
And grace to your neck.
23 Then you will walk safely in your way,
And your foot will not stumble.
24 When you lie down, you will not be afraid;
Yes, you will lie down and your sleep will be sweet.
25 Do not be afraid of sudden terror,
Nor of trouble from the wicked when it comes;
26 For the LORD will be your confidence,
And will keep your foot from being caught.

27 Do not withhold good from those to whom it is due,
When it is in the power of your hand to do *so*.
28 Do not say to your neighbor,
"Go, and come back,
And tomorrow I will give *it*,"
When *you have* it with you.
29 Do not devise evil against your neighbor,
For he dwells by you for safety's sake.
30 Do not strive with a man without cause,
If he has done you no harm.

31 Do not envy the oppressor,
And choose none of his ways;
32 For the perverse *person is* an abomination to the LORD,
But His secret counsel *is* with the upright.
33 The curse of the LORD *is* on the house of the wicked,
But He blesses the home of the just.
34 Surely He scorns the scornful,

After a lot of trial and error, God, I think I've learned something about Your will in my life. And the key is so simple. So often I have stubbornly knocked and banged my head against a door of decision or opportunity I wanted to push open. And so often nothing happened. The door just wouldn't budge. At other times when You and I were tuned in to the same channel, I barely touched the latch, and the door swung open. Everything poured out: happinesses, opportunities for creativity, spiritual presents, deeper relationships with friends, and, when the timing was right, a chance to share Your love with someone. . . . Your guidance kind of snowballs, God, from relying on You for dozens of little actions and decisions, we learn to seek Your guidance in times of big events, even tragedies, in our lives. Gradually we begin to rely on You in everything we do, no matter how insignificant.

(From *Struggles of a Sinner-Saint* by Lucille Lavender)

APPLICATION Is your life like a hotel, with certain rooms marked "Do Not Disturb"? Open one of those rooms to God. If you are a pianist, give your practice or performance to God. If you are a basketball referee, give your game to God. No matter what your role in life or your occupation, live every aspect of your life to honor God.

EXPLORATION Guidance—Joshua 1:9; Psalm 48:14; 118:8; Proverbs 2:1-5; Matthew 2:13; Luke 9:24-25; John 4:13-14; Acts 8:26.

LIFE LESSON

Proverbs 4:1-27

SITUATION The author emphasized that God's wisdom has been tested through the generations. These time-tested truths can help everyone avoid evil.

OBSERVATION Listening and following the words of a wise father help children learn how to act.

INSPIRATION Many passages in the Old Testament deal with the concept of wisdom. The book of Proverbs is especially concerned with it. Here are some general comments:

"Only the LORD gives wisdom; he gives knowledge and understanding. He stores up wisdom for those who are honest. Like a shield he protects the innocent" (Proverbs 2:6-7).

"Happy is the person who finds wisdom, the one who gets understanding. Wisdom is worth more than silver; it brings more profit than gold" (Proverbs 3:13-14).

"My child, hold on to wisdom and good sense. Don't let them out of your sight" (Proverbs 3:20-21).

There are really too many to include here. The book of Proverbs itself is worthy of a study on this subject, but I think you get some idea of what it has to say about wisdom.

But gives grace to the humble.
35 The wise shall inherit glory,
But shame shall be the legacy of fools.

Security in Wisdom

4 Hear, *my* children, the instruction of a father,
And give attention to know understanding;
2 For I give you good doctrine:
Do not forsake my law.
3 When I was my father's son,
Tender and the only one in the sight of my mother,
4 He also taught me, and said to me:
"Let your heart retain my words;
Keep my commands, and live.
5 Get wisdom! Get understanding!
Do not forget, nor turn away from the words of my mouth.
6 Do not forsake her, and she will preserve you;
Love her, and she will keep you.
7 Wisdom *is* the principal thing;
Therefore get wisdom.
And in all your getting, get understanding.
8 Exalt her, and she will promote you;
She will bring you honor, when you embrace her.
9 She will place on your head an ornament of grace;
A crown of glory she will deliver to you."

10 Hear, my son, and receive my sayings,
And the years of your life will be many.
11 I have taught you in the way of wisdom;
I have led you in right paths.
12 When you walk, your steps will not be hindered,
And when you run, you will not stumble.
13 Take firm hold of instruction, do not let go;
Keep her, for she *is* your life.

14 Do not enter the path of the wicked,
And do not walk in the way of evil.
15 Avoid it, do not travel on it;
Turn away from it and pass on.
16 For they do not sleep unless they have done evil;
And their sleep is taken away unless they make *someone* fall.
17 For they eat the bread of wickedness,
And drink the wine of violence.

18 But the path of the just *is* like the shining sun,[f]
That shines ever brighter unto the perfect day.
19 The way of the wicked *is* like darkness;
They do not know what makes them stumble.

20 My son, give attention to my words;
Incline your ear to my sayings.
21 Do not let them depart from your eyes;

4:18 [f] Literally *light*

Keep them in the midst of your heart;
22 For they *are* life to those who find them,
And health to all their flesh.
23 Keep your heart with all diligence,
For out of it *spring* the issues of life.
24 Put away from you a deceitful mouth,
And put perverse lips far from you.
25 Let your eyes look straight ahead,
And your eyelids look right before you.
26 Ponder the path of your feet,
And let all your ways be established.
27 Do not turn to the right or the left;
Remove your foot from evil.

The Peril of Adultery

5 My son, pay attention to my wisdom;
Lend your ear to my understanding,
2 That you may preserve discretion,
And your lips may keep knowledge.
3 For the lips of an immoral woman drip honey,
And her mouth *is* smoother than oil;
4 But in the end she is bitter as wormwood,
Sharp as a two-edged sword.
5 Her feet go down to death,
Her steps lay hold of hell.[g]
6 Lest you ponder *her* path of life—
Her ways are unstable;
You do not know *them.*

7 Therefore hear me now, *my* children,
And do not depart from the words of my mouth.
8 Remove your way far from her,
And do not go near the door of her house,
9 Lest you give your honor to others,
And your years to the cruel *one;*
10 Lest aliens be filled with your wealth,
And your labors *go* to the house of a foreigner;
11 And you mourn at last,
When your flesh and your body are consumed,
12 And say:
"How I have hated instruction,
And my heart despised correction!
13 I have not obeyed the voice of my teachers,
Nor inclined my ear to those who instructed me!
14 I was on the verge of total ruin,
In the midst of the assembly and congregation."

15 Drink water from your own cistern,
And running water from your own well.
16 Should your fountains be dispersed abroad,

One of the best passages dealing with this concept, however, is found in the New Testament. In Ephesians 5:3-14, the apostle Paul exhorted the Ephesian believers to live moral lives. He made it clear to them that they where neither to participate in evil nor to speak of it. On the contrary, he commanded them to expose immoral deeds of evil persons.

. . . Practically speaking, our goal as believers cannot simply be not to sin. Rather it must be to walk wisely because walking wisely is the means by which moral living is carried out. Wise living provides a safety factor. It is like putting a fence around a pit with a Keep Out sign on it. The fence serves as a means of keeping people out of the pit. As the fence is to the pit, so wisdom is to sin. When followed, wisdom keeps us out of trouble by eliminating the possibility in the first place.

(From *How to Keep Your Kids on Your Team* by Charles Stanley)

APPLICATION Did you ever read about different thinkers or philosophers? Did you ever notice that their ideas seem to go out of style after a few years? God's wisdom doesn't! Make living by God's Word your highest priority. Read it, memorize it, think about it often, and let it change your life every day.

EXPLORATION Listen and Obey—Proverbs 30:5; Isaiah 30:21.

5:5 [g] Or *Sheol*

LIFE LESSON

Proverbs 5:1-23

SITUATION Solomon warned his son of the sin of adultery. He urged him to remember what he was taught and to avoid the temptation of having sex outside of marriage. Rather, he encouraged him to enjoy the love of his own wife.

OBSERVATION Do not be seduced by lust. Falling prey to lust only leads to moral ruin and spiritual death.

INSPIRATION As the national sales manager for his securities firm, Jeremy was on the road at least three days out of every five. After two years of countless hotel rooms, he found the boredom setting in. Retiring to his hotel room at night, he began channel surfing with the television, searching for something to catch his interest. Like a moth to a flame, he became increasingly curious about the X-rated cable channels.

Not wanting to give in, he asked the men in his Saturday morning Bible study to hold him accountable to three things. When he arrived at the hotel, he would ask the desk clerk to disconnect his television. The second was that he would maintain a list of and be accountable about the books and magazines that he bought and was currently reading. Finally, whenever he felt tempted morally, he asked permission to call one of the other men, regardless of where he was or the time of day.

(From *A Dad's Blessing* by Gary Smalley and John Trent)

APPLICATION When do you struggle with lust? How can you avoid those situations? Don't allow sexual thoughts to occupy your mind. If you are married, avoid anything that causes you to desire anyone other than your own spouse and take extra time to demonstrate love to your spouse.

EXPLORATION Lust—Proverbs 6:23; Matthew 5:27-30; Colossians 3:5; 1 Thessalonians 4:3; 1 John 2:16.

Streams of water in the streets?
17 Let them be only your own,
And not for strangers with you.
18 Let your fountain be blessed,
And rejoice with the wife of your youth.
19 *As a* loving deer and a graceful doe,
Let her breasts satisfy you at all times;
And always be enraptured with her love.
20 For why should you, my son, be enraptured by an immoral woman,
And be embraced in the arms of a seductress?

21 For the ways of man *are* before the eyes of the LORD,
And He ponders all his paths.
22 His own iniquities entrap the wicked *man*,
And he is caught in the cords of his sin.
23 He shall die for lack of instruction,
And in the greatness of his folly he shall go astray.

Dangerous Promises

6 My son, if you become surety for your friend,
If you have shaken hands in pledge for a stranger,
2 You are snared by the words of your mouth;
You are taken by the words of your mouth.
3 So do this, my son, and deliver yourself;
For you have come into the hand of your friend:
Go and humble yourself;
Plead with your friend.
4 Give no sleep to your eyes,
Nor slumber to your eyelids.
5 Deliver yourself like a gazelle from the hand *of the hunter*,
And like a bird from the hand of the fowler.[h]

The Folly of Indolence

6 Go to the ant, you sluggard!
Consider her ways and be wise,
7 Which, having no captain,
Overseer or ruler,
8 Provides her supplies in the summer,
And gathers her food in the harvest.
9 How long will you slumber, O sluggard?
When will you rise from your sleep?
10 A little sleep, a little slumber,
A little folding of the hands to sleep—
11 So shall your poverty come on you like a prowler,
And your need like an armed man.

The Wicked Man

12 A worthless person, a wicked man,
Walks with a perverse mouth;
13 He winks with his eyes,

6:5 *h* That is, one who catches birds in a trap or snare

He shuffles his feet,
He points with his fingers;
14 Perversity *is* in his heart,
He devises evil continually,
He sows discord.
15 Therefore his calamity shall come suddenly;
Suddenly he shall be broken without remedy.

16 These six *things* the LORD hates,
Yes, seven *are* an abomination to Him:
17 A proud look,
A lying tongue,
Hands that shed innocent blood,
18 A heart that devises wicked plans,
Feet that are swift in running to evil,
19 A false witness *who* speaks lies,
And one who sows discord among brethren.

Beware of Adultery

20 My son, keep your father's command,
And do not forsake the law of your mother.
21 Bind them continually upon your heart;
Tie them around your neck.
22 When you roam, they[i] will lead you;
When you sleep, they will keep you;
And *when* you awake, they will speak with you.
23 For the commandment *is* a lamp,
And the law a light;
Reproofs of instruction *are* the way of life,
24 To keep you from the evil woman,
From the flattering tongue of a seductress.
25 Do not lust after her beauty in your heart,
Nor let her allure you with her eyelids.
26 For by means of a harlot
A man is reduced to a crust of bread;
And an adulteress[j] will prey upon his precious life.
27 Can a man take fire to his bosom,
And his clothes not be burned?
28 Can one walk on hot coals,
And his feet not be seared?
29 So *is* he who goes in to his neighbor's wife;
Whoever touches her shall not be innocent.

30 *People* do not despise a thief
If he steals to satisfy himself when he is starving.
31 Yet *when* he is found, he must restore sevenfold;
He may have to give up all the substance of his house.
32 Whoever commits adultery with a woman lacks understanding;
He *who* does so destroys his own soul.
33 Wounds and dishonor he will get,
And his reproach will not be wiped away.

6:22 [i] Literally *it*
6:26 [j] Literally *a man's wife*, that is, of another

LIFE LESSON

Proverbs 6:1-35

SITUATION Solomon gave advice to his son: avoid adultery and foolishness.

OBSERVATION Often, wisdom can be found by simply saying no to temptation.

INSPIRATION It is never too late to say no. The freedom offered in Christ is that we can say no, and when we say it there comes the opposite resounding yes. And out of that yes God builds a life more beautiful, more complete, more satisfying than anything that we could ever create for ourselves. He wants that for each of us.

For more than ten years, first on an eastern campus and then in the midwest, I ministered to university students. We would meet regularly to pray for each other, "How can I pray for you to be the obedient man or woman God wants you to be? What are the blocks that need to be eliminated, and what are the changes that need to be made?" And as we prayed specifically for obedience and holiness and faith, I could see God take those young lives and develop them.

I see how he has honored those times of serious prayer. Wherever I go now, I meet these students with whom I once prayed or who prayed for me, and I see what God is doing in their lives. I compare them to others who missed that time of praying because they were not willing to let God have them—to be all that God wanted them to be—and I see the difference.

(From *Enjoying the Closeness of God* by Roger Palms)

APPLICATION Develop one or two friends who will ask you often, "How can I pray for you to be the obedient man or woman God wants you to be? What are the blocks that need to be eliminated, and what are the changes that need to be made?" Pray for them daily, too. Slip them a note, reminding them that you are supporting them in prayer.

EXPLORATION Folly—Mark 7:22; Adultery—Exodus 20:14; Matthew 5:27-30; Avoiding Evil—1 Thessalonians 5:21-22.

Life Lesson

Proverbs 7:1-27

SITUATION The writer of Proverbs warned against yielding to the temptation of extramarital sex and other sins.

OBSERVATION Beware of being entrapped in the lies of the world that promise sensuality as the means of happiness and significance.

INSPIRATION As I work on this manuscript, I'm seated at a desk in a hotel room. I'm away from home. Away from people who know me.

Voices that encourage and affirm are distant.

But voices that tantalize and entice are near. Although the room is quiet, if I listen, their voices are crystal clear.

A placard on my nightstand invites me to a lounge in the lobby, where I can "make new friends in a relaxing atmosphere." An advertisement on top of the television promises me that with the request of a late-night adult movie my "fantasies will come true." In the phone book, several columns of escort services offer "love away from home." . . . On television a talk-show host discusses the day's topic: "How to succeed at sex in the office."

Voices. Some for pleasure. Some for power.

The world rams at your door; Jesus taps at your door. The voices scream for your allegiance; Jesus softly and tenderly requests it. The world promises flashy pleasure; Jesus promises a quiet dinner . . . with God. "I will come in and eat."

Which voice do you hear?

(From *In the Eye of the Storm* by Max Lucado)

APPLICATION We cannot stand firm against the lies of the world unless we are firmly grounded in Christ. Be diligent to read God's Word, and pray often. Promise yourself to pray at three different times today.

EXPLORATION Follow the Lord—Deuteronomy 4:30; Psalm 111:10; Proverbs 8; Luke 9:35; Revelation 3:20.

34 For jealousy *is* a husband's fury;
Therefore he will not spare in the day of vengeance.
35 He will accept no recompense,
Nor will he be appeased though you give many gifts.

7 My son, keep my words,
And treasure my commands within you.
2 Keep my commands and live,
And my law as the apple of your eye.
3 Bind them on your fingers;
Write them on the tablet of your heart.
4 Say to wisdom, "You *are* my sister,"
And call understanding *your* nearest kin,
5 That they may keep you from the immoral woman,
From the seductress *who* flatters with her words.

The Crafty Harlot

6 For at the window of my house
I looked through my lattice,
7 And saw among the simple,
I perceived among the youths,
A young man devoid of understanding,
8 Passing along the street near her corner;
And he took the path to her house
9 In the twilight, in the evening,
In the black and dark night.

10 And there a woman met him,
With the attire of a harlot, and a crafty heart.
11 She *was* loud and rebellious,
Her feet would not stay at home.
12 At times *she was* outside, at times in the open square,
Lurking at every corner.
13 So she caught him and kissed him;
With an impudent face she said to him:
14 "*I have* peace offerings with me;
Today I have paid my vows.
15 So I came out to meet you,
Diligently to seek your face,
And I have found you.
16 I have spread my bed with tapestry,
Colored coverings of Egyptian linen.
17 I have perfumed my bed
With myrrh, aloes, and cinnamon.
18 Come, let us take our fill of love until morning;
Let us delight ourselves with love.
19 For my husband *is* not at home;
He has gone on a long journey;
20 He has taken a bag of money with him,
And will come home on the appointed day."

21 With her enticing speech she caused him to yield,
With her flattering lips she seduced him.

22 Immediately he went after her, as an ox goes to the slaughter,
Or as a fool to the correction of the stocks,[k]
23 Till an arrow struck his liver.
As a bird hastens to the snare,
He did not know it *would cost* his life.

24 Now therefore, listen to me, *my* children;
Pay attention to the words of my mouth:
25 Do not let your heart turn aside to her ways,
Do not stray into her paths;
26 For she has cast down many wounded,
And all who were slain by her were strong *men.*
27 Her house *is* the way to hell,[l]
Descending to the chambers of death.

The Excellence of Wisdom

8 Does not wisdom cry out,
And understanding lift up her voice?
2 She takes her stand on the top of the high hill,
Beside the way, where the paths meet.
3 She cries out by the gates, at the entry of the city,
At the entrance of the doors:
4 "To you, O men, I call,
And my voice *is* to the sons of men.
5 O you simple ones, understand prudence,
And you fools, be of an understanding heart.
6 Listen, for I will speak of excellent things,
And from the opening of my lips *will come* right things;
7 For my mouth will speak truth;
Wickedness *is* an abomination to my lips.
8 All the words of my mouth *are* with righteousness;
Nothing crooked or perverse *is* in them.
9 They *are* all plain to him who understands,
And right to those who find knowledge.
10 Receive my instruction, and not silver,
And knowledge rather than choice gold;
11 For wisdom *is* better than rubies,
And all the things one may desire cannot
be compared with her.

12 "I, wisdom, dwell with prudence,
And find out knowledge *and* discretion.
13 The fear of the LORD *is* to hate evil;
Pride and arrogance and the evil way
And the perverse mouth I hate.
14 Counsel *is* mine, and sound wisdom;
I *am* understanding, I have strength.
15 By me kings reign,
And rulers decree justice.

Life Lesson

Proverbs 8:1-36

SITUATION God's wisdom called the readers of Proverbs to make right choices rather than wicked ones.

OBSERVATION God always makes his wisdom available to us. Human wisdom will fail.

INSPIRATION Everything God made—even human beings—has as its key purpose the reflection of the honor of God.

Unfortunately, the power of sin has tarnished the capacity of some aspects of creation to reflect that honor. In fact, sin first appears to have done its job on humanity; then, through men and women, sin systematically tarnished everything else in creation. But where man has not been able to confuse the issue, the creation continues to shout out its message: God the Creator be praised!

The growing mind, filled with the love of Christ, searches creation for these messages. Because of our spiritual and natural gifts, each of us is able to see and hear them in particular areas more than in others. And we are enabled to take this creation material and identify it, shape it, reconfigure it, or in other ways use it so that God is further glorified. The carpenter works with wood; the physician listens to the body; the musician shapes sounds; the executive manages people; the educator trains youth; the researcher analyzes, innovates, and implements with the elements of the universe.

We develop our minds for these tasks and rejoice as we do them for all that God is revealing to us out of His loving heart.

(From *Ordering Your Private World* by Gordon MacDonald)

APPLICATION What is your toughest decision today? After you have prayed and searched God's Word for advice, call a Christian friend who can help.

EXPLORATION Wisdom's Call—Psalm 119:97-104; Proverbs 1:20-28; 2:3-6; 4:5-8.

7:22 [k] Septuagint, Syriac, and Targum read *as a dog to bonds;* Vulgate reads *as a lamb . . . to bonds.*
7:27 [l] Or *Sheol*

LIFE LESSON

Proverbs 9:1-18

SITUATION By contrasting the invitations of wisdom and foolishness, chapter 9 provides a summary statement of the first eight chapters of Proverbs.

OBSERVATION God's wisdom leads to life. Foolishness, personified by the adulteress, leads to death.

INSPIRATION "If Satan were to blow you out of the water," he asked, "how do you think he would do it?"

"I'm not sure I know," I answered. "All sorts of ways, I suppose; but I know there's one way he wouldn't get me."

"What's that?"

"He'd never get me in the area of my personal relationships. That's one place where I have no doubt that I'm as strong as you can get."

A few years after that conversation my world broke wide open. A chain of seemingly innocent choices became destructive, and it was my fault. And then my world broke—in the very area I had predicted I was safe—and my world had to be rebuilt. . . .

I wondered why until I realized from personal experience that where we perceive ourselves to be the strongest is where we're least likely to be prepared for a battle that isn't psychological or emotional. It's spiritual! Let no person ever say, "I can't be taken." Or as St. Paul wrote, "So, if you think you are standing firm, be careful that you don't fall!" (1 Cor. 10:12).

(From *Rebuilding Your Broken World* by Gordon MacDonald)

APPLICATION Have you been nurturing a "harmless" habit? If so, you are like the man who continually passes in front of the harlot's house, thinking he can withstand her alluring invitations! Stop that compromising habit today and return to God before it is too late!

EXPLORATION Avoiding Sin—Job 31:1; Proverbs 4:14-15; 6:20-26; 8:13; 1 Corinthians 10:12-13; 2 Timothy 2:22; James 1:13-15.

16 By me princes rule, and nobles,
All the judges of the earth.[m]
17 I love those who love me,
And those who seek me diligently will find me.
18 Riches and honor *are* with me,
Enduring riches and righteousness.
19 My fruit *is* better than gold, yes, than fine gold,
And my revenue than choice silver.
20 I traverse the way of righteousness,
In the midst of the paths of justice,
21 That I may cause those who love me to inherit wealth,
That I may fill their treasuries.

22 "The LORD possessed me at the beginning of His way,
Before His works of old.
23 I have been established from everlasting,
From the beginning, before there was ever an earth.
24 When *there were* no depths I was brought forth,
When *there were* no fountains abounding with water.
25 Before the mountains were settled,
Before the hills, I was brought forth;
26 While as yet He had not made the
earth or the fields,
Or the primal dust of the world.
27 When He prepared the heavens, I *was* there,
When He drew a circle on the face of the deep,
28 When He established the clouds above,
When He strengthened the fountains of the deep,
29 When He assigned to the sea its limit,
So that the waters would not transgress
His command,
When He marked out the foundations of the earth,
30 Then I was beside Him *as* a master craftsman;[n]
And I was daily *His* delight,
Rejoicing always before Him,
31 Rejoicing in His inhabited world,
And my delight *was* with the sons of men.

32 "Now therefore, listen to me, *my* children,
For blessed *are those who* keep my ways.
33 Hear instruction and be wise,
And do not disdain *it.*
34 Blessed is the man who listens to me,
Watching daily at my gates,
Waiting at the posts of my doors.
35 For whoever finds me finds life,
And obtains favor from the LORD;
36 But he who sins against me wrongs his own soul;
All those who hate me love death."

8:16 [m] Masoretic Text, Syriac, Targum, and Vulgate read *righteousness;* Septuagint, Bomberg, and some manuscripts and editions read *earth.*
8:30 [n] A Jewish tradition reads *one brought up.*

The Way of Wisdom

9 Wisdom has built her house,
She has hewn out her seven pillars;
2 She has slaughtered her meat,
She has mixed her wine,
She has also furnished her table.
3 She has sent out her maidens,
She cries out from the highest places of the city,
4 "Whoever *is* simple, let him turn in here!"
As for him who lacks understanding, she says to him,
5 "Come, eat of my bread
And drink of the wine I have mixed.
6 Forsake foolishness and live,
And go in the way of understanding.

7 "He who corrects a scoffer gets shame for himself,
And he who rebukes a wicked *man only* harms himself.
8 Do not correct a scoffer, lest he hate you;
Rebuke a wise *man,* and he will love you.
9 Give *instruction* to a wise *man,* and he will be still wiser;
Teach a just *man,* and he will increase in learning.

10 "The fear of the LORD *is* the beginning of wisdom,
And the knowledge of the Holy One *is* understanding.
11 For by me your days will be multiplied,
And years of life will be added to you.
12 If you are wise, you are wise for yourself,
And *if* you scoff, you will bear *it* alone."

The Way of Folly

13 A foolish woman is clamorous;
She is simple, and knows nothing.
14 For she sits at the door of her house,
On a seat *by* the highest places of the city,
15 To call to those who pass by,
Who go straight on their way:
16 "Whoever *is* simple, let him turn in here";
And *as for* him who lacks understanding,
she says to him,
17 "Stolen water is sweet,
And bread *eaten* in secret is pleasant."
18 But he does not know that the dead *are* there,
That her guests *are* in the depths of hell.[o]

Wise Sayings of Solomon

10 The proverbs of Solomon:

A wise son makes a glad father,
But a foolish son *is* the grief of his mother.

2 Treasures of wickedness profit nothing,
But righteousness delivers from death.

9:18 [o] Or *Sheol*

LIFE LESSON

Proverbs 10:1-32

SITUATION This chapter begins a collection of proverbs attributed to Solomon.

OBSERVATION The actions of wise and good people are contrasted with the deeds of foolish and evil people. Solomon emphasizes the need for honesty and the wise choice of words.

INSPIRATION Insensitivity makes a wound that heals slowly.

If someone hurts your feelings intentionally, you know how to react. You know the source of the pain. But if someone accidentally bruises your soul, it's difficult to know how to respond.

Someone at work criticizes the new boss, who also happens to be your dear friend. "Oh, I'm sorry—I forgot the two of you were so close."

A joke is told at a party about overweight people. You're overweight. You hear the joke. You smile politely while your heart sinks.

What was intended to be a reprimand for a decision or action becomes a personal attack. "You have a history of poor decisions, John."

Someone chooses to wash your dirty laundry in public. "Sue, is it true that you and Jim are separated?"

Insensitive comments. Thoughts that should have remained thoughts. Feelings which had no business being expressed. Opinions carelessly tossed like a grenade into a crowd.

And if you were to tell the one who threw these thoughtless darts about the pain they caused, his response would be "Oh, but I had no intention. . . . I didn't realize you were so sensitive!" or "I forgot you were here."

In a way, the words are comforting, until you stop to think about them (which is not recommended). For when you start to think about insensitive slurs, you realize they come from an infamous family whose father has breeded generations of pain. His name? Egotism. His children? Three sisters: disregard, disrespect, and disappointment.

Continued

These three witches have combined to poison countless relationships and break innumerable hearts. Listed among their weapons are Satan's cruelest artillery: gossip, accusations, resentment, impatience, and on and on. . . .

God's Word has strong medicine for those who carelessly wag their tongues. The message is clear: He who dares to call himself God's ambassador is not afforded the luxury of idle words. Excuses such as "I didn't know you were here" or "I didn't realize this was so touchy" are shallow when they come from those who claim to be followers and imitators of the Great Physician. We have an added responsibility to guard our tongues. (From *God Came Near* by Max Lucado)

APPLICATION Evaluate the words you have spoken in the past week. What statements have been sinful or harmful? Did your words build up or tear down? Were they critical? Were they vulgar? If so, ask for God's forgiveness and seek the forgiveness of anyone you have offended. Ask for God's help to use your words wisely.

EXPLORATION Helpful Words—Proverbs 16:24; 25:11; Ecclesiastes 10:12; Isaiah 50:4; Ephesians 4:29; Colossians 4:6.

3 The LORD will not allow the righteous soul to famish,
But He casts away the desire of the wicked.

4 He who has a slack hand becomes poor,
But the hand of the diligent makes rich.
5 He who gathers in summer *is* a wise son;
He who sleeps in harvest *is* a son who causes shame.

6 Blessings *are* on the head of the righteous,
But violence covers the mouth of the wicked.
7 The memory of the righteous *is* blessed,
But the name of the wicked will rot.

8 The wise in heart will receive commands,
But a prating fool will fall.

9 He who walks with integrity walks securely,
But he who perverts his ways will become known.

10 He who winks with the eye causes trouble,
But a prating fool will fall.

11 The mouth of the righteous *is* a well of life,
But violence covers the mouth of the wicked.

12 Hatred stirs up strife,
But love covers all sins.

13 Wisdom is found on the lips of him who has understanding,
But a rod *is* for the back of him who is devoid of understanding.

14 Wise *people* store up knowledge,
But the mouth of the foolish *is* near destruction.

15 The rich man's wealth *is* his strong city;
The destruction of the poor *is* their poverty.

16 The labor of the righteous *leads* to life,
The wages of the wicked to sin.

17 He who keeps instruction *is in* the way of life,
But he who refuses correction goes astray.

18 Whoever hides hatred *has* lying lips,
And whoever spreads slander *is* a fool.

19 In the multitude of words sin is not lacking,
But he who restrains his lips *is* wise.
20 The tongue of the righteous *is* choice silver;
The heart of the wicked *is worth* little.
21 The lips of the righteous feed many,
But fools die for lack of wisdom.[p]

22 The blessing of the LORD makes *one* rich,
And He adds no sorrow with it.

23 To do evil *is* like sport to a fool,
But a man of understanding has wisdom.

10:21 *p* Literally *heart*

24 The fear of the wicked will come upon him,
And the desire of the righteous will be granted.
25 When the whirlwind passes by, the wicked *is* no *more*,
But the righteous *has* an everlasting foundation.

26 As vinegar to the teeth and smoke to the eyes,
So *is* the lazy *man* to those who send him.

27 The fear of the LORD prolongs days,
But the years of the wicked will be shortened.
28 The hope of the righteous *will be* gladness,
But the expectation of the wicked will perish.
29 The way of the LORD *is* strength for the upright,
But destruction *will come* to the workers of iniquity.
30 The righteous will never be removed,
But the wicked will not inhabit the earth.
31 The mouth of the righteous brings forth wisdom,
But the perverse tongue will be cut out.
32 The lips of the righteous know what is acceptable,
But the mouth of the wicked *what is* perverse.

11

Dishonest scales *are* an abomination to the LORD,
But a just weight *is* His delight.

2 When pride comes, then comes shame;
But with the humble *is* wisdom.

3 The integrity of the upright will guide them,
But the perversity of the unfaithful will destroy them.
4 Riches do not profit in the day of wrath,
But righteousness delivers from death.
5 The righteousness of the blameless will
direct[q] his way aright,
But the wicked will fall by his own wickedness.
6 The righteousness of the upright will deliver them,
But the unfaithful will be caught by *their* lust.
7 When a wicked man dies, *his* expectation will perish,
And the hope of the unjust perishes.
8 The righteous is delivered from trouble,
And it comes to the wicked instead.
9 The hypocrite with *his* mouth destroys his neighbor,
But through knowledge the righteous will be delivered.
10 When it goes well with the righteous, the city rejoices;
And when the wicked perish, *there is* jubilation.
11 By the blessing of the upright the city is exalted,
But it is overthrown by the mouth of the wicked.

12 He who is devoid of wisdom despises his neighbor,
But a man of understanding holds his peace.

13 A talebearer reveals secrets,
But he who is of a faithful spirit conceals a matter.

11:5 [q] Or *make smooth* or *straight*

LIFE LESSON

Proverbs 11:1-31

SITUATION Solomon gave practical words of wisdom that would ensure long life to those who heed them.

OBSERVATION Solomon contrasted righteous and wicked behavior, paying special attention to the best use of money.

INSPIRATION I know two men who work for a nonprofit organization. Both travel on expense accounts. One lives as a friend of God; the other does not. Circumstances are the same for both, but their responses to those circumstances are opposite. This is how the difference shows:

"Go ahead and order the steak."

"But I don't eat like this at home; I can't afford it."

"You're not at home; it's going on your expense account."

"No."

"You work hard; you've earned it."

"I'm paid to work hard. I am not paid to exploit."

When those two men started their work, both had strong convictions about the high calling of their vocations. They felt a sense of mission in a worthwhile organization, one that helped people in need. They kept costs down so that the money could be used as the donors expected it to be used. But then they began to notice that others in their group weren't so fussy. After a while it became easier for one of those men to change from a high view of commitment to the rationalization, "You won't be appreciated any more if you don't take." Even worse, he gave in to the charge, "You make the rest of us look bad when we turn in our expenses."

. . . But the other man won't bend. . . .

He just goes on, one day at a time, trying to do what is expected of him by God. And usually that's all we have to go on as we try to be a friend of God. What others say cannot be the measure of what is ethical, moral, or right, even if it is legal. The view of the majority is not necessarily the view of God.

(From *Enjoying the Closeness of God* by Roger Palms)

Continued

APPLICATION Take a minute to look through your checkbook. How do you spend your money? Where does extra money go—eating out, golf, movies? Over the next month, skip one of these extras and give the money you save to a Christian ministry.

EXPLORATION The Rich Ruler—Luke 18:18-30. The Faithful, Wise Servant—Luke 12:42-48.

14 Where *there is* no counsel, the people fall;
But in the multitude of counselors *there is* safety.

15 He who is surety for a stranger will suffer,
But one who hates being surety is secure.

16 A gracious woman retains honor,
But ruthless *men* retain riches.
17 The merciful man does good for his own soul,
But *he who is* cruel troubles his own flesh.
18 The wicked *man* does deceptive work,
But he who sows righteousness *will have* a sure reward.
19 As righteousness *leads* to life,
So he who pursues evil *pursues it* to his own death.
20 Those who are of a perverse heart *are* an abomination to the LORD,
But *the* blameless in their ways *are* His delight.
21 *Though they join* forces,[r] the wicked will not go unpunished;
But the posterity of the righteous will be delivered.

22 *As* a ring of gold in a swine's snout,
So is a lovely woman who lacks discretion.

23 The desire of the righteous *is* only good,
But the expectation of the wicked *is* wrath.

24 There is *one* who scatters, yet increases more;
And there is *one* who withholds more than is right,
But it *leads* to poverty.
25 The generous soul will be made rich,
And he who waters will also be watered himself.
26 The people will curse him who withholds grain,
But blessing *will be* on the head of him who sells *it.*

27 He who earnestly seeks good finds favor,
But trouble will come to him who seeks *evil.*

28 He who trusts in his riches will fall,
But the righteous will flourish like foliage.

29 He who troubles his own house will inherit the wind,
And the fool *will be* servant to the wise of heart.

30 The fruit of the righteous *is a* tree of life,
And he who wins souls *is* wise.

31 If the righteous will be recompensed on the earth,
How much more the ungodly and the sinner.

12 Whoever loves instruction loves knowledge,
But he who hates correction *is* stupid.

2 A good *man* obtains favor from the LORD,
But a man of wicked intentions He will condemn.

3 A man is not established by wickedness,
But the root of the righteous cannot be moved.

11:21 [r] Literally *hand to hand*

BIBLE

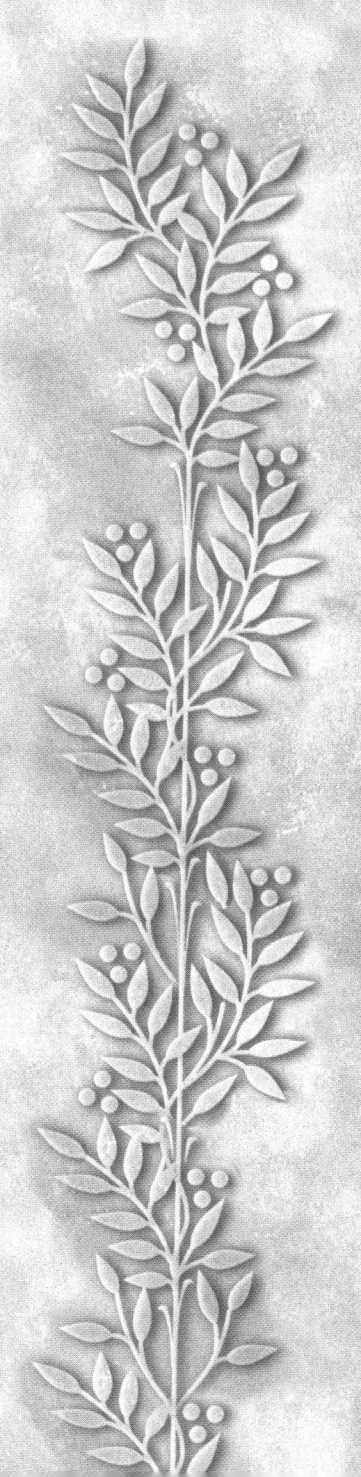

We go to the Word of God for comfort, and when we do, the words pierce like a surgeon's scalpel, both cutting and healing. The Word of God cuts to the very place where thoughts and attitudes come together, at the juncture of soul and spirit, providing a healing that can be obtained in no other way on earth.

The Bible was provided for us as a vehicle to carry us so that we might be able to see Jesus Christ.

If you want to grow in the Word of God, become a person with a chisel and quarry the Word—look, explore, seek. Let the Word become your Word, and you will grow.

I challenge you to rediscover the Bible in your own life . . . to regain the same hunger and enthusiasm you felt when you first heard the name of Jesus!

Father, we're amazed at how practical your Bible is. Who would have thought that daily help could be found in a book so old. Every time we open it we find it's not old at all. Help us to look for your guidance in that precious book. Make us aware of how precious your Word is. Bless those who transport your Word to far-off places, to people who haven't been able to open your Word. Thank you, Father, for giving us this source of light and strength, and for giving us the opportunity to uncover the jewels waiting to be discovered in your holy pages.

Busyness

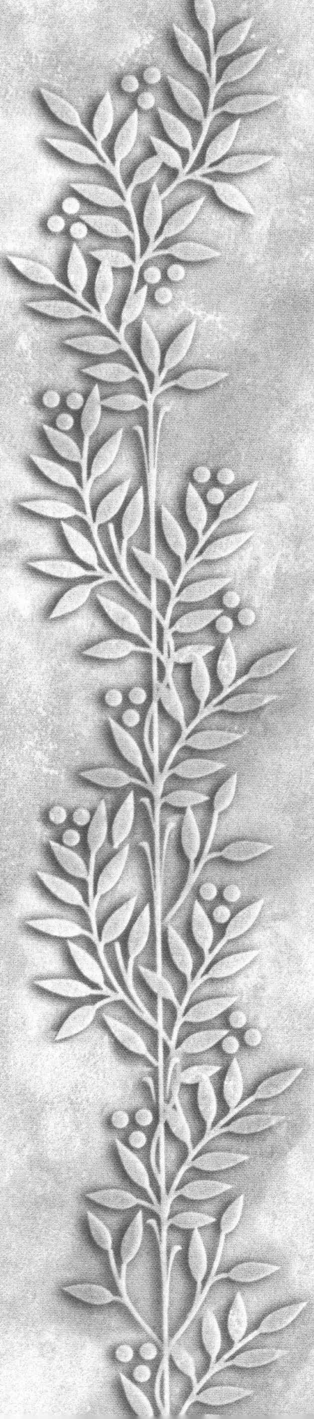

Being busy is not a sin. Jesus was busy. Paul was busy. Peter was busy. Nothing of significance is achieved without effort and hard work and weariness. That, in and of itself, is not a sin. But being busy in an endless pursuit of *things* that leave us empty and hollow and broken inside—that cannot be pleasing to God.

In the midst of a busy life on the freeway of humanity, it seems that the faster we go, the emptier we become. When we're always in a hurry trying to get ahead, never taking time to pause and reflect, we sacrifice a lot to stay on top. Sometimes it takes hard decisions to bring our life under control and realign our priorities, focusing on the Father and letting everything else take a backseat.

In the midst of your busyness, the Cross is still there. In the midst of your emptiness, the Cross is still there. The promises of Jesus still stand today. You can claim peace in the midst of a hectic life—not without sacrifice or concentration, but you can do it.

FATHER, *help us to say no to the world and yes to you. Help us to hear the true voice of Jesus Christ amid the voices of pressure and success and power. We don't really know how, unless you come and help us.*

FAITH

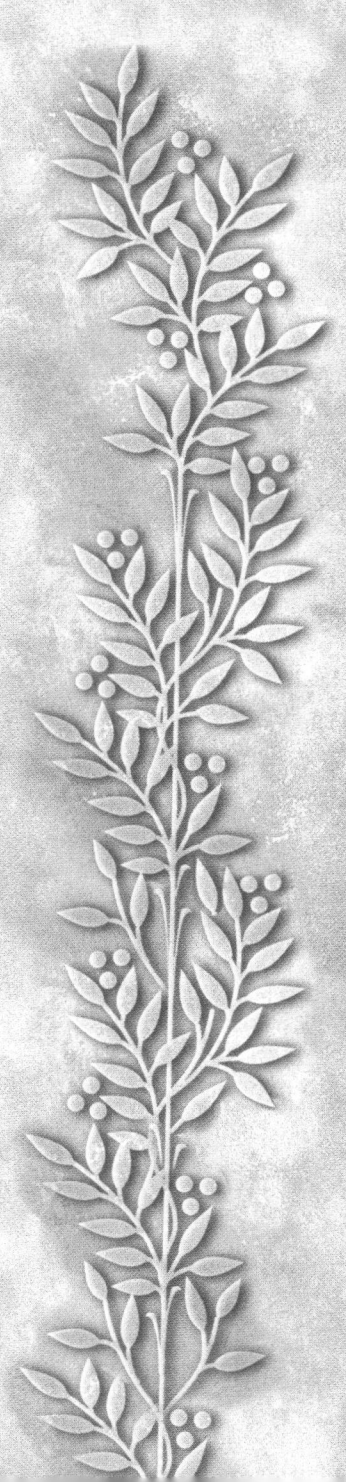

Don't build your house on a career. Don't build your house on a thrill. Don't build your house on a talent. Don't build your house on one solitary earthly relationship. Don't pursue things that don't last. Build your house on the only thing that can last: faith.

Do you have faith? If you have faith, then you have what it takes to tackle your problems before they tackle you. If you have that confident hope, then you will know how to handle whatever life brings you.

One thing no one can take away from you is your faith. This world can and may take everything you have. But no one can take away your faith. Grab that faith; clutch tightly that anchor of the soul.

Make your faith an independent dogged faith, firmly planted in God's sacrificed Son on the hill of Calvary. It can never be taken away from you.

FATHER, help us renew our commitment to you, to release everything and to be owned and possessed by you. We long to submit ourselves to you so that we might know the holy freedom available to us only through your grace.

Decisions

Anchor your convictions to the Word of God to help prevent crises from occurring in your life. When facing tough decisions, employ dogged and determined prayer and thinking grounded in the Word.

Do what is right this week, whatever it is, whatever comes down the path, whatever problems and dilemmas you face—just do what's right. Maybe no one else is doing what's right, but you do what's right. You be honest. You take a stand. You be true. After all, regardless of what you do, God does what is right: he saves you with his grace.

Never let your decisions be made on the basis of the blowings of the winds of opinion and popularity.

The majority is not always right. If the majority had ruled, the children of Israel never would have left Egypt. They would have voted to stay in bondage. If the majority had ruled, David never would have fought Goliath. His brothers would have voted for him to stay with the sheep. What's the point? You must listen to your own heart.

God says you're on your way to becoming a disciple when you can keep a clear head and a pure heart.

Do you ever wonder if everything will turn out right as long as you do everything right? Do you ever try to do something right and yet nothing seems to turn out like you planned? Take heart—when people do what is right, God remembers.

FATHER, we invite you to be our guide through life. Lord, we don't ask that you take from us the worries of this life but that you surface the worries of this life so that we can share them with you and turn them over to you.

4 An excellent[s] wife *is* the crown of her husband,
But she who causes shame *is* like rottenness in his bones.

5 The thoughts of the righteous *are* right,
But the counsels of the wicked *are* deceitful.
6 The words of the wicked *are*, "Lie in wait for blood,"
But the mouth of the upright will deliver them.

7 The wicked are overthrown and *are* no more,
But the house of the righteous will stand.

8 A man will be commended according to his wisdom,
But he who is of a perverse heart will be despised.

9 Better *is the one* who is slighted but has a servant,
Than he who honors himself but lacks bread.

10 A righteous *man* regards the life of his animal,
But the tender mercies of the wicked *are* cruel.

11 He who tills his land will be satisfied with bread,
But he who follows frivolity *is* devoid of understanding.[t]

12 The wicked covet the catch of evil *men*,
But the root of the righteous yields *fruit*.
13 The wicked is ensnared by the transgression of *his* lips,
But the righteous will come through trouble.
14 A man will be satisfied with good by the fruit of *his* mouth,
And the recompense of a man's hands will be rendered to him.

15 The way of a fool *is* right in his own eyes,
But he who heeds counsel *is* wise.
16 A fool's wrath is known at once,
But a prudent *man* covers shame.

17 He *who* speaks truth declares righteousness,
But a false witness, deceit.
18 There is one who speaks like the piercings of a sword,
But the tongue of the wise *promotes* health.
19 The truthful lip shall be established forever,
But a lying tongue *is* but for a moment.
20 Deceit is in the heart of those who devise evil,
But counselors of peace have joy.
21 No grave trouble will overtake the righteous,
But the wicked shall be filled with evil.
22 Lying lips *are* an abomination to the LORD,
But those who deal truthfully *are* His delight.

23 A prudent man conceals knowledge,
But the heart of fools proclaims foolishness.

24 The hand of the diligent will rule,
But the lazy *man* will be put to forced labor.

25 Anxiety in the heart of man causes depression,
But a good word makes it glad.

12:4 [s] Literally *A wife of valor*
12:11 [t] Literally *heart*

LIFE LESSON

Proverbs 12:1-28

SITUATION Solomon gave instruction about life. He contrasted good with evil, wisdom with foolishness, and labor with laziness.

OBSERVATION Do right and you will succeed. Wickedness leads to failure and death. Foolishness and laziness lead to ruin.

INSPIRATION You want success? Here's your model. You want achievement? Here's your prototype. You want bright lights, pageants and media attention? Consider the front-page, center article of the nation's largest daily newspaper.

It is a caricature of "Miss America." The vital data of the fifty-one participants has been compiled to present the perfect woman. She has brown hair. She has brown eyes. She knows how to sing and has a perfect figure: 35-24-35. She is Miss America.

The message trumpets off the page: "This is the standard for American women." The implication is clear: Do what it takes to be like her. Firm your thighs. Deepen your cleavage. Pamper your hair. Improve your walk.

No reference is made to her convictions. . . to her honesty. . . to her. . . faith. . . or to her God. But you are told her hip size.

In a small photo, four inches to the left, is another woman. Her face is thin. Her skin is wrinkled, almost leathery. No makeup . . . no blush . . . no lipstick. There is a faint smile on her lips and a glint in her eyes. She looks pale. Perhaps it's my imagination or perhaps it's time. The caption read, "Mother Teresa: In serious condition."

Mother Teresa. You know her story. When she won the Nobel Peace Prize in 1985, she gave the two hundred thousand dollars to the poor of Calcutta. When a business man bought her a new car, she sold it and gave the money to the underprivileged. She owns nothing. She owes nothing.

Two women: Miss America and Mother Teresa. One walks the boardwalk; the other walks the alley. Two voices. One promises crowns, flowers, and crowds. The other promises service, surrender, and joy.

Continued

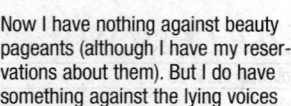

Now I have nothing against beauty pageants (although I have my reservations about them). But I do have something against the lying voices that noise our world.

You've heard them. They tell you to swap your integrity for a new sale. To barter your convictions for an easy deal. To exchange your devotion for a quick thrill.

They whisper. They woo. They taunt. They tantalize. They flirt. They flatter. "Go ahead, it's O.K." "Just wait until tomorrow." "Don't worry, no one will know." "How could anything that feels so right be so wrong?"

For amidst the fleeting promises of pleasure is the timeless promise of [God's] presence.

"Surely I am with you always, to the very end of the age."

"Never will I leave you; never will I forsake you'"

There is no chorus so loud that the voice of God cannot be heard . . . if we will but listen.

(From *In the Eye of the Storm* by Max Lucado)

APPLICATION What matters to you: looks or love, your job or service to God, wealth or sacrifice? Pattern your life after wise, spiritual, and devoted workers.

EXPLORATION Righteousness —Psalm 1; Proverbs 10:2; Romans 4:3.

26 The righteous should choose his friends carefully,
For the way of the wicked leads them astray.

27 The lazy *man* does not roast what he took in hunting,
But diligence *is* man's precious possession.

28 In the way of righteousness *is* life,
And in *its* pathway *there is* no death.

13 A wise son *heeds* his father's instruction,
But a scoffer does not listen to rebuke.

2 A man shall eat well by the fruit of *his* mouth,
But the soul of the unfaithful feeds on violence.

3 He who guards his mouth preserves his life,
But he who opens wide his lips shall have destruction.

4 The soul of a lazy *man* desires, and *has* nothing;
But the soul of the diligent shall be made rich.

5 A righteous *man* hates lying,
But a wicked *man* is loathsome and comes to shame.

6 Righteousness guards *him whose* way is blameless,
But wickedness overthrows the sinner.

7 There is one who makes himself rich, yet *has* nothing;
And one who makes himself poor, yet *has* great riches.

8 The ransom of a man's life *is* his riches,
But the poor does not hear rebuke.

9 The light of the righteous rejoices,
But the lamp of the wicked will be put out.

10 By pride comes nothing but strife,
But with the well-advised *is* wisdom.

11 Wealth *gained by* dishonesty will be diminished,
But he who gathers by labor will increase.

12 Hope deferred makes the heart sick,
But *when* the desire comes, *it is* a tree of life.

13 He who despises the word will be destroyed,
But he who fears the commandment will be rewarded.

14 The law of the wise *is* a fountain of life,
To turn *one* away from the snares of death.

15 Good understanding gains favor,
But the way of the unfaithful *is* hard.

16 Every prudent *man* acts with knowledge,
But a fool lays open *his* folly.

17 A wicked messenger falls into trouble,
But a faithful ambassador *brings* health.

18 Poverty and shame *will come* to him who disdains correction,
But he who regards a rebuke will be honored.

19 A desire accomplished is sweet to the soul,
But *it is* an abomination to fools to depart from evil.

20 He who walks with wise *men* will be wise,
But the companion of fools will be destroyed.

21 Evil pursues sinners,
But to the righteous, good shall be repaid.

22 A good *man* leaves an inheritance to his children's children,
But the wealth of the sinner is stored up for the righteous.

23 Much food *is in* the fallow *ground* of the poor,
And for lack of justice there is waste.[u]

24 He who spares his rod hates his son,
But he who loves him disciplines him promptly.

25 The righteous eats to the satisfying of his soul,
But the stomach of the wicked shall be in want.

14 The wise woman builds her house,
But the foolish pulls it down with her hands.

2 He who walks in his uprightness fears the LORD,
But *he who is* perverse in his ways despises Him.

3 In the mouth of a fool *is* a rod of pride,
But the lips of the wise will preserve them.

4 Where no oxen *are,* the trough *is* clean;
But much increase *comes* by the strength of an ox.

5 A faithful witness does not lie,
But a false witness will utter lies.

6 A scoffer seeks wisdom and does not *find it,*
But knowledge *is* easy to him who understands.

7 Go from the presence of a foolish man,
When you do not perceive *in him* the lips of knowledge.

8 The wisdom of the prudent *is* to understand his way,
But the folly of fools *is* deceit.

9 Fools mock at sin,
But among the upright *there is* favor.

10 The heart knows its own bitterness,
And a stranger does not share its joy.

11 The house of the wicked will be overthrown,
But the tent of the upright will flourish.

12 There is a way *that seems* right to a man,
But its end *is* the way of death.

13 Even in laughter the heart may sorrow,
And the end of mirth *may be* grief.

14 The backslider in heart will be filled with his own ways,
But a good man *will be satisfied* from above.[v]

15 The simple believes every word,
But the prudent considers well his steps.

LIFE LESSON

Proverbs 13:1-25

SITUATION Solomon wrote wise sayings for people who loyally followed God.

OBSERVATION People who follow God's wisdom allow his instructions to change their daily lives.

INSPIRATION Scripture:
[1] . . . varies in texture and substance, and correspondingly, in ease of digestion. The more you develop spiritually, the better able you will be to stomach the meat of Scripture. Strong truth makes strong Christians stronger.
[2] . . . gives you clear moral guidelines to live by. They will not always be in the form of simple do's and don'ts. God designed Scripture to give moral orientation to people living in any culture, in any age, and in any moral climate. [3] . . . will make you wise: wiser than people around you . . . notice I said wiser, not more knowledgeable. A wise man is one who can distinguish what is fundamental from what is trivial, who knows what life is about and who acts appropriately whatever the circumstances.
(From *The Fight* by John White)

APPLICATION Write down a particularly meaningful proverb from this chapter and put it in your wallet or purse. Pull the proverb out throughout the day. Take time to read it and relate it to your life.

EXPLORATION Spiritual Milk and Meat—Hebrews 5:13-14; 1 Peter 2:2. Applying God's Word—Psalm 119:9, 11; 2 Timothy 3:16-17.

13:23 [u] Literally *what is swept away*
14:14 [v] Literally *from above himself*

LIFE LESSON

Proverbs 14:1-35

SITUATION Each proverb in this section was written to capture interest through contrast. Each one highlights the life of the wise and righteous person in contrast to life of the foolish and wicked.

OBSERVATION If we choose to live by God's standards, we will be righteous. But if we choose to live by our own standards, we will be wicked and will face God's wrath.

INSPIRATION The natural man is spiritually dead, separated from God. He has neither the presence of God in His life nor the knowledge of God's ways. He has learned to live his life independently of God. Essentially, this is what constitutes the "flesh." His mind has been conformed to this world. The brain, which is physical and part of the body, functions like a computer. The mind is the programmer. The body picks up data from the world through its five senses. The mind chooses and interprets the data, and the brain stores it. The emotions are essentially a product of how the mind chooses to think and interpret life's events.

When we are born again, the Holy Spirit takes up residence in our life. Because we are now spiritually alive and united with Christ, we have the mind of Christ. We have become a partaker of the divine nature. However, nobody pushed the clear button in the computer. The brain is still programmed to live independently of God. . . .

The battle is for the mind: "For the flesh sets its desire against the Spirit, and the Spirit against the flesh; for these are in opposition to one another" (Galatians 5:17). God has given us the responsibility to choose. The carnal

16 A wise *man* fears and departs from evil,
But a fool rages and is self-confident.
17 A quick-tempered *man* acts foolishly,
And a man of wicked intentions is hated.
18 The simple inherit folly,
But the prudent are crowned with knowledge.
19 The evil will bow before the good,
And the wicked at the gates of the righteous.

20 The poor *man* is hated even by his own neighbor,
But the rich *has* many friends.
21 He who despises his neighbor sins;
But he who has mercy on the poor, happy *is* he.

22 Do they not go astray who devise evil?
But mercy and truth *belong* to those who devise good.

23 In all labor there is profit,
But idle chatter[w] *leads* only to poverty.

24 The crown of the wise is their riches,
But the foolishness of fools *is* folly.

25 A true witness delivers souls,
But a deceitful *witness* speaks lies.

26 In the fear of the LORD *there is* strong confidence,
And His children will have a place of refuge.
27 The fear of the LORD *is* a fountain of life,
To turn *one* away from the snares of death.

28 In a multitude of people *is* a king's honor,
But in the lack of people *is* the downfall of a prince.

29 *He who is* slow to wrath has great understanding,
But *he who is* impulsive[x] exalts folly.

30 A sound heart *is* life to the body,
But envy *is* rottenness to the bones.

31 He who oppresses the poor reproaches his Maker,
But he who honors Him has mercy on the needy.

32 The wicked is banished in his wickedness,
But the righteous has a refuge in his death.

33 Wisdom rests in the heart of him who has understanding,
But *what is* in the heart of fools is made known.

34 Righteousness exalts a nation,
But sin *is* a reproach to *any* people.

35 The king's favor *is* toward a wise servant,
But his wrath *is against* him who causes shame.

15 A soft answer turns away wrath,
But a harsh word stirs up anger.
2 The tongue of the wise uses knowledge rightly,
But the mouth of fools pours forth foolishness.

14:23 [w] Literally *talk of the lips*
14:29 [x] Literally *short of spirit*

3 The eyes of the LORD *are* in every place,
Keeping watch on the evil and the good.

4 A wholesome tongue *is* a tree of life,
But perverseness in it breaks the spirit.

5 A fool despises his father's instruction,
But he who receives correction is prudent.

6 *In* the house of the righteous *there is* much treasure,
But in the revenue of the wicked is trouble.

7 The lips of the wise disperse knowledge,
But the heart of the fool *does* not *do* so.

8 The sacrifice of the wicked *is* an abomination to the LORD,
But the prayer of the upright *is* His delight.
9 The way of the wicked *is* an abomination to the LORD,
But He loves him who follows righteousness.

10 Harsh discipline *is* for him who forsakes the way,
And he who hates correction will die.

11 Hell[y] and Destruction[z] *are* before the LORD;
So how much more the hearts of the sons of men.

12 A scoffer does not love one who corrects him,
Nor will he go to the wise.

13 A merry heart makes a cheerful countenance,
But by sorrow of the heart the spirit is broken.

14 The heart of him who has understanding seeks knowledge,
But the mouth of fools feeds on foolishness.

15 All the days of the afflicted *are* evil,
But he who is of a merry heart *has* a continual feast.

16 Better *is* a little with the fear of the LORD,
Than great treasure with trouble.
17 Better *is* a dinner of herbs[a] where love is,
Than a fatted calf with hatred.

18 A wrathful man stirs up strife,
But *he who is* slow to anger allays contention.

19 The way of the lazy *man is* like a hedge of thorns,
But the way of the upright *is* a highway.

20 A wise son makes a father glad,
But a foolish man despises his mother.

21 Folly *is* joy *to him who is* destitute of discernment,
But a man of understanding walks uprightly.

22 Without counsel, plans go awry,
But in the multitude of counselors they are established.

23 A man has joy by the answer of his mouth,
And a word *spoken* in due season, how good *it is!*

Christian chooses to walk according to the flesh. What governs his behavior are the old habit patterns and thoughts that were programmed over time. The spiritually defeated Christian fails to put on the armor of God, and ends up paying attention to deceiving spirits. The spiritual man has crucified the flesh and put on the armor of God; he chooses to think upon that which is true.

We are to be renewed in the spirit of our minds (Ephesians 4:23). The Holy Spirit discloses the mind of Christ. We must choose to no longer be conformed to this world. We are to be diligent to present ourselves approved to God as a workman who does not need to be ashamed, handling accurately the word of truth (2 Timothy 2:15). When we do, we are transformed by the renewing of our minds. We choose to think the truth, and the Holy Spirit enables our thoughts and renews our minds with the *logos.* Then the peace of God guards our hearts and minds. We let the peace of Christ rule in our hearts by letting the word of Christ richly dwell in us (Colossians 3:15,16). We are now equipped to discern.

(From *Walking in the Light* by Neil Anderson)

APPLICATION Do you have a quick temper? Do you respond selfishly to others? Reread this chapter substituting the word "I" for the subject in sentences that deal with righteousness ("I strengthen my family. . . I live a good life. . . I am a truthful witness"). With each statement, ask, "Is this true of me?" When you answer no, look for ways to make it true!

EXPLORATION Wisdom—1 Kings 3:6-9, 12; Psalm 119:97-104; Proverbs 1:23-28; 2:3-6, 9-10; Ecclesiastes 8:1; Obadiah 8; Luke 2:40; James 1:5.

15:11 [y] Or *Sheol* [z] Hebrew *Abaddon*
15:17 [a] Or *vegetables*

LIFE LESSON

Proverbs 15:1-33

SITUATION Wise and prudent followers of God solve their problems while pleasing God. The corrupt and foolish may gain wealth, but they also gain God's wrath.

OBSERVATION We should seek God's wisdom in every part of life. A wise person solves problems peacefully.

INSPIRATION "Those who are peacemakers will plant seeds of peace and reap a harvest of goodness."

The principle for peace is the same as the principle for crops: Never underestimate the power of a seed.

The story of Heinz is a good example. Europe, 1934. Hitler's plague of anti-Semitism was infecting a continent. Some would escape it. Some would die from it. But eleven-year-old Heinz would learn from it. He would learn the power of sowing seeds of peace. Heinz was a Jew.

The Bavarian village of Furth, where Heinz lived, was being overrun by Hitler's young thugs. Heinz's father, a schoolteacher, lost his job. Recreational activities ceased. Tension mounted on the streets.

The Jewish families clutched the traditions that held them together—the observance of the Sabbath, of Rosh Hashanah, of Yom Kippur. Old ways took on new significance. As the clouds of persecution swelled and blackened, these ancient precepts were a precious cleft in a mighty rock.

And as the streets became a battleground, such security meant survival.

Hitler youth roamed the neighborhoods looking for trouble. Young Heinz learned to keep his eyes open. When he saw a band of troublemakers, he would step to the other side of the street. Sometimes he would escape a fight—sometimes not.

24 The way of life *winds* upward for the wise,
That he may turn away from hell[b] below.

25 The LORD will destroy the house of the proud,
But He will establish the boundary of the widow.

26 The thoughts of the wicked *are* an abomination to the LORD,
But *the words* of the pure *are* pleasant.

27 He who is greedy for gain troubles his own house,
But he who hates bribes will live.

28 The heart of the righteous studies how to answer,
But the mouth of the wicked pours forth evil.

29 The LORD *is* far from the wicked,
But He hears the prayer of the righteous.

30 The light of the eyes rejoices the heart,
And a good report makes the bones healthy.[c]

31 The ear that hears the rebukes of life
Will abide among the wise.

32 He who disdains instruction despises his own soul,
But he who heeds rebuke gets understanding.

33 The fear of the LORD *is* the instruction of wisdom,
And before honor *is* humility.

16 The preparations of the heart *belong* to man,
But the answer of the tongue *is* from the LORD.

2 All the ways of a man *are* pure in his own eyes,
But the LORD weighs the spirits.

3 Commit your works to the LORD,
And your thoughts will be established.

4 The LORD has made all for Himself,
Yes, even the wicked for the day of doom.

5 Everyone proud in heart *is* an abomination to the LORD;
Though they join forces,[d] none will go unpunished.

6 In mercy and truth
Atonement is provided for iniquity;
And by the fear of the LORD *one* departs from evil.

7 When a man's ways please the LORD,
He makes even his enemies to be at peace with him.

8 Better *is* a little with righteousness,
Than vast revenues without justice.

9 A man's heart plans his way,
But the LORD directs his steps.

10 Divination *is* on the lips of the king;
His mouth must not transgress in judgment.

15:24 [b] Or *Sheol*
15:30 [c] Literally *fat*
16:5 [d] Literally *hand to hand*

11 Honest weights and scales *are* the LORD's;
All the weights in the bag *are* His work.
12 *It is* an abomination for kings to commit wickedness,
For a throne is established by righteousness.
13 Righteous lips *are* the delight of kings,
And they love him who speaks *what is* right.
14 As messengers of death *is* the king's wrath,
But a wise man will appease it.
15 In the light of the king's face *is* life,
And his favor *is* like a cloud of the latter rain.

16 How much better to get wisdom than gold!
And to get understanding is to be chosen rather than silver.

17 The highway of the upright *is* to depart from evil;
He who keeps his way preserves his soul.

18 Pride *goes* before destruction,
And a haughty spirit before a fall.
19 Better *to be* of a humble spirit with the lowly,
Than to divide the spoil with the proud.

20 He who heeds the word wisely will find good,
And whoever trusts in the LORD, happy *is* he.

21 The wise in heart will be called prudent,
And sweetness of the lips increases learning.

22 Understanding *is* a wellspring of life to him who has it.
But the correction of fools *is* folly.

23 The heart of the wise teaches his mouth,
And adds learning to his lips.

24 Pleasant words *are like* a honeycomb,
Sweetness to the soul and health to the bones.

25 There is a way *that seems* right to a man,
But its end *is* the way of death.

26 The person who labors, labors for himself,
For his *hungry* mouth drives him *on.*

27 An ungodly man digs up evil,
And *it is* on his lips like a burning fire.
28 A perverse man sows strife,
And a whisperer separates the best of friends.
29 A violent man entices his neighbor,
And leads him in a way *that is* not good.
30 He winks his eye to devise perverse things;
He purses his lips *and* brings about evil.

31 The silver-haired head *is* a crown of glory,
If it is found in the way of righteousness.

32 *He who is* slow to anger *is* better than the mighty,
And he who rules his spirit than he who takes a city.

33 The lot is cast into the lap,
But its every decision *is* from the LORD.

One day, in 1934, a pivotal confrontation occurred. Heinz found himself face-to-face with a Hitler bully. A beating appeared inevitable. This time, however, he walked away unhurt—not because of what he did, but because of what he said. He didn't fight back; he spoke up. He convinced the troublemakers that a fight was not necessary. His words kept battle at bay. And Heinz saw firsthand how the tongue can create peace.

He learned the skill of using words to avoid conflict. And for a young Jew in Hitler-ridden Europe, that skill had many opportunities to be honed.

Fortunately, Heinz's family escaped from Bavaria and made their way to America. Later in life, he would downplay the impact those adolescent experiences had on his development.

But one has to wonder. For after Heinz grew up, his name became synonymous with peace negotiations. His legacy became that of a bridge-builder. Somewhere he had learned the power of the properly placed word of peace. And one has to wonder if his training didn't come on the streets of Bavaria.

You don't know him as Heinz. You know him by his Anglicized name, Henry. Henry Kissinger.

Never underestimate the power of a seed.

(From *The Applause of Heaven* by Max Lucado)

APPLICATION This chapter has nine proverbs that deal directly with your relationship with God. Select three of them to help you improve your relationship with him.

EXPLORATION Continual Devotion—Psalm 119:147-148; Matthew 13:44-46; Mark 12:28-30; Romans 12:11-12; Galatians 6:9.

LIFE LESSON

Proverbs 16:1-33

SITUATION Solomon knew that when his actions and motives pleased God, God rewarded him with peace. When pride and greed entered his heart, he began to travel down the road to chaos and destruction.

OBSERVATION No matter what good we do, God knows our motivation for doing it. God judges our motives, not simply our actions.

INSPIRATION Conscience is like a compass. If a compass is faulty, you'll quickly get off course. A conscience gets its signals from the heart, which can be dulled, hardened, or calloused. Furthermore, a conscience can be overly sensitive or can even drive one mad. . . .

In order for one's conscience to be a good guide, one the Spirit can direct, it needs to be healthy, sensitive, and capable of getting God's message and truth.

. . . When one realizes the true condition of the heart without God and ponders the impact of his or her sinfulness, there is an emotional reaction—greater in some than in others. But there is an emotional reaction. *I have offended. I have grieved the heart of God. I have driven nails into Christ's hands with my sins.* That does something to my emotions when I, as a sinner, realize that. When the truth of forgiveness and grace and

17

Better *is* a dry morsel with quietness,
Than a house full of feasting[e] *with* strife.

2 A wise servant will rule over a son who causes shame,
And will share an inheritance among the brothers.

3 The refining pot *is* for silver and the furnace for gold,
But the LORD tests the hearts.

4 An evildoer gives heed to false lips;
A liar listens eagerly to a spiteful tongue.

5 He who mocks the poor reproaches his Maker;
He who is glad at calamity will not go unpunished.

6 Children's children *are* the crown of old men,
And the glory of children *is* their father.

7 Excellent speech is not becoming to a fool,
Much less lying lips to a prince.

8 A present *is* a precious stone in the eyes of its possessor;
Wherever he turns, he prospers.

9 He who covers a transgression seeks love,
But he who repeats a matter separates friends.

10 Rebuke is more effective for a wise *man*
Than a hundred blows on a fool.

11 An evil *man* seeks only rebellion;
Therefore a cruel messenger will be sent against him.

12 Let a man meet a bear robbed of her cubs,
Rather than a fool in his folly.

13 Whoever rewards evil for good,
Evil will not depart from his house.

14 The beginning of strife *is like* releasing water;
Therefore stop contention before a quarrel starts.

15 He who justifies the wicked, and he who condemns the just,
Both of them alike *are* an abomination to the LORD.

16 Why *is there* in the hand of a fool the purchase price of wisdom,
Since *he has* no heart *for it?*

17 A friend loves at all times,
And a brother is born for adversity.

18 A man devoid of understanding shakes hands in a pledge,
And becomes surety for his friend.

19 He who loves transgression loves strife,
And he who exalts his gate seeks destruction.

20 He who has a deceitful heart finds no good,
And he who has a perverse tongue falls into evil.

17:1 [e] Or *sacrificial meals*

21 He who begets a scoffer *does so* to his sorrow,
And the father of a fool has no joy.

22 A merry heart does good, *like* medicine,[f]
But a broken spirit dries the bones.

23 A wicked *man* accepts a bribe behind the back[g]
To pervert the ways of justice.

24 Wisdom *is* in the sight of him who has understanding,
But the eyes of a fool *are* on the ends of the earth.

25 A foolish son *is* a grief to his father,
And bitterness to her who bore him.

26 Also, to punish the righteous *is* not good,
Nor to strike princes for *their* uprightness.

27 He who has knowledge spares his words,
And a man of understanding is of a calm spirit.
28 Even a fool is counted wise when he holds his peace;
When he shuts his lips, *he is considered* perceptive.

18 A man who isolates himself seeks his own desire;
He rages against all wise judgment.

2 A fool has no delight in understanding,
But in expressing his own heart.

3 When the wicked comes, contempt comes also;
And with dishonor *comes* reproach.

4 The words of a man's mouth *are* deep waters;
The wellspring of wisdom *is* a flowing brook.

5 *It is* not good to show partiality to the wicked,
Or to overthrow the righteous in judgment.

6 A fool's lips enter into contention,
And his mouth calls for blows.
7 A fool's mouth *is* his destruction,
And his lips *are* the snare of his soul.
8 The words of a talebearer *are* like tasty trifles,[h]
And they go down into the inmost body.

9 He who is slothful in his work
Is a brother to him who is a great destroyer.

10 The name of the LORD *is* a strong tower;
The righteous run to it and are safe.
11 The rich man's wealth *is* his strong city,
And like a high wall in his own esteem.

12 Before destruction the heart of a man is haughty,
And before honor *is* humility.

13 He who answers a matter before he hears *it*,
It *is* folly and shame to him.

God's overwhelming love pour over me, there is an emotional reaction. And I must admit that. When I realize that God has reserved a home in heaven for me—a reprobate sinner who was running in the other direction when He stopped me, turned me around in grace, and brought me to Himself—that brings an emotional response. Don't deny those emotions! . . .

God gave you a mind. Use it to know Him better. Study the doctrines that put steal into the cement of your faith. Exercise your mind!

God gave you a will. Use it to obey Him. Make decisions that honor Him and please Him. Exercise your will!

And God gave you emotions. Don't be afraid of them. Let them out. Allow your heart to show through. Exercise your emotions!

If we refuse to open up, to allow the full prism of His love and truth to shine through our lives, we will miss much of the color life has to offer.

(From *Flying Closer to the Flame* by Charles Swindoll)

APPLICATION Are you fooling God? It can't be done! You can't just "go through the motions." Live a genuine life of faith today by praying that God will guide your heart and mind. Then he will direct your actions.

EXPLORATION Heart—1 Samuel 16:7; Psalm 95:8; Proverbs 4:23; Jeremiah 17:9-10; Luke 6:45.

17:22 *f* Or *makes medicine even better*
17:23 *g* Literally *from the bosom*
18:8 *h* A Jewish tradition reads *wounds.*

Life Lesson

Proverbs 17:1-28

SITUATION God judges every person by the same standard. He condemns evil.

OBSERVATION Wisdom does not come naturally. We gain it by respecting God and making careful choices.

INSPIRATION The God who has shown himself to be for us, wills also to be with us. He is infinitely capable and desirous of relating himself to every person who freely opens himself to such a relationship. God wills this as the means of fulfilling his purpose in us, enabling us to become the kind of persons he intends us to be.

The divine capacity to be personally related to us is rooted in the richness and complexity of the very being of God. "God in Three Persons!" Transcendent above and immanent in all that exists. Disclosing himself dramatically and painfully in our history. Intimately and profoundly present with each who will open himself to the Spirit.

And we are built so that we may deeply receive his Spirit. We bear his image. Our person is patterned after his Person. Our spirit, at its deepest level, is kin to his Spirit.

As we, then, accept the loving knowledge of God made possible through Christ, we are drawn by the Spirit into a deeper knowledge which becomes trust, commitment, growth, fulfillment.

(From *With Good Reason* by Chester A. Pennington)

APPLICATION Avoid the mistakes others have made. Spend time with a Christian older than you. Gain wisdom by hearing of that person's success and failures. Find answers to questions like: "What has helped you get to know God better? How do you resist temptation? How do you respond to stress?"

EXPLORATION Faith—Psalm 20:7; John 14:14-17; Hebrews 11:1.

14 The spirit of a man will sustain him in sickness,
But who can bear a broken spirit?

15 The heart of the prudent acquires knowledge,
And the ear of the wise seeks knowledge.

16 A man's gift makes room for him,
And brings him before great men.

17 The first *one* to plead his cause *seems* right,
Until his neighbor comes and examines him.

18 Casting lots causes contentions to cease,
And keeps the mighty apart.

19 A brother offended *is harder to win* than a strong city,
And contentions *are* like the bars of a castle.

20 A man's stomach shall be satisfied from the fruit of his mouth;
From the produce of his lips he shall be filled.

21 Death and life *are* in the power of the tongue,
And those who love it will eat its fruit.

22 *He who* finds a wife finds a good *thing,*
And obtains favor from the LORD.

23 The poor *man* uses entreaties,
But the rich answers roughly.

24 A man *who has* friends must himself be friendly,[i]
But there is a friend *who* sticks closer than a brother.

19

Better *is* the poor who walks in his integrity
Than *one who is* perverse in his lips, and is a fool.

2 Also it is not good *for* a soul *to be* without knowledge,
And he sins who hastens with *his* feet.

3 The foolishness of a man twists his way,
And his heart frets against the LORD.

4 Wealth makes many friends,
But the poor is separated from his friend.

5 A false witness will not go unpunished,
And *he who* speaks lies will not escape.

6 Many entreat the favor of the nobility,
And every man *is* a friend to one who gives gifts.

7 All the brothers of the poor hate him;
How much more do his friends go far from him!
He may pursue *them with* words, *yet* they abandon *him.*

8 He who gets wisdom loves his own soul;
He who keeps understanding will find good.

9 A false witness will not go unpunished,
And *he who* speaks lies shall perish.

18:24 [i] Following Greek manuscripts, Syriac, Targum, and Vulgate; Masoretic Text reads *may come to ruin.*

10 Luxury is not fitting for a fool,
Much less for a servant to rule over princes.

11 The discretion of a man makes him slow to anger,
And his glory *is* to overlook a transgression.

12 The king's wrath *is* like the roaring of a lion,
But his favor *is* like dew on the grass.

13 A foolish son *is* the ruin of his father,
And the contentions of a wife *are* a continual dripping.

14 Houses and riches *are* an inheritance from fathers,
But a prudent wife *is* from the LORD.

15 Laziness casts *one* into a deep sleep,
And an idle person will suffer hunger.

16 He who keeps the commandment keeps his soul,
But he who is careless[j] of his ways will die.

17 He who has pity on the poor lends to the LORD,
And He will pay back what he has given.

18 Chasten your son while there is hope,
And do not set your heart on his destruction.[k]

19 *A man of* great wrath will suffer punishment;
For if you rescue *him,* you will have to do it again.

20 Listen to counsel and receive instruction,
That you may be wise in your latter days.

21 There are many plans in a man's heart,
Nevertheless the LORD's counsel—that will stand.

22 What is desired in a man is kindness,
And a poor man is better than a liar.

23 The fear of the LORD *leads* to life,
And *he who has it* will abide in satisfaction;
He will not be visited with evil.

24 A lazy *man* buries his hand in the bowl,[l]
And will not so much as bring it to his mouth again.

25 Strike a scoffer, and the simple will become wary;
Rebuke one who has understanding, *and* he
will discern knowledge.

26 He who mistreats *his* father *and* chases away *his* mother
Is a son who causes shame and brings reproach.

27 Cease listening to instruction, my son,
And you will stray from the words of knowledge.

28 A disreputable witness scorns justice,
And the mouth of the wicked devours iniquity.

19:16 *j* Literally *despises,* figurative of recklessness or carelessness
19:18 *k* Literally *to put him to death;* a Jewish tradition reads *on his crying.*
19:24 *l* Septuagint and Syriac read *bosom;* Targum and Vulgate read *armpit.*

LIFE LESSON

Proverbs 18:1-24

SITUATION For Jews, the individual was not separate from the community. Antisocial behavior was considered a terrible crime in Israel and Judah.

OBSERVATION It is better to be humble and discerning than proud and foolish. This better mindset can be applied in several areas of life, such as speech, wealth, decision-making, and arguments.

INSPIRATION It is an old and common saying, that "coming events cast their shadows before them"; the wise man teaches us that a haughty heart is the prophetic prelude of evil. . . . When men have ridden the high horse, destruction has always overtaken them. Let David's aching heart show that there is an eclipse of a man's glory when he dotes upon his own greatness. . . . See Nebuchadnezzar, the mighty builder of Babylon, creeping on the earth, devouring grass like oxen. . . . Pride made the boaster a beast, as once before it made an angel a devil. God hates high looks, and never fails to bring them down. . . . O Christian, is thine heart haughty this evening? For pride can get into the Christian's heart as well as into the sinner's; it can delude him into dreaming. . . . Art thou glorying in thy graces or thy talents? Art thou proud of thyself? . . . If we forget to live at the foot of the cross in deepest lowliness of spirit, God will not forget to make us smart under His rod. . . . Wherefore, "He that glorieth, let him glory in the Lord."

(From *Morning and Evening* by Charles H. Spurgeon)

APPLICATION What do you take pride in? Whom do you praise when you do well? Whom do you blame when events do not go your way? Take inventory in prayer and repent as needed. If necessary, restore a relationship with a friend, family member, or co-worker where pride has damaged your relationship.

EXPLORATION Foolish Words: Psalm 12:3; 94:4; Proverbs 10:14; 13:3; 17:7; 27:1-2; James 3:5-6.

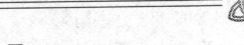

LIFE LESSON

Proverbs 19:1-29

SITUATION Solomon contrasted foolishness with wisdom, wealth with poverty, and falsehood with truth.

OBSERVATION Keep the highest standards for God in your thoughts and actions.

INSPIRATION Jesus summarized the Christian life in the simplest summation of all: "Just as you want men to do to you, you also do to them likewise" (Luke 6:31). This we call the Golden Rule—the law of gold, a gold more precious than diamonds and rubies. Any child can recite the Golden Rule, but to make it an active part of daily living is no mean feat.

. . . Our response to petty criticism is often to retaliate in kind, instead of in kindness. This is where the Golden Rule touches life. Here is where Jesus spoke of not returning evil for evil. Doing to others what we want others to do to us is simply a matter of kindness. It involves being thoughtful and considerate. But it is more than mere politeness. It is doing what is right. It is doing what pleases God.

Righteousness means right living. It means treating people right. It means living with personal integrity. A righteous person is one whom we can trust. His integrity is consistent. It is not for sale. A righteous person is moral without being moralistic. He is pious without being pietistic. He has a sense of concern for other people's feelings. He wants to treat people right because he has the over-arching desire to please a loving God.

(From *Pleasing God* by R.C. Sproul)

APPLICATION Do you give more than you take in your family, at church, and with friends? Do you look at any of these as people who "owe you" rather than you "owing them"? Put their needs ahead of your own. Practice the principles of Proverbs 19 with each of them.

EXPLORATION Obeying God's Principles—Matthew 7:24-27; 1 Corinthians 2:14-16; James 1:22-25; 1 Peter 1:13-16.

29 Judgments are prepared for scoffers,
And beatings for the backs of fools.

20

Wine *is* a mocker,
Strong drink *is* a brawler,
And whoever is led astray by it is not wise.

2 The wrath[m] of a king *is* like the roaring of a lion;
Whoever provokes him to anger sins *against* his own life.

3 *It is* honorable for a man to stop striving,
Since any fool can start a quarrel.

4 The lazy *man* will not plow because of winter;
He will beg during harvest and *have* nothing.

5 Counsel in the heart of man *is like* deep water,
But a man of understanding will draw it out.

6 Most men will proclaim each his own goodness,
But who can find a faithful man?

7 The righteous *man* walks in his integrity;
His children *are* blessed after him.

8 A king who sits on the throne of judgment
Scatters all evil with his eyes.

9 Who can say, "I have made my heart clean,
I am pure from my sin"?

10 Diverse weights *and* diverse measures,
They *are* both alike, an abomination to the LORD.

11 Even a child is known by his deeds,
Whether what he does *is* pure and right.

12 The hearing ear and the seeing eye,
The LORD has made them both.

13 Do not love sleep, lest you come to poverty;
Open your eyes, *and* you will be satisfied with bread.

14 "*It is* good for nothing,"[n] cries the buyer;
But when he has gone his way, then he boasts.

15 There is gold and a multitude of rubies,
But the lips of knowledge *are* a precious jewel.

16 Take the garment of one who is surety *for* a stranger,
And hold it as a pledge *when it* is for a seductress.

17 Bread gained by deceit *is* sweet to a man,
But afterward his mouth will be filled with gravel.

18 Plans are established by counsel;
By wise counsel wage war.

19 He who goes about *as* a talebearer reveals secrets;
Therefore do not associate with one who flatters with his lips.

20:2 [m] Literally *fear* or *terror* which is produced by the king's wrath
20:14 [n] Literally *evil, evil*

20 Whoever curses his father or his mother,
His lamp will be put out in deep darkness.

21 An inheritance gained hastily at the beginning
Will not be blessed at the end.

22 Do not say, "I will recompense evil";
Wait for the LORD, and He will save you.

23 Diverse weights *are* an abomination to the LORD,
And dishonest scales *are* not good.

24 A man's steps *are* of the LORD;
How then can a man understand his own way?

25 *It is* a snare for a man to devote rashly *something as* holy,
And afterward to reconsider *his* vows.

26 A wise king sifts out the wicked,
And brings the threshing wheel over them.

27 The spirit of a man *is* the lamp of the LORD,
Searching all the inner depths of his heart.[o]

28 Mercy and truth preserve the king,
And by lovingkindness he upholds his throne.

29 The glory of young men *is* their strength,
And the splendor of old men *is* their gray head.

30 Blows that hurt cleanse away evil,
As *do* stripes the inner depths of the heart.[p]

21 The king's heart *is* in the hand of the LORD,
Like the rivers of water; He turns it wherever He wishes.

2 Every way of a man *is* right in his own eyes,
But the LORD weighs the hearts.

3 To do righteousness and justice
Is more acceptable to the LORD than sacrifice.

4 A haughty look, a proud heart,
And the plowing[q] of the wicked *are* sin.

5 The plans of the diligent *lead* surely to plenty,
But *those of* everyone *who is* hasty, surely to poverty.

6 Getting treasures by a lying tongue
Is the fleeting fantasy of those who seek death.[r]

7 The violence of the wicked will destroy them,[s]
Because they refuse to do justice.

8 The way of a guilty man *is* perverse;[t]
But *as for* the pure, his work *is* right.

20:27 [o] Literally *the rooms of the belly*
20:30 [p] Literally *the rooms of the belly*
21:4 [q] Or *lamp*
21:6 [r] Septuagint reads *Pursue vanity on the snares of death;* Vulgate reads *Is vain and foolish, and shall stumble on the snares of death;* Targum reads *They shall be destroyed, and they shall fall who seek death.*
21:7 [s] Literally *drag them away*
21:8 [t] Or *The way of a man is perverse and strange*

LIFE LESSON

Proverbs 20:1-30

SITUATION Solomon wrote more proverbs. If readers followed these words of wisdom, Solomon promised that God would approve of their life.

OBSERVATION Sin takes many forms: gossip, laziness, drunkenness, and dishonesty.

INSPIRATION My spiritual battleground is not over a pack of cigarettes or a bottle of port. It's not in a disco or a movie theater. My spiritual battleground is not a backyard fence over which I gossip to my neighbor, nor is it a fast car I race past the speed limit. My paralysis prevents me from reaching for the common temptations. That's why my spiritual battleground is on the field of my thoughts.

I possess a very unlovely trait: I waste precious time in idle daydreams. I hate it because wasteful fantasies distract me from the real concerns of life, causing me to feel restless and dissatisfied with the way things are.

. . . The very fact that I am ashamed of myself drives me to God. I lie in the dust of my self-despair at His feet and find safety and acceptance. My lazy thoughts make me contrite and repentant, and I am humbled that I have to come so often to God for cleansing.

If we are to have power with the Lord, to be dear to Him, if our prayers are to prevail and if we are to be most useful to Him, we must jerk right-side up those wrong and unlovely traits in our lives.

Amy Carmichael has said, "No word can declare with what longings Divine Love waits until the heart, all weary and sick of itself, turns to the Lord and says, 'Take full possession.'"

(From *Diamonds in the Dust* by Joni Eareckson Tada)

APPLICATION What sin do you wrestle with? How long has it been a problem? Seek God for victory. Ask him to help you throw that habit out of your life today.

EXPLORATION Victory over Sin and Temptation—Proverbs 1:10; Daniel 1:8; Romans 6:13; 1 Corinthians 10:13; 1 John 5:3-5.

LIFE LESSON

Proverbs 21:1-31

SITUATION Solomon gave advice to moral people and warnings to the wicked ones. A God-honoring lifestyle will bring God's reward, but a selfish, wicked lifestyle leads to ruin.

OBSERVATION When we live in a way that honors God, we will receive our reward from him. He knows and will judge evildoers.

INSPIRATION In my pocket as I write these words is a card I always carry with me. It came to me many years ago, and I have it retyped occasionally because it gets ragged and worn. On it are five lines, as follows:

The light of God surrounds me

The love of God enfolds me

The power of God protects me

The presence of God watches over me

Wherever I am, God is!

Why do I carry this card? Because the image that it evokes of a loving, caring God is the prefect antidote to fear, to worry, to anxiety, to just about every problem under the sun. . . .

This is the greatest concept that the human mind can hold. The more intensely you image it, the happier you are going to be, because you will never feel abandoned or alone. That's what religion is all about, that's what churches are all about, that's what Christ came to teach us—that the love of God is available to us uncertain, groping, unsure, human beings, all the time, no matter where we may be.

(From *Positive Imaging* by Norman Vincent Peale)

APPLICATION It can be difficult to keep a God-honoring lifestyle with pressures and temptations surrounding us daily. What pushes you toward the ungodly: music, magazine covers, someone else's wealth, feelings of inferiority? Make a bold move to resist all that does not honor God.

EXPLORATION Righteousness—Exodus 1:17-21; Esther 3:2; 1 Samuel 14:44-45; Psalm 1:1-3; Romans 1:17; 2 Corinthians 5:21.

9 Better to dwell in a corner of a housetop,
Than in a house shared with a contentious woman.

10 The soul of the wicked desires evil;
His neighbor finds no favor in his eyes.

11 When the scoffer is punished, the simple is made wise;
But when the wise is instructed, he receives knowledge.

12 The righteous *God* wisely considers the house of the wicked,
Overthrowing the wicked for *their* wickedness.

13 Whoever shuts his ears to the cry of the poor
Will also cry himself and not be heard.

14 A gift in secret pacifies anger,
And a bribe behind the back,[u] strong wrath.

15 *It is* a joy for the just to do justice,
But destruction *will come* to the workers of iniquity.

16 A man who wanders from the way of understanding
Will rest in the assembly of the dead.

17 He who loves pleasure *will be* a poor man;
He who loves wine and oil will not be rich.

18 The wicked *shall be* a ransom for the righteous,
And the unfaithful for the upright.

19 Better to dwell in the wilderness,
Than with a contentious and angry woman.

20 *There is* desirable treasure,
And oil in the dwelling of the wise,
But a foolish man squanders it.

21 He who follows righteousness and mercy
Finds life, righteousness and honor.

22 A wise *man* scales the city of the mighty,
And brings down the trusted stronghold.

23 Whoever guards his mouth and tongue
Keeps his soul from troubles.

24 A proud *and* haughty *man*—"Scoffer" *is* his name;
He acts with arrogant pride.

25 The desire of the lazy *man* kills him,
For his hands refuse to labor.
26 He covets greedily all day long,
But the righteous gives and does not spare.

27 The sacrifice of the wicked *is* an abomination;
How much more *when* he brings it with wicked intent!

28 A false witness shall perish,
But the man who hears *him* will speak endlessly.

21:14 [u] Literally *in the bosom*

29 A wicked man hardens his face,
But *as for* the upright, he establishes[v] his way.

30 *There is* no wisdom or understanding
Or counsel against the LORD.

31 The horse *is* prepared for the day of battle,
But deliverance *is* of the LORD.

22 A *good* name is to be chosen rather than great riches,
Loving favor rather than silver and gold.

2 The rich and the poor have this in common,
The LORD *is* the maker of them all.

3 A prudent *man* foresees evil and hides himself,
But the simple pass on and are punished.

4 By humility *and* the fear of the LORD
Are riches and honor and life.

5 Thorns *and* snares *are* in the way of the perverse;
He who guards his soul will be far from them.

6 Train up a child in the way he should go,
And when he is old he will not depart from it.

7 The rich rules over the poor,
And the borrower *is* servant to the lender.

8 He who sows iniquity will reap sorrow,
And the rod of his anger will fail.

9 He who has a generous eye will be blessed,
For he gives of his bread to the poor.

10 Cast out the scoffer, and contention will leave;
Yes, strife and reproach will cease.

11 He who loves purity of heart
And has grace on his lips,
The king *will be* his friend.

12 The eyes of the LORD preserve knowledge,
But He overthrows the words of the faithless.

13 The lazy *man* says, "*There is* a lion outside!
I shall be slain in the streets!"

14 The mouth of an immoral woman *is* a deep pit;
He who is abhorred by the LORD will fall there.

15 Foolishness *is* bound up in the heart of a child;
The rod of correction will drive it far from him.

16 He who oppresses the poor to increase his *riches,*
And he who gives to the rich, *will* surely
come to poverty.

21:29 [v] Qere and Septuagint read *understands.*

LIFE LESSON

Proverbs 22:1-29

SITUATION The proverbs in this chapter point to the way for proper living. The promised rewards are more than just earthly accolades.

OBSERVATION Having a good reputation is wise. People should desire to have a good name, not because this brings status but because it honors God.

INSPIRATION Each year we have a student recognition day at our church. On the Sunday between Christmas and New Year's Day, we ask the young people of our church who are students at colleges and universities to give us reports of how their educational experiences have been going. It is a very special Sunday because ours is a Black Baptist church. The older members of our congregation have not had the educational opportunities that our young people enjoy. Consequently, they love to hear about what their children and grandchildren are learning.

On one such Sunday, after half a dozen students had given their reports, my pastor got up and delivered some closing words. "Children," he said, "you are going to die! You may not think you're going to die. But you're going to die. One of these days, they're going to take you out to the cemetery, drop you in a hole, throw some dirt on your face, and go back to the church and eat potato salad."

"When you were born," he said, "you alone were crying and everybody else was happy. The important question I want to ask is this: When you die are you alone going to be happy, leaving everybody else crying? The answer depends on whether you live to get titles or you live to get testimonies. When they lay you in the grave, are people going to stand around reciting the fancy titles you earned, or are they going to stand around giving testimonies of the good things you did for them? Will they list your degrees and awards, or will they tell about what a blessing you were to them? Will you leave behind just a newspaper column telling people how important you were, or will you leave crying people who give testimonies of how

Continued

they've lost the best friend they ever had? There's nothing wrong with titles. Titles are good things to have. But if it ever comes down to a choice between a title or a testimony—go for the testimony."
(From *Who Switched the Price Tags?* by Tony Campolo)

APPLICATION What are some of your goals for the next five years? Do they promise human recognition or a life that is faithful to God? Remember that a good, respected name does not always mean one of status, but rather one of stature and accomplishment for God.

EXPLORATION A Good Name—1 Samuel 18:30; Ecclesiastes 7:1; Acts 6:3; 10:22; 16:2; 22:12; 2 Corinthians 8:18; 3 John 12.

Sayings of the Wise

17 Incline your ear and hear the words of the wise,
And apply your heart to my knowledge;
18 For *it is* a pleasant thing if you keep them within you;
Let them all be fixed upon your lips,
19 So that your trust may be in the LORD;
I have instructed you today, even you.
20 Have I not written to you excellent things
Of counsels and knowledge,
21 That I may make you know the certainty of the words of truth,
That you may answer words of truth
To those who send to you?

22 Do not rob the poor because he *is* poor,
Nor oppress the afflicted at the gate;
23 For the LORD will plead their cause,
And plunder the soul of those who plunder them.

24 Make no friendship with an angry man,
And with a furious man do not go,
25 Lest you learn his ways
And set a snare for your soul.

26 Do not be one of those who shakes hands in a pledge,
One of those who is surety for debts;
27 If you have nothing *with which* to pay,
Why should he take away your bed from under you?

28 Do not remove the ancient landmark
Which your fathers have set.

29 Do you see a man *who* excels in his work?
He will stand before kings;
He will not stand before unknown *men.*

23 When you sit down to eat with a ruler,
Consider carefully what *is* before you;
2 And put a knife to your throat
If you *are* a man given to appetite.
3 Do not desire his delicacies,
For they *are* deceptive food.

4 Do not overwork to be rich;
Because of your own understanding, cease!
5 Will you set your eyes on that which is not?
For *riches* certainly make themselves wings;
They fly away like an eagle *toward* heaven.

6 Do not eat the bread of a miser,[w]
Nor desire his delicacies;
7 For as he thinks in his heart, so *is* he.
"Eat and drink!" he says to you,
But his heart is not with you.

23:6 [w] Literally *one who has an evil eye*

8 The morsel you have eaten, you will vomit up,
And waste your pleasant words.

9 Do not speak in the hearing of a fool,
For he will despise the wisdom of your words.

10 Do not remove the ancient landmark,
Nor enter the fields of the fatherless;
11 For their Redeemer *is* mighty;
He will plead their cause against you.

12 Apply your heart to instruction,
And your ears to words of knowledge.

13 Do not withhold correction from a child,
For *if* you beat him with a rod, he will not die.
14 You shall beat him with a rod,
And deliver his soul from hell.[x]

15 My son, if your heart is wise,
My heart will rejoice—indeed, I myself;
16 Yes, my inmost being will rejoice
When your lips speak right things.

17 Do not let your heart envy sinners,
But *be zealous* for the fear of the LORD all the day;
18 For surely there is a hereafter,
And your hope will not be cut off.

19 Hear, my son, and be wise;
And guide your heart in the way.
20 Do not mix with winebibbers,
Or with gluttonous eaters of meat;
21 For the drunkard and the glutton will come to poverty,
And drowsiness will clothe *a man* with rags.

22 Listen to your father who begot you,
And do not despise your mother when she is old.

23 Buy the truth, and do not sell *it*,
Also wisdom and instruction and understanding.

24 The father of the righteous will greatly rejoice,
And he who begets a wise *child* will delight in him.
25 Let your father and your mother be glad,
And let her who bore you rejoice.

26 My son, give me your heart,
And let your eyes observe my ways.
27 For a harlot *is* a deep pit,
And a seductress *is* a narrow well.
28 She also lies in wait as *for* a victim,
And increases the unfaithful among men.

29 Who has woe?
Who has sorrow?

23:14 [x] Or *Sheol*

LIFE LESSON

Proverbs 23:1-35

SITUATION Solomon exhorted his hearers to avoid gluttony and drunkenness. He also advised them to respect older people.

OBSERVATION Younger people can gain wisdom by learning from those who are older.

INSPIRATION Don't you hate it when someone else reminds you?

The barber: "Getting a little thin on top here, Joe."

The stylist: "Next time you come in, Sue, we'll do something about these gray streaks."

The invitation: "You are invited to your thirtieth high school reunion."

Your doctor: "Nothing to worry about, Bill. Your condition is common for folks in their mid-age."

The dawning of old age. The first pages of the final chapters. A golden speck appears on the green leaves of your life, and you are brought face to wrinkled face with the fact that you are getting older. . . .

Everything hurts when you wake up. What doesn't hurt, doesn't work.

Your parents begin acting like your children.

The smile lines don't go away when you stop smiling.

And then—boom! The rain becomes a torrent. The gentle taps become thunder. Cardiac arrest. Empty nest. Forty candles. Bifocals. Boom. Boom! BOOM! Now there is no denial. Ponce de Leon didn't find the fountain of youth, and neither will you. Oh, but how we try. Barbells get pumped. Black hair gone gray goes black again, or better yet, blond. The van is traded in on a truck, a four-wheel-drive monster that will tackle the treacherous ravines of the interstate. The face gets stretched. The chin gets tucked. Breasts get a lift.

But try as we might, the calendar pages still turn. The clocks still tick. And the body still grows older. And with every new pill we take we are reminded that growing old is a pill that has to be swallowed. . . .

But the real pain is deeper. For some it is the hollowness of success. Life at the

Continued

top of the ladder can be lonely. Mahogany desks grow cold. Sales awards tarnish. Diplomas fade. Sometimes a dream-come-true world has come true and it's less than you'd hoped. . . .

It can get even worse. Regret can lead to rebellion. Rebellion against the demands. Rebellion against the mundane. Rebellion against the ho-hum. Rebellion against whatever ties you down: your job, your government, your station wagon, or worse still . . . your family. . . .

Let me be very clear with my point: Growing old can be dangerous. The trail is treacherous and the pitfalls are many. One is wise to be prepared. You know it's coming. It's not like God kept the process a secret. It's not like you are blazing a trail as you grow older. It's not as if no one has ever done it before. Look around you. You have ample opportunity to prepare and ample case studies to consider. If growing old catches you by surprise, don't blame God. He gave you plenty of warning. He also gave you plenty of advice. . . .

Read Jesus' admonition. "Whoever tries to keep his life will lose it, and the man who is prepared to lose his life will preserve it." . . .

Your last chapters can be your best. Your final song can be your greatest. It could be that all of your life has prepared you for a grand exit. God's oldest have always been among his choicest. . . .

As we get older, our vision should improve. Not our vision of earth but our vision of heaven. Those who have spent their life looking for heaven gain a skip in their step as the city comes into view. . . .

And I hope you'll be ready when you get home. For you, age is no enemy. Age is a mile-marker—a gentle reminder that home has never been so near.

Tell that to your barber.

(From *He Still Moves Stones* by Max Lucado)

APPLICATION Do you listen to the wisdom of the elderly? Take time this week to talk with an older person and gain wisdom from that individual.

EXPLORATION Overindulgence —Deuteronomy 21:20-21; Proverbs 20:1; 28:7; Isaiah 5:11; 22; Habakkuk 2:15-16; Luke 21:34; Romans 13:13-14; 1 Thessalonians 5:7-8.

Who has contentions?
Who has complaints?
Who has wounds without cause?
Who has redness of eyes?
30 Those who linger long at the wine,
Those who go in search of mixed wine.
31 Do not look on the wine when it is red,
When it sparkles in the cup,
When it swirls around smoothly;
32 At the last it bites like a serpent,
And stings like a viper.
33 Your eyes will see strange things,
And your heart will utter perverse things.
34 Yes, you will be like one who lies down in the midst of the sea,
Or like one who lies at the top of the mast, *saying:*
35 "They have struck me, *but* I was not hurt;
They have beaten me, but I did not feel *it.*
When shall I awake, that I may seek another *drink?*"

24 Do not be envious of evil men,
Nor desire to be with them;
2 For their heart devises violence,
And their lips talk of troublemaking.

3 Through wisdom a house is built,
And by understanding it is established;
4 By knowledge the rooms are filled
With all precious and pleasant riches.

5 A wise man *is* strong,
Yes, a man of knowledge increases strength;
6 For by wise counsel you will wage your own war,
And in a multitude of counselors *there is* safety.

7 Wisdom *is* too lofty for a fool;
He does not open his mouth in the gate.

8 He who plots to do evil
Will be called a schemer.
9 The devising of foolishness *is* sin,
And the scoffer *is* an abomination to men.

10 *If* you faint in the day of adversity,
Your strength *is* small.

11 Deliver *those who* are drawn toward death,
And hold back *those* stumbling to the slaughter.
12 If you say, "Surely we did not know this,"
Does not He who weighs the hearts consider *it?*
He who keeps your soul, does He *not* know *it?*
And will He *not* render to *each* man according to his deeds?

13 My son, eat honey because *it is* good,
And the honeycomb *which is* sweet to your taste;

14 So *shall* the knowledge of wisdom *be* to your soul;
If you have found *it,* there is a prospect,
And your hope will not be cut off.

15 Do not lie in wait, O wicked *man,* against the dwelling
of the righteous;
Do not plunder his resting place;
16 For a righteous *man* may fall seven times
And rise again,
But the wicked shall fall by calamity.

17 Do not rejoice when your enemy falls,
And do not let your heart be glad when he stumbles;
18 Lest the LORD see *it,* and it displease Him,
And He turn away His wrath from him.

19 Do not fret because of evildoers,
Nor be envious of the wicked;
20 For there will be no prospect for the evil *man;*
The lamp of the wicked will be put out.

21 My son, fear the LORD and the king;
Do not associate with those given to change;
22 For their calamity will rise suddenly,
And who knows the ruin those two can bring?

Further Sayings of the Wise

23 These *things* also *belong* to the wise:

It is not good to show partiality in judgment.
24 He who says to the wicked, "You *are* righteous,"
Him the people will curse;
Nations will abhor him.
25 But those who rebuke *the wicked* will have delight,
And a good blessing will come upon them.

26 He who gives a right answer kisses the lips.

27 Prepare your outside work,
Make it fit for yourself in the field;
And afterward build your house.

28 Do not be a witness against your neighbor without cause,
For would you deceive[y] with your lips?
29 Do not say, "I will do to him just as he has done to me;
I will render to the man according to his work."

30 I went by the field of the lazy *man,*
And by the vineyard of the man devoid of understanding;
31 And there it was, all overgrown with thorns;
Its surface was covered with nettles;
Its stone wall was broken down.
32 When I saw *it,* I considered *it* well;
I looked on *it and* received instruction:

24:28 [y] Septuagint and Vulgate read *Do not deceive.*

LIFE LESSON

Proverbs 24:1-34

SITUATION Solomon admonished and warned, but he also motivated and encouraged.

OBSERVATION Don't be jealous of evil people. Instead, live wisely—exemplify justice, honesty, and hard work.

INSPIRATION The sluggard never seems to have time for the things that really matter, especially things that require discipline. But before he realizes it, his time and opportunities are lost. As Proverbs 24:33-34 observes, "A little sleep, a little slumber, . . . " Notice that it's just a "little" sleep, a "little" slumber, a "little" folding of the hands to rest that brought the ruin of lost time and opportunity. It's so easy to lose so much. You don't have to do anything to lose time.

Many people value time as silver was appraised in the days of Solomon. It is said of him in 1 Kings 10:27, "The king made silver as common in Jerusalem as stones." Time appears to be so plentiful that losing much of it seems inconsequential. But money is easily wasted as well. And if people threw away their money as thoughtlessly as they throw away their time, we would think them insane. Yet time is infinitely more precious than money because money can't buy time. But you can minimize the loss and waste of time by disciplining yourself for the purpose of Godliness. . . .

If you suddenly realized that you had no more time, would you regret how you have spent your time in the past and how you spend it now? The way you have used your time *can* be of comfort to you in your last hour. You may not be happy with some of the ways you used your time, but won't you be pleased then for all the times of Spirit-filled living, for all occasions when you have obeyed Christ? Won't you be glad then for those parts of your life that you spent in the Scriptures, prayer, worship, evangelism, serving, fasting, etc., for the purpose of becoming more like the One before whom you are about to stand in judgment (John 5:22-29)? What great wisdom there is in living as Jonathan Edwards resolved to live: "Resolved,

Continued

that I will live so, as I shall wish I had done when I come to die."

Why not do something about it while you still have time?
(From *Spiritual Disciplines for the Christian Life* by Donald S. Whitney)

APPLICATION Approach your day in a new way. How much time do you spend driving, working, or eating? What time is wasted? Replace wasted time with an activity that has value in the kingdom of God.

EXPLORATION Laziness—
Proverbs 6:6-11; 18:9;
Ecclesiastes 10:18; Romans 12:11;
2 Thessalonians 3:11-12;
Hebrews 6:11-12.

33 A little sleep, a little slumber,
A little folding of the hands to rest;
34 So shall your poverty come *like* a prowler,
And your need like an armed man.

Further Wise Sayings of Solomon

25 These also *are* proverbs of Solomon which the men of Hezekiah king of Judah copied:

2 *It is* the glory of God to conceal a matter,
But the glory of kings *is* to search out a matter.

3 *As* the heavens for height and the earth for depth,
So the heart of kings *is* unsearchable.

4 Take away the dross from silver,
And it will go to the silversmith *for* jewelry.
5 Take away the wicked from before the king,
And his throne will be established in righteousness.

6 Do not exalt yourself in the presence of the king,
And do not stand in the place of the great;
7 For *it is* better that he say to you,
"Come up here,"
Than that you should be put lower in the presence of the prince,
Whom your eyes have seen.

8 Do not go hastily to court;
For what will you do in the end,
When your neighbor has put you to shame?
9 Debate your case with your neighbor,
And do not disclose the secret to another;
10 Lest he who hears *it* expose your shame,
And your reputation be ruined.

11 A word fitly spoken *is like* apples of gold
In settings of silver.
12 *Like* an earring of gold and an ornament of fine gold
Is a wise rebuker to an obedient ear.

13 Like the cold of snow in time of harvest
Is a faithful messenger to those who send him,
For he refreshes the soul of his masters.

14 Whoever falsely boasts of giving
Is like clouds and wind without rain.

15 By long forbearance a ruler is persuaded,
And a gentle tongue breaks a bone.

16 Have you found honey?
Eat only as much as you need,
Lest you be filled with it and vomit.

17 Seldom set foot in your neighbor's house,
Lest he become weary of you and hate you.

18 A man who bears false witness against his neighbor
Is like a club, a sword, and a sharp arrow.

19 Confidence in an unfaithful *man* in time of trouble
Is like a bad tooth and a foot out of joint.

20 *Like* one who takes away a garment in cold weather,
And like vinegar on soda,
Is one who sings songs to a heavy heart.

21 If your enemy is hungry, give him bread to eat;
And if he is thirsty, give him water to drink;
22 For *so* you will heap coals of fire on his head,
And the LORD will reward you.

23 The north wind brings forth rain,
And a backbiting tongue an angry countenance.

24 *It is* better to dwell in a corner of a housetop,
Than in a house shared with a contentious woman.

25 *As* cold water to a weary soul,
So *is* good news from a far country.

26 A righteous *man* who falters before the wicked
Is like a murky spring and a polluted well.

27 *It is* not good to eat much honey;
So to seek one's own glory *is not* glory.

28 Whoever *has* no rule over his own spirit
Is like a city broken down, without walls.

26 As snow in summer and rain in harvest,
So honor is not fitting for a fool.

2 Like a flitting sparrow, like a flying swallow,
So a curse without cause shall not alight.

3 A whip for the horse,
A bridle for the donkey,
And a rod for the fool's back.
4 Do not answer a fool according to his folly,
Lest you also be like him.
5 Answer a fool according to his folly,
Lest he be wise in his own eyes.
6 He who sends a message by the hand of a fool
Cuts off *his own* feet *and* drinks violence.
7 *Like* the legs of the lame that hang limp
Is a proverb in the mouth of fools.
8 Like one who binds a stone in a sling
Is he who gives honor to a fool.
9 *Like* a thorn *that* goes into the hand of a drunkard
Is a proverb in the mouth of fools.
10 The great *God* who formed everything
Gives the fool *his* hire and the transgressor *his* wages.[z]

26:10 [z] The Hebrew is difficult; ancient and modern translators differ greatly.

LIFE LESSON

Proverbs 25:1-28

SITUATION Solomon encouraged his hearers to be wise and careful in their conversations.

OBSERVATION Learning to control the tongue is an important step in self-control.

INSPIRATION The tongue—what a study in contrasts! To the physician it's merely a two-ounce slab of mucous membrane enclosing a complex array of muscles and nerves that enable our bodies to chew, taste, and swallow. How helpful! Equally significant, it is the major organ of communication that enables us to articulate distinct sounds so we can understand each other. How essential! . . . But the tongue is as volatile as it is vital. It was Washington Irving who first said, "A sharp tongue is the only edge tool that grows keener with constant use." It was James, the half brother of Jesus, who first warned:

The tongue is a fire . . . a restless evil and full of deadly poison (James 3:6, 8).

Verbal cyanide. A lethal, relentless, flaming missile which assaults with hellish power, blistering and destroying at will.

And yet it doesn't look anything like the brutal beast it is. Neatly hidden behind ivory palace gates, its movements are an intriguing study of coordination. It can curl itself either into a cheery whistle or manipulate a lazy, afternoon yawn. With no difficulty it can flick a husk of popcorn from between two jaw teeth or hold a thermometer just so. And it is *tricky*! It can help you enjoy the flavor of a stick of peppermint as it switches from side to side without once getting nipped. Moments later it can follow the directions of a trumpeter, allowing him to play "Flight of the Bumble Bee" without a single miscue.

But watch out! Let your thumb get smashed with a hammer or your toe get clobbered on a chair and that slippery creature in your mouth will suddenly play the flip side of its nature.

Not only is the tongue untamed, it's *untamable*! Meaning what? Meaning as long as you live it will never gain control of itself. It defies being tamed.

Continued

Incredible! We can tame Flipper and Trigger and Shamu and Lassie . . . but the tongue? Impossible to train!

. . . [I]t takes . . . a tight, conscious muzzle on the muscle in your mouth. Harnessing such a wily creature requires a determined mindset. . . . It's a project you've put off long enough.

(From *Growing Old in the Seasons of Life* by Charles Swindoll)

APPLICATION Have words ever popped out of your mouth before you thought about them? Think before you respond. Never just blurt out an answer. Don't insult someone or carelessly criticize. Never be sarcastic, and be careful how you tease.

EXPLORATION The Tongue and Self-control—Psalm 34:13; Proverbs 10:19; 21:23; Galatians 5:22-23; James 1:26; 3:5-10; 2 Peter 1:5-7.

11 As a dog returns to his own vomit,
So a fool repeats his folly.
12 Do you see a man wise in his own eyes?
There is more hope for a fool than for him.

13 The lazy *man* says, "*There is* a lion in the road!
A fierce lion *is* in the streets!"
14 *As* a door turns on its hinges,
So *does* the lazy *man* on his bed.
15 The lazy *man* buries his hand in the bowl;[a]
It wearies him to bring it back to his mouth.
16 The lazy *man is* wiser in his own eyes
Than seven men who can answer sensibly.

17 He who passes by *and* meddles in a quarrel not his own
Is like one who takes a dog by the ears.

18 Like a madman who throws firebrands, arrows, and death,
19 *Is* the man *who* deceives his neighbor,
And says, "I was only joking!"

20 Where *there is* no wood, the fire goes out;
And where *there is* no talebearer, strife ceases.
21 *As* charcoal *is* to burning coals, and wood to fire,
So *is* a contentious man to kindle strife.
22 The words of a talebearer *are* like tasty trifles,
And they go down into the inmost body.

23 Fervent lips with a wicked heart
Are like earthenware covered with silver dross.

24 He who hates, disguises *it* with his lips,
And lays up deceit within himself;
25 When he speaks kindly, do not believe him,
For *there are* seven abominations in his heart;
26 *Though his* hatred is covered by deceit,
His wickedness will be revealed before the assembly.

27 Whoever digs a pit will fall into it,
And he who rolls a stone will have it roll back on him.

28 A lying tongue hates *those who are* crushed by it,
And a flattering mouth works ruin.

27

Do not boast about tomorrow,
For you do not know what a day may bring forth.

2 Let another man praise you, and not your own mouth;
A stranger, and not your own lips.

3 A stone *is* heavy and sand *is* weighty,
But a fool's wrath *is* heavier than both of them.

4 Wrath *is* cruel and anger a torrent,
But who *is* able to stand before jealousy?

5 Open rebuke *is* better
Than love carefully concealed.

26:15 [a] Compare 19:24

6 Faithful *are* the wounds of a friend,
But the kisses of an enemy *are* deceitful.

7 A satisfied soul loathes the honeycomb,
But to a hungry soul every bitter thing *is* sweet.

8 Like a bird that wanders from its nest
Is a man who wanders from his place.

9 Ointment and perfume delight the heart,
And the sweetness of a man's friend *gives delight* by
hearty counsel.

10 Do not forsake your own friend or your father's friend,
Nor go to your brother's house in the day of your calamity;
Better *is* a neighbor nearby than a brother far away.

11 My son, be wise, and make my heart glad,
That I may answer him who reproaches me.

12 A prudent *man* foresees evil *and* hides himself;
The simple pass on *and* are punished.

13 Take the garment of him who is surety for a stranger,
And hold it in pledge *when* he is surety for a seductress.

14 He who blesses his friend with a loud voice, rising
early in the morning,
It will be counted a curse to him.

15 A continual dripping on a very rainy day
And a contentious woman are alike;
16 Whoever restrains her restrains the wind,
And grasps oil with his right hand.

17 *As* iron sharpens iron,
So a man sharpens the countenance of his friend.

18 Whoever keeps the fig tree will eat its fruit;
So he who waits on his master will be honored.

19 As in water face *reflects* face,
So a man's heart *reveals* the man.

20 Hell[b] and Destruction[c] are never full;
So the eyes of man are never satisfied.

21 The refining pot *is* for silver and the furnace for gold,
And a man *is valued* by what others say of him.

22 Though you grind a fool in a mortar with a pestle
along with crushed grain,
Yet his foolishness will not depart from him.

23 Be diligent to know the state of your flocks,
And attend to your herds;
24 For riches *are* not forever,
Nor does a crown *endure* to all generations.

27:20 [b] Or *Sheol* [c] Hebrew *Abaddon*

LIFE LESSON

Proverbs 26:1-28

SITUATION Solomon warned: Beware of negative people who can hurt you. The fool, the lazy, and the gossip bring nothing but damage to your life.

OBSERVATION If you can't help them change, detach yourself from people with a negative attitude.

INSPIRATION If it were not for the restraining presence of the Spirit, you and I would be the personification of wickedness. No sin would be too extreme. No act of disobedience too rebellious. . . .

Before we go further, perhaps I should clarify the meaning of the phrase, "those who practice such things shall not inherit the kingdom of God."

Paul selects words very carefully. For example, "practice." The tense of the original verb suggests "habitually practice." In other words, it refers to one whose entire life is consumed by such evil. . . .

But before we cluck our tongues at those who "habitually practice" such things, let's keep in mind that our old nature remains just as dark and depraved as theirs, even though the Spirit resides within us. Were it not for the presence of God's Spirit, our wickedness would know no bounds.

. . . The good news is: We don't have to serve the old master any longer! Now that we have our Lord's divine, dynamic presence perpetually living within us, we can live above all that . . . and we can do so on a consistent basis. By the Spirit's filling, evidences of our new nature emerge.

. . . By turning the controls of our life over to Him who lives within, we begin to model the life Christ modeled when He lived and walked on earth. . . .

(From *Flying Closer to the Flame* by Charles Swindoll)

APPLICATION Put the brakes on gossip this week. Squash it like an intruding spider.

EXPLORATION Negative People—Leviticus 26:14-35; Nehemiah 13:25-29; Psalm 57:4; Matthew 7:1-5.

LIFE LESSON

Proverbs 27:1-27

SITUATION Many of these proverbs affirm the value of friends who will be honest about one's strengths and weaknesses.

OBSERVATION Wise friends facilitate growth. Be a wise friend and help others grow.

INSPIRATION Inwardly my soul was crying out for someone who would listen—someone who could listen without responding—without judging. Someone who could help me translate the meaningless jumble of scrambled thoughts without taking offense of being critical.

I was too closed, too masked, too threatened. I had never really bared my soul to anyone, not even myself. I was so afraid to take it out that again I slammed the lid shut and guarded it with all the emotional strength I had at my disposal.

Emery then told me a story.

"A man was walking in a wilderness. He became lost and was unable to find his way out. Another man met him. 'Sir, I am lost, can you show me the way out of this wilderness?' 'No,' said the stranger, 'I cannot show you the way out of this wilderness, but maybe if I walk with you, we can find our way out together.'"

(From *Depression* by Donald Baker and Emery Nester)

APPLICATION You can benefit from a close friend in your Christian life. Find a friend who will share your deepest concerns. Share together over lunch and commit to helping each other.

EXPLORATION Christian Friendships—Proverbs 15:31; 16:21, 24; Ecclesiastes 4:9-12; Romans 15:14; Galatians 2:11-16; Colossians 1:28-29; Hebrews 10:24-25; 13:7.

25 *When* the hay is removed, and the tender grass shows itself,
And the herbs of the mountains are gathered in,
26 The lambs *will provide* your clothing,
And the goats the price of a field;
27 *You shall have* enough goats' milk for your food,
For the food of your household,
And the nourishment of your maidservants.

28 The wicked flee when no one pursues,
But the righteous are bold as a lion.

2 Because of the transgression of a land, many *are* its princes;
But by a man of understanding *and* knowledge
Right will be prolonged.

3 A poor man who oppresses the poor
Is like a driving rain which leaves no food.

4 Those who forsake the law praise the wicked,
But such as keep the law contend with them.

5 Evil men do not understand justice,
But those who seek the LORD understand all.

6 Better *is* the poor who walks in his integrity
Than one perverse *in his* ways, though he *be* rich.

7 Whoever keeps the law *is* a discerning son,
But a companion of gluttons shames his father.

8 One who increases his possessions by usury and extortion
Gathers it for him who will pity the poor.

9 One who turns away his ear from hearing the law,
Even his prayer *is* an abomination.

10 Whoever causes the upright to go astray in an evil way,
He himself will fall into his own pit;
But the blameless will inherit good.

11 The rich man *is* wise in his own eyes,
But the poor who has understanding searches him out.

12 When the righteous rejoice, *there is* great glory;
But when the wicked arise, men hide themselves.

13 He who covers his sins will not prosper,
But whoever confesses and forsakes *them* will have mercy.

14 Happy *is* the man who is always reverent,
But he who hardens his heart will fall into calamity.

15 *Like* a roaring lion and a charging bear
Is a wicked ruler over poor people.

16 A ruler who lacks understanding *is* a great oppressor,
But he who hates covetousness will prolong *his* days.

17 A man burdened with bloodshed will flee into a pit;
Let no one help him.

18 Whoever walks blamelessly will be saved,
But *he who is* perverse *in his* ways will suddenly fall.

19 He who tills his land will have plenty of bread,
But he who follows frivolity will have poverty enough!

20 A faithful man will abound with blessings,
But he who hastens to be rich will not go unpunished.

21 To show partiality *is* not good,
Because for a piece of bread a man will transgress.

22 A man with an evil eye hastens after riches,
And does not consider that poverty will come upon him.

23 He who rebukes a man will find more favor afterward
Than he who flatters with the tongue.

24 Whoever robs his father or his mother,
And says, "*It is* no transgression,"
The same *is* companion to a destroyer.

25 He who is of a proud heart stirs up strife,
But he who trusts in the LORD will be prospered.

26 He who trusts in his own heart is a fool,
But whoever walks wisely will be delivered.

27 He who gives to the poor will not lack,
But he who hides his eyes will have many curses.

28 When the wicked arise, men hide themselves;
But when they perish, the righteous increase.

29 He who is often rebuked, *and* hardens *his* neck,
Will suddenly be destroyed, and that without remedy.

2 When the righteous are in authority, the people rejoice;
But when a wicked *man* rules, the people groan.

3 Whoever loves wisdom makes his father rejoice,
But a companion of harlots wastes *his* wealth.

4 The king establishes the land by justice,
But he who receives bribes overthrows it.

5 A man who flatters his neighbor
Spreads a net for his feet.

6 By transgression an evil man is snared,
But the righteous sings and rejoices.

7 The righteous considers the cause of the poor,
But the wicked does not understand *such* knowledge.

8 Scoffers set a city aflame,
But wise *men* turn away wrath.

9 *If* a wise man contends with a foolish man,
Whether *the fool* rages or laughs, *there is* no peace.

LIFE LESSON

Proverbs 28:1-28

SITUATION God wanted the Israelites to govern themselves with justice and wisdom.

OBSERVATION When you lead others, have a high moral standard. Don't let any part of your life be questionable.

INSPIRATION "Whoever wishes to become great among you shall be your servant."

Forgotten words.

Yes, these seem to be forgotten words, even in many churches with their smooth pastors, high powered executives, and superstar singers. Unfortunately, there doesn't seem to be much of the servant mentality in such settings. Even in our church life we tend to get so caught up in a success and size race that we lose sight of our primary calling as followers of Christ. The "celebrity syndrome" so present in our Christian thought and activities just doesn't square with the attitudes and messages of Jesus. We have skidded into a pattern whereby the celebrities and top dogs in our church life call the shots, and it is difficult to be a servant when you're used to telling others what to do. . . .

You're probably saying, "But there must be leadership to get the job done." Yes, I agree. But it must be servant-hearted leadership among *all.* You see, I am not interested in which form of government you or your church may embrace, but only that every one involved in that ministry (whether leader or not) sees himself as one who serves, one who gives. It's the *attitude* that's most important.

(From *Improving Your Serve* by Charles Swindoll)

APPLICATION Do you try to control others by your tone of voice? Do your words make them want to follow you? Are you trustworthy? Develop a friendly attitude that causes others to want to follow you.

EXPLORATION Leadership—Job 34:30; Colossians 3:15; Titus 3:1.

LIFE LESSON

Proverbs 29:1-27

SITUATION Without the love and fear of God, Israel made mistakes. Without restraint and discipline, sin took over.

OBSERVATION God's standards are crucial to our lives. Those who ignore them drift apart from God, but loving, God-fearing people prosper.

INSPIRATION I used to wonder how to remember all the commandments of God. As a child I memorized the Ten Commandments in the Bible, but there are so many other commandments in the Bible—hundreds of them. Then I discovered a wonderful fact, that the first and greatest commandment is to love God. . . .

So it isn't as complicated as I had thought! Love God completely, and do to your neighbor as you, in your best moments, want him or her to do to you. If we obey only these two basic laws, we will be obeying all the others, too. It is wonderful of God to tell us what He allows and what He prohibits, what He likes and dislikes, for we might otherwise be unsure of ourselves, and unsure whether or not we are loving God by obeying Him.

(From *Next Steps for New Christians* by Kenneth Taylor)

APPLICATION God has set the example for parents. Children need rules to guide and protect them. If you are a parent, set clear, fair guidelines. Then be firm in implementing them.

EXPLORATION Law of God—Exodus 15:25; 31:18; Deuteronomy 4:8; Galatians 2:15-16.

10 The bloodthirsty hate the blameless,
But the upright seek his well-being.[d]

11 A fool vents all his feelings,[e]
But a wise *man* holds them back.

12 If a ruler pays attention to lies,
All his servants *become* wicked.

13 The poor *man* and the oppressor have this in common:
The LORD gives light to the eyes of both.

14 The king who judges the poor with truth,
His throne will be established forever.

15 The rod and rebuke give wisdom,
But a child left *to himself* brings shame to his mother.

16 When the wicked are multiplied, transgression increases;
But the righteous will see their fall.

17 Correct your son, and he will give you rest;
Yes, he will give delight to your soul.

18 Where *there is* no revelation,[f] the people cast off restraint;
But happy *is* he who keeps the law.

19 A servant will not be corrected by mere words;
For though he understands, he will not respond.

20 Do you see a man hasty in his words?
There is more hope for a fool than for him.

21 He who pampers his servant from childhood
Will have him as a son in the end.

22 An angry man stirs up strife,
And a furious man abounds in transgression.

23 A man's pride will bring him low,
But the humble in spirit will retain honor.

24 Whoever is a partner with a thief hates his own life;
He swears to tell the truth,[g] but reveals nothing.

25 The fear of man brings a snare,
But whoever trusts in the LORD shall be safe.

26 Many seek the ruler's favor,
But justice for man *comes* from the LORD.

27 An unjust man *is* an abomination to the righteous,
And *he who is* upright in the way *is* an abomination to the wicked.

The Wisdom of Agur

30 The words of Agur the son of Jakeh, *his* utterance. This man declared to Ithiel—to Ithiel and Ucal:

29:10 [d] Literally *soul*
29:11 [e] Literally *spirit*
29:18 [f] Or *prophetic vision*
29:24 [g] Literally *hears the adjuration*

2 Surely I *am* more stupid than *any* man,
And do not have the understanding of a man.
3 I neither learned wisdom
Nor have knowledge of the Holy One.

4 Who has ascended into heaven, or descended?
Who has gathered the wind in His fists?
Who has bound the waters in a garment?
Who has established all the ends of the earth?
What *is* His name, and what *is* His Son's name,
If you know?

5 Every word of God *is* pure;
He *is* a shield to those who put their trust in Him.
6 Do not add to His words,
Lest He rebuke you, and you be found a liar.

7 Two *things* I request of You
(Deprive me not before I die):
8 Remove falsehood and lies far from me;
Give me neither poverty nor riches—
Feed me with the food allotted to me;
9 Lest I be full and deny *You,*
And say, "Who *is* the LORD?"
Or lest I be poor and steal,
And profane the name of my God.

10 Do not malign a servant to his master,
Lest he curse you, and you be found guilty.

11 *There is* a generation *that* curses its father,
And does not bless its mother.
12 *There is* a generation *that is* pure in its own eyes,
Yet is not washed from its filthiness.
13 *There is* a generation—oh, how lofty are their eyes!
And their eyelids are lifted up.
14 *There is* a generation whose teeth *are like* swords,
And whose fangs *are like* knives,
To devour the poor from off the earth,
And the needy from *among* men.

15 The leech has two daughters—
Give *and* Give!

There are three *things that* are never satisfied,
Four never say, "Enough!":
16 The grave,[h]
The barren womb,
The earth *that* is not satisfied with water—
And the fire never says, "Enough!"

17 The eye *that* mocks *his* father,
And scorns obedience to *his* mother,
The ravens of the valley will pick it out,
And the young eagles will eat it.

LIFE LESSON

Proverbs 30:1-33

SITUATION Agur was a descendant from Abraham's son, Ishmael. Agur came from the Ancient Near East, which was famous for its wisdom.

OBSERVATION Many people, although they may have different backgrounds, understand common moral laws.

INSPIRATION Many Christians admit that they do not really *know* God. For other believers, lack of knowledge of God is the cause of vacillating spirituality, inconsistency between the talk and walk of faith, and ineffectiveness in prayer. For still others, inadequate knowledge of God accounts for the reluctant response to holy living and moral responsibility. . . .

What does it mean to know God and live with a knowledge of Him? It involves both intimacy and integrity. The intimacy of the Thou-I relationship we were created to experience with God requires the opening of our innermost being to Him just as He has revealed His innermost nature to us. The word *intimacy* means "proceeding from within, inward, internal." In Hebrew the word for knowledge has the same root as "to know." It is also the physical and spiritual oneness of a husband and wife.

Knowledge of God is more than ideas about Him. It involves our total inner selves: intellect, emotion, and will.

(From *Climbing the Rainbow* by Lloyd J. Ogilvie)

APPLICATION What evil does society allow now that it used to frown on? What moral standard seems to be falling away? Follow God's morals rather than society's. When questioned about your uncompromising morals, find a way to introduce that person to Jesus.

EXPLORATION Knowing God—Genesis 3:8-9; Exodus 9:29; Psalm 46:8-10; Matthew 11:27; Romans 1:19-20; 1 Corinthians 2:9-16; Ephesians 1:17.

30:16 [h] Or *Sheol*

18 There are three *things which* are too
wonderful for me,
Yes, four *which* I do not understand:
19 The way of an eagle in the air,
The way of a serpent on a rock,
The way of a ship in the midst of the sea,
And the way of a man with a virgin.

20 This *is* the way of an adulterous woman:
She eats and wipes her mouth,
And says, "I have done no wickedness."

21 For three *things* the earth is perturbed,
Yes, for four it cannot bear up:
22 For a servant when he reigns,
A fool when he is filled with food,
23 A hateful *woman* when she is married,
And a maidservant who succeeds her
mistress.

24 There are four *things which* are little on the
earth,
But they *are* exceedingly wise:
25 The ants *are* a people not strong,
Yet they prepare their food in the summer;
26 The rock badgers[i] are a feeble folk,
Yet they make their homes in the crags;
27 The locusts have no king,
Yet they all advance in ranks;
28 The spider[j] skillfully grasps with its hands,
And it is in kings' palaces.

29 There are three *things which* are majestic in
pace,
Yes, four *which* are stately in walk:
30 A lion, *which is* mighty among beasts
And does not turn away from any;
31 A greyhound,[k]
A male goat also,
And a king *whose* troops *are* with him.[l]

32 If you have been foolish in exalting yourself,
Or if you have devised evil, *put your* hand on
your mouth.
33 For *as* the churning of milk produces butter,
And wringing the nose produces blood,
So the forcing of wrath produces strife.

The Words of King Lemuel's Mother

31 The words of King Lemuel, the utterance
which his mother taught him:

2 What, my son?
And what, son of my womb?
And what, son of my vows?
3 Do not give your strength to women,
Nor your ways to that which destroys kings.

4 *It is* not for kings, O Lemuel,
It is not for kings to drink wine,
Nor for princes intoxicating drink;
5 Lest they drink and forget the law,
And pervert the justice of all the afflicted.
6 Give strong drink to him who is perishing,
And wine to those who are bitter of heart.
7 Let him drink and forget his poverty,
And remember his misery no more.

8 Open your mouth for the speechless,
In the cause of all *who are* appointed to die.[m]
9 Open your mouth, judge righteously,
And plead the cause of the poor and needy.

The Virtuous Wife

10 Who[n] can find a virtuous[o] wife?
For her worth *is* far above rubies.
11 The heart of her husband safely trusts her;
So he will have no lack of gain.
12 She does him good and not evil
All the days of her life.
13 She seeks wool and flax,
And willingly works with her hands.
14 She is like the merchant ships,
She brings her food from afar.
15 She also rises while it is yet night,
And provides food for her household,
And a portion for her maidservants.
16 She considers a field and buys it;
From her profits she plants a vineyard.
17 She girds herself with strength,
And strengthens her arms.
18 She perceives that her merchandise *is* good,
And her lamp does not go out by night.
19 She stretches out her hands to the distaff,
And her hand holds the spindle.
20 She extends her hand to the poor,

30:26 [i] Or *hyraxes*
30:28 [j] Or *lizard*
30:31 [k] Exact identity unknown [l] A Jewish tradition reads *a king against whom there is no uprising.*
31:8 [m] Literally *sons of passing away*
31:10 [n] Verses 10 through 31 are an alphabetic acrostic in Hebrew (compare Psalm 119). [o] Literally *a wife of valor,* in the sense of all forms of excellence

Yes, she reaches out her hands to the needy.
21 She is not afraid of snow for her household,
For all her household *is* clothed with scarlet.
22 She makes tapestry for herself;
Her clothing *is* fine linen and purple.
23 Her husband is known in the gates,
When he sits among the elders of the land.
24 She makes linen garments and sells *them,*
And supplies sashes for the merchants.
25 Strength and honor *are* her clothing;
She shall rejoice in time to come.
26 She opens her mouth with wisdom,
And on her tongue *is* the law of kindness.
27 She watches over the ways of her household,
And does not eat the bread of idleness.
28 Her children rise up and call her blessed;
Her husband *also,* and he praises her:
29 "Many daughters have done well,
But you excel them all."
30 Charm *is* deceitful and beauty *is* passing,
But a woman *who* fears the LORD, she
shall be praised.
31 Give her of the fruit of her hands,
And let her own works praise her in the gates.

The Book of

ECCLESIASTES

INTRODUCTION

She didn't want to share her name, just her pain. So I cradled the phone against my shoulder and listened. Her husband had cheated. She was angry. Angry at him. Angry at God. Angry at herself for being angry. In two months she'd gone through three bottles of antidepressants. She didn't want to leave her room or see her friends. Weak and bitter she finally asked, "Max, will I ever be happy again?"

She's not the first to wonder.

As the drinker orders a double, he wonders.

As the achiever logs another eighteen-hour day, she wonders.

As the boss reaches for his secretary's hand, both wonder.

"Will I ever be happy again?"

There is a great dissatisfaction across the land. Hand after hand reaching out to quench thirsts and scratch itches. But the thirst lingers, the itch remains. As one man told me, "I learned that once I had what I wanted, I found I didn't want what I had."

Solomon could have said those words. He was unlimited in what he could do. Unbridled in what he could own. Unharnessed in what he could experience. So he set out to do it all.

He tried knowledge (1:13), pleasure, possessions and projects (2:3–8). He was serious about each. He built a temple and a palace. He owned forty thousand horses with twelve thousand horsemen. He married the daughter of Pharaoh and built her a house (which was good because he had six hundred and ninety-nine more wives so *his* place was crowded).

In spite of it all, or because of it all, he was restless. "I hated life," he journaled. He was isolated (3:22), frustrated (5:17), and longed for the good old days when things were simpler and the wine was sweeter.

For some reason, Solomon kept a record of his longings. And somehow, they became public. Maybe he knew that he wasn't the only one to get to the top of the ladder only to find it against the wrong building.

If that's where you are, or might be, this book is for you.

LIFE LESSON

Ecclesiastes 1:1–2:26

SITUATION The writer of Ecclesiastes wanted to help those who would live after him lead a fulfilling life. He taught lessons learned from his own life.

OBSERVATION Without God, all of our work, pleasure, and wisdom are useless. Lasting fulfillment comes from honoring God in all we do.

INSPIRATION It is as if we are on an ocean beach called Earth. We are frantic. We build castles—or at least we think we do. But what we are really doing is just throwing up sand piles as fast as we can before the next big wave comes in. And that wave is coming. We can't run from it; there's no escaping it. We will stay on the beach building our castles higher, bigger, more elaborate. We won't enjoy them. There will be no time for that. The wave is coming. . . .

People have always built sand castles, and those castles have always crumbled. There have always been those who grabbed for things that break. But now it is like the beginning of the end, like the first moments of a stock market crash, and the scramble is on. . . .

We have made Jesus to be our Jesus, and we are so accustomed to responding to "our" Jesus that we have forgotten how to respond to the Son of the living God.

His teachings have been taken with the pragmatic view of "helping me," not followed because we must obey and can do nothing else. His words

The Vanity of Life

The words of the Preacher, the son of David, king in Jerusalem.

2 "Vanity[a] of vanities," says the Preacher;
"Vanity of vanities, all *is* vanity."

3 What profit has a man from all his labor
In which he toils under the sun?
4 *One* generation passes away, and *another* generation comes;
But the earth abides forever.
5 The sun also rises, and the sun goes down,
And hastens to the place where it arose.
6 The wind goes toward the south,
And turns around to the north;
The wind whirls about continually,
And comes again on its circuit.
7 All the rivers run into the sea,
Yet the sea *is* not full;
To the place from which the rivers come,
There they return again.
8 All things *are* full of labor;
Man cannot express *it*.
The eye is not satisfied with seeing,
Nor the ear filled with hearing.

9 That which has been *is* what will be,
That which *is* done is what will be done,
And *there is* nothing new under the sun.
10 Is there anything of which it may be said,
"See, this *is* new"?
It has already been in ancient times before us.
11 *There is* no remembrance of former *things*,
Nor will there be any remembrance of *things* that are to come
By *those* who will come after.

The Grief of Wisdom

12I, the Preacher, was king over Israel in Jerusalem. 13And I set my heart
to seek and search out by wisdom concerning all that is done under
heaven; this burdensome task God has given to the sons of man, by which
they may be exercised. 14I have seen all the works that are done under the
sun; and indeed, all *is* vanity and grasping for the wind.

15 *What is* crooked cannot be made straight,
And what is lacking cannot be numbered.

16I communed with my heart, saying, "Look, I have attained greatness,
and have gained more wisdom than all who were before me in Jerusalem.
My heart has understood great wisdom and knowledge." 17And I set my
heart to know wisdom and to know madness and folly. I perceived that
this also is grasping for the wind.

18 For in much wisdom *is* much grief,
And he who increases knowledge increases sorrow.

1:2 [a] Or *Absurdity, Frustration, Futility, Nonsense;* and so throughout this book

The Vanity of Pleasure

2 I said in my heart, "Come now, I will test you with mirth; therefore
enjoy pleasure"; but surely, this also *was* vanity. [2]I said of laughter—
"Madness!"; and of mirth, "What does it accomplish?" [3]I searched in my
heart *how* to gratify my flesh with wine, while guiding my heart with wisdom, and how to lay hold on folly, till I might see what *was* good for the
sons of men to do under heaven all the days of their lives.
[4]I made my works great, I built myself houses, and planted myself vineyards. [5]I made myself gardens and orchards, and I planted all *kinds* of
fruit trees in them. [6]I made myself water pools from which to water the
growing trees of the grove. [7]I acquired male and female servants, and had
servants born in my house. Yes, I had greater possessions of herds and
flocks than all who were in Jerusalem before me. [8]I also gathered for myself silver and gold and the special treasures of kings and of the provinces.
I acquired male and female singers, the delights of the sons of men, *and*
musical instruments[b] of all kinds.
[9]So I became great and excelled more than all who were before me in Jerusalem. Also my wisdom remained with me.

10 Whatever my eyes desired I did not keep from them.
I did not withhold my heart from any pleasure,
For my heart rejoiced in all my labor;
And this was my reward from all my labor.
11 Then I looked on all the works that my hands had done
And on the labor in which I had toiled;
And indeed all *was* vanity and grasping for the wind.
There was no profit under the sun.

The End of the Wise and the Fool

12 Then I turned myself to consider wisdom and madness and folly;
For what *can* the man *do* who succeeds the king?—
Only what he has already done.
13 Then I saw that wisdom excels folly
As light excels darkness.
14 The wise man's eyes *are* in his head,
But the fool walks in darkness.
Yet I myself perceived
That the same event happens to them all.

15 So I said in my heart,
"As it happens to the fool,
It also happens to me,
And why was I then more wise?"
Then I said in my heart,
"This also *is* vanity."
16 For *there is* no more remembrance of the wise than
of the fool forever,
Since all that now *is* will be forgotten in the days to come.
And how does a wise *man* die?
As the fool!

2:8 *b* Exact meaning unknown

have been diluted by so many diverse therapies that all we know to respond to is a "feel-good" deity, a piece of religious plastic which we label "God."

To reject God out of hand is one thing, but to acknowledge Him and then to live as if He is neither Lord nor God is a horrible existence. Then all we have left is sand.

God expects us to be disciplined. It is not the unnatural but rather the natural thing to be. We were created to be disciplined, put on this earth by God at this time and in this place not for personal gain or personal pleasure but for His purpose.

God is here in our world now. He has been all the time. He calls to scrambling, grasping people like us through the words of Jesus Christ. He says, "Come unto me."

It is time for us to do what he asks.

(From *Enjoying the Closeness of God* by Roger Palms)

APPLICATION How do you seek intellectual knowledge? What pleasures do you seek? Solomon warns that these activities will never bring fulfillment by themselves. Learn to live your life so every detail pleases God. Mow the lawn, clean up your house, or enjoy a hobby in order to please God.

EXPLORATION Coming to God—Matthew 11:28-30. Persevering—Jude 20-25. Heavenly Wisdom—James 3:17-18.

LIFE LESSON

Ecclesiastes 3:1–5:17

SITUATION The author gives insights on values. He encourages the reader to use time wisely by making right choices.

OBSERVATION God has planned a time for every thing and every action. Our choices should reflect what we value.

INSPIRATION The central principle of all personal organization of time is simple: *time must be budgeted!*

Most of us learned this about money a long time ago. When we discovered that we rarely had enough money to do all the things we wanted to do with it, we found it prudent to sit down and think through our financial priorities. When money is limited, one budgets. And when time is in limited supply, the same principle holds. The disorganized person must have a budgeting perspective. And that means determining the difference between the fixed—what one *must* do—and the discretionary—what one would *like* to do. . . . Years ago my father wisely shared with me that one of the great tests of human character is found in making critical choices of selection and rejection amidst all of the opportunities that lurk in life's path. "Your challenge," he told me, "will not be in separating out the good from the bad, but in grabbing the best out of all the possible good." He was absolutely correct. I did indeed have to learn, sometimes the hard way, that I had to say no to things I really wanted to do in order to say yes to the very best things.

Heeding that counsel has meant saying an occasional no to dinner parties

[17]Therefore I hated life because the work that was done under the sun *was*
distressing to me, for all *is* vanity and grasping for the wind.
[18]Then I hated all my labor in which I had toiled under the sun, because
I must leave it to the man who will come after me. [19]And who knows
whether he will be wise or a fool? Yet he will rule over all my labor in which
I toiled and in which I have shown myself wise under the sun. This also *is*
vanity. [20]Therefore I turned my heart and despaired of all the labor in
which I had toiled under the sun. [21]For there is a man whose labor *is* with
wisdom, knowledge, and skill; yet he must leave his heritage to a man who
has not labored for it. This also *is* vanity and a great evil. [22]For what has
man for all his labor, and for the striving of his heart with which he has
toiled under the sun? [23]For all his days *are* sorrowful, and his work burdensome;
even in the night his heart takes no rest. This also is vanity.
[24]Nothing *is* better for a man *than* that he should eat and drink, and *that*
his soul should enjoy good in his labor. This also, I saw, was from the hand
of God. [25]For who can eat, or who can have enjoyment, more than I?[c] [26]For
God gives wisdom and knowledge and joy to a man who *is* good in His
sight; but to the sinner He gives the work of gathering and collecting, that
he may give to *him who is* good before God. This also *is* vanity and grasping
for the wind.

Everything Has Its Time

3 To everything *there is* a season,
A time for every purpose under heaven:

2 A time to be born,
And a time to die;
A time to plant,
And a time to pluck *what is* planted;
3 A time to kill,
And a time to heal;
A time to break down,
And a time to build up;
4 A time to weep,
And a time to laugh;
A time to mourn,
And a time to dance;
5 A time to cast away stones,
And a time to gather stones;
A time to embrace,
And a time to refrain from embracing;
6 A time to gain,
And a time to lose;
A time to keep,
And a time to throw away;
7 A time to tear,
And a time to sew;
A time to keep silence,
And a time to speak;

2:25 [c] Following Masoretic Text, Targum, and Vulgate; some Hebrew manuscripts, Septuagint, and Syriac read *without Him.*

8 A time to love,
And a time to hate;
A time of war,
And a time of peace.

The God-Given Task

9What profit has the worker from that in which he labors? 10I have seen
the God-given task with which the sons of men are to be occupied. 11He
has made everything beautiful in its time. Also He has put eternity in their
hearts, except that no one can find out the work that God does from beginning to end.
12I know that nothing *is* better for them than to rejoice, and to do good
in their lives, 13and also that every man should eat and drink and enjoy the
good of all his labor—it *is* the gift of God.

14 I know that whatever God does,
It shall be forever.
Nothing can be added to it,
And nothing taken from it.
God does *it,* that men should fear before Him.
15 That which is has already been,
And what is to be has already been;
And God requires an account of what is past.

Injustice Seems to Prevail

16Moreover I saw under the sun:

In the place of judgment,
Wickedness *was* there;
And *in* the place of righteousness,
Iniquity *was* there.

17I said in my heart,

"God shall judge the righteous and the wicked,
For *there is* a time there for every purpose and for every work."

18I said in my heart, "Concerning the condition of the sons of men, God
tests them, that they may see that they themselves are *like* animals." 19For
what happens to the sons of men also happens to animals; one thing befalls them: as one dies, so dies the other. Surely, they all have one breath;
man has no advantage over animals, for all *is* vanity. 20All go to one place:
all are from the dust, and all return to dust. 21Who knows the spirit of the
sons of men, which goes upward, and the spirit of the animal, which goes
down to the earth?[d] 22So I perceived that nothing *is* better than that a man
should rejoice in his own works, for that *is* his heritage. For who can bring
him to see what will happen after him?

4 Then I returned and considered all the oppression that is done under
the sun:

And look! The tears of the oppressed,
But they have no comforter—

3:21 [d] Septuagint, Syriac, Targum, and Vulgate read *Who knows whether the spirit . . . goes upward, and whether . . . goes downward to the earth?*

and sporting events on Saturday night so that I could be fresh mentally and physically on Sunday morning. It has meant saying *no* to certain speaking dates when I really wanted to say *yes.*

Sometimes I find such choices hard to make, simply because I like people to approve of me. When a person learns to say *no* to good things, he runs the risk of making enemies and gaining critics; and who needs more of those? So I find it hard to say *no.*

I have discovered that most people whose lives are centered on forms of leadership have the same problem. But if we are to command our time, we will have to bite the bullet and say a firm but courteous *no* to opportunities that are good but not the best.

Once again that demands, as it did in the ministry of our Lord, a sense of our mission. What are we called to do? What do we do best with our time? What are the necessities without which we cannot get along? Everything else has to be considered negotiable: discretionary, not necessary.

(From *Ordering Your Private World* by Gordon MacDonald)

APPLICATION Reflect on your use of time. What activities require more time than they are worth? What relationships could use a bigger time investment? How could you use time with your family better? After you evaluate your schedule, reorganize it so that it accurately reflects your priorities.

EXPLORATION Decisions—Exodus 4:1; Ruth 2:20; Psalm 119:105, 133.

On the side of their oppressors *there is* power,
But they have no comforter.
2 Therefore I praised the dead who were
already dead,
More than the living who are still alive.
3 Yet, better than both *is he* who has
never existed,
Who has not seen the evil work that is done
under the sun.

The Vanity of Selfish Toil

4 Again, I saw that for all toil and every skillful work a man is envied by his neighbor. This also *is* vanity and grasping for the wind.

5 The fool folds his hands
And consumes his own flesh.
6 Better a handful *with* quietness
Than both hands full, *together with* toil and
grasping for the wind.

7 Then I returned, and I saw vanity under the sun:

8 There is one alone, without companion:
He has neither son nor brother.
Yet *there is* no end to all his labors,
Nor is his eye satisfied with riches.
But he never asks,
"For whom do I toil and deprive myself
of good?"
This also *is* vanity and a grave misfortune.

The Value of a Friend

9 Two *are* better than one,
Because they have a good reward for
their labor.
10 For if they fall, one will lift up his companion.
But woe to him *who is* alone when he falls,
For *he has* no one to help him up.
11 Again, if two lie down together, they will
keep warm;
But how can one be warm *alone?*
12 Though one may be overpowered by another,
two can withstand him.
And a threefold cord is not quickly broken.

Popularity Passes Away

13 Better a poor and wise youth
Than an old and foolish king who will be
admonished no more.
14 For he comes out of prison to be king,
Although he was born poor in his kingdom.
15 I saw all the living who walk under the sun;
They were with the second youth who stands
in his place.
16 *There was* no end of all the people over whom
he was made king;
Yet those who come afterward will not
rejoice in him.
Surely this also *is* vanity and grasping for
the wind.

Fear God, Keep Your Vows

5 Walk prudently when you go to the house of God;
and draw near to hear rather than to give the sacrifice of fools, for they do not know that they do evil.

2 Do not be rash with your mouth,
And let not your heart utter anything hastily
before God.
For God *is* in heaven, and you on earth;
Therefore let your words be few.
3 For a dream comes through much activity,
And a fool's voice *is known* by *his* many words.

4 When you make a vow to God, do not
delay to pay it;
For *He has* no pleasure in fools.
Pay what you have vowed—
5 Better not to vow than to vow
and not pay.

6 Do not let your mouth cause your flesh to sin, nor say
before the messenger *of God* that it *was* an error. Why
should God be angry at your excuse[e] and destroy the
work of your hands? 7 For in the multitude of dreams
and many words *there is* also vanity. But fear God.

The Vanity of Gain and Honor

8 If you see the oppression of the poor, and the violent
perversion of justice and righteousness in a province,
do not marvel at the matter; for high official watches
over high official, and higher officials are over them.
9 Moreover the profit of the land is for all; *even* the
king is served from the field.

10 He who loves silver will not be satisfied
with silver;
Nor he who loves abundance, with increase.
This also *is* vanity.
11 When goods increase,
They increase who eat them;

5:6 [e] Literally *voice*

So what profit have the owners
Except to see *them* with their eyes?

12 The sleep of a laboring man *is* sweet,
Whether he eats little or much;
But the abundance of the rich will not permit him to sleep.

13 There is a severe evil *which* I have seen under the sun:
Riches kept for their owner to his hurt.
14 But those riches perish through misfortune;
When he begets a son, *there is* nothing in his hand.
15 As he came from his mother's womb, naked shall he return,
To go as he came;
And he shall take nothing from his labor
Which he may carry away in his hand.

16 And this also *is* a severe evil—
Just exactly as he came, so shall he go.
And what profit has he who has labored for the wind?
17 All his days he also eats in darkness,
And *he has* much sorrow and sickness and anger.

18Here is what I have seen: *It is* good and fitting *for one* to eat and drink,
and to enjoy the good of all his labor in which he toils under the sun all the
days of his life which God gives him; for it *is* his heritage. 19As for every
man to whom God has given riches and wealth, and given him power to
eat of it, to receive his heritage and rejoice in his labor—this *is* the gift of
God. 20For he will not dwell unduly on the days of his life, because God
keeps *him* busy with the joy of his heart.

6 There is an evil which I have seen under the sun, and it *is* common
among men: 2A man to whom God has given riches and wealth and
honor, so that he lacks nothing for himself of all he desires; yet God does
not give him power to eat of it, but a foreigner consumes it. This *is* vanity,
and it *is* an evil affliction.

3If a man begets a hundred *children* and lives many years, so that the
days of his years are many, but his soul is not satisfied with goodness, or
indeed he has no burial, I say *that* a stillborn child *is* better than he— 4for
it comes in vanity and departs in darkness, and its name is covered with
darkness. 5Though it has not seen the sun or known *anything*, this has
more rest than that man, 6even if he lives a thousand years twice—but has
not seen goodness. Do not all go to one place?

7 All the labor of man *is* for his mouth,
And yet the soul is not satisfied.
8 For what more has the wise *man* than the fool?
What does the poor man have,
Who knows *how* to walk before the living?
9 Better *is* the sight of the eyes than the
wandering of desire.
This also *is* vanity and grasping for the wind.

10 Whatever one is, he has been named already,
For it is known that he *is* man;
And he cannot contend with Him who is mightier than he.

LIFE LESSON

Ecclesiastes 5:18–8:17

SITUATION Although people cannot fully understand all of God's plan, the author of Ecclesiastes believed people could find some of God's goodness.

OBSERVATION No one can understand all the ways of God. However, by studying the Bible and his creation, we can serve him and find fulfillment in our work.

INSPIRATION Look (says the preacher) at the sort of world we live in. Take off your rose-coloured spectacles, rub your eyes, and look at it long and hard. . . . You see death coming to everyone sooner or later, but coming haphazard; its coming bears no relation to good or ill desert. . . . You see evil running rampant. . . .

Seeing all this, you realize that God's order of events is inscrutable, much as you want to make it out, you cannot do so. . . . For the truth is that God in His wisdom, to make and keep us humble and to teach us to walk by faith, has hidden from us almost everything that we should like to know about the providential purposes which He is working out in the churches and in our lives.

We can be sure that the God who made this marvelously complex world-order, and who compassed the great redemption from Egypt, and later compassed the even greater redemption from sin and Satan, knows what He is doing and "doeth all things well," even if for the moment He hides His hand. We can trust Him and rejoice in Him, even when we cannot discern His path.

(From *Knowing God* by J. I. Packer)

APPLICATION Many people are afraid to die. But those who believe in Christ can anticipate death as the doorway to heaven. While you are alive, invest your time in projects and people for a heavenly purpose.

EXPLORATION Obeying God—1 Samuel 22. Greatness of God—Psalm 8:3-9. Wisdom of God—Job 9. Jesus and the Holy Spirit—Matthew 12:15-21. God and Christ—John 1:1-5; Acts 2:36.

11 Since there are many things that
increase vanity,
How *is* man the better?

12For who knows what *is* good for man in life, all the
days of his vain life which he passes like a shadow?
Who can tell a man what will happen after him under
the sun?

The Value of Practical Wisdom

7 A good name *is* better than precious ointment,
And the day of death than the day of one's birth;
2 Better to go to the house of mourning
Than to go to the house of feasting,
For that *is* the end of all men;
And the living will take *it* to heart.
3 Sorrow *is* better than laughter,
For by a sad countenance the heart is
made better.
4 The heart of the wise *is* in the house
of mourning,
But the heart of fools *is* in the house of mirth.
5 *It is* better to hear the rebuke of the wise
Than for a man to hear the song of fools.
6 For like the crackling of thorns under a pot,
So *is* the laughter of the fool.
This also is vanity.
7 Surely oppression destroys a wise *man's* reason,
And a bribe debases the heart.

8 The end of a thing *is* better than its beginning;
The patient in spirit *is* better than the proud
in spirit.
9 Do not hasten in your spirit to be angry,
For anger rests in the bosom of fools.
10 Do not say,
"Why were the former days better than these?"
For you do not inquire wisely concerning this.

11 Wisdom *is* good with an inheritance,
And profitable to those who see the sun.
12 For wisdom *is* a defense *as* money *is*
a defense,
But the excellence of knowledge *is that*
wisdom gives life to those who have it.

13 Consider the work of God;
For who can make straight what He has
made crooked?
14 In the day of prosperity be joyful,
But in the day of adversity consider:
Surely God has appointed the one as well as
the other,
So that man can find out nothing *that will*
come after him.

15I have seen everything in my days of vanity:
There is a just *man* who perishes in
his righteousness,
And there is a wicked *man* who prolongs *life*
in his wickedness.

16 Do not be overly righteous,
Nor be overly wise:
Why should you destroy yourself?
17 Do not be overly wicked,
Nor be foolish:
Why should you die before your time?
18 *It is* good that you grasp this,
And also not remove your hand from
the other;
For he who fears God will escape them all.

19 Wisdom strengthens the wise
More than ten rulers of the city.

20 For *there is* not a just man on earth who
does good
And does not sin.

21 Also do not take to heart everything people say,
Lest you hear your servant cursing you.
22 For many times, also, your own heart
has known
That even you have cursed others.

23 All this I have proved by wisdom.
I said, "I will be wise";
But it *was* far from me.
24 As for that which is far off and exceedingly deep,
Who can find it out?
25 I applied my heart to know,
To search and seek out wisdom and the
reason *of things,*
To know the wickedness of folly,
Even of foolishness *and* madness.

26 And I find more bitter than death
The woman whose heart *is* snares and nets,
Whose hands *are* fetters.
He who pleases God shall escape from her,
But the sinner shall be trapped by her.

27 "Here is what I have found," says the Preacher,
"*Adding* one thing to the other to find out
the reason,
28 Which my soul still seeks but I cannot find:

One man among a thousand I have found,
But a woman among all these I have
not found.
29 Truly, this only I have found:
That God made man upright,
But they have sought out many schemes."

8 Who *is* like a wise *man?*
And who knows the interpretation of a thing?
A man's wisdom makes his face shine,
And the sternness of his face is changed.

Obey Authorities for God's Sake

2I *say,* "Keep the king's commandment for the sake
of your oath to God. 3Do not be hasty to go from his
presence. Do not take your stand for an evil thing, for
he does whatever pleases him."

4 Where the word of a king *is, there is* power;
And who may say to him, "What are
you doing?"
5 He who keeps his command will experience
nothing harmful;
And a wise man's heart discerns both time
and judgment,
6 Because for every matter there is a time
and judgment,
Though the misery of man increases greatly.
7 For he does not know what will happen;
So who can tell him when it will occur?
8 No one has power over the spirit to retain
the spirit,
And no one has power in the day of death.
There is no release from that war,
And wickedness will not deliver those who are
given to it.

9All this I have seen, and applied my heart to every
work that is done under the sun: *There is* a time in
which one man rules over another to his own hurt.

Death Comes to All

10Then I saw the wicked buried, who had come and
gone from the place of holiness, and they were forgotten[f] in the city where they had so done. This also *is*
vanity. 11Because the sentence against an evil work is
not executed speedily, therefore the heart of the sons
of men is fully set in them to do evil. 12Though a sinner
does evil a hundred *times,* and his *days* are prolonged,
yet I surely know that it will be well with those who fear
God, who fear before Him. 13But it will not be well with
the wicked; nor will he prolong *his* days, *which are* as a
shadow, because he does not fear before God.

14There is a vanity which occurs on earth, that there
are just *men* to whom it happens according to the
work of the wicked; again, there are wicked *men* to
whom it happens according to the work of the righteous. I said that this also *is* vanity.

15So I commended enjoyment, because a man has
nothing better under the sun than to eat, drink, and
be merry; for this will remain with him in his labor *all*
the days of his life which God gives him under the sun.

16When I applied my heart to know wisdom and to
see the business that is done on earth, even though one
sees no sleep day or night, 17then I saw all the work of
God, that a man cannot find out the work that is done
under the sun. For though a man labors to discover *it,*
yet he will not find *it;* moreover, though a wise *man*
attempts to know *it,* he will not be able to find *it.*

9 For I considered all this in my heart, so that I
could declare it all: that the righteous and the wise
and their works *are* in the hand of God. People know
neither love nor hatred *by* anything *they see* before
them. 2All things *come* alike to all:

One event *happens* to the righteous and
the wicked;
To the good,[g] the clean, and the unclean;
To him who sacrifices and him who does
not sacrifice.
As is the good, so *is* the sinner;
He who takes an oath as *he* who fears an oath.

3This *is* an evil in all that is done under the sun: that
one thing *happens* to all. Truly the hearts of the sons of
men are full of evil; madness *is* in their hearts while
they live, and after that *they go* to the dead. 4But for
him who is joined to all the living there is hope, for a
living dog is better than a dead lion.

5 For the living know that they will die;
But the dead know nothing,
And they have no more reward,
For the memory of them is forgotten.
6 Also their love, their hatred, and their envy
have now perished;
Nevermore will they have a share
In anything done under the sun.

7 Go, eat your bread with joy,
And drink your wine with a merry heart;

8:10 *f* Some Hebrew manuscripts, Septuagint, and Vulgate read *praised.*
9:2 *g* Septuagint, Syriac, and Vulgate read *good and bad.*

LIFE LESSON

Ecclesiastes 9:1–12:14

SITUATION Every person must face death. Those who are righteous and wise rest in God's hands.

OBSERVATION Work hard, enjoy what you have in life, and seek wisdom. Wisdom provides greater assets than power. Although you still face death, you can be comforted to know that those who follow God will live forever with him.

INSPIRATION Remarkable.

Each morning I climb into a truck that weighs half a ton and take it out on an interstate where I—and a thousand other drivers—turn our vehicles into sixty-mile-per-hour missiles. Although I've had a few scares and mishaps, I still whistle while I drive at a speed that would have caused my great-grandfather to pass out.

Remarkable.

Every day I have the honor of sitting down with a book that contains the words of the One who created me. Every day I have the opportunity to let him give me a thought or two on how to live.

If I don't do what he says, he doesn't burn the book or cancel my subscription. If I disagree with what he says, lightning doesn't split my swivel chair or an angel doesn't mark my name off the holy list. If I don't understand what he says, he doesn't call me a dummy. In fact, he calls me "Son," and on a different page explains what I don't understand.

Remarkable.

At the end of the day when I walk through the house, I step into the bedrooms of three little girls. Their covers are usually kicked off, so I cover them up. Their hair usually hides their faces, so I brush it back. And one by one, I bend over and kiss the foreheads of the angels God has loaned me. Then I stand in the door-

For God has already accepted your works.
8 Let your garments always be white,
And let your head lack no oil.

[9]Live joyfully with the wife whom you love all the days of your vain life
which He has given you under the sun, all your days of vanity; for that *is*
your portion in life, and in the labor which you perform under the sun.
[10]Whatever your hand finds to do, do *it* with your might; for *there is* no
work or device or knowledge or wisdom in the grave where you are going.
[11]I returned and saw under the sun that—

The race *is* not to the swift,
Nor the battle to the strong,
Nor bread to the wise,
Nor riches to men of understanding,
Nor favor to men of skill;
But time and chance happen to them all.
12 For man also does not know his time:
Like fish taken in a cruel net,
Like birds caught in a snare,
So the sons of men *are* snared in an evil time,
When it falls suddenly upon them.

Wisdom Superior to Folly

[13]This wisdom I have also seen under the sun, and it *seemed* great to me:
[14]*There was* a little city with few men in it; and a great king came against it,
besieged it, and built great snares[h] around it. [15]Now there was found in it a
poor wise man, and he by his wisdom delivered the city. Yet no one remembered that same poor man.
[16]Then I said:

"Wisdom *is* better than strength.
Nevertheless the poor man's wisdom *is* despised,
And his words are not heard.
17 Words of the wise, *spoken* quietly, *should be* heard
Rather than the shout of a ruler of fools.
18 Wisdom *is* better than weapons of war;
But one sinner destroys much good."

10 Dead flies putrefy[i] the perfumer's ointment,
And cause it to give off a foul odor;
So does a little folly to one respected for wisdom *and* honor.
2 A wise man's heart *is* at his right hand,
But a fool's heart at his left.
3 Even when a fool walks along the way,
He lacks wisdom,
And he shows everyone *that* he *is* a fool.
4 If the spirit of the ruler rises against you,
Do not leave your post;
For conciliation pacifies great offenses.

9:14 *h* Septuagint, Syriac, and Vulgate read *bulwarks*.
10:1 *i* Targum and Vulgate omit *putrefy*.

5 There is an evil I have seen under the sun,
As an error proceeding from the ruler:
6 Folly is set in great dignity,
While the rich sit in a lowly place.
7 I have seen servants on horses,
While princes walk on the ground like servants.

8 He who digs a pit will fall into it,
And whoever breaks through a wall will be bitten by a serpent.
9 He who quarries stones may be hurt by them,
And he who splits wood may be endangered by it.
10 If the ax is dull,
And one does not sharpen the edge,
Then he must use more strength;
But wisdom brings success.
11 A serpent may bite when *it is* not charmed;
The babbler is no different.
12 The words of a wise man's mouth *are* gracious,
But the lips of a fool shall swallow him up;
13 The words of his mouth begin with foolishness,
And the end of his talk *is* raving madness.
14 A fool also multiplies words.
No man knows what is to be;
Who can tell him what will be after him?
15 The labor of fools wearies them,
For they do not even know how to go to the city!

16 Woe to you, O land, when your king *is* a child,
And your princes feast in the morning!
17 Blessed *are* you, O land, when your king *is* the son of nobles,
And your princes feast at the proper time—
For strength and not for drunkenness!
18 Because of laziness the building decays,
And through idleness of hands the house leaks.
19 A feast is made for laughter,
And wine makes merry;
But money answers everything.

20 Do not curse the king, even in your thought;
Do not curse the rich, even in your bedroom;
For a bird of the air may carry your voice,
And a bird in flight may tell the matter.

The Value of Diligence

11 Cast your bread upon the waters,
For you will find it after many days.
2 Give a serving to seven, and also to eight,
For you do not know what evil will be on the earth.

3 If the clouds are full of rain,
They empty *themselves* upon the earth;
And if a tree falls to the south or the north,
In the place where the tree falls, there it shall lie.

way and wonder why in the world he would entrust a stumbling, fumbling fellow like me with the task of loving and leading such treasures. Remarkable.

Then I go and crawl into bed with a woman far wiser than I . . . a woman who deserves a man much better looking than I . . . but a woman who would argue that fact and tell me from the bottom of her heart that I'm the best thing to come down her pike.

After I think about the wife I have, and when I think that I get to be with her for a lifetime, I shake my head and thank the God of grace for grace and think, *Remarkable.*

In the morning, I'll do it all again. I'll drive down the same road. Go to the same office. Call on the same bank. Kiss the same girls. And crawl into bed with the same woman. But I'm learning not to take these everyday miracles for granted. . . .

I'm discovering many things: traffic jams eventually clear up, sunsets are for free, Little League is a work of art, and most planes take off and arrive on time. I'm learning that most folks are good folks who are just as timid as I am about starting a conversation. . . . I'm learning that if I look . . . if I open my eyes and observe . . . there are many reasons to take off my hat, look at the source of it all, and just say thanks.

(From *In the Eye of the Storm* by Max Lucado)

APPLICATION Do you feel like you are falling behind in the rat race? Do you wonder how you will catch up? Look at your remarkable blessings, and give God thanks for what you *do* have.

EXPLORATION Life—Genesis 9:5-6; Deuteronomy 8:3; Psalm 90:12; 144:3-4; Matthew 10:39; Mark 8:35-37; John 4:13-14; Acts 20:24.

4 He who observes the wind will not sow,
And he who regards the clouds will not reap.

5 As you do not know what *is* the way of the wind,[j]
Or how the bones *grow* in the womb of her
who is with child,
So you do not know the works of God who
makes everything.

6 In the morning sow your seed,
And in the evening do not withhold your hand;
For you do not know which will prosper,
Either this or that,
Or whether both alike *will be* good.

7 Truly the light is sweet,
And *it is* pleasant for the eyes to behold the sun;
8 But if a man lives many years
And rejoices in them all,
Yet let him remember the days of darkness,
For they will be many.
All that is coming *is* vanity.

Seek God in Early Life

9 Rejoice, O young man, in your youth,
And let your heart cheer you in the days of
your youth;
Walk in the ways of your heart,
And in the sight of your eyes;
But know that for all these
God will bring you into judgment.
10 Therefore remove sorrow from your heart,
And put away evil from your flesh,
For childhood and youth *are* vanity.

12 Remember now your Creator in the days of
your youth,
Before the difficult days come,
And the years draw near when you say,
"I have no pleasure in them":
2 While the sun and the light,
The moon and the stars,
Are not darkened,
And the clouds do not return after the rain;
3 In the day when the keepers of the
house tremble,
And the strong men bow down;
When the grinders cease because they are few,
And those that look through the windows
grow dim;
4 When the doors are shut in the streets,
And the sound of grinding is low;
When one rises up at the sound of a bird,
And all the daughters of music are brought low.
5 Also they are afraid of height,
And of terrors in the way;
When the almond tree blossoms,
The grasshopper is a burden,
And desire fails.
For man goes to his eternal home,
And the mourners go about the streets.

6 *Remember your Creator* before the
silver cord is loosed,[k]
Or the golden bowl is broken,
Or the pitcher shattered at the fountain,
Or the wheel broken at the well.
7 Then the dust will return to the earth as it was,
And the spirit will return to God who gave it.

8 "Vanity of vanities," says the Preacher,
"All *is* vanity."

The Whole Duty of Man

9And moreover, because the Preacher was wise, he
still taught the people knowledge; yes, he pondered
and sought out *and* set in order many proverbs. 10The
Preacher sought to find acceptable words; and *what*
was written *was* upright—words of truth. 11The words
of the wise are like goads, and the words of scholars[l]
are like well-driven nails, given by one Shepherd.
12And further, my son, be admonished by these. Of
making many books *there is* no end, and much study
is wearisome to the flesh.

13Let us hear the conclusion of the whole matter:

Fear God and keep His commandments,
For this is man's all.
14 For God will bring every work into judgment,
Including every secret thing,
Whether good or evil.

11:5 [j] Or *spirit*
12:6 [k] Following Qere and Targum; Kethib reads *removed;* Septuagint and Vulgate read *broken.*
12:11 [l] Literally *masters of the assemblies*

The

SONG OF SOLOMON

INTRODUCTION

Remember your love notes of young romance?

Come on, now. Think about it.

Flip back through the scrapbook of your heart. You'll find one.

You thought *he* was the only one. You knew *she* was the reason for creation. And with youthful passion, you expressed your love.

"I'll love you forever."

"You are my one and only."

"Had I the pen of a poet, had I the stars to give you, even then I couldn't show it . . ."

Ahhh, the words of romance. (That last verse? That was mine, proving that even a crusty West Texan can be romantic.)

But the most daring Romeos will blush at what you are about to read—"The Song of Songs." A love poem that chronicles the passion between starstruck Solomon and his spellbound bride.

It's unlike anything in the Bible. For that reason, it should be read differently than any book in the Bible. Don't take it literally. Don't search for hidden codes or submerged messages. Love letters are to be appreciated, not analyzed.

Appreciate this one. Don't get hung up on the ancient terms of affection. Sure, they sound strange. My wife wouldn't appreciate being told her neck was like David's tower (4:4) or that her limbs were like pomegranates (4:13). Just remember that these words were not written for you.

You are opening someone else's shoebox of letters and reading the correspondence between two people madly in love.

I guess God knew we needed a reminder that romance was his idea.

LIFE LESSON

Song of Solomon 1:1–2:7

SITUATION Solomon's Song describes a relationship between a bride and groom. Solomon and the Shulammite woman were about to be married in the king's palace. The woman was a peasant worker from Shunem, a farming town sixty miles north of Jerusalem.

OBSERVATION God gives marriage as a gift. It is a gift based on unquestioning commitment and unconditional acceptance.

INSPIRATION I sensed it as we were lying on the bed. It blew over me mixed with the sweet fragrance of fresh rain. My wife was lying silently at my side. Jenna was using my stomach for a pillow. She, too, was quiet. Our second child, only a month from birth, rested within the womb of her mother. They must have sensed it, for no one spoke. It entered our presence as if introduced by God himself. And no one dared stir for fear it leave prematurely.

What was it? An eternal instant.

An instant in time that had no time. A picture that froze in mid-frame, demanding to be savored. A minute that refused to die after sixty seconds. A moment that was lifted off the timeline and amplified into a forever so all the angels could witness its majesty.

An eternal instant.

A moment that reminds you of the treasures surrounding you. Your home. Your peace of mind. Your health. A moment that tenderly rebukes you for spending so much time on temporal preoccupations such as savings accounts, houses, and punctuality. A moment that can bring a mist to the manliest of eyes and perspective to the darkest life.

Eternal instants have dotted history.

It was an eternal instant when the Creator smiled and said, "It is good."

The song of songs, which *is* Solomon's.

The Banquet

THE SHULAMITE[a]

2 Let him kiss me with the kisses of his mouth—
For your[b] love *is* better than wine.
3 Because of the fragrance of your good ointments,
Your name *is* ointment poured forth;
Therefore the virgins love you.
4 Draw me away!

THE DAUGHTERS OF JERUSALEM

We will run after you.[c]

THE SHULAMITE

The king has brought me into his chambers.

THE DAUGHTERS OF JERUSALEM

We will be glad and rejoice in you.[d]
We will remember your[e] love more than wine.

THE SHULAMITE

Rightly do they love you.[f]

5 I *am* dark, but lovely,
O daughters of Jerusalem,
Like the tents of Kedar,
Like the curtains of Solomon.
6 Do not look upon me, because I *am* dark,
Because the sun has tanned me.
My mother's sons were angry with me;
They made me the keeper of the vineyards,
But my own vineyard I have not kept.

(TO HER BELOVED)

7 Tell me, O you whom I love,
Where you feed *your flock,*
Where you make *it* rest at noon.
For why should I be as one who veils herself[g]
By the flocks of your companions?

THE BELOVED

8 If you do not know, O fairest among women,
Follow in the footsteps of the flock,
And feed your little goats

1:2 [a] A Palestinian young woman *(compare 6:13)*. The speaker and audience are identified according to the number, gender, and person of the Hebrew words. Occasionally the identity is not certain. [b] Masculine singular, that is, the Beloved
1:4 [c] Masculine singular, that is, the Beloved [d] Feminine singular, that is, the Shulamite [e] Masculine singular, that is, the Beloved [f] Masculine singular, that is, the Beloved
1:7 [g] Septuagint, Syriac, and Vulgate read *wanders*.

Beside the shepherds' tents.
9 I have compared you, my love,
To my filly among Pharaoh's chariots.
10 Your cheeks are lovely with ornaments,
Your neck with chains *of gold.*

THE DAUGHTERS OF JERUSALEM

11 We will make you[h] ornaments of gold
With studs of silver.

THE SHULAMITE

12 While the king *is* at his table,
My spikenard sends forth its fragrance.
13 A bundle of myrrh *is* my beloved to me,
That lies all night between my breasts.
14 My beloved *is* to me a cluster of henna *blooms*
In the vineyards of En Gedi.

THE BELOVED

15 Behold, you *are* fair, my love!
Behold, you *are* fair!
You *have* dove's eyes.

THE SHULAMITE

16 Behold, you *are* handsome, my beloved!
Yes, pleasant!
Also our bed *is* green.
17 The beams of our houses *are* cedar,
And our rafters of fir.

2 I *am* the rose of Sharon,
And the lily of the valleys.

THE BELOVED

2 Like a lily among thorns,
So is my love among the daughters.

THE SHULAMITE

3 Like an apple tree among the
trees of the woods,
So *is* my beloved among the sons.
I sat down in his shade with great delight,
And his fruit *was* sweet to my taste.

THE SHULAMITE TO THE DAUGHTERS OF JERUSALEM

4 He brought me to the banqueting house,
And his banner over me *was* love.
5 Sustain me with cakes of raisins,
Refresh me with apples,
For I *am* lovesick.

1:11 *h* Feminine singular, that is, the Shulamite

It was a timeless moment when Abraham pleaded for mercy from the God of mercy, "But if there are just ten faithful." It was a moment without time when Noah pushed open the rain-soaked hatch and breathed in the clean air. And it was a moment in the "fullness of time" when a carpenter, some smelly shepherds, and an exhausted young mother stood in silent awe at the sight of the infant in the manger.

Eternal instants. You've had them. We all have.

Sharing a porch swing on a summer evening with your grandchild.

Seeing *her* face in the glow of a candle.

Putting your arm into your husband's as you stroll through the golden leaves and breathe the brisk autumn air.

Listening to your six year old thank God for everything from goldfish to Grandma.

Such moments are necessary because they remind us that everything is okay. The King is still on the throne and life is still worth living. Eternal instants remind us that love is still the greatest possession and the future is nothing to fear.

The next time an instant in your life begins to be eternal, let it. Put your head back on the pillow and soak it in. Resist the urge to cut it short. Don't interrupt the silence or shatter the solemnity. You are, in a very special way, on holy ground.

(From *God Came Near* by Max Lucado)

APPLICATION Schedule a night to get away from pressing commitments. Create a time when you put the cares of the world on hold, and simply enjoy your family.

EXPLORATION Husbands and Wives—Genesis 2:23-24; Proverbs 5:15-19; Ecclesiastes 9:9; 1 Corinthians 7:3-5; Ephesians 5:21-29, 33.

LIFE LESSON

Song of Solomon 2:8–3:4

SITUATION Solomon's lover recalled their early courtship days and even remembered a dream that caused her concern about Solomon's whereabouts.

OBSERVATION Good memories of courtship can keep fresh and alive the gift of love that God has given to partners in a marriage relationship.

INSPIRATION Stacy and I rarely make big occasions out of anniversaries, but two years ago we took an exception. We decided to cash in airline mileage on a special trip to England to celebrate our fifteen years together.

The grandparents came to take care of their grandchildren, and we gathered our travel brochures and camera and headed off for a week. . . . And we did have a good time. . . . But I had to admit that our trip hardly resembled the pictures in the advertisements.

For one thing, the prices were almost double those we remembered from ten years previous. Rain or unexpected crowds canceled a number of our plans. And those little Cotswald cottages had beds made for two of the seven dwarfs. . . . Not exactly a second honeymoon. . . .

Our trip—and our marriage—had been different from what we expected. . . . Having children and renovating houses, straining to find each of our career niches—our relationship was more than the sum of those parts, just as our vacation couldn't be defined by the places we visited. . . .

The point was, we had made the trip *together.* We were beginning to learn something about what it meant to keep company on cold nights. . . .

We discovered a love that is valuable precisely because it has been costly.

(From *The Cleavers Don't Live Here Anymore* by Paula Rinehart)

APPLICATION What could you do to strengthen your relationship? Ask God to show you how.

EXPLORATION Married Love —Genesis 2:23-24; 24:67; 29:20; Ruth 2-4; Proverbs 18:22; 1 Corinthians 11:11; Ephesians 5:25-30.

6 His left hand *is* under my head,
And his right hand embraces me.
7 I charge you, O daughters of Jerusalem,
By the gazelles or by the does of the field,
Do not stir up nor awaken love
Until it pleases.

The Beloved's Request

THE SHULAMITE

8 The voice of my beloved!
Behold, he comes
Leaping upon the mountains,
Skipping upon the hills.
9 My beloved is like a gazelle
or a young stag.
Behold, he stands behind our wall;
He is looking through the windows,
Gazing through the lattice.

10 My beloved spoke, and said to me:
"Rise up, my love, my fair one,
And come away.
11 For lo, the winter is past,
The rain is over *and* gone.
12 The flowers appear on the earth;
The time of singing has come,
And the voice of the turtledove
Is heard in our land.
13 The fig tree puts forth her green figs,
And the vines *with* the tender grapes
Give a good smell.
Rise up, my love, my fair one,
And come away!

14 "O my dove, in the clefts of the rock,
In the secret *places* of the cliff,
Let me see your face,
Let me hear your voice;
For your voice *is* sweet,
And your face *is* lovely."

HER BROTHERS

15 Catch us the foxes,
The little foxes that spoil the vines,
For our vines *have* tender grapes.

THE SHULAMITE

16 My beloved *is* mine, and I *am* his.
He feeds *his flock* among the lilies.

(TO HER BELOVED)

17 Until the day breaks

And the shadows flee away,
Turn, my beloved,
And be like a gazelle
Or a young stag
Upon the mountains of Bether.[i]

A Troubled Night

THE SHULAMITE

3 By night on my bed I sought the one I love;
I sought him, but I did not find him.
2 "I will rise now," *I said,*
"And go about the city;
In the streets and in the squares
I will seek the one I love."
I sought him, but I did not find him.
3 The watchmen who go about the city found me;
I said,
"Have you seen the one I love?"

4 Scarcely had I passed by them,
When I found the one I love.
I held him and would not let him go,
Until I had brought him to the house of my mother,
And into the chamber of her who conceived me.

5 I charge you, O daughters of Jerusalem,
By the gazelles or by the does of the field,
Do not stir up nor awaken love
Until it pleases.

The Coming of Solomon

THE SHULAMITE

6 Who *is* this coming out of the wilderness
Like pillars of smoke,
Perfumed with myrrh and frankincense,
With all the merchant's fragrant powders?
7 Behold, it *is* Solomon's couch,
With sixty valiant men around it,
Of the valiant of Israel.
8 They all hold swords,
Being expert in war.
Every man *has* his sword on his thigh
Because of fear in the night.

9 Of the wood of Lebanon
Solomon the King
Made himself a palanquin:[j]
10 He made its pillars *of* silver,

2:17 [i] Literally *Separation*
3:9 [j] A portable enclosed chair

LIFE LESSON

Song of Solomon 3:5–5:1

SITUATION Solomon recalled the occasion when he declared his love to his bride. He offered his hand in marriage, and she accepted.

OBSERVATION The Song of Solomon attests to the joy that comes from following guidelines from God.

INSPIRATION The Song of Solomon is a beautiful record of the love a man and woman can feel for each other. The lover's fantasies of his beloved are interwoven with her fantasies of him in one of the world's greatest love songs. Their words describe the physical love between them, yet the song is striking for its absence of lewdness. The essence of their fantasies is not physical sensuality. Instead, the strong love and honor in which they hold each other pulses underneath and gives vibrancy to their physical enjoyment of each other. They yearn for each other as persons; their bodies are the vehicles for expressing their love for each other. Their fantasies of each other—the images of each other that they carry inside—ache for expression in physical union, not as an end in itself but as a demonstration of their deep, internal bonding with each other. . . .

The sexual relationship between a man and woman is a tangible demonstration that marriage is different, more intimate than any other relationship can possibly be. . . . As a husband and wife give themselves freely and exclusively to each other in a sexual relationship, they are affirming the unique and special place each holds in the other's heart, and are preserving a unity that demonstrates God's own love. And this is certainly something to celebrate!

(From *Making Marriage Work* by Truman Esau and Beverly Burch)

APPLICATION Strive to maintain God's standard: sex only within the bonds of marriage. Ask the Lord to help you resist the influences of secular society to disregard God's sexual standard.

EXPLORATION Sexual Intimacy—Genesis 2:24; Job 31:1; Proverbs 5:15, 18-20; Matthew 5:27-28; 1 Corinthians 7:1-5; 7:32-35; Ephesians 5:25; 1 Thessalonians 4:3-5; Hebrews 13:4.

Its support *of* gold,
Its seat *of* purple,
Its interior paved *with* love
By the daughters of Jerusalem.
11 Go forth, O daughters of Zion,
And see King Solomon with the crown
With which his mother crowned him
On the day of his wedding,
The day of the gladness of his heart.

THE BELOVED

4 Behold, you *are* fair, my love!
Behold, you *are* fair!
You *have* dove's eyes behind your veil.
Your hair *is* like a flock of goats,
Going down from Mount Gilead.
2 Your teeth *are* like a flock of shorn *sheep*
Which have come up from the washing,
Every one of which bears twins,
And none *is* barren among them.
3 Your lips *are* like a strand of scarlet,
And your mouth is lovely.
Your temples behind your veil
Are like a piece of pomegranate.
4 Your neck *is* like the tower of David,
Built for an armory,
On which hang a thousand bucklers,
All shields of mighty men.
5 Your two breasts *are* like two fawns,
Twins of a gazelle,
Which feed among the lilies.
6 Until the day breaks
And the shadows flee away,
I will go my way to the mountain of myrrh
And to the hill of frankincense.

7 You *are* all fair, my love,
And *there is* no spot in you.
8 Come with me from Lebanon, *my* spouse,
With me from Lebanon.
Look from the top of Amana,
From the top of Senir and Hermon,
From the lions' dens,
From the mountains of the leopards.
9 You have ravished my heart,
My sister, *my* spouse;
You have ravished my heart
With one *look* of your eyes,
With one link of your necklace.
10 How fair is your love,
My sister, *my* spouse!
How much better than wine is your love,
And the scent of your perfumes
Than all spices!
11 Your lips, O *my* spouse,
Drip as the honeycomb;
Honey and milk *are* under your tongue;
And the fragrance of your garments
Is like the fragrance of Lebanon.

12 A garden enclosed
Is my sister, *my* spouse,
A spring shut up,
A fountain sealed.
13 Your plants *are* an orchard of pomegranates
With pleasant fruits,
Fragrant henna with spikenard,
14 Spikenard and saffron,
Calamus and cinnamon,
With all trees of frankincense,
Myrrh and aloes,
With all the chief spices—
15 A fountain of gardens,
A well of living waters,
And streams from Lebanon.

THE SHULAMITE

16 Awake, O north *wind*,
And come, O south!
Blow upon my garden,
That its spices may flow out.
Let my beloved come to his garden
And eat its pleasant fruits.

THE BELOVED

5 I have come to my garden, my sister, *my* spouse;
I have gathered my myrrh with my spice;
I have eaten my honeycomb with my honey;
I have drunk my wine with my milk.

(TO HIS FRIENDS)

Eat, O friends!
Drink, yes, drink deeply,
O beloved ones!

The Shulamite's Troubled Evening

THE SHULAMITE

2 I sleep, but my heart is awake;
It is the voice of my beloved!
He knocks, *saying*,
"Open for me, my sister, my love,
My dove, my perfect one;

For my head is covered with dew,
My locks with the drops of the night."
3 I have taken off my robe;
How can I put it on *again?*
I have washed my feet;
How can I defile them?
4 My beloved put his hand
By the latch *of the door,*
And my heart yearned for him.
5 I arose to open for my beloved,
And my hands dripped *with* myrrh,
My fingers with liquid myrrh,
On the handles of the lock.

6 I opened for my beloved,
But my beloved had turned away *and* was gone.
My heart leaped up when he spoke.
I sought him, but I could not find him;
I called him, but he gave me no answer.
7 The watchmen who went about the city found me.
They struck me, they wounded me;
The keepers of the walls
Took my veil away from me.
8 I charge you, O daughters of Jerusalem,
If you find my beloved,
That you tell him I *am* lovesick!

THE DAUGHTERS OF JERUSALEM

9 What *is* your beloved
More than *another* beloved,
O fairest among women?
What *is* your beloved
More than *another* beloved,
That you so charge us?

THE SHULAMITE

10 My beloved *is* white and ruddy,
Chief among ten thousand.
11 His head *is like* the finest gold;
His locks *are* wavy,
And black as a raven.
12 His eyes *are* like doves
By the rivers of waters,
Washed with milk,
And fitly set.
13 His cheeks *are* like a bed of spices,
Banks of scented herbs.
His lips *are* lilies,
Dripping liquid myrrh.

14 His hands *are* rods of gold
Set with beryl.

LIFE LESSON

Song of Solomon 5:2–6:3

SITUATION Misunderstandings sprang up between Solomon and his wife. The bride took steps to heal the marriage breach. The growing maturity in this marriage was indicated by references to friendship and an understanding that Solomon and his bride belong exclusively to each other.

OBSERVATION Marriage has several elements: love, commitment, sexual desire, admiration, and friendship. As a marriage matures, so does the commitment to resolve problems and to deepen the friendship.

INSPIRATION The other night I fell into bed with a miserable cold. Mind you, I am not able to blow my nose because I can't use my hands, and I can't really cough because I have no chest muscles. I knew I was going to face a rough night. But not as rough as Ken.

I woke up at 3:00 a.m. and groaned, "Ken, please get up. Help me sit up so I can cough." The poor guy threw back the covers, stumbled out of bed, and sat me up to pound on my back. He held a tissue to my nose as I coughed and sputtered.

An hour-and-a-half later, we repeated the routine. We were both dead tired and somewhere in between squeezing my ribs and reaching for another tissue, he moaned, "Did our wedding vows include this stuff?"

I sniffed and reminded him, "Remember that part about 'for better or for worse'? Well, this is the worst part. And remember when we said we'd love each other through thick and thin?"

"I know, I know," Ken sighed. "This is the thin part."

Every couple agrees that marriage has its ups and downs. The up times are when love is as plain as day and fully visible. The down times are when love goes undercover and incognito. So commonplace are the ups and downs that one wonders why they aren't written into the wedding vows. But they are. When a husband and wife vow to love for better or for worse, it includes the full extent of the ups and downs.

Continued

Marriage will always ask you to prove love. To be married is not to be taken off the front lines of love but to be plunged into the thick and thin of the ups and downs.

(From *Diamonds in the Dust* by Joni Eareckson Tada)

APPLICATION Marriage—and every other relationship in our lives—has ups and downs. How do you respond to problems or challenges in your friendships or in your marriage? It may be hard to work through problems, but it is the right way! Work it out. Don't give up!

EXPLORATION Commitment—Ruth 1:16-17; 1 Samuel 20:17; Proverbs 17:17; 18:24; 27:17; Ecclesiastes 4:9-10; Mark 10:6-9; John 15:13; Romans 12:5; Ephesians 5:25-33.

His body *is* carved ivory
Inlaid *with* sapphires.
15 His legs *are* pillars of marble
Set on bases of fine gold.
His countenance *is* like Lebanon,
Excellent as the cedars.
16 His mouth *is* most sweet,
Yes, he *is* altogether lovely.
This *is* my beloved,
And this *is* my friend,
O daughters of Jerusalem!

THE DAUGHTERS OF JERUSALEM

6 Where has your beloved gone,
O fairest among women?
Where has your beloved turned aside,
That we may seek him with you?

THE SHULAMITE

2 My beloved has gone to his garden,
To the beds of spices,
To feed *his flock* in the gardens,
And to gather lilies.
3 I *am* my beloved's,
And my beloved *is* mine.
He feeds *his flock* among the lilies.

Praise of the Shulamite's Beauty

THE BELOVED

4 O my love, you *are as* beautiful as Tirzah,
Lovely as Jerusalem,
Awesome as *an army* with banners!
5 Turn your eyes away from me,
For they have overcome me.
Your hair *is* like a flock of goats
Going down from Gilead.
6 Your teeth *are* like a flock of sheep
Which have come up from the washing;
Every one bears twins,
And none *is* barren among them.
7 Like a piece of pomegranate
Are your temples behind your veil.

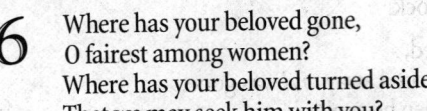

8 There are sixty queens
And eighty concubines,
And virgins without number.
9 My dove, my perfect one,
Is the only one,
The only one of her mother,
The favorite of the one who bore her.
The daughters saw her

And called her blessed,
The queens and the concubines,
And they praised her.

10 Who is she who looks forth as the morning,
Fair as the moon,
Clear as the sun,
Awesome as *an army* with banners?

THE SHULAMITE

11 I went down to the garden of nuts
To see the verdure of the valley,
To see whether the vine had budded
And the pomegranates had bloomed.
12 Before I was even aware,
My soul had made me
As the chariots of my noble people.[k]

THE BELOVED AND HIS FRIENDS

13 Return, return, O Shulamite;
Return, return, that we may look upon you!

THE SHULAMITE

What would you see in the Shulamite—
As it were, the dance of the two camps?[l]

Expressions of Praise

THE BELOVED

7 How beautiful are your feet in sandals,
O prince's daughter!
The curves of your thighs *are* like jewels,
The work of the hands of a skillful workman.
2 Your navel *is* a rounded goblet;
It lacks no blended beverage.
Your waist *is* a heap of wheat
Set about with lilies.
3 Your two breasts *are* like two fawns,
Twins of a gazelle.
4 Your neck *is* like an ivory tower,
Your eyes *like* the pools in Heshbon
By the gate of Bath Rabbim.
Your nose *is* like the tower of Lebanon
Which looks toward Damascus.
5 Your head *crowns* you like *Mount* Carmel,
And the hair of your head *is* like purple;
A king *is* held captive by *your* tresses.

6 How fair and how pleasant you are,
O love, with your delights!
7 This stature of yours is like a palm tree,

LIFE LESSON

Song of Solomon 6:4–7:9

SITUATION King Solomon expressed his love for his bride.

OBSERVATION The Song of Solomon is traditionally considered to be a love poem. God used marriage as an illustration of Christ's love for the church.

INSPIRATION What is more beautiful than a bride? One of the side benefits of being a minister is that I get an early glimpse of the bride as she stands at the top of the aisle. And I have to say that I have never seen an ugly bride. I've seen some grooms that could use an alteration or two, but never a bride. Maybe it is the aura of whiteness that clings to her as dew clings to a rose. Or perhaps it is the diamonds that glisten in her eyes. Or maybe it's the blush of love that pinks her cheeks or the bouquet of promises she carries. Whatever it is, there is the feeling that when you see a bride you are seeing the purest beauty the world can boast.

A bride. A commitment robed in elegance. "I'll be with you forever." Tomorrow bringing hope to today. Promised purity faithfully delivered.

When you read that our heavenly home is similar to a bride, tell me, doesn't it make you want to go home? (From *The Applause of Heaven* by Max Lucado)

APPLICATION What are you doing to get ready for your spiritual wedding with Christ? Will you be pure, sinless, clean, without a spot? Get ready by being faithful today. When someone asks you to compromise your standards, say no. If they ask you to help them with something questionable, refuse.

EXPLORATION Bride and Bridegroom—Isaiah 62:5; Jeremiah 3:14; Ezekiel 16:8.

6:12 [k] Hebrew *Ammi Nadib*
6:13 [l] Hebrew *Mahanaim*
7:9 [m] Septuagint, Syriac, and Vulgate read *lips and teeth.*

LIFE LESSON

Song of Solomon 7:10–8:4

SITUATION King Solomon knew that love between a husband and wife should be enjoyed and celebrated. God made human bodies to be enjoyable to their spouses.

OBSERVATION Enjoy your spouse! Celebrate love! Never awaken these passions outside of marriage, and never let anything interfere with your enjoyment.

INSPIRATION We all have some hurt that loves to come back and steal our joy. It sits on the back of our memory waiting for an opportunity to be recalled. It's always there, and no matter how hard we try, we can't remove it. There are a myriad of advantages of being human rather than a computer, but sometimes it would be nice to have all of our painful memories stored on a floppy disc stuck in the side of our head. A simple command could erase the hurt.

Even though we can't erase the hurts that lie stored in the file drawers of our memory, we *can* offset their negative impact. In chemistry, if I want to neutralize an acid, I must counter with the equivalent of an opposite substance. Forgiveness works like that. It's an alkaline nullifying the acidic nature of bitterness. It's that balancing presence that says "You can remind me of my pain, but you can't rob me of my rest."

If we don't deal with our unresolved conflicts, they'll deal with us. Bitterness is a slavemaster. It controls us. It demands too much.

(From *Little House on the Freeway* by Tim Kimmel)

APPLICATION When you think about a memory with your spouse does it still make you angry? It is time to resolve the conflict. True love cannot hold a grudge.

EXPLORATION Forgiveness—Matthew 6:12-15; 18:21-35; Luke 17:3.

And your breasts *like* its clusters.
8 I said, "I will go up to the palm tree,
I will take hold of its branches."
Let now your breasts be like clusters of the vine,
The fragrance of your breath like apples,
9 And the roof of your mouth like the best wine.

THE SHULAMITE

The wine goes *down* smoothly for my beloved,
Moving gently the lips of sleepers.*m*
10 I *am* my beloved's,
And his desire *is* toward me.

11 Come, my beloved,
Let us go forth to the field;
Let us lodge in the villages.
12 Let us get up early to the vineyards;
Let us see if the vine has budded,
Whether the grape blossoms are open,
And the pomegranates are in bloom.
There I will give you my love.
13 The mandrakes give off a fragrance,
And at our gates *are* pleasant *fruits,*
All manner, new and old,
Which I have laid up for you, my beloved.

8 Oh, that you were like my brother,
Who nursed at my mother's breasts!
If I should find you outside,
I would kiss you;
I would not be despised.
2 I would lead you *and* bring you
Into the house of my mother,
She *who* used to instruct me.
I would cause you to drink of spiced wine,
Of the juice of my pomegranate.

(TO THE DAUGHTERS OF JERUSALEM)

3 His left hand *is* under my head,
And his right hand embraces me.
4 I charge you, O daughters of Jerusalem,
Do not stir up nor awaken love
Until it pleases.

Love Renewed in Lebanon

A RELATIVE

5 Who *is* this coming up from the wilderness,
Leaning upon her beloved?

I awakened you under the apple tree.
There your mother brought you forth;
There she *who* bore you brought *you* forth.

8:6 *n* Or *Sheol* *o* Literally *A flame of* YAH (a poetic form of *YHWH, the* LORD)

The Shulamite to Her Beloved

6 Set me as a seal upon your heart,
As a seal upon your arm;
For love *is as* strong as death,
Jealousy *as* cruel as the grave;[n]
Its flames *are* flames of fire,
A most vehement[o] flame.

7 Many waters cannot quench love,
Nor can the floods drown it.
If a man would give for love
All the wealth of his house,
It would be utterly despised.

The Shulamite's Brothers

8 We have a little sister,
And she has no breasts.
What shall we do for our sister
In the day when she is spoken for?
9 If she *is* a wall,
We will build upon her
A battlement of silver;
And if she *is* a door,
We will enclose her
With boards of cedar.

The Shulamite

10 I *am* a wall,
And my breasts like towers;
Then I became in his eyes
As one who found peace.
11 Solomon had a vineyard at Baal Hamon;
He leased the vineyard to keepers;
Everyone was to bring for its fruit
A thousand silver coins.

(To Solomon)

12 My own vineyard *is* before me.
You, O Solomon, *may have* a thousand,
And those who tend its fruit two hundred.

The Beloved

13 You who dwell in the gardens,
The companions listen for your voice—
Let me hear it!

The Shulamite

14 Make haste, my beloved,
And be like a gazelle
Or a young stag
On the mountains of spices.

The Book of

ISAIAH

INTRODUCTION

Isaiah was a blueblood among the prophets. His Hebrew was classic. His style was noble. His circles were influential. But his message was bare-knuckled.

Through the reigns of four kings he proclaimed one message: God will not forever wink at wrong.

He spoke with a grit in his gut and a fire in his eyes like one who had stood in hell and seen heaven, for that is exactly what had happened. Isaiah saw God.

Whether what he saw was in the sky or in his head matters little compared to the truth that it was in his heart. The lights danced and the angels chanted back and forth, "Holy, Holy, Holy," as if they had nothing else to say, and they didn't—for that is all you can say before him who is holy.

There are those who boast about having a vision of God like they boast about seeing the president. Not so with Isaiah. When he saw God he didn't update his resume, he begged for mercy.

"Woe is me, for I am undone! Because I am a man of unclean lips, and I dwell in the midst of a people of unclean lips; for my eyes have seen the king, the LORD of hosts" (6:5).

No sooner is the mercy requested than it is received. An angel purges his mouth with a hot coal, teaching us that the only mouth worthy of speaking for God is the one cleansed by God.

Isaiah was never the same after that. *Send me!* he volunteered. And so God sent. And so Isaiah preached. He preached with the passion and fury of a man who'd seen his life pass before his eyes.

For he had. He preached with the passion and fury of a man sent by God. For he was.

And he preached with the passion and fury of a man who longed to join the angels and spend eternity singing, "Holy, Holy, Holy" at the top of his lungs.

Something tells me that's what he is doing right now.

LIFE LESSON

Isaiah 1:1-31

SITUATION Isaiah revealed Judah's impending doom. God vowed not to listen to the prayers of his people because of their excessive sin. But God assured he would restore Israel after purging it of sin.

OBSERVATION A loving and patient God continued to offer hope to the Israelites. He offered forgiveness if they repented.

INSPIRATION In fact, it seems [God's] favorite word is *come*.

"*Come*, let us talk about these things. Though your sins are like scarlet, they can be as white as snow."

"All you who are thirsty, *come* and drink."

"*Come* to me all, all of you who are tired and have heavy loads, and I will give you rest."

"*Come* to the wedding feast."

"*Come* follow me, and I will make you fish for people."

"Let anyone who is thirsty *come* to me and drink."

God is a God who invites. God is a God who calls. God is a God who opens the door and waves his hand pointing pilgrims to a full table.

His invitation is not just for a meal, however, it is for life. An invitation to come into his kingdom and take up residence in a tearless, graveless, painless world. Who can come? Whoever wishes. The invitation is at once universal and personal.

(From *And the Angels Were Silent* by Max Lucado)

APPLICATION To repent means being both remorseful for your sin and also acting so that you do not repeat the sin again. What sin are you enjoying? Repent of it. Then put the past behind and live a new day.

EXPLORATION God's Forgiveness—Genesis 50:15-21; 1 Chronicles 21:8; Luke 11:4; Acts 8:18-23; Romans 12:17-21; 1 John 1:9.

The vision of Isaiah the son of Amoz, which he saw concerning Judah and Jerusalem in the days of Uzziah, Jotham, Ahaz, *and* Hezekiah, kings of Judah.

The Wickedness of Judah

2 Hear, O heavens, and give ear, O earth!
For the LORD has spoken:
"I have nourished and brought up children,
And they have rebelled against Me;
3 The ox knows its owner
And the donkey its master's crib;
But Israel does not know,
My people do not consider."

4 Alas, sinful nation,
A people laden with iniquity,
A brood of evildoers,
Children who are corrupters!
They have forsaken the LORD,
They have provoked to anger
The Holy One of Israel,
They have turned away backward.

5 Why should you be stricken again?
You will revolt more and more.
The whole head is sick,
And the whole heart faints.
6 From the sole of the foot even to the head,
There is no soundness in it,
But wounds and bruises and putrefying sores;
They have not been closed or bound up,
Or soothed with ointment.

7 Your country *is* desolate,
Your cities *are* burned with fire;
Strangers devour your land in your presence;
And *it is* desolate, as overthrown by strangers.
8 So the daughter of Zion is left as a booth in a vineyard,
As a hut in a garden of cucumbers,
As a besieged city.
9 Unless the LORD of hosts
Had left to us a very small remnant,
We would have become like Sodom,
We would have been made like Gomorrah.

10 Hear the word of the LORD,
You rulers of Sodom;
Give ear to the law of our God,
You people of Gomorrah:
11 "To what purpose *is* the multitude of your sacrifices to Me?"
Says the LORD.

"I have had enough of burnt offerings of rams
And the fat of fed cattle.
I do not delight in the blood of bulls,
Or of lambs or goats.

12 "When you come to appear before Me,
Who has required this from your hand,
To trample My courts?
13 Bring no more futile sacrifices;
Incense is an abomination to Me.
The New Moons, the Sabbaths, and the calling
of assemblies—
I cannot endure iniquity and
the sacred meeting.
14 Your New Moons and your appointed feasts
My soul hates;
They are a trouble to Me,
I am weary of bearing *them.*
15 When you spread out your hands,
I will hide My eyes from you;
Even though you make many prayers,
I will not hear.
Your hands are full of blood.

16 "Wash yourselves, make yourselves clean;
Put away the evil of your doings from
before My eyes.
Cease to do evil,
17 Learn to do good;
Seek justice,
Rebuke the oppressor;[a]
Defend the fatherless,
Plead for the widow.

18 "Come now, and let us reason together,"
Says the LORD,
"Though your sins are like scarlet,
They shall be as white as snow;
Though they are red like crimson,
They shall be as wool.
19 If you are willing and obedient,
You shall eat the good of the land;
20 But if you refuse and rebel,
You shall be devoured by the sword";
For the mouth of the LORD has spoken.

The Degenerate City

21 How the faithful city has become a harlot!
It was full of justice;
Righteousness lodged in it,
But now murderers.
22 Your silver has become dross,
Your wine mixed with water.
23 Your princes *are* rebellious,
And companions of thieves;
Everyone loves bribes,
And follows after rewards.
They do not defend the fatherless,
Nor does the cause of the widow
come before them.

24 Therefore the Lord says,
The LORD of hosts, the Mighty One of Israel,
"Ah, I will rid Myself of My adversaries,
And take vengeance on My enemies.
25 I will turn My hand against you,
And thoroughly purge away your dross,
And take away all your alloy.
26 I will restore your judges as at the first,
And your counselors as at the beginning.
Afterward you shall be called the city of
righteousness, the faithful city."

27 Zion shall be redeemed with justice,
And her penitents with righteousness.
28 The destruction of transgressors and of
sinners *shall be* together,
And those who forsake the LORD
shall be consumed.
29 For they[b] shall be ashamed of the
terebinth trees
Which you have desired;
And you shall be embarrassed because
of the gardens
Which you have chosen.
30 For you shall be as a terebinth
whose leaf fades,
And as a garden that has no water.
31 The strong shall be as tinder,
And the work of it as a spark;
Both will burn together,
And no one shall quench *them.*

The Future House of God

2 The word that Isaiah the son of Amoz saw concerning Judah and Jerusalem.

2 Now it shall come to pass in the latter days
That the mountain of the LORD's house
Shall be established on the top
of the mountains,

1:17 [a] Some ancient versions read *the oppressed.*
1:29 [b] Following Masoretic Text, Septuagint, and Vulgate; some Hebrew manuscripts and Targum read *you.*

LIFE LESSON

Isaiah 2:1–5:30

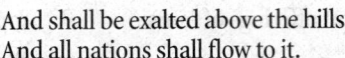

SITUATION Isaiah's vision told both of God's judgment of the wicked and the promise of his coming kingdom for the righteous.

OBSERVATION God can never approve of sin, but he longs to reward those who follow him.

INSPIRATION In the moral conflict now raging around us, whoever is on God's side is on the winning side and cannot lose; whoever is on the other side is on the losing side and cannot win. Here there is no chance, no gamble. There is freedom to choose which side we shall be on but no freedom to negotiate the results of the choice once it is made. By the mercy of God we may repent a wrong choice and alter the consequences by making a new and right choice. Beyond that we cannot go.

The whole matter of moral choice centers around Jesus Christ. Christ stated it plainly: "He that is not with me is against me," and "No man cometh unto the Father, but by me." The gospel message embodies three distinct elements: an announcement, a command, and a call. It announces the good news of redemption accomplished in mercy; it commands all men everywhere to repent, and it calls all men to surrender to the terms of grace by believing on Jesus Christ as Lord and Saviour.

We must all choose whether we will obey the gospel or turn away in unbelief and reject its authority. Our choice is our own, but the consequences of the choice have already been determined by the sovereign will of God, and from this there is no appeal.

(From *The Knowledge of the Holy* by A. W. Tozer)

APPLICATION Are you inside God's kingdom or do you find yourself peeking in, to see if it is for you? You cannot have one foot in and one foot out. Choose to be in God's kingdom. It will mean eternal rewards and fellowship with God.

EXPLORATION Wickedness or Righteousness—Psalm 1; Proverbs 3:33; Ezekiel 18:20-21; Malachi 3:18; Matthew 25:46; 1 Peter 3:12.

And shall be exalted above the hills;
And all nations shall flow to it.
3 Many people shall come and say,
"Come, and let us go up to the mountain of the LORD,
To the house of the God of Jacob;
He will teach us His ways,
And we shall walk in His paths."
For out of Zion shall go forth the law,
And the word of the LORD from Jerusalem.
4 He shall judge between the nations,
And rebuke many people;
They shall beat their swords into plowshares,
And their spears into pruning hooks;
Nation shall not lift up sword against nation,
Neither shall they learn war anymore.

The Day of the LORD

5 O house of Jacob, come and let us walk
In the light of the LORD.

6 For You have forsaken Your people, the house of Jacob,
Because they are filled with eastern ways;
They *are* soothsayers like the Philistines,
And they are pleased with the children of foreigners.
7 Their land is also full of silver and gold,
And there is no end to their treasures;
Their land is also full of horses,
And there is no end to their chariots.
8 Their land is also full of idols;
They worship the work of their own hands,
That which their own fingers have made.
9 People bow down,
And each man humbles himself;
Therefore do not forgive them.

10 Enter into the rock, and hide in the dust,
From the terror of the LORD
And the glory of His majesty.
11 The lofty looks of man shall be humbled,
The haughtiness of men shall be bowed down,
And the LORD alone shall be exalted in that day.

12 For the day of the LORD of hosts
Shall come upon everything proud and lofty,
Upon everything lifted up—
And it shall be brought low—
13 Upon all the cedars of Lebanon *that are* high and lifted up,
And upon all the oaks of Bashan;
14 Upon all the high mountains,
And upon all the hills *that are* lifted up;
15 Upon every high tower,
And upon every fortified wall;

16 Upon all the ships of Tarshish,
And upon all the beautiful sloops.
17 The loftiness of man shall be bowed down,
And the haughtiness of men shall
be brought low;
The LORD alone will be exalted in that day,
18 But the idols He shall utterly abolish.

19 They shall go into the holes of the rocks,
And into the caves of the earth,
From the terror of the LORD
And the glory of His majesty,
When He arises to shake the earth mightily.

20 In that day a man will cast away his
idols of silver
And his idols of gold,
Which they made, *each* for himself to worship,
To the moles and bats,
21 To go into the clefts of the rocks,
And into the crags of the rugged rocks,
From the terror of the LORD
And the glory of His majesty,
When He arises to shake the earth mightily.

22 Sever yourselves from such a man,
Whose breath *is* in his nostrils;
For of what account is he?

Judgment on Judah and Jerusalem

3 For behold, the Lord, the LORD of hosts,
Takes away from Jerusalem and from Judah
The stock and the store,
The whole supply of bread and the whole
supply of water;
2 The mighty man and the man of war,
The judge and the prophet,
And the diviner and the elder;
3 The captain of fifty and the honorable man,
The counselor and the skillful artisan,
And the expert enchanter.

4 "I will give children *to be* their princes,
And babes shall rule over them.
5 The people will be oppressed,
Every one by another and every one
by his neighbor;
The child will be insolent toward the elder,
And the base toward the honorable."

6 When a man takes hold of his brother
In the house of his father, *saying,*
"You have clothing;
You be our ruler,
And *let* these ruins *be* under your power,"[c]
7 In that day he will protest, saying,
"I cannot cure *your* ills,
For in my house *is* neither food nor clothing;
Do not make me a ruler of the people."

8 For Jerusalem stumbled,
And Judah is fallen,
Because their tongue and their doings
Are against the LORD,
To provoke the eyes of His glory.
9 The look on their countenance witnesses
against them,
And they declare their sin as Sodom;
They do not hide *it.*
Woe to their soul!
For they have brought evil upon themselves.

10 "Say to the righteous that *it shall be*
well *with them,*
For they shall eat the fruit of their doings.
11 Woe to the wicked! *It shall be* ill *with him,*
For the reward of his hands shall be given him.
12 *As for* My people, children *are* their oppressors,
And women rule over them.
O My people! Those who lead you cause
you to err,
And destroy the way of your paths."

Oppression and Luxury Condemned

13 The LORD stands up to plead,
And stands to judge the people.
14 The LORD will enter into judgment
With the elders of His people
And His princes:
"For you have eaten up the vineyard;
The plunder of the poor *is* in your houses.
15 What do you mean by crushing My people
And grinding the faces of the poor?"
Says the Lord GOD of hosts.

16 Moreover the LORD says:

"Because the daughters of Zion are haughty,
And walk with outstretched necks
And wanton eyes,
Walking and mincing *as* they go,
Making a jingling with their feet,

3:6 [c] Literally *hand*

17 Therefore the Lord will strike with a scab
The crown of the head of the daughters of Zion,
And the LORD will uncover their secret parts."

18 In that day the Lord will take away the finery:
The jingling anklets, the scarves,
and the crescents;
19 The pendants, the bracelets, and the veils;
20 The headdresses, the leg ornaments,
and the headbands;
The perfume boxes, the charms,
21 and the rings;
The nose jewels,
22 the festal apparel, and the mantles;
The outer garments, the purses,
23 and the mirrors;
The fine linen, the turbans, and the robes.

24And so it shall be:

Instead of a sweet smell there will be a stench;
Instead of a sash, a rope;
Instead of well-set hair, baldness;
Instead of a rich robe, a girding of sackcloth;
And branding instead of beauty.
25 Your men shall fall by the sword,
And your mighty in the war.

26 Her gates shall lament and mourn,
And she *being* desolate shall sit on the ground.

4 And in that day seven women shall take hold
of one man, saying,
"We will eat our own food and wear
our own apparel;
Only let us be called by your name,
To take away our reproach."

The Renewal of Zion

2 In that day the Branch of the LORD shall be
beautiful and glorious;
And the fruit of the earth *shall be* excellent
and appealing
For those of Israel who have escaped.

3And it shall come to pass that *he who is* left in Zion
and remains in Jerusalem will be called holy—everyone who is recorded among the living in Jerusalem.
4When the Lord has washed away the filth of the
daughters of Zion, and purged the blood of Jerusalem
from her midst, by the spirit of judgment and by the
spirit of burning, 5then the LORD will create above
every dwelling place of Mount Zion, and above her
assemblies, a cloud and smoke by day and the shining of a flaming fire by night. For over all the glory
there *will be* a covering. 6And there will be a tabernacle for shade in the daytime from the heat, for a place
of refuge, and for a shelter from storm and rain.

God's Disappointing Vineyard

5 Now let me sing to my Well-beloved
A song of my Beloved regarding His vineyard:

My Well-beloved has a vineyard
On a very fruitful hill.
2 He dug it up and cleared out its stones,
And planted it with the choicest vine.
He built a tower in its midst,
And also made a winepress in it;
So He expected *it* to bring forth *good* grapes,
But it brought forth wild grapes.

3 "And now, O inhabitants of Jerusalem and
men of Judah,
Judge, please, between Me and My vineyard.
4 What more could have been done
to My vineyard
That I have not done in it?
Why then, when I expected *it* to bring
forth *good* grapes,
Did it bring forth wild grapes?
5 And now, please let Me tell you what I will do
to My vineyard:
I will take away its hedge, and it shall be burned;
And break down its wall, and it shall be
trampled down.
6 I will lay it waste;
It shall not be pruned or dug,
But there shall come up briers and thorns.
I will also command the clouds
That they rain no rain on it."

7 For the vineyard of the LORD of hosts *is* the
house of Israel,
And the men of Judah are His pleasant plant.
He looked for justice, but behold, oppression;
For righteousness, but behold, a cry *for help.*

Impending Judgment on Excesses

8 Woe to those who join house to house;
They add field to field,
Till *there is* no place
Where they may dwell alone in the midst of
the land!

9 In my hearing the LORD of hosts *said*,
"Truly, many houses shall be desolate,
Great and beautiful ones, without inhabitant.
10 For ten acres of vineyard shall yield one bath,
And a homer of seed shall yield one ephah."

11 Woe to those who rise early in the morning,
That they may follow intoxicating drink;
Who continue until night, *till*
wine inflames them!
12 The harp and the strings,
The tambourine and flute,
And wine are in their feasts;
But they do not regard the work of the LORD,
Nor consider the operation of His hands.

13 Therefore my people have gone into captivity,
Because *they have* no knowledge;
Their honorable men *are* famished,
And their multitude dried up with thirst.
14 Therefore Sheol has enlarged itself
And opened its mouth beyond measure;
Their glory and their multitude
and their pomp,
And he who is jubilant, shall descend into it.
15 People shall be brought down,
Each man shall be humbled,
And the eyes of the lofty shall be humbled.
16 But the LORD of hosts shall be
exalted in judgment,
And God who is holy shall be hallowed
in righteousness.
17 Then the lambs shall feed in their pasture,
And in the waste places of the fat ones
strangers shall eat.

18 Woe to those who draw iniquity with
cords of vanity,
And sin as if with a cart rope;
19 That say, "Let Him make speed *and*
hasten His work,
That we may see *it*;
And let the counsel of the Holy One of Israel
draw near and come,
That we may know *it*."

20 Woe to those who call evil good, and good evil;
Who put darkness for light, and
light for darkness;
Who put bitter for sweet, and sweet for bitter!

21 Woe to *those who are* wise in their own eyes,
And prudent in their own sight!

22 Woe to men mighty at drinking wine,
Woe to men valiant for mixing
intoxicating drink,
23 Who justify the wicked for a bribe,
And take away justice from the righteous man!

24 Therefore, as the fire devours the stubble,
And the flame consumes the chaff,
So their root will be as rottenness,
And their blossom will ascend like dust;
Because they have rejected the law of the
LORD of hosts,
And despised the word of the Holy
One of Israel.
25 Therefore the anger of the LORD is aroused
against His people;
He has stretched out His hand against them
And stricken them,
And the hills trembled.
Their carcasses *were* as refuse in the midst
of the streets.

For all this His anger is not turned away,
But His hand *is* stretched out still.

26 He will lift up a banner to the nations from afar,
And will whistle to them from the end
of the earth;
Surely they shall come with speed, swiftly.
27 No one will be weary or stumble among them,
No one will slumber or sleep;
Nor will the belt on their loins be loosed,
Nor the strap of their sandals be broken;
28 Whose arrows *are* sharp,
And all their bows bent;
Their horses' hooves will seem like flint,
And their wheels like a whirlwind.
29 Their roaring *will be* like a lion,
They will roar like young lions;
Yes, they will roar
And lay hold of the prey;
They will carry *it* away safely,
And no one will deliver.
30 In that day they will roar against them
Like the roaring of the sea.
And if *one* looks to the land,
Behold, darkness *and* sorrow;
And the light is darkened by the clouds.

Isaiah Called to Be a Prophet

6 In the year that King Uzziah died, I saw the Lord
sitting on a throne, high and lifted up, and the

LIFE LESSON

Isaiah 6:1–7:25

SITUATION Isaiah recalled the commission God had given him. Isaiah carried a message of both hope and judgment. He described and predicted the coming Messiah: Jesus Christ.

OBSERVATION We are commissioned to tell others about God and his plan for salvation.

INSPIRATION It is no frivolous matter to hear the voice of God; and certainly it is an awesome trust to deign to speak for Him. Luther said that preaching made his knees knock. Spurgeon, the brilliant British preacher, said he "trembled" lest he should misinterpret the Word.

So, the only way we can ever speak with confidence is to speak from the Word. Jesus gives us the best example; He knew the Scriptures, drew His authority from them, and based His words upon them. Those who follow Him must do the same . . . [T]he quiet, often unnoticed actions of "ordinary" Christians who believe and obey speak far more loudly than all the bombast of so-called religious leaders. Who speaks for God? He does quite nicely for Himself. Through His holy and infallible Word—and the quiet obedience of His servants.
(From *Who Speaks for God?* by Charles Colson)

APPLICATION Have you known someone for some time but have never shared Christ with that person? Create an opportunity to share about the most important aspect of your life.

EXPLORATION The Road to Salvation—Romans 3:23; 5:8; 6:23; 10:10-13.

train of His *robe* filled the temple. 2 Above it stood seraphim; each one had
six wings: with two he covered his face, with two he covered his feet, and
with two he flew. 3 And one cried to another and said:

"Holy, holy, holy *is* the LORD of hosts;
The whole earth *is* full of His glory!"

4 And the posts of the door were shaken by the voice of him who cried out,
and the house was filled with smoke.
5 So I said:

"Woe *is* me, for I am undone!
Because I *am* a man of unclean lips,
And I dwell in the midst of a people of unclean lips;
For my eyes have seen the King,
The LORD of hosts."

6 Then one of the seraphim flew to me, having in his hand a live coal
which he had taken with the tongs from the altar. 7 And he touched my
mouth *with it,* and said:

"Behold, this has touched your lips;
Your iniquity is taken away,
And your sin purged."

8 Also I heard the voice of the Lord, saying:

"Whom shall I send,
And who will go for Us?"

Then I said, "Here *am* I! Send me."
9 And He said, "Go, and tell this people:

'Keep on hearing, but do not understand;
Keep on seeing, but do not perceive.'

10 "Make the heart of this people dull,
And their ears heavy,
And shut their eyes;
Lest they see with their eyes,
And hear with their ears,
And understand with their heart,
And return and be healed."

11 Then I said, "Lord, how long?"
And He answered:

"Until the cities are laid waste and without inhabitant,
The houses are without a man,
The land is utterly desolate,
12 The LORD has removed men far away,
And the forsaken places *are* many in the midst of the land.
13 But yet a tenth *will be* in it,
And will return and be for consuming,
As a terebinth tree or as an oak,
Whose stump *remains* when it is cut down.
So the holy seed *shall be* its stump."

Isaiah Sent to King Ahaz

7 Now it came to pass in the days of Ahaz the son of
Jotham, the son of Uzziah, king of Judah, *that*
Rezin king of Syria and Pekah the son of Remaliah,
king of Israel, went up to Jerusalem to *make* war
against it, but could not prevail against it. 2And it was
told to the house of David, saying, "Syria's forces are
deployed in Ephraim." So his heart and the heart of
his people were moved as the trees of the woods are
moved with the wind.
3Then the LORD said to Isaiah, "Go out now to meet
Ahaz, you and Shear-Jashub[d] your son, at the end of
the aqueduct from the upper pool, on the highway to
the Fuller's Field, 4and say to him: 'Take heed, and be
quiet; do not fear or be fainthearted for these two stubs
of smoking firebrands, for the fierce anger of Rezin
and Syria, and the son of Remaliah. 5Because Syria,
Ephraim, and the son of Remaliah have plotted evil
against you, saying, 6"Let us go up against Judah and
trouble it, and let us make a gap in its wall for ourselves, and set a king over them, the son of Tabel"—
7thus says the Lord GOD:

"It shall not stand,
Nor shall it come to pass.
8 For the head of Syria *is* Damascus,
And the head of Damascus *is* Rezin.
Within sixty-five years Ephraim will be broken,
So that it will not *be* a people.
9 The head of Ephraim *is* Samaria,
And the head of Samaria *is* Remaliah's son.
If you will not believe,
Surely you shall not be established." ' "

The Immanuel Prophecy

10Moreover the LORD spoke again to Ahaz, saying,
11"Ask a sign for yourself from the LORD your God; ask
it either in the depth or in the height above."
12But Ahaz said, "I will not ask, nor will I test the
LORD!"
13Then he said, "Hear now, O house of David! *Is it* a
small thing for you to weary men, but will you weary
my God also? 14Therefore the Lord Himself will give
you a sign: Behold, the virgin shall conceive and bear
a Son, and shall call His name Immanuel.[e] 15Curds
and honey He shall eat, that He may know to refuse
the evil and choose the good. 16For before the Child
shall know to refuse the evil and choose the good, the
land that you dread will be forsaken by both her kings.
17The LORD will bring the king of Assyria upon you and
your people and your father's house—days that have
not come since the day that Ephraim departed from
Judah."

18 And it shall come to pass in that day
That the LORD will whistle for the fly
That *is* in the farthest part of the rivers of Egypt,
And for the bee that *is* in the land of Assyria.
19 They will come, and all of them will rest
In the desolate valleys and in the clefts
of the rocks,
And on all thorns and in all pastures.

20 In the same day the Lord will shave with a
hired razor,
With those from beyond the River,[f] with the
king of Assyria,
The head and the hair of the legs,
And will also remove the beard.

21 It shall be in that day
That a man will keep alive a young cow
and two sheep;
22 So it shall be, from the abundance of
milk they give,
That he will eat curds;
For curds and honey everyone will eat who is
left in the land.

23 It shall happen in that day,
That wherever there could be a thousand vines
Worth a thousand *shekels* of silver,
It will be for briers and thorns.
24 With arrows and bows men will come there,
Because all the land will become
briers and thorns.
25 And to any hill which could be dug with the hoe,
You will not go there for fear of
briers and thorns;
But it will become a range for oxen
And a place for sheep to roam.

Assyria Will Invade the Land

8 Moreover the LORD said to me, "Take a large scroll,
and write on it with a man's pen concerning
Maher-Shalal-Hash-Baz.[g] 2And I will take for Myself
faithful witnesses to record, Uriah the priest and
Zechariah the son of Jeberechiah."

7:3 [d] Literally *A Remnant Shall Return*
7:14 [e] Literally *God-With-Us*
7:20 [f] That is, the Euphrates
8:1 [g] Literally *Speed the Spoil, Hasten the Booty*

LIFE LESSON

Isaiah 8:1–10:34

SITUATION Isaiah brought a shocking announcement that God planned to deliver Israel into the hands of Assyria. Israel would experience difficult days ahead. But during these hard times, God would not forget about his people.

OBSERVATION God judges sin. But he also restores his people into a peaceful relationship with himself.

INSPIRATION The struggle we have with a holy God is rooted in the conflict between God's righteousness and our unrighteousness. He is just and we are unjust. This tension creates fear, hostility, and anger within us toward God. The unjust person does not desire the company of a just judge. We become fugitives fleeing from the presence of One whose glory can blind us and whose justice can condemn us. We are at war with Him unless or until we are justified. . . .

I remember the sultry summer day in 1945 when I was busy playing stickball in the streets of Chicago. At that time my world consisted of the piece of real estate that extended from one manhole cover to the next. All that was important to me was that my turn at bat had finally come. I was most annoyed when the first pitch was interrupted by an outbreak of chaos and noise all around me. People started running out of apartment doors screaming and beating dishpans with wooden spoons. I thought for a moment it might be the end of the world. It was certainly the end of my stickball game. In the riotous confusion I saw my mother rushing toward me with tears streaming down her face. She scooped me up in her arms and squeezed me, sobbing over and over again, "It's over, it's over, it's over!"

3Then I went to the prophetess, and she conceived and bore a son. Then
the LORD said to me, "Call his name Maher-Shalal-Hash-Baz; 4for before
the child shall have knowledge to cry 'My father' and 'My mother,' the
riches of Damascus and the spoil of Samaria will be taken away before the
king of Assyria."
5The LORD also spoke to me again, saying:

6 "Inasmuch as these people refused
The waters of Shiloah that flow softly,
And rejoice in Rezin and in Remaliah's son;
7 Now therefore, behold, the Lord brings up over them
The waters of the River,[h] strong and mighty—
The king of Assyria and all his glory;
He will go up over all his channels
And go over all his banks.
8 He will pass through Judah,
He will overflow and pass over,
He will reach up to the neck;
And the stretching out of his wings
Will fill the breadth of Your land, O Immanuel.[i]

9 "Be shattered, O you peoples, and be broken in pieces!
Give ear, all you from far countries.
Gird yourselves, but be broken in pieces;
Gird yourselves, but be broken in pieces.
10 Take counsel together, but it will come to nothing;
Speak the word, but it will not stand,
For God *is* with us."[j]

Fear God, Heed His Word

11For the LORD spoke thus to me with a strong hand, and instructed me
that I should not walk in the way of this people, saying:

12 "Do not say, 'A conspiracy,'
Concerning all that this people call a conspiracy,
Nor be afraid of their threats, nor be troubled.
13 The LORD of hosts, Him you shall hallow;
Let Him *be* your fear,
And *let* Him *be* your dread.
14 He will be as a sanctuary,
But a stone of stumbling and a rock of offense
To both the houses of Israel,
As a trap and a snare to the inhabitants of Jerusalem.
15 And many among them shall stumble;
They shall fall and be broken,
Be snared and taken."

16 Bind up the testimony,
Seal the law among my disciples.

8:7 *h* That is, the Euphrates
8:8 *i* Literally *God-With-Us*
8:10 *j* Hebrew *Immanuel*

17 And I will wait on the LORD,
Who hides His face from the house of Jacob;
And I will hope in Him.
18 Here am I and the children whom the LORD has given me!
We are for signs and wonders in Israel
From the LORD of hosts,
Who dwells in Mount Zion.

19 And when they say to you, "Seek those who are mediums and wizards,
who whisper and mutter," should not a people seek their God? *Should they*
seek the dead on behalf of the living? 20 To the law and to the testimony! If
they do not speak according to this word, *it is* because *there is* no light in them.
21 They will pass through it hard-pressed and hungry; and it shall happen,
when they are hungry, that they will be enraged and curse their king and
their God, and look upward. 22 Then they will look to the earth, and see trouble and darkness, gloom of anguish; and *they will be* driven into darkness.

The Government of the Promised Son

9 Nevertheless the gloom *will* not *be* upon her who *is* distressed,
As when at first He lightly esteemed
The land of Zebulun and the land of Naphtali,
And afterward more heavily oppressed *her,*
By the way of the sea, beyond the Jordan,
In Galilee of the Gentiles.
2 The people who walked in darkness
Have seen a great light;
Those who dwelt in the land of the shadow of death,
Upon them a light has shined.

3 You have multiplied the nation
And increased its joy;[k]
They rejoice before You
According to the joy of harvest,
As *men* rejoice when they divide the spoil.
4 For You have broken the yoke of his burden
And the staff of his shoulder,
The rod of his oppressor,
As in the day of Midian.
5 For every warrior's sandal from the noisy battle,
And garments rolled in blood,
Will be used for burning *and* fuel of fire.

6 For unto us a Child is born,
Unto us a Son is given;
And the government will be upon His shoulder.
And His name will be called
Wonderful, Counselor, Mighty God,
Everlasting Father, Prince of Peace.
7 Of the increase of *His* government and peace
There will be no end,

9:3 [k] Following Qere and Targum; Kethib and Vulgate read *not increased joy;* Septuagint reads *Most of the people You brought down in Your joy.*

It was VJ Day, 1945. I wasn't sure what it all meant, but one thing was clear. It meant that the war had ended and my father was coming home. No more airmail to far-away countries. No more listening to the daily news reports about battle casualties. . . . The war was over and peace had come at last.

That moment of jubilation left a lasting impression in my childhood brain. I learned that peace was an important thing, a cause for unbridled celebration when it was established and for bitter remorse when it was lost. . . .

When God signs a peace treaty, it is a sign for perpetuity. The war is over forever and ever. Of course we still sin; we still rebel; we still commit acts of hostility toward God. But God is not a co-belligerent. He will not be drawn into warfare with us. We have an advocate with the Father. We have a mediator who keeps the peace. He rules over the peace because He is both the Prince of Peace and He is our peace.

(From *The Holiness of God* by R. C. Sproul)

APPLICATION Rejoice because you have peace with God! Celebrate God's forgiveness for you. Demonstrate God's peace to others through your relationships. Help your co-workers and family to meet their needs. Relieve the disappointments of others.

EXPLORATION Peace—Psalm 29:11; 119:165; Isaiah 26:3; 48:18; 53:5; John 16:13; Romans 5:1; Ephesians 2:14; Philippians 4:7; Colossians 1:20.

Upon the throne of David and
over His kingdom,
To order it and establish it with judgment
and justice
From that time forward, even forever.
The zeal of the LORD of hosts will perform this.

The Punishment of Samaria

8 The Lord sent a word against Jacob,
And it has fallen on Israel.
9 All the people will know—
Ephraim and the inhabitant of Samaria—
Who say in pride and arrogance of heart:
10 "The bricks have fallen down,
But we will rebuild with hewn stones;
The sycamores are cut down,
But we will replace *them* with cedars."
11 Therefore the LORD shall set up
The adversaries of Rezin against him,
And spur his enemies on,
12 The Syrians before and the Philistines behind;
And they shall devour Israel with
an open mouth.

For all this His anger is not turned away,
But His hand *is* stretched out still.

13 For the people do not turn to Him
who strikes them,
Nor do they seek the LORD of hosts.
14 Therefore the LORD will cut off head and
tail from Israel,
Palm branch and bulrush in one day.
15 The elder and honorable, he *is* the head;
The prophet who teaches lies, he *is* the tail.
16 For the leaders of this people cause *them* to err,
And *those who are* led by them are destroyed.
17 Therefore the Lord will have no joy in
their young men,
Nor have mercy on their fatherless
and widows;
For everyone *is* a hypocrite and an evildoer,
And every mouth speaks folly.

For all this His anger is not turned away,
But His hand *is* stretched out still.

18 For wickedness burns as the fire;
It shall devour the briers and thorns,
And kindle in the thickets of the forest;
They shall mount up *like* rising smoke.
19 Through the wrath of the LORD of hosts
The land is burned up,
And the people shall be as fuel for the fire;
No man shall spare his brother.
20 And he shall snatch on the right hand
And be hungry;
He shall devour on the left hand
And not be satisfied;
Every man shall eat the flesh of his own arm.
21 Manasseh *shall devour* Ephraim,
and Ephraim Manasseh;
Together they *shall be* against Judah.

For all this His anger is not turned away,
But His hand *is* stretched out still.

10 "Woe to those who decree unrighteous decrees,
Who write misfortune,
Which they have prescribed
2 To rob the needy of justice,
And to take what is right from the poor
of My people,
That widows may be their prey,
And *that* they may rob the fatherless.
3 What will you do in the day of punishment,
And in the desolation *which* will
come from afar?
To whom will you flee for help?
And where will you leave your glory?
4 Without Me they shall bow down
among the prisoners,
And they shall fall among the slain."

For all this His anger is not turned away,
But His hand *is* stretched out still.

Arrogant Assyria Also Judged

5 "Woe to Assyria, the rod of My anger
And the staff in whose hand is My indignation.
6 I will send him against an ungodly nation,
And against the people of My wrath
I will give him charge,
To seize the spoil, to take the prey,
And to tread them down like the mire
of the streets.
7 Yet he does not mean so,
Nor does his heart think so;
But *it is* in his heart to destroy,
And cut off not a few nations.
8 For he says,
'*Are* not my princes altogether kings?

9 *Is* not Calno like Carchemish?
Is not Hamath like Arpad?
Is not Samaria like Damascus?
10 As my hand has found the kingdoms
of the idols,
Whose carved images excelled those
of Jerusalem and Samaria,
11 As I have done to Samaria and her idols,
Shall I not do also to Jerusalem and her idols?' "

12Therefore it shall come to pass, when the Lord has
performed all His work on Mount Zion and on Jerusalem, *that He will say,* "I will punish the fruit of the
arrogant heart of the king of Assyria, and the glory of
his haughty looks."
13For he says:

"By the strength of my hand I have done *it,*
And by my wisdom, for I am prudent;
Also I have removed the boundaries
of the people,
And have robbed their treasuries;
So I have put down the inhabitants like
a valiant *man.*
14 My hand has found like a nest the riches
of the people,
And as one gathers eggs *that are* left,
I have gathered all the earth;
And there was no one who moved *his* wing,
Nor opened *his* mouth with even a peep."

15 Shall the ax boast itself against him who
chops with it?
Or shall the saw exalt itself against him who
saws with it?
As if a rod could wield *itself* against those who
lift it up,
Or as if a staff could lift up, *as if it*
were not wood!
16 Therefore the Lord, the Lord[l] of hosts,
Will send leanness among his fat ones;
And under his glory
He will kindle a burning
Like the burning of a fire.
17 So the Light of Israel will be for a fire,
And his Holy One for a flame;
It will burn and devour
His thorns and his briers in one day.
18 And it will consume the glory of his forest and
of his fruitful field,
Both soul and body;
And they will be as when a sick
man wastes away.
19 Then the rest of the trees of his forest
Will be so few in number
That a child may write them.

The Returning Remnant of Israel

20 And it shall come to pass in that day
That the remnant of Israel,
And such as have escaped of the
house of Jacob,
Will never again depend on him
who defeated them,
But will depend on the LORD, the Holy One of
Israel, in truth.
21 The remnant will return, the remnant of Jacob,
To the Mighty God.
22 For though your people, O Israel, be as the
sand of the sea,
A remnant of them will return;
The destruction decreed shall overflow
with righteousness.
23 For the Lord GOD of hosts
Will make a determined end
In the midst of all the land.

24Therefore thus says the Lord GOD of hosts: "O My
people, who dwell in Zion, do not be afraid of the Assyrian. He shall strike you with a rod and lift up his
staff against you, in the manner of Egypt. 25For yet a
very little while and the indignation will cease, as will
My anger in their destruction." 26And the LORD of hosts
will stir up a scourge for him like the slaughter of
Midian at the rock of Oreb; *as* His rod was on the sea,
so will He lift it up in the manner of Egypt.

27 It shall come to pass in that day
That his burden will be taken away
from your shoulder,
And his yoke from your neck,
And the yoke will be destroyed because of the
anointing oil.

28 He has come to Aiath,
He has passed Migron;
At Michmash he has attended
to his equipment.
29 They have gone along the ridge,
They have taken up lodging at Geba.

10:16 [l] Following Bomberg; Masoretic Text and Dead Sea Scrolls read *YHWH* (*the* LORD).

LIFE LESSON

Isaiah 11:1–12:6

SITUATION Isaiah prophesied about Jesus, who would establish a kingdom of peace and prosperity.

OBSERVATION Jesus Christ ushered in a kingdom where God reigns in righteousness and justice. We will realize it fully when he comes again.

INSPIRATION The government in God's kingdom is *unique.* It is not a democracy where the people govern, but a Christocracy where Christ is the supreme Authority. In a government of unredeemed men, democracy is the only fair and equitable system. But no democracy can ever be better than the people who make it up. When men are selfishly motivated, the government will be inequitable. When men are dishonest, the government will be the same. When everyone wants his own way, someone is going to get hurt.

But in God's kingdom, Christ is King. He is compassionate, fair, merciful, and just. When He is sovereign in men's hearts, anguish turns to peace, hatred is transformed into love, and misunderstanding into understanding.

Not only this, but God's kingdom is *lasting.* The history of man has been a continuous series of half successes and total failures. Prosperity exists for a time, only to be followed by war and depression. Twenty-six civilizations have come and gone, and man still battles with the same problems, over and over again.

But the kingdom of God will abide forever. The fluctuations of time, the swinging of the pendulum from war to peace, from starvation to plenty, from chaos to order, will end forever. The Bible says, "And of his kingdom there shall be no end" (Luke 1:33).

(From *Unto the Hills* by Billy Graham)

APPLICATION Is your behavior appropriate for a citizen of God's kingdom? Make adjustments so that you are fair in your business, loving to your family, considerate to your friends, and honest in everything you do.

EXPLORATION The Kingdom of God—Matthew 6:33; Luke 12:32-34; 1 Corinthians 15:23-28; Hebrews 12:28; James 2:5.

Ramah is afraid,
Gibeah of Saul has fled.
30 Lift up your voice,
O daughter of Gallim!
Cause it to be heard as far as Laish—
O poor Anathoth![m]
31 Madmenah has fled,
The inhabitants of Gebim seek refuge.
32 As yet he will remain at Nob that day;
He will shake his fist at the mount of the daughter of Zion,
The hill of Jerusalem.

33 Behold, the Lord,
The LORD of hosts,
Will lop off the bough with terror;
Those of high stature *will be* hewn down,
And the haughty will be humbled.
34 He will cut down the thickets of the forest with iron,
And Lebanon will fall by the Mighty One.

The Reign of Jesse's Offspring

11 There shall come forth a Rod from the stem of Jesse,
And a Branch shall grow out of his roots.
2 The Spirit of the LORD shall rest upon Him,
The Spirit of wisdom and understanding,
The Spirit of counsel and might,
The Spirit of knowledge and of the fear of the LORD.

3 His delight *is* in the fear of the LORD,
And He shall not judge by the sight of His eyes,
Nor decide by the hearing of His ears;
4 But with righteousness He shall judge the poor,
And decide with equity for the meek of the earth;
He shall strike the earth with the rod of His mouth,
And with the breath of His lips He shall slay the wicked.
5 Righteousness shall be the belt of His loins,
And faithfulness the belt of His waist.

6 "The wolf also shall dwell with the lamb,
The leopard shall lie down with the young goat,
The calf and the young lion and the fatling together;
And a little child shall lead them.
7 The cow and the bear shall graze;
Their young ones shall lie down together;
And the lion shall eat straw like the ox.
8 The nursing child shall play by the cobra's hole,
And the weaned child shall put his hand in the viper's den.
9 They shall not hurt nor destroy in all My holy mountain,
For the earth shall be full of the knowledge of the LORD
As the waters cover the sea.

10:30 [m] Following Masoretic Text, Targum, and Vulgate; Septuagint and Syriac read *Listen to her, O Anathoth.*

10 "And in that day there shall be a Root of Jesse,
Who shall stand as a banner to the people;
For the Gentiles shall seek Him,
And His resting place shall be glorious."

11 It shall come to pass in that day
That the Lord shall set His hand again
the second time
To recover the remnant of His people
who are left,
From Assyria and Egypt,
From Pathros and Cush,
From Elam and Shinar,
From Hamath and the islands of the sea.

12 He will set up a banner for the nations,
And will assemble the outcasts of Israel,
And gather together the dispersed of Judah
From the four corners of the earth.
13 Also the envy of Ephraim shall depart,
And the adversaries of Judah shall be cut off;
Ephraim shall not envy Judah,
And Judah shall not harass Ephraim.
14 But they shall fly down upon the shoulder of
the Philistines toward the west;
Together they shall plunder the people
of the East;
They shall lay their hand on Edom and Moab;
And the people of Ammon shall obey them.
15 The LORD will utterly destroy[n] the tongue of
the Sea of Egypt;
With His mighty wind He will shake His fist
over the River,[o]
And strike it in the seven streams,
And make *men* cross over dryshod.
16 There will be a highway for the remnant
of His people
Who will be left from Assyria,
As it was for Israel
In the day that he came up from the
land of Egypt.

A Hymn of Praise

12 And in that day you will say:

"O LORD, I will praise You;
Though You were angry with me,
Your anger is turned away, and You
comfort me.
2 Behold, God *is* my salvation,
I will trust and not be afraid;
'For YAH, the LORD, *is* my strength and song;
He also has become my salvation.' "[p]

3 Therefore with joy you will draw water
From the wells of salvation.
4 And in that day you will say:

"Praise the LORD, call upon His name;
Declare His deeds among the peoples,
Make mention that His name is exalted.
5 Sing to the LORD,
For He has done excellent things;
This *is* known in all the earth.
6 Cry out and shout, O inhabitant of Zion,
For great *is* the Holy One of Israel
in your midst!"

Proclamation Against Babylon

13 The burden against Babylon which Isaiah the
son of Amoz saw.

2 "Lift up a banner on the high mountain,
Raise your voice to them;
Wave your hand, that they may enter the gates
of the nobles.
3 I have commanded My sanctified ones;
I have also called My mighty ones
for My anger—
Those who rejoice in My exaltation."

4 The noise of a multitude in the mountains,
Like that of many people!
A tumultuous noise of the kingdoms of
nations gathered together!
The LORD of hosts musters
The army for battle.
5 They come from a far country,
From the end of heaven—
The LORD and His weapons of indignation,
To destroy the whole land.

6 Wail, for the day of the LORD *is* at hand!
It will come as destruction from the Almighty.
7 Therefore all hands will be limp,
Every man's heart will melt,
8 And they will be afraid.
Pangs and sorrows will take hold of *them;*
They will be in pain as a woman in childbirth;
They will be amazed at one another;
Their faces *will be like* flames.

11:15 [n] Following Masoretic Text and Vulgate; Septuagint, Syriac, and Targum read *dry up.* [o] That is, the Euphrates
12:2 [p] Exodus 15:2

LIFE LESSON

Isaiah 13:1–21:17

SITUATION Isaiah reminded Israel not to make alliances with pagan nations. If the people sought God, his strength would be adequate to protect them. God promised to punish each neighboring country for its arrogance, rebellion, and immorality.

OBSERVATION God expects his people as a group to stand up for truth.

INSPIRATION It was May Day, 1990. The place, Moscow's Red Square.

"Is it straight, Father?" one Orthodox priest asked another, shifting the heavy, eight-foot crucifix on his shoulder.

"Yes," said the other. "It is straight."

Together the two priests, along with a group of parishioners holding ropes that steadied the beams of the huge cross, walked the parade route. Before them had passed the official might of the Union of Soviet Socialist Republics: the usual May Day procession of tanks, missiles, troops, and salutes to the Communist party elite.

Behind the tanks surged a giant crowd of protesters, shouting up at Mikhail Gorbachev. "Bread! . . . Freedom! . . . Truth!"

As the throng passed directly in front of the Soviet leader standing in his place of honor, the priests hoisted their

9 Behold, the day of the LORD comes,
Cruel, with both wrath and fierce anger,
To lay the land desolate;
And He will destroy its sinners from it.
10 For the stars of heaven and their constellations
Will not give their light;
The sun will be darkened in its going forth,
And the moon will not cause its light to shine.

11 "I will punish the world for *its* evil,
And the wicked for their iniquity;
I will halt the arrogance of the proud,
And will lay low the haughtiness of the terrible.
12 I will make a mortal more rare than fine gold,
A man more than the golden wedge of Ophir.
13 Therefore I will shake the heavens,
And the earth will move out of her place,
In the wrath of the LORD of hosts
And in the day of His fierce anger.
14 It shall be as the hunted gazelle,
And as a sheep that no man takes up;
Every man will turn to his own people,
And everyone will flee to his own land.
15 Everyone who is found will be thrust through,
And everyone who is captured will fall by the sword.
16 Their children also will be dashed to pieces before their eyes;
Their houses will be plundered
And their wives ravished.

17 "Behold, I will stir up the Medes against them,
Who will not regard silver;
And *as for* gold, they will not delight in it.
18 Also *their* bows will dash the young men to pieces,
And they will have no pity on the fruit of the womb;
Their eye will not spare children.
19 And Babylon, the glory of kingdoms,
The beauty of the Chaldeans' pride,
Will be as when God overthrew Sodom and Gomorrah.
20 It will never be inhabited,
Nor will it be settled from generation to generation;
Nor will the Arabian pitch tents there,
Nor will the shepherds make their sheepfolds there.
21 But wild beasts of the desert will lie there,
And their houses will be full of owls;
Ostriches will dwell there,
And wild goats will caper there.
22 The hyenas will howl in their citadels,
And jackals in their pleasant palaces.
Her time *is* near to come,
And her days will not be prolonged."

Mercy on Jacob

14 For the LORD will have mercy on Jacob, and will still choose Israel,
and settle them in their own land. The strangers will be joined with
them, and they will cling to the house of Jacob. 2Then people will take them
and bring them to their place, and the house of Israel will possess them for
servants and maids in the land of the LORD; they will take them captive
whose captives they were, and rule over their oppressors.

Fall of the King of Babylon

3It shall come to pass in the day the LORD gives you rest from your sorrow,
and from your fear and the hard bondage in which you were made to serve,
4that you will take up this proverb against the king of Babylon, and say:

"How the oppressor has ceased,
The golden[q] city ceased!
5 The LORD has broken the staff of the wicked,
The scepter of the rulers;
6 He who struck the people in wrath with a continual stroke,
He who ruled the nations in anger,
Is persecuted *and* no one hinders.
7 The whole earth is at rest *and* quiet;
They break forth into singing.
8 Indeed the cypress trees rejoice over you,
And the cedars of Lebanon,
Saying, 'Since you were cut down,
No woodsman has come up against us.'

9 "Hell from beneath is excited about you,
To meet *you* at your coming;
It stirs up the dead for you,
All the chief ones of the earth;
It has raised up from their thrones
All the kings of the nations.
10 They all shall speak and say to you:
'Have you also become as weak as we?
Have you become like us?
11 Your pomp is brought down to Sheol,
And the sound of your stringed instruments;
The maggot is spread under you,
And worms cover you.'

The Fall of Lucifer

12 "How you are fallen from heaven,
O Lucifer,[r] son of the morning!
How you are cut down to the ground,
You who weakened the nations!
13 For you have said in your heart:
'I will ascend into heaven,
I will exalt my throne above the stars of God;

heavy burden toward the sky. The cross emerged from the crowd. As it did, the figure of Jesus Christ obscured the giant poster faces of Karl Marx, Friedrich Engels, and Vladimir Lenin that provided the backdrop for Gorbachev's reviewing stand.

"Mikhail Sergeyevich!" one of the priests shouted, his deep voice cleaving the clamor of the protesters and piercing straight toward the angry Soviet leader. "Mikhail Sergeyevich! Christ is risen!"

In a matter of months after that final May Day celebration, the Soviet Union was officially dissolved. Christ is risen indeed and is building His church, " . . . and the gates of hell shall not prevail against it."

(From *The Body* by Charles Colson)

APPLICATION Do you know how your representatives in Congress have voted on moral issues? Do their votes align with God's desires? Write your representatives in Congress. Ask their position on specific issues. Write them with your support or concerns. Next election, know the position of all the candidates.

EXPLORATION Nations—Exodus 19:5; Deuteronomy 16:18-20; Isaiah 3:14.

14:4 q Or *insolent*
14:12 r Literally *Day Star*

I will also sit on the mount of the congregation
On the farthest sides of the north;
14 I will ascend above the heights of the clouds,
I will be like the Most High.'
15 Yet you shall be brought down to Sheol,
To the lowest depths of the Pit.

16 "Those who see you will gaze at you,
And consider you, *saying*:
'*Is* this the man who made the earth tremble,
Who shook kingdoms,
17 Who made the world as a wilderness
And destroyed its cities,
Who did not open the house of his prisoners?'

18 "All the kings of the nations,
All of them, sleep in glory,
Everyone in his own house;
19 But you are cast out of your grave
Like an abominable branch,
Like the garment of those who are slain,
Thrust through with a sword,
Who go down to the stones of the pit,
Like a corpse trodden underfoot.
20 You will not be joined with them in burial,
Because you have destroyed your land
And slain your people.
The brood of evildoers shall never be named.
21 Prepare slaughter for his children
Because of the iniquity of their fathers,
Lest they rise up and possess the land,
And fill the face of the world with cities."

Babylon Destroyed

22 "For I will rise up against them," says the LORD
of hosts,
"And cut off from Babylon the name
and remnant,
And offspring and posterity," says the LORD.
23 "I will also make it a possession for
the porcupine,
And marshes of muddy water;
I will sweep it with the broom of destruction,"
says the LORD of hosts.

Assyria Destroyed

24 The LORD of hosts has sworn, saying,
"Surely, as I have thought, so it shall
come to pass,
And as I have purposed, *so* it shall stand:
25 That I will break the Assyrian in My land,
And on My mountains tread him underfoot.
Then his yoke shall be removed from them,
And his burden removed from their shoulders.
26 This *is* the purpose that is purposed against
the whole earth,
And this *is* the hand that is stretched out over
all the nations.
27 For the LORD of hosts has purposed,
And who will annul *it?*
His hand *is* stretched out,
And who will turn it back?"

Philistia Destroyed

28 This is the burden which came in the year that
King Ahaz died.

29 "Do not rejoice, all you of Philistia,
Because the rod that struck you is broken;
For out of the serpent's roots will come
forth a viper,
And its offspring *will be* a fiery flying serpent.
30 The firstborn of the poor will feed,
And the needy will lie down in safety;
I will kill your roots with famine,
And it will slay your remnant.
31 Wail, O gate! Cry, O city!
All you of Philistia *are* dissolved;
For smoke will come from the north,
And no one *will be* alone in
his appointed times."

32 What will they answer the messengers
of the nation?
That the LORD has founded Zion,
And the poor of His people shall take
refuge in it.

Proclamation Against Moab

15 The burden against Moab.

Because in the night Ar of Moab is laid waste
And destroyed,
Because in the night Kir of Moab is laid waste
And destroyed,
2 He has gone up to the temple[s] and Dibon,
To the high places to weep.
Moab will wail over Nebo and over Medeba;
On all their heads *will be* baldness,
And every beard cut off.

15:2 [s] Hebrew *bayith,* literally *house*

3 In their streets they will clothe themselves
with sackcloth;
On the tops of their houses
And in their streets
Everyone will wail, weeping bitterly.
4 Heshbon and Elealeh will cry out,
Their voice shall be heard as far as Jahaz;
Therefore the armed soldiers[t] of
Moab will cry out;
His life will be burdensome to him.

5 "My heart will cry out for Moab;
His fugitives *shall flee* to Zoar,
Like a three-year-old heifer.[u]
For by the Ascent of Luhith
They will go up with weeping;
For in the way of Horonaim
They will raise up a cry of destruction,
6 For the waters of Nimrim will be desolate,
For the green grass has withered away;
The grass fails, there is nothing green.
7 Therefore the abundance they have gained,
And what they have laid up,
They will carry away to the Brook
of the Willows.
8 For the cry has gone all around the
borders of Moab,
Its wailing to Eglaim
And its wailing to Beer Elim.
9 For the waters of Dimon[v] will be full of blood;
Because I will bring more upon Dimon,[w]
Lions upon him who escapes from Moab,
And on the remnant of the land."

Moab Destroyed

16 Send the lamb to the ruler of the land,
From Sela to the wilderness,
To the mount of the daughter of Zion.
2 For it shall be as a wandering bird thrown out
of the nest;
So shall be the daughters of Moab at the fords
of the Arnon.

3 "Take counsel, execute judgment;
Make your shadow like the night in the middle
of the day;
Hide the outcasts,
Do not betray him who escapes.
4 Let My outcasts dwell with you, O Moab;
Be a shelter to them from the face of the spoiler.
For the extortioner is at an end,
Devastation ceases,
The oppressors are consumed out of the land.
5 In mercy the throne will be established;
And One will sit on it in truth, in the tabernacle
of David,
Judging and seeking justice and hastening
righteousness."

6 We have heard of the pride of Moab—
He is very proud—
Of his haughtiness and his pride
and his wrath;
But his lies *shall* not *be* so.
7 Therefore Moab shall wail for Moab;
Everyone shall wail.
For the foundations of Kir Hareseth
you shall mourn;
Surely *they are* stricken.

8 For the fields of Heshbon languish,
And the vine of Sibmah;
The lords of the nations have broken down its
choice plants,
Which have reached to Jazer
And wandered through the wilderness.
Her branches are stretched out,
They are gone over the sea.
9 Therefore I will bewail the vine of Sibmah,
With the weeping of Jazer;
I will drench you with my tears,
O Heshbon and Elealeh;
For battle cries have fallen
Over your summer fruits and your harvest.

10 Gladness is taken away,
And joy from the plentiful field;
In the vineyards there will be no singing,
Nor will there be shouting;
No treaders will tread out wine in the presses;
I have made their shouting cease.
11 Therefore my heart shall resound like a
harp for Moab,
And my inner being for Kir Heres.

12 And it shall come to pass,
When it is seen that Moab is weary on the
high place,

15:4 [t] Following Masoretic Text, Targum, and Vulgate; Septuagint and Syriac read *loins.*
15:5 [u] Or *The Third Eglath,* an unknown city (compare Jeremiah 48:34)
15:9 [v] Following Masoretic Text and Targum; Dead Sea Scrolls and Vulgate read *Dibon;* Septuagint reads *Rimon.* [w] Following Masoretic Text and Targum; Dead Sea Scrolls and Vulgate read *Dibon;* Septuagint reads *Rimon.*

That he will come to his sanctuary to pray;
But he will not prevail.

13This *is* the word which the LORD has spoken concerning Moab since that time. 14But now the LORD has
spoken, saying, "Within three years, as the years of a
hired man, the glory of Moab will be despised with all
that great multitude, and the remnant *will be* very
small *and* feeble."

Proclamation Against Syria and Israel

17 The burden against Damascus.

"Behold, Damascus will cease from *being* a city,
And it will be a ruinous heap.
2 The cities of Aroer *are* forsaken;[x]
They will be for flocks
Which lie down, and no one will
make *them* afraid.
3 The fortress also will cease from Ephraim,
The kingdom from Damascus,
And the remnant of Syria;
They will be as the glory of the children
of Israel,"
Says the LORD of hosts.

4 "In that day it shall come to pass
That the glory of Jacob will wane,
And the fatness of his flesh grow lean.
5 It shall be as when the harvester
gathers the grain,
And reaps the heads with his arm;
It shall be as he who gathers heads of grain
In the Valley of Rephaim.
6 Yet gleaning grapes will be left in it,
Like the shaking of an olive tree,
Two *or* three olives at the top of the
uppermost bough,
Four *or* five in its most fruitful branches,"
Says the LORD God of Israel.

7 In that day a man will look to his Maker,
And his eyes will have respect for the Holy
One of Israel.
8 He will not look to the altars,
The work of his hands;
He will not respect what his fingers have made,
Nor the wooden images[y] nor the incense altars.

9 In that day his strong cities will be
as a forsaken bough[z]
And an uppermost branch,[a]
Which they left because of the
children of Israel;
And there will be desolation.

10 Because you have forgotten the God
of your salvation,
And have not been mindful of the Rock of
your stronghold,
Therefore you will plant pleasant plants
And set out foreign seedlings;
11 In the day you will make your plant to grow,
And in the morning you will make your
seed to flourish;
But the harvest *will be* a heap of ruins
In the day of grief and desperate sorrow.

12 Woe to the multitude of many people
Who make a noise like the roar of the seas,
And to the rushing of nations
That make a rushing like the rushing of
mighty waters!
13 The nations will rush like the rushing
of many waters;
But *God* will rebuke them and they
will flee far away,
And be chased like the chaff of the mountains
before the wind,
Like a rolling thing before the whirlwind.
14 Then behold, at eventide, trouble!
And before the morning, he *is* no more.
This *is* the portion of those who plunder us,
And the lot of those who rob us.

Proclamation Against Ethiopia

18 Woe to the land shadowed with
buzzing wings,
Which *is* beyond the rivers of Ethiopia,
2 Which sends ambassadors by sea,
Even in vessels of reed on the waters, *saying,*
"Go, swift messengers, to a nation tall and
smooth *of skin,*
To a people terrible from their
beginning onward,
A nation powerful and treading down,
Whose land the rivers divide."

17:2 [x] Following Masoretic Text and Vulgate; Septuagint reads *It shall be forsaken forever;* Targum reads *Its cities shall be forsaken and desolate.*
17:8 [y] Hebrew *Asherim,* Canaanite deities
17:9 [z] Septuagint reads *Hivites;* Targum reads *laid waste;* Vulgate reads *as the plows.* [a] Septuagint reads *Amorites;* Targum reads *in ruins;* Vulgate reads *corn.*

3 All inhabitants of the world and dwellers
on the earth:
When he lifts up a banner on the mountains,
you see *it;*
And when he blows a trumpet, you hear *it.*
4 For so the LORD said to me,
"I will take My rest,
And I will look from My dwelling place
Like clear heat in sunshine,
Like a cloud of dew in the heat of harvest."
5 For before the harvest, when the bud is perfect
And the sour grape is ripening in the flower,
He will both cut off the sprigs
with pruning hooks
And take away *and* cut down the branches.
6 They will be left together for the mountain
birds of prey
And for the beasts of the earth;
The birds of prey will summer on them,
And all the beasts of the earth will
winter on them.

7 In that time a present will be brought to the
LORD of hosts
From[b] a people tall and smooth *of skin,*
And from a people terrible from
their beginning onward,
A nation powerful and treading down,
Whose land the rivers divide—
To the place of the name of the LORD of hosts,
To Mount Zion.

Proclamation Against Egypt

19 The burden against Egypt.

Behold, the LORD rides on a swift cloud,
And will come into Egypt;
The idols of Egypt will totter at His presence,
And the heart of Egypt will melt in its midst.

2 "I will set Egyptians against Egyptians;
Everyone will fight against his brother,
And everyone against his neighbor,
City against city, kingdom against kingdom.
3 The spirit of Egypt will fail in its midst;
I will destroy their counsel,
And they will consult the idols
and the charmers,
The mediums and the sorcerers.
4 And the Egyptians I will give
Into the hand of a cruel master,
And a fierce king will rule over them,"
Says the Lord, the LORD of hosts.

5 The waters will fail from the sea,
And the river will be wasted and dried up.
6 The rivers will turn foul;
The brooks of defense will be emptied
and dried up;
The reeds and rushes will wither.
7 The papyrus reeds by the River,[c] by the mouth
of the River,
And everything sown by the River,
Will wither, be driven away, and be no more.
8 The fishermen also will mourn;
All those will lament who cast hooks
into the River,
And they will languish who spread nets
on the waters.
9 Moreover those who work in fine flax
And those who weave fine fabric
will be ashamed;
10 And its foundations will be broken.
All who make wages *will be* troubled of soul.

11 Surely the princes of Zoan *are* fools;
Pharaoh's wise counselors give foolish counsel.
How do you say to Pharaoh, "I *am* the son
of the wise,
The son of ancient kings?"
12 Where *are* they?
Where are your wise men?
Let them tell you now,
And let them know what the LORD of hosts has
purposed against Egypt.
13 The princes of Zoan have become fools;
The princes of Noph[d] are deceived;
They have also deluded Egypt,
Those who are the mainstay of its tribes.
14 The LORD has mingled a perverse spirit
in her midst;
And they have caused Egypt to err in
all her work,
As a drunken man staggers in his vomit.
15 Neither will there be *any* work for Egypt,
Which the head or tail,
Palm branch or bulrush, may do.[e]

18:7 [b] Following Dead Sea Scrolls, Septuagint, and Vulgate; Masoretic Text omits *From;* Targum reads *To.*
19:7 [c] That is, the Nile
19:13 [d] That is, ancient Memphis
19:15 [e] Compare Isaiah 9:14–16

16 In that day Egypt will be like women, and will be
afraid and fear because of the waving of the hand of
the LORD of hosts, which He waves over it. 17 And the
land of Judah will be a terror to Egypt; everyone who
makes mention of it will be afraid in himself, because
of the counsel of the LORD of hosts which He has determined against it.

Egypt, Assyria, and Israel Blessed

18 In that day five cities in the land of Egypt will speak
the language of Canaan and swear by the LORD of
hosts; one will be called the City of Destruction.[f]
19 In that day there will be an altar to the LORD in the
midst of the land of Egypt, and a pillar to the LORD at its
border. 20 And it will be for a sign and for a witness to
the LORD of hosts in the land of Egypt; for they will cry
to the LORD because of the oppressors, and He will send
them a Savior and a Mighty One, and He will deliver
them. 21 Then the LORD will be known to Egypt, and the
Egyptians will know the LORD in that day, and will make
sacrifice and offering; yes, they will make a vow to the
LORD and perform *it.* 22 And the LORD will strike Egypt,
He will strike and heal *it;* they will return to the LORD,
and He will be entreated by them and heal them.
23 In that day there will be a highway from Egypt to
Assyria, and the Assyrian will come into Egypt and the
Egyptian into Assyria, and the Egyptians will serve
with the Assyrians.
24 In that day Israel will be one of three with Egypt
and Assyria—a blessing in the midst of the land,
25 whom the LORD of hosts shall bless, saying, "Blessed
is Egypt My people, and Assyria the work of My
hands, and Israel My inheritance."

The Sign Against Egypt and Ethiopia

20 In the year that Tartan[g] came to Ashdod, when
Sargon the king of Assyria sent him, and he
fought against Ashdod and took it, 2 at the same time the
LORD spoke by Isaiah the son of Amoz, saying, "Go, and
remove the sackcloth from your body, and take your
sandals off your feet." And he did so, walking naked
and barefoot.
3 Then the LORD said, "Just as My servant Isaiah has
walked naked and barefoot three years *for* a sign and a
wonder against Egypt and Ethiopia, 4 so shall the king
of Assyria lead away the Egyptians as prisoners and
the Ethiopians as captives, young and old, naked and
barefoot, with their buttocks uncovered, to the shame
of Egypt. 5 Then they shall be afraid and ashamed of
Ethiopia their expectation and Egypt their glory. 6 And
the inhabitant of this territory will say in that day,
'Surely such *is* our expectation, wherever we flee for
help to be delivered from the king of Assyria; and how
shall we escape?' "

The Fall of Babylon Proclaimed

21 The burden against the Wilderness of the Sea.

As whirlwinds in the South pass through,
So it comes from the desert, from
a terrible land.
2 A distressing vision is declared to me;
The treacherous dealer deals treacherously,
And the plunderer plunders.
Go up, O Elam!
Besiege, O Media!
All its sighing I have made to cease.

3 Therefore my loins are filled with pain;
Pangs have taken hold of me, like the pangs of
a woman in labor.
I was distressed when *I* heard *it;*
I was dismayed when *I* saw *it.*
4 My heart wavered, fearfulness frightened me;
The night for which I longed He turned into
fear for me.
5 Prepare the table,
Set a watchman in the tower,
Eat and drink.
Arise, you princes,
Anoint the shield!

6 For thus has the Lord said to me:
"Go, set a watchman,
Let him declare what he sees."
7 And he saw a chariot *with* a pair of horsemen,
A chariot of donkeys, *and* a chariot of camels,
And he listened earnestly with great care.
8 Then he cried, "A lion,[h] my Lord!
I stand continually on the watchtower
in the daytime;
I have sat at my post every night.
9 And look, here comes a chariot of men *with* a
pair of horsemen!"
Then he answered and said,
"Babylon is fallen, is fallen!
And all the carved images of her gods
He has broken to the ground."

19:18 [f] Some Hebrew manuscripts, Arabic, Dead Sea Scrolls, Targum, and Vulgate read *Sun;* Septuagint reads *Asedek* (literally *Righteousness*).
20:1 [g] Or *the Commander in Chief*
21:8 [h] Dead Sea Scrolls read *Then the observer cried.*

10 Oh, my threshing and the grain of my floor!
That which I have heard from the LORD of hosts,
The God of Israel,
I have declared to you.

Proclamation Against Edom

11 The burden against Dumah.

He calls to me out of Seir,
"Watchman, what of the night?
Watchman, what of the night?"
12 The watchman said,
"The morning comes, and also the night.
If you will inquire, inquire;
Return! Come back!"

Proclamation Against Arabia

13 The burden against Arabia.

In the forest in Arabia you will lodge,
O you traveling companies of Dedanites.
14 O inhabitants of the land of Tema,
Bring water to him who is thirsty;
With their bread they met him who fled.
15 For they fled from the swords, from the drawn sword,
From the bent bow, and from the distress of war.

16 For thus the LORD has said to me: "Within a year, according to the year
of a hired man, all the glory of Kedar will fail; 17 and the remainder of the
number of archers, the mighty men of the people of Kedar, will be diminished; for the LORD God of Israel has spoken *it*."

Proclamation Against Jerusalem

22 The burden against the Valley of Vision.

What ails you now, that you have all gone up to the housetops,
2 You who are full of noise,
A tumultuous city, a joyous city?
Your slain *men are* not slain with the sword,
Nor dead in battle.
3 All your rulers have fled together;
They are captured by the archers.
All who are found in you are bound together;
They have fled from afar.
4 Therefore I said, "Look away from me,
I will weep bitterly;
Do not labor to comfort me
Because of the plundering of the daughter of my people."

5 For *it is* a day of trouble and treading down and perplexity
By the Lord GOD of hosts

LIFE LESSON

Isaiah 22:1–23:18

SITUATION Isaiah foretold the destruction of Jerusalem and Tyre. Both cities would be destroyed for ignoring God and trusting in their own ingenuity.

OBSERVATION When faced with a dilemma, ask God for his help and guidance rather than depending on your own resources.

INSPIRATION It is the same now as of old. Christ in His visible presence has left us, but the Ark of His Covenant remains, His sacramental presence. "Lo, I am with you always, even unto the end of the world." Remember that word, "always." Regardless of circumstances, He is still there. Another word in your New Testament says, "I will not leave you destitute, I will come to you." . . .

Who cares? To whom can you go? Where are decisions of right and wrong made? How can I fight on if there is no prevailing power of righteousness to check the erosion of sin?

How are we to go against our enemies? Shall we try it in our own strength?

. . .You can't do it by yourself! You can't overcome Satan in your own strength. *Divine help is always available.*

Live the life, and call on God. That's the combination that spells victory.

. . . If we go against our spiritual foes, we must go in the strength of God, having first put away from our hearts the evil we have done, through sincere repentance. *Faith and a conscience void of offense toward God and man make a winning combination.*

Are you in trouble? Has temptation backed you into a corner? Is your marriage partner unsaved? Has the one who promised to love you, honor you, and protect you, deserted you?

. . . Seek refuge and strength in God! . . . You are not alone. Another shares your battle. He will support you and bring you through to victory. . . .

None of us can make it through without God's help. *I need an abiding sense of God's presence.* I need a "cloud" by day and a "pillar of fire" by night. In the gloomiest hour, when the lights of this

Continued

world have gone out, I need to know that He is there watching over me. . . .

Sinner, what is your hope? *Who will open a path for you at death*? What friend will part the waters and let you through? . . . You'll need to know that Jesus never fails. I ask you to turn toward Him now.

(From *Revivaltime Pulpit* compiled by C. M. Ward)

APPLICATION Pride can keep us from asking God for help. Are you too self-confident? Too self-assured? God asks you to give up your self-dependence and give him your heart.

EXPLORATION God's Help—Genesis 18:14; Exodus 4:14; Leviticus 20:22-23; Deuteronomy 7:21-24; Psalm 9:13-14; 115:9-11; Jeremiah 14:1; Matthew 9:23-26; Luke 18:35.

In the Valley of Vision—
Breaking down the walls
And of crying to the mountain.
6 Elam bore the quiver
With chariots of men *and* horsemen,
And Kir uncovered the shield.
7 It shall come to pass *that* your choicest valleys
Shall be full of chariots,
And the horsemen shall set themselves in array at the gate.

8 He removed the protection of Judah.
You looked in that day to the armor of the House of the Forest;
9 You also saw the damage to the city of David,
That it was great;
And you gathered together the waters of the lower pool.
10 You numbered the houses of Jerusalem,
And the houses you broke down
To fortify the wall.
11 You also made a reservoir between the two walls
For the water of the old pool.
But you did not look to its Maker,
Nor did you have respect for Him who fashioned it long ago.

12 And in that day the Lord GOD of hosts
Called for weeping and for mourning,
For baldness and for girding with sackcloth.
13 But instead, joy and gladness,
Slaying oxen and killing sheep,
Eating meat and drinking wine:
"Let us eat and drink, for tomorrow we die!"

14 Then it was revealed in my hearing by the LORD of hosts,
"Surely for this iniquity there will be no atonement for you,
Even to your death," says the Lord GOD of hosts.

The Judgment on Shebna

15 Thus says the Lord GOD of hosts:

"Go, proceed to this steward,
To Shebna, who *is* over the house, *and say:*
16 'What have you here, and whom have you here,
That you have hewn a sepulcher here,
As he who hews himself a sepulcher on high,
Who carves a tomb for himself in a rock?
17 Indeed, the LORD will throw you away violently,
O mighty man,
And will surely seize you.
18 He will surely turn violently and toss you like a ball
Into a large country;
There you shall die, and there your glorious chariots
Shall be the shame of your master's house.

19 So I will drive you out of your office,
And from your position he will pull you down.[i]

20 'Then it shall be in that day,
That I will call My servant Eliakim the
son of Hilkiah;
21 I will clothe him with your robe
And strengthen him with your belt;
I will commit your responsibility into his hand.
He shall be a father to the inhabitants
of Jerusalem
And to the house of Judah.
22 The key of the house of David
I will lay on his shoulder;
So he shall open, and no one shall shut;
And he shall shut, and no one shall open.
23 I will fasten him *as* a peg in a secure place,
And he will become a glorious throne to his
father's house.

24 'They will hang on him all the glory of his father's
house, the offspring and the posterity, all vessels of
small quantity, from the cups to all the pitchers. 25 In
that day,' says the LORD of hosts, 'the peg that is fastened in the secure place will be removed and be cut
down and fall, and the burden that *was* on it will be
cut off; for the LORD has spoken.' "

Proclamation Against Tyre

23 The burden against Tyre.

Wail, you ships of Tarshish!
For it is laid waste,
So that there is no house, no harbor;
From the land of Cyprus[j] it is revealed to them.

2 Be still, you inhabitants of the coastland,
You merchants of Sidon,
Whom those who cross the sea have filled.[k]
3 And on great waters the grain of Shihor,
The harvest of the River,[l] *is* her revenue;
And she is a marketplace for the nations.

4 Be ashamed, O Sidon;
For the sea has spoken,
The strength of the sea, saying,
"I do not labor, nor bring forth children;
Neither do I rear young men,
Nor bring up virgins."

5 When the report *reaches* Egypt,
They also will be in agony at the report of Tyre.

6 Cross over to Tarshish;
Wail, you inhabitants of the coastland!
7 *Is* this your joyous *city,*
Whose antiquity *is* from ancient days,
Whose feet carried her far off to dwell?
8 Who has taken this counsel against Tyre,
the crowning *city,*
Whose merchants *are* princes,
Whose traders *are* the honorable of the earth?
9 The LORD of hosts has purposed it,
To bring to dishonor the pride of all glory,
To bring into contempt all the honorable
of the earth.

10 Overflow through your land like the River,[m]
O daughter of Tarshish;
There is no more strength.
11 He stretched out His hand over the sea,
He shook the kingdoms;
The LORD has given a commandment
against Canaan
To destroy its strongholds.
12 And He said, "You will rejoice no more,
O you oppressed virgin daughter of Sidon.
Arise, cross over to Cyprus;
There also you will have no rest."

13 Behold, the land of the Chaldeans,
This people *which* was not;
Assyria founded it for wild beasts
of the desert.
They set up its towers,
They raised up its palaces,
And brought it to ruin.

14 Wail, you ships of Tarshish!
For your strength is laid waste.

15 Now it shall come to pass in that day that Tyre will
be forgotten seventy years, according to the days of
one king. At the end of seventy years it will happen to
Tyre as *in* the song of the harlot:

16 "Take a harp, go about the city,
You forgotten harlot;
Make sweet melody, sing many songs,
That you may be remembered."

22:19 [i] Septuagint omits *he will pull you down;* Syriac, Targum, and Vulgate read *I will pull you down.*
23:1 [j] Hebrew *Kittim,* western lands, especially Cyprus
23:2 [k] Following Masoretic Text and Vulgate; Septuagint and Targum read *Passing over the water;* Dead Sea Scrolls read *Your messengers passing over the sea.*
23:3 [l] That is, the Nile
23:10 [m] That is, the Nile

LIFE LESSON
Isaiah 24:1–27:13

SITUATION God would step in and judge sin. Life would not be business as usual. God, the deliverer and comforter of Zion, would punish oppressors and preserve his people.

OBSERVATION Sin corrupts the world. But God will judge the world and destroy death. God's people will enjoy eternity with him.

INSPIRATION You were created in the image and likeness of God. You were made for God's fellowship and your heart can never be satisfied without His communion. Just as iron is attracted to a magnet, the soul in its state of hunger is drawn to God. Though you, like thousands of others, may feel in the state of sin that the world is more alluring and more to your liking, some day—perhaps even now as you read these words—you will acknowledge that there is something deep down inside you which cannot be satisfied by the alloy of earth. Then with David, the Psalmist who had sampled the delicacies of sin and had found them unsatisfying, you will say, "Oh God, you are my God; early will I seek you: my soul thirsteth for you, my flesh longs for you in a dry and thirsty land, where there is no water."

(*From Day by Day with Billy Graham* by Joan W. Brown)

APPLICATION How has moral sin entered your community? Find ways to stand for what is right: rent movies from stores that do not carry adult movies. Shop at the convenience store that does not carry pornography. Call your mayor and share that you do not want any more adult book shops. Make your godly preference known through your wallet and your voice.

EXPLORATION Sin—Genesis 3:6-7; 9:20-27; Joshua 7:24-25; Judges 4:1; 1 Chronicles 9:1.

17 And it shall be, at the end of seventy years, that the LORD will deal with
Tyre. She will return to her hire, and commit fornication with all the kingdoms of the world on the face of the earth. 18 Her gain and her pay will be set
apart for the LORD; it will not be treasured nor laid up, for her gain will be for
those who dwell before the LORD, to eat sufficiently, and for fine clothing.

Impending Judgment on the Earth

24 Behold, the LORD makes the earth empty and makes it waste,
Distorts its surface
And scatters abroad its inhabitants.
2 And it shall be:
As with the people, so with the priest;
As with the servant, so with his master;
As with the maid, so with her mistress;
As with the buyer, so with the seller;
As with the lender, so with the borrower;
As with the creditor, so with the debtor.
3 The land shall be entirely emptied and utterly plundered,
For the LORD has spoken this word.

4 The earth mourns *and* fades away,
The world languishes *and* fades away;
The haughty people of the earth languish.
5 The earth is also defiled under its inhabitants,
Because they have transgressed the laws,
Changed the ordinance,
Broken the everlasting covenant.
6 Therefore the curse has devoured the earth,
And those who dwell in it are desolate.
Therefore the inhabitants of the earth are burned,
And few men *are* left.

7 The new wine fails, the vine languishes,
All the merry-hearted sigh.
8 The mirth of the tambourine ceases,
The noise of the jubilant ends,
The joy of the harp ceases.
9 They shall not drink wine with a song;
Strong drink is bitter to those who drink it.
10 The city of confusion is broken down;
Every house is shut up, so that none may go in.
11 *There is* a cry for wine in the streets,
All joy is darkened,
The mirth of the land is gone.
12 In the city desolation is left,
And the gate is stricken with destruction.
13 When it shall be thus in the midst of the land among the people,
It shall be like the shaking of an olive tree,
Like the gleaning of grapes when the vintage is done.

14 They shall lift up their voice, they shall sing;
For the majesty of the LORD
They shall cry aloud from the sea.
15 Therefore glorify the LORD in the dawning light,

The name of the LORD God of Israel in the
coastlands of the sea.
16 From the ends of the earth we
have heard songs:
"Glory to the righteous!"
But I said, "I am ruined, ruined!
Woe to me!
The treacherous dealers have
dealt treacherously,
Indeed, the treacherous dealers have dealt
very treacherously."
17 Fear and the pit and the snare
Are upon you, O inhabitant of the earth.
18 And it shall be
That he who flees from the noise of the fear
Shall fall into the pit,
And he who comes up from the midst
of the pit
Shall be caught in the snare;
For the windows from on high are open,
And the foundations of the earth are shaken.
19 The earth is violently broken,
The earth is split open,
The earth is shaken exceedingly.
20 The earth shall reel to and fro like a drunkard,
And shall totter like a hut;
Its transgression shall be heavy upon it,
And it will fall, and not rise again.
21 It shall come to pass in that day
That the LORD will punish on high the host
of exalted ones,
And on the earth the kings of the earth.
22 They will be gathered together,
As prisoners are gathered in the pit,
And will be shut up in the prison;
After many days they will be punished.
23 Then the moon will be disgraced
And the sun ashamed;
For the LORD of hosts will reign
On Mount Zion and in Jerusalem
And before His elders, gloriously.

Praise to God

25 O LORD, You *are* my God.
I will exalt You,
I will praise Your name,
For You have done wonderful *things;*
Your counsels of old *are* faithfulness *and* truth.
2 For You have made a city a ruin,
A fortified city a ruin,
A palace of foreigners to be a city no more;
It will never be rebuilt.
3 Therefore the strong people will glorify You;
The city of the terrible nations will fear You.
4 For You have been a strength to the poor,
A strength to the needy in his distress,
A refuge from the storm,
A shade from the heat;
For the blast of the terrible ones *is* as a storm
against the wall.
5 You will reduce the noise of aliens,
As heat in a dry place;
As heat in the shadow of a cloud,
The song of the terrible ones
will be diminished.
6 And in this mountain
The LORD of hosts will make for all people
A feast of choice pieces,
A feast of wines on the lees,
Of fat things full of marrow,
Of well-refined wines on the lees.
7 And He will destroy on this mountain
The surface of the covering cast over all people,
And the veil that is spread over all nations.
8 He will swallow up death forever,
And the Lord GOD will wipe away tears
from all faces;
The rebuke of His people
He will take away from all the earth;
For the LORD has spoken.
9 And it will be said in that day:
"Behold, this *is* our God;
We have waited for Him, and He will save us.
This *is* the LORD;
We have waited for Him;
We will be glad and rejoice in His salvation."
10 For on this mountain the hand of the
LORD will rest,
And Moab shall be trampled down
under Him,
As straw is trampled down for the refuse heap.
11 And He will spread out His hands
in their midst
As a swimmer reaches out to swim,
And He will bring down their pride
Together with the trickery of their hands.
12 The fortress of the high fort of your walls
He will bring down, lay low,
And bring to the ground, down to the dust.

A Song of Salvation

26 In that day this song will be sung in the land of Judah:
"We have a strong city;
God will appoint salvation *for* walls
and bulwarks.
2 Open the gates,
That the righteous nation which keeps the
truth may enter in.
3 You will keep *him* in perfect peace,
Whose mind *is* stayed *on You,*
Because he trusts in You.
4 Trust in the LORD forever,
For in YAH, the LORD, *is* everlasting strength.[n]
5 For He brings down those who dwell on high,
The lofty city;
He lays it low,
He lays it low to the ground,
He brings it down to the dust.
6 The foot shall tread it down—
The feet of the poor
And the steps of the needy."

7 The way of the just *is* uprightness;
O Most Upright,
You weigh the path of the just.
8 Yes, in the way of Your judgments,
O LORD, we have waited for You;
The desire of *our* soul *is* for Your name
And for the remembrance of You.
9 With my soul I have desired You in the night,
Yes, by my spirit within me I will
seek You early;
For when Your judgments *are* in the earth,
The inhabitants of the world will
learn righteousness.

10 Let grace be shown to the wicked,
Yet he will not learn righteousness;
In the land of uprightness he will deal unjustly,
And will not behold the majesty of the LORD.
11 LORD, *when* Your hand is lifted up, they
will not see.
But they will see and be ashamed
For *their* envy of people;
Yes, the fire of Your enemies shall devour them.

12 LORD, You will establish peace for us,
For You have also done all our works in us.
13 O LORD our God, masters besides You
Have had dominion over us;
But by You only we make mention
of Your name.
14 *They are* dead, they will not live;
They are deceased, they will not rise.
Therefore You have punished
and destroyed them,
And made all their memory to perish.
15 You have increased the nation, O LORD,
You have increased the nation;
You are glorified;
You have expanded all the borders of the land.

16 LORD, in trouble they have visited You,
They poured out a prayer *when* Your
chastening *was* upon them.
17 As a woman with child
Is in pain and cries out in her pangs,
When she draws near the time of her delivery,
So have we been in Your sight, O LORD.
18 We have been with child, we have been in pain;
We have, as it were, brought forth wind;
We have not accomplished any deliverance
in the earth,
Nor have the inhabitants of the world fallen.

19 Your dead shall live;
Together with my dead body[o] they shall arise.
Awake and sing, you who dwell in dust;
For your dew *is like* the dew of herbs,
And the earth shall cast out the dead.

Take Refuge from the Coming Judgment

20 Come, my people, enter your chambers,
And shut your doors behind you;
Hide yourself, as it were, for a little moment,
Until the indignation is past.
21 For behold, the LORD comes out of His place
To punish the inhabitants of the earth
for their iniquity;
The earth will also disclose her blood,
And will no more cover her slain.

27 In that day the LORD with His severe sword,
great and strong,
Will punish Leviathan the fleeing serpent,
Leviathan that twisted serpent;
And He will slay the reptile that *is* in the sea.

26:4 [n] Or *Rock of Ages*
26:19 [o] Following Masoretic Text and Vulgate; Syriac and Targum read *their dead bodies;* Septuagint reads *those in the tombs.*

The Restoration of Israel

2 In that day sing to her,
"A vineyard of red wine![p]
3 I, the LORD, keep it,
I water it every moment;
Lest any hurt it,
I keep it night and day.
4 Fury *is* not in Me.
Who would set briers *and* thorns
Against Me in battle?
I would go through them,
I would burn them together.
5 Or let him take hold of My strength,
That he may make peace with Me;
And he shall make peace with Me."

6 Those who come He shall cause to take
root in Jacob;
Israel shall blossom and bud,
And fill the face of the world with fruit.

7 Has He struck Israel as He struck those
who struck him?
Or has He been slain according to the
slaughter of those who were slain by Him?
8 In measure, by sending it away,
You contended with it.
He removes *it* by His rough wind
In the day of the east wind.
9 Therefore by this the iniquity of Jacob
will be covered;
And this *is* all the fruit of taking away his sin:
When he makes all the stones of the altar
Like chalkstones that are beaten to dust,
Wooden images[q] and incense altars
shall not stand.

10 Yet the fortified city *will be* desolate,
The habitation forsaken and left like
a wilderness;
There the calf will feed, and there it will lie down
And consume its branches.
11 When its boughs are withered, they will
be broken off;
The women come *and* set them on fire.
For it *is* a people of no understanding;
Therefore He who made them will not have
mercy on them,
And He who formed them will show
them no favor.

12 And it shall come to pass in that day
That the LORD will thresh,
From the channel of the River[r] to the Brook
of Egypt;
And you will be gathered one by one,
O you children of Israel.

13 So it shall be in that day:
The great trumpet will be blown;
They will come, who are about to perish
in the land of Assyria,
And they who are outcasts in the land
of Egypt,
And shall worship the LORD in the holy mount
at Jerusalem.

Woe to Ephraim and Jerusalem

28 Woe to the crown of pride, to the
drunkards of Ephraim,
Whose glorious beauty *is* a fading flower
Which *is* at the head of the verdant valleys,
To those who are overcome with wine!
2 Behold, the Lord has a mighty and strong one,
Like a tempest of hail and a destroying storm,
Like a flood of mighty waters overflowing,
Who will bring *them* down to the earth with
His hand.
3 The crown of pride, the drunkards of
Ephraim,
Will be trampled underfoot;
4 And the glorious beauty is a fading flower
Which *is* at the head of the verdant valley,
Like the first fruit before the summer,
Which an observer sees;
He eats it up while it is still in his hand.

5 In that day the LORD of hosts will be
For a crown of glory and a diadem of beauty
To the remnant of His people,
6 For a spirit of justice to him who sits
in judgment,
And for strength to those who turn back the
battle at the gate.

7 But they also have erred through wine,
And through intoxicating drink are
out of the way;

27:2 [p] Following Masoretic Text (Kittel's *Biblia Hebraica*), Bomberg, and Vulgate; Masoretic Text (*Biblia Hebraica Stuttgartensia*), some Hebrew manuscripts, and Septuagint read *delight;* Targum reads *choice vineyard.*
27:9 [q] Hebrew *Asherim,* Canaanite deities
27:12 [r] That is, the Euphrates

Life Lesson

Isaiah 28:1–31:9

SITUATION God warned Judah by using Israel as an example. God offered peace and protection if Israel repented and turned to him, but the people jeered and scoffed at God's Word. They preferred to trust Assyria and Egypt.

OBSERVATION God punishes those who reject him and rebel against him. But the repentant will experience his blessings.

INSPIRATION Very few people know the power of surrender. Most of us know only the power of resistance. We derive a kind of negative energy from holding out.

For example, we may resist our parents. We feel strong when we break the family's rules or defy our parents' admonitions. If they tell us not to stay out too late, we assert ourselves by coming home later than they advised. In a similar manner, we may defy spouses, teachers, bosses, the police, and even God.

God asks us to love him and obey his commandments (John 14:15; the book of 1 John), but we find power in "doing it our way." I remember one physically large person who stood on a chair in my office so he could get closer to God. Then he shook his fist and yelled, "I dare you, God!" Most of

The priest and the prophet have erred through intoxicating drink,
They are swallowed up by wine,
They are out of the way through intoxicating drink;
They err in vision, they stumble *in* judgment.
8 For all tables are full of vomit *and* filth;
No place *is clean.*

9 "Whom will he teach knowledge?
And whom will he make to understand the message?
Those *just* weaned from milk?
Those *just* drawn from the breasts?
10 For precept *must be* upon precept, precept upon precept,
Line upon line, line upon line,
Here a little, there a little."

11 For with stammering lips and another tongue
He will speak to this people,
12 To whom He said, "This *is* the rest *with which*
You may cause the weary to rest,"
And, "This *is* the refreshing";
Yet they would not hear.
13 But the word of the LORD was to them,
"Precept upon precept, precept upon precept,
Line upon line, line upon line,
Here a little, there a little,"
That they might go and fall backward, and be broken
And snared and caught.

14 Therefore hear the word of the LORD, you scornful men,
Who rule this people who *are* in Jerusalem,
15 Because you have said, "We have made a covenant with death,
And with Sheol we are in agreement.
When the overflowing scourge passes through,
It will not come to us,
For we have made lies our refuge,
And under falsehood we have hidden ourselves."

A Cornerstone in Zion

16 Therefore thus says the Lord GOD:

"Behold, I lay in Zion a stone for a foundation,
A tried stone, a precious cornerstone, a sure foundation;
Whoever believes will not act hastily.
17 Also I will make justice the measuring line,
And righteousness the plummet;
The hail will sweep away the refuge of lies,
And the waters will overflow the hiding place.
18 Your covenant with death will be annulled,
And your agreement with Sheol will not stand;
When the overflowing scourge passes through,
Then you will be trampled down by it.

19 As often as it goes out it will take you;
For morning by morning it will pass over,
And by day and by night;
It will be a terror just to understand the report."

20 For the bed is too short to stretch out *on*,
And the covering so narrow that one cannot wrap himself *in it*.
21 For the LORD will rise up as *at* Mount Perazim,
He will be angry as in the Valley of Gibeon—
That He may do His work, His awesome work,
And bring to pass His act, His unusual act.
22 Now therefore, do not be mockers,
Lest your bonds be made strong;
For I have heard from the Lord GOD of hosts,
A destruction determined even upon the whole earth.

Listen to the Teaching of God

23 Give ear and hear my voice,
Listen and hear my speech.
24 Does the plowman keep plowing all day to sow?
Does he keep turning his soil and breaking the clods?
25 When he has leveled its surface,
Does he not sow the black cummin
And scatter the cummin,
Plant the wheat in rows,
The barley in the appointed place,
And the spelt in its place?
26 For He instructs him in right judgment,
His God teaches him.

27 For the black cummin is not threshed with a threshing sledge,
Nor is a cartwheel rolled over the cummin;
But the black cummin is beaten out with a stick,
And the cummin with a rod.
28 Bread *flour* must be ground;
Therefore he does not thresh it forever,
Break *it with* his cartwheel,
Or crush it *with* his horsemen.
29 This also comes from the LORD of hosts,
Who is wonderful in counsel *and* excellent in guidance.

Woe to Jerusalem

29 "Woe to Ariel,[s] to Ariel, the city *where* David dwelt!
Add year to year;
Let feasts come around.
2 Yet I will distress Ariel;
There shall be heaviness and sorrow,
And it shall be to Me as Ariel.
3 I will encamp against you all around,
I will lay siege against you with a mound,
And I will raise siegeworks against you.

29:1 [s] That is, Jerusalem

us choose more subtle ways to defy God, but we defy him nonetheless.

. . . God looks the same upon all those who submit to him. God knows he made people in different ways: some short, some tall; some outgoing, some reflective; some emotional, some intellectual. The blessed part is that God made all of us, and he knows we will come to him in different ways. What is important is that we arrive.

When I surrender to a purpose I gain power, because once I surrender I am freed from the conflict of indecision. After I surrender to Jesus Christ, no longer is part of me resisting his call. I am able to be twice as forceful, because all of me is now headed in the same direction.

(From "How Do I Submit to Jesus Christ?" by David and Cheryl Aspy in *Practical Christianity*)

APPLICATION How does your life say "God, I don't trust you": in money matters, relationships, honesty, entertainment choices? Tell God all of your worries. Admit your defiance and ask him for help.

EXPLORATION Repentance—1 Kings 21:29; 1 Chronicles 21:8; Ezra 10:2-4; Psalm 80:3, 7, 19; Matthew 3:1-6; Luke 19:1-8; Acts 3:19-20; 2 Corinthians 7:10.

4 You shall be brought down,
You shall speak out of the ground;
Your speech shall be low, out of the dust;
Your voice shall be like a medium's,
out of the ground;
And your speech shall whisper out of the dust.
5 "Moreover the multitude of your foes
Shall be like fine dust,
And the multitude of the terrible ones
Like chaff that passes away;
Yes, it shall be in an instant, suddenly.
6 You will be punished by the LORD of hosts
With thunder and earthquake and great noise,
With storm and tempest
And the flame of devouring fire.
7 The multitude of all the nations who fight
against Ariel,
Even all who fight against her and
her fortress,
And distress her,
Shall be as a dream of a night vision.
8 It shall even be as when a hungry man dreams,
And look—he eats;
But he awakes, and his soul is still empty;
Or as when a thirsty man dreams,
And look—he drinks;
But he awakes, and indeed *he is* faint,
And his soul still craves:
So the multitude of all the nations shall be,
Who fight against Mount Zion."

The Blindness of Disobedience

9 Pause and wonder!
Blind yourselves and be blind!
They are drunk, but not with wine;
They stagger, but not with intoxicating drink.
10 For the LORD has poured out on you
The spirit of deep sleep,
And has closed your eyes, namely,
the prophets;
And He has covered your heads, *namely,*
the seers.

11 The whole vision has become to you like the
words of a book that is sealed, which *men* deliver to
one who is literate, saying, "Read this, please."
And he says, "I cannot, for it *is* sealed."
12 Then the book is delivered to one who is illiterate,
saying, "Read this, please."
And he says, "I am not literate."

13 Therefore the Lord said:

"Inasmuch as these people draw near with
their mouths
And honor Me with their lips,
But have removed their hearts far from Me,
And their fear toward Me is taught by the
commandment of men,
14 Therefore, behold, I will again do
a marvelous work
Among this people,
A marvelous work and a wonder;
For the wisdom of their wise *men* shall perish,
And the understanding of their prudent *men*
shall be hidden."

15 Woe to those who seek deep to hide their
counsel far from the LORD,
And their works are in the dark;
They say, "Who sees us?" and,
"Who knows us?"
16 Surely you have things turned around!
Shall the potter be esteemed as the clay;
For shall the thing made say of him
who made it,
"He did not make me"?
Or shall the thing formed say of him who
formed it,
"He has no understanding"?

Future Recovery of Wisdom

17 *Is* it not yet a very little while
Till Lebanon shall be turned into
a fruitful field,
And the fruitful field be esteemed as a forest?
18 In that day the deaf shall hear the words
of the book,
And the eyes of the blind shall see out of
obscurity and out of darkness.
19 The humble also shall increase *their* joy
in the LORD,
And the poor among men shall rejoice
In the Holy One of Israel.
20 For the terrible one is brought to nothing,
The scornful one is consumed,
And all who watch for iniquity are cut off—
21 Who make a man an offender by a word,
And lay a snare for him who reproves
in the gate,
And turn aside the just by empty words.

[22]Therefore thus says the LORD, who redeemed Abraham, concerning the house of Jacob:

"Jacob shall not now be ashamed,
Nor shall his face now grow pale;
23 But when he sees his children,
The work of My hands, in his midst,
They will hallow My name,
And hallow the Holy One of Jacob,
And fear the God of Israel.
24 These also who erred in spirit will
come to understanding,
And those who complained will
learn doctrine."

Futile Confidence in Egypt

30 "Woe to the rebellious children," says
the LORD,
"Who take counsel, but not of Me,
And who devise plans, but not of My Spirit,
That they may add sin to sin;
2 Who walk to go down to Egypt,
And have not asked My advice,
To strengthen themselves in the strength
of Pharaoh,
And to trust in the shadow of Egypt!
3 Therefore the strength of Pharaoh
Shall be your shame,
And trust in the shadow of Egypt
Shall be *your* humiliation.
4 For his princes were at Zoan,
And his ambassadors came to Hanes.
5 They were all ashamed of a people *who* could
not benefit them,
Or be help or benefit,
But a shame and also a reproach."

[6]The burden against the beasts of the South.

Through a land of trouble and anguish,
From which *came* the lioness and lion,
The viper and fiery flying serpent,
They will carry their riches on the backs of
young donkeys,
And their treasures on the humps of camels,
To a people *who* shall not profit;
7 For the Egyptians shall help in vain and to
no purpose.
Therefore I have called her
Rahab-Hem-Shebeth.[t]

A Rebellious People

8 Now go, write it before them on a tablet,
And note it on a scroll,
That it may be for time to come,
Forever and ever:
9 That this *is* a rebellious people,
Lying children,
Children *who* will not hear the law of the LORD;
10 Who say to the seers, "Do not see,"
And to the prophets, "Do not prophesy to us
right things;
Speak to us smooth things, prophesy deceits.
11 Get out of the way,
Turn aside from the path,
Cause the Holy One of Israel
To cease from before us."

[12]Therefore thus says the Holy One of Israel:

"Because you despise this word,
And trust in oppression and perversity,
And rely on them,
13 Therefore this iniquity shall be to you
Like a breach ready to fall,
A bulge in a high wall,
Whose breaking comes suddenly, in an instant.
14 And He shall break it like the breaking of the
potter's vessel,
Which is broken in pieces;
He shall not spare.
So there shall not be found among
its fragments
A shard to take fire from the hearth,
Or to take water from the cistern."

[15]For thus says the Lord GOD, the Holy One of Israel:

"In returning and rest you shall be saved;
In quietness and confidence shall
be your strength."
But you would not,
16 And you said, "No, for we will flee
on horses"—
Therefore you shall flee!
And, "We will ride on swift *horses*"—
Therefore those who pursue you
shall be swift!
17 One thousand *shall flee* at the threat of one,
At the threat of five you shall flee,
Till you are left as a pole on top of a mountain
And as a banner on a hill.

30:7 [t] Literally *Rahab Sits Idle*

God Will Be Gracious

18 Therefore the LORD will wait, that He may be
gracious to you;
And therefore He will be exalted, that He may
have mercy on you.
For the LORD *is* a God of justice;
Blessed *are* all those who wait for Him.

19 For the people shall dwell in Zion at Jerusalem;
You shall weep no more.
He will be very gracious to you at the sound
of your cry;
When He hears it, He will answer you.
20 And *though* the Lord gives you
The bread of adversity and the water
of affliction,
Yet your teachers will not be moved into
a corner anymore,
But your eyes shall see your teachers.
21 Your ears shall hear a word behind you, saying,
"This *is* the way, walk in it,"
Whenever you turn to the right hand
Or whenever you turn to the left.
22 You will also defile the covering of your
images of silver,
And the ornament of your molded
images of gold.
You will throw them away as an unclean thing;
You will say to them, "Get away!"

23 Then He will give the rain for your seed
With which you sow the ground,
And bread of the increase of the earth;
It will be fat and plentiful.
In that day your cattle will feed
In large pastures.
24 Likewise the oxen and the young donkeys that
work the ground
Will eat cured fodder,
Which has been winnowed with the shovel
and fan.
25 There will be on every high mountain
And on every high hill
Rivers *and* streams of waters,
In the day of the great slaughter,
When the towers fall.
26 Moreover the light of the moon will be as the
light of the sun,
And the light of the sun will be sevenfold,
As the light of seven days,
In the day that the LORD binds up the bruise of
His people
And heals the stroke of their wound.

Judgment on Assyria

27 Behold, the name of the LORD comes from afar,
Burning *with* His anger,
And *His* burden *is* heavy;
His lips are full of indignation,
And His tongue like a devouring fire.
28 His breath is like an overflowing stream,
Which reaches up to the neck,
To sift the nations with the sieve of futility;
And *there shall be* a bridle in the jaws
of the people,
Causing *them* to err.

29 You shall have a song
As in the night *when* a holy festival is kept,
And gladness of heart as when one goes
with a flute,
To come into the mountain of the LORD,
To the Mighty One of Israel.
30 The LORD will cause His glorious voice
to be heard,
And show the descent of His arm,
With the indignation of *His* anger
And the flame of a devouring fire,
With scattering, tempest, and hailstones.
31 For through the voice of the LORD
Assyria will be beaten down,
As He strikes with the rod.
32 And *in* every place where the staff
of punishment passes,
Which the LORD lays on him,
It will be with tambourines and harps;
And in battles of brandishing He will
fight with it.
33 For Tophet *was* established of old,
Yes, for the king it is prepared.
He has made *it* deep and large;
Its pyre *is* fire with much wood;
The breath of the LORD, like a stream
of brimstone,
Kindles it.

The Folly of Not Trusting God

31 Woe to those who go down to Egypt for help,
And rely on horses,
Who trust in chariots because *they are* many,
And in horsemen because they
are very strong,

But who do not look to the Holy One of Israel,
Nor seek the LORD!
2 Yet He also *is* wise and will bring disaster,
And will not call back His words,
But will arise against the house of evildoers,
And against the help of those who work iniquity.
3 Now the Egyptians *are* men, and not God;
And their horses are flesh, and not spirit.
When the LORD stretches out His hand,
Both he who helps will fall,
And he who is helped will fall down;
They all will perish together.

God Will Deliver Jerusalem

4For thus the LORD has spoken to me:

"As a lion roars,
And a young lion over his prey
(When a multitude of shepherds is summoned against him,
He will not be afraid of their voice
Nor be disturbed by their noise),
So the LORD of hosts will come down
To fight for Mount Zion and for its hill.
5 Like birds flying about,
So will the LORD of hosts defend Jerusalem.
Defending, He will also deliver *it;*
Passing over, He will preserve *it.*"

6Return *to Him* against whom the children of Israel have deeply revolted. 7For in that day every man shall throw away his idols of silver and
his idols of gold—sin, which your own hands have made for yourselves.

8 "Then Assyria shall fall by a sword not of man,
And a sword not of mankind shall devour him.
But he shall flee from the sword,
And his young men shall become forced labor.
9 He shall cross over to his stronghold for fear,
And his princes shall be afraid of the banner,"
Says the LORD,
Whose fire *is* in Zion
And whose furnace *is* in Jerusalem.

A Reign of Righteousness

32 Behold, a king will reign in righteousness,
And princes will rule with justice.
2 A man will be as a hiding place from the wind,
And a cover from the tempest,
As rivers of water in a dry place,
As the shadow of a great rock in a weary land.
3 The eyes of those who see will not be dim,
And the ears of those who hear will listen.
4 Also the heart of the rash will understand knowledge,
And the tongue of the stammerers will be ready to speak plainly.

LIFE LESSON

Isaiah 32:1–35:10

SITUATION Isaiah spoke of God's coming judgment on both individuals and nations surrounding Judah. People's motives were clear to God, and he rewarded those who lived by his commandments and were honest. He punished sinners.

OBSERVATION Although slow to anger, God punishes sin. Only the faithful will know God's bounty and security.

INSPIRATION Almost every headline, every television news report, and every radio bulletin these days proclaims one essential truth: The modern world is in chaos and no one has a realistic solution. . . .

The whole world is crying out for some word of hope, but all we hear is the babble of wishful thinkers and charlatans. Psychologists, educators, social scientists, physicians, and media wizards of every stripe offer pronouncements and preachments, but even the best ideas generally collapse under closer scrutiny. So far, our modern secular society has produced no positive answers; yet we continue to reach out in hope.

Actually, there is still good reason to hope; there is still time. For with society's failure comes the chance to repent and seek renewal. If we recognize the failures of living without God and turn from our foolishness and disobedience, we may yet be able to receive God's mercy and forgiveness.

Today's headlines are God's warning to a sinful world. The television news flashes are a shadow of His loving hand at work, pushing for the world's redemption. The radio bulletins are a reminder that in spite of our compulsive determination to ruin the earth and destroy God's program of salvation, He has not given up on us completely. Until that day when God's final judgment affixes each of us into place for eternity, there is a chance to begin again. Jesus said, "You must be born again" (John 3:7). That is the last best hope for this world. Ultimately it is our only hope.

(From *Storm Warning* by Billy Graham)

Continued

APPLICATION Have you ever surrendered your life to God? Have you ever asked him to forgive your sins? Pray and ask him to be your Lord and Savior. Tell him you are sorry for your sins. Tell your pastor that you accept Christ as your Savior.

EXPLORATION Judgment—Deuteronomy 7:2; Matthew 3:10; 13:30.

5 The foolish person will no longer be called generous,
Nor the miser said *to be* bountiful;
6 For the foolish person will speak foolishness,
And his heart will work iniquity:
To practice ungodliness,
To utter error against the LORD,
To keep the hungry unsatisfied,
And he will cause the drink of the thirsty to fail.
7 Also the schemes of the schemer *are* evil;
He devises wicked plans
To destroy the poor with lying words,
Even when the needy speaks justice.
8 But a generous man devises generous things,
And by generosity he shall stand.

Consequences of Complacency

9 Rise up, you women who are at ease,
Hear my voice;
You complacent daughters,
Give ear to my speech.
10 In a year and *some* days
You will be troubled, you complacent women;
For the vintage will fail,
The gathering will not come.
11 Tremble, you *women* who are at ease;
Be troubled, you complacent ones;
Strip yourselves, make yourselves bare,
And gird *sackcloth* on *your* waists.

12 People shall mourn upon their breasts
For the pleasant fields, for the fruitful vine.
13 On the land of my people will come up thorns *and* briers,
Yes, on all the happy homes *in* the joyous city;
14 Because the palaces will be forsaken,
The bustling city will be deserted.
The forts and towers will become lairs forever,
A joy of wild donkeys, a pasture of flocks—
15 Until the Spirit is poured upon us from on high,
And the wilderness becomes a fruitful field,
And the fruitful field is counted as a forest.

The Peace of God's Reign

16 Then justice will dwell in the wilderness,
And righteousness remain in the fruitful field.
17 The work of righteousness will be peace,
And the effect of righteousness, quietness and assurance forever.
18 My people will dwell in a peaceful habitation,
In secure dwellings, and in quiet resting places,
19 Though hail comes down on the forest,
And the city is brought low in humiliation.

20 Blessed *are* you who sow beside all waters,
Who send out freely the feet of the ox and the donkey.

A Prayer in Deep Distress

33 Woe to you who plunder, though you *have* not
been plundered;
And you who deal treacherously, though
they have not dealt
treacherously with you!
When you cease plundering,
You will be plundered;
When you make an end of dealing
treacherously,
They will deal treacherously with you.

2 O LORD, be gracious to us;
We have waited for You.
Be their[u] arm every morning,
Our salvation also in the time of trouble.
3 At the noise of the tumult the people shall flee;
When You lift Yourself up, the nations
shall be scattered;
4 And Your plunder shall be gathered
Like the gathering of the caterpillar;
As the running to and fro of locusts,
He shall run upon them.

5 The LORD is exalted, for He dwells on high;
He has filled Zion with justice and
righteousness.
6 Wisdom and knowledge will be the stability
of your times,
And the strength of salvation;
The fear of the LORD *is* His treasure.

7 Surely their valiant ones shall cry outside,
The ambassadors of peace shall weep bitterly.
8 The highways lie waste,
The traveling man ceases.
He has broken the covenant,
He has despised the cities,[v]
He regards no man.
9 The earth mourns *and* languishes,
Lebanon is shamed *and* shriveled;
Sharon is like a wilderness,
And Bashan and Carmel shake off *their fruits.*

Impending Judgment on Zion

10 "Now I will rise," says the LORD;
"Now I will be exalted,
Now I will lift Myself up.
11 You shall conceive chaff,
You shall bring forth stubble;
Your breath, *as* fire, shall devour you.
12 And the people shall be *like* the burnings
of lime;
Like thorns cut up they shall be burned
in the fire.
13 Hear, you *who are* afar off, what I have done;
And you *who are* near, acknowledge
My might."
14 The sinners in Zion are afraid;
Fearfulness has seized the hypocrites:
"Who among us shall dwell with the
devouring fire?
Who among us shall dwell with everlasting
burnings?"
15 He who walks righteously and
speaks uprightly,
He who despises the gain of oppressions,
Who gestures with his hands, refusing bribes,
Who stops his ears from hearing of bloodshed,
And shuts his eyes from seeing evil:
16 He will dwell on high;
His place of defense *will be* the fortress of rocks;
Bread will be given him,
His water *will be* sure.

The Land of the Majestic King

17 Your eyes will see the King in His beauty;
They will see the land that is very far off.
18 Your heart will meditate on terror:
"Where *is* the scribe?
Where *is* he who weighs?
Where *is* he who counts the towers?"
19 You will not see a fierce people,
A people of obscure speech, beyond perception,
Of a stammering tongue *that you*
cannot understand.
20 Look upon Zion, the city of our
appointed feasts;
Your eyes will see Jerusalem, a quiet home,
A tabernacle *that* will not be taken down;
Not one of its stakes will ever be removed,
Nor will any of its cords be broken.
21 But there the majestic LORD *will be* for us
A place of broad rivers *and* streams,
In which no galley with oars will sail,
Nor majestic ships pass by

33:2 [u] Septuagint omits *their;* Syriac, Targum, and Vulgate read *our.*
33:8 [v] Following Masoretic Text and Vulgate; Dead Sea Scrolls read *witnesses;* Septuagint omits *cities;* Targum reads *They have been removed from their cities.*

22 (For the LORD *is* our Judge,
The LORD *is* our Lawgiver,
The LORD *is* our King;
He will save us);
23 Your tackle is loosed,
They could not strengthen their mast,
They could not spread the sail.

Then the prey of great plunder is divided;
The lame take the prey.
24 And the inhabitant will not say, "I am sick";
The people who dwell in it *will be* forgiven
their iniquity.

Judgment on the Nations

34 Come near, you nations, to hear;
And heed, you people!
Let the earth hear, and all that is in it,
The world and all things that come
forth from it.
2 For the indignation of the LORD *is* against
all nations,
And *His* fury against all their armies;
He has utterly destroyed them,
He has given them over to the slaughter.
3 Also their slain shall be thrown out;
Their stench shall rise from their corpses,
And the mountains shall be melted
with their blood.
4 All the host of heaven shall be dissolved,
And the heavens shall be rolled up like a scroll;
All their host shall fall down
As the leaf falls from the vine,
And as *fruit* falling from a fig tree.

5 "For My sword shall be bathed in heaven;
Indeed it shall come down on Edom,
And on the people of My curse, for judgment.
6 The sword of the LORD is filled with blood,
It is made overflowing with fatness,
With the blood of lambs and goats,
With the fat of the kidneys of rams.
For the LORD has a sacrifice in Bozrah,
And a great slaughter in the land of Edom.
7 The wild oxen shall come down with them,
And the young bulls with the mighty bulls;
Their land shall be soaked with blood,
And their dust saturated with fatness."

8 For *it is* the day of the LORD's vengeance,
The year of recompense for the cause of Zion.
9 Its streams shall be turned into pitch,
And its dust into brimstone;
Its land shall become burning pitch.
10 It shall not be quenched night or day;
Its smoke shall ascend forever.
From generation to generation it
shall lie waste;
No one shall pass through it forever and ever.
11 But the pelican and the porcupine
shall possess it,
Also the owl and the raven shall dwell in it.
And He shall stretch out over it
The line of confusion and the stones
of emptiness.
12 They shall call its nobles to the kingdom,
But none *shall be* there, and all its princes
shall be nothing.
13 And thorns shall come up in its palaces,
Nettles and brambles in its fortresses;
It shall be a habitation of jackals,
A courtyard for ostriches.
14 The wild beasts of the desert shall also meet
with the jackals,
And the wild goat shall bleat to
its companion;
Also the night creature shall rest there,
And find for herself a place of rest.
15 There the arrow snake shall make her nest
and lay *eggs*
And hatch, and gather *them* under
her shadow;
There also shall the hawks be gathered,
Every one with her mate.

16 "Search from the book of the LORD, and read:
Not one of these shall fail;
Not one shall lack her mate.
For My mouth has commanded it, and His
Spirit has gathered them.
17 He has cast the lot for them,
And His hand has divided it among them
with a measuring line.
They shall possess it forever;
From generation to generation they shall
dwell in it."

The Future Glory of Zion

35 The wilderness and the wasteland shall be
glad for them,
And the desert shall rejoice and blossom
as the rose;
2 It shall blossom abundantly and rejoice,

Even with joy and singing.
The glory of Lebanon shall be given to it,
The excellence of Carmel and Sharon.
They shall see the glory of the LORD,
The excellency of our God.

3 Strengthen the weak hands,
And make firm the feeble knees.
4 Say to those *who are* fearful-hearted,
"Be strong, do not fear!
Behold, your God will come *with* vengeance,
With the recompense of God;
He will come and save you."

5 Then the eyes of the blind shall be opened,
And the ears of the deaf shall be unstopped.
6 Then the lame shall leap like a deer,
And the tongue of the dumb sing.
For waters shall burst forth in the wilderness,
And streams in the desert.
7 The parched ground shall become a pool,
And the thirsty land springs of water;
In the habitation of jackals, where each lay,
There shall be grass with reeds and rushes.

8 A highway shall be there, and a road,
And it shall be called the Highway of Holiness.
The unclean shall not pass over it,
But it *shall be* for others.
Whoever walks the road, although a fool,
Shall not go astray.
9 No lion shall be there,
Nor shall *any* ravenous beast go up on it;
It shall not be found there.
But the redeemed shall walk *there,*
10 And the ransomed of the LORD shall return,
And come to Zion with singing,
With everlasting joy on their heads.
They shall obtain joy and gladness,
And sorrow and sighing shall flee away.

Sennacherib Boasts Against the LORD

36 Now it came to pass in the fourteenth year of King Hezekiah *that*
Sennacherib king of Assyria came up against all the fortified cities of
Judah and took them.
2Then the king of Assyria sent *the* Rabshakeh[w] with a
great army from Lachish to King Hezekiah at Jerusalem. And he stood by
the aqueduct from the upper pool, on the highway to the Fuller's Field.
3And
Eliakim the son of Hilkiah, who was over the household, Shebna the scribe,
and Joah the son of Asaph, the recorder, came out to him.
4Then *the* Rabshakeh said to them, "Say now to Hezekiah, 'Thus says
the great king, the king of Assyria: "What confidence is this in which you

36:2 [w] A title, probably *Chief of Staff* or *Governor*

LIFE LESSON

Isaiah 36:1–39:8

SITUATION King Hezekiah reigned in Israel during a time when the people had forgotten about God. Unlike his predecessors, Hezekiah tried to restore the worship of God. During these reforms, the expanding Assyrian empire threatened his kingdom.

OBSERVATION Don't be afraid of the enemy. Trust God. God will save you from all kinds of difficult situations.

INSPIRATION My first lesson in stepping out on trust came in connection with the problem of financing a college education. . . . Something I had dreamed of as far back as I could remember—a college education—now seemed out of the question. The dream even included a particular college—Agnes Scott in Decatur, Georgia.

Agnes Scott accepted me. Although the school was accustomed to ministers' and missionaries' daughters whose ambitions outstripped their pocket books, the financial burden nevertheless looked hopelessly heavy. Even with the promise of a small work scholarship and the $125 I had saved from high school essay and debating prizes, we were several hundred dollars short.

It was frightening to see that my parents were helpless in this situation. It was in their faces, in their voices. Through all my growing-up years, in every childish emergency they had been equal to anything. What now? Did this mean that I was going to have to relinquish my heart's desire?

One evening Mother found me lying across my bed, sobbing. She sat down beside me, put her cool hand on my forehead. No words were needed. She knew what the trouble was. Presently she said quietly, "You and I are going to pray about this. Let's go into the guest room where we won't be disturbed."

We sat down on the old-fashioned golden-oak bed, the one that Mother and Father had bought for their first home. "Let's talk about this a minute before we pray," Mother said slowly. "I believe that it is God's will for you to go to college, or else He would not have given you the mental equipment. Furthermore, all resources are at

Continued

God's disposal. Do you believe that, Catherine?"

"Yes—I think I do."

"All right. Now here's another fact I want you to think about. Everybody has faith. We're born with it. Much of what happens to us in life depends on where we place our faith. If we deposit it in God, then we're on sure ground. If we place our trust in poverty or failure or fear, then we're investing it poorly.

Whenever we ask God for something that is His will, He hears us. If He hears us, then He grants the request that we have made. So you and I can rest on that promise. Let's claim it right now for the resources of your college." And so we knelt by the bed and prayed about it. . . .

When [the answer] came, it was the offer of a job for Mother with the Federal Writers' project. Would she be willing to write the history of the county? Her salary would cover the amount needed for my college expenses with a little to spare.

. . .That's how I learned that we must have faith before the fact, not after, if we are to function as human beings at all. The only question is—faith in whom? Faith in what?

God challenges us to place it in Him rather than in fallible human beings. (From *Beyond Ourselves* by Catherine Marshall)

APPLICATION Have you been given a difficult assignment? Rewrite Hezekiah's prayer in 37:16-20. Lay your problems before God and trust in God to answer.

EXPLORATION Trusting God—Exodus 14:13; Proverbs 3:5-6; Isaiah 43:1-2; Mark 11:22-24.

trust? 5I say you speak of having plans and power for war; but *they are*
mere words. Now in whom do you trust, that you rebel against me? 6Look!
You are trusting in the staff of this broken reed, Egypt, on which if a man
leans, it will go into his hand and pierce it. So *is* Pharaoh king of Egypt to
all who trust in him.

7"But if you say to me, 'We trust in the LORD our God,' *is it* not He whose
high places and whose altars Hezekiah has taken away, and said to Judah
and Jerusalem, 'You shall worship before this altar'?" ' 8Now therefore, I
urge you, give a pledge to my master the king of Assyria, and I will give
you two thousand horses—if you are able on your part to put riders on
them! 9How then will you repel one captain of the least of my master's servants, and put your trust in Egypt for chariots and horsemen? 10Have I
now come up without the LORD against this land to destroy it? The LORD
said to me, 'Go up against this land, and destroy it.' "

11Then Eliakim, Shebna, and Joah said to *the* Rabshakeh, "Please speak
to your servants in Aramaic, for we understand *it;* and do not speak to us
in Hebrew[x] in the hearing of the people who *are* on the wall."

12But *the* Rabshakeh said, "Has my master sent me to your master and
to you to speak these words, and not to the men who sit on the wall, who
will eat and drink their own waste with you?"

13Then *the* Rabshakeh stood and called out with a loud voice in Hebrew,
and said, "Hear the words of the great king, the king of Assyria! 14Thus says
the king: 'Do not let Hezekiah deceive you, for he will not be able to deliver
you; 15nor let Hezekiah make you trust in the LORD, saying, "The LORD will
surely deliver us; this city will not be given into the hand of the king of Assyria." ' 16Do not listen to Hezekiah; for thus says the king of Assyria: 'Make
peace with me *by a* present and come out to me; and every one of you eat
from his own vine and every one from his own fig tree, and every one of
you drink the waters of his own cistern; 17until I come and take you away to
a land like your own land, a land of grain and new wine, a land of bread and
vineyards. 18*Beware* lest Hezekiah persuade you, saying, "The LORD will deliver us." Has any one of the gods of the nations delivered its land from the
hand of the king of Assyria? 19Where *are* the gods of Hamath and Arpad?
Where *are* the gods of Sepharvaim? Indeed, have they delivered Samaria
from my hand? 20Who among all the gods of these lands have delivered
their countries from my hand, that the LORD should deliver Jerusalem from
my hand?' "

21But they held their peace and answered him not a word; for the king's
commandment was, "Do not answer him." 22Then Eliakim the son of
Hilkiah, who *was* over the household, Shebna the scribe, and Joah the son
of Asaph, the recorder, came to Hezekiah with *their* clothes torn, and told
him the words of *the* Rabshakeh.

Isaiah Assures Deliverance

37 And so it was, when King Hezekiah heard *it,* that he tore his clothes,
covered himself with sackcloth, and went into the house of the LORD.
2Then he sent Eliakim, who *was* over the household, Shebna the scribe,
and the elders of the priests, covered with sackcloth, to Isaiah the prophet,
the son of Amoz. 3And they said to him, "Thus says Hezekiah: 'This day *is*
a day of trouble and rebuke and blasphemy; for the children have come to

36:11 [x] Literally *Judean*

birth, but *there is* no strength to bring them forth. 4It
may be that the LORD your God will hear the words of
the Rabshakeh, whom his master the king of Assyria
has sent to reproach the living God, and will rebuke
the words which the LORD your God has heard. Therefore
lift up *your* prayer for the remnant that is left.' "
5So the servants of King Hezekiah came to Isaiah.
6And Isaiah said to them, "Thus you shall say to your
master, 'Thus says the LORD: "Do not be afraid of the
words which you have heard, with which the servants
of the king of Assyria have blasphemed Me. 7Surely I
will send a spirit upon him, and he shall hear a rumor
and return to his own land; and I will cause him to fall
by the sword in his own land." ' "

Sennacherib's Threat and Hezekiah's Prayer

8Then *the* Rabshakeh returned, and found the king
of Assyria warring against Libnah, for he heard that he
had departed from Lachish. 9And the king heard concerning Tirhakah king of Ethiopia, "He has come out
to make war with you." So when he heard *it,* he sent
messengers to Hezekiah, saying, 10"Thus you shall speak
to Hezekiah king of Judah, saying: 'Do not let your God
in whom you trust deceive you, saying, "Jerusalem shall
not be given into the hand of the king of Assyria."
11Look! You have heard what the kings of Assyria have
done to all lands by utterly destroying them; and shall
you be delivered? 12Have the gods of the nations delivered those whom my fathers have destroyed, Gozan
and Haran and Rezeph, and the people of Eden who
were in Telassar? 13Where *is* the king of Hamath, the
king of Arpad, and the king of the city of Sepharvaim,
Hena, and Ivah?' "
14And Hezekiah received the letter from the hand of
the messengers, and read it; and Hezekiah went up to
the house of the LORD, and spread it before the LORD.
15Then Hezekiah prayed to the LORD, saying: 16"O LORD
of hosts, God of Israel, *the One* who dwells *between* the
cherubim, You *are* God, You alone, of all the kingdoms
of the earth. You have made heaven and earth. 17Incline
Your ear, O LORD, and hear; open Your eyes, O LORD,
and see; and hear all the words of Sennacherib, which
he has sent to reproach the living God. 18Truly, LORD,
the kings of Assyria have laid waste all the nations and
their lands, 19and have cast their gods into the fire; for
they *were* not gods, but the work of men's hands—
wood and stone. Therefore they destroyed them. 20Now
therefore, O LORD our God, save us from his hand, that
all the kingdoms of the earth may know that You *are*
the LORD, You alone."

The Word of the LORD Concerning Sennacherib

21Then Isaiah the son of Amoz sent to Hezekiah,
saying, "Thus says the LORD God of Israel, 'Because
you have prayed to Me against Sennacherib king of
Assyria, 22this *is* the word which the LORD has spoken
concerning him:

"The virgin, the daughter of Zion,
Has despised you, laughed you to scorn;
The daughter of Jerusalem
Has shaken *her* head behind your back!

23 "Whom have you reproached and blasphemed?
Against whom have you raised *your* voice,
And lifted up your eyes on high?
Against the Holy One of Israel.
24 By your servants you have reproached
the Lord,
And said, 'By the multitude of my chariots
I have come up to the height of the mountains,
To the limits of Lebanon;
I will cut down its tall cedars
And its choice cypress trees;
I will enter its farthest height,
To its fruitful forest.
25 I have dug and drunk water,
And with the soles of my feet I have dried up
All the brooks of defense.'

26 "Did you not hear long ago
How I made it,
From ancient times that I formed it?
Now I have brought it to pass,
That you should be
For crushing fortified cities *into* heaps of ruins.
27 Therefore their inhabitants *had* little power;
They were dismayed and confounded;
They were *as* the grass of the field
And the green herb,
As the grass on the housetops
And grain blighted before it is grown.

28 "But I know your dwelling place,
Your going out and your coming in,
And your rage against Me.
29 Because your rage against Me
and your tumult
Have come up to My ears,
Therefore I will put My hook in your nose
And My bridle in your lips,
And I will turn you back
By the way which you came." '

30"This *shall be* a sign to you:

You shall eat this year such as grows of itself,
And the second year what springs from the same;
Also in the third year sow and reap,
Plant vineyards and eat the fruit of them.
31 And the remnant who have escaped of the house of Judah
Shall again take root downward,
And bear fruit upward.
32 For out of Jerusalem shall go a remnant,
And those who escape from Mount Zion.
The zeal of the LORD of hosts will do this.

33"Therefore thus says the LORD concerning the king of Assyria:

'He shall not come into this city,
Nor shoot an arrow there,
Nor come before it with shield,
Nor build a siege mound against it.
34 By the way that he came,
By the same shall he return;
And he shall not come into this city,'
Says the LORD.
35 'For I will defend this city, to save it
For My own sake and for My servant David's sake.' "

Sennacherib's Defeat and Death

36Then the angel[y] of the LORD went out, and killed in
the camp of the Assyrians one hundred and eighty-five
thousand; and when *people* arose early in the morning,
there were the corpses—all dead. 37So Sennacherib
king of Assyria departed and went away, returned
home, and remained at Nineveh. 38Now it came to pass,
as he was worshiping in the house of Nisroch his god,
that his sons Adrammelech and Sharezer struck him
down with the sword; and they escaped into the land of
Ararat. Then Esarhaddon his son reigned in his place.

Hezekiah's Life Extended

38 In those days Hezekiah was sick and near death.
And Isaiah the prophet, the son of Amoz, went
to him and said to him, "Thus says the LORD: 'Set your
house in order, for you shall die and not live.' "

2Then Hezekiah turned his face toward the wall,
and prayed to the LORD, 3and said, "Remember now,
O LORD, I pray, how I have walked before You in truth
and with a loyal heart, and have done *what is* good in
Your sight." And Hezekiah wept bitterly.

4And the word of the LORD came to Isaiah, saying,
5"Go and tell Hezekiah, 'Thus says the LORD, the God
of David your father: "I have heard your prayer, I have
seen your tears; surely I will add to your days fifteen
years. 6I will deliver you and this city from the hand of
the king of Assyria, and I will defend this city." ' 7And
this *is* the sign to you from the LORD, that the LORD will
do this thing which He has spoken: 8Behold, I will
bring the shadow on the sundial, which has gone
down with the sun on the sundial of Ahaz, ten degrees
backward." So the sun returned ten degrees on the
dial by which it had gone down.

9This is the writing of Hezekiah king of Judah, when
he had been sick and had recovered from his sickness:

10 I said,
"In the prime of my life
I shall go to the gates of Sheol;
I am deprived of the remainder of my years."
11 I said,
"I shall not see YAH,
The LORD[z] in the land of the living;
I shall observe man no more among the inhabitants of the world.[a]
12 My life span is gone,
Taken from me like a shepherd's tent;
I have cut off my life like a weaver.
He cuts me off from the loom;
From day until night You make an end of me.
13 I have considered until morning—
Like a lion,
So He breaks all my bones;
From day until night You make an end of me.
14 Like a crane *or* a swallow, so I chattered;
I mourned like a dove;
My eyes fail *from looking* upward.
O LORD,[b] I am oppressed;
Undertake for me!
15 "What shall I say?
He has both spoken to me,[c]
And He Himself has done *it.*
I shall walk carefully all my years
In the bitterness of my soul.
16 O Lord, by these *things men* live;
And in all these *things is* the life of my spirit;

37:36 [y] Or *Angel*
38:11 [z] Hebrew *YAH, YAH* [a] Following some Hebrew manuscripts; Masoretic Text and Vulgate read *rest;* Septuagint omits *among the inhabitants of the world;* Targum reads *land.*
38:14 [b] Following Bomberg; Masoretic Text and Dead Sea Scrolls read *Lord.*
38:15 [c] Following Masoretic Text and Vulgate; Dead Sea Scrolls and Targum read *And shall I say to Him;* Septuagint omits first half of this verse.

So You will restore me and make me live.
17 Indeed *it was* for *my own* peace
That I had great bitterness;
But You have lovingly *delivered* my soul from
the pit of corruption,
For You have cast all my sins behind Your back.
18 For Sheol cannot thank You,
Death cannot praise You;
Those who go down to the pit cannot hope for
Your truth.
19 The living, the living man, he shall praise You,
As I *do* this day;
The father shall make known Your truth to
the children.

20 "The LORD *was ready* to save me;
Therefore we will sing my songs with
stringed instruments
All the days of our life, in the house
of the LORD."

21 Now Isaiah had said, "Let them take a lump of
figs, and apply *it* as a poultice on the boil, and he shall
recover."
22 And Hezekiah had said, "What *is* the sign that I
shall go up to the house of the LORD?"

The Babylonian Envoys

39 At that time Merodach-Baladan[d] the son of
Baladan, king of Babylon, sent letters and a
present to Hezekiah, for he heard that he had been sick
and had recovered. 2 And Hezekiah was pleased with
them, and showed them the house of his treasures—the
silver and gold, the spices and precious ointment, and
all his armory—all that was found among his treasures.
There was nothing in his house or in all his dominion
that Hezekiah did not show them.
3 Then Isaiah the prophet went to King Hezekiah,
and said to him, "What did these men say, and from
where did they come to you?"
So Hezekiah said, "They came to me from a far
country, from Babylon."
4 And he said, "What have they seen in your house?"
So Hezekiah answered, "They have seen all that *is*
in my house; there is nothing among my treasures
that I have not shown them."
5 Then Isaiah said to Hezekiah, "Hear the word of
the LORD of hosts: 6 'Behold, the days are coming when
all that *is* in your house, and what your fathers have
accumulated until this day, shall be carried to Babylon;
nothing shall be left,' says the LORD. 7 'And they shall
take away *some* of your sons who will descend from
you, whom you will beget; and they shall be eunuchs
in the palace of the king of Babylon.' "
8 So Hezekiah said to Isaiah, "The word of the LORD
which you have spoken *is* good!" For he said, "At least
there will be peace and truth in my days."

God's People Are Comforted

40 "Comfort, yes, comfort My people!"
Says your God.
2 "Speak comfort to Jerusalem, and cry out to her,
That her warfare is ended,
That her iniquity is pardoned;
For she has received from the LORD's hand
Double for all her sins."

3 The voice of one crying in the wilderness:
"Prepare the way of the LORD;
Make straight in the desert[e]
A highway for our God.
4 Every valley shall be exalted
And every mountain and hill brought low;
The crooked places shall be made straight
And the rough places smooth;
5 The glory of the LORD shall be revealed,
And all flesh shall see *it* together;
For the mouth of the LORD has spoken."

6 The voice said, "Cry out!"
And he[f] said, "What shall I cry?"

"All flesh *is* grass,
And all its loveliness *is* like the flower
of the field.
7 The grass withers, the flower fades,
Because the breath of the LORD blows upon it;
Surely the people *are* grass.
8 The grass withers, the flower fades,
But the word of our God stands forever."

9 O Zion,
You who bring good tidings,
Get up into the high mountain;
O Jerusalem,
You who bring good tidings,
Lift up your voice with strength,
Lift *it* up, be not afraid;
Say to the cities of Judah, "Behold your God!"

39:1 [d] Spelled *Berodach-Baladan* in 2 Kings 20:12
40:3 [e] Following Masoretic Text, Targum, and Vulgate; Septuagint omits *in the desert.*
40:6 [f] Following Masoretic Text and Targum; Dead Sea Scrolls, Septuagint, and Vulgate read *I.*

Life Lesson

Isaiah 40:1–41:29

SITUATION God promised to remain faithful to his people. The Jews felt that God had ignored them, but God would rescue them from captivity.

OBSERVATION Because he is perfect, all powerful, and knows everything, God transcends nature. Mysteriously, though, he still concerns himself with our lives.

INSPIRATION God is always first, and God will surely be last.

To say this is not to draw God downward into the stream of time and involve Him in the flux and flow of the world. He stands above His own creation and outside of time; but for the convenience of His creatures, who are children of time, He makes free use of time-words when refering to Himself. So He says that He is the Alpha and Omega, the beginning and the ending, the first and the last.

Man in the plan of God has been granted considerable say; but never is he permitted to utter the first word nor the last. That is the prerogative of the Deity, and one which He will never surrender to His creatures.

Man has no say about the time or place of his birth; God determines that without consulting the man himself. One day the little man finds himself in consciousness and accepts the fact that he is. There his volitional life begins. Before that he had nothing to say about anything. After that he struts

10 Behold, the Lord GOD shall come with a strong *hand,*
And His arm shall rule for Him;
Behold, His reward *is* with Him,
And His work before Him.
11 He will feed His flock like a shepherd;
He will gather the lambs with His arm,
And carry *them* in His bosom,
And gently lead those who are with young.

12 Who has measured the waters[g] in the hollow of His hand,
Measured heaven with a span
And calculated the dust of the earth in a measure?
Weighed the mountains in scales
And the hills in a balance?
13 Who has directed the Spirit of the LORD,
Or *as* His counselor has taught Him?
14 With whom did He take counsel, and *who* instructed Him,
And taught Him in the path of justice?
Who taught Him knowledge,
And showed Him the way of understanding?

15 Behold, the nations *are* as a drop in a bucket,
And are counted as the small dust on the scales;
Look, He lifts up the isles as a very little thing.
16 And Lebanon *is* not sufficient to burn,
Nor its beasts sufficient for a burnt offering.
17 All nations before Him *are* as nothing,
And they are counted by Him less than nothing and worthless.

18 To whom then will you liken God?
Or what likeness will you compare to Him?
19 The workman molds an image,
The goldsmith overspreads it with gold,
And the silversmith casts silver chains.
20 Whoever *is* too impoverished for *such* a contribution
Chooses a tree *that* will not rot;
He seeks for himself a skillful workman
To prepare a carved image *that* will not totter.

21 Have you not known?
Have you not heard?
Has it not been told you from the beginning?
Have you not understood from the foundations of the earth?
22 *It is* He who sits above the circle of the earth,
And its inhabitants *are* like grasshoppers,
Who stretches out the heavens like a curtain,
And spreads them out like a tent to dwell in.
23 He brings the princes to nothing;
He makes the judges of the earth useless.

40:12 *g* Following Masoretic Text, Septuagint, and Vulgate; Dead Sea Scrolls read *waters of the sea;* Targum reads *waters of the world.*

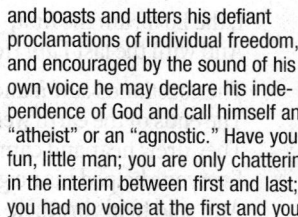

24 Scarcely shall they be planted,
Scarcely shall they be sown,
Scarcely shall their stock take root in the earth,
When He will also blow on them,
And they will wither,
And the whirlwind will take them away like stubble.
25 "To whom then will you liken Me,
Or *to whom* shall I be equal?" says the Holy One.
26 Lift up your eyes on high,
And see who has created these *things,*
Who brings out their host by number;
He calls them all by name,
By the greatness of His might
And the strength of *His* power;
Not one is missing.

27 Why do you say, O Jacob,
And speak, O Israel:
"My way is hidden from the LORD,
And my just claim is passed over by my God"?
28 Have you not known?
Have you not heard?
The everlasting God, the LORD,
The Creator of the ends of the earth,
Neither faints nor is weary.
His understanding is unsearchable.
29 He gives power to the weak,
And to *those who have* no might He increases strength.
30 Even the youths shall faint and be weary,
And the young men shall utterly fall,
31 But those who wait on the LORD
Shall renew *their* strength;
They shall mount up with wings like eagles,
They shall run and not be weary,
They shall walk and not faint.

Israel Assured of God's Help

41 "Keep silence before Me, O coastlands,
And let the people renew *their* strength!
Let them come near, then let them speak;
Let us come near together for judgment.

2 "Who raised up one from the east?
Who in righteousness called him to His feet?
Who gave the nations before him,
And made *him* rule over kings?
Who gave *them* as the dust *to* his sword,
As driven stubble to his bow?
3 Who pursued them, *and* passed safely
By the way *that* he had not gone with his feet?
4 Who has performed and done *it,*
Calling the generations from the beginning?

and boasts and utters his defiant proclamations of individual freedom, and encouraged by the sound of his own voice he may declare his independence of God and call himself an "atheist" or an "agnostic." Have your fun, little man; you are only chattering in the interim between first and last; you had no voice at the first and you will have none at the last. God reserves the right to take up at the last where He began at the first, and you are in the hands of God whether you will or not.

This knowledge should humble us and encourage us, too. It should humble us when we remember how frail we are, how utterly dependent on God; and it should encourage us to know that when everything else has passed we may still have God no less surely than before.

(From *The Root of Righteousness* by A. W. Tozer)

APPLICATION Is anything in your life guaranteed? Is your career unshakable, your family immortal, your money eternal? Do not base your comfort and enjoyment on what could be gone tomorrow. Only God and his Word will last for ever—let these be the basis of everything in your life.

EXPLORATION Waiting—Isaiah 52:10; 2 Corinthians 4:1; Hebrews 12:1-3.

'I, the LORD, am the first;
And with the last I *am* He.' "

5 The coastlands saw *it* and feared,
The ends of the earth were afraid;
They drew near and came.
6 Everyone helped his neighbor,
And said to his brother,
"Be of good courage!"
7 So the craftsman encouraged the goldsmith;
He who smooths *with* the hammer *inspired*
him who strikes the anvil,
Saying, "It *is* ready for the soldering";
Then he fastened it with pegs,
That it might not totter.

8 "But you, Israel, *are* My servant,
Jacob whom I have chosen,
The descendants of Abraham My friend.
9 *You* whom I have taken from the ends of
the earth,
And called from its farthest regions,
And said to you,
'You *are* My servant,
I have chosen you and have not cast you away:
10 Fear not, for I *am* with you;
Be not dismayed, for I *am* your God.
I will strengthen you,
Yes, I will help you,
I will uphold you with My righteous right hand.'

11 "Behold, all those who were incensed
against you
Shall be ashamed and disgraced;
They shall be as nothing,
And those who strive with you shall perish.
12 You shall seek them and not find them—
Those who contended with you.
Those who war against you
Shall be as nothing,
As a nonexistent thing.
13 For I, the LORD your God, will hold your
right hand,
Saying to you, 'Fear not, I will help you.'

14 "Fear not, you worm Jacob,
You men of Israel!
I will help you," says the LORD
And your Redeemer, the Holy One of Israel.
15 "Behold, I will make you into a new threshing
sledge with sharp teeth;
You shall thresh the mountains and beat
them small,
And make the hills like chaff.
16 You shall winnow them, the wind shall carry
them away,
And the whirlwind shall scatter them;
You shall rejoice in the LORD,
And glory in the Holy One of Israel.

17 "The poor and needy seek water, but *there*
is none,
Their tongues fail for thirst.
I, the LORD, will hear them;
I, the God of Israel, will not forsake them.
18 I will open rivers in desolate heights,
And fountains in the midst of the valleys;
I will make the wilderness a pool of water,
And the dry land springs of water.
19 I will plant in the wilderness the cedar and the
acacia tree,
The myrtle and the oil tree;
I will set in the desert the cypress tree *and*
the pine
And the box tree together,
20 That they may see and know,
And consider and understand together,
That the hand of the LORD has done this,
And the Holy One of Israel has created it.

The Futility of Idols

21 "Present your case," says the LORD.
"Bring forth your strong *reasons*," says the
King of Jacob.
22 "Let them bring forth and show us what
will happen;
Let them show the former things, what
they *were*,
That we may consider them,
And know the latter end of them;
Or declare to us things to come.
23 Show the things that are to come hereafter,
That we may know that you *are* gods;
Yes, do good or do evil,
That we may be dismayed and see *it* together.
24 Indeed you *are* nothing,
And your work *is* nothing;
He who chooses you *is* an abomination.

25 "I have raised up one from the north,
And he shall come;
From the rising of the sun he shall call
on My name;
And he shall come against princes as
though mortar,
As the potter treads clay.

26 Who has declared from the beginning,
that we may know?
And former times, that we may say, '*He is* righteous'?
Surely *there is* no one who shows,
Surely *there is* no one who declares,
Surely *there is* no one who hears your words.
27 The first time *I said* to Zion,
'Look, there they are!'
And I will give to Jerusalem one who brings good tidings.
28 For I looked, and *there was* no man;
I looked among them, but *there was* no counselor,
Who, when I asked of them, could answer a word.
29 Indeed they *are* all worthless;[h]
Their works *are* nothing;
Their molded images *are* wind and confusion.

The Servant of the LORD

42 "Behold! My Servant whom I uphold,
My Elect One *in whom* My soul delights!
I have put My Spirit upon Him;
He will bring forth justice to the Gentiles.
2 He will not cry out, nor raise *His voice,*
Nor cause His voice to be heard in the street.
3 A bruised reed He will not break,
And smoking flax He will not quench;
He will bring forth justice for truth.
4 He will not fail nor be discouraged,
Till He has established justice in the earth;
And the coastlands shall wait for His law."

5 Thus says God the LORD,
Who created the heavens and stretched them out,
Who spread forth the earth and that which comes from it,
Who gives breath to the people on it,
And spirit to those who walk on it:
6 "I, the LORD, have called You in righteousness,
And will hold Your hand;
I will keep You and give You as a covenant
to the people,
As a light to the Gentiles,
7 To open blind eyes,
To bring out prisoners from the prison,
Those who sit in darkness from the prison house.
8 I *am* the LORD, that *is* My name;
And My glory I will not give to another,
Nor My praise to carved images.
9 Behold, the former things have come to pass,
And new things I declare;
Before they spring forth I tell you of them."

41:29 *h* Following Masoretic Text and Vulgate; Dead Sea Scrolls, Syriac, and Targum read *nothing;* Septuagint omits the first line.

LIFE LESSON

Isaiah 42:1–43:28

SITUATION Isaiah looked ahead to the time when Jesus would bring justice to the world. Isaiah pointed out that although the Israelites were unfaithful to God, God would still deliver them from captivity (43:8-28).

OBSERVATION God never gives up on us. He always pursues us when we wander from him.

INSPIRATION As for his chosen people of Israel, whatever shame and humiliation they endured, God also endured. The Israelites watched in horror as Babylonian axmen hacked apart the cedar beams of the temple—but it was God's own house they were invading, and he felt that invasion as a personal desecration. . . .

A single, elegant sentence from Isaiah summarizes God's point of view: "In all their distresses he too was distressed." God may have hidden his face, but that face was streaked with tears. . . .

In choosing Israel, God was seeking such a relationship. He wanted what any parent wants: a happy household of children who return their parent's love. His voice sings with pride as he reminisces about the early days: "Is not Ephraim my dear son, the child in whom I delight?" But the joy fades away as God abruptly shifts from the perspective of a parent to that of a lover, a wounded lover. *What have I done wrong*? he demands in a tone of sadness, and horror, and rage. . . .

"What else can I do?" God's poignant question to Jeremiah points up the dilemma of an omnipotent God who has made room for freedom. The stork in the sky knows her seasons, the ocean tide rolls in on schedule, snow always covers the high mountains, but human beings are like nothing else in nature. God cannot control them. Yet he cannot simply thrust them aside either. He cannot get humanity out of his mind.

(From *Disappointment with God* by Philip Yancey)

Continued

APPLICATION God goes everywhere you go. Wherever you go today, imagine God going with you. Imagine him walking or sitting with you. Remind yourself that whenever you succeed, he is there. Whenever you share Christ, he is there. Whenever you sin—he is there.

EXPLORATION God's Love—Deuteronomy 7:8; Jeremiah 31:3; John 3:16; Romans 5:8; Ephesians 2:4-5; 2 Peter 3:9; 1 John 3:1.

Praise to the LORD

10 Sing to the LORD a new song,
And His praise from the ends of the earth,
You who go down to the sea, and all that is in it,
You coastlands and you inhabitants of them!
11 Let the wilderness and its cities lift up *their voice,*
The villages *that* Kedar inhabits.
Let the inhabitants of Sela sing,
Let them shout from the top of the mountains.
12 Let them give glory to the LORD,
And declare His praise in the coastlands.
13 The LORD shall go forth like a mighty man;
He shall stir up *His* zeal like a man of war.
He shall cry out, yes, shout aloud;
He shall prevail against His enemies.

Promise of the LORD's Help

14 "I have held My peace a long time,
I have been still and restrained Myself.
Now I will cry like a woman in labor,
I will pant and gasp at once.
15 I will lay waste the mountains and hills,
And dry up all their vegetation;
I will make the rivers coastlands,
And I will dry up the pools.
16 I will bring the blind by a way they did not know;
I will lead them in paths they have not known.
I will make darkness light before them,
And crooked places straight.
These things I will do for them,
And not forsake them.
17 They shall be turned back,
They shall be greatly ashamed,
Who trust in carved images,
Who say to the molded images,
'You *are* our gods.'

18 "Hear, you deaf;
And look, you blind, that you may see.
19 Who *is* blind but My servant,
Or deaf as My messenger *whom* I send?
Who *is* blind as *he who is* perfect,
And blind as the LORD's servant?
20 Seeing many things, but you do not observe;
Opening the ears, but he does not hear."

Israel's Obstinate Disobedience

21 The LORD is well pleased for His righteousness' sake;
He will exalt the law and make *it* honorable.
22 But this *is* a people robbed and plundered;
All of them are snared in holes,
And they are hidden in prison houses;

They are for prey, and no one delivers;
For plunder, and no one says, "Restore!"
23 Who among you will give ear to this?
Who will listen and hear for the time to come?
24 Who gave Jacob for plunder, and Israel to the robbers?
Was it not the LORD,
He against whom we have sinned?
For they would not walk in His ways,
Nor were they obedient to His law.
25 Therefore He has poured on him the fury of His anger
And the strength of battle;
It has set him on fire all around,
Yet he did not know;
And it burned him,
Yet he did not take *it* to heart.

The Redeemer of Israel

43 But now, thus says the LORD, who created you, O Jacob,
And He who formed you, O Israel:
"Fear not, for I have redeemed you;
I have called *you* by your name;
You *are* Mine.
2 When you pass through the waters, I *will be* with you;
And through the rivers, they shall not overflow you.
When you walk through the fire, you shall not be burned,
Nor shall the flame scorch you.
3 For I *am* the LORD your God,
The Holy One of Israel, your Savior;
I gave Egypt for your ransom,
Ethiopia and Seba in your place.
4 Since you were precious in My sight,
You have been honored,
And I have loved you;
Therefore I will give men for you,
And people for your life.
5 Fear not, for I *am* with you;
I will bring your descendants from the east,
And gather you from the west;
6 I will say to the north, 'Give them up!'
And to the south, 'Do not keep them back!'
Bring My sons from afar,
And My daughters from the ends of the earth—
7 Everyone who is called by My name,
Whom I have created for My glory;
I have formed him, yes, I have made him."
8 Bring out the blind people who have eyes,
And the deaf who have ears.
9 Let all the nations be gathered together,
And let the people be assembled.
Who among them can declare this,
And show us former things?
Let them bring out their witnesses, that they may be justified;
Or let them hear and say, "*It is* truth."
10 "You *are* My witnesses," says the LORD,
"And My servant whom I have chosen,
That you may know and believe Me,
And understand that I *am* He.
Before Me there was no God formed,
Nor shall there be after Me.
11 I, *even* I, *am* the LORD,
And besides Me *there is* no savior.
12 I have declared and saved,
I have proclaimed,
And *there was* no foreign *god* among you;
Therefore you *are* My witnesses,"
Says the LORD, "that I *am* God.
13 Indeed before the day *was*, I *am* He;
And *there is* no one who can deliver out of My hand;
I work, and who will reverse it?"

14 Thus says the LORD, your Redeemer,
The Holy One of Israel:
"For your sake I will send to Babylon,
And bring them all down as fugitives—
The Chaldeans, who rejoice in their ships.
15 I *am* the LORD, your Holy One,
The Creator of Israel, your King."

16 Thus says the LORD, who makes a way in the sea
And a path through the mighty waters,
17 Who brings forth the chariot and horse,
The army and the power
(They shall lie down together, they shall not rise;
They are extinguished, they are quenched like a wick):
18 "Do not remember the former things,
Nor consider the things of old.
19 Behold, I will do a new thing,
Now it shall spring forth;
Shall you not know it?
I will even make a road in the wilderness
And rivers in the desert.
20 The beast of the field will honor Me,
The jackals and the ostriches,

Life Lesson

Isaiah 44:1–46:13

SITUATION God reaffirmed Israel as his chosen people. He warned them that practicing idolatry was foolish.

OBSERVATION God reminded the Israelites that worshiping an inanimate object, such as a piece of firewood, as a god was not only futile but stupid.

INSPIRATION You can make an idol out of anything or anyone in life. A church building can become an idol to us, when all the while it is simply a place to meet and worship our Lord—nothing more. Your child can become your idol . . . in subtle ways you can so adore that little one that your whole life revolves around the child. Your mate or date can be given first place in your life and literally idolized. Your work can easily become your God . . . as can some pursuit in life. A house, a lawn, an antique car, a letter sport, an education, a trip abroad, and even that goal of "retirement." . . .

Your Lord and Savior wants to occupy first place. Matthew 6:33 says that when He *has* it, everything else will be added to you. How long has it been since you've enlisted your Lord's help in a private, personal temple-cleansing session? It's so easy to get attached to idols—good things, inappropriately adored. But when you have Jesus in the center of the room, everything else only junks up the decor.

(From *Come Before Winter* by Charles Swindoll)

APPLICATION Who created you? Who can you ultimatly depend on? Where can you find supreme truth? Where can you find happiness? Did you answer anything but God for these questions? If so, you may be in danger of falling into idolatry. Pull yourself out of that trap and let God be the one you rely on.

EXPLORATION Idolatry—Exodus 20:3; 1 Samuel 15:23; 1 Corinthians 6:9.

Because I give waters in the wilderness
And rivers in the desert,
To give drink to My people, My chosen.
21 This people I have formed for Myself;
They shall declare My praise.

Pleading with Unfaithful Israel

22 "But you have not called upon Me, O Jacob;
And you have been weary of Me, O Israel.
23 You have not brought Me the sheep for your burnt offerings,
Nor have you honored Me with your sacrifices.
I have not caused you to serve with grain offerings,
Nor wearied you with incense.
24 You have bought Me no sweet cane with money,
Nor have you satisfied Me with the fat of your sacrifices;
But you have burdened Me with your sins,
You have wearied Me with your iniquities.

25 "I, *even* I, *am* He who blots out your transgressions
for My own sake;
And I will not remember your sins.
26 Put Me in remembrance;
Let us contend together;
State your *case,* that you may be acquitted.
27 Your first father sinned,
And your mediators have transgressed against Me.
28 Therefore I will profane the princes of the sanctuary;
I will give Jacob to the curse,
And Israel to reproaches.

God's Blessing on Israel

44 "Yet hear me now, O Jacob My servant,
And Israel whom I have chosen.
2 Thus says the LORD who made you
And formed you from the womb, *who* will help you:
'Fear not, O Jacob My servant;
And you, Jeshurun, whom I have chosen.
3 For I will pour water on him who is thirsty,
And floods on the dry ground;
I will pour My Spirit on your descendants,
And My blessing on your offspring;
4 They will spring up among the grass
Like willows by the watercourses.'
5 One will say, 'I *am* the LORD's';
Another will call *himself* by the name of Jacob;
Another will write *with* his hand, 'The LORD's,'
And name *himself* by the name of Israel.

There Is No Other God

6 "Thus says the LORD, the King of Israel,
And his Redeemer, the LORD of hosts:
'I *am* the First and I *am* the Last;
Besides Me *there is* no God.

7 And who can proclaim as I do?
Then let him declare it and set it in order for Me,
Since I appointed the ancient people.
And the things that are coming and shall come,
Let them show these to them.
8 Do not fear, nor be afraid;
Have I not told you from that time, and declared *it?*
You *are* My witnesses.
Is there a God besides Me?
Indeed *there is* no other Rock;
I know not *one.*' "

Idolatry Is Foolishness

9 Those who make an image, all of them *are* useless,
And their precious things shall not profit;
They *are* their own witnesses;
They neither see nor know, that they may be ashamed.
10 Who would form a god or mold an image
That profits him nothing?
11 Surely all his companions would be ashamed;
And the workmen, they *are* mere men.
Let them all be gathered together,
Let them stand up;
Yet they shall fear,
They shall be ashamed together.
12 The blacksmith with the tongs works one in the coals,
Fashions it with hammers,
And works it with the strength of his arms.
Even so, he is hungry, and his strength fails;
He drinks no water and is faint.

13 The craftsman stretches out *his* rule,
He marks one out with chalk;
He fashions it with a plane,
He marks it out with the compass,
And makes it like the figure of a man,
According to the beauty of a man, that it may remain in the house.
14 He cuts down cedars for himself,
And takes the cypress and the oak;
He secures *it* for himself among the trees of the forest.
He plants a pine, and the rain nourishes *it.*

15 Then it shall be for a man to burn,
For he will take some of it and warm himself;
Yes, he kindles *it* and bakes bread;
Indeed he makes a god and worships *it;*
He makes it a carved image, and falls down to it.
16 He burns half of it in the fire;
With this half he eats meat;
He roasts a roast, and is satisfied.
He even warms *himself* and says,
"Ah! I am warm,
I have seen the fire."
17 And the rest of it he makes into a god,
His carved image.
He falls down before it and worships *it,*
Prays to it and says,
"Deliver me, for you *are* my god!"

18 They do not know nor understand;
For He has shut their eyes, so that they cannot see,
And their hearts, so that they cannot understand.
19 And no one considers in his heart,
Nor *is there* knowledge nor understanding to say,
"I have burned half of it in the fire,
Yes, I have also baked bread on its coals;
I have roasted meat and eaten *it;*
And shall I make the rest of it an abomination?
Shall I fall down before a block of wood?"
20 He feeds on ashes;
A deceived heart has turned him aside;
And he cannot deliver his soul,
Nor say, "*Is there* not a lie in my right hand?"

Israel Is Not Forgotten

21 "Remember these, O Jacob,
And Israel, for you *are* My servant;
I have formed you, you *are* My servant;
O Israel, you will not be forgotten by Me!
22 I have blotted out, like a thick cloud, your transgressions,
And like a cloud, your sins.
Return to Me, for I have redeemed you."

23 Sing, O heavens, for the LORD has done *it!*
Shout, you lower parts of the earth;
Break forth into singing, you mountains,
O forest, and every tree in it!
For the LORD has redeemed Jacob,
And glorified Himself in Israel.

Judah Will Be Restored

24 Thus says the LORD, your Redeemer,
And He who formed you from the womb:
"I *am* the LORD, who makes all *things*,
Who stretches out the heavens all alone,
Who spreads abroad the earth by Myself;
25 Who frustrates the signs of the babblers,
And drives diviners mad;
Who turns wise men backward,
And makes their knowledge foolishness;
26 Who confirms the word of His servant,
And performs the counsel of His messengers;
Who says to Jerusalem, 'You shall
be inhabited,'
To the cities of Judah, 'You shall be built,'
And I will raise up her waste places;
27 Who says to the deep, 'Be dry!
And I will dry up your rivers';
28 Who says of Cyrus, '*He is* My shepherd,
And he shall perform all My pleasure,
Saying to Jerusalem, "You shall be built,"
And to the temple, "Your foundation
shall be laid." '

Cyrus, God's Instrument

45 "Thus says the LORD to His anointed,
To Cyrus, whose right hand I have held—
To subdue nations before him
And loose the armor of kings,
To open before him the double doors,
So that the gates will not be shut:
2 'I will go before you
And make the crooked places[i] straight;
I will break in pieces the gates of bronze
And cut the bars of iron.
3 I will give you the treasures of darkness
And hidden riches of secret places,
That you may know that I, the LORD,
Who call *you* by your name,
Am the God of Israel.
4 For Jacob My servant's sake,
And Israel My elect,
I have even called you by your name;
I have named you, though you have not
known Me.
5 I *am* the LORD, and *there is* no other;
There is no God besides Me.
I will gird you, though you have
not known Me,
6 That they may know from the rising of the sun
to its setting
That *there is* none besides Me.
I *am* the LORD, and *there is* no other;
7 I form the light and create darkness,
I make peace and create calamity;
I, the LORD, do all these *things*.'

8 "Rain down, you heavens, from above,
And let the skies pour down righteousness;
Let the earth open, let them bring
forth salvation,
And let righteousness spring up together.
I, the LORD, have created it.

9 "Woe to him who strives with his Maker!
Let the potsherd *strive* with the potsherds
of the earth!
Shall the clay say to him who forms it, 'What
are you making?'
Or shall your handiwork *say*, 'He has
no hands'?
10 Woe to him who says to *his* father, 'What are
you begetting?'
Or to the woman, 'What have you
brought forth?' "

11 Thus says the LORD,
The Holy One of Israel, and his Maker:
"Ask Me of things to come concerning
My sons;
And concerning the work of My hands, you
command Me.
12 I have made the earth,
And created man on it.
I—My hands—stretched out the heavens,
And all their host I have commanded.
13 I have raised him up in righteousness,
And I will direct all his ways;
He shall build My city
And let My exiles go free,
Not for price nor reward,"
Says the LORD of hosts.

The LORD, the Only Savior

14 Thus says the LORD:

"The labor of Egypt and merchandise of Cush
And of the Sabeans, men of stature,
Shall come over to you, and they shall
be yours;
They shall walk behind you,

45:2 [i] Dead Sea Scrolls and Septuagint read *mountains;* Targum reads *I will trample down the walls;* Vulgate reads *I will humble the great ones of the earth.*

They shall come over in chains;
And they shall bow down to you.
They will make supplication to you, *saying,*
'Surely God *is* in you,
And *there is* no other;
There is no other God.' "

15 Truly You *are* God, who hide Yourself,
O God of Israel, the Savior!
16 They shall be ashamed
And also disgraced, all of them;
They shall go in confusion together,
Who are makers of idols.
17 *But* Israel shall be saved by the LORD
With an everlasting salvation;
You shall not be ashamed or disgraced
Forever and ever.

18 For thus says the LORD,
Who created the heavens,
Who is God,
Who formed the earth and made it,
Who has established it,
Who did not create it in vain,
Who formed it to be inhabited:
"I *am* the LORD, and *there is* no other.
19 I have not spoken in secret,
In a dark place of the earth;
I did not say to the seed of Jacob,
'Seek Me in vain';
I, the LORD, speak righteousness,
I declare things that are right.

20 "Assemble yourselves and come;
Draw near together,
You *who have* escaped from the nations.
They have no knowledge,
Who carry the wood of their carved image,
And pray to a god *that* cannot save.
21 Tell and bring forth *your case;*
Yes, let them take counsel together.
Who has declared this from ancient time?
Who has told it from that time?
Have not I, the LORD?
And *there is* no other God besides Me,
A just God and a Savior;
There is none besides Me.

22 "Look to Me, and be saved,
All you ends of the earth!
For I *am* God, and *there is* no other.
23 I have sworn by Myself;
The word has gone out of My mouth
in righteousness,
And shall not return,
That to Me every knee shall bow,
Every tongue shall take an oath.
24 He shall say,
'Surely in the LORD I have righteousness
and strength.
To Him *men* shall come,
And all shall be ashamed
Who are incensed against Him.
25 In the LORD all the descendants of Israel
Shall be justified, and shall glory.' "

Dead Idols and the Living God

46 Bel bows down, Nebo stoops;
Their idols were on the beasts and on the cattle.
Your carriages *were* heavily loaded,
A burden to the weary *beast.*
2 They stoop, they bow down together;
They could not deliver the burden,
But have themselves gone into captivity.

3 "Listen to Me, O house of Jacob,
And all the remnant of the house of Israel,
Who have been upheld *by Me* from birth,
Who have been carried from the womb:
4 Even to *your* old age, I *am* He,
And *even* to gray hairs I will carry *you!*
I have made, and I will bear;
Even I will carry, and will deliver *you.*

5 "To whom will you liken Me, and make
Me equal
And compare Me, that we should be alike?
6 They lavish gold out of the bag,
And weigh silver on the scales;
They hire a goldsmith, and he makes it a god;
They prostrate themselves, yes, they worship.
7 They bear it on the shoulder, they carry it
And set it in its place, and it stands;
From its place it shall not move.
Though *one* cries out to it, yet it cannot answer
Nor save him out of his trouble.

8 "Remember this, and show yourselves men;
Recall to mind, O you transgressors.
9 Remember the former things of old,
For I *am* God, and *there is* no other;
I *am* God, and *there is* none like Me,

10 Declaring the end from the beginning,
And from ancient times *things* that are not *yet* done,
Saying, 'My counsel shall stand,
And I will do all My pleasure,'
11 Calling a bird of prey from the east,
The man who executes My counsel, from a far country.
Indeed I have spoken *it;*
I will also bring it to pass.
I have purposed *it;*
I will also do it.

12 "Listen to Me, you stubborn-hearted,
Who *are* far from righteousness:
13 I bring My righteousness near, it shall not be far off;
My salvation shall not linger.
And I will place salvation in Zion,
For Israel My glory.

The Humiliation of Babylon

47 "Come down and sit in the dust,
O virgin daughter of Babylon;
Sit on the ground without a throne,
O daughter of the Chaldeans!
For you shall no more be called
Tender and delicate.
2 Take the millstones and grind meal.
Remove your veil,
Take off the skirt,
Uncover the thigh,
Pass through the rivers.
3 Your nakedness shall be uncovered,
Yes, your shame will be seen;
I will take vengeance,
And I will not arbitrate with a man."

4 *As for* our Redeemer, the LORD of hosts *is* His name,
The Holy One of Israel.

5 "Sit in silence, and go into darkness,
O daughter of the Chaldeans;
For you shall no longer be called
The Lady of Kingdoms.
6 I was angry with My people;
I have profaned My inheritance,
And given them into your hand.
You showed them no mercy;
On the elderly you laid your yoke very heavily.
7 And you said, 'I shall be a lady forever,'
So that you did not take these *things* to heart,
Nor remember the latter end of them.

LIFE LESSON

Isaiah 47:1–48:22

SITUATION Isaiah celebrated the overthrow of Babylon with a song of victory. God continued to rebuke Israel for its stubbornness.

OBSERVATION Israel had a history of unyielding stubbornness in its relationship with God. This led to idolatry and unnecessary suffering.

INSPIRATION When we are yielded to God and His will, we are filled with the Holy Spirit. The Holy Spirit controls and dominates us. Now we are to *act* on that truth and *walk* or live with full assurance that God has already filled us, and we are under His control. . . .

Personally, I find it helpful to begin each day silently committing that day into God's hands. I thank Him that I belong to Him, and I thank Him that He knows what the day holds for me. I ask Him to take my life that day and use it for His glory. I ask Him to cleanse me from anything which would hinder His work in my life. And then I step out in faith, knowing that His Holy Spirit is filling me continually as I trust in Him and obey His Word. Sometimes during the day I may not be aware of His presence; sometimes I am. But at the end of the day, I can look back and thank Him, because I see His hand at work. He promised to be with me that day—and He has been!
(From *The Holy Spirit* by Billy Graham)

APPLICATION Does your family name give you confidence? Can you rely on your upstanding church? Does your house make you feel secure? All securities in this life will fail. Trust completely in God. Let him be your unfailing security.

EXPLORATION Repentance—Psalm 32:5; Ezekiel 18:23; 1 John 1:9.

8 "Therefore hear this now, *you who are* given
to pleasures,
Who dwell securely,
Who say in your heart, 'I *am,* and *there is* no
one else besides me;
I shall not sit *as* a widow,
Nor shall I know the loss of children';
9 But these two *things* shall come to you
In a moment, in one day:
The loss of children, and widowhood.
They shall come upon you in their fullness
Because of the multitude of your sorceries,
For the great abundance of
your enchantments.

10 "For you have trusted in your wickedness;
You have said, 'No one sees me';
Your wisdom and your knowledge have
warped you;
And you have said in your heart,
'I *am,* and *there is* no one else besides me.'
11 Therefore evil shall come upon you;
You shall not know from where it arises.
And trouble shall fall upon you;
You will not be able to put it off.
And desolation shall come upon
you suddenly,
Which you shall not know.

12 "Stand now with your enchantments
And the multitude of your sorceries,
In which you have labored from your youth—
Perhaps you will be able to profit,
Perhaps you will prevail.
13 You are wearied in the multitude
of your counsels;
Let now the astrologers, the stargazers,
And the monthly prognosticators
Stand up and save you
From what shall come upon you.
14 Behold, they shall be as stubble,
The fire shall burn them;
They shall not deliver themselves
From the power of the flame;
It shall not *be* a coal to be warmed by,
Nor a fire to sit before!
15 Thus shall they be to you
With whom you have labored,
Your merchants from your youth;
They shall wander each one to his quarter.
No one shall save you.

Israel Refined for God's Glory

48 "Hear this, O house of Jacob,
Who are called by the name of Israel,
And have come forth from the wellsprings
of Judah;
Who swear by the name of the LORD,
And make mention of the God of Israel,
But not in truth or in righteousness;
2 For they call themselves after the holy city,
And lean on the God of Israel;
The LORD of hosts *is* His name:

3 "I have declared the former things from
the beginning;
They went forth from My mouth, and I caused
them to hear it.
Suddenly I did *them,* and they came to pass.
4 Because I knew that you *were* obstinate,
And your neck *was* an iron sinew,
And your brow bronze,
5 Even from the beginning I have declared
it to you;
Before it came to pass I proclaimed *it* to you,
Lest you should say, 'My idol has done them,
And my carved image and my molded image
Have commanded them.'

6 "You have heard;
See all this.
And will you not declare *it?*
I have made you hear new things from
this time,
Even hidden things, and you did not
know them.
7 They are created now and not from
the beginning;
And before this day you have not heard them,
Lest you should say, 'Of course I knew them.'
8 Surely you did not hear,
Surely you did not know;
Surely from long ago your ear was
not opened.
For I knew that you would deal
very treacherously,
And were called a transgressor
from the womb.

9 "For My name's sake I will defer My anger,
And *for* My praise I will restrain it from you,
So that I do not cut you off.
10 Behold, I have refined you, but not as silver;
I have tested you in the furnace of affliction.

11 For My own sake, for My own sake, I will do *it;*
For how should *My name* be profaned?
And I will not give My glory to another.

God's Ancient Plan to Redeem Israel

12 "Listen to Me, O Jacob,
And Israel, My called:
I *am* He, I *am* the First,
I *am* also the Last.
13 Indeed My hand has laid the foundation
of the earth,
And My right hand has stretched out
the heavens;
When I call to them,
They stand up together.

14 "All of you, assemble yourselves, and hear!
Who among them has declared these *things?*
The LORD loves him;
He shall do His pleasure on Babylon,
And His arm *shall be against* the Chaldeans.
15 I, *even* I, have spoken;
Yes, I have called him,
I have brought him, and his way will prosper.

16 "Come near to Me, hear this:
I have not spoken in secret from
the beginning;
From the time that it was, I *was* there.
And now the Lord GOD and His Spirit
Have[j] sent Me."

17 Thus says the LORD, your Redeemer,
The Holy One of Israel:
"I *am* the LORD your God,
Who teaches you to profit,
Who leads you by the way you should go.
18 Oh, that you had heeded My commandments!
Then your peace would have been like a river,
And your righteousness like the waves
of the sea.
19 Your descendants also would have been
like the sand,
And the offspring of your body like the
grains of sand;
His name would not have been cut off
Nor destroyed from before Me."

20 Go forth from Babylon!
Flee from the Chaldeans!
With a voice of singing,
Declare, proclaim this,
Utter it to the end of the earth;
Say, "The LORD has redeemed
His servant Jacob!"
21 And they did not thirst
When He led them through the deserts;
He caused the waters to flow from the rock
for them;
He also split the rock, and the waters
gushed out.

22 "*There is* no peace," says the LORD,
"for the wicked."

The Servant, the Light to the Gentiles

49 "Listen, O coastlands, to Me,
And take heed, you peoples from afar!
The LORD has called Me from the womb;
From the matrix of My mother He has made
mention of My name.
2 And He has made My mouth like
a sharp sword;
In the shadow of His hand He has hidden Me,
And made Me a polished shaft;
In His quiver He has hidden Me."

3 "And He said to me,
'You *are* My servant, O Israel,
In whom I will be glorified.'
4 Then I said, 'I have labored in vain,
I have spent my strength for nothing
and in vain;
Yet surely my just reward *is* with the LORD,
And my work with my God.' "

5 "And now the LORD says,
Who formed Me from the womb *to be*
His Servant,
To bring Jacob back to Him,
So that Israel is gathered to Him[k]
(For I shall be glorious in the eyes of the LORD,
And My God shall be My strength),
6 Indeed He says,
'It is too small a thing that You should be
My Servant
To raise up the tribes of Jacob,
And to restore the preserved ones of Israel;
I will also give You as a light to the Gentiles,
That You should be My salvation to the ends
of the earth.' "

48:16 [j] The Hebrew verb is singular.
49:5 [k] Qere, Dead Sea Scrolls, and Septuagint read *is gathered to Him;* Kethib reads *is not gathered.*

7 Thus says the LORD,
The Redeemer of Israel, their Holy One,
To Him whom man despises,
To Him whom the nation abhors,
To the Servant of rulers:
"Kings shall see and arise,
Princes also shall worship,
Because of the LORD who is faithful,
The Holy One of Israel;
And He has chosen You."

8Thus says the LORD:

"In an acceptable time I have heard You,
And in the day of salvation I have helped You;
I will preserve You and give You
As a covenant to the people,
To restore the earth,
To cause them to inherit the desolate heritages;
9 That You may say to the prisoners, 'Go forth,'
To those who *are* in darkness, 'Show yourselves.'

"They shall feed along the roads,
And their pastures *shall be* on all desolate heights.
10 They shall neither hunger nor thirst,
Neither heat nor sun shall strike them;
For He who has mercy on them will lead them,
Even by the springs of water He will guide them.
11 I will make each of My mountains a road,
And My highways shall be elevated.
12 Surely these shall come from afar;
Look! Those from the north and the west,
And these from the land of Sinim."

13 Sing, O heavens!
Be joyful, O earth!
And break out in singing, O mountains!
For the LORD has comforted His people,
And will have mercy on His afflicted.

God Will Remember Zion

14 But Zion said, "The LORD has forsaken me,
And my Lord has forgotten me."

15 "Can a woman forget her nursing child,
And not have compassion on the son of her womb?
Surely they may forget,
Yet I will not forget you.
16 See, I have inscribed you on the palms *of My hands;*
Your walls *are* continually before Me.
17 Your sons[l] shall make haste;

49:17 [l] Dead Sea Scrolls, Septuagint, Targum, and Vulgate read *builders*.

LIFE LESSON

Isaiah 49:1–52:12

SITUATION Isaiah introduced the purpose of the Servant-Messiah. Isaiah reminded the Israelites of God's previous rescue of them and of the Messiah's future saving work.

OBSERVATION God has a long history when it comes to being faithful. He has kept his people safe for thousands of years.

INSPIRATION We have already seen that the Bible teaches that God was a God of love. He wanted to do something for man. He wanted to save man. He wanted to free man from the curse of sin. How could He do it? God was a just God. He was righteous, and holy. He had warned man from the beginning that if he obeyed the Devil and disobeyed God, he would die physically and spiritually. . . .

All through the Old Testament, God gave man the promise of salvation if by faith he would believe in the coming Redeemer. Therefore God began to teach His people that man could only be saved by substitution. Someone else would have to pay the bill for man's redemption. . . .

Thanks be to God—that is exactly what happened! Looking down over the battlements of heaven He saw this planet swinging in space—doomed, damned, crushed, and bound for hell. He saw you and me struggling beneath our load of sin and bound in the chains and ropes of sin. He made His decision in the council halls of God. The angelic hosts bowed in humility and awe as heaven's Prince of Princes and Lord of Lords, who could speak worlds into space, got into His jeweled chariot, went through pearly gates, across the steep of the skies, and on a black Judean night, while the stars sang together and the escorting angels chanted praises, stepped out of the chariot, threw off His robes, and became man!

(From *Peace with God* by Billy Graham)

Continued

APPLICATION Meditate on the things God has saved you from: hell, drugs, despair, alcohol, sinful habits, hopelessness, restlessness, and selfishness. Thank God for this most wonderful gift of redemption.

EXPLORATION Redemption—Psalm 31:5; 130:7; Luke 1:68; Romans 3:24; Ephesians 4:30; Titus 2:14; 1 Peter 1:18, 19.

Your destroyers and those who laid you waste
Shall go away from you.
18 Lift up your eyes, look around and see;
All these gather together *and* come to you.
As I live," says the LORD,
"You shall surely clothe yourselves with them all as an ornament,
And bind them *on you* as a bride *does.*

19 "For your waste and desolate places,
And the land of your destruction,
Will even now be too small for the inhabitants;
And those who swallowed you up will be far away.
20 The children you will have,
After you have lost the others,
Will say again in your ears,
'The place *is* too small for me;
Give me a place where I may dwell.'
21 Then you will say in your heart,
'Who has begotten these for me,
Since I have lost my children and am desolate,
A captive, and wandering to and fro?
And who has brought these up?
There I was, left alone;
But these, where *were* they?' "

22 Thus says the Lord GOD:

"Behold, I will lift My hand in an oath to the nations,
And set up My standard for the peoples;
They shall bring your sons in *their* arms,
And your daughters shall be carried on *their* shoulders;
23 Kings shall be your foster fathers,
And their queens your nursing mothers;
They shall bow down to you with *their* faces to the earth,
And lick up the dust of your feet.
Then you will know that I *am* the LORD,
For they shall not be ashamed who wait for Me."

24 Shall the prey be taken from the mighty,
Or the captives of the righteous[m] be delivered?

25 But thus says the LORD:

"Even the captives of the mighty shall be taken away,
And the prey of the terrible be delivered;
For I will contend with him who contends with you,
And I will save your children.
26 I will feed those who oppress you with their own flesh,
And they shall be drunk with their own blood as with sweet wine.
All flesh shall know
That I, the LORD, *am* your Savior,
And your Redeemer, the Mighty One of Jacob."

49:24 [m] Following Masoretic Text and Targum; Dead Sea Scrolls, Syriac, and Vulgate read *the mighty;* Septuagint reads *unjustly*.

The Servant, Israel's Hope

50 Thus says the LORD:

"Where *is* the certificate of your
mother's divorce,
Whom I have put away?
Or which of My creditors *is it* to whom I have
sold you?
For your iniquities you have sold yourselves,
And for your transgressions your mother has
been put away.
2 Why, when I came, *was there* no man?
Why, when I called, *was there* none to answer?
Is My hand shortened at all that it
cannot redeem?
Or have I no power to deliver?
Indeed with My rebuke I dry up the sea,
I make the rivers a wilderness;
Their fish stink because *there is* no water,
And die of thirst.
3 I clothe the heavens with blackness,
And I make sackcloth their covering."

4 "The Lord GOD has given Me
The tongue of the learned,
That I should know how to speak
A word in season to *him who is* weary.
He awakens Me morning by morning,
He awakens My ear
To hear as the learned.
5 The Lord GOD has opened My ear;
And I was not rebellious,
Nor did I turn away.
6 I gave My back to those who struck *Me,*
And My cheeks to those who plucked out
the beard;
I did not hide My face from
shame and spitting.

7 "For the Lord GOD will help Me;
Therefore I will not be disgraced;
Therefore I have set My face like a flint,
And I know that I will not be ashamed.
8 *He is* near who justifies Me;
Who will contend with Me?
Let us stand together.
Who *is* My adversary?
Let him come near Me.
9 Surely the Lord GOD will help Me;
Who *is* he *who* will condemn Me?
Indeed they will all grow old like a garment;
The moth will eat them up.

10 "Who among you fears the LORD?
Who obeys the voice of His Servant?
Who walks in darkness
And has no light?
Let him trust in the name of the LORD
And rely upon his God.
11 Look, all you who kindle a fire,
Who encircle *yourselves* with sparks:
Walk in the light of your fire and in the sparks
you have kindled—
This you shall have from My hand:
You shall lie down in torment.

The LORD Comforts Zion

51 "Listen to Me, you who follow after
righteousness,
You who seek the LORD:
Look to the rock *from which* you were hewn,
And to the hole of the pit *from which*
you were dug.
2 Look to Abraham your father,
And to Sarah *who* bore you;
For I called him alone,
And blessed him and increased him."

3 For the LORD will comfort Zion,
He will comfort all her waste places;
He will make her wilderness like Eden,
And her desert like the garden of the LORD;
Joy and gladness will be found in it,
Thanksgiving and the voice of melody.

4 "Listen to Me, My people;
And give ear to Me, O My nation:
For law will proceed from Me,
And I will make My justice rest
As a light of the peoples.
5 My righteousness *is* near,
My salvation has gone forth,
And My arms will judge the peoples;
The coastlands will wait upon Me,
And on My arm they will trust.
6 Lift up your eyes to the heavens,
And look on the earth beneath.
For the heavens will vanish away like smoke,
The earth will grow old like a garment,
And those who dwell in it will die in
like manner;
But My salvation will be forever,
And My righteousness will not be abolished.

7 "Listen to Me, you who know righteousness,
You people in whose heart *is* My law:
Do not fear the reproach of men,
Nor be afraid of their insults.
8 For the moth will eat them up like
a garment,
And the worm will eat them like wool;
But My righteousness will be forever,
And My salvation from generation
to generation."

9 Awake, awake, put on strength,
O arm of the LORD!
Awake as in the ancient days,
In the generations of old.
Are You not *the arm* that cut Rahab apart,
And wounded the serpent?

10 *Are* You not *the One* who dried up the sea,
The waters of the great deep;
That made the depths of the sea a road
For the redeemed to cross over?
11 So the ransomed of the LORD shall return,
And come to Zion with singing,
With everlasting joy on their heads.
They shall obtain joy and gladness;
Sorrow and sighing shall flee away.

12 "I, *even* I, *am* He who comforts you.
Who *are* you that you should be afraid
Of a man *who* will die,
And of the son of a man *who* will be made
like grass?
13 And you forget the LORD your Maker,
Who stretched out the heavens
And laid the foundations of the earth;
You have feared continually every day
Because of the fury of the oppressor,
When *he has* prepared to destroy.
And where *is* the fury of the oppressor?
14 The captive exile hastens, that he
may be loosed,
That he should not die in the pit,
And that his bread should not fail.
15 But I *am* the LORD your God,
Who divided the sea whose waves roared—
The LORD of hosts *is* His name.
16 And I have put My words in your mouth;
I have covered you with the shadow
of My hand,
That I may plant the heavens,
Lay the foundations of the earth,
And say to Zion, 'You *are* My people.' "

God's Fury Removed

17 Awake, awake!
Stand up, O Jerusalem,
You who have drunk at the hand of the LORD
The cup of His fury;
You have drunk the dregs of the cup
of trembling,
And drained *it* out.
18 *There is* no one to guide her
Among all the sons she has brought forth;
Nor *is there any* who takes her by the hand
Among all the sons she has brought up.
19 These two *things* have come to you;
Who will be sorry for you?—
Desolation and destruction, famine
and sword—
By whom will I comfort you?
20 Your sons have fainted,
They lie at the head of all the streets,
Like an antelope in a net;
They are full of the fury of the LORD,
The rebuke of your God.

21 Therefore please hear this, you afflicted,
And drunk but not with wine.
22 Thus says your Lord,
The LORD and your God,
Who pleads the cause of His people:
"See, I have taken out of your hand
The cup of trembling,
The dregs of the cup of My fury;
You shall no longer drink it.
23 But I will put it into the hand of those
who afflict you,
Who have said to you,[n]
'Lie down, that we may walk over you.'
And you have laid your body like the ground,
And as the street, for those who walk over."

God Redeems Jerusalem

52 Awake, awake!
Put on your strength, O Zion;
Put on your beautiful garments,
O Jerusalem, the holy city!
For the uncircumcised and the unclean
Shall no longer come to you.

51:23 [n] Literally *your soul*

2 Shake yourself from the dust, arise;
Sit down, O Jerusalem!
Loose yourself from the bonds of your neck,
O captive daughter of Zion!

3 For thus says the LORD:

"You have sold yourselves for nothing,
And you shall be redeemed without money."

4 For thus says the Lord GOD:

"My people went down at first
Into Egypt to dwell there;
Then the Assyrian oppressed them without cause.
5 Now therefore, what have I here," says the LORD,
"That My people are taken away for nothing?
Those who rule over them
Make them wail,"[o] says the LORD,
"And My name *is* blasphemed continually every day.
6 Therefore My people shall know My name;
Therefore *they shall know* in that day
That I *am* He who speaks:
'Behold, *it is* I.' "

7 How beautiful upon the mountains
Are the feet of him who brings good news,
Who proclaims peace,
Who brings glad tidings of good *things*,
Who proclaims salvation,
Who says to Zion,
"Your God reigns!"
8 Your watchmen shall lift up *their* voices,
With their voices they shall sing together;
For they shall see eye to eye
When the LORD brings back Zion.
9 Break forth into joy, sing together,
You waste places of Jerusalem!
For the LORD has comforted His people,
He has redeemed Jerusalem.
10 The LORD has made bare His holy arm
In the eyes of all the nations;
And all the ends of the earth shall see
The salvation of our God.

11 Depart! Depart! Go out from there,
Touch no unclean *thing;*
Go out from the midst of her,
Be clean,
You who bear the vessels of the LORD.

52:5 *o* Dead Sea Scrolls read *Mock;* Septuagint reads *Marvel and wail;* Targum reads *Boast themselves;* Vulgate reads *Treat them unjustly.*

LIFE LESSON

Isaiah 52:13–53:12

SITUATION Isaiah prophesied about the coming of the Messiah, the suffering servant—Jesus Christ. He referred to the Servant's lowly existence, agonizing death, and honorable purpose.

OBSERVATION Because he did not want to see us suffer in hell, God suffered for us.

INSPIRATION My friend and associate, Cliff Barrows, told me this story about bearing punishment. He recalled the time when he took the punishment for his children when they had disobeyed. "They had done something I had forbidden them to do. I told them if they did the same thing again I would have to discipline them. When I returned from work and found that they hadn't minded me, the heart went out of me. I just couldn't discipline them."

A loving father can understand Cliff's dilemma. Most of us have been in the same position. He continued with the story: "Bobby and Bettie Ruth were very small. I called them into my room, took off my belt and my shirt, and with a bare back, knelt down at the bed. I made them both strap me with the belt ten times each. You should have heard the crying! From them, I mean! They didn't want to do it. But I told them the penalty had to be paid and so through their sobs and tears they did what I told them."

Cliff smiled when he remembered the incident. "I must admit I wasn't much of a hero. It hurt. I haven't offered to do that again, but I never had to spank them again, either, because they got the point. We kissed each other when it was over and prayed together."

In that infinite way that staggers our hearts and minds, we know that Christ paid the penalty for our sins, past, present, and future.

That is why He died on the cross.

(From *How to Be Born Again* by Billy Graham)

Continued

APPLICATION Read the account of Jesus' death in one of the Gospels. Consider the pain he felt because of your sins. Thank him, praise him, sing with joy. Then tell others about him.

EXPLORATION Forgiveness of Sins—Isaiah 43:25; 44:22; Micah 7:18; Matthew 26:28; Acts 2:38; 13:38; Romans 6:23; Ephesians 1:7; Hebrews 9:22; 1 John 1:9.

12 For you shall not go out with haste,
Nor go by flight;
For the LORD will go before you,
And the God of Israel *will be* your rear guard.

The Sin-Bearing Servant

13 Behold, My Servant shall deal prudently;
He shall be exalted and extolled and be very high.
14 Just as many were astonished at you,
So His visage was marred more than any man,
And His form more than the sons of men;
15 So shall He sprinkle[p] many nations.
Kings shall shut their mouths at Him;
For what had not been told them they shall see,
And what they had not heard they shall consider.

53 Who has believed our report?
And to whom has the arm of the LORD been revealed?
2 For He shall grow up before Him as a tender plant,
And as a root out of dry ground.
He has no form or comeliness;
And when we see Him,
There is no beauty that we should desire Him.
3 He is despised and rejected by men,
A Man of sorrows and acquainted with grief.
And we hid, as it were, *our* faces from Him;
He was despised, and we did not esteem Him.

4 Surely He has borne our griefs
And carried our sorrows;
Yet we esteemed Him stricken,
Smitten by God, and afflicted.
5 But He *was* wounded for our transgressions,
He was bruised for our iniquities;
The chastisement for our peace *was* upon Him,
And by His stripes we are healed.
6 All we like sheep have gone astray;
We have turned, every one, to his own way;
And the LORD has laid on Him the iniquity of us all.

7 He was oppressed and He was afflicted,
Yet He opened not His mouth;
He was led as a lamb to the slaughter,
And as a sheep before its shearers is silent,
So He opened not His mouth.
8 He was taken from prison and from judgment,
And who will declare His generation?
For He was cut off from the land of the living;
For the transgressions of My people He was stricken.
9 And they[q] made His grave with the wicked—
But with the rich at His death,
Because He had done no violence,

52:15 [p] Or *startle*
53:9 [q] Literally *he* or *He*

Nor *was any* deceit in His mouth.
10 Yet it pleased the LORD to bruise Him;
He has put *Him* to grief.
When You make His soul an offering for sin,
He shall see *His* seed, He shall prolong *His* days,
And the pleasure of the LORD shall prosper in His hand.
11 He shall see the labor of His soul,[r] *and* be satisfied.
By His knowledge My righteous Servant shall justify many,
For He shall bear their iniquities.
12 Therefore I will divide Him a portion with the great,
And He shall divide the spoil with the strong,
Because He poured out His soul unto death,
And He was numbered with the transgressors,
And He bore the sin of many,
And made intercession for the transgressors.

A Perpetual Covenant of Peace

54 "Sing, O barren,
You *who* have not borne!
Break forth into singing, and cry aloud,
You *who* have not labored with child!
For more *are* the children of the desolate
Than the children of the married woman," says the LORD.
2 "Enlarge the place of your tent,
And let them stretch out the curtains of your dwellings;
Do not spare;
Lengthen your cords,
And strengthen your stakes.
3 For you shall expand to the right and to the left,
And your descendants will inherit the nations,
And make the desolate cities inhabited.
4 "Do not fear, for you will not be ashamed;
Neither be disgraced, for you will not be put to shame;
For you will forget the shame of your youth,
And will not remember the reproach of your widowhood anymore.
5 For your Maker *is* your husband,
The LORD of hosts *is* His name;
And your Redeemer *is* the Holy One of Israel;
He is called the God of the whole earth.
6 For the LORD has called you
Like a woman forsaken and grieved in spirit,
Like a youthful wife when you were refused,"
Says your God.
7 "For a mere moment I have forsaken you,
But with great mercies I will gather you.
8 With a little wrath I hid My face from you for a moment;
But with everlasting kindness I will have mercy on you,"
Says the LORD, your Redeemer.

LIFE LESSON

Isaiah 54:1–55:13

SITUATION Isaiah comforted the Israelites by telling them of God's power.

OBSERVATION Because God encourages and rescues his people, we can call him the great Comforter and Redeemer.

INSPIRATION Mercy is an attribute of God, an infinite and inexhaustible energy within the divine nature which disposes God to be actively compassionate. Both the Old and the New Testaments proclaim the mercy of God. . . . If we could remember that the divine mercy is not a temporary mood but an attribute of God's eternal being, we would no longer fear that it will someday cease to be. Mercy never began to be, but from eternity was; so it will never cease to be. It will never be more since it is itself infinite; and it will never be less because the infinite cannot suffer diminution. Nothing that has occurred or will occur in heaven or earth or hell can change the tender mercies of our God. Forever His mercy stands, a boundless, overwhelming immensity of divine pity and compassion. . . .
And it is not enough to believe that He once showed mercy to Noah or Abraham or David and will again show mercy in some happy future day. We must believe that God's mercy is boundless, free and, through Jesus Christ our Lord, available to us now in our present situation.
(From *The Knowledge of the Holy* by A. W. Tozer)

APPLICATION Do you know someone who is hard to get along with? Read these chapters again and brainstorm how you can be kind and gentle to that person. Pick one of these actions and ask God to help you do it.

EXPLORATION God's Mercy—Lamentations 3:19-24; Doing Good—Galatians 6:9; James 1:22-25.

53:11 [r] Following Masoretic Text, Targum, and Vulgate; Dead Sea Scrolls and Septuagint read *From the labor of His soul He shall see light.*

9 "For this *is* like the waters of Noah to Me;
For as I have sworn
That the waters of Noah would no longer
cover the earth,
So have I sworn
That I would not be angry with you,
nor rebuke you.
10 For the mountains shall depart
And the hills be removed,
But My kindness shall not depart from you,
Nor shall My covenant of peace be removed,"
Says the LORD, who has mercy on you.

11 "O you afflicted one,
Tossed with tempest, *and* not comforted,
Behold, I will lay your stones
with colorful gems,
And lay your foundations with sapphires.
12 I will make your pinnacles of rubies,
Your gates of crystal,
And all your walls of precious stones.
13 All your children *shall be* taught by the LORD,
And great *shall be* the peace of your children.
14 In righteousness you shall be established;
You shall be far from oppression, for you
shall not fear;
And from terror, for it shall not
come near you.
15 Indeed they shall surely assemble, *but* not
because of Me.
Whoever assembles against you shall fall
for your sake.

16 "Behold, I have created the blacksmith
Who blows the coals in the fire,
Who brings forth an instrument for his work;
And I have created the spoiler to destroy.
17 No weapon formed against you shall prosper,
And every tongue *which* rises against
you in judgment
You shall condemn.
This *is* the heritage of the servants of the LORD,
And their righteousness *is* from Me,"
Says the LORD.

An Invitation to Abundant Life

55 "Ho! Everyone who thirsts,
Come to the waters;
And you who have no money,
Come, buy and eat.
Yes, come, buy wine and milk
Without money and without price.
2 Why do you spend money for *what is* not bread,
And your wages for *what* does not satisfy?
Listen carefully to Me, and eat *what is* good,
And let your soul delight itself in abundance.
3 Incline your ear, and come to Me.
Hear, and your soul shall live;
And I will make an everlasting covenant
with you—
The sure mercies of David.
4 Indeed I have given him *as* a witness
to the people,
A leader and commander for the people.
5 Surely you shall call a nation you do not know,
And nations *who* do not know you
shall run to you,
Because of the LORD your God,
And the Holy One of Israel;
For He has glorified you."

6 Seek the LORD while He may be found,
Call upon Him while He is near.
7 Let the wicked forsake his way,
And the unrighteous man his thoughts;
Let him return to the LORD,
And He will have mercy on him;
And to our God,
For He will abundantly pardon.

8 "For My thoughts *are* not your thoughts,
Nor *are* your ways My ways," says the LORD.
9 "For *as* the heavens are higher than the earth,
So are My ways higher than your ways,
And My thoughts than your thoughts.

10 "For as the rain comes down, and the snow
from heaven,
And do not return there,
But water the earth,
And make it bring forth and bud,
That it may give seed to the sower
And bread to the eater,
11 So shall My word be that goes forth
from My mouth;
It shall not return to Me void,
But it shall accomplish what I please,
And it shall prosper *in the thing* for
which I sent it.

12 "For you shall go out with joy,
And be led out with peace;
The mountains and the hills
Shall break forth into singing before you,
And all the trees of the field shall clap
their hands.

13 Instead of the thorn shall come up the cypress tree,
And instead of the brier shall come up
the myrtle tree;
And it shall be to the LORD for a name,
For an everlasting sign *that* shall not be cut off."

Salvation for the Gentiles

56 Thus says the LORD:

"Keep justice, and do righteousness,
For My salvation *is* about to come,
And My righteousness to be revealed.
2 Blessed *is* the man *who* does this,
And the son of man *who* lays hold on it;
Who keeps from defiling the Sabbath,
And keeps his hand from doing any evil."

3 Do not let the son of the foreigner
Who has joined himself to the LORD
Speak, saying,
"The LORD has utterly separated me from His people";
Nor let the eunuch say,
"Here I am, a dry tree."
4 For thus says the LORD:
"To the eunuchs who keep My Sabbaths,
And choose what pleases Me,
And hold fast My covenant,
5 Even to them I will give in My house
And within My walls a place and a name
Better than that of sons and daughters;
I will give them[s] an everlasting name
That shall not be cut off.

6 "Also the sons of the foreigner
Who join themselves to the LORD, to serve Him,
And to love the name of the LORD, to be His servants—
Everyone who keeps from defiling the Sabbath,
And holds fast My covenant—
7 Even them I will bring to My holy mountain,
And make them joyful in My house of prayer.
Their burnt offerings and their sacrifices
Will be accepted on My altar;
For My house shall be called a house of prayer
for all nations."
8 The Lord GOD, who gathers the outcasts of Israel, says,
"Yet I will gather to him
Others besides those who are gathered to him."

Israel's Irresponsible Leaders

9 All you beasts of the field, come to devour,
All you beasts in the forest.

56:5 [s] Literally *him*

LIFE LESSON

Isaiah 56:1–57:21

SITUATION Isaiah reported God's message to Israel. He exhorted the people to observe God's laws concerning the Sabbath.

OBSERVATION God gives peace and satisfaction to those who love him, but he punishes the wicked for their sins.

INSPIRATION Read what Jesus did during the last Sabbath of his life. . . . Looks like Jesus was quiet that day.

"Wait a minute. That's it?" That's it.

"You mean with one week left to live, Jesus observed the Sabbath?" As far as we can tell.

"You mean with all those apostles to train and people to teach, he took a day to rest and worship?" Apparently so.

"You're telling me that Jesus thought worship was more important than work?" That's exactly what I'm telling you.

For such is the purpose of the Sabbath. And such was the practice of Jesus. "On the Sabbath day he went to the synagogue, *as he always did,* and stood up to read." Should we do any less?

If Jesus found time in the midst of a racing agenda to stop the rush and sit in the silence, do you think we could, too?

Ahh, I know what you're thinking. I can see it in your face. There you are. Looking at me from my monitor with dubious eyes and furrowed brows. "But, Max, Sunday is the only day I have to get caught up at the office." Or, "Good idea, Max, but have you heard our preacher? He provides the rest all right—I fall asleep! But the worship?" Or, "That's easy for you to say, Max. You're a preacher. If you were a housewife like me and had four kids like mine. . . . " It's not easy to slow down.

It's almost as if activity is a sign of maturity. After all, isn't there a beatitude which reads, "Blessed are the busy?" No, there isn't. But there is a verse which summarizes many lives: "Man is a mere phantom as he goes

Continued

to and fro: He bustles about, but only in vain; he heaps up wealth, not knowing who will get it."

Does that sound like your life? Are you so seldom in one place that your friends regard you as a phantom? Are you so constantly on the move that your family is beginning to question your existence? Do you take pride in your frenzy at the expense of your faith?

Are [these] words yours? "I don't remember how to stop." If so, you are headed for a crash.

Slow down. If God commanded it, you need it. If Jesus modeled it, you need it. God still provides the manna. Trust him. Take a day to say no to work and yes to worship.

(From *And the Angels Were Silent* by Max Lucado)

APPLICATION Do you need to slow down? Why not leave Sunday agenda-free? Do something you find relaxing. Take the day off. Take a nap. Read a book. Spend it doing . . . nothing.

EXPLORATION Peace/Comfort —Psalm 29:11; Isaiah 26:3-4; 32:17; Habakkuk 3:17-19; John 14:27; Romans 2:10; 5:1.

10 His watchmen *are* blind,
They are all ignorant;
They *are* all dumb dogs,
They cannot bark;
Sleeping, lying down, loving to slumber.
11 Yes, *they are* greedy dogs
Which never have enough.
And they *are* shepherds
Who cannot understand;
They all look to their own way,
Every one for his own gain,
From his *own* territory.
12 "Come," *one says,* "I will bring wine,
And we will fill ourselves with intoxicating drink;
Tomorrow will be as today,
And much more abundant."

Israel's Futile Idolatry

57 The righteous perishes,
And no man takes *it* to heart;
Merciful men *are* taken away,
While no one considers
That the righteous is taken away from evil.
2 He shall enter into peace;
They shall rest in their beds,
Each one walking *in* his uprightness.

3 "But come here,
You sons of the sorceress,
You offspring of the adulterer and the harlot!
4 Whom do you ridicule?
Against whom do you make a wide mouth
And stick out the tongue?
Are you not children of transgression,
Offspring of falsehood,
5 Inflaming yourselves with gods under every green tree,
Slaying the children in the valleys,
Under the clefts of the rocks?
6 Among the smooth *stones* of the stream
Is your portion;
They, they, *are* your lot!
Even to them you have poured a drink offering,
You have offered a grain offering.
Should I receive comfort in these?

7 "On a lofty and high mountain
You have set your bed;
Even there you went up
To offer sacrifice.
8 Also behind the doors and their posts
You have set up your remembrance;
For you have uncovered yourself *to those other* than Me,

And have gone up to them;
You have enlarged your bed
And made *a covenant* with them;
You have loved their bed,
Where you saw *their* nudity.[t]
9 You went to the king with ointment,
And increased your perfumes;
You sent your messengers far off,
And *even* descended to Sheol.
10 You are wearied in the length of your way;
Yet you did not say, 'There is no hope.'
You have found the life of your hand;
Therefore you were not grieved.

11 "And of whom have you been afraid,
or feared,
That you have lied
And not remembered Me,
Nor taken *it* to your heart?
Is it not because I have held My peace
from of old
That you do not fear Me?
12 I will declare your righteousness
And your works,
For they will not profit you.
13 When you cry out,
Let your collection *of idols* deliver you.
But the wind will carry them all away,
A breath will take *them.*
But he who puts his trust in Me shall
possess the land,
And shall inherit My holy mountain."

Healing for the Backslider

14 And one shall say,
"Heap it up! Heap it up!
Prepare the way,
Take the stumbling block out of the way
of My people."

15 For thus says the High and Lofty One
Who inhabits eternity, whose name *is* Holy:
"I dwell in the high and holy *place,*
With him *who* has a contrite
and humble spirit,
To revive the spirit of the humble,
And to revive the heart of the contrite ones.
16 For I will not contend forever,
Nor will I always be angry;
For the spirit would fail before Me,
And the souls *which* I have made.
17 For the iniquity of his covetousness
I was angry and struck him;
I hid and was angry,
And he went on backsliding in the way
of his heart.
18 I have seen his ways, and will heal him;
I will also lead him,
And restore comforts to him
And to his mourners.
19 "I create the fruit of the lips:
Peace, peace to *him who is* far off and to *him
who is* near,"
Says the LORD,
"And I will heal him."
20 But the wicked *are* like the troubled sea,
When it cannot rest,
Whose waters cast up mire and dirt.
21 "*There is* no peace,"
Says my God, "for the wicked."

Fasting that Pleases God

58 "Cry aloud, spare not;
Lift up your voice like a trumpet;
Tell My people their transgression,
And the house of Jacob their sins.
2 Yet they seek Me daily,
And delight to know My ways,
As a nation that did righteousness,
And did not forsake the ordinance
of their God.
They ask of Me the ordinances of justice;
They take delight in approaching God.
3 'Why have we fasted,' *they say,* 'and You
have not seen?
Why have we afflicted our souls, and You
take no notice?'

"In fact, in the day of your fast you find pleasure,
And exploit all your laborers.
4 Indeed you fast for strife and debate,
And to strike with the fist of wickedness.
You will not fast as *you do* this day,
To make your voice heard on high.
5 Is it a fast that I have chosen,
A day for a man to afflict his soul?
Is it to bow down his head like a bulrush,
And to spread out sackcloth and ashes?
Would you call this a fast,
And an acceptable day to the LORD?

57:8 [t] Literally *hand,* a euphemism

LIFE LESSON

Isaiah 58:1–59:21

SITUATION God ordered Isaiah to remind the people of their rebellion. Even their efforts to be religious had selfish motivations.

OBSERVATION Seek God with pure motives. Do good works because you love God, not because others expect them.

INSPIRATION Holy living demands constant examination of our actions and motives. But in doing so we must guard against the tendency to focus totally on self, which is easy to do—especially as the culture's egocentric values invade the church. In fact, this self-indulgent character of our times is a major reason the topic of true holiness is so neglected today by Christian teachers, leaders, writers, and speakers. We have, perhaps unconsciously, substituted a secularized self-centered message in its place. For when we speak of "victory" in the Christian life, we all-too-often mean personal victory—how God will conquer sin FOR US (at least those sins we would like to be rid of—those extra ten pounds, that annoying habit, maybe a quick temper). This reflects not only egocentricity but an incorrect view of sin.

. . .The Christian life begins with obedience, depends on obedience, and results in obedience. We can't escape it. The orders from our commander-in-chief are plain: "Whoever has my commandments and obeys them, he is the one who loves me."

Loving God—really loving Him—means living out His commands no matter what the cost.

(From *Loving God* by Charles Colson)

APPLICATION The next time you sing at church, during the second stanza ask yourself, "Why am I doing this? Why am I here? Why am I singing? Why did I bring my Bible?" Examine your motives!

EXPLORATION Obey from Your Heart—Isaiah 1:11-20; Hosea 6:6; Joel 2:12-13; Amos 5:23-24; Matthew 15:6-9.

6 "*Is* this not the fast that I have chosen:
To loose the bonds of wickedness,
To undo the heavy burdens,
To let the oppressed go free,
And that you break every yoke?
7 *Is it* not to share your bread with the hungry,
And that you bring to your house the poor who are cast out;
When you see the naked, that you cover him,
And not hide yourself from your own flesh?
8 Then your light shall break forth like the morning,
Your healing shall spring forth speedily,
And your righteousness shall go before you;
The glory of the LORD shall be your rear guard.
9 Then you shall call, and the LORD will answer;
You shall cry, and He will say, 'Here I *am.*'

"If you take away the yoke from your midst,
The pointing of the finger, and speaking wickedness,
10 *If* you extend your soul to the hungry
And satisfy the afflicted soul,
Then your light shall dawn in the darkness,
And your darkness shall *be* as the noonday.
11 The LORD will guide you continually,
And satisfy your soul in drought,
And strengthen your bones;
You shall be like a watered garden,
And like a spring of water, whose waters do not fail.
12 Those from among you
Shall build the old waste places;
You shall raise up the foundations of many generations;
And you shall be called the Repairer of the Breach,
The Restorer of Streets to Dwell In.

13 "If you turn away your foot from the Sabbath,
From doing your pleasure on My holy day,
And call the Sabbath a delight,
The holy *day* of the LORD honorable,
And shall honor Him, not doing your own ways,
Nor finding your own pleasure,
Nor speaking *your own* words,
14 Then you shall delight yourself in the LORD;
And I will cause you to ride on the high hills of the earth,
And feed you with the heritage of Jacob your father.
The mouth of the LORD has spoken."

Separated from God

59 Behold, the LORD's hand is not shortened,
That it cannot save;
Nor His ear heavy,
That it cannot hear.
2 But your iniquities have separated you from your God;
And your sins have hidden *His* face from you,
So that He will not hear.

3 For your hands are defiled with blood,
And your fingers with iniquity;
Your lips have spoken lies,
Your tongue has muttered perversity.
4 No one calls for justice,
Nor does *any* plead for truth.
They trust in empty words and speak lies;
They conceive evil and bring forth iniquity.
5 They hatch vipers' eggs and weave
the spider's web;
He who eats of their eggs dies,
And *from* that which is crushed a
viper breaks out.
6 Their webs will not become garments,
Nor will they cover themselves with
their works;
Their works *are* works of iniquity,
And the act of violence *is* in their hands.
7 Their feet run to evil,
And they make haste to shed innocent blood;
Their thoughts *are* thoughts of iniquity;
Wasting and destruction *are* in their paths.
8 The way of peace they have not known,
And *there is* no justice in their ways;
They have made themselves crooked paths;
Whoever takes that way shall not know peace.

Sin Confessed

9 Therefore justice is far from us,
Nor does righteousness overtake us;
We look for light, but there is darkness!
For brightness, *but* we walk in blackness!
10 We grope for the wall like the blind,
And we grope as if *we had* no eyes;
We stumble at noonday as at twilight;
We are as dead *men* in desolate places.
11 We all growl like bears,
And moan sadly like doves;
We look for justice, but *there is* none;
For salvation, *but* it is far from us.
12 For our transgressions are multiplied
before You,
And our sins testify against us;
For our transgressions *are* with us,
And *as for* our iniquities, we know them:
13 In transgressing and lying against the LORD,
And departing from our God,
Speaking oppression and revolt,
Conceiving and uttering from the heart words
of falsehood.
14 Justice is turned back,
And righteousness stands afar off;
For truth is fallen in the street,
And equity cannot enter.
15 So truth fails,
And he *who* departs from evil makes
himself a prey.

The Redeemer of Zion

Then the LORD saw *it,* and it displeased Him
That *there was* no justice.
16 He saw that *there was* no man,
And wondered that *there was* no intercessor;
Therefore His own arm brought
salvation for Him;
And His own righteousness, it
sustained Him.
17 For He put on righteousness as
a breastplate,
And a helmet of salvation on His head;
He put on the garments of vengeance
for clothing,
And was clad with zeal as a cloak.
18 According to *their* deeds, accordingly
He will repay,
Fury to His adversaries,
Recompense to His enemies;
The coastlands He will fully repay.
19 So shall they fear
The name of the LORD from the west,
And His glory from the rising of the sun;
When the enemy comes in like a flood,
The Spirit of the LORD will lift up a standard
against him.

20 "The Redeemer will come to Zion,
And to those who turn from
transgression in Jacob,"
Says the LORD.

21 "As for Me," says the LORD, "this *is* My covenant
with them: My Spirit who *is* upon you, and My words
which I have put in your mouth, shall not depart from
your mouth, nor from the mouth of your descendants,
nor from the mouth of your descendants' descendants," says the LORD, "from this time and forevermore."

The Gentiles Bless Zion

60 Arise, shine;
For your light has come!
And the glory of the LORD is risen upon you.

LIFE LESSON

Isaiah 60:1–61:11

SITUATION Isaiah continued to prophesy. He reported the deliverance that the Messiah would bring to Israel.

OBSERVATION God's Messiah would bring in a new kingdom in which Jerusalem would regain her glory. The people mistook this kingdom to be only earthly, therefore they missed Jesus' mission.

INSPIRATION When John's disciples asked Jesus who he was, the burden of proof was on him to provide the answer. Jesus did not answer John's question with mere words; he authenticated his messianic claim by his actions. In fact, his deeds that followed—healing the blind and lame and lepers and preaching good news to the poor—were in fulfillment of the prophecy in Isaiah 61 concerning the Messiah and the favorable year of the Lord.

This same Scripture was the basis for Jesus' "inaugural address," his first public sermon in which he announced himself and his mission to the Jews: "The Spirit of the Lord is on me, because he has annointed me to preach good news to the poor. He has sent me to proclaim freedom for the prisoners and recovery of sight for the blind, to release the oppressed, to proclaim the year of the Lord's favor" (Luke 4:18-19).

As Jesus sent John's disciples away, echoing the prophecy of Isaiah 61 once again, (Luke 7:22-23), they knew exactly what he was saying, even though he never gave a straight-out "yes." Jesus' actions in answer to John's questions recalled the Old Testament prophecy about the ministry of the Messiah. Among the poor, Jesus authenticated his claim to be the Son of God. John's disciples returned to his prison cell as eyewitnesses of the proof of Jesus' lordship. Now, no matter what happened to him, John could die in peace. He had

2 For behold, the darkness shall cover the earth,
And deep darkness the people;
But the LORD will arise over you,
And His glory will be seen upon you.
3 The Gentiles shall come to your light,
And kings to the brightness of your rising.

4 "Lift up your eyes all around, and see:
They all gather together, they come to you;
Your sons shall come from afar,
And your daughters shall be nursed at *your* side.
5 Then you shall see and become radiant,
And your heart shall swell with joy;
Because the abundance of the sea shall be turned to you,
The wealth of the Gentiles shall come to you.
6 The multitude of camels shall cover your *land,*
The dromedaries of Midian and Ephah;
All those from Sheba shall come;
They shall bring gold and incense,
And they shall proclaim the praises of the LORD.
7 All the flocks of Kedar shall be gathered together to you,
The rams of Nebaioth shall minister to you;
They shall ascend with acceptance on My altar,
And I will glorify the house of My glory.

8 "Who *are* these *who* fly like a cloud,
And like doves to their roosts?
9 Surely the coastlands shall wait for Me;
And the ships of Tarshish *will come* first,
To bring your sons from afar,
Their silver and their gold with them,
To the name of the LORD your God,
And to the Holy One of Israel,
Because He has glorified you.

10 "The sons of foreigners shall build up your walls,
And their kings shall minister to you;
For in My wrath I struck you,
But in My favor I have had mercy on you.
11 Therefore your gates shall be open continually;
They shall not be shut day or night,
That *men* may bring to you the wealth of the Gentiles,
And their kings in procession.
12 For the nation and kingdom which will not serve
you shall perish,
And *those* nations shall be utterly ruined.

13 "The glory of Lebanon shall come to you,
The cypress, the pine, and the box tree together,
To beautify the place of My sanctuary;
And I will make the place of My feet glorious.

14 Also the sons of those who afflicted you
Shall come bowing to you,
And all those who despised you shall fall prostrate at
the soles of your feet;
And they shall call you The City of the LORD,
Zion of the Holy One of Israel.

15 "Whereas you have been forsaken and hated,
So that no one went through *you*,
I will make you an eternal excellence,
A joy of many generations.
16 You shall drink the milk of the Gentiles,
And milk the breast of kings;
You shall know that I, the LORD, *am* your Savior
And your Redeemer, the Mighty One of Jacob.

17 "Instead of bronze I will bring gold,
Instead of iron I will bring silver,
Instead of wood, bronze,
And instead of stones, iron.
I will also make your officers peace,
And your magistrates righteousness.
18 Violence shall no longer be heard in your land,
Neither wasting nor destruction within your borders;
But you shall call your walls Salvation,
And your gates Praise.

God the Glory of His People

19 "The sun shall no longer be your light by day,
Nor for brightness shall the moon give light to you;
But the LORD will be to you an everlasting light,
And your God your glory.
20 Your sun shall no longer go down,
Nor shall your moon withdraw itself;
For the LORD will be your everlasting light,
And the days of your mourning shall be ended.
21 Also your people *shall* all *be* righteous;
They shall inherit the land forever,
The branch of My planting,
The work of My hands,
That I may be glorified.
22 A little one shall become a thousand,
And a small one a strong nation.
I, the LORD, will hasten it in its time."

The Good News of Salvation

61 "The Spirit of the Lord GOD *is* upon Me,
Because the LORD has anointed Me
To preach good tidings to the poor;
He has sent Me to heal the brokenhearted,
To proclaim liberty to the captives,
And the opening of the prison to *those who are* bound;

fulfilled his task; he had prepared the way for the Messiah. . . .

Today the burden of proof is on the church of Jesus Christ, the people of God. . . .

We the church face a crisis in terms of the gospel we preach because we have not authenticated ourselves to the world around us. It amazes me how we can be so versed in the Scriptures yet never get around to asking ourselves the right questions. The proof of the burden is on us just as it was on Jesus. When Jesus was asked by the disciples of John to give proof of his messianic claims, he did so by his actions. He said to go and tell John not only what they heard but also what they saw: "the blind see, the lame walk, the lepers are cleansed, the deaf hear, the dead are raised, to the poor the gospel is preached" (see Matt. 11:5). If we are to be Jesus' replacement on earth then we should constantly ask ourselves this same question: How do we as Christians demonstrate the proof of our claims to the world? If the church will ever authenticate its claim to be "the answer," "the way," "the good news," then we will prove that claim, as Jesus did, among the poor and oppressed.

(From *Beyond Charity* by John Perkins)

APPLICATION Can people see that you are a Christian by the way you help the poor and oppressed, or do they only hear by your words? Consider becoming involved in your church's visitation ministry. Visit the poor, sick, and shut-ins. Commit to one year of service.

EXPLORATION Helping the Poor—Deuteronomy 15:7-11; Psalm 82:3; Proverbs 19:17; 21:13; Jeremiah 22:16; Galatians 2:10.

LIFE LESSON

Isaiah 62:1–64:12

SITUATION Isaiah prophesied that God would one day be proud of his people—a day to long for, prepare for, and pray for. Recollecting God's past favors and faithfulness, Isaiah passionately pleaded for God's compassion and mercy. He asked that Israel's enemies be punished.

OBSERVATION When Jesus Christ came and provided a way for salvation, God would exalt his people. God would see his children as people without sin because Jesus paid their penalty.

INSPIRATION The holiness we are to exhibit is not our own, but the holiness of Christ in us. We are not holy, and we will not become holy humans. Christ in us can manifest His holiness if we will yield our flesh to Him. This is not a human operation; it is a spiritual one. Jesus installs His holiness in us by grace. Not a once-for-all-time transaction, this is a daily, moment-by-moment striving to live more by the Spirit and less by the flesh.

. . . A friend bought his daughter a new car, but it must sit in the garage until she reaches the legal driving age. Until her sixteenth birthday she only has partial use of the car, when accompanied by an adult. Similarly, holiness is like a gift already purchased for us (by the blood of Christ), but we cannot have full use of it until a certain date in the future (our glorification).

Becoming holy is a process which includes God's part and our part. On

2 To proclaim the acceptable year of the LORD,
And the day of vengeance of our God;
To comfort all who mourn,
3 To console those who mourn in Zion,
To give them beauty for ashes,
The oil of joy for mourning,
The garment of praise for the spirit of heaviness;
That they may be called trees of righteousness,
The planting of the LORD, that He may be glorified."

4 And they shall rebuild the old ruins,
They shall raise up the former desolations,
And they shall repair the ruined cities,
The desolations of many generations.
5 Strangers shall stand and feed your flocks,
And the sons of the foreigner
Shall be your plowmen and your vinedressers.
6 But you shall be named the priests of the LORD,
They shall call you the servants of our God.
You shall eat the riches of the Gentiles,
And in their glory you shall boast.
7 Instead of your shame *you shall have* double *honor,*
And *instead of* confusion they shall rejoice in their portion.
Therefore in their land they shall possess double;
Everlasting joy shall be theirs.

8 "For I, the LORD, love justice;
I hate robbery for burnt offering;
I will direct their work in truth,
And will make with them an everlasting covenant.
9 Their descendants shall be known among the Gentiles,
And their offspring among the people.
All who see them shall acknowledge them,
That they *are* the posterity *whom* the LORD has blessed."

10 I will greatly rejoice in the LORD,
My soul shall be joyful in my God;
For He has clothed me with the garments of salvation,
He has covered me with the robe of righteousness,
As a bridegroom decks *himself* with ornaments,
And as a bride adorns *herself* with her jewels.
11 For as the earth brings forth its bud,
As the garden causes the things that are sown in it
to spring forth,
So the Lord GOD will cause righteousness and praise to spring
forth before all the nations.

Assurance of Zion's Salvation

62 For Zion's sake I will not hold My peace,
And for Jerusalem's sake I will not rest,
Until her righteousness goes forth as brightness,
And her salvation as a lamp *that* burns.

2 The Gentiles shall see your righteousness,
And all kings your glory.
You shall be called by a new name,
Which the mouth of the LORD will name.
3 You shall also be a crown of glory
In the hand of the LORD,
And a royal diadem
In the hand of your God.
4 You shall no longer be termed Forsaken,
Nor shall your land any more be termed Desolate;
But you shall be called Hephzibah,[u] and your land Beulah;[v]
For the LORD delights in you,
And your land shall be married.
5 For *as* a young man marries a virgin,
So shall your sons marry you;
And *as* the bridegroom rejoices over the bride,
So shall your God rejoice over you.

6 I have set watchmen on your walls, O Jerusalem;
They shall never hold their peace day or night.
You who make mention of the LORD, do not keep silent,
7 And give Him no rest till He establishes
And till He makes Jerusalem a praise in the earth.

8 The LORD has sworn by His right hand
And by the arm of His strength:
"Surely I will no longer give your grain
As food for your enemies;
And the sons of the foreigner shall not drink your new wine,
For which you have labored.
9 But those who have gathered it shall eat it,
And praise the LORD;
Those who have brought it together shall drink
it in My holy courts."

10 Go through,
Go through the gates!
Prepare the way for the people;
Build up,
Build up the highway!
Take out the stones,
Lift up a banner for the peoples!
11 Indeed the LORD has proclaimed
To the end of the world:
"Say to the daughter of Zion,
'Surely your salvation is coming;
Behold, His reward *is* with Him,
And His work before Him.' "
12 And they shall call them The Holy People,
The Redeemed of the LORD;
And you shall be called Sought Out,
A City Not Forsaken.

one hand, our part is to stay out of God's part—to yield, to surrender, to stop seeking God on our own terms. But our part also is to obey. It is to enter His rehabilitation program. When you put yourself under a doctor's care, he cannot help you if you don't follow his instructions. As the patient surrenders his own good ideas and obeys the doctor's instruction, he becomes well. The same is true in sanctification. If you and I want to be made holy, then we must willingly surrender ourselves to His care, and we must also actively obey His instructions. We have no more power to make ourselves holy than a dying man has to save himself. We are weak and tired, and we cannot offer much help. However, we can submit to His rehabilitation program—sanctification. The key to our part is faith—to seek Him in obedience.

(From *Walking with Christ in the Details of Life* by Patrick Morley)

APPLICATION Are you working for God's kingdom? Are you active in spreading the gospel of Jesus Christ? Do you tell others what God has done for you? All these things are done by those who desire to see God's kingdom come. Be an active member of God's kingdom.

EXPLORATION Holiness—Exodus 20:1; Leviticus 11:44-45; Psalm 93:5; Isaiah 4:2-4; John 17:17; Hebrews 10:14; 1 Peter 1:14-16.

62:4 [u] Literally *My Delight Is in Her* [v] Literally *Married*

The Lord *in Judgment and Salvation*

63 Who *is* this who comes from Edom,
With dyed garments from Bozrah,
This *One who is* glorious in His apparel,
Traveling in the greatness of His strength?—

"I who speak in righteousness, mighty to save."

2 Why *is* Your apparel red,
And Your garments like one who treads
in the winepress?

3 "I have trodden the winepress alone,
And from the peoples no one *was* with Me.
For I have trodden them in My anger,
And trampled them in My fury;
Their blood is sprinkled upon My garments,
And I have stained all My robes.
4 For the day of vengeance *is* in My heart,
And the year of My redeemed has come.
5 I looked, but *there was* no one to help,
And I wondered
That *there was* no one to uphold;
Therefore My own arm brought
salvation for Me;
And My own fury, it sustained Me.
6 I have trodden down the peoples
in My anger,
Made them drunk in My fury,
And brought down their strength
to the earth."

God's Mercy Remembered

7 I will mention the lovingkindnesses
of the Lord
And the praises of the Lord,
According to all that the Lord has
bestowed on us,
And the great goodness toward the
house of Israel,
Which He has bestowed on them according
to His mercies,
According to the multitude of
His lovingkindnesses.
8 For He said, "Surely they *are* My people,
Children *who* will not lie."
So He became their Savior.
9 In all their affliction He was afflicted,
And the Angel of His Presence saved them;
In His love and in His pity He redeemed them;
And He bore them and carried them
All the days of old.

10 But they rebelled and grieved His Holy Spirit;
So He turned Himself against them
as an enemy,
And He fought against them.

11 Then he remembered the days of old,
Moses *and* his people, *saying:*
"Where *is* He who brought them up
out of the sea
With the shepherd of His flock?
Where *is* He who put His Holy
Spirit within them,
12 Who led *them* by the right hand of Moses,
With His glorious arm,
Dividing the water before them
To make for Himself an everlasting name,
13 Who led them through the deep,
As a horse in the wilderness,
That they might not stumble?"
14 As a beast goes down into the valley,
And the Spirit of the Lord causes him to rest,
So You lead Your people,
To make Yourself a glorious name.

A Prayer of Penitence

15 Look down from heaven,
And see from Your habitation,
holy and glorious.
Where *are* Your zeal and Your strength,
The yearning of Your heart and Your
mercies toward me?
Are they restrained?
16 Doubtless You *are* our Father,
Though Abraham was ignorant of us,
And Israel does not acknowledge us.
You, O Lord, *are* our Father;
Our Redeemer from Everlasting *is* Your name.
17 O Lord, why have You made us stray
from Your ways,
And hardened our heart from Your fear?
Return for Your servants' sake,
The tribes of Your inheritance.
18 Your holy people have possessed *it*
but a little while;
Our adversaries have trodden down
Your sanctuary.
19 We have become *like* those of old, over whom
You never ruled,
Those who were never called by Your name.

64 Oh, that You would rend the heavens!
That You would come down!
That the mountains might shake
at Your presence—

RESURRECTION

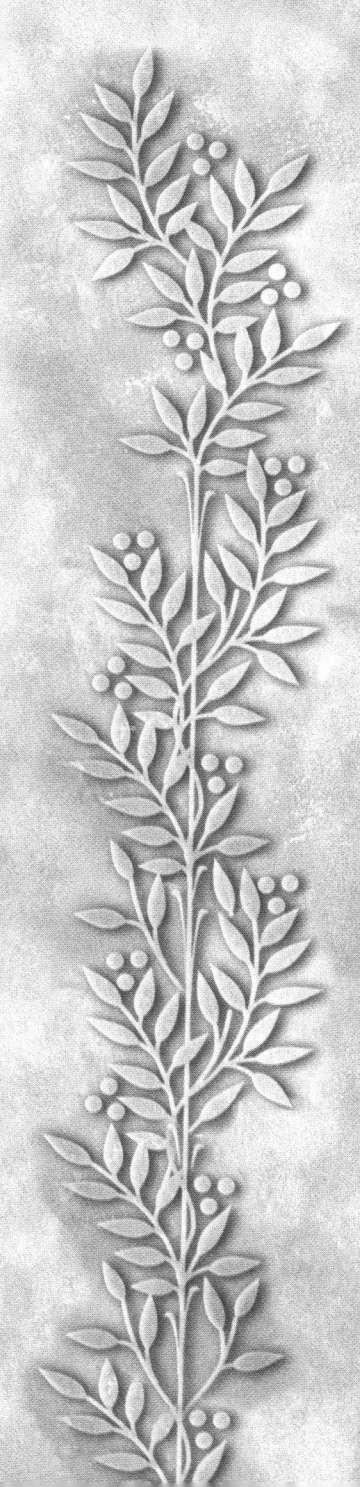

The fire that lit the boiler of the New Testament church was an unquenchable belief that if Jesus had been only a man, he would have stayed in the tomb. They couldn't stay silent about the fact that the one they saw hung on a cross walked again on the earth and appeared to five hundred people. I wonder if sometimes we stay silent because we've forgotten the one who was on that cross.

Let us ask our Father humbly, yet confidently in the name of Jesus, to remind us of the empty tomb. Let us see the victorious Jesus: the conqueror of the tomb, the one who defied death. And let us be reminded that we, too, will be granted that same victory!

THANK YOU *for the sweet surprise of Easter morning. We are thankful that when you arose from your sleep of death, you didn't go immediately to heaven, but instead you went and visited people. This visit of love reminds us that it was for people that you died. We praise your name for that sweet surprise.*

HOPE

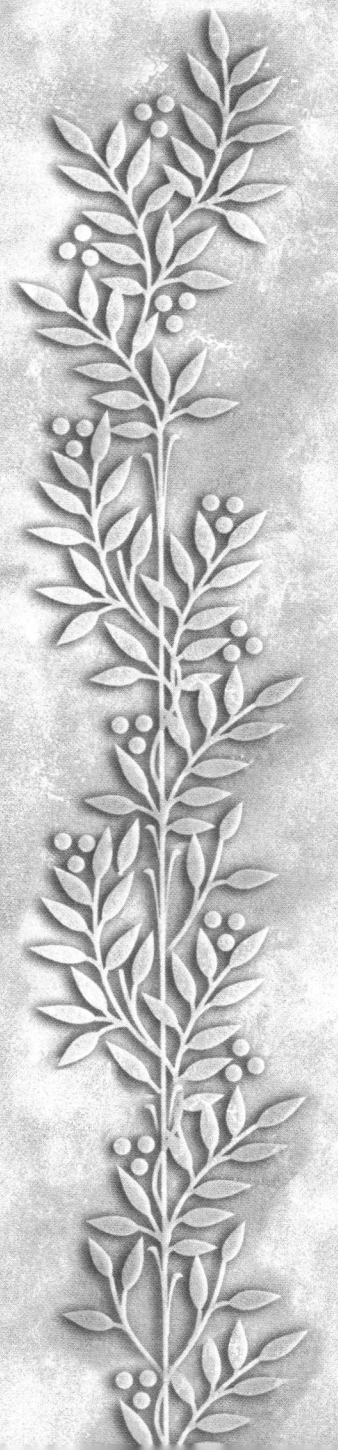

What do you need most today? Do you need just a word of hope? That's what we all need. And that's what the Word of God does that nothing and no one else can. The Word of God says to us that there is no hopeless situation, no hopeless illness, no hopeless marriage. If there were hopeless situations, then God would have given up long ago.

Having a Savior in Christ means that the hopeless have hope, the dead have life, and the abandoned have Good News.

Our hope is the anchor for the soul. "Where's your hope?" Jesus asks. It is the confident hope of the return of Christ.

YOU NEVER promised us that this world would be easy. And yet, all of us can look ahead to the city that's set on a hill, to the lights that call us to eternity. And we take hope.

THANKFULNESS

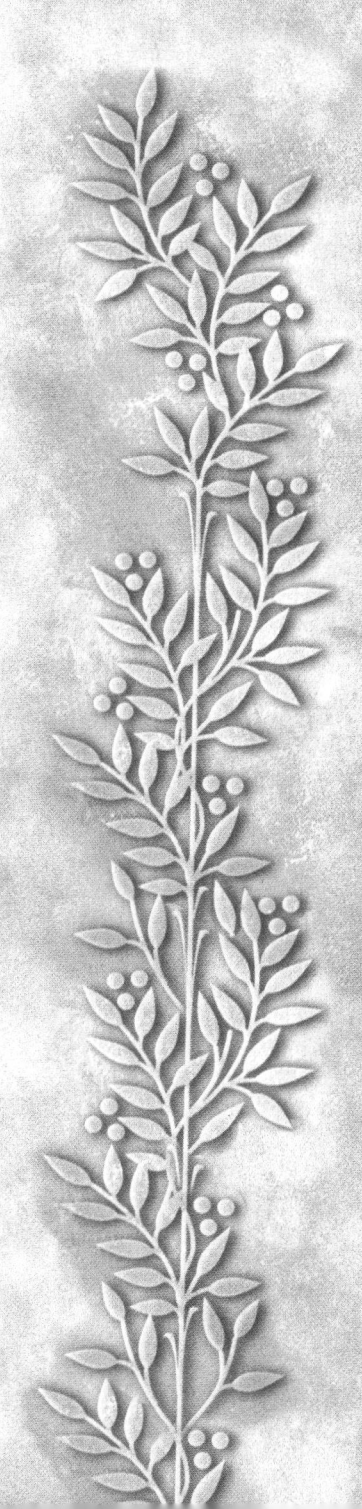

Gratitude comes from having the right perspective. It's being able to look at what you have and being thankful for that, rather than longing for what you don't have.

Do you know why you should feel grateful? You are a part of God's plan, you are touched by God's tenderness, and you are a victor in God's victory. What greater blessing could there be?

It's incredible that anyone could look at the kindness of God, the faithfulness of God, and the goodness of God and not feel any emotion of gratitude.

Remember the Lord. Remember who is in control. Remember his goodness in the past. Remember God's closeness in the present. Remember his power for the future.

FATHER, we want to see you and know you better. We ask you, Father, to help us see Jesus and to deepen our faith upon seeing him more clearly.

PRAYER

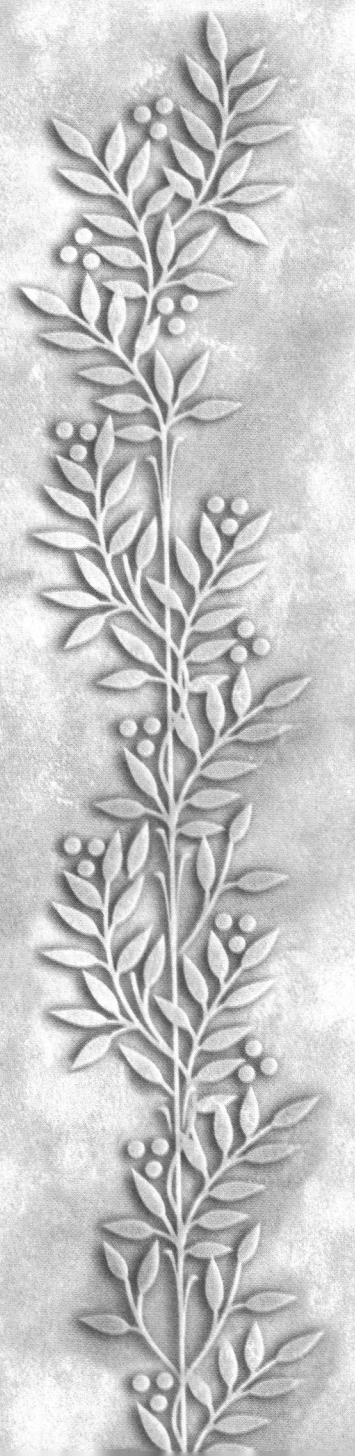

When God says to pray, he really means it. To pray is the most commonly mentioned command in Scripture. It is mentioned more than "love your neighbor," more than "go to church," and more than "evangelize." More than anything else, God calls us to pray.

We should be people of great prayer. We should be prayer warriors. We should be people who use the ministry of prayer to its fullest capacity. The highest and greatest calling of Christians is the ministry of prayer.

I would like to encourage you, admonish you to make a decision to pray more and to set up some specific plans to support that decision. Will you determine in your heart to pray more? Will you start a prayer group in your home? Pray continually—live in a spirit of prayer.

FATHER, *when you were on earth, you prayed. You prayed in the morning, you prayed at night, you prayed alone, you prayed with people. In your hours of distress, you retreated into times of prayer. In your hours of joy, you lifted your heart and hands to the Father in prayer. Help us to be more like you in this way... help us to make prayer a priority in our daily lives.*

2 As fire burns brushwood,
As fire causes water to boil—
To make Your name known
to Your adversaries,
That the nations may tremble at Your presence!
3 When You did awesome things *for which* we
did not look,
You came down,
The mountains shook at Your presence.
4 For since the beginning of the world
Men have not heard nor perceived by the ear,
Nor has the eye seen any God besides You,
Who acts for the one who waits for Him.
5 You meet him who rejoices
and does righteousness,
Who remembers You in Your ways.
You are indeed angry, for we have sinned—
In these ways we continue;
And we need to be saved.

6 But we are all like an unclean *thing,*
And all our righteousnesses *are*
like filthy rags;
We all fade as a leaf,
And our iniquities, like the wind,
Have taken us away.
7 And *there is* no one who calls on Your name,
Who stirs himself up to take hold of You;
For You have hidden Your face from us,
And have consumed us because
of our iniquities.

8 But now, O LORD,
You *are* our Father;
We *are* the clay, and You our potter;
And all we *are* the work of Your hand.
9 Do not be furious, O LORD,
Nor remember iniquity forever;
Indeed, please look—we all
are Your people!
10 Your holy cities are a wilderness,
Zion is a wilderness,
Jerusalem a desolation.
11 Our holy and beautiful temple,
Where our fathers praised You,
Is burned up with fire;
And all our pleasant things are laid waste.
12 Will You restrain Yourself because of these
things, O LORD?
Will You hold Your peace, and
afflict us very severely?

The Righteousness of God's Judgment

65 "I was sought by *those who* did not ask *for Me;*
I was found by *those who* did not seek Me.
I said, 'Here I am, here I am,'
To a nation *that* was not called by My name.
2 I have stretched out My hands all day long
to a rebellious people,
Who walk in a way *that is* not good,
According to their own thoughts;
3 A people who provoke Me to anger
continually to My face;
Who sacrifice in gardens,
And burn incense on altars of brick;
4 Who sit among the graves,
And spend the night in the tombs;
Who eat swine's flesh,
And the broth of abominable things
is *in* their vessels;
5 Who say, 'Keep to yourself,
Do not come near me,
For I am holier than you!'
These *are* smoke in My nostrils,
A fire that burns all the day.

6 "Behold, *it is* written before Me:
I will not keep silence, but will repay—
Even repay into their bosom—
7 Your iniquities and the iniquities of your
fathers together,"
Says the LORD,
"Who have burned incense on
the mountains
And blasphemed Me on the hills;
Therefore I will measure their former work
into their bosom."

8 Thus says the LORD:

"As the new wine is found in the cluster,
And *one* says, 'Do not destroy it,
For a blessing *is* in it,'
So will I do for My servants' sake,
That I may not destroy them all.
9 I will bring forth descendants from Jacob,
And from Judah an heir of My mountains;
My elect shall inherit it,
And My servants shall dwell there.
10 Sharon shall be a fold of flocks,
And the Valley of Achor a place for
herds to lie down,
For My people who have sought Me.

LIFE LESSON

Isaiah 65:1–66:24

SITUATION God answered the prayers of his people. Those who remained faithful would receive life, joy, and peace beyond imagination. The disobedient would receive judgment and death.

OBSERVATION God cannot overlook sin, and he will punish it; but the faithful will know the eternal blessings of God's new kingdom.

INSPIRATION While the kingdom is full of righteousness, peace, and joy, it isn't a physical, tangible thing. It isn't something we touch or see. . . .

Furthermore, this kingdom isn't verbal, something we can actually hear with our ears, even though it is powerful. . . .

If that isn't mysterious enough, I should add that while it is unshakable, it isn't visible either!

. . . How about that! We're supposed to seek something we cannot feel, or hear. And we're expected to embrace something that is intangible, inaudible, and invisible.

. . . *God's kingdom is a synonym for God's rule.* Those who choose to live in His kingdom (though still very much alive on Planet Earth) choose to live under His authority.

Maybe a super-simple outline of the Bible will help us understand the definition of God's kingdom even better. But first let me warn you—it's so basic you'll probably sneer!

I. God creates the heavens and earth and all things in them, including mankind. That's Genesis 1 and 2.

II. Mankind, alone, rebels against God's authority. That's covered in Genesis 3.

III. God moves through history to reestablish His authority over all creation. That's Genesis 4 through Revelation 22.

11 "But you *are* those who forsake the LORD,
Who forget My holy mountain,
Who prepare a table for Gad,[w]
And who furnish a drink offering for Meni.[x]
12 Therefore I will number you for the sword,
And you shall all bow down to the slaughter;
Because, when I called, you did not answer;
When I spoke, you did not hear,
But did evil before My eyes,
And chose *that* in which I do not delight."

13 Therefore thus says the Lord GOD:

"Behold, My servants shall eat,
But you shall be hungry;
Behold, My servants shall drink,
But you shall be thirsty;
Behold, My servants shall rejoice,
But you shall be ashamed;
14 Behold, My servants shall sing for joy of heart,
But you shall cry for sorrow of heart,
And wail for grief of spirit.
15 You shall leave your name as a curse to My chosen;
For the Lord GOD will slay you,
And call His servants by another name;
16 So that he who blesses himself in the earth
Shall bless himself in the God of truth;
And he who swears in the earth
Shall swear by the God of truth;
Because the former troubles are forgotten,
And because they are hidden from My eyes.

The Glorious New Creation

17 "For behold, I create new heavens and a new earth;
And the former shall not be remembered or come to mind.
18 But be glad and rejoice forever in what I create;
For behold, I create Jerusalem *as* a rejoicing,
And her people a joy.
19 I will rejoice in Jerusalem,
And joy in My people;
The voice of weeping shall no longer be heard in her,
Nor the voice of crying.

20 "No more shall an infant from there *live but a few* days,
Nor an old man who has not fulfilled his days;
For the child shall die one hundred years old,
But the sinner *being* one hundred years old
shall be accursed.
21 They shall build houses and inhabit *them;*
They shall plant vineyards and eat their fruit.

65:11 [w] Literally *Troop* or *Fortune,* a pagan deity [x] Literally *Number* or *Destiny,* a pagan deity

22 They shall not build and another inhabit;
They shall not plant and another eat;
For as the days of a tree, *so shall be* the days of My people,
And My elect shall long enjoy the work of their hands.
23 They shall not labor in vain,
Nor bring forth children for trouble;
For they *shall be* the descendants of the blessed of the LORD,
And their offspring with them.

24 "It shall come to pass
That before they call, I will answer;
And while they are still speaking, I will hear.
25 The wolf and the lamb shall feed together,
The lion shall eat straw like the ox,
And dust *shall be* the serpent's food.
They shall not hurt nor destroy in all My holy mountain,"
Says the LORD.

True Worship and False

66 Thus says the LORD:
"Heaven *is* My throne,
And earth *is* My footstool.
Where *is* the house that you will build Me?
And where *is* the place of My rest?
2 For all those *things* My hand has made,
And all those *things* exist,"
Says the LORD.
"But on this *one* will I look:
On *him who is* poor and of a contrite spirit,
And who trembles at My word.

3 "He who kills a bull *is as if* he slays a man;
He who sacrifices a lamb, *as if* he breaks a dog's neck;
He who offers a grain offering, *as if he offers* swine's blood;
He who burns incense, *as if* he blesses an idol.
Just as they have chosen their own ways,
And their soul delights in their abominations,
4 So will I choose their delusions,
And bring their fears on them;
Because, when I called, no one answered,
When I spoke they did not hear;
But they did evil before My eyes,
And chose *that* in which I do not delight."

The LORD Vindicates Zion

5 Hear the word of the LORD,
You who tremble at His word:
"Your brethren who hated you,
Who cast you out for My name's sake, said,
'Let the LORD be glorified,
That we may see your joy.'
But they shall be ashamed."

. . . If you are wondering where you and I fit into this outline, take a look at category three. For centuries God has been at work reestablishing His rulership. . . .

All this leads me to some helpful news, some bad news, and some good news! The kingdom is the invisible realm where God rules as supreme authority. That's *helpful news.* The bad news is that we, by nature, don't want Him to rule over us; we much prefer to please ourselves. We'd much rather serve mammon (the word means "money") than the Master. . . . More bad news is this: Most people do serve mammon. Just look around. Who's in charge, God or mammon? What's happening? The mediocre majority have bought into a mammon lifestyle.

Now, the good news. We don't have to live that way. God has given us an avenue of escape. It's called a birth from above. . . . Not until we experience a spiritual rebirth will we submit to God's rule.

So when I write of God's kingdom, I'm referring to His right-authority over our lives. Only then can we experience true excellence.

(From *Living Above the Level of Mediocrity* by Charles Swindoll)

APPLICATION Become a citizen in God's kingdom today by trusting in Jesus Christ as Lord and Savior. Reserve your place in his new creation. You can have permanent hope and eternal life! There is no better way to live than by following him.

EXPLORATION Kingdom of God—Matthew 5:3-12; 6:10; Luke 4:43; 9:2; John 3:3; Acts 1:3; 1 Corinthians 1:2.

6 The sound of noise from the city!
A voice from the temple!
The voice of the LORD,
Who fully repays His enemies!

7 "Before she was in labor, she gave birth;
Before her pain came,
She delivered a male child.
8 Who has heard such a thing?
Who has seen such things?
Shall the earth be made to give birth
in one day?
Or shall a nation be born at once?
For as soon as Zion was in labor,
She gave birth to her children.
9 Shall I bring to the time of birth, and not
cause delivery?" says the LORD.
"Shall I who cause delivery shut up *the womb?*"
says your God.
10 "Rejoice with Jerusalem,
And be glad with her, all you who love her;
Rejoice for joy with her, all you
who mourn for her;
11 That you may feed and be satisfied
With the consolation of her bosom,
That you may drink deeply and be delighted
With the abundance of her glory."

12 For thus says the LORD:

"Behold, I will extend peace to her like a river,
And the glory of the Gentiles
like a flowing stream.
Then you shall feed;
On *her* sides shall you be carried,
And be dandled on *her* knees.
13 As one whom his mother comforts,
So I will comfort you;
And you shall be comforted in Jerusalem."

The Reign and Indignation of God

14 When you see *this*, your heart shall rejoice,
And your bones shall flourish like grass;
The hand of the LORD shall be known
to His servants,
And *His* indignation to His enemies.
15 For behold, the LORD will come with fire
And with His chariots, like a whirlwind,
To render His anger with fury,
And His rebuke with flames of fire.
16 For by fire and by His sword
The LORD will judge all flesh;
And the slain of the LORD shall be many.

17 "Those who sanctify themselves and
purify themselves,
To go to the gardens
After an *idol* in the midst,
Eating swine's flesh and the abomination and
the mouse,
Shall be consumed together," says the LORD.

18 "For I *know* their works and their thoughts. It shall
be that I will gather all nations and tongues; and they
shall come and see My glory. 19 I will set a sign among
them; and those among them who escape I will send
to the nations: *to* Tarshish and Pul[y] and Lud, who
draw the bow, and Tubal and Javan, *to* the coastlands
afar off who have not heard My fame nor seen My
glory. And they shall declare My glory among the
Gentiles. 20 Then they shall bring all your brethren for
an offering to the LORD out of all nations, on horses
and in chariots and in litters, on mules and on camels,
to My holy mountain Jerusalem," says the LORD, "as
the children of Israel bring an offering in a clean vessel
into the house of the LORD. 21 And I will also take some
of them for priests *and* Levites," says the LORD.

22 "For as the new heavens and the new earth
Which I will make shall remain before Me,"
says the LORD,
"So shall your descendants and your
name remain.
23 And it shall come to pass
That from one New Moon to another,
And from one Sabbath to another,
All flesh shall come to worship before Me,"
says the LORD.

24 "And they shall go forth and look
Upon the corpses of the men
Who have transgressed against Me.
For their worm does not die,
And their fire is not quenched.
They shall be an abhorrence to all flesh."

66:19 *y* Following Masoretic Text and Targum; Septuagint reads *Put* (compare Jeremiah 46:9).

The Book of

JEREMIAH

INTRODUCTION

No church would hire Jeremiah. He wouldn't make it past the first interview. Better still, he wouldn't even make it to the interview.

He had little stomach for organized religion. One can hardly blame him. What he saw would nauseate the worst of us.

He saw raging immorality. He saw blatant idolatry. He saw unbridled hypocrisy. He saw priests who sold out to the highest bidder. He saw kings who lived out his worst nightmare.

Were his head a Niagara, it wouldn't generate enough tears for him to weep. Like Job, he cursed the day he was born, and again, you can hardly blame him. It was a rotten day in which to live.

He could see the writing on the Babylonian wall, but you'd think he was the only one who knew how to read.

In the end, the walls fell, just like he said. The Temple was raided, just like he prophesied. And the people were bound like slaves and led into Babylon.

To his credit, he never said, "I told you so."

He remained behind and walked among the ruins and did what he did most of his life. He wept.

LIFE LESSON

Jeremiah 1:1-19

SITUATION Jeremiah, the weeping prophet, was called to minister to Judah during the reigns of its last five kings: Josiah, Jehoahaz, Jehoiakim, Jehoiachin, and Zedekiah (627-586 B.C.). Other prophets, Habakkuk and Zephaniah, ministered during Jeremiah's time.

OBSERVATION Just as Jeremiah was appointed by God "as a prophet to the nations" (v. 5), so every Believer has a unique purpose in serving God. God provides the strength and resources for us to do what He asks.

INSPIRATION There is no royal road to becoming a worker for God. The only way is to let God in His mighty providence lift the life by a great tide, or break it from its moorings in some storm, and in one way or another get the life out to sea in reckless abandon to God. When once God's purpose is begun He seems to put His hand upon the life and uproot and detach it in every way, and there is darkness and mystery and very often kicking. We can be impertinent to God's providence the moment we choose; there is no punishment, we have simply chosen not to be workers for God in that particular [situation]. . . . The value to God of one man or woman right out in supreme sanctification is incalculable. The value of a life can only be estimated by its spiritual relationship to God. . . . The greatest service we can render God is to fulfill our spiritual destiny. It is the despised crown God is counting on, insignificant but holy.

(From *God's Workmanship* by Oswald Chambers)

APPLICATION Do you feel inadequate because of your age, education, or talents? Have you kept quiet because you are not a skilled speaker? The next time you are tempted to bypass an opportunity, remember God will not lead you where he cannot help you. Thank God that he is your strength.

EXPLORATION Confidence in God—Psalm 27:1-3; 71:5; 112:7-8; Jeremiah 17:7; Philippians 1:3-6; Hebrews 13:6; 1 Peter 3:12-14.

The words of Jeremiah the son of Hilkiah, of the priests who
were in Anathoth in the land of Benjamin, 2to whom the
word of the LORD came in the days of Josiah the son of Amon, king
of Judah, in the thirteenth year of his reign. 3It came also in the days
of Jehoiakim the son of Josiah, king of Judah, until the end of the eleventh
year of Zedekiah the son of Josiah, king of Judah, until the carrying away
of Jerusalem captive in the fifth month.

The Prophet Is Called

4Then the word of the LORD came to me, saying:

5 "Before I formed you in the womb I knew you;
Before you were born I sanctified you;
I ordained you a prophet to the nations."

6Then said I:

"Ah, Lord GOD!
Behold, I cannot speak, for I *am* a youth."

7But the LORD said to me:

"Do not say, 'I *am* a youth,'
For you shall go to all to whom I send you,
And whatever I command you, you shall speak.
8 Do not be afraid of their faces,
For I *am* with you to deliver you," says the LORD.

9Then the LORD put forth His hand and touched my mouth, and the
LORD said to me:

"Behold, I have put My words in your mouth.
10 See, I have this day set you over the nations and over the kingdoms,
To root out and to pull down,
To destroy and to throw down,
To build and to plant."

11Moreover the word of the LORD came to me, saying, "Jeremiah, what
do you see?"

And I said, "I see a branch of an almond tree."

12Then the LORD said to me, "You have seen well, for I am ready to perform My word."

13And the word of the LORD came to me the second time, saying, "What
do you see?"

And I said, "I see a boiling pot, and it is facing away from the north."

14Then the LORD said to me:

"Out of the north calamity shall break forth
On all the inhabitants of the land.
15 For behold, I am calling
All the families of the kingdoms of the north," says the LORD;
"They shall come and each one set his throne
At the entrance of the gates of Jerusalem,
Against all its walls all around,
And against all the cities of Judah.
16 I will utter My judgments

Against them concerning all their wickedness,
Because they have forsaken Me,
Burned incense to other gods,
And worshiped the works of their own hands.

17 "Therefore prepare yourself and arise,
And speak to them all that I command you.
Do not be dismayed before their faces,
Lest I dismay you before them.
18 For behold, I have made you this day
A fortified city and an iron pillar,
And bronze walls against the whole land—
Against the kings of Judah,
Against its princes,
Against its priests,
And against the people of the land.
19 They will fight against you,
But they shall not prevail against you.
For I *am* with you," says the LORD,
"to deliver you."

God's Case Against Israel

2 Moreover the word of the LORD came to me, saying,
2"Go and cry in the hearing of Jerusalem, saying,
'Thus says the LORD:

"I remember you,
The kindness of your youth,
The love of your betrothal,
When you went after Me in the wilderness,
In a land not sown.
3 Israel *was* holiness to the LORD,
The firstfruits of His increase.
All that devour him will offend;
Disaster will come upon them," says the LORD.'"

4Hear the word of the LORD, O house of Jacob and all
the families of the house of Israel. 5Thus says the LORD:

"What injustice have your fathers found in Me,
That they have gone far from Me,
Have followed idols,
And have become idolaters?
6 Neither did they say, 'Where *is* the LORD,
Who brought us up out of the land of Egypt,
Who led us through the wilderness,
Through a land of deserts and pits,
Through a land of drought and the
shadow of death,
Through a land that no one crossed
And where no one dwelt?'
7 I brought you into a bountiful country,
To eat its fruit and its goodness.
But when you entered, you defiled My land
And made My heritage an abomination.
8 The priests did not say, 'Where *is* the LORD?'
And those who handle the law
did not know Me;
The rulers also transgressed against Me;
The prophets prophesied by Baal,
And walked after *things that* do not profit.

9 "Therefore I will yet bring charges against
you," says the LORD,
"And against your children's children I will
bring charges.
10 For pass beyond the coasts of Cyprus[a] and see,
Send to Kedar[b] and consider diligently,
And see if there has been such *a* thing.
11 Has a nation changed *its* gods,
Which *are* not gods?
But My people have changed their Glory
For *what* does not profit.
12 Be astonished, O heavens, at this,
And be horribly afraid;
Be very desolate," says the LORD.
13 "For My people have committed two evils:
They have forsaken Me, the fountain
of living waters,
And hewn themselves cisterns—broken
cisterns that can hold no water.

14 "*Is* Israel a servant?
Is he a homeborn *slave?*
Why is he plundered?
15 The young lions roared at him, *and* growled;
They made his land waste;
His cities are burned, without inhabitant.
16 Also the people of Noph[c] and Tahpanhes
Have broken the crown of your head.
17 Have you not brought this on yourself,
In that you have forsaken the LORD your God
When He led you in the way?
18 And now why take the road to Egypt,
To drink the waters of Sihor?
Or why take the road to Assyria,
To drink the waters of the River?[d]
19 Your own wickedness will correct you,
And your backslidings will rebuke you.

2:10 [a] Hebrew *Kittim,* western lands, especially Cyprus [b] In the northern Arabian desert, representative of the eastern cultures
2:16 [c] That is, Memphis in ancient Egypt
2:18 [d] That is, the Euphrates

LIFE LESSON

Jeremiah 2:1–6:30

SITUATION Many sinful kings led the people astray in both Judah and the Northern Kingdom. Eventually, the Assyrians captured the Northern Kingdom (722 B.C.). Judah was on the verge of similar punishment from Babylon. Jeremiah began his prophecy against Judah by outlining the people's unfaithfulness to God and urging them to repent or face strong punishment.

OBSERVATION Any severe and prolonged pattern of sin, practiced by people who claim to be devoted to God, invites punishment from God.

INSPIRATION Many people will profess faithfulness, but very few will demonstrate it. The virtue of faithfulness is often costly, and few people are willing to pay the price. But for the godly person, faithfulness is an absolutely essential quality of his character, regardless of what it might cost.

What is faithfulness? How do we practice it, and when do we exhibit it in our lives? The biblical word denotes that which is firm and can be counted upon. . . . The faithful person is one who is dependable, trustworthy, and loyal, who can be depended upon in all of his relationships, and who is absolutely honest and ethical in all of his affairs. . . .

If we are careful to be honest in the little things, we will certainly be careful to be honest in the more important

Know therefore and see that *it is* an evil and bitter *thing*
That you have forsaken the LORD your God,
And the fear of Me *is* not in you,"
Says the Lord GOD of hosts.

20 "For of old I have broken your yoke *and* burst your bonds;
And you said, 'I will not transgress,'
When on every high hill and under every green tree
You lay down, playing the harlot.
21 Yet I had planted you a noble vine, a seed of highest quality.
How then have you turned before Me
Into the degenerate plant of an alien vine?
22 For though you wash yourself with lye, and use much soap,
Yet your iniquity is marked before Me," says the Lord GOD.

23 "How can you say, 'I am not polluted,
I have not gone after the Baals'?
See your way in the valley;
Know what you have done:
You are a swift dromedary breaking loose in her ways,
24 A wild donkey used to the wilderness,
That sniffs at the wind in her desire;
In her time of mating, who can turn her away?
All those who seek her will not weary themselves;
In her month they will find her.
25 Withhold your foot from being unshod, and your throat from thirst.
But you said, 'There is no hope.
No! For I have loved aliens, and after them I will go.'

26 "As the thief is ashamed when he is found out,
So is the house of Israel ashamed;
They and their kings and their princes, and their
priests and their prophets,
27 Saying to a tree, 'You *are* my father,'
And to a stone, 'You gave birth to me.'
For they have turned *their* back to Me, and not *their* face.
But in the time of their trouble
They will say, 'Arise and save us.'
28 But where *are* your gods that you have made for yourselves?
Let them arise,
If they can save you in the time of your trouble;
For *according to* the number of your cities
Are your gods, O Judah.

29 "Why will you plead with Me?
You all have transgressed against Me," says the LORD.
30 "In vain I have chastened your children;
They received no correction.
Your sword has devoured your prophets
Like a destroying lion.

31 "O generation, see the word of the LORD!
Have I been a wilderness to Israel,
Or a land of darkness?

Why do My people say, 'We are lords;
We will come no more to You'?
32 Can a virgin forget her ornaments,
Or a bride her attire?
Yet My people have forgotten Me days without number.

33 "Why do you beautify your way to seek love?
Therefore you have also taught
The wicked women your ways.
34 Also on your skirts is found
The blood of the lives of the poor innocents.
I have not found it by secret search,
But plainly on all these things.
35 Yet you say, 'Because I am innocent,
Surely His anger shall turn from me.'
Behold, I will plead My case against you,
Because you say, 'I have not sinned.'
36 Why do you gad about so much to change your way?
Also you shall be ashamed of Egypt as you were ashamed of Assyria.
37 Indeed you will go forth from him
With your hands on your head;
For the LORD has rejected your trusted allies,
And you will not prosper by them.

Israel Is Shameless

3 "They say, 'If a man divorces his wife,
And she goes from him
And becomes another man's,
May he return to her again?'
Would not that land be greatly polluted?
But you have played the harlot with many lovers;
Yet return to Me," says the LORD.

2 "Lift up your eyes to the desolate heights and see:
Where have you not lain *with men?*
By the road you have sat for them
Like an Arabian in the wilderness;
And you have polluted the land
With your harlotries and your wickedness.
3 Therefore the showers have been withheld,
And there has been no latter rain.
You have had a harlot's forehead;
You refuse to be ashamed.
4 Will you not from this time cry to Me,
'My Father, You *are* the guide of my youth?
5 Will He remain angry forever?
Will He keep it to the end?'
Behold, you have spoken and done evil things,
As you were able."

A Call to Repentance

6The LORD said also to me in the days of Josiah the king: "Have you seen

things of life. . . . If our society needs to reemphasize the virtue of honesty, it certainly needs to place great importance on dependability. . . .

Reliability is not just a social obligation; it is a spiritual obligation. God is even more concerned about our faithfulness than the person who is relying on us in some particular situation. . . . The faithful person is not only honest and dependable, but also loyal. . . .

Whether it be in honesty or dependability or loyalty, faithfulness is frequently a costly virtue. Only the Holy Spirit can enable us to pay that price. (From *The Practice of Godliness* by Jerry Bridges)

APPLICATION Do you gossip about others? Do you criticize others? Do you lustfully think about someone? Last April, did you cheat the government? Do you work hard on your job, or do you waste time? If you repeat sin again and again, you will experience God's discipline! Consider your life and ask the Holy Spirit to help you get rid of sin.

EXPLORATION Backsliding—Psalm 78:56-58; Jeremiah 17:5; Ezekiel 18:24-26; Matthew 5:13; Galatians 5:7-9; Hebrews 5:11-13.

what backsliding Israel has done? She has gone up on
every high mountain and under every green tree, and
there played the harlot. 7And I said, after she had done
all these *things*, 'Return to Me.' But she did not return.
And her treacherous sister Judah saw it. 8Then I saw that
for all the causes for which backsliding Israel had committed adultery, I had put her away and given her a certificate of divorce; yet her treacherous sister Judah did
not fear, but went and played the harlot also. 9So it came
to pass, through her casual harlotry, that she defiled the
land and committed adultery with stones and trees.
10And yet for all this her treacherous sister Judah has
not turned to Me with her whole heart, but in pretense," says the LORD.

11Then the LORD said to me, "Backsliding Israel has
shown herself more righteous than treacherous Judah. 12Go and proclaim these words toward the north,
and say:

'Return, backsliding Israel,' says the LORD;
'I will not cause My anger to fall on you.
For I *am* merciful,' says the LORD;
'I will not remain angry forever.
13 Only acknowledge your iniquity,
That you have transgressed against
the LORD your God,
And have scattered your charms
To alien deities under every green tree,
And you have not obeyed My voice,'
says the LORD.

14"Return, O backsliding children," says the LORD;
"for I am married to you. I will take you, one from a city
and two from a family, and I will bring you to Zion. 15And
I will give you shepherds according to My heart, who
will feed you with knowledge and understanding.

16"Then it shall come to pass, when you are multiplied
and increased in the land in those days," says the LORD,
"that they will say no more, 'The ark of the covenant
of the LORD.' It shall not come to mind, nor shall they
remember it, nor shall they visit *it*, nor shall it be
made anymore.

17"At that time Jerusalem shall be called The Throne
of the LORD, and all the nations shall be gathered to it,
to the name of the LORD, to Jerusalem. No more shall
they follow the dictates of their evil hearts.

18"In those days the house of Judah shall walk with
the house of Israel, and they shall come together out
of the land of the north to the land that I have given as
an inheritance to your fathers.

19"But I said:

'How can I put you among the children
And give you a pleasant land,
A beautiful heritage of the hosts of nations?'

"And I said:

'You shall call Me, "My Father,"
And not turn away from Me.'
20 Surely, *as* a wife treacherously departs
from her husband,
So have you dealt treacherously with Me,
O house of Israel," says the LORD.

21 A voice was heard on the desolate heights,
Weeping *and* supplications of the
children of Israel.
For they have perverted their way;
They have forgotten the LORD their God.

22 "Return, you backsliding children,
And I will heal your backslidings."

"Indeed we do come to You,
For You are the LORD our God.
23 Truly, in vain *is salvation hoped for*
from the hills,
And from the multitude of mountains;
Truly, in the LORD our God
Is the salvation of Israel.
24 For shame has devoured
The labor of our fathers from our youth—
Their flocks and their herds,
Their sons and their daughters.
25 We lie down in our shame,
And our reproach covers us.
For we have sinned against the LORD our God,
We and our fathers,
From our youth even to this day,
And have not obeyed the voice of
the LORD our God."

4 "If you will return, O Israel," says the LORD,
"Return to Me;
And if you will put away your abominations
out of My sight,
Then you shall not be moved.
2 And you shall swear, 'The LORD lives,'
In truth, in judgment, and in righteousness;
The nations shall bless themselves in Him,
And in Him they shall glory."

3For thus says the LORD to the men of Judah and Jerusalem:

"Break up your fallow ground,
And do not sow among thorns.

4 Circumcise yourselves to the LORD,
And take away the foreskins of your hearts,
You men of Judah and inhabitants of Jerusalem,
Lest My fury come forth like fire,
And burn so that no one can quench *it*,
Because of the evil of your doings."

An Imminent Invasion

5Declare in Judah and proclaim in Jerusalem, and say:

"Blow the trumpet in the land;
Cry, 'Gather together,'
And say, 'Assemble yourselves,
And let us go into the fortified cities.'
6 Set up the standard toward Zion.
Take refuge! Do not delay!
For I will bring disaster from the north,
And great destruction."

7 The lion has come up from his thicket,
And the destroyer of nations is on his way.
He has gone forth from his place
To make your land desolate.
Your cities will be laid waste,
Without inhabitant.
8 For this, clothe yourself with sackcloth,
Lament and wail.
For the fierce anger of the LORD
Has not turned back from us.

9 "And it shall come to pass in that day,"
says the LORD,
"*That* the heart of the king shall perish,
And the heart of the princes;
The priests shall be astonished,
And the prophets shall wonder."

10 Then I said, "Ah, Lord GOD!
Surely You have greatly deceived
this people and Jerusalem,
Saying, 'You shall have peace,'
Whereas the sword reaches to the heart."

11 At that time it will be said
To this people and to Jerusalem,
"A dry wind of the desolate heights
blows in the wilderness
Toward the daughter of My people—
Not to fan or to cleanse—
12 A wind too strong for these will come for Me;
Now I will also speak judgment against them."

13 "Behold, he shall come up like clouds,
And his chariots like a whirlwind.
His horses are swifter than eagles.
Woe to us, for we are plundered!"

14 O Jerusalem, wash your heart from wickedness,
That you may be saved.
How long shall your evil thoughts lodge
within you?
15 For a voice declares from Dan
And proclaims affliction from Mount Ephraim:
16 "Make mention to the nations,
Yes, proclaim against Jerusalem,
That watchers come from a far country
And raise their voice against the cities of Judah.
17 Like keepers of a field they are against
her all around,
Because she has been rebellious against Me,"
says the LORD.
18 "Your ways and your doings
Have procured these *things* for you.
This *is* your wickedness,
Because it is bitter,
Because it reaches to your heart."

Sorrow for the Doomed Nation

19 O my soul, my soul!
I am pained in my very heart!
My heart makes a noise in me;
I cannot hold my peace,
Because you have heard, O my soul,
The sound of the trumpet,
The alarm of war.
20 Destruction upon destruction is cried,
For the whole land is plundered.
Suddenly my tents are plundered,
And my curtains in a moment.
21 How long will I see the standard,
And hear the sound of the trumpet?

22 "For My people *are* foolish,
They have not known Me.
They *are* silly children,
And they have no understanding.
They *are* wise to do evil,
But to do good they have no knowledge."

23 I beheld the earth, and indeed *it*
was without form, and void;
And the heavens, they *had* no light.
24 I beheld the mountains, and
indeed they trembled,
And all the hills moved back and forth.

25 I beheld, and indeed *there was* no man,
And all the birds of the heavens had fled.
26 I beheld, and indeed the fruitful land
was a wilderness,
And all its cities were broken down
At the presence of the LORD,
By His fierce anger.

27 For thus says the LORD:

"The whole land shall be desolate;
Yet I will not make a full end.
28 For this shall the earth mourn,
And the heavens above be black,
Because I have spoken.
I have purposed and will not relent,
Nor will I turn back from it.
29 The whole city shall flee from the noise of the
horsemen and bowmen.
They shall go into thickets and climb
up on the rocks.
Every city *shall be* forsaken,
And not a man shall dwell in it.

30 "And *when* you *are* plundered,
What will you do?
Though you clothe yourself with crimson,
Though you adorn *yourself* with
ornaments of gold,
Though you enlarge your eyes with paint,
In vain you will make yourself fair;
Your lovers will despise you;
They will seek your life.

31 "For I have heard a voice as of a woman in labor,
The anguish as of her who brings forth
her first child,
The voice of the daughter of Zion
bewailing herself;
She spreads her hands, *saying*,
'Woe *is* me now, for my soul is weary
Because of murderers!'

The Justice of God's Judgment

5 "Run to and fro through the streets of Jerusalem;
See now and know;
And seek in her open places
If you can find a man,
If there is *anyone* who executes judgment,
Who seeks the truth,
And I will pardon her.
2 Though they say, '*As* the LORD lives,'
Surely they swear falsely."

3 O LORD, *are* not Your eyes on the truth?
You have stricken them,
But they have not grieved;
You have consumed them,
But they have refused to receive correction.
They have made their faces harder than rock;
They have refused to return.

4 Therefore I said, "Surely these *are* poor.
They are foolish;
For they do not know the way of the LORD,
The judgment of their God.
5 I will go to the great men and speak to them,
For they have known the way of the LORD,
The judgment of their God."

But these have altogether broken the yoke
And burst the bonds.
6 Therefore a lion from the forest
shall slay them,
A wolf of the deserts shall destroy them;
A leopard will watch over their cities.
Everyone who goes out from there shall be
torn in pieces,
Because their transgressions are many;
Their backslidings have increased.

7 "How shall I pardon you for this?
Your children have forsaken Me
And sworn by *those that are* not gods.
When I had fed them to the full,
Then they committed adultery
And assembled themselves by troops
in the harlots' houses.
8 They were *like* well-fed lusty stallions;
Every one neighed after his neighbor's wife.
9 Shall I not punish *them* for these *things?*"
says the LORD.
"And shall I not avenge Myself on
such a nation as this?

10 "Go up on her walls and destroy,
But do not make a complete end.
Take away her branches,
For they *are* not the LORD's.
11 For the house of Israel and the house of Judah
Have dealt very treacherously with Me,"
says the LORD.

12 They have lied about the LORD,
And said, "*It is* not He.
Neither will evil come upon us,
Nor shall we see sword or famine.
13 And the prophets become wind,

For the word *is* not in them.
Thus shall it be done to them."

14 Therefore thus says the LORD God of hosts:
"Because you speak this word,
Behold, I will make My words in your mouth fire,
And this people wood,
And it shall devour them.
15 Behold, I will bring a nation against you from afar,
O house of Israel," says the LORD.
"It *is* a mighty nation,
It *is* an ancient nation,
A nation whose language you do not know,
Nor can you understand what they say.
16 Their quiver *is* like an open tomb;
They *are* all mighty men.
17 And they shall eat up your harvest and your bread,
Which your sons and daughters should eat.
They shall eat up your flocks and your herds;
They shall eat up your vines and your fig trees;
They shall destroy your fortified cities,
In which you trust, with the sword.

18 "Nevertheless in those days," says the LORD, "I will
not make a complete end of you. 19 And it will be when
you say, 'Why does the LORD our God do all these *things*
to us?' then you shall answer them, 'Just as you have
forsaken Me and served foreign gods in your land, so
you shall serve aliens in a land *that is* not yours.'

20 "Declare this in the house of Jacob
And proclaim it in Judah, saying,
21 'Hear this now, O foolish people,
Without understanding,
Who have eyes and see not,
And who have ears and hear not:
22 Do you not fear Me?' says the LORD.
'Will you not tremble at My presence,
Who have placed the sand as the bound of the sea,
By a perpetual decree, that it cannot pass beyond it?
And though its waves toss to and fro,
Yet they cannot prevail;
Though they roar, yet they cannot pass over it.
23 But this people has a defiant and rebellious heart;
They have revolted and departed.
24 They do not say in their heart,
"Let us now fear the LORD our God,
Who gives rain, both the former and the latter, in its season.
He reserves for us the appointed weeks of the harvest."
25 Your iniquities have turned these *things* away,
And your sins have withheld good from you.

26 'For among My people are found wicked *men;*
They lie in wait as one who sets snares;
They set a trap;
They catch men.
27 As a cage is full of birds,
So their houses *are* full of deceit.
Therefore they have become great and grown rich.
28 They have grown fat, they are sleek;
Yes, they surpass the deeds of the wicked;
They do not plead the cause,
The cause of the fatherless;
Yet they prosper,
And the right of the needy they do not defend.
29 Shall I not punish *them* for these *things?*
says the LORD.
'Shall I not avenge Myself on such a nation as this?'

30 "An astonishing and horrible thing
Has been committed in the land:
31 The prophets prophesy falsely,
And the priests rule by their *own* power;
And My people love *to have it* so.
But what will you do in the end?

Impending Destruction from the North

6 "O you children of Benjamin,
Gather yourselves to flee from the midst of Jerusalem!
Blow the trumpet in Tekoa,
And set up a signal-fire in Beth Haccerem;
For disaster appears out of the north,
And great destruction.
2 I have likened the daughter of Zion
To a lovely and delicate woman.
3 The shepherds with their flocks shall come to her.
They shall pitch *their* tents against her all around.
Each one shall pasture in his own place."

4 "Prepare war against her;
Arise, and let us go up at noon.
Woe to us, for the day goes away,

For the shadows of the evening are lengthening.
5 Arise, and let us go by night,
And let us destroy her palaces."

6For thus has the LORD of hosts said:

"Cut down trees,
And build a mound against Jerusalem.
This *is* the city to be punished.
She *is* full of oppression in her midst.
7 As a fountain wells up with water,
So she wells up with her wickedness.
Violence and plundering are heard in her.
Before Me continually *are* grief and wounds.
8 Be instructed, O Jerusalem,
Lest My soul depart from you;
Lest I make you desolate,
A land not inhabited."

9Thus says the LORD of hosts:

"They shall thoroughly glean as a vine
the remnant of Israel;
As a grape-gatherer, put your hand
back into the branches."

10 To whom shall I speak and give warning,
That they may hear?
Indeed their ear *is* uncircumcised,
And they cannot give heed.
Behold, the word of the LORD is
a reproach to them;
They have no delight in it.
11 Therefore I am full of the fury of the LORD.
I am weary of holding *it* in.
"I will pour it out on the children outside,
And on the assembly of young men together;
For even the husband shall be
taken with the wife,
The aged with *him who is* full of days.
12 And their houses shall be turned over to others,
Fields and wives together;
For I will stretch out My hand
Against the inhabitants of the land,"
says the LORD.
13 "Because from the least of them even to the
greatest of them,
Everyone *is* given to covetousness;
And from the prophet even to the priest,
Everyone deals falsely.
14 They have also healed the hurt of
My people slightly,
Saying, 'Peace, peace!'
When *there is* no peace.
15 Were they ashamed when they had
committed abomination?
No! They were not at all ashamed;
Nor did they know how to blush.
Therefore they shall fall among those who fall;
At the time I punish them,
They shall be cast down," says the LORD.

16Thus says the LORD:

"Stand in the ways and see,
And ask for the old paths, where the good way *is*,
And walk in it;
Then you will find rest for your souls.
But they said, 'We will not walk *in it*.'
17 Also, I set watchmen over you, *saying*,
'Listen to the sound of the trumpet!'
But they said, 'We will not listen.'
18 Therefore hear, you nations,
And know, O congregation, what
is among them.
19 Hear, O earth!
Behold, I will certainly bring calamity
on this people—
The fruit of their thoughts,
Because they have not heeded My words
Nor My law, but rejected it.
20 For what purpose to Me
Comes frankincense from Sheba,
And sweet cane from a far country?
Your burnt offerings *are* not acceptable,
Nor your sacrifices sweet to Me."

21Therefore thus says the LORD:

"Behold, I will lay stumbling blocks
before this people,
And the fathers and the sons together
shall fall on them.
The neighbor and his friend shall perish."

22Thus says the LORD:

"Behold, a people comes from the north country,
And a great nation will be raised from
the farthest parts of the earth.
23 They will lay hold on bow and spear;
They *are* cruel and have no mercy;
Their voice roars like the sea;
And they ride on horses,
As men of war set in array against you,
O daughter of Zion."

24 We have heard the report of it;
Our hands grow feeble.

Anguish has taken hold of us,
Pain as of a woman in labor.
25 Do not go out into the field,
Nor walk by the way.
Because of the sword of the enemy,
Fear *is* on every side.
26 O daughter of my people,
Dress in sackcloth
And roll about in ashes!
Make mourning *as for* an only son,
most bitter lamentation;
For the plunderer will suddenly come upon us.

27 "I have set you *as* an assayer *and* a fortress
among My people,
That you may know and test their way.
28 They *are* all stubborn rebels, walking
as slanderers.
They are bronze and iron,
They *are* all corrupters;
29 The bellows blow fiercely,
The lead is consumed by the fire;
The smelter refines in vain,
For the wicked are not drawn off.
30 *People* will call them rejected silver,
Because the LORD has rejected them."

Trusting in Lying Words

7 The word that came to Jeremiah from the LORD,
saying, 2"Stand in the gate of the LORD's house, and
proclaim there this word, and say, 'Hear the word of
the LORD, all *you of* Judah who enter in at these gates to
worship the LORD!' " 3Thus says the LORD of hosts, the
God of Israel: "Amend your ways and your doings, and
I will cause you to dwell in this place. 4Do not trust in
these lying words, saying, 'The temple of the LORD, the
temple of the LORD, the temple of the LORD *are* these.'
5"For if you thoroughly amend your ways and your
doings, if you thoroughly execute judgment between a
man and his neighbor, 6*if* you do not oppress the stranger, the fatherless, and the widow, and do not shed innocent blood in this place, or walk after other gods to
your hurt, 7then I will cause you to dwell in this place,
in the land that I gave to your fathers forever and ever.
8"Behold, you trust in lying words that cannot profit.
9Will you steal, murder, commit adultery, swear falsely,
burn incense to Baal, and walk after other gods whom
you do not know, 10and *then* come and stand before
Me in this house which is called by My name, and say,
'We are delivered to do all these abominations'? 11Has
this house, which is called by My name, become a den
of thieves in your eyes? Behold, I, even I, have seen *it*,"
says the LORD.
12"But go now to My place which *was* in Shiloh,
where I set My name at the first, and see what I did to
it because of the wickedness of My people Israel. 13And
now, because you have done all these works," says the
LORD, "and I spoke to you, rising up early and speaking,
but you did not hear, and I called you, but you did not
answer, 14therefore I will do to the house which is called
by My name, in which you trust, and to this place which
I gave to you and your fathers, as I have done to Shiloh.
15And I will cast you out of My sight, as I have cast out
all your brethren—the whole posterity of Ephraim.
16"Therefore do not pray for this people, nor lift up
a cry or prayer for them, nor make intercession to Me;
for I will not hear you. 17Do you not see what they do in
the cities of Judah and in the streets of Jerusalem? 18The
children gather wood, the fathers kindle the fire, and
the women knead dough, to make cakes for the queen
of heaven; and *they* pour out drink offerings to other
gods, that they may provoke Me to anger. 19Do they provoke Me to anger?" says the LORD. "*Do they* not *provoke*
themselves, to the shame of their own faces?"
20Therefore thus says the Lord GOD: "Behold, My
anger and My fury will be poured out on this place—
on man and on beast, on the trees of the field and on
the fruit of the ground. And it will burn and not be
quenched."
21Thus says the LORD of hosts, the God of Israel: "Add
your burnt offerings to your sacrifices and eat meat.
22For I did not speak to your fathers, or command them
in the day that I brought them out of the land of Egypt,
concerning burnt offerings or sacrifices. 23But this is
what I commanded them, saying, 'Obey My voice, and
I will be your God, and you shall be My people. And walk
in all the ways that I have commanded you, that it may
be well with you.' 24Yet they did not obey or incline their
ear, but followed the counsels *and* the dictates of their
evil hearts, and went backward and not forward. 25Since
the day that your fathers came out of the land of Egypt
until this day, I have even sent to you all My servants
the prophets, daily rising up early and sending *them*.
26Yet they did not obey Me or incline their ear, but
stiffened their neck. They did worse than their fathers.
27"Therefore you shall speak all these words to
them, but they will not obey you. You shall also call to
them, but they will not answer you.

Judgment on Obscene Religion

28"So you shall say to them, 'This *is* a nation that does
not obey the voice of the LORD their God nor receive

LIFE LESSON

Jeremiah 7:1–10:25

SITUATION Jeremiah prophesied from the Temple gates and challenged the people. He told them that even if it meant destroying the temple, God would bring discipline on Jerusalem. The nation had forgotten God after the death of good King Josiah.

OBSERVATION True religion must have substance, integrity, and purity. God will uncover and rebuke sin, especially when people minimize it or let it go unacknowledged.

INSPIRATION Habits are the thought and emotional patterns engraved on our minds. These internal habit patterns play just as forceful a role as external influences on our actions—in fact, perhaps more so. . . .

As unbelievers, we formerly gave ourselves to developing habits of unholiness—what Paul called "ever-increasing wickedness" (Romans 6:19). Every time we sinned—every time we lusted, coveted, hated, cheated, or lied—we were developing habits of ever increasing wickedness. These repeated acts of unrighteousness became habits that made us, in fact, slaves to sin. . . .

Though we are to deal with these habits of unholiness, we must not try to do it in our own strength. Breaking sinful habits must be done in cooperation with the Holy Spirit and in dependence upon Him. The determination that "I'll not do that anymore," based upon sheer human resolve, has never once broken the shackles of sin. But there are practical principles which we can follow to train ourselves in godliness.

The first principle is that habits are developed and reinforced by *frequent*

correction. Truth has perished and has been cut off from their mouth.
29Cut off your hair and cast *it* away, and take up a lamentation on the desolate heights; for the LORD has rejected and forsaken the generation of His
wrath.' 30For the children of Judah have done evil in My sight," says the LORD.
"They have set their abominations in the house which is called by My name,
to pollute it. 31And they have built the high places of Tophet, which *is* in the
Valley of the Son of Hinnom, to burn their sons and their daughters in the
fire, which I did not command, nor did it come into My heart.
32"Therefore behold, the days are coming," says the LORD, "when it will
no more be called Tophet, or the Valley of the Son of Hinnom, but the
Valley of Slaughter; for they will bury in Tophet until there is no room. 33The
corpses of this people will be food for the birds of the heaven and for the
beasts of the earth. And no one will frighten *them away.* 34Then I will cause
to cease from the cities of Judah and from the streets of Jerusalem the
voice of mirth and the voice of gladness, the voice of the bridegroom and
the voice of the bride. For the land shall be desolate.

8 "At that time," says the LORD, "they shall bring out the bones of the
kings of Judah, and the bones of its princes, and the bones of the
priests, and the bones of the prophets, and the bones of the inhabitants of
Jerusalem, out of their graves. 2They shall spread them before the sun and
the moon and all the host of heaven, which they have loved and which they
have served and after which they have walked, which they have sought and
which they have worshiped. They shall not be gathered nor buried; they
shall be like refuse on the face of the earth. 3Then death shall be chosen
rather than life by all the residue of those who remain of this evil family, who
remain in all the places where I have driven them," says the LORD of hosts.

The Peril of False Teaching

4"Moreover you shall say to them, 'Thus says the LORD:

"Will they fall and not rise?
Will one turn away and not return?
5 Why has this people slidden back,
Jerusalem, in a perpetual backsliding?
They hold fast to deceit,
They refuse to return.
6 I listened and heard,
But they do not speak aright.
No man repented of his wickedness,
Saying, 'What have I done?'
Everyone turned to his own course,
As the horse rushes into the battle.

7 "Even the stork in the heavens
Knows her appointed times;
And the turtledove, the swift, and the swallow
Observe the time of their coming.
But My people do not know the judgment of the LORD.

8 "How can you say, 'We *are* wise,
And the law of the LORD *is* with us'?
Look, the false pen of the scribe certainly works falsehood.
9 The wise men are ashamed,

They are dismayed and taken.
Behold, they have rejected the word of the LORD;
So what wisdom do they have?
10 Therefore I will give their wives to others,
And their fields to those who will inherit *them;*
Because from the least even to the greatest
Everyone is given to covetousness;
From the prophet even to the priest
Everyone deals falsely.
11 For they have healed the hurt of the daughter of My people slightly,
Saying, 'Peace, peace!'
When *there is* no peace.
12 Were they ashamed when they had committed abomination?
No! They were not at all ashamed,
Nor did they know how to blush.
Therefore they shall fall among those who fall;
In the time of their punishment
They shall be cast down," says the LORD.

13 "I will surely consume them," says the LORD.
"No grapes *shall be* on the vine,
Nor figs on the fig tree,
And the leaf shall fade;
And *the things* I have given them shall pass away from them." ' "

14 "Why do we sit still?
Assemble yourselves,
And let us enter the fortified cities,
And let us be silent there.
For the LORD our God has put us to silence
And given us water of gall to drink,
Because we have sinned against the LORD.
15 "*We* looked for peace, but no good *came;*
And for a time of health, and there was trouble!
16 The snorting of His horses was heard from Dan.
The whole land trembled at the sound of the
neighing of His strong ones;
For they have come and devoured the land and all that is in it,
The city and those who dwell in it."

17 "For behold, I will send serpents among you,
Vipers which cannot be charmed,
And they shall bite you," says the LORD.

The Prophet Mourns for the People

18 I would comfort myself in sorrow;
My heart *is* faint in me.
19 Listen! The voice,
The cry of the daughter of my people
From a far country:
"*Is* not the LORD in Zion?
Is not her King in her?"

repetition. . . . This is the principle underlying the fact that the more we sin the more we are inclined to sin. But the converse is also true. The more we say no to sin, the more we are inclined to say no.

Therefore, in dependence on the Holy Spirit, we must systematically work at acquiring the habit of saying no to the sins that so easily entangle us. We all know what these sins are; the sins to which we are particularly vulnerable. We begin by concentrating on saying no to these. Then God will lead us to work on other sins which we may not even be aware of at this time. The more we succeed in saying no to our sinful desires, the easier it becomes to say no.

In the same manner we can develop positive habits of holiness. We can develop the habit of thinking thoughts that are pure, true, and good. We can develop the habits of prayer and meditating on the Scriptures. But these habits will only be developed through frequent repetition.

(From *The Pursuit of Holiness* by Jerry Bridges)

APPLICATION Are you a person of integrity? How do you work without supervision? Do you work harder if your boss is around? Do you cut corners you know your supervisor will never notice? Work for your employer as you would for Jesus Christ. Work hard, with or without supervision.

EXPLORATION Idolatry Punished—Exodus 22:20; Deuteronomy 4:25-28; 8:19-20; 1 Kings 9:6-7; Psalm 97:7; Ezekiel 7:20-22; Romans 1:22-25; Revelation 14:9-10.

"Why have they provoked Me to anger
With their carved images—
With foreign idols?"

20 "The harvest is past,
The summer is ended,
And we are not saved!"

21 For the hurt of the daughter of my
people I am hurt.
I am mourning;
Astonishment has taken hold of me.
22 *Is there* no balm in Gilead,
Is there no physician there?
Why then is there no recovery
For the health of the daughter of my people?

9 Oh, that my head were waters,
And my eyes a fountain of tears,
That I might weep day and night
For the slain of the daughter of my people!
2 Oh, that I had in the wilderness
A lodging place for travelers;
That I might leave my people,
And go from them!
For they *are* all adulterers,
An assembly of treacherous men.

3 "And *like* their bow they have bent their
tongues *for* lies.
They are not valiant for the truth on the earth.
For they proceed from evil to evil,
And they do not know Me," says the LORD.
4 "Everyone take heed to his neighbor,
And do not trust any brother;
For every brother will utterly supplant,
And every neighbor will walk with slanderers.
5 Everyone will deceive his neighbor,
And will not speak the truth;
They have taught their tongue to speak lies;
They weary themselves to commit iniquity.
6 Your dwelling place *is* in the midst of deceit;
Through deceit they refuse to know Me,"
says the LORD.

7 Therefore thus says the LORD of hosts:

"Behold, I will refine them and try them;
For how shall I deal with the daughter
of My people?
8 Their tongue *is* an arrow shot out;
It speaks deceit;
One speaks peaceably to his neighbor
with his mouth,
But in his heart he lies in wait.
9 Shall I not punish them for these *things?*"
says the LORD.
"Shall I not avenge Myself on such a
nation as this?"

10 I will take up a weeping and wailing
for the mountains,
And for the dwelling places of the wilderness
a lamentation,
Because they are burned up,
So that no one can pass through;
Nor can *men* hear the voice of the cattle.
Both the birds of the heavens and the
beasts have fled;
They are gone.

11 "I will make Jerusalem a heap of ruins,
a den of jackals.
I will make the cities of Judah desolate,
without an inhabitant."

12 Who *is* the wise man who may understand this?
And *who is he* to whom the mouth of the LORD has
spoken, that he may declare it? Why does the land
perish *and* burn up like a wilderness, so that no one
can pass through?
13 And the LORD said, "Because they have forsaken
My law which I set before them, and have not obeyed
My voice, nor walked according to it, 14 but they have
walked according to the dictates of their own hearts
and after the Baals, which their fathers taught them,"
15 therefore thus says the LORD of hosts, the God of Israel:
"Behold, I will feed them, this people, with wormwood,
and give them water of gall to drink. 16 I will scatter them
also among the Gentiles, whom neither they nor their
fathers have known. And I will send a sword after
them until I have consumed them."

The People Mourn in Judgment

17 Thus says the LORD of hosts:

"Consider and call for the mourning women,
That they may come;
And send for skillful wailing women,
That they may come.
18 Let them make haste
And take up a wailing for us,
That our eyes may run with tears,
And our eyelids gush with water.
19 For a voice of wailing is heard from Zion:
'How we are plundered!
We are greatly ashamed,

Because we have forsaken the land,
Because we have been cast out
of our dwellings.' "

20 Yet hear the word of the LORD, O women,
And let your ear receive the word of His mouth;
Teach your daughters wailing,
And everyone her neighbor a lamentation.
21 For death has come through our windows,
Has entered our palaces,
To kill off the children—*no longer to be* outside!
And the young men—*no longer* on the streets!

22 Speak, "Thus says the LORD:

'Even the carcasses of men shall fall as refuse
on the open field,
Like cuttings after the harvester,
And no one shall gather *them.*' "

23 Thus says the LORD:

"Let not the wise *man* glory in his wisdom,
Let not the mighty *man* glory in his might,
Nor let the rich *man* glory in his riches;
24 But let him who glories glory in this,
That he understands and knows Me,
That I *am* the LORD, exercising lovingkindness,
judgment, and righteousness in the earth.
For in these I delight," says the LORD.

25 "Behold, the days are coming," says the LORD, "that
I will punish all *who are* circumcised with the uncircumcised— 26 Egypt, Judah, Edom, the people of
Ammon, Moab, and all *who are* in the farthest corners,
who dwell in the wilderness. For all *these* nations *are*
uncircumcised, and all the house of Israel *are* uncircumcised in the heart."

Idols and the True God

10 Hear the word which the LORD speaks to you,
O house of Israel.
2 Thus says the LORD:

"Do not learn the way of the Gentiles;
Do not be dismayed at the signs of heaven,
For the Gentiles are dismayed at them.
3 For the customs of the peoples *are* futile;
For *one* cuts a tree from the forest,
The work of the hands of the workman,
with the ax.
4 They decorate it with silver and gold;
They fasten it with nails and hammers
So that it will not topple.
5 They *are* upright, like a palm tree,
And they cannot speak;
They must be carried,
Because they cannot go *by themselves.*
Do not be afraid of them,
For they cannot do evil,
Nor can they do any good."

6 Inasmuch as *there is* none like You, O LORD
(You *are* great, and Your name *is* great in might),
7 Who would not fear You, O King of the nations?
For this is Your rightful due.
For among all the wise *men* of the nations,
And in all their kingdoms,
There is none like You.
8 But they are altogether dull-hearted and foolish;
A wooden idol *is* a worthless doctrine.
9 Silver is beaten into plates;
It is brought from Tarshish,
And gold from Uphaz,
The work of the craftsman
And of the hands of the metalsmith;
Blue and purple *are* their clothing;
They *are* all the work of skillful *men.*
10 But the LORD *is* the true God;
He *is* the living God and the everlasting King.
At His wrath the earth will tremble,
And the nations will not be able to
endure His indignation.

11 Thus you shall say to them: "The gods that have
not made the heavens and the earth shall perish from
the earth and from under these heavens."

12 He has made the earth by His power,
He has established the world by His wisdom,
And has stretched out the heavens
at His discretion.
13 When He utters His voice,
There is a multitude of waters in the heavens:
"And He causes the vapors to ascend
from the ends of the earth.
He makes lightning for the rain,
He brings the wind out of His treasuries."[e]

14 Everyone is dull-hearted, without knowledge;
Every metalsmith is put to shame
by an image;
For his molded image *is* falsehood,
And *there is* no breath in them.
15 They *are* futile, a work of errors;

10:13 [e] Psalm 135:7

LIFE LESSON
Jeremiah 11:1–13:27

SITUATION God would bring disaster on Israel if they did not repent; He would refuse to hear their prayers and let foreigners invade who would kill and exile many. God granted the Israelites an opportunity to acknowledge their sin and repent.

OBSERVATION God's demands are not unreasonable. He does not destroy us every time we sin. He shows patience with our human frailty, but he cannot tolerate repeated, rebellious sin.

INSPIRATION Have I ever come to a place in my experience where I can say—"I indeed—but He"? Until that moment does come, I will never know what the baptism of the Holy Ghost means. I indeed am at an end, I cannot do a thing: but He begins just there—He does the thing no one else can ever do. Am I prepared for His coming? Jesus cannot come as long as there is anything in the way either of goodness or badness. When He comes, am I prepared for Him to drag into the light every wrong thing I have done? It is just there that He comes. Wherever I know I am unclean, He will put His feet: Wherever I think I am clean, He will withdraw them.

In the time of their punishment they shall perish.
16 The Portion of Jacob *is* not like them,
For He *is* the Maker of all *things*,
And Israel *is* the tribe of His inheritance;
The LORD of hosts *is* His name.

The Coming Captivity of Judah

17 Gather up your wares from the land,
O inhabitant of the fortress!

18 For thus says the LORD:

"Behold, I will throw out at this time
The inhabitants of the land,
And will distress them,
That they may find *it so*."

19 Woe is me for my hurt!
My wound is severe.
But I say, "Truly this *is* an infirmity,
And I must bear it."
20 My tent is plundered,
And all my cords are broken;
My children have gone from me,
And they *are* no more.
There is no one to pitch my tent anymore,
Or set up my curtains.

21 For the shepherds have become dull-hearted,
And have not sought the LORD;
Therefore they shall not prosper,
And all their flocks shall be scattered.
22 Behold, the noise of the report has come,
And a great commotion out of the north country,
To make the cities of Judah desolate, a den of jackals.

23 O LORD, I know the way of man *is* not in himself;
It is not in man who walks to direct his own steps.
24 O LORD, correct me, but with justice;
Not in Your anger, lest You bring me to nothing.
25 Pour out Your fury on the Gentiles, who do not know You,
And on the families who do not call on Your name;
For they have eaten up Jacob,
Devoured him and consumed him,
And made his dwelling place desolate.

The Broken Covenant

11 The word that came to Jeremiah from the LORD, saying, 2 "Hear the
words of this covenant, and speak to the men of Judah and to the
inhabitants of Jerusalem; 3 and say to them, 'Thus says the LORD God of Israel:
"Cursed *is* the man who does not obey the words of this covenant 4 which I
commanded your fathers in the day I brought them out of the land of Egypt,
from the iron furnace, saying, 'Obey My voice, and do according to all that I
command you; so shall you be My people, and I will be your God,' 5 that I

may establish the oath which I have sworn to your fathers, to give them 'a
land flowing with milk and honey,'[f] as *it is* this day." ' "
And I answered and said, "So be it, LORD."
6Then the LORD said to me, "Proclaim all these words in the cities of Judah
and in the streets of Jerusalem, saying: 'Hear the words of this covenant
and do them. 7For I earnestly exhorted your fathers in the day I brought
them up out of the land of Egypt, until this day, rising early and exhorting,
saying, "Obey My voice." 8Yet they did not obey or incline their ear, but
everyone followed the dictates of his evil heart; therefore I will bring upon
them all the words of this covenant, which I commanded *them* to do, but
which they have not done.' "
9And the LORD said to me, "A conspiracy has been found among the men
of Judah and among the inhabitants of Jerusalem. 10They have turned back
to the iniquities of their forefathers who refused to hear My words, and
they have gone after other gods to serve them; the house of Israel and the
house of Judah have broken My covenant which I made with their fathers."
11Therefore thus says the LORD: "Behold, I will surely bring calamity on
them which they will not be able to escape; and though they cry out to Me,
I will not listen to them. 12Then the cities of Judah and the inhabitants of
Jerusalem will go and cry out to the gods to whom they offer incense, but
they will not save them at all in the time of their trouble. 13For *according to*
the number of your cities were your gods, O Judah; and *according to* the
number of the streets of Jerusalem you have set up altars to *that* shameful
thing, altars to burn incense to Baal.
14"So do not pray for this people, or lift up a cry or prayer for them; for I will
not hear *them* in the time that they cry out to Me because of their trouble.

15 "What has My beloved to do in My house,
Having done lewd deeds with many?
And the holy flesh has passed from you.
When you do evil, then you rejoice.
16 The LORD called your name,
Green Olive Tree, Lovely *and* of Good Fruit.
With the noise of a great tumult
He has kindled fire on it,
And its branches are broken.

17"For the LORD of hosts, who planted you, has pronounced doom against
you for the evil of the house of Israel and of the house of Judah, which they
have done against themselves to provoke Me to anger in offering incense
to Baal."

Jeremiah's Life Threatened

18Now the LORD gave me knowledge *of it*, and I know *it*; for You showed
me their doings. 19But I *was* like a docile lamb brought to the slaughter;
and I did not know that they had devised schemes against me, *saying*, "Let
us destroy the tree with its fruit, and let us cut him off from the land of the
living, that his name may be remembered no more."

20 But, O LORD of hosts,
You who judge righteously,

11:5 [f] Exodus 3:8

Repentance does not bring a sense of sin, but a sense of unutterable unworthiness. When I repent, I realize that I am utterly helpless; I know all through me that I am not worthy even to bear His shoes. Have I repented like that? Or is there a lingering suggestion of standing up for myself? The reason God cannot come into my life is because I am not through into repentance.

"He shall baptize you with the Holy Ghost and fire." John does not speak of the baptism of the Holy Ghost as an experience, but as a work performed by Jesus Christ. "He shall baptize you." The only conscious experience those who are baptized with the Holy Ghost ever have is a sense of absolute unworthiness.

(From *My Utmost for His Highest* by Oswald Chambers)

APPLICATION Are you burnt out? Have you had more than you can take? Is your relationship with God suffering because of it? Take a break. Take a vacation—a restful one. Sit back and refresh your love for God, his Word, and your family.

EXPLORATION Repentance—1 Kings 21:29; 1 Chronicles 21:8.

Testing the mind and the heart,
Let me see Your vengeance on them,
For to You I have revealed my cause.

21"Therefore thus says the LORD concerning the
men of Anathoth who seek your life, saying, 'Do not
prophesy in the name of the LORD, lest you die by our
hand'— 22therefore thus says the LORD of hosts: 'Behold,
I will punish them. The young men shall die by the
sword, their sons and their daughters shall die by
famine; 23and there shall be no remnant of them, for I
will bring catastrophe on the men of Anathoth, *even*
the year of their punishment.' "

Jeremiah's Question

12 Righteous *are* You, O LORD, when I plead with
You;
Yet let me talk with You about *Your* judgments.
Why does the way of the wicked prosper?
Why are those happy who deal
so treacherously?
2 You have planted them, yes, they
have taken root;
They grow, yes, they bear fruit.
You *are* near in their mouth
But far from their mind.

3 But You, O LORD, know me;
You have seen me,
And You have tested my heart toward You.
Pull them out like sheep for the slaughter,
And prepare them for the day of slaughter.
4 How long will the land mourn,
And the herbs of every field wither?
The beasts and birds are consumed,
For the wickedness of those
who dwell there,
Because they said, "He will not
see our final end."

The LORD Answers Jeremiah

5 "If you have run with the footmen, and they
have wearied you,
Then how can you contend with horses?
And *if* in the land of peace,
In which you trusted, *they wearied you,*
Then how will you do in the floodplain[g]
of the Jordan?
6 For even your brothers, the house of
your father,
Even they have dealt treacherously with you;
Yes, they have called a multitude after you.
Do not believe them,
Even though they speak smooth words to you.

7 "I have forsaken My house, I have
left My heritage;
I have given the dearly beloved of My soul into
the hand of her enemies.
8 My heritage is to Me like a lion in the forest;
It cries out against Me;
Therefore I have hated it.
9 My heritage *is* to Me *like* a speckled vulture;
The vultures all around *are* against her.
Come, assemble all the beasts of the field,
Bring them to devour!

10 "Many rulers[h] have destroyed My vineyard,
They have trodden My portion underfoot;
They have made My pleasant portion
a desolate wilderness.
11 They have made it desolate;
Desolate, it mourns to Me;
The whole land is made desolate,
Because no one takes *it* to heart.
12 The plunderers have come
On all the desolate heights in the wilderness,
For the sword of the LORD shall devour
From *one* end of the land to the
other end of the land;
No flesh shall have peace.
13 They have sown wheat but reaped thorns;
They have put themselves to pain
but do not profit.
But be ashamed of your harvest
Because of the fierce anger of the LORD."

14Thus says the LORD: "Against all My evil neighbors
who touch the inheritance which I have caused My people Israel to inherit—behold, I will pluck them out of
their land and pluck out the house of Judah from
among them. 15Then it shall be, after I have plucked
them out, that I will return and have compassion on
them and bring them back, everyone to his heritage
and everyone to his land. 16And it shall be, if they will
learn carefully the ways of My people, to swear by My
name, 'As the LORD lives,' as they taught My people to
swear by Baal, then they shall be established in the midst
of My people. 17But if they do not obey, I will utterly
pluck up and destroy that nation," says the LORD.

12:5 [g] Or *thicket*
12:10 [h] Literally *shepherds* or *pastors*

Symbol of the Linen Sash

13 Thus the LORD said to me: "Go and get yourself
a linen sash, and put it around your waist, but
do not put it in water." 2So I got a sash according to
the word of the LORD, and put *it* around my waist.
3And the word of the LORD came to me the second
time, saying, 4"Take the sash that you acquired, which
is around your waist, and arise, go to the Euphrates,[i]
and hide it there in a hole in the rock." 5So I went and
hid it by the Euphrates, as the LORD commanded me.
6Now it came to pass after many days that the LORD
said to me, "Arise, go to the Euphrates, and take from
there the sash which I commanded you to hide there."
7Then I went to the Euphrates and dug, and I took the
sash from the place where I had hidden it; and there
was the sash, ruined. It was profitable for nothing.
8Then the word of the LORD came to me, saying,
9"Thus says the LORD: 'In this manner I will ruin the
pride of Judah and the great pride of Jerusalem. 10This
evil people, who refuse to hear My words, who follow
the dictates of their hearts, and walk after other gods
to serve them and worship them, shall be just like this
sash which is profitable for nothing. 11For as the sash
clings to the waist of a man, so I have caused the
whole house of Israel and the whole house of Judah to
cling to Me,' says the LORD, 'that they may become My
people, for renown, for praise, and for glory; but they
would not hear.'

Symbol of the Wine Bottles

12"Therefore you shall speak to them this word:
'Thus says the LORD God of Israel: "Every bottle shall
be filled with wine." '
"And they will say to you, 'Do we not certainly
know that every bottle will be filled with wine?'
13"Then you shall say to them, 'Thus says the LORD:
"Behold, I will fill all the inhabitants of this land—
even the kings who sit on David's throne, the priests,
the prophets, and all the inhabitants of Jerusalem—
with drunkenness! 14And I will dash them one against
another, even the fathers and the sons together," says
the LORD. "I will not pity nor spare nor have mercy,
but will destroy them." ' "

Pride Precedes Captivity

15 Hear and give ear:
Do not be proud,
For the LORD has spoken.
16 Give glory to the LORD your God
Before He causes darkness,
And before your feet stumble
On the dark mountains,
And while you are looking for light,
He turns it into the shadow of death
And makes *it* dense darkness.
17 But if you will not hear it,
My soul will weep in secret for *your* pride;
My eyes will weep bitterly
And run down with tears,
Because the LORD's flock has been taken captive.

18 Say to the king and to the queen mother,
"Humble yourselves;
Sit down,
For your rule shall collapse, the
crown of your glory."
19 The cities of the South shall be shut up,
And no one shall open *them;*
Judah shall be carried away captive, all of it;
It shall be wholly carried away captive.

20 Lift up your eyes and see
Those who come from the north.
Where *is* the flock *that* was given to you,
Your beautiful sheep?
21 What will you say when He punishes you?
For you have taught them
To be chieftains, to be head over you.
Will not pangs seize you,
Like a woman in labor?
22 And if you say in your heart,
"Why have these things come upon me?"
For the greatness of your iniquity
Your skirts have been uncovered,
Your heels made bare.
23 Can the Ethiopian change his skin
or the leopard its spots?
Then may you also do good who are
accustomed to do evil.

24 "Therefore I will scatter them like stubble
That passes away by the wind of the wilderness.
25 This is your lot,
The portion of your measures from Me,"
says the LORD,
"Because you have forgotten Me
And trusted in falsehood.
26 Therefore I will uncover your skirts
over your face,
That your shame may appear.

13:4 [i] Hebrew *Perath*

LIFE LESSON

Jeremiah 14:1–17:27

SITUATION Jeremiah prophesied drought, famine, and days of disaster for God's people.

OBSERVATION Sin requires judgment. Sin can distort our judgment of good and evil. God calls us to repent and to have moral outrage for violations of his holiness.

INSPIRATION Where is our sense of moral outrage? Perhaps our moral sensibilities have been dulled because of today's dazzling instant communications. We sit mesmerized in front of our TVs, unable to turn the sets off, so we turn our minds off instead.

Over time, so much trash is heaped upon us that we come to expect and accept it; the bizarre becomes commonplace. Morally exhausted, we lose our capacity to discern good from evil.

The brilliant essayist Charles Krauthammer, citing economist Thomas Sowell, sums up our predicament beautifully: "The inability to make moral distinctions is the AIDS of the intellectuals: an acquired immune deficiency syndrome . . . moral blindness of this caliber requires practice. It has to be learned."

In a culture with moral AIDS, words lose all meaning; or they are manipulated to obscure meaning. . . . But when

27 I have seen your adulteries
And your *lustful* neighings,
The lewdness of your harlotry,
Your abominations on the hills in the fields.
Woe to you, O Jerusalem!
Will you still not be made clean?"

Sword, Famine, and Pestilence

14 The word of the LORD that came to Jeremiah concerning the droughts.

2 "Judah mourns,
And her gates languish;
They mourn for the land,
And the cry of Jerusalem has gone up.
3 Their nobles have sent their lads for water;
They went to the cisterns *and* found no water.
They returned with their vessels empty;
They were ashamed and confounded
And covered their heads.
4 Because the ground is parched,
For there was no rain in the land,
The plowmen were ashamed;
They covered their heads.
5 Yes, the deer also gave birth in the field,
But left because there was no grass.
6 And the wild donkeys stood in the desolate heights;
They sniffed at the wind like jackals;
Their eyes failed because *there was* no grass."

7 O LORD, though our iniquities testify against us,
Do it for Your name's sake;
For our backslidings are many,
We have sinned against You.
8 O the Hope of Israel, his Savior in time of trouble,
Why should You be like a stranger in the land,
And like a traveler *who* turns aside to tarry for a night?
9 Why should You be like a man astonished,
Like a mighty one *who* cannot save?
Yet You, O LORD, *are* in our midst,
And we are called by Your name;
Do not leave us!

10 Thus says the LORD to this people:

"Thus they have loved to wander;
They have not restrained their feet.
Therefore the LORD does not accept them;
He will remember their iniquity now,
And punish their sins."

11 Then the LORD said to me, "Do not pray for this people, for *their* good.
12 When they fast, I will not hear their cry; and when they offer burnt offering and grain offering, I will not accept them. But I will consume them by the sword, by the famine, and by the pestilence."

13 Then I said, "Ah, Lord GOD! Behold, the prophets say to them, 'You shall
not see the sword, nor shall you have famine, but I will give you assured
peace in this place.' "
14 And the LORD said to me, "The prophets prophesy lies in My name. I
have not sent them, commanded them, nor spoken to them; they prophesy
to you a false vision, divination, a worthless thing, and the deceit of their
heart. 15 Therefore thus says the LORD concerning the prophets who prophesy in My name, whom I did not send, and who say, 'Sword and famine
shall not be in this land'—'By sword and famine those prophets shall be
consumed! 16 And the people to whom they prophesy shall be cast out in
the streets of Jerusalem because of the famine and the sword; they will
have no one to bury them—them nor their wives, their sons nor their
daughters—for I will pour their wickedness on them.'
17 "Therefore you shall say this word to them:

'Let my eyes flow with tears night and day,
And let them not cease;
For the virgin daughter of my people
Has been broken with a mighty stroke, with a very severe blow.
18 If I go out to the field,
Then behold, those slain with the sword!
And if I enter the city,
Then behold, those sick from famine!
Yes, both prophet and priest go about in a land they do not know.' "

The People Plead for Mercy

19 Have You utterly rejected Judah?
Has Your soul loathed Zion?
Why have You stricken us so that *there is* no healing for us?
We looked for peace, but *there was* no good;
And for the time of healing, and there was trouble.
20 We acknowledge, O LORD, our wickedness
And the iniquity of our fathers,
For we have sinned against You.
21 Do not abhor *us*, for Your name's sake;
Do not disgrace the throne of Your glory.
Remember, do not break Your covenant with us.
22 Are there any among the idols of the nations
that can cause rain?
Or can the heavens give showers?
Are You not He, O LORD our God?
Therefore we will wait for You,
Since You have made all these.

The LORD Will Not Relent

15 Then the LORD said to me, "*Even* if Moses and Samuel stood before
Me, My mind *would* not *be* favorable toward this people. Cast *them*
out of My sight, and let them go forth. 2 And it shall be, if they say to you,
'Where should we go?' then you shall tell them, 'Thus says the LORD:

"Such as *are* for death, to death;
And such as *are* for the sword, to the sword;

words lose their meaning, it is nearly impossible for the Word of God to be received. If sin and repentance mean nothing, then God's grace is irrelevant. Our preaching falls on deaf ears.

This moral deafness leads to disaster. The Scriptures tell us it was when people accepted King Ahab's gross evils as "trivial" that fearsome judgment befell ancient Israel.

Certainly evil is to be expected in a fallen world. What is not expected is for a holy people to accept it. If Christ is Lord of all, Christians must recapture their sense of moral outrage.
(From *Who Speaks for God* by Charles Colson)

APPLICATION What views about sin have softened so that they are even acceptable among Christians? What areas of life has this affected? Male-female relationships? Social settings? Family life? Don't be drawn in by the world's standards. Be morally pure in your dating or marriage relationship. Be bold in keeping a high standard. Don't let Satan wear down your defenses.

EXPLORATION Endurance—Philippians 3:12-16; 4:11-13; Jude 17-25.

And such as *are* for the famine,
to the famine;
And such as *are* for the captivity,
to the captivity." '

3 "And I will appoint over them four forms *of destruc-*
tion," says the LORD: "the sword to slay, the dogs to drag,
the birds of the heavens and the beasts of the earth to
devour and destroy. 4 I will hand them over to trouble, to
all kingdoms of the earth, because of Manasseh the son
of Hezekiah, king of Judah, for what he did in Jerusalem.

5 "For who will have pity on you, O Jerusalem?
Or who will bemoan you?
Or who will turn aside to ask
how you are doing?
6 You have forsaken Me," says the LORD,
"You have gone backward.
Therefore I will stretch out My hand against
you and destroy you;
I am weary of relenting!
7 And I will winnow them with a winnowing
fan in the gates of the land;
I will bereave *them* of children;
I will destroy My people,
Since they do not return from their ways.
8 Their widows will be increased to Me more
than the sand of the seas;
I will bring against them,
Against the mother of the young men,
A plunderer at noonday;
I will cause anguish and terror to fall
on them suddenly.

9 "She languishes who has borne seven;
She has breathed her last;
Her sun has gone down
While *it was* yet day;
She has been ashamed and confounded.
And the remnant of them I will
deliver to the sword
Before their enemies," says the LORD.

Jeremiah's Dejection

10 Woe is me, my mother,
That you have borne me,
A man of strife and a man of contention to the
whole earth!
I have neither lent for interest,
Nor have men lent to me for interest.
Every one of them curses me.

11 The LORD said:

"Surely it will be well with your remnant;
Surely I will cause the enemy to
intercede with you
In the time of adversity and in the
time of affliction.
12 Can anyone break iron,
The northern iron and the bronze?
13 Your wealth and your treasures
I will give as plunder without price,
Because of all your sins,
Throughout your territories.
14 And I will make *you* cross over
with[j] your enemies
Into a land *which* you do not know;
For a fire is kindled in My anger,
Which shall burn upon you."

15 O LORD, You know;
Remember me and visit me,
And take vengeance for me on my persecutors.
In Your enduring patience, do not take me away.
Know that for Your sake I have suffered rebuke.
16 Your words were found, and I ate them,
And Your word was to me the joy and
rejoicing of my heart;
For I am called by Your name,
O LORD God of hosts.
17 I did not sit in the assembly of the mockers,
Nor did I rejoice;
I sat alone because of Your hand,
For You have filled me with indignation.
18 Why is my pain perpetual
And my wound incurable,
Which refuses to be healed?
Will You surely be to me like an
unreliable stream,
As waters *that* fail?

The LORD Reassures Jeremiah

19 Therefore thus says the LORD:

"If you return,
Then I will bring you back;
You shall stand before Me;
If you take out the precious
from the vile,
You shall be as My mouth.
Let them return to you,
But you must not return to them.

15:14 [j] Following Masoretic Text and Vulgate; Septuagint, Syriac, and Targum read *cause you to serve* (compare 17:4).

20 And I will make you to this people a fortified
bronze wall;
And they will fight against you,
But they shall not prevail against you;
For I *am* with you to save you
And deliver you," says the LORD.
21 "I will deliver you from the hand of the wicked,
And I will redeem you from the
grip of the terrible."

Jeremiah's Life-Style and Message

16 The word of the LORD also came to me, saying,
2"You shall not take a wife, nor shall you have
sons or daughters in this place." 3For thus says the LORD
concerning the sons and daughters who are born in
this place, and concerning their mothers who bore them
and their fathers who begot them in this land: 4"They
shall die gruesome deaths; they shall not be lamented
nor shall they be buried, *but* they shall be like refuse on
the face of the earth. They shall be consumed by the
sword and by famine, and their corpses shall be meat
for the birds of heaven and for the beasts of the earth."
5For thus says the LORD: "Do not enter the house of
mourning, nor go to lament or bemoan them; for I
have taken away My peace from this people," says the
LORD, "lovingkindness and mercies. 6Both the great
and the small shall die in this land. They shall not be
buried; neither shall men lament for them, cut themselves, nor make themselves bald for them. 7Nor shall
men break *bread* in mourning for them, to comfort
them for the dead; nor shall *men* give them the cup of
consolation to drink for their father or their mother.
8Also you shall not go into the house of feasting to sit
with them, to eat and drink."
9For thus says the LORD of hosts, the God of Israel:
"Behold, I will cause to cease from this place, before
your eyes and in your days, the voice of mirth and the
voice of gladness, the voice of the bridegroom and the
voice of the bride.
10"And it shall be, when you show this people all
these words, and they say to you, 'Why has the LORD
pronounced all this great disaster against us? Or what
is our iniquity? Or what *is* our sin that we have committed against the LORD our God?' 11then you shall say
to them, 'Because your fathers have forsaken Me,'
says the LORD; 'they have walked after other gods and
have served them and worshiped them, and have forsaken Me and not kept My law. 12And you have done
worse than your fathers, for behold, each one follows
the dictates of his own evil heart, so that no one listens
to Me. 13Therefore I will cast you out of this land into a
land that you do not know, neither you nor your fathers; and there you shall serve other gods day and
night, where I will not show you favor.'

God Will Restore Israel

14"Therefore behold, the days are coming," says the
LORD, "that it shall no more be said, 'The LORD lives
who brought up the children of Israel from the land of
Egypt,' 15but, 'The LORD lives who brought up the children of Israel from the land of the north and from all
the lands where He had driven them.' For I will bring
them back into their land which I gave to their fathers.
16"Behold, I will send for many fishermen," says the
LORD, "and they shall fish them; and afterward I will
send for many hunters, and they shall hunt them from
every mountain and every hill, and out of the holes of
the rocks. 17For My eyes *are* on all their ways; they are
not hidden from My face, nor is their iniquity hidden
from My eyes. 18And first I will repay double for their
iniquity and their sin, because they have defiled My
land; they have filled My inheritance with the carcasses of their detestable and abominable idols."

19 O LORD, my strength and my fortress,
My refuge in the day of affliction,
The Gentiles shall come to You
From the ends of the earth and say,
"Surely our fathers have inherited lies,
Worthlessness and unprofitable *things.*"
20 Will a man make gods for himself,
Which *are* not gods?

21 "Therefore behold, I will this once
cause them to know,
I will cause them to know
My hand and My might;
And they shall know that My
name *is* the LORD.

Judah's Sin and Punishment

17 "The sin of Judah *is* written with a pen of iron;
With the point of a diamond *it is* engraved
On the tablet of their heart,
And on the horns of your altars,
2 While their children remember
Their altars and their wooden images[k]
By the green trees on the high hills.
3 O My mountain in the field,
I will give as plunder your wealth,
all your treasures,

17:2 [k] Hebrew *Asherim,* Canaanite deities

And your high places of sin within
all your borders.
4 And you, even yourself,
Shall let go of your heritage which I gave you;
And I will cause you to serve your enemies
In the land which you do not know;
For you have kindled a fire in My anger *which*
shall burn forever."

5Thus says the LORD:
"Cursed *is* the man who trusts in man
And makes flesh his strength,
Whose heart departs from the LORD.
6 For he shall be like a shrub in the desert,
And shall not see when good comes,
But shall inhabit the parched
places in the wilderness,
In a salt land *which is* not inhabited.
7 "Blessed *is* the man who trusts in the LORD,
And whose hope is the LORD.
8 For he shall be like a tree planted
by the waters,
Which spreads out its roots by the river,
And will not fear[l] when heat comes;
But its leaf will be green,
And will not be anxious in the
year of drought,
Nor will cease from yielding fruit.

9 "The heart *is* deceitful above all *things,*
And desperately wicked;
Who can know it?
10 I, the LORD, search the heart,
I test the mind,
Even to give every man according to his ways,
According to the fruit of his doings.

11 "*As* a partridge that broods but does not hatch,
So is he who gets riches, but not by right;
It will leave him in the midst of his days,
And at his end he will be a fool."

12 A glorious high throne from the beginning
Is the place of our sanctuary.
13 O LORD, the hope of Israel,
All who forsake You shall be ashamed.

"Those who depart from Me
Shall be written in the earth,
Because they have forsaken the LORD,
The fountain of living waters."

Jeremiah Prays for Deliverance

14 Heal me, O LORD, and I shall be healed;
Save me, and I shall be saved,
For You *are* my praise.
15 Indeed they say to me,
"Where *is* the word of the LORD?
Let it come now!"
16 As for me, I have not hurried away from *being*
a shepherd *who* follows You,
Nor have I desired the woeful day;
You know what came out of my lips;
It was right there before You.
17 Do not be a terror to me;
You *are* my hope in the day of doom.
18 Let them be ashamed who persecute me,
But do not let me be put to shame;
Let them be dismayed,
But do not let me be dismayed.
Bring on them the day of doom,
And destroy them with double destruction!

Hallow the Sabbath Day

19Thus the LORD said to me: "Go and stand in the gate
of the children of the people, by which the kings of Judah
come in and by which they go out, and in all the gates of
Jerusalem; 20and say to them, 'Hear the word of the LORD,
you kings of Judah, and all Judah, and all the inhabitants of Jerusalem, who enter by these gates. 21Thus
says the LORD: "Take heed to yourselves, and bear no
burden on the Sabbath day, nor bring *it* in by the gates
of Jerusalem; 22nor carry a burden out of your houses
on the Sabbath day, nor do any work, but hallow the
Sabbath day, as I commanded your fathers. 23But they
did not obey nor incline their ear, but made their neck
stiff, that they might not hear nor receive instruction.
24"And it shall be, if you heed Me carefully," says
the LORD, "to bring no burden through the gates of this
city on the Sabbath day, but hallow the Sabbath day, to
do no work in it, 25then shall enter the gates of this city
kings and princes sitting on the throne of David, riding in chariots and on horses, they and their princes,
accompanied by the men of Judah and the inhabitants of Jerusalem; and this city shall remain forever.
26And they shall come from the cities of Judah and
from the places around Jerusalem, from the land of
Benjamin and from the lowland, from the mountains
and from the South, bringing burnt offerings and sacrifices, grain offerings and incense, bringing sacrifices of praise to the house of the LORD.

17:8 *l* Qere and Targum read *see.*

27"But if you will not heed Me to hallow the Sabbath
day, such as not carrying a burden when entering the
gates of Jerusalem on the Sabbath day, then I will kindle a fire in its gates, and it shall devour the palaces of
Jerusalem, and it shall not be quenched." ' "

The Potter and the Clay

18 The word which came to Jeremiah from the
LORD, saying: 2"Arise and go down to the potter's house, and there I will cause you to hear My
words." 3Then I went down to the potter's house, and
there he was, making something at the wheel. 4And
the vessel that he made of clay was marred in the
hand of the potter; so he made it again into another
vessel, as it seemed good to the potter to make.
5Then the word of the LORD came to me, saying: 6"O
house of Israel, can I not do with you as this potter?"
says the LORD. "Look, as the clay *is* in the potter's hand,
so *are* you in My hand, O house of Israel! 7The instant
I speak concerning a nation and concerning a kingdom, to pluck up, to pull down, and to destroy *it,* 8if
that nation against whom I have spoken turns from
its evil, I will relent of the disaster that I thought to
bring upon it. 9And the instant I speak concerning a
nation and concerning a kingdom, to build and to
plant *it,* 10if it does evil in My sight so that it does not
obey My voice, then I will relent concerning the good
with which I said I would benefit it.
11"Now therefore, speak to the men of Judah and to
the inhabitants of Jerusalem, saying, 'Thus says the
LORD: "Behold, I am fashioning a disaster and devising
a plan against you. Return now every one from his evil
way, and make your ways and your doings good." ' "

God's Warning Rejected

12And they said, "That is hopeless! So we will walk
according to our own plans, and we will every one
obey the dictates of his evil heart."
13Therefore thus says the LORD:

"Ask now among the Gentiles,
Who has heard such things?
The virgin of Israel has done a
very horrible thing.
14 Will *a man* leave the snow water of Lebanon,
Which comes from the rock of the field?
Will the cold flowing waters be forsaken for
strange waters?
15 "Because My people have forgotten Me,
They have burned incense to worthless idols.
And they have caused themselves to
stumble in their ways,
From the ancient paths,
To walk in pathways and not on a highway,
16 To make their land desolate *and* a
perpetual hissing;
Everyone who passes by it will be astonished
And shake his head.
17 I will scatter them as with an east
wind before the enemy;
I will show them[m] the back and not the face
In the day of their calamity."

Jeremiah Persecuted

18Then they said, "Come and let us devise plans
against Jeremiah; for the law shall not perish from the
priest, nor counsel from the wise, nor the word from
the prophet. Come and let us attack him with the
tongue, and let us not give heed to any of his words."

19 Give heed to me, O LORD,
And listen to the voice of those who
contend with me!
20 Shall evil be repaid for good?
For they have dug a pit for my life.
Remember that I stood before You
To speak good for them,
To turn away Your wrath from them.
21 Therefore deliver up their children
to the famine,
And pour out their *blood*
By the force of the sword;
Let their wives *become* widows
And bereaved of their children.
Let their men be put to death,
Their young men *be* slain
By the sword in battle.
22 Let a cry be heard from their houses,
When You bring a troop
suddenly upon them;
For they have dug a pit to take me,
And hidden snares for my feet.
23 Yet, LORD, You know all their counsel
Which is against me, to slay *me.*
Provide no atonement for their iniquity,
Nor blot out their sin from Your sight;
But let them be overthrown before You.
Deal *thus* with them
In the time of Your anger.

18:17 *m* Following Septuagint, Syriac, Targum, and Vulgate; Masoretic Text reads *look them in.*

LIFE LESSON

Jeremiah 18:1–20:18

SITUATION God sent Jeremiah to a potter's shop. While there, God told him that Jerusalem would be destroyed as easily as a clay pot. The people persecuted Jeremiah for his unpopular message.

OBSERVATION God shapes our lives like a potter shapes clay.

INSPIRATION The prophet was in the pits. Literally. Like Poe's fanciful character, he was "sick, sick unto death." Swamped with disillusionment and drowning in despair, he cursed the day he was born and wondered why an abortion wasn't performed, killing him prior to his birth. . . .

An exaggeration? Not hardly. Read the record for yourself. Jeremiah's journal holds nothing back. In chapter 20 the chief officer in the temple had him beaten (forty lashes), then placed in stocks. That means his feet, hands, and neck were secured in a torturous device that caused the body to be bent almost double. That happened after he was beaten! Why? Had he committed some crime? No. He had simply declared the truth. He had done what was right—and this is what he got in return. It hurt him deeply.

On top of all that, sarcastic whisperings swirled about. His once-trusted friends tagged him with a nickname—MAGOR-MISSABIB—meaning "terror on every side." That also hurt. He must have felt like a limp rag doll in the mouth of a snarling Doberman. . . .

The man is in anguish. Prophet or not, he is struggling with God's justice, His strange treatment. Deep down he is questioning His presence. "Where is He? Why has Jehovah vanished at a time when I need Him the most?" . . .

What desperate feelings!

And one need not be . . . doubled over in stocks and beaten with rods. No, sometimes they come in the dark, long tunnel of suffering when pain won't go away. Or when a marriage partner who promised to stay "for better or worse" breaks that vow. Or when a long-sought-after dream goes up in smoke. Or when we kiss a loved one goodbye for the last time.

The Sign of the Broken Flask

19 Thus says the LORD: "Go and get a potter's earthen flask, and *take*
some of the elders of the people and some of the elders of the
priests. 2And go out to the Valley of the Son of Hinnom, which *is* by the
entry of the Potsherd Gate; and proclaim there the words that I will tell
you, 3and say, 'Hear the word of the LORD, O kings of Judah and inhabitants of Jerusalem. Thus says the LORD of hosts, the God of Israel: "Behold, I will bring such a catastrophe on this place, that whoever hears of it,
his ears will tingle.
4"Because they have forsaken Me and made this an alien place, because
they have burned incense in it to other gods whom neither they, their fathers, nor the kings of Judah have known, and have filled this place with
the blood of the innocents 5(they have also built the high places of Baal, to
burn their sons with fire *for* burnt offerings to Baal, which I did not command or speak, nor did it come into My mind), 6therefore behold, the days
are coming," says the LORD, "that this place shall no more be called Tophet
or the Valley of the Son of Hinnom, but the Valley of Slaughter. 7And I will
make void the counsel of Judah and Jerusalem in this place, and I will
cause them to fall by the sword before their enemies and by the hands of
those who seek their lives; their corpses I will give as meat for the birds of
the heaven and for the beasts of the earth. 8I will make this city desolate and
a hissing; everyone who passes by it will be astonished and hiss because of
all its plagues. 9And I will cause them to eat the flesh of their sons and the
flesh of their daughters, and everyone shall eat the flesh of his friend in the
siege and in the desperation with which their enemies and those who seek
their lives shall drive them to despair." '
10"Then you shall break the flask in the sight of the men who go with
you, 11and say to them, 'Thus says the LORD of hosts: "Even so I will break this
people and this city, as *one* breaks a potter's vessel, which cannot be made
whole again; and they shall bury *them* in Tophet till *there is* no place to
bury. 12Thus I will do to this place," says the LORD, "and to its inhabitants,
and make this city like Tophet. 13And the houses of Jerusalem and the
houses of the kings of Judah shall be defiled like the place of Tophet, because of all the houses on whose roofs they have burned incense to all the
host of heaven, and poured out drink offerings to other gods." ' "
14Then Jeremiah came from Tophet, where the LORD had sent him to
prophesy; and he stood in the court of the Lord's house and said to all the
people, 15"Thus says the LORD of hosts, the God of Israel: 'Behold, I will
bring on this city and on all her towns all the doom that I have pronounced
against it, because they have stiffened their necks that they might not hear
My words.' "

The Word of God to Pashhur

20 Now Pashhur the son of Immer, the priest who *was* also chief governor in the house of the LORD, heard that Jeremiah prophesied
these things. 2Then Pashhur struck Jeremiah the prophet, and put him in
the stocks that *were* in the high gate of Benjamin, which *was* by the house
of the LORD.
3And it happened on the next day that Pashhur brought Jeremiah out of
the stocks. Then Jeremiah said to him, "The LORD has not called your

name Pashhur, but Magor-Missabib.[n] 4 For thus says the LORD: 'Behold, I
will make you a terror to yourself and to all your friends; and they shall fall
by the sword of their enemies, and your eyes shall see *it.* I will give all Judah
into the hand of the king of Babylon, and he shall carry them captive to
Babylon and slay them with the sword. 5 Moreover I will deliver all the wealth
of this city, all its produce, and all its precious things; all the treasures of
the kings of Judah I will give into the hand of their enemies, who will plunder them, seize them, and carry them to Babylon. 6 And you, Pashhur, and
all who dwell in your house, shall go into captivity. You shall go to Babylon,
and there you shall die, and be buried there, you and all your friends, to
whom you have prophesied lies.' "

Jeremiah's Unpopular Ministry

7 O LORD, You induced me, and I was persuaded;
You are stronger than I, and have prevailed.
I am in derision daily;
Everyone mocks me.
8 For when I spoke, I cried out;
I shouted, "Violence and plunder!"
Because the word of the LORD was made to me
A reproach and a derision daily.
9 Then I said, "I will not make mention of Him,
Nor speak anymore in His name."
But *His word* was in my heart like a burning fire
Shut up in my bones;
I was weary of holding *it* back,
And I could not.
10 For I heard many mocking:
"Fear on every side!"
"Report," *they say,* "and we will report it!"
All my acquaintances watched for my stumbling, *saying,*
"Perhaps he can be induced;
Then we will prevail against him,
And we will take our revenge on him."
11 But the LORD *is* with me as a mighty, awesome One.
Therefore my persecutors will stumble, and will not prevail.
They will be greatly ashamed, for they will not prosper.
Their everlasting confusion will never be forgotten.
12 But, O LORD of hosts,
You who test the righteous,
And see the mind and heart,
Let me see Your vengeance on them;
For I have pleaded my cause before You.

13 Sing to the LORD! Praise the LORD!
For He has delivered the life of the poor
From the hand of evildoers.

14 Cursed *be* the day in which I was born!
Let the day not be blessed in which my mother bore me!

20:3 [n] Literally *Fear on Every Side*

Not always . . . but sometimes (usually unmuttered and hidden away in the secret vaults of our minds) we question Jehovah's justice. We ask, "Is He absent today?" . . .

At those times I'm tempted to say what the prophet said:
I will not remember Him or speak anymore in His name . . . (20:9a).

"That's it! I'm tossing in my collar. No more sermons or devotionals for this preacher. Secular job here I come!" But right about the time I start to jump I experience what Jeremiah admitted:
. . . Then in my heart it becomes like a burning fire shut up in my bones; and I am weary of holding it in, and I cannot endure it (20:9b).

Directly sent from God is this surge of hope, this cleansing fire of confidence, this renewed sense of determination swelling up within me. And the disillusionment is quietly replaced with His reassurance as He reminds me of that glorious climax to the hymn I often sing back to Him in full volume:
"All is well, all is well!"

Thank God, it is. Recently, I doubted that—like Jeremiah. But not today. Reassurance has returned. Divine perspective has provided a fresh breeze of hope in the pits. I have determined that disillusionment must go. Now . . . not later.

(From *Growing Strong in the Seasons of Life* by Charles Swindoll)

APPLICATION Is your minister close to being burned out? Does he ever feel like throwing in the towel? Look for ways to encourage him. After church on Sunday, tell him what you learned from the message. During the week, call, write, or stop by the church office and share what makes his ministry helpful to you.

EXPLORATION Trusting God in Difficult Times—Psalm 27:5; Matthew 5:4;10; Romans 8:28; 2 Timothy 1:11-12.

Life Lesson

Jeremiah 21:1–23:40

SITUATION God had allowed many disobedient kings to continue ruling. But now God forewarned the people of his plan for a harsh discipline if they once again refused to return to him. Nebuchadnezzar, the Babylonian king, attacked Jerusalem between 588 and 586 B.C. When he destroyed the city, he was fulfilling God's prophecy.

OBSERVATION God makes clear what is right and wrong. When people choose to do wrong, God helps them see their sin. God's discipline arises from his love for his people.

INSPIRATION Oftentimes we do not recognize the disciplining hand of God. When there are personal consequences resulting from our sin, such as an injury or a financial loss, we can usually recognize those right away. But sometimes God's discipline comes in forms that at first seem to have no relationship to what we have done. In time, however, the truth usually becomes apparent.

People who accept the discipline of God realize that His discipline is for their own protection. They do not view it as something negative. They see it as an expression of His love, for that is exactly what it is.

Imagine for a moment a child who has been told repeatedly not to play in the street. But he goes right ahead and does it anyway. His parents, if they are

15 Let the man *be* cursed
Who brought news to my father, saying,
"A male child has been born to you!"
Making him very glad.
16 And let that man be like the cities
Which the LORD overthrew, and did not relent;
Let him hear the cry in the morning
And the shouting at noon,
17 Because he did not kill me from the womb,
That my mother might have been my grave,
And her womb always enlarged *with me.*
18 Why did I come forth from the womb to see labor and sorrow,
That my days should be consumed with shame?

Jerusalem's Doom Is Sealed

21 The word which came to Jeremiah from the LORD when King
Zedekiah sent to him Pashhur the son of Melchiah, and Zephaniah
the son of Maaseiah, the priest, saying, 2"Please inquire of the LORD for us,
for Nebuchadnezzar[o] king of Babylon makes war against us. Perhaps the
LORD will deal with us according to all His wonderful works, that *the king*
may go away from us."
3Then Jeremiah said to them, "Thus you shall say to Zedekiah, 4'Thus
says the LORD God of Israel: "Behold, I will turn back the weapons of war
that *are* in your hands, with which you fight against the king of Babylon
and the Chaldeans[p] who besiege you outside the walls; and I will assemble
them in the midst of this city. 5I Myself will fight against you with an outstretched hand and with a strong arm, even in anger and fury and great
wrath. 6I will strike the inhabitants of this city, both man and beast; they shall
die of a great pestilence. 7And afterward," says the LORD, "I will deliver
Zedekiah king of Judah, his servants and the people, and such as are left in
this city from the pestilence and the sword and the famine, into the hand
of Nebuchadnezzar king of Babylon, into the hand of their enemies, and
into the hand of those who seek their life; and he shall strike them with the
edge of the sword. He shall not spare them, or have pity or mercy." '
8"Now you shall say to this people, 'Thus says the LORD: "Behold, I set
before you the way of life and the way of death. 9He who remains in this
city shall die by the sword, by famine, and by pestilence; but he who goes
out and defects to the Chaldeans who besiege you, he shall live, and his life
shall be as a prize to him. 10For I have set My face against this city for adversity and not for good," says the LORD. "It shall be given into the hand of
the king of Babylon, and he shall burn it with fire." '

Message to the House of David

11"And concerning the house of the king of Judah, *say,* 'Hear the word of
the LORD, 12O house of David! Thus says the LORD:

"Execute judgment in the morning;
And deliver *him who is* plundered
Out of the hand of the oppressor,
Lest My fury go forth like fire

21:2 [o] Hebrew *Nebuchadrezzar,* and so elsewhere
21:4 [p] Or *Babylonians*

And burn so that no one can quench *it,*
Because of the evil of your doings.

13 "Behold, I *am* against you, O inhabitant of the valley,
And rock of the plain," says the LORD,
"Who say, 'Who shall come down against us?
Or who shall enter our dwellings?'
14 But I will punish you according to the fruit of your doings,"
says the LORD;
"I will kindle a fire in its forest,
And it shall devour all things around it." ' "

22 Thus says the LORD: "Go down to the house of the king of Judah,
and there speak this word, 2and say, 'Hear the word of the LORD, O
king of Judah, you who sit on the throne of David, you and your servants
and your people who enter these gates! 3Thus says the LORD: "Execute
judgment and righteousness, and deliver the plundered out of the hand of
the oppressor. Do no wrong and do no violence to the stranger, the fatherless, or the widow, nor shed innocent blood in this place. 4For if you indeed
do this thing, then shall enter the gates of this house, riding on horses and
in chariots, accompanied by servants and people, kings who sit on the throne
of David. 5But if you will not hear these words, I swear by Myself," says the
LORD, "that this house shall become a desolation." ' "
6For thus says the LORD to the house of the king of Judah:

"You *are* Gilead to Me,
The head of Lebanon;
Yet I surely will make you a wilderness,
Cities *which* are not inhabited.
7 I will prepare destroyers against you,
Everyone with his weapons;
They shall cut down your choice cedars
And cast *them* into the fire.

8And many nations will pass by this city; and everyone will say to his neighbor, 'Why has the LORD done so to this great city?' 9Then they will answer,
'Because they have forsaken the covenant of the LORD their God, and worshiped other gods and served them.' "

10 Weep not for the dead, nor bemoan him;
Weep bitterly for him who goes away,
For he shall return no more,
Nor see his native country.

Message to the Sons of Josiah

11For thus says the LORD concerning Shallum[q] the son of Josiah, king of
Judah, who reigned instead of Josiah his father, who went from this place:
"He shall not return here anymore, 12but he shall die in the place where
they have led him captive, and shall see this land no more.

13 "Woe to him who builds his house by unrighteousness
And his chambers by injustice,
Who uses his neighbor's service without wages
And gives him nothing for his work,

wise, will discipline him. Why? Because they are the parents and he is just a child and how dare he break their rules? No. They know that if he doesn't learn to stay out of the street, he could be killed or crippled. The disciplinary action they choose may seem painful to their child, but a simple spanking is far better than being hit by a car. A lesser evil is used to guard the child from a much greater evil. So it is when God disciplines us. He is trying to keep us from the greater harm that comes from involvement with sin. We will not fully appreciate the love God has expressed toward us through His discipline until we get to heaven.

(From *Winning the War Within* by Charles Stanley)

APPLICATION Do you love your children? Don't be afraid to discipline them! Your thankless work will help them to become respected adults. Are you still a young person at home? When you are disciplined, realize that your parents want to help you become a respected adult. Thank them for it!

EXPLORATION God's Discipline—Deuteronomy 8:2-5; Proverbs 10:17; Jeremiah 32:33; Hosea 6:1-3; 14:1-2, 4; Joel 2:13; Micah 7:18-19; Haggai 2:17; 2 Corinthians 7:10; Philippians 1:6; Hebrews 12:5-11.

22:11 [q] Also called *Jehoahaz*

14 Who says, 'I will build myself a wide house
with spacious chambers,
And cut out windows for it,
Paneling *it* with cedar
And painting *it* with vermilion.'
15 "Shall you reign because you enclose
yourself in cedar?
Did not your father eat and drink,
And do justice and righteousness?
Then *it was* well with him.
16 He judged the cause of the poor and needy;
Then *it was* well.
Was not this knowing Me?" says the LORD.
17 "Yet your eyes and your heart *are* for nothing
but your covetousness,
For shedding innocent blood,
And practicing oppression and violence."

18 Therefore thus says the LORD concerning Jehoiakim the son of Josiah, king of Judah:

"They shall not lament for him,
Saying, 'Alas, my brother!' or 'Alas, my sister!'
They shall not lament for him,
Saying, 'Alas, master!' or 'Alas, his glory!'
19 He shall be buried with the burial of a donkey,
Dragged and cast out beyond the
gates of Jerusalem.

20 "Go up to Lebanon, and cry out,
And lift up your voice in Bashan;
Cry from Abarim,
For all your lovers are destroyed.
21 I spoke to you in your prosperity,
But you said, 'I will not hear.'
This *has been* your manner from your youth,
That you did not obey My voice.
22 The wind shall eat up all your rulers,
And your lovers shall go into captivity;
Surely then you will be ashamed
and humiliated
For all your wickedness.
23 O inhabitant of Lebanon,
Making your nest in the cedars,
How gracious will you be when pangs
come upon you,
Like the pain of a woman in labor?

Message to Coniah

24 "*As* I live," says the LORD, "though Coniah[r] the son
of Jehoiakim, king of Judah, were the signet on My
right hand, yet I would pluck you off; 25 and I will give
you into the hand of those who seek your life, and into
the hand *of those* whose face you fear—the hand of
Nebuchadnezzar king of Babylon and the hand of the
Chaldeans. 26 So I will cast you out, and your mother who
bore you, into another country where you were not born;
and there you shall die. 27 But to the land to which they
desire to return, there they shall not return.

28 "Is this man Coniah a despised, broken idol—
A vessel in which *is* no pleasure?
Why are they cast out, he and his descendants,
And cast into a land which they do not know?
29 O earth, earth, earth,
Hear the word of the LORD!
30 Thus says the LORD:
'Write this man down as childless,
A man *who* shall not prosper in his days;
For none of his descendants shall prosper,
Sitting on the throne of David,
And ruling anymore in Judah.'"

The Branch of Righteousness

23 "Woe to the shepherds who destroy and scatter
the sheep of My pasture!" says the LORD. 2 Therefore thus says the LORD God of Israel against the shepherds who feed My people: "You have scattered My
flock, driven them away, and not attended to them.
Behold, I will attend to you for the evil of your doings," says the LORD. 3 "But I will gather the remnant of
My flock out of all countries where I have driven
them, and bring them back to their folds; and they
shall be fruitful and increase. 4 I will set up shepherds
over them who will feed them; and they shall fear no
more, nor be dismayed, nor shall they be lacking,"
says the LORD.

5 "Behold, *the* days are coming," says the LORD,
"That I will raise to David a Branch
of righteousness;
A King shall reign and prosper,
And execute judgment and righteousness
in the earth.
6 In His days Judah will be saved,
And Israel will dwell safely;
Now this *is* His name by which
He will be called:

THE LORD OUR RIGHTEOUSNESS.[s]

22:24 [r] Also called *Jeconiah* and *Jehoiachin*
23:6 [s] Hebrew *YHWH Tsidkenu*

7"Therefore, behold, *the* days are coming," says the
LORD, "that they shall no longer say, 'As the LORD lives
who brought up the children of Israel from the land of
Egypt,' 8but, 'As the LORD lives who brought up and led
the descendants of the house of Israel from the north
country and from all the countries where I had driven
them.' And they shall dwell in their own land."

False Prophets and Empty Oracles

9 My heart within me is broken
Because of the prophets;
All my bones shake.
I am like a drunken man,
And like a man whom wine has overcome,
Because of the LORD,
And because of His holy words.
10 For the land is full of adulterers;
For because of a curse the land mourns.
The pleasant places of the wilderness
are dried up.
Their course of life is evil,
And their might *is* not right.

11 "For both prophet and priest are profane;
Yes, in My house I have found their
wickedness," says the LORD.

12 "Therefore their way shall be to them
Like slippery *ways;*
In the darkness they shall be driven on
And fall in them;
For I will bring disaster on them,
The year of their punishment," says the LORD.

13 "And I have seen folly in the
prophets of Samaria:
They prophesied by Baal
And caused My people Israel to err.
14 Also I have seen a horrible thing in the
prophets of Jerusalem:
They commit adultery and walk in lies;
They also strengthen the hands of evildoers,
So that no one turns back from
his wickedness.
All of them are like Sodom to Me,
And her inhabitants like Gomorrah.

15"Therefore thus says the LORD of hosts concerning
the prophets:

'Behold, I will feed them with wormwood,
And make them drink the water of gall;
For from the prophets of Jerusalem
Profaneness has gone out into all the land.' "

16Thus says the LORD of hosts:

"Do not listen to the words of the prophets
who prophesy to you.
They make you worthless;
They speak a vision of their own heart,
Not from the mouth of the LORD.
17 They continually say to those who despise Me,
'The LORD has said, "You shall have peace" ';
And *to* everyone who walks according to the
dictates of his own heart, they say,
'No evil shall come upon you.' "

18 For who has stood in the counsel of the LORD,
And has perceived and heard His word?
Who has marked His word and heard *it?*
19 Behold, a whirlwind of the LORD has
gone forth in fury—
A violent whirlwind!
It will fall violently on the head of the wicked.
20 The anger of the LORD will not turn back
Until He has executed and performed the
thoughts of His heart.
In the latter days you will understand
it perfectly.

21 "I have not sent these prophets, yet they ran.
I have not spoken to them, yet they prophesied.
22 But if they had stood in My counsel,
And had caused My people to hear My words,
Then they would have turned them
from their evil way
And from the evil of their doings.

23 "*Am* I a God near at hand," says the LORD,
"And not a God afar off?
24 Can anyone hide himself in secret places,
So I shall not see him?" says the LORD;
"Do I not fill heaven and earth?" says the LORD.

25"I have heard what the prophets have said who
prophesy lies in My name, saying, 'I have dreamed, I
have dreamed!' 26How long will *this* be in the heart of the
prophets who prophesy lies? Indeed *they are* prophets of
the deceit of their own heart, 27who try to make My people forget My name by their dreams which everyone tells
his neighbor, as their fathers forgot My name for Baal.

28 "The prophet who has a dream, let
him tell a dream;
And he who has My word, let him
speak My word faithfully.
What *is* the chaff to the wheat?" says the LORD.
29 "*Is* not My word like a fire?" says the LORD,

LIFE LESSON

Jeremiah 24:1–26:24

SITUATION Unless they turned from their sins, God vowed to exile Judah into Babylon for seventy years. Although the king threatened Jeremiah, the priests gradually believed that Jeremiah spoke with God's authority.

OBSERVATION God promised protection for his people if they turned from their sin. If not, they would suffer his fierce wrath.

INSPIRATION Conviction of sin is one of the rarest things that ever strikes a man. It is the threshold of an understanding of God. Jesus Christ said that when the Holy Spirit came He would convict of sin, and when the Holy Spirit rouses a man's conscience and brings him into the presence of God, it is not his relationship with men that bothers him, but his relationship with God—"against Thee, Thee only, have I sinned, and done this evil in Thy sight." The marvels of conviction of sin, forgiveness, and holiness are so interwoven that it is only the forgiven man who is the holy man, he proves he is forgiven by being the opposite to what he was, by God's grace. Repentance always brings a man to this point: I have sinned. The surest sign that God is at work is when a man says that and means it.

"And like a hammer *that* breaks the rock in pieces?

30"Therefore behold, I *am* against the prophets," says the LORD, "who steal
My words every one from his neighbor. 31Behold, I *am* against the prophets,"
says the LORD, "who use their tongues and say, 'He says.' 32Behold, I *am*
against those who prophesy false dreams," says the LORD, "and tell them,
and cause My people to err by their lies and by their recklessness. Yet I did
not send them or command them; therefore they shall not profit this people at all," says the LORD.

33"So when these people or the prophet or the priest ask you, saying,
'What is the oracle of the LORD?' you shall then say to them, 'What oracle?'[t]
I will even forsake you," says the LORD. 34"And *as for* the prophet and the
priest and the people who say, 'The oracle of the LORD!' I will even punish
that man and his house. 35Thus every one of you shall say to his neighbor,
and every one to his brother, 'What has the LORD answered?' and, 'What
has the LORD spoken?' 36And the oracle of the LORD you shall mention no
more. For every man's word will be his oracle, for you have perverted the
words of the living God, the LORD of hosts, our God. 37Thus you shall say to
the prophet, 'What has the LORD answered you?' and, 'What has the LORD
spoken?' 38But since you say, 'The oracle of the LORD!' therefore thus says
the LORD: 'Because you say this word, "The oracle of the LORD!" and I have
sent to you, saying, "Do not say, 'The oracle of the LORD!' " 39therefore behold,
I, even I, will utterly forget you and forsake you, and the city that I gave you
and your fathers, and *will cast you* out of My presence. 40And I will bring
an everlasting reproach upon you, and a perpetual shame, which shall not
be forgotten.' "

The Sign of Two Baskets of Figs

24 The LORD showed me, and there were two baskets of figs set before
the temple of the LORD, after Nebuchadnezzar king of Babylon had
carried away captive Jeconiah the son of Jehoiakim, king of Judah, and the
princes of Judah with the craftsmen and smiths, from Jerusalem, and had
brought them to Babylon. 2One basket *had* very good figs, like the figs *that*
are first ripe; and the other basket *had* very bad figs which could not be eaten,
they were so bad. 3Then the LORD said to me, "What do you see, Jeremiah?"

And I said, "Figs, the good figs, very good; and the bad, very bad, which
cannot be eaten, they are so bad."

4Again the word of the LORD came to me, saying, 5"Thus says the LORD,
the God of Israel: 'Like these good figs, so will I acknowledge those who
are carried away captive from Judah, whom I have sent out of this place
for *their own* good, into the land of the Chaldeans. 6For I will set My eyes
on them for good, and I will bring them back to this land; I will build them
and not pull *them* down, and I will plant them and not pluck *them* up.
7Then I will give them a heart to know Me, that I *am* the LORD; and they
shall be My people, and I will be their God, for they shall return to Me with
their whole heart.

8'And as the bad figs which cannot be eaten, they are so bad'—surely
thus says the LORD—'so will I give up Zedekiah the king of Judah, his
princes, the residue of Jerusalem who remain in this land, and those who
dwell in the land of Egypt. 9I will deliver them to trouble into all the king-

23:33 [t] Septuagint, Targum, and Vulgate read '*You are the burden.*'

doms of the earth, for *their* harm, *to be* a reproach and a byword, a taunt
and a curse, in all places where I shall drive them. 10And I will send the
sword, the famine, and the pestilence among them, till they are consumed
from the land that I gave to them and their fathers.' "

Seventy Years of Desolation

25 The word that came to Jeremiah concerning all the people of Judah, in
the fourth year of Jehoiakim the son of Josiah, king of Judah (which
was the first year of Nebuchadnezzar king of Babylon), 2which Jeremiah the
prophet spoke to all the people of Judah and to all the inhabitants of Jerusalem, saying: 3"From the thirteenth year of Josiah the son of Amon, king of
Judah, even to this day, this *is* the twenty-third year in which the word of
the LORD has come to me; and I have spoken to you, rising early and speaking,
but you have not listened. 4And the LORD has sent to you all His servants the
prophets, rising early and sending *them,* but you have not listened nor inclined
your ear to hear. 5They said, 'Repent now everyone of his evil way and his evil
doings, and dwell in the land that the LORD has given to you and your fathers
forever and ever. 6Do not go after other gods to serve them and worship them,
and do not provoke Me to anger with the works of your hands; and I will not
harm you.' 7Yet you have not listened to Me," says the LORD, "that you might
provoke Me to anger with the works of your hands to your own hurt.
8"Therefore thus says the LORD of hosts: 'Because you have not heard My
words, 9behold, I will send and take all the families of the north,' says the
LORD, 'and Nebuchadnezzar the king of Babylon, My servant, and will bring
them against this land, against its inhabitants, and against these nations
all around, and will utterly destroy them, and make them an astonishment,
a hissing, and perpetual desolations. 10Moreover I will take from them the
voice of mirth and the voice of gladness, the voice of the bridegroom and
the voice of the bride, the sound of the millstones and the light of the lamp.
11And this whole land shall be a desolation *and* an astonishment, and
these nations shall serve the king of Babylon seventy years.
12'Then it will come to pass, when seventy years are completed, *that* I
will punish the king of Babylon and that nation, the land of the Chaldeans,
for their iniquity,' says the LORD; 'and I will make it a perpetual desolation.
13So I will bring on that land all My words which I have pronounced
against it, all that is written in this book, which Jeremiah has prophesied
concerning all the nations. 14(For many nations and great kings shall be
served by them also; and I will repay them according to their deeds and
according to the works of their own hands.)' "

Judgment on the Nations

15For thus says the LORD God of Israel to me: "Take this wine cup of fury
from My hand, and cause all the nations, to whom I send you, to drink it.
16And they will drink and stagger and go mad because of the sword that I
will send among them."
17Then I took the cup from the LORD's hand, and made all the nations
drink, to whom the LORD had sent me: 18Jerusalem and the cities of Judah,
its kings and its princes, to make them a desolation, an astonishment, a
hissing, and a curse, as *it is* this day; 19Pharaoh king of Egypt, his servants,
his princes, and all his people; 20all the mixed multitude, all the kings of
the land of Uz, all the kings of the land of the Philistines (namely,

Anything less than this is remorse for having made blunders, the reflex action of disgust at himself.

The entrance into the Kingdom is through the panging pains of repentance crashing into a man's respectable goodness; then the Holy Ghost, Who produces these agonies, begins the formation of the Son of God in the life. The new life will manifest itself in conscious repentance and unconscious holiness, never the other way about. The bedrock of Christianity is repentance. Strictly speaking, a man cannot repent when he chooses; repentance is a gift of God. The old Puritans used to pray for "the gift of tears." If ever you cease to know the virtue of repentance, you are in darkness. Examine yourself and see if you have forgotten how to be sorry.

(From *My Utmost for His Highest* by Oswald Chambers)

APPLICATION Be thankful for a loving and patient God who forgives you when you are willing to honor and obey him. But don't take his graciousness lightly. Express your gratefulness for his mercy.

EXPLORATION Repentance—Exodus 9:27-34; Jonah 3:10; Luke 15:8-10.

Ashkelon, Gaza, Ekron, and the remnant of Ashdod);
21Edom, Moab, and the people of Ammon; 22all the
kings of Tyre, all the kings of Sidon, and the kings of
the coastlands which *are* across the sea; 23Dedan,
Tema, Buz, and all *who are* in the farthest corners; 24all
the kings of Arabia and all the kings of the mixed multitude who dwell in the desert; 25all the kings of Zimri,
all the kings of Elam, and all the kings of the Medes; 26all
the kings of the north, far and near, one with another;
and all the kingdoms of the world which *are* on the
face of the earth. Also the king of Sheshach[u] shall
drink after them.

27"Therefore you shall say to them, 'Thus says the
LORD of hosts, the God of Israel: "Drink, be drunk, and
vomit! Fall and rise no more, because of the sword
which I will send among you." ' 28And it shall be, if they
refuse to take the cup from your hand to drink, then
you shall say to them, 'Thus says the LORD of hosts:
"You shall certainly drink! 29For behold, I begin to bring
calamity on the city which is called by My name, and
should you be utterly unpunished? You shall not be
unpunished, for I will call for a sword on all the inhabitants of the earth," says the LORD of hosts.'

30"Therefore prophesy against them all these words,
and say to them:

'The LORD will roar from on high,
And utter His voice from His holy habitation;
He will roar mightily against His fold.
He will give a shout, as those who
tread *the grapes*,
Against all the inhabitants of the earth.
31 A noise will come to the ends of the earth—
For the LORD has a controversy with the nations;
He will plead His case with all flesh.
He will give those *who are* wicked to the
sword,' says the LORD."

32Thus says the LORD of hosts:

"Behold, disaster shall go forth
From nation to nation,
And a great whirlwind shall be raised up
From the farthest parts of the earth.

33"And at that day the slain of the LORD shall be from
one end of the earth even to the *other* end of the earth.
They shall not be lamented, or gathered, or buried;
they shall become refuse on the ground.

34 "Wail, shepherds, and cry!
Roll about *in the ashes*,
You leaders of the flock!
For the days of your slaughter and
your dispersions are fulfilled;
You shall fall like a precious vessel.
35 And the shepherds will have no way to flee,
Nor the leaders of the flock to escape.
36 A voice of the cry of the shepherds,
And a wailing of the leaders to the
flock *will be heard*.
For the LORD has plundered their pasture,
37 And the peaceful dwellings are cut down
Because of the fierce anger of the LORD.
38 He has left His lair like the lion;
For their land is desolate
Because of the fierceness of the Oppressor,
And because of His fierce anger."

Jeremiah Saved from Death

26 In the beginning of the reign of Jehoiakim the
son of Josiah, king of Judah, this word came
from the LORD, saying, 2"Thus says the LORD: 'Stand in
the court of the LORD's house, and speak to all the cities
of Judah, which come to worship *in* the LORD's house,
all the words that I command you to speak to them.
Do not diminish a word. 3Perhaps everyone will listen
and turn from his evil way, that I may relent concerning the calamity which I purpose to bring on them because of the evil of their doings.' 4And you shall say to
them, 'Thus says the LORD: "If you will not listen to
Me, to walk in My law which I have set before you, 5to
heed the words of My servants the prophets whom I
sent to you, both rising up early and sending *them*
(but you have not heeded), 6then I will make this
house like Shiloh, and will make this city a curse to all
the nations of the earth." ' "

7So the priests and the prophets and all the people
heard Jeremiah speaking these words in the house of
the LORD. 8Now it happened, when Jeremiah had made
an end of speaking all that the LORD had commanded
him to speak to all the people, that the priests and the
prophets and all the people seized him, saying, "You
will surely die! 9Why have you prophesied in the name
of the LORD, saying, 'This house shall be like Shiloh,
and this city shall be desolate, without an inhabitant'?"
And all the people were gathered against Jeremiah in
the house of the LORD.

10When the princes of Judah heard these things,
they came up from the king's house to the house of
the LORD and sat down in the entry of the New Gate of

25:26 [u] A code word for Babylon (compare 51:41)

the LORD's *house.* [11]And the priests and the prophets
spoke to the princes and all the people, saying, "This
man deserves to die! For he has prophesied against
this city, as you have heard with your ears."
[12]Then Jeremiah spoke to all the princes and all the
people, saying: "The LORD sent me to prophesy against
this house and against this city with all the words that
you have heard. [13]Now therefore, amend your ways
and your doings, and obey the voice of the LORD your
God; then the LORD will relent concerning the doom
that He has pronounced against you. [14]As for me, here
I am, in your hand; do with me as seems good and
proper to you. [15]But know for certain that if you put
me to death, you will surely bring innocent blood on
yourselves, on this city, and on its inhabitants; for
truly the LORD has sent me to you to speak all these
words in your hearing."
[16]So the princes and all the people said to the priests
and the prophets, "This man does not deserve to die. For
he has spoken to us in the name of the LORD our God."
[17]Then certain of the elders of the land rose up and
spoke to all the assembly of the people, saying: [18]"Micah
of Moresheth prophesied in the days of Hezekiah king
of Judah, and spoke to all the people of Judah, saying,
'Thus says the LORD of hosts:

"Zion shall be plowed *like* a field,
Jerusalem shall become heaps of ruins,
And the mountain of the temple[v]
Like the bare hills of the forest." '[w]

[19]Did Hezekiah king of Judah and all Judah ever put
him to death? Did he not fear the LORD and seek the
LORD's favor? And the LORD relented concerning the
doom which He had pronounced against them. But
we are doing great evil against ourselves."
[20]Now there was also a man who prophesied in the
name of the LORD, Urijah the son of Shemaiah of Kirjath
Jearim, who prophesied against this city and against
this land according to all the words of Jeremiah.
[21]And when Jehoiakim the king, with all his mighty
men and all the princes, heard his words, the king
sought to put him to death; but when Urijah heard *it,*
he was afraid and fled, and went to Egypt. [22]Then
Jehoiakim the king sent men to Egypt: Elnathan the
son of Achbor, and *other* men *who went* with him to
Egypt. [23]And they brought Urijah from Egypt and
brought him to Jehoiakim the king, who killed him
with the sword and cast his dead body into the graves
of the common people.
[24]Nevertheless the hand of Ahikam the son of Shaphan was with Jeremiah, so that they should not give
him into the hand of the people to put him to death.

Symbol of the Bonds and Yokes

27 In the beginning of the reign of Jehoiakim[x] the
son of Josiah, king of Judah, this word came to
Jeremiah from the LORD, saying,[y] [2]"Thus says the LORD
to me: 'Make for yourselves bonds and yokes, and put
them on your neck, [3]and send them to the king of Edom,
the king of Moab, the king of the Ammonites, the king
of Tyre, and the king of Sidon, by the hand of the messengers who come to Jerusalem to Zedekiah king of
Judah. [4]And command them to say to their masters,
"Thus says the LORD of hosts, the God of Israel—thus
you shall say to your masters: [5]'I have made the earth,
the man and the beast that *are* on the ground, by My
great power and by My outstretched arm, and have
given it to whom it seemed proper to Me. [6]And now I
have given all these lands into the hand of Nebuchadnezzar the king of Babylon, My servant; and the
beasts of the field I have also given him to serve him.
[7]So all nations shall serve him and his son and his
son's son, until the time of his land comes; and then
many nations and great kings shall make him serve
them. [8]And it shall be, *that* the nation and kingdom
which will not serve Nebuchadnezzar the king of
Babylon, and which will not put its neck under the
yoke of the king of Babylon, that nation I will punish,'
says the LORD, 'with the sword, the famine, and the
pestilence, until I have consumed them by his hand.
[9]Therefore do not listen to your prophets, your diviners, your dreamers, your soothsayers, or your sorcerers, who speak to you, saying, "You shall not serve the
king of Babylon." [10]For they prophesy a lie to you, to
remove you far from your land; and I will drive you
out, and you will perish. [11]But the nations that bring
their necks under the yoke of the king of Babylon and
serve him, I will let them remain in their own land,'
says the LORD, 'and they shall till it and dwell in it.' " ' "
[12]I also spoke to Zedekiah king of Judah according
to all these words, saying, "Bring your necks under
the yoke of the king of Babylon, and serve him and his
people, and live! [13]Why will you die, you and your
people, by the sword, by the famine, and by the pestilence, as the LORD has spoken against the nation that
will not serve the king of Babylon? [14]Therefore do not
listen to the words of the prophets who speak to you,
saying, 'You shall not serve the king of Babylon,' for

26:18 [v] Literally *house* [w] Compare Micah 3:12
27:1 [x] Following Masoretic Text, Targum, and Vulgate; some Hebrew manuscripts, Arabic, and Syriac read *Zedekiah* (compare 27:3, 12; 28:1). [y] Septuagint omits verse 1.

LIFE LESSON

Jeremiah 27:1–29:32

SITUATION Jeremiah responded to the false prophets. One false prophet, Hananiah, said that the "yoke" of Babylon would be broken in two years.

OBSERVATION After seventy years the people would seek for God and would find him (29:10-14). Daniel wrote of the fulfillment of this promise seventy years later (Daniel 9).

INSPIRATION As I write this I'm at 35,000 feet. It's 5:45 p.m., Saturday. It should be 4:15. The airliner was an hour and a half late . . . It all started with the *delay*. "Mechanical trouble," they said. "Inexcusable," responded a couple of passengers. Frankly, I'd rather they fix it before we leave than decide to do something about it en route. But we Americans don't like to wait. Delays are irritating. Aggravating. Nerve-jangling. With impatient predictability we are consistently—and I might add *obnoxiously*—demanding. We want what we want *when* we want it. Not a one of us finds a delay easy to accept. . . . You're a little late to work. The freeway's full so you decide to slip through traffic using a rarely-known shortcut only Daniel Boone could have figured out. You hit all green lights as you slide around trucks and slow drivers. Just about the time you start feeling foxy, an ominous clang, clang, clang strikes your ears. A train. You're delayed. How's your response? The rubber of Christianity meets the road of proof at just such intersections of life. As the expression goes, our faith is "fleshed out" at times like that. The best test of my Christian growth occurs in the mainstream of life, not in the quietness of my study. *Anybody* can walk in victory when surrounded by books, silence, and the warm waves of sunshine splashing through the window. But those late takeoffs, those grocery lines, those busy restaurants, those trains! That's where faith is usually "flushed out." . . .

they prophesy a lie to you; [15]for I have not sent them," says the LORD, "yet
they prophesy a lie in My name, that I may drive you out, and that you may
perish, you and the prophets who prophesy to you."
[16]Also I spoke to the priests and to all this people, saying, "Thus says the
LORD: 'Do not listen to the words of your prophets who prophesy to you,
saying, "Behold, the vessels of the LORD's house will now shortly be
brought back from Babylon"; for they prophesy a lie to you. [17]Do not listen
to them; serve the king of Babylon, and live! Why should this city be laid
waste? [18]But if they *are* prophets, and if the word of the LORD is with them,
let them now make intercession to the LORD of hosts, that the vessels
which are left in the house of the LORD, *in* the house of the king of Judah,
and at Jerusalem, do not go to Babylon.'
[19]"For thus says the LORD of hosts concerning the pillars, concerning the
Sea, concerning the carts, and concerning the remainder of the vessels
that remain in this city, [20]which Nebuchadnezzar king of Babylon did not
take, when he carried away captive Jeconiah the son of Jehoiakim, king of
Judah, from Jerusalem to Babylon, and all the nobles of Judah and Jerusalem— [21]yes, thus says the LORD of hosts, the God of Israel, concerning the
vessels that remain in the house of the LORD, and in the house of the king
of Judah and of Jerusalem: [22]'They shall be carried to Babylon, and there
they shall be until the day that I visit them,' says the LORD. 'Then I will
bring them up and restore them to this place.' "

Hananiah's Falsehood and Doom

28 And it happened in the same year, at the beginning of the reign of
Zedekiah king of Judah, in the fourth year *and* in the fifth month,
that Hananiah the son of Azur the prophet, who *was* from Gibeon, spoke
to me in the house of the LORD in the presence of the priests and of all the
people, saying, [2]"Thus speaks the LORD of hosts, the God of Israel, saying:
'I have broken the yoke of the king of Babylon. [3]Within two full years I will
bring back to this place all the vessels of the LORD's house, that
Nebuchadnezzar king of Babylon took away from this place and carried to
Babylon. [4]And I will bring back to this place Jeconiah the son of
Jehoiakim, king of Judah, with all the captives of Judah who went to
Babylon,' says the LORD, 'for I will break the yoke of the king of Babylon.' "
[5]Then the prophet Jeremiah spoke to the prophet Hananiah in the presence of the priests and in the presence of all the people who stood in the
house of the LORD, [6]and the prophet Jeremiah said, "Amen! The LORD do
so; the LORD perform your words which you have prophesied, to bring
back the vessels of the LORD's house and all who were carried away captive,
from Babylon to this place. [7]Nevertheless hear now this word that I speak
in your hearing and in the hearing of all the people: [8]The prophets who have
been before me and before you of old prophesied against many countries
and great kingdoms—of war and disaster and pestilence. [9]As for the
prophet who prophesies of peace, when the word of the prophet comes to
pass, the prophet will be known *as* one whom the LORD has truly sent."
[10]Then Hananiah the prophet took the yoke off the prophet Jeremiah's
neck and broke it. [11]And Hananiah spoke in the presence of all the people,
saying, "Thus says the LORD: 'Even so I will break the yoke of Nebuchadnezzar
king of Babylon from the neck of all nations within the space of two full
years.' " And the prophet Jeremiah went his way.

12 Now the word of the LORD came to Jeremiah, after Hananiah the prophet
had broken the yoke from the neck of the prophet Jeremiah, saying, 13 "Go
and tell Hananiah, saying, 'Thus says the LORD: "You have broken the yokes
of wood, but you have made in their place yokes of iron." 14 For thus says
the LORD of hosts, the God of Israel: "I have put a yoke of iron on the neck
of all these nations, that they may serve Nebuchadnezzar king of Babylon;
and they shall serve him. I have given him the beasts of the field also." ' "
15 Then the prophet Jeremiah said to Hananiah the prophet, "Hear now,
Hananiah, the LORD has not sent you, but you make this people trust in a
lie. 16 Therefore thus says the LORD: 'Behold, I will cast you from the face of
the earth. This year you shall die, because you have taught rebellion against
the LORD.' "
17 So Hananiah the prophet died the same year in the seventh month.

Jeremiah's Letter to the Captives

29 Now these *are* the words of the letter that Jeremiah the prophet sent
from Jerusalem to the remainder of the elders who were carried away
captive—to the priests, the prophets, and all the people whom Nebuchadnezzar had carried away captive from Jerusalem to Babylon. 2 (This happened after Jeconiah the king, the queen mother, the eunuchs, the princes
of Judah and Jerusalem, the craftsmen, and the smiths had departed from
Jerusalem.) 3 *The letter was sent* by the hand of Elasah the son of Shaphan,
and Gemariah the son of Hilkiah, whom Zedekiah king of Judah sent to
Babylon, to Nebuchadnezzar king of Babylon, saying,

4 Thus says the LORD of hosts, the God of Israel, to all who were carried
away captive, whom I have caused to be carried away from
Jerusalem to Babylon:
5 Build houses and dwell *in them;* plant gardens and eat their fruit.
6 Take wives and beget sons and daughters; and take wives for your
sons and give your daughters to husbands, so that they may bear sons
and daughters—that you may be increased there, and not
diminished. 7 And seek the peace of the city where I have caused
you to be carried away captive, and pray to the LORD for it; for in its
peace you will have peace. 8 For thus says the LORD of hosts, the
God of Israel: Do not let your prophets and your diviners who are
in your midst deceive you, nor listen to your dreams which you
cause to be dreamed. 9 For they prophesy falsely to you in My
name; I have not sent them, says the LORD.
10 For thus says the LORD: After seventy years are completed at
Babylon, I will visit you and perform My good word toward you,
and cause you to return to this place. 11 For I know the thoughts
that I think toward you, says the LORD, thoughts of peace and not
of evil, to give you a future and a hope. 12 Then you will call upon
Me and go and pray to Me, and I will listen to you. 13 And you will
seek Me and find *Me,* when you search for Me with all your heart.
14 I will be found by you, says the LORD, and I will bring you back
from your captivity; I will gather you from all the nations and from
all the places where I have driven you, says the LORD, and I will bring
you to the place from which I cause you to be carried away captive.

The ability to accept delay graciously. Calmly. Quietly. Understandingly. With a smile. If the robe of purity is far above rubies, the garment of patience is even beyond that. Why? Because its threads of unselfishness and kindness are woven on the Lord's loom, guided within our lives by the Spirit of God. But, alas, the garment seldom clothes us!

Remember the verse?

But the fruit of the Spirit is love, joy, peace . . .

And what else? The first three are the necessary style along with the buttons and zipper of the garment. The rest give it color and beauty:

. . . patience, kindness, goodness, faithfulness, gentleness, self-control . . . (Galatians 5:22-23).

The ability to accept delay. Or disappointment. To smile back at setbacks and respond with a pleasant, understanding spirit. To cool it while others around you curse it. For a change, I refused to be hassled by today's delay. I asked God to keep me calm and cheerful, relaxed and refreshed. Know what? He did. He *really* did! No pills. No booze. No hocus-pocus. Just relaxing in the power of Jesus.
(From *Growing Strong in the Seasons of Life* by Charles Swindoll)

APPLICATION Are you impatient with your present situation in life? Are you wanting to move on to graduate, get married, get promoted, or get a new house? Remember, God calls you to be content and compliant. Ask him to help you accept his perfect timing for the changes you desire.

EXPLORATION Patience in Circumstances—Psalm 37:7; Isaiah 33:2; Acts 1:4; Romans 12:12; 2 Thessalonians 1:4; Hebrews 10:36; James 1:2-4; 5:7-11.

15 Because you have said, "The LORD has raised
up prophets for us in Babylon"— [16]therefore
thus says the LORD concerning the king who
sits on the throne of David, concerning all the
people who dwell in this city, and concerning
your brethren who have not gone out with you
into captivity— [17]thus says the LORD of hosts:
Behold, I will send on them the sword, the
famine, and the pestilence, and will make
them like rotten figs that cannot be eaten, they
are so bad. [18]And I will pursue them with the
sword, with famine, and with pestilence; and I
will deliver them to trouble among all the
kingdoms of the earth—to be a curse, an
astonishment, a hissing, and a reproach
among all the nations where I have driven
them, [19]because they have not heeded My
words, says the LORD, which I sent to them by
My servants the prophets, rising up early and
sending *them;* neither would you heed, says
the LORD. [20]Therefore hear the word of the
LORD, all you of the captivity, whom I have
sent from Jerusalem to Babylon.

21 Thus says the LORD of hosts, the God of Israel,
concerning Ahab the son of Kolaiah, and
Zedekiah the son of Maaseiah, who prophesy
a lie to you in My name: Behold, I will deliver
them into the hand of Nebuchadnezzar king
of Babylon, and he shall slay them before your
eyes. [22]And because of them a curse shall be
taken up by all the captivity of Judah who *are*
in Babylon, saying, "The LORD make you like
Zedekiah and Ahab, whom the king of
Babylon roasted in the fire"; [23]because they
have done disgraceful things in Israel, have
committed adultery with their neighbors'
wives, and have spoken lying words in My
name, which I have not commanded them.
Indeed I know, and *am* a witness, says the LORD.

24 You shall also speak to Shemaiah the
Nehelamite, saying, [25]Thus speaks the LORD of
hosts, the God of Israel, saying: You have sent
letters in your name to all the people who *are*
at Jerusalem, to Zephaniah the son of
Maaseiah the priest, and to all the priests,
saying, [26]"The LORD has made you priest
instead of Jehoiada the priest, so that there
should be officers *in* the house of the LORD over
every man *who* is demented and considers
himself a prophet, that you should put him in
prison and in the stocks. [27]Now therefore, why
have you not rebuked Jeremiah of Anathoth
who makes himself a prophet to you? [28]For he
has sent to us *in* Babylon, saying, 'This *captivity*
is long; build houses and dwell *in them,* and
plant gardens and eat their fruit.' "

29 Now Zephaniah the priest read this letter in
the hearing of Jeremiah the prophet. [30]Then
the word of the LORD came to Jeremiah,
saying: [31]Send to all those in captivity, saying,
Thus says the LORD concerning Shemaiah the
Nehelamite: Because Shemaiah has
prophesied to you, and I have not sent him,
and he has caused you to trust in a lie—
[32]therefore thus says the LORD: Behold, I will
punish Shemaiah the Nehelamite and his family:
he shall not have anyone to dwell among this
people, nor shall he see the good that I will do
for My people, says the LORD, because he has
taught rebellion against the LORD.

Restoration of Israel and Judah

30 The word that came to Jeremiah from the LORD,
saying, [2]"Thus speaks the LORD God of Israel,
saying: 'Write in a book for yourself all the words that
I have spoken to you. [3]For behold, the days are coming,' says the LORD, 'that I will bring back from captivity My people Israel and Judah,' says the LORD. 'And I
will cause them to return to the land that I gave to
their fathers, and they shall possess it.' "

[4]Now these *are* the words that the LORD spoke concerning Israel and Judah.

[5]"For thus says the LORD:

'We have heard a voice of trembling,
Of fear, and not of peace.
6 Ask now, and see,
Whether a man is ever in labor with child?
So why do I see every man *with* his
hands on his loins
Like a woman in labor,
And all faces turned pale?
7 Alas! For that day *is* great,
So that none *is* like it;
And it *is* the time of Jacob's trouble,
But he shall be saved out of it.

8 'For it shall come to pass in that day,'
Says the LORD of hosts,
'*That* I will break his yoke from your neck,
And will burst your bonds;
Foreigners shall no more enslave them.

9 But they shall serve the LORD their God,
And David their king,
Whom I will raise up for them.

10 'Therefore do not fear, O My servant Jacob,' says the LORD,
'Nor be dismayed, O Israel;
For behold, I will save you from afar,
And your seed from the land of their captivity.
Jacob shall return, have rest and be quiet,
And no one shall make *him* afraid.
11 For I *am* with you,' says the LORD, 'to save you;
Though I make a full end of all nations where I have scattered you,
Yet I will not make a complete end of you.
But I will correct you in justice,
And will not let you go altogether unpunished.'

12 "For thus says the LORD:
'Your affliction *is* incurable,
Your wound *is* severe.
13 *There is* no one to plead your cause,
That you may be bound up;
You have no healing medicines.
14 All your lovers have forgotten you;
They do not seek you;
For I have wounded you with the wound of an enemy,
With the chastisement of a cruel one,
For the multitude of your iniquities,
Because your sins have increased.
15 Why do you cry about your affliction?
Your sorrow *is* incurable.
Because of the multitude of your iniquities,
Because your sins have increased,
I have done these things to you.

16 'Therefore all those who devour you shall be devoured;
And all your adversaries, every one of them, shall go into captivity;
Those who plunder you shall become plunder,
And all who prey upon you I will make a prey.
17 For I will restore health to you
And heal you of your wounds,' says the LORD,
'Because they called you an outcast *saying:*
"This *is* Zion;
No one seeks her." '

18 "Thus says the LORD:

'Behold, I will bring back the captivity of Jacob's tents,
And have mercy on his dwelling places;
The city shall be built upon its own mound,
And the palace shall remain according to its own plan.
19 Then out of them shall proceed thanksgiving
And the voice of those who make merry;
I will multiply them, and they shall not diminish;

LIFE LESSON

Jeremiah 30:1–33:26

SITUATION Jeremiah did not just preach doom and gloom. He told the people to hope in God, who would restore them.

OBSERVATION Christians must never lose all hope. Our belief in Jesus Christ gives us hope for the future.

INSPIRATION For thousands of years, using his wit and charm, man had tried to be friends with God. And for thousands of years he had let God down more than he had lifted him up. He's done the very thing he promised he'd never do. It was a fiasco. Even the holiest of the heroes sometimes forgot whose side they were on. Some of the scenarios in the Bible look more like the adventures of Sinbad the sailor than stories for vacation Bible school. Remember these characters?

Aaron. Right-hand man to Moses. Witness of the plagues. Member of the "Red Sea Riverbed Expedition." Holy priest of God. But if he was so saintly, what is he doing leading the Israelites in fireside aerobics in front of the golden calf?

The sons of Jacob. The fathers of the tribes of Israel. Great-grandsons of Abraham. Yet, if they were so special, why were they gagging their younger brother and sending him to Egypt?

David. The man after God's own heart. The King's king. The giant-slayer and songwriter. He's also the guy whose glasses got steamy as a result of a bath on a roof. Unfortunately, the water wasn't his, nor was the woman he was watching.

And Samson. Swooning on Delilah's couch, drunk on the wine, perfume, and soft lights. He's thinking, *She's putting on something more comfortable.* She's thinking, *I know I put those shears in here somewhere.*

Adam adorned in fig leaves and stains of forbidden fruit. Moses throwing both a staff and a temper tantrum. King Saul looking into a crystal ball for the will of God. Noah, drunk and naked in his own tent.

These are the chosen ones of God? This is the royal lineage of the King? These are the ones who were to carry out God's mission?

Continued

It's easy to see the absurdity.

Why didn't he give up? Why didn't he let the globe spin off its axis?

Even after generations of people had spit in his face, he still loved them. After a nation of chosen ones had stripped him naked and ripped his incarnated flesh, he still died for them. And even today, after billions have chosen to prostitute themselves before the pimps of power, fame, and wealth, he still waits for them.

It *is* inexplicable. It doesn't have a drop of logic nor a thread of rationality.

And yet, it is that very irrationality that gives the gospel its greatest defense. For only God could love like that.

(From *God Came Near* by Max Lucado)

APPLICATION Do this project with someone close to you: spend an hour on your own making a list of all God has done for you. Then share together and rejoice in his goodness and faithfulness.

EXPLORATION Hope—Proverbs 13:12; Isaiah 40:31; Jeremiah 29:11; Romans 15:13; Hebrews 11:1.

I will also glorify them, and they shall not be small.
20 Their children also shall be as before,
And their congregation shall be established before Me;
And I will punish all who oppress them.
21 Their nobles shall be from among them,
And their governor shall come from their midst;
Then I will cause him to draw near,
And he shall approach Me;
For who *is* this who pledged his heart to approach Me?' says the LORD.
22 'You shall be My people,
And I will be your God.' "

23 Behold, the whirlwind of the LORD
Goes forth with fury,
A continuing whirlwind;
It will fall violently on the head of the wicked.
24 The fierce anger of the LORD will not return until He has done it,
And until He has performed the intents of His heart.

In the latter days you will consider it.

The Remnant of Israel Saved

31 "At the same time," says the LORD, "I will be the God of all the families of Israel, and they shall be My people."
2 Thus says the LORD:

"The people who survived the sword
Found grace in the wilderness—
Israel, when I went to give him rest."

3 The LORD has appeared of old to me, *saying:*
"Yes, I have loved you with an everlasting love;
Therefore with lovingkindness I have drawn you.
4 Again I will build you, and you shall be rebuilt,
O virgin of Israel!
You shall again be adorned with your tambourines,
And shall go forth in the dances of those who rejoice.
5 You shall yet plant vines on the mountains of Samaria;
The planters shall plant and eat *them* as ordinary food.
6 For there shall be a day
When the watchmen will cry on Mount Ephraim,
'Arise, and let us go up *to* Zion,
To the LORD our God.' "

7 For thus says the LORD:

"Sing with gladness for Jacob,
And shout among the chief of the nations;
Proclaim, give praise, and say,
'O LORD, save Your people,
The remnant of Israel!'
8 Behold, I will bring them from the north country,
And gather them from the ends of the earth,
Among them the blind and the lame,

The woman with child
And the one who labors with child, together;
A great throng shall return there.
9 They shall come with weeping,
And with supplications I will lead them.
I will cause them to walk by the rivers of waters,
In a straight way in which they
shall not stumble;
For I am a Father to Israel,
And Ephraim *is* My firstborn.

10 "Hear the word of the LORD, O nations,
And declare *it* in the isles afar off, and say,
'He who scattered Israel will gather him,
And keep him as a shepherd *does* his flock.'
11 For the LORD has redeemed Jacob,
And ransomed him from the hand of one
stronger than he.
12 Therefore they shall come and sing in the
height of Zion,
Streaming to the goodness of the LORD—
For wheat and new wine and oil,
For the young of the flock and the herd;
Their souls shall be like a
well-watered garden,
And they shall sorrow no more at all.
13 "Then shall the virgin rejoice in the dance,
And the young men and the old, together;
For I will turn their mourning to joy,
Will comfort them,
And make them rejoice rather than sorrow.
14 I will satiate the soul of the priests
with abundance,
And My people shall be satisfied with My
goodness, says the LORD."

Mercy on Ephraim

15Thus says the LORD:

"A voice was heard in Ramah,
Lamentation *and* bitter weeping,
Rachel weeping for her children,
Refusing to be comforted for her children,
Because they *are* no more."

16Thus says the LORD:

"Refrain your voice from weeping,
And your eyes from tears;
For your work shall be rewarded,
says the LORD,
And they shall come back from the
land of the enemy.
17 There is hope in your future, says the LORD,
That *your* children shall come back
to their own border.

18 "I have surely heard Ephraim
bemoaning himself:
'You have chastised me, and I was chastised,
Like an untrained bull;
Restore me, and I will return,
For You *are* the LORD my God.
19 Surely, after my turning, I repented;
And after I was instructed, I struck
myself on the thigh;
I was ashamed, yes, even humiliated,
Because I bore the reproach of my youth.'
20 *Is* Ephraim My dear son?
Is he a pleasant child?
For though I spoke against him,
I earnestly remember him still;
Therefore My heart yearns for him;
I will surely have mercy on him, says the LORD.

21 "Set up signposts,
Make landmarks;
Set your heart toward the highway,
The way in *which* you went.
Turn back, O virgin of Israel,
Turn back to these your cities.
22 How long will you gad about,
O you backsliding daughter?
For the LORD has created a new
thing in the earth—
A woman shall encompass a man."

Future Prosperity of Judah

23Thus says the LORD of hosts, the God of Israel: "They
shall again use this speech in the land of Judah and in
its cities, when I bring back their captivity: 'The LORD
bless you, O home of justice, *and* mountain of holiness!' 24And there shall dwell in Judah itself, and in all
its cities together, farmers and those going out with
flocks. 25For I have satiated the weary soul, and I have
replenished every sorrowful soul."

26After this I awoke and looked around, and my
sleep was sweet to me.

27"Behold, the days are coming, says the LORD, that I
will sow the house of Israel and the house of Judah with
the seed of man and the seed of beast. 28And it shall
come to pass, *that* as I have watched over them to pluck
up, to break down, to throw down, to destroy, and to
afflict, so I will watch over them to build and to plant,
says the LORD. 29In those days they shall say no more:

'The fathers have eaten sour grapes,
And the children's teeth are set on edge.'

30But every one shall die for his own iniquity; every man
who eats the sour grapes, his teeth shall be set on edge.

A New Covenant

31"Behold, the days are coming, says the LORD, when
I will make a new covenant with the house of Israel
and with the house of Judah— 32not according to the
covenant that I made with their fathers in the day *that*
I took them by the hand to lead them out of the land of
Egypt, My covenant which they broke, though I was a
husband to them,[z] says the LORD. 33But this *is* the
covenant that I will make with the house of Israel after
those days, says the LORD: I will put My law in their
minds, and write it on their hearts; and I will be their
God, and they shall be My people. 34No more shall
every man teach his neighbor, and every man his
brother, saying, 'Know the LORD,' for they all shall
know Me, from the least of them to the greatest of
them, says the LORD. For I will forgive their iniquity,
and their sin I will remember no more."

35 Thus says the LORD,
Who gives the sun for a light by day,
The ordinances of the moon and the
stars for a light by night,
Who disturbs the sea,
And its waves roar
(The LORD of hosts *is* His name):

36 "If those ordinances depart
From before Me, says the LORD,
Then the seed of Israel shall also cease
From being a nation before Me forever."

37Thus says the LORD:
"If heaven above can be measured,
And the foundations of the earth
searched out beneath,
I will also cast off all the seed of Israel
For all that they have done, says the LORD.

38"Behold, the days are coming, says the LORD, that
the city shall be built for the LORD from the Tower of
Hananel to the Corner Gate. 39The surveyor's line shall
again extend straight forward over the hill Gareb; then
it shall turn toward Goath. 40And the whole valley of
the dead bodies and of the ashes, and all the fields as
far as the Brook Kidron, to the corner of the Horse
Gate toward the east, *shall be* holy to the LORD. It shall
not be plucked up or thrown down anymore forever."

Jeremiah Buys a Field

32 The word that came to Jeremiah from the LORD
in the tenth year of Zedekiah king of Judah,
which was the eighteenth year of Nebuchadnezzar.
2For then the king of Babylon's army besieged Jerusalem, and Jeremiah the prophet was shut up in the
court of the prison, which *was in* the king of Judah's
house. 3For Zedekiah king of Judah had shut him up,
saying, "Why do you prophesy and say, 'Thus says the
LORD: "Behold, I will give this city into the hand of the
king of Babylon, and he shall take it; 4and Zedekiah
king of Judah shall not escape from the hand of the
Chaldeans, but shall surely be delivered into the hand
of the king of Babylon, and shall speak with him face
to face,[a] and see him eye to eye; 5then he shall lead
Zedekiah to Babylon, and there he shall be until I visit
him," says the LORD; "though you fight with the
Chaldeans, you shall not succeed"'?"

6And Jeremiah said, "The word of the LORD came to
me, saying, 7'Behold, Hanamel the son of Shallum your
uncle will come to you, saying, "Buy my field which *is*
in Anathoth, for the right of redemption *is* yours to
buy *it*."' 8Then Hanamel my uncle's son came to me
in the court of the prison according to the word of the
LORD, and said to me, 'Please buy my field that *is* in
Anathoth, which *is* in the country of Benjamin; for the
right of inheritance *is* yours, and the redemption yours;
buy *it* for yourself.' Then I knew that this was the word
of the LORD. 9So I bought the field from Hanamel, the
son of my uncle who *was* in Anathoth, and weighed
out to him the money—seventeen shekels of silver.
10And I signed the deed and sealed *it,* took witnesses,
and weighed the money on the scales. 11So I took the
purchase deed, *both* that which was sealed *according*
to the law and custom, and that which was open; 12and
I gave the purchase deed to Baruch the son of Neriah,
son of Mahseiah, in the presence of Hanamel my
uncle's *son,* and in the presence of the witnesses who
signed the purchase deed, before all the Jews who sat
in the court of the prison.

13"Then I charged Baruch before them, saying,
14'Thus says the LORD of hosts, the God of Israel: "Take
these deeds, both this purchase deed which is sealed
and this deed which is open, and put them in an
earthen vessel, that they may last many days." 15For
thus says the LORD of hosts, the God of Israel: "Houses

31:32 [z] Following Masoretic Text, Targum, and Vulgate; Septuagint and Syriac read *and I turned away from them.*
32:4 [a] Literally *mouth to mouth*

and fields and vineyards shall be possessed again in this land." ' "

Jeremiah Prays for Understanding

16"Now when I had delivered the purchase deed to Baruch the son of Neriah, I prayed to the LORD, saying: 17'Ah, Lord GOD! Behold, You have made the heavens and the earth by Your great power and outstretched arm. There is nothing too hard for You. 18*You* show lovingkindness to thousands, and repay the iniquity of the fathers into the bosom of their children after them—the Great, the Mighty God, whose name *is* the LORD of hosts. 19*You are* great in counsel and mighty in work, for Your eyes *are* open to all the ways of the sons of men, to give everyone according to his ways and according to the fruit of his doings. 20You have set signs and wonders in the land of Egypt, to this day, and in Israel and among *other* men; and You have made Yourself a name, as it is this day. 21You have brought Your people Israel out of the land of Egypt with signs and wonders, with a strong hand and an outstretched arm, and with great terror; 22You have given them this land, of which You swore to their fathers to give them—"a land flowing with milk and honey."[b] 23And they came in and took possession of it, but they have not obeyed Your voice or walked in Your law. They have done nothing of all that You commanded them to do; therefore You have caused all this calamity to come upon them.

24'Look, the siege mounds! They have come to the city to take it; and the city has been given into the hand of the Chaldeans who fight against it, because of the sword and famine and pestilence. What You have spoken has happened; there You see *it!* 25And You have said to me, O Lord GOD, "Buy the field for money, and take witnesses"!—yet the city has been given into the hand of the Chaldeans.' "

God's Assurance of the People's Return

26Then the word of the LORD came to Jeremiah, saying, 27"Behold, I *am* the LORD, the God of all flesh. Is there anything too hard for Me? 28Therefore thus says the LORD: 'Behold, I will give this city into the hand of the Chaldeans, into the hand of Nebuchadnezzar king of Babylon, and he shall take it. 29And the Chaldeans who fight against this city shall come and set fire to this city and burn it, with the houses on whose roofs they have offered incense to Baal and poured out drink offerings to other gods, to provoke Me to anger; 30because the children of Israel and the children of Judah have done only evil before Me from their youth. For the children of Israel have provoked Me only to anger with the work of their hands,' says the LORD. 31'For this city has been to Me *a provocation of* My anger and My fury from the day that they built it, even to this day; so I will remove it from before My face 32because of all the evil of the children of Israel and the children of Judah, which they have done to provoke Me to anger—they, their kings, their princes, their priests, their prophets, the men of Judah, and the inhabitants of Jerusalem. 33And they have turned to Me the back, and not the face; though I taught them, rising up early and teaching *them,* yet they have not listened to receive instruction. 34But they set their abominations in the house which is called by My name, to defile it. 35And they built the high places of Baal which *are* in the Valley of the Son of Hinnom, to cause their sons and their daughters to pass through *the fire* to Molech, which I did not command them, nor did it come into My mind that they should do this abomination, to cause Judah to sin.'

36"Now therefore, thus says the LORD, the God of Israel, concerning this city of which you say, 'It shall be delivered into the hand of the king of Babylon by the sword, by the famine, and by the pestilence: 37Behold, I will gather them out of all countries where I have driven them in My anger, in My fury, and in great wrath; I will bring them back to this place, and I will cause them to dwell safely. 38They shall be My people, and I will be their God; 39then I will give them one heart and one way, that they may fear Me forever, for the good of them and their children after them. 40And I will make an everlasting covenant with them, that I will not turn away from doing them good; but I will put My fear in their hearts so that they will not depart from Me. 41Yes, I will rejoice over them to do them good, and I will assuredly plant them in this land, with all My heart and with all My soul.'

42"For thus says the LORD: 'Just as I have brought all this great calamity on this people, so I will bring on them all the good that I have promised them. 43And fields will be bought in this land of which you say, "*It is* desolate, without man or beast; it has been given into the hand of the Chaldeans." 44Men will buy fields for money, sign deeds and seal *them,* and take witnesses, in the land of Benjamin, in the places around Jerusalem, in the cities of Judah, in the cities of the mountains, in the cities of the lowland, and in the cities of the South; for I will cause their captives to return,' says the LORD."

32:22 [b] Exodus 3:8

Excellence of the Restored Nation

33 Moreover the word of the LORD came to
Jeremiah a second time, while he was still shut
up in the court of the prison, saying, 2"Thus says the
LORD who made it, the LORD who formed it to establish it (the LORD *is* His name): 3'Call to Me, and I will
answer you, and show you great and mighty things,
which you do not know.'
4"For thus says the LORD, the God of Israel, concerning the houses of this city and the houses of the
kings of Judah, which have been pulled down *to fortify*[c]
against the siege mounds and the sword: 5'They come
to fight with the Chaldeans, but *only* to fill their
places[d] with the dead bodies of men whom I will slay
in My anger and My fury, all for whose wickedness I
have hidden My face from this city. 6Behold, I will
bring it health and healing; I will heal them and reveal
to them the abundance of peace and truth. 7And I will
cause the captives of Judah and the captives of Israel
to return, and will rebuild those places as at the first. 8I
will cleanse them from all their iniquity by which they
have sinned against Me, and I will pardon all their iniquities by which they have sinned and by which they
have transgressed against Me. 9Then it shall be to Me
a name of joy, a praise, and an honor before all nations of the earth, who shall hear all the good that I do
to them; they shall fear and tremble for all the goodness and all the prosperity that I provide for it.'
10"Thus says the LORD: 'Again there shall be heard
in this place—of which you say, "It *is* desolate, without man and without beast"—in the cities of Judah,
in the streets of Jerusalem that are desolate, without
man and without inhabitant and without beast, 11the
voice of joy and the voice of gladness, the voice of the
bridegroom and the voice of the bride, the voice of
those who will say:

"Praise the LORD of hosts,
For the LORD *is* good,
For His mercy *endures* forever"—

and of those *who will* bring the sacrifice of praise into
the house of the LORD. For I will cause the captives of
the land to return as at the first,' says the LORD.
12"Thus says the LORD of hosts: 'In this place which
is desolate, without man and without beast, and in all
its cities, there shall again be a dwelling place of shepherds causing *their* flocks to lie down. 13In the cities of
the mountains, in the cities of the lowland, in the
cities of the South, in the land of Benjamin, in the
places around Jerusalem, and in the cities of Judah,
the flocks shall again pass under the hands of him
who counts *them*,' says the LORD.
14'Behold, the days are coming,' says the LORD, 'that
I will perform that good thing which I have promised
to the house of Israel and to the house of Judah:

15 'In those days and at that time
I will cause to grow up to David
A Branch of righteousness;
He shall execute judgment and righteousness
in the earth.
16 In those days Judah will be saved,
And Jerusalem will dwell safely.
And this *is the name* by which she will be called:

THE LORD OUR RIGHTEOUSNESS.'[e]

17"For thus says the LORD: 'David shall never lack a
man to sit on the throne of the house of Israel; 18nor
shall the priests, the Levites, lack a man to offer burnt
offerings before Me, to kindle grain offerings, and to
sacrifice continually.' "

The Permanence of God's Covenant

19And the word of the LORD came to Jeremiah, saying, 20"Thus says the LORD: 'If you can break My
covenant with the day and My covenant with the
night, so that there will not be day and night in their
season, 21then My covenant may also be broken with
David My servant, so that he shall not have a son to
reign on his throne, and with the Levites, the priests,
My ministers. 22As the host of heaven cannot be numbered, nor the sand of the sea measured, so will I multiply the descendants of David My servant and the
Levites who minister to Me.' "
23Moreover the word of the LORD came to Jeremiah,
saying, 24"Have you not considered what these people
have spoken, saying, 'The two families which the LORD
has chosen, He has also cast them off'? Thus they
have despised My people, as if they should no more
be a nation before them.
25"Thus says the LORD: 'If My covenant *is* not with day
and night, *and if* I have not appointed the ordinances
of heaven and earth, 26then I will cast away the descendants of Jacob and David My servant, *so* that I
will not take *any* of his descendants *to be* rulers over
the descendants of Abraham, Isaac, and Jacob. For I

33:4 [c] Compare Isaiah 22:10
33:5 [d] Compare 2 Kings 23:14
33:16 [e] Compare 23:5, 6

will cause their captives to return, and will have mercy on them.’ ”

Zedekiah Warned by God

34 The word which came to Jeremiah from the LORD, when Nebuchadnezzar king of Babylon and all his army, all the kingdoms of the
earth under his dominion, and all the people, fought against Jerusalem and
all its cities, saying, 2“Thus says the LORD, the God of Israel: ‘Go and speak
to Zedekiah king of Judah and tell him, “Thus says the LORD: ‘Behold, I will
give this city into the hand of the king of Babylon, and he shall burn it with
fire. 3And you shall not escape from his hand, but shall surely be taken and
delivered into his hand; your eyes shall see the eyes of the king of Babylon,
he shall speak with you face to face,[f] and you shall go to Babylon.’ ” ’ 4Yet
hear the word of the LORD, O Zedekiah king of Judah! Thus says the LORD
concerning you: ‘You shall not die by the sword. 5You shall die in peace; as
in the ceremonies of your fathers, the former kings who were before you,
so they shall burn incense for you and lament for you, *saying,* “Alas, lord!”
For I have pronounced the word, says the LORD.’ ”
6Then Jeremiah the prophet spoke all these words to Zedekiah king of
Judah in Jerusalem, 7when the king of Babylon’s army fought against Jerusalem and all the cities of Judah that were left, against Lachish and
Azekah; for *only* these fortified cities remained of the cities of Judah.

Treacherous Treatment of Slaves

8*This is* the word that came to Jeremiah from the LORD, after King Zedekiah had made a covenant with all the people who *were* at Jerusalem to
proclaim liberty to them: 9that every man should set free his male and female slave—a Hebrew man or woman—that no one should keep a Jewish brother in bondage. 10Now when all the princes and all the people, who
had entered into the covenant, heard that everyone should set free his
male and female slaves, that no one should keep them in bondage anymore, they obeyed and let *them* go. 11But afterward they changed their
minds and made the male and female slaves return, whom they had set
free, and brought them into subjection as male and female slaves.
12Therefore the word of the LORD came to Jeremiah from the LORD, saying, 13“Thus says the LORD, the God of Israel: ‘I made a covenant with your
fathers in the day that I brought them out of the land of Egypt, out of the
house of bondage, saying, 14“At the end of seven years let every man set
free his Hebrew brother, who has been sold to him; and when he has
served you six years, you shall let him go free from you.” But your fathers
did not obey Me nor incline their ear. 15Then you recently turned and did
what was right in My sight—every man proclaiming liberty to his neighbor; and you made a covenant before Me in the house which is called by
My name. 16Then you turned around and profaned My name, and every
one of you brought back his male and female slaves, whom you had set at
liberty, at their pleasure, and brought them back into subjection, to be
your male and female slaves.’
17“Therefore thus says the LORD: ‘You have not obeyed Me in proclaiming
liberty, every one to his brother and every one to his neighbor. Behold, I
proclaim liberty to you,’ says the LORD—‘to the sword, to pestilence, and

34:3 *f* Literally *mouth to mouth*

LIFE LESSON

Jeremiah 34:1–35:19

SITUATION Nebuchadnezzar attacked Jerusalem with a huge army. King Zedekiah of Judah fought for survival.

OBSERVATION Keep the commandments of God. Listen and obey him. Obedience brings blessing.

INSPIRATION We don’t consciously and deliberately disobey God—we simply don’t listen to Him. God has given His commands to us, but we pay no attention to them—not because of willful disobedience, but because we do not truly love and respect Him.

We show how little love we have for God by preferring to listen to His servants rather that to Him. We like to listen to personal testimonies, but we don’t want God Himself to speak to us. Why are we so terrified for God to speak to us? It is because we know that when God speaks we must either do what He asks or tell Him we will not obey. But if it is simply one of God’s servants speaking to us, we feel obedience is optional, not imperative. We respond by saying, “Well, that’s only your own idea, even though I don’t deny that what you said is probably God’s truth.”

Am I constantly humiliating God by ignoring Him, while He lovingly continues to treat me as His child? Once I finally do hear Him, the humiliation I have heaped on Him returns to me. My response then becomes, “Lord, why was I so insensitive and obstinate?” This is always the result once we hear God. But our real delight in finally hearing Him is tempered with the shame we feel for having taken so long to do so.

(From *My Utmost for His Highest* by Oswald Chambers)

APPLICATION When was the last time you told the story of how God saved you and began to mold your character? Have lunch with someone you don’t know very well and ask to hear that person’s story—then tell yours.

EXPLORATION Listening—Isaiah 30:21; 51:7; Hebrews 3:7-11.

to famine! And I will deliver you to trouble among all
the kingdoms of the earth. 18And I will give the men
who have transgressed My covenant, who have not
performed the words of the covenant which they made
before Me, when they cut the calf in two and passed
between the parts of it— 19the princes of Judah, the
princes of Jerusalem, the eunuchs, the priests, and all
the people of the land who passed between the parts
of the calf— 20I will give them into the hand of their
enemies and into the hand of those who seek their
life. Their dead bodies shall be for meat for the birds
of the heaven and the beasts of the earth. 21And I will
give Zedekiah king of Judah and his princes into the
hand of their enemies, into the hand of those who seek
their life, and into the hand of the king of Babylon's
army which has gone back from you. 22Behold, I will
command,' says the LORD, 'and cause them to return
to this city. They will fight against it and take it and
burn it with fire; and I will make the cities of Judah a
desolation without inhabitant.' "

The Obedient Rechabites

35 The word which came to Jeremiah from the LORD
in the days of Jehoiakim the son of Josiah, king of
Judah, saying, 2"Go to the house of the Rechabites, speak
to them, and bring them into the house of the LORD, into
one of the chambers, and give them wine to drink."
3Then I took Jaazaniah the son of Jeremiah, the son
of Habazziniah, his brothers and all his sons, and the
whole house of the Rechabites, 4and I brought them into
the house of the LORD, into the chamber of the sons of
Hanan the son of Igdaliah, a man of God, which *was* by
the chamber of the princes, above the chamber of Maaseiah the son of Shallum, the keeper of the door. 5Then
I set before the sons of the house of the Rechabites bowls
full of wine, and cups; and I said to them, "Drink wine."
6But they said, "We will drink no wine, for Jonadab
the son of Rechab, our father, commanded us, saying,
'You shall drink no wine, you nor your sons, forever.
7You shall not build a house, sow seed, plant a vineyard,
nor have *any of these;* but all your days you shall dwell
in tents, that you may live many days in the land where
you are sojourners.' 8Thus we have obeyed the voice of
Jonadab the son of Rechab, our father, in all that he
charged us, to drink no wine all our days, we, our wives,
our sons, or our daughters, 9nor to build ourselves
houses to dwell in; nor do we have vineyard, field, or
seed. 10But we have dwelt in tents, and have obeyed and
done according to all that Jonadab our father commanded us. 11But it came to pass, when Nebuchadnezzar king of Babylon came up into the land, that we
said, 'Come, let us go to Jerusalem for fear of the army
of the Chaldeans and for fear of the army of the Syrians.' So we dwell at Jerusalem."
12Then came the word of the LORD to Jeremiah, saying, 13"Thus says the LORD of hosts, the God of Israel:
'Go and tell the men of Judah and the inhabitants of
Jerusalem, "Will you not receive instruction to obey
My words?" says the LORD. 14"The words of Jonadab
the son of Rechab, which he commanded his sons,
not to drink wine, are performed; for to this day they
drink none, and obey their father's commandment.
But although I have spoken to you, rising early and
speaking, you did not obey Me. 15I have also sent to
you all My servants the prophets, rising up early and
sending *them,* saying, 'Turn now everyone from his
evil way, amend your doings, and do not go after other
gods to serve them; then you will dwell in the land
which I have given you and your fathers.' But you have
not inclined your ear, nor obeyed Me. 16Surely the sons
of Jonadab the son of Rechab have performed the
commandment of their father, which he commanded
them, but this people has not obeyed Me." '
17"Therefore thus says the LORD God of hosts, the
God of Israel: 'Behold, I will bring on Judah and on all
the inhabitants of Jerusalem all the doom that I have
pronounced against them; because I have spoken to
them but they have not heard, and I have called to
them but they have not answered.' "
18And Jeremiah said to the house of the Rechabites,
"Thus says the LORD of hosts, the God of Israel: 'Because
you have obeyed the commandment of Jonadab your
father, and kept all his precepts and done according to all
that he commanded you, 19therefore thus says the LORD
of hosts, the God of Israel: "Jonadab the son of Rechab
shall not lack a man to stand before Me forever." ' "

The Scroll Read in the Temple

36 Now it came to pass in the fourth year of Jehoiakim the son of Josiah, king of Judah, *that* this
word came to Jeremiah from the LORD, saying: 2"Take a
scroll of a book and write on it all the words that I have
spoken to you against Israel, against Judah, and against
all the nations, from the day I spoke to you, from the days
of Josiah even to this day. 3It may be that the house of
Judah will hear all the adversities which I purpose to
bring upon them, that everyone may turn from his evil
way, that I may forgive their iniquity and their sin."
4Then Jeremiah called Baruch the son of Neriah;
and Baruch wrote on a scroll of a book, at the instruction of Jeremiah,[g] all the words of the LORD which He
had spoken to him. 5And Jeremiah commanded

Baruch, saying, "I *am* confined, I cannot go into the house of the LORD.
6You go, therefore, and read from the scroll which you have written at my
instruction,[h] the words of the LORD, in the hearing of the people in the
LORD's house on the day of fasting. And you shall also read them in the
hearing of all Judah who come from their cities. 7It may be that they will
present their supplication before the LORD, and everyone will turn from
his evil way. For great *is* the anger and the fury that the LORD has pronounced against this people." 8And Baruch the son of Neriah did according to all that Jeremiah the prophet commanded him, reading from the
book the words of the LORD in the LORD's house.

9Now it came to pass in the fifth year of Jehoiakim the son of Josiah,
king of Judah, in the ninth month, *that* they proclaimed a fast before the
LORD to all the people in Jerusalem, and to all the people who came from
the cities of Judah to Jerusalem. 10Then Baruch read from the book the
words of Jeremiah in the house of the LORD, in the chamber of Gemariah
the son of Shaphan the scribe, in the upper court at the entry of the New
Gate of the LORD's house, in the hearing of all the people.

The Scroll Read in the Palace

11When Michaiah the son of Gemariah, the son of Shaphan, heard all the
words of the LORD from the book, 12he then went down to the king's house,
into the scribe's chamber; and there all the princes were sitting—Elishama
the scribe, Delaiah the son of Shemaiah, Elnathan the son of Achbor, Gemariah the son of Shaphan, Zedekiah the son of Hananiah, and all the princes.
13Then Michaiah declared to them all the words that he had heard when
Baruch read the book in the hearing of the people. 14Therefore all the princes
sent Jehudi the son of Nethaniah, the son of Shelemiah, the son of Cushi,
to Baruch, saying, "Take in your hand the scroll from which you have read
in the hearing of the people, and come." So Baruch the son of Neriah took
the scroll in his hand and came to them. 15And they said to him, "Sit down
now, and read it in our hearing." So Baruch read *it* in their hearing.

16Now it happened, when they had heard all the words, that they looked
in fear from one to another, and said to Baruch, "We will surely tell the king
of all these words." 17And they asked Baruch, saying, "Tell us now, how did
you write all these words—at his instruction?"[i]

18So Baruch answered them, "He proclaimed with his mouth all these
words to me, and I wrote *them* with ink in the book."

19Then the princes said to Baruch, "Go and hide, you and Jeremiah; and
let no one know where you are."

The King Destroys Jeremiah's Scroll

20And they went to the king, into the court; but they stored the scroll in
the chamber of Elishama the scribe, and told all the words in the hearing
of the king. 21So the king sent Jehudi to bring the scroll, and he took it from
Elishama the scribe's chamber. And Jehudi read it in the hearing of the
king and in the hearing of all the princes who stood beside the king. 22Now
the king was sitting in the winter house in the ninth month, with *a fire*
burning on the hearth before him. 23And it happened, when Jehudi had

36:4 [g] Literally *from Jeremiah's mouth*
36:6 [h] Literally *from my mouth*
36:17 [i] Literally *with his mouth*

LIFE LESSON

Jeremiah 36:1-32

SITUATION When he heard Jeremiah's prophecy, King Jehoiakim instructed his aide to burn Jeremiah's message. The king also issued a decree to arrest Jeremiah and Baruch the scribe, but God aided them.

OBSERVATION Pride blinds people and can endanger a person's spiritual life.

INSPIRATION Thousands of years before Jesus was called the Lamb of God, God promised forgiveness.

"Someday," God confided to Jeremiah, "these people will be my people and I will be their God."

"And someday," wrote David, "the mistakes of men will be tossed, not under a rug, or behind the sofa, but far, far away. As far as the east is from the west."

And do you know what? That someday came. On a garbage heap outside of Jerusalem.

Someday the almighty God, who has every right to make me burn forever, will look past my apathy, point to the cross and invite me to come home . . . forgiven . . . forever.

(From *On the Anvil* by Max Lucado)

APPLICATION Do you know someone who has asked God for forgiveness, yet still dwells in guilt? Write that person a note with a fitting Scripture verse and a word of encouragement that God forgives first, then he forgets.

EXPLORATION God Provided a Way—Psalm 68:18; Isaiah 63:9; Titus 3:5; 1 Peter 1:23.

LIFE LESSON

Jeremiah 37:1–38:28

SITUATION When Jeremiah prophesied against the king, the king imprisoned him on the false charge of treason. After a lengthy stay in prison, King Zedekiah released Jeremiah.

OBSERVATION The world hates to hear what God says. As a result, unbelievers will sometimes accuse God's servants falsely.

INSPIRATION Honestly—have you said, "Thanks, Lord, for this test"? Have you finally stopped struggling and expressed to Him how much you appreciate His loving sovereignty over your life? I submit that one of the reasons our suffering is prolonged is that we take so long saying "Thank you Lord" with an attitude of genuine appreciation.

How unfinished and rebellious and proud and unconcerned we would be without suffering! Here are two statements on suffering I heard years ago and shall never forget:

Pain plants the flag of reality in the fortress of a rebel heart.

When God wants to do an impossible task, He takes an impossible individual—and crushes him.

May these things encourage you the next time God heats up the furnace!

(From *Come Before Winter* by Charles Swindoll)

APPLICATION While you are free to come and go, some people are imprisoned behind bars. Most deserve to be there. But we all deserve punishment for our sins, yet Christ forgave us through his death on the cross. Show Christ's love by becoming a pen-pal to a prisoner. By your speech and action, share God's love.

EXPLORATION Unjust Suffering—Philippians 1:29; James 5:10; I Peter 5:10.

read three or four columns, *that the king* cut it with the scribe's knife and
cast *it* into the fire that *was* on the hearth, until all the scroll was consumed
in the fire that *was* on the hearth. [24]Yet they were not afraid, nor did they
tear their garments, the king nor any of his servants who heard all these
words. [25]Nevertheless Elnathan, Delaiah, and Gemariah implored the king
not to burn the scroll; but he would not listen to them. [26]And the king commanded Jerahmeel the king's[j] son, Seraiah the son of Azriel, and Shelemiah
the son of Abdeel, to seize Baruch the scribe and Jeremiah the prophet,
but the LORD hid them.

Jeremiah Rewrites the Scroll

[27]Now after the king had burned the scroll with the words which Baruch
had written at the instruction of Jeremiah,[k] the word of the LORD came to
Jeremiah, saying: [28]"Take yet another scroll, and write on it all the former
words that were in the first scroll which Jehoiakim the king of Judah has
burned. [29]And you shall say to Jehoiakim king of Judah, 'Thus says the
LORD: "You have burned this scroll, saying, 'Why have you written in it that
the king of Babylon will certainly come and destroy this land, and cause
man and beast to cease from here?' " [30]Therefore thus says the LORD concerning Jehoiakim king of Judah: "He shall have no one to sit on the
throne of David, and his dead body shall be cast out to the heat of the day
and the frost of the night. [31]I will punish him, his family, and his servants
for their iniquity; and I will bring on them, on the inhabitants of Jerusalem, and on the men of Judah all the doom that I have pronounced against
them; but they did not heed." ' "

[32]Then Jeremiah took another scroll and gave it to Baruch the scribe, the
son of Neriah, who wrote on it at the instruction of Jeremiah[l] all the words
of the book which Jehoiakim king of Judah had burned in the fire. And besides, there were added to them many similar words.

Zedekiah's Vain Hope

37 Now King Zedekiah the son of Josiah reigned instead of Coniah the son
of Jehoiakim, whom Nebuchadnezzar king of Babylon made king in
the land of Judah. [2]But neither he nor his servants nor the people of the land
gave heed to the words of the LORD which He spoke by the prophet Jeremiah.

[3]And Zedekiah the king sent Jehucal the son of Shelemiah, and Zephaniah the son of Maaseiah, the priest, to the prophet Jeremiah, saying, "Pray
now to the LORD our God for us." [4]Now Jeremiah was coming and going
among the people, for they had not *yet* put him in prison. [5]Then Pharaoh's
army came up from Egypt; and when the Chaldeans who were besieging
Jerusalem heard news of them, they departed from Jerusalem.

[6]Then the word of the LORD came to the prophet Jeremiah, saying,
[7]"Thus says the LORD, the God of Israel, 'Thus you shall say to the king of
Judah, who sent you to Me to inquire of Me: "Behold, Pharaoh's army
which has come up to help you will return to Egypt, to their own land.
[8]And the Chaldeans shall come back and fight against this city, and take it
and burn it with fire." ' [9]Thus says the LORD: 'Do not deceive yourselves,
saying, "The Chaldeans will surely depart from us," for they will not de-

36:26 [j] Hebrew *Hammelech*
36:27 [k] Literally *from Jeremiah's mouth*
36:32 [l] Literally *from Jeremiah's mouth*

part. 10For though you had defeated the whole army of
the Chaldeans who fight against you, and there remained *only* wounded men among them, they would
rise up, every man in his tent, and burn the city with
fire.' "

Jeremiah Imprisoned

11And it happened, when the army of the Chaldeans
left *the siege* of Jerusalem for fear of Pharaoh's army,
12that Jeremiah went out of Jerusalem to go into the
land of Benjamin to claim his property there among
the people. 13And when he was in the Gate of Benjamin, a captain of the guard *was* there whose name
was Irijah the son of Shelemiah, the son of Hananiah;
and he seized Jeremiah the prophet, saying, "You are
defecting to the Chaldeans!"

14Then Jeremiah said, "False! I am not defecting to
the Chaldeans." But he did not listen to him.

So Irijah seized Jeremiah and brought him to the
princes. 15Therefore the princes were angry with
Jeremiah, and they struck him and put him in prison
in the house of Jonathan the scribe. For they had
made that the prison.

16When Jeremiah entered the dungeon and the
cells, and Jeremiah had remained there many days,
17then Zedekiah the king sent and took him *out*. The
king asked him secretly in his house, and said, "Is
there *any* word from the LORD?"

And Jeremiah said, "There is." Then he said, "You
shall be delivered into the hand of the king of Babylon!"

18Moreover Jeremiah said to King Zedekiah, "What
offense have I committed against you, against your
servants, or against this people, that you have put me
in prison? 19Where now *are* your prophets who prophesied to you, saying, 'The king of Babylon will not come
against you or against this land'? 20Therefore please
hear now, O my lord the king. Please, let my petition
be accepted before you, and do not make me return to
the house of Jonathan the scribe, lest I die there."

21Then Zedekiah the king commanded that they
should commit Jeremiah to the court of the prison, and
that they should give him daily a piece of bread from
the bakers' street, until all the bread in the city was gone.
Thus Jeremiah remained in the court of the prison.

Jeremiah in the Dungeon

38 Now Shephatiah the son of Mattan, Gedaliah
the son of Pashhur, Jucal[m] the son of Shelemiah,
and Pashhur the son of Malchiah heard the words that
Jeremiah had spoken to all the people, saying, 2"Thus
says the LORD: 'He who remains in this city shall die by
the sword, by famine, and by pestilence; but he who
goes over to the Chaldeans shall live; his life shall be as
a prize to him, and he shall live.'[n] 3Thus says the LORD:
'This city shall surely be given into the hand of the
king of Babylon's army, which shall take it.' "

4Therefore the princes said to the king, "Please, let
this man be put to death, for thus he weakens the
hands of the men of war who remain in this city, and
the hands of all the people, by speaking such words to
them. For this man does not seek the welfare of this
people, but their harm."

5Then Zedekiah the king said, "Look, he *is* in your
hand. For the king can *do* nothing against you." 6So
they took Jeremiah and cast him into the dungeon of
Malchiah the king's[o] son, which *was* in the court of the
prison, and they let Jeremiah down with ropes. And
in the dungeon *there was* no water, but mire. So
Jeremiah sank in the mire.

7Now Ebed-Melech the Ethiopian, one of the eunuchs,
who was in the king's house, heard that they had put
Jeremiah in the dungeon. When the king was sitting at
the Gate of Benjamin, 8Ebed-Melech went out of the
king's house and spoke to the king, saying: 9"My lord the
king, these men have done evil in all that they have done
to Jeremiah the prophet, whom they have cast into the
dungeon, and he is likely to die from hunger in the place
where he is. For *there is* no more bread in the city." 10Then
the king commanded Ebed-Melech the Ethiopian, saying, "Take from here thirty men with you, and lift Jeremiah the prophet out of the dungeon before he dies."
11So Ebed-Melech took the men with him and went into
the house of the king under the treasury, and took from
there old clothes and old rags, and let them down by
ropes into the dungeon to Jeremiah. 12Then Ebed-Melech
the Ethiopian said to Jeremiah, "Please put these old
clothes and rags under your armpits, under the ropes."
And Jeremiah did so. 13So they pulled Jeremiah up
with ropes and lifted him out of the dungeon. And
Jeremiah remained in the court of the prison.

Zedekiah's Fears and Jeremiah's Advice

14Then Zedekiah the king sent and had Jeremiah
the prophet brought to him at the third entrance of the
house of the LORD. And the king said to Jeremiah, "I will
ask you something. Hide nothing from me."

38:1 *m* Same as *Jehucal* (compare 37:3)
38:2 *n* Compare 21:9
38:6 *o* Hebrew *Hammelech*

LIFE LESSON

Jeremiah 39:1-18

SITUATION After Zedekiah had ruled Judah for eleven years, the Babylonians captured Jerusalem. The Babylonians deported the rich and powerful from the conquered land and left the poor behind.

OBSERVATION Servants of God who are called to proclaim an unpopular message will be protected in difficulty.

INSPIRATION An average view of the Christian life is that it means deliverance from trouble. It is deliverance in trouble, which is very different. . . . If you are a child of God, there certainly will be troubles to meet, but Jesus says do not be surprised when they come. . . . God does not give us overcoming life: He gives us life as we overcome. The strain is the strength. If there is no strain, there is no strength. Are you asking God to give you life and liberty and joy? He cannot, unless you will accept the strain. Immediately, when you face the strain, you will get the strength. Overcome your own timidity and take the step, and God will give you to eat of the tree of life and you will get nourishment. If you spend yourself physically, you become exhausted; but spend yourself spiritually, and you get more strength. God never gives strength for tomorrow, or for the next hour, but only for the strain of the minute. The temptation is to face difficulties from a common-sense standpoint. The saint is hilarious when he is crushed with difficulties because the thing is so ludicrously impossible to anyone but God.

(From *My Utmost for His Highest* by Oswald Chambers)

APPLICATION God promises to protect us, but he also calls us to proclaim his message. Do you break the law to proclaim God's message? Are you militant when you stand up for what you believe God's standard to be? Be careful that opponents to your cause are not needlessly offended by your actions.

EXPLORATION Protection—Genesis 15:1; Job 5:11; Psalm 9:9; 16:5; 91:1-4; Proverbs 3:25-26; 2 Thessalonians 3:3; Hebrews 13:6.

15Jeremiah said to Zedekiah, "If I declare *it* to you, will you not surely
put me to death? And if I give you advice, you will not listen to me."
16So Zedekiah the king swore secretly to Jeremiah, saying, "*As* the LORD
lives, who made our very souls, I will not put you to death, nor will I give
you into the hand of these men who seek your life."
17Then Jeremiah said to Zedekiah, "Thus says the LORD, the God of hosts,
the God of Israel: 'If you surely surrender to the king of Babylon's princes,
then your soul shall live; this city shall not be burned with fire, and you and
your house shall live. 18But if you do not surrender to the king of Babylon's
princes, then this city shall be given into the hand of the Chaldeans; they
shall burn it with fire, and you shall not escape from their hand.'"
19And Zedekiah the king said to Jeremiah, "I am afraid of the Jews who
have defected to the Chaldeans, lest they deliver me into their hand, and
they abuse me."
20But Jeremiah said, "They shall not deliver *you.* Please, obey the voice of the
LORD which I speak to you. So it shall be well with you, and your soul shall live.
21But if you refuse to surrender, this *is* the word that the LORD has shown me:
22'Now behold, all the women who are left in the king of Judah's house *shall
be* surrendered to the king of Babylon's princes, and those *women* shall say:

"Your close friends have set upon you
And prevailed against you;
Your feet have sunk in the mire,
And they have turned away again."

23'So they shall surrender all your wives and children to the Chaldeans.
You shall not escape from their hand, but shall be taken by the hand of the
king of Babylon. And you shall cause this city to be burned with fire.'"
24Then Zedekiah said to Jeremiah, "Let no one know of these words,
and you shall not die. 25But if the princes hear that I have talked with you,
and they come to you and say to you, 'Declare to us now what you have
said to the king, and also what the king said to you; do not hide *it* from us,
and we will not put you to death,' 26then you shall say to them, 'I presented
my request before the king, that he would not make me return to Jonathan's house to die there.'"
27Then all the princes came to Jeremiah and asked him. And he told
them according to all these words that the king had commanded. So they
stopped speaking with him, for the conversation had not been heard.
28Now Jeremiah remained in the court of the prison until the day that Jerusalem was taken. And he was *there* when Jerusalem was taken.

The Fall of Jerusalem

39 In the ninth year of Zedekiah king of Judah, in the tenth month,
Nebuchadnezzar king of Babylon and all his army came against Jerusalem, and besieged it. 2In the eleventh year of Zedekiah, in the fourth
month, on the ninth *day* of the month, the city was penetrated.
3Then all the princes of the king of Babylon came in and sat in the Middle
Gate: Nergal-Sharezer, Samgar-Nebo, Sarsechim, Rabsaris,[p] Nergal-
Sarezer, Rabmag,[q] with the rest of the princes of the king of Babylon.
4So it was, when Zedekiah the king of Judah and all the men of war saw
them, that they fled and went out of the city by night, by way of the king's

39:3 [p] A title, probably *Chief Officer;* also verse 13 [q] A title, probably *Troop Commander;* also verse 13

garden, by the gate between the two walls. And he
went out by way of the plain.[r] 5But the Chaldean army
pursued them and overtook Zedekiah in the plains of
Jericho. And when they had captured him, they
brought him up to Nebuchadnezzar king of Babylon,
to Riblah in the land of Hamath, where he pronounced judgment on him. 6Then the king of Babylon
killed the sons of Zedekiah before his eyes in Riblah;
the king of Babylon also killed all the nobles of Judah.
7Moreover he put out Zedekiah's eyes, and bound
him with bronze fetters to carry him off to Babylon.
8And the Chaldeans burned the king's house and the
houses of the people with fire, and broke down the
walls of Jerusalem. 9Then Nebuzaradan the captain of
the guard carried away captive to Babylon the remnant of the people who remained in the city and those
who defected to him, with the rest of the people who
remained. 10But Nebuzaradan the captain of the
guard left in the land of Judah the poor people, who
had nothing, and gave them vineyards and fields at
the same time.

Jeremiah Goes Free

11Now Nebuchadnezzar king of Babylon gave charge
concerning Jeremiah to Nebuzaradan the captain of
the guard, saying, 12"Take him and look after him, and
do him no harm; but do to him just as he says to you."
13So Nebuzaradan the captain of the guard sent
Nebushasban, Rabsaris, Nergal-Sharezer, Rabmag,
and all the king of Babylon's chief officers; 14then they
sent *someone* to take Jeremiah from the court of the
prison, and committed him to Gedaliah the son of
Ahikam, the son of Shaphan, that he should take him
home. So he dwelt among the people.

15Meanwhile the word of the LORD had come to
Jeremiah while he was shut up in the court of the prison,
saying, 16"Go and speak to Ebed-Melech the Ethiopian, saying, 'Thus says the LORD of hosts, the God of
Israel: "Behold, I will bring My words upon this city
for adversity and not for good, and they shall be *per-*
formed in that day before you. 17But I will deliver you
in that day," says the LORD, "and you shall not be given
into the hand of the men of whom you *are* afraid. 18For
I will surely deliver you, and you shall not fall by the
sword; but your life shall be as a prize to you, because
you have put your trust in Me," says the LORD.' "

Jeremiah with Gedaliah the Governor

40 The word that came to Jeremiah from the
LORD after Nebuzaradan the captain of the
guard had let him go from Ramah, when he had taken
him bound in chains among all who were carried
away captive from Jerusalem and Judah, who were
carried away captive to Babylon.

2And the captain of the guard took Jeremiah and
said to him: "The LORD your God has pronounced this
doom on this place. 3Now the LORD has brought *it*,
and has done just as He said. Because you *people* have
sinned against the LORD, and not obeyed His voice,
therefore this thing has come upon you. 4And now
look, I free you this day from the chains that *were* on
your hand. If it seems good to you to come with me to
Babylon, come, and I will look after you. But if it seems
wrong for you to come with me to Babylon, remain
here. See, all the land *is* before you; wherever it seems
good and convenient for you to go, go there."

5Now while Jeremiah had not yet gone back, *Nebu-*
zaradan said, "Go back to Gedaliah the son of Ahikam,
the son of Shaphan, whom the king of Babylon has
made governor over the cities of Judah, and dwell
with him among the people. Or go wherever it seems
convenient for you to go." So the captain of the guard
gave him rations and a gift and let him go. 6Then
Jeremiah went to Gedaliah the son of Ahikam, to
Mizpah, and dwelt with him among the people who
were left in the land.

7And when all the captains of the armies who *were*
in the fields, they and their men, heard that the king of
Babylon had made Gedaliah the son of Ahikam governor in the land, and had committed to him men,
women, children, and the poorest of the land who
had not been carried away captive to Babylon, 8then
they came to Gedaliah at Mizpah—Ishmael the son of
Nethaniah, Johanan and Jonathan the sons of
Kareah, Seraiah the son of Tanhumeth, the sons of
Ephai the Netophathite, and Jezaniah[s] the son of a
Maachathite, they and their men. 9And Gedaliah the son
of Ahikam, the son of Shaphan, took an oath before
them and their men, saying, "Do not be afraid to serve
the Chaldeans. Dwell in the land and serve the king of
Babylon, and it shall be well with you. 10As for me, I
will indeed dwell at Mizpah and serve the Chaldeans
who come to us. But you, gather wine and summer
fruit and oil, put *them* in your vessels, and dwell in
your cities that you have taken." 11Likewise, when all
the Jews who *were* in Moab, among the Ammonites,

39:4 [r] Or *the Arabah,* that is, the Jordan Valley
40:8 [s] Spelled *Jaazaniah* in 2 Kings 25:23

in Edom, and who *were* in all the countries, heard that
the king of Babylon had left a remnant of Judah, and
that he had set over them Gedaliah the son of Ahikam,
the son of Shaphan, 12then all the Jews returned out of
all places where they had been driven, and came to
the land of Judah, to Gedaliah at Mizpah, and gathered wine and summer fruit in abundance.

13Moreover Johanan the son of Kareah and all the
captains of the forces that *were* in the fields came to
Gedaliah at Mizpah, 14and said to him, "Do you certainly know that Baalis the king of the Ammonites has
sent Ishmael the son of Nethaniah to murder you?"
But Gedaliah the son of Ahikam did not believe them.
15Then Johanan the son of Kareah spoke secretly to
Gedaliah in Mizpah, saying, "Let me go, please, and I
will kill Ishmael the son of Nethaniah, and no one will
know *it*. Why should he murder you, so that all the
Jews who are gathered to you would be scattered, and
the remnant in Judah perish?"

16But Gedaliah the son of Ahikam said to Johanan
the son of Kareah, "You shall not do this thing, for you
speak falsely concerning Ishmael."

Insurrection Against Gedaliah

41 Now it came to pass in the seventh month *that*
Ishmael the son of Nethaniah, the son of
Elishama, of the royal family and of the officers of the
king, came with ten men to Gedaliah the son of
Ahikam, at Mizpah. And there they ate bread together
in Mizpah. 2Then Ishmael the son of Nethaniah, and
the ten men who were with him, arose and struck
Gedaliah the son of Ahikam, the son of Shaphan, with
the sword, and killed him whom the king of Babylon
had made governor over the land. 3Ishmael also
struck down all the Jews who were with him, *that is,*
with Gedaliah at Mizpah, and the Chaldeans who
were found there, the men of war.

4And it happened, on the second day after he had
killed Gedaliah, when as yet no one knew *it*, 5that certain men came from Shechem, from Shiloh, and from
Samaria, eighty men with their beards shaved and their
clothes torn, having cut themselves, with offerings
and incense in their hand, to bring *them* to the house
of the LORD. 6Now Ishmael the son of Nethaniah went
out from Mizpah to meet them, weeping as he went
along; and it happened as he met them that he said to
them, "Come to Gedaliah the son of Ahikam!" 7So it
was, when they came into the midst of the city, that
Ishmael the son of Nethaniah killed them *and cast*
them into the midst of a pit, he and the men who were
with him. 8But ten men were found among them who
said to Ishmael, "Do not kill us, for we have treasures of
wheat, barley, oil, and honey in the field." So he desisted
and did not kill them among their brethren. 9Now the
pit into which Ishmael had cast all the dead bodies of
the men whom he had slain, because of Gedaliah, *was*
the same one Asa the king had made for fear of
Baasha king of Israel. Ishmael the son of Nethaniah
filled it with *the* slain. 10Then Ishmael carried away
captive all the rest of the people who *were* in Mizpah,
the king's daughters and all the people who remained
in Mizpah, whom Nebuzaradan the captain of the
guard had committed to Gedaliah the son of Ahikam.
And Ishmael the son of Nethaniah carried them away
captive and departed to go over to the Ammonites.

11But when Johanan the son of Kareah and all the
captains of the forces that *were* with him heard of all
the evil that Ishmael the son of Nethaniah had done,
12they took all the men and went to fight with Ishmael
the son of Nethaniah; and they found him by the great
pool that *is* in Gibeon. 13So it was, when all the people
who *were* with Ishmael saw Johanan the son of
Kareah, and all the captains of the forces who *were*
with him, that they were glad. 14Then all the people
whom Ishmael had carried away captive from
Mizpah turned around and came back, and went to
Johanan the son of Kareah. 15But Ishmael the son of
Nethaniah escaped from Johanan with eight men and
went to the Ammonites.

16Then Johanan the son of Kareah, and all the captains of the forces that were with him, took from
Mizpah all the rest of the people whom he had recovered from Ishmael the son of Nethaniah after he had
murdered Gedaliah the son of Ahikam—the mighty
men of war and the women and the children and the
eunuchs, whom he had brought back from Gibeon.
17And they departed and dwelt in the habitation of
Chimham, which is near Bethlehem, as they went on
their way to Egypt, 18because of the Chaldeans; for
they were afraid of them, because Ishmael the son of
Nethaniah had murdered Gedaliah the son of
Ahikam, whom the king of Babylon had made governor in the land.

The Flight to Egypt Forbidden

42 Now all the captains of the forces, Johanan the
son of Kareah, Jezaniah the son of Hoshaiah,
and all the people, from the least to the greatest, came
near 2and said to Jeremiah the prophet, "Please, let
our petition be acceptable to you, and pray for us to
the LORD your God, for all this remnant (since we are
left *but* a few of many, as you can see), 3that the LORD

your God may show us the way in which we should
walk and the thing we should do."
[4]Then Jeremiah the prophet said to them, "I have
heard. Indeed, I will pray to the LORD your God according to your words, and it shall be, *that* whatever the
LORD answers you, I will declare *it* to you. I will keep
nothing back from you."
[5]So they said to Jeremiah, "Let the LORD be a true and
faithful witness between us, if we do not do according to
everything which the LORD your God sends us by you.
[6]Whether *it is* pleasing or displeasing, we will obey the
voice of the LORD our God to whom we send you, that it
may be well with us when we obey the voice of the LORD
our God."
[7]And it happened after ten days that the word of the
LORD came to Jeremiah. [8]Then he called Johanan the
son of Kareah, all the captains of the forces which
were with him, and all the people from the least even
to the greatest, [9]and said to them, "Thus says the
LORD, the God of Israel, to whom you sent me to present your petition before Him: [10]'If you will still remain in this land, then I will build you and not pull
you down, and I will plant you and not pluck *you* up.
For I relent concerning the disaster that I have
brought upon you. [11]Do not be afraid of the king of
Babylon, of whom you are afraid; do not be afraid of
him,' says the LORD, 'for I *am* with you, to save you and
deliver you from his hand. [12]And I will show you
mercy, that he may have mercy on you and cause you
to return to your own land.'
[13]"But if you say, 'We will not dwell in this land,' disobeying the voice of the LORD your God, [14]saying, 'No,
but we will go to the land of Egypt where we shall see
no war, nor hear the sound of the trumpet, nor be hungry for bread, and there we will dwell'— [15]Then hear
now the word of the LORD, O remnant of Judah! Thus
says the LORD of hosts, the God of Israel: 'If you wholly
set your faces to enter Egypt, and go to dwell there,
[16]then it shall be *that* the sword which you feared shall
overtake you there in the land of Egypt; the famine of
which you were afraid shall follow close after you
there *in* Egypt; and there you shall die. [17]So shall it be
with all the men who set their faces to go to Egypt to
dwell there. They shall die by the sword, by famine,
and by pestilence. And none of them shall remain or
escape from the disaster that I will bring upon them.'
[18]"For thus says the LORD of hosts, the God of Israel:
'As My anger and My fury have been poured out on the
inhabitants of Jerusalem, so will My fury be poured
out on you when you enter Egypt. And you shall be an
oath, an astonishment, a curse, and a reproach; and
you shall see this place no more.'
[19]"The LORD has said concerning you, O remnant of
Judah, 'Do not go to Egypt!' Know certainly that I
have admonished you this day. [20]For you were hypocrites in your hearts when you sent me to the LORD
your God, saying, 'Pray for us to the LORD our God,
and according to all that the LORD your God says, so
declare to us and we will do *it*.' [21]And I have this day
declared *it* to you, but you have not obeyed the voice
of the LORD your God, or anything which He has sent
you by me. [22]Now therefore, know certainly that you
shall die by the sword, by famine, and by pestilence in
the place where you desire to go to dwell."

Jeremiah Taken to Egypt

43 Now it happened, when Jeremiah had stopped
speaking to all the people all the words of the
LORD their God, for which the LORD their God had sent
him to them, all these words, [2]that Azariah the son of
Hoshaiah, Johanan the son of Kareah, and all the proud
men spoke, saying to Jeremiah, "You speak falsely! The
LORD our God has not sent you to say, 'Do not go to Egypt
to dwell there.' [3]But Baruch the son of Neriah has set you
against us, to deliver us into the hand of the Chaldeans,
that they may put us to death or carry us away captive
to Babylon." [4]So Johanan the son of Kareah, all the captains of the forces, and all the people would not obey the
voice of the LORD, to remain in the land of Judah. [5]But
Johanan the son of Kareah and all the captains of the
forces took all the remnant of Judah who had returned
to dwell in the land of Judah, from all nations where they
had been driven— [6]men, women, children, the king's
daughters, and every person whom Nebuzaradan the
captain of the guard had left with Gedaliah the son of
Ahikam, the son of Shaphan, and Jeremiah the
prophet and Baruch the son of Neriah. [7]So they went
to the land of Egypt, for they did not obey the voice of
the LORD. And they went as far as Tahpanhes.
[8]Then the word of the LORD came to Jeremiah in
Tahpanhes, saying, [9]"Take large stones in your hand,
and hide them in the sight of the men of Judah, in the
clay in the brick courtyard which *is* at the entrance to
Pharaoh's house in Tahpanhes; [10]and say to them,
'Thus says the LORD of hosts, the God of Israel: "Behold, I will send and bring Nebuchadnezzar the king
of Babylon, My servant, and will set his throne above
these stones that I have hidden. And he will spread his
royal pavilion over them. [11]When he comes, he shall
strike the land of Egypt *and deliver* to death *those
appointed* for death, and to captivity *those appointed*
for captivity, and to the sword *those appointed* for the

43:12 *t* Following Masoretic Text and Targum; Septuagint, Syriac, and Vulgate read *He*.

LIFE LESSON

Jeremiah 40:1–45:5

SITUATION Except for chapter 52:31-34, chapters 40—44 are chronologically the last writings in the book of Jeremiah. They recount the fall of Jerusalem (in 586 B.C.) and its aftermath of devastation.

OBSERVATION God can see the whole picture, while our vision is limited. Be careful not to disregard what he says.

INSPIRATION When I lived in the forest of Ecuador, I usually traveled on foot. Except for one occasion when I went off alone (and quickly learned what a bad mistake that was), I always had with me a guide who knew the way or new much better than I did how to find it. Trails often led through streams and rivers that we had to wade, but sometimes there was a log laid high above the water we had to cross.

I dreaded those logs and was always tempted to take the steep, hard way down the ravine and up the other side. But the Indians would say, "Just walk across, senorita," and over they would go, confident and lightfooted. I was barefoot as they were, but it was not enough. On the log, I could not keep from looking down at the river below. I knew I would slip. I had never been any good at balancing myself on the tops of walls and things, and the log looked impossible. So my guide would stretch out a hand, and the touch of it was all I needed. I stopped worrying about slipping. I stopped looking down at the river or even at the log, and looked at the guide, who held my hand with only the lightest touch. When I reached the other side, I realized that

sword. [12]I[t] will kindle a fire in the houses of the gods of Egypt, and he shall burn them and carry them away captive. And he shall array himself with the land of Egypt, as a shepherd puts on his garment, and he shall go out from there in peace. [13]He shall also break the sacred pillars of Beth Shemesh[u] that *are* in the land of Egypt; and the houses of the gods of the Egyptians he shall burn with fire." ' "

Israelites Will Be Punished in Egypt

44 The word that came to Jeremiah concerning all the Jews who dwell in the land of Egypt, who dwell at Migdol, at Tahpanhes, at Noph,[v] and in the country of Pathros, saying, [2]"Thus says the LORD of hosts, the God of Israel: 'You have seen all the calamity that I have brought on Jerusalem and on all the cities of Judah; and behold, this day they *are* a desolation, and no one dwells in them, [3]because of their wickedness which they have committed to provoke Me to anger, in that they went to burn incense *and* to serve other gods whom they did not know, they nor you nor your fathers. [4]However I have sent to you all My servants the prophets, rising early and sending *them,* saying, "Oh, do not do this abominable thing that I hate!" [5]But they did not listen or incline their ear to turn from their wickedness, to burn no incense to other gods. [6]So My fury and My anger were poured out and kindled in the cities of Judah and in the streets of Jerusalem; and they are wasted *and* desolate, as it is this day.'

[7]"Now therefore, thus says the LORD, the God of hosts, the God of Israel: 'Why do you commit *this* great evil against yourselves, to cut off from you man and woman, child and infant, out of Judah, leaving none to remain, [8]in that you provoke Me to wrath with the works of your hands, burning incense to other gods in the land of Egypt where you have gone to dwell, that you may cut yourselves off and be a curse and a reproach among all the nations of the earth? [9]Have you forgotten the wickedness of your fathers, the wickedness of the kings of Judah, the wickedness of their wives, your own wickedness, and the wickedness of your wives, which they committed in the land of Judah and in the streets of Jerusalem? [10]They have not been humbled, to this day, nor have they feared; they have not walked in My law or in My statutes that I set before you and your fathers.'

[11]"Therefore thus says the LORD of hosts, the God of Israel: 'Behold, I will set My face against you for catastrophe and for cutting off all Judah. [12]And I will take the remnant of Judah who have set their faces to go into the land of Egypt to dwell there, and they shall all be consumed *and* fall in the land of Egypt. They shall be consumed by the sword *and* by famine. They shall die, from the least to the greatest, by the sword and by famine; and they shall be an oath, an astonishment, a curse and a reproach! [13]For I will punish those who dwell in the land of Egypt, as I have punished Jerusalem, by the sword, by famine, and by pestilence, [14]so that none of the remnant of Judah who have gone into the land of Egypt to dwell there shall escape or survive, lest they return to the land of Judah, to which they desire to return and dwell. For none shall return except those who escape.' "

[15]Then all the men who knew that their wives had burned incense to other gods, with all the women who stood by, a great multitude, and all the people who dwelt in the land of Egypt, in Pathros, answered Jeremiah,

43:13 [u] Literally *House of the Sun,* ancient On; later called Heliopolis
44:1 [v] That is, ancient Memphis

saying: 16“*As for* the word that you have spoken to us in the name of the
LORD, we will not listen to you! 17But we will certainly do whatever has gone
out of our own mouth, to burn incense to the queen of heaven and pour out
drink offerings to her, as we have done, we and our fathers, our kings and
our princes, in the cities of Judah and in the streets of Jerusalem. For *then* we
had plenty of food, were well-off, and saw no trouble. 18But since we
stopped burning incense to the queen of heaven and pouring out drink offerings to her, we have lacked everything and have been consumed by the
sword and by famine.”

19*The women also said,* “And when we burned incense to the queen of
heaven and poured out drink offerings to her, did we make cakes for her,
to worship her, and pour out drink offerings to her without our husbands’
permission?”

20Then Jeremiah spoke to all the people—the men, the women, and all
the people who had given him *that* answer—saying: 21“The incense that
you burned in the cities of Judah and in the streets of Jerusalem, you and
your fathers, your kings and your princes, and the people of the land, did
not the LORD remember them, and did it *not* come into His mind? 22So the
LORD could no longer bear *it,* because of the evil of your doings *and* because
of the abominations which you committed. Therefore your land is a desolation, an astonishment, a curse, and without an inhabitant, as *it is* this
day. 23Because you have burned incense and because you have sinned
against the LORD, and have not obeyed the voice of the LORD or walked in
His law, in His statutes or in His testimonies, therefore this calamity has
happened to you, as *at* this day.”

24Moreover Jeremiah said to all the people and to all the women, “Hear
the word of the LORD, all Judah who *are* in the land of Egypt! 25Thus says
the LORD of hosts, the God of Israel, saying: ‘You and your wives have spoken
with your mouths and fulfilled with your hands, saying, “We will surely
keep our vows that we have made, to burn incense to the queen of heaven
and pour out drink offerings to her.” You will surely keep your vows and
perform your vows!’ 26Therefore hear the word of the LORD, all Judah who
dwell in the land of Egypt: ‘Behold, I have sworn by My great name,’ says
the LORD, ‘that My name shall no more be named in the mouth of any man
of Judah in all the land of Egypt, saying, “The Lord GOD lives.” 27Behold, I
will watch over them for adversity and not for good. And all the men of Judah
who *are* in the land of Egypt shall be consumed by the sword and by famine,
until there is an end to them. 28Yet a small number who escape the sword
shall return from the land of Egypt to the land of Judah; and all the remnant of Judah, who have gone to the land of Egypt to dwell there, shall
know whose words will stand, Mine or theirs. 29And this *shall be* a sign to
you,’ says the LORD, ‘that I will punish you in this place, that you may know
that My words will surely stand against you for adversity.’

30“Thus says the LORD: ‘Behold, I will give Pharaoh Hophra king of
Egypt into the hand of his enemies and into the hand of those who seek
his life, as I gave Zedekiah king of Judah into the hand of Nebuchadnezzar
king of Babylon, his enemy who sought his life.’ ”

Assurance to Baruch

45 The word that Jeremiah the prophet spoke to Baruch the son of
Neriah, when he had written these words in a book at the instruction

if I had slipped he could not have held me. But his being there and his touch were all I needed.

The analogy breaks down, of course. If our guide is God, he can hold us from any slipping. He could, if he chose, carry us across bodily. But the lesson the Indians taught me was that of trust. The only thing I really needed, the touch of a steady hand, they could provide. If I had been inclined to come to a halt in the middle of the log and raise nasty questions or argue their ability to keep me from falling, my trust would have collapsed and so would I.

The truth is that the whole thing has been done for us—Jesus is our Guide, and He is himself the way. My sins are those ravines, the gaps I cannot cross by myself, the interruptions along the way. But there is a way across. Logs have been laid and Someone is there to help me walk on them. However, we don't need to cross all of the logs at once. We take them as they come, and it is the same Guide who helps us over each one. We go with Him.

(From *A Slow and Certain Light* by Elisabeth Elliot)

APPLICATION Are you facing difficult decisions about your future? What goals have you set for your life? Take a day to spend time alone with God in prayer and in his Word. Ask him to help you understand his goals for your life.

EXPLORATION Guidance—Psalm 23:3; 25:4-5; Isaiah 58:11; John 16:12-13.

of Jeremiah,[w] in the fourth year of Jehoiakim the son
of Josiah, king of Judah, saying, 2"Thus says the LORD,
the God of Israel, to you, O Baruch: 3'You said, "Woe is
me now! For the LORD has added grief to my sorrow. I
fainted in my sighing, and I find no rest." '
4"Thus you shall say to him, 'Thus says the LORD:
"Behold, what I have built I will break down, and what
I have planted I will pluck up, that is, this whole land.
5And do you seek great things for yourself? Do not
seek *them;* for behold, I will bring adversity on all
flesh," says the LORD. "But I will give your life to you as
a prize in all places, wherever you go." ' "

Judgment on Egypt

46 The word of the LORD which came to Jeremiah
the prophet against the nations. 2Against Egypt.
Concerning the army of Pharaoh Necho, king of
Egypt, which was by the River Euphrates in Carchemish, and which Nebuchadnezzar king of Babylon
defeated in the fourth year of Jehoiakim the son of
Josiah, king of Judah:

3 "Order the buckler and shield,
And draw near to battle!
4 Harness the horses,
And mount up, you horsemen!
Stand forth with *your* helmets,
Polish the spears,
Put on the armor!
5 Why have I seen them dismayed
and turned back?
Their mighty ones are beaten down;
They have speedily fled,
And did not look back,
For fear *was* all around," says the LORD.
6 "Do not let the swift flee away,
Nor the mighty man escape;
They will stumble and fall
Toward the north, by the River Euphrates.

7 "Who *is* this coming up like a flood,
Whose waters move like the rivers?
8 Egypt rises up like a flood,
And *its* waters move like the rivers;
And he says, 'I will go up *and* cover the earth,
I will destroy the city and its inhabitants.'
9 Come up, O horses, and rage, O chariots!
And let the mighty men come forth:
The Ethiopians and the Libyans who
handle the shield,
And the Lydians who handle
and bend the bow.
10 For this *is* the day of the Lord GOD of hosts,
A day of vengeance,
That He may avenge Himself
on His adversaries.
The sword shall devour;
It shall be satiated and made drunk
with their blood;
For the Lord GOD of hosts has a sacrifice
In the north country by the River Euphrates.

11 "Go up to Gilead and take balm,
O virgin, the daughter of Egypt;
In vain you will use many medicines;
You shall not be cured.
12 The nations have heard of your shame,
And your cry has filled the land;
For the mighty man has stumbled
against the mighty;
They both have fallen together."

Babylonia Will Strike Egypt

13The word that the LORD spoke to Jeremiah the
prophet, how Nebuchadnezzar king of Babylon would
come *and* strike the land of Egypt.

14 "Declare in Egypt, and proclaim in Migdol;
Proclaim in Noph[x] and in Tahpanhes;
Say, 'Stand fast and prepare yourselves,
For the sword devours all around you.'
15 Why are your valiant *men* swept away?
They did not stand
Because the LORD drove them away.
16 He made many fall;
Yes, one fell upon another.
And they said, 'Arise!
Let us go back to our own people
And to the land of our nativity
From the oppressing sword.'
17 They cried there,
'Pharaoh, king of Egypt, *is but* a noise.
He has passed by the appointed time!'

18 "*As* I live," says the King,
Whose name *is* the LORD of hosts,
"Surely as Tabor *is* among the mountains
And as Carmel by the sea, *so* he shall come.
19 O you daughter dwelling in Egypt,
Prepare yourself to go into captivity!

45:1 [w] Literally *from Jeremiah's mouth*
46:14 [x] That is, ancient Memphis

For Noph[y] shall be waste and desolate,
without inhabitant.

20 "Egypt *is* a very pretty heifer,
But destruction comes, it comes
from the north.
21 Also her mercenaries are in her
midst like fat bulls,
For they also are turned back,
They have fled away together.
They did not stand,
For the day of their calamity had
come upon them,
The time of their punishment.
22 Her noise shall go like a serpent,
For they shall march with an army
And come against her with axes,
Like those who chop wood.

23 "They shall cut down her forest," says the LORD,
"Though it cannot be searched,
Because they *are* innumerable,
And more numerous than grasshoppers.
24 The daughter of Egypt shall be ashamed;
She shall be delivered into the hand
Of the people of the north."

25The LORD of hosts, the God of Israel, says: "Behold,
I will bring punishment on Amon[z] of No,[a] and Pharaoh
and Egypt, with their gods and their kings—Pharaoh
and those who trust in him. 26And I will deliver them
into the hand of those who seek their lives, into the
hand of Nebuchadnezzar king of Babylon and the
hand of his servants. Afterward it shall be inhabited
as in the days of old," says the LORD.

God Will Preserve Israel

27 "But do not fear, O My servant Jacob,
And do not be dismayed, O Israel!
For behold, I will save you from afar,
And your offspring from the land of
their captivity;
Jacob shall return, have rest and be at ease;
No one shall make *him* afraid.
28 Do not fear, O Jacob My servant," says the LORD,
"For I *am* with you;
For I will make a complete end of all the nations
To which I have driven you,
But I will not make a complete end of you.
I will rightly correct you,
For I will not leave you wholly unpunished."

Judgment on Philistia

47 The word of the LORD that came to Jeremiah the
prophet against the Philistines, before Pharaoh
attacked Gaza.

2Thus says the LORD:

"Behold, waters rise out of the north,
And shall be an overflowing flood;
They shall overflow the land and all that is in it,
The city and those who dwell within;
Then the men shall cry,
And all the inhabitants of the land shall wail.
3 At the noise of the stamping hooves of his
strong horses,
At the rushing of his chariots,
At the rumbling of his wheels,
The fathers will not look back for *their* children,
Lacking courage,
4 Because of the day that comes to plunder all
the Philistines,
To cut off from Tyre and Sidon every helper
who remains;
For the LORD shall plunder the Philistines,
The remnant of the country of Caphtor.
5 Baldness has come upon Gaza,
Ashkelon is cut off
With the remnant of their valley.
How long will you cut yourself?

6 "O you sword of the LORD,
How long until you are quiet?
Put yourself up into your scabbard,
Rest and be still!
7 How can it be quiet,
Seeing the LORD has given it a charge
Against Ashkelon and against the seashore?
There He has appointed it."

Judgment on Moab

48 Against Moab.

Thus says the LORD of hosts, the God of Israel:

"Woe to Nebo!
For it is plundered,
Kirjathaim is shamed *and* taken;
The high stronghold[b] is shamed
and dismayed—

46:19 [y] That is, ancient Memphis
46:25 [z] A sun god [a] That is, ancient Thebes
48:1 [b] Hebrew *Misgab*

LIFE LESSON

Jeremiah 46:1–49:39

SITUATION Since the book of Jeremiah is not arranged chronologically, this section of Scripture would historically follow the events of Jeremiah 25. Jeremiah anticipated Nebuchadnezzar's conquest (25:9).

OBSERVATION God not only ruled Judah, but all nations. God doesn't just rule over Christians, but over the whole world.

INSPIRATION You and I are called upon, at times, to announce coming judgment. There is no way that we can be faithful to God and avoid the judgmental aspects of our ministry. We must recognize that sin must be dealt with. It is impossible to be biblical and at the same time sugar-coat the message of the Gospel. The Gospel cuts right into the heart of man and into his sinfulness. As Oswald Chambers has put it, "If there is no tragedy at the back of human life, no gap between God and man, then the Redemption of Jesus Christ is 'much ado about nothing.'"

. . .When you and I are called upon to minister for God, one part of our message has to be to pluck up and to break down, to overthrow and destroy, to announce the coming judgment of God against sin.

2 No more praise of Moab.
In Heshbon they have devised evil against her:
'Come, and let us cut her off as a nation.'
You also shall be cut down, O Madmen![c]
The sword shall pursue you;
3 A voice of crying *shall be* from Horonaim:
'Plundering and great destruction!'

4 "Moab is destroyed;
Her little ones have caused a cry to be heard;[d]
5 For in the Ascent of Luhith they ascend with continual weeping;
For in the descent of Horonaim the enemies have
heard a cry of destruction.

6 "Flee, save your lives!
And be like the juniper[e] in the wilderness.
7 For because you have trusted in your works and your treasures,
You also shall be taken.
And Chemosh shall go forth into captivity,
His priests and his princes together.
8 And the plunderer shall come against every city;
No one shall escape.
The valley also shall perish,
And the plain shall be destroyed,
As the LORD has spoken.

9 "Give wings to Moab,
That she may flee and get away;
For her cities shall be desolate,
Without any to dwell in them.
10 Cursed *is* he who does the work of the LORD deceitfully,
And cursed *is* he who keeps back his sword from blood.

11 "Moab has been at ease from his[f] youth;
He has settled on his dregs,
And has not been emptied from vessel to vessel,
Nor has he gone into captivity.
Therefore his taste remained in him,
And his scent has not changed.

12 "Therefore behold, the days are coming," says the LORD,
"That I shall send him wine-workers
Who will tip him over
And empty his vessels
And break the bottles.
13 Moab shall be ashamed of Chemosh,
As the house of Israel was ashamed of Bethel, their confidence.

14 "How can you say, 'We *are* mighty
And strong men for the war'?
15 Moab is plundered and gone up *from* her cities;

48:2 [c] A city of Moab
48:4 [d] Following Masoretic Text, Targum, and Vulgate; Septuagint reads *Proclaim it in Zoar.*
48:6 [e] Or *Aroer,* a city of Moab
48:11 [f] The Hebrew uses masculine and feminine pronouns interchangeably in this chapter.

Her chosen young men have gone down to
the slaughter," says the King,
Whose name *is* the LORD of hosts.

16 "The calamity of Moab *is* near at hand,
And his affliction comes quickly.
17 Bemoan him, all you who are around him;
And all you who know his name,
Say, 'How the strong staff is broken,
The beautiful rod!'

18 "O daughter inhabiting Dibon,
Come down from *your* glory,
And sit in thirst;
For the plunderer of Moab has come against you,
He has destroyed your strongholds.
19 O inhabitant of Aroer,
Stand by the way and watch;
Ask him who flees
And her who escapes;
Say, 'What has happened?'
20 Moab is shamed, for he is broken down.
Wail and cry!
Tell it in Arnon, that Moab is plundered.

21 "And judgment has come on the plain country:
On Holon and Jahzah and Mephaath,
22 On Dibon and Nebo and Beth Diblathaim,
23 On Kirjathaim and Beth Gamul and Beth Meon,
24 On Kerioth and Bozrah,
On all the cities of the land of Moab,
Far or near.
25 The horn of Moab is cut off,
And his arm is broken," says the LORD.

26 "Make him drunk,
Because he exalted *himself* against the LORD.
Moab shall wallow in his vomit,
And he shall also be in derision.
27 For was not Israel a derision to you?
Was he found among thieves?
For whenever you speak of him,
You shake *your head in* scorn.
28 You who dwell in Moab,
Leave the cities and dwell in the rock,
And be like the dove *which* makes her nest
In the sides of the cave's mouth.

29 "We have heard the pride of Moab
(He *is* exceedingly proud),
Of his loftiness and arrogance and pride,
And of the haughtiness of his heart."

30 "I know his wrath," says the LORD,

Jeremiah's message did not end there. He was also called upon to build and to plant. There was also the message of mercy. Whenever God announces judgment, there is always also the great truth that righteousness and peace have met together. There is the merciful aspect of God. Mercy and truth have kissed each other, because those two things come together in the Cross of Jesus Christ.

. . . You and I are called upon, in our ministry in witnessing to others, to make clear the judgment of God against sin and the mercy of God who has provided the way out of that sin. (From *Words of Fire, Rivers of Tears* by David M. Howard)

APPLICATION Is there someone God wants you to witness to? As he brings people into your life, take time to get to know them. Let them get to know you. As you become friends, ask God to show you the right time to share Christ with them. And let your life portray the truth of what you say.

EXPLORATION God's Power—Job 38—41; God's Justice and Righteousness—Romans 3:9-26; Christian Witness—Romans 8:35-39; Ephesians 3:20-21.

"But it *is* not right;
His lies have made nothing right.
31 Therefore I will wail for Moab,
And I will cry out for all Moab;
I[g] will mourn for the men of Kir Heres.
32 O vine of Sibmah! I will weep for you with the weeping of Jazer.
Your plants have gone over the sea,
They reach to the sea of Jazer.
The plunderer has fallen on your summer fruit and your vintage.
33 Joy and gladness are taken
From the plentiful field
And from the land of Moab;
I have caused wine to fail from the winepresses;
No one will tread with joyous shouting—
Not joyous shouting!

34 "From the cry of Heshbon to Elealeh and to Jahaz
They have uttered their voice,
From Zoar to Horonaim,
Like a three-year-old heifer;[h]
For the waters of Nimrim also shall be desolate.

35 "Moreover," says the LORD,
"I will cause to cease in Moab
The one who offers *sacrifices* in the high places
And burns incense to his gods.
36 Therefore My heart shall wail like flutes for Moab,
And like flutes My heart shall wail
For the men of Kir Heres.
Therefore the riches they have acquired have perished.

37 "For every head *shall be* bald, and every beard clipped;
On all the hands *shall be* cuts, and on the loins sackcloth—
38 A general lamentation
On all the housetops of Moab,
And in its streets;
For I have broken Moab like a vessel in which *is* no pleasure," says the LORD.
39 "They shall wail:
'How she is broken down!
How Moab has turned her back with shame!'
So Moab shall be a derision
And a dismay to all those about her."

40 For thus says the LORD:

"Behold, one shall fly like an eagle,
And spread his wings over Moab.
41 Kerioth is taken,
And the strongholds are surprised;
The mighty men's hearts in Moab on that day shall be
Like the heart of a woman in birth pangs.
42 And Moab shall be destroyed as a people,
Because he exalted *himself* against the LORD.
43 Fear and the pit and the snare *shall be* upon you,
O inhabitant of Moab," says the LORD.
44 "He who flees from the fear shall fall into the pit,
And he who gets out of the pit shall be caught in the snare.
For upon Moab, upon it I will bring
The year of their punishment," says the LORD.

45 "Those who fled stood under the shadow of Heshbon
Because of exhaustion.
But a fire shall come out of Heshbon,
A flame from the midst of Sihon,
And shall devour the brow of Moab,
The crown of the head of the sons of tumult.
46 Woe to you, O Moab!
The people of Chemosh perish;
For your sons have been taken captive,
And your daughters captive.

47 "Yet I will bring back the captives of Moab
In the latter days," says the LORD.
Thus far *is* the judgment of Moab.

Judgment on Ammon

49 Against the Ammonites.
Thus says the LORD:

"Has Israel no sons?
Has he no heir?
Why *then* does Milcom[i] inherit Gad,
And his people dwell in its cities?
2 Therefore behold, the days are coming," says the LORD,
"That I will cause to be heard an alarm of war

48:31 [g] Following Dead Sea Scrolls, Septuagint, and Vulgate; Masoretic Text reads *He*.
48:34 [h] Or *The Third Eglath*, an unknown city (compare Isaiah 15:5)
49:1 [i] Hebrew *Malcam*, literally *their king*, a god of the Ammonites; also called *Molech* (compare verse 3)

In Rabbah of the Ammonites;
It shall be a desolate mound,
And her villages shall be burned with fire.
Then Israel shall take possession of
his inheritance," says the LORD.

3 "Wail, O Heshbon, for Ai is plundered!
Cry, you daughters of Rabbah,
Gird yourselves with sackcloth!
Lament and run to and fro by the walls;
For Milcom shall go into captivity
With his priests and his princes together.
4 Why do you boast in the valleys,
Your flowing valley, O backsliding daughter?
Who trusted in her treasures, *saying*,
'Who will come against me?'
5 Behold, I will bring fear upon you,"
Says the Lord GOD of hosts,
"From all those who are around you;
You shall be driven out, everyone headlong,
And no one will gather those who wander off.
6 But afterward I will bring back
The captives of the people of Ammon,"
says the LORD.

Judgment on Edom

7 Against Edom.
Thus says the LORD of hosts:

"*Is* wisdom no more in Teman?
Has counsel perished from the prudent?
Has their wisdom vanished?
8 Flee, turn back, dwell in the depths,
O inhabitants of Dedan!
For I will bring the calamity of Esau upon him,
The time *that* I will punish him.
9 If grape-gatherers came to you,
Would they not leave *some* gleaning grapes?
If thieves by night,
Would they not destroy until they have enough?
10 But I have made Esau bare;
I have uncovered his secret places,[j]
And he shall not be able to hide himself.
His descendants are plundered,
His brethren and his neighbors,
And he *is* no more.
11 Leave your fatherless children,
I will preserve *them* alive;
And let your widows trust in Me."

12 For thus says the LORD: "Behold, those whose judgment *was* not to drink of the cup have assuredly drunk.
And *are* you the one who will altogether go unpunished? You shall not go unpunished, but you shall
surely drink *of it*. 13 For I have sworn by Myself," says
the LORD, "that Bozrah shall become a desolation, a
reproach, a waste, and a curse. And all its cities shall
be perpetual wastes."

14 I have heard a message from the LORD,
And an ambassador has been
sent to the nations:
"Gather together, come against her,
And rise up to battle!

15 "For indeed, I will make you small
among nations,
Despised among men.
16 Your fierceness has deceived you,
The pride of your heart,
O you who dwell in the clefts of the rock,
Who hold the height of the hill!
Though you make your nest as high as the eagle,
I will bring you down from there,"
says the LORD.[k]

17 "Edom also shall be an astonishment;
Everyone who goes by it will be astonished
And will hiss at all its plagues.
18 As in the overthrow of Sodom and Gomorrah
And their neighbors," says the LORD,
"No one shall remain there,
Nor shall a son of man dwell in it.

19 "Behold, he shall come up like a lion from the
floodplain[l] of the Jordan
Against the dwelling place of the strong;
But I will suddenly make him run
away from her.
And who *is* a chosen *man that* I
may appoint over her?
For who *is* like Me?
Who will arraign Me?
And who *is* that shepherd
Who will withstand Me?"

20 Therefore hear the counsel of the LORD that
He has taken against Edom,
And His purposes that He has proposed
against the inhabitants of Teman:
Surely the least of the flock shall draw them out;

49:10 *j* Compare Obadiah 5, 6
49:16 *k* Compare Obadiah 3, 4
49:19 *l* Or *thicket*

Surely He shall make their dwelling places
desolate with them.
21 The earth shakes at the noise of their fall;
At the cry its noise is heard at the Red Sea.
22 Behold, He shall come up and fly like the eagle,
And spread His wings over Bozrah;
The heart of the mighty men of Edom in
that day shall be
Like the heart of a woman in birth pangs.

Judgment on Damascus

23 Against Damascus.

"Hamath and Arpad are shamed,
For they have heard bad news.
They are fainthearted;
There is trouble on the sea;
It cannot be quiet.
24 Damascus has grown feeble;
She turns to flee,
And fear has seized *her*.
Anguish and sorrows have taken her
like a woman in labor.
25 Why is the city of praise not deserted,
the city of My joy?
26 Therefore her young men shall fall
in her streets,
And all the men of war shall be cut off in that
day," says the LORD of hosts.
27 "I will kindle a fire in the wall of Damascus,
And it shall consume the palaces
of Ben-Hadad."[m]

Judgment on Kedar and Hazor

28 Against Kedar and against the kingdoms of Hazor, which Nebuchadnezzar king of Babylon shall strike.
Thus says the LORD:

"Arise, go up to Kedar,
And devastate the men of the East!
29 Their tents and their flocks they shall take away.
They shall take for themselves their curtains,
All their vessels and their camels;
And they shall cry out to them,
'Fear *is* on every side!'
30 "Flee, get far away! Dwell in the depths,
O inhabitants of Hazor!" says the LORD.
"For Nebuchadnezzar king of Babylon has
taken counsel against you,
And has conceived a plan against you.
31 "Arise, go up to the wealthy nation that dwells
securely," says the LORD,
"Which has neither gates nor bars,
Dwelling alone.
32 Their camels shall be for booty,
And the multitude of their cattle for plunder.
I will scatter to all winds those in
the farthest corners,
And I will bring their calamity from all its
sides," says the LORD.
33 "Hazor shall be a dwelling for jackals,
a desolation forever;
No one shall reside there,
Nor son of man dwell in it."

Judgment on Elam

34 The word of the LORD that came to Jeremiah the prophet against Elam, in the beginning of the reign of Zedekiah king of Judah, saying, 35 "Thus says the LORD of hosts:

'Behold, I will break the bow of Elam,
The foremost of their might.
36 Against Elam I will bring the four winds
From the four quarters of heaven,
And scatter them toward all those winds;
There shall be no nations where the outcasts
of Elam will not go.
37 For I will cause Elam to be dismayed before
their enemies
And before those who seek their life.
I will bring disaster upon them,
My fierce anger,' says the LORD;
'And I will send the sword after them
Until I have consumed them.
38 I will set My throne in Elam,
And will destroy from there the king and the
princes,' says the LORD.
39 'But it shall come to pass in the latter days:
I will bring back the captives of Elam,'
says the LORD."

Judgment on Babylon and Babylonia

50 The word that the LORD spoke against Babylon *and* against the land of the Chaldeans by Jeremiah the prophet.

2 "Declare among the nations,
Proclaim, and set up a standard;
Proclaim—do not conceal *it*—

49:27 m Compare Amos 1:4

Say, 'Babylon is taken, Bel is shamed.
Merodach[n] is broken in pieces;
Her idols are humiliated,
Her images are broken in pieces.'
3 For out of the north a nation comes up against her,
Which shall make her land desolate,
And no one shall dwell therein.
They shall move, they shall depart,
Both man and beast.

4 "In those days and in that time," says the LORD,
"The children of Israel shall come,
They and the children of Judah together;
With continual weeping they shall come,
And seek the LORD their God.
5 They shall ask the way to Zion,
With their faces toward it, *saying*,
'Come and let us join ourselves to the LORD
In a perpetual covenant
That will not be forgotten.'

6 "My people have been lost sheep.
Their shepherds have led them astray;
They have turned them away *on* the mountains.
They have gone from mountain to hill;
They have forgotten their resting place.
7 All who found them have devoured them;
And their adversaries said, 'We have not offended,
Because they have sinned against the LORD, the habitation of justice,
The LORD, the hope of their fathers.'

8 "Move from the midst of Babylon,
Go out of the land of the Chaldeans;
And be like the rams before the flocks.
9 For behold, I will raise and cause to come up against Babylon
An assembly of great nations from the north country,
And they shall array themselves against her;
From there she shall be captured.
Their arrows *shall be* like *those* of an expert warrior;[o]
None shall return in vain.
10 And Chaldea shall become plunder;
All who plunder her shall be satisfied," says the LORD.

11 "Because you were glad, because you rejoiced,
You destroyers of My heritage,
Because you have grown fat like a heifer threshing grain,
And you bellow like bulls,
12 Your mother shall be deeply ashamed;
She who bore you shall be ashamed.
Behold, the least of the nations *shall be* a wilderness,

50:2 [n] A Babylonian god; sometimes spelled *Marduk*
50:9 [o] Following some Hebrew manuscripts, Septuagint, and Syriac; Masoretic Text, Targum, and Vulgate read *a warrior who makes childless.*

LIFE LESSON

Jeremiah 50:1-46

SITUATION Jeremiah foretold the fall of Babylon. The powerful and arrogant Babylonians would be conquered by a power from the north. Under the Messiah, Israel would rise again and would regain her preeminent status among nations.

OBSERVATION God gave his people something in which to place their hope. A new Israel, led by God's chosen Messiah, would arrive after Babylon was crushed.

INSPIRATION Do you have the hope of the coming again of the Lord Jesus Christ? Then you should live it—a pure life, a godly life, a surrendered life, a consecrated life. There's a sense in which we're sanctified when we receive Christ. There's a sense in which we grow in the grace and knowledge of Christ in progressive sanctification. But one day we shall see Jesus face to face, and total sanctification is when we're perfect, as He is perfect. We shall see Him as He is.

. . . I know sometimes we get a little anxious and wonder if Jesus is really going to come back. . . . He has appointed a day. God knows the day. It's all set. He will be back right on time—He won't be an hour late or an hour early.

. . . We are to be constantly thinking about His coming. . . .

. . . People say, "Well, Christ is coming back—let's quit all these activities that we're involved in." No! He may not come in our lifetime. Let's do our best to help reach our fellow man for Christ. His return should be our incentive toward work.

(From *Peace with God* by Billy Graham)

APPLICATION Trusting Jesus gives us hope. Did you trust him to work out your day's worth of headaches, to get you to work safely, to help you get your homework done, or to get along with your spouse? When you pray, go over each detail of your day. Who will you see and talk to? What projects need to get done? Where will you drive . . . ? Don't live any part of your day without letting God know you are looking to him for stamina.

EXPLORATION Hope—Leviticus 26:40-45; Mark 5:35, 36; 1 Corinthians 15:54-57; 2 Corinthians 4:8.

A dry land and a desert.
13 Because of the wrath of the LORD
She shall not be inhabited,
But she shall be wholly desolate.
Everyone who goes by Babylon
shall be horrified
And hiss at all her plagues.

14 "Put yourselves in array against
Babylon all around,
All you who bend the bow;
Shoot at her, spare no arrows,
For she has sinned against the LORD.
15 Shout against her all around;
She has given her hand,
Her foundations have fallen,
Her walls are thrown down;
For it *is* the vengeance of the LORD.
Take vengeance on her.
As she has done, so do to her.
16 Cut off the sower from Babylon,
And him who handles the sickle
at harvest time.
For fear of the oppressing sword
Everyone shall turn to his own people,
And everyone shall flee to his own land.

17 "Israel *is* like scattered sheep;
The lions have driven *him* away.
First the king of Assyria devoured him;
Now at last this Nebuchadnezzar king of
Babylon has broken his bones."

18 Therefore thus says the LORD of hosts, the God of Israel:

"Behold, I will punish the king of Babylon
and his land,
As I have punished the king of Assyria.
19 But I will bring back Israel to his home,
And he shall feed on Carmel and Bashan;
His soul shall be satisfied on Mount
Ephraim and Gilead.
20 In those days and in that time," says the LORD,
"The iniquity of Israel shall be sought, but *there*
shall be none;
And the sins of Judah, but they
shall not be found;
For I will pardon those whom I preserve.

21 "Go up against the land of Merathaim, against it,
And against the inhabitants of Pekod.
Waste and utterly destroy them," says the LORD,
"And do according to all that I
have commanded you.
22 A sound of battle *is* in the land,
And of great destruction.
23 How the hammer of the whole earth has been
cut apart and broken!
How Babylon has become a desolation
among the nations!
I have laid a snare for you;
24 You have indeed been trapped, O Babylon,
And you were not aware;
You have been found and also caught,
Because you have contended against the LORD.
25 The LORD has opened His armory,
And has brought out the weapons
of His indignation;
For this *is* the work of the Lord GOD of hosts
In the land of the Chaldeans.
26 Come against her from the farthest border;
Open her storehouses;
Cast her up as heaps of ruins,
And destroy her utterly;
Let nothing of her be left.
27 Slay all her bulls,
Let them go down to the slaughter.
Woe to them!
For their day has come, the time
of their punishment.
28 The voice of those who flee and escape from
the land of Babylon
Declares in Zion the vengeance of
the LORD our God,
The vengeance of His temple.

29 "Call together the archers against Babylon.
All you who bend the bow, encamp
against it all around;
Let none of them escape.[p]
Repay her according to her work;
According to all she has done, do to her;
For she has been proud against the LORD,
Against the Holy One of Israel.
30 Therefore her young men shall
fall in the streets,
And all her men of war shall be cut off
in that day," says the LORD.

31 "Behold, I *am* against you,

50:29 *p* Qere, some Hebrew manuscripts, Septuagint, and Targum add *to her.*

O most haughty one!" says the Lord
GOD of hosts;
"For your day has come,
The time *that* I will punish you.[q]
32 The most proud shall stumble and fall,
And no one will raise him up;
I will kindle a fire in his cities,
And it will devour all around him."

33 Thus says the LORD of hosts:

"The children of Israel *were* oppressed,
Along with the children of Judah;
All who took them captive have held them fast;
They have refused to let them go.
34 Their Redeemer *is* strong;
The LORD of hosts *is* His name.
He will thoroughly plead their case,
That He may give rest to the land,
And disquiet the inhabitants of Babylon.

35 "A sword *is* against the Chaldeans,"
says the LORD,
"Against the inhabitants of Babylon,
And against her princes and her wise men.
36 A sword *is* against the soothsayers,
and they will be fools.
A sword *is* against her mighty men,
and they will be dismayed.
37 A sword *is* against their horses,
Against their chariots,
And against all the mixed peoples
who *are* in her midst;
And they will become like women.
A sword *is* against her treasures, and
they will be robbed.
38 A drought[r] *is* against her waters, and
they will be dried up.
For it *is* the land of carved images,
And they are insane with *their* idols.

39 "Therefore the wild desert beasts shall dwell
there with the jackals,
And the ostriches shall dwell in it.
It shall be inhabited no more forever,
Nor shall it be dwelt in from generation
to generation.
40 As God overthrew Sodom and Gomorrah
And their neighbors," says the LORD,
"*So* no one shall reside there,
Nor son of man dwell in it.

41 "Behold, a people shall come from the north,
And a great nation and many kings
Shall be raised up from the ends of the earth.
42 They shall hold the bow and the lance;
They *are* cruel and shall not show mercy.
Their voice shall roar like the sea;
They shall ride on horses,
Set in array, like a man for the battle,
Against you, O daughter of Babylon.

43 "The king of Babylon has heard
the report about them,
And his hands grow feeble;
Anguish has taken hold of him,
Pangs as of a woman in childbirth.

44 "Behold, he shall come up like a lion from the
floodplain[s] of the Jordan
Against the dwelling place of the strong;
But I will make them suddenly run
away from her.
And who *is* a chosen *man that* I may
appoint over her?
For who *is* like Me?
Who will arraign Me?
And who *is* that shepherd
Who will withstand Me?"

45 Therefore hear the counsel of the LORD that He
has taken against Babylon,
And His purposes that He has proposed
against the land of the Chaldeans:
Surely the least of the flock shall draw them out;
Surely He will make their dwelling
place desolate with them.
46 At the noise of the taking of Babylon
The earth trembles,
And the cry is heard among the nations.

The Utter Destruction of Babylon

51 Thus says the LORD:

"Behold, I will raise up against Babylon,
Against those who dwell in Leb Kamai,[t]
A destroying wind.
2 And I will send winnowers to Babylon,
Who shall winnow her and empty her land.
For in the day of doom

50:31 [q] Following Masoretic Text and Targum; Septuagint and Vulgate read *The time of your punishment.*
50:38 [r] Following Masoretic Text, Targum, and Vulgate; Syriac reads *sword;* Septuagint omits *A drought is.*
50:44 [s] Or *thicket*
51:1 [t] A code word for Chaldea (Babylonia); may be translated *The Midst of Those Who Rise Up Against Me*

They shall be against her all around.
3 Against *her* let the archer bend his bow,
And lift himself up against *her* in his armor.
Do not spare her young men;
Utterly destroy all her army.
4 Thus the slain shall fall in the
land of the Chaldeans,
And *those* thrust through in her streets.
5 For Israel is not forsaken, nor Judah,
By his God, the LORD of hosts,
Though their land was filled with sin against
the Holy One of Israel."

6 Flee from the midst of Babylon,
And every one save his life!
Do not be cut off in her iniquity,
For this *is* the time of the LORD's vengeance;
He shall recompense her.
7 Babylon *was* a golden cup in the LORD's hand,
That made all the earth drunk.
The nations drank her wine;
Therefore the nations are deranged.
8 Babylon has suddenly fallen and been destroyed.
Wail for her!
Take balm for her pain;
Perhaps she may be healed.

9 We would have healed Babylon,
But she is not healed.
Forsake her, and let us go everyone to his own
country;
For her judgment reaches to heaven
and is lifted up to the skies.
10 The LORD has revealed our righteousness.
Come and let us declare in Zion the
work of the LORD our God.

11 Make the arrows bright!
Gather the shields!
The LORD has raised up the spirit of
the kings of the Medes.
For His plan *is* against Babylon to destroy it,
Because it *is* the vengeance of the LORD,
The vengeance for His temple.
12 Set up the standard on the walls of Babylon;
Make the guard strong,
Set up the watchmen,
Prepare the ambushes.
For the LORD has both devised and done
What He spoke against the inhabitants
of Babylon.
13 O you who dwell by many waters,
Abundant in treasures,
Your end has come,
The measure of your covetousness.
14 The LORD of hosts has sworn by Himself:
"Surely I will fill you with men, as with locusts,
And they shall lift up a shout against you."

15 He has made the earth by His power;
He has established the world by His wisdom,
And stretched out the heaven by
His understanding.
16 When He utters *His* voice—
There is a multitude of waters in the heavens:
"He causes the vapors to ascend from the ends
of the earth;
He makes lightnings for the rain;
He brings the wind out of His treasuries."[u]

17 Everyone is dull-hearted, without knowledge;
Every metalsmith is put to shame by the
carved image;
For his molded image *is* falsehood,
And *there is* no breath in them.
18 They *are* futile, a work of errors;
In the time of their punishment
they shall perish.
19 The Portion of Jacob *is* not like them,
For He *is* the Maker of all things;
And *Israel is* the tribe of His inheritance.
The LORD of hosts *is* His name.

20 "You *are* My battle-ax *and* weapons of war:
For with you I will break the nation in pieces;
With you I will destroy kingdoms;
21 With you I will break in pieces the
horse and its rider;
With you I will break in pieces the chariot and
its rider;
22 With you also I will break in pieces
man and woman;
With you I will break in pieces old and young;
With you I will break in pieces the young
man and the maiden;
23 With you also I will break in pieces
the shepherd and his flock;
With you I will break in pieces the
farmer and his yoke of oxen;
And with you I will break in pieces
governors and rulers.

24 "And I will repay Babylon

51:16 [u] Psalm 135:7

And all the inhabitants of Chaldea
For all the evil they have done
In Zion in your sight," says the LORD.

25 "Behold, I *am* against you,
O destroying mountain,
Who destroys all the earth," says the LORD.
"And I will stretch out My hand against you,
Roll you down from the rocks,
And make you a burnt mountain.
26 They shall not take from you a
stone for a corner
Nor a stone for a foundation,
But you shall be desolate forever," says the LORD.

27 Set up a banner in the land,
Blow the trumpet among the nations!
Prepare the nations against her,
Call the kingdoms together against her:
Ararat, Minni, and Ashkenaz.
Appoint a general against her;
Cause the horses to come up like
the bristling locusts.
28 Prepare against her the nations,
With the kings of the Medes,
Its governors and all its rulers,
All the land of his dominion.
29 And the land will tremble and sorrow;
For every purpose of the LORD shall
be performed against Babylon,
To make the land of Babylon a desolation
without inhabitant.
30 The mighty men of Babylon
have ceased fighting,
They have remained in their strongholds;
Their might has failed,
They became *like* women;
They have burned her dwelling places,
The bars of her *gate* are broken.
31 One runner will run to meet another,
And one messenger to meet another,
To show the king of Babylon that his city is
taken on *all* sides;
32 The passages are blocked,
The reeds they have burned with fire,
And the men of war are terrified.

33 For thus says the LORD of hosts, the God of Israel:

"The daughter of Babylon *is* like
a threshing floor
When it is time to thresh her;
Yet a little while
And the time of her harvest will come."

34 "Nebuchadnezzar the king of Babylon
Has devoured me, he has crushed me;
He has made me an empty vessel,
He has swallowed me up like a monster;
He has filled his stomach with my delicacies,
He has spit me out.
35 Let the violence *done* to me and my
flesh *be* upon Babylon,"
The inhabitant of Zion will say;
"And my blood be upon the inhabitants
of Chaldea!"
Jerusalem will say.

36 Therefore thus says the LORD:

"Behold, I will plead your case and take
vengeance for you.
I will dry up her sea and make her springs dry.
37 Babylon shall become a heap,
A dwelling place for jackals,
An astonishment and a hissing,
Without an inhabitant.
38 They shall roar together like lions,
They shall growl like lions' whelps.
39 In their excitement I will prepare their feasts;
I will make them drunk,
That they may rejoice,
And sleep a perpetual sleep
And not awake," says the LORD.
40 "I will bring them down
Like lambs to the slaughter,
Like rams with male goats.

41 "Oh, how Sheshach[v] is taken!
Oh, how the praise of the whole
earth is seized!
How Babylon has become desolate
among the nations!
42 The sea has come up over Babylon;
She is covered with the multitude of its waves.
43 Her cities are a desolation,
A dry land and a wilderness,
A land where no one dwells,
Through which no son of man passes.
44 I will punish Bel in Babylon,
And I will bring out of his mouth
what he has swallowed;

51:41 [v] A code word for Babylon (compare Jeremiah 25:26)

And the nations shall not stream
to him anymore.
Yes, the wall of Babylon shall fall.

45 "My people, go out of the midst of her!
And let everyone deliver himself from the
fierce anger of the LORD.
46 And lest your heart faint,
And you fear for the rumor that *will be*
heard in the land
(A rumor will come *one* year,
And after that, in *another* year
A rumor *will come,*
And violence in the land,
Ruler against ruler),
47 Therefore behold, the days are coming
That I will bring judgment on the carved
images of Babylon;
Her whole land shall be ashamed,
And all her slain shall fall in her midst.
48 Then the heavens and the earth and
all that *is* in them
Shall sing joyously over Babylon;
For the plunderers shall come to her from
the north," says the LORD.

49 As Babylon *has caused* the slain of Israel to fall,
So at Babylon the slain of all the earth shall fall.
50 You who have escaped the sword,
Get away! Do not stand still!
Remember the LORD afar off,
And let Jerusalem come to your mind.

51 We are ashamed because we
have heard reproach.
Shame has covered our faces,
For strangers have come into the sanctuaries
of the LORD's house.

52 "Therefore behold, the days are coming,"
says the LORD,
"That I will bring judgment on her
carved images,
And throughout all her land the
wounded shall groan.
53 Though Babylon were to mount up to heaven,
And though she were to fortify the height of
her strength,
Yet from Me plunderers would come to her,"
says the LORD.

54 The sound of a cry *comes* from Babylon,
And great destruction from the
land of the Chaldeans,
55 Because the LORD is plundering Babylon
And silencing her loud voice,
Though her waves roar like great waters,
And the noise of their voice is uttered,
56 Because the plunderer comes against her,
against Babylon,
And her mighty men are taken.
Every one of their bows is broken;
For the LORD *is* the God of recompense,
He will surely repay.

57 "And I will make drunk
Her princes and wise men,
Her governors, her deputies, and
her mighty men.
And they shall sleep a perpetual sleep
And not awake," says the King,
Whose name *is* the LORD of hosts.

58Thus says the LORD of hosts:

"The broad walls of Babylon shall
be utterly broken,
And her high gates shall be burned with fire;
The people will labor in vain,
And the nations, because of the fire;
And they shall be weary."

Jeremiah's Command to Seraiah

59The word which Jeremiah the prophet commanded
Seraiah the son of Neriah, the son of Mahseiah, when
he went with Zedekiah the king of Judah to Babylon in
the fourth year of his reign. And Seraiah *was* the
quartermaster. 60So Jeremiah wrote in a book all the
evil that would come upon Babylon, all these words
that are written against Babylon. 61And Jeremiah said
to Seraiah, "When you arrive in Babylon and see it,
and read all these words, 62then you shall say, 'O LORD,
You have spoken against this place to cut it off, so that
none shall remain in it, neither man nor beast, but it
shall be desolate forever.' 63Now it shall be, when you
have finished reading this book, *that* you shall tie a
stone to it and throw it out into the Euphrates. 64Then
you shall say, 'Thus Babylon shall sink and not rise
from the catastrophe that I will bring upon her. And
they shall be weary.' "

Thus far *are* the words of Jeremiah.

The Fall of Jerusalem Reviewed

52 Zedekiah *was* twenty-one years old when he
became king, and he reigned eleven years in
Jerusalem. His mother's name *was* Hamutal the
daughter of Jeremiah of Libnah. 2He also did evil in

the sight of the LORD, according to all that Jehoiakim had done. 3For because
of the anger of the LORD *this* happened in Jerusalem and Judah, till He finally
cast them out from His presence. Then Zedekiah rebelled against the king
of Babylon.

4Now it came to pass in the ninth year of his reign, in the tenth month,
on the tenth *day* of the month, *that* Nebuchadnezzar king of Babylon and
all his army came against Jerusalem and encamped against it; and *they* built
a siege wall against it all around. 5So the city was besieged until the eleventh
year of King Zedekiah. 6By the fourth month, on the ninth day of the month,
the famine had become so severe in the city that there was no food for the
people of the land. 7Then the city wall was broken through, and all the men
of war fled and went out of the city at night by way of the gate between the
two walls, which *was* by the king's garden, even though the Chaldeans *were*
near the city all around. And they went by way of the plain.[w]

8But the army of the Chaldeans pursued the king, and they overtook
Zedekiah in the plains of Jericho. All his army was scattered from him. 9So
they took the king and brought him up to the king of Babylon at Riblah in
the land of Hamath, and he pronounced judgment on him. 10Then the
king of Babylon killed the sons of Zedekiah before his eyes. And he killed
all the princes of Judah in Riblah. 11He also put out the eyes of Zedekiah;
and the king of Babylon bound him in bronze fetters, took him to Babylon,
and put him in prison till the day of his death.

The Temple and City Plundered and Burned

12Now in the fifth month, on the tenth *day* of the month (which *was* the
nineteenth year of King Nebuchadnezzar king of Babylon), Nebuzaradan,
the captain of the guard, *who* served the king of Babylon, came to Jerusalem. 13He burned the house of the LORD and the king's house; all the houses
of Jerusalem, that is, all the houses of the great, he burned with fire. 14And
all the army of the Chaldeans who *were* with the captain of the guard broke
down all the walls of Jerusalem all around. 15Then Nebuzaradan the captain
of the guard carried away captive *some* of the poor people, the rest of the people who remained in the city, the defectors who had deserted to the king of
Babylon, and the rest of the craftsmen. 16But Nebuzaradan the captain of
the guard left *some* of the poor of the land as vinedressers and farmers.

17The bronze pillars that *were* in the house of the LORD, and the carts and
the bronze Sea that *were* in the house of the LORD, the Chaldeans broke in
pieces, and carried all their bronze to Babylon. 18They also took away the
pots, the shovels, the trimmers, the bowls, the spoons, and all the bronze
utensils with which the priests ministered. 19The basins, the firepans, the
bowls, the pots, the lampstands, the spoons, and the cups, whatever *was*
solid gold and whatever *was* solid silver, the captain of the guard took
away. 20The two pillars, one Sea, the twelve bronze bulls which *were* under
it, and the carts, which King Solomon had made for the house of the
LORD—the bronze of all these articles was beyond measure. 21Now *concerning* the pillars: the height of one pillar *was* eighteen cubits, a measuring line of twelve cubits could measure its circumference, and its thickness
was four fingers; *it was* hollow. 22A capital of bronze *was* on it; and the
height of one capital *was* five cubits, with a network and pomegranates all

52:7 [w] Or *the Arabah,* that is, the Jordan Valley

LIFE LESSON

Jeremiah 52:1-34

SITUATION Jerusalem fell to the Babylonians after a two-year siege. The Babylonians blinded King Zedekiah, looted the temple, and destroyed the city. Many Israelites were exiled to Babylon. God completely fulfilled Jeremiah's prophecy.

OBSERVATION True to his word, God punished unrepentant Israel through conquest by Babylon.

INSPIRATION There is a window in your heart through which you can see God. Once upon a time that window was clear. Your view of God was crisp. You could see God as vividly as you could see a gentle valley or hillside. The glass was clean, the pane unbroken.

You knew God. You knew how he worked. You knew what he wanted you to do. No surprises. Nothing unexpected. You knew that God had a will, and you continually discovered what it was.

Then, suddenly, the window cracked. A pebble broke the window. A pebble of pain.

Perhaps the stone struck when you were a child and a parent left home—forever. Maybe the rock hit in adolescence when your heart was broken. Maybe you made it into adulthood before the window was cracked. But then the pebble came. . . .

Whatever the pebble's form, the result was the same—a shattered window. The pebble missiled into the pane and shattered it. The crash echoed down the halls of your heart. Cracks shot out from the point of impact, creating a spider web of fragmented pieces.

And suddenly God was not so easy to see. The view that had been so crisp had changed. You turned to see God, and his figure was distorted. It was hard to see him through the pain. It was hard to see him through the fragments of hurt.

You were puzzled. God wouldn't allow something like this to happen, would he? Tragedy and travesty weren't on the agenda of the One you had seen, were they? Had you been fooled? Had you been blind?

Continued

The moment the pebble struck, the glass became a reference point for you. From then on, there was life before the pain and life after the pain. Before your pain, the view was clear; God seemed so near. After your pain, well, he was harder to see. He seemed a bit distant . . . harder to perceive. Your pain distorted the view—not eclipsed it, but distorted it. . . .

When you can't see him, trust him. The figure you see is not a ghost. The voice you hear is not the wind.

Jesus is closer than you've ever dreamed.

(From *In the Eye of the Storm* by Max Lucado)

APPLICATION Is someone in your family anxious? In a panic? Help that person to face the chaos, to work through the pain with God's help, to face the problems peacefully.

EXPLORATION Punishment—Genesis 3:14-19; 9:11-15; Exodus 32:34; 2 Samuel 20:7-10; Psalm 38:2-4; Isaiah 13:11; Jeremiah 52.

around the capital, all of bronze. The second pillar, with pomegranates was the same. 23There were ninety-six pomegranates on the sides; all the pomegranates, all around on the network, *were* one hundred.

The People Taken Captive to Babylonia

24The captain of the guard took Seraiah the chief priest, Zephaniah the second priest, and the three doorkeepers. 25He also took out of the city an officer who had charge of the men of war, seven men of the king's close associates who were found in the city, the principal scribe of the army who mustered the people of the land, and sixty men of the people of the land who were found in the midst of the city. 26And Nebuzaradan the captain of the guard took these and brought them to the king of Babylon at Riblah. 27Then the king of Babylon struck them and put them to death at Riblah in the land of Hamath. Thus Judah was carried away captive from its own land.

28These *are* the people whom Nebuchadnezzar carried away captive: in the seventh year, three thousand and twenty-three Jews; 29in the eighteenth year of Nebuchadnezzar he carried away captive from Jerusalem eight hundred and thirty-two persons; 30in the twenty-third year of Nebuchadnezzar, Nebuzaradan the captain of the guard carried away captive of the Jews seven hundred and forty-five persons. All the persons *were* four thousand six hundred.

Jehoiachin Released from Prison

31Now it came to pass in the thirty-seventh year of the captivity of Jehoiachin king of Judah, in the twelfth month, on the twenty-fifth *day* of the month, *that* Evil-Merodach[x] king of Babylon, in the first *year* of his reign, lifted up the head of Jehoiachin king of Judah and brought him out of prison. 32And he spoke kindly to him and gave him a more prominent seat than those of the kings who *were* with him in Babylon. 33So Jehoiachin changed from his prison garments, and he ate bread regularly before the king all the days of his life. 34And as for his provisions, there was a regular ration given him by the king of Babylon, a portion for each day until the day of his death, all the days of his life.

52:31 [x] Or *Awil-Marduk*

The Book of LAMENTATIONS

INTRODUCTION

You're looking for Jeremiah? Come, look out the window. That's him. That's him walking through the rubble. Shoulders stooped, step slow.

He's a tired man. I knew him when he was young.

But that was long ago.

That was before the walls fell.

That was before the enemy came.

Look at him sort through the stones. He does this all day. He'll spot a dish that once sat on a table or a sandal once worn by a child. Each item he clutches, not to keep but to mourn. He'll hold the plate to his chest and fall on his knees and wail. Sobbing erupts like cloudbursts. He'll stay there and weep until he has mourned the memory of the object, and then he'll place it back on the pile and move on.

Soon he sees another item, and the weeping starts all over again.

Some people think he's crazy. Some people think he's lost what little sense he had.

I don't. I don't think him insane. After all, didn't he tell us this would happen? No, he's not crazy. He's just sad.

I told him the other day, I said, "Jeremiah, write these things down. These feelings that you have. This sorrow that you feel—write it down."

He looked at me from under those bushy eyebrows and said, "Maybe you're right . . . maybe you're right. I just don't want the people to forget."

I told him to write it down. I hope he will.

Life Lesson

Lamentations 1:1-22

SITUATION Lamentations was read publicly each year to remind the Jews that their sin had caused the destruction of Jerusalem. The book recorded both the faithfulness of God and the repentance of the people.

OBSERVATION Sin brings punishment. But sorrow, confession, and repentance bring healing and wholeness.

INSPIRATION A vast number and variety of human emotional experiences come under the general label, "sorrow." Marie, a friend of mine and a member of my congregation, shared these intimate feelings with me upon the death of her husband: "No two sorrows are the same. I lost my son as a teenager; I lost my daughter in her twenties. Now my husband has passed away. Each grief has been painful, but each grief has been different."

Over and over I've seen sorrow, and over and over again I have witnessed this one fact: *God does comfort good people when bad things happen to them.* It *is* possible to be happy even in a world where sorrow casts its long, gray shadow.

Trouble never leaves us where it finds us; sorrow will change our tomorrow. But God inspires us to become better people, not bitter ones. He shows us the negative can be turned into a positive, a minus into a plus, and that's what the cross is all about.

How can we find relief from grief? How can we turn our mourning into a morning? (1) Realize what you can do for yourself! (2) Realize what God can do for you!

(From *The Be (Happy) Attitudes* by Robert Schuller)

APPLICATION What sorrows have you known? Have you experienced the death of a loved one, a ruined life, or regrettable mistakes? If your heart is grieving, turn to God for comfort and assurance. He hears your cries, tears, and disappointments.

EXPLORATION Comfort from God—Psalm 23:1-4; 94:19; 119:50, 52; Isaiah 66:13; 2 Corinthians 1:3-5; Philippians 2:1; 2 Thessalonians 2:16-17.

Jerusalem in Affliction

How lonely sits the city
That was full of people!
How like a widow is she,
Who *was* great among the nations!
The princess among the provinces
Has become a slave!

2 She weeps bitterly in the night,
Her tears *are* on her cheeks;
Among all her lovers
She has none to comfort *her.*
All her friends have dealt treacherously with her;
They have become her enemies.

3 Judah has gone into captivity,
Under affliction and hard servitude;
She dwells among the nations,
She finds no rest;
All her persecutors overtake her in dire straits.

4 The roads to Zion mourn
Because no one comes to the set feasts.
All her gates are desolate;
Her priests sigh,
Her virgins are afflicted,
And she *is* in bitterness.

5 Her adversaries have become the master,
Her enemies prosper;
For the LORD has afflicted her
Because of the multitude of her transgressions.
Her children have gone into captivity before the enemy.

6 And from the daughter of Zion
All her splendor has departed.
Her princes have become like deer
That find no pasture,
That flee without strength
Before the pursuer.

7 In the days of her affliction and roaming,
Jerusalem remembers all her pleasant things
That she had in the days of old.
When her people fell into the hand of the enemy,
With no one to help her,
The adversaries saw her
And mocked at her downfall.[a]

8 Jerusalem has sinned gravely,
Therefore she has become vile.[b]

1:7 [a] Vulgate reads *her Sabbaths.*
1:8 [b] Septuagint and Vulgate read *moved* or *removed.*

All who honored her despise her
Because they have seen her nakedness;
Yes, she sighs and turns away.

9 Her uncleanness *is* in her skirts;
She did not consider her destiny;
Therefore her collapse was awesome;
She had no comforter.
"O LORD, behold my affliction,
For *the* enemy is exalted!"

10 The adversary has spread his hand
Over all her pleasant things;
For she has seen the nations enter her sanctuary,
Those whom You commanded
Not to enter Your assembly.

11 All her people sigh,
They seek bread;
They have given their valuables for
food to restore life.
"See, O LORD, and consider,
For I am scorned."

12 "*Is it* nothing to you, all you who pass by?
Behold and see
If there is any sorrow like my sorrow,
Which has been brought on me,
Which the LORD has inflicted
In the day of His fierce anger.

13 "From above He has sent fire into my bones,
And it overpowered them;
He has spread a net for my feet
And turned me back;
He has made me desolate
And faint all the day.

14 "The yoke of my transgressions was bound;[c]
They were woven together by His hands,
And thrust upon my neck.
He made my strength fail;
The Lord delivered me into the hands of *those*
whom I am not able to withstand.

15 "The Lord has trampled underfoot all my
mighty *men* in my midst;
He has called an assembly against me
To crush my young men;
The Lord trampled *as* in a winepress
The virgin daughter of Judah.

16 "For these *things* I weep;
My eye, my eye overflows with water;
Because the comforter, who should
restore my life,
Is far from me.
My children are desolate
Because the enemy prevailed."

17 Zion spreads out her hands,
But no one comforts her;
The LORD has commanded concerning Jacob
That those around him *become*
his adversaries;
Jerusalem has become an unclean thing
among them.

18 "The LORD is righteous,
For I rebelled against His commandment.
Hear now, all peoples,
And behold my sorrow;
My virgins and my young men
Have gone into captivity.

19 "I called for my lovers,
But they deceived me;
My priests and my elders
Breathed their last in the city,
While they sought food
To restore their life.

20 "See, O LORD, that I *am* in distress;
My soul is troubled;
My heart is overturned within me,
For I have been very rebellious.
Outside the sword bereaves,
At home *it is* like death.

21 "They have heard that I sigh,
But no one comforts me.
All my enemies have heard of my trouble;
They are glad that You have done *it*.
Bring on the day You have announced,
That they may become like me.

22 "Let all their wickedness come before You,
And do to them as You have done to me
For all my transgressions;
For my sighs *are* many,
And my heart *is* faint."

God's Anger with Jerusalem

2 How the Lord has covered the daughter of Zion
With a cloud in His anger!
He cast down from heaven to the earth
The beauty of Israel,

1:14 [c] Following Masoretic Text and Targum; Septuagint, Syriac, and Vulgate read *watched over.*

LIFE LESSON

Lamentations 2:1-22

SITUATION Jeremiah's second lament spoke of affliction and deliverance. Solomon's temple symbolized God's presence in Israel. Its destruction represented God's rejection of his people because of their stubborn sinfulness.

OBSERVATION God cares more about how we worship him than where we worship him.

INSPIRATION If we ponder who God really is before we carelessly utter any remark before or about Him, surely we will render a more considered, respectful utterance. This is no different from the respect we would show the distinguished stranger if we knew his true identity. When once we see Him as He really is, the trite or casual remark no longer seems appropriate.

In fact, when we know the God who is, our first reaction is to hide from the awfulness of His presence. We want to see the face of God, until the presence of His glory draws near. Then, we want Him to hide us in the cleft of a rock. His presence is like peals of thunder and fierce winds of a violent storm, and we reconsider the foolishness of our whim to see Him. He is a holy God. Not only holy—but holy, holy, holy. "Holy, holy, holy is the Lord God Almighty, who was, and is, and is to come" (Revelation 4:8).

. . . Let us reconsider who God is—His power, His wealth, His wisdom, His glory, His honor, His Praise. Let us take our cue from the living creatures, elders, and the angels. Let us

And did not remember His footstool
In the day of His anger.

2 The Lord has swallowed up and has not pitied
All the dwelling places of Jacob.
He has thrown down in His wrath
The strongholds of the daughter of Judah;
He has brought *them* down to the ground;
He has profaned the kingdom and its princes.

3 He has cut off in fierce anger
Every horn of Israel;
He has drawn back His right hand
From before the enemy.
He has blazed against Jacob like a flaming fire
Devouring all around.

4 Standing like an enemy, He has bent His bow;
With His right hand, like an adversary,
He has slain all *who were* pleasing to His eye;
On the tent of the daughter of Zion,
He has poured out His fury like fire.

5 The Lord was like an enemy.
He has swallowed up Israel,
He has swallowed up all her palaces;
He has destroyed her strongholds,
And has increased mourning and lamentation
In the daughter of Judah.

6 He has done violence to His tabernacle,
As if it were a garden;
He has destroyed His place of assembly;
The LORD has caused
The appointed feasts and Sabbaths to be forgotten in Zion.
In His burning indignation He has spurned
the king and the priest.

7 The Lord has spurned His altar,
He has abandoned His sanctuary;
He has given up the walls of her palaces
Into the hand of the enemy.
They have made a noise in the house of the LORD
As on the day of a set feast.

8 The LORD has purposed to destroy
The wall of the daughter of Zion.
He has stretched out a line;
He has not withdrawn His hand from destroying;
Therefore He has caused the rampart and wall to lament;
They languished together.

9 Her gates have sunk into the ground;
He has destroyed and broken her bars.
Her king and her princes *are* among the nations;

The Law *is* no *more,*
And her prophets find no vision from the LORD.

10 The elders of the daughter of Zion
Sit on the ground *and* keep silence;
They throw dust on their heads
And gird themselves with sackcloth.
The virgins of Jerusalem
Bow their heads to the ground.

11 My eyes fail with tears,
My heart is troubled;
My bile is poured on the ground
Because of the destruction of the daughter of my people,
Because the children and the infants
Faint in the streets of the city.

12 They say to their mothers,
"Where *is* grain and wine?"
As they swoon like the wounded
In the streets of the city,
As their life is poured out
In their mothers' bosom.

13 How shall I console you?
To what shall I liken you,
O daughter of Jerusalem?
What shall I compare with you, that I may comfort you,
O virgin daughter of Zion?
For your ruin *is* spread wide as the sea;
Who can heal you?

14 Your prophets have seen for you
False and deceptive visions;
They have not uncovered your iniquity,
To bring back your captives,
But have envisioned for you false prophecies and delusions.

15 All who pass by clap *their* hands at you;
They hiss and shake their heads
At the daughter of Jerusalem:
"*Is* this the city that is called
'The perfection of beauty,
The joy of the whole earth'?"

16 All your enemies have opened their mouth against you;
They hiss and gnash *their* teeth.
They say, "We have swallowed *her* up!
Surely this *is* the day we have waited for;
We have found *it,* we have seen *it!*"

17 The LORD has done what He purposed;
He has fulfilled His word
Which He commanded in days of old.
He has thrown down and has not pitied,

not approach the God who is holy, holy, holy with caprice or unthinking casualness.

Let us come into His presence with praise and thanksgiving, but also in sober recognition that we are in the presence of the Holy. "Let us then approach the throne of grace with confidence" (Hebrews 4:16), but with the bearing and respect we would show to the One whose identity we have learned: the God who is, who created all things, in whom we have our being.

When you come apart to meet with God, consider these statements as you begin your time in His presence. Pause and meditate upon them:

- Father, I come to meet with You. . . . Meet with me.
- Lord Jesus, I come to meet with You. . . . Meet with me.
- Holy Spirit, I come to meet with You. . . . Meet with me.

Enter into the presence of God who is with the respect and honor and praise He is due.

(From *Walking with Christ in the Details of Life* by Patrick Morley)

APPLICATION Worship God in prayer and song. Find a song that lifts your heart to God; sing it throughout the day. Thank God often for his help and love for you.

EXPLORATION Worship—Nehemiah 9:2-3; Psalm 122:1; Isaiah 29:13-14; Jeremiah 7:2-3; John 4: 21-24; 1 Corinthians 11:2-16.

And He has caused an enemy to
rejoice over you;
He has exalted the horn of your adversaries.

18 Their heart cried out to the Lord,
"O wall of the daughter of Zion,
Let tears run down like a river day and night;
Give yourself no relief;
Give your eyes no rest.

19 "Arise, cry out in the night,
At the beginning of the watches;
Pour out your heart like water before the face
of the Lord.
Lift your hands toward Him
For the life of your young children,
Who faint from hunger at the
head of every street."

20 "See, O LORD, and consider!
To whom have You done this?
Should the women eat their offspring,
The children they have cuddled?[d]
Should the priest and prophet be slain
In the sanctuary of the Lord?

21 "Young and old lie
On the ground in the streets;
My virgins and my young men
Have fallen by the sword;
You have slain *them* in the day of Your anger,
You have slaughtered *and* not pitied.

22 "You have invited as to a feast day
The terrors that surround me.
In the day of the LORD's anger
There was no refugee or survivor.
Those whom I have borne and brought up
My enemies have destroyed."

The Prophet's Anguish and Hope

3 I *am* the man *who* has seen affliction by the rod
of His wrath.
2 He has led me and made *me* walk
In darkness and not *in* light.
3 Surely He has turned His hand against me
Time and time again throughout the day.

4 He has aged my flesh and my skin,
And broken my bones.
5 He has besieged me
And surrounded *me* with bitterness and woe.
6 He has set me in dark places
Like the dead of long ago.

7 He has hedged me in so that I cannot get out;
He has made my chain heavy.
8 Even when I cry and shout,
He shuts out my prayer.
9 He has blocked my ways with hewn stone;
He has made my paths crooked.

10 He *has been* to me a bear lying in wait,
Like a lion in ambush.
11 He has turned aside my ways and
torn me in pieces;
He has made me desolate.
12 He has bent His bow
And set me up as a target for the arrow.

13 He has caused the arrows of His quiver
To pierce my loins.[e]
14 I have become the ridicule of all my people—
Their taunting song all the day.
15 He has filled me with bitterness,
He has made me drink wormwood.

16 He has also broken my teeth with gravel,
And covered me with ashes.
17 You have moved my soul far from peace;
I have forgotten prosperity.
18 And I said, "My strength and my hope
Have perished from the LORD."

19 Remember my affliction and roaming,
The wormwood and the gall.
20 My soul still remembers
And sinks within me.
21 This I recall to my mind,
Therefore I have hope.

22 *Through* the LORD's mercies we are
not consumed,
Because His compassions fail not.
23 *They are* new every morning;
Great *is* Your faithfulness.
24 "The LORD *is* my portion," says my soul,
"Therefore I hope in Him!"

25 The LORD *is* good to those who wait for Him,
To the soul *who* seeks Him.
26 *It is* good that *one* should hope and wait quietly
For the salvation of the LORD.
27 *It is* good for a man to bear
The yoke in his youth.

2:20 [d] Vulgate reads *a span long*.
3:13 [e] Literally *kidneys*

28 Let him sit alone and keep silent,
Because *God* has laid *it* on him;
29 Let him put his mouth in the dust—
There may yet be hope.
30 Let him give *his* cheek to the one who strikes him,
And be full of reproach.

31 For the Lord will not cast off forever.
32 Though He causes grief,
Yet He will show compassion
According to the multitude of His mercies.
33 For He does not afflict willingly,
Nor grieve the children of men.

34 To crush under one's feet
All the prisoners of the earth,
35 To turn aside the justice *due* a man
Before the face of the Most High,
36 Or subvert a man in his cause—
The Lord does not approve.

37 Who *is* he *who* speaks and it comes to pass,
When the Lord has not commanded *it*?
38 *Is it* not from the mouth of the Most High
That woe and well-being proceed?
39 Why should a living man complain,
A man for the punishment of his sins?

40 Let us search out and examine our ways,
And turn back to the LORD;
41 Let us lift our hearts and hands
To God in heaven.
42 We have transgressed and rebelled;
You have not pardoned.

43 You have covered *Yourself* with anger
And pursued us;
You have slain *and* not pitied.
44 You have covered Yourself with a cloud,
That prayer should not pass through.
45 You have made us an offscouring and refuse
In the midst of the peoples.

46 All our enemies
Have opened their mouths against us.
47 Fear and a snare have come upon us,
Desolation and destruction.
48 My eyes overflow with rivers of water
For the destruction of the
daughter of my people.

49 My eyes flow and do not cease,
Without interruption,
50 Till the LORD from heaven
Looks down and sees.

LIFE LESSON

Lamentations 3:1-66

SITUATION Jeremiah's sorrow and consolation represented the nation's agony. Surrounded by sin and sorrow, Jeremiah saw hope in God's steadfast love and mercy.

OBSERVATION God renews our lives day by day.

INSPIRATION The fog of the broken heart.

It's a dark fog that slyly imprisons the soul and refuses easy escape. It's a silent mist that eclipses the sun and beckons the darkness. It's a heavy cloud that honors no hour and respects no person. Depression, discouragement, disappointment, doubt . . . all are companions of this dreaded presence.

The fog of the broken heart disorients our life. It makes it hard to see the road. Dim your lights. Wipe off the windshield. Slow down. Do what you wish, nothing helps. When this fog encircles us, our vision is blocked and tomorrow is a forever away. When this billowy blackness envelops us, the most earnest words of help and hope are but vacant phrases.

If you have ever been betrayed by a friend, you know what I mean. If you have ever been dumped by a spouse or abandoned by a parent, you have seen this fog. If you have ever placed a spade of dirt on a loved one's casket or kept vigil at a dear one's bedside, you, too, recognize this cloud.

If you have been in this fog, or are in it now, you can be sure of one thing—you are not alone. Even the saltiest of sea captains have lost their bearings because of the appearance of this unwanted cloud. . . .

Think back over the last two or three months. How many broken hearts did you encounter? How many wounded spirits did you witness? How many stories of tragedy did you read about? . . .

The list goes on and on, doesn't it? Foggy tragedies. How they blind our vision and destroy our dreams. Forget any great hopes of reaching the world. Forget any plans of changing

Continued

society. Forget any aspirations of moving mountains. Forget all that. Just help me make it through the night!

The suffering of the broken heart. . . . Seeing God . . . does wonders for our own suffering. God was never more human than at this hour. God was never nearer to us than when he hurt. The Incarnation was never so fulfilled as in the garden.

As a result, time spent in the fog of pain could be God's greatest gift. It could be the hour that we finally see our Maker. . . . Maybe in our suffering we can see God like never before.

The next time you are called to suffer, pay attention. It may be the closest you'll ever get to God. Watch closely. It could very well be that the hand that extends itself to lead you out of the fog is a pierced one.

(From *No Wonder They Call Him the Savior* by Max Lucado)

APPLICATION Send a note to someone who is overwhelmed by his or her lot in life. Assure that friend of your prayers. Include a Scripture verse that tells of God's love.

EXPLORATION God's Love—Proverbs 13:24; Luke 12:7; John 13:27-38; Romans 8:35-39; Ephesians 3:17-19; 1 John 4:9-10.

51 My eyes bring suffering to my soul
Because of all the daughters of my city.

52 My enemies without cause
Hunted me down like a bird.
53 They silenced[f] my life in the pit
And threw stones at me.
54 The waters flowed over my head;
I said, "I am cut off!"

55 I called on Your name, O LORD,
From the lowest pit.
56 You have heard my voice:
"Do not hide Your ear
From my sighing, from my cry for help."
57 You drew near on the day I called on You,
And said, "Do not fear!"

58 O Lord, You have pleaded the case for my soul;
You have redeemed my life.
59 O LORD, You have seen *how* I am wronged;
Judge my case.
60 You have seen all their vengeance,
All their schemes against me.

61 You have heard their reproach, O LORD,
All their schemes against me,
62 The lips of my enemies
And their whispering against me all the day.
63 Look at their sitting down and their rising up;
I *am* their taunting song.

64 Repay them, O LORD,
According to the work of their hands.
65 Give them a veiled[g] heart;
Your curse *be* upon them!
66 In Your anger,
Pursue and destroy them
From under the heavens of the LORD.

The Degradation of Zion

4 How the gold has become dim!
How changed the fine gold!
The stones of the sanctuary are scattered
At the head of every street.

2 The precious sons of Zion,
Valuable as fine gold,
How they are regarded as clay pots,
The work of the hands of the potter!

3 Even the jackals present their breasts
To nurse their young;

3:53 [f] Septuagint reads *put to death.*
3:65 [g] A Jewish tradition reads *sorrow of.*

But the daughter of my people *is* cruel,
Like ostriches in the wilderness.

4 The tongue of the infant clings
To the roof of its mouth for thirst;
The young children ask for bread,
But no one breaks *it* for them.

5 Those who ate delicacies
Are desolate in the streets;
Those who were brought up in scarlet
Embrace ash heaps.

6 The punishment of the iniquity of the
daughter of my people
Is greater than the punishment of the sin of Sodom,
Which was overthrown in a moment,
With no hand to help her!

7 Her Nazirites[h] were brighter than snow
And whiter than milk;
They were more ruddy in body than rubies,
Like sapphire in their appearance.

8 *Now* their appearance is blacker than soot;
They go unrecognized in the streets;
Their skin clings to their bones,
It has become as dry as wood.

9 *Those* slain by the sword are better off
Than *those* who die of hunger;
For these pine away,
Stricken *for lack* of the fruits of the field.

10 The hands of the compassionate women
Have cooked their own children;
They became food for them
In the destruction of the daughter of my people.

11 The LORD has fulfilled His fury,
He has poured out His fierce anger.
He kindled a fire in Zion,
And it has devoured its foundations.

12 The kings of the earth,
And all inhabitants of the world,
Would not have believed
That the adversary and the enemy
Could enter the gates of Jerusalem—

13 Because of the sins of her prophets
And the iniquities of her priests,
Who shed in her midst
The blood of the just.

14 They wandered blind in the streets;

4:7 *h* Or *nobles*

LIFE LESSON

Lamentations 4:1-22

SITUATION Jeremiah described the people's fate. He also told what they had done to deserve such punishment. The sins of the prophets, priests, and people had brought about the city's destruction.

OBSERVATION God does not leave his people in destruction and judgment. God will restore.

INSPIRATION I came into this world physically alive but spiritually dead; I learned to live my life independent of God. Essentially, that is what constitutes the flesh. I had neither the presence of God in my life nor the knowledge of God's ways, so I learned to cope and defend myself as I was being conformed to this world. This learned independence is what makes the flesh hostile toward God. That is why the flesh and the Spirit are in opposition to one another.

Being children of God, the presence of the Holy Spirit restrains us so we will not do the things that we please. If there were no moral restraints and no boundaries to govern our behavior, we would drive ourselves into moral decadence. Imagine the air traffic controller saying to the pilot, "You have my permission to land any time and any place you want." . . .

God wants us free, but freedom is not license. I believe we are free by the grace of God to live a responsible life. In the early part of the twentieth century, a rigid fundamentalism had left our churches frozen in legalism. In the '50s it began to thaw, and the Jesus People movement of the '60s and '70s melted it into license for many. The pendulum had swung from the justice of God to the mercy of God. . . . There's always a price to pay for license. True freedom doesn't lie in the exercise of choices, but in the consequences of the choices made. You may reserve the right to tell a lie, but you'll be in

Continued

bondage to it because you'll have to remember the nature of the lie and to whom you told it. You may choose to rob a bank, but you will always be looking over your shoulder, fearing you may be caught. That's bondage. (From *Walking with Christ in the Details of Life* by Patrick Morley)

APPLICATION What tempts you to neglect or ignore God? Take a walk in a quiet place. Fellowship with God. Spend time in his presence every day.

EXPLORATION Carnal Life—Judges 3:5-7; Psalm 49:1; 119:9; Romans 13:12-14; 1 Corinthians 6:9-11; 1 John 2:15-16; Revelation 9:20-21.

They have defiled themselves with blood,
So that no one would touch their garments.

15 They cried out to them,
"Go away, unclean!
Go away, go away,
Do not touch us!"
When they fled and wandered,
Those among the nations said,
"They shall no longer dwell *here*."

16 The face[i] of the LORD scattered them;
He no longer regards them.
The people do not respect the priests
Nor show favor to the elders.

17 Still our eyes failed us,
Watching vainly for our help;
In our watching we watched
For a nation *that* could not save *us*.

18 They tracked our steps
So that we could not walk in our streets.
Our end was near;
Our days were over,
For our end had come.

19 Our pursuers were swifter
Than the eagles of the heavens.
They pursued us on the mountains
And lay in wait for us in the wilderness.

20 The breath of our nostrils, the anointed of the LORD,
Was caught in their pits,
Of whom we said, "Under his shadow
We shall live among the nations."

21 Rejoice and be glad, O daughter of Edom,
You who dwell in the land of Uz!
The cup shall also pass over to you
And you shall become drunk and make yourself naked.

22 *The punishment of* your iniquity is accomplished,
O daughter of Zion;
He will no longer send you into captivity.
He will punish your iniquity,
O daughter of Edom;
He will uncover your sins!

A Prayer for Restoration

5 Remember, O LORD, what has come upon us;
Look, and behold our reproach!
2 Our inheritance has been turned over to aliens,
And our houses to foreigners.

4:16 [i] Targum reads *anger*.

3 We have become orphans and waifs,
Our mothers *are* like widows.

4 We pay for the water we drink,
And our wood comes at a price.
5 *They* pursue at our heels;[j]
We labor *and* have no rest.
6 We have given our hand *to* the Egyptians
And the Assyrians, to be satisfied with bread.

7 Our fathers sinned *and are* no more,
But we bear their iniquities.
8 Servants rule over us;
There is none to deliver *us* from their hand.
9 We get our bread *at the risk* of our lives,
Because of the sword in the wilderness.

10 Our skin is hot as an oven,
Because of the fever of famine.
11 They ravished the women in Zion,
The maidens in the cities of Judah.
12 Princes were hung up by their hands,
And elders were not respected.
13 Young men ground at the millstones;
Boys staggered under *loads of* wood.
14 The elders have ceased *gathering at* the gate,
And the young men from their music.

15 The joy of our heart has ceased;
Our dance has turned into mourning.
16 The crown has fallen *from* our head.
Woe to us, for we have sinned!
17 Because of this our heart is faint;
Because of these *things* our eyes grow dim;
18 Because of Mount Zion which is desolate,
With foxes walking about on it.

19 You, O LORD, remain forever;
Your throne from generation to generation.
20 Why do You forget us forever,
And forsake us for so long a time?
21 Turn us back to You, O LORD, and we will be restored;
Renew our days as of old,
22 Unless You have utterly rejected us,
And are very angry with us!

5:5 *j* Literally *necks*

LIFE LESSON

Lamentations 5:1-22

SITUATION After four mournful chants, in the final lament Jeremiah prayed for mercy. The poet sketched the loss of freedom, land, and respect, as well as the increase in rape, cruelty, forced labor, and starvation. Weary of chastening and longing for renewal, the people prayed for restoration.

OBSERVATION Grief should turn us to God. He alone can heal and restore.

INSPIRATION We live in a profoundly religious country, and we are a prosperous people. But we are also a broken people—a people who have pursued the God of our own imaginations, believing we can re-create His character to suit our own practical problems. The result? We are the most religious nation in the world, but [spiritually] lukewarm.

Prosperous Christians become lukewarm. Lukewarm Christians rely upon themselves and forget the terms of their surrender to Christ. Instead of living by the will of God, they live according to the self-will and break fellowship with God. . . .

. . . Jesus offers to reestablish fellowship with broken, lukewarm, cultural Christians. He cries out His offer to the church: . . . "Those whom I love I rebuke and discipline. So be earnest, and repent. Here I am! I stand at the door and knock. If anyone hears my voice and opens the door, I will come in and eat with him, and he with me" (Revelation 3:19-20).

He is the way back. When we become complacent, when we stop walking with Him, He still loves us. He despises our behavior, but He wants to restore fellowship with us.

(From *Walking with Christ in the Details of Life* by Patrick Morley)

APPLICATION Do you think you are too old for renewal? Too young? Don't believe it! God offers new qualities of life, new hope, and a bright future at every age. Put the past in God's hands, and grasp his new day for you.

EXPLORATION Renewal—2 Chronicles 31:20-21; Nehemiah 2:17-18; Mark 6:31; John 6:63, 65.

The Book of

EZEKIEL

INTRODUCTION

Out of the ruins of Jerusalem came a gutsy preacher named Ezekiel. He was among the Jews taken to Babylon after the fall of his country. He left behind his city. He left behind his Temple. He left behind his home.

But he didn't leave his faith.

He announced it to everyone who would listen. For twenty-two years he paced the streets proclaiming both sides of the faith.

The bad side? Turn or burn. Forgive me for being so direct, but Ezekiel was.

The good side? Turn and learn. God has a great plan for his people. A great city. Justice will reign and worship will be restored. Unlike Jerusalem, God's city is eternal. Who will be in God's city? Ezekiel answers that with the final words of the book—*THE LORD IS THERE.*

Out of the ruins came Ezekiel. Out of the ruins came the promise. Out of the ruins came the new hope.

Is your life in ruins? Look ahead to God's city: *THE LORD IS THERE.*

Life Lesson

Ezekiel 1:1–3:27

SITUATION Ezekiel, a priest who had favor in God's eyes, suffered because of the sin of the whole nation. In exile, he preached to fellow Jewish captives.

OBSERVATION God ordains our position so that we can show God's love to those around us.

INSPIRATION What we *want* is relief. We want our problem or heartache to just go away. And yet the biblical message of rest is that your relief may come from the power you gain when you accept your suffering. Your relief may come from the strength you develop from serving in spite of it.

Remember, Jesus said, "Take My yoke (suffering) upon you and learn of Me, for I am meek and lowly in heart and you shall *find* rest for your souls."

If you are bewildered, badgered, broken, or battered as you try to make your way along the freeways of life, take a rest. You'll find a quiet calm awaiting you when you accept what you cannot change, and serve the very people who contribute to your pain.

(From *Little House on the Freeway* by Tim Kimmel)

APPLICATION Is your life discouraging? Is the difficulty unavoidable? God has placed you where you can help others. Encourage others who have the same illness you have. Share Christ with those who have also experienced the loss of a loved one. Get to know others who are recovering from a problem you have faced and share with them what has helped you.

EXPLORATION Preaching without a Response—Isaiah 6:9-12; Jeremiah 1:17-19.

Ezekiel's Vision of God

Now it came to pass in the thirtieth year, in the fourth *month,* on the fifth *day* of the month, as I *was* among the captives by the River Chebar, *that* the heavens were opened and I saw visions[a] of God. 2On the fifth *day* of the month, which *was* in the fifth year of King Jehoiachin's captivity, 3the word of the LORD came expressly to Ezekiel the priest, the son of Buzi, in the land of the Chaldeans[b] by the River Chebar; and the hand of the LORD was upon him there.

4Then I looked, and behold, a whirlwind was coming out of the north, a great cloud with raging fire engulfing itself; and brightness *was* all around it and radiating out of its midst like the color of amber, out of the midst of the fire. 5Also from within it *came* the likeness of four living creatures. And this *was* their appearance: they had the likeness of a man. 6Each one had four faces, and each one had four wings. 7Their legs *were* straight, and the soles of their feet *were* like the soles of calves' feet. They sparkled like the color of burnished bronze. 8The hands of a man *were* under their wings on their four sides; and each of the four had faces and wings. 9Their wings touched one another. *The creatures* did not turn when they went, but each one went straight forward.

10As for the likeness of their faces, *each* had the face of a man; each of the four had the face of a lion on the right side, each of the four had the face of an ox on the left side, and each of the four had the face of an eagle. 11Thus *were* their faces. Their wings stretched upward; two *wings* of each one touched one another, and two covered their bodies. 12And each one went straight forward; they went wherever the spirit wanted to go, and they did not turn when they went.

13As for the likeness of the living creatures, their appearance *was* like burning coals of fire, like the appearance of torches going back and forth among the living creatures. The fire was bright, and out of the fire went lightning. 14And the living creatures ran back and forth, in appearance like a flash of lightning.

15Now as I looked at the living creatures, behold, a wheel *was* on the earth beside each living creature with its four faces. 16The appearance of the wheels and their workings *was* like the color of beryl, and all four had the same likeness. The appearance of their workings *was,* as it were, a wheel in the middle of a wheel. 17When they moved, they went toward any one of four directions; they did not turn aside when they went. 18As for their rims, they were so high they were awesome; and their rims *were* full of eyes, all around the four of them. 19When the living creatures went, the wheels went beside them; and when the living creatures were lifted up from the earth, the wheels were lifted up. 20Wherever the spirit wanted to go, they went, *because* there the spirit went; and the wheels were lifted together with them, for the spirit of the living creatures[c] *was* in the wheels. 21When those went, *these* went; when those stood, *these* stood; and when those were lifted up from the earth, the wheels were lifted up together with them, for the spirit of the living creatures[d] *was* in the wheels.

1:1 [a] Following Masoretic Text, Septuagint, and Vulgate; Syriac and Targum read *a vision.*
1:3 [b] Or *Babylonians,* and so elsewhere in this book
1:20 [c] Literally *living creature;* Septuagint and Vulgate read *spirit of life;* Targum reads *creatures.*
1:21 [d] Literally *living creature;* Septuagint and Vulgate read *spirit of life;* Targum reads *creatures.*

22The likeness of the firmament above the heads of the living creatures[e] *was* like the color of an awesome crystal, stretched out over their heads. 23And under the firmament their wings *spread out* straight, one toward another. Each one had two which covered one side, and each one had two which covered the other side of the body. 24When they went, I heard the noise of their wings, like the noise of many waters, like the voice of the Almighty, a tumult like the noise of an army; and when they stood still, they let down their wings. 25A voice came from above the firmament that *was* over their heads; whenever they stood, they let down their wings.

26And above the firmament over their heads *was* the likeness of a throne, in appearance like a sapphire stone; on the likeness of the throne *was* a likeness with the appearance of a man high above it. 27Also from the appearance of His waist and upward I saw, as it were, the color of amber with the appearance of fire all around within it; and from the appearance of His waist and downward I saw, as it were, the appearance of fire with brightness all around. 28Like the appearance of a rainbow in a cloud on a rainy day, so *was* the appearance of the brightness all around it. This *was* the appearance of the likeness of the glory of the LORD.

Ezekiel Sent to Rebellious Israel

So when I saw *it,* I fell on my face, and I heard a voice of One speaking.

2 And He said to me, "Son of man, stand on your feet, and I will speak to you." 2Then the Spirit entered me when He spoke to me, and set me on my feet; and I heard Him who spoke to me. 3And He said to me: "Son of man, I am sending you to the children of Israel, to a rebellious nation that has rebelled against Me; they and their fathers have transgressed against Me to this very day. 4For *they are* impudent and stubborn children. I am sending you to them, and you shall say to them, 'Thus says the Lord GOD.' 5As for them, whether they hear or whether they refuse—for they *are* a rebellious house—yet they will know that a prophet has been among them.

6"And you, son of man, do not be afraid of them nor be afraid of their words, though briers and thorns *are* with you and you dwell among scorpions; do not be afraid of their words or dismayed by their looks, though they *are* a rebellious house. 7You shall speak My words to them, whether they hear or whether they refuse, for they *are* rebellious. 8But you, son of man, hear what I say to you. Do not be rebellious like that rebellious house; open your mouth and eat what I give you."

9Now when I looked, there was a hand stretched out to me; and behold, a scroll of a book *was* in it. 10Then He spread it before me; and *there was* writing on the inside and on the outside, and written on it *were* lamentations and mourning and woe.

3 Moreover He said to me, "Son of man, eat what you find; eat this scroll, and go, speak to the house of Israel." 2So I opened my mouth, and He caused me to eat that scroll.

3And He said to me, "Son of man, feed your belly, and fill your stomach with this scroll that I give you." So I ate, and it was in my mouth like honey in sweetness.

4Then He said to me: "Son of man, go to the house of Israel and speak with My words to them. 5For you *are* not sent to a people of unfamiliar speech and of hard language, *but* to the house of Israel, 6not to many people of unfamiliar speech and of hard language, whose words you cannot understand. Surely, had I sent you to them, they would have listened to you. 7But the house of Israel will not listen to you, because they will not listen to Me; for all the house of Israel *are* impudent and hard-hearted. 8Behold, I have made your face strong against their faces, and your forehead strong against their foreheads. 9Like adamant stone, harder than flint, I have made your forehead; do not be afraid of them, nor be dismayed at their looks, though they *are* a rebellious house."

10Moreover He said to me: "Son of man, receive into your heart all My words that I speak to you, and hear with your ears. 11And go, get to the captives, to the children of your people, and speak to them and tell them, 'Thus says the Lord GOD,' whether they hear, or whether they refuse."

12Then the Spirit lifted me up, and I heard behind me a great thunderous voice: "Blessed *is* the glory of the LORD from His place!" 13*I* also *heard* the noise of the wings of the living creatures that touched one another, and the noise of the wheels beside them, and a great thunderous noise. 14So the Spirit lifted me up and took me away, and I went in bitterness, in the heat of my spirit; but the hand of the LORD was strong upon me. 15Then I came to the captives at Tel Abib, who dwelt by the River Chebar; and I sat where they sat, and remained there astonished among them seven days.

1:22 [e] Following Septuagint, Targum, and Vulgate; Masoretic Text reads *living creature.*

LIFE LESSON

Ezekiel 4:1–7:27

SITUATION Before the fall of Jerusalem in 586 B.C., God told Ezekiel about the impending judgment.

OBSERVATION Israel's idolatry needed to be judged. God will not tolerate anything that displaces him in our lives.

INSPIRATION What is idolatry? Idolatry is anything that comes between us and God. Joshua told his people that their nation would be destroyed if they persisted in idolatry, and their souls would suffer eternal death. He said, "You must make your decision today. You must decide whether you want to serve the idols of this life, or the living God." "Choose you this day," said Joshua, "as for me and my house, we will serve the Lord." What about you? Are you taking your stand with Joshua? No matter what the cost? I am asking you to choose this day whom you will serve. Our families cannot choose Christ for us. Our friends cannot do it. God is a great God, but even God can't make the decision for us. He can help, but only we can decide. We have to make our own choice.

(From *Day by Day with Billy Graham* by Joan W. Brown)

APPLICATION We don't see many people worshiping idols today. However, we do see career, cars, money, and pleasure crowding God out of people's lives. No one is immune from such temptation. Be aware of selfish desires for material wealth or social status. Have only one concern: a right relationship with God.

EXPLORATION Idolatry/Sin—Exodus 20:1-6; Joshua 24:23; Job 31:24-28; Jeremiah 1:16; Luke 16:10-15; Revelation 21:8.

Ezekiel Is a Watchman

[16]Now it came to pass at the end of seven days that the word of the LORD
came to me, saying, [17]"Son of man, I have made you a watchman for the
house of Israel; therefore hear a word from My mouth, and give them
warning from Me: [18]When I say to the wicked, 'You shall surely die,' and
you give him no warning, nor speak to warn the wicked from his wicked
way, to save his life, that same wicked *man* shall die in his iniquity; but his
blood I will require at your hand. [19]Yet, if you warn the wicked, and he does
not turn from his wickedness, nor from his wicked way, he shall die in his
iniquity; but you have delivered your soul.
[20]"Again, when a righteous *man* turns from his righteousness and commits iniquity, and I lay a stumbling block before him, he shall die; because
you did not give him warning, he shall die in his sin, and his righteousness
which he has done shall not be remembered; but his blood I will require at
your hand. [21]Nevertheless if you warn the righteous *man* that the righteous
should not sin, and he does not sin, he shall surely live because he took
warning; also you will have delivered your soul."
[22]Then the hand of the LORD was upon me there, and He said to me,
"Arise, go out into the plain, and there I shall talk with you."
[23]So I arose and went out into the plain, and behold, the glory of the
LORD stood there, like the glory which I saw by the River Chebar; and I fell
on my face. [24]Then the Spirit entered me and set me on my feet, and spoke
with me and said to me: "Go, shut yourself inside your house. [25]And you,
O son of man, surely they will put ropes on you and bind you with them,
so that you cannot go out among them. [26]I will make your tongue cling to
the roof of your mouth, so that you shall be mute and not be one to rebuke
them, for they *are* a rebellious house. [27]But when I speak with you, I will
open your mouth, and you shall say to them, 'Thus says the Lord GOD.' He
who hears, let him hear; and he who refuses, let him refuse; for they *are* a
rebellious house.

The Siege of Jerusalem Portrayed

4 "You also, son of man, take a clay tablet and lay it before you, and portray on it a city, Jerusalem. [2]Lay siege against it, build a siege wall
against it, and heap up a mound against it; set camps against it also, and
place battering rams against it all around. [3]Moreover take for yourself an
iron plate, and set it *as* an iron wall between you and the city. Set your face
against it, and it shall be besieged, and you shall lay siege against it. This
will be a sign to the house of Israel.
[4]"Lie also on your left side, and lay the iniquity of the house of Israel
upon it. *According* to the number of the days that you lie on it, you shall
bear their iniquity. [5]For I have laid on you the years of their iniquity, according to the number of the days, three hundred and ninety days; so you
shall bear the iniquity of the house of Israel. [6]And when you have completed them, lie again on your right side; then you shall bear the iniquity of
the house of Judah forty days. I have laid on you a day for each year.
[7]"Therefore you shall set your face toward the siege of Jerusalem; your
arm *shall be* uncovered, and you shall prophesy against it. [8]And surely I
will restrain you so that you cannot turn from one side to another till you
have ended the days of your siege.

9“Also take for yourself wheat, barley, beans,
lentils, millet, and spelt; put them into one vessel, and
make bread of them for yourself. *During* the number
of days that you lie on your side, three hundred and
ninety days, you shall eat it. 10And your food which
you eat *shall be* by weight, twenty shekels a day; from
time to time you shall eat it. 11You shall also drink
water by measure, one-sixth of a hin; from time to time
you shall drink. 12And you shall eat it *as* barley cakes;
and bake it using fuel of human waste in their sight.”
13Then the LORD said, “So shall the children of Israel
eat their defiled bread among the Gentiles, where I
will drive them.”
14So I said, “Ah, Lord GOD! Indeed I have never defiled myself from my youth till now; I have never
eaten what died of itself or was torn by beasts, nor has
abominable flesh ever come into my mouth.”
15Then He said to me, “See, I am giving you cow
dung instead of human waste, and you shall prepare
your bread over it.”
16Moreover He said to me, “Son of man, surely I
will cut off the supply of bread in Jerusalem; they shall
eat bread by weight and with anxiety, and shall drink
water by measure and with dread, 17that they may lack
bread and water, and be dismayed with one another,
and waste away because of their iniquity.

A Sword Against Jerusalem

5 “And you, son of man, take a sharp sword, take it
as a barber’s razor, and pass *it* over your head and
your beard; then take scales to weigh and divide the
hair. 2You shall burn with fire one-third in the midst
of the city, when the days of the siege are finished;
then you shall take one-third and strike around *it*
with the sword, and one-third you shall scatter in the
wind: I will draw out a sword after them. 3You shall
also take a small number of them and bind them in
the edge of your *garment.* 4Then take some of them
again and throw them into the midst of the fire, and
burn them in the fire. From there a fire will go out into
all the house of Israel.
5“Thus says the Lord GOD: ‘This *is* Jerusalem; I have
set her in the midst of the nations and the countries
all around her. 6She has rebelled against My judgments by doing wickedness more than the nations,
and against My statutes more than the countries that
are all around her; for they have refused My judgments, and they have not walked in My statutes.’
7Therefore thus says the Lord GOD: ‘Because you have
multiplied *disobedience* more than the nations that
are all around you, have not walked in My statutes nor
kept My judgments, nor even done[f] according to the
judgments of the nations that *are* all around you’—
8therefore thus says the Lord GOD: ‘Indeed I, even I,
am against you and will execute judgments in your
midst in the sight of the nations. 9And I will do among
you what I have never done, and the like of which I
will never do again, because of all your abominations.
10Therefore fathers shall eat *their* sons in your midst,
and sons shall eat their fathers; and I will execute
judgments among you, and all of you who remain I
will scatter to all the winds.
11‘Therefore, *as* I live,’ says the Lord GOD, ‘surely, because you have defiled My sanctuary with all your detestable things and with all your abominations,
therefore I will also diminish *you;* My eye will not
spare, nor will I have any pity. 12One-third of you shall
die of the pestilence, and be consumed with famine in
your midst; and one-third shall fall by the sword all
around you; and I will scatter another third to all the
winds, and I will draw out a sword after them.
13‘Thus shall My anger be spent, and I will cause
My fury to rest upon them, and I will be avenged; and
they shall know that I, the LORD, have spoken *it* in My
zeal, when I have spent My fury upon them. 14More-
over I will make you a waste and a reproach among
the nations that *are* all around you, in the sight of all
who pass by.
15‘So it[g] shall be a reproach, a taunt, a lesson, and an
astonishment to the nations that *are* all around you,
when I execute judgments among you in anger and in
fury and in furious rebukes. I, the LORD, have spoken.
16When I send against them the terrible arrows of
famine which shall be for destruction, which I will
send to destroy you, I will increase the famine upon
you and cut off your supply of bread. 17So I will send
against you famine and wild beasts, and they will bereave you. Pestilence and blood shall pass through
you, and I will bring the sword against you. I, the
LORD, have spoken.’ ”

Judgment on Idolatrous Israel

6 Now the word of the LORD came to me, saying:
2“Son of man, set your face toward the mountains
of Israel, and prophesy against them, 3and say, ‘O
mountains of Israel, hear the word of the Lord GOD!
Thus says the Lord GOD to the mountains, to the hills,
to the ravines, and to the valleys: “Indeed I, *even* I, will

5:7 [f] Following Masoretic Text, Septuagint, Targum, and Vulgate; many Hebrew manuscripts and Syriac read *but have done* (compare 11:12).
5:15 [g] Septuagint, Syriac, Targum, and Vulgate read *you.*

bring a sword against you, and I will destroy your
high places. 4Then your altars shall be desolate, your
incense altars shall be broken, and I will cast down
your slain *men* before your idols. 5And I will lay the
corpses of the children of Israel before their idols, and
I will scatter your bones all around your altars. 6In all
your dwelling places the cities shall be laid waste, and
the high places shall be desolate, so that your altars
may be laid waste and made desolate, your idols may
be broken and made to cease, your incense altars may
be cut down, and your works may be abolished. 7The
slain shall fall in your midst, and you shall know that
I *am* the LORD.

8"Yet I will leave a remnant, so that you may have
some who escape the sword among the nations, when
you are scattered through the countries. 9Then those
of you who escape will remember Me among the nations where they are carried captive, because I was
crushed by their adulterous heart which has departed
from Me, and by their eyes which play the harlot after
their idols; they will loathe themselves for the evils
which they committed in all their abominations. 10And
they shall know that I *am* the LORD; I have not said in
vain that I would bring this calamity upon them."

11"Thus says the Lord GOD: "Pound your fists and
stamp your feet, and say, 'Alas, for all the evil
abominations of the house of Israel! For they shall fall
by the sword, by famine, and by pestilence. 12He who
is far off shall die by the pestilence, he who is near
shall fall by the sword, and he who remains and is besieged shall die by the famine. Thus will I spend My
fury upon them. 13Then you shall know that I *am* the
LORD, when their slain are among their idols all
around their altars, on every high hill, on all the
mountaintops, under every green tree, and under
every thick oak, wherever they offered sweet incense
to all their idols. 14So I will stretch out My hand
against them and make the land desolate, yes, more
desolate than the wilderness toward Diblah, in all
their dwelling places. Then they shall know that I *am*
the LORD.' " ' "

Judgment on Israel Is Near

7 Moreover the word of the LORD came to me, saying, 2"And you, son of man, thus says the Lord
GOD to the land of Israel:

'An end! The end has come upon the four
corners of the land.
3 Now the end *has come* upon you,
And I will send My anger against you;
I will judge you according to your ways,
And I will repay you for all
your abominations.
4 My eye will not spare you,
Nor will I have pity;
But I will repay your ways,
And your abominations will be in your midst;
Then you shall know that I *am* the LORD!'

5"Thus says the Lord GOD:
'A disaster, a singular disaster;
Behold, it has come!
6 An end has come,
The end has come;
It has dawned for you;
Behold, it has come!
7 Doom has come to you, you who dwell
in the land;
The time has come,
A day of trouble *is* near,
And not of rejoicing in the mountains.
8 Now upon you I will soon pour out My fury,
And spend My anger upon you;
I will judge you according to your ways,
And I will repay you for all
your abominations.

9 'My eye will not spare,
Nor will I have pity;
I will repay you according to your ways,
And your abominations will be in your midst.
Then you shall know that I *am* the LORD
who strikes.
10 'Behold, the day!
Behold, it has come!
Doom has gone out;
The rod has blossomed,
Pride has budded.
11 Violence has risen up into a rod
of wickedness;
None of them *shall remain,*
None of their multitude,
None of them;
Nor *shall there be* wailing for them.
12 The time has come,
The day draws near.

'Let not the buyer rejoice,
Nor the seller mourn,
For wrath *is* on their whole multitude.
13 For the seller shall not return to what
has been sold,

Though he may still be alive;
For the vision concerns the whole multitude,
And it shall not turn back;
No one will strengthen himself
Who lives in iniquity.

14 'They have blown the trumpet and made
everyone ready,
But no one goes to battle;
For My wrath *is* on all their multitude.
15 The sword *is* outside,
And the pestilence and famine within.
Whoever *is* in the field
Will die by the sword;
And whoever *is* in the city,
Famine and pestilence will devour him.

16 'Those who survive will escape and be
on the mountains
Like doves of the valleys,
All of them mourning,
Each for his iniquity.
17 Every hand will be feeble,
And every knee will be *as* weak *as* water.
18 They will also be girded with sackcloth;
Horror will cover them;
Shame *will be* on every face,
Baldness on all their heads.

19 'They will throw their silver into the streets,
And their gold will be like refuse;
Their silver and their gold will not be able to
deliver them
In the day of the wrath of the LORD;
They will not satisfy their souls,
Nor fill their stomachs,
Because it became their stumbling block
of iniquity.

20 'As for the beauty of his ornaments,
He set it in majesty;
But they made from it
The images of their abominations—
Their detestable things;
Therefore I have made it
Like refuse to them.
21 I will give it as plunder
Into the hands of strangers,
And to the wicked of the earth as spoil;
And they shall defile it.
22 I will turn My face from them,
And they will defile My secret place;
For robbers shall enter it and defile it.
23 'Make a chain,
For the land is filled with crimes of blood,
And the city is full of violence.
24 Therefore I will bring the worst of the Gentiles,
And they will possess their houses;
I will cause the pomp of the strong to cease,
And their holy places shall be defiled.
25 Destruction comes;
They will seek peace, but *there shall be* none.
26 Disaster will come upon disaster,
And rumor will be upon rumor.
Then they will seek a vision from a prophet;
But the law will perish from the priest,
And counsel from the elders.

27 'The king will mourn,
The prince will be clothed with desolation,
And the hands of the common people
will tremble.
I will do to them according to their way,
And according to what they deserve I will
judge them;
Then they shall know that I *am* the LORD!'"

Abominations in the Temple

8 And it came to pass in the sixth year, in the sixth
month, on the fifth *day* of the month, as I sat in my
house with the elders of Judah sitting before me, that
the hand of the Lord GOD fell upon me there. 2Then I
looked, and there was a likeness, like the appearance
of fire—from the appearance of His waist and downward, fire; and from His waist and upward, like the
appearance of brightness, like the color of amber. 3He
stretched out the form of a hand, and took me by a
lock of my hair; and the Spirit lifted me up between
earth and heaven, and brought me in visions of God
to Jerusalem, to the door of the north gate of the inner
court, where the seat of the image of jealousy *was,*
which provokes to jealousy. 4And behold, the glory of
the God of Israel *was* there, like the vision that I saw in
the plain.

5Then He said to me, "Son of man, lift your eyes
now toward the north." So I lifted my eyes toward the
north, and there, north of the altar gate, was this
image of jealousy in the entrance.

6Furthermore He said to me, "Son of man, do you
see what they are doing, the great abominations that
the house of Israel commits here, to make Me go far
away from My sanctuary? Now turn again, you will
see greater abominations." 7So He brought me to the

LIFE LESSON

Ezekiel 8:1–11:25

SITUATION God spoke through his servant Ezekiel. He showed the Israelites the reason for their exile.

OBSERVATION God hates idolatry. He hates anything that gets in the way of a relationship with him.

INSPIRATION The real test of spiritual focus is being able to bring your mind and thoughts under control. Is your mind focused on the face of an idol? Is the idol yourself? Is it your work? Is it your idea of what a servant should be or maybe your experience of salvation and sanctification? If so, then your ability to see God is blinded. You will be powerless when faced with difficulties and will be forced to endure in darkness. If your power to see has been blinded, don't look back on your experiences, but look to God. It is God you need. Go beyond yourself and away from everything else that has been blinding your thinking. . . . Deliberately turn your thoughts and your eyes to God.

(From *My Utmost for His Highest* by Oswald Chambers)

APPLICATION Idols come in attractive packages today. You can identify them when they keep you from worship, consume your tithe, or become what you are most proud of. What to do? Let your most important task today honor God, don't spend money designated for the offering plate, and thank God for your successes.

EXPLORATION Idolatry—Leviticus 26:1; Isaiah 42:8; 1 John 5:21.

door of the court; and when I looked, there was a hole in the wall. 8Then He said to me, "Son of man, dig into the wall"; and when I dug into the wall, there was a door.

9And He said to me, "Go in, and see the wicked abominations which they are doing there." 10So I went in and saw, and there—every sort of creeping thing, abominable beasts, and all the idols of the house of Israel, portrayed all around on the walls. 11And there stood before them seventy men of the elders of the house of Israel, and in their midst stood Jaazaniah the son of Shaphan. Each man had a censer in his hand, and a thick cloud of incense went up. 12Then He said to me, "Son of man, have you seen what the elders of the house of Israel do in the dark, every man in the room of his idols? For they say, 'The LORD does not see us, the LORD has forsaken the land.' "

13And He said to me, "Turn again, *and* you will see greater abominations that they are doing." 14So He brought me to the door of the north gate of the LORD's house; and to my dismay, women were sitting there weeping for Tammuz.

15Then He said to me, "Have you seen *this,* O son of man? Turn again, you will see greater abominations than these." 16So He brought me into the inner court of the LORD's house; and there, at the door of the temple of the LORD, between the porch and the altar, *were* about twenty-five men with their backs toward the temple of the LORD and their faces toward the east, and they were worshiping the sun toward the east.

17And He said to me, "Have you seen *this,* O son of man? Is it a trivial thing to the house of Judah to commit the abominations which they commit here? For they have filled the land with violence; then they have returned to provoke Me to anger. Indeed they put the branch to their nose. 18Therefore I also will act in fury. My eye will not spare nor will I have pity; and though they cry in My ears with a loud voice, I will not hear them."

The Wicked Are Slain

9 Then He called out in my hearing with a loud voice, saying, "Let those who have charge over the city draw near, each *with* a deadly weapon in his hand." 2And suddenly six men came from the direction of the upper gate, which faces north, each with his battle-ax in his hand. One man among them *was* clothed with linen and had a writer's inkhorn at his side. They went in and stood beside the bronze altar.

3Now the glory of the God of Israel had gone up from the cherub, where it had been, to the threshold of the temple.[h] And He called to the man clothed with linen, who *had* the writer's inkhorn at his side; 4and the LORD said to him, "Go through the midst of the city, through the midst of Jerusalem, and put a mark on the foreheads of the men who sigh and cry over all the abominations that are done within it."

5To the others He said in my hearing, "Go after him through the city and kill; do not let your eye spare, nor have any pity. 6Utterly slay old *and* young men, maidens and little children and women; but do not come near anyone on whom *is* the mark; and begin at My sanctuary." So they began with the elders who *were* before the temple. 7Then He said to them, "Defile the temple, and fill the courts with the slain. Go out!" And they went out and killed in the city.

8So it was, that while they were killing them, I was left *alone;* and I fell on

9:3 *h* Literally *house*

my face and cried out, and said, "Ah, Lord GOD! Will You destroy all the remnant of Israel in pouring out Your fury on Jerusalem?"

9Then He said to me, "The iniquity of the house of Israel and Judah *is* exceedingly great, and the land is full of bloodshed, and the city full of perversity; for they say, 'The LORD has forsaken the land, and the LORD does not see!' 10And as for Me also, My eye will neither spare, nor will I have pity, *but* I will recompense their deeds on their own head."

11Just then, the man clothed with linen, who *had* the inkhorn at his side, reported back and said, "I have done as You commanded me."

The Glory Departs from the Temple

10 And I looked, and there in the firmament that was above the head of the cherubim, there appeared something like a sapphire stone, having the appearance of the likeness of a throne. 2Then He spoke to the man clothed with linen, and said, "Go in among the wheels, under the cherub, fill your hands with coals of fire from among the cherubim, and scatter *them* over the city." And he went in as I watched.

3Now the cherubim were standing on the south side of the temple[i] when the man went in, and the cloud filled the inner court. 4Then the glory of the LORD went up from the cherub, *and paused* over the threshold of the temple; and the house was filled with the cloud, and the court was full of the brightness of the LORD's glory. 5And the sound of the wings of the cherubim was heard *even* in the outer court, like the voice of Almighty God when He speaks.

6Then it happened, when He commanded the man clothed in linen, saying, "Take fire from among the wheels, from among the cherubim," that he went in and stood beside the wheels. 7And the cherub stretched out his hand from among the cherubim to the fire that *was* among the cherubim, and took *some of it* and put *it* into the hands of the *man* clothed with linen, who took *it* and went out. 8The cherubim appeared to have the form of a man's hand under their wings.

9And when I looked, there were four wheels by the cherubim, one wheel by one cherub and another wheel by each other cherub; the wheels appeared *to have* the color of a beryl stone. 10*As for* their appearance, all four looked alike—as it were, a wheel in the middle of a wheel. 11When they went, they went toward *any of* their four directions; they did not turn aside when they went, but followed in the direction the head was facing. They did not turn aside when they went. 12And their whole body, with their back, their hands, their wings, and the wheels that the four had, *were* full of eyes all around. 13As for the wheels, they were called in my hearing, "Wheel."

14Each one had four faces: the first face *was* the face of a cherub, the second face the face of a man, the third the face of a lion, and the fourth the face of an eagle. 15And the cherubim were lifted up. This *was* the living creature I saw by the River Chebar. 16When the cherubim went, the wheels went beside them; and when the cherubim lifted their wings to mount up from the earth, the same wheels also did not turn from beside them. 17When *the cherubim*[j] stood still, *the wheels* stood still, and when *one*[k] was lifted up, *the other*[l] lifted itself up, for the spirit of the living creature *was* in them.

18Then the glory of the LORD departed from the threshold of the temple and stood over the cherubim. 19And the cherubim lifted their wings and mounted up from the earth in my sight. When they went out, the wheels *were* beside them; and they stood at the door of the east gate of the LORD's house, and the glory of the God of Israel *was* above them.

20This *is* the living creature I saw under the God of Israel by the River Chebar, and I knew they *were* cherubim. 21Each one had four faces and each one four wings, and the likeness of the hands of a man *was* under their wings. 22And the likeness of their faces *was* the same *as* the faces which I had seen by the River Chebar, their appearance and their persons. They each went straight forward.

Judgment on Wicked Counselors

11 Then the Spirit lifted me up and brought me to the East Gate of the LORD's house, which faces eastward; and there at the door of the gate were twenty-five men, among whom I saw Jaazaniah the son of Azzur, and Pelatiah the son of Benaiah, princes of the people. 2And He said to me: "Son of man, these *are* the men who devise iniquity and give wicked counsel in this city, 3who say, '*The time is* not near to build houses; this *city is* the caldron, and we *are* the meat.' 4Therefore prophesy against them, prophesy, O son of man!"

5Then the Spirit of the LORD fell upon me, and said to me, "Speak! 'Thus says the LORD: "Thus you have said, O house of Israel; for I know the things that come into your mind. 6You have multiplied your slain

10:3 [i] Literally *house,* also in verses 4 and 18
10:17 [j] Literally *they* [k] Literally *they* [l] Literally *they*

Life Lesson

Ezekiel 12:1-28

SITUATION Although Jerusalem was about to be destroyed, the Jews remained blind to their own disobedience and rebellion.

OBSERVATION The Israelites refused to obey God. They would not believe that God's warnings of destruction applied to them.

INSPIRATION The people heard, but few really listened. . . .

It was not a new message from a prophet of God that "All we like sheep have gone astray." . . . The throne of David was gone! And the throne of Solomon! And when at last some time after Isaiah's death, Judah also collapsed and was no more, who but a few thoughtful ones could have taken the message of Isaiah seriously? Isaiah's prophetic message [like Ezekiel's] poured itself relentlessly into the time of the final decay of Judah, like a Bach fugue coloring its main theme with the bright counterpoint of new motifs. The main theme cried that God was not limited to human history! That human affairs are not governed ultimately by historical events, fate or chance, but by God. He saw the whole stream of history through God's eyes, with Redemption as much a part of God's responsibility as Creation. Isaiah saw history in the bright light of divine purpose moving steadily from beginning to end.

(From *Beloved World: The Story of God and People* by Eugenia Price)

APPLICATION Learn from victorious Christians. Note and imitate the habits that make them victorious. Read a biography of a well-known Christian this week.

EXPLORATION Obedience to God—1 Samuel 15:22; Psalm 1; John 14:15; Romans 3:21-26; 2 Corinthians 5:18-21; Hebrews 12:4-29.

in this city, and you have filled its streets with the slain." [7]Therefore thus
says the Lord GOD: "Your slain whom you have laid in its midst, they *are*
the meat, and this *city is* the caldron; but I shall bring you out of the midst
of it. [8]You have feared the sword; and I will bring a sword upon you," says
the Lord GOD. [9]"And I will bring you out of its midst, and deliver you into
the hands of strangers, and execute judgments on you. [10]You shall fall by
the sword. I will judge you at the border of Israel. Then you shall know that
I *am* the LORD. [11]This *city* shall not be your caldron, nor shall you be the
meat in its midst. I will judge you at the border of Israel. [12]And you shall
know that I *am* the LORD; for you have not walked in My statutes nor executed
My judgments, but have done according to the customs of the
Gentiles which *are* all around you." ' "

[13]Now it happened, while I was prophesying, that Pelatiah the son of
Benaiah died. Then I fell on my face and cried with a loud voice, and said,
"Ah, Lord GOD! Will You make a complete end of the remnant of Israel?"

God Will Restore Israel

[14]Again the word of the LORD came to me, saying, [15]"Son of man, your
brethren, your relatives, your countrymen, and all the house of Israel in its
entirety, *are* those about whom the inhabitants of Jerusalem have said,
'Get far away from the LORD; this land has been given to us as a possession.'
[16]Therefore say, 'Thus says the Lord GOD: "Although I have cast them
far off among the Gentiles, and although I have scattered them among the
countries, yet I shall be a little sanctuary for them in the countries where
they have gone." ' [17]Therefore say, 'Thus says the Lord GOD: "I will gather
you from the peoples, assemble you from the countries where you have
been scattered, and I will give you the land of Israel." ' [18]And they will go
there, and they will take away all its detestable things and all its abominations
from there. [19]Then I will give them one heart, and I will put a new
spirit within them,[m] and take the stony heart out of their flesh, and give
them a heart of flesh, [20]that they may walk in My statutes and keep My
judgments and do them; and they shall be My people, and I will be their
God. [21]But *as for those* whose hearts follow the desire for their detestable
things and their abominations, I will recompense their deeds on their own
heads," says the Lord GOD.

[22]So the cherubim lifted up their wings, with the wheels beside them,
and the glory of the God of Israel *was* high above them. [23]And the glory of
the LORD went up from the midst of the city and stood on the mountain,
which *is* on the east side of the city.

[24]Then the Spirit took me up and brought me in a vision by the Spirit of
God into Chaldea,[n] to those in captivity. And the vision that I had seen
went up from me. [25]So I spoke to those in captivity of all the things the
LORD had shown me.

Judah's Captivity Portrayed

12 Now the word of the LORD came to me, saying: [2]"Son of man, you dwell
in the midst of a rebellious house, which has eyes to see but does not
see, and ears to hear but does not hear; for they *are* a rebellious house.

[3]"Therefore, son of man, prepare your belongings for captivity, and go
into captivity by day in their sight. You shall go from your place into captiv-

11:19 [m] Literally *you*
11:24 [n] Or *Babylon,* and so elsewhere in this book

ity to another place in their sight. It may be that they
will consider, though they *are* a rebellious house. 4By
day you shall bring out your belongings in their sight,
as though going into captivity; and at evening you shall
go in their sight, like those who go into captivity. 5Dig
through the wall in their sight, and carry your belongings out through it. 6In their sight you shall bear *them*
on *your* shoulders *and* carry *them* out at twilight; you
shall cover your face, so that you cannot see the ground,
for I have made you a sign to the house of Israel."

7So I did as I was commanded. I brought out my
belongings by day, as though going into captivity, and
at evening I dug through the wall with my hand. I
brought *them* out at twilight, *and* I bore *them* on *my*
shoulder in their sight.

8And in the morning the word of the LORD came to
me, saying, 9"Son of man, has not the house of Israel,
the rebellious house, said to you, 'What are you
doing?' 10Say to them, 'Thus says the Lord GOD: "This
burden *concerns* the prince in Jerusalem and all the
house of Israel who are among them." ' 11Say, 'I *am* a
sign to you. As I have done, so shall it be done to
them; they shall be carried away into captivity.' 12And
the prince who *is* among them shall bear *his belongings* on *his* shoulder at twilight and go out. They shall
dig through the wall to carry *them* out through it. He
shall cover his face, so that he cannot see the ground
with *his* eyes. 13I will also spread My net over him, and
he shall be caught in My snare. I will bring him to
Babylon, *to* the land of the Chaldeans; yet he shall not
see it, though he shall die there. 14I will scatter to every
wind all who *are* around him to help him, and all his
troops; and I will draw out the sword after them.

15"Then they shall know that I *am* the LORD, when I
scatter them among the nations and disperse them
throughout the countries. 16But I will spare a few of
their men from the sword, from famine, and from
pestilence, that they may declare all their abominations among the Gentiles wherever they go. Then they
shall know that I *am* the LORD."

Judgment Not Postponed

17Moreover the word of the LORD came to me, saying, 18"Son of man, eat your bread with quaking, and
drink your water with trembling and anxiety. 19And
say to the people of the land, 'Thus says the Lord GOD
to the inhabitants of Jerusalem *and* to the land of Israel: "They shall eat their bread with anxiety, and
drink their water with dread, so that her land may be
emptied of all who are in it, because of the violence of
all those who dwell in it. 20Then the cities that are inhabited shall be laid waste, and the land shall become
desolate; and you shall know that I *am* the LORD." ' "

21And the word of the LORD came to me, saying,
22"Son of man, what *is* this proverb *that* you *people*
have about the land of Israel, which says, 'The days
are prolonged, and every vision fails'? 23Tell them
therefore, 'Thus says the Lord GOD: "I will lay this
proverb to rest, and they shall no more use it as a
proverb in Israel." But say to them, "The days are at
hand, and the fulfillment of every vision. 24For no
more shall there be any false vision or flattering
divination within the house of Israel. 25For I *am* the
LORD. I speak, and the word which I speak will come
to pass; it will no more be postponed; for in your days,
O rebellious house, I will say the word and perform
it," says the Lord GOD.' "

26Again the word of the LORD came to me, saying,
27"Son of man, look, the house of Israel is saying, 'The
vision that he sees *is* for many days *from now,* and he
prophesies of times far off.' 28Therefore say to them,
'Thus says the Lord GOD: "None of My words will be
postponed any more, but the word which I speak will
be done," says the Lord GOD.' "

Woe to Foolish Prophets

13 And the word of the LORD came to me, saying,
2"Son of man, prophesy against the prophets of
Israel who prophesy, and say to those who prophesy
out of their own heart, 'Hear the word of the LORD!' "

3Thus says the Lord GOD: "Woe to the foolish
prophets, who follow their own spirit and have seen
nothing! 4O Israel, your prophets are like foxes in the
deserts. 5You have not gone up into the gaps to build a
wall for the house of Israel to stand in battle on the
day of the LORD. 6They have envisioned futility and
false divination, saying, 'Thus says the LORD!' But the
LORD has not sent them; yet they hope that the word
may be confirmed. 7Have you not seen a futile vision,
and have you not spoken false divination? You say,
'The LORD says,' but I have not spoken."

8Therefore thus says the Lord GOD: "Because you
have spoken nonsense and envisioned lies, therefore
I *am* indeed against you," says the Lord GOD. 9"My
hand will be against the prophets who envision futility and who divine lies; they shall not be in the assembly of My people, nor be written in the record of the
house of Israel, nor shall they enter into the land of Israel. Then you shall know that I *am* the Lord GOD.

10"Because, indeed, because they have seduced My
people, saying, 'Peace!' when *there is* no peace—and
one builds a wall, and they plaster it with untempered

Life Lesson

Ezekiel 13:1–14:23

SITUATION Ezekiel continued to prophesy about the destruction of Israel. He warned the people not to listen to false prophets or to worship idols.

OBSERVATION Israel abandoned God's covenant.

INSPIRATION Everything begins with God the Father. The initiative of grace is his alone. It is he who in sheer love desired both to show himself to mankind (which is "revelation") and to bring mankind to himself (which is "redemption").

In both he acted through Jesus Christ. It is through Christ that he has revealed himself to us, and it is through Christ that he has redeemed us for himself.

It is inconceivable, therefore, that there could ever be either a higher revelation than God has given through the person of Jesus Christ his son, or a fuller redemption than he has achieved through the work of Jesus Christ our Saviour. Both are perfect and complete.

(From *Understanding Christ* by John Stott)

APPLICATION Do you demonstrate your right relationship with God even in small areas—like driving? Do you observe the speed limit? Does your driving change when you see a police car? Be diligent to obey God even in small areas.

EXPLORATION Judgment—Matthew 11:20-24; Acts 17:30-31; 2 Peter 2.

mortar— 11say to those who plaster *it* with untempered *mortar,* that it will
fall. There will be flooding rain, and you, O great hailstones, shall fall; and
a stormy wind shall tear *it* down. 12Surely, when the wall has fallen, will it
not be said to you, 'Where *is* the mortar with which you plastered *it?*' "
13Therefore thus says the Lord GOD: "I will cause a stormy wind to break
forth in My fury; and there shall be a flooding rain in My anger, and great
hailstones in fury to consume *it.* 14So I will break down the wall you have
plastered with untempered *mortar,* and bring it down to the ground, so
that its foundation will be uncovered; it will fall, and you shall be consumed in the midst of it. Then you shall know that I *am* the LORD.
15"Thus will I accomplish My wrath on the wall and on those who have
plastered it with untempered *mortar;* and I will say to you, 'The wall *is* no
more, nor those who plastered it, 16*that is,* the prophets of Israel who
prophesy concerning Jerusalem, and who see visions of peace for her
when *there is* no peace,' " says the Lord GOD.
17"Likewise, son of man, set your face against the daughters of your people, who prophesy out of their own heart; prophesy against them, 18and
say, 'Thus says the Lord GOD: "Woe to the *women* who sew *magic* charms
on their sleeves[o] and make veils for the heads of people of every height to
hunt souls! Will you hunt the souls of My people, and keep yourselves
alive? 19And will you profane Me among My people for handfuls of barley
and for pieces of bread, killing people who should not die, and keeping people alive who should not live, by your lying to My people who listen to lies?"
20"Therefore thus says the Lord GOD: "Behold, I *am* against your *magic*
charms by which you hunt souls there like birds. I will tear them from
your arms, and let the souls go, the souls you hunt like birds. 21I will also
tear off your veils and deliver My people out of your hand, and they shall
no longer be as prey in your hand. Then you shall know that I *am* the LORD.
22"Because with lies you have made the heart of the righteous sad,
whom I have not made sad; and you have strengthened the hands of the
wicked, so that he does not turn from his wicked way to save his life.
23Therefore you shall no longer envision futility nor practice divination;
for I will deliver My people out of your hand, and you shall know that I *am*
the LORD." ' "

Idolatry Will Be Punished

14 Now some of the elders of Israel came to me and sat before me.
2And the word of the LORD came to me, saying, 3"Son of man, these
men have set up their idols in their hearts, and put before them that which
causes them to stumble into iniquity. Should I let Myself be inquired of at
all by them?
4"Therefore speak to them, and say to them, 'Thus says the Lord GOD:
"Everyone of the house of Israel who sets up his idols in his heart, and
puts before him what causes him to stumble into iniquity, and then comes
to the prophet, I the LORD will answer him who comes, according to the
multitude of his idols, 5that I may seize the house of Israel by their heart,
because they are all estranged from Me by their idols." '
6"Therefore say to the house of Israel, 'Thus says the Lord GOD: "Repent,
turn away from your idols, and turn your faces away from all your

13:18 [o] Literally *over all the joints of My hands;* Vulgate reads *under every elbow;* Septuagint and Targum read *on all elbows of the hands.*

abominations. 7For anyone of the house of Israel, or
of the strangers who dwell in Israel, who separates
himself from Me and sets up his idols in his heart and
puts before him what causes him to stumble into iniquity, then comes to a prophet to inquire of him concerning Me, I the LORD will answer him by Myself. 8I
will set My face against that man and make him a sign
and a proverb, and I will cut him off from the midst of
My people. Then you shall know that I *am* the LORD.
9"And if the prophet is induced to speak anything, I
the LORD have induced that prophet, and I will stretch
out My hand against him and destroy him from
among My people Israel. 10And they shall bear their
iniquity; the punishment of the prophet shall be the
same as the punishment of the one who inquired,
11that the house of Israel may no longer stray from
Me, nor be profaned anymore with all their transgressions, but that they may be My people and I may
be their God," says the Lord GOD.' "

Judgment on Persistent Unfaithfulness

12The word of the LORD came again to me, saying:
13"Son of man, when a land sins against Me by persistent unfaithfulness, I will stretch out My hand against
it; I will cut off its supply of bread, send famine on it,
and cut off man and beast from it. 14Even *if* these
three men, Noah, Daniel, and Job, were in it, they
would deliver *only* themselves by their righteousness," says the Lord GOD.
15"If I cause wild beasts to pass through the land,
and they empty it, and make it so desolate that no
man may pass through because of the beasts, 16*even
though* these three men *were* in it, *as* I live," says the
Lord GOD, "they would deliver neither sons nor
daughters; only they would be delivered, and the land
would be desolate.
17"Or *if* I bring a sword on that land, and say,
'Sword, go through the land,' and I cut off man and
beast from it, 18even *though* these three men *were* in it,
as I live," says the Lord GOD, "they would deliver neither sons nor daughters, but only they themselves
would be delivered.
19"Or *if* I send a pestilence into that land and pour
out My fury on it in blood, and cut off from it man
and beast, 20even *though* Noah, Daniel, and Job *were*
in it, *as* I live," says the Lord GOD, "they would deliver
neither son nor daughter; they would deliver *only*
themselves by their righteousness."
21For thus says the Lord GOD: "How much more it
shall be when I send My four severe judgments on
Jerusalem—the sword and famine and wild beasts
and pestilence—to cut off man and beast from it? 22Yet
behold, there shall be left in it a remnant who will be
brought out, *both* sons and daughters; surely they will
come out to you, and you will see their ways and their
doings. Then you will be comforted concerning the
disaster that I have brought upon Jerusalem, all that I
have brought upon it. 23And they will comfort you,
when you see their ways and their doings; and you
shall know that I have done nothing without cause
that I have done in it," says the Lord GOD.

The Outcast Vine

15 Then the word of the LORD came to me, saying:
2"Son of man, how is the wood of the vine *better*
than any other wood, the vine branch which is among
the trees of the forest? 3Is wood taken from it to make
any object? Or can *men* make a peg from it to hang
any vessel on? 4Instead, it is thrown into the fire for
fuel; the fire devours both ends of it, and its middle is
burned. Is it useful for *any* work? 5Indeed, when it was
whole, no object could be made from it. How much
less will it be useful for *any* work when the fire has devoured it, and it is burned?
6"Therefore thus says the Lord GOD: 'Like the wood
of the vine among the trees of the forest, which I have
given to the fire for fuel, so I will give up the inhabitants
of Jerusalem; 7and I will set My face against them.
They will go out from *one* fire, but *another* fire shall
devour them. Then you shall know that I *am* the LORD,
when I set My face against them. 8Thus I will make the
land desolate, because they have persisted in unfaithfulness,' says the Lord GOD."

God's Love for Jerusalem

16 Again the word of the LORD came to me, saying,
2"Son of man, cause Jerusalem to know her
abominations, 3and say, 'Thus says the Lord GOD to
Jerusalem: "Your birth and your nativity *are* from the
land of Canaan; your father *was* an Amorite and your
mother a Hittite. 4*As for* your nativity, on the day you
were born your navel cord was not cut, nor were you
washed in water to cleanse *you;* you were not rubbed
with salt nor wrapped in swaddling cloths. 5No eye
pitied you, to do any of these things for you, to have
compassion on you; but you were thrown out into the
open field, when you yourself were loathed on the day
you were born.
6"And when I passed by you and saw you struggling in your own blood, I said to you in your blood,
'Live!' Yes, I said to you in your blood, 'Live!' 7I made
you thrive like a plant in the field; and you grew, matured, and became very beautiful. *Your* breasts were
formed, your hair grew, but you *were* naked and bare.

Life Lesson

Ezekiel 15:1–20:44

SITUATION God intended to destroy Jerusalem for its idolatry and rebellion. He compared the idol-worshiping city to a useless vine. God told Ezekiel that he would burn the city into a charred stalk.

OBSERVATION Lack of faith leads to disaster.

INSPIRATION During the reign of Oliver Cromwell, the British government began to run low on silver for coins. Lord Cromwell sent his men on an investigation of the local cathedral to see if they could find any precious metal there. After investigating, they reported: The only silver we could find is in the statues of the saints standing in the corners.

To which the radical soldier and statesman of England replied: Good! We'll melt down the saints and put them into circulation!

Not bad theology for a proper, strait-laced, Lord Protector of the Isles, huh? In a few words the direct order states the essence . . . the kernel . . . the practical goal of authentic Christianity. Not rows of silver saints, highly polished, frequently dusted, crammed into the corners of elegant cathedrals. Not plaster people cloaked in thin layers of untarnished silver and topped with a metallic halo. But real persons. Melted saints circulating through the main stream of humanity. Bringing worth and value down where life transpires in the raw. . . .

It's easy to kid ourselves. So easy. The Christian must guard against self-deception. We can begin to consider ourselves martyrs because we are in church twice on Sunday—really sacrificing by investing a few hours on

8“When I passed by you again and looked upon you, indeed your time
was the time of love; so I spread My wing over you and covered your
nakedness. Yes, I swore an oath to you and entered into a covenant with
you, and you became Mine,” says the Lord GOD.
9“Then I washed you in water; yes, I thoroughly washed off your blood,
and I anointed you with oil. 10I clothed you in embroidered cloth and gave
you sandals of badger skin; I clothed you with fine linen and covered you
with silk. 11I adorned you with ornaments, put bracelets on your wrists,
and a chain on your neck. 12And I put a jewel in your nose, earrings in your
ears, and a beautiful crown on your head. 13Thus you were adorned with
gold and silver, and your clothing *was of* fine linen, silk, and embroidered
cloth. You ate *pastry of* fine flour, honey, and oil. You were exceedingly
beautiful, and succeeded to royalty. 14Your fame went out among the nations because of your beauty, for it *was* perfect through My splendor
which I had bestowed on you,” says the Lord GOD.

Jerusalem's Harlotry

15“But you trusted in your own beauty, played the harlot because of your
fame, and poured out your harlotry on everyone passing by who *would
have* it. 16You took some of your garments and adorned multicolored high
places for yourself, and played the harlot on them. *Such* things should not
happen, nor be. 17You have also taken your beautiful jewelry from My gold
and My silver, which I had given you, and made for yourself male images
and played the harlot with them. 18You took your embroidered garments
and covered them, and you set My oil and My incense before them. 19Also
My food which I gave you—the pastry of fine flour, oil, and honey *which* I
fed you—you set it before them as sweet incense; and *so* it was,” says the
Lord GOD.
20“Moreover you took your sons and your daughters, whom you bore to
Me, and these you sacrificed to them to be devoured. *Were* your *acts* of
harlotry a small matter, 21that you have slain My children and offered
them up to them by causing them to pass through *the fire?* 22And in all
your abominations and acts of harlotry you did not remember the days of
your youth, when you were naked and bare, struggling in your blood.
23“Then it was so, after all your wickedness—‘Woe, woe to you!’ says the
Lord GOD— 24*that* you also built for yourself a shrine, and made a high
place for yourself in every street. 25You built your high places at the head of
every road, and made your beauty to be abhorred. You offered yourself to
everyone who passed by, and multiplied your acts of harlotry. 26You also
committed harlotry with the Egyptians, your very fleshly neighbors, and
increased your acts of harlotry to provoke Me to anger.
27“Behold, therefore, I stretched out My hand against you, diminished
your allotment, and gave you up to the will of those who hate you, the
daughters of the Philistines, who were ashamed of your lewd behavior.
28You also played the harlot with the Assyrians, because you were insatiable; indeed you played the harlot with them and still were not satisfied.
29Moreover you multiplied your acts of harlotry as far as the land of the
trader, Chaldea; and even then you were not satisfied.
30“How degenerate is your heart!” says the Lord GOD, “seeing you do all
these *things,* the deeds of a brazen harlot.

Jerusalem's Adultery

31“You erected your shrine at the head of every road, and built your high
place in every street. Yet you were not like a harlot, because you scorned
payment. 32*You are* an adulterous wife, *who* takes strangers instead of her
husband. 33Men make payment to all harlots, but you made your pay-
ments to all your lovers, and hired them to come to you from all around
for your harlotry. 34You are the opposite of *other* women in your harlotry,
because no one solicited you to be a harlot. In that you gave payment but
no payment was given you, therefore you are the opposite.”

Jerusalem's Lovers Will Abuse Her

35“Now then, O harlot, hear the word of the LORD! 36Thus says the Lord
GOD: “Because your filthiness was poured out and your nakedness uncovered in your harlotry with your lovers, and with all your abominable idols,
and because of the blood of your children which you gave to them,
37surely, therefore, I will gather all your lovers with whom you took pleasure, all those you loved, *and* all those you hated; I will gather them from
all around against you and will uncover your nakedness to them, that they
may see all your nakedness. 38And I will judge you as women who break
wedlock or shed blood are judged; I will bring blood upon you in fury and
jealousy. 39I will also give you into their hand, and they shall throw down
your shrines and break down your high places. They shall also strip you of
your clothes, take your beautiful jewelry, and leave you naked and bare.
40“They shall also bring up an assembly against you, and they shall
stone you with stones and thrust you through with their swords. 41They
shall burn your houses with fire, and execute judgments on you in the
sight of many women; and I will make you cease playing the harlot, and
you shall no longer hire lovers. 42So I will lay to rest My fury toward you,
and My jealousy shall depart from you. I will be quiet, and be angry no
more. 43Because you did not remember the days of your youth, but agitated Me[p] with all these *things,* surely I will also recompense your deeds on
your own head,” says the Lord GOD. “And you shall not commit lewdness
in addition to all your abominations.

More Wicked than Samaria and Sodom

44“Indeed everyone who quotes proverbs will use *this* proverb against
you: ‘Like mother, like daughter!’ 45You *are* your mother's daughter, loath-
ing husband and children; and you *are* the sister of your sisters, who
loathed their husbands and children; your mother *was* a Hittite and your
father an Amorite.
46“Your elder sister *is* Samaria, who dwells with her daughters to the
north of you; and your younger sister, who dwells to the south of you, *is*
Sodom and her daughters. 47You did not walk in their ways nor act according to their abominations; but, as *if that were* too little, you became more
corrupt than they in all your ways.
48“*As* I live,” says the Lord GOD, “neither your sister Sodom nor her
daughters have done as you and your daughters have done. 49Look, this
was the iniquity of your sister Sodom: She and her daughter had pride,
fullness of food, and abundance of idleness; neither did she strengthen the

16:43 *p* Following Septuagint, Syriac, Targum, and Vulgate; Masoretic Text reads *were agitated with Me.*

the “day of rest.” Listen, my friend, being among the saints is no sacrifice . . . it's a brief, choice privilege. The cost factor occurs on Monday or Tuesday . . . and during the rest of the week. That's when we're “melted down and put into circulation.” That's when they go for the jugular. And it is remarkable how that monotonous work-week test discolors many a silver saint. “Sunday religion” may seem sufficient, but it isn't. . . .

Doing battle in the steaming jungle calls for shock troops in super shape. No rhinestone cowboys can cut it among the swamps and insects of the gross world system. Sunday-go-to-meetin' silver saints in shining armor are simply out of circulation if that's the limit to their faith. Waging wilderness warfare calls for sweat . . . energy . . . keen strategy . . . determination . . . a good supply of ammunition . . . willingness to fight . . . refusal to surrender, even with the elephants tromping on your airhose.

And that is why we must be melted! It's all part of being “in circulation.” Those who successfully wage war with silent heroism under relentless secular pressure—ah, they are the saints who know what it means to be melted.

(From *Encourage Me* by Charles Swindoll)

APPLICATION If you were melted down to your essence, what impurities would you find? Think of one area of weakness and work this week to become faithful where once you were faithless. Trust God to supply your needs.

EXPLORATION Following Christ—Mark 8:34-38; John 8:12; 10:25; Romans 15:5.

hand of the poor and needy. 50 And they were haughty
and committed abomination before Me; therefore I
took them away as I saw *fit*.[q]
51 "Samaria did not commit half of your sins; but
you have multiplied your abominations more than
they, and have justified your sisters by all the
abominations which you have done. 52 You who judged
your sisters, bear your own shame also, because the
sins which you committed were more abominable
than theirs; they are more righteous than you. Yes, be
disgraced also, and bear your own shame, because
you justified your sisters.
53 "When I bring back their captives, the captives of
Sodom and her daughters, and the captives of Samaria and her daughters, then *I will also bring back*
the captives of your captivity among them, 54 that you
may bear your own shame and be disgraced by all
that you did when you comforted them. 55 When your
sisters, Sodom and her daughters, return to their former state, and Samaria and her daughters return to
their former state, then you and your daughters will
return to your former state. 56 For your sister Sodom
was not a byword in your mouth in the days of your
pride, 57 before your wickedness was uncovered. It
was like the time of the reproach of the daughters of
Syria[r] and all *those* around her, and of the daughters
of the Philistines, who despise you everywhere. 58 You
have paid for your lewdness and your abominations,"
says the LORD. 59 For thus says the Lord GOD: "I will
deal with you as you have done, who despised the
oath by breaking the covenant.

An Everlasting Covenant

60 "Nevertheless I will remember My covenant with
you in the days of your youth, and I will establish an
everlasting covenant with you. 61 Then you will remember your ways and be ashamed, when you receive your older and your younger sisters; for I will
give them to you for daughters, but not because of My
covenant with you. 62 And I will establish My covenant
with you. Then you shall know that I *am* the LORD,
63 that you may remember and be ashamed, and never
open your mouth anymore because of your shame,
when I provide you an atonement for all you have
done," says the Lord GOD.' "

The Eagles and the Vine

17 And the word of the LORD came to me, saying,
2 "Son of man, pose a riddle, and speak a parable to the house of Israel, 3 and say, 'Thus says the Lord
GOD:

"A great eagle with large wings and long pinions,
Full of feathers of various colors,
Came to Lebanon
And took from the cedar the highest branch.
4 He cropped off its topmost young twig
And carried it to a land of trade;
He set it in a city of merchants.
5 Then he took some of the seed of the land
And planted it in a fertile field;
He placed *it* by abundant waters
And set it like a willow tree.
6 And it grew and became a spreading vine of low stature;
Its branches turned toward him,
But its roots were under it.
So it became a vine,
Brought forth branches,
And put forth shoots.

7 "But there was another[s] great eagle with large wings and many feathers;
And behold, this vine bent its roots toward him,
And stretched its branches toward him,
From the garden terrace where it had been planted,
That he might water it.
8 It was planted in good soil by many waters,
To bring forth branches, bear fruit,
And become a majestic vine." '

9 "Say, 'Thus says the Lord GOD:

"Will it thrive?
Will he not pull up its roots,
Cut off its fruit,
And leave it to wither?
All of its spring leaves will wither,
And no great power or many people
Will be needed to pluck it up by its roots.
10 Behold, *it is* planted,
Will it thrive?
Will it not utterly wither when the east wind touches it?
It will wither in the garden terrace where it grew." ' "

16:50 [q] Vulgate reads *you saw;* Septuagint reads *he saw;* Targum reads *as was revealed to Me.*
16:57 [r] Following Masoretic Text, Septuagint, Targum, and Vulgate; many Hebrew manuscripts and Syriac read *Edom.*
17:7 [s] Following Septuagint, Syriac, and Vulgate; Masoretic Text and Targum read *one.*

11 Moreover the word of the LORD came to me, saying, 12 "Say now to the rebellious house: 'Do you not
know what these *things mean?*' Tell *them,* 'Indeed the
king of Babylon went to Jerusalem and took its king
and princes, and led them with him to Babylon. 13 And
he took the king's offspring, made a covenant with
him, and put him under oath. He also took away the
mighty of the land, 14 that the kingdom might be
brought low and not lift itself up, *but* that by keeping
his covenant it might stand. 15 But he rebelled against
him by sending his ambassadors to Egypt, that they
might give him horses and many people. Will he
prosper? Will he who does such *things* escape? Can he
break a covenant and still be delivered?

16 '*As* I live,' says the Lord GOD, 'surely in the place
where the king *dwells* who made him king, whose oath
he despised and whose covenant he broke—with him
in the midst of Babylon he shall die. 17 Nor will Pharaoh
with *his* mighty army and great company do anything
in the war, when they heap up a siege mound and build
a wall to cut off many persons. 18 Since he despised the
oath by breaking the covenant, and in fact gave his
hand and still did all these *things,* he shall not escape.' "

19 Therefore thus says the Lord GOD: "*As* I live, surely
My oath which he despised, and My covenant which he
broke, I will recompense on his own head. 20 I will
spread My net over him, and he shall be taken in My
snare. I will bring him to Babylon and try him there for
the treason which he committed against Me. 21 All his
fugitives[t] with all his troops shall fall by the sword, and
those who remain shall be scattered to every wind; and
you shall know that I, the LORD, have spoken."

Israel Exalted at Last

22 Thus says the Lord GOD: "I will take also *one* of the
highest branches of the high cedar and set *it* out. I will
crop off from the topmost of its young twigs a tender
one, and will plant *it* on a high and prominent mountain. 23 On the mountain height of Israel I will plant it;
and it will bring forth boughs, and bear fruit, and be a
majestic cedar. Under it will dwell birds of every sort;
in the shadow of its branches they will dwell. 24 And all
the trees of the field shall know that I, the LORD, have
brought down the high tree and exalted the low tree,
dried up the green tree and made the dry tree flourish; I, the LORD, have spoken and have done *it.*"

A False Proverb Refuted

18 The word of the LORD came to me again, saying,
2 "What do you mean when you use this
proverb concerning the land of Israel, saying:

'The fathers have eaten sour grapes,
And the children's teeth are set on edge'?

3 "*As* I live," says the Lord GOD, "you shall no longer
use this proverb in Israel.

4 "Behold, all souls are Mine;
The soul of the father
As well as the soul of the son is Mine;
The soul who sins shall die.
5 But if a man is just
And does what is lawful and right;
6 If he has not eaten on the mountains,
Nor lifted up his eyes to the idols of
the house of Israel,
Nor defiled his neighbor's wife,
Nor approached a woman during her impurity;
7 If he has not oppressed anyone,
But has restored to the debtor his pledge;
Has robbed no one by violence,
But has given his bread to the hungry
And covered the naked with clothing;
8 If he has not exacted usury
Nor taken any increase,
But has withdrawn his hand from iniquity
And executed true judgment between man
and man;
9 *If* he has walked in My statutes
And kept My judgments faithfully—
He *is* just;
He shall surely live!"
Says the Lord GOD.

10 "If he begets a son *who is* a robber
Or a shedder of blood,
Who does any of these *things*
11 And does none of those *duties,*
But has eaten on the mountains
Or defiled his neighbor's wife;
12 If he has oppressed the poor and needy,
Robbed by violence,
Not restored the pledge,
Lifted his eyes to the idols,
Or committed abomination;
13 If he has exacted usury
Or taken increase—
Shall he then live?
He shall not live!
If he has done any of these abominations,
He shall surely die;
His blood shall be upon him.

17:21 [t] Following Masoretic Text and Vulgate; many Hebrew manuscripts and Syriac read *choice men;* Targum reads *mighty men;* Septuagint omits *All his fugitives.*

14 "*If*, however, he begets a son
Who sees all the sins which his father
has done,
And considers but does not do likewise;
15 *Who* has not eaten on the mountains,
Nor lifted his eyes to the idols of
the house of Israel,
Nor defiled his neighbor's wife;
16 Has not oppressed anyone,
Nor withheld a pledge,
Nor robbed by violence,
But has given his bread to the hungry
And covered the naked with clothing;
17 *Who* has withdrawn his hand from the poor[u]
And not received usury or increase,
But has executed My judgments
And walked in My statutes—
He shall not die for the iniquity of his father;
He shall surely live!
18 "*As for* his father,
Because he cruelly oppressed,
Robbed his brother by violence,
And did what *is* not good among his people,
Behold, he shall die for his iniquity.

Turn and Live

19"Yet you say, 'Why should the son not bear the
guilt of the father?' Because the son has done what is
lawful and right, and has kept all My statutes and observed them, he shall surely live. 20The soul who sins
shall die. The son shall not bear the guilt of the father,
nor the father bear the guilt of the son. The righteousness of the righteous shall be upon himself, and the
wickedness of the wicked shall be upon himself.
21"But if a wicked man turns from all his sins which he
has committed, keeps all My statutes, and does what is
lawful and right, he shall surely live; he shall not die.
22None of the transgressions which he has committed
shall be remembered against him; because of the righteousness which he has done, he shall live. 23Do I have any
pleasure at all that the wicked should die?" says the Lord
GOD, "*and* not that he should turn from his ways and live?
24"But when a righteous man turns away from his
righteousness and commits iniquity, and does according to all the abominations that the wicked *man*
does, shall he live? All the righteousness which he has
done shall not be remembered; because of the
unfaithfulness of which he is guilty and the sin which
he has committed, because of them he shall die.

25"Yet you say, 'The way of the Lord is not fair.' Hear
now, O house of Israel, is it not My way which is fair,
and your ways which are not fair? 26When a righteous
man turns away from his righteousness, commits iniquity, and dies in it, it is because of the iniquity which
he has done that he dies. 27Again, when a wicked *man*
turns away from the wickedness which he committed,
and does what is lawful and right, he preserves himself alive. 28Because he considers and turns away from
all the transgressions which he committed, he shall
surely live; he shall not die. 29Yet the house of Israel
says, 'The way of the Lord is not fair.' O house of Israel, is it not My ways which are fair, and your ways
which are not fair?
30"Therefore I will judge you, O house of Israel,
every one according to his ways," says the Lord GOD.
"Repent, and turn from all your transgressions, so
that iniquity will not be your ruin. 31Cast away from
you all the transgressions which you have committed,
and get yourselves a new heart and a new spirit. For
why should you die, O house of Israel? 32For I have no
pleasure in the death of one who dies," says the Lord
GOD. "Therefore turn and live!"

Israel Degraded

19 "Moreover take up a lamentation for the
princes of Israel, 2and say:

'What *is* your mother? A lioness:
She lay down among the lions;
Among the young lions she nourished
her cubs.
3 She brought up one of her cubs,
And he became a young lion;
He learned to catch prey,
And he devoured men.
4 The nations also heard of him;
He was trapped in their pit,
And they brought him with chains
to the land of Egypt.

5 'When she saw that she waited, *that* her
hope was lost,
She took another of her cubs *and* made
him a young lion.
6 He roved among the lions,
And became a young lion;
He learned to catch prey;
He devoured men.

18:17 [u] Following Masoretic Text, Targum, and Vulgate; Septuagint reads *iniquity* (compare verse 8).

7 He knew their desolate places,[v]
And laid waste their cities;
The land with its fullness was desolated
By the noise of his roaring.
8 Then the nations set against him from the
provinces on every side,
And spread their net over him;
He was trapped in their pit.
9 They put him in a cage with chains,
And brought him to the king of Babylon;
They brought him in nets,
That his voice should no longer be heard on the
mountains of Israel.

10 'Your mother *was* like a vine in
your bloodline,[w]
Planted by the waters,
Fruitful and full of branches
Because of many waters.
11 She had strong branches for scepters of rulers.
She towered in stature above
the thick branches,
And was seen in her height amid
the dense foliage.
12 But she was plucked up in fury,
She was cast down to the ground,
And the east wind dried her fruit.
Her strong branches were
broken and withered;
The fire consumed them.
13 And now she *is* planted in the wilderness,
In a dry and thirsty land.
14 Fire has come out from a rod of her branches
And devoured her fruit,
So that she has no strong branch— a scepter
for ruling.' "

This *is* a lamentation, and has become a lamentation.

The Rebellions of Israel

20 It came to pass in the seventh year, in the fifth
month, on the tenth *day* of the month, *that* certain of the elders of Israel came to inquire of the LORD,
and sat before me. 2 Then the word of the LORD came to
me, saying, 3 "Son of man, speak to the elders of Israel,
and say to them, 'Thus says the Lord GOD: "Have you
come to inquire of Me? *As* I live," says the Lord GOD, "I
will not be inquired of by you." ' 4 Will you judge
them, son of man, will you judge *them?* Then make
known to them the abominations of their fathers.
5 "Say to them, 'Thus says the Lord GOD: "On the day
when I chose Israel and raised My hand in an oath to
the descendants of the house of Jacob, and made
Myself known to them in the land of Egypt, I raised
My hand in an oath to them, saying, 'I *am* the LORD
your God.' 6 On that day I raised My hand in an oath to
them, to bring them out of the land of Egypt into a
land that I had searched out for them, 'flowing with
milk and honey,'[x] the glory of all lands. 7 Then I said to
them, 'Each of you, throw away the abominations
which are before his eyes, and do not defile yourselves with the idols of Egypt. I *am* the LORD your
God.' 8 But they rebelled against Me and would not
obey Me. They did not all cast away the abominations
which were before their eyes, nor did they forsake the
idols of Egypt. Then I said, 'I will pour out My fury on
them and fulfill My anger against them in the midst of
the land of Egypt.' 9 But I acted for My name's sake,
that it should not be profaned before the Gentiles
among whom they *were,* in whose sight I had made
Myself known to them, to bring them out of the land
of Egypt.
10 "Therefore I made them go out of the land of
Egypt and brought them into the wilderness. 11 And I
gave them My statutes and showed them My judgments, 'which, *if* a man does, he shall live by them.'[y]
12 Moreover I also gave them My Sabbaths, to be a sign
between them and Me, that they might know that I
am the LORD who sanctifies them. 13 Yet the house of
Israel rebelled against Me in the wilderness; they did
not walk in My statutes; they despised My judgments,
'which, *if* a man does, he shall live by them';[z] and they
greatly defiled My Sabbaths. Then I said I would pour
out My fury on them in the wilderness, to consume
them. 14 But I acted for My name's sake, that it should
not be profaned before the Gentiles, in whose sight I
had brought them out. 15 So I also raised My hand in
an oath to them in the wilderness, that I would not
bring them into the land which I had given *them,*
'flowing with milk and honey,'[a] the glory of all lands,
16 because they despised My judgments and did not
walk in My statutes, but profaned My Sabbaths; for

19:7 [v] Septuagint reads *He stood in insolence;* Targum reads *He destroyed its palaces;* Vulgate reads *He learned to make widows.*
19:10 [w] Literally *blood,* following Masoretic Text, Syriac, and Vulgate; Septuagint reads *like a flower on a pomegranate tree;* Targum reads *in your likeness.*
20:6 [x] Exodus 3:8
20:11 [y] Leviticus 18:5
20:13 [z] Leviticus 18:5
20:15 [a] Exodus 3:8

LIFE LESSON

Ezekiel 20:45–24:27

SITUATION God told Ezekiel of Jerusalem's impending judgment. He compared Jerusalem to a woman who has prostituted herself for pleasure and money. As punishment, Jerusalem would suffer greatly from foreign invaders. Despite the punishment brought upon Jerusalem, some righteous Israelites would survive and honor God.

OBSERVATION God planned severe judgment for the Israelites because of their godless and immoral lifestyles. This was their last chance to repent.

INSPIRATION People with marital problems have told me they have found it more difficult to forget than to forgive. With the best will in the world, they have tried to forgive and forget, but it has not always been possible. "Time is a great healer," as they say, and gradually the wounds heal in most cases. And it takes a considerable amount of concentration on the past for a person with a failing memory to remember all the things he is supposed to forget. They just tend to drip away in the end, or become so confused with other things that there is more fantasy than reality left.

Now, think of something else. God doesn't have a failing memory. He doesn't overlook sin and He is eternal, so that what we call the past is the

their heart went after their idols. 17Nevertheless My eye spared them from
destruction. I did not make an end of them in the wilderness.

18"But I said to their children in the wilderness, 'Do not walk in the
statutes of your fathers, nor observe their judgments, nor defile yourselves
with their idols. 19I *am* the LORD your God: Walk in My statutes, keep My
judgments, and do them; 20hallow My Sabbaths, and they will be a sign between Me and you, that you may know that I *am* the LORD your God.'

21"Notwithstanding, the children rebelled against Me; they did not walk
in My statutes, and were not careful to observe My judgments, 'which, *if* a
man does, he shall live by them';[b] but they profaned My Sabbaths. Then I
said I would pour out My fury on them and fulfill My anger against them
in the wilderness. 22Nevertheless I withdrew My hand and acted for My
name's sake, that it should not be profaned in the sight of the Gentiles, in
whose sight I had brought them out. 23Also I raised My hand in an oath to
those in the wilderness, that I would scatter them among the Gentiles and
disperse them throughout the countries, 24because they had not executed
My judgments, but had despised My statutes, profaned My Sabbaths, and
their eyes were fixed on their fathers' idols.

25"Therefore I also gave them up to statutes *that were* not good, and
judgments by which they could not live; 26and I pronounced them unclean
because of their ritual gifts, in that they caused all their firstborn to pass
through *the fire,* that I might make them desolate and that they might
know that I am the LORD." '

27"Therefore, son of man, speak to the house of Israel, and say to them,
'Thus says the Lord GOD: "In this too your fathers have blasphemed Me, by
being unfaithful to Me. 28When I brought them into the land *concerning*
which I had raised My hand in an oath to give them, and they saw all the
high hills and all the thick trees, there they offered their sacrifices and provoked Me with their offerings. There they also sent up their sweet aroma
and poured out their drink offerings. 29Then I said to them, 'What *is* this
high place to which you go?' So its name is called Bamah[c] to this day." '
30Therefore say to the house of Israel, 'Thus says the Lord GOD: "Are you
defiling yourselves in the manner of your fathers, and committing harlotry according to their abominations? 31For when you offer your gifts and
make your sons pass through the fire, you defile yourselves with all your
idols, even to this day. So shall I be inquired of by you, O house of Israel?
As I live," says the Lord GOD, "I will not be inquired of by you. 32What you
have in your mind shall never be, when you say, 'We will be like the
Gentiles, like the families in other countries, serving wood and stone.'

God Will Restore Israel

33"*As* I live," says the Lord GOD, "surely with a mighty hand, with an outstretched arm, and with fury poured out, I will rule over you. 34I will bring
you out from the peoples and gather you out of the countries where you
are scattered, with a mighty hand, with an outstretched arm, and with
fury poured out. 35And I will bring you into the wilderness of the peoples,
and there I will plead My case with you face to face. 36Just as I pleaded My
case with your fathers in the wilderness of the land of Egypt, so I will plead
My case with you," says the Lord GOD.

20:21 [b] Leviticus 18:5
20:29 [c] Literally *High Place*

[37]"I will make you pass under the rod, and I will bring you into the bond
of the covenant; [38]I will purge the rebels from among you, and those who
transgress against Me; I will bring them out of the country where they
dwell, but they shall not enter the land of Israel. Then you will know that I
am the LORD.

[39]"As for you, O house of Israel," thus says the Lord GOD: "Go, serve
every one of you his idols—and hereafter—if you will not obey Me; but
profane My holy name no more with your gifts and your idols. [40]For on
My holy mountain, on the mountain height of Israel," says the Lord GOD,
"there all the house of Israel, all of them in the land, shall serve Me; there I
will accept them, and there I will require your offerings and the firstfruits
of your sacrifices, together with all your holy things. [41]I will accept you as a
sweet aroma when I bring you out from the peoples and gather you out of
the countries where you have been scattered; and I will be hallowed in you
before the Gentiles. [42]Then you shall know that I *am* the LORD, when I bring
you into the land of Israel, into the country *for* which I raised My hand in
an oath to give to your fathers. [43]And there you shall remember your ways
and all your doings with which you were defiled; and you shall loathe
yourselves in your own sight because of all the evils that you have committed. [44]Then you shall know that I *am* the LORD, when I have dealt with
you for My name's sake, not according to your wicked ways nor according
to your corrupt doings, O house of Israel," says the Lord GOD.' "

Fire in the Forest

[45]Furthermore the word of the LORD came to me, saying, [46]"Son of man,
set your face toward the south; preach against the south and prophesy
against the forest land, the South,[d] [47]and say to the forest of the South,
'Hear the word of the LORD! Thus says the Lord GOD: "Behold, I will kindle
a fire in you, and it shall devour every green tree and every dry tree in you;
the blazing flame shall not be quenched, and all faces from the south to the
north shall be scorched by it. [48]All flesh shall see that I, the LORD, have kindled it; it shall not be quenched." ' "

[49]Then I said, "Ah, Lord GOD! They say of me, 'Does he not speak parables?' "

Babylon, the Sword of God

21 And the word of the LORD came to me, saying, [2]"Son of man, set
your face toward Jerusalem, preach against the holy places, and
prophesy against the land of Israel; [3]and say to the land of Israel, 'Thus
says the LORD: "Behold, I *am* against you, and I will draw My sword out of
its sheath and cut off both righteous and wicked from you. [4]Because I will
cut off both righteous and wicked from you, therefore My sword shall go
out of its sheath against all flesh from south *to* north, [5]that all flesh may
know that I, the LORD, have drawn My sword out of its sheath; it shall not
return anymore." ' [6]Sigh therefore, son of man, with a breaking heart, and
sigh with bitterness before their eyes. [7]And it shall be when they say to you,
'Why are you sighing?' that you shall answer, 'Because of the news; when it
comes, every heart will melt, all hands will be feeble, every spirit will faint,
and all knees will be weak *as* water. Behold, it is coming and shall be
brought to pass,' says the Lord GOD."

[8]Again the word of the LORD came to me, saying, [9]"Son of man, prophesy and say, 'Thus says the LORD!' Say:

present to Him, and what hasn't happened yet is in the now with Him. If this is confusing, it is also sobering, because it means the considerable mind of God is fully aware of all that has gone by in our lives. And all that has gone past includes an awful lot of sin—"a multitude of sins."

This is serious beyond description because people are responsible beings who must stand before God and give an answer for their sins. No evasion, no postponement, no tricky defense lawyer. Just man and God and a multitude of sins. But one thing we need to remember: God can "put away sin," "hide it in the depths of the sea," "remove it as far as the east is from the west," and "remember it no more." All because Christ's sacrifice for sin is applicable to all who come to Him in repentance and faith. (From *Getting Into God* by Stuart Briscoe)

APPLICATION If secret sins mar your relationship with God, deal with them immediately. Confess your sin, get it out of your life, seek help, and ask God to free your spirit from guilt.

EXPLORATION Judgment—Deuteronomy 7:2; 1 Samuel 2:25; 1 Kings 22:34; Isaiah 1:2-4; Matthew 3:10; Romans 2:12-15.

20:46 [d] Hebrew *Negev*

'A sword, a sword is sharpened
And also polished!
10 Sharpened to make a dreadful slaughter,
Polished to flash like lightning!
Should we then make mirth?
It despises the scepter of My son,
As it does all wood.
11 And He has given it to be polished,
That it may be handled;
This sword is sharpened, and it is polished
To be given into the hand of the slayer.'

12 "Cry and wail, son of man;
For it will be against My people,
Against all the princes of Israel.
Terrors including the sword will be against
My people;
Therefore strike *your* thigh.
13 "Because *it is* a testing,
And what if *the sword* despises even
the scepter?
The scepter shall be no *more*,"

says the Lord GOD.

14 "You therefore, son of man, prophesy,
And strike *your* hands together.
The third time let the sword do double *damage*.
It *is* the sword *that* slays,
The sword that slays the great *men*,
That enters their private chambers.
15 I have set the point of the sword against all
their gates,
That the heart may melt and many
may stumble.
Ah! *It is* made bright;
It is grasped for slaughter:
16 "Swords at the ready!
Thrust right!
Set your blade!
Thrust left—
Wherever your edge is ordered!

17 "I also will beat My fists together,
And I will cause My fury to rest;
I, the LORD, have spoken."

18 The word of the LORD came to me again, saying:
19 "And son of man, appoint for yourself two ways for
the sword of the king of Babylon to go; both of them
shall go from the same land. Make a sign; put *it* at the
head of the road to the city. 20 Appoint a road for the
sword to go to Rabbah of the Ammonites, and to Judah, into fortified Jerusalem. 21 For the king of
Babylon stands at the parting of the road, at the fork
of the two roads, to use divination: he shakes the arrows, he consults the images, he looks at the liver. 22 In
his right hand is the divination for Jerusalem: to set
up battering rams, to call for a slaughter, to lift the voice
with shouting, to set battering rams against the gates, to
heap up a *siege* mound, and to build a wall. 23 And it will
be to them like a false divination in the eyes of those
who have sworn oaths with them; but he will bring their
iniquity to remembrance, that they may be taken.
24 "Therefore thus says the Lord GOD: 'Because you
have made your iniquity to be remembered, in that
your transgressions are uncovered, so that in all your
doings your sins appear—because you have come to
remembrance, you shall be taken in hand.
25 'Now to you, O profane, wicked prince of Israel,
whose day has come, whose iniquity *shall* end, 26 thus
says the Lord GOD:

"Remove the turban, and take off the crown;
Nothing *shall remain* the same.
Exalt the humble, and humble the exalted.
27 Overthrown, overthrown,
I will make it overthrown!
It shall be no *longer*,
Until He comes whose right it is,
And I will give it *to* Him." '

A Sword Against the Ammonites

28 "And you, son of man, prophesy and say, 'Thus
says the Lord GOD concerning the Ammonites and
concerning their reproach,' and say:

'A sword, a sword *is* drawn,
Polished for slaughter,
For consuming, for flashing—
29 While they see false visions for you,
While they divine a lie to you,
To bring you on the necks of the wicked,
the slain
Whose day has come,
Whose iniquity *shall* end.

30 'Return *it* to its sheath.
I will judge you
In the place where you were created,
In the land of your nativity.
31 I will pour out My indignation on you;
I will blow against you with the fire of
My wrath,
And deliver you into the hands of brutal men
who are skillful to destroy.

32 You shall be fuel for the fire;
Your blood shall be in the midst of the land.
You shall not be remembered,
For I the LORD have spoken.’ ”

Sins of Jerusalem

22 Moreover the word of the LORD came to me,
saying, 2“Now, son of man, will you judge, will
you judge the bloody city? Yes, show her all her
abominations! 3Then say, ‘Thus says the Lord GOD:
“The city sheds blood in her own midst, that her time
may come; and she makes idols within herself to defile
herself. 4You have become guilty by the blood which you
have shed, and have defiled yourself with the idols which
you have made. You have caused your days to draw near,
and have come to *the end of* your years; therefore I have
made you a reproach to the nations, and a mockery to all
countries. 5*Those* near and *those* far from you will mock
you as infamous *and* full of tumult.

6“Look, the princes of Israel: each one has used his
power to shed blood in you. 7In you they have made
light of father and mother; in your midst they have
oppressed the stranger; in you they have mistreated
the fatherless and the widow. 8You have despised My
holy things and profaned My Sabbaths. 9In you are
men who slander to cause bloodshed; in you are
those who eat on the mountains; in your midst they
commit lewdness. 10In you men uncover their fathers’
nakedness; in you they violate women who are set
apart during their impurity. 11One commits abomination with his neighbor’s wife; another lewdly defiles
his daughter-in-law; and another in you violates his
sister, his father’s daughter. 12In you they take bribes
to shed blood; you take usury and increase; you have
made profit from your neighbors by extortion, and
have forgotten Me,” says the Lord GOD.

13“Behold, therefore, I beat My fists at the dishonest
profit which you have made, and at the bloodshed
which has been in your midst. 14Can your heart endure, or can your hands remain strong, in the days
when I shall deal with you? I, the LORD, have spoken,
and will do *it.* 15I will scatter you among the nations,
disperse you throughout the countries, and remove
your filthiness completely from you. 16You shall defile
yourself in the sight of the nations; then you shall
know that I *am* the LORD.” ’ ”

Israel in the Furnace

17The word of the LORD came to me, saying, 18“Son
of man, the house of Israel has become dross to Me;
they *are* all bronze, tin, iron, and lead, in the midst of a
furnace; they have become dross from silver. 19There-
fore thus says the Lord GOD: ‘Because you have all become dross, therefore behold, I will gather you into
the midst of Jerusalem. 20*As men* gather silver, bronze,
iron, lead, and tin into the midst of a furnace, to blow
fire on it, to melt *it;* so I will gather *you* in My anger
and in My fury, and I will leave *you there* and melt you.
21Yes, I will gather you and blow on you with the fire of
My wrath, and you shall be melted in its midst. 22As
silver is melted in the midst of a furnace, so shall you
be melted in its midst; then you shall know that I, the
LORD, have poured out My fury on you.’ ”

Israel’s Wicked Leaders

23And the word of the LORD came to me, saying,
24“Son of man, say to her: ‘You *are* a land that is not
cleansed[e] or rained on in the day of indignation.’
25The conspiracy of her prophets[f] in her midst is like a
roaring lion tearing the prey; they have devoured people; they have taken treasure and precious things;
they have made many widows in her midst. 26Her
priests have violated My law and profaned My holy
things; they have not distinguished between the holy
and unholy, nor have they made known *the difference*
between the unclean and the clean; and they have hidden their eyes from My Sabbaths, so that I am profaned among them. 27Her princes in her midst *are* like
wolves tearing the prey, to shed blood, to destroy people, and to get dishonest gain. 28Her prophets plastered them with untempered *mortar,* seeing false
visions, and divining lies for them, saying, ‘Thus says
the Lord GOD,’ when the LORD had not spoken. 29The
people of the land have used oppressions, committed
robbery, and mistreated the poor and needy; and they
wrongfully oppress the stranger. 30So I sought for a
man among them who would make a wall, and stand
in the gap before Me on behalf of the land, that I
should not destroy it; but I found no one. 31Therefore I
have poured out My indignation on them; I have consumed them with the fire of My wrath; and I have recompensed their deeds on their own heads,” says the
Lord GOD.

Two Harlot Sisters

23 The word of the LORD came again to me,
saying:

2 “Son of man, there were two women,
The daughters of one mother.

22:24 [e] Following Masoretic Text, Syriac, and Vulgate; Septuagint reads *showered upon.*
22:25 [f] Following Masoretic Text and Vulgate; Septuagint reads *princes;* Targum reads *scribes.*

3 They committed harlotry in Egypt,
They committed harlotry in their youth;
Their breasts were there embraced,
Their virgin bosom was there pressed.
4 Their names: Oholah[g] the elder and Oholibah[h]
her sister;
They were Mine,
And they bore sons and daughters.
As for their names,
Samaria *is* Oholah, and Jerusalem *is* Oholibah.

The Older Sister, Samaria

5 "Oholah played the harlot even though
she was Mine;
And she lusted for her lovers, the
neighboring Assyrians,
6 *Who were* clothed in purple,
Captains and rulers,
All of them desirable young men,
Horsemen riding on horses.
7 Thus she committed her harlotry with them,
All of them choice men of Assyria;
And with all for whom she lusted,
With all their idols, she defiled herself.
8 She has never given up her harlotry *brought*
from Egypt,
For in her youth they had lain with her,
Pressed her virgin bosom,
And poured out their immorality upon her.
9 "Therefore I have delivered her
Into the hand of her lovers,
Into the hand of the Assyrians,
For whom she lusted.
10 They uncovered her nakedness,
Took away her sons and daughters,
And slew her with the sword;
She became a byword among women,
For they had executed judgment on her.

The Younger Sister, Jerusalem

11 "Now although her sister Oholibah saw *this,* she became more corrupt in her lust than she, and in her harlotry more corrupt than her sister's harlotry.

12 "She lusted for the neighboring Assyrians,
Captains and rulers,
Clothed most gorgeously,
Horsemen riding on horses,
All of them desirable young men.
13 Then I saw that she was defiled;
Both *took* the same way.
14 But she increased her harlotry;
She looked at men portrayed on the wall,
Images of Chaldeans portrayed in vermilion,
15 Girded with belts around their waists,
Flowing turbans on their heads,
All of them looking like captains,
In the manner of the Babylonians of Chaldea,
The land of their nativity.
16 As soon as her eyes saw them,
She lusted for them
And sent messengers to them in Chaldea.

17 "Then the Babylonians came to her, into the
bed of love,
And they defiled her with their immorality;
So she was defiled by them, and alienated
herself from them.
18 She revealed her harlotry and uncovered
her nakedness.
Then I alienated Myself from her,
As I had alienated Myself from her sister.

19 "Yet she multiplied her harlotry
In calling to remembrance the days
of her youth,
When she had played the harlot in the
land of Egypt.
20 For she lusted for her paramours,
Whose flesh *is like* the flesh of donkeys,
And whose issue *is like* the issue of horses.
21 Thus you called to remembrance the lewdness
of your youth,
When the Egyptians pressed your bosom
Because of your youthful breasts.

Judgment on Jerusalem

22 "Therefore, Oholibah, thus says the Lord GOD:

'Behold, I will stir up your lovers against you,
From whom you have alienated yourself,
And I will bring them against you from
every side:
23 The Babylonians,
All the Chaldeans,
Pekod, Shoa, Koa,
All the Assyrians with them,

23:4 [g] Literally *Her Own Tabernacle* [h] Literally *My Tabernacle Is in Her*

All of them desirable young men,
Governors and rulers,
Captains and men of renown,
All of them riding on horses.
24 And they shall come against you
With chariots, wagons, and war-horses,
With a horde of people.
They shall array against you
Buckler, shield, and helmet all around.

'I will delegate judgment to them,
And they shall judge you according to
their judgments.
25 I will set My jealousy against you,
And they shall deal furiously with you;
They shall remove your nose and your ears,
And your remnant shall fall by the sword;
They shall take your sons and your daughters,
And your remnant shall be devoured by fire.
26 They shall also strip you of your clothes
And take away your beautiful jewelry.

27 'Thus I will make you cease your lewdness and
your harlotry
Brought from the land of Egypt,
So that you will not lift your eyes to them,
Nor remember Egypt anymore.'

28 "For thus says the Lord GOD: 'Surely I will deliver
you into the hand of those you hate, into the hand *of*
those from whom you alienated yourself. 29 They will
deal hatefully with you, take away all you have worked
for, and leave you naked and bare. The nakedness of
your harlotry shall be uncovered, both your lewdness
and your harlotry. 30 I will do these *things* to you because you have gone as a harlot after the Gentiles, because you have become defiled by their idols. 31 You
have walked in the way of your sister; therefore I will
put her cup in your hand.'

32 "Thus says the Lord GOD:

'You shall drink of your sister's cup,
The deep and wide one;
You shall be laughed to scorn
And held in derision;
It contains much.
33 You will be filled with drunkenness
and sorrow,
The cup of horror and desolation,
The cup of your sister Samaria.
34 You shall drink and drain it,
You shall break its shards,
And tear at your own breasts;
For I have spoken,'
Says the Lord GOD.

35 "Therefore thus says the Lord GOD:

'Because you have forgotten Me and cast Me
behind your back,
Therefore you shall bear the *penalty*
Of your lewdness and your harlotry.' "

Both Sisters Judged

36 The LORD also said to me: "Son of man, will you
judge Oholah and Oholibah? Then declare to them
their abominations. 37 For they have committed adultery, and blood *is* on their hands. They have committed adultery with their idols, and even sacrificed their
sons whom they bore to Me, passing them through
the fire, to devour *them.* 38 Moreover they have done
this to Me: They have defiled My sanctuary on the
same day and profaned My Sabbaths. 39 For after they
had slain their children for their idols, on the same
day they came into My sanctuary to profane it; and
indeed thus they have done in the midst of My house.

40 "Furthermore you sent for men to come from
afar, to whom a messenger *was* sent; and there they
came. And you washed yourself for them, painted
your eyes, and adorned yourself with ornaments.
41 You sat on a stately couch, with a table prepared before it, on which you had set My incense and My oil.
42 The sound of a carefree multitude *was* with her, and
Sabeans *were* brought from the wilderness with men
of the common sort, who put bracelets on their wrists
and beautiful crowns on their heads. 43 Then I said
concerning *her who had grown* old in adulteries, 'Will
they commit harlotry with her now, and she *with*
them?' 44 Yet they went in to her, as men go in to a
woman who plays the harlot; thus they went in to
Oholah and Oholibah, the lewd women. 45 But righteous men will judge them after the manner of adulteresses, and after the manner of women who shed
blood, because they *are* adulteresses, and blood *is* on
their hands.

46 "For thus says the Lord GOD: 'Bring up an assembly against them, give them up to trouble and plunder. 47 The assembly shall stone them with stones and
execute them with their swords; they shall slay their
sons and their daughters, and burn their houses with
fire. 48 Thus I will cause lewdness to cease from the
land, that all women may be taught not to practice
your lewdness. 49 They shall repay you for your lewdness, and you shall pay for your idolatrous sins. Then
you shall know that I *am* the Lord GOD.' "

Symbol of the Cooking Pot

24 Again, in the ninth year, in the tenth month, on the tenth *day* of the month, the word of the
LORD came to me, saying, 2"Son of man, write down
the name of the day, this very day—the king of
Babylon started his siege against Jerusalem this very
day. 3And utter a parable to the rebellious house, and
say to them, 'Thus says the Lord GOD:

"Put on a pot, set *it* on,
And also pour water into it.
4 Gather pieces *of meat* in it,
Every good piece,
The thigh and the shoulder.
Fill *it* with choice cuts;
5 Take the choice of the flock.
Also pile *fuel* bones under it,
Make it boil well,
And let the cuts simmer in it."

6"Therefore thus says the Lord GOD:

"Woe to the bloody city,
To the pot whose scum *is* in it,
And whose scum is not gone from it!
Bring it out piece by piece,
On which no lot has fallen.
7 For her blood is in her midst;
She set it on top of a rock;
She did not pour it on the ground,
To cover it with dust.
8 That it may raise up fury and take vengeance,
I have set her blood on top of a rock,
That it may not be covered."

9"Therefore thus says the Lord GOD:

"Woe to the bloody city!
I too will make the pyre great.
10 Heap on the wood,
Kindle the fire;
Cook the meat well,
Mix in the spices,
And let the cuts be burned up.

11 "Then set the pot empty on the coals,
That it may become hot and its bronze may burn,
That its filthiness may be melted in it,
That its scum may be consumed.
12 She has grown weary with lies,
And her great scum has not gone from her.
Let her scum *be* in the fire!
13 In your filthiness *is* lewdness.
Because I have cleansed you, and you were not cleansed,
You will not be cleansed of your filthiness anymore,
Till I have caused My fury to rest upon you.
14 I, the LORD, have spoken *it;*
It shall come to pass, and I will do *it;*
I will not hold back,
Nor will I spare,
Nor will I relent;
According to your ways
And according to your deeds
They[i] will judge you,"
Says the Lord GOD.'"

The Prophet's Wife Dies

15Also the word of the LORD came to me, saying,
16"Son of man, behold, I take away from you the desire of your eyes with one stroke; yet you shall neither
mourn nor weep, nor shall your tears run down.
17Sigh in silence, make no mourning for the dead;
bind your turban on your head, and put your sandals
on your feet; do not cover *your* lips, and do not eat
man's bread *of sorrow*."
18So I spoke to the people in the morning, and at
evening my wife died; and the next morning I did as I
was commanded.
19And the people said to me, "Will you not tell us
what these *things signify* to us, that you behave so?"
20Then I answered them, "The word of the LORD
came to me, saying, 21'Speak to the house of Israel,
"Thus says the Lord GOD: 'Behold, I will profane My
sanctuary, your arrogant boast, the desire of your
eyes, the delight of your soul; and your sons and
daughters whom you left behind shall fall by the
sword. 22And you shall do as I have done; you shall
not cover *your* lips nor eat man's bread *of sorrow*.
23Your turbans shall be on your heads and your sandals on your feet; you shall neither mourn nor weep,
but you shall pine away in your iniquities and mourn
with one another. 24Thus Ezekiel is a sign to you; according to all that he has done you shall do; and when
this comes, you shall know that I *am* the Lord GOD.'"
25'And you, son of man—*will it* not *be* in the day
when I take from them their stronghold, their joy and

24:14 [i] Septuagint, Syriac, Targum, and Vulgate read *I*.

their glory, the desire of their eyes, and that on which they set their minds,
their sons and their daughters: 26on that day one who escapes will come to
you to let *you* hear *it* with *your* ears; 27on that day your mouth will be
opened to him who has escaped; you shall speak and no longer be mute.
Thus you will be a sign to them, and they shall know that I *am* the LORD.' "

Proclamation Against Ammon

25 The word of the LORD came to me, saying, 2"Son of man, set your
face against the Ammonites, and prophesy against them. 3Say to
the Ammonites, 'Hear the word of the Lord GOD! Thus says the Lord GOD:
"Because you said, 'Aha!' against My sanctuary when it was profaned, and
against the land of Israel when it was desolate, and against the house of Judah when they went into captivity, 4indeed, therefore, I will deliver you as
a possession to the men of the East, and they shall set their encampments
among you and make their dwellings among you; they shall eat your fruit,
and they shall drink your milk. 5And I will make Rabbah a stable for
camels and Ammon a resting place for flocks. Then you shall know that I
am the LORD."

6"For thus says the Lord GOD: "Because you clapped *your* hands,
stamped your feet, and rejoiced in heart with all your disdain for the land
of Israel, 7indeed, therefore, I will stretch out My hand against you, and
give you as plunder to the nations; I will cut you off from the peoples, and
I will cause you to perish from the countries; I will destroy you, and you
shall know that I *am* the LORD."

Proclamation Against Moab

8"Thus says the Lord GOD: "Because Moab and Seir say, 'Look! The
house of Judah *is* like all the nations,' 9therefore, behold, I will clear the territory of Moab of cities, of the cities on its frontier, the glory of the country,
Beth Jeshimoth, Baal Meon, and Kirjathaim. 10To the men of the East I will
give it as a possession, together with the Ammonites, that the Ammonites
may not be remembered among the nations. 11And I will execute judgments upon Moab, and they shall know that I *am* the LORD."

Proclamation Against Edom

12"Thus says the Lord GOD: "Because of what Edom did against the
house of Judah by taking vengeance, and has greatly offended by avenging
itself on them," 13therefore thus says the Lord GOD: "I will also stretch out
My hand against Edom, cut off man and beast from it, and make it desolate from Teman; Dedan shall fall by the sword. 14I will lay My vengeance
on Edom by the hand of My people Israel, that they may do in Edom according to My anger and according to My fury; and they shall know My
vengeance," says the Lord GOD.

Proclamation Against Philistia

15"Thus says the Lord GOD: "Because the Philistines dealt vengefully and
took vengeance with a spiteful heart, to destroy because of the old hatred,"
16therefore thus says the Lord GOD: "I will stretch out My hand against the
Philistines, and I will cut off the Cherethites and destroy the remnant of the
seacoast. 17I will execute great vengeance on them with furious rebukes; and
they shall know that I *am* the LORD, when I lay My vengeance upon them." ' "

LIFE LESSON

Ezekiel 25:1–32:32

SITUATION The prophets knew that God reigned over all the world. When these seven nations failed to acknowledge God as their king, they were punished.

OBSERVATION We are never beyond the reach of God's judgment. God condemns pride and arrogance wherever it appears.

INSPIRATION There are two kinds of pride. One is the opposite of humility; it is very bad. The other is the opposite of shame; it is very good.

The kind of pride that is the opposite of humility leaves God and other circumstances out of our successes. It claims that whatever we have achieved, we have achieved by our own virtue.

The essence of this kind of pride is self-centeredness and selfishness and it is condemned by Scripture. This does not mean, however, that the Bible is opposed to the self. The self is one of God's good creations; selfishness is worshiping the creation rather than the creator.

Bad pride is the kind of selfishness that always wants to be center stage, that takes all the credit, that leaves God out, that gives no thanks to other people, that goes it alone. It is the opposite of what God desires for us. . . .

By contrast, the kind of pride that is the opposite of shame has to do with a job well done, with excellence, with striving for the best, with rising above mediocrity. In a Christian, this kind of pride attempts to give of its best to the Master.

People who misunderstand the difference between the two kinds of pride may have a misimpression of the Christian faith. Christianity is not opposed to excellence. It is not opposed to putting forth your best effort, excelling, and achieving. No, it is only opposed to a person's thinking he can excel without God's help.

Selfish pride is the opposite of thankfulness and gratitude. It shows no gratitude to God for a healthy body, a healthy mind, good parents, a good national heritage, a good diet, and a thousand other blessings over which

Continued

the person has no control. A person filled with selfish pride thinks he has created himself through his own efforts. . . .

The other kind of pride, the kind that is opposite to shame, doesn't crawl out between the mattress and springs and say, "I'm a worm; step on me." It doesn't finish playing a solo and say, "It was nothing." It is not unable to accept a compliment.

The pride that is opposite to shame can say thank you and give credit where credit is due. It can thank God for his gifts and, at the same time, acknowledge good work when it is done. The person who can accept a compliment is not arrogant. He knows where his dexterous fingers come from, who gave him his mind and his sense of rhythm. . . .

When Michelangelo walked away from the Sistine Chapel, he knew he had done a beautiful work, and he was proud of it. Yet when a person looks at the ceiling of that chapel, he is always drawn toward God. He is inspired to worship God, not Michelangelo. The art is great, but because it is aimed at glorifying the heavenly Father, the observer is moved to worship.

(From "Two Kinds of Pride" by Jay Kesler in *Practical Christianity*)

APPLICATION Have you been successful? Do people praise your achievements? Give credit to God in thankful prayer for each gift he has given you.

EXPLORATION Pride—Mark 9:34; Luke 18:11-14; 1 Peter 5:5-6.

Proclamation Against Tyre

26 And it came to pass in the eleventh year, on the first *day* of the
month, *that* the word of the LORD came to me, saying, 2"Son of
man, because Tyre has said against Jerusalem, 'Aha! She is broken who
was the gateway of the peoples; now she is turned over to me; I shall be
filled; she is laid waste.'
3"Therefore thus says the Lord GOD: 'Behold, I *am* against you, O Tyre,
and will cause many nations to come up against you, as the sea causes its
waves to come up. 4And they shall destroy the walls of Tyre and break
down her towers; I will also scrape her dust from her, and make her like the
top of a rock. 5It shall be *a place for* spreading nets in the midst of the sea,
for I have spoken,' says the Lord GOD; 'it shall become plunder for the nations. 6Also her daughter *villages* which *are* in the fields shall be slain by
the sword. Then they shall know that I *am* the LORD.'
7"For thus says the Lord GOD: 'Behold, I will bring against Tyre from the
north Nebuchadnezzar[j] king of Babylon, king of kings, with horses, with
chariots, and with horsemen, and an army with many people. 8He will
slay with the sword your daughter *villages* in the fields; he will heap up a
siege mound against you, build a wall against you, and raise a defense
against you. 9He will direct his battering rams against your walls, and with
his axes he will break down your towers. 10Because of the abundance of his
horses, their dust will cover you; your walls will shake at the noise of the
horsemen, the wagons, and the chariots, when he enters your gates, as
men enter a city that has been breached. 11With the hooves of his horses he
will trample all your streets; he will slay your people by the sword, and
your strong pillars will fall to the ground. 12They will plunder your riches
and pillage your merchandise; they will break down your walls and destroy your pleasant houses; they will lay your stones, your timber, and
your soil in the midst of the water. 13I will put an end to the sound of your
songs, and the sound of your harps shall be heard no more. 14I will make
you like the top of a rock; you shall be *a place for* spreading nets, and you
shall never be rebuilt, for I the LORD have spoken,' says the Lord GOD.
15"Thus says the Lord GOD to Tyre: 'Will the coastlands not shake at the
sound of your fall, when the wounded cry, when slaughter is made in the
midst of you? 16Then all the princes of the sea will come down from their
thrones, lay aside their robes, and take off their embroidered garments;
they will clothe themselves with trembling; they will sit on the ground,
tremble *every* moment, and be astonished at you. 17And they will take up a
lamentation for you, and say to you:

"How you have perished,
O one inhabited by seafaring men,
O renowned city,
Who was strong at sea,
She and her inhabitants,
Who caused their terror *to be* on all her inhabitants!
18 Now the coastlands tremble on the day of your fall;
Yes, the coastlands by the sea are troubled at your departure." '

19"For thus says the Lord GOD: 'When I make you a desolate city, like
cities that are not inhabited, when I bring the deep upon you, and great

26:7 *j* Hebrew *Nebuchadrezzar,* and so elsewhere in this book

waters cover you, [20]then I will bring you down with
those who descend into the Pit, to the people of old,
and I will make you dwell in the lowest part of the
earth, in places desolate from antiquity, with those
who go down to the Pit, so that you may never be inhabited; and I shall establish glory in the land of the
living. [21]I will make you a terror, and you *shall be* no
more; though you are sought for, you will never be
found again,' says the Lord GOD."

Lamentation for Tyre

27 The word of the LORD came again to me, saying,
[2]"Now, son of man, take up a lamentation for
Tyre, [3]and say to Tyre, 'You who are situated at the entrance of the sea, merchant of the peoples on many
coastlands, thus says the Lord GOD:

"O Tyre, you have said,
'I *am* perfect in beauty.'
4 Your borders *are* in the midst of the seas.
Your builders have perfected your beauty.
5 They made all *your* planks of fir trees
from Senir;
They took a cedar from Lebanon to make
you a mast.
6 *Of* oaks from Bashan they made your oars;
The company of Ashurites have inlaid
your planks
With ivory from the coasts of Cyprus.[k]
7 Fine embroidered linen from Egypt was what
you spread for your sail;
Blue and purple from the coasts of Elishah
was what covered you.

8 "Inhabitants of Sidon and Arvad were
your oarsmen;
Your wise men, O Tyre, were in you;
They became your pilots.
9 Elders of Gebal and its wise men
Were in you to caulk your seams;
All the ships of the sea
And their oarsmen were in you
To market your merchandise.

10 "Those from Persia, Lydia,[l] and Libya[m]
Were in your army as men of war;
They hung shield and helmet in you;
They gave splendor to you.
11 Men of Arvad with your army *were* on your
walls *all* around,
And the men of Gammad were in your towers;
They hung their shields on your walls
all around;
They made your beauty perfect.

[12]"Tarshish *was* your merchant because of your
many luxury goods. They gave you silver, iron, tin,
and lead for your goods. [13]Javan, Tubal, and Meshech
were your traders. They bartered human lives and
vessels of bronze for your merchandise. [14]Those from
the house of Togarmah traded for your wares with
horses, steeds, and mules. [15]The men of Dedan *were*
your traders; many isles *were* the market of your
hand. They brought you ivory tusks and ebony as
payment. [16]Syria *was* your merchant because of the
abundance of goods you made. They gave you for
your wares emeralds, purple, embroidery, fine linen,
corals, and rubies. [17]Judah and the land of Israel *were*
your traders. They traded for your merchandise
wheat of Minnith, millet, honey, oil, and balm. [18]Da-
mascus *was* your merchant because of the abundance
of goods you made, because of your many luxury
items, with the wine of Helbon and with white wool.
[19]Dan and Javan paid for your wares, traversing back
and forth. Wrought iron, cassia, and cane were
among your merchandise. [20]Dedan *was* your merchant in saddlecloths for riding. [21]Arabia and all the
princes of Kedar *were* your regular merchants. They
traded with you in lambs, rams, and goats. [22]The merchants of Sheba and Raamah *were* your merchants.
They traded for your wares the choicest spices, all
kinds of precious stones, and gold. [23]Haran, Canneh,
Eden, the merchants of Sheba, Assyria, *and* Chilmad
were your merchants. [24]These *were* your merchants in
choice items—in purple clothes, in embroidered garments, in chests of multicolored apparel, in sturdy
woven cords, which were in your marketplace.

25 "The ships of Tarshish were carriers
of your merchandise.
You were filled and very glorious in the
midst of the seas.
26 Your oarsmen brought you into many waters,
But the east wind broke you in the midst
of the seas.

27 "Your riches, wares, and merchandise,
Your mariners and pilots,
Your caulkers and merchandisers,
All your men of war who *are* in you,
And the entire company which *is* in
your midst,

27:6 [k] Hebrew *Kittim,* western lands, especially Cyprus
27:10 [l] Hebrew *Lud* [m] Hebrew *Put*

Will fall into the midst of the seas on the day
of your ruin.
28 The common-land will shake at the sound of
the cry of your pilots.
29 "All who handle the oar,
The mariners,
All the pilots of the sea
Will come down from their ships *and* stand
on the shore.
30 They will make their voice heard because
of you;
They will cry bitterly and cast dust on
their heads;
They will roll about in ashes;
31 They will shave themselves completely bald
because of you,
Gird themselves with sackcloth,
And weep for you
With bitterness of heart *and* bitter wailing.
32 In their wailing for you
They will take up a lamentation,
And lament for you:
'What *city is* like Tyre,
Destroyed in the midst of the sea?
33 'When your wares went out by sea,
You satisfied many people;
You enriched the kings of the earth
With your many luxury goods and
your merchandise.
34 But you are broken by the seas in the depths
of the waters;
Your merchandise and the entire company
will fall in your midst.
35 All the inhabitants of the isles will be
astonished at you;
Their kings will be greatly afraid,
And *their* countenance will be troubled.
36 The merchants among the peoples will
hiss at you;
You will become a horror, and *be* no
more forever.' " ' "

Proclamation Against the King of Tyre

28 The word of the LORD came to me again, saying, 2"Son of man, say to the prince of Tyre,
'Thus says the Lord GOD:

"Because your heart *is* lifted up,
And you say, 'I *am* a god,
I sit *in* the seat of gods,
In the midst of the seas,'
Yet you *are* a man, and not a god,
Though you set your heart as the heart
of a god
3 (Behold, you *are* wiser than Daniel!
There is no secret that can be hidden
from you!
4 With your wisdom and your understanding
You have gained riches for yourself,
And gathered gold and silver into
your treasuries;
5 By your great wisdom in trade you have
increased your riches,
And your heart is lifted up because of
your riches),"

6"Therefore thus says the Lord GOD:

"Because you have set your heart as the
heart of a god,
7 Behold, therefore, I will bring strangers
against you,
The most terrible of the nations;
And they shall draw their swords against the
beauty of your wisdom,
And defile your splendor.
8 They shall throw you down into the Pit,
And you shall die the death of the slain
In the midst of the seas.
9 "Will you still say before him who slays you,
'I *am* a god?'
But you *shall be* a man, and not a god,
In the hand of him who slays you.
10 You shall die the death of the uncircumcised
By the hand of aliens;
For I have spoken," says the Lord GOD.' "

Lamentation for the King of Tyre

11Moreover the word of the LORD came to me, saying, 12"Son of man, take up a lamentation for the king of Tyre, and say to him, 'Thus says the Lord GOD:

"You *were* the seal of perfection,
Full of wisdom and perfect in beauty.
13 You were in Eden, the garden of God;
Every precious stone *was* your covering:
The sardius, topaz, and diamond,
Beryl, onyx, and jasper,
Sapphire, turquoise, and emerald with gold.
The workmanship of your timbrels and pipes
Was prepared for you on the day you
were created.

14 "You *were* the anointed cherub who covers;
I established you;
You were on the holy mountain of God;
You walked back and forth in the midst of fiery stones.
15 You *were* perfect in your ways from the day you were created,
Till iniquity was found in you.

16 "By the abundance of your trading
You became filled with violence within,
And you sinned;
Therefore I cast you as a profane thing
Out of the mountain of God;
And I destroyed you, O covering cherub,
From the midst of the fiery stones.

17 "Your heart was lifted up because of your beauty;
You corrupted your wisdom for the sake of your splendor;
I cast you to the ground,
I laid you before kings,
That they might gaze at you.

18 "You defiled your sanctuaries
By the multitude of your iniquities,
By the iniquity of your trading;
Therefore I brought fire from your midst;
It devoured you,
And I turned you to ashes upon the earth
In the sight of all who saw you.
19 All who knew you among the peoples are astonished at you;
You have become a horror,
And *shall be* no more forever." ' "

Proclamation Against Sidon

20 Then the word of the LORD came to me, saying,
21 "Son of man, set your face toward Sidon, and prophesy against her, 22 and say, 'Thus says the Lord GOD:

"Behold, I *am* against you, O Sidon;
I will be glorified in your midst;
And they shall know that I *am* the LORD,
When I execute judgments in her and am hallowed in her.
23 For I will send pestilence upon her,
And blood in her streets;
The wounded shall be judged in her midst
By the sword against her on every side;
Then they shall know that I *am* the LORD.

24 "And there shall no longer be a pricking brier or a painful thorn for the house of Israel from among all *who are* around them, who despise them. Then they shall know that I *am* the Lord GOD."

Israel's Future Blessing

25 "Thus says the Lord GOD: "When I have gathered the house of Israel from the peoples among whom they are scattered, and am hallowed in them in the sight of the Gentiles, then they will dwell in their own land which I gave to My servant Jacob.
26 And they will dwell safely there, build houses, and plant vineyards; yes, they will dwell securely, when I execute judgments on all those around them who despise them. Then they shall know that I *am* the LORD their God." ' "

Proclamation Against Egypt

29 In the tenth year, in the tenth *month,* on the twelfth *day* of the month, the word of the LORD came to me, saying,
2 "Son of man, set your face against Pharaoh king of Egypt, and prophesy against him, and against all Egypt.
3 Speak, and say, 'Thus says the Lord GOD:

"Behold, I *am* against you,
O Pharaoh king of Egypt,
O great monster who lies in the midst of his rivers,
Who has said, 'My River[n] *is* my own;
I have made *it* for myself.'
4 But I will put hooks in your jaws,
And cause the fish of your rivers to stick to your scales;
I will bring you up out of the midst of your rivers,
And all the fish in your rivers will stick to your scales.
5 I will leave you in the wilderness,
You and all the fish of your rivers;
You shall fall on the open field;
You shall not be picked up or gathered.[o]
I have given you as food
To the beasts of the field
And to the birds of the heavens.

6 "Then all the inhabitants of Egypt
Shall know that I *am* the LORD,

29:3 [n] That is, the Nile
29:5 [o] Following Masoretic Text, Septuagint, and Vulgate; some Hebrew manuscripts and Targum read *buried*.

Because they have been a staff of reed to the
house of Israel.
7 When they took hold of you with the hand,
You broke and tore all their shoulders;[p]
When they leaned on you,
You broke and made all their backs quiver."

8"Therefore thus says the Lord GOD: "Surely I will
bring a sword upon you and cut off from you man
and beast. 9And the land of Egypt shall become desolate and waste; then they will know that I *am* the LORD,
because he said, 'The River *is* mine, and I have made
it.' 10Indeed, therefore, I *am* against you and against
your rivers, and I will make the land of Egypt utterly
waste and desolate, from Migdol[q] *to* Syene, as far as
the border of Ethiopia. 11Neither foot of man shall
pass through it nor foot of beast pass through it, and
it shall be uninhabited forty years. 12I will make the
land of Egypt desolate in the midst of the countries
that are desolate; and among the cities *that are* laid
waste, her cities shall be desolate forty years; and I will
scatter the Egyptians among the nations and disperse
them throughout the countries."

13"Yet, thus says the Lord GOD: "At the end of forty
years I will gather the Egyptians from the peoples
among whom they were scattered. 14I will bring back
the captives of Egypt and cause them to return to the
land of Pathros, to the land of their origin, and there
they shall be a lowly kingdom. 15It shall be the lowliest
of kingdoms; it shall never again exalt itself above the
nations, for I will diminish them so that they will not
rule over the nations anymore. 16No longer shall it be
the confidence of the house of Israel, but will remind
them of *their* iniquity when they turned to follow them.
Then they shall know that I *am* the Lord GOD." ' "

Babylonia Will Plunder Egypt

17And it came to pass in the twenty-seventh year, in
the first *month*, on the first *day* of the month, *that* the
word of the LORD came to me, saying, 18"Son of man,
Nebuchadnezzar king of Babylon caused his army to
labor strenuously against Tyre; every head *was* made
bald, and every shoulder rubbed raw; yet neither he
nor his army received wages from Tyre, for the labor
which they expended on it. 19Therefore thus says the
Lord GOD: 'Surely I will give the land of Egypt to
Nebuchadnezzar king of Babylon; he shall take away
her wealth, carry off her spoil, and remove her pillage;
and that will be the wages for his army. 20I have given
him the land of Egypt *for* his labor, because they
worked for Me,' says the Lord GOD.

21'In that day I will cause the horn of the house of Israel
to spring forth, and I will open your mouth to speak in
their midst. Then they shall know that I *am* the LORD.' "

Egypt and Her Allies Will Fall

30 The word of the LORD came to me again, saying, 2"Son of man, prophesy and say, 'Thus
says the Lord GOD:

"Wail, 'Woe to the day!'
3 For the day *is* near,
Even the day of the LORD *is* near;
It will be a day of clouds, the time
of the Gentiles.
4 The sword shall come upon Egypt,
And great anguish shall be in Ethiopia,
When the slain fall in Egypt,
And they take away her wealth,
And her foundations are broken down.

5"Ethiopia, Libya,[r] Lydia,[s] all the mingled people,
Chub, and the men of the lands who are allied, shall
fall with them by the sword."

6"Thus says the LORD:

"Those who uphold Egypt shall fall,
And the pride of her power shall come down.
From Migdol *to* Syene
Those within her shall fall by the sword,"
Says the Lord GOD.

7 "They shall be desolate in the midst of the
desolate countries,
And her cities shall be in the midst of the
cities *that are* laid waste.
8 Then they will know that I *am* the LORD,
When I have set a fire in Egypt
And all her helpers are destroyed.
9 On that day messengers shall go forth
from Me in ships
To make the careless Ethiopians afraid,
And great anguish shall come upon them,
As on the day of Egypt;
For indeed it is coming!"

29:7 [p] Following Masoretic Text and Vulgate; Septuagint and Syriac read *hand*.
29:10 [q] Or *tower*
30:5 [r] Hebrew *Put* [s] Hebrew *Lud*

[10]"Thus says the Lord GOD:
"I will also make a multitude of Egypt to cease
By the hand of Nebuchadnezzar king
of Babylon.
11 He and his people with him, the most
terrible of the nations,
Shall be brought to destroy the land;
They shall draw their swords against Egypt,
And fill the land with the slain.
12 I will make the rivers dry,
And sell the land into the hand of the wicked;
I will make the land waste, and all that is in it,
By the hand of aliens.
I, the LORD, have spoken."

[13]"Thus says the Lord GOD:
"I will also destroy the idols,
And cause the images to cease from Noph;[t]
There shall no longer be princes from
the land of Egypt;
I will put fear in the land of Egypt.
14 I will make Pathros desolate,
Set fire to Zoan,
And execute judgments in No.[u]
15 I will pour My fury on Sin,[v] the strength
of Egypt;
I will cut off the multitude of No,
16 And set a fire in Egypt;
Sin shall have great pain,
No shall be split open,
And Noph *shall be in* distress daily.
17 The young men of Aven[w] and Pi Beseth shall
fall by the sword,
And these *cities* shall go into captivity.
18 At Tehaphnehes[x] the day shall also
be darkened,[y]
When I break the yokes of Egypt there.
And her arrogant strength shall cease in her;
As for her, a cloud shall cover her,
And her daughters shall go into captivity.
19 Thus I will execute judgments on Egypt,
Then they shall know that I *am* the LORD." ' "

Proclamation Against Pharaoh

[20]And it came to pass in the eleventh year, in the
first *month,* on the seventh *day* of the month, *that* the
word of the LORD came to me, saying, [21]"Son of man, I
have broken the arm of Pharaoh king of Egypt; and
see, it has not been bandaged for healing, nor a splint
put on to bind it, to make it strong enough to hold a
sword. [22]Therefore thus says the Lord GOD: 'Surely I
am against Pharaoh king of Egypt, and will break his
arms, both the strong one and the one that was broken; and I will make the sword fall out of his hand. [23]I
will scatter the Egyptians among the nations, and disperse them throughout the countries. [24]I will
strengthen the arms of the king of Babylon and put
My sword in his hand; but I will break Pharaoh's
arms, and he will groan before him with the groanings of a mortally wounded *man.* [25]Thus I will
strengthen the arms of the king of Babylon, but the
arms of Pharaoh shall fall down; they shall know that
I *am* the LORD, when I put My sword into the hand of
the king of Babylon and he stretches it out against the
land of Egypt. [26]I will scatter the Egyptians among the
nations and disperse them throughout the countries.
Then they shall know that I *am* the LORD.' "

Egypt Cut Down Like a Great Tree

31 Now it came to pass in the eleventh year, in the
third *month,* on the first *day* of the month, *that*
the word of the LORD came to me, saying, [2]"Son of man,
say to Pharaoh king of Egypt and to his multitude:

'Whom are you like in your greatness?
3 Indeed Assyria *was* a cedar in Lebanon,
With fine branches that shaded the forest,
And of high stature;
And its top was among the thick boughs.
4 The waters made it grow;
Underground waters gave it height,
With their rivers running around the place
where it was planted,
And sent out rivulets to all the trees
of the field.

5 'Therefore its height was exalted above all the
trees of the field;
Its boughs were multiplied,
And its branches became long because of the
abundance of water,
As it sent them out.

30:13 [t] That is, ancient Memphis
30:14 [u] That is, ancient Thebes
30:15 [v] That is, ancient Pelusium
30:17 [w] That is, ancient On (Heliopolis)
30:18 [x] Spelled *Tahpanhes* in Jeremiah 43:7 and elsewhere [y] Following many Hebrew manuscripts, Bomberg, Septuagint, Syriac, Targum, and Vulgate; Masoretic Text reads *refrained.*

6 All the birds of the heavens made their nests
in its boughs;
Under its branches all the beasts of the field
brought forth their young;
And in its shadow all great nations made
their home.

7 'Thus it was beautiful in greatness and in the
length of its branches,
Because its roots reached to abundant waters.
8 The cedars in the garden of God could not
hide it;
The fir trees were not like its boughs,
And the chestnut[z] trees were not like
its branches;
No tree in the garden of God was like
it in beauty.
9 I made it beautiful with a multitude
of branches,
So that all the trees of Eden envied it,
That *were* in the garden of God.'

10"Therefore thus says the Lord GOD: 'Because you have increased in height, and it set its top among the thick boughs, and its heart was lifted up in its height, 11therefore I will deliver it into the hand of the mighty one of the nations, and he shall surely deal with it; I have driven it out for its wickedness. 12And aliens, the most terrible of the nations, have cut it down and left it; its branches have fallen on the mountains and in all the valleys; its boughs lie broken by all the rivers of the land; and all the peoples of the earth have gone from under its shadow and left it.

13 'On its ruin will remain all the birds
of the heavens,
And all the beasts of the field will come
to its branches—

14'So that no trees by the waters may ever again exalt themselves for their height, nor set their tops among the thick boughs, that no tree which drinks water may ever be high enough to reach up to them.

'For they have all been delivered to death,
To the depths of the earth,
Among the children of men who go
down to the Pit.'

15"Thus says the Lord GOD: 'In the day when it went down to hell, I caused mourning. I covered the deep because of it. I restrained its rivers, and the great waters were held back. I caused Lebanon to mourn for it, and all the trees of the field wilted because of it. 16I
made the nations shake at the sound of its fall, when I cast it down to hell together with those who descend into the Pit; and all the trees of Eden, the choice and best of Lebanon, all that drink water, were comforted in the depths of the earth. 17They also went down to
hell with it, with those *slain* by the sword; and *those who were* its *strong* arm dwelt in its shadows among the nations.

18"To which of the trees in Eden will you then be likened in glory and greatness? Yet you shall be brought down with the trees of Eden to the depths of the earth; you shall lie in the midst of the uncircumcised, with *those* slain by the sword. This *is* Pharaoh and all his multitude,' says the Lord GOD."

Lamentation for Pharaoh and Egypt

32 And it came to pass in the twelfth year, in the twelfth *month,* on the first *day* of the month, *that* the word of the LORD came to me, saying, 2"Son of
man, take up a lamentation for Pharaoh king of Egypt, and say to him:

'You are like a young lion among the nations,
And you *are* like a monster in the seas,
Bursting forth in your rivers,
Troubling the waters with your feet,
And fouling their rivers.'

3"Thus says the Lord GOD:

'I will therefore spread My net over you with a
company of many people,
And they will draw you up in My net.
4 Then I will leave you on the land;
I will cast you out on the open fields,
And cause to settle on you all the birds
of the heavens.
And with you I will fill the beasts of
the whole earth.
5 I will lay your flesh on the mountains,
And fill the valleys with your carcass.

6 'I will also water the land with the flow
of your blood,
Even to the mountains;
And the riverbeds will be full of you.
7 When *I* put out your light,

31:8 [z] Hebrew *armon*

I will cover the heavens, and make its
stars dark;
I will cover the sun with a cloud,
And the moon shall not give her light.
8 All the bright lights of the heavens I will make
dark over you,
And bring darkness upon your land,'
Says the Lord GOD.

9"I will also trouble the hearts of many peoples, when
I bring your destruction among the nations, into the
countries which you have not known. 10Yes, I will make
many peoples astonished at you, and their kings shall
be horribly afraid of you when I brandish My sword
before them; and they shall tremble *every* moment,
every man for his own life, in the day of your fall.'
11"For thus says the Lord GOD: 'The sword of the
king of Babylon shall come upon you. 12By the swords
of the mighty warriors, all of them the most terrible of
the nations, I will cause your multitude to fall.

'They shall plunder the pomp of Egypt,
And all its multitude shall be destroyed.
13 Also I will destroy all its animals
From beside its great waters;
The foot of man shall muddy them no more,
Nor shall the hooves of animals muddy them.
14 Then I will make their waters clear,
And make their rivers run like oil,'
Says the Lord GOD.
15 'When I make the land of Egypt desolate,
And the country is destitute of all that
once filled it,
When I strike all who dwell in it,
Then they shall know that I *am* the LORD.
16 'This *is* the lamentation
With which they shall lament her;
The daughters of the nations shall lament her;
They shall lament for her, for Egypt,
And for all her multitude,'
Says the Lord GOD."

Egypt and Others Consigned to the Pit

17It came to pass also in the twelfth year, on the fifteenth *day* of the month, *that* the word of the LORD
came to me, saying:

18 "Son of man, wail over the multitude of Egypt,
And cast them down to the depths
of the earth,
Her and the daughters of the famous nations,
With those who go down to the Pit:
19 'Whom do you surpass in beauty?
Go down, be placed with the uncircumcised.'
20 "They shall fall in the midst of *those* slain
by the sword;
She is delivered to the sword,
Drawing her and all her multitudes.
21 The strong among the mighty
Shall speak to him out of the midst of hell
With those who help him:
'They have gone down,
They lie with the uncircumcised, slain
by the sword.'

22 "Assyria *is* there, and all her company,
With their graves all around her,
All of them slain, fallen by the sword.
23 Her graves are set in the recesses of the Pit,
And her company is all around her grave,
All of them slain, fallen by the sword,
Who caused terror in the land of the living.

24 "There *is* Elam and all her multitude,
All around her grave,
All of them slain, fallen by the sword,
Who have gone down uncircumcised to the
lower parts of the earth,
Who caused their terror in the land of
the living;
Now they bear their shame with those who go
down to the Pit.
25 They have set her bed in the midst of the slain,
With all her multitude,
With her graves all around it,
All of them uncircumcised, slain by
the sword;
Though their terror was caused
In the land of the living,
Yet they bear their shame
With those who go down to the Pit;
It was put in the midst of the slain.

26 "There *are* Meshech and Tubal and all
their multitudes,
With all their graves around it,
All of them uncircumcised, slain by
the sword,
Though they caused their terror in the land of
the living.
27 They do not lie with the mighty
Who are fallen of the uncircumcised,
Who have gone down to hell with their
weapons of war;

LIFE LESSON

Ezekiel 33:1–36:38

SITUATION Ezekiel acted as a watchman and preached about hope, comfort, and restoration. The people felt bad about their sins but refused to quit sinning. They treated Ezekiel's message as entertainment.

OBSERVATION God promises to forgive and restore if we turn to him in repentance.

INSPIRATION Without any question, forgiveness is the key relational issue in the Bible. It is essential to our relationship with God, with others, and even with ourselves. Forgiveness is central to emotional and spiritual growth.

Scripture teaches us that grace and salvation are unconditional. This is absolutely true in the sense that there is no way we can earn God's grace or love; there's nothing we can do in order to achieve it; there are no conditions of merit we must meet in order to receive it. Our salvation is given to us freely as the gift of God's love. But when we read Scripture carefully, we discover that before God forgives us, he expects us to forgive others. It seems as if God has made us psychologically so that we are not able to receive his forgiveness unless we first forgive.

In Luke 6:37, Jesus states this principle: "Forgive, and you will be forgiven." Again and again he stresses this. In what we call the Lord's Prayer, he said, "Forgive us our debts, as we also have forgiven our debtors" (Matthew 6:12). A couple of verses later, he explains, "If you forgive men when they sin against you, your heavenly Father will also forgive you. But if you do not forgive men their sins, your Father will not forgive your sins" (vv. 14, 15).

. . . Again and again we get this message that Jesus expects us to be as willing to forgive others as he is to forgive us. This . . . points to a basic

They have laid their swords under their heads,
But their iniquities will be on their bones,
Because of the terror of the mighty in the land of the living.
28 Yes, you shall be broken in the midst of the uncircumcised,
And lie with *those* slain by the sword.

29 "There *is* Edom,
Her kings and all her princes,
Who despite their might
Are laid beside *those* slain by the sword;
They shall lie with the uncircumcised,
And with those who go down to the Pit.
30 There *are* the princes of the north,
All of them, and all the Sidonians,
Who have gone down with the slain
In shame at the terror which they caused by their might;
They lie uncircumcised with *those* slain by the sword,
And bear their shame with those who go down to the Pit.

31 "Pharaoh will see them
And be comforted over all his multitude,
Pharaoh and all his army,
Slain by the sword,"
Says the Lord GOD.

32 "For I have caused My terror in the land of the living;
And he shall be placed in the midst of the uncircumcised
With *those* slain by the sword,
Pharaoh and all his multitude,"
Says the Lord GOD.

The Watchman and His Message

33 Again the word of the LORD came to me, saying, 2"Son of man, speak
to the children of your people, and say to them: 'When I bring the
sword upon a land, and the people of the land take a man from their territory and make him their watchman, 3when he sees the sword coming
upon the land, if he blows the trumpet and warns the people, 4then whoever hears the sound of the trumpet and does not take warning, if the
sword comes and takes him away, his blood shall be on his *own* head. 5He
heard the sound of the trumpet, but did not take warning; his blood shall
be upon himself. But he who takes warning will save his life. 6But if the
watchman sees the sword coming and does not blow the trumpet, and the
people are not warned, and the sword comes and takes *any* person from
among them, he is taken away in his iniquity; but his blood I will require at
the watchman's hand.'

7"So you, son of man: I have made you a watchman for the house of Israel; therefore you shall hear a word from My mouth and warn them for
Me. 8When I say to the wicked, 'O wicked *man*, you shall surely die!' and you
do not speak to warn the wicked from his way, that wicked *man* shall die in
his iniquity; but his blood I will require at your hand. 9Nevertheless if you
warn the wicked to turn from his way, and he does not turn from his way,
he shall die in his iniquity; but you have delivered your soul.

10"Therefore you, O son of man, say to the house of Israel: 'Thus you say,

"If our transgressions and our sins *lie* upon us, and we pine away in them,
how can we then live?" ' 11Say to them: '*As* I live,' says the Lord GOD, 'I have
no pleasure in the death of the wicked, but that the wicked turn from his
way and live. Turn, turn from your evil ways! For why should you die, O
house of Israel?'

The Fairness of God's Judgment

12"Therefore you, O son of man, say to the children of your people: 'The
righteousness of the righteous man shall not deliver him in the day of his
transgression; as for the wickedness of the wicked, he shall not fall because
of it in the day that he turns from his wickedness; nor shall the righteous
be able to live because of *his righteousness* in the day that he sins.' 13When I
say to the righteous *that* he shall surely live, but he trusts in his own righteousness and commits iniquity, none of his righteous works shall be remembered; but because of the iniquity that he has committed, he shall
die. 14Again, when I say to the wicked, 'You shall surely die,' if he turns
from his sin and does what is lawful and right, 15*if* the wicked restores the
pledge, gives back what he has stolen, and walks in the statutes of life without committing iniquity, he shall surely live; he shall not die. 16None of his
sins which he has committed shall be remembered against him; he has
done what is lawful and right; he shall surely live.

17"Yet the children of your people say, 'The way of the LORD is not fair.'
But it is their way which is not fair! 18When the righteous turns from his
righteousness and commits iniquity, he shall die because of it. 19But when
the wicked turns from his wickedness and does what is lawful and right,
he shall live because of it. 20Yet you say, 'The way of the LORD is not fair.' O
house of Israel, I will judge every one of you according to his own ways."

The Fall of Jerusalem

21And it came to pass in the twelfth year of our captivity, in the tenth
month, on the fifth *day* of the month, *that* one who had escaped from Jerusalem came to me and said, "The city has been captured!"

22Now the hand of the LORD had been upon me the evening before the man
came who had escaped. And He had opened my mouth; so when he came to
me in the morning, my mouth was opened, and I was no longer mute.

The Cause of Judah's Ruin

23Then the word of the LORD came to me, saying: 24"Son of man, they
who inhabit those ruins in the land of Israel are saying, 'Abraham was
only one, and he inherited the land. But we *are* many; the land has been
given to us as a possession.'

25"Therefore say to them, 'Thus says the Lord GOD: "You eat *meat* with
blood, you lift up your eyes toward your idols, and shed blood. Should you
then possess the land? 26You rely on your sword, you commit abominations,
and you defile one another's wives. Should you then possess the land?" '

27"Say thus to them, 'Thus says the Lord GOD: "*As* I live, surely those
who *are* in the ruins shall fall by the sword, and the one who *is* in the open
field I will give to the beasts to be devoured, and those who *are* in the
strongholds and caves shall die of the pestilence. 28For I will make the land
most desolate, her arrogant strength shall cease, and the mountains of Israel shall be so desolate that no one will pass through. 29Then they shall

biblical, emotional, psychological, and spiritual principle—if we want to receive forgiveness without giving forgiveness, we're asking God to violate his own moral nature. We're asking him to violate principles he has built into us.

If you find it hard to believe that forgiveness is a need God has built into us, look at the opposite of forgiveness—resentment. When we resent someone, we destroy our relationship with that person, of course. We also destroy our own physical health. Any doctor [will] tell you about diseases and physical disorders that are closely tied to resentment. It literally eats holes in us, and that's a living metaphor of what it does to our relationships.

God's laws are a given of existence. They are built into our muscles, brains, personalities, and social interactions. His highest law, love, is what brought the world into being, and love is nourished by forgiveness. The opposite of love is hate, and hate is kept alive through resentment.

So if we're looking for emotional, spiritual, and physical well-being, forgiveness is central.

(From "Forgiveness: The Cure for Resentment" by David Seamands in *Practical Christianity*)

APPLICATION The tough part of forgiveness is actually doing it. Merely thinking about forgiving someone accomplishes nothing. Forgiveness requires action. Ask God to help you forgive someone. Show you have forgiven that person by your actions. God will bless you.

EXPLORATION Forgiveness—Leviticus 26:13; 1 Chronicles 21:8; Matthew 6:14-15; John 20:23; Romans 12:17-21.

know that I *am* the LORD, when I have made the land
most desolate because of all their abominations
which they have committed." '

Hearing and Not Doing

30"As for you, son of man, the children of your people are talking about you beside the walls and in the
doors of the houses; and they speak to one another,
everyone saying to his brother, 'Please come and hear
what the word is that comes from the LORD.' 31So they
come to you as people do, they sit before you *as* My
people, and they hear your words, but they do not do
them; for with their mouth they show much love, *but*
their hearts pursue their *own* gain. 32Indeed you *are* to
them as a very lovely song of one who has a pleasant
voice and can play well on an instrument; for they
hear your words, but they do not do them. 33And
when this comes to pass—surely it will come—then
they will know that a prophet has been among them."

Irresponsible Shepherds

34 And the word of the LORD came to me, saying,
2"Son of man, prophesy against the shepherds
of Israel, prophesy and say to them, 'Thus says the
Lord GOD to the shepherds: "Woe to the shepherds of
Israel who feed themselves! Should not the shepherds
feed the flocks? 3You eat the fat and clothe yourselves
with the wool; you slaughter the fatlings, *but* you do
not feed the flock. 4The weak you have not strengthened, nor have you healed those who were sick, nor
bound up the broken, nor brought back what was
driven away, nor sought what was lost; but with force
and cruelty you have ruled them. 5So they were scattered because *there was* no shepherd; and they became food for all the beasts of the field when they
were scattered. 6My sheep wandered through all the
mountains, and on every high hill; yes, My flock was
scattered over the whole face of the earth, and no one
was seeking or searching *for them.*"

7"Therefore, you shepherds, hear the word of the
LORD: 8"*As* I live," says the Lord GOD, "surely because
My flock became a prey, and My flock became food
for every beast of the field, because *there was* no shepherd, nor did My shepherds search for My flock, but
the shepherds fed themselves and did not feed My
flock"— 9therefore, O shepherds, hear the word of the
LORD! 10Thus says the Lord GOD: "Behold, I *am* against
the shepherds, and I will require My flock at their
hand; I will cause them to cease feeding the sheep,
and the shepherds shall feed themselves no more; for
I will deliver My flock from their mouths, that they
may no longer be food for them."

God, the True Shepherd

11"For thus says the Lord GOD: "Indeed I Myself will
search for My sheep and seek them out. 12As a shepherd seeks out his flock on the day he is among his
scattered sheep, so will I seek out My sheep and deliver
them from all the places where they were scattered on
a cloudy and dark day. 13And I will bring them out
from the peoples and gather them from the countries,
and will bring them to their own land; I will feed them
on the mountains of Israel, in the valleys and in all the
inhabited places of the country. 14I will feed them in
good pasture, and their fold shall be on the high
mountains of Israel. There they shall lie down in a
good fold and feed in rich pasture on the mountains
of Israel. 15I will feed My flock, and I will make them lie
down," says the Lord GOD. 16"I will seek what was lost
and bring back what was driven away, bind up the
broken and strengthen what was sick; but I will destroy
the fat and the strong, and feed them in judgment."

17"And *as for* you, O My flock, thus says the Lord
GOD: "Behold, I shall judge between sheep and sheep,
between rams and goats. 18*Is it* too little for you to have
eaten up the good pasture, that you must tread down
with your feet the residue of your pasture—and to
have drunk of the clear waters, that you must foul the
residue with your feet? 19And *as for* My flock, they eat
what you have trampled with your feet, and they
drink what you have fouled with your feet."

20"Therefore thus says the Lord GOD to them: "Behold, I Myself will judge between the fat and the lean
sheep. 21Because you have pushed with side and
shoulder, butted all the weak ones with your horns,
and scattered them abroad, 22therefore I will save My
flock, and they shall no longer be a prey; and I will
judge between sheep and sheep. 23I will establish one
shepherd over them, and he shall feed them—My
servant David. He shall feed them and be their shepherd. 24And I, the LORD, will be their God, and My servant David a prince among them; I, the LORD, have
spoken.

25"I will make a covenant of peace with them, and
cause wild beasts to cease from the land; and they will
dwell safely in the wilderness and sleep in the woods.
26I will make them and the places all around My hill a
blessing; and I will cause showers to come down in
their season; there shall be showers of blessing. 27Then
the trees of the field shall yield their fruit, and the
earth shall yield her increase. They shall be safe in
their land; and they shall know that I *am* the LORD,
when I have broken the bands of their yoke and deliv-

ered them from the hand of those who enslaved them.
28And they shall no longer be a prey for the nations, nor
shall beasts of the land devour them; but they shall
dwell safely, and no one shall make *them* afraid. 29I will
raise up for them a garden of renown, and they shall no
longer be consumed with hunger in the land, nor bear
the shame of the Gentiles anymore. 30Thus they shall
know that I, the LORD their God, *am* with them, and they,
the house of Israel, *are* My people," says the Lord GOD.' "
31"You are My flock, the flock of My pasture; you *are*
men, *and* I *am* your God," says the Lord GOD.

Judgment on Mount Seir

35 Moreover the word of the LORD came to me,
saying, 2"Son of man, set your face against
Mount Seir and prophesy against it, 3and say to it,
'Thus says the Lord GOD:

"Behold, O Mount Seir, I *am* against you;
I will stretch out My hand against you,
And make you most desolate;
4 I shall lay your cities waste,
And you shall be desolate.
Then you shall know that I *am* the LORD.

5"Because you have had an ancient hatred, and
have shed *the blood of* the children of Israel by the
power of the sword at the time of their calamity, *when*
their iniquity *came to an* end, 6therefore, *as* I live,"
says the Lord GOD, "I will prepare you for blood, and
blood shall pursue you; since you have not hated
blood, therefore blood shall pursue you. 7Thus I will
make Mount Seir most desolate, and cut off from it
the one who leaves and the one who returns. 8And I
will fill its mountains with the slain; on your hills and
in your valleys and in all your ravines those who are
slain by the sword shall fall. 9I will make you perpetually desolate, and your cities shall be uninhabited;
then you shall know that I *am* the LORD.
10"Because you have said, 'These two nations and
these two countries shall be mine, and we will possess
them,' although the LORD was there, 11therefore, *as* I
live," says the Lord GOD, "I will do according to your
anger and according to the envy which you showed in
your hatred against them; and I will make Myself
known among them when I judge you. 12Then you
shall know that I *am* the LORD. I have heard all your
blasphemies which you have spoken against the
mountains of Israel, saying, 'They are desolate; they
are given to us to consume.' 13Thus with your mouth
you have boasted against Me and multiplied your
words against Me; I have heard *them.*"
14"Thus says the Lord GOD: "The whole earth will rejoice when I make you desolate. 15As you rejoiced because the inheritance of the house of Israel was
desolate, so I will do to you; you shall be desolate, O
Mount Seir, as well as all of Edom—all of it! Then
they shall know that I *am* the LORD." '

Blessing on Israel

36 "And you, son of man, prophesy to the mountains of Israel, and say, 'O mountains of Israel,
hear the word of the LORD! 2Thus says the Lord GOD:
"Because the enemy has said of you, 'Aha! The ancient
heights have become our possession,' " ' 3therefore
prophesy, and say, 'Thus says the Lord GOD: "Because
they made *you* desolate and swallowed you up on
every side, so that you became the possession of the
rest of the nations, and you are taken up by the lips of
talkers and slandered by the people"— 4therefore, O
mountains of Israel, hear the word of the Lord GOD!
Thus says the Lord GOD to the mountains, the hills,
the rivers, the valleys, the desolate wastes, and the
cities that have been forsaken, which became plunder
and mockery to the rest of the nations all around—
5therefore thus says the Lord GOD: "Surely I have spoken
in My burning jealousy against the rest of the nations
and against all Edom, who gave My land to themselves
as a possession, with wholehearted joy *and* spiteful
minds, in order to plunder its open country." '
6"Therefore prophesy concerning the land of Israel,
and say to the mountains, the hills, the rivers, and the
valleys, 'Thus says the Lord GOD: "Behold, I have spoken in My jealousy and My fury, because you have
borne the shame of the nations." 7Therefore thus says
the Lord GOD: "I have raised My hand in an oath that
surely the nations that *are* around you shall bear their
own shame. 8But you, O mountains of Israel, you shall
shoot forth your branches and yield your fruit to My
people Israel, for they are about to come. 9For indeed
I *am* for you, and I will turn to you, and you shall be
tilled and sown. 10I will multiply men upon you, all the
house of Israel, all of it; and the cities shall be inhabited and the ruins rebuilt. 11I will multiply upon you
man and beast; and they shall increase and bear
young; I will make you inhabited as in former times,
and do better *for you* than at your beginnings. Then
you shall know that I *am* the LORD. 12Yes, I will cause
men to walk on you, My people Israel; they shall take
possession of you, and you shall be their inheritance;
no more shall you bereave them *of children.*"
13"Thus says the Lord GOD: "Because they say to you,
'You devour men and bereave your nation *of children,*'

14therefore you shall devour men no more, nor bereave
your nation anymore," says the Lord GOD. 15Nor will I let
you hear the taunts of the nations anymore, nor bear the
reproach of the peoples anymore, nor shall you cause
your nation to stumble anymore," says the Lord GOD.' "

The Renewal of Israel

16Moreover the word of the LORD came to me, saying: 17"Son of man, when the house of Israel dwelt in
their own land, they defiled it by their own ways and
deeds; to Me their way was like the uncleanness of a
woman in her customary impurity. 18Therefore I poured
out My fury on them for the blood they had shed on
the land, and for their idols *with which* they had defiled it. 19So I scattered them among the nations, and
they were dispersed throughout the countries; I
judged them according to their ways and their deeds.
20When they came to the nations, wherever they went,
they profaned My holy name—when they said of
them, 'These *are* the people of the LORD, *and* yet they
have gone out of His land.' 21But I had concern for My
holy name, which the house of Israel had profaned
among the nations wherever they went.

22"Therefore say to the house of Israel, 'Thus says the
Lord GOD: "I do not do *this* for your sake, O house of
Israel, but for My holy name's sake, which you have
profaned among the nations wherever you went. 23And
I will sanctify My great name, which has been profaned
among the nations, which you have profaned in their
midst; and the nations shall know that I *am* the LORD,"
says the Lord GOD, "when I am hallowed in you before
their eyes. 24For I will take you from among the nations,
gather you out of all countries, and bring you into your
own land. 25Then I will sprinkle clean water on you, and
you shall be clean; I will cleanse you from all your filthiness and from all your idols. 26I will give you a new
heart and put a new spirit within you; I will take the
heart of stone out of your flesh and give you a heart of
flesh. 27I will put My Spirit within you and cause you to
walk in My statutes, and you will keep My judgments
and do *them.* 28Then you shall dwell in the land that I
gave to your fathers; you shall be My people, and I will be
your God. 29I will deliver you from all your unclean-
nesses. I will call for the grain and multiply it, and bring
no famine upon you. 30And I will multiply the fruit of
your trees and the increase of your fields, so that you
need never again bear the reproach of famine among
the nations. 31Then you will remember your evil ways
and your deeds that *were* not good; and you will loathe
yourselves in your own sight, for your iniquities and
your abominations. 32Not for your sake do I do *this,*" says
the Lord GOD, "let it be known to you. Be ashamed and
confounded for your own ways, O house of Israel!"

33"Thus says the Lord GOD: "On the day that I cleanse
you from all your iniquities, I will also enable *you* to
dwell in the cities, and the ruins shall be rebuilt. 34The
desolate land shall be tilled instead of lying desolate in
the sight of all who pass by. 35So they will say, 'This
land that was desolate has become like the garden of
Eden; and the wasted, desolate, and ruined cities *are*
now fortified *and* inhabited.' 36Then the nations which
are left all around you shall know that I, the LORD,
have rebuilt the ruined places *and* planted what was
desolate. I, the LORD, have spoken *it,* and I will do *it.*"

37"Thus says the Lord GOD: "I will also let the house
of Israel inquire of Me to do this for them: I will increase their men like a flock. 38Like a flock *offered as*
holy *sacrifices,* like the flock at Jerusalem on its feast
days, so shall the ruined cities be filled with flocks of
men. Then they shall know that I *am* the LORD." ' "

The Dry Bones Live

37 The hand of the LORD came upon me and
brought me out in the Spirit of the LORD, and set
me down in the midst of the valley; and it *was* full of
bones. 2Then He caused me to pass by them all
around, and behold, *there were* very many in the open
valley; and indeed *they were* very dry. 3And He said to
me, "Son of man, can these bones live?"

So I answered, "O Lord GOD, You know."

4Again He said to me, "Prophesy to these bones,
and say to them, 'O dry bones, hear the word of the
LORD! 5Thus says the Lord GOD to these bones: "Surely
I will cause breath to enter into you, and you shall live.
6I will put sinews on you and bring flesh upon you,
cover you with skin and put breath in you; and you
shall live. Then you shall know that I *am* the LORD." ' "

7So I prophesied as I was commanded; and as I
prophesied, there was a noise, and suddenly a rattling; and the bones came together, bone to bone. 8In-
deed, as I looked, the sinews and the flesh came upon
them, and the skin covered them over; but *there was*
no breath in them.

9Also He said to me, "Prophesy to the breath,
prophesy, son of man, and say to the breath, 'Thus
says the Lord GOD: "Come from the four winds, O
breath, and breathe on these slain, that they may
live." ' " 10So I prophesied as He commanded me, and
breath came into them, and they lived, and stood
upon their feet, an exceedingly great army.

11Then He said to me, "Son of man, these bones are
the whole house of Israel. They indeed say, 'Our bones

are dry, our hope is lost, and we ourselves are cut off!' 12 Therefore prophesy and say to them, 'Thus says the Lord GOD: "Behold, O My people, I will
open your graves and cause you to come up from your graves, and bring
you into the land of Israel. 13 Then you shall know that I *am* the LORD, when
I have opened your graves, O My people, and brought you up from your
graves. 14 I will put My Spirit in you, and you shall live, and I will place you
in your own land. Then you shall know that I, the LORD, have spoken *it* and
performed *it*," says the LORD.' "

One Kingdom, One King

15 Again the word of the LORD came to me, saying, 16 "As for you, son of
man, take a stick for yourself and write on it: 'For Judah and for the children of Israel, his companions.' Then take another stick and write on it,
'For Joseph, the stick of Ephraim, and *for* all the house of Israel, his companions.' 17 Then join them one to another for yourself into one stick, and
they will become one in your hand.
18 "And when the children of your people speak to you, saying, 'Will you
not show us what you *mean* by these?'— 19 say to them, 'Thus says the Lord
GOD: "Surely I will take the stick of Joseph, which *is* in the hand of Ephraim,
and the tribes of Israel, his companions; and I will join them with it, with the
stick of Judah, and make them one stick, and they will be one in My hand." '
20 And the sticks on which you write will be in your hand before their eyes.
21 "Then say to them, 'Thus says the Lord GOD: "Surely I will take the children of Israel from among the nations, wherever they have gone, and will
gather them from every side and bring them into their own land; 22 and I
will make them one nation in the land, on the mountains of Israel; and
one king shall be king over them all; they shall no longer be two nations,
nor shall they ever be divided into two kingdoms again. 23 They shall not
defile themselves anymore with their idols, nor with their detestable
things, nor with any of their transgressions; but I will deliver them from
all their dwelling places in which they have sinned, and will cleanse them.
Then they shall be My people, and I will be their God.
24 "David My servant *shall be* king over them, and they shall all have one
shepherd; they shall also walk in My judgments and observe My statutes,
and do them. 25 Then they shall dwell in the land that I have given to Jacob
My servant, where your fathers dwelt; and they shall dwell there, they, their
children, and their children's children, forever; and My servant David
shall be their prince forever. 26 Moreover I will make a covenant of peace
with them, and it shall be an everlasting covenant with them; I will establish
them and multiply them, and I will set My sanctuary in their midst forevermore. 27 My tabernacle also shall be with them; indeed I will be their God,
and they shall be My people. 28 The nations also will know that I, the LORD,
sanctify Israel, when My sanctuary is in their midst forevermore." ' "

Gog and Allies Attack Israel

38 Now the word of the LORD came to me, saying, 2 "Son of man, set
your face against Gog, of the land of Magog, the prince of Rosh,[a]
Meshech, and Tubal, and prophesy against him, 3 and say, 'Thus says the
Lord GOD: "Behold, I *am* against you, O Gog, the prince of Rosh, Meshech,

38:2 [a] Targum, Vulgate, and Aquila read *chief prince of* (also verse 3).

LIFE LESSON

Ezekiel 37:1–39:29

SITUATION Ezekiel preached a message of hope to the exiles in Babylon. Yet, they were as unresponsive as dead bones.

OBSERVATION God miraculously restores and reunites his people. He shows ultimate triumph over the evils of world powers. His might always prevails in world affairs.

INSPIRATION Instead of seeing [God's sovereignty] as doing away with our free will, we should rejoice. God is in total control. No move of nation against nation is done apart from His choosing. God looks at our past lives from a completely different perspective. God was accomplishing His will even through our own failures and sin. Are people free to choose for or against God? They are not free in the sense that they are unbiased toward God. Everyone is born with a bias against God. It certainly is not a fifty-fifty choice; that is, one does not grow up with as good a chance to choose for God as against Him. A person will choose against Him every time unless God moves first. Within His sovereignty there is clear indication of man's freedom throughout the Scriptures, but man's freedom has boundaries whereas God's sovereignty does not.

It is foolish to think that a man could turn aside the purposes of God. If you were standing on the top of a cliff with the water rushing in from the ocean, could you imagine yourself jumping down and pushing back the waves into the ocean? Of course not. Could you stand in a storm and as the bolt of lightning came through the sky, grab it and change its course? Of course not. Still more foolish is the thought that you could push back or change the determination of the Almighty.

Not only is God's will sovereign, but His power is, as well. That power may be called the creative energy of His nature. The sovereign power of God and God's other attributes work together. God's great power works within the realm of His holiness. My son once asked me why the Lord did

Continued

not go ahead and save the devil—we would all be better off! That sounds good when you consider God's sovereign power, but does not fit with God's holiness. It might fit with God's mercy but not with His justice. God, being totally just, will have all things made right and fair when we see Him face to face. My failure, sin and confusion do not change His chosen ends. What would it profit a man to spend any time trying to buck God's will? Could he win? Never!
(From *The God You Can Know* by Dan DeHaan)

APPLICATION Are you unified with your family? Take each of your children out for a special one-on-one time during the next month. If you are a young person, take your Dad or Mom out to breakfast—you pay!

EXPLORATION Rebirth—Jeremiah 24:7; 31:31-34; Ezekiel 11:19-20; John 3:3-8; 16-21; 1 Peter 1:23.

and Tubal. 4I will turn you around, put hooks into your jaws, and lead you
out, with all your army, horses, and horsemen, all splendidly clothed, a
great company *with* bucklers and shields, all of them handling swords.
5Persia, Ethiopia,[b] and Libya[c] are with them, all of them *with* shield and
helmet; 6Gomer and all its troops; the house of Togarmah *from* the far
north and all its troops—many people *are* with you.
7"Prepare yourself and be ready, you and all your companies that are
gathered about you; and be a guard for them. 8After many days you will be
visited. In the latter years you will come into the land of those brought back
from the sword *and* gathered from many people on the mountains of Israel,
which had long been desolate; they were brought out of the nations, and now
all of them dwell safely. 9You will ascend, coming like a storm, covering the
land like a cloud, you and all your troops and many peoples with you."
10"Thus says the Lord GOD: "On that day it shall come to pass *that* thoughts
will arise in your mind, and you will make an evil plan: 11You will say, 'I will
go up against a land of unwalled villages; I will go to a peaceful people,
who dwell safely, all of them dwelling without walls, and having neither
bars nor gates'— 12to take plunder and to take booty, to stretch out your
hand against the waste places *that are again* inhabited, and against a people gathered from the nations, who have acquired livestock and goods,
who dwell in the midst of the land. 13Sheba, Dedan, the merchants of
Tarshish, and all their young lions will say to you, 'Have you come to take
plunder? Have you gathered your army to take booty, to carry away silver
and gold, to take away livestock and goods, to take great plunder?' " '
14"Therefore, son of man, prophesy and say to Gog, 'Thus says the Lord
GOD: "On that day when My people Israel dwell safely, will you not know *it?*
15Then you will come from your place out of the far north, you and many
peoples with you, all of them riding on horses, a great company and a
mighty army. 16You will come up against My people Israel like a cloud, to
cover the land. It will be in the latter days that I will bring you against My
land, so that the nations may know Me, when I am hallowed in you, O Gog,
before their eyes." 17Thus says the Lord GOD: "Are *you* he of whom I have
spoken in former days by My servants the prophets of Israel, who prophesied for years in those days that I would bring you against them?

Judgment on Gog

18"And it will come to pass at the same time, when Gog comes against
the land of Israel," says the Lord GOD, "*that* My fury will show in My face.
19For in My jealousy *and* in the fire of My wrath I have spoken: 'Surely in
that day there shall be a great earthquake in the land of Israel, 20so that the
fish of the sea, the birds of the heavens, the beasts of the field, all creeping
things that creep on the earth, and all men who *are* on the face of the earth
shall shake at My presence. The mountains shall be thrown down, the
steep places shall fall, and every wall shall fall to the ground.' 21I will call for
a sword against Gog throughout all My mountains," says the Lord GOD.
"Every man's sword will be against his brother. 22And I will bring him to
judgment with pestilence and bloodshed; I will rain down on him, on his
troops, and on the many peoples who *are* with him, flooding rain, great
hailstones, fire, and brimstone. 23Thus I will magnify Myself and sanctify

38:5 [b] Hebrew *Cush* [c] Hebrew *Put*

HOME

The power of a strong relationship sustains us and gives us strength—it's that power in knowing, *If* I fail, my friend is still there, or, *If* I fail, I have a wife who still loves me. It's the power in knowing that—no matter what—we have a Father who still loves us.

In repairing a relationship, it's essential to realize that no friendship is perfect, no marriage is perfect, no person is perfect. With the resolve that you are going to make a relationship work, you can develop peace treaties of love and tolerance and harmony to transform a difficult situation into something beautiful.

God's goal for your home is harmony. That means a family of individuals singing different notes, but with the same score of music, with the same goal.

Your home is simply a means to take you to a greater end—a heavenly end. Working together as coheirs of eternal salvation is the foundation for the home.

GOD, give us strength as we try to be more like Jesus in our homes. We ask you to keep the evil one away from us; keep us close. Let our homes be testimonies of your love for us, that when people see our homes, they would see how you have loved the world.

MATERIALISM

One source of man's weariness is the pursuit of things that can never satisfy, but which one of us has not been caught up in that pursuit at some time in our life? Our passions, possessions, and pride—these are all *dead* things. When you try to get life out of dead things, the result is only weariness and dissatisfaction.

Do you feel that you've spent your life in endless pursuit of contentment? Do you reach the top of the ladder, and discover you don't want to be there any more? Do you dream about having the perfect mate, and once you marry, you realize he or she isn't perfect? Contentment is not found in things of this world; the only path to contentment is through Christ.

Here's something that's important to remember: Forget tomorrow's material pleasures because giving in to them can spoil your long-term devotion to your family with the burden of needless debt. You need to be dogged, determined, and full of discipline to avoid this trap.

I am frightened by our ability in America to convince ourselves that we don't need Jesus. We can amass fortunes, we can get degrees, we can own our house all on our own. And yet, there's a certain affluence that we can attain when we become poverty-stricken—a certain humility that comes with trials, that brings us face to face with the Savior.

FATHER, keep us from being so blinded by possessions we cannot keep that we would fail to see the eternal treasure we cannot lose.

GUIDANCE

It's not easy to hear the voice of God when popular opinion tells you it's okay to be immoral, or when your friends cheat on their income tax. But if you remain true to what you know to be right and godly, God says you will be blessed.

The Christian is the one who seeks to discern the voice of God amidst the many voices that come our way. One of the greatest challenges that we have is to learn to hear the voice of truth.

HELP US to see what is important, what is eternal, and what is lasting. Let us make decisions based on our eternal life and not on temporary possessions. Help us to put into practice the timeless truths found in your Word. And most of all, Father, thank you for loving us.

FAILURE

I wonder if we stay so busy because we're trying to forget yesterday's failures. We do need to forget those failures of the past, but if we never stop to deal with them, the guilt over those old mistakes will hound us and nip at our heels like an ill-behaved puppy.

When we avoid dealing with our mistakes and pretend they don't exist, they usually express themselves in ways that we would not anticipate: anger at someone else, frustration at something else, lack of control.

Sometimes we try to deal with a mistake by covering it up with more mistakes, or by repressing it, or by justifying it. That's like walking around with a pebble in our shoe—it causes us so much frustration that our whole body compensates for its presence, when all we have to do is take it out and toss it away.

God can take our mistakes and turn them into opportunities. He's shown us, over and over, through the lives of people like David, Paul, Peter. He can do the same for us.

FATHER, *help us to forgive ourselves—even as you have forgiven us—that we might not live burdened and shackled by yesterday's failures, but that we might live set free by your grace.*

Myself, and I will be known in the eyes of many nations. Then they shall know that I *am* the LORD." '

Gog's Armies Destroyed

39 "And you, son of man, prophesy against Gog,
and say, 'Thus says the Lord GOD: "Behold, I *am*
against you, O Gog, the prince of Rosh,[d] Meshech, and
Tubal; 2 and I will turn you around and lead you on,
bringing you up from the far north, and bring you
against the mountains of Israel. 3 Then I will knock the
bow out of your left hand, and cause the arrows to fall
out of your right hand. 4 You shall fall upon the mountains of Israel, you and all your troops and the peoples
who *are* with you; I will give you to birds of prey of
every sort and *to* the beasts of the field to be devoured. 5 You shall fall on the open field; for I have
spoken," says the Lord GOD. 6 "And I will send fire on
Magog and on those who live in security in the coastlands. Then they shall know that I *am* the LORD. 7 So I
will make My holy name known in the midst of My
people Israel, and I will not *let them* profane My holy
name anymore. Then the nations shall know that *I*
am the LORD, the Holy One in Israel. 8 Surely it is coming, and it shall be done," says the Lord GOD. "This *is*
the day of which I have spoken.

9 "Then those who dwell in the cities of Israel will go
out and set on fire and burn the weapons, both the
shields and bucklers, the bows and arrows, the javelins and spears; and they will make fires with them for
seven years. 10 They will not take wood from the field
nor cut down *any* from the forests, because they will
make fires with the weapons; and they will plunder
those who plundered them, and pillage those who pil-
laged them," says the Lord GOD.

The Burial of Gog

11 "It will come to pass in that day *that* I will give Gog
a burial place there in Israel, the valley of those who
pass by east of the sea; and it will obstruct travelers,
because there they will bury Gog and all his multitude. Therefore they will call *it* the Valley of Hamon
Gog.[e] 12 For seven months the house of Israel will be
burying them, in order to cleanse the land. 13 Indeed
all the people of the land will be burying, and they will
gain renown for it on the day that I am glorified," says
the Lord GOD. 14 "They will set apart men regularly employed, with the help of a search party,[f] to pass
through the land and bury those bodies remaining on
the ground, in order to cleanse it. At the end of seven
months they will make a search. 15 The search party
will pass through the land; and *when anyone* sees a
man's bone, he shall set up a marker by it, till the
buriers have buried it in the Valley of Hamon Gog.
16 *The* name of *the* city *will* also *be* Hamonah. Thus
they shall cleanse the land." '

A Triumphant Festival

17 "And as for you, son of man, thus says the Lord
GOD, 'Speak to every sort of bird and to every beast of
the field:

"Assemble yourselves and come;
Gather together from all sides to
My sacrificial meal
Which I am sacrificing for you,
A great sacrificial meal on the
mountains of Israel,
That you may eat flesh and drink blood.
18 You shall eat the flesh of the mighty,
Drink the blood of the princes of the earth,
Of rams and lambs,
Of goats and bulls,
All of them fatlings of Bashan.
19 You shall eat fat till you are full,
And drink blood till you are drunk,
At My sacrificial meal
Which I am sacrificing for you.
20 You shall be filled at My table
With horses and riders,
With mighty men
And with all the men of war," says the Lord GOD.

Israel Restored to the Land

21 "I will set My glory among the nations; all the nations shall see My judgment which I have executed,
and My hand which I have laid on them. 22 So the house
of Israel shall know that I *am* the LORD their God from
that day forward. 23 The Gentiles shall know that the
house of Israel went into captivity for their iniquity;
because they were unfaithful to Me, therefore I hid My
face from them. I gave them into the hand of their enemies, and they all fell by the sword. 24 According to their
uncleanness and according to their transgressions I
have dealt with them, and hidden My face from them." '

25 "Therefore thus says the Lord GOD: 'Now I will
bring back the captives of Jacob, and have mercy on
the whole house of Israel; and I will be jealous for My

39:1 [d] Targum, Vulgate and Aquila read *chief prince of.*
39:11 [e] Literally *The Multitude of Gog*
39:14 [f] Literally *those who pass through*

LIFE LESSON

Ezekiel 40:1–42:20

SITUATION God gave Ezekiel, a priest, the measurements of Solomon's Temple. The Temple had been destroyed at the beginning of the captivity.

OBSERVATION God reveals his perfect kingdom. The details of his vision gave the Jews hope for a restored worship and show us the importance of true God-centered worship.

INSPIRATION Why did Christ come? Why was He conceived? Why was He born? Why was He crucified? Why did He rise again? Why is He now at the right hand of the Father? The answer to all these questions is, "In order that He might make worshipers out of rebels; in order that He might restore us again to the place of worship we knew when we were first created." Now because we were created to worship, worship is the normal employment of moral beings. . . . It is something that is built into human nature. Every glimpse of heaven shows them worshiping. . . . Worship is a moral imperative. . . .

What are the factors that you will find present in worship? . . . First, there is boundless confidence. . . . Worship rises or falls in any church altogether depending upon the attitude we take toward God, whether we see God big or whether we see Him little. . . .

holy name— [26]after they have borne their shame, and all their unfaithfulness in which they were unfaithful to Me, when they dwelt safely in their *own* land and no one made *them* afraid. [27]When I have brought them back from the peoples and gathered them out of their enemies' lands, and I am hallowed in them in the sight of many nations, [28]then they shall know that I *am* the LORD their God, who sent them into captivity among the nations, but also brought them back to their land, and left none of them captive any longer. [29]And I will not hide My face from them anymore; for I shall have poured out My Spirit on the house of Israel,' says the Lord GOD."

A New City, a New Temple

40 In the twenty-fifth year of our captivity, at the beginning of the year, on the tenth *day* of the month, in the fourteenth year after the city was captured, on the very same day the hand of the LORD was upon me; and He took me there. [2]In the visions of God He took me into the land of Israel and set me on a very high mountain; on it toward the south *was* something like the structure of a city. [3]He took me there, and behold, *there was* a man whose appearance *was* like the appearance of bronze. He had a line of flax and a measuring rod in his hand, and he stood in the gateway.

[4]And the man said to me, "Son of man, look with your eyes and hear with your ears, and fix your mind on everything I show you; for you *were* brought here so that I might show *them* to you. Declare to the house of Israel everything you see." [5]Now there was a wall all around the outside of the temple.[g] In the man's hand was a measuring rod six cubits *long, each being a* cubit and a handbreadth; and he measured the width of the wall structure, one rod; and the height, one rod.

The Eastern Gateway of the Temple

[6]Then he went to the gateway which faced east; and he went up its stairs and measured the threshold of the gateway, *which was* one rod wide, and the other threshold *was* one rod wide. [7]Each gate chamber *was* one rod long and one rod wide; between the gate chambers *was a space of* five cubits; and the threshold of the gateway by the vestibule of the inside gate *was* one rod. [8]He also measured the vestibule of the inside gate, one rod. [9]Then he measured the vestibule of the gateway, eight cubits; and the gateposts, two cubits. The vestibule of the gate *was* on the inside. [10]In the eastern gateway *were* three gate chambers on one side and three on the other; the three *were* all the same size; also the gateposts were of the same size on this side and that side.

[11]He measured the width of the entrance to the gateway, ten cubits; *and* the length of the gate, thirteen cubits. [12]*There was* a space in front of the gate chambers, one cubit *on this side* and one cubit on that side; the gate chambers *were* six cubits on this side and six cubits on that side. [13]Then he measured the gateway from the roof of *one* gate chamber to the roof of the other; the width *was* twenty-five cubits, as door faces door. [14]He measured the gateposts, sixty cubits high, and the court all around the gateway *extended* to the gatepost. [15]*From* the front of the entrance gate to the front of the vestibule of the inner gate *was* fifty cubits. [16]*There were* beveled window *frames* in the gate chambers and in their intervening archways on the in-

40:5 *g* Literally *house,* and so elsewhere in this book

side of the gateway all around, and likewise in the vestibules. *There were*
windows all around on the inside. And on each gatepost *were* palm trees.

The Outer Court

17Then he brought me into the outer court; and *there were* chambers and
a pavement made all around the court; thirty chambers faced the pavement. 18The pavement was by the side of the gateways, corresponding to
the length of the gateways; *this was* the lower pavement. 19Then he measured the width from the front of the lower gateway to the front of the
inner court exterior, one hundred cubits toward the east and the north.

The Northern Gateway

20On the outer court was also a gateway facing north, and he measured
its length and its width. 21Its gate chambers, three on this side and three on
that side, its gateposts and its archways, had the same measurements as
the first gate; its length *was* fifty cubits and its width twenty-five cubits.
22Its windows and those of its archways, and also its palm trees, *had* the
same measurements as the gateway facing east; it was ascended by seven
steps, and its archway *was* in front of it. 23A gate of the inner court was opposite the northern gateway, just as the eastern *gateway;* and he measured
from gateway to gateway, one hundred cubits.

The Southern Gateway

24After that he brought me toward the south, and there a gateway was
facing south; and he measured its gateposts and archways according to
these same measurements. 25*There were* windows in it and in its archways
all around like those windows; its length *was* fifty cubits and its width
twenty-five cubits. 26Seven steps led up to it, and its archway *was* in front
of them; and it had palm trees on its gateposts, one on this side and one on
that side. 27*There was* also a gateway on the inner court, facing south; and he
measured from gateway to gateway toward the south, one hundred cubits.

Gateways of the Inner Court

28Then he brought me to the inner court through the southern gateway;
he measured the southern gateway according to these same measurements. 29Also its gate chambers, its gateposts, and its archways *were* according to these same measurements; *there were* windows in it and in its
archways all around; *it was* fifty cubits long and twenty-five cubits wide.
30*There were* archways all around, twenty-five cubits long and five cubits
wide. 31Its archways faced the outer court, palm trees *were* on its gateposts,
and going up to it *were* eight steps.

32And he brought me into the inner court facing east; he measured the
gateway according to these same measurements. 33Also its gate chambers,
its gateposts, and its archways *were* according to these same measurements; and *there were* windows in it and in its archways all around; *it was*
fifty cubits long and twenty-five cubits wide. 34Its archways faced the outer
court, and palm trees *were* on its gateposts on this side and on that side;
and going up to it *were* eight steps.

35Then he brought me to the north gateway and measured *it* according
to these same measurements— 36also its gate chambers, its gateposts,
and its archways. It had windows all around; its length *was* fifty cubits and

Worship, I say, rises or falls with our concept of God. . . . And if there is one terrible disease in the Church it is that we do not see God as great as He is. We're too familiar with God. . . . Then there is admiration, that is, appreciation of the excellency of God. . . . Fascination is another element in true worship. . . . entranced with who God is, and struck with astonished wonder at the inconceivable elevation and magnitude and splendor of Almighty God. . . . Next is adoration, to love God with all the power within us. . . . Now when the mental and emotional and spiritual factors that I've spoken to you about are present and, as I've admitted, in varying degrees of intensity, in some, in praise, in prayer . . . you are worshiping.
(From *The Best of Tozer* compiled by Warren Wiersbe)

APPLICATION What is the center of worship for you—music? Prayer? Sermon? Communion? How can you focus better on bringing glory to God in worship? Do something different. Kneel when you pray or take notes during the sermon.

EXPLORATION Temple—
1 Chronicles 22:19; 29:6-13;
2 Chronicles 7:1-6; Ezra 3:10-13;
Luke 1:8-10.

its width twenty-five cubits. 37Its gateposts faced the
outer court, palm trees *were* on its gateposts on this side
and on that side, and going up to it *were* eight steps.

Where Sacrifices Were Prepared

38*There was* a chamber and its entrance by the
gateposts of the gateway, where they washed the burnt
offering. 39In the vestibule of the gateway *were* two tables on this side and two tables on that side, on which
to slay the burnt offering, the sin offering, and the trespass offering. 40At the outer side of the vestibule, as one
goes up to the entrance of the northern gateway, *were*
two tables; and on the other side of the vestibule of the
gateway *were* two tables. 41Four tables *were* on this side
and four tables on that side, by the side of the gateway,
eight tables on which they slaughtered *the sacrifices.*
42*There were* also four tables of hewn stone for the burnt
offering, one cubit and a half long, one cubit and a
half wide, and one cubit high; on these they laid the
instruments with which they slaughtered the burnt
offering and the sacrifice. 43Inside *were* hooks, a handbreadth wide, fastened all around; and the flesh of the
sacrifices *was* on the tables.

Chambers for Singers and Priests

44Outside the inner gate *were* the chambers for the
singers in the inner court, one facing south at the side
of the northern gateway, and the other facing north at
the side of the southern gateway. 45Then he said to me,
"This chamber which faces south *is* for the priests
who have charge of the temple. 46The chamber which
faces north *is* for the priests who have charge of the
altar; these *are* the sons of Zadok, from the sons of Levi,
who come near the LORD to minister to Him."

Dimensions of the Inner Court and Vestibule

47And he measured the court, one hundred cubits
long and one hundred cubits wide, foursquare. The
altar *was* in front of the temple. 48Then he brought me
to the vestibule of the temple and measured the doorposts of the vestibule, five cubits on this side and five
cubits on that side; and the width of the gateway was
three cubits on this side and three cubits on that side.
49The length of the vestibule *was* twenty cubits, and
the width eleven cubits; and by the steps which led up
to it *there were* pillars by the doorposts, one on this
side and another on that side.

Dimensions of the Sanctuary

41 Then he brought me into the sanctuary[h] and
measured the doorposts, six cubits wide on
one side and six cubits wide on the other side—the
width of the tabernacle. 2The width of the entryway
was ten cubits, and the side walls of the entrance *were*
five cubits on this side and five cubits on the other
side; and he measured its length, forty cubits, and its
width, twenty cubits.

3Also he went inside and measured the doorposts,
two cubits; and the entrance, six cubits *high;* and the
width of the entrance, seven cubits. 4He measured the
length, twenty cubits; and the width, twenty cubits,
beyond the sanctuary; and he said to me, "This *is* the
Most Holy *Place.*"

The Side Chambers on the Wall

5Next, he measured the wall of the temple, six cubits. The width of each side chamber all around the
temple *was* four cubits on every side. 6The side chambers *were* in three stories, one above the other, thirty
chambers in each story; they rested on ledges which
were for the side chambers all around, that they might
be supported, but not fastened to the wall of the temple. 7As one went up from story to story, the side
chambers became wider all around, because their
supporting ledges in the wall of the temple ascended
like steps; therefore the width of the structure increased as one went up *from* the lowest *story* to the
highest by way of the middle one. 8I also saw an elevation all around the temple; it was the foundation of
the side chambers, a full rod, *that is,* six cubits *high.*
9The thickness of the outer wall of the side chambers
was five cubits, and so also the remaining terrace by
the place of the side chambers of the temple. 10And
between *it and* the *wall* chambers was a width of
twenty cubits all around the temple on every side.
11The doors of the side chambers opened on the terrace, one door toward the north and another toward
the south; and the width of the terrace *was* five cubits
all around.

The Building at the Western End

12The building that faced the separating courtyard
at its western end *was* seventy cubits wide; the wall of
the building *was* five cubits thick all around, and its
length ninety cubits.

Dimensions and Design of the Temple Area

13So he measured the temple, one hundred cubits
long; and the separating courtyard with the building
and its walls *was* one hundred cubits long; 14also the
width of the eastern face of the temple, including the

41:1 [h] Hebrew *heykal,* here the main room of the temple, sometimes called the *holy place* (compare Exodus 26:33)

separating courtyard, *was* one hundred cubits. 15He
measured the length of the building behind it, facing
the separating courtyard, with its galleries on the one
side and on the other side, one hundred cubits, as
well as the inner temple and the porches of the court,
16their doorposts and the beveled window frames.
And the galleries all around their three stories opposite the threshold were paneled with wood from the
ground to the windows—the windows were covered— 17from the space above the door, even to the
inner room,[i] as well as outside, and on every wall all
around, inside and outside, by measure.

18And *it was* made with cherubim and palm trees, a
palm tree between cherub and cherub. *Each* cherub
had two faces, 19so that the face of a man *was* toward a
palm tree on one side, and the face of a young lion toward a palm tree on the other side; thus *it was* made
throughout the temple all around. 20From the floor to
the space above the door, and on the wall of the sanctuary, cherubim and palm trees *were* carved.

21The doorposts of the temple *were* square, *as was*
the front of the sanctuary; their appearance was similar. 22The altar *was* of wood, three cubits high, and its
length two cubits. Its corners, its length, and its sides
were of wood; and he said to me, "This *is* the table that
is before the LORD."

23The temple and the sanctuary had two doors.
24The doors had two panels *apiece,* two folding panels: two *panels* for one door and two panels for the
other *door.* 25Cherubim and palm trees *were* carved on
the doors of the temple just as they *were* carved on the
walls. A wooden canopy *was* on the front of the
vestibule outside. 26*There were* beveled window
frames and palm trees on one side and on the other,
on the sides of the vestibule—also on the side chambers of the temple and on the canopies.

The Chambers for the Priests

42 Then he brought me out into the outer court,
by the way toward the north; and he brought
me into the chamber which *was* opposite the separating courtyard, and which *was* opposite the building
toward the north. 2Facing the length, *which was* one
hundred cubits (the width was fifty cubits), was the
north door. 3Opposite the inner court of twenty *cubits,*
and opposite the pavement of the outer court, *was*
gallery against gallery in three *stories.* 4In front of the
chambers, toward the inside, *was* a walk ten cubits
wide, at a distance of one cubit; and their doors faced
north. 5Now the upper chambers *were* shorter, because the galleries took away *space* from them more
than from the lower and middle stories of the building. 6For they *were* in three *stories* and did not have
pillars like the pillars of the courts; therefore *the upper
level* was shortened more than the lower and middle
levels from the ground up. 7And a wall which *was* outside ran parallel to the chambers, at the front of the
chambers, toward the outer court; its length *was* fifty
cubits. 8The length of the chambers toward the outer
court *was* fifty cubits, whereas that facing the temple
was one hundred cubits. 9At the lower chambers *was*
the entrance on the east side, as one goes into them
from the outer court.

10Also *there were* chambers in the thickness of the
wall of the court toward the east, opposite the separating courtyard and opposite the building. 11*There was* a
walk in front of them also, and their appearance *was*
like the chambers which *were* toward the north; they
were as long and as wide as the others, and all their
exits and entrances *were* according to plan. 12And corresponding to the doors of the chambers that *were*
facing south, as one enters them, *there was* a door in
front of the walk, the way directly in front of the wall
toward the east.

13Then he said to me, "The north chambers *and* the
south chambers, which *are* opposite the separating
courtyard, *are* the holy chambers where the priests
who approach the LORD shall eat the most holy offerings. There they shall lay the most holy offerings—
the grain offering, the sin offering, and the trespass
offering—for the place *is* holy. 14When the priests
enter them, they shall not go out of the holy *chamber*
into the outer court; but there they shall leave their
garments in which they minister, for they *are* holy.
They shall put on other garments; then they may approach *that* which *is* for the people."

Outer Dimensions of the Temple

15Now when he had finished measuring the inner
temple, he brought me out through the gateway that
faces toward the east, and measured it all around. 16He
measured the east side with the measuring rod,[j] five
hundred rods by the measuring rod all around. 17He
measured the north side, five hundred rods by the
measuring rod all around. 18He measured the south
side, five hundred rods by the measuring rod. 19He
came around to the west side *and* measured five hundred rods by the measuring rod. 20He measured it on

41:17 [i] Literally *house,* here *the Most Holy Place*
42:16 [j] Compare 40:5

the four sides; it had a wall all around, five hundred *cubits* long and five
hundred wide, to separate the holy areas from the common.

The Temple, the LORD's Dwelling Place

43 Afterward he brought me to the gate, the gate that faces toward the
east. 2And behold, the glory of the God of Israel came from the way
of the east. His voice *was* like the sound of many waters; and the earth
shone with His glory. 3*It was* like the appearance of the vision which I
saw—like the vision which I saw when I[k] came to destroy the city. The visions *were* like the vision which I saw by the River Chebar; and I fell on my
face. 4And the glory of the LORD came into the temple by way of the gate
which faces toward the east. 5The Spirit lifted me up and brought me into
the inner court; and behold, the glory of the LORD filled the temple.
6Then I heard *Him* speaking to me from the temple, while a man stood
beside me. 7And He said to me, "Son of man, *this is* the place of My throne
and the place of the soles of My feet, where I will dwell in the midst of the
children of Israel forever. No more shall the house of Israel defile My holy
name, they nor their kings, by their harlotry or with the carcasses of their
kings on their high places. 8When they set their threshold by My threshold,
and their doorpost by My doorpost, with a wall between them and Me,
they defiled My holy name by the abominations which they committed;
therefore I have consumed them in My anger. 9Now let them put their harlotry and the carcasses of their kings far away from Me, and I will dwell in
their midst forever.
10"Son of man, describe the temple to the house of Israel, that they may
be ashamed of their iniquities; and let them measure the pattern. 11And if
they are ashamed of all that they have done, make known to them the design of the temple and its arrangement, its exits and its entrances, its entire
design and all its ordinances, all its forms and all its laws. Write *it* down in
their sight, so that they may keep its whole design and all its ordinances,
and perform them. 12This *is* the law of the temple: The whole area surrounding the mountaintop *is* most holy. Behold, this *is* the law of the temple.

Dimensions of the Altar

13"These are the measurements of the altar in cubits (the *cubit is* one
cubit and a handbreadth): the base one cubit high and one cubit wide, with
a rim all around its edge of one span. This *is* the height of the altar: 14from the
base on the ground to the lower ledge, two cubits; the width of the ledge,
one cubit; from the smaller ledge to the larger ledge, four cubits; and the
width of the ledge, *one* cubit. 15The altar hearth *is* four cubits high, with
four horns extending upward from the hearth. 16The altar hearth *is* twelve
cubits long, twelve wide, square at its four corners; 17the ledge, fourteen
cubits long and fourteen wide on its four sides, with a rim of half a cubit
around it; its base, one cubit all around; and its steps face toward the east."

Consecrating the Altar

18And He said to me, "Son of man, thus says the Lord GOD: 'These *are* the
ordinances for the altar on the day when it is made, for sacrificing burnt
offerings on it, and for sprinkling blood on it. 19You shall give a young bull

LIFE LESSON

Ezekiel 43:1–48:35

SITUATION God's glory had been present in Solomon's Temple (2 Chronicles 2–7), but it departed before Jerusalem fell to the Babylonians.

OBSERVATION God requires his people to be holy (v. 12). Therefore, as believers, we should be completely devoted to him and separated from sin.

INSPIRATION It is possible to establish convictions regarding a life of holiness, and even make a definite commitment to that end, yet fail to achieve the goal. . . . This is what we must do if we pursue holiness: We must correct, mold, and train our moral character.

Discipline toward holiness begins with the Word of God. . . . Discipline toward holiness begins then with the Scriptures—with a disciplined plan for regular intake of the Scriptures and a disciplined plan for applying them to our daily lives. . . . Every Christian who makes progress in holiness is a person who has disciplined his life so that he spends regular time in the Bible. There simply is no other way.

Satan will always battle us at this point. . . . A disciplined intake of the Word of God not only involves a planned

43:3 *k* Some Hebrew manuscripts and Vulgate read *He*.

for a sin offering to the priests, the Levites, who are of the seed of Zadok,
who approach Me to minister to Me,' says the Lord GOD. 20You shall take
some of its blood and put *it* on the four horns of the altar, on the four corners of the ledge, and on the rim around it; thus you shall cleanse it and
make atonement for it. 21Then you shall also take the bull of the sin offering, and burn it in the appointed place of the temple, outside the sanctuary.
22On the second day you shall offer a kid of the goats without blemish for a
sin offering; and they shall cleanse the altar, as they cleansed *it* with the
bull. 23When you have finished cleansing *it,* you shall offer a young bull
without blemish, and a ram from the flock without blemish. 24When you
offer them before the LORD, the priests shall throw salt on them, and they
will offer them up *as* a burnt offering to the LORD. 25Every day for seven
days you shall prepare a goat *for* a sin offering; they shall also prepare a
young bull and a ram from the flock, both without blemish. 26Seven days
they shall make atonement for the altar and purify it, and so consecrate *it.*
27When these days are over it shall be, on the eighth day and thereafter, that
the priests shall offer your burnt offerings and your peace offerings on the
altar; and I will accept you,' says the Lord GOD."

The East Gate and the Prince

44 Then He brought me back to the outer gate of the sanctuary which
faces toward the east, but it *was* shut. 2And the LORD said to me,
"This gate shall be shut; it shall not be opened, and no man shall enter by it,
because the LORD God of Israel has entered by it; therefore it shall be shut.
3*As for* the prince, *because* he *is* the prince, he may sit in it to eat bread before the LORD; he shall enter by way of the vestibule of the gateway, and go
out the same way."

Those Admitted to the Temple

4Also He brought me by way of the north gate to the front of the temple;
so I looked, and behold, the glory of the LORD filled the house of the LORD;
and I fell on my face. 5And the LORD said to me, "Son of man, mark well,
see with your eyes and hear with your ears, all that I say to you concerning
all the ordinances of the house of the LORD and all its laws. Mark well who
may enter the house and all who go out from the sanctuary.
6"Now say to the rebellious, to the house of Israel, 'Thus says the Lord
GOD: "O house of Israel, let Us have no more of all your abominations.
7When you brought in foreigners, uncircumcised in heart and uncircumcised in flesh, to be in My sanctuary to defile it—My house—and when
you offered My food, the fat and the blood, then they broke My covenant
because of all your abominations. 8And you have not kept charge of My
holy things, but you have set *others* to keep charge of My sanctuary for
you." 9Thus says the Lord GOD: "No foreigner, uncircumcised in heart or
uncircumcised in flesh, shall enter My sanctuary, including any foreigner
who *is* among the children of Israel.

Laws Governing Priests

10"And the Levites who went far from Me, when Israel went astray, who
strayed away from Me after their idols, they shall bear their iniquity. 11Yet they
shall be ministers in My sanctuary, *as* gatekeepers of the house and ministers of the house; they shall slay the burnt offering and the sacrifice for the

time; it also involves a planned method. . . . But if we are to pursue holiness with discipline, we must do more than hear, read, study, or memorize Scripture. We must meditate on it. . . . simply thinking about it and its application to life—is a practice we develop through discipline. . . . The most important part of this process is the specific application of the Scripture to specific life situations. . . . You can readily see that this structured training in holiness is a lifelong process. So a necessary ingredient of discipline is perseverance. . . . If we would succeed in our pursuit of holiness we must persevere in spite of failure. (From *The Pursuit of Holiness* by Jerry Bridges)

APPLICATION Are you completely dedicated to God? Is there an area of life you have not committed to him? What sin still stays with you? Lust, gossip, selfishness, an unrepentant or unforgiving heart? Talk to your pastor about how you can overcome these sins.

EXPLORATION Glory of God—Exodus 15:11; 40:34-35; Deuteronomy 5:24; Psalm 8:1; Luke 2:9, 14; Hebrews 1:3; Revelation 21:23.

Continued

people, and they shall stand before them to minister to them. 12Because they ministered to them before their idols and caused the house of Israel to fall into iniquity, therefore I have raised My hand in an oath against them," says the Lord GOD, "that they shall bear their iniquity. 13And they shall not come near Me to minister to Me as priest, nor come near any of My holy things, nor into the Most Holy *Place;* but they shall bear their shame and their abominations which they have committed. 14Nevertheless I will make them keep charge of the temple, for all its work, and for all that has to be done in it.

15"But the priests, the Levites, the sons of Zadok, who kept charge of My sanctuary when the children of Israel went astray from Me, they shall come near Me to minister to Me; and they shall stand before Me to offer to Me the fat and the blood," says the Lord GOD. 16"They shall enter My sanctuary, and they shall come near My table to minister to Me, and they shall keep My charge. 17And it shall be, whenever they enter the gates of the inner court, that they shall put on linen garments; no wool shall come upon them while they minister within the gates of the inner court or within the house. 18They shall have linen turbans on their heads and linen trousers on their bodies; they shall not clothe themselves with *anything that causes* sweat. 19When they go out to the outer court, to the *outer* court to the people, they shall take off their garments in which they have ministered, leave them in the holy chambers, and put on other garments; and in their holy garments they shall not sanctify the people.

20"They shall neither shave their heads, nor let their hair grow long, but they shall keep their hair well trimmed. 21No priest shall drink wine when he enters the inner court. 22They shall not take as wife a widow or a divorced woman, but take virgins of the descendants of the house of Israel, or widows of priests.

23"And they shall teach My people *the difference* between the holy and the unholy, and cause them to discern between the unclean and the clean. 24In controversy they shall stand as judges, *and* judge it according to My judgments. They shall keep My laws and My statutes in all My appointed meetings, and they shall hallow My Sabbaths.

25"They shall not defile *themselves* by coming near a dead person. Only for father or mother, for son or daughter, for brother or unmarried sister may they defile themselves. 26After he is cleansed, they shall count seven days for him. 27And on the day that he goes to the sanctuary to minister in the sanctuary, he must offer his sin offering in the inner court," says the Lord GOD.

28"It shall be, in regard to their inheritance, *that* I *am* their inheritance. You shall give them no possession in Israel, for I *am* their possession. 29They shall eat the grain offering, the sin offering, and the trespass offering; every dedicated thing in Israel shall be theirs. 30The best of all firstfruits of any kind, and every sacrifice of any kind from all your sacrifices, shall be the priest's; also you shall give to the priest the first of your ground meal, to cause a blessing to rest on your house. 31The priests shall not eat anything, bird or beast, that died naturally or was torn *by wild beasts.*

The Holy District

45 "Moreover, when you divide the land by lot into inheritance, you shall set apart a district for the LORD, a holy section of the land; its length *shall be* twenty-five thousand *cubits,* and the width ten thousand. It *shall be* holy throughout its territory all around. 2Of this there shall be a square plot for the sanctuary, five hundred by five hundred *rods,* with fifty cubits around it for an open space. 3So this is the district you shall measure: twenty-five thousand *cubits* long and ten thousand wide; in it shall be the sanctuary, the Most Holy *Place.* 4It shall be a holy *section* of the land, belonging to the priests, the ministers of the sanctuary, who come near to minister to the LORD; it shall be a place for their houses and a holy place for the sanctuary. 5*An area* twenty-five thousand *cubits* long and ten thousand wide shall belong to the Levites, the ministers of the temple; they shall have twenty chambers as a possession.[l]

Properties of the City and the Prince

6"You shall appoint as the property of the city *an area* five thousand *cubits* wide and twenty-five thousand long, adjacent to the district of the holy *section;* it shall belong to the whole house of Israel.

7"The prince shall have *a section* on one side and the other of the holy district and the city's property; and bordering on the holy district and the city's property, extending westward on the west side and eastward on the east side, the length *shall be* side by side with one of the *tribal* portions, from the west border to the east border. 8The land shall be his possession in Israel; and My princes shall no more oppress My people, but they shall give *the rest of* the land to the house of Israel, according to their tribes."

45:5 [l] Following Masoretic Text, Targum, and Vulgate; Septuagint reads *a possession, cities of dwelling.*

Laws Governing the Prince

9 “Thus says the Lord GOD: “Enough, O princes of Israel! Remove violence and plundering, execute justice
and righteousness, and stop dispossessing My people,”
says the Lord GOD. 10 “You shall have honest scales, an
honest ephah, and an honest bath. 11 The ephah and the
bath shall be of the same measure, so that the bath
contains one-tenth of a homer, and the ephah one-
tenth of a homer; their measure shall be according to
the homer. 12 The shekel *shall be* twenty gerahs; twenty
shekels, twenty-five shekels, *and* fifteen shekels shall
be your mina.

13 “This *is* the offering which you shall offer: you shall
give one-sixth of an ephah from a homer of wheat, and
one-sixth of an ephah from a homer of barley. 14 The
ordinance concerning oil, the bath of oil, *is* one-tenth
of a bath from a kor. A kor *is* a homer or ten baths, for
ten baths *are* a homer. 15 And one lamb shall be given
from a flock of two hundred, from the rich pastures of
Israel. These shall be for grain offerings, burnt offerings,
and peace offerings, to make atonement for them,” says
the Lord GOD. 16 “All the people of the land shall give this
offering for the prince in Israel. 17 Then it shall be the
prince’s part *to give* burnt offerings, grain offerings,
and drink offerings, at the feasts, the New Moons, the
Sabbaths, and at all the appointed seasons of the
house of Israel. He shall prepare the sin offering, the
grain offering, the burnt offering, and the peace offerings to make atonement for the house of Israel.”

Keeping the Feasts

18 ‘Thus says the Lord GOD: “In the first *month,* on the
first *day* of the month, you shall take a young bull without blemish and cleanse the sanctuary. 19 The priest shall
take some of the blood of the sin offering and put *it* on
the doorposts of the temple, on the four corners of the
ledge of the altar, and on the gateposts of the gate of
the inner court. 20 And so you shall do on the seventh
day of the month for everyone who has sinned unintentionally or in ignorance. Thus you shall make
atonement for the temple.

21 “In the first *month,* on the fourteenth day of the
month, you shall observe the Passover, a feast of seven
days; unleavened bread shall be eaten. 22 And on that
day the prince shall prepare for himself and for all the
people of the land a bull *for* a sin offering. 23 On the
seven days of the feast he shall prepare a burnt offering to the LORD, seven bulls and seven rams without
blemish, daily for seven days, and a kid of the goats
daily *for* a sin offering. 24 And he shall prepare a grain
offering of one ephah for each bull and one ephah for
each ram, together with a hin of oil for each ephah.

25 “In the seventh *month,* on the fifteenth day of the
month, at the feast, he shall do likewise for seven days,
according to the sin offering, the burnt offering, the
grain offering, and the oil.”

The Manner of Worship

46 ‘Thus says the Lord GOD: “The gateway of the
inner court that faces toward the east shall be
shut the six working days; but on the Sabbath it shall
be opened, and on the day of the New Moon it shall be
opened. 2 The prince shall enter by way of the vestibule
of the gateway from the outside, and stand by the
gatepost. The priests shall prepare his burnt offering
and his peace offerings. He shall worship at the threshold of the gate. Then he shall go out, but the gate shall
not be shut until evening. 3 Likewise the people of the
land shall worship at the entrance to this gateway before
the LORD on the Sabbaths and the New Moons. 4 The
burnt offering that the prince offers to the LORD on the
Sabbath day *shall be* six lambs without blemish, and a
ram without blemish; 5 and the grain offering *shall be*
one ephah for a ram, and the grain offering for the
lambs, as much as he wants to give, as well as a hin of
oil with every ephah. 6 On the day of the New Moon *it*
shall be a young bull without blemish, six lambs, and
a ram; they shall be without blemish. 7 He shall prepare a grain offering of an ephah for a bull, an ephah
for a ram, as much as he wants to give for the lambs,
and a hin of oil with every ephah. 8 When the prince
enters, he shall go in by way of the vestibule of the
gateway, and go out the same way.

9 “But when the people of the land come before the
LORD on the appointed feast days, whoever enters by way
of the north gate to worship shall go out by way of the
south gate; and whoever enters by way of the south gate
shall go out by way of the north gate. He shall not return
by way of the gate through which he came, but shall go
out through the opposite gate. 10 The prince shall then be
in their midst. When they go in, he shall go in; and when
they go out, he shall go out. 11 At the festivals and the appointed feast days the grain offering shall be an ephah
for a bull, an ephah for a ram, as much as he wants to
give for the lambs, and a hin of oil with every ephah.

12 “Now when the prince makes a voluntary burnt
offering or voluntary peace offering to the LORD, the gate
that faces toward the east shall then be opened for him;
and he shall prepare his burnt offering and his peace
offerings as he did on the Sabbath day. Then he shall
go out, and after he goes out the gate shall be shut.

[13]"You shall daily make a burnt offering to the LORD
of a lamb of the first year without blemish; you shall
prepare it every morning. [14]And you shall prepare a
grain offering with it every morning, a sixth of an
ephah, and a third of a hin of oil to moisten the fine
flour. This grain offering is a perpetual ordinance, to
be made regularly to the LORD. [15]Thus they shall prepare the lamb, the grain offering, and the oil, *as* a regular burnt offering every morning."

The Prince and Inheritance Laws

[16]"Thus says the Lord GOD: "If the prince gives a gift
of some of his inheritance to any of his sons, it shall
belong to his sons; it is their possession by inheritance.
[17]But if he gives a gift of some of his inheritance to one
of his servants, it shall be his until the year of liberty,
after which it shall return to the prince. But his inheritance shall belong to his sons; it shall become theirs.
[18]Moreover the prince shall not take any of the people's inheritance by evicting them from their property; he shall provide an inheritance for his sons from
his own property, so that none of My people may be
scattered from his property." ' "

How the Offerings Were Prepared

[19]Now he brought me through the entrance, which
was at the side of the gate, into the holy chambers of
the priests which face toward the north; and there a
place *was* situated at their extreme western end. [20]And
he said to me, "This *is* the place where the priests shall
boil the trespass offering and the sin offering, *and*
where they shall bake the grain offering, so that they
do not bring *them* out into the outer court to sanctify
the people."

[21]Then he brought me out into the outer court and
caused me to pass by the four corners of the court;
and in fact, in every corner of the court *there was another* court. [22]In the four corners of the court *were* enclosed courts, forty *cubits* long and thirty wide; all
four corners *were* the same size. [23]*There was* a row *of
building stones* all around in them, all around the four
of them; and cooking hearths were made under the
rows of stones all around. [24]And he said to me, "These
are the kitchens where the ministers of the temple
shall boil the sacrifices of the people."

The Healing Waters and Trees

47 Then he brought me back to the door of the
temple; and there was water, flowing from
under the threshold of the temple toward the east, for
the front of the temple faced east; the water was flowing from under the right side of the temple, south of
the altar. [2]He brought me out by way of the north gate,
and led me around on the outside to the outer gateway that faces east; and there was water, running out
on the right side.

[3]And when the man went out to the east with the
line in his hand, he measured one thousand cubits,
and he brought me through the waters; the water *came
up to my* ankles. [4]Again he measured one thousand
and brought me through the waters; the water *came
up to my* knees. Again he measured one thousand and
brought me through; the water *came up to my* waist.
[5]Again he measured one thousand, *and it was* a river
that I could not cross; for the water was too deep, water
in which one must swim, a river that could not be
crossed. [6]He said to me, "Son of man, have you seen
this?" Then he brought me and returned me to the
bank of the river.

[7]When I returned, there, along the bank of the river,
were very many trees on one side and the other. [8]Then
he said to me: "This water flows toward the eastern region, goes down into the valley, and enters the sea.
When it reaches the sea, *its* waters are healed. [9]And it
shall be *that* every living thing that moves, wherever
the rivers go, will live. There will be a very great multitude of fish, because these waters go there; for they
will be healed, and everything will live wherever the
river goes. [10]It shall be *that* fishermen will stand by it
from En Gedi to En Eglaim; they will be *places* for
spreading their nets. Their fish will be of the same
kinds as the fish of the Great Sea, exceedingly many.
[11]But its swamps and marshes will not be healed; they
will be given over to salt. [12]Along the bank of the river,
on this side and that, will grow all *kinds of* trees used
for food; their leaves will not wither, and their fruit
will not fail. They will bear fruit every month, because
their water flows from the sanctuary. Their fruit will
be for food, and their leaves for medicine."

Borders of the Land

[13]Thus says the Lord GOD: "These *are* the borders by
which you shall divide the land as an inheritance among
the twelve tribes of Israel. Joseph *shall have two* portions. [14]You shall inherit it equally with one another;
for I raised My hand in an oath to give it to your fathers,
and this land shall fall to you as your inheritance.

[15]"This *shall be* the border of the land on the north:
from the Great Sea, *by* the road to Hethlon, as one
goes to Zedad, [16]Hamath, Berothah, Sibraim (which *is*
between the border of Damascus and the border of
Hamath), to Hazar Hatticon (which *is* on the border

of Hauran). 17Thus the boundary shall be from the Sea to Hazar Enan, the border of Damascus; and as for the north, northward, it is the border of Hamath. *This is* the north side.

18"On the east side you shall mark out the border from between Hauran and Damascus, and between Gilead and the land of Israel, along the Jordan, and along the eastern side of the sea. *This is* the east side.

19"The south side, toward the South,[m] *shall be* from Tamar to the waters of Meribah by Kadesh, along the brook to the Great Sea. *This is* the south side, toward the South.

20"The west side *shall be* the Great Sea, from the *southern* boundary until one comes to a point opposite Hamath. This *is* the west side.

21"Thus you shall divide this land among yourselves according to the tribes of Israel. 22It shall be that you will divide it by lot as an inheritance for yourselves, and for the strangers who dwell among you and who bear children among you. They shall be to you as native-born among the children of Israel; they shall have an inheritance with you among the tribes of Israel. 23And it shall be *that* in whatever tribe the stranger dwells, there you shall give *him* his inheritance," says the Lord GOD.

Division of the Land

48 "Now these *are* the names of the tribes: From the northern border along the road to Hethlon at the entrance of Hamath, to Hazar Enan, the border of Damascus northward, in the direction of Hamath, *there shall be* one *section for* Dan from its east to its west side; 2by the border of Dan, from the east side to the west, one *section for* Asher; 3by the border of Asher, from the east side to the west, one *section for* Naphtali; 4by the border of Naphtali, from the east side to the west, one *section for* Manasseh; 5by the border of Manasseh, from the east side to the west, one *section for* Ephraim; 6by the border of Ephraim, from the east side to the west, one *section for* Reuben; 7by the border of Reuben, from the east side to the west, one *section for* Judah; 8by the border of Judah, from the east side to the west, shall be the district which you shall set apart, twenty-five thousand *cubits* in width, and *in* length the same as one of the *other* portions, from the east side to the west, with the sanctuary in the center.

9"The district that you shall set apart for the LORD *shall be* twenty-five thousand *cubits* in length and ten thousand in width. 10To these—to the priests—the holy district shall belong: on the north twenty-five thousand *cubits in length,* on the west ten thousand in width, on the east ten thousand in width, and on the south twenty-five thousand in length. The sanctuary of the LORD shall be in the center. 11*It shall be* for the priests of the sons of Zadok, who are sanctified, who have kept My charge, who did not go astray when the children of Israel went astray, as the Levites went astray. 12And *this* district of land that is set apart shall be to them a thing most holy by the border of the Levites.

13"Opposite the border of the priests, the Levites *shall have an area* twenty-five thousand *cubits* in length and ten thousand in width; its entire length *shall be* twenty-five thousand and its width ten thousand. 14And they shall not sell or exchange any of it; they may not alienate this best *part* of the land, for *it is* holy to the LORD.

15"The five thousand *cubits* in width that remain, along the edge of the twenty-five thousand, shall be for general use by the city, for dwellings and common-land; and the city shall be in the center. 16These *shall be* its measurements: the north side four thousand five hundred *cubits,* the south side four thousand five hundred, the east side four thousand five hundred, and the west side four thousand five hundred. 17The common-land of the city shall be: to the north two hundred and fifty *cubits,* to the south two hundred and fifty, to the east two hundred and fifty, and to the west two hundred and fifty. 18The rest of the length, alongside the district of the holy *section, shall be* ten thousand *cubits* to the east and ten thousand to the west. It shall be adjacent to the district of the holy *section,* and its produce shall be food for the workers of the city. 19The workers of the city, from all the tribes of Israel, shall cultivate it. 20The entire district *shall be* twenty-five thousand *cubits* by twenty-five thousand *cubits,* foursquare. You shall set apart the holy district with the property of the city.

21"The rest *shall belong* to the prince, on one side and on the other of the holy district and of the city's property, next to the twenty-five thousand *cubits* of the *holy* district as far as the eastern border, and westward next to the twenty-five thousand as far as the western border, adjacent to the *tribal* portions; *it shall belong* to the prince. It shall be the holy district, and the sanctuary of the temple *shall be* in the center. 22Moreover, apart from the possession of the Levites and the possession of the city *which are* in the midst of what *belongs* to the prince, *the area* between the border of Judah and the border of Benjamin shall belong to the prince.

23"As for the rest of the tribes, from the east side to the west, Benjamin *shall have* one *section;* 24by the border

47:19 [m] Hebrew *Negev*

of Benjamin, from the east side to the west, Simeon
shall have one *section;* 25by the border of Simeon, from
the east side to the west, Issachar *shall have* one *section;*
26by the border of Issachar, from the east side to the
west, Zebulun *shall have* one *section;* 27by the border of
Zebulun, from the east side to the west, Gad *shall have*
one *section;* 28by the border of Gad, on the south side,
toward the South,[n] the border shall be from Tamar *to*
the waters of Meribah *by* Kadesh, along the brook to
the Great Sea. 29This *is* the land which you shall divide
by lot as an inheritance among the tribes of Israel, and
these *are* their portions," says the Lord GOD.

The Gates of the City and Its Name

30"These *are* the exits of the city. On the north side,
measuring four thousand five hundred *cubits* 31(the
gates of the city *shall be* named after the tribes of Israel),
the three gates northward: one gate for Reuben, one
gate for Judah, and one gate for Levi; 32on the east side,
four thousand five hundred *cubits,* three gates: one gate
for Joseph, one gate for Benjamin, and one gate for
Dan; 33on the south side, measuring four thousand
five hundred *cubits,* three gates: one gate for Simeon,
one gate for Issachar, and one gate for Zebulun; 34on
the west side, four thousand five hundred *cubits* with
their three gates: one gate for Gad, one gate for Asher,
and one gate for Naphtali. 35All the way around *shall
be* eighteen thousand *cubits;* and the name of the city
from *that* day *shall be:* THE LORD *IS* THERE."[o]

48:28 [n] Hebrew *Negev*
48:35 [o] Hebrew *YHWH Shammah*

The Book of

DANIEL

INTRODUCTION

If you are a Jew in Babylon, you've got reason to be depressed. Jeremiah was right all along. All those times you thought he was one taco short of a platter, he was telling the truth!

Jerusalem is in ashes. The Temple is in ruins. And you and the rest of your people are in captivity.

Your captors mock you, "Sing us one of the songs of Zion!" (Psalm 137:3). But you don't sing. You hang your harps on the poplar trees and sit on the banks of the river, watching the water and your days pass by.

Who can sing songs about the Lord in a foreign country?

Daniel can.

Though he was only a teenager when taken captive, he remembers well the songs of his youth. Somewhere in his early years he came to believe that God was sovereign. Nothing happens without his permission. Nothing happens outside of his plan.

But even Daniel could not have imagined the plans God had for him. Prime minister of the court. Interpreter of dreams. Prophet. Teacher. Ruler. A lifelong voice for God among pagan people.

But though the central character of the book is Daniel, the hero is God. "There is a God in heaven ...," Daniel told the king (2:28), and it was that God in heaven who sustained Daniel and the people while in captivity.

That God, by the way, still reigns.

And anytime God's people have hung up their harps, listen carefully.

God always has a Daniel who remembers how to sing.

Life Lesson

Daniel 1:1-21

SITUATION Daniel and his Israelite friends were exiled to Babylon. Servants of the king prepared them to serve in the royal court.

OBSERVATION It is possible to be obedient to God even when surrounded by people who are disobedient to his Word.

INSPIRATION Whereas Ezekiel spent his days preaching (and acting out) sermons to the Jewish exiles, Daniel was recruited for a job in the king's palace.

In fact, Daniel's life in the palace more closely resembles that of the ancient character Joseph, who also rose to a position of prominence in a foreign government. As this chapter underscores, Daniel achieved success without bending his own principles of integrity. Somehow he managed to thrive in an environment marked by ambition and intrigue, while still holding to his high-minded Jewish ideals. . . .

Taken together, the Biblical prophets offer not one, but many models of how a person can serve both God and the state. On the one extreme stand men like Amos and Elijah, who, as outsiders, railed against the evils of society. Others, such as Jeremiah and Nathan, gave occasional counsel to kings, but kept a safe distance. Isaiah and Samuel, however, became official advisors of kings. And in this book the prophet Daniel shows that a person can keep pure even while working within a tyrannical regime.

For at least sixty-six years, Daniel served pagan kings with great diligence and resourcefulness. Yet he never once compromised his faith, even when threatened with death. The Bible offers no better model of how to live among people who do not share or respect your beliefs.

(From *Discovering God* by Philip Yancey)

APPLICATION Are you ever in a situation where you are too embarrassed to do what is right? Plan how you will handle those situations to bring honor to God. Ask him for strength to respond correctly. Be bold!

EXPLORATION Unwavering Witness—Daniel 3:28; Matthew 5:16; Philippians 1:27-30.

Daniel and His Friends Obey God

In the third year of the reign of Jehoiakim king of Judah,
Nebuchadnezzar king of Babylon came to Jerusalem and
besieged it. 2 And the Lord gave Jehoiakim king of Judah into
his hand, with some of the articles of the house of God, which he
carried into the land of Shinar to the house of his god; and he brought the
articles into the treasure house of his god.
3 Then the king instructed Ashpenaz, the master of his eunuchs, to bring
some of the children of Israel and some of the king's descendants and some
of the nobles, 4 young men in whom *there was* no blemish, but good-looking,
gifted in all wisdom, possessing knowledge and quick to understand, who *had*
ability to serve in the king's palace, and whom they might teach the language
and literature of the Chaldeans. 5 And the king appointed for them a daily
provision of the king's delicacies and of the wine which he drank, and three
years of training for them, so that at the end of *that time* they might serve
before the king. 6 Now from among those of the sons of Judah were Daniel,
Hananiah, Mishael, and Azariah. 7 To them the chief of the eunuchs gave
names: he gave Daniel *the name* Belteshazzar; to Hananiah, Shadrach; to
Mishael, Meshach; and to Azariah, Abed-Nego.
8 But Daniel purposed in his heart that he would not defile himself with
the portion of the king's delicacies, nor with the wine which he drank;
therefore he requested of the chief of the eunuchs that he might not defile
himself. 9 Now God had brought Daniel into the favor and goodwill of the
chief of the eunuchs. 10 And the chief of the eunuchs said to Daniel, "I fear
my lord the king, who has appointed your food and drink. For why should
he see your faces looking worse than the young men who *are* your age?
Then you would endanger my head before the king."
11 So Daniel said to the steward[a] whom the chief of the eunuchs had set
over Daniel, Hananiah, Mishael, and Azariah, 12 "Please test your servants
for ten days, and let them give us vegetables to eat and water to drink.
13 Then let our appearance be examined before you, and the appearance of
the young men who eat the portion of the king's delicacies; and as you see
fit, *so* deal with your servants." 14 So he consented with them in this matter,
and tested them ten days.
15 And at the end of ten days their features appeared better and fatter in
flesh than all the young men who ate the portion of the king's delicacies.
16 Thus the steward took away their portion of delicacies and the wine that
they were to drink, and gave them vegetables.
17 As for these four young men, God gave them knowledge and skill in all
literature and wisdom; and Daniel had understanding in all visions and
dreams.
18 Now at the end of the days, when the king had said that they should be
brought in, the chief of the eunuchs brought them in before Nebuchadnezzar.
19 Then the king interviewed[b] them, and among them all none was found
like Daniel, Hananiah, Mishael, and Azariah; therefore they served before
the king. 20 And in all matters of wisdom *and* understanding about which
the king examined them, he found them ten times better than all the magicians *and* astrologers who *were* in all his realm. 21 Thus Daniel continued
until the first year of King Cyrus.

1:11 [a] Hebrew *Melzar,* also in verse 16
1:19 [b] Literally *talked with them*

Nebuchadnezzar's Dream

2 Now in the second year of Nebuchadnezzar's reign, Nebuchadnezzar
had dreams; and his spirit was *so* troubled that his sleep left him.
2Then the king gave the command to call the magicians, the astrologers,
the sorcerers, and the Chaldeans to tell the king his dreams. So they came
and stood before the king. 3And the king said to them, "I have had a
dream, and my spirit is anxious to know the dream."
4Then the Chaldeans spoke to the king in Aramaic,[c] "O king, live forever! Tell your servants the dream, and we will give the interpretation."
5The king answered and said to the Chaldeans, "My decision is firm: if
you do not make known the dream to me, and its interpretation, you shall
be cut in pieces, and your houses shall be made an ash heap. 6However, if
you tell the dream and its interpretation, you shall receive from me gifts,
rewards, and great honor. Therefore tell me the dream and its interpretation."
7They answered again and said, "Let the king tell his servants the dream,
and we will give its interpretation."
8The king answered and said, "I know for certain that you would gain
time, because you see that my decision is firm: 9if you do not make known
the dream to me, *there is only* one decree for you! For you have agreed to
speak lying and corrupt words before me till the time has changed. Therefore
tell me the dream, and I shall know that you can give me its interpretation."
10The Chaldeans answered the king, and said, "There is not a man on
earth who can tell the king's matter; therefore no king, lord, or ruler has
ever asked such things of any magician, astrologer, or Chaldean. 11*It is* a
difficult thing that the king requests, and there is no other who can tell it to
the king except the gods, whose dwelling is not with flesh."
12For this reason the king was angry and very furious, and gave the
command to destroy all the wise *men* of Babylon. 13So the decree went out,
and they began killing the wise *men;* and they sought Daniel and his companions, to kill *them.*

God Reveals Nebuchadnezzar's Dream

14Then with counsel and wisdom Daniel answered Arioch, the captain
of the king's guard, who had gone out to kill the wise *men* of Babylon; 15he
answered and said to Arioch the king's captain, "Why is the decree from
the king so urgent?" Then Arioch made the decision known to Daniel.
16So Daniel went in and asked the king to give him time, that he might
tell the king the interpretation. 17Then Daniel went to his house, and made
the decision known to Hananiah, Mishael, and Azariah, his companions,
18that they might seek mercies from the God of heaven concerning this secret, so that Daniel and his companions might not perish with the rest of
the wise *men* of Babylon. 19Then the secret was revealed to Daniel in a
night vision. So Daniel blessed the God of heaven.
20Daniel answered and said:

"Blessed be the name of God forever and ever,
For wisdom and might are His.
21 And He changes the times and the seasons;
He removes kings and raises up kings;
He gives wisdom to the wise

2:4 [c] The original language of Daniel 2:4b through 7:28 is Aramaic.

LIFE LESSON

Daniel 2:1-49

SITUATION Because the astrologers were unable to interpret his dream, King Nebuchadnezzar ordered all of the wise men to be killed.

OBSERVATION Even though astrologers and psychics don't have all the answers, God does.

INSPIRATION It is one thing to thank God privately for a specific answer to prayer, but what would Daniel say in the presence of the king? Would he be a different man in the presence of Nebuchadnezzar than in his own room and among his friends? He had an opportunity to acquire tremendous prestige and advance his professional life. He was a man of gifts and abilities who now had the opportunity of receiving praise from the ruler of the then-known world.

Yet as he stood in the presence of the pagan king Nebuchadnezzar, Daniel's first statement was much like what he prayed alone. He kept the king waiting to hear the dream and the interpretation until he had given praise to God. "There is a God in heaven who reveals secrets," he told the king (Dan. 2:28).

Throughout the Jews' captivity in Babylon, the phrase *the God of heaven* apparently was the main designation used for the living God, and it contrasted Him with all other gods. He is not a god who is stuck in a temple or a god of one nation. He cannot be limited. He is the God of all the heavens, the God of the universe, the Creator.

We must remember that Daniel's using this term was an affront to Nebuchadnezzar because Daniel was saying in effect, "You have overcome Jerusalem, but the God of heaven, the God that the Jews worship, is a greater God than your god, O Nebuchadnezzar." It took great courage to make this speech.

And having so much opportunity for personal aggrandizement, Daniel discounted his own cleverness . . . ,"The understanding did not come because I am wise and clever, but because the God of Heaven, who is a living God, revealed it to me." One of the big dangers and temptations in

Continued

Christianity today is to be infiltrated with the cult of cleverness, but Daniel carefully removed the praise from himself and placed it upon God.

We now see clearly the answer to our earlier question. Daniel's first action, not only when he was alone but also when he was in the presence of the king and the surrounding culture, was to praise God.

(From *The Complete Works of Francis Schaeffer* by Francis Schaeffer)

APPLICATION Have you ever visited a psychic or fortune-teller? Do you even glance at your horoscope, just for fun? Put the newspaper down. Trust God to lead your future and fulfill his promises to you. He alone knows what the future holds.

EXPLORATION Giving Credit to God—Joshua 6:16; 1 Samuel 1:27; Luke 19:37; John 9:24-33; 11:40-41; Acts 14:8-15.

And knowledge to those who have understanding.
22 He reveals deep and secret things;
He knows what *is* in the darkness,
And light dwells with Him.
23 "I thank You and praise You,
O God of my fathers;
You have given me wisdom and might,
And have now made known to me what we asked of You,
For You have made known to us the king's demand."

Daniel Explains the Dream

24 Therefore Daniel went to Arioch, whom the king had appointed to destroy the wise *men* of Babylon. He went and said thus to him: "Do not destroy
the wise *men* of Babylon; take me before the king, and I will tell the king
the interpretation."
25 Then Arioch quickly brought Daniel before the king, and said thus to
him, "I have found a man of the captives[d] of Judah, who will make known
to the king the interpretation."
26 The king answered and said to Daniel, whose name *was* Belteshazzar,
"Are you able to make known to me the dream which I have seen, and its
interpretation?"
27 Daniel answered in the presence of the king, and said, "The secret
which the king has demanded, the wise *men,* the astrologers, the magicians, and the soothsayers cannot declare to the king. 28 But there is a God
in heaven who reveals secrets, and He has made known to King Nebuchadnezzar what will be in the latter days. Your dream, and the visions of
your head upon your bed, were these: 29 As for you, O king, thoughts came
to your *mind while* on your bed, *about* what would come to pass after this;
and He who reveals secrets has made known to you what will be. 30 But as
for me, this secret has not been revealed to me because I have more wisdom than anyone living, but for *our* sakes who make known the interpretation to the king, and that you may know the thoughts of your heart.
31 "You, O king, were watching; and behold, a great image! This great
image, whose splendor *was* excellent, stood before you; and its form *was*
awesome. 32 This image's head *was* of fine gold, its chest and arms of silver,
its belly and thighs[e] of bronze, 33 its legs of iron, its feet partly of iron and
partly of clay.[f] 34 You watched while a stone was cut out without hands, which
struck the image on its feet of iron and clay, and broke them in pieces.
35 Then the iron, the clay, the bronze, the silver, and the gold were crushed
together, and became like chaff from the summer threshing floors; the
wind carried them away so that no trace of them was found. And the stone
that struck the image became a great mountain and filled the whole earth.
36 "This *is* the dream. Now we will tell the interpretation of it before the
king. 37 You, O king, *are* a king of kings. For the God of heaven has given you
a kingdom, power, strength, and glory; 38 and wherever the children of
men dwell, or the beasts of the field and the birds of the heaven, He has
given *them* into your hand, and has made you ruler over them all—you
are this head of gold. 39 But after you shall arise another kingdom inferior

2:25 [d] Literally *of the sons of the captivity*
2:32 [e] Or *sides*
2:33 [f] Or *baked clay,* and so in verses 34, 35, and 42

to yours; then another, a third kingdom of bronze, which shall rule over all
the earth. 40And the fourth kingdom shall be as strong as iron, inasmuch as
iron breaks in pieces and shatters everything; and like iron that crushes, *that*
kingdom will break in pieces and crush all the others. 41Whereas you saw the
feet and toes, partly of potter's clay and partly of iron, the kingdom shall be
divided; yet the strength of the iron shall be in it, just as you saw the iron
mixed with ceramic clay. 42And *as* the toes of the feet *were* partly of iron and
partly of clay, *so* the kingdom shall be partly strong and partly fragile. 43As you
saw iron mixed with ceramic clay, they will mingle with the seed of men; but
they will not adhere to one another, just as iron does not mix with clay. 44And
in the days of these kings the God of heaven will set up a kingdom which
shall never be destroyed; and the kingdom shall not be left to other people;
it shall break in pieces and consume all these kingdoms, and it shall stand
forever. 45Inasmuch as you saw that the stone was cut out of the mountain
without hands, and that it broke in pieces the iron, the bronze, the clay, the
silver, and the gold—the great God has made known to the king what will
come to pass after this. The dream is certain, and its interpretation is sure."

Daniel and His Friends Promoted

46Then King Nebuchadnezzar fell on his face, prostrate before Daniel,
and commanded that they should present an offering and incense to him.
47The king answered Daniel, and said, "Truly your God *is* the God of gods,
the Lord of kings, and a revealer of secrets, since you could reveal this secret." 48Then the king promoted Daniel and gave him many great gifts;
and he made him ruler over the whole province of Babylon, and chief administrator over all the wise *men* of Babylon. 49Also Daniel petitioned the
king, and he set Shadrach, Meshach, and Abed-Nego over the affairs of the
province of Babylon; but Daniel *sat* in the gate[g] of the king.

The Image of Gold

3 Nebuchadnezzar the king made an image of gold, whose height *was*
sixty cubits *and* its width six cubits. He set it up in the plain of Dura, in
the province of Babylon. 2And King Nebuchadnezzar sent *word* to gather
together the satraps, the administrators, the governors, the counselors, the
treasurers, the judges, the magistrates, and all the officials of the provinces,
to come to the dedication of the image which King Nebuchadnezzar had
set up. 3So the satraps, the administrators, the governors, the counselors,
the treasurers, the judges, the magistrates, and all the officials of the
provinces gathered together for the dedication of the image that King
Nebuchadnezzar had set up; and they stood before the image that
Nebuchadnezzar had set up. 4Then a herald cried aloud: "To you it is commanded, O peoples, nations, and languages, 5*that* at the time you hear the
sound of the horn, flute, harp, lyre, *and* psaltery, in symphony with all
kinds of music, you shall fall down and worship the gold image that King
Nebuchadnezzar has set up; 6and whoever does not fall down and worship
shall be cast immediately into the midst of a burning fiery furnace."
7So at that time, when all the people heard the sound of the horn, flute,
harp, *and* lyre, in symphony with all kinds of music, all the people, nations, and languages fell down *and* worshiped the gold image which King
Nebuchadnezzar had set up.

2:49 *g* That is, the king's court

LIFE LESSON

Daniel 3:1-30

SITUATION Although at one time he praised God, Nebuchadnezzar still promoted idolatry in his kingdom.

OBSERVATION God displayed his surpassing power over all the Babylonian gods when he delievered his people from danger.

INSPIRATION Daniel and his friends were men who stuck their necks out. This was not foolhardiness. They knew what they were doing. They had counted the cost. They had measured the risk. They were well aware what the outcome of their actions would be unless God miraculously intervened, as in fact He did. But these things did not move them. Once they were convinced that their stand was *right*, and that loyalty to their God required them to take it, then, in Oswald Chambers' phrase, they "smilingly washed their hands of the consequences". "We ought to obey God rather than men," said the apostles (Acts 5:29). "Neither count I my life dear unto myself, so that I might finish my course with joy," said Paul (Acts 20:24). This was precisely the spirit of Daniel, Shadrach, Meshach, and Abednego. It is the spirit of all who know God. They may find the determination of the right course to take agonisingly difficult, but once they are clear on it they embrace it boldly and without hesitation. It does not worry them that others of God's people see the matter differently, and do not stand with them. (Were Shadrach, Meshach, and Abednego the only Jews who declined to worship Nebuchadnezzar's image? Nothing in their recorded words suggests that they either knew, or, in the final analysis, cared. They were clear as to what they personally had to do, and that was enough for them.) By this test also we may measure our own knowledge of God.

(From *Knowing God* by J. I. Packer)

Continued

APPLICATION Imagine yourself in a situation, perhaps in another country, where you are on trial for believing in Jesus. Would you stand firm in your faith in threatening circumstances? What would help you to be strong?

EXPLORATION Faithful During Persecution—Acts 5:40-42; Romans 8:17-18; 2 Corinthians 4:10-11; Hebrews 11:24-25; 11:24-25, 35-39; James 5:10-11.

Daniel's Friends Disobey the King

[8]Therefore at that time certain Chaldeans came forward and accused
the Jews. [9]They spoke and said to King Nebuchadnezzar, "O king, live forever! [10]You, O king, have made a decree that everyone who hears the sound
of the horn, flute, harp, lyre, *and* psaltery, in symphony with all kinds of
music, shall fall down and worship the gold image; [11]and whoever does
not fall down and worship shall be cast into the midst of a burning fiery
furnace. [12]There are certain Jews whom you have set over the affairs of the
province of Babylon: Shadrach, Meshach, and Abed-Nego; these men, O king, have not paid due regard to you. They do not serve your gods or worship the gold image which you have set up."

[13]Then Nebuchadnezzar, in rage and fury, gave the command to bring
Shadrach, Meshach, and Abed-Nego. So they brought these men before
the king. [14]Nebuchadnezzar spoke, saying to them, "*Is it* true, Shadrach,
Meshach, and Abed-Nego, *that* you do not serve my gods or worship the
gold image which I have set up? [15]Now if you are ready at the time you hear
the sound of the horn, flute, harp, lyre, *and* psaltery, in symphony with all kinds of music, and you fall down and worship the image which I have made, *good!* But if you do not worship, you shall be cast immediately into the midst of a burning fiery furnace. And who *is* the god who will deliver you from my hands?"

[16]Shadrach, Meshach, and Abed-Nego answered and said to the king,
"O Nebuchadnezzar, we have no need to answer you in this matter. [17]If that
is the case, our God whom we serve is able to deliver us from the burning
fiery furnace, and He will deliver *us* from your hand, O king. [18]But if not,
let it be known to you, O king, that we do not serve your gods, nor will we worship the gold image which you have set up."

Saved in Fiery Trial

[19]Then Nebuchadnezzar was full of fury, and the expression on his face
changed toward Shadrach, Meshach, and Abed-Nego. He spoke and commanded that they heat the furnace seven times more than it was usually
heated. [20]And he commanded certain mighty men of valor who *were* in his
army to bind Shadrach, Meshach, and Abed-Nego, *and* cast *them* into the
burning fiery furnace. [21]Then these men were bound in their coats, their
trousers, their turbans, and their *other* garments, and were cast into the
midst of the burning fiery furnace. [22]Therefore, because the king's command was urgent, and the furnace exceedingly hot, the flame of the fire
killed those men who took up Shadrach, Meshach, and Abed-Nego. [23]And
these three men, Shadrach, Meshach, and Abed-Nego, fell down bound into the midst of the burning fiery furnace.

[24]Then King Nebuchadnezzar was astonished; and he rose in haste *and* spoke, saying to his counselors, "Did we not cast three men bound into the midst of the fire?"

They answered and said to the king, "True, O king."

[25]"Look!" he answered, "I see four men loose, walking in the midst of the fire; and they are not hurt, and the form of the fourth is like the Son of God."[h]

Nebuchadnezzar Praises God

[26]Then Nebuchadnezzar went near the mouth of the burning fiery furnace

3:25 [h] Or *a son of the gods*

and spoke, saying, "Shadrach, Meshach, and Abed-Nego, servants of the
Most High God, come out, and come *here*." Then Shadrach, Meshach, and
Abed-Nego came from the midst of the fire. 27 And the satraps, administrators, governors, and the king's counselors gathered together, and they
saw these men on whose bodies the fire had no power; the hair of their
head was not singed nor were their garments affected, and the smell of fire
was not on them.
28 Nebuchadnezzar spoke, saying, "Blessed be the God of Shadrach,
Meshach, and Abed-Nego, who sent His Angel[i] and delivered His servants
who trusted in Him, and they have frustrated the king's word, and yielded
their bodies, that they should not serve nor worship any god except their
own God! 29 Therefore I make a decree that any people, nation, or language
which speaks anything amiss against the God of Shadrach, Meshach, and
Abed-Nego shall be cut in pieces, and their houses shall be made an ash
heap; because there is no other God who can deliver like this."
30 Then the king promoted Shadrach, Meshach, and Abed-Nego in the
province of Babylon.

Nebuchadnezzar's Second Dream

4 Nebuchadnezzar the king,

To all peoples, nations, and languages that dwell in
all the earth:

Peace be multiplied to you.

2 I thought it good to declare the signs and wonders that the Most
High God has worked for me.

3 How great *are* His signs,
And how mighty His wonders!
His kingdom *is* an everlasting kingdom,
And His dominion *is* from generation to generation.

4 I, Nebuchadnezzar, was at rest in my house, and flourishing in my
palace. 5 I saw a dream which made me afraid, and the thoughts on
my bed and the visions of my head troubled me. 6 Therefore I issued
a decree to bring in all the wise *men* of Babylon before me, that
they might make known to me the interpretation of the dream.
7 Then the magicians, the astrologers, the Chaldeans, and the
soothsayers came in, and I told them the dream; but they did not
make known to me its interpretation. 8 But at last Daniel came
before me (his name *is* Belteshazzar, according to the name of my
god; in him *is* the Spirit of the Holy God), and I told the dream
before him, *saying*: 9 "Belteshazzar, chief of the magicians, because
I know that the Spirit of the Holy God *is* in you, and no secret
troubles you, explain to me the visions of my dream that I have
seen, and its interpretation.

10 "These *were* the visions of my head *while* on my bed:
I was looking, and behold,
A tree in the midst of the earth,

3:28 [i] Or *angel*

LIFE LESSON

Daniel 4:1-37

SITUATION When King Nebuchadnezzar had a strange dream, he asked Daniel to interpret it.

OBSERVATION God has an eternal kingdom. He brings earthly kings under his control.

INSPIRATION It is quite evident that Daniel loved this reprobate. God had revealed to him the future of his friend, Nebuchadnezzar, through this tragic, terrible dream. As he wrestled with the meaning of the dream, he didn't want to tell the king what he had learned. He was undoubtedly very troubled when he said, "My lord, if only the dream applied to your enemies and its meaning to your adversaries!" (Daniel 4:19).

Daniel gives us a superb pattern of how to teach the judgment of God to people. It needs to be done with a broken heart, with a true concern, pointing out the consequences with mercy. I have a lot of friends in the ministry who can't wait to get to the passages on judgment, because they come on with great vengeance. One thing is missing—the tears.

Years ago in London there was a large gathering of notables for a concert. One of the invited guests was a famous preacher, Caesar Milan. A young lady charmed the audience that night with her singing. After the concert Milan went up to her and graciously, but very boldly, said to her, "I thought as I listened to you tonight how tremendously the cause of Christ would be benefited if your talents were dedicated to His cause. You know, young lady, you are a sinner in the sight of God, but I am glad to tell you that the blood of Jesus can cleanse you from all sin."

The lady became so angry at the preacher that she stomped her feet and walked away. As she was leaving he said, "I mean no offense. I will pray that God's Spirit will convict you."

Now that's not exactly my style of witnessing, but here's the rest of the story. The young lady went home, but she couldn't sleep. The face of the preacher appeared before her, and his words rang through her mind. About

Continued

two o'clock in the morning she got out of bed, took a pencil and piece of paper, and with tears rolling down her face, Charlotte Elliot wrote:

Just as I am without one plea,
But that Thy blood was shed for me,
And that Thou bidst me come to Thee,
O Lamb of God, I come, I come.

That song has been sung by choirs throughout the world as an invitation to accept Jesus Christ. . . . A few words by a man who preached the judgment of God with a broken heart resulted in tens of thousands of new Christians declaring their faith. I wonder what would happen if that would be our modus operandi in the ministry today. (From *The Handwriting on the Wall* by David Jeremiah)

APPLICATION Choose one or two people you have read about in the newspaper the past week and pray for God's Holy Spirit to convict them of sin and reveal Christ to them.

EXPLORATION Concern for Others—Luke 19:41; Galatians 6:1; Hebrews 3:12-13; 12:14-16; James 5:19-20.

And its height was great.
11 The tree grew and became strong;
Its height reached to the heavens,
And it could be seen to the ends of all the earth.
12 Its leaves *were* lovely,
Its fruit abundant,
And in it *was* food for all.
The beasts of the field found shade under it,
The birds of the heavens dwelt in its branches,
And all flesh was fed from it.

13 "I saw in the visions of my head *while* on my bed, and there was a
watcher, a holy one, coming down from heaven. 14 He cried aloud
and said thus:

'Chop down the tree and cut off its branches,
Strip off its leaves and scatter its fruit.
Let the beasts get out from under it,
And the birds from its branches.
15 Nevertheless leave the stump and roots in the earth,
Bound with a band of iron and bronze,
In the tender grass of the field.
Let it be wet with the dew of heaven,
And *let* him graze with the beasts
On the grass of the earth.
16 Let his heart be changed from *that of* a man,
Let him be given the heart of a beast,
And let seven times[j] pass over him.

17 'This decision *is* by the decree of the watchers,
And the sentence by the word of the holy ones,
In order that the living may know
That the Most High rules in the kingdom of men,
Gives it to whomever He will,
And sets over it the lowest of men.'

18 "This dream I, King Nebuchadnezzar, have seen. Now you,
Belteshazzar, declare its interpretation, since all the wise *men* of
my kingdom are not able to make known to me the interpretation;
but you *are* able, for the Spirit of the Holy God *is* in you."

Daniel Explains the Second Dream

19 Then Daniel, whose name was Belteshazzar, was astonished for a
time, and his thoughts troubled him. *So* the king spoke, and said,
"Belteshazzar, do not let the dream or its interpretation trouble you."
Belteshazzar answered and said, "My lord, *may* the dream concern
those who hate you, and its interpretation concern your enemies!

20 "The tree that you saw, which grew and became strong, whose
height reached to the heavens and which *could be seen* by all the
earth, 21 whose leaves *were* lovely and its fruit abundant, in which
was food for all, under which the beasts of the field dwelt, and in

4:16 *j* Possibly *seven years,* and so in verses 23, 25, and 32

whose branches the birds of the heaven had
their home— [22]it *is* you, O king, who have
grown and become strong; for your greatness
has grown and reaches to the heavens, and
your dominion to the end of the earth.

23 "And inasmuch as the king saw a watcher, a
holy one, coming down from heaven and
saying, 'Chop down the tree and destroy it, but
leave its stump and roots in the earth, *bound*
with a band of iron and bronze in the tender
grass of the field; let it be wet with the dew of
heaven, and let him graze with the beasts of the
field, till seven times pass over him'; [24]this is
the interpretation, O king, and this is the decree
of the Most High, which has come upon my
lord the king: [25]They shall drive you from men,
your dwelling shall be with the beasts of the
field, and they shall make you eat grass like oxen.
They shall wet you with the dew of heaven,
and seven times shall pass over you, till you
know that the Most High rules in the kingdom
of men, and gives it to whomever He chooses.

26 "And inasmuch as they gave the command to
leave the stump *and* roots of the tree, your
kingdom shall be assured to you, after you come
to know that Heaven rules. [27]Therefore, O king,
let my advice be acceptable to you; break off
your sins by *being* righteous, and your iniquities
by showing mercy to *the* poor. Perhaps there
may be a lengthening of your prosperity."

Nebuchadnezzar's Humiliation

28 All *this* came upon King Nebuchadnezzar. [29]At
the end of the twelve months he was walking
about the royal palace of Babylon. [30]The king
spoke, saying, "Is not this great Babylon, that I
have built for a royal dwelling by my mighty
power and for the honor of my majesty?"

31 While the word *was still* in the king's mouth, a
voice fell from heaven: "King Nebuchadnezzar,
to you it is spoken: the kingdom has departed
from you! [32]And they shall drive you from
men, and your dwelling *shall be* with the
beasts of the field. They shall make you eat
grass like oxen; and seven times shall pass
over you, until you know that the Most High
rules in the kingdom of men, and gives it to
whomever He chooses."

33 That very hour the word was fulfilled concerning
Nebuchadnezzar; he was driven from men
and ate grass like oxen; his body was wet with
the dew of heaven till his hair had grown like
eagles' *feathers* and his nails like birds' *claws.*

Nebuchadnezzar Praises God

34 And at the end of the time[k] I, Nebuchadnezzar,
lifted my eyes to heaven, and my understanding
returned to me; and I blessed the Most High
and praised and honored Him who lives forever:

For His dominion *is* an everlasting dominion,
And His kingdom *is* from generation
to generation.

35 All the inhabitants of the earth *are* reputed
as nothing;
He does according to His will in the army
of heaven
And *among* the inhabitants of the earth.
No one can restrain His hand
Or say to Him, "What have You done?"

36 At the same time my reason returned to me,
and for the glory of my kingdom, my honor
and splendor returned to me. My counselors
and nobles resorted to me, I was restored to
my kingdom, and excellent majesty was added
to me. [37]Now I, Nebuchadnezzar, praise and
extol and honor the King of heaven, all of whose
works *are* truth, and His ways justice. And
those who walk in pride He is able to put down.

Belshazzar's Feast

5 Belshazzar the king made a great feast for a thousand of his lords, and drank wine in the presence
of the thousand. [2]While he tasted the wine, Belshazzar
gave the command to bring the gold and silver vessels
which his father Nebuchadnezzar had taken from the
temple which *had been* in Jerusalem, that the king
and his lords, his wives, and his concubines might
drink from them. [3]Then they brought the gold vessels
that had been taken from the temple of the house of
God which *had been* in Jerusalem; and the king and
his lords, his wives, and his concubines drank from
them. [4]They drank wine, and praised the gods of gold
and silver, bronze and iron, wood and stone.
[5]In the same hour the fingers of a man's hand appeared and wrote opposite the lampstand on the plaster of the wall of the king's palace; and the king saw

4:34 [k] Literally *days*

Life Lesson
Daniel 5:1-31

SITUATION At the height of his power, Belshazzar, King of Assyria, was judged by God for his corrupt and worldly lifestyle, which included desecrating the temple goblets in a wild party. A mysterious hand wrote a cryptic message on the wall of the Assyrian palace. Only Daniel could translate the message. The message told of the imminent fall of the Assyrian Empire.

OBSERVATION Materialism is not the answer to a fulfilled life. Trust only in God.

INSPIRATION Not far from where I live are some of the most luxurious beach communities in all the world. The finest in homes, furnishings, clothing, automobiles, restaurants, artworks, yachts, and craftsmanship can be found in the Newport Beach-Balboa Island-Laguna Beach region. If you ever want to witness materialism on parade, just visit that elegant stretch of real estate.

While driving on the Balboa Peninsula to meet a man for lunch one day, I found myself momentarily behind a bright red Porsche, a beautiful little German-made sports car, meticulously cared for by the owner, who was whipping in and out of traffic. Obviously, he was familiar with the road. As I pulled up behind him to wait for a traffic light, I noticed several appointments on him and his car that revealed he was very much at home in

the part of the hand that wrote. 6Then the king's countenance changed,
and his thoughts troubled him, so that the joints of his hips were loosened
and his knees knocked against each other. 7The king cried aloud to bring
in the astrologers, the Chaldeans, and the soothsayers. The king spoke,
saying to the wise *men* of Babylon, "Whoever reads this writing, and tells
me its interpretation, shall be clothed with purple and *have* a chain of gold
around his neck; and he shall be the third ruler in the kingdom." 8Now all
the king's wise *men* came, but they could not read the writing, or make
known to the king its interpretation. 9Then King Belshazzar was greatly
troubled, his countenance was changed, and his lords were astonished.
10The queen, because of the words of the king and his lords, came to the
banquet hall. The queen spoke, saying, "O king, live forever! Do not let your
thoughts trouble you, nor let your countenance change. 11There is a man
in your kingdom in whom *is* the Spirit of the Holy God. And in the days of
your father, light and understanding and wisdom, like the wisdom of the
gods, were found in him; and King Nebuchadnezzar your father—your father the king—made him chief of the magicians, astrologers, Chaldeans,
and soothsayers. 12Inasmuch as an excellent spirit, knowledge, understanding, interpreting dreams, solving riddles, and explaining enigmas[l]
were found in this Daniel, whom the king named Belteshazzar, now let
Daniel be called, and he will give the interpretation."

The Writing on the Wall Explained

13Then Daniel was brought in before the king. The king spoke, and said
to Daniel, "*Are* you that Daniel who is one of the captives[m] from Judah,
whom my father the king brought from Judah? 14I have heard of you, that
the Spirit of God *is* in you, and *that* light and understanding and excellent
wisdom are found in you. 15Now the wise *men,* the astrologers, have been
brought in before me, that they should read this writing and make known
to me its interpretation, but they could not give the interpretation of the
thing. 16And I have heard of you, that you can give interpretations and explain enigmas. Now if you can read the writing and make known to me its
interpretation, you shall be clothed with purple and *have* a chain of gold
around your neck, and shall be the third ruler in the kingdom."
17Then Daniel answered, and said before the king, "Let your gifts be for
yourself, and give your rewards to another; yet I will read the writing to the
king, and make known to him the interpretation. 18O king, the Most High
God gave Nebuchadnezzar your father a kingdom and majesty, glory and
honor. 19And because of the majesty that He gave him, all peoples, nations,
and languages trembled and feared before him. Whomever he wished, he
executed; whomever he wished, he kept alive; whomever he wished, he set
up; and whomever he wished, he put down. 20But when his heart was lifted
up, and his spirit was hardened in pride, he was deposed from his kingly
throne, and they took his glory from him. 21Then he was driven from the
sons of men, his heart was made like the beasts, and his dwelling *was* with
the wild donkeys. They fed him with grass like oxen, and his body was wet
with the dew of heaven, till he knew that the Most High God rules in the
kingdom of men, and appoints over it whomever He chooses.
22"But you his son, Belshazzar, have not humbled your heart, although

5:12 [l] Literally *untying knots,* and so in verse 16
5:13 [m] Literally *of the sons of the captivity*

you knew all this. 23And you have lifted yourself up against the Lord of heaven.
They have brought the vessels of His house before you, and you and your
lords, your wives and your concubines, have drunk wine from them. And
you have praised the gods of silver and gold, bronze and iron, wood and
stone, which do not see or hear or know; and the God who *holds* your
breath in His hand and owns all your ways, you have not glorified. 24Then
the fingers[n] of the hand were sent from Him, and this writing was written.
25"And this is the inscription that was written:

MENE,[o] MENE, TEKEL,[p] UPHARSIN.[q]

26This *is* the interpretation of *each* word. MENE: God has numbered your
kingdom, and finished it; 27TEKEL: You have been weighed in the balances,
and found wanting; 28PERES: Your kingdom has been divided, and given to
the Medes and Persians."[r] 29Then Belshazzar gave the command, and they
clothed Daniel with purple and *put* a chain of gold around his neck, and
made a proclamation concerning him that he should be the third ruler in
the kingdom.

Belshazzar's Fall

30That very night Belshazzar, king of the Chaldeans, was slain. 31And
Darius the Mede received the kingdom, *being* about sixty-two years old.

The Plot Against Daniel

6 It pleased Darius to set over the kingdom one hundred and twenty
satraps, to be over the whole kingdom; 2and over these, three governors,
of whom Daniel *was* one, that the satraps might give account to them, so
that the king would suffer no loss. 3Then this Daniel distinguished himself
above the governors and satraps, because an excellent spirit *was* in him;
and the king gave thought to setting him over the whole realm. 4So the
governors and satraps sought to find *some* charge against Daniel concerning the kingdom; but they could find no charge or fault, because he *was*
faithful; nor was there any error or fault found in him. 5Then these men said,
"We shall not find any charge against this Daniel unless we find *it* against
him concerning the law of his God."
6So these governors and satraps thronged before the king, and said thus to
him: "King Darius, live forever! 7All the governors of the kingdom, the administrators and satraps, the counselors and advisors, have consulted together
to establish a royal statute and to make a firm decree, that whoever petitions any god or man for thirty days, except you, O king, shall be cast into
the den of lions. 8Now, O king, establish the decree and sign the writing, so
that it cannot be changed, according to the law of the Medes and Persians,
which does not alter." 9Therefore King Darius signed the written decree.

Daniel in the Lions' Den

10Now when Daniel knew that the writing was signed, he went home.
And in his upper room, with his windows open toward Jerusalem, he
knelt down on his knees three times that day, and prayed and gave thanks
before his God, as was his custom since early days.

5:24 [n] Literally *palm*
5:25 [o] Literally *a mina* (50 shekels) from the verb "to number" [p] Literally *a shekel* from the verb "to weigh" [q] Literally *and half-shekels* from the verb "to divide"
5:28 [r] Aramaic *Paras,* consonant with *Peres*

the chic scene. As I smiled at his clever license plate, personalized, of course, I caught a glimpse of the lettered frame that bordered it—which told me volumes about the man's lifestyle, had I had any doubt up to that point. It contained eight words: *He who dies with the most toys wins!* That, friends and neighbors, is "materialism to the max," as some teenagers would say. Before we can ever expect to build a life that is meaningful and fulfilling, we must see the futility of materialism. . . .

The idea, then, is to live a pure and godly life, walking in righteousness and letting the power of the Spirit flow through us. Because God's grace frees us from the guilt of sin, we can be plugged into His liberating power. We are free! Now that is the way to walk. And I'll tell you, it is a marvelous way to live. Talk about having a blast!

(From *Living on the Ragged Edge* by Charles Swindoll)

APPLICATION Give God the respect and honor he is due. Look for his help in difficult times, rather than relying on worldly goods and answers whose value is only temporary. Today, pray for help with a problem that material resources cannot solve.

EXPLORATION Materialism—Proverbs 11:28; Ecclesiastes 5:10; Matthew 6:24; Revelation 18:9-10.

Life Lesson

Daniel 6:1-28

SITUATION Daniel's enemies coveted his job and sought to destroy him. They developed a clever scheme to force the king to kill Daniel, but God rescued him.

OBSERVATION God protects those who remain faithful to him. Daniel was not ashamed of his faith and did his best to serve God and the king faithfully.

INSPIRATION I recently read a story of a woman who for years was married to a harsh husband. Each day he would leave her a list of chores to complete before he returned at the end of the day. "Clean the yard. Stack the firewood. Wash the windows. . . ."

If she didn't complete the tasks, she would be greeted with his explosive anger. But even if she did complete the list, he was never satisfied; he would always find inadequacies in her work.

After several years, the husband passed away. Some time later she remarried, this time to a man who lavished her with tenderness and adoration.

One day, while going through a box of old papers, the wife discovered one of her first husband's lists. And as she read the sheet, a realization caused a tear of joy to splash on the paper.

"I'm still doing all these things, and no one has to tell me. I do it because I love him."

That is the unique characteristic of the new kingdom. Its subjects don't work in order to go to heaven; they work because they are going to heaven. Arrogance and fear are replaced with gratitude and joy.

(From *The Applause of Heaven* by Max Lucado)

APPLICATION Because you love God, give honor to those in positions of leadership. Avoid telling cutting jokes about the president. Don't gossip about your boss. Give policemen proper respect. In this way, others may see your love for God.

EXPLORATION Faith—Psalm 27:1; 118:5-9; Habakkuk 2:4; Mark 9:23.

11 Then these men assembled and found Daniel praying and making
supplication before his God. 12 And they went before the king, and spoke
concerning the king's decree: "Have you not signed a decree that every
man who petitions any god or man within thirty days, except you, O king,
shall be cast into the den of lions?"
The king answered and said, "The thing *is* true, according to the law of
the Medes and Persians, which does not alter."
13 So they answered and said before the king, "That Daniel, who is one of
the captives[s] from Judah, does not show due regard for you, O king, or for
the decree that you have signed, but makes his petition three times a day."
14 And the king, when he heard *these* words, was greatly displeased with
himself, and set *his* heart on Daniel to deliver him; and he labored till the
going down of the sun to deliver him. 15 Then these men approached the king,
and said to the king, "Know, O king, that *it is* the law of the Medes and Persians
that no decree or statute which the king establishes may be changed."
16 So the king gave the command, and they brought Daniel and cast *him*
into the den of lions. *But* the king spoke, saying to Daniel, "Your God, whom
you serve continually, He will deliver you." 17 Then a stone was brought and
laid on the mouth of the den, and the king sealed it with his own signet
ring and with the signets of his lords, that the purpose concerning Daniel
might not be changed.

Daniel Saved from the Lions

18 Now the king went to his palace and spent the night fasting; and no
musicians[t] were brought before him. Also his sleep went from him. 19 Then
the king arose very early in the morning and went in haste to the den of
lions. 20 And when he came to the den, he cried out with a lamenting voice
to Daniel. The king spoke, saying to Daniel, "Daniel, servant of the living
God, has your God, whom you serve continually, been able to deliver you
from the lions?"
21 Then Daniel said to the king, "O king, live forever! 22 My God sent His
angel and shut the lions' mouths, so that they have not hurt me, because I
was found innocent before Him; and also, O king, I have done no wrong
before you."
23 Now the king was exceedingly glad for him, and commanded that they
should take Daniel up out of the den. So Daniel was taken up out of the den,
and no injury whatever was found on him, because he believed in his God.

Darius Honors God

24 And the king gave the command, and they brought those men who
had accused Daniel, and they cast *them* into the den of lions—them, their
children, and their wives; and the lions overpowered them, and broke all
their bones in pieces before they ever came to the bottom of the den.
25 Then King Darius wrote:

> To all peoples, nations, and languages that dwell in all the earth:
> Peace be multiplied to you.
>
> 26 I make a decree that in every dominion of my kingdom *men must*
> tremble and fear before the God of Daniel.

6:13 [s] Literally *of the sons of the captivity*
6:18 [t] Exact meaning unknown

For He *is* the living God,
And steadfast forever;
His kingdom *is the one* which shall not be destroyed,
And His dominion *shall endure* to the end.
27 He delivers and rescues,
And He works signs and wonders
In heaven and on earth,
Who has delivered Daniel from the power of the lions.

28So this Daniel prospered in the reign of Darius and in the reign of
Cyrus the Persian.

Vision of the Four Beasts

7 In the first year of Belshazzar king of Babylon, Daniel had a dream and
visions of his head *while* on his bed. Then he wrote down the dream,
telling the main facts.[u]
2Daniel spoke, saying, "I saw in my vision by night, and behold, the four
winds of heaven were stirring up the Great Sea.
3And four great beasts
came up from the sea, each different from the other.
4The first *was* like a
lion, and had eagle's wings. I watched till its wings were plucked off; and it
was lifted up from the earth and made to stand on two feet like a man, and
a man's heart was given to it.
5"And suddenly another beast, a second, like a bear. It was raised up on
one side, and *had* three ribs in its mouth between its teeth. And they said
thus to it: 'Arise, devour much flesh!'
6"After this I looked, and there was another, like a leopard, which had
on its back four wings of a bird. The beast also had four heads, and dominion was given to it.
7"After this I saw in the night visions, and behold, a fourth beast, dreadful and terrible, exceedingly strong. It had huge iron teeth; it was devouring, breaking in pieces, and trampling the residue with its feet. It *was*
different from all the beasts that *were* before it, and it had ten horns.
8I was
considering the horns, and there was another horn, a little one, coming up
among them, before whom three of the first horns were plucked out by the
roots. And there, in this horn, *were* eyes like the eyes of a man, and a
mouth speaking pompous words.

Vision of the Ancient of Days

9 "I watched till thrones were put in place,
And the Ancient of Days was seated;
His garment *was* white as snow,
And the hair of His head *was* like pure wool.
His throne *was* a fiery flame,
Its wheels a burning fire;
10 A fiery stream issued
And came forth from before Him.
A thousand thousands ministered to Him;
Ten thousand times ten thousand stood before Him.
The court[v] was seated,
And the books were opened.

7:1 [u] Literally *the head* (or *chief*) *of the words*
7:10 [v] Or *judgment*

LIFE LESSON

Daniel 7:1-28

SITUATION Through a vision, God told Daniel about the coming of the Messiah and the final judgment. Daniel didn't understand everything he saw, because some of the events would take place five hundred years later.

OBSERVATION God always fulfills his prophecies. Christians can have confidence in him no matter how bleak the world situation may seem.

INSPIRATION Thousands of people today are excited about Bible prophecy. The revelation of what the Bible says about events past, present, and future, has become more prominent in the themes of books, sermons, and conferences. The Second Coming of Christ is becoming a closer and closer reality for those of us who study the Bible and the world scene.

The entire plan for the future has its key in the resurrection. Unless Christ was raised from the dead, there can be no kingdom and no returning King. When the disciples stood at the place Jesus left this earth, which is called the place of ascension, they were given assurance by angels that the Christ of resurrection would be the Christ of returning glory. . . .

The resurrection is an event which prepares us and confirms for us that future event when He will return again. Yes, Jesus Christ is alive.

Obviously Christ's physical resurrection is an essential part of God's plan to save us. Have you given yourself to this living Christ? . . .

If you trust the resurrected Christ as your Lord and Savior, He will be with you when you die, and will give you life with Him forever. Because of the resurrection, you can be "Born Again."

(From *How to Be Born Again* by Billy Graham)

APPLICATION Who tries to predict the future for you? What forecasts do you rely on? If your biggest fears and problems could be solved, would the future really make you happier? Pray that God would fill your heart with assurance of his love and care.

EXPLORATION Prophecy—Deuteronomy 18:21-22; 1 Corinthians 14:1; Revelation 1:3.

11“I watched then because of the sound of the
pompous words which the horn was speaking; I
watched till the beast was slain, and its body destroyed
and given to the burning flame. 12As for the rest of the
beasts, they had their dominion taken away, yet their
lives were prolonged for a season and a time.

13 “I was watching in the night visions,
And behold, *One* like the Son of Man,
Coming with the clouds of heaven!
He came to the Ancient of Days,
And they brought Him near before Him.
14 Then to Him was given dominion and glory
and a kingdom,
That all peoples, nations, and languages
should serve Him.
His dominion *is* an everlasting dominion,
Which shall not pass away,
And His kingdom *the one*
Which shall not be destroyed.

Daniel's Visions Interpreted

15“I, Daniel, was grieved in my spirit within *my* body,
and the visions of my head troubled me. 16I came near
to one of those who stood by, and asked him the truth
of all this. So he told me and made known to me the
interpretation of these things: 17‘Those great beasts,
which are four, *are* four kings[w] *which* arise out of the
earth. 18But the saints of the Most High shall receive the
kingdom, and possess the kingdom forever, even forever and ever.’

19“Then I wished to know the truth about the fourth
beast, which was different from all the others, exceedingly dreadful, *with* its teeth of iron and its nails of
bronze, *which* devoured, broke in pieces, and trampled the residue with its feet; 20and the ten horns that
were on its head, and the other *horn* which came up,
before which three fell, namely, that horn which had
eyes and a mouth which spoke pompous words,
whose appearance *was* greater than his fellows.

21“I was watching; and the same horn was making
war against the saints, and prevailing against them,
22until the Ancient of Days came, and a judgment was
made *in favor* of the saints of the Most High, and the
time came for the saints to possess the kingdom.

23“Thus he said:

‘The fourth beast shall be
A fourth kingdom on earth,
Which shall be different from all
other kingdoms,
And shall devour the whole earth,
Trample it and break it in pieces.
24 The ten horns *are* ten kings
Who shall arise from this kingdom.
And another shall rise after them;
He shall be different from the first *ones,*
And shall subdue three kings.
25 He shall speak *pompous* words against the
Most High,
Shall persecute[x] the saints of the Most High,
And shall intend to change times and law.
Then *the saints* shall be given into his hand
For a time and times and half a time.

26 ‘But the court shall be seated,
And they shall take away his dominion,
To consume and destroy *it* forever.
27 Then the kingdom and dominion,
And the greatness of the kingdoms under the
whole heaven,
Shall be given to the people, the saints of the
Most High.
His kingdom *is* an everlasting kingdom,
And all dominions shall serve and obey Him.’

28“This *is* the end of the account.[y] As for me, Daniel,
my thoughts greatly troubled me, and my countenance changed; but I kept the matter in my heart.”

Vision of a Ram and a Goat

8 In the third year of the reign of King Belshazzar a
vision appeared *to* me—to me, Daniel—after the
one that appeared to me the first time. 2I saw in the vision, and it so happened while I was looking, that I
was in Shushan, the citadel, which *is* in the province
of Elam; and I saw in the vision that I was by the River
Ulai. 3Then I lifted my eyes and saw, and there, standing beside the river, was a ram which had two horns
and the two horns *were* high; but one *was* higher than
the other, and the higher *one* came up last. 4I saw the
ram pushing westward, northward, and southward
so that no animal could withstand him; nor *was there*
any that could deliver from his hand, but he did ac
cording to his will and became great.

5And as I was considering, suddenly a male goa
came from the west, across the surface of the whol
earth, without touching the ground; and the goat *ha*

7:17 [w] Representing their kingdoms (compare verse 23)
7:25 [x] Literally *wear out*
7:28 [y] Literally *the word*

a notable horn between his eyes. [6]Then he came to the ram that had two
horns, which I had seen standing beside the river, and ran at him with furious
power. [7]And I saw him confronting the ram; he was moved with rage against
him, attacked the ram, and broke his two horns. There was no power in the
ram to withstand him, but he cast him down to the ground and trampled
him; and there was no one that could deliver the ram from his hand.
[8]Therefore the male goat grew very great; but when he became strong,
the large horn was broken, and in place of it four notable ones came up toward the four winds of heaven. [9]And out of one of them came a little horn
which grew exceedingly great toward the south, toward the east, and toward the Glorious *Land.* [10]And it grew up to the host of heaven; and it cast
down *some* of the host and *some* of the stars to the ground, and trampled
them. [11]He even exalted *himself* as high as the Prince of the host; and by
him the daily *sacrifices* were taken away, and the place of His sanctuary
was cast down. [12]Because of transgression, an army was given over *to the
horn* to oppose the daily *sacrifices;* and he cast truth down to the ground.
He did *all this* and prospered.
[13]Then I heard a holy one speaking; and *another* holy one said to that
certain *one* who was speaking, "How long *will* the vision *be, concerning* the
daily *sacrifices* and the transgression of desolation, the giving of both the
sanctuary and the host to be trampled underfoot?"
[14]And he said to me, "For two thousand three hundred days;[z] then the
sanctuary shall be cleansed."

Gabriel Interprets the Vision

[15]Then it happened, when I, Daniel, had seen the vision and was seeking
the meaning, that suddenly there stood before me one having the appearance of a man. [16]And I heard a man's voice between *the banks of* the Ulai,
who called, and said, "Gabriel, make this *man* understand the vision."
[17]So he came near where I stood, and when he came I was afraid and fell on
my face; but he said to me, "Understand, son of man, that the vision *refers*
to the time of the end."
[18]Now, as he was speaking with me, I was in a deep sleep with my face to
the ground; but he touched me, and stood me upright. [19]And he said,
"Look, I am making known to you what shall happen in the latter time of
the indignation; for at the appointed time the end *shall be.* [20]The ram
which you saw, having the two horns—*they are* the kings of Media and
Persia. [21]And the male goat *is* the kingdom[a] of Greece. The large horn that
is between its eyes *is* the first king. [22]As for the broken *horn* and the four
that stood up in its place, four kingdoms shall arise out of that nation, but
not with its power.

23 "And in the latter time of their kingdom,
When the transgressors have reached their fullness,
A king shall arise,
Having fierce features,
Who understands sinister schemes.
24 His power shall be mighty, but not by his own power;
He shall destroy fearfully,

8:14 [z] Literally *evening-mornings*
8:21 [a] Literally *king,* representing his kingdom (compare 7:17, 23)

LIFE LESSON

Daniel 8:1-27

SITUATION Daniel's dreams symbolized the future rise and fall of Greece. By overthrowing human power, God would triumph and establish his kingdom.

OBSERVATION God selected certain people to be his prophets in the Old Testament. Through their message, we come to know more about God.

INSPIRATION A further indication that the Bible is the Word of God is in the remarkable number of fulfilled prophecies it contains. These are not vague generalities like those given by modern fortunetellers: "A handsome man will soon come into your life." Such predictions are susceptible to easy misinterpration. Many Bible prophecies are specific in their details, and the authentication and veracity of the prophet rests on them. The Scripture itself makes it clear that fulfilled prophecy is one of the evidences of the supernatural origin of the word of its prophets. . . .

There are various kinds of prophecies. One group has to do with predictions of a coming Messiah, the Lord Jesus Christ. Others have to do with specific historical events, and still others with the Jews. It is very significant that the early disciples quoted the Old Testament prophecies frequently to show that Jesus fulfilled in detail the prophecies made many years earlier. . . . Then there are the remarkable prophecies about the Jewish people, the Israelites. . . .

One cannot gainsay the force of fulfilled prophecy. Many prophecies could not possibly have been written after the event predicted. There are, then, a number of pieces of evidence on which one can reasonably base his belief that the Bible is the Word of God.

(From *Know Why You Believe* by Paul Little)

APPLICATION Many people like to predict the second coming of Jesus Christ, but we cannot rely on radio programs and books that tell the exact date of Christ's return. As interesting as they may be, no guess has ever been right. God alone knows the time of Christ's return. Live every day as if Christ would come back.

EXPLORATION Prophecy—Genesis 41:8; 42:8-9; Daniel 2:1-11; Matthew 2:13.

LIFE LESSON

Daniel 9:1-27

SITUATION While Daniel was in exile, he read Jeremiah 25:11-12 and Jeremiah 29:10. He realized that Israel's seventy-year punishment was almost over. Daniel knew his people had been unfaithful, but he asked God to forgive them. Daniel received another vision about the end times and the fate of Israel.

OBSERVATION God answers our prayers and reveals his plan for us when we ask for guidance.

INSPIRATION How can we worship in prayer? By first reflecting upon who God is and thanking Him for the things He has revealed about Himself. To worship in prayer is to allow our spirits to feast upon what God has revealed concerning His acts in the distant and recent past, and what He has told us about Himself. Slowly, as we review these things in a spirit of thanksgiving and recognition, we can sense our spirits beginning to expand, to take in the broader reality of God's presence and being. Slowly our consciousness is able to accept the fact that the universe about us is not closed or limited, but is in fact as expansive as the Creator meant for it to be. As we enter into worship we remind ourselves of how great He is.

And shall prosper and thrive;
He shall destroy the mighty, and *also* the holy people.

25 "Through his cunning
He shall cause deceit to prosper under his rule;[b]
And he shall exalt *himself* in his heart.
He shall destroy many in *their* prosperity.
He shall even rise against the Prince of princes;
But he shall be broken without *human* means.[c]

26 "And the vision of the evenings and mornings
Which was told is true;
Therefore seal up the vision,
For *it refers* to many days *in the future.*"

27And I, Daniel, fainted and was sick for days; afterward I arose and
went about the king's business. I was astonished by the vision, but no one
understood it.

Daniel's Prayer for the People

9 In the first year of Darius the son of Ahasuerus, of the lineage of the
Medes, who was made king over the realm of the Chaldeans— 2in the
first year of his reign I, Daniel, understood by the books the number of the
years *specified* by the word of the LORD through Jeremiah the prophet, that
He would accomplish seventy years in the desolations of Jerusalem.
3Then I set my face toward the Lord God to make request by prayer and
supplications, with fasting, sackcloth, and ashes. 4And I prayed to the LORD
my God, and made confession, and said, "O Lord, great and awesome
God, who keeps His covenant and mercy with those who love Him, and
with those who keep His commandments, 5we have sinned and committed iniquity, we have done wickedly and rebelled, even by departing from
Your precepts and Your judgments. 6Neither have we heeded Your servants the prophets, who spoke in Your name to our kings and our princes,
to our fathers and all the people of the land. 7O Lord, righteousness *belongs*
to You, but to us shame of face, as *it is* this day—to the men of Judah, to
the inhabitants of Jerusalem and all Israel, those near and those far off in
all the countries to which You have driven them, because of the unfaithfulness which they have committed against You.
8"O Lord, to us *belongs* shame of face, to our kings, our princes, and our
fathers, because we have sinned against You. 9To the Lord our God *belong*
mercy and forgiveness, though we have rebelled against Him. 10We have
not obeyed the voice of the LORD our God, to walk in His laws, which He set
before us by His servants the prophets. 11Yes, all Israel has transgressed
Your law, and has departed so as not to obey Your voice; therefore the
curse and the oath written in the Law of Moses the servant of God have
been poured out on us, because we have sinned against Him. 12And He has
confirmed His words, which He spoke against us and against our judges
who judged us, by bringing upon us a great disaster; for under the whole
heaven such has never been done as what has been done to Jerusalem.
13"As *it is* written in the Law of Moses, all this disaster has come upon us;
yet we have not made our prayer before the LORD our God, that we might

8:25 [b] Literally *hand* [c] Literally *hand*

turn from our iniquities and understand Your truth. 14Therefore the LORD
has kept the disaster in mind, and brought it upon us; for the LORD our God
is righteous in all the works which He does, though we have not obeyed
His voice. 15And now, O Lord our God, who brought Your people out of the
land of Egypt with a mighty hand, and made Yourself a name, as *it is* this
day—we have sinned, we have done wickedly!
16"O Lord, according to all Your righteousness, I pray, let Your anger and
Your fury be turned away from Your city Jerusalem, Your holy mountain;
because for our sins, and for the iniquities of our fathers, Jerusalem and Your
people *are* a reproach to all *those* around us. 17Now therefore, our God, hear
the prayer of Your servant, and his supplications, and for the Lord's sake
cause Your face to shine on Your sanctuary, which is desolate. 18O my God,
incline Your ear and hear; open Your eyes and see our desolations, and the city
which is called by Your name; for we do not present our supplications before
You because of our righteous deeds, but because of Your great mercies. 19O
Lord, hear! O Lord, forgive! O Lord, listen and act! Do not delay for Your own
sake, my God, for Your city and Your people are called by Your name."

The Seventy-Weeks Prophecy

20Now while I *was* speaking, praying, and confessing my sin and the sin
of my people Israel, and presenting my supplication before the LORD my God
for the holy mountain of my God, 21yes, while I *was* speaking in prayer, the
man Gabriel, whom I had seen in the vision at the beginning, being caused
to fly swiftly, reached me about the time of the evening offering. 22And he
informed *me,* and talked with me, and said, "O Daniel, I have now come
forth to give you skill to understand. 23At the beginning of your supplications the command went out, and I have come to tell *you,* for you *are*
greatly beloved; therefore consider the matter, and understand the vision:

24 "Seventy weeks[d] are determined
For your people and for your holy city,
To finish the transgression,
To make an end of[e] sins,
To make reconciliation for iniquity,
To bring in everlasting righteousness,
To seal up vision and prophecy,
And to anoint the Most Holy.

25 "Know therefore and understand,
That from the going forth of the command
To restore and build Jerusalem
Until Messiah the Prince,
There shall be seven weeks and sixty-two weeks;
The street[f] shall be built again, and the wall,[g]
Even in troublesome times.

26 "And after the sixty-two weeks
Messiah shall be cut off, but not for Himself;
And the people of the prince who is to come
Shall destroy the city and the sanctuary.

In the light of God's majesty, we are called to an honesty about ourselves: what we are by contrast. This is the second aspect of prayer: confession. Spiritual discipline calls for a regular acknowledgment of our true nature and the specific acts and attitudes of the recent past that have not been pleasurable to God as He has sought our fellowship and our obedience.

"God be merciful to me a sinner" is an abbreviated version of the prayer of confession. We need the daily humbling experience of being broken before God as we face up to our imperfection, our propensity to seek evil ways. (From *Ordering Your Private World* by Gordon MacDonald)

APPLICATION Fasting reminds us that we are dependent on God. When you need guidance, fast and pray. Whether you fast for part of a day or an entire day, spend the time in prayer and meditation of God's Word.

EXPLORATION Prayer—Genesis 25:21; 2 Chronicles 7:12; Ezra 8:23; Daniel 6:10; Mark 9:29; Philippians 4:6-7.

9:24 [d] Literally *sevens,* and so throughout the chapter [e] Following Qere, Septuagint, Syriac, and Vulgate; Kethib and Theodotion read *To seal up.*
9:25 [f] Or *open square* [g] Or *moat*

The end of it *shall be* with a flood,
And till the end of the war desolations
are determined.
27 Then he shall confirm a covenant with many
for one week;
But in the middle of the week
He shall bring an end to sacrifice and offering.
And on the wing of abominations shall be one
who makes desolate,
Even until the consummation, which
is determined,
Is poured out on the desolate."

Vision of the Glorious Man

10 In the third year of Cyrus king of Persia a message was revealed to Daniel, whose name was
called Belteshazzar. The message *was* true, but the appointed time *was* long;[h] and he understood the message, and had understanding of the vision. 2 In those
days I, Daniel, was mourning three full weeks. 3 I ate
no pleasant food, no meat or wine came into my
mouth, nor did I anoint myself at all, till three whole
weeks were fulfilled.
4 Now on the twenty-fourth day of the first month,
as I was by the side of the great river, that *is,* the Tigris,[i]
5 I lifted my eyes and looked, and behold, a certain man
clothed in linen, whose waist *was* girded with gold of
Uphaz! 6 His body *was* like beryl, his face like the appearance of lightning, his eyes like torches of fire, his arms
and feet like burnished bronze in color, and the sound
of his words like the voice of a multitude.
7 And I, Daniel, alone saw the vision, for the men who
were with me did not see the vision; but a great terror
fell upon them, so that they fled to hide themselves.
8 Therefore I was left alone when I saw this great vision,
and no strength remained in me; for my vigor was
turned to frailty in me, and I retained no strength. 9 Yet
I heard the sound of his words; and while I heard the
sound of his words I was in a deep sleep on my face,
with my face to the ground.

Prophecies Concerning Persia and Greece

10 Suddenly, a hand touched me, which made me
tremble on my knees and *on* the palms of my hands.
11 And he said to me, "O Daniel, man greatly beloved,
understand the words that I speak to you, and stand
upright, for I have now been sent to you." While he
was speaking this word to me, I stood trembling.
12 Then he said to me, "Do not fear, Daniel, for from
the first day that you set your heart to understand, and
to humble yourself before your God, your words were
heard; and I have come because of your words. 13 But the
prince of the kingdom of Persia withstood me twenty-
one days; and behold, Michael, one of the chief princes,
came to help me, for I had been left alone there with the
kings of Persia. 14 Now I have come to make you understand what will happen to your people in the latter
days, for the vision *refers* to *many* days yet *to come.*"
15 When he had spoken such words to me, I turned
my face toward the ground and became speechless.
16 And suddenly, *one* having the likeness of the sons[j] of
men touched my lips; then I opened my mouth and
spoke, saying to him who stood before me, "My lord,
because of the vision my sorrows have overwhelmed
me, and I have retained no strength. 17 For how can
this servant of my lord talk with you, my lord? As for
me, no strength remains in me now, nor is any breath
left in me."
18 Then again, *the one* having the likeness of a man
touched me and strengthened me. 19 And he said, "O
man greatly beloved, fear not! Peace *be* to you; be strong,
yes, be strong!"
So when he spoke to me I was strengthened, and said,
"Let my lord speak, for you have strengthened me."
20 Then he said, "Do you know why I have come to
you? And now I must return to fight with the prince of
Persia; and when I have gone forth, indeed the prince
of Greece will come. 21 But I will tell you what is noted
in the Scripture of Truth. (No one upholds me against
these, except Michael your prince.
11 "Also in the first year of Darius the Mede, I, *even*
I, stood up to confirm and strengthen him.)
2 And now I will tell you the truth: Behold, three more
kings will arise in Persia, and the fourth shall be far
richer than *them* all; by his strength, through his
riches, he shall stir up all against the realm of Greece.
3 Then a mighty king shall arise, who shall rule with
great dominion, and do according to his will. 4 And
when he has arisen, his kingdom shall be broken up
and divided toward the four winds of heaven, but not
among his posterity nor according to his dominion
with which he ruled; for his kingdom shall be uprooted, even for others besides these.

Warring Kings of North and South

5 "Also the king of the South shall become strong, as

10:1 [h] Or *and of great conflict*
10:4 [i] Hebrew *Hiddekel*
10:16 [j] Theodotion and Vulgate read *the son;* Septuagint reads *a hand.*

well as *one* of his princes; and he shall gain power over him and have dominion. His dominion *shall be* a great dominion. 6 And at the end of *some* years
they shall join forces, for the daughter of the king of the South shall go to
the king of the North to make an agreement; but she shall not retain the
power of her authority,[k] and neither he nor his authority[l] shall stand; but
she shall be given up, with those who brought her, and with him who begot
her, and with him who strengthened her in *those* times. 7 But from a branch
of her roots *one* shall arise in his place, who shall come with an army, enter
the fortress of the king of the North, and deal with them and prevail. 8 And
he shall also carry their gods captive to Egypt, with their princes[m] *and* their
precious articles of silver and gold; and he shall continue *more* years than
the king of the North.

9 "Also *the king of the North* shall come to the kingdom of the king of the
South, but shall return to his own land. 10 However his sons shall stir up
strife, and assemble a multitude of great forces; and *one* shall certainly come
and overwhelm and pass through; then he shall return to his fortress and
stir up strife.

11 "And the king of the South shall be moved with rage, and go out and fight
with him, with the king of the North, who shall muster a great multitude;
but the multitude shall be given into the hand of his *enemy.* 12 When he has
taken away the multitude, his heart will be lifted up; and he will cast down
tens of thousands, but he will not prevail. 13 For the king of the North will
return and muster a multitude greater than the former, and shall certainly
come at the end of some years with a great army and much equipment.

14 "Now in those times many shall rise up against the king of the South.
Also, violent men[n] of your people shall exalt themselves in fulfillment of
the vision, but they shall fall. 15 So the king of the North shall come and
build a siege mound, and take a fortified city; and the forces[o] of the South
shall not withstand *him.* Even his choice troops *shall have* no strength to
resist. 16 But he who comes against him shall do according to his own will,
and no one shall stand against him. He shall stand in the Glorious Land
with destruction in his power.[p]

17 "He shall also set his face to enter with the strength of his whole kingdom, and upright ones[q] with him; thus shall he do. And he shall give him
the daughter of women to destroy it; but she shall not stand *with him,* or
be for him. 18 After this he shall turn his face to the coastlands, and shall take
many. But a ruler shall bring the reproach against them to an end; and with
the reproach removed, he shall turn back on him. 19 Then he shall turn his
face toward the fortress of his own land; but he shall stumble and fall, and
not be found.

20 "There shall arise in his place one who imposes taxes *on* the glorious
kingdom; but within a few days he shall be destroyed, but not in anger or
in battle. 21 And in his place shall arise a vile person, to whom they will not
give the honor of royalty; but he shall come in peaceably, and seize the
kingdom by intrigue. 22 With the force[r] of a flood they shall be swept away
from before him and be broken, and also the prince of the covenant. 23 And

11:6 [k] Literally *arm* [l] Literally *arm*
11:8 [m] Or *molded images*
11:14 [n] Or *robbers,* literally *sons of breakage*
11:15 [o] Literally *arms*
11:16 [p] Literally *hand*
11:17 [q] Or *bring equitable terms*
11:22 [r] Literally *arms*

LIFE LESSON

Daniel 10:1–12:13

SITUATION Daniel lived in a time of persecution, but he found comfort in knowing that God transcended the political limits and destiny of Israel.

OBSERVATION Daniel realized that there are events that take place beyond human understanding. Daniel was comforted to know that God will not forget those who follow him.

INSPIRATION In their high expectations of politics, many Christians also misjudge the source of true societal reform. In reality, it is impossible to effect genuine political reform without reforming individual, and eventually, national character.

While it has a moral responsibility to restrain evil, government can never change the hearts and minds of its citizens. Attitudes are forged by spiritual forces, not by legislation. "All history, once you strip the rind off the kernel, is really spiritual," said historian Arnold Toynbee. Values change when spiritual movements stir the hearts of people and when fresh winds of reason stir their minds.
(From *Against the Night* by Charles Colson)

APPLICATION Use your godly values to influence society for good. Become involved in local, state, or national government. Many mayors are eager to appoint local citizens to city boards. Call today and find out how to become more involved.

EXPLORATION God's Power and Love—Lamentations 3:1-24; Psalm 36; John 13:1; 1 John 3:1-3.

after the league *is made* with him he shall act deceitfully, for he shall come up and become strong with a small *number of* people. 24 He shall enter peaceably, even into the richest places of the province; and he shall do *what* his fathers have not done, nor his forefathers: he shall disperse among them the plunder, spoil, and riches; and he shall devise his plans against the strongholds, but *only* for a time.

25 "He shall stir up his power and his courage against the king of the South with a great army. And the king of the South shall be stirred up to battle with a very great and mighty army; but he shall not stand, for they shall devise plans against him. 26 Yes, those who eat of the portion of his delicacies shall destroy him; his army shall be swept away, and many shall fall down slain. 27 Both these kings' hearts *shall be* bent on evil, and they shall speak lies at the same table; but it shall not prosper, for the end *will* still *be* at the appointed time. 28 While returning to his land with great riches, his heart shall be *moved* against the holy covenant; so he shall do *damage* and return to his own land.

The Northern King's Blasphemies

29 "At the appointed time he shall return and go toward the south; but it shall not be like the former or the latter. 30 For ships from Cyprus[s] shall come against him; therefore he shall be grieved, and return in rage against the holy covenant, and do *damage.*

"So he shall return and show regard for those who forsake the holy covenant. 31 And forces[t] shall be mustered by him, and they shall defile the sanctuary fortress; then they shall take away the daily *sacrifices,* and place *there* the abomination of desolation. 32 Those who do wickedly against the covenant he shall corrupt with flattery; but the people who know their God shall be strong, and carry out *great exploits.* 33 And those of the people who understand shall instruct many; yet *for many* days they shall fall by sword and flame, by captivity and plundering. 34 Now when they fall, they shall be aided with a little help; but many shall join with them by intrigue. 35 And *some* of those of understanding shall fall, to refine them, purify *them,* and make *them* white, *until* the time of the end; because *it is* still for the appointed time.

36 "Then the king shall do according to his own will: he shall exalt and magnify himself above every god, shall speak blasphemies against the God of gods, and shall prosper till the wrath has been accomplished; for what has been determined shall be done. 37 He shall regard neither the God[u] of his fathers nor the desire of women, nor regard any god; for he shall exalt himself above *them* all. 38 But in their place he shall honor a god of fortresses; and a god which his fathers did not know he shall honor with gold and silver, with precious stones and pleasant things. 39 Thus he shall act against the strongest fortresses with a foreign god, which he shall acknowledge, *and* advance *its* glory; and he shall cause them to rule over many, and divide the land for gain.

The Northern King's Conquests

40 "At the time of the end the king of the South shall attack him; and the king of the North shall come against him like a whirlwind, with chariots, horsemen, and with many ships; and he shall enter the countries, overwhelm *them,* and pass through. 41 He shall also enter the Glorious Land, and many *countries* shall be overthrown; but these shall escape from his hand: Edom, Moab, and the prominent people of Ammon. 42 He shall stretch out his hand against the countries, and the land of Egypt shall not escape. 43 He shall have power over the treasures of gold and silver, and over all the precious things of Egypt; also the Libyans and Ethiopians *shall follow* at his heels. 44 But news from the east and the north shall trouble him; therefore he shall go out with great fury to destroy and annihilate many. 45 And he shall plant the tents of his palace between the seas and the glorious holy mountain; yet he shall come to his end, and no one will help him.

Prophecy of the End Time

12 "At that time Michael shall stand up,
The great prince who stands *watch* over the sons of your people;
And there shall be a time of trouble,
Such as never was since there was a nation,
Even to that time.
And at that time your people shall be delivered,
Every one who is found written in the book.
2 And many of those who sleep in the dust of the earth shall awake,
Some to everlasting life,
Some to shame *and* everlasting contempt.
3 Those who are wise shall shine
Like the brightness of the firmament,
And those who turn many to righteousness
Like the stars forever and ever.

11:30 [s] Hebrew *Kittim,* western lands, especially Cyprus
11:31 [t] Literally *arms*
11:37 [u] Or *gods*

4"But you, Daniel, shut up the words, and seal the
book until the time of the end; many shall run to and
fro, and knowledge shall increase."

5Then I, Daniel, looked; and there stood two others,
one on this riverbank and the other on that riverbank.
6And *one* said to the man clothed in linen, who *was*
above the waters of the river, "How long shall the fulfillment of these wonders *be?*"

7Then I heard the man clothed in linen, who *was*
above the waters of the river, when he held up his right
hand and his left hand to heaven, and swore by Him who
lives forever, that *it shall be* for a time, times, and half *a
time;* and when the power of the holy people has been
completely shattered, all these *things* shall be finished.

8Although I heard, I did not understand. Then I said,
"My lord, what *shall be* the end of these *things?*"

9And he said, "Go *your way,* Daniel, for the words
are closed up and sealed till the time of the end. 10Many
shall be purified, made white, and refined, but the
wicked shall do wickedly; and none of the wicked
shall understand, but the wise shall understand.

11"And from the time *that* the daily *sacrifice* is taken
away, and the abomination of desolation is set up,
there shall be one thousand two hundred and ninety
days. 12Blessed *is* he who waits, and comes to the one
thousand three hundred and thirty-five days.

13"But you, go *your way* till the end; for you shall rest,
and will arise to your inheritance at the end of the days."

The Book of

HOSEA

INTRODUCTION

"It's only puppy love," adults used to say, commenting on your early love life. You wanted to shout back, "No! This is the real thing!" And it *was* real for you, the puppy. But soon you forgot that love and moved on to another.

A few years later in high school, you found another and were head-over-heels-in-love and going steady. You pledged devotion to each other—emotions and sexual attraction pulled you two together. And when the breakup occurred, you thought you would die . . . but you didn't. In fact, you survived to experience several other relationships, some pretty serious. Through each experience you learned a bit more about love—true love.

Today you chuckle at youthful infatuation and have to bite your tongue to avoid saying something about puppy love. Over the years, you have learned that real love—true love—is more than emotions, sex, fun, dating, and feeling good. Real love—lasting love—involves giving, serving, listening, and being there. At the foundation lies commitment: the solid decision to stick with that person through everything—no matter what.

The book of Hosea is a love story involving a very unlikely couple: Hosea, the prophet of God, and Gomer, a prostitute. Hosea marries Gomer, even though he knows that she will be unfaithful to him. And when she is . . . well, I'll let you read for yourself.

This profound book, however, holds a deeper love story—God's love for his people, mirrored by this very human couple. As you read, look for traces of yourself in Gomer and her actions. And watch God, through Hosea, display true love.

LIFE LESSON
Hosea 1:1–3:5

SITUATION Hosea illustrates God's enduring desire for his people. The first three chapters, Hosea's personal life story, symbolize God's relationship with Israel.

OBSERVATION When we turn away from God, he does not wait for us to come back to him. He pursues us and desires that we be reunited with him.

INSPIRATION In his book, *Sky Pilot*, Ralph Conner tells of a young man who wandered from a good home in Scotland to one of the ranches in the wild west. One day, as the pilot was making his rounds and going from shack to shack, he heard someone singing Psalm 23. He made his way to the shack from whence the sound was coming, and there found the young man dying. He had been brought up in a good Christian home, but now he lay dying an early death through the sins he had committed.

The pilot spoke tenderly to the lad, and then he was asked to read a letter which had come to the boy from his mother that very day. He read it, and the letter closed something like this: "And oh! Davie laddie, if ever your heart should turn homeward, remember the door stands widely open, and there is nothing but joy that you will bring to us all."

That is the distinctive message of the parable of the prodigal son. There is joy in the presence of the angels of God over one sinner who repents.

(Told by F. W. Boreham in *The Prodigal*. From *Prodigals and Those Who Love Them* by Ruth Bell Graham)

APPLICATION Have you ever wandered from God the way Gomer did from Hosea? How did God initiate reconciliation with you? Did he convict you or use friends to encourage you? Thank God for his faithfulness to bring you back into fellowship with him.

EXPLORATION Endurance—Matthew 10:22; Mark 13:13; Hebrews 3:6; 2 Timothy 4:5-8; Revelation 14:12.

The word of the LORD that came to Hosea the son of Beeri, in the days of Uzziah, Jotham, Ahaz, *and* Hezekiah, kings of Judah, and in the days of Jeroboam the son of Joash, king of Israel.

The Family of Hosea

2When the LORD began to speak by Hosea, the LORD said to Hosea:

"Go, take yourself a wife of harlotry
And children of harlotry,
For the land has committed great harlotry
By departing from the LORD."

3So he went and took Gomer the daughter of Diblaim, and she conceived
and bore him a son. 4Then the LORD said to him:

"Call his name Jezreel,
For in a little *while*
I will avenge the bloodshed of Jezreel on the house of Jehu,
And bring an end to the kingdom of the house of Israel.
5 It shall come to pass in that day
That I will break the bow of Israel in the Valley of Jezreel."

6And she conceived again and bore a daughter. Then *God* said to him:

"Call her name Lo-Ruhamah,[a]
For I will no longer have mercy on the house of Israel,
But I will utterly take them away.[b]
7 Yet I will have mercy on the house of Judah,
Will save them by the LORD their God,
And will not save them by bow,
Nor by sword or battle,
By horses or horsemen."

8Now when she had weaned Lo-Ruhamah, she conceived and bore a
son. 9Then *God* said:

"Call his name Lo-Ammi,[c]
For you *are* not My people,
And I will not be your *God.*

The Restoration of Israel

10 "Yet the number of the children of Israel
Shall be as the sand of the sea,
Which cannot be measured or numbered.
And it shall come to pass
In the place where it was said to them,
'You *are* not My people,'[d]
There it shall be said to them,
'*You are* sons of the living God.'
11 Then the children of Judah and the children of Israel
Shall be gathered together,
And appoint for themselves one head;

1:6 [a] Literally *No-Mercy* [b] Or *That I may forgive them at all*
1:9 [c] Literally *Not-My-People*
1:10 [d] Hebrew *lo-ammi* (compare verse 9)

And they shall come up out of the land,
For great *will be* the day of Jezreel!

2 Say to your brethren, 'My people,'[e]
And to your sisters, 'Mercy[f] *is shown*.'

God's Unfaithful People

2 "Bring charges against your mother, bring charges;
For she *is* not My wife, nor *am* I her Husband!
Let her put away her harlotries from her sight,
And her adulteries from between her breasts;
3 Lest I strip her naked
And expose her, as in the day she was born,
And make her like a wilderness,
And set her like a dry land,
And slay her with thirst.

4 "I will not have mercy on her children,
For they *are* the children of harlotry.
5 For their mother has played the harlot;
She who conceived them has behaved shamefully.
For she said, 'I will go after my lovers,
Who give *me* my bread and my water,
My wool and my linen,
My oil and my drink.'

6 "Therefore, behold,
I will hedge up your way with thorns,
And wall her in,
So that she cannot find her paths.
7 She will chase her lovers,
But not overtake them;
Yes, she will seek them, but not find *them*.
Then she will say,
'I will go and return to my first husband,
For then *it was* better for me than now.'
8 For she did not know
That I gave her grain, new wine, and oil,
And multiplied her silver and gold—
Which they prepared for Baal.

9 "Therefore I will return and take away
My grain in its time
And My new wine in its season,
And will take back My wool and My linen,
Given to cover her nakedness.
10 Now I will uncover her lewdness in the sight of her lovers,
And no one shall deliver her from My hand.
11 I will also cause all her mirth to cease,
Her feast days,
Her New Moons,
Her Sabbaths—
All her appointed feasts.

12 "And I will destroy her vines and her fig trees,
Of which she has said,
'These *are* my wages that my lovers have given me.'
So I will make them a forest,
And the beasts of the field shall eat them.
13 I will punish her
For the days of the Baals to which she burned incense.
She decked herself with her earrings and jewelry,
And went after her lovers;
But Me she forgot," says the LORD.

God's Mercy on His People

14 "Therefore, behold, I will allure her,
Will bring her into the wilderness,
And speak comfort to her.
15 I will give her her vineyards from there,
And the Valley of Achor as a door of hope;
She shall sing there,
As in the days of her youth,
As in the day when she came up from the land of Egypt.

16 "And it shall be, in that day,"
Says the LORD,
"*That* you will call Me 'My Husband,'[g]
And no longer call Me 'My Master,'[h]
17 For I will take from her mouth the names of the Baals,
And they shall be remembered by their name no more.
18 In that day I will make a covenant for them
With the beasts of the field,
With the birds of the air,
And *with* the creeping things of the ground.
Bow and sword of battle I will shatter from the earth,
To make them lie down safely.

19 "I will betroth you to Me forever;
Yes, I will betroth you to Me
In righteousness and justice,
In lovingkindness and mercy;

2:1 [e] Hebrew *Ammi* (compare 1:9, 10) [f] Hebrew *Ruhamah* (compare 1:6)
2:16 [g] Hebrew *Ishi* [h] Hebrew *Baali*

20 I will betroth you to Me in faithfulness,
And you shall know the LORD.

21 "It shall come to pass in that day
That I will answer," says the LORD;
"I will answer the heavens,
And they shall answer the earth.
22 The earth shall answer
With grain,
With new wine,
And with oil;
They shall answer Jezreel.[i]
23 Then I will sow her for Myself in the earth,
And I will have mercy on *her who had*
not obtained mercy;[j]
Then I will say to *those who were*
not My people,[k]
'You *are* My people!'
And they shall say, '*You are* my God!'"

Israel Will Return to God

3 Then the LORD said to me, "Go again, love a woman
who is loved by a lover[l] and is committing adultery, just like the love of the LORD for the children of Israel, who look to other gods and love *the* raisin cakes
of the pagans."
2So I bought her for myself for fifteen *shekels* of silver,
and one and one-half homers of barley. 3And I said to
her, "You shall stay with me many days; you shall not
play the harlot, nor shall you have a man—so, too, *will*
I *be* toward you."
4For the children of Israel shall abide many days without king or prince, without sacrifice or sacred pillar,
without ephod or teraphim. 5Afterward the children
of Israel shall return and seek the LORD their God and
David their king. They shall fear the LORD and His
goodness in the latter days.

God's Charge Against Israel

4 Hear the word of the LORD,
You children of Israel,
For the LORD *brings* a charge against
the inhabitants of the land:

"There is no truth or mercy
Or knowledge of God in the land.
2 *By* swearing and lying,
Killing and stealing and committing adultery,
They break all restraint,
With bloodshed upon bloodshed.
3 Therefore the land will mourn;
And everyone who dwells there will waste away
With the beasts of the field
And the birds of the air;
Even the fish of the sea will be taken away.

4 "Now let no man contend, or rebuke another;
For your people *are* like those who contend
with the priest.
5 Therefore you shall stumble in the day;
The prophet also shall stumble with you
in the night;
And I will destroy your mother.
6 My people are destroyed for lack of knowledge.
Because you have rejected knowledge,
I also will reject you from being priest for Me;
Because you have forgotten the law of your God,
I also will forget your children.

7 "The more they increased,
The more they sinned against Me;
I will change[m] their glory[n] into shame.
8 They eat up the sin of My people;
They set their heart on their iniquity.
9 And it shall be: like people, like priest.
So I will punish them for their ways,
And reward them for their deeds.
10 For they shall eat, but not have enough;
They shall commit harlotry, but not increase;
Because they have ceased obeying the LORD.

The Idolatry of Israel

11 "Harlotry, wine, and new wine enslave the heart.
12 My people ask counsel from their wooden *idols,*
And their staff informs them.
For the spirit of harlotry has caused
them to stray,
And they have played the harlot against
their God.
13 They offer sacrifices on the mountaintops,
And burn incense on the hills,
Under oaks, poplars, and terebinths,
Because their shade *is* good.
Therefore your daughters commit harlotry,
And your brides commit adultery.

2:22 [i] Literally *God Will Sow*
2:23 [j] Hebrew *lo-ruhamah* [k] Hebrew *lo-ammi*
3:1 [l] Literally *friend* or *husband*
4:7 [m] Following Masoretic Text, Septuagint, and Vulgate; scribal tradition, Syriac, and Targum read *They will change.* [n] Following Masoretic Text, Septuagint, Syriac, Targum, and Vulgate; scribal tradition reads *My glory.*

14 "I will not punish your daughters when they commit harlotry,
Nor your brides when they commit adultery;
For *the men* themselves go apart with harlots,
And offer sacrifices with a ritual harlot.[o]
Therefore people *who* do not understand will be trampled.

15 "Though you, Israel, play the harlot,
Let not Judah offend.
Do not come up to Gilgal,
Nor go up to Beth Aven,
Nor swear an oath, *saying,* 'As the LORD lives'—

16 "For Israel is stubborn
Like a stubborn calf;
Now the LORD will let them forage
Like a lamb in open country.

17 "Ephraim *is* joined to idols,
Let him alone.
18 Their drink is rebellion,
They commit harlotry continually.
Her rulers dearly love dishonor.[p]
19 The wind has wrapped her up in its wings,
And they shall be ashamed because of their sacrifices.

Impending Judgment on Israel and Judah

5 "Hear this, O priests!
Take heed, O house of Israel!
Give ear, O house of the king!
For yours *is* the judgment,
Because you have been a snare to Mizpah
And a net spread on Tabor.
2 The revolters are deeply involved in slaughter,
Though I rebuke them all.
3 I know Ephraim,
And Israel is not hidden from Me;
For now, O Ephraim, you commit harlotry;
Israel is defiled.

4 "They do not direct their deeds
Toward turning to their God,
For the spirit of harlotry is in their midst,
And they do not know the LORD.
5 The pride of Israel testifies to his face;
Therefore Israel and Ephraim stumble in their iniquity;
Judah also stumbles with them.

6 "With their flocks and herds
They shall go to seek the LORD,
But they will not find *Him;*
He has withdrawn Himself from them.
7 They have dealt treacherously with the LORD,

4:14 [o] Compare Deuteronomy 23:18
4:18 [p] Hebrew is difficult; a Jewish tradition reads *Her rulers shamefully love, 'Give!'*

LIFE LESSON

Hosea 4:1–5:15

SITUATION Israel disobeyed. The national leaders had failed to teach God's Law to the people. Many of God's chosen people sold their bodies in prostitution, which in turn led to national destruction.

OBSERVATION People who have genuine faith and love for God will try to obey God.

INSPIRATION To be a Christian is, in a sense, to be a man without a country. If you truly are obedient to Christ—if you take the Scriptures to heart and attempt to live them—you will inevitably come into conflict with the world. You belong to no one but Christ, while those in the world give themselves to people, possessions, institutions, and idols other than to Christ. To be a Christian is to stand apart and yet to remain within—to dare to be different. You look at everything through the prism of Scripture, and things look different when viewed biblically.

Success in the world means power, influence, money, prestige. But in the Christian world, it means pleasing God. This quest for obedience may lead you to do things that are wholly contrary to what the world wants and rewards. . . .

Obeying his commandments means reading and understanding Scripture, then determining that you are going to live exactly as Scripture teaches. I don't believe anybody can do that, because it is almost impossible not to be caught up every day in the ways of the world. But you can make an effort to live biblically. That is how the process of sanctification works—learning how to obey God, how to listen for his commands in your life. It is reading the Scripture and allowing it to soak into you. It is understanding the requirements of God's commandments and then gradually, day by day, in large ways and small, allowing that understanding to control the actions of your life. . . .

If I had to pick the one thing . . . that has caused the most failure in obeying God, it would be that we figure God's time is our Bible study, our prayer

Continued

For they have begotten pagan children.
Now a New Moon shall devour them and their heritage.

8 "Blow the ram's horn in Gibeah,
The trumpet in Ramah!
Cry aloud *at* Beth Aven,
'*Look* behind you, O Benjamin!'
9 Ephraim shall be desolate in the day of rebuke;
Among the tribes of Israel I make known what is sure.

10 "The princes of Judah are like those who remove a landmark;
I will pour out My wrath on them like water.
11 Ephraim is oppressed *and* broken in judgment,
Because he willingly walked by *human* precept.
12 Therefore I *will be* to Ephraim like a moth,
And to the house of Judah like rottenness.

13 "When Ephraim saw his sickness,
And Judah *saw* his wound,
Then Ephraim went to Assyria
And sent to King Jareb;
Yet he cannot cure you,
Nor heal you of your wound.
14 For I *will be* like a lion to Ephraim,
And like a young lion to the house of Judah.
I, *even* I, will tear *them* and go away;
I will take *them* away, and no one shall rescue.
15 I will return again to My place
Till they acknowledge their offense.
Then they will seek My face;
In their affliction they will earnestly seek Me."

A Call to Repentance

6 Come, and let us return to the LORD;
For He has torn, but He will heal us;
He has stricken, but He will bind us up.
2 After two days He will revive us;
On the third day He will raise us up,
That we may live in His sight.
3 Let us know,
Let us pursue the knowledge of the LORD.
His going forth is established as the morning;
He will come to us like the rain,
Like the latter *and* former rain to the earth.

Impenitence of Israel and Judah

4 "O Ephraim, what shall I do to you?
O Judah, what shall I do to you?
For your faithfulness is like a morning cloud,
And like the early dew it goes away.
5 Therefore I have hewn *them* by the prophets,
I have slain them by the words of My mouth;
And your judgments *are like* light *that* goes forth.

time, the meeting with our prayer group, and Sunday morning church service. That's just not true. God's time is every moment of our lives. Bible study and church simply prepare us for the rest of the moments of our lives. . . . We don't put him on and take him off like a suit of clothes. . . . If we would "wear" him all day long, we would discover obedience becoming a reflex reaction. (From "The Quest for Obedience" by Charles Colson in *Practical Christianity)*

APPLICATION Does obedience to God come easier—or harder—at certain times of the week? In certain places? Among certain people? In order to obey God faithfully, you may need to make changes in your heart and in your life. Make a change and declare a new start today.

EXPLORATION Obedience—Genesis 2:16-17; Exodus 8:25-29; Joshua 1:6-8; 1 Samuel 15:22; Matthew 23:23-24; Luke 17:7-10.

6 For I desire mercy and not sacrifice,
And the knowledge of God more than
burnt offerings.
7 "But like men[q] they transgressed the covenant;
There they dealt treacherously with Me.
8 Gilead *is* a city of evildoers
And defiled with blood.
9 As bands of robbers lie in wait for a man,
So the company of priests murder on the way
to Shechem;
Surely they commit lewdness.
10 I have seen a horrible thing in the
house of Israel:
There *is* the harlotry of Ephraim;
Israel is defiled.
11 Also, O Judah, a harvest is appointed for you,
When I return the captives of My people.

7 "When I would have healed Israel,
Then the iniquity of Ephraim
was uncovered,
And the wickedness of Samaria.
For they have committed fraud;
A thief comes in;
A band of robbers takes spoil outside.
2 They do not consider in their hearts
That I remember all their wickedness;
Now their own deeds have surrounded them;
They are before My face.
3 They make a king glad with
their wickedness,
And princes with their lies.

4 "They *are* all adulterers.
Like an oven heated by a baker—
He ceases stirring *the fire* after kneading
the dough,
Until it is leavened.
5 In the day of our king
Princes have made *him* sick, inflamed
with wine;
He stretched out his hand with scoffers.
6 They prepare their heart like an oven,
While they lie in wait;
Their baker[r] sleeps all night;
In the morning it burns like a flaming fire.
7 They are all hot, like an oven,
And have devoured their judges;
All their kings have fallen.
None among them calls upon Me.

8 "Ephraim has mixed himself
among the peoples;
Ephraim is a cake unturned.
9 Aliens have devoured his strength,
But he does not know *it;*
Yes, gray hairs are here and there on him,
Yet he does not know *it.*
10 And the pride of Israel testifies to his face,
But they do not return to the LORD their God,
Nor seek Him for all this.

Futile Reliance on the Nations

11 "Ephraim also is like a silly dove,
without sense—
They call to Egypt,
They go to Assyria.
12 Wherever they go, I will spread My
net on them;
I will bring them down like birds of the air;
I will chastise them
According to what their congregation
has heard.

13 "Woe to them, for they have
fled from Me!
Destruction to them,
Because they have transgressed against Me!
Though I redeemed them,
Yet they have spoken lies against Me.
14 They did not cry out to Me with their heart
When they wailed upon their beds.

"They assemble together for[s] grain and
new wine,
They rebel against Me;[t]
15 Though I disciplined *and* strengthened
their arms,
Yet they devise evil against Me;
16 They return, *but* not to the Most High;[u]
They are like a treacherous bow.
Their princes shall fall by the sword
For the cursings of their tongue.
This *shall be* their derision in
the land of Egypt.

6:7 [q] Or *like Adam*
7:6 [r] Following Masoretic Text and Vulgate; Syriac and Targum read *Their anger;* Septuagint reads *Ephraim.*
7:14 [s] Following Masoretic Text and Targum; Vulgate reads *thought upon;* Septuagint reads *slashed themselves for* (compare 1 Kings 18:28). [t] Following Masoretic Text, Syriac, and Targum; Septuagint omits *They rebel against Me;* Vulgate reads *They departed from Me.*
7:16 [u] Or *upward*

LIFE LESSON

Hosea 6:1–10:15

SITUATION God called Hosea to be a living parable to Israel. God loved his people despite their unfaithfulness.

OBSERVATION God wants us to be faithful to him. It hurts him to see us wander away.

INSPIRATION [God] demands from those whom He has loved and redeemed utter and absolute loyalty, and will vindicate His claim by stern action against them if they betray His love by unfaithfulness. Calvin hit the nail on the head when he explained the sanction of the second commandment as follows:

"The Lord very frequently addresses us in the character of a husband . . . As He performs all the offices of a true and faithful husband, so He requires love and chastity from us; that is, that we do not prostitute our souls to Satan . . . As the purer and chaster a husband is, the more grievously he is offended when he sees his wife inclining to a rival; so the Lord, who has betrothed us to Himself in truth, declares that He burns with the hottest jealousy whenever, neglecting the purity of His holy marriage, we defile ourselves with abominable lusts, and especially when the worship of His deity, which ought to have been most carefully kept unimpaired, is transferred to another,

The Apostasy of Israel

8 "*Set* the trumpet[v] to your mouth!
He shall come like an eagle against the house of the LORD,
Because they have transgressed My covenant
And rebelled against My law.
2 Israel will cry to Me,
'My God, we know You!'
3 Israel has rejected the good;
The enemy will pursue him.

4 "They set up kings, but not by Me;
They made princes, but I did not acknowledge *them.*
From their silver and gold
They made idols for themselves—
That they might be cut off.
5 Your calf is rejected, O Samaria!
My anger is aroused against them—
How long until they attain to innocence?
6 For from Israel *is* even this:
A workman made it, and it *is* not God;
But the calf of Samaria shall be broken to pieces.

7 "They sow the wind,
And reap the whirlwind.
The stalk has no bud;
It shall never produce meal.
If it should produce,
Aliens would swallow it up.
8 Israel is swallowed up;
Now they are among the Gentiles
Like a vessel in which *is* no pleasure.
9 For they have gone up to Assyria,
Like a wild donkey alone by itself;
Ephraim has hired lovers.
10 Yes, though they have hired among the nations,
Now I will gather them;
And they shall sorrow a little,[w]
Because of the burden[x] of the king of princes.

11 "Because Ephraim has made many altars for sin,
They have become for him altars for sinning.
12 I have written for him the great things of My law,
But they were considered a strange thing.
13 *For* the sacrifices of My offerings they sacrifice flesh and eat *it,*
But the LORD does not accept them.
Now He will remember their iniquity and punish their sins.
They shall return to Egypt.

14 "For Israel has forgotten his Maker,
And has built temples;[y]

8:1 [v] Hebrew *shophar,* ram's horn
8:10 [w] Or *begin to diminish* [x] Or *oracle*
8:14 [y] Or *palaces*

Judah also has multiplied fortified cities;
But I will send fire upon his cities,
And it shall devour his palaces."

Judgment of Israel's Sin

9 Do not rejoice, O Israel, with joy like *other* peoples,
For you have played the harlot against your God.
You have made love *for* hire on every threshing floor.
2 The threshing floor and the winepress
Shall not feed them,
And the new wine shall fail in her.

3 They shall not dwell in the LORD's land,
But Ephraim shall return to Egypt,
And shall eat unclean *things* in Assyria.
4 They shall not offer wine *offerings* to the LORD,
Nor shall their sacrifices be pleasing to Him.
It shall be like bread of mourners to them;
All who eat it shall be defiled.
For their bread *shall be* for their *own* life;
It shall not come into the house of the LORD.
5 What will you do in the appointed day,
And in the day of the feast of the LORD?
6 For indeed they are gone because of destruction.
Egypt shall gather them up;
Memphis shall bury them.
Nettles shall possess their valuables of silver;
Thorns *shall be* in their tents.

7 The days of punishment have come;
The days of recompense have come.
Israel knows!
The prophet *is* a fool,
The spiritual man *is* insane,
Because of the greatness of your iniquity and great enmity.
8 The watchman of Ephraim *is* with my God;
But the prophet *is* a fowler's[z] snare in all his ways—
Enmity in the house of his God.
9 They are deeply corrupted,
As in the days of Gibeah.
He will remember their iniquity;
He will punish their sins.

10 "I found Israel
Like grapes in the wilderness;
I saw your fathers
As the firstfruits on the fig tree in its first season.
But they went to Baal Peor,
And separated themselves *to that* shame;
They became an abomination like the thing they loved.
11 *As for* Ephraim, their glory shall fly away like a bird—

9:8 [z] That is, one who catches birds in a trap or snare

or adulterated with some superstition; since in this way we not only violate our plighted troth, but defile the nuptial couch, by giving access to adulterers" (*Institutes,* II, viii, 18).

The jealousy of God requires us to be zealous for God. As our right response to God's love for us is love for Him, so our right response to His jealousy over us is zeal for Him. His concern for us is great; ours for Him must be great too. What the prohibition of idolatry in the second commandment implies is that God's people should be positively and passionately devoted to His person, His cause, and His honour. The Bible word for such devotion is zeal, sometimes actually called jealousy for God. God Himself, as we saw, manifests this zeal, and the godly must manifest it too.

(From *Knowing God* by J. I. Packer)

APPLICATION Encourage your friends to be zealous for God. Look for ways you can build them up, when so much in our culture tends to tear them down. Who is a specific person you can contact and encourage?

EXPLORATION Marital Responsibilities—Ephesians 5:21-33; Jealousy—Exodus 20:4-6; 34:14; 2 Corinthians 11:2.

No birth, no pregnancy, and no conception!
12 Though they bring up their children,
Yet I will bereave them to the last man.
Yes, woe to them when I depart from them!
13 Just as I saw Ephraim like Tyre, planted in a pleasant place,
So Ephraim will bring out his children to the murderer."

14 Give them, O LORD—
What will You give?
Give them a miscarrying womb
And dry breasts!
15 "All their wickedness *is* in Gilgal,
For there I hated them.
Because of the evil of their deeds
I will drive them from My house;
I will love them no more.
All their princes *are* rebellious.
16 Ephraim is stricken,
Their root is dried up;
They shall bear no fruit.
Yes, were they to bear children,
I would kill the darlings of their womb."

17 My God will cast them away,
Because they did not obey Him;
And they shall be wanderers among the nations.

Israel's Sin and Captivity

10 Israel empties *his* vine;
He brings forth fruit for himself.
According to the multitude of his fruit
He has increased the altars;
According to the bounty of his land
They have embellished *his* sacred pillars.
2 Their heart is divided;
Now they are held guilty.
He will break down their altars;
He will ruin their sacred pillars.

3 For now they say,
"We have no king,
Because we did not fear the LORD.
And as for a king, what would he do for us?"
4 They have spoken words,
Swearing falsely in making a covenant.
Thus judgment springs up like hemlock in the furrows of the field.

5 The inhabitants of Samaria fear
Because of the calf[a] of Beth Aven.
For its people mourn for it,
And its priests shriek for it—
Because its glory has departed from it.
6 *The idol* also shall be carried to Assyria
As a present for King Jareb.
Ephraim shall receive shame,
And Israel shall be ashamed of his own counsel.

7 *As for* Samaria, her king is cut off
Like a twig on the water.
8 Also the high places of Aven, the sin of Israel,
Shall be destroyed.
The thorn and thistle shall grow on their altars;
They shall say to the mountains, "Cover us!"
And to the hills, "Fall on us!"

9 "O Israel, you have sinned from the days of Gibeah;
There they stood.
The battle in Gibeah against the children of iniquity[b]
Did not overtake them.
10 When *it is* My desire, I will chasten them.
Peoples shall be gathered against them
When I bind them for their two transgressions.[c]
11 Ephraim *is* a trained heifer
That loves to thresh *grain;*
But I harnessed her fair neck,
I will make Ephraim pull *a plow.*
Judah shall plow;
Jacob shall break his clods."

12 Sow for yourselves righteousness;
Reap in mercy;
Break up your fallow ground,
For *it is* time to seek the LORD,
Till He comes and rains righteousness on you.

13 You have plowed wickedness;
You have reaped iniquity.
You have eaten the fruit of lies,
Because you trusted in your own way,
In the multitude of your mighty men.
14 Therefore tumult shall arise among your people,
And all your fortresses shall be plundered
As Shalman plundered Beth Arbel in the day of battle—

10:5 [a] Literally *calves*
10:9 [b] So read many Hebrew manuscripts, Septuagint, and Vulgate; Masoretic Text reads *unruliness.*
10:10 [c] Or *in their two habitations*

A mother dashed in pieces upon *her* children.
15 Thus it shall be done to you, O Bethel,
Because of your great wickedness.
At dawn the king of Israel
Shall be cut off utterly.

God's Continuing Love for Israel

11 "When Israel *was* a child, I loved him,
And out of Egypt I called My son.
2 *As* they called them,[d]
So they went from them;[e]
They sacrificed to the Baals,
And burned incense to carved images.

3 "I taught Ephraim to walk,
Taking them by their arms;[f]
But they did not know that I healed them.
4 I drew them with gentle cords,[g]
With bands of love,
And I was to them as those who take the yoke
from their neck.[h]
I stooped *and* fed them.

5 "He shall not return to the land of Egypt;
But the Assyrian shall be his king,
Because they refused to repent.
6 And the sword shall slash in his cities,
Devour his districts,
And consume *them,*
Because of their own counsels.
7 My people are bent on backsliding from Me.
Though they call to the Most High,[i]
None at all exalt *Him.*

8 "How can I give you up, Ephraim?
How can I hand you over, Israel?
How can I make you like Admah?
How can I set you like Zeboiim?
My heart churns within Me;
My sympathy is stirred.
9 I will not execute the fierceness of My anger;
I will not again destroy Ephraim.
For I *am* God, and not man,
The Holy One in your midst;
And I will not come with terror.[j]

10 "They shall walk after the LORD.
He will roar like a lion.
When He roars,
Then *His* sons shall come trembling
from the west;
11 They shall come trembling like a
bird from Egypt,
Like a dove from the land of Assyria.
And I will let them dwell in their houses,"
Says the LORD.

God's Charge Against Ephraim

12 "Ephraim has encircled Me with lies,
And the house of Israel with deceit;
But Judah still walks with God,
Even with the Holy One[k] *who is* faithful.

12 "Ephraim feeds on the wind,
And pursues the east wind;
He daily increases lies and desolation.
Also they make a covenant with the Assyrians,
And oil is carried to Egypt.

2 "The LORD also *brings* a charge against Judah,
And will punish Jacob according to his ways;
According to his deeds He will recompense him.
3 He took his brother by the heel in the womb,
And in his strength he struggled with God.[l]
4 Yes, he struggled with the Angel and prevailed;
He wept, and sought favor from Him.
He found Him *in* Bethel,
And there He spoke to us—
5 That is, the LORD God of hosts.
The LORD *is* His memorable name.
6 So you, by *the help of* your God, return;
Observe mercy and justice,
And wait on your God continually.

7 "A cunning Canaanite!
Deceitful scales *are* in his hand;
He loves to oppress.
8 And Ephraim said,
'Surely I have become rich,
I have found wealth for myself;
In all my labors
They shall find in me no
iniquity that *is* sin.'

11:2 [d] Following Masoretic Text and Vulgate; Septuagint reads *Just as I called them;* Targum interprets as *I sent prophets to a thousand of them.* [e] Following Masoretic Text, Targum, and Vulgate; Septuagint reads *from My face.*
11:3 [f] Some Hebrew manuscripts, Septuagint, Syriac, and Vulgate read *My arms.*
11:4 [g] Literally *cords of a man* [h] Literally *jaws*
11:7 [i] Or *upward*
11:9 [j] Or *I will not enter a city*
11:12 [k] Or *holy ones*
12:3 [l] Compare Genesis 32:28

LIFE LESSON

Hosea 11:1–14:9

SITUATION Although Israel abandoned God, God still loved the nation. Through anger and punishment, God desired to show favor to Israel.

OBSERVATION Although at times we tend to be ungrateful, faithless, and loveless toward God, he remains devoted to us.

INSPIRATION The parables of Jesus reveal a God who is consistently overgenerous with His forgiveness and grace. He portrays God as the lender magnanimously canceling a debt, as the shepherd seeking a strayed sheep, as the judge hearing the prayer of the tax collector. In Jesus' stories, divine forgiveness does not depend upon our repentance, or on our ability to love our enemies, or our doing heroic, virtuous deeds. God's forgiveness depends only on the love out of which He fashioned the human race.

The God of Judaism forgives the person who has changed his ways, done penance, and shown that he is leading a better life. But under the old covenant there is no forgiveness for those who remain sinners: the sinner faces judgement. But the Father of Jesus does not judge us, for He loves even those who are evil. In a word, the Father of Jesus loves sinners. He is the only God man has ever heard of who behaves this way. Unreal gods, the inventions of men, despise sinners. But the Father of Jesus loves all, no matter what they do. And this, of course, is almost too incredible for us to accept.

9 "But I *am* the LORD your God,
Ever since the land of Egypt;
I will again make you dwell in tents,
As in the days of the appointed feast.
10 I have also spoken by the prophets,
And have multiplied visions;
I have given symbols through the witness of the prophets."

11 Though Gilead *has* idols—
Surely they are vanity—
Though they sacrifice bulls in Gilgal,
Indeed their altars *shall be* heaps in the furrows of the field.

12 Jacob fled to the country of Syria;
Israel served for a spouse,
And for a wife he tended *sheep.*
13 By a prophet the LORD brought Israel out of Egypt,
And by a prophet he was preserved.
14 Ephraim provoked *Him* to anger most bitterly;
Therefore his Lord will leave the guilt of his bloodshed upon him,
And return his reproach upon him.

Relentless Judgment on Israel

13 When Ephraim spoke, trembling,
He exalted *himself* in Israel;
But when he offended through
Baal *worship,* he died.
2 Now they sin more and more,
And have made for themselves molded images,
Idols of their silver, according to their skill;
All of it *is* the work of craftsmen.
They say of them,
"Let the men who sacrifice[m] kiss the calves!"
3 Therefore they shall be like the morning cloud
And like the early dew that passes away,
Like chaff blown off from a threshing floor
And like smoke from a chimney.

4 "Yet I *am* the LORD your God
Ever since the land of Egypt,
And you shall know no God but Me;
For *there is* no savior besides Me.
5 I knew you in the wilderness,
In the land of great drought.
6 When they had pasture, they were filled;
They were filled and their heart was exalted;
Therefore they forgot Me.

7 "So I will be to them like a lion;
Like a leopard by the road I will lurk;
8 I will meet them like a bear deprived *of her cubs;*
I will tear open their rib cage,

13:2 [m] Or *those who offer human sacrifice*

And there I will devour them like a lion.
The wild beast shall tear them.

9 "O Israel, you are destroyed,[n]
But your help[o] *is* from Me.
10 I will be your King;[p]
Where *is any other,*
That he may save you in all your cities?
And your judges to whom you said,
'Give me a king and princes'?
11 I gave you a king in My anger,
And took *him* away in My wrath.

12 "The iniquity of Ephraim *is* bound up;
His sin *is* stored up.
13 The sorrows of a woman in childbirth
shall come upon him.
He *is* an unwise son,
For he should not stay long where children are born.

14 "I will ransom them from the power of the grave;[q]
I will redeem them from death.
O Death, I will be your plagues![r]
O Grave,[s] I will be your destruction![t]
Pity is hidden from My eyes."

15 Though he is fruitful among *his* brethren,
An east wind shall come;
The wind of the LORD shall come up from the wilderness.
Then his spring shall become dry,
And his fountain shall be dried up.
He shall plunder the treasury of every desirable prize.
16 Samaria is held guilty,[u]
For she has rebelled against her God.
They shall fall by the sword,
Their infants shall be dashed in pieces,
And their women with child ripped open.

Israel Restored at Last

14 O Israel, return to the LORD your God,
For you have stumbled because of your iniquity;
2 Take words with you,
And return to the LORD.
Say to Him,
"Take away all iniquity;
Receive *us* graciously,
For we will offer the sacrifices[v] of our lips.
3 Assyria shall not save us,
We will not ride on horses,

God does not condemn but forgives. The sinner is accepted even before he repents. Forgiveness is granted to him, he need only accept the gift. This is real amnesty. . . . The Gospel of Jesus Christ is the love story of God with us. It begins with unconditional forgiveness: the sole condition is trusting faith. Christianity happens when men and women experience the unwavering trust and reckless confidence that come from knowing the God of Jesus. There is no reason for being wary, scrupulous, cautious, or afraid with this God. As John writes in his first letter: "In love there can be no fear, but fear is driven out by perfect love: because to fear is to expect punishment, and anyone who is afraid is still imperfect in love" (1 John 4:18 JB). (From *Lion and Lamb* by Brennan Manning)

APPLICATION How have you seen God's faithfulness during a time of difficulty and discouragment? Did he send you a friend, see that your bills were paid, bring some type of comfort, let you know him in a deeper way? Take advantage of discouraging times and see God's hand at work. Praise God for his faithfulness. By doing this, you may encourage others.

EXPLORATION God Comforts—John 14:16-17; Acts 9:31.

13:9 [n] Literally *it* or *he destroyed you* [o] Literally *in your help*
13:10 [p] Septuagint, Syriac, Targum, and Vulgate read *Where is your king?*
13:14 [q] Or *Sheol* [r] Septuagint reads *where is your punishment?* [s] Or *Sheol* [t] Septuagint reads *where is your sting?*
13:16 [u] Septuagint reads *shall be disfigured*
14:2 [v] Literally *bull calves;* Septuagint reads *fruit.*

Nor will we say anymore to the work of our
hands, '*You are* our gods.'
For in You the fatherless finds mercy."

4 "I will heal their backsliding,
I will love them freely,
For My anger has turned away from him.
5 I will be like the dew to Israel;
He shall grow like the lily,
And lengthen his roots like Lebanon.
6 His branches shall spread;
His beauty shall be like an olive tree,
And his fragrance like Lebanon.
7 Those who dwell under his
shadow shall return;
They shall be revived *like* grain,
And grow like a vine.
Their scent[w] *shall be* like the wine of Lebanon.

8 "Ephraim *shall say,* 'What have I to do
anymore with idols?'
I have heard and observed him.
I *am* like a green cypress tree;
Your fruit is found in Me."

9 Who *is* wise?
Let him understand these things.
Who is prudent?
Let him know them.
For the ways of the LORD *are* right;
The righteous walk in them,
But transgressors stumble in them.

14:7 [w] Literally *remembrance*

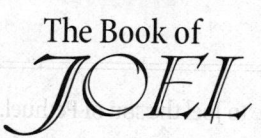

The Book of JOEL

INTRODUCTION

Hey!"

"Listen up!" "I'm talking to you!"

What gets your attention? For some, a touch on the arm. For others, a shout from the street. But some people seem oblivious to everything and everyone.

Distractions, daydreams, worries, and concerns can consume us. They make it difficult to hear or think about anything else. Sometimes we need a wake-up call, something to grab our attention and put us on the right track.

The people of Judah needed such a call. They were coasting.

Prosperous and complacent, they had become self-centered. Taking God for granted, they had turned to idols. So, through Joel, God sends a wake-up call, a divine attention-getter, to shake them out of their lethargy and sin. Joel predicts a devastating plague of locusts that will destroy the land unless the people repent and turn back to God.

God does what it takes to get our attention. Does he have yours?

LIFE LESSON

Joel 1:1–3:21

SITUATION The prophet Joel cautioned Israel about God's impending judgment for its spiritual complacency and religious neglect. When the people prospered, they abandoned God or minimized the importance of him in their life.

OBSERVATION God always gives us a chance to repent before he inflicts discipline. Like a loving parent, God's purpose is not to punish but to correct and nurture.

INSPIRATION I'd seen that silly light burning on the car panel for days. And for days I'd ignored it. Too busy. "I'll take the car to the mechanic tomorrow." But tomorrow never became today. The light continued to burn, vainly waving red flags before my blind eyes. Something was wrong, but I had too many things to do.

"Next time I'll pay attention," I mumbled to myself. The flashlight I was waving must have looked like a dancing firefly to the oncoming traffic. The situation was not pretty: a cold winter night, stranded on a lonely highway in rural Brazil with my daughter and pregnant wife.

My breath became smoke as I stood on the shoulder flagging cars. I promised myself I would never ignore a warning again.

Warnings. Red lights in life that signal us of impending danger. They exist in all parts of life. Sirens scream as a marriage starts to sour; alarms blare when a faith weakens; flares go up to alert us of morals being compromised.

The word of the LORD that came to Joel the son of Pethuel.

The Land Laid Waste

2 Hear this, you elders,
And give ear, all you inhabitants of the land!
Has *anything like* this happened in your days,
Or even in the days of your fathers?
3 Tell your children about it,
Let your children *tell* their children,
And their children another generation.

4 What the chewing locust[a] left, the swarming locust has eaten;
What the swarming locust left, the crawling locust has eaten;
And what the crawling locust left, the consuming locust has eaten.

5 Awake, you drunkards, and weep;
And wail, all you drinkers of wine,
Because of the new wine,
For it has been cut off from your mouth.
6 For a nation has come up against My land,
Strong, and without number;
His teeth *are* the teeth of a lion,
And he has the fangs of a fierce lion.
7 He has laid waste My vine,
And ruined My fig tree;
He has stripped it bare and thrown *it* away;
Its branches are made white.

8 Lament like a virgin girded with sackcloth
For the husband of her youth.
9 The grain offering and the drink offering
Have been cut off from the house of the LORD;
The priests mourn, who minister to the LORD.
10 The field is wasted,
The land mourns;
For the grain is ruined,
The new wine is dried up,
The oil fails.

11 Be ashamed, you farmers,
Wail, you vinedressers,
For the wheat and the barley;
Because the harvest of the field has perished.
12 The vine has dried up,
And the fig tree has withered;
The pomegranate tree,
The palm tree also,
And the apple tree—
All the trees of the field are withered;
Surely joy has withered away from the sons of men.

1:4 [a] Exact identity of these locusts is unknown.

Mourning for the Land

13 Gird yourselves and lament, you priests;
Wail, you who minister before the altar;
Come, lie all night in sackcloth,
You who minister to my God;
For the grain offering and the drink offering
Are withheld from the house of your God.
14 Consecrate a fast,
Call a sacred assembly;
Gather the elders
And all the inhabitants of the land
Into the house of the LORD your God,
And cry out to the LORD.

15 Alas for the day!
For the day of the LORD *is* at hand;
It shall come as destruction from the Almighty.
16 Is not the food cut off before our eyes,
Joy and gladness from the house of our God?
17 The seed shrivels under the clods,
Storehouses are in shambles;
Barns are broken down,
For the grain has withered.
18 How the animals groan!
The herds of cattle are restless,
Because they have no pasture;
Even the flocks of sheep suffer punishment.[b]

19 O LORD, to You I cry out;
For fire has devoured the open pastures,
And a flame has burned all the trees of the field.
20 The beasts of the field also cry out to You,
For the water brooks are dried up,
And fire has devoured the open pastures.

The Day of the LORD

2 Blow the trumpet in Zion,
And sound an alarm in My holy mountain!
Let all the inhabitants of the land tremble;
For the day of the LORD is coming,
For it is at hand:
2 A day of darkness and gloominess,
A day of clouds and thick darkness,
Like the morning *clouds* spread over the mountains.
A people *come*, great and strong,
The like of whom has never been;
Nor will there ever be any *such* after them,
Even for many successive generations.

3 A fire devours before them,
And behind them a flame burns;

They manifest themselves in a variety of ways: guilt, depression, rationalizations. A friend might confront. A Scripture might sting. A burden might prove too heavy. Regardless of how they may arrive, warnings come with the same purpose: To alert. To wake up.

Unfortunately, they are not always heeded. All of us have learned to cover our ears and shield our eyes at the right moment. It's amazing how adept we can be at keeping them out. Warnings can be as blunt as a sledgehammer and we still turn our heads and whistle them away. We have just enough of the rascal in us to believe we are the proverbial exception to the rule.

Are you close to the falls? Are your senses numb? Are your eyes trained to turn and roll when they should pause and observe?

Then maybe you need to repair your warning detector.

Divine warnings. All inspired by God and tested by time. They're yours to do with as you wish. They are red lights on your dashboard. Heed them and safety is yours to enjoy. Ignore them and I'll be looking for you on the side of the road.

(From *God Came Near* by Max Lucado)

APPLICATION What warning signs should alert you to trouble? What attitude or action have you failed to confront ? Is it hard to persevere? Yes! But it is so important.

EXPLORATION Warnings—Deuteronomy 27:15-26; Ezekiel 3:18-19; 1 Timothy 4:1-6.

1:18 *b* Septuagint and Vulgate read *are made desolate.*

The land *is* like the Garden of Eden
before them,
And behind them a desolate wilderness;
Surely nothing shall escape them.
4 Their appearance is like the appearance
of horses;
And like swift steeds, so they run.
5 With a noise like chariots
Over mountaintops they leap,
Like the noise of a flaming fire that devours
the stubble,
Like a strong people set in battle array.

6 Before them the people writhe in pain;
All faces are drained of color.[c]
7 They run like mighty men,
They climb the wall like men of war;
Every one marches in formation,
And they do not break ranks.
8 They do not push one another;
Every one marches in his own column.[d]
Though they lunge between the weapons,
They are not cut down.[e]
9 They run to and fro in the city,
They run on the wall;
They climb into the houses,
They enter at the windows like a thief.

10 The earth quakes before them,
The heavens tremble;
The sun and moon grow dark,
And the stars diminish their brightness.
11 The LORD gives voice before His army,
For His camp is very great;
For strong *is the One* who executes His word.
For the day of the LORD *is* great and
very terrible;
Who can endure it?

A Call to Repentance

12 "Now, therefore," says the LORD,
"Turn to Me with all your heart,
With fasting, with weeping, and
with mourning."
13 So rend your heart, and not your garments;
Return to the LORD your God,
For He *is* gracious and merciful,
Slow to anger, and of great kindness;
And He relents from doing harm.
14 Who knows *if* He will turn and relent,
And leave a blessing behind Him—
A grain offering and a drink offering
For the LORD your God?

15 Blow the trumpet in Zion,
Consecrate a fast,
Call a sacred assembly;
16 Gather the people,
Sanctify the congregation,
Assemble the elders,
Gather the children and nursing babes;
Let the bridegroom go out from his chamber,
And the bride from her dressing room.
17 Let the priests, who minister to the LORD,
Weep between the porch and the altar;
Let them say, "Spare Your people, O LORD,
And do not give Your heritage to reproach,
That the nations should rule over them.
Why should they say among the peoples,
'Where *is* their God?' "

The Land Refreshed

18 Then the LORD will be zealous for His land,
And pity His people.
19 The LORD will answer and say to His people,
"Behold, I will send you grain and new wine
and oil,
And you will be satisfied by them;
I will no longer make you a reproach among
the nations.
20 "But I will remove far from you the
northern *army*,
And will drive him away into a barren and
desolate land,
With his face toward the eastern sea
And his back toward the western sea;
His stench will come up,
And his foul odor will rise,
Because he has done monstrous things."

21 Fear not, O land;
Be glad and rejoice,
For the LORD has done marvelous things!
22 Do not be afraid, you beasts of the field;
For the open pastures are springing up,
And the tree bears its fruit;
The fig tree and the vine yield their strength.
23 Be glad then, you children of Zion,

2:6 [c] Septuagint, Targum, and Vulgate read *gather blackness.*
2:8 [d] Literally *his own highway* [e] That is, they are not halted by losses

And rejoice in the LORD your God;
For He has given you the former
rain faithfully,[f]
And He will cause the rain to come down
for you—
The former rain,
And the latter rain in the first *month*.
24 The threshing floors shall be full of wheat,
And the vats shall overflow with new wine
and oil.

25 "So I will restore to you the years that the
swarming locust has eaten,
The crawling locust,
The consuming locust,
And the chewing locust,[g]
My great army which I sent among you.
26 You shall eat in plenty and be satisfied,
And praise the name of the LORD your God,
Who has dealt wondrously with you;
And My people shall never be put to shame.
27 Then you shall know that I *am* in the midst
of Israel:
I *am* the LORD your God
And there is no other.
My people shall never be put to shame.

God's Spirit Poured Out

28 "And it shall come to pass afterward
That I will pour out My Spirit on all flesh;
Your sons and your daughters shall prophesy,
Your old men shall dream dreams,
Your young men shall see visions.
29 And also on *My* menservants and on
My maidservants
I will pour out My Spirit in those days.

30 "And I will show wonders in the heavens
and in the earth:
Blood and fire and pillars of smoke.
31 The sun shall be turned into darkness,
And the moon into blood,
Before the coming of the great and awesome
day of the LORD.
32 And it shall come to pass
That whoever calls on the name
of the LORD
Shall be saved.
For in Mount Zion and in Jerusalem there
shall be deliverance,
As the LORD has said,
Among the remnant whom the LORD calls.

God Judges the Nations

3 "For behold, in those days and at that time,
When I bring back the captives of Judah
and Jerusalem,
2 I will also gather all nations,
And bring them down to the Valley of
Jehoshaphat;
And I will enter into judgment with
them there
On account of My people, My heritage Israel,
Whom they have scattered among the nations;
They have also divided up My land.
3 They have cast lots for My people,
Have given a boy *as payment* for a harlot,
And sold a girl for wine, that they may drink.

4 "Indeed, what have you to do with Me,
O Tyre and Sidon, and all the coasts
of Philistia?
Will you retaliate against Me?
But if you retaliate against Me,
Swiftly and speedily I will return your
retaliation upon your own head;
5 Because you have taken My silver and
My gold,
And have carried into your temples My prized
possessions.
6 Also the people of Judah and the people
of Jerusalem
You have sold to the Greeks,
That you may remove them far from
their borders.

7 "Behold, I will raise them
Out of the place to which you have sold them,
And will return your retaliation upon your
own head.
8 I will sell your sons and your daughters
Into the hand of the people of Judah,
And they will sell them to the Sabeans,[h]
To a people far off;
For the LORD has spoken."

9 Proclaim this among the nations:
"Prepare for war!
Wake up the mighty men,
Let all the men of war draw near,

2:23 [f] Or *the teacher of righteousness*
2:25 [g] Compare 1:4
3:8 [h] Literally *Shebaites* (compare Isaiah 60:6 and Ezekiel 27:22)

Let them come up.
10 Beat your plowshares into swords
And your pruning hooks into spears;
Let the weak say, 'I *am* strong.' "
11 Assemble and come, all you nations,
And gather together all around.
Cause Your mighty ones to go down there,
O LORD.

12 "Let the nations be wakened, and come up to
the Valley of Jehoshaphat;
For there I will sit to judge all the
surrounding nations.
13 Put in the sickle, for the harvest is ripe.
Come, go down;
For the winepress is full,
The vats overflow—
For their wickedness *is* great."
14 Multitudes, multitudes in the valley
of decision!
For the day of the LORD *is* near in the valley
of decision.
15 The sun and moon will grow dark,
And the stars will diminish their brightness.
16 The LORD also will roar from Zion,
And utter His voice from Jerusalem;
The heavens and earth will shake;
But the LORD will be a shelter for His people,
And the strength of the children of Israel.

17 "So you shall know that I *am* the LORD your God,
Dwelling in Zion My holy mountain.
Then Jerusalem shall be holy,
And no aliens shall ever pass through
her again."

God Blesses His People

18 And it will come to pass in that day
That the mountains shall drip
with new wine,
The hills shall flow with milk,
And all the brooks of Judah shall be flooded
with water;
A fountain shall flow from the house of
the LORD
And water the Valley of Acacias.

19 "Egypt shall be a desolation,
And Edom a desolate wilderness,
Because of violence *against* the people
of Judah,
For they have shed innocent blood in
their land.
20 But Judah shall abide forever,
And Jerusalem from generation
to generation.
21 For I will acquit them of the guilt of
bloodshed, whom I had not acquitted;
For the LORD dwells in Zion."

The Book of

AMOS

INTRODUCTION

Ever met a "justa"? "Just a salesman." "Just a secretary." "Just a farmer." or "Just a custodian." "Just a" implies that one's calling or occupation is fairly insignificant, not very important in the grand scheme of things. We would feel much better if we could say with pride: world-class athlete, high-powered politician, best-selling author, brain surgeon, dynamic evangelist, CEO, television star, or rocket scientist. Self-esteem would soar, people would take notice, and God could use us to change the world. Being a "justa" feels small and ordinary.

By most standards, Amos would be considered a "justa." After all, he wasn't a prophet or priest or the son of either. He was just a shepherd, a small businessman in Judah. Who would listen to him?

But instead of making excuses, Amos obeyed and became God's powerful voice for change.

God has no "justa's."

God has often used "justa's"—shepherds, carpenters, fishermen . . . Whatever your station in life, God can use you. Check out Amos's example and God's message and be willing to be used by your Lord.

Amos wasn't much. He was a "justa" . . . just a servant of God. But that was enough.

The words of Amos, who was among the sheepbreeders[a] of Tekoa, which he saw concerning Israel in the days of Uzziah king of Judah, and in the days of Jeroboam the son of Joash, king of Israel, two years before the earthquake.

2 And he said:

"The LORD roars from Zion,
And utters His voice from Jerusalem;
The pastures of the shepherds mourn,
And the top of Carmel withers."

Judgment on the Nations

3 Thus says the LORD:

"For three transgressions of Damascus, and for four,
I will not turn away its *punishment*,
Because they have threshed Gilead with implements of iron.
4 But I will send a fire into the house of Hazael,
Which shall devour the palaces of Ben-Hadad.
5 I will also break the *gate* bar of Damascus,
And cut off the inhabitant from the Valley of Aven,
And the one who holds the scepter from Beth Eden.
The people of Syria shall go captive to Kir,"
Says the LORD.

6 Thus says the LORD:

"For three transgressions of Gaza, and for four,
I will not turn away its *punishment*,
Because they took captive the whole captivity
To deliver *them* up to Edom.
7 But I will send a fire upon the wall of Gaza,
Which shall devour its palaces.
8 I will cut off the inhabitant from Ashdod,
And the one who holds the scepter from Ashkelon;
I will turn My hand against Ekron,
And the remnant of the Philistines shall perish,"
Says the Lord GOD.

9 Thus says the LORD:

"For three transgressions of Tyre, and for four,
I will not turn away its *punishment*,
Because they delivered up the whole captivity to Edom,
And did not remember the covenant of brotherhood.
10 But I will send a fire upon the wall of Tyre,
Which shall devour its palaces."

11 Thus says the LORD:

"For three transgressions of Edom, and for four,
I will not turn away its *punishment*,
Because he pursued his brother with the sword,
And cast off all pity;

LIFE LESSON

Amos 1:1–2:16

SITUATION God called Amos, a shepherd from Judah, to prophesy against the Northern Kingdom (Israel). Amos's prophecy preceded the Assyrian captivity.

OBSERVATION God holds people accountable for their actions. He judged the Israelites for their evil works, and he will also examine our works.

INSPIRATION Amos is convinced that God has spoken. Read Amos 1:2. . . . He likens God's voice to the sound of a roaring lion. The prophet has a tremendous sense of the majesty of God and the authority of his Word. As far as he is concerned, he has left his normal job to proclaim the majesty of God and the authority of his Word. Amos has become obsessed with listening to God.

God's roaring like a lion does not fit our image of God today. We have various images of God: 1) He is our friend. 2) He is our Father. 3) He is our Creator. 4) He is our Savior. All these are valid concepts. But they should not be our only pictures of God. He is also like a roaring lion, demanding attention.

It is obvious that Amos's ministry never recovers from hearing the roar of the Lord. Over and over he proclaims, "This is what the Lord says" (see verses 3, 6, 9, 11, and 13). This

1:1 [a] Compare 2 Kings 3:4

His anger tore perpetually,
And he kept his wrath forever.
12 But I will send a fire upon Teman,
Which shall devour the palaces of Bozrah."

13Thus says the LORD:

"For three transgressions of the people of Ammon, and for four,
I will not turn away its *punishment*,
Because they ripped open the women with child in Gilead,
That they might enlarge their territory.
14 But I will kindle a fire in the wall of Rabbah,
And it shall devour its palaces,
Amid shouting in the day of battle,
And a tempest in the day of the whirlwind.
15 Their king shall go into captivity,
He and his princes together,"
Says the LORD.

2 Thus says the LORD:

"For three transgressions of Moab, and for four,
I will not turn away its *punishment*,
Because he burned the bones of the king of Edom to lime.
2 But I will send a fire upon Moab,
And it shall devour the palaces of Kerioth;
Moab shall die with tumult,
With shouting *and* trumpet sound.
3 And I will cut off the judge from its midst,
And slay all its princes with him,"
Says the LORD.

Judgment on Judah

4Thus says the LORD:

"For three transgressions of Judah, and for four,
I will not turn away its *punishment*,
Because they have despised the law of the LORD,
And have not kept His commandments.
Their lies lead them astray,
Lies which their fathers followed.
5 But I will send a fire upon Judah,
And it shall devour the palaces of Jerusalem."

Judgment on Israel

6Thus says the LORD:

"For three transgressions of Israel, and for four,
I will not turn away its *punishment*,
Because they sell the righteous for silver,
And the poor for a pair of sandals.
7 They pant after[b] the dust of the earth *which is*
on the head of the poor,

2:7 [b] Or *trample on*

same phrase appears three times in chapter 2 also. Repetition can be an evidence that the preacher is unprepared, or it can demonstrate that he had a point worth emphasizing. When Amos says eight consecutive times in a very carefully structured piece of writing, "This is what the Lord says," he is obviously trying to get a point across. The people need to listen! . . . When God speaks, do I listen? When God roars from heaven and wants my attention, do I stop talking and listen? Or is my life so busy that I only listen now and then? Do I only listen to God when it doesn't interfere with the normal course of events? Or have I been so arrested by what God says that I stop dead in my tracks and listen? (From *Hearing God's Voice Above the Noise* by Stuart Briscoe)

APPLICATION Do you obey God's word quickly, or are you slow to act? Do you consider God's expectation two or three times before acting on it? Whatever God requires of you, whether it be asking forgiveness or helping a friend, be quick to obey.

EXPLORATION Obedience—Deuteronomy 5:29; Joshua 11:15; 1 Samuel 15:22; John 14:23; Acts 5:29.

LIFE LESSON

Amos 3:1–6:14

SITUATION Through Amos, God warned Israel of the judgment that would come upon the nation for its disobedience.

OBSERVATION Despite continued discipline, Israel continued to turn away from God.

INSPIRATION When my family lived in Rio de Janiero, I owned a ham radio. I kept it in the utility room on top of the freezer. When we traveled, I always unplugged the radio and disconnected the antenna.

Once, when we were leaving for a week-long trip, I remembered I hadn't unplugged the radio. I ran back in the house, pulled the plug, and dashed out again.

But I pulled the wrong plug. I unplugged the freezer. . . . For seven days, then, a freezer full of food sat in a sweltering apartment with the power off.

When we came home, . . . guess who got fingered as the one who had unplugged the freezer—and who therefore would be responsible for cleaning it? You got it. So I got to work.

What is the best way to clean out a rotten interior? I knew exactly what to do. I got a rag and a bucket of soapy water and began cleaning the outside of the appliance. I was sure the odor would disappear with a good shine, so I polished and buffed and wiped. When I was through, the freezer could have passed a Marine boot-camp inspection. It was sparkling.

But when I opened the door, that freezer was revolting.

(Are you wondering, "Now what kind of fool would do that?" Read on and you'll see.)

No problem, I thought. I knew what to do. This freezer needs some friends. I'd stink, too, if I had the social life of a machine in a utility room. So, I threw a party. I invited all the appliances from the neighborhood kitchens. It was hard work, but we filled our apartment with refrigerators, stoves, microwaves, and washing machines. It was a great party. A couple of toasters recognized each other from the appliance store. Everyone played pin the plug on the socket and had a few laughs about limited warranties.

And pervert the way of the humble.
A man and his father go in to the *same* girl,
To defile My holy name.
8 They lie down by every altar on clothes taken in pledge,
And drink the wine of the condemned *in* the house of their god.

9 "Yet *it was* I *who* destroyed the Amorite before them,
Whose height *was* like the height of the cedars,
And he *was as* strong as the oaks;
Yet I destroyed his fruit above
And his roots beneath.
10 Also *it was* I *who* brought you up from the land of Egypt,
And led you forty years through the wilderness,
To possess the land of the Amorite.
11 I raised up some of your sons as prophets,
And some of your young men as Nazirites.
Is it not so, O you children of Israel?"
Says the LORD.
12 "But you gave the Nazirites wine to drink,
And commanded the prophets saying,
'Do not prophesy!'

13 "Behold, I am weighed down by you,
As a cart full of sheaves is weighed down.
14 Therefore flight shall perish from the swift,
The strong shall not strengthen his power,
Nor shall the mighty deliver himself;
15 He shall not stand who handles the bow,
The swift of foot shall not escape,
Nor shall he who rides a horse deliver himself.
16 The most courageous men of might
Shall flee naked in that day,"
Says the LORD.

Authority of the Prophet's Message

3 Hear this word that the LORD has spoken against you, O children of
Israel, against the whole family which I brought up from the land of
Egypt, saying:

2 "You only have I known of all the families of the earth;
Therefore I will punish you for all your iniquities."

3 Can two walk together, unless they are agreed?
4 Will a lion roar in the forest, when he has no prey?
Will a young lion cry out of his den, if he has caught nothing?
5 Will a bird fall into a snare on the earth, where
there is no trap for it?
Will a snare spring up from the earth, if it
has caught nothing at all?
6 If a trumpet is blown in a city, will not the people be afraid?
If there is calamity in a city, will not the LORD have done *it?*

7 Surely the Lord GOD does nothing,
Unless He reveals His secret to His servants the prophets.

8 A lion has roared!
Who will not fear?
The Lord GOD has spoken!
Who can but prophesy?

Punishment of Israel's Sins

9 "Proclaim in the palaces at Ashdod,[c]
And in the palaces in the land of Egypt, and say:
'Assemble on the mountains of Samaria;
See great tumults in her midst,
And the oppressed within her.
10 For they do not know to do right,'
Says the LORD,
'Who store up violence and robbery in their palaces.' "

11 Therefore thus says the Lord GOD:

"An adversary *shall be* all around the land;
He shall sap your strength from you,
And your palaces shall be plundered."

12 Thus says the LORD:

"As a shepherd takes from the mouth of a lion
Two legs or a piece of an ear,
So shall the children of Israel be taken out
Who dwell in Samaria—
In the corner of a bed and on the edge[d] of a couch!
13 Hear and testify against the house of Jacob,"
Says the Lord GOD, the God of hosts,
14 "That in the day I punish Israel for their transgressions,
I will also visit *destruction* on the altars of Bethel;
And the horns of the altar shall be cut off
And fall to the ground.
15 I will destroy the winter house along with the summer house;
The houses of ivory shall perish,
And the great houses shall have an end,"
Says the LORD.

4 Hear this word, you cows of Bashan, who
are on the mountain of Samaria,
Who oppress the poor,
Who crush the needy,
Who say to your husbands,[e] "Bring *wine*, let us drink!"
2 The Lord GOD has sworn by His holiness:
"Behold, the days shall come upon you
When He will take you away with fishhooks,
And your posterity with fishhooks.
3 You will go out *through* broken *walls*,
Each one straight ahead of her,
And you will be cast into Harmon,"
Says the LORD.

3:9 [c] Following Masoretic Text; Septuagint reads *Assyria*.
3:12 [d] The Hebrew is uncertain.
4:1 [e] Literally *their lords* or *their masters*

The blenders were the hit, though; they really mixed well.

I was sure the social interaction would cure the inside of my freezer, but I was wrong. I opened it up, and the stink was even worse!

Now what?

I had an idea. If a polish job wouldn't do it and social life didn't help, I'd give the freezer some status!

I bought a Mercedes sticker and stuck it on the door. I painted a paisley tie down the front. I put a "Save the Whales" bumper sticker on the rear and installed a cellular phone on the side. That freezer was classy. It was stylish. It was . . . cool. I splashed it with cologne and gave it a credit card for clout. . . .

Then I opened the door, expecting to see a clean inside, but what I saw was putrid—a stinky and repulsive interior. I could think of only one other option. My freezer needed some high-voltage pleasure! I immediately bought it some copies of *Playfridge* magazines—the publication that displays freezers with their doors open. I rented some films about foxy appliances. . . . I even tried to get my freezer a date with the Westinghouse next door, but she gave him the cold shoulder.

After a few days of supercharged, after-hours entertainment, I opened the door. And I nearly got sick.

I know what you're thinking. The only thing worse than Max's humor is his common sense. Who would concentrate on the outside when the problem is on the inside?

Do you really want to know?

A homemaker battles with depression. What is the solution suggested by some well-meaning friend? Buy a new dress.

A husband is involved in an affair that brings him as much guilt as it does adventure. The solution? Change peer groups. Hang out with people who don't make you feel guilty!

A young professional is plagued with loneliness. His obsession with success has left him with no friends. His boss gives him an idea: Change your style. Get a new haircut. Flash some cash.

Case after case of treating the outside while ignoring the inside—polishing the case while ignoring the interior. And what is the result?

Continued

The homemaker gets a new dress, and the depression disappears . . . for a day, maybe. Then the shadow returns. The husband finds a bunch of buddies who sanction his adultery. The result? Peace . . . until the crowd is gone. Then the guilt is back.

The young professional gets a new look and the people notice . . . until the styles change. Then he has to scurry out and buy more stuff so he won't appear outdated.

The exterior polished; the interior corroding. The outside altered; the inside faltering. One thing is clear: Cosmetic changes are only skin deep.

By now you could write the message of the beatitude. It's a clear one: You change your life by changing your heart.

(From *The Applause of Heaven* by Max Lucado)

APPLICATION No one enjoys being disciplined. Yet, it is often through the discomfort of chastisement that we return to the right path. Make your life easier: repent of your sin before God must bring discipline. If you are being disciplined, correct the wrong quickly.

EXPLORATION Discipline—Job 5:17; Psalm 39:11; 94:12; Proverbs 3:11-12; Jeremiah 30:11; Hebrews 12:7-10.

4 "Come to Bethel and transgress,
At Gilgal multiply transgression;
Bring your sacrifices every morning,
Your tithes every three days.[f]
5 Offer a sacrifice of thanksgiving with leaven,
Proclaim *and* announce the freewill offerings;
For this you love,
You children of Israel!"
Says the Lord GOD.

Israel Did Not Accept Correction

6 "Also I gave you cleanness of teeth in all your cities.
And lack of bread in all your places;
Yet you have not returned to Me,"
Says the LORD.

7 "I also withheld rain from you,
When *there were* still three months to the harvest.
I made it rain on one city,
I withheld rain from another city.
One part was rained upon,
And where it did not rain the part withered.
8 So two *or* three cities wandered to another city to drink water,
But they were not satisfied;
Yet you have not returned to Me,"
Says the LORD.

9 "I blasted you with blight and mildew.
When your gardens increased,
Your vineyards,
Your fig trees,
And your olive trees,
The locust devoured *them;*
Yet you have not returned to Me,"
Says the LORD.

10 "I sent among you a plague after the manner of Egypt;
Your young men I killed with a sword,
Along with your captive horses;
I made the stench of your camps come up into your nostrils;
Yet you have not returned to Me,"
Says the LORD.

11 "I overthrew *some* of you,
As God overthrew Sodom and Gomorrah,
And you were like a firebrand plucked from the burning;
Yet you have not returned to Me,"
Says the LORD.

12 "Therefore thus will I do to you, O Israel;
Because I will do this to you,

4:4 *f* Or *years* (compare Deuteronomy 14:28)

Prepare to meet your God, O Israel!"
13 For behold,
He who forms mountains,
And creates the wind,
Who declares to man what his[g] thought *is*,
And makes the morning darkness,
Who treads the high places of the earth—
The LORD God of hosts *is* His name.

A Lament for Israel

5 Hear this word which I take up against you, a
lamentation, O house of Israel:

2 The virgin of Israel has fallen;
She will rise no more.
She lies forsaken on her land;
There is no one to raise her up.

3 For thus says the Lord GOD:

"The city that goes out by a thousand
Shall have a hundred left,
And that which goes out by a hundred
Shall have ten left to the house of Israel."

A Call to Repentance

4 For thus says the LORD to the house of Israel:

"Seek Me and live;
5 But do not seek Bethel,
Nor enter Gilgal,
Nor pass over to Beersheba;
For Gilgal shall surely go into captivity,
And Bethel shall come to nothing.
6 Seek the LORD and live,
Lest He break out like fire *in* the house
of Joseph,
And devour *it*,
With no one to quench *it* in Bethel—
7 You who turn justice to wormwood,
And lay righteousness to rest in the earth!"
8 He made the Pleiades and Orion;
He turns the shadow of death into morning
And makes the day dark as night;
He calls for the waters of the sea
And pours them out on the face of the earth;
The LORD *is* His name.
9 He rains ruin upon the strong,
So that fury comes upon the fortress.

10 They hate the one who rebukes in the gate,
And they abhor the one who speaks uprightly.
11 Therefore, because you tread down the poor
And take grain taxes from him,
Though you have built houses of hewn stone,
Yet you shall not dwell in them;
You have planted pleasant vineyards,
But you shall not drink wine from them.
12 For I know your manifold transgressions
And your mighty sins:
Afflicting the just *and* taking bribes;
Diverting the poor *from justice* at the gate.
13 Therefore the prudent keep silent at that time,
For it *is* an evil time.

14 Seek good and not evil,
That you may live;
So the LORD God of hosts will be with you,
As you have spoken.
15 Hate evil, love good;
Establish justice in the gate.
It may be that the LORD God of hosts
Will be gracious to the remnant of Joseph.

The Day of the LORD

16 Therefore the LORD God of hosts, the Lord,
says this:

"*There shall be* wailing in all streets,
And they shall say in all the highways,
'Alas! Alas!'
They shall call the farmer to mourning,
And skillful lamenters to wailing.
17 In all vineyards *there shall be* wailing,
For I will pass through you,"
Says the LORD.

18 Woe to you who desire the day of the LORD!
For what good *is* the day of the LORD to you?
It *will be* darkness, and not light.
19 It *will be* as though a man fled from a lion,
And a bear met him!
Or *as though* he went into the house,
Leaned his hand on the wall,
And a serpent bit him!
20 *Is* not the day of the LORD darkness, and
not light?
Is it not very dark, with no brightness in it?
21 "I hate, I despise your feast days,
And I do not savor your sacred assemblies.
22 Though you offer Me burnt offerings and your
grain offerings,
I will not accept *them*,

4:13 g Or *His*

Nor will I regard your fattened peace offerings.
23 Take away from Me the noise of your songs,
For I will not hear the melody of your
stringed instruments.
24 But let justice run down like water,
And righteousness like a mighty stream.

25 "Did you offer Me sacrifices and offerings
In the wilderness forty years, O house
of Israel?
26 You also carried Sikkuth[h] your king[i]
And Chiun,[j] your idols,
The star of your gods,
Which you made for yourselves.
27 Therefore I will send you into captivity
beyond Damascus,"
Says the LORD, whose name *is* the God
of hosts.

Warnings to Zion and Samaria

6 Woe to you *who are* at ease in Zion,
And trust in Mount Samaria,
Notable persons in the chief nation,
To whom the house of Israel comes!
2 Go over to Calneh and see;
And from there go to Hamath the great;
Then go down to Gath of the Philistines.
Are you better than these kingdoms?
Or is their territory greater than
your territory?
3 *Woe to* you who put far off the day of doom,
Who cause the seat of violence to come near;
4 Who lie on beds of ivory,
Stretch out on your couches,
Eat lambs from the flock
And calves from the midst of the stall;
5 Who sing idly to the sound of
stringed instruments,
And invent for yourselves musical
instruments like David;
6 Who drink wine from bowls,
And anoint yourselves with the
best ointments,
But are not grieved for the affliction of Joseph.
7 Therefore they shall now go captive as the first
of the captives,
And those who recline at banquets shall
be removed.

8 The Lord GOD has sworn by Himself,
The LORD God of hosts says:
"I abhor the pride of Jacob,
And hate his palaces;
Therefore I will deliver up *the* city
And all that is in it."

9 Then it shall come to pass, that if ten men remain
in one house, they shall die. 10 And when a relative *of the*
dead, with one who will burn *the bodies,* picks up the
bodies[k] to take them out of the house, he will say to
one inside the house, "*Are there* any more with you?"
Then someone will say, "None."
And he will say, "Hold your tongue! For we dare not
mention the name of the LORD."

11 For behold, the LORD gives
a command:
He will break the great house into bits,
And the little house into pieces.
12 Do horses run on rocks?
Does *one* plow *there* with oxen?
Yet you have turned justice into gall,
And the fruit of righteousness
into wormwood,
13 You who rejoice over Lo Debar,[l]
Who say, "Have we not taken
Karnaim[m] for ourselves
By our own strength?"
14 "But, behold, I will raise up a nation
against you,
O house of Israel,"
Says the LORD God of hosts;
"And they will afflict you from the entrance
of Hamath
To the Valley of the Arabah."

Vision of the Locusts

7 Thus the Lord GOD showed me: Behold, He
formed locust swarms at the beginning of the late
crop; indeed *it was* the late crop after the king's mow-
ings. 2 And so it was, when they had finished eating the
grass of the land, that I said:

"O Lord GOD, forgive, I pray!
Oh, that Jacob may stand,
For he *is* small!"
3 *So* the LORD relented concerning this.
"It shall not be," said the LORD.

5:26 [h] A pagan deity [i] Septuagint and Vulgate read *tabernacle of Moloch.* [j] A pagan deity
6:10 [k] Literally *bones*
6:13 [l] Literally *Nothing* [m] Literally *Horns,* symbol of strength

Vision of the Fire

[4]Thus the Lord GOD showed me: Behold, the Lord GOD called for conflict by
fire, and it consumed the great deep and devoured the territory. [5]Then I said:

"O Lord GOD, cease, I pray!
Oh, that Jacob may stand,
For he *is* small!"
6 *So* the LORD relented concerning this.
"This also shall not be," said the Lord GOD.

Vision of the Plumb Line

[7]Thus He showed me: Behold, the Lord stood on a wall *made* with a
plumb line, with a plumb line in His hand. [8]And the LORD said to me,
"Amos, what do you see?"

And I said, "A plumb line."

Then the Lord said:

"Behold, I am setting a plumb line
In the midst of My people Israel;
I will not pass by them anymore.
9 The high places of Isaac shall be desolate,
And the sanctuaries of Israel shall be laid waste.
I will rise with the sword against the house of Jeroboam."

Amaziah's Complaint

[10]Then Amaziah the priest of Bethel sent to Jeroboam king of Israel, saying, "Amos has conspired against you in the midst of the house of Israel.
The land is not able to bear all his words. [11]For thus Amos has said:

'Jeroboam shall die by the sword,
And Israel shall surely be led away captive
From their own land.'"

[12]Then Amaziah said to Amos:

"Go, you seer!
Flee to the land of Judah.
There eat bread,
And there prophesy.
13 But never again prophesy at Bethel,
For it *is* the king's sanctuary,
And it *is* the royal residence."

[14]Then Amos answered, and said to Amaziah:

"I *was* no prophet,
Nor *was* I a son of a prophet,
But I *was* a sheepbreeder[n]
And a tender of sycamore fruit.
15 Then the LORD took me as I followed the flock,
And the LORD said to me,
'Go, prophesy to My people Israel.'
16 Now therefore, hear the word of the LORD:

7:14 [n] Compare 2 Kings 3:4

LIFE LESSON

Amos 7:1–9:15

SITUATION Amos saw God's coming judgments on Israel through two visions. After each vision, he prayed that God would be merciful.

OBSERVATION God sent his prophet Amos to warn the people of Israel to repent of their sins. God gives us these examples to teach us that he hates sin.

INSPIRATION The task of the prophet is to nurture, nourish, and evoke a vision of an alternative to the dominant system. The prophet must generate hope for something that lies beyond the present order. We need a vision of an alternative future that will energize us and motivate us to act, a vision of possibilities that will make our blood run hot and give us the courage to revolt against the way things are.

A prophet's vision can replace people's numbness with energy. The possibility of a glorious "might be" can enable us to live in ways that appear dangerous to the custodians of the status quo. With vision, the dead bones can come alive. The psychically dead can be resurrected. The spiritual sleepers can be awakened. Out of sorrow for the death of the old can come a new dynamism to us; through the message of the prophet we can come to believe in a new heaven and a new earth. The apathy that works in people in dying societies can be dispelled. There can be passion. There can be a "new song" (Isaiah 42:10), and the fatigue that is so evident among those in the present order can be overcome. . . .

All of this energy comes from the message of the prophet. The people of the dying society can be "born again." The prophet's hope can generate the dynamism for change.

(From *Wake Up America* by Tony Campolo)

APPLICATION Use Sundays as a chance to get to know God better. Go to church faithfully. Worship and listen attentively. Spend Sunday building relationships with others in your church or spending time with your family.

EXPLORATION Bold Witnesses—Matthew 5:13-16; Mark 4:21-25; John 3:21; Acts 1:8; Galatians 6:9.

You say, 'Do not prophesy against Israel,
And do not spout against the house of Isaac.'

17 "Therefore thus says the LORD:
'Your wife shall be a harlot in the city;
Your sons and daughters shall fall by
the sword;
Your land shall be divided by *survey* line;
You shall die in a defiled land;
And Israel shall surely be led away captive
From his own land.' "

Vision of the Summer Fruit

8 Thus the Lord GOD showed me: Behold, a basket
of summer fruit. 2 And He said, "Amos, what do
you see?"
So I said, "A basket of summer fruit."
Then the LORD said to me:

"The end has come upon My people Israel;
I will not pass by them anymore.
3 And the songs of the temple
Shall be wailing in that day,"
Says the Lord GOD—
"Many dead bodies everywhere,
They shall be thrown out in silence."

4 Hear this, you who swallow up[o] the needy,
And make the poor of the land fail,

5 Saying:
"When will the New Moon be past,
That we may sell grain?
And the Sabbath,
That we may trade wheat?
Making the ephah small and the shekel large,
Falsifying the scales by deceit,
6 That we may buy the poor for silver,
And the needy for a pair of sandals—
Even sell the bad wheat?"

7 The LORD has sworn by the pride of Jacob:
"Surely I will never forget any of their works.
8 Shall the land not tremble for this,
And everyone mourn who dwells in it?
All of it shall swell like the River,[p]
Heave and subside
Like the River of Egypt.

9 "And it shall come to pass in that day," says the
Lord GOD,
"That I will make the sun go down at noon,
And I will darken the earth in
broad daylight;
10 I will turn your feasts into mourning,
And all your songs into lamentation;
I will bring sackcloth on every waist,
And baldness on every head;
I will make it like mourning for an only *son*,
And its end like a bitter day.

11 "Behold, the days are coming," says the
Lord GOD,
"That I will send a famine on the land,
Not a famine of bread,
Nor a thirst for water,
But of hearing the words of the LORD.
12 They shall wander from sea to sea,
And from north to east;
They shall run to and fro, seeking the
word of the LORD,
But shall not find *it*.

13 "In that day the fair virgins
And strong young men
Shall faint from thirst.
14 Those who swear by the sin[q] of Samaria,
Who say,
'As your god lives, O Dan!'
And, 'As the way of Beersheba lives!'
They shall fall and never rise again."

The Destruction of Israel

9 I saw the Lord standing by the altar, and He said:

"Strike the doorposts, that the thresholds
may shake,
And break them on the heads of them all.
I will slay the last of them with the sword.
He who flees from them shall not get away,
And he who escapes from them shall not
be delivered.

2 "Though they dig into hell,[r]
From there My hand shall take them;
Though they climb up to heaven,
From there I will bring them down;
3 And though they hide themselves on top
of Carmel,
From there I will search and take them;

8:4 [o] Or *trample on* (compare 2:7)
8:8 [p] That is, the Nile; some Hebrew manuscripts, Septuagint, Syriac, Targum, and Vulgate read *River;* Masoretic Text reads *the light.*
8:14 [q] Or *Ashima,* a Syrian goddess
9:2 [r] Or *Sheol*

Though they hide from My sight at the bottom
of the sea,
From there I will command the serpent, and it
shall bite them;
4 Though they go into captivity before
their enemies,
From there I will command the sword,
And it shall slay them.
I will set My eyes on them for harm
and not for good."

5 The Lord GOD of hosts,
He who touches the earth and it melts,
And all who dwell there mourn;
All of it shall swell like the River,[s]
And subside like the River of Egypt.
6 He who builds His layers in the sky,
And has founded His strata in the earth;
Who calls for the waters of the sea,
And pours them out on the face of the earth—
The LORD *is* His name.

7 "*Are* you not like the people of Ethiopia to Me,
O children of Israel?" says the LORD.
"Did I not bring up Israel from the land
of Egypt,
The Philistines from Caphtor,
And the Syrians from Kir?

8 "Behold, the eyes of the Lord GOD *are* on the
sinful kingdom,
And I will destroy it from the face of the earth;
Yet I will not utterly destroy the house
of Jacob,"
Says the LORD.

9 "For surely I will command,
And will sift the house of Israel among
all nations,
As *grain* is sifted in a sieve;
Yet not the smallest grain shall fall to
the ground.
10 All the sinners of My people shall die by
the sword,
Who say, 'The calamity shall not overtake nor
confront us.'

Israel Will Be Restored

11 "On that day I will raise up
The tabernacle[t] of David, which has
fallen down,
And repair its damages;
I will raise up its ruins,
And rebuild it as in the days of old;
12 That they may possess the remnant of Edom,[u]
And all the Gentiles who are called by
My name,"
Says the LORD who does this thing.

13 "Behold, the days are coming," says the LORD,
"When the plowman shall overtake the reaper,
And the treader of grapes him who sows seed;
The mountains shall drip with sweet wine,
And all the hills shall flow *with it.*
14 I will bring back the captives of My
people Israel;
They shall build the waste cities and
inhabit *them;*
They shall plant vineyards and drink wine
from them;
They shall also make gardens and eat fruit
from them.
15 I will plant them in their land,
And no longer shall they be pulled up
From the land I have given them,"
Says the LORD your God.

9:5 [s] That is, the Nile
9:11 [t] Literally *booth,* figure of a deposed dynasty
9:12 [u] Septuagint reads *mankind.*

The Book of

OBADIAH

INTRODUCTION

I know how to make you mad. I don't want to. I don't intend to. But if I desired to, I would know how to do it.

I would insult your family.

I wouldn't insult you. I would insult your family. I'd mock your mother. I'd make fun of your father. I'd criticize your kids. Again, I'm not going to. But if I did, I know what would happen.

You'd get angry. If there is any shred of loyalty in your heart, you'd tell me to mind my own business.

Even if I were right.

Even if my accusations were accurate. No matter. You'd tell me to quit sticking my nose in your business. When it comes to the family, we look out for our own. God does the same.

God's children, the Jews, weren't the best of children. They were stubborn, rebellious, and forgetful. Over the years God dished out the discipline and correction. But through all the stresses and strains, God's love for his children was stubborn.

Edom, a powerful nation, enjoyed picking on Israel. Here in Obadiah, we see God rising to the defense of his children. He says, in effect, *Mess with them and you mess with me.*

It's a small book with a huge message. God cares for his children.

LIFE LESSON

Obadiah 1–21

SITUATION A bloody feud between Edom and Israel continued from the days of Esau and Jacob (Genesis 25:19-34). Obadiah denounced Edom's cruelty and pride, and then prophesied about its destruction. He also prophesied that Israel would be restored as a nation with extended territory.

OBSERVATION God always protects and takes care of his children. With God on their side, his children are never the underdog.

INSPIRATION I have never met a Christian who had lost his salvation. However, I have met plenty who had lost their assurance. Our *security* rests in the hands of an unconditionally loving heavenly Father. One who gave His best to insure our fellowship with Him forever. Our *assurance* rests in understanding and acceptance of these glorious truths.

For some people, the problem is erroneous teaching; for others, the problem is guilt. But whatever the reason, the result is the same, a lack of assurance. And when assurance goes, the basic building blocks of the relationship go also.

More is at stake than assurance. The very gospel itself comes under attack when the eternal security of the believer is questioned. Placing the responsibility for maintaining salvation on the believer is adding works to grace. Salvation would no longer be a gift. It would become trade—our faithfulness for His faithfulness.

The Coming Judgment on Edom

The vision of Obadiah.
Thus says the Lord GOD concerning Edom
(We have heard a report from the LORD,
And a messenger has been sent among the nations, *saying,*
"Arise, and let us rise up against her for battle"):

2 "Behold, I will make you small among the nations;
You shall be greatly despised.
3 The pride of your heart has deceived you,
You who dwell in the clefts of the rock,
Whose habitation is high;
You who say in your heart, 'Who will bring me down to the ground?'
4 Though you ascend *as* high as the eagle,
And though you set your nest among the stars,
From there I will bring you down," says the LORD.

5 "If thieves had come to you,
If robbers by night—
Oh, how you will be cut off!—
Would they not have stolen till they had enough?
If grape-gatherers had come to you,
Would they not have left *some* gleanings?

6 "Oh, how Esau shall be searched out!
How his hidden treasures shall be sought after!
7 All the men in your confederacy
Shall force you to the border;
The men at peace with you
Shall deceive you *and* prevail against you.
Those who eat your bread shall lay a trap[a] for you.
No one is aware of it.

8 "Will I not in that day," says the LORD,
"Even destroy the wise *men* from Edom,
And understanding from the mountains of Esau?
9 Then your mighty men, O Teman, shall be dismayed,
To the end that everyone from the mountains of Esau
May be cut off by slaughter.

Edom Mistreated His Brother

10 "For violence against your brother Jacob,
Shame shall cover you,
And you shall be cut off forever.
11 In the day that you stood on the other side—
In the day that strangers carried captive his forces,
When foreigners entered his gates
And cast lots for Jerusalem—
Even you *were* as one of them.

12 "But you should not have gazed on the day of your brother
In the day of his captivity;[b]

7 [a] Or *wound,* or *plot*
12 [b] Literally *On the day he became a foreigner*

Nor should you have rejoiced over the children of Judah
In the day of their destruction;
Nor should you have spoken proudly
In the day of distress.
13 You should not have entered the gate of My people
In the day of their calamity.
Indeed, you should not have gazed on their affliction
In the day of their calamity,
Nor laid *hands* on their substance
In the day of their calamity.
14 You should not have stood at the crossroads
To cut off those among them who escaped;
Nor should you have delivered up those among them who remained
In the day of distress.

15 "For the day of the LORD upon all the nations *is* near;
As you have done, it shall be done to you;
Your reprisal shall return upon your own head.
16 For as you drank on My holy mountain,
So shall all the nations drink continually;
Yes, they shall drink, and swallow,
And they shall be as though they had never been.

Israel's Final Triumph

17 "But on Mount Zion there shall be deliverance,
And there shall be holiness;
The house of Jacob shall possess their possessions.
18 The house of Jacob shall be a fire,
And the house of Joseph a flame;
But the house of Esau *shall be* stubble;
They shall kindle them and devour them,
And no survivor shall *remain* of the house of Esau,"
For the LORD has spoken.

19 The South[c] shall possess the mountains of Esau,
And the Lowland shall possess Philistia.
They shall possess the fields of Ephraim
And the fields of Samaria.
Benjamin *shall possess* Gilead.
20 And the captives of this host of the children of Israel
Shall possess the land of the Canaanites
As far as Zarephath.
The captives of Jerusalem who are in Sepharad
Shall possess the cities of the South.[d]
21 Then saviors[e] shall come to Mount Zion
To judge the mountains of Esau,
And the kingdom shall be the LORD's.

This is a far cry from the good news Jesus preached and Paul heralded. Their gospel was salvation by faith—and only by faith.

The salvation spoken of by Jesus and Paul takes place at one moment in time yet seals the believer for all time. This faith moves the Judge not only to forgive and pardon the sinner, but to adopt him into His own family as well.

. . . Why the mercy? Why the kindness? The only answer is love—love of such magnitude that all human illustrations fall short, love that is unconditional at its core with no hidden agendas and no fine print. God's love is such that He accepts us just the way we are but refuses to leave us there. . . .

God has gone to great lengths to make our relationship with Him possible. Doing so cost Him His Son. But the sacrifice of His Son did far more than merely provide us with the possibility of such a relationship; it guaranteed the permanency of that relationship as well.

Your salvation is secure. My prayer is that you would experience the assurance of this precious and costly gift.

(From *Eternal Security* by Charles Stanley)

APPLICATION Have you ever felt that you were out of favor with God? Did you try to ask Jesus into your heart again, and again? Jesus comes the first time! He stays! Be confident that he will never leave you for you are his child.

EXPLORATION Security—Psalm 17:8-9; 18:2-3; 27:1; Proverbs 18:10; 1 Peter 1:3-4.

19 c Hebrew *Negev*
20 d Hebrew *Negev*
21 e Or *deliverers*

The Book of

JONAH

INTRODUCTION

He had every right to run (he thought). Why should he go to that stinking city? He hated the place. Why should he warn the Ninevites about God's judgment? After how they had treated his people, they deserved to be wiped out. The last thing Jonah wanted was for his enemies to receive God's blessing.

So he ran . . . as fast and as far as he could away from what God wanted him to do.

But God had other plans.

You know the story: God stirred up a storm. Jonah bailed out of the boat and ended up in the belly of the fish.

God gave Jonah time to think over his actions and attitudes. For the first time Jonah didn't complain, he prayed. (Probably the only time anyone ever prayed for a fish-burp.)

The prayer was answered and Jonah eventually traveled to hated Nineveh. He preached to the people there. Though his odor wasn't appealing, his message was and the Ninevites repented. God relented (as Jonah knew he would), and Jonah fumed, furious over the turn of events. He sulked.

We can be so difficult.

But God can be so patient.

The book of Jonah is more than a fascinating account of one man's futile attempt to run away from God. It is a story of God's love for even the most unlovable, despicable people we can imagine—and of our responsibility to tell them the Good News.

LIFE LESSON

Jonah 1:1–2:10

SITUATION God told Jonah to preach to the Assyrians in Nineveh. Jonah knew that if he preached to them, they would have an opportunity to avoid God's wrath. Jonah hoped to see these enemies punished by God, so he ran away.

OBSERVATION Running away from God can't be done. Jonah discovered that. God's dominion extends everywhere.

INSPIRATION How infinitely more difficult it is for us to grasp what Jesus meant when He said: "God is Spirit." Jesus knew! His mind was not limited as our minds are limited. His eyes were not focused on the mud puddle of life. He knew full well the borderless reaches of the Spirit, and He came to try to give us some understanding of its wonders, its comfort, and its peace.

The spirit is not something bound in a body. The Bible declares that God is a Spirit—that He is not limited to body; He is not limited to shape; He is not limited to boundaries or bonds; He is absolutely immeasurable and undiscernible by eyes that can see only physical things. The Bible tells us that because He has no such limitations He can be everywhere at once—that He can hear all, see all, and know all.

Jonah's Disobedience

Now the word of the LORD came to Jonah the son of
Amittai, saying, 2"Arise, go to Nineveh, that great city,
and cry out against it; for their wickedness has come up
before Me." 3But Jonah arose to flee to Tarshish from the
presence of the LORD. He went down to Joppa, and found a ship going to
Tarshish; so he paid the fare, and went down into it, to go with them to
Tarshish from the presence of the LORD.

The Storm at Sea

4But the LORD sent out a great wind on the sea, and there was a mighty
tempest on the sea, so that the ship was about to be broken up.
5Then the mariners were afraid; and every man cried out to his god, and
threw the cargo that *was* in the ship into the sea, to lighten the load.[a] But
Jonah had gone down into the lowest parts of the ship, had lain down, and
was fast asleep.
6So the captain came to him, and said to him, "What do you mean,
sleeper? Arise, call on your God; perhaps your God will consider us, so that
we may not perish."
7And they said to one another, "Come, let us cast lots, that we may know
for whose cause this trouble *has come* upon us." So they cast lots, and the
lot fell on Jonah. 8Then they said to him, "Please tell us! For whose cause *is*
this trouble upon us? What is your occupation? And where do you come
from? What is your country? And of what people are you?"
9So he said to them, "I *am* a Hebrew; and I fear the LORD, the God of heaven,
who made the sea and the dry *land*."

Jonah Thrown into the Sea

10Then the men were exceedingly afraid, and said to him, "Why have
you done this?" For the men knew that he fled from the presence of the
LORD, because he had told them. 11Then they said to him, "What shall we
do to you that the sea may be calm for us?"—for the sea was growing
more tempestuous.
12And he said to them, "Pick me up and throw me into the sea; then the sea
will become calm for you. For I know that this great tempest *is* because of me."
13Nevertheless the men rowed hard to return to land, but they could not,
for the sea continued to grow more tempestuous against them. 14Therefore
they cried out to the LORD and said, "We pray, O LORD, please do not let us
perish for this man's life, and do not charge us with innocent blood; for You,
O LORD, have done as it pleased You." 15So they picked up Jonah and threw
him into the sea, and the sea ceased from its raging. 16Then the men feared
the LORD exceedingly, and offered a sacrifice to the LORD and took vows.

Jonah's Prayer and Deliverance

17Now the LORD had prepared a great fish to swallow Jonah. And Jonah
was in the belly of the fish three days and three nights.
2 Then Jonah prayed to the LORD his God from the fish's belly. 2And he
said:

"I cried out to the LORD because of my affliction,
And He answered me.

1:5 [a] Literally *from upon them*

"Out of the belly of Sheol I cried,
And You heard my voice.
3 For You cast me into the deep,
Into the heart of the seas,
And the floods surrounded me;
All Your billows and Your waves passed over me.
4 Then I said, 'I have been cast out of Your sight;
Yet I will look again toward Your holy temple.'
5 The waters surrounded me, *even* to my soul;
The deep closed around me;
Weeds were wrapped around my head.
6 I went down to the moorings of the mountains;
The earth with its bars *closed* behind me forever;
Yet You have brought up my life from the pit,
O LORD, my God.

7 "When my soul fainted within me,
I remembered the LORD;
And my prayer went *up* to You,
Into Your holy temple.
8 "Those who regard worthless idols
Forsake their own Mercy.
9 But I will sacrifice to You
With the voice of thanksgiving;
I will pay what I have vowed.
Salvation *is* of the LORD."

10 So the LORD spoke to the fish, and it vomited Jonah onto dry *land*.

Jonah Preaches at Nineveh

3 Now the word of the LORD came to Jonah the second time, saying,
2 "Arise, go to Nineveh, that great city, and preach to it the message that
I tell you." 3 So Jonah arose and went to Nineveh, according to the word of
the LORD. Now Nineveh was an exceedingly great city, a three-day journey[b]
in extent. 4 And Jonah began to enter the city on the first day's walk. Then
he cried out and said, "Yet forty days, and Nineveh shall be overthrown!"

The People of Nineveh Believe

5 So the people of Nineveh believed God, proclaimed a fast, and put on
sackcloth, from the greatest to the least of them. 6 Then word came to the
king of Nineveh; and he arose from his throne and laid aside his robe, covered *himself* with sackcloth and sat in ashes. 7 And he caused *it* to be proclaimed and published throughout Nineveh by the decree of the king and
his nobles, saying,

> Let neither man nor beast, herd nor flock, taste anything; do not
> let them eat, or drink water. 8 But let man and beast be covered
> with sackcloth, and cry mightily to God; yes, let every one turn
> from his evil way and from the violence that is in his hands. 9 Who
> can tell *if* God will turn and relent, and turn away from His fierce
> anger, so that we may not perish?

He can be everywhere at once, heeding the prayers of all who call out in the name of Christ; performing the mighty miracles that keep the stars in their places and the plants bursting up through the earth and the fish swimming in the sea. There is no limit to God. There is no limit to His wisdom. There is no limit to His power. There is no limit to His love.

If you have been trying to limit God—stop it! You wouldn't try to limit the ocean. You cannot limit the universe. You wouldn't be bold enough to try to change the course of the moon, or to stop the earth as it turns on its axis! How everlastingly more foolish it is to try to limit the God who created and controls all these wonders!

(From *Peace with God* by Billy Graham)

APPLICATION Did you ever try to run away from your shadow as a child? You can't run from God either. When God tells you to go somewhere, listen and follow. Where is God sending you to tell others about him—to your family, next door, your co-workers? Will you run from God's call?

EXPLORATION Sovereignty—Job 37:23; 38:1; Revelation 19:16.

3:3 *b* Exact meaning unknown

Life Lesson

Jonah 3:1–4:11

SITUATION Jonah finally obeyed God and preached in Nineveh. The people and their king responded immediately, and God had compassion on them.

OBSERVATION God's words can have a transforming effect on people, causing them to repent of their sins.

INSPIRATION Violent strife and conflict have haunted the human race to one degree or another since the day Adam and Eve first chose to rebel against God.

At those times, death rides through every city and town bringing suffering and death. But sometimes, just as suddenly, we enter a time of peace and relative calm. Why? . . . because many have listened to His message of warning and turned to Him in repentance and faith.

A good example of this is seen in God's dealings with the people of the ancient Assyrian capital of Nineveh. They were an evil, pagan people who worshiped idols and often fought against God's people. God sent the prophet Jonah to Nineveh to proclaim His coming judgment to them: "Go to the great city of Nineveh and proclaim to it the message I give you. . . . Forty more days and Nineveh will be overturned." But when the king of Nineveh heard Jonah's message, he repented and ordered the whole people to repent as well. As a result God's judgment was averted. Only later, when evil increased in the generations after Jonah and the people failed to repent, did God's judgment finally fall on Nineveh. God's judgment is often this way. Some day it will come in all its fullness and finality, but in the meantime it may be that God's hand of judgment will pause when we repent.

(From *Storm Warning* by Billy Graham)

APPLICATION If God tells you to speak to others about their actions, take courage. You might be surprised at how many accept your words and repent.

EXPLORATION Repentance—2 Kings 22:19; Matthew 3:8; Acts 17:30.

10 Then God saw their works, that they turned from their evil way; and
God relented from the disaster that He had said He would bring upon
them, and He did not do it.

Jonah's Anger and God's Kindness

4 But it displeased Jonah exceedingly, and he became angry. 2 So he
prayed to the LORD, and said, "Ah, LORD, was not this what I said when
I was still in my country? Therefore I fled previously to Tarshish; for I know
that You *are* a gracious and merciful God, slow to anger and abundant in
lovingkindness, One who relents from doing harm. 3 Therefore now, O
LORD, please take my life from me, for *it is* better for me to die than to live!"
4 Then the LORD said, "*Is it* right for you to be angry?"
5 So Jonah went out of the city and sat on the east side of the city. There
he made himself a shelter and sat under it in the shade, till he might see
what would become of the city. 6 And the LORD God prepared a plant[c] and
made it come up over Jonah, that it might be shade for his head to deliver
him from his misery. So Jonah was very grateful for the plant. 7 But as
morning dawned the next day God prepared a worm, and it *so* damaged
the plant that it withered. 8 And it happened, when the sun arose, that God
prepared a vehement east wind; and the sun beat on Jonah's head, so that
he grew faint. Then he wished death for himself, and said, "*It is* better for
me to die than to live."
9 Then God said to Jonah, "*Is it* right for you to be angry about the plant?"
And he said, "*It is* right for me to be angry, even to death!"
10 But the LORD said, "You have had pity on the plant for which you have
not labored, nor made it grow, which came up in a night and perished in a
night. 11 And should I not pity Nineveh, that great city, in which are more
than one hundred and twenty thousand persons who cannot discern between their right hand and their left—and much livestock?"

4:6 [c] Hebrew *kikayon,* exact identity unknown

The Book of

MICAH

INTRODUCTION

Some time ago I did something I hadn't done in years. I listened to the airline attendant as she gave her warnings. I normally tune her out. I usually bury my nose in a book or magazine and ignore her cautions. But this time I didn't.

I didn't, because the day before a commercial plane had gone down. As I boarded the flight I realized that if this plane crashed I would not know what to do.

So I listened. As she held up a seat belt, I buckled mine. As she described the oxygen mask, I looked up to see where it was stored. When she pointed to the exit doors, I turned to find them. That's when I noticed what she notices on every flight. No one was listening!

No one was paying attention. I was shocked. I seriously considered standing up and getting everyone's attention and shouting, "You guys better listen up. One mishap and this plane becomes a flaming mausoleum. What this lady is telling you might save your life!"

I wondered what would happen if she used more drastic means. What if she took a gasoline drenched doll and set it on fire? What if the in-flight screen portrayed images of desperate people scrambling to deboard a blazing plane? What if she marched up and down the aisle yanking away the papers and snatching the magazines, demanding that the passengers listen if they wanted to survive this flying inferno?

She would lose her job. But she would be doing us a favor. Love cautions the loved.

The Book of Micah is a warning. God's prophet warns of the terrible judgment which awaits all who ignore God. "Be prepared," he pleads, and then explains how to prepare.

I wonder if he noticed what I noticed on the plane. Most people don't listen to warnings. Let's be the exception.

LIFE LESSON

Micah 1:1–2:13

SITUATION Micah, a prophet from Judah, prophesied to both Israel and Judah. The people told him to be quiet.

OBSERVATION Micah's message to the sinful people was not well received; people don't like to be reminded of their sin.

INSPIRATION Micah had the same experience as the other prophets who came before him, and those who followed him. The people did not want to hear what he had to say. People rarely want to be told of judgment; they seldom want to be warned of what is happening. They prefer not that someone interprets the events unfolding on an international scale and show that God is intervening in men's affairs. Note this as well: Often those who can predict, prophesy, and interpret, who would bring a message from the Lord, find that it is like pulling teeth to get people to listen to the warnings. Accordingly, Micah finds it necessary to use a dramatic means of conveying his message. He goes around Jerusalem weeping and wailing, barefoot and partially clothed. He howls like a jackel and moans like an owl. It must have been exciting to have Micah around!

I have a very good friend in a Third World country, a Rhodes scholar, an absolutely brilliant man. He was the pastor of the largest church of his denomination. I remember he once debated a leading political figure on national television on the issue of legalized lotteries and gambling. He totally routed him. It was a national humiliation for that dignitary. My young pastor friend was particularly concerned that the people of his homeland were not listening to the Word of the Lord. As long as he told them what they wanted to hear it was great. As long as he preached that all was good and bright, that they would be prosperous and peaceful, that was super. But the

The word of the LORD that came to Micah of Moresheth in the days of Jotham, Ahaz, *and* Hezekiah, kings of Judah, which he saw concerning Samaria and Jerusalem.

The Coming Judgment on Israel

2 Hear, all you peoples!
Listen, O earth, and all that is in it!
Let the Lord GOD be a witness against you,
The Lord from His holy temple.

3 For behold, the LORD is coming out of His place;
He will come down
And tread on the high places of the earth.
4 The mountains will melt under Him,
And the valleys will split
Like wax before the fire,
Like waters poured down a steep place.
5 All this is for the transgression of Jacob
And for the sins of the house of Israel.
What *is* the transgression of Jacob?
Is it not Samaria?
And what *are* the high places of Judah?
Are they not Jerusalem?

6 "Therefore I will make Samaria a heap of ruins in the field,
Places for planting a vineyard;
I will pour down her stones into the valley,
And I will uncover her foundations.
7 All her carved images shall be beaten to pieces,
And all her pay as a harlot shall be
burned with the fire;
All her idols I will lay desolate,
For she gathered *it* from the pay of a harlot,
And they shall return to the pay of a harlot."

Mourning for Israel and Judah

8 Therefore I will wail and howl,
I will go stripped and naked;
I will make a wailing like the jackals
And a mourning like the ostriches,
9 For her wounds *are* incurable.
For it has come to Judah;
It has come to the gate of My people—
To Jerusalem.

10 Tell *it* not in Gath,
Weep not at all;
In Beth Aphrah[a]
Roll yourself in the dust.
11 Pass by in naked shame, you inhabitant of Shaphir;
The inhabitant of Zaanan[b] does not go out.

1:10 [a] Literally *House of Dust*
1:11 [b] Literally *Going Out*

Beth Ezel mourns;
Its place to stand is taken away from you.

12 For the inhabitant of Maroth pined[c] for good,
But disaster came down from the LORD
To the gate of Jerusalem.

13 O inhabitant of Lachish,
Harness the chariot to the swift steeds
(She *was* the beginning of sin to the daughter of Zion),
For the transgressions of Israel were found in you.

14 Therefore you shall give presents to Moresheth Gath;[d]
The houses of Achzib[e] *shall be* a lie to the kings of Israel.

15 I will yet bring an heir to you, O inhabitant of Mareshah;[f]
The glory of Israel shall come to Adullam.

16 Make yourself bald and cut off your hair,
Because of your precious children;
Enlarge your baldness like an eagle,
For they shall go from you into captivity.

Woe to Evildoers

2 Woe to those who devise iniquity,
And work out evil on their beds!
At morning light they practice it,
Because it is in the power of their hand.

2 They covet fields and take *them* by violence,
Also houses, and seize *them.*
So they oppress a man and his house,
A man and his inheritance.

3 Therefore thus says the LORD:
"Behold, against this family I am devising disaster,
From which you cannot remove your necks;
Nor shall you walk haughtily,
For this *is* an evil time.

4 In that day *one* shall take up a proverb against you,
And lament with a bitter lamentation, saying:
'We are utterly destroyed!
He has changed the heritage of my people;
How He has removed *it* from me!
To a turncoat He has divided our fields.' "

5 Therefore you will have no one to determine boundaries[g] by lot
In the assembly of the LORD.

Lying Prophets

6 "Do not prattle," *you say to those* who prophesy.
So they shall not prophesy to you;[h]
They shall not return insult for insult.[i]

young pastor was convinced that things were bad in his country and something needed to be done about it. People needed to be brought to repentance and take God seriously.

He felt as if he had been hammering his head against a brick wall. So one day he came into church late for the Sunday morning service, to get the people's attention. He came in the back door instead of the front. That also aroused their attention. Instead of wearing his pulpit gown, he dressed himself in sackcloth and ashes. Instead of carrying a Bible he carried a bell. He came in ringing his bell, dressed in sackcloth and ashes. As a result, they fired him as their pastor and put him in a home for the mentally unstable. One day I talked to him and asked, "Did you have a nervous breakdown?"

"No," he said. "They decided that was what I had, but in actual fact I was trying hard to get their attention. I got it," he went on, "and when they gave me their full attention, they locked me up. They didn't want to know."

Such has always been the lot of the prophet. The person who tells people what is really happening in the world is not always welcome. . . . When a prophet comes with a hard message, he is bound to be unpopular. A prophet is one who warns of God's impending wrath. If people refuse to heed the message, if they refuse to repent, if they remain complacent, then the judgment eventually will fall. (From *Hearing God's Voice Above the Noise* by Stuart Briscoe)

APPLICATION Expect sinners to sin. Do not be offended when someone sins against you. Extend a caring arm to people whose sin makes them unbearable.

EXPLORATION Respect for Spiritual Leaders—Joshua 1:16-18; 1 Thessalonians 5:12-13; 1 Timothy 5:17-20; Hebrews 13:7.

1:12 [c] Literally *was sick*
1:14 [d] Literally *Possession of Gath* [e] Literally *Lie*
1:15 [f] Literally *Inheritance*
2:5 [g] Literally *one casting a surveyor's line*
2:6 [h] Literally *to these* [i] Vulgate reads *He shall not take shame.*

LIFE LESSON

Micah 3:1–5:15

SITUATION Micah continued his prophecies to Judah and Jerusalem. He rebuked the present leaders but promised a perfect future leader, Christ.

OBSERVATION God promises that one day all weapons of war will be done away with and God's people will live in total peace.

INSPIRATION The Lord's promise that in "the last days" there will be peace symbolized by turning weapons into productive tools has been a hope of many Christians through the centuries including Toyohiko Kagawa, who was born in Japan in 1888.

At the age of fourteen, he enrolled in an English class taught by a Presbyterian missionary. Although he had been warned by relatives not to be influenced by Christianity, he could not resist. One year later he confessed his faith in Christ and was baptized. The real test of his faith came when Japan declared war on Russia. He was conscripted into the military along with other students, but his conscience would not permit him to train with a rifle. "All he could hear in his mind were the words of Jesus, 'Love your enemies,' and all he could see was Christ dying without resistance on the cross." His stand created an uproar. His instructor physically assaulted him, and he was attacked by fellow students.

Following his college years, Kagawa took seminary training. But he soon left his studies in order to reach out with the gospel to the impoverished and destitute slums in the city of Kobe. He lived with the people in a tin hut with a dirt floor and bamboo walls, and quickly became known among the people as "the Christian." But despite all his sacrifice, Kagawa realized that what the impoverished people in the inner-city needed most

7 *You who are* named the house of Jacob:
"Is the Spirit of the LORD restricted?
Are these His doings?
Do not My words do good
To him who walks uprightly?

8 "Lately My people have risen up as an enemy—
You pull off the robe with the garment
From those who trust *you,* as they pass by,
Like men returned from war.
9 The women of My people you cast out
From their pleasant houses;
From their children
You have taken away My glory forever.

10 "Arise and depart,
For this *is* not *your* rest;
Because it is defiled, it shall destroy,
Yes, with utter destruction.
11 If a man should walk in a false spirit
And speak a lie, *saying,*
'I will prophesy to you of wine and drink,'
Even he would be the prattler of this people.

Israel Restored

12 "I will surely assemble all of you, O Jacob,
I will surely gather the remnant of Israel;
I will put them together like sheep of the fold,[j]
Like a flock in the midst of their pasture;
They shall make a loud noise because of *so many* people.
13 The one who breaks open will come up before them;
They will break out,
Pass through the gate,
And go out by it;
Their king will pass before them,
With the LORD at their head."

Wicked Rulers and Prophets

3 And I said:

"Hear now, O heads of Jacob,
And you rulers of the house of Israel:
Is it not for you to know justice?
2 You who hate good and love evil;
Who strip the skin from *My* people,[k]
And the flesh from their bones;
3 Who also eat the flesh of My people,
Flay their skin from them,
Break their bones,
And chop *them* in pieces

2:12 [j] Hebrew *Bozrah*
3:2 [k] Literally *them*

Like *meat* for the pot,
Like flesh in the caldron."

4 Then they will cry to the LORD,
But He will not hear them;
He will even hide His face from them at that time,
Because they have been evil in their deeds.

5 Thus says the LORD concerning the prophets
Who make my people stray;
Who chant "Peace"
While they chew with their teeth,
But who prepare war against him
Who puts nothing into their mouths:
6 "Therefore you shall have night without vision,
And you shall have darkness without divination;
The sun shall go down on the prophets,
And the day shall be dark for them.
7 So the seers shall be ashamed,
And the diviners abashed;
Indeed they shall all cover their lips;
For *there is* no answer from God."

8 But truly I am full of power by the Spirit of the LORD,
And of justice and might,
To declare to Jacob his transgression
And to Israel his sin.
9 Now hear this,
You heads of the house of Jacob
And rulers of the house of Israel,
Who abhor justice
And pervert all equity,
10 Who build up Zion with bloodshed
And Jerusalem with iniquity:
11 Her heads judge for a bribe,
Her priests teach for pay,
And her prophets divine for money.
Yet they lean on the LORD, and say,
"Is not the LORD among us?
No harm can come upon us."
12 Therefore because of you
Zion shall be plowed *like* a field,
Jerusalem shall become heaps of ruins,
And the mountain of the temple[l]
Like the bare hills of the forest.

The LORD's Reign in Zion

4 Now it shall come to pass in the latter days
That the mountain of the LORD's house
Shall be established on the top of the mountains,
And shall be exalted above the hills;

3:12 [l] Literally *house*

was not handouts but organizational strength. After studying for a time in America, he returned to Japan and organized labor unions and relief programs. Then, "in 1928 he initiated the 'Kingdom of God Movement,' a daring nationwide evangelistic campaign to win a million Japanese to Christ."

Once again, however, Kagawa's faith was tested by nationalism and militarism. When Japan attacked Manchuria in 1931, he made a public apology: "To my brethren in China, Forgive the sin of Japan. Though Japanese Christians have not the power to oppose military force, some of them regret the sin of Japan. I wish the day of reconciliation may soon come." He was even more distressed by the bombing of Pearl Harbor in 1941 and the U.S. retaliation—a retaliation that seemed incomprehensible to him because it was coming from a "Christian" nation.

Kagawa lived out his life seeking to beat swords into plowshares. He wanted to stop the senseless killing and to raise the standard of living of the poor. He seemed to meet with little success in light of the military build-up in both the East and the West. At times he seemed to be one lone Christian against the rest of the world—a man whose motto was the hymn, "Jesus Keep Me Near the Cross."

(From *Stories of Faith* by Ruth A. Tucker)

APPLICATION Christians should pray for peace and harmony in the world. Pick up today's newspaper and pray for an area of the world where people are suffering from the horrible consequences of war. Pray that your fellow Christians there will stand strong in their difficult circumstances.

EXPLORATION Pursue Peace—Psalm 34:14; Matthew 5:9; Mark 9:50; Romans 12:18; Colossians 3:15; Hebrews 12:14.

And peoples shall flow to it.
2 Many nations shall come and say,
"Come, and let us go up to the mountain
of the LORD,
To the house of the God of Jacob;
He will teach us His ways,
And we shall walk in His paths."
For out of Zion the law shall go forth,
And the word of the LORD from Jerusalem.
3 He shall judge between many peoples,
And rebuke strong nations afar off;
They shall beat their swords into plowshares,
And their spears into pruning hooks;
Nation shall not lift up sword against nation,
Neither shall they learn war anymore.[m]
4 But everyone shall sit under his vine and
under his fig tree,
And no one shall make *them* afraid;
For the mouth of the LORD of hosts has spoken.
5 For all people walk each in the name of his god,
But we will walk in the name of the LORD
our God
Forever and ever.

Zion's Future Triumph

6 "In that day," says the LORD,
"I will assemble the lame,
I will gather the outcast
And those whom I have afflicted;
7 I will make the lame a remnant,
And the outcast a strong nation;
So the LORD will reign over them in Mount Zion
From now on, even forever.
8 And you, O tower of the flock,
The stronghold of the daughter of Zion,
To you shall it come,
Even the former dominion shall come,
The kingdom of the daughter of Jerusalem."
9 Now why do you cry aloud?
Is there no king in your midst?
Has your counselor perished?
For pangs have seized you like a
woman in labor.
10 Be in pain, and labor to bring forth,
O daughter of Zion,
Like a woman in birth pangs.
For now you shall go forth from the city,
You shall dwell in the field,
And to Babylon you shall go.
There you shall be delivered;
There the LORD will redeem you
From the hand of your enemies.
11 Now also many nations have gathered
against you,
Who say, "Let her be defiled,
And let our eye look upon Zion."
12 But they do not know the thoughts of the LORD,
Nor do they understand His counsel;
For He will gather them like sheaves to the
threshing floor.
13 "Arise and thresh, O daughter of Zion;
For I will make your horn iron,
And I will make your hooves bronze;
You shall beat in pieces many peoples;
I will consecrate their gain to the LORD,
And their substance to the Lord of
the whole earth."

5 Now gather yourself in troops,
O daughter of troops;
He has laid siege against us;
They will strike the judge of Israel with a rod
on the cheek.

The Coming Messiah

2 "But you, Bethlehem Ephrathah,
Though you are little among the thousands
of Judah,
Yet out of you shall come forth to Me
The One to be Ruler in Israel,
Whose goings forth *are* from of old,
From everlasting."
3 Therefore He shall give them up,
Until the time *that* she who is in labor has
given birth;
Then the remnant of His brethren
Shall return to the children of Israel.
4 And He shall stand and feed *His flock*
In the strength of the LORD,
In the majesty of the name of the LORD His God;
And they shall abide,
For now He shall be great
To the ends of the earth;
5 And this *One* shall be peace.

Judgment on Israel's Enemies

When the Assyrian comes into our land,
And when he treads in our palaces,

4:3 *m* Compare Isaiah 2:2–4

Then we will raise against him
Seven shepherds and eight princely men.
6 They shall waste with the sword the
land of Assyria,
And the land of Nimrod at its entrances;
Thus He shall deliver *us* from the Assyrian,
When he comes into our land
And when he treads within our borders.

7 Then the remnant of Jacob
Shall be in the midst of many peoples,
Like dew from the LORD,
Like showers on the grass,
That tarry for no man
Nor wait for the sons of men.
8 And the remnant of Jacob
Shall be among the Gentiles,
In the midst of many peoples,
Like a lion among the beasts of the forest,
Like a young lion among flocks of sheep,
Who, if he passes through,
Both treads down and tears in pieces,
And none can deliver.
9 Your hand shall be lifted against
your adversaries,
And all your enemies shall be cut off.

10 "And it shall be in that day," says the LORD,
"That I will cut off your horses from your midst
And destroy your chariots.
11 I will cut off the cities of your land
And throw down all your strongholds.
12 I will cut off sorceries from your hand,
And you shall have no soothsayers.
13 Your carved images I will also cut off,
And your sacred pillars from your midst;
You shall no more worship the work
of your hands;
14 I will pluck your wooden images[n] from
your midst;
Thus I will destroy your cities.
15 And I will execute vengeance in
anger and fury
On the nations that have not heard."[o]

God Pleads with Israel

6 Hear now what the LORD says:

"Arise, plead your case before the mountains,
And let the hills hear your voice.

2 Hear, O you mountains, the LORD's complaint,
And you strong foundations of the earth;
For the LORD has a complaint against His people,
And He will contend with Israel.

3 "O My people, what have I done to you?
And how have I wearied you?
Testify against Me.
4 For I brought you up from the land of Egypt,
I redeemed you from the house of bondage;
And I sent before you Moses, Aaron,
and Miriam.
5 O My people, remember now
What Balak king of Moab counseled,
And what Balaam the son of Beor answered him,
From Acacia Grove[p] to Gilgal,
That you may know the righteousness
of the LORD."

6 With what shall I come before the LORD,
And bow myself before the High God?
Shall I come before Him with burnt offerings,
With calves a year old?
7 Will the LORD be pleased with
thousands of rams,
Ten thousand rivers of oil?
Shall I give my firstborn *for* my transgression,
The fruit of my body *for* the sin of my soul?
8 He has shown you, O man, what *is* good;
And what does the LORD require of you
But to do justly,
To love mercy,
And to walk humbly with your God?

Punishment of Israel's Injustice

9 The LORD's voice cries to the city—
Wisdom shall see Your name:

"Hear the rod!
Who has appointed it?
10 Are there yet the treasures of wickedness
In the house of the wicked,
And the short measure *that is* an abomination?
11 Shall I count pure *those* with the wicked scales,
And with the bag of deceitful weights?
12 For her rich men are full of violence,
Her inhabitants have spoken lies,
And their tongue is deceitful in their mouth.

5:14 [n] Hebrew *Asherim,* Canaanite deities
5:15 [o] Or *obeyed*
6:5 [p] Hebrew *Shittim* (compare Numbers 25:1; Joshua 2:1; 3:1)

13 "Therefore I will also make *you* sick
by striking you,
By making *you* desolate because
of your sins.
14 You shall eat, but not be satisfied;
Hunger[q] *shall be* in your midst.
You may carry *some* away,[r] but shall
not save *them;*
And what you do rescue I will give
over to the sword.

15 "You shall sow, but not reap;
You shall tread the olives, but not anoint
yourselves with oil;
And *make* sweet wine, but not drink wine.
16 For the statutes of Omri are kept;
All the works of Ahab's house *are done;*
And you walk in their counsels,
That I may make you a desolation,
And your inhabitants a hissing.
Therefore you shall bear the reproach
of My people."[s]

Sorrow for Israel's Sins

7 Woe is me!
For I am like those who gather summer fruits,
Like those who glean vintage grapes;
There is no cluster to eat
Of the first-ripe fruit *which* my soul desires.
2 The faithful *man* has perished from the earth,
And *there is* no one upright among men.
They all lie in wait for blood;
Every man hunts his brother with a net.

3 That they may successfully do evil
with both hands—
The prince asks *for gifts,*
The judge *seeks* a bribe,
And the great *man* utters his evil desire;
So they scheme together.
4 The best of them *is* like a brier;
The most upright *is sharper* than a thorn hedge;
The day of your watchman and your
punishment comes;
Now shall be their perplexity.

5 Do not trust in a friend;
Do not put your confidence in a companion;
Guard the doors of your mouth
From her who lies in your bosom.
6 For son dishonors father,
Daughter rises against her mother,
Daughter-in-law against her
mother-in-law;
A man's enemies *are* the men of his
own household.
7 Therefore I will look to the LORD;
I will wait for the God of my salvation;
My God will hear me.

Israel's Confession and Comfort

8 Do not rejoice over me, my enemy;
When I fall, I will arise;
When I sit in darkness,
The LORD *will be* a light to me.
9 I will bear the indignation of the LORD,
Because I have sinned against Him,
Until He pleads my case
And executes justice for me.
He will bring me forth to the light;
I will see His righteousness.
10 Then *she who is* my enemy will see,
And shame will cover her who
said to me,
"Where is the LORD your God?"
My eyes will see her;
Now she will be trampled down
Like mud in the streets.

11 *In* the day when your walls are to be built,
In that day the decree shall go far and wide.[t]
12 *In* that day they[u] shall come to you
From Assyria and the fortified cities,[v]
From the fortress[w] to the River,[x]
From sea to sea,
And mountain *to* mountain.
13 Yet the land shall be desolate
Because of those who dwell in it,
And for the fruit of their deeds.

God Will Forgive Israel

14 Shepherd Your people with Your staff,
The flock of Your heritage,
Who dwell solitarily *in* a woodland,
In the midst of Carmel;
Let them feed *in* Bashan and Gilead,
As in days of old.

6:14 [q] Or *Emptiness* or *Humiliation* [r] Targum and Vulgate read *You shall take hold.*
6:16 [s] Following Masoretic Text, Targum, and Vulgate; Septuagint reads *of nations.*
7:11 [t] Or *the boundary shall be extended*
7:12 [u] Literally *he,* collective of the captives [v] Hebrew *arey mazor,* possibly *cities of Egypt* [w] Hebrew *mazor,* possibly *Egypt* [x] That is, the Euphrates

15 "As in the days when you came out of the
land of Egypt,
I will show them[y] wonders."

16 The nations shall see and be ashamed
of all their might;
They shall put *their* hand over *their* mouth;
Their ears shall be deaf.
17 They shall lick the dust like a serpent;
They shall crawl from their holes like
snakes of the earth.
They shall be afraid of the LORD our God,
And shall fear because of You.
18 Who *is* a God like You,
Pardoning iniquity
And passing over the transgression
of the remnant of His heritage?

He does not retain His anger forever,
Because He delights *in* mercy.
19 He will again have compassion on us,
And will subdue our iniquities.

You will cast all our[z] sins
Into the depths of the sea.
20 You will give truth to Jacob
And mercy to Abraham,
Which You have sworn to our fathers
From days of old.

7:15 [y] Literally *him,* collective for the captives
7:19 [z] Literally *their*

The Book of

NAHUM

INTRODUCTION

Remember the playground bully? He was big and tough and he enjoyed pushing kids around. Everyone was afraid of him (even some of the teachers, you thought)—he seemed invincible. But over the next few years, the other boys grew past him—bigger, stronger, faster. Then the bully didn't seem so tough or frightening as before.

Assyria was the bully of the Middle East, the conqueror of many nations including Israel. This nation's power, epitomized by Nineveh, the capital city, was awesome and overwhelming. Proud and defiant, Assyria plundered, oppressed, and slaughtered its victims.

Enter Nahum, the prophet.

Nahum pronounced God's judgment upon this prideful and wicked people, exclaiming that powerful Assyria would be utterly destroyed. His prediction was fulfilled within fifty years.

This book provides strong testimony to God's ultimate power and justice—he calls all people to live under his rule: nations, cities, parents, neighborhood bullies . . . and you.

Perhaps you don't have to *remember* a bully. There may be one in your world today. Huge debt, ugly guilt. Bossy employer. If so, remember what Nahum announced thousands of years ago: Your Father is bigger than any bully.

LIFE LESSON

Nahum 1:1–3:19

SITUATION The Assyrian Empire conquered Israel and harassed Judah. God offered to free Judah from Assyrian oppression by destroying Assyria's wicked capital, Nineveh.

OBSERVATION God doesn't want people to fail, rather he gives them opportunities to repent and enter Heaven. But if they persist in sin, they will be punished.

INSPIRATION God has no needs. Human love, as Plato teaches us, is the child of Poverty—of want or lack; it is caused by a real or supposed good in its beloved which the lover needs and desires. But God's love, far from being caused by goodness in the object, causes all the goodness which the object has, loving it first into existence and then into real, though derivative, loveability. God is Goodness. He can give good, but cannot need or get it. In that sense all His love is, as it were, bottomlessly selfless by very definition; it has everything to give and nothing to receive.
(From *The Problem of Pain* by C. S. Lewis as quoted in *The Quotable Lewis*)

APPLICATION Do you feel empty? Overwhelmed? Do you wonder why you have to face difficult trials? Memorize Nahum 1:7 and take confidence in God who remains good.

EXPLORATION God's Judgment—1 Chronicles 13:10-14; Psalm 75:8; Matthew 24:51; Romans 2:5-11.

The burden[a] against Nineveh. The book of the vision of Nahum the Elkoshite.

God's Wrath on His Enemies

2 God *is* jealous, and the LORD avenges;
The LORD avenges and *is* furious.
The LORD will take vengeance on His adversaries,
And He reserves *wrath* for His enemies;
3 The LORD *is* slow to anger and great in power,
And will not at all acquit *the wicked.*

The LORD has His way
In the whirlwind and in the storm,
And the clouds *are* the dust of His feet.
4 He rebukes the sea and makes it dry,
And dries up all the rivers.
Bashan and Carmel wither,
And the flower of Lebanon wilts.
5 The mountains quake before Him,
The hills melt,
And the earth heaves[b] at His presence,
Yes, the world and all who dwell in it.

6 Who can stand before His indignation?
And who can endure the fierceness of His anger?
His fury is poured out like fire,
And the rocks are thrown down by Him.

7 The LORD *is* good,
A stronghold in the day of trouble;
And He knows those who trust in Him.
8 But with an overflowing flood
He will make an utter end of its place,
And darkness will pursue His enemies.

9 What do you conspire against the LORD?
He will make an utter end *of it.*
Affliction will not rise up a second time.
10 For while tangled *like* thorns,
And while drunken *like* drunkards,
They shall be devoured like stubble fully dried.
11 From you comes forth *one*
Who plots evil against the LORD,
A wicked counselor.

12 Thus says the LORD:

"Though *they are* safe, and likewise many,
Yet in this manner they will be cut down
When he passes through.
Though I have afflicted you,
I will afflict you no more;

1:1 [a] Or *oracle*
1:5 [b] Targum reads *burns.*

13 For now I will break off his yoke from you,
And burst your bonds apart."
14 The LORD has given a command
concerning you:
"Your name shall be perpetuated no longer.
Out of the house of your gods
I will cut off the carved image and
the molded image.
I will dig your grave,
For you are vile."

15 Behold, on the mountains
The feet of him who brings good tidings,
Who proclaims peace!
O Judah, keep your appointed feasts,
Perform your vows.
For the wicked one shall no more pass
through you;
He is utterly cut off.

The Destruction of Nineveh

2 He who scatters[c] has come up before your face.
Man the fort!
Watch the road!
Strengthen *your* flanks!
Fortify *your* power mightily.
2 For the LORD will restore the excellence of Jacob
Like the excellence of Israel,
For the emptiers have emptied them out
And ruined their vine branches.

3 The shields of his mighty men *are* made red,
The valiant men *are* in scarlet.
The chariots *come* with flaming torches
In the day of his preparation,
And the spears are brandished.[d]
4 The chariots rage in the streets,
They jostle one another in the broad roads;
They seem like torches,
They run like lightning.

5 He remembers his nobles;
They stumble in their walk;
They make haste to her walls,
And the defense is prepared.
6 The gates of the rivers are opened,
And the palace is dissolved.
7 It is decreed:[e]
She shall be led away captive,
She shall be brought up;
And her maidservants shall lead *her* as with
the voice of doves,
Beating their breasts.

8 Though Nineveh of old *was* like a pool of water,
Now they flee away.
"Halt! Halt!" *they cry;*
But no one turns back.
9 Take spoil of silver!
Take spoil of gold!
There is no end of treasure,
Or wealth of every desirable prize.
10 She is empty, desolate, and waste!
The heart melts, and the knees shake;
Much pain *is* in every side,
And all their faces are drained of color.[f]

11 Where *is* the dwelling of the lions,
And the feeding place of the young lions,
Where the lion walked, the lioness
and lion's cub,
And no one made *them* afraid?
12 The lion tore in pieces enough for his cubs,
Killed for his lionesses,
Filled his caves with prey,
And his dens with flesh.

13 "Behold, I *am* against you," says the LORD of hosts,
"I will burn your[g] chariots in smoke, and the sword
shall devour your young lions; I will cut off your prey
from the earth, and the voice of your messengers shall
be heard no more."

The Woe of Nineveh

3 Woe to the bloody city!
It *is* all full of lies
and robbery.
2 The noise of a whip
And the noise of rattling wheels,
Of galloping horses,
Of clattering chariots!
3 Horsemen charge with bright sword
and glittering spear.
There is a multitude of slain,
A great number of bodies,
Countless corpses—
They stumble over the corpses—

2:1 [c] Vulgate reads *he who destroys.*
2:3 [d] Literally *the cypresses are shaken;* Septuagint and Syriac read *the horses rush about;* Vulgate reads *the drivers are stupefied.*
2:7 [e] Hebrew *Huzzab*
2:10 [f] Compare Joel 2:6
2:13 [g] Literally *her*

4 Because of the multitude of harlotries of the
seductive harlot,
The mistress of sorceries,
Who sells nations through her harlotries,
And families through her sorceries.

5 "Behold, I *am* against you," says the
LORD of hosts;
"I will lift your skirts over your face,
I will show the nations your nakedness,
And the kingdoms your shame.

6 I will cast abominable filth upon you,
Make you vile,
And make you a spectacle.

7 It shall come to pass *that* all who look upon you
Will flee from you, and say,
'Nineveh is laid waste!
Who will bemoan her?'
Where shall I seek comforters for you?"

8 Are you better than No Amon[h]
That was situated by the River,[i]
That had the waters around her,
Whose rampart *was* the sea,
Whose wall *was* the sea?

9 Ethiopia and Egypt *were* her strength,
And *it was* boundless;
Put and Lubim were your[j] helpers.

10 Yet she *was* carried away,
She went into captivity;
Her young children also were dashed to pieces
At the head of every street;
They cast lots for her honorable men,
And all her great men were bound in chains.

11 You also will be drunk;
You will be hidden;
You also will seek refuge from the enemy.

12 All your strongholds *are* fig trees
with ripened figs:
If they are shaken,
They fall into the mouth of the eater.

13 Surely, your people in your midst *are* women!
The gates of your land are wide open
for your enemies;
Fire shall devour the bars of your *gates.*

14 Draw your water for the siege!
Fortify your strongholds!
Go into the clay and tread the mortar!
Make strong the brick kiln!

15 There the fire will devour you,
The sword will cut you off;
It will eat you up like a locust.

Make yourself many—like the locust!
Make yourself many— like the
swarming locusts!

16 You have multiplied your merchants more
than the stars of heaven.
The locust plunders and flies away.

17 Your commanders *are* like *swarming* locusts,
And your generals like great grasshoppers,
Which camp in the hedges on a cold day;
When the sun rises they flee away,
And the place where they *are* is not known.

18 Your shepherds slumber, O king of Assyria;
Your nobles rest *in the dust.*
Your people are scattered on the mountains,
And no one gathers them.

19 Your injury *has* no healing,
Your wound is severe.
All who hear news of you
Will clap *their* hands over you,
For upon whom has not your wickedness
passed continually?

3:8 [h] That is, ancient Thebes; Targum and Vulgate read *populous Alexandria.* [i] Literally *rivers,* that is, the Nile and the surrounding canals
3:9 [j] Septuagint reads *her.*

The Book of

HABAKKUK

INTRODUCTION

Here's a challenge. Find one sincere seeker whom God ignored. Search the Bible for one honest person spurned by heaven. Go ahead. Flip the pages. Examine the Scriptures. Read the stories. Where in the Bible did God turn away the genuine heart? Where in history did God spurn the authentic soul?

Thomas came with doubts. Did Christ turn him away?

Moses had his reservations. Did God tell him to go home?

Job had his struggles. Did God avoid him?

Paul had his hard times. Did God abandon him?

And Habakkuk had his questions. Tough questions. Get-down-and-get-honest type of questions.

O LORD, how long shall I cry, and You will not hear? (1:2)

Why do You look on those who deal treacherously, and hold Your tongue when the wicked devours a person more righteous than he? (1:13)

Did God tell him to talk to someone else?

No. God never turns away the sincere heart. Tough questions don't stump God. He invites our probing. And that is what Habakkuk did. He probed. As well as speaking for God, he spoke to God. He dared to ask his own troubling questions.

Were all his questions answered? I don't know. But I do know Habakkuk was satisfied. You might want to underline his declaration of devotion found in chapter three:

Though the fig tree may not blossom, nor fruit be on the vines; though the labor of the olive may fail, and the fields yield no food; though the flock may be cut off from the fold, and there be no herd in the stalls—yet I will rejoice in the LORD, I will joy in the God of my salvation (vv. 17, 18).

Mark it down. God never turns away the honest seeker. Go to God with your questions. You may not find all the answers, but in finding God, you know the One who does.

LIFE LESSON

Habakkuk 1:1–3:19

SITUATION Judah was making alliances with other nations. God was bringing judgment on Judah through the Babylonians. Habakkuk prophesied at the same time as Jeremiah.

OBSERVATION In the face of great trouble, Habakkuk brought his questions to God. After hearing God's answer, he responded with a prayer of faith (3:2). He asked God to do great miracles.

INSPIRATION Have you ever seen someone unconscious? Such a person will usually have vital signs but is not aware of anything that is occurring. There is also a lack of any perception of reality.

There is a difference between revival and resuscitation. *Resuscitation* is used on a person who is dead and whom the doctors are trying to bring back to life. *Revival* is for a person who is alive but unconscious. Spiritually, we can be unconscious and completely out of touch with the Spirit of God. We may be unaware of the God who made us and what He wants to do in and through us.

When one comes to Christ in faith and is born again, he or she is brought

The burden[a] which the prophet Habakkuk saw.

The Prophet's Question

2 O LORD, how long shall I cry,
And You will not hear?
Even cry out to You, "Violence!"
And You will not save.
3 Why do You show me iniquity,
And cause *me* to see trouble?
For plundering and violence *are* before me;
There is strife, and contention arises.
4 Therefore the law is powerless,
And justice never goes forth.
For the wicked surround the righteous;
Therefore perverse judgment proceeds.

The LORD's Reply

5 "Look among the nations and watch—
Be utterly astounded!
For *I will* work a work in your days
Which you would not believe, though it were told *you.*
6 For indeed I am raising up the Chaldeans,
A bitter and hasty nation
Which marches through the breadth of the earth,
To possess dwelling places *that are* not theirs.
7 They are terrible and dreadful;
Their judgment and their dignity proceed from themselves.
8 Their horses also are swifter than leopards,
And more fierce than evening wolves.
Their chargers charge ahead;
Their cavalry comes from afar;
They fly as the eagle *that* hastens to eat.
9 "They all come for violence;
Their faces are set *like* the east wind.
They gather captives like sand.
10 They scoff at kings,
And princes are scorned by them.
They deride every stronghold,
For they heap up earthen *mounds* and seize it.
11 Then *his* mind[b] changes, and he transgresses;
He commits offense,
Ascribing this power to his god."

The Prophet's Second Question

12 Are You not from everlasting,
O LORD my God, my Holy One?
We shall not die.
O LORD, You have appointed them for judgment;
O Rock, You have marked them for correction.

1:1 [a] Or *oracle*
1:11 [b] Literally *spirit* or *wind*

13 *You are* of purer eyes than to behold evil,
And cannot look on wickedness.
Why do You look on those who deal treacherously,
And hold Your tongue when the wicked devours
A *person* more righteous than he?
14 *Why* do You make men like fish of the sea,
Like creeping things *that have* no ruler over them?
15 They take up all of them with a hook,
They catch them in their net,
And gather them in their dragnet.
Therefore they rejoice and are glad.
16 Therefore they sacrifice to their net,
And burn incense to their dragnet;
Because by them their share *is* sumptuous
And their food plentiful.
17 Shall they therefore empty their net,
And continue to slay nations without pity?

2 I will stand my watch
And set myself on the rampart,
And watch to see what He will say to me,
And what I will answer when I am corrected.

The Just Live by Faith

2 Then the LORD answered me and said:

"Write the vision
And make *it* plain on tablets,
That he may run who reads it.
3 For the vision *is* yet for an appointed time;
But at the end it will speak, and it will not lie.
Though it tarries, wait for it;
Because it will surely come,
It will not tarry.
4 "Behold the proud,
His soul is not upright in him;
But the just shall live by his faith.

Woe to the Wicked

5 "Indeed, because he transgresses by wine,
He is a proud man,
And he does not stay at home.
Because he enlarges his desire as hell,[c]
And he *is* like death, and cannot be satisfied,
He gathers to himself all nations
And heaps up for himself all peoples.

6 "Will not all these take up a proverb against him,
And a taunting riddle against him, and say,
'Woe to him who increases

back from the dead into life. But when revival occurs, a person who is already a Christian is brought back from the brink of apathy, of taking God for granted, of ignoring God and trying to live under one's own power and strength. This can be deadly for others, because the Christian in need of revival is not producing any fruit for God.

We have not seen a revival in America since shortly after the turn of the twentieth century. But, as the hymn says, "Lord, send a revival and let it begin with me." If we are to see a revival in our nation, it must begin in the hearts of individual believers. What are you doing in your daily walk with God that will bring revival to your life?
(From *Unto the Hills* by Billy Graham)

APPLICATION What are three situations that could depress you or make you anxious today? Give them to God in prayer. Ask God to help you trust him and give you the strength to do his will.

EXPLORATION Strength through Prayer—Matthew 21:21-22; James 1:5-6.

2:5 [c] Or *Sheol*

What is not his—how long?
And to him who loads himself with
many pledges'?[d]
7 Will not your creditors[e] rise up suddenly?
Will they not awaken who oppress you?
And you will become their booty.
8 Because you have plundered many nations,
All the remnant of the people shall plunder you,
Because of men's blood
And the violence of the land *and* the city,
And of all who dwell in it.

9 "Woe to him who covets evil gain for his house,
That he may set his nest on high,
That he may be delivered from the power
of disaster!
10 You give shameful counsel to your house,
Cutting off many peoples,
And sin *against* your soul.
11 For the stone will cry out from the wall,
And the beam from the timbers will answer it.

12 "Woe to him who builds a town with bloodshed,
Who establishes a city by iniquity!
13 Behold, *is it* not of the LORD of hosts
That the peoples labor to feed the fire,[f]
And nations weary themselves in vain?
14 For the earth will be filled
With the knowledge of the glory of the LORD,
As the waters cover the sea.

15 "Woe to him who gives drink to his neighbor,
Pressing[g] *him to* your bottle,
Even to make *him* drunk,
That you may look on his nakedness!
16 You are filled with shame instead of glory.
You also—drink!
And be exposed as uncircumcised![h]
The cup of the LORD's right hand *will be*
turned against you,
And utter shame will be on your glory.
17 For the violence *done to* Lebanon will
cover you,
And the plunder of beasts *which* made
them afraid,
Because of men's blood
And the violence of the land *and* the city,
And of all who dwell in it.

18 "What profit is the image, that its maker
should carve it,
The molded image, a teacher of lies,
That the maker of its mold should trust in it,
To make mute idols?
19 Woe to him who says to wood, 'Awake!'
To silent stone, 'Arise! It shall teach!'
Behold, it is overlaid with gold and silver,
Yet in it there is no breath at all.

20 "But the LORD is in His holy temple.
Let all the earth keep silence before Him."

The Prophet's Prayer

3 A prayer of Habakkuk the prophet, on Shigionoth.[i]

2 O LORD, I have heard Your speech
and was afraid;
O LORD, revive Your work in the midst of
the years!
In the midst of the years make *it* known;
In wrath remember mercy.
3 God came from Teman,
The Holy One from Mount Paran. Selah

His glory covered the heavens,
And the earth was full of His praise.
4 *His* brightness was like the light;
He had rays *flashing* from His hand,
And there His power *was* hidden.
5 Before Him went pestilence,
And fever followed at His feet.
6 He stood and measured the earth;
He looked and startled the nations.
And the everlasting mountains were scattered,
The perpetual hills bowed.
His ways *are* everlasting.
7 I saw the tents of Cushan in affliction;
The curtains of the land of Midian trembled.

8 O LORD, were *You* displeased with the rivers,
Was Your anger against the rivers,
Was Your wrath against the sea,
That You rode on Your horses,
Your chariots of salvation?
9 Your bow was made quite ready;
Oaths were sworn over *Your* arrows.[j] Selah

2:6 [d] Syriac and Vulgate read *thick clay.*
2:7 [e] Literally *those who bite you*
2:13 [f] Literally *for what satisfies fire,* that is, for what is of no lasting value
2:15 [g] Literally *Attaching* or *Joining*
2:16 [h] Dead Sea Scrolls and Septuagint read *And reel!;* Syriac and Vulgate read *And fall fast asleep!*
3:1 [i] Exact meaning unknown
3:9 [j] Literally *rods* or *tribes* (compare verse 14)

You divided the earth with rivers.
10 The mountains saw You *and* trembled;
The overflowing of the water passed by.
The deep uttered its voice,
And lifted its hands on high.
11 The sun and moon stood still in
their habitation;
At the light of Your arrows they went,
At the shining of Your glittering spear.

12 You marched through the land in indignation;
You trampled the nations in anger.
13 You went forth for the salvation of
Your people,
For salvation with Your Anointed.
You struck the head from the house of
the wicked,
By laying bare from foundation
to neck. Selah

14 You thrust through with his own arrows
The head of his villages.
They came out like a whirlwind to scatter me;
Their rejoicing was like feasting on the poor
in secret.

15 You walked through the sea with Your horses,
Through the heap of great waters.

16 When I heard, my body trembled;
My lips quivered at *the* voice;
Rottenness entered my bones;
And I trembled in myself,
That I might rest in the day of trouble.
When he comes up to the people,
He will invade them with his troops.

A Hymn of Faith

17 Though the fig tree may not blossom,
Nor fruit be on the vines;
Though the labor of the olive may fail,
And the fields yield no food;
Though the flock may be cut off from the fold,
And there be no herd in the stalls—
18 Yet I will rejoice in the LORD,
I will joy in the God of my salvation.

19 The LORD God[k] is my strength;
He will make my feet like deer's *feet*,
And He will make me walk on my high hills.

To the Chief Musician. With my stringed instruments.

3:19 ***k*** Hebrew *YHWH Adonai*

The Book of ZEPHANIAH

INTRODUCTION

Rain can be depressing—constant dripping, wet clothes, mud, gray skies, and distant thunder. After many days of rain, we listen intently for positive clues in weather reports and search the skies for a sunny break in the clouds. We look for signs of change.

God's spokesman, Zephaniah, had nothing but doom and gloom to tell the people of Judah. Most of his prophecies, and thus most of this book (two and one-half chapters to be exact), tell of God's terrible judgment upon the nations, including Judah herself. His words, like the steady pounding of rain, continued to beat the depressing truth that God was not happy with the way people had flaunted his laws and had worshiped idols and he would punish their sin, wiping out entire nations.

That constant negative, and truthful, message would be enough to depress even the most positive optimist.

Suddenly, a ray of hope broke through the clouds. Check out the last eleven verses of the book. God says: *"At that time I will bring you back, even at the time I gather you; for I will give you fame and praise among all the peoples of the earth, when I return your captives before your eyes"* (3:20).

Hear God's Word through his faithful prophet—surely he will judge sin. But there is hope, deliverance, and salvation for those who trust in him. The storm is over; take a walk in the sun!

LIFE LESSON

Zephaniah 1:1–3:20

SITUATION Zephaniah prophesied during the reign of King Josiah and warned the Israelites that their sins would bring God's approaching judgment.

OBSERVATION God does not want to destroy people or nations, but God's moral perfection means that he cannot overlook sin.

INSPIRATION The man they mocked was half-dead. The man they mocked was beaten. But the man they mocked was at peace. "Father, forgive them, because they don't know what they are doing" (Luke 23:34).

After Jesus' prayer, one of the criminals began to shout insults at him: "Aren't you the Christ? Then save yourself and us."

The heart of this thief remains hard. The presence of Christ crucified meant nothing to him. Jesus is worthy of ridicule, so the thief ridicules. He expects his chorus to be harmonized from the other cross. It isn't. Instead it is challenged.

"You should fear God! You are getting the same punishment he is. We are punished justly, getting what we deserve for what we did. But this man has done nothing wrong" (vv. 40-41).

Unbelievable. The same mouth that cursed Christ now defends Christ. What has happened? What has he seen since he has been on the cross? Did he witness a miracle? Did he hear a lecture? Was he read a treatise on the trinity?

No, of course not. According to Luke, all he heard was a prayer, a prayer of grace. . . . But this man has done nothing wrong.

The word of the LORD which came to Zephaniah the son of Cushi, the son of Gedaliah, the son of Amariah, the son of Hezekiah, in the days of Josiah the son of Amon, king of Judah.

The Great Day of the LORD

2 "I will utterly consume everything
From the face of the land,"
Says the LORD;
3 "I will consume man and beast;
I will consume the birds of the heavens,
The fish of the sea,
And the stumbling blocks[a] along with the wicked.
I will cut off man from the face of the land,"
Says the LORD.
4 "I will stretch out My hand against Judah,
And against all the inhabitants of Jerusalem.
I will cut off every trace of Baal from this place,
The names of the idolatrous priests[b] with
the *pagan* priests—
5 Those who worship the host of heaven
on the housetops;
Those who worship and swear *oaths* by the LORD,
But who *also* swear by Milcom;[c]
6 Those who have turned back from *following* the LORD,
And have not sought the LORD, nor inquired of Him."

7 Be silent in the presence of the Lord GOD;
For the day of the LORD *is* at hand,
For the LORD has prepared a sacrifice;
He has invited[d] His guests.

8 "And it shall be,
In the day of the LORD's sacrifice,
That I will punish the princes and the king's children,
And all such as are clothed with foreign apparel.
9 In the same day I will punish
All those who leap over the threshold,[e]
Who fill their masters' houses with
violence and deceit.

10 "And there shall be on that day," says the LORD,
"The sound of a mournful cry from the Fish Gate,
A wailing from the Second Quarter,
And a loud crashing from the hills.
11 Wail, you inhabitants of Maktesh![f]
For all the merchant people are cut down;
All those who handle money are cut off.

1:3 [a] Figurative of idols
1:4 [b] Hebrew *chemarim*
1:5 [c] Or *Malcam,* an Ammonite god, also called *Molech* (compare Leviticus 18:21)
1:7 [d] Literally *set apart, consecrated*
1:9 [e] Compare 1 Samuel 5:5
1:11 [f] Literally *Mortar,* a market district of Jerusalem

12 "And it shall come to pass at that time
That I will search Jerusalem with lamps,
And punish the men
Who are settled in complacency,[g]
Who say in their heart,
'The LORD will not do good,
Nor will He do evil.'
13 Therefore their goods shall become booty,
And their houses a desolation;
They shall build houses, but not inhabit *them;*
They shall plant vineyards, but not drink their wine."
14 The great day of the LORD *is* near;
It is near and hastens quickly.
The noise of the day of the LORD is bitter;
There the mighty men shall cry out.
15 That day *is* a day of wrath,
A day of trouble and distress,
A day of devastation and desolation,
A day of darkness and gloominess,
A day of clouds and thick darkness,
16 A day of trumpet and alarm
Against the fortified cities
And against the high towers.

17 "I will bring distress upon men,
And they shall walk like blind men,
Because they have sinned against the LORD;
Their blood shall be poured out like dust,
And their flesh like refuse."

18 Neither their silver nor their gold
Shall be able to deliver them
In the day of the LORD's wrath;
But the whole land shall be devoured
By the fire of His jealousy,
For He will make speedy riddance
Of all those who dwell in the land.

A Call to Repentance

2 Gather yourselves together, yes, gather together,
O undesirable[h] nation,
2 Before the decree is issued,
Or the day passes like chaff,
Before the LORD's fierce anger comes upon you,
Before the day of the LORD's anger comes upon you!
3 Seek the LORD, all you meek of the earth,
Who have upheld His justice.
Seek righteousness, seek humility.
It may be that you will be hidden
In the day of the LORD's anger.

1:12 [g] Literally *on their lees,* that is, settled like the dregs of wine
2:1 [h] Or *shameless*

The core of the gospel in one sentence. The essence of eternity through the mouth of a crook:

I am wrong; Jesus is right.

I have failed; Jesus has not.

I deserve to die; Jesus deserves to live.

The thief knew precious little about Christ, but what he knew was precious indeed. He knew that an innocent man was dying an unjust death with no complaint on his lips. And if Jesus can do that, he just might be who he says he is.

So the thief asks for help: "Jesus, remember me when you come into your kingdom."

. . . Who is he to beg for forgiveness? . . . What right does he have to pray this prayer?

Do you really want to know? The same right you have to pray yours.

You see, that is you and me on the cross. Naked, desolate, hopeless, and estranged. That is us. That is us asking, "In spite of what I've done, in spite of what you see, is there any way you could remember me when we all get home?"

. . . We, like the thief, hear the voice of grace. Today you will be with me in my kingdom.

(From *He Still Moves Stones* by Max Lucado)

APPLICATION What makes you angry: traffic jams, your boss, demanding parents? When you feel anger approaching, ask God for patience. Remember how patient he has been with you.

EXPLORATION Repentance—Psalm 51:1-4; Luke 15:11-24; 5:8-10; Acts 2:37-42.

Judgment on Nations

4 For Gaza shall be forsaken,
And Ashkelon desolate;
They shall drive out Ashdod at noonday,
And Ekron shall be uprooted.
5 Woe to the inhabitants of the seacoast,
The nation of the Cherethites!
The word of the LORD *is* against you,
O Canaan, land of the Philistines:
"I will destroy you;
So there shall be no inhabitant."

6 The seacoast shall be pastures,
With shelters[i] for shepherds and folds
for flocks.
7 The coast shall be for the remnant of the
house of Judah;
They shall feed *their* flocks there;
In the houses of Ashkelon they shall lie down
at evening.
For the LORD their God will intervene
for them,
And return their captives.

8 "I have heard the reproach of Moab,
And the insults of the people of Ammon,
With which they have reproached My people,
And made arrogant threats against
their borders.
9 Therefore, as I live,"
Says the LORD of hosts, the God of Israel,
"Surely Moab shall be like Sodom,
And the people of Ammon like Gomorrah—
Overrun with weeds and saltpits,
And a perpetual desolation.
The residue of My people shall plunder them,
And the remnant of My people
shall possess them."

10 This they shall have for their pride,
Because they have reproached and
made arrogant threats
Against the people of the LORD of hosts.
11 The LORD *will be* awesome to them,
For He will reduce to nothing all the
gods of the earth;
People shall worship Him,
Each one from his place,
Indeed all the shores of the nations.

12 "You Ethiopians also,
You shall be slain by My sword."

13 And He will stretch out His hand
against the north,
Destroy Assyria,
And make Nineveh a desolation,
As dry as the wilderness.
14 The herds shall lie down in her midst,
Every beast of the nation.
Both the pelican and the bittern
Shall lodge on the capitals *of* her *pillars;*
Their voice shall sing in the windows;
Desolation *shall be* at the threshold;
For He will lay bare the cedar work.
15 This is the rejoicing city
That dwelt securely,
That said in her heart,
"I *am it,* and *there is* none besides me."
How has she become a desolation,
A place for beasts to lie down!
Everyone who passes by her
Shall hiss and shake his fist.

The Wickedness of Jerusalem

3 Woe to her who is rebellious and polluted,
To the oppressing city!
2 She has not obeyed *His* voice,
She has not received correction;
She has not trusted in the LORD,
She has not drawn near to her God.

3 Her princes in her midst *are* roaring lions;
Her judges *are* evening wolves
That leave not a bone till morning.
4 Her prophets are insolent, treacherous people;
Her priests have polluted the sanctuary,
They have done violence to the law.
5 The LORD *is* righteous in her midst,
He will do no unrighteousness.
Every morning He brings His justice to light;
He never fails,
But the unjust knows no shame.

6 "I have cut off nations,
Their fortresses are devastated;
I have made their streets desolate,
With none passing by.
Their cities are destroyed;
There is no one, no inhabitant.
7 I said, 'Surely you will fear Me,
You will receive instruction'—

2:6 [i] Literally *excavations,* either underground huts *or cisterns*

So that her dwelling would not be cut off,
Despite everything for which I punished her.
But they rose early and corrupted all
their deeds.

A Faithful Remnant

8 "Therefore wait for Me," says the LORD,
"Until the day I rise up for plunder;[j]
My determination *is* to gather the nations
To My assembly of kingdoms,
To pour on them My indignation,
All My fierce anger;
All the earth shall be devoured
With the fire of My jealousy.

9 "For then I will restore to the peoples
a pure language,
That they all may call on the name
of the LORD,
To serve Him with one accord.
10 From beyond the rivers of Ethiopia
My worshipers,
The daughter of My dispersed ones,
Shall bring My offering.
11 In that day you shall not be shamed for
any of your deeds
In which you transgress against Me;
For then I will take away from your midst
Those who rejoice in your pride,
And you shall no longer be haughty
In My holy mountain.
12 I will leave in your midst
A meek and humble people,
And they shall trust in the name of the LORD.
13 The remnant of Israel shall do
no unrighteousness
And speak no lies,
Nor shall a deceitful tongue be found
in their mouth;
For they shall feed *their* flocks and lie down,
And no one shall make *them* afraid."

Joy in God's Faithfulness

14 Sing, O daughter of Zion!
Shout, O Israel!
Be glad and rejoice with all *your* heart,
O daughter of Jerusalem!
15 The LORD has taken away your judgments,
He has cast out your enemy.
The King of Israel, the LORD, *is* in your midst;
You shall see[k] disaster no more.

16 In that day it shall be said to Jerusalem:
"Do not fear;
Zion, let not your hands be weak.
17 The LORD your God in your midst,
The Mighty One, will save;
He will rejoice over you with gladness,
He will quiet *you* with His love,
He will rejoice over you with singing."

18 "I will gather those who sorrow over the
appointed assembly,
Who are among you,
To whom its reproach *is* a burden.
19 Behold, at that time
I will deal with all who afflict you;
I will save the lame,
And gather those who were driven out;
I will appoint them for praise and fame
In every land where they were put to shame.
20 At that time I will bring you back,
Even at the time I gather you;
For I will give you fame and praise
Among all the peoples of the earth,
When I return your captives before your
eyes,"
Says the LORD.

3:8 [j] Septuagint and Syriac read *for witness;* Targum reads *for the day of My revelation for judgment;* Vulgate reads *for the day of My resurrection that is to come.*
3:15 [k] Some Hebrew manuscripts, Septuagint, and Bomberg read *see;* Masoretic Text and Vulgate read *fear.*

The Book of

HAGGAI

INTRODUCTION

C. S. Lewis wrote, "You can't get second things by putting them first; you can get second things only by putting first things first" (*God in the Dock*). Wise advice about setting priorities. Unfortunately, it's easy to focus on second, third, fourth, fifth, or sixth "things" instead.

What should be first? A person's relationship with God.

God's message through the prophet Haggai hit the Jews where it hurt—right in their priorities. They had returned to Jerusalem from exile in Babylon with the challenge of rebuilding the Temple. They had begun the work but somewhere along the line had left the task.

The Temple was not just another building or church edifice; it was the holy place where sacrifices were made and people met with God. And it symbolized the nation's close relationship with the Almighty.

A shabby Temple indicated a break in that relationship. And that's exactly what had happened—the people had built fine homes for themselves while leaving God's house in ruins.

Priorities. Values. God's people had it wrong.

Have you made a value check lately? Discover what God told the Jerusalem Jews through Haggai and make sure you are putting first things first.

LIFE LESSON

Haggai 1:1–2:23

SITUATION Twenty years passed since Israel's return from Babylon. But the people quickly forgot the lessons exile had taught them. They worked hard, but their crops failed. They earned money, but it was never enough.

OBSERVATION If God gives you a task, follow it through. Don't make excuses or settle for halfhearted work.

INSPIRATION In deciding my life's priorities, I should keep three things in mind—my relationship to God, my relationship to other people, and my relationship to myself.

Priority 1: Glorifying God. . . . [Our] chief purpose is to know God and to glorify him forever. The first commandment says, "You shall have no other gods before me" (Exodus 20:3). God should come first in everything. This does not mean our faith should be a fanatical pursuit of heaven to the detriment of everything else in the world. But the first question we should always ask is, Does this glorify God? If it doesn't glorify God, don't do it.

Priority 2: Loving others. God cares for the world so much that he gave his only Son to save it (John 3:16). Because of this, we can serve him by caring for the people around us. This means living the life of Christ. How do we do that? By being gentle, humble, kind, and forgiving (Colossians 3:12-17).

The Command to Build God's House

In the second year of King Darius, in the sixth month, on the
first day of the month, the word of the LORD came by Haggai
the prophet to Zerubbabel the son of Shealtiel, governor of
Judah, and to Joshua the son of Jehozadak, the high priest, saying,
2"Thus speaks the LORD of hosts, saying: 'This people says, "The time has
not come, the time that the LORD's house should be built." ' "
3Then the word of the LORD came by Haggai the prophet, saying, 4"*Is it* time
for you yourselves to dwell in your paneled houses, and this temple[a] *to lie* in
ruins?" 5Now therefore, thus says the LORD of hosts: "Consider your ways!

6 "You have sown much, and bring in little;
You eat, but do not have enough;
You drink, but you are not filled with drink;
You clothe yourselves, but no one is warm;
And he who earns wages,
Earns wages *to put* into a bag with holes."

7Thus says the LORD of hosts: "Consider your ways! 8Go up to the mountains and bring wood and build the temple, that I may take pleasure in it
and be glorified," says the LORD. 9"*You* looked for much, but indeed *it came
to* little; and when you brought it home, I blew it away. Why?" says the LORD
of hosts. "Because of My house that *is in* ruins, while every one of you runs to
his own house. 10Therefore the heavens above you withhold the dew, and the
earth withholds its fruit. 11For I called for a drought on the land and the
mountains, on the grain and the new wine and the oil, on whatever the ground
brings forth, on men and livestock, and on all the labor of *your* hands."

The People's Obedience

12Then Zerubbabel the son of Shealtiel, and Joshua the son of Jehozadak, the high priest, with all the remnant of the people, obeyed the voice
of the LORD their God, and the words of Haggai the prophet, as the LORD their
God had sent him; and the people feared the presence of the LORD. 13Then
Haggai, the LORD's messenger, spoke the LORD's message to the people,
saying, "I *am* with you, says the LORD." 14So the LORD stirred up the spirit
of Zerubbabel the son of Shealtiel, governor of Judah, and the spirit of
Joshua the son of Jehozadak, the high priest, and the spirit of all the remnant of the people; and they came and worked on the house of the LORD of
hosts, their God, 15on the twenty-fourth day of the sixth month, in the second year of King Darius.

The Coming Glory of God's House

2 In the seventh *month*, on the twenty-first of the month, the word of the
LORD came by Haggai the prophet, saying: 2"Speak now to Zerubbabel the
son of Shealtiel, governor of Judah, and to Joshua the son of Jehozadak,
the high priest, and to the remnant of the people, saying: 3'Who is left
among you who saw this temple[b] in its former glory? And how do you see
it now? In comparison with it, *is this* not in your eyes as nothing? 4Yet now
be strong, Zerubbabel,' says the LORD; 'and be strong, Joshua, son of
Jehozadak, the high priest; and be strong, all you people of the land,' says

1:4 [a] Literally *house,* and so in verse 8
2:3 [b] Literally *house,* and so in verses 7 and 9

the LORD, 'and work; for I *am* with you,' says the LORD of hosts. 5'*According
to* the word that I covenanted with you when you came out of Egypt, so My
Spirit remains among you; do not fear!'
6"For thus says the LORD of hosts: 'Once more (it *is* a little while) I will
shake heaven and earth, the sea and dry land; 7and I will shake all nations,
and they shall come to the Desire of All Nations,[c] and I will fill this temple
with glory,' says the LORD of hosts. 8'The silver *is* Mine, and the gold *is*
Mine,' says the LORD of hosts. 9'The glory of this latter temple shall be
greater than the former,' says the LORD of hosts. 'And in this place I will
give peace,' says the LORD of hosts."

The People Are Defiled

10On the twenty-fourth *day* of the ninth *month,* in the second year of Darius,
the word of the LORD came by Haggai the prophet, saying, 11"Thus says the
LORD of hosts: 'Now, ask the priests *concerning the* law, saying, 12"If one
carries holy meat in the fold of his garment, and with the edge he touches
bread or stew, wine or oil, or any food, will it become holy?" ' "
Then the priests answered and said, "No."
13And Haggai said, "If *one who is* unclean *because* of a dead body touches
any of these, will it be unclean?"
So the priests answered and said, "It shall be unclean."
14Then Haggai answered and said, " 'So is this people, and so is this nation before Me,' says the LORD, 'and so is every work of their hands; and
what they offer there is unclean.

Promised Blessing

15'And now, carefully consider from this day forward: from before stone
was laid upon stone in the temple of the LORD— 16since those *days,* when
one came to a heap of twenty ephahs, there were *but* ten; when *one* came to
the wine vat to draw out fifty baths from the press, there were *but* twenty.
17I struck you with blight and mildew and hail in all the labors of your
hands; yet you did not *turn* to Me,' says the LORD. 18'Consider now from
this day forward, from the twenty-fourth day of the ninth month, from the
day that the foundation of the LORD's temple was laid—consider it: 19Is the
seed still in the barn? As yet the vine, the fig tree, the pomegranate, and the
olive tree have not yielded *fruit. But* from this day I will bless *you.*' "

Zerubbabel Chosen as a Signet

20And again the word of the LORD came to Haggai on the twenty-fourth day
of the month, saying, 21"Speak to Zerubbabel, governor of Judah, saying:

'I will shake heaven and earth.
22 I will overthrow the throne of kingdoms;
I will destroy the strength of the Gentile kingdoms.
I will overthrow the chariots
And those who ride in them;
The horses and their riders shall come down,
Every one by the sword of his brother.

23'In that day,' says the LORD of hosts, 'I will take you, Zerubbabel My
servant, the son of Shealtiel,' says the LORD, 'and will make you like a signet
ring; for I have chosen you,' says the LORD of hosts."

2:7 [c] Or *the desire of all nations*

Priority 3: Living in the light. Paul said, "Let the peace of Christ rule your hearts, . . . [and] let the word of Christ dwell in you richly" (Colossians 3:15, 16). We should choose activities that enable us to be conscious of God all the time. We don't have to walk around with our hands folded. But we should worship God on Sunday and carry the experience with us into Monday.

In deciding what to do . . . these three priorities should guide us. But we have to use our judgment, which we can do through education, practice, and experience. Then, like Jesus, we will grow in wisdom and stature (Luke 2:52).

(From "Deciding Life's Priorities" by Oswald Hoffman in *Practical Christianity*)

APPLICATION List your top ten priorities for today. Where does Bible reading and prayer fall on the list? Did you plan time just to enjoy the world around you (the world God gave you)? Shift and sort your priorities until your schedule reflects his desires.

EXPLORATION Priorities—Deuteronomy 17:1; 2 Chronicles 1:11-12; Malachi 2:1-2; Matthew 6:33; 8:21-22; Revelation 3:17.

The Book of ZECHARIAH

INTRODUCTION

You wake with a start, sweating profusely. You aren't sure what the dream was about, you just know it was bad. You remember trying to run in the dream, but not being able to move your legs. It was pure fantasy, but it felt real and it was enough to wake you up.

Dreams can be caused by indigestion, anxiety, desires, concerns, and other mental and emotional conditions. Dreams can be fun, entertaining, and even enlightening. But they can also invoke fear, stress, and outright terror.

Zechariah, God's prophet in Jerusalem more than five hundred years before Christ, had a series of nighttime experiences that kept him awake for a week. More than mere dreams, these were visions of God's future plans for his people, including a description of the Messiah. Through these visions God gave his message to Zechariah, who then faithfully relayed them to his family, friends, neighbors, countrymen . . . and us.

As you read Zechariah, take hope in knowing that God controls the future, *your* future, and that the King is coming. Then get a good night's sleep.

LIFE LESSON

Zechariah 1:1–6:8

SITUATION The exiles returned from Babylon to rebuild the temple. Enemies, however, thwarted and stalled the project. Zechariah motivated the people and encouraged them to resume their work.

OBSERVATION God provides the strength we need to accomplish great deeds for him.

INSPIRATION There is great power in dreaming big. Such vision implies a long-term approach to ministry. Many leaders suffer from having to constantly rethink their vision because it was so small they accomplished it quickly, or so insignificant it barely seemed worth the effort. God's vision for your life, though, is grand. His vision is not one you are likely to accomplish in a year or two. A few Christian visionaries have learned that once you catch His vision, it will outlive you. Your role is to grasp it, articulate it, and see that it gets acted upon. Your responsibility is not to see it come to a conclusion. Work toward that end, but do not feel incomplete if it is not fully accomplished in your lifetime. Along the way, simply being part of making that vision become reality will seem like sufficient reward.

Dreaming big, through God's enablement, is also one means of allowing the Church to see and to flaunt God's power and majesty. His desires are so much better and more meaningful than our own that when we envision them and fully support them, the spiritual and emotional empowerment is incredible. People become genuinely excited over the grand possibilities. The magnitude of the task is dwarfed by the realization that He wants to do it, and He intends to make it happen through you.

(From *The Power of Vision* by George Barna)

APPLICATION Do you have a friend who works hard in service to the church? Send that person an unexpected note of encouragement. Cheer your friend on in his or her work. Add that name to your prayer list.

EXPLORATION The Need for Vision—Proverbs 29:18. Faithfulness—2 Timothy 1:3-7.

A Call to Repentance

In the eighth month of the second year of Darius, the word of
the LORD came to Zechariah the son of Berechiah, the son of
Iddo the prophet, saying, 2"The LORD has been very angry with
your fathers. 3Therefore say to them, 'Thus says the LORD of hosts:
"Return to Me," says the LORD of hosts, "and I will return to you," says the
LORD of hosts. 4"Do not be like your fathers, to whom the former prophets
preached, saying, 'Thus says the LORD of hosts: "Turn now from your evil ways
and your evil deeds." ' But they did not hear nor heed Me," says the LORD.

5 "Your fathers, where *are* they?
And the prophets, do they live forever?
6 Yet surely My words and My statutes,
Which I commanded My servants the prophets,
Did they not overtake your fathers?

"So they returned and said:

'Just as the LORD of hosts determined to do to us,
According to our ways and according to our deeds,
So He has dealt with us.' " ' "

Vision of the Horses

7On the twenty-fourth day of the eleventh month, which is the month
Shebat, in the second year of Darius, the word of the LORD came to Zechariah
the son of Berechiah, the son of Iddo the prophet: 8I saw by night, and behold, a man riding on a red horse, and it stood among the myrtle trees in
the hollow; and behind him *were* horses: red, sorrel, and white. 9Then I
said, "My lord, what *are* these?" So the angel who talked with me said to
me, "I will show you what they *are*."

10And the man who stood among the myrtle trees answered and said,
"These *are the ones* whom the LORD has sent to walk to and fro throughout
the earth."

11So they answered the Angel of the LORD, who stood among the myrtle
trees, and said, "We have walked to and fro throughout the earth, and behold, all the earth is resting quietly."

The LORD Will Comfort Zion

12Then the Angel of the LORD answered and said, "O LORD of hosts, how
long will You not have mercy on Jerusalem and on the cities of Judah, against
which You were angry these seventy years?"

13And the LORD answered the angel who talked to me, *with* good *and*
comforting words. 14So the angel who spoke with me said to me, "Proclaim, saying, 'Thus says the LORD of hosts:

"I am zealous for Jerusalem
And for Zion with great zeal.
15 I am exceedingly angry with the nations at ease;
For I was a little angry,
And they helped—*but* with evil *intent*."

16'Therefore thus says the LORD:

"I am returning to Jerusalem with mercy;

My house shall be built in it," says the
LORD of hosts,
"And a *surveyor's* line shall be stretched
out over Jerusalem." '

17 "Again proclaim, saying, 'Thus says the LORD of hosts:

"My cities shall again spread out
through prosperity;
The LORD will again comfort Zion,
And will again choose Jerusalem." ' "

Vision of the Horns

18 Then I raised my eyes and looked, and there *were* four horns. 19 And I said to the angel who talked with me, "What *are* these?"

So he answered me, "These *are* the horns that have scattered Judah, Israel, and Jerusalem."

20 Then the LORD showed me four craftsmen. 21 And I said, "What are these coming to do?"

So he said, "These *are* the horns that scattered Judah, so that no one could lift up his head; but the craftsmen[a] are coming to terrify them, to cast out the horns of the nations that lifted up *their* horn against the land of Judah to scatter it."

Vision of the Measuring Line

2 Then I raised my eyes and looked, and behold, a man with a measuring line in his hand. 2 So I said, "Where are you going?"

And he said to me, "To measure Jerusalem, to see what *is* its width and what *is* its length."

3 And there *was* the angel who talked with me, going out; and another angel was coming out to meet him, 4 who said to him, "Run, speak to this young man, saying: 'Jerusalem shall be inhabited *as* towns without walls, because of the multitude of men and livestock in it. 5 For I,' says the LORD, 'will be a wall of fire all around her, and I will be the glory in her midst.' "

Future Joy of Zion and Many Nations

6 "Up, up! Flee from the land of the north," says the LORD; "for I have spread you abroad like the four winds of heaven," says the LORD. 7 "Up, Zion! Escape, you who dwell with the daughter of Babylon."

8 For thus says the LORD of hosts: "He sent Me after glory, to the nations which plunder you; for he who touches you touches the apple of His eye. 9 For surely I will shake My hand against them, and they shall become spoil for their servants. Then you will know that the LORD of hosts has sent Me.

10 "Sing and rejoice, O daughter of Zion! For behold, I am coming and I will dwell in your midst," says the LORD. 11 "Many nations shall be joined to the LORD in that day, and they shall become My people. And I will dwell in your midst. Then you will know that the LORD of hosts has sent Me to you. 12 And the LORD will take possession of Judah as His inheritance in the Holy Land, and will again choose Jerusalem. 13 Be silent, all flesh, before the LORD, for He is aroused from His holy habitation!"

Vision of the High Priest

3 Then he showed me Joshua the high priest standing before the Angel of the LORD, and Satan standing at his right hand to oppose him. 2 And the LORD said to Satan, "The LORD rebuke you, Satan! The LORD who has chosen Jerusalem rebuke you! *Is* this not a brand plucked from the fire?"

3 Now Joshua was clothed with filthy garments, and was standing before the Angel.

4 Then He answered and spoke to those who stood before Him, saying, "Take away the filthy garments from him." And to him He said, "See, I have removed your iniquity from you, and I will clothe you with rich robes."

5 And I said, "Let them put a clean turban on his head."

So they put a clean turban on his head, and they put the clothes on him. And the Angel of the LORD stood by.

The Coming Branch

6 Then the Angel of the LORD admonished Joshua, saying, 7 "Thus says the LORD of hosts:

'If you will walk in My ways,
And if you will keep My command,
Then you shall also judge My house,
And likewise have charge of My courts;
I will give you places to walk
Among these who stand here.

8 'Hear, O Joshua, the high priest,
You and your companions who
sit before you,
For they are a wondrous sign;
For behold, I am bringing forth My Servant
the BRANCH.
9 For behold, the stone
That I have laid before Joshua:
Upon the stone *are* seven eyes.
Behold, I will engrave its inscription,'

1:21 [a] Literally *these*

Says the LORD of hosts,
'And I will remove the iniquity of that
land in one day.
10 In that day,' says the LORD of hosts,
'Everyone will invite his neighbor
Under his vine and under his fig tree.' "

Vision of the Lampstand and Olive Trees

4 Now the angel who talked with me came back and
wakened me, as a man who is wakened out of his
sleep. 2And he said to me, "What do you see?"
So I said, "I am looking, and there *is* a lampstand of
solid gold with a bowl on top of it, and on the *stand*
seven lamps with seven pipes to the seven lamps. 3Two
olive trees *are* by it, one at the right of the bowl and the
other at its left." 4So I answered and spoke to the angel
who talked with me, saying, "What *are* these, my lord?"
5Then the angel who talked with me answered and
said to me, "Do you not know what these are?"
And I said, "No, my lord."
6So he answered and said to me:

"This *is* the word of the LORD to Zerubbabel:
'Not by might nor by power, but
by My Spirit,'
Says the LORD of hosts.
7 'Who *are* you, O great mountain?
Before Zerubbabel *you shall become* a plain!
And he shall bring forth the capstone
With shouts of "Grace, grace to it!" ' "

8Moreover the word of the LORD came to me, saying:
9 "The hands of Zerubbabel
Have laid the foundation of this temple;[b]
His hands shall also finish *it*.
Then you will know
That the LORD of hosts has sent Me to you.
10 For who has despised the day of small things?
For these seven rejoice to see
The plumb line in the hand of Zerubbabel.
They are the eyes of the LORD,
Which scan to and fro throughout
the whole earth."

11Then I answered and said to him, "What *are* these
two olive trees—at the right of the lampstand and at
its left?" 12And I further answered and said to him,
"What *are these* two olive branches that *drip* into the
receptacles[c] of the two gold pipes from which the
golden *oil* drains?"
13Then he answered me and said, "Do you not know
what these *are?*"
And I said, "No, my lord."
14So he said, "These *are* the two anointed ones, who
stand beside the Lord of the whole earth."

Vision of the Flying Scroll

5 Then I turned and raised my eyes, and saw there a
flying scroll.
2And he said to me, "What do you see?"
So I answered, "I see a flying scroll. Its length *is*
twenty cubits and its width ten cubits."
3Then he said to me, "This *is* the curse that goes out
over the face of the whole earth: 'Every thief shall be
expelled,' according *to* this side of *the scroll;* and,
'Every perjurer shall be expelled,' according *to* that
side of it."

4 "I will send out *the curse,*" says the LORD of hosts;
"It shall enter the house of the thief
And the house of the one who swears falsely
by My name.
It shall remain in the midst of his house
And consume it, with its timber and stones."

Vision of the Woman in a Basket

5Then the angel who talked with me came out and
said to me, "Lift your eyes now, and see what this *is* that
goes forth."
6So I asked, "What *is* it?" And he said, "It *is* a basket[d]
that is going forth."
He also said, "This *is* their resemblance throughout the earth: 7Here *is* a lead disc lifted up, and this *is*
a woman sitting inside the basket"; 8then he said,
"This *is* Wickedness!" And he thrust her down into
the basket, and threw the lead cover[e] over its mouth.
9Then I raised my eyes and looked, and there *were* two
women, coming with the wind in their wings; for they
had wings like the wings of a stork, and they lifted up
the basket between earth and heaven.
10So I said to the angel who talked with me, "Where
are they carrying the basket?"
11And he said to me, "To build a house for it in the
land of Shinar;[f] when it is ready, *the basket* will be set
there on its base."

4:9 [b] Literally *house*
4:12 [c] Literally *into the hands of*
5:6 [d] Hebrew *ephah,* a measuring container, and so elsewhere
5:8 [e] Literally *stone*
5:11 [f] That is, Babylon

Vision of the Four Chariots

6 Then I turned and raised my eyes and looked, and behold, four chariots
were coming from between two mountains, and the mountains *were*
mountains of bronze. 2With the first chariot *were* red horses, with the second chariot black horses, 3with the third chariot white horses, and with
the fourth chariot dappled horses—strong *steeds.* 4Then I answered and
said to the angel who talked with me, "What *are* these, my lord?"

5And the angel answered and said to me, "These *are* four spirits of
heaven, who go out from *their* station before the Lord of all the earth. 6The
one with the black horses is going to the north country, the white are going
after them, and the dappled are going toward the south country." 7Then
the strong *steeds* went out, eager to go, that they might walk to and fro
throughout the earth. And He said, "Go, walk to and fro throughout the
earth." So they walked to and fro throughout the earth. 8And He called to
me, and spoke to me, saying, "See, those who go toward the north country
have given rest to My Spirit in the north country."

The Command to Crown Joshua

9Then the word of the LORD came to me, saying: 10"Receive *the gift* from
the captives—from Heldai, Tobijah, and Jedaiah, who have come from
Babylon—and go the same day and enter the house of Josiah the son of
Zephaniah. 11Take the silver and gold, make an elaborate crown, and set *it*
on the head of Joshua the son of Jehozadak, the high priest. 12Then speak
to him, saying, 'Thus says the LORD of hosts, saying:

"Behold, the Man whose name *is* the BRANCH!
From His place He shall branch out,
And He shall build the temple of the LORD;
13 Yes, He shall build the temple of the LORD.
He shall bear the glory,
And shall sit and rule on His throne;
So He shall be a priest on His throne,
And the counsel of peace shall be between them both." '

14"Now the elaborate crown shall be for a memorial in the temple of the
LORD for Helem,[g] Tobijah, Jedaiah, and Hen the son of Zephaniah. 15Even
those from afar shall come and build the temple of the LORD. Then you
shall know that the LORD of hosts has sent Me to you. And *this* shall come
to pass if you diligently obey the voice of the LORD your God."

Obedience Better than Fasting

7 Now in the fourth year of King Darius it came to pass *that* the word of
the LORD came to Zechariah, on the fourth day of the ninth month,
Chislev, 2when *the people*[h] sent Sherezer,[i] with Regem-Melech and his men,
to the house of God,[j] to pray before the LORD, 3*and* to ask the priests who
were in the house of the LORD of hosts, and the prophets, saying, "Should I
weep in the fifth month and fast as I have done for so many years?"

4Then the word of the LORD of hosts came to me, saying, 5"Say to all the
people of the land, and to the priests: 'When you fasted and mourned in

6:14 [g] Following Masoretic Text, Targum, and Vulgate; Syriac reads *for Heldai* (compare verse 10); Septuagint reads *for the patient ones.*
7:2 [h] Literally *they* (compare verse 5) [i] Or *Sar-Ezer* [j] Hebrew *Bethel*

LIFE LESSON

Zechariah 6:9–8:23

SITUATION God wanted his people to enjoy life. He gave many encouraging promises that would allow Israel to rejoice because of God's love for them.

OBSERVATION Religious ceremonies, while sacred and orderly, are meant to make us rejoice in God.

INSPIRATION Worship is a function of the spiritual health of a congregation. A church may have a beautiful choir singing uplifting songs with theologically correct words, a tremendous organ, and a beautiful sanctuary. But if the people's hearts are far from God and there is no foundation of prayer, worship does not take place. It is an empty experience. A healthy spiritual life results from a church's individual and corporate prayer life, the presenting of the gospel in both word and action, the presence of community and theological soundness.

Our experience of God in worship depends on our commitment and attitude toward God. Developing an attitude of worship is not a matter of aesthetics or strategy, but an awareness of the presence of God's Spirit. A service that fosters this attitude includes no parts simply as aesthetic decoration. Every part helps concentrate people's attention on their union with Christ. In fact, the beauty of a service often has little to do with how conducive it is to worship. In many simple forms of worship, aesthetic elements are missing, but worship takes place because God is pleased to be there.

Our personal receptivity also affects our worship experience. We can go into a service one morning and get nothing out of it, not because the service is mediocre but because we are not open to receiving God's Spirit. If we are not ready to listen and worship, it doesn't matter how wonderful the service is.

Our individual backgrounds also influence our experience. We can get tired of one style of worship. If I were shut up in a room and listened to nothing but the nine Beethoven symphonies for three years, I would become utterly

Continued

immune to them. People who attended unstructured church services as children may go to a liturgical service and discover a tremendous freedom in that style of worship. Other people who have been hardened by a liturgical pattern will come alive in a freestyle situation. . . .

We need to find the style of worship that scratches where we itch, and we should not be afraid of changing worship styles if we find ourselves in a rut. The psalmist said, "Sing to the Lord a new song" (Psalm 149:1). God is a fountain of endless novelty. He is a source of constant freshness, like a symphony that uses the same themes but constantly unfolds new meanings, new ways of combining things.

(From "Developing an Attitude of Worship" by Richard Lovelace in *Practical Christianity)*

APPLICATION What forms of worship do you enjoy most? Are there some forms that bore you? What can you contribute to worship? Let your heart be open to God's direction.

EXPLORATION Worship—Leviticus 7:38; Numbers 29:1-2; 2 Kings 17:27-29; Nehemiah 9:2-3; Psalm 100:4; Jeremiah 7:2-3; John 4:23-24.

the fifth and seventh *months* during those seventy years, did you really fast
for Me—for Me? 6 When you eat and when you drink, do you not eat and
drink *for yourselves?* 7 *Should you* not *have obeyed* the words which the LORD
proclaimed through the former prophets when Jerusalem and the cities
around it were inhabited and prosperous, and the South[k] and the Lowland
were inhabited?' "

Disobedience Resulted in Captivity

8 Then the word of the LORD came to Zechariah, saying, 9 "Thus says the
LORD of hosts:

'Execute true justice,
Show mercy and compassion
Everyone to his brother.
10 Do not oppress the widow or the fatherless,
The alien or the poor.
Let none of you plan evil in his heart
Against his brother.'

11 "But they refused to heed, shrugged their shoulders, and stopped their
ears so that they could not hear. 12 Yes, they made their hearts like flint, refusing to hear the law and the words which the LORD of hosts had sent by
His Spirit through the former prophets. Thus great wrath came from the
LORD of hosts. 13 Therefore it happened, *that* just as He proclaimed and they
would not hear, so they called out and I would not listen," says the LORD of
hosts. 14 "But I scattered them with a whirlwind among all the nations which
they had not known. Thus the land became desolate after them, so that no
one passed through or returned; for they made the pleasant land desolate."

Jerusalem, Holy City of the Future

8 Again the word of the LORD of hosts came, saying, 2 "Thus says the LORD
of hosts:

'I am zealous for Zion with great zeal;
With great fervor I am zealous for her.'

3 "Thus says the LORD:

'I will return to Zion,
And dwell in the midst of Jerusalem.
Jerusalem shall be called the City of Truth,
The Mountain of the LORD of hosts,
The Holy Mountain.'

4 "Thus says the LORD of hosts:

'Old men and old women shall again sit
In the streets of Jerusalem,
Each one with his staff in his hand
Because of great age.
5 The streets of the city
Shall be full of boys and girls
Playing in its streets.'

7:7 k Hebrew *Negev*

6"Thus says the LORD of hosts:

'If it is marvelous in the eyes of the remnant of
this people in these days,
Will it also be marvelous in My eyes?'
Says the LORD of hosts.

7"Thus says the LORD of hosts:

'Behold, I will save My people from the land of
the east
And from the land of the west;
8 I will bring them *back*,
And they shall dwell in the midst
of Jerusalem.
They shall be My people
And I will be their God,
In truth and righteousness.'

9"Thus says the LORD of hosts:

'Let your hands be strong,
You who have been hearing in these days
These words by the mouth of the prophets,
Who *spoke* in the day the foundation was laid
For the house of the LORD of hosts,
That the temple might be built.
10 For before these days
There were no wages for man nor any hire
for beast;
There was no peace from the enemy for
whoever went out or came in;
For I set all men, everyone, against
his neighbor.

11But now I *will* not *treat* the remnant of this people as
in the former days,' says the LORD of hosts.

12 'For the seed *shall be* prosperous,
The vine shall give its fruit,
The ground shall give her increase,
And the heavens shall give their dew—
I will cause the remnant of this people
To possess all these.
13 And it shall come to pass
That just as you were a curse among
the nations,
O house of Judah and house of Israel,
So I will save you, and you shall be a blessing.
Do not fear,
Let your hands be strong.'

14"For thus says the LORD of hosts:

'Just as I determined to punish you
When your fathers provoked Me to wrath,'
Says the LORD of hosts,
'And I would not relent,
15 So again in these days
I am determined to do good
To Jerusalem and to the house of Judah.
Do not fear.
16 These *are* the things you shall do:
Speak each man the truth to his neighbor;
Give judgment in your gates for truth, justice,
and peace;
17 Let none of you think evil in your[l] heart
against your neighbor;
And do not love a false oath.
For all these *are things* that I hate,'
Says the LORD."

18Then the word of the LORD of hosts came to me,
saying, 19"Thus says the LORD of hosts:

'The fast of the fourth *month*,
The fast of the fifth,
The fast of the seventh,
And the fast of the tenth,
Shall be joy and gladness and cheerful feasts
For the house of Judah.
Therefore love truth and peace.'

20"Thus says the LORD of hosts:

'Peoples shall yet come,
Inhabitants of many cities;
21 The inhabitants of one *city* shall go to
another, saying,
"Let us continue to go and pray before
the LORD,
And seek the LORD of hosts.
I myself will go also."
22 Yes, many peoples and strong nations
Shall come to seek the LORD of hosts
in Jerusalem,
And to pray before the LORD.'

23"Thus says the LORD of hosts: 'In those days ten
men from every language of the nations shall grasp
the sleeve of a Jewish man, saying, "Let us go with
you, for we have heard *that* God *is* with you." ' "

Israel Defended Against Enemies

9 The burden[m] of the word of the LORD
Against the land of Hadrach,
And Damascus its resting place

8:17 [l] Literally *his*
9:1 [m] Or *oracle*

(For the eyes of men
And all the tribes of Israel
Are on the LORD);
2 Also *against* Hamath, *which* borders on it,
And *against* Tyre and Sidon, though they are very wise.

3 For Tyre built herself a tower,
Heaped up silver like the dust,
And gold like the mire of the streets.
4 Behold, the LORD will cast her out;
He will destroy her power in the sea,
And she will be devoured by fire.

5 Ashkelon shall see *it* and fear;
Gaza also shall be very sorrowful;
And Ekron, for He dried up her expectation.
The king shall perish from Gaza,
And Ashkelon shall not be inhabited.

6 "A mixed race shall settle in Ashdod,
And I will cut off the pride of the Philistines.
7 I will take away the blood from his mouth,
And the abominations from between his teeth.
But he who remains, even he *shall be* for our God,
And shall be like a leader in Judah,
And Ekron like a Jebusite.
8 I will camp around My house
Because of the army,
Because of him who passes by and him who returns.
No more shall an oppressor pass through them,
For now I have seen with My eyes.

The Coming King

9 "Rejoice greatly, O daughter of Zion!
Shout, O daughter of Jerusalem!
Behold, your King is coming to you;
He *is* just and having salvation,
Lowly and riding on a donkey,
A colt, the foal of a donkey.
10 I will cut off the chariot from Ephraim
And the horse from Jerusalem;
The battle bow shall be cut off.
He shall speak peace to the nations;
His dominion *shall be* 'from sea to sea,
And from the River to the ends of the earth.'[n]

God Will Save His People

11 "As for you also,
Because of the blood of your covenant,
I will set your prisoners free from the waterless pit.
12 Return to the stronghold,
You prisoners of hope.
Even today I declare
That I will restore double to you.
13 For I have bent Judah, My *bow*,
Fitted the bow with Ephraim,
And raised up your sons, O Zion,
Against your sons, O Greece,
And made you like the sword of a mighty man."

14 Then the LORD will be seen over them,
And His arrow will go forth like lightning.
The Lord GOD will blow the trumpet,
And go with whirlwinds from the south.
15 The LORD of hosts will defend them;
They shall devour and subdue with slingstones.
They shall drink *and* roar as if with wine;
They shall be filled *with blood* like basins,
Like the corners of the altar.
16 The LORD their God will save them in that day,
As the flock of His people.
For they *shall be like* the jewels of a crown,
Lifted like a banner over His land—
17 For how great is its[o] goodness
And how great its[p] beauty!
Grain shall make the young men thrive,
And new wine the young women.

Restoration of Judah and Israel

10 Ask the LORD for rain
In the time of the latter rain.[q]
The LORD will make flashing clouds;
He will give them showers of rain,
Grass in the field for everyone.

2 For the idols[r] speak delusion;
The diviners envision lies,
And tell false dreams;
They comfort in vain.
Therefore *the people* wend their way like sheep;
They are in trouble because *there is* no shepherd.

3 "My anger is kindled against the shepherds,
And I will punish the goatherds.

9:10 [n] Psalm 72:8
9:17 [o] Or *His* [p] Or *His*
10:1 [q] That is, spring rain
10:2 [r] Hebrew *teraphim*

For the LORD of hosts will visit His flock,
The house of Judah,
And will make them as His royal horse in the battle.
4 From him comes the cornerstone,
From him the tent peg,
From him the battle bow,
From him every ruler[s] together.
5 They shall be like mighty men,
Who tread down *their enemies*
In the mire of the streets in the battle.
They shall fight because the LORD is with them,
And the riders on horses shall be put to shame.

6 "I will strengthen the house of Judah,
And I will save the house of Joseph.
I will bring them back,
Because I have mercy on them.
They shall be as though I had not cast them aside;
For I *am* the LORD their God,
And I will hear them.
7 *Those of* Ephraim shall be like a mighty man,
And their heart shall rejoice as if with wine.
Yes, their children shall see *it* and be glad;
Their heart shall rejoice in the LORD.
8 I will whistle for them and gather them,
For I will redeem them;
And they shall increase as they once increased.

9 "I will sow them among the peoples,
And they shall remember Me in far countries;
They shall live, together with their children,
And they shall return.
10 I will also bring them back from the land of Egypt,
And gather them from Assyria.
I will bring them into the land of Gilead and Lebanon,
Until no *more room* is found for them.
11 He shall pass through the sea with affliction,
And strike the waves of the sea:
All the depths of the River[t] shall dry up.
Then the pride of Assyria shall be brought down,
And the scepter of Egypt shall depart.

12 "So I will strengthen them in the LORD,
And they shall walk up and down in His name,"
Says the LORD.

Desolation of Israel

11 Open your doors, O Lebanon,
That fire may devour your cedars.
2 Wail, O cypress, for the cedar has fallen,

10:4 [s] Or *despot*
10:11 [t] That is, the Nile

Life Lesson

Zechariah 9:1–14:21

SITUATION Zechariah prophesied that the key to Israel's future was the coming Messiah, whose gentle leadership would triumph through suffering.

OBSERVATION Greatness emerges through struggle and suffering. This was an important message for the early church to understand.

INSPIRATION "There lies the most perfect ruler of men the world has ever seen . . . [and] now he belongs to the ages."

Of whom was this said?

One of the Caesars? No. Napoleon? No. Alexander the Great? No. Eisenhower? Patton? MacArthur . . . or some earlier military strategist like Grant or Lee or Pershing? No, none of the above. How about Rockne or Lombardi? No. Or Luther? Calvin? Knox? Wesley? Spurgeon? Again, the answer is no.

Well, it was no doubt said of a great leader, a powerful and persuasive personality, was it not? Certainly one admired for his success. That depends, I suppose.

When he was seven years old, his family was forced out of their home because of a legal technicality. He had to work to help support them.

At age nine, while still a backward, shy little boy, his mother died.

At twenty-two, he lost his job as a store clerk. He wanted to go to law school, but his education was not good enough.

At twenty-three, he went into debt to become a partner in a small store.

Three years later his business partner died, leaving him a huge debt that took years to repay.

At twenty-eight, after developing a romantic relationship with a young lady for four years, he asked her to marry him. She said no. An earlier youthful love he shared with a lovely girl ended in heartache at her death.

Continued

At thirty-seven, on his third try, he was finally elected to Congress. Two years later he ran again and failed to be reelected. I should add it was about this time he had what some today would call a nervous breakdown.

At forty-one, adding additional heartache to an already unhappy marriage, his four-year-old son died.

The next year he was rejected for Land Officer.

At forty-five, he ran for the Senate and lost.

Two years later, he was defeated for nomination for Vice-President.

At forty-nine he ran for the Senate again . . . and lost again.

Add to this an endless barrage of criticism, misunderstanding, ugly and false rumors, and deep periods of depression and you realize it's no wonder he was snubbed by his peers and despised by multitudes, hardly the envy of his day.

At fifty-one, however, he was elected President of the United States . . . but his second term in office was cut short by his assassination. As he lay dying in a little rooming house across from the place where he was shot, a former detractor (Edwin Stanton) spoke the fitting tribute I quoted at the top of this column. By now you know it was spoken of the most inspirational and highly regarded president in American history, Abraham Lincoln. . . .

What a strange lot we are! Enamored of the dazzling lights, the fickle applause of the public, the splash of success, we seldom trace the lines that led to that flimsy and fleeting pinnacle. Bitter hardship. Unfair and undeserved

Because the mighty *trees* are ruined.
Wail, O oaks of Bashan,
For the thick forest has come down.
3 *There is* the sound of wailing shepherds!
For their glory is in ruins.
There is the sound of roaring lions!
For the pride[u] of the Jordan is in ruins.

Prophecy of the Shepherds

4Thus says the LORD my God, "Feed the flock for slaughter, 5whose owners
slaughter them and feel no guilt; those who sell them say, 'Blessed be the
LORD, for I am rich'; and their shepherds do not pity them. 6For I will no
longer pity the inhabitants of the land," says the LORD. "But indeed I will
give everyone into his neighbor's hand and into the hand of his king. They
shall attack the land, and I will not deliver *them* from their hand."

7So I fed the flock for slaughter, in particular the poor of the flock.[v] I
took for myself two staffs: the one I called Beauty,[w] and the other I called
Bonds;[x] and I fed the flock. 8I dismissed the three shepherds in one month.
My soul loathed them, and their soul also abhorred me. 9Then I said, "I will
not feed you. Let what is dying die, and what is perishing perish. Let those
that are left eat each other's flesh." 10And I took my staff, Beauty, and cut it
in two, that I might break the covenant which I had made with all the peoples. 11So it was broken on that day. Thus the poor[y] of the flock, who were
watching me, knew that it *was* the word of the LORD. 12Then I said to them,
"If it is agreeable to you, give *me* my wages; and if not, refrain." So they
weighed out for my wages thirty *pieces* of silver.

13And the LORD said to me, "Throw it to the potter"—that princely price
they set on me. So I took the thirty *pieces* of silver and threw them into the
house of the LORD for the potter. 14Then I cut in two my other staff, Bonds,
that I might break the brotherhood between Judah and Israel.

15And the LORD said to me, "Next, take for yourself the implements of a
foolish shepherd. 16For indeed I will raise up a shepherd in the land *who*
will not care for those who are cut off, nor seek the young, nor heal those
that are broken, nor feed those that still stand. But he will eat the flesh of
the fat and tear their hooves in pieces.

17 "Woe to the worthless shepherd,
Who leaves the flock!
A sword *shall be* against his arm
And against his right eye;
His arm shall completely wither,
And his right eye shall be totally blinded."

The Coming Deliverance of Judah

12 The burden[z] of the word of the LORD against Israel. Thus says the
LORD, who stretches out the heavens, lays the foundation of the earth,
and forms the spirit of man within him: 2"Behold, I will make Jerusalem a

11:3 [u] Or *floodplain, thicket*
11:7 [v] Following Masoretic Text, Targum, and Vulgate; Septuagint reads *for the Canaanites.* [w] Or *Grace,* and so in verse 10 [x] Or *Unity,* and so in verse 14
11:11 [y] Following Masoretic Text, Targum, and Vulgate; Septuagint reads *the Canaanites.*
12:1 [z] Or *oracle*

cup of drunkenness to all the surrounding peoples, when they lay siege against Judah and Jerusalem. [3]And it shall happen in that day that I will make Jerusalem a very heavy stone for all peoples; all who would heave it away will surely be cut in pieces, though all nations of the earth are gathered against it. [4]In that day," says the LORD, "I will strike every horse with confusion, and its rider with madness; I will open My eyes on the house of Judah, and will strike every horse of the peoples with blindness. [5]And the governors of Judah shall say in their heart, 'The inhabitants of Jerusalem *are* my strength in the LORD of hosts, their God.' [6]In that day I will make the governors of Judah like a firepan in the woodpile, and like a fiery torch in the sheaves; they shall devour all the surrounding peoples on the right hand and on the left, but Jerusalem shall be inhabited again in her own place—Jerusalem.

[7]"The LORD will save the tents of Judah first, so that the glory of the house of David and the glory of the inhabitants of Jerusalem shall not become greater than that of Judah. [8]In that day the LORD will defend the inhabitants of Jerusalem; the one who is feeble among them in that day shall be like David, and the house of David *shall be* like God, like the Angel of the LORD before them. [9]It shall be in that day *that* I will seek to destroy all the nations that come against Jerusalem.

Mourning for the Pierced One

[10]"And I will pour on the house of David and on the inhabitants of Jerusalem the Spirit of grace and supplication; then they will look on Me whom they pierced. Yes, they will mourn for Him as one mourns for *his* only *son*, and grieve for Him as one grieves for a firstborn. [11]In that day there shall be a great mourning in Jerusalem, like the mourning at Hadad Rimmon in the plain of Megiddo.[a] [12]And the land shall mourn, every family by itself: the family of the house of David by itself, and their wives by themselves; the family of the house of Nathan by itself, and their wives by themselves; [13]the family of the house of Levi by itself, and their wives by themselves; the family of Shimei by itself, and their wives by themselves; [14]all the families that remain, every family by itself, and their wives by themselves.

Idolatry Cut Off

13 "In that day a fountain shall be opened for the house of David and for the inhabitants of Jerusalem, for sin and for uncleanness.

[2]"It shall be in that day," says the LORD of hosts, "*that* I will cut off the names of the idols from the land, and they shall no longer be remembered. I will also cause the prophets and the unclean spirit to depart from the land. [3]It shall come to pass *that* if anyone still prophesies, then his father and mother who begot him will say to him, 'You shall not live, because you have spoken lies in the name of the LORD.' And his father and mother who begot him shall thrust him through when he prophesies.

[4]"And it shall be in that day *that* every prophet will be ashamed of his vision when he prophesies; they will not wear a robe of coarse hair to deceive. [5]But he will say, 'I *am* no prophet, I *am* a farmer; for a man taught me to keep cattle from my youth.' [6]And *one* will say to him, 'What are these wounds between your arms?[b] Then he will answer, '*Those* with which I was wounded in the house of my friends.'

12:11 [a] Hebrew *Megiddon*
13:6 [b] Or *hands*

abuses. Loneliness and loss. Humiliating failures. Debilitating disappointments. Agony beyond comprehension suffered in the valley and crevices of the climb from bottom to top.

How short sighted! Instead of accepting the fact that no one deserves the right to lead without first persevering through pain and heartache and failure, we resent those intruders. We treat them as enemies, not friends. We forget that the marks of greatness are not delivered in a paper sack by capricious gods. They are not hurriedly stuck onto skin like a tattoo.

No, those who are really worth following have paid their dues. They have come through the furnace melted, beaten, reshaped, and tempered. To use the words of the teacher from Tarsus, they bear in their bodies "the brand-marks of Jesus" (Galatians 6:17). Or, as one paraphrases it, they carry "the scars of the whipping and wounds" which link them to all mankind.

Small wonder when such people move from time to eternity they "belong to the ages."

(From *Growing Old in the Seasons of Life* by Charles Swindoll)

APPLICATION You may face trials and trying circumstances in life. But don't give up. Take courage! Your strength rests in your Savior, Jesus Christ. Your stamina for future service to God will come through these trials.

EXPLORATION Greatness—2 Samuel 5:12; Mark 10:42-45; John 1:30; Matthew 23:11-12.

The Shepherd Savior

7 "Awake, O sword, against My Shepherd,
Against the Man who is My Companion,"
Says the LORD of hosts.
"Strike the Shepherd,
And the sheep will be scattered;
Then I will turn My hand against the little ones.
8 And it shall come to pass in all the land,"
Says the LORD,
"*That* two-thirds in it shall be cut off *and* die,
But *one*-third shall be left in it:
9 I will bring the *one*-third through the fire,
Will refine them as silver is refined,
And test them as gold is tested.
They will call on My name,
And I will answer them.
I will say, 'This *is* My people';
And each one will say, 'The LORD *is* my God.' "

The Day of the LORD

14 Behold, the day of the LORD is coming,
And your spoil will be divided in your midst.
2 For I will gather all the nations to battle
against Jerusalem;
The city shall be taken,
The houses rifled,
And the women ravished.
Half of the city shall go into captivity,
But the remnant of the people shall not be cut
off from the city.

3 Then the LORD will go forth
And fight against those nations,
As He fights in the day of battle.
4 And in that day His feet will stand on the
Mount of Olives,
Which faces Jerusalem on the east.
And the Mount of Olives shall be split in two,
From east to west,
Making a very large valley;
Half of the mountain shall move
toward the north
And half of it toward the south.

5 Then you shall flee *through* My mountain valley,
For the mountain valley shall reach to Azal.
Yes, you shall flee
As you fled from the earthquake
In the days of Uzziah king of Judah.
Thus the LORD my God will come,
And all the saints with You.[c]
6 It shall come to pass in that day
That there will be no light;
The lights will diminish.
7 It shall be one day
Which is known to the LORD—
Neither day nor night.
But at evening time it shall happen
That it will be light.
8 And in that day it shall be
That living waters shall flow from Jerusalem,
Half of them toward the eastern sea
And half of them toward the western sea;
In both summer and winter it shall occur.
9 And the LORD shall be King over all the earth.
In that day it shall be—
"The LORD *is* one,"[d]
And His name one.

10 All the land shall be turned into a plain from Geba
to Rimmon south of Jerusalem. *Jerusalem*[e] shall be
raised up and inhabited in her place from Benjamin's
Gate to the place of the First Gate and the Corner Gate,
and *from* the Tower of Hananel to the king's winepresses.

11 *The people* shall dwell in it;
And no longer shall there be utter destruction,
But Jerusalem shall be safely inhabited.

12 And this shall be the plague with which the LORD
will strike all the people who fought against Jerusalem:

Their flesh shall dissolve while they
stand on their feet,
Their eyes shall dissolve in their sockets,
And their tongues shall dissolve
in their mouths.
13 It shall come to pass in that day
That a great panic from the LORD will be
among them.
Everyone will seize the hand of his neighbor,
And raise his hand against his neighbor's hand;
14 Judah also will fight at Jerusalem.
And the wealth of all the surrounding nations
Shall be gathered together:
Gold, silver, and apparel in great abundance.

15 Such also shall be the plague
On the horse *and* the mule,

14:5 [c] Or *you;* Septuagint, Targum, and Vulgate read *Him.*
14:9 [d] Compare Deuteronomy 6:4
14:10 [e] Literally *She*

On the camel and the donkey,
And on all the cattle that will be in those camps.
So *shall* this plague *be.*

The Nations Worship the King

16And it shall come to pass *that* everyone who is left
of all the nations which came against Jerusalem shall
go up from year to year to worship the King, the LORD of
hosts, and to keep the Feast of Tabernacles. 17And it shall
be *that* whichever of the families of the earth do not
come up to Jerusalem to worship the King, the LORD
of hosts, on them there will be no rain. 18If the family
of Egypt will not come up and enter in, they *shall have*
no *rain;* they shall receive the plague with which the
LORD strikes the nations who do not come up to keep
the Feast of Tabernacles. 19This shall be the punishment of Egypt and the punishment of all the nations
that do not come up to keep the Feast of Tabernacles.

20In that day "HOLINESS TO THE LORD" shall be
engraved on the bells of the horses. The pots in the
LORD's house shall be like the bowls before the altar.
21Yes, every pot in Jerusalem and Judah shall be holiness to the LORD of hosts.[f] Everyone who sacrifices
shall come and take them and cook in them. In that
day there shall no longer be a Canaanite in the house
of the LORD of hosts.

14:21 [f] Or *on every pot . . . shall be (engraved) "HOLINESS TO THE LORD OF HOSTS"*

The Book of MALACHI

INTRODUCTION

You offer defiled food on My altar, but say, "In what way have we defiled You?" (1:7).

The image is vivid. A family on their way to the temple realizes they have forgotten the sheep. He turns to her and says "Did you bring a sacrifice?" "No, I thought you did," she replies. He stops the wagon and says, "You go ahead and take the kids, I'll go back."

He goes back to the pen and begins to sort through the sheep looking for the one to be sacrificed. He picks up a big fat one with thick wool. "Too valuable," he decides and puts it down. He picks up another fat one. "No, I want to enter this one in a contest." He finds another healthy one. "No, I need to save this one for breeding."

Finally comes upon a frail lamb with a broken leg and spotted wool. "Ahh," he says. "This will be a good one to get rid of . . ."

What the fellow doesn't know is that God has been watching the process. God has been observing the choosing. What God has heard the man say is, "I will give a token, but I won't give my heart."

Such an attitude angers God. And such anger is found in this, the last book of the Old Testament.

"You bring the stolen, the lame, and the sick; thus you bring an offering! Should I accept this from your hand?" (1:13)

We don't offer sheep, but every Sunday we have an opportunity to give. Some people arrive at the altar with no thought given at all to their financial responsibility before God. As the plate comes she elbows him and says, "What do you want to give?"

He says, "Let me see what I've got."

Wallets come out and the process of proclamation begins. We begin to sort through the sheep pen. We consider that big sheep with the picture of Franklin, no, that's too much. We think about writing a check with a couple of zeros. "Better not," we decide.

We forget that the process itself is a statement.

We forget that God is watching.

We forget that God has challenged us to challenge him.

"Bring all the tithes into the storehouse, that there may be food in My house, and try Me now in this," says the LORD of hosts, "if I will not open for you the windows of heaven and pour out for you such blessing that there will not be room enough to receive it" (3:10).

The Book of Malachi is a challenge to take God seriously, not just in giving but in every aspect of life.

LIFE LESSON

Malachi 1:1–4:6

SITUATION God condemned Israel's complacent and contemptuous attitude toward him. The priests withheld their best animals from the sacrifice, and the people got tired of waiting for the Messiah.

OBSERVATION We can learn the most from God when we give him our undivided attention.

INSPIRATION I wish there were some way to announce over a loudspeaker system outside every worship gathering, "The pew zone is for learning and listening and changing only. No parking." God is saying, "Guard your steps! You're about to take a risk. Watch out! Be alert! Listen carefully. Truth will be deposited in your head that is designed to change your life." But chances are good that even though a loudspeaker made such an announcement, the same thing would occur—folks would still "park" and turn a deaf ear to the recording.

You see why that's important? Because our favorite place to park is in a pew. Just come, sit ("Whew! Finally got a seat!"), listen, and leave. . . .

So much of today's worship is dull-edge stuff—meaningless words, clichés that sit like tombstones over dead ideas. God is speaking. That's the reason for the command. The living God is communicating.

The burden[a] of the word of the LORD to Israel by Malachi.

Israel Beloved of God

2 "I have loved you," says the LORD.
"Yet you say, 'In what way have You loved us?'
Was not Esau Jacob's brother?"
Says the LORD.
"Yet Jacob I have loved;
3 But Esau I have hated,
And laid waste his mountains and his heritage
For the jackals of the wilderness."

4 Even though Edom has said,
"We have been impoverished,
But we will return and build the desolate places,"

Thus says the LORD of hosts:
"They may build, but I will throw down;
They shall be called the Territory of Wickedness,
And the people against whom the LORD
will have indignation forever.
5 Your eyes shall see,
And you shall say,
'The LORD is magnified beyond the border of Israel.'

Polluted Offerings

6 "A son honors *his* father,
And a servant *his* master.
If then I am the Father,
Where *is* My honor?
And if I *am* a Master,
Where *is* My reverence?
Says the LORD of hosts
To you priests who despise My name.
Yet you say, 'In what way have we despised Your name?'
7 "You offer defiled food on My altar,
But say,
'In what way have we defiled You?'
By saying,
'The table of the LORD is contemptible.'
8 And when you offer the blind as a sacrifice,
Is it not evil?
And when you offer the lame and sick,
Is it not evil?
Offer it then to your governor!
Would he be pleased with you?
Would he accept you favorably?"
Says the LORD of hosts.

9 "But now entreat God's favor,
That He may be gracious to us.

1:1 [a] Or *oracle*

While this is being *done* by your hands,
Will He accept you favorably?"
Says the LORD of hosts.
10 "Who *is there* even among you who would shut the doors,
So that you would not kindle fire *on* My altar in vain?
I have no pleasure in you,"
Says the LORD of hosts,
"Nor will I accept an offering from your hands.
11 For from the rising of the sun, even to its going down,
My name *shall be* great among the Gentiles;
In every place incense *shall be* offered to My name,
And a pure offering;
For My name shall be great among the nations,"
Says the LORD of hosts.

12 "But you profane it,
In that you say,
'The table of the LORD[b] is defiled;
And its fruit, its food, *is* contemptible.'
13 You also say,
'Oh, what a weariness!'
And you sneer at it,"
Says the LORD of hosts.
"And you bring the stolen, the lame, and the sick;
Thus you bring an offering!
Should I accept this from your hand?"
Says the LORD.
14 "But cursed *be* the deceiver
Who has in his flock a male,
And takes a vow,
But sacrifices to the Lord what is blemished—
For I *am* a great King,"
Says the LORD of hosts,
"And My name *is to be* feared among the nations.

Corrupt Priests

2 "And now, O priests, this commandment
is for you.
2 If you will not hear,
And if you will not take *it* to heart,
To give glory to My name,"
Says the LORD of hosts,
"I will send a curse upon you,
And I will curse your blessings.
Yes, I have cursed them already,
Because you do not take *it* to heart.

3 "Behold, I will rebuke your descendants
And spread refuse on your faces,
The refuse of your solemn feasts;
And *one* will take you away with it.

Henry David Thoreau once wrote: "It takes two to speak the truth. One to speak and another to listen." Walt Whitman confessed: "To have great poets there must be great audiences." I like that!—someone to write and someone to appreciate. To have great messages from God, there must be a well-prepared spokesman and there must be an equally well-prepared congregation. They work in tandem with each other.

Come to terms with your lips, with your ears, as you envision yourself preparing for worship. Experiment with something different for a change. Be quiet. Try silence.

From the first strains of music to the last word of the benediction . . . learn to hitchhike on God's thoughts. Sometimes those thoughts come in the silence of the offertory. Sometimes they come as someone else is leading in prayer. Occasionally they come in the singing of a hymn. Draw near. Listen well, because God is communicating.

(From *Living on the Ragged Edge* by Charles Swindoll)

APPLICATION What steals your attention during worship? Do your thoughts wander toward the day's demands? Do you become preoccupied with later activities? What are some strategies you could employ to help keep your mind focused?

EXPLORATION Faithful Worship—Joshua 22:27; Psalm 95:6; Daniel 3:16-18; John 4:23-24.

1:12 [b] Following Bomberg; Masoretic Text reads *Lord.*

4 Then you shall know that I have sent this
commandment to you,
That My covenant with Levi may continue,"
Says the LORD of hosts.
5 "My covenant was with him, *one* of life
and peace,
And I gave them to him *that he might* fear *Me;*
So he feared Me
And was reverent before My name.
6 The law of truth[c] was in his mouth,
And injustice was not found on his lips.
He walked with Me in peace and equity,
And turned many away from iniquity.

7 "For the lips of a priest should keep knowledge,
And *people* should seek the law from
his mouth;
For he is the messenger of the LORD of hosts.
8 But you have departed from the way;
You have caused many to stumble at the law.
You have corrupted the covenant of Levi,"
Says the LORD of hosts.
9 "Therefore I also have made you contemptible
and base
Before all the people,
Because you have not kept My ways
But have shown partiality in the law."

Treachery of Infidelity

10 Have we not all one Father?
Has not one God created us?
Why do we deal treacherously with one
another
By profaning the covenant of the fathers?
11 Judah has dealt treacherously,
And an abomination has been committed in
Israel and in Jerusalem,
For Judah has profaned
The LORD's holy *institution* which He loves:
He has married the daughter of a foreign god.
12 May the LORD cut off from the tents of Jacob
The man who does this, being awake
and aware,[d]
Yet who brings an offering to the LORD of hosts!

13 And this is the second thing you do:
You cover the altar of the LORD with tears,
With weeping and crying;
So He does not regard the offering anymore,
Nor receive *it* with goodwill from your hands.

14 Yet you say, "For what reason?"
Because the LORD has been witness
Between you and the wife of your youth,
With whom you have dealt treacherously;
Yet she is your companion
And your wife by covenant.
15 But did He not make *them* one,
Having a remnant of the Spirit?
And why one?
He seeks godly offspring.
Therefore take heed to your spirit,
And let none deal treacherously with the wife
of his youth.

16 "For the LORD God of Israel says
That He hates divorce,
For it covers one's garment with violence,"
Says the LORD of hosts.
"Therefore take heed to your spirit,
That you do not deal treacherously."

17 You have wearied the LORD with your words;
Yet you say,
"In what way have we wearied *Him?*"
In that you say,
"Everyone who does evil
Is good in the sight of the LORD,
And He delights in them,"
Or, "Where *is* the God of justice?"

The Coming Messenger

3 "Behold, I send My messenger,
And he will prepare the way before Me.
And the Lord, whom you seek,
Will suddenly come to His temple,
Even the Messenger of the covenant,
In whom you delight.
Behold, He is coming,"
Says the LORD of hosts.

2 "But who can endure the day of His coming?
And who can stand when He appears?
For He *is* like a refiner's fire
And like launderers' soap.
3 He will sit as a refiner and a purifier of silver;
He will purify the sons of Levi,
And purge them as gold and silver,
That they may offer to the LORD
An offering in righteousness.

2:6 [c] Or *true instruction*
2:12 [d] Talmud and Vulgate read *teacher and student.*

4 "Then the offering of Judah and Jerusalem
Will be pleasant to the LORD,
As in the days of old,
As in former years.
5 And I will come near you for judgment;
I will be a swift witness
Against sorcerers,
Against adulterers,
Against perjurers,
Against those who exploit wage earners and widows and orphans,
And against those who turn away an alien—
Because they do not fear Me,"
Says the LORD of hosts.

6 "For I *am* the LORD, I do not change;
Therefore you are not consumed, O sons of Jacob.
7 Yet from the days of your fathers
You have gone away from My ordinances
And have not kept *them.*
Return to Me, and I will return to you,"
Says the LORD of hosts.
"But you said,
'In what way shall we return?'

Do Not Rob God

8 "Will a man rob God?
Yet you have robbed Me!
But you say,
'In what way have we robbed You?'
In tithes and offerings.
9 You are cursed with a curse,
For you have robbed Me,
Even this whole nation.
10 Bring all the tithes into the storehouse,
That there may be food in My house,
And try Me now in this,"
Says the LORD of hosts,
"If I will not open for you the windows of heaven
And pour out for you *such* blessing
That *there will* not *be room* enough *to receive it.*

11 "And I will rebuke the devourer for your sakes,
So that he will not destroy the fruit of your ground,
Nor shall the vine fail to bear fruit for you in the field,"
Says the LORD of hosts;
12 And all nations will call you blessed,
For you will be a delightful land,"
Says the LORD of hosts.

The People Complain Harshly

13 "Your words have been harsh against Me,"
Says the LORD,
"Yet you say,
'What have we spoken against You?'
14 You have said,
'It is useless to serve God;
What profit *is it* that we have kept His ordinance,
And that we have walked as mourners
Before the LORD of hosts?
15 So now we call the proud blessed,
For those who do wickedness are raised up;
They even tempt God and go free.' "

A Book of Remembrance

16 Then those who feared the LORD spoke to one another,
And the LORD listened and heard *them;*
So a book of remembrance was written before Him
For those who fear the LORD
And who meditate on His name.

17 "They shall be Mine," says the LORD of hosts,
"On the day that I make them My jewels.[e]
And I will spare them
As a man spares his own son who serves him."
18 Then you shall again discern
Between the righteous and the wicked,
Between one who serves God
And one who does not serve Him.

The Great Day of God

4 "For behold, the day is coming,
Burning like an oven,
And all the proud, yes, all who do wickedly will be stubble.
And the day which is coming shall burn them up,"
Says the LORD of hosts,
"That will leave them neither root nor branch.
2 But to you who fear My name
The Sun of Righteousness shall arise
With healing in His wings;
And you shall go out
And grow fat like stall-fed calves.

3:17 [e] Literally *special treasure*

3 You shall trample the wicked,
For they shall be ashes under the soles
of your feet
On the day that I do *this*,"
Says the LORD of hosts.

4 "Remember the Law of Moses, My servant,
Which I commanded him in Horeb for
all Israel,
With the statutes and judgments.

5 Behold, I will send you Elijah the prophet
Before the coming of the great and dreadful
day of the LORD.

6 And he will turn
The hearts of the fathers to the children,
And the hearts of the children to their fathers,
Lest I come and strike the earth with a curse."

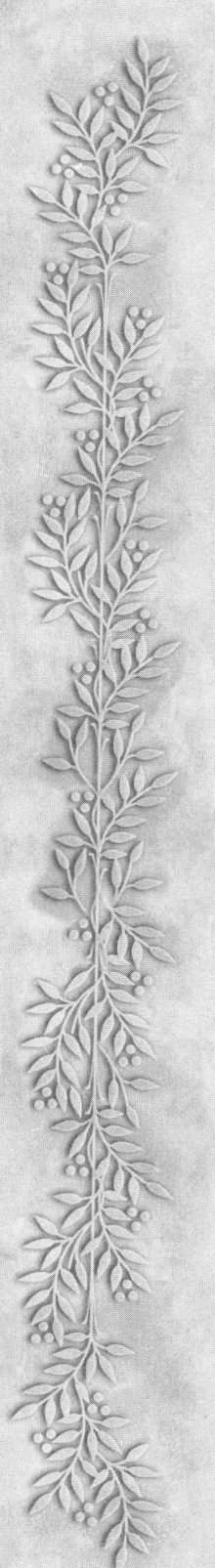

I will plant them and not pluck them up. Then I will give them a heart to know Me, that I am the LORD; and they shall be My people, and I will be their God, for they shall return to Me with their whole heart.

Jeremiah 24:6, 7

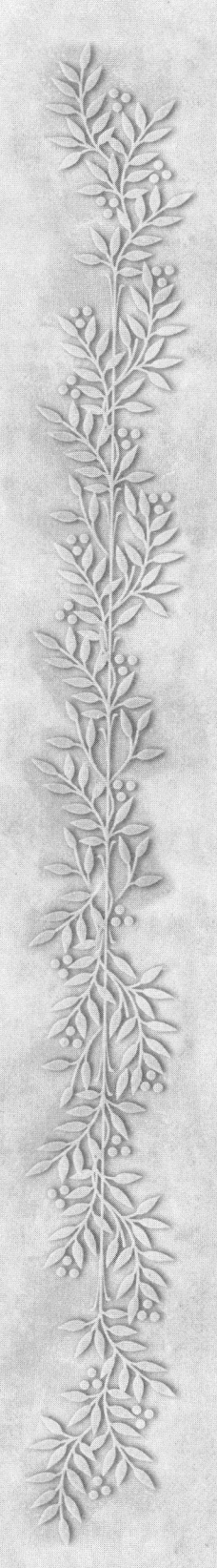

The
INSPIRATIONAL
STUDY BIBLE

THE NEW TESTAMENT

Jesus

When Jesus says, "Come to me," he doesn't say come to religion, come to a system, or come to a certain doctrine. This is a very personal invitation to a God, an invitation to a Savior.

In essence, Christianity is nothing more, nothing less than a desire and an effort to see Jesus. That's all it is. We're trying to catch a glimpse of a man, not a program, not a plan, not a system, not a doctrine. We're trying to see a man who called himself the Son of God.

Our God is not aloof—he's not so far above us that he can't see and understand our problems. Jesus isn't a God who stayed on the mountaintop—he's a Savior who came down and lived and worked with the people. Everywhere he went, the crowds followed, drawn together by the magnet that was—and is—the Savior.

The life of Jesus Christ is a message of hope, a message of mercy, a message of life in a dark world.

BLESSED LORD and God, we come to you, aware that you have pierced our world. You became flesh, you dwelled among us, you saw us in our fallen state, you reached in and pulled us out. You offered us salvation, you offered us mercy. And we are ever thankful.

SUFFERING

Folks, if you're expecting to be given a fair shake in your life, forget it! You won't be. You're going to face illness. And your body is going to wear out. You may be the victim of someone else's mistake. But you can get through those tough times if you prepare your heart now, living to know and serve the Savior who loves you and died so that you might have an eternal home free of pain and sorrow.

The struggles that you're going through now—don't discard them. Listen to God as he teaches you so that you can teach others. You see, a time of suffering teaches us something we never knew before and may prepare us for a time of counsel that we will give someone years from now.

God is with you. God is with you! The same God that guided his Son through death and back to life said he will never leave us or forsake us. He is right there with you, perhaps even more in times of crisis than any other time.

FATHER, we believe that when we see you, any suffering that we endured on the face of this earth will be worth it. We believe that the first five minutes we stand in heaven we will know that anything we endured on this globe will be forgotten. Father, help us to understand. And when we cannot understand, help us to trust.

HOSPITALITY

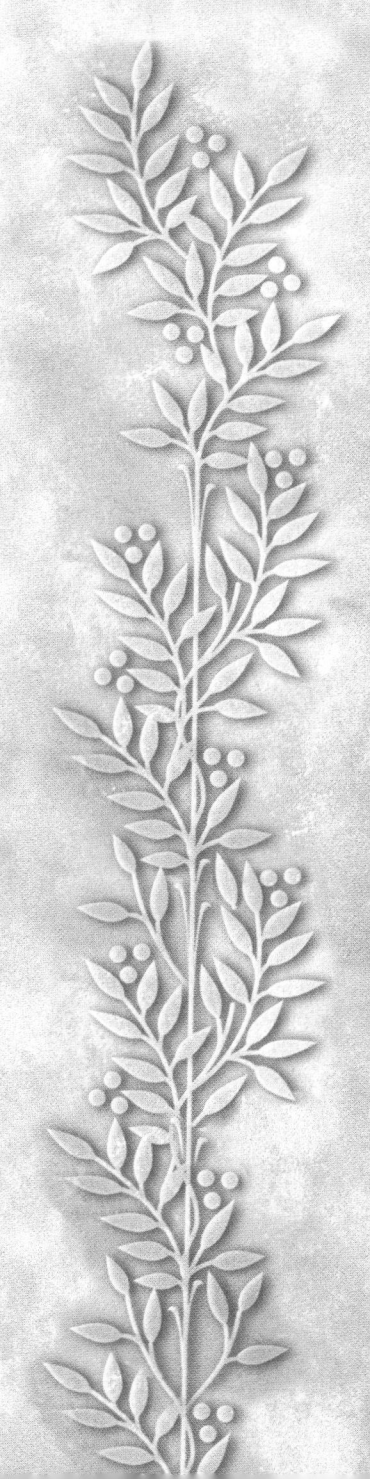

Here's a suggestion: We should all wear antennas to work, to church, to school—antennas that pick up on people who seem out of place, whose loneliness shows. Why not be the one to approach these folks and extend friendship to them? Maybe you think the last thing you need is another friend. But friendliness—hospitality—is a virtue that brings as much joy to the giver as to the receiver.

When you extend hospitality to others, you're not trying to impress people, you're trying to reflect God to them. You don't have to be rich to be hospitable. A wise friend once told me, "If you won't give people hot dogs when you're poor, you won't give them steaks when you're rich." We shouldn't let our pride get in the way of being hospitable.

We are here on earth to be God's people. We are here to show others the same God who came to be a friend to the earth—that's our task. Maybe today you will meet someone who really needs a friend—and you can fill that need. Maybe you can make an eternal difference in that person's life, just because you choose to be friendly today.

FATHER, as we set about the task of trying to be your people, we pray that you'll help us. May we glorify your name, may we be open-minded, may we be sincere, may we be willing to change and grow. We thank you, Lord, for the privilege of being your people.

HURT

Where is God when we hurt? Where is he when sleep won't come? Where is he when we awaken in a hospital bed with pain that won't subside? He's right here! He hung on the gallows to prove once and for all, with pierced hands and blood-stained face—that he's here—that he didn't create the hurt, but he came to take it away.

When you hurt, God hurts with you. When no one listens to you, God listens to you. When you wipe away tears of loneliness or frustration or anguish, in heaven there's a pierced hand approaching a heavenly face wiping away a tear.

Sometimes storms of life come to teach us that God is in control, that we must lean on him and learn to be thankful for the richness of his blessings to us.

We should serve God even if there is darkness enveloping our life and even if we don't understand what's happening . . . even when the circumstances of our life don't make sense: Because he is worthy of praise, *because* he is God.

FATHER, nothing is louder than the silence of our God. But Father, forgive us for the times we've interpreted your silence as a lack of love. Give us patience, for we know you'll answer, Father, if only we'll wait.

The Gospel According to

MATTHEW

INTRODUCTION

You gotta wonder what Jesus saw in Matthew.

He was a tax collector. The profession hasn't been too popular in any era, but especially not in the days of Christ. Tax collectors were the quislings of Palestine. They took from their own people and gave to Rome. As long as they met their quota, they could tax whatever they wanted and as much as they wanted.

People ducked when they saw these guys coming.

Not only was Matthew a tax collector, he was a public tax collector. Some collectors did their business underground. They hired runners to do their dirty work. Matthew did his own. He was the leech at the bottom of the pit. He pulled his stretch limo right into the greasiest parts of town and set up his table and held out his hand.

That's where he was when Jesus called him.

You gotta wonder what Jesus saw in Matthew. At the same time, you gotta wonder what Matthew saw in Jesus. I mean, look at him. Dirt under his nails. Calloused hands. Holes in his sandals. No headquarters. No office. No committee. No clout with the local church.

The clergy won't give him the time of day. His followers look more like dockhands or pool sharks than seminarians.

This guy claims to be the Messiah?

Quite a pair, these two. You gotta wonder what they saw in each other. Whatever it was, it must've been something. Matthew heard the call and never went back. He spent the rest of his life convincing folks that the carpenter was the King. Jesus gave the call and never took it back. He spent his life dying for people like Matthew, convincing a lot of us that if he had a place for Matthew, he just might have a place for us.

LIFE LESSON

Matthew 1:1-24

SITUATION Because Matthew wrote for a Jewish audience, he began his Gospel by showing through family records that Jesus was a descendant of both King David and Abraham.

OBSERVATION Joseph found it difficult to understand the supernatural conception and birth of Jesus Christ.

INSPIRATION Perhaps changes are in the air right now. Maybe you're in the midst of a decision. It's disrupting, isn't it? You like your branch. . . . And, like Joseph, you've been a pretty good branch-sitter. And then you hear the call. "I need you to go out on the limb and

. . . move. Take your family and move overseas, I have a special work for you."

. . . forgive. It doesn't matter who hurt who first. What matters is that you go and build the bridge."

. . . evangelize. That new family down the block? They don't know anyone in town. Go meet them."

. . . sacrifice. The orphanage has a mortgage payment due this month. They can't meet it. Remember the bonus you received last week?"

Regardless of the nature of the call, the consequences are the same: civil war. Though your heart may say yes, your feet say no. Excuses blow numerously as golden leaves in an autumn wind. "That's not my talent." "It's time for someone else to take charge." "Not now. I'll get to it tomorrow."

But eventually you're left staring at a bare tree and a hard choice: His will or yours?

(From *God Came Near* by Max Lucado)

APPLICATION God's plan encompasses your personality, your talents, and your future. Ask God today to help you be a witness, open to new assignments, and eager to grow in faith.

EXPLORATION Family History of Jesus—Ruth 4:18-22; 1 Chronicles 3:10-17; Luke 3:23-28. Virgin Birth of Jesus—Isaiah 7:14.

The Genealogy of Jesus Christ

The book of the genealogy of Jesus Christ, the Son of David, the
Son of Abraham:
2Abraham begot Isaac, Isaac begot Jacob, and Jacob begot Judah
and his brothers. 3Judah begot Perez and Zerah by Tamar, Perez
begot Hezron, and Hezron begot Ram. 4Ram begot Amminadab,
Amminadab begot Nahshon, and Nahshon begot Salmon. 5Salmon begot
Boaz by Rahab, Boaz begot Obed by Ruth, Obed begot Jesse, 6and Jesse
begot David the king.
David the king begot Solomon by her *who had been the wife*[a] of Uriah.
7Solomon begot Rehoboam, Rehoboam begot Abijah, and Abijah begot
Asa.[b] 8Asa begot Jehoshaphat, Jehoshaphat begot Joram, and Joram begot
Uzziah. 9Uzziah begot Jotham, Jotham begot Ahaz, and Ahaz begot
Hezekiah. 10Hezekiah begot Manasseh, Manasseh begot Amon,[c] and
Amon begot Josiah. 11Josiah begot Jeconiah and his brothers about the
time they were carried away to Babylon.
12And after they were brought to Babylon, Jeconiah begot Shealtiel, and
Shealtiel begot Zerubbabel. 13Zerubbabel begot Abiud, Abiud begot
Eliakim, and Eliakim begot Azor. 14Azor begot Zadok, Zadok begot Achim,
and Achim begot Eliud. 15Eliud begot Eleazar, Eleazar begot Matthan, and
Matthan begot Jacob. 16And Jacob begot Joseph the husband of Mary, of
whom was born Jesus who is called Christ.
17So all the generations from Abraham to David *are* fourteen generations, from David until the captivity in Babylon *are* fourteen generations,
and from the captivity in Babylon until the Christ *are* fourteen generations.

Christ Born of Mary

18Now the birth of Jesus Christ was as follows: After His mother Mary
was betrothed to Joseph, before they came together, she was found with
child of the Holy Spirit. 19Then Joseph her husband, being a just *man,* and
not wanting to make her a public example, was minded to put her away secretly. 20But while he thought about these things, behold, an angel of the
Lord appeared to him in a dream, saying, "Joseph, son of David, do not be
afraid to take to you Mary your wife, for that which is conceived in her is of
the Holy Spirit. 21And she will bring forth a Son, and you shall call His
name JESUS, for He will save His people from their sins."
22So all this was done that it might be fulfilled which was spoken by the
Lord through the prophet, saying: 23"*Behold, the virgin shall be with child,
and bear a Son, and they shall call His name Immanuel,*"[d] which is translated, "God with us."
24Then Joseph, being aroused from sleep, did as the angel of the Lord
commanded him and took to him his wife, 25and did not know her till she
had brought forth her firstborn Son.[e] And he called His name JESUS.

Wise Men from the East

2 Now after Jesus was born in Bethlehem of Judea in the days of Herod
the king, behold, wise men from the East came to Jerusalem, 2saying,

1:6 [a] Words in italic type have been added for clarity. They are not found in the original Greek.
1:7 [b] NU-Text reads *Asaph.*
1:10 [c] NU-Text reads *Amos.*
1:23 [d] Isaiah 7:14. Words in oblique type in the New Testament are quoted from the Old Testament.
1:25 [e] NU-Text reads *a Son.*

"Where is He who has been born King of the Jews? For we have seen His
star in the East and have come to worship Him."
3When Herod the king heard *this,* he was troubled, and all Jerusalem
with him. 4And when he had gathered all the chief priests and scribes of
the people together, he inquired of them where the Christ was to be born.
5So they said to him, "In Bethlehem of Judea, for thus it is written by the
prophet:

6 *'But you, Bethlehem, in the land of Judah,*
Are not the least among the rulers of Judah;
For out of you shall come a Ruler
Who will shepherd My people Israel.'"[f]

7Then Herod, when he had secretly called the wise men, determined
from them what time the star appeared. 8And he sent them to Bethlehem
and said, "Go and search carefully for the young Child, and when you have
found *Him,* bring back word to me, that I may come and worship Him also."
9When they heard the king, they departed; and behold, the star which
they had seen in the East went before them, till it came and stood over
where the young Child was. 10When they saw the star, they rejoiced with
exceedingly great joy. 11And when they had come into the house, they saw
the young Child with Mary His mother, and fell down and worshiped Him.
And when they had opened their treasures, they presented gifts to Him:
gold, frankincense, and myrrh.
12Then, being divinely warned in a dream that they should not return to
Herod, they departed for their own country another way.

The Flight into Egypt

13Now when they had departed, behold, an angel of the Lord appeared
to Joseph in a dream, saying, "Arise, take the young Child and His mother,
flee to Egypt, and stay there until I bring you word; for Herod will seek the
young Child to destroy Him."
14When he arose, he took the young Child and His mother by night and
departed for Egypt, 15and was there until the death of Herod, that it might
be fulfilled which was spoken by the Lord through the prophet, saying,
"Out of Egypt I called My Son."[g]

Massacre of the Innocents

16Then Herod, when he saw that he was deceived by the wise men, was
exceedingly angry; and he sent forth and put to death all the male children
who were in Bethlehem and in all its districts, from two years old and
under, according to the time which he had determined from the wise men.
17Then was fulfilled what was spoken by Jeremiah the prophet, saying:

18 *"A voice was heard in Ramah,*
Lamentation, weeping, and great mourning,
Rachel weeping for her children,
Refusing to be comforted,
Because they are no more."[h]

2:6 *f* Micah 5:2
2:15 *g* Hosea 11:1
2:18 *h* Jeremiah 31:15

Life Lesson

Matthew 2:1-23

SITUATION Jesus was born a descendent of King David during the reign of King Herod. The Roman Senate had appointed Herod to rule Judea.

OBSERVATION Reaction to Jesus' birth was mixed. The Magi came to worship Jesus, while King Herod tried to kill him.

INSPIRATION Have you ever been at a party where an attempt was made to celebrate just for the sake of celebration? I have, and I found it to be exceptionally contrived and boring. A true celebration must be rooted in an event.

In both the Old and New Testaments, worship is rooted in an actual event. The content of Old Testament worship is determined by the Exodus-event, while the content of New Testament worship is determined by the Christ-event. In either case, biblical worship celebrates the event and makes it come alive again.

. . . We don't go to worship to celebrate what we have done. We don't say, "Look, Lord, isn't it wonderful that I believe in you!" No! We go to worship to praise and thank God for what *he* has done, is doing, and will do. God's work in Christ is the focus of worship. And it is the focus we need to recapture as we seek to renew our public worship experience.
(From *Worship Is a Verb* by Robert E. Webber)

APPLICATION How do I respond to Jesus, the King? Do I worship him? Do I celebrate his birth, life, death, and resurrection? What do I bring to give to him? Bring a gift to Jesus in your prayer, worship, or service.

EXPLORATION Prophecies about Jesus—Jeremiah 31:15; Micah 5:2.

LIFE LESSON

Matthew 3:1-17

SITUATION Two major religious groups existed in Israel at the time of Jesus. The Pharisees were more religiously minded, while the Sadducees were more politically minded. These groups were united in their hatred of Jesus.

OBSERVATION True repentance prepares the way for Jesus in our lives.

INSPIRATION Then there was what John the Baptist said—that he had come to prepare the way for the Lord. And everyone got excited. They knew their prophecies, and were watching out for God to come and visit and redeem his people. Then Jesus suddenly appears on the scene. And John seems to have known something about Jesus—something that made him hesitate before baptizing him. That seems significant. It was as if he knew that Jesus didn't *need* to be baptized. It was as if he had no sin to be washed away. If anybody needed to baptize anyone else, it was John who needed to be baptized by Jesus. . . .

What seemed ridiculous if Jesus was just a man makes perfect sense if he really was God. . . . Jesus conveyed the impression that he had the authority to act and speak as God. It is almost as if he anticipated the verdict of the resurrection—that he was *authorized* to speak and act in this way. And didn't people say that he taught with authority?

Suppose it were true. . . . If Jesus is God, it means we have a revelation of God which goes far beyond anything and everything we have ever had in the past. . . .

It means that the great gulf between God and ourselves has been bridged. . . .

And it would mean that any idea of God as some distant and remote figure would have to go.

(From *What Was God Doing on the Cross?* by Alister E. McGrath)

APPLICATION Have you followed this example of Jesus through baptism? Give it prayerful consideration.

EXPLORATION Baptism of Jesus—Mark 1:1-11; Luke 3:1-22.

The Home in Nazareth

19Now when Herod was dead, behold, an angel of the Lord appeared in
a dream to Joseph in Egypt, 20saying, "Arise, take the young Child and His
mother, and go to the land of Israel, for those who sought the young
Child's life are dead." 21Then he arose, took the young Child and His
mother, and came into the land of Israel.
22But when he heard that Archelaus was reigning over Judea instead of
his father Herod, he was afraid to go there. And being warned by God in a
dream, he turned aside into the region of Galilee. 23And he came and dwelt
in a city called Nazareth, that it might be fulfilled which was spoken by the
prophets, "He shall be called a Nazarene."

John the Baptist Prepares the Way

3 In those days John the Baptist came preaching in the wilderness of
Judea, 2and saying, "Repent, for the kingdom of heaven is at hand!"
3For this is he who was spoken of by the prophet Isaiah, saying:

"The voice of one crying in the wilderness:
'Prepare the way of the LORD;
Make His paths straight.'"[i]

4Now John himself was clothed in camel's hair, with a leather belt
around his waist; and his food was locusts and wild honey. 5Then Jerusalem, all Judea, and all the region around the Jordan went out to him 6and
were baptized by him in the Jordan, confessing their sins.
7But when he saw many of the Pharisees and Sadducees coming to his
baptism, he said to them, "Brood of vipers! Who warned you to flee from
the wrath to come? 8Therefore bear fruits worthy of repentance, 9and do
not think to say to yourselves, 'We have Abraham as *our* father.' For I say
to you that God is able to raise up children to Abraham from these stones.
10And even now the ax is laid to the root of the trees. Therefore every tree
which does not bear good fruit is cut down and thrown into the fire. 11I indeed baptize you with water unto repentance, but He who is coming after
me is mightier than I, whose sandals I am not worthy to carry. He will
baptize you with the Holy Spirit and fire.[j] 12His winnowing fan *is* in His
hand, and He will thoroughly clean out His threshing floor, and gather His
wheat into the barn; but He will burn up the chaff with unquenchable fire."

John Baptizes Jesus

13Then Jesus came from Galilee to John at the Jordan to be baptized by
him. 14And John *tried to* prevent Him, saying, "I need to be baptized by
You, and are You coming to me?"
15But Jesus answered and said to him, "Permit *it to be so* now, for thus it
is fitting for us to fulfill all righteousness." Then he allowed Him.
16When He had been baptized, Jesus came up immediately from the
water; and behold, the heavens were opened to Him, and He[k] saw the
Spirit of God descending like a dove and alighting upon Him. 17And suddenly a voice *came* from heaven, saying, "This is My beloved Son, in
whom I am well pleased."

3:3 [i] Isaiah 40:3
3:11 [j] M-Text omits *and fire.*
3:16 [k] Or *he*

Satan Tempts Jesus

4 Then Jesus was led up by the Spirit into the wilderness to be tempted
by the devil. 2And when He had fasted forty days and forty nights, afterward He was hungry. 3Now when the tempter came to Him, he said, "If
You are the Son of God, command that these stones become bread."
4But He answered and said, "It is written, *'Man shall not live by bread
alone, but by every word that proceeds from the mouth of God.'* "[l]
5Then the devil took Him up into the holy city, set Him on the pinnacle
of the temple, 6and said to Him, "If You are the Son of God, throw Yourself
down. For it is written:

'He shall give His angels charge over you,'

and,

'In their hands they shall bear you up,
Lest you dash your foot against a stone.' "[m]

7Jesus said to him, "It is written again, *'You shall not tempt the* LORD
your God.' "[n]
8Again, the devil took Him up on an exceedingly high mountain, and
showed Him all the kingdoms of the world and their glory. 9And he said to
Him, "All these things I will give You if You will fall down and worship me."
10Then Jesus said to him, "Away with you,[o] Satan! For it is written, *'You
shall worship the* LORD *your God, and Him only you shall serve.'* "[p]
11Then the devil left Him, and behold, angels came and ministered to Him.

Jesus Begins His Galilean Ministry

12Now when Jesus heard that John had been put in prison, He departed
to Galilee. 13And leaving Nazareth, He came and dwelt in Capernaum,
which is by the sea, in the regions of Zebulun and Naphtali, 14that it might
be fulfilled which was spoken by Isaiah the prophet, saying:

15 *"The land of Zebulun and the land of Naphtali,*
By the way of the sea, beyond the Jordan,
Galilee of the Gentiles:
16 *The people who sat in darkness have seen a great light,*
And upon those who sat in the region and shadow of death
Light has dawned."[q]

17From that time Jesus began to preach and to say, "Repent, for the
kingdom of heaven is at hand."

Four Fishermen Called as Disciples

18And Jesus, walking by the Sea of Galilee, saw two brothers, Simon
called Peter, and Andrew his brother, casting a net into the sea; for they
were fishermen. 19Then He said to them, "Follow Me, and I will make you
fishers of men." 20They immediately left *their* nets and followed Him.
21Going on from there, He saw two other brothers, James *the son* of
Zebedee, and John his brother, in the boat with Zebedee their father,

4:4 [l] Deuteronomy 8:3
4:6 [m] Psalm 91:11, 12
4:7 [n] Deuteronomy 6:16
4:10 [o] M-Text reads *Get behind Me.* [p] Deuteronomy 6:13
4:16 [q] Isaiah 9:1, 2

LIFE LESSON

Matthew 4:1-25

SITUATION Jesus told John the Baptist, "We should do all things that are God's will" (Matthew 3:15). Jesus followed God's will by resisting the devil's temptations and by teaching, preaching, and healing.

OBSERVATION Jesus gave his disciples the most rewarding job. He taught them to reach out to people with the Good News of God.

INSPIRATION When I was in high school, our family used to fish every year during spring break. One year my brother and my mom couldn't go, so my dad let me invite a friend. I asked Mark. He was a good pal and a great sport. He got permission from his parents, and we began planning our trip. . . .

We loaded our camper and set out for the lake.

We arrived late at night, unfolded the camper, and went to bed—dreaming of tomorrow's day in the sun. But during the night, an unseasonably strong norther blew in. It got cold fast! The wind was so strong that we could barely open the camper door the next morning. The sky was gray. The lake was a mountain range of white-topped waves. There was no way we could fish in that weather.

"No problem," we said. "We'll spend the day in the camper. After all, we have Monopoly. We have *Reader's Digest.* We all know a few jokes. It's not what we came to do, but we'll make the best of it and fish tomorrow."

We were in for a surprise. The next morning it wasn't the wind that made the door hard to open, it was the ice!

It was a long day. It was a long, cold night.

When we awoke the next morning to the sound of sleet slapping the canvas, we didn't even pretend to be cheerful. We were flat-out grumpy. Mark became more of a jerk with each passing moment; I wondered what spell of ignorance I must have been in when I invited him. Dad couldn't do anything right; I wondered how someone so irritable could have such an even-tempered son. We sat in misery the whole day, our fishing equipment still unpacked.

Continued

The next day was even colder. "We're going home" were my father's first words. No one objected.

I learned a hard lesson that week. Not about fishing, but about people.

When those who are called to fish don't fish, they fight.

But note the other side of this fish tale: When those who are called to fish, fish—they flourish!

Leave soldiers inside the barracks with no time on the front line and see what happens to their attitude. The soldiers will invent things to complain about. Bunks will be too hard. Food will be too cold. Leadership will be too tough. The company will be too stale. Yet place those same soldiers in the trench and let them duck a few bullets, and what was a boring barracks will seem like a haven. The beds will feel great. The food will be almost ideal. The leadership will be courageous. The company will be exciting.

When those who are called to fish, fish—they flourish!

(From *In the Eye of the Storm* by Max Lucado)

APPLICATION Are you a faithful worker in God's service? Is it easier for you to share your faith or argue with another Christian? Ask God to help you become a successful fisher of people.

EXPLORATION Temptation of Jesus—Mark 1:12-13; Luke 4:1-13. Jesus' Preaching—Mark 12:14-15; Luke 4:14-15; John 4:42-45. Jesus' Followers—Mark 1:16-20.

mending their nets. He called them, 22 and immediately they left the boat
and their father, and followed Him.

Jesus Heals a Great Multitude

23 And Jesus went about all Galilee, teaching in their synagogues,
preaching the gospel of the kingdom, and healing all kinds of sickness and
all kinds of disease among the people. 24 Then His fame went throughout
all Syria; and they brought to Him all sick people who were afflicted with
various diseases and torments, and those who were demon-possessed,
epileptics, and paralytics; and He healed them. 25 Great multitudes followed Him—from Galilee, and *from* Decapolis, Jerusalem, Judea, and beyond the Jordan.

The Beatitudes

5 And seeing the multitudes, He went up on a mountain, and when He
was seated His disciples came to Him. 2 Then He opened His mouth
and taught them, saying:

3 "Blessed *are* the poor in spirit,
For theirs is the kingdom of heaven.
4 Blessed *are* those who mourn,
For they shall be comforted.
5 Blessed *are* the meek,
For they shall inherit the earth.
6 Blessed *are* those who hunger and thirst for righteousness,
For they shall be filled.
7 Blessed *are* the merciful,
For they shall obtain mercy.
8 Blessed *are* the pure in heart,
For they shall see God.
9 Blessed *are* the peacemakers,
For they shall be called sons of God.
10 Blessed *are* those who are persecuted for righteousness' sake,
For theirs is the kingdom of heaven.

11 "Blessed are you when they revile and persecute you, and say all kinds of
evil against you falsely for My sake. 12 Rejoice and be exceedingly glad, for
great *is* your reward in heaven, for so they persecuted the prophets who
were before you.

Believers Are Salt and Light

13 "You are the salt of the earth; but if the salt loses its flavor, how shall it
be seasoned? It is then good for nothing but to be thrown out and trampled underfoot by men.
14 "You are the light of the world. A city that is set on a hill cannot be hidden.
15 Nor do they light a lamp and put it under a basket, but on a lampstand, and
it gives light to all *who are* in the house. 16 Let your light so shine before men,
that they may see your good works and glorify your Father in heaven.

Christ Fulfills the Law

17 "Do not think that I came to destroy the Law or the Prophets. I did not
come to destroy but to fulfill. 18 For assuredly, I say to you, till heaven and

earth pass away, one jot or one tittle will by no means pass from the law till
all is fulfilled. 19Whoever therefore breaks one of the least of these commandments, and teaches men so, shall be called least in the kingdom of
heaven; but whoever does and teaches *them,* he shall be called great in the
kingdom of heaven. 20For I say to you, that unless your righteousness exceeds *the righteousness* of the scribes and Pharisees, you will by no means
enter the kingdom of heaven.

Murder Begins in the Heart

21"You have heard that it was said to those of old, '*You shall not murder,*[r] and whoever murders will be in danger of the judgment.' 22But I say
to you that whoever is angry with his brother without a cause[s] shall be in
danger of the judgment. And whoever says to his brother, 'Raca!' shall be
in danger of the council. But whoever says, 'You fool!' shall be in danger of
hell fire. 23Therefore if you bring your gift to the altar, and there remember
that your brother has something against you, 24leave your gift there before
the altar, and go your way. First be reconciled to your brother, and then
come and offer your gift. 25Agree with your adversary quickly, while you
are on the way with him, lest your adversary deliver you to the judge, the
judge hand you over to the officer, and you be thrown into prison. 26As-
suredly, I say to you, you will by no means get out of there till you have
paid the last penny.

Adultery in the Heart

27"You have heard that it was said to those of old,[t] '*You shall not commit
adultery.*'[u] 28But I say to you that whoever looks at a woman to lust for her
has already committed adultery with her in his heart. 29If your right eye
causes you to sin, pluck it out and cast *it* from you; for it is more profitable
for you that one of your members perish, than for your whole body to be
cast into hell. 30And if your right hand causes you to sin, cut it off and cast
it from you; for it is more profitable for you that one of your members perish, than for your whole body to be cast into hell.

Marriage Is Sacred and Binding

31"Furthermore it has been said, 'Whoever divorces his wife, let him
give her a certificate of divorce.' 32But I say to you that whoever divorces his
wife for any reason except sexual immorality[v] causes her to commit adultery; and whoever marries a woman who is divorced commits adultery.

Jesus Forbids Oaths

33"Again you have heard that it was said to those of old, 'You shall not
swear falsely, but shall perform your oaths to the Lord.' 34But I say to you,
do not swear at all: neither by heaven, for it is God's throne; 35nor by the
earth, for it is His footstool; nor by Jerusalem, for it is the city of the great
King. 36Nor shall you swear by your head, because you cannot make one
hair white or black. 37But let your 'Yes' be 'Yes,' and your 'No,' 'No.' For
whatever is more than these is from the evil one.

5:21 [r] Exodus 20:13; Deuteronomy 5:17
5:22 [s] NU-Text omits *without a cause.*
5:27 [t] NU-Text and M-Text omit *to those of old.* [u] Exodus 20:14; Deuteronomy 5:18
5:32 [v] Or *fornication*

LIFE LESSON

Matthew 5:1-48

SITUATION Jesus gave this sermon (chapters 5–7) on a hillside near the town of Capernaum. Matthew presented four other great discourses of Jesus (Matthew 10; 13; 18; 24–25).

OBSERVATION Jesus did not come to destroy the law of Moses or the teaching of the prophets, but to fulfill what they said. Jesus told us to be perfect, just as our Father in heaven is perfect.

INSPIRATION Sacred delight is good news coming through the back door of your heart. It's what you'd always dreamed but never expected. It's the too-good-to-be-true coming true. It's having God as your pinch-hitter, your lawyer, your dad, your biggest fan, and your best friend. God on your side, in your heart, out in front, and protecting your back. It's hope where you least expected it: a flower in life's sidewalk.

It is *sacred* because only God can grant it. It is a *delight* because it thrills. Since it is sacred, it can't be stolen. And since it is delightful, it can't be predicted.

It was this gladness that danced through the Red Sea. It was this joy that blew the trumpet at Jericho. It was this secret that made Mary sing. It was this surprise that put the spring-time into Easter morning. . . .

It is this sacred delight that Jesus promises in the Sermon on the Mount. Nine times he promises it. And he promises it to an unlikely crowd:

"The poor in spirit . . . Those who mourn . . . The meek . . . Those who hunger and thirst . . . The merciful . . . The pure in heart . . . The peacemak-ers . . . The persecuted . . . "

It is to this band of pilgrims that God promises a special blessing. A heav-enly joy. A sacred delight.

(From *The Applause of Heaven* by Max Lucado)

Continued

APPLICATION How are you fulfilling Jesus' command to be perfect before God? Do you fall short by lying, lusting, cheating, coveting, or gossiping? When you battle one of these temptations, instead of giving in, pray, sing a worshipful song, or think of a memorized verse. Praise God instead of giving in.

EXPLORATION Happiness—Luke 6:17-49. The Law—Exodus 19–24.

Go the Second Mile

38"You have heard that it was said, '*An eye for an eye and a tooth for a*
tooth.'[w] 39But I tell you not to resist an evil person. But whoever slaps you
on your right cheek, turn the other to him also. 40If anyone wants to sue
you and take away your tunic, let him have your cloak also. 41And whoever
compels you to go one mile, go with him two. 42Give to him who asks you,
and from him who wants to borrow from you do not turn away.

Love Your Enemies

43"You have heard that it was said, '*You shall love your neighbor*[x] and
hate your enemy.' 44But I say to you, love your enemies, bless those who
curse you, do good to those who hate you, and pray for those who spitefully use you and persecute you,[y] 45that you may be sons of your Father in
heaven; for He makes His sun rise on the evil and on the good, and sends
rain on the just and on the unjust. 46For if you love those who love you,
what reward have you? Do not even the tax collectors do the same? 47And if
you greet your brethren[z] only, what do you do more *than others?* Do not
even the tax collectors[a] do so? 48Therefore you shall be perfect, just as your
Father in heaven is perfect.

Do Good to Please God

6 "Take heed that you do not do your charitable deeds before men, to be
seen by them. Otherwise you have no reward from your Father in
heaven. 2Therefore, when you do a charitable deed, do not sound a trumpet before you as the hypocrites do in the synagogues and in the streets,
that they may have glory from men. Assuredly, I say to you, they have their
reward. 3But when you do a charitable deed, do not let your left hand know
what your right hand is doing, 4that your charitable deed may be in secret;
and your Father who sees in secret will Himself reward you openly.[b]

The Model Prayer

5"And when you pray, you shall not be like the hypocrites. For they love to
pray standing in the synagogues and on the corners of the streets, that they
may be seen by men. Assuredly, I say to you, they have their reward. 6But you,
when you pray, go into your room, and when you have shut your door, pray
to your Father who *is* in the secret *place;* and your Father who sees in secret
will reward you openly.[c] 7And when you pray, do not use vain repetitions as
the heathen *do*. For they think that they will be heard for their many words.
8"Therefore do not be like them. For your Father knows the things you
have need of before you ask Him. 9In this manner, therefore, pray:

Our Father in heaven,
Hallowed be Your name.
10 Your kingdom come.
Your will be done
On earth as *it is* in heaven.

5:38 [w] Exodus 21:24; Leviticus 24:20; Deuteronomy 19:21
5:43 [x] Compare Leviticus 19:18
5:44 [y] NU-Text omits three clauses from this verse, leaving, *"But I say to you, love your enemies and pray for those who persecute you."*
5:47 [z] M-Text reads *friends.* [a] NU-Text reads *Gentiles.*
6:4 [b] NU-Text omits *openly.*
6:6 [c] NU-Text omits *openly.*

11 Give us this day our daily bread.
12 And forgive us our debts,
As we forgive our debtors.
13 And do not lead us into temptation,
But deliver us from the evil one.
For Yours is the kingdom and the power and the glory forever. Amen.[d]

14“For if you forgive men their trespasses, your heavenly Father will also
forgive you. 15But if you do not forgive men their trespasses, neither will
your Father forgive your trespasses.

Fasting to Be Seen Only by God

16“Moreover, when you fast, do not be like the hypocrites, with a sad
countenance. For they disfigure their faces that they may appear to men to
be fasting. Assuredly, I say to you, they have their reward. 17But you, when
you fast, anoint your head and wash your face, 18so that you do not appear
to men to be fasting, but to your Father who *is* in the secret *place;* and your
Father who sees in secret will reward you openly.[e]

Lay Up Treasures in Heaven

19“Do not lay up for yourselves treasures on earth, where moth and rust
destroy and where thieves break in and steal; 20but lay up for yourselves
treasures in heaven, where neither moth nor rust destroys and where
thieves do not break in and steal. 21For where your treasure is, there your
heart will be also.

The Lamp of the Body

22“The lamp of the body is the eye. If therefore your eye is good, your
whole body will be full of light. 23But if your eye is bad, your whole body
will be full of darkness. If therefore the light that is in you is darkness, how
great *is* that darkness!

You Cannot Serve God and Riches

24“No one can serve two masters; for either he will hate the one and love
the other, or else he will be loyal to the one and despise the other. You cannot serve God and mammon.

Do Not Worry

25“Therefore I say to you, do not worry about your life, what you will eat
or what you will drink; nor about your body, what you will put on. Is not
life more than food and the body more than clothing? 26Look at the birds
of the air, for they neither sow nor reap nor gather into barns; yet your
heavenly Father feeds them. Are you not of more value than they? 27Which
of you by worrying can add one cubit to his stature?
28“So why do you worry about clothing? Consider the lilies of the field,
how they grow: they neither toil nor spin; 29and yet I say to you that even
Solomon in all his glory was not arrayed like one of these. 30Now if God so
clothes the grass of the field, which today is, and tomorrow is thrown into
the oven, *will He* not much more *clothe* you, O you of little faith?

6:13 *d* NU-Text omits *For Yours* through *Amen.*
6:18 *e* NU-Text and M-Text omit *openly.*

LIFE LESSON

Matthew 6:1-34

SITUATION After teaching about happiness and honoring the Law, Jesus taught about giving, praying, and worshiping.

OBSERVATION God sees everything we do, and he will reward us even for the good works we do that no one else notices.

INSPIRATION Various incentives are held out by Jesus as he recommends the way of the kingdom of God as the path to be followed. They include the prospect of reward or retribution at the last judgment or in the course of history. Any courting of human applause is discouraged: actions which are in themselves good are deprived of any virtue if they are done “before men in order to be seen by them” (Matthew 6:1). But the highest of all incentives is the example of God himself: his children should reflect their Father’s character. This incentive is clearly set forth in the Old Testament: one section of the book of Leviticus is commonly called “the law of holiness” because of its recurring refrain: “I am the Lord your God . . . you shall therefore be holy, for I am holy” (Leviticus 11:44, 45). “You, therefore, must be perfect,” says Jesus in the sermon on the mount, “as your heavenly Father is perfect” (Matthew 5:48). In this context “perfect” means something like “all-embracing in your love.” . . . There was nothing, then, in this part of the sermon which Jesus’ Jewish hearers would find unfamiliar. They would readily appreciate his argument that, if God does not discriminate between the good and the bad in sending his gifts of sunshine and rain, his children should equally show kindness to all. It is, of course, one thing to appreciate the argument; it is another thing, whether for Jews or for Christians, to act accordingly.

The Gospels bear witness to the fact that Jesus’ own life was the practical manifestation of his teaching. This testimony is specially explicit with regard to service and sacrifice. Repeatedly he insisted that the highest honour lies in humble service—not as a reward for it, but in the service itself. In the kingdoms of the

Continued

31“Therefore do not worry, saying, ‘What shall we eat?’ or ‘What shall we
drink?’ or ‘What shall we wear?’ 32For after all these things the Gentiles
seek. For your heavenly Father knows that you need all these things. 33But
seek first the kingdom of God and His righteousness, and all these things
shall be added to you. 34Therefore do not worry about tomorrow, for tomorrow will worry about its own things. Sufficient for the day *is* its own trouble.

Do Not Judge

7 “Judge not, that you be not judged. 2For with what judgment you
judge, you will be judged; and with the measure you use, it will be measured back to you. 3And why do you look at the speck in your brother’s eye,
but do not consider the plank in your own eye? 4Or how can you say to
your brother, ‘Let me remove the speck from your eye’; and look, a plank *is*
in your own eye? 5Hypocrite! First remove the plank from your own eye,
and then you will see clearly to remove the speck from your brother’s eye.
6“Do not give what is holy to the dogs; nor cast your pearls before swine,
lest they trample them under their feet, and turn and tear you in pieces.

Keep Asking, Seeking, Knocking

7“Ask, and it will be given to you; seek, and you will find; knock, and it
will be opened to you. 8For everyone who asks receives, and he who seeks
finds, and to him who knocks it will be opened. 9Or what man is there
among you who, if his son asks for bread, will give him a stone? 10Or if he
asks for a fish, will he give him a serpent? 11If you then, being evil, know how
to give good gifts to your children, how much more will your Father who is
in heaven give good things to those who ask Him! 12Therefore, whatever you
want men to do to you, do also to them, for this is the Law and the Prophets.

The Narrow Way

13“Enter by the narrow gate; for wide *is* the gate and broad *is* the way that
leads to destruction, and there are many who go in by it. 14Because[f] narrow *is*
the gate and difficult *is* the way which leads to life, and there are few who find it.

You Will Know Them by Their Fruits

15“Beware of false prophets, who come to you in sheep’s clothing, but
inwardly they are ravenous wolves. 16You will know them by their fruits.
Do men gather grapes from thornbushes or figs from thistles? 17Even so,
every good tree bears good fruit, but a bad tree bears bad fruit. 18A good
tree cannot bear bad fruit, nor *can* a bad tree bear good fruit. 19Every tree
that does not bear good fruit is cut down and thrown into the fire. 20There-
fore by their fruits you will know them.

I Never Knew You

21“Not everyone who says to Me, ‘Lord, Lord,’ shall enter the kingdom of
heaven, but he who does the will of My Father in heaven. 22Many will say to
Me in that day, ‘Lord, Lord, have we not prophesied in Your name, cast out
demons in Your name, and done many wonders in Your name?’ 23And
then I will declare to them, ‘I never knew you; depart from Me, you who
practice lawlessness!’

7:14 *f* NU-Text and M-Text read *How . . . !*

world the high and mighty received service; this was a sign of the honour in which they were held. Jesus’ disciples found it difficult to grasp the thought that it is quite otherwise in the kingdom of God. “It shall not be so among you,” he said to them, “but whoever would be great among you must be your servant, and whoever would be first among you must be slave of all. For the Son of Man also came not to be served but to serve, and to give his life as a ransom for many” (Mark 10:43-45).

(From *Jesus: Lord and Savior* by F. F. Bruce)

APPLICATION How can you anonymously give to someone in need today? What changes need to be made in your prayer life? How can you make worship a higher priority? Identify the needed changes and make them.

EXPLORATION Prayer—Luke 11:2-4. Money—Luke 11:34-36. Worry—Luke 12:22-31.

Build on the Rock

24“Therefore whoever hears these sayings of Mine, and does them, I will
liken him to a wise man who built his house on the rock: 25and the rain descended, the floods came, and the winds blew and beat on that house; and
it did not fall, for it was founded on the rock.
26“But everyone who hears these sayings of Mine, and does not do
them, will be like a foolish man who built his house on the sand: 27and the
rain descended, the floods came, and the winds blew and beat on that
house; and it fell. And great was its fall.”
28And so it was, when Jesus had ended these sayings, that the people
were astonished at His teaching, 29for He taught them as one having authority, and not as the scribes.

Jesus Cleanses a Leper

8 When He had come down from the mountain, great multitudes followed Him. 2And behold, a leper came and worshiped Him, saying,
“Lord, if You are willing, You can make me clean.”
3Then Jesus put out *His* hand and touched him, saying, “I am willing; be
cleansed.” Immediately his leprosy was cleansed.
4And Jesus said to him, “See that you tell no one; but go your way, show
yourself to the priest, and offer the gift that Moses commanded, as a testimony to them.”

Jesus Heals a Centurion’s Servant

5Now when Jesus had entered Capernaum, a centurion came to Him,
pleading with Him, 6saying, “Lord, my servant is lying at home paralyzed,
dreadfully tormented.”
7And Jesus said to him, “I will come and heal him.”
8The centurion answered and said, “Lord, I am not worthy that You
should come under my roof. But only speak a word, and my servant will
be healed. 9For I also am a man under authority, having soldiers under
me. And I say to this *one,* ‘Go,’ and he goes; and to another, ‘Come,’ and he
comes; and to my servant, ‘Do this,’ and he does *it.*”
10When Jesus heard *it,* He marveled, and said to those who followed,
“Assuredly, I say to you, I have not found such great faith, not even in Israel! 11And I say to you that many will come from east and west, and sit
down with Abraham, Isaac, and Jacob in the kingdom of heaven. 12But the
sons of the kingdom will be cast out into outer darkness. There will be
weeping and gnashing of teeth.” 13Then Jesus said to the centurion, “Go
your way; and as you have believed, *so* let it be done for you.” And his servant was healed that same hour.

Peter’s Mother-in-Law Healed

14Now when Jesus had come into Peter’s house, He saw his wife’s
mother lying sick with a fever. 15So He touched her hand, and the fever left
her. And she arose and served them.[g]

Many Healed After Sabbath Sunset

16When evening had come, they brought to Him many who were

8:15 *g* NU-Text and M-Text read *Him.*

LIFE LESSON

Matthew 7:1-29

SITUATION Matthew recorded the ending of Jesus’ sermon. Jesus called his hearers to put his teaching into practice.

OBSERVATION Jesus advised: do to others what you want them to do to you. If you hear and obey Jesus’ words, you are like a wise man who builds his house on a rock.

INSPIRATION God saves men by His sovereign grace through the Atonement of Jesus; He works in us to will and to do of His good pleasure; but we have to work out that salvation in practical living. If once we start on the basis of His Redemption to do what He commands, we find that we can do it. If we fail, it is because we have not practised. The crisis will reveal whether we have been practising or not. If we obey the Spirit of God and practise in our physical life what God has put in us by His Spirit, then when the crisis comes, we shall find that our own nature as well as the grace of God will stand by us.

Thank God He does give us difficult things to do! His salvation is a glad thing, but it is also a heroic, holy thing. It tests us for all we are worth. Jesus is bringing many “sons” unto glory, and God will not shield us from the requirements of a son. God’s grace turns out men and women with a strong family likeness to Jesus Christ, not milksops. It takes a tremendous amount of discipline to live the noble life of a disciple of Jesus in actual things. It is always necessary to make an effort to be noble.

(From *My Utmost for His Highest* by Oswald Chambers)

APPLICATION Are you a champion of the Golden Rule, or are you a rookie? Try to apply the rule while on the phone with a client, after work with friends, at the Little-League baseball game, or wherever else you encounter people today. Try to enrich each relationship with it.

EXPLORATION Judging—Luke 6:37-42. Fruit of Our Lives—Luke 6:43-45. Obeying Jesus—Luke 6:46-49.

demon-possessed. And He cast out the spirits with a word, and healed all who were sick, [17]that it might be fulfilled which was spoken by Isaiah the prophet, saying:

> *"He Himself took our infirmities*
> *And bore our sicknesses."*[h]

The Cost of Discipleship

[18]And when Jesus saw great multitudes about Him, He gave a command to depart to the other side. [19]Then a certain scribe came and said to Him, "Teacher, I will follow You wherever You go."

[20]And Jesus said to him, "Foxes have holes and birds of the air *have* nests, but the Son of Man has nowhere to lay *His* head."

[21]Then another of His disciples said to Him, "Lord, let me first go and bury my father."

[22]But Jesus said to him, "Follow Me, and let the dead bury their own dead."

Wind and Wave Obey Jesus

[23]Now when He got into a boat, His disciples followed Him. [24]And suddenly a great tempest arose on the sea, so that the boat was covered with the waves. But He was asleep. [25]Then His disciples came to *Him* and awoke Him, saying, "Lord, save us! We are perishing!"

[26]But He said to them, "Why are you fearful, O you of little faith?" Then He arose and rebuked the winds and the sea, and there was a great calm. [27]So the men marveled, saying, "Who can this be, that even the winds and the sea obey Him?"

Two Demon-Possessed Men Healed

[28]When He had come to the other side, to the country of the Gergesenes,[i] there met Him two demon-possessed *men,* coming out of the tombs, exceedingly fierce, so that no one could pass that way. [29]And suddenly they cried out, saying, "What have we to do with You, Jesus, You Son of God? Have You come here to torment us before the time?"

[30]Now a good way off from them there was a herd of many swine feeding. [31]So the demons begged Him, saying, "If You cast us out, permit us to go away[j] into the herd of swine."

[32]And He said to them, "Go." So when they had come out, they went into the herd of swine. And suddenly the whole herd of swine ran violently down the steep place into the sea, and perished in the water.

[33]Then those who kept *them* fled; and they went away into the city and told everything, including what *had happened* to the demon-possessed *men.* [34]And behold, the whole city came out to meet Jesus. And when they saw Him, they begged *Him* to depart from their region.

Jesus Forgives and Heals a Paralytic

9 So He got into a boat, crossed over, and came to His own city. [2]Then behold, they brought to Him a paralytic lying on a bed. When Jesus saw their faith, He said to the paralytic, "Son, be of good cheer; your sins are forgiven you."

8:17 *h* Isaiah 53:4
8:28 *i* NU-Text reads *Gadarenes.*
8:31 *j* NU-Text reads *send us.*

Life Lesson

Matthew 8:1-34

SITUATION Matthew recorded Jesus' miracles involving people who were sick and diseased.

OBSERVATION Jesus takes our suffering on himself and carries our diseases. But it takes faith to see that Jesus can help us.

INSPIRATION I heard about a man some years ago who was rolling a wheelbarrow back and forth across Niagara River on a tightrope. Thousands of people were shouting him on. He put a two-hundred pound sack of dirt in the wheelbarrow and rolled it over, and then he rolled it back. Then he turned to the crowd and said, "How many of you believe I can roll a man across?"

Everybody shouted! One man in the front was very excited about his professed belief. The man pointed to this excited professor and said, "You're next!"

You couldn't see the man for dust! . . . He said he believed it, he thought he believed it—but he was not willing to get in the wheelbarrow.

Just so with Christ. There are many people who say they believe on Him, who say they will follow Him. But they never have gotten into the wheelbarrow. . . .

There are many people who ask, "Well, how much faith does it take?" Jesus said only the faith as a of "a grain of mustard seed."

Others ask, "What kind of faith?" . . . There is only one kind, really. It is the object of the faith that counts. What is the object of your faith? The object of your faith must be Christ. Not faith in ritual, not faith in sacrifices, not faith in morals, not faith in yourself—not faith in anything but Christ!

(From *Peace with God* by Billy Graham)

APPLICATION The centurion placed himself under Jesus' authority. As you come to Jesus now, do you believe he can and will change your life? Ask, believe, and obey him. Be confident in Jesus' authority, even in the details of your day.

EXPLORATION Skin Diseases—Leviticus 14. Suffering Servant—Isaiah 52:13–53:12.

3And at once some of the scribes said within themselves, "This Man
blasphemes!"
4But Jesus, knowing their thoughts, said, "Why do you think evil in
your hearts? 5For which is easier, to say, '*Your* sins are forgiven you,' or to
say, 'Arise and walk'? 6But that you may know that the Son of Man has
power on earth to forgive sins"—then He said to the paralytic, "Arise,
take up your bed, and go to your house." 7And he arose and departed to
his house.
8Now when the multitudes saw *it,* they marveled[k] and glorified God,
who had given such power to men.

Matthew the Tax Collector

9As Jesus passed on from there, He saw a man named Matthew sitting at the
tax office. And He said to him, "Follow Me." So he arose and followed Him.
10Now it happened, as Jesus sat at the table in the house, *that* behold,
many tax collectors and sinners came and sat down with Him and His disciples. 11And when the Pharisees saw *it,* they said to His disciples, "Why
does your Teacher eat with tax collectors and sinners?"
12When Jesus heard *that,* He said to them, "Those who are well have no
need of a physician, but those who are sick. 13But go and learn what *this*
means: '*I desire mercy and not sacrifice.*'[l] For I did not come to call the
righteous, but sinners, to repentance."[m]

Jesus Is Questioned About Fasting

14Then the disciples of John came to Him, saying, "Why do we and the
Pharisees fast often,[n] but Your disciples do not fast?"
15And Jesus said to them, "Can the friends of the bridegroom mourn as
long as the bridegroom is with them? But the days will come when the
bridegroom will be taken away from them, and then they will fast. 16No
one puts a piece of unshrunk cloth on an old garment; for the patch pulls
away from the garment, and the tear is made worse. 17Nor do they put new
wine into old wineskins, or else the wineskins break, the wine is spilled,
and the wineskins are ruined. But they put new wine into new wineskins,
and both are preserved."

A Girl Restored to Life and a Woman Healed

18While He spoke these things to them, behold, a ruler came and worshiped Him, saying, "My daughter has just died, but come and lay Your
hand on her and she will live." 19So Jesus arose and followed him, and so
did His disciples.
20And suddenly, a woman who had a flow of blood for twelve years
came from behind and touched the hem of His garment. 21For she said to
herself, "If only I may touch His garment, I shall be made well." 22But Jesus turned around, and when He saw her He said, "Be of good cheer,
daughter; your faith has made you well." And the woman was made well
from that hour.
23When Jesus came into the ruler's house, and saw the flute players and
the noisy crowd wailing, 24He said to them, "Make room, for the girl is not

9:8 [k] NU-Text reads *were afraid.*
9:13 [l] Hosea 6:6 [m] NU-Text omits *to repentance.*
9:14 [n] NU-Text brackets *often* as disputed.

Life Lesson

Matthew 9:1-38

SITUATION Although he was neither rude nor arrogant, Jesus aggravated the teachers of the Law when he exercised his privileges as Son of God. When he forgave sins, mingled with sinners, raised the dead, and healed the sick, the teachers thought his actions were either inappropriate or unexplainable.

OBSERVATION The Kingdom of God had come. Jesus used his power over sickness and death to show his compassion for needy humanity. As a true friend, he meets the needs we bring him. He asks us to join his mission and reach out to those around us.

INSPIRATION Tell me, why are these stories in the Bible? Why are the Gospels full of such people? Such hopeless people? Though their situations vary, their conditions don't. They are trapped. Estranged. Rejected. They have nowhere to turn. On their lips, a desperate prayer. In their hearts, desolate dreams. And in their hands, a broken rope. But before their eyes a never-say-die Galilean who majors in stepping in when everyone else steps out.

Surprisingly simple, the actions of this man. Just words of mercy or touches of kindness. Fingers on sightless eyes. A hand on a weary shoulder. Words for sad hearts . . . all fulfilling the prophecy: "A bruised reed he will not break, and a smoldering wick he will not snuff out."

Again I ask. Why are these portraits in the Bible? . . . Why did God leave us one tale after another of wounded lives being restored? So we could be grateful for the past? So we could look back with amazement at what Jesus did?

No. No. No. A thousand times no. The purpose of these stories is not to tell us what Jesus *did.* Their purpose is to tell us what Jesus *does.*

"Everything that was written in the past was written to teach us," Paul penned. "The Scriptures give us patience and encouragement so that we can have hope" (Rom. 15:4).

These are not just Sunday school stories. Not romantic fables. Not somewhere-over-the-rainbow illusions.

Continued

They are historic moments in which a real God met real pain so we could answer the question, "Where is God when I hurt?"

How does God react to dashed hopes? Read the story of Jairus. How does the Father feel about those who are ill? Stand with him at the pool of Bethesda. Do you long for God to speak to your lonely heart? Then listen as he speaks to the Emmaus-bound disciples. What is God's word for the shameful? Watch as his finger draws in the dirt of the Jerusalem courtyard.

He's not doing it just for them. He's doing it for me. He's doing it for you. . . . I know there used to be a stone in front of a tomb. And I do know it was moved. And I also know that there are stones in your path. Stones that trip and stones that trap. Stones too big for you.

Please remember, the goal of these stories is not to help us look back with amazement, but forward with faith. The God who spoke still speaks. The God who forgave still forgives. The God who came still comes. He comes into our world. He comes into your world. He comes to do what you can't. He comes to move the stones you can't budge.

Stones are no match for God. Not then and not now. He still moves stones. (From *He Still Moves Stones* by Max Lucado)

APPLICATION Do you see Jesus as a close friend or far away? Jesus desires to relate to us as a friend. Talk with him. Tell him all of your needs.

EXPLORATION God Cares—Deuteronomy 7:9; Nehemiah 1:5; 1 Chronicles 16:31; Psalm 9:2; 67:4; Habakkuk 3:17-19.

dead, but sleeping." And they ridiculed Him. 25But when the crowd was put outside, He went in and took her by the hand, and the girl arose. 26And the report of this went out into all that land.

Two Blind Men Healed

27When Jesus departed from there, two blind men followed Him, crying out and saying, "Son of David, have mercy on us!"

28And when He had come into the house, the blind men came to Him. And Jesus said to them, "Do you believe that I am able to do this?"

They said to Him, "Yes, Lord."

29Then He touched their eyes, saying, "According to your faith let it be to you." 30And their eyes were opened. And Jesus sternly warned them, saying, "See *that* no one knows *it.*" 31But when they had departed, they spread the news about Him in all that country.

A Mute Man Speaks

32As they went out, behold, they brought to Him a man, mute and demon-possessed. 33And when the demon was cast out, the mute spoke. And the multitudes marveled, saying, "It was never seen like this in Israel!"

34But the Pharisees said, "He casts out demons by the ruler of the demons."

The Compassion of Jesus

35Then Jesus went about all the cities and villages, teaching in their synagogues, preaching the gospel of the kingdom, and healing every sickness and every disease among the people.[o] 36But when He saw the multitudes, He was moved with compassion for them, because they were weary[p] and scattered, like sheep having no shepherd. 37Then He said to His disciples, "The harvest truly *is* plentiful, but the laborers *are* few. 38Therefore pray the Lord of the harvest to send out laborers into His harvest."

The Twelve Apostles

10 And when He had called His twelve disciples to *Him,* He gave them power *over* unclean spirits, to cast them out, and to heal all kinds of sickness and all kinds of disease. 2Now the names of the twelve apostles are these: first, Simon, who is called Peter, and Andrew his brother; James the *son* of Zebedee, and John his brother; 3Philip and Bartholomew; Thomas and Matthew the tax collector; James the *son* of Alphaeus, and Lebbaeus, whose surname was[q] Thaddaeus; 4Simon the Cananite,[r] and Judas Iscariot, who also betrayed Him.

Sending Out the Twelve

5These twelve Jesus sent out and commanded them, saying: "Do not go into the way of the Gentiles, and do not enter a city of the Samaritans. 6But go rather to the lost sheep of the house of Israel. 7And as you go, preach, saying, 'The kingdom of heaven is at hand.' 8Heal the sick, cleanse the lepers, raise the dead,[s] cast out demons. Freely you have received, freely give. 9Provide neither gold nor silver nor copper in your money belts, 10nor bag

9:35 [o] NU-Text omits *among the people.*
9:36 [p] NU-Text and M-Text read *harassed.*
10:3 [q] NU-Text omits *Lebbaeus, whose surname was.*
10:4 [r] NU-Text reads *Cananaean.*
10:8 [s] NU-Text reads *raise the dead, cleanse the lepers;* M-Text omits *raise the dead.*

for *your* journey, nor two tunics, nor sandals, nor staffs; for a worker is
worthy of his food.
[11]"Now whatever city or town you enter, inquire who in it is worthy, and
stay there till you go out. [12]And when you go into a household, greet it. [13]If
the household is worthy, let your peace come upon it. But if it is not worthy, let your peace return to you. [14]And whoever will not receive you nor
hear your words, when you depart from that house or city, shake off the
dust from your feet. [15]Assuredly, I say to you, it will be more tolerable for
the land of Sodom and Gomorrah in the day of judgment than for that city!

Persecutions Are Coming

[16]"Behold, I send you out as sheep in the midst of wolves. Therefore be
wise as serpents and harmless as doves. [17]But beware of men, for they will
deliver you up to councils and scourge you in their synagogues. [18]You will
be brought before governors and kings for My sake, as a testimony to
them and to the Gentiles. [19]But when they deliver you up, do not worry
about how or what you should speak. For it will be given to you in that
hour what you should speak; [20]for it is not you who speak, but the Spirit of
your Father who speaks in you.
[21]"Now brother will deliver up brother to death, and a father *his* child;
and children will rise up against parents and cause them to be put to
death. [22]And you will be hated by all for My name's sake. But he who endures to the end will be saved. [23]When they persecute you in this city, flee
to another. For assuredly, I say to you, you will not have gone through the
cities of Israel before the Son of Man comes.
[24]"A disciple is not above *his* teacher, nor a servant above his master. [25]It
is enough for a disciple that he be like his teacher, and a servant like his
master. If they have called the master of the house Beelzebub,[t] how much
more *will they call* those of his household! [26]Therefore do not fear them.
For there is nothing covered that will not be revealed, and hidden that will
not be known.

Jesus Teaches the Fear of God

[27]"Whatever I tell you in the dark, speak in the light; and what you hear
in the ear, preach on the housetops. [28]And do not fear those who kill the
body but cannot kill the soul. But rather fear Him who is able to destroy
both soul and body in hell. [29]Are not two sparrows sold for a copper coin?
And not one of them falls to the ground apart from your Father's will. [30]But
the very hairs of your head are all numbered. [31]Do not fear therefore; you
are of more value than many sparrows.

Confess Christ Before Men

[32]"Therefore whoever confesses Me before men, him I will also confess
before My Father who is in heaven. [33]But whoever denies Me before men,
him I will also deny before My Father who is in heaven.

Christ Brings Division

[34]"Do not think that I came to bring peace on earth. I did not come to
bring peace but a sword. [35]For I have come to '*set a man against his father,*
a daughter against her mother, and a daughter-in-law against her

10:25 [t] NU-Text and M-Text read *Beelzebul.*

Life Lesson

Matthew 10:1-42

SITUATION The Jews viewed suffering as God's punishment. The disciples could not understand Jesus' message that they would suffer for being obedient.

OBSERVATION Although believers will be persecuted, they can trust that God has a plan for all difficult circumstances.

INSPIRATION Could you use some courage? Are you backing down more than you are standing up? If so, let the Master lead you up the mountain again. Let him remind you why you should "fear not." Listen to the time Jesus scattered the butterflies out of the stomachs of his nervous disciples and see if his words help you.

We need to remember that the disciples were common men given a compelling task. Before they were the stained-glassed saints in the windows of cathedrals, they were somebody's next-door-neighbors trying to make a living and raise a family. They weren't cut from theological cloth or raised on supernatural milk. But they were an ounce more devoted than they were afraid and, as a result, did some extraordinary things. . . .

Earthly fears are no fears at all. All the mystery is revealed. The final destination is guaranteed. Answer the big question of eternity, and the little questions of life fall into perspective. (From *The Applause of Heaven* by Max Lucado)

APPLICATION Jesus promised hard times, but he also promised comfort. Are you experiencing opposition for being a Christian but neglecting to accept his comfort? Look forward to the day when you will no longer be persecuted but will be rewarded for persevering. Let the reality of that reward encourage you.

EXPLORATION Do Not Be Afraid—Joshua 1:9; 2 Kings 6:15-17; Psalm 37:7, 13, 28; Isaiah 41:10; 43:1-2; Luke 12:32; Hebrews 13:6; 1 Peter 5:7.

LIFE LESSON

Matthew 11:1-30

SITUATION Very few people recognized or accepted John as the forerunner to the Messiah, but Jesus confirmed what his listeners eagerly waited to hear—that the Messiah's time had come.

OBSERVATION John the Baptist fulfilled Malachi's prophecy that someone would come in the spirit of the prophet Elijah. This prophet would prepare hearts to accept the Messiah. Many people, however, got sidetracked by John's behavior and the uniqueness of his ministry rather than focusing on his message.

INSPIRATION Could someone build a temple and forget why? Could someone construct a palace, yet forget the king? Could someone sculpt a tribute and forget the hero?

You answer those questions. Answer them in a church. The next time you enter an assembly of worship, position yourself where you can see the people. Then decide.

You can tell the ones who remember the slain one. They're wide-eyed and expectant. They're children watching the unwrapping of a gift. They're servants standing still as a king passes. You don't doze in the presence of royalty. And you don't yawn while receiving a gift, especially when the giver is the king himself!

You can also tell the ones who see only the temple. Their eyes wander. Their feet shuffle. Their hands doodle, and their mouths open—not to sing, but to yawn. For no matter how hard they try to stay amazed, their eyes start to glaze over. All temples, even the Taj Mahal, lose their luster after a while.

mother-in-law'; 36and *'a man's enemies will be those of his own house-*
hold.'[u] 37He who loves father or mother more than Me is not worthy of Me.
And he who loves son or daughter more than Me is not worthy of Me. 38And
he who does not take his cross and follow after Me is not worthy of Me. 39He
who finds his life will lose it, and he who loses his life for My sake will find it.

A Cup of Cold Water

40"He who receives you receives Me, and he who receives Me receives
Him who sent Me. 41He who receives a prophet in the name of a prophet
shall receive a prophet's reward. And he who receives a righteous man in
the name of a righteous man shall receive a righteous man's reward. 42And
whoever gives one of these little ones only a cup of cold *water* in the name
of a disciple, assuredly, I say to you, he shall by no means lose his reward."

John the Baptist Sends Messengers to Jesus

11 Now it came to pass, when Jesus finished commanding His twelve disciples, that He departed from there to teach and to preach in their cities.
2And when John had heard in prison about the works of Christ, he sent
two of[v] his disciples 3and said to Him, "Are You the Coming One, or do we
look for another?"

4Jesus answered and said to them, "Go and tell John the things which
you hear and see: 5*The* blind see and *the* lame walk; *the* lepers are cleansed
and *the* deaf hear; *the* dead are raised up and *the* poor have the gospel
preached to them. 6And blessed is he who is not offended because of Me."

7As they departed, Jesus began to say to the multitudes concerning
John: "What did you go out into the wilderness to see? A reed shaken by
the wind? 8But what did you go out to see? A man clothed in soft garments?
Indeed, those who wear soft *clothing* are in kings' houses. 9But what did
you go out to see? A prophet? Yes, I say to you, and more than a prophet.
10For this is *he* of whom it is written:

> *'Behold, I send My messenger before Your face,*
> *Who will prepare Your way before You.'*[w]

11"Assuredly, I say to you, among those born of women there has not
risen one greater than John the Baptist; but he who is least in the kingdom of
heaven is greater than he. 12And from the days of John the Baptist until now
the kingdom of heaven suffers violence, and the violent take it by force. 13For
all the prophets and the law prophesied until John. 14And if you are willing to
receive *it*, he is Elijah who is to come. 15He who has ears to hear, let him hear!

16"But to what shall I liken this generation? It is like children sitting in
the marketplaces and calling to their companions, 17and saying:

> 'We played the flute for you,
> And you did not dance;
> We mourned to you,
> And you did not lament.'

18For John came neither eating nor drinking, and they say, 'He has a
demon.' 19The Son of Man came eating and drinking, and they say, 'Look,

10:36 [u] Micah 7:6
11:2 [v] NU-Text reads *by* for *two of*.
11:10 [w] Malachi 3:1

a glutton and a winebibber, a friend of tax collectors and sinners!' But wisdom is justified by her children."[x]

Woe to the Impenitent Cities

20Then He began to rebuke the cities in which most of His mighty works
had been done, because they did not repent: 21"Woe to you, Chorazin! Woe
to you, Bethsaida! For if the mighty works which were done in you had
been done in Tyre and Sidon, they would have repented long ago in sackcloth and ashes. 22But I say to you, it will be more tolerable for Tyre and
Sidon in the day of judgment than for you. 23And you, Capernaum, who
are exalted to heaven, will be[y] brought down to Hades; for if the mighty
works which were done in you had been done in Sodom, it would have remained until this day. 24But I say to you that it shall be more tolerable for
the land of Sodom in the day of judgment than for you."

Jesus Gives True Rest

25At that time Jesus answered and said, "I thank You, Father, Lord of
heaven and earth, that You have hidden these things from *the* wise and
prudent and have revealed them to babes. 26Even so, Father, for so it
seemed good in Your sight. 27All things have been delivered to Me by My
Father, and no one knows the Son except the Father. Nor does anyone
know the Father except the Son, and *the one* to whom the Son wills to reveal *Him.* 28Come to Me, all *you* who labor and are heavy laden, and I will
give you rest. 29Take My yoke upon you and learn from Me, for I am gentle
and lowly in heart, and you will find rest for your souls. 30For My yoke *is*
easy and My burden is light."

Jesus Is Lord of the Sabbath

12 At that time Jesus went through the grainfields on the Sabbath. And
His disciples were hungry, and began to pluck heads of grain and to
eat. 2And when the Pharisees saw *it,* they said to Him, "Look, Your disciples are doing what is not lawful to do on the Sabbath!"

3But He said to them, "Have you not read what David did when he was
hungry, he and those who were with him: 4how he entered the house of
God and ate the showbread which was not lawful for him to eat, nor for
those who were with him, but only for the priests? 5Or have you not read in
the law that on the Sabbath the priests in the temple profane the Sabbath,
and are blameless? 6Yet I say to you that in this place there is *One* greater
than the temple. 7But if you had known what *this* means, *'I desire mercy
and not sacrifice,'*[z] you would not have condemned the guiltless. 8For the
Son of Man is Lord even[a] of the Sabbath."

Healing on the Sabbath

9Now when He had departed from there, He went into their synagogue.
10And behold, there was a man who had a withered hand. And they asked
Him, saying, "Is it lawful to heal on the Sabbath?"—that they might accuse Him.

11:19 [x] NU-Text reads *works.*
11:23 [y] NU-Text reads *will you be exalted to heaven? No, you will be.*
12:7 [z] Hosea 6:6
12:8 [a] NU-Text and M-Text omit *even.*

The temple gazers don't mean to be bored. They love the church. They can cite its programs and praise its pastors. They don't mean to grow stale. They put on hats and hose and coats and ties and come every week. But still, something is missing. The one they once planned to honor hasn't been seen in a while.

But those who have seen him can't seem to forget him. They find him, often in spite of the temple rather than because of it. They brush the dust away and stand ever impressed before his tomb—his empty tomb.

The temple builders and the Savior seekers. You'll find them both in the same church, on the same pew—at times, even in the same suit. One sees the structure and says, "O What a great church." The other sees the Savior and says, "O What a great Christ!"

Which do you see?

(From *The Applause of Heaven* by Max Lucado)

APPLICATION Examine the ministries you support or take part in—missions, service opportunities, and your choice of church. Are you involved with them because God uses them to help others, or because of some element of glamour, visibility, or uniqueness? Do you focus on the reason for the ministry, or are you supportive because of a bandwagon influence—the temptation to join in just because it is popular?

EXPLORATION Elijah and John—Isaiah 40:3-5; Malachi 3:1; 4:5-6; Matthew 3:1-15; Mark 1:2-8; 9:11-13; Luke 1:5-17, 76; 3:2-18; John 1:19-34.

LIFE LESSON

Matthew 12:1-50

SITUATION Fourteen hundred years before Jesus' birth, Israel received God's command to keep the Sabbath holy. In their zeal to obey this command, the Jewish leaders gradually developed many rules and traditions to avoid working on the Sabbath. Jesus overruled the traditions and focused on God's purpose in establishing this command.

OBSERVATION When God commanded the Israelites not to work on the Sabbath, Jesus knew that law was given to relieve the people. Jesus focused on the purpose of the Sabbath. Therefore, he knew it was not sin to take care of one's needs or to help others on the Sabbath.

INSPIRATION The purpose of Sabbath rest is physical and emotional renewal, but it is also fellowship—a delightful space on the weekly calendar reserved for becoming better acquainted with ourselves, others, and God; it is a time for good talk, holy laughter, serious ideas, and shared intimacies between Creator and creature. Our souls are replenished, quieted, nurtured, caressed. Rest without spiritual rest is incomplete. One of the reasons for the frantic search for leisure activities in our culture (the rushing off to one weekend event or

11Then He said to them, "What man is there among you who has one sheep,
and if it falls into a pit on the Sabbath, will not lay hold of it and lift *it* out? 12Of
how much more value then is a man than a sheep? Therefore it is lawful to do
good on the Sabbath." 13Then He said to the man, "Stretch out your hand."
And he stretched *it* out, and it was restored as whole as the other. 14Then the
Pharisees went out and plotted against Him, how they might destroy Him.

Behold, My Servant

15But when Jesus knew *it,* He withdrew from there. And great multitudes[b] followed Him, and He healed them all. 16Yet He warned them not to
make Him known, 17that it might be fulfilled which was spoken by Isaiah
the prophet, saying:

18 *"Behold! My Servant whom I have chosen,*
My Beloved in whom My soul is well pleased!
I will put My Spirit upon Him,
And He will declare justice to the Gentiles.
19 *He will not quarrel nor cry out,*
Nor will anyone hear His voice in the streets.
20 *A bruised reed He will not break,*
And smoking flax He will not quench,
Till He sends forth justice to victory;
21 *And in His name Gentiles will trust."*[c]

A House Divided Cannot Stand

22Then one was brought to Him who was demon-possessed, blind and
mute; and He healed him, so that the blind and[d] mute man both spoke
and saw. 23And all the multitudes were amazed and said, "Could this be
the Son of David?"

24Now when the Pharisees heard *it* they said, "This *fellow* does not cast
out demons except by Beelzebub,[e] the ruler of the demons."

25But Jesus knew their thoughts, and said to them: "Every kingdom divided against itself is brought to desolation, and every city or house divided against itself will not stand. 26If Satan casts out Satan, he is divided
against himself. How then will his kingdom stand? 27And if I cast out
demons by Beelzebub, by whom do your sons cast *them* out? Therefore
they shall be your judges. 28But if I cast out demons by the Spirit of God,
surely the kingdom of God has come upon you. 29Or how can one enter a
strong man's house and plunder his goods, unless he first binds the
strong man? And then he will plunder his house. 30He who is not with Me
is against Me, and he who does not gather with Me scatters abroad.

The Unpardonable Sin

31"Therefore I say to you, every sin and blasphemy will be forgiven men,
but the blasphemy *against* the Spirit will not be forgiven men. 32Anyone
who speaks a word against the Son of Man, it will be forgiven him; but
whoever speaks against the Holy Spirit, it will not be forgiven him, either
in this age or in the *age* to come.

12:15 *b* NU-Text brackets *multitudes* as disputed.
12:21 *c* Isaiah 42:1–4
12:22 *d* NU-Text omits *blind and.*
12:24 *e* NU-Text and M-Text read *Beelzebul.*

A Tree Known by Its Fruit

33"Either make the tree good and its fruit good, or else make the tree
bad and its fruit bad; for a tree is known by *its* fruit. 34Brood of vipers! How
can you, being evil, speak good things? For out of the abundance of the
heart the mouth speaks. 35A good man out of the good treasure of his
heart[f] brings forth good things, and an evil man out of the evil treasure
brings forth evil things. 36But I say to you that for every idle word men may
speak, they will give account of it in the day of judgment. 37For by your
words you will be justified, and by your words you will be condemned."

The Scribes and Pharisees Ask for a Sign

38Then some of the scribes and Pharisees answered, saying, "Teacher,
we want to see a sign from You."
39But He answered and said to them, "An evil and adulterous generation seeks after a sign, and no sign will be given to it except the sign of the
prophet Jonah. 40For as Jonah was three days and three nights in the belly
of the great fish, so will the Son of Man be three days and three nights in
the heart of the earth. 41The men of Nineveh will rise up in the judgment
with this generation and condemn it, because they repented at the preaching of Jonah; and indeed a greater than Jonah *is* here. 42The queen of the
South will rise up in the judgment with this generation and condemn it,
for she came from the ends of the earth to hear the wisdom of Solomon;
and indeed a greater than Solomon *is* here.

An Unclean Spirit Returns

43"When an unclean spirit goes out of a man, he goes through dry
places, seeking rest, and finds none. 44Then he says, 'I will return to my
house from which I came.' And when he comes, he finds *it* empty, swept,
and put in order. 45Then he goes and takes with him seven other spirits
more wicked than himself, and they enter and dwell there; and the last
state of that man is worse than the first. So shall it also be with this wicked
generation."

Jesus' Mother and Brothers Send for Him

46While He was still talking to the multitudes, behold, His mother and
brothers stood outside, seeking to speak with Him. 47Then one said to
Him, "Look, Your mother and Your brothers are standing outside, seeking
to speak with You."
48But He answered and said to the one who told Him, "Who is My
mother and who are My brothers?" 49And He stretched out His hand toward
His disciples and said, "Here are My mother and My brothers! 50For whoever
does the will of My Father in heaven is My brother and sister and mother."

The Parable of the Sower

13 On the same day Jesus went out of the house and sat by the sea.
2And great multitudes were gathered together to Him, so that He
got into a boat and sat; and the whole multitude stood on the shore.
3Then He spoke many things to them in parables, saying: "Behold, a
sower went out to sow. 4And as he sowed, some *seed* fell by the wayside;

another, then breathlessly returning when Sunday is ended) is that we cannot find true renewal when we deny the spiritual. . . .

When we cease from our work and let Christ do His work within us, we realize that our work is not so important. We can stop and the world goes on. It is God's activity that is important, not ours. It is finally the death and resurrection of Christ that allowed fellowship with God to be a perpetual covenant. When we participate in his resurrected life by the memorial of Sunday, when we bring to that memorial day a Sabbath understanding, "We should," as Jonathan Edwards says, "have sympathy with Christ in His joy. He was refreshed on this day; we should be refreshed as those whose hearts are united with His."

(From *Making Sunday Special* by Karen Burton Mains)

APPLICATION How do you keep the Sabbath command? What makes Sunday a unique day for you? How can you avoid "business as usual" on Sunday?

EXPLORATION Sabbath—Exodus 20:8-11; 35:1-3; Deuteronomy 5:12-15; Isaiah 58:13-14; Luke 6:1-10; 13:10-17; John 7:22-24; 9:13-16; Colossians 2:16-17.

12:35 *f* NU-Text and M-Text omit *of his heart.*

and the birds came and devoured them. 5Some fell on stony places, where
they did not have much earth; and they immediately sprang up because
they had no depth of earth. 6But when the sun was up they were scorched,
and because they had no root they withered away. 7And some fell among
thorns, and the thorns sprang up and choked them. 8But others fell on
good ground and yielded a crop: some a hundredfold, some sixty, some
thirty. 9He who has ears to hear, let him hear!"

The Purpose of Parables

10And the disciples came and said to Him, "Why do You speak to them
in parables?"

11He answered and said to them, "Because it has been given to you to
know the mysteries of the kingdom of heaven, but to them it has not been
given. 12For whoever has, to him more will be given, and he will have abundance; but whoever does not have, even what he has will be taken away
from him. 13Therefore I speak to them in parables, because seeing they do
not see, and hearing they do not hear, nor do they understand. 14And in
them the prophecy of Isaiah is fulfilled, which says:

'Hearing you will hear and shall not understand,
And seeing you will see and not perceive;
15 *For the hearts of this people have grown dull.*
Their ears are hard of hearing,
And their eyes they have closed,
Lest they should see with their eyes and hear with their ears,
Lest they should understand with their hearts and turn,
So that I should[g] heal them.'[h]

16But blessed *are* your eyes for they see, and your ears for they hear; 17for
assuredly, I say to you that many prophets and righteous *men* desired to
see what you see, and did not see *it,* and to hear what you hear, and did not
hear *it.*

The Parable of the Sower Explained

18"Therefore hear the parable of the sower: 19When anyone hears the
word of the kingdom, and does not understand *it,* then the wicked *one*
comes and snatches away what was sown in his heart. This is he who received seed by the wayside. 20But he who received the seed on stony places,
this is he who hears the word and immediately receives it with joy; 21yet he
has no root in himself, but endures only for a while. For when tribulation
or persecution arises because of the word, immediately he stumbles.
22Now he who received seed among the thorns is he who hears the word,
and the cares of this world and the deceitfulness of riches choke the word,
and he becomes unfruitful. 23But he who received seed on the good
ground is he who hears the word and understands *it,* who indeed bears
fruit and produces: some a hundredfold, some sixty, some thirty."

The Parable of the Wheat and the Tares

24Another parable He put forth to them, saying: "The kingdom of
heaven is like a man who sowed good seed in his field; 25but while men
slept, his enemy came and sowed tares among the wheat and went his

13:15 [g] NU-Text and M-Text read *would.* [h] Isaiah 6:9, 10

LIFE LESSON

Matthew 13:1-58

SITUATION The Jewish people eagerly looked forward to the Kingdom of Heaven but also had some mistaken ideas about it. Jesus' teaching told about this Kingdom.

OBSERVATION Jesus taught about the Kingdom of Heaven through parables in order to clear up wrong ideas. Many explanations in the Gospels show that the Kingdom of Heaven (or Kingdom of God) means we must recognize God's authority and work to do his will.

INSPIRATION The natural inclination in Christian living is to act on the impulse of a good idea. Not every good idea is from God. Sometimes good ideas get in the way of God ideas.

Where does your inspiration come from? The vision of the transfigured Christ inspired Peter: "O Lord, it is good for us to be here. If you wish, I will put up three shelters—one for you, one for Moses and one for Elijah" (Matthew 17:4). Our natural impulse is to do something good for God and suggest it to Him.

The tendency of the well-meaning person is to prepare a plan to do some good idea, and then pray, "Jesus, this is my plan. It is a good plan. It hurts no one, and I want it to please You. Lord, please bless my plan." It is plan, then pray.

So many of our ideas are impetuous. They are not what the Lord wants to do. They do not resemble in any way the things which concern Him. We have good ideas, but they are not God ideas. His agenda and our agenda conflict. We want to build Him a shelter, but that is not what He wants. . . .

When Peter, James, and John heard the voice of the Lord . . . they abandoned their inventive-but-self-made

way. 26But when the grain had sprouted and produced a crop, then the
tares also appeared. 27So the servants of the owner came and said to him,
'Sir, did you not sow good seed in your field? How then does it have tares?'
28He said to them, 'An enemy has done this.' The servants said to him, 'Do
you want us then to go and gather them up?' 29But he said, 'No, lest while
you gather up the tares you also uproot the wheat with them. 30Let both
grow together until the harvest, and at the time of harvest I will say to the
reapers, "First gather together the tares and bind them in bundles to burn
them, but gather the wheat into my barn." ' "

The Parable of the Mustard Seed

31Another parable He put forth to them, saying: "The kingdom of
heaven is like a mustard seed, which a man took and sowed in his field,
32which indeed is the least of all the seeds; but when it is grown it is greater
than the herbs and becomes a tree, so that the birds of the air come and
nest in its branches."

The Parable of the Leaven

33Another parable He spoke to them: "The kingdom of heaven is like
leaven, which a woman took and hid in three measures[i] of meal till it was
all leavened."

Prophecy and the Parables

34All these things Jesus spoke to the multitude in parables; and without
a parable He did not speak to them, 35that it might be fulfilled which was
spoken by the prophet, saying:

"I will open My mouth in parables;
I will utter things kept secret from the foundation of the world."[j]

The Parable of the Tares Explained

36Then Jesus sent the multitude away and went into the house. And His disciples came to Him, saying, "Explain to us the parable of the tares of the field."
37He answered and said to them: "He who sows the good seed is the Son
of Man. 38The field is the world, the good seeds are the sons of the kingdom, but the tares are the sons of the wicked *one.* 39The enemy who sowed
them is the devil, the harvest is the end of the age, and the reapers are the
angels. 40Therefore as the tares are gathered and burned in the fire, so it
will be at the end of this age. 41The Son of Man will send out His angels,
and they will gather out of His kingdom all things that offend, and those
who practice lawlessness, 42and will cast them into the furnace of fire.
There will be wailing and gnashing of teeth. 43Then the righteous will shine
forth as the sun in the kingdom of their Father. He who has ears to hear, let
him hear!

The Parable of the Hidden Treasure

44"Again, the kingdom of heaven is like treasure hidden in a field, which
a man found and hid; and for joy over it he goes and sells all that he has
and buys that field.

13:33 [i] Greek *sata,* approximately two pecks in all
13:35 [j] Psalm 78:2

idea. The presence of the Lord magnified, and His holiness brought them to their senses. Jesus gained their attention, not by subduing them with a stern scolding, but by magnifying His presence until all the genius of their human ideas was bleached out by His refulgent face.

When they abandoned their good idea and fell facedown before the Lord, He could work with them again. . . .

When you and I abandon our good idea and fall to our face before the Lord, then He will come and touch us, too. When we pursue our own plan, He cannot use us. We must abandon our good idea and fall facedown before Him. Then He will be able to use us again. Then He will reveal what He is doing—a God idea. . . . It is pray, then plan. Through prayer, Jesus instructs of His plan, a God idea.

Prayer removes the impulse of the good idea, the good idea born of human ingenuity but not of God. Pray, then plan. It is the habit of the surrendered saint.

(From *Walking with Christ in the Details of Life* by Patrick M. Morley)

APPLICATION In what ways are you supporting God's Kingdom? Are you looking for God's plan and following it? Or are you following your own plan and asking God to bless it? Allow God to adjust your dreams to match his plans.

EXPLORATION Kingdom of Heaven—Isaiah 24:23; Daniel 2:44; Matthew 3:2; 6:9-10, 33; Mark 10:14-15, 23-25; Luke 9:61-62; 12:31; 17:20-21; John 3:3; 18:36.

LIFE LESSON

Matthew 14:1-36

SITUATION Jesus demonstrated his power over the laws of nature when he fed the five thousand and walked on the water.

OBSERVATION John's unfair execution disturbed Jesus deeply, but he could not escape either the crowds of people or his disciples. Yet, Jesus showed compassion on the people and met their needs.

INSPIRATION "Come on" is the invitation.

And Peter doesn't have to be told twice. It's not every day that you walk on water through waves that are taller than you are. . . .

The first few steps go well. But a few strides out onto the water, and he forgets to look to the One who got him there in the first place, and down he plunges. . . .

Peter knows better than to bite the hand that can save him. His response may lack class—it probably wouldn't get him on the cover of *Gentleman's Quarterly* or even *Sports Illustrated*—but it gets him out of some deep water: "Help me!"

And since Peter would rather swallow pride than water, a hand comes through the rain and pulls him up.

The message is clear.

As long as Jesus is one of many options, he is no option. As long as you can carry your burdens alone, you don't need a burden bearer. As long as your situation brings you no grief, you will receive no comfort. And as long as you can take him or leave him, you might as well leave him, because he won't be taken half-heartedly.

(From *The Applause of Heaven* by Max Lucado)

APPLICATION Imitate Christ's compassion by putting the needs of others ahead of your own. Be willing to stay up late with a disappointed friend rather than getting your sleep. Let your schedule be interrupted to comfort or listen to somebody else.

EXPLORATION Jesus' Compassion—Matthew 20:30-34; 23:37; Mark 1:40-42; 8:1-3; Luke 7:12-15; John 11:33-36.

The Parable of the Pearl of Great Price

45“Again, the kingdom of heaven is like a merchant seeking beautiful
pearls, 46who, when he had found one pearl of great price, went and sold
all that he had and bought it.

The Parable of the Dragnet

47“Again, the kingdom of heaven is like a dragnet that was cast into the
sea and gathered some of every kind, 48which, when it was full, they drew
to shore; and they sat down and gathered the good into vessels, but threw
the bad away. 49So it will be at the end of the age. The angels will come
forth, separate the wicked from among the just, 50and cast them into the
furnace of fire. There will be wailing and gnashing of teeth.”
51Jesus said to them,[k] “Have you understood all these things?”
They said to Him, “Yes, Lord.”[l]
52Then He said to them, “Therefore every scribe instructed concerning[m]
the kingdom of heaven is like a householder who brings out of his treasure *things* new and old.”

Jesus Rejected at Nazareth

53Now it came to pass, when Jesus had finished these parables, that He
departed from there. 54When He had come to His own country, He taught
them in their synagogue, so that they were astonished and said, “Where
did this *Man* get this wisdom and *these* mighty works? 55Is this not the
carpenter’s son? Is not His mother called Mary? And His brothers James,
Joses,[n] Simon, and Judas? 56And His sisters, are they not all with us? Where
then did this *Man* get all these things?” 57So they were offended at Him.
But Jesus said to them, “A prophet is not without honor except in his
own country and in his own house.” 58Now He did not do many mighty
works there because of their unbelief.

John the Baptist Beheaded

14 At that time Herod the tetrarch heard the report about Jesus 2and
said to his servants, “This is John the Baptist; he is risen from the
dead, and therefore these powers are at work in him.” 3For Herod had laid
hold of John and bound him, and put *him* in prison for the sake of
Herodias, his brother Philip’s wife. 4Because John had said to him, “It is
not lawful for you to have her.” 5And although he wanted to put him to
death, he feared the multitude, because they counted him as a prophet.
6But when Herod’s birthday was celebrated, the daughter of Herodias
danced before them and pleased Herod. 7Therefore he promised with an
oath to give her whatever she might ask.
8So she, having been prompted by her mother, said, “Give me John the
Baptist’s head here on a platter.”
9And the king was sorry; nevertheless, because of the oaths and because
of those who sat with him, he commanded *it* to be given to *her*. 10So he sent
and had John beheaded in prison. 11And his head was brought on a platter
and given to the girl, and she brought *it* to her mother. 12Then his disciples
came and took away the body and buried it, and went and told Jesus.

13:51 [k] NU-Text omits *Jesus said to them.* [l] NU-Text omits *Lord.*
13:52 [m] Or *for*
13:55 [n] NU-Text reads *Joseph.*

Feeding the Five Thousand

13When Jesus heard *it,* He departed from there by
boat to a deserted place by Himself. But when the multitudes heard it, they followed Him on foot from the
cities. 14And when Jesus went out He saw a great multitude; and He was moved with compassion for them,
and healed their sick. 15When it was evening, His disciples came to Him, saying, "This is a deserted place, and
the hour is already late. Send the multitudes away, that
they may go into the villages and buy themselves food."
16But Jesus said to them, "They do not need to go
away. You give them something to eat."
17And they said to Him, "We have here only five
loaves and two fish."
18He said, "Bring them here to Me." 19Then He commanded the multitudes to sit down on the grass. And
He took the five loaves and the two fish, and looking
up to heaven, He blessed and broke and gave the
loaves to the disciples; and the disciples gave to the
multitudes. 20So they all ate and were filled, and they
took up twelve baskets full of the fragments that remained. 21Now those who had eaten were about five
thousand men, besides women and children.

Jesus Walks on the Sea

22Immediately Jesus made His disciples get into the
boat and go before Him to the other side, while He
sent the multitudes away. 23And when He had sent the
multitudes away, He went up on the mountain by
Himself to pray. Now when evening came, He was
alone there. 24But the boat was now in the middle of
the sea,[o] tossed by the waves, for the wind was contrary.
25Now in the fourth watch of the night Jesus went to
them, walking on the sea. 26And when the disciples
saw Him walking on the sea, they were troubled, saying, "It is a ghost!" And they cried out for fear.
27But immediately Jesus spoke to them, saying, "Be
of good cheer! It is I; do not be afraid."
28And Peter answered Him and said, "Lord, if it is
You, command me to come to You on the water."
29So He said, "Come." And when Peter had come
down out of the boat, he walked on the water to go to
Jesus. 30But when he saw that the wind *was* boisterous,[p] he was afraid; and beginning to sink he cried
out, saying, "Lord, save me!"
31And immediately Jesus stretched out *His* hand
and caught him, and said to him, "O you of little faith,
why did you doubt?" 32And when they got into the
boat, the wind ceased.
33Then those who were in the boat came and[q] worshiped Him, saying, "Truly You are the Son of God."

Many Touch Him and Are Made Well

34When they had crossed over, they came to the
land of[r] Gennesaret. 35And when the men of that place
recognized Him, they sent out into all that surrounding region, brought to Him all who were sick, 36and
begged Him that they might only touch the hem of
His garment. And as many as touched *it* were made
perfectly well.

Defilement Comes from Within

15 Then the scribes and Pharisees who were from
Jerusalem came to Jesus, saying, 2"Why do
Your disciples transgress the tradition of the elders?
For they do not wash their hands when they eat bread."
3He answered and said to them, "Why do you also
transgress the commandment of God because of your
tradition? 4For God commanded, saying, *'Honor your
father and your mother';*[s] and, *'He who curses father
or mother, let him be put to death.'*[t] 5But you say,
'Whoever says to his father or mother, "Whatever
profit you might have received from me *is* a gift *to
God*"— 6then he need not honor his father or mother.'[u]
Thus you have made the commandment[v] of God of
no effect by your tradition. 7Hypocrites! Well did Isaiah
prophesy about you, saying:

8 *'These people draw near to Me with*
their mouth,
And[w] *honor Me with their lips,*
But their heart is far from Me.
9 *And in vain they worship Me,*
Teaching as doctrines the commandments
of men.' "[x]

10When He had called the multitude to *Himself,* He
said to them, "Hear and understand: 11Not what goes
into the mouth defiles a man; but what comes out of
the mouth, this defiles a man."
12Then His disciples came and said to Him, "Do

14:24 [o] NU-Text reads *many furlongs away from the land.*
14:30 [p] NU-Text brackets *that* and *boisterous* as disputed.
14:33 [q] NU-Text omits *came and.*
14:34 [r] NU-Text reads *came to land at.*
15:4 [s] Exodus 20:12; Deuteronomy 5:16 [t] Exodus 21:17
15:6 [u] NU-Text omits *or mother.* [v] NU-Text reads *word.*
15:8 [w] NU-Text omits *draw near to Me with their mouth, And.*
15:9 [x] Isaiah 29:13

LIFE LESSON

Matthew 15:1-39

SITUATION Although Pharisees were experts in God's Law, they lacked proper understanding of the purpose of the Law. Most importantly, they lacked faith in God.

OBSERVATION The Pharisees had faith in the religious system. Jesus pointed to God who was beyond the system.

INSPIRATION The disciples are annoyed. As Jesus sits in silence, they grow more smug. "Send her away," they demand. The spotlight is put on Jesus. He looks at the disciples, then looks at the woman. And what follows is one of the most intriguing dialogues in the New Testament.

"I was sent only to the lost sheep of Israel," he says.

"Lord, help me!"

"It is not right to take the children's bread and toss it to their dogs," he answers.

"But even the dogs eat the crumbs that fall from their masters' tables," she responds.

Is Jesus being rude? Is he worn-out? Is he frustrated? Is he calling this woman a dog? How do we explain this dialogue? . . .

Could it be that Jesus' tongue is poking his cheek? Could it be that he and the woman are engaging in satirical banter? Is it wry exchange in which God's unlimited grace is being highlighted? Could Jesus be so delighted to have

You know that the Pharisees were offended when they heard this saying?"
13But He answered and said, "Every plant which My heavenly Father has not planted will be uprooted.
14Let them alone. They are blind leaders of the blind. And if the blind leads the blind, both will fall into a ditch."
15Then Peter answered and said to Him, "Explain this parable to us."
16So Jesus said, "Are you also still without understanding?
17Do you not yet understand that whatever enters the mouth goes into the stomach and is eliminated?
18But those things which proceed out of the mouth come from the heart, and they defile a man.
19For out of the heart proceed evil thoughts, murders, adulteries, fornications, thefts, false witness, blasphemies.
20These are *the things* which defile a man, but to eat with unwashed hands does not defile a man."

A Gentile Shows Her Faith

21Then Jesus went out from there and departed to the region of Tyre and Sidon.
22And behold, a woman of Canaan came from that region and cried out to Him, saying, "Have mercy on me, O Lord, Son of David! My daughter is severely demon-possessed."
23But He answered her not a word.
And His disciples came and urged Him, saying, "Send her away, for she cries out after us."
24But He answered and said, "I was not sent except to the lost sheep of the house of Israel."
25Then she came and worshiped Him, saying, "Lord, help me!"
26But He answered and said, "It is not good to take the children's bread and throw *it* to the little dogs."
27And she said, "Yes, Lord, yet even the little dogs eat the crumbs which fall from their masters' table."
28Then Jesus answered and said to her, "O woman, great *is* your faith! Let it be to you as you desire." And her daughter was healed from that very hour.

Jesus Heals Great Multitudes

29Jesus departed from there, skirted the Sea of Galilee, and went up on the mountain and sat down there.
30Then great multitudes came to Him, having with them *the* lame, blind, mute, maimed, and many others; and they laid them down at Jesus' feet, and He healed them.
31So the multitude marveled when they saw *the* mute speaking, *the* maimed made whole, *the* lame walking, and *the* blind seeing; and they glorified the God of Israel.

Feeding the Four Thousand

32Now Jesus called His disciples to *Himself* and said, "I have compassion on the multitude, because they have now continued with Me three days and have nothing to eat. And I do not want to send them away hungry, lest they faint on the way."
33Then His disciples said to Him, "Where could we get enough bread in the wilderness to fill such a great multitude?"
34Jesus said to them, "How many loaves do you have?"
And they said, "Seven, and a few little fish."
35So He commanded the multitude to sit down on the ground.
36And He took the seven loaves and the fish and gave thanks, broke *them* and gave *them* to His disciples; and the disciples *gave* to the multitude.
37So they all

ate and were filled, and they took up seven large baskets full of the fragments that were left. 38Now those who ate were four thousand men, besides women and children. 39And He sent away the multitude, got into the
boat, and came to the region of Magdala.[y]

The Pharisees and Sadducees Seek a Sign

16 Then the Pharisees and Sadducees came, and testing Him asked
that He would show them a sign from heaven. 2He answered and
said to them, "When it is evening you say, '*It will be* fair weather, for the
sky is red'; 3and in the morning, '*It will be* foul weather today, for the sky is
red and threatening.' Hypocrites![z] You know how to discern the face of the
sky, but you cannot *discern* the signs of the times. 4A wicked and adulterous generation seeks after a sign, and no sign shall be given to it except the
sign of the prophet[a] Jonah." And He left them and departed.

The Leaven of the Pharisees and Sadducees

5Now when His disciples had come to the other side, they had forgotten
to take bread. 6Then Jesus said to them, "Take heed and beware of the
leaven of the Pharisees and the Sadducees."
7And they reasoned among themselves, saying, "*It is* because we have
taken no bread."
8But Jesus, being aware of *it,* said to them, "O you of little faith, why do
you reason among yourselves because you have brought no bread?[b] 9Do
you not yet understand, or remember the five loaves of the five thousand
and how many baskets you took up? 10Nor the seven loaves of the four
thousand and how many large baskets you took up? 11How is it you do not
understand that I did not speak to you concerning bread?—*but* to beware
of the leaven of the Pharisees and Sadducees." 12Then they understood
that He did not tell *them* to beware of the leaven of bread, but of the doctrine of the Pharisees and Sadducees.

Peter Confesses Jesus as the Christ

13When Jesus came into the region of Caesarea Philippi, He asked His
disciples, saying, "Who do men say that I, the Son of Man, am?"
14So they said, "Some *say* John the Baptist, some Elijah, and others
Jeremiah or one of the prophets."
15He said to them, "But who do you say that I am?"
16Simon Peter answered and said, "You are the Christ, the Son of the living God."
17Jesus answered and said to him, "Blessed are you, Simon Bar-Jonah, for
flesh and blood has not revealed *this* to you, but My Father who is in heaven.
18And I also say to you that you are Peter, and on this rock I will build My
church, and the gates of Hades shall not prevail against it. 19And I will give you
the keys of the kingdom of heaven, and whatever you bind on earth will be
bound in heaven, and whatever you loose on earth will be loosed[c] in heaven."
20Then He commanded His disciples that they should tell no one that
He was Jesus the Christ.

15:39 [y] NU-Text reads *Magadan.*
16:3 [z] NU-Text omits *Hypocrites.*
16:4 [a] NU-Text omits *the prophet.*
16:8 [b] NU-Text reads *you have no bread.*
16:19 [c] Or *will have been bound . . . will have been loosed*

found one who is not bartering with a religious system or proud of a heritage that he can't resist a bit of satire?

He knows he can heal her daughter. He knows he isn't bound by a plan. He knows her heart is good. So he decides to engage in a humorous moment with a faithful woman. In essence, here's what they said:

"Now, you know that God only cares about Jews," he says smiling.

And when she catches on, she volleys back, "But your bread is so precious, I'll be happy to eat the crumbs."

In a spirit of exuberance, he bursts out, "Never have I seen such faith! Your daughter is healed."

This story does not portray a contemptuous God. It portrays a willing One who delights in a sincere seeker. Aren't you glad he does?
(From *In the Eye of the Storm* by Max Lucado)

APPLICATION When you obey certain rules today, think through *why* you obey. "I don't speed because. . . ." "I don't falsify expense reports because. . . ." "I honor my parents because. . . ."

EXPLORATION The Spirit and Letter of The Law—1 Samuel 15:22; Psalm 51:17; Isaiah 1:13-17; 29:13; Hosea 6:6; Matthew 23:23; Mark 12:29-31; Acts 15:5-11; 2 Corinthians 3:6; Galatians 2:16; 3:2-5; 6:2.

Jesus Predicts His Death and Resurrection

21 From that time Jesus began to show to His disciples that He must go to
Jerusalem, and suffer many things from the elders and chief priests and
scribes, and be killed, and be raised the third day.
22 Then Peter took Him aside and began to rebuke Him, saying, "Far be it
from You, Lord; this shall not happen to You!"
23 But He turned and said to Peter, "Get behind Me, Satan! You are an offense
to Me, for you are not mindful of the things of God, but the things of men."

Take Up the Cross and Follow Him

24 Then Jesus said to His disciples, "If anyone desires to come after Me,
let him deny himself, and take up his cross, and follow Me. 25 For whoever
desires to save his life will lose it, but whoever loses his life for My sake will
find it. 26 For what profit is it to a man if he gains the whole world, and loses
his own soul? Or what will a man give in exchange for his soul? 27 For the
Son of Man will come in the glory of His Father with His angels, and then
He will reward each according to his works.

Jesus Transfigured on the Mount

28 Assuredly, I say to you, there are some standing here who shall not taste
death till they see the Son of Man coming in His kingdom."

17 Now after six days Jesus took Peter, James, and John his brother, led
them up on a high mountain by themselves; 2 and He was transfigured before them. His face shone like the sun, and His clothes became as
white as the light. 3 And behold, Moses and Elijah appeared to them, talking with Him. 4 Then Peter answered and said to Jesus, "Lord, it is good for
us to be here; if You wish, let us[d] make here three tabernacles: one for You,
one for Moses, and one for Elijah."
5 While he was still speaking, behold, a bright cloud overshadowed
them; and suddenly a voice came out of the cloud, saying, "This is My
beloved Son, in whom I am well pleased. Hear Him!" 6 And when the disciples heard *it,* they fell on their faces and were greatly afraid. 7 But Jesus
came and touched them and said, "Arise, and do not be afraid." 8 When
they had lifted up their eyes, they saw no one but Jesus only.
9 Now as they came down from the mountain, Jesus commanded them,
saying, "Tell the vision to no one until the Son of Man is risen from the dead."
10 And His disciples asked Him, saying, "Why then do the scribes say
that Elijah must come first?"
11 Jesus answered and said to them, "Indeed, Elijah is coming first[e] and
will restore all things. 12 But I say to you that Elijah has come already, and
they did not know him but did to him whatever they wished. Likewise the
Son of Man is also about to suffer at their hands." 13 Then the disciples understood that He spoke to them of John the Baptist.

A Boy Is Healed

14 And when they had come to the multitude, a man came to Him,
kneeling down to Him and saying, 15 "Lord, have mercy on my son, for he
is an epileptic[f] and suffers severely; for he often falls into the fire and

17:4 [d] NU-Text reads *I will.*
17:11 [e] NU-Text omits *first.*
17:15 [f] Literally *moonstruck*

LIFE LESSON

Matthew 16:1-28

SITUATION The Pharisees and the Sadducees were two prestigious groups of Jewish teachers who jockeyed for influence and power. Leaders in both groups failed to recognize Jesus as the Messiah.

OBSERVATION Jesus did not seek to have earthly power like the Pharisees and Sadducees. He sought to build a kingdom that would last into eternity.

INSPIRATION The pole of power is greasy.

The Roman emperor Charlemagne knew that. An interesting story surrounds the burial of this famous king. Legend has it that he asked to be entombed sitting upright in his throne. He asked that his crown be placed on his head and his scepter in his hand. He requested that the royal cape be draped around his shoulders and an open book be placed in his lap.

That was A.D. 814. Nearly two hundred years later, Emperor Othello determined to see if the burial request had been carried out. He allegedly sent a team of men to open the tomb and make a report. They found the body just as Charlemagne had requested. Only now, nearly two centuries later, the scene was gruesome. . . . But open on the skeletal thighs was the book Charlemagne had requested—the Bible. One bony finger pointed to Matthew 16:26: "What good will it be for a man if he gains the whole world, yet forfeits his soul?"

You can answer that one.

(From *The Applause of Heaven* by Max Lucado)

APPLICATION It is easy for us to be wary of false teachers who don't know Christ at all—such as people from other world religions. But we must also guard against those teachers who claim to follow Christ, yet misinterpret his Word.

EXPLORATION False Teaching—Jeremiah 50:6; Matthew 7:15-20; Romans 16:17-18; 2 Corinthians 11:13-15; 1 Timothy 1:6-7; 4:1-2; 2 Timothy 4:3-4; 2 Peter 2:1-3.

often into the water. 16So I brought him to Your disciples, but they could not
cure him."
17Then Jesus answered and said, "O faithless and perverse generation,
how long shall I be with you? How long shall I bear with you? Bring him
here to Me." 18And Jesus rebuked the demon, and it came out of him; and
the child was cured from that very hour.
19Then the disciples came to Jesus privately and said, "Why could we
not cast it out?"
20So Jesus said to them, "Because of your unbelief;[g] for assuredly, I say
to you, if you have faith as a mustard seed, you will say to this mountain,
'Move from here to there,' and it will move; and nothing will be impossible
for you. 21However, this kind does not go out except by prayer and fasting."[h]

Jesus Again Predicts His Death and Resurrection

22Now while they were staying[i] in Galilee, Jesus said to them, "The Son
of Man is about to be betrayed into the hands of men, 23and they will kill
Him, and the third day He will be raised up." And they were exceedingly
sorrowful.

Peter and His Master Pay Their Taxes

24When they had come to Capernaum,[j] those who received the *temple*
tax came to Peter and said, "Does your Teacher not pay the *temple* tax?"
25He said, "Yes."
And when he had come into the house, Jesus anticipated him, saying,
"What do you think, Simon? From whom do the kings of the earth take
customs or taxes, from their sons or from strangers?"
26Peter said to Him, "From strangers."
Jesus said to him, "Then the sons are free. 27Nevertheless, lest we offend
them, go to the sea, cast in a hook, and take the fish that comes up first.
And when you have opened its mouth, you will find a piece of money;[k]
take that and give it to them for Me and you."

Who Is the Greatest?

18 At that time the disciples came to Jesus, saying, "Who then is greatest in the kingdom of heaven?"
2Then Jesus called a little child to Him, set him in the midst of them,
3and said, "Assuredly, I say to you, unless you are converted and become
as little children, you will by no means enter the kingdom of heaven.
4Therefore whoever humbles himself as this little child is the greatest in
the kingdom of heaven. 5Whoever receives one little child like this in My
name receives Me.

Jesus Warns of Offenses

6"Whoever causes one of these little ones who believe in Me to sin, it
would be better for him if a millstone were hung around his neck, and he
were drowned in the depth of the sea. 7Woe to the world because of offenses!
For offenses must come, but woe to that man by whom the offense comes!

17:20 [g] NU-Text reads *little faith.*
17:21 [h] NU-Text omits this verse.
17:22 [i] NU-Text reads *gathering together.*
17:24 [j] NU-Text reads *Capharnaum* (here and elsewhere).
17:27 [k] Greek *stater,* the exact amount to pay the temple tax (didrachma) for two

LIFE LESSON

Matthew 17:1-27

SITUATION Jesus' followers took a risk when they believed that Jesus was the Messiah and the Son of God.

OBSERVATION Though they had seen Jesus' power and authority daily, this transformation of Jesus proved that Jesus was God's Son—the Messiah.

INSPIRATION How deity and humanity can coexist in one person is beyond our understanding. Let me give an example. We know that God cannot die, and we know that Jesus is God. Yet Jesus died. How can that be? . . . He did not lay aside the glory of deity; rather, He veiled that glory in a garb of flesh. If a prince leaves the royal palace to go and live in the slums, his position has changed, but he is still the same person. He can empty himself of his privileged place and veil his true identity, but he cannot empty himself of his personhood. So it was with the Lord Jesus. He did not consider His position with the Father in heaven something He had to hold on to at all costs. He came as a man so that He might die for humankind.

. . . We hold to the truth that "in Him dwells all the fullness of the Godhead bodily" (Col. 2:9), and that means He always possessed all the attributes of deity.

(From *Alone in Majesty* by William MacDonald)

APPLICATION When did God open your eyes to accept him? Recount the experience when God took your heart and made it new. Thank him for his grace. In your daily routine today, look for a way to tell someone your story.

EXPLORATION Jesus Glorified—Mark 9:2-8; 16:19; Luke 9:28-36; John 1:14; 17:5, 24; Ephesians 1:21-22; Philippians 2:9-10; Colossians 1:15-18; 1 Peter 3:22; Revelation 5:7-14; 19:11-16.

LIFE LESSON
Matthew 18:1-35

SITUATION The Roman Empire occupied the nation of Israel. Only Roman citizens had privileges. The average Jewish person in Jesus' day could not expect much honor or power. The disciples needed to hear Jesus' encouraging message about who they should honor.

OBSERVATION Who is great in God's eyes? God honors the lost, the weak, the humble, children, and the merciful. Status in the eyes of society, government, or even the church does not equate to status in God's eyes.

INSPIRATION A boy went into a pet shop, looking for a puppy. The store owner showed him a litter in a box. The boy looked at the puppies. He picked each one up, examined it, and put it back into the box.

After several minutes, he walked back to the owner and said, "I picked one out. How much will it cost?"

The man gave him the price, and the boy promised to be back in a few days with the money. . . .

The boy went to work—weeding, washing windows, cleaning yards. He worked hard and saved his money. When he had enough for the puppy, he returned to the store.

He walked up to the counter and laid down a pocketful of wadded bills. The store owner sorted and counted the cash. . . . "All right, son, you can go get your puppy."

The boy reached into the back of the box, pulled out a skinny dog with a limp leg, and started to leave.

The owner stopped him.

"Don't take that puppy," he objected. "He's crippled. He can't play. He'll never run with you. He can't fetch. Get one of the healthy pups."

8"If your hand or foot causes you to sin, cut it off and cast *it* from you. It
is better for you to enter into life lame or maimed, rather than having two
hands or two feet, to be cast into the everlasting fire. 9And if your eye causes
you to sin, pluck it out and cast *it* from you. It is better for you to enter into
life with one eye, rather than having two eyes, to be cast into hell fire.

The Parable of the Lost Sheep

10"Take heed that you do not despise one of these little ones, for I say to
you that in heaven their angels always see the face of My Father who is in
heaven. 11For the Son of Man has come to save that which was lost.[l]
12"What do you think? If a man has a hundred sheep, and one of them
goes astray, does he not leave the ninety-nine and go to the mountains to
seek the one that is straying? 13And if he should find it, assuredly, I say to
you, he rejoices more over that *sheep* than over the ninety-nine that did
not go astray. 14Even so it is not the will of your Father who is in heaven that
one of these little ones should perish.

Dealing with a Sinning Brother

15"Moreover if your brother sins against you, go and tell him his fault
between you and him alone. If he hears you, you have gained your brother.
16But if he will not hear, take with you one or two more, that *'by the mouth
of two or three witnesses every word may be established.'*[m] 17And if he refuses to hear them, tell *it* to the church. But if he refuses even to hear the
church, let him be to you like a heathen and a tax collector.
18"Assuredly, I say to you, whatever you bind on earth will be bound in
heaven, and whatever you loose on earth will be loosed in heaven.
19"Again I say[n] to you that if two of you agree on earth concerning anything
that they ask, it will be done for them by My Father in heaven. 20For where two
or three are gathered together in My name, I am there in the midst of them."

The Parable of the Unforgiving Servant

21Then Peter came to Him and said, "Lord, how often shall my brother
sin against me, and I forgive him? Up to seven times?"
22Jesus said to him, "I do not say to you, up to seven times, but up to seventy times seven. 23Therefore the kingdom of heaven is like a certain king
who wanted to settle accounts with his servants. 24And when he had begun
to settle accounts, one was brought to him who owed him ten thousand
talents. 25But as he was not able to pay, his master commanded that he be
sold, with his wife and children and all that he had, and that payment be
made. 26The servant therefore fell down before him, saying, 'Master, have
patience with me, and I will pay you all.' 27Then the master of that servant
was moved with compassion, released him, and forgave him the debt.
28"But that servant went out and found one of his fellow servants who
owed him a hundred denarii; and he laid hands on him and took *him* by
the throat, saying, 'Pay me what you owe!' 29So his fellow servant fell down
at his feet[o] and begged him, saying, 'Have patience with me, and I will pay
you all.'[p] 30And he would not, but went and threw him into prison till he

18:11 [l] NU-Text omits this verse.
18:16 [m] Deuteronomy 19:15
18:19 [n] NU-Text and M-Text read *Again, assuredly, I say.*
18:29 [o] NU-Text omits *at his feet.* [p] NU-Text and M-Text omit *all.*

should pay the debt. 31So when his fellow servants saw what had been
done, they were very grieved, and came and told their master all that had
been done. 32Then his master, after he had called him, said to him, 'You
wicked servant! I forgave you all that debt because you begged me.
33Should you not also have had compassion on your fellow servant, just as
I had pity on you?' 34And his master was angry, and delivered him to the
torturers until he should pay all that was due to him.
35"So My heavenly Father also will do to you if each of you, from his
heart, does not forgive his brother his trespasses."[q]

Marriage and Divorce

19 Now it came to pass, when Jesus had finished these sayings, *that* He
departed from Galilee and came to the region of Judea beyond the
Jordan. 2And great multitudes followed Him, and He healed them there.
3The Pharisees also came to Him, testing Him, and saying to Him, "Is it
lawful for a man to divorce his wife for *just* any reason?"
4And He answered and said to them, "Have you not read that He who
made[r] *them* at the beginning *'made them male and female,'*[s] 5and said, *'For
this reason a man shall leave his father and mother and be joined to his wife,
and the two shall become one flesh'* ?[t] 6So then, they are no longer two but
one flesh. Therefore what God has joined together, let not man separate."
7They said to Him, "Why then did Moses command to give a certificate
of divorce, and to put her away?"
8He said to them, "Moses, because of the hardness of your hearts, permitted you to divorce your wives, but from the beginning it was not so.
9And I say to you, whoever divorces his wife, except for sexual immorality,[u] and marries another, commits adultery; and whoever marries her
who is divorced commits adultery."
10His disciples said to Him, "If such is the case of the man with *his* wife,
it is better not to marry."

Jesus Teaches on Celibacy

11But He said to them, "All cannot accept this saying, but only *those* to
whom it has been given: 12For there are eunuchs who were born thus from
their mother's womb, and there are eunuchs who were made eunuchs by
men, and there are eunuchs who have made themselves eunuchs for the
kingdom of heaven's sake. He who is able to accept *it,* let him accept *it.*"

Jesus Blesses Little Children

13Then little children were brought to Him that He might put *His* hands
on them and pray, but the disciples rebuked them. 14But Jesus said, "Let the
little children come to Me, and do not forbid them; for of such is the kingdom of heaven." 15And He laid *His* hands on them and departed from there.

Jesus Counsels the Rich Young Ruler

16Now behold, one came and said to Him, "Good[v] Teacher, what good
thing shall I do that I may have eternal life?"

18:35 [q] NU-Text omits *his trespasses.*
19:4 [r] NU-Text reads *created.* [s] Genesis 1:27; 5:2
19:5 [t] Genesis 2:24
19:9 [u] Or *fornication*
19:16 [v] NU-Text omits *Good.*

"No thank you, sir," the boy replied. "This is exactly the kind of dog I've been looking for."

As the boy turned to leave, the store owner started to speak but remained silent. Suddenly he understood. For extending from the bottom of the boy's trousers was a brace—a brace for his crippled leg.

Why did the boy want the dog? Because he knew how it felt. And he knew it was very special. . . .

Jesus knows how you feel. You're under the gun at work? Jesus knows how you feel. You've got more to do than is humanly possible? So did he. You've got children who make a "piranha hour" out of your dinner hour? Jesus knows what that's like. People take more from you than they give? Jesus understands. . . .

When you struggle, he listens. When you yearn, he responds. When you question, he hears. He has been there. You've heard that before, but you need to hear it again. . . .

He understands you with the compassion of the crippled boy. . . . And, like the boy, he paid a great price to take you home.

(From *In the Eye of the Storm* by Max Lucado)

APPLICATION Refuse to focus on your weaknesses even if people keep reminding you of them. Instead, sing a little about God's great blessings to you—especially his gift of eternal life.

EXPLORATION Great in God's Sight—Isaiah 57:15; Matthew 25:37-40; Mark 10:43-45; Luke 16:15; 18:16; 22:26; 1 Corinthians 1:26-28; James 2:5; 4:10.

LIFE LESSON

Matthew 19:1-30

SITUATION Jesus crossed the Jordan River into Perea before coming back through Jericho to Jerusalem. Herod imprisoned and killed John the Baptist for expressing his opinion publicly on Herod's marriage. The Jews hoped to trap Jesus also.

OBSERVATION Jesus taught about the demands of discipleship. Disciples must honor marriage vows, have childlike humility, and refuse to be dominated by wealth.

INSPIRATION Humility is a fruit of the Spirit, the result of his ministry in our hearts. But this ministry does not occur without deliberate, conscious effort on our part. The Spirit does not make us humble; he enables us to humble ourselves in these difficult situations. . . . A very common occasion for showing humility is through *serving one another.* In this area Jesus is our greatest teacher and pacesetter. . . . Jesus' whole life was one of serving others. He said he did not come to be served but to serve; he went around doing good for others. . . . Jesus also taught us the importance of serving one another. . . . He promised blessing to those who followed his example in serving others. . . . Dependence upon the grace of God results in God being glorified; it also makes it possible for those who are not natural servants to practice humility. His grace is sufficient for all of our needs. We can, by his ennoblement, *learn* to serve one another.

(From *The Practice of Godliness* by Jerry Bridges)

APPLICATION Judge yourself: When do you put your needs ahead of your spouse or your parents or your children? What step can you take to put their needs ahead of yours?

EXPLORATION Humility—Luke 14:7-11; Romans 12:3; Ephesians 4:2; Philippians 2:3-4.

17 So He said to him, "Why do you call Me good?[w] No one *is* good but One,
that is, God.[x] But if you want to enter into life, keep the commandments."
18 He said to Him, "Which ones?"
Jesus said, "'*You shall not murder,*' '*You shall not commit adultery,*'
'*You shall not steal,*' '*You shall not bear false witness,*' 19 '*Honor your father and your mother,*'[y] and, '*You shall love your neighbor as yourself.*' "[z]
20 The young man said to Him, "All these things I have kept from my
youth.[a] What do I still lack?"
21 Jesus said to him, "If you want to be perfect, go, sell what you have and
give to the poor, and you will have treasure in heaven; and come, follow Me."
22 But when the young man heard that saying, he went away sorrowful,
for he had great possessions.

With God All Things Are Possible

23 Then Jesus said to His disciples, "Assuredly, I say to you that it is hard
for a rich man to enter the kingdom of heaven. 24 And again I say to you, it
is easier for a camel to go through the eye of a needle than for a rich man
to enter the kingdom of God."
25 When His disciples heard *it,* they were greatly astonished, saying,
"Who then can be saved?"
26 But Jesus looked at *them* and said to them, "With men this is impossible, but with God all things are possible."
27 Then Peter answered and said to Him, "See, we have left all and followed You. Therefore what shall we have?"
28 So Jesus said to them, "Assuredly I say to you, that in the regeneration,
when the Son of Man sits on the throne of His glory, you who have followed
Me will also sit on twelve thrones, judging the twelve tribes of Israel. 29 And
everyone who has left houses or brothers or sisters or father or mother or
wife[b] or children or lands, for My name's sake, shall receive a hundredfold,
and inherit eternal life. 30 But many *who are* first will be last, and the last first.

The Parable of the Workers in the Vineyard

20 "For the kingdom of heaven is like a landowner who went out early
in the morning to hire laborers for his vineyard. 2 Now when he had
agreed with the laborers for a denarius a day, he sent them into his vineyard.
3 And he went out about the third hour and saw others standing idle in the
marketplace, 4 and said to them, 'You also go into the vineyard, and whatever is
right I will give you.' So they went. 5 Again he went out about the sixth and the
ninth hour, and did likewise. 6 And about the eleventh hour he went out and
found others standing idle,[c] and said to them, 'Why have you been standing
here idle all day?' 7 They said to him, 'Because no one hired us.' He said to them,
'You also go into the vineyard, and whatever is right you will receive.'[d]
8 "So when evening had come, the owner of the vineyard said to his steward, 'Call the laborers and give them *their* wages, beginning with the last to
the first.' 9 And when those came who *were hired* about the eleventh hour,
they each received a denarius. 10 But when the first came, they supposed

19:17 [w] NU-Text reads *Why do you ask Me about what is good?* [x] NU-Text reads *There is One who is good.*
19:19 [y] Exodus 20:12–16; Deuteronomy 5:16–20 [z] Leviticus 19:18
19:20 [a] NU-Text omits *from my youth.*
19:29 [b] NU-Text omits *or wife.*
20:6 [c] NU-Text omits *idle.*
20:7 [d] NU-Text omits the last clause of this verse.

that they would receive more; and they likewise received each a denarius. [11]And when they had received *it,* they complained against the landowner, [12]saying, 'These last *men* have worked *only* one hour, and you made them equal to us who have borne the burden and the heat of the day.' [13]But he answered one of them and said, 'Friend, I am doing you no wrong. Did you not agree with me for a denarius? [14]Take *what is* yours and go your way. I wish to give to this last man *the same* as to you. [15]Is it not lawful for me to do what I wish with my own things? Or is your eye evil because I am good?' [16]So the last will be first, and the first last. For many are called, but few chosen."[e]

Jesus a Third Time Predicts His Death and Resurrection

[17]Now Jesus, going up to Jerusalem, took the twelve disciples aside on the road and said to them, [18]"Behold, we are going up to Jerusalem, and the Son of Man will be betrayed to the chief priests and to the scribes; and they will condemn Him to death, [19]and deliver Him to the Gentiles to mock and to scourge and to crucify. And the third day He will rise again."

Greatness Is Serving

[20]Then the mother of Zebedee's sons came to Him with her sons, kneeling down and asking something from Him.

[21]And He said to her, "What do you wish?"

She said to Him, "Grant that these two sons of mine may sit, one on Your right hand and the other on the left, in Your kingdom."

[22]But Jesus answered and said, "You do not know what you ask. Are you able to drink the cup that I am about to drink, and be baptized with the baptism that I am baptized with?"[f]

They said to Him, "We are able."

[23]So He said to them, "You will indeed drink My cup, and be baptized with the baptism that I am baptized with;[g] but to sit on My right hand and on My left is not Mine to give, but *it is for those* for whom it is prepared by My Father."

[24]And when the ten heard *it,* they were greatly displeased with the two brothers. [25]But Jesus called them to *Himself* and said, "You know that the rulers of the Gentiles lord it over them, and those who are great exercise authority over them. [26]Yet it shall not be so among you; but whoever desires to become great among you, let him be your servant. [27]And whoever desires to be first among you, let him be your slave— [28]just as the Son of Man did not come to be served, but to serve, and to give His life a ransom for many."

Two Blind Men Receive Their Sight

[29]Now as they went out of Jericho, a great multitude followed Him. [30]And behold, two blind men sitting by the road, when they heard that Jesus was passing by, cried out, saying, "Have mercy on us, O Lord, Son of David!"

[31]Then the multitude warned them that they should be quiet; but they cried out all the more, saying, "Have mercy on us, O Lord, Son of David!"

[32]So Jesus stood still and called them, and said, "What do you want Me to do for you?"

20:16 [e]NU-Text omits the last sentence of this verse.
20:22 [f]NU-Text omits *and be baptized with the baptism that I am baptized with.*
20:23 [g]NU-Text omits *and be baptized with the baptism that I am baptized with.*

LIFE LESSON

Matthew 20:1-34

SITUATION Jesus traveled toward Jerusalem for the last time. He refuted the Jewish leaders' ideas that their heritage would ensure them membership in heaven. His disciples were also slow to learn and argued over kingdom status for themselves.

OBSERVATION Jesus emphasized that salvation depends on God's love, mercy, and kindness. No one deserves it.

INSPIRATION A certain landowner needs workers. At 6:00 A.M. he picks his crew, they agree on a wage, and he puts them to work. At 9:00 he is back at the unemployment agency and picks a few more. At noon he is back and at 3:00 in the afternoon he is back and at 5:00, you guessed it. He's back again.

Now, the punchline of the story is the anger the twelve-hour laborers felt when the other guys got the same wage. That's a great message, but we'll save it for another book.

I want to hone in on an often forgotten scene in the story: the choosing. Can you see it? It happened at 9:00. It happened at noon. It happened at 3:00. But most passionately, it happened at 5:00.

Five in the afternoon. Tell me. What is a worker still doing in the yard at 5:00 in the afternoon? The best have long since gone. The mediocre workers went at lunch. The last string went at 3:00. What kind of worker is left at 5:00 p.m.?

All day they get passed by. They are unskilled. Untrained. Uneducated. They are hanging with one hand from the bottom of the ladder. They are absolutely dependent upon a merciful boss giving them a chance they don't deserve.

So, by the way, were we. Lest we get a bit cocky, we might take Paul's advice and look at what we were when God called us. Do you remember?

Some of us were polished and sharp but papier-mâché thin. Others of us didn't even try to hide our despair. We drank it. We smelled it. We shot it. We sold it. Life was a passion-pursuit. We were on a treasure hunt for an empty chest in a dead-end canyon.

Continued

Do you remember how you felt? Do you remember the perspiration on your forehead and the crack in your soul? Do you remember how you tried to hide the loneliness until it got bigger than you and then you just tried to survive?

Hold that picture for a moment. Now answer this. Why did he choose you? Why did he choose me? Honestly. Why? What do we have that he needs?

Intellect? Do we honestly think for one minute that we have—or ever will have—a thought he hasn't had?

Willpower? I can respect that. Some of us are stubborn enough to walk on water if we feel called to do so . . . but to think God's kingdom would have done a belly-up without our determination?

How about money? We came into the kingdom with a nice little nest egg. Perhaps that's why we were chosen. Perhaps the creator of heaven and earth could use a little of our cash. Maybe the owner of every breath and every person and the author of history was getting low on capital and he saw us and our black ink and. . . .

Get the point?

We were chosen for the same reason the five o'clock workers were. You and me? We are the five o'clock workers. That's us leaning against the orchard fence sucking cigarettes we can't afford and betting beers we'll never buy on a game of penny-toss. Migrant workers with no jobs and no futures. The tattoo on your arm reads "Betty." The one on my biceps is nameless but her hips bounce when I flex. We should have given up and gone home after the lunch whistle but home is a one-bedroom motel with a wife whose first question will be, "Did you get on or not?"

So we wait. The too little, too lates.

33 They said to Him, "Lord, that our eyes may be opened." 34 So Jesus had
compassion and touched their eyes. And immediately their eyes received
sight, and they followed Him.

The Triumphal Entry

21 Now when they drew near Jerusalem, and came to Bethphage,[h] at
the Mount of Olives, then Jesus sent two disciples, 2 saying to them,
"Go into the village opposite you, and immediately you will find a donkey
tied, and a colt with her. Loose *them* and bring *them* to Me. 3 And if anyone
says anything to you, you shall say, 'The Lord has need of them,' and immediately he will send them."

4 All[i] this was done that it might be fulfilled which was spoken by the
prophet, saying:

5 *"Tell the daughter of Zion,*
'Behold, your King is coming to you,
Lowly, and sitting on a donkey,
A colt, the foal of a donkey.'"[j]

6 So the disciples went and did as Jesus commanded them. 7 They brought
the donkey and the colt, laid their clothes on them, and set *Him*[k] on them.
8 And a very great multitude spread their clothes on the road; others cut
down branches from the trees and spread *them* on the road. 9 Then the multitudes who went before and those who followed cried out, saying:

"Hosanna to the Son of David!
'Blessed is He who comes in the name of the LORD!'[l]
Hosanna in the highest!"

10 And when He had come into Jerusalem, all the city was moved, saying,
"Who is this?"

11 So the multitudes said, "This is Jesus, the prophet from Nazareth of Galilee."

Jesus Cleanses the Temple

12 Then Jesus went into the temple of God[m] and drove out all those who
bought and sold in the temple, and overturned the tables of the money
changers and the seats of those who sold doves. 13 And He said to them, "It
is written, *'My house shall be called a house of prayer,'*[n] but you have
made it a *'den of thieves.'*"[o]

14 Then *the* blind and *the* lame came to Him in the temple, and He healed
them. 15 But when the chief priests and scribes saw the wonderful things
that He did, and the children crying out in the temple and saying,
"Hosanna to the Son of David!" they were indignant 16 and said to Him,
"Do You hear what these are saying?"

And Jesus said to them, "Yes. Have you never read,

'Out of the mouth of babes and nursing infants
You have perfected praise'?"[p]

17 Then He left them and went out of the city to Bethany, and He lodged there.

21:1 [h] M-Text reads *Bethsphage.*
21:4 [i] NU-Text omits *All.*
21:5 [j] Zechariah 9:9
21:7 [k] NU-Text reads *and He sat.*
21:9 [l] Psalm 118:26
21:12 [m] NU-Text omits *of God.*
21:13 [n] Isaiah 56:7 [o] Jeremiah 7:11
21:16 [p] Psalm 8:2

The Fig Tree Withered

18Now in the morning, as He returned to the city, He was hungry. 19And seeing a fig tree by the road, He came to it and found nothing on it but leaves, and said to it, "Let no fruit grow on you ever again." Immediately the fig tree withered away.

The Lesson of the Withered Fig Tree

20And when the disciples saw *it,* they marveled, saying, "How did the fig tree wither away so soon?"

21So Jesus answered and said to them, "Assuredly, I say to you, if you have faith and do not doubt, you will not only do what was done to the fig tree, but also if you say to this mountain, 'Be removed and be cast into the sea,' it will be done. 22And whatever things you ask in prayer, believing, you will receive."

Jesus' Authority Questioned

23Now when He came into the temple, the chief priests and the elders of the people confronted Him as He was teaching, and said, "By what authority are You doing these things? And who gave You this authority?"

24But Jesus answered and said to them, "I also will ask you one thing, which if you tell Me, I likewise will tell you by what authority I do these things: 25The baptism of John—where was it from? From heaven or from men?"

And they reasoned among themselves, saying, "If we say, 'From heaven,' He will say to us, 'Why then did you not believe him?' 26But if we say, 'From men,' we fear the multitude, for all count John as a prophet." 27So they answered Jesus and said, "We do not know."

And He said to them, "Neither will I tell you by what authority I do these things.

The Parable of the Two Sons

28"But what do you think? A man had two sons, and he came to the first and said, 'Son, go, work today in my vineyard.' 29He answered and said, 'I will not,' but afterward he regretted it and went. 30Then he came to the second and said likewise. And he answered and said, 'I *go,* sir,' but he did not go. 31Which of the two did the will of *his* father?"

They said to Him, "The first."

Jesus said to them, "Assuredly, I say to you that tax collectors and harlots enter the kingdom of God before you. 32For John came to you in the way of righteousness, and you did not believe him; but tax collectors and harlots believed him; and when you saw *it,* you did not afterward relent and believe him.

The Parable of the Wicked Vinedressers

33"Hear another parable: There was a certain landowner who planted a vineyard and set a hedge around it, dug a winepress in it and built a tower. And he leased it to vinedressers and went into a far country. 34Now when vintage-time drew near, he sent his servants to the vinedressers, that they might receive its fruit. 35And the vinedressers took his servants, beat one, killed one, and stoned another. 36Again he sent other servants, more than the first, and they did likewise to them. 37Then last of all he sent his son to them, saying, 'They will respect my son.' 38But when the vinedressers saw the son, they said among themselves, 'This is the heir. Come, let us kill him

And Jesus? Well, Jesus is the guy in the black pickup who owns the hillside acreage. He's the fellow who noticed us as he drove by leaving us in his dust. He's the one who stopped the truck, put it in reverse, and backed up to where we were standing.

He's the one you'll tell your wife about tonight as you walk to the grocery with a jingle in your pocket. "I'd never seen this guy before. He just stopped, rolled down his window, and asked us if we wanted to work. It was already near quitting time, but he said he had some work that wouldn't wait. I swear, Martha, I only worked one hour and he paid me for the full day."

"No, I don't know his name."

"Of course, I'm gonna find out. Too good to be true, that guy."

Why did he pick you? He wanted to. After all, you are his. He made you. He brought you home. He owns you. And once upon a time, he tapped you on the shoulder and reminded you of that fact. No matter how long you'd waited or how much time you'd wasted, you are his and he has a place for you.

(From *And the Angels Were Silent* by Max Lucado)

APPLICATION If you are a Christian ask yourself, "What are my special skills or abilities?" List your answers: administration, technical work, or cooking. Now that God has brought you to work in his Kingdom, how can you use these gifts for him?

EXPLORATION Kingdom Citizens—Matthew 7:13-23; 21:28-32; James 2:5; 1 Corinthians 4:20; 2 Peter 1:5-11.

LIFE LESSON

Matthew 21:1-46

SITUATION A week after Jesus entered Jerusalem as a king, the Jews killed him. Jesus' dynamic entrance into Jerusalem fulfilled prophecy (Zechariah 9:9), affirmed his messianic royalty, and set the stage for his crucifixion.

OBSERVATION During this last week, Jesus taught about faithful workers in the Kingdom of God. He encouraged all to work faithfully without procrastinating.

INSPIRATION As the husband looks in the jewelry case, he rationalizes, "Sure she would want the watch, but it's too expensive. She's a practical woman, she'll understand. I'll just get the bracelet today. I'll buy the watch . . . someday."

Someday. The enemy of risky love is a snake whose tongue has mastered the talk of deception. "Someday," he hisses.

"Someday, I can take her on the cruise."

"Someday, I will have time to call and chat."

"Someday, the children will understand why I was so busy."

But you know the truth, don't you? You know even before I write it. You could say it better than I.
Some days never come.

And the price of practicality is sometimes higher than extravagance.

But the rewards of risky love are always greater than its cost.

Go to the effort. Invest the time. Write the letter. Make the apology. Take the trip. Purchase the gift. Do it. The seized opportunity renders joy. The neglected brings regret.

(From *And the Angels Were Silent* by Max Lucado)

APPLICATION If you died today, would you be happy with the level of service you have given to God's Kingdom? If not, plan to be more involved in serving others.

EXPLORATION Jesus the King—Psalm 118; Zechariah 9:9; Luke 19:28-44; Ephesians 1:19-23; Colossians 1:17-18; 2:10; Philippians 2:5-11; Revelation 4:9–5:14.

and seize his inheritance.' [39]So they took him and cast *him* out of the vineyard
and killed *him.*
[40]"Therefore, when the owner of the vineyard comes, what will he do to
those vinedressers?"
[41]They said to Him, "He will destroy those wicked men miserably, and lease *his*
vineyard to other vinedressers who will render to him the fruits in their seasons."
[42]Jesus said to them, "Have you never read in the Scriptures:

'The stone which the builders rejected
Has become the chief cornerstone.
This was the LORD*'s doing,*
And it is marvelous in our eyes' ?[q]

[43]"Therefore I say to you, the kingdom of God will be taken from you
and given to a nation bearing the fruits of it. [44]And whoever falls on this
stone will be broken; but on whomever it falls, it will grind him to powder."
[45]Now when the chief priests and Pharisees heard His parables, they perceived that He was speaking of them. [46]But when they sought to lay hands on
Him, they feared the multitudes, because they took Him for a prophet.

The Parable of the Wedding Feast

22 And Jesus answered and spoke to them again by parables and said:
[2]"The kingdom of heaven is like a certain king who arranged a marriage for his son, [3]and sent out his servants to call those who were invited
to the wedding; and they were not willing to come. [4]Again, he sent out
other servants, saying, 'Tell those who are invited, "See, I have prepared
my dinner; my oxen and fatted cattle *are* killed, and all things *are* ready.
Come to the wedding." ' [5]But they made light of it and went their ways, one
to his own farm, another to his business. [6]And the rest seized his servants,
treated *them* spitefully, and killed *them.* [7]But when the king heard *about it,*
he was furious. And he sent out his armies, destroyed those murderers,
and burned up their city. [8]Then he said to his servants, 'The wedding is
ready, but those who were invited were not worthy. [9]Therefore go into the
highways, and as many as you find, invite to the wedding.' [10]So those servants went out into the highways and gathered together all whom they
found, both bad and good. And the wedding *hall* was filled with guests.
[11]"But when the king came in to see the guests, he saw a man there who did
not have on a wedding garment. [12]So he said to him, 'Friend, how did you
come in here without a wedding garment?' And he was speechless. [13]Then
the king said to the servants, 'Bind him hand and foot, take him away, and[r]
cast *him* into outer darkness; there will be weeping and gnashing of teeth.'
[14]"For many are called, but few *are* chosen."

The Pharisees: Is It Lawful to Pay Taxes to Caesar?

[15]Then the Pharisees went and plotted how they might entangle Him in
His talk. [16]And they sent to Him their disciples with the Herodians, saying,
"Teacher, we know that You are true, and teach the way of God in truth; nor
do You care about anyone, for You do not regard the person of men. [17]Tell
us, therefore, what do You think? Is it lawful to pay taxes to Caesar, or not?"
[18]But Jesus perceived their wickedness, and said, "Why do you test Me,
you hypocrites? [19]Show Me the tax money."

21:42 [q] Psalm 118:22, 23
22:13 [r] NU-Text omits *take him away, and.*

So they brought Him a denarius.
20And He said to them, "Whose image and inscription *is* this?"
21They said to Him, "Caesar's."
And He said to them, "Render therefore to Caesar the things that are Caesar's, and to God the things that are God's." 22When they had heard *these words,* they marveled, and left Him and went their way.

The Sadducees: What About the Resurrection?

23The same day the Sadducees, who say there is no resurrection, came to Him and asked Him, 24saying: "Teacher, Moses said that if a man dies, having no children, his brother shall marry his wife and raise up offspring for his brother. 25Now there were with us seven brothers. The first died after he had married, and having no offspring, left his wife to his brother. 26Likewise the second also, and the third, even to the seventh. 27Last of all the woman died also. 28Therefore, in the resurrection, whose wife of the seven will she be? For they all had her."

29Jesus answered and said to them, "You are mistaken, not knowing the Scriptures nor the power of God. 30For in the resurrection they neither marry nor are given in marriage, but are like angels of God[s] in heaven. 31But concerning the resurrection of the dead, have you not read what was spoken to you by God, saying, 32'*I am the God of Abraham, the God of Isaac, and the God of Jacob*'?[t] God is not the God of the dead, but of the living." 33And when the multitudes heard *this,* they were astonished at His teaching.

The Scribes: Which Is the First Commandment of All?

34But when the Pharisees heard that He had silenced the Sadducees, they gathered together. 35Then one of them, a lawyer, asked *Him a question,* testing Him, and saying, 36"Teacher, which *is* the great commandment in the law?"

37Jesus said to him, "'*You shall love the* LORD *your God with all your heart, with all your soul, and with all your mind.*'[u] 38This is *the* first and great commandment. 39And *the* second *is* like it: '*You shall love your neighbor as yourself.*'[v] 40On these two commandments hang all the Law and the Prophets."

Jesus: How Can David Call His Descendant Lord?

41While the Pharisees were gathered together, Jesus asked them, 42saying, "What do you think about the Christ? Whose Son is He?"
They said to Him, "*The Son* of David."
43He said to them, "How then does David in the Spirit call Him '*Lord,*' saying:

44 '*The* LORD *said to my Lord,*
"*Sit at My right hand,*
Till I make Your enemies Your footstool"'?[w]

45If David then calls Him '*Lord,*' how is He his Son?" 46And no one was able to answer Him a word, nor from that day on did anyone dare question Him anymore.

22:30 [s] NU-Text omits *of God.*
22:32 [t] Exodus 3:6, 15
22:37 [u] Deuteronomy 6:5
22:39 [v] Leviticus 19:18
22:44 [w] Psalm 110:1

LIFE LESSON

Matthew 22:1-46

SITUATION Three Jewish factions confronted Jesus. The Pharisees opposed Roman occupation of Palestine. The Herodians supported Herod Antipas and Roman policies. The Sadducees did not believe in the resurrection, because they could not find it directly taught in the books of the Law.

OBSERVATION Jesus continued to show that God's Word was superior to the Jewish leaders' human reasoning.

INSPIRATION No doubt you've had your share of words that wound. You've felt the sting of a well-aimed gibe. Maybe you're still feeling it. Someone you love or respect slams you to the floor with a slur or slip of the tongue. And there you lie, wounded and bleeding. Perhaps the words were intended to hurt you, perhaps not; but that doesn't matter. The wound is deep. The injuries are internal. Broken heart, wounded pride, bruised feelings. Or maybe your wound is old. . . . The old pain flares unpredictably and decisively, reminding you of harsh words yet unforgiven. If you have suffered or are suffering because of someone else's words, you'll be glad to know there is a balm for this laceration. . . .

Did you see what Jesus did not do? He did not retaliate. He did not bite back. He did not say, "I'll get you!" . . . . He left the judging to God. He did not take on the task of seeking revenge. He demanded no apology. He hired no bounty hunters and sent out no posse. . . . If ever a person deserved a shot at revenge, Jesus did. But he didn't take it. Instead he died for them. How could he do it? I don't know. But I do know that all of a sudden my wounds seem very painless. My grudges and hard feelings are suddenly childish.

(From *No Wonder They Call Him the Savior* by Max Lucado)

Continued

APPLICATION When someone challenges your integrity, disregards your opinion, and ignores your work, how do you respond? Do you lose your temper, hold a grudge, or put the person down? Next time you face criticism, consider how Jesus carefully chose his words and used Scripture to answer his opponents.

EXPLORATION Jesus' Wisdom—Matthew 11:27; John 2:24-25; Acts 1:24; 1 Corinthians 4-5; Revelation 2:19.

Woe to the Scribes and Pharisees

23 Then Jesus spoke to the multitudes and to His disciples, 2saying: "The scribes and the Pharisees sit in Moses' seat. 3Therefore whatever they tell you to observe,[x] *that* observe and do, but do not do according to their works; for they say, and do not do. 4For they bind heavy burdens, hard to bear, and lay *them* on men's shoulders; but they *themselves* will not move them with one of their fingers. 5But all their works they do to be seen by men. They make their phylacteries broad and enlarge the borders of their garments. 6They love the best places at feasts, the best seats in the synagogues, 7greetings in the marketplaces, and to be called by men, 'Rabbi, Rabbi.' 8But you, do not be called 'Rabbi'; for One is your Teacher, the Christ,[y] and you are all brethren. 9Do not call anyone on earth your father; for One is your Father, He who is in heaven. 10And do not be called teachers; for One is your Teacher, the Christ. 11But he who is greatest among you shall be your servant. 12And whoever exalts himself will be humbled, and he who humbles himself will be exalted.

13"But woe to you, scribes and Pharisees, hypocrites! For you shut up the kingdom of heaven against men; for you neither go in *yourselves,* nor do you allow those who are entering to go in. 14Woe to you, scribes and Pharisees, hypocrites! For you devour widows' houses, and for a pretense make long prayers. Therefore you will receive greater condemnation.[z]

15"Woe to you, scribes and Pharisees, hypocrites! For you travel land and sea to win one proselyte, and when he is won, you make him twice as much a son of hell as yourselves.

16"Woe to you, blind guides, who say, 'Whoever swears by the temple, it is nothing; but whoever swears by the gold of the temple, he is obliged *to perform it.*' 17Fools and blind! For which is greater, the gold or the temple that sanctifies[a] the gold? 18And, 'Whoever swears by the altar, it is nothing; but whoever swears by the gift that is on it, he is obliged *to perform it.*' 19Fools and blind! For which is greater, the gift or the altar that sanctifies the gift? 20Therefore he who swears by the altar, swears by it and by all things on it. 21He who swears by the temple, swears by it and by Him who dwells[b] in it. 22And he who swears by heaven, swears by the throne of God and by Him who sits on it.

23"Woe to you, scribes and Pharisees, hypocrites! For you pay tithe of mint and anise and cummin, and have neglected the weightier *matters* of the law: justice and mercy and faith. These you ought to have done, without leaving the others undone. 24Blind guides, who strain out a gnat and swallow a camel!

25"Woe to you, scribes and Pharisees, hypocrites! For you cleanse the outside of the cup and dish, but inside they are full of extortion and self-indulgence.[c] 26Blind Pharisee, first cleanse the inside of the cup and dish, that the outside of them may be clean also.

27"Woe to you, scribes and Pharisees, hypocrites! For you are like whitewashed tombs which indeed appear beautiful outwardly, but inside are full of dead *men's* bones and all uncleanness. 28Even so you also outwardly appear righteous to men, but inside you are full of hypocrisy and lawlessness.

23:3 [x] NU-Text omits *to observe.*
23:8 [y] NU-Text omits *the Christ.*
23:14 [z] NU-Text omits this verse.
23:17 [a] NU-Text reads *sanctified.*
23:21 [b] M-Text reads *dwelt.*
23:25 [c] M-Text reads *unrighteousness.*

29“Woe to you, scribes and Pharisees, hypocrites! Because you build the
tombs of the prophets and adorn the monuments of the righteous, 30and
say, ‘If we had lived in the days of our fathers, we would not have been partakers with them in the blood of the prophets.’
31“Therefore you are witnesses against yourselves that you are sons of
those who murdered the prophets. 32Fill up, then, the measure of your fathers’ *guilt.* 33Serpents, brood of vipers! How can you escape the
condemnation of hell? 34Therefore, indeed, I send you prophets, wise men,
and scribes: *some* of them you will kill and crucify, and *some* of them you
will scourge in your synagogues and persecute from city to city, 35that on
you may come all the righteous blood shed on the earth, from the blood of
righteous Abel to the blood of Zechariah, son of Berechiah, whom you
murdered between the temple and the altar. 36Assuredly, I say to you, all
these things will come upon this generation.

Jesus Laments over Jerusalem

37“O Jerusalem, Jerusalem, the one who kills the prophets and stones
those who are sent to her! How often I wanted to gather your children together, as a hen gathers her chicks under *her* wings, but you were not willing!
38See! Your house is left to you desolate; 39for I say to you, you shall see Me no
more till you say, *‘Blessed is He who comes in the name of the LORD!’* ”[d]

Jesus Predicts the Destruction of the Temple

24 Then Jesus went out and departed from the temple, and His disciples came up to show Him the buildings of the temple. 2And Jesus
said to them, “Do you not see all these things? Assuredly, I say to you, not
one stone shall be left here upon another, that shall not be thrown down.”

The Signs of the Times and the End of the Age

3Now as He sat on the Mount of Olives, the disciples came to Him privately, saying, “Tell us, when will these things be? And what *will be* the sign
of Your coming, and of the end of the age?”
4And Jesus answered and said to them: “Take heed that no one deceives
you. 5For many will come in My name, saying, ‘I am the Christ,’ and will
deceive many. 6And you will hear of wars and rumors of wars. See that you
are not troubled; for all[e] *these things* must come to pass, but the end is not
yet. 7For nation will rise against nation, and kingdom against kingdom.
And there will be famines, pestilences,[f] and earthquakes in various places.
8All these *are* the beginning of sorrows.
9“Then they will deliver you up to tribulation and kill you, and you will
be hated by all nations for My name’s sake. 10And then many will be offended, will betray one another, and will hate one another. 11Then many
false prophets will rise up and deceive many. 12And because lawlessness
will abound, the love of many will grow cold. 13But he who endures to the
end shall be saved. 14And this gospel of the kingdom will be preached in all
the world as a witness to all the nations, and then the end will come.

23:39 [d] Psalm 118:26
24:6 [e] NU-Text omits *all.*
24:7 [f] NU-Text omits *pestilences.*

LIFE LESSON

Matthew 23:1-39

SITUATION Human rules, practices, and interpretations became more important than God’s Law; Jesus condemned the Pharisees as hypocrites.

OBSERVATION God hates religious hypocrisy.

INSPIRATION Consider for a moment a few brief epithets that Jesus reserved for the Pharisees: “You snakes!” “You brood of vipers!” “Blind guides!” “Children of hell!” “Blind fools!” These forms of address can hardly be considered compliments. Jesus spared no invectives in his denunciations of these men. His words were uncharacteristically harsh, though not unjustifiably harsh. They were different from His usual style. The normal form of rebuke He made to sinners was gentle. He spoke tenderly, though firmly to the woman caught in adultery, and to the woman at the well. It seems that Jesus saved his severe comments for the big boys, the theological professionals. With them he asked no quarter and gave none.

It has been said that nothing dispels a lie faster than the truth; nothing exposes the counterfeit faster than the genuine. Clever counterfeit dollars may be unnoticed by the untrained eye. What every counterfeiter fears is that someone will examine his bogus bill while holding a genuine one next to it. The presence of Jesus represented the presence of the genuine in the midst of the bogus. Here authentic holiness appeared.

(From *The Holiness of God* by R.C. Sproul)

APPLICATION Do you practice what you preach? Or do people snicker when you announce a new set of resolutions? Pray for strength to live what you claim to believe.

EXPLORATION Hypocrisy—Isaiah 29:13; Ezekiel 33:30-32; Malachi 1:6-14; Matthew 16:5-12; Romans 2:17-24; Titus 1:16.

LIFE LESSON

Matthew 24:1-51

SITUATION Jesus prophesied about the second coming. He delivered this teaching from the Mount of Olives, where the prophet Zechariah predicted that the Messiah would stand when he came to establish his Kingdom.

OBSERVATION Christians need to be watchful and prepare for Jesus' return, because we don't know when it will be.

INSPIRATION If you lose your faith, you will probably do so gradually. In tiny increments you will get spiritually sloppy. You will let a few days slip by without consulting your compass. Your sails will go untrimmed. Your rigging will go unprepared. And worst of all, you will forget to anchor your boat. And, before you know it, you'll be bouncing from wave to wave in stormy seas. . . .

Stability in the storm comes not from seeking a new message, but from understanding an old one. The most reliable anchor points are not recent discoveries, but are time-tested truths that have held their ground against the winds of change. . . .

Attach your soul to these boulders and no wave is big enough to wash you under.

(From *Six Hours One Friday* by Max Lucado)

APPLICATION How faithfully do you pray, read the Bible, attend church? Are prayer and Bible study regular parts of your life, or do you just resort to them in emergency situations? Ask God to help you be more faithful in anchoring your life in Jesus, even when there are no storms on the horizon.

EXPLORATION Jesus' Return—Mark 13:1-23; Luke 21:5-24; Acts 1:10-12; 1 Corinthians 15:50-57; 2 Timothy 3:1-5; 2 Thessalonians 2:1-10; Revelation 19.

The Great Tribulation

15“Therefore when you see the ‘*abomination of desolation*,’[g] spoken of
by Daniel the prophet, standing in the holy place” (whoever reads, let him
understand), 16“then let those who are in Judea flee to the mountains. 17Let
him who is on the housetop not go down to take anything out of his house.
18And let him who is in the field not go back to get his clothes. 19But woe to
those who are pregnant and to those who are nursing babies in those
days! 20And pray that your flight may not be in winter or on the Sabbath.
21For then there will be great tribulation, such as has not been since the beginning of the world until this time, no, nor ever shall be. 22And unless
those days were shortened, no flesh would be saved; but for the elect's
sake those days will be shortened.

23“Then if anyone says to you, ‘Look, here *is* the Christ!’ or ‘There!’ do
not believe *it*. 24For false christs and false prophets will rise and show great
signs and wonders to deceive, if possible, even the elect. 25See, I have told
you beforehand.

26“Therefore if they say to you, ‘Look, He is in the desert!’ do not go out; *or*
‘Look, *He is* in the inner rooms!’ do not believe *it*. 27For as the lightning comes
from the east and flashes to the west, so also will the coming of the Son of Man
be. 28For wherever the carcass is, there the eagles will be gathered together.

The Coming of the Son of Man

29“Immediately after the tribulation of those days the sun will be darkened, and the moon will not give its light; the stars will fall from heaven,
and the powers of the heavens will be shaken. 30Then the sign of the Son of
Man will appear in heaven, and then all the tribes of the earth will mourn,
and they will see the Son of Man coming on the clouds of heaven with
power and great glory. 31And He will send His angels with a great sound of
a trumpet, and they will gather together His elect from the four winds,
from one end of heaven to the other.

The Parable of the Fig Tree

32“Now learn this parable from the fig tree: When its branch has already
become tender and puts forth leaves, you know that summer *is* near. 33So
you also, when you see all these things, know that it[h] is near—at the doors!
34Assuredly, I say to you, this generation will by no means pass away till all
these things take place. 35Heaven and earth will pass away, but My words
will by no means pass away.

No One Knows the Day or Hour

36“But of that day and hour no one knows, not even the angels of
heaven,[i] but My Father only. 37But as the days of Noah *were*, so also will the
coming of the Son of Man be. 38For as in the days before the flood, they
were eating and drinking, marrying and giving in marriage, until the day
that Noah entered the ark, 39and did not know until the flood came and
took them all away, so also will the coming of the Son of Man be. 40Then two
men will be in the field: one will be taken and the other left. 41Two *women will
be* grinding at the mill: one will be taken and the other left. 42Watch therefore,

24:15 [g] Daniel 11:31; 12:11
24:33 [h] Or *He*
24:36 [i] NU-Text adds *nor the Son*.

for you do not know what hour[j] your Lord is coming. 43But know this, that if
the master of the house had known what hour the thief would come, he
would have watched and not allowed his house to be broken into. 44Therefore
you also be ready, for the Son of Man is coming at an hour you do not expect.

The Faithful Servant and the Evil Servant

45"Who then is a faithful and wise servant, whom his master made ruler
over his household, to give them food in due season? 46Blessed *is* that servant whom his master, when he comes, will find so doing. 47Assuredly, I
say to you that he will make him ruler over all his goods. 48But if that evil
servant says in his heart, 'My master is delaying his coming,'[k] 49and begins to
beat *his* fellow servants, and to eat and drink with the drunkards, 50the master of that servant will come on a day when he is not looking for *him* and at an
hour that he is not aware of, 51and will cut him in two and appoint *him* his
portion with the hypocrites. There shall be weeping and gnashing of teeth.

The Parable of the Wise and Foolish Virgins

25 "Then the kingdom of heaven shall be likened to ten virgins who took
their lamps and went out to meet the bridegroom. 2Now five of them
were wise, and five *were* foolish. 3Those who *were* foolish took their lamps
and took no oil with them, 4but the wise took oil in their vessels with their
lamps. 5But while the bridegroom was delayed, they all slumbered and slept.
6"And at midnight a cry was *heard:* 'Behold, the bridegroom is coming;[l]
go out to meet him!' 7Then all those virgins arose and trimmed their
lamps. 8And the foolish said to the wise, 'Give us *some* of your oil, for our
lamps are going out.' 9But the wise answered, saying, '*No,* lest there should
not be enough for us and you; but go rather to those who sell, and buy for
yourselves.' 10And while they went to buy, the bridegroom came, and those
who were ready went in with him to the wedding; and the door was shut.
11"Afterward the other virgins came also, saying, 'Lord, Lord, open to us!'
12But he answered and said, 'Assuredly, I say to you, I do not know you.'
13"Watch therefore, for you know neither the day nor the hour[m] in which
the Son of Man is coming.

The Parable of the Talents

14"For *the kingdom of heaven is* like a man traveling to a far country, *who*
called his own servants and delivered his goods to them. 15And to one he
gave five talents, to another two, and to another one, to each according to
his own ability; and immediately he went on a journey. 16Then he who had
received the five talents went and traded with them, and made another
five talents. 17And likewise he who *had received* two gained two more also.
18But he who had received one went and dug in the ground, and hid his
lord's money. 19After a long time the lord of those servants came and settled accounts with them.
20"So he who had received five talents came and brought five other talents, saying, 'Lord, you delivered to me five talents; look, I have gained
five more talents besides them.' 21His lord said to him, 'Well *done,* good

Life Lesson

Matthew 25:1-46

SITUATION Jesus used parables to teach his disciples to be ready for his return.

OBSERVATION Jesus wants his followers to be busy in service and in sharing the good news right up until the day of his return. Watchfulness and active service go hand in hand.

INSPIRATION I don't have to be afraid of Judgment Day because all my sins are forgiven and forgotten. They are blotted out and remembered no more. . . . All the things in my life that are rotten and filthy, and all the things that are so shameful that I have never dared to share them with anyone, will be erased from my records. In place of all that garbage will be recorded all the magnificent things that Jesus did. . . .

The joy that comes from thinking about glory is a joy available to all who have surrendered their lives to Christ. All they have to do is just stop and *reflect* on it all from time to time.

(From *Who Switched the Price Tags?* by Tony Campolo)

APPLICATION Do you know the joy of being forgiven? If not, come to Jesus and lay your past as well as your future in his hands. Take comfort in knowing that no matter what the circumstances, Christ remains within you.

EXPLORATION Faithfulness to the End—Luke 12:35-40; 1 Timothy 6:12-14; Titus 2:11-13; James 5:7-9; 1 Peter 1:13-15.

24:42 *j* NU-Text reads *day.*
24:48 *k* NU-Text omits *his coming.*
25:6 *l* NU-Text omits *is coming.*
25:13 *m* NU-Text omits the rest of this verse.

and faithful servant; you were faithful over a few things, I will make you ruler over many things. Enter into the joy of your lord.' 22He also who had received two talents came and said, 'Lord, you delivered to me two talents; look, I have gained two more talents besides them.' 23His lord said to him, 'Well *done,* good and faithful servant; you have been faithful over a few things, I will make you ruler over many things. Enter into the joy of your lord.'

24"Then he who had received the one talent came and said, 'Lord, I knew you to be a hard man, reaping where you have not sown, and gathering where you have not scattered seed. 25And I was afraid, and went and hid your talent in the ground. Look, *there* you have *what is* yours.'

26"But his lord answered and said to him, 'You wicked and lazy servant, you knew that I reap where I have not sown, and gather where I have not scattered seed. 27So you ought to have deposited my money with the bankers, and at my coming I would have received back my own with interest. 28So take the talent from him, and give *it* to him who has ten talents.

29'For to everyone who has, more will be given, and he will have abundance; but from him who does not have, even what he has will be taken away. 30And cast the unprofitable servant into the outer darkness. There will be weeping and gnashing of teeth.'

The Son of Man Will Judge the Nations

31"When the Son of Man comes in His glory, and all the holy[n] angels with Him, then He will sit on the throne of His glory. 32All the nations will be gathered before Him, and He will separate them one from another, as a shepherd divides *his* sheep from the goats. 33And He will set the sheep on His right hand, but the goats on the left. 34Then the King will say to those on His right hand, 'Come, you blessed of My Father, inherit the kingdom prepared for you from the foundation of the world: 35for I was hungry and you gave Me food; I was thirsty and you gave Me drink; I was a stranger and you took Me in; 36I *was* naked and you clothed Me; I was sick and you visited Me; I was in prison and you came to Me.'

37"Then the righteous will answer Him, saying, 'Lord, when did we see You hungry and feed *You,* or thirsty and give *You* drink? 38When did we see You a stranger and take *You* in, or naked and clothe *You?* 39Or when did we see You sick, or in prison, and come to You?' 40And the King will answer and say to them, 'Assuredly, I say to you, inasmuch as you did *it* to one of the least of these My brethren, you did *it* to Me.'

41"Then He will also say to those on the left hand, 'Depart from Me, you cursed, into the everlasting fire prepared for the devil and his angels: 42for I was hungry and you gave Me no food; I was thirsty and you gave Me no drink; 43I was a stranger and you did not take Me in, naked and you did not clothe Me, sick and in prison and you did not visit Me.'

44"Then they also will answer Him,[o] saying, 'Lord, when did we see You hungry or thirsty or a stranger or naked or sick or in prison, and did not minister to You?' 45Then He will answer them, saying, 'Assuredly, I say to you, inasmuch as you did not do *it* to one of the least of these, you did not do *it* to Me.' 46And these will go away into everlasting punishment, but the righteous into eternal life."

The Plot to Kill Jesus

26 Now it came to pass, when Jesus had finished all these sayings, *that* He said to His disciples, 2"You know that after two days is the Passover, and the Son of Man will be delivered up to be crucified."

3Then the chief priests, the scribes,[p] and the elders of the people assembled at the palace of the high priest, who was called Caiaphas, 4and plotted to take Jesus by trickery and kill *Him.* 5But they said, "Not during the feast, lest there be an uproar among the people."

The Anointing at Bethany

6And when Jesus was in Bethany at the house of Simon the leper, 7a woman came to Him having an alabaster flask of very costly fragrant oil, and she poured *it* on His head as He sat *at the table.* 8But when His disciples saw *it,* they were indignant, saying, "Why this waste? 9For this fragrant oil might have been sold for much and given to *the* poor."

10But when Jesus was aware of *it,* He said to them, "Why do you trouble the woman? For she has done a good work for Me. 11For you have the poor with you always, but Me you do not have always. 12For in pouring this fragrant oil on My body, she did *it* for My burial. 13Assuredly, I say to you, wherever this gospel is preached in the whole world, what this woman has done will also be told as a memorial to her."

Judas Agrees to Betray Jesus

14Then one of the twelve, called Judas Iscariot, went to the chief priests 15and said, "What are you willing

25:31 [n] NU-Text omits *holy.*
25:44 [o] NU-Text and M-Text omit *Him.*
26:3 [p] NU-Text omits *the scribes.*

to give me if I deliver Him to you?" And they counted out to him thirty
pieces of silver. 16So from that time he sought opportunity to betray Him.

Jesus Celebrates Passover with His Disciples

17Now on the first *day of the Feast* of the Unleavened Bread the disciples
came to Jesus, saying to Him, "Where do You want us to prepare for You to
eat the Passover?"
18And He said, "Go into the city to a certain man, and say to him, 'The
Teacher says, "My time is at hand; I will keep the Passover at your house
with My disciples." ' "
19So the disciples did as Jesus had directed them; and they prepared the
Passover.
20When evening had come, He sat down with the twelve. 21Now as they
were eating, He said, "Assuredly, I say to you, one of you will betray Me."
22And they were exceedingly sorrowful, and each of them began to say
to Him, "Lord, is it I?"
23He answered and said, "He who dipped *his* hand with Me in the dish
will betray Me. 24The Son of Man indeed goes just as it is written of Him,
but woe to that man by whom the Son of Man is betrayed! It would have
been good for that man if he had not been born."
25Then Judas, who was betraying Him, answered and said, "Rabbi, is it I?"
He said to him, "You have said it."

Jesus Institutes the Lord's Supper

26And as they were eating, Jesus took bread, blessed[q] and broke *it,* and
gave *it* to the disciples and said, "Take, eat; this is My body."
27Then He took the cup, and gave thanks, and gave *it* to them, saying,
"Drink from it, all of you. 28For this is My blood of the new[r] covenant,
which is shed for many for the remission of sins. 29But I say to you, I will
not drink of this fruit of the vine from now on until that day when I drink
it new with you in My Father's kingdom."
30And when they had sung a hymn, they went out to the Mount
of Olives.

Jesus Predicts Peter's Denial

31Then Jesus said to them, "All of you will be made to stumble because
of Me this night, for it is written:

'I will strike the Shepherd,
And the sheep of the flock will be scattered.'[s]

32But after I have been raised, I will go before you to Galilee."
33Peter answered and said to Him, "Even if all are made to stumble because of You, I will never be made to stumble."
34Jesus said to him, "Assuredly, I say to you that this night, before the
rooster crows, you will deny Me three times."
35Peter said to Him, "Even if I have to die with You, I will not deny You!"
And so said all the disciples.

26:26 [q] M-Text reads *gave thanks for.*
26:28 [r] NU-Text omits *new.*
26:31 [s] Zechariah 13:7

Life Lesson

Matthew 26:1-75

SITUATION Jesus looked toward the Passover and his death. He prepared his disciples by teaching them and spending time alone in prayer.

OBSERVATION Jesus willingly obeyed God during the events leading up to his death. This obedience made salvation possible.

INSPIRATION Consider the holiness of Christ. We need this first of all *to be firmly grounded in our security in Christ.* . . . It is important therefore that we understand the righteousness of Christ, and the fact that His righteousness is credited to us.

On numerous occasions the Scriptures testify that Jesus during His time on earth lived a perfectly holy life. . . .

But the holiness of Jesus was more than simply the absence of actual sin. It was also a perfect conformity to the will of His Father. . . .

It is possible to do the right action from the wrong motive, but this does not please God. Holiness has to do with more than mere acts. Our motives must be holy, that is, arising from a desire to do something simply because it is the will of God. . . .

Consider the holiness of Christ, because His life is meant to be an example of holiness for us. . . .

Consider then His statement, "I always do what pleases Him." Do we dare take that as our personal goal in life? Are we truly willing to scrutinize all our activities, our goals and plans, and all of our impulsive actions in the light of this statement: "I am doing this to please God"? . . .

This is the example we are to follow. In all of our thoughts, all of our actions, in every part of our character, the ruling principle that motivates and guides us should be the desire to follow Christ in doing the will of the Father. This is the high road we must follow in the pursuit of holiness.

(From *The Pursuit of Holiness* by Jerry Bridges)

Continued

APPLICATION Do you really want to follow Christ's example by doing the will of the Father? Are you ready and willing to submit your plans, thoughts, and behavior to him? If submitting is difficult for you in a particular area, pray specifically that God will help you.

EXPLORATION Loyalty and Obedience—Joshua 22:2-5; Psalm 119:33-37; John 21:15-17; Philippians 4:3; 1 Peter 1:14-16.

The Prayer in the Garden

[36]Then Jesus came with them to a place called Gethsemane, and said to
the disciples, "Sit here while I go and pray over there." [37]And He took with
Him Peter and the two sons of Zebedee, and He began to be sorrowful and
deeply distressed. [38]Then He said to them, "My soul is exceedingly sorrowful, even to death. Stay here and watch with Me."

[39]He went a little farther and fell on His face, and prayed, saying, "O My
Father, if it is possible, let this cup pass from Me; nevertheless, not as I will,
but as You *will*."

[40]Then He came to the disciples and found them sleeping, and said to
Peter, "What! Could you not watch with Me one hour? [41]Watch and pray, lest
you enter into temptation. The spirit indeed *is* willing, but the flesh *is* weak."

[42]Again, a second time, He went away and prayed, saying, "O My Father,
if this cup cannot pass away from Me unless[t] I drink it, Your will be done."
[43]And He came and found them asleep again, for their eyes were heavy.

[44]So He left them, went away again, and prayed the third time, saying
the same words. [45]Then He came to His disciples and said to them, "Are
you still sleeping and resting? Behold, the hour is at hand, and the Son of
Man is being betrayed into the hands of sinners. [46]Rise, let us be going.
See, My betrayer is at hand."

Betrayal and Arrest in Gethsemane

[47]And while He was still speaking, behold, Judas, one of the twelve, with
a great multitude with swords and clubs, came from the chief priests and
elders of the people.

[48]Now His betrayer had given them a sign, saying, "Whomever I kiss,
He is the One; seize Him." [49]Immediately he went up to Jesus and said,
"Greetings, Rabbi!" and kissed Him.

[50]But Jesus said to him, "Friend, why have you come?"

Then they came and laid hands on Jesus and took Him. [51]And suddenly,
one of those *who were* with Jesus stretched out *his* hand and drew his
sword, struck the servant of the high priest, and cut off his ear.

[52]But Jesus said to him, "Put your sword in its place, for all who take the
sword will perish[u] by the sword. [53]Or do you think that I cannot now pray to
My Father, and He will provide Me with more than twelve legions of angels?
[54]How then could the Scriptures be fulfilled, that it must happen thus?"

[55]In that hour Jesus said to the multitudes, "Have you come out, as
against a robber, with swords and clubs to take Me? I sat daily with you,
teaching in the temple, and you did not seize Me. [56]But all this was done
that the Scriptures of the prophets might be fulfilled."

Then all the disciples forsook Him and fled.

Jesus Faces the Sanhedrin

[57]And those who had laid hold of Jesus led *Him* away to Caiaphas the
high priest, where the scribes and the elders were assembled. [58]But Peter
followed Him at a distance to the high priest's courtyard. And he went in
and sat with the servants to see the end.

[59]Now the chief priests, the elders,[v] and all the council sought false testimony against Jesus to put Him to death, [60]but found none. Even though

26:42 [t] NU-Text reads *if this may not pass away unless.*
26:52 [u] M-Text reads *die.*
26:59 [v] NU-Text omits *the elders.*

many false witnesses came forward, they found none.[w] But at last two false
witnesses[x] came forward 61 and said, "This *fellow* said, 'I am able to destroy
the temple of God and to build it in three days.'"
62 And the high priest arose and said to Him, "Do You answer nothing?
What *is it* these men testify against You?" 63 But Jesus kept silent. And the
high priest answered and said to Him, "I put You under oath by the living
God: Tell us if You are the Christ, the Son of God!"
64 Jesus said to him, "*It is as* you said. Nevertheless, I say to you, hereafter you will see the Son of Man sitting at the right hand of the Power, and
coming on the clouds of heaven."
65 Then the high priest tore his clothes, saying, "He has spoken blasphemy! What further need do we have of witnesses? Look, now you have
heard His blasphemy! 66 What do you think?"
They answered and said, "He is deserving of death."
67 Then they spat in His face and beat Him; and others struck *Him* with
the palms of their hands, 68 saying, "Prophesy to us, Christ! Who is the one
who struck You?"

Peter Denies Jesus, and Weeps Bitterly

69 Now Peter sat outside in the courtyard. And a servant girl came to
him, saying, "You also were with Jesus of Galilee."
70 But he denied it before *them* all, saying, "I do not know what you are
saying."
71 And when he had gone out to the gateway, another *girl* saw him and
said to those *who were* there, "This *fellow* also was with Jesus of Nazareth."
72 But again he denied with an oath, "I do not know the Man!"
73 And a little later those who stood by came up and said to Peter, "Surely
you also are *one* of them, for your speech betrays you."
74 Then he began to curse and swear, *saying,* "I do not know the Man!"
Immediately a rooster crowed. 75 And Peter remembered the word of Jesus who had said to him, "Before the rooster crows, you will deny Me three
times." So he went out and wept bitterly.

Jesus Handed Over to Pontius Pilate

27 When morning came, all the chief priests and elders of the people
plotted against Jesus to put Him to death. 2 And when they had bound
Him, they led Him away and delivered Him to Pontius[y] Pilate the governor.

Judas Hangs Himself

3 Then Judas, His betrayer, seeing that He had been condemned, was remorseful and brought back the thirty pieces of silver to the chief priests
and elders, 4 saying, "I have sinned by betraying innocent blood."
And they said, "What *is that* to us? You see *to it!*"
5 Then he threw down the pieces of silver in the temple and departed,
and went and hanged himself.
6 But the chief priests took the silver pieces and said, "It is not lawful to
put them into the treasury, because they are the price of blood." 7 And they
consulted together and bought with them the potter's field, to bury strangers in. 8 Therefore that field has been called the Field of Blood to this day.

26:60 [w] NU-Text puts a comma after *but found none,* does not capitalize *Even,* and omits *they found none.* [x] NU-Text omits *false witnesses.*
27:2 [y] NU-Text omits *Pontius.*

Life Lesson

Matthew 27:1-66

SITUATION The Jewish leaders decided that Jesus must die. Because they were not allowed to execute anyone, they turned him over to the Romans. Jesus appeared before Pontius Pilate (governor of Samaria and Judea from A.D. 26-36) prior to his crucifixion.

OBSERVATION Jewish leaders refused to believe Jesus was the Messiah and insisted that Pilate execute him. Yet Jesus died for their sins, and ours too.

INSPIRATION Six hours. One Friday.

Let me ask you a question: What do you do with that day in history? What do you do with its claims?

If it really happened . . . if God did commandeer his own crucifixion . . . if he did turn his back on his own son . . . if he did storm Satan's gate, then those six hours that Friday were packed with tragic triumph. If that was God on that cross, then the hill called Skull is a granite studded with stakes to which you can anchor.

Those six hours were no normal six hours. They were the most critical hours in history. For during those six hours on that Friday, God embedded in the earth three anchor points sturdy enough to withstand any hurricane.

Anchor point #1—*My life is not futile.* This rock secures the hull of your heart. Its sole function is to give you something which you can grip when facing the surging tides of futility and relativism. . . . Someone is in control and I have a purpose.

Anchor point #2—*My failures are not fatal.* It's not that he loves what you did, but he loves who you are. . . . The one who has the right to condemn you has provided the way to acquit you. You make mistakes. God doesn't. And he made you.

Anchor point #3—*My death is not final.* There is one more stone to which you should tie. . . . It blocked the door of a grave. It wasn't big enough, though. . . . He only went in to prove he could come out. And on

Continued

the way out he took the stone with him and turned it into an anchor point. . . . Tie it to his rock and the typhoon of the tomb becomes a spring breeze on Easter Sunday. There they are. Three anchor points. The anchor points of the cross. (From *Six Hours One Friday* by Max Lucado)

APPLICATION Some people would rather see Jesus dead than controlling their lives. What room in the castle of your life (career, family, church) needs to be placed under Christ's control? Don't hesitate a day. Pray now. Give your life fully to him.

EXPLORATION Jesus' Death Saves Us—John 3:14-17; 11:25-26; Romans 3:23-26; 1 Corinthians 1:18; Colossians 1:20-22; Titus 3:3-7.

9Then was fulfilled what was spoken by Jeremiah the prophet, saying,
"*And they took the thirty pieces of silver, the value of Him who was*
priced, whom they of the children of Israel priced, 10*and gave them for the*
potter's field, as the LORD *directed me.*"[z]

Jesus Faces Pilate

11Now Jesus stood before the governor. And the governor asked Him,
saying, "Are You the King of the Jews?"
Jesus said to him, "*It is as* you say." 12And while He was being accused
by the chief priests and elders, He answered nothing.
13Then Pilate said to Him, "Do You not hear how many things they testify against You?" 14But He answered him not one word, so that the governor marveled greatly.

Taking the Place of Barabbas

15Now at the feast the governor was accustomed to releasing to the multitude one prisoner whom they wished. 16And at that time they had a noto-
rious prisoner called Barabbas.[a] 17Therefore, when they had gathered
together, Pilate said to them, "Whom do you want me to release to you?
Barabbas, or Jesus who is called Christ?" 18For he knew that they had
handed Him over because of envy.
19While he was sitting on the judgment seat, his wife sent to him, saying,
"Have nothing to do with that just Man, for I have suffered many things
today in a dream because of Him."
20But the chief priests and elders persuaded the multitudes that they
should ask for Barabbas and destroy Jesus. 21The governor answered and
said to them, "Which of the two do you want me to release to you?"
They said, "Barabbas!"
22Pilate said to them, "What then shall I do with Jesus who is called Christ?"
They all said to him, "Let Him be crucified!"
23Then the governor said, "Why, what evil has He done?"
But they cried out all the more, saying, "Let Him be crucified!"
24When Pilate saw that he could not prevail at all, but rather *that* a tumult was rising, he took water and washed *his* hands before the multitude,
saying, "I am innocent of the blood of this just Person.[b] You see *to it*."
25And all the people answered and said, "His blood *be* on us and on our
children."
26Then he released Barabbas to them; and when he had scourged Jesus,
he delivered *Him* to be crucified.

The Soldiers Mock Jesus

27Then the soldiers of the governor took Jesus into the Praetorium and
gathered the whole garrison around Him. 28And they stripped Him and
put a scarlet robe on Him. 29When they had twisted a crown of thorns, they
put *it* on His head, and a reed in His right hand. And they bowed the knee
before Him and mocked Him, saying, "Hail, King of the Jews!" 30Then they
spat on Him, and took the reed and struck Him on the head. 31And when
they had mocked Him, they took the robe off Him, put His *own* clothes on
Him, and led Him away to be crucified.

27:10 [z] Jeremiah 32:6–9
27:16 [a] NU-Text reads *Jesus Barabbas.*
27:24 [b] NU-Text omits *just.*

The King on a Cross

[32]Now as they came out, they found a man of Cyrene, Simon by name. Him they compelled to bear His cross. [33]And when they had come to a place called Golgotha, that is to say, Place of a Skull, [34]they gave Him sour[c] wine mingled with gall to drink. But when He had tasted *it,* He would not drink.

[35]Then they crucified Him, and divided His garments, casting lots,[d] that it might be fulfilled which was spoken by the prophet:

> *"They divided My garments among them,*
> *And for My clothing they cast lots."*[e]

[36]Sitting down, they kept watch over Him there. [37]And they put up over His head the accusation written against Him:

THIS IS JESUS THE KING OF THE JEWS.

[38]Then two robbers were crucified with Him, one on the right and another on the left.

[39]And those who passed by blasphemed Him, wagging their heads [40]and saying, "You who destroy the temple and build *it* in three days, save Yourself! If You are the Son of God, come down from the cross."

[41]Likewise the chief priests also, mocking with the scribes and elders,[f] said, [42]"He saved others; Himself He cannot save. If He is the King of Israel,[g] let Him now come down from the cross, and we will believe Him.[h] [43]He trusted in God; let Him deliver Him now if He will have Him; for He said, 'I am the Son of God.' "

[44]Even the robbers who were crucified with Him reviled Him with the same thing.

Jesus Dies on the Cross

[45]Now from the sixth hour until the ninth hour there was darkness over all the land. [46]And about the ninth hour Jesus cried out with a loud voice, saying, "Eli, Eli, lama sabachthani?" that is, *"My God, My God, why have You forsaken Me?"*[i]

[47]Some of those who stood there, when they heard *that,* said, "This Man is calling for Elijah!" [48]Immediately one of them ran and took a sponge, filled *it* with sour wine and put *it* on a reed, and offered it to Him to drink.

[49]The rest said, "Let Him alone; let us see if Elijah will come to save Him."

[50]And Jesus cried out again with a loud voice, and yielded up His spirit.

[51]Then, behold, the veil of the temple was torn in two from top to bottom; and the earth quaked, and the rocks were split, [52]and the graves were opened; and many bodies of the saints who had fallen asleep were raised; [53]and coming out of the graves after His resurrection, they went into the holy city and appeared to many.

[54]So when the centurion and those with him, who were guarding Jesus, saw the earthquake and the things that had happened, they feared greatly, saying, "Truly this was the Son of God!"

[55]And many women who followed Jesus from Galilee, ministering to Him, were there looking on from afar, [56]among whom were Mary Magdalene, Mary the mother of James and Joses,[j] and the mother of Zebedee's sons.

Jesus Buried in Joseph's Tomb

[57]Now when evening had come, there came a rich man from Arimathea, named Joseph, who himself had also become a disciple of Jesus. [58]This man went to Pilate and asked for the body of Jesus. Then Pilate commanded the body to be given to him. [59]When Joseph had taken the body, he wrapped it in a clean linen cloth, [60]and laid it in his new tomb which he had hewn out of the rock; and he rolled a large stone against the door of the tomb, and departed. [61]And Mary Magdalene was there, and the other Mary, sitting opposite the tomb.

Pilate Sets a Guard

[62]On the next day, which followed the Day of Preparation, the chief priests and Pharisees gathered together to Pilate, [63]saying, "Sir, we remember, while He was still alive, how that deceiver said, 'After three days I will rise.' [64]Therefore command that the tomb be made secure until the third day, lest His disciples come by night[k] and steal Him *away,* and say to the people, 'He has risen from the dead.' So the last deception will be worse than the first."

[65]Pilate said to them, "You have a guard; go your way, make *it* as secure as you know how." [66]So they went and made the tomb secure, sealing the stone and setting the guard.

27:34 [c] NU-Text omits *sour.*
27:35 [d] NU-Text and M-Text omit the rest of this verse. [e] Psalm 22:18
27:41 [f] M-Text reads *with the scribes, the Pharisees, and the elders.*
27:42 [g] NU-Text reads *He is the King of Israel!* [h] NU-Text and M-Text read *we will believe in Him.*
27:46 [i] Psalm 22:1
27:56 [j] NU-Text reads *Joseph.*
27:64 [k] NU-Text omits *by night.*

He Is Risen

28 Now after the Sabbath, as the first *day* of the week
began to dawn, Mary Magdalene and the other
Mary came to see the tomb. 2And behold, there was a
great earthquake; for an angel of the Lord descended
from heaven, and came and rolled back the stone from
the door,[l] and sat on it. 3His countenance was like lightning, and his clothing as white as snow. 4And the guards
shook for fear of him, and became like dead *men.*
5But the angel answered and said to the women,
"Do not be afraid, for I know that you seek Jesus who
was crucified. 6He is not here; for He is risen, as He
said. Come, see the place where the Lord lay. 7And go
quickly and tell His disciples that He is risen from the
dead, and indeed He is going before you into Galilee;
there you will see Him. Behold, I have told you."
8So they went out quickly from the tomb with fear
and great joy, and ran to bring His disciples word.

The Women Worship the Risen Lord

9And as they went to tell His disciples,[m] behold, Jesus
met them, saying, "Rejoice!" So they came and held
Him by the feet and worshiped Him. 10Then Jesus said
to them, "Do not be afraid. Go *and* tell My brethren to
go to Galilee, and there they will see Me."

The Soldiers Are Bribed

11Now while they were going, behold, some of the
guard came into the city and reported to the chief
priests all the things that had happened. 12When they
had assembled with the elders and consulted together, they gave a large sum of money to the soldiers,
13saying, "Tell them, 'His disciples came at night and
stole Him *away* while we slept.' 14And if this comes to
the governor's ears, we will appease him and make
you secure." 15So they took the money and did as they
were instructed; and this saying is commonly reported among the Jews until this day.

The Great Commission

16Then the eleven disciples went away into Galilee,
to the mountain which Jesus had appointed for them.
17When they saw Him, they worshiped Him; but some
doubted.
18And Jesus came and spoke to them, saying, "All
authority has been given to Me in heaven and on
earth. 19Go therefore[n] and make disciples of all the nations, baptizing them in the name of the Father and of
the Son and of the Holy Spirit, 20teaching them to observe all things that I have commanded you; and lo, I
am with you always, *even* to the end of the age." Amen.[o]

28:2 [l] NU-Text omits *from the door.*
28:9 [m] NU-Text omits the first clause of this verse.
28:19 [n] M-Text omits *therefore.*
28:20 [o] NU-Text omits *Amen.*

The Gospel According to MARK

INTRODUCTION

The drama of Mark's Gospel peaks in Caesarea Philippi.

It's a religious mecca. Every major religion can be found here. Temples dot the landscape. Priests stride the streets.

Jesus and his followers are here? Why? If Jesus preached a sermon, it's not recorded. If he performed a miracle, we don't know it. As far as we know, all he did was ask two questions.

The first, "Who do people say that I am?"

The disciples are quick to respond. They've overheard the chatter. "Some say you are John the Baptist. Others say you are Elijah, and others say you are one of the prophets."

Good answers. True answers. But wrong answers.

Jesus then turns and asks them the question. *The* question. "But who do you say that I am?"

He doesn't ask, "What do you think about what I've done?" He asks, "Who do you say that I am?"

He doesn't ask, "Who *did* you think I was when the crowds were great and the miracles were many?" He asks, "Who *do* you think I am? Here against the backdrop of religion. Me, a penniless itinerant surrounded by affluent temples. Who do you say I am?"

He doesn't ask, "Who do your friends think? … Who do your parents think? … Who do your peers think?" He poses instead a starkly personal query, "Who do *you* think I am?"

The disciples aren't as quick to respond. One ducks his eyes. Another shuffles his feet. A third clears his throat. But Peter lifts his head. He lifts his head and looks at the Nazarene and speaks the words heaven has longed to hear. "You are the Christ."

You have been asked some important questions in your life:

Will you marry me?

Would you be interested in a transfer?

What would you think if I told you I was pregnant?

You've been asked some important questions. But the grandest of them is an anthill compared to the Everest found in the eighth chapter of Mark.

Who do you say that I am?

Life Lesson

Mark 1:1-45

SITUATION Persecution and martyrdom in Rome created a dangerous environment for Christians. Mark wrote this Gospel to the Christians in Rome to encourage and strengthen their faith. He recorded Christ's baptism, temptation, and the beginning of his ministry with his disciples.

OBSERVATION Jesus came to be active and compassionate to the people around him. He exemplified tenderness when he healed the leper by touching him.

INSPIRATION Jesus was a master at communicating love and personal acceptance. He did so when He blessed and held . . . little children. But another time His sensitivity to touch someone was even more graphic. This was when Jesus met a grown man's need for meaningful touch, a man who was barred by law from ever touching anyone again. . . .

To touch a leper was unthinkable. Banishing lepers from society, people would not get within a stone's throw of them. (In fact, they would throw stones at them if they did come close!) . . . With their open sores and dirty bandages, lepers were the last

John the Baptist Prepares the Way

The beginning of the gospel of Jesus Christ, the Son of God. 2As it is written in the Prophets:[a]

"Behold, I send My messenger before Your face,
Who will prepare Your way before You." [b]
3 *The voice of one crying in the wilderness:*
'Prepare the way of the Lord;
Make His paths straight.' "[c]

4John came baptizing in the wilderness and preaching a baptism of repentance for the remission of sins. 5Then all the land of Judea, and those from Jerusalem, went out to him and were all baptized by him in the Jordan River, confessing their sins.

6Now John was clothed with camel's hair and with a leather belt around his waist, and he ate locusts and wild honey. 7And he preached, saying, "There comes One after me who is mightier than I, whose sandal strap I am not worthy to stoop down and loose. 8I indeed baptized you with water, but He will baptize you with the Holy Spirit."

John Baptizes Jesus

9It came to pass in those days *that* Jesus came from Nazareth of Galilee, and was baptized by John in the Jordan. 10And immediately, coming up from[d] the water, He saw the heavens parting and the Spirit descending upon Him like a dove. 11Then a voice came from heaven, "You are My beloved Son, in whom I am well pleased."

Satan Tempts Jesus

12Immediately the Spirit drove Him into the wilderness. 13And He was there in the wilderness forty days, tempted by Satan, and was with the wild beasts; and the angels ministered to Him.

Jesus Begins His Galilean Ministry

14Now after John was put in prison, Jesus came to Galilee, preaching the gospel of the kingdom[e] of God, 15and saying, "The time is fulfilled, and the kingdom of God is at hand. Repent, and believe in the gospel."

Four Fishermen Called as Disciples

16And as He walked by the Sea of Galilee, He saw Simon and Andrew his brother casting a net into the sea; for they were fishermen. 17Then Jesus said to them, "Follow Me, and I will make you become fishers of men." 18They immediately left their nets and followed Him.

19When He had gone a little farther from there, He saw James the *son* of Zebedee, and John his brother, who also *were* in the boat mending their nets. 20And immediately He called them, and they left their father Zebedee in the boat with the hired servants, and went after Him.

Jesus Casts Out an Unclean Spirit

21Then they went into Capernaum, and immediately on the Sabbath He

1:2 [a] NU-Text reads *Isaiah the prophet.* [b] *Malachi 3:1*
1:3 [c] Isaiah 40:3
1:10 [d] NU-Text reads *out of.*
1:14 [e] NU-Text omits *of the kingdom.*

entered the synagogue and taught. 22And they were astonished at His teaching, for He taught them as one having authority, and not as the scribes.
23Now there was a man in their synagogue with an unclean spirit. And he
cried out, 24saying, "Let *us* alone! What have we to do with You, Jesus of Nazareth? Did You come to destroy us? I know who You are—the Holy One of God!"
25But Jesus rebuked him, saying, "Be quiet, and come out of him!" 26And
when the unclean spirit had convulsed him and cried out with a loud
voice, he came out of him. 27Then they were all amazed, so that they questioned among themselves, saying, "What is this? What new doctrine *is*
this? For with authority[f] He commands even the unclean spirits, and they
obey Him." 28And immediately His fame spread throughout all the region
around Galilee.

Peter's Mother-in-Law Healed

29Now as soon as they had come out of the synagogue, they entered the
house of Simon and Andrew, with James and John. 30But Simon's wife's
mother lay sick with a fever, and they told Him about her at once. 31So He
came and took her by the hand and lifted her up, and immediately the
fever left her. And she served them.

Many Healed After Sabbath Sunset

32At evening, when the sun had set, they brought to Him all who were
sick and those who were demon-possessed. 33And the whole city was
gathered together at the door. 34Then He healed many who were sick with
various diseases, and cast out many demons; and He did not allow the
demons to speak, because they knew Him.

Preaching in Galilee

35Now in the morning, having risen a long while before daylight, He went
out and departed to a solitary place; and there He prayed. 36And Simon
and those *who were* with Him searched for Him. 37When they found Him,
they said to Him, "Everyone is looking for You."
38But He said to them, "Let us go into the next towns, that I may preach
there also, because for this purpose I have come forth."
39And He was preaching in their synagogues throughout all Galilee, and
casting out demons.

Jesus Cleanses a Leper

40Now a leper came to Him, imploring Him, kneeling down to Him and
saying to Him, "If You are willing, You can make me clean."
41Then Jesus, moved with compassion, stretched out *His* hand and touched
him, and said to him, "I am willing; be cleansed." 42As soon as He had spoken, immediately the leprosy left him, and he was cleansed. 43And He
strictly warned him and sent him away at once, 44and said to him, "See
that you say nothing to anyone; but go your way, show yourself to the
priest, and offer for your cleansing those things which Moses commanded,
as a testimony to them."
45However, he went out and began to proclaim *it* freely, and to spread
the matter, so that Jesus could no longer openly enter the city, but was outside in deserted places; and they came to Him from every direction.

1:27 [f]NU-Text reads *What is this? A new doctrine with authority.*

persons anyone would want to touch. Yet the first thing Christ did for this man was touch him.

Even before Jesus spoke to him, He reached out His hand and touched him. Can you imagine what that scene must have looked like? Think how this man must have longed for someone to touch him, not throw stones at him to drive him away. Jesus could have healed him first and then touched him. But recognizing his deepest need, Jesus stretched out His hand even before He spoke words of physical and spiritual healing.

(From *The Gift of the Blessing* by Gary Smalley and John Trent)

APPLICATION Jesus shows us the power of gentle compassion. Who do you have trouble "touching" because they are not attractive in any way? Compassion requires more than words; compassion requires action. Look for ways to express compassion to those who are starving for a tender touch.

EXPLORATION Compassion of Christ—Matthew 8:3,15; 9:36; 14:14; 15:32; 17:7; 20:34; 23:37; Mark 10:13-16; Luke 7:13; 22:51; John 11:35.

Jesus Forgives and Heals a Paralytic

2 And again He entered Capernaum after *some* days, and it was heard that
He was in the house. 2Immediately[g] many gathered together, so that there
was no longer room to receive *them,* not even near the door. And He preached
the word to them. 3Then they came to Him, bringing a paralytic who was
carried by four *men.* 4And when they could not come near Him because of
the crowd, they uncovered the roof where He was. So when they had broken through, they let down the bed on which the paralytic was lying.
5When Jesus saw their faith, He said to the paralytic, "Son, your sins are
forgiven you."
6And some of the scribes were sitting there and reasoning in their
hearts, 7"Why does this *Man* speak blasphemies like this? Who can forgive
sins but God alone?"
8But immediately, when Jesus perceived in His spirit that they reasoned
thus within themselves, He said to them, "Why do you reason about these
things in your hearts? 9Which is easier, to say to the paralytic, '*Your* sins
are forgiven you,' or to say, 'Arise, take up your bed and walk'? 10But that
you may know that the Son of Man has power on earth to forgive sins"—
He said to the paralytic, 11"I say to you, arise, take up your bed, and go to
your house." 12Immediately he arose, took up the bed, and went out in the
presence of them all, so that all were amazed and glorified God, saying,
"We never saw *anything* like this!"

Matthew the Tax Collector

13Then He went out again by the sea; and all the multitude came to Him,
and He taught them. 14As He passed by, He saw Levi the *son* of Alphaeus
sitting at the tax office. And He said to him, "Follow Me." So he arose and
followed Him.
15Now it happened, as He was dining in *Levi's* house, that many tax collectors and sinners also sat together with Jesus and His disciples; for there
were many, and they followed Him. 16And when the scribes and[h] Pharisees
saw Him eating with the tax collectors and sinners, they said to His disciples, "How *is it* that He eats and drinks with tax collectors and sinners?"
17When Jesus heard *it,* He said to them, "Those who are well have no
need of a physician, but those who are sick. I did not come to call *the* righteous, but sinners, to repentance."[i]

Jesus Is Questioned About Fasting

18The disciples of John and of the Pharisees were fasting. Then they came
and said to Him, "Why do the disciples of John and of the Pharisees fast,
but Your disciples do not fast?"
19And Jesus said to them, "Can the friends of the bridegroom fast while
the bridegroom is with them? As long as they have the bridegroom with
them they cannot fast. 20But the days will come when the bridegroom will
be taken away from them, and then they will fast in those days. 21No one
sews a piece of unshrunk cloth on an old garment; or else the new piece
pulls away from the old, and the tear is made worse. 22And no one puts
new wine into old wineskins; or else the new wine bursts the wineskins,

2:2 [g] NU-Text omits *Immediately.*
2:16 [h] NU-Text reads *of the.*
2:17 [i] NU-Text omits *to repentance.*

LIFE LESSON

Mark 2:1-28

SITUATION Jesus' power over illness and evil spirits quickly became exciting news to the people around him. They came to him from everywhere, looking for help.

OBSERVATION Jesus offers hope, healing, and new life to all who come to him in faith.

INSPIRATION I'll never forget Steven. I met him in St. Louis. His twenty-three years had been hard on him, his arm scarred from the needle and his wrist scarred from the knife. His pride was his fist and his weakness was his girl. . . .

He wanted to change.

But his girlfriend would have none of it. Oh, she would listen politely and would be very sweet, but her heart was gripped by darkness. Any changes Steve made would be quickly muffled as she would craftily maneuver him back into his old habits. She was the last thing between him and the Kingdom. We begged him to leave her. He was trying to put new wine into an old wineskin.

He wrestled for days trying to decide what to do. Finally, he reached a conclusion. He couldn't leave her.

The last time I saw Steve he wept . . . uncontrollably. I held big, tough, macho Steve in my arms. The prophecy of Jesus was true. By putting his new wine into an old skin, it was lost.

. . . No friendship or romance is worth your soul. Repentance means change. And change means purging your heart of anything that can't coexist with Christ.

You can't put new life into an old lifestyle. The inevitable tragedy occurs. The new life is lost.

(From *On the Anvil* by Max Lucado)

APPLICATION Do you need a big change to put your life on course? Boldly put your life in Christ's hands and let God do a miracle!

EXPLORATION Bringing People to Jesus for Miracles—Matthew 4:24; 8:16; Mark 9:17-20; Luke 5:18-19.

the wine is spilled, and the wineskins are ruined. But new wine must be
put into new wineskins."

Jesus Is Lord of the Sabbath

23Now it happened that He went through the grainfields on the Sabbath;
and as they went His disciples began to pluck the heads of grain. 24And the
Pharisees said to Him, "Look, why do they do what is not lawful on the
Sabbath?"
25But He said to them, "Have you never read what David did when he
was in need and hungry, he and those with him: 26how he went into the
house of God *in the days* of Abiathar the high priest, and ate the showbread, which is not lawful to eat except for the priests, and also gave some
to those who were with him?"
27And He said to them, "The Sabbath was made for man, and not man
for the Sabbath. 28Therefore the Son of Man is also Lord of the Sabbath."

Healing on the Sabbath

3 And He entered the synagogue again, and a man was there who had a
withered hand. 2So they watched Him closely, whether He would heal
him on the Sabbath, so that they might accuse Him. 3And He said to the
man who had the withered hand, "Step forward." 4Then He said to them,
"Is it lawful on the Sabbath to do good or to do evil, to save life or to kill?"
But they kept silent. 5And when He had looked around at them with anger,
being grieved by the hardness of their hearts, He said to the man, "Stretch
out your hand." And he stretched *it* out, and his hand was restored as
whole as the other.[j] 6Then the Pharisees went out and immediately plotted
with the Herodians against Him, how they might destroy Him.

A Great Multitude Follows Jesus

7But Jesus withdrew with His disciples to the sea. And a great multitude
from Galilee followed Him, and from Judea 8and Jerusalem and Idumea
and beyond the Jordan; and those from Tyre and Sidon, a great multitude,
when they heard how many things He was doing, came to Him. 9So He
told His disciples that a small boat should be kept ready for Him because
of the multitude, lest they should crush Him. 10For He healed many, so that
as many as had afflictions pressed about Him to touch Him. 11And the unclean spirits, whenever they saw Him, fell down before Him and cried out,
saying, "You are the Son of God." 12But He sternly warned them that they
should not make Him known.

The Twelve Apostles

13And He went up on the mountain and called to *Him* those He Himself
wanted. And they came to Him. 14Then He appointed twelve,[k] that they
might be with Him and that He might send them out to preach, 15and to
have power to heal sicknesses and[l] to cast out demons: 16Simon,[m] to whom
He gave the name Peter; 17James the *son* of Zebedee and John the brother
of James, to whom He gave the name Boanerges, that is, "Sons of
Thunder"; 18Andrew, Philip, Bartholomew, Matthew, Thomas, James the

3:5 [j] NU-Text omits *as whole as the other.*
3:14 [k] NU-Text adds *whom He also named apostles.*
3:15 [l] NU-Text omits *to heal sicknesses and.*
3:16 [m] NU-Text reads *and He appointed the twelve: Simon, ...*

LIFE LESSON

Mark 3:1-35

SITUATION Mark affirmed the spiritual authority and power present in Jesus' ministry. Jesus properly interpreted the Mosaic Law. His power was greater than evil spirits. This passage also revealed Jesus' ministry to call his spiritual brothers and sisters to do the will of God.

OBSERVATION Jesus demonstrated remarkable patience. Though many questioned his authority, he patiently refuted them. When his immediate family thought that Jesus was a lunatic, he expanded the concept of his family to include the kinship of people who love God.

INSPIRATION Can you still remember? Are you still in love with Him? . . . Remember Jesus. Before you remember anything, remember Him. If you forget anything, don't forget Him.

Oh, but how quickly we forget. So much happens through the years. So many changes within. So many alterations without. And, somewhere, back there, we leave Him. We don't turn away from Him . . . we just don't take Him with us. Assignments come. Promotions come. Budgets are made. Kids are born, and the Christ . . . the Christ is forgotten.

Has it been a while since you stared at the heavens in speechless amazement? Has it been a while since you realized God's divinity and your carnality?

If it has, then you need to know something. He is still there. He hasn't left. Under all those papers and books and reports and years. In the midst of all those voices and faces and memories and pictures, He is still there.

(From *Six Hours One Friday* by Max Lucado)

APPLICATION Have you forgotten Jesus? Has your love for him slipped through time? Let Christ renew your love and let it flow freely again, as it once did.

EXPLORATION Spiritual Family—Isaiah 63:16; John 1:12; Galatians 4:6; Ephesians 2:19; Hebrews 2:11.

LIFE LESSON
Mark 4:1-41

SITUATION Jesus used parables to teach. These stories contained great truths and insights about God and man. While quoting from Isaiah, Jesus also demonstrated how he fulfilled prophecy through his stories. Mark related not only the power of Jesus in stories but also his authority over creation in his command of the weather at sea.

OBSERVATION Even in the middle of a dangerous sea, when Jesus patiently calmed the storm, he showed the fearful disciples that he truly cared for them. Sometimes even those close to Jesus were slow to realize how much he loved them.

INSPIRATION "God, don't you care?"

Such an honest cry, a doggedly painful cry. I've asked that one before, haven't you? It's been screamed countless times. . . .

A mother weeps over a stillborn child. A husband is torn from his wife by a tragic accident. The tears of an eight-year-old fall on a daddy's casket. And the question wails.

"God, don't you care?" "Why me?" "Why my friend?" "Why my business?" "Don't you care?"

It's the timeless question. The question asked by literally every person that has stalked this globe. There has never been a president, a worker, or a businessman who hasn't asked it. There has never been a soul who hasn't wrestled with this aching question. Does my God care? Or is my pain God's great goof?

son of Alphaeus, Thaddaeus, Simon the Cananite; [19]and Judas Iscariot, who also betrayed Him. And they went into a house.

A House Divided Cannot Stand

[20]Then the multitude came together again, so that they could not so much as eat bread. [21]But when His own people heard *about this,* they went out to lay hold of Him, for they said, "He is out of His mind."

[22]And the scribes who came down from Jerusalem said, "He has Beelzebub," and, "By the ruler of the demons He casts out demons."

[23]So He called them to *Himself* and said to them in parables: "How can Satan cast out Satan? [24]If a kingdom is divided against itself, that kingdom cannot stand. [25]And if a house is divided against itself, that house cannot stand. [26]And if Satan has risen up against himself, and is divided, he cannot stand, but has an end. [27]No one can enter a strong man's house and plunder his goods, unless he first binds the strong man. And then he will plunder his house.

The Unpardonable Sin

[28]"Assuredly, I say to you, all sins will be forgiven the sons of men, and whatever blasphemies they may utter; [29]but he who blasphemes against the Holy Spirit never has forgiveness, but is subject to eternal condemnation"— [30]because they said, "He has an unclean spirit."

Jesus' Mother and Brothers Send for Him

[31]Then His brothers and His mother came, and standing outside they sent to Him, calling Him. [32]And a multitude was sitting around Him; and they said to Him, "Look, Your mother and Your brothers[n] are outside seeking You."

[33]But He answered them, saying, "Who is My mother, or My brothers?" [34]And He looked around in a circle at those who sat about Him, and said, "Here are My mother and My brothers! [35]For whoever does the will of God is My brother and My sister and mother."

The Parable of the Sower

4 And again He began to teach by the sea. And a great multitude was gathered to Him, so that He got into a boat and sat *in it* on the sea; and the whole multitude was on the land facing the sea. [2]Then He taught them many things by parables, and said to them in His teaching:

[3]"Listen! Behold, a sower went out to sow. [4]And it happened, as he sowed, *that* some *seed* fell by the wayside; and the birds of the air[o] came and devoured it. [5]Some fell on stony ground, where it did not have much earth; and immediately it sprang up because it had no depth of earth. [6]But when the sun was up it was scorched, and because it had no root it withered away. [7]And some *seed* fell among thorns; and the thorns grew up and choked it, and it yielded no crop. [8]But other *seed* fell on good ground and yielded a crop that sprang up, increased and produced: some thirtyfold, some sixty, and some a hundred."

[9]And He said to them,[p] "He who has ears to hear, let him hear!"

3:32 [n] NU-Text and M-Text add *and Your sisters.*
4:4 [o] NU-Text and M-Text omit *of the air.*
4:9 [p] NU-Text and M-Text omit *to them.*

The Purpose of Parables

[10]But when He was alone, those around Him with the twelve asked Him
about the parable. [11]And He said to them, "To you it has been given to know
the mystery of the kingdom of God; but to those who are outside, all things
come in parables, [12]so that

> *'Seeing they may see and not perceive,*
> *And hearing they may hear and not understand;*
> *Lest they should turn,*
> *And their sins be forgiven them.'* "[q]

The Parable of the Sower Explained

[13]And He said to them, "Do you not understand this parable? How then will
you understand all the parables? [14]The sower sows the word. [15]And these are
the ones by the wayside where the word is sown. When they hear, Satan comes
immediately and takes away the word that was sown in their hearts. [16]These
likewise are the ones sown on stony ground who, when they hear the word,
immediately receive it with gladness; [17]and they have no root in themselves, and so endure only for a time. Afterward, when tribulation or persecution arises for the word's sake, immediately they stumble. [18]Now these
are the ones sown among thorns; *they are* the ones who hear the word,
[19]and the cares of this world, the deceitfulness of riches, and the desires for
other things entering in choke the word, and it becomes unfruitful. [20]But
these are the ones sown on good ground, those who hear the word, accept
it, and bear fruit: some thirtyfold, some sixty, and some a hundred."

Light Under a Basket

[21]Also He said to them, "Is a lamp brought to be put under a basket or
under a bed? Is it not to be set on a lampstand? [22]For there is nothing hidden which will not be revealed, nor has anything been kept secret but that
it should come to light. [23]If anyone has ears to hear, let him hear."
[24]Then He said to them, "Take heed what you hear. With the same measure you use, it will be measured to you; and to you who hear, more will be
given. [25]For whoever has, to him more will be given; but whoever does not
have, even what he has will be taken away from him."

The Parable of the Growing Seed

[26]And He said, "The kingdom of God is as if a man should scatter seed on
the ground, [27]and should sleep by night and rise by day, and the seed should
sprout and grow, he himself does not know how. [28]For the earth yields
crops by itself: first the blade, then the head, after that the full grain in the
head. [29]But when the grain ripens, immediately he puts in the sickle, because the harvest has come."

The Parable of the Mustard Seed

[30]Then He said, "To what shall we liken the kingdom of God? Or with
what parable shall we picture it? [31]*It is* like a mustard seed which, when it
is sown on the ground, is smaller than all the seeds on earth; [32]but when it
is sown, it grows up and becomes greater than all herbs, and shoots out
large branches, so that the birds of the air may nest under its shade."

As the winds howled and the sea raged, the impatient and frightened disciples screamed their fear at the sleeping Jesus. "Teacher, don't you care that we are about to die?" He could have kept on sleeping. He could have told them to shut up. He could have impatiently jumped up and angrily dismissed the storm. He could have pointed out their immaturity. . . . But he didn't.

With all the patience that only one who cares can have, he answered the question. He hushed the storm so the shivering disciples wouldn't miss his response. Jesus answered once and for all the aching dilemma of man—"Where is God when I hurt?"

Listening and healing. That's where he is. He cares.

(From *On the Anvil* by Max Lucado,)

APPLICATION What stories of Jesus' love and ministry can you share with others? Consider the impact of stories that have taught you. Dare yourself to discover the ways God shows he cares for you in the storms of your life.

EXPLORATION Christ as a Teacher—Matthew 4:23; 5:2; 7:29; Mark 6:34; Luke 4:15; 5:3; John 3:2; 7:14; 8:2. Divine Power—Exodus 4:21; 15:11; Joshua 3:5; Psalm 77:14; Daniel 4:3; Joel 2:30; Acts 6:8.

4:12 *q* Isaiah 6:9, 10

LIFE LESSON

Mark 5:1-43

SITUATION Jesus ministered to the most important people and the most despised people in town. His power surpassed demons, sickness, and death.

OBSERVATION Although Jesus brought life to those who were physically dead, he spent most of his energy reaching those who were spiritually dead. He wanted to give them a new spiritual life.

INSPIRATION The funeral had begun. The people thought the best Jesus could do was offer some kind words about Jairus's girl. Jesus had some words all right. Not about the girl, but for the girl.

"My child, stand up!" . . .

The next thing the father knew, she was eating, Jesus was laughing, and the hired mourners were sent home early. . . .

He'll do it again, you know. He's promised he would. And he's shown that he can.

"The Lord himself will come down from heaven with a loud command" (1 Thess. 4:16).

The same voice that awoke the boy near Nain, that stirred the still daughter of Jairus, that awakened the corpse of Lazarus—the same voice will speak again. The earth and the sea will give up their dead. There will be no more death.

Jesus made sure of that.

(From *He Still Moves Stones* by Max Lucado)

APPLICATION What could you do to show love and acceptance for a homeless beggar in rags? Could you share God's love with an alcoholic, a street gang member, an AIDS victim? These people are worthy of God's love, and your love too. Join with other Christians this week in an effort to share God's Word with people you would not normally approach.

EXPLORATION Impartiality—Ruth 1:16; Luke 5:13; Galatians 3:28.

Jesus' Use of Parables

33 And with many such parables He spoke the word to them as they were
able to hear *it.* 34 But without a parable He did not speak to them. And
when they were alone, He explained all things to His disciples.

Wind and Wave Obey Jesus

35 On the same day, when evening had come, He said to them, "Let us cross
over to the other side." 36 Now when they had left the multitude, they took
Him along in the boat as He was. And other little boats were also with Him.
37 And a great windstorm arose, and the waves beat into the boat, so that it
was already filling. 38 But He was in the stern, asleep on a pillow. And they
awoke Him and said to Him, "Teacher, do You not care that we are perishing?"
39 Then He arose and rebuked the wind, and said to the sea, "Peace, be
still!" And the wind ceased and there was a great calm. 40 But He said to them,
"Why are you so fearful? How *is it* that you have no faith?"[r] 41 And they feared
exceedingly, and said to one another, "Who can this be, that even the wind
and the sea obey Him!"

A Demon-Possessed Man Healed

5 Then they came to the other side of the sea, to the country of the Gadarenes.[s] 2 And when He had come out of the boat, immediately there met
Him out of the tombs a man with an unclean spirit, 3 who had *his* dwelling
among the tombs; and no one could bind him,[t] not even with chains, 4 because
he had often been bound with shackles and chains. And the chains had
been pulled apart by him, and the shackles broken in pieces; neither could
anyone tame him. 5 And always, night and day, he was in the mountains
and in the tombs, crying out and cutting himself with stones.
6 When he saw Jesus from afar, he ran and worshiped Him. 7 And he cried
out with a loud voice and said, "What have I to do with You, Jesus, Son of
the Most High God? I implore You by God that You do not torment me."
8 For He said to him, "Come out of the man, unclean spirit!" 9 Then He
asked him, "What *is* your name?"
And he answered, saying, "My name *is* Legion; for we are many." 10 Also
he begged Him earnestly that He would not send them out of the country.
11 Now a large herd of swine was feeding there near the mountains. 12 So
all the demons begged Him, saying, "Send us to the swine, that we may enter
them." 13 And at once Jesus[u] gave them permission. Then the unclean spirits
went out and entered the swine (there were about two thousand); and the
herd ran violently down the steep place into the sea, and drowned in the sea.
14 So those who fed the swine fled, and they told *it* in the city and in the
country. And they went out to see what it was that had happened. 15 Then
they came to Jesus, and saw the one *who had been* demon-possessed and
had the legion, sitting and clothed and in his right mind. And they were
afraid. 16 And those who saw it told them how it happened to him *who had
been* demon-possessed, and about the swine. 17 Then they began to plead
with Him to depart from their region.
18 And when He got into the boat, he who had been demon-possessed

4:40 [r] NU-Text reads *Have you still no faith?*
5:1 [s] NU-Text reads *Gerasenes.*
5:3 [t] NU-Text adds *anymore.*
5:13 [u] NU-Text reads *And He gave.*

begged Him that he might be with Him. 19However,
Jesus did not permit him, but said to him, "Go home
to your friends, and tell them what great things the
Lord has done for you, and how He has had compassion on you." 20And he departed and began to proclaim in Decapolis all that Jesus had done for him;
and all marveled.

A Girl Restored to Life and a Woman Healed

21Now when Jesus had crossed over again by boat to
the other side, a great multitude gathered to Him; and
He was by the sea. 22And behold, one of the rulers of
the synagogue came, Jairus by name. And when he saw
Him, he fell at His feet 23and begged Him earnestly, saying, "My little daughter lies at the point of death. Come
and lay Your hands on her, that she may be healed,
and she will live." 24So *Jesus* went with him, and a
great multitude followed Him and thronged Him.

25Now a certain woman had a flow of blood for
twelve years, 26and had suffered many things from
many physicians. She had spent all that she had and
was no better, but rather grew worse. 27When she
heard about Jesus, she came behind *Him* in the crowd
and touched His garment. 28For she said, "If only I
may touch His clothes, I shall be made well."

29Immediately the fountain of her blood was dried
up, and she felt in *her* body that she was healed of the
affliction. 30And Jesus, immediately knowing in Himself
that power had gone out of Him, turned around in the
crowd and said, "Who touched My clothes?"

31But His disciples said to Him, "You see the multitude thronging You, and You say, 'Who touched Me?' "

32And He looked around to see her who had done
this thing. 33But the woman, fearing and trembling,
knowing what had happened to her, came and fell
down before Him and told Him the whole truth.
34And He said to her, "Daughter, your faith has made
you well. Go in peace, and be healed of your affliction."

35While He was still speaking, *some* came from the
ruler of the synagogue's *house* who said, "Your daughter is dead. Why trouble the Teacher any further?"

36As soon as Jesus heard the word that was spoken,
He said to the ruler of the synagogue, "Do not be afraid;
only believe." 37And He permitted no one to follow Him
except Peter, James, and John the brother of James.
38Then He came to the house of the ruler of the synagogue, and saw a tumult and those who wept and
wailed loudly. 39When He came in, He said to them,
"Why make this commotion and weep? The child is
not dead, but sleeping."

40And they ridiculed Him. But when He had put them
all outside, He took the father and the mother of the
child, and those *who were* with Him, and entered where
the child was lying. 41Then He took the child by the hand,
and said to her, "Talitha, cumi," which is translated,
"Little girl, I say to you, arise." 42Immediately the girl
arose and walked, for she was twelve years *of age.* And
they were overcome with great amazement. 43But He
commanded them strictly that no one should know
it, and said that *something* should be given her to eat.

Jesus Rejected at Nazareth

6 Then He went out from there and came to His
own country, and His disciples followed Him.
2And when the Sabbath had come, He began to teach
in the synagogue. And many hearing *Him* were astonished, saying, "Where *did* this Man *get* these things?
And what wisdom *is* this which is given to Him, that
such mighty works are performed by His hands! 3Is
this not the carpenter, the Son of Mary, and brother of
James, Joses, Judas, and Simon? And are not His sisters here with us?" So they were offended at Him.

4But Jesus said to them, "A prophet is not without
honor except in his own country, among his own relatives, and in his own house." 5Now He could do no
mighty work there, except that He laid His hands on a
few sick people and healed *them.* 6And He marveled
because of their unbelief. Then He went about the villages in a circuit, teaching.

Sending Out the Twelve

7And He called the twelve to *Himself,* and began to
send them out two *by* two, and gave them power over
unclean spirits. 8He commanded them to take nothing for the journey except a staff—no bag, no bread,
no copper in *their* money belts— 9but to wear sandals, and not to put on two tunics.

10Also He said to them, "In whatever place you enter
a house, stay there till you depart from that place.
11And whoever[v] will not receive you nor hear you, when
you depart from there, shake off the dust under your
feet as a testimony against them.[w] Assuredly, I say to
you, it will be more tolerable for Sodom and Gomorrah
in the day of judgment than for that city!"

12So they went out and preached that *people* should
repent. 13And they cast out many demons, and anointed
with oil many who were sick, and healed *them.*

John the Baptist Beheaded

14Now King Herod heard *of Him,* for His name had

6:11 [v] NU-Text reads *whatever place.* [w] NU-Text omits the rest of this verse.

LIFE LESSON
Mark 6:1-56

SITUATION This record of a particularly busy day is found in all four Gospels. Particularly significant is the feeding of the five thousand.

OBSERVATION Jesus experienced stressful, chaotic days like ours. He knows what the pace of our life is like.

INSPIRATION A day in the life of Christ. . . .

[A] day in which Jesus experiences more stress than he will any other day of his life—aside from his crucifixion. Before the morning becomes evening, he has reason to weep . . . run . . . shout . . . curse . . . praise . . . doubt.

From calm to chaos. From peace to perplexity. Within moments his world is turned upside down. . . .

The morning has been a jungle trail of the unexpected. First Jesus grieves over the death of a dear friend and relative. Then his life is threatened. Next he celebrates the triumphant return of his followers. Then he is nearly suffocated by a brouhaha of humanity.

Bereavement . . . jeopardy . . . jubilation . . . bedlam. . . .

Ponder this the next time your world goes from calm to chaos. . . .

Jesus knows how you feel.

A friend of mine was recently trying to teach his six-year-old son how to shoot a basket. The boy would take

become well known. And he said, "John the Baptist is risen from the dead,
and therefore these powers are at work in him."
[15]Others said, "It is Elijah."
And others said, "It is the Prophet, or[x] like one of the prophets."
[16]But when Herod heard, he said, "This is John, whom I beheaded; he
has been raised from the dead!" [17]For Herod himself had sent and laid
hold of John, and bound him in prison for the sake of Herodias, his
brother Philip's wife; for he had married her. [18]Because John had said to
Herod, "It is not lawful for you to have your brother's wife."
[19]Therefore Herodias held it against him and wanted to kill him, but she
could not; [20]for Herod feared John, knowing that he *was* a just and holy
man, and he protected him. And when he heard him, he did many things,
and heard him gladly.
[21]Then an opportune day came when Herod on his birthday gave a feast
for his nobles, the high officers, and the chief *men* of Galilee. [22]And when
Herodias' daughter herself came in and danced, and pleased Herod and
those who sat with him, the king said to the girl, "Ask me whatever you
want, and I will give *it* to you." [23]He also swore to her, "Whatever you ask
me, I will give you, up to half my kingdom."
[24]So she went out and said to her mother, "What shall I ask?"
And she said, "The head of John the Baptist!"
[25]Immediately she came in with haste to the king and asked, saying, "I
want you to give me at once the head of John the Baptist on a platter."
[26]And the king was exceedingly sorry; *yet,* because of the oaths and because
of those who sat with him, he did not want to refuse her. [27]Immediately the
king sent an executioner and commanded his head to be brought. And he
went and beheaded him in prison, [28]brought his head on a platter, and
gave it to the girl; and the girl gave it to her mother. [29]When his disciples
heard *of it,* they came and took away his corpse and laid it in a tomb.

Feeding the Five Thousand

[30]Then the apostles gathered to Jesus and told Him all things, both what
they had done and what they had taught. [31]And He said to them, "Come
aside by yourselves to a deserted place and rest a while." For there were
many coming and going, and they did not even have time to eat. [32]So they
departed to a deserted place in the boat by themselves.
[33]But the multitudes[y] saw them departing, and many knew Him and
ran there on foot from all the cities. They arrived before them and came together to Him. [34]And Jesus, when He came out, saw a great multitude and
was moved with compassion for them, because they were like sheep not
having a shepherd. So He began to teach them many things. [35]When the
day was now far spent, His disciples came to Him and said, "This is a deserted place, and already the hour *is* late. [36]Send them away, that they may
go into the surrounding country and villages and buy themselves bread;[z]
for they have nothing to eat."
[37]But He answered and said to them, "You give them something to eat."
And they said to Him, "Shall we go and buy two hundred denarii worth
of bread and give them *something* to eat?"

6:15 [x] NU-Text and M-Text omit *or.*
6:33 [y] NU-Text and M-Text read *they.*
6:36 [z] NU-Text reads *something to eat* and omits the rest of this verse.

38But He said to them, "How many loaves do you have? Go and see."
And when they found out they said, "Five, and two fish."
39Then He commanded them to make them all sit down in groups on
the green grass. 40So they sat down in ranks, in hundreds and in fifties. 41And
when He had taken the five loaves and the two fish, He looked up to heaven,
blessed and broke the loaves, and gave *them* to His disciples to set before
them; and the two fish He divided among *them* all. 42So they all ate and
were filled. 43And they took up twelve baskets full of fragments and of the
fish. 44Now those who had eaten the loaves were about[a] five thousand men.

Jesus Walks on the Sea

45Immediately He made His disciples get into the boat and go before
Him to the other side, to Bethsaida, while He sent the multitude away. 46And
when He had sent them away, He departed to the mountain to pray. 47Now
when evening came, the boat was in the middle of the sea; and He *was*
alone on the land. 48Then He saw them straining at rowing, for the wind was
against them. Now about the fourth watch of the night He came to them,
walking on the sea, and would have passed them by. 49And when they saw
Him walking on the sea, they supposed it was a ghost, and cried out; 50for
they all saw Him and were troubled. But immediately He talked with them
and said to them, "Be of good cheer! It is I; do not be afraid." 51Then He
went up into the boat to them, and the wind ceased. And they were greatly
amazed in themselves beyond measure, and marveled. 52For they had not
understood about the loaves, because their heart was hardened.

Many Touch Him and Are Made Well

53When they had crossed over, they came to the land of Gennesaret and
anchored there. 54And when they came out of the boat, immediately the
people recognized Him, 55ran through that whole surrounding region, and
began to carry about on beds those who were sick to wherever they heard
He was. 56Wherever He entered, into villages, cities, or the country, they laid
the sick in the marketplaces, and begged Him that they might just touch
the hem of His garment. And as many as touched Him were made well.

Defilement Comes from Within

7 Then the Pharisees and some of the scribes came together to Him, having come from Jerusalem. 2Now when[b] they saw some of His disciples
eat bread with defiled, that is, with unwashed hands, they found fault. 3For
the Pharisees and all the Jews do not eat unless they wash *their* hands in a
special way, holding the tradition of the elders. 4*When they come* from the
marketplace, they do not eat unless they wash. And there are many other
things which they have received and hold, *like* the washing of cups, pitchers, copper vessels, and couches.
5Then the Pharisees and scribes asked Him, "Why do Your disciples not
walk according to the tradition of the elders, but eat bread with unwashed
hands?"
6He answered and said to them, "Well did Isaiah prophesy of you hypocrites, as it is written:

6:44 [a] NU-Text and M-Text omit *about*.
7:2 [b] NU-Text omits *when* and *they found fault*.

the basketball and push it as hard as he could toward the goal, but it always fell short. The father would then take the ball and toss it toward the basket, saying something like, "Just do it like this, son. It's easy."

Then the boy would try, and miss, again. My friend would then take the ball and make another basket, encouraging his son to push the ball a bit harder.

After several minutes and many misses, the boy responded to his father's encouragement by saying, "Yeah, but it's easy for you up there. You don't know how hard it is from down here."

You and I can never say that about God. Of the many messages Jesus taught us that day about stress, the first one is this: "God knows how you feel."

(From *In the Eye of the Storm* by Max Lucado)

APPLICATION Follow Jesus' example in handling stress. If today starts to get hectic, take five minutes to be alone with God. If your work gets interrupted, ask God for patience to deal with the interruption and for endurance to finish the task.

EXPLORATION Stress—Isaiah 26:3; Matthew 11:28; Luke 10:38-42; Philippians 4:6; 2 Peter 3:8.

'This people honors Me with their lips,
But their heart is far from Me.
7 *And in vain they worship Me,*
Teaching as doctrines the commandments of men.'[c]
8For laying aside the commandment of God, you hold the tradition of men[d]—
the washing of pitchers and cups, and many other such things you do."
9He said to them, "*All too* well you reject the commandment of God,
that you may keep your tradition. 10For Moses said, *'Honor your father*
and your mother';[e] and, *'He who curses father or mother, let him be put to*
death.'[f] 11But you say, 'If a man says to his father or mother, "Whatever
profit you might have received from me *is* Corban"—' (that is, a gift *to*
God), 12then you no longer let him do anything for his father or his mother,
13making the word of God of no effect through your tradition which you
have handed down. And many such things you do."
14When He had called all the multitude to *Himself,* He said to them, "Hear
Me, everyone, and understand: 15There is nothing that enters a man from
outside which can defile him; but the things which come out of him, those
are the things that defile a man. 16If anyone has ears to hear, let him hear!"[g]
17When He had entered a house away from the crowd, His disciples asked
Him concerning the parable. 18So He said to them, "Are you thus without
understanding also? Do you not perceive that whatever enters a man from
outside cannot defile him, 19because it does not enter his heart but his
stomach, and is eliminated, *thus* purifying all foods?"[h] 20And He said, "What
comes out of a man, that defiles a man. 21For from within, out of the heart
of men, proceed evil thoughts, adulteries, fornications, murders, 22thefts,
covetousness, wickedness, deceit, lewdness, an evil eye, blasphemy, pride,
foolishness. 23All these evil things come from within and defile a man."

A Gentile Shows Her Faith

24From there He arose and went to the region of Tyre and Sidon.[i] And
He entered a house and wanted no one to know *it,* but He could not be
hidden. 25For a woman whose young daughter had an unclean spirit heard
about Him, and she came and fell at His feet. 26The woman was a Greek, a
Syro-Phoenician by birth, and she kept asking Him to cast the demon out
of her daughter. 27But Jesus said to her, "Let the children be filled first, for
it is not good to take the children's bread and throw *it* to the little dogs."
28And she answered and said to Him, "Yes, Lord, yet even the little dogs
under the table eat from the children's crumbs."
29Then He said to her, "For this saying go your way; the demon has gone
out of your daughter."
30And when she had come to her house, she found the demon gone out,
and her daughter lying on the bed.

Jesus Heals a Deaf-Mute

31Again, departing from the region of Tyre and Sidon, He came through

7:7 [c] Isaiah 29:13
7:8 [d] NU-Text omits the rest of this verse.
7:10 [e] Exodus 20:12; Deuteronomy 5:16 [f] Exodus 21:17
7:16 [g] NU-Text omits this verse.
7:19 [h] NU-Text ends quotation with *eliminated,* setting off the final clause as Mark's comment that Jesus has declared all foods clean.
7:24 [i] NU-Text omits *and Sidon.*

Life Lesson

Mark 7:1-37

SITUATION Many Pharisees of Jesus' day believed that their rituals demonstrated respect for God. Hundreds of laws and rituals prescribed exactly how Jews should live, including the consumption of clean and unclean foods. Jesus showed that faith was more important.

OBSERVATION Jesus amazed the people by his teaching and dumbfounded them by his actions.

INSPIRATION Quite a passage, isn't it?

Jesus is presented with a man who is deaf and has a speech impediment. Perhaps he stammered. Maybe he spoke with a lisp. Perhaps, because of his deafness, he never learned to articulate words properly.

Jesus, refusing to exploit the situation, took the man aside. He looked him in the face. Knowing it would be useless to talk, he explained what he was about to do through gestures. He spat and touched the man's tongue, telling him that whatever restricted his speech was about to be removed. He touched his ears. They, for the first time, were about to hear.

But before the man said a word or heard a sound, Jesus did something I never would have anticipated.

He sighed. . . .

Sigh. The word seemed out of place.

I'd never thought of God as one who sighs. I'd thought of God as one who commands. I'd thought of God as one who weeps. I'd thought of God as one who called forth the dead with a command or created the universe with a word . . . but a God who sighs?

Perhaps this phrase caught my eye because I do my share of sighing.

I sighed yesterday when I visited a lady whose invalid husband had deteriorated so much he didn't recognize me. He thought I was trying to sell him something.

I sighed when the dirty-faced, scantily dressed, six-year-old girl in the grocery store asked me for some change.

And I sighed today listening to a husband tell how his wife won't forgive him.

the midst of the region of Decapolis to the Sea of Galilee. 32Then they
brought to Him one who was deaf and had an impediment in his speech,
and they begged Him to put His hand on him. 33And He took him aside
from the multitude, and put His fingers in his ears, and He spat and
touched his tongue. 34Then, looking up to heaven, He sighed, and said to
him, "Ephphatha," that is, "Be opened."

35Immediately his ears were opened, and the impediment of his tongue
was loosed, and he spoke plainly. 36Then He commanded them that they
should tell no one; but the more He commanded them, the more widely they
proclaimed *it.* 37And they were astonished beyond measure, saying, "He has
done all things well. He makes both the deaf to hear and the mute to speak."

Feeding the Four Thousand

8 In those days, the multitude being very great and having nothing to
eat, Jesus called His disciples *to Him* and said to them, 2"I have compassion on the multitude, because they have now continued with Me three
days and have nothing to eat. 3And if I send them away hungry to their own
houses, they will faint on the way; for some of them have come from afar."

4Then His disciples answered Him, "How can one satisfy these people
with bread here in the wilderness?"

5He asked them, "How many loaves do you have?"

And they said, "Seven."

6So He commanded the multitude to sit down on the ground. And He
took the seven loaves and gave thanks, broke *them* and gave *them* to His
disciples to set before *them;* and they set *them* before the multitude. 7They
also had a few small fish; and having blessed them, He said to set them
also before *them.* 8So they ate and were filled, and they took up seven large
baskets of leftover fragments. 9Now those who had eaten were about four
thousand. And He sent them away, 10immediately got into the boat with
His disciples, and came to the region of Dalmanutha.

The Pharisees Seek a Sign

11Then the Pharisees came out and began to dispute with Him, seeking
from Him a sign from heaven, testing Him. 12But He sighed deeply in His
spirit, and said, "Why does this generation seek a sign? Assuredly, I say to
you, no sign shall be given to this generation."

Beware of the Leaven of the Pharisees and Herod

13And He left them, and getting into the boat again, departed to the other
side. 14Now the disciples[j] had forgotten to take bread, and they did not have
more than one loaf with them in the boat. 15Then He charged them, saying,
"Take heed, beware of the leaven of the Pharisees and the leaven of Herod."

16And they reasoned among themselves, saying, "*It is* because we have
no bread."

17But Jesus, being aware of *it,* said to them, "Why do you reason because
you have no bread? Do you not yet perceive nor understand? Is your heart
still[k] hardened? 18Having eyes, do you not see? And having ears, do you not
hear? And do you not remember? 19When I broke the five loaves for the five
thousand, how many baskets full of fragments did you take up?"

8:14 *j* NU-Text and M-Text read *they.*
8:17 *k* NU-Text omits *still.*

No doubt you've done your share of sighing.

If you have teenagers, you've probably sighed. If you're tried to resist temptation, you've probably sighed. If you've had your motives questioned or your best acts of love rejected, you have been forced to take a deep breath and let escape a painful sigh. . . .

All these sighs come from the same anxiety; a recognition of pain that was never intended, or of hope deferred.

Man was not created to be separated from his creator; hence he sighs, longing for home. The creation was never intended to be inhabited by evil; hence she sighs, yearning for the Garden. . . .

And when Jesus looked into the eyes of Satan's victim, the only appropriate thing to do was sigh. "It was never intended to be this way," the sigh said. "Your ears weren't made to be deaf, your tongue wasn't made to stumble." The imbalance of it all caused the Master to languish.

So, I found a place for the word. You might think it strange, but I placed it beside the word *comfort,* for in an indirect way, God's pain is our comfort.

And in the agony of Jesus lies our hope. Had he not sighed, had he not felt the burden for what was not intended, we would be in a pitiful condition. Had he simply chalked it all up to the inevitable or washed his hands of the whole stinking mess, what hope would we have?

But he didn't. That holy sigh assures us that God still groans for his people. He groans for the day when all sighs will cease, when what was intended to be will be.

(From *God Came Near* by Max Lucado)

APPLICATION What situations cause you to need comfort? A broken relationship, a lost loved one, or overwhelming anxiety? Pray, thanking God that he still groans for his people.

EXPLORATION Comfort—Job 15:11; Psalm 23; 71:19-21; 86:17; 94:19; 119:50, 76; Isaiah 12:1; 40:1; 2 Corinthians 1:3; Hebrews 6:18.

LIFE LESSON

Mark 8:1-38

SITUATION The Pharisees doubted Jesus' divine nature. They asked him for a sign from heaven that would proclaim him as Messiah.

OBSERVATION To see God's presence at work, we must look at the power behind the miracle first—God.

INSPIRATION His lunch wasn't much. In fact, it wasn't anything compared to what was needed for more than five thousand people.

He probably wrestled with the silliness of it all. What was one lunch for so many?

How far could one lunch go?

I think that's why he didn't give the lunch to the crowd. Instead he gave it to Jesus. Something told him that if he would plant the seed, God would grant the crop.

So he did.

He summoned his courage, got up off the grass, and walked into the circle of grownups. He must have been nervous. No one likes to appear silly.

Someone probably snickered at him.

If they didn't snicker, they shook their heads. "The little fellow doesn't know any better."

If they didn't shake their heads, they rolled their eyes. "Here we have a hunger crisis, and this little boy thinks that a sack lunch will solve it."

But it wasn't the men's heads or eyes that the boy saw; he saw only Jesus.

(From *In the Eye of the Storm* by Max Lucado)

APPLICATION What do you believe about miracles? Look for the amazing things that have happened in your life: at work, at home, and with friends. They are all God's blessings. Help meet the needs of another, and be a part of God's miracle in that life.

EXPLORATION Miracles—Matthew 8:23-27; Mark 3:20-30; Luke 18:35-43; John 2:1-11; 11:1-44; 4:43-54.

They said to Him, "Twelve."

20 "Also, when I broke the seven for the four thousand, how many large baskets full of fragments did you take up?"

And they said, "Seven."

21 So He said to them, "How *is it* you do not understand?"

A Blind Man Healed at Bethsaida

22 Then He came to Bethsaida; and they brought a blind man to Him, and begged Him to touch him. 23 So He took the blind man by the hand and led him out of the town. And when He had spit on his eyes and put His hands on him, He asked him if he saw anything.

24 And he looked up and said, "I see men like trees, walking."

25 Then He put *His* hands on his eyes again and made him look up. And he was restored and saw everyone clearly. 26 Then He sent him away to his house, saying, "Neither go into the town, nor tell anyone in the town."[l]

Peter Confesses Jesus as the Christ

27 Now Jesus and His disciples went out to the towns of Caesarea Philippi; and on the road He asked His disciples, saying to them, "Who do men say that I am?"

28 So they answered, "John the Baptist; but some *say,* Elijah; and others, one of the prophets."

29 He said to them, "But who do you say that I am?"

Peter answered and said to Him, "You are the Christ."

30 Then He strictly warned them that they should tell no one about Him.

Jesus Predicts His Death and Resurrection

31 And He began to teach them that the Son of Man must suffer many things, and be rejected by the elders and chief priests and scribes, and be killed, and after three days rise again. 32 He spoke this word openly. Then Peter took Him aside and began to rebuke Him. 33 But when He had turned around and looked at His disciples, He rebuked Peter, saying, "Get behind Me, Satan! For you are not mindful of the things of God, but the things of men."

Take Up the Cross and Follow Him

34 When He had called the people to *Himself,* with His disciples also, He said to them, "Whoever desires to come after Me, let him deny himself, and take up his cross, and follow Me. 35 For whoever desires to save his life will lose it, but whoever loses his life for My sake and the gospel's will save it. 36 For what will it profit a man if he gains the whole world, and loses his own soul? 37 Or what will a man give in exchange for his soul? 38 For whoever is ashamed of Me and My words in this adulterous and sinful generation, of him the Son of Man also will be ashamed when He comes in the glory of His Father with the holy angels."

Jesus Transfigured on the Mount

9 And He said to them, "Assuredly, I say to you that there are some standing here who will not taste death till they see the kingdom of God present with power."

8:26 [l] NU-Text reads *"Do not even go into the town."*

[2]Now after six days Jesus took Peter, James, and John, and led them up
on a high mountain apart by themselves; and He was transfigured before
them. [3]His clothes became shining, exceedingly white, like snow, such as
no launderer on earth can whiten them. [4]And Elijah appeared to them
with Moses, and they were talking with Jesus. [5]Then Peter answered and
said to Jesus, "Rabbi, it is good for us to be here; and let us make three
tabernacles: one for You, one for Moses, and one for Elijah"— [6]because he
did not know what to say, for they were greatly afraid.
[7]And a cloud came and overshadowed them; and a voice came out of the
cloud, saying, "This is My beloved Son. Hear Him!" [8]Suddenly, when they had
looked around, they saw no one anymore, but only Jesus with themselves.
[9]Now as they came down from the mountain, He commanded them
that they should tell no one the things they had seen, till the Son of Man
had risen from the dead. [10]So they kept this word to themselves, questioning what the rising from the dead meant.
[11]And they asked Him, saying, "Why do the scribes say that Elijah must
come first?"
[12]Then He answered and told them, "Indeed, Elijah is coming first and
restores all things. And how is it written concerning the Son of Man, that
He must suffer many things and be treated with contempt? [13]But I say to
you that Elijah has also come, and they did to him whatever they wished,
as it is written of him."

A Boy Is Healed

[14]And when He came to the disciples, He saw a great multitude around
them, and scribes disputing with them. [15]Immediately, when they saw
Him, all the people were greatly amazed, and running to *Him,* greeted
Him. [16]And He asked the scribes, "What are you discussing with them?"
[17]Then one of the crowd answered and said, "Teacher, I brought You my
son, who has a mute spirit. [18]And wherever it seizes him, it throws him
down; he foams at the mouth, gnashes his teeth, and becomes rigid. So I
spoke to Your disciples, that they should cast it out, but they could not."
[19]He answered him and said, "O faithless generation, how long shall I be
with you? How long shall I bear with you? Bring him to Me." [20]Then they
brought him to Him. And when he saw Him, immediately the spirit convulsed him, and he fell on the ground and wallowed, foaming at the mouth.
[21]So He asked his father, "How long has this been happening to him?"
And he said, "From childhood. [22]And often he has thrown him both into
the fire and into the water to destroy him. But if You can do anything, have
compassion on us and help us."
[23]Jesus said to him, "If you can believe,[m] all things *are* possible to him
who believes."
[24]Immediately the father of the child cried out and said with tears,
"Lord, I believe; help my unbelief!"
[25]When Jesus saw that the people came running together, He rebuked
the unclean spirit, saying to it, "Deaf and dumb spirit, I command you,
come out of him and enter him no more!" [26]Then *the spirit* cried out, convulsed him greatly, and came out of him. And he became as one dead, so
that many said, "He is dead." [27]But Jesus took him by the hand and lifted
him up, and he arose.

9:23 *m* NU-Text reads "*'If You can!' All things . . . .*"

Life Lesson

Mark 9:1-50

SITUATION Jesus explained what God's Kingdom was about. The disciples could not fathom God's eternal plan. Jesus brought Peter, James, and John up on a mountain top. There Jesus' true glory was revealed, and Elijah and Moses appeared to the disciples as God spoke to them.

OBSERVATION Even the majestic son of God sympathizes with our most desperate cries.

INSPIRATION Some of you pray like a Concorde jet—smooth, sleek, high, and mighty. Your words reverberate in the clouds and send sonic booms throughout the heavens. If you pray like a Concorde, I salute you. If you don't, I understand.

Maybe you are like me, more a crop duster than a Concorde. You aren't flashy, you fly low, you seem to cover the same ground a lot, and some mornings it's tough to get the old engine cranked up.

Most of us are like that. Most of our prayer lives could use a tune-up.

Some prayer lives lack consistency. They're either a desert or an oasis. . . . We go days or weeks without consistent prayer, but then something happens—we hear a sermon, read a book, experience a tragedy—something leads us to pray, so we dive in. We submerge ourselves in prayer and leave refreshed and renewed. But as the journey resumes, our prayers don't.

Others of us need sincerity. Our prayers are a bit hollow, memorized, and rigid. More liturgy than life. And though they are daily, they are dull.

Still others lack, well, honesty. We honestly wonder if prayer makes a difference. Why on earth would God in heaven want to talk to me? . . .

If you struggle with prayer, I've got just the guy for you. Don't worry, he's not a monastic saint. He's not a calloused-kneed apostle. Nor is he a prophet whose middle name is meditation. He's not a too-holy-to-be-you reminder of how far you need to go in prayer. He's just the opposite. A fellow crop duster. A parent with a sick son in need of a miracle. The father's prayer isn't much, but the answer is,

Continued

and the result reminds us: The power is not in the prayer; it's in the one who hears it.

He prayed out of desperation. His son, his only son, was demon-possessed. Not only was he a deaf mute and an epileptic, he was also possessed by an evil spirit. Ever since the boy was young, the demon had thrown him into fires and water.

Imagine the pain of the father. Other dads could watch their children grow and mature; he could only watch his suffer. While others were teaching their sons an occupation, he was just trying to keep his son alive. . . .

He was desperate and tired, and his prayer reflects both.

"If you can do anything for him, please have pity on us and help us."

Listen to that prayer. Does it sound courageous? Confident? Strong? Hardly.

One word would have made a lot of difference. Instead of *if*, what if he'd said *since? "Since* you can do anything for him, please have pity on us and help us."

But that's not what he said. He said *if.* The Greek is even more emphatic. The tense implies doubt. It's as if the man were saying, "This one's probably out of your league, but if you can. . . ."

A classic crop-duster appeal. More meek than might. More timid than towering. More like a crippled lamb coming to a shepherd than a proud lion roaring in the jungle. If his prayer sounds like yours, then don't be discouraged, for that's where prayer begins.

It begins as a yearning. An honest appeal. Ordinary people staring at Mount Everest. No pretense. No boasting. No posturing. Just prayer. Feeble prayer, but prayer nonetheless. (From *He Still Moves Stones* by Max Lucado)

APPLICATION What is your most desperate prayer? Does a rebellious child cause you grief? Is a parent dying without Christ? Are you frantic about tomorrow's bills? Tell God about your grief and anxiety.

EXPLORATION Accepting Christ—Luke 2:9-10; 9:7-8; John 3:3.

28 And when He had come into the house, His disciples asked Him privately, "Why could we not cast it out?"

29 So He said to them, "This kind can come out by nothing but prayer and fasting."[n]

Jesus Again Predicts His Death and Resurrection

30 Then they departed from there and passed through Galilee, and He did not want anyone to know *it.* 31 For He taught His disciples and said to them, "The Son of Man is being betrayed into the hands of men, and they will kill Him. And after He is killed, He will rise the third day." 32 But they did not understand this saying, and were afraid to ask Him.

Who Is the Greatest?

33 Then He came to Capernaum. And when He was in the house He asked them, "What was it you disputed among yourselves on the road?" 34 But they kept silent, for on the road they had disputed among themselves who *would be the* greatest. 35 And He sat down, called the twelve, and said to them, "If anyone desires to be first, he shall be last of all and servant of all." 36 Then He took a little child and set him in the midst of them. And when He had taken him in His arms, He said to them, 37 "Whoever receives one of these little children in My name receives Me; and whoever receives Me, receives not Me but Him who sent Me."

Jesus Forbids Sectarianism

38 Now John answered Him, saying, "Teacher, we saw someone who does not follow us casting out demons in Your name, and we forbade him because he does not follow us."

39 But Jesus said, "Do not forbid him, for no one who works a miracle in My name can soon afterward speak evil of Me. 40 For he who is not against us is on our[o] side. 41 For whoever gives you a cup of water to drink in My name, because you belong to Christ, assuredly, I say to you, he will by no means lose his reward.

Jesus Warns of Offenses

42 "But whoever causes one of these little ones who believe in Me to stumble, it would be better for him if a millstone were hung around his neck, and he were thrown into the sea. 43 If your hand causes you to sin, cut it off. It is better for you to enter into life maimed, rather than having two hands, to go to hell, into the fire that shall never be quenched— 44 where

'Their worm does not die
And the fire is not quenched.'[p]

45 And if your foot causes you to sin, cut it off. It is better for you to enter life lame, rather than having two feet, to be cast into hell, into the fire that shall never be quenched— 46 where

'Their worm does not die
And the fire is not quenched.'[q]

9:29 [n] NU-Text omits *and fasting.*
9:40 [o] M-Text reads *against you is on your side.*
9:44 [p] NU-Text omits this verse.
9:46 [q] NU-Text omits the last clause of verse 45 and all of verse 46.

47And if your eye causes you to sin, pluck it out. It is better for you to enter
the kingdom of God with one eye, rather than having two eyes, to be cast
into hell fire— 48where

'Their worm does not die
And the fire is not quenched.'[r]

Tasteless Salt Is Worthless

49"For everyone will be seasoned with fire,[s] and every sacrifice will be
seasoned with salt. 50Salt *is* good, but if the salt loses its flavor, how will you
season it? Have salt in yourselves, and have peace with one another."

Marriage and Divorce

10 Then He arose from there and came to the region of Judea by the
other side of the Jordan. And multitudes gathered to Him again, and
as He was accustomed, He taught them again.
2The Pharisees came and asked Him, "Is it lawful for a man to divorce
his wife?" testing Him.
3And He answered and said to them, "What did Moses command you?"
4They said, "Moses permitted *a man* to write a certificate of divorce, and
to dismiss *her.*"
5And Jesus answered and said to them, "Because of the hardness of
your heart he wrote you this precept. 6But from the beginning of the creation, God *'made them male and female.'*[t] 7*'For this reason a man shall
leave his father and mother and be joined to his wife,* 8*and the two shall
become one flesh';*[u] so then they are no longer two, but one flesh. 9Therefore
what God has joined together, let not man separate."
10In the house His disciples also asked Him again about the same *matter.*
11So He said to them, "Whoever divorces his wife and marries another commits adultery against her. 12And if a woman divorces her husband and marries another, she commits adultery."

Jesus Blesses Little Children

13Then they brought little children to Him, that He might touch them;
but the disciples rebuked those who brought *them.* 14But when Jesus saw
it, He was greatly displeased and said to them, "Let the little children come
to Me, and do not forbid them; for of such is the kingdom of God. 15Assuredly,
I say to you, whoever does not receive the kingdom of God as a little child
will by no means enter it." 16And He took them up in His arms, laid *His*
hands on them, and blessed them.

Jesus Counsels the Rich Young Ruler

17Now as He was going out on the road, one came running, knelt before
Him, and asked Him, "Good Teacher, what shall I do that I may inherit
eternal life?"
18So Jesus said to him, "Why do you call Me good? No one *is* good but
One, *that is,* God. 19You know the commandments: *'Do not commit adultery,' 'Do not murder,' 'Do not steal,' 'Do not bear false witness,'* 'Do not
defraud,' *'Honor your father and your mother.'* "[v]

9:48 [r] Isaiah 66:24
9:49 [s] NU-Text omits the rest of this verse.
10:6 [t] Genesis 1:27; 5:2
10:8 [u] Genesis 2:24
10:19 [v] Exodus 20:12–16; Deuteronomy 5:16–20

LIFE LESSON

Mark 10:1-52

SITUATION To serve others rather than to be served best exemplified Jesus' message to humanity. People, then as now, often hoped that others would meet their needs. They committed to ideals such as marriage and trust in God as long as these seemed convenient. Giving up personal freedoms, wealth, and status to serve others was too great a price for many people.

OBSERVATION Jesus urges us to discard material security to follow him. By sacrificing the treasures of this world, we gain the treasures of Heaven.

INSPIRATION Jesus gets to the point. "If you want to be perfect, then go sell your possessions and give to the poor, and you will have treasure in heaven."

The statement leaves the young man distraught and the disciples bewildered. Their question could be ours: "Who then can be saved?"

Jesus' answer shell-shocks the listeners, "With man this is impossible. . . ." Impossible.

He doesn't say improbable. He doesn't say unlikely. He doesn't even say it will be tough. He says it is "impossible." . . .

Does that strike you as cold? All your life you've been rewarded according to your performance. You get grades according to your study. You get commendations according to your success. You get money in response to your work.

That's why the rich young ruler thought heaven was just a payment away. It only made sense. You work hard, you pay your dues, and "zap"—your account is credited as paid in full. Jesus says, "No way." What you want costs far more than what you can pay. You don't need a system, you need a Savior. You don't need a resumé, you need a Redeemer. For "what is impossible with men is possible with God."

. . . You see, it wasn't the money that hindered the rich man; it was the self-sufficiency. It wasn't the possessions; it was the pomp. It wasn't the big bucks; it was the big head. . . .

Continued

Astounding. These people are standing before the throne of God and bragging about themselves. The great trumpet has sounded, and they are still tooting their own horns. Rather than sing his praises, they sing their own. Rather than worship God, they read their resumés. When they should be speechless, they speak. In the very aura of the King they boast of self. What is worse—their arrogance or their blindness?

. . . God does not save us because of what we've done. . . .

And only a great God does for his children what they can't do for themselves.

That is the message of Paul: "For what the law was powerless to do . . . God did."

And that is the message of the first beatitude.

"Blessed are the poor in spirit . . ."

The jewel of joy is given to the impoverished spirits, not the affluent. God's delight is received upon surrender, not awarded upon conquest.

(From *The Applause of Heaven* by Max Lucado)

APPLICATION Don't let money stand between you and God. You can't buy a ticket into heaven, you only have to ask in faith. Think about the rich value of faith throughout the day.

EXPLORATION Selfishness—Proverbs 28:25; Matthew 19:21; Mark 8:36-37; Luke 12:15-21; 16:19-31; Philippians 2:3.

20 And he answered and said to Him, "Teacher, all these things I have
kept from my youth."
21 Then Jesus, looking at him, loved him, and said to him, "One thing
you lack: Go your way, sell whatever you have and give to the poor, and you
will have treasure in heaven; and come, take up the cross, and follow Me."
22 But he was sad at this word, and went away sorrowful, for he had great
possessions.

With God All Things Are Possible

23 Then Jesus looked around and said to His disciples, "How hard it is for
those who have riches to enter the kingdom of God!"
24 And the disciples
were astonished at His words. But Jesus answered again and said to them,
"Children, how hard it is for those who trust in riches[w] to enter the kingdom of God!
25 It is easier for a camel to go through the eye of a needle than
for a rich man to enter the kingdom of God."
26 And they were greatly astonished, saying among themselves, "Who
then can be saved?"
27 But Jesus looked at them and said, "With men *it is* impossible, but not
with God; for with God all things are possible."
28 Then Peter began to say to Him, "See, we have left all and followed You."
29 So Jesus answered and said, "Assuredly, I say to you, there is no one
who has left house or brothers or sisters or father or mother or wife[x] or
children or lands, for My sake and the gospel's,
30 who shall not receive a
hundredfold now in this time—houses and brothers and sisters and
mothers and children and lands, with persecutions—and in the age to
come, eternal life.
31 But many *who are* first will be last, and the last first."

Jesus a Third Time Predicts His Death and Resurrection

32 Now they were on the road, going up to Jerusalem, and Jesus was
going before them; and they were amazed. And as they followed they were
afraid. Then He took the twelve aside again and began to tell them the
things that would happen to Him:
33 "Behold, we are going up to Jerusalem,
and the Son of Man will be betrayed to the chief priests and to the scribes;
and they will condemn Him to death and deliver Him to the Gentiles;
34 and
they will mock Him, and scourge Him, and spit on Him, and kill Him. And
the third day He will rise again."

Greatness Is Serving

35 Then James and John, the sons of Zebedee, came to Him, saying,
"Teacher, we want You to do for us whatever we ask."
36 And He said to them, "What do you want Me to do for you?"
37 They said to Him, "Grant us that we may sit, one on Your right hand
and the other on Your left, in Your glory."
38 But Jesus said to them, "You do not know what you ask. Are you able
to drink the cup that I drink, and be baptized with the baptism that I am
baptized with?"
39 They said to Him, "We are able."
So Jesus said to them, "You will indeed drink the cup that I drink, and

10:24 [w] NU-Text omits *for those who trust in riches.*
10:29 [x] NU-Text omits *or wife.*

PAIN

Sometimes people question God—"Is pain my punishment?" You've heard the expression "The rain falls on the just and the unjust"—or better, the unjust and the unjust, for we are all sinners. All of us are or will be victims of pain—it's simply a fact of our existence, regardless of how good or how bad we are. Life isn't fair? No, but there is one who justifies life and understands that pain.

When we face struggles, we often wonder, *Why?* Years from now, though, we may realize that it was those struggles that taught us something we could not have otherwise learned—that there was a purpose in our pain.

God's purpose is greater than your pain, and he has a greater purpose than your problems. Your crises are not going to slow down the purpose of God—have confidence in that.

TEACH US to set our hopes on heaven, to hold firmly to the promise of eternal life, so that we can withstand the struggles and storms of this world. May your holy Word be a soothing medicine to the wounded heart.

FAILURES

We enjoy many freedoms in the United States. But unless you've been freed by God Almighty, there is one bondage you still carry, regardless of the country you're in. And that's the freedom of yesterday's regrets, yesterday's failures. All of us need to have that capacity and strength to stand tall with the confidence that God has released us from that bondage of regret.

Perhaps the heaviest burden we try to carry is the burden of mistakes, failures. What do you do with your failures?

Even if you've fallen, even if you've failed, even if everyone else has rejected you, Christ will not turn away from you. He came first and foremost to those who have no hope. He goes to those no one else would go to and says, "I'll give you eternity."

Only you can surrender your concerns to the Father. No one else can take those away and give them to God. Only you can cast all your anxieties on the one who cares for you. What better way to start the day than laying your cares at his feet?

Regardless of what you've done, it's not too late. It doesn't matter how low the mistake is, it's not too late to dig down, pull out that mistake, and then let it go—and be free.

Father in heaven, help us as we cope and grapple with yesterday's failures. They dog at our heels like irritations. They follow us around. They cling to our ankles like fifteen-pound ball weights. Help us to release those regrets in the right way, and keep us close.

Mercy

The first step in finding your place in God's plan is to see his mercy—instead of looking inside yourself, look up to him and reflect upon and understand his mercy. How great is the call of God!

God forgave us before we even asked it. He extended mercy to us before we even knew we needed it. Why? Because the God of mercy took pity on us—a band of creatures who are incapable of saving themselves without his gift of mercy.

FATHER, you have expressed toward us unlimited mercy. The only reason this world continues is because you have mercy upon us. Millions of people today are receiving food for which they'll never give thanks. We're breathing air that we take for granted. Somehow, though, you continue to feed us with your mercy and forgiveness. Thank you for the unimaginable gifts of your love.

CONFLICT

Conflict is inevitable, but combat is optional. Use your God-given creative energy to solve conflict before it escalates into combat.

Perhaps the seeds you sow in your areas of conflict won't reach maturity tomorrow, next week, or even for a generation. Does that mean you shouldn't sow the seeds? No! It means you should sow the seeds *immediately.* Never underestimate the power of a seed of peace: the power of a kind word, a seed of apology, a phone call, an explanation. This is the way we serve a God of peace.

GOD OF PEACE, Father of comfort, we pray that your kingdom would come into our hearts and that peace would rule. Teach us what it means to be peacemakers. Help us cultivate peace between others and you—in our neighborhoods, offices, schoolrooms. Teach us the art of building bridges and not walls. We glorify your name, the great God of peace.

with the baptism I am baptized with you will be baptized; 40but to sit on
My right hand and on My left is not Mine to give, but *it is for those* for
whom it is prepared."
41And when the ten heard *it,* they began to be greatly displeased with James
and John. 42But Jesus called them to *Himself* and said to them, "You know that
those who are considered rulers over the Gentiles lord it over them, and their
great ones exercise authority over them. 43Yet it shall not be so among you; but
whoever desires to become great among you shall be your servant. 44And whoever of you desires to be first shall be slave of all. 45For even the Son of Man did
not come to be served, but to serve, and to give His life a ransom for many."

Jesus Heals Blind Bartimaeus

46Now they came to Jericho. As He went out of Jericho with His disciples
and a great multitude, blind Bartimaeus, the son of Timaeus, sat by the
road begging. 47And when he heard that it was Jesus of Nazareth, he began
to cry out and say, "Jesus, Son of David, have mercy on me!"
48Then many warned him to be quiet; but he cried out all the more, "Son
of David, have mercy on me!"
49So Jesus stood still and commanded him to be called.
Then they called the blind man, saying to him, "Be of good cheer. Rise,
He is calling you."
50And throwing aside his garment, he rose and came to Jesus.
51So Jesus answered and said to him, "What do you want Me to do for you?"
The blind man said to Him, "Rabboni, that I may receive my sight."
52Then Jesus said to him, "Go your way; your faith has made you well."
And immediately he received his sight and followed Jesus on the road.

The Triumphal Entry

11 Now when they drew near Jerusalem, to Bethphage[y] and Bethany, at
the Mount of Olives, He sent two of His disciples; 2and He said to
them, "Go into the village opposite you; and as soon as you have entered it
you will find a colt tied, on which no one has sat. Loose it and bring *it.*
3And if anyone says to you, 'Why are you doing this?' say, 'The Lord has
need of it,' and immediately he will send it here."
4So they went their way, and found the[z] colt tied by the door outside on
the street, and they loosed it. 5But some of those who stood there said to
them, "What are you doing, loosing the colt?"
6And they spoke to them just as Jesus had commanded. So they let them
go. 7Then they brought the colt to Jesus and threw their clothes on it, and
He sat on it. 8And many spread their clothes on the road, and others cut
down leafy branches from the trees and spread *them* on the road. 9Then
those who went before and those who followed cried out, saying:

"Hosanna!
'Blessed is He who comes in the name of the LORD!'[a]
10 Blessed *is* the kingdom of our father David
That comes in the name of the Lord![b]
Hosanna in the highest!"

11:1 [y] M-Text reads *Bethsphage.*
11:4 [z] NU-Text and M-Text read *a.*
11:9 [a] Psalm 118:26
11:10 [b] NU-Text omits *in the name of the Lord.*

Life Lesson

Mark 11:1-33

SITUATION Jesus and his disciples made a pilgrimage to the Temple in Jerusalem during the Passover. The people heralded Jesus, calling him the Messiah. He threw merchants and money changers out of the Temple for profiting from people's worship. During this week, he traveled between Bethany and Jerusalem frequently.

OBSERVATION Have faith in God. He always fulfills his word. Jesus promised that through faith his disciples would accomplish great things.

INSPIRATION The story is told about the time Napoleon's steed got away from him. An alert private jumped on his own horse and chased down the general's horse. When he presented the reins of the animal to Napoleon, the ruler took them, smiled at his willing private, and said, "Thank you, Captain."

The soldier's eyes widened at what he had heard. He then straightened. Saluted. And snapped, "Thank you, sir!"

He immediately went to the barracks. Got his bags. Moved into the officers' quarters. Took his uniform to the quartermaster and exchanged it for that of a captain. By the general's word, he had become a private-turned-commissioned officer. He didn't argue. He didn't shrug. He didn't doubt. He knew that the one who had the power to do it had done it. And he accepted that.

If only we would do the same. If only we would have the faith of the private. . . . If only, when God smiles and says we are saved, we'd salute him, and live like those who have just received a gift from the commander in chief.

(From *In the Eye of the Storm* by Max Lucado)

APPLICATION Develop regular prayer times when you tell both your troubles and your joys to God.

EXPLORATION Faith—Matthew 21:21; Hebrews 11:1-6; James 5:13-18; 1 John 5:14.

11 And Jesus went into Jerusalem and into the temple. So when He had looked around at all things, as the hour was already late, He went out to Bethany with the twelve.

The Fig Tree Withered

12 Now the next day, when they had come out from Bethany, He was hungry. 13 And seeing from afar a fig tree having leaves, He went to see if perhaps He would find something on it. When He came to it, He found nothing but leaves, for it was not the season for figs. 14 In response Jesus said to it, "Let no one eat fruit from you ever again."

And His disciples heard *it.*

Jesus Cleanses the Temple

15 So they came to Jerusalem. Then Jesus went into the temple and began to drive out those who bought and sold in the temple, and overturned the tables of the money changers and the seats of those who sold doves. 16 And He would not allow anyone to carry wares through the temple. 17 Then He taught, saying to them, "Is it not written, *'My house shall be called a house of prayer for all nations'* ?[c] But you have made it a *'den of thieves.'* "[d]

18 And the scribes and chief priests heard it and sought how they might destroy Him; for they feared Him, because all the people were astonished at His teaching. 19 When evening had come, He went out of the city.

The Lesson of the Withered Fig Tree

20 Now in the morning, as they passed by, they saw the fig tree dried up from the roots. 21 And Peter, remembering, said to Him, "Rabbi, look! The fig tree which You cursed has withered away."

22 So Jesus answered and said to them, "Have faith in God. 23 For assuredly, I say to you, whoever says to this mountain, 'Be removed and be cast into the sea,' and does not doubt in his heart, but believes that those things he says will be done, he will have whatever he says. 24 Therefore I say to you, whatever things you ask when you pray, believe that you receive *them,* and you will have *them.*

Forgiveness and Prayer

25 "And whenever you stand praying, if you have anything against anyone, forgive him, that your Father in heaven may also forgive you your trespasses. 26 But if you do not forgive, neither will your Father in heaven forgive your trespasses."[e]

Jesus' Authority Questioned

27 Then they came again to Jerusalem. And as He was walking in the temple, the chief priests, the scribes, and the elders came to Him. 28 And they said to Him, "By what authority are You doing these things? And who gave You this authority to do these things?"

29 But Jesus answered and said to them, "I also will ask you one question; then answer Me, and I will tell you by what authority I do these things: 30 The baptism of John—was it from heaven or from men? Answer Me."

31 And they reasoned among themselves, saying, "If we say, 'From heaven,' He will say, 'Why then did you not believe him?' 32 But if we say, 'From men' "—they feared the people, for all counted John to have been a prophet indeed. 33 So they answered and said to Jesus, "We do not know."

And Jesus answered and said to them, "Neither will I tell you by what authority I do these things."

The Parable of the Wicked Vinedressers

12 Then He began to speak to them in parables: "A man planted a vineyard and set a hedge around *it,* dug *a place for* the wine vat and built a tower. And he leased it to vinedressers and went into a far country. 2 Now at vintage-time he sent a servant to the vinedressers, that he might receive some of the fruit of the vineyard from the vinedressers. 3 And they took *him* and beat him and sent *him* away empty-handed. 4 Again he sent them another servant, and at him they threw stones,[f] wounded *him* in the head, and sent *him* away shamefully treated. 5 And again he sent another, and him they killed; and many others, beating some and killing some. 6 Therefore still having one son, his beloved, he also sent him to them last, saying, 'They will respect my son.' 7 But those vinedressers said among themselves, 'This is the heir. Come, let us kill him, and the inheritance will be ours.' 8 So they took him and killed *him* and cast *him* out of the vineyard.

9 "Therefore what will the owner of the vineyard do? He will come and destroy the vinedressers, and give the vineyard to others. 10 Have you not even read this Scripture:

> *'The stone which the builders rejected*
> *Has become the chief cornerstone.*

11:17 [c] Isaiah 56:7 [d] Jeremiah 7:11
11:26 [e] NU-Text omits this verse.
12:4 [f] NU-Text omits *and at him they threw stones.*

11 *This was the* LORD's *doing,*
And it is marvelous in our eyes'?"[g]
12 And they sought to lay hands on Him, but feared the multitude, for they knew
He had spoken the parable against them. So they left Him and went away.

The Pharisees: Is It Lawful to Pay Taxes to Caesar?

13 Then they sent to Him some of the Pharisees and the Herodians, to
catch Him in *His* words. 14 When they had come, they said to Him, "Teacher,
we know that You are true, and care about no one; for You do not regard
the person of men, but teach the way of God in truth. Is it lawful to pay
taxes to Caesar, or not? 15 Shall we pay, or shall we not pay?"
But He, knowing their hypocrisy, said to them, "Why do you test Me?
Bring Me a denarius that I may see *it.*" 16 So they brought *it.*
And He said to them, "Whose image and inscription *is* this?" They said
to Him, "Caesar's."
17 And Jesus answered and said to them, "Render to Caesar the things
that are Caesar's, and to God the things that are God's."
And they marveled at Him.

The Sadducees: What About the Resurrection?

18 Then *some* Sadducees, who say there is no resurrection, came to Him;
and they asked Him, saying: 19 "Teacher, Moses wrote to us that if a man's
brother dies, and leaves *his* wife behind, and leaves no children, his brother
should take his wife and raise up offspring for his brother. 20 Now there
were seven brothers. The first took a wife; and dying, he left no offspring.
21 And the second took her, and he died; nor did he leave any offspring. And
the third likewise. 22 So the seven had her and left no offspring. Last of all
the woman died also. 23 Therefore, in the resurrection, when they rise,
whose wife will she be? For all seven had her as wife."
24 Jesus answered and said to them, "Are you not therefore mistaken,
because you do not know the Scriptures nor the power of God? 25 For when
they rise from the dead, they neither marry nor are given in marriage, but
are like angels in heaven. 26 But concerning the dead, that they rise, have
you not read in the book of Moses, in the *burning* bush *passage,* how God
spoke to him, saying, '*I am* the God of Abraham, the God of Isaac, and the
God of Jacob'?[h] 27 He is not the God of the dead, but the God of the living.
You are therefore greatly mistaken."

The Scribes: Which Is the First Commandment of All?

28 Then one of the scribes came, and having heard them reasoning together, perceiving[i] that He had answered them well, asked Him, "Which is
the first commandment of all?"
29 Jesus answered him, "The first of all the commandments *is: 'Hear, O*
Israel, the LORD *our God, the* LORD *is one.* 30 *And you shall love the* LORD
your God with all your heart, with all your soul, with all your mind, and
with all your strength.'[j] This *is* the first commandment.[k] 31 And the second,
like *it, is* this: '*You shall love your neighbor as yourself.*'[l] There is no other
commandment greater than these."

12:11 [g] Psalm 118:22, 23
12:26 [h] Exodus 3:6, 15
12:28 [i] NU-Text reads *seeing.*
12:30 [j] Deuteronomy 6:4, 5 [k] NU-Text omits this sentence.
12:31 [l] Leviticus 19:18

LIFE LESSON

Mark 12:1-44

SITUATION The time for Jesus' death was approaching quickly. Nearing his final hour, Jesus wanted God's love to be made clear through his teaching and example.

OBSERVATION As a result of God's love for us, we can love God and others. God's love also gives us hope that we have eternal life.

INSPIRATION Love for the Master is not some sweet sentimental emotion that sweeps over the soul in moments of special piety. Love for Christ is a deliberate setting of the will to carry out His commands at any cost. It is the fixed attitude of heart that decides to do His will at all times. It is the desire and delight of accomplishing our Father's highest purposes, no matter how challenging. . . .

In our highly permissive society, where the so-called "me" generation is encouraged to be so self-centered and so self-preoccupied, the call to obey Christ and comply with His commands cuts across our culture and our cynical conduct.

It simply is not normal nor natural for most of us to "love" God or "love" others in the drastic discipline of a laid-down life. We are a selfish, self-serving people. And when called upon to serve others we feel insulted. We have the strange, worldly idea that to be of lowly service is to be "used" or "abused."

Yet God, very God, in Christ came among us in lowly service. He came to minister to us. He came to give Himself to us. And so, because He first "loved" us, we in turn are to be willing and ready to "love" Him and others.

(From *Lessons from a Sheep Dog* by Phillip Keller)

APPLICATION When you are fed up with life and utterly exhausted, look for a way to love someone around you. Being patient and maintaining a caring attitude when you don't feel like it shows that you have experienced God's love.

EXPLORATION God's Sacrifice— Romans 5:8; Ephesians 5:2; 1 John 4:10.

[32]So the scribe said to Him, "Well *said,* Teacher. You have spoken the truth, for there is one God, and there is no other but He. [33]And to love Him with all the heart, with all the understanding, with all the soul,[m] and with all the strength, and to love one's neighbor as oneself, is more than all the whole burnt offerings and sacrifices."

[34]Now when Jesus saw that he answered wisely, He said to him, "You are not far from the kingdom of God."

But after that no one dared question Him.

Jesus: How Can David Call His Descendant Lord?

[35]Then Jesus answered and said, while He taught in the temple, "How *is it* that the scribes say that the Christ is the Son of David? [36]For David himself said by the Holy Spirit:

> *'The LORD said to my Lord,*
> *"Sit at My right hand,*
> *Till I make Your enemies Your footstool."'*[n]

[37]Therefore David himself calls Him '*Lord*'; how is He *then* his Son?"

And the common people heard Him gladly.

Beware of the Scribes

[38]Then He said to them in His teaching, "Beware of the scribes, who desire to go around in long robes, *love* greetings in the marketplaces, [39]the best seats in the synagogues, and the best places at feasts, [40]who devour widows' houses, and for a pretense make long prayers. These will receive greater condemnation."

The Widow's Two Mites

[41]Now Jesus sat opposite the treasury and saw how the people put money into the treasury. And many *who were* rich put in much. [42]Then one poor widow came and threw in two mites,[o] which make a quadrans. [43]So He called His disciples to *Himself* and said to them, "Assuredly, I say to you that this poor widow has put in more than all those who have given to the treasury; [44]for they all put in out of their abundance, but she out of her poverty put in all that she had, her whole livelihood."

Jesus Predicts the Destruction of the Temple

13 Then as He went out of the temple, one of His disciples said to Him, "Teacher, see what manner of stones and what buildings *are here!*"

[2]And Jesus answered and said to him, "Do you see these great buildings? Not *one* stone shall be left upon another, that shall not be thrown down."

The Signs of the Times and the End of the Age

[3]Now as He sat on the Mount of Olives opposite the temple, Peter, James, John, and Andrew asked Him privately, [4]"Tell us, when will these things be? And what *will be* the sign when all these things will be fulfilled?"

[5]And Jesus, answering them, began to say: "Take heed that no one deceives you. [6]For many will come in My name, saying, 'I am *He,*' and will deceive many. [7]But when you hear of wars and rumors of wars, do not be troubled; for *such things* must happen, but the end *is* not yet. [8]For nation will rise against nation, and kingdom against kingdom. And there will be earthquakes in various places, and there will be famines and troubles.[p] These *are* the beginnings of sorrows.

[9]"But watch out for yourselves, for they will deliver you up to councils, and you will be beaten in the synagogues. You will be brought[q] before rulers and kings for My sake, for a testimony to them. [10]And the gospel must first be preached to all the nations. [11]But when they arrest *you* and deliver you up, do not worry beforehand, or premeditate[r] what you will speak. But whatever is given you in that hour, speak that; for it is not you who speak, but the Holy Spirit. [12]Now brother will betray brother to death, and a father *his* child; and children will rise up against parents and cause them to be put to death. [13]And you will be hated by all for My name's sake. But he who endures to the end shall be saved.

The Great Tribulation

[14]"So when you see the '*abomination of desolation,*'[s] spoken of by Daniel the prophet,[t] standing where it ought not" (let the reader understand), "then let those who are in Judea flee to the mountains. [15]Let him who is on the housetop not go down into the house, nor enter to take anything out of his house. [16]And let him who is in the field not go back to get his clothes. [17]But woe to those who are pregnant and to those who are

12:33 [m] NU-Text omits *with all the soul.*
12:36 [n] Psalm 110:1
12:42 [o] Greek *lepta,* very small copper coins worth a fraction of a penny
13:8 [p] NU-Text omits *and troubles.*
13:9 [q] NU-Text and M-Text read *will stand.*
13:11 [r] NU-Text omits *or premeditate.*
13:14 [s] Daniel 11:31; 12:11 [t] NU-Text omits *spoken of by Daniel the prophet.*

nursing babies in those days! 18And pray that your flight may not be in
winter. 19For *in* those days there will be tribulation, such as has not been since
the beginning of the creation which God created until this time, nor ever
shall be. 20And unless the Lord had shortened those days, no flesh would
be saved; but for the elect's sake, whom He chose, He shortened the days.
21"Then if anyone says to you, 'Look, here *is* the Christ!' or, 'Look, *He is*
there!' do not believe it. 22For false christs and false prophets will rise and
show signs and wonders to deceive, if possible, even the elect. 23But take
heed; see, I have told you all things beforehand.

The Coming of the Son of Man

24"But in those days, after that tribulation, the sun will be darkened, and
the moon will not give its light; 25the stars of heaven will fall, and the powers in the heavens will be shaken. 26Then they will see the Son of Man coming in the clouds with great power and glory. 27And then He will send His
angels, and gather together His elect from the four winds, from the farthest part of earth to the farthest part of heaven.

The Parable of the Fig Tree

28"Now learn this parable from the fig tree: When its branch has already
become tender, and puts forth leaves, you know that summer is near. 29So
you also, when you see these things happening, know that it[u] is near—at
the doors! 30Assuredly, I say to you, this generation will by no means pass
away till all these things take place. 31Heaven and earth will pass away, but
My words will by no means pass away.

No One Knows the Day or Hour

32"But of that day and hour no one knows, not even the angels in
heaven, nor the Son, but only the Father. 33Take heed, watch and pray; for
you do not know when the time is. 34*It is* like a man going to a far country,
who left his house and gave authority to his servants, and to each his work,
and commanded the doorkeeper to watch. 35Watch therefore, for you do
not know when the master of the house is coming—in the evening, at
midnight, at the crowing of the rooster, or in the morning— 36lest, coming
suddenly, he find you sleeping. 37And what I say to you, I say to all: Watch!"

The Plot to Kill Jesus

14 After two days it was the Passover and *the Feast* of Unleavened
Bread. And the chief priests and the scribes sought how they might
take Him by trickery and put *Him* to death. 2But they said, "Not during the
feast, lest there be an uproar of the people."

The Anointing at Bethany

3And being in Bethany at the house of Simon the leper, as He sat at the
table, a woman came having an alabaster flask of very costly oil of spikenard. Then she broke the flask and poured *it* on His head. 4But there were
some who were indignant among themselves, and said, "Why was this
fragrant oil wasted? 5For it might have been sold for more than three hundred denarii and given to the poor." And they criticized her sharply.

13:29 [u] Or *He*

LIFE LESSON

Mark 13:1-37

SITUATION Jesus taught his disciples about the signs of the end times. While he taught, he stood on the Mount of Olives directly opposite the temple in Jerusalem. Peter, James, John, and Andrew asked him to explain when the end would come.

OBSERVATION Be ready for the return of Christ. Some of the signs that will precede his coming are war, hunger, earthquakes, false Christs, false prophets, rumors of wars, loss of faith, persecution of believers, the increase of evil, and the preaching of the Good News to all the world.

INSPIRATION I was with American soldiers, near the front line at Danang. Can you imagine what it meant to them that an old lady came to see them? Their wives and mothers were far away in America. . . . At first I made them laugh heartily. Americans have a great sense of humor. But then I spoke to them very seriously. "Boys," I said, "we all know that you are in danger of your lives. It is possible that tomorrow you will be killed. Are you ready to look a righteous God in the eyes? It is possible if you repent and take your sins to Jesus. He wants to forgive you and to cleanse your heart with His blood and fill it with His spirit. He said: 'Come to Me: and him that cometh to me I will in no wise cast out (John 6:37).'" Many of these boys and men came. It is quite possible that now they are in heaven.
What about you who are reading this? Perhaps you will say: I am not on the front line of a war; my life is not in danger. But we all know that every person will have to die one day and after that the judgment—everyone, whether he wants it or not. Are you ready?
(From *Not I but Christ* by Corrie ten Boom)

APPLICATION If Jesus returned today, would you be among those who welcome him or who dread his coming? Reconsider your priorities and stand ready to go at a moment's notice.

EXPLORATION Ready for Jesus Christ's Return—Matthew 24; 25:1-13; Luke 21:5-36; 1 Thessalonians 5:1-11.

LIFE LESSON

Mark 14:1-72

SITUATION Jesus neared the time of his death. He triumphantly entered Jerusalem and chased men from the Temple who exploited worship. Excitement filled the air in Jerusalem because the people considered Jesus to be the conquering Messiah. Instead, Jesus prepared to face the cross.

OBSERVATION The people thought that Jesus would be a glorious hero and give the nation a majestic destiny. Instead, Jesus humbled himself according to God's plan and won our salvation.

INSPIRATION Are you willing to be offered for the work of the faithful—to pour out your life blood as a libation on the sacrifice of the faith of others? Or do you say— "I am not going to be offered up just yet, I do not want God to choose my work. I want to choose the scenery of my own sacrifice; I want to have the right kind of people watching and saying 'Well done.'"

It is one thing to go on the lonely way with dignified heroism, but quite another thing if the line mapped out for you by God means being a doormat under other people's feet. Suppose God wants to teach you to say, "I know how to be abased"—are you ready to be offered up like that? Are you ready to be not so much as a drop in a bucket—to be so hopelessly insignificant that you are never thought of again in connection with the life you served? Are you willing to spend and be spent; not seeking to be ministered unto, but to minister? Some saints cannot do menial work and remain saints because it is beneath their dignity.

(From *My Utmost for His Highest* by Oswald Chambers)

APPLICATION Instead of campaigning at work or church for a high and honored office, commit six months to doing what everyone else avoids. Look for ways to identify with the Servant Messiah, Jesus.

EXPLORATION Servanthood—Matthew 20:26-28; Luke 18:14; John 13:13-17; Philippians 2:5-11.

6But Jesus said, "Let her alone. Why do you trouble her? She has done a
good work for Me. 7For you have the poor with you always, and whenever
you wish you may do them good; but Me you do not have always. 8She has
done what she could. She has come beforehand to anoint My body for
burial. 9Assuredly, I say to you, wherever this gospel is preached in the whole
world, what this woman has done will also be told as a memorial to her."

Judas Agrees to Betray Jesus

10Then Judas Iscariot, one of the twelve, went to the chief priests to betray Him to them. 11And when they heard *it,* they were glad, and promised
to give him money. So he sought how he might conveniently betray Him.

Jesus Celebrates the Passover with His Disciples

12Now on the first day of Unleavened Bread, when they killed the Passover
lamb, His disciples said to Him, "Where do You want us to go and prepare,
that You may eat the Passover?"
13And He sent out two of His disciples and said to them, "Go into the city,
and a man will meet you carrying a pitcher of water; follow him. 14Wher-
ever he goes in, say to the master of the house, 'The Teacher says, "Where
is the guest room in which I may eat the Passover with My disciples?" '
15Then he will show you a large upper room, furnished *and* prepared; there
make ready for us."
16So His disciples went out, and came into the city, and found it just as
He had said to them; and they prepared the Passover.
17In the evening He came with the twelve. 18Now as they sat and ate, Jesus
said, "Assuredly, I say to you, one of you who eats with Me will betray Me."
19And they began to be sorrowful, and to say to Him one by one, "*Is* it I?"
And another *said,* "*Is* it I?"[v]
20He answered and said to them, "*It is* one of the twelve, who dips with
Me in the dish. 21The Son of Man indeed goes just as it is written of Him,
but woe to that man by whom the Son of Man is betrayed! It would have
been good for that man if he had never been born."

Jesus Institutes the Lord's Supper

22And as they were eating, Jesus took bread, blessed and broke *it,* and
gave *it* to them and said, "Take, eat;[w] this is My body."
23Then He took the cup, and when He had given thanks He gave *it* to
them, and they all drank from it. 24And He said to them, "This is My blood
of the new[x] covenant, which is shed for many. 25Assuredly, I say to you, I
will no longer drink of the fruit of the vine until that day when I drink it
new in the kingdom of God."
26And when they had sung a hymn, they went out to the Mount of Olives.

Jesus Predicts Peter's Denial

27Then Jesus said to them, "All of you will be made to stumble because
of Me this night,[y] for it is written:

'I will strike the Shepherd,
And the sheep will be scattered.'[z]

14:19 [v] NU-Text omits this sentence.
14:22 [w] NU-Text omits *eat.*
14:24 [x] NU-Text omits *new.*
14:27 [y] NU-Text omits *because of Me this night.* [z] Zechariah 13:7

28“But after I have been raised, I will go before you
to Galilee.”
29Peter said to Him, “Even if all are made to stumble, yet I *will* not *be*.”
30Jesus said to him, “Assuredly, I say to you that
today, *even* this night, before the rooster crows twice,
you will deny Me three times.”
31But he spoke more vehemently, “If I have to die
with You, I will not deny You!”
And they all said likewise.

The Prayer in the Garden

32Then they came to a place which was named Gethsemane; and He said to His disciples, “Sit here while I
pray.” 33And He took Peter, James, and John with Him,
and He began to be troubled and deeply distressed.
34Then He said to them, “My soul is exceedingly sorrowful, *even* to death. Stay here and watch.”
35He went a little farther, and fell on the ground, and
prayed that if it were possible, the hour might pass
from Him. 36And He said, “Abba, Father, all things *are*
possible for You. Take this cup away from Me; nevertheless, not what I will, but what You *will*.”
37Then He came and found them sleeping, and said
to Peter, “Simon, are you sleeping? Could you not watch
one hour? 38Watch and pray, lest you enter into temptation. The spirit indeed *is* willing, but the flesh *is* weak.”
39Again He went away and prayed, and spoke the
same words. 40And when He returned, He found them
asleep again, for their eyes were heavy; and they did
not know what to answer Him.
41Then He came the third time and said to them,
“Are you still sleeping and resting? It is enough! The
hour has come; behold, the Son of Man is being betrayed into the hands of sinners. 42Rise, let us be
going. See, My betrayer is at hand.”

Betrayal and Arrest in Gethsemane

43And immediately, while He was still speaking, Judas, one of the twelve, with a great multitude with
swords and clubs, came from the chief priests and the
scribes and the elders. 44Now His betrayer had given
them a signal, saying, “Whomever I kiss, He is the
One; seize Him and lead *Him* away safely.”
45As soon as he had come, immediately he went up to
Him and said to Him, “Rabbi, Rabbi!” and kissed Him.
46Then they laid their hands on Him and took Him.
47And one of those who stood by drew his sword and
struck the servant of the high priest, and cut off his ear.
48Then Jesus answered and said to them, “Have you
come out, as against a robber, with swords and clubs
to take Me? 49I was daily with you in the temple teaching, and you did not seize Me. But the Scriptures must
be fulfilled.”
50Then they all forsook Him and fled.

A Young Man Flees Naked

51Now a certain young man followed Him, having a
linen cloth thrown around *his* naked *body*. And the
young men laid hold of him, 52and he left the linen
cloth and fled from them naked.

Jesus Faces the Sanhedrin

53And they led Jesus away to the high priest; and with
him were assembled all the chief priests, the elders,
and the scribes. 54But Peter followed Him at a distance,
right into the courtyard of the high priest. And he sat
with the servants and warmed himself at the fire.
55Now the chief priests and all the council sought
testimony against Jesus to put Him to death, but found
none. 56For many bore false witness against Him, but
their testimonies did not agree.
57Then some rose up and bore false witness against
Him, saying, 58“We heard Him say, ‘I will destroy this
temple made with hands, and within three days I will
build another made without hands.’ ” 59But not even
then did their testimony agree.
60And the high priest stood up in the midst and
asked Jesus, saying, “Do You answer nothing? What *is*
it these men testify against You?” 61But He kept silent
and answered nothing.
Again the high priest asked Him, saying to Him,
“Are You the Christ, the Son of the Blessed?”
62Jesus said, “I am. And you will see the Son of Man
sitting at the right hand of the Power, and coming with
the clouds of heaven.”
63Then the high priest tore his clothes and said, “What
further need do we have of witnesses? 64You have
heard the blasphemy! What do you think?”
And they all condemned Him to be deserving of
death.
65Then some began to spit on Him, and to blindfold
Him, and to beat Him, and to say to Him, “Prophesy!”
And the officers struck Him with the palms of their
hands.[a]

Peter Denies Jesus, and Weeps

66Now as Peter was below in the courtyard, one of
the servant girls of the high priest came. 67And when
she saw Peter warming himself, she looked at him and
said, “You also were with Jesus of Nazareth.”

14:65 *a* NU-Text reads *received Him with slaps.*

LIFE LESSON

Mark 15:1-47

SITUATION Judas betrayed Jesus, and the religious authorities arrested God's Son. The disciples scattered, and Peter denied him three times. Jesus, beaten and mocked throughout the night, provided salvation through his death and resurrection.

OBSERVATION The hours before Jesus' crucifixion were extremely painful for him, yet he faced the sacrifice with love, courage, and conviction so great that he willingly gave up his life for us!

INSPIRATION He looked around the hill and foresaw a scene. Three figures hung on three crosses. Arms spread. Heads fallen forward. They moaned with the wind.

Men clad in soldiers' garb sat on the ground near the trio. They played games in the dirt and laughed.

Men clad in religion stood off to one side. They smiled. Arrogant, cocky. They had protected God, they thought, by killing this false one.

Women clad in sorrow huddled at the foot of the hill. Speechless. Faces tear streaked. Eyes downward. One put her arm around another and tried to lead her away. She wouldn't leave. "I will stay," she said softly. "I will stay."

All heaven stood to fight. All nature rose to rescue. All eternity poised to protect. But the Creator gave no command.

"It must be done . . . ," he said, and withdrew.

But as he stepped back in time, he heard the cry that he would someday scream: "My God, my God, why have you forsaken me?" He wrenched at tomorrow's agony.

The angel spoke again. "It would be less painful . . . "

The Creator interrupted softly. "But it wouldn't be love."

(From *In the Eye of the Storm* by Max Lucado)

APPLICATION What have you given up for others recently? Remember how great Christ's generosity was to you as you think of these "sacrifices."

EXPLORATION Christ's Sacrifice—John 3:16; Romans 5:6-8; Philippians 2:5-8; Hebrews 12:1-3.

68But he denied it, saying, "I neither know nor understand what you are
saying." And he went out on the porch, and a rooster crowed.
69And the servant girl saw him again, and began to say to those who
stood by, "This is one of them." 70But he denied it again.
And a little later those who stood by said to Peter again, "Surely you are
one of them; for you are a Galilean, and your speech shows *it*."[b]
71Then he began to curse and swear, "I do not know this Man of whom
you speak!"
72A second time *the* rooster crowed. Then Peter called to mind the word
that Jesus had said to him, "Before the rooster crows twice, you will deny
Me three times." And when he thought about it, he wept.

Jesus Faces Pilate

15 Immediately, in the morning, the chief priests held a consultation
with the elders and scribes and the whole council; and they bound
Jesus, led *Him* away, and delivered *Him* to Pilate. 2Then Pilate asked Him,
"Are You the King of the Jews?"
He answered and said to him, "*It is as* you say."
3And the chief priests accused Him of many things, but He answered
nothing. 4Then Pilate asked Him again, saying, "Do You answer nothing?
See how many things they testify against You!"[c] 5But Jesus still answered
nothing, so that Pilate marveled.

Taking the Place of Barabbas

6Now at the feast he was accustomed to releasing one prisoner to them,
whomever they requested. 7And there was one named Barabbas, *who was*
chained with his fellow rebels; they had committed murder in the rebellion. 8Then the multitude, crying aloud,[d] began to ask *him to do* just as he
had always done for them. 9But Pilate answered them, saying, "Do you
want me to release to you the King of the Jews?" 10For he knew that the
chief priests had handed Him over because of envy.
11But the chief priests stirred up the crowd, so that he should rather release Barabbas to them. 12Pilate answered and said to them again, "What
then do you want me to do *with Him* whom you call the King of the Jews?"
13So they cried out again, "Crucify Him!"
14Then Pilate said to them, "Why, what evil has He done?"
But they cried out all the more, "Crucify Him!"
15So Pilate, wanting to gratify the crowd, released Barabbas to them; and
he delivered Jesus, after he had scourged *Him*, to be crucified.

The Soldiers Mock Jesus

16Then the soldiers led Him away into the hall called Praetorium, and
they called together the whole garrison. 17And they clothed Him with purple; and they twisted a crown of thorns, put it on His *head*, 18and began to
salute Him, "Hail, King of the Jews!" 19Then they struck Him on the head
with a reed and spat on Him; and bowing the knee, they worshiped Him.
20And when they had mocked Him, they took the purple off Him, put His
own clothes on Him, and led Him out to crucify Him.

14:70 [b] NU-Text omits *and your speech shows it.*
15:4 [c] NU-Text reads *of which they accuse You.*
15:8 [d] NU-Text reads *going up.*

The King on a Cross

21 Then they compelled a certain man, Simon a Cyrenian, the father of Alexander and Rufus, as he was coming out of the country and passing by, to bear
His cross. 22 And they brought Him to the place Golgotha, which is translated,
Place of a Skull. 23 Then they gave Him wine mingled with myrrh to drink,
but He did not take *it.* 24 And when they crucified Him, they divided His
garments, casting lots for them to determine what every man should take.
25 Now it was the third hour, and they crucified Him. 26 And the inscription of His accusation was written above:

THE KING OF THE JEWS.

27 With Him they also crucified two robbers, one on His right and the other
on His left. 28 So the Scripture was fulfilled[e] which says, *"And He was numbered with the transgressors."*[f]
29 And those who passed by blasphemed Him, wagging their heads and
saying, "Aha! *You* who destroy the temple and build *it* in three days, 30 save
Yourself, and come down from the cross!"
31 Likewise the chief priests also, mocking among themselves with the
scribes, said, "He saved others; Himself He cannot save. 32 Let the Christ,
the King of Israel, descend now from the cross, that we may see and believe."[g]
Even those who were crucified with Him reviled Him.

Jesus Dies on the Cross

33 Now when the sixth hour had come, there was darkness over the
whole land until the ninth hour. 34 And at the ninth hour Jesus cried out
with a loud voice, saying, "Eloi, Eloi, lama sabachthani?" which is translated, *"My God, My God, why have You forsaken Me?"*[h]
35 Some of those who stood by, when they heard *that,* said, "Look, He is
calling for Elijah!" 36 Then someone ran and filled a sponge full of sour wine,
put *it* on a reed, and offered *it* to Him to drink, saying, "Let Him alone; let
us see if Elijah will come to take Him down."
37 And Jesus cried out with a loud voice, and breathed His last.
38 Then the veil of the temple was torn in two from top to bottom. 39 So
when the centurion, who stood opposite Him, saw that He cried out like
this and breathed His last,[i] he said, "Truly this Man was the Son of God!"
40 There were also women looking on from afar, among whom were
Mary Magdalene, Mary the mother of James the Less and of Joses, and
Salome, 41 who also followed Him and ministered to Him when He was in
Galilee, and many other women who came up with Him to Jerusalem.

Jesus Buried in Joseph's Tomb

42 Now when evening had come, because it was the Preparation Day, that
is, the day before the Sabbath, 43 Joseph of Arimathea, a prominent council
member, who was himself waiting for the kingdom of God, coming and
taking courage, went in to Pilate and asked for the body of Jesus. 44 Pilate
marveled that He was already dead; and summoning the centurion, he
asked him if He had been dead for some time. 45 So when he found out

15:28 [e] Isaiah 53:12 [f] NU-Text omits this verse.
15:32 [g] M-Text reads *believe Him.*
15:34 [h] Psalm 22:1
15:39 [i] NU-Text reads *that He thus breathed His last.*

Life Lesson

Mark 16:1-20

SITUATION Jesus was crucified and his body buried. His followers were dismayed because he did not create a kingdom on earth. Because he died so close to the Sabbath (a day on which Israelites could do no work), his body was not embalmed. Once the Sabbath was over some women set out to embalm his body.

OBSERVATION Jesus was not simply a man who led a good life and died. He rose from the dead. Death cannot hold him or his followers. God conquered death, and gave us hope.

INSPIRATION The year 1899 marked the deaths of two well-known men—Dwight L. Moody, the acclaimed evangelist, and Robert Ingersoll, the famous lawyer, orator, and political leader.

The two men had many similarities. Both were raised in Christian homes. Both were skilled orators. . . . Both drew immense crowds when they spoke and attracted loyal followings. But there was one striking difference between them—their view of God.

Ingersoll was an agnostic; he had no belief in the eternal, but stressed the importance of living only in the here and now. Ingersoll made light of the Bible. . . . The Bible was "a fable, an obscenity, a humbug, a sham and a lie." . . .

Dwight L. Moody, had different convictions. He dedicated his life to presenting a resurrected King to a dying people. He embraced the Bible as the hope for humanity and the cross as the turning point of history. He left behind a legacy of written and spoken words, institutions of education, churches, and changed lives.

Two men. Both powerful speakers and influential leaders. One rejected God; the other embraced him. The impact of their decisions is seen most clearly in the way they died. . . .

Ingersoll died suddenly. The news of his death stunned his family. His body was kept at home for several days because his wife was reluctant to part with it. It was eventually removed for the sake of the family's health.

Continued

Ingersoll's remains were cremated, and the public response to his passing was altogether dismal. For a man who put all his hopes on the world, death was tragic and came without the consolation of hope. . . .

Moody's legacy was different. On December 22, 1899, Moody awoke to his last winter dawn. Having grown increasingly weak during the night, he began to speak in slow measured words. "Earth recedes, heaven opens before me!" Son Will, who was nearby, hurried across the room to his father's side.

"Father, you are dreaming," he said.

"No. This is no dream, Will," Moody said. "It is beautiful. It is like a trance. If this is death, it is sweet. God is calling me, and I must go. Don't call me back."

At that point, the family gathered around, and moments later the great evangelist died. It was his coronation day—a day he had looked forward to for many years. He was with his Lord.

. . . There was no despair. Loved ones gathered to sing praise to God at a triumphant home-going service. Many remembered the words the evangelist had spoken earlier that year in New York City: "Someday you will read in the papers that Moody is dead. Don't you believe a word of it. At that moment I shall be more alive than I am now. . . . I was born of the flesh in 1837, I was born of the spirit in 1855. That which is born of the flesh may die. That which is born of the Spirit shall live forever."

(From *The Applause of Heaven* by Max Lucado)

APPLICATION What do you fear about death? Remember that Jesus did the impossible by rising from the dead. One day your body and spirit will rise from the dead.

EXPLORATION Victory over Death—Psalm 23:4; Hosea 13:14; Romans 8:2; 1 Corinthians 15:54-57; Ephesians 2:4-5; Revelation 1:18.

from the centurion, he granted the body to Joseph. 46Then he bought fine linen, took Him down, and wrapped Him in the linen. And he laid Him in a tomb which had been hewn out of the rock, and rolled a stone against the door of the tomb. 47And Mary Magdalene and Mary *the mother* of Joses observed where He was laid.

He Is Risen

16 Now when the Sabbath was past, Mary Magdalene, Mary *the mother* of James, and Salome bought spices, that they might come and anoint Him. 2Very early in the morning, on the first *day* of the week, they came to the tomb when the sun had risen. 3And they said among themselves, "Who will roll away the stone from the door of the tomb for us?" 4But when they looked up, they saw that the stone had been rolled away—for it was very large. 5And entering the tomb, they saw a young man clothed in a long white robe sitting on the right side; and they were alarmed.

6But he said to them, "Do not be alarmed. You seek Jesus of Nazareth, who was crucified. He is risen! He is not here. See the place where they laid Him. 7But go, tell His disciples—and Peter—that He is going before you into Galilee; there you will see Him, as He said to you."

8So they went out quickly[j] and fled from the tomb, for they trembled and were amazed. And they said nothing to anyone, for they were afraid.

Mary Magdalene Sees the Risen Lord

9Now when *He* rose early on the first *day* of the week, He appeared first to Mary Magdalene, out of whom He had cast seven demons. 10She went and told those who had been with Him, as they mourned and wept. 11And when they heard that He was alive and had been seen by her, they did not believe.

Jesus Appears to Two Disciples

12After that, He appeared in another form to two of them as they walked and went into the country. 13And they went and told *it* to the rest, *but* they did not believe them either.

The Great Commission

14Later He appeared to the eleven as they sat at the table; and He rebuked their unbelief and hardness of heart, because they did not believe those who had seen Him after He had risen. 15And He said to them, "Go into all the world and preach the gospel to every creature. 16He who believes and is baptized will be saved; but he who does not believe will be condemned. 17And these signs will follow those who believe: In My name they will cast out demons; they will speak with new tongues; 18they[k] will take up serpents; and if they drink anything deadly, it will by no means hurt them; they will lay hands on the sick, and they will recover."

Christ Ascends to God's Right Hand

19So then, after the Lord had spoken to them, He was received up into heaven, and sat down at the right hand of God. 20And they went out and preached everywhere, the Lord working with *them* and confirming the word through the accompanying signs. Amen.[l]

16:8 *j* NU-Text and M-Text omit *quickly.*
16:18 *k* NU-Text reads *and in their hands they will.*
16:20 *l* Verses 9–20 are bracketed in NU-Text as not original. They are lacking in Codex Sinaiticus and Codex Vaticanus, although nearly all other manuscripts of Mark contain them.

The Gospel According to

LUKE

INTRODUCTION

Nearly two thousand years ago a doctor named Luke began a letter to a friend with these words:

Inasmuch as many have taken in hand to set in order a narrative of those things which have been fulfilled among us, just as those who from the beginning were eyewitnesses and ministers of the word delivered them to us, it seemed good to me also, having had perfect understanding of all things from the very first, to write to you an orderly account, most excellent Theophilus, that you may know the certainty of those things in which you were instructed (1:1–4).

Luke and Theophilus shared two loves: a love for Christ and a love for the facts. They didn't want legends, they wanted truth. And so Dr. Luke begins to sort the truth and report the facts to Theophilus. The result is part letter and part research paper.

It is part letter because it was written for a friend. What a bond must have existed between these two that Luke would labor so! It is part research paper, because Luke had studied everything carefully from the beginning and he wanted Theophilus to benefit from his study.

Can't you envision him in the home of Mary, "Tell me again what happened in Bethlehem." Can't you see him peppering Matthew with questions? "Let me see if I got this parable right." Or on long walks with Peter, "When you denied him the third time, did Jesus know?" With the skill of a surgeon, Luke probes for truth.

Why?

So his friend could know that what he had been taught was true.

Did Luke have any idea that millions of us would benefit from his study? I doubt it. All he did was share the truth with a friend.

Can you imagine what would happen if we all did the same?

LIFE LESSON

Luke 1:1-80

SITUATION Scholars have suggested that these events took place around 6 B.C. during the rule of Herod the Great. God set the stage for the coming of Jesus into the world.

OBSERVATION The events leading up to Jesus' birth can be summarized by the angel's words: "God can do anything!"

INSPIRATION Hope is not what you expect; it is what you would never dream. It is a wild, improbable tale with a pinch-me-I'm-dreaming ending. It's Abraham adjusting his bifocals so he can see not his grandson, but his son. It's Moses standing in the Promised Land not with Aaron or Miriam at his side, but with Elijah and the transfigured Christ. It's Zechariah left speechless at the sight of wife Elizabeth, gray-headed and pregnant. And it is the two Emmaus-bound pilgrims reaching out to take a piece of bread only to see the hands from which it is offered are pierced. Hope is not a granted wish or a favor performed; no, it is far greater than that. It is a zany, unpredictable dependence on a God who loves to surprise us out of our socks and be there in the flesh to see our reaction.

(From *God Came Near* by Max Lucado)

APPLICATION What are your greatest dreams? Remember, God can do anything, and he loves to fulfill dreams. Ask God to show you what he wants you to do, and then ask him for the power and courage to do it.

EXPLORATION Ability of God—Joshua 3:5; Job 42:2; Psalm 77:14; Daniel 4:3; Matthew 19:26; Romans 16:25; Ephesians 3:20.

Dedication to Theophilus

Inasmuch as many have taken in hand to set in order a narrative of
those things which have been fulfilled[a] among us, 2just as those
who from the beginning were eyewitnesses and ministers of the
word delivered them to us, 3it seemed good to me also, having had perfect understanding of all things from the very first, to write to you an orderly
account, most excellent Theophilus, 4that you may know the certainty of those
things in which you were instructed.

John's Birth Announced to Zacharias

5There was in the days of Herod, the king of Judea, a certain priest
named Zacharias, of the division of Abijah. His wife *was* of the daughters
of Aaron, and her name *was* Elizabeth. 6And they were both righteous before God, walking in all the commandments and ordinances of the Lord
blameless. 7But they had no child, because Elizabeth was barren, and they
were both well advanced in years.

8So it was, that while he was serving as priest before God in the order of
his division, 9according to the custom of the priesthood, his lot fell to burn
incense when he went into the temple of the Lord. 10And the whole multitude of the people was praying outside at the hour of incense. 11Then an
angel of the Lord appeared to him, standing on the right side of the altar of incense. 12And when Zacharias saw *him,* he was troubled, and fear fell upon him.

13But the angel said to him, "Do not be afraid, Zacharias, for your prayer
is heard; and your wife Elizabeth will bear you a son, and you shall call his
name John. 14And you will have joy and gladness, and many will rejoice at
his birth. 15For he will be great in the sight of the Lord, and shall drink neither wine nor strong drink. He will also be filled with the Holy Spirit, even
from his mother's womb. 16And he will turn many of the children of Israel
to the Lord their God. 17He will also go before Him in the spirit and power
of Elijah, '*to turn the hearts of the fathers to the children,*'[b] and the disobedient to the wisdom of the just, to make ready a people prepared for the Lord."
18And Zacharias said to the angel, "How shall I know this? For I am an
old man, and my wife is well advanced in years."

19And the angel answered and said to him, "I am Gabriel, who stands in
the presence of God, and was sent to speak to you and bring you these glad
tidings. 20But behold, you will be mute and not able to speak until the day
these things take place, because you did not believe my words which will
be fulfilled in their own time."

21And the people waited for Zacharias, and marveled that he lingered so
long in the temple. 22But when he came out, he could not speak to them;
and they perceived that he had seen a vision in the temple, for he beckoned
to them and remained speechless.

23So it was, as soon as the days of his service were completed, that he departed to his own house. 24Now after those days his wife Elizabeth conceived;
and she hid herself five months, saying, 25"Thus the Lord has dealt with me, in
the days when He looked on *me,* to take away my reproach among people."

Christ's Birth Announced to Mary

26Now in the sixth month the angel Gabriel was sent by God to a city of

1:1 [a] Or *are most surely believed*
1:17 [b] Malachi 4:5, 6

Galilee named Nazareth, [27]to a virgin betrothed to a man whose name was Joseph, of the house of David. The virgin's name *was* Mary. [28]And having come in, the angel said to her, "Rejoice, highly favored *one,* the Lord *is* with you; blessed *are* you among women!"[c]

[29]But when she saw *him,*[d] she was troubled at his saying, and considered what manner of greeting this was. [30]Then the angel said to her, "Do not be afraid, Mary, for you have found favor with God. [31]And behold, you will conceive in your womb and bring forth a Son, and shall call His name JESUS. [32]He will be great, and will be called the Son of the Highest; and the Lord God will give Him the throne of His father David. [33]And He will reign over the house of Jacob forever, and of His kingdom there will be no end."

[34]Then Mary said to the angel, "How can this be, since I do not know a man?"

[35]And the angel answered and said to her, "*The* Holy Spirit will come upon you, and the power of the Highest will overshadow you; therefore, also, that Holy One who is to be born will be called the Son of God. [36]Now indeed, Elizabeth your relative has also conceived a son in her old age; and this is now the sixth month for her who was called barren. [37]For with God nothing will be impossible."

[38]Then Mary said, "Behold the maidservant of the Lord! Let it be to me according to your word." And the angel departed from her.

Mary Visits Elizabeth

[39]Now Mary arose in those days and went into the hill country with haste, to a city of Judah, [40]and entered the house of Zacharias and greeted Elizabeth. [41]And it happened, when Elizabeth heard the greeting of Mary, that the babe leaped in her womb; and Elizabeth was filled with the Holy Spirit. [42]Then she spoke out with a loud voice and said, "Blessed *are* you among women, and blessed *is* the fruit of your womb! [43]But why *is* this *granted* to me, that the mother of my Lord should come to me? [44]For indeed, as soon as the voice of your greeting sounded in my ears, the babe leaped in my womb for joy. [45]Blessed *is* she who believed, for there will be a fulfillment of those things which were told her from the Lord."

The Song of Mary

[46]And Mary said:

"My soul magnifies the Lord,
47 And my spirit has rejoiced in God my Savior.
48 For He has regarded the lowly state of
His maidservant;
For behold, henceforth all generations
will call me blessed.
49 For He who is mighty has done
great things for me,
And holy *is* His name.
50 And His mercy *is* on those who fear Him
From generation to generation.
51 He has shown strength with His arm;
He has scattered *the* proud in the imagination
of their hearts.
52 He has put down the mighty from *their* thrones,
And exalted *the* lowly.
53 He has filled *the* hungry with good things,
And *the* rich He has sent away empty.
54 He has helped His servant Israel,
In remembrance of *His* mercy,
55 As He spoke to our fathers,
To Abraham and to his seed forever."

[56]And Mary remained with her about three months, and returned to her house.

Birth of John the Baptist

[57]Now Elizabeth's full time came for her to be delivered, and she brought forth a son. [58]When her neighbors and relatives heard how the Lord had shown great mercy to her, they rejoiced with her.

Circumcision of John the Baptist

[59]So it was, on the eighth day, that they came to circumcise the child; and they would have called him by the name of his father, Zacharias. [60]His mother answered and said, "No; he shall be called John."

[61]But they said to her, "There is no one among your relatives who is called by this name." [62]So they made signs to his father—what he would have him called.

[63]And he asked for a writing tablet, and wrote, saying, "His name is John." So they all marveled. [64]Immediately his mouth was opened and his tongue *loosed,* and he spoke, praising God. [65]Then fear came on all who dwelt around them; and all these sayings were discussed throughout all the hill country of Judea. [66]And all those who heard *them* kept *them* in their hearts, saying, "What kind of child will this be?" And the hand of the Lord was with him.

Zacharias' Prophecy

[67]Now his father Zacharias was filled with the Holy Spirit, and prophesied, saying:

1:28 [c]NU-Text omits *blessed are you among women.*
1:29 [d]NU-Text omits *when she saw him.*

LIFE LESSON

Luke 2:1-52

SITUATION Luke gave an account of the birth of Jesus and his early life. In his culture, boys were considered responsible adults around the age of twelve. It was not, therefore, irresponsible of Joseph and Mary to accidentally leave Jesus behind. They must have thought he was traveling with another part of the group.

OBSERVATION God's son became a person and lived with us for a while. During his life he was sad, happy, excited, and disappointed. God knows what life on earth is like.

INSPIRATION The implications of the name *Immanuel* are both comforting and unsettling. Comforting, because He has come to share the danger as well as the drudgery of our everyday lives. He desires to weep with us and to wipe away our tears. And what seems most bizarre, Jesus Christ, the Son of God, longs to share in and to be the source of the laughter and the joy we all too rarely know.

The implications are unsettling. It is one thing to claim that God looks down upon us, from a safe distance, and speaks to us (via long distance, we hope). But to say that He is right here, is to put ourselves and Him in a totally new situation. He is no longer the calm and benevolent observer in the sky, the kindly old caricature with the beard. His image becomes that of Jesus, who wept and laughed, who fasted and feasted, and who, above all, was fully present to those He loved. He was there with them. He is here with us. . . .

Most incredible, however, are the times we know He is with us in the midst of our daily, routine lives. In the middle of cleaning the house or driving somewhere in the pick-up, He stops

68 "Blessed *is* the Lord God of Israel,
For He has visited and redeemed His people,
69 And has raised up a horn of salvation for us
In the house of His servant David,
70 As He spoke by the mouth of His holy prophets,
Who *have been* since the world began,
71 That we should be saved from our enemies
And from the hand of all who hate us,
72 To perform the mercy *promised* to our fathers
And to remember His holy covenant,
73 The oath which He swore to our father Abraham:
74 To grant us that we,
Being delivered from the hand of our enemies,
Might serve Him without fear,
75 In holiness and righteousness before Him all the days of our life.

76 "And you, child, will be called the prophet of the Highest;
For you will go before the face of the Lord to prepare His ways,
77 To give knowledge of salvation to His people
By the remission of their sins,
78 Through the tender mercy of our God,
With which the Dayspring from on high has visited[e] us;
79 To give light to those who sit in darkness and the shadow of death,
To guide our feet into the way of peace."

80 So the child grew and became strong in spirit, and was in the deserts
till the day of his manifestation to Israel.

Christ Born of Mary

2 And it came to pass in those days *that* a decree went out from Caesar
Augustus that all the world should be registered. 2 This census first
took place while Quirinius was governing Syria. 3 So all went to be registered, everyone to his own city.
4 Joseph also went up from Galilee, out of the city of Nazareth, into
Judea, to the city of David, which is called Bethlehem, because he was of
the house and lineage of David, 5 to be registered with Mary, his betrothed
wife,[f] who was with child. 6 So it was, that while they were there, the days
were completed for her to be delivered. 7 And she brought forth her firstborn Son, and wrapped Him in swaddling cloths, and laid Him in a manger, because there was no room for them in the inn.

Glory in the Highest

8 Now there were in the same country shepherds living out in the fields,
keeping watch over their flock by night. 9 And behold,[g] an angel of the Lord
stood before them, and the glory of the Lord shone around them, and they
were greatly afraid. 10 Then the angel said to them, "Do not be afraid, for
behold, I bring you good tidings of great joy which will be to all people.
11 For there is born to you this day in the city of David a Savior, who is
Christ the Lord. 12 And this *will be* the sign to you: You will find a Babe
wrapped in swaddling cloths, lying in a manger."

1:78 [e] NU-Text reads *shall visit.*
2:5 [f] NU-Text omits *wife.*
2:9 [g] NU-Text omits *behold.*

13And suddenly there was with the angel a multitude of the heavenly
host praising God and saying:

14 "Glory to God in the highest,
And on earth peace, goodwill toward men!"[h]

15So it was, when the angels had gone away from them into heaven, that
the shepherds said to one another, "Let us now go to Bethlehem and see
this thing that has come to pass, which the Lord has made known to us."
16And they came with haste and found Mary and Joseph, and the Babe
lying in a manger. 17Now when they had seen *Him,* they made widely[i]
known the saying which was told them concerning this Child. 18And all
those who heard *it* marveled at those things which were told them by the
shepherds. 19But Mary kept all these things and pondered *them* in her
heart. 20Then the shepherds returned, glorifying and praising God for all
the things that they had heard and seen, as it was told them.

Circumcision of Jesus

21And when eight days were completed for the circumcision of the
Child,[j] His name was called JESUS, the name given by the angel before He
was conceived in the womb.

Jesus Presented in the Temple

22Now when the days of her purification according to the law of Moses
were completed, they brought Him to Jerusalem to present *Him* to the
Lord 23(as it is written in the law of the Lord, *"Every male who opens the
womb shall be called holy to the LORD"*),[k] 24and to offer a sacrifice according to what is said in the law of the Lord, *"A pair of turtledoves or two
young pigeons."*[l]

Simeon Sees God's Salvation

25And behold, there was a man in Jerusalem whose name was Simeon,
and this man was just and devout, waiting for the Consolation of Israel,
and the Holy Spirit was upon him. 26And it had been revealed to him by
the Holy Spirit that he would not see death before he had seen the Lord's
Christ. 27So he came by the Spirit into the temple. And when the parents
brought in the Child Jesus, to do for Him according to the custom of the
law, 28he took Him up in his arms and blessed God and said:

29 "Lord, now You are letting Your servant depart in peace,
According to Your word;
30 For my eyes have seen Your salvation
31 Which You have prepared before the face of all peoples,
32 A light to *bring* revelation to the Gentiles,
And the glory of Your people Israel."

33And Joseph and His mother[m] marveled at those things which were
spoken of Him. 34Then Simeon blessed them, and said to Mary His

us . . . in our tracks and makes His presence known. Often it's in the middle of the most mundane task that He lets us know He is there with us. We realize, then, that there can be no "ordinary" moments for people who live their lives with Jesus.

Jesus paid a tremendous price to be with us. Certainly the cross was the most obvious cost. But I believe more is in view.

We focus so much on the fact that Jesus died for us, we sometimes forget that He also lived for us and lives for us still. If Jesus had simply come as Himself, and not as one of us, the Bible makes it quite clear that we could not have borne the sight of His presence, any more than Moses could have looked directly at the face of God.

Imagine what it would be like to be at the Father's side one moment and struggling to sleep in a cattle trough the next. Imagine what it would be like to go from hearing the praise of angels to suffering the taunts of stupid men. The cost to Jesus is an indication of the incredible value of what He came to give us. And because no one will ever fully know what that cost Jesus, we can only begin to understand the incredible value of His gift to us.

(From *Immanuel* by Michael Card)

APPLICATION Take a moment and reflect on what "Immanuel—God with us" means to you in your daily life. Make it a point to seek God even in the mundane tasks of your life.

EXPLORATION God with Us—Exodus 33:20-23; Isaiah 7:14; Matthew 1:23; John 14:19; Acts 17:28; 2 Corinthians 6:16.

2:14 [h] NU-Text reads *toward men of goodwill.*
2:17 [i] NU-Text omits *widely.*
2:21 [j] NU-Text reads *for His circumcision.*
2:23 [k] Exodus 13:2, 12, 15
2:24 [l] Leviticus 12:8
2:33 [m] NU-Text reads *And His father and mother.*

LIFE LESSON

Luke 3:1-38

SITUATION John the Baptist began his ministry and called people to repent of their sins.

OBSERVATION John was a humble man who submitted to God. Not concerned with his own popularity, he knew that his ministry was to point people to Jesus Christ.

INSPIRATION John the Baptizer is a powerful example of a called man. . . . John seems to have had from the very beginning a vivid sense of destiny, the result of a heavenly assignment that came from deep inside himself. . . .

To those who questioned him regarding his feelings about the growing popularity of the Man from Nazareth, he likened his purpose to that of the best man at a wedding: "He who has the bride is the Bridegroom; but the friend [that's John] of the bridegroom, who stands and hears him, rejoices greatly because of the bridegroom's voice" (John 3:29). The purpose of the best man is simply to stand with the groom, to make sure that all attention is riveted upon him. The best man would be a fool if in the middle of the wedding processional he suddenly turned to the wedding guests and began to sing a song or engage in a humorous monologue. The best man has fulfilled his purpose most admirably when he draws no attention to himself but focuses all attention upon the bride and groom.

And that is what John did. If Jesus Christ was the groom, to use John's metaphor, then the Baptizer was committed to being the best man *and nothing else.* That was the purpose that flowed from his call, and he had no desire to aspire to anything beyond. Thus to see the crowd headed toward Christ was all the affirmation John needed; his purpose had been fulfilled.

(From *Ordering Your Private World* by Gordon MacDonald)

APPLICATION Like John, Believers should point people to Jesus Christ. Who are the people God is placing on your heart to pray for, to witness to, and to help?

EXPLORATION Witnesses for Christ—Matthew 5:13-16; 28:18-20; Mark 16:15; John 15:26-27; 2 Timothy 4:2.

mother, "Behold, this *Child* is destined for the fall and rising of many in Israel, and for a sign which will be spoken against 35(yes, a sword will pierce through your own soul also), that the thoughts of many hearts may be revealed."

Anna Bears Witness to the Redeemer

36Now there was one, Anna, a prophetess, the daughter of Phanuel, of the tribe of Asher. She was of a great age, and had lived with a husband seven years from her virginity; 37and this woman was a widow of about eighty-four years,[n] who did not depart from the temple, but served God with fastings and prayers night and day. 38And coming in that instant she gave thanks to the Lord,[o] and spoke of Him to all those who looked for redemption in Jerusalem.

The Family Returns to Nazareth

39So when they had performed all things according to the law of the Lord, they returned to Galilee, to their *own* city, Nazareth. 40And the Child grew and became strong in spirit,[p] filled with wisdom; and the grace of God was upon Him.

The Boy Jesus Amazes the Scholars

41His parents went to Jerusalem every year at the Feast of the Passover. 42And when He was twelve years old, they went up to Jerusalem according to the custom of the feast. 43When they had finished the days, as they returned, the Boy Jesus lingered behind in Jerusalem. And Joseph and His mother[q] did not know *it;* 44but supposing Him to have been in the company, they went a day's journey, and sought Him among *their* relatives and acquaintances. 45So when they did not find Him, they returned to Jerusalem, seeking Him. 46Now so it was *that* after three days they found Him in the temple, sitting in the midst of the teachers, both listening to them and asking them questions. 47And all who heard Him were astonished at His understanding and answers. 48So when they saw Him, they were amazed; and His mother said to Him, "Son, why have You done this to us? Look, Your father and I have sought You anxiously."

49And He said to them, "Why did you seek Me? Did you not know that I must be about My Father's business?" 50But they did not understand the statement which He spoke to them.

Jesus Advances in Wisdom and Favor

51Then He went down with them and came to Nazareth, and was subject to them, but His mother kept all these things in her heart. 52And Jesus increased in wisdom and stature, and in favor with God and men.

John the Baptist Prepares the Way

3 Now in the fifteenth year of the reign of Tiberius Caesar, Pontius Pilate being governor of Judea, Herod being tetrarch of Galilee, his brother Philip tetrarch of Iturea and the region of Trachonitis, and Lysanias tetrarch of Abilene, 2while Annas and Caiaphas were high priests,[r] the word of God came to John the son of Zacharias in the wilderness. 3And he

2:37 [n] NU-Text reads *a widow until she was eighty-four.*
2:38 [o] NU-Text reads *to God.*
2:40 [p] NU-Text omits *in spirit.*
2:43 [q] NU-Text reads *And His parents.*
3:2 [r] NU-Text and M-Text read *in the high priesthood of Annas and Caiaphas.*

went into all the region around the Jordan, preaching a baptism of repentance for the remission of sins, 4as it is written in the book of the words of Isaiah the prophet, saying:

"The voice of one crying in the wilderness:
'Prepare the way of the LORD;
Make His paths straight.
5 *Every valley shall be filled*
And every mountain and hill brought low;
The crooked places shall be made straight
And the rough ways smooth;
6 *And all flesh shall see the salvation of God.' "*[s]

John Preaches to the People

7Then he said to the multitudes that came out to be baptized by him, "Brood of vipers! Who warned you to flee from the wrath to come? 8Therefore bear fruits worthy of repentance, and do not begin to say to yourselves, 'We have Abraham as *our* father.' For I say to you that God is able to raise up children to Abraham from these stones. 9And even now the ax is laid to the root of the trees. Therefore every tree which does not bear good fruit is cut down and thrown into the fire."

10So the people asked him, saying, "What shall we do then?"

11He answered and said to them, "He who has two tunics, let him give to him who has none; and he who has food, let him do likewise."

12Then tax collectors also came to be baptized, and said to him, "Teacher, what shall we do?"

13And he said to them, "Collect no more than what is appointed for you."

14Likewise the soldiers asked him, saying, "And what shall we do?"

So he said to them, "Do not intimidate anyone or accuse falsely, and be content with your wages."

15Now as the people were in expectation, and all reasoned in their hearts about John, whether he was the Christ *or* not, 16John answered, saying to all, "I indeed baptize you with water; but One mightier than I is coming, whose sandal strap I am not worthy to loose. He will baptize you with the Holy Spirit and fire. 17His winnowing fan *is* in His hand, and He will thoroughly clean out His threshing floor, and gather the wheat into His barn; but the chaff He will burn with unquenchable fire."

18And with many other exhortations he preached to the people. 19But Herod the tetrarch, being rebuked by him concerning Herodias, his brother Philip's wife,[t] and for all the evils which Herod had done, 20also added this, above all, that he shut John up in prison.

John Baptizes Jesus

21When all the people were baptized, it came to pass that Jesus also was baptized; and while He prayed, the heaven was opened. 22And the Holy Spirit descended in bodily form like a dove upon Him, and a voice came from heaven which said, "You are My beloved Son; in You I am well pleased."

The Genealogy of Jesus Christ

23Now Jesus Himself began *His ministry at* about thirty years of age, being (as was supposed) *the* son of Joseph, *the son* of Heli, 24*the son* of Matthat,[u] *the son* of Levi, *the son* of Melchi, *the son* of Janna, *the son* of Joseph, 25*the son* of Mattathiah, *the son* of Amos, *the son* of Nahum, *the son* of Esli, *the son* of Naggai, 26*the son* of Maath, *the son* of Mattathiah, *the son* of Semei, *the son* of Joseph, *the son* of Judah, 27*the son* of Joannas, *the son* of Rhesa, *the son* of Zerubbabel, *the son* of Shealtiel, *the son* of Neri, 28*the son* of Melchi, *the son* of Addi, *the son* of Cosam, *the son* of Elmodam, *the son* of Er, 29*the son* of Jose, *the son* of Eliezer, *the son* of Jorim, *the son* of Matthat, *the son* of Levi, 30*the son* of Simeon, *the son* of Judah, *the son* of Joseph, *the son* of Jonan, *the son* of Eliakim, 31*the son* of Melea, *the son* of Menan, *the son* of Mattathah, *the son* of Nathan, *the son* of David, 32*the son* of Jesse, *the son* of Obed, *the son* of Boaz, *the son* of Salmon, *the son* of Nahshon, 33*the son* of Amminadab, *the son* of Ram, *the son* of Hezron, *the son* of Perez, *the son* of Judah, 34*the son* of Jacob, *the son* of Isaac, *the son* of Abraham, *the son* of Terah, *the son* of Nahor, 35*the son* of Serug, *the son* of Reu, *the son* of Peleg, *the son* of Eber, *the son* of Shelah, 36*the son* of Cainan, *the son* of Arphaxad, *the son* of Shem, *the son* of Noah, *the son* of Lamech, 37*the son* of Methuselah, *the son* of Enoch, *the son* of Jared, *the son* of Mahalalel, *the son* of Cainan, 38*the son* of Enosh, *the son* of Seth, *the son* of Adam, *the son* of God.

Satan Tempts Jesus

4 Then Jesus, being filled with the Holy Spirit, returned from the Jordan and was led by the Spirit into[v] the wilderness, 2being tempted for forty days by

3:6 [s] Isaiah 40:3–5
3:19 [t] NU-Text reads *his brother's wife.*
3:24 [u] This and several other names in the genealogy are spelled somewhat differently in the NU-Text. Since the New King James Version uses the Old Testament spelling for persons mentioned in the New Testament, these variations, which come from the Greek, have not been footnoted.
4:1 [v] NU-Text reads *in.*

the devil. And in those days He ate nothing, and afterward, when they had
ended, He was hungry.
3 And the devil said to Him, "If You are the Son of God, command this
stone to become bread."
4 But Jesus answered him, saying,[w] "It is written, *'Man shall not live by
bread alone, but by every word of God.'* "[x]
5 Then the devil, taking Him up on a high mountain, showed Him[y] all the
kingdoms of the world in a moment of time. 6 And the devil said to Him,
"All this authority I will give You, and their glory; for *this* has been delivered to me, and I give it to whomever I wish. 7 Therefore, if You will worship before me, all will be Yours."
8 And Jesus answered and said to him, "Get behind Me, Satan![z] For[a] it is written, *'You shall worship the LORD your God, and Him only you shall serve.'* "[b]
9 Then he brought Him to Jerusalem, set Him on the pinnacle of the temple, and said to Him, "If You are the Son of God, throw Yourself down from
here. 10 For it is written:

'He shall give His angels charge over you,
To keep you,'

11 and,

'In their hands they shall bear you up,
Lest you dash your foot against a stone.' "[c]

12 And Jesus answered and said to him, "It has been said, *'You shall not
tempt the LORD your God.'* "[d]
13 Now when the devil had ended every temptation, he departed from
Him until an opportune time.

Jesus Begins His Galilean Ministry

14 Then Jesus returned in the power of the Spirit to Galilee, and news of
Him went out through all the surrounding region. 15 And He taught in their
synagogues, being glorified by all.

Jesus Rejected at Nazareth

16 So He came to Nazareth, where He had been brought up. And as His
custom was, He went into the synagogue on the Sabbath day, and stood up
to read. 17 And He was handed the book of the prophet Isaiah. And when
He had opened the book, He found the place where it was written:

18 *"The Spirit of the LORD is upon Me,*
Because He has anointed Me
To preach the gospel to the poor;
He has sent Me to heal the brokenhearted,[e]
To proclaim liberty to the captives
And recovery of sight to the blind,
To set at liberty those who are oppressed;
19 *To proclaim the acceptable year of the LORD."*[f]

LIFE LESSON

Luke 4:1-44

SITUATION The Jewish people had been expecting the Messiah for a long time. They believed that he would free Israel from foreign rule and restore the nation to its prominence and greatness. As Jesus served, performed miracles, and spoke words with wisdom, the people were amazed and confused. Jesus was not the type of messiah they had been expecting.

OBSERVATION Because the Jews assumed they knew what the Messiah would look like, they had a difficult time recognizing Jesus as God's Messiah.

INSPIRATION Early one Saturday morning Jesus returned to Nazareth to speak in the synagogue. His friends and relatives and neighbors gathered in great excitement. They had watched Him grow to manhood; they knew His parents, Mary and Joseph. So they were astonished at His air of authority as He strode to the center of the crowded stone room and was handed the book of the prophet Isaiah from the Torah shrine. He found the passage He wanted, then read the ancient prophecy: "The Spirit of the Lord is on me, because he has anointed me to preach good news to the poor. He has sent me to proclaim freedom for the prisoners and recovery of sight for the blind, to release the oppressed, to proclaim the year of the Lord's favor."

Jesus handed the Scriptures back to the attendant and stared quietly at the rows of townspeople. "Today," He said slowly, "this Scripture is fulfilled in your hearing."

At first there were gasps, then excited murmurings. Was Jesus claiming that their hopes were to be realized? Had the long-dreamed-of day of the Lord—the coming of Messiah—arrived?

4:4 [w] Deuteronomy 8:3 [x] NU-Text omits *but by every word of God.*
4:5 [y] NU-Text reads *And taking Him up, he showed Him.*
4:8 [z] NU-Text omits *Get behind Me, Satan.* [a] NU-Text and M-Text omit *For.* [b] Deuteronomy 6:13
4:11 [c] Psalm 91:11, 12
4:12 [d] Deuteronomy 6:16
4:18 [e] NU-Text omits *to heal the brokenhearted.*
4:19 [f] Isaiah 61:1, 2

20Then He closed the book, and gave *it* back to the attendant and sat down.
And the eyes of all who were in the synagogue were fixed on Him. 21And
He began to say to them, "Today this Scripture is fulfilled in your hearing."
22So all bore witness to Him, and marveled at the gracious words which
proceeded out of His mouth. And they said, "Is this not Joseph's son?"
23He said to them, "You will surely say this proverb to Me, 'Physician,
heal yourself! Whatever we have heard done in Capernaum,[g] do also here
in Your country.' " 24Then He said, "Assuredly, I say to you, no prophet is
accepted in his own country. 25But I tell you truly, many widows were in Israel
in the days of Elijah, when the heaven was shut up three years and six months,
and there was a great famine throughout all the land; 26but to none of them
was Elijah sent except to Zarephath,[h] *in the region* of Sidon, to a woman *who*
was a widow. 27And many lepers were in Israel in the time of Elisha the
prophet, and none of them was cleansed except Naaman the Syrian."
28So all those in the synagogue, when they heard these things, were filled
with wrath, 29and rose up and thrust Him out of the city; and they led Him to the
brow of the hill on which their city was built, that they might throw Him down
over the cliff. 30Then passing through the midst of them, He went His way.

Jesus Casts Out an Unclean Spirit

31Then He went down to Capernaum, a city of Galilee, and was teaching
them on the Sabbaths. 32And they were astonished at His teaching, for His
word was with authority. 33Now in the synagogue there was a man who
had a spirit of an unclean demon. And he cried out with a loud voice,
34saying, "Let *us* alone! What have we to do with You, Jesus of Nazareth?
Did You come to destroy us? I know who You are—the Holy One of God!"
35But Jesus rebuked him, saying, "Be quiet, and come out of him!" And
when the demon had thrown him in *their* midst, it came out of him and
did not hurt him. 36Then they were all amazed and spoke among themselves, saying, "What a word this *is!* For with authority and power He
commands the unclean spirits, and they come out." 37And the report
about Him went out into every place in the surrounding region.

Peter's Mother-in-Law Healed

38Now He arose from the synagogue and entered Simon's house. But Simon's wife's mother was sick with a high fever, and they made request of
Him concerning her. 39So He stood over her and rebuked the fever, and it
left her. And immediately she arose and served them.

Many Healed After Sabbath Sunset

40When the sun was setting, all those who had any that were sick with
various diseases brought them to Him; and He laid His hands on every
one of them and healed them. 41And demons also came out of many, crying out and saying, "You are the Christ,[i] the Son of God!"
And He, rebuking *them,* did not allow them to speak, for they knew that
He was the Christ.

Jesus Preaches in Galilee

42Now when it was day, He departed and went into a deserted place. And
the crowd sought Him and came to Him, and tried to keep Him from leaving

Jesus knew what they were thinking. "No prophet," He said steadily, "is accepted in his hometown." Then He reminded them of two stories they knew well from their heritage: During a great drought, the prophet Elijah had brought water not to the dying widows of Israel, but to a heathen widow; and his successor Elisha had ignored Jewish lepers and cleansed a Syrian instead.

His words were like a dash of cold water in the faces of the crowd. They expected liberation for the Jews and judgment for all others. Now this arrogant young man was extending the long-awaited promise of their liberation with one hand and insinuating their own judgment with the other.

The crowd surged forward and dragged Jesus out of the building, shoving Him to the brow of the hill on which the synagogue perched. But when they reached the edge, they discovered that in the confusion, Jesus had slipped away.

This humble message at the remote Nazareth synagogue was the inaugural address for Jesus' entire ministry. Through it He formally announced His messiahship and the rule of God in this world. As a result, human history was forever altered.

The Kingdom of God had come.

(From *Kingdoms in Conflict* by Charles Colson)

APPLICATION Who is Jesus? Don't try to squeeze him into your own mold of a Savior. The Bible gives a clear picture. Study the Word of God and discover the real Jesus: God in the flesh who wants to change lives.

EXPLORATION The Messiah—Matthew 3:17; John 1:1-18; 10:30; Colossians 1:15-20.

4:23 [g] Here and elsewhere the NU-Text spelling is *Capharnaum.*
4:26 [h] Greek *Sarepta*
4:41 [i] NU-Text omits *the Christ.*

Life Lesson

Luke 5:1-39

SITUATION Luke continued to tell about what Jesus did on earth. Jesus began to call his disciples and perform various miracles.

OBSERVATION Luke emphasized how people responded in faith to Jesus and were rewarded by blessings greater than they could imagine.

INSPIRATION Whether he was born paralyzed or became paralyzed—the end result was the same: total dependence on others. . . . When people looked at him, they didn't see the man; they saw a body in need of a miracle. That's not what Jesus saw, but that's what the people saw. And that's certainly what his friends saw. So they did what any of us would do for a friend. They tried to get him some help. . . .

By the time his friends arrived at the place, the house was full. People jammed the doorways. Kids sat in the windows. Others peeked over shoulders. How would this small band of friends ever attract Jesus' attention? They had to make a choice. Do we go in or give up?

What would have happened had the friends given up? What if they had shrugged their shoulders and mumbled something about the crowd being big and dinner getting cold and turned and left? After all, they had done a good deed in coming this far. Who could fault them for turning back? You can only do so much for somebody. But these friends hadn't done enough.

One said that he had an idea. The four huddled over the paralytic and listened to the plan to climb to the top of the house, cut through the roof, and lower their friend down with their sashes.

It was risky—they could fall. It was dangerous—*he* could fall. It was

them; 43but He said to them, "I must preach the kingdom of God to the
other cities also, because for this purpose I have been sent." 44And He was
preaching in the synagogues of Galilee.[j]

Four Fishermen Called as Disciples

5 So it was, as the multitude pressed about Him to hear the word of God,
that He stood by the Lake of Gennesaret, 2and saw two boats standing
by the lake; but the fishermen had gone from them and were washing *their*
nets. 3Then He got into one of the boats, which was Simon's, and asked
him to put out a little from the land. And He sat down and taught the multitudes from the boat.
4When He had stopped speaking, He said to Simon, "Launch out into
the deep and let down your nets for a catch."
5But Simon answered and said to Him, "Master, we have toiled all night
and caught nothing; nevertheless at Your word I will let down the net."
6And when they had done this, they caught a great number of fish, and
their net was breaking. 7So they signaled to *their* partners in the other boat
to come and help them. And they came and filled both the boats, so that
they began to sink. 8When Simon Peter saw *it,* he fell down at Jesus' knees,
saying, "Depart from me, for I am a sinful man, O Lord!"
9For he and all who were with him were astonished at the catch of fish
which they had taken; 10and so also *were* James and John, the sons of
Zebedee, who were partners with Simon. And Jesus said to Simon, "Do
not be afraid. From now on you will catch men." 11So when they had
brought their boats to land, they forsook all and followed Him.

Jesus Cleanses a Leper

12And it happened when He was in a certain city, that behold, a man
who was full of leprosy saw Jesus; and he fell on *his* face and implored
Him, saying, "Lord, if You are willing, You can make me clean."
13Then He put out *His* hand and touched him, saying, "I am willing; be
cleansed." Immediately the leprosy left him. 14And He charged him to tell
no one, "But go and show yourself to the priest, and make an offering for
your cleansing, as a testimony to them, just as Moses commanded."
15However, the report went around concerning Him all the more; and
great multitudes came together to hear, and to be healed by Him of their
infirmities. 16So He Himself *often* withdrew into the wilderness and prayed.

Jesus Forgives and Heals a Paralytic

17Now it happened on a certain day, as He was teaching, that there were
Pharisees and teachers of the law sitting by, who had come out of every
town of Galilee, Judea, and Jerusalem. And the power of the Lord was
present to heal them.[k] 18Then behold, men brought on a bed a man who
was paralyzed, whom they sought to bring in and lay before Him. 19And
when they could not find how they might bring him in, because of the
crowd, they went up on the housetop and let him down with *his* bed
through the tiling into the midst before Jesus.
20When He saw their faith, He said to him, "Man, your sins are forgiven
you."

4:44 [j] NU-Text reads *Judea.*
5:17 [k] NU-Text reads *present with Him to heal.*

21 And the scribes and the Pharisees began to reason, saying, "Who is this who speaks blasphemies? Who can forgive sins but God alone?"

22 But when Jesus perceived their thoughts, He answered and said to them, "Why are you reasoning in your hearts? 23 Which is easier, to say, 'Your sins are forgiven you,' or to say, 'Rise up and walk'? 24 But that you may know that the Son of Man has power on earth to forgive sins"—He said to the man who was paralyzed, "I say to you, arise, take up your bed, and go to your house."

25 Immediately he rose up before them, took up what he had been lying on, and departed to his own house, glorifying God. 26 And they were all amazed, and they glorified God and were filled with fear, saying, "We have seen strange things today!"

Matthew the Tax Collector

27 After these things He went out and saw a tax collector named Levi, sitting at the tax office. And He said to him, "Follow Me." 28 So he left all, rose up, and followed Him.

29 Then Levi gave Him a great feast in his own house. And there were a great number of tax collectors and others who sat down with them. 30 And their scribes and the Pharisees[l] complained against His disciples, saying, "Why do You eat and drink with tax collectors and sinners?"

31 Jesus answered and said to them, "Those who are well have no need of a physician, but those who are sick. 32 I have not come to call *the* righteous, but sinners, to repentance."

Jesus Is Questioned About Fasting

33 Then they said to Him, "Why do[m] the disciples of John fast often and make prayers, and likewise those of the Pharisees, but Yours eat and drink?"

34 And He said to them, "Can you make the friends of the bridegroom fast while the bridegroom is with them? 35 But the days will come when the bridegroom will be taken away from them; then they will fast in those days."

36 Then He spoke a parable to them: "No one puts a piece from a new garment on an old one;[n] otherwise the new makes a tear, and also the piece that was *taken* out of the new does not match the old. 37 And no one puts new wine into old wineskins; or else the new wine will burst the wineskins and be spilled, and the wineskins will be ruined. 38 But new wine must be put into new wineskins, and both are preserved.[o] 39 And no one, having drunk old *wine*, immediately[p] desires new; for he says, 'The old is better.' "[q]

Jesus Is Lord of the Sabbath

6 Now it happened on the second Sabbath after the first[r] that He went through the grainfields. And His disciples plucked the heads of grain and ate *them,* rubbing *them* in *their* hands. 2 And some of the Pharisees said to them, "Why are you doing what is not lawful to do on the Sabbath?"

3 But Jesus answering them said, "Have you not even read this, what David did when he was hungry, he and those who were with him: 4 how he

unorthodox—de-roofing is antisocial. It was intrusive—Jesus was busy. But it was their only chance to see Jesus. So they climbed to the roof. Faith does these things. Faith does the unexpected. And faith gets God's attention. . . .

Jesus was moved by the scene of faith. So he applauds—if not with his hands, at least with his heart. And not only does he applaud, he blesses. And we witness a divine loveburst.

The friends want him to heal their friend. But Jesus won't settle for a simple healing of the body—he wants to heal the soul. He leapfrogs the physical and deals with the spiritual. To heal the body is temporal; to heal the soul is eternal. . . . So strong was his love for this crew of faith that he went beyond their appeal and went straight to the cross.

Jesus already knows the cost of grace. He already knows the price of forgiveness. But he offers it anyway. Love bursts in his heart. . . .

And though we can't hear it here, the angels can hear him there. All of heaven must pause as another burst of love declares the only words that really matter: "Your sins are forgiven." (From *He Still Moves Stones* by Max Lucado)

APPLICATION Do you believe God knows your problem? Do you have a disability or lack of resources that robs your faith? Remember, you don't have to go it alone. Find a group of Christians at school, work, or church who will get together weekly with you to present your requests to God.

EXPLORATION Faith—Habakkuk 2:4; Matthew 7:7; Mark 9:24; Galatians 2:20.

5:30 [l] NU-Text reads *But the Pharisees and their scribes.*
5:33 [m] NU-Text omits *Why do,* making the verse a statement.
5:36 [n] NU-Text reads *No one tears a piece from a new garment and puts it on an old one.*
5:38 [o] NU-Text omits *and both are preserved.*
5:39 [p] NU-Text omits *immediately.* [q] NU-Text reads *good.*
6:1 [r] NU-Text reads *on a Sabbath.*

went into the house of God, took and ate the showbread, and also gave
some to those with him, which is not lawful for any but the priests to eat?"
5 And He said to them, "The Son of Man is also Lord of the Sabbath."

Healing on the Sabbath

6 Now it happened on another Sabbath, also, that He entered the synagogue and taught. And a man was there whose right hand was withered.
7 So the scribes and Pharisees watched Him closely, whether He would heal
on the Sabbath, that they might find an accusation against Him. 8 But He
knew their thoughts, and said to the man who had the withered hand,
"Arise and stand here." And he arose and stood. 9 Then Jesus said to them,
"I will ask you one thing: Is it lawful on the Sabbath to do good or to do
evil, to save life or to destroy?"[s] 10 And when He had looked around at them
all, He said to the man,[t] "Stretch out your hand." And he did so, and his
hand was restored as whole as the other.[u] 11 But they were filled with rage,
and discussed with one another what they might do to Jesus.

The Twelve Apostles

12 Now it came to pass in those days that He went out to the mountain to
pray, and continued all night in prayer to God. 13 And when it was day, He
called His disciples to *Himself;* and from them He chose twelve whom He
also named apostles: 14 Simon, whom He also named Peter, and Andrew
his brother; James and John; Philip and Bartholomew; 15 Matthew and
Thomas; James the *son* of Alphaeus, and Simon called the Zealot; 16 Judas
the son of James, and Judas Iscariot who also became a traitor.

Jesus Heals a Great Multitude

17 And He came down with them and stood on a level place with a crowd
of His disciples and a great multitude of people from all Judea and Jerusalem, and from the seacoast of Tyre and Sidon, who came to hear Him and
be healed of their diseases, 18 as well as those who were tormented with unclean spirits. And they were healed. 19 And the whole multitude sought to
touch Him, for power went out from Him and healed *them* all.

The Beatitudes

20 Then He lifted up His eyes toward His disciples, and said:

"Blessed *are you* poor,
For yours is the kingdom of God.
21 Blessed *are you* who hunger now,
For you shall be filled.
Blessed *are you* who weep now,
For you shall laugh.
22 Blessed are you when men hate you,
And when they exclude you,
And revile *you,* and cast out your name as evil,
For the Son of Man's sake.
23 Rejoice in that day and leap for joy!
For indeed your reward *is* great in heaven,

LIFE LESSON

Luke 6:1-49

SITUATION Jesus called and appointed his apostles. He spent the next three years teaching them.

OBSERVATION The night before Jesus appointed the Twelve Apostles, he prayed.

INSPIRATION "He went up on a mountainside by Himself to pray." . . .

Maybe he didn't ask for anything. Maybe he just stood quietly in the presence of Presence and basked in the Majesty. Perhaps he placed his war-weary self before the throne and rested.

Maybe he lifted his head out of the confusion of earth long enough to hear the solution of heaven. Perhaps he was reminded that hard hearts don't faze the Father. That problem people don't perturb the Eternal One.

We don't know what he did or what he said. But we do know the result. The hill became a steppingstone; the storm became a path. And the disciples saw Jesus as they had never seen him before.

During the storm, Jesus prayed. The sky darkened. The winds howled. Yet he prayed. The people grumbled. The disciples doubted. Yet he prayed. When forced to choose between the muscles of men and the mountain of prayer, he prayed.

Jesus did not try to do it by himself. Why should you?

There are crevasses in your life that you cannot cross alone. There are hearts in your world that you cannot change without help. There are mountains that you cannot climb until you climb His mountain.

Climb it. You will be amazed.

(From *In the Eye of the Storm* by Max Lucado)

APPLICATION All around you people are hurting, even Christian brothers and sisters. Think of how you can meet their needs and encourage them. Follow Jesus' example and pray for them.

EXPLORATION Discipleship—Matthew 10:42; 28:19; Luke 14:33; John 8:31-32; 13:35; 15:8.

6:9 [s] M-Text reads *to kill.*
6:10 [t] NU-Text and M-Text read *to him.* [u] NU-Text omits *as whole as the other.*

For in like manner their fathers did to
the prophets.

Jesus Pronounces Woes

24 “But woe to you who are rich,
For you have received your consolation.
25 Woe to you who are full,
For you shall hunger.
Woe to you who laugh now,
For you shall mourn and weep.
26 Woe to you[v] when all[w] men speak well of you,
For so did their fathers to the
false prophets.

Love Your Enemies

27“But I say to you who hear: Love your enemies, do
good to those who hate you, 28bless those who curse
you, and pray for those who spitefully use you. 29To
him who strikes you on the *one* cheek, offer the other
also. And from him who takes away your cloak, do
not withhold *your* tunic either. 30Give to everyone who
asks of you. And from him who takes away your
goods do not ask *them* back. 31And just as you want
men to do to you, you also do to them likewise.
32“But if you love those who love you, what credit is
that to you? For even sinners love those who love
them. 33And if you do good to those who do good to
you, what credit is that to you? For even sinners do the
same. 34And if you lend *to those* from whom you hope
to receive back, what credit is that to you? For even
sinners lend to sinners to receive as much back. 35But
love your enemies, do good, and lend, hoping for
nothing in return; and your reward will be great, and
you will be sons of the Most High. For He is kind to
the unthankful and evil. 36Therefore be merciful, just
as your Father also is merciful.

Do Not Judge

37“Judge not, and you shall not be judged.
Condemn not, and you shall not be condemned. Forgive, and you will be forgiven. 38Give, and it will be
given to you: good measure, pressed down, shaken
together, and running over will be put into your bosom. For with the same measure that you use, it will
be measured back to you.”
39And He spoke a parable to them: “Can the blind
lead the blind? Will they not both fall into the ditch?
40A disciple is not above his teacher, but everyone who
is perfectly trained will be like his teacher. 41And why
do you look at the speck in your brother’s eye, but do
not perceive the plank in your own eye? 42Or how can
you say to your brother, ‘Brother, let me remove the
speck that *is* in your eye,’ when you yourself do not
see the plank that *is* in your own eye? Hypocrite! First
remove the plank from your own eye, and then you
will see clearly to remove the speck that is in your
brother’s eye.

A Tree Is Known by Its Fruit

43“For a good tree does not bear bad fruit, nor does
a bad tree bear good fruit. 44For every tree is known
by its own fruit. For *men* do not gather figs from
thorns, nor do they gather grapes from a bramble
bush. 45A good man out of the good treasure of his
heart brings forth good; and an evil man out of the
evil treasure of his heart[x] brings forth evil. For out of
the abundance of the heart his mouth speaks.

Build on the Rock

46“But why do you call Me ‘Lord, Lord,’ and not do
the things which I say? 47Whoever comes to Me, and
hears My sayings and does them, I will show you
whom he is like: 48He is like a man building a house,
who dug deep and laid the foundation on the rock.
And when the flood arose, the stream beat vehemently against that house, and could not shake it, for
it was founded on the rock.[y] 49But he who heard and
did nothing is like a man who built a house on the
earth without a foundation, against which the stream
beat vehemently; and immediately it fell.[z] And the
ruin of that house was great.”

Jesus Heals a Centurion’s Servant

7 Now when He concluded all His sayings in the
hearing of the people, He entered Capernaum.
2And a certain centurion’s servant, who was dear to
him, was sick and ready to die. 3So when he heard
about Jesus, he sent elders of the Jews to Him, pleading
with Him to come and heal his servant. 4And when they
came to Jesus, they begged Him earnestly, saying that
the one for whom He should do this was deserving,
5“for he loves our nation, and has built us a synagogue.”
6Then Jesus went with them. And when He was already not far from the house, the centurion sent
friends to Him, saying to Him, “Lord, do not trouble

6:26 [v] NU-Text and M-Text omit *to you.* [w] M-Text omits *all.*
6:45 [x] NU-Text omits *treasure of his heart.*
6:48 [y] NU-Text reads *for it was well built.*
6:49 [z] NU-Text reads *collapsed.*

LIFE LESSON

Luke 7:1-50

SITUATION People heard about the signs and wonders Jesus was performing and came to meet him. Jesus' popularity kept increasing.

OBSERVATION Jesus pointed to people who had great faith in order to show what God desires from his people.

INSPIRATION Two crowds. One entering the city and one leaving. They couldn't be more diverse. The group arriving buzzes with laughter and conversation. They follow Jesus. The group leaving the city is solemn—a herd of sadness hypnotized by the requiem of death. Above them rides the reason for their grief—a cold body on a wicker stretcher.

The woman at the back of the procession is the mother. She has walked this trail before. It seems like just yesterday she buried the body of her husband. Her son walked with her then. Now she walks alone, quarantined in her sadness. She is the victim of this funeral.

She is the one with no arm around her shoulder. She is the one who will sleep in the empty house tonight. She is the one who will make dinner for one and conversation with none. She is the one most violated. The thief stole her most treasured diamond—companionship.

The followers of Jesus stop and step aside as the procession shadows by. The blanket of mourning muffles the laughter of the disciples. No one spoke. What could they say? . . .

Jesus, however, knew what to say and what to do. When he saw the mother, his heart began to break . . . and his lips began to tighten. He glared at the angel of death that hovered over the body of the boy. "Not this time, Satan. This boy is mine."

At that moment the mother walked in front of him. Jesus spoke to her.

Yourself, for I am not worthy that You should enter under my roof. 7There-
fore I did not even think myself worthy to come to You. But say the word,
and my servant will be healed. 8For I also am a man placed under authority, having soldiers under me. And I say to one, 'Go,' and he goes; and to
another, 'Come,' and he comes; and to my servant, 'Do this,' and he does *it*."
9When Jesus heard these things, He marveled at him, and turned
around and said to the crowd that followed Him, "I say to you, I have not
found such great faith, not even in Israel!" 10And those who were sent, returning to the house, found the servant well who had been sick.[a]

Jesus Raises the Son of the Widow of Nain

11Now it happened, the day after, *that* He went into a city called Nain;
and many of His disciples went with Him, and a large crowd. 12And when
He came near the gate of the city, behold, a dead man was being carried
out, the only son of his mother; and she was a widow. And a large crowd
from the city was with her. 13When the Lord saw her, He had compassion
on her and said to her, "Do not weep." 14Then He came and touched the
open coffin, and those who carried *him* stood still. And He said, "Young
man, I say to you, arise." 15So he who was dead sat up and began to speak.
And He presented him to his mother.
16Then fear came upon all, and they glorified God, saying, "A great prophet
has risen up among us"; and, "God has visited His people." 17And this report
about Him went throughout all Judea and all the surrounding region.

John the Baptist Sends Messengers to Jesus

18Then the disciples of John reported to him concerning all these things.
19And John, calling two of his disciples to *him,* sent *them* to Jesus,[b] saying,
"Are You the Coming One, or do we look for another?"
20When the men had come to Him, they said, "John the Baptist has sent
us to You, saying, 'Are You the Coming One, or do we look for another?' "
21And that very hour He cured many of infirmities, afflictions, and evil
spirits; and to many blind He gave sight.
22Jesus answered and said to them, "Go and tell John the things you
have seen and heard: that *the* blind see, *the* lame walk, *the* lepers are
cleansed, *the* deaf hear, *the* dead are raised, *the* poor have the gospel
preached to them. 23And blessed is *he* who is not offended because of Me."
24When the messengers of John had departed, He began to speak to the
multitudes concerning John: "What did you go out into the wilderness to
see? A reed shaken by the wind? 25But what did you go out to see? A man
clothed in soft garments? Indeed those who are gorgeously appareled and
live in luxury are in kings' courts. 26But what did you go out to see? A prophet?
Yes, I say to you, and more than a prophet. 27This is *he* of whom it is written:

> *'Behold, I send My messenger before Your face,*
> *Who will prepare Your way before You.'*[c]

28For I say to you, among those born of women there is not a greater
prophet than John the Baptist;[d] but he who is least in the kingdom of God is
greater than he."

7:10 [a] NU-Text omits *who had been sick.*
7:19 [b] NU-Text reads *the Lord.*
7:27 [c] Malachi 3:1
7:28 [d] NU-Text reads *there is none greater than John.*

29 And when all the people heard *Him,* even the tax collectors justified
God, having been baptized with the baptism of John. 30 But the Pharisees
and lawyers rejected the will of God for themselves, not having been baptized by him.
31 And the Lord said,[e] "To what then shall I liken the men of this generation, and what are they like? 32 They are like children sitting in the marketplace and calling to one another, saying:

'We played the flute for you,
And you did not dance;
We mourned to you,
And you did not weep.'

33 For John the Baptist came neither eating bread nor drinking wine, and
you say, 'He has a demon.' 34 The Son of Man has come eating and drinking, and you say, 'Look, a glutton and a winebibber, a friend of tax collectors and sinners!' 35 But wisdom is justified by all her children."

A Sinful Woman Forgiven

36 Then one of the Pharisees asked Him to eat with him. And He went to
the Pharisee's house, and sat down to eat. 37 And behold, a woman in the
city who was a sinner, when she knew that *Jesus* sat at the table in the
Pharisee's house, brought an alabaster flask of fragrant oil, 38 and stood at
His feet behind *Him* weeping; and she began to wash His feet with her
tears, and wiped *them* with the hair of her head; and she kissed His feet
and anointed *them* with the fragrant oil. 39 Now when the Pharisee who
had invited Him saw *this,* he spoke to himself, saying, "This Man, if He
were a prophet, would know who and what manner of woman *this is* who
is touching Him, for she is a sinner."
40 And Jesus answered and said to him, "Simon, I have something to say
to you."
So he said, "Teacher, say it."
41 "There was a certain creditor who had two debtors. One owed five
hundred denarii, and the other fifty. 42 And when they had nothing with
which to repay, he freely forgave them both. Tell Me, therefore, which of
them will love him more?"
43 Simon answered and said, "I suppose the *one* whom he forgave more."
And He said to him, "You have rightly judged." 44 Then He turned to the
woman and said to Simon, "Do you see this woman? I entered your house;
you gave Me no water for My feet, but she has washed My feet with her
tears and wiped *them* with the hair of her head. 45 You gave Me no kiss, but
this woman has not ceased to kiss My feet since the time I came in. 46 You
did not anoint My head with oil, but this woman has anointed My feet
with fragrant oil. 47 Therefore I say to you, her sins, *which are* many, are
forgiven, for she loved much. But to whom little is forgiven, *the same*
loves little."
48 Then He said to her, "Your sins are forgiven."
49 And those who sat at the table with Him began to say to themselves,
"Who is this who even forgives sins?"
50 Then He said to the woman, "Your faith has saved you. Go in peace."

7:31 *e* NU-Text and M-Text omit *And the Lord said.*

"Don't cry." She stopped and looked into this stranger's face. If she wasn't shocked by his presumption, you can bet some of the witnesses were.

Don't cry? Don't cry? What kind of request is that?

A request only God can make.

Jesus stepped toward the bier and touched it. The pall-bearers stopped marching. The mourners ceased moaning. As Jesus stared at the boy, the crowd was silent. . . .

Jesus turned his attention to the dead boy. "Young man," his voice was calm, "come back to life again."

The living stood motionless as the dead came to life. Wooden fingers moved. Gray-pale cheeks blushed. The dead man sat up. . . .

Jesus must have smiled as the two embraced. Stunned, the crowd broke into cheers and applause. They hugged each other and slapped Jesus on the back. Someone proclaimed the undeniable, "God has come to help his people."

Jesus gave the woman much more than her son. He gave her a secret—a whisper that was overheard by us. "That," he said pointing at the cot, "that is fantasy. This," he grinned, putting an arm around the boy, "this is reality."

(From *Six Hours One Friday* by Max Lucado)

APPLICATION What can you do to demonstrate your faith? Is there something you are afraid to do? Someone you don't want to see? A relationship that needs repair? Ask God to help you do it. Believe he will, then step out and act.

EXPLORATION Faith—1 Samuel 17:37; 2 Chronicles 20:20; John 6:28-29; Romans 10:9; 10:17; Ephesians 6:16; Hebrews 11:1, 6; James 2:17.

LIFE LESSON

Luke 8:1-56

SITUATION Because of increasing hostility from the Pharisees and Sadducees, Jesus stopped going to the synagogues. Instead, he began to preach in the countryside.

OBSERVATION Jesus emphasized that not only must we hear God's words, but we must act on them too.

INSPIRATION Only when I reach the point where I solemnly place great store upon what he says will it ever become a powerful force in my life.

Only when I really take Him seriously will His word be made Spirit and life (supernatural life) to me.

Only when I recognize that what I am hearing is in fact and in truth divine revelation designed by deity for my own good, will I hear it as a word from above.

God has chosen to articulate Himself to me as a man in four ways: through the natural created universe around me; through His word expressed by inspired men who reported it in human language I can read and understand; through the person of Jesus Christ, the Word made flesh, exemplified in human form; through those other men and women in whom He deigns to reside by His own Gracious Spirit.

He may speak to me deliberately and distinctly through any one or all of these ways. It is my responsibility then to recognize: "O God, You are communicating with me. I will listen. I do recognize Your voice communing with me." . . .

I must set aside whatever else preoccupies my thoughts and give my undivided attention to the Lord.

Many Women Minister to Jesus

8 Now it came to pass, afterward, that He went through every city and
village, preaching and bringing the glad tidings of the kingdom of God.
And the twelve *were* with Him, 2and certain women who had been healed of
evil spirits and infirmities—Mary called Magdalene, out of whom had come
seven demons, 3and Joanna the wife of Chuza, Herod's steward, and Susanna,
and many others who provided for Him[f] from their substance.

The Parable of the Sower

4And when a great multitude had gathered, and they had come to Him
from every city, He spoke by a parable: 5"A sower went out to sow his seed.
And as he sowed, some fell by the wayside; and it was trampled down, and
the birds of the air devoured it. 6Some fell on rock; and as soon as it sprang
up, it withered away because it lacked moisture. 7And some fell among
thorns, and the thorns sprang up with it and choked it. 8But others fell on
good ground, sprang up, and yielded a crop a hundredfold." When He
had said these things He cried, "He who has ears to hear, let him hear!"

The Purpose of Parables

9Then His disciples asked Him, saying, "What does this parable mean?"
10And He said, "To you it has been given to know the mysteries of the
kingdom of God, but to the rest *it is given* in parables, that

'Seeing they may not see,
And hearing they may not understand.'[g]

The Parable of the Sower Explained

11"Now the parable is this: The seed is the word of God. 12Those by the wayside are the ones who hear; then the devil comes and takes away the word out
of their hearts, lest they should believe and be saved. 13But the ones on the rock
are those who, when they hear, receive the word with joy; and these have no
root, who believe for a while and in time of temptation fall away. 14Now the
ones *that* fell among thorns are those who, when they have heard, go out and
are choked with cares, riches, and pleasures of life, and bring no fruit to maturity. 15But the ones *that* fell on the good ground are those who, having heard
the word with a noble and good heart, keep *it* and bear fruit with patience.

The Parable of the Revealed Light

16"No one, when he has lit a lamp, covers it with a vessel or puts *it* under
a bed, but sets *it* on a lampstand, that those who enter may see the light.
17For nothing is secret that will not be revealed, nor *anything* hidden that
will not be known and come to light. 18Therefore take heed how you hear.
For whoever has, to him *more* will be given; and whoever does not have,
even what he seems to have will be taken from him."

Jesus' Mother and Brothers Come to Him

19Then His mother and brothers came to Him, and could not approach
Him because of the crowd. 20And it was told Him *by some,* who said, "Your
mother and Your brothers are standing outside, desiring to see You."
21But He answered and said to them, "My mother and My brothers are
these who hear the word of God and do it."

8:3 [f] NU-Text and M-Text read *them.*
8:10 [g] Isaiah 6:9

Wind and Wave Obey Jesus

22Now it happened, on a certain day, that He got into a boat with His disciples. And He said to them, "Let us cross over to the other side of the
lake." And they launched out. 23But as they sailed He fell asleep. And a
windstorm came down on the lake, and they were filling *with water,* and
were in jeopardy. 24And they came to Him and awoke Him, saying, "Master, Master, we are perishing!"
Then He arose and rebuked the wind and the raging of the water. And they
ceased, and there was a calm. 25But He said to them, "Where is your faith?"
And they were afraid, and marveled, saying to one another, "Who can
this be? For He commands even the winds and water, and they obey Him!"

A Demon-Possessed Man Healed

26Then they sailed to the country of the Gadarenes,[h] which is opposite
Galilee. 27And when He stepped out on the land, there met Him a certain
man from the city who had demons for a long time. And he wore no
clothes,[i] nor did he live in a house but in the tombs. 28When he saw Jesus,
he cried out, fell down before Him, and with a loud voice said, "What have
I to do with You, Jesus, Son of the Most High God? I beg You, do not torment me!" 29For He had commanded the unclean spirit to come out of the
man. For it had often seized him, and he was kept under guard, bound
with chains and shackles; and he broke the bonds and was driven by the
demon into the wilderness.
30Jesus asked him, saying, "What is your name?"
And he said, "Legion," because many demons had entered him. 31And
they begged Him that He would not command them to go out into the abyss.
32Now a herd of many swine was feeding there on the mountain. So they
begged Him that He would permit them to enter them. And He permitted
them. 33Then the demons went out of the man and entered the swine, and
the herd ran violently down the steep place into the lake and drowned.
34When those who fed *them* saw what had happened, they fled and told
it in the city and in the country. 35Then they went out to see what had happened, and came to Jesus, and found the man from whom the demons
had departed, sitting at the feet of Jesus, clothed and in his right mind.
And they were afraid. 36They also who had seen *it* told them by what
means he who had been demon-possessed was healed. 37Then the whole
multitude of the surrounding region of the Gadarenes[j] asked Him to depart from them, for they were seized with great fear. And He got into the
boat and returned.
38Now the man from whom the demons had departed begged Him that
he might be with Him. But Jesus sent him away, saying, 39"Return to your
own house, and tell what great things God has done for you." And he went
his way and proclaimed throughout the whole city what great things Jesus
had done for him.

A Girl Restored to Life and a Woman Healed

40So it was, when Jesus returned, that the multitude welcomed Him, for
they were all waiting for Him. 41And behold, there came a man named

It is not good enough to "half listen" to God. He demands my total concentration on what He is conveying to me. He knows that anything less will leave me half-hearted. . . .

My positive response results in immediate action on my part. His will is done. His wishes are carried out. His desires are complied with happily. His commands are executed without delay or debate.

In short I simply do what He asks me to do.

This is faith in action—the faith of obedience.

This is the gateway into the good ground of God's garden.

This is to "hear" the Word and have it come alive.

This is to have Him implant the good seed of His good intentions for me in the good, warm, open, prepared soil of my responsive soul.

The seed will germinate. The young plants will prosper and grow vigorously. There will be fruit production of His choosing—a harvest that delights Him and refreshes others.

(From *A Gardener Looks at the Fruits of the Spirit* by Phillip Keller)

APPLICATION As you read God's Word, listen to the Holy Spirit. What is God telling you to *do*? Don't ignore his prodding—obey him now.

EXPLORATION Hearing—Exodus 22:27; 2 Chronicles 7:14; Isaiah 59:1; John 5:24; Romans 2:13; 10:17; Revelation 3:20.

8:26 [h] NU-Text reads *Gerasenes.*
8:27 [i] NU-Text reads *who had demons and for a long time wore no clothes.*
8:37 [j] NU-Text reads *Gerasenes.*

LIFE LESSON

Luke 9:1-62

SITUATION Jesus' teaching, preaching, and miracles stirred up interest among the people. They wondered if Jesus was a prophet or the Messiah.

OBSERVATION Not only is Jesus the Messiah, at the same time he is mysteriously God and man.

INSPIRATION One of the most dramatic scenes in the New Testament occurred in a city known as Caesarea Philippi. . . . It was indeed a dramatic picture. In the midst of this carnival of marble columns and golden idols, a penniless, homeless, nameless Nazarene asks his band of followers, "Who do you say that I am?"

The immensity of the question is staggering. I would imagine that Peter's answer did not come without some hesitation. Shuffling of feet. Anxious silence. How absurd that this man should be the Son of God. No trumpets. No purple robes. No armies. Yet there was that glint of determination in his eye and that edge of certainty in his message. Peter's response sliced the silence. "I believe that you are . . . the Son of God."

Many have looked at Jesus; but few have seen him. Many have seen his shadow, his people, his story. But only a handful have seen Jesus. Only a few have looked through the fog of religiosity and found him. Only a few have dared to stand eye to eye and heart to heart with Jesus and say, "I believe that you are the Son of God."

(From *On the Anvil* by Max Lucado)

APPLICATION Who is Jesus to you? Does your answer depend on who is asking? On your feelings or circumstances? Worship your Messiah, the Son of God.

EXPLORATION Identity of Christ—Matthew 16:13-20; Luke 1:30-35; John 4:25-26; 9:35-38.

Jairus, and he was a ruler of the synagogue. And he fell down at Jesus' feet
and begged Him to come to his house, 42for he had an only daughter about
twelve years of age, and she was dying.
But as He went, the multitudes thronged Him. 43Now a woman, having
a flow of blood for twelve years, who had spent all her livelihood on physicians and could not be healed by any, 44came from behind and touched the
border of His garment. And immediately her flow of blood stopped.
45And Jesus said, "Who touched Me?"
When all denied it, Peter and those with him[k] said, "Master, the multitudes throng and press You, and You say, 'Who touched Me?' "[l]
46But Jesus said, "Somebody touched Me, for I perceived power going
out from Me." 47Now when the woman saw that she was not hidden, she
came trembling; and falling down before Him, she declared to Him in the
presence of all the people the reason she had touched Him and how she
was healed immediately.
48And He said to her, "Daughter, be of good cheer;[m] your faith has made
you well. Go in peace."
49While He was still speaking, someone came from the ruler of the synagogue's *house,* saying to him, "Your daughter is dead. Do not trouble the
Teacher."[n]
50But when Jesus heard *it,* He answered him, saying, "Do not be afraid;
only believe, and she will be made well." 51When He came into the house,
He permitted no one to go in[o] except Peter, James, and John,[p] and the father and mother of the girl. 52Now all wept and mourned for her; but He
said, "Do not weep; she is not dead, but sleeping." 53And they ridiculed
Him, knowing that she was dead.
54But He put them all outside,[q] took her by the hand and called, saying,
"Little girl, arise." 55Then her spirit returned, and she arose immediately.
And He commanded that she be given *something* to eat. 56And her parents
were astonished, but He charged them to tell no one what had happened.

Sending Out the Twelve

9 Then He called His twelve disciples together and gave them power and
authority over all demons, and to cure diseases. 2He sent them to
preach the kingdom of God and to heal the sick. 3And He said to them,
"Take nothing for the journey, neither staffs nor bag nor bread nor money;
and do not have two tunics apiece.
4"Whatever house you enter, stay there, and from there depart. 5And
whoever will not receive you, when you go out of that city, shake off the
very dust from your feet as a testimony against them."
6So they departed and went through the towns, preaching the gospel
and healing everywhere.

Herod Seeks to See Jesus

7Now Herod the tetrarch heard of all that was done by Him; and he was
perplexed, because it was said by some that John had risen from the dead,
8and by some that Elijah had appeared, and by others that one of the old

8:45 [k] NU-Text omits *and those with him.* [l] NU-Text omits *and You say, 'Who touched Me?'*
8:48 [m] NU-Text omits *be of good cheer.*
8:49 [n] NU-Text adds *anymore.*
8:51 [o] NU-Text adds *with Him.* [p] NU-Text and M-Text read *Peter, John, and James.*
8:54 [q] NU-Text omits *put them all outside.*

prophets had risen again. 9Herod said, "John I have beheaded, but who is this of whom I hear such things?" So he sought to see Him.

Feeding the Five Thousand

10And the apostles, when they had returned, told Him all that they had done. Then He took them and went aside privately into a deserted place belonging to the city called Bethsaida. 11But when the multitudes knew *it,* they followed Him; and He received them and spoke to them about the kingdom of God, and healed those who had need of healing. 12When the day began to wear away, the twelve came and said to Him, "Send the multitude away, that they may go into the surrounding towns and country, and lodge and get provisions; for we are in a deserted place here."

13But He said to them, "You give them something to eat."

And they said, "We have no more than five loaves and two fish, unless we go and buy food for all these people." 14For there were about five thousand men.

Then He said to His disciples, "Make them sit down in groups of fifty." 15And they did so, and made them all sit down.

16Then He took the five loaves and the two fish, and looking up to heaven, He blessed and broke *them,* and gave *them* to the disciples to set before the multitude. 17So they all ate and were filled, and twelve baskets of the leftover fragments were taken up by them.

Peter Confesses Jesus as the Christ

18And it happened, as He was alone praying, *that* His disciples joined Him, and He asked them, saying, "Who do the crowds say that I am?"

19So they answered and said, "John the Baptist, but some *say* Elijah; and others *say* that one of the old prophets has risen again."

20He said to them, "But who do you say that I am?"

Peter answered and said, "The Christ of God."

Jesus Predicts His Death and Resurrection

21And He strictly warned and commanded them to tell this to no one, 22saying, "The Son of Man must suffer many things, and be rejected by the elders and chief priests and scribes, and be killed, and be raised the third day."

Take Up the Cross and Follow Him

23Then He said to *them* all, "If anyone desires to come after Me, let him deny himself, and take up his cross daily,[r] and follow Me. 24For whoever desires to save his life will lose it, but whoever loses his life for My sake will save it. 25For what profit is it to a man if he gains the whole world, and is himself destroyed or lost? 26For whoever is ashamed of Me and My words, of him the Son of Man will be ashamed when He comes in His *own* glory, and *in His* Father's, and of the holy angels.

Jesus Transfigured on the Mount

27But I tell you truly, there are some standing here who shall not taste death till they see the kingdom of God."

28Now it came to pass, about eight days after these sayings, that He took Peter, John, and James and went up on the mountain to pray. 29As He prayed, the appearance of His face was altered, and His robe *became* white *and* glistening. 30And behold, two men talked with Him, who were Moses and Elijah, 31who appeared in glory and spoke of His decease which He was about to accomplish at Jerusalem. 32But Peter and those with him were heavy with sleep; and when they were fully awake, they saw His glory and the two men who stood with Him. 33Then it happened, as they were parting from Him, *that* Peter said to Jesus, "Master, it is good for us to be here; and let us make three tabernacles: one for You, one for Moses, and one for Elijah"—not knowing what he said.

34While he was saying this, a cloud came and overshadowed them; and they were fearful as they entered the cloud. 35And a voice came out of the cloud, saying, "This is My beloved Son.[s] Hear Him!" 36When the voice had ceased, Jesus was found alone. But they kept quiet, and told no one in those days any of the things they had seen.

A Boy Is Healed

37Now it happened on the next day, when they had come down from the mountain, that a great multitude met Him. 38Suddenly a man from the multitude cried out, saying, "Teacher, I implore You, look on my son, for he is my only child. 39And behold, a spirit seizes him, and he suddenly cries out; it convulses him so that he foams *at the mouth;* and it departs from him with great difficulty, bruising him. 40So I implored Your disciples to cast it out, but they could not."

41Then Jesus answered and said, "O faithless and perverse generation, how long shall I be with you and bear with you? Bring your son here." 42And as he was still coming, the demon threw him down and convulsed *him.* Then Jesus rebuked the unclean spirit, healed the child, and gave him back to his father.

9:23 [r] M-Text omits *daily.*
9:35 [s] NU-Text reads *This is My Son, the Chosen One.*

Jesus Again Predicts His Death

43And they were all amazed at the majesty of God.
But while everyone marveled at all the things which
Jesus did, He said to His disciples, 44"Let these words
sink down into your ears, for the Son of Man is about
to be betrayed into the hands of men." 45But they did
not understand this saying, and it was hidden from
them so that they did not perceive it; and they were
afraid to ask Him about this saying.

Who Is the Greatest?

46Then a dispute arose among them as to which of
them would be greatest. 47And Jesus, perceiving the
thought of their heart, took a little child and set him
by Him, 48and said to them, "Whoever receives this
little child in My name receives Me; and whoever receives Me receives Him who sent Me. For he who is
least among you all will be great."

Jesus Forbids Sectarianism

49Now John answered and said, "Master, we saw
someone casting out demons in Your name, and we
forbade him because he does not follow with us."
50But Jesus said to him, "Do not forbid *him,* for he
who is not against us[t] is on our[u] side."

A Samaritan Village Rejects the Savior

51Now it came to pass, when the time had come for
Him to be received up, that He steadfastly set His face
to go to Jerusalem, 52and sent messengers before His
face. And as they went, they entered a village of the Samaritans, to prepare for Him. 53But they did not receive Him, because His face was *set* for the journey to
Jerusalem. 54And when His disciples James and John
saw *this,* they said, "Lord, do You want us to command fire to come down from heaven and consume
them, just as Elijah did?"[v]
55But He turned and rebuked them,[w] and said, "You
do not know what manner of spirit you are of. 56For the
Son of Man did not come to destroy men's lives but to
save *them.*"[x] And they went to another village.

The Cost of Discipleship

57Now it happened as they journeyed on the road,
that someone said to Him, "Lord, I will follow You
wherever You go."
58And Jesus said to him, "Foxes have holes and
birds of the air *have* nests, but the Son of Man has
nowhere to lay *His* head."
59Then He said to another, "Follow Me."
But he said, "Lord, let me first go and bury my father."
60Jesus said to him, "Let the dead bury their own
dead, but you go and preach the kingdom of God."
61And another also said, "Lord, I will follow You,
but let me first go *and* bid them farewell who are at
my house."
62But Jesus said to him, "No one, having put his
hand to the plow, and looking back, is fit for the kingdom of God."

The Seventy Sent Out

10 After these things the Lord appointed seventy
others also,[y] and sent them two by two before
His face into every city and place where He Himself
was about to go. 2Then He said to them, "The harvest
truly *is* great, but the laborers *are* few; therefore pray
the Lord of the harvest to send out laborers into His
harvest. 3Go your way; behold, I send you out as
lambs among wolves. 4Carry neither money bag,
knapsack, nor sandals; and greet no one along the
road. 5But whatever house you enter, first say, 'Peace
to this house.' 6And if a son of peace is there, your
peace will rest on it; if not, it will return to you. 7And
remain in the same house, eating and drinking such
things as they give, for the laborer is worthy of his
wages. Do not go from house to house. 8Whatever city
you enter, and they receive you, eat such things as are
set before you. 9And heal the sick there, and say to
them, 'The kingdom of God has come near to you.'
10But whatever city you enter, and they do not receive
you, go out into its streets and say, 11'The very dust of
your city which clings to us[z] we wipe off against you.
Nevertheless know this, that the kingdom of God has
come near you.' 12But[a] I say to you that it will be more
tolerable in that Day for Sodom than for that city.

Woe to the Impenitent Cities

13"Woe to you, Chorazin! Woe to you, Bethsaida!
For if the mighty works which were done in you had
been done in Tyre and Sidon, they would have repented long ago, sitting in sackcloth and ashes. 14But
it will be more tolerable for Tyre and Sidon at the

9:50 [t] NU-Text reads *you.* [u] NU-Text reads *your.*
9:54 [v] NU-Text omits *just as Elijah did.*
9:55 [w] NU-Text omits the rest of this verse.
9:56 [x] NU-Text omits the first sentence of this verse.
10:1 [y] NU-Text reads *seventy-two others.*
10:11 [z] NU-Text reads *our feet.*
10:12 [a] NU-Text and M-Text omit *But.*

judgment than for you. 15And you, Capernaum, who are exalted to heaven, will be brought down to Hades.[b] 16He who hears you hears Me, he who rejects you rejects Me, and he who rejects Me rejects Him who sent Me."

The Seventy Return with Joy

17Then the seventy[c] returned with joy, saying, "Lord, even the demons are subject to us in Your name."

18And He said to them, "I saw Satan fall like lightning from heaven. 19Behold, I give you the authority to trample on serpents and scorpions, and over all the power of the enemy, and nothing shall by any means hurt you. 20Nevertheless do not rejoice in this, that the spirits are subject to you, but rather[d] rejoice because your names are written in heaven."

Jesus Rejoices in the Spirit

21In that hour Jesus rejoiced in the Spirit and said, "I thank You, Father, Lord of heaven and earth, that You have hidden these things from *the* wise and prudent and revealed them to babes. Even so, Father, for so it seemed good in Your sight. 22All[e] things have been delivered to Me by My Father, and no one knows who the Son is except the Father, and who the Father is except the Son, and *the one* to whom the Son wills to reveal *Him.*"

23Then He turned to *His* disciples and said privately, "Blessed *are* the eyes which see the things you see; 24for I tell you that many prophets and kings have desired to see what you see, and have not seen *it*, and to hear what you hear, and have not heard *it.*"

The Parable of the Good Samaritan

25And behold, a certain lawyer stood up and tested Him, saying, "Teacher, what shall I do to inherit eternal life?"

26He said to him, "What is written in the law? What is your reading *of it?*"

27So he answered and said, "'*You shall love the* LORD *your God with all your heart, with all your soul, with all your strength, and with all your mind,*'[f] and '*your neighbor as yourself.*'"[g]

28And He said to him, "You have answered rightly; do this and you will live."

29But he, wanting to justify himself, said to Jesus, "And who is my neighbor?"

30Then Jesus answered and said: "A certain *man* went down from Jerusalem to Jericho, and fell among thieves, who stripped him of his clothing, wounded *him*, and departed, leaving *him* half dead. 31Now by chance a certain priest came down that road. And when he saw him, he passed by on the other side. 32Likewise a Levite, when he arrived at the place, came and looked, and passed by on the other side. 33But a certain Samaritan, as he journeyed, came where he was. And when he saw him, he had compassion. 34So he went to *him* and bandaged his wounds, pouring on oil and wine; and he set him on his own animal, brought him to an inn, and took care of him. 35On the next day, when he departed,[h] he took out two denarii,

10:15 [b] NU-Text reads *will you be exalted to heaven? You will be thrust down to Hades!*
10:17 [c] NU-Text reads *seventy-two.*
10:20 [d] NU-Text and M-Text omit *rather.*
10:22 [e] M-Text reads *And turning to the disciples He said, "All . . . .*
10:27 [f] Deuteronomy 6:5 [g] Leviticus 19:18
10:35 [h] NU-Text omits *when he departed.*

LIFE LESSON

Luke 10:1-42

SITUATION Luke recorded the stories of busy people. Religious leaders neglected the injured Samaritan because they were too busy. Martha was too busy to merely listen to Jesus. He encouraged his hearers never to be too busy to love God or serve others.

OBSERVATION Demonstrate your love for God by showing love to those who are difficult to love.

INSPIRATION A driving rainstorm in an area suffering from drought does not discriminate. All receive the benefits. The same can be said for the sun. It bathes all homes alike with warmth and light. Why? Because God is love. Grace is His style. That is why Christ would minister so graciously to those who hated Him. Love and grace prompt the rain to fall on all the ground and the sun to shine on all the homes. For love to replace hate and grace to replace prejudice, playing favorites must cease. Love and grace befit those who are Fatherlike.

Then how far do we take this love-your-neighbor stuff? Do we love atheists? Yes! Scoffers? Yes! Criminals? Yes! Love, remember, sees the soul and focuses on the heart.

(From *Simple Faith* by Charles Swindoll)

APPLICATION Name someone you see often who is unlovely or neglected. What can you do this week to help reach out to that person with God's love?

EXPLORATION Love the Poor—Proverbs 31:20; 1 Corinthians 13:3.

Life Lesson

Luke 11:1-54

SITUATION Jesus gave the disciples a good example by praying constantly. The disciples asked Jesus to teach them how to pray.

OBSERVATION Prayer reminds us that only God is perfectly holy. Prayer also keeps us dependent on God to meet our needs and to forgive our sins.

INSPIRATION We complain before God, and sometimes we are apologetic or indifferent to Him, but we actually ask Him for very few things. Yet a child exhibits a magnificent boldness to ask! Our Lord said, ". . . unless you . . . become as little children . . ." (Matthew 18:3). Ask and God will do. Give Jesus Christ the opportunity and the room to work. The problem is that no one will ever do this until he is at his wits' end. When a person is at his wits' end, it no longer seems to be the cowardly thing to pray; in fact, it is the only way he can get in touch with the truth and the reality of God Himself. Be yourself before God and present Him with your problems—the very things that have brought you to your wits' end. But as long as you think you are self-sufficient, you do not need to ask God for anything.

(From *My Utmost for His Highest* by Oswald Chambers)

APPLICATION Describe your prayer life. How often do you pray? What do you pray about? How can you increase the time you spend in prayer? Develop a plan, then have a family member help you stick to it.

EXPLORATION Prayer—Matthew 7:7-11; John 14:13-14; 15:7; Philippians 4:6.

gave *them* to the innkeeper, and said to him, 'Take care of him; and whatever more you spend, when I come again, I will repay you.' 36 So which of
these three do you think was neighbor to him who fell among the thieves?"
37 And he said, "He who showed mercy on him."
Then Jesus said to him, "Go and do likewise."

Mary and Martha Worship and Serve

38 Now it happened as they went that He entered a certain village; and a
certain woman named Martha welcomed Him into her house. 39 And she
had a sister called Mary, who also sat at Jesus'[i] feet and heard His word.
40 But Martha was distracted with much serving, and she approached Him
and said, "Lord, do You not care that my sister has left me to serve alone?
Therefore tell her to help me."
41 And Jesus[j] answered and said to her, "Martha, Martha, you are worried and troubled about many things. 42 But one thing is needed, and Mary
has chosen that good part, which will not be taken away from her."

The Model Prayer

11 Now it came to pass, as He was praying in a certain place, when He
ceased, *that* one of His disciples said to Him, "Lord, teach us to pray,
as John also taught his disciples."
2 So He said to them, "When you pray, say:

Our Father in heaven,[k]
Hallowed be Your name.
Your kingdom come.[l]
Your will be done
On earth as *it is* in heaven.
3 Give us day by day our daily bread.
4 And forgive us our sins,
For we also forgive everyone who is indebted to us.
And do not lead us into temptation,
But deliver us from the evil one." [m]

A Friend Comes at Midnight

5 And He said to them, "Which of you shall have a friend, and go to him
at midnight and say to him, 'Friend, lend me three loaves; 6 for a friend of
mine has come to me on his journey, and I have nothing to set before him';
7 and he will answer from within and say, 'Do not trouble me; the door is now
shut, and my children are with me in bed; I cannot rise and give to you'? 8 I
say to you, though he will not rise and give to him because he is his friend,
yet because of his persistence he will rise and give him as many as he needs.

Keep Asking, Seeking, Knocking

9 "So I say to you, ask, and it will be given to you; seek, and you will find;
knock, and it will be opened to you. 10 For everyone who asks receives, and
he who seeks finds, and to him who knocks it will be opened. 11 If a son
asks for bread[n] from any father among you, will he give him a stone? Or if

10:39 [i] NU-Text reads *the Lord's.*
10:41 [j] NU-Text reads *the Lord.*
11:2 [k] NU-Text omits *Our* and *in heaven.* [l] NU-Text omits the rest of this verse.
11:4 [m] NU-Text omits *But deliver us from the evil one.*
11:11 [n] NU-Text omits the words from *bread* through *for* in the next sentence.

he asks for a fish, will he give him a serpent instead of
a fish? 12Or if he asks for an egg, will he offer him a scorpion? 13If you then, being evil, know how to give good
gifts to your children, how much more will *your* heavenly Father give the Holy Spirit to those who ask Him!"

A House Divided Cannot Stand

14And He was casting out a demon, and it was
mute. So it was, when the demon had gone out, that
the mute spoke; and the multitudes marveled. 15But
some of them said, "He casts out demons by
Beelzebub,[o] the ruler of the demons."
16Others, testing *Him*, sought from Him a sign from
heaven. 17But He, knowing their thoughts, said to
them: "Every kingdom divided against itself is brought
to desolation, and a house *divided* against a house falls.
18If Satan also is divided against himself, how will his
kingdom stand? Because you say I cast out demons by
Beelzebub. 19And if I cast out demons by Beelzebub, by
whom do your sons cast *them* out? Therefore they will
be your judges. 20But if I cast out demons with the finger of God, surely the kingdom of God has come upon
you. 21When a strong man, fully armed, guards his own
palace, his goods are in peace. 22But when a stronger
than he comes upon him and overcomes him, he takes
from him all his armor in which he trusted, and divides
his spoils. 23He who is not with Me is against Me, and he
who does not gather with Me scatters.

An Unclean Spirit Returns

24"When an unclean spirit goes out of a man, he goes
through dry places, seeking rest; and finding none, he
says, 'I will return to my house from which I came.' 25And
when he comes, he finds *it* swept and put in order. 26Then
he goes and takes with *him* seven other spirits more
wicked than himself, and they enter and dwell there; and
the last *state* of that man is worse than the first."

Keeping the Word

27And it happened, as He spoke these things, that a
certain woman from the crowd raised her voice and
said to Him, "Blessed *is* the womb that bore You, and
the breasts which nursed You!"
28But He said, "More than that, blessed *are* those
who hear the word of God and keep it!"

Seeking a Sign

29And while the crowds were thickly gathered together, He began to say, "This is an evil generation. It
seeks a sign, and no sign will be given to it except the
sign of Jonah the prophet.[p] 30For as Jonah became a
sign to the Ninevites, so also the Son of Man will be to
this generation. 31The queen of the South will rise up
in the judgment with the men of this generation and
condemn them, for she came from the ends of the
earth to hear the wisdom of Solomon; and indeed a
greater than Solomon *is* here. 32The men of Nineveh
will rise up in the judgment with this generation and
condemn it, for they repented at the preaching of Jonah; and indeed a greater than Jonah *is* here.

The Lamp of the Body

33"No one, when he has lit a lamp, puts *it* in a secret
place or under a basket, but on a lampstand, that
those who come in may see the light. 34The lamp of
the body is the eye. Therefore, when your eye is good,
your whole body also is full of light. But when *your eye*
is bad, your body also *is* full of darkness. 35Therefore
take heed that the light which is in you is not darkness. 36If then your whole body *is* full of light, having
no part dark, *the* whole *body* will be full of light, as
when the bright shining of a lamp gives you light."

Woe to the Pharisees and Lawyers

37And as He spoke, a certain Pharisee asked Him to
dine with him. So He went in and sat down to eat.
38When the Pharisee saw *it,* he marveled that He had
not first washed before dinner.
39Then the Lord said to him, "Now you Pharisees
make the outside of the cup and dish clean, but your
inward part is full of greed and wickedness. 40Foolish
ones! Did not He who made the outside make the inside also? 41But rather give alms of such things as you
have; then indeed all things are clean to you.
42"But woe to you Pharisees! For you tithe mint and
rue and all manner of herbs, and pass by justice and
the love of God. These you ought to have done, without leaving the others undone. 43Woe to you
Pharisees! For you love the best seats in the synagogues and greetings in the marketplaces. 44Woe to
you, scribes and Pharisees, hypocrites![q] For you are
like graves which are not seen, and the men who walk
over *them* are not aware *of them.*"
45Then one of the lawyers answered and said to Him,
"Teacher, by saying these things You reproach us also."
46And He said, "Woe to you also, lawyers! For you load
men with burdens hard to bear, and you yourselves do

11:15 [o] NU-Text and M-Text read *Beelzebul.*
11:29 [p] NU-Text omits *the prophet.*
11:44 [q] NU-Text omits *scribes and Pharisees, hypocrites.*

LIFE LESSON

Luke 12:1-59

SITUATION Thousands of people gathered around Jesus. Yet he spoke to his disciples, letting the crowd overhear.

OBSERVATION Believers shouldn't worry about the basic necessities of life. If we keep God first in our lives, he will sustain us. He is in control.

INSPIRATION Be honest. Are we glad he says no to what we want and yes to what we need? Not always. If we ask for a new marriage, and he says honor the one you've got, we aren't happy. If we ask for healing, and he says learn through the pain, we aren't happy. If we ask for more money, and he says treasure the unseen, we aren't always happy.

When God doesn't do what we want, it's not easy. Never has been. Never will be. But faith is the conviction that God knows more than we do about this life and he will get us through it.

Remember, disappointment is caused by unmet expectations. Disappointment is cured by revamped expectations.

I like that story about the fellow who went to the pet store in search of a singing parakeet. Seems he was a bachelor and his house was too quiet. The store owner had just the bird for him, so the man bought it. The next day the bachelor came home from work to a house full of music. He

not touch the burdens with one of your fingers. 47Woe to you! For you
build the tombs of the prophets, and your fathers killed them. 48In fact,
you bear witness that you approve the deeds of your fathers; for they indeed killed them, and you build their tombs. 49Therefore the wisdom of
God also said, 'I will send them prophets and apostles, and *some* of them
they will kill and persecute,' 50that the blood of all the prophets which was
shed from the foundation of the world may be required of this generation,
51from the blood of Abel to the blood of Zechariah who perished between the
altar and the temple. Yes, I say to you, it shall be required of this generation.
52"Woe to you lawyers! For you have taken away the key of knowledge. You
did not enter in yourselves, and those who were entering in you hindered."
53And as He said these things to them,[r] the scribes and the Pharisees
began to assail *Him* vehemently, and to cross-examine Him about many
things, 54lying in wait for Him, and seeking to catch Him in something He
might say, that they might accuse Him.[s]

Beware of Hypocrisy

12 In the meantime, when an innumerable multitude of people had
gathered together, so that they trampled one another, He began to
say to His disciples first *of all*, "Beware of the leaven of the Pharisees,
which is hypocrisy. 2For there is nothing covered that will not be revealed,
nor hidden that will not be known. 3Therefore whatever you have spoken
in the dark will be heard in the light, and what you have spoken in the ear
in inner rooms will be proclaimed on the housetops.

Jesus Teaches the Fear of God

4"And I say to you, My friends, do not be afraid of those who kill the
body, and after that have no more that they can do. 5But I will show you
whom you should fear: Fear Him who, after He has killed, has power to
cast into hell; yes, I say to you, fear Him!
6"Are not five sparrows sold for two copper coins?[t] And not one of them
is forgotten before God. 7But the very hairs of your head are all numbered.
Do not fear therefore; you are of more value than many sparrows.

Confess Christ Before Men

8"Also I say to you, whoever confesses Me before men, him the Son of
Man also will confess before the angels of God. 9But he who denies Me before men will be denied before the angels of God.
10"And anyone who speaks a word against the Son of Man, it will be forgiven
him; but to him who blasphemes against the Holy Spirit, it will not be forgiven.
11"Now when they bring you to the synagogues and magistrates and authorities, do not worry about how or what you should answer, or what you
should say. 12For the Holy Spirit will teach you in that very hour what you
ought to say."

The Parable of the Rich Fool

13Then one from the crowd said to Him, "Teacher, tell my brother to divide the inheritance with me."

11:53 [r] NU-Text reads *And when He left there.*
11:54 [s] NU-Text omits *and seeking* and *that they might accuse Him.*
12:6 [t] Greek *assarion,* a coin of very small value

14 But He said to him, "Man, who made Me a judge or an arbitrator over
you?" 15 And He said to them, "Take heed and beware of covetousness,[u] for
one's life does not consist in the abundance of the things he possesses."
16 Then He spoke a parable to them, saying: "The ground of a certain rich
man yielded plentifully. 17 And he thought within himself, saying, 'What
shall I do, since I have no room to store my crops?' 18 So he said, 'I will do
this: I will pull down my barns and build greater, and there I will store all
my crops and my goods. 19 And I will say to my soul, "Soul, you have many
goods laid up for many years; take your ease; eat, drink, *and* be merry." '
20 But God said to him, 'Fool! This night your soul will be required of you;
then whose will those things be which you have provided?'
21 "So *is* he who lays up treasure for himself, and is not rich toward God."

Do Not Worry

22 Then He said to His disciples, "Therefore I say to you, do not worry
about your life, what you will eat; nor about the body, what you will put on.
23 Life is more than food, and the body *is more* than clothing. 24 Consider the
ravens, for they neither sow nor reap, which have neither storehouse nor
barn; and God feeds them. Of how much more value are you than the
birds? 25 And which of you by worrying can add one cubit to his stature? 26 If
you then are not able to do *the* least, why are you anxious for the rest?
27 Consider the lilies, how they grow: they neither toil nor spin; and yet I say
to you, even Solomon in all his glory was not arrayed like one of these. 28 If
then God so clothes the grass, which today is in the field and tomorrow is
thrown into the oven, how much more *will He clothe* you, O *you* of little faith?
29 "And do not seek what you should eat or what you should drink, nor
have an anxious mind. 30 For all these things the nations of the world seek
after, and your Father knows that you need these things. 31 But seek the
kingdom of God, and all these things[v] shall be added to you.
32 "Do not fear, little flock, for it is your Father's good pleasure to give you
the kingdom. 33 Sell what you have and give alms; provide yourselves
money bags which do not grow old, a treasure in the heavens that does not
fail, where no thief approaches nor moth destroys. 34 For where your treasure is, there your heart will be also.

The Faithful Servant and the Evil Servant

35 "Let your waist be girded and *your* lamps burning; 36 and you yourselves be like men who wait for their master, when he will return from the
wedding, that when he comes and knocks they may open to him immediately. 37 Blessed *are* those servants whom the master, when he comes, will
find watching. Assuredly, I say to you that he will gird himself and have
them sit down *to eat,* and will come and serve them. 38 And if he should
come in the second watch, or come in the third watch, and find *them* so,
blessed are those servants. 39 But know this, that if the master of the house
had known what hour the thief would come, he would have watched and[w]
not allowed his house to be broken into. 40 Therefore you also be ready, for
the Son of Man is coming at an hour you do not expect."
41 Then Peter said to Him, "Lord, do You speak this parable *only* to us, or
to all *people?*"

12:15 [u] NU-Text reads *all covetousness.*
12:31 [v] NU-Text reads *His kingdom, and these things.*
12:39 [w] NU-Text reads *he would not have allowed.*

went to the cage to feed the bird and noticed for the first time that the parakeet had only one leg.

He felt cheated that he'd been sold a one-legged bird, so he called and complained.

"What do you want," the store owner responded, "a bird who can sing or a bird who can dance?" . . .

We need to hear that God is still in control. We need to hear that it's not over until he says so. We need to hear that life's mishaps and tragedies are not a reason to bail out. They are simply a reason to sit tight.

Corrie ten Boom used to say, "When the train goes through a tunnel and the world gets dark, do you jump out? Of course not. You sit still and trust the engineer to get you through." . . .

Next time you're disappointed, don't panic. Don't jump out. Don't give up. Just be patient and let God remind you he's still in control. It ain't over till it's over.

(From *He Still Moves Stones* by Max Lucado)

APPLICATION What worries consume your thoughts? Turn them over to God . . . then breathe a sigh of relief and live for him. Let God carry your burdens.

EXPLORATION Strong Faith—Proverbs 3:6; Matthew 6:33; Mark 8:14-21.

42 And the Lord said, "Who then is that faithful and wise steward, whom
his master will make ruler over his household, to give *them their* portion of
food in due season? 43 Blessed *is* that servant whom his master will find so
doing when he comes. 44 Truly, I say to you that he will make him ruler over
all that he has. 45 But if that servant says in his heart, 'My master is delaying
his coming,' and begins to beat the male and female servants, and to eat
and drink and be drunk, 46 the master of that servant will come on a day
when he is not looking for *him,* and at an hour when he is not aware, and
will cut him in two and appoint *him* his portion with the unbelievers.
47 And that servant who knew his master's will, and did not prepare *himself*
or do according to his will, shall be beaten with many *stripes.* 48 But he who
did not know, yet committed things deserving of stripes, shall be beaten with
few. For everyone to whom much is given, from him much will be required;
and to whom much has been committed, of him they will ask the more.

Christ Brings Division

49 "I came to send fire on the earth, and how I wish it were already kindled! 50 But I have a baptism to be baptized with, and how distressed I am
till it is accomplished! 51 Do *you* suppose that I came to give peace on earth?
I tell you, not at all, but rather division. 52 For from now on five in one
house will be divided: three against two, and two against three. 53 Father
will be divided against son and son against father, mother against daughter and daughter against mother, mother-in-law against her daughter-in-
law and daughter-in-law against her mother-in-law."

Discern the Time

54 Then He also said to the multitudes, "Whenever *you see* a cloud rising
out of the west, immediately you say, 'A shower is coming'; and so it is.
55 And when you see the south wind blow, you say, 'There will be hot
weather'; and there is. 56 Hypocrites! You can discern the face of the sky and
of the earth, but how *is it* you do not discern this time?

Make Peace with Your Adversary

57 "Yes, and why, even of yourselves, do you not judge what is right?
58 When you go with your adversary to the magistrate, make every effort
along the way to settle with him, lest he drag you to the judge, the judge deliver you to the officer, and the officer throw you into prison. 59 I tell you,
you shall not depart from there till you have paid the very last mite."

Repent or Perish

13 There were present at that season some who told Him about the
Galileans whose blood Pilate had mingled with their sacrifices.
2 And Jesus answered and said to them, "Do you suppose that these Galileans were worse sinners than all *other* Galileans, because they suffered
such things? 3 I tell you, no; but unless you repent you will all likewise perish. 4 Or those eighteen on whom the tower in Siloam fell and killed them,
do you think that they were worse sinners than all *other* men who dwelt in
Jerusalem? 5 I tell you, no; but unless you repent you will all likewise perish."

The Parable of the Barren Fig Tree

6 He also spoke this parable: "A certain *man* had a fig tree planted in his
vineyard, and he came seeking fruit on it and found none. 7 Then he said to

LIFE LESSON

Luke 13:1-35

SITUATION Many Jews believed that good fortune, health, and wealth were signs of God's approval and that hardships or tragedies were signs of God's judgment.

OBSERVATION When others experience hardship, it is easy to judge them. Jesus taught that the best response is compassion.

INSPIRATION God has a beautiful way of taking what is negative and turning it around for His glory—if we let Him. . . . If we will respond properly to our failure, God can use it to bring Himself glory and to better prepare us for His service.

The first stage in the recovery process is *repentance.* . . .

Genuine repentance involves several things. First of all, confession. Not just, "Lord I am sorry for my mistake," but, "Lord, I have sinned against You." Confession acknowledges guilt. Second, repentance involves the recognition that the sin was against God. . . .

Last, repentance requires total honesty with God. You know, we won't always be holy, but we can always be honest. I believe God is looking for us to be honest about our sin—honest about our weaknesses, our failures, and our frustrations. Honesty promotes fellowship. As long as we continue to be open and honest with God, He can continue to work with us, even after we have committed our most grievous sin.

(From *Winning the War Within* by Charles Stanley)

APPLICATION Don't fool yourself by thinking that sins will be ignored. Confess your sins today, and enjoy the freedom that God wants for you.

EXPLORATION Repentance—2 Chronicles 7:14; Psalm 51:17; Proverbs 28:13; Ezekiel 18:30-32; Matthew 3:2; Acts 3:19; 2 Corinthians 7:10; 1 John 1:9.

the keeper of his vineyard, 'Look, for three years I have come seeking fruit on this fig tree and find none. Cut it down; why does it use up the ground?' 8But he answered and said to him, 'Sir, let it alone this year also, until I dig around it and fertilize *it.* 9And if it bears fruit, *well.* But if not, after that[x] you can cut it down.' "

A Spirit of Infirmity

10Now He was teaching in one of the synagogues on the Sabbath. 11And behold, there was a woman who had a spirit of infirmity eighteen years, and was bent over and could in no way raise *herself* up. 12But when Jesus saw her, He called *her* to *Him* and said to her, "Woman, you are loosed from your infirmity." 13And He laid *His* hands on her, and immediately she was made straight, and glorified God.

14But the ruler of the synagogue answered with indignation, because Jesus had healed on the Sabbath; and he said to the crowd, "There are six days on which men ought to work; therefore come and be healed on them, and not on the Sabbath day."

15The Lord then answered him and said, "Hypocrite![y] Does not each one of you on the Sabbath loose his ox or donkey from the stall, and lead *it* away to water it? 16So ought not this woman, being a daughter of Abraham, whom Satan has bound—think of it—for eighteen years, be loosed from this bond on the Sabbath?" 17And when He said these things, all His adversaries were put to shame; and all the multitude rejoiced for all the glorious things that were done by Him.

The Parable of the Mustard Seed

18Then He said, "What is the kingdom of God like? And to what shall I compare it? 19It is like a mustard seed, which a man took and put in his garden; and it grew and became a large[z] tree, and the birds of the air nested in its branches."

The Parable of the Leaven

20And again He said, "To what shall I liken the kingdom of God? 21It is like leaven, which a woman took and hid in three measures[a] of meal till it was all leavened."

The Narrow Way

22And He went through the cities and villages, teaching, and journeying toward Jerusalem. 23Then one said to Him, "Lord, are there few who are saved?"

And He said to them, 24"Strive to enter through the narrow gate, for many, I say to you, will seek to enter and will not be able. 25When once the Master of the house has risen up and shut the door, and you begin to stand outside and knock at the door, saying, 'Lord, Lord, open for us,' and He will answer and say to you, 'I do not know you, where you are from,' 26then you will begin to say, 'We ate and drank in Your presence, and You taught in our streets.' 27But He will say, 'I tell you I do not know you, where you are from. Depart from Me, all you workers of iniquity.' 28There will be weeping and gnashing of teeth, when you see Abraham and Isaac and Jacob and all the prophets in the kingdom of God, and yourselves thrust out. 29They will come from the east and the west, from the north and the south, and sit down in the kingdom of God. 30And indeed there are last who will be first, and there are first who will be last."

31On that very day[b] some Pharisees came, saying to Him, "Get out and depart from here, for Herod wants to kill You."

32And He said to them, "Go, tell that fox, 'Behold, I cast out demons and perform cures today and tomorrow, and the third *day* I shall be perfected.' 33Nevertheless I must journey today, tomorrow, and the *day* following; for it cannot be that a prophet should perish outside of Jerusalem.

Jesus Laments over Jerusalem

34"O Jerusalem, Jerusalem, the one who kills the prophets and stones those who are sent to her! How often I wanted to gather your children together, as a hen *gathers* her brood under *her* wings, but you were not willing! 35See! Your house is left to you desolate; and assuredly,[c] I say to you, you shall not see Me until *the time* comes when you say, '*Blessed is He who comes in the name of the* LORD!' "[d]

A Man with Dropsy Healed on the Sabbath

14 Now it happened, as He went into the house of one of the rulers of the Pharisees to eat bread on the Sabbath, that they watched Him closely. 2And behold, there was a certain man before Him who had dropsy. 3And Jesus, answering, spoke to the lawyers and Pharisees, saying, "Is it lawful to heal on the Sabbath?"[e]

13:9 [x] NU-Text reads *And if it bears fruit after that, well. But if not, you can cut it down.*
13:15 [y] NU-Text and M-Text read *Hypocrites.*
13:19 [z] NU-Text omits *large.*
13:21 [a] Greek *sata,* approximately two pecks in all
13:31 [b] NU-Text reads *In that very hour.*
13:35 [c] NU-Text and M-Text omit *assuredly.* [d] Psalm 118:26
14:3 [e] NU-Text adds *or not.*

LIFE LESSON

Luke 14:1-35

SITUATION While these characteristics are all too common, Jesus' stories explain that pride, laziness, and the desire for honor have no place among his disciples.

OBSERVATION Being a disciple of Christ requires humility, commitment, and servanthood.

INSPIRATION They splashed and they flopped, those aspiring wind surfers. Day after day we chronicled their struggles. It looked simple enough: a surfboard, a detachable sail with a length of rope tied to it, water, wind and, of course, instruction. . . .

The following summer we discovered a few surfers who had more or less mastered the art. They skimmed about with surprising skill even on rough days. One had so much confidence that he even sailed with his jacket on, maneuvering his craft skillfully wherever he wished it to go. He was so cocky. I kept hoping he would flop just once, but he had learned well.

He was, we discovered, the instructor. . . .

Like wind surfing, the Christian life is simple but not easy. . . .

We who are older in the Christian walk and those who, through experience, have earned the status of instructor should be quick to encourage, quick to help the one who has fallen.

We who have not yet mastered the art of Christian living need to keep carefully studying our Book of Instructions, listening attentively when our Instructor speaks, and promptly following His instructions.

Alexander Whyte of Edinburgh once said: "The perseverance of the saints consists in ever new beginnings." (From *The Legacy of a Pack Rat* by Ruth Bell Graham)

APPLICATION Putting Christ first in all things takes practice and persistence. Day after day we learn to follow him.

EXPLORATION Discipleship—Deuteronomy 6:5; Matthew 6:33; 16:24; Mark 10:28; John 15:8; Galatians 5:24; Colossians 3:1-3; 2 Timothy 2:15; Revelation 3:19.

[4]But they kept silent. And He took *him* and healed him, and let him go. [5]Then He answered them, saying, "Which of you, having a donkey[f] or an ox that has fallen into a pit, will not immediately pull him out on the Sabbath day?" [6]And they could not answer Him regarding these things.

Take the Lowly Place

[7]So He told a parable to those who were invited, when He noted how they chose the best places, saying to them: [8]"When you are invited by anyone to a wedding feast, do not sit down in the best place, lest one more honorable than you be invited by him; [9]and he who invited you and him come and say to you, 'Give place to this man,' and then you begin with shame to take the lowest place. [10]But when you are invited, go and sit down in the lowest place, so that when he who invited you comes he may say to you, 'Friend, go up higher.' Then you will have glory in the presence of those who sit at the table with you. [11]For whoever exalts himself will be humbled, and he who humbles himself will be exalted."

[12]Then He also said to him who invited Him, "When you give a dinner or a supper, do not ask your friends, your brothers, your relatives, nor rich neighbors, lest they also invite you back, and you be repaid. [13]But when you give a feast, invite *the* poor, *the* maimed, *the* lame, *the* blind. [14]And you will be blessed, because they cannot repay you; for you shall be repaid at the resurrection of the just."

The Parable of the Great Supper

[15]Now when one of those who sat at the table with Him heard these things, he said to Him, "Blessed *is* he who shall eat bread[g] in the kingdom of God!"

[16]Then He said to him, "A certain man gave a great supper and invited many, [17]and sent his servant at supper time to say to those who were invited, 'Come, for all things are now ready.' [18]But they all with one *accord* began to make excuses. The first said to him, 'I have bought a piece of ground, and I must go and see it. I ask you to have me excused.' [19]And another said, 'I have bought five yoke of oxen, and I am going to test them. I ask you to have me excused.' [20]Still another said, 'I have married a wife, and therefore I cannot come.' [21]So that servant came and reported these things to his master. Then the master of the house, being angry, said to his servant, 'Go out quickly into the streets and lanes of the city, and bring in here *the* poor and *the* maimed and *the* lame and *the* blind.' [22]And the servant said, 'Master, it is done as you commanded, and still there is room.' [23]Then the master said to the servant, 'Go out into the highways and hedges, and compel *them* to come in, that my house may be filled. [24]For I say to you that none of those men who were invited shall taste my supper.' "

Leaving All to Follow Christ

[25]Now great multitudes went with Him. And He turned and said to them, [26]"If anyone comes to Me and does not hate his father and mother, wife and children, brothers and sisters, yes, and his own life also, he cannot be My disciple. [27]And whoever does not bear his cross and come after Me cannot be My disciple. [28]For which of you, intending to build a tower,

14:5 [f] NU-Text and M-Text read *son.*
14:15 [g] M-Text reads *dinner.*

does not sit down first and count the cost, whether he has *enough* to finish
it— 29lest, after he has laid the foundation, and is not able to finish, all
who see *it* begin to mock him, 30saying, 'This man began to build and was
not able to finish.' 31Or what king, going to make war against another king,
does not sit down first and consider whether he is able with ten thousand
to meet him who comes against him with twenty thousand? 32Or else,
while the other is still a great way off, he sends a delegation and asks conditions of peace. 33So likewise, whoever of you does not forsake all that he
has cannot be My disciple.

Tasteless Salt Is Worthless

34"Salt *is* good; but if the salt has lost its flavor, how shall it be seasoned?
35It is neither fit for the land nor for the dunghill, *but* men throw it out. He
who has ears to hear, let him hear!"

The Parable of the Lost Sheep

15 Then all the tax collectors and the sinners drew near to Him to hear
Him. 2And the Pharisees and scribes complained, saying, "This
Man receives sinners and eats with them." 3So He spoke this parable to
them, saying:
4"What man of you, having a hundred sheep, if he loses one of them,
does not leave the ninety-nine in the wilderness, and go after the one
which is lost until he finds it? 5And when he has found *it*, he lays *it* on his
shoulders, rejoicing. 6And when he comes home, he calls together *his*
friends and neighbors, saying to them, 'Rejoice with me, for I have found
my sheep which was lost!' 7I say to you that likewise there will be more joy
in heaven over one sinner who repents than over ninety-nine just persons
who need no repentance.

The Parable of the Lost Coin

8"Or what woman, having ten silver coins,[h] if she loses one coin, does
not light a lamp, sweep the house, and search carefully until she finds *it?*
9And when she has found *it*, she calls *her* friends and neighbors together,
saying, 'Rejoice with me, for I have found the piece which I lost!' 10Like-
wise, I say to you, there is joy in the presence of the angels of God over one
sinner who repents."

The Parable of the Lost Son

11Then He said: "A certain man had two sons. 12And the younger of
them said to *his* father, 'Father, give me the portion of goods that falls *to
me*.' So he divided to them *his* livelihood. 13And not many days after, the
younger son gathered all together, journeyed to a far country, and there
wasted his possessions with prodigal living. 14But when he had spent all,
there arose a severe famine in that land, and he began to be in want. 15Then
he went and joined himself to a citizen of that country, and he sent him
into his fields to feed swine. 16And he would gladly have filled his stomach
with the pods that the swine ate, and no one gave him *anything*.
17"But when he came to himself, he said, 'How many of my father's hired
servants have bread enough and to spare, and I perish with hunger! 18I will

15:8 *h* Greek *drachma*, a valuable coin often worn in a ten-piece garland by married women

Life Lesson

Luke 15:1-32

SITUATION The Pharisees and teachers of the Law were intrigued by Jesus' teaching; they were always nearby to hear him and watch him—and criticize him. The Pharisees went to great lengths to be ceremonially clean, which they believed made them righteous in God's sight. Jesus' great concern, however, was offering salvation to sinners.

OBSERVATION Jesus told three parables to correct the Pharisees' misconception about God. These parables show that God loves *all* people and wants everyone—especially sinners—to come to him. God doesn't play favorites, and he rejoices when anyone turns to him.

INSPIRATION Theresa Briones is a tender, loving mother. She also has a stout left hook that she used to punch a lady in a coin laundry. Why'd she do it?

Some kids were making fun of Theresa's daughter, Alicia.

Alicia is bald. Her knees are arthritic. Her nose is pinched. Her hips are creaky. Her hearing is bad. She has the stamina of a seventy-year-old. And she is only ten.

"Mom," the kids taunted, "come and look at the monster!"

Alicia weighs only twenty-two pounds and is shorter than most preschoolers. She suffers from progeria—a genetic aging disease that strikes one child in eight million. The life expectancy of progeria victims is twenty years. There are only fifteen known cases of this disease in the world.

"She is not an alien. She is not a monster," Theresa defended. "She is just like you and me."

Mentally, Alicia is a bubbly, fun-loving third grader. She has a long list of friends. She watches television in a toddler-sized rocking chair. She plays with Barbie dolls and teases her younger brother.

Theresa has grown accustomed to the glances and questions. She is patient with the constant curiosity. Genuine inquiries she accepts. Insensitive slanders she does not.

Continued

The mother of the finger-pointing children came to investigate. "I see 'it,'" she told the kids.

"My child is not an 'it,'" Theresa stated. Then she decked the woman.

Who could blame her? Such is the nature of parental love. Mothers and fathers have a God-given ability to love their children regardless of imperfections. Not because the parents are blind. Just the opposite. They see vividly.

Theresa sees Alicia's inability as clearly as anyone. But she also sees Alicia's value.

So does God.

God sees us with the eyes of a Father. He sees our defects, errors, and blemishes. But he also sees our value.

. . . What did Jesus know that enabled him to do what he did?

Here's part of the answer. He knew the value of people. He knew that each human being is a treasure. And because he did, people were not a source of stress, but a source of joy.

(From *In the Eye of the Storm* by Max Lucado)

APPLICATION God offers salvation to everyone. If you find yourself judging others, remember that God values them. Think of what you can do to show God's love to the unlovely.

EXPLORATION God's Impartiality—Job 34:19; Acts 10:28; 34-35; Romans 10:11-13; Galatians 3:28; 1 Timothy 2:3-4; 2 Peter 3:9; Revelation 3:20.

arise and go to my father, and will say to him, "Father, I have sinned
against heaven and before you, 19and I am no longer worthy to be called
your son. Make me like one of your hired servants." '
20"And he arose and came to his father. But when he was still a great way
off, his father saw him and had compassion, and ran and fell on his neck
and kissed him. 21And the son said to him, 'Father, I have sinned against
heaven and in your sight, and am no longer worthy to be called your son.'
22"But the father said to his servants, 'Bring[i] out the best robe and put *it* on
him, and put a ring on his hand and sandals on *his* feet. 23And bring the fatted calf here and kill *it,* and let us eat and be merry; 24for this my son was dead
and is alive again; he was lost and is found.' And they began to be merry.
25"Now his older son was in the field. And as he came and drew near to
the house, he heard music and dancing. 26So he called one of the servants
and asked what these things meant. 27And he said to him, 'Your brother
has come, and because he has received him safe and sound, your father
has killed the fatted calf.'
28"But he was angry and would not go in. Therefore his father came out
and pleaded with him. 29So he answered and said to *his* father, 'Lo, these
many years I have been serving you; I never transgressed your commandment at any time; and yet you never gave me a young goat, that I might make
merry with my friends. 30But as soon as this son of yours came, who has devoured your livelihood with harlots, you killed the fatted calf for him.'
31"And he said to him, 'Son, you are always with me, and all that I have
is yours. 32It was right that we should make merry and be glad, for your
brother was dead and is alive again, and was lost and is found.' "

The Parable of the Unjust Steward

16 He also said to His disciples: "There was a certain rich man who had a
steward, and an accusation was brought to him that this man was wasting his goods. 2So he called him and said to him, 'What is this I hear about
you? Give an account of your stewardship, for you can no longer be steward.'
3"Then the steward said within himself, 'What shall I do? For my master
is taking the stewardship away from me. I cannot dig; I am ashamed to
beg. 4I have resolved what to do, that when I am put out of the stewardship, they may receive me into their houses.'
5"So he called every one of his master's debtors to *him,* and said to the
first, 'How much do you owe my master?' 6And he said, 'A hundred measures[j] of oil.' So he said to him, 'Take your bill, and sit down quickly and
write fifty.' 7Then he said to another, 'And how much do you owe?' So he
said, 'A hundred measures[k] of wheat.' And he said to him, 'Take your bill,
and write eighty.' 8So the master commended the unjust steward because
he had dealt shrewdly. For the sons of this world are more shrewd in their
generation than the sons of light.
9"And I say to you, make friends for yourselves by unrighteous mammon, that when you fail,[l] they may receive you into an everlasting home.
10He who *is* faithful in *what is* least is faithful also in much; and he who is
unjust in *what is* least is unjust also in much. 11Therefore if you have not

15:22 [i] NU-Text reads *Quickly bring.*
16:6 [j] Greek *batos,* eight or nine gallons each (Old Testament *bath*)
16:7 [k] Greek *koros,* ten or twelve bushels each (Old Testament *kor*)
16:9 [l] NU-Text reads *it fails.*

been faithful in the unrighteous mammon, who will commit to your trust
the true *riches?* 12And if you have not been faithful in what is another
man's, who will give you what is your own?
13"No servant can serve two masters; for either he will hate the one and
love the other, or else he will be loyal to the one and despise the other. You
cannot serve God and mammon."

The Law, the Prophets, and the Kingdom

14Now the Pharisees, who were lovers of money, also heard all these
things, and they derided Him. 15And He said to them, "You are those who
justify yourselves before men, but God knows your hearts. For what is
highly esteemed among men is an abomination in the sight of God.
16"The law and the prophets *were* until John. Since that time the kingdom
of God has been preached, and everyone is pressing into it. 17And it is easier for heaven and earth to pass away than for one tittle of the law to fail.
18"Whoever divorces his wife and marries another commits adultery; and
whoever marries her who is divorced from *her* husband commits adultery.

The Rich Man and Lazarus

19"There was a certain rich man who was clothed in purple and fine
linen and fared sumptuously every day. 20But there was a certain beggar
named Lazarus, full of sores, who was laid at his gate, 21desiring to be fed
with the crumbs which fell[m] from the rich man's table. Moreover the dogs
came and licked his sores. 22So it was that the beggar died, and was carried
by the angels to Abraham's bosom. The rich man also died and was
buried. 23And being in torments in Hades, he lifted up his eyes and saw
Abraham afar off, and Lazarus in his bosom.
24"Then he cried and said, 'Father Abraham, have mercy on me, and
send Lazarus that he may dip the tip of his finger in water and cool my
tongue; for I am tormented in this flame.' 25But Abraham said, 'Son, remember that in your lifetime you received your good things, and likewise
Lazarus evil things; but now he is comforted and you are tormented.
26And besides all this, between us and you there is a great gulf fixed, so
that those who want to pass from here to you cannot, nor can those from
there pass to us.'
27"Then he said, 'I beg you therefore, father, that you would send him to
my father's house, 28for I have five brothers, that he may testify to them,
lest they also come to this place of torment.' 29Abraham said to him, 'They
have Moses and the prophets; let them hear them.' 30And he said, 'No, father Abraham; but if one goes to them from the dead, they will repent.'
31But he said to him, 'If they do not hear Moses and the prophets, neither
will they be persuaded though one rise from the dead.' "

Jesus Warns of Offenses

17 Then He said to the disciples, "It is impossible that no offenses
should come, but woe *to him* through whom they do come! 2It
would be better for him if a millstone were hung around his neck, and he
were thrown into the sea, than that he should offend one of these little
ones. 3Take heed to yourselves. If your brother sins against you,[n] rebuke

16:21 [m] NU-Text reads *with what fell.*
17:3 [n] NU-Text omits *against you.*

LIFE LESSON

Luke 17:1-37

SITUATION Jesus taught about the power of sin, forgiveness, and faith. He instilled a passion in his disciples for the Kingdom of God.

OBSERVATION Sin deceives and enslaves us, distorting the truth about ourselves and about God.

INSPIRATION After twenty years of cigarette smoking, I wanted to quit. . . .

Wanting to quit, however, I could not. Thinking I had the willpower to stop, I kept drifting back to the addiction. I tried cigars, pipes, candy, resolutions, withering self-castigation—and even prayers, which always began, "Lord, help me." They slowed but did not stop my return to cigarettes.

Slowly it began to dawn on me that I could not help myself. Worse, the more I used my willpower, the more helpless I became. I was like a fish which has hit the bait of a trolling fisherman. The more the fish struggles, the deeper the hook is embedded. The only hope for a hooked fish is that the fisherman will remove the hook and return the fish to the water.

Some God-fearing friends who are wise in the ways of fish and people advised me to abandon my willpower approach. So I gave up. Surrendered. Waited. I waited for a power other than myself. I could never save myself from addiction. Salvation would mean being saved by Another. . . .

Our power-mindedness plays great havoc in our lives. Sometimes we almost kill ourselves trying to demonstrate our great power.

(From *The Kingdom of Self* by Earl Jabay)

APPLICATION Be ruthlessly honest: Who really controls your life? If you are struggling under the illusion of your own power, ask God to show you the truth about yourself.

EXPLORATION Struggling with Sin—Romans 6:1–8:4; Galatians 3:1-14; Philippians 3:1-11.

him; and if he repents, forgive him. 4And if he sins against you seven times in a day, and seven times in a day returns to you,[o] saying, 'I repent,' you shall forgive him."

Faith and Duty

5And the apostles said to the Lord, "Increase our faith."

6So the Lord said, "If you have faith as a mustard seed, you can say to this mulberry tree, 'Be pulled up by the roots and be planted in the sea,' and it would obey you. 7And which of you, having a servant plowing or tending sheep, will say to him when he has come in from the field, 'Come at once and sit down to eat'? 8But will he not rather say to him, 'Prepare something for my supper, and gird yourself and serve me till I have eaten and drunk, and afterward you will eat and drink'? 9Does he thank that servant because he did the things that were commanded him? I think not.[p] 10So likewise you, when you have done all those things which you are commanded, say, 'We are unprofitable servants. We have done what was our duty to do.' "

Ten Lepers Cleansed

11Now it happened as He went to Jerusalem that He passed through the midst of Samaria and Galilee. 12Then as He entered a certain village, there met Him ten men who were lepers, who stood afar off. 13And they lifted up *their* voices and said, "Jesus, Master, have mercy on us!"

14So when He saw *them,* He said to them, "Go, show yourselves to the priests." And so it was that as they went, they were cleansed.

15And one of them, when he saw that he was healed, returned, and with a loud voice glorified God, 16and fell down on *his* face at His feet, giving Him thanks. And he was a Samaritan.

17So Jesus answered and said, "Were there not ten cleansed? But where *are* the nine? 18Were there not any found who returned to give glory to God except this foreigner?" 19And He said to him, "Arise, go your way. Your faith has made you well."

The Coming of the Kingdom

20Now when He was asked by the Pharisees when the kingdom of God would come, He answered them and said, "The kingdom of God does not come with observation; 21nor will they say, 'See here!' or 'See there!'[q] For indeed, the kingdom of God is within you."

22Then He said to the disciples, "The days will come when you will desire to see one of the days of the Son of Man, and you will not see *it.* 23And they will say to you, 'Look here!' or 'Look there!'[r] Do not go after *them* or follow *them.* 24For as the lightning that flashes out of one *part* under heaven shines to the other *part* under heaven, so also the Son of Man will be in His day. 25But first He must suffer many things and be rejected by this generation. 26And as it was in the days of Noah, so it will be also in the days of the Son of Man: 27They ate, they drank, they married wives, they were given in marriage, until the day that Noah entered the ark, and the flood came and destroyed them all. 28Likewise as it was also in the days of Lot: They ate, they drank, they bought, they sold, they planted, they built; 29but on the day that Lot went out of Sodom it rained fire and brimstone from heaven and destroyed *them* all. 30Even so will it be in the day when the Son of Man is revealed.

31"In that day, he who is on the housetop, and his goods *are* in the house, let him not come down to take them away. And likewise the one who is in the field, let him not turn back. 32Remember Lot's wife. 33Whoever seeks to save his life will lose it, and whoever loses his life will preserve it. 34I tell you, in that night there will be two *men* in one bed: the one will be taken and the other will be left. 35Two *women* will be grinding together: the one will be taken and the other left. 36Two *men* will be in the field: the one will be taken and the other left."[s]

37And they answered and said to Him, "Where, Lord?"

So He said to them, "Wherever the body is, there the eagles will be gathered together."

The Parable of the Persistent Widow

18 Then He spoke a parable to them, that men always ought to pray and not lose heart, 2saying: "There was in a certain city a judge who did not fear God nor regard man. 3Now there was a widow in that city; and she came to him, saying, 'Get justice for me from my adversary.' 4And he would not for a while; but afterward he said within himself, 'Though I do not fear God nor regard man, 5yet because this widow troubles me I will avenge her, lest by her continual coming she weary me.' "

17:4 [o] M-Text omits *to you.*
17:9 [p] NU-Text ends verse with *commanded;* M-Text omits *him.*
17:21 [q] NU-Text reverses *here* and *there.*
17:23 [r] NU-Text reverses *here* and *there.*
17:36 [s] NU-Text and M-Text omit verse 36.

[6]Then the Lord said, "Hear what the unjust judge said. [7]And shall God not
avenge His own elect who cry out day and night to Him, though He bears
long with them? [8]I tell you that He will avenge them speedily. Nevertheless,
when the Son of Man comes, will He really find faith on the earth?"

The Parable of the Pharisee and the Tax Collector

[9]Also He spoke this parable to some who trusted in themselves that they
were righteous, and despised others: [10]"Two men went up to the temple to
pray, one a Pharisee and the other a tax collector. [11]The Pharisee stood and
prayed thus with himself, 'God, I thank You that I am not like other
men—extortioners, unjust, adulterers, or even as this tax collector. [12]I fast
twice a week; I give tithes of all that I possess.' [13]And the tax collector,
standing afar off, would not so much as raise *his* eyes to heaven, but beat his
breast, saying, 'God, be merciful to me a sinner!' [14]I tell you, this man went
down to his house justified *rather* than the other; for everyone who exalts
himself will be humbled, and he who humbles himself will be exalted."

Jesus Blesses Little Children

[15]Then they also brought infants to Him that He might touch them; but
when the disciples saw *it,* they rebuked them. [16]But Jesus called them to
Him and said, "Let the little children come to Me, and do not forbid them;
for of such is the kingdom of God. [17]Assuredly, I say to you, whoever does
not receive the kingdom of God as a little child will by no means enter it."

Jesus Counsels the Rich Young Ruler

[18]Now a certain ruler asked Him, saying, "Good Teacher, what shall I do
to inherit eternal life?"

[19]So Jesus said to him, "Why do you call Me good? No one *is* good but
One, *that is,* God. [20]You know the commandments: *'Do not commit adultery,' 'Do not murder,' 'Do not steal,' 'Do not bear false witness,' 'Honor
your father and your mother.'* "[t]

[21]And he said, "All these things I have kept from my youth."

[22]So when Jesus heard these things, He said to him, "You still lack one
thing. Sell all that you have and distribute to the poor, and you will have
treasure in heaven; and come, follow Me."

[23]But when he heard this, he became very sorrowful, for he was very rich.

With God All Things Are Possible

[24]And when Jesus saw that he became very sorrowful, He said, "How
hard it is for those who have riches to enter the kingdom of God! [25]For it is
easier for a camel to go through the eye of a needle than for a rich man to
enter the kingdom of God."

[26]And those who heard it said, "Who then can be saved?"

[27]But He said, "The things which are impossible with men are possible
with God."

[28]Then Peter said, "See, we have left all[u] and followed You."

[29]So He said to them, "Assuredly, I say to you, there is no one who has
left house or parents or brothers or wife or children, for the sake of the
kingdom of God, [30]who shall not receive many times more in this present
time, and in the age to come eternal life."

18:20 [t] Exodus 20:12–16; Deuteronomy 5:16–20
18:28 [u] NU-Text reads *our own.*

LIFE LESSON

Luke 18:1-43

SITUATION Through a series of short illustrations, Jesus taught the people how to obtain eternal life and how to pray so that God would hear.

OBSERVATION When we pray we must be persistent and humble. Most of all, we can't depend on our own resources to get us through problems. We need to trust God and his strength.

INSPIRATION One of my favorite stories concerns a bishop who was traveling by ship to visit a church across the ocean. While en route, the ship stopped at an island for a day. He went for a walk on a beach. He came upon three fishermen mending their nets.

Curious about their trade he asked them some questions. Curious about his ecclesiastical robes, they asked him some questions. When they found out he was a Christian leader, they got excited. "We Christians!" they said, proudly pointing to one another.

The bishop was impressed but cautious. Did they know the Lord's Prayer? They had never heard of it.

"What do you say, then, when you pray?"

"We pray, O We are three, you are three, have mercy on us.'"

The bishop was appalled at the primitive nature of the prayer. "That will not do." So he spent the day teaching them the Lord's Prayer. The fishermen were poor but willing learners. And before the bishop sailed away the next day, they could recite the prayer with no mistakes.

The bishop was proud.

On the return trip the bishop's ship drew near the island again. When the island came into view the bishop came to the deck and recalled with pleasure the men he had taught and resolved to go see them again. As he was thinking a light appeared on the horizon near the island. It seemed to be getting nearer. As the bishop gazed in wonder he realized the three fishermen were walking toward him on the water. Soon all the passengers and crew were on the deck to see the sight.

Continued

When they were within speaking distance, the fisherman cried out, "Bishop, we come hurry to meet you."

"What is it you want?" asked the stunned bishop.

"We are so sorry. We forget lovely prayer. We say, 'O Our Father, who art in heaven, hallowed be your name . . .' and then we forget. Please tell us prayer again."

The bishop was humbled. "Go back to your homes, my friends, and when you pray say, O We are three, you are three, have mercy on us.'"

(From *And the Angels Were Silent* by Max Lucado)

APPLICATION Do you mean what you pray? Do you get caught up in just saying words and miss their meaning? Continue to pray often—but do so out of a humble, honest heart. If the fancy prayers and big words aren't you—use your own. God wants to hear what you honestly pray.

EXPLORATION Prayer—Psalm 5:1-3; 55:17; 116:2.

Jesus a Third Time Predicts His Death and Resurrection

31 Then He took the twelve aside and said to them, "Behold, we are going
up to Jerusalem, and all things that are written by the prophets concerning
the Son of Man will be accomplished. 32 For He will be delivered to the
Gentiles and will be mocked and insulted and spit upon. 33 They will
scourge *Him* and kill Him. And the third day He will rise again."
34 But they understood none of these things; this saying was hidden
from them, and they did not know the things which were spoken.

A Blind Man Receives His Sight

35 Then it happened, as He was coming near Jericho, that a certain blind
man sat by the road begging. 36 And hearing a multitude passing by, he
asked what it meant. 37 So they told him that Jesus of Nazareth was passing
by. 38 And he cried out, saying, "Jesus, Son of David, have mercy on me!"
39 Then those who went before warned him that he should be quiet; but
he cried out all the more, "Son of David, have mercy on me!"
40 So Jesus stood still and commanded him to be brought to Him. And
when he had come near, He asked him, 41 saying, "What do you want Me to
do for you?"
He said, "Lord, that I may receive my sight."
42 Then Jesus said to him, "Receive your sight; your faith has made you
well." 43 And immediately he received his sight, and followed Him, glorifying God. And all the people, when they saw *it,* gave praise to God.

Jesus Comes to Zacchaeus' House

19 Then *Jesus* entered and passed through Jericho. 2 Now behold, *there
was* a man named Zacchaeus who was a chief tax collector, and he
was rich. 3 And he sought to see who Jesus was, but could not because of
the crowd, for he was of short stature. 4 So he ran ahead and climbed up
into a sycamore tree to see Him, for He was going to pass that *way.* 5 And
when Jesus came to the place, He looked up and saw him,[v] and said to
him, "Zacchaeus, make haste and come down, for today I must stay at
your house." 6 So he made haste and came down, and received Him joyfully. 7 But when they saw *it,* they all complained, saying, "He has gone to
be a guest with a man who is a sinner."
8 Then Zacchaeus stood and said to the Lord, "Look, Lord, I give half of
my goods to the poor; and if I have taken anything from anyone by false
accusation, I restore fourfold."
9 And Jesus said to him, "Today salvation has come to this house, because he also is a son of Abraham; 10 for the Son of Man has come to seek
and to save that which was lost."

The Parable of the Minas

11 Now as they heard these things, He spoke another parable, because He
was near Jerusalem and because they thought the kingdom of God would
appear immediately. 12 Therefore He said: "A certain nobleman went into a
far country to receive for himself a kingdom and to return. 13 So he called
ten of his servants, delivered to them ten minas,[w] and said to them, 'Do

19:5 [v] NU-Text omits *and saw him.*
19:13 [w] The *mina* (Greek *mna,* Hebrew *minah*) was worth about three months' salary.

business till I come.' 14But his citizens hated him, and sent a delegation
after him, saying, 'We will not have this *man* to reign over us.'
15"And so it was that when he returned, having received the kingdom,
he then commanded these servants, to whom he had given the money, to
be called to him, that he might know how much every man had gained by
trading. 16Then came the first, saying, 'Master, your mina has earned ten
minas.' 17And he said to him, 'Well *done,* good servant; because you were
faithful in a very little, have authority over ten cities.' 18And the second
came, saying, 'Master, your mina has earned five minas.' 19Likewise he
said to him, 'You also be over five cities.'
20"Then another came, saying, 'Master, here is your mina, which I have
kept put away in a handkerchief. 21For I feared you, because you are an
austere man. You collect what you did not deposit, and reap what you did
not sow.' 22And he said to him, 'Out of your own mouth I will judge you,
you wicked servant. You knew that I was an austere man, collecting what I
did not deposit and reaping what I did not sow. 23Why then did you not
put my money in the bank, that at my coming I might have collected it
with interest?'
24"And he said to those who stood by, 'Take the mina from him, and give
it to him who has ten minas.' 25(But they said to him, 'Master, he has ten
minas.') 26'For I say to you, that to everyone who has will be given; and
from him who does not have, even what he has will be taken away from
him. 27But bring here those enemies of mine, who did not want me to
reign over them, and slay *them* before me.'"

The Triumphal Entry

28When He had said this, He went on ahead, going up to Jerusalem.
29And it came to pass, when He drew near to Bethphage[x] and Bethany, at
the mountain called Olivet, *that* He sent two of His disciples, 30saying, "Go
into the village opposite *you,* where as you enter you will find a colt tied, on
which no one has ever sat. Loose it and bring *it here.* 31And if anyone asks
you, 'Why are you loosing *it?*' thus you shall say to him, 'Because the Lord
has need of it.'"
32So those who were sent went their way and found *it* just as He had said
to them. 33But as they were loosing the colt, the owners of it said to them,
"Why are you loosing the colt?"
34And they said, "The Lord has need of him." 35Then they brought him
to Jesus. And they threw their own clothes on the colt, and they set Jesus
on him. 36And as He went, *many* spread their clothes on the road.
37Then, as He was now drawing near the descent of the Mount of Olives,
the whole multitude of the disciples began to rejoice and praise God with
a loud voice for all the mighty works they had seen, 38saying:

"'*Blessed is the King who comes in the name of the* LORD!'[y]
Peace in heaven and glory in the highest!"

39And some of the Pharisees called to Him from the crowd, "Teacher, rebuke Your disciples."
40But He answered and said to them, "I tell you that if these should keep
silent, the stones would immediately cry out."

19:29 [x] M-Text reads *Bethsphage.*
19:38 [y] Psalm 118:26

LIFE LESSON

Luke 19:1-48

SITUATION The testimony of Zacchaeus as well as Jesus' tears for Jerusalem demonstrate that God desires genuine faith from his people.

OBSERVATION God will judge those who peddle the faith and those who prevent people from worshiping.

INSPIRATION It's tough to be let down. It's disappointing when you think someone is interested in you, only to find they are interested in your money. When salespeople do it, it's irritating—but when people of faith do it, it can be devastating.

It's a sad but true fact of the faith: religion is used for profit and prestige. When it is there are two results: people are exploited and God is infuriated.

There's no better example of this than what happened at the temple. After he had entered the city on the back of a donkey, Jesus "went into the Temple. After he had looked at everything, since it was already late, he went out to Bethany with the twelve apostles." . . .

Want to know what he saw? Then read what he did on Monday, the next morning when he returned. "Jesus went into the Temple and threw out all the people who were buying and selling there. He turned over the tables of those who were exchanging different kinds of money, and he upset the benches of those who were selling doves. Jesus said to all the people there, 'O It is written in the Scriptures, "My temple will be called a house for prayer." But you are changing it into a "hideout for robbers."'"

What did he see? Hucksters. Faith peddlers. What lit the fire under Jesus' broiler? What was his first thought on Monday? People in the temple making a franchise out of the faith.

It was Passover week. The Passover was the highlight of the Jewish calendar. People came from all regions and many countries to be present for the celebration. Upon arriving they were obligated to meet two requirements.

First, an animal sacrifice, usually a dove. The dove had to be perfect, without blemish. The animal could be

Continued

brought in from anywhere, but odds were that if you brought a sacrifice from another place, yours would be considered insufficient by the authorities in the temple. So, under the guise of keeping the sacrifice pure, the dove sellers sold doves—at their price.

Second, the people had to pay a tax, a temple tax. It was due every year. During Passover the tax had to be rendered in local currency. Knowing many foreigners would be in Jerusalem to pay the tax, money changers conveniently set up tables and offered to exchange the foreign money for local—for a modest fee, of course.

It's not difficult to see what angered Jesus. Pilgrims journeyed days to see God, to witness the holy, to worship His Majesty. But before they were taken into the presence of God, they were taken to the cleaners. What was promised and what was delivered were two different things. . . .

"I've had enough," was written all over the Messiah's face. In he stormed. Doves flapped and tables flew. People scampered and traders scattered.

This was not an impulsive show. This was not a temper tantrum. It was a deliberate act with an intentional message. Jesus had seen the money-changers the day before. He went to sleep with pictures of this midway and its barkers in his memory. And when he woke up the next morning, knowing his days were drawing to a close, he chose to make a point: "You cash in on my people and you've got me to answer to." God will never hold guiltless those who exploit the privilege of worship.

(From *And the Angels Were Silent* by Max Lucado)

APPLICATION Be careful that you are motivated to attend church to worship and get to know God better. We can become like the people in this chapter if we attend church in order to meet business contacts.

EXPLORATION God's Compassion—Exodus 33:19; Psalm 84:11; Nahum 1:7; Matthew 9:36; Romans 8:32.

Jesus Weeps over Jerusalem

41Now as He drew near, He saw the city and wept over it, 42saying, "If you
had known, even you, especially in this your day, the things *that make* for
your peace! But now they are hidden from your eyes. 43For days will come
upon you when your enemies will build an embankment around you, surround you and close you in on every side, 44and level you, and your children within you, to the ground; and they will not leave in you one stone
upon another, because you did not know the time of your visitation."

Jesus Cleanses the Temple

45Then He went into the temple and began to drive out those who
bought and sold in it,[z] 46saying to them, "It is written, *'My house is*[a] *a
house of prayer,'*[b] but you have made it a *'den of thieves.'* "[c]
47And He was teaching daily in the temple. But the chief priests, the
scribes, and the leaders of the people sought to destroy Him, 48and were
unable to do anything; for all the people were very attentive to hear Him.

Jesus' Authority Questioned

20 Now it happened on one of those days, as He taught the people in
the temple and preached the gospel, *that* the chief priests and the
scribes, together with the elders, confronted *Him* 2and spoke to Him, saying, "Tell us, by what authority are You doing these things? Or who is he
who gave You this authority?"
3But He answered and said to them, "I also will ask you one thing, and
answer Me: 4The baptism of John—was it from heaven or from men?"
5And they reasoned among themselves, saying, "If we say, 'From heaven,'
He will say, 'Why then[d] did you not believe him?' 6But if we say, 'From men,'
all the people will stone us, for they are persuaded that John was a prophet."
7So they answered that they did not know where *it was* from.
8And Jesus said to them, "Neither will I tell you by what authority I do
these things."

The Parable of the Wicked Vinedressers

9Then He began to tell the people this parable: "A certain man planted a
vineyard, leased it to vinedressers, and went into a far country for a long time.
10Now at vintage-time he sent a servant to the vinedressers, that they might
give him some of the fruit of the vineyard. But the vinedressers beat him and
sent *him* away empty-handed. 11Again he sent another servant; and they beat
him also, treated *him* shamefully, and sent *him* away empty-handed. 12And
again he sent a third; and they wounded him also and cast *him* out.
13"Then the owner of the vineyard said, 'What shall I do? I will send my
beloved son. Probably they will respect *him* when they see him.' 14But
when the vinedressers saw him, they reasoned among themselves, saying,
'This is the heir. Come, let us kill him, that the inheritance may be ours.'
15So they cast him out of the vineyard and killed *him.* Therefore what will
the owner of the vineyard do to them? 16He will come and destroy those
vinedressers and give the vineyard to others."
And when they heard *it* they said, "Certainly not!"

19:45 [z] NU-Text reads *those who were selling.*
19:46 [a] NU-Text reads *shall be.* [b] Isaiah 56:7 [c] Jeremiah 7:11
20:5 [d] NU-Text and M-Text omit *then.*

17Then He looked at them and said, "What then is this that is written:

'The stone which the builders rejected
Has become the chief cornerstone'?[e]

18Whoever falls on that stone will be broken; but on whomever it falls, it will grind him to powder."

19And the chief priests and the scribes that very hour sought to lay hands on Him, but they feared the people[f]—for they knew He had spoken this parable against them.

The Pharisees: Is It Lawful to Pay Taxes to Caesar?

20So they watched *Him,* and sent spies who pretended to be righteous, that they might seize on His words, in order to deliver Him to the power and the authority of the governor.

21Then they asked Him, saying, "Teacher, we know that You say and teach rightly, and You do not show personal favoritism, but teach the way of God in truth: 22Is it lawful for us to pay taxes to Caesar or not?"

23But He perceived their craftiness, and said to them, "Why do you test Me?[g] 24Show Me a denarius. Whose image and inscription does it have?"

They answered and said, "Caesar's."

25And He said to them, "Render therefore to Caesar the things that are Caesar's, and to God the things that are God's."

26But they could not catch Him in His words in the presence of the people. And they marveled at His answer and kept silent.

The Sadducees: What About the Resurrection?

27Then some of the Sadducees, who deny that there is a resurrection, came to *Him* and asked Him, 28saying: "Teacher, Moses wrote to us *that* if a man's brother dies, having a wife, and he dies without children, his brother should take his wife and raise up offspring for his brother. 29Now there were seven brothers. And the first took a wife, and died without children. 30And the second[h] took her as wife, and he died childless. 31Then the third took her, and in like manner the seven also; and they left no children,[i] and died. 32Last of all the woman died also. 33Therefore, in the resurrection, whose wife does she become? For all seven had her as wife."

34Jesus answered and said to them, "The sons of this age marry and are given in marriage. 35But those who are counted worthy to attain that age, and the resurrection from the dead, neither marry nor are given in marriage; 36nor can they die anymore, for they are equal to the angels and are sons of God, being sons of the resurrection. 37But even Moses showed in the *burning* bush *passage* that the dead are raised, when he called the Lord *'the God of Abraham, the God of Isaac, and the God of Jacob.'*[j] 38For He is not the God of the dead but of the living, for all live to Him."

39Then some of the scribes answered and said, "Teacher, You have spoken well." 40But after that they dared not question Him anymore.

Jesus: How Can David Call His Descendant Lord?

41And He said to them, "How can they say that the Christ is the Son of David? 42Now David himself said in the Book of Psalms:

'The LORD said to my Lord,
"Sit at My right hand,
43 *Till I make Your enemies Your footstool."'*[k]

44Therefore David calls Him *'Lord'*; how is He then his Son?"

Beware of the Scribes

45Then, in the hearing of all the people, He said to His disciples, 46"Beware of the scribes, who desire to go around in long robes, love greetings in the marketplaces, the best seats in the synagogues, and the best places at feasts, 47who devour widows' houses, and for a pretense make long prayers. These will receive greater condemnation."

The Widow's Two Mites

21 And He looked up and saw the rich putting their gifts into the treasury, 2and He saw also a certain poor widow putting in two mites. 3So He said, "Truly I say to you that this poor widow has put in more than all; 4for all these out of their abundance have put in offerings for God,[l] but she out of her poverty put in all the livelihood that she had."

Jesus Predicts the Destruction of the Temple

5Then, as some spoke of the temple, how it was adorned with beautiful stones and donations, He

20:17 [e] Psalm 118:22
20:19 [f] M-Text reads *but they were afraid.*
20:23 [g] NU-Text omits *Why do you test Me?*
20:30 [h] NU-Text ends verse 30 here.
20:31 [i] NU-Text and M-Text read *the seven also left no children.*
20:37 [j] Exodus 3:6, 15
20:43 [k] Psalm 110:1
21:4 [l] NU-Text omits *for God.*

LIFE LESSON

Luke 21:1-38

SITUATION The Temple was rebuilt about 516 B.C. In addition, Herod had undertaken a massive renovation and enlargement of the Temple. Jesus prophesied that persecution would come and the Temple would be destroyed.

OBSERVATION As Jesus' disciples, we should be prepared for persecution and be discerning about world events. In this world's turmoil, we can also have great comfort that Jesus will return.

INSPIRATION When my wife flew to Canada to celebrate her parents' fiftieth wedding anniversary, my two sons and I remained at home. None of us was particularly adept at household things, proved by our initial meal of pizza and ice cream floats. There was one particular problem—we didn't know when my wife would return home. We divided the household responsibilities: preparing meals, doing the dishes, and washing the laundry. As we anticipated when she might be coming, we cleaned the house in earnest; we even decorated the living room with colorful streamers. She was coming at anytime, and we wanted to be ready.

The teaching that Christ can come at anytime is called the "imminent" return of Christ. It does not say He is coming soon, but rather that He may come at any moment. What is the significance? Does that affect the way we live?

Reflecting on the trials and sufferings in this present age, Paul said we are "waiting eagerly" for the completion of our redemption (Romans 8:23, 25).

said, 6"These things which you see—the days will come in which not *one*
stone shall be left upon another that shall not be thrown down."

The Signs of the Times and the End of the Age

7So they asked Him, saying, "Teacher, but when will these things be?
And what sign *will there be* when these things are about to take place?"
8And He said: "Take heed that you not be deceived. For many will come
in My name, saying, 'I am *He*,' and, 'The time has drawn near.' Therefore[m]
do not go after them. 9But when you hear of wars and commotions, do not
be terrified; for these things must come to pass first, but the end *will not come* immediately."
10Then He said to them, "Nation will rise against nation, and kingdom
against kingdom. 11And there will be great earthquakes in various places,
and famines and pestilences; and there will be fearful sights and great
signs from heaven. 12But before all these things, they will lay their hands
on you and persecute *you*, delivering *you* up to the synagogues and prisons. You will be brought before kings and rulers for My name's sake. 13But
it will turn out for you as an occasion for testimony. 14Therefore settle *it* in
your hearts not to meditate beforehand on what you will answer; 15for I
will give you a mouth and wisdom which all your adversaries will not be
able to contradict or resist. 16You will be betrayed even by parents and
brothers, relatives and friends; and they will put *some* of you to death.
17And you will be hated by all for My name's sake. 18But not a hair of your
head shall be lost. 19By your patience possess your souls.

The Destruction of Jerusalem

20"But when you see Jerusalem surrounded by armies, then know that
its desolation is near. 21Then let those who are in Judea flee to the mountains, let those who are in the midst of her depart, and let not those who
are in the country enter her. 22For these are the days of vengeance, that all
things which are written may be fulfilled. 23But woe to those who are pregnant and to those who are nursing babies in those days! For there will be
great distress in the land and wrath upon this people. 24And they will fall by
the edge of the sword, and be led away captive into all nations. And Jerusalem will be trampled by Gentiles until the times of the Gentiles are fulfilled.

The Coming of the Son of Man

25"And there will be signs in the sun, in the moon, and in the stars; and
on the earth distress of nations, with perplexity, the sea and the waves
roaring; 26men's hearts failing them from fear and the expectation of those
things which are coming on the earth, for the powers of the heavens will be
shaken. 27Then they will see the Son of Man coming in a cloud with power
and great glory. 28Now when these things begin to happen, look up and lift
up your heads, because your redemption draws near."

The Parable of the Fig Tree

29Then He spoke to them a parable: "Look at the fig tree, and all the trees.
30When they are already budding, you see and know for yourselves that
summer is now near. 31So you also, when you see these things happening,

21:8 [m] NU-Text omits *Therefore.*

know that the kingdom of God is near. 32Assuredly, I say to you, this generation will by no means pass away till all things take place. 33Heaven and earth
will pass away, but My words will by no means pass away.

The Importance of Watching

34"But take heed to yourselves, lest your hearts be weighed down with
carousing, drunkenness, and cares of this life, and that Day come on you
unexpectedly. 35For it will come as a snare on all those who dwell on the
face of the whole earth. 36Watch therefore, and pray always that you may
be counted worthy[n] to escape all these things that will come to pass, and to
stand before the Son of Man."
37And in the daytime He was teaching in the temple, but at night He
went out and stayed on the mountain called Olivet. 38Then early in the
morning all the people came to Him in the temple to hear Him.

The Plot to Kill Jesus

22 Now the Feast of Unleavened Bread drew near, which is called
Passover. 2And the chief priests and the scribes sought how they
might kill Him, for they feared the people.
3Then Satan entered Judas, surnamed Iscariot, who was numbered
among the twelve. 4So he went his way and conferred with the chief priests
and captains, how he might betray Him to them. 5And they were glad, and
agreed to give him money. 6So he promised and sought opportunity to betray Him to them in the absence of the multitude.

Jesus and His Disciples Prepare the Passover

7Then came the Day of Unleavened Bread, when the Passover must be
killed. 8And He sent Peter and John, saying, "Go and prepare the Passover
for us, that we may eat."
9So they said to Him, "Where do You want us to prepare?"
10And He said to them, "Behold, when you have entered the city, a man
will meet you carrying a pitcher of water; follow him into the house which
he enters. 11Then you shall say to the master of the house, 'The Teacher says
to you, "Where is the guest room where I may eat the Passover with My
disciples?" ' 12Then he will show you a large, furnished upper room; there
make ready."
13So they went and found it just as He had said to them, and they prepared the Passover.

Jesus Institutes the Lord's Supper

14When the hour had come, He sat down, and the twelve[o] apostles with
Him. 15Then He said to them, "With *fervent* desire I have desired to eat this
Passover with you before I suffer; 16for I say to you, I will no longer eat of it
until it is fulfilled in the kingdom of God."
17Then He took the cup, and gave thanks, and said, "Take this and divide *it* among yourselves; 18for I say to you,[p] I will not drink of the fruit of
the vine until the kingdom of God comes."
19And He took bread, gave thanks and broke *it*, and gave *it* to them, saying,
"This is My body which is given for you; do this in remembrance of Me."

21:36 [n] NU-Text reads *may have strength.*
22:14 [o] NU-Text omits *twelve.*
22:18 [p] NU-Text adds *from now on.*

As a pregnant mother anticipates the birth of her child, so all creation is groaning with labor pains, waiting for release. Paul exhorted the Philippians not to center their attention on earthly things because "our citizenship is in heaven, from which also we eagerly wait for a Savior, the Lord Jesus Christ" (Philippians 3:20).

We eagerly wait for our Savior because He can come at any moment. If we know His coming is far off, we don't wait eagerly. As we look for Him, we want to be pleasing to Him when He returns; therefore we are instructed to "deny ungodliness and worldly desires and to live sensibly, righteously and godly in this present age" (Titus 2:12-13). The Thessalonian believers left their idolatry to search for the true God and "to wait for His Son from heaven" (1 Thessalonians 1:10). What a simple, beautiful statement. Are you waiting for your Savior each day? As G. Campbell Morgan said, "I never begin my work in the morning without thinking that perhaps He may interrupt my work and begin His own. I am not looking for death—I am looking for Him." He may come today—what a glorious hope!

(From *Approaching God* by Paul Enns)

APPLICATION We have all eagerly waited for one event or another in our lives. Do you look forward to Christ's return? Do you get more excited anticipating a birthday or anniversary? Why or why not? What can you do to prepare for Christ's return?

EXPLORATION Signs of Christ's Return—Mark 13:6; 3:1-5; 2 Timothy 4:3-4; 2 Peter 3:3-4; Revelation 13:1-8.

[20]Likewise He also *took* the cup after supper, saying, "This cup *is* the
new covenant in My blood, which is shed for you. [21]But behold, the hand of
My betrayer *is* with Me on the table. [22]And truly the Son of Man goes as it
has been determined, but woe to that man by whom He is betrayed!"
[23]Then they began to question among themselves, which of them it was
who would do this thing.

The Disciples Argue About Greatness

[24]Now there was also a dispute among them, as to which of them should
be considered the greatest. [25]And He said to them, "The kings of the
Gentiles exercise lordship over them, and those who exercise authority
over them are called 'benefactors.' [26]But not so *among* you; on the contrary, he who is greatest among you, let him be as the younger, and he who
governs as he who serves. [27]For who *is* greater, he who sits at the table, or
he who serves? *Is* it not he who sits at the table? Yet I am among you as the
One who serves.
[28]"But you are those who have continued with Me in My trials. [29]And I
bestow upon you a kingdom, just as My Father bestowed *one* upon Me,
[30]that you may eat and drink at My table in My kingdom, and sit on
thrones judging the twelve tribes of Israel."

Jesus Predicts Peter's Denial

[31]And the Lord said,[q] "Simon, Simon! Indeed, Satan has asked for you, that
he may sift *you* as wheat. [32]But I have prayed for you, that your faith should
not fail; and when you have returned to *Me,* strengthen your brethren."
[33]But he said to Him, "Lord, I am ready to go with You, both to prison
and to death."
[34]Then He said, "I tell you, Peter, the rooster shall not crow this day before you will deny three times that you know Me."

Supplies for the Road

[35]And He said to them, "When I sent you without money bag, knapsack,
and sandals, did you lack anything?"
So they said, "Nothing."
[36]Then He said to them, "But now, he who has a money bag, let him take
it, and likewise a knapsack; and he who has no sword, let him sell his garment and buy one. [37]For I say to you that this which is written must still be
accomplished in Me: *'And He was numbered with the transgressors.'*[r] For
the things concerning Me have an end."
[38]So they said, "Lord, look, here *are* two swords."
And He said to them, "It is enough."

The Prayer in the Garden

[39]Coming out, He went to the Mount of Olives, as He was accustomed,
and His disciples also followed Him. [40]When He came to the place, He said
to them, "Pray that you may not enter into temptation."
[41]And He was withdrawn from them about a stone's throw, and He knelt
down and prayed, [42]saying, "Father, if it is Your will, take this cup away
from Me; nevertheless not My will, but Yours, be done." [43]Then an angel

22:31 [q] NU-Text omits *And the Lord said.*
22:37 [r] Isaiah 53:12

LIFE LESSON

Luke 22:1-71

SITUATION Jesus prophesied about his coming death and tried to prepare his disciples. Christ's death signaled the rebirth of humanity and redemption from sin.

OBSERVATION Jesus was determined to obey his father and to die in our place for our sins.

INSPIRATION Jesus. The man. The bronzed Galilean who spoke with such thunderous authority and loved with such childlike humility.

The God. The one who claimed to be older than time and greater than death.

Gone is the pomp of religion; dissipated is the fog of theology. Momentarily lifted is the opaque curtain of controversy and opinion. Erased are our own blinding errors and egotism. And there he stands.

Jesus. Have you seen him? Those who first did were never the same.

"My Lord and my God!" cried Thomas.

"I have seen the Lord," exclaimed Mary Magdalene.

"We have seen his glory," declared John.

"Were not our hearts burning within us while he talked?" rejoiced the two Emmaus-bound disciples.

But Peter said it best. "We were eyewitnesses of his majesty."

His Majesty. The emperor of Judah. The soaring eagle of eternity. The noble admiral of the Kingdom. All the splendor of heaven revealed in a human body. For a period ever so brief, the doors to the throne room were open and God came near. His Majesty was seen. Heaven touched the earth and, as a result, earth can know heaven. In astounding tandem a human body housed divinity. Holiness and earthliness intertwined.

This is no run-of-the-mill messiah. His story was extraordinary. He called himself divine, yet allowed a minimum-wage Roman soldier to drive a nail into his wrist. He demanded purity, yet stood for the rights of a repentant whore. He called men to march, yet

appeared to Him from heaven, strengthening Him. 44And being in agony,
He prayed more earnestly. Then His sweat became like great drops of
blood falling down to the ground.[s]
45When He rose up from prayer, and had come to His disciples, He
found them sleeping from sorrow. 46Then He said to them, "Why do you
sleep? Rise and pray, lest you enter into temptation."

Betrayal and Arrest in Gethsemane

47And while He was still speaking, behold, a multitude; and he who was
called Judas, one of the twelve, went before them and drew near to Jesus to
kiss Him. 48But Jesus said to him, "Judas, are you betraying the Son of Man
with a kiss?"
49When those around Him saw what was going to happen, they said to
Him, "Lord, shall we strike with the sword?" 50And one of them struck the
servant of the high priest and cut off his right ear.
51But Jesus answered and said, "Permit even this." And He touched his
ear and healed him.
52Then Jesus said to the chief priests, captains of the temple, and the elders who had come to Him, "Have you come out, as against a robber, with
swords and clubs? 53When I was with you daily in the temple, you did not
try to seize Me. But this is your hour, and the power of darkness."

Peter Denies Jesus, and Weeps Bitterly

54Having arrested Him, they led *Him* and brought Him into the high
priest's house. But Peter followed at a distance. 55Now when they had kindled a fire in the midst of the courtyard and sat down together, Peter sat
among them. 56And a certain servant girl, seeing him as he sat by the fire,
looked intently at him and said, "This man was also with Him."
57But he denied Him,[t] saying, "Woman, I do not know Him."
58And after a little while another saw him and said, "You also are of them."
But Peter said, "Man, I am not!"
59Then after about an hour had passed, another confidently affirmed,
saying, "Surely this *fellow* also was with Him, for he is a Galilean."
60But Peter said, "Man, I do not know what you are saying!"
Immediately, while he was still speaking, the rooster[u] crowed. 61And the
Lord turned and looked at Peter. Then Peter remembered the word of the
Lord, how He had said to him, "Before the rooster crows,[v] you will deny
Me three times." 62So Peter went out and wept bitterly.

Jesus Mocked and Beaten

63Now the men who held Jesus mocked Him and beat Him. 64And having blindfolded Him, they struck Him on the face and asked Him,[w] saying,
"Prophesy! Who is the one who struck You?" 65And many other things
they blasphemously spoke against Him.

Jesus Faces the Sanhedrin

66As soon as it was day, the elders of the people, both chief priests and
scribes, came together and led Him into their council, saying, 67"If You are the
Christ, tell us."

refused to allow them to call him King. He sent men into all the world, yet equipped them with only bended knees and memories of a resurrected carpenter.

We can't regard him as simply a good teacher. His claims are too outrageous to limit him to the company of Socrates or Aristotle. Nor can we categorize him as one of many prophets sent to reveal eternal truths. His own claims eliminate that possibility.

Then who is he?

Let's try to find out. Let's follow his sandal prints. Let's sit on the cold, hard floor of the cave in which he was born. Let's smell the sawdust of the carpentry shop. Let's hear his sandals slap the hard trails of Galilee. Let's sigh as we touch the healed sores of the leper. Let's smile as we see his compassion with the woman at the well. Let's cringe as we hear the hissing of hell's Satan. Let's let our voices soar with the praises of the multitudes. Let's try to see him.

Has it been a while since you have seen him? If your prayers seem stale, it probably has. If your faith seems to be trembling, perhaps your vision of him has blurred. If you can't find power to face your problems, perhaps it is time to face him.

One warning. Something happens to a person who has witnessed his Majesty. He becomes addicted. One glimpse of the King and you are consumed by a desire to see more of him and say more about him. Pew-warming is no longer an option. Junk religion will no longer suffice. Sensation-seeking is needless. Once you have seen his face you will forever long to see it again.

(From *God Came Near* by Max Lucado)

APPLICATION When was the last time you saw Jesus or considered what he has done for you? Have you ever? If not, ask God to show you Jesus as you read his Word.

EXPLORATION Redemption—Exodus 15:13; Luke 1:68; Galatians 3:13-14; Ephesians. 1:7; 1 Peter 1:18-19.

22:44 [s] NU-Text brackets verses 43 and 44 as not in the original text.
22:57 [t] NU-Text reads *denied it.*
22:60 [u] NU-Text and M-Text read *a rooster.*
22:61 [v] NU-Text adds *today.*
22:64 [w] NU-Text reads *And having blindfolded Him, they asked Him.*

LIFE LESSON

Luke 23:1-56

SITUATION Incited by the Temple priests, an angry mob demanded that Pilate crucify Jesus. Pilate knew that he did not have justification for using the death penalty.

OBSERVATION Through his sacrifice on the cross, Jesus fulfilled his earthly mission and atoned for sin.

INSPIRATION The King swallowed. . . .

He looked at the Prince of Light. "The darkness will be great." He passed his hand over the spotless face of his Son. "The pain will be awful." Then he paused and looked at his darkened dominion. When he looked up, his eyes were moist. "But there is no other way."

The Son looked into the stars as he heard the answer. "Then, let it be done."

Slowly the words that would kill the Son began to come from the lips of the Father.

"Hour of death, moment of sacrifice, it is your moment. Rehearsed a million times on false altars with false lambs; the moment of truth has come. . . .

"Oh, my Son, my Child. Look up into the heavens and see my face before I turn it. Hear my voice before I silence it. Would that I could save you and them. But they don't see and they don't hear.

"The living must die so that the dying can live. The time has come to kill the Lamb." . . .

But He said to them, "If I tell you, you will by no means believe. 68And if
I also ask *you,* you will by no means answer Me or let *Me* go.[x] 69Hereafter
the Son of Man will sit on the right hand of the power of God."
70Then they all said, "Are You then the Son of God?"
So He said to them, "You *rightly* say that I am."
71And they said, "What further testimony do we need? For we have
heard it ourselves from His own mouth."

Jesus Handed Over to Pontius Pilate

23 Then the whole multitude of them arose and led Him to Pilate.
2And they began to accuse Him, saying, "We found this *fellow* perverting the[y] nation, and forbidding to pay taxes to Caesar, saying that He
Himself is Christ, a King."
3Then Pilate asked Him, saying, "Are You the King of the Jews?"
He answered him and said, "*It is as* you say."
4So Pilate said to the chief priests and the crowd, "I find no fault in this
Man."
5But they were the more fierce, saying, "He stirs up the people, teaching
throughout all Judea, beginning from Galilee to this place."

Jesus Faces Herod

6When Pilate heard of Galilee,[z] he asked if the Man were a Galilean. 7And
as soon as he knew that He belonged to Herod's jurisdiction, he sent Him
to Herod, who was also in Jerusalem at that time. 8Now when Herod saw
Jesus, he was exceedingly glad; for he had desired for a long *time* to see
Him, because he had heard many things about Him, and he hoped to see
some miracle done by Him. 9Then he questioned Him with many words,
but He answered him nothing. 10And the chief priests and scribes stood
and vehemently accused Him. 11Then Herod, with his men of war, treated
Him with contempt and mocked *Him,* arrayed Him in a gorgeous robe, and
sent Him back to Pilate. 12That very day Pilate and Herod became friends
with each other, for previously they had been at enmity with each other.

Taking the Place of Barabbas

13Then Pilate, when he had called together the chief priests, the rulers,
and the people, 14said to them, "You have brought this Man to me, as one
who misleads the people. And indeed, having examined *Him* in your presence, I have found no fault in this Man concerning those things of which
you accuse Him; 15no, neither did Herod, for I sent you back to him;[a] and
indeed nothing deserving of death has been done by Him. 16I will therefore
chastise Him and release *Him*" 17(for it was necessary for him to release
one to them at the feast).[b]
18And they all cried out at once, saying, "Away with this *Man,* and release to us Barabbas"— 19who had been thrown into prison for a certain
rebellion made in the city, and for murder.
20Pilate, therefore, wishing to release Jesus, again called out to them.
21But they shouted, saying, "Crucify *Him,* crucify Him!"
22Then he said to them the third time, "Why, what evil has He done? I

22:68 [x] NU-Text omits *also* and *Me or let Me go.*
23:2 [y] NU-Text reads *our.*
23:6 [z] NU-Text omits *of Galilee.*
23:15 [a] NU-Text reads *for he sent Him back to us.*
23:17 [b] NU-Text omits verse 17.

have found no reason for death in Him. I will therefore chastise Him and
let *Him* go."
23But they were insistent, demanding with loud voices that He be crucified. And the voices of these men and of the chief priests prevailed.[c] 24So
Pilate gave sentence that it should be as they requested. 25And he released
to them[d] the one they requested, who for rebellion and murder had been
thrown into prison; but he delivered Jesus to their will.

The King on a Cross

26Now as they led Him away, they laid hold of a certain man, Simon a
Cyrenian, who was coming from the country, and on him they laid the
cross that he might bear *it* after Jesus.
27And a great multitude of the people followed Him, and women who
also mourned and lamented Him. 28But Jesus, turning to them, said,
"Daughters of Jerusalem, do not weep for Me, but weep for yourselves and
for your children. 29For indeed the days are coming in which they will say,
'Blessed *are* the barren, wombs that never bore, and breasts which never
nursed!' 30Then they will begin *'to say to the mountains, "Fall on us!" and
to the hills, "Cover us!"'*[e] 31For if they do these things in the green wood,
what will be done in the dry?"
32There were also two others, criminals, led with Him to be put to death.
33And when they had come to the place called Calvary, there they crucified
Him, and the criminals, one on the right hand and the other on the left.
34Then Jesus said, "Father, forgive them, for they do not know what they do."[f]
And they divided His garments and cast lots. 35And the people stood
looking on. But even the rulers with them sneered, saying, "He saved others; let Him save Himself if He is the Christ, the chosen of God."
36The soldiers also mocked Him, coming and offering Him sour wine,
37and saying, "If You are the King of the Jews, save Yourself."
38And an inscription also was written over Him in letters of Greek, Latin,
and Hebrew:[g]

THIS IS THE KING OF THE JEWS.

39Then one of the criminals who were hanged blasphemed Him, saying,
"If You are the Christ,[h] save Yourself and us."
40But the other, answering, rebuked him, saying, "Do you not even fear
God, seeing you are under the same condemnation? 41And we indeed
justly, for we receive the due reward of our deeds; but this Man has done
nothing wrong." 42Then he said to Jesus, "Lord,[i] remember me when You
come into Your kingdom."
43And Jesus said to him, "Assuredly, I say to you, today you will be with
Me in Paradise."

Jesus Dies on the Cross

44Now it was[j] about the sixth hour, and there was darkness over all the

23:23 [c] NU-Text omits *and of the chief priests.*
23:25 [d] NU-Text and M-Text omit *to them.*
23:30 [e] Hosea 10:8
23:34 [f] NU-Text brackets the first sentence as a later addition.
23:38 [g] NU-Text omits *written* and *in letters of Greek, Latin, and Hebrew.*
23:39 [h] NU-Text reads *Are You not the Christ?*
23:42 [i] NU-Text reads *And he said, "Jesus, remember me.*
23:44 [j] NU-Text adds *already.*

God must have wept as he performed his task. Every lie, every lure, every act done in shadows was in that cup. Slowly, hideously they were absorbed into the body of the Son. The final act of incarnation.

The throne room is dark and cavernous. The eyes of the King are closed. He is resting.

In his dream he is again in the Garden. The cool of the evening floats across the river as the three walk. They speak of the Garden—of how it is, of how it will be.

"Father . . . " the Son begins. The King replays the word again. Father. Father. The word was a flower, petal-delicate, yet so easily crushed. Oh, how he longed for his children to call him Father again.

A noise snaps him from his dream. He opens his eyes and sees a transcendent figure gleaming in the doorway. "It is finished, Father. I have come home."

(From *Six Hours One Friday* by Max Lucado)

APPLICATION By faith in Christ, we gain access to all of God's treasures—joy, peace, and eternal life. Don't wait another minute. Receive Christ as your Savior and Lord. Commit the rest of your life to following his teachings.

EXPLORATION Sacrifice—Psalm 50:5-9; 51:17; 1 Samuel 15:22.

LIFE LESSON

Luke 24:1-53

SITUATION The disciples failed to understand what Jesus was saying when he told them he would rise again.

OBSERVATION Jesus rose from the dead. He is alive!

INSPIRATION We were buried in darkness and the shadow of death, but a light shone out from heaven, purer than the sun, and everyone who opens himself to the light lives.

The darkness is the black night of sin, and that light is eternal life. The darkness cannot hold back the light, and like night giving way to the first rays of the sun, the day of the Lord has dawned. In the bright light of this gospel morning people everywhere are waking up! The dying of the night has become the resurrection of the day. That is what Paul meant by the "new creation," the dawning of another First Day.

The "sun of righteousness" shines upon every person quite impartially, just as the Father "makes his sun rise on good and bad alike." All are flooded with the light of truth, though not all receive it.

And all of this comes from Christ himself, the Light of the world, who by dying crucified death, and by his resurrection changed the setting into a rising sun, the blackness of night into the radiance of the morning.

(From Clement of Alexander in *Faith Under Fire* paraphrased by David Winter)

APPLICATION You serve a risen Savior. Live with the confidence that Jesus is true and your salvation is sure.

EXPLORATION Resurrection—Matthew 28:1-10; Acts 2:24-32; 1 Peter 1:3-5.

earth until the ninth hour. 45Then the sun was darkened,[k] and the veil of
the temple was torn in two. 46And when Jesus had cried out with a loud
voice, He said, "Father, *'into Your hands I commit My spirit.'* "[l] Having
said this, He breathed His last.
47So when the centurion saw what had happened, he glorified God, saying, "Certainly this was a righteous Man!"
48And the whole crowd who came together to that sight, seeing what
had been done, beat their breasts and returned. 49But all His acquaintances, and the women who followed Him from Galilee, stood at a distance, watching these things.

Jesus Buried in Joseph's Tomb

50Now behold, *there was* a man named Joseph, a council member, a
good and just man. 51He had not consented to their decision and deed. *He
was* from Arimathea, a city of the Jews, who himself was also waiting[m] for
the kingdom of God. 52This man went to Pilate and asked for the body of
Jesus. 53Then he took it down, wrapped it in linen, and laid it in a tomb *that
was* hewn out of the rock, where no one had ever lain before. 54That day
was the Preparation, and the Sabbath drew near.
55And the women who had come with Him from Galilee followed after,
and they observed the tomb and how His body was laid. 56Then they returned and prepared spices and fragrant oils. And they rested on the Sabbath according to the commandment.

He Is Risen

24 Now on the first *day* of the week, very early in the morning, they,
and certain *other women* with them,[n] came to the tomb bringing
the spices which they had prepared. 2But they found the stone rolled away
from the tomb. 3Then they went in and did not find the body of the Lord
Jesus. 4And it happened, as they were greatly[o] perplexed about this, that
behold, two men stood by them in shining garments. 5Then, as they were
afraid and bowed *their* faces to the earth, they said to them, "Why do you
seek the living among the dead? 6He is not here, but is risen! Remember
how He spoke to you when He was still in Galilee, 7saying, 'The Son of Man
must be delivered into the hands of sinful men, and be crucified, and the third day rise again.' "
8And they remembered His words. 9Then they returned from the tomb
and told all these things to the eleven and to all the rest. 10It was Mary
Magdalene, Joanna, Mary *the mother* of James, and the other *women* with
them, who told these things to the apostles. 11And their words seemed to
them like idle tales, and they did not believe them. 12But Peter arose and
ran to the tomb; and stooping down, he saw the linen cloths lying[p] by themselves; and he departed, marveling to himself at what had happened.

The Road to Emmaus

13Now behold, two of them were traveling that same day to a village
called Emmaus, which was seven miles[q] from Jerusalem. 14And they

23:45 [k] NU-Text reads *obscured.*
23:46 [l] Psalm 31:5
23:51 [m] NU-Text reads *who was waiting.*
24:1 [n] NU-Text omits *and certain other women with them.*
24:4 [o] NU-Text omits *greatly.*
24:12 [p] NU-Text omits *lying.*
24:13 [q] Literally *sixty stadia*

talked together of all these things which had happened. [15]So it was, while they conversed and reasoned, that Jesus Himself drew near and went with them. [16]But their eyes were restrained, so that they did not know Him.

[17]And He said to them, "What kind of conversation *is* this that you have with one another as you walk and are sad?"[r]

[18]Then the one whose name was Cleopas answered and said to Him, "Are You the only stranger in Jerusalem, and have You not known the things which happened there in these days?"

[19]And He said to them, "What things?"

So they said to Him, "The things concerning Jesus of Nazareth, who was a Prophet mighty in deed and word before God and all the people, [20]and how the chief priests and our rulers delivered Him to be condemned to death, and crucified Him. [21]But we were hoping that it was He who was going to redeem Israel. Indeed, besides all this, today is the third day since these things happened. [22]Yes, and certain women of our company, who arrived at the tomb early, astonished us. [23]When they did not find His body, they came saying that they had also seen a vision of angels who said He was alive. [24]And certain of those *who were* with us went to the tomb and found *it* just as the women had said; but Him they did not see."

[25]Then He said to them, "O foolish ones, and slow of heart to believe in all that the prophets have spoken! [26]Ought not the Christ to have suffered these things and to enter into His glory?" [27]And beginning at Moses and all the Prophets, He expounded to them in all the Scriptures the things concerning Himself.

The Disciples' Eyes Opened

[28]Then they drew near to the village where they were going, and He indicated that He would have gone farther. [29]But they constrained Him, saying, "Abide with us, for it is toward evening, and the day is far spent." And He went in to stay with them.

[30]Now it came to pass, as He sat at the table with them, that He took bread, blessed and broke *it*, and gave it to them. [31]Then their eyes were opened and they knew Him; and He vanished from their sight.

[32]And they said to one another, "Did not our heart burn within us while He talked with us on the road, and while He opened the Scriptures to us?" [33]So they rose up that very hour and returned to Jerusalem, and found the eleven and those *who were* with them gathered together, [34]saying, "The Lord is risen indeed, and has appeared to Simon!" [35]And they told about the things *that had happened* on the road, and how He was known to them in the breaking of bread.

Jesus Appears to His Disciples

[36]Now as they said these things, Jesus Himself stood in the midst of them, and said to them, "Peace to you." [37]But they were terrified and frightened, and supposed they had seen a spirit. [38]And He said to them, "Why are you troubled? And why do doubts arise in your hearts? [39]Behold My hands and My feet, that it is I Myself. Handle Me and see, for a spirit does not have flesh and bones as you see I have."

[40]When He had said this, He showed them His hands and His feet.[s] [41]But while they still did not believe for joy, and marveled, He said to them, "Have you any food here?" [42]So they gave Him a piece of a broiled fish and some honeycomb.[t] [43]And He took *it* and ate in their presence.

The Scriptures Opened

[44]Then He said to them, "These *are* the words which I spoke to you while I was still with you, that all things must be fulfilled which were written in the Law of Moses and *the* Prophets and *the* Psalms concerning Me." [45]And He opened their understanding, that they might comprehend the Scriptures.

[46]Then He said to them, "Thus it is written, and thus it was necessary for the Christ to suffer and to rise[u] from the dead the third day, [47]and that repentance and remission of sins should be preached in His name to all nations, beginning at Jerusalem. [48]And you are witnesses of these things. [49]Behold, I send the Promise of My Father upon you; but tarry in the city of Jerusalem[v] until you are endued with power from on high."

The Ascension

[50]And He led them out as far as Bethany, and He lifted up His hands and blessed them. [51]Now it came to pass, while He blessed them, that He was parted from them and carried up into heaven. [52]And they worshiped Him, and returned to Jerusalem with great joy, [53]and were continually in the temple praising and[w] blessing God. Amen.[x]

24:17 [r] NU-Text reads *as you walk? And they stood still, looking sad.*
24:40 [s] Some printed New Testaments omit this verse. It is found in nearly all Greek manuscripts.
24:42 [t] NU-Text omits *and some honeycomb.*
24:46 [u] NU-Text reads *written, that the Christ should suffer and rise.*
24:49 [v] NU-Text omits *of Jerusalem.*
24:53 [w] NU-Text omits *praising and.* [x] NU-Text omits *Amen.*

The Gospel According to JOHN

INTRODUCTION

He's an old man, this one who sits on the stool and leans against the wall. Eyes closed and face soft, were it not for his hand stroking his beard, you'd think he was asleep.

Some in the room assume he is. He does this often during worship. As the people sing, his eyes will close and his chin will fall until it rests on his chest, and there he will remain motionless. Silent.

Those who know him well know better. They know he is not resting. He is traveling. Atop the music he journeys back, back, back until he is young again. Strong again. There again. There on the seashore with James and the apostles. There on the trail with the disciples and the women. There in the Temple with Caiaphas and the accusers.

It's been sixty years, but John sees him still. The decades took John's strength, but they didn't take his memory. The years dulled his sight, but they didn't dull his vision. The seasons may have wrinkled his face, but they didn't soften his love.

He had been with God. God had been with him. How could he forget?

- The wine that moments before had been water—John could still taste it.
- The mud placed on the eyes of the blind man in Jerusalem—John could still remember it.
- The aroma of Mary's perfume as it filled the room—John could still smell it.

And the voice. Oh, the voice. His voice. John could still hear it.

I am the light of the world, it rang . . . I am the door . . . I am the way, the truth, the life.

I will come back, it promised, and take you to be with me.

Those who believe in me, it assured, will have life even if they die.

John could hear him. John could see him. Scenes branded on his heart. Words seared into his soul. John would never forget. How could he? He had been there.

He opens his eyes and blinks. The singing has stopped. The teaching has begun. John looks at the listeners and listens to the teacher.

If only you could have been there, he thinks.

But he wasn't. Most weren't. Most weren't even born. And most who were there are dead. Peter is. So is James. Nathanael, Martha, Philip. They are all gone. Even Paul, the apostle who came late, is dead.

Only John remains.

He looks again at the church. Small but earnest. They lean forward to hear the teacher. John listens to him. What a task. Speaking of one he never saw. Explaining words he never heard. John is there if the teacher needs him.

But what will happen when John is gone? What will the teacher do then? When John's voice is silent and his tongue stilled? Who will tell them how Jesus silenced the waves? Will they hear how he fed the thousands? Will they remember how he prayed for unity?

How will they know? If only they could have been there.

Suddenly, in his heart he knows what to do.

Later, under the light of a sunlit shaft, the old fisherman unfolds the scroll and begins to write the story of his life . . .

In the beginning was the Word . . .

LIFE LESSON

John 1:1-51

SITUATION The Greeks and the Jews were familiar with the concept of the *word.* For the Jews it was an expression of God's wisdom, and for the Greeks it meant reason and intellect.

OBSERVATION Leaving his heavenly home, Jesus put on human flesh to bring us God's Good News.

INSPIRATION It all happened in a moment, a most remarkable moment. . . . that was like none other. For through that segment of time a spectacular thing occurred. God became a man. While the creatures of earth walked unaware, Divinity arrived. Heaven opened herself and placed her most precious one in a human womb. . . .

God as a fetus. Holiness sleeping in a womb. The creator of life being created.

God was given eyebrows, elbows, two kidneys, and a spleen. He stretched against the walls and floated in the amniotic fluids of his mother.

God had come near. . . .

The hands that first held him were unmanicured, calloused, and dirty.

No silk. No ivory. No hype. No party. No hoopla.

Were it not for the shepherds, there would have been no reception. And were it not for a group of star-gazers, there would have been no gifts. . . .

The Eternal Word

In the beginning was the Word, and the Word was with God, and the Word was God. 2He was in the beginning with God. 3All things were made through Him, and without Him nothing was made that was made. 4In Him was life, and the life was the light of men. 5And the light shines in the darkness, and the darkness did not comprehend[a] it.

John's Witness: The True Light

6There was a man sent from God, whose name *was* John. 7This man came for a witness, to bear witness of the Light, that all through him might believe. 8He was not that Light, but *was sent* to bear witness of that Light. 9That was the true Light which gives light to every man coming into the world.[b]

10He was in the world, and the world was made through Him, and the world did not know Him. 11He came to His own,[c] and His own[d] did not receive Him. 12But as many as received Him, to them He gave the right to become children of God, to those who believe in His name: 13who were born, not of blood, nor of the will of the flesh, nor of the will of man, but of God.

The Word Becomes Flesh

14And the Word became flesh and dwelt among us, and we beheld His glory, the glory as of the only begotten of the Father, full of grace and truth.

15John bore witness of Him and cried out, saying, "This was He of whom I said, 'He who comes after me is preferred before me, for He was before me.' "

16And[e] of His fullness we have all received, and grace for grace. 17For the law was given through Moses, *but* grace and truth came through Jesus Christ. 18No one has seen God at any time. The only begotten Son,[f] who is in the bosom of the Father, He has declared *Him.*

A Voice in the Wilderness

19Now this is the testimony of John, when the Jews sent priests and Levites from Jerusalem to ask him, "Who are you?"

20He confessed, and did not deny, but confessed, "I am not the Christ."

21And they asked him, "What then? Are you Elijah?"

He said, "I am not."

"Are you the Prophet?"

And he answered, "No."

22Then they said to him, "Who are you, that we may give an answer to those who sent us? What do you say about yourself?"

23He said: "I *am*

> *'The voice of one crying in the wilderness:*
> *"Make straight the way of the LORD," '*[g]

as the prophet Isaiah said."

24Now those who were sent were from the Pharisees. 25And they asked him, saying, "Why then do you baptize if you are not the Christ, nor Elijah, nor the Prophet?"

1:5 [a] Or *overcome*
1:9 [b] Or *That was the true Light which, coming into the world, gives light to every man.*
1:11 [c] That is, His own things or domain [d] That is, His own people
1:16 [e] NU-Text reads *For.*
1:18 [f] NU-Text reads *only begotten God.*
1:23 [g] Isaiah 40:3

26 John answered them, saying, "I baptize with water, but there stands
One among you whom you do not know. 27 It is He who, coming after me,
is preferred before me, whose sandal strap I am not worthy to loose."
28 These things were done in Bethabara[h] beyond the Jordan, where John
was baptizing.

The Lamb of God

29 The next day John saw Jesus coming toward him, and said, "Behold!
The Lamb of God who takes away the sin of the world! 30 This is He of
whom I said, 'After me comes a Man who is preferred before me, for He was
before me.' 31 I did not know Him; but that He should be revealed to Israel,
therefore I came baptizing with water."
32 And John bore witness, saying, "I saw the Spirit descending from heaven
like a dove, and He remained upon Him. 33 I did not know Him, but He
who sent me to baptize with water said to me, 'Upon whom you see the
Spirit descending, and remaining on Him, this is He who baptizes with
the Holy Spirit.' 34 And I have seen and testified that this is the Son of God."

The First Disciples

35 Again, the next day, John stood with two of his disciples. 36 And looking at Jesus as He walked, he said, "Behold the Lamb of God!"
37 The two disciples heard him speak, and they followed Jesus. 38 Then Jesus turned, and seeing them following, said to them, "What do you seek?"
They said to Him, "Rabbi" (which is to say, when translated, Teacher),
"where are You staying?"
39 He said to them, "Come and see." They came and saw where He was
staying, and remained with Him that day (now it was about the tenth hour).
40 One of the two who heard John *speak,* and followed Him, was Andrew,
Simon Peter's brother. 41 He first found his own brother Simon, and said to
him, "We have found the Messiah" (which is translated, the Christ). 42 And
he brought him to Jesus.
Now when Jesus looked at him, He said, "You are Simon the son of Jonah.[i]
You shall be called Cephas" (which is translated, A Stone).

Philip and Nathanael

43 The following day Jesus wanted to go to Galilee, and He found Philip
and said to him, "Follow Me." 44 Now Philip was from Bethsaida, the city of
Andrew and Peter. 45 Philip found Nathanael and said to him, "We have
found Him of whom Moses in the law, and also the prophets, wrote—Jesus
of Nazareth, the son of Joseph."
46 And Nathanael said to him, "Can anything good come out of Nazareth?"
Philip said to him, "Come and see."
47 Jesus saw Nathanael coming toward Him, and said of him, "Behold,
an Israelite indeed, in whom is no deceit!"
48 Nathanael said to Him, "How do You know me?"
Jesus answered and said to him, "Before Philip called you, when you
were under the fig tree, I saw you."
49 Nathanael answered and said to Him, "Rabbi, You are the Son of God!
You are the King of Israel!"

1:28 [h] NU-Text and M-Text read *Bethany.*
1:42 [i] NU-Text reads *John.*

For thirty-three years he would feel everything you and I have ever felt. He felt weak. He grew weary. He was afraid of failure. He was susceptible to wooing women. He got colds, burped, and had body odor. His feelings got hurt. His feet got tired. And his head ached.

To think of Jesus in such a light is—well, it seems almost irreverent, doesn't it? It's not something we like to do; it's uncomfortable. It is much easier to keep the humanity out of the incarnation.He's easier to stomach that way. . . .

But don't do it. For heaven's sake, don't. Let him be as human as he intended to be. Let him into the mire and muck of our world. For only if we let him in can he pull us out.

(From *God Came Near* by Max Lucado)

APPLICATION If people want to know what God is like, they can look at Jesus. If they want to know what Jesus is like, they should be able to look at his followers. Can people see Christ in you?

EXPLORATION The Word is Born—John 14:6-7; 1 Corinthians 8:5-6; Galatians 4:4; Philippians 2:7, 8; 1 Timothy 3:16; Hebrews 2:14; 13:8; 1 John 1:1-2; 4:2.

LIFE LESSON

John 2:1-25

SITUATION Weddings were an important part of Jewish culture. An entire village or town often participated in the festivities. Jesus performed his first miracle at this wedding in Cana.

OBSERVATION Jesus is concerned about us because we are his children and his friends.

INSPIRATION Picture six men walking on a narrow road. . . .

The men's faces are eager, but common. Their leader is confident, but unknown. They call him Rabbi. . . .

Where are they going? . . . They haven't been told, but they each have their own idea. . . .

Then a chorus of confusion breaks out and ends only when Jesus lifts his hand and says softly, "We're on our way to a wedding." . . .

"Why would we go to a wedding?". . .

The answer? It's found in the second verse of John 2. "Jesus and his followers were also invited to the wedding." . . .

Big deal? I think so. I think it's significant that common folk in a little town enjoyed being with Jesus. . . . Jesus was a likable fellow. And his disciples should be the same. I'm not talking debauchery, drunkenness, and adultery. I'm not endorsing compromise, coarseness, or obscenity. I am simply crusading for the freedom to enjoy a good joke, enliven a dull party, and appreciate a fun evening. . . .

(From *When God Whispers Your Name* by Max Lucado)

APPLICATION How long has it been since you had a good laugh? A hilarious time of fun with Christian friends? Jesus wants us to rejoice and enjoy life. Celebrate!

EXPLORATION God's Care and Concern—2 Kings 13:23; Matthew 7:9-11; John 11:33-38; Acts 15:14.

50 Jesus answered and said to him, "Because I said to you, 'I saw you under the fig tree,' do you believe? You will see greater things than these." 51 And He said to him, "Most assuredly, I say to you, hereafter[j] you shall see heaven open, and the angels of God ascending and descending upon the Son of Man."

Water Turned to Wine

2 On the third day there was a wedding in Cana of Galilee, and the mother of Jesus was there. 2 Now both Jesus and His disciples were invited to the wedding. 3 And when they ran out of wine, the mother of Jesus said to Him, "They have no wine."

4 Jesus said to her, "Woman, what does your concern have to do with Me? My hour has not yet come."

5 His mother said to the servants, "Whatever He says to you, do *it*."

6 Now there were set there six waterpots of stone, according to the manner of purification of the Jews, containing twenty or thirty gallons apiece. 7 Jesus said to them, "Fill the waterpots with water." And they filled them up to the brim. 8 And He said to them, "Draw *some* out now, and take *it* to the master of the feast." And they took *it*. 9 When the master of the feast had tasted the water that was made wine, and did not know where it came from (but the servants who had drawn the water knew), the master of the feast called the bridegroom. 10 And he said to him, "Every man at the beginning sets out the good wine, and when the *guests* have well drunk, then the inferior. You have kept the good wine until now!"

11 This beginning of signs Jesus did in Cana of Galilee, and manifested His glory; and His disciples believed in Him.

12 After this He went down to Capernaum, He, His mother, His brothers, and His disciples; and they did not stay there many days.

Jesus Cleanses the Temple

13 Now the Passover of the Jews was at hand, and Jesus went up to Jerusalem. 14 And He found in the temple those who sold oxen and sheep and doves, and the money changers doing business. 15 When He had made a whip of cords, He drove them all out of the temple, with the sheep and the oxen, and poured out the changers' money and overturned the tables. 16 And He said to those who sold doves, "Take these things away! Do not make My Father's house a house of merchandise!" 17 Then His disciples remembered that it was written, *"Zeal for Your house has eaten[k] Me up."*[l]

18 So the Jews answered and said to Him, "What sign do You show to us, since You do these things?"

19 Jesus answered and said to them, "Destroy this temple, and in three days I will raise it up."

20 Then the Jews said, "It has taken forty-six years to build this temple, and will You raise it up in three days?"

21 But He was speaking of the temple of His body. 22 Therefore, when He had risen from the dead, His disciples remembered that He had said this to them;[m] and they believed the Scripture and the word which Jesus had said.

1:51 [j] NU-Text omits *hereafter.*
2:17 [k] NU-Text and M-Text read *will eat.* [l] Psalm 69:9
2:22 [m] NU-Text and M-Text omit *to them.*

The Discerner of Hearts

23Now when He was in Jerusalem at the Passover, during the feast, many
believed in His name when they saw the signs which He did. 24But Jesus
did not commit Himself to them, because He knew all *men,* 25and had no
need that anyone should testify of man, for He knew what was in man.

The New Birth

3 There was a man of the Pharisees named Nicodemus, a ruler of the
Jews. 2This man came to Jesus by night and said to Him, "Rabbi, we
know that You are a teacher come from God; for no one can do these signs
that You do unless God is with him."
3Jesus answered and said to him, "Most assuredly, I say to you, unless
one is born again, he cannot see the kingdom of God."
4Nicodemus said to Him, "How can a man be born when he is old? Can
he enter a second time into his mother's womb and be born?"
5Jesus answered, "Most assuredly, I say to you, unless one is born of
water and the Spirit, he cannot enter the kingdom of God. 6That which is
born of the flesh is flesh, and that which is born of the Spirit is spirit. 7Do
not marvel that I said to you, 'You must be born again.' 8The wind blows
where it wishes, and you hear the sound of it, but cannot tell where it
comes from and where it goes. So is everyone who is born of the Spirit."
9Nicodemus answered and said to Him, "How can these things be?"
10Jesus answered and said to him, "Are you the teacher of Israel, and do
not know these things? 11Most assuredly, I say to you, We speak what We
know and testify what We have seen, and you do not receive Our witness.
12If I have told you earthly things and you do not believe, how will you believe if I tell you heavenly things? 13No one has ascended to heaven but He
who came down from heaven, *that is,* the Son of Man who is in heaven.[n]
14And as Moses lifted up the serpent in the wilderness, even so must the
Son of Man be lifted up, 15that whoever believes in Him should not perish
but[o] have eternal life. 16For God so loved the world that He gave His only
begotten Son, that whoever believes in Him should not perish but have
everlasting life. 17For God did not send His Son into the world to condemn
the world, but that the world through Him might be saved.
18"He who believes in Him is not condemned; but he who does not believe is condemned already, because he has not believed in the name of the
only begotten Son of God. 19And this is the condemnation, that the light
has come into the world, and men loved darkness rather than light, because their deeds were evil. 20For everyone practicing evil hates the light
and does not come to the light, lest his deeds should be exposed. 21But he
who does the truth comes to the light, that his deeds may be clearly seen,
that they have been done in God."

John the Baptist Exalts Christ

22After these things Jesus and His disciples came into the land of Judea,
and there He remained with them and baptized. 23Now John also was baptizing in Aenon near Salim, because there was much water there. And they
came and were baptized. 24For John had not yet been thrown into prison.

3:13 [n] NU-Text omits *who is in heaven.*
3:15 [o] NU-Text omits *not perish but.*

LIFE LESSON

John 3:1-36

SITUATION Nicodemus belonged to the highest governing body of the Jewish people, the Sanhedrin. Many of these Jewish leaders were bound by tradition and legalism.

OBSERVATION Jesus came to free men and women from slavery to sin and from the chains of legalism.

INSPIRATION The meeting between Jesus and Nicodemus was more than an encounter between two religious figures. It was a collision between two philosophies. Two opposing views on salvation.

Nicodemus thought the person did the work; Jesus says God does the work. . . .

These two views encompass all views. All the world religions can be placed in one of two camps: legalism or grace. . . .

A legalist believes the supreme force behind salvation is you. If you look right, speak right, and belong to the right segment of the right group, you will be saved. The brunt of responsibility doesn't lie with God; it lies within you. . . .

Spirituality, Jesus says, comes not from church attendance or good deeds or correct doctrine, but from heaven itself. Such words must have set Nicodemus back on his heels. But Jesus was just getting started. . . .

Salvation is God's business. Grace is his idea, his work, and his expense. He offers it to whom he desires, when he desires. Our job in the process is to inform the people, not screen the people.

The question must have been written all over Nicodemus's face. Why would God do this? What would motivate him to offer such a gift? What Jesus told Nicodemus, Nicodemus could never have imagined. The motive behind the gift of new birth? Love. "God loved the world so much that he gave his one and only Son so that whoever believes in him may not be lost, but have eternal life" (v.16).

Nicodemus has never heard such words. Never. He has had many discussions of salvation. But this is the first in which no rules were given.

Continued

No system was offered. No code or ritual. "Everyone who believes can have eternal life in him," Jesus told him. Could God be so generous?

(From *He Still Moves Stones* by Max Lucado)

APPLICATION Are there religious "rules" you observe but do not understand? Did God command them, or did mere men create them? Do they help you feel close to God? If so, keep them. Are some confusing to you? Ask your pastor to explain them to you.

EXPLORATION Legalism—Matthew 5:17, 21-22; 12:10-12; 1 Corinthians 10:25-27.

[25]Then there arose a dispute between *some* of John's disciples and the
Jews about purification. [26]And they came to John and said to him, "Rabbi,
He who was with you beyond the Jordan, to whom you have testified—behold, He is baptizing, and all are coming to Him!"
[27]John answered and said, "A man can receive nothing unless it has been
given to him from heaven. [28]You yourselves bear me witness, that I said, 'I
am not the Christ,' but, 'I have been sent before Him.' [29]He who has the
bride is the bridegroom; but the friend of the bridegroom, who stands and
hears him, rejoices greatly because of the bridegroom's voice. Therefore this
joy of mine is fulfilled. [30]He must increase, but I *must* decrease. [31]He who
comes from above is above all; he who is of the earth is earthly and speaks
of the earth. He who comes from heaven is above all. [32]And what He has
seen and heard, that He testifies; and no one receives His testimony. [33]He
who has received His testimony has certified that God is true. [34]For He
whom God has sent speaks the words of God, for God does not give the
Spirit by measure. [35]The Father loves the Son, and has given all things into
His hand. [36]He who believes in the Son has everlasting life; and he who does
not believe the Son shall not see life, but the wrath of God abides on him."

A Samaritan Woman Meets Her Messiah

4 Therefore, when the Lord knew that the Pharisees had heard that Jesus
made and baptized more disciples than John [2](though Jesus Himself
did not baptize, but His disciples), [3]He left Judea and departed again to
Galilee. [4]But He needed to go through Samaria.
[5]So He came to a city of Samaria which is called Sychar, near the plot of
ground that Jacob gave to his son Joseph. [6]Now Jacob's well was there. Jesus therefore, being wearied from *His* journey, sat thus by the well. It was
about the sixth hour.
[7]A woman of Samaria came to draw water. Jesus said to her, "Give Me a
drink." [8]For His disciples had gone away into the city to buy food.
[9]Then the woman of Samaria said to Him, "How is it that You, being a
Jew, ask a drink from me, a Samaritan woman?" For Jews have no dealings
with Samaritans.
[10]Jesus answered and said to her, "If you knew the gift of God, and who
it is who says to you, 'Give Me a drink,' you would have asked Him, and He
would have given you living water."
[11]The woman said to Him, "Sir, You have nothing to draw with, and the
well is deep. Where then do You get that living water? [12]Are You greater
than our father Jacob, who gave us the well, and drank from it himself, as
well as his sons and his livestock?"
[13]Jesus answered and said to her, "Whoever drinks of this water will thirst
again, [14]but whoever drinks of the water that I shall give him will never
thirst. But the water that I shall give him will become in him a fountain of
water springing up into everlasting life."
[15]The woman said to Him, "Sir, give me this water, that I may not thirst,
nor come here to draw."
[16]Jesus said to her, "Go, call your husband, and come here."
[17]The woman answered and said, "I have no husband."
Jesus said to her, "You have well said, 'I have no husband,' [18]for you have
had five husbands, and the one whom you now have is not your husband;
in that you spoke truly."

19 The woman said to Him, "Sir, I perceive that You are a prophet. 20 Our
fathers worshiped on this mountain, and you *Jews* say that in Jerusalem is
the place where one ought to worship."
21 Jesus said to her, "Woman, believe Me, the hour is coming when you
will neither on this mountain, nor in Jerusalem, worship the Father. 22 You
worship what you do not know; we know what we worship, for salvation is
of the Jews. 23 But the hour is coming, and now is, when the true worshipers
will worship the Father in spirit and truth; for the Father is seeking such to
worship Him. 24 God *is* Spirit, and those who worship Him must worship
in spirit and truth."
25 The woman said to Him, "I know that Messiah is coming" (who is
called Christ). "When He comes, He will tell us all things."
26 Jesus said to her, "I who speak to you am *He.*"

The Whitened Harvest

27 And at this *point* His disciples came, and they marveled that He talked
with a woman; yet no one said, "What do You seek?" or, "Why are You
talking with her?"
28 The woman then left her waterpot, went her way into the city, and said
to the men, 29 "Come, see a Man who told me all things that I ever did. Could
this be the Christ?" 30 Then they went out of the city and came to Him.
31 In the meantime His disciples urged Him, saying, "Rabbi, eat."
32 But He said to them, "I have food to eat of which you do not know."
33 Therefore the disciples said to one another, "Has anyone brought Him
anything to eat?"
34 Jesus said to them, "My food is to do the will of Him who sent Me, and
to finish His work. 35 Do you not say, 'There are still four months and *then*
comes the harvest'? Behold, I say to you, lift up your eyes and look at the
fields, for they are already white for harvest! 36 And he who reaps receives
wages, and gathers fruit for eternal life, that both he who sows and he who
reaps may rejoice together. 37 For in this the saying is true: 'One sows and
another reaps.' 38 I sent you to reap that for which you have not labored;
others have labored, and you have entered into their labors."

The Savior of the World

39 And many of the Samaritans of that city believed in Him because of
the word of the woman who testified, "He told me all that I *ever* did." 40 So
when the Samaritans had come to Him, they urged Him to stay with them;
and He stayed there two days. 41 And many more believed because of His
own word.
42 Then they said to the woman, "Now we believe, not because of what
you said, for we ourselves have heard *Him* and we know that this is indeed
the Christ,[p] the Savior of the world."

Welcome at Galilee

43 Now after the two days He departed from there and went to Galilee.
44 For Jesus Himself testified that a prophet has no honor in his own country.
45 So when He came to Galilee, the Galileans received Him, having seen all
the things He did in Jerusalem at the feast; for they also had gone to the feast.

4:42 *p* NU-Text omits *the Christ.*

LIFE LESSON

John 4:1-54

SITUATION Although the Jews did not like the Samaritans, Jesus purposely went through their territory. His disciples were amazed to find Jesus talking with a Samaritan—especially a woman!

OBSERVATION Jesus knows everything about us before we tell him.

INSPIRATION Remarkable. . . . It wasn't within the colonnades of a Roman court that he announced his identity.

No, it was in the shade of a well in a rejected land to an ostracized woman. His eyes must have danced as he whispered the secret.

"I am the Messiah." . . .

Don't miss the drama of the moment. Look at her eyes, wide with amazement. Listen to her as she struggles for words. "Y-y-y-you a-a-a-are the M-m-m-messiah!" . . .

Suddenly the insignificance of her life was swallowed by the significance of the moment. "God is here! God has come! God cares . . . for me!" . . .

That is why she grabbed the first person she saw and announced her discovery, "I just talked to a man who knows everything I ever did . . . and he loves me anyway!"

The disciples offered Jesus some food. He refused it—he was too excited! He had just done what he does best. He had taken a life that was drifting and given it direction.

He was exuberant!

(From *Six Hours One Friday* by Max Lucado)

APPLICATION What doubts and misgivings about Jesus do you have that hinder your faith? First, realize that even the disciples doubted, right up to the end (Matt. 28:17). Second, commit your doubts to the Lord, and ask for faith to live for Christ. Third, have confidence in Jesus the living Word. He will refresh your faith.

EXPLORATION Doubts—Genesis 3:1-6; 21:7; Numbers 11:21-22; Mark 8:17-18; Luke 1:18; 4:3; John 3:18; 20:25-28; James 1:5-8.

LIFE LESSON
John 5:1-47

SITUATION While he was traveling to Jerusalem to attend the feast of the Passover, Jesus made a detour to Bethesda to meet the needs of the people.

OBSERVATION Jesus had special concern for the suffering and the neglected.

INSPIRATION Picture a battleground strewn with wounded bodies, and you see Bethesda. Imagine a nursing home overcrowded and understaffed, and you see the pool. Call to mind the orphans in Bangladesh or the abandoned in New Delhi, and you will see what people saw when they passed Bethesda. As they passed, what did they hear? An endless wave of groans. What did they witness? A field of faceless need. What did they do? Most walked past, ignoring the people.

But not Jesus. . . .

He is alone. . . . The people need him—so he's there.

Can you picture it? Jesus walking among the suffering. . . .

It's worth the telling of the story if all we do is watch him walk. It's worth it

A Nobleman's Son Healed

46So Jesus came again to Cana of Galilee where He had made the water wine.
And there was a certain nobleman whose son was sick at Capernaum.
47When he heard that Jesus had come out of Judea into Galilee, he went to
Him and implored Him to come down and heal his son, for he was at the
point of death. 48Then Jesus said to him, "Unless you *people* see signs and
wonders, you will by no means believe."
49The nobleman said to Him, "Sir, come down before my child dies!"
50Jesus said to him, "Go your way; your son lives." So the man believed the
word that Jesus spoke to him, and he went his way. 51And as he was now
going down, his servants met him and told *him*, saying, "Your son lives!"
52Then he inquired of them the hour when he got better. And they said to
him, "Yesterday at the seventh hour the fever left him." 53So the father
knew that *it was* at the same hour in which Jesus said to him, "Your son
lives." And he himself believed, and his whole household.
54This again *is* the second sign Jesus did when He had come out of Judea
into Galilee.

A Man Healed at the Pool of Bethesda

5 After this there was a feast of the Jews, and Jesus went up to Jerusalem.
2Now there is in Jerusalem by the Sheep *Gate* a pool, which is called in
Hebrew, Bethesda,[q] having five porches. 3In these lay a great multitude of
sick people, blind, lame, paralyzed, waiting for the moving of the water.
4For an angel went down at a certain time into the pool and stirred up the
water; then whoever stepped in first, after the stirring of the water, was
made well of whatever disease he had.[r] 5Now a certain man was there who
had an infirmity thirty-eight years. 6When Jesus saw him lying there, and
knew that he already had been *in that condition* a long time, He said to
him, "Do you want to be made well?"
7The sick man answered Him, "Sir, I have no man to put me into the
pool when the water is stirred up; but while I am coming, another steps
down before me."
8Jesus said to him, "Rise, take up your bed and walk." 9And immediately the man was made well, took up his bed, and walked.
And that day was the Sabbath. 10The Jews therefore said to him who was
cured, "It is the Sabbath; it is not lawful for you to carry your bed."
11He answered them, "He who made me well said to me, 'Take up your
bed and walk.' "
12Then they asked him, "Who is the Man who said to you, 'Take up your
bed and walk'?" 13But the one who was healed did not know who it was, for
Jesus had withdrawn, a multitude being in *that* place. 14Afterward Jesus
found him in the temple, and said to him, "See, you have been made well.
Sin no more, lest a worse thing come upon you."
15The man departed and told the Jews that it was Jesus who had made
him well.

Honor the Father and the Son

16For this reason the Jews persecuted Jesus, and sought to kill Him,[s]

5:2 [q] NU-Text reads *Bethzatha.*
5:4 [r] NU-Text omits *waiting for the moving of the water* at the end of verse 3, and all of verse 4.
5:16 [s] NU-Text omits *and sought to kill Him.*

because He had done these things on the Sabbath. 17But Jesus answered
them, "My Father has been working until now, and I have been working."

18Therefore the Jews sought all the more to kill Him, because He not only
broke the Sabbath, but also said that God was His Father, making Himself
equal with God. 19Then Jesus answered and said to them, "Most assuredly, I
say to you, the Son can do nothing of Himself, but what He sees the Father do;
for whatever He does, the Son also does in like manner. 20For the Father loves
the Son, and shows Him all things that He Himself does; and He will show
Him greater works than these, that you may marvel. 21For as the Father
raises the dead and gives life to *them,* even so the Son gives life to whom
He will. 22For the Father judges no one, but has committed all judgment to
the Son, 23that all should honor the Son just as they honor the Father. He
who does not honor the Son does not honor the Father who sent Him.

Life and Judgment Are Through the Son

24"Most assuredly, I say to you, he who hears My word and believes in
Him who sent Me has everlasting life, and shall not come into judgment,
but has passed from death into life. 25Most assuredly, I say to you, the hour
is coming, and now is, when the dead will hear the voice of the Son of God;
and those who hear will live. 26For as the Father has life in Himself, so He
has granted the Son to have life in Himself, 27and has given Him authority
to execute judgment also, because He is the Son of Man. 28Do not marvel at
this; for the hour is coming in which all who are in the graves will hear His
voice 29and come forth—those who have done good, to the resurrection of
life, and those who have done evil, to the resurrection of condemnation. 30I
can of Myself do nothing. As I hear, I judge; and My judgment is righteous,
because I do not seek My own will but the will of the Father who sent Me.

The Fourfold Witness

31"If I bear witness of Myself, My witness is not true. 32There is another
who bears witness of Me, and I know that the witness which He witnesses
of Me is true. 33You have sent to John, and he has borne witness to the
truth. 34Yet I do not receive testimony from man, but I say these things
that you may be saved. 35He was the burning and shining lamp, and you
were willing for a time to rejoice in his light. 36But I have a greater witness
than John's; for the works which the Father has given Me to finish—the
very works that I do—bear witness of Me, that the Father has sent Me.
37And the Father Himself, who sent Me, has testified of Me. You have neither heard His voice at any time, nor seen His form. 38But you do not have
His word abiding in you, because whom He sent, Him you do not believe.
39You search the Scriptures, for in them you think you have eternal life;
and these are they which testify of Me. 40But you are not willing to come to
Me that you may have life.

41"I do not receive honor from men. 42But I know you, that you do not
have the love of God in you. 43I have come in My Father's name, and you do
not receive Me; if another comes in his own name, him you will receive. 44How
can you believe, who receive honor from one another, and do not seek the
honor that *comes* from the only God? 45Do not think that I shall accuse you
to the Father; there is *one* who accuses you—Moses, in whom you trust.
46For if you believed Moses, you would believe Me; for he wrote about Me.
47But if you do not believe his writings, how will you believe My words?"

just to know he even came. He didn't have to, you know. Surely there are more sanitary crowds in Jerusalem. Surely there are more enjoyable activities. After all, this is the Passover feast. It's an exciting time in the holy city. People have come from miles around to meet God in the temple.

Little do they know that God is with the sick.

Little do they know that God is walking slowly, stepping carefully between the beggars and the blind.

Little do they know that the strong young carpenter who surveys the ragged landscape of pain is God.

(From *He Still Moves Stones* by Max Lucado)

APPLICATION Do you spend much time among suffering people? Think of how you can meet the needs of those who suffer, and with God's help, do it.

EXPLORATION Meeting Needs— Exodus 20:11; Numbers 10:29-32; 35:2-3; 2 Kings 6:1-7; Matthew 25:34-40.

LIFE LESSON

John 6:1-71

SITUATION Jesus demonstrated his power to meet spiritual and physical needs.

OBSERVATION To gain eternal life, we must be nourished with God's Word, drawn to Christ, and united with him.

INSPIRATION The stress seen that day is not on Jesus' face, but on the faces of the disciples. "Send the crowds away," they demand. Fair request. "After all," they are saying, "You've taught them. You've healed them. You've accommodated them. And now they're getting hungry. If we don't send them away, they'll want you to feed them, too!"

I wish I could have seen the expression on the disciples' faces when they heard the Master's response. . . .

"You give them something to eat." . . .

Rather than look to God, they looked in their wallets. "That would take eight months of a man's wages! Are we to go and spend that much on bread and give it to them to eat?"

"Y-y-y-you've got to be kidding."

"He can't be serious."

"It's one of Jesus' jokes."

"Do you know how many people are out there?"

Eyes watermelon-wide. Jaws dangling open. One ear hearing the din of the crowd, the other the command of God.

Don't miss the contrasting views. When Jesus saw the people, he saw an opportunity to love and affirm value. When the disciples saw the people they saw thousands of problems.

Feeding the Five Thousand

6 After these things Jesus went over the Sea of Galilee, which is *the Sea* of Tiberias. 2 Then a great multitude followed Him, because they saw His signs which He performed on those who were diseased. 3 And Jesus went up on the mountain, and there He sat with His disciples.

4 Now the Passover, a feast of the Jews, was near. 5 Then Jesus lifted up *His* eyes, and seeing a great multitude coming toward Him, He said to Philip, "Where shall we buy bread, that these may eat?" 6 But this He said to test him, for He Himself knew what He would do.

7 Philip answered Him, "Two hundred denarii worth of bread is not sufficient for them, that every one of them may have a little."

8 One of His disciples, Andrew, Simon Peter's brother, said to Him, 9 "There is a lad here who has five barley loaves and two small fish, but what are they among so many?"

10 Then Jesus said, "Make the people sit down." Now there was much grass in the place. So the men sat down, in number about five thousand. 11 And Jesus took the loaves, and when He had given thanks He distributed *them* to the disciples, and the disciples[t] to those sitting down; and likewise of the fish, as much as they wanted. 12 So when they were filled, He said to His disciples, "Gather up the fragments that remain, so that nothing is lost." 13 Therefore they gathered *them* up, and filled twelve baskets with the fragments of the five barley loaves which were left over by those who had eaten. 14 Then those men, when they had seen the sign that Jesus did, said, "This is truly the Prophet who is to come into the world."

Jesus Walks on the Sea

15 Therefore when Jesus perceived that they were about to come and take Him by force to make Him king, He departed again to the mountain by Himself alone.

16 Now when evening came, His disciples went down to the sea, 17 got into the boat, and went over the sea toward Capernaum. And it was already dark, and Jesus had not come to them. 18 Then the sea arose because a great wind was blowing. 19 So when they had rowed about three or four miles,[u] they saw Jesus walking on the sea and drawing near the boat; and they were afraid. 20 But He said to them, "It is I; do not be afraid." 21 Then they willingly received Him into the boat, and immediately the boat was at the land where they were going.

The Bread from Heaven

22 On the following day, when the people who were standing on the other side of the sea saw that there was no other boat there, except that one which His disciples had entered,[v] and that Jesus had not entered the boat with His disciples, but His disciples had gone away alone— 23 however, other boats came from Tiberias, near the place where they ate bread after the Lord had given thanks— 24 when the people therefore saw that Jesus was not there, nor His disciples, they also got into boats and came to Capernaum, seeking Jesus. 25 And when they found Him on the other side of the sea, they said to Him, "Rabbi, when did You come here?"

6:11 [t] NU-Text omits *to the disciples, and the disciples.*
6:19 [u] Literally *twenty-five or thirty stadia*
6:22 [v] NU-Text omits *that* and *which His disciples had entered.*

26Jesus answered them and said, "Most assuredly, I say to you, you seek
Me, not because you saw the signs, but because you ate of the loaves and
were filled. 27Do not labor for the food which perishes, but for the food
which endures to everlasting life, which the Son of Man will give you, because God the Father has set His seal on Him."
28Then they said to Him, "What shall we do, that we may work the works
of God?"
29Jesus answered and said to them, "This is the work of God, that you
believe in Him whom He sent."
30Therefore they said to Him, "What sign will You perform then, that we
may see it and believe You? What work will You do? 31Our fathers ate the
manna in the desert; as it is written, *'He gave them bread from heaven to
eat.'* "[w]
32Then Jesus said to them, "Most assuredly, I say to you, Moses did not
give you the bread from heaven, but My Father gives you the true bread
from heaven. 33For the bread of God is He who comes down from heaven
and gives life to the world."
34Then they said to Him, "Lord, give us this bread always."
35And Jesus said to them, "I am the bread of life. He who comes to Me
shall never hunger, and he who believes in Me shall never thirst. 36But I
said to you that you have seen Me and yet do not believe. 37All that the
Father gives Me will come to Me, and the one who comes to Me I will by no
means cast out. 38For I have come down from heaven, not to do My own
will, but the will of Him who sent Me. 39This is the will of the Father who
sent Me, that of all He has given Me I should lose nothing, but should raise
it up at the last day. 40And this is the will of Him who sent Me, that everyone who sees the Son and believes in Him may have everlasting life; and I
will raise him up at the last day."

Rejected by His Own

41The Jews then complained about Him, because He said, "I am the bread
which came down from heaven." 42And they said, "Is not this Jesus, the
son of Joseph, whose father and mother we know? How is it then that He
says, 'I have come down from heaven'?"
43Jesus therefore answered and said to them, "Do not murmur among
yourselves. 44No one can come to Me unless the Father who sent Me draws
him; and I will raise him up at the last day. 45It is written in the prophets,
'And they shall all be taught by God.'[x] Therefore everyone who has heard
and learned[y] from the Father comes to Me. 46Not that anyone has seen the
Father, except He who is from God; He has seen the Father. 47Most assuredly, I say to you, he who believes in Me[z] has everlasting life. 48I am the
bread of life. 49Your fathers ate the manna in the wilderness, and are dead.
50This is the bread which comes down from heaven, that one may eat of it
and not die. 51I am the living bread which came down from heaven. If anyone eats of this bread, he will live forever; and the bread that I shall give is
My flesh, which I shall give for the life of the world."
52The Jews therefore quarreled among themselves, saying, "How can
this Man give us *His* flesh to eat?"

6:31 [w] Exodus 16:4; Nehemiah 9:15; Psalm 78:24
6:45 [x] Isaiah 54:13 [y] M-Text reads *hears and has learned.*
6:47 [z] NU-Text omits *in Me.*

Also, don't miss the irony. In the midst of a bakery—in the presence of the Eternal Baker—they tell the "Bread of Life" that there is no bread. How silly we must appear to God.

Here's where Jesus should have given up. This is the point in the pressure-packed day where Jesus should have exploded. The sorrow, the life threats, the exuberance, the crowds, the interruptions, the demands, and now this. His own disciples can't do what he asks them. In front of five thousand men, they let him down.

"Beam me up, Father," should have been Jesus' next words. But they weren't. Instead he inquires, "How many loaves do you have?"

The disciples bring him a little boy's lunch. A lunch pail becomes a banquet, and all are fed. No word of reprimand is given. No furrowed brow of anger is seen. No "I-told-you-so" speech is delivered. The same compassion Jesus extends to the crowd is extended to his friends.

(From *In the Eye of the Storm* by Max Lucado)

APPLICATION What is the source of your spiritual nourishment? Movies, television, or music? Do you need to change your diet so that Christ becomes the strong force in your life? Do this by Bible reading, prayer, and worship.

EXPLORATION Choices—Genesis 2:15-17; Matthew 9:9; Romans 1:24-32.

LIFE LESSON

John 7:1-52

SITUATION Jesus prepared his followers for his death, and the leading priests and Pharisees became more determined than ever to arrest him.

OBSERVATION Jesus knows how it feels to be persecuted and threatened. His own family did not believe in him. When we encounter difficult times, Jesus knows how we feel.

INSPIRATION These are distressing times for a new Christian, but they will make you a better person and prepare you for something magnificent. For a brief effort, you will receive an everlasting reward, and for a passing difficulty, infinite glory.

Will you always enjoy spiritual comfort? No, even my most devoted saints had problems, temptations, and feelings of desolation. But they endured it all patiently, trusting me rather than themselves, knowing that the suffering of "this present time cannot be compared at all with the glory that is going to be revealed" (Rom: 8:18). It is ridiculous for you to expect to receive instantly what others have barely obtained after many tears and great spiritual fatigue.

Wait patiently for me. Control your behavior. Take courage and never stop serving me because of suffering or fear. Offer your very life for my glory. I will reward you for it, and I will not desert you when you are in trouble.

(From *Growing in His Image* by Bernard Bangley)

APPLICATION Does Jesus have a slot in your schedule? Do you plan your day around your time with him, or does he get whatever time is left? Give Jesus priority by praying often and by making decisions you believe he would make.

EXPLORATION Gift of Faith—1 Corinthians 12:7-13; Ephesians 2:8-9.

53Then Jesus said to them, "Most assuredly, I say to you, unless you eat
the flesh of the Son of Man and drink His blood, you have no life in you.
54Whoever eats My flesh and drinks My blood has eternal life, and I will
raise him up at the last day. 55For My flesh is food indeed,[a] and My blood is
drink indeed. 56He who eats My flesh and drinks My blood abides in Me,
and I in him. 57As the living Father sent Me, and I live because of the
Father, so he who feeds on Me will live because of Me. 58This is the bread
which came down from heaven—not as your fathers ate the manna, and
are dead. He who eats this bread will live forever."
59These things He said in the synagogue as He taught in Capernaum.

Many Disciples Turn Away

60Therefore many of His disciples, when they heard *this,* said, "This is a
hard saying; who can understand it?"
61When Jesus knew in Himself that His disciples complained about this,
He said to them, "Does this offend you? 62*What* then if you should see the
Son of Man ascend where He was before? 63It is the Spirit who gives life; the
flesh profits nothing. The words that I speak to you are spirit, and *they* are
life. 64But there are some of you who do not believe." For Jesus knew from
the beginning who they were who did not believe, and who would betray
Him. 65And He said, "Therefore I have said to you that no one can come to
Me unless it has been granted to him by My Father."
66From that *time* many of His disciples went back and walked with Him
no more. 67Then Jesus said to the twelve, "Do you also want to go away?"
68But Simon Peter answered Him, "Lord, to whom shall we go? You have
the words of eternal life. 69Also we have come to believe and know that You
are the Christ, the Son of the living God."[b]
70Jesus answered them, "Did I not choose you, the twelve, and one of
you is a devil?" 71He spoke of Judas Iscariot, *the son* of Simon, for it was he
who would betray Him, being one of the twelve.

Jesus' Brothers Disbelieve

7 After these things Jesus walked in Galilee; for He did not want to walk
in Judea, because the Jews[c] sought to kill Him. 2Now the Jews' Feast of
Tabernacles was at hand. 3His brothers therefore said to Him, "Depart from
here and go into Judea, that Your disciples also may see the works that You
are doing. 4For no one does anything in secret while he himself seeks to be
known openly. If You do these things, show Yourself to the world." 5For
even His brothers did not believe in Him.
6Then Jesus said to them, "My time has not yet come, but your time is
always ready. 7The world cannot hate you, but it hates Me because I testify
of it that its works are evil. 8You go up to this feast. I am not yet[d] going up
to this feast, for My time has not yet fully come." 9When He had said these
things to them, He remained in Galilee.

The Heavenly Scholar

10But when His brothers had gone up, then He also went up to the feast,
not openly, but as it were in secret. 11Then the Jews sought Him at the feast,

6:55 [a] NU-Text reads *true food* and *true drink.*
6:69 [b] NU-Text reads *You are the Holy One of God.*
7:1 [c] That is, the ruling authorities
7:8 [d] NU-Text omits *yet.*

and said, "Where is He?" 12And there was much complaining among the people concerning Him. Some
said, "He is good"; others said, "No, on the contrary,
He deceives the people." 13However, no one spoke
openly of Him for fear of the Jews.
14Now about the middle of the feast Jesus went up into
the temple and taught. 15And the Jews marveled, saying,
"How does this Man know letters, having never studied?"
16Jesus[e] answered them and said, "My doctrine is
not Mine, but His who sent Me. 17If anyone wills to do
His will, he shall know concerning the doctrine,
whether it is from God or *whether* I speak on My own
authority. 18He who speaks from himself seeks his
own glory; but He who seeks the glory of the One who
sent Him is true, and no unrighteousness is in Him.
19Did not Moses give you the law, yet none of you
keeps the law? Why do you seek to kill Me?"
20The people answered and said, "You have a demon.
Who is seeking to kill You?"
21Jesus answered and said to them, "I did one work,
and you all marvel. 22Moses therefore gave you circumcision (not that it is from Moses, but from the fathers),
and you circumcise a man on the Sabbath. 23If a man
receives circumcision on the Sabbath, so that the law
of Moses should not be broken, are you angry with
Me because I made a man completely well on the
Sabbath? 24Do not judge according to appearance, but
judge with righteous judgment."

Could This Be the Christ?

25Now some of them from Jerusalem said, "Is this
not He whom they seek to kill? 26But look! He speaks
boldly, and they say nothing to Him. Do the rulers
know indeed that this is truly[f] the Christ? 27However,
we know where this Man is from; but when the Christ
comes, no one knows where He is from."
28Then Jesus cried out, as He taught in the temple,
saying, "You both know Me, and you know where I
am from; and I have not come of Myself, but He who
sent Me is true, whom you do not know. 29But[g] I know
Him, for I am from Him, and He sent Me."
30Therefore they sought to take Him; but no one
laid a hand on Him, because His hour had not yet
come. 31And many of the people believed in Him, and
said, "When the Christ comes, will He do more signs
than these which this *Man* has done?"

Jesus and the Religious Leaders

32The Pharisees heard the crowd murmuring these
things concerning Him, and the Pharisees and the chief
priests sent officers to take Him. 33Then Jesus said to
them,[h] "I shall be with you a little while longer, and
then I go to Him who sent Me. 34You will seek Me and
not find *Me,* and where I am you cannot come."
35Then the Jews said among themselves, "Where
does He intend to go that we shall not find Him? Does
He intend to go to the Dispersion among the Greeks
and teach the Greeks? 36What is this thing that He
said, 'You will seek Me and not find Me, and where I
am you cannot come'?"

The Promise of the Holy Spirit

37On the last day, that great *day* of the feast, Jesus
stood and cried out, saying, "If anyone thirsts, let him
come to Me and drink. 38He who believes in Me, as the
Scripture has said, out of his heart will flow rivers of
living water." 39But this He spoke concerning the Spirit,
whom those believing[i] in Him would receive; for the
Holy[j] Spirit was not yet *given,* because Jesus was not
yet glorified.

Who Is He?

40Therefore many[k] from the crowd, when they heard
this saying, said, "Truly this is the Prophet." 41Others
said, "This is the Christ."
But some said, "Will the Christ come out of Galilee?
42Has not the Scripture said that the Christ comes from
the seed of David and from the town of Bethlehem,
where David was?" 43So there was a division among
the people because of Him. 44Now some of them wanted
to take Him, but no one laid hands on Him.

Rejected by the Authorities

45Then the officers came to the chief priests and
Pharisees, who said to them, "Why have you not
brought Him?"
46The officers answered, "No man ever spoke like
this Man!"
47Then the Pharisees answered them, "Are you also
deceived? 48Have any of the rulers or the Pharisees believed in Him? 49But this crowd that does not know
the law is accursed."

7:16 [e] NU-Text and M-Text read *So Jesus.*
7:26 [f] NU-Text omits *truly.*
7:29 [g] NU-Text and M-Text omit *But.*
7:33 [h] NU-Text and M-Text omit *to them.*
7:39 [i] NU-Text reads *who believed.* [j] NU-Text omits *Holy.*
7:40 [k] NU-Text reads *some.*

Life Lesson

John 8:1-59

SITUATION Jesus convinced the Pharisees that God could forgive the most hideous sins. He also tried to convince them of his divine lineage, but they assumed he was demon-possessed or mad. The Pharisees grew angry when Jesus told them that they had fallen out of favor with God.

OBSERVATION We must seek God's wisdom to overcome difficult situations in life.

INSPIRATION Sightless and heartless redeemers. . . . That's not the Redeemer of the New Testament.

Compare the blind Christ I saw in Rio to the compassionate one seen by a frightened woman early one morning in Jerusalem.

Jesus sits surrounded by a horseshoe of listeners. Some nod their heads in agreement and open their hearts in obedience. . . .

We don't know his topic that morning. Prayer, perhaps. Or maybe kindness or anxiety. But whatever it was, it was soon interrupted when people burst into the courtyard. . . .

The listeners scramble to get out of the way. The mob is made up of religious leaders, the elders and deacons of their day. . . . And struggling to keep her balance on the crest of this angry wave is a scantily-clad woman. Only moments before she had been in bed with a man who was not her husband. Was this how she made her living? Maybe. Maybe not. We don't know.

But we do know that a door was jerked open and she was yanked from a bed. . . .

And now, with holy strides, the mob storms toward the teacher. They throw the woman in his direction. . . .

"We found this woman in bed with a man!" cries the leader. "The law says to stone her. What do you say?" . . .

The accusers are persistent. "Tell us teacher! What do you want us to do with her?"

He just raised his head and offered an invitation, "I guess if you've never made a mistake, then you have a

50 Nicodemus (he who came to Jesus by night,[l] being one of them) said to
them, 51 "Does our law judge a man before it hears him and knows what he
is doing?"
52 They answered and said to him, "Are you also from Galilee? Search
and look, for no prophet has arisen[m] out of Galilee."

An Adulteress Faces the Light of the World

53 And everyone went to his *own* house.[n]

8 But Jesus went to the Mount of Olives.
2 Now early[o] in the morning He came again into the temple, and all the
people came to Him; and He sat down and taught them. 3 Then the scribes
and Pharisees brought to Him a woman caught in adultery. And when
they had set her in the midst, 4 they said to Him, "Teacher, this woman was
caught[p] in adultery, in the very act. 5 Now Moses, in the law, commanded[q]
us that such should be stoned.[r] But what do You say?"[s] 6 This they said,
testing Him, that they might have *something* of which to accuse Him. But
Jesus stooped down and wrote on the ground with *His* finger, as though
He did not hear.[t]
7 So when they continued asking Him, He raised Himself up[u] and said to
them, "He who is without sin among you, let him throw a stone at her
first." 8 And again He stooped down and wrote on the ground. 9 Then those
who heard *it,* being convicted by *their* conscience,[v] went out one by one,
beginning with the oldest *even* to the last. And Jesus was left alone, and the
woman standing in the midst. 10 When Jesus had raised Himself up and saw
no one but the woman, He said to her,[w] "Woman, where are those accusers
of yours?[x] Has no one condemned you?"
11 She said, "No one, Lord."
And Jesus said to her, "Neither do I condemn you; go and[y] sin no more."
12 Then Jesus spoke to them again, saying, "I am the light of the world.
He who follows Me shall not walk in darkness, but have the light of life."

Jesus Defends His Self-Witness

13 The Pharisees therefore said to Him, "You bear witness of Yourself;
Your witness is not true."
14 Jesus answered and said to them, "Even if I bear witness of Myself, My
witness is true, for I know where I came from and where I am going; but
you do not know where I come from and where I am going. 15 You judge according to the flesh; I judge no one. 16 And yet if I do judge, My judgment is
true; for I am not alone, but I *am* with the Father who sent Me. 17 It is also
written in your law that the testimony of two men is true. 18 I am One who
bears witness of Myself, and the Father who sent Me bears witness of Me."

7:50 [l] NU-Text reads *before.*
7:52 [m] NU-Text reads *is to rise.*
7:53 [n] The words *And everyone* through *sin no more* (8:11) are bracketed by NU-Text as not original. They are present in over 900 manuscripts.
8:2 [o] M-Text reads *very early.*
8:4 [p] M-Text reads *we found this woman.*
8:5 [q] M-Text reads *in our law Moses commanded.* [r] NU-Text and M-Text read *to stone such.* [s] M-Text adds *about her.*
8:6 [t] NU-Text and M-Text omit *as though He did not hear.*
8:7 [u] M-Text reads *He looked up.*
8:9 [v] NU-Text and M-Text omit *being convicted by their conscience.*
8:10 [w] NU-Text omits *and saw no one but the woman;* M-Text reads *He saw her and said.* [x] NU-Text and M-Text omit *of yours.*
8:11 [y] NU-Text and M-Text add *from now on.*

19Then they said to Him, "Where is Your Father?"
Jesus answered, "You know neither Me nor My Father. If you had known
Me, you would have known My Father also."
20These words Jesus spoke in the treasury, as He taught in the temple;
and no one laid hands on Him, for His hour had not yet come.

Jesus Predicts His Departure

21Then Jesus said to them again, "I am going away, and you will seek Me,
and will die in your sin. Where I go you cannot come."
22So the Jews said, "Will He kill Himself, because He says, 'Where I go
you cannot come'?"
23And He said to them, "You are from beneath; I am from above. You are
of this world; I am not of this world. 24Therefore I said to you that you will die
in your sins; for if you do not believe that I am *He,* you will die in your sins."
25Then they said to Him, "Who are You?"
And Jesus said to them, "Just what I have been saying to you from the
beginning. 26I have many things to say and to judge concerning you, but
He who sent Me is true; and I speak to the world those things which I heard
from Him."
27They did not understand that He spoke to them of the Father.
28Then Jesus said to them, "When you lift up the Son of Man, then you
will know that I am *He,* and *that* I do nothing of Myself; but as My Father
taught Me, I speak these things. 29And He who sent Me is with Me. The
Father has not left Me alone, for I always do those things that please Him."
30As He spoke these words, many believed in Him.

The Truth Shall Make You Free

31Then Jesus said to those Jews who believed Him, "If you abide in My
word, you are My disciples indeed. 32And you shall know the truth, and
the truth shall make you free."
33They answered Him, "We are Abraham's descendants, and have never
been in bondage to anyone. How *can* You say, 'You will be made free'?"
34Jesus answered them, "Most assuredly, I say to you, whoever commits
sin is a slave of sin. 35And a slave does not abide in the house forever, *but* a son
abides forever. 36Therefore if the Son makes you free, you shall be free indeed.

Abraham's Seed and Satan's

37"I know that you are Abraham's descendants, but you seek to kill Me,
because My word has no place in you. 38I speak what I have seen with My
Father, and you do what you have seen with[z] your father."
39They answered and said to Him, "Abraham is our father."
Jesus said to them, "If you were Abraham's children, you would do the
works of Abraham. 40But now you seek to kill Me, a Man who has told you
the truth which I heard from God. Abraham did not do this. 41You do the
deeds of your father."
Then they said to Him, "We were not born of fornication; we have one
Father—God."
42Jesus said to them, "If God were your Father, you would love Me, for I
proceeded forth and came from God; nor have I come of Myself, but He
sent Me. 43Why do you not understand My speech? Because you are not

8:38 [z] NU-Text reads *heard from.*

right to stone this woman." He looked back down and began to draw on the earth again.

Someone cleared his throat as if to speak, but no one spoke. Feet shuffled. Eyes dropped. Then thud . . . thud . . . thud . . . rocks fell to the ground. . . . And they walked away. They came as one, but they left one by one.

Jesus told the woman to look up. "Is there no one to condemn you?" Maybe she expected him to scold her. . . . I'm not sure, but I do know this: What she got, she never expected. She got a promise and a commission.

The promise: "Then neither do I condemn you."

The commission: "Go and sin no more."

The woman turns and walks into anonymity. . . . But we can be confident of one thing: On that morning in Jerusalem, she saw Jesus and Jesus saw her. And could we somehow transport her to Rio de Janeiro and let her stand at the base of the *Cristo Redentor*, I know what her response would be.

"That's not the Jesus I saw," she would say. For the Jesus she saw didn't have a hard heart. And the Jesus that saw her didn't have blind eyes.

However, if we could somehow transport her to Calvary and let her stand at the base of the cross . . . you know what she would say. "That's him."

She would recognize his voice. It's raspier and weaker, but the words are the same, "Father, forgive them. . . ." And she would recognize his eyes. Eyes that saw her not as she was, but as she was intended to be.

(From *Six Hours One Friday* by Max Lucado)

APPLICATION Discerning right from wrong is sometimes easy, sometimes hard. How about those who have made the wrong choice? How do you judge people? Seek God's wisdom so that you are slow to condemn and quick to show compassion.

EXPLORATION Judgment—Isaiah 11:3-5; Matthew 13:40-43; Romans 2:12-15; Acts 11:2-18.

LIFE LESSON

John 9:1-41

SITUATION Jesus restored sight to a man born blind. The Pharisees questioned the man, but refused to believe that Jesus had healed him. Despite the obvious evidence, the scoffing Pharisees threw the healed man out of the Temple.

OBSERVATION Some people doubt Christ's work, not for lack of evidence but because they don't want to believe it. Jesus' mission is often missed by the "wise" people of this world.

INSPIRATION What about the blind man Jesus and the disciples discovered?

The followers thought he was a great theological case study.

"Why do you think he's blind?" one asked.

"He must have sinned."

"No, it's his folks' fault."

"Jesus, what do you think? Why is he blind?"

"He's blind to show what God can do." The apostles knew what was coming; they had seen this look in Jesus' eyes before. They knew what he was going to do, but they didn't know how he was going to do it. "Lightning? Thunder? A shout? A clap of the hands?" They all watched.

Jesus began to work his mouth a little. The onlookers stared. "What is he doing?" He moved his jaw as if he were chewing on something.

Some of the people began to get restless. Jesus just chewed. His jaw rotated around until he had what he wanted. Spit. Ordinary saliva.

able to listen to My word. 44You are of *your* father the devil, and the desires of
your father you want to do. He was a murderer from the beginning, and does
not stand in the truth, because there is no truth in him. When he speaks a lie,
he speaks from his own *resources,* for he is a liar and the father of it. 45But
because I tell the truth, you do not believe Me. 46Which of you convicts Me
of sin? And if I tell the truth, why do you not believe Me? 47He who is of God
hears God's words; therefore you do not hear, because you are not of God."

Before Abraham Was, I AM

48Then the Jews answered and said to Him, "Do we not say rightly that
You are a Samaritan and have a demon?"
49Jesus answered, "I do not have a demon; but I honor My Father, and
you dishonor Me. 50And I do not seek My *own* glory; there is One who seeks
and judges. 51Most assuredly, I say to you, if anyone keeps My word he
shall never see death."
52Then the Jews said to Him, "Now we know that You have a demon!
Abraham is dead, and the prophets; and You say, 'If anyone keeps My word
he shall never taste death.' 53Are You greater than our father Abraham, who
is dead? And the prophets are dead. Who do You make Yourself out to be?"
54Jesus answered, "If I honor Myself, My honor is nothing. It is My
Father who honors Me, of whom you say that He is your[a] God. 55Yet you
have not known Him, but I know Him. And if I say, 'I do not know Him,' I
shall be a liar like you; but I do know Him and keep His word. 56Your father
Abraham rejoiced to see My day, and he saw *it* and was glad."
57Then the Jews said to Him, "You are not yet fifty years old, and have
You seen Abraham?"
58Jesus said to them, "Most assuredly, I say to you, before Abraham was,
I AM."
59Then they took up stones to throw at Him; but Jesus hid Himself and
went out of the temple,[b] going through the midst of them, and so passed by.

A Man Born Blind Receives Sight

9 Now as *Jesus* passed by, He saw a man who was blind from birth. 2And
His disciples asked Him, saying, "Rabbi, who sinned, this man or his
parents, that he was born blind?"
3Jesus answered, "Neither this man nor his parents sinned, but that the
works of God should be revealed in him. 4I[c] must work the works of Him
who sent Me while it is day; *the* night is coming when no one can work. 5As
long as I am in the world, I am the light of the world."
6When He had said these things, He spat on the ground and made clay
with the saliva; and He anointed the eyes of the blind man with the clay.
7And He said to him, "Go, wash in the pool of Siloam" (which is translated, Sent). So he went and washed, and came back seeing.
8Therefore the neighbors and those who previously had seen that he
was blind[d] said, "Is not this he who sat and begged?"
9Some said, "This is he." Others *said,* "He is like him."[e]
He said, "I am *he.*"

8:54 [a] NU-Text and M-Text read *our.*
8:59 [b] NU-Text omits the rest of this verse.
9:4 [c] NU-Text reads *We.*
9:8 [d] NU-Text reads *a beggar.*
9:9 [e] NU-Text reads *"No, but he is like him."*

10Therefore they said to him, "How were your eyes opened?"
11He answered and said, "A Man called Jesus made clay and anointed
my eyes and said to me, 'Go to the pool of[f] Siloam and wash.' So I went
and washed, and I received sight."
12Then they said to him, "Where is He?"
He said, "I do not know."

The Pharisees Excommunicate the Healed Man

13They brought him who formerly was blind to the Pharisees. 14Now it
was a Sabbath when Jesus made the clay and opened his eyes. 15Then the
Pharisees also asked him again how he had received his sight. He said to
them, "He put clay on my eyes, and I washed, and I see."
16Therefore some of the Pharisees said, "This Man is not from God, because He does not keep the Sabbath."
Others said, "How can a man who is a sinner do such signs?" And there
was a division among them.
17They said to the blind man again, "What do you say about Him because He opened your eyes?"
He said, "He is a prophet."
18But the Jews did not believe concerning him, that he had been blind
and received his sight, until they called the parents of him who had received
his sight. 19And they asked them, saying, "Is this your son, who you say
was born blind? How then does he now see?"
20His parents answered them and said, "We know that this is our son,
and that he was born blind; 21but by what means he now sees we do not
know, or who opened his eyes we do not know. He is of age; ask him. He
will speak for himself." 22His parents said these *things* because they feared
the Jews, for the Jews had agreed already that if anyone confessed *that* He
was Christ, he would be put out of the synagogue. 23Therefore his parents
said, "He is of age; ask him."
24So they again called the man who was blind, and said to him, "Give
God the glory! We know that this Man is a sinner."
25He answered and said, "Whether He is a sinner *or not* I do not know.
One thing I know: that though I was blind, now I see."
26Then they said to him again, "What did He do to you? How did He
open your eyes?"
27He answered them, "I told you already, and you did not listen. Why do
you want to hear *it* again? Do you also want to become His disciples?"
28Then they reviled him and said, "You are His disciple, but we are Moses'
disciples. 29We know that God spoke to Moses; *as for* this *fellow,* we do not
know where He is from."
30The man answered and said to them, "Why, this is a marvelous thing,
that you do not know where He is from; yet He has opened my eyes! 31Now
we know that God does not hear sinners; but if anyone is a worshiper of
God and does His will, He hears him. 32Since the world began it has been
unheard of that anyone opened the eyes of one who was born blind. 33If
this Man were not from God, He could do nothing."
34They answered and said to him, "You were completely born in sins,
and are you teaching us?" And they cast him out.

9:11 *f* NU-Text omits *the pool of.*

If no one said it, somebody had to be thinking it: "Yuk!"

Jesus spat on the ground, stuck his finger into the puddle, and stirred. Soon it was a mud pie, and he smeared some of the mud across the blind man's eyes.

The same One who'd turned a stick into a scepter and a pebble into a missile now turned saliva and mud into a balm for the blind.

Once again, the mundane became majestic. Once again the dull became divine, the humdrum holy. Once again God's power was seen, not through the ability of the instrument, but through its availability.

"Blessed are the meek," Jesus explained. Blessed are the available. Blessed are the conduits, the tunnels, the tools. Deliriously joyful are the ones who believe that if God has used sticks, rocks, and spit to do his will, then he can use us.

(From *The Applause of Heaven* by Max Lucado)

APPLICATION Do Jesus' miracles seem hard to believe? God can defy the laws of time and space because he created them. Miracles are easily within God's power to perform. Remember, you serve a powerful God. Go ahead, then, and tell him how you need his help today.

EXPLORATION Belief—2 Kings 5:12; Matthew 8:5-10; Mark 4:35-41; 9:17-27; 10:15.

LIFE LESSON

John 10:1-42

SITUATION The parable of the Good Shepherd described Jesus' role perfectly. Unlike a hired worker, Jesus, through love and affection, offered to lay down his life for his flock. Believers trust and know him.

OBSERVATION Christ is our faithful shepherd. Put your trust in him.

INSPIRATION By the end of July 1941, Auschwitz was working like a well organized killing machine, and the Nazis congratulated themselves on their efficiency. . . .

About the only problem was the occasional prisoner from the work side of the camp who would figure out a way to escape. When these escapees were caught, as they usually were, they would be hung with special nooses that slowly choked out their miserable lives—a grave warning to others who might be tempted to try.

Then one July night as the frogs and insects in the marshy land surrounding the camp began their evening chorus, the air was suddenly filled with the baying of dogs, the curses of soldiers, and the roar of motorcycles. A man had escaped from Barracks 14.

The next morning there was a peculiar tension as the ranks of phantom-thin prisoners lined up for morning roll call in the central square, their eyes on the large gallows before them. But there was no condemned man standing there, his hands bound behind him, his face bloodied from blows and dog bites. That meant the prisoner had made it out of Auschwitz. And that meant death for some of those who remained. . . .

Soon there were ten men—ten numbers neatly listed on the death roll.

The chosen groaned, sweating with fear. "My poor wife!" one man cried. "My poor children! What will they do?" . . .

Suddenly there was a commotion in the ranks. A prisoner had broken out of line, calling for the commandant. . . .

The prisoners gasped. It was their beloved Father Kolbe, the priest who shared his last crust, who comforted the dying, who heard their confessions and nourished their souls.

True Vision and True Blindness

35 Jesus heard that they had cast him out; and when He had found him, He said to him, "Do you believe in the Son of God?"[g]

36 He answered and said, "Who is He, Lord, that I may believe in Him?"

37 And Jesus said to him, "You have both seen Him and it is He who is talking with you."

38 Then he said, "Lord, I believe!" And he worshiped Him.

39 And Jesus said, "For judgment I have come into this world, that those who do not see may see, and that those who see may be made blind."

40 Then *some* of the Pharisees who were with Him heard these words, and said to Him, "Are we blind also?"

41 Jesus said to them, "If you were blind, you would have no sin; but now you say, 'We see.' Therefore your sin remains.

Jesus the True Shepherd

10 "Most assuredly, I say to you, he who does not enter the sheepfold by the door, but climbs up some other way, the same is a thief and a robber. 2 But he who enters by the door is the shepherd of the sheep. 3 To him the doorkeeper opens, and the sheep hear his voice; and he calls his own sheep by name and leads them out. 4 And when he brings out his own sheep, he goes before them; and the sheep follow him, for they know his voice. 5 Yet they will by no means follow a stranger, but will flee from him, for they do not know the voice of strangers." 6 Jesus used this illustration, but they did not understand the things which He spoke to them.

Jesus the Good Shepherd

7 Then Jesus said to them again, "Most assuredly, I say to you, I am the door of the sheep. 8 All who *ever* came before Me[h] are thieves and robbers, but the sheep did not hear them. 9 I am the door. If anyone enters by Me, he will be saved, and will go in and out and find pasture. 10 The thief does not come except to steal, and to kill, and to destroy. I have come that they may have life, and that they may have *it* more abundantly.

11 "I am the good shepherd. The good shepherd gives His life for the sheep. 12 But a hireling, *he who is* not the shepherd, one who does not own the sheep, sees the wolf coming and leaves the sheep and flees; and the wolf catches the sheep and scatters them. 13 The hireling flees because he is a hireling and does not care about the sheep. 14 I am the good shepherd; and I know My *sheep,* and am known by My own. 15 As the Father knows Me, even so I know the Father; and I lay down My life for the sheep. 16 And other sheep I have which are not of this fold; them also I must bring, and they will hear My voice; and there will be one flock *and* one shepherd.

17 "Therefore My Father loves Me, because I lay down My life that I may take it again. 18 No one takes it from Me, but I lay it down of Myself. I have power to lay it down, and I have power to take it again. This command I have received from My Father."

19 Therefore there was a division again among the Jews because of these sayings. 20 And many of them said, "He has a demon and is mad. Why do you listen to Him?"

9:35 [g] NU-Text reads *Son of Man.*
10:8 [h] M-Text omits *before Me.*

21Others said, "These are not the words of one who has a demon. Can a
demon open the eyes of the blind?"

The Shepherd Knows His Sheep

22Now it was the Feast of Dedication in Jerusalem, and it was winter.
23And Jesus walked in the temple, in Solomon's porch. 24Then the Jews
surrounded Him and said to Him, "How long do You keep us in doubt? If
You are the Christ, tell us plainly."

25Jesus answered them, "I told you, and you do not believe. The works that
I do in My Father's name, they bear witness of Me. 26But you do not believe,
because you are not of My sheep, as I said to you.[i] 27My sheep hear My voice,
and I know them, and they follow Me. 28And I give them eternal life, and
they shall never perish; neither shall anyone snatch them out of My hand.
29My Father, who has given *them* to Me, is greater than all; and no one is
able to snatch *them* out of My Father's hand. 30I and *My* Father are one."

Renewed Efforts to Stone Jesus

31Then the Jews took up stones again to stone Him. 32Jesus answered
them, "Many good works I have shown you from My Father. For which of
those works do you stone Me?"

33The Jews answered Him, saying, "For a good work we do not stone You,
but for blasphemy, and because You, being a Man, make Yourself God."

34Jesus answered them, "Is it not written in your law, *'I said, "You are
gods"'*?[j] 35If He called them gods, to whom the word of God came (and the
Scripture cannot be broken), 36do you say of Him whom the Father sanctified and sent into the world, 'You are blaspheming,' because I said, 'I am
the Son of God'? 37If I do not do the works of My Father, do not believe Me;
38but if I do, though you do not believe Me, believe the works, that you may
know and believe[k] that the Father *is* in Me, and I in Him." 39Therefore they
sought again to seize Him, but He escaped out of their hand.

The Believers Beyond Jordan

40And He went away again beyond the Jordan to the place where John
was baptizing at first, and there He stayed. 41Then many came to Him and
said, "John performed no sign, but all the things that John spoke about
this Man were true." 42And many believed in Him there.

The Death of Lazarus

11 Now a certain *man* was sick, Lazarus of Bethany, the town of Mary
and her sister Martha. 2It was *that* Mary who anointed the Lord with
fragrant oil and wiped His feet with her hair, whose brother Lazarus was
sick. 3Therefore the sisters sent to Him, saying, "Lord, behold, he whom
You love is sick."

4When Jesus heard *that,* He said, "This sickness is not unto death, but
for the glory of God, that the Son of God may be glorified through it."

5Now Jesus loved Martha and her sister and Lazarus. 6So, when He
heard that he was sick, He stayed two more days in the place where He was.
7Then after this He said to *the* disciples, "Let us go to Judea again."

10:26 [i] NU-Text omits *as I said to you.*
10:34 [j] Psalm 82:6
10:38 [k] NU-Text reads *understand.*

The frail priest spoke softly, even calmly, to the Nazi butcher. "I would like to die in place of one of the men you condemned." . . .

"Why?" snapped the commandant. . . .

"I am an old man, sir, and good for nothing. My life will serve no purpose."

His ploy triggered the response Kolbe wanted. "In whose place do you want to die?" asked Fritsch.

"For that one," Kolbe responded, pointing to the weeping prisoner who had bemoaned his wife and children. . . .

Kolbe's place on the death ledger was set. . . .

Kolbe wasn't looking for gratitude. If he was to lay down his life for another, the fulfillment had to be in the act of obedience itself. The joy must be found in submitting his small will to the will of One more grand. . . .

In the basement the ten men were herded into a dark, windowless cell. As the hours and days passed, however, the camp became aware of something extraordinary happening in the death cell. . . . Coming from the death box, those outside heard the faint sounds of singing. For this time the prisoners had a shepherd to gently lead them through the shadows of the valley of death, pointing them to the Great Shepherd. And perhaps for that reason Father Kolbe was the last to die. . . .

For those with eyes to see, it points to the Man who laid down His life for His friends, on the cross. To the only King in history who died for His subjects.

(From *The Body* by Charles Colson)

APPLICATION Think of people who are greatly trusted. How many of them would you entrust with your life? Or your family's life? Do you have the same trust in Christ as your shepherd? Put your self-centered wishes behind and learn what Christ's wishes are for you.

EXPLORATION Shepherd—Genesis 48:15; Psalm 23:1-6.

Life Lesson

John 11:1-57

SITUATION Jesus traveled from villages beyond the Jordan River to Bethany to raise Lazarus from the dead. Bethany was about two miles east of Jerusalem, and this miracle attracted the attention of many people, including the chief priests and Pharisees. As a result, the people welcomed him into Jerusalem like a king, but the Pharisees sought to kill him.

OBSERVATION Jesus knew Lazarus would die, but he showed his power by raising him from the dead. Before seeing him perform this great miracle, however, we see that Jesus was sensitive to grief and pain.

INSPIRATION Have you been there? Have you been called to stand at the thin line that separates the living from the dead? Have you lain awake at night listening to machines pumping air in and out of your lungs? Have you watched sickness corrode and atrophy the body of a friend? Have you lingered behind at the cemetery long after the others have left, gazing in disbelief at the metal casket that contains the body that contained the soul of the one you can't believe is gone?

If so, then this canyon is not unfamiliar to you. . . . Standing on the edge of the canyon draws all of life into perspective. What matters and what doesn't are easily distinguished. . . .

It is possible that I'm addressing someone who is walking the canyon wall. . . . If this is the case, please read the rest of this piece very carefully. Look carefully at the scene described in John 11.

In this scene there are two people: Martha and Jesus. And for all practical purposes they are the only two people in the universe.

Her words were full of despair. "If you had been here. . . ." She stares into the Master's face with confused eyes. . . . Lazarus was dead. And the one man who could have made a difference didn't. He hadn't even made it for the burial. . . .

You see, if God is God anywhere, he has to be God in the face of death. Pop psychology can deal with depression. Pep talks can deal with pessimism. Prosperity can handle hunger.

8*The* disciples said to Him, "Rabbi, lately the Jews sought to stone You,
and are You going there again?"
9Jesus answered, "Are there not twelve hours in the day? If anyone
walks in the day, he does not stumble, because he sees the light of this
world. 10But if one walks in the night, he stumbles, because the light is not
in him." 11These things He said, and after that He said to them, "Our friend
Lazarus sleeps, but I go that I may wake him up."
12Then His disciples said, "Lord, if he sleeps he will get well." 13However,
Jesus spoke of his death, but they thought that He was speaking about taking rest in sleep.
14Then Jesus said to them plainly, "Lazarus is dead. 15And I am glad for your
sakes that I was not there, that you may believe. Nevertheless let us go to him."
16Then Thomas, who is called the Twin, said to his fellow disciples, "Let
us also go, that we may die with Him."

I Am the Resurrection and the Life

17So when Jesus came, He found that he had already been in the tomb
four days. 18Now Bethany was near Jerusalem, about two miles[l] away. 19And
many of the Jews had joined the women around Martha and Mary, to
comfort them concerning their brother.
20Now Martha, as soon as she heard that Jesus was coming, went and met
Him, but Mary was sitting in the house. 21Now Martha said to Jesus, "Lord,
if You had been here, my brother would not have died. 22But even now I
know that whatever You ask of God, God will give You."
23Jesus said to her, "Your brother will rise again."
24Martha said to Him, "I know that he will rise again in the resurrection
at the last day."
25Jesus said to her, "I am the resurrection and the life. He who believes
in Me, though he may die, he shall live. 26And whoever lives and believes in
Me shall never die. Do you believe this?"
27She said to Him, "Yes, Lord, I believe that You are the Christ, the Son of
God, who is to come into the world."

Jesus and Death, the Last Enemy

28And when she had said these things, she went her way and secretly
called Mary her sister, saying, "The Teacher has come and is calling for
you." 29As soon as she heard *that,* she arose quickly and came to Him. 30Now
Jesus had not yet come into the town, but was[m] in the place where Martha
met Him. 31Then the Jews who were with her in the house, and comforting
her, when they saw that Mary rose up quickly and went out, followed her,
saying, "She is going to the tomb to weep there."[n]
32Then, when Mary came where Jesus was, and saw Him, she fell down
at His feet, saying to Him, "Lord, if You had been here, my brother would
not have died."
33Therefore, when Jesus saw her weeping, and the Jews who came with
her weeping, He groaned in the spirit and was troubled. 34And He said,
"Where have you laid him?"
They said to Him, "Lord, come and see."

11:18 [l] Literally *fifteen stadia*
11:30 [m] NU-Text adds *still.*
11:31 [n] NU-Text reads *supposing that she was going to the tomb to weep there.*

35Jesus wept. 36Then the Jews said, "See how He loved him!"
37And some of them said, "Could not this Man, who opened the eyes of
the blind, also have kept this man from dying?"

Lazarus Raised from the Dead

38Then Jesus, again groaning in Himself, came to the tomb. It was a
cave, and a stone lay against it. 39Jesus said, "Take away the stone."
Martha, the sister of him who was dead, said to Him, "Lord, by this time
there is a stench, for he has been *dead* four days."
40Jesus said to her, "Did I not say to you that if you would believe you
would see the glory of God?" 41Then they took away the stone *from the*
place where the dead man was lying.[o] And Jesus lifted up *His* eyes and said,
"Father, I thank You that You have heard Me. 42And I know that You always
hear Me, but because of the people who are standing by I said *this,* that
they may believe that You sent Me." 43Now when He had said these things,
He cried with a loud voice, "Lazarus, come forth!" 44And he who had died
came out bound hand and foot with graveclothes, and his face was wrapped
with a cloth. Jesus said to them, "Loose him, and let him go."

The Plot to Kill Jesus

45Then many of the Jews who had come to Mary, and had seen the things
Jesus did, believed in Him. 46But some of them went away to the Pharisees
and told them the things Jesus did. 47Then the chief priests and the Pharisees
gathered a council and said, "What shall we do? For this Man works many
signs. 48If we let Him alone like this, everyone will believe in Him, and the
Romans will come and take away both our place and nation."
49And one of them, Caiaphas, being high priest that year, said to them,
"You know nothing at all, 50nor do you consider that it is expedient for us[p]
that one man should die for the people, and not that the whole nation
should perish." 51Now this he did not say on his own *authority;* but being
high priest that year he prophesied that Jesus would die for the nation,
52and not for that nation only, but also that He would gather together in
one the children of God who were scattered abroad.
53Then, from that day on, they plotted to put Him to death. 54Therefore
Jesus no longer walked openly among the Jews, but went from there into
the country near the wilderness, to a city called Ephraim, and there remained with His disciples.
55And the Passover of the Jews was near, and many went from the country up to Jerusalem before the Passover, to purify themselves. 56Then they
sought Jesus, and spoke among themselves as they stood in the temple,
"What do you think—that He will not come to the feast?" 57Now both the
chief priests and the Pharisees had given a command, that if anyone knew
where He was, he should report *it,* that they might seize Him.

The Anointing at Bethany

12 Then, six days before the Passover, Jesus came to Bethany, where
Lazarus was who had been dead,[q] whom He had raised from the
dead. 2There they made Him a supper; and Martha served, but Lazarus

11:41 [o] NU-Text omits *from the place where the dead man was lying.*
11:50 [p] NU-Text reads *you.*
12:1 [q] NU-Text omits *who had been dead.*

But only God can deal with our ultimate dilemma—death. And only the God of the Bible has dared to stand on the canyon's edge and offer an answer. . . . Jesus then made one of those claims that place him either on the throne or in the asylum: "Your brother will rise again."

Martha misunderstood. (Who wouldn't have?) "I know he will rise again in the resurrection at the last day."

That wasn't what Jesus meant. . . . Imagine the setting: Jesus has intruded on the enemy's turf; he's standing in Satan's territory, Death Canyon. His stomach turns as he smells the sulfuric stench of the ex-angel, and he winces as he hears the oppressed wails of those trapped in the prison. Satan has been here. He has violated one of God's creations.

With his foot planted on the serpent's head, Jesus speaks loudly enough that his words echo off the canyon walls. "I am the resurrection and the life. He who believes in me will live, even though he dies; and whoever lives and believes in me will never die" (John 11:25). . . .

. . . Life confronts death—and wins! The wind stops. A cloud blocks the sun and a bird chirps in the distance while a humiliated snake slithers between the rocks and disappears into the ground. . . .

But Jesus isn't through with Martha. With eyes locked on hers he asks the greatest question found in Scripture, a question meant as much for you and me as for Martha.

"Do you believe this?" . . .

This is a canyon question. . . . For then we must face ourselves as we really are: rudderless humans tailspinning toward disaster. And we are forced to see him for what he claims to be: our only hope.

(From *God Came Near* by Max Lucado)

APPLICATION Are there ways to imitate Jesus' care and compassion for others in times of deep hurt? Responding to grief with your own emotion offers greater comfort than words.

EXPLORATION Responding to Emotion—Job 6:26; 8:2; Romans 12:15. Jesus' Compassion—Matthew 9:36; 15:32; 20:34; 2 Corinthians 1:3.

Life Lesson

John 12:1-50

SITUATION Several groups turned out to see Jesus in the days just prior to his death. Some Jews still believed he was about to set up an earthly political kingdom. Others, especially the Pharisees, opposed Jesus.

OBSERVATION Jesus proclaimed his kingship with an entry suitable for a king. In Jerusalem, he engaged the leaders and common folks alike in final words of teaching. He explained why he had to die and summarized his overall message.

INSPIRATION "We would see Jesus." . . . It is a blessed thing for a man, when he has brought all his desires into a focus, so that they all center on one object. When he has fifty different desires, his heart resembles a mere of stagnant water, spread out into a marsh, breeding miasma and pestilence; but when all his desires are brought into one channel, his heart becomes like a river of pure water. . . . Happy is he who hath one desire, if that desire be set on Christ, though it may not yet have been realized. If Jesus be a soul's desire, it is a blessed sign of divine work within. . . .

was one of those who sat at the table with Him. 3Then Mary took a pound of
very costly oil of spikenard, anointed the feet of Jesus, and wiped His feet with
her hair. And the house was filled with the fragrance of the oil.
4But one of His disciples, Judas Iscariot, Simon's *son,* who would betray
Him, said, 5"Why was this fragrant oil not sold for three hundred denarii[r] and
given to the poor?" 6This he said, not that he cared for the poor, but because he
was a thief, and had the money box; and he used to take what was put in it.
7But Jesus said, "Let her alone; she has kept[s] this for the day of My burial.
8For the poor you have with you always, but Me you do not have always."

The Plot to Kill Lazarus

9Now a great many of the Jews knew that He was there; and they came,
not for Jesus' sake only, but that they might also see Lazarus, whom He
had raised from the dead. 10But the chief priests plotted to put Lazarus to
death also, 11because on account of him many of the Jews went away and
believed in Jesus.

The Triumphal Entry

12The next day a great multitude that had come to the feast, when they
heard that Jesus was coming to Jerusalem, 13took branches of palm trees
and went out to meet Him, and cried out:

"Hosanna!
'Blessed is He who comes in the name of the LORD!'[t]
The King of Israel!"

14Then Jesus, when He had found a young donkey, sat on it; as it is written:

15 *"Fear not, daughter of Zion;*
Behold, your King is coming,
Sitting on a donkey's colt."[u]

16His disciples did not understand these things at first; but when Jesus
was glorified, then they remembered that these things were written about
Him and *that* they had done these things to Him.
17Therefore the people, who were with Him when He called Lazarus out
of his tomb and raised him from the dead, bore witness. 18For this reason
the people also met Him, because they heard that He had done this sign.
19The Pharisees therefore said among themselves, "You see that you are
accomplishing nothing. Look, the world has gone after Him!"

The Fruitful Grain of Wheat

20Now there were certain Greeks among those who came up to worship
at the feast. 21Then they came to Philip, who was from Bethsaida of Galilee,
and asked him, saying, "Sir, we wish to see Jesus."
22Philip came and told Andrew, and in turn Andrew and Philip told Jesus.
23But Jesus answered them, saying, "The hour has come that the Son of
Man should be glorified. 24Most assuredly, I say to you, unless a grain of
wheat falls into the ground and dies, it remains alone; but if it dies, it produces much grain. 25He who loves his life will lose it, and he who hates his

12:5 [r] About one year's wages for a worker
12:7 [s] NU-Text reads *that she may keep.*
12:13 [t] Psalm 118:26
12:15 [u] Zechariah 9:9

life in this world will keep it for eternal life. 26 If anyone serves Me, let him
follow Me; and where I am, there My servant will be also. If anyone serves
Me, him *My* Father will honor.

Jesus Predicts His Death on the Cross

27 "Now My soul is troubled, and what shall I say? 'Father, save Me from this
hour'? But for this purpose I came to this hour. 28 Father, glorify Your name."
Then a voice came from heaven, *saying,* "I have both glorified *it* and will
glorify *it* again."
29 Therefore the people who stood by and heard *it* said that it had thundered. Others said, "An angel has spoken to Him."
30 Jesus answered and said, "This voice did not come because of Me, but
for your sake. 31 Now is the judgment of this world; now the ruler of this
world will be cast out. 32 And I, if I am lifted up from the earth, will draw all
peoples to Myself." 33 This He said, signifying by what death He would die.
34 The people answered Him, "We have heard from the law that the
Christ remains forever; and how *can* You say, 'The Son of Man must be
lifted up'? Who is this Son of Man?"
35 Then Jesus said to them, "A little while longer the light is with you.
Walk while you have the light, lest darkness overtake you; he who walks in
darkness does not know where he is going. 36 While you have the light, believe in the light, that you may become sons of light." These things Jesus
spoke, and departed, and was hidden from them.

Who Has Believed Our Report?

37 But although He had done so many signs before them, they did not
believe in Him, 38 that the word of Isaiah the prophet might be fulfilled,
which he spoke:

> *"Lord, who has believed our report?*
> *And to whom has the arm of the LORD been revealed?"*[v]

39 Therefore they could not believe, because Isaiah said again:

40 *"He has blinded their eyes and hardened their hearts,*
Lest they should see with their eyes,
Lest they should understand with their hearts and turn,
So that I should heal them." [w]

41 These things Isaiah said when[x] he saw His glory and spoke of Him.

Walk in the Light

42 Nevertheless even among the rulers many believed in Him, but because
of the Pharisees they did not confess *Him,* lest they should be put out of the
synagogue; 43 for they loved the praise of men more than the praise of God.
44 Then Jesus cried out and said, "He who believes in Me, believes not in Me
but in Him who sent Me. 45 And he who sees Me sees Him who sent Me. 46 I
have come *as* a light into the world, that whoever believes in Me should not
abide in darkness. 47 And if anyone hears My words and does not believe,[y]
I do not judge him; for I did not come to judge the world but to save the
world. 48 He who rejects Me, and does not receive My words, has that

12:38 [v] Isaiah 53:1
12:40 [w] Isaiah 6:10
12:41 [x] NU-Text reads *because.*
12:47 [y] NU-Text reads *keep them.*

Is this thy condition, my reader, at this moment? Hast thou but one desire, and that is after Christ? Then thou are not far from the kingdom of heaven. Hast thou but one wish in thy heart, and that one wish that thou mayest be washed from all thy sins in Jesus' blood? Canst thou really say, "I would give all I have to be a Christian; I would give up everything I have and hope for, if I might but feel that I have an interest in Christ"? Then, despite all thy fears, be of good cheer, the Lord loveth thee, and thou shalt come out into daylight soon, and rejoice in the liberty wherewith Christ makes men free.

(From *Morning and Evening* by Charles H. Spurgeon)

APPLICATION In what circumstances do you find it most difficult to believe that Jesus will protect and provide for you? Let today be your prayer-day. At the top of each hour, commit yourself more completely to the Savior by taking a moment to pray.

EXPLORATION Unbelief—Numbers 14:11-12; 2 Kings 17:14; 18-20; Luke 12:8-9; John 3:18, 36; Romans 9:30-32; Hebrews 4:2-3, 6, 11.

LIFE LESSON

John 13:1-38

SITUATION Jesus began to teach in the upper room the night before his death. He looked forward to spending this last Passover with his disciples.

OBSERVATION Jesus washed his disciples' feet, giving us a significant lesson in servanthood. If Jesus had an attitude to serve, certainly his followers ought to demonstrate a similar heart.

INSPIRATION What kind of life did those first Christians live? When they were together, they devoted themselves to four things. . . .

First, they gave themselves to "the apostles' teaching." That was everything the apostles had seen Jesus do and heard him say. Eventually they got it all written down; now we call it the New Testament. Our equivalent today of the "apostles' teaching" would be Bible study.

Second, they devoted themselves to the fellowship. That was simply being together for the joy of being together. Why draw your stimuli for life, they must have been thinking, from non-Christians who have nothing to contribute, when you could be absorbing more and more of the life of Christ from within your Christian friends? This was no deliberate cut-off from worldlings to be exclusive. Their fellowship was the strong base from which they reached out to others. But there was far more power for evangelism in this close-knit community than we find today—we, whose spirits are diluted by so much exposure to the world—even though we may say it's to win them for Christ!

Third, they devoted themselves to breaking bread together. I'm sure this meant Communion, but I think it meant other meals, too. How did it happen? Well, I'll use my imagination. Here was Thomas with a roomful of new believers in a home together. They were singing, praying, laughing

which judges him—the word that I have spoken will judge him in the last
day. 49For I have not spoken on My own *authority;* but the Father who sent
Me gave Me a command, what I should say and what I should speak.
50And I know that His command is everlasting life. Therefore, whatever I
speak, just as the Father has told Me, so I speak."

Jesus Washes the Disciples' Feet

13 Now before the Feast of the Passover, when Jesus knew that His
hour had come that He should depart from this world to the Father,
having loved His own who were in the world, He loved them to the end.
2And supper being ended,[z] the devil having already put it into the heart
of Judas Iscariot, Simon's *son,* to betray Him, 3Jesus, knowing that the
Father had given all things into His hands, and that He had come from
God and was going to God, 4rose from supper and laid aside His garments,
took a towel and girded Himself. 5After that, He poured water into a basin
and began to wash the disciples' feet, and to wipe *them* with the towel with
which He was girded. 6Then He came to Simon Peter. And *Peter* said to
Him, "Lord, are You washing my feet?"
7Jesus answered and said to him, "What I am doing you do not understand now, but you will know after this."
8Peter said to Him, "You shall never wash my feet!"
Jesus answered him, "If I do not wash you, you have no part with Me."
9Simon Peter said to Him, "Lord, not my feet only, but also *my* hands
and *my* head!"
10Jesus said to him, "He who is bathed needs only to wash *his* feet, but is
completely clean; and you are clean, but not all of you." 11For He knew
who would betray Him; therefore He said, "You are not all clean."
12So when He had washed their feet, taken His garments, and sat down
again, He said to them, "Do you know what I have done to you? 13You call
Me Teacher and Lord, and you say well, for *so* I am. 14If I then, *your* Lord
and Teacher, have washed your feet, you also ought to wash one another's
feet. 15For I have given you an example, that you should do as I have done
to you. 16Most assuredly, I say to you, a servant is not greater than his master; nor is he who is sent greater than he who sent him. 17If you know these
things, blessed are you if you do them.

Jesus Identifies His Betrayer

18"I do not speak concerning all of you. I know whom I have chosen; but
that the Scripture may be fulfilled, *'He who eats bread with Me[a] has lifted
up his heel against Me.'*[b] 19Now I tell you before it comes, that when it does
come to pass, you may believe that I am *He.* 20Most assuredly, I say to you,
he who receives whomever I send receives Me; and he who receives Me receives Him who sent Me."
21When Jesus had said these things, He was troubled in spirit, and testified
and said, "Most assuredly, I say to you, one of you will betray Me." 22Then
the disciples looked at one another, perplexed about whom He spoke.
23Now there was leaning on Jesus' bosom one of His disciples, whom Jesus
loved. 24Simon Peter therefore motioned to him to ask who it was of whom
He spoke.

13:2 [z] NU-Text reads *And during supper.*
13:18 [a] NU-Text reads *My bread.* [b] Psalm 41:9

25Then, leaning back[c] on Jesus' breast, he said to Him, "Lord, who is it?"
26Jesus answered, "It is he to whom I shall give a piece of bread when I
have dipped *it*." And having dipped the bread, He gave *it* to Judas Iscariot,
the son of Simon. 27Now after the piece of bread, Satan entered him. Then
Jesus said to him, "What you do, do quickly." 28But no one at the table knew
for what reason He said this to him. 29For some thought, because Judas
had the money box, that Jesus had said to him, "Buy *those things* we need
for the feast," or that he should give something to the poor.
30Having received the piece of bread, he then went out immediately.
And it was night.

The New Commandment

31So, when he had gone out, Jesus said, "Now the Son of Man is glorified, and God is glorified in Him. 32If God is glorified in Him, God will also
glorify Him in Himself, and glorify Him immediately. 33Little children, I
shall be with you a little while longer. You will seek Me; and as I said to the
Jews, 'Where I am going, you cannot come,' so now I say to you. 34A new
commandment I give to you, that you love one another; as I have loved
you, that you also love one another. 35By this all will know that you are My
disciples, if you have love for one another."

Jesus Predicts Peter's Denial

36Simon Peter said to Him, "Lord, where are You going?"
Jesus answered him, "Where I am going you cannot follow Me now, but
you shall follow Me afterward."
37Peter said to Him, "Lord, why can I not follow You now? I will lay down
my life for Your sake."
38Jesus answered him, "Will you lay down your life for My sake? Most
assuredly, I say to you, the rooster shall not crow till you have denied Me
three times.

The Way, the Truth, and the Life

14 "Let not your heart be troubled; you believe in God, believe also in
Me. 2In My Father's house are many mansions;[d] if *it were* not *so*, I
would have told you. I go to prepare a place for you.[e] 3And if I go and prepare
a place for you, I will come again and receive you to Myself; that where I am,
there you may be also. 4And where I go you know, and the way you know."
5Thomas said to Him, "Lord, we do not know where You are going, and
how can we know the way?"
6Jesus said to him, "I am the way, the truth, and the life. No one comes to
the Father except through Me.

The Father Revealed

7"If you had known Me, you would have known My Father also; and
from now on you know Him and have seen Him."
8Philip said to Him, "Lord, show us the Father, and it is sufficient for us."
9Jesus said to him, "Have I been with you so long, and yet you have not

13:25 [c] NU-Text and M-Text add *thus*.
14:2 [d] Literally *dwellings* [e] NU-Text adds a word which would cause the text to read either *if it were not so, would I have told you that I go to prepare a place for you?* or *if it were not so I would have told you; for I go to prepare a place for you.*

together, sharing their trials, and listening to Thomas teach. Finally one of them slaps his forehead.

"I don't believe it!" he says. "The sun's gone down. I hadn't even noticed. The children must be starving."

Everybody looks shocked and frustrated. The lady of the house says, "Oh, Thomas, just keep talking, and I'll break out something for us, somehow." . . .

My bet is that the meals just *happened* that way at first, and they added so much to the fun and close feelings, besides extending the time, that they began to be planned for!

Number four ingredient in their new life together: "the prayers." That's right, the Greek has the article *the* in front of it, and it's the same word as in Acts 3:1: "One day Peter and John were going up to the temple at the time of the prayers." In other words, "the prayers" were the stated times for worship at the temple, and all believers went together. . . .

No doubt a lot of former activities had to go, for the early Christians. They "eliminated" and they "concentrated"; they "continually devoted themselves" to these four things.

Friends, let's check our lifestyles. Have we eliminated a lot of clutter from our lives so that we, and the ones around us who want to go hard after God, can give ourselves to Bible study, to fellowship, to eating together, and to the regular services of the church?

(From *Discipling One Another* by Anne Ortlund)

APPLICATION Host a party. Spend part of your time praying together. Have fun talking. Brainstorm with your friends ways to help the church and community.

EXPLORATION Fellowship—Psalm 133:1-3; Mark 10:42-45; Acts 20:35; Philippians 2:1-2; 1 John 1:3-7.

LIFE LESSON

John 14:1-31

SITUATION Jesus knew that the disciples were troubled at the thought of his departure. He reassured them by teaching about the Holy Spirit, who would help them.

OBSERVATION Jesus sent the Holy Spirit to be our helper during our service to God.

INSPIRATION Whenever I teach on the subject of personal holiness, I always stress that we are *responsible* to obey the will of God, but that we are *dependent* upon the Holy Spirit for the enabling power to do it. The same principle applies in the realm of trusting God. We are responsible to trust Him in times of adversity but we are dependent upon the Holy Spirit to enable us to do so.

Again, let me emphasize that trusting God does not mean we do not experience pain. It means that we believe God is at work through the occasion of our pain for our ultimate good. It means we work back through the Scriptures regarding His sovereignty, wisdom, and goodness and ask Him to use those Scriptures to bring peace and comfort to our Hearts. It means, above all, that we do not sin against God by allowing distrustful and hard thoughts about Him to hold sway in our minds. It will often mean that we may have to say, "God, I don't understand, but I trust You."

(From *Trusting God* by Jerry Bridges)

APPLICATION The Holy Spirit won't always remove your obstacles, but he will give you the strength to overcome them. What obstacles do you face as you try to serve God? Are you weak, bashful, unorganized, or alone in your work? Take a bold step and let the Holy Spirit guide you through.

EXPLORATION The Counselor— Ezekiel 39:29; Luke 24:49; Acts 1:8; Romans 8:26-27; 1 Corinthians 12:4-11; Ephesians 6:18.

known Me, Philip? He who has seen Me has seen the Father; so how can
you say, 'Show us the Father'? 10Do you not believe that I am in the Father,
and the Father in Me? The words that I speak to you I do not speak on My
own *authority;* but the Father who dwells in Me does the works. 11Believe
Me that I *am* in the Father and the Father in Me, or else believe Me for the
sake of the works themselves.

The Answered Prayer

12"Most assuredly, I say to you, he who believes in Me, the works that I
do he will do also; and greater *works* than these he will do, because I go to My
Father. 13And whatever you ask in My name, that I will do, that the Father
may be glorified in the Son. 14If you ask[f] anything in My name, I will do *it.*

Jesus Promises Another Helper

15"If you love Me, keep[g] My commandments. 16And I will pray the Father,
and He will give you another Helper, that He may abide with you forever— 17the Spirit of truth, whom the world cannot receive, because it neither sees Him nor knows Him; but you know Him, for He dwells with you
and will be in you. 18I will not leave you orphans; I will come to you.

Indwelling of the Father and the Son

19"A little while longer and the world will see Me no more, but you will
see Me. Because I live, you will live also. 20At that day you will know that I
am in My Father, and you in Me, and I in you. 21He who has My commandments and keeps them, it is he who loves Me. And he who loves Me
will be loved by My Father, and I will love him and manifest Myself to him."
22Judas (not Iscariot) said to Him, "Lord, how is it that You will manifest
Yourself to us, and not to the world?"
23Jesus answered and said to him, "If anyone loves Me, he will keep My
word; and My Father will love him, and We will come to him and make
Our home with him. 24He who does not love Me does not keep My words;
and the word which you hear is not Mine but the Father's who sent Me.

The Gift of His Peace

25"These things I have spoken to you while being present with you. 26But
the Helper, the Holy Spirit, whom the Father will send in My name, He will
teach you all things, and bring to your remembrance all things that I said
to you. 27Peace I leave with you, My peace I give to you; not as the world gives
do I give to you. Let not your heart be troubled, neither let it be afraid.
28You have heard Me say to you, 'I am going away and coming *back* to you.'
If you loved Me, you would rejoice because I said,[h] 'I am going to the
Father,' for My Father is greater than I.
29"And now I have told you before it comes, that when it does come to
pass, you may believe. 30I will no longer talk much with you, for the ruler
of this world is coming, and he has nothing in Me. 31But that the world
may know that I love the Father, and as the Father gave Me commandment, so I do. Arise, let us go from here.

14:14 [f] NU-Text adds *Me.*
14:15 [g] NU-Text reads *you will keep.*
14:28 [h] NU-Text omits *I said.*

The True Vine

15 "I am the true vine, and My Father is the vinedresser. 2Every branch
in Me that does not bear fruit He takes away;[i] and every *branch* that
bears fruit He prunes, that it may bear more fruit. 3You are already clean
because of the word which I have spoken to you. 4Abide in Me, and I in
you. As the branch cannot bear fruit of itself, unless it abides in the vine,
neither can you, unless you abide in Me.

5"I am the vine, you *are* the branches. He who abides in Me, and I in
him, bears much fruit; for without Me you can do nothing. 6If anyone does
not abide in Me, he is cast out as a branch and is withered; and they gather
them and throw *them* into the fire, and they are burned. 7If you abide in
Me, and My words abide in you, you will[j] ask what you desire, and it shall
be done for you. 8By this My Father is glorified, that you bear much fruit;
so you will be My disciples.

Love and Joy Perfected

9"As the Father loved Me, I also have loved you; abide in My love. 10If you
keep My commandments, you will abide in My love, just as I have kept My
Father's commandments and abide in His love.

11"These things I have spoken to you, that My joy may remain in you,
and *that* your joy may be full. 12This is My commandment, that you love
one another as I have loved you. 13Greater love has no one than this, than
to lay down one's life for his friends. 14You are My friends if you do whatever I command you. 15No longer do I call you servants, for a servant does
not know what his master is doing; but I have called you friends, for all
things that I heard from My Father I have made known to you. 16You did
not choose Me, but I chose you and appointed you that you should go and
bear fruit, and *that* your fruit should remain, that whatever you ask the
Father in My name He may give you. 17These things I command you, that
you love one another.

The World's Hatred

18"If the world hates you, you know that it hated Me before *it hated* you.
19If you were of the world, the world would love its own. Yet because you
are not of the world, but I chose you out of the world, therefore the world
hates you. 20Remember the word that I said to you, 'A servant is not greater
than his master.' If they persecuted Me, they will also persecute you. If they
kept My word, they will keep yours also. 21But all these things they will do
to you for My name's sake, because they do not know Him who sent Me.
22If I had not come and spoken to them, they would have no sin, but now
they have no excuse for their sin. 23He who hates Me hates My Father also.
24If I had not done among them the works which no one else did, they
would have no sin; but now they have seen and also hated both Me and My
Father. 25But *this happened* that the word might be fulfilled which is written in their law, '*They hated Me without a cause.*'[k]

The Coming Rejection

26"But when the Helper comes, whom I shall send to you from the

15:2 [i] Or *lifts up*
15:7 [j] NU-Text omits *you will.*
15:25 [k] Psalm 69:4

LIFE LESSON

John 15:1–16:4a

SITUATION The Old Testament referred to Israel as the vine. The Jews in Jesus' day believed that because they belonged to Israel, they were connected to God. But Israel often failed to produce the fruit God looked for. Jesus made a radical statement by claiming to be the vine.

OBSERVATION Jesus emphasized that Christians must produce fruit. By comparing believers to branches on a grape vine, Jesus explained that we do not produce fruit through our own efforts. We bear fruit *only* by uniting with him and letting him work through us.

INSPIRATION Christ expected His followers then and now to bear fruit. Notice He did not expect them to *produce* fruit, just *bear* it. And not just *some* fruit, but *much* fruit. The amount of fruit we bear correlates with how apparent it is to others that we are believers (see John 15:8). Our faith is known to others through the good deeds that overflow from our character (see Matt. 5:16), or the fruit we bear.

You know as well as I do that for others to be impressed with our life-styles or good deeds, they must be consistent. Unbelievers are very sensitive to our inconsistencies. Oftentimes they look for them. So if we are to bear the kind of fruit Jesus is talking about—the kind that draws others to our way of believing—there must be a regular harvest.

The second thing that is clear from these verses is that what Jesus calls us to do is impossible. It's not merely difficult. It's not simply a struggle. It's not just hard. IT'S IMPOSSIBLE! "For apart from Me you can do *nothing*." Not a *little*. Not a *few things*. NOTHING. This should come as good news. . . . No one can live the Christian life apart from Christ—at least not with the consistency necessary to accomplish what Jesus has called us to accomplish.

In essence, He was saying to His followers, "Men, if you think you are dependent on Me now, wait until I'm gone!" . . . After He was gone, they would conduct themselves as soldiers

Continued

Father, the Spirit of truth who proceeds from the Father, He will testify of
Me. 27 And you also will bear witness, because you have been with Me from
the beginning.

16 "These things I have spoken to you, that you should not be made to
stumble. 2 They will put you out of the synagogues; yes, the time is
coming that whoever kills you will think that he offers God service. 3 And
these things they will do to you[l] because they have not known the Father
nor Me. 4 But these things I have told you, that when the[m] time comes, you
may remember that I told you of them.

"And these things I did not say to you at the beginning, because I was
with you.

The Work of the Holy Spirit

5 "But now I go away to Him who sent Me, and none of you asks Me,
'Where are You going?' 6 But because I have said these things to you, sorrow
has filled your heart. 7 Nevertheless I tell you the truth. It is to your advantage that I go away; for if I do not go away, the Helper will not come to you;
but if I depart, I will send Him to you. 8 And when He has come, He will
convict the world of sin, and of righteousness, and of judgment: 9 of sin,
because they do not believe in Me; 10 of righteousness, because I go to My
Father and you see Me no more; 11 of judgment, because the ruler of this
world is judged.

12 "I still have many things to say to you, but you cannot bear *them* now.
13 However, when He, the Spirit of truth, has come, He will guide you into
all truth; for He will not speak on His own *authority,* but whatever He
hears He will speak; and He will tell you things to come. 14 He will glorify
Me, for He will take of what is Mine and declare *it* to you. 15 All things that the
Father has are Mine. Therefore I said that He will take of Mine and declare
it to you.[n]

Sorrow Will Turn to Joy

16 "A little while, and you will not see Me; and again a little while, and you
will see Me, because I go to the Father."

17 Then *some* of His disciples said among themselves, "What is this that
He says to us, 'A little while, and you will not see Me; and again a little
while, and you will see Me'; and, 'because I go to the Father'?" 18 They said
therefore, "What is this that He says, 'A little while'? We do not know what
He is saying."

19 Now Jesus knew that they desired to ask Him, and He said to them,
"Are you inquiring among yourselves about what I said, 'A little while,
and you will not see Me; and again a little while, and you will see Me'?
20 Most assuredly, I say to you that you will weep and lament, but the world
will rejoice; and you will be sorrowful, but your sorrow will be turned into
joy. 21 A woman, when she is in labor, has sorrow because her hour has
come; but as soon as she has given birth to the child, she no longer remembers the anguish, for joy that a human being has been born into the
world. 22 Therefore you now have sorrow; but I will see you again and your
heart will rejoice, and your joy no one will take from you.

16:3 [l] NU-Text and M-Text omit *to you.*
16:4 [m] NU-Text reads *their.*
16:15 [n] NU-Text and M-Text read *He takes of Mine and will declare it to you.*

who had been given orders. They would strike out to fulfill their mission of righteousness.

He wanted them to understand that though He was not going to be with them physically, He still expected them to depend on Him. And the same holds true for us today.

To put it in more practical terms, if you do not learn to abide in Christ, you will never have a marriage characterized by love, joy, and peace. You will never have the self-control necessary to consistently overcome temptation. And you will always be an emotional hostage of your circumstances. Why? Because apart from abiding in Christ, you can do nothing. Jesus makes a clear delineation between the vine and the branch. The two are not the same. *He* is the vine; *we* are the branches. The two are joined but not one. The common denominator in nature is the sap. The sap is the life of the vine and its branches. Cut off the flow of sap to the branch, and it slowly withers and dies.

As the branch draws its life from the vine, so we draw life from Christ. *To abide in Christ is to draw upon His life.*

(From *The Wonderful Spirit-Filled Life* by Charles Stanley)

APPLICATION What fruit do you see in your life? Are people brought to Christ through you? Do you encourage others in their Christian walk? Do you see more fruit in your life as you follow Christ year after year? The key to producing fruit is growing closer to Jesus, knowing him more accurately, loving him more, and obeying him in more detail and with more joy.

EXPLORATION Bearing Fruit—Psalm 1:2-3; Micah 3:8; Zechariah 4:6; Matthew 13:23; 2 Corinthians 3:18; Galatians 5:22-23; Ephesians 3:16-17; Philippians 1:6; 2 Peter 1:5-8; 1 John 3:6.

23"And in that day you will ask Me nothing. Most assuredly, I say to you,
whatever you ask the Father in My name He will give you. 24Until now you
have asked nothing in My name. Ask, and you will receive, that your joy
may be full.

Jesus Christ Has Overcome the World

25"These things I have spoken to you in figurative language; but the time
is coming when I will no longer speak to you in figurative language, but I
will tell you plainly about the Father. 26In that day you will ask in My name,
and I do not say to you that I shall pray the Father for you; 27for the Father
Himself loves you, because you have loved Me, and have believed that I
came forth from God. 28I came forth from the Father and have come into
the world. Again, I leave the world and go to the Father."
29His disciples said to Him, "See, now You are speaking plainly, and
using no figure of speech! 30Now we are sure that You know all things, and
have no need that anyone should question You. By this we believe that You
came forth from God."
31Jesus answered them, "Do you now believe? 32Indeed the hour is coming,
yes, has now come, that you will be scattered, each to his own, and will leave
Me alone. And yet I am not alone, because the Father is with Me. 33These things
I have spoken to you, that in Me you may have peace. In the world you will[o]
have tribulation; but be of good cheer, I have overcome the world."

Jesus Prays for Himself

17 Jesus spoke these words, lifted up His eyes to heaven, and said: "Father,
the hour has come. Glorify Your Son, that Your Son also may glorify
You, 2as You have given Him authority over all flesh, that He should[p] give
eternal life to as many as You have given Him. 3And this is eternal life, that
they may know You, the only true God, and Jesus Christ whom You have
sent. 4I have glorified You on the earth. I have finished the work which You
have given Me to do. 5And now, O Father, glorify Me together with Yourself,
with the glory which I had with You before the world was.

Jesus Prays for His Disciples

6"I have manifested Your name to the men whom You have given Me
out of the world. They were Yours, You gave them to Me, and they have
kept Your word. 7Now they have known that all things which You have
given Me are from You. 8For I have given to them the words which You
have given Me; and they have received *them,* and have known surely that I
came forth from You; and they have believed that You sent Me.
9"I pray for them. I do not pray for the world but for those whom You
have given Me, for they are Yours. 10And all Mine are Yours, and Yours are
Mine, and I am glorified in them. 11Now I am no longer in the world, but
these are in the world, and I come to You. Holy Father, keep through Your
name those whom You have given Me,[q] that they may be one as We *are.*
12While I was with them in the world,[r] I kept them in Your name. Those
whom You gave Me I have kept;[s] and none of them is lost except the son of

16:33 [o] NU-Text and M-Text omit *will.*
17:2 [p] M-Text reads *shall.*
17:11 [q] NU-Text and M-Text read *keep them through Your name which You have given Me.*
17:12 [r] NU-Text omits *in the world.* [s] NU-Text reads *in Your name which You gave Me. And I guarded them;* (or *it;*).

Life Lesson

John 17:1-26

SITUATION This is the longest prayer of Jesus recorded in the Bible. It marked the end of Jesus' earthly ministry but looked forward to the ongoing ministry of the immediate and future disciples. Prayer was an important aspect of Jesus' ministry. Whenever a strategic time approached, Jesus spent time in prayer.

OBSERVATION The world is a battleground. Constant spiritual and physical warfare wages between the forces of God and Satan. Jesus prayed that God would keep his people pure, give them abundant joy, give them peace and unity, and protect them from Satan's power.

INSPIRATION Jesus frequently prayed alone, separating Himself from every earthly distraction. I would strongly urge you to select a place—a room or corner in your home, place of work, or in your yard or garden—where you can regularly meet God alone. . . .

A missionary and his family were forced to camp outside on a hill. They had money with them and were fearful of an attack by roving thieves. After praying, they went to sleep. Months later an injured man was brought into the mission hospital. He asked the missionary if he had soldiers guarding him on that special night. "We intended to rob you," he said, "but we were afraid of the twenty-seven soldiers."

When the missionary returned to his homeland, he related this strange story, and a member of his church said, "We had a prayer meeting that night, and I took the roll. There were just twenty-seven of us present."

(From *Hope for the Troubled Heart* by Billy Graham)

APPLICATION Do you have special times reserved only for praying? Remember, Jesus regularly went to a quiet place and talked to God. Set up a prayer plan, keep it for a week, and ask God to bless it.

EXPLORATION Prayer—Deuteronomy 4:7; Psalm 32:6; Matthew 14:23; 26:36; Luke 6:28; Ephesians 6:18.

LIFE LESSON
John 18:1-27

SITUATION Events surrounding the crucifixion and the resurrection of Jesus form the climax of all four Gospels. The arrest of Jesus has the stamp of divine plan. Jesus suffered to give us eternal life.

OBSERVATION The way of the cross provides the way to glory and victory, not defeat and humiliation.

INSPIRATION "Dear friends, do not be surprised at the painful trial you are suffering, as though something strange were happening to you. But rejoice that you participate in the sufferings of Christ, so that you may be overjoyed when his glory is revealed" (1 Pet. 4:12-13).

God works through pain to bring glory! All of us have to understand that God's fabulous treasures aren't bought with cash and credit, slapping down a contract on a bargaining table and scratching a signature and a date. They just don't come that way!

Our Lord Jesus suffered too, to show us the way. He suffered first and most—to purchase for himself glory in our eyes (Phil. 2:5-11). First the pain, and then the prize.

"Come, let us return to the Lord," says the prophet Hosea:

"He has torn us to pieces, but he will heal us;

perdition, that the Scripture might be fulfilled. 13But now I come to You,
and these things I speak in the world, that they may have My joy fulfilled in
themselves. 14I have given them Your word; and the world has hated them
because they are not of the world, just as I am not of the world. 15I do not
pray that You should take them out of the world, but that You should keep
them from the evil one. 16They are not of the world, just as I am not of the
world. 17Sanctify them by Your truth. Your word is truth. 18As You sent Me
into the world, I also have sent them into the world. 19And for their sakes I
sanctify Myself, that they also may be sanctified by the truth.

Jesus Prays for All Believers

20"I do not pray for these alone, but also for those who will[t] believe in Me
through their word; 21that they all may be one, as You, Father, *are* in Me,
and I in You; that they also may be one in Us, that the world may believe
that You sent Me. 22And the glory which You gave Me I have given them,
that they may be one just as We are one: 23I in them, and You in Me; that
they may be made perfect in one, and that the world may know that You
have sent Me, and have loved them as You have loved Me.

24"Father, I desire that they also whom You gave Me may be with Me
where I am, that they may behold My glory which You have given Me; for
You loved Me before the foundation of the world. 25O righteous Father! The
world has not known You, but I have known You; and these have known
that You sent Me. 26And I have declared to them Your name, and will declare
it, that the love with which You loved Me may be in them, and I in them."

Betrayal and Arrest in Gethsemane

18 When Jesus had spoken these words, He went out with His disciples
over the Brook Kidron, where there was a garden, which He and His
disciples entered. 2And Judas, who betrayed Him, also knew the place; for
Jesus often met there with His disciples. 3Then Judas, having received a
detachment *of troops,* and officers from the chief priests and Pharisees,
came there with lanterns, torches, and weapons. 4Jesus therefore, knowing all things that would come upon Him, went forward and said to them,
"Whom are you seeking?"

5They answered Him, "Jesus of Nazareth."

Jesus said to them, "I am *He.*" And Judas, who betrayed Him, also stood
with them. 6Now when He said to them, "I am *He,*" they drew back and fell
to the ground.

7Then He asked them again, "Whom are you seeking?"

And they said, "Jesus of Nazareth."

8Jesus answered, "I have told you that I am *He.* Therefore, if you seek
Me, let these go their way," 9that the saying might be fulfilled which He
spoke, "Of those whom You gave Me I have lost none."

10Then Simon Peter, having a sword, drew it and struck the high priest's
servant, and cut off his right ear. The servant's name was Malchus.

11So Jesus said to Peter, "Put your sword into the sheath. Shall I not
drink the cup which My Father has given Me?"

Before the High Priest

12Then the detachment *of troops* and the captain and the officers of the

17:20 [t] NU-Text and M-Text omit *will.*

Jews arrested Jesus and bound Him. 13And they led Him away to Annas
first, for he was the father-in-law of Caiaphas who was high priest that
year. 14Now it was Caiaphas who advised the Jews that it was expedient
that one man should die for the people.

Peter Denies Jesus

15And Simon Peter followed Jesus, and so *did* another[u] disciple. Now that
disciple was known to the high priest, and went with Jesus into the courtyard of the high priest. 16But Peter stood at the door outside. Then the other
disciple, who was known to the high priest, went out and spoke to her who
kept the door, and brought Peter in. 17Then the servant girl who kept the
door said to Peter, "You are not also *one* of this Man's disciples, are you?"
He said, "I am not."
18Now the servants and officers who had made a fire of coals stood
there, for it was cold, and they warmed themselves. And Peter stood with
them and warmed himself.

Jesus Questioned by the High Priest

19The high priest then asked Jesus about His disciples and His doctrine.
20Jesus answered him, "I spoke openly to the world. I always taught in
synagogues and in the temple, where the Jews always meet,[v] and in secret
I have said nothing. 21Why do you ask Me? Ask those who have heard Me
what I said to them. Indeed they know what I said."
22And when He had said these things, one of the officers who stood by
struck Jesus with the palm of his hand, saying, "Do You answer the high
priest like that?"
23Jesus answered him, "If I have spoken evil, bear witness of the evil; but
if well, why do you strike Me?"
24Then Annas sent Him bound to Caiaphas the high priest.

Peter Denies Twice More

25Now Simon Peter stood and warmed himself. Therefore they said to
him, "You are not also *one* of His disciples, are you?"
He denied *it* and said, "I am not!"
26One of the servants of the high priest, a relative *of him* whose ear Peter
cut off, said, "Did I not see you in the garden with Him?" 27Peter then denied
again; and immediately a rooster crowed.

In Pilate's Court

28Then they led Jesus from Caiaphas to the Praetorium, and it was early
morning. But they themselves did not go into the Praetorium, lest they
should be defiled, but that they might eat the Passover. 29Pilate then went
out to them and said, "What accusation do you bring against this Man?"
30They answered and said to him, "If He were not an evildoer, we would
not have delivered Him up to you."
31Then Pilate said to them, "You take Him and judge Him according to
your law."
Therefore the Jews said to him, "It is not lawful for us to put anyone to
death," 32that the saying of Jesus might be fulfilled which He spoke, signifying by what death He would die.

18:15 [u] M-Text reads *the other.*
18:20 [v] NU-Text reads *where all the Jews meet.*

he has injured us,
but he will bind up our wounds.
After two days he will revive us;
on the third day he will restore us,
that we may live in his
presence." (6:1-2)

Do you catch something here? It's as if the shadow of a cross is falling across these words. God is totally involved in our suffering, as we will be totally involved in His ultimate triumph. The two processes are inseparable.

(From *My Sacrifice, His Fire* by Anne Ortlund)

APPLICATION Think of specific instances when you have kept your Christian identity secret. Don't be ashamed—Jesus paid such a high price for your life. Remember, God joins our suffering—strengthening and lifting us up so that we can share in his glory.

EXPLORATION Suffering—Exodus 5:4-9; Leviticus 26:40-45; Job 3:23-26; Psalm 44:9-22; Mark 8:31-32; Romans 8:17; Philippians 1:29; Hebrews 2:10, 18; James 1:2-4; Revelation 2:10-11.

Life Lesson

John 18:22–19:42

SITUATION Jewish leaders hoped to crucify Jesus but did not have the authority to do this, so they brought him to the Roman governor, Pilate. Shrewd Pilate knew that the Jewish leaders wanted him to act as their executioner. He pronounced Jesus innocent and tried to save him, but finally consented to the crucifixion because of public pressure.

OBSERVATION Jesus knew that his trial was according to God's will and faced it with humility and self-control. In his cry, "It is finished," we hear the triumphant recognition that he has now fully accomplished God's will and paid for our sins in full.

INSPIRATION Pilate wants to let Jesus go. *Just give me a reason*, he thinks, almost aloud. *I'll set you free.*

His thoughts are interrupted by a tap on the shoulder. A messenger leans and whispers. Strange. Pilate's wife has sent word not to get involved in the case. Something about a dream she had.

Pilate walks back to his chair, sits, and stares at Jesus. "Even the gods are on your side?" he states with no explanation. . . .

How many wide eyes have stared at him, pleading for mercy, begging for acquittal?

But the eyes of this Nazarene are calm, silent. . . .

33Then Pilate entered the Praetorium again, called Jesus, and said to
Him, "Are You the King of the Jews?"
34Jesus answered him, "Are you speaking for yourself about this, or did
others tell you this concerning Me?"
35Pilate answered, "Am I a Jew? Your own nation and the chief priests
have delivered You to me. What have You done?"
36Jesus answered, "My kingdom is not of this world. If My kingdom
were of this world, My servants would fight, so that I should not be delivered to the Jews; but now My kingdom is not from here."
37Pilate therefore said to Him, "Are You a king then?"
Jesus answered, "You say *rightly* that I am a king. For this cause I was
born, and for this cause I have come into the world, that I should bear witness to the truth. Everyone who is of the truth hears My voice."
38Pilate said to Him, "What is truth?" And when he had said this, he
went out again to the Jews, and said to them, "I find no fault in Him at all.

Taking the Place of Barabbas

39"But you have a custom that I should release someone to you at the
Passover. Do you therefore want me to release to you the King of the Jews?"
40Then they all cried again, saying, "Not this Man, but Barabbas!" Now
Barabbas was a robber.

The Soldiers Mock Jesus

19 So then Pilate took Jesus and scourged *Him.* 2And the soldiers
twisted a crown of thorns and put *it* on His head, and they put on
Him a purple robe. 3Then they said,[w] "Hail, King of the Jews!" And they
struck Him with their hands.
4Pilate then went out again, and said to them, "Behold, I am bringing
Him out to you, that you may know that I find no fault in Him."

Pilate's Decision

5Then Jesus came out, wearing the crown of thorns and the purple robe.
And *Pilate* said to them, "Behold the Man!"
6Therefore, when the chief priests and officers saw Him, they cried out,
saying, "Crucify *Him,* crucify *Him!*"
Pilate said to them, "You take Him and crucify *Him,* for I find no fault in
Him."
7The Jews answered him, "We have a law, and according to our[x] law He
ought to die, because He made Himself the Son of God."
8Therefore, when Pilate heard that saying, he was the more afraid, 9and
went again into the Praetorium, and said to Jesus, "Where are You from?"
But Jesus gave him no answer.
10Then Pilate said to Him, "Are You not speaking to me? Do You not
know that I have power to crucify You, and power to release You?"
11Jesus answered, "You could have no power at all against Me unless it
had been given you from above. Therefore the one who delivered Me to
you has the greater sin."
12From then on Pilate sought to release Him, but the Jews cried out, saying, "If you let this Man go, you are not Caesar's friend. Whoever makes
himself a king speaks against Caesar."

19:3 [w] NU-Text reads *And they came up to Him and said.*
19:7 [x] NU-Text reads *the law.*

13When Pilate therefore heard that saying, he brought Jesus out and sat
down in the judgment seat in a place that is called *The* Pavement, but in
Hebrew, Gabbatha. 14Now it was the Preparation Day of the Passover, and
about the sixth hour. And he said to the Jews, "Behold your King!"
15But they cried out, "Away with *Him,* away with *Him!* Crucify Him!"
Pilate said to them, "Shall I crucify your King?"
The chief priests answered, "We have no king but Caesar!"
16Then he delivered Him to them to be crucified. Then they took Jesus
and led *Him* away.[y]

The King on a Cross

17And He, bearing His cross, went out to a place called *the Place* of a
Skull, which is called in Hebrew, Golgotha, 18where they crucified Him,
and two others with Him, one on either side, and Jesus in the center. 19Now
Pilate wrote a title and put *it* on the cross. And the writing was:

JESUS OF NAZARETH, THE KING OF THE JEWS.

20Then many of the Jews read this title, for the place where Jesus was crucified was near the city; and it was written in Hebrew, Greek, *and* Latin.
21Therefore the chief priests of the Jews said to Pilate, "Do not write, 'The
King of the Jews,' but, 'He said, "I am the King of the Jews." ' "
22Pilate answered, "What I have written, I have written."
23Then the soldiers, when they had crucified Jesus, took His garments
and made four parts, to each soldier a part, and also the tunic. Now the
tunic was without seam, woven from the top in one piece. 24They said
therefore among themselves, "Let us not tear it, but cast lots for it, whose
it shall be," that the Scripture might be fulfilled which says:

"They divided My garments among them,
And for My clothing they cast lots."[z]

Therefore the soldiers did these things.

Behold Your Mother

25Now there stood by the cross of Jesus His mother, and His mother's
sister, Mary the *wife* of Clopas, and Mary Magdalene. 26When Jesus therefore
saw His mother, and the disciple whom He loved standing by, He said to His
mother, "Woman, behold your son!" 27Then He said to the disciple, "Behold
your mother!" And from that hour that disciple took her to his own *home.*

It Is Finished

28After this, Jesus, knowing[a] that all things were now accomplished,
that the Scripture might be fulfilled, said, "I thirst!" 29Now a vessel full of
sour wine was sitting there; and they filled a sponge with sour wine, put *it*
on hyssop, and put *it* to His mouth. 30So when Jesus had received the sour
wine, He said, "It is finished!" And bowing His head, He gave up His spirit.

Jesus' Side Is Pierced

31Therefore, because it was the Preparation *Day,* that the bodies should

19:16 [y] NU-Text omits *and led Him away.*
19:24 [z] Psalm 22:18
19:28 [a] M-Text reads *seeing.*

He's not angry with me. He's not afraid . . . he seems to understand. . . .

"What should I do with Jesus, the one called the Christ?" . . .

What do you do with a man who claims to be God, yet hates religion? . . . What do you do with a man who knows the place and time of his death, yet goes there anyway? . . .

You can reject him. . . .

Or you can accept him. You can journey with him. You can listen for his voice amidst the hundreds of voices and follow him.

(From *And the Angels Were Silent* by Max Lucado)

APPLICATION What resources do you call upon to make tough decisions? Where do you go for advice? How do you process the options? Next time you need to make a decision, pray first. Then pray again all along the way until you decide.

EXPLORATION God's Will—Psalm 40:8; 143:10; Micah 6:8; Matthew 6:10; 7:21; John 6:38; Philippians 2:13; 1 Thessalonians 4:3; Hebrews 10:1.

LIFE LESSON

John 20:1-31

SITUATION Tombs in ancient times were closed by a circular stone across the mouth of a cave. Matthew tells us that authorities sealed the tomb and guarded it (Matthew 27:66). When Mary saw the stone rolled away, she was shocked and amazed. She ran to tell Peter and John.

OBSERVATION The resurrection of Jesus is true. We worship a living Savior and can live forever because he does.

INSPIRATION There is something about a living testimony that gives us courage. Once we see someone else emerging from life's dark tunnels we realize that we, too, can overcome. . . .

In the eyes of humanity, death was still the black veil that separated them from joy. There was no victory over this hooded foe. Its putrid odor invaded the nostrils of every human, convincing them that life was only meant to end abruptly and senselessly.

It was left to the Son of God to disclose the true nature of this force. It was on the cross that the showdown occurred. Christ called for Satan's cards. Weary of seeing humanity fooled by a coverup, he entered the tunnel death to prove that there was indeed an exit. And, as the world darkened, creation held her breath. . . .

Christ emerged from death's tunnel, lifted a triumphant fist toward the sky, and freed all from the fear of death.

"Death has been swallowed up in victory!"

(From *On the Anvil* by Max Lucado)

APPLICATION Pretend for a moment that you are a prisoner of a heartless regime, working in a labor camp, awaiting your execution. Overnight you are liberated, almost miraculously. Life is yours again. Describe the feelings. Now be glad, for Jesus has done that for you.

EXPLORATION Resurrection—Matthew 22:31-32; John 11:25; Acts 1:22; 4:2; 4:33; Romans 1:4; 6:5; 1 Peter 1:3; 3:21.

not remain on the cross on the Sabbath (for that Sabbath was a high day), the Jews asked Pilate that their legs might be broken, and *that* they might be taken away. 32Then the soldiers came and broke the legs of the first and of the other who was crucified with Him. 33But when they came to Jesus and saw that He was already dead, they did not break His legs. 34But one of the soldiers pierced His side with a spear, and immediately blood and water came out. 35And he who has seen has testified, and his testimony is true; and he knows that he is telling the truth, so that you may believe. 36For these things were done that the Scripture should be fulfilled, *"Not one of His bones shall be broken."*[b] 37And again another Scripture says, *"They shall look on Him whom they pierced."*[c]

Jesus Buried in Joseph's Tomb

38After this, Joseph of Arimathea, being a disciple of Jesus, but secretly, for fear of the Jews, asked Pilate that he might take away the body of Jesus; and Pilate gave *him* permission. So he came and took the body of Jesus. 39And Nicodemus, who at first came to Jesus by night, also came, bringing a mixture of myrrh and aloes, about a hundred pounds. 40Then they took the body of Jesus, and bound it in strips of linen with the spices, as the custom of the Jews is to bury. 41Now in the place where He was crucified there was a garden, and in the garden a new tomb in which no one had yet been laid. 42So there they laid Jesus, because of the Jews' Preparation *Day,* for the tomb was nearby.

The Empty Tomb

20 Now the first *day* of the week Mary Magdalene went to the tomb early, while it was still dark, and saw *that* the stone had been taken away from the tomb. 2Then she ran and came to Simon Peter, and to the other disciple, whom Jesus loved, and said to them, "They have taken away the Lord out of the tomb, and we do not know where they have laid Him."

3Peter therefore went out, and the other disciple, and were going to the tomb. 4So they both ran together, and the other disciple outran Peter and came to the tomb first. 5And he, stooping down and looking in, saw the linen cloths lying *there;* yet he did not go in. 6Then Simon Peter came, following him, and went into the tomb; and he saw the linen cloths lying *there,* 7and the handkerchief that had been around His head, not lying with the linen cloths, but folded together in a place by itself. 8Then the other disciple, who came to the tomb first, went in also; and he saw and believed. 9For as yet they did not know the Scripture, that He must rise again from the dead. 10Then the disciples went away again to their own homes.

Mary Magdalene Sees the Risen Lord

11But Mary stood outside by the tomb weeping, and as she wept she stooped down *and looked* into the tomb. 12And she saw two angels in white sitting, one at the head and the other at the feet, where the body of Jesus had lain. 13Then they said to her, "Woman, why are you weeping?"

She said to them, "Because they have taken away my Lord, and I do not know where they have laid Him."

14Now when she had said this, she turned around and saw Jesus standing

19:36 [b] Exodus 12:46; Numbers 9:12; Psalm 34:20
19:37 [c] Zechariah 12:10

there, and did not know that it was Jesus. 15Jesus said to her, "Woman, why are you weeping? Whom are you seeking?"

She, supposing Him to be the gardener, said to Him, "Sir, if You have carried Him away, tell me where You have laid Him, and I will take Him away."

16Jesus said to her, "Mary!"

She turned and said to Him,[d] "Rabboni!" (which is to say, Teacher).

17Jesus said to her, "Do not cling to Me, for I have not yet ascended to My Father; but go to My brethren and say to them, 'I am ascending to My Father and your Father, and *to* My God and your God.' "

18Mary Magdalene came and told the disciples that she had seen the Lord,[e] and *that* He had spoken these things to her.

The Apostles Commissioned

19Then, the same day at evening, being the first *day* of the week, when the doors were shut where the disciples were assembled,[f] for fear of the Jews, Jesus came and stood in the midst, and said to them, "Peace *be* with you." 20When He had said this, He showed them *His* hands and His side. Then the disciples were glad when they saw the Lord.

21So Jesus said to them again, "Peace to you! As the Father has sent Me, I also send you." 22And when He had said this, He breathed on *them,* and said to them, "Receive the Holy Spirit. 23If you forgive the sins of any, they are forgiven them; if you retain the *sins* of any, they are retained."

Seeing and Believing

24Now Thomas, called the Twin, one of the twelve, was not with them when Jesus came. 25The other disciples therefore said to him, "We have seen the Lord."

So he said to them, "Unless I see in His hands the print of the nails, and put my finger into the print of the nails, and put my hand into His side, I will not believe."

26And after eight days His disciples were again inside, and Thomas with them. Jesus came, the doors being shut, and stood in the midst, and said, "Peace to you!" 27Then He said to Thomas, "Reach your finger here, and look at My hands; and reach your hand *here,* and put *it* into My side. Do not be unbelieving, but believing."

28And Thomas answered and said to Him, "My Lord and my God!"

29Jesus said to him, "Thomas,[g] because you have seen Me, you have believed. Blessed *are* those who have not seen and *yet* have believed."

That You May Believe

30And truly Jesus did many other signs in the presence of His disciples, which are not written in this book; 31but these are written that you may believe that Jesus is the Christ, the Son of God, and that believing you may have life in His name.

Breakfast by the Sea

21 After these things Jesus showed Himself again to the disciples at the Sea of Tiberias, and in this way He showed *Himself:* 2Simon Peter, Thomas called the Twin, Nathanael of Cana in Galilee, the *sons* of Zebedee, and two others of His disciples were together. 3Simon Peter said to them, "I am going fishing."

They said to him, "We are going with you also." They went out and immediately[h] got into the boat, and that night they caught nothing. 4But when the morning had now come, Jesus stood on the shore; yet the disciples did not know that it was Jesus. 5Then Jesus said to them, "Children, have you any food?"

They answered Him, "No."

6And He said to them, "Cast the net on the right side of the boat, and you will find *some.*" So they cast, and now they were not able to draw it in because of the multitude of fish.

7Therefore that disciple whom Jesus loved said to Peter, "It is the Lord!" Now when Simon Peter heard that it was the Lord, he put on *his* outer garment (for he had removed it), and plunged into the sea. 8But the other disciples came in the little boat (for they were not far from land, but about two hundred cubits), dragging the net with fish. 9Then, as soon as they had come to land, they saw a fire of coals there, and fish laid on it, and bread. 10Jesus said to them, "Bring some of the fish which you have just caught."

11Simon Peter went up and dragged the net to land, full of large fish, one hundred and fifty-three; and although there were so many, the net was not broken. 12Jesus said to them, "Come *and* eat breakfast." Yet none of the disciples dared ask Him, "Who are You?"—knowing that it was the Lord. 13Jesus then came and took the bread and gave it to them, and likewise the fish.

14This *is* now the third time Jesus showed Himself to His disciples after He was raised from the dead.

20:16 [d] NU-Text adds *in Hebrew.*
20:18 [e] NU-Text reads *disciples, "I have seen the Lord," . . . .*
20:19 [f] NU-Text omits *assembled.*
20:29 [g] NU-Text and M-Text omit *Thomas.*
21:3 [h] NU-Text omits *immediately.*

Jesus Restores Peter

15 So when they had eaten breakfast, Jesus said to Simon Peter, "Simon, *son* of Jonah,[i] do you love Me more
than these?"

He said to Him, "Yes, Lord; You know that I love You."
He said to him, "Feed My lambs."

16 He said to him again a second time, "Simon, *son* of
Jonah,[j] do you love Me?"

He said to Him, "Yes, Lord; You know that I love You."
He said to him, "Tend My sheep."

17 He said to him the third time, "Simon, *son* of Jonah,[k]
do you love Me?" Peter was grieved because He said to
him the third time, "Do you love Me?"

And he said to Him, "Lord, You know all things; You
know that I love You."

Jesus said to him, "Feed My sheep. 18 Most assuredly,
I say to you, when you were younger, you girded your-
self and walked where you wished; but when you are
old, you will stretch out your hands, and another will
gird you and carry *you* where you do not wish." 19 This
He spoke, signifying by what death he would glorify
God. And when He had spoken this, He said to him,
"Follow Me."

The Beloved Disciple and His Book

20 Then Peter, turning around, saw the disciple whom
Jesus loved following, who also had leaned on His
breast at the supper, and said, "Lord, who is the one
who betrays You?" 21 Peter, seeing him, said to Jesus,
"But Lord, what *about* this man?"

22 Jesus said to him, "If I will that he remain till I
come, what *is that* to you? You follow Me."

23 Then this saying went out among the brethren
that this disciple would not die. Yet Jesus did not say
to him that he would not die, but, "If I will that he remain till I come, what *is that* to you?"

24 This is the disciple who testifies of these things,
and wrote these things; and we know that his testimony is true.

25 And there are also many other things that Jesus
did, which if they were written one by one, I suppose
that even the world itself could not contain the books
that would be written. Amen.

21:15 [i] NU-Text reads *John.*
21:16 [j] NU-Text reads *John.*
21:17 [k] NU-Text reads *John.*

ACTS of the Apostles

INTRODUCTION

They aren't the same men.

Oh, I know they look like it. They have the same names. The same faces. The same mannerisms. They look the same. But they aren't. On the surface they appear no different. Peter is still brazen. Nathanael is still reflective. Philip is still calculating.

They look the same. But they aren't. They aren't the same men you read about in the last four books. The fellows you got to know in the Gospels? These are the ones, but they're different.

You'll see it. As you read you'll see it. In their eyes. You hear it in their voices. You feel it in their passion. These men have changed.

As you read you'll wonder—are these the same guys? The ones who doubted in Galilee? The ones who argued in Capernaum? The ones who ran for their lives in Gethsemane? You'll wonder, "Are these the same men?"

The answer is no. They are different. They have stood face to face with God. They have sat at the feet of the resurrected King. They are different.

Within them dwells a fire not found on earth. Christ has taught them. The Father has forgiven them. The Spirit indwells them. They are not the same.

And because they are different, so is the world.

Read their adventures and be encouraged. Read their adventures and be listening. What God did to them, he longs to do for you.

Life Lesson

Acts 1:1-26

SITUATION The Book of Acts was written to give an accurate report of what happened to Jesus' followers and how the early church began and spread. It was written by Luke, the physician and historian, as a sequel to the Gospel that bears his name. Luke told how the gospel spread from Jerusalem to Samaria and finally to every part of the world.

OBSERVATION God planned that the Holy Spirit would come to empower Believers. Jesus gave this plan to the apostles, his last promise before he ascended to heaven.

INSPIRATION If the Christian life is simply a matter of doing our best, there was no need for God to send the Holy Spirit to help us. After all, our best is our best. How do we improve on that? Since God is omniscient, as we certainly believe He is, He knows when we have done all we can do. Why complicate matters?

Jesus let it be known, however, that God was looking for more than our best. He was looking for a life-style and attitude that superseded our best, a life-style and attitude that we could never attain through our own efforts. . . .

Think about this. If we don't need any help, why send a Helper? The promise of a Helper presupposes that we need help. The promise of a Helper was Jesus' way of tipping us off to one of the most profound truths concerning the Christian life—it's impossible! The quality of life Jesus expects from His followers is unattainable apart from outside intervention.

(From *The Wonderful Spirit-Filled Life* by Charles Stanley)

APPLICATION Are you nervous about sharing your faith? Be bold. Open your mouth to share and let the reliable Holy Spirit direct your conversation.

EXPLORATION Promises about the Spirit—John 14:16, 26; 15:26-27; 16:7-8, 13; Romans 8:11, 26; 2 Corinthians 1:21-22; 5:5; Ephesians 1:13-14; Hebrews 10:23.

Prologue

The former account I made, O Theophilus, of all that Jesus
began both to do and teach, [2]until the day in which He was
taken up, after He through the Holy Spirit had given commandments
to the apostles whom He had chosen, [3]to whom He also presented
Himself alive after His suffering by many infallible proofs, being seen by them
during forty days and speaking of the things pertaining to the kingdom of God.

The Holy Spirit Promised

[4]And being assembled together with *them,* He commanded them not to
depart from Jerusalem, but to wait for the Promise of the Father, "which,"
He said, "you have heard from Me; [5]for John truly baptized with water, but
you shall be baptized with the Holy Spirit not many days from now."
[6]Therefore, when they had come together, they asked Him, saying, "Lord,
will You at this time restore the kingdom to Israel?" [7]And He said to them,
"It is not for you to know times or seasons which the Father has put in His
own authority. [8]But you shall receive power when the Holy Spirit has come
upon you; and you shall be witnesses to Me[a] in Jerusalem, and in all Judea
and Samaria, and to the end of the earth."

Jesus Ascends to Heaven

[9]Now when He had spoken these things, while they watched, He was
taken up, and a cloud received Him out of their sight. [10]And while they
looked steadfastly toward heaven as He went up, behold, two men stood
by them in white apparel, [11]who also said, "Men of Galilee, why do you stand
gazing up into heaven? This *same* Jesus, who was taken up from you into
heaven, will so come in like manner as you saw Him go into heaven."

The Upper Room Prayer Meeting

[12]Then they returned to Jerusalem from the mount called Olivet, which
is near Jerusalem, a Sabbath day's journey. [13]And when they had entered,
they went up into the upper room where they were staying: Peter, James,
John, and Andrew; Philip and Thomas; Bartholomew and Matthew; James
the son of Alphaeus and Simon the Zealot; and Judas *the son* of James. [14]These
all continued with one accord in prayer and supplication,[b] with the women
and Mary the mother of Jesus, and with His brothers.

Matthias Chosen

[15]And in those days Peter stood up in the midst of the disciples[c] (altogether the number of names was about a hundred and twenty), and said,
[16]"Men *and* brethren, this Scripture had to be fulfilled, which the Holy Spirit
spoke before by the mouth of David concerning Judas, who became a guide
to those who arrested Jesus; [17]for he was numbered with us and obtained a
part in this ministry."

[18](Now this man purchased a field with the wages of iniquity; and
falling headlong, he burst open in the middle and all his entrails gushed
out. [19]And it became known to all those dwelling in Jerusalem; so that field
is called in their own language, Akel Dama, that is, Field of Blood.)

1:8 [a] NU-Text reads *My witnesses.*
1:14 [b] NU-Text omits *and supplication.*
1:15 [c] NU-Text reads *brethren.*

20"For it is written in the Book of Psalms:

'Let his dwelling place be desolate,
And let no one live in it';[d]

and,

'Let[e] *another take his office.'*[f]

21"Therefore, of these men who have accompanied us all the time that
the Lord Jesus went in and out among us, 22beginning from the baptism of
John to that day when He was taken up from us, one of these must become
a witness with us of His resurrection."
23And they proposed two: Joseph called Barsabas, who was surnamed
Justus, and Matthias. 24And they prayed and said, "You, O Lord, who know
the hearts of all, show which of these two You have chosen 25to take part in
this ministry and apostleship from which Judas by transgression fell, that
he might go to his own place." 26And they cast their lots, and the lot fell on
Matthias. And he was numbered with the eleven apostles.

Coming of the Holy Spirit

2 When the Day of Pentecost had fully come, they were all with one accord[g]
in one place. 2And suddenly there came a sound from heaven, as of a
rushing mighty wind, and it filled the whole house where they were sitting.
3Then there appeared to them divided tongues, as of fire, and *one* sat upon
each of them. 4And they were all filled with the Holy Spirit and began to
speak with other tongues, as the Spirit gave them utterance.

The Crowd's Response

5And there were dwelling in Jerusalem Jews, devout men, from every
nation under heaven. 6And when this sound occurred, the multitude came
together, and were confused, because everyone heard them speak in his own
language. 7Then they were all amazed and marveled, saying to one another,
"Look, are not all these who speak Galileans? 8And how *is it that* we hear,
each in our own language in which we were born? 9Parthians and Medes and
Elamites, those dwelling in Mesopotamia, Judea and Cappadocia, Pontus
and Asia, 10Phrygia and Pamphylia, Egypt and the parts of Libya adjoining
Cyrene, visitors from Rome, both Jews and proselytes, 11Cretans and
Arabs—we hear them speaking in our own tongues the wonderful works
of God." 12So they were all amazed and perplexed, saying to one another,
"Whatever could this mean?"
13Others mocking said, "They are full of new wine."

Peter's Sermon

14But Peter, standing up with the eleven, raised his voice and said to
them, "Men of Judea and all who dwell in Jerusalem, let this be known to you,
and heed my words. 15For these are not drunk, as you suppose, since it is *only*
the third hour of the day. 16But this is what was spoken by the prophet Joel:

17 *'And it shall come to pass in the last days, says God,*
That I will pour out of My Spirit on all flesh;
Your sons and your daughters shall prophesy,

1:20 [d] Psalm 69:25 [e] Psalm 109:8 [f] Greek *episkopen,* position of overseer
2:1 [g] NU-Text reads *together.*

LIFE LESSON

Acts 2:1-47

SITUATION In Old Testament times, God's Spirit did not permanently remain in people who trusted him. Instead, God usually sent his Spirit to inspire specific people at specific times. Though Jesus had talked with his disciples about the new role of the Spirit, the Jews were amazed at the outpouring of God's Spirit on the day of Pentecost and the fulfillment of Joel's prophecy.

OBSERVATION Christ's Spirit lives in us. The indwelling Spirit enables us to live out our faith. He guides, teaches, convicts, counsels, inspires, empowers, and bears fruit—all so that God may be glorified.

INSPIRATION Picture the scene. Peter, John, James. They came back. Banking on some zany possibility that the well of forgiveness still had a few drops, they came back. Daring to dream that the master had left them some word, some plan, some direction, they came back.

But little did they know, their wildest dream wasn't wild enough. Just as someone mumbles, "It's no use," they hear a noise. They hear a voice.

"Peace be with you."

Every head lifted. Every eye turned. Every mouth dropped open. Someone looked at the door.

It was still locked.

It was a moment the apostles would never forget, a story they would never cease to tell. The stone of the tomb was not enough to keep him *in.* The walls of the room were not enough to keep him *out.*

The one betrayed sought his betrayers. What did he say to them? Not "What a bunch of flops!" Not "I told you so." No "Where-were-you-when-I-needed-you?" speeches. But simply one phrase, "Peace be with you." The very thing they didn't have was the very thing he offered: peace.

It was too good to be true! So amazing was the appearance that some were saying, "Pinch me, I'm dreaming" even at the ascension. No wonder they returned to Jerusalem with great joy! No wonder they were always in the temple praising God!

Continued

A transformed group stood beside a transformed Peter as he announced some weeks later: "Therefore let all Israel be assured of this: God has made this Jesus, whom you crucified, both Lord and Christ."

No timidity in his words. No reluctance. About three thousand people believed his message.

The apostles sparked a movement. The people became followers of the death-conqueror. They couldn't hear enough or say enough about him. . . . Christ was their model, their message. They preached "Jesus Christ and him crucified," not for the lack of another topic, but because they couldn't exhaust this one.

What unlocked the doors of the apostles' hearts?

Simple. They saw Jesus. They encountered the Christ. Their sins collided with their Savior and their Savior won! . . .

A lot of things would happen to them over the next few decades. Many nights would be spent away from home. Hunger would gnaw at their bellies. Rain would soak their skin. Stones would bruise their bodies. Shipwrecks, lashings, martyrdom. But there was a scene in the repertoire of memories that caused them to never look back: the betrayed coming back to find his betrayers; not to scourge them, but to send them. Not to criticize them for forgetting, but to commission them to remember. *Remember* that he who was dead is alive and they who were guilty have been forgiven.

(From *Six Hours One Friday* by Max Lucado)

APPLICATION To change is not easy and not common. Most of us develop comfortable ruts. In your life today, where is change needed? What comfortable ruts are you in? Ask God to change your life through the power of the Holy Spirit.

EXPLORATION God's Spirit Living in Us—John 14:17; Romans 8:9, 15; 1 Corinthians 3:16; 6:19; 2 Corinthians 4:6-7, 16; Galatians 2:20; Ephesians 3:16-17; Colossians 1:27; 1 John 3:24; 4:4, 13.

Your young men shall see visions,
Your old men shall dream dreams.
18 *And on My menservants and on My maidservants*
I will pour out My Spirit in those days;
And they shall prophesy.
19 *I will show wonders in heaven above*
And signs in the earth beneath:
Blood and fire and vapor of smoke.
20 *The sun shall be turned into darkness,*
And the moon into blood,
Before the coming of the great and awesome day of the LORD.
21 *And it shall come to pass*
That whoever calls on the name of the LORD
Shall be saved.'[h]

22"Men of Israel, hear these words: Jesus of Nazareth, a Man attested by
God to you by miracles, wonders, and signs which God did through Him
in your midst, as you yourselves also know— 23Him, being delivered by the
determined purpose and foreknowledge of God, you have taken[i] by lawless hands, have crucified, and put to death; 24whom God raised up, having
loosed the pains of death, because it was not possible that He should be
held by it. 25For David says concerning Him:

'I foresaw the LORD always before my face,
For He is at my right hand, that I may not be shaken.
26 *Therefore my heart rejoiced, and my tongue was glad;*
Moreover my flesh also will rest in hope.
27 *For You will not leave my soul in Hades,*
Nor will You allow Your Holy One to see corruption.
28 *You have made known to me the ways of life;*
You will make me full of joy in Your presence.'[j]

29"Men *and* brethren, let *me* speak freely to you of the patriarch David,
that he is both dead and buried, and his tomb is with us to this day.
30Therefore, being a prophet, and knowing that God had sworn with an oath
to him that of the fruit of his body, according to the flesh, He would raise
up the Christ to sit on his throne,[k] 31he, foreseeing this, spoke concerning
the resurrection of the Christ, that His soul was not left in Hades, nor did
His flesh see corruption. 32This Jesus God has raised up, of which we are
all witnesses. 33Therefore being exalted to the right hand of God, and having received from the Father the promise of the Holy Spirit, He poured out
this which you now see and hear.
34"For David did not ascend into the heavens, but he says himself:

'The LORD said to my Lord,
"Sit at My right hand,
35 *Till I make Your enemies Your footstool."'*[l]

36"Therefore let all the house of Israel know assuredly that God has
made this Jesus, whom you crucified, both Lord and Christ."

2:21 [h] Joel 2:28–32
2:23 [i] NU-Text omits *have taken.*
2:28 [j] Psalm 16:8–11
2:30 [k] NU-Text omits *according to the flesh, He would raise up the Christ* and completes the verse with *He would seat one on his throne.*
2:35 [l] Psalm 110:1

37Now when they heard *this,* they were cut to the heart, and said to Peter and the rest of the apostles, "Men *and* brethren, what shall we do?"

38Then Peter said to them, "Repent, and let every one of you be baptized in the name of Jesus Christ for the remission of sins; and you shall receive the gift of the Holy Spirit. 39For the promise is to you and to your children, and to all who are afar off, as many as the Lord our God will call."

A Vital Church Grows

40And with many other words he testified and exhorted them, saying, "Be saved from this perverse generation." 41Then those who gladly[m] received his word were baptized; and that day about three thousand souls were added *to them.* 42And they continued steadfastly in the apostles' doctrine and fellowship, in the breaking of bread, and in prayers. 43Then fear came upon every soul, and many wonders and signs were done through the apostles. 44Now all who believed were together, and had all things in common, 45and sold their possessions and goods, and divided them among all, as anyone had need.

46So continuing daily with one accord in the temple, and breaking bread from house to house, they ate their food with gladness and simplicity of heart, 47praising God and having favor with all the people. And the Lord added to the church[n] daily those who were being saved.

A Lame Man Healed

3 Now Peter and John went up together to the temple at the hour of prayer, the ninth *hour.* 2And a certain man lame from his mother's womb was carried, whom they laid daily at the gate of the temple which is called Beautiful, to ask alms from those who entered the temple; 3who, seeing Peter and John about to go into the temple, asked for alms. 4And fixing his eyes on him, with John, Peter said, "Look at us." 5So he gave them his attention, expecting to receive something from them. 6Then Peter said, "Silver and gold I do not have, but what I do have I give you: In the name of Jesus Christ of Nazareth, rise up and walk." 7And he took him by the right hand and lifted *him* up, and immediately his feet and ankle bones received strength. 8So he, leaping up, stood and walked and entered the temple with them—walking, leaping, and praising God. 9And all the people saw him walking and praising God. 10Then they knew that it was he who sat begging alms at the Beautiful Gate of the temple; and they were filled with wonder and amazement at what had happened to him.

Preaching in Solomon's Portico

11Now as the lame man who was healed held on to Peter and John, all the people ran together to them in the porch which is called Solomon's, greatly amazed. 12So when Peter saw *it,* he responded to the people: "Men of Israel, why do you marvel at this? Or why look so intently at us, as though by our own power or godliness we had made this man walk? 13The God of Abraham, Isaac, and Jacob, the God of our fathers, glorified His Servant Jesus, whom you delivered up and denied in the presence of Pilate, when he was determined to let *Him* go. 14But you denied the Holy One and the Just, and asked for a murderer to be granted to you, 15and killed the Prince of life, whom God raised from the dead, of which we are witnesses. 16And His name, through faith in His name, has made this man strong, whom you see and know. Yes, the faith which comes through Him has given him this perfect soundness in the presence of you all.

17"Yet now, brethren, I know that you did *it* in ignorance, as *did* also your rulers. 18But those things which God foretold by the mouth of all His prophets, that the Christ would suffer, He has thus fulfilled. 19Repent therefore and be converted, that your sins may be blotted out, so that times of refreshing may come from the presence of the Lord, 20and that He may send Jesus Christ, who was preached to you before,[o] 21whom heaven must receive until the times of restoration of all things, which God has spoken by the mouth of all His holy prophets since the world began. 22For Moses truly said to the fathers, *'The LORD your God will raise up for you a Prophet like me from your brethren. Him you shall hear in all things, whatever He says to you.* 23*And it shall be that every soul who will not hear that Prophet shall be utterly destroyed from among the people.'*[p] 24Yes, and all the prophets, from Samuel and those who follow, as many as have spoken, have also foretold[q] these days. 25You are sons of the prophets, and of the covenant which God made with our fathers, saying to Abraham, *'And in your seed all the families of the earth shall be blessed.'*[r] 26To you first,

2:41 [m] NU-Text omits *gladly.*
2:47 [n] NU-Text omits *to the church.*
3:20 [o] NU-Text and M-Text read *Christ Jesus, who was ordained for you before.*
3:23 [p] Deuteronomy 18:15, 18, 19
3:24 [q] NU-Text and M-Text read *proclaimed.*
3:25 [r] Genesis 22:18; 26:4; 28:14

LIFE LESSON

Acts 4:1-37

SITUATION Because so many Jews longed for a political messiah to save them from Roman rule, they failed to recognize the Messiah who suffered instead.

OBSERVATION The world offers many religions, opinions, and philosophies, but the Bible teaches that only Jesus Christ can reconcile people to God through his death and resurrection.

INSPIRATION Jesus was alone. He had come to His own, and His own received Him not. . . . The crowds who had so recently shouted, "Hosanna," had that very day shouted, "Crucify him. Crucify him." Now even His loyal twelve had left.

And at last we hear Him cry out, "My God, my God, why hast thou forsaken me?" Not only had He been forsaken by His human companions, but now in that desperate and lonely hour, He—because He was bearing our sins in His own body on the cross—had been forsaken by God as well. Jesus was enduring the suffering and judgment of hell for you and me.

Hell, essentially, is separation from God. . . . Jesus suffered its agony for you, in your place. Now God says, Repent, believe on Christ, receive Christ, and you will never know the sorrow, the loneliness and the agony of hell. . . .

Christ can give you power to overcome every sin and habit in your life. He can break the ropes, fetters and chains of sin; but you must repent, confess, commit and surrender yourself to Him first. Right now, it can be settled, and you can know the peace, joy and fellowship of Christ.

(From *Peace with God* by Billy Graham)

APPLICATION Does "one way" to God seem unfair and narrow-minded? Not when you realize the generosity, compassion, and initiative that God's way involved. Try to be equally compassionate (and even knowledgeable) about other beliefs, by sharing God's Good News with people heading the wrong way.

EXPLORATION Salvation in Christ Alone—John 14:6; Romans 3:21-24; 5:1, 6-10; 1 Corinthians 3:11; 2 Corinthians 5:21; 1 Timothy 2:5; 1 Peter 2:24; 1 John 2:22-23.

God, having raised up His Servant Jesus, sent Him to bless you, in turning away every one *of you* from your iniquities."

Peter and John Arrested

4 Now as they spoke to the people, the priests, the captain of the temple, and the Sadducees came upon them, 2being greatly disturbed that they taught the people and preached in Jesus the resurrection from the dead. 3And they laid hands on them, and put *them* in custody until the next day, for it was already evening. 4However, many of those who heard the word believed; and the number of the men came to be about five thousand.

Addressing the Sanhedrin

5And it came to pass, on the next day, that their rulers, elders, and scribes, 6as well as Annas the high priest, Caiaphas, John, and Alexander, and as many as were of the family of the high priest, were gathered together at Jerusalem. 7And when they had set them in the midst, they asked, "By what power or by what name have you done this?"

8Then Peter, filled with the Holy Spirit, said to them, "Rulers of the people and elders of Israel: 9If we this day are judged for a good deed *done* to a helpless man, by what means he has been made well, 10let it be known to you all, and to all the people of Israel, that by the name of Jesus Christ of Nazareth, whom you crucified, whom God raised from the dead, by Him this man stands here before you whole. 11This is the *'stone which was rejected by you builders, which has become the chief cornerstone.'*[s] 12Nor is there salvation in any other, for there is no other name under heaven given among men by which we must be saved."

The Name of Jesus Forbidden

13Now when they saw the boldness of Peter and John, and perceived that they were uneducated and untrained men, they marveled. And they realized that they had been with Jesus. 14And seeing the man who had been healed standing with them, they could say nothing against it. 15But when they had commanded them to go aside out of the council, they conferred among themselves, 16saying, "What shall we do to these men? For, indeed, that a notable miracle has been done through them *is* evident to all who dwell in Jerusalem, and we cannot deny *it*. 17But so that it spreads no further among the people, let us severely threaten them, that from now on they speak to no man in this name."

18So they called them and commanded them not to speak at all nor teach in the name of Jesus. 19But Peter and John answered and said to them, "Whether it is right in the sight of God to listen to you more than to God, you judge. 20For we cannot but speak the things which we have seen and heard." 21So when they had further threatened them, they let them go, finding no way of punishing them, because of the people, since they all glorified God for what had been done. 22For the man was over forty years old on whom this miracle of healing had been performed.

Prayer for Boldness

23And being let go, they went to their own *companions* and reported all that the chief priests and elders had said to them. 24So when they heard

4:11 [s] Psalm 118:22

that, they raised their voice to God with one accord and said: "Lord, You
are God, who made heaven and earth and the sea, and all that is in them,
[25]who by the mouth of Your servant David[t] have said:

'Why did the nations rage,
And the people plot vain things?
26 *The kings of the earth took their stand,*
And the rulers were gathered together
Against the L*ORD and against His Christ.'*[u]

[27]"For truly against Your holy Servant Jesus, whom You anointed, both
Herod and Pontius Pilate, with the Gentiles and the people of Israel, were
gathered together [28]to do whatever Your hand and Your purpose determined
before to be done. [29]Now, Lord, look on their threats, and grant to Your
servants that with all boldness they may speak Your word, [30]by stretching
out Your hand to heal, and that signs and wonders may be done through
the name of Your holy Servant Jesus."
[31]And when they had prayed, the place where they were assembled together was shaken; and they were all filled with the Holy Spirit, and they
spoke the word of God with boldness.

Sharing in All Things

[32]Now the multitude of those who believed were of one heart and one
soul; neither did anyone say that any of the things he possessed was his
own, but they had all things in common. [33]And with great power the apostles gave witness to the resurrection of the Lord Jesus. And great grace was
upon them all. [34]Nor was there anyone among them who lacked; for all
who were possessors of lands or houses sold them, and brought the proceeds of the things that were sold, [35]and laid *them* at the apostles' feet; and
they distributed to each as anyone had need.
[36]And Joses,[v] who was also named Barnabas by the apostles (which is
translated Son of Encouragement), a Levite of the country of Cyprus, [37]hav-
ing land, sold *it,* and brought the money and laid *it* at the apostles' feet.

Lying to the Holy Spirit

5 But a certain man named Ananias, with Sapphira his wife, sold a possession. [2]And he kept back *part* of the proceeds, his wife also being aware
of it, and brought a certain part and laid *it* at the apostles' feet. [3]But Peter said,
"Ananias, why has Satan filled your heart to lie to the Holy Spirit and keep
back *part* of the price of the land for yourself? [4]While it remained, was it not
your own? And after it was sold, was it not in your own control? Why have you
conceived this thing in your heart? You have not lied to men but to God."
[5]Then Ananias, hearing these words, fell down and breathed his last. So
great fear came upon all those who heard these things. [6]And the young
men arose and wrapped him up, carried *him* out, and buried *him.*
[7]Now it was about three hours later when his wife came in, not knowing
what had happened. [8]And Peter answered her, "Tell me whether you sold
the land for so much?"
She said, "Yes, for so much."

4:25 [t] NU-Text reads *who through the Holy Spirit, by the mouth of our father, Your servant David.*
4:26 [u] Psalm 2:1, 2
4:36 [v] NU-Text reads *Joseph.*

LIFE LESSON

Acts 5:1-42

SITUATION When God empowered the apostles to perform miracles and amazing signs, the disciples caught the attention of jealous and skeptical religious leaders. Even some Pharisees came to believe in Jesus.

OBSERVATION Jesus' followers can find comfort and even joy in knowing that suffering for Jesus makes us more like him.

INSPIRATION On God's anvil. Perhaps you've been there.

Melted down. Formless. Undone.

I know. I've been on it. It's rough. It's a spiritual slump, a famine. The fire goes out. Although the fire may flame for a moment, it soon disappears. We drift downward. Downward into the foggy valley of question, the misty lowland of discouragement. . . .

Passion? It slips out the door.

Enthusiasm? Are you kidding?

Anvil time. . . .

Pound, pound, pound.

I hope you're not on the anvil. (Unless you need to be and, if so, I hope you are.) Anvil time is not to be avoided; it's to be experienced. . . . To escape it could be to escape God.

God sees our life from beginning to end. He may lead us through a storm at age thirty so we can endure a hurricane at age sixty. An instrument is useful only if it's in the right shape. A dull ax or a bent screwdriver needs attention, and so do we. A good blacksmith keeps his tools in shape. So does God.

Should God place you on his anvil, be thankful. It means he thinks you're still worth reshaping.

(From *On the Anvil* by Max Lucado)

APPLICATION As a result of your faith, relatives may give you a hard time or friends may write you off. Remember that you are following Jesus' footsteps. Pray for the joy that overcomes troubles, given by God, just for you.

EXPLORATION Attitudes During Trouble—Matthew 5:10-12; 10:22; Romans 8:17; 2 Corinthians 4:8-9, 16-17; Hebrews 10:32-34; James 5:10; 1 Peter 2:20-21; 4:12-13; 5:10.

9 Then Peter said to her, "How is it that you have agreed together to test the Spirit of the Lord? Look, the feet of those who have buried your husband *are* at the door, and they will carry you out." 10 Then immediately she fell down at his feet and breathed her last. And the young men came in and found her dead, and carrying *her* out, buried *her* by her husband. 11 So great fear came upon all the church and upon all who heard these things.

Continuing Power in the Church

12 And through the hands of the apostles many signs and wonders were done among the people. And they were all with one accord in Solomon's Porch. 13 Yet none of the rest dared join them, but the people esteemed them highly. 14 And believers were increasingly added to the Lord, multitudes of both men and women, 15 so that they brought the sick out into the streets and laid *them* on beds and couches, that at least the shadow of Peter passing by might fall on some of them. 16 Also a multitude gathered from the surrounding cities to Jerusalem, bringing sick people and those who were tormented by unclean spirits, and they were all healed.

Imprisoned Apostles Freed

17 Then the high priest rose up, and all those who *were* with him (which is the sect of the Sadducees), and they were filled with indignation, 18 and laid their hands on the apostles and put them in the common prison. 19 But at night an angel of the Lord opened the prison doors and brought them out, and said, 20 "Go, stand in the temple and speak to the people all the words of this life."

21 And when they heard *that,* they entered the temple early in the morning and taught. But the high priest and those with him came and called the council together, with all the elders of the children of Israel, and sent to the prison to have them brought.

Apostles on Trial Again

22 But when the officers came and did not find them in the prison, they returned and reported, 23 saying, "Indeed we found the prison shut securely, and the guards standing outside[w] before the doors; but when we opened them, we found no one inside!" 24 Now when the high priest,[x] the captain of the temple, and the chief priests heard these things, they wondered what the outcome would be. 25 So one came and told them, saying,[y] "Look, the men whom you put in prison are standing in the temple and teaching the people!"

26 Then the captain went with the officers and brought them without violence, for they feared the people, lest they should be stoned. 27 And when they had brought them, they set *them* before the council. And the high priest asked them, 28 saying, "Did we not strictly command you not to teach in this name? And look, you have filled Jerusalem with your doctrine, and intend to bring this Man's blood on us!"

29 But Peter and the *other* apostles answered and said: "We ought to obey God rather than men. 30 The God of our fathers raised up Jesus whom you murdered by hanging on a tree. 31 Him God has exalted to His right hand *to be* Prince and Savior, to give repentance to Israel and forgiveness of sins. 32 And we are His witnesses to these things, and *so* also *is* the Holy Spirit whom God has given to those who obey Him."

Gamaliel's Advice

33 When they heard *this,* they were furious and plotted to kill them. 34 Then one in the council stood up, a Pharisee named Gamaliel, a teacher of the law held in respect by all the people, and commanded them to put the apostles outside for a little while. 35 And he said to them: "Men of Israel, take heed to yourselves what you intend to do regarding these men. 36 For some time ago Theudas rose up, claiming to be somebody. A number of men, about four hundred, joined him. He was slain, and all who obeyed him were scattered and came to nothing. 37 After this man, Judas of Galilee rose up in the days of the census, and drew away many people after him. He also perished, and all who obeyed him were dispersed. 38 And now I say to you, keep away from these men and let them alone; for if this plan or this work is of men, it will come to nothing; 39 but if it is of God, you cannot overthrow it—lest you even be found to fight against God."

40 And they agreed with him, and when they had called for the apostles and beaten *them,* they commanded that they should not speak in the name of Jesus, and let them go. 41 So they departed from the presence of the council, rejoicing that they were counted worthy to suffer shame for His[z] name. 42 And daily in the temple, and in every house, they did not cease teaching and preaching Jesus *as* the Christ.

Seven Chosen to Serve

6 Now in those days, when *the number of* the disciples was multiplying, there arose a complaint against the Hebrews by the Hellenists,[a] because their

5:23 [w] NU-Text and M-Text omit *outside.*
5:24 [x] NU-Text omits *the high priest.*
5:25 [y] NU-Text and M-Text omit *saying.*
5:41 [z] NU-Text reads *the name;* M-Text reads *the name of Jesus.*
6:1 [a] That is, Greek-speaking Jews

widows were neglected in the daily distribution. 2Then the twelve summoned the multitude of the disciples and said, "It is not desirable that we
should leave the word of God and serve tables. 3Therefore, brethren, seek
out from among you seven men of *good* reputation, full of the Holy Spirit
and wisdom, whom we may appoint over this business; 4but we will give
ourselves continually to prayer and to the ministry of the word."
5And the saying pleased the whole multitude. And they chose Stephen, a
man full of faith and the Holy Spirit, and Philip, Prochorus, Nicanor, Timon,
Parmenas, and Nicolas, a proselyte from Antioch, 6whom they set before
the apostles; and when they had prayed, they laid hands on them.
7Then the word of God spread, and the number of the disciples multiplied greatly in Jerusalem, and a great many of the priests were obedient
to the faith.

Stephen Accused of Blasphemy

8And Stephen, full of faith[b] and power, did great wonders and signs among
the people. 9Then there arose some from what is called the Synagogue of
the Freedmen (Cyrenians, Alexandrians, and those from Cilicia and Asia),
disputing with Stephen. 10And they were not able to resist the wisdom and
the Spirit by which he spoke. 11Then they secretly induced men to say, "We
have heard him speak blasphemous words against Moses and God." 12And
they stirred up the people, the elders, and the scribes; and they came upon
him, seized him, and brought *him* to the council. 13They also set up false
witnesses who said, "This man does not cease to speak blasphemous[c]
words against this holy place and the law; 14for we have heard him say that
this Jesus of Nazareth will destroy this place and change the customs
which Moses delivered to us." 15And all who sat in the council, looking
steadfastly at him, saw his face as the face of an angel.

Stephen's Address: The Call of Abraham

7 Then the high priest said, "Are these things so?"
2And he said, "Brethren and fathers, listen: The God of glory appeared
to our father Abraham when he was in Mesopotamia, before he dwelt in
Haran, 3and said to him, *'Get out of your country and from your relatives,
and come to a land that I will show you.'*[d] 4Then he came out of the land of
the Chaldeans and dwelt in Haran. And from there, when his father was
dead, He moved him to this land in which you now dwell. 5And *God* gave
him no inheritance in it, not even *enough* to set his foot on. But even when
Abraham had no child, He promised to give it to him for a possession, and
to his descendants after him. 6But God spoke in this way: that his descendants would dwell in a foreign land, and that they would bring them into
bondage and oppress *them* four hundred years. 7*'And the nation to whom
they will be in bondage I will judge,'*[e] said God, *'and after that they shall
come out and serve Me in this place.'*[f] 8Then He gave him the covenant of
circumcision; and so *Abraham* begot Isaac and circumcised him on the
eighth day; and Isaac *begot* Jacob, and Jacob begot the twelve patriarchs.

The Patriarchs in Egypt

9"And the patriarchs, becoming envious, sold Joseph into Egypt. But

6:8 [b] NU-Text reads *grace.*
6:13 [c] NU-Text omits *blasphemous.*
7:3 [d] Genesis 12:1
7:7 [e] Genesis 15:14 [f] Exodus 3:12

LIFE LESSON

Acts 6:1-15

SITUATION Jewish Christians of different ethnic backgrounds were living in Jerusalem, and some disagreements split along ethnic lines. The leadership of the early church resolved these differences in a fair way.

OBSERVATION A point of contention arose among the early group of Christians over an important issue. Church leaders sought to honor God and gave a wise solution to the problem.

INSPIRATION Who are the people you know who appear to get along well with others? . . . The people I know who get along well with others are enjoyable to be with. They show genuine interest in others. When they are with you, they are really with you.

I think of a man I know who is very gracious, friendly, and refined in his dealings with people, whether they are his friends, his co-workers, or the waiters who serve him. His pleasant manner is not put on; it's genuine. . . .

A man who encourages and builds up others, he is compassionate and empathetic, touching people in times of joy and sorrow. He fits the description of a likable character I read about recently in a novel. This man was described as "large-hearted with everyone." The way my friend treats the people in his life is how most people want to be treated.

Do these qualities describe how you would like to be treated? Are these qualities evident in your dealings with others? It takes time to develop the qualities I find in my friend. I'm still working on them in my life. Fortunately, we all have the capacity to learn them and put them into practice.

(From *How to Get Along with Almost Anyone* by H. Norman Wright)

APPLICATION When disagreements with other Believers come up, work for solutions that help both sides, respecting opinions that differ while maintaining unity.

EXPLORATION Disagreements among Believers—Proverbs 17:14; 1 Corinthians 1:10; 3:3; 6:1-7; 2 Corinthians 12:20; Ephesians 4:2-4; Philippians 2:3; 1 Peter 3:8-9.

God was with him [10]and delivered him out of all his
troubles, and gave him favor and wisdom in the presence of Pharaoh, king of Egypt; and he made him governor over Egypt and all his house. [11]Now a famine
and great trouble came over all the land of Egypt and
Canaan, and our fathers found no sustenance. [12]But
when Jacob heard that there was grain in Egypt, he
sent out our fathers first. [13]And the second *time* Joseph was made known to his brothers, and Joseph's
family became known to the Pharaoh. [14]Then Joseph
sent and called his father Jacob and all his relatives to
him, seventy-five[g] people. [15]So Jacob went down to
Egypt; and he died, he and our fathers. [16]And they
were carried back to Shechem and laid in the tomb
that Abraham bought for a sum of money from the
sons of Hamor, *the father* of Shechem.

God Delivers Israel by Moses

[17]"But when the time of the promise drew near which
God had sworn to Abraham, the people grew and
multiplied in Egypt [18]till another king arose who did
not know Joseph. [19]This man dealt treacherously with
our people, and oppressed our forefathers, making
them expose their babies, so that they might not live.
[20]At this time Moses was born, and was well pleasing
to God; and he was brought up in his father's house for
three months. [21]But when he was set out, Pharaoh's
daughter took him away and brought him up as her
own son. [22]And Moses was learned in all the wisdom
of the Egyptians, and was mighty in words and deeds.

[23]"Now when he was forty years old, it came into his
heart to visit his brethren, the children of Israel. [24]And
seeing one of *them* suffer wrong, he defended and
avenged him who was oppressed, and struck down the
Egyptian. [25]For he supposed that his brethren would
have understood that God would deliver them by his
hand, but they did not understand. [26]And the next day
he appeared to two of them as they were fighting, and
tried to reconcile them, saying, 'Men, you are brethren;
why do you wrong one another?' [27]But he who did his
neighbor wrong pushed him away, saying, *'Who
made you a ruler and a judge over us? [28]Do you want
to kill me as you did the Egyptian yesterday?'*[h] [29]Then,
at this saying, Moses fled and became a dweller in the
land of Midian, where he had two sons.

[30]"And when forty years had passed, an Angel of
the Lord[i] appeared to him in a flame of fire in a bush,
in the wilderness of Mount Sinai. [31]When Moses saw
it, he marveled at the sight; and as he drew near to observe, the voice of the Lord came to him, [32]*saying, 'I
am the God of your fathers—the God of Abraham,
the God of Isaac, and the God of Jacob.'*[j] And Moses
trembled and dared not look. [33]*'Then the LORD said to
him, "Take your sandals off your feet, for the place
where you stand is holy ground. [34]I have surely seen
the oppression of My people who are in Egypt; I have
heard their groaning and have come down to deliver
them. And now come, I will send you to Egypt." '*[k]

[35]"This Moses whom they rejected, saying, *'Who
made you a ruler and a judge?'*[l] is the one God sent *to
be* a ruler and a deliverer by the hand of the Angel who
appeared to him in the bush. [36]He brought them out,
after he had shown wonders and signs in the land of
Egypt, and in the Red Sea, and in the wilderness forty
years.

Israel Rebels Against God

[37]"This is that Moses who said to the children of Israel,[m] *'The LORD your God will raise up for you a Prophet
like me from your brethren. Him you shall hear.'*[n]

[38]"This is he who was in the congregation in the
wilderness with the Angel who spoke to him on Mount
Sinai, and *with* our fathers, the one who received the living oracles to give to us, [39]whom our fathers would not
obey, but rejected. And in their hearts they turned back
to Egypt, [40]saying to Aaron, *'Make us gods to go before
us; as for this Moses who brought us out of the land of
Egypt, we do not know what has become of him.'*[o] [41]And
they made a calf in those days, offered sacrifices to the
idol, and rejoiced in the works of their own hands.
[42]Then God turned and gave them up to worship the host
of heaven, as it is written in the book of the Prophets:

'Did you offer Me slaughtered animals
and sacrifices during forty years
in the wilderness,
O house of Israel?
43 *You also took up the tabernacle of Moloch,*
And the star of your god Remphan,
Images which you made to worship;
And I will carry you away beyond Babylon.'[p]

7:14 [g] Or *seventy* (compare Exodus 1:5)
7:28 [h] Exodus 2:14
7:30 [i] NU-Text omits *of the Lord.*
7:32 [j] Exodus 3:6, 15
7:34 [k] Exodus 3:5, 7, 8, 10
7:35 [l] Exodus 2:14
7:37 [m] Deuteronomy 18:15 [n] NU-Text and M-Text omit *Him you shall hear.*
7:40 [o] Exodus 32:1, 23
7:43 [p] Amos 5:25–27

God's True Tabernacle

44"Our fathers had the tabernacle of witness in the wilderness, as He appointed, instructing Moses to make it according to the pattern that he had
seen, 45which our fathers, having received it in turn, also brought with Joshua
into the land possessed by the Gentiles, whom God drove out before the face
of our fathers until the days of David, 46who found favor before God and asked
to find a dwelling for the God of Jacob. 47But Solomon built Him a house.
48"However, the Most High does not dwell in temples made with hands,
as the prophet says:

49 *'Heaven is My throne,*
And earth is My footstool.
What house will you build for Me? says the LORD,
Or what is the place of My rest?
50 *Has My hand not made all these things?'*[q]

Israel Resists the Holy Spirit

51"*You* stiff-necked and uncircumcised in heart and ears! You always resist
the Holy Spirit; as your fathers *did,* so *do* you. 52Which of the prophets did your
fathers not persecute? And they killed those who foretold the coming of the
Just One, of whom you now have become the betrayers and murderers, 53who
have received the law by the direction of angels and have not kept *it.*"

Stephen the Martyr

54When they heard these things they were cut to the heart, and they
gnashed at him with *their* teeth. 55But he, being full of the Holy Spirit, gazed
into heaven and saw the glory of God, and Jesus standing at the right hand
of God, 56and said, "Look! I see the heavens opened and the Son of Man
standing at the right hand of God!"
57Then they cried out with a loud voice, stopped their ears, and ran at
him with one accord; 58and they cast *him* out of the city and stoned *him.*
And the witnesses laid down their clothes at the feet of a young man named
Saul. 59And they stoned Stephen as he was calling on *God* and saying,
"Lord Jesus, receive my spirit." 60Then he knelt down and cried out with a
loud voice, "Lord, do not charge them with this sin." And when he had
said this, he fell asleep.

Saul Persecutes the Church

8 Now Saul was consenting to his death.
At that time a great persecution arose against the church which was at
Jerusalem; and they were all scattered throughout the regions of Judea
and Samaria, except the apostles. 2And devout men carried Stephen *to his*
burial, and made great lamentation over him.
3As for Saul, he made havoc of the church, entering every house, and
dragging off men and women, committing *them* to prison.

Christ Is Preached in Samaria

4Therefore those who were scattered went everywhere preaching the
word. 5Then Philip went down to the[r] city of Samaria and preached Christ

7:50 [q] Isaiah 66:1, 2
8:5 [r] Or *a*

Life Lesson

Acts 7:1–8:1a

SITUATION Stephen's speech summarized Jewish history. God had blessed the Hebrew nation magnificently, Stephen recalled, but once again their leaders had turned against God.

OBSERVATION Stephen's speech repeatedly referred to human rebelliousness toward God. It shows how desperately we try to avoid God's truth—even to the extent of killing the messenger. At his death, Stephen looked to Christ.

INSPIRATION The story of young Matthew Huffman came across my desk the week I was writing this chapter. He was the six-year-old son of missionaries in Salvador, Brazil. One morning he began to complain of fever. As his temperature went up, he began losing his eyesight. His mother and father put him in the car and raced him to the hospital.

As they were driving and he was lying on his mother's lap, he did something his parents will never forget. He extended his hand in the air. His mother took it and he pulled it away. He extended it again. She again took it and he, again, pulled it back and reached into the air. Confused, the mother asked her son, "What are you reaching for, Matthew?"

"I'm reaching for Jesus' hand," he answered. And with those words he closed his eyes and slid into a coma from which he never would awaken. He died two days later, a victim of bacterial meningitis.

Of all the things he didn't learn in his short life, he'd learned the most important: who to reach for in the hour of death.

(From *And the Angels Were Silent* by Max Lucado)

APPLICATION Have you developed the practice of constantly looking to Jesus? If you have, you will reach to him during your most difficult hour. If you haven't, ask him to accompany you in all your thoughts.

EXPLORATION Spiritual Battle—Ephesians 6:10-16; Philippians 1:27-28; 1 Thessalonians 5:8; 1 Timothy 6:12; James 1:2-4; 1 Peter 1:6-7.

LIFE LESSON

Acts 8:1b-40

SITUATION Persecution against the church after Stephen's death forced Believers to go beyond Jerusalem to share the gospel. Philip was the first example of such missionary activity.

OBSERVATION The gospel is for everyone regardless of ethnic group. Therefore, Believers should be ready to witness to anyone who may be seeking.

INSPIRATION You've heard the voice whispering your name, haven't you? You've felt the nudge to go and sensed the urge to speak. Hasn't it occurred to you?

You invite a couple over for coffee. Nothing heroic, just a nice evening with old friends. But from the moment you enter, you can feel the tension. Colder than glaciers, they are. You can tell something is wrong. Typically you're not one to inquire, but you feel a concern that won't be silent. So you ask.

You are in a business meeting where one of your co-workers gets raked over the coals. Everyone else is thinking, *I'm glad that wasn't me.* But the Holy Spirit is leading you to think, *How hard this must be.* So, after the meeting you approach the employee and express your concern.

You notice the fellow on the other side of the church auditorium. He looks a bit out of place, what with his strange clothing and all. You learn that he is from Africa, in town on business. The next Sunday he is back. And the third Sunday he is present. You introduce yourself. He tells you how he is fascinated by the faith and how he wants to learn more. Rather than offer to teach him, you simply urge him to read the Bible.

to them. [6]And the multitudes with one accord heeded the things spoken by Philip, hearing and seeing the miracles which he did. [7]For unclean spirits, crying with a loud voice, came out of many who were possessed; and many who were paralyzed and lame were healed. [8]And there was great joy in that city.

The Sorcerer's Profession of Faith

[9]But there was a certain man called Simon, who previously practiced sorcery in the city and astonished the people of Samaria, claiming that he was someone great, [10]to whom they all gave heed, from the least to the greatest, saying, "This man is the great power of God." [11]And they heeded him because he had astonished them with his sorceries for a long time. [12]But when they believed Philip as he preached the things concerning the kingdom of God and the name of Jesus Christ, both men and women were baptized. [13]Then Simon himself also believed; and when he was baptized he continued with Philip, and was amazed, seeing the miracles and signs which were done.

The Sorcerer's Sin

[14]Now when the apostles who were at Jerusalem heard that Samaria had received the word of God, they sent Peter and John to them, [15]who, when they had come down, prayed for them that they might receive the Holy Spirit. [16]For as yet He had fallen upon none of them. They had only been baptized in the name of the Lord Jesus. [17]Then they laid hands on them, and they received the Holy Spirit.

[18]And when Simon saw that through the laying on of the apostles' hands the Holy Spirit was given, he offered them money, [19]saying, "Give me this power also, that anyone on whom I lay hands may receive the Holy Spirit."

[20]But Peter said to him, "Your money perish with you, because you thought that the gift of God could be purchased with money! [21]You have neither part nor portion in this matter, for your heart is not right in the sight of God. [22]Repent therefore of this your wickedness, and pray God if perhaps the thought of your heart may be forgiven you. [23]For I see that you are poisoned by bitterness and bound by iniquity."

[24]Then Simon answered and said, "Pray to the Lord for me, that none of the things which you have spoken may come upon me."

[25]So when they had testified and preached the word of the Lord, they returned to Jerusalem, preaching the gospel in many villages of the Samaritans.

Christ Is Preached to an Ethiopian

[26]Now an angel of the Lord spoke to Philip, saying, "Arise and go toward the south along the road which goes down from Jerusalem to Gaza." This is desert. [27]So he arose and went. And behold, a man of Ethiopia, a eunuch of great authority under Candace the queen of the Ethiopians, who had charge of all her treasury, and had come to Jerusalem to worship, [28]was returning. And sitting in his chariot, he was reading Isaiah the prophet. [29]Then the Spirit said to Philip, "Go near and overtake this chariot."

[30]So Philip ran to him, and heard him reading the prophet Isaiah, and said, "Do you understand what you are reading?"

[31]And he said, "How can I, unless someone guides me?" And he asked Philip to come up and sit with him. [32]The place in the Scripture which he read was this:

"He was led as a sheep to the slaughter;
And as a lamb before its shearer is silent,
So He opened not His mouth.
33 *In His humiliation His justice was taken away,*
And who will declare His generation?
For His life is taken from the earth."[s]

34 So the eunuch answered Philip and said, "I ask you, of whom does the
prophet say this, of himself or of some other man?" 35 Then Philip opened
his mouth, and beginning at this Scripture, preached Jesus to him. 36 Now
as they went down the road, they came to some water. And the eunuch
said, "See, *here is* water. What hinders me from being baptized?"
37 Then Philip said, "If you believe with all your heart, you may."
And he answered and said, "I believe that Jesus Christ is the Son of God."[t]
38 So he commanded the chariot to stand still. And both Philip and the
eunuch went down into the water, and he baptized him. 39 Now when they
came up out of the water, the Spirit of the Lord caught Philip away, so that
the eunuch saw him no more; and he went on his way rejoicing. 40 But Philip
was found at Azotus. And passing through, he preached in all the cities till
he came to Caesarea.

The Damascus Road: Saul Converted

9 Then Saul, still breathing threats and murder against the disciples of
the Lord, went to the high priest 2 and asked letters from him to the
synagogues of Damascus, so that if he found any who were of the Way,
whether men or women, he might bring them bound to Jerusalem.
3 As he journeyed he came near Damascus, and suddenly a light shone
around him from heaven. 4 Then he fell to the ground, and heard a voice
saying to him, "Saul, Saul, why are you persecuting Me?"
5 And he said, "Who are You, Lord?"
Then the Lord said, "I am Jesus, whom you are persecuting.[u] It *is* hard
for you to kick against the goads."
6 So he, trembling and astonished, said, "Lord, what do You want me to do?"
Then the Lord *said* to him, "Arise and go into the city, and you will be
told what you must do."
7 And the men who journeyed with him stood speechless, hearing a voice
but seeing no one. 8 Then Saul arose from the ground, and when his eyes were
opened he saw no one. But they led him by the hand and brought *him* into
Damascus. 9 And he was three days without sight, and neither ate nor drank.

Ananias Baptizes Saul

10 Now there was a certain disciple at Damascus named Ananias; and to
him the Lord said in a vision, "Ananias."
And he said, "Here I am, Lord."
11 So the Lord *said* to him, "Arise and go to the street called Straight, and
inquire at the house of Judas for *one* called Saul of Tarsus, for behold, he is
praying. 12 And in a vision he has seen a man named Ananias coming in
and putting *his* hand on him, so that he might receive his sight."

8:33 [s] Isaiah 53:7, 8
8:37 [t] NU-Text and M-Text omit this verse. It is found in Western texts, including the Latin tradition.
9:5 [u] NU-Text and M-Text omit the last sentence of verse 5 and begin verse 6 with *But arise and go.*

Later in the week, you regret not being more direct. You call the office where he is consulting and learn that he is leaving today for home. You know in your heart you can't let him leave. So you rush to the airport and find him awaiting his flight, with a Bible open on his lap.

"Do you understand what you are reading?" you inquire.

"How can I, unless someone explains it to me?"

And so you, like Philip, explain. And he, like the Ethiopian, believes. Baptism is requested and baptism is offered. He catches a later flight and you catch a glimpse of what it means to be led by the Spirit.

Were there lights? You just lit one. Were there voices? You just were one. Was there a miracle? You just witnessed one. Who knows? If the Bible were being written today, that might be your name in the eighth chapter of Acts.

(From *When God Whispers Your Name* by Max Lucado)

APPLICATION Is there anyone you are not willing to tell about Jesus? Is there any place you are not willing to take the Good News? Ask God to give you the willingness and the courage. Let him direct you where he wants, not where you want.

EXPLORATION Witnessing—Acts 13:46-47; Romans 1:14-16; 10:8-9; 1 Corinthians 15:1-4; 2 Timothy 1:8; 1 Peter 1:23-25; Galatians 2:7-9.

Life Lesson

Acts 9:1-43

SITUATION Saul (later known as Paul) continued his aggressive persecution of the church. Many Believers had fled Jerusalem to seek refuge in other cities. Saul went as far as Damascus, Syria (150 miles from Jerusalem) to track down Christians. It was on this trip that God saved him. After Saul's conversion, the church enjoyed a time of peace during which Peter ministered in Lydda and Joppa.

OBSERVATION Even such an unlikely prospect as Saul, who was a fanatical enemy of the church, can be saved by God's power.

INSPIRATION Before he encountered Christ, Paul had been somewhat of a hero among the Pharisees. . . .

Blue-blooded and wild-eyed, this young zealot was hellbent on keeping the kingdom pure—and that meant keeping the Christians out. He marched through the countryside like a general demanding that backslidden Jews salute the flag of the motherland or kiss their family and hopes good-bye.

All this came to a halt, however, on the shoulder of a highway. . . . That's when someone slammed on the stadium lights, and he heard the voice.

When he found out whose voice it was, his jaw hit the ground, and his body followed. He braced himself for the worst. He knew it was all over. . . . He prayed that death would be quick and painless.

But all he got was silence and the first of a lifetime of surprises.

He ended up bewildered and befuddled in a borrowed bedroom. God left him there a few days with scales on

[13]Then Ananias answered, "Lord, I have heard from many about this
man, how much harm he has done to Your saints in Jerusalem. [14]And here
he has authority from the chief priests to bind all who call on Your name."
[15]But the Lord said to him, "Go, for he is a chosen vessel of Mine to bear
My name before Gentiles, kings, and the children of Israel. [16]For I will
show him how many things he must suffer for My name's sake."
[17]And Ananias went his way and entered the house; and laying his
hands on him he said, "Brother Saul, the Lord Jesus,[v] who appeared to you on
the road as you came, has sent me that you may receive your sight and be
filled with the Holy Spirit." [18]Immediately there fell from his eyes *something*
like scales, and he received his sight at once; and he arose and was baptized.
[19]So when he had received food, he was strengthened. Then Saul spent
some days with the disciples at Damascus.

Saul Preaches Christ

[20]Immediately he preached the Christ[w] in the synagogues, that He is the
Son of God.
[21]Then all who heard were amazed, and said, "Is this not he who destroyed
those who called on this name in Jerusalem, and has come here for that
purpose, so that he might bring them bound to the chief priests?"
[22]But Saul increased all the more in strength, and confounded the Jews
who dwelt in Damascus, proving that this *Jesus* is the Christ.

Saul Escapes Death

[23]Now after many days were past, the Jews plotted to kill him. [24]But their
plot became known to Saul. And they watched the gates day and night, to
kill him. [25]Then the disciples took him by night and let *him* down through
the wall in a large basket.

Saul at Jerusalem

[26]And when Saul had come to Jerusalem, he tried to join the disciples;
but they were all afraid of him, and did not believe that he was a disciple.
[27]But Barnabas took him and brought *him* to the apostles. And he declared
to them how he had seen the Lord on the road, and that He had spoken to
him, and how he had preached boldly at Damascus in the name of Jesus.
[28]So he was with them at Jerusalem, coming in and going out. [29]And he spoke
boldly in the name of the Lord Jesus and disputed against the Hellenists,
but they attempted to kill him. [30]When the brethren found out, they brought
him down to Caesarea and sent him out to Tarsus.

The Church Prospers

[31]Then the churches[x] throughout all Judea, Galilee, and Samaria had peace
and were edified. And walking in the fear of the Lord and in the comfort of
the Holy Spirit, they were multiplied.

Aeneas Healed

[32]Now it came to pass, as Peter went through all *parts of the country,* that
he also came down to the saints who dwelt in Lydda. [33]There he found a

9:17 [v] M-Text omits *Jesus.*
9:20 [w] NU-Text reads *Jesus.*
9:31 [x] NU-Text reads *church . . . was edified.*

certain man named Aeneas, who had been bedridden eight years and was
paralyzed. 34And Peter said to him, "Aeneas, Jesus the Christ heals you.
Arise and make your bed." Then he arose immediately. 35So all who dwelt
at Lydda and Sharon saw him and turned to the Lord.

Dorcas Restored to Life

36At Joppa there was a certain disciple named Tabitha, which is translated
Dorcas. This woman was full of good works and charitable deeds which
she did. 37But it happened in those days that she became sick and died.
When they had washed her, they laid *her* in an upper room. 38And since
Lydda was near Joppa, and the disciples had heard that Peter was there,
they sent two men to him, imploring *him* not to delay in coming to them.
39Then Peter arose and went with them. When he had come, they brought
him to the upper room. And all the widows stood by him weeping, showing the tunics and garments which Dorcas had made while she was with
them. 40But Peter put them all out, and knelt down and prayed. And turning to the body he said, "Tabitha, arise." And she opened her eyes, and
when she saw Peter she sat up. 41Then he gave her *his* hand and lifted her
up; and when he had called the saints and widows, he presented her alive.
42And it became known throughout all Joppa, and many believed on the
Lord. 43So it was that he stayed many days in Joppa with Simon, a tanner.

Cornelius Sends a Delegation

10 There was a certain man in Caesarea called Cornelius, a centurion
of what was called the Italian Regiment, 2a devout *man* and one who
feared God with all his household, who gave alms generously to the people,
and prayed to God always. 3About the ninth hour of the day he saw clearly
in a vision an angel of God coming in and saying to him, "Cornelius!"
4And when he observed him, he was afraid, and said, "What is it, lord?"
So he said to him, "Your prayers and your alms have come up for a memorial before God. 5Now send men to Joppa, and send for Simon whose surname is Peter. 6He is lodging with Simon, a tanner, whose house is by the
sea.[y] He will tell you what you must do." 7And when the angel who spoke
to him had departed, Cornelius called two of his household servants and a
devout soldier from among those who waited on him continually. 8So
when he had explained all *these* things to them, he sent them to Joppa.

Peter's Vision

9The next day, as they went on their journey and drew near the city, Peter
went up on the housetop to pray, about the sixth hour. 10Then he became
very hungry and wanted to eat; but while they made ready, he fell into a
trance 11and saw heaven opened and an object like a great sheet bound at
the four corners, descending to him and let down to the earth. 12In it were
all kinds of four-footed animals of the earth, wild beasts, creeping things,
and birds of the air. 13And a voice came to him, "Rise, Peter; kill and eat."
14But Peter said, "Not so, Lord! For I have never eaten anything common
or unclean."
15And a voice *spoke* to him again the second time, "What God has cleansed
you must not call common." 16This was done three times. And the object
was taken up into heaven again.

10:6 *y* NU-Text and M-Text omit the last sentence of this verse.

his eyes so thick that the only direction he could look was inside himself. And he didn't like what he saw.

He saw himself for what he really was—to use his own words, the worst of sinners.

. . . Alone in the room with his sins on his conscience and blood on his hands, he asked to be cleansed.

. . . The legalist Saul was buried, and the liberator Paul was born. He was never the same afterwards. And neither was the world. . . .

The message is gripping: Show a man his failures without Jesus, and the result will be found in the roadside gutter. Give a man religion without reminding him of his filth, and the result will be arrogance in a three-piece suit. But get the two in the same heart—get sin to meet Savior and Savior to meet sin—and the result just might be another Pharisee turned preacher who sets the world on fire.

(From *The Applause of Heaven* by Max Lucado)

APPLICATION Have you met people who are hostile to Christians? Maybe a popular celebrity or prominent people in your community make a stand against the church. Pray for these people by name. Ask God to save them. Look at people who oppose your faith as needy people—not enemies.

EXPLORATION Conversion—John 3:3-8, 16-21; 6:44, 65; 11:25-26; Acts 22:13-16; Romans 10:9-10; Galatians 6:12-16.

Summoned to Caesarea

17Now while Peter wondered within himself what this vision which he had seen meant, behold, the men who had been sent from Cornelius had made inquiry for Simon's house, and stood before the gate. 18And they called and asked whether Simon, whose surname was Peter, was lodging there.

19While Peter thought about the vision, the Spirit said to him, "Behold, three men are seeking you. 20Arise therefore, go down and go with them, doubting nothing; for I have sent them."

21Then Peter went down to the men who had been sent to him from Cornelius,[z] and said, "Yes, I am he whom you seek. For what reason have you come?"

22And they said, "Cornelius *the* centurion, a just man, one who fears God and has a good reputation among all the nation of the Jews, was divinely instructed by a holy angel to summon you to his house, and to hear words from you." 23Then he invited them in and lodged *them.*

On the next day Peter went away with them, and some brethren from Joppa accompanied him.

Peter Meets Cornelius

24And the following day they entered Caesarea. Now Cornelius was waiting for them, and had called together his relatives and close friends. 25As Peter was coming in, Cornelius met him and fell down at his feet and worshiped *him.* 26But Peter lifted him up, saying, "Stand up; I myself am also a man." 27And as he talked with him, he went in and found many who had come together. 28Then he said to them, "You know how unlawful it is for a Jewish man to keep company with or go to one of another nation. But God has shown me that I should not call any man common or unclean. 29Therefore I came without objection as soon as I was sent for. I ask, then, for what reason have you sent for me?"

30So Cornelius said, "Four days ago I was fasting until this hour; and at the ninth hour[a] I prayed in my house, and behold, a man stood before me in bright clothing, 31and said, 'Cornelius, your prayer has been heard, and your alms are remembered in the sight of God. 32Send therefore to Joppa and call Simon here, whose surname is Peter. He is lodging in the house of Simon, a tanner, by the sea.[b] When he comes, he will speak to you.' 33So I sent to you immediately, and you have done well to come. Now therefore, we are all present before God, to hear all the things commanded you by God."

Preaching to Cornelius' Household

34Then Peter opened *his* mouth and said: "In truth I perceive that God shows no partiality. 35But in every nation whoever fears Him and works righteousness is accepted by Him. 36The word which *God* sent to the children of Israel, preaching peace through Jesus Christ—He is Lord of all—37that word you know, which was proclaimed throughout all Judea, and began from Galilee after the baptism which John preached: 38how God anointed Jesus of Nazareth with the Holy Spirit and with power, who went about doing good and healing all who were oppressed by the devil, for God was with Him. 39And we are witnesses of all things which He did both in

10:21 [z] NU-Text and M-Text omit *who had been sent to him from Cornelius.*
10:30 [a] NU-Text reads *Four days ago to this hour, at the ninth hour.*
10:32 [b] NU-Text omits the last sentence of this verse.

LIFE LESSON

Acts 10:1-48

SITUATION One of the first non-Jews to embrace the gospel was Cornelius, a Roman centurion stationed at Palestinian Caesarea. God gave visions to Cornelius and Peter to set the stage for their meeting and to show Peter that Gentiles are included in God's plan.

OBSERVATION The gospel and the church transcend ethnic and racial distinction.

INSPIRATION There was some dice-throwing that went on at the foot of the cross. . . . I've wondered what that scene must have looked like to Jesus. As he looked downward past his bloody feet at the circle of gamblers, what did he think? What emotions did he feel? He must have been amazed. Here are common soldiers witnessing the world's most uncommon event and they don't know it. As far as they're concerned, it's just another Friday morning and he is just another criminal. "Come on, hurry up; it's my turn!"

"All right, all right—this throw is for the sandals."

Casting lots for the possessions of Christ. Heads ducked. Eyes downward. Cross forgotten.

The symbolism is striking. Do you see it?

It makes me think of us. The religious. Those who claim heritage at the cross. I'm thinking of all of us. Every believer in the land. The stuffy. The loose. The strict. The simple. Upper church. Lower church. "Spirit-filled." Millennialists. Evangelical. Political. Mystical. Literal. Cynical. Robes. Collars. Three-piece suits. Born-againers. Ameners.

I'm thinking of us.

I'm thinking that we aren't so unlike those soldiers. (I'm sorry to say.)

We, too, play games at the foot of the cross. We compete for members. We scramble for status. We deal our judgments and condemnations. Competition. Selfishness. Personal gain. It's all there. We don't like what the other did so we take the sandal we won and walk away in a huff.

So close to the timbers yet so far from the blood.

the land of the Jews and in Jerusalem, whom they [c] killed by hanging on a tree.
40Him God raised up on the third day, and showed Him openly, 41not to all the
people, but to witnesses chosen before by God, *even* to us who ate and drank
with Him after He arose from the dead. 42And He commanded us to preach
to the people, and to testify that it is He who was ordained by God *to be* Judge
of the living and the dead. 43To Him all the prophets witness that, through
His name, whoever believes in Him will receive remission of sins."

The Holy Spirit Falls on the Gentiles

44While Peter was still speaking these words, the Holy Spirit fell upon all
those who heard the word. 45And those of the circumcision who believed
were astonished, as many as came with Peter, because the gift of the Holy
Spirit had been poured out on the Gentiles also. 46For they heard them
speak with tongues and magnify God.
Then Peter answered, 47"Can anyone forbid water, that these should not
be baptized who have received the Holy Spirit just as we *have?*" 48And he
commanded them to be baptized in the name of the Lord. Then they asked
him to stay a few days.

Peter Defends God's Grace

11 Now the apostles and brethren who were in Judea heard that the
Gentiles had also received the word of God. 2And when Peter came
up to Jerusalem, those of the circumcision contended with him, 3saying,
"You went in to uncircumcised men and ate with them!"
4But Peter explained *it* to them in order from the beginning, saying: 5"I
was in the city of Joppa praying; and in a trance I saw a vision, an object
descending like a great sheet, let down from heaven by four corners; and it
came to me. 6When I observed it intently and considered, I saw four-footed
animals of the earth, wild beasts, creeping things, and birds of the air. 7And
I heard a voice saying to me, 'Rise, Peter; kill and eat.' 8But I said, 'Not so,
Lord! For nothing common or unclean has at any time entered my mouth.'
9But the voice answered me again from heaven, 'What God has cleansed
you must not call common.' 10Now this was done three times, and all were
drawn up again into heaven. 11At that very moment, three men stood before
the house where I was, having been sent to me from Caesarea. 12Then the
Spirit told me to go with them, doubting nothing. Moreover these six brethren
accompanied me, and we entered the man's house. 13And he told us how
he had seen an angel standing in his house, who said to him, 'Send men to
Joppa, and call for Simon whose surname is Peter, 14who will tell you words
by which you and all your household will be saved.' 15And as I began to
speak, the Holy Spirit fell upon them, as upon us at the beginning. 16Then
I remembered the word of the Lord, how He said, 'John indeed baptized
with water, but you shall be baptized with the Holy Spirit.' 17If therefore
God gave them the same gift as *He gave* us when we believed on the Lord
Jesus Christ, who was I that I could withstand God?"
18When they heard these things they became silent; and they glorified
God, saying, "Then God has also granted to the Gentiles repentance to life."

Barnabas and Saul at Antioch

19Now those who were scattered after the persecution that arose over

We are so close to the world's most uncommon event, but we act like common crapshooters huddled in bickering groups and fighting over silly opinions.

How many pulpit hours have been wasted on preaching the trivial? How many churches have tumbled at the throes of minuscuity? How many leaders have saddled their pet peeves, drawn their swords of bitterness and launched into battle against brethren over issues that are not worth discussing?

So close to the cross but so far from the Christ.

We specialize in "I am right" rallies. We write books about what the other does wrong. We major in finding gossip and become experts in unveiling weaknesses. We split into little huddles and then, God forbid, we split again. . . .

Are our differences that divisive? Are our opinions that obtrusive? Are our walls that wide? Is it *that* impossible to find a common cause?

"May they all be one," Jesus prayed.

One. Not one in groups of two thousand. But one in One. *One* church. *One* faith. *One* Lord. Not Baptist, not Methodist, not Adventist. Just Christian. No denominations. No hierarchies. No traditions. Just Christ.

Too idealistic? Impossible to achieve? I don't think so. Harder things have been done, you know. For example, once upon a tree, a Creator gave his life for his creation. Maybe all we need are a few hearts that are willing to follow suit.

(From *No Wonder They Call Him the Savior* by Max Lucado)

APPLICATION Who would be less than welcome at your church this Sunday? Do your part to overcome lingering prejudice against people whose race or language is different from your own.

EXPLORATION Christian Freedom—1 Corinthians 8:1-13; Galatians 4:8-11; Colossians 2:20-23; 1 Timothy 4:1-5.

10:39 [c] NU-Text and M-Text add *also.*

LIFE LESSON

Acts 11:1-30

SITUATION Peter explained to Jewish Believers what happened to Cornelius. They needed clarification because they mistakenly thought that salvation was only for Jews.

OBSERVATION Peter convinced the Jewish church leaders of the rightness of reaching out to the Gentiles, and many Gentiles were subsequently added to the church, notably at Antioch.

INSPIRATION The first communication of his message to non-Jews was the work of anonymous Christians, who without any special commissioning began to share the Good News with their Gentile neighbours. The place where they started to do this was Antioch, a great city in the north of Syria. The Gentiles with whom they shared the Good News took to it like ducks to water: this was the very message they had been waiting for, the very thing that met their need. It was among those people, at Antioch, that the disciples of Jesus first came to be called Christians.

Since that time, in one generation after another and progressively in all parts of the world, men, women and children who have heard the story of Jesus have recognized in it something completely suited to their condition and have welcomed Jesus as their all-sufficient Lord and deliverer. There is no cultural climate in which Jesus cannot make himself at home, which he cannot claim for himself, where his saving grace and power cannot be experienced. His message of liberation is for the whole human family. (From *Jesus: Lord and Savior* by F. F. Bruce)

APPLICATION Has another Christian ever criticized you because you associated with the "wrong" people? What was your response? Find a way to help your critic understand everyone is equal in God's eyes.

EXPLORATION God's Family—Isaiah 53:12; John 2:1-2; Acts 13:47; 28:28; 2 Corinthians 5:14-15; 1 Timothy 2:3-4.

Stephen traveled as far as Phoenicia, Cyprus, and Antioch, preaching the
word to no one but the Jews only. 20But some of them were men from Cyprus
and Cyrene, who, when they had come to Antioch, spoke to the Hellenists,
preaching the Lord Jesus. 21And the hand of the Lord was with them, and a
great number believed and turned to the Lord.
22Then news of these things came to the ears of the church in Jerusalem,
and they sent out Barnabas to go as far as Antioch. 23When he came and
had seen the grace of God, he was glad, and encouraged them all that with
purpose of heart they should continue with the Lord. 24For he was a good
man, full of the Holy Spirit and of faith. And a great many people were
added to the Lord.
25Then Barnabas departed for Tarsus to seek Saul. 26And when he had
found him, he brought him to Antioch. So it was that for a whole year they
assembled with the church and taught a great many people. And the disciples were first called Christians in Antioch.

Relief to Judea

27And in these days prophets came from Jerusalem to Antioch. 28Then one
of them, named Agabus, stood up and showed by the Spirit that there was
going to be a great famine throughout all the world, which also happened
in the days of Claudius Caesar. 29Then the disciples, each according to his
ability, determined to send relief to the brethren dwelling in Judea. 30This
they also did, and sent it to the elders by the hands of Barnabas and Saul.

Herod's Violence to the Church

12 Now about that time Herod the king stretched out *his* hand to harass
some from the church. 2Then he killed James the brother of John
with the sword. 3And because he saw that it pleased the Jews, he proceeded
further to seize Peter also. Now it was *during* the Days of Unleavened
Bread. 4So when he had arrested him, he put *him* in prison, and delivered
him to four squads of soldiers to keep him, intending to bring him before
the people after Passover.

Peter Freed from Prison

5Peter was therefore kept in prison, but constant[d] prayer was offered to
God for him by the church. 6And when Herod was about to bring him out,
that night Peter was sleeping, bound with two chains between two soldiers;
and the guards before the door were keeping the prison. 7Now behold, an
angel of the Lord stood by *him*, and a light shone in the prison; and he struck
Peter on the side and raised him up, saying, "Arise quickly!" And his chains
fell off *his* hands. 8Then the angel said to him, "Gird yourself and tie on your
sandals"; and so he did. And he said to him, "Put on your garment and follow
me." 9So he went out and followed him, and did not know that what was done
by the angel was real, but thought he was seeing a vision. 10When they were
past the first and the second guard posts, they came to the iron gate that
leads to the city, which opened to them of its own accord; and they went out
and went down one street, and immediately the angel departed from him.
11And when Peter had come to himself, he said, "Now I know for certain
that the Lord has sent His angel, and has delivered me from the hand of
Herod and *from* all the expectation of the Jewish people."

12:5 [d] NU-Text reads *constantly* (or *earnestly*).

12 So, when he had considered *this,* he came to the house of Mary, the mother
of John whose surname was Mark, where many were gathered together
praying. 13 And as Peter knocked at the door of the gate, a girl named Rhoda
came to answer. 14 When she recognized Peter's voice, because of *her* gladness she did not open the gate, but ran in and announced that Peter stood
before the gate. 15 But they said to her, "You are beside yourself!" Yet she
kept insisting that it was so. So they said, "It is his angel."
16 Now Peter continued knocking; and when they opened *the door* and
saw him, they were astonished. 17 But motioning to them with his hand to
keep silent, he declared to them how the Lord had brought him out of the
prison. And he said, "Go, tell these things to James and to the brethren."
And he departed and went to another place.
18 Then, as soon as it was day, there was no small stir among the soldiers
about what had become of Peter. 19 But when Herod had searched for him
and not found him, he examined the guards and commanded that *they*
should be put to death.

And he went down from Judea to Caesarea, and stayed *there.*

Herod's Violent Death

20 Now Herod had been very angry with the people of Tyre and Sidon;
but they came to him with one accord, and having made Blastus the king's
personal aide their friend, they asked for peace, because their country was
supplied with food by the king's *country.*
21 So on a set day Herod, arrayed in royal apparel, sat on his throne and
gave an oration to them. 22 And the people kept shouting, "The voice of a
god and not of a man!" 23 Then immediately an angel of the Lord struck him,
because he did not give glory to God. And he was eaten by worms and died.
24 But the word of God grew and multiplied.

Barnabas and Saul Appointed

25 And Barnabas and Saul returned from[e] Jerusalem when they had fulfilled *their* ministry, and they also took with them John whose surname
was Mark.

13 Now in the church that was at Antioch there were certain prophets
and teachers: Barnabas, Simeon who was called Niger, Lucius of
Cyrene, Manaen who had been brought up with Herod the tetrarch, and Saul.
2 As they ministered to the Lord and fasted, the Holy Spirit said, "Now separate to Me Barnabas and Saul for the work to which I have called them." 3 Then,
having fasted and prayed, and laid hands on them, they sent *them* away.

Preaching in Cyprus

4 So, being sent out by the Holy Spirit, they went down to Seleucia, and
from there they sailed to Cyprus. 5 And when they arrived in Salamis, they
preached the word of God in the synagogues of the Jews. They also had
John as *their* assistant.
6 Now when they had gone through the island[f] to Paphos, they found a
certain sorcerer, a false prophet, a Jew whose name *was* Bar-Jesus, 7 who
was with the proconsul, Sergius Paulus, an intelligent man. This man called
for Barnabas and Saul and sought to hear the word of God. 8 But Elymas

12:25 [e] NU-Text and M-Text read *to.*
13:6 [f] NU-Text reads *the whole island.*

Life Lesson

Acts 12:1-25

SITUATION The Romans appointed Herod Agrippa I, grandson of Herod the Great, to rule much of Palestine during this time. He persecuted Christians, killed James, and planned to kill Peter.

OBSERVATION God can rescue Believers, like Peter, from the most difficult situations.

INSPIRATION We must not measure our spiritual capacity by education or intellect; our capacity in spiritual things is measured by the promises of God. If we get less than God wants us to have, before long we will slander Him as the servant slandered his master: "You expect more than You give me power to do; You demand too much of me, I cannot stand true to You where I am placed." When it is a question of God's Almighty Spirit, never say "I can't." Never let the limitation of natural ability come in. If we have received the Holy Spirit, God expects the work of the Holy Spirit to be manifested in us.

The servant justified himself in everything he did and condemned his lord on every point. . . . Have we been slandering God by daring to worry? Worrying means exactly what this servant implied—"I know You mean to leave me in the lurch."

. . . Never forget that our capacity in spiritual matters is measured by the promises of God. Is God able to fulfil His promises?

(From *My Utmost for His Highest* by Oswald Chambers)

APPLICATION God answered prayer and set Peter free. How has God answered your prayers? Write down your requests so you can thank him for all his answers. Thank God today that prayer is an open channel to his heart.

EXPLORATION Power of Prayer—Psalm 40:1-3; Matthew 7:8-11; 18:19-20; Hebrews 4:14-16; James 5:16.

LIFE LESSON

Acts 13:1-52

SITUATION Luke shifts the focus of his book to Paul's ministry and the worldwide spread of the church. Paul stopped at key population and cultural centers, and spoke to both Jews and Gentiles.

OBSERVATION God desires that the church will reach new people with the message of Jesus' hope. The preaching of the gospel will always draw new converts, in spite of difficulties and opposition.

INSPIRATION The priority of spiritual awakening was so important that the Holy Spirit breathed on Luke to record His dealings with the early church. That first church was initiated and sustained by a prayer movement. The glory of God covered that early church.

Jesus told the disciples to wait in Jerusalem for the promise of the Father. The first call upon the New Testament church was prayer. Intense praying resulted in the powerful proclamation of Christ. In Acts 1:14 the church is found seeking the face of God: "These all with one mind were continually devoting themselves to prayer." In Acts 2:4-41 the church is empowered to proclaim the resurrection of Christ. Three thousand people were converted in this mighty visitation of God.

This incited the church to move forward in prayer. Acts 2:42 says, "They were continually devoting themselves to the apostles' teaching and to fellowship, to the breaking of bread and to prayer." The results were phenomenal. People came to know Christ daily. Peter and John are on their way to a prayer meeting in Acts 3, and five thousand are converted before they

the sorcerer (for so his name is translated) withstood them, seeking to
turn the proconsul away from the faith. 9Then Saul, who also *is called* Paul,
filled with the Holy Spirit, looked intently at him 10and said, "O full of all
deceit and all fraud, *you* son of the devil, *you* enemy of all righteousness,
will you not cease perverting the straight ways of the Lord? 11And now, indeed,
the hand of the Lord *is* upon you, and you shall be blind, not seeing the
sun for a time."

And immediately a dark mist fell on him, and he went around seeking
someone to lead him by the hand. 12Then the proconsul believed, when he
saw what had been done, being astonished at the teaching of the Lord.

At Antioch in Pisidia

13Now when Paul and his party set sail from Paphos, they came to Perga
in Pamphylia; and John, departing from them, returned to Jerusalem. 14But
when they departed from Perga, they came to Antioch in Pisidia, and went
into the synagogue on the Sabbath day and sat down. 15And after the reading of the Law and the Prophets, the rulers of the synagogue sent to them,
saying, "Men *and* brethren, if you have any word of exhortation for the
people, say on."

16Then Paul stood up, and motioning with *his* hand said, "Men of Israel,
and you who fear God, listen: 17The God of this people Israel[g] chose our fathers,
and exalted the people when they dwelt as strangers in the land of Egypt,
and with an uplifted arm He brought them out of it. 18Now for a time of
about forty years He put up with their ways in the wilderness. 19And when
He had destroyed seven nations in the land of Canaan, He distributed their
land to them by allotment.

20"After that He gave *them* judges for about four hundred and fifty years,
until Samuel the prophet. 21And afterward they asked for a king; so God
gave them Saul the son of Kish, a man of the tribe of Benjamin, for forty
years. 22And when He had removed him, He raised up for them David as
king, to whom also He gave testimony and said, *'I have found David*[h] the
son of Jesse, *a man after My own heart,* who will do all My will.'[i] 23From this
man's seed, according to *the* promise, God raised up for Israel a Savior—
Jesus—[j] 24after John had first preached, before His coming, the baptism
of repentance to all the people of Israel. 25And as John was finishing his
course, he said, 'Who do you think I am? I am not *He.* But behold, there
comes One after me, the sandals of whose feet I am not worthy to loose.'

26"Men *and* brethren, sons of the family of Abraham, and those among
you who fear God, to you the word of this salvation has been sent. 27For
those who dwell in Jerusalem, and their rulers, because they did not know
Him, nor even the voices of the Prophets which are read every Sabbath,
have fulfilled *them* in condemning *Him.* 28And though they found no
cause for death *in Him,* they asked Pilate that He should be put to death.
29Now when they had fulfilled all that was written concerning Him, they
took *Him* down from the tree and laid *Him* in a tomb. 30But God raised
Him from the dead. 31He was seen for many days by those who came up
with Him from Galilee to Jerusalem, who are His witnesses to the people.
32And we declare to you glad tidings—that promise which was made to

13:17 [g] M-Text omits *Israel.*
13:22 [h] Psalm 89:20 [i] 1 Samuel 13:14
13:23 [j] M-Text reads *for Israel salvation.*

the fathers. 33God has fulfilled this for us their children, in that He has
raised up Jesus. As it is also written in the second Psalm:

'You are My Son,
Today I have begotten You.'[k]

34And that He raised Him from the dead, no more to return to corruption,
He has spoken thus:

'I will give you the sure mercies of David.'[l]

35Therefore He also says in another *Psalm:*

'You will not allow Your Holy One to see corruption.'[m]

36"For David, after he had served his own generation by the will of God,
fell asleep, was buried with his fathers, and saw corruption; 37but He whom
God raised up saw no corruption. 38Therefore let it be known to you, brethren,
that through this Man is preached to you the forgiveness of sins; 39and by
Him everyone who believes is justified from all things from which you could
not be justified by the law of Moses. 40Beware therefore, lest what has been
spoken in the prophets come upon you:

41 *'Behold, you despisers,*
Marvel and perish!
For I work a work in your days,
A work which you will by no means believe,
Though one were to declare it to you.'"[n]

Blessing and Conflict at Antioch

42So when the Jews went out of the synagogue,[o] the Gentiles begged that
these words might be preached to them the next Sabbath. 43Now when the
congregation had broken up, many of the Jews and devout proselytes followed Paul and Barnabas, who, speaking to them, persuaded them to continue in the grace of God.
44On the next Sabbath almost the whole city came together to hear the
word of God. 45But when the Jews saw the multitudes, they were filled with
envy; and contradicting and blaspheming, they opposed the things spoken
by Paul. 46Then Paul and Barnabas grew bold and said, "It was necessary
that the word of God should be spoken to you first; but since you reject it,
and judge yourselves unworthy of everlasting life, behold, we turn to the
Gentiles. 47For so the Lord has commanded us:

'I have set you as a light to the Gentiles,
That you should be for salvation to the ends of the earth.' "[p]

48Now when the Gentiles heard this, they were glad and glorified the word
of the Lord. And as many as had been appointed to eternal life believed.
49And the word of the Lord was being spread throughout all the region.
50But the Jews stirred up the devout and prominent women and the chief men
of the city, raised up persecution against Paul and Barnabas, and expelled

even arrive. The church continues to pray in Acts 4, which results in an even more powerful proclamation of the gospel. In Acts 5:14 they stop counting those who are being saved, simply stating, "All the more believers in the Lord, multitudes of men and women, were constantly added to their number."

This should be ample evidence of the relationship between prayer and the phenomenal growth of the New Testament church. But we should also look at the apostle Paul. Paul's ministry grew out of a prayer meeting. All of Europe and North America should be grateful for five humble men of prayer. The history of both continents would never be the same because of that prayer meeting, where a ministry was born that would ultimately shape much of Western civilization. The early church's motto was "pray and proclaim." It was said of them that they were "men who have upset the world" (Acts 17:6).

(From *The Prayer Factor* by Sammy Tippet)

APPLICATION Imagine that you are a missionary in a far off country. Imagine that you have seen no one from your culture in months. How excited would you be to receive a letter from someone back in your own country? Help encourage a missionary by writing a letter. Your letter might arrive at an opportune time.

EXPLORATION Universality of Gospel—Isaiah 53:12; Matthew 28:18-20; Acts 1:8; 16:9-10; 2 Corinthians 10:15-16; 1 Timothy 2:3-6.

13:33 [k] Psalm 2:7
13:34 [l] Isaiah 55:3
13:35 [m] Psalm 16:10
13:41 [n] Habakkuk 1:5
13:42 [o] Or *And when they went out of the synagogue of the Jews;* NU-Text reads *And when they went out of the synagogue, they begged.*
13:47 [p] Isaiah 49:6

Life Lesson

Acts 14:1-28

SITUATION After being expelled from Antioch, Paul and Barnabas continued to preach the gospel. They ventured into Iconium, Lystra, and Derbe performing great miracles and winning over great multitudes for Christ. Their adversaries, however, continued to oppose them in every city.

OBSERVATION Their higher calling would not let Paul and Barnabas quit. They even went into hostile regions to deliver God's message of salvation.

INSPIRATION I fear our generation has come dangerously near the "I'm-getting-tired-so-let's-quit" mentality. And not just in the spiritual realm. Dieting is a discipline, so we stay fat. Finishing school is a hassle, so we bail out. Cultivating a close relationship is painful, so we back off. Getting a book written is demanding, so we stop short. Working through conflicts in marriage is a tiring struggle, so we walk away. Sticking with an occupation is tough, so we start looking elsewhere. . . .

Ignace Jan Paderewski, the famous composer-pianist, was scheduled to perform at a great concert hall in America. It was an evening to remember– black tuxedoes and long evening dresses, a high society extravaganza. Present in the audience that evening was a mother with her fidgety nine-year-old son. Weary of waiting, he squirmed constantly in his seat. His mother was in hopes that her boy would be encouraged to practice the piano if he could just hear the immortal Paderewski at the keyboard. So—against his wishes—he had come.

As she turned to talk with friends, her son could stay seated no longer. He slipped away from her side, strangely drawn to the ebony concert grand Steinway and its leather tufted stool, staring wide-eyed at the black and white keys. He placed his small, trembling fingers in the right location

them from their region. 51 But they shook off the dust from their feet against
them, and came to Iconium. 52 And the disciples were filled with joy and
with the Holy Spirit.

At Iconium

14 Now it happened in Iconium that they went together to the synagogue of the Jews, and so spoke that a great multitude both of the
Jews and of the Greeks believed. 2 But the unbelieving Jews stirred up the
Gentiles and poisoned their minds against the brethren. 3 Therefore they
stayed there a long time, speaking boldly in the Lord, who was bearing
witness to the word of His grace, granting signs and wonders to be done
by their hands.
4 But the multitude of the city was divided: part sided with the Jews, and
part with the apostles. 5 And when a violent attempt was made by both the
Gentiles and Jews, with their rulers, to abuse and stone them, 6 they became
aware of it and fled to Lystra and Derbe, cities of Lycaonia, and to the surrounding region. 7 And they were preaching the gospel there.

Idolatry at Lystra

8 And in Lystra a certain man without strength in his feet was sitting, a
cripple from his mother's womb, who had never walked. 9 *This* man heard
Paul speaking. Paul, observing him intently and seeing that he had faith to
be healed, 10 said with a loud voice, "Stand up straight on your feet!" And
he leaped and walked. 11 Now when the people saw what Paul had done,
they raised their voices, saying in the Lycaonian *language,* "The gods have
come down to us in the likeness of men!" 12 And Barnabas they called Zeus,
and Paul, Hermes, because he was the chief speaker. 13 Then the priest of
Zeus, whose temple was in front of their city, brought oxen and garlands to
the gates, intending to sacrifice with the multitudes.
14 But when the apostles Barnabas and Paul heard this, they tore their
clothes and ran in among the multitude, crying out 15 and saying, "Men, why
are you doing these things? We also are men with the same nature as you,
and preach to you that you should turn from these useless things to the
living God, who made the heaven, the earth, the sea, and all things that are
in them, 16 who in bygone generations allowed all nations to walk in their
own ways. 17 Nevertheless He did not leave Himself without witness, in that
He did good, gave us rain from heaven and fruitful seasons, filling our hearts
with food and gladness." 18 And with these sayings they could scarcely restrain the multitudes from sacrificing to them.

Stoning, Escape to Derbe

19 Then Jews from Antioch and Iconium came there; and having persuaded
the multitudes, they stoned Paul *and* dragged *him* out of the city, supposing
him to be dead. 20 However, when the disciples gathered around him, he rose
up and went into the city. And the next day he departed with Barnabas to
Derbe.

Strengthening the Converts

21 And when they had preached the gospel to that city and made many
disciples, they returned to Lystra, Iconium, and Antioch, 22 strengthening
the souls of the disciples, exhorting *them* to continue in the faith, and *saying,*

"We must through many tribulations enter the kingdom of God." 23So
when they had appointed elders in every church, and prayed with fasting,
they commended them to the Lord in whom they had believed. 24And after
they had passed through Pisidia, they came to Pamphylia. 25Now when
they had preached the word in Perga, they went down to Attalia. 26From
there they sailed to Antioch, where they had been commended to the grace
of God for the work which they had completed.
27Now when they had come and gathered the church together, they reported all that God had done with them, and that He had opened the door
of faith to the Gentiles. 28So they stayed there a long time with the disciples.

Conflict over Circumcision

15 And certain *men* came down from Judea and taught the brethren,
"Unless you are circumcised according to the custom of Moses, you
cannot be saved." 2Therefore, when Paul and Barnabas had no small dissension and dispute with them, they determined that Paul and Barnabas
and certain others of them should go up to Jerusalem, to the apostles and
elders, about this question.
3So, being sent on their way by the church, they passed through Phoenicia
and Samaria, describing the conversion of the Gentiles; and they caused
great joy to all the brethren. 4And when they had come to Jerusalem, they
were received by the church and the apostles and the elders; and they reported all things that God had done with them. 5But some of the sect of the
Pharisees who believed rose up, saying, "It is necessary to circumcise them,
and to command *them* to keep the law of Moses."

The Jerusalem Council

6Now the apostles and elders came together to consider this matter.
7And when there had been much dispute, Peter rose up and said to them:
"Men and brethren, you know that a good while ago God chose among us,
that by my mouth the Gentiles should hear the word of the gospel and believe. 8So God, who knows the heart, acknowledged them by giving them
the Holy Spirit, just as *He did* to us, 9and made no distinction between us
and them, purifying their hearts by faith. 10Now therefore, why do you test
God by putting a yoke on the neck of the disciples which neither our fathers nor we were able to bear? 11But we believe that through the grace of
the Lord Jesus Christ[q] we shall be saved in the same manner as they."
12Then all the multitude kept silent and listened to Barnabas and Paul
declaring how many miracles and wonders God had worked through
them among the Gentiles. 13And after they had become silent, James answered, saying, "Men *and* brethren, listen to me: 14Simon has declared
how God at the first visited the Gentiles to take out of them a people for His
name. 15And with this the words of the prophets agree, just as it is written:

16 *'After this I will return*
And will rebuild the tabernacle of David, which has fallen down;
I will rebuild its ruins,
And I will set it up;
17 *So that the rest of mankind may seek the* LORD,

15:11 [q] NU-Text and M-Text omit *Christ.*

and began to play "chopsticks." The roar of the crowd was hushed as hundreds of frowning faces turned in his direction. Irritated and embarrassed, they began to shout:

"Get that boy away from there!"

"Who'd bring a kid that young in here?"

"Where's his mother?"

"Somebody stop him!"

Backstage, the master overheard the sounds out front and quickly put together in his mind what was happening. Hurriedly, he grabbed his coat and rushed toward the stage. Without one word of announcement he stooped over behind the boy, reached around both sides, and began to improvise a counter melody to harmonize and enhance "chopsticks." As the two of them played together, Paderewski kept whispering in the boy's ear:

Keep going. Don't quit, son. Keep on playing . . . don't stop . . . don't quit.

And so it is with us. We hammer away on our project, which seems about as significant as "chopsticks" in a concert hall. And about the time we are ready to give up, along comes the Master, who leans over and whispers:

Now keep going; don't quit. Keep on . . . don't stop; don't quit.

(From *Growing Strong in the Seasons of Life* by Charles Swindoll)

APPLICATION Is there a project in your life that you've given up on because of discouragement? No matter how great the task, God promises to help us through if we are obedient to him. Today, get back on track with your project and hold fast to the promise that God will see you through it.

EXPLORATION Perseverance—1 Corinthians 15:58; Galatians 6:9; Philippians 3:12-14; 2 Timothy 3:11-14; Hebrews 3:6; 1 Peter 5:8, 10.

LIFE LESSON

Acts 15:1-41

SITUATION Many Jewish Christians insisted that Gentile Christians had to follow Jewish traditions in order to become true Christians. The Jerusalem Council decided that only God's grace and individual faith in Jesus was neccessary for salvation.

OBSERVATION The Law can never save you. God saves only by grace through faith in Jesus Christ.

INSPIRATION What exactly is grace? And is it limited to Jesus' life and ministry? You may be surprised to know that Jesus never used the word itself. He just taught it and, equally important, lived it. Furthermore, the Bible never gives us a one-statement definition, though grace appears throughout its pages . . . not only the word itself but numerous demonstrations of it. Understanding what grace means requires our going back to an old Hebrew term that meant "to bend, to stoop." By and by, it came to include the idea of "condescending favor."

If you have traveled to London, you have perhaps seen royalty. If so, you must have noticed sophistication, aloofness, distance. On occasion, royalty in England will make the news because someone in the ranks of nobility will stop, kneel down and touch or bless a commoner. That is grace. There is nothing in the commoner that deserves being noticed or touched or blessed by the royal family. But because of grace in the heart of the queen, there is the desire at that moment to pause, to stoop, to touch, even to bless.

The late pastor and Bible scholar Donald Barnhouse perhaps said it best: "Love that goes upward is worship; love that goes outward is affection; love that stoops is grace."

Even all the Gentiles who are called by My name,
Says the LORD who does all these things.'[r]

18"Known to God from eternity are all His works.[s] 19Therefore I judge that
we should not trouble those from among the Gentiles who are turning to God,
20but that we write to them to abstain from things polluted by idols, *from*
sexual immorality,[t] *from* things strangled, and *from* blood. 21For Moses
has had throughout many generations those who preach him in every city,
being read in the synagogues every Sabbath."

The Jerusalem Decree

22Then it pleased the apostles and elders, with the whole church, to send
chosen men of their own company to Antioch with Paul and Barnabas,
namely, Judas who was also named Barsabas,[u] and Silas, leading men among
the breathren.
23They wrote this, *letter* by them:

The apostles, the elders, and the brethren,

To the brethren who are of the Gentiles in Antioch, Syria, and Cilicia:

Greetings.

24 Since we have heard that some who went out from us have troubled
you with words, unsettling your souls, saying, "*You must* be
circumcised and keep the law"[v]—to whom we gave no *such*
commandment—25it seemed good to us, being assembled with
one accord, to send chosen men to you with our beloved Barnabas
and Paul, 26men who have risked their lives for the name of our
Lord Jesus Christ. 27We have therefore sent Judas and Silas, who will
also report the same things by word of mouth. 28For it seemed good
to the Holy Spirit, and to us, to lay upon you no greater burden than
these necessary things: 29that you abstain from things offered to idols,
from blood, from things strangled, and from sexual immorality.[w]
If you keep yourselves from these, you will do well.

Farewell.

Continuing Ministry in Syria

30So when they were sent off, they came to Antioch; and when they had
gathered the multitude together, they delivered the letter. 31When they had
read it, they rejoiced over its encouragement. 32Now Judas and Silas, themselves being prophets also, exhorted and strengthened the brethren with
many words. 33And after they had stayed *there* for a time, they were sent
back with greetings from the brethren to the apostles.[x]
34However, it seemed good to Silas to remain there.[y] 35Paul and Barnabas
also remained in Antioch, teaching and preaching the word of the Lord,
with many others also.

15:17 [r] Amos 9:11, 12
15:18 [s] NU-Text (combining with verse 17) reads *Says the Lord, who makes these things known from eternity (of old).*
15:20 [t] Or *fornication*
15:22 [u] NU-Text and M-Text read *Barsabbas.*
15:24 [v] NU-Text omits *saying, "You must be circumcised and keep the law."*
15:29 [w] Or *fornication*
15:33 [x] NU-Text reads *to those who had sent them.*
15:34 [y] NU-Text and M-Text omit this verse.

Division over John Mark

[36]Then after some days Paul said to Barnabas, "Let us now go back and
visit our brethren in every city where we have preached the word of the
Lord, *and see* how they are doing." [37]Now Barnabas was determined to take
with them John called Mark. [38]But Paul insisted that they should not take
with them the one who had departed from them in Pamphylia, and had
not gone with them to the work. [39]Then the contention became so sharp
that they parted from one another. And so Barnabas took Mark and sailed
to Cyprus; [40]but Paul chose Silas and departed, being commended by the
brethren to the grace of God. [41]And he went through Syria and Cilicia,
strengthening the churches.

Timothy Joins Paul and Silas

16 Then he came to Derbe and Lystra. And behold, a certain disciple
was there, named Timothy, *the* son of a certain Jewish woman who
believed, but his father *was* Greek. [2]He was well spoken of by the brethren
who were at Lystra and Iconium. [3]Paul wanted to have him go on with
him. And he took *him* and circumcised him because of the Jews who were
in that region, for they all knew that his father was Greek. [4]And as they
went through the cities, they delivered to them the decrees to keep, which
were determined by the apostles and elders at Jerusalem. [5]So the churches
were strengthened in the faith, and increased in number daily.

The Macedonian Call

[6]Now when they had gone through Phrygia and the region of Galatia,
they were forbidden by the Holy Spirit to preach the word in Asia. [7]After
they had come to Mysia, they tried to go into Bithynia, but the Spirit[z] did
not permit them. [8]So passing by Mysia, they came down to Troas. [9]And a
vision appeared to Paul in the night. A man of Macedonia stood and pleaded
with him, saying, "Come over to Macedonia and help us." [10]Now after he
had seen the vision, immediately we sought to go to Macedonia, concluding
that the Lord had called us to preach the gospel to them.

Lydia Baptized at Philippi

[11]Therefore, sailing from Troas, we ran a straight course to Samothrace,
and the next *day* came to Neapolis, [12]and from there to Philippi, which is
the foremost city of that part of Macedonia, a colony. And we were staying
in that city for some days. [13]And on the Sabbath day we went out of the city
to the riverside, where prayer was customarily made; and we sat down and
spoke to the women who met *there.* [14]Now a certain woman named Lydia
heard *us.* She was a seller of purple from the city of Thyatira, who worshiped God. The Lord opened her heart to heed the things spoken by Paul.
[15]And when she and her household were baptized, she begged *us,* saying,
"If you have judged me to be faithful to the Lord, come to my house and
stay." So she persuaded us.

Paul and Silas Imprisoned

[16]Now it happened, as we went to prayer, that a certain slave girl possessed
with a spirit of divination met us, who brought her masters much profit

To show grace is to extend favor or kindness to one who doesn't deserve it and can never earn it. Receiving God's acceptance by grace always stands in sharp contrast to earning it on the basis *of* works. Every time the thought of grace appears, there is the idea of its being undeserved. In no way is the recipient getting what he or she deserves. Favor is being extended simply out of the goodness of the heart of the giver. . . .

One more thing should be emphasized about grace: It is absolutely and totally free. You will never be asked to pay it back. You couldn't even if you tried. Most of us have trouble with that thought, because we work for everything we get. The old saying goes, "There ain't no free lunch." But in this case, grace comes to us free and clear, no strings attached. We should not even try to repay it; to do so is insulting. . . .

And now that Christ has come and died and thereby satisfied the Father's demands on sin, all we need to do is claim His grace by accepting the free gift of eternal life. Period. He smiles on us because of His Son's death and resurrection. It's grace, my friend, amazing grace. That is enough to give anybody a "Yes" face!

(From *The Grace Awakening* by Charles Swindoll)

APPLICATION How do you react to Christians whose worship style is different from your own? Remember God's gift of eternal life is free and for everybody, whatever the color, race, or worship preference. Have the same gracious attitude toward others that Jesus had.

EXPLORATION Grace—Romans 3:24; Galatians 2:16; Ephesians 2:5-8.

16:7 [z] NU-Text adds *of Jesus.*

Life Lesson

Acts 16:1-40

SITUATION During his second missionary journey, Paul visited and encouraged churches established during his first journey. Despite persecution, Paul boldly shared the gospel wherever he went.

OBSERVATION Even when we are persecuted for the sake of the gospel, God can make us a powerful testimony. His Holy Spirit will work through us as we reach out to those around us.

INSPIRATION Prayer Of Saint Patrick

I establish myself today in:
The power of God to guide me,
The might of God to uphold me,
The wisdom of God to teach me,
The eye of God to watch over me,
The ear of God to hear me,
The word of God to speak to me,
The hand of God to protect me,
The way of God to lie before me,
The shield of God to shelter me,
The hosts of God to defend me,
Christ with me, Christ before me,
Christ behind me, Christ within me,
Christ beneath me, Christ above me,
Christ at my right, Christ at my left,
Christ in breadth, Christ in length,
Christ in height, Christ in the heart
of every man who thinks of me,
Christ in the mouth of every man
who speaks to me,
Christ in the ear of every man
who hears me.
Confident in Christ.
(From *My Sacrifice, His Fire* by Anne Ortlund)

APPLICATION Where can you witness for Christ today: your home, church, school, community? Put your trust in him. Say a word for Jesus.

EXPLORATION Trust—Psalm 9:10; 22:4; 37:5; 125:1; Proverbs 28:25; 29:25; Isaiah 28:16; Nahum 1:7; 1 Corinthians 4:2.

by fortune-telling. 17 This girl followed Paul and us, and cried out, saying,
"These men are the servants of the Most High God, who proclaim to us the
way of salvation." 18 And this she did for many days.
But Paul, greatly annoyed, turned and said to the spirit, "I command you in
the name of Jesus Christ to come out of her." And he came out that very hour.
19 But when her masters saw that their hope of profit was gone, they seized
Paul and Silas and dragged *them* into the marketplace to the authorities.
20 And they brought them to the magistrates, and said, "These men, being
Jews, exceedingly trouble our city; 21 and they teach customs which are not
lawful for us, being Romans, to receive or observe." 22 Then the multitude
rose up together against them; and the magistrates tore off their clothes
and commanded *them* to be beaten with rods. 23 And when they had laid
many stripes on them, they threw *them* into prison, commanding the
jailer to keep them securely. 24 Having received such a charge, he put them
into the inner prison and fastened their feet in the stocks.

The Philippian Jailer Saved

25 But at midnight Paul and Silas were praying and singing hymns to God,
and the prisoners were listening to them. 26 Suddenly there was a great earthquake, so that the foundations of the prison were shaken; and immediately
all the doors were opened and everyone's chains were loosed. 27 And the keeper
of the prison, awaking from sleep and seeing the prison doors open, supposing the prisoners had fled, drew his sword and was about to kill himself. 28 But
Paul called with a loud voice, saying, "Do yourself no harm, for we are all here."
29 Then he called for a light, ran in, and fell down trembling before Paul and
Silas. 30 And he brought them out and said, "Sirs, what must I do to be saved?"
31 So they said, "Believe on the Lord Jesus Christ, and you will be saved,
you and your household." 32 Then they spoke the word of the Lord to him
and to all who were in his house. 33 And he took them the same hour of the
night and washed *their* stripes. And immediately he and all his family were
baptized. 34 Now when he had brought them into his house, he set food before them; and he rejoiced, having believed in God with all his household.

Paul Refuses to Depart Secretly

35 And when it was day, the magistrates sent the officers, saying, "Let those
men go."
36 So the keeper of the prison reported these words to Paul, saying, "The
magistrates have sent to let you go. Now therefore depart, and go in peace."
37 But Paul said to them, "They have beaten us openly, uncondemned
Romans, *and* have thrown *us* into prison. And now do they put us out secretly? No indeed! Let them come themselves and get us out."
38 And the officers told these words to the magistrates, and they were afraid
when they heard that they were Romans. 39 Then they came and pleaded
with them and brought *them* out, and asked *them* to depart from the city.
40 So they went out of the prison and entered *the house of* Lydia; and when
they had seen the brethren, they encouraged them and departed.

Preaching Christ at Thessalonica

17 Now when they had passed through Amphipolis and Apollonia,
they came to Thessalonica, where there was a synagogue of the Jews.
2 Then Paul, as his custom was, went in to them, and for three Sabbaths

reasoned with them from the Scriptures, 3explaining and demonstrating
that the Christ had to suffer and rise again from the dead, and *saying,* "This
Jesus whom I preach to you is the Christ." 4And some of them were persuaded; and a great multitude of the devout Greeks, and not a few of the
leading women, joined Paul and Silas.

Assault on Jason's House

5But the Jews who were not persuaded, becoming envious,[a] took some
of the evil men from the marketplace, and gathering a mob, set all the city
in an uproar and attacked the house of Jason, and sought to bring them
out to the people. 6But when they did not find them, they dragged Jason
and some brethren to the rulers of the city, crying out, "These who have
turned the world upside down have come here too. 7Jason has harbored
them, and these are all acting contrary to the decrees of Caesar, saying there
is another king—Jesus." 8And they troubled the crowd and the rulers of
the city when they heard these things. 9So when they had taken security
from Jason and the rest, they let them go.

Ministering at Berea

10Then the brethren immediately sent Paul and Silas away by night to
Berea. When they arrived, they went into the synagogue of the Jews. 11These
were more fair-minded than those in Thessalonica, in that they received
the word with all readiness, and searched the Scriptures daily *to find out*
whether these things were so. 12Therefore many of them believed, and also
not a few of the Greeks, prominent women as well as men. 13But when the
Jews from Thessalonica learned that the word of God was preached by
Paul at Berea, they came there also and stirred up the crowds. 14Then immediately the brethren sent Paul away, to go to the sea; but both Silas and
Timothy remained there. 15So those who conducted Paul brought him to
Athens; and receiving a command for Silas and Timothy to come to him
with all speed, they departed.

The Philosophers at Athens

16Now while Paul waited for them at Athens, his spirit was provoked within
him when he saw that the city was given over to idols. 17Therefore he reasoned in the synagogue with the Jews and with the *Gentile* worshipers,
and in the marketplace daily with those who happened to be there. 18Then[b]
certain Epicurean and Stoic philosophers encountered him. And some
said, "What does this babbler want to say?"

Others said, "He seems to be a proclaimer of foreign gods," because he
preached to them Jesus and the resurrection.

19And they took him and brought him to the Areopagus, saying, "May we
know what this new doctrine *is* of which you speak? 20For you are bringing
some strange things to our ears. Therefore we want to know what these things
mean." 21For all the Athenians and the foreigners who were there spent
their time in nothing else but either to tell or to hear some new thing.

Addressing the Areopagus

22Then Paul stood in the midst of the Areopagus and said, "Men of
Athens, I perceive that in all things you are very religious; 23for as I was

17:5 [a] NU-Text omits *who were not persuaded;* M-Text omits *becoming envious.*
17:18 [b] NU-Text and M-Text add *also.*

LIFE LESSON

Acts 17:1-34

SITUATION Banished from Philippi, Paul and his companions visited the cities of Thessalonica and Athens. In both places Paul boldly testified to the saving grace of God.

OBSERVATION When we speak about Jesus, we should understand our audience well.

INSPIRATION The prevailing world-view denies the existence of absolute truth. So when the Christian message, which is essentially historical and propositional, is proclaimed, modern listeners hear what they interpret as simply one person's preference—another autonomous human choice of lifestyle or belief. . . .

What does this tell us? . . . To evangelize today we must address the human condition at its point of felt need—conscience, guilt, dealing with others, finding a purpose for staying alive. . . .

So we must be familiar enough with the prevailing world-view to look for points of contact and discern points of disagreement.

It is no different than if you or I were talking with a Hindu, for example, about issues of life and religion. We wouldn't assume that he or she was coming from a Judeo-Christian perspective. We would start from the Hindu presuppositions about the world, probe their world-view, find the points of contact and concern, and then begin to challenge or question those presuppositions. Only then could we begin to present our case effectively. . . .

Our handy prepackaged God-talk won't do. Before we tell them what the Bible says, we may have to tell them why they should believe the Bible (there is a great case to be made). And we need a Christian apologetic that doesn't just make the case for us; it must touch the chords within our unbelieving friends and neighbors and begin to alter their view of reality.

(From *The Body* by Charles Colson)

Continued

APPLICATION When you were introduced to the faith, what kind of testimony intrigued you? Is there someone in your life who may be in the same situation you were in? How can you share with them what you have found? If there is no one, find a circle of friends where you can share what Christ has done for you.

EXPLORATION God Communicates—Isaiah 1:1; Daniel 5:5-9; Matthew 1:20; 2:12-13; 3:13-17; Luke 1:13, 30; 2:10; Acts 18:9; Hebrews 1:1-2.

passing through and considering the objects of your worship, I even
found an altar with this inscription:

TO THE UNKNOWN GOD.

Therefore, the One whom you worship without knowing, Him I proclaim
to you: [24]God, who made the world and everything in it, since He is Lord of
heaven and earth, does not dwell in temples made with hands. [25]Nor is He
worshiped with men's hands, as though He needed anything, since He
gives to all life, breath, and all things. [26]And He has made from one blood[c]
every nation of men to dwell on all the face of the earth, and has determined their preappointed times and the boundaries of their dwellings,
[27]so that they should seek the Lord, in the hope that they might grope for
Him and find Him, though He is not far from each one of us; [28]for in Him
we live and move and have our being, as also some of your own poets have
said, 'For we are also His offspring.' [29]Therefore, since we are the offspring
of God, we ought not to think that the Divine Nature is like gold or silver or
stone, something shaped by art and man's devising. [30]Truly, these times of
ignorance God overlooked, but now commands all men everywhere to repent, [31]because He has appointed a day on which He will judge the world
in righteousness by the Man whom He has ordained. He has given assurance of this to all by raising Him from the dead."

[32]And when they heard of the resurrection of the dead, some mocked,
while others said, "We will hear you again on this *matter.*" [33]So Paul departed from among them. [34]However, some men joined him and believed,
among them Dionysius the Areopagite, a woman named Damaris, and
others with them.

Ministering at Corinth

18 After these things Paul departed from Athens and went to Corinth.
[2]And he found a certain Jew named Aquila, born in Pontus, who
had recently come from Italy with his wife Priscilla (because Claudius had
commanded all the Jews to depart from Rome); and he came to them. [3]So,
because he was of the same trade, he stayed with them and worked; for by
occupation they were tentmakers. [4]And he reasoned in the synagogue every
Sabbath, and persuaded both Jews and Greeks.

[5]When Silas and Timothy had come from Macedonia, Paul was compelled by the Spirit, and testified to the Jews *that* Jesus *is* the Christ. [6]But
when they opposed him and blasphemed, he shook *his* garments and said
to them, "Your blood *be* upon your *own* heads; I *am* clean. From now on I
will go to the Gentiles." [7]And he departed from there and entered the house
of a certain *man* named Justus,[d] *one* who worshiped God, whose house
was next door to the synagogue. [8]Then Crispus, the ruler of the synagogue,
believed on the Lord with all his household. And many of the Corinthians,
hearing, believed and were baptized.

[9]Now the Lord spoke to Paul in the night by a vision, "Do not be afraid,
but speak, and do not keep silent; [10]for I am with you, and no one will attack you to hurt you; for I have many people in this city." [11]And he continued *there* a year and six months, teaching the word of God among them.

17:26 [c] NU-Text omits *blood.*
18:7 [d] NU-Text reads *Titius Justus.*

12When Gallio was proconsul of Achaia, the Jews with one accord rose
up against Paul and brought him to the judgment seat, 13saying, "This *fel-*
low persuades men to worship God contrary to the law."
14And when Paul was about to open *his* mouth, Gallio said to the Jews,
"If it were a matter of wrongdoing or wicked crimes, O Jews, there would
be reason why I should bear with you. 15But if it is a question of words and
names and your own law, look *to it* yourselves; for I do not want to be a
judge of such *matters.*" 16And he drove them from the judgment seat. 17Then
all the Greeks[e] took Sosthenes, the ruler of the synagogue, and beat *him*
before the judgment seat. But Gallio took no notice of these things.

Paul Returns to Antioch

18So Paul still remained a good while. Then he took leave of the brethren
and sailed for Syria, and Priscilla and Aquila *were* with him. He had *his*
hair cut off at Cenchrea, for he had taken a vow. 19And he came to Ephesus,
and left them there; but he himself entered the synagogue and reasoned
with the Jews. 20When they asked *him* to stay a longer time with them, he
did not consent, 21but took leave of them, saying, "I must by all means
keep this coming feast in Jerusalem;[f] but I will return again to you, God
willing." And he sailed from Ephesus.
22And when he had landed at Caesarea, and gone up and greeted the
church, he went down to Antioch. 23After he had spent some time *there,* he
departed and went over the region of Galatia and Phrygia in order, strengthening all the disciples.

Ministry of Apollos

24Now a certain Jew named Apollos, born at Alexandria, an eloquent
man *and* mighty in the Scriptures, came to Ephesus. 25This man had been
instructed in the way of the Lord; and being fervent in spirit, he spoke and
taught accurately the things of the Lord, though he knew only the baptism of
John. 26So he began to speak boldly in the synagogue. When Aquila and
Priscilla heard him, they took him aside and explained to him the way of God
more accurately. 27And when he desired to cross to Achaia, the brethren wrote,
exhorting the disciples to receive him; and when he arrived, he greatly
helped those who had believed through grace; 28for he vigorously refuted
the Jews publicly, showing from the Scriptures that Jesus is the Christ.

Paul at Ephesus

19 And it happened, while Apollos was at Corinth, that Paul, having
passed through the upper regions, came to Ephesus. And finding
some disciples 2he said to them, "Did you receive the Holy Spirit when you
believed?"
So they said to him, "We have not so much as heard whether there is a
Holy Spirit."
3And he said to them, "Into what then were you baptized?"
So they said, "Into John's baptism."
4Then Paul said, "John indeed baptized with a baptism of repentance,
saying to the people that they should believe on Him who would come
after him, that is, on Christ Jesus."

18:17 [e] NU-Text reads *they all.*
18:21 [f] NU-Text omits *I must* through *Jerusalem.*

LIFE LESSON

Acts 18:1-28

SITUATION Corinth, the commercial center of Greece, was a haven of corruption. It also held great ministry opportunities.

OBSERVATION We must rejoice in the victories Jesus gives us and remain positive during persecution and suffering.

INSPIRATION Today's world is joyless, full of shadows, disillusionment, and fear. Freedom is rapidly disappearing from the face of the earth. Along with the loss of freedom, a great many of the superficial joys and pleasures of life are also disappearing, but God, by His Spirit, directs His joy to our bleak, problem-riddled lives, making it possible for us to be filled with joy regardless of our circumstances. . . .

I once visited Dohnavur in South India where Amy Carmichael had lived for fifty years, caring for hundreds of girls originally dedicated to temple service. She was bedridden for the last twenty years of her life, during which time she wrote books that have blessed millions. Joy filled her sick room so that everyone who visited her came away praising God. . . .

Even after her death, when I visited the room where she had served the Lord for twenty years, writing from her bed, I was asked by her former nurse to lead in prayer. I began, but was so overwhelmed by a sense of God's presence I broke down (a thing I seldom ever do). . . . As I left that room, I sensed the joy of the Lord in my own heart. Many times I have visited sick people to encourage them. Some suffered from terminal illnesses. Strangely enough, I have come away blessed in my own soul by their contagious joy.

(From *The Holy Spirit* by Billy Graham)

APPLICATION It's not generated in your own mind or heart, it's not bought at a store. True joy is God's gift.

EXPLORATION Joy—
Nehemiah 8:10; Psalm 94:19; Proverbs 10:28; Isaiah 35:10; Habakkuk 3:17-19; John 15:11; 1 Thessalonians 1:6.

LIFE LESSON

Acts 19:1-41

SITUATION On Paul's third missionary journey he corrected doctrinal misunderstandings that had been creeping into the churches.

OBSERVATION The power to change comes from God. Magical formulas and magic words cannot secure this power. Christ conquered evil.

INSPIRATION At the center of the occult, either openly or disguised as an "angel of light," is Satan. Peter exhorts believers concerning our chief foe when he writes, "Be of sober spirit, be on the alert. Your adversary, the devil, prowls about like a roaring lion, seeking someone to devour" (1 Peter 5:8, NASB).

Christians often have the tendency to "blame it all on the devil," when in fact it was their own carelessness or fleshly nature which led to the sin or error. It can also be said, however, that even when it is our fleshly nature or the world which draws us from the Lord—and not the devil directly—it is nevertheless true that Satan and his army of demons desire that we be drawn to the world's standards.

Satan is the one who ultimately desires that we pursue the lusts of the flesh, and it is he who sits as the "god of this world" (Ephesians 2:1-10). Though not always directly involved, Satan's prime objective is the defeat of God, and for us that means our defeat. . . .

As you study the Old Testament, you see that men and women were in a constant struggle with Satan, fighting many spiritual battles. As you study the life of Christ, and Paul, and the other Apostles, you see a constant spiritual struggle. Christians today face many spiritual battles.

I'm so glad I learned the authority of the believer before I went to South America. The authority of the believer is a possession that belongs to every true child of God. And it gives so much authority over the enemy that Satan has tried to blind most believers to the authority they have.

During Easter week at Balboa, I first learned of the authority of the believer. About 50,000 high school and college students came down for Easter. With Andre Kole, the illusionist, we packed out a big ballroom several nights in a

5When they heard *this,* they were baptized in the name of the Lord Jesus.
6And when Paul had laid hands on them, the Holy Spirit came upon them,
and they spoke with tongues and prophesied. 7Now the men were about
twelve in all.
8And he went into the synagogue and spoke boldly for three months,
reasoning and persuading concerning the things of the kingdom of God.
9But when some were hardened and did not believe, but spoke evil of the
Way before the multitude, he departed from them and withdrew the disciples, reasoning daily in the school of Tyrannus. 10And this continued for
two years, so that all who dwelt in Asia heard the word of the Lord Jesus,
both Jews and Greeks.

Miracles Glorify Christ

11Now God worked unusual miracles by the hands of Paul, 12so that even
handkerchiefs or aprons were brought from his body to the sick, and the
diseases left them and the evil spirits went out of them. 13Then some of the
itinerant Jewish exorcists took it upon themselves to call the name of the
Lord Jesus over those who had evil spirits, saying, "We[g] exorcise you by
the Jesus whom Paul preaches." 14Also there were seven sons of Sceva, a
Jewish chief priest, who did so.
15And the evil spirit answered and said, "Jesus I know, and Paul I know;
but who are you?"
16Then the man in whom the evil spirit was leaped on them, overpowered[h]
them, and prevailed against them,[i] so that they fled out of that house naked
and wounded. 17This became known both to all Jews and Greeks dwelling
in Ephesus; and fear fell on them all, and the name of the Lord Jesus was
magnified. 18And many who had believed came confessing and telling their
deeds. 19Also, many of those who had practiced magic brought their books
together and burned *them* in the sight of all. And they counted up the
value of them, and *it* totaled fifty thousand *pieces* of silver. 20So the word of
the Lord grew mightily and prevailed.

The Riot at Ephesus

21When these things were accomplished, Paul purposed in the Spirit,
when he had passed through Macedonia and Achaia, to go to Jerusalem,
saying, "After I have been there, I must also see Rome." 22So he sent into
Macedonia two of those who ministered to him, Timothy and Erastus, but
he himself stayed in Asia for a time.
23And about that time there arose a great commotion about the Way.
24For a certain man named Demetrius, a silversmith, who made silver shrines
of Diana,[j] brought no small profit to the craftsmen. 25He called them together
with the workers of similar occupation, and said: "Men, you know that we
have our prosperity by this trade. 26Moreover you see and hear that not only
at Ephesus, but throughout almost all Asia, this Paul has persuaded and
turned away many people, saying that they are not gods which are made
with hands. 27So not only is this trade of ours in danger of falling into disrepute, but also the temple of the great goddess Diana may be despised
and her magnificence destroyed,[k] whom all Asia and the world worship."

19:13 [g] NU-Text reads *I.*
19:16 [h] M-Text reads *and they overpowered.* [i] NU-Text reads *both of them.*
19:24 [j] Greek *Artemis*
19:27 [k] NU-Text reads *she be deposed from her magnificence.*

28Now when they heard *this,* they were full of wrath and cried out, saying, "Great *is* Diana of the Ephesians!" 29So the whole city was filled with confusion, and rushed into the theater with one accord, having seized Gaius and Aristarchus, Macedonians, Paul's travel companions. 30And when Paul wanted to go in to the people, the disciples would not allow him. 31Then some of the officials of Asia, who were his friends, sent to him pleading that he would not venture into the theater. 32Some therefore cried one thing and some another, for the assembly was confused, and most of them did not know why they had come together. 33And they drew Alexander out of the multitude, the Jews putting him forward. And Alexander motioned with his hand, and wanted to make his defense to the people. 34But when they found out that he was a Jew, all with one voice cried out for about two hours, "Great *is* Diana of the Ephesians!"

35And when the city clerk had quieted the crowd, he said: "Men of Ephesus, what man is there who does not know that the city of the Ephesians is temple guardian of the great goddess Diana, and of the *image* which fell down from Zeus? 36Therefore, since these things cannot be denied, you ought to be quiet and do nothing rashly. 37For you have brought these men here who are neither robbers of temples nor blasphemers of your[l] goddess. 38Therefore, if Demetrius and his fellow craftsmen have a case against anyone, the courts are open and there are proconsuls. Let them bring charges against one another. 39But if you have any other inquiry to make, it shall be determined in the lawful assembly. 40For we are in danger of being called in question for today's uproar, there being no reason which we may give to account for this disorderly gathering." 41And when he had said these things, he dismissed the assembly.

Journeys in Greece

20 After the uproar had ceased, Paul called the disciples to *himself,* embraced *them,* and departed to go to Macedonia. 2Now when he had gone over that region and encouraged them with many words, he came to Greece 3and stayed three months. And when the Jews plotted against him as he was about to sail to Syria, he decided to return through Macedonia. 4And Sopater of Berea accompanied him to Asia—also Aristarchus and Secundus of the Thessalonians, and Gaius of Derbe, and Timothy, and Tychicus and Trophimus of Asia. 5These men, going ahead, waited for us at Troas. 6But we sailed away from Philippi after the Days of Unleavened Bread, and in five days joined them at Troas, where we stayed seven days.

Ministering at Troas

7Now on the first *day* of the week, when the disciples came together to break bread, Paul, ready to depart the next day, spoke to them and continued his message until midnight. 8There were many lamps in the upper room where they[m] were gathered together. 9And in a window sat a certain young man named Eutychus, who was sinking into a deep sleep. He was overcome by sleep; and as Paul continued speaking, he fell down from the third story and was taken up dead. 10But Paul went down, fell on him, and embracing *him* said, "Do not trouble yourselves, for his life is in him." 11Now when he had come up, had broken bread and eaten, and talked a

row—for two or three meetings a night. So many people were coming to our meetings, in fact, that many of the bars were empty. It really irritated some of the people. The second night, one of the men from a night club came over to break up our meeting. They figured if they broke up one of them, that would finish it for us.

As Andre was performing, this guy pulled up with his Dodge Dart all souped up. With a deafening sound, he popped the clutch and went roaring down the street. Everyone inside, of course, turned around and looked out to see the commotion. Finally, Andre got them settled down.

Then the guy went around the block again. As he stopped out front, he revved it up again and roared down the street. By this time everyone was whispering and wondering what was going on. Some stood up, trying to look out the window.

When the guy went back around the block again, I knew that if he repeated his performance one more time, it would break up the meeting. Turning to Gene Huntsman, one of our staff members, I said, "I think Satan is trying to break up this meeting. Let's step out in the doorway and exercise the authority of the believer." So we stepped out and prayed a very simple prayer.

When the guy came back, he started to rev it up again, and as he popped the clutch—pow! The rear end of his car blew all over the street. By that time, we just thanked the Lord and went over and pushed him off the street. As I shared the *Four Spiritual Laws* with him, it reminded me that Jesus said all authority is given to the believer in heaven and in earth.

(From *Understanding the Occult* by Josh McDowell and Don Stewart)

APPLICATION Occult practice is loathsome to God. By delving in the occult, people deny the victory God has over the powers of evil. Let the power of the resurrected Christ give you freedom from any and all forms of occultism.

EXPLORATION Occult—Leviticus 19:31; 20:6, 27; Deuteronomy 18:10-12.

19:37 [l] NU-Text reads *our.*
20:8 [m] NU-Text and M-Text read *we.*

long while, even till daybreak, he departed. [12]And they
brought the young man in alive, and they were not a
little comforted.

From Troas to Miletus

[13]Then we went ahead to the ship and sailed to Assos,
there intending to take Paul on board; for so he had
given orders, intending himself to go on foot. [14]And
when he met us at Assos, we took him on board and
came to Mitylene. [15]We sailed from there, and the next
day came opposite Chios. The following *day* we arrived
at Samos and stayed at Trogyllium. The next *day* we
came to Miletus. [16]For Paul had decided to sail past
Ephesus, so that he would not have to spend time in
Asia; for he was hurrying to be at Jerusalem, if possible, on the Day of Pentecost.

The Ephesian Elders Exhorted

[17]From Miletus he sent to Ephesus and called for
the elders of the church. [18]And when they had come to
him, he said to them: "You know, from the first day that
I came to Asia, in what manner I always lived among
you, [19]serving the Lord with all humility, with many tears
and trials which happened to me by the plotting of the
Jews; [20]how I kept back nothing that was helpful, but
proclaimed it to you, and taught you publicly and from
house to house, [21]testifying to Jews, and also to Greeks,
repentance toward God and faith toward our Lord Jesus
Christ. [22]And see, now I go bound in the spirit to Jerusalem, not knowing the things that will happen to me
there, [23]except that the Holy Spirit testifies in every
city, saying that chains and tribulations await me.
[24]But none of these things move me; nor do I count
my life dear to myself,[n] so that I may finish my race
with joy, and the ministry which I received from the
Lord Jesus, to testify to the gospel of the grace of God.
[25]"And indeed, now I know that you all, among
whom I have gone preaching the kingdom of God, will
see my face no more. [26]Therefore I testify to you this
day that I *am* innocent of the blood of all *men.* [27]For I
have not shunned to declare to you the whole counsel
of God. [28]Therefore take heed to yourselves and to all
the flock, among which the Holy Spirit has made you
overseers, to shepherd the church of God[o] which He
purchased with His own blood. [29]For I know this, that
after my departure savage wolves will come in among
you, not sparing the flock. [30]Also from among yourselves
men will rise up, speaking perverse things, to draw
away the disciples after themselves. [31]Therefore watch,
and remember that for three years I did not cease to
warn everyone night and day with tears.
[32]"So now, brethren, I commend you to God and to
the word of His grace, which is able to build you up
and give you an inheritance among all those who are
sanctified. [33]I have coveted no one's silver or gold or
apparel. [34]Yes,[p] you yourselves know that these hands
have provided for my necessities, and for those who
were with me. [35]I have shown you in every way, by laboring like this, that you must support the weak. And
remember the words of the Lord Jesus, that He said,
'It is more blessed to give than to receive.' "
[36]And when he had said these things, he knelt down
and prayed with them all. [37]Then they all wept freely,
and fell on Paul's neck and kissed him, [38]sorrowing
most of all for the words which he spoke, that they
would see his face no more. And they accompanied
him to the ship.

Warnings on the Journey to Jerusalem

21 Now it came to pass, that when we had departed
from them and set sail, running a straight course
we came to Cos, the following *day* to Rhodes, and from
there to Patara. [2]And finding a ship sailing over to
Phoenicia, we went aboard and set sail. [3]When we had
sighted Cyprus, we passed it on the left, sailed to Syria,
and landed at Tyre; for there the ship was to unload
her cargo. [4]And finding disciples,[q] we stayed there seven
days. They told Paul through the Spirit not to go up to
Jerusalem. [5]When we had come to the end of those
days, we departed and went on our way; and they all
accompanied us, with wives and children, till *we were*
out of the city. And we knelt down on the shore and
prayed. [6]When we had taken our leave of one another,
we boarded the ship, and they returned home.
[7]And when we had finished *our* voyage from Tyre,
we came to Ptolemais, greeted the brethren, and stayed
with them one day. [8]On the next *day* we who were
Paul's companions[r] departed and came to Caesarea,
and entered the house of Philip the evangelist, who
was *one* of the seven, and stayed with him. [9]Now this
man had four virgin daughters who prophesied. [10]And
as we stayed many days, a certain prophet named Agabus came down from Judea. [11]When he had come to
us, he took Paul's belt, bound his *own* hands and feet,

20:24 [n] NU-Text reads *But I do not count my life of any value or dear to myself.*
20:28 [o] M-Text reads *of the Lord and God.*
20:34 [p] NU-Text and M-Text omit *Yes.*
21:4 [q] NU-Text reads *the disciples.*
21:8 [r] NU-Text omits *who were Paul's companions.*

and said, "Thus says the Holy Spirit, 'So shall the Jews at Jerusalem bind the
man who owns this belt, and deliver *him* into the hands of the Gentiles.' "
12 Now when we heard these things, both we and those from that place
pleaded with him not to go up to Jerusalem. 13 Then Paul answered, "What
do you mean by weeping and breaking my heart? For I am ready not only
to be bound, but also to die at Jerusalem for the name of the Lord Jesus."
14 So when he would not be persuaded, we ceased, saying, "The will of
the Lord be done."

Paul Urged to Make Peace

15 And after those days we packed and went up to Jerusalem. 16 Also some
of the disciples from Caesarea went with us and brought with them a certain Mnason of Cyprus, an early disciple, with whom we were to lodge.
17 And when we had come to Jerusalem, the brethren received us gladly.
18 On the following *day* Paul went in with us to James, and all the elders
were present. 19 When he had greeted them, he told in detail those things
which God had done among the Gentiles through his ministry. 20 And
when they heard *it*, they glorified the Lord. And they said to him, "You see,
brother, how many myriads of Jews there are who have believed, and they
are all zealous for the law; 21 but they have been informed about you that
you teach all the Jews who are among the Gentiles to forsake Moses, saying
that they ought not to circumcise *their* children nor to walk according to
the customs. 22 What then? The assembly must certainly meet, for they
will[s] hear that you have come. 23 Therefore do what we tell you: We have
four men who have taken a vow. 24 Take them and be purified with them,
and pay their expenses so that they may shave *their* heads, and that all may
know that those things of which they were informed concerning you are
nothing, but *that* you yourself also walk orderly and keep the law. 25 But
concerning the Gentiles who believe, we have written *and* decided that
they should observe no such thing,[t] except that they should keep themselves from *things* offered to idols, from blood, from things strangled, and
from sexual immorality."

Arrested in the Temple

26 Then Paul took the men, and the next day, having been purified with
them, entered the temple to announce the expiration of the days of purification, at which time an offering should be made for each one of them.
27 Now when the seven days were almost ended, the Jews from Asia, seeing him in the temple, stirred up the whole crowd and laid hands on him,
28 crying out, "Men of Israel, help! This is the man who teaches all *men*
everywhere against the people, the law, and this place; and furthermore he
also brought Greeks into the temple and has defiled this holy place." 29 (For
they had previously[u] seen Trophimus the Ephesian with him in the city,
whom they supposed that Paul had brought into the temple.)
30 And all the city was disturbed; and the people ran together, seized
Paul, and dragged him out of the temple; and immediately the doors were
shut. 31 Now as they were seeking to kill him, news came to the commander of the garrison that all Jerusalem was in an uproar. 32 He immediately

21:22 [s] NU-Text reads *What then is to be done? They will certainly.*
21:25 [t] NU-Text omits *that they should observe no such thing, except.*
21:29 [u] M-Text omits *previously.*

Life Lesson

Acts 21:1-40

SITUATION After an emotional good-bye, Paul continued to visit many other churches throughout the region. When he was warned that he would be captured by the Jews and imprisoned, Paul assured the people that he was ready to die for the sake of the gospel.

OBSERVATION Paul met hardships with the confidence that God's will would be accomplished.

INSPIRATION In Poland, . . . Father Jerzy felt a call to lay down his own life for his brothers.

Soon after the birth of Solidarity, Father Jerzy preached among the striking workers in Warsaw's huge steel works. He showed them how alcohol contributed to their oppression: If their drinking caused absenteeism or mistakes at work, it could be used to blackmail them. After that, alcoholism dropped dramatically.

. . . Not long after martial law was imposed and his foray into the night with Christmas peace for the soldiers, Father Jerzy instituted a monthly "Mass for the Homeland," dedicated to all victims of the repressive regime. Eventually thousands, then tens of thousands, attended these services at St. Stanislaw Kostka, with Father Jerzy ministering from a balcony and the people fanned out in the courtyard and streets below.

. . . Father Jerzy's influence did not escape the notice of the authorities. He was far too popular, far too independent, far too threatening to the regime's control. He must be silenced.

The secret police followed Father Jerzy everywhere. He received unsigned, threatening letters. On the first anniversary of martial law, a pipe bomb sailed through the front window of his small flat, exploding in his sitting room.

Then, on October 19, 1984, while driving back to Warsaw from Bydgoszcz where he had celebrated a special mass and delivered a homily called "Overcome Evil with Good," Father Jerzy disappeared.

Continued

On the last Sunday of October, as fifty thousand people filled St. Stanislaw Kostka in an emotional Mass for the Homeland and listened in tears to a tape of Father Jerzy's final sermon, Father Antoni Lewek, one of the thirty priests at the altar, received word: "Just a moment ago it was announced on the television that Father Jerzy's body has been found in the Vistula River." Months later Father Lewek recalled the scene as he told the people the dreaded news.

"I shall never forget what happened," he said. "In a second, people went down on their knees, crying and shouting; what they had feared the most had happened . . .

"And then something very moving happened. This crying crowd managed to show that they could forgive. Three times they repeated after the priest: 'And forgive us our trespasses as we forgive them that trespass against us.' It was a Christian answer to the unchristian deed of the murders."

. . . On November 2, the day after Father Jerzy's funeral, people marched the streets past the secret police headquarters bearing banners reading, "We forgive."

Regardless of their expertise in murdering the body, the executioners could not kill the soul. Father Jerzy had taught his people well.

(From *The Body* by Charles Colson)

APPLICATION How bold are you to share your faith? Have you known people for years but have never shared Christ with them? Do your neighbors know you are a Christian? Look for an opportunity to share with someone new.

EXPLORATION Persecution—Matthew 10:22; John 7:7; 15:21; Acts 9:16; 20:24.

took soldiers and centurions, and ran down to them. And when they saw the commander and the soldiers, they stopped beating Paul. 33Then the commander came near and took him, and commanded *him* to be bound with two chains; and he asked who he was and what he had done. 34And some among the multitude cried one thing and some another.

So when he could not ascertain the truth because of the tumult, he commanded him to be taken into the barracks. 35When he reached the stairs, he had to be carried by the soldiers because of the violence of the mob. 36For the multitude of the people followed after, crying out, "Away with him!"

Addressing the Jerusalem Mob

37Then as Paul was about to be led into the barracks, he said to the commander, "May I speak to you?"

He replied, "Can you speak Greek? 38Are you not the Egyptian who some time ago stirred up a rebellion and led the four thousand assassins out into the wilderness?"

39But Paul said, "I am a Jew from Tarsus, in Cilicia, a citizen of no mean city; and I implore you, permit me to speak to the people."

40So when he had given him permission, Paul stood on the stairs and motioned with his hand to the people. And when there was a great silence, he spoke to *them* in the Hebrew language, saying,

22 "Brethren and fathers, hear my defense before you now." 2And when they heard that he spoke to them in the Hebrew language, they kept all the more silent.

Then he said: 3"I am indeed a Jew, born in Tarsus of Cilicia, but brought up in this city at the feet of Gamaliel, taught according to the strictness of our fathers' law, and was zealous toward God as you all are today. 4I persecuted this Way to the death, binding and delivering into prisons both men and women, 5as also the high priest bears me witness, and all the council of the elders, from whom I also received letters to the brethren, and went to Damascus to bring in chains even those who were there to Jerusalem to be punished.

6"Now it happened, as I journeyed and came near Damascus at about noon, suddenly a great light from heaven shone around me. 7And I fell to the ground and heard a voice saying to me, 'Saul, Saul, why are you persecuting Me?' 8So I answered, 'Who are You, Lord?' And He said to me, 'I am Jesus of Nazareth, whom you are persecuting.'

9"And those who were with me indeed saw the light and were afraid,[v] but they did not hear the voice of Him who spoke to me. 10So I said, 'What shall I do, Lord?' And the Lord said to me, 'Arise and go into Damascus, and there you will be told all things which are appointed for you to do.' 11And since I could not see for the glory of that light, being led by the hand of those who were with me, I came into Damascus.

12"Then a certain Ananias, a devout man according to the law, having a good testimony with all the Jews who dwelt *there,* 13came to me; and he stood and said to me, 'Brother Saul, receive your sight.' And at that same hour I looked up at him. 14Then he said, 'The God of our fathers has chosen you that you should know His will, and see the Just One, and hear the voice of His mouth. 15For you will be His witness to all men of what you have

22:9 [v] NU-Text omits *and were afraid.*

seen and heard. 16And now why are you waiting? Arise and be baptized,
and wash away your sins, calling on the name of the Lord.'
17"Now it happened, when I returned to Jerusalem and was praying in
the temple, that I was in a trance 18and saw Him saying to me, 'Make haste
and get out of Jerusalem quickly, for they will not receive your testimony
concerning Me.' 19So I said, 'Lord, they know that in every synagogue I
imprisoned and beat those who believe on You. 20And when the blood of
Your martyr Stephen was shed, I also was standing by consenting to his
death,[w] and guarding the clothes of those who were killing him.' 21Then He
said to me, 'Depart, for I will send you far from here to the Gentiles.' "

Paul's Roman Citizenship

22And they listened to him until this word, and *then* they raised their
voices and said, "Away with such a *fellow* from the earth, for he is not fit to
live!" 23Then, as they cried out and tore off *their* clothes and threw dust
into the air, 24the commander ordered him to be brought into the barracks,
and said that he should be examined under scourging, so that he might
know why they shouted so against him. 25And as they bound him with
thongs, Paul said to the centurion who stood by, "Is it lawful for you to
scourge a man who is a Roman, and uncondemned?"
26When the centurion heard *that,* he went and told the commander, saying, "Take care what you do, for this man is a Roman."
27Then the commander came and said to him, "Tell me, are you a Roman?"
He said, "Yes."
28The commander answered, "With a large sum I obtained this citizenship."
And Paul said, "But I was born *a citizen.*"
29Then immediately those who were about to examine him withdrew
from him; and the commander was also afraid after he found out that he
was a Roman, and because he had bound him.

The Sanhedrin Divided

30The next day, because he wanted to know for certain why he was accused by the Jews, he released him from *his* bonds, and commanded the
chief priests and all their council to appear, and brought Paul down and
set him before them.

23 Then Paul, looking earnestly at the council, said, "Men *and* brethren,
I have lived in all good conscience before God until this day." 2And
the high priest Ananias commanded those who stood by him to strike him
on the mouth. 3Then Paul said to him, "God will strike you, *you* whitewashed wall! For you sit to judge me according to the law, and do you command me to be struck contrary to the law?"
4And those who stood by said, "Do you revile God's high priest?"
5Then Paul said, "I did not know, brethren, that he was the high priest;
for it is written, '*You shall not speak evil of a ruler of your people.*' "[x]
6But when Paul perceived that one part were Sadducees and the other
Pharisees, he cried out in the council, "Men *and* brethren, I am a Pharisee,
the son of a Pharisee; concerning the hope and resurrection of the dead I
am being judged!"
7And when he had said this, a dissension arose between the Pharisees

22:20 [w] NU-Text omits *to his death.*
23:5 [x] Exodus 22:28

LIFE LESSON

Acts 22:1-29

SITUATION Paul was saved from the angry mob in Jerusalem by the Roman garrison commander. Then he was placed in prison.

OBSERVATION God can work in unconventional or unusual ways to accomplish his will.

INSPIRATION The sword of God's Holy Spirit is the Bible, the Word of God. When the Holy Spirit goes into action in your life, more than dust flies! Your bad thoughts come under control, your bad actions wither and decline, and all the good things within you flourish and blossom. Good intentions that were never put into effect can now become a way of life. Bad habits you couldn't conquer come under the knife of the Master Surgeon.

All this from Bible reading? Yes, but there is one vital factor I haven't mentioned: Read to discover what God wants you to do, and do it. Those who read the Bible as interesting literature will not find it very exciting; those who read it as God's guidebook for their lives will find it to be a fascinating adventure. . . .

The Bible is "the sword of the Spirit" that cuts deep into our lives, opening the festering spiritual sores so that the healing of the Spirit can occur. Thus new life grows and flourishes.

(From *Next Steps for New Christians* by Kenneth Taylor)

APPLICATION Have you ever found refuge or support in an unexpected place? Have problems resolved themselves in ways you didn't expect? Ask God today to make you the unexpected solution to someone else's problem—God's miracle channel.

EXPLORATION God's Will—2 Chronicles 18:33; Esther 4:13-14; Acts 16:6.

Life Lesson

Acts 22:30–23:35

SITUATION In Jerusalem, Paul escaped a flogging by asserting his Roman citizenship. Claudius Lysias, the commander who stopped the riot and was about to flog him, brought Paul before the Sanhedrin (Jewish council) to further investigate the incident.

OBSERVATION Even if the civil rights of a Believer are abused, God still holds the situation in his hand.

INSPIRATION Among presidents, Abraham Lincoln stands head and shoulders above the rest. . . . [He said] "I desire to so conduct the affairs of this administration that if, at the end, when I come to lay down the reins of power, I have lost every other friend on earth, I shall at least have one friend left, and that friend shall be deep down inside me. . . . I am not bound to succeed, but I am bound to live up to the light I have. . . . Let us have the faith that right makes might, and in that faith, let us, to the end, dare to do our duty as we understand it. . . .

Intelligence, patriotism, Christianity, and a firm reliance on Him, who has never forsaken this favored land, are still competent to adjust, in the best way, our present difficulties. . . ."

The "present difficulties" of Lincoln's day were hard but no harder than the present difficulties of our day. The power that Lincoln knew a faithful God could supply is still available. But Christians also have the same responsibility that Lincoln had—to stand for the right. It is a lonely, risky position, but as we stand for the right, God will supply the might.

(From *Plus Living* by Vicki Huffman)

APPLICATION Set your mind on a course to become more dedicated to God. Don't let excuses, a new crisis, or a busy day make you put your time with God on hold. Find something else to skip before you skip your time in prayer or reading from the Bible.

EXPLORATION Determination—Philippians 3:12-14.
Faithfulness—2 Samuel 22:26.
Steadfastness—Psalm 51:10.

and the Sadducees; and the assembly was divided. 8For Sadducees say
that there is no resurrection—and no angel or spirit; but the Pharisees
confess both. 9Then there arose a loud outcry. And the scribes of the
Pharisees' party arose and protested, saying, "We find no evil in this man;
but if a spirit or an angel has spoken to him, let us not fight against God."[y]
10Now when there arose a great dissension, the commander, fearing lest
Paul might be pulled to pieces by them, commanded the soldiers to go down
and take him by force from among them, and bring *him* into the barracks.

The Plot Against Paul

11But the following night the Lord stood by him and said, "Be of good
cheer, Paul; for as you have testified for Me in Jerusalem, so you must also
bear witness at Rome."
12And when it was day, some of the Jews banded together and bound
themselves under an oath, saying that they would neither eat nor drink till
they had killed Paul. 13Now there were more than forty who had formed
this conspiracy. 14They came to the chief priests and elders, and said, "We
have bound ourselves under a great oath that we will eat nothing until we
have killed Paul. 15Now you, therefore, together with the council, suggest to
the commander that he be brought down to you tomorrow,[z] as though you
were going to make further inquiries concerning him; but we are ready to
kill him before he comes near."
16So when Paul's sister's son heard of their ambush, he went and entered
the barracks and told Paul. 17Then Paul called one of the centurions to *him*
and said, "Take this young man to the commander, for he has something
to tell him." 18So he took him and brought *him* to the commander and
said, "Paul the prisoner called me to *him* and asked *me* to bring this young
man to you. He has something to say to you."
19Then the commander took him by the hand, went aside, and asked
privately, "What is it that you have to tell me?"
20And he said, "The Jews have agreed to ask that you bring Paul down to
the council tomorrow, as though they were going to inquire more fully
about him. 21But do not yield to them, for more than forty of them lie in
wait for him, men who have bound themselves by an oath that they will
neither eat nor drink till they have killed him; and now they are ready,
waiting for the promise from you."
22So the commander let the young man depart, and commanded *him,*
"Tell no one that you have revealed these things to me."

Sent to Felix

23And he called for two centurions, saying, "Prepare two hundred soldiers,
seventy horsemen, and two hundred spearmen to go to Caesarea at the third
hour of the night; 24and provide mounts to set Paul on, and bring *him*
safely to Felix the governor." 25He wrote a letter in the following manner:

26 Claudius Lysias,

To the most excellent governor Felix:

Greetings.

23:9 [y] NU-Text omits last clause and reads *what if a spirit or an angel has spoken to him?*
23:15 [z] NU-Text omits *tomorrow.*

PRAISE

Praise is the highest occupation of any being. What happens when we praise the Father? We reestablish the proper chain of command; we recognize that the King is on the throne and that he has saved his people.

The whole purpose of coming before the King is to praise him, to live in recognition of his splendor. Praise—lifting up our heart and hands, exulting with our voices, singing his praises—is the occupation of those who dwell in the kingdom.

I believe that praise and prayer develop us for what we will do when we arrive in heaven. What's your picture of what you'll be doing there—sitting on a cloud? Polishing your halo? Playing your harp? That's not what you're going to be doing. You're going to be involved in the ongoing process of coreigning with God.

WE GIVE YOU PRAISE. We honor and glorify your name. You truly are the King of kings and the Lord of lords. We thank you and worship you and glorify your name forever and ever.

PARENTS

Never underestimate the ponderings of a Christian parent. Never underestimate the power that comes when a parent pleads with God on behalf of a child. Who knows how many prayers are being answered right now because of the faithful ponderings of a parent ten or twenty years ago? God listens to thoughtful parents.

Praying for our children is a noble task. If what we are doing, in this fast-paced society, is taking us away from prayer time for our children, we're doing too much. There is nothing more special, more precious than that time that a parent spends struggling and pondering with God on behalf of a child.

It's not too late for the child who has brought only tears. Think of Jesus' parents; the mother who had to watch her son crucified saw her son raised from the dead. Though you may go to the grave wondering if your prayers will ever be answered, don't stop praying. God blesses faithfulness.

FATHER, in the midst of hectic schedules, we come to you. What was supposed to give us more time seems to take more time to run. What was supposed to free us up seems to imprison us. And, Lord, there are times when the only stability in the world is the Cross of Christ. So to that Cross we turn, praying that you would give us the courage to do only what needs to be done in your eyes, through your power.

RESENTMENT

Resentment is when you allow your hurts to turn into hates. When those hates simmer in your heart, they create bitterness, and you are the one who suffers. Forget those hurts!

When you have a relationship in need of repair, the first key to improvement is to examine your own heart. Look at your own heart—remember who you are and who God called you to be. Did the Father call you to be angry? to be bitter? Or did he call you to be loving and forgiving?

An itinerant preacher from Nazareth can do something for the hurt that is in your heart. Maybe you're trying to rebuild an estranged relationship. . . . Maybe you've been trying to find God for longer than you can remember. There was something about this Nazarene preacher that made people cluster around him like he was God's gift to humanity. He is your gift as well.

Father, we know that resentment and bitterness don't belong in Christian hearts. But sometimes, like little children, we hold onto our hurts. Help us turn them over to you, Father. Remind us that your touch can make us stronger at our broken places.

FORGIVENESS

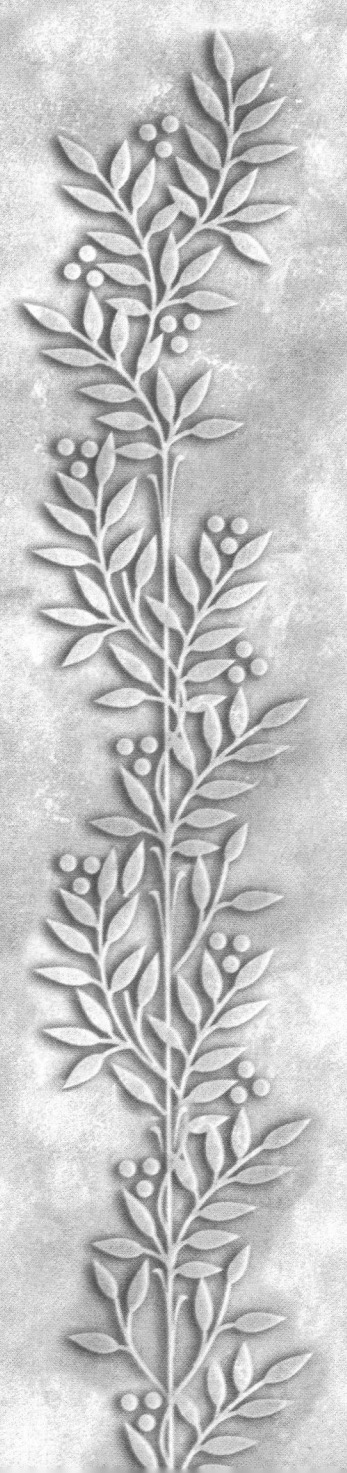

What do you do when people mistreat you or those you love? Does the fire of anger boil within you, with leaping flames consuming your emotions? Or do you reach somewhere, to some source of cool water and pull out a bucket of mercy—to free yourself? Is there any emotion that imprisons the soul more than the unwillingness to forgive?

Don't get on the roller coaster of resentment and anger. You be the one who says, "Yes, he mistreated me, but I am going to be like Christ. I'll be the one who says, 'Forgive them, Father, they don't know what they're doing.'"

The first step toward forgiveness is to see the other person as a human being, not as a source of hurt. That's how God treated us with mercy—he became one of us, he felt as we feel, he understood our frustrations. And as a result, when he hung on the cross, he could look at those crucifying him and ask God to forgive them.

When you forgive someone, you are as close to God as you will ever be, because in that forgiveness you are demonstrating the very heart of God, the merciful King. If you want to understand God, if you want to draw closer to him, then forgive someone today.

FATHER, sometimes forgiving others seems impossible. Forgive us when we hesitate to extend grace to others. And remind us that revisiting the cross is the first step in knowing how to forgive.

27This man was seized by the Jews and was about to be killed by
them. Coming with the troops I rescued him, having learned that
he was a Roman. 28And when I wanted to know the reason they
accused him, I brought him before their council. 29I found out that
he was accused concerning questions of their law, but had nothing
charged against him deserving of death or chains. 30And when it
was told me that the Jews lay in wait for the man,[a] I sent him
immediately to you, and also commanded his accusers to state
before you the charges against him.

Farewell.

31Then the soldiers, as they were commanded, took Paul and brought
him by night to Antipatris. 32The next day they left the horsemen to go on
with him, and returned to the barracks. 33When they came to Caesarea
and had delivered the letter to the governor, they also presented Paul to
him. 34And when the governor had read *it*, he asked what province he was
from. And when he understood that *he was* from Cilicia, 35he said, "I will
hear you when your accusers also have come." And he commanded him
to be kept in Herod's Praetorium.

Accused of Sedition

24 Now after five days Ananias the high priest came down with the elders
and a certain orator *named* Tertullus. These gave evidence to the
governor against Paul.

2And when he was called upon, Tertullus began his accusation, saying:
"Seeing that through you we enjoy great peace, and prosperity is being
brought to this nation by your foresight, 3we accept *it* always and in all
places, most noble Felix, with all thankfulness. 4Nevertheless, not to be tedious to you any further, I beg you to hear, by your courtesy, a few words
from us. 5For we have found this man a plague, a creator of dissension among
all the Jews throughout the world, and a ringleader of the sect of the Naza-
renes. 6He even tried to profane the temple, and we seized him,[b] and wanted
to judge him according to our law. 7But the commander Lysias came by and
with great violence took *him* out of our hands, 8commanding his accusers
to come to you. By examining him yourself you may ascertain all these
things of which we accuse him." 9And the Jews also assented,[c] maintaining that these things were so.

The Defense Before Felix

10Then Paul, after the governor had nodded to him to speak, answered:
"Inasmuch as I know that you have been for many years a judge of this nation, I do the more cheerfully answer for myself, 11because you may ascertain that it is no more than twelve days since I went up to Jerusalem to
worship. 12And they neither found me in the temple disputing with anyone nor inciting the crowd, either in the synagogues or in the city. 13Nor
can they prove the things of which they now accuse me. 14But this I confess
to you, that according to the Way which they call a sect, so I worship the
God of my fathers, believing all things which are written in the Law and in

23:30 [a] NU-Text reads *there would be a plot against the man.*
24:6 [b] NU-Text ends the sentence here and omits the rest of verse 6, all of verse 7, and the first clause of verse 8.
24:9 [c] NU-Text and M-Text read *joined the attack.*

Life Lesson

Acts 24:1-27

SITUATION Foiled in their attempts to kill Paul, the priests hoped to manipulate the law against him before the Roman governor. Paul became Christ's mouthpiece; he defended himself and his faith against their accusations. Paul's powerful arguments thwarted the priests and won new converts at the governor's court, although some remained hesitant to receive God's Word.

OBSERVATION Although God's wisdom is wiser than any other type of wisdom, some non-Christians will never accept it.

INSPIRATION Most people I know look forward to payday. You do too, right? For a week, or perhaps a two-week period, you give time and effort to your job. When payday arrives, you receive a hard-earned, well-deserved paycheck. . . .

But with God the economy is altogether different. There is no wage relationship with God. Spiritually speaking, you and I haven't earned anything but death. . . .

Everyone who hopes to be eternally justified must come to God the same way: on the basis of grace; it is a gift. And that gift comes to us absolutely free. Any other view of salvation is heresy, plain and simple. . . .

We being justified by faith, not works, get the one thing we've longed for—peace with God. Is it through our merits? Not at all. The verse states we've been justified by faith. It is through Jesus Christ our Lord who paid the absolute, final payment for sin when He died in our place at the Cross. Sin against God required the payment of death. And Jesus Christ, the perfect Substitute, made the ultimate, once-and-for-all payment on our behalf. It cost Him His life. As a result, God gives the free gift of salvation to all who believe in His Son. . . .

Wonderful! Marvelous reassurance!

"You're telling me, Chuck, that by simply believing in Jesus Christ I can have eternal life with God, my sins forgiven, a destiny secure in heaven, all of this and much more without my

Continued

working for that?" Yes, that is precisely what Scripture teaches. I remind you, it is called grace.

(From *The Grace Awakening* by Charles Swindoll)

APPLICATION You've probably met people who attend church regularly but are unmoved by the preaching of God's Word. Their attendance seems more of a social obligation than a means for sharing and being enriched with God's Word. Is that how life is for you or your family? Think about your relationship with Christ. Does it have a true and real meaning? Make your goal next Sunday to worship God through active participation and listening.

EXPLORATION Acceptance—Judges 11:3; Luke 4:24; 9:7-8.

the Prophets. 15I have hope in God, which they themselves also accept, that
there will be a resurrection of *the* dead,[d] both of *the* just and *the* unjust.
16This *being* so, I myself always strive to have a conscience without offense
toward God and men.

17"Now after many years I came to bring alms and offerings to my nation,
18in the midst of which some Jews from Asia found me purified in the temple, neither with a mob nor with tumult. 19They ought to have been here
before you to object if they had anything against me. 20Or else let those
who are *here* themselves say if they found any wrongdoing[e] in me while I
stood before the council, 21unless *it is* for this one statement which I cried
out, standing among them, 'Concerning the resurrection of the dead I am
being judged by you this day.' "

Felix Procrastinates

22But when Felix heard these things, having more accurate knowledge
of *the* Way, he adjourned the proceedings and said, "When Lysias the commander comes down, I will make a decision on your case." 23So he commanded the centurion to keep Paul and to let *him* have liberty, and told him
not to forbid any of his friends to provide for or visit him.

24And after some days, when Felix came with his wife Drusilla, who was
Jewish, he sent for Paul and heard him concerning the faith in Christ. 25Now
as he reasoned about righteousness, self-control, and the judgment to come,
Felix was afraid and answered, "Go away for now; when I have a convenient
time I will call for you." 26Meanwhile he also hoped that money would be
given him by Paul, that he might release him.[f] Therefore he sent for him
more often and conversed with him.

27But after two years Porcius Festus succeeded Felix; and Felix, wanting
to do the Jews a favor, left Paul bound.

Paul Appeals to Caesar

25 Now when Festus had come to the province, after three days he
went up from Caesarea to Jerusalem. 2Then the high priest[g] and the
chief men of the Jews informed him against Paul; and they petitioned him,
3asking a favor against him, that he would summon him to Jerusalem—
while *they* lay in ambush along the road to kill him. 4But Festus answered
that Paul should be kept at Caesarea, and that he himself was going *there*
shortly. 5"Therefore," he said, "let those who have authority among you go
down with *me* and accuse this man, to see if there is any fault in him."

6And when he had remained among them more than ten days, he went
down to Caesarea. And the next day, sitting on the judgment seat, he commanded Paul to be brought. 7When he had come, the Jews who had come
down from Jerusalem stood about and laid many serious complaints
against Paul, which they could not prove, 8while he answered for himself,
"Neither against the law of the Jews, nor against the temple, nor against
Caesar have I offended in anything at all."

9But Festus, wanting to do the Jews a favor, answered Paul and said,
"Are you willing to go up to Jerusalem and there be judged before me concerning these things?"

24:15 [d] NU-Text omits *of the dead.*
24:20 [e] NU-Text and M-Text read *say what wrongdoing they found.*
24:26 [f] NU-Text omits *that he might release him.*
25:2 [g] NU-Text reads *chief priests.*

10So Paul said, "I stand at Caesar's judgment seat, where I ought to be
judged. To the Jews I have done no wrong, as you very well know. 11For if I
am an offender, or have committed anything deserving of death, I do not
object to dying; but if there is nothing in these things of which these men
accuse me, no one can deliver me to them. I appeal to Caesar."
12Then Festus, when he had conferred with the council, answered, "You
have appealed to Caesar? To Caesar you shall go!"

Paul Before Agrippa

13And after some days King Agrippa and Bernice came to Caesarea to
greet Festus. 14When they had been there many days, Festus laid Paul's
case before the king, saying: "There is a certain man left a prisoner by
Felix, 15about whom the chief priests and the elders of the Jews informed
me, when I was in Jerusalem, asking for a judgment against him. 16To them
I answered, 'It is not the custom of the Romans to deliver any man to destruction[h] before the accused meets the accusers face to face, and has opportunity
to answer for himself concerning the charge against him.' 17Therefore when
they had come together, without any delay, the next day I sat on the judgment seat and commanded the man to be brought in. 18When the accusers
stood up, they brought no accusation against him of such things as I supposed, 19but had some questions against him about their own religion and
about a certain Jesus, who had died, whom Paul affirmed to be alive. 20And
because I was uncertain of such questions, I asked whether he was willing
to go to Jerusalem and there be judged concerning these matters. 21But when
Paul appealed to be reserved for the decision of Augustus, I commanded
him to be kept till I could send him to Caesar."
22Then Agrippa said to Festus, "I also would like to hear the man myself."
"Tomorrow," he said, "you shall hear him."
23So the next day, when Agrippa and Bernice had come with great pomp,
and had entered the auditorium with the commanders and the prominent
men of the city, at Festus' command Paul was brought in. 24And Festus
said: "King Agrippa and all the men who are here present with us, you see
this man about whom the whole assembly of the Jews petitioned me, both
at Jerusalem and here, crying out that he was not fit to live any longer.
25But when I found that he had committed nothing deserving of death,
and that he himself had appealed to Augustus, I decided to send him. 26I
have nothing certain to write to my lord concerning him. Therefore I have
brought him out before you, and especially before you, King Agrippa, so
that after the examination has taken place I may have something to write.
27For it seems to me unreasonable to send a prisoner and not to specify
the charges against him."

Paul's Early Life

26 Then Agrippa said to Paul, "You are permitted to speak for yourself."
So Paul stretched out his hand and answered for himself: 2"I think
myself happy, King Agrippa, because today I shall answer for myself before you concerning all the things of which I am accused by the Jews, 3es-
pecially because you are expert in all customs and questions which have
to do with the Jews. Therefore I beg you to hear me patiently.

25:16 [h] NU-Text omits *to destruction,* although it is implied.

LIFE LESSON

Acts 25:1-27

SITUATION After two years in prison, Paul awaited a new trial before the Romans and the Jews. He hoped his appeal to be heard by Caesar would fulfill part of his task to spread the gospel.

OBSERVATION Paul never lost hope or vision and made the most of his situation to obtain safe passage to Rome to await trial. While preaching to everyone he came in touch with, Paul developed a positive and respected reputation among those he met.

INSPIRATION Earl Palmer, in a fine little book entitled *The Enormous Exception*, tells the story of a pre-med student at the University of California, Berkeley "who became a Christian after a long journey through doubts and questions." When Palmer asked the young man why he had chosen Jesus Christ, he answered that what had "tipped the scales" in his spiritual journey were the actions of a classmate who happened to be a Christian. During the previous term the pre-med student had been very ill with the flu and, as a result, had missed ten days of school. "Without any fanfare or complaints," his Christian classmate carefully collected all his class assignments and took time away from his own studies to help him catch up.

The pre-med student told Palmer, "You know, this kind of thing just isn't done. I wanted to know what made this guy act the way he did. I even found myself asking if I could go to church with him."

(From *Simple Faith* by Charles Swindoll)

APPLICATION Perhaps you have been in a discouraging rut that caused you to lose your Christian witness. Did you stop being a good Christian because you had a bad day? Make the most of every situation, even the bad times. Your dark cloud may have a surprise silver lining.

EXPLORATION Opportunities—Exodus 2:7-8; 2 Corinthians 4:17; Philippians 1:12-14.

LIFE LESSON

Acts 26:1-32

SITUATION Festus asked Agrippa for advice on Paul's case. When Agrippa asked to hear Paul's case, Paul recounted how Jesus had changed his life.

OBSERVATION Christ fills a Believer's new life with joy, hope, love, and peace. People still in the "old life" can see the difference but do not always understand it.

INSPIRATION It is possible for God's people to live in moderation, wisdom, and exuberant joy. We can so conduct ourselves amid a corrupt society and sick culture that we are a credit to our Master. . . .

My walk with God need not in any sense be a spectacular display of special dedication. It need not have any carnival atmosphere about it to be convincing. I don't have to indulge in theatrics to impress either Him or other human beings.

What He desires most is that I walk with Him humbly, quietly, and obediently. The communion between shepherd and sheep is sweet and secure because He knows me and I know Him!

(From *A Shepherd Looks at the Good Shepherd and His Sheep* by Phillip Keller)

APPLICATION Do you just say, "I believe"? Or, do your actions prove it? Consider volunteering to meet one of your church's needs.

EXPLORATION Witnessing—Acts 1:8, 21, 22; 1 Corinthians 1:18-31.

4"My manner of life from my youth, which was spent from the beginning among my own nation at Jerusalem, all the Jews know. 5They knew
me from the first, if they were willing to testify, that according to the
strictest sect of our religion I lived a Pharisee. 6And now I stand and am
judged for the hope of the promise made by God to our fathers. 7To this
promise our twelve tribes, earnestly serving *God* night and day, hope to attain. For this hope's sake, King Agrippa, I am accused by the Jews. 8Why
should it be thought incredible by you that God raises the dead?
9"Indeed, I myself thought I must do many things contrary to the name
of Jesus of Nazareth. 10This I also did in Jerusalem, and many of the saints I
shut up in prison, having received authority from the chief priests; and when
they were put to death, I cast my vote against *them.* 11And I punished them
often in every synagogue and compelled *them* to blaspheme; and being exceedingly enraged against them, I persecuted *them* even to foreign cities.

Paul Recounts His Conversion

12"While thus occupied, as I journeyed to Damascus with authority and
commission from the chief priests, 13at midday, O king, along the road I
saw a light from heaven, brighter than the sun, shining around me and those
who journeyed with me. 14And when we all had fallen to the ground, I heard
a voice speaking to me and saying in the Hebrew language, 'Saul, Saul, why
are you persecuting Me? *It is* hard for you to kick against the goads.' 15So I
said, 'Who are You, Lord?' And He said, 'I am Jesus, whom you are persecuting. 16But rise and stand on your feet; for I have appeared to you for this
purpose, to make you a minister and a witness both of the things which you
have seen and of the things which I will yet reveal to you. 17I will deliver
you from the *Jewish* people, as well as *from* the Gentiles, to whom I now[i]
send you, 18to open their eyes, *in order* to turn *them* from darkness to light,
and *from* the power of Satan to God, that they may receive forgiveness of
sins and an inheritance among those who are sanctified by faith in Me.'

Paul's Post-Conversion Life

19"Therefore, King Agrippa, I was not disobedient to the heavenly vision,
20but declared first to those in Damascus and in Jerusalem, and throughout
all the region of Judea, and *then* to the Gentiles, that they should repent,
turn to God, and do works befitting repentance. 21For these reasons the Jews
seized me in the temple and tried to kill *me.* 22Therefore, having obtained
help from God, to this day I stand, witnessing both to small and great, saying no other things than those which the prophets and Moses said would
come— 23that the Christ would suffer, that He would be the first to rise from
the dead, and would proclaim light to the *Jewish* people and to the Gentiles."

Agrippa Parries Paul's Challenge

24Now as he thus made his defense, Festus said with a loud voice, "Paul,
you are beside yourself! Much learning is driving you mad!"
25But he said, "I am not mad, most noble Festus, but speak the words of
truth and reason. 26For the king, before whom I also speak freely, knows
these things; for I am convinced that none of these things escapes his attention, since this thing was not done in a corner. 27King Agrippa, do you
believe the prophets? I know that you do believe."

26:17 [i] NU-Text and M-Text omit *now.*

28 Then Agrippa said to Paul, "You almost persuade me to become a
Christian."
29 And Paul said, "I would to God that not only you, but also all who hear
me today, might become both almost and altogether such as I am, except
for these chains."
30 When he had said these things, the king stood up, as well as the governor and Bernice and those who sat with them; 31 and when they had gone
aside, they talked among themselves, saying, "This man is doing nothing
deserving of death or chains."
32 Then Agrippa said to Festus, "This man might have been set free if he
had not appealed to Caesar."

The Voyage to Rome Begins

27 And when it was decided that we should sail to Italy, they delivered
Paul and some other prisoners to *one* named Julius, a centurion of
the Augustan Regiment. 2 So, entering a ship of Adramyttium, we put to
sea, meaning to sail along the coasts of Asia. Aristarchus, a Macedonian of
Thessalonica, was with us. 3 And the next *day* we landed at Sidon. And Julius
treated Paul kindly and gave *him* liberty to go to his friends and receive care.
4 When we had put to sea from there, we sailed under *the shelter of* Cyprus,
because the winds were contrary. 5 And when we had sailed over the sea
which is off Cilicia and Pamphylia, we came to Myra, *a city* of Lycia. 6 There the
centurion found an Alexandrian ship sailing to Italy, and he put us on board.
7 When we had sailed slowly many days, and arrived with difficulty off
Cnidus, the wind not permitting us to proceed, we sailed under *the shelter
of* Crete off Salmone. 8 Passing it with difficulty, we came to a place called
Fair Havens, near the city *of* Lasea.

Paul's Warning Ignored

9 Now when much time had been spent, and sailing was now dangerous
because the Fast was already over, Paul advised them, 10 saying, "Men, I
perceive that this voyage will end with disaster and much loss, not only of
the cargo and ship, but also our lives." 11 Nevertheless the centurion was
more persuaded by the helmsman and the owner of the ship than by the
things spoken by Paul. 12 And because the harbor was not suitable to winter
in, the majority advised to set sail from there also, if by any means they
could reach Phoenix, a harbor of Crete opening toward the southwest and
northwest, *and* winter *there*.

In the Tempest

13 When the south wind blew softly, supposing that they had obtained
their desire, putting out to sea, they sailed close by Crete. 14 But not long
after, a tempestuous head wind arose, called Euroclydon.[j] 15 So when the ship
was caught, and could not head into the wind, we let *her* drive. 16 And running
under *the shelter of* an island called Clauda,[k] we secured the skiff with difficulty. 17 When they had taken it on board, they used cables to undergird
the ship; and fearing lest they should run aground on the Syrtis[l] *Sands*,
they struck sail and so were driven. 18 And because we were exceedingly

27:14 [j] NU-Text reads *Euraquilon*.
27:16 [k] NU-Text reads *Cauda*.
27:17 [l] M-Text reads *Syrtes*.

LIFE LESSON

Acts 27:1-44

SITUATION Paul proved to be a calming presence on board the ship as he was taken to Rome. His faith and confidence remained like a rock when trouble engulfed the ship.

OBSERVATION Trust in God to fulfill his promises. He provides hope when there seems to be no way out.

INSPIRATION The love of God is a subject that can never be exhausted. No human mind will ever be able to fathom it. . . .

Think of all the hymns and poems that have been composed in praise of the love of God, the books that have been written, the messages that have been preached. And yet that is not enough. God's will is that His love be manifested in our lives! The world today is dying for lack of love, and only Christians can really fill the need.

We should never lose a sense of wonder that God's love for us is so undeserved.

We should love Him with a love that is undivided, obedient, and worshipful, allowing no rival to share the throne with Him.

We should love our brothers and sisters in Christ without regard to denominations or religious labels. John insists that if we do not love our brothers whom we have seen we cannot love God whom we have not seen.

When this is our spiritual craving, we are getting close to Calvary love.

(From *Alone in Majesty* by William MacDonald)

APPLICATION Imagine yourself on a plane flying through rough weather with engine trouble. Would you be bold enough to provide hope to the person next to you? Would you quickly share Christ with that person? Anyone you know could be close to death. An unfortunate accident could claim the lives of a couple of your friends. What keeps you from sharing Christ with them?

EXPLORATION God's Love—Psalm 136:1-26; Jeremiah 31:3; John 3:16; 11:33-38; 1 John 3:1; Revelation 3:20.

tempest-tossed, the next *day* they lightened the ship. 19On the third *day* we threw the ship's tackle overboard with our own hands. 20Now when neither sun nor stars appeared for many days, and no small tempest beat on *us,* all hope that we would be saved was finally given up.

21But after long abstinence from food, then Paul stood in the midst of them and said, "Men, you should have listened to me, and not have sailed from Crete and incurred this disaster and loss. 22And now I urge you to take heart, for there will be no loss of life among you, but only of the ship. 23For there stood by me this night an angel of the God to whom I belong and whom I serve, 24saying, 'Do not be afraid, Paul; you must be brought before Caesar; and indeed God has granted you all those who sail with you.' 25Therefore take heart, men, for I believe God that it will be just as it was told me. 26However, we must run aground on a certain island."

27Now when the fourteenth night had come, as we were driven up and down in the Adriatic *Sea,* about midnight the sailors sensed that they were drawing near some land. 28And they took soundings and found *it* to be twenty fathoms; and when they had gone a little farther, they took soundings again and found *it* to be fifteen fathoms. 29Then, fearing lest we should run aground on the rocks, they dropped four anchors from the stern, and prayed for day to come. 30And as the sailors were seeking to escape from the ship, when they had let down the skiff into the sea, under pretense of putting out anchors from the prow, 31Paul said to the centurion and the soldiers, "Unless these men stay in the ship, you cannot be saved." 32Then the soldiers cut away the ropes of the skiff and let it fall off.

33And as day was about to dawn, Paul implored *them* all to take food, saying, "Today is the fourteenth day you have waited and continued without food, and eaten nothing. 34Therefore I urge you to take nourishment, for this is for your survival, since not a hair will fall from the head of any of you." 35And when he had said these things, he took bread and gave thanks to God in the presence of them all; and when he had broken *it* he began to eat. 36Then they were all encouraged, and also took food themselves. 37And in all we were two hundred and seventy-six persons on the ship. 38So when they had eaten enough, they lightened the ship and threw out the wheat into the sea.

Shipwrecked on Malta

39When it was day, they did not recognize the land; but they observed a bay with a beach, onto which they planned to run the ship if possible. 40And they let go the anchors and left *them* in the sea, meanwhile loosing the rudder ropes; and they hoisted the mainsail to the wind and made for shore. 41But striking a place where two seas met, they ran the ship aground; and the prow stuck fast and remained immovable, but the stern was being broken up by the violence of the waves.

42And the soldiers' plan was to kill the prisoners, lest any of them should swim away and escape. 43But the centurion, wanting to save Paul, kept them from *their* purpose, and commanded that those who could swim should jump *overboard* first and get to land, 44and the rest, some on boards and some on *parts* of the ship. And so it was that they all escaped safely to land.

Paul's Ministry on Malta

28 Now when they had escaped, they then found out that the island was called Malta. 2And the natives showed us unusual kindness; for they kindled a fire and made us all welcome, because of the rain that was falling and because of the cold. 3But when Paul had gathered a bundle of sticks and laid *them* on the fire, a viper came out because of the heat, and fastened on his hand. 4So when the natives saw the creature hanging from his hand, they said to one another, "No doubt this man is a murderer, whom, though he has escaped the sea, yet justice does not allow to live." 5But he shook off the creature into the fire and suffered no harm. 6However, they were expecting that he would swell up or suddenly fall down dead. But after they had looked for a long time and saw no harm come to him, they changed their minds and said that he was a god.

7In that region there was an estate of the leading citizen of the island, whose name was Publius, who received us and entertained us courteously for three days. 8And it happened that the father of Publius lay sick of a fever and dysentery. Paul went in to him and prayed, and he laid his hands on him and healed him. 9So when this was done, the rest of those on the island who had diseases also came and were healed. 10They also honored us in many ways; and when we departed, they provided such things as were necessary.

Arrival at Rome

11After three months we sailed in an Alexandrian ship whose figurehead was the Twin Brothers, which had wintered at the island. 12And landing at Syracuse, we stayed three days. 13From there we circled round and reached Rhegium. And after one day the south wind blew; and the next day we came to Puteoli, 14where we

found brethren, and were invited to stay with them seven days. And so we
went toward Rome. 15 And from there, when the brethren heard about us,
they came to meet us as far as Appii Forum and Three Inns. When Paul
saw them, he thanked God and took courage.
16 Now when we came to Rome, the centurion delivered the prisoners to
the captain of the guard; but Paul was permitted to dwell by himself with
the soldier who guarded him.

Paul's Ministry at Rome

17 And it came to pass after three days that Paul called the leaders of the
Jews together. So when they had come together, he said to them: "Men *and*
brethren, though I have done nothing against our people or the customs
of our fathers, yet I was delivered as a prisoner from Jerusalem into the
hands of the Romans, 18 who, when they had examined me, wanted to let
me go, because there was no cause for putting me to death. 19 But when the
Jews[m] spoke against *it,* I was compelled to appeal to Caesar, not that I had
anything of which to accuse my nation. 20 For this reason therefore I have
called for you, to see *you* and speak with *you,* because for the hope of Israel
I am bound with this chain."
21 Then they said to him, "We neither received letters from Judea concerning you, nor have any of the brethren who came reported or spoken
any evil of you. 22 But we desire to hear from you what you think; for concerning this sect, we know that it is spoken against everywhere."
23 So when they had appointed him a day, many came to him at *his* lodging,
to whom he explained and solemnly testified of the kingdom of God, persuading them concerning Jesus from both the Law of Moses and the Prophets,
from morning till evening. 24 And some were persuaded by the things which
were spoken, and some disbelieved. 25 So when they did not agree among
themselves, they departed after Paul had said one word: "The Holy Spirit
spoke rightly through Isaiah the prophet to our[n] fathers, 26 saying,

'Go to this people and say:
"Hearing you will hear, and shall not understand;
And seeing you will see, and not perceive;
27 *For the hearts of this people have grown dull.*
Their ears are hard of hearing,
And their eyes they have closed,
Lest they should see with their eyes and hear with their ears,
Lest they should understand with their hearts and turn,
So that I should heal them."'[o]

28 "Therefore let it be known to you that the salvation of God has been
sent to the Gentiles, and they will hear it!" 29 And when he had said these
words, the Jews departed and had a great dispute among themselves.[p]
30 Then Paul dwelt two whole years in his own rented house, and received all who came to him, 31 preaching the kingdom of God and teaching
the things which concern the Lord Jesus Christ with all confidence, no one
forbidding him.

LIFE LESSON

Acts 28:1-31

SITUATION Paul, Luke, and the others survived the crash. Paul arrived in Rome and attempted to bring the message of Jesus to the Jewish community in Rome, but they rejected the message.

OBSERVATION The message of God is meant for all people. It cannot be limited by race or culture.

INSPIRATION There, then, is the watchword of those men of the New Testament and the secret of their amazing, indomitable vitality—never "We are able," but always "He is able." God is able! Christ is able! Able to succour the tempted, able to save to the uttermost, able to support and keep you from failing, able to subdue all things to Himself, able to secure you in death's decisive hour, able to surpass your dreams of immortality. All this is yours and mine, if we are Christ's. . . . Why should we not believe it and confide in it, and lift up our hearts to its splendour? . . . come, and let us walk in the light of the Lord!

(From *The Wind of the Spirit* by James Stewart)

APPLICATION Give thanks to God for the sacrifice of the early Christians who spread the Good News from Judea. Learn a little bit more this month about someone who helped pass on the gospel throughout the centuries—Augustine, Luther, Wesley, Carey, or Zinzendorf for starters.

EXPLORATION Good News for Everyone—Isaiah 40:28; John 3:31-35; Titus 2:11-12; Philippians 2:5-11; Revelation 14:6.

28:19 *m* That is, the ruling authorities
28:25 *n* NU-Text reads *your.*
28:27 *o* Isaiah 6:9, 10
28:29 *p* NU-Text omits this verse.

The Epistle of Paul to the

ROMANS

INTRODUCTION

At the moment I don't feel too smart. I just got off the wrong plane that took me to the wrong city and left me at the wrong airport. I went east instead of west and ended up in Houston instead of Denver.

It didn't look like the wrong plane, but it was. I walked through the wrong gate, dozed off on the wrong flight, and ended up in the wrong place.

Paul says we've all done the same thing. Not with airplanes and airports, but with our lives and God. He tells the Roman readers,

There is none righteous, no, not one (3:10).

All have sinned and fall short of the glory of God (3:23).

We are all on the wrong plane, he says. All of us. Gentile and Jew. Every person has taken the wrong turn. And we need help.

In this profound Epistle, Paul explores all the wrong options and takes us to the only correct one. The wrong solutions are pleasure and pride (chapters 1 and 2), the correct solution is Christ Jesus (3:21–26). According to Paul, we are saved by grace, (undeserved, unearned favor) through faith (complete trust) in Jesus and his work.

The letter concludes with practical instruction for a growing church, including thoughts on spiritual gifts (12:3–8); genuine love (12:9–21); good citizenship (13:1–14). The final chapters provide brilliant instruction for dealing with everything from church division to difficult brethren.

Romans is a life-changing letter for people who are willing to admit they are sinners. For those who admit they are on the wrong plane, the letter provides the correct itinerary.

Read it and take note. That flight home is one you don't want to miss.

LIFE LESSON

Romans 1:1-32

SITUATION Paul wrote this letter to teach the Christian faith to the first Believers in Rome. He taught that no one deserves God's love.

OBSERVATION Sin paints an ugly picture in people and in a culture. Without God's intervention, we have no way to deal with sin.

INSPIRATION What does it mean to be righteous? . . .

Righteousness has nothing to do with doing good works, though good works are a byproduct of being righteous. Jesus spoke of God as the only one who is truly good. The word "good" is a synonym for righteous, so it follows that to be righteous is to be like God. But how can anyone be like God, who is holy and perfect?

. . . Righteousness, meaning to be right or just, begins with believing God. It sounds so simple, but how many times do we disbelieve God? God's formulas are so simple that we ignore them because we think there must be more to it than that.

All sin is rooted in unbelief. All righteousness is rooted in belief. Believe God for all His promises and He will count it unto you as righteousness. Believe on the Lord Jesus Christ, God's ultimate standard and incarnation of righteousness, and be saved. Believe in Jesus Christ to deliver you in your day of trouble and learn what the righteousness of Christ can do in and through you.

(From *Unto the Hills* by Billy Graham)

APPLICATION How does the bleak side of life reflect your experience? Is that where you were? Is that where you are? If it is, switch sides—join God's side. If you already have, then thank him throughout the day for his mercy.

EXPLORATION Righteousness—1 Samuel 26:23; 1 Kings 10:9; Psalm 111:3; Zephaniah 2:3; Habakkuk 2:4; Malachi 4:2; Romans 3:21; 8:10; Galatians 3:11; 2 Timothy 3:16.

Greeting

Paul, a bondservant of Jesus Christ, called *to be* an apostle, separated to the gospel of God [2]which He promised before through
His prophets in the Holy Scriptures, [3]concerning His Son Jesus
Christ our Lord, who was born of the seed of David according to the
flesh, [4]*and* declared *to be* the Son of God with power according to the Spirit of
holiness, by the resurrection from the dead. [5]Through Him we have received grace and apostleship for obedience to the faith among all nations
for His name, [6]among whom you also are the called of Jesus Christ;

[7]To all who are in Rome, beloved of God, called *to be* saints:

Grace to you and peace from God our Father and the Lord Jesus Christ.

Desire to Visit Rome

[8]First, I thank my God through Jesus Christ for you all, that your faith is
spoken of throughout the whole world. [9]For God is my witness, whom I
serve with my spirit in the gospel of His Son, that without ceasing I make
mention of you always in my prayers, [10]making request if, by some means,
now at last I may find a way in the will of God to come to you. [11]For I long
to see you, that I may impart to you some spiritual gift, so that you may be
established— [12]that is, that I may be encouraged together with you by the
mutual faith both of you and me.

[13]Now I do not want you to be unaware, brethren, that I often planned to
come to you (but was hindered until now), that I might have some fruit
among you also, just as among the other Gentiles. [14]I am a debtor both to
Greeks and to barbarians, both to wise and to unwise. [15]So, as much as is
in me, *I am* ready to preach the gospel to you who are in Rome also.

The Just Live by Faith

[16]For I am not ashamed of the gospel of Christ,[a] for it is the power of God
to salvation for everyone who believes, for the Jew first and also for the
Greek. [17]For in it the righteousness of God is revealed from faith to faith; as
it is written, *"The just shall live by faith."*[b]

God's Wrath on Unrighteousness

[18]For the wrath of God is revealed from heaven against all ungodliness
and unrighteousness of men, who suppress the truth in unrighteousness,
[19]because what may be known of God is manifest in them, for God has
shown *it* to them. [20]For since the creation of the world His invisible *attributes* are clearly seen, being understood by the things that are made, *even*
His eternal power and Godhead, so that they are without excuse, [21]because,
although they knew God, they did not glorify *Him* as God, nor were thankful,
but became futile in their thoughts, and their foolish hearts were darkened.
[22]Professing to be wise, they became fools, [23]and changed the glory of the
incorruptible God into an image made like corruptible man—and birds
and four-footed animals and creeping things.

[24]Therefore God also gave them up to uncleanness, in the lusts of their
hearts, to dishonor their bodies among themselves, [25]who exchanged the
truth of God for the lie, and worshiped and served the creature rather than
the Creator, who is blessed forever. Amen.

1:16 [a] NU-Text omits *of Christ.*
1:17 [b] Habakkuk 2:4

26For this reason God gave them up to vile passions. For even their women
exchanged the natural use for what is against nature. 27Likewise also the men,
leaving the natural use of the woman, burned in their lust for one another,
men with men committing what is shameful, and receiving in themselves
the penalty of their error which was due.
28And even as they did not like to retain God in *their* knowledge, God gave
them over to a debased mind, to do those things which are not fitting; 29being
filled with all unrighteousness, sexual immorality,[c] wickedness, covetousness,
maliciousness; full of envy, murder, strife, deceit, evil-mindedness; *they are*
whisperers, 30backbiters, haters of God, violent, proud, boasters, inven-
tors of evil things, disobedient to parents, 31undiscerning, untrustworthy,
unloving, unforgiving,[d] unmerciful; 32who, knowing the righteous judgment of God, that those who practice such things are deserving of death,
not only do the same but also approve of those who practice them.

God's Righteous Judgment

2 Therefore you are inexcusable, O man, whoever you are who judge, for
in whatever you judge another you condemn yourself; for you who
judge practice the same things. 2But we know that the judgment of God is
according to truth against those who practice such things. 3And do you
think this, O man, you who judge those practicing such things, and doing
the same, that you will escape the judgment of God? 4Or do you despise the
riches of His goodness, forbearance, and longsuffering, not knowing that
the goodness of God leads you to repentance? 5But in accordance with
your hardness and your impenitent heart you are treasuring up for yourself wrath in the day of wrath and revelation of the righteous judgment of
God, 6who *"will render to each one according to his deeds"*:[e] 7eternal life to
those who by patient continuance in doing good seek for glory, honor, and
immortality; 8but to those who are self-seeking and do not obey the truth,
but obey unrighteousness—indignation and wrath, 9tribulation and anguish, on every soul of man who does evil, of the Jew first and also of the
Greek; 10but glory, honor, and peace to everyone who works what is good,
to the Jew first and also to the Greek. 11For there is no partiality with God.
12For as many as have sinned without law will also perish without law,
and as many as have sinned in the law will be judged by the law 13(for not
the hearers of the law *are* just in the sight of God, but the doers of the law
will be justified; 14for when Gentiles, who do not have the law, by nature do
the things in the law, these, although not having the law, are a law to themselves, 15who show the work of the law written in their hearts, their conscience also bearing witness, and between themselves *their* thoughts
accusing or else excusing *them*) 16in the day when God will judge the secrets of men by Jesus Christ, according to my gospel.

The Jews Guilty as the Gentiles

17Indeed[f] you are called a Jew, and rest on the law, and make your boast
in God, 18and know *His* will, and approve the things that are excellent,
being instructed out of the law, 19and are confident that you yourself are a
guide to the blind, a light to those who are in darkness, 20an instructor of

1:29 [c] NU-Text omits *sexual immorality.*
1:31 [d] NU-Text omits *unforgiving.*
2:6 [e] Psalm 62:12; Proverbs 24:12
2:17 [f] NU-Text reads *But if.*

LIFE LESSON

Romans 2:1–3:8

SITUATION Paul encouraged the church in Rome to be set apart from the world. God made a right relationship with him available to all people.

OBSERVATION God hates sin and desires all to follow him in word and action.

INSPIRATION I've wondered, at times, what kind of man this Judas was. What he looked like, how he acted, who his friends were. . . .

But for all the things we don't know about Judas, there is one thing we know for sure: he had no relationship with the Master. He had seen Jesus, but he did not know him. He had heard Jesus, but he did not understand him. He had religion, but no relationship.

As Satan worked his way around the table in the Upper Room, he needed a special kind of man to betray our Lord. He needed a man who had seen Jesus, but did not know him. He needed a man who knew the actions of Jesus, but had missed out on the mission of Jesus. Judas was this man. He knew the empire but had never known the Man.

We learn this timeless lesson from the betrayer. Satan's best tools of destruction are not from outside the church, they are from within the church. A church will never die from the immorality in Hollywood or the corruption in Washington. But it will die from corrosion within—from those who bear the name of Jesus but have never met him, and from those who have religion, but no relationship.

Judas bore the cloak of religion, but he never knew the heart of Christ. Let's make it our goal to know . . . deeply.

(From *On the Anvil* by Max Lucado)

APPLICATION Spend uninterrupted time with Christ today. Tell him your thoughts, dreams, worries, sins.

EXPLORATION Relationship with Christ—Matthew 12:50; John 1:12; 15:5; Romans 8:15-17; 2 Corinthians 5:17; 6:18; Philippians 3:8.

LIFE LESSON

Romans 3:9-31

SITUATION Paul showed that no one can claim innocence. Everyone has sinned. But through Christ's death on the cross God has redeemed us.

OBSERVATION Willing and ready, God will forgive us if we come to him in faith.

INSPIRATION Salvation is free! God puts no price tag on the Gift of gifts—it's free! Preachers are not salesmen for they have nothing to sell. They are bearers of Good News, the good tidings that "Christ died for our sins according to the Scriptures." Money can't buy it. Man's righteousness can't earn it. Social prestige can't help you acquire it. Morality can't purchase it. It is, as Isaiah said, "without money and without price." God is not a bargaining God. You cannot barter with Him. You must do business with Him on His own terms. He holds in His omnipotent hand the priceless, precious, eternal gift of salvation, and He bids you to take it without money and without price. The best things in life are free, are they not? The air we breathe is not sold by the cubic foot. The water which flows crystal clear from the mountain stream is free for the taking. Love is free, faith is free, hope is free.

(From *Day by Day with Billy Graham* by Joan W. Brown)

APPLICATION Have you accepted the free gift of God, forgiveness and eternal life, won for you by Christ? Submit to Christ's rule in your life and kneel to his lordship. Don't wait.

EXPLORATION Faith—Acts 13:39; Romans 4:25; 5:16, 18; 10:10; Galatians 2:16; Titus 3:7.

the foolish, a teacher of babes, having the form of knowledge and truth in
the law. 21You, therefore, who teach another, do you not teach yourself? You
who preach that a man should not steal, do you steal? 22You who say, "Do
not commit adultery," do you commit adultery? You who abhor idols, do
you rob temples? 23You who make your boast in the law, do you dishonor
God through breaking the law? 24For *"the name of God is blasphemed
among the Gentiles because of you,"*[g] as it is written.

Circumcision of No Avail

25For circumcision is indeed profitable if you keep the law; but if you are a
breaker of the law, your circumcision has become uncircumcision. 26There-
fore, if an uncircumcised man keeps the righteous requirements of the law,
will not his uncircumcision be counted as circumcision? 27And will not the
physically uncircumcised, if he fulfills the law, judge you who, *even* with *your*
written *code* and circumcision, *are* a transgressor of the law? 28For he is not a
Jew who *is one* outwardly, nor *is* circumcision that which *is* outward in the
flesh; 29but *he is* a Jew who *is one* inwardly; and circumcision *is that* of the heart,
in the Spirit, not in the letter; whose praise *is* not from men but from God.

God's Judgment Defended

3 What advantage then has the Jew, or what *is* the profit of circumcision?
2Much in every way! Chiefly because to them were committed the oracles of God. 3For what if some did not believe? Will their unbelief make the
faithfulness of God without effect? 4Certainly not! Indeed, let God be true
but every man a liar. As it is written:

"That You may be justified in Your words,
And may overcome when You are judged."[h]

5But if our unrighteousness demonstrates the righteousness of God, what
shall we say? *Is* God unjust who inflicts wrath? (I speak as a man.) 6Certainly
not! For then how will God judge the world?

7For if the truth of God has increased through my lie to His glory, why
am I also still judged as a sinner? 8And *why* not *say,* "Let us do evil that
good may come"?—as we are slanderously reported and as some affirm
that we say. Their condemnation is just.

All Have Sinned

9What then? Are we better *than they?* Not at all. For we have previously
charged both Jews and Greeks that they are all under sin.
10As it is written:

"There is none righteous, no, not one;
11 *There is none who understands;*
There is none who seeks after God.
12 *They have all turned aside;*
They have together become unprofitable;
There is none who does good, no, not one."[i]
13 *"Their throat is an open tomb;*
With their tongues they have practiced deceit";[j]
"The poison of asps is under their lips";[k]

2:24 [g] Isaiah 52:5; Ezekiel 36:22
3:4 [h] Psalm 51:4
3:12 [i] Psalms 14:1–3; 53:1–3; Ecclesiastes 7:20
3:13 [j] Psalm 5:9 [k] Psalm 140:3

14 *"Whose mouth is full of cursing and bitterness."*[l]
15 *"Their feet are swift to shed blood;*
16 *Destruction and misery are in their ways;*
17 *And the way of peace they have not known."*[m]
18 *"There is no fear of God before their eyes."*[n]

19Now we know that whatever the law says, it says to those who are under
the law, that every mouth may be stopped, and all the world may become
guilty before God. 20Therefore by the deeds of the law no flesh will be justified
in His sight, for by the law *is* the knowledge of sin.

God's Righteousness Through Faith

21But now the righteousness of God apart from the law is revealed, being
witnessed by the Law and the Prophets, 22even the righteousness of God,
through faith in Jesus Christ, to all and on all[o] who believe. For there is no
difference; 23for all have sinned and fall short of the glory of God, 24being
justified freely by His grace through the redemption that is in Christ Jesus,
25whom God set forth *as* a propitiation by His blood, through faith, to demonstrate His righteousness, because in His forbearance God had passed over
the sins that were previously committed, 26to demonstrate at the present
time His righteousness, that He might be just and the justifier of the one
who has faith in Jesus.

Boasting Excluded

27Where *is* boasting then? It is excluded. By what law? Of works? No, but
by the law of faith. 28Therefore we conclude that a man is justified by faith
apart from the deeds of the law. 29Or *is He* the God of the Jews only? *Is He*
not also the God of the Gentiles? Yes, of the Gentiles also, 30since *there is* one
God who will justify the circumcised by faith and the uncircumcised through
faith. 31Do we then make void the law through faith? Certainly not! On the
contrary, we establish the law.

Abraham Justified by Faith

4 What then shall we say that Abraham our father has found according
to the flesh?[p] 2For if Abraham was justified by works, he has *something* to
boast about, but not before God. 3For what does the Scripture say? *"Abraham
believed God, and it was accounted to him for righteousness."*[q] 4Now to
him who works, the wages are not counted as grace but as debt.

David Celebrates the Same Truth

5But to him who does not work but believes on Him who justifies the
ungodly, his faith is accounted for righteousness, 6just as David also describes the blessedness of the man to whom God imputes righteousness
apart from works:

7 *"Blessed are those whose lawless deeds are forgiven,*
And whose sins are covered;
8 *Blessed is the man to whom the LORD shall not impute sin."*[r]

3:14 *l* Psalm 10:7
3:17 *m* Isaiah 59:7, 8
3:18 *n* Psalm 36:1
3:22 *o* NU-Text omits *and on all.*
4:1 *p* Or *Abraham our (fore)father according to the flesh has found?*
4:3 *q* Genesis 15:6
4:8 *r* Psalm 32:1, 2

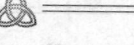

LIFE LESSON

Romans 4:1-25

SITUATION Paul showed that Abraham's leadership in God's family was due to faith.

OBSERVATION We accept God's gift by faith; we cannot earn it by good works.

INSPIRATION Henry Drummond [writes:] "You will find, if you think for a moment, that the people who influence you are people who believe in you. In an atmosphere of suspicion men shrivel up; but in that atmosphere they expand and find encouragement and educative fellowship. It is a wonderful thing that here and there in this hard uncharitable world there should still be left a few rare souls who think no evil. This is the great unworldliness. Love sees the bright side, puts the best construction on every action. What a delightful state of mind to live in! What a stimulus and benediction even to meet with it for a day! To be trusted is to be saved. And if we try to influence or elevate others, we shall soon see that success is in proportion to their belief of our belief in them. For the respect of another is the first restoration of the self-respect a man has lost; our ideal of what he is becomes to him the hope and pattern of what he may become."

This faith moves mountains of inertia in other people. It pulverizes prejudices and impossibilities. This faith is the fruit of God's Gracious Spirit that sweetens a sour world. It replaces suspicion and distrust with friendship and hope and good cheer. It makes our friends, family, and casual acquaintances stand tall.

(From *A Gardener Looks at the Fruits of the Spirit* by Phillip Keller)

APPLICATION Picture yourself at a department store. On the shelf you see something you've wanted for years, but the price is still too high. How would you feel if a caring friend or relative bought the item, wrapped it, and gave it to you? Thank God for giving you a gift you could never afford.

EXPLORATION Faith—Genesis 15:6; Psalm 32:1, 2; 2 Chronicles 20:20; Isaiah 7:9; Habakkuk 2:4; Matthew 9:29; Acts 15:9; Romans 4:16; 5:1; 10:17.

Abraham Justified Before Circumcision

9 *Does* this blessedness then *come* upon the circumcised *only,* or upon the uncircumcised also? For we say that faith was accounted to Abraham for righteousness. 10 How then was it accounted? While he was circumcised, or uncircumcised? Not while circumcised, but while uncircumcised. 11 And he received the sign of circumcision, a seal of the righteousness of the faith which *he had while still* uncircumcised, that he might be the father of all those who believe, though they are uncircumcised, that righteousness might be imputed to them also, 12 and the father of circumcision to those who not only *are* of the circumcision, but who also walk in the steps of the faith which our father Abraham *had while still* uncircumcised.

The Promise Granted Through Faith

13 For the promise that he would be the heir of the world *was* not to Abraham or to his seed through the law, but through the righteousness of faith. 14 For if those who are of the law *are* heirs, faith is made void and the promise made of no effect, 15 because the law brings about wrath; for where there is no law *there is* no transgression.

16 Therefore *it is* of faith that *it might be* according to grace, so that the promise might be sure to all the seed, not only to those who are of the law, but also to those who are of the faith of Abraham, who is the father of us all 17 (as it is written, *"I have made you a father of many nations"*[s]) in the presence of Him whom he believed—God, who gives life to the dead and calls those things which do not exist as though they did; 18 who, contrary to hope, in hope believed, so that he became the father of many nations, according to what was spoken, *"So shall your descendants be."*[t] 19 And not being weak in faith, he did not consider his own body, already dead (since he was about a hundred years old), and the deadness of Sarah's womb. 20 He did not waver at the promise of God through unbelief, but was strengthened in faith, giving glory to God, 21 and being fully convinced that what He had promised He was also able to perform. 22 And therefore *"it was accounted to him for righteousness."*[u]

23 Now it was not written for his sake alone that it was imputed to him, 24 but also for us. It shall be imputed to us who believe in Him who raised up Jesus our Lord from the dead, 25 who was delivered up because of our offenses, and was raised because of our justification.

Faith Triumphs in Trouble

5 Therefore, having been justified by faith, we have[v] peace with God through our Lord Jesus Christ, 2 through whom also we have access by faith into this grace in which we stand, and rejoice in hope of the glory of God. 3 And not only *that,* but we also glory in tribulations, knowing that tribulation produces perseverance; 4 and perseverance, character; and character, hope. 5 Now hope does not disappoint, because the love of God has been poured out in our hearts by the Holy Spirit who was given to us.

Christ in Our Place

6 For when we were still without strength, in due time Christ died for the ungodly. 7 For scarcely for a righteous man will one die; yet perhaps for a good man someone would even dare to die. 8 But God demonstrates His own love toward us, in that while we were still sinners, Christ died for us. 9 Much more then, having now been justified by His blood, we shall be saved from wrath through Him. 10 For if when we were enemies we were reconciled to God through the death of His Son, much more, having been reconciled, we shall be saved by His life. 11 And not only *that,* but we also rejoice in God through our Lord Jesus Christ, through whom we have now received the reconciliation.

Death in Adam, Life in Christ

12 Therefore, just as through one man sin entered the world, and death through sin, and thus death spread to all men, because all sinned— 13 (For until the law sin was in the world, but sin is not imputed when there is no law. 14 Nevertheless death reigned from Adam to Moses, even over those who had not sinned according to the likeness of the transgression of Adam, who is a type of Him who was to come. 15 But the free gift *is* not like the offense. For if by the one man's offense many died, much more the grace of God and the gift by the grace of the one Man, Jesus Christ, abounded to many. 16 And the gift *is* not like *that which came* through the one who sinned. For the judgment *which came* from one *offense resulted* in condemnation, but the free gift *which came* from many offenses *resulted* in justification. 17 For if by the one man's offense death reigned through the one, much more those who receive abundance of grace and of the gift of righteousness will reign in life through the One, Jesus Christ.)

4:17 [s] Genesis 17:5
4:18 [t] Genesis 15:5
4:22 [u] Genesis 15:6
5:1 [v] Another ancient reading is, *let us have peace.*

18Therefore, as through one man's offense *judgment* came to all men,
resulting in condemnation, even so through one Man's righteous act *the
free gift came* to all men, resulting in justification of life. 19For as by one man's
disobedience many were made sinners, so also by one Man's obedience
many will be made righteous.
20Moreover the law entered that the offense might abound. But where
sin abounded, grace abounded much more, 21so that as sin reigned in
death, even so grace might reign through righteousness to eternal life
through Jesus Christ our Lord.

Dead to Sin, Alive to God

6 What shall we say then? Shall we continue in sin that grace may abound?
2Certainly not! How shall we who died to sin live any longer in it? 3Or
do you not know that as many of us as were baptized into Christ Jesus
were baptized into His death? 4Therefore we were buried with Him
through baptism into death, that just as Christ was raised from the dead
by the glory of the Father, even so we also should walk in newness of life.
5For if we have been united together in the likeness of His death, certainly
we also shall be *in the likeness* of *His* resurrection, 6knowing this, that our
old man was crucified with *Him,* that the body of sin might be done away
with, that we should no longer be slaves of sin. 7For he who has died has
been freed from sin. 8Now if we died with Christ, we believe that we shall also
live with Him, 9knowing that Christ, having been raised from the dead, dies
no more. Death no longer has dominion over Him. 10For *the death* that He
died, He died to sin once for all; but *the life* that He lives, He lives to God.
11Likewise you also, reckon yourselves to be dead indeed to sin, but alive to
God in Christ Jesus our Lord.
12Therefore do not let sin reign in your mortal body, that you should
obey it in its lusts. 13And do not present your members *as* instruments of
unrighteousness to sin, but present yourselves to God as being alive from
the dead, and your members as instruments of righteousness to God. 14For sin
shall not have dominion over you, for you are not under law but under grace.

From Slaves of Sin to Slaves of God

15What then? Shall we sin because we are not under law but under
grace? Certainly not! 16Do you not know that to whom you present yourselves slaves to obey, you are that one's slaves whom you obey, whether of
sin *leading* to death, or of obedience *leading* to righteousness? 17But God
be thanked that *though* you were slaves of sin, yet you obeyed from the
heart that form of doctrine to which you were delivered. 18And having been
set free from sin, you became slaves of righteousness. 19I speak in human
terms because of the weakness of your flesh. For just as you presented
your members *as* slaves of uncleanness, and of lawlessness *leading* to
more lawlessness, so now present your members *as* slaves *of* righteousness for holiness.
20For when you were slaves of sin, you were free in regard to righteousness. 21What fruit did you have then in the things of which you are now
ashamed? For the end of those things *is* death. 22But now having been set
free from sin, and having become slaves of God, you have your fruit to holiness, and the end, everlasting life. 23For the wages of sin *is* death, but the
gift of God *is* eternal life in Christ Jesus our Lord.

Life Lesson

Romans 6:1-23

SITUATION Since Christ's righteousness brought us into a favored relationship with God, we should live by God's standards.

OBSERVATION Christians are not slaves to sin but can overcome by the power of God.

INSPIRATION Imagine being thrown in jail on suspicion of a charge, left there, virtually forgotten, while the system, ever so slowly caught up with you. You get sick. You're treated harshly. Abused. Assaulted. Would you begin to entertain that feeling of lostness and hopelessness?

Back to the question: "How shall we who died to sin still live in it?" Who would volunteer to be dumped in a jail for another series of months, having been there and suffered the consequences of such a setting? His point: Then why would emancipated slaves who have been freed from sin and shame return to live under that same domination any longer? . . .

We have been programmed to think, I know I am going to sin, to fail . . . to fall short today. Since this is true I need to be ready to find cleansing. You have not been programmed to yield yourself unto God as those who have power over sin.

How much better to begin each day thinking victory, not defeat; to awake to grace, not shame; to encounter each temptation with thoughts like, Jesus, You are my Lord and Savior. I am your child—liberated and depending on Your power. Therefore, Christ, this is Your day, to be lived for Your glory. Work through my eyes, my mouth, and through my thoughts and actions to carry out Your victory. And, Lord, do that all day long.

(From *The Grace Awakening* by Charles Swindoll)

APPLICATION Select a habit that you'd like to kick, a habit that hurts your life. Pray for help. Now, kick the sin out of your life and enjoy grace. Do it today—enjoy your new life.

EXPLORATION Freedom—Psalm 68:19-21; John 8:32; Galatians 5:1; 1 Corinthians 8:10-13.

LIFE LESSON

Romans 7:1-25

SITUATION Paul taught the Romans that the Law could never guarantee eternal life. He proved again that Jesus Christ could save.

OBSERVATION The Bible teaches us how sinful we have become, but Jesus Christ and his Holy Spirit provide the power to overcome sin.

INSPIRATION Our country imprisons more people per capita than any other nation except the Soviet Union and South Africa; yet we have the highest crime rate in the world. If that's law and order, spare us any more.

Baffling? Yes, but nothing new. Eighteenth-century British officials tried to cut crime by promoting large crowds to witness the hanging of pickpockets. There was a problem, however. Other thieves had a field day stealing the wallets of those gathered to watch the execution of their fellow pickpockets.

The paradox makes no sense to the secular mind—but the Christian should understand. For where is the anguish of the human soul more poignantly expressed than in Paul's letter to the Romans? "The good I wish, I do not do; but I practice the very evil that I do not wish." He never wanted to covet, Paul explains in Chapter 7, until the law said "thou shalt not covet." Then he found himself filled with covetousness of every kind.

Why? The sin within us uses the law itself to produce the very offense the law is intended to prevent. But in the next chapter the apostle answers the dilemma: though the law alone could not restrain sin, through Christ we are set free, rescued from the sin which controls us.

(From *Who Speaks for God* by Charles Colson)

APPLICATION What sin do you struggle to avoid? Thank God that he will one day rescue you from the struggle. Until then, let a prayer for strength be a reflex reaction to temptations.

EXPLORATION Victory over Sin—Genesis 4:7; Psalm 119:33; 1 John 3:4-6.

Freed from the Law

7 Or do you not know, brethren (for I speak to those who know the law),
that the law has dominion over a man as long as he lives? [2]For the
woman who has a husband is bound by the law to *her* husband as long as
he lives. But if the husband dies, she is released from the law of *her* husband. [3]So then if, while *her* husband lives, she marries another man, she
will be called an adulteress; but if her husband dies, she is free from that
law, so that she is no adulteress, though she has married another man.
[4]Therefore, my brethren, you also have become dead to the law through
the body of Christ, that you may be married to another—to Him who was
raised from the dead, that we should bear fruit to God. [5]For when we were
in the flesh, the sinful passions which were aroused by the law were at
work in our members to bear fruit to death. [6]But now we have been delivered from the law, having died to what we were held by, so that we should
serve in the newness of the Spirit and not *in* the oldness of the letter.

Sin's Advantage in the Law

[7]What shall we say then? *Is* the law sin? Certainly not! On the contrary, I
would not have known sin except through the law. For I would not have
known covetousness unless the law had said, *"You shall not covet."*[w] [8]But
sin, taking opportunity by the commandment, produced in me all *man-*
ner of evil desire. For apart from the law sin *was* dead. [9]I was alive once
without the law, but when the commandment came, sin revived and I
died. [10]And the commandment, which *was* to *bring* life, I found to *bring*
death. [11]For sin, taking occasion by the commandment, deceived me, and
by it killed *me.* [12]Therefore the law is holy, and the commandment holy
and just and good.

Law Cannot Save from Sin

[13]Has then what is good become death to me? Certainly not! But sin, that
it might appear sin, was producing death in me through what is good, so
that sin through the commandment might become exceedingly sinful.
[14]For we know that the law is spiritual, but I am carnal, sold under sin.
[15]For what I am doing, I do not understand. For what I will to do, that I do
not practice; but what I hate, that I do. [16]If, then, I do what I will not to do,
I agree with the law that *it is* good. [17]But now, *it is* no longer I who do it, but
sin that dwells in me. [18]For I know that in me (that is, in my flesh) nothing
good dwells; for to will is present with me, but *how* to perform what is
good I do not find. [19]For the good that I will *to do,* I do not do; but the evil I
will not *to do,* that I practice. [20]Now if I do what I will not *to do,* it is no
longer I who do it, but sin that dwells in me.

[21]I find then a law, that evil is present with me, the one who wills to do
good. [22]For I delight in the law of God according to the inward man. [23]But
I see another law in my members, warring against the law of my mind,
and bringing me into captivity to the law of sin which is in my members.
[24]O wretched man that I am! Who will deliver me from this body of death?
[25]I thank God—through Jesus Christ our Lord!

So then, with the mind I myself serve the law of God, but with the flesh
the law of sin.

7:7 [w] Exodus 20:17; Deuteronomy 5:21

Free from Indwelling Sin

8 *There is* therefore now no condemnation to those who are in Christ Jesus,[x] who do not walk according to the flesh, but according to the
Spirit. 2For the law of the Spirit of life in Christ Jesus has made me free
from the law of sin and death. 3For what the law could not do in that it was
weak through the flesh, God *did* by sending His own Son in the likeness of
sinful flesh, on account of sin: He condemned sin in the flesh, 4that the
righteous requirement of the law might be fulfilled in us who do not walk
according to the flesh but according to the Spirit. 5For those who live according to the flesh set their minds on the things of the flesh, but those *who live*
according to the Spirit, the things of the Spirit. 6For to be carnally minded
is death, but to be spiritually minded *is* life and peace. 7Because the carnal
mind *is* enmity against God; for it is not subject to the law of God, nor indeed can be. 8So then, those who are in the flesh cannot please God.
9But you are not in the flesh but in the Spirit, if indeed the Spirit of God
dwells in you. Now if anyone does not have the Spirit of Christ, he is not
His. 10And if Christ *is* in you, the body *is* dead because of sin, but the Spirit
is life because of righteousness. 11But if the Spirit of Him who raised Jesus
from the dead dwells in you, He who raised Christ from the dead will also
give life to your mortal bodies through His Spirit who dwells in you.

Sonship Through the Spirit

12Therefore, brethren, we are debtors—not to the flesh, to live according
to the flesh. 13For if you live according to the flesh you will die; but if by the
Spirit you put to death the deeds of the body, you will live. 14For as many as
are led by the Spirit of God, these are sons of God. 15For you did not receive
the spirit of bondage again to fear, but you received the Spirit of adoption
by whom we cry out, "Abba, Father." 16The Spirit Himself bears witness
with our spirit that we are children of God, 17and if children, then heirs—
heirs of God and joint heirs with Christ, if indeed we suffer with *Him,* that
we may also be glorified together.

From Suffering to Glory

18For I consider that the sufferings of this present time are not worthy *to
be compared* with the glory which shall be revealed in us. 19For the earnest
expectation of the creation eagerly waits for the revealing of the sons of
God. 20For the creation was subjected to futility, not willingly, but because
of Him who subjected *it* in hope; 21because the creation itself also will be
delivered from the bondage of corruption into the glorious liberty of the
children of God. 22For we know that the whole creation groans and labors
with birth pangs together until now. 23Not only *that,* but we also who have
the firstfruits of the Spirit, even we ourselves groan within ourselves, eagerly waiting for the adoption, the redemption of our body. 24For we were
saved in this hope, but hope that is seen is not hope; for why does one still
hope for what he sees? 25But if we hope for what we do not see, we eagerly
wait for *it* with perseverance.
26Likewise the Spirit also helps in our weaknesses. For we do not know
what we should pray for as we ought, but the Spirit Himself makes intercession for us[y] with groanings which cannot be uttered. 27Now He who searches

8:1 [x] NU-Text omits the rest of this verse.
8:26 [y] NU-Text omits *for us.*

LIFE LESSON

Romans 8:1-39

SITUATION Although Christians still struggle with sin, the threat of judgment for their sin was removed at the cross.

OBSERVATION In God's eyes, Christians are not guilty! Jesus' sacrifice removed our certain punishment.

INSPIRATION The Bible says the judgment for sin that I deserved is already passed. Christ took my judgment on the cross. Every demand of the law has been met. The law was completely satisfied in the offering that Christ made of Himself for sins. . . .

I deserved judgment and hell, but Christ took that judgment and hell for me. . . .

We shall never understand the extent of God's love in Christ at the cross until we understand that we shall never have to stand before the judgment of God for our sins. Christ took our sins. He finished the work of redemption. I am not saved through any works or merit of my own. I have preached to thousands of people on every continent, but I shall not go to heaven because I am a preacher. I am going to heaven entirely on the merit of the work of Christ. I shall never stand at God's judgment bar. That is all past.

(From *Unto the Hills* by Billy Graham)

APPLICATION Would you like to be free from your deserved judgment? Ask Jesus to forgive your sins and allow him to direct your life. Study the Bible to find what God expects you to do. Find ways to put God's plan for you before your own plan.

EXPLORATION Not Guilty—Isaiah 50:9; John 5:22-24; Hebrews 10:17.

LIFE LESSON

Romans 9:1-33

SITUATION Paul reminded the Romans that no good work could bring salvation. Rather, God saves his people through his love.

OBSERVATION We know God's love will never fail. Therefore, we can be certain that he will save those who believe in him.

INSPIRATION God's love is based on nothing, and the fact that it is based on nothing makes us secure. Were it based on anything we do, and that "anything" were to collapse, then God's love would crumble as well. But with the God of Jesus no such thing can possibly happen. People who realize this can live freely and to the full. Remember Atlas, who carries the whole world? We have Christian Atlases who mistakenly carry the burden of trying to deserve God's love. Even the mere watching of this lifestyle is depressing. I'd like to say to Atlas: "Put that globe down and dance on it. That's why God made it." And to these weary Christian Atlases: "Lay down your load and build your life on God's love." We don't have to earn this love; neither do we have to support it. It is a free gift. Jesus calls out: "Come to Me, all you Atlases who are weary and find life burdensome, and I will refresh you."

(From *Lion and Lamb* by Brennan Manning)

APPLICATION Do you trust God for salvation? Trust him then for smaller things, too. Trust him for the money for bills, the right job, for your spouse and children. If you can trust him for salvation, certainly you can trust him to direct your everyday activities.

EXPLORATION Trust—Job 13:15; Psalm 131:2; Isaiah 45:9; Habakkuk 3:17-19; Hebrews 11:1; 1 Peter 5:7.

the hearts knows what the mind of the Spirit *is,* because He makes intercession for the saints according to *the will of* God.
28And we know that all things work together for good to those who love
God, to those who are the called according to *His* purpose. 29For whom He
foreknew, He also predestined *to be* conformed to the image of His Son,
that He might be the firstborn among many brethren. 30Moreover whom
He predestined, these He also called; whom He called, these He also justified; and whom He justified, these He also glorified.

God's Everlasting Love

31What then shall we say to these things? If God *is* for us, who *can be*
against us? 32He who did not spare His own Son, but delivered Him up for
us all, how shall He not with Him also freely give us all things? 33Who shall
bring a charge against God's elect? *It is* God who justifies. 34Who *is* he who
condemns? *It is* Christ who died, and furthermore is also risen, who is
even at the right hand of God, who also makes intercession for us. 35Who
shall separate us from the love of Christ? *Shall* tribulation, or distress, or
persecution, or famine, or nakedness, or peril, or sword? 36As it is written:

"For Your sake we are killed all day long;
We are accounted as sheep for the slaughter."[z]

37Yet in all these things we are more than conquerors through Him who
loved us. 38For I am persuaded that neither death nor life, nor angels nor principalities nor powers, nor things present nor things to come, 39nor height
nor depth, nor any other created thing, shall be able to separate us from
the love of God which is in Christ Jesus our Lord.

Israel's Rejection of Christ

9 I tell the truth in Christ, I am not lying, my conscience also bearing me
witness in the Holy Spirit, 2that I have great sorrow and continual grief
in my heart. 3For I could wish that I myself were accursed from Christ for
my brethren, my countrymen[a] according to the flesh, 4who are Israelites,
to whom *pertain* the adoption, the glory, the covenants, the giving of the law,
the service *of God,* and the promises; 5of whom *are* the fathers and from
whom, according to the flesh, Christ *came,* who is over all, *the* eternally
blessed God. Amen.

Israel's Rejection and God's Purpose

6But it is not that the word of God has taken no effect. For they *are* not all
Israel who *are* of Israel, 7nor *are they* all children because they are the seed of
Abraham; but, *"In Isaac your seed shall be called."*[b] 8That is, those who *are*
the children of the flesh, these *are* not the children of God; but the children
of the promise are counted as the seed. 9For this *is* the word of promise:
"At this time I will come and Sarah shall have a son."[c]
10And not only *this,* but when Rebecca also had conceived by one man,
even by our father Isaac 11(for *the children* not yet being born, nor having
done any good or evil, that the purpose of God according to election might
stand, not of works but of Him who calls), 12it was said to her, *"The older*

8:36 [z] Psalm 44:22
9:3 [a] Or *relatives*
9:7 [b] Genesis 21:12
9:9 [c] Genesis 18:10, 14

shall serve the younger."[d] 13 As it is written, *"Jacob I*
have loved, but Esau I have hated."[e]

Israel's Rejection and God's Justice

14 What shall we say then? *Is there* unrighteousness
with God? Certainly not! 15 For He says to Moses, *"I will*
have mercy on whomever I will have mercy, and I will
have compassion on whomever I will have compas-
sion."[f] 16 So then *it is* not of him who wills, nor of him
who runs, but of God who shows mercy. 17 For the
Scripture says to the Pharaoh, *"For this very purpose*
I have raised you up, that I may show My power in
you, and that My name may be declared in all the
earth."[g] 18 Therefore He has mercy on whom He wills,
and whom He wills He hardens.

19 You will say to me then, "Why does He still find
fault? For who has resisted His will?" 20 But indeed, O
man, who are you to reply against God? Will the thing
formed say to him who formed *it,* "Why have you
made me like this?" 21 Does not the potter have power
over the clay, from the same lump to make one vessel
for honor and another for dishonor?

22 *What* if God, wanting to show *His* wrath and to
make His power known, endured with much longsuffering the vessels of wrath prepared for destruction,
23 and that He might make known the riches of His
glory on the vessels of mercy, which He had prepared
beforehand for glory, 24 *even* us whom He called, not
of the Jews only, but also of the Gentiles?

25 As He says also in Hosea:

"I will call them My people, who were
not My people,
And her beloved, who was not beloved."[h]

26 *"And it shall come to pass in the place*
where it was said to them,
'You are not My people,'
There they shall be called sons of
the living God."[i]

27 Isaiah also cries out concerning Israel:[j]

"Though the number of the children of Israel
be as the sand of the sea,
The remnant will be saved.

28 *For He will finish the work and cut it*
short in righteousness,
Because the LORD will make a short work
upon the earth."[k]

29 And as Isaiah said before:

"Unless the LORD of Sabaoth[l] *had left us a seed,*
We would have become like Sodom,
And we would have been made
like Gomorrah."[m]

Present Condition of Israel

30 What shall we say then? That Gentiles, who did not
pursue righteousness, have attained to righteousness,
even the righteousness of faith; 31 but Israel, pursuing
the law of righteousness, has not attained to the law of
righteousness.[n] 32 Why? Because *they did* not *seek it* by
faith, but as it were, by the works of the law.[o] For they
stumbled at that stumbling stone. 33 As it is written:

"Behold, I lay in Zion a stumbling stone
and rock of offense,
And whoever believes on Him will not
be put to shame."[p]

Israel Needs the Gospel

10 Brethren, my heart's desire and prayer to God for
Israel[q] is that they may be saved. 2 For I bear them
witness that they have a zeal for God, but not according
to knowledge. 3 For they being ignorant of God's righteousness, and seeking to establish their own righteousness, have not submitted to the righteousness of God.
4 For Christ *is* the end of the law for righteousness to
everyone who believes.

5 For Moses writes about the righteousness which is
of the law, *"The man who does those things shall live*
by them."[r] 6 But the righteousness of faith speaks in this
way, *"Do not say in your heart, 'Who will ascend into*

9:12 [d] Genesis 25:23
9:13 [e] Malachi 1:2, 3
9:15 [f] Exodus 33:19
9:17 [g] Exodus 9:16
9:25 [h] Hosea 2:23
9:26 [i] Hosea 1:10
9:27 [j] Isaiah 10:22, 23
9:28 [k] NU-Text reads *For the LORD will finish the work and cut it short upon the earth.*
9:29 [l] Literally, in Hebrew, *Hosts* [m] Isaiah 1:9
9:31 [n] NU-Text omits *of righteousness.*
9:32 [o] NU-Text reads *by works.*
9:33 [p] Isaiah 8:14; 28:16
10:1 [q] NU-Text reads *them.*
10:5 [r] Leviticus 18:5

LIFE LESSON

Romans 10:1-21

SITUATION Though the Old Testament emphasized God's mercy and pointed to God's salvation by faith, many first-century Jews preferred to count on their own righteousness to make them acceptable to God. Paul admires their zeal but is heartbroken that they have failed to understand God's plan for salvation.

OBSERVATION God offers salvation to every individual, regardless of ethnic background. Salvation comes through believing in Jesus—no amount of good works can ever be sufficient to win God's approval.

INSPIRATION Remember when your mother caught you disobeying one of her orders? You were guilty, caught red-handed, and you knew it. And you had to accept your punishment.

Over the years, the situations have changed drastically, but the results are the same—disobedience and guilt. The reality is that the deserved punishment for our sins is death—eternal death, separation from God forever. But this passage says we have been . . . declared "not guilty." No matter what we have done, we have been acquitted and forgiven because of Jesus. Thus we have "peace with God" and stand in a place of highest privilege. Not only has God declared us "not guilty," he has drawn us close to himself. Instead of being his enemies, we have become his friends—in fact, his very own children.

Being freed from the shackles of sin and the burden of guilt, we are now free to serve our loving Lord. Thank you Jesus.

(From *On Eagles' Wings* by Dave Veerman)

APPLICATION Have you understood God's plan for salvation? God welcomes you with open arms when you come to him in faith. Trust God's mercy, because it brings the joy of a relationship with God.

EXPLORATION Salvation through Faith—Genesis 15:6; John 3:16; 5:24; 20:31; Galatians 2:16; Ephesians 2:8-9; Philippians 3:9.

heaven?' "[s] (that is, to bring Christ down *from above*) 7 or, " *'Who will descend*
into the abyss?' "[t] (that is, to bring Christ up from the dead). 8 But what does
it say? *"The word is near you, in your mouth and in your heart"*[u] (that is,
the word of faith which we preach): 9 that if you confess with your mouth
the Lord Jesus and believe in your heart that God has raised Him from the
dead, you will be saved. 10 For with the heart one believes unto righteousness,
and with the mouth confession is made unto salvation. 11 For the Scripture
says, *"Whoever believes on Him will not be put to shame."*[v] 12 For there is no
distinction between Jew and Greek, for the same Lord over all is rich to all who
call upon Him. 13 For *"whoever calls on the name of the LORD shall be saved."*[w]

Israel Rejects the Gospel

14 How then shall they call on Him in whom they have not believed? And
how shall they believe in Him of whom they have not heard? And how shall
they hear without a preacher? 15 And how shall they preach unless they are
sent? As it is written:

"How beautiful are the feet of those who preach the gospel of peace,[x]
Who bring glad tidings of good things!"[y]

16 But they have not all obeyed the gospel. For Isaiah says, *"LORD, who has be-*
lieved our report?"[z] 17 So then faith *comes* by hearing, and hearing by the
word of God.

18 But I say, have they not heard? Yes indeed:

"Their sound has gone out to all the earth,
And their words to the ends of the world."[a]

19 But I say, did Israel not know? First Moses says:

"I will provoke you to jealousy by those who are not a nation,
I will move you to anger by a foolish nation."[b]

20 But Isaiah is very bold and says:

"I was found by those who did not seek Me;
I was made manifest to those who did not ask for Me."[c]

21 But to Israel he says:

"All day long I have stretched out My hands
To a disobedient and contrary people."[d]

Israel's Rejection Not Total

11 I say then, has God cast away His people? Certainly not! For I also
am an Israelite, of the seed of Abraham, *of* the tribe of Benjamin.
2 God has not cast away His people whom He foreknew. Or do you not know
what the Scripture says of Elijah, how he pleads with God against Israel,

10:6 [s] Deuteronomy 30:12
10:7 [t] Deuteronomy 30:13
10:8 [u] Deuteronomy 30:14
10:11 [v] Isaiah 28:16
10:13 [w] Joel 2:32
10:15 [x] NU-Text omits *preach the gospel of peace, Who.* [y] Isaiah 52:7; Nahum 1:15
10:16 [z] Isaiah 53:1
10:18 [a] Psalm 19:4
10:19 [b] Deuteronomy 32:21
10:20 [c] Isaiah 65:1
10:21 [d] Isaiah 65:2

saying, 3"*LORD, they have killed Your prophets and torn down Your altars,*
and I alone am left, and they seek my life"?[e] 4But what does the divine response say to him? "*I have reserved for Myself seven thousand men who*
have not bowed the knee to Baal."[f] 5Even so then, at this present time
there is a remnant according to the election of grace. 6And if by grace, then
it is no longer of works; otherwise grace is no longer grace.[g] But if *it is* of
works, it is no longer grace; otherwise work is no longer work.
7What then? Israel has not obtained what it seeks; but the elect have obtained it, and the rest were blinded. 8Just as it is written:

"*God has given them a spirit of stupor,*
Eyes that they should not see
And ears that they should not hear,
To this very day."[h]

9And David says:

"*Let their table become a snare and a trap,*
A stumbling block and a recompense to them.
10 *Let their eyes be darkened, so that they do not see,*
And bow down their back always."[i]

Israel's Rejection Not Final

11I say then, have they stumbled that they should fall? Certainly not! But
through their fall, to provoke them to jealousy, salvation *has come* to the
Gentiles. 12Now if their fall *is* riches for the world, and their failure riches
for the Gentiles, how much more their fullness!
13For I speak to you Gentiles; inasmuch as I am an apostle to the Gentiles,
I magnify my ministry, 14if by any means I may provoke to jealousy *those who*
are my flesh and save some of them. 15For if their being cast away *is* the reconciling of the world, what *will* their acceptance *be* but life from the dead?
16For if the firstfruit *is* holy, the lump *is* also *holy;* and if the root *is* holy,
so *are* the branches. 17And if some of the branches were broken off, and
you, being a wild olive tree, were grafted in among them, and with them
became a partaker of the root and fatness of the olive tree, 18do not boast
against the branches. But if you do boast, *remember that* you do not support the root, but the root supports you.
19You will say then, "Branches were broken off that I might be grafted in."
20Well *said.* Because of unbelief they were broken off, and you stand by
faith. Do not be haughty, but fear. 21For if God did not spare the natural
branches, He may not spare you either. 22Therefore consider the goodness
and severity of God: on those who fell, severity; but toward you, goodness,[j]
if you continue in *His* goodness. Otherwise you also will be cut off. 23And
they also, if they do not continue in unbelief, will be grafted in, for God is
able to graft them in again. 24For if you were cut out of the olive tree which
is wild by nature, and were grafted contrary to nature into a cultivated
olive tree, how much more will these, who *are* natural *branches,* be grafted
into their own olive tree?

11:3 [e] 1 Kings 19:10, 14
11:4 [f] 1 Kings 19:18
11:6 [g] NU-Text omits the rest of this verse.
11:8 [h] Deuteronomy 29:4; Isaiah 29:10
11:10 [i] Psalm 69:22, 23
11:22 [j] NU-Text adds *of God.*

LIFE LESSON

Romans 11:1-36

SITUATION Were the Jews still God's chosen people? What role did the Gentiles have? Paul set out to answer these questions.

OBSERVATION Christians often feel superior to other groups—as if we had done something great to earn our acceptance before God. Instead, God's gift of salvation should make us humble and grateful.

INSPIRATION The fact that God has chosen some to be saved does not mean that He has chosen the rest to be lost. The world is already lost and dead in sins. If left to ourselves, all of us would be condemned eternally. The question is, Does God have a right to stoop down, take a handful of already doomed clay, and fashion a vessel of beauty out of it? Of course He does. C. R. Erdman put it in right perspective when he said, "God's sovereignty is never exercised in condemning men who ought to be saved, but rather it has resulted in the salvation of men who ought to be lost."

The only way people can know if they are among the elect is by trusting Jesus Christ as Lord and Savior (1 Thessalonians 1:4-7). God holds people responsible to accept the Savior by an act of the will. In reproving those Jews who did not believe, Jesus placed the blame on their will. He did *not* say, "You cannot come to Me because you are not chosen." Rather, He *did* say, "You *are not willing* to come to Me that you may have life" (John 5:40, emphasis added).

The real question of a believer is not, Does the sovereign God have the right to choose people to be saved? Rather, it is, Why did He choose *me*? This should make a person a worshiper for all eternity.

(From *Alone in Majesty* by William MacDonald)

APPLICATION Though we have a responsibility to follow Christ, we need to recognize we could only achieve it by God's Spirit.

EXPLORATION God's Choice in Salvation—Deuteronomy 9:4-5; Romans 2:4; 8:28-29; Ephesians 1:4-5, 11; 2:8-9; 1 Timothy 2:3-4; Titus 3:5.

25 For I do not desire, brethren, that you should be ignorant of this mystery, lest you should be wise in your own opinion, that blindness in part
has happened to Israel until the fullness of the Gentiles has come in. 26 And
so all Israel will be saved,[k] as it is written:

"The Deliverer will come out of Zion,
And He will turn away ungodliness from Jacob;
27 *For this is My covenant with them,*
When I take away their sins."[l]

28 Concerning the gospel *they are* enemies for your sake, but concerning
the election *they are* beloved for the sake of the fathers. 29 For the gifts and
the calling of God *are* irrevocable. 30 For as you were once disobedient to God,
yet have now obtained mercy through their disobedience, 31 even so these
also have now been disobedient, that through the mercy shown you they
also may obtain mercy. 32 For God has committed them all to disobedience,
that He might have mercy on all.
33 Oh, the depth of the riches both of the wisdom and knowledge of God!
How unsearchable *are* His judgments and His ways past finding out!

34 *"For who has known the mind of the LORD?*
Or who has become His counselor?"[m]
35 *"Or who has first given to Him*
And it shall be repaid to him?"[n]

36 For of Him and through Him and to Him *are* all things, to whom *be*
glory forever. Amen.

Living Sacrifices to God

12 I beseech you therefore, brethren, by the mercies of God, that you
present your bodies a living sacrifice, holy, acceptable to God, *which*
is your reasonable service. 2 And do not be conformed to this world, but be
transformed by the renewing of your mind, that you may prove what *is*
that good and acceptable and perfect will of God.

Serve God with Spiritual Gifts

3 For I say, through the grace given to me, to everyone who is among you,
not to think *of himself* more highly than he ought to think, but to think
soberly, as God has dealt to each one a measure of faith. 4 For as we have
many members in one body, but all the members do not have the same
function, 5 so we, *being* many, are one body in Christ, and individually members of one another. 6 Having then gifts differing according to the grace that
is given to us, *let us use them:* if prophecy, *let us prophesy* in proportion to
our faith; 7 or ministry, *let us use it* in *our* ministering; he who teaches, in
teaching; 8 he who exhorts, in exhortation; he who gives, with liberality; he
who leads, with diligence; he who shows mercy, with cheerfulness.

Behave Like a Christian

9 *Let* love *be* without hypocrisy. Abhor what is evil. Cling to what is good.
10 *Be* kindly affectionate to one another with brotherly love, in honor giving

11:26 [k] Or *delivered*
11:27 [l] Isaiah 59:20, 21
11:34 [m] Isaiah 40:13; Jeremiah 23:18
11:35 [n] Job 41:11

LIFE LESSON

Romans 12:1-21

SITUATION Paul told the Roman Christians how to live so that their behavior would be worshipful to God.

OBSERVATION God desires you to surrender every part of your life to him.

INSPIRATION Would you buy a house if you were only allowed to see one of its rooms? Would you purchase a car if you were permitted to see only its tires and a taillight? Would you pass judgment on a book after reading only one paragraph?

Nor would I.

Good judgment requires a broad picture. Not only is that true in purchasing houses, cars, and books, it's true in evaluating life. One failure doesn't make a person a failure; one achievement doesn't make a person a success.

"The end of the matter is better than its beginning," penned the sage.

"Be . . . patient in affliction," echoed the apostle Paul. . . .

We only have a fragment. Life's mishaps and horrors are only a page out of a grand book. We must be slow about drawing conclusions. We must reserve judgment on life's storms until we know the whole story. . . .

"Do not worry about tomorrow, for tomorrow will worry about itself."

He should know. He is the Author of our story. And he has already written the final chapter.

(From *In the Eye of the Storm* by Max Lucado)

APPLICATION What particular sin stalks you? When does it seize you with temptation? As a safeguard, memorize Romans 12:1-2. Whenever you feel tempted, repeat these verses in your mind and by God's power plan not to sin.

EXPLORATION Honoring God—Matthew 16:24-25; Galatians 1:10; 1 Corinthians 6:20; 2 Corinthians 5:15.

preference to one another; 11not lagging in diligence, fervent in spirit, serving
the Lord; 12rejoicing in hope, patient in tribulation, continuing steadfastly
in prayer; 13distributing to the needs of the saints, given to hospitality.
14Bless those who persecute you; bless and do not curse. 15Rejoice with
those who rejoice, and weep with those who weep. 16Be of the same mind
toward one another. Do not set your mind on high things, but associate
with the humble. Do not be wise in your own opinion.
17Repay no one evil for evil. Have regard for good things in the sight of all
men. 18If it is possible, as much as depends on you, live peaceably with all men.
19Beloved, do not avenge yourselves, but *rather* give place to wrath; for it is
written, *"Vengeance is Mine, I will repay,"*[o] says the Lord. 20Therefore

"If your enemy is hungry, feed him;
If he is thirsty, give him a drink;
For in so doing you will heap coals of fire on his head."[p]

21Do not be overcome by evil, but overcome evil with good.

Submit to Government

13 Let every soul be subject to the governing authorities. For there is no
authority except from God, and the authorities that exist are appointed
by God. 2Therefore whoever resists the authority resists the ordinance of
God, and those who resist will bring judgment on themselves. 3For rulers
are not a terror to good works, but to evil. Do you want to be unafraid of the
authority? Do what is good, and you will have praise from the same. 4For
he is God's minister to you for good. But if you do evil, be afraid; for he does
not bear the sword in vain; for he is God's minister, an avenger to *execute*
wrath on him who practices evil. 5Therefore *you* must be subject, not only
because of wrath but also for conscience' sake. 6For because of this you
also pay taxes, for they are God's ministers attending continually to this very
thing. 7Render therefore to all their due: taxes to whom taxes *are due,* customs to whom customs, fear to whom fear, honor to whom honor.

Love Your Neighbor

8Owe no one anything except to love one another, for he who loves another has fulfilled the law. 9For the commandments, *"You shall not commit
adultery," "You shall not murder," "You shall not steal," "You shall not
bear false witness,"*[q] *"You shall not covet,"*[r] and if *there is* any other commandment, are *all* summed up in this saying, namely, *"You shall love your
neighbor as yourself."*[s] 10Love does no harm to a neighbor; therefore love *is*
the fulfillment of the law.

Put on Christ

11And *do* this, knowing the time, that now *it is* high time to awake out of
sleep; for now our salvation *is* nearer than when we *first* believed. 12The
night is far spent, the day is at hand. Therefore let us cast off the works of
darkness, and let us put on the armor of light. 13Let us walk properly, as in
the day, not in revelry and drunkenness, not in lewdness and lust, not in
strife and envy. 14But put on the Lord Jesus Christ, and make no provision
for the flesh, to *fulfill its* lusts.

12:19 [o] Deuteronomy 32:35
12:20 [p] Proverbs 25:21, 22
13:9 [q] NU-Text omits *"You shall not bear false witness."* [r] Exodus 20:13–15, 17; Deuteronomy 5:17–19, 21
[s] Leviticus 19:18

LIFE LESSON

Romans 13:1-14

SITUATION Paul encouraged Christians to obey the government even though submitting to a pagan government would be difficult. He also encouraged Christians to love each other.

OBSERVATION Christians should be well-known in their communities for their obedience to government and their love for each other.

INSPIRATION Let us pray for each other so that we grow in tender love, that we allow God to love us, and that we allow God to love others through us.

Where does that showing of love begin? At home; so let us bring that love to the sick, to the old, to the lonely, to the unwanted. For people do not hunger only for bread; they hunger for love, they hunger to be somebody to somebody.

I will never forget that I once met a man in the street who looked very lonely and miserable. So I walked right up to him, and I shook his hand. My hands are always very warm; and he looked up, gave me a beautiful smile, and he said, "Oh, it has been such a long, long time since I felt the warmth of a human hand!" How very wonderful and very beautiful that our simple actions can show love in that way.

And let us remember to bring that kind of love into our family. We can do this through prayer; for where there is prayer, there is love. And where there is love, there is the complete oneness that Jesus was talking about when he said, "Be one, as the Father and I are one. And love one another as I love you. As the Father loved me, I have loved you."

(From *Who Is for Life?* by Mother Teresa)

APPLICATION Have you received love in an unusual way from someone? Look for a new way to show love to those who normally hear you say, "I love you."

EXPLORATION Love—
1 Corinthians 13; 1 John 3:16; 4:7-8.

LIFE LESSON

Romans 14:1–15:13

SITUATION Paul continued to call Christians to unity and love, particularly between those who were weak or strong in their faith and walk with God. Paul addressed the habit of holy days and the eating of meat sacrificed to idols.

OBSERVATION The church should be marked by how we love each other rather than how we judge each other.

INSPIRATION Accepting others is basic to letting them be. Those who didn't eat [meat] (called here "weak in the faith") were exhorted to accept and not judge those who ate. And those who ate were exhorted to accept and not regard with contempt those who did not eat. The secret lies in accepting one another. All of this is fairly easy to read so long as I stay on the issue of eating meat. That one is safe because it isn't a current taboo. It's easy to accept those folks today because they don't exist!

How about those in our life who may disagree with us on issues that are taboos in evangelical Christian circles today? . . . Going to movies . . . Playing cards . . . Not having a "quiet time" every morning . . . Going to a restaurant that sells liquor . . . Listening to certain music . . . Dancing . . . Drinking coffee . . .

There are a dozen other things I could list, some of which would make you smile. But believe me, in various areas of our country or the world some or all of these things may be taboo. . . . [D]on't assume that all areas are identical when it comes to taboos. . . . (Remember, our goal is acceptance, the basis of a grace state of mind.)

(From *Grace Awakening* by Charles Swindoll*)*

APPLICATION Examine your own taboos and look for some that may be unnecessary points of contention with other Christians.

EXPLORATION Personal Responsibilities—Deuteronomy 24:16; Job 19:4; Proverbs 9:12; Jeremiah 31:30; Ezekiel 18:20.

The Law of Liberty

14 Receive one who is weak in the faith, *but* not to disputes over doubtful
things. 2For one believes he may eat all things, but he who is weak eats
only vegetables. 3Let not him who eats despise him who does not eat, and let
not him who does not eat judge him who eats; for God has received him.
4Who are you to judge another's servant? To his own master he stands or
falls. Indeed, he will be made to stand, for God is able to make him stand.
5One person esteems *one* day above another; another esteems every day
alike. Let each be fully convinced in his own mind. 6He who observes the
day, observes *it* to the Lord;[t] and he who does not observe the day, to the
Lord he does not observe *it.* He who eats, eats to the Lord, for he gives God
thanks; and he who does not eat, to the Lord he does not eat, and gives
God thanks. 7For none of us lives to himself, and no one dies to himself. 8For
if we live, we live to the Lord; and if we die, we die to the Lord. Therefore,
whether we live or die, we are the Lord's. 9For to this end Christ died and
rose[u] and lived again, that He might be Lord of both the dead and the living. 10But why do you judge your brother? Or why do you show contempt
for your brother? For we shall all stand before the judgment seat of Christ.[v]
11For it is written:

"As I live, says the LORD,
Every knee shall bow to Me,
And every tongue shall confess to God."[w]

12So then each of us shall give account of himself to God. 13Therefore let
us not judge one another anymore, but rather resolve this, not to put a
stumbling block or a cause to fall in *our* brother's way.

The Law of Love

14I know and am convinced by the Lord Jesus that *there is* nothing unclean of itself; but to him who considers anything to be unclean, to him *it*
is unclean. 15Yet if your brother is grieved because of *your* food, you are no
longer walking in love. Do not destroy with your food the one for whom
Christ died. 16Therefore do not let your good be spoken of as evil; 17for the
kingdom of God is not eating and drinking, but righteousness and peace
and joy in the Holy Spirit. 18For he who serves Christ in these things[x] *is*
acceptable to God and approved by men.
19Therefore let us pursue the things *which make* for peace and the things
by which one may edify another. 20Do not destroy the work of God for the
sake of food. All things indeed *are* pure, but *it is* evil for the man who eats
with offense. 21*It is* good neither to eat meat nor drink wine nor *do anything*
by which your brother stumbles or is offended or is made weak.[y] 22Do you
have faith?[z] Have *it* to yourself before God. Happy *is* he who does not condemn
himself in what he approves. 23But he who doubts is condemned if he eats,
because *he does* not *eat* from faith; for whatever *is* not from faith is sin.[a]

14:6 [t] NU-Text omits the rest of this sentence.
14:9 [u] NU-Text omits *and rose.*
14:10 [v] NU-Text reads *of God.*
14:11 [w] Isaiah 45:23
14:18 [x] NU-Text reads *this.*
14:21 [y] NU-Text omits *or is offended or is made weak.*
14:22 [z] NU-Text reads *The faith which you have—have.*
14:23 [a] M-Text puts Romans 16:25–27 here.

Bearing Others' Burdens

15 We then who are strong ought to bear with the scruples of the weak,
and not to please ourselves. 2Let each of us please *his* neighbor for
his good, leading to edification. 3For even Christ did not please Himself; but
as it is written, *"The reproaches of those who reproached You fell on Me."*[b]
4For whatever things were written before were written for our learning, that
we through the patience and comfort of the Scriptures might have hope.
5Now may the God of patience and comfort grant you to be like-minded
toward one another, according to Christ Jesus, 6that you may with one
mind *and* one mouth glorify the God and Father of our Lord Jesus Christ.

Glorify God Together

7Therefore receive one another, just as Christ also received us,[c] to the
glory of God. 8Now I say that Jesus Christ has become a servant to the circumcision for the truth of God, to confirm the promises *made* to the fathers,
9and that the Gentiles might glorify God for *His* mercy, as it is written:

> *"For this reason I will confess to You among the Gentiles,*
> *And sing to Your name."*[d]

10And again he says:

> *"Rejoice, O Gentiles, with His people!"*[e]

11And again:

> *"Praise the LORD, all you Gentiles!*
> *Laud Him, all you peoples!"*[f]

12And again, Isaiah says:

> *"There shall be a root of Jesse;*
> *And He who shall rise to reign over the Gentiles,*
> *In Him the Gentiles shall hope."*[g]

13Now may the God of hope fill you with all joy and peace in believing,
that you may abound in hope by the power of the Holy Spirit.

From Jerusalem to Illyricum

14Now I myself am confident concerning you, my brethren, that you
also are full of goodness, filled with all knowledge, able also to admonish
one another.[h] 15Nevertheless, brethren, I have written more boldly to you
on *some* points, as reminding you, because of the grace given to me by
God, 16that I might be a minister of Jesus Christ to the Gentiles, ministering the gospel of God, that the offering of the Gentiles might be acceptable,
sanctified by the Holy Spirit. 17Therefore I have reason to glory in Christ
Jesus in the things *which pertain* to God. 18For I will not dare to speak of
any of those things which Christ has not accomplished through me, in
word and deed, to make the Gentiles obedient— 19in mighty signs and
wonders, by the power of the Spirit of God, so that from Jerusalem and

15:3 [b] Psalm 69:9
15:7 [c] NU-Text and M-Text read *you.*
15:9 [d] 2 Samuel 22:50; Psalm 18:49
15:10 [e] Deuteronomy 32:43
15:11 [f] Psalm 117:1
15:12 [g] Isaiah 11:10
15:14 [h] M-Text reads *others.*

LIFE LESSON

Romans 15:14-33

SITUATION Having concluded his presentation of the gospel and its impact on those who believe, Paul turned his focus to his ministry.

OBSERVATION Paul expressed his passion for the unsaved and his love for Christians.

INSPIRATION A few nights ago a peculiar thing happened.

An electrical storm caused a blackout in our neighborhood. When the lights went out, I felt my way through the darkness into the storage closet where we keep the candles for nights like this. . . . I took my match and lit four of them. . . .

I was turning to leave with the large candle in my hand when I heard a voice, "Now, hold it right there."

"Who said that?"

"I did." The voice was near my hand.

"Who are you? What are you?"

"I'm a candle."

I lifted up the candle to take a closer look. You won't believe what I saw. There was a tiny face in the wax . . . a moving, functioning, flesh-like face full of expression and life.

"Don't take me out of here!"

"What?"

"I said, Don't take me out of this room."

"What do you mean? I have to take you out. You're a candle. Your job is to give light. It's dark out there."

"But you can't take me out. I'm not ready," the candle explained with pleading eyes. "I need more prepara-tion."

I couldn't believe my ears. "More preparation?"

"Yeah, I've decided I need to research this job of light-giving so I won't go out and make a bunch of mistakes. You'd be surprised how distorted the glow of an untrained candle can be. . . . "

"All right then, " I said. "You're not the only candle on the shelf. I'll blow you out and take the others!"

But just as I got my cheeks full of air, I heard other voices.

Continued

round about to Illyricum I have fully preached the gospel of Christ. 20 And
so I have made it my aim to preach the gospel, not where Christ was named,
lest I should build on another man's foundation, 21 but as it is written:

"To whom He was not announced, they shall see;
And those who have not heard shall understand."[i]

Plan to Visit Rome

22 For this reason I also have been much hindered from coming to you.
23 But now no longer having a place in these parts, and having a great desire
these many years to come to you, 24 whenever I journey to Spain, I shall
come to you.[j] For I hope to see you on my journey, and to be helped on my
way there by you, if first I may enjoy your *company* for a while. 25 But now I
am going to Jerusalem to minister to the saints. 26 For it pleased those from
Macedonia and Achaia to make a certain contribution for the poor among
the saints who are in Jerusalem. 27 It pleased them indeed, and they are their
debtors. For if the Gentiles have been partakers of their spiritual things,
their duty is also to minister to them in material things. 28 Therefore, when
I have performed this and have sealed to them this fruit, I shall go by way
of you to Spain. 29 But I know that when I come to you, I shall come in the
fullness of the blessing of the gospel[k] of Christ.

30 Now I beg you, brethren, through the Lord Jesus Christ, and through
the love of the Spirit, that you strive together with me in prayers to God for
me, 31 that I may be delivered from those in Judea who do not believe, and
that my service for Jerusalem may be acceptable to the saints, 32 that I may
come to you with joy by the will of God, and may be refreshed together
with you. 33 Now the God of peace *be* with you all. Amen.

Sister Phoebe Commended

16 I commend to you Phoebe our sister, who is a servant of the church
in Cenchrea, 2 that you may receive her in the Lord in a manner worthy of the saints, and assist her in whatever business she has need of you;
for indeed she has been a helper of many and of myself also.

Greeting Roman Saints

3 Greet Priscilla and Aquila, my fellow workers in Christ Jesus, 4 who risked
their own necks for my life, to whom not only I give thanks, but also all the
churches of the Gentiles. 5 Likewise *greet* the church that is in their house.

Greet my beloved Epaenetus, who is the firstfruits of Achaia[l] to Christ.
6 Greet Mary, who labored much for us. 7 Greet Andronicus and Junia, my
countrymen and my fellow prisoners, who are of note among the apostles,
who also were in Christ before me.

8 Greet Amplias, my beloved in the Lord. 9 Greet Urbanus, our fellow
worker in Christ, and Stachys, my beloved. 10 Greet Apelles, approved in Christ.
Greet those who are of the *household* of Aristobulus. 11 Greet Herodion, my
countryman.[m] Greet those who are of the *household* of Narcissus who are
in the Lord.

15:21 [i] Isaiah 52:15
15:24 [j] NU-Text omits *I shall come to you* (and joins *Spain* with the next sentence).
15:29 [k] NU-Text omits *of the gospel.*
16:5 [l] NU-Text reads *Asia.*
16:11 [m] Or *relative*

"We aren't going either!"

. . . I turned around and looked at the three other candles. . . . "You are candles and your job is to light dark places!"

"Well, that may be what you think," said the candle on the far left. . . . "You may think we have to go, but I'm busy. . . . I'm meditating on the importance of light. It's really enlightening." . . .

"And you other two," I asked, "are you going to stay in here as well?"

A short, fat, purple candle with plump cheeks that reminded me of Santa Claus spoke up. "I'm waiting to get my life together. I'm not stable enough."

The last candle had a female voice, very pleasant to the ear. "I'd like to help," she explain, "but lighting the darkness is not my gift. . . . I'm a singer. I sing to other candles to encourage them to burn more brightly."

. . . She began a rendition of "This Little Light of Mine.". . .The other three joined in, filling the storage room with singing. . . . I took a step back and considered the absurdity of it all. Four perfectly healthy candles singing to each other about light but refusing to come out of the closet.

(From *God Came Near* by Max Lucado)

APPLICATION When was the last time you presented the gospel to someone? Are you scared to be the light-giver that God has created you to be? Pray today that God would bring you opportunities to share your faith and give you the courage to take them. Now step out in faith and keep your eyes open!

EXPLORATION Evangelism—Matthew 5:13-16; 28:18-20; Acts 1:8; 2 Corinthians 2:14-17; 1 Thessalonians 2:8; 1 Peter 3:15-16.

[12]Greet Tryphena and Tryphosa, who have labored
in the Lord. Greet the beloved Persis, who labored much
in the Lord. [13]Greet Rufus, chosen in the Lord, and his
mother and mine. [14]Greet Asyncritus, Phlegon, Hermas,
Patrobas, Hermes, and the brethren who are with them.
[15]Greet Philologus and Julia, Nereus and his sister,
and Olympas, and all the saints who are with them.
[16]Greet one another with a holy kiss. The[n] churches
of Christ greet you.

Avoid Divisive Persons

[17]Now I urge you, brethren, note those who cause
divisions and offenses, contrary to the doctrine which
you learned, and avoid them. [18]For those who are
such do not serve our Lord Jesus[o] Christ, but their
own belly, and by smooth words and flattering speech
deceive the hearts of the simple. [19]For your obedience
has become known to all. Therefore I am glad on your
behalf; but I want you to be wise in what is good, and
simple concerning evil. [20]And the God of peace will
crush Satan under your feet shortly.
The grace of our Lord Jesus Christ *be* with you. Amen.

Greetings from Paul's Friends

[21]Timothy, my fellow worker, and Lucius, Jason, and
Sosipater, my countrymen, greet you.
[22]I, Tertius, who wrote *this* epistle, greet you in the
Lord.
[23]Gaius, my host and *the host* of the whole church,
greets you. Erastus, the treasurer of the city, greets you,
and Quartus, a brother. [24]The grace of our Lord Jesus
Christ *be* with you all. Amen.[p]

Benediction

[25]Now to Him who is able to establish you according to my gospel and the preaching of Jesus Christ,
according to the revelation of the mystery kept secret
since the world began [26]but now made manifest, and
by the prophetic Scriptures made known to all nations,
according to the commandment of the everlasting
God, for obedience to the faith— [27]to God, alone wise,
be glory through Jesus Christ forever. Amen.[q]

16:16 [n] NU-Text reads *All the churches.*
16:18 [o] NU-Text and M-Text omit *Jesus.*
16:24 [p] NU-Text omits this verse.
16:27 [q] M-Text puts Romans 16:25–27 after Romans 14:23.

The First Epistle of Paul to the CORINTHIANS

INTRODUCTION

An Indian was walking up a mountain when he heard a voice.

"Carry me with you," it requested.

The Indian turned and saw a snake. He refused. "If I carry you up the mountain you will bite me."

"I wouldn't do that," the snake assured. "All I need is some help. I am slow and you are fast, please be kind and carry me to the top of the mountain."

It was against his better judgment, but the Indian agreed. He picked up the snake, put him in his shirt, and resumed the journey. When they reached the top, he reached in his shirt to remove the snake and got bit.

He fell to the ground, and the snake slithered away.

"You lied!" the Indian cried, "You said you wouldn't bite me."

The snake stopped and looked back, "I didn't lie. You knew who I was when you picked me up."

We hear the legend and shake our heads. He should have known better, we bemoan. And we are right. He should have.

And so should we. But don't we do the same? Don't we believe the lies of the snake? Don't we pick up what we should leave alone?

The Corinthian Christians did. One snake after another had hissed his lies in their ears, and they had believed it. How many lies did they believe?

How much time do you have?

The list is long and ugly: sectarianism, disunity, sexual immorality. And that is only the first six chapters.

But First Corinthians is more than a list of sins, it is an epistle of patience. Paul initiates the letter by calling these Christians "brothers." He could have called them heretics or hypocrites or skirt-chasers (and in so many words he does), but not before he calls them brothers.

He patiently teaches them about worship, unity, the role of women, and the Lord's Supper. He writes as if he can see them face to face. He is disturbed but not despondent. Angry but not desperate. His driving passion is love. And his treatise on love in chapter 13 remains the greatest essay ever penned.

The letter, however personal, is not just for Corinth. It is for all who have heard the whisper and felt the fangs.

We, like the Indian, should have known better. We, like the Corinthians, sometimes need a second chance.

Life Lesson

1 Corinthians 1:1-31

SITUATION In a constructive manner, Paul admonished Christians in Corinth for being divisive. Paul reminded them about the limits of human wisdom.

OBSERVATION Christians must focus on Christ to understand God's will. Human wisdom won't do it.

INSPIRATION Throughout the expanse of creation God has hidden things for humankind to discover, to enjoy, and with which to perceive the nature of the Creator Himself. . . .

The work of the first man and woman was to discover and identify things God had made. Because of their disobedience against God's laws, some of the opportunity for that kind of marvelous work was forfeited. They now had to worry more about surviving in a hostile world than continuing to discover what was in it. The nature of work abruptly changed. I have a conviction that the heavenly life will in some way recover that original form of work.

But the principle and privilege of discovery still prevails in part. . . .

And much of the exploration of creation is done purely within the mind. We dig, as it were, and uncover ideas and truths; then we turn around to express them artistically, worshipfully, and inventively.

Thinking is a great work. It is best done with a mind that has trained and is in shape just as competitive running is done with a body that has trained and is in shape. The best kind of thinking is accomplished when it is done in the context of reverence for God's kingly reign over all creation.

(From *Ordering Your Private World* by Gordon MacDonald)

APPLICATION Human wisdom tells us to get as much as we can, believe only what we can see, enjoy pleasure, and avoid pain. God's wisdom tells us to give all we can, believe what we can't see, enjoy service, and expect persecution. See that your life reflects the difference.

EXPLORATION Wisdom—Job 28:13; Proverbs 1:7; 9:1; Ecclesiastes 8:1; Obadiah 8.

Greeting

Paul, called *to be* an apostle of Jesus Christ through the will of
God, and Sosthenes *our* brother,
[2]To the church of God which is at Corinth, to those who are sanctified in Christ Jesus, called *to be* saints, with all who in every place call on
the name of Jesus Christ our Lord, both theirs and ours:
[3]Grace to you and peace from God our Father and the Lord Jesus Christ.

Spiritual Gifts at Corinth

[4]I thank my God always concerning you for the grace of God which was
given to you by Christ Jesus, [5]that you were enriched in everything by Him
in all utterance and all knowledge, [6]even as the testimony of Christ was
confirmed in you, [7]so that you come short in no gift, eagerly waiting for
the revelation of our Lord Jesus Christ, [8]who will also confirm you to the
end, *that you may be* blameless in the day of our Lord Jesus Christ. [9]God *is*
faithful, by whom you were called into the fellowship of His Son, Jesus
Christ our Lord.

Sectarianism Is Sin

[10]Now I plead with you, brethren, by the name of our Lord Jesus Christ,
that you all speak the same thing, and *that* there be no divisions among
you, but *that* you be perfectly joined together in the same mind and in the
same judgment. [11]For it has been declared to me concerning you, my
brethren, by those of Chloe's *household,* that there are contentions among
you. [12]Now I say this, that each of you says, "I am of Paul," or "I am of
Apollos," or "I am of Cephas," or "I am of Christ." [13]Is Christ divided? Was
Paul crucified for you? Or were you baptized in the name of Paul?
[14]I thank God that I baptized none of you except Crispus and Gaius,
[15]lest anyone should say that I had baptized in my own name. [16]Yes, I also
baptized the household of Stephanas. Besides, I do not know whether I
baptized any other. [17]For Christ did not send me to baptize, but to preach
the gospel, not with wisdom of words, lest the cross of Christ should be
made of no effect.

Christ the Power and Wisdom of God

[18]For the message of the cross is foolishness to those who are perishing,
but to us who are being saved it is the power of God. [19]For it is written:

"I will destroy the wisdom of the wise,
And bring to nothing the understanding of the prudent."[a]

[20]Where *is* the wise? Where *is* the scribe? Where *is* the disputer of this
age? Has not God made foolish the wisdom of this world? [21]For since, in
the wisdom of God, the world through wisdom did not know God, it
pleased God through the foolishness of the message preached to save
those who believe. [22]For Jews request a sign, and Greeks seek after wisdom;
[23]but we preach Christ crucified, to the Jews a stumbling block and to the
Greeks[b] foolishness, [24]but to those who are called, both Jews and Greeks,
Christ the power of God and the wisdom of God. [25]Because the foolishness
of God is wiser than men, and the weakness of God is stronger than men.

1:19 *a* Isaiah 29:14
1:23 *b* NU-Text reads *Gentiles.*

Glory Only in the Lord

26For you see your calling, brethren, that not many wise according to the
flesh, not many mighty, not many noble, *are called.* 27But God has chosen
the foolish things of the world to put to shame the wise, and God has chosen
the weak things of the world to put to shame the things which are mighty;
28and the base things of the world and the things which are despised God
has chosen, and the things which are not, to bring to nothing the things
that are, 29that no flesh should glory in His presence. 30But of Him you are
in Christ Jesus, who became for us wisdom from God—and righteousness and sanctification and redemption— 31that, as it is written, *"He who
glories, let him glory in the LORD."*[c]

Christ Crucified

2 And I, brethren, when I came to you, did not come with excellence of
speech or of wisdom declaring to you the testimony[d] of God. 2For I determined not to know anything among you except Jesus Christ and Him
crucified. 3I was with you in weakness, in fear, and in much trembling.
4And my speech and my preaching *were* not with persuasive words of human[e] wisdom, but in demonstration of the Spirit and of power, 5that your
faith should not be in the wisdom of men but in the power of God.

Spiritual Wisdom

6However, we speak wisdom among those who are mature, yet not the
wisdom of this age, nor of the rulers of this age, who are coming to nothing.
7But we speak the wisdom of God in a mystery, the hidden *wisdom* which God
ordained before the ages for our glory, 8which none of the rulers of this age
knew; for had they known, they would not have crucified the Lord of glory.
9But as it is written:

> *"Eye has not seen, nor ear heard,*
> *Nor have entered into the heart of man*
> *The things which God has prepared for those who love Him."*[f]

10But God has revealed *them* to us through His Spirit. For the Spirit
searches all things, yes, the deep things of God. 11For what man knows the
things of a man except the spirit of the man which is in him? Even so no
one knows the things of God except the Spirit of God. 12Now we have received, not the spirit of the world, but the Spirit who is from God, that we
might know the things that have been freely given to us by God.
13These things we also speak, not in words which man's wisdom teaches
but which the Holy[g] Spirit teaches, comparing spiritual things with spiritual. 14But the natural man does not receive the things of the Spirit of God,
for they are foolishness to him; nor can he know *them,* because they are
spiritually discerned. 15But he who is spiritual judges all things, yet he
himself is *rightly* judged by no one. 16For *"who has known the mind of the
LORD that he may instruct Him?"*[h] But we have the mind of Christ.

1:31 [c] Jeremiah 9:24
2:1 [d] NU-Text reads *mystery.*
2:4 [e] NU-Text omits *human.*
2:9 [f] Isaiah 64:4
2:13 [g] NU-Text omits *Holy.*
2:16 [h] Isaiah 40:13

LIFE LESSON

1 Corinthians 2:1-16

SITUATION The world cannot understand God's wisdom, nor can it comprehend that God's Son had to die to bring sinners back to God.

OBSERVATION God reveals the mystery of the gospel to us when the Holy Spirit opens our spiritual eyes.

INSPIRATION Men are always seeking for greater wisdom, but they usually bypass the Ultimate Source of wisdom. The Scriptures clearly point this direction. They reveal, "The fear of the Lord is the beginning of wisdom, and the knowledge of the Holy One is understanding" (Proverbs 9:10). But what has man done with this tremendous resource at his fingertips? Ignored it! "For even though they knew God, they did not honor Him as God, or give thanks; but they became futile in their speculations, and their foolish heart was darkened. Professing to be wise, they became fools" (Rom. 1:21-22).

Since God's wisdom resides in His Word, it is imperative to know what He has revealed, but even many Christians ignore a regular time reading and studying the Scriptures. Therefore, many of their decisions are foolish, because they've not consulted the Ultimate Source of wisdom.

(From *Finding Time* by Rick Yohn)

APPLICATION Do you read God's Word faithfully? Create a notebook of observations. Keep track of new discoveries and old truths. Let them strengthen your faith and share them in your conversations.

EXPLORATION Renew Your Mind—Proverbs 15:14; Romans 12:2; Philippians 4:8.

LIFE LESSON

1 Corinthians 3:1-23

SITUATION Paul wrote to a church that was young and immature. He corrected some misunderstandings in the Corinthian church and outlined how the people should act, live, and relate.

OBSERVATION Growing spiritually requires that we look to Christ for our identity.

INSPIRATION True spirituality manifests itself in certain desires. . . . First is the desire to be holy rather than happy. . . . The truly spiritual man knows that God will give abundance of joy after we have become able to receive it without injury to our soul, but he does not demand it at once. . . . Again, a Christian is spiritual when he sees everything from God's viewpoint. The ability to weigh all things in the divine scale and place the same value upon them as God does is the mark of a Spirit-filled life. . . . The desire to see others advance at his expense is another mark of the spiritual man. He wants to see other Christians above him and is happy when they are promoted and he is overlooked. . . .

And all of this must be by the operation of the Holy Spirit within him. No man can become spiritual by himself. Only the free Spirit can make a man spiritual.

(From *The Best of Tozer* compiled by Warren Wiersbe)

APPLICATION Read the Gospels to find out how Christ lived, what he said, and how he responded to people and situations. Follow his examples as you face challenges in your life. Encourage others with what you are learning from Jesus' life.

EXPLORATION Abiding in Christ—Matthew 6:33; John 15:4-7; Romans 14:8; Galatians 2:20; Ephesians 3:17-19; 1 Timothy 4:10; 1 John 2:6; 3:6.

Sectarianism Is Carnal

3 And I, brethren, could not speak to you as to spiritual *people* but as to
carnal, as to babes in Christ. 2I fed you with milk and not with solid food;
for until now you were not able *to receive it,* and even now you are still not able;
3for you are still carnal. For where *there are* envy, strife, and divisions among
you, are you not carnal and behaving like *mere* men? 4For when one says,
"I am of Paul," and another, "I *am* of Apollos," are you not carnal?

Watering, Working, Warning

5Who then is Paul, and who *is* Apollos, but ministers through whom you
believed, as the Lord gave to each one? 6I planted, Apollos watered, but God
gave the increase. 7So then neither he who plants is anything, nor he who waters, but God who gives the increase. 8Now he who plants and he who waters
are one, and each one will receive his own reward according to his own labor.
9For we are God's fellow workers; you are God's field, *you are* God's building. 10According to the grace of God which was given to me, as a wise master
builder I have laid the foundation, and another builds on it. But let each
one take heed how he builds on it. 11For no other foundation can anyone
lay than that which is laid, which is Jesus Christ. 12Now if anyone builds on
this foundation *with* gold, silver, precious stones, wood, hay, straw, 13each
one's work will become clear; for the Day will declare it, because it will be
revealed by fire; and the fire will test each one's work, of what sort it is. 14If
anyone's work which he has built on *it* endures, he will receive a reward.
15If anyone's work is burned, he will suffer loss; but he himself will be
saved, yet so as through fire.
16Do you not know that you are the temple of God and *that* the Spirit of
God dwells in you? 17If anyone defiles the temple of God, God will destroy
him. For the temple of God is holy, which *temple* you are.

Avoid Worldly Wisdom

18Let no one deceive himself. If anyone among you seems to be wise in
this age, let him become a fool that he may become wise. 19For the wisdom
of this world is foolishness with God. For it is written, "*He catches the wise
in their own craftiness*";[i] 20and again, "*The* LORD *knows the thoughts of
the wise, that they are futile.*"[j] 21Therefore let no one boast in men. For all
things are yours: 22whether Paul or Apollos or Cephas, or the world or life
or death, or things present or things to come—all are yours. 23And you *are*
Christ's, and Christ *is* God's.

Stewards of the Mysteries of God

4 Let a man so consider us, as servants of Christ and stewards of the
mysteries of God. 2Moreover it is required in stewards that one be found
faithful. 3But with me it is a very small thing that I should be judged by you
or by a human court.[k] In fact, I do not even judge myself. 4For I know of
nothing against myself, yet I am not justified by this; but He who judges
me is the Lord. 5Therefore judge nothing before the time, until the Lord
comes, who will both bring to light the hidden things of darkness and reveal the counsels of the hearts. Then each one's praise will come from God.

3:19 [i] Job 5:13
3:20 [j] Psalm 94:11
4:3 [k] Literally *day*

Fools for Christ's Sake

6Now these things, brethren, I have figuratively transferred to myself and Apollos for your sakes, that you may learn in us not to think beyond what is written, that none of you may be puffed up on behalf of one against the other. 7For who makes you differ *from another?* And what do you have that you did not receive? Now if you did indeed receive *it,* why do you boast as if you had not received *it?*

8You are already full! You are already rich! You have reigned as kings without us—and indeed I could wish you did reign, that we also might reign with you! 9For I think that God has displayed us, the apostles, last, as men condemned to death; for we have been made a spectacle to the world, both to angels and to men. 10We *are* fools for Christ's sake, but you *are* wise in Christ! We *are* weak, but you *are* strong! You *are* distinguished, but we *are* dishonored! 11To the present hour we both hunger and thirst, and we are poorly clothed, and beaten, and homeless. 12And we labor, working with our own hands. Being reviled, we bless; being persecuted, we endure; 13being defamed, we entreat. We have been made as the filth of the world, the offscouring of all things until now.

Paul's Paternal Care

14I do not write these things to shame you, but as my beloved children I warn *you.* 15For though you might have ten thousand instructors in Christ, yet *you do* not *have* many fathers; for in Christ Jesus I have begotten you through the gospel. 16Therefore I urge you, imitate me. 17For this reason I have sent Timothy to you, who is my beloved and faithful son in the Lord, who will remind you of my ways in Christ, as I teach everywhere in every church.

18Now some are puffed up, as though I were not coming to you. 19But I will come to you shortly, if the Lord wills, and I will know, not the word of those who are puffed up, but the power. 20For the kingdom of God *is* not in word but in power. 21What do you want? Shall I come to you with a rod, or in love and a spirit of gentleness?

Immorality Defiles the Church

5 It is actually reported *that there is* sexual immorality among you, and such sexual immorality as is not even named[l] among the Gentiles—that a man has his father's wife! 2And you are puffed up, and have not rather mourned, that he who has done this deed might be taken away from among you. 3For I indeed, as absent in body but present in spirit, have already judged (as though I were present) him who has so done this deed. 4In the name of our Lord Jesus Christ, when you are gathered together, along with my spirit, with the power of our Lord Jesus Christ, 5deliver such a one to Satan for the destruction of the flesh, that his spirit may be saved in the day of the Lord Jesus.[m]

6Your glorying *is* not good. Do you not know that a little leaven leavens the whole lump? 7Therefore purge out the old leaven, that you may be a new lump, since you truly are unleavened. For indeed Christ, our Passover, was sacrificed for us.[n] 8Therefore let us keep the feast, not with old leaven, nor with the leaven of malice and wickedness, but with the unleavened *bread* of sincerity and truth.

5:1 [l] NU-Text omits *named.*
5:5 [m] NU-Text omits *Jesus.*
5:7 [n] NU-Text omits *for us.*

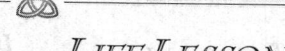

Life Lesson

1 Corinthians 4:1-21

SITUATION Paul hoped church leaders in Corinth would regard him and other apostles as fellow servants of God. Paul sought to correct the church, not abandon or demean it.

OBSERVATION We should never elevate our spiritual leaders too highly. Doing so creates division and places an unfair expectation on them.

INSPIRATION "Think it not strange concerning the fiery trial which is to try you," says Peter. If we do think it strange concerning the things we meet with, it is because we are craven-hearted. We have discreet affinities that keep us out of the mire—I won't stoop, I won't bend. You do not need to, you can be saved by the skin of your teeth if you like; you can refuse to let God count you as one separated unto the gospel. Or you may say—"I do not care if I am treated as the offscourging of the earth as long as the Gospel is proclaimed." A servant of Jesus Christ is one who is willing to go to martyrdom for the reality of the gospel of God. When a merely moral man or woman comes in contact with baseness and immorality and treachery, the recoil is so desperately offensive to human goodness that the heart shuts up in despair. The marvel of the Redemptive Reality of God is that the worst and the vilest can never get to the bottom of His love. Paul did not say that God separated him to show what a wonderful man He could make of him, but "*to reveal His Son in me.*"

(From *My Utmost for His Highest* by Oswald Chambers)

APPLICATION How are capable spiritual leaders being developed in your church? What steps can you take today to develop your leadership skills? Pray for God to lead you to mature faith and service.

EXPLORATION Leaders—Exodus 6:9-12; 17:10-13; Judges 1:1; 1 Kings 2:5-7; Hebrews 13:7, 17.

LIFE LESSON

1 Corinthians 5:1-13

SITUATION Paul never permitted sexually immoral behavior in the church. Yet he remained compassionate when dealing with people.

OBSERVATION Immoral behavior in the church must be handled firmly but sensitively.

INSPIRATION So, do not look to prompt lust. Do not touch to stimulate lust. In today's terms, do not undress a man or woman in your mind as you stare at the physical appearance. Do not linger at the magazine rack or rent X-rated videos or watch films that stir your sensual desires. And, ladies, you can cooperate by refusing to wear seductive attire. By saying no to such things, you "tear out your eye" and you "cut off your hand." One of the best ways I have found to obey Jesus' instruction is simply to replace sensual thoughts with wholesome ones . . . to occupy my mind with things that are pure, lovely, healthy, and positive rather than lurid, provocative and questionable. Scripture memory works wonders, frankly. I find it impossible to simultaneously lust and repeat verses on moral purity.

(From *Simple Faith* by Charles Swindoll)

APPLICATION Sexual desire must be directed and disciplined if we are to live as God intended. What is your strategy for curbing and controlling sexual appetite? Develop a strategy and stick to it. What is the cost of failure to control? Behave as Christ would on this sensitive subject.

EXPLORATION Immorality—Judges 3:5-7; 18:31; Job 31:1; 1 Corinthians 6:9-11; Revelation 9:20-21.

Immorality Must Be Judged

9I wrote to you in my epistle not to keep company with sexually immoral people. 10Yet *I* certainly *did* not *mean* with the sexually immoral
people of this world, or with the covetous, or extortioners, or idolaters,
since then you would need to go out of the world. 11But now I have written
to you not to keep company with anyone named a brother, who is sexually
immoral, or covetous, or an idolater, or a reviler, or a drunkard, or an extortioner—not even to eat with such a person.
12For what *have* I *to do* with judging those also who are outside? Do you
not judge those who are inside? 13But those who are outside God judges.
Therefore "*put away from yourselves the evil person.*"[o]

Do Not Sue the Brethren

6 Dare any of you, having a matter against another, go to law before the
unrighteous, and not before the saints? 2Do you not know that the
saints will judge the world? And if the world will be judged by you, are you
unworthy to judge the smallest matters? 3Do you not know that we shall
judge angels? How much more, things that pertain to this life? 4If then you
have judgments concerning things pertaining to this life, do you appoint
those who are least esteemed by the church to judge? 5I say this to your
shame. Is it so, that there is not a wise man among you, not even one, who
will be able to judge between his brethren? 6But brother goes to law
against brother, and that before unbelievers!
7Now therefore, it is already an utter failure for you that you go to law
against one another. Why do you not rather accept wrong? Why do you
not rather *let yourselves* be cheated? 8No, you yourselves do wrong and
cheat, and *you do* these things *to your* brethren! 9Do you not know that the
unrighteous will not inherit the kingdom of God? Do not be deceived. Neither fornicators, nor idolaters, nor adulterers, nor homosexuals,[p] nor sodomites, 10nor thieves, nor covetous, nor drunkards, nor revilers, nor
extortioners will inherit the kingdom of God. 11And such were some of
you. But you were washed, but you were sanctified, but you were justified
in the name of the Lord Jesus and by the Spirit of our God.

Glorify God in Body and Spirit

12All things are lawful for me, but all things are not helpful. All things
are lawful for me, but I will not be brought under the power of any. 13Foods
for the stomach and the stomach for foods, but God will destroy both it
and them. Now the body *is* not for sexual immorality but for the Lord, and
the Lord for the body. 14And God both raised up the Lord and will also
raise us up by His power.
15Do you not know that your bodies are members of Christ? Shall I then
take the members of Christ and make *them* members of a harlot?
Certainly not! 16Or do you not know that he who is joined to a harlot is one
body *with her?* For "*the two,*" He says, "*shall become one flesh.*"[q] 17But he
who is joined to the Lord is one spirit *with Him.*
18Flee sexual immorality. Every sin that a man does is outside the body,
but he who commits sexual immorality sins against his own body. 19Or do

5:13 *o* Deuteronomy 17:7; 19:19; 22:21, 24; 24:7
6:9 *p* That is, catamites
6:16 *q* Genesis 2:24

you not know that your body is the temple of the Holy Spirit *who is* in you,
whom you have from God, and you are not your own? 20For you were
bought at a price; therefore glorify God in your body[r] and in your spirit,
which are God's.

Principles of Marriage

7 Now concerning the things of which you wrote to me:
It is good for a man not to touch a woman. 2Nevertheless, because of
sexual immorality, let each man have his own wife, and let each woman
have her own husband. 3Let the husband render to his wife the affection due
her, and likewise also the wife to her husband. 4The wife does not have authority over her own body, but the husband *does.* And likewise the husband does
not have authority over his own body, but the wife *does.* 5Do not deprive one
another except with consent for a time, that you may give yourselves to
fasting and prayer; and come together again so that Satan does not tempt
you because of your lack of self-control. 6But I say this as a concession, not
as a commandment. 7For I wish that all men were even as I myself. But each
one has his own gift from God, one in this manner and another in that.
8But I say to the unmarried and to the widows: It is good for them if they
remain even as I am; 9but if they cannot exercise self-control, let them
marry. For it is better to marry than to burn *with passion.*

Keep Your Marriage Vows

10Now to the married I command, *yet* not I but the Lord: A wife is not to
depart from *her* husband. 11But even if she does depart, let her remain unmarried or be reconciled to *her* husband. And a husband is not to divorce
his wife.
12But to the rest I, not the Lord, say: If any brother has a wife who does
not believe, and she is willing to live with him, let him not divorce her. 13And
a woman who has a husband who does not believe, if he is willing to live
with her, let her not divorce him. 14For the unbelieving husband is sanctified by the wife, and the unbelieving wife is sanctified by the husband;
otherwise your children would be unclean, but now they are holy. 15But if
the unbeliever departs, let him depart; a brother or a sister is not under
bondage in such *cases.* But God has called us to peace. 16For how do you
know, O wife, whether you will save *your* husband? Or how do you know, O
husband, whether you will save *your* wife?

Live as You Are Called

17But as God has distributed to each one, as the Lord has called each
one, so let him walk. And so I ordain in all the churches. 18Was anyone called
while circumcised? Let him not become uncircumcised. Was anyone called
while uncircumcised? Let him not be circumcised. 19Circumcision is nothing and uncircumcision is nothing, but keeping the commandments of
God *is what matters.* 20Let each one remain in the same calling in which he
was called. 21Were you called *while* a slave? Do not be concerned about it; but
if you can be made free, rather use *it.* 22For he who is called in the Lord *while*
a slave is the Lord's freedman. Likewise he who is called *while* free is Christ's
slave. 23You were bought at a price; do not become slaves of men. 24Brethren,
let each one remain with God in that *state* in which he was called.

6:20 [r] NU-Text ends the verse at *body.*

LIFE LESSON

1 Corinthians 7:1-40

SITUATION Since the residents of Corinth were renowned for godlessness, Paul explained how to honor God in Christian relationships, specifically sexual relations. Paul's teaching contrasted with the majority opinion in Corinth.

OBSERVATION Whether single or married, we must live devoted to the Lord. God's design for marriage will glorify him, but Paul also points out advantages of being unmarried.

INSPIRATION Marriage is like a ship going out to sea. Anyone setting sail knows buffeting will come, sometimes externally and other times internally. . . .

When we exchange marriage vows, we vow a lifetime of mutual commitment. Nowhere else on earth is there an agreement quite like marriage vows. These vows are binding, and that is why they are so serious. . . .

An ideal marriage is, of all things, a love triangle. In one corner is the wife; in the other, her husband. At the apex of the triangle is God Himself. The closer our communion which is expressed in loving and abiding with God, the closer our communion with each other. Many marriages are already a triangle. God is not at the apex, however. Instead, the third party may be money. Or career(s). Or golf. Or another person.

Does this mean that every marital problem has a spiritual solution? Human relationships are not quite that simplistic.

It does mean, however, that if you and your mate allow lifestyle worship to permeate your marriage, you will save yourselves a lot of grief and anxiety and give yourselves a lot of joy and peace. And God will be glorified in you.

(From *Lifestyle Worship* by John Garmo)

Continued

APPLICATION To honor God in all of our relationships, we must know what the Bible teaches and then obey. Are you familiar with the Bible's teachings on marriage, singleness, and sexuality? How can you take a step closer to God in this vulnerable area? Begin with the verses below and then do a thorough study.

EXPLORATION Marriage and Singleness—Genesis 2:24; Matthew 19:3-12; Romans 12:10; 1 Corinthians 6:9-10, 18-20; Ephesians 5:21-31; Colossians 3:12, 23; 1 Timothy 5:5-6; Hebrews 13:4; 1 Peter 3:1, 7.

To the Unmarried and Widows

25Now concerning virgins: I have no commandment from the Lord; yet
I give judgment as one whom the Lord in His mercy *has made* trustworthy. 26I suppose therefore that this is good because of the present distress—that *it is* good for a man to remain as he is: 27Are you bound to a
wife? Do not seek to be loosed. Are you loosed from a wife? Do not seek a
wife. 28But even if you do marry, you have not sinned; and if a virgin marries, she has not sinned. Nevertheless such will have trouble in the flesh,
but I would spare you.
29But this I say, brethren, the time *is* short, so that from now on even
those who have wives should be as though they had none, 30those who weep
as though they did not weep, those who rejoice as though they did not rejoice, those who buy as though they did not possess, 31and those who use
this world as not misusing *it*. For the form of this world is passing away.
32But I want you to be without care. He who is unmarried cares for the
things of the Lord—how he may please the Lord. 33But he who is married
cares about the things of the world—how he may please *his* wife. 34There
is[s] a difference between a wife and a virgin. The unmarried woman cares
about the things of the Lord, that she may be holy both in body and in
spirit. But she who is married cares about the things of the world—how
she may please *her* husband. 35And this I say for your own profit, not that
I may put a leash on you, but for what is proper, and that you may serve
the Lord without distraction.
36But if any man thinks he is behaving improperly toward his virgin, if
she is past the flower of youth, and thus it must be, let him do what he
wishes. He does not sin; let them marry. 37Nevertheless he who stands
steadfast in his heart, having no necessity, but has power over his own will,
and has so determined in his heart that he will keep his virgin,[t] does well.
38So then he who gives *her*[u] in marriage does well, but he who does not give
her in marriage does better.
39A wife is bound by law as long as her husband lives; but if her husband
dies, she is at liberty to be married to whom she wishes, only in the Lord.
40But she is happier if she remains as she is, according to my judgment—
and I think I also have the Spirit of God.

Be Sensitive to Conscience

8 Now concerning things offered to idols: We know that we all have
knowledge. Knowledge puffs up, but love edifies. 2And if anyone thinks
that he knows anything, he knows nothing yet as he ought to know. 3But if
anyone loves God, this one is known by Him.
4Therefore concerning the eating of things offered to idols, we know
that an idol *is* nothing in the world, and that *there is* no other God but one.
5For even if there are so-called gods, whether in heaven or on earth (as
there are many gods and many lords), 6yet for us *there is* one God, the
Father, of whom *are* all things, and we for Him; and one Lord Jesus Christ,
through whom *are* all things, and through whom we *live*.
7However, *there is* not in everyone that knowledge; for some, with consciousness of the idol, until now eat *it* as a thing offered to an idol; and

7:34 [s] M-Text adds *also*.
7:37 [t] Or *virgin daughter*
7:38 [u] NU-Text reads *his own virgin*.

their conscience, being weak, is defiled. 8But food does not commend us to
God; for neither if we eat are we the better, nor if we do not eat are we the worse.
9But beware lest somehow this liberty of yours become a stumbling
block to those who are weak. 10For if anyone sees you who have knowledge
eating in an idol's temple, will not the conscience of him who is weak be
emboldened to eat those things offered to idols? 11And because of your
knowledge shall the weak brother perish, for whom Christ died? 12But
when you thus sin against the brethren, and wound their weak conscience,
you sin against Christ. 13Therefore, if food makes my brother stumble, I will
never again eat meat, lest I make my brother stumble.

A Pattern of Self-Denial

9 Am I not an apostle? Am I not free? Have I not seen Jesus Christ our Lord?
Are you not my work in the Lord? 2If I am not an apostle to others, yet
doubtless I am to you. For you are the seal of my apostleship in the Lord.
3My defense to those who examine me is this: 4Do we have no right to
eat and drink? 5Do we have no right to take along a believing wife, as *do*
also the other apostles, the brothers of the Lord, and Cephas? 6Or *is it* only
Barnabas and I *who* have no right to refrain from working? 7Who ever
goes to war at his own expense? Who plants a vineyard and does not eat of
its fruit? Or who tends a flock and does not drink of the milk of the flock?
8Do I say these things as a *mere* man? Or does not the law say the same
also? 9For it is written in the law of Moses, *"You shall not muzzle an ox
while it treads out the grain."*[v] Is it oxen God is concerned about? 10Or does
He say *it* altogether for our sakes? For our sakes, no doubt, *this* is written,
that he who plows should plow in hope, and he who threshes in hope
should be partaker of his hope. 11If we have sown spiritual things for you,
is it a great thing if we reap your material things? 12If others are partakers
of *this* right over you, *are* we not even more?
Nevertheless we have not used this right, but endure all things lest we
hinder the gospel of Christ. 13Do you not know that those who minister the
holy things eat *of the things* of the temple, and those who serve at the altar
partake of *the offerings of* the altar? 14Even so the Lord has commanded
that those who preach the gospel should live from the gospel.
15But I have used none of these things, nor have I written these things
that it should be done so to me; for it *would be* better for me to die than
that anyone should make my boasting void. 16For if I preach the gospel, I
have nothing to boast of, for necessity is laid upon me; yes, woe is me if I do
not preach the gospel! 17For if I do this willingly, I have a reward; but if against
my will, I have been entrusted with a stewardship. 18What is my reward
then? That when I preach the gospel, I may present the gospel of Christ[w]
without charge, that I may not abuse my authority in the gospel.

Serving All Men

19For though I am free from all *men,* I have made myself a servant to all,
that I might win the more; 20and to the Jews I became as a Jew, that I might
win Jews; to those *who are* under the law, as under the law,[x] that I might
win those *who are* under the law; 21to those *who are* without law, as without
law (not being without law toward God,[y] but under law toward Christ[z]),

9:9 [v] Deuteronomy 25:4
9:18 [w] NU-Text omits *of Christ.*
9:20 [x] NU-Text adds *though not being myself under the law.*
9:21 [y] NU-Text reads *God's law.* [z] NU-Text reads *Christ's law.*

LIFE LESSON

1 Corinthians 9:1-27

SITUATION Some Believers questioned Paul's rights as an apostle. Paul responded by pointing out that the rights apostles claimed were very reasonable, yet he himself didn't claim them. To Paul, nothing was more important than spreading the gospel, so giving up his rights was a worthwhile sacrifice.

OBSERVATION One of our top priorities should be enabling others to understand the gospel. Though God has given us many blessings and rights, we should be willing to give them up if it would help someone to know Christ.

INSPIRATION I could see the blond head of "Big Daddy," England's most famous wrestler. He was taking his daily constitutional in the deep, choppy waters of the Mediterranean when suddenly I heard him shout to his daughter, "Jan! Jan! A jellyfish just got me. Help!"

Rolling over in the water, I watched to see how tiny Jan could help her enormous daddy.

"He got me again!" his voice boomed.

Suddenly I was struck. It was as if my right arm touched a high-voltage wire. Spinning violently, my leg caught in a viselike cramp, I glimpsed the tiny blue jellyfish swimming away. Grateful for the safety rope beside me, I hung on, weak with shock and the incredible stinging, my right calf painfully knotted. It seemed an eternity before I was able to make it back the short distance to the beach, petrified that there might be a second close encounter of the first kind. It wasn't long before ugly welts rose around my right forearm and a livid red line crossed my back. By dinner time the pain had subsided to a bone-deep ache; the swelling lasted six weeks; the scars will last my lifetime.

Later, as "Big Daddy" and I compared stings, he inquired solicitously, "I hope you won't let this keep you from going into the water, will you?" His voice was both compassionate and concerned, and his granite face, with its blue eyes, was friendly and kind. I hadn't the heart to tell him I'd lost all taste for the sea, all trust of its "critters."

Continued

that I might win those *who are* without law; 22to the weak I became as[a] weak, that I might win the weak. I have become all things to all *men,* that I might by all means save some. 23Now this I do for the gospel's sake, that I may be partaker of it with *you.*

Striving for a Crown

24Do you not know that those who run in a race all run, but one receives the prize? Run in such a way that you may obtain *it.* 25And everyone who competes *for the prize* is temperate in all things. Now they *do it* to obtain a perishable crown, but we *for* an imperishable *crown.* 26Therefore I run thus: not with uncertainty. Thus I fight: not as *one who* beats the air. 27But I discipline my body and bring *it* into subjection, lest, when I have preached to others, I myself should become disqualified.

Old Testament Examples

10 Moreover, brethren, I do not want you to be unaware that all our fathers were under the cloud, all passed through the sea, 2all were baptized into Moses in the cloud and in the sea, 3all ate the same spiritual food, 4and all drank the same spiritual drink. For they drank of that spiritual Rock that followed them, and that Rock was Christ. 5But with most of them God was not well pleased, for *their bodies* were scattered in the wilderness.

6Now these things became our examples, to the intent that we should not lust after evil things as they also lusted. 7And do not become idolaters as *were* some of them. As it is written, *"The people sat down to eat and drink, and rose up to play."*[b] 8Nor let us commit sexual immorality, as some of them did, and in one day twenty-three thousand fell; 9nor let us tempt Christ, as some of them also tempted, and were destroyed by serpents; 10nor complain, as some of them also complained, and were destroyed by the destroyer. 11Now all[c] these things happened to them as examples, and they were written for our admonition, upon whom the ends of the ages have come.

12Therefore let him who thinks he stands take heed lest he fall. 13No temptation has overtaken you except such as is common to man; but God *is* faithful, who will not allow you to be tempted beyond what you are able, but with the temptation will also make the way of escape, that you may be able to bear *it.*

Flee from Idolatry

14Therefore, my beloved, flee from idolatry. 15I speak as to wise men; judge for yourselves what I say. 16The cup of blessing which we bless, is it not the communion of the blood of Christ? The bread which we break, is it not the communion of the body of Christ? 17For we, *though* many, are one bread *and* one body; for we all partake of that one bread.

18Observe Israel after the flesh: Are not those who eat of the sacrifices partakers of the altar? 19What am I saying then? That an idol is anything, or what is offered to idols is anything? 20Rather, that the things which the Gentiles sacrifice they sacrifice to demons and not to God, and I do not want you to have fellowship with demons. 21You cannot drink the cup of the Lord and the cup of demons; you cannot partake of the Lord's table

9:22 [a] NU-Text omits *as.*
10:7 [b] Exodus 32:6
10:11 [c] NU-Text omits *all.*

But two painful days later, assured by the beachboys and bathers that the sea was clear, I ventured another swim. Suddenly a familiar voice boomed, "Good for you! Didn't let that jellyfish put you off, did you?"

It was "Big Daddy" out for his hourly workout in the deep water, shouting encouragement to this one timid swimmer. "Good girl!" he responded to my wave. "Keep it up!" Here was a professional athlete, a giant of a man, an experienced swimmer, looking out for one of the poorest, least enthusiastic swimmers in the sea.

Life is a lot like the sea: full of unseen hazards and venomous creatures that attack without warning. I kept thinking of baby Christians who, after that first painful encounter, lose heart. Hurting and fearful, they call it quits unless some more experienced, stronger Christian offers a word of sympathetic advice, a shout of encouragement, and a note of praise.

Long after I'd forgotten the jellyfish attack and its painful aftermath, I remembered those words, "You won't let it keep you from going into the water, will you?" And later, "Good for you! Keep it up!"

Has anybody around you been stung lately?

(From *Legacy of a Pack Rat* by Ruth Bell Graham)

APPLICATION Our culture encourages us to stand up for ourselves and demand our rights, even at the expense of others. Yet Jesus and the New Testament writers repeatedly point to the joy we receive from humility and self-sacrifice. Why not give up your right for free time or watching a movie and use the time to share with a new Christian a lesson you have learned recently.

EXPLORATION Self-Sacrifice—Micah 6:8; Matthew 16:24-25; 18:4; Mark 10:28; Luke 14:33; 1 Corinthians 10:24, 33; 2 Corinthians 8:9; Philippians 2:4-8; 3:8.

and of the table of demons. 22Or do we provoke the Lord to jealousy? Are
we stronger than He?

All to the Glory of God

23All things are lawful for me,[d] but not all things are helpful; all things
are lawful for me,[e] but not all things edify. 24Let no one seek his own, but
each one the other's *well-being.*
25Eat whatever is sold in the meat market, asking no questions for conscience' sake; 26for *"the earth is the LORD's, and all its fullness."*[f]
27If any of those who do not believe invites you *to dinner,* and you desire
to go, eat whatever is set before you, asking no question for conscience'
sake. 28But if anyone says to you, "This was offered to idols," do not eat it
for the sake of the one who told you, and for conscience' sake;[g] for *"the
earth is the LORD's, and all its fullness."*[h] 29"Conscience," I say, not your
own, but that of the other. For why is my liberty judged by another *man's*
conscience? 30But if I partake with thanks, why am I evil spoken of for *the
food* over which I give thanks?
31Therefore, whether you eat or drink, or whatever you do, do all to the
glory of God. 32Give no offense, either to the Jews or to the Greeks or to the
church of God, 33just as I also please all *men* in all *things,* not seeking my
own profit, but the *profit* of many, that they may be saved.

11 Imitate me, just as I also *imitate* Christ.

Head Coverings

2Now I praise you, brethren, that you remember me in all things and
keep the traditions just as I delivered *them* to you. 3But I want you to know
that the head of every man is Christ, the head of woman *is* man, and the
head of Christ *is* God. 4Every man praying or prophesying, having *his* head
covered, dishonors his head. 5But every woman who prays or prophesies
with *her* head uncovered dishonors her head, for that is one and the same
as if her head were shaved. 6For if a woman is not covered, let her also be
shorn. But if it is shameful for a woman to be shorn or shaved, let her be
covered. 7For a man indeed ought not to cover *his* head, since he is the
image and glory of God; but woman is the glory of man. 8For man is not
from woman, but woman from man. 9Nor was man created for the
woman, but woman for the man. 10For this reason the woman ought to have
a symbol of authority on *her* head, because of the angels. 11Nevertheless,
neither *is* man independent of woman, nor woman independent of man,
in the Lord. 12For as woman *came* from man, even so man also *comes*
through woman; but all things are from God.
13Judge among yourselves. Is it proper for a woman to pray to God with
her head uncovered? 14Does not even nature itself teach you that if a man
has long hair, it is a dishonor to him? 15But if a woman has long hair, it is a
glory to her; for *her* hair is given to her[i] for a covering. 16But if anyone seems
to be contentious, we have no such custom, nor *do* the churches of God.

Conduct at the Lord's Supper

17Now in giving these instructions I do not praise *you,* since you come

10:23 *d* NU-Text omits *for me.* *e* NU-Text omits *for me.*
10:26 *f* Psalm 24:1
10:28 *g* NU-Text omits the rest of this verse. *h* Psalm 24:1
11:15 *i* M-Text omits *to her.*

LIFE LESSON

1 Corinthians 10:1–11:1

SITUATION Paul taught the Corinthians about the dangers of idol worship and petty arguments using lessons from history and faith.

OBSERVATION In everything that we do, whether we relate to each other or worship, we ought to give glory to God. Though mindful not to offend other Christians, we should be focused on bringing praise to God.

INSPIRATION Loving others requires us to express our liberty wisely. In other words, love must rule. I'm not my own, I'm bought with a price. My goal is not to please me, it is to please my Lord Jesus, my God. It is not to please you, it is to please my Lord. The same is true for you. So the bottom line is this: I don't adapt my life according to what you may say, I adapt my life according to the basis of my love for you because I answer to Christ. And so do you.

. . . Even if you personally would not do what another is doing, let it be. And you who feel the freedom to do so, don't flaunt it or mock those who disagree. We are in the construction business, not destruction. And let's all remember that God's big-picture kingdom plan is not being shaped by small things like what one person prefers over another, but by large things, like righteousness and peace and joy.

(From *Grace Awakening* by Charles Swindoll)

APPLICATION What is your motivation for your daily tasks? Who gets the glory—you or God? Even the smallest decisions and the briefest interpersonal encounters should be done so that God receives glory.

EXPLORATION Bringing Glory to God—Psalm 22:23; Matthew 5:16; John 15:8; Romans 15:6; 1 Corinthians 6:20.

LIFE LESSON

1 Corinthians 11:2-34

SITUATION The Corinthians allowed some parts of their worship services to become times of selfishness and bickering. Lack of respect and concern for others undermined their gathering for worship.

OBSERVATION Careful self-examination of our motives along with a good dose of courtesy and love are necessary to worship with other believers and bring glory to God.

INSPIRATION Self is like the cuckoo. Cuckoos lay their eggs in other birds' nests. A baby cuckoo in a sparrow's nest may be three times the size of its foster parents. I will never forget the comic-tragic sight of a pair of hedge sparrows, frantically darting to and from their nest to supply an enormous baby cuckoo with bits of food. It amazed me to see what power the cuckoo held to keep the sparrows on the move. His lusty cries could be heard for a quarter of a mile. The sparrows had grown thin and weary in their endless haste to cram food into his insatiable gullet.

Self is a cuckoo in the nest of your heart. Like the sparrows, you are driven mercilessly by his cries to be satisfied. And the bigger he gets, the hungrier he grows; while the hungrier he grows, the louder he shrieks.

But there's another aspect to the problem. So long as the cuckoo in the nest gets preference, the weak cries of the baby sparrows are less effective in securing food from their parents. In the same way, so long as the strident voice of self enslaves you, the real you, the redeemed you, the new creation in Christ, will have little chance to grow. You'll be too busy feeding self. (From *The Race* by John White)

APPLICATION Do you dislike a certain hymn, a chorus, or a piece of liturgy? Don't gripe about it. Accept it. Realize that as you put aside your preference, another Christian is able to worship better through it.

EXPLORATION Self-Examination—Lamentations 3:40; Psalm 51:10-12; Matthew 7:5; Romans 12:1-2; 2 Corinthians 13:5.

together not for the better but for the worse. [18]For first of all, when you
come together as a church, I hear that there are divisions among you, and
in part I believe it. [19]For there must also be factions among you, that those
who are approved may be recognized among you. [20]Therefore when you
come together in one place, it is not to eat the Lord's Supper. [21]For in eating, each one takes his own supper ahead of *others;* and one is hungry and
another is drunk. [22]What! Do you not have houses to eat and drink in? Or
do you despise the church of God and shame those who have nothing?
What shall I say to you? Shall I praise you in this? I do not praise *you.*

Institution of the Lord's Supper

[23]For I received from the Lord that which I also delivered to you: that the
Lord Jesus on the *same* night in which He was betrayed took bread; [24]and
when He had given thanks, He broke *it* and said, "Take, eat;[j] this is My
body which is broken[k] for you; do this in remembrance of Me." [25]In the
same manner *He* also *took* the cup after supper, saying, "This cup is the
new covenant in My blood. This do, as often as you drink *it,* in remembrance of Me."
[26]For as often as you eat this bread and drink this cup, you proclaim the
Lord's death till He comes.

Examine Yourself

[27]Therefore whoever eats this bread or drinks *this* cup of the Lord in an
unworthy manner will be guilty of the body and blood[l] of the Lord. [28]But
let a man examine himself, and so let him eat of the bread and drink of the
cup. [29]For he who eats and drinks in an unworthy manner[m] eats and
drinks judgment to himself, not discerning the Lord's[n] body. [30]For this
reason many *are* weak and sick among you, and many sleep. [31]For if we
would judge ourselves, we would not be judged. [32]But when we are judged, we
are chastened by the Lord, that we may not be condemned with the world.
[33]Therefore, my brethren, when you come together to eat, wait for one
another. [34]But if anyone is hungry, let him eat at home, lest you come together for judgment. And the rest I will set in order when I come.

Spiritual Gifts: Unity in Diversity

12 Now concerning spiritual *gifts,* brethren, I do not want you to be ignorant: [2]You know that[o] you were Gentiles, carried away to these
dumb idols, however you were led. [3]Therefore I make known to you that
no one speaking by the Spirit of God calls Jesus accursed, and no one can
say that Jesus is Lord except by the Holy Spirit.
[4]There are diversities of gifts, but the same Spirit. [5]There are differences
of ministries, but the same Lord. [6]And there are diversities of activities,
but it is the same God who works all in all. [7]But the manifestation of the
Spirit is given to each one for the profit *of all:* [8]for to one is given the word
of wisdom through the Spirit, to another the word of knowledge through
the same Spirit, [9]to another faith by the same Spirit, to another gifts of
healings by the same[p] Spirit, [10]to another the working of miracles, to an-

11:24 [j] NU-Text omits *Take, eat.* [k] NU-Text omits *broken.*
11:27 [l] NU-Text and M-Text read *the blood.*
11:29 [m] NU-Text omits *in an unworthy manner.* [n] NU-Text omits *Lord's.*
12:2 [o] NU-Text and M-Text add *when.*
12:9 [p] NU-Text reads *one.*

other prophecy, to another discerning of spirits, to another *different* kinds of tongues, to another the interpretation of tongues. 11 But one and the same Spirit works all these things, distributing to each one individually as He wills.

Unity and Diversity in One Body

12 For as the body is one and has many members, but all the members of that one body, being many, are one body, so also *is* Christ. 13 For by one Spirit we were all baptized into one body—whether Jews or Greeks, whether slaves or free—and have all been made to drink into[q] one Spirit. 14 For in fact the body is not one member but many.

15 If the foot should say, "Because I am not a hand, I am not of the body," is it therefore not of the body? 16 And if the ear should say, "Because I am not an eye, I am not of the body," is it therefore not of the body? 17 If the whole body *were* an eye, where *would be* the hearing? If the whole *were* hearing, where *would be* the smelling? 18 But now God has set the members, each one of them, in the body just as He pleased. 19 And if they *were* all one member, where *would* the body *be?*

20 But now indeed *there are* many members, yet one body. 21 And the eye cannot say to the hand, "I have no need of you"; nor again the head to the feet, "I have no need of you." 22 No, much rather, those members of the body which seem to be weaker are necessary. 23 And those *members* of the body which we think to be less honorable, on these we bestow greater honor; and our unpresentable *parts* have greater modesty, 24 but our presentable *parts* have no need. But God composed the body, having given greater honor to that *part* which lacks it, 25 that there should be no schism in the body, but *that* the members should have the same care for one another. 26 And if one member suffers, all the members suffer with *it;* or if one member is honored, all the members rejoice with *it.*

27 Now you are the body of Christ, and members individually. 28 And God has appointed these in the church: first apostles, second prophets, third teachers, after that miracles, then gifts of healings, helps, administrations, varieties of tongues. 29 *Are* all apostles? *Are* all prophets? *Are* all teachers? *Are* all workers of miracles? 30 Do all have gifts of healings? Do all speak with tongues? Do all interpret? 31 But earnestly desire the best[r] gifts. And yet I show you a more excellent way.

The Greatest Gift

13 Though I speak with the tongues of men and of angels, but have not love, I have become sounding brass or a clanging cymbal. 2 And though I have *the gift of* prophecy, and understand all mysteries and all knowledge, and though I have all faith, so that I could remove mountains, but have not love, I am nothing. 3 And though I bestow all my goods to feed *the poor,* and though I give my body to be burned,[s] but have not love, it profits me nothing.

4 Love suffers long *and* is kind; love does not envy; love does not parade itself, is not puffed up; 5 does not behave rudely, does not seek its own, is not provoked, thinks no evil; 6 does not rejoice in iniquity, but rejoices in the truth; 7 bears all things, believes all things, hopes all things, endures all things.

12:13 [q] NU-Text omits *into.*
12:31 [r] NU-Text reads *greater.*
13:3 [s] NU-Text reads *so I may boast.*

LIFE LESSON

1 Corinthians 12:1-31a

SITUATION The Corinthians struggled with petty disagreements and offenses. Once again, Paul emphasized the need for unity in the church.

OBSERVATION Though the church is a universal body, the gifts and skills of each Christian are unique. We can achieve unity by appreciating different abilities in others and empathizing with each other's joys and sorrows.

INSPIRATION Abraham Lincoln once said, characteristically: "I am sorry for the man who can't feel the whip when it is laid on the other man's back. . . ."

Jesus wept tears of compassion at the graveside of a friend. He mourned over Jerusalem because as a city it had lost its appreciation of the things of the spirit. His great heart was sensitive to the needs of others.

Tears shed for self are tears of weakness, but tears of love shed for others are a sign of strength. I am not as sensitive as I ought to be until I am able to "weep o'er the erring one and lift up the fallen." And until I have learned the value of compassionately sharing others' sorrow, distress, and misfortune, I cannot know real happiness.

(From *The Secret of Happiness* by Billy Graham)

APPLICATION Are there fellow Believers around you who need someone to share in their sorrow or joy? Do you have trouble being happy with some, or sad with others? Look for challenging opportunities to share the emotions of other people's lives.

EXPLORATION Sympathy for Others—Isaiah 58:7; Acts 20:35; Romans 15:1; Galatians 6:2; Hebrews 13:3; James 1:27.

LIFE LESSON

1 Corinthians 12:31b–13:13

SITUATION The Corinthians compared spiritual gifts and ministries. They rated a person's value to the church by that person's gifts.

OBSERVATION All spiritual gifts are equally valuable to the church. But love is even greater than all of them combined.

INSPIRATION Paul used the metaphor of the body to illustrate the interdependence of individual Christians (1 Cor 12:12-13). When one part of our physical body suffers, the other parts suffer; when one part accomplishes its duty, it is always a cooperative effort. . . .

This interdependence results in a cooperative concern for the various parts of the body. . . . Similarly, we as Christians are connected in Christ. When one Christian fails, we share his failure and care for his needs. When he is restored to fellowship, we rejoice with him.

We can't afford to believe that it doesn't matter whether we are actively involved in the struggles against the world or whether we are drifting aimlessly with the tide. When we lose our passion for the church (Christ's Body) and are preoccupied with our own concerns, our witness will be submerged. We will drown in the icy waters of indifference. . . .

The same is true in the local church. A church preoccupied with its own differences or torn by schism is a good candidate for ultimate oblivion. . . . Differences must be held without bitterness, self-righteousness, and pride. In this way, a church can work out its differences and exercise discipline without diminishing its impact on the world.

(From *How in the World Can I be Holy?* by Erwin W. Lutzer)

APPLICATION Teamwork is important, whether on the job or in a ministry. How are you doing as a team player? Are you using your spiritual gifts as well as you can? (If you're not sure about your gift, ask the Lord what contribution you can make.)

EXPLORATION Harmony of Believers—Leviticus 19:18; Psalm 133:1; Romans 15:5-7; 1 Corinthians 1:10; Philippians 2:1-2; 1 Peter 3:8.

[8]Love never fails. But whether *there are* prophecies, they will fail;
whether *there are* tongues, they will cease; whether *there is* knowledge, it
will vanish away. [9]For we know in part and we prophesy in part. [10]But when
that which is perfect has come, then that which is in part will be done away.
[11]When I was a child, I spoke as a child, I understood as a child, I
thought as a child; but when I became a man, I put away childish things.
[12]For now we see in a mirror, dimly, but then face to face. Now I know in
part, but then I shall know just as I also am known.
[13]And now abide faith, hope, love, these three; but the greatest of these *is*
love.

Prophecy and Tongues

14 Pursue love, and desire spiritual *gifts,* but especially that you may
prophesy. [2]For he who speaks in a tongue does not speak to men but to
God, for no one understands *him;* however, in the spirit he speaks mysteries.
[3]But he who prophesies speaks edification and exhortation and comfort to
men. [4]He who speaks in a tongue edifies himself, but he who prophesies edifies the church. [5]I wish you all spoke with tongues, but even more that you
prophesied; for[t] he who prophesies *is* greater than he who speaks with
tongues, unless indeed he interprets, that the church may receive edification.

Tongues Must Be Interpreted

[6]But now, brethren, if I come to you speaking with tongues, what shall I
profit you unless I speak to you either by revelation, by knowledge, by
prophesying, or by teaching? [7]Even things without life, whether flute or
harp, when they make a sound, unless they make a distinction in the
sounds, how will it be known what is piped or played? [8]For if the trumpet
makes an uncertain sound, who will prepare for battle? [9]So likewise you,
unless you utter by the tongue words easy to understand, how will it be
known what is spoken? For you will be speaking into the air. [10]There are, it
may be, so many kinds of languages in the world, and none of them *is*
without significance. [11]Therefore, if I do not know the meaning of the language, I shall be a foreigner to him who speaks, and he who speaks *will be*
a foreigner to me. [12]Even so you, since you are zealous for spiritual *gifts, let
it be* for the edification of the church *that* you seek to excel.
[13]Therefore let him who speaks in a tongue pray that he may interpret.
[14]For if I pray in a tongue, my spirit prays, but my understanding is
unfruitful. [15]What is *the conclusion* then? I will pray with the spirit, and I
will also pray with the understanding. I will sing with the spirit, and I will
also sing with the understanding. [16]Otherwise, if you bless with the spirit,
how will he who occupies the place of the uninformed say "Amen" at your
giving of thanks, since he does not understand what you say? [17]For you indeed give thanks well, but the other is not edified.
[18]I thank my God I speak with tongues more than you all; [19]yet in the
church I would rather speak five words with my understanding, that I
may teach others also, than ten thousand words in a tongue.

Tongues a Sign to Unbelievers

[20]Brethren, do not be children in understanding; however, in malice be
babes, but in understanding be mature.

14:5 [t] NU-Text reads *and.*

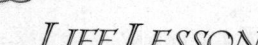

21 In the law it is written:

"With men of other tongues and other lips
I will speak to this people;
And yet, for all that, they will not hear Me,"[u]

says the Lord.
22 Therefore tongues are for a sign, not to those who believe but to unbelievers; but prophesying is not for unbelievers but for those who believe.
23 Therefore if the whole church comes together in one place, and all speak
with tongues, and there come in *those who are* uninformed or unbelievers,
will they not say that you are out of your mind? 24 But if all prophesy, and
an unbeliever or an uninformed person comes in, he is convinced by all,
he is convicted by all. 25 And thus[v] the secrets of his heart are revealed; and
so, falling down on *his* face, he will worship God and report that God is
truly among you.

Order in Church Meetings

26 How is it then, brethren? Whenever you come together, each of you
has a psalm, has a teaching, has a tongue, has a revelation, has an interpretation. Let all things be done for edification. 27 If anyone speaks in a
tongue, *let there be* two or at the most three, *each* in turn, and let one interpret. 28 But if there is no interpreter, let him keep silent in church, and let
him speak to himself and to God. 29 Let two or three prophets speak, and
let the others judge. 30 But if *anything* is revealed to another who sits by, let
the first keep silent. 31 For you can all prophesy one by one, that all may
learn and all may be encouraged. 32 And the spirits of the prophets are subject to the prophets. 33 For God is not *the author* of confusion but of peace,
as in all the churches of the saints.
34 Let your[w] women keep silent in the churches, for they are not permitted to speak; but *they are* to be submissive, as the law also says. 35 And if
they want to learn something, let them ask their own husbands at home;
for it is shameful for women to speak in church.
36 Or did the word of God come *originally* from you? Or *was it* you only
that it reached? 37 If anyone thinks himself to be a prophet or spiritual, let
him acknowledge that the things which I write to you are the commandments of the Lord. 38 But if anyone is ignorant, let him be ignorant.[x]
39 Therefore, brethren, desire earnestly to prophesy, and do not forbid to
speak with tongues. 40 Let all things be done decently and in order.

The Risen Christ, Faith's Reality

15 Moreover, brethren, I declare to you the gospel which I preached to
you, which also you received and in which you stand, 2 by which also
you are saved, if you hold fast that word which I preached to you—unless
you believed in vain.
3 For I delivered to you first of all that which I also received: that Christ
died for our sins according to the Scriptures, 4 and that He was buried, and
that He rose again the third day according to the Scriptures, 5 and that He
was seen by Cephas, then by the twelve. 6 After that He was seen by over five

14:21 [u] Isaiah 28:11, 12
14:25 [v] NU-Text omits *And thus.*
14:34 [w] NU-Text omits *your.*
14:38 [x] NU-Text reads *if anyone does not recognize this, he is not recognized.*

LIFE LESSON

1 Corinthians 14:1-40

SITUATION The Corinthian Believers were so impressed by the glitz and wonder of spiritual gifts that they lost their perspective and forgot the purpose of these gifts.

OBSERVATION Spiritual gifts glorify God and build up the Body of Christ. Gifts should never be misused, envied, or cause division.

INSPIRATION The mark of Spirit-filled men and women is the fruit they bear. Fruit is the standard by which our walk with God can be measured. The Bible is crystal clear at this point. Yet it never ceases to amaze me how prone believers are to substitute other measuring devices or standards. . . .

The two most popular substitutes for fruit are (1) spiritual gifts and (2) natural talent. . . .

It's not hard to figure out why gifts and talents are so readily substituted for fruit. It's easier to exercise a gift than to walk in the Spirit. Not only that, certain gifts and talents have a high entertainment value. When exploited in the right way, gifts and talents can be real crowd pleasers. . . . But none of these things are indications that a man or woman is under the control of the Holy Spirit. . . .

Giftedness does not determine greatness in God's book. Jesus said, "You will know them by their fruits." Not by how anointed they may appear to be. Not by the miracles they perform. Not by the revelation knowledge they claim to have. You will recognize God's hand of blessing on men and women by the fruit they bear. A man who claims to be doing miracles by the power of the Spirit but who exhibits no fruit of the Spirit in his life is either lying or confused. . . .

(From *The Wonderful Spirit-Filled Life* by Charles Stanley)

APPLICATION What is your priority: becoming like Christ or getting a chance to use your gifts? Your gifts, talents, and abilities should build up other Believers and bring unity in the church. If they're not quite doing that, check your attitudes.

EXPLORATION Spiritual Gifts and Unity—Romans 12:3-8; 14:19; 15:1-6; 2 Corinthians 12:19-20; Galatians 5:22-26; Ephesians 4:3-7, 11-16.

Life Lesson

1 Corinthians 15:1-58

SITUATION Because of their culture, the Corinthians did not believe in the resurrection. Instead, they thought only the soul would rise from the dead, leaving behind the body.

OBSERVATION Because Jesus rose from the dead, we have hope, salvation, victory, and purpose. We can be confident in faith and diligent in work for him.

INSPIRATION A sudden breeze, surprisingly warm, whistles through the leaves scattering dust from the lifeless form. And with the breath of fresh air comes the difference. Winging on the warm wind is his image. Laughter is laid in the sculpted cheeks. A reservoir of tears is stored in the soul. A sprinkling of twinkle for the eyes. Poetry for the spirit. Logic. Loyalty. Like leaves on an autumn breeze, they float and land and are absorbed. His gifts become a part of him.

His Majesty smiles at his image. "It is good."

The eyes open.

Oneness. Creator and created walking on the river bank. Laughter. Purity. Innocent joy. Life unending.

Then the tree.

The struggle. The snake. The lie. The enticement. Heart torn, lured. Soul drawn to pleasure, to independence, to importance. Inner agony. Whose will?

The choice. Death of innocence. Entrance of death. The fall.

Tearstains mingling with fruit-stains. . . .

[Then,] The Quest.

"Abram, you will father a nation! And Abram—tell the people I love them."

"Moses, you will deliver my people! And Moses—tell the people I love them."

"Joshua, you will lead the chosen ones! And Joshua—tell the people I love them."

hundred brethren at once, of whom the greater part remain to the present, but
some have fallen asleep. 7After that He was seen by James, then by all the apostles. 8Then last of all He was seen by me also, as by one born out of due time.
9For I am the least of the apostles, who am not worthy to be called an
apostle, because I persecuted the church of God. 10But by the grace of God
I am what I am, and His grace toward me was not in vain; but I labored
more abundantly than they all, yet not I, but the grace of God *which was* with
me. 11Therefore, whether *it was* I or they, so we preach and so you believed.

The Risen Christ, Our Hope

12Now if Christ is preached that He has been raised from the dead, how
do some among you say that there is no resurrection of the dead? 13But if
there is no resurrection of the dead, then Christ is not risen. 14And if Christ
is not risen, then our preaching *is* empty and your faith *is* also empty.
15Yes, and we are found false witnesses of God, because we have testified of
God that He raised up Christ, whom He did not raise up—if in fact the
dead do not rise. 16For if *the* dead do not rise, then Christ is not risen. 17And
if Christ is not risen, your faith *is* futile; you are still in your sins! 18Then
also those who have fallen asleep in Christ have perished. 19If in this life
only we have hope in Christ, we are of all men the most pitiable.

The Last Enemy Destroyed

20But now Christ is risen from the dead, *and* has become the firstfruits
of those who have fallen asleep. 21For since by man *came* death, by Man
also *came* the resurrection of the dead. 22For as in Adam all die, even so in
Christ all shall be made alive. 23But each one in his own order: Christ the
firstfruits, afterward those *who are* Christ's at His coming. 24Then *comes* the
end, when He delivers the kingdom to God the Father, when He puts an end to
all rule and all authority and power. 25For He must reign till He has put all enemies under His feet. 26The last enemy *that* will be destroyed *is* death. 27For
"*He has put all things under His feet.*"[y] But when He says "all things are put
under *Him*," it is evident that He who put all things under Him is excepted.
28Now when all things are made subject to Him, then the Son Himself will also
be subject to Him who put all things under Him, that God may be all in all.

Effects of Denying the Resurrection

29Otherwise, what will they do who are baptized for the dead, if the dead
do not rise at all? Why then are they baptized for the dead? 30And why do
we stand in jeopardy every hour? 31I affirm, by the boasting in you which I
have in Christ Jesus our Lord, I die daily. 32If, in the manner of men, I have
fought with beasts at Ephesus, what advantage *is it* to me? If *the* dead do
not rise, "*Let us eat and drink, for tomorrow we die!*"[z]
33Do not be deceived: "Evil company corrupts good habits." 34Awake to
righteousness, and do not sin; for some do not have the knowledge of God.
I speak *this* to your shame.

A Glorious Body

35But someone will say, "How are the dead raised up? And with what
body do they come?" 36Foolish one, what you sow is not made alive unless

15:27 [y] Psalm 8:6
15:32 [z] Isaiah 22:13

it dies. 37 And what you sow, you do not sow that body that shall be, but
mere grain—perhaps wheat or some other *grain*. 38 But God gives it a
body as He pleases, and to each seed its own body.
39 All flesh *is* not the same flesh, but *there is* one *kind of* flesh[a] of men, another flesh of animals, another of fish, *and* another of birds.
40 *There are* also celestial bodies and terrestrial bodies; but the glory of
the celestial *is* one, and the *glory* of the terrestrial *is* another. 41 *There is* one
glory of the sun, another glory of the moon, and another glory of the stars;
for *one* star differs from *another* star in glory.
42 So also *is* the resurrection of the dead. *The body* is sown in corruption,
it is raised in incorruption. 43 It is sown in dishonor, it is raised in glory. It
is sown in weakness, it is raised in power. 44 It is sown a natural body, it is
raised a spiritual body. There is a natural body, and there is a spiritual
body. 45 And so it is written, *"The first man Adam became a living being."*[b]
The last Adam *became* a life-giving spirit.
46 However, the spiritual is not first, but the natural, and afterward the
spiritual. 47 The first man *was* of the earth, *made* of dust; the second Man *is*
the Lord[c] from heaven. 48 As *was* the *man* of dust, so also *are* those *who are*
made of dust; and as *is* the heavenly *Man*, so also *are* those *who are* heavenly. 49 And as we have borne the image of the *man* of dust, we shall also
bear[d] the image of the heavenly *Man*.

Our Final Victory

50 Now this I say, brethren, that flesh and blood cannot inherit the kingdom of God; nor does corruption inherit incorruption. 51 Behold, I tell you
a mystery: We shall not all sleep, but we shall all be changed— 52 in a moment, in the twinkling of an eye, at the last trumpet. For the trumpet will
sound, and the dead will be raised incorruptible, and we shall be changed.
53 For this corruptible must put on incorruption, and this mortal *must* put
on immortality. 54 So when this corruptible has put on incorruption, and
this mortal has put on immortality, then shall be brought to pass the saying that is written: *"Death is swallowed up in victory."*[e]

55 *"O Death, where is your sting?*[f]
O Hades, where is your victory?"[g]

56 The sting of death *is* sin, and the strength of sin *is* the law. 57 But thanks *be*
to God, who gives us the victory through our Lord Jesus Christ.
58 Therefore, my beloved brethren, be steadfast, immovable, always
abounding in the work of the Lord, knowing that your labor is not in vain
in the Lord.

Collection for the Saints

16 Now concerning the collection for the saints, as I have given orders
to the churches of Galatia, so you must do also: 2 On the first *day* of
the week let each one of you lay something aside, storing up as he may
prosper, that there be no collections when I come. 3 And when I come,

"David, you will reign over the people! And David—tell the people I love them."

"Jeremiah, you will bear tidings of bondage! But Jeremiah, remind my children, remind my children that I love them."

. . . God watching, never turning, ever loving, ever yearning for the Garden again. . . .

[Finally,] Empty throne. Spirit descending. Hushed angels.

A girl . . . a womb . . . an egg.

The same Divine Artist again forms a body. This time his own. Fleshly divinity. Skin layered on spirit. Omnipotence with hair. Toenails. Knuckles. Molars. Kneecaps. Once again he walks with man. Yet the Garden is now thorny. Thorns that cut, thorns that poison, thorns that remain lodged, leaving bitter wounds. Disharmony. Sickness. Betrayal. Fear. Guilt. . . .

And once again, a tree.

Once again the struggle. The snake. The enticement. Heart torn, lured. Once again the question, "Whose will?"

Then the choice. Tearstains mingle with bloodstains. Relationship restored. Bridge erected.

Once again he smiles. "It is good."

"For just as death came by the means of a man, in the same way the rising from death comes by means of a man. For just as all people die because of their union with Adam, in the same way all will be raised to life because of their union with Christ" (1 Corinthians 15:21-22 TEV).

(From *God Came Near* by Max Lucado)

APPLICATION Be confident today in your faith because of what Jesus has done. He broke the power of death so that you might have eternal life with him.

EXPLORATION Confidence—John 6:40; 11:25; Romans 1:16; Galatians 5:1; 6:9; Philippians 1:6; 2 Timothy 1:8-10; Hebrews 4:16; 11:1; 1 John 2:28.

15:39 [a] NU-Text and M-Text omit *of flesh.*
15:45 [b] Genesis 2:7
15:47 [c] NU-Text omits *the Lord.*
15:49 [d] M-Text reads *let us also bear.*
15:54 [e] Isaiah 25:8
15:55 [f] Hosea 13:14 [g] NU-Text reads *O Death, where is your victory? O Death, where is your sting?*

whomever you approve by *your* letters I will send to
bear your gift to Jerusalem. 4But if it is fitting that I go
also, they will go with me.

Personal Plans

5Now I will come to you when I pass through
Macedonia (for I am passing through Macedonia).
6And it may be that I will remain, or even spend the
winter with you, that you may send me on my journey, wherever I go. 7For I do not wish to see you now
on the way; but I hope to stay a while with you, if the
Lord permits.
8But I will tarry in Ephesus until Pentecost. 9For a
great and effective door has opened to me, and *there*
are many adversaries.
10And if Timothy comes, see that he may be with
you without fear; for he does the work of the Lord, as I
also *do.* 11Therefore let no one despise him. But send
him on his journey in peace, that he may come to me;
for I am waiting for him with the brethren.
12Now concerning *our* brother Apollos, I strongly
urged him to come to you with the brethren, but he
was quite unwilling to come at this time; however, he
will come when he has a convenient time.

Final Exhortations

13Watch, stand fast in the faith, be brave, be strong.
14Let all *that* you *do* be done with love.
15I urge you, brethren—you know the household of
Stephanas, that it is the firstfruits of Achaia, and *that*
they have devoted themselves to the ministry of the
saints— 16that you also submit to such, and to everyone who works and labors with *us.*
17I am glad about the coming of Stephanas,
Fortunatus, and Achaicus, for what was lacking on
your part they supplied. 18For they refreshed my spirit
and yours. Therefore acknowledge such men.

Greetings and a Solemn Farewell

19The churches of Asia greet you. Aquila and
Priscilla greet you heartily in the Lord, with the
church that is in their house. 20All the brethren greet
you.

Greet one another with a holy kiss.
21The salutation with my own hand—Paul's.
22If anyone does not love the Lord Jesus Christ, let
him be accursed.[h] O Lord, come![i]
23The grace of our Lord Jesus Christ *be* with you.
24My love *be* with you all in Christ Jesus. Amen.

16:22 [h] Greek *anathema* [i] Aramaic *Maranatha*

The Second Epistle of Paul to the

CORINTHIANS

INTRODUCTION

Once there was a school in a village. Atop the school was a bell which was rung every morning to call the children to class. The boys and girls arrived reluctantly and precisely at the hour. Never a minute early. The bell would ring again in the afternoon, liberating the children to their play. The children bolted out the door at the ringing of the bell. Never lingering a minute late. This is how it was with each child.

Except one.

There was a girl who came early. She helped the teacher prepare the room for the day. The same girl would stay late—cleaning the board and dusting the erasers. During class she was attentive. She sat close to the teacher, absorbing the lessons.

One day when the other children were unruly and inattentive, the teacher used the girl as an example. "Why can't you be like her? She listens. She works. She comes early. She stays late."

"It isn't fair to ask us to be like her," a boy blurted out from the rear of the room.

"Why?" asked the teacher.

The boy was uncomfortable, wishing he hadn't spoken. "She has an advantage," he shrugged.

"And what's that?"

"She is an orphan," he almost whispered as he sat down.

The boy was right. The girl had an advantage. An advantage of knowing that school, as tedious as it was, was better than the orphanage. Since she knew that, she appreciated what the others took for granted.

We, too, were orphans.

Alone.

No name. No future. No hope.

Were it not for our adoption as his children, we would have no place to belong. We sometimes forget that.

The Corinthians forgot.

They had grown puffy in their achievements and divisive in their fellowship. They argued over the correct leader, the greater gifts. They rebelled against Paul's leadership. They were indifferent to sin and insensitive in worship.

Paul defends his ministry and admonishes the Christians to remember to whom they belong. "Examine yourselves," Paul says (13:5). His words are clear. "If anyone is in Christ, he is a new creation; old things have passed away; behold, all things have become new" (5:17).

Good reminder.

Not just for them but for us as well. For if we forget, we too will be like the students who did just enough to pass the grade and never enough to show their thanks.

LIFE LESSON

2 Corinthians 1:1–2:4

SITUATION Second Corinthians was written less than a year after First Corinthians. Paul wrote because he was delayed in his visit to Corinth. Paul began explaining his actions among the Corinthians by reviewing his relationship with them.

OBSERVATION God's comfort and deliverance are certainties, even in the middle of difficult trials. We can confidently rely upon him as we make our plans.

INSPIRATION "Why?" we wonder as we struggle to put the pieces back in a broken relationship.

"Why?" we think as we read of a devastating earthquake halfway around the world.

"Why?" we cry as we stand at the grave of a loved one.

Life is short and sometimes tragic, and each day we are reminded of our finiteness. We don't know the future, we don't know the relationship between events, and we certainly don't know *why.*

But we do know that God is good and all-knowing—nothing catches him by surprise, not the car out of control, the malignant tumor, the hurricane, or the disease. So even as we wonder and question the reason and cause for each event, we can be confident that God knows and that in everything, even the senseless tragedy, he is working.

(From *On Eagles' Wings* by Dave Veerman)

APPLICATION What season of suffering have you known? What helped you move through it? Use the experience to help others whose hearts grieve. Write or call a friend today with encouragement.

EXPLORATION God's Comfort—Psalm 23:1-4; 119:50, 52; John 14:16-17; 2 Corinthians 1:3-5; Philippians 2:1-2.

Greeting

Paul, an apostle of Jesus Christ by the will of God, and Timothy
our brother,
To the church of God which is at Corinth, with all the saints who
are in all Achaia:
2 Grace to you and peace from God our Father and the Lord Jesus Christ.

Comfort in Suffering

3 Blessed *be* the God and Father of our Lord Jesus Christ, the Father of
mercies and God of all comfort, 4 who comforts us in all our tribulation, that
we may be able to comfort those who are in any trouble, with the comfort
with which we ourselves are comforted by God. 5 For as the sufferings of
Christ abound in us, so our consolation also abounds through Christ. 6 Now
if we are afflicted, *it is* for your consolation and salvation, which is effective
for enduring the same sufferings which we also suffer. Or if we are comforted,
it is for your consolation and salvation. 7 And our hope for you *is* steadfast,
because we know that as you are partakers of the sufferings, so also *you will*
partake of the consolation.

Delivered from Suffering

8 For we do not want you to be ignorant, brethren, of our trouble which
came to us in Asia: that we were burdened beyond measure, above strength,
so that we despaired even of life. 9 Yes, we had the sentence of death in ourselves, that we should not trust in ourselves but in God who raises the
dead, 10 who delivered us from so great a death, and does[a] deliver us; in
whom we trust that He will still deliver *us,* 11 you also helping together in
prayer for us, that thanks may be given by many persons on our[b] behalf
for the gift *granted* to us through many.

Paul's Sincerity

12 For our boasting is this: the testimony of our conscience that we conducted ourselves in the world in simplicity and godly sincerity, not with
fleshly wisdom but by the grace of God, and more abundantly toward you.
13 For we are not writing any other things to you than what you read or understand. Now I trust you will understand, even to the end 14 (as also you have
understood us in part), that we are your boast as you also *are* ours, in the
day of the Lord Jesus.

Sparing the Church

15 And in this confidence I intended to come to you before, that you
might have a second benefit— 16 to pass by way of you to Macedonia, to
come again from Macedonia to you, and be helped by you on my way to
Judea. 17 Therefore, when I was planning this, did I do it lightly? Or the
things I plan, do I plan according to the flesh, that with me there should be
Yes, Yes, and No, No? 18 But *as* God *is* faithful, our word to you was not Yes
and No. 19 For the Son of God, Jesus Christ, who was preached among you
by us—by me, Silvanus, and Timothy—was not Yes and No, but in Him
was Yes. 20 For all the promises of God in Him *are* Yes, and in Him Amen, to

1:10 [a] NU-Text reads *shall.*
1:11 [b] M-Text reads *your behalf.*

the glory of God through us. 21Now He who establishes us with you in Christ
and has anointed us *is* God, 22who also has sealed us and given us the Spirit
in our hearts as a guarantee.
23Moreover I call God as witness against my soul, that to spare you I
came no more to Corinth. 24Not that we have dominion over your faith,
but are fellow workers for your joy; for by faith you stand.

2 But I determined this within myself, that I would not come again to
you in sorrow. 2For if I make you sorrowful, then who is he who makes
me glad but the one who is made sorrowful by me?

Forgive the Offender

3And I wrote this very thing to you, lest, when I came, I should have sorrow over those from whom I ought to have joy, having confidence in you
all that my joy is *the joy* of you all. 4For out of much affliction and anguish
of heart I wrote to you, with many tears, not that you should be grieved,
but that you might know the love which I have so abundantly for you.
5But if anyone has caused grief, he has not grieved me, but all of you to
some extent—not to be too severe. 6This punishment which *was inflicted*
by the majority *is* sufficient for such a man, 7so that, on the contrary, you
ought rather to forgive and comfort *him,* lest perhaps such a one be swallowed up with too much sorrow. 8Therefore I urge you to reaffirm *your* love
to him. 9For to this end I also wrote, that I might put you to the test, whether
you are obedient in all things. 10Now whom you forgive anything, I also
forgive. For if indeed I have forgiven anything, I have forgiven that one[c] for
your sakes in the presence of Christ, 11lest Satan should take advantage of
us; for we are not ignorant of his devices.

Triumph in Christ

12Furthermore, when I came to Troas to *preach* Christ's gospel, and a door
was opened to me by the Lord, 13I had no rest in my spirit, because I did not
find Titus my brother; but taking my leave of them, I departed for Macedonia.
14Now thanks *be* to God who always leads us in triumph in Christ, and
through us diffuses the fragrance of His knowledge in every place. 15For we are to
God the fragrance of Christ among those who are being saved and among
those who are perishing. 16To the one *we are* the aroma of death *leading* to
death, and to the other the aroma of life *leading* to life. And who *is* sufficient
for these things? 17For we are not, as so many,[d] peddling the word of God;
but as of sincerity, but as from God, we speak in the sight of God in Christ.

Christ's Epistle

3 Do we begin again to commend ourselves? Or do we need, as some *others,*
epistles of commendation to you or *letters* of commendation from you?
2You are our epistle written in our hearts, known and read by all men; 3clearly
you are an epistle of Christ, ministered by us, written not with ink but by
the Spirit of the living God, not on tablets of stone but on tablets of flesh,
that is, of the heart.

The Spirit, Not the Letter

4And we have such trust through Christ toward God. 5Not that we are
sufficient of ourselves to think of anything as *being* from ourselves, but

2:10 [c] NU-Text reads *For indeed, what I have forgiven, if I have forgiven anything, I did it.*
2:17 [d] M-Text reads *the rest.*

LIFE LESSON

2 Corinthians 2:5-17

SITUATION In his previous letter, Paul urged the Corinthians to put a particular unrepentant sinner out of the church (1 Corinthians 5). Perhaps this man repented and was the individual mentioned in this letter.

OBSERVATION God eagerly forgives a repentant sinner. God puts forgiven sins out of his view.

INSPIRATION We all find forgiveness exceedingly difficult. Sometimes forgiveness comes so hard that we can release our grudges only one level at a time. This means forgiveness is often granted only at superficial levels. These are *qualified* forgiveness. A key word is *if.* "I'll forgive you, *if* you show proper remorse. . . ."

Another key word is *when.* "I'll forgive you *when* I am able. You've got to give me some time to work through this. . . ."

A second level is *partial* forgiveness. The key word here is *but.* "I'll forgive you, *but* . . . please get out of my life. . . ."

You must *do* forgiveness. We *do* our way into better feelings. We do not feel our way into better doing. If we wait until all that bitterness is swept out of the corners of our feelings before we do right by someone who has hurt us, we might just as well give up. The bad feelings may never completely go away. But if we begin now dealing with that person, as if he had been totally forgiven and as if all the bad feelings were gone, giving him full personhood and affirmation, somehow the bitterness eventually dissipates. Jesus didn't just *tell* us how to forgive, he *showed* us how on the cross.

(From *Finding the Heart to Go On* by Lynn Anderson)

APPLICATION Are you holding on to a grudge? Pray, then go and make peace.

EXPLORATION Victory—John 15:5; 1 Corinthians 1:7-8; 2 Corinthians 12:9; Galatians 2:20; Ephesians 3:16-17.

LIFE LESSON

1 Corinthians 3:1-18

SITUATION False teachers confused the Corinthian church and undermined Paul's ministry.

OBSERVATION As a minister of the New Covenant, Paul defended the sincerity of his ministry. Paul also illustrated that salvation was received by accepting the gospel rather than by trying to keep the Jewish Law.

INSPIRATION The outstanding characteristic of a Christian is this unveiled frankness before God so that the life becomes a mirror for other lives. . . . Beware of anything which would sully that mirror in you; it is nearly always a good thing, the good that is not the best.

The golden rule for your life and mine is this concentrated keeping of the life open towards God. . . . The rush of other things always tends to obscure this concentration on God. . . . Let other things come and go as they may, let other people criticize as they will, but never let anything obscure the life that is hid with Christ in God.

(From *My Utmost for His Highest* by Oswald Chambers)

APPLICATION Our first reactions to people and circumstances tell who we really are. If someone cuts you off on the road, what is your first reaction? If someone corrects you, what is your first reaction? What will be your first reactions to the people and places you encounter today? Which ones need a make-over?

EXPLORATION New Covenant Glory—Exodus 34:28-35; Jeremiah 31:33; Ezekiel 36:26; Hebrews 8.

our sufficiency *is* from God, 6who also made us sufficient as ministers of
the new covenant, not of the letter but of the Spirit;[e] for the letter kills, but
the Spirit gives life.

Glory of the New Covenant

7But if the ministry of death, written *and* engraved on stones, was glorious,
so that the children of Israel could not look steadily at the face of Moses
because of the glory of his countenance, which *glory* was passing away, 8how
will the ministry of the Spirit not be more glorious? 9For if the ministry of
condemnation *had* glory, the ministry of righteousness exceeds much more
in glory. 10For even what was made glorious had no glory in this respect,
because of the glory that excels. 11For if what is passing away *was* glorious,
what remains *is* much more glorious.

12Therefore, since we have such hope, we use great boldness of speech—
13unlike Moses, *who* put a veil over his face so that the children of Israel could
not look steadily at the end of what was passing away. 14But their minds
were blinded. For until this day the same veil remains unlifted in the reading
of the Old Testament, because the *veil* is taken away in Christ. 15But even to
this day, when Moses is read, a veil lies on their heart. 16Nevertheless when
one turns to the Lord, the veil is taken away. 17Now the Lord is the Spirit; and
where the Spirit of the Lord *is,* there *is* liberty. 18But we all, with unveiled
face, beholding as in a mirror the glory of the Lord, are being transformed
into the same image from glory to glory, just as by the Spirit of the Lord.

The Light of Christ's Gospel

4 Therefore, since we have this ministry, as we have received mercy, we
do not lose heart. 2But we have renounced the hidden things of shame,
not walking in craftiness nor handling the word of God deceitfully, but by
manifestation of the truth commending ourselves to every man's conscience
in the sight of God. 3But even if our gospel is veiled, it is veiled to those who are
perishing, 4whose minds the god of this age has blinded, who do not believe,
lest the light of the gospel of the glory of Christ, who is the image of God,
should shine on them. 5For we do not preach ourselves, but Christ Jesus the
Lord, and ourselves your bondservants for Jesus' sake. 6For it is the God who
commanded light to shine out of darkness, who has shone in our hearts to
give the light of the knowledge of the glory of God in the face of Jesus Christ.

Cast Down but Unconquered

7But we have this treasure in earthen vessels, that the excellence of the
power may be of God and not of us. 8*We are* hard-pressed on every side,
yet not crushed; *we are* perplexed, but not in despair; 9persecuted, but not
forsaken; struck down, but not destroyed— 10always carrying about in the
body the dying of the Lord Jesus, that the life of Jesus also may be manifested in our body. 11For we who live are always delivered to death for Jesus'
sake, that the life of Jesus also may be manifested in our mortal flesh. 12So
then death is working in us, but life in you.

13And since we have the same spirit of faith, according to what is written,
"I believed and therefore I spoke,"[f] we also believe and therefore speak,
14knowing that He who raised up the Lord Jesus will also raise us up with

3:6 [e] Or *spirit*
4:13 [f] Psalm 116:10

Jesus, and will present *us* with you. 15 For all things *are* for your sakes, that
grace, having spread through the many, may cause thanksgiving to
abound to the glory of God.

Seeing the Invisible

16 Therefore we do not lose heart. Even though our outward man is perishing, yet the inward *man* is being renewed day by day. 17 For our light affliction, which is but for a moment, is working for us a far more exceeding
and eternal weight of glory, 18 while we do not look at the things which are
seen, but at the things which are not seen. For the things which are seen
are temporary, but the things which are not seen *are* eternal.

Assurance of the Resurrection

5 For we know that if our earthly house, *this* tent, is destroyed, we have a
building from God, a house not made with hands, eternal in the heavens.
2 For in this we groan, earnestly desiring to be clothed with our habitation
which is from heaven, 3 if indeed, having been clothed, we shall not be found
naked. 4 For we who are in *this* tent groan, being burdened, not because we
want to be unclothed, but further clothed, that mortality may be swallowed up by life. 5 Now He who has prepared us for this very thing *is* God,
who also has given us the Spirit as a guarantee.
6 So *we are* always confident, knowing that while we are at home in the
body we are absent from the Lord. 7 For we walk by faith, not by sight. 8 We
are confident, yes, well pleased rather to be absent from the body and to
be present with the Lord.

The Judgment Seat of Christ

9 Therefore we make it our aim, whether present or absent, to be well
pleasing to Him. 10 For we must all appear before the judgment seat of Christ,
that each one may receive the things *done* in the body, according to what
he has done, whether good or bad. 11 Knowing, therefore, the terror of the
Lord, we persuade men; but we are well known to God, and I also trust are
well known in your consciences.

Be Reconciled to God

12 For we do not commend ourselves again to you, but give you opportunity to boast on our behalf, that you may have *an answer* for those who
boast in appearance and not in heart. 13 For if we are beside ourselves, *it is*
for God; or if we are of sound mind, *it is* for you. 14 For the love of Christ
compels us, because we judge thus: that if One died for all, then all died;
15 and He died for all, that those who live should live no longer for themselves, but for Him who died for them and rose again.
16 Therefore, from now on, we regard no one according to the flesh. Even
though we have known Christ according to the flesh, yet now we know
Him thus no longer. 17 Therefore, if anyone *is* in Christ, *he is* a new creation;
old things have passed away; behold, all things have become new. 18 Now
all things *are* of God, who has reconciled us to Himself through Jesus
Christ, and has given us the ministry of reconciliation, 19 that is, that God
was in Christ reconciling the world to Himself, not imputing their trespasses to them, and has committed to us the word of reconciliation.

LIFE LESSON

2 Corinthians 4:1-15

SITUATION Smooth-talking, slick-operating teachers impressed the Corinthians. Paul contrasted these teachers with humble and honest ones who gave credit to God.

OBSERVATION People who minister in Christ's name must be honest. Phonies are disqualified.

INSPIRATION Have you "renounced the hidden things of dishonesty"—the things that your sense of honor will not allow to come to light? . . . Is there a thought in your heart about anyone which you would not like to be dragged into the light? Renounce it as soon as it springs up; renounce the whole thing until there is no hidden thing of dishonesty or craftiness about you. . . . Maintain a continual watchfulness so that nothing of which you would be ashamed arises in your life.
(From *My Utmost for His Highest* by Oswald Chambers)

APPLICATION Countless reasons and excuses can justify a lie. Tell the truth. Don't let anything persuade you into compromising.

EXPLORATION Strength from God—John 15:1-2; 1 Corinthians 4:10; 2 Corinthians 5:7; James 1:2-6; 1 John 5:15.

20 Now then, we are ambassadors for Christ, as though God were pleading
through us: we implore *you* on Christ's behalf, be reconciled to God. 21 For
He made Him who knew no sin *to be* sin for us, that we might become the
righteousness of God in Him.

Marks of the Ministry

6 We then, *as* workers together *with Him* also plead with *you* not to receive
the grace of God in vain. 2 For He says:

"In an acceptable time I have heard you,
And in the day of salvation I have helped you."[g]

Behold, now *is* the accepted time; behold, now *is* the day of salvation.
3 We give no offense in anything, that our ministry may not be blamed.
4 But in all *things* we commend ourselves as ministers of God: in much patience, in tribulations, in needs, in distresses, 5 in stripes, in imprisonments,
in tumults, in labors, in sleeplessness, in fastings; 6 by purity, by knowledge, by longsuffering, by kindness, by the Holy Spirit, by sincere love, 7 by
the word of truth, by the power of God, by the armor of righteousness on
the right hand and on the left, 8 by honor and dishonor, by evil report and
good report; as deceivers, and *yet* true; 9 as unknown, and *yet* well known;
as dying, and behold we live; as chastened, and *yet* not killed; 10 as sorrowful,
yet always rejoicing; as poor, yet making many rich; as having nothing,
and *yet* possessing all things.

Be Holy

11 O Corinthians! We have spoken openly to you, our heart is wide open.
12 You are not restricted by us, but you are restricted by your *own* affections.
13 Now in return for the same (I speak as to children), you also be open.
14 Do not be unequally yoked together with unbelievers. For what fellowship has righteousness with lawlessness? And what communion has light
with darkness? 15 And what accord has Christ with Belial? Or what part has
a believer with an unbeliever? 16 And what agreement has the temple of
God with idols? For you[h] are the temple of the living God. As God has said:

"I will dwell in them
And walk among them.
I will be their God,
And they shall be My people."[i]

17 Therefore

"Come out from among them
And be separate, says the Lord.
Do not touch what is unclean,
And I will receive you."[j]

18 *"I will be a Father to you,*
And you shall be My sons and daughters,
Says the LORD *Almighty."*[k]

6:2 [g] Isaiah 49:8
6:16 [h] NU-Text reads *we.* [i] Leviticus 26:12; Jeremiah 32:38; Ezekiel 37:27
6:17 [j] Isaiah 52:11; Ezekiel 20:34, 41
6:18 [k] 2 Samuel 7:14

LIFE LESSON

2 Corinthians 4:16–5:10

SITUATION Paul stressed that the Corinthians could have confidence in the bodily resurrection and afterlife. This contrasted with contemporary ideas that some Corinthians held—that bodily resurrection would not happen and that the soul was separate from the body.

OBSERVATION Jesus' followers know that God reserves bodily resurrection and a heavenly dwelling place for them.

INSPIRATION It's not easy for us to see a City we've never seen, either, especially when the road is bumpy . . . the hour is late . . . and companions are wanting to cancel the trip and take up residence in a motel. It's not easy to fix our eyes on what is unseen. But it is necessary. . . .

For some of you, the journey has been long. Very long and stormy. In no way do I wish to minimize the difficulties that you have had to face along the way. . . .

And you are tired.

It's hard for you to see the City in the midst of the storms. The desire to pull over to the side of the road and get out entices you. You want to go on, but some days the road seems so long.

Let me encourage you . . . *It's worth it.*

(From *In the Eye of the Storm* by Max Lucado)

APPLICATION You may be tempted to throw in the towel and walk away when life gets hard. When this impulse hits you: stop, relax, pray, and take that next step. Discover new faith and hope.

EXPLORATION Hope of Heaven—Job 19:25-27; Psalm 73:24-26; John 15:1-4; 1 Corinthians 4:10; 1 Thessalonians 4:13-18; Revelation 21:27; 22:14.

7 Therefore, having these promises, beloved, let us cleanse ourselves from
all filthiness of the flesh and spirit, perfecting holiness in the fear of God.

The Corinthians' Repentance

2Open *your hearts* to us. We have wronged no one, we have corrupted no
one, we have cheated no one. 3I do not say *this* to condemn; for I have said
before that you are in our hearts, to die together and to live together. 4Great
is my boldness of speech toward you, great *is* my boasting on your behalf.
I am filled with comfort. I am exceedingly joyful in all our tribulation.
5For indeed, when we came to Macedonia, our bodies had no rest, but
we were troubled on every side. Outside *were* conflicts, inside *were* fears.
6Nevertheless God, who comforts the downcast, comforted us by the coming of Titus, 7and not only by his coming, but also by the consolation with
which he was comforted in you, when he told us of your earnest desire,
your mourning, your zeal for me, so that I rejoiced even more.
8For even if I made you sorry with my letter, I do not regret it; though I
did regret it. For I perceive that the same epistle made you sorry, though
only for a while. 9Now I rejoice, not that you were made sorry, but that your
sorrow led to repentance. For you were made sorry in a godly manner,
that you might suffer loss from us in nothing. 10For godly sorrow produces
repentance *leading* to salvation, not to be regretted; but the sorrow of the
world produces death. 11For observe this very thing, that you sorrowed in
a godly manner: What diligence it produced in you, *what* clearing *of yourselves, what* indignation, *what* fear, *what* vehement desire, *what* zeal, *what*
vindication! In all *things* you proved yourselves to be clear in this matter.
12Therefore, although I wrote to you, *I did* not *do it* for the sake of him who
had done the wrong, nor for the sake of him who suffered wrong, but that
our care for you in the sight of God might appear to you.

The Joy of Titus

13Therefore we have been comforted in your comfort. And we rejoiced
exceedingly more for the joy of Titus, because his spirit has been refreshed
by you all. 14For if in anything I have boasted to him about you, I am not
ashamed. But as we spoke all things to you in truth, even so our boasting to
Titus was found true. 15And his affections are greater for you as he remembers the obedience of you all, how with fear and trembling you received
him. 16Therefore I rejoice that I have confidence in you in everything.

Excel in Giving

8 Moreover, brethren, we make known to you the grace of God bestowed
on the churches of Macedonia: 2that in a great trial of affliction the
abundance of their joy and their deep poverty abounded in the riches of their
liberality. 3For I bear witness that according to *their* ability, yes, and beyond
their ability, *they were* freely willing, 4imploring us with much urgency that
we would receive[l] the gift and the fellowship of the ministering to the
saints. 5And not *only* as we had hoped, but they first gave themselves to
the Lord, and *then* to us by the will of God. 6So we urged Titus, that as he
had begun, so he would also complete this grace in you as well. 7But as you
abound in everything—in faith, in speech, in knowledge, in all diligence,
and in your love for us—*see* that you abound in this grace also.

8:4 [l] NU-Text and M-Text omit *that we would receive,* thus changing text to *urgency for the favor and fellowship . . . .*

Life Lesson

2 Corinthians 6:14–7:16

SITUATION Paul warned Christians that intimate relationships with unbelievers are dangerous. He was glad that the Corinthians would apply his advice.

OBSERVATION Christians should not marry unbelievers. Spiritually incompatible relationships weaken faith.

INSPIRATION I *love* ocean sailing. Not long ago I took five men from my church . . . ocean sailing for a week. . . .

The first day out of the harbor was a sailor's dream: twenty-five-knot winds, clear sky, six- to eight-foot seas. . . . A couple hours out, I was standing at the helm singing at the top of my lungs—laughing, joking, having the time of my life. "Does it get any better than this?" I shouted. "Are we having fun, or what?"

No response. In fact, I noticed that some of the guys were looking a little green. . . . They both experienced "unplanned protein spills." . . . I tried to maintain my euphoria at sea, but with no one to share it, it faded. So, with a perfect wind still blowing, I headed back toward protected waters.

As much as I love ocean sailing, it is no match for how I feel about my relationship with Jesus Christ. . . . My wife . . . loves Christ with a passion every bit as strong as mine. It would be torture for me not to able to share the greatest treasure in my life with my wife. And that is nothing unique to me. To have a spouse yawn about that which means more than anything else in life would bring heartache to any true Believer.

(From *Fit to Be Tied* by Bill and Lynne Hybels)

APPLICATION Are you in a relationship that shifts your loyalty away from God? Do you ever compromise God's desire in order to keep the relationship? What does God expect from you?

EXPLORATION Spiritually Compatible Relationships—Hosea 1–3; 1 Corinthians 5:9-13; 7:12-16; Ephesians 4:2-6; 5:3-11; Colossians 3:11-17.

LIFE LESSON

2 Corinthians 8:1-24

SITUATION Paul expressed confidence in the Corinthian church. He asked them to complete their collection for the Jerusalem church, which they had promised a year before.

OBSERVATION We give as a natural response to our love for Jesus. We should give according to our abilities, voluntarily and generously. God gives to us so that we can share with others.

INSPIRATION Our tithes and offerings are God's by right, for the firstfruits belong to Him. Tithing is God's key to your successful personal finances.

Christians live under grace and, therefore, their tithing is not a legal requirement but a response of grace to God. Jesus Himself fulfilled the Old Testament Law including tithing, but He never revised the law downward.

God owns everything. When billionaire Howard Hughes died, naked and terrified of flies, someone asked how much he left. The answer, of course, was, "All of it!" The ultimate measure of a man's wealth is how much he is worth when he has lost everything. Naked we come into this world and naked we depart. Our wealth consists not in the abundance of our possessions, but in who we are as children of God. How we must remember, "The earth is the Lord's and everything in it, the world, and all who live in it" (Psalm 24:1). We may possess things, but God owns them.

(From "God's Call for Responsible Giving" by Gordon K. Moyes in *Money for Ministries*)

APPLICATION Do you plan giving so that you can give regularly? Is it spontaneous enough so you can respond to needs right away or generous enough to show something of God's self-sacrifice? Today, make your gratitude to God tangible with a gift to your church or another trustworthy ministry.

EXPLORATION Giving—Deuteronomy 15:10-11; Isaiah 1:13; Malachi 3:8; Matthew 10:8; Luke 6:38; Romans 12:8; Acts 20:35.

Christ Our Pattern

[8]I speak not by commandment, but I am testing the sincerity of your love by the diligence of others. [9]For you know the grace of our Lord Jesus Christ, that though He was rich, yet for your sakes He became poor, that you through His poverty might become rich.

[10]And in this I give advice: It is to your advantage not only to be doing what you began and were desiring to do a year ago; [11]but now you also must complete the doing *of it;* that as *there was* a readiness to desire *it,* so *there* also *may be* a completion out of what *you* have. [12]For if there is first a willing mind, *it is* accepted according to what one has, *and* not according to what he does not have.

[13]For *I do* not *mean* that others should be eased and you burdened; [14]but by an equality, *that* now at this time your abundance *may supply* their lack, that their abundance also may supply your lack—that there may be equality. [15]As it is written, *"He who gathered much had nothing left over, and he who gathered little had no lack."*[m]

Collection for the Judean Saints

[16]But thanks *be* to God who puts[n] the same earnest care for you into the heart of Titus. [17]For he not only accepted the exhortation, but being more diligent, he went to you of his own accord. [18]And we have sent with him the brother whose praise *is* in the gospel throughout all the churches, [19]and not only *that,* but who was also chosen by the churches to travel with us with this gift, which is administered by us to the glory of the Lord Himself and *to show* your ready mind, [20]avoiding this: that anyone should blame us in this lavish gift which is administered by us— [21]providing honorable things, not only in the sight of the Lord, but also in the sight of men.

[22]And we have sent with them our brother whom we have often proved diligent in many things, but now much more diligent, because of the great confidence which *we have* in you. [23]If *anyone inquires* about Titus, *he is* my partner and fellow worker concerning you. Or if our brethren *are inquired about, they are* messengers of the churches, the glory of Christ. [24]Therefore show to them, and[o] before the churches, the proof of your love and of our boasting on your behalf.

Administering the Gift

9 Now concerning the ministering to the saints, it is superfluous for me to write to you; [2]for I know your willingness, about which I boast of you to the Macedonians, that Achaia was ready a year ago; and your zeal has stirred up the majority. [3]Yet I have sent the brethren, lest our boasting of you should be in vain in this respect, that, as I said, you may be ready; [4]lest if *some* Macedonians come with me and find you unprepared, we (not to mention you!) should be ashamed of this confident boasting.[p] [5]Therefore I thought it necessary to exhort the brethren to go to you ahead of time, and prepare your generous gift beforehand, which *you had* previously promised, that it may be ready as *a matter of* generosity and not as a grudging obligation.

8:15 [m] Exodus 16:18
8:16 [n] NU-Text reads *has put.*
8:24 [o] NU-Text and M-Text omit *and.*
9:4 [p] NU-Text reads *this confidence.*

The Cheerful Giver

6But this *I say:* He who sows sparingly will also reap sparingly, and he
who sows bountifully will also reap bountifully. 7*So let* each one *give* as he
purposes in his heart, not grudgingly or of necessity; for God loves a
cheerful giver. 8And God *is* able to make all grace abound toward you, that
you, always having all sufficiency in all *things,* may have an abundance for
every good work. 9As it is written:

"He has dispersed abroad,
He has given to the poor;
His righteousness endures forever."[q]

10Now may[r] He who supplies seed to the sower, and bread for food, supply and multiply the seed you have *sown* and increase the fruits of your
righteousness, 11while *you are* enriched in everything for all liberality, which
causes thanksgiving through us to God. 12For the administration of this
service not only supplies the needs of the saints, but also is abounding
through many thanksgivings to God, 13while, through the proof of this
ministry, they glorify God for the obedience of your confession to the gospel
of Christ, and for *your* liberal sharing with them and all *men,* 14and by their
prayer for you, who long for you because of the exceeding grace of God in
you. 15Thanks *be* to God for His indescribable gift!

The Spiritual War

10 Now I, Paul, myself am pleading with you by the meekness and gentleness of Christ—who in presence *am* lowly among you, but being
absent am bold toward you. 2But I beg *you* that when I am present I may not
be bold with that confidence by which I intend to be bold against some, who
think of us as if we walked according to the flesh. 3For though we walk in the
flesh, we do not war according to the flesh. 4For the weapons of our warfare
are not carnal but mighty in God for pulling down strongholds, 5casting down
arguments and every high thing that exalts itself against the knowledge of
God, bringing every thought into captivity to the obedience of Christ, 6and
being ready to punish all disobedience when your obedience is fulfilled.

Reality of Paul's Authority

7Do you look at things according to the outward appearance? If anyone
is convinced in himself that he is Christ's, let him again consider this in
himself, that just as he *is* Christ's, even so we *are* Christ's.[s] 8For even if I
should boast somewhat more about our authority, which the Lord gave
us[t] for edification and not for your destruction, I shall not be ashamed—
9lest I seem to terrify you by letters. 10"For *his* letters," they say, "*are* weighty
and powerful, but *his* bodily presence *is* weak, and *his* speech contemptible."
11Let such a person consider this, that what we are in word by letters when
we are absent, such *we will* also *be* in deed when we are present.

Limits of Paul's Authority

12For we dare not class ourselves or compare ourselves with those who
commend themselves. But they, measuring themselves by themselves,

9:9 [q] Psalm 112:9
9:10 [r] NU-Text reads *Now He who supplies . . . will supply . . . .*
10:7 [s] NU-Text reads *even as we are.*
10:8 [t] NU-Text omits *us.*

Life Lesson

2 Corinthians 10:1-18

SITUATION Paul learned that certain rival preachers had succeeded in their attempt to discredit him before a few Corinthian Christians. Paul responded to the charges and accusations raised by them; he warned that he would exercise strict discipline, if that became necessary.

OBSERVATION God gives spiritual leaders to provide order and direction. Be sure to uphold and respect these leaders.

INSPIRATION We sometimes think that power comes only through aggressive self-promotion, but Jesus made it clear that this was not so. He explained to his disciples very bluntly that power and authority in his kingdom is based on servanthood.

Dee Jepson, who served as an assistant to her husband, a U. S. senator, quickly became aware of the power-hungry atmosphere of Washington, D.C. Political wheeling and dealing was the name of the game—always with an eye on gaining influence with high-ranking officials. Jesus' message of servanthood seemed entirely out of place, until one day when Dee observed an honored guest's visit to the city.

"The unimportance of sophistication was brought home to me," she writes, "at a Capitol Hill luncheon for Mother Teresa . . . . In came this tiny woman, even smaller than I had expected, wearing that familiar blue and white habit, over it a gray sweater that had seen many better days, which she wore again to the White House the next day. As that little woman walked into the room, her bare feet in worn sandals, I saw some of the most powerful leaders in this country stand to their feet with tears in their eyes just to be in her presence."

"As I listened that afternoon, I thought, 'Don't forget this, Dee. Here in this little woman who doesn't want a thing, never asked for anything for herself; never demanded anything, or shook her fist in anger, here's real power.' It was a paradox. She has reached down into the gutter and loved and given. She has loved those the world

Continued

sees as unlovable—the desolate, the dying—because they are created in the image of the God she serves. Ironically, seeking nothing for herself, she has been raised to the pinnacle of world recognition, received the Nobel Peace Prize, and is a figure known to most people, at least in the Western world, and revered by many. She has nothing, yet in a strange way, she has everything."

(From *Stories of Faith* by Ruth A. Tucker)

APPLICATION Participate in conversations that encourage and build up leaders rather than criticize or demean them. If you have a legitimate complaint, go directly to the leader before you complain to others.

EXPLORATION Authority—Genesis 1:26-27; Romans 13:1; 2 Corinthians 13:10.

and comparing themselves among themselves, are not wise. 13We, however, will not boast beyond measure, but within the limits of the sphere
which God appointed us—a sphere which especially includes you. 14For
we are not overextending ourselves (as though *our authority* did not extend
to you), for it was to you that we came with the gospel of Christ; 15not boasting of things beyond measure, *that is,* in other men's labors, but having
hope, *that* as your faith is increased, we shall be greatly enlarged by you in
our sphere, 16to preach the gospel in the *regions* beyond you, *and* not to
boast in another man's sphere of accomplishment.
17But "*he who glories, let him glory in the* LORD."[u] 18For not he who commends himself is approved, but whom the Lord commends.

Concern for Their Faithfulness

11 Oh, that you would bear with me in a little folly—and indeed you do
bear with me. 2For I am jealous for you with godly jealousy. For I
have betrothed you to one husband, that I may present *you as* a chaste virgin
to Christ. 3But I fear, lest somehow, as the serpent deceived Eve by his craftiness, so your minds may be corrupted from the simplicity[v] that is in Christ.
4For if he who comes preaches another Jesus whom we have not preached,
or *if* you receive a different spirit which you have not received, or a different gospel which you have not accepted—you may well put up with it!

Paul and False Apostles

5For I consider that I am not at all inferior to the most eminent apostles.
6Even though *I am* untrained in speech, yet *I am* not in knowledge. But we
have been thoroughly manifested[w] among you in all things.
7Did I commit sin in humbling myself that you might be exalted, because
I preached the gospel of God to you free of charge? 8I robbed other churches,
taking wages *from them* to minister to you. 9And when I was present with
you, and in need, I was a burden to no one, for what I lacked the brethren
who came from Macedonia supplied. And in everything I kept myself
from being burdensome to you, and so I will keep *myself.* 10As the truth of
Christ is in me, no one shall stop me from this boasting in the regions of
Achaia. 11Why? Because I do not love you? God knows!
12But what I do, I will also continue to do, that I may cut off the opportunity from those who desire an opportunity to be regarded just as we are
in the things of which they boast. 13For such *are* false apostles, deceitful
workers, transforming themselves into apostles of Christ. 14And no wonder!
For Satan himself transforms himself into an angel of light. 15Therefore *it
is* no great thing if his ministers also transform themselves into ministers
of righteousness, whose end will be according to their works.

Reluctant Boasting

16I say again, let no one think me a fool. If otherwise, at least receive me
as a fool, that I also may boast a little. 17What I speak, I speak not according to the Lord, but as it were, foolishly, in this confidence of boasting.
18Seeing that many boast according to the flesh, I also will boast. 19For you
put up with fools gladly, since you *yourselves* are wise! 20For you put up

10:17 [u] Jeremiah 9:24
11:3 [v] NU-Text adds *and purity.*
11:6 [w] NU-Text omits *been.*

with it if one brings you into bondage, if one devours *you,* if one takes *from*
you, if one exalts himself, if one strikes you on the face. 21To *our* shame I
say that we were too weak for that! But in whatever anyone is bold—I
speak foolishly—I am bold also.

Suffering for Christ

22Are they Hebrews? So *am* I. Are they Israelites? So *am* I. Are they the
seed of Abraham? So *am* I. 23Are they ministers of Christ?—I speak as a
fool—I *am* more: in labors more abundant, in stripes above measure, in
prisons more frequently, in deaths often. 24From the Jews five times I received
forty *stripes* minus one. 25Three times I was beaten with rods; once I was
stoned; three times I was shipwrecked; a night and a day I have been in the
deep; 26*in* journeys often, *in* perils of waters, *in* perils of robbers, *in* perils of
my own countrymen, *in* perils of the Gentiles, *in* perils in the city, *in* perils in
the wilderness, *in* perils in the sea, *in* perils among false brethren; 27in weariness and toil, in sleeplessness often, in hunger and thirst, in fastings often,
in cold and nakedness— 28besides the other things, what comes upon me
daily: my deep concern for all the churches. 29Who is weak, and I am not
weak? Who is made to stumble, and I do not burn *with indignation?*
30If I must boast, I will boast in the things which concern my infirmity.
31The God and Father of our Lord Jesus Christ, who is blessed forever,
knows that I am not lying. 32In Damascus the governor, under Aretas the
king, was guarding the city of the Damascenes with a garrison, desiring to
arrest me; 33but I was let down in a basket through a window in the wall,
and escaped from his hands.

The Vision of Paradise

12 It is doubtless[x] not profitable for me to boast. I will come to visions
and revelations of the Lord: 2I know a man in Christ who fourteen
years ago—whether in the body I do not know, or whether out of the body I
do not know, God knows—such a one was caught up to the third heaven.
3And I know such a man—whether in the body or out of the body I do not
know, God knows— 4how he was caught up into Paradise and heard inexpressible words, which it is not lawful for a man to utter. 5Of such a one I
will boast; yet of myself I will not boast, except in my infirmities. 6For
though I might desire to boast, I will not be a fool; for I will speak the truth.
But I refrain, lest anyone should think of me above what he sees me *to be*
or hears from me.

The Thorn in the Flesh

7And lest I should be exalted above measure by the abundance of the
revelations, a thorn in the flesh was given to me, a messenger of Satan to
buffet me, lest I be exalted above measure. 8Concerning this thing I pleaded
with the Lord three times that it might depart from me. 9And He said to
me, "My grace is sufficient for you, for My strength is made perfect in weakness." Therefore most gladly I will rather boast in my infirmities, that the
power of Christ may rest upon me. 10Therefore I take pleasure in infirmities,
in reproaches, in needs, in persecutions, in distresses, for Christ's sake. For
when I am weak, then I am strong.

12:1 [x] NU-Text reads *necessary, though not profitable, to boast.*

LIFE LESSON

2 Corinthians 12:1-21

SITUATION Paul promised to come to the Corinthians with the love of a father, but he feared that he might have to deal with troublemakers harshly.

OBSERVATION God does not spare us trials, but he helps us overcome them. God works in our weakness, because when we are weak his strength accomplishes the task.

INSPIRATION They aren't exactly what you'd call a list of "Who's Who in Purity and Sainthood." In fact, some of their antics and attitudes would make you think of the Saturday night crowd at the county jail. What few halos there are among this befuddled bunch could probably use a bit of straightening and polish. Yet, strange as it may seem, it is this very humanness that makes these people refreshing. They are so refreshing that should you ever need a reminder of God's tolerance, you'd find it in these people. If you ever wonder how in the world God could use you to change the world, look at these people. . . .

What people? The people God used to change history. A ragbag of ne'er-do-wells and has-beens who found hope, not in their performance, but in God's proverbially open arms.

What can you say about a fellow whose lust got so lusty that he got a woman pregnant, tried to blame it on her husband, had her husband killed, and then went on living like nothing ever happened? Well, you could say he was a man after God's own heart. David's track record left a little to be desired, but his repentant spirit was unquestionable.

Then comes Jonah. God's ambassador to Nineveh. Jonah, however, had other ideas. He had no desire to go to that heathen city. So he hopped on another boat while God wasn't looking (or at least that's what Jonah thought). God put him in a whale's belly to bring him back to his senses. But even the whale couldn't stomach this missionary for too long. A good burp and Jonah went flying over the surf and landed big-eyed and repentant on the beach. (Which just goes to

Continued

show that you can't keep a good man down.)

And on and on the stories go: Elijah, the prophet who pouted; Solomon, the king who knew too much; Jacob, the wheeler-dealer; Gomer, the prostitute; Sarah, the woman who giggled at God. One story after another of God using man's best and overcoming man's worst.

Even the genealogy of Jesus is salted with a dubious character or two—Tamar the adulteress, Rahab the harlot, and Bathsheba, who tended to take baths in questionable locations.

The reassuring lesson is clear. God used (and uses!) people to change the world. People! Not saints or superhumans or geniuses, but people. Crooks, creeps, lovers, and liars—he uses them all. And what they may lack in perfection, God makes up for in love.

(From *No Wonder They Call Him the Savior* by Max Lucado)

APPLICATION When your weakness surfaces, remember that God still uses you. Volunteer for a form of service that requires you to depend on God's strength. Depend on him every step of the way.

EXPLORATION Strength in Weakness—Psalm 82:3; Romans 8:26; 1 Corinthians 1:25-31; 9:22; 2 Corinthians 12:9-10; 13:4; 15:43; Hebrews 5:2; 11:34.

Signs of an Apostle

11 I have become a fool in boasting;[y] you have compelled me. For I ought to
have been commended by you; for in nothing was I behind the most eminent apostles, though I am nothing. 12 Truly the signs of an apostle were
accomplished among you with all perseverance, in signs and wonders and
mighty deeds. 13 For what is it in which you were inferior to other churches,
except that I myself was not burdensome to you? Forgive me this wrong!

Love for the Church

14 Now *for* the third time I am ready to come to you. And I will not be
burdensome to you; for I do not seek yours, but you. For the children ought
not to lay up for the parents, but the parents for the children. 15 And I will very
gladly spend and be spent for your souls; though the more abundantly I
love you, the less I am loved.
16 But be that *as it may,* I did not burden you. Nevertheless, being crafty, I
caught you by cunning! 17 Did I take advantage of you by any of those whom
I sent to you? 18 I urged Titus, and sent our brother with *him.* Did Titus take
advantage of you? Did we not walk in the same spirit? Did *we* not *walk* in
the same steps?
19 Again, do you think[z] that we excuse ourselves to you? We speak before
God in Christ. But *we do* all things, beloved, for your edification. 20 For I fear
lest, when I come, I shall not find you such as I wish, and *that* I shall be found
by you such as you do not wish; lest *there be* contentions, jealousies, outbursts
of wrath, selfish ambitions, backbitings, whisperings, conceits, tumults;
21 lest, when I come again, my God will humble me among you, and I shall
mourn for many who have sinned before and have not repented of the
uncleanness, fornication, and lewdness which they have practiced.

Coming with Authority

13 This *will be* the third *time* I am coming to you. *"By the mouth of two
or three witnesses every word shall be established."*[a] 2 I have told you
before, and foretell as if I were present the second time, and now being absent I write[b] to those who have sinned before, and to all the rest, that if I
come again I will not spare— 3 since you seek a proof of Christ speaking in
me, who is not weak toward you, but mighty in you. 4 For though He was
crucified in weakness, yet He lives by the power of God. For we also are
weak in Him, but we shall live with Him by the power of God toward you.
5 Examine yourselves *as to* whether you are in the faith. Test yourselves.
Do you not know yourselves, that Jesus Christ is in you?—unless indeed you
are disqualified. 6 But I trust that you will know that we are not disqualified.

Paul Prefers Gentleness

7 Now I[c] pray to God that you do no evil, not that we should appear approved,
but that you should do what is honorable, though we may seem disqualified. 8 For we can do nothing against the truth, but for the truth. 9 For we are
glad when we are weak and you are strong. And this also we pray, that you

12:11 [y] NU-Text omits *in boasting.*
12:19 [z] NU-Text reads *You have been thinking for a long time . . . .*
13:1 [a] Deuteronomy 19:15
13:2 [b] NU-Text omits *I write.*
13:7 [c] NU-Text reads *we.*

may be made complete. 10 Therefore I write these
things being absent, lest being present I should use
sharpness, according to the authority which the Lord
has given me for edification and not for destruction.

Greetings and Benediction

11 Finally, brethren, farewell. Become complete. Be of
good comfort, be of one mind, live in peace; and the
God of love and peace will be with you.
12 Greet one another with a holy kiss.
13 All the saints greet you.
14 The grace of the Lord Jesus Christ, and the love of
God, and the communion of the Holy Spirit *be* with
you all. Amen.

The Epistle of Paul to the GALATIANS

INTRODUCTION

The Emancipation Proclamation was ready to be signed. The papers were complete. All that was lacking was the signature of the president. But Abraham Lincoln was not ready. He had spent the morning at a reception and his hand was swollen from greeting visitors.

"Let me wait until my hand is better," he reportedly requested. "I don't want my signature to be shaky. I want people to know I set the slaves free in confidence."

Galatians states that Christ did the same for us. "He set the slaves free in confidence." No hesitation. No reservation. No reluctance. No exceptions.

The Book of Galatians is the Emancipation Proclamation for the church. Written by the confident hand of one who had known slavery, it declares and defines Christian liberty. Paul wrote it to combat those in the church who were insisting that it was necessary to follow a law or code in order to be saved.

Many of the early Christians were Jewish Christians who were accustomed to following a law. Though they had accepted the gift of grace offered by Christ on the cross, some were falling away—substituting God's gift with man's works. Paul recognized this for what it was—legalism.

Legalism is not unique to the Galatians. Any time the gospel has been preached, there have been those who contend it is too good to be true. It's not enough to be saved by faith, argues the legalist, we must earn God's approval. Some teach that we earn God's favor by what we know (intellectualism). Others insist we are saved by what we do (moralism). Still others claim that salvation is determined by what we feel (emotionalism).

However you package it, Paul contests, legalism is heresy. Any gospel other than the pure gospel is *anathema*. Salvation comes only through the cross—no additions, no alterations.

We are free in Christ. "Stand fast therefore in the liberty by which Christ has made us free, and do not be entangled again with a yoke of bondage" (5:1). Galatians is a document of freedom. As you read, note the confidence of the writer. His hand doesn't shake, his conviction doesn't waver, his belief doesn't falter.

And so neither should ours.

LIFE LESSON

Galatians 1:1-24

SITUATION Paul and Barnabas established churches in several cities in the Roman province of Galatia (in the south-central part of modern Turkey). These churches began to grow but needed to be reminded of certain lessons.

OBSERVATION Paul vigorously condemned the teaching that would require Gentiles to embrace Jewish laws and customs.

INSPIRATION It is my intention to set forth here a method by which we may test the spirits and prove all things religious and moral that come to us or are brought or offered to us by anyone. . . . Briefly stated the test is this: This new doctrine, this new religious habit, this new view of truth, this new spiritual experience—how has it affected my attitude toward and my relationship to God, Christ, the Holy Scriptures, self, other Christians, the world and sin? . . . Whatever makes Christ dear to us is pretty sure to be from God. . . . Whatever originates outside the Scriptures should for that very reason be suspect until it can be shown to be in accord with them. . . . "To the word and to the testimony" must always be the last and final proof. . . . All true Christian experience will deepen our love for other Christians. Therefore we conclude that whatever tends to separate us in person or in heart from our fellow Christians is not of God . . . . It may be stated unequivocally that any spirit that permits compromise with the world is a false spirit. . . .
(From *The Best of Tozer* compiled by Warren Wiersbe)

APPLICATION Will you believe anything you hear from a Christian radio preacher? Will a book by a Christian author convince you of right and wrong? Confirm what you hear or read with what the Bible says. Is the teacher right? What does the Bible say?

EXPLORATION Gospel of Grace—Acts 15:11; 20:24; Romans 3:22-24; 6:17; Ephesians 2:4-10; Titus 3:4-7.

Greeting

Paul, an apostle (not from men nor through man, but through
Jesus Christ and God the Father who raised Him from the
dead), 2and all the brethren who are with me,

To the churches of Galatia:

3Grace to you and peace from God the Father and our Lord Jesus Christ,
4who gave Himself for our sins, that He might deliver us from this present
evil age, according to the will of our God and Father, 5to whom *be* glory forever and ever. Amen.

Only One Gospel

6I marvel that you are turning away so soon from Him who called you in
the grace of Christ, to a different gospel, 7which is not another; but there
are some who trouble you and want to pervert the gospel of Christ. 8But
even if we, or an angel from heaven, preach any other gospel to you than
what we have preached to you, let him be accursed. 9As we have said before, so now I say again, if anyone preaches any other gospel to you than
what you have received, let him be accursed.
10For do I now persuade men, or God? Or do I seek to please men? For if
I still pleased men, I would not be a bondservant of Christ.

Call to Apostleship

11But I make known to you, brethren, that the gospel which was
preached by me is not according to man. 12For I neither received it from
man, nor was I taught *it,* but *it came* through the revelation of Jesus Christ.
13For you have heard of my former conduct in Judaism, how I persecuted the church of God beyond measure and *tried to* destroy it. 14And I
advanced in Judaism beyond many of my contemporaries in my own nation, being more exceedingly zealous for the traditions of my fathers.
15But when it pleased God, who separated me from my mother's womb
and called *me* through His grace, 16to reveal His Son in me, that I might
preach Him among the Gentiles, I did not immediately confer with flesh
and blood, 17nor did I go up to Jerusalem to those *who were* apostles before
me; but I went to Arabia, and returned again to Damascus.

Contacts at Jerusalem

18Then after three years I went up to Jerusalem to see Peter,[a] and remained with him fifteen days. 19But I saw none of the other apostles except
James, the Lord's brother. 20(Now *concerning* the things which I write to
you, indeed, before God, I do not lie.)
21Afterward I went into the regions of Syria and Cilicia. 22And I was unknown by face to the churches of Judea which *were* in Christ. 23But they
were hearing only, "He who formerly persecuted us now preaches the faith
which he once *tried to* destroy." 24And they glorified God in me.

Defending the Gospel

2 Then after fourteen years I went up again to Jerusalem with Barnabas, and
also took Titus with *me.* 2And I went up by revelation, and communicated
to them that gospel which I preach among the Gentiles, but privately to

1:18 [a] NU-Text reads *Cephas.*

those who were of reputation, lest by any means I might run, or had run,
in vain. 3Yet not even Titus who *was* with me, being a Greek, was compelled to be circumcised. 4And *this occurred* because of false brethren secretly brought in (who came in by stealth to spy out our liberty which we
have in Christ Jesus, that they might bring us into bondage), 5to whom we
did not yield submission even for an hour, that the truth of the gospel
might continue with you.
6But from those who seemed to be something—whatever they were, it
makes no difference to me; God shows personal favoritism to no man—
for those who seemed *to be something* added nothing to me. 7But on the
contrary, when they saw that the gospel for the uncircumcised had been
committed to me, as *the gospel* for the circumcised *was* to Peter 8(for He
who worked effectively in Peter for the apostleship to the circumcised also
worked effectively in me toward the Gentiles), 9and when James, Cephas,
and John, who seemed to be pillars, perceived the grace that had been given
to me, they gave me and Barnabas the right hand of fellowship, that we
should go to the Gentiles and they to the circumcised. 10*They desired* only that
we should remember the poor, the very thing which I also was eager to do.

No Return to the Law

11Now when Peter[b] had come to Antioch, I withstood him to his face, because he was to be blamed; 12for before certain men came from James, he
would eat with the Gentiles; but when they came, he withdrew and separated himself, fearing those who were of the circumcision. 13And the rest
of the Jews also played the hypocrite with him, so that even Barnabas was
carried away with their hypocrisy.
14But when I saw that they were not straightforward about the truth of
the gospel, I said to Peter before *them* all, "If you, being a Jew, live in the
manner of Gentiles and not as the Jews, why do you[c] compel Gentiles to
live as Jews?[d] 15We *who are* Jews by nature, and not sinners of the Gentiles,
16knowing that a man is not justified by the works of the law but by faith in
Jesus Christ, even we have believed in Christ Jesus, that we might be justified by faith in Christ and not by the works of the law; for by the works of
the law no flesh shall be justified.
17"But if, while we seek to be justified by Christ, we ourselves also are
found sinners, *is* Christ therefore a minister of sin? Certainly not! 18For if I
build again those things which I destroyed, I make myself a transgressor.
19For I through the law died to the law that I might live to God. 20I have
been crucified with Christ; it is no longer I who live, but Christ lives in me;
and the *life* which I now live in the flesh I live by faith in the Son of God,
who loved me and gave Himself for me. 21I do not set aside the grace of
God; for if righteousness *comes* through the law, then Christ died in vain."

Justification by Faith

3 O foolish Galatians! Who has bewitched you that you should not obey
the truth,[e] before whose eyes Jesus Christ was clearly portrayed among
you[f] as crucified? 2This only I want to learn from you: Did you receive the
Spirit by the works of the law, or by the hearing of faith? 3Are you so foolish?

2:11 [b] NU-Text reads *Cephas.*
2:14 [c] NU-Text reads *how can you.* [d] Some interpreters stop the quotation here.
3:1 [e] NU-Text omits *that you should not obey the truth.* [f] NU-Text omits *among you.*

Life Lesson

Galatians 2:1-21

SITUATION When Paul visited Jerusalem he explained that God saves Gentiles, too. Later, when Peter showed favoritism to Jews, Paul corrected him.

OBSERVATION Keeping thousands of laws does not save us. Because of this, God sent Jesus. Jesus paid the price that our actions never could.

INSPIRATION There is a great deal of difference between law and grace. . . . There is no peace until we see the finished work of Jesus Christ—until we can look back and see the cross of Christ between us and our sins. . . .

Then there is glory for the time to come. A great many people seem to forget that the best is before us. . . . The kingdom we are going to inherit is glorious: our crown is to be a "crown of glory"; the city we are going to inhabit is the city of the glorified; the songs we are to sing are the songs of the glorified; we are to wear garments of "glory and beauty." . . .

Many are always looking on the backward path and mourning over the troubles through which they have passed. They keep lugging up the cares and anxieties they have been called on to bear and are forever looking at them. Why should we go reeling and staggering under the burdens and cares of life when we have such prospects before us?

If there is nothing but glory beyond, our faces ought to shine brightly all the time.

(From "Peace, Grace, and Glory" by D. L. Moody in *They Walked with God*)

APPLICATION Do you wonder if God approves of you? If Jesus reigns in your life, then God looks on you with favor. Rejoice! But, if you are trying to call the shots in your life, then you have disregarded his claim on your life. Surrender the remaining areas in your life to God.

EXPLORATION Grace—Psalm 130:3; Romans 3:19-24; Ephesians 1:3-14.

LIFE LESSON

Galatians 3:1-4:7

SITUATION Some Galatian Believers were in Jerusalem on Pentecost (Acts 2). They already knew that God freely gave the Holy Spirit.

OBSERVATION Paul used Abraham's example (Genesis 15) to prove that Old Testament Believers were also saved by faith.

INSPIRATION I have often been asked by young Christians: "Why is it that I fail so? I did so solemnly vow with my whole heart, and did desire to serve God; why have I failed?" To such I always give the one answer: "My dear friend, you are trying to do in your own strength what Christ alone can do in you." And when they tell me: "I am sure I knew Christ alone could do it, I was not trusting in myself," my answer always is: "You were trusting in yourself or you could not have failed. If you had trusted Christ, He could not have failed." Oh, this perfecting in the flesh what was begun in the Spirit runs far deeper through us than we knew. Let us ask God to reveal to us that it is only when we are brought to utter shame and emptiness that we shall be prepared to receive the blessing that comes from on high. . . . I ask it of every member of Christ's church and of every believer: Are you living a life under the power of the Holy Spirit day by day, or are you attempting to live without that? Remember you cannot. Are you consecrated, given up to the Spirit to work and live in you? Oh, come and confess every failure of temper, every failure of the tongue however small, every failure owing to the absence of the Holy Spirit and the presence of the power of self.

(From "Having Begun in the Spirit" by Andrew Murray in *They Walked with God*)

APPLICATION Paul warned: Don't be tricked. Don't let anyone think that you must win God's approval. Rejoice that if you are God's child his love toward you is endless.

EXPLORATION Law's Inferiority—Romans 3:19-20; 4:13-25; 8:3; Galatians 5:4-6; Hebrews 3:1-6; 8:7-13.

Having begun in the Spirit, are you now being made perfect by the flesh?
4 Have you suffered so many things in vain—if indeed *it was* in vain?
5 Therefore He who supplies the Spirit to you and works miracles among
you, *does He do it* by the works of the law, or by the hearing of faith?— 6 just as
Abraham *"believed God, and it was accounted to him for righteousness."*[g]
7 Therefore know that *only* those who are of faith are sons of Abraham. 8 And
the Scripture, foreseeing that God would justify the Gentiles by faith, preached
the gospel to Abraham beforehand, *saying, "In you all the nations shall be
blessed."*[h] 9 So then those who *are* of faith are blessed with believing Abraham.

The Law Brings a Curse

10 For as many as are of the works of the law are under the curse; for it is
written, *"Cursed is everyone who does not continue in all things which are
written in the book of the law, to do them."*[i] 11 But that no one is justified by
the law in the sight of God *is* evident, for *"the just shall live by faith."*[j] 12 Yet
the law is not of faith, but *"the man who does them shall live by them."*[k]
13 Christ has redeemed us from the curse of the law, having become a
curse for us (for it is written, *"Cursed is everyone who hangs on a tree"*[l]),
14 that the blessing of Abraham might come upon the Gentiles in Christ Jesus, that we might receive the promise of the Spirit through faith.

The Changeless Promise

15 Brethren, I speak in the manner of men: Though *it is* only a man's
covenant, yet *if it is* confirmed, no one annuls or adds to it. 16 Now to Abraham and his Seed were the promises made. He does not say, "And to
seeds," as of many, but as of one, *"And to your Seed,"*[m] who is Christ.
17 And this I say, *that* the law, which was four hundred and thirty years later,
cannot annul the covenant that was confirmed before by God in Christ,[n]
that it should make the promise of no effect. 18 For if the inheritance *is* of
the law, *it is* no longer of promise; but God gave *it* to Abraham by promise.

Purpose of the Law

19 What purpose then *does* the law *serve?* It was added because of transgressions, till the Seed should come to whom the promise was made; *and
it was* appointed through angels by the hand of a mediator. 20 Now a mediator does not *mediate* for one *only,* but God is one.
21 *Is* the law then against the promises of God? Certainly not! For if there
had been a law given which could have given life, truly righteousness
would have been by the law. 22 But the Scripture has confined all under sin,
that the promise by faith in Jesus Christ might be given to those who believe. 23 But before faith came, we were kept under guard by the law, kept
for the faith which would afterward be revealed. 24 Therefore the law was
our tutor *to bring us* to Christ, that we might be justified by faith. 25 But
after faith has come, we are no longer under a tutor.

3:6 [g] Genesis 15:6
3:8 [h] Genesis 12:3; 18:18; 22:18; 26:4; 28:14
3:10 [i] Deuteronomy 27:26
3:11 [j] Habakkuk 2:4
3:12 [k] Leviticus 18:5
3:13 [l] Deuteronomy 21:23
3:16 [m] Genesis 12:7; 13:15; 24:7
3:17 [n] NU-Text omits *in Christ.*

Sons and Heirs

[26]For you are all sons of God through faith in Christ Jesus. [27]For as many
of you as were baptized into Christ have put on Christ. [28]There is neither
Jew nor Greek, there is neither slave nor free, there is neither male nor female; for you are all one in Christ Jesus. [29]And if you *are* Christ's, then you
are Abraham's seed, and heirs according to the promise.

4 Now I say *that* the heir, as long as he is a child, does not differ at all
from a slave, though he is master of all, [2]but is under guardians and
stewards until the time appointed by the father. [3]Even so we, when we were
children, were in bondage under the elements of the world. [4]But when the
fullness of the time had come, God sent forth His Son, born[o] of a woman,
born under the law, [5]to redeem those who were under the law, that we
might receive the adoption as sons.

[6]And because you are sons, God has sent forth the Spirit of His Son into
your hearts, crying out, "Abba, Father!" [7]Therefore you are no longer a
slave but a son, and if a son, then an heir of[p] God through Christ.

Fears for the Church

[8]But then, indeed, when you did not know God, you served those which
by nature are not gods. [9]But now after you have known God, or rather are
known by God, how *is it that* you turn again to the weak and beggarly elements, to which you desire again to be in bondage? [10]You observe days and
months and seasons and years. [11]I am afraid for you, lest I have labored
for you in vain.

[12]Brethren, I urge you to become like me, for I *became* like you. You have
not injured me at all. [13]You know that because of physical infirmity I
preached the gospel to you at the first. [14]And my trial which was in my
flesh you did not despise or reject, but you received me as an angel of God,
even as Christ Jesus. [15]What[q] then was the blessing you *enjoyed?* For I bear
you witness that, if possible, you would have plucked out your own eyes
and given them to me. [16]Have I therefore become your enemy because I
tell you the truth?

[17]They zealously court you, *but* for no good; yes, they want to exclude
you, that you may be zealous for them. [18]But it is good to be zealous in a
good thing always, and not only when I am present with you. [19]My little
children, for whom I labor in birth again until Christ is formed in you, [20]I
would like to be present with you now and to change my tone; for I have
doubts about you.

Two Covenants

[21]Tell me, you who desire to be under the law, do you not hear the law?
[22]For it is written that Abraham had two sons: the one by a bondwoman,
the other by a freewoman. [23]But he *who was* of the bondwoman was born
according to the flesh, and he of the freewoman through promise, [24]which
things are symbolic. For these are the[r] two covenants: the one from Mount
Sinai which gives birth to bondage, which is Hagar— [25]for this Hagar is
Mount Sinai in Arabia, and corresponds to Jerusalem which now is, and is

4:4 [o] Or *made*
4:7 [p] NU-Text reads *through God* and omits *through Christ.*
4:15 [q] NU-Text reads *Where.*
4:24 [r] NU-Text and M-Text omit *the.*

LIFE LESSON

Galatians 4:8-31

SITUATION Judaizers taught that Gentile Believers had to obey Jewish laws in order to be saved. Paul wrote to correct this false teaching.

OBSERVATION As a result of God's promise, Christians are children of God. God expects faith from his children.

INSPIRATION Paul is not dealing with sin in this chapter of Galatians, but with the relation of the natural to the spiritual. The natural must be turned into the spiritual by sacrifice, otherwise a tremendous divorce will be produced in the actual life. Why should God ordain the natural to be sacrificed? God did not. It is not God's order, but His permissive will. God's order was that the natural should be transformed into the spiritual by obedience; it is sin that made it necessary for the natural to be sacrificed. . . .

If we do not sacrifice the natural to the spiritual, the natural life will mock at the life of the Son of God in us and produce a continual swither. This is always the result of an undisciplined spiritual nature. We go wrong because we stubbornly refuse to discipline ourselves, physically, morally or mentally. "I wasn't disciplined when I was a child." You must discipline yourself now. If you do not, you will ruin the whole of your personal life for God. God is not with our natural life while we pamper it; but when we put it out in the desert and resolutely keep it under, then God will be with it; and He will open up wells and oases, and fulfil all His promises for the natural.

(From *My Utmost for His Highest* by Oswald Chambers)

APPLICATION You can become God's child by trusting in Jesus. Don't try to win God's approval through your behavior. Trust God to save, guide, and strengthen you.

EXPLORATION Hagar and Ishmael—Genesis 16. Sarah and Isaac—Genesis 21.

LIFE LESSON

Galatians 5:1-26

SITUATION Christians in Galatia faced a problem. Should they embrace the Jewish Law? Paul emphasized the importance of faith and warned about the danger of emphasizing law above faith.

OBSERVATION Paul taught that if you begin to keep the Law, you are obligated to keep all of it. Instead, Christians ought to trust Jesus who makes them righteous.

INSPIRATION The way we live, the things we say, the attitudes we entertain, the lifestyle we adopt, the enterprises in which we engage are all continuously producing either positive or negative results in society. Far too many people assume they can adopt a neutral stance. They feel they can be noncommittal. They try to remain detached, uninvolved with the trauma, turmoil and tension of their times.

Again and again Jesus pointed out that this was impossible. "Either you are for me, or against me," He said. "You cannot serve two masters at once. Either you hate one and love the other or vice-versa. . . ."

We live in an atmosphere of antagonism, an environment of enmity. Yet amid such adversity Christ calls us to produce peace.

This peace is love quietly, strongly, persistently meeting every onslaught against it with good will. It is that inner attitude of tranquillity and tolerance in the face of angry attacks. It is the willingness to accept the assaults of others even at the price of personal humiliation. It implies that even though my enemies and detractors may be at war with me, I can be at peace with them.

(From *Salt for Society* by Phillip Keller)

APPLICATION How do you exhibit your faith? Do you hurry out the door after church on Sundays? Or, do you take the time to greet and listen to the concerns of others? Next Sunday, stay and listen. Remember that listening begins to help those in need.

EXPLORATION Faith—
1 Corinthians 13:2; Romans 8:1-39; James 2:14.

in bondage with her children— 26but the Jerusalem above is free, which is
the mother of us all. 27For it is written:

> *"Rejoice, O barren,*
> *You who do not bear!*
> *Break forth and shout,*
> *You who are not in labor!*
> *For the desolate has many more children*
> *Than she who has a husband."*[s]

28Now we, brethren, as Isaac *was,* are children of promise. 29But, as he
who was born according to the flesh then persecuted him *who was born*
according to the Spirit, even so *it is* now. 30Nevertheless what does the
Scripture say? *"Cast out the bondwoman and her son, for the son of the
bondwoman shall not be heir with the son of the freewoman."*[t] 31So then,
brethren, we are not children of the bondwoman but of the free.

Christian Liberty

5 Stand fast therefore in the liberty by which Christ has made us free,[u]
and do not be entangled again with a yoke of bondage. 2Indeed I, Paul,
say to you that if you become circumcised, Christ will profit you nothing.
3And I testify again to every man who becomes circumcised that he is a
debtor to keep the whole law. 4You have become estranged from Christ,
you who *attempt to* be justified by law; you have fallen from grace. 5For we
through the Spirit eagerly wait for the hope of righteousness by faith. 6For
in Christ Jesus neither circumcision nor uncircumcision avails anything,
but faith working through love.

Love Fulfills the Law

7You ran well. Who hindered you from obeying the truth? 8This persua-
sion does not *come* from Him who calls you. 9A little leaven leavens the
whole lump. 10I have confidence in you, in the Lord, that you will have no
other mind; but he who troubles you shall bear his judgment, whoever he is.
11And I, brethren, if I still preach circumcision, why do I still suffer persecution? Then the offense of the cross has ceased. 12I could wish that
those who trouble you would even cut themselves off!
13For you, brethren, have been called to liberty; only do not *use* liberty as
an opportunity for the flesh, but through love serve one another. 14For all
the law is fulfilled in one word, *even* in this: *"You shall love your neighbor
as yourself."*[v] 15But if you bite and devour one another, beware lest you be
consumed by one another!

Walking in the Spirit

16I say then: Walk in the Spirit, and you shall not fulfill the lust of the
flesh. 17For the flesh lusts against the Spirit, and the Spirit against the flesh;
and these are contrary to one another, so that you do not do the things that
you wish. 18But if you are led by the Spirit, you are not under the law.
19Now the works of the flesh are evident, which are: adultery,[w] fornication,
uncleanness, lewdness, 20idolatry, sorcery, hatred, contentions, jealousies,

4:27 [s] Isaiah 54:1
4:30 [t] Genesis 21:10
5:1 [u] NU-Text reads *For freedom Christ has made us free; stand fast therefore.*
5:14 [v] Leviticus 19:18
5:19 [w] NU-Text omits *adultery.*

outbursts of wrath, selfish ambitions, dissensions, heresies, 21envy, murders,[x]
drunkenness, revelries, and the like; of which I tell you beforehand, just as
I also told *you* in time past, that those who practice such things will not inherit the kingdom of God.
22But the fruit of the Spirit is love, joy, peace, longsuffering, kindness,
goodness, faithfulness, 23gentleness, self-control. Against such there is no
law. 24And those *who are* Christ's have crucified the flesh with its passions
and desires. 25If we live in the Spirit, let us also walk in the Spirit. 26Let us
not become conceited, provoking one another, envying one another.

Bear and Share the Burdens

6 Brethren, if a man is overtaken in any trespass, you who *are* spiritual
restore such a one in a spirit of gentleness, considering yourself lest
you also be tempted. 2Bear one another's burdens, and so fulfill the law of
Christ. 3For if anyone thinks himself to be something, when he is nothing,
he deceives himself. 4But let each one examine his own work, and then he
will have rejoicing in himself alone, and not in another. 5For each one shall
bear his own load.

Be Generous and Do Good

6Let him who is taught the word share in all good things with him who
teaches.
7Do not be deceived, God is not mocked; for whatever a man sows, that
he will also reap. 8For he who sows to his flesh will of the flesh reap corruption, but he who sows to the Spirit will of the Spirit reap everlasting life.
9And let us not grow weary while doing good, for in due season we shall
reap if we do not lose heart. 10Therefore, as we have opportunity, let us do
good to all, especially to those who are of the household of faith.

Glory Only in the Cross

11See with what large letters I have written to you with my own hand!
12As many as desire to make a good showing in the flesh, these *would* compel you to be circumcised, only that they may not suffer persecution for
the cross of Christ. 13For not even those who are circumcised keep the law,
but they desire to have you circumcised that they may boast in your flesh.
14But God forbid that I should boast except in the cross of our Lord Jesus
Christ, by whom[y] the world has been crucified to me, and I to the world.
15For in Christ Jesus neither circumcision nor uncircumcision avails anything, but a new creation.

Blessing and a Plea

16And as many as walk according to this rule, peace and mercy *be* upon
them, and upon the Israel of God.
17From now on let no one trouble me, for I bear in my body the marks of
the Lord Jesus.
18Brethren, the grace of our Lord Jesus Christ *be* with your spirit. Amen.

5:21 [x] NU-Text omits *murders.*
6:14 [y] Or *by which* (the cross)

LIFE LESSON

Galatians 6:1-18

SITUATION Paul warned the Galatians not to compare themselves with others. Rather, they had to be concerned with their own responsibility before God.

OBSERVATION God transformed you into a new person. Live like it!

INSPIRATION The Bible reveals that God has a plan for every life, and that if we live in constant fellowship with Him, He will direct and lead us in the fulfillment of this plan.

Many of us have God's second or third best. However, if you have substituted the good for the best, do not despair. Wherever you are at this moment, yield your life unconditionally to God, and He can still make it a thing of beauty and an honor to His name.

You cannot know the will of God for your life unless you first come to the cross and confess that you are a sinner and receive Christ as Lord and Savior. If you want the perfect plan that God has for your life, you will have to go by way of Calvary to get it. It is only through Christ that we can be on speaking terms with God and know God's plan for our lives.

(From *Unto the Hills* by Billy Graham)

APPLICATION Both legalism and sin end in frustration. But your freedom from sin and your desire to please God frees you to do your best before him. You can help others. You can do good.

EXPLORATION Paul's Suffering—Acts 14:19; 16:22; 2 Corinthians 11:23-29; 12:7; Galatians 4:13-14.

The Epistle of Paul to the EPHESIANS

INTRODUCTION

I just witnessed a beautiful wedding. The most beautiful I've ever seen. That says a lot since I've seen a lot. Ministers see many weddings. It's a perk of the profession.

Is there anything more elegant than a wedding? Candles bathe a chapel in gold. Families fill the pews in love. Groomsmen and bridesmaids descend the aisles with bouquets of newness and rings of promise. What an occasion.

And nothing quite compares with that moment when the bride stands at the top of the aisle. Arm entwined with her father's, she takes those final steps with him and steps toward a new life with *him.*

Ahhh, the glory of a wedding. So to say I just saw the most beautiful one is no small thing. What made these nuptials so unforgettable? The groom. Usually the groom is not the star of the wedding. The fellow is typically upstaged by the girl. But this wedding was made special by the groom.

It was enhanced by something he did.

And who he was made what he did even more startling. You see, he's a cowboy: a stocky fellow who went to college on a rodeo scholarship. But what stood by me was not a macho calf roper, but a pinch-me-I'm-dreaming boy who'd never seen a bride so gorgeous.

He was composed as he walked down the aisle. He was fine as he took his place at the altar. But when he saw the bride, he wept.

It was the moment he'd dreamed of. It was as if he'd been given life's greatest gift—a bride in all her beauty. By the way, those are the very words Paul uses to describe the church: a bride in all her beauty.

"*Christ also loved the church and gave Himself for her, that He might sanctify and cleanse her with the washing of water by the word, that He might present her to Himself a glorious church, not having a spot or wrinkle or any such thing, but that she should be holy and without blemish*" (5:25–27).

Ponder that verse. Jesus died for a bride. He died so he could be married. This passage anticipates the day when the groom will see his bride—when Christ will receive his church. Jesus' fondest longing will be fulfilled. His bride will arrive.

The letter to the Ephesians celebrates the beauty of the church—the Bride of Christ. From our perspective, the church isn't so pretty. We see the backbiting, the squabbling, the divisions. Heaven sees that, as well. But heaven sees more. Heaven sees the church as cleansed and made holy by Christ.

Heaven sees the church ascending to heaven. Heaven sees the Bride wearing the spotless gown of Jesus Christ.

It's enough to make one weep.

LIFE LESSON

Ephesians 1:1-23

SITUATION In a city with many sinful distractions, Paul wrote so that Christians would know what God thought of his people.

OBSERVATION God cherishes us. The more we know him, the more we will understand his love toward us.

INSPIRATION We all desire relationships in which we are accepted, valued, and wanted. We desperately long for this esteem from our peers, but seldom experience the "real thing." Countless stories are written about teenagers who accept life-threatening dares in the hopes of being accepted by their peers, or business people who compromise their integrity and ethics to join an elite, inner circle. We read of men and women who are driven to succeed because they believe the lie that says their value is determined by the quality and level of their performance. Or how about the teenager or lonely single who sacrifices his virginity for the chance to experience closeness and the feeling of being wanted.

For the Christian, none of this futile struggle is necessary because we have been chosen by God before time ever began. We belong, we matter, we have been accepted. No longer outcasts or second-class citizens, we are part of his family.

(From *A Dad's Blessing* by Gary Smalley and John Trent)

APPLICATION Tell someone what you've learned about who you are in Christ. Write a note, make a phone call, go to lunch, or share together on a walk.

EXPLORATION Adopted by God—Isaiah 43:6; 63:8; John 1:12; Romans 8:15; 2 Corinthians 6:17; Galatians 3:26; 4:6; Ephesians 2:19; 5:1; Hebrews 12:9.

Greeting

Paul, an apostle of Jesus Christ by the will of God,

To the saints who are in Ephesus, and faithful in Christ Jesus:
2Grace to you and peace from God our Father and the Lord Jesus Christ.

Redemption in Christ

3Blessed *be* the God and Father of our Lord Jesus Christ, who has
blessed us with every spiritual blessing in the heavenly *places* in Christ,
4just as He chose us in Him before the foundation of the world, that we
should be holy and without blame before Him in love, 5having predestined us to adoption as sons by Jesus Christ to Himself, according to the
good pleasure of His will, 6to the praise of the glory of His grace, by which
He made us accepted in the Beloved.
7In Him we have redemption through His blood, the forgiveness of sins,
according to the riches of His grace 8which He made to abound toward us
in all wisdom and prudence, 9having made known to us the mystery of His
will, according to His good pleasure which He purposed in Himself, 10that
in the dispensation of the fullness of the times He might gather together in
one all things in Christ, both[a] which are in heaven and which are on
earth—in Him. 11In Him also we have obtained an inheritance, being predestined according to the purpose of Him who works all things according
to the counsel of His will, 12that we who first trusted in Christ should be to
the praise of His glory.
13In Him you also *trusted,* after you heard the word of truth, the gospel
of your salvation; in whom also, having believed, you were sealed with the
Holy Spirit of promise, 14who[b] is the guarantee of our inheritance until the
redemption of the purchased possession, to the praise of His glory.

Prayer for Spiritual Wisdom

15Therefore I also, after I heard of your faith in the Lord Jesus and your
love for all the saints, 16do not cease to give thanks for you, making mention
of you in my prayers: 17that the God of our Lord Jesus Christ, the Father of
glory, may give to you the spirit of wisdom and revelation in the knowledge of Him, 18the eyes of your understanding[c] being enlightened; that you
may know what is the hope of His calling, what are the riches of the glory
of His inheritance in the saints, 19and what *is* the exceeding greatness of His
power toward us who believe, according to the working of His mighty power
20which He worked in Christ when He raised Him from the dead and
seated *Him* at His right hand in the heavenly *places,* 21far above all principality and power and might and dominion, and every name that is named,
not only in this age but also in that which is to come.
22And He put all *things* under His feet, and gave Him *to be* head over all
things to the church, 23which is His body, the fullness of Him who fills all in all.

By Grace Through Faith

2 And you *He made alive,* who were dead in trespasses and sins, 2in
which you once walked according to the course of this world, according
to the prince of the power of the air, the spirit who now works in the sons

1:10 [a] NU-Text and M-Text omit *both.*
1:14 [b] NU-Text reads *which.*
1:18 [c] NU-Text and M-Text read *hearts.*

of disobedience, 3among whom also we all once conducted ourselves in
the lusts of our flesh, fulfilling the desires of the flesh and of the mind, and
were by nature children of wrath, just as the others.
4But God, who is rich in mercy, because of His great love with which He
loved us, 5even when we were dead in trespasses, made us alive together
with Christ (by grace you have been saved), 6and raised *us* up together, and
made *us* sit together in the heavenly *places* in Christ Jesus, 7that in the ages
to come He might show the exceeding riches of His grace in *His* kindness
toward us in Christ Jesus. 8For by grace you have been saved through faith,
and that not of yourselves; *it is* the gift of God, 9not of works, lest anyone
should boast. 10For we are His workmanship, created in Christ Jesus for
good works, which God prepared beforehand that we should walk in them.

Brought Near by His Blood

11Therefore remember that you, once Gentiles in the flesh—who are
called Uncircumcision by what is called the Circumcision made in the
flesh by hands— 12that at that time you were without Christ, being aliens
from the commonwealth of Israel and strangers from the covenants of
promise, having no hope and without God in the world. 13But now in
Christ Jesus you who once were far off have been brought near by the
blood of Christ.

Christ Our Peace

14For He Himself is our peace, who has made both one, and has broken
down the middle wall of separation, 15having abolished in His flesh the enmity,
that is, the law of commandments *contained* in ordinances, so as to create
in Himself one new man *from* the two, *thus* making peace, 16and that He
might reconcile them both to God in one body through the cross, thereby
putting to death the enmity. 17And He came and preached peace to you
who were afar off and to those who were near. 18For through Him we both
have access by one Spirit to the Father.

Christ Our Cornerstone

19Now, therefore, you are no longer strangers and foreigners, but fellow
citizens with the saints and members of the household of God, 20having
been built on the foundation of the apostles and prophets, Jesus Christ
Himself being the chief corner*stone,* 21in whom the whole building, being
fitted together, grows into a holy temple in the Lord, 22in whom you also
are being built together for a dwelling place of God in the Spirit.

The Mystery Revealed

3 For this reason I, Paul, the prisoner of Christ Jesus for you Gentiles—
2if indeed you have heard of the dispensation of the grace of God which
was given to me for you, 3how that by revelation He made known to me the
mystery (as I have briefly written already, 4by which, when you read, you
may understand my knowledge in the mystery of Christ), 5which in other
ages was not made known to the sons of men, as it has now been revealed
by the Spirit to His holy apostles and prophets: 6that the Gentiles should be
fellow heirs, of the same body, and partakers of His promise in Christ
through the gospel, 7of which I became a minister according to the gift of
the grace of God given to me by the effective working of His power.

Life Lesson

Ephesians 2:1-22

SITUATION The Ephesians forgot what God did to save them and to make them a part of his Body.

OBSERVATION God's mercy plucks us from the destruction of our countless sins and places us in Jesus Christ's righteousness.

INSPIRATION When I read a verse like Ephesians 2:4, I feel I have discovered God's roadblock on one's way to hell—[But God's mercy is great]. He is so rich in mercy that none need perish, but individuals must come to God in his appointed way. I adore the mercy that had lovingkindness, pity and compassion on me. . . .

Let me give you a modern illustration of mercy in action. One day, a Christian named Paul went into a coffee shop, sat on a stool, and ordered his lunch. When he began speaking to the man next to him, he realized that Fred was in deep spiritual need. After sharing the gospel with him, Paul arranged to meet him again. It was at the second meeting that Fred was converted. Then Paul began to disciple him on a one-on-one basis, and Fred grew in grace and in knowledge of the Lord Jesus. But it wasn't long before Fred learned that he had a life-threatening disease. He had to go to a convalescent hospital that was sadly substandard. Paul visited him regularly, bathed him, changed the sheets, and did other chores that the staff should have been doing. The night Fred died, Paul was holding him in his arms, whispering verses of Scripture in his ear. That's mercy. It's a wonderful thing to see that Godlike quality in a human life.

(From *Alone in Majesty* by William MacDonald)

APPLICATION Are there some people around you who slip through the cracks unnoticed? Is there a lonely widow? An insecure junior-high student? A struggling single mother? Pay these people a visit—bring flowers or another gift; invest some time in their lives.

EXPLORATION Mercy—Matthew 5:7; Luke 6:36; 1 Peter 3:9.

LIFE LESSON

Ephesians 3:1-21

SITUATION Paul told the Ephesians his goals for them. He shared his prayer for their growth in insight and strength.

OBSERVATION Although God's love for us cannot be measured by any comprehensible standards, God wants us to know this ocean of love.

INSPIRATION The promises of God's love and forgiveness are as real, as sure, as positive as human words can make them. But like describing the ocean, its total beauty cannot be understood until it is actually seen. It is the same with God's love. Until you actually accept it, until you actually experience it, until you actually posses true peace with God, no one can describe its wonders to you.

It is not something that you can do with your mind. Your finite mind is not capable of dealing with anything as great as the love of God. Your mind might have difficulty explaining how a black cow can eat green grass and give white milk—but you drink the milk and are nourished by it. Your mind can't reason through all the intricate processes that take place when you plant a small flat seed that produces a huge vine bearing luscious red and green watermelons—but you eat them and enjoy them! You can't understand radio, but you listen. Your mind can't explain the electricity that may be creating the light by which you are reading at this very moment—but you know that it's there and that it is making it possible for you to read!

(From *Peace with God* by Billy Graham)

APPLICATION Learn to see God's love for you in the details of daily life. Read 1 John and get a firmer grasp on understanding God's love.

EXPLORATION God's Love—Psalm 6:4; John 3:16; 15:12; Romans 5:8; 8:35-37; 1 John 3:1.

Purpose of the Mystery

8To me, who am less than the least of all the saints, this grace was given,
that I should preach among the Gentiles the unsearchable riches of Christ,
9and to make all see what *is* the fellowship[d] of the mystery, which from the
beginning of the ages has been hidden in God who created all things
through Jesus Christ;[e] 10to the intent that now the manifold wisdom of God
might be made known by the church to the principalities and powers in
the heavenly *places,* 11according to the eternal purpose which He accomplished in Christ Jesus our Lord, 12in whom we have boldness and access
with confidence through faith in Him. 13Therefore I ask that you do not
lose heart at my tribulations for you, which is your glory.

Appreciation of the Mystery

14For this reason I bow my knees to the Father of our Lord Jesus Christ,[f]
15from whom the whole family in heaven and earth is named, 16that He
would grant you, according to the riches of His glory, to be strengthened
with might through His Spirit in the inner man, 17that Christ may dwell in
your hearts through faith; that you, being rooted and grounded in love,
18may be able to comprehend with all the saints what *is* the width and
length and depth and height— 19to know the love of Christ which passes
knowledge; that you may be filled with all the fullness of God.

20Now to Him who is able to do exceedingly abundantly above all that
we ask or think, according to the power that works in us, 21to Him *be* glory
in the church by Christ Jesus to all generations, forever and ever. Amen.

Walk in Unity

4 I, therefore, the prisoner of the Lord, beseech you to walk worthy of the
calling with which you were called, 2with all lowliness and gentleness,
with longsuffering, bearing with one another in love, 3endeavoring to keep
the unity of the Spirit in the bond of peace. 4*There is* one body and one
Spirit, just as you were called in one hope of your calling; 5one Lord, one
faith, one baptism; 6one God and Father of all, who *is* above all, and through
all, and in you[g] all.

Spiritual Gifts

7But to each one of us grace was given according to the measure of
Christ's gift. 8Therefore He says:

> *"When He ascended on high,*
> *He led captivity captive,*
> *And gave gifts to men."*[h]

9(Now this, *"He ascended"*—what does it mean but that He also first[i] descended into the lower parts of the earth? 10He who descended is also the
One who ascended far above all the heavens, that He might fill all things.)

11And He Himself gave some *to be* apostles, some prophets, some evangelists, and some pastors and teachers, 12for the equipping of the saints for
the work of ministry, for the edifying of the body of Christ, 13till we all come

3:9 [d] NU-Text and M-Text read *stewardship* (dispensation). [e] NU-Text omits *through Jesus Christ.*
3:14 [f] NU-Text omits *of our Lord Jesus Christ.*
4:6 [g] NU-Text omits *you;* M-Text reads *us.*
4:8 [h] Psalm 68:18
4:9 [i] NU-Text omits *first.*

to the unity of the faith and of the knowledge of the Son of God, to a perfect
man, to the measure of the stature of the fullness of Christ; 14that we should
no longer be children, tossed to and fro and carried about with every wind
of doctrine, by the trickery of men, in the cunning craftiness of deceitful
plotting, 15but, speaking the truth in love, may grow up in all things into
Him who is the head—Christ— 16from whom the whole body, joined and
knit together by what every joint supplies, according to the effective working by which every part does its share, causes growth of the body for the
edifying of itself in love.

The New Man

17This I say, therefore, and testify in the Lord, that you should no longer
walk as the rest of[j] the Gentiles walk, in the futility of their mind, 18having
their understanding darkened, being alienated from the life of God, because
of the ignorance that is in them, because of the blindness of their heart;
19who, being past feeling, have given themselves over to lewdness, to work
all uncleanness with greediness.
20But you have not so learned Christ, 21if indeed you have heard Him
and have been taught by Him, as the truth is in Jesus: 22that you put off,
concerning your former conduct, the old man which grows corrupt according to the deceitful lusts, 23and be renewed in the spirit of your mind, 24and
that you put on the new man which was created according to God, in true
righteousness and holiness.

Do Not Grieve the Spirit

25Therefore, putting away lying, *"Let each one of you speak truth with his
neighbor,"*[k] for we are members of one another. 26*"Be angry, and do not sin"*:[l]
do not let the sun go down on your wrath, 27nor give place to the devil.
28Let him who stole steal no longer, but rather let him labor, working with
his hands what is good, that he may have something to give him who has
need. 29Let no corrupt word proceed out of your mouth, but what is good
for necessary edification, that it may impart grace to the hearers. 30And do
not grieve the Holy Spirit of God, by whom you were sealed for the day of
redemption. 31Let all bitterness, wrath, anger, clamor, and evil speaking be
put away from you, with all malice. 32And be kind to one another, tenderhearted, forgiving one another, even as God in Christ forgave you.

Walk in Love

5 Therefore be imitators of God as dear children. 2And walk in love, as
Christ also has loved us and given Himself for us, an offering and a sacrifice to God for a sweet-smelling aroma.
3But fornication and all uncleanness or covetousness, let it not even be
named among you, as is fitting for saints; 4neither filthiness, nor foolish
talking, nor coarse jesting, which are not fitting, but rather giving of
thanks. 5For this you know,[m] that no fornicator, unclean person, nor covetous man, who is an idolater, has any inheritance in the kingdom of
Christ and God. 6Let no one deceive you with empty words, for because of
these things the wrath of God comes upon the sons of disobedience.
7Therefore do not be partakers with them.

4:17 [j] NU-Text omits *the rest of.*
4:25 [k] Zechariah 8:16
4:26 [l] Psalm 4:4
5:5 [m] NU-Text reads *For know this.*

LIFE LESSON

Ephesians 4:1-32

SITUATION Paul labored to bring unity between Gentiles and Jews. He urgently defended the need for a unified and God-honoring lifestyle.

OBSERVATION In Jesus Christ's church, many cultures become unified. Paul explained how the Holy Spirit exhibits this unifying work.

INSPIRATION Forgiveness embraces suffering. Saint Francis of Assisi prayed, "Lord, make me an instrument of Thy peace. Where there is injury let me sow pardon."

Sometimes we can be sinned against and not notice it or notice it hardly at all. But there are times when it hurts sharply. There is real injury. It is human nature to want revenge of some sort, even if it is only making sure that the person is aware of having hurt us—and that, I am convinced, is sometimes a form of revenge. It is not human nature to forgive. I have found in my own heart, at times, the sinful lust to see the other person "come crawling."

One who is truly an instrument of God's peace offers, in return for injury, only one thing: pardon, remembering the millions of pounds he himself owed to the King, and how utterly he was pardoned.

(From *The Mark of a Man* by Elisabeth Elliot)

APPLICATION How many different cultures make up your church? Are the people generally the same race and class? Consider becoming involved in or beginning an outreach ministry that will touch people outside your culture and bring diversity to your church.

EXPLORATION Forgiveness—Mark 11:25; Luke 17:4; Colossians 3:13.

Life Lesson

Ephesians 6:1-24

SITUATION To fight effectively in their spiritual battle, the Ephesians must know Christ, obey his standards, and be prepared to fight.

OBSERVATION Each Christian has a responsibility to love, honor, and respect. If faithful to these duties, Christians will find themselves united against the spiritual power of evil.

INSPIRATION What does it mean to honor your parents? We can see that if we will look at the word *honor* in the Scriptures. In Hebrew, the word for "honor" is *kabed*. This word literally means, "to be heavy, weighty, to honor." Even today, we still link the idea of being heavy with honoring a person.

When the President of the United States or some other important person speaks, people often say that his words "carry a lot of weight." Someone whose words are weighty is someone worthy of honor and respect. However, we can learn even more about what it means to honor someone by looking at its opposite in Scriptures.

. . . [T]he literal meaning of the word *curse (qalal)* was "to make light, of little weight, to dishonor." If we go back to our example above, if we dishonor a person we would say, "Their words carry little weight." The contrast is striking!

Walk in Light

[8]For you were once darkness, but now *you are* light in the Lord. Walk as children of light [9](for the fruit of the Spirit[n] *is* in all goodness, righteousness, and truth), [10]finding out what is acceptable to the Lord. [11]And have no fellowship with the unfruitful works of darkness, but rather expose *them.* [12]For it is shameful even to speak of those things which are done by them in secret. [13]But all things that are exposed are made manifest by the light, for whatever makes manifest is light. [14]Therefore He says:

"Awake, you who sleep,
Arise from the dead,
And Christ will give you light."

Walk in Wisdom

[15]See then that you walk circumspectly, not as fools but as wise, [16]redeeming the time, because the days are evil.

[17]Therefore do not be unwise, but understand what the will of the Lord *is.* [18]And do not be drunk with wine, in which is dissipation; but be filled with the Spirit, [19]speaking to one another in psalms and hymns and spiritual songs, singing and making melody in your heart to the Lord, [20]giving thanks always for all things to God the Father in the name of our Lord Jesus Christ, [21]submitting to one another in the fear of God.[o]

Marriage—Christ and the Church

[22]Wives, submit to your own husbands, as to the Lord. [23]For the husband is head of the wife, as also Christ is head of the church; and He is the Savior of the body. [24]Therefore, just as the church is subject to Christ, so *let* the wives *be* to their own husbands in everything.

[25]Husbands, love your wives, just as Christ also loved the church and gave Himself for her, [26]that He might sanctify and cleanse her with the washing of water by the word, [27]that He might present her to Himself a glorious church, not having spot or wrinkle or any such thing, but that she should be holy and without blemish. [28]So husbands ought to love their own wives as their own bodies; he who loves his wife loves himself. [29]For no one ever hated his own flesh, but nourishes and cherishes it, just as the Lord *does* the church. [30]For we are members of His body,[p] of His flesh and of His bones. [31]*"For this reason a man shall leave his father and mother and be joined to his wife, and the two shall become one flesh."*[q] [32]This is a great mystery, but I speak concerning Christ and the church. [33]Nevertheless let each one of you in particular so love his own wife as himself, and let the wife see that she respects her husband.

Children and Parents

6 Children, obey your parents in the Lord, for this is right. [2]*"Honor your father and mother,"* which is the first commandment with promise: [3]*"that it may be well with you and you may live long on the earth."*[r]

[4]And you, fathers, do not provoke your children to wrath, but bring them up in the training and admonition of the Lord.

5:9 [n] NU-Text reads *light.*
5:21 [o] NU-Text reads *Christ.*
5:30 [p] NU-Text omits the rest of this verse.
5:31 [q] Genesis 2:24
6:3 [r] Deuteronomy 5:16

Bondservants and Masters

[5]Bondservants, be obedient to those who are your masters according to
the flesh, with fear and trembling, in sincerity of heart, as to Christ; [6]not
with eyeservice, as men-pleasers, but as bondservants of Christ, doing the
will of God from the heart, [7]with goodwill doing service, as to the Lord,
and not to men, [8]knowing that whatever good anyone does, he will receive
the same from the Lord, whether *he is* a slave or free.
[9]And you, masters, do the same things to them, giving up threatening,
knowing that your own Master also[s] is in heaven, and there is no partiality
with Him.

The Whole Armor of God

[10]Finally, my brethren, be strong in the Lord and in the power of His
might. [11]Put on the whole armor of God, that you may be able to stand
against the wiles of the devil. [12]For we do not wrestle against flesh and blood,
but against principalities, against powers, against the rulers of the darkness
of this age,[t] against spiritual *hosts* of wickedness in the heavenly *places.*
[13]Therefore take up the whole armor of God, that you may be able to withstand in the evil day, and having done all, to stand.
[14]Stand therefore, having girded your waist with truth, having put on
the breastplate of righteousness, [15]and having shod your feet with the
preparation of the gospel of peace; [16]above all, taking the shield of faith
with which you will be able to quench all the fiery darts of the wicked one.
[17]And take the helmet of salvation, and the sword of the Spirit, which is the
word of God; [18]praying always with all prayer and supplication in the Spirit,
being watchful to this end with all perseverance and supplication for all
the saints— [19]and for me, that utterance may be given to me, that I may
open my mouth boldly to make known the mystery of the gospel, [20]for
which I am an ambassador in chains; that in it I may speak boldly, as I
ought to speak.

A Gracious Greeting

[21]But that you also may know my affairs *and* how I am doing, Tychicus,
a beloved brother and faithful minister in the Lord, will make all things
known to you; [22]whom I have sent to you for this very purpose, that you
may know our affairs, and *that* he may comfort your hearts.
[23]Peace to the brethren, and love with faith, from God the Father and the
Lord Jesus Christ. [24]Grace *be* with all those who love our Lord Jesus Christ
in sincerity. Amen.

When Paul tells us to honor our parents, he is telling us that they are worthy of high value and respect. In modern-day terms, we could call them a heavyweight in our lives! Just the opposite is true if we choose to dishonor our parents.

Some people treat their parents as if they are a layer of dust on a table. Dust weighs almost nothing and can be swept away with a brush of the hand. Dust is a nuisance and an eyesore that clouds any real beauty the table might have. Paul tells us that such an attitude should not be a part of how any child views his or her parents, and for good reason. If we fail to honor our parents, we not only do what is wrong and dishonor God, but we also literally drain ourselves of life! (From *The Gift of the Blessing* by Gary Smalley and John Trent)

APPLICATION In what ways do you honor your boss, parents, children, or employees? How have you dishonored them? Pinpoint areas in which you need to improve. Honor others not only with your actions but with your thoughts, too.

EXPLORATION Obedience to Parents—Proverbs 1:8; 6:20; Colossians 3:20. Parental Duties—Deuteronomy 6:7; Proverbs 22:6; 2 Corinthians 12:14; 1 Timothy 3:4; Titus 2:4.

6:9 [s] NU-Text reads *He who is both their Master and yours.*
6:12 [t] NU-Text reads *rulers of this darkness.*

The Epistle of Paul to the

PHILIPPIANS

INTRODUCTION

Perhaps the symbol of this generation is the exercise bike.

It represents what most have—excess weight.

It represents what most want—to be different.

It represents what most people spend most their time doing—pedaling furiously and getting nowhere. High activity but low achievement. Car pools, diapers, bills, time clocks. Office walls painted grey with routine. Houses framed with wooden humdrum. For many, life is lived on the exercise bicycle. Day after day in the same seat, doing the same thing but seeing the same scenery. Is there any end to this tunnel of greyness?

There is.

Go with me back in history a couple of thousand years. Let's go to the city of Rome. The thrilling metropolis of gladiators, chariots, and empires. But don't stop at the coliseum or palace. Go rather to a drab little room, surrounded by high walls. Let's imagine that we can peek into the room and look. Inside we see a man seated on the floor. He's an older fellow, shoulders stooped, and balding. Chains are on his hands and feet. And chained to him is a guard from the Roman army.

It is the apostle Paul. The apostle who has traveled all over the world. The apostle who has liberated people in every port. The apostle who was bound only by the will of God is now in chains—stuck in a dingy house—attached to a Roman officer.

Here is a fellow who has every reason to be in a slump!

He is restricted by walls. He is afflicted by friends (v. 15). He is conflicted by danger (v. 21).

He is writing a letter. No doubt it is a complaint letter to God. No doubt it is a list of grievances. No doubt he is writing the New Testament version of Lamentations. He has every reason to be bitter and complain. But he doesn't. Instead, he writes a letter that two thousand years later is still known as the treatise on joy.

Sound interesting? Of course it does. Who couldn't use a guide to joy in this world? Why don't you spend some time with it? Dismount the bicycle to nowhere and follow Paul as he guides you down the trail to peace.

LIFE LESSON

Philippians 1:1–2:4

SITUATION Paul wrote this epistle to the Philippians as an expression of joy and gratitude. Looking beyond his Roman imprisonment, Paul reflected on the joy of his ministry: serving Christ and others.

OBSERVATION Regardless of circumstances, you can have real joy. Paul noted that living wholeheartedly for Christ and selflessly for others brings joy.

INSPIRATION Should a man see only popularity, he becomes a mirror, reflecting whatever needs to be reflected to gain acceptance. . . . He is everyone and no one.

Should a man see only power, he becomes a wolf—prowling, hunting, and stalking the elusive game. Recognition is his prey and people are his prizes. His quest is endless. . . . As a result, he who sees only power is degraded to an animal, an insatiable scavenger, controlled not by a will from within, but by luring from without.

Should a man see only pleasure, he becomes a carnival thrill-seeker, alive only in bright lights, wild rides, and titillating entertainment. With lustful fever he races from ride to ride, satisfying his insatiable passion for sensations only long enough to look for another. . . .

Seekers of popularity, power, and pleasure. The end result is the same: painful unfulfillment.

Only in seeking his Maker does a man truly become man. For in seeing his Creator man catches a glimpse of what he was intended to be. He who would see his God would then see the reason for death and the purpose of time. Destiny? Tomorrow? Truth? All are questions within the reach of the man who knows his source. . . .

(From *God Came Near* by Max Lucado)

APPLICATION How can you encourage others in their walk with Christ this week? Choose two friends you will encounter this week and encourage them toward a closer walk with Christ.

EXPLORATION Unselfishness —Genesis 13:9; 50:21; Numbers 11:29; 1 Samuel 18:4; 1 Corinthians 10:33; 2 Corinthians 8:9.

Greeting

Paul and Timothy, bondservants of Jesus Christ,

To all the saints in Christ Jesus who are in Philippi, with the bishops[a] and deacons:

[2]Grace to you and peace from God our Father and the Lord Jesus Christ.

Thankfulness and Prayer

[3]I thank my God upon every remembrance of you, [4]always in every prayer of mine making request for you all with joy, [5]for your fellowship in the gospel from the first day until now, [6]being confident of this very thing, that He who has begun a good work in you will complete *it* until the day of Jesus Christ; [7]just as it is right for me to think this of you all, because I have you in my heart, inasmuch as both in my chains and in the defense and confirmation of the gospel, you all are partakers with me of grace. [8]For God is my witness, how greatly I long for you all with the affection of Jesus Christ.

[9]And this I pray, that your love may abound still more and more in knowledge and all discernment, [10]that you may approve the things that are excellent, that you may be sincere and without offense till the day of Christ, [11]being filled with the fruits of righteousness which *are* by Jesus Christ, to the glory and praise of God.

Christ Is Preached

[12]But I want you to know, brethren, that the things *which happened* to me have actually turned out for the furtherance of the gospel, [13]so that it has become evident to the whole palace guard, and to all the rest, that my chains are in Christ; [14]and most of the brethren in the Lord, having become confident by my chains, are much more bold to speak the word without fear.

[15]Some indeed preach Christ even from envy and strife, and some also from goodwill: [16]The former[b] preach Christ from selfish ambition, not sincerely, supposing to add affliction to my chains; [17]but the latter out of love, knowing that I am appointed for the defense of the gospel. [18]What then? Only *that* in every way, whether in pretense or in truth, Christ is preached; and in this I rejoice, yes, and will rejoice.

To Live Is Christ

[19]For I know that this will turn out for my deliverance through your prayer and the supply of the Spirit of Jesus Christ, [20]according to my earnest expectation and hope that in nothing I shall be ashamed, but with all boldness, as always, so now also Christ will be magnified in my body, whether by life or by death. [21]For to me, to live *is* Christ, and to die *is* gain. [22]But if *I* live on in the flesh, this *will mean* fruit from *my* labor; yet what I shall choose I cannot tell. [23]For[c] I am hard-pressed between the two, having a desire to depart and be with Christ, *which is* far better. [24]Nevertheless to remain in the flesh *is* more needful for you. [25]And being confident of this, I know that I shall remain and continue with you all for your progress and joy of faith, [26]that your rejoicing for me may be more abundant in Jesus Christ by my coming to you again.

1:1 [a] Literally *overseers*
1:16 [b] NU-Text reverses the contents of verses 16 and 17.
1:23 [c] NU-Text and M-Text read *But.*

Striving and Suffering for Christ

27Only let your conduct be worthy of the gospel of Christ, so that whether
I come and see you or am absent, I may hear of your affairs, that you stand
fast in one spirit, with one mind striving together for the faith of the gospel,
28and not in any way terrified by your adversaries, which is to them a proof
of perdition, but to you of salvation,[d] and that from God. 29For to you it has
been granted on behalf of Christ, not only to believe in Him, but also to
suffer for His sake, 30having the same conflict which you saw in me and
now hear *is* in me.

Unity Through Humility

2 Therefore if *there is* any consolation in Christ, if any comfort of love, if
any fellowship of the Spirit, if any affection and mercy, 2fulfill my joy
by being like-minded, having the same love, *being* of one accord, of one mind.
3*Let* nothing *be done* through selfish ambition or conceit, but in lowliness
of mind let each esteem others better than himself. 4Let each of you look
out not only for his own interests, but also for the interests of others.

The Humbled and Exalted Christ

5Let this mind be in you which was also in Christ Jesus, 6who, being in
the form of God, did not consider it robbery to be equal with God, 7but made
Himself of no reputation, taking the form of a bondservant, *and* coming in
the likeness of men. 8And being found in appearance as a man, He humbled Himself and became obedient to *the point of* death, even the death of
the cross. 9Therefore God also has highly exalted Him and given Him the
name which is above every name, 10that at the name of Jesus every knee
should bow, of those in heaven, and of those on earth, and of those under
the earth, 11and *that* every tongue should confess that Jesus Christ *is* Lord,
to the glory of God the Father.

Light Bearers

12Therefore, my beloved, as you have always obeyed, not as in my presence only, but now much more in my absence, work out your own salvation
with fear and trembling; 13for it is God who works in you both to will and
to do for *His* good pleasure.
14Do all things without complaining and disputing, 15that you may become
blameless and harmless, children of God without fault in the midst of a
crooked and perverse generation, among whom you shine as lights in the
world, 16holding fast the word of life, so that I may rejoice in the day of
Christ that I have not run in vain or labored in vain.
17Yes, and if I am being poured out *as a drink offering* on the sacrifice
and service of your faith, I am glad and rejoice with you all. 18For the same
reason you also be glad and rejoice with me.

Timothy Commended

19But I trust in the Lord Jesus to send Timothy to you shortly, that I also
may be encouraged when I know your state. 20For I have no one like-
minded, who will sincerely care for your state. 21For all seek their own, not
the things which are of Christ Jesus. 22But you know his proven character,

1:28 [d] NU-Text reads *of your salvation.*

LIFE LESSON

Philippians 2:5-30

SITUATION Paul pointed to Jesus as the ultimate example of servanthood and selflessness.

OBSERVATION Imitate Jesus Christ, the humble servant of God. Jesus gave up his rights so that we could be saved.

INSPIRATION Jesus deliberately stripped Himself of everything—His divine rights and privileges—and crossed the unthinkable chasm between God and man.

Try to imagine the span of that chasm. . . . The unlimited God became limited man. . . . Jesus Christ is God.

. . . From the world's viewpoint, Jesus had descended as low as a man—to say nothing of God—could go.

But there was one more downward step, in heaven's eyes the deepest descent of all: from sinless to sin stained. . . . Truly, He could go no lower.

. . . He knowingly and actively embraced a life of giving, serving, losing, and dying.

What was, and is, really hard for Jesus' followers to swallow is that we are called to do the same. To make ourselves nothing. . . . We must believe that as painful as it sometimes feels, descending is the only way to greatness. . . . Jesus obeyed for the sake of love.

And we, His followers and the recipients of His love, are called to do the same. When asked about the two greatest commands, Jesus replied: to love God and to love others. That is what motivated Jesus, and that is what is to motivate us.

(From *Descending into Greatness* by Bill Hybels)

APPLICATION God views service and humility as strengths, not weaknesses. What steps in your relationships can you take to show greater humility? How can you expand your service to others?

EXPLORATION Humility of Jesus—Zechariah 9:9; Matthew 11:29; John 13:5; 2 Corinthians 8:9.

LIFE LESSON

Philippians 3:1-21

SITUATION Paul reminded the Philippians that Christ guaranteed their position through faith alone.

OBSERVATION As we know Christ more, we discover the insignificance of worldly treasures. Our true goal should be to know Christ and his power.

INSPIRATION I was glad to see the plastic ball pit. . . . It's a large, covered, shady, cool, soothing pavilion. . . . But rather than being filled with water, it is loaded with balls—thousands and thousands of plastic, colorful, light-weight balls.

Three-year-old Andrea, however, had a few difficulties. As soon as she took one step into the pit, she filled her arms with balls. . . .

Andrea took a step and fell. . . . She began to cry. I walked over to the edge of the pit. "Andrea," I said gently, "let go of the balls, and you can walk."

"No!" she screamed, wiggling and submerging herself beneath the balls. I reached in and pulled her up. She was still clutching her armful of treasures. . . .

Andrea's determination to hold those balls is nothing compared to the vise-grips we put on life. . . . Try prying our fingers away from our earthly treasures. . . . The way we clutch our possessions and our pennies, you'd think we couldn't live without them.

Ouch.

Jesus' promise is comprehensive: "Blessed are those who hunger and thirst for righteousness, for they will be filled." . . .

Blessed are those, then, who hold their earthly possessions in open palms. . . . Blessed are those who are totally dependent upon Jesus for their joy. (From *The Applause of Heaven* by Max Lucado)

APPLICATION Do you find yourself taking pride in your friends, career, talents, abilities, or position? Tell God today that you treasure him most of all.

EXPLORATION Treasures on Earth—Matthew 6:21; 13:44; Luke 14:33; 2 Corinthians 4:18.

that as a son with *his* father he served with me in the gospel. 23Therefore I
hope to send him at once, as soon as I see how it goes with me. 24But I trust
in the Lord that I myself shall also come shortly.

Epaphroditus Praised

25Yet I considered it necessary to send to you Epaphroditus, my brother,
fellow worker, and fellow soldier, but your messenger and the one who
ministered to my need; 26since he was longing for you all, and was distressed
because you had heard that he was sick. 27For indeed he was sick almost
unto death; but God had mercy on him, and not only on him but on me also,
lest I should have sorrow upon sorrow. 28Therefore I sent him the more eagerly, that when you see him again you may rejoice, and I may be less sorrowful. 29Receive him therefore in the Lord with all gladness, and hold such
men in esteem; 30because for the work of Christ he came close to death, not
regarding his life, to supply what was lacking in your service toward me.

All for Christ

3 Finally, my brethren, rejoice in the Lord. For me to write the same things
to you *is* not tedious, but for you *it is* safe.
2Beware of dogs, beware of evil workers, beware of the mutilation! 3For
we are the circumcision, who worship God in the Spirit,[e] rejoice in Christ
Jesus, and have no confidence in the flesh, 4though I also might have confidence in the flesh. If anyone else thinks he may have confidence in the
flesh, I more so: 5circumcised the eighth day, of the stock of Israel, *of* the tribe
of Benjamin, a Hebrew of the Hebrews; concerning the law, a Pharisee;
6concerning zeal, persecuting the church; concerning the righteousness
which is in the law, blameless.
7But what things were gain to me, these I have counted loss for Christ.
8Yet indeed I also count all things loss for the excellence of the knowledge
of Christ Jesus my Lord, for whom I have suffered the loss of all things,
and count them as rubbish, that I may gain Christ 9and be found in Him,
not having my own righteousness, which *is* from the law, but that which *is*
through faith in Christ, the righteousness which is from God by faith;
10that I may know Him and the power of His resurrection, and the fellowship of His sufferings, being conformed to His death, 11if, by any means, I
may attain to the resurrection from the dead.

Pressing Toward the Goal

12Not that I have already attained, or am already perfected; but I press
on, that I may lay hold of that for which Christ Jesus has also laid hold of
me. 13Brethren, I do not count myself to have apprehended; but one thing
I do, forgetting those things which are behind and reaching forward to
those things which are ahead, 14I press toward the goal for the prize of the
upward call of God in Christ Jesus.
15Therefore let us, as many as are mature, have this mind; and if in anything you think otherwise, God will reveal even this to you. 16Nevertheless,
to *the degree* that we have already attained, let us walk by the same rule,[f] let
us be of the same mind.

3:3 [e] NU-Text and M-Text read *who worship in the Spirit of God.*
3:16 [f] NU-Text omits *rule* and the rest of the verse.

Our Citizenship in Heaven

17Brethren, join in following my example, and note those who so walk,
as you have us for a pattern. 18For many walk, of whom I have told you
often, and now tell you even weeping, *that they are* the enemies of the cross
of Christ: 19whose end *is* destruction, whose god *is their* belly, and *whose*
glory *is* in their shame—who set their mind on earthly things. 20For our
citizenship is in heaven, from which we also eagerly wait for the Savior, the
Lord Jesus Christ, 21who will transform our lowly body that it may be conformed to His glorious body, according to the working by which He is able
even to subdue all things to Himself.

4 Therefore, my beloved and longed-for brethren, my joy and crown, so
stand fast in the Lord, beloved.

Be United, Joyful, and in Prayer

2I implore Euodia and I implore Syntyche to be of the same mind in the
Lord. 3And[g] I urge you also, true companion, help these women who labored
with me in the gospel, with Clement also, and the rest of my fellow workers,
whose names *are* in the Book of Life.

4Rejoice in the Lord always. Again I will say, rejoice!

5Let your gentleness be known to all men. The Lord *is* at hand.

6Be anxious for nothing, but in everything by prayer and supplication,
with thanksgiving, let your requests be made known to God; 7and the peace
of God, which surpasses all understanding, will guard your hearts and minds
through Christ Jesus.

Meditate on These Things

8Finally, brethren, whatever things are true, whatever things *are* noble,
whatever things *are* just, whatever things *are* pure, whatever things *are*
lovely, whatever things *are* of good report, if *there is* any virtue and if *there*
is anything praiseworthy—meditate on these things. 9The things which
you learned and received and heard and saw in me, these do, and the God
of peace will be with you.

Philippian Generosity

10But I rejoiced in the Lord greatly that now at last your care for me has
flourished again; though you surely did care, but you lacked opportunity.
11Not that I speak in regard to need, for I have learned in whatever state I
am, to be content: 12I know how to be abased, and I know how to abound.
Everywhere and in all things I have learned both to be full and to be hungry, both to abound and to suffer need. 13I can do all things through Christ[h]
who strengthens me.

14Nevertheless you have done well that you shared in my distress. 15Now
you Philippians know also that in the beginning of the gospel, when I departed from Macedonia, no church shared with me concerning giving and
receiving but you only. 16For even in Thessalonica you sent *aid* once and
again for my necessities. 17Not that I seek the gift, but I seek the fruit that
abounds to your account. 18Indeed I have all and abound. I am full, having

4:3 [g] NU-Text and M-Text read *Yes.*
4:13 [h] NU-Text reads *Him who.*

Life Lesson

Philippians 4:1-23

SITUATION Paul expressed joy and thanked the Philippians for their support. In addition to earlier gifts, they willingly sent financial support with Epaphroditus for Paul during his imprisonment.

OBSERVATION God knows our needs and promises to provide for them. We know if we bring our requests to him, he will give us strength to live through any difficulty.

INSPIRATION No matter where we are, God is as close as a prayer. He is our support and strength. He will help us make our way up again from whatever depths we have fallen.

We don't often consider that sometimes Jesus is our strength simply to sit still. "Be still, and know that I am God" (Psalm 46:10). Our natural tendency when we have a painful happening in our lives is to go into action—do something. Sometimes it is wiser to wait and just be still. The answers will come.

. . . We may be sure that God is true to His word and answers all sincere prayers offered in the name of the Lord Jesus Christ. His answer may be yes, or it may be no, or it may be "Wait." If it is no or "Wait," we cannot say that God has not answered our prayer. It simply means that the answer is different from what we expected.

When we pray for help in trouble, or for healing in sickness, or for deliverance in persecution, God may not give us what we ask for because that may not be His wise and loving will for us. He will answer our prayer in His own way, and He will not let us down in our hour of need.

(From *Hope for the Troubled Heart* by Billy Graham)

APPLICATION Are you worried or in need? Bring your requests before God. Be specific. Let God know your feelings. Praise him for his help. Share your prayer concerns with friends who will also pray for you.

EXPLORATION Provision—Matthew 7:11; Mark 11:22-24; 2 Corinthians 9:8; 11:9. Prayer—Ephesians 6:18; 1 Peter 5:7. Contentment—Psalm 23:1; Matthew 6:25-34; 1 Timothy 6:6-8.

received from Epaphroditus the things *sent* from you, a sweet-smelling aroma, an acceptable sacrifice, well pleasing to God. [19]And my God shall supply all your need according to His riches in glory by Christ Jesus. [20]Now to our God and Father *be* glory forever and ever. Amen.

Greeting and Blessing

[21]Greet every saint in Christ Jesus. The brethren who are with me greet you. [22]All the saints greet you, but especially those who are of Caesar's household.

[23]The grace of our Lord Jesus Christ be with you all.[i] Amen.

4:23 [i] NU-Text reads *your spirit.*

The Epistle of Paul to the COLOSSIANS

INTRODUCTION

To qualify for welfare, you have to admit you're poor.

To qualify for bankruptcy, you have to admit you are broke.

To be admitted to a hospital, you have to admit you're sick.

And to go to heaven, you have to admit you are hellbound.

We're willing to do the first three, but the fourth? That's a tough one. That's enough to trip up a fellow. Not easy for a decent guy to admit he's a sinner. Hard for a pretty good girl to confess spiritual destitution.

Oh, it isn't at first. When we first meet Christ. When life is a mess and the future is bleak. When we don't have anything to lose because we've lost it all. It's not hard to admit it at first.

But then, by God's grace, things get better. Bills get paid. The dog comes home. The pantry gets full. The face we see in the morning mirror has a smile on it. And with time, the person in the mirror grows a bit proud. A bit puffy. A bit, shall we say . . . cocky?

We forget where we were. We forget what God gave. We gradually begin to think that God is lucky to have us on his side. We begin to see salvation not as a toss of the life preserver to the sinking but as a journey in a rowboat: God's grace handling one oar and our good deeds handling the other. It's not that Jesus isn't necessary, it's just that Jesus isn't enough.

Slowly, deftly, we begin believing in the doctrine of *salvation by Jesus plus.* Jesus plus good deeds. Jesus plus the right doctrine. Jesus plus the right Bible translation. Jesus plus the right charitable activities.

Or in the case of the church in Colosse, Jesus plus the right religious feast, New Moon Festival, and Sabbath Day. To the Christians in Colosse, the right ritual was just as important as the right Savior.

Paul would have none of this. He denounced the philosophy as heretical and stated in no uncertain terms that if we are saved it is because God rescued us and not because we learned to swim. God is the verb and we are the noun. God does the saving and we do the receiving.

All we do is accept it. We might as well admit it.

Life Lesson

Colossians 1:1-29

SITUATION Paul's letter gave tribute to the power and glory of Christ. While commending the Colossians for their actions, he reminded them that Christ's power comes not from what we know, but who we know—Jesus Christ.

OBSERVATION God provides salvation for anyone who will take it. God doesn't require that we know hidden secrets or certain inside information to accept Christ's message and enjoy eternal life.

INSPIRATION When God chose to reveal himself, he did so (surprise of surprises) through a human body. The tongue that called forth the dead was a human one. The hand that touched the leper had dirt under its nails. The feet upon which the woman wept were calloused and dusty. And his tears . . . oh, don't miss the tears . . . they came from a heart as broken as yours or mine ever has been.

So, people came to him. My, how they came to him! They came at night; they touched him as he walked down the street; they followed him around the sea; they invited him into their homes and placed their children at his feet. Why? Because he refused to be a statue in a cathedral or a priest in an elevated pulpit. He chose instead to be Jesus.

. . . There were those who revered him. But there was not one person who considered him too holy, too divine, or too celestial to touch. There was not one person who was reluctant to approach him for fear of being rejected.

Remember. It is man who creates the distance. It is Jesus who builds the bridge.

(From *God Came Near* by Max Lucado)

APPLICATION Pray this week that God will spark new love for him in your heart. Don't let this next week pass without finding a way of telling someone else about the Good News of God's love.

EXPLORATION Love—Ephesians 3:15-18; John 3:16; 13:34; 1 John 4:9-10.

Greeting

1 Paul, an apostle of Jesus Christ by the will of God, and Timothy our
brother,

[2]To the saints and faithful brethren in Christ *who are* in Colosse:

Grace to you and peace from God our Father and the Lord Jesus Christ.[a]

Their Faith in Christ

[3]We give thanks to the God and Father of our Lord Jesus Christ, praying
always for you, [4]since we heard of your faith in Christ Jesus and of your
love for all the saints; [5]because of the hope which is laid up for you in
heaven, of which you heard before in the word of the truth of the gospel,
[6]which has come to you, as *it has* also in all the world, and is bringing forth
fruit,[b] as *it is* also among you since the day you heard and knew the grace
of God in truth; [7]as you also learned from Epaphras, our dear fellow servant, who is a faithful minister of Christ on your behalf, [8]who also declared to us your love in the Spirit.

Preeminence of Christ

[9]For this reason we also, since the day we heard it, do not cease to pray
for you, and to ask that you may be filled with the knowledge of His will in
all wisdom and spiritual understanding; [10]that you may walk worthy of
the Lord, fully pleasing *Him,* being fruitful in every good work and increasing in the knowledge of God; [11]strengthened with all might, according to His glorious power, for all patience and longsuffering with joy;
[12]giving thanks to the Father who has qualified us to be partakers of the inheritance of the saints in the light. [13]He has delivered us from the power of
darkness and conveyed *us* into the kingdom of the Son of His love, [14]in
whom we have redemption through His blood,[c] the forgiveness of sins.
[15]He is the image of the invisible God, the firstborn over all creation.
[16]For by Him all things were created that are in heaven and that are on
earth, visible and invisible, whether thrones or dominions or principalities or powers. All things were created through Him and for Him. [17]And
He is before all things, and in Him all things consist. [18]And He is the head
of the body, the church, who is the beginning, the firstborn from the dead,
that in all things He may have the preeminence.

Reconciled in Christ

[19]For it pleased *the Father that* in Him all the fullness should dwell, [20]and
by Him to reconcile all things to Himself, by Him, whether things on earth
or things in heaven, having made peace through the blood of His cross.
[21]And you, who once were alienated and enemies in your mind by
wicked works, yet now He has reconciled [22]in the body of His flesh
through death, to present you holy, and blameless, and above reproach in
His sight— [23]if indeed you continue in the faith, grounded and steadfast,
and are not moved away from the hope of the gospel which you heard,
which was preached to every creature under heaven, of which I, Paul, became a minister.

1:2 [a] NU-Text omits *and the Lord Jesus Christ.*
1:6 [b] NU-Text and M-Text add *and growing.*
1:14 [c] NU-Text and M-Text omit *through His blood.*

Sacrificial Service for Christ

24I now rejoice in my sufferings for you, and fill up in my flesh what is lacking in the afflictions of Christ, for the sake of His body, which is the church,
25of which I became a minister according to the stewardship from God which
was given to me for you, to fulfill the word of God, 26the mystery which has
been hidden from ages and from generations, but now has been revealed to
His saints. 27To them God willed to make known what are the riches of the
glory of this mystery among the Gentiles: which[d] is Christ in you, the hope of
glory. 28Him we preach, warning every man and teaching every man in all wisdom, that we may present every man perfect in Christ Jesus. 29To this *end* I
also labor, striving according to His working which works in me mightily.

Not Philosophy but Christ

2 For I want you to know what a great conflict I have for you and those in
Laodicea, and *for* as many as have not seen my face in the flesh, 2that
their hearts may be encouraged, being knit together in love, and *attaining*
to all riches of the full assurance of understanding, to the knowledge of the
mystery of God, both of the Father and[e] of Christ, 3in whom are hidden all
the treasures of wisdom and knowledge.
4Now this I say lest anyone should deceive you with persuasive words.
5For though I am absent in the flesh, yet I am with you in spirit, rejoicing
to see your *good* order and the steadfastness of your faith in Christ.
6As you therefore have received Christ Jesus the Lord, so walk in Him,
7rooted and built up in Him and established in the faith, as you have been
taught, abounding in it[f] with thanksgiving.
8Beware lest anyone cheat you through philosophy and empty deceit,
according to the tradition of men, according to the basic principles of the
world, and not according to Christ. 9For in Him dwells all the fullness of
the Godhead bodily; 10and you are complete in Him, who is the head of all
principality and power.

Not Legalism but Christ

11In Him you were also circumcised with the circumcision made without hands, by putting off the body of the sins[g] of the flesh, by the circumcision of Christ, 12buried with Him in baptism, in which you also were
raised with *Him* through faith in the working of God, who raised Him
from the dead. 13And you, being dead in your trespasses and the uncircumcision of your flesh, He has made alive together with Him, having forgiven
you all trespasses, 14having wiped out the handwriting of requirements that
was against us, which was contrary to us. And He has taken it out of the way,
having nailed it to the cross. 15Having disarmed principalities and powers,
He made a public spectacle of them, triumphing over them in it.
16So let no one judge you in food or in drink, or regarding a festival or a
new moon or sabbaths, 17which are a shadow of things to come, but the
substance is of Christ. 18Let no one cheat you of your reward, taking delight in *false* humility and worship of angels, intruding into those things
which he has not[h] seen, vainly puffed up by his fleshly mind, 19and not

1:27 [d] M-Text reads *who.*
2:2 [e] NU-Text omits *both of the Father and.*
2:7 [f] NU-Text omits *in it.*
2:11 [g] NU-Text omits *of the sins.*
2:18 [h] NU-Text omits *not.*

Life Lesson

Colossians 2:6-23

SITUATION Many distractions surround us, even religious ones or church-centered activities. The center of our faith, however, should always be Jesus Christ.

OBSERVATION Followers of Christ do not become sidetracked by the insights of religious cults or modern philosophies. Only one person warrants our allegiance and trust—Jesus.

INSPIRATION *When you are not sure that something is from the Spirit, tread softly.* Back off. Use the Scriptures as your guide. If they are of the Lord, those unidentified inner promptings won't contradict anything biblically. Peace will remain your companion. The Lord doesn't lead against His own revealed Word. So don't get on a hobbyhorse over something that is questionable or clearly unbiblical.

. . . *When you are confident that it's of God, stand firm, even against other people's doubts.* Be strong and resolute. That's a part of walking by faith. There are times when other people will say, "There is no way in the world God could be in this"; yet you know absolutely in your heart that He is. At times like that, simply stand firm. You won't be able to convince them, but that's all right. God is still doing unusual things. BUT don't get weird. You can be confident in God without becoming spooky or seeing lots of things no one else can see. (From *Flying Closer to the Flame* by Charles Swindoll)

APPLICATION If unusual religious rituals have made you feel uneasy, or scholars have put your mind in a maze, don't be troubled. Keep your focus on Christ through prayer, Bible reading, and Christian fellowship.

EXPLORATION Obedience—Luke 17:7-10; 1 John 2:6.

holding fast to the Head, from whom all the body, nourished and knit together by joints and ligaments, grows with the increase *that is* from God.
20Therefore,[i] if you died with Christ from the basic principles of the
world, why, as *though* living in the world, do you subject yourselves to regulations— 21"Do not touch, do not taste, do not handle," 22which all concern
things which perish with the using—according to the commandments
and doctrines of men? 23These things indeed have an appearance of wisdom
in self-imposed religion, *false* humility, and neglect of the body, *but are* of
no value against the indulgence of the flesh.

Not Carnality but Christ

3 If then you were raised with Christ, seek those things which are above,
where Christ is, sitting at the right hand of God. 2Set your mind on
things above, not on things on the earth. 3For you died, and your life is
hidden with Christ in God. 4When Christ *who is* our life appears, then you
also will appear with Him in glory.
5Therefore put to death your members which are on the earth: fornication,
uncleanness, passion, evil desire, and covetousness, which is idolatry.
6Because of these things the wrath of God is coming upon the sons of disobedience, 7in which you yourselves once walked when you lived in them.
8But now you yourselves are to put off all these: anger, wrath, malice,
blasphemy, filthy language out of your mouth. 9Do not lie to one another,
since you have put off the old man with his deeds, 10and have put on the
new *man* who is renewed in knowledge according to the image of Him who
created him, 11where there is neither Greek nor Jew, circumcised nor uncircumcised, barbarian, Scythian, slave *nor* free, but Christ *is* all and in all.

Character of the New Man

12Therefore, as *the* elect of God, holy and beloved, put on tender mercies, kindness, humility, meekness, longsuffering; 13bearing with one another, and forgiving one another, if anyone has a complaint against
another; even as Christ forgave you, so you also *must do.* 14But above all
these things put on love, which is the bond of perfection. 15And let the
peace of God rule in your hearts, to which also you were called in one
body; and be thankful. 16Let the word of Christ dwell in you richly in all
wisdom, teaching and admonishing one another in psalms and hymns
and spiritual songs, singing with grace in your hearts to the Lord. 17And
whatever you do in word or deed, *do* all in the name of the Lord Jesus, giving thanks to God the Father through Him.

The Christian Home

18Wives, submit to your own husbands, as is fitting in the Lord.
19Husbands, love your wives and do not be bitter toward them.
20Children, obey your parents in all things, for this is well pleasing to the
Lord.
21Fathers, do not provoke your children, lest they become discouraged.
22Bondservants, obey in all things your masters according to the flesh,
not with eyeservice, as men-pleasers, but in sincerity of heart, fearing
God. 23And whatever you do, do it heartily, as to the Lord and not to men,

2:20 [i] NU-Text and M-Text omit *Therefore.*

Life Lesson

Colossians 3:1–4:1

SITUATION Paul provided the Colossian church with guidelines for proper conduct. Paul needed to remind the Colossians whom they served.

OBSERVATION A deep personal relationship with God through Jesus Christ will transform every area of our lives.

INSPIRATION If people love you at 6:30 in the morning, one thing is sure: They love *you.* They don't love your title. They don't love your style. They don't love your accomplishments. They just love you. . . .

Sounds like God's love.

"He has made perfect forever those who are being made holy," wrote another.

Underline the word *perfect.* Note that the word is not *better.* Not *improving.* Not *on the upswing.* God doesn't improve; he perfects. He doesn't enhance; he completes. What does the perfect person lack?

Now I realize that there's a sense in which we're imperfect. We still err. We still stumble. We still do exactly what we don't want to do. And that part of us is, according to the verse, "being made holy."

But when it comes to our position before God, we're perfect. When he sees each of us, he sees one who has been made perfect through the One who is perfect—Jesus Christ. . . .

You are absolute perfection. Flawless. Without defects or mistakes. Unsullied. Unrivaled. Unmarred. Peerless. Virgin pure. Undeserved yet unreserved perfection.

No wonder heaven applauds when you wake up. A masterpiece has stirred.

(From *In the Eye of the Storm* by Max Lucado)

APPLICATION Is your relationship with Jesus noticeable by your words? Ask God for a vocabulary that reflects love for others without any bitterness or hate.

EXPLORATION Becoming Like Christ—Acts 3:19; Romans 5:1-5; 1 Corinthians 6:9-11; 2 Corinthians 1:21-22; 1 Peter 3:8.

24knowing that from the Lord you will receive the reward of the inheritance; for[j] you serve the Lord Christ. 25But he who does wrong will be repaid for what he has done, and there is no partiality.
4 Masters, give your bondservants what is just and fair, knowing that
you also have a Master in heaven.

Christian Graces

2Continue earnestly in prayer, being vigilant in it with thanksgiving;
3meanwhile praying also for us, that God would open to us a door for the
word, to speak the mystery of Christ, for which I am also in chains, 4that I
may make it manifest, as I ought to speak.
5Walk in wisdom toward those *who are* outside, redeeming the time.
6*Let* your speech always *be* with grace, seasoned with salt, that you may
know how you ought to answer each one.

Final Greetings

7Tychicus, a beloved brother, faithful minister, and fellow servant in the
Lord, will tell you all the news about me. 8I am sending him to you for this
very purpose, that he[k] may know your circumstances and comfort your
hearts, 9with Onesimus, a faithful and beloved brother, who is *one* of you.
They will make known to you all things which *are happening* here.
10Aristarchus my fellow prisoner greets you, with Mark the cousin of
Barnabas (about whom you received instructions: if he comes to you,
welcome him), 11and Jesus who is called Justus. These *are my* only fellow
workers for the kingdom of God who are of the circumcision; they have
proved to be a comfort to me.
12Epaphras, who is *one* of you, a bondservant of Christ, greets you,
always laboring fervently for you in prayers, that you may stand perfect
and complete[l] in all the will of God. 13For I bear him witness that he has a
great zeal[m] for you, and those who are in Laodicea, and those in Hierapolis.
14Luke the beloved physician and Demas greet you. 15Greet the brethren
who are in Laodicea, and Nymphas and the church that *is* in his[n] house.

Closing Exhortations and Blessing

16Now when this epistle is read among you, see that it is read also in the
church of the Laodiceans, and that you likewise read the epistle from
Laodicea. 17And say to Archippus, "Take heed to the ministry which you
have received in the Lord, that you may fulfill it."
18This salutation by my own hand—Paul. Remember my chains. Grace
be with you. Amen.

LIFE LESSON

Colossians 4:2-18

SITUATION Paul concluded his letter with some final practical advice and greetings.

OBSERVATION Christians who desire to share their faith must pray and watch for opportunities.

INSPIRATION Disciplined thought and planning should go into evangelism. . . . We must think about evangelism whenever we talk with outsiders—wisely making the most of every opportunity. . . .

Whether with someone you're around frequently or with someone you've met for the first time, the best way I've found to turn the conversation toward spiritual matters is to ask the person how you can pray for him or her. Although it's almost routine to the Christian, most non-Christians don't know of anyone who is praying for them. I've discovered that unbelievers are often deeply moved by this unusual expression of concern. . . .

But the point in all these possibilities is that you will have to discipline yourself to bring them about. They won't just happen. You'll have to discipline yourself to ask your neighbors how you can pray for them or when you can share a meal with them. You'll have to discipline yourself to get with your coworkers during off-hours. Many such opportunities for evangelism will never take place if you wait for them to occur spontaneously. The world, the flesh, and the Devil will do their best to see to that. You, however, backed by the invincible power of the Holy Spirit, can make sure that these enemies of the gospel do not win.

(From *Spiritual Disciplines of the Christian Life* by Donald S. Whitney)

APPLICATION Do you share the message of the Lord Jesus with others? Pray and ask God to give you opportunities to tell others about Jesus, especially those you encounter regularly. Be sure that nothing in your daily conversation contradicts the message you proclaim. Be set apart from non-Christians by what you say.

EXPLORATION Making the Most of Opportunity—John 9:4; Acts 21:37–22:1; Ephesians 5:15-16.

3:24 *j* NU-Text omits *for.*
4:8 *k* NU-Text reads *you may know our circumstances and he may.*
4:12 *l* NU-Text reads *fully assured.*
4:13 *m* NU-Text reads *concern.*
4:15 *n* NU-Text reads *Nympha . . . her house.*

3:24 NU-Text omits *for*.

Colossians 4:2–18

The First Epistle of Paul to the

THESSALONIANS

INTRODUCTION

In the third century, St. Cyprian wrote to a friend named Donatus:

This seems a cheerful world, Donatus, when I view it from this fair garden under the shadow of these vines. But if I climbed some great mountain and looked out over the wide lands, you know very well what I would see; brigands on the high road, pirates on the seas, in the amphitheaters men murdered to please the applauding crowds, under all roofs misery and selfishness. It really is a bad world, Donatus, an incredibly bad world.

Yet, in the midst of it, I have found a quiet and holy people. They have discovered a joy which is a thousand times better than any pleasure of this sinful life. They are despised and persecuted, but they care not. They have overcome the world. These people, Donatus, are Christians . . . and I am one of them. (Gordon MacDonald, *Forging a Realworld Faith.*)

What a compliment! *A quiet and holy people.* Is there any phrase which captures the essence of the faith any better? *A quiet and holy people.*

Quiet.

Not obnoxious. Not boastful. Not demanding. Just quiet. Contagiously quiet.

Holy.

Set apart. Pure. Decent. Honest. Wholesome. Holy. A quiet and holy people.

Paul urges the same from us.

"Aspire to lead a quiet life, to mind your own business, and to work with your own hands, as we commanded you, that you may walk properly toward those who are outside, and that you may lack nothing" (4:11, 12).

A quiet and holy people. That describes the church in Thessalonica. May that describe the church today.

LIFE LESSON

1 Thessalonians 1:1-10

SITUATION Paul and Silas preached in Thessalonica and helped many new Christians. They left quickly because of persecution from the Jews (Acts 17) and could not return. The church in Thessalonica faced persecution. Paul wrote with encouragement and instructions for proper living.

OBSERVATION The Thessalonians were commended for their faith and good works. They became an example of faith and love to all Believers.

INSPIRATION I have found that the casual Christian has little or no influence upon others. I am finding that it is only the Christian who refuses to compromise in matters of honesty, integrity and morality who is bearing an effective witness for Christ. The worldly Christian is prepared to do as the world does and will condone practices which are dishonest and unethical because he is afraid of the world's displeasure. Only by a life of obedience to the voice of the Spirit, by daily dying to self, by a full dedication to Christ and constant fellowship with Him, are we able to live a godly life and have a positive influence in this present ungodly world.

(From *Unto the Hills* by Billy Graham)

APPLICATION Are you an example of faith and love to the people around you? Do you have a reputation for being faithful? What attitudes are typical of people whose faith you respect?

EXPLORATION Being an Example—Acts 17:1-9; 1 Corinthians 11:1; 2 Corinthians 2:14-17; 4:1-3; 1 Timothy 4:12.

Greeting

Paul, Silvanus, and Timothy,

To the church of the Thessalonians in God the Father and the
Lord Jesus Christ:

Grace to you and peace from God our Father and the Lord Jesus Christ.[a]

Their Good Example

2We give thanks to God always for you all, making mention of you in our
prayers, 3remembering without ceasing your work of faith, labor of love,
and patience of hope in our Lord Jesus Christ in the sight of our God and
Father, 4knowing, beloved brethren, your election by God. 5For our gospel
did not come to you in word only, but also in power, and in the Holy Spirit
and in much assurance, as you know what kind of men we were among
you for your sake.
6And you became followers of us and of the Lord, having received the word
in much affliction, with joy of the Holy Spirit, 7so that you became examples
to all in Macedonia and Achaia who believe. 8For from you the word of the
Lord has sounded forth, not only in Macedonia and Achaia, but also in every
place. Your faith toward God has gone out, so that we do not need to say anything. 9For they themselves declare concerning us what manner of entry we
had to you, and how you turned to God from idols to serve the living and
true God, 10and to wait for His Son from heaven, whom He raised from the
dead, *even* Jesus who delivers us from the wrath to come.

Paul's Conduct

2 For you yourselves know, brethren, that our coming to you was not in
vain. 2But even[b] after we had suffered before and were spitefully treated
at Philippi, as you know, we were bold in our God to speak to you the gospel
of God in much conflict. 3For our exhortation *did* not *come* from error or
uncleanness, nor *was it* in deceit.
4But as we have been approved by God to be entrusted with the gospel,
even so we speak, not as pleasing men, but God who tests our hearts. 5For
neither at any time did we use flattering words, as you know, nor a cloak
for covetousness—God *is* witness. 6Nor did we seek glory from men, either
from you or from others, when we might have made demands as apostles
of Christ. 7But we were gentle among you, just as a nursing *mother* cherishes her own children. 8So, affectionately longing for you, we were well
pleased to impart to you not only the gospel of God, but also our own lives,
because you had become dear to us. 9For you remember, brethren, our labor and toil; for laboring night and day, that we might not be a burden to
any of you, we preached to you the gospel of God.
10You *are* witnesses, and God *also,* how devoutly and justly and blamelessly we behaved ourselves among you who believe; 11as you know how
we exhorted, and comforted, and charged[c] every one of you, as a father
does his own children, 12that you would walk worthy of God who calls you
into His own kingdom and glory.

1:1 [a] NU-Text omits *from God our Father and the Lord Jesus Christ.*
2:2 [b] NU-Text and M-Text omit *even.*
2:11 [c] NU-Text and M-Text read *implored.*

Their Conversion

[13]For this reason we also thank God without ceasing, because when you
received the word of God which you heard from us, you welcomed *it* not *as*
the word of men, but as it is in truth, the word of God, which also effectively
works in you who believe. [14]For you, brethren, became imitators of the
churches of God which are in Judea in Christ Jesus. For you also suffered the
same things from your own countrymen, just as they *did* from the Judeans,
[15]who killed both the Lord Jesus and their own prophets, and have persecuted
us; and they do not please God and are contrary to all men, [16]forbidding us
to speak to the Gentiles that they may be saved, so as always to fill up *the
measure of* their sins; but wrath has come upon them to the uttermost.

Longing to See Them

[17]But we, brethren, having been taken away from you for a short time in
presence, not in heart, endeavored more eagerly to see your face with great
desire. [18]Therefore we wanted to come to you—even I, Paul, time and
again—but Satan hindered us. [19]For what *is* our hope, or joy, or crown of
rejoicing? *Is it* not even you in the presence of our Lord Jesus Christ at His
coming? [20]For you are our glory and joy.

Concern for Their Faith

3 Therefore, when we could no longer endure it, we thought it good to be
left in Athens alone, [2]and sent Timothy, our brother and minister of God,
and our fellow laborer in the gospel of Christ, to establish you and encourage you concerning your faith, [3]that no one should be shaken by these afflictions; for you yourselves know that we are appointed to this. [4]For, in
fact, we told you before when we were with you that we would suffer tribulation, just as it happened, and you know. [5]For this reason, when I could no
longer endure it, I sent to know your faith, lest by some means the tempter
had tempted you, and our labor might be in vain.

Encouraged by Timothy

[6]But now that Timothy has come to us from you, and brought us good
news of your faith and love, and that you always have good remembrance of
us, greatly desiring to see us, as we also *to see* you— [7]therefore, brethren, in
all our affliction and distress we were comforted concerning you by your
faith. [8]For now we live, if you stand fast in the Lord.

[9]For what thanks can we render to God for you, for all the joy with which
we rejoice for your sake before our God, [10]night and day praying exceedingly that we may see your face and perfect what is lacking in your faith?

Prayer for the Church

[11]Now may our God and Father Himself, and our Lord Jesus Christ, direct our way to you. [12]And may the Lord make you increase and abound in
love to one another and to all, just as we *do* to you, [13]so that He may establish your hearts blameless in holiness before our God and Father at the
coming of our Lord Jesus Christ with all His saints.

Plea for Purity

4 Finally then, brethren, we urge and exhort in the Lord Jesus that you
should abound more and more, just as you received from us how you
ought to walk and to please God; [2]for you know what commandments we
gave you through the Lord Jesus.

LIFE LESSON

1 Thessalonians 2:1-16

SITUATION Paul encouraged Believers to be dedicated to God despite trying circumstances.

OBSERVATION Dedicate your life to God. Speak with empathy, give with generosity, treat others gently.

INSPIRATION Each of us should lead a life stirring enough to start a movement. We should yearn to change the world. We should love unquenchably, dream unfalteringly, and work unceasingly.

We should close our ears to the manifold voices of compromise and perch ourselves on the branch of truth. We should champion the value of people, proclaim the forgiveness of God, and claim the promise of heaven.

Will we see a movement occur? Perhaps and perhaps not. Movements never run their course in one generation. The great revivals and reformations that dot the history of humanity were never the work of just one person. Every movement is the sum of visionaries who have gone before, generations of uncompromised lives and non-negotiated truths. Let's live lives stirring and forceful enough to cause a movement. A true mark of a visionary is his willingness to lay down his life for those whom he'll never see.

(From *On the Anvil* by Max Lucado)

APPLICATION What gets you excited: your team winning the World Series? Your country winning the Olympic gold? Getting elected to the PTA presidency? Do you get as excited about seeing others take steps in their Christian journey? Pray that God would direct your natural passions to rejoice in his successes.

EXPLORATION Right Living—Colossians 2:6-7; 3:2; 1 Timothy 4:12; Titus 3:8.

LIFE LESSON

1 Thessalonians 4:1-18

SITUATION Paul expressed to the Thessalonians that their lives should remain pure as they watched for the second coming of Jesus.

OBSERVATION Be pure in all that you do. We are commanded to keep ourselves busy. By doing this, we can keep ourselves from evil.

INSPIRATION An intriguing verse is found in 1 Thessalonians 4:16, "The Lord himself will come down from heaven with a loud command."

Have you ever wondered what that command will be? It will be the inaugural word of heaven. It will be the first audible message most have heard from God. It will be the word which closes one age and opens a new one.

I think I know what the command will be. I could very well be wrong, but I think the command which puts an end to the pains of the earth and initiates the joys of heaven will be two words: "No more."

The King of kings will raise his pierced hand and proclaim, "No more."

The angels will stand and the Father will speak, "No more."

Every person who lives and who ever lived will turn toward the sky and hear God announce, "No more."

No more loneliness. No more tears. No more death. No more sadness. No more crying. No more pain.

As John sat on the Island of Patmos surrounded by sea and separated

3For this is the will of God, your sanctification: that you should abstain from sexual immorality; 4that each of you should know how to possess his own vessel in sanctification and honor, 5not in passion of lust, like the Gentiles who do not know God; 6that no one should take advantage of and defraud his brother in this matter, because the Lord *is* the avenger of all such, as we also forewarned you and testified. 7For God did not call us to uncleanness, but in holiness. 8Therefore he who rejects *this* does not reject man, but God, who has also given[d] us His Holy Spirit.

A Brotherly and Orderly Life

9But concerning brotherly love you have no need that I should write to you, for you yourselves are taught by God to love one another; 10and indeed you do so toward all the brethren who are in all Macedonia. But we urge you, brethren, that you increase more and more; 11that you also aspire to lead a quiet life, to mind your own business, and to work with your own hands, as we commanded you, 12that you may walk properly toward those who are outside, and *that* you may lack nothing.

The Comfort of Christ's Coming

13But I do not want you to be ignorant, brethren, concerning those who have fallen asleep, lest you sorrow as others who have no hope. 14For if we believe that Jesus died and rose again, even so God will bring with Him those who sleep in Jesus.[e]

15For this we say to you by the word of the Lord, that we who are alive *and* remain until the coming of the Lord will by no means precede those who are asleep. 16For the Lord Himself will descend from heaven with a shout, with the voice of an archangel, and with the trumpet of God. And the dead in Christ will rise first. 17Then we who are alive *and* remain shall be caught up together with them in the clouds to meet the Lord in the air. And thus we shall always be with the Lord. 18Therefore comfort one another with these words.

The Day of the Lord

5 But concerning the times and the seasons, brethren, you have no need that I should write to you. 2For you yourselves know perfectly that the day of the Lord so comes as a thief in the night. 3For when they say, "Peace and safety!" then sudden destruction comes upon them, as labor pains upon a pregnant woman. And they shall not escape. 4But you, brethren, are not in darkness, so that this Day should overtake you as a thief. 5You are all sons of light and sons of the day. We are not of the night nor of darkness. 6Therefore let us not sleep, as others *do,* but let us watch and be sober. 7For those who sleep, sleep at night, and those who get drunk are drunk at night. 8But let us who are of the day be sober, putting on the breastplate of faith and love, and *as* a helmet the hope of salvation. 9For God did not appoint us to wrath, but to obtain salvation through our Lord Jesus Christ, 10who died for us, that whether we wake or sleep, we should live together with Him.

11Therefore comfort each other and edify one another, just as you also are doing.

4:8 [d] NU-Text reads *who also gives.*
4:14 [e] Or *those who through Jesus sleep*

Various Exhortations

[12]And we urge you, brethren, to recognize those who labor among you,
and are over you in the Lord and admonish you, [13]and to esteem them very
highly in love for their work's sake. Be at peace among yourselves.
[14]Now we exhort you, brethren, warn those who are unruly, comfort the
fainthearted, uphold the weak, be patient with all. [15]See that no one renders evil for evil to anyone, but always pursue what is good both for yourselves and for all.
[16]Rejoice always, [17]pray without ceasing, [18]in everything give thanks; for
this is the will of God in Christ Jesus for you.
[19]Do not quench the Spirit. [20]Do not despise prophecies. [21]Test all things;
hold fast what is good. [22]Abstain from every form of evil.

Blessing and Admonition

[23]Now may the God of peace Himself sanctify you completely; and may
your whole spirit, soul, and body be preserved blameless at the coming of
our Lord Jesus Christ. [24]He who calls you *is* faithful, who also will do *it.*
[25]Brethren, pray for us.
[26]Greet all the brethren with a holy kiss.
[27]I charge you by the Lord that this epistle be read to all the holy[f] brethren.
[28]The grace of our Lord Jesus Christ *be* with you. Amen.

from friends he dreamt of the day when God would say, "No more."

This same disciple who had heard Jesus speak these words of assurance over a half a century before now knew what they meant. I wonder if he could hear the voice of Jesus in his memory.

"The end will come."

For those who live for this world, that's bad news. But for those who live for the world to come, it's an encouraging promise.

You're on a land mine, my friend, and it's only a matter of time: "For in this world you will have trouble. . . . " Next time you are tossed into a river as you ride the rapids of life, remember his words of assurance.

Those who endure will be saved. The gospel will be preached. The end will come.

You can count on it.

(From *And the Angels Were Silent* by Max Lucado)

APPLICATION What are the extras in your life? A little extra money? A little extra time? Please God by using your money to help further his kingdom. Spend your extra time building lasting friendships that honor him.

EXPLORATION Flee Sin—1 Corinthians 6:18. Strength—Ephesians 4:28; 1 Thessalonians 3:12; 2 Thessalonians 3:10-12.

5:27 *f* NU-Text omits *holy.*

The Second Epistle of Paul to the

THESSALONIANS

INTRODUCTION

I'm seated on an airplane. A grounded airplane.

I'm surrounded by kids. Restless kids.

The kids are mine. The plane is not. The plane is late, however, and my kids are restless. I took them with me on a trip so we'd have a bit of time together. This is more than I had in mind.

They ask the questions you'd expect of a five- and eight-year-old. "Are they bringing drinks yet?"

"When are we going to leave?"

"How much more time?"

"Are we nearly home?"

"Why is it taking so long?"

Questions. Lots of questions. The kind of questions that were circulating through the church at Thessalonica. They, too, were restless. Somewhere they got the idea that Jesus was returning tomorrow so they got ready. Some were selling their homes, others were quitting their work, and all were twiddling their thumbs while awaiting the return of Christ.

Paul gets wind of their assumption and writes them this letter. He urges them not to buy into the reports that the final days have already begun (2:1, 2). Several things still need to occur first (2:3–12), and until they do, their task is to be patient and alert.

No easy task. Human nature tends to one or the other. We tend to be so patient we aren't alert, or so alert we aren't patient. The church becomes a hybrid of the restless and the resting. The result can be squabbling kids. Just like mine. They've done their best to be patient, but after a while a person can only take so much.

"Hang in there," I say.

"We'll be home soon," I urge.

"Try to get along," I exhort.

(I'm starting to sound a lot like Paul.)

LIFE LESSON

2 Thessalonians 1:1-12

SITUATION Paul wrote a second letter to the Thessalonians less than a year after the first. The Thessalonians continued to grow in their new faith, but Paul needed to correct misunderstandings that resulted from his teaching on Christ's second coming.

OBSERVATION Paul thanks God for the Thessalonians' spiritual growth, and he also urges them to persevere through persecution while they await Jesus' return.

INSPIRATION All of us need encouragement—somebody to believe in us. To reassure and reinforce us. To help us pick up the pieces and go on. To provide us with increased determination in spite of the odds.

When you stop to analyze the concept, "encourage" takes on new meaning. It's the act of inspiring others with renewed courage, spirit, hope. When we encourage others we spur them on, we stimulate and affirm them. . . . Most of us need massive doses of it as we slug it out in the trenches. But we are usually too proud to admit it. Unfortunately, this pride is as prevalent among members of God's family as it is on the streets of the world. . . .

The beautiful part about encouragement is this: *Anybody* can do it. You don't need a lot of money to carry it out. You don't even need to be a certain age. In fact, some of the most encouraging actions or words I've received have come from my own children at a time when my heart was heavy. They saw the need and moved right in. . . . They "came alongside and helped."

(From *Strengthening Your Grip* by Charles Swindoll)

APPLICATION How would you feel if someone sent a letter to you thanking God for you, boasting of you, and telling you that they were praying for you? We could all use this kind of mail. Write a letter of encouragement to someone this week.

EXPLORATION Encouragement—Ezra 5:1-2; Acts 11:23-24; 14:21-22; 1 Corinthians 14:3; 1 Thessalonians 5:9-11.

Greeting

Paul, Silvanus, and Timothy,

To the church of the Thessalonians in God our Father and the Lord Jesus Christ:

2Grace to you and peace from God our Father and the Lord Jesus
Christ.

God's Final Judgment and Glory

3We are bound to thank God always for you, brethren, as it is fitting, because your faith grows exceedingly, and the love of every one of you all
abounds toward each other, 4so that we ourselves boast of you among the
churches of God for your patience and faith in all your persecutions and
tribulations that you endure, 5*which is* manifest evidence of the righteous
judgment of God, that you may be counted worthy of the kingdom of God,
for which you also suffer; 6since *it is* a righteous thing with God to repay
with tribulation those who trouble you, 7and to *give* you who are troubled
rest with us when the Lord Jesus is revealed from heaven with His mighty
angels, 8in flaming fire taking vengeance on those who do not know God,
and on those who do not obey the gospel of our Lord Jesus Christ. 9These
shall be punished with everlasting destruction from the presence of the
Lord and from the glory of His power, 10when He comes, in that Day, to be
glorified in His saints and to be admired among all those who believe,[a] because our testimony among you was believed.

11Therefore we also pray always for you that our God would count you
worthy of *this* calling, and fulfill all the good pleasure of *His* goodness and
the work of faith with power, 12that the name of our Lord Jesus Christ may
be glorified in you, and you in Him, according to the grace of our God and
the Lord Jesus Christ.

The Great Apostasy

2 Now, brethren, concerning the coming of our Lord Jesus Christ and
our gathering together to Him, we ask you, 2not to be soon shaken in
mind or troubled, either by spirit or by word or by letter, as if from us, as
though the day of Christ[b] had come. 3Let no one deceive you by any
means; for *that Day will not come* unless the falling away comes first, and
the man of sin[c] is revealed, the son of perdition, 4who opposes and exalts
himself above all that is called God or that is worshiped, so that he sits as
God[d] in the temple of God, showing himself that he is God.

5Do you not remember that when I was still with you I told you these
things? 6And now you know what is restraining, that he may be revealed in
his own time. 7For the mystery of lawlessness is already at work; only He[e]
who now restrains *will do so* until He[f] is taken out of the way. 8And then the
lawless one will be revealed, whom the Lord will consume with the breath
of His mouth and destroy with the brightness of His coming. 9The coming
of the *lawless one* is according to the working of Satan, with all power,
signs, and lying wonders, 10and with all unrighteous deception among

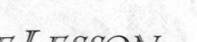

1:10 [a] NU-Text and M-Text read *have believed.*
2:2 [b] NU-Text reads *the Lord.*
2:3 [c] NU-Text reads *lawlessness.*
2:4 [d] NU-Text omits *as God.*
2:7 [e] Or *he* [f] Or *he*

those who perish, because they did not receive the
love of the truth, that they might be saved. [11]And for
this reason God will send them strong delusion, that
they should believe the lie, [12]that they all may be condemned who did not believe the truth but had pleasure in unrighteousness.

Stand Fast

[13]But we are bound to give thanks to God always for
you, brethren beloved by the Lord, because God from
the beginning chose you for salvation through sanctification by the Spirit and belief in the truth, [14]to which
He called you by our gospel, for the obtaining of the
glory of our Lord Jesus Christ. [15]Therefore, brethren,
stand fast and hold the traditions which you were
taught, whether by word or our epistle.
[16]Now may our Lord Jesus Christ Himself, and our
God and Father, who has loved us and given *us* everlasting consolation and good hope by grace, [17]comfort your
hearts and establish you in every good word and work.

Pray for Us

3 Finally, brethren, pray for us, that the word of the
Lord may run *swiftly* and be glorified, just as *it is*
with you, [2]and that we may be delivered from unreasonable and wicked men; for not all have faith.
[3]But the Lord is faithful, who will establish you and
guard *you* from the evil one. [4]And we have confidence
in the Lord concerning you, both that you do and will
do the things we command you.
[5]Now may the Lord direct your hearts into the love
of God and into the patience of Christ.

Warning Against Idleness

[6]But we command you, brethren, in the name of
our Lord Jesus Christ, that you withdraw from every
brother who walks disorderly and not according to
the tradition which he[g] received from us. [7]For you
yourselves know how you ought to follow us, for we
were not disorderly among you; [8]nor did we eat anyone's bread free of charge, but worked with labor and
toil night and day, that we might not be a burden to
any of you, [9]not because we do not have authority, but
to make ourselves an example of how you should
follow us.
[10]For even when we were with you, we commanded
you this: If anyone will not work, neither shall he eat.
[11]For we hear that there are some who walk among
you in a disorderly manner, not working at all, but are
busybodies. [12]Now those who are such we command
and exhort through our Lord Jesus Christ that they
work in quietness and eat their own bread.
[13]But *as for* you, brethren, do not grow weary *in*
doing good. [14]And if anyone does not obey our word
in this epistle, note that person and do not keep company with him, that he may be ashamed. [15]Yet do not
count *him* as an enemy, but admonish *him* as a brother.

Benediction

[16]Now may the Lord of peace Himself give you
peace always in every way. The Lord *be* with you all.
[17]The salutation of Paul with my own hand, which
is a sign in every epistle; so I write.
[18]The grace of our Lord Jesus Christ *be* with you all.
Amen.

3:6 *g* NU-Text and M-Text read *they.*

The First Epistle of Paul to

TIMOTHY

INTRODUCTION

Watch a small boy follow his dad through the snow. He stretches to step where his dad stepped. Not an easy task. His small legs extend as far as they can so his feet can fall in his father's prints.

The father, seeing what the son is doing, smiles and begins taking shorter steps, so the son can follow.

It's a picture of discipleship.

In our faith we follow in someone's steps. A parent, a teacher, a hero—none of us are the first to walk the trail. All of us have someone we follow.

In our faith we leave footprints to guide others. A child, a friend, a recent convert. None should be left to walk the trail alone.

It's the principle of discipleship.

Timothy didn't walk the trail alone. He followed in the steps of Paul, his father in the faith. Paul knew he was following. He also knew the snow was getting deep. So he slowed his pace to help. He penned a letter to Timothy, giving him practical advice on how to lead a church.

As a young minister, Timothy was faced with all sorts of challenges. Step by step, Paul patiently instructs him, and in doing so, he instructs us.

A few questions to consider as you read. Who are you following? When you get where you are going, will it be where you intended? Also, what kind of trail are you leaving? If someone follows your steps, will they arrive at the right place?

The message of First Timothy urges you: Watch your step.

LIFE LESSON

1 Timothy 2:1-15

SITUATION Paul laid down guidelines for proper worship. He emphasized the importance of prayer and orderly worship.

OBSERVATION Prayer is an important part of public worship.

INSPIRATION We live in a society that is reasonably organized. Put a letter in the box, and it usually ends up where you want it to go. Order an item from a catalog, and it usually comes to you in the right size, color, and model. Ask someone to provide you a service, and it is reasonable to expect that it will work out that way. In other words, we are used to results in response to our arrangements. That is why prayer can be discouraging for some of us. How can we predict the result? We are tempted to abandon prayer as a viable exercise and try getting the results ourselves.

But the fact is that my prayer life cannot be directly tied to the results I expect or demand. I have had many opportunities by now to see that the things I want God to do in response to my prayers can be unhealthy for me. I have begun to see that *worship and intercession are far more the business of aligning myself with God's purposes than asking Him to align with mine.*

Henri Nouwen says it best when he writes:

"Prayer is a radical conversion of all our mental processes because in prayer we move away from ourselves, our worries, preoccupation, and self-gratification—and direct all that we recognize as ours to God in the simple trust that through His love all will be made new."

(From *Ordering Your Private World* by Gordon MacDonald)

APPLICATION Worship God today and join with other Christians this Sunday in public prayer, singing, and Bible teaching. Let corporate worship become a first priority to you.

EXPLORATION Worship—1 Chronicles 16:29; Nehemiah 9:2-3; Psalm 100:2; Jeremiah 7:2-3; John 4:24.

Greeting

Paul, an apostle of Jesus Christ, by the commandment of God
our Savior and the Lord Jesus Christ, our hope,
2To Timothy, a true son in the faith:
Grace, mercy, *and* peace from God our Father and Jesus
Christ our Lord.

No Other Doctrine

3As I urged you when I went into Macedonia—remain in Ephesus that
you may charge some that they teach no other doctrine, 4nor give heed to
fables and endless genealogies, which cause disputes rather than godly
edification which is in faith. 5Now the purpose of the commandment is
love from a pure heart, *from* a good conscience, and *from* sincere faith,
6from which some, having strayed, have turned aside to idle talk, 7desiring
to be teachers of the law, understanding neither what they say nor the
things which they affirm.
8But we know that the law *is* good if one uses it lawfully, 9knowing this:
that the law is not made for a righteous person, but for *the* lawless and insubordinate, for *the* ungodly and for sinners, for *the* unholy and profane,
for murderers of fathers and murderers of mothers, for manslayers, 10for
fornicators, for sodomites, for kidnappers, for liars, for perjurers, and if
there is any other thing that is contrary to sound doctrine, 11according to
the glorious gospel of the blessed God which was committed to my trust.

Glory to God for His Grace

12And I thank Christ Jesus our Lord who has enabled me, because He
counted me faithful, putting *me* into the ministry, 13although I was formerly a blasphemer, a persecutor, and an insolent man; but I obtained
mercy because I did *it* ignorantly in unbelief. 14And the grace of our Lord
was exceedingly abundant, with faith and love which are in Christ Jesus.
15This *is* a faithful saying and worthy of all acceptance, that Christ Jesus
came into the world to save sinners, of whom I am chief. 16However, for
this reason I obtained mercy, that in me first Jesus Christ might show all
longsuffering, as a pattern to those who are going to believe on Him for
everlasting life. 17Now to the King eternal, immortal, invisible, to God who
alone is wise,[a] *be* honor and glory forever and ever. Amen.

Fight the Good Fight

18This charge I commit to you, son Timothy, according to the prophecies
previously made concerning you, that by them you may wage the good warfare, 19having faith and a good conscience, which some having rejected, concerning the faith have suffered shipwreck, 20of whom are Hymenaeus and
Alexander, whom I delivered to Satan that they may learn not to blaspheme.

Pray for All Men

2 Therefore I exhort first of all that supplications, prayers, intercessions,
and giving of thanks be made for all men, 2for kings and all who are in
authority, that we may lead a quiet and peaceable life in all godliness and

1:17 [a] NU-Text reads *to the only God.*

reverence. [3]For this *is* good and acceptable in the sight of God our Savior,
[4]who desires all men to be saved and to come to the knowledge of the
truth. [5]For *there is* one God and one Mediator between God and men, *the*
Man Christ Jesus, [6]who gave Himself a ransom for all, to be testified in due
time, [7]for which I was appointed a preacher and an apostle—I am speaking the truth in Christ[b] *and* not lying—a teacher of the Gentiles in faith
and truth.

Men and Women in the Church

[8]I desire therefore that the men pray everywhere, lifting up holy hands,
without wrath and doubting; [9]in like manner also, that the women adorn
themselves in modest apparel, with propriety and moderation, not with
braided hair or gold or pearls or costly clothing, [10]but, which is proper for
women professing godliness, with good works. [11]Let a woman learn in silence with all submission. [12]And I do not permit a woman to teach or to
have authority over a man, but to be in silence. [13]For Adam was formed
first, then Eve. [14]And Adam was not deceived, but the woman being deceived, fell into transgression. [15]Nevertheless she will be saved in
childbearing if they continue in faith, love, and holiness, with self-control.

Qualifications of Overseers

3 This *is* a faithful saying: If a man desires the position of a bishop,[c] he
desires a good work. [2]A bishop then must be blameless, the husband
of one wife, temperate, sober-minded, of good behavior, hospitable, able
to teach; [3]not given to wine, not violent, not greedy for money,[d] but gentle,
not quarrelsome, not covetous; [4]one who rules his own house well, having
his children in submission with all reverence [5](for if a man does not know
how to rule his own house, how will he take care of the church of God?);
[6]not a novice, lest being puffed up with pride he fall into the *same*
condemnation as the devil. [7]Moreover he must have a good testimony
among those who are outside, lest he fall into reproach and the snare of
the devil.

Qualifications of Deacons

[8]Likewise deacons *must be* reverent, not double-tongued, not given to
much wine, not greedy for money, [9]holding the mystery of the faith with a
pure conscience. [10]But let these also first be tested; then let them serve as
deacons, being *found* blameless. [11]Likewise, *their* wives *must be* reverent,
not slanderers, temperate, faithful in all things. [12]Let deacons be the husbands of one wife, ruling *their* children and their own houses well. [13]For
those who have served well as deacons obtain for themselves a good
standing and great boldness in the faith which is in Christ Jesus.

The Great Mystery

[14]These things I write to you, though I hope to come to you shortly; [15]but
if I am delayed, *I write* so that you may know how you ought to conduct
yourself in the house of God, which is the church of the living God, the pillar and ground of the truth. [16]And without controversy great is the mystery
of godliness:

2:7 [b] NU-Text omits *in Christ.*
3:1 [c] Literally *overseer*
3:3 [d] NU-Text omits *not greedy for money.*

LIFE LESSON

1 Timothy 3:1-16

SITUATION Paul laid down certain qualifications for selecting leaders in the church. These qualifications would help the church weed out undeserving candidates, develop Christian maturity, and bring glory and honor to God.

OBSERVATION Leaders must know God's Word and have a mature Christian lifestyle. Every Christian ought to pursue these characteristics. Leaders must already have them.

INSPIRATION How do we tear down the pedestals? How do we vigorously assert the biblical mind-set of servant leadership, so radically at odds with the celebrity-crazed culture in which we live? Like everything else, it begins with each of us coming under the conviction of God's truth. All of us—pastors and lay leaders and parishioners—need to take a hard look at ourselves.

First, we must reassess our objectives. . . .

The church, as a witness to the kingdom of God, is to be a community that worships God and equips men and women to be disciples, growing in holiness and service. How can the church fulfill these functions if it is not a servant church—from pulpit to pew? And this being the case, the principal job of the pastor is to equip others to serve. . . .

Our second task is to consciously strive to avoid the snares. This is not easy. Temptations surround us every day—both our natural inclinations and the world's style of authoritarian leadership. But there are ways to protect ourselves. . . .

William Booth, founder and first general of the Salvation Army, sent a command to all of his missionaries in India: "Go to the Indian as a brother, which indeed you are, and show the love which none can doubt you feel . . . eat and drink and dress and live by his side. Speak his language, share his sorrow." . . .

As Dietrich Bonhoeffer put it: "The church is herself only when she exists for humanity. . . . She must

Continued

take her part in the social life of the world, not lording it over men, but helping and serving them. She must tell men, whatever their calling, what it means to live in Christ, to exist for others."

If the church can only be the church when it exists for others, then the Christian can only be truly Christian when he or she is willing to be emptied out for others. There are no harder words in all of Scripture than Jesus' commandment that we love one another as He loved us—which means love that lays down its life for another.

(From *The Body* by Charles Colson)

APPLICATION Make a list of all the qualifications Paul gave Timothy for Christian leadership. Rate yourself on each item. What three need your attention most? What steps can you take toward maturity? Pray that your family and friends would notice a difference in the next weeks as you sharpen your character.

EXPLORATION Leadership—Exodus 15:13; Numbers 27:15-17; Deuteronomy 1:9-18; Luke 22:24-27; Titus 1:5-9; Hebrews 13:17-19.

God[e] was manifested in the flesh,
Justified in the Spirit,
Seen by angels,
Preached among the Gentiles,
Believed on in the world,
Received up in glory.

The Great Apostasy

4 Now the Spirit expressly says that in latter times some will depart from the faith, giving heed to deceiving spirits and doctrines of demons, 2speaking lies in hypocrisy, having their own conscience seared with a hot iron, 3forbidding to marry, *and commanding* to abstain from foods which God created to be received with thanksgiving by those who believe and know the truth. 4For every creature of God *is* good, and nothing is to be refused if it is received with thanksgiving; 5for it is sanctified by the word of God and prayer.

A Good Servant of Jesus Christ

6If you instruct the brethren in these things, you will be a good minister of Jesus Christ, nourished in the words of faith and of the good doctrine which you have carefully followed. 7But reject profane and old wives' fables, and exercise yourself toward godliness. 8For bodily exercise profits a little, but godliness is profitable for all things, having promise of the life that now is and of that which is to come. 9This *is* a faithful saying and worthy of all acceptance. 10For to this *end* we both labor and suffer reproach,[f] because we trust in the living God, who is *the* Savior of all men, especially of those who believe. 11These things command and teach.

Take Heed to Your Ministry

12Let no one despise your youth, but be an example to the believers in word, in conduct, in love, in spirit,[g] in faith, in purity. 13Till I come, give attention to reading, to exhortation, to doctrine. 14Do not neglect the gift that is in you, which was given to you by prophecy with the laying on of the hands of the eldership. 15Meditate on these things; give yourself entirely to them, that your progress may be evident to all. 16Take heed to yourself and to the doctrine. Continue in them, for in doing this you will save both yourself and those who hear you.

Treatment of Church Members

5 Do not rebuke an older man, but exhort *him* as a father, younger men as brothers, 2older women as mothers, younger women as sisters, with all purity.

Honor True Widows

3Honor widows who are really widows. 4But if any widow has children or grandchildren, let them first learn to show piety at home and to repay their parents; for this is good and[h] acceptable before God. 5Now she who is

3:16 [e] NU-Text reads *Who.*
4:10 [f] NU-Text reads *we labor and strive.*
4:12 [g] NU-Text omits *in spirit.*
5:4 [h] NU-Text and M-Text omit *good and.*

really a widow, and left alone, trusts in God and continues in supplications
and prayers night and day. 6But she who lives in pleasure is dead while she
lives. 7And these things command, that they may be blameless. 8But if
anyone does not provide for his own, and especially for those of his household, he has denied the faith and is worse than an unbeliever.
9Do not let a widow under sixty years old be taken into the number, *and
not unless* she has been the wife of one man, 10well reported for good
works: if she has brought up children, if she has lodged strangers, if she
has washed the saints' feet, if she has relieved the afflicted, if she has diligently followed every good work.
11But refuse *the* younger widows; for when they have begun to grow
wanton against Christ, they desire to marry, 12having condemnation because they have cast off their first faith. 13And besides they learn *to be* idle,
wandering about from house to house, and not only idle but also gossips
and busybodies, saying things which they ought not. 14Therefore I desire
that *the* younger *widows* marry, bear children, manage the house, give no
opportunity to the adversary to speak reproachfully. 15For some have already turned aside after Satan. 16If any believing man or[i] woman has widows, let them relieve them, and do not let the church be burdened, that it
may relieve those who are really widows.

Honor the Elders

17Let the elders who rule well be counted worthy of double honor, especially those who labor in the word and doctrine. 18For the Scripture says,
"*You shall not muzzle an ox while it treads out the grain,*"[j] and, "The laborer *is* worthy of his wages."[k] 19Do not receive an accusation against an
elder except from two or three witnesses. 20Those who are sinning rebuke
in the presence of all, that the rest also may fear.
21I charge *you* before God and the Lord Jesus Christ and the elect angels
that you observe these things without prejudice, doing nothing with partiality. 22Do not lay hands on anyone hastily, nor share in other people's
sins; keep yourself pure.
23No longer drink only water, but use a little wine for your stomach's
sake and your frequent infirmities.
24Some men's sins are clearly evident, preceding *them* to judgment, but
those of some *men* follow later. 25Likewise, the good works *of some* are
clearly evident, and those that are otherwise cannot be hidden.

Honor Masters

6 Let as many bondservants as are under the yoke count their own masters worthy of all honor, so that the name of God and *His* doctrine may
not be blasphemed. 2And those who have believing masters, let them not despise *them* because they are brethren, but rather serve *them* because those
who are benefited are believers and beloved. Teach and exhort these things.

Error and Greed

3If anyone teaches otherwise and does not consent to wholesome
words, *even* the words of our Lord Jesus Christ, and to the doctrine which
accords with godliness, 4he is proud, knowing nothing, but is obsessed

5:16 [i] NU-Text omits *man or.*
5:18 [j] Deuteronomy 25:4 [k] Luke 10:7

Life Lesson

1 Timothy 4:1-16

SITUATION False teachers have always blemished the church. The false teachers in the Ephesian church did not believe Jesus was really human. They contradicted Scripture while appearing to be self-disciplined and morally righteous.

OBSERVATION Christian leaders must be disciplined. They must guard their motives, be faithful to God and his Word, and live commendable lives. A false teacher can easily be detected if the teacher's message differs from the Bible's truth.

INSPIRATION For you to rest—that is, to live in total acceptance of God's way—demands quiet. . . .

To rest in God permanently means to hand over each activity, each situation of your life, to Him and to learn the habit of trusting Him to work for you.

We don't naturally rest. Naturally we are stewers, tinkerers, and fussers. . . . Have you too much to do? Are you pushed, rushed, harried?

Said George Fox long ago, "Come out of the bustlings you that are bustling."

To guard your inner life, you must guard your outer life. How's your pace? Are you too busy? . . .

Does your pace allow you to keep in touch with yourself—with your inner needs and feelings and longings? Does it allow you time to think, plan, make changes? Does it allow you time to observe carefully the dear ones around you and care for their needs—physical and emotional? Do you have time to really live? . . .

Asian theologian Kosuke Koyama says that in human affairs God moves at something like three miles an hour, the pace at which a person walks, not runs! Are you synchronized to your world, maybe even to your Christian world, but out of sync with God? . . .

You will change when your inner life changes. But I just said your inner life is affected by your outer life! Then is the whole thing a vicious circle that can't be stopped?

No, the change begins with a decision. Your heart is your headquarters.

Continued

with disputes and arguments over words, from which come envy, strife,
reviling, evil suspicions, 5useless wranglings[l] of men of corrupt minds
and destitute of the truth, who suppose that godliness is a *means of* gain.
From such withdraw yourself.[m]

6Now godliness with contentment is great gain. 7For we brought nothing into *this* world, *and it is* certain[n] we can carry nothing out. 8And having
food and clothing, with these we shall be content. 9But those who desire to
be rich fall into temptation and a snare, and *into* many foolish and harmful lusts which drown men in destruction and perdition. 10For the love of
money is a root of all *kinds of* evil, for which some have strayed from the faith
in their greediness, and pierced themselves through with many sorrows.

The Good Confession

11But you, O man of God, flee these things and pursue righteousness,
godliness, faith, love, patience, gentleness. 12Fight the good fight of faith,
lay hold on eternal life, to which you were also called and have confessed
the good confession in the presence of many witnesses. 13I urge you in the
sight of God who gives life to all things, and *before* Christ Jesus who witnessed the good confession before Pontius Pilate, 14that you keep *this* commandment without spot, blameless until our Lord Jesus Christ's
appearing, 15which He will manifest in His own time, *He who is* the blessed
and only Potentate, the King of kings and Lord of lords, 16who alone has
immortality, dwelling in unapproachable light, whom no man has seen or
can see, to whom *be* honor and everlasting power. Amen.

Instructions to the Rich

17Command those who are rich in this present age not to be haughty,
nor to trust in uncertain riches but in the living God, who gives us richly all
things to enjoy. 18*Let them* do good, that they be rich in good works, ready
to give, willing to share, 19storing up for themselves a good foundation for
the time to come, that they may lay hold on eternal life.

Guard the Faith

20O Timothy! Guard what was committed to your trust, avoiding the
profane *and* idle babblings and contradictions of what is falsely called
knowledge— 21by professing it some have strayed concerning the faith.
Grace *be* with you. Amen.

Even as you read this chapter, make the decision, by a conscious act of your will, that you will learn to rest in God both in your inner life and your outer life. Once the decision is made—and you implement it as God opens your eyes to ways to implement it—gradually, gradually over the weeks or years, the changes will come. Your heart will start listening to a different pulse deep within you, and with joy you'll begin to match your steps to that lovely, restful beat.

(From *Disciplines of the Heart* by Anne Ortlund)

APPLICATION Are you satisfied with God's plans for you? Are you discontent because you are too young or too old? Impatient because you are not advancing as high as you would like? Frustrated with your restrictions? Be content where God has placed you. Live your life as an example to others. Speak boldly of what Christ has done for you and what he can do for others.

EXPLORATION Discipline—Proverbs 3:11-12; 12:1; 1 Corinthians 5:1; 2 Corinthians 2:5-11; Hebrews 12:5-11; Revelation 3:19.

6:5 [l] NU-Text and M-Text read *constant friction.* [m] NU-Text omits this sentence.
6:7 [n] NU-Text omits *and it is certain.*

The Second Epistle of Paul to

TIMOTHY

INTRODUCTION

I have kept the faith.

They have taken everything else. They have taken his freedom—he's locked in a Roman prison. They have taken his possessions—he hasn't even a shawl to keep him warm. They have taken his churches—he will not see them again. They have taken his future—he is sentenced to die.

What do you have left, Paul? What do you have left to show for your life? Had you stayed a Jew in Jerusalem, you'd have a seat of status and a house of retirement. Had you been more compromising, you might have gone unnoticed by the Romans. Had you been less passionate, you might have pastored a church and stayed in one city. But you were too convinced to compromise—too convicted to stay home.

And now, with the end in sight, with the verdict rendered and the end in sight, what do you have left?

The old apostle leans forward with eyes twinkling and says, *I have kept the faith.*

That was the heart of the apostle. And that is the heart of this Epistle. As far as we know, this is the last one he ever wrote. Paul picks up his pen one final time. He knows the end is near. "I am already being poured out as a drink offering," he tells Timothy, his son in the faith.

But he has no regrets, only counsel—practical, inspirational counsel for young Timothy, who has been left to lead the church in Ephesus. His tenderness for the young minister peeks out from behind every word. "Be diligent," he urges, "to present yourself approved to God, a worker who does not need to be ashamed, rightly dividing the word of truth" (2:15).

Timothy never had another teacher like Paul. The world has never had another teacher like Paul. He was convinced of two facts—he was once lost but then saved. He spent a lifetime telling every person who would listen.

In the end it cost him everything. For in the end, all he had was his faith. But in the end, his faith was all he needed.

LIFE LESSON

2 Timothy 1:1-18

SITUATION Paul gave hope and encouragement to Timothy. Christians came under increasing persecution from Romans throughout the empire. The pressure to abandon the faith was strong.

OBSERVATION We must seek strength from the Lord to deal with daily stresses and the pressure to abandon our faith.

INSPIRATION In our house we call 5:00 p.m. the piranha hour. That's the time of day when everyone wants a piece of Mom. Sara, the baby, is hungry. Andrea wants Mom to read her a book. Jenna wants help with her homework. And I–the ever-loving, ever-sensitive husband–want Denalyn to drop everything and talk to me about my day.

When is your piranha hour? When do people in your world demand much and offer little?

Every boss has had a day in which the requests outnumber the results. There's not a businessperson alive who hasn't groaned as an armada of assignments docks at his or her desk. For the teacher, the piranha hour often begins when the first student enters and ends when the last student leaves.

Piranha hours: parents have them, bosses endure them, secretaries dread them, teachers are besieged by them, and Jesus taught us how to live through them successfully.

When hands extended and voices demanded, Jesus responded with love. He did so because the code within him disarmed the alarm. The code is worth noting: "People are precious."

(From *In the Eye of the Storm* by Max Lucado)

APPLICATION Do daily stresses cause you to doubt the power of God? Guard your heart against the external influences that attack your faith.Turn to the Lord for wisdom and strength to counter these challenges.

EXPLORATION Pressure—Genesis 25:32-33; Judges 6:25-30; Proverbs 4:23; Matthew 4:1; James 1:2-4.

Greeting

Paul, an apostle of Jesus Christ[a] by the will of God, according to
the promise of life which is in Christ Jesus,
[2]To Timothy, a beloved son:
Grace, mercy, *and* peace from God the Father and Christ Jesus our Lord.

Timothy's Faith and Heritage

[3]I thank God, whom I serve with a pure conscience, as *my* forefathers *did*,
as without ceasing I remember you in my prayers night and day, [4]greatly
desiring to see you, being mindful of your tears, that I may be filled with joy,
[5]when I call to remembrance the genuine faith that is in you, which dwelt
first in your grandmother Lois and your mother Eunice, and I am persuaded
is in you also. [6]Therefore I remind you to stir up the gift of God which is in
you through the laying on of my hands. [7]For God has not given us a spirit of
fear, but of power and of love and of a sound mind.

Not Ashamed of the Gospel

[8]Therefore do not be ashamed of the testimony of our Lord, nor of me
His prisoner, but share with me in the sufferings for the gospel according
to the power of God, [9]who has saved us and called *us* with a holy calling,
not according to our works, but according to His own purpose and grace
which was given to us in Christ Jesus before time began, [10]but has now been
revealed by the appearing of our Savior Jesus Christ, *who* has abolished
death and brought life and immortality to light through the gospel, [11]to which
I was appointed a preacher, an apostle, and a teacher of the Gentiles.[b] [12]For
this reason I also suffer these things; nevertheless I am not ashamed, for I
know whom I have believed and am persuaded that He is able to keep
what I have committed to Him until that Day.

Be Loyal to the Faith

[13]Hold fast the pattern of sound words which you have heard from me,
in faith and love which are in Christ Jesus. [14]That good thing which was
committed to you, keep by the Holy Spirit who dwells in us.
[15]This you know, that all those in Asia have turned away from me,
among whom are Phygellus and Hermogenes. [16]The Lord grant mercy to
the household of Onesiphorus, for he often refreshed me, and was not
ashamed of my chain; [17]but when he arrived in Rome, he sought me out
very zealously and found *me*. [18]The Lord grant to him that he may find
mercy from the Lord in that Day—and you know very well how many
ways he ministered *to me*[c] at Ephesus.

Be Strong in Grace

2 You therefore, my son, be strong in the grace that is in Christ Jesus.
[2]And the things that you have heard from me among many witnesses,
commit these to faithful men who will be able to teach others also. [3]You
therefore must endure[d] hardship as a good soldier of Jesus Christ. [4]No one

1:1 [a] NU-Text and M-Text read *Christ Jesus.*
1:11 [b] NU-Text omits *of the Gentiles.*
1:18 [c] *To me* is from the Vulgate and a few Greek manuscripts.
2:3 [d] NU-Text reads *You must share.*

engaged in warfare entangles himself with the affairs of *this* life, that he
may please him who enlisted him as a soldier. 5 And also if anyone competes
in athletics, he is not crowned unless he competes according to the rules.
6 The hardworking farmer must be first to partake of the crops. 7 Consider
what I say, and may[e] the Lord give you understanding in all things.
8 Remember that Jesus Christ, of the seed of David, was raised from the
dead according to my gospel, 9 for which I suffer trouble as an evildoer, *even*
to the point of chains; but the word of God is not chained. 10 Therefore I endure
all things for the sake of the elect, that they also may obtain the salvation
which is in Christ Jesus with eternal glory.
11 *This is* a faithful saying:

For if we died with *Him,*
We shall also live with *Him.*
12 If we endure,
We shall also reign with *Him.*
If we deny *Him,*
He also will deny us.
13 If we are faithless,
He remains faithful;
He cannot deny Himself.

Approved and Disapproved Workers

14 Remind *them* of these things, charging *them* before the Lord not to
strive about words to no profit, to the ruin of the hearers. 15 Be diligent to
present yourself approved to God, a worker who does not need to be
ashamed, rightly dividing the word of truth. 16 But shun profane *and* idle
babblings, for they will increase to more ungodliness. 17 And their message
will spread like cancer. Hymenaeus and Philetus are of this sort, 18 who have
strayed concerning the truth, saying that the resurrection is already past;
and they overthrow the faith of some. 19 Nevertheless the solid foundation
of God stands, having this seal: "The Lord knows those who are His," and,
"Let everyone who names the name of Christ[f] depart from iniquity."
20 But in a great house there are not only vessels of gold and silver, but
also of wood and clay, some for honor and some for dishonor. 21 Therefore
if anyone cleanses himself from the latter, he will be a vessel for honor,
sanctified and useful for the Master, prepared for every good work. 22 Flee
also youthful lusts; but pursue righteousness, faith, love, peace with those
who call on the Lord out of a pure heart. 23 But avoid foolish and ignorant
disputes, knowing that they generate strife. 24 And a servant of the Lord
must not quarrel but be gentle to all, able to teach, patient, 25 in humility cor-
recting those who are in opposition, if God perhaps will grant them repentance, so that they may know the truth, 26 and *that* they may come to their
senses *and escape* the snare of the devil, having been taken captive by him
to *do* his will.

Perilous Times and Perilous Men

3 But know this, that in the last days perilous times will come: 2 For men will
be lovers of themselves, lovers of money, boasters, proud, blasphemers, disobedient to parents, unthankful, unholy, 3 unloving, unforgiving,

2:7 [e] NU-Text reads *the Lord will give you.*
2:19 [f] NU-Text and M-Text read *the Lord.*

LIFE LESSON

2 Timothy 2:1-26

SITUATION Believers in Timothy's church had lost their focus on Christ. Paul knew that concentrating on Christ and ignoring personal annoyances would help Timothy's problems.

OBSERVATION Christians, even those enduring suffering, must focus on Jesus the Savior and avoid being distracted by worldly problems.

INSPIRATION In the shop of a blacksmith, there are three types of tools.

There are tools on the junkpile: outdated, broken, dull, rusty. . . .

There are tools on the anvil: melted down, molten hot, moldable, changeable. . . .

There are tools of usefulness: sharpened, primed, defined, mobile. They lie ready in the blacksmith's toolchest, available to their master, fulfilling their calling. . . .

We are all somewhere in the blacksmith's shop. We are either on the scrap pile, on the anvil, in the Master's hands, or in the toolchest. (Some of us have been in all three.) . . .

From the shelves to the workbench, from the water to the fire. . . .

I'm sure that somewhere you'll see yourself. . . .

The rubbish pile of broken tools, the anvil of recasting, the hands of the Master—it's a simultaneously joyful and painful voyage.

And for you who make the journey—who leave the heap and enter the fire, dare to be pounded on God's anvil, and doggedly seek to discover your own purpose—take courage, for you await the privilege of being called "God's chosen instruments."

(From *On the Anvil* by Max Lucado)

APPLICATION Is your walk with the Lord obscured by day-to-day annoyances? Remember the priority of your relationship with the Lord and get back on track through prayer, Bible study, and worship.

EXPLORATION Focus—Judges 15:18; Nehemiah 13:25-29; 2 Corinthians 11:3.

LIFE LESSON

2 Timothy 3:1–4:8

SITUATION Paul warned that godlessness and evil schemes would increase as the end of history approached. People would follow false teachers who would tell them what they wanted to hear. Paul's words warned and encouraged Timothy to teach the Scriptures soundly.

OBSERVATION Christians must guard against deceit by knowing what Scripture teaches.

INSPIRATION The apostle Paul warned that many will follow the false teachers, not knowing that in feeding upon what these people say they are taking the devil's poison into their own lives. Thousands of people in every walk of life are being deceived today. False teachers use high-sounding words that seem like the height of logic, scholarship, and sophistication. They are intellectually clever and crafty in their sophistry. They are adept at beguiling men and women whose spiritual foundations are weak.

These false teachers have departed from the faith of God revealed in the Scripture. . . .

Writing to Timothy, the apostle Paul warned, "Now the Spirit expressly says that in latter times some will depart from the faith, giving heed to deceiving spirits and doctrines of demons, speaking lies in hypocrisy, having their own conscience seared with a hot iron."

Paul later wrote to Timothy, "For the time will come when they will not endure sound doctrine, but according to their own desires, because they have itching ears, they will heap up for themselves teachers; and they will turn their ears away from the truth, and be turned aside to fables." Doesn't this sound familiar today? . . .

God's plan is not abstract or unclear. It is not a secret. He says very clearly, "I love you!" He has called tens of thousands all over the world to proclaim His love to the world and to call every man, woman, and child to His

slanderers, without self-control, brutal, despisers of good, 4traitors, head-
strong, haughty, lovers of pleasure rather than lovers of God, 5having a
form of godliness but denying its power. And from such people turn away!
6For of this sort are those who creep into households and make captives of
gullible women loaded down with sins, led away by various lusts, 7always
learning and never able to come to the knowledge of the truth. 8Now as
Jannes and Jambres resisted Moses, so do these also resist the truth: men of
corrupt minds, disapproved concerning the faith; 9but they will progress
no further, for their folly will be manifest to all, as theirs also was.

The Man of God and the Word of God

10But you have carefully followed my doctrine, manner of life, purpose,
faith, longsuffering, love, perseverance, 11persecutions, afflictions, which
happened to me at Antioch, at Iconium, at Lystra—what persecutions I
endured. And out of *them* all the Lord delivered me. 12Yes, and all who desire to live godly in Christ Jesus will suffer persecution. 13But evil men and
impostors will grow worse and worse, deceiving and being deceived. 14But
you must continue in the things which you have learned and been assured
of, knowing from whom you have learned *them,* 15and that from childhood you have known the Holy Scriptures, which are able to make you
wise for salvation through faith which is in Christ Jesus.
16All Scripture *is* given by inspiration of God, and *is* profitable for doctrine, for reproof, for correction, for instruction in righteousness, 17that the
man of God may be complete, thoroughly equipped for every good work.

Preach the Word

4 I charge *you* therefore before God and the Lord Jesus Christ, who will
judge the living and the dead at[g] His appearing and His kingdom:
2Preach the word! Be ready in season *and* out of season. Convince, rebuke,
exhort, with all longsuffering and teaching. 3For the time will come when
they will not endure sound doctrine, but according to their own desires,
because they have itching ears, they will heap up for themselves teachers;
4and they will turn *their* ears away from the truth, and be turned aside to
fables. 5But you be watchful in all things, endure afflictions, do the work of
an evangelist, fulfill your ministry.

Paul's Valedictory

6For I am already being poured out as a drink offering, and the time of
my departure is at hand. 7I have fought the good fight, I have finished the
race, I have kept the faith. 8Finally, there is laid up for me the crown of
righteousness, which the Lord, the righteous Judge, will give to me on that
Day, and not to me only but also to all who have loved His appearing.

The Abandoned Apostle

9Be diligent to come to me quickly; 10for Demas has forsaken me, having
loved this present world, and has departed for Thessalonica—Crescens
for Galatia, Titus for Dalmatia. 11Only Luke is with me. Get Mark and bring
him with you, for he is useful to me for ministry. 12And Tychicus I have
sent to Ephesus. 13Bring the cloak that I left with Carpus at Troas when you
come—and the books, especially the parchments.

4:1 [g] NU-Text omits *therefore* and reads *and by* for *at.*

14 Alexander the coppersmith did me much harm. May the Lord repay
him according to his works. 15 You also must beware of him, for he has
greatly resisted our words.
16 At my first defense no one stood with me, but all forsook me. May it
not be charged against them.

The Lord Is Faithful

17 But the Lord stood with me and strengthened me, so that the message
might be preached fully through me, and *that* all the Gentiles might hear.
Also I was delivered out of the mouth of the lion. 18 And the Lord will deliver
me from every evil work and preserve *me* for His heavenly kingdom. To
Him *be* glory forever and ever. Amen!

Come Before Winter

19 Greet Prisca and Aquila, and the household of Onesiphorus. 20 Erastus
stayed in Corinth, but Trophimus I have left in Miletus sick.
21 Do your utmost to come before winter.
Eubulus greets you, as well as Pudens, Linus, Claudia, and all the brethren.

Farewell

22 The Lord Jesus Christ[h] be with your spirit. Grace be with you. Amen.

loving arms. To exemplify the army of God that is going forth at this moment into the world I can think of no better example than the thousands of "barefoot preachers" and other itinerant evangelists we helped train in Amsterdam during the past decade. . . .

Preachers, teachers, students, and mission helpers came from all over the world. Thousands came from Africa. . . . They came from all over Asia, Latin America, and Eastern Europe, and they went out into the streets of Amsterdam to see and learn and share the love of Jesus Christ with others.

Today that mighty army of traveling preachers from every corner of the world is traveling from village to village and house to house preaching the good news of God's love. Why do they do it? For the money? No, they receive almost no support for what they do. Many are lucky if they have a bicycle, a Bible, and a change of clothes. Do they do it for fame and fortune? There is none. In most cases only God knows what good works these humble, sincere pastors have done.

They do it because Jesus Christ is alive! He is living in their hearts, and that good news is something worthy to share with the world. They are compelled by the life that is in them to tell everyone that Jesus is Lord. If Jesus Christ is *not* the son of God, nothing matters. But if He is, *nothing else matters!*

(From *Storm Warning* by Billy Graham)

APPLICATION False religious teachers today still deceive people with twisted versions of "truth" that hurt people and sidetrack lives. Keep such people away from your family and church. You will find strength in the true gospel, not in phony substitutes.

EXPLORATION False Teachers—Deuteronomy 13:1-3; Matthew 7:15; 24:11; Mark 13:22-23; 2 Corinthians 11:3-4; 1 John 1:8-10; 1 Timothy 4:1-2.

4:22 *h* NU-Text omits *Jesus Christ.*

The Epistle of Paul to

TITUS

INTRODUCTION

The letter to Titus was the result of two storms.

The first was a storm which left Paul on the Island of Crete (Acts 27). The second was a storm of relativism which left the Cretans with little values.

"Cretans are always liars, evil beasts, lazy gluttons." The words didn't originate with Paul but might as well have. He used them to summarize the state of affairs on the island (1:12).

He had reason to lament. By the time of Paul the society had a despicable reputation. Greed was god. Schemers were admired. Cheating was wrong only if you got caught. Right and wrong were determined by the situation, and rape was not a crime.

The economy was so bad that boys were sold as mercenaries as young as the age of twelve. Hence, the people were left with few male role models and fewer abiding beliefs.

Paul established the church in the society and sent Titus to "set in order the things that [were] lacking" (1:5). Since Paul had definite ideas as to what still needed to be done, we are given definite principles of a healthy church. Strong leadership is the first item. Titus is instructed to select elders and to do so carefully (1:4–16).

Strong character is the next. Judging from the style of life in Crete, it would have been easy for the Cretan Christians to compromise their convictions. Paul urges them not to.

Judging from the style of life in our world, we could do with the same reminder.

By the way, don't miss Paul's eloquent paragraph on grace (2:11–14). We're familiar with grace which saves, but grace does much more. It trains us to, "live soberly, righteously, and godly in the present age."

Something told Paul the Cretans needed such instruction. Something tells me, we do too.

Life Lesson

Titus 2:1-15

SITUATION The Christians in Titus' church needed role models. Imitating those who lived a God-honoring life would help them be morally distinct from their culture.

OBSERVATION As we grow to become more like Christ, our behavior grows more distinctive from the world.

INSPIRATION Now I see why powerful people often wear sunglasses—the spotlight blinds them to reality. . . . They are under the impression that earthly authority will make a heavenly difference (it won't).

Can I prove my point? Take this quiz.

Name the ten wealthiest men in the world.

Name the last ten Heisman trophy winners.

Name the last ten winners of the Miss America contest.

Name eight people who have won the Nobel or Pulitzer prize. . . .

How did you do? I didn't do well either. With the exception of you trivia hounds, none of us remember the headliners of yesterday too well. . . . Awards tarnish. Achievements are forgotten. Accolades and certificates are buried with their owners.

Here's another quiz. See how you do on this one.

Think of three people you enjoy spending time with. . . .

List a few teachers who have aided your journey through school.

Name half-a-dozen heroes whose stories have inspired you.

Easier? It was for me, too. The lesson? The people who make a difference are not the ones with the credentials, but the ones with the concern.

(From *And the Angels Were Silent* by Max Lucado)

APPLICATION Ask God in the coming month to lead you to a friend of a different generation, race, or ethnic group . . . someone to sharpen your faith.

EXPLORATION Role Models—Matthew 5:13-16; 2 Peter 1:5-7; Ephesians 4:29; Colossians 3:16; Romans 15:14; 2 Timothy 2:24-26; Hebrews 10:24-25.

Greeting

Paul, a bondservant of God and an apostle of Jesus Christ, according to the faith of God's elect and the acknowledgment of the
truth which accords with godliness, 2in hope of eternal life
which God, who cannot lie, promised before time began, 3but has
in due time manifested His word through preaching, which was committed
to me according to the commandment of God our Savior;

4To Titus, a true son in *our* common faith:

Grace, mercy, *and* peace from God the Father and the Lord Jesus Christ[a]
our Savior.

Qualified Elders

5For this reason I left you in Crete, that you should set in order the things
that are lacking, and appoint elders in every city as I commanded you— 6if
a man is blameless, the husband of one wife, having faithful children not
accused of dissipation or insubordination. 7For a bishop[b] must be blameless,
as a steward of God, not self-willed, not quick-tempered, not given to wine,
not violent, not greedy for money, 8but hospitable, a lover of what is good,
sober-minded, just, holy, self-controlled, 9holding fast the faithful word as
he has been taught, that he may be able, by sound doctrine, both to exhort
and convict those who contradict.

The Elders' Task

10For there are many insubordinate, both idle talkers and deceivers, especially those of the circumcision, 11whose mouths must be stopped, who subvert whole households, teaching things which they ought not, for the sake of
dishonest gain. 12One of them, a prophet of their own, said, "Cretans *are* always
liars, evil beasts, lazy gluttons." 13This testimony is true. Therefore rebuke
them sharply, that they may be sound in the faith, 14not giving heed to Jewish
fables and commandments of men who turn from the truth. 15To the pure
all things are pure, but to those who are defiled and unbelieving nothing
is pure; but even their mind and conscience are defiled. 16They profess to
know God, but in works they deny Him, being abominable, disobedient,
and disqualified for every good work.

Qualities of a Sound Church

2 But as for you, speak the things which are proper for sound doctrine:
2that the older men be sober, reverent, temperate, sound in faith, in
love, in patience; 3the older women likewise, that they be reverent in behavior, not slanderers, not given to much wine, teachers of good things—
4that they admonish the young women to love their husbands, to love their
children, 5to be discreet, chaste, homemakers, good, obedient to their own
husbands, that the word of God may not be blasphemed.

6Likewise, exhort the young men to be sober-minded, 7in all things
showing yourself *to be* a pattern of good works; in doctrine *showing* integrity, reverence, incorruptibility,[c] 8sound speech that cannot be condemned, that one who is an opponent may be ashamed, having nothing
evil to say of you.[d]

1:4 [a] NU-Text reads *and Christ Jesus.*
1:7 [b] Literally *overseer*
2:7 [c] NU-Text omits *incorruptibility.*
2:8 [d] NU-Text and M-Text read *us.*

9*Exhort* bondservants to be obedient to their own masters, to be well pleasing in all *things,* not answering back, 10not pilfering, but showing all good fidelity, that they may adorn the doctrine of God our Savior in all things.

Trained by Saving Grace

11For the grace of God that brings salvation has appeared to all men, 12teaching us that, denying ungodliness and worldly lusts, we should live soberly, righteously, and godly in the present age, 13looking for the blessed hope and glorious appearing of our great God and Savior Jesus Christ, 14who gave Himself for us, that He might redeem us from every lawless deed and purify for Himself *His* own special people, zealous for good works.

15Speak these things, exhort, and rebuke with all authority. Let no one despise you.

Graces of the Heirs of Grace

3 Remind them to be subject to rulers and authorities, to obey, to be ready for every good work, 2to speak evil of no one, to be peaceable, gentle, showing all humility to all men. 3For we ourselves were also once foolish, disobedient, deceived, serving various lusts and pleasures, living in malice and envy, hateful and hating one another. 4But when the kindness and the love of God our Savior toward man appeared, 5not by works of righteousness which we have done, but according to His mercy He saved us, through the washing of regeneration and renewing of the Holy Spirit, 6whom He poured out on us abundantly through Jesus Christ our Savior, 7that having been justified by His grace we should become heirs according to the hope of eternal life.

8This is a faithful saying, and these things I want you to affirm constantly, that those who have believed in God should be careful to maintain good works. These things are good and profitable to men.

Avoid Dissension

9But avoid foolish disputes, genealogies, contentions, and strivings about the law; for they are unprofitable and useless. 10Reject a divisive man after the first and second admonition, 11knowing that such a person is warped and sinning, being self-condemned.

Final Messages

12When I send Artemas to you, or Tychicus, be diligent to come to me at Nicopolis, for I have decided to spend the winter there. 13Send Zenas the lawyer and Apollos on their journey with haste, that they may lack nothing. 14And let our *people* also learn to maintain good works, to *meet* urgent needs, that they may not be unfruitful.

Farewell

15All who *are* with me greet you. Greet those who love us in the faith.

Grace *be* with you all. Amen.

LIFE LESSON

Titus 3:1-15

SITUATION Paul reminded Christians that Christ saved them from sin and death. Paul's teaching opposed false teachers who tried to win converts.

OBSERVATION Christians need to be reminded of God's great forgiveness.

INSPIRATION What's the toughest stain to remove? grape juice? coffee? mud? After soaking, scrubbing, and soaking some more, we often give up in frustration. It just won't come out, and the shirt is ruined!

The effects of sin run profoundly deeper than juice-soiled clothing, affecting all of life and staining the soul, with real guilt and painful estrangement from God. And this sin-stain resists every human effort to remove it. No matter how hard we work or hope, or even pray, the contaminating stain remains.

The truth is that only God can cleanse us and make us truly clean. And he promises to do just that . . . through faith, faith in the Son.

Are you struggling with guilt from transgressions and omissions—the whole spectrum of God-ignoring or God-defying attitudes and acts? You can be forgiven, released, and set on the path of righteousness. For a new start and a new life, confess your sins to God and trust in Christ. His stain-remover works!

(From *On Eagle's Wings* by Dave Veerman)

APPLICATION Good works are a sign that we are grateful to God and that we love him. What service project in your community or church could you join? Ask the Lord to guide you to service that pleases him.

EXPLORATION Service—Joshua 24:14-15; Matthew 25:35-45; 1 Corinthians 15:58; Colossians 3:23; 1 Timothy 1:12; 1 Peter 4:10-11.

The Epistle of Paul to

PHILEMON

INTRODUCTION

Philemon had every reason to be angry. His slave, Onesimus, had stolen from him and run away. He had escaped to Rome, where he met Paul and became a believer.

Now Onesimus is returning to Philemon. Under normal circumstances, Philemon has the right to exact revenge. But these are not normal circumstances, Paul explains. Onesimus fled as a slave, he returns as a believer.

Paul doesn't ask Philemon to free Onesimus from slavery, but to free him from anger. He urges Philemon to offer grace rather than demand justice.

Does this short letter have any application for your life? It does if there is an Onesimus in your world. It does if someone has betrayed you or offended you or turned away from you. What they did wasn't right. And to demand justice is only natural, which is precisely the problem. Getting even is natural, it's not spiritual.

As you consider how to respond, consider a higher law. A law which sets all men, slave or nonslave, free.

Life Lesson

Philemon 1-25

SITUATION Both Christians and non-Christians owned slaves in the Roman Empire. Onesimus, a slave from Colosse, stole from his owner, Philemon. After stealing, Onesimus ran away to Rome where Paul met him. Paul led Onesimus to Jesus.

OBSERVATION Paul asked Philemon to forgive and accept his runaway slave back without punishment.

INSPIRATION Among the most wonderful gifts in the forgiveness of sins is this one, that God permits us poor children of the earth to become co-workers in His Kingdom. We are to help spread the knowledge of the availability of this forgiveness to our neighbor next door and in faraway places. . . . We are to speak a word for Him to those who need His comfort and courage. . . . We are to help promote understanding and goodwill. We are to help build the Kingdom of kindness. We are to live redeemed.

(From *Trustful Living* by Carla Holtermann)

APPLICATION Remember that time someone took advantage of you, misled you, or even cheated you? Ask God to help you put the offense out of your mind. Next time you interact with that person, treat the person with love and show that you don't hold a grudge.

EXPLORATION Respect—Job 31:13-15; Proverbs 22:2; Micah 6:8; Romans 13:7; Galatians 3:28; 1 Peter 2:17.

Greeting

Paul, a prisoner of Christ Jesus, and Timothy *our* brother,

To Philemon our beloved *friend* and fellow laborer, 2to the beloved[a] Apphia, Archippus our fellow soldier, and to the church in your house:

3Grace to you and peace from God our Father and the Lord Jesus Christ.

Philemon's Love and Faith

4I thank my God, making mention of you always in my prayers, 5hearing of your love and faith which you have toward the Lord Jesus and toward all the saints, 6that the sharing of your faith may become effective by the acknowledgment of every good thing which is in you[b] in Christ Jesus. 7For we have[c] great joy[d] and consolation in your love, because the hearts of the saints have been refreshed by you, brother.

The Plea for Onesimus

8Therefore, though I might be very bold in Christ to command you what is fitting, 9*yet* for love's sake I rather appeal *to you*—being such a one as Paul, the aged, and now also a prisoner of Jesus Christ— 10I appeal to you for my son Onesimus, whom I have begotten *while* in my chains, 11who once was unprofitable to you, but now is profitable to you and to me.

12I am sending him back.[e] You therefore receive him, that is, my own heart, 13whom I wished to keep with me, that on your behalf he might minister to me in my chains for the gospel. 14But without your consent I wanted to do nothing, that your good deed might not be by compulsion, as it were, but voluntary.

15For perhaps he departed for a while for this *purpose,* that you might receive him forever, 16no longer as a slave but more than a slave—a beloved brother, especially to me but how much more to you, both in the flesh and in the Lord.

Philemon's Obedience Encouraged

17If then you count me as a partner, receive him as *you would* me. 18But if he has wronged you or owes anything, put that on my account. 19I, Paul, am writing with my own hand. I will repay—not to mention to you that you owe me even your own self besides. 20Yes, brother, let me have joy from you in the Lord; refresh my heart in the Lord.

21Having confidence in your obedience, I write to you, knowing that you will do even more than I say. 22But, meanwhile, also prepare a guest room for me, for I trust that through your prayers I shall be granted to you.

Farewell

23Epaphras, my fellow prisoner in Christ Jesus, greets you, 24*as do* Mark, Aristarchus, Demas, Luke, my fellow laborers.

25The grace of our Lord Jesus Christ *be* with your spirit. Amen.

2 [a] NU-Text reads *to our sister Apphia.*
6 [b] NU-Text and M-Text read *us.*
7 [c] NU-Text reads *had.* [d] M-Text reads *thanksgiving.*
12 [e] NU-Text reads *back to you in person, that is, my own heart.*

The Epistle to the HEBREWS

INTRODUCTION

The best just got better—it's a favorite slogan with advertisers.

It's not that our previous product was poor. It's just that the current one is superior.

The Book of Hebrews might well use the same slogan. The best just got better.

There was nothing inferior about the Jewish religion. It was given by God and designed by God. Every principle, rule, and ritual had a wealth of meaning. The Old Testament served as a faithful guide for thousands of people over thousands of years. It was the best offered to man.

But when Christ came, the best got better.

Hebrews was written for Jewish believers who were torn between their new faith and their old ways. The temptation was to slip back into familiar routines and rituals, settling for second best.

The author skillfully makes a case against such a digression. He argues that Jesus is better than every form of the old faith—better than the angels (1:4–2:18), better than their leaders (3:1–4:13), and better than their priests (4:14–7:28). When it comes to comparing the two, there is simply no comparison. Christianity has a better covenant (8:1–13), a better sanctuary, (9:1–10), and a better sacrifice for sins (9:11– 10:18).

It's not that the old law was bad, it's just that the new law—salvation by faith in Christ—is better. Once you've known the best, why settle for second rate?

It's doubtful that you will ever be tempted to exchange your faith for an ancient system of priests and sacrifices. But you will be tempted to exchange it for something inferior.

If you are reading Hebrews, be reminded: Once you've known the best, why settle for anything less? (Hmmm, there's another catchy slogan.)

LIFE LESSON

Hebrews 2:1-18

SITUATION As God's Son, Jesus' authority surpassed any prophet or angel. He is God, yet he became man.

OBSERVATION Because Jesus became man, we know he understands our human frustrations.

INSPIRATION It is an undeniable fact that usually it is those who have suffered most who are best able to comfort others who are passing through suffering. I know of pastors whose ministries have been enriched by suffering. Through their trials they have learned to "live through" the difficulties of the people in their parish. They are able to empathize as well as sympathize with the afflictions of others because of what they have experienced in their own lives.

Our sufferings may be rough and hard to bear, but they teach us lessons which in turn equip and enable us to help others. Our attitutude toward suffering should not be, "Grit your teeth and bear it," hoping it will pass as quickly as possible. Rather, our goal should be to learn all we can from what we are called upon to endure, so that we can fulfill a ministry of comfort—as Jesus did. "Because he himself suffered when he was tempted, he is able to help those who are being tempted" (Hebrews 2:18, NIV). The sufferer becomes the comforter or helper in the service of the Lord.

By the way, by "enduring" suffering, God led me to my wonderful wife, Ruth, who was His intended one for me.

(From *Unto the Hills* by Billy Graham)

APPLICATION Jesus knows all about life on earth. Tell him what will be your biggest temptations and struggles today. Ask him to provide you with strength and encouragement. He knows how you feel.

EXPLORATION Christ's Victory over Sin and Death—Romans 6:5-11.

God's Supreme Revelation

God, who at various times and in various ways spoke in time
past to the fathers by the prophets, 2 has in these last days spoken to us by *His* Son, whom He has appointed heir of all
things, through whom also He made the worlds; 3 who being
the brightness of *His* glory and the express image of His person, and up-
holding all things by the word of His power, when He had by Himself[a]
purged our[b] sins, sat down at the right hand of the Majesty on high, 4 having become so much better than the angels, as He has by inheritance obtained a more excellent name than they.

The Son Exalted Above Angels

5 For to which of the angels did He ever say:

"You are My Son,
Today I have begotten You"?[c]

And again:

"I will be to Him a Father,
And He shall be to Me a Son"?[d]

6 But when He again brings the firstborn into the world, He says:

"Let all the angels of God worship Him."[e]

7 And of the angels He says:

"Who makes His angels spirits
And His ministers a flame of fire."[f]

8 But to the Son *He says:*

"Your throne, O God, is forever and ever;
A scepter of righteousness is the scepter of Your kingdom.
9 *You have loved righteousness and hated lawlessness;*
Therefore God, Your God, has anointed You
With the oil of gladness more than Your companions."[g]

10 And:

"You, LORD, in the beginning laid the foundation of the earth,
And the heavens are the work of Your hands.
11 *They will perish, but You remain;*
And they will all grow old like a garment;
12 *Like a cloak You will fold them up,*
And they will be changed.
But You are the same,
And Your years will not fail."[h]

13 But to which of the angels has He ever said:

"Sit at My right hand,
Till I make Your enemies Your footstool"?[i]

1:3 [a] NU-Text omits *by Himself.* [b] NU-Text omits *our.*
1:5 [c] Psalm 2:7 [d] 2 Samuel 7:14
1:6 [e] Deuteronomy 32:43 (Septuagint, Dead Sea Scrolls); Psalm 97:7
1:7 [f] Psalm 104:4
1:9 [g] Psalm 45:6, 7
1:12 [h] Psalm 102:25–27
1:13 [i] Psalm 110:1

14Are they not all ministering spirits sent forth to minister for those who will inherit salvation?

Do Not Neglect Salvation

2 Therefore we must give the more earnest heed to
the things we have heard, lest we drift away. 2For if
the word spoken through angels proved steadfast, and
every transgression and disobedience received a just
reward, 3how shall we escape if we neglect so great a
salvation, which at the first began to be spoken by the
Lord, and was confirmed to us by those who heard
Him, 4God also bearing witness both with signs and
wonders, with various miracles, and gifts of the Holy
Spirit, according to His own will?

The Son Made Lower than Angels

5For He has not put the world to come, of which we
speak, in subjection to angels. 6But one testified in a
certain place, saying:

"What is man that You are mindful of him,
Or the son of man that You take care of him?
7 *You have made him a little lower than*
the angels;
You have crowned him with glory and honor,[j]
And set him over the works of Your hands.
8 *You have put all things in subjection under*
his feet."[k]

For in that He put all in subjection under him, He left
nothing *that is* not put under him. But now we do not
yet see all things put under him. 9But we see Jesus, who
was made a little lower than the angels, for the suffering
of death crowned with glory and honor, that He, by the
grace of God, might taste death for everyone.

Bringing Many Sons to Glory

10For it was fitting for Him, for whom *are* all things
and by whom *are* all things, in bringing many sons to
glory, to make the captain of their salvation perfect
through sufferings. 11For both He who sanctifies and
those who are being sanctified *are* all of one, for
which reason He is not ashamed to call them
brethren, 12saying:

"I will declare Your name to My brethren;
In the midst of the assembly I will sing praise
to You."[l]

13And again:

"I will put My trust in Him."[m]

And again:

"Here am I and the children whom God has
given Me."[n]

14Inasmuch then as the children have partaken of flesh
and blood, He Himself likewise shared in the same, that
through death He might destroy him who had the power
of death, that is, the devil, 15and release those who
through fear of death were all their lifetime subject to
bondage. 16For indeed He does not give aid to angels, but
He does give aid to the seed of Abraham. 17Therefore, in
all things He had to be made like *His* brethren, that He
might be a merciful and faithful High Priest in things
pertaining to God, to make propitiation for the sins of the
people. 18For in that He Himself has suffered, being
tempted, He is able to aid those who are tempted.

The Son Was Faithful

3 Therefore, holy brethren, partakers of the heavenly calling, consider the Apostle and High Priest
of our confession, Christ Jesus, 2who was faithful to
Him who appointed Him, as Moses also *was faithful* in
all His house. 3For this One has been counted worthy of
more glory than Moses, inasmuch as He who built the
house has more honor than the house. 4For every house
is built by someone, but He who built all things *is* God.
5And Moses indeed *was* faithful in all His house as a servant, for a testimony of those things which would be
spoken *afterward,* 6but Christ as a Son over His own
house, whose house we are if we hold fast the confidence and the rejoicing of the hope firm to the end.[o]

Be Faithful

7Therefore, as the Holy Spirit says:

"Today, if you will hear His voice,
8 *Do not harden your hearts as in the rebellion,*
In the day of trial in the wilderness,
9 *Where your fathers tested Me, tried Me,*
And saw My works forty years.
10 *Therefore I was angry with that generation,*
And said, 'They always go astray in
their heart,
And they have not known My ways.'
11 *So I swore in My wrath,*
'They shall not enter My rest.' "[p]

2:7 [j] NU-Text and M-Text omit the rest of verse 7.
2:8 [k] Psalm 8:4–6
2:12 [l] Psalm 22:22
2:13 [m] 2 Samuel 22:3; Isaiah 8:17 [n] Isaiah 8:18
3:6 [o] NU-Text omits *firm to the end.*
3:11 [p] Psalm 95:7–11

Life Lesson

Hebrews 3:1–4:13

SITUATION To the Jews, Moses was God's greatest prophet. He delivered them from Egyptian bondage, brought them to the land promised by God, and wrote the first five books of the Bible.

OBSERVATION Although Moses was God's faithful servant, Christ is God's faithful Son. Christ's ministry surpasses all of Moses' work.

INSPIRATION Sleep is determined to bring the day to a close and joy is determined to stretch the day out as long as possible. One last enchanted kingdom. One last giggle. One last game.

Maybe you are like that. Maybe, if you had your way, your day would never end. Every moment demands to be savored. You resist sleep as long as possible because you love being awake so much. If you are like that, congratulations. If not, welcome to the majority.

Most of us have learned another way of going to bed, haven't we? It's called crash and burn. Life is so full of games that the last thing we want is another one as we are trying to sleep. So, for most of us, it's good-bye world, hello pillow. Sleep, for many, is not a robber but a refuge; eight hours of relief for our wounded souls.

And if you are kept awake, it's not by counting your fingers, but by counting your debts, tasks, or even your tears.

You are tired.

You are weary.

Weary of being slapped by the waves of broken dreams.

Weary of being stepped on and run over in the endless marathon to the top.

Weary of trusting in someone only to have that trust returned in an envelope with no return address.

Weary of staring into the future and seeing only futility.

12Beware, brethren, lest there be in any of you an evil heart of unbelief in
departing from the living God; 13but exhort one another daily, while it is
called *"Today,"* lest any of you be hardened through the deceitfulness of
sin. 14For we have become partakers of Christ if we hold the beginning of
our confidence steadfast to the end, 15while it is said:

"Today, if you will hear His voice,
Do not harden your hearts as in the rebellion."[q]

Failure of the Wilderness Wanderers

16For who, having heard, rebelled? Indeed, *was it* not all who came out
of Egypt, *led* by Moses? 17Now with whom was He angry forty years? *Was it*
not with those who sinned, whose corpses fell in the wilderness? 18And to
whom did He swear that they would not enter His rest, but to those who
did not obey? 19So we see that they could not enter in because of unbelief.

The Promise of Rest

4 Therefore, since a promise remains of entering His rest, let us fear lest
any of you seem to have come short of it. 2For indeed the gospel was
preached to us as well as to them; but the word which they heard did not
profit them,[r] not being mixed with faith in those who heard *it*. 3For we
who have believed do enter that rest, as He has said:

"So I swore in My wrath,
'They shall not enter My rest,'"[s]

although the works were finished from the foundation of the world. 4For
He has spoken in a certain place of the seventh *day* in this way: *"And God*
rested on the seventh day from all His works";[t] 5and again in this *place:*
"They shall not enter My rest."[u]

6Since therefore it remains that some *must* enter it, and those to whom
it was first preached did not enter because of disobedience, 7again He designates a certain day, saying in David, *"Today,"* after such a long time, as it
has been said:

"Today, if you will hear His voice,
Do not harden your hearts."[v]

8For if Joshua had given them rest, then He would not afterward have
spoken of another day. 9There remains therefore a rest for the people of
God. 10For he who has entered His rest has himself also ceased from his
works as God *did* from His.

The Word Discovers Our Condition

11Let us therefore be diligent to enter that rest, lest anyone fall according
to the same example of disobedience. 12For the word of God *is* living and
powerful, and sharper than any two-edged sword, piercing even to the
division of soul and spirit, and of joints and marrow, and is a discerner of

3:15 [q] Psalm 95:7, 8
4:2 [r] NU-Text and M-Text read *profit them, since they were not united by faith with those who heeded it.*
4:3 [s] Psalm 95:11
4:4 [t] Genesis 2:2
4:5 [u] Psalm 95:11
4:7 [v] Psalm 95:7, 8

the thoughts and intents of the heart. 13And there is no creature hidden
from His sight, but all things *are* naked and open to the eyes of Him to
whom we *must give* account.

Our Compassionate High Priest

14Seeing then that we have a great High Priest who has passed through
the heavens, Jesus the Son of God, let us hold fast *our* confession. 15For we
do not have a High Priest who cannot sympathize with our weaknesses,
but was in all *points* tempted as *we are, yet* without sin. 16Let us therefore
come boldly to the throne of grace, that we may obtain mercy and find
grace to help in time of need.

Qualifications for High Priesthood

5 For every high priest taken from among men is appointed for men in
things *pertaining* to God, that he may offer both gifts and sacrifices for
sins. 2He can have compassion on those who are ignorant and going astray,
since he himself is also subject to weakness. 3Because of this he is required
as for the people, so also for himself, to offer *sacrifices* for sins. 4And no man
takes this honor to himself, but he who is called by God, just as Aaron *was.*

A Priest Forever

5So also Christ did not glorify Himself to become High Priest, *but it* was
He who said to Him:

"You are My Son,
Today I have begotten You."[w]

6As *He* also *says* in another *place:*

"You are a priest forever
According to the order of Melchizedek"; [x]

7who, in the days of His flesh, when He had offered up prayers and supplications, with vehement cries and tears to Him who was able to save Him
from death, and was heard because of His godly fear, 8though He was a
Son, *yet* He learned obedience by the things which He suffered. 9And having been perfected, He became the author of eternal salvation to all who
obey Him, 10called by God as High Priest *"according to the order of
Melchizedek,"* 11of whom we have much to say, and hard to explain, since
you have become dull of hearing.

Spiritual Immaturity

12For though by this time you ought to be teachers, you need *someone* to
teach you again the first principles of the oracles of God; and you have
come to need milk and not solid food. 13For everyone who partakes *only* of
milk *is* unskilled in the word of righteousness, for he is a babe. 14But solid
food belongs to those who are of full age, *that is,* those who by reason of
use have their senses exercised to discern both good and evil.

The Peril of Not Progressing

6 Therefore, leaving the discussion of the elementary *principles* of
Christ, let us go on to perfection, not laying again the foundation of repentance from dead works and of faith toward God, 2of the doctrine of

What steals our childhood zeal? . . .

It is this weariness that makes the words of the carpenter so compelling. Listen to them. "Come to me, all you who are weary and burdened and I will give you rest."

Come to me. . . . The invitation is to come to him. Why him?

He offers the invitation as a penniless rabbi in an oppressed nation. He has no connections with the authorities in Rome. He hasn't written a best-seller or earned a diploma.

Yet, he dares to look into the leathery faces of farmers and tired faces of housewives and offer rest. He looks into the disillusioned eyes of a bar-tender and makes this paradoxical promise: "Take my yoke upon you and learn from me, for I am gentle and humble in heart, and you will find rest for your souls."

The people came. They came out of the cul-de-sacs and office complexes of their existence and he gave them, not religion, not doctrine, not systems, but rest.

As a result, they called him Lord.

As a result, they called him Savior.

Not so much because of what he said, but because of what he did.

What he did on the cross during six hours, one Friday.

(From *Six Hours One Friday* by Max Lucado)

APPLICATION Jesus provides rest for your soul. Rather than be disheartened by bills, quotas, deadlines, and turmoil in the home, let Jesus give you his rest. Ask him to give you peace.

EXPLORATION Unbelieving Heart—Numbers 13; 14; 20; Psalm 95; God's Rest—Genesis 2:2; Deuteronomy 12:8-12; Psalm 95; Matthew 12:28; John 14:1-4.

5:5 [w] Psalm 2:7
5:6 [x] Psalm 110:4

Life Lesson

Hebrews 4:14–5:10

SITUATION Just as Jesus surpassed Moses, he also surpassed Aaron, God's high priest. The author of Hebrews continued presenting the reasons for Jesus' superiority.

OBSERVATION Jesus intercedes for us before God.

INSPIRATION Life is difficult . . . really very little more than an endless series of problems. Do we want to moan and groan about them or face them? Do we want to teach the next generation the disciplines involved in accepting and solving them or encourage them to run and hide from them? . . .

The tragedy, of course, is that the substitute itself ultimately becomes more painful than the "legitimate suffering" it was trying to avoid. And, adding insult to injury, the avoidance of legitimate suffering means we also avoid the *growth* that problems demand of us. Our determination to push pain away instead of meeting it head on creates a vicious circle.

Could this explain why God's wisest saints are often people who endure pain rather than escape it? Like their Savior, they are men and women " acquainted with grief." I recall that Jesus "learned obedience *from* the things which he suffered" (Hebrews 5:8), not in *spite* of those things.

Do you have a problem? You're smiling back at me. "A problem? Would you believe *several dozen* problems?" If you listen to the voices around you, you'll search for a substitute—an escape route. You'll miss the fact that each one of those problems is a God-appointed instructor ready to stretch you and challenge you and deepen your walk with Him. Growth and wisdom await you at the solution of each one, the pain and mess notwithstanding.

(From *Growing Strong in the Seasons of Life* by Charles Swindoll)

APPLICATION Because of Jesus, you can ask God to meet your needs.

EXPLORATION Aaron—Leviticus 8; Numbers 12; Melchizedek—Genesis 14; Hebrews 7.

baptisms, of laying on of hands, of resurrection of the dead, and of eternal
judgment. [3]And this we will[y] do if God permits.
[4]For *it is* impossible for those who were once enlightened, and have
tasted the heavenly gift, and have become partakers of the Holy Spirit,
[5]and have tasted the good word of God and the powers of the age to come,
[6]if they fall away,[z] to renew them again to repentance, since they crucify
again for themselves the Son of God, and put *Him* to an open shame.
[7]For the earth which drinks in the rain that often comes upon it, and
bears herbs useful for those by whom it is cultivated, receives blessing
from God; [8]but if it bears thorns and briers, *it is* rejected and near to being
cursed, whose end *is* to be burned.

A Better Estimate

[9]But, beloved, we are confident of better things concerning you, yes,
things that accompany salvation, though we speak in this manner. [10]For
God *is* not unjust to forget your work and labor of[a] love which you have
shown toward His name, *in that* you have ministered to the saints, and do
minister. [11]And we desire that each one of you show the same diligence to
the full assurance of hope until the end, [12]that you do not become sluggish,
but imitate those who through faith and patience inherit the promises.

God's Infallible Purpose in Christ

[13]For when God made a promise to Abraham, because He could swear by
no one greater, He swore by Himself, [14]saying, "*Surely blessing I will bless
you, and multiplying I will multiply you.*"[b] [15]And so, after he had patiently
endured, he obtained the promise. [16]For men indeed swear by the greater,
and an oath for confirmation *is* for them an end of all dispute. [17]Thus God,
determining to show more abundantly to the heirs of promise the immuta-
bility of His counsel, confirmed *it* by an oath, [18]that by two immutable
things, in which it *is* impossible for God to lie, we might[c] have strong consolation, who have fled for refuge to lay hold of the hope set before *us*.
[19]This *hope* we have as an anchor of the soul, both sure and steadfast,
and which enters the *Presence* behind the veil, [20]where the forerunner has
entered for us, *even* Jesus, having become High Priest forever according to
the order of Melchizedek.

The King of Righteousness

7 For this Melchizedek, king of Salem, priest of the Most High God, who
met Abraham returning from the slaughter of the kings and blessed
him, [2]to whom also Abraham gave a tenth part of all, first being translated
"king of righteousness," and then also king of Salem, meaning "king of
peace," [3]without father, without mother, without genealogy, having neither beginning of days nor end of life, but made like the Son of God, remains
a priest continually.
[4]Now consider how great this man *was*, to whom even the patriarch
Abraham gave a tenth of the spoils. [5]And indeed those who are of the sons
of Levi, who receive the priesthood, have a commandment to receive tithes
from the people according to the law, that is, from their brethren, though
they have come from the loins of Abraham; [6]but he whose genealogy is not

6:3 [y] M-Text reads *let us do.*
6:6 [z] Or *and have fallen away*
6:10 [a] NU-Text omits *labor of.*
6:14 [b] Genesis 22:17
6:18 [c] M-Text omits *might.*

derived from them received tithes from Abraham and blessed him who
had the promises. 7Now beyond all contradiction the lesser is blessed by
the better. 8Here mortal men receive tithes, but there he *receives them,* of
whom it is witnessed that he lives. 9Even Levi, who receives tithes, paid
tithes through Abraham, so to speak, 10for he was still in the loins of his father when Melchizedek met him.

Need for a New Priesthood

11Therefore, if perfection were through the Levitical priesthood (for
under it the people received the law), what further need *was there* that another priest should rise according to the order of Melchizedek, and not be
called according to the order of Aaron? 12For the priesthood being
changed, of necessity there is also a change of the law. 13For He of whom
these things are spoken belongs to another tribe, from which no man has
officiated at the altar.

14For *it is* evident that our Lord arose from Judah, of which tribe Moses
spoke nothing concerning priesthood.[d] 15And it is yet far more evident if,
in the likeness of Melchizedek, there arises another priest 16who has come,
not according to the law of a fleshly commandment, but according to the
power of an endless life. 17For He testifies:[e]

"You are a priest forever
According to the order of Melchizedek."[f]

18For on the one hand there is an annulling of the former commandment because of its weakness and unprofitableness, 19for the law made
nothing perfect; on the other hand, *there is the* bringing in of a better hope,
through which we draw near to God.

Greatness of the New Priest

20And inasmuch as *He was* not *made priest* without an oath 21(for they
have become priests without an oath, but He with an oath by Him who
said to Him:

"The LORD has sworn
And will not relent,
'You are a priest forever[g]
According to the order of Melchizedek'"),[h]

22by so much more Jesus has become a surety of a better covenant.
23Also there were many priests, because they were prevented by
death from continuing. 24But He, because He continues forever, has an
unchangeable priesthood. 25Therefore He is also able to save to the uttermost those who come to God through Him, since He always lives to make
intercession for them.

26For such a High Priest was fitting for us, *who is* holy, harmless, undefiled, separate from sinners, and has become higher than the heavens;
27who does not need daily, as those high priests, to offer up sacrifices, first
for His own sins and then for the people's, for this He did once for all when
He offered up Himself. 28For the law appoints as high priests men who
have weakness, but the word of the oath, which came after the law, *appoints* the Son who has been perfected forever.

7:14 [d] NU-Text reads *priests.*
7:17 [e] NU-Text reads *it is testified.* [f] Psalm 110:4
7:21 [g] NU-Text ends the quotation here. [h] Psalm 110:4

LIFE LESSON

Hebrews 7:1-28

SITUATION Melchizedek, king of Salem, was greater than Abraham. Abraham, the father of all Jews, offered sacrifices to God through Melchizedek. Yet Jesus even surpassed Melchizedek's service.

OBSERVATION "Jesus is the kind of high priest we need." He is able to save those who come to God through him.

INSPIRATION God wants praying people who will vicariously take on the difficulties of the various churches and denominations and communities in which they live. He wants us to present these difficulties before God, being identified with them.

The New Testament teaches that we are raised up "together" to sit "in heavenly places in Christ Jesus"—not raised in isolation, but together. God grant that we may learn the tremendous meaning of intercessory prayer!

Intercession includes vicarious repentance—feeling all the distress and all the pain of the sins of the people to whom we belong, as if they were really our own. Are you willing to make this your ministry?

(From *Devotions for a Deeper Life* by Oswald Chambers)

APPLICATION Have you come to God through Jesus, your High Priest? There is no other way of being saved. By his design, God made Jesus the only way. Come to Jesus today. Submit your plans and future to God. Let him be more important than any earthly tie.

EXPLORATION Melchizedek—Genesis 14; Hebrews 4:14–5:10.

LIFE LESSON

Hebrews 8:1-13

SITUATION Jewish Christians struggled to understand the relationship between God's free salvation and the Mosaic Law. The author explained that Jesus Christ was superior to the Law of Moses.

OBSERVATION God does not keep a record of our sins in order to use them against us. Rather, he forgives and loves us even as we suffer through the consequences of our sins.

INSPIRATION I was thanking the Father today for his mercy. I began listing the sins he'd forgiven. One by one I thanked God for forgiving my stumbles and tumbles. My motives were pure and my heart was thankful, but my understanding of God was wrong. It was when I used the word "remember" that it hit me. . . .

God doesn't just forgive, he forgets. He erases the board. He destroys the evidence. He burns the microfilm. He clears the computer. . . .

No, he doesn't remember. But I do, you do. You still remember. You're like me. You still remember what you did before you changed. In the cellar of your heart lurk the ghosts of yesterday's sins. Sins you've confessed; errors of which you've repented; damage you've done your best to repair.

And though you're a different person, the ghosts still linger. Though you've locked the basement door, they still haunt you. They float to meet you, spooking your soul and robbing your joy. With wordless whispers they remind you of moments when you forgot whose child you were. . . .

The New Priestly Service

8 Now *this is* the main point of the things we are saying: We have such a High Priest, who is seated at the right hand of the throne of the Majesty in the heavens, [2]a Minister of the sanctuary and of the true tabernacle which the Lord erected, and not man.

[3]For every high priest is appointed to offer both gifts and sacrifices. Therefore *it is* necessary that this One also have something to offer. [4]For if He were on earth, He would not be a priest, since there are priests who offer the gifts according to the law; [5]who serve the copy and shadow of the heavenly things, as Moses was divinely instructed when he was about to make the tabernacle. For He said, *"See that you make all things according to the pattern shown you on the mountain."*[i] [6]But now He has obtained a more excellent ministry, inasmuch as He is also Mediator of a better covenant, which was established on better promises.

A New Covenant

[7]For if that first *covenant* had been faultless, then no place would have been sought for a second. [8]Because finding fault with them, He says: *"Behold, the days are coming, says the LORD, when I will make a new covenant with the house of Israel and with the house of Judah—* [9]*not according to the covenant that I made with their fathers in the day when I took them by the hand to lead them out of the land of Egypt; because they did not continue in My covenant, and I disregarded them, says the LORD.* [10]*For this is the covenant that I will make with the house of Israel after those days, says the LORD: I will put My laws in their mind and write them on their hearts; and I will be their God, and they shall be My people.* [11]*None of them shall teach his neighbor, and none his brother, saying, 'Know the LORD,' for all shall know Me, from the least of them to the greatest of them.* [12]*For I will be merciful to their unrighteousness, and their sins and their lawless deeds*[j] *I will remember no more."*[k]

[13]In that He says, *"A new covenant,"* He has made the first obsolete. Now what is becoming obsolete and growing old is ready to vanish away.

The Earthly Sanctuary

9 Then indeed, even the first *covenant* had ordinances of divine service and the earthly sanctuary. [2]For a tabernacle was prepared: the first *part,* in which *was* the lampstand, the table, and the showbread, which is called the sanctuary; [3]and behind the second veil, the part of the tabernacle which is called the Holiest of All, [4]which had the golden censer and the ark of the covenant overlaid on all sides with gold, in which *were* the golden pot that had the manna, Aaron's rod that budded, and the tablets of the covenant; [5]and above it were the cherubim of glory overshadowing the mercy seat. Of these things we cannot now speak in detail.

Limitations of the Earthly Service

[6]Now when these things had been thus prepared, the priests always went into the first part of the tabernacle, performing *the services.* [7]But into the second part the high priest *went* alone once a year, not without blood,

8:5 [i] Exodus 25:40
8:12 [j] NU-Text omits *and their lawless deeds.* [k] Jeremiah 31:31–34

which he offered for himself and *for* the people's sins *committed* in ignorance; 8the Holy Spirit indicating this, that the way into the Holiest of All was not yet made manifest while the first tabernacle was still standing. 9It *was* symbolic for the present time in which both gifts and sacrifices are offered which cannot make him who performed the service perfect in regard to the conscience— 10*concerned* only with foods and drinks, various washings, and fleshly ordinances imposed until the time of reformation.

The Heavenly Sanctuary

11But Christ came *as* High Priest of the good things to come,[l] with the greater and more perfect tabernacle not made with hands, that is, not of this creation. 12Not with the blood of goats and calves, but with His own blood He entered the Most Holy Place once for all, having obtained eternal redemption. 13For if the blood of bulls and goats and the ashes of a heifer, sprinkling the unclean, sanctifies for the purifying of the flesh, 14how much more shall the blood of Christ, who through the eternal Spirit offered Himself without spot to God, cleanse your conscience from dead works to serve the living God? 15And for this reason He is the Mediator of the new covenant, by means of death, for the redemption of the transgressions under the first covenant, that those who are called may receive the promise of the eternal inheritance.

The Mediator's Death Necessary

16For where there *is* a testament, there must also of necessity be the death of the testator. 17For a testament *is* in force after men are dead, since it has no power at all while the testator lives. 18Therefore not even the first *covenant* was dedicated without blood. 19For when Moses had spoken every precept to all the people according to the law, he took the blood of calves and goats, with water, scarlet wool, and hyssop, and sprinkled both the book itself and all the people, 20saying, *"This is the blood of the covenant which God has commanded you."*[m] 21Then likewise he sprinkled with blood both the tabernacle and all the vessels of the ministry. 22And according to the law almost all things are purified with blood, and without shedding of blood there is no remission.

Greatness of Christ's Sacrifice

23Therefore *it was* necessary that the copies of the things in the heavens should be purified with these, but the heavenly things themselves with better sacrifices than these. 24For Christ has not entered the holy places made with hands, *which are* copies of the true, but into heaven itself, now to appear in the presence of God for us; 25not that He should offer Himself often, as the high priest enters the Most Holy Place every year with blood of another— 26He then would have had to suffer often since the foundation of the world; but now, once at the end of the ages, He has appeared to put away sin by the sacrifice of Himself. 27And as it is appointed for men to die once, but after this the judgment, 28so Christ was offered once to bear the sins of many. To those who eagerly wait for Him He will appear a second time, apart from sin, for salvation.

9:11 [l] NU-Text reads *that have come.*
9:20 [m] Exodus 24:8

Poltergeists from yesterday's pitfalls. Spiteful specters that slyly suggest, "Are you really forgiven? Sure God forgets most of our mistakes, but do you think he could actually forget the time you. . .?"

. . . Was [God] exaggerating when he said he would cast our sins as far as the east is from the west? Do you actually believe he would make a statement like "I will not hold their iniquities against them" and then rub our noses in them whenever we ask for help? . . .

You see, God is either the God of perfect grace . . . or he is not God. Grace forgets. Period. He who is perfect love cannot hold grudges. If he does, then he isn't perfect love. And if he isn't perfect love, you might as well put this book down and go fishing, because both of us are chasing fairy tales.

But I believe in his loving forgetfulness. And I believe he has a graciously terrible memory.

(From *God Came Near* by Max Lucado)

APPLICATION Because of Jesus' perfect sacrifice, God forgets our sins. Jesus paid the penalty for sins. We must no longer feel guilty for sins that God forgave.

EXPLORATION Promised Pardon of God—Isaiah 43:25; 44:22; 55:7; Micah 7:18; 1 John 1:9.

Animal Sacrifices Insufficient

10 For the law, having a shadow of the good things to come, *and* not the very image of the things, can never with these same sacrifices, which they offer continually year by year, make those who approach perfect. 2For then would they not have ceased to be offered? For the worshipers, once purified, would have had no more consciousness of sins. 3But in those *sacrifices there is* a reminder of sins every year. 4For *it is* not possible that the blood of bulls and goats could take away sins.

Christ's Death Fulfills God's Will

5Therefore, when He came into the world, He said:

"Sacrifice and offering You did not desire,
But a body You have prepared for Me.
6 *In burnt offerings and sacrifices for sin*
You had no pleasure.
7 *Then I said, 'Behold, I have come—*
In the volume of the book it is written of Me—
To do Your will, O God.'"[n]

8Previously saying, *"Sacrifice and offering, burnt offerings, and offerings for sin You did not desire, nor had pleasure in them"* (which are offered according to the law), 9then He said, *"Behold, I have come to do Your will, O God."*[o] He takes away the first that He may establish the second. 10By that will we have been sanctified through the offering of the body of Jesus Christ once *for all.*

Christ's Death Perfects the Sanctified

11And every priest stands ministering daily and offering repeatedly the same sacrifices, which can never take away sins. 12But this Man, after He had offered one sacrifice for sins forever, sat down at the right hand of God, 13from that time waiting till His enemies are made His footstool. 14For by one offering He has perfected forever those who are being sanctified.

15But the Holy Spirit also witnesses to us; for after He had said before, 16*"This is the covenant that I will make with them after those days, says the LORD: I will put My laws into their hearts, and in their minds I will write them,"*[p] 17*then He adds, "Their sins and their lawless deeds I will remember no more."*[q] 18Now where there is remission of these, *there is* no longer an offering for sin.

Hold Fast Your Confession

19Therefore, brethren, having boldness to enter the Holiest by the blood of Jesus, 20by a new and living way which He consecrated for us, through the veil, that is, His flesh, 21and *having* a High Priest over the house of God, 22let us draw near with a true heart in full assurance of faith, having our hearts sprinkled from an evil conscience and our bodies washed with pure water. 23Let us hold fast the confession of *our* hope without wavering, for He who promised *is* faithful. 24And let us consider one another in order to stir up love and good works, 25not forsaking the assembling of ourselves

10:7 [n] Psalm 40:6–8
10:9 [o] NU-Text and M-Text omit *O God.*
10:16 [p] Jeremiah 31:33
10:17 [q] Jeremiah 31:34

LIFE LESSON

Hebrews 9:1-22

SITUATION The writer of Hebrews emphasized that Christ's sacrifice surpassed the sacrifices of the Old Testament. There will never be a greater sacrifice.

OBSERVATION The Old Testament helps us understand why Jesus died. When we understand the Old Testament laws and traditions, we can gain a deeper appreciation for our new High Priest, Jesus.

INSPIRATION To those with ears to hear and eyes to see, there will be very great release from unbearable burdens in the language of autumn trees, for example, when they dress most gloriously in preparation for death. The red of the leaves is the sign of the cross. Winter follows, when snow closes everything in frozen silence. The trees then are skeletons, but wonders are being performed under the surface of things. Spring comes, and the hidden wonders burst out all at once—tiny shoots, swelling buds, touches of green and red where all seemed hopeless the day before. . . . Plain lessons for us, if we'll open our eyes.

If the leaves had not been let go to fall and wither, if the tree had not consented to be a skeleton for many months, there would be no new life rising, no bud, no flower, no fruit, no seed, no new generation.

(From *Passion and Purity* by Elisabeth Elliot)

APPLICATION Can anything be as encouraging as how Jesus saved us? Offer your praise and thanksgiving for what He has done! Set up some reminders for yourself to remember to praise God throughout the day.

EXPLORATION Sacrifice of Christ—John 15:13; Galatians 1:4; Ephesians 5:2; Titus 2:14; 1 Peter 3:18.

together, as *is* the manner of some, but exhorting *one another,* and so
much the more as you see the Day approaching.

The Just Live by Faith

26For if we sin willfully after we have received the knowledge of the
truth, there no longer remains a sacrifice for sins, 27but a certain fearful
expectation of judgment, and fiery indignation which will devour the adversaries. 28Anyone who has rejected Moses' law dies without mercy on
the testimony of two or three witnesses. 29Of how much worse punishment, do you suppose, will he be thought worthy who has trampled the
Son of God underfoot, counted the blood of the covenant by which he was
sanctified a common thing, and insulted the Spirit of grace? 30For we
know Him who said, *"Vengeance is Mine, I will repay,"*[r] says the Lord.[s]
And again, *"The LORD will judge His people."*[t] 31It is a fearful thing to fall
into the hands of the living God.

32But recall the former days in which, after you were illuminated, you
endured a great struggle with sufferings: 33partly while you were made a
spectacle both by reproaches and tribulations, and partly while you became companions of those who were so treated; 34for you had compassion
on me[u] in my chains, and joyfully accepted the plundering of your goods,
knowing that you have a better and an enduring possession for yourselves
in heaven.[v] 35Therefore do not cast away your confidence, which has great
reward. 36For you have need of endurance, so that after you have done the
will of God, you may receive the promise:

37 *"For yet a little while,*
And He[w] *who is coming will come and will not tarry.*
38 *Now the*[x] *just shall live by faith;*
But if anyone draws back,
My soul has no pleasure in him."[y]

39But we are not of those who draw back to perdition, but of those who believe to the saving of the soul.

By Faith We Understand

11 Now faith is the substance of things hoped for, the evidence of
things not seen. 2For by it the elders obtained a *good* testimony.
3By faith we understand that the worlds were framed by the word of God,
so that the things which are seen were not made of things which are visible.

Faith at the Dawn of History

4By faith Abel offered to God a more excellent sacrifice than Cain,
through which he obtained witness that he was righteous, God testifying
of his gifts; and through it he being dead still speaks.
5By faith Enoch was taken away so that he did not see death, *"and was
not found, because God had taken him"*;[z] for before he was taken he had
this testimony, that he pleased God. 6But without faith *it is* impossible to
please *Him,* for he who comes to God must believe that He is, and *that* He
is a rewarder of those who diligently seek Him.

10:30 [r] Deuteronomy 32:35 [s] NU-Text omits *says the Lord.* [t] Deuteronomy 32:36
10:34 [u] NU-Text reads *the prisoners* instead of *me in my chains.* [v] NU-Text omits *in heaven.*
10:37 [w] Or *that which*
10:38 [x] NU-Text reads *My just one.* [y] Habakkuk 2:3, 4
11:5 [z] Genesis 5:24

LIFE LESSON

Hebrews 9:23–10:39

SITUATION Once the author told that Jesus' death surpassed any earthly sacrifice, he encouraged the Hebrew Christians to have confidence.

OBSERVATION Jesus' death not only provides salvation, but also great confidence for Christians. We can step boldly before the Lord in prayer, and boldly into the world in service and witness. Jesus has already won the battle!

INSPIRATION Picture it this way. Imagine that you are an ice skater in competition. You are in first place with one more round to go. If you perform well, the trophy is yours. You are nervous, anxious, and frightened.

Then, only minutes before your performance, your trainer rushes to you with the thrilling news: "You've already won! The judges tabulated the scores, and the person in second place can't catch you. You are too far ahead."

Upon hearing that news, how will you feel? Exhilarated!

And how will you skate? Timidly? Cautiously? Of course not. How about courageously and confidently? You bet you will. You will do your best because the prize is yours. You will skate like a champion because that is what you are! You will hear the applause of victory. . . .

The point is clear: the truth will triumph. The Father of truth will win, and the followers of truth will be saved.

(From *The Applause of Heaven* by Max Lucado)

APPLICATION If you are a child of God, claim your victory over sin! Be confident. Nothing can ever take you out of God's hand. No one can ever take away your salvation. No matter what happens, you are *always* his.

EXPLORATION Spiritual Boldness—Ephesians 3:12; 1 Timothy 3:13; Hebrews 4:16; 1 John 4:17.

Life Lesson

Hebrews 11:1-40

SITUATION Old Testament heroes provided examples of faith and obedience to God.

OBSERVATION Faith is more than a belief in God. It is also a way of life. Heroes of faith, although imperfect, trusted God and gave their lives to him.

INSPIRATION Faith is the belief that God is real and that God is good. . . . It is a choice to believe that the one who made it all hasn't left it all and that he still sends light into the shadows and responds to gestures of faith. . . .

Faith is the belief that God will do what is right.

"Blessed are the dirt-poor, nothing-to-give, trapped-in-a-corner, destitute, diseased," Jesus said, "for theirs is the kingdom of heaven" (Matt. 5:6, my translation). . . .

God says that the more hopeless your circumstances, the more likely your salvation. The greater your cares, the more genuine your prayers. The darker the room, the greater the need for light. . . .

God's help is near and always available, but it is only given to those who seek it. Nothing results from apathy. . . .

Compared to God's part, our part is minuscule but necessary. . . . Write a letter. Ask forgiveness. Call a counselor. Confess. Call Mom. Visit a doctor. Be baptized. Feed a hungry person. Pray. Teach. Go.

Do something that demonstrates faith. For faith with no effort is no faith at all. *God will respond.* He has never rejected a genuine gesture of faith. Never.

(From *He Still Moves Stones* by Max Lucado)

APPLICATION Hebrews chapter 11 can encourage you by telling about people's faith in the Old Testament. These examples encourage you. What are you doing to encourage others? Who will you tell?

EXPLORATION Remembering the Faithful—Proverbs 10:7; Matthew 26:13; 2 Timothy 1:5.

7By faith Noah, being divinely warned of things not yet seen, moved
with godly fear, prepared an ark for the saving of his household, by which
he condemned the world and became heir of the righteousness which is
according to faith.

Faithful Abraham

8By faith Abraham obeyed when he was called to go out to the place
which he would receive as an inheritance. And he went out, not knowing
where he was going. 9By faith he dwelt in the land of promise as *in* a foreign country, dwelling in tents with Isaac and Jacob, the heirs with him of
the same promise; 10for he waited for the city which has foundations,
whose builder and maker *is* God.
11By faith Sarah herself also received strength to conceive seed, and she
bore a child[a] when she was past the age, because she judged Him faithful
who had promised. 12Therefore from one man, and him as good as dead,
were born *as many* as the stars of the sky in multitude—innumerable as
the sand which is by the seashore.

The Heavenly Hope

13These all died in faith, not having received the promises, but having
seen them afar off were assured of them,[b] embraced *them* and confessed
that they were strangers and pilgrims on the earth. 14For those who say
such things declare plainly that they seek a homeland. 15And truly if they
had called to mind that *country* from which they had come out, they would
have had opportunity to return. 16But now they desire a better, that is, a
heavenly *country.* Therefore God is not ashamed to be called their God, for
He has prepared a city for them.

The Faith of the Patriarchs

17By faith Abraham, when he was tested, offered up Isaac, and he who
had received the promises offered up his only begotten *son,* 18of whom it
was said, *"In Isaac your seed shall be called,"*[c] 19concluding that God *was*
able to raise *him* up, even from the dead, from which he also received him
in a figurative sense.
20By faith Isaac blessed Jacob and Esau concerning things to come.
21By faith Jacob, when he was dying, blessed each of the sons of Joseph,
and worshiped, *leaning* on the top of his staff.
22By faith Joseph, when he was dying, made mention of the departure of
the children of Israel, and gave instructions concerning his bones.

The Faith of Moses

23By faith Moses, when he was born, was hidden three months by his
parents, because they saw *he was* a beautiful child; and they were not
afraid of the king's command.
24By faith Moses, when he became of age, refused to be called the son of
Pharaoh's daughter, 25choosing rather to suffer affliction with the people of
God than to enjoy the passing pleasures of sin, 26esteeming the reproach of
Christ greater riches than the treasures in[d] Egypt; for he looked to the reward.

11:11 [a] NU-Text omits *she bore a child.*
11:13 [b] NU-Text and M-Text omit *were assured of them.*
11:18 [c] Genesis 21:12
11:26 [d] NU-Text and M-Text read *of.*

Forgiveness

When Jesus told us to pray for forgiveness of our debts as we forgive our own debtors, he knew who would be the one to pay the debt. As he would hang on the cross he would say, "It is finished" . . . *the* debt is paid!

There are some facts that will never change. One fact is that you are forgiven. If you are in Christ, when he sees you, your sins are covered—he doesn't see them. He sees you better than you see yourself. And that is a glorious fact of your life.

Our forgiveness of others is a signal of our awareness of how much God has given us.

Isn't it presumptuous to come to the throne of grace if we haven't been gracious to the people in our life? How can we approach a God of mercy if we ourselves have hearts full of bitterness or anger? We must take care of relationship problems—make up with a spouse, get along with fellow church members, love our neighbors—then we will be fully united in prayer with the Father.

FATHER, we want to come home to you. But sometimes we're afraid that we've done something unforgivable, afraid that we've made you angry. And we wonder how you can forgive us. But Father, your Word teaches us that you will forgive us and that there's no sin too deep for your hand of forgiveness to reach.

Sorrow

We serve the God who designed the universe and set our world in motion. But those hands that hung the stars in the heavens also wiped away the tears of the widow and the leper. And they will wipe away your tears as well.

There has never been a time in the history of this globe when there was not a rain cloud somewhere on the earth. There may be blue skies for us occasionally, but the rain always comes. So, instead of looking for ways to escape problems, look for methods to face them head on.

Father, you are God and Creator, but we come to you as children coming to their father, as children who would ask their father to hold and comfort them, hoping to receive words of wisdom.

AS YOU STILLED the storm on the Sea of Galilee, will you still the storms that rage within our hearts? Will you calm the whirling winds of fear and hurt that threaten our faith? Will you, Father, draw us ever closer to you?

PRAYER

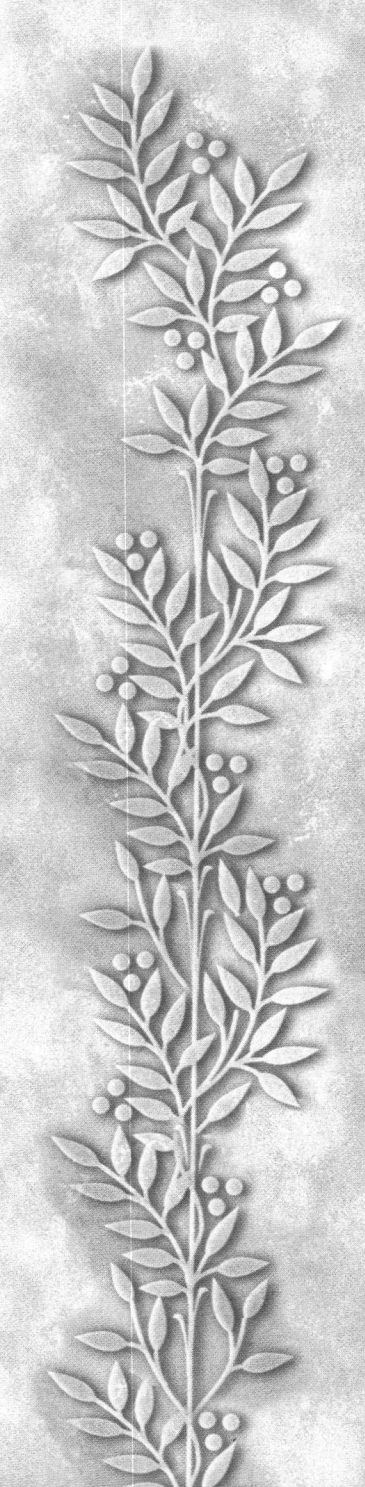

You know, we really don't know what to pray for, do we? What if God had answered every prayer that you ever prayed? Just think who you'd be married to. Just think where you'd be living. Just think what you'd be doing.

God loves us so much that sometimes he gives us what we need and not what we ask.

Prayer is the recognition that if God had not engaged himself in our problems, we would still be lost in the blackness. It is by his mercy that we have been lifted up. Prayer is that whole process that reminds us of who God is and who we are.

I believe there's great power in prayer. I believe God heals the wounded, and that he can raise the dead. But I don't believe we tell God what to do and when to do it. You see, there's a difference between faith and presumption. There's a difference between believing he's the almighty God and demanding he become our divine servant.

God knows that we, with our limited vision, don't even know that for which we should pray. And we are praying for things right now that God knows would not be best for us. When we entrust our requests to him, we trust him to honor our prayers with holy judgment.

LORD, we want only to please you. We cherish your promise to take care of your children. And yet we often come to you with muddled ideas, unsure of what is best, uncertain of your will. Thank you, Father, for the assurance that our imperfect prayers cannot hinder your incredible power.

SURRENDER

In our "bootstrap" society, where you tough it up and do it on your own and take pride in being a rugged individualist, the one thing that seems to escape us is being before God on our knees—being before God, aware that we are helpless and *allowing* him to assist us.

Can you say to Jesus, "This burden's too heavy for me. I want you to be my co-worker. I want you to carry this burden with me. I cannot do it any longer." He says if you will come to him, if you'll allow him to carry that burden with you, his promise is that you will receive rest.

Surrendering our life to Christ means going to him and saying, "I'm yours; use me however you want to." Once you've done this, you can begin to seek his will for your life.

Once we're honest with ourselves about who we are, then God can begin to remold our hearts . . . in total surrender.

FATHER, *we invite your assistance and guidance and powerful indwelling, because we do not have the strength to be transformed into your likeness and not be conformed to this world. May we understand more of what it means to say, "It is well with my soul."*

27By faith he forsook Egypt, not fearing the wrath of the king; for he endured as seeing Him who is invisible. 28By faith he kept the Passover and the
sprinkling of blood, lest he who destroyed the firstborn should touch them.
29By faith they passed through the Red Sea as by dry *land, whereas* the
Egyptians, attempting *to do* so, were drowned.

By Faith They Overcame

30By faith the walls of Jericho fell down after they were encircled for
seven days. 31By faith the harlot Rahab did not perish with those who did
not believe, when she had received the spies with peace.
32And what more shall I say? For the time would fail me to tell of Gideon
and Barak and Samson and Jephthah, also *of* David and Samuel and the
prophets: 33who through faith subdued kingdoms, worked righteousness,
obtained promises, stopped the mouths of lions, 34quenched the violence
of fire, escaped the edge of the sword, out of weakness were made strong,
became valiant in battle, turned to flight the armies of the aliens. 35Women
received their dead raised to life again.
Others were tortured, not accepting deliverance, that they might obtain
a better resurrection. 36Still others had trial of mockings and scourgings,
yes, and of chains and imprisonment. 37They were stoned, they were sawn
in two, were tempted,[e] were slain with the sword. They wandered about in
sheepskins and goatskins, being destitute, afflicted, tormented— 38of
whom the world was not worthy. They wandered in deserts and mountains, *in* dens and caves of the earth.
39And all these, having obtained a good testimony through faith, did not
receive the promise, 40God having provided something better for us, that
they should not be made perfect apart from us.

The Race of Faith

12 Therefore we also, since we are surrounded by so great a cloud of
witnesses, let us lay aside every weight, and the sin which so easily
ensnares *us,* and let us run with endurance the race that is set before us,
2looking unto Jesus, the author and finisher of *our* faith, who for the joy
that was set before Him endured the cross, despising the shame, and has
sat down at the right hand of the throne of God.

The Discipline of God

3For consider Him who endured such hostility from sinners against
Himself, lest you become weary and discouraged in your souls. 4You have
not yet resisted to bloodshed, striving against sin. 5And you have forgotten
the exhortation which speaks to you as to sons:

"My son, do not despise the chastening of the LORD,
Nor be discouraged when you are rebuked by Him;
6 *For whom the LORD loves He chastens,*
And scourges every son whom He receives."[f]

7If[g] you endure chastening, God deals with you as with sons; for what
son is there whom a father does not chasten? 8But if you are without chastening, of which all have become partakers, then you are illegitimate and
not sons. 9Furthermore, we have had human fathers who corrected *us,*

11:37 [e] NU-Text omits *were tempted.*
12:6 [f] Proverbs 3:11, 12
12:7 [g] NU-Text and M-Text read *It is for discipline that you endure; God. . . .*

LIFE LESSON

Hebrews 12:1-29

SITUATION The Hebrew readers of this book needed encouragement to face persecution. They were called to follow the perfect example of Jesus, who overcame difficult circumstances.

OBSERVATION Jesus, the perfect model of faith, obeyed God to the point of death. He looked beyond his immediate, painful circumstances and knew that his sacrifice would bring life to others.

INSPIRATION He looked around the carpentry shop. He stood for a moment in the refuge of the little room that housed so many sweet memories. He balanced the hammer in his hand. He ran his fingers across the sharp teeth of the saw. He stroked the smoothly worn wood of the sawhorse. He had come to say good-bye.

It was time for him to leave. He had heard something that made him know it was time to go. So he came one last time to smell the sawdust and lumber.

Life was peaceful here. Life was so . . . safe. . . .

I wonder if he wanted to stay. . . . I wonder because I know he had already read the last chapter. He knew that the feet that would step out of the safe shadow of the carpentry shop would not rest until they'd been pierced and placed on a Roman cross.

. . . If there was any hesitation on the part of his humanity, it was overcome by the compassion of his divinity. His divinity heard the voices. . . .

And his divinity saw the faces. . . . From the face of Adam to the face of the infant born somewhere in the world as you read these words, he saw them all.

And you can be sure of one thing. Among the voices that found their way into that carpentry shop in Nazareth was your voice. . . .

And not only did he hear you, he saw you. He saw your face aglow the hour you first knew him. He saw your face in shame the hour you first fell. The same face that looked back at you from this morning's mirror, looked at him. And it was enough to kill him.

Continued

He left because of you.

He laid his security down with his hammer. He hung tranquillity on the peg with his nail apron. He closed the window shutters on the sunshine of his youth and locked the door on the comfort and ease of anonymity.

Since he could bear your sins more easily than he could bear the thought of your hopelessness, he chose to leave.

It wasn't easy. Leaving the carpentry shop never has been.

(From *God Came Near* by Max Lucado)

APPLICATION Look for joy in difficult times. How can others benefit from your struggle? Look beyond the pain and find God's purpose for your struggle.

EXPLORATION Joy in Troubled Times—Psalm 126:2; Luke 15:5; John 15:11.

and we paid *them* respect. Shall we not much more readily be in subjection to the Father of spirits and live? 10 For they indeed for a few days chastened *us* as seemed *best* to them, but He for *our* profit, that *we* may be
partakers of His holiness. 11 Now no chastening seems to be joyful for the
present, but painful; nevertheless, afterward it yields the peaceable fruit of
righteousness to those who have been trained by it.

Renew Your Spiritual Vitality

12 Therefore strengthen the hands which hang down, and the feeble
knees, 13 and make straight paths for your feet, so that what is lame may
not be *dislocated,* but rather be healed.
14 Pursue peace with all *people,* and holiness, without which no one will
see the Lord: 15 looking carefully lest anyone fall short of the grace of God;
lest any root of bitterness springing up cause trouble, and by this many
become defiled; 16 lest there *be* any fornicator or profane person like Esau,
who for one morsel of food sold his birthright. 17 For you know that afterward, when he wanted to inherit the blessing, he was rejected, for he found
no place for repentance, though he sought it diligently with tears.

The Glorious Company

18 For you have not come to the mountain that[h] may be touched and that
burned with fire, and to blackness and darkness[i] and tempest, 19 and the
sound of a trumpet and the voice of words, so that those who heard *it*
begged that the word should not be spoken to them anymore. 20 (For they
could not endure what was commanded: *"And if so much as a beast touches
the mountain, it shall be stoned*[j] *or shot with an arrow."*[k] 21 And so terrifying
was the sight *that* Moses said, *"I am exceedingly afraid* and trembling."[l])
22 But you have come to Mount Zion and to the city of the living God, the
heavenly Jerusalem, to an innumerable company of angels, 23 to the general assembly and church of the firstborn *who are* registered in heaven, to
God the Judge of all, to the spirits of just men made perfect, 24 to Jesus the
Mediator of the new covenant, and to the blood of sprinkling that speaks
better things than *that of* Abel.

Hear the Heavenly Voice

25 See that you do not refuse Him who speaks. For if they did not escape
who refused Him who spoke on earth, much more *shall we not escape* if we
turn away from Him who *speaks* from heaven, 26 whose voice then shook
the earth; but now He has promised, saying, *"Yet once more I shake*[m] *not
only the earth, but also heaven."*[n] 27 Now this, *"Yet once more,"* indicates
the removal of those things that are being shaken, as of things that are
made, that the things which cannot be shaken may remain.
28 Therefore, since we are receiving a kingdom which cannot be shaken,
let us have grace, by which we may[o] serve God acceptably with reverence
and godly fear. 29 For our God *is* a consuming fire.

12:18 [h] NU-Text reads *to that which.* [i] NU-Text reads *gloom.*
12:20 [j] NU-Text and M-Text omit the rest of this verse. [k] Exodus 19:12, 13
12:21 [l] Deuteronomy 9:19
12:26 [m] NU-Text reads *will shake.*
12:26 [n] Haggai 2:6
12:28 [o] M-Text omits *may.*

Concluding Moral Directions

13 Let brotherly love continue. [2]Do not forget to
entertain strangers, for by so *doing* some have
unwittingly entertained angels. [3]Remember the prisoners as if chained with them—those who are mistreated—since you yourselves are in the body also.
[4]Marriage *is* honorable among all, and the bed undefiled; but fornicators and adulterers God will judge.
[5]*Let your* conduct *be* without covetousness; *be* content with such things as you have. For He Himself has
said, *"I will never leave you nor forsake you."*[p] [6]So we
may boldly say:

> *"The LORD is my helper;*
> *I will not fear.*
> *What can man do to me?"*[q]

Concluding Religious Directions

[7]Remember those who rule over you, who have
spoken the word of God to you, whose faith follow,
considering the outcome of *their* conduct. [8]Jesus
Christ *is* the same yesterday, today, and forever. [9]Do
not be carried about[r] with various and strange doctrines. For *it is* good that the heart be established by
grace, not with foods which have not profited those
who have been occupied with them.
[10]We have an altar from which those who serve the
tabernacle have no right to eat. [11]For the bodies of
those animals, whose blood is brought into the sanctuary by the high priest for sin, are burned outside the
camp. [12]Therefore Jesus also, that He might sanctify
the people with His own blood, suffered outside the
gate. [13]Therefore let us go forth to Him, outside the
camp, bearing His reproach. [14]For here we have no
continuing city, but we seek the one to come. [15]There-
fore by Him let us continually offer the sacrifice of
praise to God, that is, the fruit of *our* lips, giving
thanks to His name. [16]But do not forget to do good and
to share, for with such sacrifices God is well pleased.
[17]Obey those who rule over you, and be submissive,
for they watch out for your souls, as those who must
give account. Let them do so with joy and not with
grief, for that would be unprofitable for you.

Prayer Requested

[18]Pray for us; for we are confident that we have a
good conscience, in all things desiring to live honorably. [19]But I especially urge *you* to do this, that I may
be restored to you the sooner.

Benediction, Final Exhortation, Farewell

[20]Now may the God of peace who brought up our Lord
Jesus from the dead, that great Shepherd of the sheep,
through the blood of the everlasting covenant, [21]make
you complete in every good work to do His will, working in you[s] what is well pleasing in His sight, through
Jesus Christ, to whom *be* glory forever and ever. Amen.
[22]And I appeal to you, brethren, bear with the word
of exhortation, for I have written to you in few words.
[23]Know that *our* brother Timothy has been set free,
with whom I shall see you if he comes shortly.
[24]Greet all those who rule over you, and all the
saints. Those from Italy greet you.
[25]Grace *be* with you all. Amen.

13:5 *p* Deuteronomy 31:6, 8; Joshua 1:5
13:6 *q* Psalm 118:6
13:9 *r* NU-Text and M-Text read *away.*
13:21 *s* NU-Text and M-Text read *us.*

The Epistle of

JAMES

INTRODUCTION

Here is a story James would have liked.

Francis of Assisi once invited an apprentice to go with him to a nearby village to preach. The young monk quickly agreed, seizing an opportunity to hear his teacher speak. When they arrived in the village, St. Francis began to visit with the people.

First he stopped in on the butcher. Next a visit with the cobbler. Then a short walk to the home of a woman who'd recently buried her husband. After that a stop at the school to chat with the teacher. This continued throughout the morning. After some time, Francis told his disciple that it was time to return to the abbey.

The student didn't understand. "But we came to preach," he reminded. "We haven't preached a sermon."

"Haven't we?" questioned the elder. "People have watched us, listened to us, responded to us. Every word we have spoken, every deed we have done has been a sermon. We have preached all morning."

James would have liked that. As far as he was concerned, Christianity was more action on Monday than worship on Sunday. "What does it profit, my brethren, if someone says he has faith but does not have works? Can faith save him?" (2:14).

His message is bare-knuckled; his style is bare-boned. Talk is cheap, he argues. Service is invaluable.

It's not that works save the Christian, but that works mark the Christian. In James's book of logic, it only makes sense that we who have been given much should give much. Not just with words. But with our lives.

Or as St. Francis is noted as saying, "Preach without ceasing. If you must, use words."

James would have liked that, too.

Greeting to the Twelve Tribes

James, a bondservant of God and of the Lord Jesus Christ,

To the twelve tribes which are scattered abroad:

Greetings.

Profiting from Trials

[2]My brethren, count it all joy when you fall into various trials, [3]knowing that the testing of your faith produces patience. [4]But let patience have *its* perfect work, that you may be perfect and complete, lacking nothing. [5]If any of you lacks wisdom, let him ask of God, who gives to all liberally and without reproach, and it will be given to him. [6]But let him ask in faith, with no doubting, for he who doubts is like a wave of the sea driven and tossed by the wind. [7]For let not that man suppose that he will receive anything from the Lord; [8]*he is* a double-minded man, unstable in all his ways.

The Perspective of Rich and Poor

[9]Let the lowly brother glory in his exaltation, [10]but the rich in his humiliation, because as a flower of the field he will pass away. [11]For no sooner has the sun risen with a burning heat than it withers the grass; its flower falls, and its beautiful appearance perishes. So the rich man also will fade away in his pursuits.

Loving God Under Trials

[12]Blessed *is* the man who endures temptation; for when he has been approved, he will receive the crown of life which the Lord has promised to those who love Him. [13]Let no one say when he is tempted, "I am tempted by God"; for God cannot be tempted by evil, nor does He Himself tempt anyone. [14]But each one is tempted when he is drawn away by his own desires and enticed. [15]Then, when desire has conceived, it gives birth to sin; and sin, when it is full-grown, brings forth death.

[16]Do not be deceived, my beloved brethren. [17]Every good gift and every perfect gift is from above, and comes down from the Father of lights, with whom there is no variation or shadow of turning. [18]Of His own will He brought us forth by the word of truth, that we might be a kind of firstfruits of His creatures.

Qualities Needed in Trials

[19]So then,[a] my beloved brethren, let every man be swift to hear, slow to speak, slow to wrath; [20]for the wrath of man does not produce the righteousness of God.

Doers—Not Hearers Only

[21]Therefore lay aside all filthiness and overflow of wickedness, and receive with meekness the implanted word, which is able to save your souls.

[22]But be doers of the word, and not hearers only, deceiving yourselves. [23]For if anyone is a hearer of the word and not a doer, he is like a man observing his natural face in a mirror; [24]for he observes himself, goes away, and immediately forgets what kind of man he was. [25]But he who looks into the perfect law of liberty and continues *in it,* and is not a forgetful hearer but a doer of the work, this one will be blessed in what he does.

1:19 [a] NU-Text reads *Know this* or *This you know.*

Life Lesson

James 1:1-27

SITUATION James knew that Christians scattered all over the world would face challenges to their faith. If they were to remain faithful, their beliefs needed to be not only intellectual, but also very practical. He urged his readers to put their faith into action.

OBSERVATION God allows tough situations in our lives in order to refine us and bring us closer to him. We should approach these times with a right attitude and seek wisdom from God.

INSPIRATION When a potter bakes a pot, he checks its solidity by pulling it out of the oven and thumping it. If it "sings" it's ready. If it "thuds," it's placed back in the oven. The character of a person is also checked by thumping.

Been thumped lately?

Late-night phone calls. Grouchy teacher. Grumpy moms. Burnt meals. Flat tires. "You've got to be kidding" deadlines. Those are thumps. Thumps are those irritating inconveniences that trigger the worst in us. They catch us off guard. Flat footed. They aren't big enough to be crises, but if you get enough of them, watch out! Traffic jams. Long lines. Empty mailboxes. Dirty clothes on the floor . . . Thump. Thump. Thump. How do I respond? Do I sing? Or do I thud? Jesus said that out of the nature of the heart a man speaks (Luke 6:45). There's nothing like a good thump to reveal the nature of a heart. The true character of a person is seen not in momentary heroics, but in the thump-packed humdrum of day-to-day living.

(From *On the Anvil* by Max Lucado)

APPLICATION How do you respond when you are "thumped" from people at work, school, family, or people at the grocery store? Your initial reaction during these times reflects who you are. What responses need to change? Make the changes today.

EXPLORATION Perseverance—Romans 2:7; 8:24-25; 2 Corinthians 6:3-7.

26If anyone among you[b] thinks he is religious, and does not bridle his
tongue but deceives his own heart, this one's religion *is* useless. 27Pure and
undefiled religion before God and the Father is this: to visit orphans and
widows in their trouble, *and* to keep oneself unspotted from the world.

Beware of Personal Favoritism

2 My brethren, do not hold the faith of our Lord Jesus Christ, *the Lord* of
glory, with partiality. 2For if there should come into your assembly a
man with gold rings, in fine apparel, and there should also come in a poor
man in filthy clothes, 3and you pay attention to the one wearing the fine
clothes and say to him, "You sit here in a good place," and say to the poor
man, "You stand there," or, "Sit here at my footstool," 4have you not shown
partiality among yourselves, and become judges with evil thoughts?
5Listen, my beloved brethren: Has God not chosen the poor of this
world *to be* rich in faith and heirs of the kingdom which He promised to
those who love Him? 6But you have dishonored the poor man. Do not the
rich oppress you and drag you into the courts? 7Do they not blaspheme
that noble name by which you are called?
8If you really fulfill *the* royal law according to the Scripture, *"You shall
love your neighbor as yourself,"*[c] you do well; 9but if you show partiality,
you commit sin, and are convicted by the law as transgressors. 10For whoever
shall keep the whole law, and yet stumble in one *point,* he is guilty of all. 11For
He who said, *"Do not commit adultery,"*[d] also said, *"Do not murder."*[e]
Now if you do not commit adultery, but you do murder, you have become
a transgressor of the law. 12So speak and so do as those who will be judged
by the law of liberty. 13For judgment is without mercy to the one who has
shown no mercy. Mercy triumphs over judgment.

Faith Without Works Is Dead

14What *does it* profit, my brethren, if someone says he has faith but does
not have works? Can faith save him? 15If a brother or sister is naked and
destitute of daily food, 16and one of you says to them, "Depart in peace, be
warmed and filled," but you do not give them the things which are needed
for the body, what *does it* profit? 17Thus also faith by itself, if it does not
have works, is dead.
18But someone will say, "You have faith, and I have works." Show me your
faith without your[f] works, and I will show you my faith by my[g] works. 19You
believe that there is one God. You do well. Even the demons believe—and
tremble! 20But do you want to know, O foolish man, that faith without
works is dead?[h] 21Was not Abraham our father justified by works when he
offered Isaac his son on the altar? 22Do you see that faith was working together with his works, and by works faith was made perfect? 23And the
Scripture was fulfilled which says, *"Abraham believed God, and it was accounted to him for righteousness."*[i] And he was called the friend of God.
24You see then that a man is justified by works, and not by faith only.
25Likewise, was not Rahab the harlot also justified by works when she
received the messengers and sent *them* out another way?

1:26 [b] NU-Text omits *among you.*
2:8 [c] Leviticus 19:18
2:11 [d] Exodus 20:14; Deuteronomy 5:18 [e] Exodus 20:13; Deuteronomy 5:17
2:18 [f] NU-Text omits *your.* [g] NU-Text omits *my.*
2:20 [h] NU-Text reads *useless.*
2:23 [i] Genesis 15:6

LIFE LESSON

James 2:1-26

SITUATION These Christians drew social lines among themselves. Certain cliques were more popular and more important in the church.

OBSERVATION Christians should avoid forming cliques. God sees no difference between the social elite and the lowest class. All are called to serve and worship side-by-side.

INSPIRATION Grant's church was beginning a ministry to people suffering from AIDS. At the initial planning session, an expert on this type of ministry was going to be present to speak to the group about the *Dos* and *Don'ts* of such a task. The catch was that the person who was coming had AIDS.

As he drove to the meeting, Grant struggled with what his response would be. "How should I address this individual? Would I shake hands with this person? Would I sit next to him? Would I pry into his lifestyle, demanding to know how he contracted the disease? How would I react if he volunteered that information? Is this a ministry that I should be involved in personally?" These questions and countless others were swirling through his mind.

As he pondered these issues, he was reminded of James 2:1 and the fact that favoritism is sin. The issue is not whether the distinction is made over economic, social, educational, physical, spiritual, or health concerns or differences. The issue is that our motives for making the distinction are immediately called into question because favoritism is sin.

(From *A Dad's Blessing* by Gary Smalley and John Trent)

APPLICATION Do you attend a church regularly? Are you involved enough to see which people are on the "outside"? If not, become more involved, then help break down walls by bringing people on the fringe into your circle.

EXPLORATION Unity—Psalm 133:1; John 10:16; 17:23; Acts 4:32; Romans 12:4; 15:5; 1 Corinthians 1:10; 10:17; Ephesians 2:14-20; Philippians 2:1-2.

LIFE LESSON

James 3:1-18

SITUATION James described how faith works in everyday life. Everyday speech and actions should correspond with inward faith.

OBSERVATION The tongue can build others up or tear them down. It needs to be controlled.

INSPIRATION Each of us has a tongue and a voice. These instruments of speech can be used destructively or employed constructively. I can use my tongue to slander, to gripe, to scold, to nag, and to quarrel; or I can bring it under the control of God's Spirit and make it an instrument of blessing and praise. . . . Only God can control it, as we yield it to Him.

The twentieth-century version of James 3:3 says, "When we put bits into the horses' mouths to make them obey us, we control the rest of their bodies also." Just so, when we submit to the claims of Christ upon our lives, our untamed natures are brought under His control. We become meek, tamed, and "fit for the Master's service."

(From *The Secret of Happiness* by Billy Graham)

APPLICATION Today, use your tongue to bring joy, peace, and happiness into the lives of others. Thank others for their friendship. Encourage those who are struggling. Tell others of your love for them. Most of all, use your words to praise God throughout today.

EXPLORATION Restraining the Tongue—Psalm 34:13; Proverbs 13:3; 21:23; Titus 3:2; James 1:26; 1 Peter 3:10.

26For as the body without the spirit is dead, so faith without works is
dead also.

The Untamable Tongue

3 My brethren, let not many of you become teachers, knowing that we
shall receive a stricter judgment. 2For we all stumble in many things. If
anyone does not stumble in word, he *is* a perfect man, able also to bridle
the whole body. 3Indeed,[j] we put bits in horses' mouths that they may obey
us, and we turn their whole body. 4Look also at ships: although they are so
large and are driven by fierce winds, they are turned by a very small rudder wherever the pilot desires. 5Even so the tongue is a little member and
boasts great things.

See how great a forest a little fire kindles! 6And the tongue *is* a fire, a
world of iniquity. The tongue is so set among our members that it defiles
the whole body, and sets on fire the course of nature; and it is set on fire by
hell. 7For every kind of beast and bird, of reptile and creature of the sea, is
tamed and has been tamed by mankind. 8But no man can tame the tongue.
It is an unruly evil, full of deadly poison. 9With it we bless our God and
Father, and with it we curse men, who have been made in the similitude of
God. 10Out of the same mouth proceed blessing and cursing. My brethren,
these things ought not to be so. 11Does a spring send forth fresh *water* and
bitter from the same opening? 12Can a fig tree, my brethren, bear olives, or
a grapevine bear figs? Thus no spring yields both salt water and fresh.[k]

Heavenly Versus Demonic Wisdom

13Who *is* wise and understanding among you? Let him show by good
conduct *that* his works *are done* in the meekness of wisdom. 14But if you have
bitter envy and self-seeking in your hearts, do not boast and lie against the
truth. 15This wisdom does not descend from above, but *is* earthly, sensual,
demonic. 16For where envy and self-seeking *exist,* confusion and every evil
thing *are* there. 17But the wisdom that is from above is first pure, then
peaceable, gentle, willing to yield, full of mercy and good fruits, without
partiality and without hypocrisy. 18Now the fruit of righteousness is sown
in peace by those who make peace.

Pride Promotes Strife

4 Where do wars and fights *come* from among you? Do *they* not *come*
from your *desires for* pleasure that war in your members? 2You lust and
do not have. You murder and covet and cannot obtain. You fight and war. Yet[l]
you do not have because you do not ask. 3You ask and do not receive, because
you ask amiss, that you may spend *it* on your pleasures. 4Adulterers and[m]
adulteresses! Do you not know that friendship with the world is enmity
with God? Whoever therefore wants to be a friend of the world makes
himself an enemy of God. 5Or do you think that the Scripture says in vain,
"The Spirit who dwells in us yearns jealously"?

6But He gives more grace. Therefore He says:

> *"God resists the proud,*
> *But gives grace to the humble."*[n]

3:3 [j] NU-Text reads *Now if.*
3:12 [k] NU-Text reads *Neither can a salty spring produce fresh water.*
4:2 [l] NU-Text and M-Text omit *Yet.*
4:4 [m] NU-Text omits *Adulterers and.*
4:6 [n] Proverbs 3:34

Humility Cures Worldliness

7 Therefore submit to God. Resist the devil and he will flee from you. 8 Draw near to God and He will draw near to you. Cleanse *your* hands, *you* sinners; and purify *your* hearts, *you* double-minded. 9 Lament and mourn and weep! Let your laughter be turned to mourning and *your* joy to gloom. 10 Humble yourselves in the sight of the Lord, and He will lift you up.

Do Not Judge a Brother

11 Do not speak evil of one another, brethren. He who speaks evil of a brother and judges his brother, speaks evil of the law and judges the law. But if you judge the law, you are not a doer of the law but a judge. 12 There is one Lawgiver,[o] who is able to save and to destroy. Who[p] are you to judge another?[q]

Do Not Boast About Tomorrow

13 Come now, you who say, "Today or tomorrow we will[r] go to such and such a city, spend a year there, buy and sell, and make a profit"; 14 whereas you do not know what *will happen* tomorrow. For what *is* your life? It is even a vapor that appears for a little time and then vanishes away. 15 Instead you *ought* to say, "If the Lord wills, we shall live and do this or that." 16 But now you boast in your arrogance. All such boasting is evil.

17 Therefore, to him who knows to do good and does not do *it,* to him it is sin.

Rich Oppressors Will Be Judged

5 Come now, *you* rich, weep and howl for your miseries that are coming upon *you!* 2 Your riches are corrupted, and your garments are moth-eaten. 3 Your gold and silver are corroded, and their corrosion will be a witness against you and will eat your flesh like fire. You have heaped up treasure in the last days. 4 Indeed the wages of the laborers who mowed your fields, which you kept back by fraud, cry out; and the cries of the reapers have reached the ears of the Lord of Sabaoth.[s] 5 You have lived on the earth in pleasure and luxury; you have fattened your hearts as[t] in a day of slaughter. 6 You have condemned, you have murdered the just; he does not resist you.

Be Patient and Persevering

7 Therefore be patient, brethren, until the coming of the Lord. See *how* the farmer waits for the precious fruit of the earth, waiting patiently for it until it receives the early and latter rain. 8 You also be patient. Establish your hearts, for the coming of the Lord is at hand.

9 Do not grumble against one another, brethren, lest you be condemned.[u] Behold, the Judge is standing at the door! 10 My brethren, take the prophets, who spoke in the name of the Lord, as an example of suffering and patience. 11 Indeed we count them blessed who endure. You have heard of the perseverance of Job and seen the end *intended by* the Lord—that the Lord is very compassionate and merciful.

12 But above all, my brethren, do not swear, either by heaven or by earth or with any other oath. But let your "Yes" be "Yes," and *your* "No," "No," lest you fall into judgment.[v]

4:12 [o] NU-Text adds *and Judge.* [p] NU-Text and M-Text read *But who.* [q] NU-Text reads *a neighbor.*
4:13 [r] M-Text reads *let us.*
5:4 [s] Literally, in Hebrew, *Hosts*
5:5 [t] NU-Text omits *as.*
5:9 [u] NU-Text and M-Text read *judged.*
5:12 [v] M-Text reads *hypocrisy.*

LIFE LESSON

James 4:1-17

SITUATION God planned for his people to be distinct by their peaceful and humble attitudes. Both words and actions mark these qualities.

OBSERVATION God can use even our weakest abilities to accomplish his plan.

INSPIRATION In order to know God's will there must be a willingness to do it.

Imagine a door in the path ahead of us. God's will is on the other side of that door. We crave to know what that is. Will God show us what's on the other side of that door? No. Why not? Because we have to resolve an issue on this side of the door first. If He is Lord, He has the right to determine what's on the other side of the door. . . .

Why do we want to know what's on the other side of the door? Isn't it because we want to reserve the right to determine whether or not we will go through it? . . .

One man probably spoke for many when he said, "I'm so used to running my own life. I'm not sure I even can or want to trust someone else. Besides, God would probably haul me off to some mission field I can't stand." What we need to realize is that if we did give our heart to the Lord, and God did call us to that mission field, by the time we got there we wouldn't want to be anywhere else.

Do you believe that the will of God is good, acceptable and perfect for you? That's the heart of the issue.

(From *Walking in the Light* by Neil Anderson)

APPLICATION List five experiences that make you proud. Now list five of your most embarrassing moments. About the first five, pray that real service would begin as God humbles you. About the second five, pray that God would exalt himself as you weakly and clumsily serve him.

EXPLORATION Submission—Luke 14:27; John 14:28; 1 Corinthians 11:3; 1 Peter 3:5.

LIFE LESSON
James 5:1-20

SITUATION Wealth can lead some into false security. Jesus and the Old Testament prophets defended the poor. James explained that instead of hoarding, exploiting, and self-indulging, Believers should share with those in need.

OBSERVATION A Christian should be more concerned with sharing and meeting the needs of others than with accumulating earthly treasures.

INSPIRATION We live at one of the great turning points in history. The present division of the World's resources dare not continue. And it will not. Either courageous pioneers will persuade reluctant nations to share the good earth's bounty, or we will enter an era of catastrophic conflict. . . .

Do Christians today have that kind of faith and courage? Will we pioneer new models of sharing for our interdependent world? Will we dare to become the vanguard in the struggle for structural change? . . .

I am not pessimistic. God regularly accomplishes his will through faithful remnants. Even in affluent nations, there are millions of Christians who love their Lord Jesus more than houses and lands. . . .

If at this moment in history a few million Christians in affluent nations dare to join hands with the poor around the world, we will decisively influence the course of world history. Together we will strive to be a biblical people ready to follow wherever Scripture leads. We must pray for the courage to bear any cross, suffer any loss and joyfully embrace any sacrifice that biblical faith requires in an Age of Hunger.

(From *Rich Christians in an Age of Hunger* by Ronald Sider)

APPLICATION Are you free to lend your possessions? Is money set aside for giving? Develop a plan today, keep it for six months, and evaluate the results.

EXPLORATION Sharing—Acts 2:44; 4:32-35.

Meeting Specific Needs

13Is anyone among you suffering? Let him pray. Is anyone cheerful? Let
him sing psalms. 14Is anyone among you sick? Let him call for the elders of
the church, and let them pray over him, anointing him with oil in the name
of the Lord. 15And the prayer of faith will save the sick, and the Lord will
raise him up. And if he has committed sins, he will be forgiven. 16Confess
your trespasses[w] to one another, and pray for one another, that you may be
healed. The effective, fervent prayer of a righteous man avails much. 17Elijah
was a man with a nature like ours, and he prayed earnestly that it would not
rain; and it did not rain on the land for three years and six months. 18And
he prayed again, and the heaven gave rain, and the earth produced its fruit.

Bring Back the Erring One

19Brethren, if anyone among you wanders from the truth, and someone
turns him back, 20let him know that he who turns a sinner from the error
of his way will save a soul[x] from death and cover a multitude of sins.

5:16 [w] NU-Text reads *Therefore confess your sins.*
5:20 [x] NU-Text reads *his soul.*

The First Epistle of

PETER

INTRODUCTION

The science teacher makes a derisive statement about God creating the world. You raise your hand and state your convictions. Your teacher rolls her eyes. The students behind you chuckle.

It's not easy being the only one in your family who goes to church. It's bad enough that they don't go. It's worse that they make fun of you for going.

If you would pad your expense account, so could the other salesmen. But if you don't, they can't. "Come on," they urge you, "just hedge a little." You refuse. The next day someone has spilled paint on your car.

Persecution. Not by firing squad. Not by death threats. Not by the government. But it's persecution nonetheless. A more subtle persecution. Persecution from friends, family, and peers. They won't take your life . . . but they will take your peace . . . and they'd like to take your faith, if you'd let them.

How do you respond? Begin with Peter's survival manual. He understood persecution. Beaten and jailed. Threatened and punished. He knew the sting of the false word and the angry whip. No doubt he'd seen some Christians stand and others fall. He'd seen enough to know what it takes to stay strong in tough times.

His counsel may surprise you.

His counsel may sustain you. It may be just what you need so that "the genuineness of your faith, being much more precious than gold that perishes, though it is tested by fire, may be found to praise, honor, and glory at the revelation of Jesus Christ" (1:7).

LIFE LESSON

1 Peter 1:1-25

SITUATION Peter reminded Christians who were scattered all over the world that they were guaranteed an inheritance. They were to base their confidence on the indestructible truth of God's Word.

OBSERVATION God promises us an inheritance that will never pass away.

INSPIRATION Hollywood, California—many people come there from around the world frantically seeking success, fame, and fortune. For most, however, the quest is a futile one.

Only a few have actually "made it" to the sidewalk along Hollywood Boulevard, where embedded bronze symbols bear the names and faces of the famous. It appears that these men and women, in worldly terms, have mastered their destinies. And yet, upon passing this way and looking at these small monuments more carefully, one cannot help but be touched with a sense of irony. The same sidewalk in which the coveted star has been firmly laid is cluttered with debris, splattered with mud, and ground over in places with patches of gum.

In stark contrast, the promise of God to His people says "I lay . . . a sure foundation.". . .

The reward of walking this "established" path is only found in God's Word. There is no bronze star waiting to be laid in concrete by the hands of man and tarnished by the passage of time. Rather, the redeemed of the Lord—those whose lives are built upon the sure foundation by God—shall shine forever.

(From *Living and Praying in Jesus' Name* by Dick Eastman and Jack Hayford)

APPLICATION How many times during the last week have you praised God because of the inheritance he has promised you?

EXPLORATION Security—Psalm 9:10; Zephaniah 2:3-7; Romans 6:6-11; 2 Corinthians 4:14; 1 John 5:13.

Greeting to the Elect Pilgrims

Peter, an apostle of Jesus Christ,

To the pilgrims of the Dispersion in Pontus, Galatia, Cappadocia, Asia, and Bithynia, [2]elect according to the foreknowledge of God the Father, in sanctification of the Spirit, for obedience and sprinkling of the blood of Jesus Christ:

Grace to you and peace be multiplied.

A Heavenly Inheritance

[3]Blessed *be* the God and Father of our Lord Jesus Christ, who according to His abundant mercy has begotten us again to a living hope through the resurrection of Jesus Christ from the dead, [4]to an inheritance incorruptible and undefiled and that does not fade away, reserved in heaven for you, [5]who are kept by the power of God through faith for salvation ready to be revealed in the last time.

[6]In this you greatly rejoice, though now for a little while, if need be, you have been grieved by various trials, [7]that the genuineness of your faith, *being* much more precious than gold that perishes, though it is tested by fire, may be found to praise, honor, and glory at the revelation of Jesus Christ, [8]whom having not seen[a] you love. Though now you do not see *Him,* yet believing, you rejoice with joy inexpressible and full of glory, [9]receiving the end of your faith—the salvation of *your* souls.

[10]Of this salvation the prophets have inquired and searched carefully, who prophesied of the grace *that would come* to you, [11]searching what, or what manner of time, the Spirit of Christ who was in them was indicating when He testified beforehand the sufferings of Christ and the glories that would follow. [12]To them it was revealed that, not to themselves, but to us[b] they were ministering the things which now have been reported to you through those who have preached the gospel to you by the Holy Spirit sent from heaven—things which angels desire to look into.

Living Before God Our Father

[13]Therefore gird up the loins of your mind, be sober, and rest *your* hope fully upon the grace that is to be brought to you at the revelation of Jesus Christ; [14]as obedient children, not conforming yourselves to the former lusts, *as* in your ignorance; [15]but as He who called you *is* holy, you also be holy in all *your* conduct, [16]because it is written, *"Be holy, for I am holy."*[c]

[17]And if you call on the Father, who without partiality judges according to each one's work, conduct yourselves throughout the time of your stay *here* in fear; [18]knowing that you were not redeemed with corruptible things, *like* silver or gold, from your aimless conduct *received* by tradition from your fathers, [19]but with the precious blood of Christ, as of a lamb without blemish and without spot. [20]He indeed was foreordained before the foundation of the world, but was manifest in these last times for you [21]who through Him believe in God, who raised Him from the dead and gave Him glory, so that your faith and hope are in God.

1:8 [a] M-Text reads *known.*
1:12 [b] NU-Text and M-Text read *you.*
1:16 [c] Leviticus 11:44, 45; 19:2; 20:7

The Enduring Word

22 Since you have purified your souls in obeying the truth through the
Spirit[d] in sincere love of the brethren, love one another fervently with a
pure heart, 23 having been born again, not of corruptible seed but incorruptible, through the word of God which lives and abides forever,[e] 24 because

"All flesh is as grass,
And all the glory of man[f] as the flower of the grass.
The grass withers,
And its flower falls away,
25 *But the word of the LORD endures forever."*[g]

Now this is the word which by the gospel was preached to you.

2 Therefore, laying aside all malice, all deceit, hypocrisy, envy, and all
evil speaking, 2 as newborn babes, desire the pure milk of the word, that
you may grow thereby,[h] 3 if indeed you have tasted that the Lord *is* gracious.

The Chosen Stone and His Chosen People

4 Coming to Him *as to* a living stone, rejected indeed by men, but chosen
by God *and* precious, 5 you also, as living stones, are being built up a spiritual house, a holy priesthood, to offer up spiritual sacrifices acceptable to
God through Jesus Christ. 6 Therefore it is also contained in the Scripture,

"Behold, I lay in Zion
A chief cornerstone, elect, precious,
And he who believes on Him will by no means be put to shame."[i]

7 Therefore, to you who believe, *He is* precious; but to those who are
disobedient,[j]

"The stone which the builders rejected
Has become the chief cornerstone,"[k]

8 and

"A stone of stumbling
And a rock of offense."[l]

They stumble, being disobedient to the word, to which they also were appointed.

9 But you *are* a chosen generation, a royal priesthood, a holy nation, His
own special people, that you may proclaim the praises of Him who called
you out of darkness into His marvelous light; 10 who once *were* not a people
but *are* now the people of God, who had not obtained mercy but now have
obtained mercy.

Living Before the World

11 Beloved, I beg *you* as sojourners and pilgrims, abstain from fleshly
lusts which war against the soul, 12 having your conduct honorable among

LIFE LESSON

1 Peter 2:1-25

SITUATION Peter knew that loyal Christians suffered from the abuse of cruel Roman practices. He told them to expect suffering. Suffering might be endured so that others could see the Lord's power to help Christians endure.

OBSERVATION Christians can encourage others who are suffering by showing mercy, humility, and kindness to them.

INSPIRATION Is there anything more frail than a bruised reed? Look at the bruised reed at the water's edge. A once slender and tall stalk of sturdy river grass, it is now bowed and bent.

Are you a bruised reed? Was it so long ago that you stood so tall, so proud? . . . Then something happened. You were bruised . . .

by harsh words

by a friend's anger

by a spouse's betrayal

by your own failure

by religion's rigidity.

. . . Your hollow reed, once erect, now stooped, and hidden in the bulrush.

And the smoldering wick on the candle. . . . Once aflame, now flickering and failing. . . . Was it that long ago you blazed with faith? Remember how you illuminated the path? . . .

Painted on canvas after canvas is the tender touch of a Creator who has a special place for the bruised and weary of the world.

(From *He Still Moves Stones* by Max Lucado)

APPLICATION Find a story of a Christian who showed grace under pressure. Read it. Pray that you, too, will endure when and if the heat in your life is turned up.

EXPLORATION Suffering—Matthew 24:9-13; Mark 8:31-33; Romans 8:17; Philippians 1:12-14; 2 Thessalonians 1:4; 1 Peter 4:12-16.

1:22 [d] NU-Text omits *through the Spirit.*
1:23 [e] NU-Text omits *forever.*
1:24 [f] NU-Text reads *all its glory.*
1:25 [g] Isaiah 40:6–8
2:2 [h] NU-Text adds *up to salvation.*
2:6 [i] Isaiah 28:16
2:7 [j] NU-Text reads *to those who disbelieve.* [k] Psalm 118:22
2:8 [l] Isaiah 8:14

the Gentiles, that when they speak against you as evildoers, they may, by
your good works which they observe, glorify God in the day of visitation.

Submission to Government

13 Therefore submit yourselves to every ordinance of man for the Lord's
sake, whether to the king as supreme, 14 or to governors, as to those who
are sent by him for the punishment of evildoers and *for the* praise of those
who do good. 15 For this is the will of God, that by doing good you may put
to silence the ignorance of foolish men— 16 as free, yet not using liberty as
a cloak for vice, but as bondservants of God. 17 Honor all *people.* Love the
brotherhood. Fear God. Honor the king.

Submission to Masters

18 Servants, *be* submissive to *your* masters with all fear, not only to the
good and gentle, but also to the harsh. 19 For this *is* commendable, if because of conscience toward God one endures grief, suffering wrongfully.
20 For what credit *is it* if, when you are beaten for your faults, you take it patiently? But when you do good and suffer, if you take it patiently, this *is*
commendable before God. 21 For to this you were called, because Christ
also suffered for us,[m] leaving us[n] an example, that you should follow
His steps:

22 *"Who committed no sin,*
Nor was deceit found in His mouth";[o]

23 who, when He was reviled, did not revile in return; when He suffered, He
did not threaten, but committed *Himself* to Him who judges righteously;
24 who Himself bore our sins in His own body on the tree, that we, having
died to sins, might live for righteousness—by whose stripes you were
healed. 25 For you were like sheep going astray, but have now returned to
the Shepherd and Overseer[p] of your souls.

Submission to Husbands

3 Wives, likewise, *be* submissive to your own husbands, that even if
some do not obey the word, they, without a word, may be won by the
conduct of their wives, 2 when they observe your chaste conduct *accompanied* by fear. 3 Do not let your adornment be *merely* outward—arranging
the hair, wearing gold, or putting on *fine* apparel— 4 rather *let it be* the hidden person of the heart, with the incorruptible *beauty* of a gentle and quiet
spirit, which is very precious in the sight of God. 5 For in this manner, in
former times, the holy women who trusted in God also adorned themselves, being submissive to their own husbands, 6 as Sarah obeyed Abraham, calling him lord, whose daughters you are if you do good and are not
afraid with any terror.

A Word to Husbands

7 Husbands, likewise, dwell with *them* with understanding, giving
honor to the wife, as to the weaker vessel, and as *being* heirs together of the
grace of life, that your prayers may not be hindered.

2:21 [m] NU-Text reads *you.* [n] NU-Text and M-Text read *you.*
2:22 [o] Isaiah 53:9
2:25 [p] Greek *Episkopos*

LIFE LESSON

1 Peter 3:1-22

SITUATION In Peter's day, women had little status. Peter encouraged wives and husbands to recognize each other's needs and respect them.

OBSERVATION Submission does not indicate weakness or inferiority. Rather, one married partner demonstrates love for the other by yielding to the other.

INSPIRATION A husband is to love his wife with the same sacrificial self-abandonment that Christ adopted toward each of us. When a man considers hardship in marriage, he needs to look at the life of Jesus. Jesus said, "The Son of Man came not to be served, but to serve" (Matthew 20:28). Jesus is presented in Scripture as both Head and Servant. He is the "head over everything for the church" (Ephesians 1:22) who took "the very nature of a servant" (Philippians 2:7). And Jesus instructed us, "The greatest among you will be your servant" (Matthew 23:11).

As believers, we are all called to servanthood as an expression of our new life in Christ. However, when it comes to marriage, modeling this attribute of God's Son is a calling extended to husbands. A husband expresses love to his wife by regarding her as a completely equal partner in everything that concerns their life together. He asserts his headship to see that this equal partnership works. Loving headship affirms and defers; it encourages and stimulates. Loving headship delights to delegate without demanding.

(From *Quiet Times for Couples* by H. Norman Wright)

APPLICATION Today, do something new to show your spouse how much you care, how happy you are together, how much God encourages you through your marriage. Do the dishes, give a flower, take a walk, or write a note. If you are unmarried, develop your character to match the one discussed by Peter. Put more attention on the beauty that comes from within rather than on physical appearance.

EXPLORATION Submission—Luke 14:27; John 14:28; 1 Corinthians 11:3, 9-12; Ephesians 5:21-24.

Called to Blessing

8Finally, all *of you be* of one mind, having compassion for one another;
love as brothers, *be* tenderhearted, *be* courteous;[q] 9not returning evil for
evil or reviling for reviling, but on the contrary blessing, knowing that you
were called to this, that you may inherit a blessing. 10For

"He who would love life
And see good days,
Let him refrain his tongue from evil,
And his lips from speaking deceit.
11 *Let him turn away from evil and do good;*
Let him seek peace and pursue it.
12 *For the eyes of the LORD are on the righteous,*
And His ears are open to their prayers;
But the face of the LORD is against those who do evil."[r]

Suffering for Right and Wrong

13And who *is* he who will harm you if you become followers of what is
good? 14But even if you should suffer for righteousness' sake, *you are*
blessed. *"And do not be afraid of their threats, nor be troubled."*[s] 15But
sanctify the Lord God[t] in your hearts, and always *be* ready to *give* a defense
to everyone who asks you a reason for the hope that is in you, with meekness and fear; 16having a good conscience, that when they defame you as
evildoers, those who revile your good conduct in Christ may be ashamed.
17For *it is* better, if it is the will of God, to suffer for doing good than for
doing evil.

Christ's Suffering and Ours

18For Christ also suffered once for sins, the just for the unjust, that He
might bring us[u] to God, being put to death in the flesh but made alive by
the Spirit, 19by whom also He went and preached to the spirits in prison,
20who formerly were disobedient, when once the Divine longsuffering
waited[v] in the days of Noah, while *the* ark was being prepared, in which a
few, that is, eight souls, were saved through water. 21There is also an anti-
type which now saves us—baptism (not the removal of the filth of the
flesh, but the answer of a good conscience toward God), through the resurrection of Jesus Christ, 22who has gone into heaven and is at the right
hand of God, angels and authorities and powers having been made subject to Him.

4 Therefore, since Christ suffered for us[w] in the flesh, arm yourselves
also with the same mind, for he who has suffered in the flesh has
ceased from sin, 2that he no longer should live the rest of *his* time in the
flesh for the lusts of men, but for the will of God. 3For we *have spent*
enough of our past lifetime[x] in doing the will of the Gentiles—when we
walked in lewdness, lusts, drunkenness, revelries, drinking parties, and

LIFE LESSON

1 Peter 4:1-19

SITUATION Christians have shed an old set of rules, and adopted a new set full of love and God's power. Following God's standards helps Christians face the difficult trials ahead.

OBSERVATION Live according to God's standards. Regardless of suffering and inconvenience, God gives us power to persevere through adversity.

INSPIRATION Now for the sake of a few idealistic souls who could assume only the best and think, I can hardly wait to live like this; this is going to be fun! I want to bring you back ever so gently to reality. When you decide to live like Christ among the selfish and strong-willed, God will honor your decision, but . . . you will encounter misunderstanding and mistreatment. You will be taken advantage of. However, don't make another wrong assumption by thinking that if you are going through tough times, you are off target. Not so. Doing what is right is never a stroll through a rose garden. Jesus' plan for living may be simple, but it is not easy. . . .

No matter how painful it may be, let us trust Him to bring good from our living His way.

The Lord Jesus Christ is the model to follow—and you remember where He wound up! But think of all those who were once His enemies, now His friends. You and I would certainly be numbered among them. The force of love is absolutely unconquerable.

(From *Simple Faith* by Charles Swindoll)

APPLICATION Has your life been spent honoring God? Evaluate the focus of your life's work. What goals do you have? Which ones have you met? Are you living for God, or for yourself? Reserve some time today to review how you have been doing.

EXPLORATION Lifestyle—Genesis 49:3-28; Matthew 25:1-46; 1 Thessalonians 5:23.

3:8 [q] NU-Text reads *humble.*
3:12 [r] Psalm 34:12–16
3:14 [s] Isaiah 8:12
3:15 [t] NU-Text reads *Christ as Lord.*
3:18 [u] NU-Text and M-Text read *you.*
3:20 [v] NU-Text and M-Text read *when the longsuffering of God waited patiently.*
4:1 [w] NU-Text omits *for us.*
4:3 [x] NU-Text reads *time.*

LIFE LESSON

1 Peter 5:1-14

SITUATION Peter challenged the elders to be good shepherds of their churches, just as Christ was a good shepherd with his disciples. He urged elders to look out for struggling Christians as shepherds would for lost sheep.

OBSERVATION Elders and leaders play a vital role in leading and protecting young Christians. Because elders face temptation, too, God will hold them accountable for their actions.

INSPIRATION The attitude Christ modeled for us is one that should typify every Christian, whether in pulpit or pew, whether leader of a vast organization or solitary prayer warrior. Not puffed up with self-importance, but poured out for others. . . .

That doesn't mean we shrink from responsibility. God calls each of us to a particular task. But when the temptation of pride comes knocking . . . as it will . . . we must lock the door against it—whatever that takes.

But the toughest question is, How do we know? Because usually the knock is very faint, and we don't listen for it. The best protection I have discovered is accountability. Since we all have blind spots, we must, as we mentioned earlier, submit ourselves to those who can see the logs floating in our eyes.

How often does your church governing body review 1 Peter 5:2? . . . Or Paul's first letter to Timothy? We must constantly check each other on how well we are measuring up to the clear biblical requirements of leadership.

(From *The Body* by Charles Colson)

APPLICATION Christians who are younger in their faith need close fellowship with those further along in their Christian life. Do you have someone who helps refine, confront, disciple, and encourage you? Do you serve in that role for someone else? Pray that God would raise up someone to help you, as you help someone else.

EXPLORATION Church Leaders—1 Timothy 3:8-13; Titus 1:5-9; Revelation 4:4.

abominable idolatries. 4 In regard to these, they think it strange that you do not run with *them* in the same flood of dissipation, speaking evil of *you.* 5 They will give an account to Him who is ready to judge the living and the dead. 6 For this reason the gospel was preached also to those who are dead, that they might be judged according to men in the flesh, but live according to God in the spirit.

Serving for God's Glory

7 But the end of all things is at hand; therefore be serious and watchful in your prayers. 8 And above all things have fervent love for one another, for *"love will cover a multitude of sins."*[y] 9 Be hospitable to one another without grumbling. 10 As each one has received a gift, minister it to one another, as good stewards of the manifold grace of God. 11 If anyone speaks, *let him speak* as the oracles of God. If anyone ministers, *let him do it* as with the ability which God supplies, that in all things God may be glorified through Jesus Christ, to whom belong the glory and the dominion forever and ever. Amen.

Suffering for God's Glory

12 Beloved, do not think it strange concerning the fiery trial which is to try you, as though some strange thing happened to you; 13 but rejoice to the extent that you partake of Christ's sufferings, that when His glory is revealed, you may also be glad with exceeding joy. 14 If you are reproached for the name of Christ, blessed *are you,* for the Spirit of glory and of God rests upon you.[z] On their part He is blasphemed, but on your part He is glorified. 15 But let none of you suffer as a murderer, a thief, an evildoer, or as a busybody in other people's matters. 16 Yet if *anyone suffers* as a Christian, let him not be ashamed, but let him glorify God in this matter.[a]

17 For the time *has come* for judgment to begin at the house of God; and if *it begins* with us first, what will *be* the end of those who do not obey the gospel of God? 18 Now

"If the righteous one is scarcely saved,
Where will the ungodly and the sinner appear?"[b]

19 Therefore let those who suffer according to the will of God commit their souls *to Him* in doing good, as to a faithful Creator.

Shepherd the Flock

5 The elders who are among you I exhort, I who am a fellow elder and a witness of the sufferings of Christ, and also a partaker of the glory that will be revealed: 2 Shepherd the flock of God which is among you, serving as overseers, not by compulsion but willingly,[c] not for dishonest gain but eagerly; 3 nor as being lords over those entrusted to you, but being examples to the flock; 4 and when the Chief Shepherd appears, you will receive the crown of glory that does not fade away.

Submit to God, Resist the Devil

5 Likewise you younger people, submit yourselves to *your* elders. Yes, all

4:8 [y] Proverbs 10:12
4:14 [z] NU-Text omits the rest of this verse.
4:16 [a] NU-Text reads *name.*
4:18 [b] Proverbs 11:31
5:2 [c] NU-Text adds *according to God.*

of *you* be submissive to one another, and be clothed
with humility, for

> *"God resists the proud,*
> *But gives grace to the humble."*[d]

6Therefore humble yourselves under the mighty hand
of God, that He may exalt you in due time, 7casting all
your care upon Him, for He cares for you.
8Be sober, be vigilant; because[e] your adversary the
devil walks about like a roaring lion, seeking whom
he may devour. 9Resist him, steadfast in the faith,
knowing that the same sufferings are experienced by
your brotherhood in the world. 10But may[f] the God of
all grace, who called us[g] to His eternal glory by Christ
Jesus, after you have suffered a while, perfect, establish, strengthen, and settle *you.* 11To Him *be* the glory
and the dominion forever and ever. Amen.

Farewell and Peace

12By Silvanus, our faithful brother as I consider
him, I have written to you briefly, exhorting and testifying that this is the true grace of God in which
you stand.
13She who is in Babylon, elect together with *you,*
greets you; and *so does* Mark my son. 14Greet one another with a kiss of love.

Peace to you all who are in Christ Jesus. Amen.

5:5 [d] Proverbs 3:34
5:8 [e] NU-Text and M-Text omit *because.*
5:10 [f] NU-Text reads *But the God of all grace . . . will perfect, establish, strengthen, and settle you.* [g] NU-Text and M-Text read *you.*

The Second Epistle of

PETER

INTRODUCTION

If a friend warns you, it's one thing. If a doctor warns you, you listen. But if your friend is your doctor, you lean forward and take note.

My friend is my doctor. My doctor is my friend. Most of my physical exams are salted with friendly chatter and jokes. There have been occasions, however, when his tone gets solemn and his voice urgent.

"We're going to have to watch this, Max."

"You haven't been exercising, have you . . ."

"With your family's history, you have to watch your diet."

When it's a warning from a friend, you listen. The second letter from Peter is a warning from a friend. His first letter was a warning about trials from without (persecution). His second caution is a warning about trials from within (heresy).

In this the last letter we have from him, he urges Christians to be careful. Avoid shortsightedness (1:2–11). Be on guard for false teachers (2:1–22). And, most importantly, be vigilant against personal complacency which will lead to a lazy faith.

The doctor's task is to detect concerns from within and urge you to take caution. Peter's task is the same. Heed his counsel.

LIFE LESSON

2 Peter 1:1-21

SITUATION The Believers had weathered persecution from the outside. Now Peter encouraged them to withstand attacks from within the church.

OBSERVATION Continue to grow in your faith and knowledge of Jesus.

INSPIRATION "Add to your faith": Supplement it, flesh it out. Being a Christian doesn't mean believing and then just sitting around. Now that you have faith in God's part, make every effort—that's your part.

That's discipline.

That's regular "holy habits."

That's pacing yourself for the cross-country run to your future.

Says Henri Nouwen, "A spiritual life without discipline is impossible." Tighten your belt. Get tough on yourself. GO FOR IT.

A woman once said to the great Paderewski, "Sir, you are truly a genius."

"Well," he answered, "before I was a genius, I was a drudge!"

To get there, to win—your life needs discipline, order, and arrangement.

"If one examines the secret behind a championship football team, a magnificent orchestra, or a successful business, the principal ingredient is invariably discipline" (James Dobson, *Disciplines of the Home*).

You will only discover excellence on the other side of hard work.

(From *My Sacrifice, His Fire* by Anne Ortlund)

APPLICATION Write down on an index card the characteristics listed in verses 5-7. Put it in a strategic position, such as on your bedroom mirror, for two weeks. Whenever you pass by, take a moment and read through the list. Which are you adding to your life? Which need more effort?

EXPLORATION Perseverance—Nehemiah 4:6; Matthew 24:13; Mark 13:13; Hebrews 3:6; 12:1-4.

Greeting the Faithful

Simon Peter, a bondservant and apostle of Jesus Christ,

To those who have obtained like precious faith with us by the righteousness of our God and Savior Jesus Christ:

2Grace and peace be multiplied to you in the knowledge of God and of Jesus our Lord, 3as His divine power has given to us all things that *pertain* to life and godliness, through the knowledge of Him who called us by glory and virtue, 4by which have been given to us exceedingly great and precious promises, that through these you may be partakers of the divine nature, having escaped the corruption *that is* in the world through lust.

Fruitful Growth in the Faith

5But also for this very reason, giving all diligence, add to your faith virtue, to virtue knowledge, 6to knowledge self-control, to self-control perseverance, to perseverance godliness, 7to godliness brotherly kindness, and to brotherly kindness love. 8For if these things are yours and abound, *you will be* neither barren nor unfruitful in the knowledge of our Lord Jesus Christ. 9For he who lacks these things is shortsighted, even to blindness, and has forgotten that he was cleansed from his old sins.

10Therefore, brethren, be even more diligent to make your call and election sure, for if you do these things you will never stumble; 11for so an entrance will be supplied to you abundantly into the everlasting kingdom of our Lord and Savior Jesus Christ.

Peter's Approaching Death

12For this reason I will not be negligent to remind you always of these things, though you know and are established in the present truth. 13Yes, I think it is right, as long as I am in this tent, to stir you up by reminding *you,* 14knowing that shortly I *must* put off my tent, just as our Lord Jesus Christ showed me. 15Moreover I will be careful to ensure that you always have a reminder of these things after my decease.

The Trustworthy Prophetic Word

16For we did not follow cunningly devised fables when we made known to you the power and coming of our Lord Jesus Christ, but were eyewitnesses of His majesty. 17For He received from God the Father honor and glory when such a voice came to Him from the Excellent Glory: "This is My beloved Son, in whom I am well pleased." 18And we heard this voice which came from heaven when we were with Him on the holy mountain.

19And so we have the prophetic word confirmed,[a] which you do well to heed as a light that shines in a dark place, until the day dawns and the morning star rises in your hearts; 20knowing this first, that no prophecy of Scripture is of any private interpretation,[b] 21for prophecy never came by the will of man, but holy men of God[c] spoke *as they were* moved by the Holy Spirit.

Destructive Doctrines

2 But there were also false prophets among the people, even as there will be false teachers among you, who will secretly bring in destructive heresies, even denying the Lord who bought them, *and* bring on themselves

1:19 [a] Or *We also have the more sure prophetic word.*
1:20 [b] Or *origin*
1:21 [c] NU-Text reads *but men spoke from God.*

swift destruction. [2]And many will follow their destructive ways, because of
whom the way of truth will be blasphemed. [3]By covetousness they will exploit
you with deceptive words; for a long time their judgment has not been
idle, and their destruction does[d] not slumber.

Doom of False Teachers

[4]For if God did not spare the angels who sinned, but cast *them* down to
hell and delivered *them* into chains of darkness, to be reserved for judgment;
[5]and did not spare the ancient world, but saved Noah, *one of* eight *people*,
a preacher of righteousness, bringing in the flood on the world of the ungodly;
[6]and turning the cities of Sodom and Gomorrah into ashes, condemned
them to destruction, making *them* an example to those who afterward
would live ungodly; [7]and delivered righteous Lot, *who was* oppressed by
the filthy conduct of the wicked [8](for that righteous man, dwelling among
them, tormented *his* righteous soul from day to day by seeing and hearing
their lawless deeds)— [9]*then* the Lord knows how to deliver the godly out
of temptations and to reserve the unjust under punishment for the day of
judgment, [10]and especially those who walk according to the flesh in the lust
of uncleanness and despise authority. *They are* presumptuous, self-willed.
They are not afraid to speak evil of dignitaries, [11]whereas angels, who are
greater in power and might, do not bring a reviling accusation against
them before the Lord.

Depravity of False Teachers

[12]But these, like natural brute beasts made to be caught and destroyed,
speak evil of the things they do not understand, and will utterly perish in
their own corruption, [13]*and* will receive the wages of unrighteousness, *as*
those who count it pleasure to carouse in the daytime. *They are* spots and
blemishes, carousing in their own deceptions while they feast with you,
[14]having eyes full of adultery and that cannot cease from sin, enticing unstable souls. *They have* a heart trained in covetous practices, *and are* accursed
children. [15]They have forsaken the right way and gone astray, following the
way of Balaam the *son* of Beor, who loved the wages of unrighteousness;
[16]but he was rebuked for his iniquity: a dumb donkey speaking with a
man's voice restrained the madness of the prophet.
[17]These are wells without water, clouds[e] carried by a tempest, for whom
is reserved the blackness of darkness forever.[f]

Deceptions of False Teachers

[18]For when they speak great swelling *words* of emptiness, they allure
through the lusts of the flesh, through lewdness, the ones who have actually
escaped[g] from those who live in error. [19]While they promise them liberty,
they themselves are slaves of corruption; for by whom a person is overcome,
by him also he is brought into bondage. [20]For if, after they have escaped
the pollutions of the world through the knowledge of the Lord and Savior
Jesus Christ, they are again entangled in them and overcome, the latter end
is worse for them than the beginning. [21]For it would have been better for
them not to have known the way of righteousness, than having known *it*,

2:3 [d] M-Text reads *will not.*
2:17 [e] NU-Text reads *and mists.* [f] NU-Text omits *forever.*
2:18 [g] NU-Text reads *are barely escaping.*

Life Lesson

2 Peter 2:1-22

SITUATION Some teachers in this church were teaching ideas that did not agree with God's Word. Peter harshly opposed them.

OBSERVATION Beware of false teachers. God will punish them severely.

INSPIRATION Jesus was warning the people of His day to be on the lookout for gifted leaders who would take advantage of them and lead them astray. They would be men who looked good on the outside but were corrupt on the inside. They would perform well. . . .

To put it bluntly, great preachers are not necessarily great Christians. The same goes for famous gospel singers and best-selling Christian writers. . . .

The best picture of what a Spirit-filled man looks like is Christ. His life was characterized by love, joy, peace, patience, and so on in the midst of a world characterized by just the opposite of those things. He was certainly no wimp. He stood up to His detractors when it was appropriate. But He knew when to be silent as well. He had the courage and wit to take on the intellectuals of His day on their turf according to their terms. He spoke with authority. People, especially children, were attracted to Him. Even sinners loved to be with Him. He was a very secure man. There was nothing pretentious or intimidating about Him. He didn't need those props. And at the end of His life He tackled the toughest account of all—death. And He won! (From *The Wonderful Spirit-Filled Life* by Charles Stanley)

APPLICATION Do you listen to preachers passively? Do you find yourself assuming the preacher is correct? Listen actively. No matter how good the message seems, compare it with the Bible. Find out what God says on the topic.

EXPLORATION Dangers of False Teachers—Isaiah 56:10-12; Jeremiah 23:2; 50:6; Ezekiel 34:2-3; Matthew 7:15-23; John 10:12; Philippians 1:15; 1 Timothy 6:3-5.

LIFE LESSON

2 Peter 3:1-18

SITUATION Peter reminded his readers that God would faithfully keep every promise.

OBSERVATION Christ's coming should motivate all Believers to live in anticipation of his arrival.

INSPIRATION The late Francis Schaeffer asked the right question, "How Should We Then Live?" What ought to occupy our time? What do we do between now and when He returns? . . .

Let me interject a telltale sign of heresy: a ministry that emphasizes the Lord's return but does not, with equal gusto, emphasize a godly life. Mark it down. Whoever highlights the coming of Christ is also responsible to teach the importance of a pure life. Why not? They mesh together, like teeth in gears. If indeed He is coming again, there is one thing we want to have in place—personal purity. . . .

"At the appointed time, the end shall be." One of these days will be "the appointed time." You are ready, aren't you?

(From *Growing Deep in the Christian Life* by Charles Swindoll)

APPLICATION Do you look forward to Christ's return? Choose actions you would want him to see and words you would want him to hear. Make decisions he would approve.

EXPLORATION Christ's Second Coming—Matthew 24:27; 26:64; Luke 12:40; 1 Thessalonians 5:2, 23; Hebrews 9:28; James 5:8; 1 John 2:28; Revelation 16:15.

to turn from the holy commandment delivered to them. 22But it has hap-
pened to them according to the true proverb: "*A dog returns to his own vomit*,"[h] and, "a sow, having washed, to her wallowing in the mire."

God's Promise Is Not Slack

3 Beloved, I now write to you this second epistle (in *both of* which I stir
up your pure minds by way of reminder), 2that you may be mindful of
the words which were spoken before by the holy prophets, and of the commandment of us,[i] the apostles of the Lord and Savior, 3knowing this first:
that scoffers will come in the last days, walking according to their own lusts,
4and saying, "Where is the promise of His coming? For since the fathers
fell asleep, all things continue as *they were* from the beginning of creation."
5For this they willfully forget: that by the word of God the heavens were of
old, and the earth standing out of water and in the water, 6by which the world
that then existed perished, being flooded with water. 7But the heavens and
the earth *which* are now preserved by the same word, are reserved for fire
until the day of judgment and perdition of ungodly men.

8But, beloved, do not forget this one thing, that with the Lord one day *is*
as a thousand years, and a thousand years as one day. 9The Lord is not
slack concerning *His* promise, as some count slackness, but is longsuffering toward us,[j] not willing that any should perish but that all should come
to repentance.

The Day of the Lord

10But the day of the Lord will come as a thief in the night, in which the
heavens will pass away with a great noise, and the elements will melt with
fervent heat; both the earth and the works that are in it will be burned up.[k]
11Therefore, since all these things will be dissolved, what manner *of persons*
ought you to be in holy conduct and godliness, 12looking for and hastening
the coming of the day of God, because of which the heavens will be dissolved,
being on fire, and the elements will melt with fervent heat? 13Nevertheless
we, according to His promise, look for new heavens and a new earth in
which righteousness dwells.

Be Steadfast

14Therefore, beloved, looking forward to these things, be diligent to be
found by Him in peace, without spot and blameless; 15and consider *that*
the longsuffering of our Lord *is* salvation—as also our beloved brother
Paul, according to the wisdom given to him, has written to you, 16as also in
all his epistles, speaking in them of these things, in which are some things
hard to understand, which untaught and unstable *people* twist to their
own destruction, as *they do* also the rest of the Scriptures.

17You therefore, beloved, since you know *this* beforehand, beware lest
you also fall from your own steadfastness, being led away with the error of
the wicked; 18but grow in the grace and knowledge of our Lord and Savior
Jesus Christ.

To Him *be* the glory both now and forever. Amen.

2:22 [h] Proverbs 26:11
3:2 [i] NU-Text and M-Text read *commandment of the apostles of your Lord and Savior* or *commandment of your apostles of the Lord and Savior.*
3:9 [j] NU-Text reads *you.*
3:10 [k] NU-Text reads *laid bare* (literally *found*).

The First Epistle of

JOHN

INTRODUCTION

Tolerance. A prized virtue today. The ability to be understanding of those with whom you differ is a sign of sophistication. Jesus, too, was a champion of tolerance:

—Tolerant of the disciples when they doubted.

—Tolerant of the crowds when they misunderstood.

—Tolerant of us when we fall.

But there is one area where Jesus was intolerant. There was one area where he was unindulgent and dogmatic. Were he to share his opinion today, he would be accused of being narrow, biased, one-sided, even bigoted.

But as far as he was concerned, when it comes to salvation, there aren't several roads ... there is only one road. There aren't several ways ... there is only one way ... there aren't several paths ... there is only one path. And that path is Jesus himself.

That is why it is so hard for people to believe in Jesus. It's much easier to consider him one of several options rather than the option. But such a philosophy is no option. Jesus closed that door. Jesus positioned himself as the peerless Savior of the world. In defining who he is, Jesus is bold and unapologetic.

His disciple John was equally firm.

First John was written to dispel doubts about Jesus. False teachers had entered the church, denying the incarnation of Christ. John steps up to the bench and makes his defense. John knew him, walked with him, lived with him. He saw him heal. He heard his words. John had been to the empty tomb and he knew ... Jesus is not one of many options. He is the only option or nothing at all.

There are times to be tolerant. And there are times to take a stand for truth. In this letter, John takes a stand.

LIFE LESSON

1 John 1:1-10

SITUATION Because John was Jesus' friend, he could speak with authority about maintaining true fellowship with God—and what hinders it!

OBSERVATION Living in fellowship with God means that we will have joy. Yet, our pride causes us to forfeit that joy when we hide our own sin. We cannot be in a right relationship with God unless we live humbly, honestly, and dependently on him.

INSPIRATION "If we confess our sins . . ." The biggest word in Scriptures just might be that two letter one, *if*. For confessing sins—admitting failure—is exactly what prisoners of pride refuse to do.

"Well, I may not be perfect, but I'm better than Hitler and certainly kinder than Idi Amin!"

"Me a sinner? Oh, sure, I get rowdy every so often, but I'm a pretty good ol' boy."

"Listen, I'm just as good as the next guy. I pay my taxes. I coach the Little League team. I even make donations to Red Cross. Why, God's probably proud to have someone like me on his team."

Justification. Rationalization. Comparison. These are the tools of the jailbird. They sound good. They sound familiar. They even sound American. But in the kingdom, they sound hollow. . . .

When you get to the point of sorrow for your sins, when you admit that you have no other option but to cast all your cares on him, and when there is truly no other one that you can call, then cast all your cares on him, for he is waiting.

(From *The Applause of Heaven* by Max Lucado)

APPLICATION What activities in your life need forgiveness? Confess them. Then remove every sinful activity from your life.

EXPLORATION Confessing Sin—2 Chronicles 7:14; Psalm 32:5; Mark 1:5.

What Was Heard, Seen, and Touched

That which was from the beginning, which we have heard, which
we have seen with our eyes, which we have looked upon, and
our hands have handled, concerning the Word of life— [2]the life
was manifested, and we have seen, and bear witness, and declare
to you that eternal life which was with the Father and was manifested to us—
[3]that which we have seen and heard we declare to you, that you also may have
fellowship with us; and truly our fellowship *is* with the Father and with His
Son Jesus Christ. [4]And these things we write to you that your[a] joy may be full.

Fellowship with Him and One Another

[5]This is the message which we have heard from Him and declare to you,
that God is light and in Him is no darkness at all. [6]If we say that we have
fellowship with Him, and walk in darkness, we lie and do not practice the
truth. [7]But if we walk in the light as He is in the light, we have fellowship with
one another, and the blood of Jesus Christ His Son cleanses us from all sin.
[8]If we say that we have no sin, we deceive ourselves, and the truth is not
in us. [9]If we confess our sins, He is faithful and just to forgive us *our* sins
and to cleanse us from all unrighteousness. [10]If we say that we have not
sinned, we make Him a liar, and His word is not in us.

2 My little children, these things I write to you, so that you may not sin.
And if anyone sins, we have an Advocate with the Father, Jesus Christ
the righteous. [2]And He Himself is the propitiation for our sins, and not for
ours only but also for the whole world.

The Test of Knowing Him

[3]Now by this we know that we know Him, if we keep His commandments.
[4]He who says, "I know Him," and does not keep His commandments, is a
liar, and the truth is not in him. [5]But whoever keeps His word, truly the love
of God is perfected in him. By this we know that we are in Him. [6]He who says
he abides in Him ought himself also to walk just as He walked.

[7]Brethren,[b] I write no new commandment to you, but an old commandment which you have had from the beginning. The old commandment is
the word which you heard from the beginning.[c] [8]Again, a new commandment
I write to you, which thing is true in Him and in you, because the darkness
is passing away, and the true light is already shining.

[9]He who says he is in the light, and hates his brother, is in darkness until
now. [10]He who loves his brother abides in the light, and there is no cause
for stumbling in him. [11]But he who hates his brother is in darkness and walks
in darkness, and does not know where he is going, because the darkness
has blinded his eyes.

Their Spiritual State

12 I write to you, little children,
Because your sins are forgiven you for His name's sake.
13 I write to you, fathers,
Because you have known Him *who is* from the beginning.
I write to you, young men,
Because you have overcome the wicked one.

1:4 [a] NU-Text and M-Text read *our.*
2:7 [b] NU-Text reads *Beloved.* [c] NU-Text omits *from the beginning.*

I write to you, little children,
Because you have known the Father.
14 I have written to you, fathers,
Because you have known Him *who is* from the beginning.
I have written to you, young men,
Because you are strong, and the word of God abides in you,
And you have overcome the wicked one.

Do Not Love the World

15 Do not love the world or the things in the world. If anyone loves the
world, the love of the Father is not in him. 16 For all that *is* in the world—the
lust of the flesh, the lust of the eyes, and the pride of life—is not of the
Father but is of the world. 17 And the world is passing away, and the lust of
it; but he who does the will of God abides forever.

Deceptions of the Last Hour

18 Little children, it is the last hour; and as you have heard that the[d]
Antichrist is coming, even now many antichrists have come, by which we
know that it is the last hour. 19 They went out from us, but they were not of
us; for if they had been of us, they would have continued with us; but *they
went out* that they might be made manifest, that none of them were of us.
20 But you have an anointing from the Holy One, and you know all things.[e]
21 I have not written to you because you do not know the truth, but because
you know it, and that no lie is of the truth.
22 Who is a liar but he who denies that Jesus is the Christ? He is antichrist
who denies the Father and the Son. 23 Whoever denies the Son does not
have the Father either; he who acknowledges the Son has the Father also.

Let Truth Abide in You

24 Therefore let that abide in you which you heard from the beginning. If
what you heard from the beginning abides in you, you also will abide in
the Son and in the Father. 25 And this is the promise that He has promised
us—eternal life.
26 These things I have written to you concerning those who *try to* deceive
you. 27 But the anointing which you have received from Him abides in you,
and you do not need that anyone teach you; but as the same anointing
teaches you concerning all things, and is true, and is not a lie, and just as it
has taught you, you will[f] abide in Him.

The Children of God

28 And now, little children, abide in Him, that when[g] He appears, we may
have confidence and not be ashamed before Him at His coming. 29 If you
know that He is righteous, you know that everyone who practices righteousness is born of Him.

3 Behold what manner of love the Father has bestowed on us, that we
should be called children of God![h] Therefore the world does not know
us,[i] because it did not know Him. 2 Beloved, now we are children of God;

2:18 [d] NU-Text omits *the.*
2:20 [e] NU-Text reads *you all know.*
2:27 [f] NU-Text reads *you abide.*
2:28 [g] NU-Text reads *if.*
3:1 [h] NU-Text adds *And we are.* [i] M-Text reads *you.*

LIFE LESSON

1 John 2:1-29

SITUATION John advised that Christians should have integrity. Obedience and repentance are the marks of those who love God.

OBSERVATION Christians avoid the temptation to compromise their standards. If we fail, however, Jesus stands ready to forgive.

INSPIRATION Adam Clarke was an assistant in a dry goods store, selling silks and satins to a cultured clientele. One day, his employer suggested to him that he try stretching the silk as he measured it out; this would increase sales and profits, and also increase Adam's value to the company. Young Clarke straightened up from his work, faced his boss courageously, and said, "Sir, your silk may stretch, but my conscience won't." Unfortunately, some of us are not so honest. The book *The Day America Told the Truth* reported the following: 91 percent of those surveyed admitted to lying about something on a regular basis; 50 percent procrastinate, in effect doing nothing, one full day out of every five; and 74 percent steal from those who will not miss it. Examples of such stealing include taking office supplies from work, long lunches, extravagant meals, accepting gifts from customers, ignoring copyright laws, claiming improper deductions, etc. But the man of integrity avoids all such temptations. He is ethically righteous.

(From *A Dad's Blessing* by Gary Smalley and John Trent)

APPLICATION Is there a situation in which you have not been completely honest? Admit to God that you have sinned and ask for his forgiveness. Then seek the forgiveness of the person you have deceived and take steps to make things right. Pray that God would keep you honest.

EXPLORATION Honesty—Psalm 51:6; Proverbs 12:22; Romans 9:1; Colossians 3:9.

LIFE LESSON

1 John 3:1-24

SITUATION John wrote that Christians should become more like Christ. Their actions should prove that they unite in love as the church of God.

OBSERVATION As God's children, Christians will be characterized as those who stop sinning and demonstrate love towards their fellow Christians.

INSPIRATION The United States Treasury Department has a special group of men whose job it is to track down counterfeiters. Naturally, these men need to know a counterfeit bill when they see it.

How do they learn to identify fake bills? Oddly enough, they are not trained by spending hours examining counterfeit money. Rather, they study *the real thing*. They become so familiar with authentic bills that they can spot a counterfeit by looking at it or, often, simply by feeling it.

This is the approach in 1 John 3, which warns us that in today's world there are counterfeit Christians—"children of the devil" (v. 10). But instead of listing the evil characteristics of Satan's children, the Scripture gives us a clear description of *God's* children. The contrast between the two is obvious.

The key verse of this chapter is verse 10: a true child of God practices righteousness and loves Christians despite differences. Verses 1-10 deal with the first topic, and verses 11-24 take up the second. . . .

An unbeliever who sins is a creature sinning against his Creator. A Christian who sins is a child sinning against his Father. The unbeliever sins against the law; the Believer sins against love. (From *Be Real* by Warren Wiersbe)

APPLICATION If God shows you sin in your life, confess that sin, asking for God's help to overcome it.

EXPLORATION Seriousness of Sin—Deuteronomy 25:13-16; 1 Chronicles 10:13-14; Proverbs 11:19; Isaiah 3:8-9; Jeremiah 14:10; Luke 16:13-15.

and it has not yet been revealed what we shall be, but we know that when
He is revealed, we shall be like Him, for we shall see Him as He is. 3And
everyone who has this hope in Him purifies himself, just as He is pure.

Sin and the Child of God

4Whoever commits sin also commits lawlessness, and sin is lawlessness. 5And you know that He was manifested to take away our sins, and in
Him there is no sin. 6Whoever abides in Him does not sin. Whoever sins
has neither seen Him nor known Him.
7Little children, let no one deceive you. He who practices righteousness
is righteous, just as He is righteous. 8He who sins is of the devil, for the
devil has sinned from the beginning. For this purpose the Son of God was
manifested, that He might destroy the works of the devil. 9Whoever has
been born of God does not sin, for His seed remains in him; and he cannot
sin, because he has been born of God.

The Imperative of Love

10In this the children of God and the children of the devil are manifest:
Whoever does not practice righteousness is not of God, nor *is* he who does not
love his brother. 11For this is the message that you heard from the beginning,
that we should love one another, 12not as Cain *who* was of the wicked one
and murdered his brother. And why did he murder him? Because his
works were evil and his brother's righteous.
13Do not marvel, my brethren, if the world hates you. 14We know that we
have passed from death to life, because we love the brethren. He who does
not love *his* brother[j] abides in death. 15Whoever hates his brother is a murderer, and you know that no murderer has eternal life abiding in him.

The Outworking of Love

16By this we know love, because He laid down His life for us. And we also
ought to lay down *our* lives for the brethren. 17But whoever has this world's
goods, and sees his brother in need, and shuts up his heart from him, how
does the love of God abide in him?
18My little children, let us not love in word or in tongue, but in deed and in
truth. 19And by this we know[k] that we are of the truth, and shall assure our
hearts before Him. 20For if our heart condemns us, God is greater than our
heart, and knows all things. 21Beloved, if our heart does not condemn us,
we have confidence toward God. 22And whatever we ask we receive from
Him, because we keep His commandments and do those things that are
pleasing in His sight. 23And this is His commandment: that we should believe on the name of His Son Jesus Christ and love one another, as He gave
us[l] commandment.

The Spirit of Truth and the Spirit of Error

24Now he who keeps His commandments abides in Him, and He in him.
And by this we know that He abides in us, by the Spirit whom He has given us.
4 Beloved, do not believe every spirit, but test the spirits, whether they
are of God; because many false prophets have gone out into the world.
2By this you know the Spirit of God: Every spirit that confesses that Jesus

3:14 [j] NU-Text omits *his brother.*
3:19 [k] NU-Text reads *we shall know.*
3:23 [l] M-Text omits *us.*

Christ has come in the flesh is of God, 3and every spirit that does not confess
that[m] Jesus Christ has come in the flesh is not of God. And this is the *spirit*
of the Antichrist, which you have heard was coming, and is now already in
the world.
4You are of God, little children, and have overcome them, because He
who is in you is greater than he who is in the world. 5They are of the world.
Therefore they speak *as* of the world, and the world hears them. 6We are of
God. He who knows God hears us; he who is not of God does not hear us.
By this we know the spirit of truth and the spirit of error.

Knowing God Through Love

7Beloved, let us love one another, for love is of God; and everyone who
loves is born of God and knows God. 8He who does not love does not know
God, for God is love. 9In this the love of God was manifested toward us, that
God has sent His only begotten Son into the world, that we might live
through Him. 10In this is love, not that we loved God, but that He loved us
and sent His Son *to be* the propitiation for our sins. 11Beloved, if God so
loved us, we also ought to love one another.

Seeing God Through Love

12No one has seen God at any time. If we love one another, God abides in
us, and His love has been perfected in us. 13By this we know that we abide
in Him, and He in us, because He has given us of His Spirit. 14And we have
seen and testify that the Father has sent the Son *as* Savior of the world.
15Whoever confesses that Jesus is the Son of God, God abides in him, and
he in God. 16And we have known and believed the love that God has for us.
God is love, and he who abides in love abides in God, and God in him.

The Consummation of Love

17Love has been perfected among us in this: that we may have boldness
in the day of judgment; because as He is, so are we in this world. 18There is
no fear in love; but perfect love casts out fear, because fear involves torment.
But he who fears has not been made perfect in love. 19We love Him[n] because
He first loved us.

Obedience by Faith

20If someone says, "I love God," and hates his brother, he is a liar; for he
who does not love his brother whom he has seen, how can[o] he love God
whom he has not seen? 21And this commandment we have from Him: that
he who loves God *must* love his brother also.

5 Whoever believes that Jesus is the Christ is born of God, and everyone
who loves Him who begot also loves him who is begotten of Him. 2By
this we know that we love the children of God, when we love God and keep
His commandments. 3For this is the love of God, that we keep His commandments. And His commandments are not burdensome. 4For whatever
is born of God overcomes the world. And this is the victory that has overcome
the world—our[p] faith. 5Who is he who overcomes the world, but he who
believes that Jesus is the Son of God?

4:3 [m] NU-Text omits *that* and *Christ has come in the flesh.*
4:19 [n] NU-Text omits *Him.*
4:20 [o] NU-Text reads *he cannot.*
5:4 [p] M-Text reads *your.*

LIFE LESSON

1 John 4:1-21

SITUATION John reminded Believers to reject the lies of false teachers. He also told them that God illustrates perfect love to us.

OBSERVATION Because of God's self-sacrificing love for us, we should love him and love others.

INSPIRATION We aren't always sure ourselves what we mean when we use the term love. That word has become one of the most widely misused words in our language. We use the word love to describe the basest as well as the most exalted of human relationships. We say we "love" to travel, we "love" to eat chocolate cake, we "love" our new car, or the pattern in the wallpaper in our home. Why, we even say we "love" our neighbors—but most of us don't do much more than just say it and let it go at that! No wonder we don't have a very clear idea of what the Bible means when it says: "God is Love."

Don't make the mistake of thinking that because God is Love that everything is going to be sweet, beautiful, and happy and that no one will be punished for his sins. God's holiness demands that all sin be punished, but God's love provides the plan and way of redemption for sinful man. God's love is the cross of Jesus, by which man can have forgiveness and cleansing. It was the love of God that sent Jesus Christ to the cross!

Never question God's great love, for it is as unchangeable a part of God as His holiness. No matter how terrible your sins, God loves you. Were it not for the love of God, none of us would ever have a chance in the future life. But God is Love and his love for us is everlasting!

(From *Peace with God* by Billy Graham)

APPLICATION Who is one person you have difficulty loving? What three steps can you take this week to show love to that person? Pray that God would give you a loving heart, then show your love.

EXPLORATION Loving Others—John 15:9-13; Galatians 5:6, 13; Ephesians 5:1; Colossians 3:12; 1 Peter 1:22; 1 John 3:11-23.

The Certainty of God's Witness

6 This is He who came by water and blood—Jesus
Christ; not only by water, but by water and blood. And
it is the Spirit who bears witness, because the Spirit is
truth. 7 For there are three that bear witness in heaven:
the Father, the Word, and the Holy Spirit; and these
three are one. 8 And there are three that bear witness
on earth:[q] the Spirit, the water, and the blood; and
these three agree as one.

9 If we receive the witness of men, the witness of
God is greater; for this is the witness of God which[r] He
has testified of His Son. 10 He who believes in the Son of
God has the witness in himself; he who does not believe
God has made Him a liar, because he has not believed
the testimony that God has given of His Son. 11 And
this is the testimony: that God has given us eternal life,
and this life is in His Son. 12 He who has the Son has
life; he who does not have the Son of God does not
have life. 13 These things I have written to you who believe
in the name of the Son of God, that you may know that
you have eternal life,[s] and that you may *continue to*
believe in the name of the Son of God.

Confidence and Compassion in Prayer

14 Now this is the confidence that we have in Him, that if
we ask anything according to His will, He hears us. 15 And
if we know that He hears us, whatever we ask, we know
that we have the petitions that we have asked of Him.

16 If anyone sees his brother sinning a sin *which*
does not *lead* to death, he will ask, and He will give
him life for those who commit sin not *leading* to
death. There is sin *leading* to death. I do not say that
he should pray about that. 17 All unrighteousness is
sin, and there is sin not *leading* to death.

Knowing the True—Rejecting the False

18 We know that whoever is born of God does not
sin; but he who has been born of God keeps himself,[t]
and the wicked one does not touch him.

19 We know that we are of God, and the whole world
lies *under the sway of* the wicked one.

20 And we know that the Son of God has come and
has given us an understanding, that we may know
Him who is true; and we are in Him who is true, in His
Son Jesus Christ. This is the true God and eternal life.
21 Little children, keep yourselves from idols. Amen.

5:8 [q] NU-Text and M-Text omit the words from *in heaven* (verse 7) through *on earth* (verse 8). Only four or five very late manuscripts contain these words in Greek.
5:9 [r] NU-Text reads *God, that.*
5:13 [s] NU-Text omits the rest of this verse.
5:18 [t] NU-Text reads *him.*

The Second Epistle of

JOHN

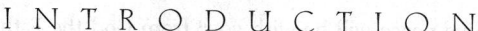

INTRODUCTION

The single most difficult pursuit is truth and love.

That sentence is grammatically correct. I know every English teacher wanted to pluralize it to read: The most difficult pursuits are those of truth and love. But that's not what I meant to say.

True, love is a difficult pursuit.

Correct, truth is a tough one, too.

But put them together, pursue truth and love at the same time and hang on baby, you're in for the ride of your life.

But that's the task of the Christian. Love in truth. Truth in love. Never one at the expense of the other. Never the embrace of love without the torch of truth. Never the heat of truth without the warmth of love.

It would be easier if we could choose between the two, but we can't. So John, in this second letter, calls for a hybrid.

"To the elect lady and her children, whom I love in truth, and not only I but also all those who have known the truth, because of the truth which abides in us and will be with us forever: Grace, mercy, and peace be with you from God the Father and from the Lord Jesus Christ, the Son of the Father, in truth and love" (vv. 1–2).

Truth and love. Love and truth. Never one without the other. To pursue both is our singular task.

LIFE LESSON

2 John 1-13

SITUATION John exhorted Christians to live in a way that pleased God and to be aware of those who did not speak God's truth.

OBSERVATION God's Word and God's spirit provide what we need to detect false teachers.

INSPIRATION The devil is declared by Scriptures to be an enemy of God and of all good men. Because he is a spirit he is able to "walk up and down in the earth" at his pleasure.

While we must not underestimate the strength of our foe, we must at the same time recognize that we need not live in constant fear of him! If he cannot make skeptics of us he will make us devil-conscious and thus throw a permanent shadow across our lives, for there is but a hairline between truth and superstition.

We should learn the truth about the enemy, but we must stand bravely against every superstitious notion he would introduce about himself. The truth will set us free but superstition will enslave us!

. . . The best way to keep the enemy out is to keep Christ in! The sheep need not be terrified by the wolf; they have but to stay close to the shepherd. The instructed Christian whose faculties have been developed by the Word and the Spirit will practice the presence of God moment by moment!

(From *Renewed Day by Day* by A. W. Tozer)

APPLICATION In order to resist Satan and his false teachers, Christians must know God's Word and depend on the Spirit for discernment. Study the Scriptures daily and become involved in a Bible study with other Christians through your local church.

EXPLORATION Truth—Psalm 25:5; 51:6; 119:160; John 14:6; Colossians 1:5-6; 2 Timothy 2:15; 2 Peter 1:12.

Greeting the Elect Lady

The Elder,

To the elect lady and her children, whom I love in truth, and not only I, but also all those who have known the truth, 2because of the truth which abides in us and will be with us forever:

3Grace, mercy, *and* peace will be with you[a] from God the Father and from the Lord Jesus Christ, the Son of the Father, in truth and love.

Walk in Christ's Commandments

4I rejoiced greatly that I have found *some* of your children walking in truth, as we received commandment from the Father. 5And now I plead with you, lady, not as though I wrote a new commandment to you, but that which we have had from the beginning: that we love one another. 6This is love, that we walk according to His commandments. This is the commandment, that as you have heard from the beginning, you should walk in it.

Beware of Antichrist Deceivers

7For many deceivers have gone out into the world who do not confess Jesus Christ *as* coming in the flesh. This is a deceiver and an antichrist. 8Look to yourselves, that we[b] do not lose those things we worked for, but *that* we[c] may receive a full reward.

9Whoever transgresses[d] and does not abide in the doctrine of Christ does not have God. He who abides in the doctrine of Christ has both the Father and the Son. 10If anyone comes to you and does not bring this doctrine, do not receive him into your house nor greet him; 11for he who greets him shares in his evil deeds.

John's Farewell Greeting

12Having many things to write to you, I did not wish *to do so* with paper and ink; but I hope to come to you and speak face to face, that our joy may be full.

13The children of your elect sister greet you. Amen.

3 [a] NU-Text and M-Text read *us.*
8 [b] NU-Text reads *you.* [c] NU-Text reads *you.*
9 [d] NU-Text reads *goes ahead.*

The Third Epistle of

JOHN

INTRODUCTION

It's like finding a postcard written from one friend to another. The writer is John, the recipient is Gaius.

John we know. We met him when he was a young man in the shadow of John the Baptist. We saw him as he stood in the shadow of the cross. We now read him as he writes as the elder statesman of the church.

He writes to Gaius. Whoever Gaius was, he had a special place in John's heart. John is writing to thank him for his hospitality. Word was out that Gaius kept his door open and pantry stocked for traveling missionaries, and John is writing to commend him.

His words are not so kind, however, for Diotrephes. Apparently, he was the opposite of Gaius. Where Gaius was accepting, Diotrephes was judgmental. Where Gaius was a servant, Diotrephes was demanding.

In a way, it's like reading a postcard that wasn't intended for you. But in another, it's like getting a personal letter from John. By the way, are you more like Gaius or Diotrephes? Or better, do you love people or love the limelight?

If John were writing a note to you, what would he say?

LIFE LESSON

3 John 1-15

SITUATION In the early church, Christians showed hospitality to traveling prophets, teachers, and evangelists. Gaius, as a church elder, was exemplary in providing hospitality and walking in truth.

OBSERVATION Believers should live by appropriate standards—be faithful to the truth and show hospitality to fellow Believers, especially teachers. John cites Gaius and Demetrius as good examples and warns against the ways of Diotrephes.

INSPIRATION The truth was in Gaius, and Gaius walked in the truth. If the first had not been the case, the second could never have occurred; and if the second could not have been said of him the first would have been a mere pretense. Truth must enter into the soul, penetrate and saturate it, or else it is of no value. . . .

Be it ours today, O gracious Spirit, to be ruled and governed by Thy divine authority, so that nothing false or sinful may reign in our hearts.

(From *Morning and Evening* by Charles H. Spurgeon)

APPLICATION How hospitable are you? Do you feel as if you can't entertain much because of poor circumstances? Fellowship with other Christians doesn't require silver, china, and fine dining. During the next three months, look for ways you can help other Christians, especially those who are traveling.

EXPLORATION Hospitality—Mark 9:41; Romans 12:13; 16:23; 2 Timothy 1:16-18; 1 Peter 4:9-11; James 2:15-16.

Greeting to Gaius

The Elder,

To the beloved Gaius, whom I love in truth:

2 Beloved, I pray that you may prosper in all things and be in health, just as your soul prospers. 3 For I rejoiced greatly when brethren came and testified of the truth *that is* in you, just as you walk in the truth. 4 I have no greater joy than to hear that my children walk in truth.[a]

Gaius Commended for Generosity

5 Beloved, you do faithfully whatever you do for the brethren and[b] for strangers, 6 who have borne witness of your love before the church. *If* you send them forward on their journey in a manner worthy of God, you will do well, 7 because they went forth for His name's sake, taking nothing from the Gentiles. 8 We therefore ought to receive[c] such, that we may become fellow workers for the truth.

Diotrephes and Demetrius

9 I wrote to the church, but Diotrephes, who loves to have the preeminence among them, does not receive us. 10 Therefore, if I come, I will call to mind his deeds which he does, prating against us with malicious words. And not content with that, he himself does not receive the brethren, and forbids those who wish to, putting *them* out of the church.

11 Beloved, do not imitate what is evil, but what is good. He who does good is of God, but[d] he who does evil has not seen God.

12 Demetrius has a *good* testimony from all, and from the truth itself. And we also bear witness, and you know that our testimony is true.

Farewell Greeting

13 I had many things to write, but I do not wish to write to you with pen and ink; 14 but I hope to see you shortly, and we shall speak face to face.

Peace to you. Our friends greet you. Greet the friends by name.

4 [a] NU-Text reads *the truth.*
5 [b] NU-Text adds *especially.*
8 [c] NU-Text reads *support.*
11 [d] NU-Text and M-Text omit *but.*

The Epistle of JUDE

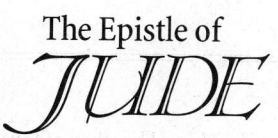

INTRODUCTION

A redwood tree fell in a California forest. Four hundred years old.

It wasn't destroyed by lightning. Storms had come and gone, but the tree stood. It wasn't felled by winds. Bent by their force, but never uprooted. The tree didn't fall to fire. It had stood when others collapsed.

What destroyed the redwood?

Insects. Termites devoured it from within. It had stood for four centuries against the elements from without, but collapsed because of an attack within.

Jude warns that the same can happen to the church.

He wanted to write about their "common salvation" (v. 3).

But he felt compelled to address a more somber issue—the danger of false teachers.

Apparently, some had entered the church, (v. 8). They were not students of the Word but, rather, promoters of sexual sin. They used God's grace as a license for passion (v. 4). The only solution? "Contend earnestly for the faith which was once for all delivered to the saints" (v. 3).

Jude is urgent in his warning. What destroyed the redwood can destroy a church. But he is equally urgent in his encouragement. "Now to Him who is able to keep you from stumbling," Jude concludes, "and to present you faultless before the presence of His glory with exceeding joy" (v. 24).

Can God really keep you from falling? To answer that, go to another tree on a barren hill. A tree older than time. A tree which covers the mistakes of your past and the problems of your future. Be assured—that tree will never fall.

Life Lesson

Jude 1-25

SITUATION Jude warned Jewish Christians about false teachers and wicked people who found their way into the church. These people taught that because God's grace was free, behavior didn't matter. Jude reminds Believers of the punishment immoral people receive.

OBSERVATION Some people claim to love God but don't obey him. Be careful that disobedience does not create a wedge between you and God.

INSPIRATION According to Gallup surveys, confirmed by other polls taken over the past fifteen years, 33 percent of all Americans over age eighteen indicate they are evangelical or "born again" Christians. That translates into 59 million Christians, or one in every three adults, who experienced a turning point in their lives as they made a personal commitment to Jesus Christ.

This information should grip us with terror. It means that the greatest revival in history has so far been impotent to change society. It's *revival* without *reformation*. It's a revival which left the country floundering in spiritual ignorance. It's a change in *belief* without a corresponding change in *behavior*. . . .

How did the building blocks of the gospel become glued together with the cement of self-centeredness? The

Greeting to the Called

Jude, a bondservant of Jesus Christ, and brother of James,

To those who are called, sanctified[a] by God the Father, and preserved in Jesus Christ:

2 Mercy, peace, and love be multiplied to you.

Contend for the Faith

3 Beloved, while I was very diligent to write to you concerning our common salvation, I found it necessary to write to you exhorting you to contend earnestly for the faith which was once for all delivered to the saints.
4 For certain men have crept in unnoticed, who long ago were marked out for this condemnation, ungodly men, who turn the grace of our God into lewdness and deny the only Lord God[b] and our Lord Jesus Christ.

Old and New Apostates

5 But I want to remind you, though you once knew this, that the Lord, having saved the people out of the land of Egypt, afterward destroyed those who did not believe. 6 And the angels who did not keep their proper domain, but left their own abode, He has reserved in everlasting chains under darkness for the judgment of the great day; 7 as Sodom and Gomorrah, and the cities around them in a similar manner to these, having given themselves over to sexual immorality and gone after strange flesh, are set forth as an example, suffering the vengeance of eternal fire.

8 Likewise also these dreamers defile the flesh, reject authority, and speak evil of dignitaries. 9 Yet Michael the archangel, in contending with the devil, when he disputed about the body of Moses, dared not bring against him a reviling accusation, but said, "The Lord rebuke you!" 10 But these speak evil of whatever they do not know; and whatever they know naturally, like brute beasts, in these things they corrupt themselves. 11 Woe to them! For they have gone in the way of Cain, have run greedily in the error of Balaam for profit, and perished in the rebellion of Korah.

Apostates Depraved and Doomed

12 These are spots in your love feasts, while they feast with you without fear, serving *only* themselves. *They are* clouds without water, carried about[c] by the winds; late autumn trees without fruit, twice dead, pulled up by the roots; 13 raging waves of the sea, foaming up their own shame; wandering stars for whom is reserved the blackness of darkness forever.

14 Now Enoch, the seventh from Adam, prophesied about these men also, saying, "Behold, the Lord comes with ten thousands of His saints, 15 to execute judgment on all, to convict all who are ungodly among them of all their ungodly deeds which they have committed in an ungodly way, and of all the harsh things which ungodly sinners have spoken against Him."

Apostates Predicted

16 These are grumblers, complainers, walking according to their own lusts; and they mouth great swelling *words,* flattering people to gain ad-

1 [a] NU-Text reads *beloved.*
4 [b] NU-Text omits *God.*
12 [c] NU-Text and M-Text read *along.*

vantage. 17But you, beloved, remember the words which were spoken before by the apostles of our Lord Jesus Christ: 18how they told you that there
would be mockers in the last time who would walk according to their own
ungodly lusts. 19These are sensual persons, who cause divisions, not having the Spirit.

Maintain Your Life with God

20But you, beloved, building yourselves up on your most holy faith,
praying in the Holy Spirit, 21keep yourselves in the love of God, looking for
the mercy of our Lord Jesus Christ unto eternal life.
22And on some have compassion, making a distinction;[d] 23but others
save with fear, pulling *them* out of the fire,[e] hating even the garment defiled by the flesh.

Glory to God

24 Now to Him who is able to keep you[f] from stumbling,
And to present *you* faultless
Before the presence of His glory with exceeding joy,
25 To God our Savior,[g]
Who alone is wise,[h]
Be glory and majesty,
Dominion and power,[i]
Both now and forever.
Amen.

American gospel has evolved into a gospel of addition without subtraction. It is the belief that we can add Christ to our lives, but not subtract sin. It is a change in belief without a change in behavior. It is a spiritual experience without any cultural impact. It is revival without reformation, without repentance. . . .

The *proof* of religious conversion is to demonstrate that we have both added a relationship with Christ and that we have subtracted sin (repentance). And we multiply proof to a weary world by what we do—our deeds, our obedience. What we do must confirm what we say. Our deeds are the proof of our repentance. . . .

A changed life is one that has added Christ and subtracted sin, that attracts a world weary of worn-out words. Obedience is the proof.

(From *Walking with Christ in the Details of Life* by Patrick Morley)

APPLICATION You may be great at obeying some commands of God but lax in obeying others. Which biblical teachings do you struggle to obey? Help others who are struggling, and let them help you. Depend on God, who can help you stand firm.

EXPLORATION Grace and Sin—Leviticus 19:2; Romans 6; 2 Corinthians 7:1; Galatians 5:13, 16-17; 6:7-8; Hebrews 12:14; 2 Peter 2:1-2, 17-20; 3:11, 14, 17.

22 [d] NU-Text reads *who are doubting* (or *making distinctions*).
23 [e] NU-Text adds *and on some have mercy with fear* and omits *with fear* in first clause.
24 [f] M-Text reads *them.*
25 [g] NU-Text reads *To the only God our Savior.* [h] NU-Text omits *Who . . . is wise* and adds *Through Jesus Christ our Lord.* [i] NU-Text adds *Before all time.*

REVELATION
of Jesus Christ

INTRODUCTION

An ancient legend tells of a general whose army was afraid to fight. The soldiers were frightened. The enemy was too strong. Its fortress was too high and weapons too mighty.

The king, however, was not afraid. He knew his men would win. How could he convince them?

He had an idea. He told his soldiers that he possessed a magical coin. A prophetic coin. A coin which would foretell the outcome of the battle. On one side was an eagle and on the other a bear. He would toss the coin. If it landed eagle-side up, they would win. If it landed with the bear up, they would lose.

The army was silent as the coin flipped in the air. Soldiers circled as it fell to the ground. They held their breath as they looked and shouted when they saw the eagle. The army would win.

Bolstered by the assurance of victory, the men marched against the castle and won.

It was only after the victory that the king showed the men the coin. The two sides were identical.

Though the story is fictional, the truth is reliable: assured victory empowers the army.

That may be the reason God gives us the Book of Revelation. In it he assures victory. We, the soldiers, are privileged a glimpse into the final battlefield. All hell breaks loose as all heaven comes forth. The two collide in the ultimate battle of good and evil. Left standing amidst the smoke and thunder is the Son of God. Jesus, born in a manger—now triumphant over Satan.

Satan is defeated. Christ is triumphant. And we, the soldiers, are assured of victory.

Let us march.

Life Lesson

Revelation 1:1-20

SITUATION John wrote Revelation to encourage Christians to resist the cult of emperor worship and to stand firm during persecution.

OBSERVATION Jesus, the Mighty One, cares for us and stands with us. No matter what we face, he gives us his love and power.

INSPIRATION As the Christian with the Bible in his hand surveys the world scene, he is aware that we do not worship an absentee God. He is aware that God is in the shadows of history and that He has a plan. The Christian is not to be disturbed by the chaos, violence, strife, bloodshed, and threat of war that fill the pages of our daily newspapers. We know that these things are the consequences of sin and greed. Every day we see a thousand evidences of the fulfillment of biblical prophecy. Every day as I read my newspaper I say: "The Bible is true."

No matter how foreboding the future, the Christian knows the end of the story. We are heading toward a glorious climax. Every writer of the New Testament believes that "the best is yet to be."

As John Baillie has said: "The Bible indicates that the future is in God's hands. If it were in our hands, we would make a mess of it. The future is not in the devil's hands, for then he would lead us to destruction. The future is not at the mercy of any historical determinism leading us blindly forward, for then life would be without meaning. But the future is in the hands of One who is preparing something better than the eye hath seen, or ear heard, or has entered into the heart of man to conceive." . . .

(From *Unto the Hills* by Billy Graham)

APPLICATION God has told you he will destroy Satan and his works that oppose you. Do your actions prove that you believe him?

EXPLORATION Sovereignty—Ezekiel 6:14; Daniel 4:25; Job 37:23; 38:1; Jude 4; Revelation 19:16.

Introduction and Benediction

The Revelation of Jesus Christ, which God gave Him to show His servants—things which must shortly take place. And He sent and signified *it* by His angel to His servant John, 2 who bore witness to the word of God, and to the testimony of Jesus Christ, to all things that he saw. 3 Blessed *is* he who reads and those who hear the words of this prophecy, and keep those things which are written in it; for the time *is* near.

Greeting the Seven Churches

4 John, to the seven churches which are in Asia:

Grace to you and peace from Him who is and who was and who is to come, and from the seven Spirits who are before His throne, 5 and from Jesus Christ, the faithful witness, the firstborn from the dead, and the ruler over the kings of the earth.

To Him who loved us and washed[a] us from our sins in His own blood, 6 and has made us kings[b] and priests to His God and Father, to Him *be* glory and dominion forever and ever. Amen.

7 Behold, He is coming with clouds, and every eye will see Him, even they who pierced Him. And all the tribes of the earth will mourn because of Him. Even so, Amen.

8 "I am the Alpha and the Omega, *the* Beginning and *the* End,"[c] says the Lord,[d] "who is and who was and who is to come, the Almighty."

Vision of the Son of Man

9 I, John, both[e] your brother and companion in the tribulation and kingdom and patience of Jesus Christ, was on the island that is called Patmos for the word of God and for the testimony of Jesus Christ. 10 I was in the Spirit on the Lord's Day, and I heard behind me a loud voice, as of a trumpet, 11 saying, "I am the Alpha and the Omega, the First and the Last," and,[f] "What you see, write in a book and send *it* to the seven churches which are in Asia:[g] to Ephesus, to Smyrna, to Pergamos, to Thyatira, to Sardis, to Philadelphia, and to Laodicea."

12 Then I turned to see the voice that spoke with me. And having turned I saw seven golden lampstands, 13 and in the midst of the seven lampstands *One* like the Son of Man, clothed with a garment down to the feet and girded about the chest with a golden band. 14 His head and hair *were* white like wool, as white as snow, and His eyes like a flame of fire; 15 His feet *were* like fine brass, as if refined in a furnace, and His voice as the sound of many waters; 16 He had in His right hand seven stars, out of His mouth went a sharp two-edged sword, and His countenance *was* like the sun shining in its strength. 17 And when I saw Him, I fell at His feet as dead. But He laid His right hand on me, saying to me,[h] "Do not be afraid; I am the First and the Last. 18 I *am* He who lives, and was dead, and behold, I am alive forevermore. Amen. And I have the keys of Hades and of Death.

1:5 [a] NU-Text reads *loves us and freed;* M-Text reads *loves us and washed.*
1:6 [b] NU-Text and M-Text read *a kingdom.*
1:8 [c] NU-Text and M-Text omit *the Beginning and the End.* [d] NU-Text and M-Text add *God.*
1:9 [e] NU-Text and M-Text omit *both.*
1:11 [f] NU-Text and M-Text omit *I am* through third *and.* [g] NU-Text and M-Text omit *which are in Asia.*
1:17 [h] NU-Text and M-Text omit *to me.*

19 Write[i] the things which you have seen, and the things which are, and the
things which will take place after this. 20 The mystery of the seven stars
which you saw in My right hand, and the seven golden lampstands: The
seven stars are the angels of the seven churches, and the seven lampstands
which you saw[j] are the seven churches.

The Loveless Church

2 "To the angel of the church of Ephesus write,
'These things says He who holds the seven stars in His right hand, who
walks in the midst of the seven golden lampstands: 2 "I know your works,
your labor, your patience, and that you cannot bear those who are evil.
And you have tested those who say they are apostles and are not, and have
found them liars; 3 and you have persevered and have patience, and have
labored for My name's sake and have not become weary. 4 Nevertheless I
have *this* against you, that you have left your first love. 5 Remember therefore from where you have fallen; repent and do the first works, or else I will
come to you quickly and remove your lampstand from its place—unless
you repent. 6 But this you have, that you hate the deeds of the Nicolaitans,
which I also hate.
7 "He who has an ear, let him hear what the Spirit says to the churches.
To him who overcomes I will give to eat from the tree of life, which is in the
midst of the Paradise of God." '

The Persecuted Church

8 "And to the angel of the church in Smyrna write,
'These things says the First and the Last, who was dead, and came to
life: 9 "I know your works, tribulation, and poverty (but you are rich); and *I
know* the blasphemy of those who say they are Jews and are not, but *are* a
synagogue of Satan. 10 Do not fear any of those things which you are about
to suffer. Indeed, the devil is about to throw *some* of you into prison, that
you may be tested, and you will have tribulation ten days. Be faithful until
death, and I will give you the crown of life.
11 "He who has an ear, let him hear what the Spirit says to the churches.
He who overcomes shall not be hurt by the second death." '

The Compromising Church

12 "And to the angel of the church in Pergamos write,
'These things says He who has the sharp two-edged sword: 13 "I know
your works, and where you dwell, where Satan's throne *is.* And you hold
fast to My name, and did not deny My faith even in the days in which
Antipas *was* My faithful martyr, who was killed among you, where Satan
dwells. 14 But I have a few things against you, because you have there those
who hold the doctrine of Balaam, who taught Balak to put a stumbling
block before the children of Israel, to eat things sacrificed to idols, and to
commit sexual immorality. 15 Thus you also have those who hold the doctrine of the Nicolaitans, which thing I hate.[k] 16 Repent, or else I will come to
you quickly and will fight against them with the sword of My mouth.
17 "He who has an ear, let him hear what the Spirit says to the churches.

1:19 [i] NU-Text and M-Text read *Therefore, write.*
1:20 [j] NU-Text and M-Text omit *which you saw.*
2:15 [k] NU-Text and M-Text read *likewise* for *which thing I hate.*

LIFE LESSON

Revelation 2:1-29

SITUATION John commended various churches in Asia Minor regarding their faithfulness and fervor for God. He highlights the importance of applying God's Word and avoiding sin.

OBSERVATION Believers remain faithful to the truth of God's Word by keeping their eyes on Jesus. Those who overcome will share in God's glory.

INSPIRATION Good things take time before they're good. . . .

Develop an attitude of trust. God can change situations; His name is Deliverer. . . .

One of the most often-repeated commands in the Bible is to "wait on the Lord." Waiting on Him "grows you up"; it keeps your eyes off yourself and on Him; it gives you staying power. . . .

John could have spent his time pacing that barren little beach, feeling bitter about what "they" did to him, and scanning the horizon every minute for a rescuer. But he didn't.

Quieted under the hand of God into a position of trust and receptivity, John received the most fabulous revelation of Jesus Christ and His future that any man has ever received, and as a result he wrote the Spirit-breathed book of Revelation.

Do you feel as if you're on a "Patmos" in your life? Are you feeling caught and trapped? Settle down. Look up. Let God decide whether He will act according to One, Two, or Three. For you, it will be perfect. . . .

(From *You Don't Have to Quit* by Anne and Ray Ortlund)

APPLICATION Remember your joy and sense of achievement when you had a problem and you continued to work on it until it was solved? God wants to give you that same feeling of joy and fulfillment as you persevere in your Christian faith. Ask God to help you endure.

EXPLORATION Perseverance —Romans 5:3-4; Hebrews 12:1; James 1:3-4, 12; 2 Peter 1:5-9.

LIFE LESSON

Revelation 3:1-22

SITUATION God continued to address the spiritual lives of his churches. He encouraged the church in the Asian city of Philadelphia to persevere through difficult times. But the churches in Sardis and Laodicea were told to repent of their sin.

OBSERVATION God does not tolerate a mediocre spiritual life. He wants all Christians to be involved in loving and serving.

INSPIRATION Consider the Laodicean church. This church was wealthy and self-sufficient. But the church had a problem—hollow, fruitless faith. "I know what you do," God spoke to this group, "that you are not hot nor cold. I wish that you were hot or cold! But because you are lukewarm—neither hot, nor cold—I am ready to spit you out of my mouth."

The literal translation is "to vomit." Why does the body vomit something? Why does it recoil violently at the presence of certain substances? Because they are incompatible with the body. Vomiting is the body's way of rejecting anything it cannot handle.

What's the point? God can't stomach lukewarm faith. He is angered by a religion that puts on a show but ignores the service.

(From *And the Angels Were Silent* by Max Lucado)

APPLICATION If God gave you a report card on your relationship with him, what would it say? Which are the areas you neglect? Continue what you are doing well; aggressively improve an area you have neglected.

EXPLORATION Hypocrisy—Job 17:1-9; Psalm 5:9; 26:4; Isaiah 29:13; Ezekiel 33:31; Matthew 16:5-12; 23:1-39; Romans 2:17-24; Titus 1:16; 1 Peter 2:1.

To him who overcomes I will give some of the hidden manna to eat. And I
will give him a white stone, and on the stone a new name written which no
one knows except him who receives *it*." '

The Corrupt Church

18"And to the angel of the church in Thyatira write,
'These things says the Son of God, who has eyes like a flame of fire, and
His feet like fine brass: 19"I know your works, love, service, faith,[l] and your
patience; and *as* for your works, the last *are* more than the first. 20Never-
theless I have a few things against you, because you allow[m] that woman[n]
Jezebel, who calls herself a prophetess, to teach and seduce[o] My servants
to commit sexual immorality and eat things sacrificed to idols. 21And I
gave her time to repent of her sexual immorality, and she did not repent.[p]
22Indeed I will cast her into a sickbed, and those who commit adultery
with her into great tribulation, unless they repent of their[q] deeds. 23I will
kill her children with death, and all the churches shall know that I am He
who searches the minds and hearts. And I will give to each one of you according to your works.
24"Now to you I say, and[r] to the rest in Thyatira, as many as do not have
this doctrine, who have not known the depths of Satan, as they say, I will[s]
put on you no other burden. 25But hold fast what you have till I come.
26And he who overcomes, and keeps My works until the end, to him I will
give power over the nations—

27 *'He shall rule them with a rod of iron;*
They shall be dashed to pieces like the potter's vessels'[t]—

as I also have received from My Father; 28and I will give him the morning
star.
29"He who has an ear, let him hear what the Spirit says to the
churches." '

The Dead Church

3 "And to the angel of the church in Sardis write,
'These things says He who has the seven Spirits of God and the seven
stars: "I know your works, that you have a name that you are alive, but you
are dead. 2Be watchful, and strengthen the things which remain, that are
ready to die, for I have not found your works perfect before God.[u] 3Re-
member therefore how you have received and heard; hold fast and repent.
Therefore if you will not watch, I will come upon you as a thief, and you
will not know what hour I will come upon you. 4You[v] have a few names
even in Sardis who have not defiled their garments; and they shall walk
with Me in white, for they are worthy. 5He who overcomes shall be clothed
in white garments, and I will not blot out his name from the Book of Life;
but I will confess his name before My Father and before His angels.

2:19 [l] NU-Text and M-Text read *faith, service.*
2:20 [m] NU-Text and M-Text read *I have against you that you tolerate.* [n] M-Text reads *your wife Jezebel.* [o] NU-Text and M-Text read *and teaches and seduces.*
2:21 [p] NU-Text and M-Text read *time to repent,* and *she does not want to repent of her sexual immorality.*
2:22 [q] NU-Text and M-Text read *her.*
2:24 [r] NU-Text and M-Text omit *and.* [s] NU-Text and M-Text omit *will.*
2:27 [t] Psalm 2:9
3:2 [u] NU-Text and M-Text read *My God.*
3:4 [v] NU-Text and M-Text read *Nevertheless you have a few names in Sardis.*

6"He who has an ear, let him hear what the Spirit says to the churches."'

The Faithful Church

7"And to the angel of the church in Philadelphia write,
'These things says He who is holy, He who is true, *"He who has the key
of David, He who opens and no one shuts, and shuts and no one opens"*:[w]
8"I know your works. See, I have set before you an open door, and no one
can shut it;[x] for you have a little strength, have kept My word, and have not
denied My name. 9Indeed I will make *those* of the synagogue of Satan, who
say they are Jews and are not, but lie—indeed I will make them come and
worship before your feet, and to know that I have loved you. 10Because you
have kept My command to persevere, I also will keep you from the hour of
trial which shall come upon the whole world, to test those who dwell on
the earth. 11Behold,[y] I am coming quickly! Hold fast what you have, that no
one may take your crown. 12He who overcomes, I will make him a pillar in
the temple of My God, and he shall go out no more. I will write on him the
name of My God and the name of the city of My God, the New Jerusalem,
which comes down out of heaven from My God. And *I will write on him*
My new name.
13"He who has an ear, let him hear what the Spirit says to the
churches."'

The Lukewarm Church

14"And to the angel of the church of the Laodiceans[z] write,
'These things says the Amen, the Faithful and True Witness, the
Beginning of the creation of God: 15"I know your works, that you are neither
cold nor hot. I could wish you were cold or hot. 16So then, because you are
lukewarm, and neither cold nor hot,[a] I will vomit you out of My mouth. 17Be-
cause you say, 'I am rich, have become wealthy, and have need of nothing'—and do not know that you are wretched, miserable, poor, blind, and
naked— 18I counsel you to buy from Me gold refined in the fire, that you
may be rich; and white garments, that you may be clothed, *that* the shame of
your nakedness may not be revealed; and anoint your eyes with eye salve,
that you may see. 19As many as I love, I rebuke and chasten. Therefore be
zealous and repent. 20Behold, I stand at the door and knock. If anyone hears
My voice and opens the door, I will come in to him and dine with him, and
he with Me. 21To him who overcomes I will grant to sit with Me on My
throne, as I also overcame and sat down with My Father on His throne.
22"He who has an ear, let him hear what the Spirit says to the
churches."'"

The Throne Room of Heaven

4 After these things I looked, and behold, a door *standing* open in
heaven. And the first voice which I heard *was* like a trumpet speaking
with me, saying, "Come up here, and I will show you things which must
take place after this."
2Immediately I was in the Spirit; and behold, a throne set in heaven, and

3:7 [w] Isaiah 22:22
3:8 [x] NU-Text and M-Text read *which no one can shut.*
3:11 [y] NU-Text and M-Text omit *Behold.*
3:14 [z] NU-Text and M-Text read *in Laodicea.*
3:16 [a] NU-Text and M-Text read *hot nor cold.*

Life Lesson

Revelation 4:1–6:17

SITUATION John reported that Jesus Christ would initiate the final conflict against Satan. At the end, God would defeat Satan and throw him into hell.

OBSERVATION For the Believers, the end will be a time of rejoicing; for the unbelievers, time to face God's judgment.

INSPIRATION The risen Christ had called John into the presence of God so that the old man could know, and through him we could know, this fact: Behind the universe there is a Power and a person worthy of our praise and of our trust. In spite of rumors to the contrary, we are not creatures abandoned on a planet spinning madly through the universe, lost in galaxies upon galaxies of gaseous flaming suns or burnt-out cinder moons. We are the children of a great and wonderful God who even now sits in power accomplishing His purposes in His creation.

At the heart of this mystery is great hope. The national powers that we see hell-bent for destruction—amassing weapons, killing, and being killed—are not the ultimate power. Nor are the individual figures who rule in our lives the ultimate powers; mothers, fathers, teachers, pastors, counselors, politicians, diplomats, bankers, police officers, social workers, wardens and jailers, probation officers, tax collectors, dictators and their soldiers, kings and presidents will all one day stand powerless before this God of John's vision.

(From *Storm Warning* by Billy Graham)

APPLICATION Were you the type of child who worried about a parent's anger? Do you worry now about God's wrath? Trust fully in Christ today as your antidote to God's punishment of sin.

EXPLORATION Judgment—Deuteronomy 32:36; Psalm 1:5; 9:8; Ecclesiastes 12:14; Jeremiah 25:31; Acts 17:31; Romans 2:16; 1 Corinthians 6:2.

One sat on the throne. 3And He who sat there was[b] like
a jasper and a sardius stone in appearance; and *there*
was a rainbow around the throne, in appearance like
an emerald. 4Around the throne *were* twenty-four
thrones, and on the thrones I saw twenty-four elders
sitting, clothed in white robes; and they had crowns[c] of
gold on their heads. 5And from the throne proceeded
lightnings, thunderings, and voices.[d] Seven lamps of
fire *were* burning before the throne, which are the[e]
seven Spirits of God.

6Before the throne *there was*[f] a sea of glass, like crystal. And in the midst of the throne, and around the
throne, *were* four living creatures full of eyes in front
and in back. 7The first living creature *was* like a lion,
the second living creature like a calf, the third living
creature had a face like a man, and the fourth living
creature was like a flying eagle. 8*The* four living creatures, each having six wings, were full of eyes around
and within. And they do not rest day or night, saying:

"Holy, holy, holy,[g]
Lord God Almighty,
Who was and is and is to come!"

9Whenever the living creatures give glory and
honor and thanks to Him who sits on the throne, who
lives forever and ever, 10the twenty-four elders fall
down before Him who sits on the throne and worship
Him who lives forever and ever, and cast their crowns
before the throne, saying:

11 "You are worthy, O Lord,[h]
To receive glory and honor and power;
For You created all things,
And by Your will they exist[i] and were created."

The Lamb Takes the Scroll

5 And I saw in the right *hand* of Him who sat on the
throne a scroll written inside and on the back,
sealed with seven seals. 2Then I saw a strong angel
proclaiming with a loud voice, "Who is worthy to open
the scroll and to loose its seals?" 3And no one in
heaven or on the earth or under the earth was able to
open the scroll, or to look at it.

4So I wept much, because no one was found worthy
to open and read[j] the scroll, or to look at it. 5But one of
the elders said to me, "Do not weep. Behold, the Lion
of the tribe of Judah, the Root of David, has prevailed
to open the scroll and to loose[k] its seven seals."

6And I looked, and behold,[l] in the midst of the
throne and of the four living creatures, and in the
midst of the elders, stood a Lamb as though it had
been slain, having seven horns and seven eyes, which
are the seven Spirits of God sent out into all the earth.
7Then He came and took the scroll out of the right
hand of Him who sat on the throne.

Worthy Is the Lamb

8Now when He had taken the scroll, the four living
creatures and the twenty-four elders fell down before
the Lamb, each having a harp, and golden bowls full
of incense, which are the prayers of the saints. 9And
they sang a new song, saying:

"You are worthy to take the scroll,
And to open its seals;
For You were slain,
And have redeemed us to God by
Your blood
Out of every tribe and tongue
and people and nation,
10 And have made us[m] kings[n] and
priests to our God;
And we[o] shall reign on the earth."

11Then I looked, and I heard the voice of many angels around the throne, the living creatures, and the
elders; and the number of them was ten thousand
times ten thousand, and thousands of thousands,
12saying with a loud voice:

"Worthy is the Lamb who was slain
To receive power and riches and wisdom,
And strength and honor and
glory and blessing!"

13And every creature which is in heaven and on the
earth and under the earth and such as are in the sea,
and all that are in them, I heard saying:

"Blessing and honor and glory and power
Be to Him who sits on the throne,

4:3 [b] M-Text omits *And He who sat there was* (which makes the description in verse 3 modify the throne rather than God).
4:4 [c] NU-Text and M-Text read *robes, with crowns.*
4:5 [d] NU-Text and M-Text read *voices, and thunderings.* [e] M-Text omits *the.*
4:6 [f] NU-Text and M-Text add *something like.*
4:8 [g] M-Text has *holy* nine times.
4:11 [h] NU-Text and M-Text read *our Lord and God.* [i] NU-Text and M-Text read *existed.*
5:4 [j] NU-Text and M-Text omit *and read.*
5:5 [k] NU-Text and M-Text omit *to loose.*
5:6 [l] NU-Text and M-Text read *I saw in the midst . . . a Lamb standing.*
5:10 [m] NU-Text and M-Text read *them.* [n] NU-Text reads *a kingdom.* [o] NU-Text and M-Text read *they.*

And to the Lamb, forever and ever!"[p]
14Then the four living creatures said, "Amen!" And
the twenty-four[q] elders fell down and worshiped Him
who lives forever and ever.[r]

First Seal: The Conqueror

6 Now I saw when the Lamb opened one of the
seals;[s] and I heard one of the four living creatures
saying with a voice like thunder, "Come and see."
2And I looked, and behold, a white horse. He who sat
on it had a bow; and a crown was given to him, and he
went out conquering and to conquer.

Second Seal: Conflict on Earth

3When He opened the second seal, I heard the second living creature saying, "Come and see."[t] 4An-
other horse, fiery red, went out. And it was granted to
the one who sat on it to take peace from the earth, and
that *people* should kill one another; and there was
given to him a great sword.

Third Seal: Scarcity on Earth

5When He opened the third seal, I heard the third
living creature say, "Come and see." So I looked, and
behold, a black horse, and he who sat on it had a pair
of scales in his hand. 6And I heard a voice in the midst
of the four living creatures saying, "A quart[u] of wheat
for a denarius,[v] and three quarts of barley for a denarius; and do not harm the oil and the wine."

Fourth Seal: Widespread Death on Earth

7When He opened the fourth seal, I heard the voice
of the fourth living creature saying, "Come and see."
8So I looked, and behold, a pale horse. And the name
of him who sat on it was Death, and Hades followed
with him. And power was given to them over a fourth
of the earth, to kill with sword, with hunger, with
death, and by the beasts of the earth.

Fifth Seal: The Cry of the Martyrs

9When He opened the fifth seal, I saw under the
altar the souls of those who had been slain for the
word of God and for the testimony which they held.
10And they cried with a loud voice, saying, "How long,
O Lord, holy and true, until You judge and avenge our
blood on those who dwell on the earth?" 11Then a white
robe was given to each of them; and it was said to them
that they should rest a little while longer, until both *the*
number of their fellow servants and their brethren,
who would be killed as they *were*, was completed.

Sixth Seal: Cosmic Disturbances

12I looked when He opened the sixth seal, and behold,[w] there was a great earthquake; and the sun became black as sackcloth of hair, and the moon[x] became
like blood. 13And the stars of heaven fell to the earth, as
a fig tree drops its late figs when it is shaken by a
mighty wind. 14Then the sky receded as a scroll when it
is rolled up, and every mountain and island was
moved out of its place. 15And the kings of the earth, the
great men, the rich men, the commanders,[y] the mighty
men, every slave and every free man, hid themselves
in the caves and in the rocks of the mountains, 16and
said to the mountains and rocks, "Fall on us and hide
us from the face of Him who sits on the throne and
from the wrath of the Lamb! 17For the great day of His
wrath has come, and who is able to stand?"

The Sealed of Israel

7 After these things I saw four angels standing at the
four corners of the earth, holding the four winds
of the earth, that the wind should not blow on the earth,
on the sea, or on any tree. 2Then I saw another angel ascending from the east, having the seal of the living God.
And he cried with a loud voice to the four angels to
whom it was granted to harm the earth and the sea,
3saying, "Do not harm the earth, the sea, or the trees till
we have sealed the servants of our God on their foreheads." 4And I heard the number of those who were
sealed. One hundred *and* forty-four thousand of all the
tribes of the children of Israel *were* sealed:

5 of the tribe of Judah twelve thousand
were sealed;[z]
of the tribe of Reuben twelve thousand
were sealed;
of the tribe of Gad twelve thousand
were sealed;
6 of the tribe of Asher twelve thousand
were sealed;
of the tribe of Naphtali twelve thousand
were sealed;
of the tribe of Manasseh twelve thousand
were sealed;

5:13 [p] M-Text adds *Amen.*
5:14 [q] NU-Text and M-Text omit *twenty-four.* [r] NU-Text and M-Text omit *Him who lives forever and ever.*
6:1 [s] NU-Text and M-Text read *seven seals.*
6:3 [t] NU-Text and M-Text omit *and see.*
6:6 [u] Greek *choinix;* that is, approximately one quart [v] This was approximately one day's wage for a worker.
6:12 [w] NU-Text and M-Text omit *behold.* [x] NU-Text and M-Text read *the whole moon.*
6:15 [y] NU-Text and M-Text read *the commanders, the rich men.*
7:5 [z] In NU-Text and M-Text *were sealed* is stated only in verses 5a and 8c; the words are understood in the remainder of the passage.

LIFE LESSON

Revelation 7:1-17

SITUATION John assured his readers that God would not lose track of his faithful people during the judgment of the world. He would rescue them.

OBSERVATION All Believers are important to God. God guarantees his protection to his followers by placing his seal over them. Nothing can remove that seal.

INSPIRATION Unlike the 144,000 mentioned in Revelation, our seal is not visible. We have been sealed "in Him." Our seal is spiritual, not physical. Instead of receiving a mark on our foreheads, we were given the Holy Spirit as a pledge of God's intent to preserve us: . . . The Holy Spirit is a pledge of God's intentions. He is not finished with us yet. But the presence of the Spirit demonstrates God's commitment to complete what He has started. If salvation is not permanent, God is simply playing games by sending the Spirit into our hearts. It would be like a man's giving a woman an engagement ring when he knows he has no intention of marrying her.

We are sealed right up through the "day of redemption." The day of redemption refers to that day when our salvation will be complete—body and spirit.

There are no exceptions. Everyone who has been sealed in Christ will remain sealed right up through the end.

Only God can break the seal (see Rev. 5:1-3). And the Scriptures clearly teach that He has already determined to leave the seal intact until our salvation is complete.

(From *Eternal Security* by Charles Stanley)

APPLICATION How have you sensed God's protection? Note three people who may be in jeopardy of God's punishment. Pray for them during the day.

EXPLORATION Protection—2 Chronicles 12:1-2; Psalm 17:8; 18:2-3; Proverbs 2:8; 2 Thessalonians 3:3.

7 of the tribe of Simeon twelve thousand *were* sealed;
of the tribe of Levi twelve thousand *were* sealed;
of the tribe of Issachar twelve thousand *were* sealed;
8 of the tribe of Zebulun twelve thousand *were* sealed;
of the tribe of Joseph twelve thousand *were* sealed;
of the tribe of Benjamin twelve thousand *were* sealed.

A Multitude from the Great Tribulation

9 After these things I looked, and behold, a great multitude which no one
could number, of all nations, tribes, peoples, and tongues, standing before
the throne and before the Lamb, clothed with white robes, with palm
branches in their hands, 10 and crying out with a loud voice, saying, "Salvation *belongs* to our God who sits on the throne, and to the Lamb!" 11 All the
angels stood around the throne and the elders and the four living creatures,
and fell on their faces before the throne and worshiped God, 12 saying:

"Amen! Blessing and glory and wisdom,
Thanksgiving and honor and power and might,
Be to our God forever and ever.
Amen."

13 Then one of the elders answered, saying to me, "Who are these arrayed in white robes, and where did they come from?"
14 And I said to him, "Sir,[a] you know."
So he said to me, "These are the ones who come out of the great tribulation, and washed their robes and made them white in the blood of the
Lamb. 15 Therefore they are before the throne of God, and serve Him day
and night in His temple. And He who sits on the throne will dwell among
them. 16 They shall neither hunger anymore nor thirst anymore; the sun
shall not strike them, nor any heat; 17 for the Lamb who is in the midst of
the throne will shepherd them and lead them to living fountains of waters.[b] And God will wipe away every tear from their eyes."

Seventh Seal: Prelude to the Seven Trumpets

8 When He opened the seventh seal, there was silence in heaven for
about half an hour. 2 And I saw the seven angels who stand before God,
and to them were given seven trumpets. 3 Then another angel, having a
golden censer, came and stood at the altar. He was given much incense,
that he should offer *it* with the prayers of all the saints upon the golden altar
which was before the throne. 4 And the smoke of the incense, with the
prayers of the saints, ascended before God from the angel's hand. 5 Then the
angel took the censer, filled it with fire from the altar, and threw *it* to the
earth. And there were noises, thunderings, lightnings, and an earthquake.
6 So the seven angels who had the seven trumpets prepared themselves
to sound.

First Trumpet: Vegetation Struck

7 The first angel sounded: And hail and fire followed, mingled with
blood, and they were thrown to the earth.[c] And a third of the trees were
burned up, and all green grass was burned up.

7:14 [a] NU-Text and M-Text read *My lord.*
7:17 [b] NU-Text and M-Text read *to fountains of the waters of life.*
8:7 [c] NU-Text and M-Text add *and a third of the earth was burned up.*

Second Trumpet: The Seas Struck

8Then the second angel sounded: And *something* like a great mountain
burning with fire was thrown into the sea, and a third of the sea became
blood. 9And a third of the living creatures in the sea died, and a third of the
ships were destroyed.

Third Trumpet: The Waters Struck

10Then the third angel sounded: And a great star fell from heaven, burning
like a torch, and it fell on a third of the rivers and on the springs of water.
11The name of the star is Wormwood. A third of the waters became wormwood, and many men died from the water, because it was made bitter.

Fourth Trumpet: The Heavens Struck

12Then the fourth angel sounded: And a third of the sun was struck, a
third of the moon, and a third of the stars, so that a third of them were
darkened. A third of the day did not shine, and likewise the night.
13And I looked, and I heard an angel[d] flying through the midst of
heaven, saying with a loud voice, "Woe, woe, woe to the inhabitants of the
earth, because of the remaining blasts of the trumpet of the three angels
who are about to sound!"

Fifth Trumpet: The Locusts from the Bottomless Pit

9 Then the fifth angel sounded: And I saw a star fallen from heaven to
the earth. To him was given the key to the bottomless pit. 2And he
opened the bottomless pit, and smoke arose out of the pit like the smoke
of a great furnace. So the sun and the air were darkened because of the
smoke of the pit. 3Then out of the smoke locusts came upon the earth. And
to them was given power, as the scorpions of the earth have power. 4They
were commanded not to harm the grass of the earth, or any green thing,
or any tree, but only those men who do not have the seal of God on their
foreheads. 5And they were not given *authority* to kill them, but to torment
them *for* five months. Their torment *was* like the torment of a scorpion
when it strikes a man. 6In those days men will seek death and will not find
it; they will desire to die, and death will flee from them.
7The shape of the locusts was like horses prepared for battle. On their
heads were crowns of something like gold, and their faces *were* like the
faces of men. 8They had hair like women's hair, and their teeth were like
lions' *teeth.* 9And they had breastplates like breastplates of iron, and the
sound of their wings *was* like the sound of chariots with many horses running into battle. 10They had tails like scorpions, and there were stings in
their tails. Their power *was* to hurt men five months. 11And they had as
king over them the angel of the bottomless pit, whose name in Hebrew *is*
Abaddon, but in Greek he has the name Apollyon.
12One woe is past. Behold, still two more woes are coming after these
things.

Sixth Trumpet: The Angels from the Euphrates

13Then the sixth angel sounded: And I heard a voice from the four horns
of the golden altar which is before God, 14saying to the sixth angel who had

8:13 *d* NU-Text and M-Text read *eagle.*

Life Lesson

Revelation 8:1–9:21

SITUATION John had a vision of a supernatural battle waged between God's and Satan's forces. Although God disciplined his own people, they refused to repent.

OBSERVATION Sin comes subtly into a person's life. Before we know it, it takes control and alienates us from God. We must repent and turn to God in faith.

INSPIRATION John was also a prophet. The prophets often held out hope for the present—hope that God's judgment could be delayed if people would repent and turn to God in faith and obedience. That does not mean that the prophets offered an easy way out of all difficulties, as if somehow all problems would vanish if people would just profess their faith in God. Instead, like Winston Churchill standing amidst the bombed ruins of London, the prophets offered "blood, sweat, and tears" for those who would follow God. It would not be easy to serve God and fight against the evil of this present, dark and sinful world, and yet the prophets knew that God would be victorious in the end and His people would share in that victory.

So John was a prophet, calling his generation—and ours—to repentance and faith and action. He knew that we could never build the kingdom of God on earth, no matter how hard we might try. Only God can do that—and someday he will, when Christ comes again. But John also knew that God's judgment on this world could be delayed if we would repent and turn to Christ.

To some, John's message of the future may have sounded gloomy and depressing. John knew, however, that the worst thing he could do would be to assure people that everything was all right and that there was no need to be concerned about the evil in the world or God's judgment. But John's message is ultimately a message of the good news of salvation in Jesus Christ.

(From *Storm Warning* by Billy Graham)

Continued

APPLICATION What is the really good news in your life right now? Tell someone about it today. What sin needs to be confessed? Pray, telling God you are sorry, and resist the temptation to give in to it again.

EXPLORATION Repentance—Deuteronomy 31:27-29; 2 Chronicles 7:14; Nehemiah 9:28-31; Isaiah 30:15; Luke 13:3; John 12:10-11; 2 Peter 3:9.

the trumpet, "Release the four angels who are bound at the great river
Euphrates." 15So the four angels, who had been prepared for the hour and
day and month and year, were released to kill a third of mankind. 16Now
the number of the army of the horsemen *was* two hundred million; I heard
the number of them. 17And thus I saw the horses in the vision: those who
sat on them had breastplates of fiery red, hyacinth blue, and sulfur yellow;
and the heads of the horses *were* like the heads of lions; and out of their
mouths came fire, smoke, and brimstone. 18By these three *plagues* a third
of mankind was killed—by the fire and the smoke and the brimstone
which came out of their mouths. 19For their power[e] is in their mouth and
in their tails; for their tails *are* like serpents, having heads; and with them
they do harm.

20But the rest of mankind, who were not killed by these plagues, did not
repent of the works of their hands, that they should not worship demons,
and idols of gold, silver, brass, stone, and wood, which can neither see nor
hear nor walk. 21And they did not repent of their murders or their sorceries[f] or their sexual immorality or their thefts.

The Mighty Angel with the Little Book

10 I saw still another mighty angel coming down from heaven, clothed
with a cloud. And a rainbow *was* on his head, his face *was* like the
sun, and his feet like pillars of fire. 2He had a little book open in his hand.
And he set his right foot on the sea and *his* left *foot* on the land, 3and cried
with a loud voice, as *when* a lion roars. When he cried out, seven thunders
uttered their voices. 4Now when the seven thunders uttered their voices,[g] I
was about to write; but I heard a voice from heaven saying to me,[h] "Seal up
the things which the seven thunders uttered, and do not write them."

5The angel whom I saw standing on the sea and on the land raised up
his hand[i] to heaven 6and swore by Him who lives forever and ever, who
created heaven and the things that are in it, the earth and the things that
are in it, and the sea and the things that are in it, that there should be delay
no longer, 7but in the days of the sounding of the seventh angel, when he is
about to sound, the mystery of God would be finished, as He declared to
His servants the prophets.

John Eats the Little Book

8Then the voice which I heard from heaven spoke to me again and said,
"Go, take the little book which is open in the hand of the angel who stands
on the sea and on the earth."

9So I went to the angel and said to him, "Give me the little book."

And he said to me, "Take and eat it; and it will make your stomach bitter, but it will be as sweet as honey in your mouth."

10Then I took the little book out of the angel's hand and ate it, and it was
as sweet as honey in my mouth. But when I had eaten it, my stomach became bitter. 11And he[j] said to me, "You must prophesy again about many
peoples, nations, tongues, and kings."

9:19 [e] NU-Text and M-Text read *the power of the horses.*
9:21 [f] NU-Text and M-Text read *drugs.*
10:4 [g] NU-Text and M-Text read *sounded.* [h] NU-Text and M-Text omit *to me.*
10:5 [i] NU-Text and M-Text read *right hand.*
10:11 [j] NU-Text and M-Text read *they.*

The Two Witnesses

11 Then I was given a reed like a measuring rod. And the angel stood,[k]
saying, "Rise and measure the temple of God, the altar, and those
who worship there. [2]But leave out the court which is outside the temple,
and do not measure it, for it has been given to the Gentiles. And they will
tread the holy city underfoot *for* forty-two months. [3]And I will give *power*
to my two witnesses, and they will prophesy one thousand two hundred
and sixty days, clothed in sackcloth."
[4]These are the two olive trees and the two lampstands standing before
the God[l] of the earth. [5]And if anyone wants to harm them, fire proceeds
from their mouth and devours their enemies. And if anyone wants to
harm them, he must be killed in this manner. [6]These have power to shut
heaven, so that no rain falls in the days of their prophecy; and they have
power over waters to turn them to blood, and to strike the earth with all
plagues, as often as they desire.

The Witnesses Killed

[7]When they finish their testimony, the beast that ascends out of the bottomless pit will make war against them, overcome them, and kill them.
[8]And their dead bodies *will lie* in the street of the great city which spiritually is called Sodom and Egypt, where also our[m] Lord was crucified. [9]Then
those from the peoples, tribes, tongues, and nations will see their dead
bodies three-and-a-half days, and not allow[n] their dead bodies to be put
into graves. [10]And those who dwell on the earth will rejoice over them,
make merry, and send gifts to one another, because these two prophets
tormented those who dwell on the earth.

The Witnesses Resurrected

[11]Now after the three-and-a-half days the breath of life from God entered them, and they stood on their feet, and great fear fell on those who
saw them. [12]And they[o] heard a loud voice from heaven saying to them,
"Come up here." And they ascended to heaven in a cloud, and their enemies saw them. [13]In the same hour there was a great earthquake, and a
tenth of the city fell. In the earthquake seven thousand people were killed,
and the rest were afraid and gave glory to the God of heaven.
[14]The second woe is past. Behold, the third woe is coming quickly.

Seventh Trumpet: The Kingdom Proclaimed

[15]Then the seventh angel sounded: And there were loud voices in
heaven, saying, "The kingdoms[p] of this world have become *the kingdoms*
of our Lord and of His Christ, and He shall reign forever and ever!" [16]And
the twenty-four elders who sat before God on their thrones fell on their
faces and worshiped God, [17]saying:

"We give You thanks, O Lord God Almighty,
The One who is and who was and who is to come,[q]
Because You have taken Your great power and reigned.

11:1 [k] NU-Text and M-Text omit *And the angel stood.*
11:4 [l] NU-Text and M-Text read *Lord.*
11:8 [m] NU-Text and M-Text read *their.*
11:9 [n] NU-Text and M-Text read *nations see . . . and will not allow.*
11:12 [o] M-Text reads *I.*
11:15 [p] NU-Text and M-Text read *kingdom . . . has become.*
11:17 [q] NU-Text and M-Text omit *and who is to come.*

LIFE LESSON

Revelation 10:1-11

SITUATION A mighty angel appeared with an open book and announced that time would end. The angel announced the final universal judgment.

OBSERVATION Although God's Word brings encouragement to the Believer, his Word also lays responsibility on the Believer to proclaim God's coming judgment.

INSPIRATION Never choose to be a worker for God, but once God has placed His call on you, woe be to you if you "turn aside to the right hand or to the left" (Deuteronomy 5:32). We are not here to work for God because we have chosen to do so, but because God has "laid hold of" us. And once He has done so, we never have this thought, "Well, I'm really not suited for this." What you are to preach is also determined by God, not by your own natural leanings or desires. Keep your soul steadfastly related to God, and remember that you are called not simply to convey your testimony but also to preach the gospel. Every Christian must testify to the truth of God, but when it comes to the call to preach, there must be the agonizing grip of God's hand on you—your life is in the grip of God for that very purpose. How many of us are held like that? Never water down the Word of God, but preach it in its undiluted sternness. There must be unflinching faithfulness to the Word of God, but when you come to personal dealings with others, remember who you are—you are not some special being created in heaven, but a sinner saved by grace.

(From *My Utmost for His Highest* by Oswald Chambers)

APPLICATION How firm is God's grip on your life? How ready are you to testify to God's Word?

EXPLORATION Scripture—Deuteronomy 18:21-22; 32:46-47; Isaiah 8:16; Jeremiah 26:2; Malachi 2:7-8; Matthew 22:29; 2 Timothy 3:16; 2 Peter 3:15.

Life Lesson

Revelation 11:1-19

SITUATION God will protect people who are faithful to him, but unbelievers do not enjoy this privilege.

OBSERVATION God will protect the faithful until the end, while preparing to judge evil once and for all.

INSPIRATION Why do I not take him seriously when he questions, "If you, then, though you are evil, know how to give good gifts to your children, how much more will your Father in Heaven give good gifts to those who ask him!"

Why don't I let my Father do for me what I am more than willing to do for my own children?

I'm learning, though. Being a parent is better than a course on theology. Being a father is teaching me that when I am criticized, injured, or afraid, there is a Father who is ready to comfort me. There is a Father who will hold me until I'm better, help me until I can live with the hurt, and who won't go to sleep when I'm afraid of waking up and seeing the dark. Ever. And that's enough.

(From *The Applause of Heaven* by Max Lucado)

APPLICATION Revelation is a great source of encouragement to Christians that the Lord will protect them from evil. Do you feel the Lord has his sheltering arm around you? Look for someone today who needs that encouragement and give it.

EXPLORATION Protection—Psalm 17:8; 18:2-3; Revelation 7:4-8.

18 The nations were angry, and Your wrath has come,
And the time of the dead, that they should be judged,
And that You should reward Your servants the
prophets and the saints,
And those who fear Your name, small and great,
And should destroy those who destroy the earth."

19Then the temple of God was opened in heaven, and the ark of His
covenant[r] was seen in His temple. And there were lightnings, noises,
thunderings, an earthquake, and great hail.

The Woman, the Child, and the Dragon

12 Now a great sign appeared in heaven: a woman clothed with the
sun, with the moon under her feet, and on her head a garland of
twelve stars. 2Then being with child, she cried out in labor and in pain to
give birth.
3And another sign appeared in heaven: behold, a great, fiery red dragon
having seven heads and ten horns, and seven diadems on his heads. 4His
tail drew a third of the stars of heaven and threw them to the earth. And
the dragon stood before the woman who was ready to give birth, to devour
her Child as soon as it was born. 5She bore a male Child who was to rule all
nations with a rod of iron. And her Child was caught up to God and His
throne. 6Then the woman fled into the wilderness, where she has a place
prepared by God, that they should feed her there one thousand two hundred and sixty days.

Satan Thrown Out of Heaven

7And war broke out in heaven: Michael and his angels fought with the
dragon; and the dragon and his angels fought, 8but they did not prevail, nor
was a place found for them[s] in heaven any longer. 9So the great dragon was
cast out, that serpent of old, called the Devil and Satan, who deceives the
whole world; he was cast to the earth, and his angels were cast out with him.
10Then I heard a loud voice saying in heaven, "Now salvation, and
strength, and the kingdom of our God, and the power of His Christ have
come, for the accuser of our brethren, who accused them before our God
day and night, has been cast down. 11And they overcame him by the blood of
the Lamb and by the word of their testimony, and they did not love their lives
to the death. 12Therefore rejoice, O heavens, and you who dwell in them! Woe
to the inhabitants of the earth and the sea! For the devil has come down to
you, having great wrath, because he knows that he has a short time."

The Woman Persecuted

13Now when the dragon saw that he had been cast to the earth, he persecuted the woman who gave birth to the male *Child.* 14But the woman was
given two wings of a great eagle, that she might fly into the wilderness to
her place, where she is nourished for a time and times and half a time,
from the presence of the serpent. 15So the serpent spewed water out of his
mouth like a flood after the woman, that he might cause her to be carried
away by the flood. 16But the earth helped the woman, and the earth opened

11:19 [r] M-Text reads *the covenant of the Lord.*
12:8 [s] M-Text reads *him.*

its mouth and swallowed up the flood which the dragon had spewed out of
his mouth. 17And the dragon was enraged with the woman, and he went to
make war with the rest of her offspring, who keep the commandments of
God and have the testimony of Jesus Christ.[t]

The Beast from the Sea

13 Then I[u] stood on the sand of the sea. And I saw a beast rising up out
of the sea, having seven heads and ten horns,[v] and on his horns ten
crowns, and on his heads a blasphemous name. 2Now the beast which I
saw was like a leopard, his feet were like *the feet of* a bear, and his mouth
like the mouth of a lion. The dragon gave him his power, his throne, and
great authority. 3And *I saw* one of his heads as if it had been mortally
wounded, and his deadly wound was healed. And all the world marveled
and followed the beast. 4So they worshiped the dragon who gave authority
to the beast; and they worshiped the beast, saying, "Who *is* like the beast?
Who is able to make war with him?"

5And he was given a mouth speaking great things and blasphemies, and
he was given authority to continue[w] for forty-two months. 6Then he
opened his mouth in blasphemy against God, to blaspheme His name, His
tabernacle, and those who dwell in heaven. 7It was granted to him to make
war with the saints and to overcome them. And authority was given him
over every tribe,[x] tongue, and nation. 8All who dwell on the earth will worship him, whose names have not been written in the Book of Life of the
Lamb slain from the foundation of the world.

9If anyone has an ear, let him hear. 10He who leads into captivity shall go
into captivity; he who kills with the sword must be killed with the sword.
Here is the patience and the faith of the saints.

The Beast from the Earth

11Then I saw another beast coming up out of the earth, and he had two
horns like a lamb and spoke like a dragon. 12And he exercises all the authority of the first beast in his presence, and causes the earth and those
who dwell in it to worship the first beast, whose deadly wound was healed.
13He performs great signs, so that he even makes fire come down from
heaven on the earth in the sight of men. 14And he deceives those[y] who
dwell on the earth by those signs which he was granted to do in the sight of
the beast, telling those who dwell on the earth to make an image to the
beast who was wounded by the sword and lived. 15He was granted *power* to
give breath to the image of the beast, that the image of the beast should
both speak and cause as many as would not worship the image of the
beast to be killed. 16He causes all, both small and great, rich and poor, free
and slave, to receive a mark on their right hand or on their foreheads,
17and that no one may buy or sell except one who has the mark or[z] the
name of the beast, or the number of his name.

18Here is wisdom. Let him who has understanding calculate the number
of the beast, for it is the number of a man: His number *is* 666.

12:17 [t] NU-Text and M-Text omit *Christ.*
13:1 [u] NU-Text reads *he.* [v] NU-Text and M-Text read *ten horns and seven heads.*
13:5 [w] M-Text reads *make war.*
13:7 [x] NU-Text and M-Text add *and people.*
13:14 [y] M-Text reads *my own people.*
13:17 [z] NU-Text and M-Text omit *or.*

LIFE LESSON

Revelation 12:1-18

SITUATION This chapter symbolizes conflict between God and Satan. The woman gave birth to Christ. The dragon, Satan, sought to destroy Christ, but his attempts were futile. A heavenly battle between Satan with his demons and God's angels resulted in Satan's defeat.

OBSERVATION The contest between good and evil is a great, cosmic battle that God will win. We can experience God's victory in our lives through faith in Jesus as Lord and Savior.

INSPIRATION Life is so short. The Bible says that we must be prepared to meet God at all times. We never know when we step into our car, walk out the door of our home, or just open our eyes to a new day, what lies ahead. "Since his days are determined, the number of his months is with Thee, and his limits Thou hast set so that he cannot pass" (Job 14:5). Millions of people on earth are walking around physically alive, but spiritually dead. When your eyes and ears become attuned to the cries of others, you hear those who say they are empty and lost. They are separated from the source of life and like a lamp which is unattached, they are dark and lifeless. The lamp may be very expensive, may have a beautiful shade which draws attention, but has no light without being plugged into the source of energy. Jesus said, "I am the life."
(From *How to Be Born Again* by Billy Graham)

APPLICATION Revelation is a beautiful, but often frightening account of the great battle for spiritual supremacy. Be sure not to take your situation for granted. Ask God to keep you aware of Satan's attacks. Depend on God for your strength and victory.

EXPLORATION Souls—
Psalm 56:3-4; John 10:28-29.

Life Lesson

Revelation 13:1-18

SITUATION Before the final battle, Christians would be challenged. God promised, though, that no spiritual harm could come to Believers, although they might have to endure persecution and pain.

OBSERVATION Christians must discern false prophets who claim to perform miracles and exercise authority from God.

INSPIRATION Counterfeit Christians, like counterfeit twenty dollar bills, are not easily detected. It takes a trained, discerning eye.

This is a good moment for me to encourage you to be a careful student of the Scriptures and a watchful follower of spiritual (perhaps a better word would be religious) leaders . . . in that order. The better you come to know God's truth, the keener will be your watchfulness. When Jesus spoke of checking the fruit of another's life, He was emphasizing the importance of paying attention to what is being taught—both what is said and what is left unsaid—as well as that which is taught as it is being lived out. In the final analysis, a tree cannot hide what it is. Take a close look. Slowly and carefully taste the fruit (if you can't tell by looking), get a respected second and even third opinion, and stay on the alert.

(From *Simple Faith* by Charles Swindoll)

APPLICATION Can you tell the difference between Christian teaching and false doctrine? Such decisions require careful discernment, ensuring that actions and words spoken are consistent with God's wisdom in the Bible. In your Bible reading this week look for ways to distinguish true teaching from false.

EXPLORATION Discernment—Philippians 1:10; James 1:5; Matthew 7:6.

The Lamb and the 144,000

14 Then I looked, and behold, a[a] Lamb standing on Mount Zion, and
with Him one hundred *and* forty-four thousand, having[b] His
Father's name written on their foreheads. 2And I heard a voice from
heaven, like the voice of many waters, and like the voice of loud thunder.
And I heard the sound of harpists playing their harps. 3They sang as it
were a new song before the throne, before the four living creatures, and
the elders; and no one could learn that song except the hundred *and* forty-
four thousand who were redeemed from the earth. 4These are the ones
who were not defiled with women, for they are virgins. These are the ones
who follow the Lamb wherever He goes. These were redeemed[c] from
among men, *being* firstfruits to God and to the Lamb. 5And in their mouth
was found no deceit,[d] for they are without fault before the throne of God.[e]

The Proclamations of Three Angels

6Then I saw another angel flying in the midst of heaven, having the everlasting gospel to preach to those who dwell on the earth—to every nation,
tribe, tongue, and people— 7saying with a loud voice, "Fear God and give
glory to Him, for the hour of His judgment has come; and worship Him
who made heaven and earth, the sea and springs of water."
8And another angel followed, saying, "Babylon[f] is fallen, is fallen, that
great city, because she has made all nations drink of the wine of the wrath
of her fornication."
9Then a third angel followed them, saying with a loud voice, "If anyone
worships the beast and his image, and receives *his* mark on his forehead
or on his hand, 10he himself shall also drink of the wine of the wrath of
God, which is poured out full strength into the cup of His indignation. He
shall be tormented with fire and brimstone in the presence of the holy angels and in the presence of the Lamb. 11And the smoke of their torment ascends forever and ever; and they have no rest day or night, who worship
the beast and his image, and whoever receives the mark of his name."
12Here is the patience of the saints; here *are* those[g] who keep the commandments of God and the faith of Jesus.
13Then I heard a voice from heaven saying to me,[h] "Write: 'Blessed *are*
the dead who die in the Lord from now on.' "

"Yes," says the Spirit, "that they may rest from their labors, and their works follow them."

Reaping the Earth's Harvest

14Then I looked, and behold, a white cloud, and on the cloud sat *One* like
the Son of Man, having on His head a golden crown, and in His hand a
sharp sickle. 15And another angel came out of the temple, crying with a
loud voice to Him who sat on the cloud, "Thrust in Your sickle and reap,
for the time has come for You[i] to reap, for the harvest of the earth is ripe."
16So He who sat on the cloud thrust in His sickle on the earth, and the earth
was reaped.

14:1 [a] NU-Text and M-Text read *the.* [b] NU-Text and M-Text add *His name and.*
14:4 [c] M-Text adds *by Jesus.*
14:5 [d] NU-Text and M-Text read *falsehood.* [e] NU-Text and M-Text omit *before the throne of God.*
14:8 [f] NU-Text reads *Babylon the great is fallen, is fallen, which has made;* M-Text reads *Babylon the great is fallen. She has made.*
14:12 [g] NU-Text and M-Text omit *here are those.*
14:13 [h] NU-Text and M-Text omit *to me.*
14:15 [i] NU-Text and M-Text omit *for You.*

Reaping the Grapes of Wrath

17Then another angel came out of the temple which is in heaven, he also
having a sharp sickle.
18And another angel came out from the altar, who had power over fire,
and he cried with a loud cry to him who had the sharp sickle, saying,
"Thrust in your sharp sickle and gather the clusters of the vine of the
earth, for her grapes are fully ripe." 19So the angel thrust his sickle into the
earth and gathered the vine of the earth, and threw *it* into the great winepress of the wrath of God. 20And the winepress was trampled outside the
city, and blood came out of the winepress, up to the horses' bridles, for
one thousand six hundred furlongs.

Prelude to the Bowl Judgments

15 Then I saw another sign in heaven, great and marvelous: seven angels having the seven last plagues, for in them the wrath of God is
complete.
2And I saw *something* like a sea of glass mingled with fire, and those
who have the victory over the beast, over his image and over his mark[j] *and*
over the number of his name, standing on the sea of glass, having harps of
God. 3They sing the song of Moses, the servant of God, and the song of the
Lamb, saying:

"Great and marvelous *are* Your works,
Lord God Almighty!
Just and true *are* Your ways,
O King of the saints![k]
4 Who shall not fear You, O Lord, and glorify Your name?
For *You* alone *are* holy.
For all nations shall come and worship before You,
For Your judgments have been manifested."

5After these things I looked, and behold,[l] the temple of the tabernacle of
the testimony in heaven was opened. 6And out of the temple came the
seven angels having the seven plagues, clothed in pure bright linen, and
having their chests girded with golden bands. 7Then one of the four living
creatures gave to the seven angels seven golden bowls full of the wrath of
God who lives forever and ever. 8The temple was filled with smoke from
the glory of God and from His power, and no one was able to enter the
temple till the seven plagues of the seven angels were completed.

16 Then I heard a loud voice from the temple saying to the seven angels, "Go and pour out the bowls[m] of the wrath of God on the earth."

First Bowl: Loathsome Sores

2So the first went and poured out his bowl upon the earth, and a foul
and loathsome sore came upon the men who had the mark of the beast
and those who worshiped his image.

15:2 *j* NU-Text and M-Text omit *over his mark.*
15:3 *k* NU-Text and M-Text read *nations.*
15:5 *l* NU-Text and M-Text omit *behold.*
16:1 *m* NU-Text and M-Text read *seven bowls.*

LIFE LESSON

Revelation 14:1-20

SITUATION God's judgment arrived. Only those who were cleansed from sin through faith in Christ remained protected from God's anger against sin. This chapter provided assurance and comfort to the faithful.

OBSERVATION God's judgment of evil will not be put off indefinitely. Only by submitting our life to him can we avoid his wrath.

INSPIRATION I'll be home soon. My plane is nearing San Antonio. I can feel the nose of the jet dipping downward. I can see the flight attendants getting ready. [My wife], Denalyn, is somewhere in the parking lot, parking the car and hustling the girls toward the terminal.

I'll be home soon. The plane will land. I'll walk down that ramp and hear my name and see their faces. I'll be home soon.

You'll be home soon, too. You may not have noticed it, but you are closer to home than ever before. Each moment is a step taken. Each breath is a page turned. Each day is a mile marked, a mountain climbed. You are closer to home than you've ever been.

Before you know it, your appointed arrival time will come; you'll descend the ramp and enter the City. You'll see faces that are waiting for you. You'll hear your name spoken by those who love you. And, maybe, just maybe—in the back, behind the crowds—the One who would rather die than live without you will remove his pierced hands from his heavenly robe and . . . applaud.

(From *The Applause of Heaven* by Max Lucado)

APPLICATION Have you accepted Christ as your Savior? Have you confessed your sins? If so, you have nothing to fear from God's judgment of the world. The judge is on our side! If you are unsure, pray to receive Christ right now.

EXPLORATION Judgment—Deuteronomy 7:2; Matthew 13:30; 16:27; Luke 11:29-32.

LIFE LESSON
Revelation 16:1-21

SITUATION The seven terrible plagues are poured out on the earth. Much sorrow and trouble await those who are not protected from God's judgment. Despite the power of the plagues, people will curse God rather than praise him.

OBSERVATION God's terrifying wrath purges the earth of evil.

INSPIRATION The Bible says that, "The fear of the Lord is the beginning of wisdom." We don't fear Him as a tyrant but as a loving and just Father who leads us in wisdom and truth to do what is good for us, what will prolong and preserve our lives. But since God is a just Father, we know He will discipline and punish us when we defy Him and break His rules. If we break those rules often enough and carelessly enough, He will take our privileges away completely. That is the risk this world faces even now. . . .
Peace with God, the peace of God, and peace between nations is possible, if we repent of our sins, listen to Him, believe in Him, and follow Him. As servants, followers, brothers, and sisters of the Savior, we are commanded to be His allies in the cause of the true and lasting peace that He can bring. . . .
We are to expect the coming of Christ at any time, but we are to work as if He were not to come for a thousand years. . . .
In the meantime, we are to work for peace and harmony among the nations of the earth and to love our neighbors even as we love ourselves.
(From *Storm Warning* by Billy Graham)

APPLICATION Before the final judgment begins, witness to friends and neighbors about God's offer of eternal life in Christ. Tell them the story of Jesus. Share how God has made a difference in your life.

EXPLORATION Wrath of God—Genesis 1:18; 18:20-33; 19:24; Romans 1:24-32.

Second Bowl: The Sea Turns to Blood

3Then the second angel poured out his bowl on the sea, and it became
blood as of a dead *man;* and every living creature in the sea died.

Third Bowl: The Waters Turn to Blood

4Then the third angel poured out his bowl on the rivers and springs of
water, and they became blood. 5And I heard the angel of the waters saying:

"You are righteous, O Lord,[n]
The One who is and who was and who is to be,[o]
Because You have judged these things.
6 For they have shed the blood of saints and prophets,
And You have given them blood to drink.
For[p] it is their just due."

7And I heard another from[q] the altar saying, "Even so, Lord God
Almighty, true and righteous *are* Your judgments."

Fourth Bowl: Men Are Scorched

8Then the fourth angel poured out his bowl on the sun, and power was
given to him to scorch men with fire. 9And men were scorched with great
heat, and they blasphemed the name of God who has power over these
plagues; and they did not repent and give Him glory.

Fifth Bowl: Darkness and Pain

10Then the fifth angel poured out his bowl on the throne of the beast,
and his kingdom became full of darkness; and they gnawed their tongues
because of the pain. 11They blasphemed the God of heaven because of their
pains and their sores, and did not repent of their deeds.

Sixth Bowl: Euphrates Dried Up

12Then the sixth angel poured out his bowl on the great river Euphrates,
and its water was dried up, so that the way of the kings from the east might
be prepared. 13And I saw three unclean spirits like frogs *coming* out of the
mouth of the dragon, out of the mouth of the beast, and out of the mouth
of the false prophet. 14For they are spirits of demons, performing signs,
which go out to the kings of the earth and[r] of the whole world, to gather
them to the battle of that great day of God Almighty.
15"Behold, I am coming as a thief. Blessed *is* he who watches, and keeps
his garments, lest he walk naked and they see his shame."
16And they gathered them together to the place called in Hebrew,
Armageddon.[s]

Seventh Bowl: The Earth Utterly Shaken

17Then the seventh angel poured out his bowl into the air, and a loud
voice came out of the temple of heaven, from the throne, saying, "It is
done!" 18And there were noises and thunderings and lightnings; and there
was a great earthquake, such a mighty and great earthquake as had not

16:5 [n] NU-Text and M-Text omit *O Lord.* [o] NU-Text and M-Text read *who was, the Holy One.*
16:6 [p] NU-Text and M-Text omit *For.*
16:7 [q] NU-Text and M-Text omit *another from.*
16:14 [r] NU-Text and M-Text omit *of the earth and.*
16:16 [s] M-Text reads *Megiddo.*

occurred since men were on the earth. 19Now the great city was divided
into three parts, and the cities of the nations fell. And great Babylon was
remembered before God, to give her the cup of the wine of the fierceness
of His wrath. 20Then every island fled away, and the mountains were not
found. 21And great hail from heaven fell upon men, *each hailstone* about
the weight of a talent. Men blasphemed God because of the plague of the
hail, since that plague was exceedingly great.

The Scarlet Woman and the Scarlet Beast

17 Then one of the seven angels who had the seven bowls came and
talked with me, saying to me,[t] "Come, I will show you the judgment
of the great harlot who sits on many waters, 2with whom the kings of the
earth committed fornication, and the inhabitants of the earth were made
drunk with the wine of her fornication."
3So he carried me away in the Spirit into the wilderness. And I saw a
woman sitting on a scarlet beast *which was* full of names of blasphemy,
having seven heads and ten horns. 4The woman was arrayed in purple and
scarlet, and adorned with gold and precious stones and pearls, having in
her hand a golden cup full of abominations and the filthiness of her fornication.[u] 5And on her forehead a name *was* written:

MYSTERY,
BABYLON THE GREAT,
THE MOTHER OF HARLOTS AND OF
THE ABOMINATIONS OF THE EARTH.

6I saw the woman, drunk with the blood of the saints and with the blood of
the martyrs of Jesus. And when I saw her, I marveled with great amazement.

The Meaning of the Woman and the Beast

7But the angel said to me, "Why did you marvel? I will tell you the mystery of the woman and of the beast that carries her, which has the seven
heads and the ten horns. 8The beast that you saw was, and is not, and will
ascend out of the bottomless pit and go to perdition. And those who dwell
on the earth will marvel, whose names are not written in the Book of Life
from the foundation of the world, when they see the beast that was, and is
not, and yet is.[v]
9"Here *is* the mind which has wisdom: The seven heads are seven
mountains on which the woman sits. 10There are also seven kings. Five
have fallen, one is, *and* the other has not yet come. And when he comes, he
must continue a short time. 11The beast that was, and is not, is himself also
the eighth, and is of the seven, and is going to perdition.
12"The ten horns which you saw are ten kings who have received no
kingdom as yet, but they receive authority for one hour as kings with the
beast. 13These are of one mind, and they will give their power and authority to the beast. 14These will make war with the Lamb, and the Lamb will
overcome them, for He is Lord of lords and King of kings; and those *who
are* with Him *are* called, chosen, and faithful."

17:1 [t] NU-Text and M-Text omit *to me.*
17:4 [u] M-Text reads *the filthiness of the fornication of the earth.*
17:8 [v] NU-Text and M-Text read *and shall be present.*

LIFE LESSON

Revelation 17:1-18

SITUATION The "great prostitute" referred to Babylon. John's readers probably equated it with the Roman Empire, but it also symbolized any system hostile to God.

OBSERVATION Using symbolic language, John described the destruction of evil and systems energized by Satan. God triumphs over evil.

INSPIRATION There is a flip side to the issue of believers who struggle. It is, "Why do I struggle when wicked people seem to be so free of trouble?"

We should not be surprised when the righteous suffer. It conforms us to the image of Christ. It gives us power in witness. It instills the valuable strength of God-sufficiency and reduces the risk in our ministry for God. It refines us to make us capable and usable. It catches the attention of a watching world so that God's glory may be seen as He becomes credible and visible through our suffering. It may even be used in a sphere far beyond ourselves to glorify God in the universe.

Don't pity the righteous who suffer. They have a divine edge. Their resource in pain is the reality that God is there and they only experience what He permits. And all that He permits is guaranteed by the kind of God He is. The righteous suffer with the knowledge that Christ has conquered and gives grace, growth, and glory in the midst of pain.

(From *The Upside of Down* by Joseph M. Stowell)

APPLICATION In the middle of struggle, God's promises are vital. Memorize verse 17; it shows that God accomplishes his plan by overcoming those who oppose him.

EXPLORATION Opposition to God—Genesis 3:1-6; Isaiah 14:13-14; Matthew 13:38-39, 41; Luke 4:5-7; Acts 26:17-18; Ephesians 2:2; Revelation 12:9.

LIFE LESSON

Revelation 18:1-24

SITUATION John pointed out that although society was built around the economy, only what was built on God would last forever.

OBSERVATION Greed and materialism will be judged and crushed. Christians must derive their security from faith in Christ.

INSPIRATION Accepting my role as a servant to properly handle the assets of the Prince brings a real-world meaning to my faith. It causes me to think ecologically about my responsibility for Christ's environment. . . .

It is enjoyable to consider what a greater world under the reign of the Prince would be like, where all things—humanity, living things, the stuff of creation—might exist as they were meant to be in the creative mind of God. Such a dream is not idle fantasy. It answers to something I believe is hidden within each one of us: a memory deep in our spiritual genes that knew of a time when God came down and walked with man, and everything was good. And the dream also answers a hope deep within us—some have called it a healthy homesickness—that one day all things will be restored to their original creative intent by the hand of God.

Believing that this is exactly what will happen when the Prince returns in glorious triumph, the servant of the kingdom makes a little history each day by claiming hunks of a spoiled creation and establishing Christ's presence in it. It cannot be done permanently (picked-up streets get dirty again, and work done well the first time has to be done over again), but it can be done with the conviction that it makes a statement and brings Christ to places where He might otherwise never have been known.

(From *Christ Followers in the Real World* by Gordon MacDonald)

APPLICATION Try listening with greater discernment to commercials on radio and television. Note how their values differ from God's.

EXPLORATION Results of Evil—Psalm 5:4-6; Proverbs 10:29-30; Zephaniah 2:13-15; Romans 1:21-32; 1 Corinthians 6:9-10; James 4:4.

15 Then he said to me, "The waters which you saw, where the harlot sits, are peoples, multitudes, nations, and tongues. 16 And the ten horns which you saw on[w] the beast, these will hate the harlot, make her desolate and naked, eat her flesh and burn her with fire. 17 For God has put it into their hearts to fulfill His purpose, to be of one mind, and to give their kingdom to the beast, until the words of God are fulfilled. 18 And the woman whom you saw is that great city which reigns over the kings of the earth."

The Fall of Babylon the Great

18 After these things I saw another angel coming down from heaven, having great authority, and the earth was illuminated with his glory. 2 And he cried mightily[x] with a loud voice, saying, "Babylon the great is fallen, is fallen, and has become a dwelling place of demons, a prison for every foul spirit, and a cage for every unclean and hated bird! 3 For all the nations have drunk of the wine of the wrath of her fornication, the kings of the earth have committed fornication with her, and the merchants of the earth have become rich through the abundance of her luxury."

4 And I heard another voice from heaven saying, "Come out of her, my people, lest you share in her sins, and lest you receive of her plagues. 5 For her sins have reached[y] to heaven, and God has remembered her iniquities. 6 Render to her just as she rendered to you,[z] and repay her double according to her works; in the cup which she has mixed, mix double for her. 7 In the measure that she glorified herself and lived luxuriously, in the same measure give her torment and sorrow; for she says in her heart, 'I sit *as* queen, and am no widow, and will not see sorrow.' 8 Therefore her plagues will come in one day—death and mourning and famine. And she will be utterly burned with fire, for strong *is* the Lord God who judges[a] her.

The World Mourns Babylon's Fall

9 "The kings of the earth who committed fornication and lived luxuriously with her will weep and lament for her, when they see the smoke of her burning, 10 standing at a distance for fear of her torment, saying, 'Alas, alas, that great city Babylon, that mighty city! For in one hour your judgment has come.'

11 "And the merchants of the earth will weep and mourn over her, for no one buys their merchandise anymore: 12 merchandise of gold and silver, precious stones and pearls, fine linen and purple, silk and scarlet, every kind of citron wood, every kind of object of ivory, every kind of object of most precious wood, bronze, iron, and marble; 13 and cinnamon and incense, fragrant oil and frankincense, wine and oil, fine flour and wheat, cattle and sheep, horses and chariots, and bodies and souls of men. 14 The fruit that your soul longed for has gone from you, and all the things which are rich and splendid have gone from you,[b] and you shall find them no more at all. 15 The merchants of these things, who became rich by her, will stand at a distance for fear of her torment, weeping and wailing, 16 and saying, 'Alas, alas, that great city that was clothed in fine linen, purple, and

17:16 [w] NU-Text and M-Text read *saw, and the beast.*
18:2 [x] NU-Text and M-Text omit *mightily.*
18:5 [y] NU-Text and M-Text read *have been heaped up.*
18:6 [z] NU-Text and M-Text omit *to you.*
18:8 [a] NU-Text and M-Text read *has judged.*
18:14 [b] NU-Text and M-Text read *been lost to you.*

scarlet, and adorned with gold and precious stones and pearls! [17]For in
one hour such great riches came to nothing.' Every shipmaster, all who
travel by ship, sailors, and as many as trade on the sea, stood at a distance
[18]and cried out when they saw the smoke of her burning, saying, 'What *is*
like this great city?'

[19]"They threw dust on their heads and cried out, weeping and wailing,
and saying, 'Alas, alas, that great city, in which all who had ships on the sea
became rich by her wealth! For in one hour she is made desolate.'

[20]"Rejoice over her, O heaven, and *you* holy apostles[c] and prophets, for
God has avenged you on her!"

Finality of Babylon's Fall

[21]Then a mighty angel took up a stone like a great millstone and threw *it*
into the sea, saying, "Thus with violence the great city Babylon shall be
thrown down, and shall not be found anymore. [22]The sound of harpists,
musicians, flutists, and trumpeters shall not be heard in you anymore. No
craftsman of any craft shall be found in you anymore, and the sound of a
millstone shall not be heard in you anymore. [23]The light of a lamp shall not
shine in you anymore, and the voice of bridegroom and bride shall not be
heard in you anymore. For your merchants were the great men of the earth,
for by your sorcery all the nations were deceived. [24]And in her was found
the blood of prophets and saints, and of all who were slain on the earth."

Heaven Exults over Babylon

19 After these things I heard[d] a loud voice of a great multitude in
heaven, saying, "Alleluia! Salvation and glory and honor and power
belong to the Lord[e] our God! [2]For true and righteous *are* His judgments,
because He has judged the great harlot who corrupted the earth with her
fornication; and He has avenged on her the blood of His servants *shed* by
her." [3]Again they said, "Alleluia! Her smoke rises up forever and ever!"
[4]And the twenty-four elders and the four living creatures fell down and
worshiped God who sat on the throne, saying, "Amen! Alleluia!" [5]Then a
voice came from the throne, saying, "Praise our God, all you His servants
and those who fear Him, both[f] small and great!"

[6]And I heard, as it were, the voice of a great multitude, as the sound of
many waters and as the sound of mighty thunderings, saying, "Alleluia!
For the[g] Lord God Omnipotent reigns! [7]Let us be glad and rejoice and give
Him glory, for the marriage of the Lamb has come, and His wife has made
herself ready." [8]And to her it was granted to be arrayed in fine linen, clean
and bright, for the fine linen is the righteous acts of the saints.

[9]Then he said to me, "Write: 'Blessed *are* those who are called to the
marriage supper of the Lamb!'" And he said to me, "These are the true
sayings of God." [10]And I fell at his feet to worship him. But he said to me,
"See *that you do* not *do that!* I am your fellow servant, and of your brethren
who have the testimony of Jesus. Worship God! For the testimony of Jesus
is the spirit of prophecy."

18:20 [c]NU-Text and M-Text read *saints and apostles.*
19:1 [d]NU-Text and M-Text add *something like.* [e]NU-Text and M-Text omit *the Lord.*
19:5 [f]NU-Text and M-Text omit *both.*
19:6 [g]NU-Text and M-Text read *our.*

LIFE LESSON

Revelation 19:1-21

SITUATION The heavenly multitude responded to God's judgment with enthusiasm and praise. Jesus, suffering Servant of the Gospels, became the righteous Judge.

OBSERVATION When Jesus returns, he will complete the work he began. He will gather his people and destroy Satan.

INSPIRATION Triumph is a precious thing. We honor the triumphant. The gallant soldier sitting astride his steed. The determined explorer returning from his discovery. The winning athlete holding aloft the triumphant trophy of victory. Yes, we love triumph. . . .

Triumph is fleeting, though. Hardly does one taste victory before it is gone; achieved, yet now history. No one remains champion forever. Time for yet another conquest, another victory. Perhaps this is the absurdity of Paul's claim: "But thanks be to God, who always leads us in triumphal procession . . . " (2 Cor. 2:14). . . .

Here is the big difference between victory in Christ and victory in the world: A victor in the world rejoices over something he did—swimming the English Channel, climbing Everest, making a million. But the believer rejoices over who he is—a child of God, a forgiven sinner, an heir of eternity. . . .

Nothing can separate us from our triumph in Christ. Nothing! Our triumph is not based upon our feelings, but upon God's gift. Our triumph is based not upon our perfection, but upon God's forgiveness. How precious is this triumph! For even though we are pressed on every side, the victory is still ours. Nothing can alter the loyalty of God. . . .

"Triumphant in Christ." It is not something we do. It's something we are.

(From *On the Anvil* by Max Lucado)

APPLICATION Christ has made you triumphant. Throughout the stress of daily living, look to Christ with joy. He has conquered sin, defeated Satan, and will one day take you home with him.

EXPLORATION Divine Judgment—Genesis 3; Isaiah 2:12; Amos 5:15; Luke 3:9; Romans 2:16; 12:19; 1 Corinthians 6:2.

Life Lesson

Revelation 20:1-15

SITUATION John described a coming time when Satan would be bound, dead Christians would be resurrected, and Satan and unrepentant sinners would be doomed to eternal destruction.

OBSERVATION Observe the final triumph of God's Kingdom over evil.

INSPIRATION When we pray, "Thy kingdom come," it is a desire expressed from our hearts for the continued forceful advancement of God's cause on the earth. Included is our request for the change of men's hearts to increase the population of the kingdom. Contained also in the petition is a longing for the supernatural defeat of sin and error with a consequent increase of truth and righteousness in the earth through his people's functioning as salt and light. And we must not exclude an expression of our earnest wish that the Lord would return from heaven with his holy angels to conduct the harvest and usher in the completed phase of his kingdom.

(From *God's Righteous Kingdom* by Walter J. Chantry)

APPLICATION Do we pray for the population of God's Kingdom to grow? Do we share the wonderful news of Christ's deliverance with those still uninformed? Set a goal to both pray and speak to this once per week!

EXPLORATION Kingdom—Psalm 145:13; Matthew 6:10; John 18:36; 2 Timothy 4:18; James 2:5.

Christ on a White Horse

11 Now I saw heaven opened, and behold, a white horse. And He who sat
on him *was* called Faithful and True, and in righteousness He judges and
makes war. 12 His eyes *were* like a flame of fire, and on His head *were* many
crowns. He had[h] a name written that no one knew except Himself. 13 He *was*
clothed with a robe dipped in blood, and His name is called The Word of
God. 14 And the armies in heaven, clothed in fine linen, white and clean,[i] followed Him on white horses. 15 Now out of His mouth goes a sharp[j] sword,
that with it He should strike the nations. And He Himself will rule them with
a rod of iron. He Himself treads the winepress of the fierceness and wrath of
Almighty God. 16 And He has on *His* robe and on His thigh a name written:

KING OF KINGS AND LORD OF LORDS.

The Beast and His Armies Defeated

17 Then I saw an angel standing in the sun; and he cried with a loud
voice, saying to all the birds that fly in the midst of heaven, "Come and
gather together for the supper of the great God,[k] 18 that you may eat the
flesh of kings, the flesh of captains, the flesh of mighty men, the flesh of
horses and of those who sit on them, and the flesh of all *people,* free[l] and
slave, both small and great."

19 And I saw the beast, the kings of the earth, and their armies, gathered
together to make war against Him who sat on the horse and against His
army. 20 Then the beast was captured, and with him the false prophet who
worked signs in his presence, by which he deceived those who received the
mark of the beast and those who worshiped his image. These two were
cast alive into the lake of fire burning with brimstone. 21 And the rest were
killed with the sword which proceeded from the mouth of Him who sat on
the horse. And all the birds were filled with their flesh.

Satan Bound 1000 Years

20 Then I saw an angel coming down from heaven, having the key to
the bottomless pit and a great chain in his hand. 2 He laid hold of
the dragon, that serpent of old, who is *the* Devil and Satan, and bound him
for a thousand years; 3 and he cast him into the bottomless pit, and shut
him up, and set a seal on him, so that he should deceive the nations no
more till the thousand years were finished. But after these things he must
be released for a little while.

The Saints Reign with Christ 1000 Years

4 And I saw thrones, and they sat on them, and judgment was committed to them. Then *I saw* the souls of those who had been beheaded for their
witness to Jesus and for the word of God, who had not worshiped the beast
or his image, and had not received *his* mark on their foreheads or on their
hands. And they lived and reigned with Christ for a[m] thousand years. 5 But

19:12 [h] M-Text adds *names written, and.*
19:14 [i] NU-Text and M-Text read *pure white linen.*
19:15 [j] M-Text adds *two-edged.*
19:17 [k] NU-Text and M-Text read *the great supper of God.*
19:18 [l] NU-Text and M-Text read *both free.*
20:4 [m] M-Text reads *the.*

the rest of the dead did not live again until the thousand years were finished.
This *is* the first resurrection. 6Blessed and holy *is* he who has part in the first
resurrection. Over such the second death has no power, but they shall be
priests of God and of Christ, and shall reign with Him a thousand years.

Satanic Rebellion Crushed

7Now when the thousand years have expired, Satan will be released
from his prison 8and will go out to deceive the nations which are in the
four corners of the earth, Gog and Magog, to gather them together to battle, whose number *is* as the sand of the sea. 9They went up on the breadth
of the earth and surrounded the camp of the saints and the beloved city.
And fire came down from God out of heaven and devoured them. 10The
devil, who deceived them, was cast into the lake of fire and brimstone
where[n] the beast and the false prophet *are.* And they will be tormented day
and night forever and ever.

The Great White Throne Judgment

11Then I saw a great white throne and Him who sat on it, from whose
face the earth and the heaven fled away. And there was found no place for
them. 12And I saw the dead, small and great, standing before God,[o] and
books were opened. And another book was opened, which is *the Book* of
Life. And the dead were judged according to their works, by the things
which were written in the books. 13The sea gave up the dead who were in it,
and Death and Hades delivered up the dead who were in them. And they
were judged, each one according to his works. 14Then Death and Hades
were cast into the lake of fire. This is the second death.[p] 15And anyone not
found written in the Book of Life was cast into the lake of fire.

All Things Made New

21 Now I saw a new heaven and a new earth, for the first heaven and
the first earth had passed away. Also there was no more sea. 2Then I,
John,[q] saw the holy city, New Jerusalem, coming down out of heaven from
God, prepared as a bride adorned for her husband. 3And I heard a loud
voice from heaven saying, "Behold, the tabernacle of God *is* with men, and
He will dwell with them, and they shall be His people. God Himself will be
with them *and be* their God. 4And God will wipe away every tear from their
eyes; there shall be no more death, nor sorrow, nor crying. There shall be
no more pain, for the former things have passed away."
5Then He who sat on the throne said, "Behold, I make all things new."
And He said to me,[r] "Write, for these words are true and faithful."
6And He said to me, "It is done![s] I am the Alpha and the Omega, the
Beginning and the End. I will give of the fountain of the water of life freely
to him who thirsts. 7He who overcomes shall inherit all things,[t] and I will
be his God and he shall be My son. 8But the cowardly, unbelieving,[u] abominable, murderers, sexually immoral, sorcerers, idolaters, and all liars shall
have their part in the lake which burns with fire and brimstone, which is
the second death."

20:10 [n] NU-Text and M-Text add *also.*
20:12 [o] NU-Text and M-Text read *the throne.*
20:14 [p] NU-Text and M-Text add *the lake of fire.*
21:2 [q] NU-Text and M-Text omit *John.*
21:5 [r] NU-Text and M-Text omit *to me.*
21:6 [s] M-Text omits *It is done.*
21:7 [t] M-Text reads *overcomes, I shall give him these things.*
21:8 [u] M-Text adds *and sinners.*

LIFE LESSON

Revelation 21:1–22:21

SITUATION John told Christians that in the end, God would triumph. Despite the obstacles Christians face in this life, all who hold Jesus as their Lord will spend eternity in fellowship with God.

OBSERVATION Finally. Sin will be destroyed. Death will die. Tears, anger, and frustrations will be gone.

INSPIRATION The most hopeful words of that passage from Revelation are those of God's resolve: "I am making everything new."

It's hard to see things grow old. The town in which I grew up is growing old. I was there recently. Some of the buildings are boarded up. Some of the houses are torn down. Some of my teachers are retired; some are buried. The old movie house where I took my dates has "For Sale" on the marquee, long since outdated by the newer theaters that give you eight choices. The only visitors to the drive-in theater are tumbleweeds and rodents. Memories of first dates and senior proms are weather-worn by the endless rain of years. High school sweethearts are divorced. A cheerleader died of an aneurysm. Our fastest halfback is buried only a few plots from my own father.

I wish I could make it all new again. I wish I could blow the dust off the streets. I wish I could walk through the familiar neighborhood, and wave at the familiar faces, and pet the familiar dogs, and hit one more home run in the Little League park. I wish I could walk down Main Street and call out to the merchants that have retired and open the doors that have been boarded up. I wish I could make everything new . . . but I can't. . . .

I can't. But God can. "He restores my soul," wrote the shepherd. He doesn't reform; he restores. He doesn't camouflage the old; he restores the new. The Master Builder will pull out the original plan and restore it. He will restore the vigor. He will restore the energy. He will restore the hope. He will restore the soul.

When you see how this world grows stooped and weary and then read of a

Continued

home where everything is made new, tell me, doesn't that make you want to go home?

What would you give in exchange for a home like that? Would you really rather have a few possessions on earth than eternal possessions in heaven? Would you really choose a life of slavery to passion over a life of freedom? Would you honestly give up all of your heavenly mansions for a second-rate sleazy motel on earth?

"Great," Jesus said, "is your reward in heaven." He must have smiled when he said that line. His eyes must have danced, and his hand must have pointed skyward.

For he should know. It was his idea. It was his home.

(From *The Applause of Heaven* by Max Lucado)

APPLICATION Are you looking forward to the day when God removes all evil? Throughout today, worship God and tell him of your love for him. As you encounter others who notice your joy, tell them about the future you have.

EXPLORATION Eternity—John 14:2-3; 1 Corinthians 2:9; 15:1-58; 1 John 3:2.

The New Jerusalem

9 Then one of the seven angels who had the seven bowls filled with the
seven last plagues came to me[v] and talked with me, saying, "Come, I will
show you the bride, the Lamb's wife."[w] 10 And he carried me away in the
Spirit to a great and high mountain, and showed me the great city, the
holy[x] Jerusalem, descending out of heaven from God, 11 having the glory of
God. Her light *was* like a most precious stone, like a jasper stone, clear as
crystal. 12 Also she had a great and high wall with twelve gates, and twelve
angels at the gates, and names written on them, which are *the names* of the
twelve tribes of the children of Israel: 13 three gates on the east, three gates
on the north, three gates on the south, and three gates on the west.
14 Now the wall of the city had twelve foundations, and on them were the
names[y] of the twelve apostles of the Lamb. 15 And he who talked with me
had a gold reed to measure the city, its gates, and its wall. 16 The city is laid
out as a square; its length is as great as its breadth. And he measured the
city with the reed: twelve thousand furlongs. Its length, breadth, and
height are equal. 17 Then he measured its wall: one hundred *and* forty-four
cubits, *according* to the measure of a man, that is, of an angel. 18 The construction of its wall was *of* jasper; and the city *was* pure gold, like clear
glass. 19 The foundations of the wall of the city *were* adorned with all kinds
of precious stones: the first foundation *was* jasper, the second sapphire,
the third chalcedony, the fourth emerald, 20 the fifth sardonyx, the sixth
sardius, the seventh chrysolite, the eighth beryl, the ninth topaz, the tenth
chrysoprase, the eleventh jacinth, and the twelfth amethyst. 21 The twelve
gates *were* twelve pearls: each individual gate was of one pearl. And the
street of the city *was* pure gold, like transparent glass.

The Glory of the New Jerusalem

22 But I saw no temple in it, for the Lord God Almighty and the Lamb are
its temple. 23 The city had no need of the sun or of the moon to shine in it,[z]
for the glory[a] of God illuminated it. The Lamb *is* its light. 24 And the nations
of those who are saved[b] shall walk in its light, and the kings of the earth
bring their glory and honor into it.[c] 25 Its gates shall not be shut at all by day
(there shall be no night there). 26 And they shall bring the glory and the
honor of the nations into it.[d] 27 But there shall by no means enter it anything that defiles, or causes[e] an abomination or a lie, but only those who
are written in the Lamb's Book of Life.

The River of Life

22 And he showed me a pure[f] river of water of life, clear as crystal, proceeding from the throne of God and of the Lamb. 2 In the middle of
its street, and on either side of the river, *was* the tree of life, which bore
twelve fruits, each *tree* yielding its fruit every month. The leaves of the tree
were for the healing of the nations. 3 And there shall be no more curse, but the
throne of God and of the Lamb shall be in it, and His servants shall serve

21:9 [v] NU-Text and M-Text omit *to me.* [w] M-Text reads *I will show you the woman, the Lamb's bride.*
21:10 [x] NU-Text and M-Text omit *the great* and read *the holy city, Jerusalem.*
21:14 [y] NU-Text and M-Text read *twelve names.*
21:23 [z] NU-Text and M-Text omit *in it.* [a] M-Text reads *the very glory.*
21:24 [b] NU-Text and M-Text omit *of those who are saved.* [c] M-Text reads *the glory and honor of the nations to Him.*
21:26 [d] M-Text adds *that they may enter in.*
21:27 [e] NU-Text and M-Text read *anything profane, nor one who causes.*
22:1 [f] NU-Text and M-Text omit *pure.*

Him. 4 They shall see His face, and His name *shall be* on
their foreheads. 5 There shall be no night there: They
need no lamp nor light of the sun, for the Lord God
gives them light. And they shall reign forever and ever.

The Time Is Near

6 Then he said to me, "These words *are* faithful and
true." And the Lord God of the holy[g] prophets sent
His angel to show His servants the things which must
shortly take place.
7 "Behold, I am coming quickly! Blessed *is* he who
keeps the words of the prophecy of this book."
8 Now I, John, saw and heard[h] these things. And
when I heard and saw, I fell down to worship before the
feet of the angel who showed me these things.
9 Then he said to me, "See *that you do* not *do that.*
For[i] I am your fellow servant, and of your brethren
the prophets, and of those who keep the words of this
book. Worship God." 10 And he said to me, "Do not
seal the words of the prophecy of this book, for the
time is at hand. 11 He who is unjust, let him be unjust
still; he who is filthy, let him be filthy still; he who is
righteous, let him be righteous[j] still; he who is holy,
let him be holy still."

Jesus Testifies to the Churches

12 "And behold, I am coming quickly, and My reward *is* with Me, to give to every one according to his
work. 13 I am the Alpha and the Omega, *the* Beginning
and *the* End, the First and the Last."[k]
14 Blessed *are* those who do His commandments,[l]
that they may have the right to the tree of life, and may
enter through the gates into the city. 15 But[m] outside *are*
dogs and sorcerers and sexually immoral and murderers and idolaters, and whoever loves and practices
a lie.
16 "I, Jesus, have sent My angel to testify to you these
things in the churches. I am the Root and the
Offspring of David, the Bright and Morning Star."
17 And the Spirit and the bride say, "Come!" And let
him who hears say, "Come!" And let him who thirsts
come. Whoever desires, let him take the water of life
freely.

A Warning

18 For[n] I testify to everyone who hears the words of
the prophecy of this book: If anyone adds to these
things, God will add[o] to him the plagues that are written in this book; 19 and if anyone takes away from the
words of the book of this prophecy, God shall take
away[p] his part from the Book[q] of Life, from the holy
city, and *from* the things which are written in this
book.

I Am Coming Quickly

20 He who testifies to these things says, "Surely I am
coming quickly."
Amen. Even so, come, Lord Jesus!
21 The grace of our Lord Jesus Christ *be* with you all.[r]
Amen.

22:6 [g] NU-Text and M-Text read *spirits of the prophets.*
22:8 [h] NU-Text and M-Text read *am the one who heard and saw.*
22:9 [i] NU-Text and M-Text omit *For.*
22:11 [j] NU-Text and M-Text read *do right.*
22:13 [k] NU-Text and M-Text read *the First and the Last, the Beginning and the End.*
22:14 [l] NU-Text reads *wash their robes.*
22:15 [m] NU-Text and M-Text omit *But.*
22:18 [n] NU-Text and M-Text omit *For.* [o] M-Text reads *may God add.*
22:19 [p] M-Text reads *may God take away.* [q] NU-Text and M-Text read *tree of life.*
22:21 [r] NU-Text reads *with all;* M-Text reads *with all the saints.*

ONE HUNDRED GREATEST THOUGHTS

ONE HUNDRED GREATEST THOUGHTS

Angels-There is joy in the presence of the angels of God over one sinner who repents. Luke 15:10

Answered Prayer-My voice You shall hear in the morning, O LORD. In the morning I will direct it to You, and I will look up. Psalm 5:3

Bible-The word of God is living and powerful, and sharper than any two-edged sword, piercing even to the division of soul and spirit, and of joints and marrow, and is a discerner of the thoughts and intents of the heart. Hebrews 4:12

Boldness-Let us therefore come boldly to the throne of grace, that we may obtain mercy and find grace to help in time of need. Hebrews 4:16

Bravery-Peace I leave with you, My peace I give to you. . . . Let not your heart be troubled, neither let it be afraid. John 14:27

Burdens-Come to Me, all you who labor and are heavy laden, and I will give you rest. Matthew 11:28

Children of God-But as many as received Him, to them He gave the right to become children of God, to those who believe in His name. John 1:12

Christ's Love-That you, being rooted and grounded in love, may be able to comprehend with all the saints what is the width and length and depth and height–to know the love of Christ which passes knowledge. Ephesians 3:17-18

Church-But you are a chosen generation, a royal priesthood, a holy nation, His own special people, that you may proclaim the praises of Him who called you out of darkness into His marvelous light. 1 Peter 2:9

Comfort-Blessed be the God and Father of our Lord Jesus Christ, the Father of mercies and God of all comfort, who comforts us in all our tribulation, that we may be able to comfort those who are in any trouble, with the comfort with which we ourselves are comforted by God. 2 Corinthians 1:3-4

Confession-If we confess our sins, He is faithful and just to forgive us our sins and to cleanse us from all unrighteousness. 1 John 1:9

Courage-Watch, stand fast in the faith, be brave, be strong. 1 Corinthians 16:13

Death of Christ-But God demonstrates His own love toward us, in that while we were still sinners, Christ died for us. Romans 5:8

Defeat-The LORD upholds all who fall, and raises up all who are bowed down. Psalm 145:14

Defender-The LORD also will be a refuge for the oppressed, a refuge in times of trouble. Psalm 9:9

Discipline-For whom the LORD loves He corrects, just as a father the son in whom he delights. Proverbs 3:12

Discouragement-The sun shall not strike you by day, nor the moon by night. The LORD shall preserve you from all evil; He shall preserve your soul. Psalm 121:6-7

Enemies-But I say to you who hear: Love your enemies, do good to those who hate you, bless those who curse you, and pray for those who spitefully use you. Luke 6:27-28

Eternal Life-And this is the testimony: that God has given us eternal life, and this life is in His Son. 1 John 5:11

Failure-All we like sheep have gone astray; we have turned everyone to his own way; and the LORD has laid on Him the iniquity of us all. Isaiah 53:6

Faith-Now faith is the substance of things hoped for, the evidence of things not seen. Hebrews 11:1

Faithfulness-I am with you always, *even* to the end of the age. Matthew 28:20

Fear-The LORD is my light and my salvation. . . . Though an army may encamp against me, my heart shall not fear; though war may rise against me, in this I *will be* confident. Psalm 27:1, 3

Forgiveness-Through His name, whoever believes in Him will receive remission of sins. Acts 10:43

Freedom in Christ-We have boldness and access with confidence through faith in Him. Ephesians 3:12

Friends-A friend loves at all times, and a brother is born for adversity. Proverbs 17:17

Friends of God-No longer do I call you servants, for a servant does not know what his master is doing; but I have called you friends, for all things that I heard from My Father I have made known to you. John 15:15

Fruit of the Spirit-The fruit of the Spirit is love, joy, peace, longsuffering, kindness, goodness, faithfulness, gentleness, self-control. Galatians 5:22-23

Glory of God-His glory covered the heavens, and the earth was full of His praise. *His* brightness was like the light; He had rays *flashing* from His hand, and there His power was hidden. Habakkuk 3:3-4

God's Favor-All have sinned and fall short of the glory of God, being justified freely by His grace through the redemption that is in Christ Jesus. Romans 3:23-24

God's Love-In this the love of God was manifested toward us, that God has sent His only begotten Son into the world, that we might live through Him. In this is love, not that we loved God, but that He loved us and sent His Son *to be* the propitiation for our sins. 1 John 4:9-10

God Created Everything-Of Him and through Him and to Him are all things, to whom *be* glory forever. Amen. Romans 11:36

Good Shepherd-He will feed His flock like a shepherd; He will gather the lambs with His arm, and carry *them* in His bosom, *and* gently lead those who are with young. Isaiah 40:11

Goodness of God-The LORD *is* good, a stronghold in the day of trouble; and He knows those who trust in Him. Nahum 1:7

Grace-My grace is sufficient for you, for My strength is made perfect in weakness. 2 Corinthians 12:9

Guidance-You in Your mercy have led forth the people whom You have redeemed; You have guided *them* in Your strength to Your holy habitation. Exodus 15:13

Happiness-But he who looks into the perfect law of liberty and continues in it, and is not a forgetful hearer but a doer of the work, this one will be blessed in what he does. James 1:25

Heart-*The LORD does* not *see* as man sees; for man looks at the outward appearance, but the LORD looks at the heart. 1 Samuel 16:7

Heaven-Our citizenship is in heaven, from which we also eagerly wait for the Savior, the Lord Jesus Christ, who will transform our lowly body that it may be conformed to His glorious body, according to the working by which He is able even to subdue all things to Himself. Philippians 3:20-21

Help-Commit your way to the LORD, trust also in Him, and He shall bring it to pass. Psalm 37:5

Honesty-The upright will dwell in the land, and the blameless will remain in it; but the wicked will be cut off from the earth, and the unfaithful will be uprooted from it. Proverbs 2:21-22

Hope-Now may the God of hope fill you with all joy and peace in believing, that you may abound in hope by the power of the Holy Spirit. Romans 15:13

Humility-Finally, all *of you* be of one mind, having compassion for one another; love as brothers, *be* tenderhearted, *be* courteous. 1 Peter 3:8

Innocence-Behold, I send you out as sheep in the midst of wolves. Therefore be wise as serpents and harmless as doves. Matthew 10:16

Justice-The LORD *is* righteous, He loves righteousness; His countenance beholds the upright. Psalm 11:7

Kindness-Be kind to one another, tenderhearted, forgiving one another, even as God in Christ forgave you. Ephesians 4:32

Knowledge of God-You know my sitting down and my rising up; You understand my thought afar off. You comprehend my path and my lying down, and are acquainted with all my ways. Psalm 139:2-3

Living Water-I am the Alpha and the Omega, the Beginning and the End. I will give of the fountain of the water of life freely to him who thirsts. Revelation 21:6

Mercy-Have mercy upon me, O God, according to Your lovingkindness; according to the multitude of Your tender mercies, blot out my transgressions. Psalm 51:1

Money-The love of money is a root of all *kinds of* evil. 1 Timothy 6:10

Mothers-She watches over the ways of her household, and does not eat the bread of idleness. Her children rise up and call her blessed; her husband *also,* and he praises her. Proverbs 31:27-28

New Life-Blessed *be* the God and Father of our Lord Jesus Christ, who according to His abundant mercy has begotten us again to a living hope through the resurrection of Jesus Christ from the dead. Peter 1:3

Overcoming-When you pass through the waters, I will be with you; and through the rivers, they shall not overflow you. Isaiah 43:2

Patience-Now may the God of patience and comfort grant you to be like-minded toward one another, according to Christ Jesus. Romans 15:5

Peace-Behold, how good and how pleasant *it is* for brethren to dwell together in unity! Psalm 133:1

Persecution-What credit *is it* if, when you are beaten for your faults, you take it patiently? But when you do good and suffer, if you take it patiently, this *is* commendable before God. 1 Peter 2:20

Perseverance-Let us not grow weary while doing good, for in due season we shall reap if we do not lose heart. Galatians 6:9

Power-Show Your marvelous lovingkindness by Your right hand, O You who save those who trust *in You* from those who rise up *against them.* Keep me as the apple of Your eye; hide me under the shadow of Your wings. Psalm 17:7-8

Praise-Give unto the LORD the glory due to His name; worship the LORD in the beauty of holiness. Psalm 29:2

Prayer-Pray without ceasing, in everything give thanks; for this is the will of God in Christ Jesus for you. 1 Thessalonians 5:17-18

Presence of God-Where can I go from Your Spirit? Or where can I flee from Your presence? If I ascend into heaven, You *are* there; if I make my bed in hell, behold, You *are there.* Psalm 139:7-8

Pride-A man's pride will bring him low, but the humble in spirit will retain honor. Proverbs 29:23

Pure-Hide Your face from my sins, and blot out all my iniquities. Create in me a clean heart, O God, and renew a steadfast spirit within me. Psalm 51:9-10

Rejoice-Alleluia! For the Lord God Omnipotent reigns! Let us be glad and rejoice and give Him glory. Revelation 19:6-7

Relax-Return to your rest, O my soul, for the LORD has dealt bountifully with you. Psalm 116:7

Repentance-If My people who are called by My name will humble themselves, and pray and seek My face, and turn from their wicked ways, then I will hear from heaven, and will forgive their sin and heal their land. 2 Chronicles 7:14

Rest-My soul, wait silently for God alone, for my expectation *is* from Him. Psalm 62:5

Resurrection-I am the resurrection and the life. He who believes in Me, though he may die, he shall live. John 11:25

Revenge-Do not say, "I will recompense evil"; wait for the LORD, and He will save you. Proverbs 20:22

Reward-I am coming quickly, and My reward *is* with Me, to give to every one according to his work. Revelation 22:12

Righteous-His delight *is* in the law of the LORD, and in His law he meditates day and night. He shall be like a tree planted by the rivers of water. Psalm 1:2-3

Rights-Open your mouth for the speechless, in the cause of all *who are* appointed to die. Open your mouth, judge righteously, and plead the cause of the poor and needy. Proverbs 31:8-9

Salvation- By grace you have been saved through faith, and that not of yourselves; *it is* the gift of God. Ephesians 2:8

Satan-Your adversary the devil walks about like a roaring lion, seeking whom he may devour. 1 Peter 5:8

Second Coming-Behold, I am coming quickly, and My reward is with Me, to give to every one according to his work. Revelation 22:12

Security-The gifts and the calling of God *are* irrevocable. Romans 11:29

Self-Control-Gird up the loins of your mind, be sober, and rest *your* hope fully upon the grace that is to be brought to you at the revelation of Jesus Christ. 1 Peter 1:13

Sharing God's Glory-Having been justified by faith, we have peace with God through our Lord Jesus Christ, through whom also we have access by faith into this grace in which we stand, and rejoice in hope of the glory of God. Romans 5:1-2

Sin-Though your sins are like scarlet, they shall be as white as snow; though they are red like crimson, they shall be as wool. Isaiah 1:18

Speech-Set a guard, O LORD, over my mouth; keep watch over the door of my lips. Do not incline my heart to any evil thing, to practice wicked works with men who work iniquity. Psalm 141:3-4

Spiritual Gifts-There are diversities of gifts, but the same Spirit. There are differences of ministries, but the same Lord. 1 Corinthians 12:4-5

Spiritual Warfare-We do not wrestle against flesh and blood, but against principalities, against powers, against the rulers of the darkness of this age, against spiritual *hosts* of wickedness in the heavenly *places.* Ephesians 6:12

Strength-The LORD God is my strength; He will make my feet like deer's *feet*, and He will make me walk on my high hills. Habakkuk 3:19

Success-Trust in the LORD with all your heart, and lean not on your own understanding; in all your ways acknowledge Him, and He shall direct your paths. Proverbs 3:5-6

Suffering-I will be glad and rejoice in Your mercy, for You have considered my trouble; You have known my soul in adversities, and have not shut me up into the hand of the enemy; You have set my feet in a wide place. Psalm 31:7-8

Temptation-God is faithful, who will not allow you to be tempted beyond what you are able. 1 Corinthians 10:13

Thankfulness-Enter into His gates with thanksgiving, *and* into His courts with praise. Be thankful to Him, *and* bless His name. Psalm 100:4

Treasures-Do not lay up for yourselves treasures on earth . . . but lay up for yourselves treasures in heaven, where neither moth nor rust destroys and where thieves do not break in and steal. For where your treasure is, there your heart will be also. Matthew 6:19-21

Troubles-As for me, I will call upon God, and the LORD shall save me. Evening and morning and at noon I will pray, and cry aloud, and He shall hear my voice. Psalm 55:16-17

Trust-Have I not commanded you? Be strong and of good courage; do not be afraid, nor be dismayed, for the LORD your God *is* with you wherever you go. Joshua 1:9

Turmoil-Peace I leave with you, My peace I give to you. . . . Let not your heart be troubled, neither let it be afraid. John 14:27

Unity-Hatred stirs up strife, but love covers all sin. Proverbs 10:12

Value of People-Are not two sparrows sold for a copper coin? And not one of them falls to the ground apart from your Father's will. But the very hairs of your head are all numbered. Do not fear therefore; you are of more value than many sparrows. Matthew 10:29-31

Victory-To him who overcomes I will grant to sit with Me on My throne, as I also overcame and sat down with My Father on His throne. Revelation 3:21

Weakness-The Spirit also helps in our weaknesses. For we do not know what we should pray for as we ought, but the Spirit Himself makes intercession for us with groanings which cannot be uttered. Romans 8:26

Weary-He gives power to the weak, and to *those who have* no might He increases strength. . . . But those who wait on the LORD shall renew *their* strength; they shall mount up with wings like eagles, they shall run and not be weary, they shall walk and not faint. Isaiah 40:29, 31

Wicked-You who love the LORD, hate evil! He preserves the souls of His saints; He delivers them out of the hand of the wicked. Psalm 97:10

Wisdom-From childhood you have known the Holy Scriptures, which are able to make you wise for salvation through faith which is in Christ Jesus. 2 Timothy 3:15

Witness-You are the light of the world. A city that is set on a hill cannot be hidden. Matthew 5:14

Worry-In the multitude of my anxieties within me, Your comforts delight my soul. Psalm 94:19

The
INSPIRATIONAL
STUDY BIBLE

INDEX
TO
SELECTED READINGS

TOPICAL INDEX TO SELECTED READINGS

The
INSPIRATIONAL
STUDY BIBLE

DICTIONARY
WITH
TOPICAL CONCORDANCE

DICTIONARY *with* TOPICAL CONCORDANCE

A

Aaron (AIR-un) The older brother of Moses (Ex 6:20; 7:7); the spokesman for Moses (Ex 7:1); brings on plagues with his rod (Ex 7:10–8:17); from him are descended the class of priests in Israel (Ex 29:9); he makes atonement and stops a plague (Num 16:41-50); his rod buds (Num 17:1-11); his death (Num 20:22-29).

Abba (AB-buh) Aramaic for "Father" (Mk 14:36; Rom 8:15; Gal 4:6).

Abed-Nego (ah-BED-nee-go) Babylonian name of one of Daniel's companions (Dan 1:7; 3:16).

Abel (AY-bull) Son of Adam; murdered by his brother Cain (Gen 4:2ff). He is described as righteous (Mt 23:35; 1 Jn 3:12). In Hebrews 11:4 he stands at the head of the heroes of faith.

abhor To despise, hate.
I hate and a. lying Ps 119:163
Nations will a. him Prov 24:24
A. what is evil Rom 12:9

abomination (ah-bom-ih-NAY-shun) Something loathsome.
Wickedness is an a. Prov 8:7
is an a. in the sight of God Lk 16:15

Abraham; Abram (AY-bruh-ham; AY-brum) Israel's first great patriarch or leader. Through faith in God's promise to make of him a great nation, he is led from Ur to Canaan (Gen 11:31–15:7). God makes a covenant with him (Gen 15:7-21); an angel of God promises that Sarah shall give birth to a son (Gen 18:10); God tests Abraham's faith (Gen 22:1-19). He stands as the father of all the faithful (Gal 3:7).

Absalom (AB-suh-lum) Son of David and Maacah; turned the people against his father; was defeated and then slain by Joab, to the great sorrow of David (2 Sam 3:3; 13:20–19:10).

Adam (ADD-um) The first man, from whom is descended all mankind. Created on the same day as the animals, he is particularly blessed by God (Gen 1:27, 28). He and Eve were driven from the Garden of Eden because of their disobedience (Gen 3:1-24).

adultery (ah-DULL-ter-ih) Unchastity; unfaithfulness to one's husband or wife.
You shall not commit a. Ex 20:14
You shall not commit a. Deut 5:18
has already committed a. with her Mt 5:28

advise To tell, inform.
I will a. you what Num 24:14

advocate One who speaks in defense of another. Christ is so called (1 Jn 2:1).

affliction Distress; pain; adversity.
God has seen my a. Gen 31:42

agape (ah-GAH-pe) A Greek word meaning "love." It is also used to denote the "love feasts" of the early Christians (Jude 12).

Agrippa (ah-GRIP-uh) King of Judea before whom Paul appeared to plead his defense (Acts 25:13–26:32).

Ahab (AY-hab) An evil king of the northern kingdom of Israel in the time of Elijah; married Jezebel, a Sidonian princess, which caused religious turmoil; robbed Naboth of his vineyard and then caused his death (1 Kgs 16:29–22:40).

Ahasuerus (ah-haz-you-EAR-us) The name of two kings in the Old Testament. 1. A king of Persia and the husband of the Jewess, Esther (Esther 1:2, 19; 2:16-17). Through her guardian, Mordecai, Esther was able to save her people, Israel, from an evil plan. 2. A king of the Medes and the father of Darius (Dan 9:1).

Ahaz (AY-haz) A name which means "he has grasped." 1. A wicked king of Judah who worshiped idols on the "high places" and even offered one of his own sons on an altar (2 Kgs 16:3-4); refused to listen to the prophet Isaiah when he encouraged the king to call on God instead of seeking foreign aid against the army of Syria (Isa 7:1-16); heard the wonderful announcement of the promised Messiah. Hosea and Micah also prophesied during the reign of Ahaz (Hos 1:1; Mic 1:1). 2. A descendant of King Saul, the son of Micah and the father of Jehoaddah (1 Chr 8:35-36; 9:42).

alien A foreigner.
give it to the a. Deut 14:21

Alleluia (al-uh-LOO-yah) Hallelujah; "Praise the Lord" (Rev 19:1, 3, 4, 6).

Almighty, the God, as being all powerful.
I am A. God Gen 17:1
as God A. Ex 6:3
Holy, holy, holy, Lord God A. Rev 4:8

Alpha and Omega (Al-fuh; oh-MEE-guh) The first and last letters of the Greek alphabet; hence, "the First and the Last." Applied to God (Rev 1:8, 11; 21:6) and to Christ (Rev 22:13).

altar Table of sacrifice.
Noah built an a. Gen 8:20
Moses built an a. Ex 17:15

Am Exist; be. The reply to Moses' question for the name of the Deity, "I AM WHO I AM" (Ex 3:14), indicates that the Lord makes Himself present as He wills.

Amen Verily; so be it (Mt 6:13; Rev 3:14).

Amos (AY-mus) A prophet of Israel; the first to proclaim that God is the ruler of the whole universe; foretold the downfall of the northern kingdom. The OT Book of Amos is the third of the 12 Minor Prophets.

Ananias (ann-uh-NIGH-us) 1. A Christian of Jerusalem who lost his life for lying and attempting to hold back part of the price of property he had sold (Acts 5:1-10). 2. A Christian of Damascus who received Paul into Christian fellowship (Acts 9:10-17; 22:12-16). 3. A Jewish high priest before whom Paul was tried in Jerusalem (Acts 23:2; 24: 1).

Ancient of Days The judge in Daniel's vision; probably intended to be God Himself (Dan 7:9, 13, 22).

Andrew One of the first of the 12 apostles of Jesus; brother of Simon Peter (Mt 4:18; 10:2-4; Mk 1:16-20, 29; 3:16-19; 13:3; 6:14-16; Jn 1:35-42, 44; 6:8; 12:20-22; 21:15-17; Acts 1:13). He was a former disciple of John the Baptist (Jn 1:35-40). *See* Simon.

angel A heavenly messenger.
an a. spoke to me 1 Kgs 13:18
a little lower than the a. Ps 8:5
a. came and ministered Mt 4:11
the a. Gabriel was sent Lk 1:26
a. of the bottomless pit Rev 9:11

Angel of the Lord The heavenly messenger whose presence is evidence of God Himself (Gen 16:7; Ex 3:2; Num 22:23; 1 Kgs 19:7; Mt 28:2; Lk 1:11; 2:9).

anoint To consecrate; to pour oil upon in a ceremony.
a. my head with oil Ps 23:5
to a. My body Mk 14:8
You did not a. Lk 7:46

answer A reply.
soft a. turns away wrath Prov 15: 1

ant An insect.
Go to the a., you sluggard Prov 6:6

antichrist (AN-tih-krist) Opponent or enemy of Christ.
He is a. who denies 1 Jn 2:22
deceiver and an a. 2 Jn 7

Antioch (ANN-tee-ock) 1. In Syria; the name "Christian" was first used here (Acts 11:26). 2. In Pisidia; visited by Paul and Barnabas (Acts 13:14-52).

anxious Worried; careful.
Be a. for nothing Phil 4:6

Apollos (uh-POLL-us) A well-educated Jew and a follower of John the Baptist; knew the Old Testament well and taught others (Acts 18:24-28); learned of the Holy Spirit from Aquila and Priscilla in Ephesus; preached in Corinth (1 Cor 1:12; 3:4-6, 22; 4:6). Some teachers think Apollos wrote the Letter to the Hebrews.

apostle (uh-POSS-ul) One of the 12 disciples chosen by Jesus (Mt 10:2-4) or certain other early Christian leaders (Acts 14:14; Rom 16:7; Gal 1:1)

apple A fruit.
a. of His eye Deut 32:10; Ps 17:8

appoint 1. To consecrate, or set apart as for the ministry.
a. elders in every church Acts 14:23
a. elders in every city Tit 1:5
2. To establish.
I will a. a place 1 Chr 17:9

Aquila (ak-WILL-uh) A Jew who lived in Rome with his wife Priscilla until the emperor ordered all Jewish people to leave; moved to Corinth where he worked as a tentmaker with Paul (Acts 18:1-3); traveled with Paul to Syria (Acts 18:18, 19).

Arabia; Arabians The NW part of the large peninsula in SW Asia; scene of many biblical events. The peoples of the area were nomads.

Arameans (air-uh-ME-uns) A Semitic people, traditionally descendants of Shem, the oldest son of Noah (Gen 10: 1, 22, 23). They were nomads, wandering along the W side of the Syrian desert.

Ararat (AIR-uh-rat) The mountain on which the ark came to rest after the Flood (Gen 8:4); the land of Ararat is Armenia.

archangel (ark-AYN-jel) An angel of the highest order.
the voice of an a. 1 Thess 4:16
Michael the a. Jude 9

ark A floating vessel; ship.
Noah's a. Gen 6:14–8:19
Noah entered the a. Mt 24:38

ark of the Testimony The chest which held the two stone tablets on which were inscribed the Ten Commandments (Ex 25:10-22). Also called the ark of the covenant (1 Kgs 8:6; 2 Chr 5:2).

Armageddon (are-muh-GED-un) The name means "mountain of Megiddo." The large valley of Jezreel or Plain of Esdraelon near the ancient fortified city of Megiddo in northern Israel. According to prophecy, this is the place where the last battle of this age will be fought between the forces of good and evil.

Artaxerxes (are-tack-SURK-sees) The name of two Persian kings: the first, mentioned in Ezra 7 and Nehemiah 2; 13; his grandson, the second, may have been the builder of the palace described in Esther 1:5, 6.

Ascension (ah-SEN-shun) The return of the risen Christ to heaven (Lk 24:51; Acts 1:9) on the fortieth day after the Resurrection.

Ascents, Song of A title given to each of Psalms 120–134; probably so called because of their use in a procession ascending to the temple or for pilgrims going up to Jerusalem.

Asher (ASH-er) The eighth son of Jacob, the second by Zilpah (Gen 30:12ff); one of the 12 tribes of Israel.

Asherah (ah-SHE-rah) The wife of the Canaanite god, Baal. Asherah often refers to a wooden pole that stood near Canaanite high places of worship ("grove"). Gideon was ordered by the Lord to destroy the wooden image beside the altar (Judg 6:25).

Asia (AY-zhuh) A Roman province in the western part of what we call Asia Minor (Acts 16:6; 20:18; 1 Pet 1:1; Rev 1:4).

ask To request.
A., and it will be given Mt 7:7
a. in prayer, believing Mt 21:22
do not know what you a. Mk 10:38

Assyria (ah-SEER-ih-uh) A kingdom between the Tigris and Euphrates Rivers in Mesopotamia; ruled over the ancient world from the 9th to the 7th centuries B.C. (before Christ). After defeating the northern kingdom of Israel in 722 B.C., the Assyrians captured and carried away thousands of Israelites to their country. In 701 B.C., Assyria attacked the southern kingdom of Judah, but did not succeed because a plague from the "Angel of the Lord" struck down the soldiers (2 Kgs 19:35). Thousands died, and Jerusalem, the capital, was saved. (Find out more about Assyria in the Book of Jonah and in Isa 10:5, Ezek 16:28, and Hos 8:9).

Athens (ATH-ins) The capital city of the ancient Greeks as well as the modern capital, located on the southern coast of Attica; center of Greek art, architecture, literature, and politics during the golden age of Grecian history. The world's most famous building—the Parthenon—stands here in ruins. During his second missionary journey, the apostle Paul preached his famous sermon on Areopagus, Mars' Hill (Acts 17:15–18:1).

Atonement, Day of An annual fast day of the Jews. Ordained in the Law as a day of humbling oneself and making amends for sins (Lev 23:27).

B

Baal (BAYL) One of the fertility gods of Canaan. There were many local Baals. Elijah met the prophets of Baal in a contest (1 Kgs 18:1-40).

Babel (BAY-bull) Hebrew form of the name "Babylon," capital of Babylonia; site of the Tower of Babel (Gen 11:1-9).

babes Infants; small children.
Out of the mouth of b. Ps 8:2; Mt 21:16

Babylon (BAB-ih-lun) An ancient walled city, once the capital of the Babylonian Empire, located between the Tigris and Euphrates Rivers. In 586 B.C., the leading citizens of Judah were taken captive by King Nebuchadnezzar and brought to Babylon where they stayed for 70 years during the period called the Exile. (You can read about this period of history in the books of Isaiah, Jeremiah, Ezekiel, and Daniel.) Here were the famous hanging gardens and, nearby, the Tower of Babel (Gen 11:1-9).

baptism A ceremony in which one enters the church family. It is a way of showing that you have been washed free of sin by the death and rising from the dead of Jesus Christ.
John's b. of Jesus Mt 3:13-17
b. by the disciples Jn 4:1, 2

Barabbas (bar-RAB-bus) A robber held in prison by the Roman authorities at the time of Jesus' trial; Pilate freed him and condemned Jesus to death (Mt 27:20-26; Mk 15:7-15; Lk 23:18-25; Jn 18:39, 40).

Barnabas (BARN-nuh-bus) The surname given by the apostles to Joses or Joseph, a Levite of Cyprus, who was sent by them to Antioch to confirm the church there. Accompanied Paul on his first missionary journey (Acts 4:36, 37; 9:27; 11:22, 25, 30; 12:25;

13:1-13, 43-52; 14:12, 14, 20; 15:2ff; 1 Cor 9:6; Gal 2:1, 9, 13; Col 4:10).

Bartholomew (bar-THAHL-uh-mew) One of the 12 apostles of Jesus (Mt 10:3; Mk 3:18; Lk 6:14; Acts 1:13).

Baruch (bar-OOK) Jeremiah's scribe, or secretary (Jer 36:4ff).

basket The container for holding a dry measure.
under a b. Mt 5:15; Mk 4:21; Lk 11:33

bath A liquid measure equal to the dry measure ephah (Ezek 45:11); about six gallons.
just ephah, and a just b. Ezek 45:10

Bathsheba (bath-SHE-bah) The wife of Uriah, the Hittite, and King David (2 Sam 11; 12:24); the woman with whom David sinned. David had her husband, Uriah, killed in battle. Then David married her and she became the mother of Solomon, who ruled after David's death.

beard The growth of hair on the lower part of a man's face. The Hebrews were forbidden to cut the edges of their beards (Lev 19:27). The shaving off of beards was an indignity (2 Sam 10:4, 5).

beast Animal (used for all living things other than man, as a general term); in the Book of Revelation the word is used of both "heavenly" beasts and "beasts from the bottomless pit."

Beatitudes (bee-AT-ih-tyoods) The blessings listed by Jesus in the Sermon on the Mount (Mt 5:3-12; Lk 6:20-23).

Beelzebub (bee-EL-zee-bub) The prince of demons whom Jesus refers to as Satan (Mt 10:25; 12:26; Mk 3:23; Lk 11:15, 18). The Jews considered this heathen god as the supreme evil spirit.

beginning Outset; start.
In the b. God created Gen 1:1
In the b. was the Word Jn 1:1

begotten Having been brought into being.
The only b. Son Jn 1:18

benediction (ben-ih-DICK-shun) An asking for God's blessing, as by a minister or priest at the conclusion of a church service; a blessing.

Benjamin The youngest son of Jacob. His mother, Rachel, died at his birth (Gen 35:18). Especially beloved by his father and by Joseph, his only full brother (Gen 42:4, 36; 43:14-16, 29, 34; 44:12; 45:12, 14, 22). Ancestor of the tribe of Benjamin, the smallest of the 12 tribes of Israel.

Bethany (BETH-uh-nee) A small village on the E slope of the Mount of Olives, about one and one-half mi. E of Jerusalem. From here Jesus made His triumphal entry into Jerusalem (Mk 11:1-11); the home of Simon the leper (Mt 26:6; Mk 14:3); home of Lazarus, Mary, and Martha (Jn 11:1-44); site of Jesus' final parting from His disciples (Lk 24:50, 51).

Bethel (BETH-ul) City 14 mi. N of Jerusalem. Near here Abraham built an altar (Gen 12:8; 13:3, 4); here Jacob's name was changed to Israel (Gen 35:10-15); the ark of the Testimony rested here (Judg 20:18-28); Jeroboam made it a place of idolatry (1 Kgs 12:29–13:32), which Josiah destroyed (2 Kgs 23:4-15).

Bethlehem A very old town about six mi. SSW of Jerusalem; the birthplace of Jesus (Mt 2:1-16; Lk 2:4-15; Jn 7:42); also associated with David (1 Sam 16:1- 13; 17:12, 15; 20:6, 28), Ruth (Ruth 1:1, 2, 19, 22; 2:4; 4:11), and other persons of the OT.

bird A winged creature.
let b. fly above Gen 1:20
b. of the air Gen 6:7; Mt 6:26

birthright Privilege of the firstborn of a family.
Esau despised his b. Gen 25:34

bishop A high-ranking minister, head of a district or diocese.
A b. then must be blameless 1 Tim 3:2

blood The life-giving fluid of the body. In the OT it is regarded as the seat of life; but since shed blood signifies death, the word is used of both life and death.
you shall not eat any b. Lev 7:26; Deut 12:16
this is My b. Mt 26:28; Mk 14:24
new covenant in My b. Lk 22:20
eats My flesh and drinks My b. Jn 6:54
redemption through His b. Eph 1:7; Col 1:14
precious b. of Christ 1 Pet 1:19

Boaz (BOH-az) A wealthy Bethlehemite who married Ruth (Ruth 2:1–4:22).

body The physical human being or animal. The church is called "the body of Christ" as the living spiritual community of which Christ is the head and all believers are members. At the Lord's Supper, Jesus broke bread to represent His body given in sacrifice for sinners.
touches the dead b. Num 19:11
lamp of the b. is the eye Mt 6:22
this is My b. Mt 26:26; Mk 14:22; Lk 22:19; 1 Cor 11:24
many members in one b. Rom 12:4
you are the b. of Christ 1 Cor 12:27

Booths, Feast of *See* Feast of Tabernacles.

bread A food made of a dough of flour or meal and water and baked; sustenance in general. Often used in offerings by OT peoples. In the NT, also used in reference to the coming of the kingdom of God or to Jesus Himself.
not live by b. alone Deut 8:3
shall eat unleavened b. Deut 16:8
Cast your b. upon the Eccles 11:1
not live by b. alone Mt 4:4
Give us this day our daily b. Mt 6:11; Lk 11:3
eat b. in the kingdom Lk 14:15
the true b. from heaven Jn 6:32
I am the b. of life Jn 6:35

bread, breaking of Since the earliest form of the Lord's Supper involved the "breaking of bread," the term has been used for worship in general (Acts 2:42).

bread from heaven The food miraculously provided by God for the Israelites in their wanderings through the wilderness (Ex 16:15).

brother A male relative of the same parents; a close associate.
Am I my b.'s keeper Gen 4:9
b. is born for adversity Prov 17:17
sticks closer than a b. Prov 18:24
is My b. and sister and Mt 12:50

C

Cain Son of Adam; murdered his brother Abel (Gen 4:2ff); prototype of wicked men (1 Jn 3:12; Jude 11).

Calvary (KAL-vuh-ree) From the Latin word meaning "skull." A place outside the second wall of Jerusalem where Jesus was crucified (Lk 23:33). Since Jerusalem has been destroyed and rebuilt so many times, no one knows for sure where this event took place, but there are at least two opinions: (1) A spot under the Church of the Holy Sepulcher; (2) "Gordon's Calvary," named for General Charles Gordon, a British soldier and explorer. The Hebrew name for the place where Jesus was crucified is *Golgotha* (Mt 27:33; Mk 15:22; Jn 19:17).

camel A large animal of desert areas.
a c. to go through Mt 19:24
and swallow a c. Mt 23:24

Canaan; Canaanites (KAY-nun; KAYnuh-nights) 1. The fourth son of Ham and grandson of Noah (Gen 9:18-27; 10:6, 15). 2. The region along the Mediterranean Sea known as the Promised Land—the land given by God to Abraham and the Children of Israel; known as Israel today; the land bridge between three continents—Africa, Europe, and Asia. Because of its position, this narrow strip of land has always been very important to invading armies as well as to traders.

Capernaum (kuh-PURR-nah-um) A city on the NW shore of the Sea of Galilee. Jesus lived there (Mk 2:1); home of Peter and Andrew (Mt 8:5, 14); here Jesus healed the man with an unclean spirit (Mk 1:21-28) and the paralytic (Mk 2:1-12) and held discussions about true greatness (Mk 9:33-37) and paying the half-shekel tax (Mt 17:24-27).

Carmel, Mount (KAR-mel) A mountain range in northern Palestine, Israel; stretches SE from the Mediterranean Sea about thirteen miles. Here Elijah held his famous contest vath the Baal priests (1 Kgs 18:19-20); saw the cloud which marked the end of a long drought (1 Kgs 18:44).

cheek The side of the face.
slaps you on your right c. Mt 5:39; Lk 6:29

cherubim (CHER-uh-bim) Winged creatures, statues of which were fixed to the mercy seat of the ark of the Testimony. Two cherubim carved from olive wood were placed within the inner room of the temple.
two c. of gold Ex 25:18
made two c. of olive 1 Kgs 6:23

child A young person of either sex
a c. is known by his Prov 20:11
unto us a C. is born Isa 9:6
little c. shall lead Isa 11:6

children Young persons of either sex.
become as little c. Mt 18:3
Let the little c. come Mt 19:14

Christians Followers of Christ.
first called C. in Antioch Acts 11:26

Christmas The holiday on December 25 which celebrates the birth of Jesus Christ.

church The people of God; those destined to inherit the kingdom of God. Also, any local group of believers.
I will build My c. Mt 16:18
Christ is head of the c. Eph 5:23
head of the body, the c. Col 1:18
the seven c. Rev 1:4, 11, 20

clean Free from defilement or dirt. Under the Hebrew law certain animals are declared clean and others unclean (Lev 11:1-47; Deut 14:3-21).
c. hands and a pure heart Ps 24:4
can make me c. Mt 8:2; Mk 1:40; Lk 5:12
c. the outside of the cup Mt 23:25; Lk 11:39
all things are c. Lk 11:41

cloud A visible mass of water particles in the air above the earth.
pillar of c. Ex 13:21; Num 12:5
c. covered the mountain Ex 24:15

Colosse; Colossians (ko-LAH-see; ko-LOSH-uns) A city in Asia Minor. Paul wrote an epistle to the Christians of this city.

commandment Any of the Ten Commandments or laws given to Moses by God at Mount Sinai (Ex 20:1-17; Deut 5:6-21); other OT laws.
keep the c. Mt 19:17
which is the great c. Mt 22:36
you love Me, keep My c. Jn 14:15

confess To admit to a fault or sin, particularly as a sign of repentance; to acknowledge God's redeeming acts and openly acknowledge that Jesus is the Messiah, Lord, and Son of God (as Peter's great confession in Mt 16:16; Mk 8:29; Lk 9:20); to offer praise and thanksgiving to God.
c. that he has sinned Lev 5:5
c. Me before men Mt 10:32; Lk 12:8
c. their sins Mk 1:5
c. that Jesus Christ is Phil 2:11
C. your trespasses to one Jas 5:16

congregation An assembly; gathering.
c. of the righteous Ps 1:5
God stands in the c. Ps 82:1
in the c. of saints Ps 149:1

converted Changed, as one's religion or belief.
unless you are c. Mt 18:3
Repent . . . and be c. Acts 3:19

Corinth (KOR-inth) Most important trade city of ancient Greece (Acts 18:1; 19:1; 1 Cor 1:2; 2 Cor 1:1; 2 Tim 4:20); situated on the Isthmus of Corinth, a narrow strip of land between the Aegean and Ionian Seas. Today a deep canal saves scores of miles of sea travel. Corinth was a very wealthy and wicked city in Paul's day. He did establish a strong church here to which he wrote letters—1 and 2 Corinthians.

Cornelius (kor-NEEL-yus) A Roman soldier stationed in Caesarea who was the first recorded Gentile convert to Christianity (Acts 10:1-33). Even before his conversion, he was a God-fearing man who believed in the Jewish teaching of one God (monotheism) and opposed the worship of idols. The apostle Peter took part in Cornelius' conversion.

counselor An adviser or teacher. Counselors seem to have been court officials of the Israelite kings (1 Chr 27:33; Job 3:14; Prov 11:14). The coming Messiah is so called (Isa 9:6).

courier Messenger.
letters were sent by c. Esther 3:13
c. who rode on royal horses Esther 8:14

covenant (KUV-uh-nunt) A binding agreement. The great covenant between God and Israel was made at Sinai (Ex 24:3-8); the tablets on which the Ten Commandments were engraved were called "the tablets of the covenant" (Deut 9:11). The chest in which these tablets were placed was called the "ark of the Testimony" (Ex 25:22). The new covenant came into being through the blood of Christ.
My blood of the new c. Mk 14:24
cup is the new c. 1 Cor 11:25

creation The act of God in making heaven and earth and bringing forth all life; the whole universe.
the story of c. Gen 1:1–2:25
c. which God created Mk 13:19
the whole c. groans Rom 8:22

creator; Creator The maker; originator; hence, **Creator:** God; the Lord.
Remember now your C. Eccles 12:1
C. of the ends of the Isa 40:28
creature rather than the C. Rom 1:25

creature Any living thing that God has made.
great sea c. Gen 1:21
called each living c. Gen 2:19
every c. of God is good I Tim 4:4

creeping thing Reptile.
every c. that creeps Gen 1:26
C. and flying fowl Ps 148:10
wild beasts, c. Acts 10:12

cross An upright post with cross-beam on which victims of execution were nailed; used by the Romans. A symbol of Christianity.
who does not take his c. Mt 10:38
take up his c. Mt 16:24; Mk 8:34
come down from the c. Mt 27:40
Simon . . . to bear His c. Mk 15:21
stood by the c. of Jesus Jn 19:25

crown A headdress of gold, precious stones, etc.; a wreath encircling the head.
A c. of glory Prov 4:9; 16:31
excellent wife is the c. Prov 12:4
c. of thorns Mt 27:29; Mk 15:17; Jn 19:2, 5
perishable c. 1 Cor 9:25

Crucifixion, the (crew-sih-FIX-shun) Jesus' execution on the Cross by the Romans at the instigation of the Jewish leaders (Mt 27; Mk 15; Lk 23; Jn 19).

crucify (CREW-sih-fy) To put to death by fastening to a cross.

scourge and to c. Mt 20:19
Let Him be c. Mt 27:22
C. Him Mk 15:13; Lk 23:21; Jn 19:6

cubit A measure of length of about 18 inches.
add one c. to Mt 6:27; Lk 12:25

cup A vessel from which to drink.
My c. runs over Ps 23:5
c. of cold water Mt 10:42; Mk 9:41
drink the c. Mt 20:22; Mk 10:39
outside of the c. Mt 23:25
took the c. Mt 26:27; Mk 14:23; Lk 22:17; 1 Cor 11:25
c. pass from Me Mt 26:39; Mk 14:36; Lk 22:42
c. which My Father Jn 18:11

curse To call on God to punish.
c. him who curses you Gen 12:3
Whoever c. his God Lev 24:15
C. God and die Job 2:9
bless those who c. you Mt 5:44; Lk 6:28
began to c. Mt 26:74; Mk 14:71
fig tree which You c. Mk 11:21

Cyrus (SIGH-rus) The powerful king of Persia (559–530 B.C.), sometimes called "Cyrus the Great." In 536 B.C., he wrote an edict or law which allowed the Jewish captives in Babylon to return to their homeland in Jerusalem; praised in the OT as God's "shepherd" and "anointed" (Isa 44:28; 45:1); encouraged the rebuilding of the temple. God often uses nonbelievers in working out His plans for His people. (Find out more about Cyrus in Ezra 3:7; 4:3, 5; 5:13, 14, 17; 6:3, 14; Dan 1:21; 6:28; 10:1.)

D

Dagon (DAY-gun) The chief god of the Philistines (1 Sam 5:2-7). When the Philistines defeated Israel, they captured the ark of the covenant and took it to the temple of Dagon in Ashdod. Samson, blinded by his captors, had been brought into the temple and tied between the two pillars which supported the roof. When he called on the Lord to return his strength, he brought down the building with his bare hands and died along with hundreds of Philistines (Judg 16:23-30).

Damascus (duh-MASK-us) A very ancient city, capital of Syria; in OT times the capital of the Aramean kingdom. Site of Saul's conversion (Acts 9:1-22).

Dan The fifth son of Jacob, born of Bilhah (Gen 30:1-6); one of the 12 tribes of Israel.

dance To move in rhythm, usually to the sound of music.
mourn, And a time to d. Eccles 3:4
you did not d. Mt 11:17; Lk 7:32

Daniel The Jewish prophet at the Babylonian court about whom the OT Book of Daniel is written. Interpreted dreams (Dan 2:1-45) and the handwriting on the wall (5:17-30); saved by God from the lions (6:16-24).

David The second and greatest king over Israel; youngest son of Jesse (1 Sam 17:12, 14); slew Goliath (1 Sam 17:41-50); friend of Jonathan (1 Sam 19:1–20:42); a fugitive from Saul's wrath (1 Sam 21–27; 30); king of Judah (2 Sam 1:1–5:5); king of Israel (2 Sam 3:6–1 Kgs 2:11); brought the ark of the Testimony to Jerusalem (2 Sam 6:1-17); his great sin in coveting Bathsheba (2 Sam 11:1-27); rebellion of his son Absalom (2 Sam 14–18); his psalm of thanksgiving (2 Sam 22); names Solomon, his son, to succeed him (1 Kgs 1:11–2:12).

day The time between sunrise and sunset; a period of 24 hours.
God called the light D. Gen 1:5
neither the d. nor Mt 25:13
D. come on you unexpectedly Lk 21:34

day of the Lord In the OT, the day when God punishes evil (Amos 5:18-20); a day of universal disaster (Isa 2; 13; 24; Zeph 1:7-18; 2:2, 3; 3:8). In the NT, the day of the Last Judgment and the end of the world (1 Cor 4:5; 5:5; 1 Thess 5:2; Rev 16:14).

deacon A servant or minister; an officer of a local church who assists the minister or priest.
with the bishops and d. Phil 1:1
d. must be reverent, not 1 Tim 3:8

Dead Sea The salt lake at the mouth of the Jordan River. Biblical names: "Salt Sea" (Gen 14:3; Num 34:3, 12; Deut 3:17; Josh 3:16; 12:3; 15:2, 5; 18:19); "eastern sea" (Joel 2:20).

death The condition of being without life; the act of dying. Symbol of the final state of the unsaved (Jn 8:51; Rom 6:23; Rev 20:6), and of the power that rules over man in the age of sin (Rom 5:14; Rev 6:8).
valley of the shadow of d. Ps 23:4
swallow up d. forever Isa 25:8
not taste d. Mt 16:28; Mk 9:1; Lk 9:27
D., where is your sting 1 Cor 15:55

Deborah 1. Rebekah's nurse and companion (Gen 35:8). 2. An early "judge" of Israel; aroused the scattered tribes to opposition to Canaanite oppression; Song of Deborah (Judg 5:2-31) celebrates her achievement.

debts Obligations; anything owed to another.
forgive us our d. Mt 6:12

Dedication, Feast of An eight-day festival observing the victories of Judas Maccabaeus and the purification and rededication of the temple (Jn 10:22). Also called Feast of Lights; Hanukkah; Chanukah.

Delilah (dih-LIE-luh) A woman from the Valley of Sorek; betrayed Samson to the Philistines (Judg 16:4-22).

deliverer, the In five OT passages (2 Sam 22:2; Ps 18:2; 40:17; 70:5; 144:2) God is referred to as "the deliverer"; but even though Christ is the instrument of God's deliverance of mankind from sin, the NT does not use the word except when Paul repeats Isaiah 59:20, using "Deliverer" instead of "Redeemer" (Rom 11:26).

demon An evil spirit.
sacrifices to d. Lev 17:7; Deut 32:17
who were d.-possessed Mt 4:24; 9:32; 12:22
He has a d. Mt 11:18; Lk 7:33

den Lair; cave of a wild animal.
into the d. of lions Dan 6:7
a 'd. of thieves Mt 21:13; Mk 11:17

detestable Abominable; loathsome.
not eat any d. thing Deut 14:3

Deuteronomy (dew-ter-ONN-oh-mee) The fifth book of the Law in the OT; teaches that God's laws are given for our own good—to help us stay close to Him in attitude and action. The name means "second law" or the second time the Law was given. (Look up Ex 20:1-17 for the first giving of the Law.)

Devil The chief demon, Satan.
Jesus . . . tempted by the d. Mt 4:1-11
serpent of old, called the D. Rev 12:9; 20:2

die Perish; lose life.
you shall surely d. Gen 2:17
born, And a time to d. Eccles 3:2
for tomorrow we d. Isa 22:13
in Me shall never d. Jn 11:26

disciple (dih-SIGH-pul) A learner; a follower, particularly one who follows Jesus Christ.
called His twelve d. Mt 10:1; Lk 6:13
sent two of his d. Mt 11:2
d. rebuked them Mt 19:13
d. were first called Christians Acts 11:26

Dispersion (dis-PURR-zhun) The widespread settlement of Jews outside of Palestine from the time of the Exile through the following centuries.

doctrine Teaching or instruction, particularly that of Jesus or the apostles concerning God's will.
My d. is pure Job 11:4
My d. is not Mine Jn 7:16
the d. of baptisms Heb 6:2

door Entrance way.
will pass over the d. Ex 12:23
and the d. was shut Mt 25:10
I am the d. Jn 10:9
d. standing open in heaven Rev 4:1

doxology A hymn, usually in a set formula, for expressing praise to God. Luke 2:14 ("Glory to God in the highest") has influenced Christian doxologies.

dreadful Awesome; feared; terrible.
d. day of the LORD Mal 4:5

dust Fine, dry, powdery earth.
God formed man of the d. Gen 2:7
d. you are, And to d. Gen 3:19

E

earth The planet on which we live; the soil.
God created the . . . e. Gen 1:1
The e. is the LORD's Ps 24:1
meek shall inherit the e. Ps 37:11
And e. is My footstool Isa 66:1
meek, . . . shall inherit the e. Mt 5:5
Your will be done On e. Mt 6:10
on e. peace, good will Lk 2:14
new heaven and a new e. Rev 21:1

Easter A Christian festival celebrating the Resurrection of Jesus; on a Sunday between March 22 and April 25.

eat To consume food.
shall not e. of every Gen 3:1
e. and drink, for tomorrow Isa 22:13
Take, e.; this is My body Mt 26:26

Ebal, Mount (EE-bull) A mountain in N Israel opposite Mt. Gerizim (Deut 11:29). It became known as the Mount of Cursing when Joshua read the curses of the Law. People on the mountain cried out with an "Amen!" When he read the blessings, people on nearby Mt. Gerizim responded in the same way. These two mountains marked the center of the land of the Samaritans in the OT. *See* Gerizim, Mount.

Eden, Garden of A garden of trees planted by the Lord (Gen 2:8) in which Adam and Eve first lived; actual site unknown; symbolically identified with Paradise.

Edom; Edomites (EE-dum; EE-duh-mights) A country to the E and S of Israel; its people had a close relationship to the Israelites, being descendants of Esau.

Egypt A land of NE Africa. Temporary home of Abraham (Gen 12:10-20); Joseph sold "into Egypt" (Gen 37:28, 36); Joseph as governor (Gen 41:37–47:26); Israel in bondage (Ex 1:1–12:36); the Exodus (Ex 12:37–14:31); Jesus taken there (Mt 2:13).

Elah, Valley of (EE-luh) A narrow valley surrounded by low hills, SW of Jerusalem, where David killed Goliath (1 Sam 17:2; 21:9).

Elohim (EL-oh-heem) One of the names of God; the other is Yahweh (YAH-way). Elohim appears first in Gen 1:1 and is plural, meaning to Christians—"Trinity"—not three gods! The abbreviated form, El, is found in many biblical names—Beth*el*, Ezeki*el*, Dani*el*, *El*izabeth.

elders Seniors; among the Jews, the old and mature men who were civil and religious leaders; in the Christian church, leaders of the local church.
seventy of the e. of Israel Ex 24:9
tradition of the e. Mt 15:2; Mk 7:3
appointed e. in every Acts 14:23
the e. who rule well 1 Tim 5:17
twenty-four e. Rev 4:4

Eli (EE-lie) The priest of Shiloh to whom the boy Samuel was brought (1 Sam 1–4).

Elijah (ih-LIE-jah) A prophet from Tishbe to Gilead in the northern kingdom; fed by ravens (1 Kgs 17:6); performs miracles (1 Kgs 17:14-24; 20:30; 2 Kgs 1:10-12; 2:8); taken up by a whirlwind into heaven (2 Kgs 2:11). Malachi prophesies his return before the day of the Lord (Mal 4:5). In NT times, some thought Jesus to be Elijah (Mt 16:14; Lk 9:8); others thought John the Baptist to be Elijah (Jn 1:21). In the early church, John was regarded as the heir to the spirit and power of Elijah (Lk 1:17) or as Elijah reborn (Mt 11:14; 17:10-13). At the Transfiguration, Elijah appears with Moses (Mt 17:3, 4; Mk 9:4, 5).

Elisha (ih-LIE-shuh) A prophet; disciple and successor to Elijah; performed many miracles (2 Kgs 2:14-24; 3:16-20; 4:2-7, 32-44; 5:10-14, 27; 6:5-7, 18-20); contact with his bones revives a dead man (2 Kgs 13:20, 21).

Elizabeth Wife of the priest, Zacharias, and mother of John the Baptist (Lk 1:5-66).

ephah (EE-fah) A dry measure equal to the liquid measure bath; estimated as three-eighths to two-thirds of a bushel.
balances, a just e. Ezek 45:10

Emmanuel (em-MAN-you-el) *See* Immanuel.

Emmaus (em-MAY-us) A village in Judea, probably NW of Jerusalem, where Jesus revealed Himself to two disciples on the road after His resurrection from the grave (Lk 24:13-29).

enemies Foes; opponents.
presence of my e. Ps 23:5
love your e. Mt 5:44; Lk 6:27, 35

enter To go or come into.
E. into His gates with Ps 100:4
E. by the narrow gate Mt 7:13; Lk 13:24

Ephesus; Ephesians (EFF-uh-sus; eeFEE-zhuns) A seaport in the Roman province of Asia; visited by Paul on his second and third journeys. Paul's NT Epistle to the Ephesians seems to be a general letter to the churches of Asia Minor.

Ephraim (EE-frah-im) The younger son of Joseph; adopted by Jacob (Gen 48: 1ff); ancestor of one of the most powerful of the 12 tribes of Israel.

epistle (ee-PIS-ul) Letter; specifically those letters written by the apostles that are included in the NT. **Pastoral Epistles:** The NT books of 1 and 2 Timothy and Titus, which are written in the name of Paul as the chief pastor of the churches. **General (Catholic) Epistles:** The NT books of James, 1 and 2 Peter, 1, 2 and 3 John, and Jude.

Esau (EE-saw) Son of Isaac and Rebekah who traded his birthright to his younger twin brother Jacob for a bowl of pottage (Gen 25:22-34; 27; 33:1-16).

Essenes A Jewish community in Palestine at the time of Jesus; strict adherents of Jewish law.

Esther A Jewess of Shushan who became Ahasuerus's queen and thwarted a plot to kill all the Jews, later commemorated by the Jewish festival of Purim. The Book of Esther tells the story.

Euphrates (you-FRAY-tees) Means "that which waters." The longest river in W Asia and one of the two major rivers in Mesopotamia; begins in the mountains of Turkey and runs down to the Persian Gulf, almost two thousand miles away. The ruins of many ancient cities, including Babylon, Nippur, and Ur of the Chaldees, are located along this river in Iraq.

Eve The first woman; wife of Adam (Gen 2:21-25); tempted by the serpent (Gen 3:1-5).

everlasting Eternal; never ending.
the E. God Gen 21:33; Isa 40:28
underneath are the e. arms Deut 33:27
into the e. fire Mt 18:8; 25:41
inherit e. life Mt 19:29
have e. life Jn 3:16, 36; 5:24

evil Wickedness; slanderous or injurious actions.
tree . . . of good and e. Gen 2:9
I will fear no e. Ps 23:4
Depart from e. Ps 37:27
deliver us from the e. Mt 6:13
what e. has He done Mt 27:23; Mk 15:14; Lk 23:22
love of money is a root of all kinds of e. 1 Tim 6:10

Exile, the A period during which most of the people of Judah and Jerusalem were forced to live in Babylonia.

Exodus The going out of Israel from Egypt as recorded in the second book of the OT. It includes the deliverance from slavery, the wandering through the wilderness, the covenant with the Lord at Mount Sinai, and the provision of the tabernacle and ark of the covenant.

eye The organ of sight.
e. of both of them were opened Gen 3:7
e. for e. Ex 21:24; Lev 24:20; Deut 19:21; Mt 5:38
lift up my e. to the hills Ps 121:1
wise in your own e. Prov 3:7
if your right e. causes you Mt 5:29; 18:9; Mk 9:47

Ezekiel (ee-ZEEK-yell) A major Jewish prophet; author of the OT Book of Ezekiel; one of the captives of the Babylonian exile. Vision of God (Ezek 1:4-28); parable of the two eagles and the vine (17:1-24); the fall of Jerusalem (24:1-27); various prophecies about other nations (25–32).

Ezra (EZ-ruh) A priest and scribe; supposed author of the OT Book of Ezra, which details the first return of the Israelites from Babylon and the rebuilding of the temple.

F

face The front of the head; the surface or top side; frequently used to indicate the presence of God. Among the Hebrews. "seeking the face of God" referred to attendance at public worship (Ps 27:8).
on the f. of the deep Gen 1:2
In the sweat of your f. you shall Gen 3:19
LORD spoke to Moses f. to f. Ex 33:11
make His f. shine upon you Num 6:25
Seek My f. Ps 27:8
f. of the LORD is against Ps 34:16
the f. of My Father Mt 18:10
My messenger before Your f. Mk 1:2
but then f. to f. 1 Cor 13:12

faith Belief or trust in someone or something. Among Christians, belief in the Holy Trinity.
your f. has made you Mt 9:22; Mk 5:34; 10:52; Lk 8:48; 17:19
f. as a mustard seed Mt 17:20; Lk 17:6
just shall live by f. Rom 1:17
man is justified by f. Rom 3:28; 5:1; Gal 2:16; 3:24
f. is accounted for righteousness Rom 4:5
saved through f. Eph 2:8
one Lord, one f., one Eph 4:5
f. is the substance of Heb 11:1
f. without works is dead Jas 2:20

Fall, the A sinking into sin; the disobedience of Adam and Eve whereby sin entered the world (Gen 3).

falsehood Lying.
love worthlessness And seek f. Ps 4:2
destroy those who speak f. Ps 5:6

fast To go without food.
when you f., do not be Mt 6:16
Pharisees f. often Mt 9:14; Mk 2:18

father The male parent or ancestor. In the OT, used of God as the One who made a covenant with the people of Israel.
be a f. of many nations Gen 17:4
Honor your f. and Ex 20:12; Lev 19:3; Deut 5:16
who curses his f. Ex 21:17; Lev 20:9
David rested with his f. 1 Kgs 2:10
f. of the fatherless, . . . Is God Ps 68:5
LORD, You are our F. Isa 64:8

Father The First Person of the Holy Trinity.
your F. in heaven Mt 5:16, 45
Our F. in Mt 6:9; Lk 11:2
Abba, F. Mk 14:36; Rom 8:15; Gal 4:6
baptizing them in the name of the F. Mt 28:19
about My F.'s business Lk 2:49
who the F. is but the Son Lk 10:22
the Promise of My F. Lk 24:49
the only begotten of the F. Jn 1:14
one F.—God Jn 8:41
I and My F. are one Jn 10:30
comes to the F. except through Me Jn 14:6
ask the F. in My name Jn 15:16

fear To dread; to be afraid of; to be anxious.
I will f. no evil Ps 23:4
Whom shall I f. Ps 27:1
F. not, for I am Isa 41:10; 43:5

fear of the LORD The term used in the OT for "religion" (Deut 6:2; 10:20; 28:58; Ps 111:10; Prov 1:7; 8:13; Eccles 12:13). In the NT, "those who fear the Lord" are the faithful (Lk 1:50; 18:4) or converts to Judaism (Acts 10:2; 13:26).

feast A festival; in ancient Israel associated with occasions of religious joy. Those mentioned in the Bible: 1. **Passover and Feast of Unleavened Bread**

(Ex 12:1-30; Lev 23:4-14; Deut 16:1-8). 2. **Feast of Weeks or Pentecost** (Lev 23:15-21; Deut 16:9-12). 3. **Feast of Tabernacles** (Lev 23:34-36; Deut 16:13-15). 4. **Purim** (Esther 9:20-28). 5. **Feast of Dedication or Feast of Lights** (Jn 10:22).

fellowship Companionship; a group of persons with a common interest. Among Christians, the common bond is their faith in Christ, particularly in partaking of the Lord's Supper.
into the f. of His Son 1 Cor 1:9
the right hand of f. Gal 2:9
any f. of the Spirit Phil 2:1
our f. is with the Father 1 Jn 1:3

fight Struggle against; do battle.
F. the good f. of faith 1 Tim 6:12

firmament Sky; heavens.
Let there be a f. in Gen 1:6
f. shows His handiwork Ps 19:1

first Before all others.
f. will be last Mt 19:30; Mk 10:31

First and the Last, the A title used by Isaiah (Isa 41:4; 44:6; 48:12) to convey the idea of God's everlasting sovereignty and eternal majesty and power. The same title is used in Revelation (1:11, 17; 2:8; 22:13) implying God's sovereign lordship manifest in Jesus Christ.

firstborn, firstfruits The eldest; the earliest fruits harvested. The consecration of the first of the male children, of animals, and of fruits was an important part of the religion of Israel.
LORD struck all the f. Ex 12:29

flesh The soft part of the human body; all mankind.
All f. is grass Isa 40:6; 1 Pet 1:24
but the f. is weak Mt 26:41; Mk 14:38
the Word became f. Jn 1:14

Flood, the The covering of the earth with water because of man's wickedness. Noah's family and the animals of the earth are saved in an ark (Gen 6:1–8:19).

fool A silly or senseless person.
f. despise wisdom Prov 1:7
f. is right in his own eyes Prov 12:15
folly of f. is deceit Prov 14:8
f. for Christ's sake 1 Cor 4:10

foolish Silly; unwise. Parables of Jesus deal with: foolish and wise virgins (Mt 25:1-13) and a foolish rich man (Lk 12:16-21).

forgive To pardon; show mercy to.
f. us . . . , As we f. Mt 6:12; Lk 11:4
F., and you will be Lk 6:37
Father, f. them Lk 23:34

fountain The source, as the spring from which water flows. The Lord is called "the fountain of living waters" (Jer 2:13; cf. Jn 4:14) and the "fountain of life" (Ps 36:9).

frankincense A fragrant incense.
spices . . . and pure f. Ex 30:34
gold, f., and myrrh Mt 2:11

friend An associate whom one likes.
the rich has many f. Prov 14:20
A f. loves at all times Prov 17:17
a f. who sticks closer Prov 18:24

G

Gabriel (GAY-brih-el) An angel of high rank (Dan 8:16; 9:21; Lk 1:19, 26).

Gad The seventh son of Jacob; born of Leah's maid Zilpah (Gen 30:10, 11); ancestor of the tribe of Gad.

Galatia; Galatians (guh-LAY-she-uh; guh-LAY-shuns) A region and Roman province in Asia Minor. Paul, in the NT Epistle to the Galatians, tells of his own conversion.

Galilee (GAL-ih-lee) A region of N Palestine, including the Sea of Galilee on the E side. OT references include: Solomon gives 20 cities of Galilee to Hiram (1 Kgs 9:11); the prophecy of Isaiah (Isa 9:1) concerning "Galilee of the Gentiles" (cf. Mt 4:13). Called "land of Gennesaret" (Mt 14:34; Mk 6:53). Jesus' active ministry was almost entirely within its borders.

Galilee, Sea of The larger of the two freshwater lakes on the Jordan River system. Site of miracles: the great catch of fish (Lk 5:1-11); Jesus stills the sea (Mt 8:23-26; Mk 4:35-39; Lk 8:22-24); Jesus walks on the sea (Mt 14:25-27; Mk 6:48-51; Jn 6:19, 20). Also called "Chinnereth" (Num 34:11; Deut 3:17; Josh 13:27); "Chinneroth" (Josh 12:3); "Gennesaret" (Lk 5:1); and "Tiberias" (Jn 6:1; 21:1).

Gamaliel (guh-MAY-lih-el) A famous member of the Jewish Sanhedrin and a teacher of the Law; taught Paul in Tarsus (Acts 22:3); advised the Sanhedrin in Jerusalem to treat well the apostles of the young Christian church. His approach was simple: If Jesus was a false prophet, Christianity would soon fail. If the movement was of God, "You cannot overthrow it!" (Acts 5:39).

gate Doorway.
Enter into His g. with Ps 100:4
Enter by the narrow g. Mt 7:13

Gaza (GAY-zuh; GAH-zuh) One of the five principal cities of the Philistines, located along the southern Mediterranean coast of Israel, on the great caravan route between Mesopotamia and Egypt. Philip preached to the Ethiopian eunuch on the road to Gaza and baptized him (Acts 8:26-40).

Gehenna (geh-HEN-uh) Or "Valley of Hinnom " in the NT. A deep, narrow, curving valley at the south end of Jerusalem, used as a garbage dump where waste and dead animals were burned; children sacrificed to the god Molech (2 Kgs 23:10); high places of heathen worship destroyed by good King Josiah; "hell" (NKJV).

Gerizim, Mount (geh-RIGH-zim) A mountain in N Israel, close to Mt. Ebal in the district of Samaria. The main north-south road through central Palestine ran between these mountains. Jacob's Well, where Jesus talked with the Samaritan woman, is situated at the foot of Mt. Gerizim (Jn 4:14). *See* Ebal, Mount.

Gethsemane (geth-SEM-uh-neh) A garden on the Mount of Olives where Jesus prayed and where He was betrayed by Judas (Mt 26:36; Mk 14:32).

Gideon (GID-ee-un) A prophet of Israel especially favored by the Lord with revelations and unusual powers (Judg 6:11–8:35).

Gilead (GILL-ih-ud) A rugged, mountainous region E of the Jordan. Possibly also a city (Judg 10:17; Hos 6:8) and a tribe (Judg 5:17).

Gilgal (GILL-gal) The name of several places in the OT, one of them a city of the tribe of Benjamin, near Jericho; site of the first encampment of the Israelites after crossing the Jordan (Josh 3–4); there Saul was made king (1 Sam 11:14, 15).

give To bestow; hand over to another.
G. us this day our daily Mt 6:11
it will be g. to you Mt 7:7; Lk 6:38; 11:9
more blessed to g. than Acts 20:35

giver One who bestows.
God loves a cheerful g. 2 Cor 9:7

glad tidings Good news; the gospel (used in Lk 1:19; 8:1; Acts 13:32; and Rom 10:15).

Gloria in Excelsis The proclamation of the heavenly host at the birth of Christ, "Glory to God in the highest" (Lk 2:14).

glory of the Lord The word *glory* is sometimes synonymous with "God" to avoid referring to God in human form (Ex 33:22). In the OT, used of the fiery presence at Sinai (Ex 24:16, 17) and of the radiance that filled the tabernacle (Ex 40:34). In the NT, used of the divine Presence (Mk 8:38; Lk 2:9), of the quality of Jesus' appearance in His transfiguration (Lk 9:29, 31), and of Jesus' Second Coming (Mt 25:31).

gnat A tiny insect.
strain out a g. and swallow Mt 23:24

God, kingdom of *See* kingdom of God; heaven, kingdom of.

gods Idols.
have no other g. before Ex 20:3

Golden Gate The eastern gate of Jerusalem, sometimes called the Gate Beautiful on the Temple Mount, directly across the Kidron Valley from the Garden of Gethsemane where Judas betrayed Jesus. According to prophecy, this gate will be opened when the Messiah, Jesus, returns the second time.

Golden Rule A commandment given by Jesus in the Sermon on the Mount (Mt 7:12; Lk 6:31).

Golgotha (GOLL-goth-uh) Place where Jesus was crucified (Mt 27:33, 35; Mk 15:22; Jn 19:17).

Goliath (go-LIE-uth) A Philistine giant about 9 ½ to 11 feet tall; from a family of giants called the Anakim, who lived in Gath (Num 13:33). David, while still a young man, killed Goliath with a stone from his sling (1 Sam 17:4-51).

Gomer (GO-mer) A prostitute whom God told the prophet Hosea to marry as a lesson to Israel about their relationship to Him. Hosea's forgiveness of his wife symbolized God's forgiving love toward Israel (Hos 1:2; 14:1-4).

Gomorrah (go-MAR-uh) One of the two cities destroyed by the Lord because of their wickedness (Gen 19:24-28).

good Virtuous; honorable.
g. name . . . rather than great Prov 22:1
No one is g. but One Mt 19:17; Lk 18:19

Good Friday The Friday before Easter; the anniversary of the Crucifixion of Jesus.

Goshen (GO-shun) A fertile part of the Nile delta in N Egypt, given to the family of Joseph by Pharaoh because of the famine in Israel (Gen 45:10-13).

gospel Good news; glad tidings. Hence, the teachings of Jesus and of the apostles. The NT books of Matthew, Mark, Luke, and John are called the Gospels.
g. of the kingdom Mt 4:23

the g. of Jesus Christ Mk 1:1
and believe in the g. Mk 1:15
preach the g. Lk 4:18
hear the word of the g. Acts 15:7
the g. of Christ Rom 1:16

grace OT usage: "favor" in the expression "found g. in the eyes of" (Gen 6:8). In NT usage: "the unmerited and abundant gift of God's love and favor to man," particularly made effective in Jesus Christ for the Christian. Used by Paul as an opening and farewell greeting (Rom 16:24; 1 Cor 1:3).
g. and truth came through Jesus Jn 1:17
g. of God and the gift by the g. Rom 5:15
G. to you and 1 Cor 1:3; Eph 1:2
by the g. of God I am 1 Cor 15:10
g. of God in vain 2 Cor 6:1
g. of our Lord Jesus 2 Cor 8:9; 13:14
by g. you have been saved Eph 2:5

guarantee A pledge.
given us the Spirit as a g. 2 Cor 5:5
who is the g. of our inheritance Eph 1:14

H

Habakkuk (huh-BACK-kuk) A prophet of Judah; the OT book which bears his name is the eighth of the 12 Minor Prophets.

Hagar (HAY-gar) The Egyptian servant of Sarah, Abraham's wife; mother of Abraham's son, Ishmael (Gen 16:1-16). When Sarah was very old, God gave her a son, Isaac, who became the father of the Jewish nation. Hagar's son Ishmael, his half-brother, became the father of the Arab nation. The two nations cannot get along to this day!

Haggai (HAG-ay-eye) A Jewish prophet contemporary with Zechariah; the tenth of the 12 Minor Prophets of the OT.

Hallelujah (hal-luh-LOO-yah) "Praise the Lord" (not used in the NKJV). *See* Alleluia.

hallowed Made sacred; consecrated.
H. be Your name Mt 6:9

hand The end of the arm.
Into Your h. I commit Ps 31:5
not let your left h. know Mt 6:3
if your h. or foot Mt 18:8; Mk 9:43

hands, laying on of A symbolic ritual: 1. Of divine blessing (Mt 19:13-15), sometimes accompanied by the gift of the Holy Spirit (Acts 19:6). 2. Of divine healing (Mk 7:32). 3. Of consecration of a man for a specific office (Acts 13:2, 3; 1 Tim 4:14). 4. Of dedication of an animal as for sacrifice (Lev 16:21).

Hannah (HAN-uh) The wife of Elkanah the priest and mother of Samuel. For many years, Hannah prayed for a child, promising God that she would dedicate him to the Lord's service. Samuel, who became a great judge, priest, and prophet, was God's answer to her prayers (1 Sam 1:11-17, 22).

Hanukkah (HAH-nuh-kah) Hebrew word for "dedication." *See* Feast of Dedication.

Haran (HAY-ran) A city of N Mesopotamia, on one of the main trade routes between Babylon and the Mediterranean Sea; home of Abraham and his father Terah (Gen 11:31-32; 12:4-5); home of Jacob and his wives, Leah and Rachel (Gen 28:10; 29:4-6).

harp A stringed musical instrument.
play the h. and flute Gen 4:21
David would take a h. and 1 Sam 16:23

haughty Overbearing; proud.
h. spirit before a fall Prov 16:18

Hazael (HAY-zay-el)A Syrian official whom the prophet Elijah anointed king of Syria at God's command (1 Kgs 19:15); sent by Ben-Hadad, king of Syria, to the prophet Elisha to ask whether the king would recover from an illness; assassinated Ben-Hadad and took the throne (2 Kgs 8:7-15); fought against God's people when the Lord's anger "became aroused against Israel" (2 Kgs 13:3).

heart The physical organ thought of as being the seat of the affections.
A broken and a contrite h. Ps 51:17
Blessed are the pure in h. Mt 5:8
not your h. be troubled Jn 14:1

heaven A term sometimes used for "God."
I have sinned against h. Lk 15:18
it has been given to him from h. Jn 3:27

heaven; heavens 1. The sky; the space in which the sun, the moon, and the stars move; the firmament.
God called the firmament H. Gen 1:8
He adorned the h. Job 26:13
h. declare the glory of God Ps 19:1
stretch out the h. Ps 104:2; Isa 40:22
saw h. opened and Acts 10:11

2. The place where God, the risen Christ, the angels, and the saints reside; the future home of the redeemed.
new h. and Isa 65:17; Rev 21:1
till h. and earth pass Mt 5:18
Father in h. Mt 6:9; Lk 11:2
looked . . . toward h. as Acts 1:10
eternal in the h. 2 Cor 5:1

heaven, kingdom of Used throughout the Gospel of Matthew for "kingdom of God." *See* kingdom of God.
the kingdom of h. is at hand Mt 3:2; 10:7
theirs is the kingdom of h. Mt 5:3, 10
least in the kingdom of h. Mt 5:19; 11:11
kingdom of h. is like Mt 13:24
such is the kingdom of h. Mt 19:14

heavenly host See host, heavenly.

Hebrews (HE-brews) The descendants of Eber (Gen 10:21); sometimes used interchangeably with "Israelites."

Hebron (HE-brun) An ancient city in the mountains of Judah, 19 mi. S of Jerusalem. Here Abraham purchased a cave for a family burial place (Gen 23:1-20). David's capital city for the first seven and one-half years of his reign (2 Sam 2:1–5:5).

Helper The Holy Spirit; the intercessor promised by Christ to help and guide believers (Jn 14:26; 15:26; 16:7).

heresy (HERR-uh-see) False doctrine or teaching which denies the truth about God or Jesus Christ. In the Book of 2 Corinthians, Paul spoke against "false apostles" and "deceitful workers" who claimed to be "apostles of Christ" (2 Cor 11:13); in 1 John, the writer also condemned a group known as the gnostics, who denied that Jesus was the Son of God (1 Jn 2:22).

Hermon, Mount (HUR-man) "Sacred mountain." The highest mountain in the area (9,232 feet), which marks the N boundary of Canaan; the major source of the Jordan River because of its melting snows and glaciers. Some scholars think Jesus' Transfiguration took place near Caesarea Philippi, at the southern base of Mt. Hermon.

Herod (HERR-ud) 1. Ruler of Jewish Palestine under Rome (37–4 B.C.); sent the wise men to search out the infant Jesus (Mt 2:1-9). 2. **Herod Antipas:** Tetrarch of Galilee (4 B.C.–A.D. 39); put John the Baptist to death (Mt 14:1-12; Mk 6:14-29; Lk 3:19, 20; 9:7-9).

Hezekiah (hez-uh-KIGH-uh) The name of four persons in the OT, one of whom was king of Judah (715–687 B.C.; 2 Kgs 18–20; 2 Chr 29–32; Isa 36–39).

Hinnom, Valley of (HEN-um) See "Gehenna," the Greek term for the same location.

Hiram (HIGH-rum) A king of Tyre and friend of both David and Solomon (2 Sam 5:11; 1 Kgs 10:11, 22; 2 Chr 8:2, 18); furnished cedar wood from the famous Cedars of Lebanon and workmen to help David build his palace; sent supplies and skilled laborers to help Solomon build the temple in Jerusalem.

Hittites (HIT-tights) A people of the ancient world who lived in Asia Minor between 1900 and 1200 B.C.; spread into N Syria and later into the land promised Abraham; had to be driven out when Israel conquered Canaan under Joshua (Ex 3:8, 17; Deut 7:1; Judg 3:5). The most famous Hittite was Uriah, the husband of Bathsheba. David had Uriah killed in battle so he could marry Bathsheba.

holy of holies The innermost room of the temple or tabernacle in which the ark of the Testimony was kept.

Holy Spirit *See* Spirit, Holy.

Holy Trinity *See* Trinity.

Holy Week The week before Easter.

honor To esteem; to give respect.
H. your father and your mother Ex 20:12; Mt 15:4
before h. is humility Prov 15:33
prophet is not without h. Mt 13:57
h. to whom h. Rom 13:7

Horeb, Mount (HOE-reb) A sacred mountain (Ex 3:1; Deut 1:2, 6, 19; 4:10; 5:2) which may be the same mountain as Mount Sinai.

Hosea (ho-ZAY-uh) A prophet of Israel; the first of the 12 Minor Prophets of the OT.

host, heavenly 1. The celestial bodies—the sun, moon, and stars.
all the h. of heaven Deut 4:19; Jer 8:2
worshiped all the h. of 2 Kgs 17:16
2. The mighty army in God's service, including the angels.
all the h. of them Gen 2:1
heavens, with all their h. Neh 9:6
the h. of them by Ps 33:6
brings out their h. Isa 40:26
worship the h. of heaven Acts 7:42

Hosts, LORD of God, first as leader of the armies of Israel (1 Sam 17:45), then as leader of the "heavenly host."
LORD of h., He is the King Ps 24:10
LORD of h. is His name Isa 47:4; 51:15; Jer 10:16; 31:35
name is the God of h. Amos 5:27

house 1. A dwelling place.
not covet your neighbor's h. Ex 20:17
Set your h. in order 2 Kgs 20:1
dwell in the h. of the LORD Ps 23:6
Father's h. are many mansions Jn 14:2

2. A family group; a nation.
h. divided against itself Mt 12:25; Lk 11:17

hypocrite (HIP-puh-krit) A person who pretends to be what he or she is not. In the Greek theater of NT times, a hypocrite was an actor who wore a mask and played a part on the stage. **hypocrisy** (hip-POCK-rih-see) Jesus spoke against the hypocrisy of many persons who opposed Him, especially the scribes and Pharisees, who tried to give the appearance of being godly, but were actually blind to the truth of God (Lk 20:19-20).
for everyone is a h. Isa 9:17
You are full of h. Mt 23:28
Let love be without h. Rom 12:9

I

idol A false god; an image or figure regarded as an object of worship.
Do not turn to i. Lev 19:4
who regard vain i. Ps 31:6
gods of the peoples are i. Ps 96:5
And with foreign i. Jer 8:19
the i. of the nations Jer 14:22
keep yourselves from i. 1 Jn 5:21

image A likeness; an idol.
make man in Our i. Gen 1:26
not make . . . any carved i. Ex 20:4

Immanuel (em-MAN-you-el) A Hebrew name meaning "God With Us," used by Isaiah in foretelling the birth of the Messiah.
call His name I. Isa 7:14
of Your land, O I. Isa 8:8
shall call His name I. Mt 1:23

Immediately Right now.
i. he stumbles Mt 13:21
end will not come i. Lk 21:9

Incarnation (in-car-NAY-shun) The taking by God of human characteristics in the person of Jesus; God's presence on earth.

iniquity (ih-NICK-kwih-tih) Sin; wickedness. *See* sin.
the i. of the fathers Ex 20:5; Deut 5:9
Pardon my i. Ps 25:11
we bear their i. Lam 5:7

intercession A plea on behalf of another; for example, Christ's prayer for His followers (Jn 17:6-26).
i. for the transgressors Isa 53:12
the Spirit Himself makes i. Rom 8:26
He ever lives to make i. Heb 7:25

Isaac (EYE-zik) The son of Abraham and Sarah, and half brother of Ishmael; by his wife Rebekah he was the father of Jacob and Esau (Gen 21:1-12; 22:1-19; 24:62-67; 25:9-11, 19, 20; 26:1–28:5; 35:27-29).

Isaiah (eye-ZAY-uh) A prophet of Israel; the first book of the OT Major Prophets.

Ishmael (ISH-may-el) The name of six persons in the OT, one of them Abraham's son by Hagar (Gen 16; 17:18-26; 21:8-21; 25:12-18).

Israel (IZ-ray-el) The name that Jacob received after his mysterious struggle at Jabbok (Gen 32:22-30); also the name of the whole people descended from him. After the separation into two kingdoms under Jeroboam, the name was confined to the northern kingdom of the ten tribes.

Israelites (IZ-ray-el-lights) A name applied to Israel (the people); also called "Hebrews," mostly by foreigners, as was the name "Jews"; the latter arose at the time when Judah, after the fall of the northern kingdom, represented the entire people.

Issachar (IZ-uh-kar) The ninth son of Jacob, the fifth by Leah (Gen 30:17, 18); ancestor of the tribe of Issachar.

J

Jacob (JAY-kob) Son of Isaac and Rebekah; younger twin brother of Esau; father of the people of Israel. Gained by craft the blessing meant for Esau; married Leah and Rachel, the daughters of his uncle Laban; received the name Israel; finally found refuge in Egypt with his favorite son, Joseph (Gen 25:21-34; 27–35; 37:1-3; 47:28–49:33).

Jacob's Well An ancient well near Shechem and Mt. Ebal and Gerizim in central Palestine; dug by hand and crude tools; site of a conversation between Jesus and a Samaritan woman, in which He told her how to find "living water" (Jn 4:5-10).

James The name of several persons in the NT. 1. "The Elder," son of Zebedee and brother of John; one of the 12 apostles; martyred under Herod Agrippa (Mt 4:21; 10:2; 17:1; 20:20; 26:37; Mk 1:19, 20, 29; 3:17; 5:37; 9:2; 10:35, 41; 13:3; 14:33; Lk 5:10; 6:14; 8:51; 9:28, 54; Acts 1:13; 12:1, 2). 2. The son of Alphaeus, also one of the 12 apostles (Mt 10:3; Mk 3:18; Lk 6:15; Acts 1:13). 3. One of the sons of Mary; known as "the Less" (Mt 27:56; Mk 15:40; 16:1; Lk 24:10). Tradition regards James (3) to be the same person as James (2). 4. The father of Judas (Lk 6:16; Acts 1:13). 5. "The brother of the Lord"; a pillar of the church at Jerusalem; called "James the Just"; traditionally the author of the Epistle of James

(Mt 13:55; Mk 6:3; Acts 12:17; 15:13; 21:18; 1 Cor 15:7; Gal 1:19; 2:9, 12; Jas 1:1; Jude 1).

jealous Envious; suspicious; full of zeal. When used of God, jealousy describes either His anger against His unfaithful people or His zeal to protect His persecuted people.

a j. God Ex 20:5; Deut 4:24

Jehovah (jeh-HOE-vuh) The LORD; God. Used by some Bible translators for the name of the covenant God of Israel (Ex 6:3; Ps 83:18; Isa 12:2; 26:4). *See* tetragrammaton.

Jephthah (JEFF-thah) A warrior of Gilead; sacrificed his daughter in fulfillment of a vow (Judg 11:1–12:7).

Jeremiah (jer-uh-MY-uh) The name of ten persons in the OT, one of them the prophet Jeremiah (c. 626–580 B.C.). His prophecies, visions, and life story are narrated in the second book of the OT Major Prophets, which bears his name. The almond rod and the boiling pot (1:11-19); the potter's wheel (18:2-10); the good and bad figs (24); Baruch records Jeremiah's prophecies (36:4-32).

Jericho (JERRY-ko) An ancient city at the S end of the Jordan Valley; the fall of the city is told in Joshua 6:1-25.

Jeroboam (jer-uh-BOW-um) 1. The first king of Israel (c. 922–901 B.C.); son of Nebat (1 Kgs 11:26–14:20; 2 Kgs 17:21, 22; 2 Chr 10:2-15; 13:1-20). 2. King of Israel (c. 786–747 B.C.); son and successor of Joash (2 Kgs 14:23-29).

Jerusalem (jeh-ROO-suh-lem) The chief city of Palestine; most sacred city of both Jews and Christians; mentioned under one name or another (Shalem; Salem; City of David; Moriah; Jebus; Zion; Ariel) in about 40 of the 66 books of the Bible. David captured the city (2 Sam 5:6-9; 1 Chr 11:4-8) and made it his capital; brought the ark of the Testimony to the city (2 Sam 6:1-17). Solomon built the temple and other buildings there (1 Kgs 5–7). Captured by Nebuchadnezzar (Jer 39); rebuilt by Ezra and Nehemiah. Several events in the life of Jesus occurred there: His presentation in the temple (Lk 2:22-38); the cleansing of the temple (Jn 2:13-25); the conversation with Nicodemus (Jn 2:23; 3:1-21); and the events of the last week of His life (Mt 21–28; Mk 11–16; Lk 19:28–24; Jn 12:12–21).

Jesse (JESS-ih) Son of Obed; grandson of Boaz and Ruth; father of David (1 Sam 16:1-13; 17:12ff).

Jesus Christ The personal name of the One whose title gave its name to the Christian religion. Since "Jesus" was a fairly common name in the first century, distinguishing phrases were used when referring to Him (Jesus of Nazareth; Jesus, Son of David; Christ Jesus; the Messiah Jesus; and Jesus Christ). The four Gospels detail His life and ministry: birth (Mt 1:18-25; Lk 2:1-20); baptism (Mt 3:13-17; Mk 1:9-11; Lk 3:21, 22); makes water into wine (Jn 2:1-12); the Sermon on the Mount (Mt 5:1–7:29; Lk 6:20-49); stilling of the storm (Mk 4:35-41; Lk 8:22-25); sending the unclean spirits into the swine (Mk 5:1-20); feeding of the 5,000 (Mt 14:13-21; Mk 6:30-44; Lk 9:10-17; Jn 6:1-14); walking on the water (Mt 14:22-33; Mk 6:45-52; Jn 6:15-21); feeding of the 4,000 (Mt 15:32-39; Mk 8:1-10); the Transfiguration (Mt 17:1-8; Mk 9:2-8; Lk 9:28-36); entry into Jerusalem (Mt 21:1-10; Mk 11:1-11; Lk 19:28-44; Jn 12:12-19); raises Lazarus from the dead (Jn 11:1-44); the Lord's Supper (Mt 26:26-29; Mk 14:22-25; Lk 22:15-20); is arrested (Mt 26:47-56; Mk 14:43-52; Lk 22:47-50; Jn 18:2-12); trial before Pilate (Mt 27:11-14; Mk 15:1-5; Lk 23:1-5; Jn 18:33-38); the Crucifixion and burial (Mt 27:32-61; Mk 15:21-47; Lk 23:26-56; Jn 19:17-42); the Resurrection and Ascension (Mt 28:1-20; Mk 16:1-20; Lk 24:1-53; Jn 20; 21).

Job (JOBE) Chief character in the OT Book of Job; unknown otherwise.

Joel (JO-ell) The name of several persons in the OT, including the prophet, son of Pethuel, author of the second book of the 12 Minor Prophets.

John The name of five persons in the NT, among them: 1. **John the apostle:** A son of Zebedee, brother of James (Mt 4:21, 22; Mk 1:19, 20; Lk 5:10); sometimes called "the beloved disciple" and "Saint John"; traditional author of the Fourth Gospel, the three epistles of John, and the Book of Revelation. 2. **John the Baptist:** The son of Elizabeth and Zacharias (Lk 1:5-25, 57-66); a prophet, called the forerunner of Jesus (Jn 1:15-28); baptized Jesus (Mt 3:13-17; Mk 1:9-11; Lk 3:21, 22; Jn 1:29-34); imprisoned by Herod and beheaded (Mt 14:3-12; Mk 6:17-29). 3. **John Mark:** *See* Mark.

Jonah (JO-nuh) The name of two persons of the OT, one of whom was the prophet about whom the fifth book of the 12 Minor Prophets is written. Swallowed by a great fish (Jonah 1:17–2:10).

Jonathan (JOHN-uh-thun) The name of 15 persons in the OT, one of whom was the oldest son of Saul; David's friend (1 Sam 13:2; 14:1-45; 19:1-7; 20).

Jordan (JOR-dun) The chief river of Palestine, flowing

from the slopes of Mount Hermon through Lake Huleh and the Sea of Galilee to the Dead Sea. The waters were miraculously stopped for the Israelites to pass (Josh 3:14–4:24). Jesus was baptized there (Mt 3:13; Mk 1:9).

Joseph; Joses (JOE-sef; JOE-sus) The name of 14 persons in the Bible, among them: 1. The son of Jacob and Rachel (Gen 30:22-24); his coat of many colors (Gen 37:3); sold into Egypt by his brothers (Gen 37:18-36); imprisoned on false accusations (Gen 39:7-23); interpreted Pharaoh's dreams, thus gaining favor (Gen 41:1-36); as administrator of Egypt (Gen 41:37–50:26); his brothers come to him for food (Gen 42–45). 2. The husband of Mary mother of Jesus; resident of Nazareth; descended from David (Mt 1:16-25; Lk 2:4-7; Jn 1:45). 3. **Joseph of Arimathea:** A member of the Sanhedrin; buried the body of Jesus on his own property (Mt 27:57-60; Mk 15:43-46; Lk 23:50-53; Jn 19:38-42).

Joshua; Jeshua (JOSH-you-ah; JESH-you-ah) The name of several persons in the OT, the most important being Joshua, son of Nun, the central figure of the Book of Joshua. This book tells the story of Moses' successor as leader of the Israelites, the conquest of Canaan, and the division of the country among the 12 tribes. His miraculous crossing of the Jordan (Josh 3:14–4:24); conquest of Jericho (Josh 6:1-21).

Josiah (jo-SIGH-uh) One of the few good kings of Judah; son of Amon and grandson of Manasseh (2 Kgs 21:23–23:30); became king at the age of 8; found the Book of the Law while the house of the Lord was being repaired (2 Chr 34:14); read the Book to the inhabitants of Judah (2 Chr 34:29-32), resulting in repentance and reform.

Judah (JEW-duh) The fourth son of Jacob, by Leah (Gen 29:31, 35); ancestor of the tribe of Judah.

Judas (JEW-dus) The name of six persons in the NT, including: 1. A brother of Jesus (Mt 13:55; Mk 6:3). *See* Jude, The General Epistle of. 2. **Judas Iscariot** (iz-CARE-ih-ut): One of the 12 apostles; the betrayer of Jesus (Mt 26:20-25, 47-50; Mk 14:18-20, 43-46; Lk 22:47, 48; Jn 13:21-26). 3. The brother of James; one of the 12 apostles (Lk 6:16; Jn 14:22; Acts 1:13). *See* Thaddaeus. 4. **Judas Barsabas** (BAR-sab-bus): A Jewish Christian (Acts 15:22, 27, 32).

Jude, The General Epistle of This NT letter designates its author as a "servant of Jesus Christ, and brother of James." *See* Judas (1).

Judea (jew-DEE-uh) An area of SW Palestine; formerly called Judah.

judge To decide; form an opinion.
J. not, that you be not Mt 7:1

judge One who forms an opinion. In the OT Book of Judges, one chosen by God to save the people from foreign oppressors; a military leader with both legislative and executive authority.
made you . . . a j. over us Ex 2:14

Judge God; Christ.
J. of all the earth Gen 18:25
J. of the living and the dead Acts 10:42
to God the J. of all Heb 12:23

justified (JUS-tih-fyed) The way sinful human beings are made acceptable to a holy God. Christianity is different from all other religions because of its teaching of being justified by grace (Rom 3:24)—an act of love from God to undeserving sinners. We can have grace and be justified when we believe and have faith that Jesus died on the Cross to save us from our sins (Rom 3:25-30; 4:3, 5, 9; Jn 6:28-29; Phil 1:29).

K

keeper One who guards or takes care of someone or something.
Am I my brother's k. Gen 4:9

Kidron Valley (KID-run) A very important valley E of the walls of Jerusalem and extending all the way to the Dead Sea; site of Nehemiah's inspection of the broken-down walls of Jerusalem (Neh 2:13-15); site of a common burial ground (2 Kgs 23:6); dumping ground for ashes of idols (1 Kgs 15:13; 2 Kgs 23:4; 2 Chron 29:16; 30:14). Jesus crossed the valley to go to the Garden of Gethsemane to pray just before He was arrested and crucified (John 18:1).

king A chief ruler; among ancient peoples, a religious leader often held to be divine. God and Jesus Christ are called "King."
trees . . . anoint a k. Judg 9:8
My K. and my God Ps 5:2; 84:3
the K. of glory shall Ps 24:7
seen the K., The LORD Isa 6:5
no k. but Caesar Jn 19:15
K. of kings and Lord 1 Tim 6:15

kingdom of God The eternal sovereignty or kingly rule of God; manifested in its acceptance by men on earth and the hope for the future; the central theme of Jesus' teaching. The phrase does not occur in the OT, but the idea is present in "Your kingdom," "My kingdom," etc., which are also sometimes used in the NT. "Kingdom of heaven" is used in Matthew's gospel; "kingdom of the Son of His love" (Col 1:13);

"kingdom of our Lord and Savior Jesus Christ" (2 Pet 1:11).
Yours is the k., O LORD 1 Chr 29:11
the scepter of Your k. Ps 45:6
Your k. come Mt 6:10; Lk 11:2
seek first the k. of God Mt 6:33; Lk 12:31
with you in My Father's k. Mt 26:29
k. of God is at hand Mk 1:15
cannot see the k. of God Jn 3:3
inherit the k. of God 1 Cor 6:10; Gal 5:21

L

Laban (LAY-bun) Brother of Rebekah and father-in-law of Jacob; lived near Haran where Abraham once lived; instrumental in two important marriages—Isaac to Rebekah (Gen 24) and Jacob to Leah and Rachel (Gen 29).

ladder A framework of uprights and crosspieces on which one may ascend or descend. Jacob dreams of a ladder (Gen 28:12).

lamb The young of a sheep, commonly used as the sacrificial animal of the Passover.
God will provide . . . l. Gen 22:8
a l. to the slaughter Isa 53:7
wolf and the l. shall feed Isa 65:25
Feed My l. Jn 21:15

Lamb (of God) Christ, whose sacrificial death removed the sins of the world. By extension of "lamb" as the most common victim of OT sacrifices, particularly the "Passover." Christ, our Passover (1 Cor 5:7).
Behold! The L. of God Jn 1:29, 36
a l. without blemish 1 Pet 1:19
stood a L. as though it had Rev 5:6
L. slain from the foundation Rev 13:8
L. will overcome them Rev 17:14

lamp A device producing light.
spirit of a man is the l. Prov 20:27
light a l. and put it Mt 5:15
ten virgins who took their l. Mt 25:1
light of a l. shall not shine Rev 18:23

lampstand Particularly the seven-branched lampstand of the tabernacle and the temple, and the symbolic one of Revelation.
make a l. of pure gold Ex 25:31
I saw seven golden l. Rev 1:12

last The final one.
first will be l. Mt 19:30; Mk 10:31
I am the First and the L. Rev 1:17

Last Supper The last meal eaten by Jesus with His apostles, on the night before His crucifixion. *See* Holy Communion.

laver (LAY-ver) A basin in which priests washed their hands for purification purposes while serving at the altar of the tabernacle or temple; made by Moses so Aaron and the priests could wash their hands and feet before offering sacrifices (Ex 30:18-21). Ten bronze lavers, decorated with lions, oxen, and cherubim, were made by Hiram for Solomon's temple (1 Kgs 7:27-39).

law Rules of conduct; particularly rules given by God to Moses by which the Israelites were to live and which were defined in the Pentateuch (the Law of Moses).
l. of the LORD is perfect Ps 19:7
not . . . to destroy the L. Mt 5:17
l. was given through Moses Jn 1:17

Lazarus (LAZ-uh-rus) 1. The beggar in a parable told by Jesus (Lk 16:19-31). 2. A friend of Jesus; brother of Martha and Mary (Jn 11:1-44; 12:1-11).

Leah (LEE-uh) Elder daughter of Laban; Jacob's first wife to whom were born six of his sons (Gen 29:16–30:21).

leaven (LEV-in) Yeast or other fermenting agent. It was forbidden to the Israelites in all offerings made with fire (Lev 2:11; 6:17) and at the Passover (Ex 12:17-19).
beware of the l. Mt 16:6
a little l. leavens 1 Cor 5:6

Lebanon (LEB-uh-nun) A nation just N of Israel (ancient Phoenicia in Bible times); named for the snow-capped range of mountains running the entire length of the country; has been conquered by the Egyptians, Assyrians, Persians, Greeks, Romans, Arabs, and Turks; famous for the Cedars of Lebanon, the wood of which was used in Solomon's temple and palace. Well-known cities include Byblos, from which we get the word "Bible," Sidon, and Tyre (Gen 10:19; Mt 15:21-28; Mk 7:24-31).

Lent The 40 weekdays preceding Easter; a period of fasting and repentance in Christian churches.

leopard (LEPP-urd) A wild animal of the cat family.
l. shall lie down with the Isa 11:6

let Allow.
l. me first go Mt 8:21
L. the little children Mt 19:14; Mk 10:14; Lk 18:16

Levi; Levites (LEE-vigh; LEE-vights) Third son of Jacob and Leah (Gen 29:31, 34); ancestor of the tribe of Levites, who were charged with the care of the tabernacle and the temple.

Leviticus (leh-VIT-ih-kus) The third book of the OT, it deals mainly with the priests and their duties.

life The union of body and soul. Christ is called the "Prince of life" (Acts 3:15).
The tree of l. was also Gen 2:9
the resurrection and the l. Jn 11:25

light Brightness; radiance.
Let there be l. Gen 1:3
my l. and my salvation Ps 27:1
the l. of the world Mt 5:14
I am the l. of the world Jn 8:12

Lights, Feast of See Dedication, Feast of

lilies Flowering plants that grow from bulbs.
He feeds his flock among the l. Song 6:3
Consider the l. of the Mt 6:28

lord One who has authority over persons or things; hence, **Lord:** God, as the supreme authority; Jesus, as leader during His ministry and as the Son of God. When large and small capitals are used, for LORD, the original Hebrew reads YHWH (*See* tetragrammaton).
L. Himself is God Deut 4:35; 1 Kgs 18:39
the L. is one Deut 6:4
L. of the whole earth Ps 97:5
says to Me, L., L. Mt 7:21
L. of heaven and earth Mt 11:25
Son of Man is also L. Mk 2:28
My L. and my God Jn 20:28
both L. and Christ Acts 2:36
crucified the L. of glory 1 Cor 2:8
is L. of l. and King Rev 17:14

LORD of Hosts *See* Hosts, LORD of.

Lord's Day Sunday (Rev 1:10).

Lord's Prayer The prayer, taught by Jesus to His disciples, that begins "Our Father" (Mt 6:9-13; Lk 11:2-4).

Lord's Supper 1. Holy Communion (1 Cor 11:20). 2. Last Supper.

lost Mislaid; not to be found.
the lost sheep Mt 18:12-14; Lk 15:4-7
the lost coin Lk 15:8-10
the lost (prodigal) son Lk 15:11-32

Lot The nephew of Abraham who came with him to Canaan (Gen 11:27-13:12). Saved from Sodom's destruction (Gen 19:1-38). His wife was turned into a pillar of salt (Gen 19:26).

love 1. A deep affection; devotion.
l. covers all sins Prov 10:12
Greater l. has no one Jn 15:13
l. of money is a root 1 Tim 6:10
God is l. 1 Jn 4:8
2. To have deep affection for someone or something.
l. your neighbor Lev 19:18; Mt 22:39; Jas 2:8
l. the LORD your God Deut 6:5; Mt 22:37
l. your enemies Mt 5:44; Lk 6:27
God so l. the world Jn 3:16

Luke Probable author of the Book of Luke and the Acts of the Apostles; Gentile, the only non-Jewish writer of a NT book; a "fellow laborer" of the apostle Paul, who accompanied him on parts of the second and third missionary journeys and the journey to Rome (2 Tim 4:11; Philem 24); a physician by profession (Col 4:14).

Lydia (LID-ee-uh) A prosperous businesswoman from the city of Thyatira in W Asia Minor (Turkey), a seller of purple cloth; lived in Philippi in N Greece, where she heard Paul preach about Jesus and became the first convert to Christianity in Europe (Acts 16:14-15, 40).

Lystra (LISS-trah) A city of Lycaonia in central Asia Minor (Turkey); home of Timothy (Acts 16:1-2). Paul preached and healed here on his first and second missionary journeys, was stoned and left for dead (Acts 14:6-21; 2 Tim 3:11).

M

Macedonia (mass-uh-DOH-nee-uh) A mountainous country N of Greece which Paul visited on his missionary journeys after receiving his "Macedonian call" (Acts 16:9); at Philippi, the first European convert to Christianity was Lydia, a businesswoman (Acts 16:14-15, 40). Philip II of Macedon, father of Alexander the Great, established his capital at Philippi and made Macedon internationally important.

Machpelah (mack-PEA-luh) The name of a field, a cave, and the surrounding land which Abraham bought as a burial place for his wife, Sarah, from Ephron the Hittite. Abraham, Sarah, Isaac, Rebekah, Jacob, and Leah are all buried in this cave (Gen 49:31; 50:13). The modern city of Hebron was built around this site, now covered by a large Muslim mosque.

Magi (MAY-ji) The wise men who came to worship the infant Jesus (Mt 2:1-12); because they offered three gifts, it is often assumed that there were three Magi.

maker One who brings into being; creator; hence, **Maker:** God.
more pure than his M. Job 4:17

man will look to his M. Isa 17:7
builder and m. is God Heb 11:10

Malachi (MAL-uh-kigh) An OT prophet, author of the last book of the OT, one of the 12 Minor Prophets.

man A male human being; the whole human race.
God is not a m. Num 23:19
m. is born to trouble Job 5:7
M. shall not live by Mt 4:4
not m. for the Sabbath Mk 2:27

Manasseh (mah-NASS-uh) 1. Joseph's eldest son, born in Egypt (Gen 41:50-51). Like his younger brother, Ephraim, Manasseh was half Hebrew and half Egyptian. Both of Joseph's sons were "adopted" by Jacob and became two of the heads of the tribes of Israel. 2. King of Judah (2 Kgs 21:1-18); reigned longer than any of the Israelite kings, but was the most wicked; rebuilt the altars to idols that had been destroyed by King Hezekiah and even sacrificed his own son to the heathen god Molech; deported to Babylon where he repented (2 Chr 33:11-13); tried to introduce reforms when he returned, but was opposed by his wicked son Amon, who succeeded him.

mark A sign.
set a m. on Cain Gen 4:15
his m. on his forehead Rev 14:9

Mark; John Mark Son of Mary of Jerusalem; companion of Paul and other early Christian missionaries; the traditional author of the Second Gospel (Acts 12:12, 25; 15:37).

marriage The union of one man and one woman. Explained by Jesus (Mk 10:6-9).
are given in m. Mt 22:30
M. is honorable among all Heb 13:4

martyr (MAR-ter) A witness. Because the early Christians often suffered for their faith, the word soon came to mean one who suffered or died because of his witness to Christ. The apostle Paul called Stephen a martyr (Acts 22:20); the Book of Revelation mentions "the martyrs of Jesus" (Rev 17:6).

Mary The name of seven persons in the NT, among them: 1. The mother of Jesus (Mt 1:16, 18-25; Lk 2:5-20). 2. **Mary Magdalene:** A Galilean follower of Jesus (Mt 27:55, 56, 61; 28:1; Mk 15:40, 47; 16:1; Lk 8:2; 24:10; Jn 19:25; 20:1, 18). 3. The sister of Martha and Lazarus (Lk 10:38-42; Jn 11:1-45; 12:1-8). 4. The mother of James "the Less" (Mt 27:55, 56, 61; 28:1-10; Mk 15:40, 41, 47; 16:1-8; Lk 24:1-11). 5. The mother of John Mark (Acts 12:12).

master A male person in authority; one who controls someone or something; owner.
is free from his m. Job 3:19
can serve two m. Mt 6:24; Lk 16:13
nor a servant above his m. Mt 10:24

Matthew (MATH-you) One of the 12 apostles; called "Levi the son of Alphaeus" in Mark 2:14; traditional author of the First Gospel.

measure A certain amount; capacity.
have a . . . just m. Deut 25:15
same m. you use Mt 7:2; Mk 4:24; Lk 6:38
good m., pressed down Lk 6:38

mediator (MEE-dee-ay-tor) One who acts as a go-between in making an agreement between two parties. Moses is so designated (Gal 3:19) in making the covenant at Sinai. Christ is called the "one Mediator between God and men" (1 Tim 2:5).

meditate To study; contemplate.
he m. day and night Ps 1:2

meek Humble; gentle.
m. shall inherit the earth Ps 37:11
Blessed are the m. Mt 5:5

Megiddo (muh-GID-oh) A fortified, walled city at the foot of the Carmel mountain range in N Israel, overlooking the Valley of Jezreel where the last battle between good and evil will be fought (Rev 16:16); a chariot city for Kings Solomon and Ahab; site of many important OT battles. Megiddo is another name for Armageddon.

Melchizedek (mel-KIZ-uh-dek) A king of Salem (Jerusalem) and priest of the Most High God (Gen 14:18-20; Ps 110:4; Heb 5:6-11; 6:20–7:21); appeared and disappeared somewhat mysteriously in the Book of Genesis; bestowed a blessing on Abraham and praised God for giving him a victory in battle (Gen 14:18-20). Melchizedek is seen as a type of Christ in both Psalm 110 and the Book of Hebrews.

"Mene, Mene, Tekel, Upharsin" (ME-neh, ME-neh, TEK-ul, you-FAR-sin) Means "numbered, numbered, weighed, and divided." An inscription that appeared on the wall of the palace of King Belshazzar in Babylon, written by a mysterious hand during a feast (Dan 5:1-29). The king ordered that the gold vessels taken from the temple of Jerusalem be brought in for the guests to use in eating and drinking. When the words appeared on the wall, Daniel was called in to interpret. Daniel told the king that God had weighed him on the scales of righteousness, and he did not measure up.

The kingdom would be divided between his enemies, the Medes and the Persians. That very night, Belshazzar was killed and his kingdom fell.

Mephibosheth (meh-FIB-oh-sheth) A son of Jonathan and grandson of King Saul; only five years old when his father and grandfather were killed on Mount Gilboa in the Battle of Jezreel (2 Sam 4:4); dropped by his nurse and crippled for the rest of his life (2 Sam 4:4); treated kindly by King David because of an agreement made between the king and his father, Jonathan (2 Sam 9:7-13).

merciful Forgiving; unwilling to punish.
LORD God, m. and gracious Ex 34:6
God be m. to us Ps 67:1
Blessed are the m. Mt 5:7
m. to me a sinner Lk 18:13

mercy Forgiveness or kindness, particularly to a wrongdoer.
His m. endures forever Ezra 3:11
they shall obtain m. Mt 5:7

mercy seat Literally, "covering." The lid of the ark of the testimony, from above which God spoke to His people (Ex 25:22).

merry Joyous; happy.
m. heart makes a cheerful Prov 15:13
m. heart does good Prov 17:22
eat, drink, and be m. Eccles 8:15; Lk 12:19

Meshach (ME-shack) The Babylonian name of one of Daniel's friends (Dan 1:7; 3:12).

Mesopotamia (mess-uh-puh-TAY-mee-uh) "Land between the rivers." A region between the Tigris and Euphrates Rivers in the modern countries of Iraq and Iran; the "cradle of civilization"; traditional site of the Garden of Eden; Ur of the Chaldees is located in the S part of the region (Acts 7:2).

Messiah (muh-SIGH-uh) Literally, "anointed one"; one sent by God to save others. In Hebrew belief, the coming savior of the Jewish people; in Christianity, Jesus.

Methuselah (meh-THOO-zuh-luh) Noah's grandfather; lived for 969 years, the oldest person mentioned in the Bible (Gen 5:27).

Micah (MY-kuh) A Judean prophet, contemporary of Isaiah, whose prophecies appear in the OT Book of Micah, the sixth of the 12 Minor Prophets.

mighty Powerful; very strong.
He was a m. hunter Gen 10:9
a great and m. nation Gen 18:18
How the m. have fallen 2 Sam 1:19
m. in deed and word Lk 24:19

ministry God's service.
to the m. of the word Acts 6:4
m. of reconciliation 2 Cor 5:18

miracle An event that exceeds the known laws of nature and science. Usually an act of God done through human agents. The OT miracles include:
ten plagues of Egypt Ex 7:14–12:30
parting of the Red Sea Ex 14:21-31
feeding with bread from heaven Ex 16:14-35
walls of Jericho fall Josh 6:1-21
strength of Samson Judg 14:1–16:30
Elijah taken by a whirlwind 2 Kgs 2:11
Elisha revives dead child 2 Kgs 4:18-37
three men saved from furnace Dan 3:19-27
Daniel saved from lions Dan 6:16-23
Jonah saved Jon 1:10–2:10
The NT miracles of Jesus include:
the leper cured Mt 8:2, 3; Mk 1:40-42; Lk 5:12, 13
centurion's servant healed Mt 8:5-13; Lk 7:1-10
the storm stilled Mt 8:23-26; Mk 4:35-39; Lk 8:22-24
demons entered into swine Mt 8:28-32; Mk 5:1-13; Lk 8:26-33
dumb demoniac healed Mt 9:32, 33
feeding the 5,000 Mt 14:15-21; Mk 6:35-44; Lk 9:10-17; Jn 6:1-14
Jesus walks on the sea Mt 14:25-27; Mk 6:48-51; Jn 6:19-21
feeding the 4,000 Mt 15:32-38; Mk 8:1-9
ten lepers cleansed Lk 17:11-19
water changed to wine Jn 2:1-11
Lazarus raised from dead Jn 11:38-44
Other NT miracles include:
the gift of tongues Acts 2:4-11
Peter restores Tabitha Acts 9:36-41
Peter's release from prison Acts 12:5-10

mite A copper coin of small value.
widow . . . threw in two m. Mk 12:42

money Riches; coins.
the tax m. Mt 22:19
no copper in their m. belts Mk 6:8
love of m. is a root of all . . . evil 1 Tim 6:10

money changers Bankers who exchanged one nation's currency for another, often charging too much for this service. Twice, Jesus found them in the temple, made a whip of cords, and drove them out, along with those who sold oxen, sheep, and doves (Jn 2:13-16; Mt 21:12-13). Jesus said, "Do not make My Father's house a house of merchandise" (Jn 2:16).

Mordecai (MOR-duh-kigh) The Jewish hero of the OT Book of Esther.

Moses (MO-zez) The great deliverer and lawgiver of Israel; born during the oppression of the Israelites in Egypt (Ex 1:22–2:2); brought up in Pharaoh's house (Ex 2:5-10); fled to Midian where he lived 40 years (Ex 2:15-25); called by God from the burning bush (Ex 3:2-5) to deliver the Israelites; after performing ten miracles of plagues (Ex 7:14–12:30) he got Pharaoh's consent to take the Israelites from Egypt; led them 40 years through the wilderness; received the Ten Commandments from God (Ex 20). The OT books of Exodus, Leviticus, Numbers, and Deuteronomy detail his life and deeds.

Most High, the A name used of God.
When the Most H. divided Deut 32:8
the Most H. rules in Dan 4:25
the Most H. does not dwell Acts 7:48

mother Female parent.
Honor . . . your m. Ex 20:12; Mt 19:19
Like m., like daughter Ezek 16:44
disciple, "Behold your m. Jn 19:27

Mount of Olives A ridge of hills E of Jerusalem, where Jesus was betrayed by Judas on the night before His crucifixion; site of Jesus' triumphal entry into Jerusalem, when He wept over the city because the people would not believe (Lk 19:37-41); traditional location of the tomb of Mary, Jesus' mother; site of Jesus' ascension (Mt 28:16).

mourn To grieve for.
Blessed are those who m. Mt 5:4

murder To kill; cause the death of.
You shall not m. Ex 20:13; Deut 5:17; Mt 5:21

myrrh An aromatic, resinous substance used in incense and perfumes.
of liquid m. Ex 30:23
frankincense, and m. Mt 2:11
wine mingled with m. Mk 15:23

N

Naaman (NAY-uh-mun) Commander of the Syrian army, who was "a great and honorable man in the eyes of his master (Ben-Hadad, king of Syria) . . . but he was a leper" (2 Kgs 5:1-27); served by a young Israelite girl who had been captured on one of Syria's frequent raids of Israel; encouraged to see the prophet Elisha, who could heal his leprosy; finally following Elisha's instructions, dipped himself seven times in the Jordan River and was healed; became a worshiper of God.

Nahum (NAY-hum) A prophet, the prophecies of whom are given in the OT Book of Nahum, the seventh of the 12 Minor Prophets.

name The word by which a person, place, or thing is called.
n. of the LORD your God in vain Ex 20:7
How excellent is Your n. Ps 8:1
Hallowed be Your n. Mt 6:9; Lk 11:2
in My n. Mt 24:5; Mk 13:6; Lk 21:8
My n. is Legion Mk 5:9
ask the Father in My n. Jn 15:16

Naomi (nay-OH-mee) The mother-in-law of Ruth, the Moabitess. After her husband and two sons died, Naomi returned to Bethlehem with her daughter-in-law Ruth, who insisted on going with her (Ruth 1: 16-17). Ruth became an ancestor of Jesus Christ when she married her kinsman, Boaz (Ruth 4:21-22; Mt 1:5).

Naphtali (NAF-tah-ligh) The sixth son of Jacob, the second born of Bilhah (Gen 30:7, 8); ancestor of one of the 12 tribes of Israel.

narrow Not wide; small in width.
n. is the gate . . . which Mt 7:14

Nathan (NAY-thun) A prophet during the reign of David and Solomon; told David that he would not be the one to build the temple at Jerusalem (1 Chr 17:1-15); confronted David after he had Uriah killed in battle so he could marry his wife, Bathsheba (2 Sam 12:9-15).

nation A group of people under one government or sharing the same history.
make you a great n. Gen 12:2
n. will rise against n. Mt 24:7; Mk 13:8

Nazareth (NAZ-uh-reth) The town in Lower Galilee where Jesus was brought up (Lk 2:39, 51).

Nazirite (NAZ-uh-right) A person who took a vow to be separated from the world and completely dedicated to God (Num 6:1-8). They promised not to touch strong drink, not to shave or cut their hair (Samson), not to touch or go near a dead body, not even to bury a relative (Num 6:5-12; Prov 20:1; Eph 5:17-18), etc.

Nebuchadnezzar (neb-you-kad-NEZ-zer) King of Babylonia (605–562 B.C.).

Nehemiah (nee-huh-MY-uh) The name of three persons in the OT, one of whom was the rebuilder of

Jerusalem after the Babylonian Exile. The Book of Nehemiah tells his story.

neighbor A person who lives near another.
false witness against your n. Ex 20:16
love your n. as yourself Lev 19:18; Mt 19:19

Nicodemus (nick-uh-DEE-mus) A wealthy, well-educated and well-respected Pharisee and member of the Sanhedrin, who probably became a disciple of Jesus; visited Jesus at night to learn more about His teachings (Jn 3:1-8; 7:50). On this visit Jesus told Him he must be "born again" (Jn 3:7), later gave him the Gospel in one verse: John 3:16! Nicodemus defended Jesus before the Sanhedrin; purchased a hundred pounds of spices to be placed between the folds of the cloth in which Jesus was buried (Jn 19:39).

night The period of darkness between sunset and sunrise.
darkness He called N. Gen 1:5
Watchman, what of the n. Isa 21:11
the n. is coming when no Jn 9:4

Nineveh (NIN-uh-vuh) One of the oldest and greatest cities of Mesopotamia; capital of Assyria; destroyed 612 B.C. (Gen 10:11, 12; 2 Kgs 19:36; Isa 37:37; Jon 1:2; 4:11; Nah 1:1; 2:8; 3:7).

Nisan (NIGH-san) The name given, after the captivity lasting 70 years, to the former month of Abib—the first month of the Jewish sacred year (Esther 3:7).

Noah (NO-uh) The ninth descendant of Adam; the survivor, with his family, of the Flood (Gen 6–9).

O

Obadiah (oh-buh-DIE-uh) The name of 11 persons in the OT, none of whom can be assumed to be the author of the Book of Obadiah, the shortest OT book and fourth of the 12 Minor Prophets.

offering Something given in worship. In the OT we find offerings of: 1. **grain:** Consisting of unleavened bread, cakes, wafers, or grain mixed with salt and, except when a sin offering, with olive oil (Lev 2:1-16; 5:11; 6:14-23; Num 15:4, 6, 9). Sometimes accepted from the poor as a sin offering in place of the burnt offering (Lev 5:11-13). 2. **drink:** Consisting of wine and used with the grain and burnt offerings, except in the sin and trespass offerings (Num 6:17; 15:5, 10). 3. **animals,** or **sacrifice:** Cattle, sheep, and goats that were free from blemish (Lev 1:3). These were used with: a. The **burnt offering** in which a male lamb, ram, goat, bull, dove, or pigeon was entirely consumed on the altar (Lev 1; 6:9-13). b. The **sin offering** in which a bull, a male or female goat, a female lamb, a dove, or a pigeon was given (Lev 4; 5:7; 6:25-30). c. The **trespass offering** in which a ram or lamb was used (Lev 5:6, 15; 6:6; 7:1-8; 14:12, 21). d. The **peace offering,** including the giving of thanks (Lev 7:12-15), the payment of a vow (Lev 7:16-20; Num 6:13-21), and the voluntary or freewill offering (Lev 7:16-20); for these any animal without blemish of either sex could be used, except birds (Lev 3; 7:11-27). In sacrifices, the term "wave offering" is used of those portions consecrated to the Lord by the rite of "waving" (Lev 7:30-34; Num 6:17-20); and the term "heave offering" is used of those portions taken away and set apart for the Lord (Lev 7:14, 32-34; Num 18:8-32).

oil Any of several greasy liquids that can be burned.
anoint my head with o. Ps 23:5

Olives, Mount of; Olivet, mount called A mountain E of Jerusalem (2 Sam 15:30; Zech 14:4). Closely associated with the last days in the life of Jesus (in the four Gospels and Acts 1:12).

P

Palestine (PAL-es-tine) The Greek and Roman names for Canaan; modern usage applies the name to the territory alloted to the 12 tribes of Israel.

Palm Sunday The Sunday before Easter; commemorates the triumphal entry of Jesus into Jerusalem (Jn 12:12, 13).

parable (PAIR-uh-bull) A short story teaching a moral lesson. Among those of the OT are:
Samson's riddle Judg 14:14
field of the slothful Prov 24:30-34
two harlots Ezek 23
healing waters Ezek 47:1-12

In the NT, parables are only by Jesus, and include:
lamp under a basket Mt 5:14-16; Mk 4:21-23; Lk 8:16-18
unshrunk cloth on an old garment Mt 9:16, 17; Mk 2:21, 22; Lk 5:36-39
weeds among wheat Mt 13:24-30
the mustard seed Mt 13:31, 32; Mk 4:30-32; Lk 13:18, 19
lost sheep Mt 18:12-14; Lk 15:4-7
laborers in vineyard Mt 20:1-16
wise and foolish virgins Mt 25:1-13
the talents Mt 25:14-30
two debtors Lk 7:41-50
Good Samaritan Lk 10:30-37
Prodigal Son Lk 15:11-32
Pharisee and tax collector Lk 18:9-14
shepherd and the sheep Jn 10:1-30

Passover 1. A seven-day Jewish festival held in March or

April, commemorating the slaying of the firstborn just before the Israelites were freed from slavery in Egypt (Ex 12); combined with the Feast of Unleavened Bread which commemorates the actual Exodus flight (Ex 13:3-16). 2. The sacrificial lamb of the Passover (Ex 12:11, 21, 27). Paul refers to Christ as the Paschal Lamb.
Christ, our P. was sacrificed 1 Cor 5:7

Pastoral Epistles The epistles to Timothy and Titus are so called because they deal chiefly with directions about the work of the pastor of a church.

pasture Grassy land where cattle and sheep graze.
me to lie down in green p. Ps 23:2

Patmos, Island of (PAT-mus) A small, rocky, irregularly shaped island off the western coast of Asia Minor or modern Turkey; used by the Romans to hold exiled criminals, one of whom was the apostle John, who received messages from the Lord, which became the Book of Revelation (Rev 1:9-11).

Paul As Saul, the son of Hebrew parents, he persecuted the followers of Jesus (Acts 8:3; Gal 1:13). Miraculously converted (Acts 9:1ff) and name changed to Paul (Acts 13:9), he became the leading missionary of early Christianity. His life is detailed in the NT Book of Acts. He founded many churches in Asia Minor and Greece and carried on extensive correspondence with them.

peace Freedom from turmoil and war.
of war, And a time of p. Eccles 3:8
is no p. . . . for the wicked Isa 57:21
not come to bring p. but a sword Mt 10:34
on earth p., good will Lk. 2:14
P. to you Lk 24:36; Jn 20:19

peeled Stripped off the bark.
rods which he had p. Gen 30:38

Pentecost (PEN-tih-cost) A Jewish festival on the fiftieth day after Passover; also called Feast of Weeks (Lev 23:15, 16). Observed by the Christian church as the day on which the gift of the Holy Spirit was given to the church (Acts 2:1).

perish To die; to be destroyed.
way of the ungodly shall p. Ps 1:6
believes in Him should not p. Jn 3:15

Peter; Simon Peter A fisherman on the Sea of Galilee who was called with his brother Andrew by Jesus (Mt 4:18-20; Mk 1:16-18; Lk 5:1-11; Jn 1:35-41). He became the "first" of the 12 apostles (Mt 10:2), and sometimes spoke for all the disciples. Jesus changed his name from Simon to Peter (Mt 16:18; Mk 3:16; Lk 6:14; Jn 1:42). His mother-in-law healed by Jesus (Mt 8:14, 15; Mk 1:30, 31; Lk 4:38, 39); his confession that Jesus is the Christ (Mt 16:16; Mk 8:29; Lk 9:20); his denial of Jesus (Mt 26:69-75; Mk 14:66-72; Lk 22:54-62). The traditional author of two NT epistles.

Pharaoh (FAY-row) A title used as a name, or prefixed to a name, of the king of Egypt. Joseph interprets Pharaoh's dream (Gen 41:1-36); the Pharaoh of the Exodus (Ex 7–14).

Pharisee (FAIR-uh-see) A member of a strict Jewish sect, holding the Mosaic Law and their own traditions as binding. The parable of the Pharisee and the publican (Lk 18:9-14).

Philemon (fih-LEE-mun) A Christian of Colosse to whom the NT Epistle to Philemon was written by Paul. In the letter Paul asks Philemon to pardon Onesimus, a runaway slave whom Paul has converted.

Philip The name of four persons in the NT, among them: 1. The apostle (Mt 10:3; Mk 3:18; Lk 6:14; Jn 1:43-48; 6:5, 7; 12:21, 22; 14:8, 9; Acts 1:13). 2. The evangelist (Acts 6:5; 8:5-40; 21:8).

Philippi; Philippians (FILL-ih-pie; fih-LIP-ih-uns) A city of Macedonia where Paul founded his first Christian congregation in Europe. The NT Epistle to the Philippians was written by Paul to the church there.

Philistines (fih-LIS-teens) The people who lived along the S coast of Palestine; often at war with the Israelites. Goliath was a champion of the Philistines (1 Sam 17:23-51).

Phoenicia (fe-NISH-she-uh) A country W of the Lebanon range and Galilee on the coast of the Mediterranean Sea (Acts 11:19; 15:3; 21:2); its chief cities were Tyre and Sidon.

physician A medical doctor.
Is there no p. there Jer 8:22
who are well have no need of a p. Mt 9:12
P, heal yourself Lk 4:23
Luke the beloved p. Col 4:14

Pilate; Pontius Pilate (PIE-lut; PON-chus) The Roman governor of Judea (A.D. 26–36); the judge in the trial and execution of Jesus (Mt 27:1-26; Mk 15:1-15; Lk 23:1-25; Jn 18:28–19:16).

pillar An upright column.
became a p. of salt Gen 19:26
by day in a p. of cloud Ex 13:21
by night in a p. of fire Ex 13:21

plank A log; a piece of timber.
remove the p. Mt 7:5

plowing
will be neither p. nor harvesting Gen 45:6
in p. time and in harvest Ex 34:21

plowshare The cutting blade of a plow.
their swords into p. Isa 2:4
Beat your p. into swords Joel 3:10

poor Needy; having little or no goods or money.
the p. shall not give less Ex 30:15
Blessed are the p. in spirit Mt 5:3
have the p. with you always Mt 26:11; Mk 14:7

prayer Words addressed to God.
house of p. Isa 56:7; Mt 21:13; Mk 11:17; Lk 19:46
by p. and fasting Mt 17:21; Mk 9:29
you ask in p. Mt 21:22

pride Conceit; vanity.
P goes before destruction Prov 16:18

priest A minister. Aaron and his sons, of the tribe of Levi, were appointed to the priesthood at Sinai; the office became hereditary and restricted to that family (Ex 28:1; 40:12-15).
p. of God Most High Gen 14:18

prince One who has authority or influence; a ruler; hence, **Prince:** the Messiah; Christ.
made you a p. . . . over us Ex 2:14
Do not put your trust in p. Ps 146:3
P. of Peace Isa 9:6
the P. of princes Dan 8:25
killed the P. of life Acts 3:15

prodigal (PROD-ih-gul) Wasteful. The parable of the Prodigal Son is given in Luke 15:11-32.

prophet (PROFF-et) A man called by God to be His spokesman.
I will raise up for them a P. Deut 18:18
p. is not without honor Mt 13:57; Mk 6:4; Jn 4:44
no p. is accepted in his Lk 4:24

propitiation (pro-pish-ee-AY-shun) Expiation; removal of guilt by atonement (Rom 3:25; 1 Jn 2:2; 4:10).

proverb (PRAH-verb); **Proverbs, the Book of** A short, meaningful saying about the nature of man and life. Proverbs in the Bible, most of which were written down by Solomon (1 Kgs 4:32), help to explain God's truths for wise and godly living.

psalm; Psalms, the Book of The hymn book of the Bible—a collection of prayers, poems, and hymns that focus the worshiper's thoughts on God in praise; the longest (150 psalms) book in the Bible. The title comes from a Greek word which means "a song sung to the accompaniment of a musical instrument." Subjects include God and His creation, war, worship, wisdom, sin and evil, judgment, justice, and the coming of the Messiah. Psalms are grouped by subject—thanksgiving, repentance, praise, confession, messianic, as well as psalms to be sung by pilgrims as they traveled to Jerusalem.

Purim (PEW-reem) A Jewish festival celebrating the deliverance from massacre (Esther 9:20-28).

R

Rabbi (RAB-eye) Master; teacher.
They said to Him, "R. Jn 1:38

Rachel (RAY-chul) The younger daughter of Laban; Jacob's second wife; mother of Joseph and Benjamin (Gen 29:1–31:35; 35:16-19).

Rebekah (ree-BECK-uh) Wife of Isaac; mother of Esau and Jacob (Gen 24:10-67; 25:20-26, 28; 26:6-11; 27:5-17).

redeemer One who buys back, rescues (as from sin), or ransoms. Jesus is called "the Redeemer," through His sacrificial death, although the word does not appear in the NT.
I know that my R. lives Job 19:25
LORD, my strength and my r. Ps 19:14
R. will come to Zion Isa 59:20

Red Sea; Sea of Reeds The body of water between Arabia and Africa; the miraculous parting of the sea (Ex 14:21-31) enabled the Israelites to escape the Egyptians.

remember To bring to mind again.
R. the Sabbath day Ex 20:8
R. Lot's wife Lk 17:32

repent To feel regret; to change one's mind about.
r. in dust and ashes Job 42:6
R., for the kingdom Mt 3:2
unless you r. you will Lk 13:3
R., and . . . be baptized Acts 2:38
R. therefore and be Acts 3:19

resurrection (rez-er-RECK-shun) A rising from the dead; a return to life; hence, **Resurrection:** The rising of Christ from the dead (Mt 28; Mk 16; Lk 24; Jn 20; 1 Cor 15).
there is no r. Mt 22:23; Mk 12:18
I am the r. and the life Jn 11:25
This is the first r. Rev 20:5

Reuben; Reubenites (ROO-bin; ROO-bin-nights) The

firstborn son of Jacob, by Leah (Gen 29:32); the ancestor of the tribe of Reuben.

revelation (rev-uh-LAY-shun) The making known of something previously concealed.
through the r. of Jesus Christ Gal 1:12
The R. of Jesus Christ Rev 1:1

reward To give payment for something done; used particularly of God's blessing upon the obedient and His punishment of the wicked.
r. in heaven Mt 5:12; Lk 6:23
receive his own r. 1 Cor 3:8

rich Wealthy; having money or property.
Do not overwork to be r. Prov 23:4
for he was very r. Lk 18:23

riches Wealth; property; material goods.
r. are not forever Prov 27:24
deceitfulness of r. Mt 13:22; Mk 4:19

righteous One who does what is right; a virtuous person.
LORD knows the way of the r. Ps 1:6
not come to call the r. Mt 9:13

righteousness Virtue; right action; particularly, conformity to God's will.
in the paths of r. Ps 23:3
hunger and thirst for r. Mt 5:6
grace might reign through r. Rom 5:21

rock A mass of stone; anything hard like a rock.
are my r. and my fortress Ps 31:3
on this r. I will build Mt 16:18

Rock The Lord.
Of the R. who begot you Deut 32:18
The LORD is my r. Ps 18:2

Rome; Romans The capital of the Roman Empire; Christianity probably came to Rome early in the apostolic age. Paul wrote the NT Epistle to the Romans to the Christian community there.

rooster
before the r. crows Mt 26:34, 75

Ruth A Moabite woman who became an ancestress of David through her second marriage, to Boaz. Her story of devotion is told in the OT Book of Ruth.

S

sabbath The day of rest ordained by God. Among Jews, the seventh day (Saturday); among Christians, the first day of the week (Sunday), the day of divine worship (1 Cor 16:2).
Remember the S. day Ex 20:8
a s. of solemn rest for you Lev 16:31
S. was made for man Mk 2:27

sacrifice (SACK-rih-fyce) An offering, usually of the life of a person or an animal, made to God.
s. to the LORD Ex 5:17
love . . . is more than . . . s. Mk 12:33
put away sin by the s. of Heb 9:26

Sadducees (SAD-you-sees) The aristocratic party of the Jews at the time of Christ. They collaborated with the Romans to maintain their favorable status.

salt A seasoning; a preservative.
became a pillar of s. Gen 19:26
You are the s. of the earth Mt 5:13

salvation (sal-VAY-shun) Deliverance from evil, danger, or trouble; God's gift, through Christ, to save men's souls.
the God of my s. Ps 25:5
to the Rock of our s. Ps 95:1
shall see the s. of God Lk 3:6
this will turn out for my s. Phil 1:19
grace of God that brings s. Tit 2:11
the author of their s. Heb 2:10

Samaria; Samaritans (suh-MARE-ee-ah; suh-MARE-ih-tuns) The capital city of the northern kingdom, Israel. Also the name of the territory near the city. The term "Samaritan" is usually applied to a member of a religious sect living in that area. The parable of the Good Samaritan told by Jesus (Lk 10:30-37).

Samson A hero of the tribe of Dan, noted for his great strength (Judg 13–16).

Samuel (SAM-you-ell) The last "judge" of Israel; a prophet of the eleventh century B.C. The two OT books of Samuel record his life and deeds and the history of Israel through the reigns of Solomon and David. The Lord calls Samuel (1 Sam 3); Samuel anoints David (1 Sam 16:11-13).

sanctify (SANK-tih-fy) To set apart as holy; to consecrate to religious use; to make holy.
seventh day and s. it Gen 2:3
s. by the Holy Spirit Rom 15:16

sanctuary (SANK-shoe-air-ih) A building or place set apart for religious worship; in the OT, the tabernacle (Ex 25:8) or the temple (1 Chr 22:19).

sandal strap Thong to fasten a sandal.
whose s.s. I am not worthy Jn 1:27

Sanhedrin (SAN-hee-drun) A council or assembly, the highest ruling body and court of justice among the

Jewish people in the time of Jesus; headed by the high priest of Israel; composed of 71 members, among whom were Joseph of Arimathea (Mk 15:43), Gamaliel, Paul's teacher (Acts 5:34), Nicodemus (Jn 3:1; 7:50), the high priests, Annas and Caiaphas (Lk 3:2) and Ananias (Acts 23:2); given limited authority over certain religious, civil, and criminal matters involving foreign nations that dominated Israel at various times in its history.

Sarah; Sarai The wife of Abraham; mother of Isaac in accord with divine promise (Gen 17:15-21; 18:1-15).

Satan (SAY-tun) The Devil; the adversary of God and Christ.
S. casts out S. Mt 12:26; Mk 3:23
forty days, tempted by S. Mk 1:13
lest S. should take advantage 2 Cor 2:11
S. will be released from Rev 20:7

Saul Son of Kish, of the tribe of Benjamin; first king over Israel. The prophet Samuel anoints him to be king (1 Sam 10:1); he disobeys the Lord (1 Sam 15); David enters his service (1 Sam 16:14-23); he tries to kill David (1 Sam 19:9, 10); David spares his life (1 Sam 26:6-24).

Saul of Tarsus *See* Paul.

Savior Literally, "one who saves or delivers"; Christ, as the One who delivers us from the sins of this life and through whom salvation is obtained; God, as the deliverer of the Israelites from oppression and as the redeemer of all peoples.
my refuge; My S. 2 Sam 22:3
A just God and a S. Isa 45:21
rejoiced in God my S. Lk 1:47
Christ, the S. of the world Jn 4:42
Christ . . . the S. of the body Eph 5:23
S., the Lord Jesus Christ Phil 3:20
God our S., Who alone is wise Jude 25

scripture; Scriptures, the Any writing, particularly that of a sacred nature; hence, the Bible. Also "Scriptures"; "Holy Scripture"; "Holy Scriptures."
Have you not read this S. Mk 12:10
search the S. Jn 5:39
S. is given by inspiration 2 Tim 3:16

seek To search for; to try to find.
s., and you will find Mt 7:7; Lk 11:9
none who s. after God Rom 3:11

Sermon on the Mount Name given to a talk by Jesus while teaching His disciples in the hill country of Galilee early in His ministry (Mt 5:3–7:27). It includes a series of blessings, the Beatitudes (5:3-12); the Lord's Prayer (6:9-13); and the Golden Rule (7:12). A similar discourse in Luke 6:17-49 is called the "Sermon on the Plain."

serpent A snake; in biblical usage, many times synonymous with "Satan."
s. was more cunning than Gen 3:1
will take up s. Mk 16:18
s. deceived Eve 2 Cor 11:3
s. of old, who is the Devil Rev 20:2

Shadrach (SHAD-rack) The Babylonian name of one of Daniel's companions (Dan 1:7; 3:12).

Sheba, queen of, (SHE-bah) A queen, probably Arabian, who came to test Solomon's wisdom (1 Kgs 10:1-13; 2 Chr 9:1-12).

Shem The eldest son of Noah who stands as the ancestor of the Semites generally and of the Hebrews specifically (Gen 5:32; 9:18-27; 10:21-31; Lk 3:36).

shepherd One who herds and takes care of sheep; by extension, the ruler or king of a people. The Lord is the shepherd of Israel; Christ is the Good Shepherd (Jn 10:7-18).
The LORD is My s. (Ps 23:1)
s. . . . keeping watch over Lk 2:8
one flock and one s. Jn 10:16
Lord Jesus . . . that great S. Heb 13:20

Silas; Silvanus (SIGH-lus; sil-VAY-nus) One of the earliest of the apostolic missionaries, associated with both Paul (Acts 16:19ff; 1 Thess 1:1; 2:1, 2) and Peter (1 Pet 5:12).

Siloam, Pool of (sigh-LOW-um) A storage pool and tunnel that provided a water supply for the residents of Jerusalem, fed by the Gihon Spring; dug through solid rock in the time of King Hezekiah of Judah (2 Chr 32:30). Water still flows through the tunnel to this day!

Simeon (SIM-ee-un) The name of six persons in the Bible, including: 1. The second son of Jacob, by Leah (Gen 29:33); ancestor of the tribe of Simeon. 2. A devout man who blessed the infant Jesus when His parents presented Him in the temple (Lk 2:25-35).

Simon (SIGH-mun) The name of nine persons in the NT, including: 1. **Simon Peter:** *See* Peter (Mt 16:17, 18; Jn 1:42). 2. **Simon the Zealot:** Also one of the 12 apostles (Lk 6:15). 3. **Simon the Pharisee,** in whose home Jesus was anointed by the sinful woman (Lk 7:36-50). 4. **Simon the leper,** in whose home Jesus was anointed by Mary (Mk 14:3-9; Jn 12:1-8). 5. **Simon of Cyrene,** who was forced to carry Jesus' cross (Mt 27:32; Mk 15:21; Lk 23:26). 6. **Simon the sorcerer,** who offered money to Peter and John for the power of the Holy Spirit (Acts 8:9-24).

sin 1. An offense or revolt against God (as Adam and Eve in the Garden of Eden); deliberate defiance; wickedness; iniquity; ungodliness.
put to death for his own s. Deut 24:16
our s. testify against us Isa 59:12
power on earth to forgive s. Mt 9:6
Who can forgive s. Mk 2:7; Lk 5:21
takes away the s. of Jn 1:29
He who is without s. Jn 8:7
gave Himself for ours. Gal 1:4
2. To commit an offense against God; to be wicked.
is no one who does not s. 1 Kgs 8:46
soul who s. shall die Ezek 18:4
S. no more, lest a Jn 5:14
cannot s., because he has been born of God 1 Jn 3:9

Sinai, Mount (SIGH-nigh) The name of a peninsula, a wilderness, and a mountain. 1. The barren, triangular-shaped peninsula stands between Egypt and Israel. 2. In the wilderness, there are no flowing streams or rivers, only wadis (dry stream beds which carry off the occasional rains). 3. The traditional mountain where Moses received the Ten Commandments (Ex 19:3-20) is in the Sinai range and is called Jebel Musa, the mountain of Moses. When the Israelites camped there, it was called Sinai (Ex 19:11), or sometimes called Horeb (Ex 3:1).

sinful Wicked; full of iniquity.
s. nation, A people laden Isa 1:4
in the likeness of s. flesh Rom 8:3

sinner One who commits an offense against God.
stands in the path of s. Ps 1:1
Why does your Teacher eat with . . . s. Mt 9:11; Mk 2:16; Lk 5:30
come to call . . . s., to repentance Mt 9:13; Mk 2:17; Lk 5:32
over one s. who repents Lk 15:7
be merciful to me a s. Lk 18:13

Sodom (SOD-um) One of the two cities destroyed by the Lord because of their wickedness (Gen 19:24-28).

Solomon Son of David and Bathsheba; third king of Israel; under his reign the kingdom reached its zenith; noted for his wisdom (1 Kgs 3:16-28) and his gift of expressing himself. The OT books of Proverbs, Ecclesiastes, and Song of Solomon, and Psalms 72 and 127 are attributed to him. He built the temple (1 Kgs 6–7; 2 Chr 3); was visited by the queen of Sheba (1 Kgs 10:1-13; 2 Chr 9:1-12).

son A male child or man as related to his parents; a male descendant.
wise s. makes a glad father Prov 10:1
Unto us a S. is given Isa 9:6
Is this not the carpenter's s. Mt 13:55

Son; Son of God The Second Person of the Trinity; Christ.
is My beloved S. Mt 3:17; 17:5; Mk 1:11; Lk 9:35
S. of the living God Mt 16:16; Jn 6:69
this is the S. of God Jn 1:34
gave His only begotten S. Jn 3:16

son of man Any human being (Ps 8:4); the prophet Ezekiel (used throughout the OT Book of Ezekiel); in the Gospels, Jesus uses "Son of Man" as a self-designation, particularly in the passages relating to His Second Coming.

sons of God Angels (Job 1:6; Dan 3:25); any human beings, as created in God's image (Hos 1:10); Christians (Rom 8:14).

soul The life principle of a human being; the immortal element of man; the spirit; the living individual.
obey . . . with all your s. Deut 30:2
Hear, and your s. shall live Isa 55:3
all s. are Mine Ezek 18:4
destroy both s. and body Mt 10:28
loses his own s. Mt 16:26; Mk 8:36
s. be subject to the governing Rom 13:1

sow To plant.
s. in tears Shall reap in joy Ps 126:5
man s., that he will also reap Gal 6:7

spirit That part of a person's being thought of as the center of life, the will, thinking, feeling; that part of man that survives death.
Into Your hand I commit my s. Ps 31:5
a haughty s. before Prov 16:18
yielded up His s. Mt 27:50; Jn 19:30
the s. indeed is willing Mt 26:41; Mk 14:38
to the s. of just men Heb 12:23

Spirit, Holy The Third Person of the Trinity; that divine Spirit, referred to in the OT as "Spirit of the LORD" or "Spirit of God," through which men receive power, particularly effective through Jesus Christ in bringing men into fellowship with God. Some Bible translators use "Holy Ghost" rather than "Holy Spirit."
in the name of the . . . Holy S. Mt 28:19
baptize you with the Holy S. Mt 3:11; Mk 1:8; Lk 3:16; Jn 1:33
be filled with the Holy S. Lk. 1:15
Holy S. was not yet given Jn 7:39
Helper, the Holy S. Jn 14:26

promise of the Holy S. Acts 2:33
witness in the Holy S. Rom 9:1
except by the Holy S. 1 Cor 12:3
communion of the Holy S. 2 Cor 13:14

Spirit of the Lord; Spirit of God; Holy Spirit The divine source of all life; a special manifestation of God's divine Presence.
S. of God was hovering Gen 1:2
S. is poured upon us Isa 32:15
S. of the Lord God is Isa 61:1; Lk 4:18
S. descending . . . like a dove Mk 1:10; Jn 1:32
God is S. Jn 4:24
not grieve the Holy S. of Eph 4:30

Stephen The first Christian martyr; one of the seven men chosen by the apostles for the special "service of tables"; his death was the signal for a general persecution of the Christians (Acts 6:1–8:3).

stew A thick soup.
Esau sells birthright for s. Gen 25:29-34

steward A manager of a household or of property; used of Christians, particularly ministers, as guardians of the affairs of God.
faithful and wise s. Lk 12:42
s. of the mysteries of God 1 Cor 4:1
s. of the manifold grace of God 1 Pet 4:10

stone A rock; a hard mineral.
dash your foot against a s. Ps 91:12; Mt 4:6; Lk 4:11
not one s. . . . upon another Mt 24:2; Mk 13:2; Lk 19:44; 21:6
s. to become bread Lk 4:3

sufficient Enough; ample.
S. for the day is its own Mt 6:34

Supper, Last *See* Last Supper.

Supper, Lord's *See* Holy Communion.

swear To declare under oath.
not s. by My name falsely Lev 19:12
not s. at all Mt 5:34

sword A sharp-bladed weapon with a hilt or handle.
beat their s. into plowshares Isa 2:4; Mic 4:3
Beat your plowshares into s. Joel 3:10
sharper than any two-edged s. Heb 4:12

synagogue (SIN-uh-gog) A building where Jewish religious services and schools and other meetings are held.
preached the word of God in the s. Acts 13:5

T

tabernacle (TAB-er-nak-kel) Literally, "tent of meeting"; the portable shelter used by the Israelites as a place of worship.
pattern of the t. Ex 25:9

Tabernacles, Feast of One of the three great joyous festivals of the Jewish year; held in autumn at the end of the harvest; celebrates a renewal of the covenant and recalls the wilderness pilgrimage (Ex 23:16; Lev 23:34-36; Deut 16:13-15). Also called "Feast of Booths" (Lev 23:42); "the Feast of Ingathering" (Ex 23:16; 34:22).

tablets Flat stones bearing inscriptions.
two t. of the Testimony Ex 31:18

talent A unit of money or of weight. Parable of the talents (Mt 25:14-30).

Tarsus (TAR-sus) The birthplace of Saul, who, after his conversion, was called Paul (Acts 9:11; 22:3); chief city of Cilicia, a province in SW Asia Minor or modern Turkey; located on the banks of the Cydnus River, about ten miles from the Mediterranean Sea; a learning center of the world. "I am a Jew from Tarsus, in Cilicia, a citizen of no mean city," declared Paul (Acts 21:39).

tax collector One who collects taxes.
Matthew the t. Mt 10:3
a friend of t. and sinners Mt 11:19
saw a t. named Levi Lk 5:27

Teacher Title, used of Jesus during His ministry.
your T., the Christ Mt 23:8, 10
trouble the T. Mk 5:35
call Me T. and Lord Jn 13:13

temple A building for the worship of a deity; hence, the temple at Jerusalem. *See* 1 Kings 5–8 for description of Solomon's temple.
Lord is in His holy t. Ps 11:4
destroy the t. of God Mt 26:61; 27:40; Mk 15:29; Jn 2:19

temptation An attempt to get someone to do something wrong; a test of character.
not lead us into t. Mt 6:13; Lk 11:4

temptations of Jesus *See* Matthew 4:1-11; Luke 4:1-13.

Ten Commandments The ten laws given by God to Moses on Mount Sinai (Ex 20:1-17; Deut 5:6-21).

tent of meeting *See* tabernacle.

testimony In OT: the divine law, especially the Ten Commandments; in NT: witness.
law and to the t. Isa 8:20
know that his t. is true Jn 21:24
to the t. of Jesus Christ Rev 1:2

Thaddaeus (THAD-ee-us) One of the twelve apostles of Jesus (Mk 3:18), also called Lebbaeus (Mt 10:3) and probably Judas. *See* Judas (3).

Thessalonica; Thessalonians (thess-uh-low-NIGH-kuh; thess-uh-LOW-nih-uns) An important city of Macedonia where Paul and his associates founded an early Christian church. The two NT epistles to the Thessalonians were among the earliest written by Paul.

Thomas One of the 12 apostles; his incredulity of Jesus' resurrection gained him the name "doubting Thomas" (Mt 10:3; Mk 3:18; Lk 6:15; Jn 11:16; 14:5; 20:24-29; Acts 1:13).

Timothy A trusted companion and assistant of Paul, from the early part of the latter's second missionary journey. According to tradition the two epistles to Timothy were written near the close of Paul's life.

tithe The tenth part of one's income paid to support God's work (Lev 27:30-32).

Titus (TIGHT-us) A gentile Christian associate of Paul (2 Cor 7:5-7); according to Titus 1:4, 5, Paul wrote the letter bearing his name in order to encourage him in his work in the churches of Crete.

tomb A place of burial.
like whitewashed t. Mt 23:27

Torah (TOE-ruh) Guidance or direction from God to His people for living the covenant relationship—a total way of life; in earlier times, a term referring directly to the first five books of Moses (*see* Pentateuch), but came to mean both the hearing and doing of the Law (Deut 32:46). Later, the Hebrew OT included the books of wisdom and prophets, and this entire collection became known as the Torah.

Transfiguration Jesus' glorious and radiant change in appearance; witnessed by three disciples (Mt 17:1-9; Mk 9:2-10; Lk 9:28-36; 2 Pet 1:16-18).

transgression A sin; rebellion against God's will.
t. of Adam Rom 5:14

Trinity The doctrine held by most Christians that there are three divine Persons (Father, Son, and Holy Spirit) united in the one Supreme Divine Being. NT teachings (Mt 12:32; 28:19; Lk 12:10; Acts 2:33; 1 Cor 12:4-6; 2 Cor 13:14) support this doctrine.

trust To have or put confidence in someone or something.
T. in the LORD with all Prov 3:5
those who t. in riches Mk 10:24

truth A proven sincerity, verity, honesty; righteousness.
A God of t. and without Deut 32:4
t. shall make you free Jn 8:32
I am the way, the t. Jn 14:6
He, the Spirit of t., has Jn 16:13

tunic An outer garment.
made him a t. of many colors Gen 37:3
do not have two t. Lk 9:3

Tyropoeon Valley (tie-ROW-pih-un) A small valley in the city of Jerusalem, which divides hill Ophel, the original City of David, from the Western Hill, or Upper City.

U

unleavened bread Bread baked from unfermented dough, or dough without yeast or "leaven" (Gen 19:3; Josh 5:11; 1 Sam 28:24); the flat bread used in the Passover celebration and the priestly rituals, recalling the Exodus, when the Hebrews left Egypt so quickly that they had no time to wait for the bread to rise (Ex 12:8, 15-20, 34, 39; 13:6-7).

Ur An ancient city on the Euphrates, called "Ur of the Chaldees"; home of Abraham (Gen 11:28).

Uzziah (uh-ZIGH-uh) The name of three persons in the OT, one of them a king of Judah (c. 783–742 B.C.).

V

vanity Futility; emptiness.
V. of v., all is v. Eccles 1:2

viper A poisonous snake.
stings like a v. Prov 23:32

vision Something seen other than by ordinary sight, as in a dream. God's revelations to the prophets were usually by visions.
They err in v. Isa 28:7
revealed to Daniel in a night v. Dan 2:19
Tell the v. to no one Mt 17:9

voice A sound uttered through the mouth as in speaking.
a still small v. 1 Kgs 19:12
v. of the turtledove is heard Song 2:12
v. of one crying Isa 40:3; Mt 3:3; Mk 1:3; Lk 3:4; Jn 1:23

W

wadi (WAH-dih) A valley, ravine, or riverbed that usually remains dry except during the rainy season; similar to an arroyo in the western United States; also "brook" (Josh 15:47; 2 Kgs 23:12) and "torrent" (Judg 5:21) in the Bible.

wages The payment for services.
be content with your w. Lk 3:14
the w. of sin is death Rom 6:23

walk To move by stepping.
w. through the valley of Ps 23:4
saw Him w. on the sea Mt 14:26
shall not w. in darkness Jn 8:12

want To lack or need (not in the sense of "to desire").
I shall not w. Ps 23:1

war Fighting with weapons between large groups.
A time of w., And a time Eccles 3:8
w. and rumors of w. Mt 24:6; Mk 13:7; Lk 21:9

wash To clean with water or other liquid.
w. His feet with her tears Lk 7:38
w. the disciples' feet Jn 13:5

water The colorless fluid that falls as rain.
over the face of the w. Gen 1:2
the flood of w. was on Gen 7:6
Planted by the rivers of w. Ps 1:3
me beside the still w. Ps 23:2
Cast your bread upon the w. Eccles 11:1
baptized you with w. Mk 1:8; Lk 3:16; Jn 1:26

way The direction; path; man's mode of living.
the w. of the righteous Ps 1:6
Train up a child in the w. Prov 22:6
Prepare the w. of the LORD Isa 40:3; Mt 3:3; Mk 1:3; Lk 3:4; Jn 1:23
I am the w., the truth Jn 14:6

Weeks, Feast of Seven weeks after Passover (Lev 23:15-21; Deut 16:9-12). Also called Feast of Harvest (Ex 23:16). *See* Pentecost.

will Desire; something wished.
Your w. be done Mt 6:10; Lk 11:2
good w. toward men Lk 2:14

wine The fermented juice of fruits.
W. is a mocker Prov 20:1
new w. into new wineskins Mt 9:17; Mk 2:22; Lk 5:37

wise Having good judgment.
tree desirable to make one w. Gen 3:6
man w. in his own eyes Prov 26:12
w. men from the East Mt 2:1

witness Someone or something that bears testimony to the truthfulness of a statement or to the occurrence of a happening.
be a w. between you Gen 31:44
as a w. to all the nations Mt 24:14
My w. is true Jn 8:14
The people . . . bore w. Jn 12:17
God is my w., whom Rom 1:9
bore w. to the word Rev 1:2

word A spoken sound having meaning.
God spoke all these w. Ex 20:1
w. fitly spoken is like Prov 25:11

Word; Word of God; word of the Lord God's revealed will; the Holy Scriptures.
the w. is very near Deut 30:14; Rom 10:8
By the w. of the LORD Ps 33:6
hear the w. of the LORD Jer 29:20
hear the w. of God Lk 8:21
for the w. of God Rev 1:9

Word; Word of God A title of Christ.
the W. was God Jn 1:1
concerning the W. of life 1 Jn 1:1
is called The W. of God Rev 19:13

work 1. Labor; effort.
God ended His w. Gen 2:2
the w. of Your fingers Ps 8:3
2. To labor; to toil.
Father has been w. Jn 5:17
all things w. together Rom 8:28
faith w. through love Gal 5:6

works Deeds; efforts.
according to his w. Mt 16:27; 2 Tim 4:14
w. which the Father Jn 5:36
its w. are evil Jn 7:7
not of w., lest anyone Eph 2:9

world The earth; the universe.
the w. is Mine, and all Ps 50:12
You are the light of the w. Mt 5:14
gains the whole w. Mt 16:26
God so loved the w. Jn 3:16
I am the light of the w. Jn 8:12
brought nothing into this w. 1 Tim 6:7

worry Be or become anxious.
by w. can add one cubit Mt 6:27
do not w. about tomorrow Mt 6:34
do not w. beforehand Mk 13:11
do not w. about your life Lk 12:22

worship To honor; to show reverence for.
you shall w. no other god Ex 34:14
w. at His footstool Ps 99:5
w. the LORD your God Mt 4:10; Lk 4:8
where one ought to w. Jn 4:20

wrath Great anger, especially God's punishment of sin.
soft answer turns away w. Prov 15:1
w. to come Mt 3:7; Lk 3:7
w. in the day of w. Rom 2:5
delivers us from the w. 1 Thess 1:10

Y

Yahweh (YAH-way) The covenant God of Israel, YHWH in the original Hebrew. According to Jewish custom, because of reverence the divine name was not to be spoken, so the Hebrew words for Lord and God were substituted. Whenever the words LORD and GOD appear in large and small capital letters, the original Hebrew reads YHWH.

Z

Zacchaeus (zack-KEY-us) Chief tax collector of Jericho at the time of one of Jesus' visits (Lk 19:2-8).

Zealot (ZELL-ut) A term used to designate the more radical Jewish rebels against foreign, particularly Roman, rule; one motivated by zeal for the Jewish law.

Zebedee (ZEB-uh-dee) The father of the apostles James and John (Mt 4:21; Mk 1:19, 20; Lk 5:10; Jn 21:2).

Zebulun (ZEB-you-lun) The tenth son of Jacob, the sixth by Leah (Gen 30:19, 20); ancestor of the tribe of Zebulun.

Zechariah; Zecher; Zacharias (zek-uh-RIGH-uh; zek-ur; zack-uh-RIGH-us) The name of 33 persons in the Bible, including: 1. Son of the priest Jehoiada (2 Chr 24:20, 21). 2. One of the OT minor prophets; contemporary of Haggai; urged the rebuilding of the temple (Ezra 5:1; 6:14; Zech 1:1, 7; 7:1, 8). 3. The father of John the Baptist (Lk 1:5-67; 3:2).

Zedekiah (zed-uh-KIGH-uh) The name three persons in the OT, including the last king of Judah (c. 597–587 B.C.). Also called Mattaniah.

Zephaniah (zef-uh-NIGH-uh) The name four persons in the OT, including a prophet during the time of Josiah; his prophecies appear in the OT Book of Zephaniah, the ninth of the 12 Minor Prophets.

Zion; Sion (ZIGH-un; SIGH-un) Originally the name of the fortified hill of pre-Israelite Jerusalem; poetically extended to refer to the religious capital of Israel.

ACKNOWLEDGMENTS

à Kempis, Thomas, *The Imitation of Christ*, reprinted in *Christian Classics in Modern English*, 1991 by Bernard Bangley. Used with permission of Harold Shaw Publishers, Wheaton, Illinois.

Anderson, Ann Kiemel, *Open Adoption, My Story of Love and Laughter*, copyright 1990 by Ann Kiemel Anderson. Used by permission of Tyndale House Publishers, Inc. All rights reserved.

Anderson, Lynn, *Finding the Heart to Go On*, copyright 1991 Thomas Nelson, Nashville, Tennessee.

Anderson, Lynn, *Heaven Came Down*, copyright 1994 Here's Life. Used by permission of Thomas Nelson, Nashville, Tennessee.

Anderson, Neil, *Walking in the Light*, copyright 1984 Thomas Nelson, Nashville, Tennessee.

Aspy, Boice, Colson, Hoffman, Hurnard, Kesler, Lovelace, McDowell, Miller, Seamands, Smedes in *Practical Christianity*. Compiled and edited by LaVonne Neff, Ron Beers, Bruce Barton, Linda Taylor, Dave Veerman, and Jim Galvin 1987 by Youth for Christ/USA. Used by permission of Tyndale House Publishers, Inc. All rights reserved.

Baker, Donald, and Emery Nester, *Depression*, copyright 1983. Used by permission.

Barclay, William, *The King and the Kingdom*, by permission of Saint Andrew Press, Board of Communication, Church of Scotland, Edinburgh.

Barna, George, *The Power of Vision*. Copyright 1992 by George Barna. Published by Regal Books, Ventura, Calif. Used by permission.

Bauman, Edward W., *Beyond Belief*, copyright 1964. Permission granted by Bauman Bible Telecasts.

Blue, Ron, and Judy Blue, *Raising Money-Smart Kids*, copyright 1992 Thomas Nelson, Nashville, Tennessee.

Boice, James, *Christ's Call to Discipleship*, Moody, copyright 1986. Used by permission.

Bounds, E. M., *Purpose in Prayer*, Moody Press, copyright 1920. Used by permission.

Bridges, Jerry, *The Practice of Godliness*, NavPress, copyright 1985. Permission granted by NavPress. For copies call 1-800-366-7788.

Bridges, Jerry, *The Pursuit of Holiness*, NavPress, copyright 1978. Permission granted by NavPress. For copies call 1-800-366-7788.

Bridges, Jerry, *Trusting God*, NavPress, copyright 1988. Permission granted by NavPress. For copies call 1-800-366-7788.

Briscoe, Stuart, *Getting into God*, World Wide Publishers, copyright 1975. Used by permission.

Briscoe, Stuart, *Hearing God's Voice Above the Noise*, published by Victor Books, 1989, SP Publications, Inc., Wheaton, Illinois 60187. Used by permission.

Brown, Joan W., *Day by Day with Billy Graham*, World Wide Publishers, copyright 1976. Used by permission.

Brownlow, Leroy, *A Psalm In My Heart*, Brownlow Publishing, copyright 1989. Used by permission.

Bruce, F. F., *Jesus: Lord and Savior*. Taken from *Jesus: Lord and Savior* by F. F. Bruce. copyright 1986 by F. F. Bruce. Used by permission of InterVarsity Press, P. O. Box 1400, Downers Grove, Illinois 60515.

Burke, Tim, and Christine Burke, *Major League Dad*, Focus On the Family Publishers, copyright 1994. Used by permission.

Buttrick, George, *God, Pain, and Evil*, Abingdon Press, copyright 1966. Used by permission.

Campolo, Tony, *It's Friday, but Sunday's Comin,'* copyright 1984 Word, Inc., Dallas, Texas.

Campolo, Tony, *Wake Up America*. HarperCollins, copyright 1991 by Anthony Campolo.

Campolo, Tony, *Who Switched the Price Tags?*, copyright 1986 Word, Inc., Dallas, Texas.

Campolo, Tony, *You Can Make a Difference*, copyright 1984 Word, Inc., Dallas, Texas.

Card, Michael, *Immanuel*, copyright 1990 Thomas Nelson, Nashville, Tennessee.

Carmichael, Amy, *Thou Givest, They Gather*, Christian Literature Crusade, copyright 1970. Used by permission.

Chambers, Oswald, *Devotions for a Deeper Life*. Copyright 1986 by Oswald Chambers. Used by permission of Zondervan Publishing House.

Chambers, Oswald, *God's Workmanship*. This quotation by Oswald Chambers is taken from *God's Workmanship*. Copyright 1953 by Oswald Chambers Publications Association, Ltd., and is used by permission of Discovery House Publishers, Box 3566, Grand Rapids, Mich. 49501. All rights reserved.

Chambers, Oswald, *My Utmost for His Highest*. The quotations by Oswald Chambers are taken from *My Utmost for His Highest: An Updated Edition in Today's Language*, Edited by James Reimann. Copyright 1935 by Dodd, Mead & Co., Inc., 1963, 1992 by Oswald Chambers Publications Association, Ltd., and are used by permission of Discovery House Publishers, Box 3566, Grand Rapids, Mich. 49501. All rights reserved.

Chantry, Walter, *God's Righteous Kingdom*, Banner of Truth, copyright 1980. Used by permission.

Chapian, Marie, *His Thoughts Toward Me*, copyright 1987, Bethany House Publishers. Used by permission.

Colson, Charles, *Against the Night*. Copyright 1989 by Fellowship Communications. Published by Servant Publications, Box 8617, Ann Arbor, Mich. 48107. Used by permission.

Colson, Charles, *The Body*, copyright 1992, Word Inc., Dallas, Texas.

Colson, Charles, *Born Again*, Fleming H. Revell Company, copyright 1977. Used by permission.

Colson, Charles, *The God of Stones and Spiders* by Chuck Colson, copyright 1990. Used by permission of Good News Publishers, Crossway Books, Wheaton, Illinois 60187.

Colson, Charles, *Kingdoms in Conflict*. Copyright 1987, by Charles Colson. Used by permission of William Morrow, Inc.

Colson, Charles, *Loving God*. Copyright 1983, 1987 by Charles W. Colson. Used by permission of Zondervan Publishing House.

Colson, Charles, *Who Speaks for God* by Charles Colson, copyright 1985, pages 21-22, 67-68. Used by permission of Good News Publishers, Crossway Books, Wheaton, Illinois 60187.

Colson, Charles, and Jack Eckerd, *Why America Doesn't Work*, copyright 1991, Word Inc., Dallas, Texas.

DeHaan, Dan, *The God You Can Know*, Moody Press, copyright 1982. Used by permission.

Dillow, Linda, *Creative Counterpart*, copyright 1977 Thomas Nelson, Nashville, Tennessee.

Dunn, Ronald, *The Faith Crises*, Tyndale House Publishers, copyright 1984 by Ronald Dunn. Used by permission of the author.

Durham, Charles, *Temptation: Help for Struggling Christians*, InterVarsity Press, copyright 1982. Used by permission.

Eastman, Dick, and Jack Hayford, *Living and Praying in Jesus' Name*, copyright 1988 by Dick Eastman and Jack Hayford. Used by permission of Tyndale House Publishers, Inc. All rights reserved.

Edman, V. Raymond, *The Disciplines of Life*, Van Kampen Press, copyright © 1948. Permission granted by David Arthur Edman.

Elliot, Elisabeth, *The Mark of a Man*, Fleming H. Revell Company, copyright 1981. Used by permission.

Elliot, Elisabeth, *Passion and Purity*, Fleming H. Revell Company, copyright 1984. Used by permission.

Elliot, Elisabeth, *The Shaping of a Christian Family*, copyright 1992 Thomas Nelson, Nashville, Tennessee.

Elliot, Elisabeth, *Slow and Certain Light*, Fleming H. Revell Company, copyright 1992. Used by permission.

Elliot, Lynda, *The Counsel of a Christian Friend*, copyright 1993 Thomas Nelson, Nashville, Tennessee.

ACKNOWLEDGMENTS

Enns, Paul, *Approaching God*, Moody Press, copyright 1991. Used by permission.

Esau, Truman and Beverly Burch, *Making Marriage Work*, published by Victor Books, 1990, SP Publications, Inc., Wheaton, Illinois 60187.

Farrar, Steve, *Point Man*, Questar Publishers, Multnomah Books, copyright 1990, by Steve Farrar. Used by permission.

Finzel, Hans, *The Top Ten Mistakes Leaders Make*, published by Victor Books, 1994, SP Publications, Inc., Wheaton, Illinois 60187. Used by permission.

Gaither, Gloria, *What My Parents Did Right*, Star Song Publishers, copyright 1991. Used by permission.

Garmo, John, *Lifestyle Worship*, copyright 1993 Thomas Nelson, Nashville, Tennessee.

Getz, Gene A., *The Measure of a Man*, copyright 1974, Regal Books, Ventura, CA 93003. Used by permission.

Graham, Billy, *Approaching Hoofbeats*, copyright 1983 Word, Inc., Dallas, Texas.

Graham, Billy, *The Holy Spirit*, copyright 1988 Word, Inc., Dallas, Texas.

Graham, Billy, *Hope for the Troubled Heart*, copyright 1991, Word Inc., Dallas, Texas.

Graham, Billy, *How to Be Born Again*, copyright 1977 Word, Inc., Dallas, Texas.

Graham, Billy, *Peace with God*, copyright 1984 Word, Inc., Dallas, Texas.

Graham, Billy, *The Secret of Happiness*, copyright 1985 Word, Inc., Dallas, Texas.

Graham, Billy, *Storm Warning*, copyright 1992, Word Inc., Dallas, Texas.

Graham, Billy, *Unto the Hills*, copyright 1986 Word, Inc., Dallas, Texas.

Graham, Ruth Bell, *The Legacy of a Pack Rat*, copyright 1989 Thomas Nelson, Nashville, Tennessee.

Graham, Ruth Bell, *Prodigals and Those Who Love Them*. "The Door Stands Open" reprinted from *Prodigals and Those Who Love Them*, by Ruth Bell Graham. Copyright 1991 Ruth Bell Graham. Used by permission of Focus on the Family.

Hansel, Tim, *You Gotta Keep Dancin',* copyright 1986 by Tim Hansel. Used by permission of Chariot Family Publishing.

Hazard, David, *Safe Within Your Love*, copyright 1992, Bethany House Publishers. Used by permission.

Holterman, Carla, *Trustful Living*, Fleming H. Revell Company, copyright 1992. Used by permission.

Howard, David M., *River of Tears, Words of Fire*, Tyndale House Publishers Inc. Copyright 1976 by David Howard. Used by permission.

Huffman, Vicki, *Plus Living*, Harold Shaw Publishers, copyright 1989. Used by permission.

Hugget, Joyce, *The Joy of Listening to God*. Taken from *The Joy of Listening to God* by Joyce Huggett. 1986 by Joyce Hugget. Used by permission of InterVarsity Press, P. O. Box 1400, Downers Grove, Illinois 60515.

Hughes, R. Kent, *James*, copyright 1991, pages 19-20. Used by permission of Good News publishers, Crossway Books, Wheaton, Illinois 60187.

Hutchcraft, Ron, *Peaceful Living in a Stressful World*, copyright 1985 Thomas Nelson, Nashville, Tennessee.

Hybels, Bill, *Descending Into Greatness*. Copyright 1993 by Bill Hybels. Used by permission of Zondervan Publishing House.

Hybels, Bill, *Who You Are When No One's Looking* by Bill Hybels, 1987 by Bill Hybels. Used by permission of InterVarsity Press, P. O. Box 1400, Downers Grove, Illinois 60515.

Hybels, Bill, and Lynne Hybels, *Fit to be Tied*. Copyright 1991 by Bill Hybels. Used by permission of Zondervan Publishing House.

Jabey, Earl, *The Kingdom of Self*, Bridge Publishing, copyright 1974. Used by permission.

Jeremiah, David, and C.C. Carlson, *The Handwriting On the Wall*, copyright 1992, Word Inc., Dallas, Texas.

Johnson, Barbara, *Stick A Geranium in Your Hat and Be Happy*, copyright 1991, Word Inc., Dallas, Texas.

Keller, Philip, *A Gardener Looks at the Fruits of the Spirit*, copyright 1986 Word, Inc., Dallas, Texas.

Keller, Philip, *Lessons from a Sheep Dog*, copyright 1983 Word, Inc., Dallas, Texas.

Keller, Philip, *Salt for Society*, copyright 1981 Word, Inc., Dallas, Texas.

Keller, Philip, *A Shepherd Looks at Psalm 23*. Copyright © 1970 by W. Philip Keller. Used by permission of Zondervan Publishing House.

Keller, Philip, *A Shepherd Looks at the Good Shepherd*. Copyright 1970 by W. Philip Keller. Used by permission of Zondervan Publishing House.

Kimmel, Tim, *Little House on the Freeway*, Questar Publishers, Multnomah Books, copyright 1987 by Tim Kimmel.

L'Engle, Madeleine, *A Cry Like A Bell*. "The Bethlehem Explosion" from *A Cry Like A Bell* by Madeleine L'Engle, copyright 1987 by Crosswicks. Used by permission of Harold Shaw Publishers, Wheaton, Illinois.

Lavender, Lucille, *Struggles of a Sinner-Saint*. Copyright 1976 by The Upper Room, 1908 Grand Avenue, P. O. Box 189, Nashville, TN 37202. Used by permission of the publisher.

Lewis, C. S., *The Quotable Lewis*, edited by Wayne Martindale and Jerry Root, copyright 1989. Used by permission of Tyndale House Publishers, Inc. All rights reserved.

Little, Paul, *Know Why You Believe*, published by Victor Books, 1984, SP Publications, Inc., Wheaton, Illinois 60187.

Littleton, Mark, *When God Seems Far Away*, copyright 1987 by Mark. R. Littleton. Used with permission of Harold Shaw Publishers, Wheaton, Illinois.

Lucado, Max, *And the Angels Were Silent*, Questar Publishers, Multnomah Books, copyright 1992 by Max Lucado.

Lucado, Max, *The Applause of Heaven*, copyright 1990, Word Inc., Dallas, Texas.

Lucado, Max, *God Came Near*, Questar Publishers, Multnomah Books, copyright 1987.

Lucado, Max, *He Still Moves Stones*, copyright 1993, Word Inc., Dallas, Texas.

Lucado, Max, *In the Eye of the Storm*, copyright 1991, Word Inc., Dallas, Texas.

Lucado, Max, *No Wonder They Call Him the Savior*, Questar Publishers, Multnomah Books, copyright 1986 by Max Lucado.

Lucado, Max, *On the Anvil*, copyright 1985 by Max Lucado. Used by permission of Tyndale House Publishers, Inc. All rights reserved.

Lucado, Max, *Six Hours One Friday*, Questar Publishers, Multnomah Books, copyright 1989 by Max Lucado.

Lucado, Max, *Tell Me the Story* by Max Lucado, copyright 1992, pages i-iv. Used by permission of Good News Publishers, Crossway Books, Wheaton, Illinois 60187.

Lucado, Max, *Walking with the Savior*. All color topical inserts were compiled from *Walking with the Savior*. Published by Tyndale House Publishers, copyright 1993 by Max Lucado.

Lucado, Max, *When God Whispers Your Name*, copyright 1994, Word Inc., Dallas, Texas.

Lutzer, Erwin, *How in the World Can I Be Holy?*, Moody Press, copyright 1974. Used by permission.

MacArthur, John,Jr., *The Ultimate Priority*, Moody Press, copyright 1983. Used by permission.

MacDonald, Gordon, *Christ Followers in the Real World*, copyright 1991 Thomas Nelson, Nashville, Tennessee.

MacDonald, Gordon, *Ordering Your Private Word*, copyright 1984 Thomas Nelson, Nashville, Tennessee.

MacDonald, Gordon, *Rebuilding Your Broken World*, copyright 1988 Thomas Nelson, Nashville, Tennessee.

MacDonald, William, *Alone in Majesty*, copyright 1994 Thomas Nelson, Nashville, Tennessee.

Mains, Karen, *Making Sunday Special*, Star Song Publications, copyright 1994. Used by permission.

Manning, Brennan, *Lion and Lamb*, Fleming H. Revell Company, copyright 1980. Used by permission.

Manning, Brennan, *The Ragamuffin Gospel*, Questar Publishers, Multnomah Books, copyright 1990 by Brennan Manning.

ACKNOWLEDGMENTS

Marshall, Catherine, *Adventures in Prayer,* Fleming H. Revell Company, copyright 1975. Used by permission.

Marshall, Catherine, *Beyond Ourselves,* Fleming H. Revell Company, copyright 1961. Used by permission.

Marshall, Catherine, *Something More,* Fleming H. Revell Company, copyright 1974. Used by permission.

McDowell, Josh, and Bob Hostetler, *Don't Check Your Brains at the Door,* copyright 1992, Word Inc., Dallas, Texas.

McDowell, Josh, and D. Stewart, *Understanding the Occult,* copyright 1992, Here's Life. Used by permission of Thomas Nelson, Nashville, Tennessee.

McGrath, Alister, *What Was God Doing on the Cross?* Copyright 1992 by Alister McGrath. Used by permission of Zondervan Publishing House.

Merton, Thomas, *Conjectures of a Guilty Bystander,* copyright 1966. Permission granted by Doubleday, a division of Bantam Doubleday Dell Publishing Group, Inc.

Meyer, Moody, Murray, Ryle, Spurgeon, et al., *They Walked with God,* Moody Press, copyright 1993. Used by permission.

Morley, Patrick, *The Man in the Mirror,* Thomas Nelson, copyright 1992.

Morley, Patrick, *Walking with Christ in the Details of Life,* copyright 1992 Thomas Nelson, Nashville, Tennessee.

Mosley, Steven, *If Only God Would Answer,* copyright 1993. Permission granted by NavPress. For copies call 1-800-366-7788.

Mother Teresa, *Who Is for Life?* copyright 1984, pages 28-30. Used by permission of Missionaries of Charity and Good News Publishers, Crossway Books, Wheaton, Illinois 60187.

Moyes, G. K., article in *Money for Ministries* compiled by W. K. Wilmer, published by Victor Books, copyright 1989, SP Publications, Inc., Wheaton, Illinois 60187.

Murray, Andrew, *The Believer's Daily Renewal,* copyright 1981, Bethany House Publishers. Used by permission.

Nouwen, Henri, *In the Name of Jesus,* copyright 1989 by Henri J. M. Nouwen. Reprinted by permission of the Crossroad Publishing Co., New York.

Ogilivie, Lloyd J., *Climbing the Rainbow,* copyright 1993, Word Inc., Dallas, Texas.

Ogilivie, Lloyd J., *Lord of the Impossible,* Abingdon Press, copyright 1984. Used by permission.

Oliver, Gary, "God is a Promise Keeper", in *What Makes a Man,* copyright 1993. Permission granted by NavPress. For copies call 1-800-366-7788.

Ortlund, Anne, *Disciplines of the Heart,* copyright 1979 Word, Inc., Dallas, Texas.

Ortlund, Anne, *Discipling One Another,* copyright 1979 Word, Inc., Dallas, Texas.

Ortlund, Anne, *My Sacrifice, His Fire,* copyright 1991 Word, Inc., Dallas, Texas.

Ortlund, Anne, and Ray Ortlund, *You Don't Have to Quit,* copyright 1986 Thomas Nelson, Nashville, Tennessee.

Packer, J. I., *God's Words,* InterVarsity Press, copyright 1981. Used by permission of J. I. Packer, Sangwoo Youtong Chee Professor of Theology, Regent College.

Packer, J. I., *Knowing God.* Taken from *Knowing God* by J. I. Packer. 1973 by J. I. Packer. Used by permission of InterVarsity Press, P. O. Box 1400, Downers Grove, Illinois 60515.

Palms, Roger, C., *Enjoying the Closeness of God,* World Wide Publishers, copyright 1976. Used by permission.

Palms, Roger, C., *God Guides Your Tomorrows,* InterVarsity Press copyright 1987. Used by permission.

Paris, Twila, with Robert Webber, *In This Sanctuary,* Star Song Publishers, copyright 1993 by Robert Webber. Used by permission.

Peale, Norman Vincent, *Positive Imaging,* Fleming H. Revell Company, copyright 1982. Used by permission.

Peale, Norman Vincent, *The Positive Power of Jesus Christ,* Tyndale House Publishers. Copyright 1980 by Norman Vincent Peale. Permission granted by Ruth S. Peale, co-trustee of the Norman Vincent Peale Trust.

Pennington, Chester, A., *With Good Reason,* Abingdon Press, copyright 1967. Used by permission.

Perkins, John, *Beyond Charity,* Fleming H. Revell Company, copyright 1993. Used by permission.

Perkins, John, *With Justice for All,* Regal Books, copyright 1982 by John M. Perkins.

Peterson, Eugene, *Run with the Horses.* Taken from *Run with the Horses* by Eugene H. Peterson. 1983 by InterVarsity Christian Fellowship of the USA. Used by permission of InterVarsity Press, P. O. Box 1400, Downers Grove, Illinois 60515.

Piper, John, *Desiring God,* Questar Publishers, Multhomah Books, copyright 1986 by John Piper. Used by permission.

Price, Eugenia, *Beloved World.* Copyright 1991 by Eugenia Price. Used by permission of Doubleday, a division of Bantam Doubleday Dell Publishing Group, Inc.

Rand, Ron, *Won by One,* copyright 1994 by Ron Rand. Used by permission of the author.

Ridenour, Fritz, *How to Be a Christian Without Being Religious,* copyright 1984, Regal Books, Ventura, CA 93003. Used by permission.

Rinehart, Paula, *The Cleavers Don't Live Here Anymore,* Moody Press, copyright 1991. Used by permission.

Robertson, Pat, *The Secret Kingdom,* copyright 1992, Word Inc., Dallas, Texas.

Schaeffer, Francis, *The Complete Works of Francis Schaeffer* by Francis Schaeffer, copyright 1982, pages 111-112. Used by permission of Good News Publishers, Crossway Books, Wheaton, Illinois 60187.

Schuller, Robert, *The Be (Happy) Attitudes,* copyright 1985 Word, Inc., Dallas, Texas.

Seamands, David, *Putting Away Childish Things,* published by Victor Books, 1982, SP Publications, Inc., Wheaton, Illinois 60187.

Sherrill, John, and Elizabeth Sherrill, *Glimpses of His Glory,* Tyndale House Publishers, copyright 1991 by Guideposts. Used by permission.

Sider, Ronald, *Rich Christians in an Age of Hunger,* copyright 1990, Word Inc., Dallas, Texas.

Smalley, Gary, and John Trent, *A Dad's Blessing,* copyright 1994 Thomas Nelson, Nashville, Tennessee.

Smalley, Gary, and John Trent, *The Gift of the Blessing,* copyright 1993 Thomas Nelson, Nashville, Tennessee.

Smith-Greer, Becky, *Keepsakes for the Heart,* Focus on the Family Publishers, copyright 1990. Used by permission.

Sproul, R. C., *The Holiness of God,* copyright 1985 by R. C. Sproul. Used by permission of Tyndale House Publishers, Inc. All rights reserved.

Sproul, R. C., *Pleasing God,* copyright 1988 by R. C. Sproul. Used by permission of Tyndale House Publishers, Inc. All rights reserved.

Spurgeon, Charles H., *Faith's Checkbook,* Moody Press, copyright 1987. Used by permission.

Spurgeon, Charles H., *Morning and Evening.* Copyright 1980 by the Zondervan Corporation. Used by permission of Zondervan Publishing House.

Stanley, Charles, *Eternal Security,* copyright 1990 Thomas Nelson, Nashville, Tennessee.

Stanley, Charles, *How to Handle Adversity,* copyright 1989 Thomas Nelson, Nashville, Tennessee.

Stanley, Charles, *How to Keep Your Kids On Your Team,* copyright 1986 Thomas Nelson, Nashville, Tennessee.

Stanley, Charles, *Winning the War Within,* copyright 1988 Thomas Nelson, Nashville, Tennessee.

Stanley, Charles, *The Wonderful Spirit-Filled Life,* copyright 1992 Thomas Nelson, Nashville, Tennessee.

Stedman, Ray, *Body Life,* Regal Books, copyright 1972 by Ray Stedman. Used by permission.

Stevens, Paul, *Disciplines of the Hungry Heart,* copyright 1993 by R. Paul Stevens. Used by permission of Harold Shaw Publishers.

ACKNOWLEDGMENTS

Stewart, James, *The Wind of the Spirit*, Abingdon Press, copyright 1968. Used by permission.

Stott, John, taken with permission from *Understanding Christ* by John Stott. Published by Zondervan Publishing House © 1981.

Stowell, Joseph, *Fan the Flame*, Moody Press, copyright 1986. Used by permission.

Stowell, Joseph, *The Upside of Down*, Moody Press, copyright 1991. Used by permission.

Swindoll, Charles, *Come Before Winter*. Copyright 1985 by Charles R. Swindoll, Inc. Used by permission of Zondervan Publishing House.

Swindoll, Charles, *Dropping Your Guard*, copyright 1983 Word, Inc., Dallas, Texas.

Swindoll, Charles, *Encourage Me*. Copyright 1982 by Charles R. Swindoll, Inc. Used by permission of Zondervan Publishing House.

Swindoll, Charles, *Flying Closer to the Flame*, copyright 1993 Word, Inc., Dallas, Texas.

Swindoll, Charles, *The Grace Awakening*, copyright 1990, Word Inc., Dallas, Texas.

Swindoll, Charles, *Growing Deep in the Christian Life*. Copyright 1986 by Charles R. Swindoll, Inc. Used by permission of Zondervan Publishing House.

Swindoll, Charles, *Growing Strong in the Seasons of Life*. Copyright 1983 by Charles R. Swindoll, Inc. Used by permission of Zondervan Publishing House.

Swindoll, Charles, *Hand Me Another Brick*, copyright 1990 Thomas Nelson, Nashville, Tennessee.

Swindoll, Charles, *Improving Your Serve*, copyright 1981 Word, Inc., Dallas, Texas.

Swindoll, Charles, *Laugh Again*, copyright 1992, Word Inc., Dallas, Texas.

Swindoll, Charles, *Living Above the Level of Mediocrity*, copyright 1987 Word, Inc., Dallas, Texas.

Swindoll, Charles, *Living on the Ragged Edge*, copyright 1985 Word, Inc., Dallas, Texas.

Swindoll, Charles, *Simple Faith*, copyright 1991, Word Inc., Dallas, Texas.

Swindoll, Charles, *Strengthening Your Grip*, copyright 1982 Word, Inc., Dallas, Texas.

Swindoll, Charles, *Three Steps Forward and Two Steps Back*, copyright 1990 Thomas Nelson, Nashville, Tennessee.

Tada, Joni Eareckson, *Diamonds in the Dust*. Copyright 1993 by Joni Eareckson Tada and Steve Estes. Used by permission of Zondervan Publishing House.

Tada, Joni Eareckson, *Secret Strength for Those Who Search*, Questar Publishers, Multnomah Books, copyright 1988 by Joni Eareckson Tada.

Tada, Joni Eareckson, and Steve Estes, *A Step Further*. Copyright 1978 by Joni Eareckson Tada and Steve Estes. Used by permission of Zondervan Publishing House.

Taylor, Daniel, *Letters to my Children*. Taken from *Letters to my Children* by Daniel Taylor. Copyright 1989 by Daniel Taylor. Used by permission of InterVarsity Press, P. O. Box 1400, Downers Grove, Illinois 60515.

Taylor, Kenneth, *Next Steps for New Christians*, copyright 1985 by Kenneth Taylor. Used by permission of Tyndale House Publishers, Inc. All rights reserved.

Ten Boom, Corrie, *Not I but Christ*, copyright 1983 Thomas Nelson, Nashville, Tennessee.

Tippet, Sammy, *Fire in Your Heart*, Moody Press, copyright 1987. Used by permission.

Tippet, Sammy, *The Prayer Factor*, Moody Press, copyright 1988. Used by permission.

Tozer, A. W., from *The Best of A. W. Tozer*, compiled by Warren W. Wiersbe, copyright 1978 Baker Book House. Used by permission.

Tozer, A. W., *Knowledge of the Holy*, Harper-Collins, copyright 1992. Used by permission.

Tozer, A. W., *The Price of Neglect*, Christian Publications, copyright 1991. Used by permission.

Tozer, A. W., *The Pursuit of God*, Christian Publications, copyright 1982. Used by permission.

Tozer, A. W., *Renewed Day by Day*, Christian Publications, copyright 1978. Used by permission.

Tozer, A. W., *The Root of Righteousness*, Christian Publications, copyright 1986. Used by permission.

Tucker, Ruth A., *Stories of Faith*. Copyright 1989 by Ruth A. Tucker. Used by permission of Zondervan Publishing House.

Veerman, Dave, *On Eagles' Wings*, copyright 1995 by The Livingstone Corporation. Used by permission of Tyndale House Publishers, Inc. All rights reserved.

Waitley, Dennis, *Timing is Everything*, copyright 1992 Thomas Nelson, Nashville, Tennessee.

Wangerin, Walter, Jr., *As for Me and My House*, copyright 1987 Walter Wangerin, Jr., Nashville, Tennessee.

Wangerin, Walter, Jr., *Mourning into Dancing*. Copyright 1992 by Walter Wangerin. Used by permission of Zondervan Publishing House.

Ward, C. M., *Revivaltime Pulpit*, book eight. General Council of the Assemblies of God, National Radio Department, copyright 1964. Used by permission.

Ward, C. M., *Revivaltime Pulpit*, book five. General Council of the Assemblies of God, National Radio Department, copyright 1961. Used by permission.

Webber, Robert, *Hand Me Another Brick*, copyright 1992 Star Song, Nashville, Tennessee. Used by permission.

Webber, Robert, *Worship Is a Verb*, copyright 1992 Star Song Nashville, Tennessee. Used by permission.

Whelchel, Mary, *Workday Meditations*, Fleming H. Revell Company, copyright 1992. Used by permission.

White, John, *The Fight*. Taken from *The Fight* by John White. 1976 by InterVarsity Christian Fellowship of the USA. Used by permission of InterVarsity Press, P. O. Box 1400, Downers Grove, Illinois 60515.

White, John, *The Race*. Taken from *The Race* by John White. 1984 by InterVarsity Christian Fellowship of the USA. Used by permission of InterVarsity Press, P. O. Box 1400, Downers Grove, Illinois 60515.

Whitney, Donald, S., *Spiritual Disciplines of the Christian Life*, copyright 1991. Permission granted by NavPress. For copies call 1-800-366-7788.

Wiersbe, Warren, *Be Real*, published by Victor Books, 1972, SP Publications, Inc., Wheaton, Illinois 60187.

Wiersbe, Warren, *Be Strong*, published by Victor Books, 1993, SP Publications, Inc., Wheaton, Illinois 60187.

Wiersbe, Warren, *Live Like a King*, Moody Press, copyright 1983. Used by permission.

Wilcox, Michael, *The Message of Judges*. Taken from *The Message of Judges* by Michael Wilcox. 1992 by Michael Wilcox. Used by permission of InterVarsity Press, P. O. Box 1400, Downers Grove, Illinois 60515.

Winter, David, from *Faith Under Fire (One Hundred Days in the Arena)* copyright by David Winter. Used by permission.

Wright, H. Norman, *How to Get Along with Almost Anyone*, copyright 1989 Word, Inc., Dallas, Texas.

Wright, H. Norman, *Quiet Times for Couples*, copyright 1990 by Harvest House Publishers. Used by permission.

Yancey, Philip, *Disappointment with God*. Copyright 1988 by Philip Yancey. Used by permission of Zondervan Publishing House.

Yancey, Philip, *Discovering God*. Copyright 1993 by Philip Yancey. Used by permission of Zondervan Publishing House.

Yancey Philip, *Guidance: Making Sense of God's Direction*, Questar Publishers, Multnomah Books, copyright 1984 by Philip Yancey. Used by persmission.

Yancey, Philip, *Where Is God When It Hurts?* Copyright 1977, 1990 by Philip Yancey. Used by permission of Zondervan Publishing House.

Yohn, Rick, *Finding Time*, copyright 1984 Thomas Nelson, Nashville, Tennessee.

NOTES

NOTES

NOTES

NOTES

NOTES

NOTES

NOTES

NOTES

NOTES

NOTES

NOTES

NOTES

NOTES

NOTES

NOTES

NOTES

NOTES